Peterson's Graduate Programs in the Physical Sciences, Mathematics, Agricultural Sciences, the Environment & Natural Resources

2011

PETERSON'S
Publishing

PETERSON'S
Publishing

About Peterson's Publishing
To succeed on your lifelong educational journey, you will need accurate, dependable, and practical tools and resources. That is why Peterson's is everywhere education happens. Because whenever and however you need education content delivered, you can rely on Peterson's to provide the information, know-how, and guidance to help you reach your goals. Tools to match the right students with the right school. It's here. Personalized resources and expert guidance. It's here. Comprehensive and dependable education content—delivered whenever and however you need it. It's all here.

For more information, contact Peterson's, 2000 Lenox Drive, Lawrenceville, NJ 08648; 800-338-3282 Ext. 54229; or find us online at www.petersonspublishing.com.

Stephen Clemente, Managing Director, Publishing and Institutional Research; Bernadette Webster, Director of Publishing; Jill C. Schwartz, Editor; Ken Britschge, Research Project Manager; Courtney Foust, Amy L. Weber, Research Associates; Phyllis Johnson, Programmer; Ray Golaszewski, Manufacturing Manager; Linda M. Williams, Composition Manager; Karen Mount, Danielle Vreeland, Shannon White, Client Relations Representatives

ISSN 1093-8443
ISBN-13: 978-0-7689-2855-6
ISBN-10: 0-7689-2855-9

Printed in the United States of America

10 9 8 7 6 5 4 3 2 1   13 12 11 10

Forty-fifth Edition

By producing this book on recycled paper (40% post-consumer waste) 56 trees were saved.

CONTENTS

A Note from the Peterson's Editors

The six volumes of Peterson's *Graduate and Professional Programs*, the only annually updated reference work of its kind, provide wide-ranging information on the graduate and professional programs offered by accredited colleges and universities in the United States, U.S. territories, and Canada and by those institutions outside the United States that are accredited by U.S. accrediting bodies. More than 44,000 individual academic and professional programs at more than 2,200 institutions are listed. Peterson's *Graduate and Professional Programs* have been used for more than forty years by prospective graduate and professional students, placement counselors, faculty advisers, and all others interested in postbaccalaureate education.

Graduate & Professional Programs: An Overview contains information on institutions as a whole, while the other books in the series are devoted to specific academic and professional fields:

Graduate Programs in the Humanities, Arts & Social Sciences
Graduate Programs in the Biological Sciences
Graduate Programs in the Physical Sciences, Mathematics, Agricultural Sciences, the Environment & Natural Resources
Graduate Programs in Engineering & Applied Sciences
Graduate Programs in Business, Education, Health, Information Studies, Law & Social Work

The books may be used individually or as a set. For example, if you have chosen a field of study but do not know what institution you want to attend or if you have a college or university in mind but have not chosen an academic field of study, it is best to begin with the Overview guide.

Graduate & Professional Programs: An Overview presents several directories to help you identify programs of study that might interest you; you can then research those programs further in the other books in the series by using the Directory of Graduate and Professional Programs by Field, which lists 500 fields and gives the names of those institutions that offer graduate degree programs in each.

For geographical or financial reasons, you may be interested in attending a particular institution and will want to know what it has to offer. You should turn to the Directory of Institutions and Their Offerings, which lists the degree programs available at each institution. As in the Directory of Graduate and Professional Programs by Field, the level of degrees offered is also indicated.

All books in the series include advice on graduate education, including topics such as admissions tests, financial aid, and accreditation. **The Graduate Adviser** includes two essays and information about accreditation. The first essay, "The Admissions Process," discusses general admission requirements, admission tests, factors to consider when selecting a graduate school or program, when and how to apply, and how admission decisions are made. Special information for international students and tips for minority students are also included. The second essay, "Financial Support," is an overview of the broad range of support available at the graduate level. Fellowships, scholarships, and grants; assistantships and internships; federal and private loan programs, as well as Federal Work-Study; and the GI bill are detailed. This essay concludes with advice on applying for need-based financial aid. "Accreditation and Accrediting Agencies" gives information on accreditation and its purpose and lists institutional accrediting agencies first and then specialized accrediting agencies relevant to each volume's specific fields of study.

With information on more than 44,000 graduate programs in 500 disciplines, Peterson's *Graduate and Professional Programs* give you all the information you need about the programs that are of interest to you in three formats: **Profiles** (capsule summaries of basic information), **Displays** (information that an institution or program wants to emphasize), and **Close-Ups** (written by administrators, with more expansive information than the **Profiles**, emphasizing different aspects of the programs). By using these various formats of program information, coupled with **Appendixes** and **Indexes** covering directories and subject areas for all six books, you will find that these guides provide the most comprehensive, accurate, and up-to-date graduate study information available.

Find Us on Facebook® and Follow Us on Twitter™

Join the grad school conversation on Facebook® and Twitter™ at www.facebook.com/usgradschools and www.twitter.com/usgradschools. Peterson's expert resources are available to help you as you search for the right graduate program for you.

Peterson's publishes a full line of resources with information you need to guide you through the graduate admissions process. Peterson's publications can be found at college libraries and career centers and your local bookstore or library—or visit us on the Web at www.petersonspublishing.com. Peterson's books are now also available as eBooks.

Colleges and universities will be pleased to know that Peterson's helped you in your selection. Admissions staff members are more than happy to answer questions, address specific problems, and help in any way they can. The editors at Peterson's wish you great success in your graduate program search!

THE GRADUATE ADVISER

The Admissions Process

Generalizations about graduate admissions practices are not always helpful because each institution has its own set of guidelines and procedures. Nevertheless, some broad statements can be made about the admissions process that may help you plan your strategy.

Factors Involved in Selecting a Graduate School or Program

Selecting a graduate school and a specific program of study is a complex matter. Quality of the faculty; program and course offerings; the nature, size, and location of the institution; admission requirements; cost; and the availability of financial assistance are among the many factors that affect one's choice of institution. Other considerations are job placement and achievements of the program's graduates and the institution's resources, such as libraries, laboratories, and computer facilities. If you are to make the best possible choice, you need to learn as much as you can about the schools and programs you are considering before you apply.

The following steps may help you narrow your choices.

- Talk to alumni of the programs or institutions you are considering to get their impressions of how well they were prepared for work in their fields of study.
- Remember that graduate school requirements change, so be sure to get the most up-to-date information possible.
- Talk to department faculty members and the graduate adviser at your undergraduate institution. They often have information about programs of study at other institutions.
- Visit the Web sites of the graduate schools in which you are interested to request a graduate catalog. Contact the department chair in your chosen field of study for additional information about the department and the field.
- Visit as many campuses as possible. Call ahead for an appointment with the graduate adviser in your field of interest and be sure to check out the facilities and talk to students.

General Requirements

Graduate schools and departments have requirements that applicants for admission must meet. Typically, these requirements include undergraduate transcripts (which provide information about undergraduate grade point average and course work applied toward a major), admission test scores, and letters of recommendation. Most graduate programs also ask for an essay or personal statement that describes your personal reasons for seeking graduate study. In some fields, such as art and music, portfolios or auditions may be required in addition to other evidence of talent. Some institutions require that the applicant have an undergraduate degree in the same subject as the intended graduate major.

Most institutions evaluate each applicant on the basis of the applicant's total record, and the weight accorded any given factor varies widely from institution to institution and from program to program.

The Application Process

You should begin the application process at least one year before you expect to begin your graduate study. Find out the application deadline for each institution (many are provided in the **Profile** section of this guide). Go to the institution's Web site and find out if you can apply online. If not, request a paper application form. Fill out this form thoroughly and neatly. Assume that the school needs all the information it is requesting and that the admissions officer will be sensitive to the neatness and overall quality of what you submit. Do not supply more information than the school requires.

The institution may ask at least one question that will require a three- or four-paragraph answer. Compose your response on the assumption that the admissions officer is interested in both what you think and how you express yourself. Keep your statement brief and to the point, but, at the same time, include all pertinent information about your past experiences and your educational goals. Individual statements vary greatly in style and content, which helps admissions officers differentiate among applicants. Many graduate departments give considerable weight to the statement in making their admissions decisions, so be sure to take the time to prepare a thoughtful and concise statement.

If recommendations are a part of the admissions requirements, carefully choose the individuals you ask to write them. It is generally best to ask current or former professors to write the recommendations, provided they are able to attest to your intellectual ability and motivation for doing the work required of a graduate student. It is advisable to provide stamped, preaddressed envelopes to people being asked to submit recommendations on your behalf.

Completed applications, including references, transcripts, and admission test scores, should be received at the institution by the specified date.

Be advised that institutions do not usually make admissions decisions until all materials have been received. Enclose a self-addressed postcard with your application, requesting confirmation of receipt. Allow at least ten days for the return of the postcard before making further inquiries.

If you plan to apply for financial support, it is imperative that you file your application early.

ADMISSION TESTS

The major testing program used in graduate admissions is the Graduate Record Examinations (GRE) testing program, sponsored by the GRE Board and administered by Educational Testing Service, Princeton, New Jersey.

The Graduate Record Examinations testing program consists of a General Test and eight Subject Tests. The General Test measures critical thinking, verbal reasoning, quantitative reasoning, and analytical writing skills. It is offered as an Internet-based test (iBT) in the United States, Canada, and many other countries.

The typical computer-based General Test consists of one 30-minute verbal reasoning section, one 45-minute quantitative reasoning sections, one 45-minute issue analysis (writing) section, and one 30-minute argument analysis (writing) section. In addition, an unidentified verbal or quantitative section that doesn't count toward a score may be included and an identified research section that is not scored may also be included.

The Subject Tests measure achievement and assume undergraduate majors or extensive background in the following eight disciplines:

- Biochemistry, Cell and Molecular Biology
- Biology
- Chemistry
- Computer Science
- Literature in English
- Mathematics
- Physics
- Psychology

The Subject Tests are available three times per year as paper-based administrations around the world. Testing time is approximately 2 hours and 50 minutes. You can obtain more information about the GRE by visiting the ETS Web site at www.ets.org or consulting the *GRE Information and Registration Bulletin*. The *Bulletin* can be obtained at many undergraduate colleges. You can also download it from the ETS Web site or obtain it by contacting Graduate Record Examinations, Educational Testing Service, P.O. Box 6000, Princeton, NJ 08541-6000; phone: 609-771-7670.

If you expect to apply for admission to a program that requires any of the GRE tests, you should select a test date well in advance of the application deadline. Scores on the computer-based General Test are reported within ten to fifteen days; scores on the paper-based Subject Tests are reported within six weeks.

Another testing program, the Miller Analogies Test (MAT), is administered at more than 500 Controlled Testing Centers, licensed by Harcourt Assessment, Inc., in the United States, Canada, and other countries. The MAT computer-based test is now available. Testing time is 60 minutes. The test consists of 120 partial analogies. You can obtain the *Candidate Information Booklet,* which contains a list of test centers and instructions for taking the test, from http://www.milleranalogies.com or by calling 800-622-3231 (toll-free).

Check the specific requirements of the programs to which you are applying.

How Admission Decisions Are Made

The program you apply to is directly involved in the admissions process. Although the final decision is usually made by the graduate dean (or an associate) or the faculty admissions committee, recommendations from faculty members in your intended field are important. At some institutions, an interview is incorporated into the decision process.

A Special Note for International Students

In addition to the steps already described, there are some special considerations for international students who intend to apply for graduate study in the United States. All graduate schools require an indication of competence in English. The purpose of the Test of English as a Foreign Language (TOEFL) is to evaluate the English proficiency of people who are nonnative speakers of English and want to study at colleges and universities where English is the language of instruction. The TOEFL is administered by Educational Testing Service (ETS) under the general direction of a policy board established by the College Board and the Graduate Record Examinations Board.

The TOEFL iBT assesses the four basic language skills: listening, reading, writing, and speaking. It was administered for the first time in September 2005, and ETS continues to introduce the TOEFL iBT in selected cities. The Internet-based test is administered at secure, official test centers. The testing time is approximately 4 hours. Because the TOEFL iBT includes a speaking section, the Test of Spoken English (TSE) is no longer needed.

The TOEFL is also offered in the paper-based format in areas of the world where Internet-based testing is not available. The paper-based TOEFL consists of three sections—listening comprehension, structure and written expression, and reading comprehension. The testing time is approximately 3 hours. The Test of Written English (TWE) is also given. The TWE is a 30-minute essay that measures the examinee's ability to compose in English. Examinees receive a TWE score separate from their TOEFL score. The *Information Bulletin* contains information on local fees and registration procedures.

Additional information and registration materials are available from TOEFL Services, Educational Testing Service, P.O. Box 6151, Princeton, New Jersey 08541-6151. Phone: 609-771-7100. Web site: www.toefl.org.

International students should apply especially early because of the number of steps required to complete the admissions process. Furthermore, many United States graduate schools have a limited number of spaces for international students, and many more students apply than the schools can accommodate.

International students may find financial assistance from institutions very limited. The U.S. government requires international applicants to submit a certification of support, which is a statement attesting to the applicant's financial resources. In addition, international students *must* have health insurance coverage.

Tips for Minority Students

Indicators of a university's values in terms of diversity are found both in its recruitment programs and its resources directed to student success. Important questions: Does the institution vigorously recruit minorities for its graduate programs? Is there funding available to help with the costs associated with visiting the school? Are minorities represented in the institution's brochures or Web site or on their faculty rolls? What campus-based resources or services (including assistance in locating housing or career counseling and placement) are available? Is funding available to members of underrepresented groups?

At the program level, it is particularly important for minority students to investigate the "climate" of a program under consideration. How many minority students are enrolled and how many have graduated? What opportunities are there to work with diverse faculty and mentors whose research interests match yours? How are conflicts resolved or concerns addressed? How interested are faculty in building strong and supportive relations with students? "Climate" concerns should be addressed by posing questions to various individuals, including faculty members, current students, and alumni.

Information is also available through various organizations, such as the Hispanic Association of Colleges & Universities (HACU), and publications such as *Diverse Issues in Higher Education* and *Hispanic Outlook* magazine. There are also books devoted to this topic, such as *The Multicultural Student's Guide to Colleges* by Robert Mitchell.

Financial Support

The range of financial support at the graduate level is very broad. The following descriptions will give you a general idea of what you might expect and what will be expected of you as a financial support recipient.

Fellowships, Scholarships, and Grants

These are usually outright awards of a few hundred to many thousands of dollars with no service to the institution required in return. Fellowships and scholarships are usually awarded on the basis of merit and are highly competitive. Grants are made on the basis of financial need or special talent in a field of study. Many fellowships, scholarships, and grants not only cover tuition, fees, and supplies but also include stipends for living expenses with allowances for dependents. However, the terms of each should be examined because some do not permit recipients to supplement their income with outside work. Fellowships, scholarships, and grants may vary in the number of years for which they are awarded.

In addition to the availability of these funds at the university or program level, many excellent fellowship programs are available at the national level and may be applied for before and during enrollment in a graduate program. A listing of many of these programs can be found at the Council of Graduate Schools' Web site: http://www.cgsnet.org. There is a wealth of information in the "Programs" and "Awards" sections.

Assistantships and Internships

Many graduate students receive financial support through assistantships, particularly involving teaching or research duties. It is important to recognize that such appointments should not be viewed simply as employment relationships but rather should constitute an integral and important part of a student's graduate education. As such, the appointments should be accompanied by strong faculty mentoring and increasingly responsible apprenticeship experiences. The specific nature of these appointments in a given program should be considered in selecting that graduate program.

TEACHING ASSISTANTSHIPS

These usually provide a salary and full or partial tuition remission and may also provide health benefits. Unlike fellowships, scholarships, and grants, which require no service to the institution, teaching assistantships require recipients to provide the institution with a specific amount of undergraduate teaching, ideally related to the student's field of study. Some teaching assistants are limited to grading papers, compiling bibliographies, taking notes, or monitoring laboratories. At some graduate schools, teaching assistants must carry lighter course loads than regular full-time students.

RESEARCH ASSISTANTSHIPS

These are very similar to teaching assistantships in the manner in which financial assistance is provided. The difference is that recipients are given basic research assignments in their disciplines rather than teaching responsibilities. The work required is normally related to the student's field of study; in most instances, the assistantship supports the student's thesis or dissertation research.

ADMINISTRATIVE INTERNSHIPS

These are similar to assistantships in application of financial assistance funds, but the student is given an assignment on a part-time basis, usually as a special assistant with one of the university's administrative offices. The assignment may not necessarily be directly related to the recipient's discipline.

RESIDENCE HALL AND COUNSELING ASSISTANTSHIPS

These assistantships are frequently assigned to graduate students in psychology, counseling, and social work, but they may be offered to students in other disciplines, especially if the student has worked in this capacity during his or her undergraduate years. Duties can vary from being available in a dean's office for a specific number of hours for consultation with undergraduates to living in campus residences and being responsible for both counseling and administrative tasks or advising student activity groups. Residence hall assistantships often include a room and board allowance and, in some cases, tuition assistance and stipends. Contact the Housing and Student Life Office for more information.

Health Insurance

The availability and affordability of health insurance is an important issue and one that should be considered in an applicant's choice of institution and program. While often included with assistantships and fellowships, this is not always the case and, even if provided, the benefits may be limited. It is important to note that the U.S. government requires international students to have health insurance.

The GI Bill

This provides financial assistance for students who are veterans of the United States armed forces. If you are a veteran, contact your local Veterans Administration office to determine your eligibility and to get full details about benefits. There are a number of programs that offer educational benefits to current military enlistees. Some states have tuition assistance programs for members of the National Guard. Contact the VA office at the college for more information.

Federal Work-Study Program (FWS)

Employment is another way some students finance their graduate studies. The federally funded Federal Work-Study Program provides eligible students with employment opportunities, usually in public and private nonprofit organizations. Federal funds pay up to 75 percent of the wages, with the remainder paid by the employing agency. FWS is available to graduate students who demonstrate financial need. Not all schools have these funds, and some only award them to undergraduates. Each school sets its application deadline and work-study earnings limits. Wages vary and are related to the type of work done. You must file the Free Application for Federal Student Aid (FAFSA) to be eligible for this program.

Loans

Many graduate students borrow to finance their graduate programs when other sources of assistance (which do not have to be repaid) prove insufficient. You should always read and understand the terms of any loan program before submitting your application.

FEDERAL DIRECT LOANS

Federal Direct Stafford Loans. The Federal Direct Stafford Loan Program offers low-interest loans to students with the Department of Education acting as the lender.

There are two components of the Federal Stafford Loan program. Under the *subsidized* component of the program, the federal government pays the interest on the loan while you are enrolled in graduate school on at least a half-time basis, during the six-month grace period after you drop below half-time enrollment, as well as during any period of deferment. Under the *unsubsidized* component of the program, you pay the interest on the loan from the day proceeds are issued. Eligibility for the federal subsidy is based on demonstrated financial need as determined by the financial aid office from the information you provide on the FAFSA. A cosigner is not required, since the loan is not based on creditworthiness.

Although *unsubsidized* Federal Direct Stafford Loans may not be as desirable as *subsidized* Federal Direct Stafford Loans from the student's perspective, they are a useful source of support for those who may not qualify for the subsidized loans or who need additional financial assistance.

Graduate students may borrow up to $20,500 per year through the Direct Stafford Loan Program, up to a cumulative maximum of $138,500, including undergraduate borrowing. This may include up to $8500 in *subsidized* Direct Stafford Loans annually, depending on eligibility, up to a cumulative maximum of $65,500, including undergraduate borrowing. The amount of the loan borrowed through the *unsubsidized* Direct Stafford Loan Program equals the total amount of the loan (as much as $20,500) minus your eligibility for a *subsidized* Direct Loan (as much as $8500). You may borrow up to the cost of attendance at the school in which you are enrolled or will attend, minus estimated financial assistance from other federal, state, and private sources, up to a maximum of $20,500.

Direct Stafford Loans made on or after July 1, 2006, carry a fixed interest rate of 6.8% both for in-school and in-repayment borrowers.

A fee is deducted from the loan proceeds upon disbursement. Loans with a first disbursement on or after July 1, 2010 have a borrower origination fee of 1 percent. The Department of Education offers a 0.5 percent origination fee rebate incentive. Borrowers must make their first twelve payments on time in order to retain the rebate.

Under the *subsidized* Federal Direct Stafford Loan Program, repayment begins six months after your last date of enrollment on at least a half-time basis. Under the *unsubsidized* program, repayment of interest begins within thirty days from disbursement of the loan proceeds, and repayment of the principal begins six months after your last enrollment on at least a half-time basis. Some borrowers may choose to defer interest payments while they are in school. The accrued interest is added to the loan balance when the borrower begins repayment. There are several repayment options.

Federal Perkins Loans. The Federal Perkins Loan is available to students demonstrating financial need and is administered directly by the school. Not all schools have these funds, and some may award them to undergraduates only. Eligibility is determined from the information you provide on the FAFSA. The school will notify you of your eligibility.

Eligible graduate students may borrow up to $6000 per year, up to a maximum of $40,000, including undergraduate borrowing (even if your previous Perkins Loans have been repaid). The interest rate for Federal Perkins Loans is 5 percent, and no interest accrues while you remain in school at least half-time. There are no guarantee, loan, or disbursement fees. Repayment begins nine months after your last date of enrollment on at least a half-time basis and may extend over a maximum of ten years with no prepayment penalty.

Federal Direct Graduate PLUS Loans. Effective July 1, 2006, graduate and professional students are eligible for Graduate PLUS loans. This program allows students to borrow up to the cost of attendance, less any other aid received. These loans have a fixed interest rate of 7.9 percent, and interest begins to accrue at the time of disbursement. The PLUS loans do involve a credit check; a PLUS borrower may obtain a loan with a cosigner if his or her credit is not good enough. Grad PLUS loans may be deferred while a student in school and for the six months following a drop below half-time enrollment. For more information, contact your college financial aid office.

Deferring Your Federal Loan Repayments. If you borrowed under the Federal Direct Stafford Loan Program, Federal Direct Loan Program, or the Federal Perkins Loan Program for previous undergraduate or graduate study, your repayments may be deferred when you return to graduate school, depending on when you borrowed and under which program.

There are other deferment options available if you are temporarily unable to repay your loan. Information about these deferments is provided at your entrance and exit interviews. If you believe you are eligible for a deferment of your loan repayments, you must contact your lender or loan servicer to request a deferment form. The deferment must be filed prior to the time your repayment is due, and it must be refiled when it expires if you remain eligible for deferment at that time.

SUPPLEMENTAL (PRIVATE) LOANS

Many lending institutions offer supplemental loan programs and other financing plans, such as the ones described here, to students seeking additional assistance in meeting their education expenses. Some loan programs target all types of graduate students; others are designed specifically for business, law, or medical students. In addition, you can use private loans not specifically designed for education to help finance your graduate degree.

If you are considering borrowing through a supplemental or private loan program, you should carefully consider the terms and be sure to "read the fine print." Check with the program sponsor for the most current terms that will be applicable to the amounts you intend to borrow for graduate study. Most supplemental loan programs for graduate study offer unsubsidized, credit-based loans. In general, a credit-ready borrower is one who has a satisfactory credit history or no credit history at all. A creditworthy borrower generally must pass a credit test to be eligible to borrow or act as a cosigner for the loan funds.

Many supplemental loan programs have minimum and maximum annual loan limits. Some offer amounts equal to the cost of attendance minus any other aid you will receive for graduate study. If you are planning to borrow for several years of graduate study, consider whether there is a cumulative or aggregate limit on the amount you may borrow. Often this cumulative or aggregate limit will include any amounts you borrowed and have not repaid for undergraduate or previous graduate study.

The combination of the annual interest rate, loan fees, and the repayment terms you choose will determine how much you will repay over time. Compare these features in combination before you decide which loan program to use. Some loans offer interest rates that are adjusted monthly, some quarterly, some annually. Some offer interest rates that are lower during the in-school, grace, and deferment periods and then increase when you begin repayment. Some programs include a loan "origination" fee, which is usually deducted from the principal amount you receive when the loan is disbursed and must be repaid along with the interest and other principal when you graduate, withdraw from school, or drop below half-time study. Sometimes the loan fees are reduced if you borrow with a qualified cosigner. Some programs allow you to defer interest and/or principal payments while you are enrolled in graduate school. Many programs allow you to capitalize your interest payments; the interest due on your loan is added to the outstanding balance of your loan, so you don't have to repay immediately, but this increases the amount you owe. Other programs allow you to pay the interest as you go, which reduces the amount you later have to repay. The private loan market is very competitive, and your financial aid office can help you evaluate these programs.

Applying for Need-Based Financial Aid

Schools that award federal and institutional financial assistance based on need will require you to complete the FAFSA and, in some cases, an institutional financial aid application.

If you are applying for federal student assistance, you **must** complete the FAFSA. A service of the U.S. Department of Education, the FAFSA is free to all applicants. Most applicants apply online at www.fafsa.ed.gov. Paper applications are available at the financial aid office of your local college.

After your FAFSA information has been processed, you will receive a Student Aid Report (SAR). If you provided an e-mail address on the FAFSA, this will be sent to you electronically; otherwise, it will be mailed to your home address.

Follow the instructions on the SAR if you need to correct information reported on your original application. If your situation changes after you file your FAFSA, contact your financial aid officer to discuss amending your information. You can also appeal your financial aid award if you have extenuating circumstances.

If you would like more information on federal student financial aid, visit the FAFSA Web site or download the most recent version of *Funding Education Beyond High School: The Guide to Federal Student Aid* at http://studentaid.ed.gov/students/publications/student_guide/index.html. This guide is also available in Spanish.

The U.S. Department of Education also has a toll-free number for questions concerning federal student aid programs. The number is 1-800-4-FED AID (1-800-433-3243). If you are hearing impaired, call toll-free, 1-800-730-8913.

Summary

Remember that these are generalized statements about financial assistance at the graduate level. Because each institution allots its aid differently, you should communicate directly with the school and the specific department of interest to you. It is not unusual, for example, to find that an endowment vested within a specific department supports one or more fellowships. You may fit its requirements and specifications precisely.

Accreditation and Accrediting Agencies

Colleges and universities in the United States, and their individual academic and professional programs, are accredited by nongovernmental agencies concerned with monitoring the quality of education in this country. Agencies with both regional and national jurisdictions grant accreditation to institutions as a whole, while specialized bodies acting on a nationwide basis—often national professional associations—grant accreditation to departments and programs in specific fields.

Institutional and specialized accrediting agencies share the same basic concerns: the purpose an academic unit—whether university or program—has set for itself and how well it fulfills that purpose, the adequacy of its financial and other resources, the quality of its academic offerings, and the level of services it provides. Agencies that grant institutional accreditation take a broader view, of course, and examine university-wide or college-wide services with which a specialized agency may not concern itself.

Both types of agencies follow the same general procedures when considering an application for accreditation. The academic unit prepares a self-evaluation, focusing on the concerns mentioned above and usually including an assessment of both its strengths and weaknesses; a team of representatives of the accrediting body reviews this evaluation, visits the campus, and makes its own report; and finally, the accrediting body makes a decision on the application. Often, even when accreditation is granted, the agency makes a recommendation regarding how the institution or program can improve. All institutions and programs are also reviewed every few years to determine whether they continue to meet established standards; if they do not, they may lose their accreditation.

Accrediting agencies themselves are reviewed and evaluated periodically by the U.S. Department of Education and the Council for Higher Education Accreditation (CHEA). Recognized agencies adhere to certain standards and practices, and their authority in matters of accreditation is widely accepted in the educational community.

This does not mean, however, that accreditation is a simple matter, either for schools wishing to become accredited or for students deciding where to apply. Indeed, in certain fields the very meaning and methods of accreditation are the subject of a good deal of debate. For their part, those applying to graduate school should be aware of the safeguards provided by regional accreditation, especially in terms of degree acceptance and institutional longevity. Beyond this, applicants should understand the role that specialized accreditation plays in their field, as this varies considerably from one discipline to another. In certain professional fields, it is necessary to have graduated from a program that is accredited in order to be eligible for a license to practice, and in some fields the federal government also makes this a hiring requirement. In other disciplines, however, accreditation is not as essential, and there can be excellent programs that are not accredited. In fact, some programs choose not to seek accreditation, although most do.

Institutions and programs that present themselves for accreditation are sometimes granted the status of candidate for accreditation, or what is known as "preaccreditation." This may happen, for example, when an academic unit is too new to have met all the requirements for accreditation. Such status signifies initial recognition and indicates that the school or program in question is working to fulfill all requirements; it does not, however, guarantee that accreditation will be granted.

Institutional Accrediting Agencies—Regional

MIDDLE STATES ASSOCIATION OF COLLEGES AND SCHOOLS
Accredits institutions in Delaware, District of Columbia, Maryland, New Jersey, New York, Pennsylvania, Puerto Rico, and the Virgin Islands.
Dr. Elizabeth Sibolski, Acting President
Middle States Commission on Higher Education
3624 Market Street, Second Floor West
Philadelphia, Pennsylvania 19104
Phone: 267-284-5000
Fax: 215-662-5501
E-mail: info@msche.org
Web: www.msche.org

NEW ENGLAND ASSOCIATION OF SCHOOLS AND COLLEGES
Accredits institutions in Connecticut, Maine, Massachusetts, New Hampshire, Rhode Island, and Vermont.
Barbara E. Brittingham, Director
Commission on Institutions of Higher Education
209 Burlington Road, Suite 201
Bedford, Massachusetts 01730-1433
Phone: 781-271-0022
Fax: 781-271-0950
E-mail: CIHE@neasc.org
Web: www.neasc.org

NORTH CENTRAL ASSOCIATION OF COLLEGES AND SCHOOLS
Accredits institutions in Arizona, Arkansas, Colorado, Illinois, Indiana, Iowa, Kansas, Michigan, Minnesota, Missouri, Nebraska, New Mexico, North Dakota, Ohio, Oklahoma, South Dakota, West Virginia, Wisconsin, and Wyoming.
Dr. Sylvia Manning, President
The Higher Learning Commission
230 South LaSalle Street, Suite 7-500
Chicago, Illinois 60604-1413
Phone: 312-263-0456
Fax: 312-263-7462
E-mail: smanning@hlcommission.org
Web: www.ncahigherlearningcommission.org

NORTHWEST COMMISSION ON COLLEGES AND UNIVERSITIES
Accredits institutions in Alaska, Idaho, Montana, Nevada, Oregon, Utah, and Washington.
Dr. Sandra E. Elman, President
8060 165th Avenue, NE, Suite 100
Redmond, Washington 98052
Phone: 425-558-4224
Fax: 425-376-0596
E-mail: selman@nwccu.org
Web: www.nwccu.org

SOUTHERN ASSOCIATION OF COLLEGES AND SCHOOLS
Accredits institutions in Alabama, Florida, Georgia, Kentucky, Louisiana, Mississippi, North Carolina, South Carolina, Tennessee, Texas, and Virginia.
Belle S. Wheelan, President
Commission on Colleges
1866 Southern Lane
Decatur, Georgia 30033-4097
Phone: 404-679-4500
Fax: 404-679-4558
E-mail: questions@sacscoc.org
Web: www.sacsoc.org

WESTERN ASSOCIATION OF SCHOOLS AND COLLEGES
Accredits institutions in California, Guam, and Hawaii.
Ralph A. Wolff, President and Executive Director
Accrediting Commission for Senior Colleges and Universities
985 Atlantic Avenue, Suite 100
Alameda, California 94501
Phone: 510-748-9001
Fax: 510-748-9797
E-mail: www.wascsenior.org
Web: www.wascweb.org/contact

Institutional Accrediting Agencies—Other

ACCREDITING COUNCIL FOR INDEPENDENT COLLEGES AND SCHOOLS
Albert C. Gray, Ph.D., Executive Director and CEO
750 First Street, NE, Suite 980
Washington, DC 20002-4241
Phone: 202-336-6780
Fax: 202-842-2593
E-mail: info@acics.org
Web: www.acics.org

DISTANCE EDUCATION AND TRAINING COUNCIL (DETC)
Accrediting Commission
Michael P. Lambert, Executive Director
1601 18th Street, NW, Suite 2
Washington, DC 20009
Phone: 202-234-5100
Fax: 202-332-1386
E-mail: detc@detc.org
Web: www.detc.org

Specialized Accrediting Agencies

[Only *Graduate & Professional Programs: An Overview* of *Peterson's Graduate and Professional Programs* Series includes the complete list of specialized accrediting groups recognized by the U.S. Department of Education and the Council on Higher Education Accreditation (CHEA). The list in this book is abridged.]

DIETETICS
Ulric K. Chung, Ph.D., Executive Director
American Dietetic Association
Commission on Accreditation for Dietetics Education (CADE-ADA)
120 South Riverside Plaza, Suite 2000
Chicago, Illinois 60606-6995
Phone: 800-877-1600
Fax: 312-899-4817
E-mail: cade@eatright.org
Web: www.eatright.org/cade

FORESTRY
Michael T. Goergen, Jr.
Executive Vice-President and CEO
Society of American Foresters (SAF)
5400 Grosvenor Lane
Bethesda, Maryland 20814-2198
Phone: 301-897-8720 Ext. 123
Fax: 301-897-3690
E-mail: goergenm@safnet.org
Web: www.safnet.org

How to Use These Guides

As you identify the particular programs and institutions that interest you, you can use both the ***Graduate & Professional Programs: An Overview*** volume and the specialized volumes in the series to obtain detailed information.

- ***Graduate Programs in the Physical Sciences, Mathematics, Agricultural Sciences, the Environment & Natural Resources***
- ***Graduate Programs in Engineering & Applied Sciences***
- ***Graduate Programs the Humanities, Arts & Social Sciences***
- ***Graduate Programs in the Biological Sciences***
- ***Graduate Programs in Business, Education, Health, Information Studies, Law & Social Work***

Each of the specialized volumes in the series is divided into sections that contain one or more directories devoted to programs in a particular field. If you do not find a directory devoted to your field of interest in a specific volume, consult "Directories and Subject Areas" (located at the end of each volume). After you have identified the correct volume, consult the "Directories and Subject Areas in This Book" index, which shows (as does the more general directory) what directories cover subjects not specifically named in a directory or section title.

Each of the specialized volumes in the series has a number of general directories. These directories have entries for the largest unit at an institution granting graduate degrees in that field. For example, the general Engineering and Applied Sciences directory in the ***Graduate Programs in Engineering & Applied Sciences*** volume consists of **Profiles** for colleges, schools, and departments of engineering and applied sciences.

General directories are followed by other directories, or sections, that give more detailed information about programs in particular areas of the general field that has been covered. The general Engineering and Applied Sciences directory, in the previous example, is followed by nineteen sections with directories in specific areas of engineering, such as Chemical Engineering, Industrial/Management Engineering, and Mechanical Engineering.

Because of the broad nature of many fields, any system of organization is bound to involve a certain amount of overlap. Environmental studies, for example, is a field whose various aspects are studied in several types of departments and schools. Readers interested in such studies will find information on relevant programs in the ***Graduate Programs in the Biological Sciences*** volume under Ecology and Environmental Biology; in the ***Graduate Programs in the Physical Sciences, Mathematics, Agricultural Sciences, the Environment & Natural Resources*** volume under Environmental Management and Policy and Natural Resources; in the ***Graduate Programs in Engineering & Applied Sciences*** volume under Energy Management and Policy and Environmental Engineering; and in the ***Graduate Programs in Business, Education, Health, Information Studies, Law & Social Work*** volume under Environmental and Occupational Health. To help you find all of the programs of interest to you, the introduction to each section within the specialized volumes includes, if applicable, a paragraph suggesting other sections and directories with information on related areas of study.

Directory of Institutions with Programs in the Physical Sciences, Mathematics, Agricultural Sciences, the Environment & Natural Resources

This directory lists institutions in alphabetical order and includes beneath each name the academic fields in which each institution offers graduate programs. The degree level in each field is also indicated, provided that the institution has supplied that information in response to Peterson's Annual Survey of Graduate and Professional Institutions.

An M indicates that a master's degree program is offered; a D indicates that a doctoral degree program is offered; a P indicates that the first professional degree is offered; an O signifies that other advanced degrees (e.g., certificates or specialist degrees) are offered; and an * (asterisk) indicates that a **Close-Up** and/or **Display** is located in this volume. See the index, "Close-Ups and Displays," for the specific page number.

Profiles of Academic and Professional Programs in the Specialized Volumes

Each section of **Profiles** has a table of contents that lists the Program Directories, **Displays**, and **Close-Ups.** Program Directories consist of the **Profiles** of programs in the relevant fields, with **Displays** following if programs have chosen to include them. **Close-Ups,** which are more individualized statements, again if programs have chosen to submit them, are also listed.

The **Profiles** found in the 500 directories in the specialized volumes provide basic data about the graduate units in capsule form for quick reference. To make these directories as useful as possible, **Profiles** are generally listed for an institution's smallest academic unit within a subject area. In other words, if an institution has a College of Liberal Arts that administers many related programs, the **Profile** for the individual program (e.g., Program in History), not the entire College, appears in the directory.

There are some programs that do not fit into any current directory and are not given individual **Profiles**. The directory structure is reviewed annually in order to keep this number to a minimum and to accommodate major trends in graduate education.

The following outline describes the **Profile** information found in the guides and explains how best to use that information. Any item that does not apply to or was not provided by a graduate unit is omitted from its listing. The format of the **Profiles** is constant, making it easy to compare one institution with another and one program with another.

Identifying Information. The institution's name, in boldface type, is followed by a complete listing of the administrative structure for that field of study. (For example, University of Akron, Buchtel College of Arts and Sciences, Department of Theoretical and Applied Mathematics, Program in Mathematics.) The last unit listed is the one to which all information in the **Profile** pertains. The institution's city, state, and zip code follow.

Offerings. Each field of study offered by the unit is listed with all postbaccalaureate degrees awarded. Degrees that are not preceded by a specific concentration are awarded in the general field listed in the unit name. Frequently, fields of study are broken down into subspecializations, and those appear following the degrees awarded; for example, "Offerings in secondary education (M.Ed.), including English education, mathematics education, science education." Students enrolled in the M.Ed. program would be able to specialize in any of the three fields mentioned.

Professional Accreditation. Some **Profiles** indicate whether a program is professionally accredited. Because it is possible for a program to receive or lose professional accreditation at any time, students entering fields in which accreditation is important to a career should verify the status of programs by contacting either the chairperson or the appropriate accrediting association.

Jointly Offered Degrees. Explanatory statements concerning programs that are offered in cooperation with other institutions are included in the list of degrees offered. This occurs most commonly on a regional basis (for example, two state universities offering a cooperative Ph.D. in special education) or where the specialized nature of the institutions encourages joint efforts (a J.D./M.B.A. offered by a law school at an institution with no formal business programs and an institution with a business school but lacking a law school). Only programs that are truly cooperative are listed; those involving only limited course work at another institution are not. Interested students should contact the heads of such units for further information.

Part-Time and Evening/Weekend Programs. When information regarding the availability of part-time or evening/weekend study appears in the **Profile**, it means that students are able to earn a degree exclusively through such study.

Postbaccalaureate Distance Learning Degrees. A postbaccalaureate distance learning degree program signifies that course requirements can be fulfilled with minimal or no on-campus study.

Faculty. Figures on the number of faculty members actively involved with graduate students through teaching or research are separated into full-and part-time as well as men and women whenever the information has been supplied.

Students. Figures for the number of students enrolled in graduate and professional programs pertain to the semester of highest enrollment from the 2009–10 academic year. These figures are broken down into full-and part-time and men and women whenever the data have been supplied. Information on the number of matriculated students enrolled in the unit who are members of a minority group or are international students appears here. The average age of the matriculated students is followed by the number of applicants, the percentage accepted, and the number enrolled for fall 2009.

Degrees Awarded. The number of degrees awarded in the calendar year is listed. Many doctoral programs offer a terminal master's degree if students leave the program after completing only part of the requirements for a doctoral degree; that is indicated here. All degrees are classified into one of four types: master's, doctoral, first professional, and other advanced degrees. A unit may award one or several degrees at a given level; however, the data are only collected by type and may therefore represent several different degree programs.

Degree Requirements. The information in this section is also broken down by type of degree, and all information for a degree level pertains to all degrees of that type unless otherwise specified. Degree requirements are collected in a simplified form to provide some very basic information on the nature of the program and on foreign language, thesis or dissertation, comprehensive exam, and registration requirements. Many units also provide a short list of additional requirements, such as fieldwork or an internship. For complete information on graduation requirements, contact the graduate school or program directly.

Entrance Requirements. Entrance requirements are broken down into the four degree levels of master's, doctoral, first professional, and other advanced degrees. Within each level, information may be provided in two basic categories: entrance exams and other requirements. The entrance exams are identified by the standard acronyms used by the testing agencies, unless they are not well known. Other entrance requirements are quite varied, but they often contain an undergraduate or graduate grade point average (GPA). Unless otherwise stated, the GPA is calculated on a 4.0 scale and is listed as a minimum required for admission. Additional exam requirements/recommendations for international students may be listed here. Application deadlines for domestic and international students, the application fee, and whether electronic applications are accepted may be listed here. Note that the deadline should be used for reference only; these dates are subject to change, and students interested in applying should always contact the graduate unit directly about application procedures and deadlines.

Expenses. The typical cost of study for the 2009–10 academic year is given in two basic categories: tuition and fees. Cost of study may be quite complex at a graduate institution. There are often sliding scales for part-time study, a different cost for first-year students, and other variables that make it impossible to completely cover the cost of study for each graduate program. To provide the most usable information, figures are given for full-time study for a full year where available and for part-time study in terms of a per-unit rate (per credit, per semester hour, etc.). Occasionally, variances may be noted in tuition and fees for reasons such as the type of program, whether courses are taken during the day or evening, whether courses are at the master's or doctoral level, or other institution-specific reasons. Expenses are usually subject to change; for exact costs at any given time, contact your chosen schools and programs directly. Keep in mind that the tuition of Canadian institutions is usually given in Canadian dollars.

Financial Support. This section contains data on the number of awards administered by the institution and given to graduate students during the 2009–10 academic year. The first figure given represents the total number of students receiving financial support enrolled in that unit. If the unit has provided information on graduate appointments, these are broken down into three major categories: fellowships give money to graduate students to cover the cost of study and living expenses and are not based on a work obligation or research commitment, research assistantships provide stipends to graduate students for assistance in a formal research project with a faculty member, and teaching assistantships provide stipends to graduate students for teaching or for assisting faculty members in teaching undergraduate classes. Within each category, figures are given for the total number of awards, the average yearly amount per award, and whether full or partial tuition reimbursements are awarded. In addition to graduate appointments, the availability of several other financial aid sources is covered in this section. Tuition waivers are routinely part of a graduate appointment, but units sometimes waive part or all of a student's tuition even if a graduate appointment is not available. Federal Work-Study is made available to students who demonstrate need and meet the federal guidelines; this form of aid normally includes 10 or more hours of work per week in an office of the institution. Institutionally sponsored loans are low-interest loans available to graduate students to cover both educational and living expenses. Career-related internships or fieldwork offer money to students who are participating in a formal off-campus research project or practicum. Grants, scholarships, traineeships, unspecified assistantships, and other awards may also be noted. The availability of financial support to part-time students is also indicated here.

Some programs list the financial aid application deadline and the forms that need to be completed for students to be eligible for financial awards. There are two forms: FAFSA, the Free Application for Federal Student Aid, which is required for federal aid, and the CSS PROFILE®.

Faculty Research. Each unit has the opportunity to list several keyword phrases describing the current research involving faculty members and graduate students. Space limitations prevent the unit from listing complete information on all research programs. The total expenditure for funded research from the previous academic year may also be included.

Unit Head and Application Contact. The head of the graduate program for each unit is listed with academic title and telephone and fax numbers and e-mail address if available. In addition to the unit head, many graduate programs list a separate contact for application and admission information, which follows the listing for the unit head. If no unit head or application contact is given, you should contact the overall institution for information on graduate admissions.

Displays and Close-Ups

The **Displays** and **Close-Ups** are supplementary insertions submitted by deans, chairs, and other administrators who wish to offer an additional, more individualized statement to readers. A number of graduate school and program administrators have attached a **Display** ad near the **Profile** listing. Here you will find information that an institution or program wants to emphasize. The **Close-Ups** are by their very nature more expansive and flexible than the **Profiles**, and the administrators who have written them may emphasize different aspects of their programs. All of the **Close-Ups** are organized in the same way (with the exception of a few that describe research and training opportunities instead of degree programs), and in each one you will find information on the same basic topics, such as programs of study, research facilities, tuition and fees, financial aid, and application procedures. If an institution or program has submitted a **Close-Up**, a boldface cross-reference appears below its **Profile**. As with the **Displays**, all of the **Close-Ups** in the guides have been submitted by choice; the absence of a **Display** or **Close-Up** does not reflect any type of editorial judgment on the part of Peterson's, and their presence in the guides should not be taken as an indication of status, quality, or approval. Statements regarding a university's objectives and accomplishments are a reflection of its own beliefs and are not the opinions of the Peterson's editors.

Appendixes

This section contains two appendixes. The first, "Institutional Changes Since the 2010 Edition," lists institutions that have closed, merged, or changed their name or status since the last edition of the guides. The second, "Abbreviations Used in the Guides," gives abbreviations of degree names, along with what those abbreviations stand for. These appendixes are identical in all six volumes of ***Peterson's Graduate and Professional Programs***.

Indexes

There are three indexes presented here. The first index, "Close-Ups and Displays," gives page references for all programs that have chosen to place **Close-Ups** and **Displays** in this volume. It is arranged alphabetically by institution; within institutions, the arrangement is alphabetical by subject area. It is not an index to all programs in the book's directories of **Profiles**; readers must refer to the directories themselves for **Profile** information on programs that have not submitted the additional, more individualized statements. The second index, "Directories and Subject Areas in Other Books in This Series", gives book references for the directories in the specialized volumes and also includes cross-references for subject area names not used in the directory structure, for example, "Computing Technology (see Computer Science)." The third index, "Directories and Subject Areas in This Book," gives page references for the directories in this volume and cross-references for subject area names not used in this volume's directory structure.

Data Collection Procedures

The information published in the directories and **Profiles** of all the books is collected through Peterson's Annual Survey of Graduate and Professional Institutions. The survey is sent each spring to more than 2,200 institutions offering postbaccalaureate degree programs, including accredited institutions in the United States, U.S. territories, and Canada and those institutions outside the United States that are accredited by U.S. accrediting bodies. Deans and other administrators complete these surveys, providing information on programs in the 500 academic and professional fields covered in the guides as well as overall institutional information. While every effort has been made to ensure the accuracy and completeness of the data, information is sometimes unavailable or changes occur after publication deadlines. All usable information received in time for publication has been included. The omission of any particular item from a directory or **Profile** signifies either that the item is not applicable to the institution or program or that information was not available. **Profiles** of programs scheduled to begin during the 2010–11 academic year cannot, obviously, include statistics on enrollment or, in many cases, the number of faculty members. If no usable data were submitted by an institution, its name, address, and program name appear in order to indicate the availability of graduate work.

Criteria for Inclusion in This Guide

To be included in this guide, an institution must have full accreditation or be a candidate for accreditation (preaccreditation) status by an institutional or specialized accrediting body recognized by the U.S. Department of Education or the Council for Higher Education Accreditation (CHEA). Institutional accrediting bodies, which review each institution as a whole, include the six regional associations of schools and colleges (Middle States, New England, North Central, Northwest, Southern, and Western), each of which is responsible for a specified portion of the United States and its territories. Other institutional accrediting bodies are national in scope and accredit specific kinds of institutions (e.g., Bible colleges, independent colleges, and rabbinical and Talmudic schools). Program registration by the New York State Board of Regents is considered to be the equivalent of institutional accreditation, since the board requires that all programs offered by an institution meet its standards before recognition is granted. A Canadian institution must be chartered and authorized to grant degrees by the provincial government, affiliated with a chartered institution, or accredited by a recognized U.S. accrediting body. This guide also includes institutions outside the United States that are accredited by these U.S. accrediting bodies. There are recognized specialized or professional accrediting bodies in more than fifty different fields, each of which is authorized to accredit institutions or specific programs in its particular field. For specialized institutions that offer programs in one field only, we designate this to be the equivalent of institutional accreditation. A full explanation of the accrediting process and complete information on recognized institutional (regional and national) and specialized accrediting bodies can be found online at www.chea.org or at www.ed.gov/admins/finaid/accred/index.html.

DIRECTORY OF INSTITUTIONS WITH PROGRAMS IN THE PHYSICAL SCIENCES, MATHEMATICS, AGRICULTURAL SCIENCES, THE ENVIRONMENT & NATURAL RESOURCES

ACADIA UNIVERSITY
- Applied Mathematics M
- Chemistry M
- Geology M
- Statistics M

ADELPHI UNIVERSITY
- Environmental Management and Policy M
- Physics M

AIR FORCE INSTITUTE OF TECHNOLOGY
- Applied Mathematics M,D
- Applied Physics M,D
- Astrophysics M,D
- Environmental Management and Policy M
- Optical Sciences M,D
- Planetary and Space Sciences M,D

ALABAMA AGRICULTURAL AND MECHANICAL UNIVERSITY
- Agricultural Sciences—General M,D
- Agronomy and Soil Sciences M,D
- Animal Sciences M,D
- Applied Physics M,D
- Environmental Sciences M,D
- Food Science and Technology M,D
- Optical Sciences M,D
- Physics M,D
- Plant Sciences M,D

ALABAMA STATE UNIVERSITY
- Mathematics M,O

ALASKA PACIFIC UNIVERSITY
- Environmental Sciences M

ALBANY STATE UNIVERSITY
- Water Resources M

ALCORN STATE UNIVERSITY
- Agricultural Sciences—General M
- Agronomy and Soil Sciences M
- Animal Sciences M

AMERICAN PUBLIC UNIVERSITY SYSTEM
- Environmental Management and Policy M

AMERICAN UNIVERSITY
- Applied Statistics M,O
- Chemistry M
- Environmental Management and Policy M,D,O
- Environmental Sciences M,O
- Marine Sciences M
- Mathematics M
- Natural Resources M,D,O
- Statistics M,O

AMERICAN UNIVERSITY OF BEIRUT
- Agronomy and Soil Sciences M
- Animal Sciences M
- Aquaculture M
- Biostatistics M
- Chemistry M
- Environmental Management and Policy M
- Environmental Sciences M,D
- Food Science and Technology M
- Geology M
- Mathematics M
- Physics M
- Plant Sciences M
- Statistics M

ANDREWS UNIVERSITY
- Mathematics M

ANGELO STATE UNIVERSITY
- Agricultural Sciences—General M
- Animal Sciences M

ANTIOCH UNIVERSITY NEW ENGLAND
- Environmental Management and Policy M,D
- Environmental Sciences M,D

ANTIOCH UNIVERSITY SEATTLE
- Environmental Management and Policy M

APPALACHIAN STATE UNIVERSITY
- Environmental Management and Policy M
- Mathematics M

ARIZONA STATE UNIVERSITY
- Applied Mathematics M,D
- Astrophysics M,D
- Chemistry M,D
- Environmental Management and Policy M
- Environmental Sciences M,D
- Geology M,D
- Geosciences M,D
- Mathematics M,D
- Physics M,D
- Statistics M,D

ARKANSAS STATE UNIVERSITY—JONESBORO
- Agricultural Sciences—General M,O
- Chemistry M,O
- Environmental Sciences M,D
- Mathematics M

ARKANSAS TECH UNIVERSITY
- Fish, Game, and Wildlife Management M

AUBURN UNIVERSITY
- Agricultural Sciences—General M,D
- Agronomy and Soil Sciences M,D
- Analytical Chemistry M,D
- Animal Sciences M,D
- Applied Mathematics M,D
- Aquaculture M,D
- Chemistry M,D
- Fish, Game, and Wildlife Management M,D
- Food Science and Technology M,D
- Forestry M,D
- Geology M*
- Horticulture M,D
- Hydrology M,D
- Inorganic Chemistry M,D
- Mathematics M,D
- Natural Resources M,D
- Organic Chemistry M,D
- Physical Chemistry M,D
- Physics M,D
- Statistics M,D

AURORA UNIVERSITY
- Mathematics M

BALL STATE UNIVERSITY
- Chemistry M
- Geology M
- Geosciences M
- Mathematics M
- Natural Resources M
- Physics M
- Statistics M

BARD COLLEGE
- Environmental Management and Policy M,O

BAYLOR UNIVERSITY
- Chemistry M,D
- Environmental Management and Policy M
- Environmental Sciences D
- Geology M,D
- Geosciences M,D
- Limnology M,D
- Mathematics M,D
- Physics M,D
- Statistics M,D

BEMIDJI STATE UNIVERSITY
- Environmental Management and Policy M

BERNARD M. BARUCH COLLEGE OF THE CITY UNIVERSITY OF NEW YORK
- Mathematical and Computational Finance M
- Statistics M

BOISE STATE UNIVERSITY
- Animal Sciences M
- Environmental Management and Policy M
- Geology M,D
- Geophysics M,D
- Geosciences M

BOSTON COLLEGE
- Chemistry M,D
- Geology M
- Geophysics M
- Inorganic Chemistry M,D
- Mathematics D
- Organic Chemistry M,D
- Physical Chemistry M,D
- Physics M,D

BOSTON UNIVERSITY
- Astronomy M,D
- Biostatistics M,D
- Chemistry M,D
- Environmental Management and Policy M,D,O
- Food Science and Technology M
- Geosciences M,D
- Mathematical and Computational Finance M,D
- Mathematics M,D
- Photonics M,D
- Physics M,D*

BOWIE STATE UNIVERSITY
- Applied Mathematics M

BOWLING GREEN STATE UNIVERSITY
- Applied Statistics M,D
- Chemistry M,D
- Geology M
- Geophysics M
- Mathematics M,D
- Physics M
- Statistics M,D

BRADLEY UNIVERSITY
- Chemistry M

BRANDEIS UNIVERSITY
- Chemistry M,D
- Inorganic Chemistry M,D
- Mathematics M,D,O
- Organic Chemistry M,D
- Physical Chemistry M,D
- Physics M,D

BRIGHAM YOUNG UNIVERSITY
- Agricultural Sciences—General M,D
- Analytical Chemistry M,D
- Animal Sciences M,D
- Applied Statistics M
- Astronomy M,D
- Chemistry M,D*
- Environmental Sciences M,D
- Fish, Game, and Wildlife Management M,D
- Food Science and Technology M
- Geology M
- Mathematics M,D
- Physics M,D
- Plant Sciences M,D
- Statistics M

BROCK UNIVERSITY
- Chemistry M,D
- Geosciences M
- Mathematics M
- Physics M
- Statistics M

BROOKLYN COLLEGE OF THE CITY UNIVERSITY OF NEW YORK
- Applied Physics M,D
- Chemistry M,D
- Geology M,D
- Geosciences M
- Mathematics M,D
- Physics M,D

BROWN UNIVERSITY
- Applied Mathematics M,D
- Biostatistics M,D
- Chemistry M,D
- Environmental Management and Policy M
- Geosciences M,D
- Mathematics M,D
- Physics M,D

BRYN MAWR COLLEGE
- Chemistry M,D
- Mathematics M,D
- Physics M,D

BUCKNELL UNIVERSITY
- Chemistry M
- Mathematics M

BUFFALO STATE COLLEGE, STATE UNIVERSITY OF NEW YORK
- Chemistry M

CALIFORNIA INSTITUTE OF TECHNOLOGY
- Applied Mathematics M,D
- Applied Physics M,D
- Astronomy D
- Chemistry M,D
- Computational Sciences M,D
- Geochemistry M,D
- Geology M,D
- Geophysics M,D
- Mathematics D
- Physics D
- Planetary and Space Sciences M,D

CALIFORNIA POLYTECHNIC STATE UNIVERSITY, SAN LUIS OBISPO
- Agricultural Sciences—General M
- Chemistry M
- Forestry M
- Mathematics M
- Natural Resources M

CALIFORNIA STATE POLYTECHNIC UNIVERSITY, POMONA
Agricultural Sciences—General M
Applied Mathematics M
Chemistry M
Environmental Sciences M
Mathematics M

CALIFORNIA STATE UNIVERSITY, BAKERSFIELD
Geology M
Hydrology M

CALIFORNIA STATE UNIVERSITY CHANNEL ISLANDS
Mathematics M

CALIFORNIA STATE UNIVERSITY, CHICO
Environmental Sciences M
Geology M
Geosciences M
Hydrogeology M
Hydrology M

CALIFORNIA STATE UNIVERSITY, DOMINGUEZ HILLS
Environmental Sciences M

CALIFORNIA STATE UNIVERSITY, EAST BAY
Biostatistics M
Chemistry M
Environmental Sciences M
Geology M
Marine Sciences M
Mathematics M
Statistics M

CALIFORNIA STATE UNIVERSITY, FRESNO
Animal Sciences M
Chemistry M
Food Science and Technology M
Geology M
Marine Sciences M
Mathematics M
Physics M
Plant Sciences M
Viticulture and Enology M

CALIFORNIA STATE UNIVERSITY, FULLERTON
Applied Mathematics M
Chemistry M
Environmental Management and Policy M
Environmental Sciences M
Geochemistry M
Geology M
Mathematics M
Physics M

CALIFORNIA STATE UNIVERSITY, LONG BEACH
Applied Mathematics M,D
Applied Statistics M
Chemistry M
Food Science and Technology M
Geology M
Geophysics M
Mathematics M
Physics M

CALIFORNIA STATE UNIVERSITY, LOS ANGELES
Analytical Chemistry M
Applied Mathematics M
Chemistry M
Geology M
Inorganic Chemistry M
Mathematics M
Organic Chemistry M
Physical Chemistry M
Physics M

CALIFORNIA STATE UNIVERSITY, MONTEREY BAY
Marine Sciences M
Water Resources M

CALIFORNIA STATE UNIVERSITY, NORTHRIDGE
Applied Mathematics M
Chemistry M
Environmental Sciences M
Geology M
Mathematics M
Physics M

CALIFORNIA STATE UNIVERSITY, SACRAMENTO
Chemistry M
Marine Sciences M
Mathematics M
Statistics M

CALIFORNIA STATE UNIVERSITY, SAN BERNARDINO
Chemistry M
Environmental Sciences M
Mathematics M

CALIFORNIA STATE UNIVERSITY, SAN MARCOS
Mathematics M

CALIFORNIA STATE UNIVERSITY, STANISLAUS
Marine Sciences M

CARLETON UNIVERSITY
Chemistry M,D
Geosciences M,D
Mathematics M,D
Physics M,D

CARNEGIE MELLON UNIVERSITY
Applied Mathematics M,D
Applied Physics M,D
Chemistry M,D
Computational Sciences M,D
Inorganic Chemistry M,D
Mathematical and Computational Finance M,D
Mathematics M,D
Organic Chemistry M,D
Physics M,D
Statistics M,D
Theoretical Chemistry M,D

CASE WESTERN RESERVE UNIVERSITY
Applied Mathematics M,D
Astronomy M,D
Biostatistics M,D
Chemistry M,D
Geology M,D
Geosciences M,D
Mathematics M,D
Physics M,D
Statistics M,D

THE CATHOLIC UNIVERSITY OF AMERICA
Environmental Management and Policy M,D,O
Optical Sciences M,D
Physics M,D

CENTRAL CONNECTICUT STATE UNIVERSITY
Chemistry M,O
Geosciences M,O
Mathematics M,O
Physics M,O
Statistics M,O

CENTRAL EUROPEAN UNIVERSITY
Applied Mathematics M,D
Environmental Management and Policy M,D

CENTRAL MICHIGAN UNIVERSITY
Chemistry M
Mathematics M,D
Physics M,D

CENTRAL WASHINGTON UNIVERSITY
Chemistry M
Geology M
Mathematics M
Natural Resources M

CHAPMAN UNIVERSITY
Food Science and Technology M

CHICAGO STATE UNIVERSITY
Mathematics M

CHRISTOPHER NEWPORT UNIVERSITY
Applied Physics M
Environmental Sciences M
Physics M

CITY COLLEGE OF THE CITY UNIVERSITY OF NEW YORK
Atmospheric Sciences M,D
Chemistry M,D
Environmental Sciences M,D
Geosciences M,D
Mathematics M
Physics M,D*

CLAREMONT GRADUATE UNIVERSITY
Applied Mathematics M,D
Computational Sciences M,D
Mathematics M,D
Statistics M,D

CLARK ATLANTA UNIVERSITY
Chemistry M,D
Mathematics M
Physics M

CLARKSON UNIVERSITY
Chemistry M,D
Environmental Sciences M,D
Mathematics M,D
Physics M,D

CLARK UNIVERSITY
Chemistry M,D
Environmental Management and Policy M
Physics M,D

CLEMSON UNIVERSITY
Agricultural Sciences—General M,D
Animal Sciences M,D
Applied Mathematics M,D
Aquaculture M,D
Astronomy M,D
Astrophysics M,D
Atmospheric Sciences M,D
Chemistry M,D
Computational Sciences M,D
Environmental Management and Policy M,D
Environmental Sciences M,D
Fish, Game, and Wildlife Management M,D
Food Science and Technology M,D
Forestry M,D
Hydrogeology M
Mathematics M,D
Physics M,D
Plant Sciences M,D
Statistics M,D

CLEVELAND STATE UNIVERSITY
Analytical Chemistry M,D
Chemistry M,D
Condensed Matter Physics M
Environmental Management and Policy M,O
Environmental Sciences M,D
Inorganic Chemistry M,D
Mathematics M
Optical Sciences M
Organic Chemistry M,D
Physical Chemistry M,D
Physics M

COASTAL CAROLINA UNIVERSITY
Marine Sciences M

THE COLLEGE AT BROCKPORT, STATE UNIVERSITY OF NEW YORK
Computational Sciences M
Environmental Sciences M
Mathematics M

COLLEGE OF CHARLESTON
Environmental Sciences M
Marine Sciences M
Mathematics M,O

COLLEGE OF STATEN ISLAND OF THE CITY UNIVERSITY OF NEW YORK
Environmental Sciences M

COLLEGE OF THE ATLANTIC
Environmental Management and Policy M

THE COLLEGE OF WILLIAM AND MARY
Chemistry M
Computational Sciences M
Marine Sciences M,D
Physics M,D

COLORADO SCHOOL OF MINES
Applied Physics M,D
Chemistry M,D
Environmental Sciences M,D
Geochemistry M,D
Geology M,D
Geophysics M,D
Mathematics M,D
Physics M,D

COLORADO STATE UNIVERSITY
Agricultural Sciences—General M,D
Agronomy and Soil Sciences M,D
Animal Sciences M,D
Atmospheric Sciences M,D
Chemistry M,D
Fish, Game, and Wildlife Management M,D
Food Science and Technology M,D
Forestry M,D
Geosciences M,D
Horticulture M,D
Hydrology M,D

*M—master's degree; P—first professional degree; D—doctorate; O—other advanced degree; *—Close-Up and/or Display*

- Mathematics M,D
- Natural Resources M,D
- Physics M,D
- Plant Sciences M,D
- Range Science M,D
- Statistics M,D
- Water Resources M,D

COLORADO STATE UNIVERSITY–PUEBLO

- Chemistry M

COLUMBIA UNIVERSITY

- Applied Mathematics M,D,O
- Applied Physics M,D,O*
- Astronomy M,D
- Atmospheric Sciences M,D
- Biostatistics M,D
- Chemical Physics M,D
- Chemistry M,D
- Environmental Management and Policy M
- Environmental Sciences M
- Geochemistry M,D
- Geodetic Sciences M,D
- Geophysics M,D
- Geosciences M,D
- Inorganic Chemistry M,D
- Mathematics M,D
- Meteorology M
- Oceanography M,D
- Organic Chemistry M,D
- Physics M,D
- Planetary and Space Sciences M,D
- Statistics M,D

COLUMBUS STATE UNIVERSITY

- Environmental Sciences M

CONCORDIA UNIVERSITY (CANADA)

- Chemistry M,D
- Environmental Management and Policy M,O
- Mathematics M,D
- Physics M,D

CORNELL UNIVERSITY

- Agronomy and Soil Sciences M,D
- Analytical Chemistry D
- Animal Sciences M,D
- Applied Mathematics M,D
- Applied Physics M,D
- Applied Statistics M,D
- Astronomy D
- Astrophysics D
- Atmospheric Sciences M,D
- Biometry M,D
- Chemical Physics D
- Chemistry D
- Computational Sciences M,D
- Environmental Management and Policy M,D
- Environmental Sciences M,D
- Fish, Game, and Wildlife Management M,D
- Food Science and Technology M,D
- Forestry M,D
- Geochemistry M,D
- Geology M,D
- Geophysics M,D
- Geosciences M,D
- Horticulture M,D
- Hydrology M,D
- Inorganic Chemistry D
- Limnology D
- Marine Geology M,D
- Marine Sciences M,D
- Mathematics D
- Mineralogy M,D
- Natural Resources M,D
- Oceanography D
- Organic Chemistry D
- Paleontology M,D
- Physical Chemistry D
- Physics M,D
- Planetary and Space Sciences D
- Plant Sciences M,D
- Statistics M,D
- Theoretical Chemistry D
- Theoretical Physics M,D

CREIGHTON UNIVERSITY

- Atmospheric Sciences M
- Physics M

DALHOUSIE UNIVERSITY

- Agricultural Sciences—General M
- Applied Mathematics M,D
- Chemistry M,D
- Environmental Management and Policy M
- Food Science and Technology M,D
- Geosciences M,D
- Marine Affairs M
- Mathematics M,D
- Natural Resources M
- Oceanography M,D
- Physics M,D
- Statistics M,D

DARTMOUTH COLLEGE

- Astronomy M,D
- Chemistry D
- Geosciences M,D
- Mathematics D
- Physics M,D

DELAWARE STATE UNIVERSITY

- Applied Mathematics M,D
- Chemistry M
- Mathematics M
- Natural Resources M
- Optical Sciences M,D
- Physics M,D
- Plant Sciences M
- Theoretical Physics D

DEPAUL UNIVERSITY

- Applied Mathematics M,O
- Applied Physics M
- Applied Statistics M,O
- Chemistry M
- Mathematical and Computational Finance M,D
- Mathematics M,O
- Physics M

DOWLING COLLEGE

- Mathematics M

DREW UNIVERSITY

- Chemistry M
- Physics M

DREXEL UNIVERSITY

- Biostatistics M,D,O
- Chemistry M,D
- Environmental Management and Policy M
- Environmental Sciences M,D
- Food Science and Technology M
- Hydrology M,D
- Mathematics M,D
- Physics M,D

DUKE UNIVERSITY

- Chemistry D
- Environmental Management and Policy M,D
- Environmental Sciences M,D
- Forestry M
- Geology M,D
- Marine Affairs M
- Marine Sciences M
- Mathematics D
- Natural Resources M,D
- Paleontology D
- Physics M,D
- Statistics D
- Water Resources M

DUQUESNE UNIVERSITY

- Chemistry M,D*
- Environmental Management and Policy M,O
- Environmental Sciences M,O
- Mathematics M

EAST CAROLINA UNIVERSITY

- Applied Mathematics M
- Chemistry M
- Geology M
- Marine Affairs D
- Mathematics M
- Natural Resources D
- Physics M,D

EASTERN ILLINOIS UNIVERSITY

- Chemistry M
- Mathematics M

EASTERN KENTUCKY UNIVERSITY

- Chemistry M
- Geology M,D
- Mathematics M

EASTERN MICHIGAN UNIVERSITY

- Applied Statistics M
- Chemistry M
- Geosciences M
- Mathematics M
- Physics M
- Water Resources M,O

EASTERN NEW MEXICO UNIVERSITY

- Chemistry M
- Mathematics M

EASTERN WASHINGTON UNIVERSITY

- Mathematics M

EAST TENNESSEE STATE UNIVERSITY

- Chemistry M
- Mathematics M

ÉCOLE POLYTECHNIQUE DE MONTRÉAL

- Applied Mathematics M,D,O
- Optical Sciences M,D,O

ELIZABETH CITY STATE UNIVERSITY

- Mathematics M

EMORY UNIVERSITY

- Biostatistics M,D
- Chemistry D
- Condensed Matter Physics D
- Mathematics M,D*
- Physics D

EMPORIA STATE UNIVERSITY

- Geosciences M,O
- Mathematics M

THE EVERGREEN STATE COLLEGE

- Environmental Management and Policy M

FAIRFIELD UNIVERSITY

- Mathematics M

FAIRLEIGH DICKINSON UNIVERSITY, COLLEGE AT FLORHAM

- Chemistry M

FAIRLEIGH DICKINSON UNIVERSITY, METROPOLITAN CAMPUS

- Chemistry M
- Mathematics M

FAYETTEVILLE STATE UNIVERSITY

- Mathematics M

FISK UNIVERSITY

- Chemistry M
- Physics M

FLORIDA AGRICULTURAL AND MECHANICAL UNIVERSITY

- Agricultural Sciences—General M
- Animal Sciences M
- Chemistry M
- Environmental Sciences M,D
- Food Science and Technology M
- Physics M,D
- Plant Sciences M

FLORIDA ATLANTIC UNIVERSITY

- Applied Mathematics M,D
- Chemistry M,D
- Environmental Management and Policy M,O
- Environmental Sciences M
- Geology M
- Geosciences M,D
- Mathematics M,D
- Physics M,D
- Statistics M,D

FLORIDA GULF COAST UNIVERSITY

- Environmental Management and Policy M
- Environmental Sciences M

FLORIDA INSTITUTE OF TECHNOLOGY

- Applied Mathematics M,D
- Chemistry M,D
- Environmental Management and Policy M,D
- Environmental Sciences M,D*
- Marine Affairs M,D
- Marine Sciences M,D
- Meteorology M,D
- Oceanography M,D*
- Physics M,D
- Planetary and Space Sciences M,D

FLORIDA INTERNATIONAL UNIVERSITY

- Biostatistics M,D
- Chemistry M,D
- Environmental Management and Policy M
- Environmental Sciences M
- Geosciences M,D
- Mathematics M
- Physics M,D
- Statistics M

FLORIDA STATE UNIVERSITY

- Analytical Chemistry M,D
- Applied Mathematics M,D
- Applied Statistics M,D
- Biostatistics M,D
- Chemistry M,D
- Food Science and Technology M,D
- Geology M,D

Geophysics	D
Inorganic Chemistry	M,D
Mathematical and Computational Finance	M,D
Mathematics	M,D
Meteorology	M,D
Oceanography	M,D
Organic Chemistry	M,D
Physical Chemistry	M,D
Physics	M,D
Statistics	M,D,O

FORT HAYS STATE UNIVERSITY

Geology	M
Geosciences	M

FORT VALLEY STATE UNIVERSITY

Animal Sciences	M

FRAMINGHAM STATE COLLEGE

Food Science and Technology	M

FROSTBURG STATE UNIVERSITY

Fish, Game, and Wildlife Management	M

FURMAN UNIVERSITY

Chemistry	M

GANNON UNIVERSITY

Environmental Sciences	M,O

GEORGE MASON UNIVERSITY

Applied Physics	M
Atmospheric Sciences	D
Biostatistics	M,D,O
Chemistry	M
Computational Sciences	M,D,O
Environmental Sciences	M,D
Geodetic Sciences	M,D,O
Mathematics	M,D
Physics	M
Statistics	M,D,O

GEORGETOWN UNIVERSITY

Analytical Chemistry	D
Biostatistics	M
Chemistry	D
Inorganic Chemistry	D
Mathematics	M
Organic Chemistry	D
Physical Chemistry	D
Statistics	M
Theoretical Chemistry	D

THE GEORGE WASHINGTON UNIVERSITY

Analytical Chemistry	M,D
Applied Mathematics	M,D
Biostatistics	M,D
Chemistry	M,D
Environmental Management and Policy	M,D
Inorganic Chemistry	M,D
Mathematics	M,D
Organic Chemistry	M,D
Physical Chemistry	M,D
Physics	M,D
Statistics	M,D,O

GEORGIA INSTITUTE OF TECHNOLOGY

Applied Mathematics	M,D
Atmospheric Sciences	M,D
Chemistry	M,D
Environmental Management and Policy	M,D
Environmental Sciences	M,D
Geochemistry	M,D
Geophysics	M,D
Geosciences	M,D
Marine Sciences	M,D
Mathematical and Computational Finance	M,D
Mathematics	M,D
Meteorology	M,D
Natural Resources	M,D
Oceanography	M,D
Physics	M,D
Planetary and Space Sciences	M,D
Statistics	M,D

GEORGIAN COURT UNIVERSITY

Mathematics	M,O

GEORGIA SOUTHERN UNIVERSITY

Biostatistics	M,D
Mathematics	M

GEORGIA STATE UNIVERSITY

Astronomy	D
Chemistry	M,D
Geology	M
Geosciences	M,O
Hydrogeology	M,O
Mathematics	M,D
Physics	M,D
Statistics	M,D

GODDARD COLLEGE

Environmental Management and Policy	M

GOVERNORS STATE UNIVERSITY

Analytical Chemistry	M

GRADUATE SCHOOL AND UNIVERSITY CENTER OF THE CITY UNIVERSITY OF NEW YORK

Chemistry	D
Environmental Sciences	D
Geosciences	D
Mathematics	D
Physics	D

GRAND VALLEY STATE UNIVERSITY

Biostatistics	M

GREEN MOUNTAIN COLLEGE

Environmental Management and Policy	M

HAMPTON UNIVERSITY

Applied Mathematics	M
Atmospheric Sciences	M,D
Chemistry	M
Computational Sciences	M
Physics	M,D
Statistics	M

HARDIN-SIMMONS UNIVERSITY

Environmental Management and Policy	M
Mathematics	M,D

HARVARD UNIVERSITY

Applied Mathematics	M,D
Applied Physics	M,D
Astronomy	D
Astrophysics	D
Biostatistics	M,D
Chemical Physics	D
Chemistry	D*
Environmental Management and Policy	M,O
Environmental Sciences	M
Forestry	M
Geosciences	M,D
Inorganic Chemistry	D
Mathematics	D
Organic Chemistry	D
Physical Chemistry	D
Physics	D
Planetary and Space Sciences	M,D
Statistics	M,D
Theoretical Physics	D

HAWAI'I PACIFIC UNIVERSITY

Marine Sciences	M

HOFSTRA UNIVERSITY

Applied Mathematics	M
Mathematics	M

HOWARD UNIVERSITY

Analytical Chemistry	M,D
Applied Mathematics	M,D
Atmospheric Sciences	M,D
Chemistry	M,D
Environmental Sciences	M,D
Inorganic Chemistry	M,D
Mathematics	M,D
Organic Chemistry	M,D
Physical Chemistry	M,D
Physics	M,D

HUMBOLDT STATE UNIVERSITY

Environmental Management and Policy	M
Environmental Sciences	M
Fish, Game, and Wildlife Management	M
Forestry	M
Geology	M
Natural Resources	M
Water Resources	M

HUNTER COLLEGE OF THE CITY UNIVERSITY OF NEW YORK

Applied Mathematics	M
Biostatistics	M
Chemistry	M,D
Environmental Sciences	M,O
Geosciences	M,O
Mathematics	M
Physics	M,D

ICR GRADUATE SCHOOL

Astrophysics	M
Geology	M
Geophysics	M

IDAHO STATE UNIVERSITY

Applied Physics	M,D
Chemistry	M
Environmental Management and Policy	M
Environmental Sciences	M,O
Geology	M,O
Geophysics	M,O
Geosciences	M,O
Hydrology	M,O
Mathematics	M,D
Physics	M,D

ILLINOIS INSTITUTE OF TECHNOLOGY

Analytical Chemistry	M,D
Applied Mathematics	M,D
Chemistry	M,D
Environmental Management and Policy	M
Food Science and Technology	M
Mathematical and Computational Finance	M
Physics	M,D

ILLINOIS STATE UNIVERSITY

Agricultural Sciences—General	M
Chemistry	M
Hydrogeology	M
Hydrology	M
Mathematics	M
Plant Sciences	M,D

INDIANA STATE UNIVERSITY

Mathematics	M

INDIANA UNIVERSITY BLOOMINGTON

Analytical Chemistry	M,D
Applied Mathematics	M,D
Astronomy	M,D
Astrophysics	M,D
Chemistry	M,D
Environmental Management and Policy	M,D,O
Environmental Sciences	M,D*
Geochemistry	M,D
Geology	M,D
Geophysics	M,D
Geosciences	M,D
Hydrogeology	M,D
Inorganic Chemistry	M,D
Mathematics	M,D
Mineralogy	M,D
Physical Chemistry	M,D
Physics	M,D
Statistics	M,D

INDIANA UNIVERSITY NORTHWEST

Environmental Sciences	M,O

INDIANA UNIVERSITY OF PENNSYLVANIA

Applied Mathematics	M
Chemistry	M
Mathematics	M
Physics	M

INDIANA UNIVERSITY–PURDUE UNIVERSITY FORT WAYNE

Applied Mathematics	M,O
Applied Statistics	M,O
Mathematics	M,O

INDIANA UNIVERSITY–PURDUE UNIVERSITY INDIANAPOLIS

Applied Mathematics	M,D
Applied Statistics	M
Chemistry	M,D
Environmental Management and Policy	M
Geology	M
Mathematics	M,D
Physics	M,D

INDIANA UNIVERSITY SOUTH BEND

Applied Mathematics	M

INSTITUTO TECNOLOGICO DE SANTO DOMINGO

Environmental Sciences	M
Food Science and Technology	M
Mathematics	M

INSTITUTO TECNOLÓGICO Y DE ESTUDIOS SUPERIORES DE MONTERREY, CAMPUS CIUDAD DE MÉXICO

Environmental Sciences	M,D

INSTITUTO TECNOLÓGICO Y DE ESTUDIOS SUPERIORES DE MONTERREY, CAMPUS ESTADO DE MÉXICO

Environmental Management and Policy	M,D

INSTITUTO TECNOLÓGICO Y DE ESTUDIOS SUPERIORES DE MONTERREY, CAMPUS IRAPUATO

Environmental Management and Policy	M,D

*M—master's degree; P—first professional degree; D—doctorate; O—other advanced degree; *—Close-Up and/or Display*

INSTITUTO TECNOLÓGICO Y DE ESTUDIOS SUPERIORES DE MONTERREY, CAMPUS MONTERREY

Agricultural Sciences—General	M,D
Applied Statistics	M,D
Chemistry	M,D
Organic Chemistry	M,D

INTER AMERICAN UNIVERSITY OF PUERTO RICO, METROPOLITAN CAMPUS

Environmental Management and Policy	M

INTER AMERICAN UNIVERSITY OF PUERTO RICO, SAN GERMÁN CAMPUS

Applied Mathematics	M
Environmental Sciences	M
Water Resources	M

IOWA STATE UNIVERSITY OF SCIENCE AND TECHNOLOGY

Agricultural Sciences—General	M,D
Agronomy and Soil Sciences	M,D
Animal Sciences	M,D
Applied Mathematics	M,D
Applied Physics	M,D
Astronomy	M,D
Astrophysics	M,D
Biostatistics	M,D
Chemistry	M,D
Condensed Matter Physics	M,D
Environmental Sciences	M,D
Fish, Game, and Wildlife Management	M,D
Food Science and Technology	M,D
Forestry	M,D
Geology	M,D
Geosciences	M,D
Horticulture	M,D
Mathematics	M,D
Meteorology	M,D
Natural Resources	M,D
Physics	M,D
Statistics	M,D

JACKSON STATE UNIVERSITY

Chemistry	M,D
Environmental Sciences	M,D
Mathematics	M

JACKSONVILLE STATE UNIVERSITY

Mathematics	M

JAMES MADISON UNIVERSITY

Mathematics	M
Statistics	M

JOHN CARROLL UNIVERSITY

Mathematics	M

THE JOHNS HOPKINS UNIVERSITY

Applied Mathematics	M,D,O
Applied Physics	M,O
Astronomy	D
Biostatistics	M,D
Chemistry	D
Environmental Management and Policy	M,O
Environmental Sciences	M
Geosciences	M,D
Mathematical and Computational Finance	M,D
Mathematics	D
Physics	D*
Statistics	M,D

KANSAS STATE UNIVERSITY

Agricultural Sciences—General	M,D
Agronomy and Soil Sciences	M,D
Analytical Chemistry	M,D
Animal Sciences	M,D
Chemistry	M,D
Food Science and Technology	M,D
Geology	M
Horticulture	M,D
Inorganic Chemistry	M,D
Mathematics	M,D
Organic Chemistry	M,D
Physical Chemistry	M,D
Range Science	M,D
Statistics	M,D

KEAN UNIVERSITY

Computational Sciences	M
Environmental Management and Policy	M
Mathematics	M
Statistics	M

KENNESAW STATE UNIVERSITY

Applied Statistics	M

KENT STATE UNIVERSITY

Analytical Chemistry	M,D
Applied Mathematics	M,D
Chemical Physics	M,D
Chemistry	M,D*
Geology	M,D
Inorganic Chemistry	M,D
Mathematics	M,D
Organic Chemistry	M,D
Physical Chemistry	M,D
Physics	M,D

KENTUCKY STATE UNIVERSITY

Aquaculture	M

LAKEHEAD UNIVERSITY

Chemistry	M
Forestry	M,D
Geology	M
Mathematics	M
Physics	M

LAMAR UNIVERSITY

Chemistry	M
Environmental Management and Policy	M,D
Mathematics	M

LAURENTIAN UNIVERSITY

Analytical Chemistry	M
Applied Physics	M
Chemistry	M
Environmental Sciences	M
Geology	M,D
Natural Resources	M,D
Organic Chemistry	M
Physical Chemistry	M
Theoretical Chemistry	M

LEHIGH UNIVERSITY

Applied Mathematics	M,D
Chemistry	M,D
Computational Sciences	M,D
Environmental Management and Policy	M
Environmental Sciences	M,D
Geology	M,D
Geosciences	M,D
Mathematics	M,D
Photonics	M,D
Physics	M,D
Statistics	M,D

LEHMAN COLLEGE OF THE CITY UNIVERSITY OF NEW YORK

Mathematics	M
Plant Sciences	D

LOMA LINDA UNIVERSITY

Biostatistics	M,D,O
Geosciences	M,D

LONG ISLAND UNIVERSITY, BROOKLYN CAMPUS

Chemistry	M

LONG ISLAND UNIVERSITY, C.W. POST CAMPUS

Applied Mathematics	M
Environmental Management and Policy	M
Geosciences	M
Mathematics	M

LOUISIANA STATE UNIVERSITY AND AGRICULTURAL AND MECHANICAL COLLEGE

Agricultural Sciences—General	M,D
Agronomy and Soil Sciences	M,D
Animal Sciences	M,D
Applied Statistics	M
Astronomy	M,D
Astrophysics	M,D
Chemistry	M,D
Environmental Management and Policy	M
Environmental Sciences	M,D
Fish, Game, and Wildlife Management	M,D
Food Science and Technology	M,D
Forestry	M,D
Geology	M,D
Geophysics	M,D
Horticulture	M,D
Marine Affairs	M,D
Mathematics	M,D
Natural Resources	M,D
Oceanography	M,D
Physics	M,D
Statistics	M

LOUISIANA STATE UNIVERSITY HEALTH SCIENCES CENTER

Biostatistics	M,D

LOUISIANA TECH UNIVERSITY

Chemistry	M
Computational Sciences	M,D
Mathematics	M
Physics	M,D
Statistics	M

LOYOLA MARYMOUNT UNIVERSITY

Environmental Sciences	M

LOYOLA UNIVERSITY CHICAGO

Applied Statistics	M
Chemistry	M,D
Mathematics	M
Statistics	M

MARQUETTE UNIVERSITY

Analytical Chemistry	M,D
Chemical Physics	M,D
Chemistry	M,D
Computational Sciences	M,D
Inorganic Chemistry	M,D
Mathematics	M,D
Organic Chemistry	M,D
Physical Chemistry	M,D

MARSHALL UNIVERSITY

Chemistry	M
Environmental Sciences	M
Mathematics	M
Physics	M

MARYLHURST UNIVERSITY

Environmental Management and Policy	M
Natural Resources	M

MASSACHUSETTS COLLEGE OF PHARMACY AND HEALTH SCIENCES

Chemistry	M,D
Organic Chemistry	M

MASSACHUSETTS INSTITUTE OF TECHNOLOGY

Atmospheric Sciences	M,D
Chemistry	D
Computational Sciences	M
Environmental Sciences	M,D,O
Geochemistry	M,D
Geology	M,D
Geophysics	M,D
Geosciences	M,D
Hydrology	M,D,O
Inorganic Chemistry	D
Marine Geology	M,D
Mathematics	D
Oceanography	M,D,O
Organic Chemistry	M,D,O
Physical Chemistry	D
Physics	M,D
Planetary and Space Sciences	M,D

MCGILL UNIVERSITY

Agricultural Sciences—General	M,D,O
Agronomy and Soil Sciences	M,D
Animal Sciences	M,D
Applied Mathematics	M,D
Atmospheric Sciences	M,D
Biostatistics	M,D,O
Chemistry	M,D
Computational Sciences	M,D
Environmental Management and Policy	M,D
Fish, Game, and Wildlife Management	M,D
Food Science and Technology	M,D
Forestry	M,D
Geosciences	M,D
Mathematics	M,D
Meteorology	M,D
Natural Resources	M,D
Oceanography	M,D
Physics	M,D
Planetary and Space Sciences	M,D
Plant Sciences	M,D,O
Statistics	M,D,O

MCMASTER UNIVERSITY

Analytical Chemistry	M,D
Applied Statistics	M
Astrophysics	D
Chemical Physics	M,D
Chemistry	M,D
Geochemistry	M,D
Geology	M,D
Geosciences	M,D
Inorganic Chemistry	M,D
Mathematics	M,D
Organic Chemistry	M,D
Physical Chemistry	M,D
Physics	D
Statistics	M

MCNEESE STATE UNIVERSITY

Agricultural Sciences—General	M
Chemistry	M
Mathematics	M
Statistics	M

MEDICAL COLLEGE OF GEORGIA
Biostatistics M,D

MEDICAL COLLEGE OF WISCONSIN
Biostatistics D*

MEDICAL UNIVERSITY OF SOUTH CAROLINA
Biostatistics M,D
Marine Sciences D

MEMORIAL UNIVERSITY OF NEWFOUNDLAND
Aquaculture M
Chemistry M,D
Computational Sciences M
Condensed Matter Physics M,D
Environmental Sciences M
Fish, Game, and Wildlife Management M,O
Food Science and Technology M,D
Geology M,D
Geophysics M,D
Geosciences M,D
Marine Affairs M,D,O
Marine Sciences M,O
Mathematics M,D
Oceanography M,D
Physics M,D
Statistics M,D

MERCER UNIVERSITY
Environmental Sciences M

MIAMI UNIVERSITY
Chemistry M,D
Computational Sciences M
Environmental Sciences M
Geology M,D
Mathematics M
Physics M
Plant Sciences M,D
Statistics M

MICHIGAN STATE UNIVERSITY
Agricultural Sciences—General M,D
Agronomy and Soil Sciences M,D
Animal Sciences M,D
Applied Mathematics M,D
Applied Statistics M,D
Astronomy M,D
Astrophysics M,D
Chemical Physics M,D
Chemistry M,D
Environmental Sciences M,D
Fish, Game, and Wildlife Management M,D
Food Science and Technology M,D
Forestry M,D
Geosciences M,D
Horticulture M,D
Mathematics M,D
Natural Resources M,D
Physics M,D
Plant Sciences M,D
Statistics M,D

MICHIGAN TECHNOLOGICAL UNIVERSITY
Atmospheric Sciences D
Chemistry M,D
Computational Sciences D
Environmental Management and Policy M
Forestry M,D
Geology M,D
Geophysics M
Mathematics M,D
Physics M,D

MIDDLE TENNESSEE STATE UNIVERSITY
Biostatistics M
Chemistry M,D
Food Science and Technology M
Geosciences O
Mathematics M

MINNESOTA STATE UNIVERSITY MANKATO
Astronomy M
Environmental Sciences M
Mathematics M
Physics M
Statistics M

MISSISSIPPI COLLEGE
Chemistry M
Mathematics M

MISSISSIPPI STATE UNIVERSITY
Agricultural Sciences—General M,D
Agronomy and Soil Sciences M,D
Animal Sciences M,D
Applied Physics M,D
Atmospheric Sciences M,D
Chemistry M,D
Fish, Game, and Wildlife Management M,D
Food Science and Technology M,D
Forestry M,D
Geosciences M,D
Horticulture M,D
Mathematics M,D
Physics M,D
Plant Sciences M,D
Statistics M,D

MISSOURI STATE UNIVERSITY
Agricultural Sciences—General M
Chemistry M
Environmental Management and Policy M
Geology M
Geosciences M
Mathematics M
Natural Resources M
Plant Sciences M

MISSOURI UNIVERSITY OF SCIENCE AND TECHNOLOGY
Applied Mathematics M,D
Chemistry M,D
Geochemistry M,D
Geology M,D
Geophysics M,D
Hydrology M,D
Mathematics M,D
Physics M,D
Statistics M,D
Water Resources M,D

MONMOUTH UNIVERSITY
Mathematical and Computational Finance M

MONTANA STATE UNIVERSITY
Agricultural Sciences—General M,D
Animal Sciences M,D
Chemistry M,D
Environmental Sciences M,D
Fish, Game, and Wildlife Management M,D
Geosciences M,D
Mathematics M,D
Natural Resources M
Physics M,D
Plant Sciences M,D
Range Science M,D
Statistics M,D

MONTANA TECH OF THE UNIVERSITY OF MONTANA
Geochemistry M
Geology M
Geosciences M
Hydrogeology M

MONTCLAIR STATE UNIVERSITY
Applied Mathematics M,D,O
Applied Statistics M,O
Chemistry M
Environmental Management and Policy M,D
Environmental Sciences M,D,O
Food Science and Technology M,O
Geosciences M,D,O
Mathematics M,D,O
Statistics M,D,O
Water Resources M,D,O

MONTEREY INSTITUTE OF INTERNATIONAL STUDIES
Environmental Management and Policy M

MOREHEAD STATE UNIVERSITY
Agricultural Sciences—General M
Environmental Management and Policy M

MORGAN STATE UNIVERSITY
Chemistry M
Mathematics M

MOUNT ALLISON UNIVERSITY
Chemistry M

MURRAY STATE UNIVERSITY
Agricultural Sciences—General M
Chemistry M
Environmental Sciences M
Geosciences M
Hydrology M
Mathematics M
Statistics M

NAROPA UNIVERSITY
Environmental Management and Policy M

NAVAL POSTGRADUATE SCHOOL
Applied Mathematics M,D
Applied Physics M,D
Mathematics M,D
Meteorology M,D
Oceanography M,D
Physics M,D

NEW JERSEY INSTITUTE OF TECHNOLOGY
Applied Mathematics M
Applied Physics M,D
Applied Statistics M
Biostatistics M
Chemistry M,D
Environmental Management and Policy M
Environmental Sciences M,D
Mathematics D

NEW MEXICO HIGHLANDS UNIVERSITY
Chemistry M
Fish, Game, and Wildlife Management M

NEW MEXICO INSTITUTE OF MINING AND TECHNOLOGY
Applied Mathematics M,D
Astrophysics M,D
Atmospheric Sciences M,D
Chemistry M,D
Environmental Sciences M,D
Geochemistry M,D
Geology M,D
Geophysics M,D
Geosciences M,D
Hydrology M,D
Mathematical Physics M,D
Mathematics M,D
Physics M,D

NEW MEXICO STATE UNIVERSITY
Agricultural Sciences—General M
Animal Sciences M,D
Applied Statistics M,D
Astronomy M,D
Chemistry M,D
Environmental Sciences M,D
Fish, Game, and Wildlife Management M
Geology M
Horticulture M,D
Mathematics M,D
Physics M,D
Plant Sciences M,D
Range Science M,D

NEW YORK INSTITUTE OF TECHNOLOGY
Environmental Management and Policy M,O

NEW YORK UNIVERSITY
Chemistry M,D
Environmental Management and Policy M
Food Science and Technology M,D
Mathematical and Computational Finance M,D
Mathematics M,D
Physics M,D
Statistics M,D

NICHOLLS STATE UNIVERSITY
Mathematics M

NORFOLK STATE UNIVERSITY
Optical Sciences M

NORTH CAROLINA AGRICULTURAL AND TECHNICAL STATE UNIVERSITY
Agricultural Sciences—General M
Agronomy and Soil Sciences M
Animal Sciences M
Chemistry M
Environmental Sciences M
Optical Sciences M,D
Plant Sciences M

NORTH CAROLINA CENTRAL UNIVERSITY
Applied Mathematics M
Chemistry M
Geosciences M
Mathematics M
Physics M

NORTH CAROLINA STATE UNIVERSITY
Agricultural Sciences—General M,D,O
Agronomy and Soil Sciences M,D
Animal Sciences M,D

*M—master's degree; P—first professional degree; D—doctorate; O—other advanced degree; *—Close-Up and/or Display*

Applied Mathematics M,D
Atmospheric Sciences M,D
Biomathematics M,D
Chemistry M,D
Fish, Game, and Wildlife Management M,D
Food Science and Technology M,D
Forestry M,D
Geosciences M,D
Horticulture M,D,O
Marine Sciences M,D
Mathematical and Computational Finance M
Mathematics M,D
Meteorology M,D
Natural Resources M,D
Oceanography M,D
Physics M,D
Statistics M,D

NORTH DAKOTA STATE UNIVERSITY

Agricultural Sciences—General M,D
Agronomy and Soil Sciences M,D
Animal Sciences M,D
Applied Mathematics M,D
Applied Statistics M,D,O
Chemistry M,D
Environmental Sciences M,D
Food Science and Technology M,D
Mathematics M,D
Natural Resources M,D
Physics M,D
Plant Sciences M,D
Range Science M,D
Statistics M,D,O

NORTHEASTERN ILLINOIS UNIVERSITY

Chemistry M
Environmental Management and Policy M
Geosciences M
Mathematics M

NORTHEASTERN UNIVERSITY

Analytical Chemistry M,D
Applied Mathematics M,D
Chemistry M,D
Inorganic Chemistry M,D
Mathematics M,D
Organic Chemistry M,D
Physical Chemistry M,D
Physics M,D*

NORTHERN ARIZONA UNIVERSITY

Applied Physics M
Atmospheric Sciences M
Chemistry M
Environmental Management and Policy M
Environmental Sciences M
Forestry M,D
Geology M
Mathematics M
Meteorology M
Physics M
Statistics M

NORTHERN ILLINOIS UNIVERSITY

Chemistry M,D
Geology M,D
Mathematics M,D
Physics M,D
Statistics M

NORTHWESTERN UNIVERSITY

Applied Mathematics M,D
Astronomy M,D
Astrophysics M,D
Chemistry D
Computational Sciences M
Geology M,D
Geosciences M,D*
Mathematics D
Physics M,D
Statistics M,D

NORTHWEST MISSOURI STATE UNIVERSITY

Agricultural Sciences—General M

NOVA SCOTIA AGRICULTURAL COLLEGE

Agricultural Sciences—General M
Agronomy and Soil Sciences M
Animal Sciences M
Aquaculture M
Environmental Management and Policy M
Environmental Sciences M
Food Science and Technology M
Horticulture M
Water Resources M

NOVA SOUTHEASTERN UNIVERSITY

Environmental Sciences M
Marine Affairs M
Marine Sciences M
Oceanography M,D

OAKLAND UNIVERSITY

Applied Mathematics M,D
Applied Statistics M
Chemistry M,D
Environmental Sciences M,D
Mathematics M
Physics M,D
Statistics O

OGI SCHOOL OF SCIENCE & ENGINEERING AT OREGON HEALTH & SCIENCE UNIVERSITY

Environmental Sciences M,D

THE OHIO STATE UNIVERSITY

Agricultural Sciences—General M,D
Agronomy and Soil Sciences M,D
Animal Sciences M,D
Astronomy M,D
Atmospheric Sciences M,D
Biostatistics D
Chemical Physics M,D
Chemistry M,D
Environmental Sciences M,D
Food Science and Technology M,D
Geodetic Sciences M,D
Geology M,D
Horticulture M,D
Mathematics M,D
Natural Resources M,D
Optical Sciences M,D
Physics M,D
Statistics M,D

OHIO UNIVERSITY

Astronomy M,D
Environmental Management and Policy M
Geochemistry M
Geology M
Geophysics M
Hydrogeology M
Mathematics M,D
Physics M,D*

OKLAHOMA STATE UNIVERSITY

Agricultural Sciences—General M,D
Agronomy and Soil Sciences M,D
Animal Sciences M,D
Chemistry M,D
Environmental Sciences M,D,O
Food Science and Technology M,D
Forestry M,D
Geology M,D
Horticulture M,D
Mathematics M,D*
Natural Resources M,D
Photonics M,D,O
Physics M,D
Plant Sciences M,D,O
Statistics M,D

OLD DOMINION UNIVERSITY

Analytical Chemistry M,D
Chemistry M,D
Marine Affairs M
Mathematics M,D
Oceanography M,D
Organic Chemistry M,D
Physical Chemistry M,D
Physics M,D

OREGON HEALTH & SCIENCE UNIVERSITY

Biostatistics M
Environmental Sciences M,D

OREGON STATE UNIVERSITY

Agricultural Sciences—General M,D
Agronomy and Soil Sciences M,D
Analytical Chemistry M,D
Animal Sciences M,D
Applied Physics M,D
Atmospheric Sciences M,D
Chemistry M,D
Environmental Sciences M,D
Fish, Game, and Wildlife Management M,D
Food Science and Technology M,D
Forestry M,D
Geology M,D
Geophysics M,D
Geosciences M,D
Horticulture M,D
Inorganic Chemistry M,D
Marine Affairs M
Marine Sciences M
Mathematics M,D
Oceanography M,D
Organic Chemistry M,D
Physical Chemistry M,D
Physics M,D
Range Science M,D
Statistics M,D

PACE UNIVERSITY

Environmental Management and Policy M
Environmental Sciences M

PENN STATE HARRISBURG

Environmental Sciences M

PENN STATE UNIVERSITY PARK

Acoustics M,D
Agricultural Sciences—General M,D,O
Agronomy and Soil Sciences M,D
Animal Sciences M,D
Applied Mathematics M,D
Astronomy M,D
Astrophysics M,D
Chemistry M,D
Environmental Management and Policy M
Environmental Sciences M
Food Science and Technology M,D
Forestry M,D
Geochemistry M,D
Geosciences M,D
Horticulture M,D
Mathematics M,D
Meteorology M,D
Natural Resources M,D
Physics M,D
Statistics M,D

PITTSBURG STATE UNIVERSITY

Applied Physics M
Chemistry M
Mathematics M
Physics M

PLYMOUTH STATE UNIVERSITY

Environmental Management and Policy M
Meteorology M

POLYTECHNIC INSTITUTE OF NYU

Chemistry M,D
Environmental Sciences M
Mathematical and Computational Finance M,O
Mathematics M,D
Physics M,D

POLYTECHNIC INSTITUTE OF NYU, LONG ISLAND GRADUATE CENTER

Chemistry M

POLYTECHNIC INSTITUTE OF NYU, WESTCHESTER GRADUATE CENTER

Chemistry M
Mathematical and Computational Finance M,O

POLYTECHNIC UNIVERSITY OF PUERTO RICO

Environmental Management and Policy M

PONTIFICAL CATHOLIC UNIVERSITY OF PUERTO RICO

Chemistry M
Environmental Sciences M

PONTIFICIA UNIVERSIDAD CATOLICA MADRE Y MAESTRA

Environmental Management and Policy M

PORTLAND STATE UNIVERSITY

Chemistry M,D
Environmental Management and Policy M,D
Environmental Sciences M,D
Geology M,D
Mathematics M,D,O
Physics M,D
Statistics M,D

PRAIRIE VIEW A&M UNIVERSITY

Agricultural Sciences—General M
Agronomy and Soil Sciences M
Animal Sciences M
Chemistry M
Mathematics M

PRESCOTT COLLEGE

Environmental Management and Policy M

PRINCETON UNIVERSITY

Applied Mathematics D
Astronomy D
Astrophysics D
Atmospheric Sciences D
Chemistry M,D*

Computational Sciences	D
Geosciences	D
Mathematics	D
Oceanography	D
Photonics	D
Physics	D
Plasma Physics	D

PURDUE UNIVERSITY

Agricultural Sciences—General	M,D
Agronomy and Soil Sciences	M,D
Analytical Chemistry	M,D
Animal Sciences	M,D
Aquaculture	M,D
Atmospheric Sciences	M,D
Chemistry	M,D
Environmental Management and Policy	M,D
Fish, Game, and Wildlife Management	M,D
Food Science and Technology	M,D
Forestry	M,D
Geosciences	M,D
Horticulture	M,D
Inorganic Chemistry	M,D
Mathematics	M,D
Natural Resources	M,D
Organic Chemistry	M,D
Physical Chemistry	M,D
Physics	M,D
Statistics	M,D,O

PURDUE UNIVERSITY CALUMET

Mathematics	M

QUEENS COLLEGE OF THE CITY UNIVERSITY OF NEW YORK

Chemistry	M
Environmental Sciences	M
Geology	M
Mathematics	M
Physics	M,D

QUEEN'S UNIVERSITY AT KINGSTON

Chemistry	M,D
Geology	M,D
Mathematics	M,D
Physics	M,D
Statistics	M,D

RENSSELAER POLYTECHNIC INSTITUTE

Acoustics	M
Analytical Chemistry	M,D
Applied Mathematics	M
Applied Physics	M,D
Astronomy	M
Astrophysics	M,D
Chemistry	M,D
Environmental Management and Policy	D
Environmental Sciences	M,D
Geochemistry	M,D
Geology	M,D
Geophysics	M,D
Geosciences	M,D
Inorganic Chemistry	M,D
Mathematics	M,D
Organic Chemistry	M,D
Physical Chemistry	M,D
Physics	M,D

RHODE ISLAND COLLEGE

Mathematics	M

RICE UNIVERSITY

Applied Mathematics	M,D
Applied Physics	M,D
Astronomy	M,D
Biostatistics	M,D
Chemistry	M,D
Computational Sciences	M,D
Environmental Management and Policy	M
Environmental Sciences	M,D
Geophysics	M
Geosciences	M,D
Inorganic Chemistry	M,D
Mathematical and Computational Finance	M,D
Mathematics	D
Organic Chemistry	M,D
Physical Chemistry	M,D
Physics	M,D
Statistics	M,D

RIVIER COLLEGE

Mathematics	M

ROCHESTER INSTITUTE OF TECHNOLOGY

Applied Mathematics	M
Applied Statistics	M,O
Astrophysics	M,D
Chemistry	M
Environmental Management and Policy	M
Environmental Sciences	M
Optical Sciences	M,D
Statistics	M,O

ROOSEVELT UNIVERSITY

Chemistry	M
Mathematics	M

ROSE-HULMAN INSTITUTE OF TECHNOLOGY

Optical Sciences	M

ROWAN UNIVERSITY

Mathematics	M

ROYAL MILITARY COLLEGE OF CANADA

Chemistry	M,D
Environmental Sciences	M,D
Mathematics	M
Physics	M

ROYAL ROADS UNIVERSITY

Environmental Management and Policy	M,O

RUTGERS, THE STATE UNIVERSITY OF NEW JERSEY, CAMDEN

Chemistry	M
Mathematics	M

RUTGERS, THE STATE UNIVERSITY OF NEW JERSEY, NEWARK

Analytical Chemistry	M,D
Applied Physics	M,D
Chemistry	M,D
Environmental Sciences	M,D
Geology	M
Inorganic Chemistry	M,D
Mathematics	D
Organic Chemistry	M,D
Physical Chemistry	M,D

RUTGERS, THE STATE UNIVERSITY OF NEW JERSEY, NEW BRUNSWICK

Animal Sciences	M,D
Applied Mathematics	M,D
Applied Statistics	M,D
Astronomy	M,D
Atmospheric Sciences	M,D
Biostatistics	M,D
Chemistry	M,D
Condensed Matter Physics	M,D
Environmental Sciences	M,D
Food Science and Technology	M,D
Geology	M,D
Horticulture	M,D
Inorganic Chemistry	M,D
Mathematics	M,D
Oceanography	M,D
Organic Chemistry	M,D
Physical Chemistry	M,D
Physics	M,D
Statistics	M,D
Theoretical Physics	M,D
Water Resources	M,D

SACRED HEART UNIVERSITY

Chemistry	M

ST. CLOUD STATE UNIVERSITY

Applied Statistics	M
Environmental Management and Policy	M
Mathematics	M

ST. FRANCIS XAVIER UNIVERSITY

Chemistry	M
Geology	M
Geosciences	M
Physics	M

ST. JOHN'S UNIVERSITY (NY)

Applied Mathematics	M
Chemistry	M
Mathematics	M
Statistics	M

SAINT JOSEPH COLLEGE

Chemistry	M

SAINT JOSEPH'S UNIVERSITY

Mathematics	M,O

SAINT LOUIS UNIVERSITY

Chemistry	M,D
Geophysics	M,D
Geosciences	M,D
Mathematics	M,D
Meteorology	M,D

SAINT MARY-OF-THE-WOODS COLLEGE

Environmental Management and Policy	M

SAINT MARY'S UNIVERSITY (CANADA)

Astronomy	M,D

ST. THOMAS UNIVERSITY

Geosciences	M,D,O
Planetary and Space Sciences	M,D,O

SAINT XAVIER UNIVERSITY

Mathematics	M

SALEM STATE COLLEGE

Mathematics	M

SAMFORD UNIVERSITY

Environmental Management and Policy	M

SAM HOUSTON STATE UNIVERSITY

Agricultural Sciences—General	M
Chemistry	M
Computational Sciences	M
Mathematics	M
Statistics	M

SAN DIEGO STATE UNIVERSITY

Applied Mathematics	M
Astronomy	M
Biometry	M
Biostatistics	M,D
Chemistry	M,D
Computational Sciences	M,D
Geology	M
Mathematics	M,D
Physics	M
Statistics	M

SAN FRANCISCO STATE UNIVERSITY

Chemistry	M
Environmental Management and Policy	M
Geosciences	M
Marine Sciences	M
Mathematics	M
Natural Resources	M
Physics	M

SAN JOSE STATE UNIVERSITY

Applied Mathematics	M
Chemistry	M
Environmental Management and Policy	M
Geology	M
Marine Sciences	M
Mathematics	M
Meteorology	M
Physics	M
Statistics	M

SANTA CLARA UNIVERSITY

Applied Mathematics	M

SAVANNAH STATE UNIVERSITY

Marine Sciences	M

THE SCRIPPS RESEARCH INSTITUTE

Chemistry	D

SETON HALL UNIVERSITY

Analytical Chemistry	M,D
Chemistry	M,D
Inorganic Chemistry	M,D
Organic Chemistry	M,D
Physical Chemistry	M,D

SHIPPENSBURG UNIVERSITY OF PENNSYLVANIA

Environmental Management and Policy	M

SIMON FRASER UNIVERSITY

Applied Mathematics	M,D
Chemical Physics	M,D
Chemistry	M,D
Computational Sciences	M,D
Environmental Management and Policy	M,D
Geosciences	M,D
Mathematics	M,D
Physics	M,D
Statistics	M,D

SLIPPERY ROCK UNIVERSITY OF PENNSYLVANIA

Environmental Management and Policy	M

SMITH COLLEGE

Chemistry	M
Mathematics	O

SOUTH DAKOTA SCHOOL OF MINES AND TECHNOLOGY

Atmospheric Sciences	M,D
Chemistry	M
Environmental Sciences	D

*M—master's degree; P—first professional degree; D—doctorate; O—other advanced degree; *—Close-Up and/or Display*

Geology M,D
Paleontology M
Physics M

SOUTH DAKOTA STATE UNIVERSITY

Agricultural Sciences—General M,D
Agronomy and Soil Sciences M,D
Animal Sciences M,D
Chemistry M,D
Computational Sciences M,D
Fish, Game, and Wildlife Management M,D
Food Science and Technology M,D
Geosciences M,D
Mathematics M,D
Physics M
Plant Sciences M,D
Statistics M,D

SOUTHEAST MISSOURI STATE UNIVERSITY

Chemistry M
Environmental Management and Policy M
Mathematics M

SOUTHERN ARKANSAS UNIVERSITY–MAGNOLIA

Agricultural Sciences—General M

SOUTHERN CONNECTICUT STATE UNIVERSITY

Chemistry M
Mathematics M

SOUTHERN ILLINOIS UNIVERSITY CARBONDALE

Agricultural Sciences—General M
Agronomy and Soil Sciences M
Animal Sciences M
Applied Physics M,D
Chemistry M,D
Environmental Sciences D
Forestry M
Geology M,D
Horticulture M
Mathematics M,D
Physics M,D
Plant Sciences M
Statistics M,D

SOUTHERN ILLINOIS UNIVERSITY EDWARDSVILLE

Chemistry M
Environmental Management and Policy M
Environmental Sciences M
Mathematics M

SOUTHERN METHODIST UNIVERSITY

Applied Mathematics M,D
Chemistry M,D
Computational Sciences M,D
Environmental Sciences M,D
Geology M,D
Geophysics M,D
Mathematics M,D
Physics M,D
Statistics M,D

SOUTHERN UNIVERSITY AND AGRICULTURAL AND MECHANICAL COLLEGE

Agricultural Sciences—General M
Analytical Chemistry M
Chemistry M
Environmental Sciences M
Forestry M
Inorganic Chemistry M
Mathematics M
Organic Chemistry M
Physical Chemistry M
Physics M

STANFORD UNIVERSITY

Applied Physics M,D
Chemistry D
Computational Sciences M,D
Environmental Management and Policy M
Environmental Sciences M,D,O
Geophysics M,D
Geosciences M,D,O
Mathematical and Computational Finance M,D
Mathematics M,D
Physics D
Statistics M,D

STATE UNIVERSITY OF NEW YORK AT BINGHAMTON

Analytical Chemistry M,D
Applied Physics M
Chemistry M,D
Geology M,D
Inorganic Chemistry M,D
Mathematics M,D
Organic Chemistry M,D
Physical Chemistry M,D
Physics M
Statistics M,D

STATE UNIVERSITY OF NEW YORK AT FREDONIA

Chemistry M
Mathematics M

STATE UNIVERSITY OF NEW YORK AT OSWEGO

Chemistry M

STATE UNIVERSITY OF NEW YORK COLLEGE AT CORTLAND

Mathematics M

STATE UNIVERSITY OF NEW YORK COLLEGE AT ONEONTA

Geosciences M

STATE UNIVERSITY OF NEW YORK COLLEGE AT POTSDAM

Mathematics M

STATE UNIVERSITY OF NEW YORK COLLEGE OF ENVIRONMENTAL SCIENCE AND FORESTRY

Chemistry M,D
Environmental Management and Policy M,D
Environmental Sciences M,D
Fish, Game, and Wildlife Management M,D
Forestry M,D
Hydrology M,D
Natural Resources M,D
Organic Chemistry M,D
Plant Sciences M,D
Water Resources M,D

STEPHEN F. AUSTIN STATE UNIVERSITY

Chemistry M
Environmental Sciences M
Forestry M,D
Geology M
Mathematics M
Physics M
Statistics M

STEVENS INSTITUTE OF TECHNOLOGY

Analytical Chemistry M,D,O
Applied Mathematics M
Applied Statistics O
Chemistry M,D,O
Hydrology M,D,O
Marine Affairs M
Mathematics M,D
Organic Chemistry M,D,O
Photonics M,D,O
Physical Chemistry M,D,O
Physics M,D,O
Statistics M,O

STONY BROOK UNIVERSITY, STATE UNIVERSITY OF NEW YORK

Applied Mathematics M,D
Astronomy D
Atmospheric Sciences M,D
Chemistry M,D
Environmental Management and Policy M,O
Geosciences M,D
Marine Sciences M,D
Mathematics M,D
Physics M,D
Statistics M,D

SUL ROSS STATE UNIVERSITY

Animal Sciences M
Fish, Game, and Wildlife Management M
Geology M*
Range Science M

SYRACUSE UNIVERSITY

Applied Statistics M
Chemistry M,D
Environmental Sciences M,D
Geology M,D
Mathematics M,D
Physics M,D

TARLETON STATE UNIVERSITY

Agricultural Sciences—General M
Environmental Sciences M
Mathematics M

TAYLOR UNIVERSITY

Environmental Sciences M

TEACHERS COLLEGE, COLUMBIA UNIVERSITY

Applied Statistics M

TEMPLE UNIVERSITY

Applied Mathematics M,D
Chemistry M,D
Computational Sciences M,D
Geology M
Mathematics M,D
Physics M,D*
Statistics M,D

TENNESSEE STATE UNIVERSITY

Agricultural Sciences—General M
Chemistry M
Mathematics M

TENNESSEE TECHNOLOGICAL UNIVERSITY

Chemistry M,D
Environmental Sciences D
Fish, Game, and Wildlife Management M
Mathematics M

TEXAS A&M INTERNATIONAL UNIVERSITY

Mathematics M
Physics M

TEXAS A&M UNIVERSITY

Agricultural Sciences—General M,D
Agronomy and Soil Sciences M,D
Animal Sciences M,D
Applied Physics M,D
Chemistry M,D
Fish, Game, and Wildlife Management M,D
Food Science and Technology M,D
Forestry M,D
Geology M,D
Geophysics M,D
Horticulture M,D
Mathematics M,D
Meteorology M,D
Natural Resources M,D
Oceanography M,D
Physics M,D
Plant Sciences M,D
Statistics M,D

TEXAS A&M UNIVERSITY AT GALVESTON

Marine Sciences M

TEXAS A&M UNIVERSITY–COMMERCE

Agricultural Sciences—General M
Chemistry M
Geosciences M
Mathematics M
Physics M

TEXAS A&M UNIVERSITY–CORPUS CHRISTI

Applied Mathematics M
Aquaculture M
Environmental Sciences M
Marine Sciences D
Mathematics M

TEXAS A&M UNIVERSITY–KINGSVILLE

Agricultural Sciences—General M,D
Agronomy and Soil Sciences M,D
Animal Sciences M
Chemistry M
Fish, Game, and Wildlife Management M,D
Geology M
Mathematics M
Plant Sciences M,D
Range Science M

TEXAS CHRISTIAN UNIVERSITY

Astrophysics M,D
Chemistry M,D
Environmental Sciences M
Geology M
Mathematics M,D
Physics M,D

TEXAS SOUTHERN UNIVERSITY

Chemistry M
Mathematics M

TEXAS STATE UNIVERSITY–SAN MARCOS

Applied Mathematics M
Chemistry M
Environmental Management and Policy M
Fish, Game, and Wildlife Management M
Mathematics M,D
Physics M

TEXAS TECH UNIVERSITY

Agricultural Sciences—General M,D
Agronomy and Soil Sciences M,D
Animal Sciences M,D

Applied Physics	M,D
Atmospheric Sciences	M,D
Chemistry	M,D
Environmental Management and Policy	D
Environmental Sciences	M,D
Fish, Game, and Wildlife Management	M,D
Food Science and Technology	M,D
Geosciences	M,D
Horticulture	M,D
Mathematics	M,D
Natural Resources	M,D
Physics	M,D
Plant Sciences	M,D
Range Science	M,D
Statistics	M

TEXAS WOMAN'S UNIVERSITY

Chemistry	M
Food Science and Technology	M,D
Mathematics	M

THOMPSON RIVERS UNIVERSITY

Environmental Sciences	M

TOWSON UNIVERSITY

Applied Mathematics	M
Environmental Management and Policy	M
Environmental Sciences	M,O

TRENT UNIVERSITY

Chemistry	M
Environmental Management and Policy	M,D
Physics	M

TROPICAL AGRICULTURE RESEARCH AND HIGHER EDUCATION CENTER

Agricultural Sciences—General	M,D
Environmental Management and Policy	M,D
Forestry	M,D
Water Resources	M,D

TROY UNIVERSITY

Environmental Management and Policy	M

TUFTS UNIVERSITY

Analytical Chemistry	M,D
Biostatistics	M,D
Chemistry	M,D
Environmental Management and Policy	M,D,O
Environmental Sciences	M,D
Inorganic Chemistry	M,D
Mathematics	M,D
Organic Chemistry	M,D
Physical Chemistry	M,D
Physics	M,D

TULANE UNIVERSITY

Applied Mathematics	M,D
Biostatistics	M,D
Chemistry	M,D
Environmental Sciences	M,D
Geology	M,D
Geosciences	M,D
Mathematics	M,D
Physics	D
Statistics	M,D

TUSKEGEE UNIVERSITY

Agronomy and Soil Sciences	M
Animal Sciences	M
Chemistry	M
Environmental Sciences	M
Food Science and Technology	M
Plant Sciences	M

UNIVERSIDAD AUTONOMA DE GUADALAJARA

Environmental Management and Policy	M,D

UNIVERSIDAD DE LAS AMÉRICAS–PUEBLA

Food Science and Technology	M

UNIVERSIDAD DEL TURABO

Chemistry	M,D
Environmental Management and Policy	M,D
Environmental Sciences	M,D

UNIVERSIDAD METROPOLITANA

Environmental Management and Policy	M
Natural Resources	M

UNIVERSITÉ DE MONCTON

Astronomy	M
Chemistry	M
Food Science and Technology	M
Mathematics	M
Physics	M

UNIVERSITÉ DE MONTRÉAL

Chemistry	M,D
Environmental Management and Policy	O
Mathematics	M,D
Physics	M,D
Statistics	M,D

UNIVERSITÉ DE SHERBROOKE

Chemistry	M,D,O
Environmental Sciences	M,O
Mathematics	M,D
Physics	M,D

UNIVERSITÉ DU QUÉBEC À CHICOUTIMI

Environmental Management and Policy	M
Geosciences	M
Mineralogy	D

UNIVERSITÉ DU QUÉBEC À MONTRÉAL

Atmospheric Sciences	M,D,O
Chemistry	M,D
Environmental Sciences	M,D,O
Geology	M,D,O
Geosciences	M,D,O
Mathematics	M,D
Meteorology	M,D,O
Mineralogy	M,D,O
Natural Resources	M,D,O

UNIVERSITÉ DU QUÉBEC À RIMOUSKI

Fish, Game, and Wildlife Management	M,D,O
Marine Affairs	M,O
Oceanography	M,D

UNIVERSITÉ DU QUÉBEC À TROIS-RIVIÈRES

Chemistry	M
Environmental Sciences	M,D
Mathematics	M
Physics	M,D

UNIVERSITÉ DU QUÉBEC EN ABITIBI-TÉMISCAMINGUE

Environmental Sciences	M,D
Forestry	M,D
Natural Resources	M,D

UNIVERSITÉ DU QUÉBEC, INSTITUT NATIONAL DE LA RECHERCHE SCIENTIFIQUE

Environmental Management and Policy	M,D
Geosciences	M,D
Hydrology	M,D

UNIVERSITÉ LAVAL

Agricultural Sciences—General	M,D
Agronomy and Soil Sciences	M,D
Animal Sciences	M,D
Chemistry	M,D
Environmental Management and Policy	M,D,O
Environmental Sciences	M,D
Food Science and Technology	M,D
Forestry	M,D
Geodetic Sciences	M,D
Geology	M,D
Geosciences	M,D
Mathematics	M,D
Oceanography	D
Physics	M,D
Statistics	M

UNIVERSITY AT ALBANY, STATE UNIVERSITY OF NEW YORK

Atmospheric Sciences	M,D
Biostatistics	M,D
Chemistry	M,D
Environmental Management and Policy	M
Environmental Sciences	M
Geology	M,D
Geosciences	M,D
Mathematics	M,D
Physics	M,D
Statistics	M,D,O

UNIVERSITY AT BUFFALO, THE STATE UNIVERSITY OF NEW YORK

Biostatistics	M,D
Chemistry	M,D
Environmental Sciences	M,D,O
Geology	M,D
Geosciences	M,D,O
Mathematics	M,D
Physics	M,D

THE UNIVERSITY OF AKRON

Applied Mathematics	M,D
Chemistry	M,D
Geology	M
Geophysics	M
Geosciences	M
Mathematics	M
Physics	M
Statistics	M

THE UNIVERSITY OF ALABAMA

Applied Mathematics	M,D
Applied Statistics	M,D
Geology	M,D
Mathematics	M,D
Physics	M,D

THE UNIVERSITY OF ALABAMA AT BIRMINGHAM

Biostatistics	M,D
Chemistry	M,D
Mathematics	M
Physics	M,D

THE UNIVERSITY OF ALABAMA IN HUNTSVILLE

Applied Mathematics	M,D
Atmospheric Sciences	M,D
Chemistry	M
Environmental Sciences	M,D
Mathematics	M,D
Optical Sciences	M,D
Photonics	M,D
Physics	M,D

UNIVERSITY OF ALASKA ANCHORAGE

Environmental Sciences	M

UNIVERSITY OF ALASKA FAIRBANKS

Astrophysics	M,D
Atmospheric Sciences	M,D
Chemistry	M,D
Computational Sciences	M,D
Environmental Management and Policy	M,D
Environmental Sciences	M,D
Fish, Game, and Wildlife Management	M,D
Geology	M,D
Geophysics	M,D
Limnology	M,D
Marine Sciences	M,D
Mathematics	M,D
Natural Resources	M,D
Oceanography	M,D
Physics	M,D
Statistics	M,D
Water Resources	M,D

UNIVERSITY OF ALBERTA

Agricultural Sciences—General	M,D
Agronomy and Soil Sciences	M,D
Applied Mathematics	M,D,O
Astrophysics	M,D
Biostatistics	M,D,O
Chemistry	M,D
Condensed Matter Physics	M,D
Environmental Management and Policy	M,D
Environmental Sciences	M,D
Forestry	M,D
Geophysics	M,D
Geosciences	M,D
Mathematical and Computational Finance	M,D,O
Mathematical Physics	M,D,O
Mathematics	M,D,O
Natural Resources	M,D
Physics	M,D
Statistics	M,D,O

THE UNIVERSITY OF ARIZONA

Agricultural Sciences—General	M,D
Agronomy and Soil Sciences	M,D
Animal Sciences	M,D
Applied Mathematics	M,D
Applied Physics	M
Astronomy	M,D
Atmospheric Sciences	M,D
Biostatistics	D
Chemistry	M,D
Environmental Sciences	M,D
Fish, Game, and Wildlife Management	M,D
Forestry	M,D
Geosciences	M,D
Hydrology	M,D
Mathematics	M,D
Optical Sciences	M,D
Physics	M,D
Planetary and Space Sciences	M,D
Plant Sciences	M,D
Range Science	M,D
Statistics	M,D
Water Resources	M,D

*M—master's degree; P—first professional degree; D—doctorate; O—other advanced degree; *—Close-Up and/or Display*

UNIVERSITY OF ARKANSAS

Agricultural Sciences—General	M,D
Agronomy and Soil Sciences	M,D
Animal Sciences	M,D
Applied Physics	M,D
Chemistry	M,D
Food Science and Technology	M,D
Geology	M
Horticulture	M
Mathematics	M,D
Photonics	M,D
Physics	M,D
Planetary and Space Sciences	M,D
Plant Sciences	D
Statistics	M

UNIVERSITY OF ARKANSAS AT LITTLE ROCK

Applied Mathematics	M,O
Applied Statistics	M,O
Chemistry	M
Geosciences	O
Mathematics	M,O

UNIVERSITY OF ARKANSAS AT MONTICELLO

Forestry	M
Natural Resources	M

UNIVERSITY OF ARKANSAS AT PINE BLUFF

Aquaculture	M
Fish, Game, and Wildlife Management	M

THE UNIVERSITY OF BRITISH COLUMBIA

Agricultural Sciences—General	M,D
Agronomy and Soil Sciences	M,D
Animal Sciences	M,D
Applied Mathematics	M,D
Astronomy	M,D
Atmospheric Sciences	M,D
Chemistry	M,D
Food Science and Technology	M,D
Forestry	M,D
Geology	M,D
Geophysics	M,D
Marine Sciences	M,D
Mathematics	M,D
Natural Resources	M,D
Oceanography	M,D
Physics	M,D
Plant Sciences	M,D
Statistics	M,D

UNIVERSITY OF CALGARY

Analytical Chemistry	M,D
Astronomy	M,D
Chemistry	M,D
Environmental Management and Policy	M,D,O
Geology	M,D
Geophysics	M,D
Inorganic Chemistry	M,D
Mathematics	M,D
Organic Chemistry	M,D
Physical Chemistry	M,D
Physics	M,D
Statistics	M,D
Theoretical Chemistry	M,D

UNIVERSITY OF CALIFORNIA, BERKELEY

Applied Mathematics	D
Astrophysics	D
Biostatistics	M,D
Chemistry	D
Environmental Management and Policy	M,D,O
Environmental Sciences	M,D
Forestry	M,D
Geology	M,D
Geophysics	M,D
Mathematics	M,D
Natural Resources	M,D
Physics	D
Range Science	M
Statistics	M,D

UNIVERSITY OF CALIFORNIA, DAVIS

Agricultural Sciences—General	M
Agronomy and Soil Sciences	M,D
Animal Sciences	M,D
Applied Mathematics	M,D
Atmospheric Sciences	M,D
Biostatistics	M,D
Chemistry	M,D
Environmental Sciences	M,D
Food Science and Technology	M,D
Geology	M,D
Horticulture	M
Hydrology	M,D
Mathematics	M,D
Physics	M,D
Statistics	M,D
Viticulture and Enology	M,D

UNIVERSITY OF CALIFORNIA, IRVINE

Chemistry	M,D
Geosciences	M,D
Mathematics	M,D
Physics	M,D

UNIVERSITY OF CALIFORNIA, LOS ANGELES

Astronomy	M,D
Astrophysics	M,D
Atmospheric Sciences	M,D
Biomathematics	M,D
Biometry	M,D
Biostatistics	M,D
Chemistry	M,D
Environmental Sciences	M,D
Geochemistry	M,D
Geology	M,D
Geophysics	M,D
Geosciences	M,D
Mathematics	M,D
Physics	M,D
Planetary and Space Sciences	M,D
Statistics	M,D

UNIVERSITY OF CALIFORNIA, MERCED

Applied Mathematics	M,D
Chemistry	M,D
Environmental Sciences	M,D
Physics	M,D

UNIVERSITY OF CALIFORNIA, RIVERSIDE

Agronomy and Soil Sciences	M,D
Applied Statistics	M,D
Chemistry	M,D
Environmental Sciences	M,D
Geology	M,D*
Mathematics	M,D
Physics	M,D
Plant Sciences	M,D
Statistics	M,D
Water Resources	M,D

UNIVERSITY OF CALIFORNIA, SAN DIEGO

Applied Mathematics	M,D
Applied Physics	M,D
Chemistry	M,D*
Geosciences	M,D
Marine Sciences	M
Mathematics	M,D
Oceanography	M,D
Photonics	M,D
Physics	M,D
Statistics	M,D

UNIVERSITY OF CALIFORNIA, SAN FRANCISCO

Chemistry	D

UNIVERSITY OF CALIFORNIA, SANTA BARBARA

Applied Mathematics	M,D
Applied Statistics	M,D
Chemistry	M,D
Computational Sciences	M,D
Environmental Management and Policy	M,D
Environmental Sciences	M,D
Geology	M,D
Geophysics	M,D
Geosciences	M,D
Marine Sciences	M,D
Mathematical and Computational Finance	M,D
Mathematics	M,D
Physics	D
Statistics	M,D

UNIVERSITY OF CALIFORNIA, SANTA CRUZ

Applied Mathematics	M,D
Astronomy	D
Astrophysics	D
Chemistry	M,D
Environmental Management and Policy	D
Geosciences	M,D
Marine Sciences	M,D
Mathematics	M,D
Physics	M,D
Planetary and Space Sciences	M,D
Statistics	M,D

UNIVERSITY OF CENTRAL ARKANSAS

Applied Mathematics	M
Mathematics	M

UNIVERSITY OF CENTRAL FLORIDA

Applied Mathematics	M,D,O
Chemistry	M,D,O
Computational Sciences	M,D
Mathematics	M,D,O
Optical Sciences	M,D
Photonics	M,D
Physics	M,D
Statistics	M,O

UNIVERSITY OF CENTRAL MISSOURI

Applied Mathematics	M,D
Environmental Management and Policy	M,D
Mathematics	M,D

UNIVERSITY OF CENTRAL OKLAHOMA

Applied Mathematics	M
Chemistry	M
Mathematics	M
Physics	M
Statistics	M

UNIVERSITY OF CHICAGO

Applied Mathematics	M,D
Astronomy	M,D
Astrophysics	M,D
Atmospheric Sciences	M,D
Chemistry	D
Environmental Management and Policy	M,D
Environmental Sciences	M,D
Geophysics	M,D
Geosciences	M,D
Mathematical and Computational Finance	M
Mathematics	M,D
Paleontology	M,D
Physics	M,D
Planetary and Space Sciences	M,D
Statistics	M,D

UNIVERSITY OF CINCINNATI

Analytical Chemistry	M,D
Applied Mathematics	M,D
Biostatistics	M,D
Chemistry	M,D
Environmental Sciences	M,D
Geology	M,D
Inorganic Chemistry	M,D
Mathematics	M,D
Organic Chemistry	M,D
Physical Chemistry	M,D
Physics	M,D
Statistics	M,D

UNIVERSITY OF COLORADO AT BOULDER

Applied Mathematics	M,D
Astrophysics	M,D
Atmospheric Sciences	M,D
Chemical Physics	M,D
Chemistry	M,D
Environmental Management and Policy	M,D
Geology	M,D
Geophysics	M,D
Hydrology	M,D
Mathematical Physics	M,D
Mathematics	M,D
Oceanography	M,D
Optical Sciences	M,D
Physics	M,D
Plasma Physics	M,D

UNIVERSITY OF COLORADO AT COLORADO SPRINGS

Applied Mathematics	M
Chemistry	M
Environmental Sciences	M
Mathematics	M
Physics	M

UNIVERSITY OF COLORADO DENVER

Applied Mathematics	M,D
Biostatistics	M,D
Chemistry	M
Environmental Sciences	M
Mathematics	M

UNIVERSITY OF CONNECTICUT

Agricultural Sciences—General	M,D
Agronomy and Soil Sciences	M,D
Animal Sciences	M,D
Applied Mathematics	M
Chemistry	M,D
Geology	M,D
Marine Sciences	M,D
Mathematical and Computational Finance	M
Mathematics	M,D
Natural Resources	M,D
Oceanography	M,D
Physics	M,D
Plant Sciences	M,D
Statistics	M,D

UNIVERSITY OF DAYTON

Applied Mathematics	M
Chemistry	M
Environmental Management and Policy	M,D

Mathematical and Computational Finance M
Optical Sciences M,D

UNIVERSITY OF DELAWARE

Agricultural Sciences—General M,D
Agronomy and Soil Sciences M,D
Animal Sciences M,D
Applied Mathematics M,D
Astronomy M,D
Atmospheric Sciences M,D
Chemistry M,D
Environmental Management and Policy M,D
Fish, Game, and Wildlife Management M,D
Food Science and Technology M,D
Geology M,D
Horticulture M
Marine Affairs M,D
Marine Geology M,D
Marine Sciences M,D
Mathematics M,D*
Natural Resources M
Oceanography M,D
Physics M,D
Plant Sciences M,D
Statistics M

UNIVERSITY OF DENVER

Applied Mathematics M,D
Applied Physics M,D
Astronomy M,D
Chemistry M,D
Environmental Management and Policy M,O
Mathematics M,D
Physics M,D
Statistics M

UNIVERSITY OF DETROIT MERCY

Chemistry M

THE UNIVERSITY OF FINDLAY

Environmental Management and Policy M

UNIVERSITY OF FLORIDA

Agricultural Sciences—General M,D
Agronomy and Soil Sciences M,D
Animal Sciences M,D
Aquaculture M,D
Astronomy M,D
Biostatistics M
Chemistry M,D
Fish, Game, and Wildlife Management M,D
Food Science and Technology M,D
Forestry M,D
Geology M,D
Geosciences M,D
Horticulture M,D
Limnology M,D
Marine Sciences M,D
Mathematics M,D
Natural Resources M,D
Physics M,D
Plant Sciences D
Statistics M,D
Water Resources M,D

UNIVERSITY OF GEORGIA

Agricultural Sciences—General M,D
Agronomy and Soil Sciences M,D
Analytical Chemistry M,D
Animal Sciences M,D
Applied Mathematics M,D
Astronomy M,D
Chemistry M,D
Food Science and Technology M,D
Forestry M,D
Geology M,D
Horticulture M,D
Inorganic Chemistry M,D
Marine Sciences M,D
Mathematics M,D
Natural Resources M,D
Oceanography M,D
Organic Chemistry M,D
Physical Chemistry M,D
Physics M,D
Statistics M,D

UNIVERSITY OF GUAM

Environmental Sciences M

UNIVERSITY OF GUELPH

Agricultural Sciences—General M,D,O
Agronomy and Soil Sciences M,D
Animal Sciences M,D
Applied Mathematics M,D
Applied Statistics M,D
Aquaculture M
Atmospheric Sciences M,D
Chemistry M,D
Environmental Management and Policy M,D
Environmental Sciences M,D
Food Science and Technology M,D
Horticulture M,D
Mathematics M,D
Natural Resources M,D
Physics M,D
Statistics M,D

UNIVERSITY OF HAWAII AT HILO

Environmental Sciences M

UNIVERSITY OF HAWAII AT MANOA

Agricultural Sciences—General M,D
Animal Sciences M
Astronomy M,D
Chemistry M,D
Environmental Management and Policy M,D,O
Food Science and Technology M
Geochemistry M,D
Geology M,D
Geophysics M,D
Horticulture M,D
Hydrogeology M,D
Marine Geology M,D
Marine Sciences O
Mathematics M,D
Meteorology M,D
Natural Resources M,D
Oceanography M,D
Physics M,D
Planetary and Space Sciences M,D
Plant Sciences M,D

UNIVERSITY OF HOUSTON

Chemistry M,D
Geology M,D
Geophysics M,D
Mathematics M,D
Physics M,D
Planetary and Space Sciences M,D

UNIVERSITY OF HOUSTON–CLEAR LAKE

Chemistry M
Environmental Management and Policy M
Environmental Sciences M
Mathematics M
Physics M
Statistics M

UNIVERSITY OF IDAHO

Agronomy and Soil Sciences M,D
Animal Sciences M,D
Chemistry M
Environmental Sciences M,D
Fish, Game, and Wildlife Management M
Food Science and Technology M,D
Forestry M
Geology M,D
Hydrology M
Mathematics M,D
Natural Resources M,D
Physics M,D
Plant Sciences M,D
Range Science M,D
Statistics M
Water Resources M,D

UNIVERSITY OF ILLINOIS AT CHICAGO

Applied Mathematics M,D
Biostatistics M,D
Chemistry M,D
Geology M,D
Geosciences M,D
Mathematical and Computational Finance M,D
Mathematics M,D
Physics M,D
Statistics M,D

UNIVERSITY OF ILLINOIS AT SPRINGFIELD

Environmental Management and Policy M
Environmental Sciences M

UNIVERSITY OF ILLINOIS AT URBANA–CHAMPAIGN

Agricultural Sciences—General M,D
Agronomy and Soil Sciences M,D
Animal Sciences M,D
Applied Mathematics M,D
Applied Statistics M,D
Astronomy M,D
Atmospheric Sciences M,D
Chemical Physics M,D
Chemistry M,D
Environmental Sciences M,D
Food Science and Technology M,D
Geology M,D
Geosciences M,D
Mathematics M,D
Natural Resources M,D
Physics M,D
Statistics M,D

THE UNIVERSITY OF IOWA

Applied Mathematics D
Astronomy M
Biostatistics M,D
Chemistry M,D
Computational Sciences D
Geosciences M,D
Mathematics M,D
Physics M,D
Statistics M,D,O

THE UNIVERSITY OF KANSAS

Astronomy M,D
Atmospheric Sciences M,D
Biostatistics M,D
Chemistry M,D
Computational Sciences M,D
Environmental Sciences M,D
Geology M,D
Mathematics M,D
Physics M,D*

UNIVERSITY OF KENTUCKY

Agricultural Sciences—General M,D
Agronomy and Soil Sciences M,D
Animal Sciences M,D
Applied Mathematics M,D
Astronomy M,D
Chemistry M,D
Forestry M
Geology M,D
Mathematics M,D
Physics M,D
Plant Sciences M
Statistics M,D

UNIVERSITY OF LETHBRIDGE

Agricultural Sciences—General M,D
Chemistry M,D
Computational Sciences M,D
Environmental Sciences M,D
Mathematics M,D
Physics M,D

UNIVERSITY OF LOUISIANA AT LAFAYETTE

Geology M
Mathematics M,D
Physics M

UNIVERSITY OF LOUISVILLE

Analytical Chemistry M,D
Applied Mathematics M,D
Biostatistics M,D
Chemical Physics M,D
Chemistry M,D
Inorganic Chemistry M,D
Mathematics M,D
Organic Chemistry M,D
Physical Chemistry M,D
Physics M,D

UNIVERSITY OF MAINE

Agricultural Sciences—General M,D,O
Agronomy and Soil Sciences M,D
Animal Sciences M
Chemistry M,D
Environmental Sciences M,D
Fish, Game, and Wildlife Management M,D
Food Science and Technology M,D
Forestry M,D
Geology M,D
Geosciences M,D
Horticulture M
Marine Affairs M
Marine Sciences M,D
Mathematics M
Natural Resources M,D
Oceanography M,D
Physics M,D
Plant Sciences M,D

UNIVERSITY OF MANITOBA

Agricultural Sciences—General M,D
Agronomy and Soil Sciences M,D
Animal Sciences M,D
Chemistry M,D
Computational Sciences M
Environmental Sciences M,D
Food Science and Technology M,D

*M—master's degree; P—first professional degree; D—doctorate; O—other advanced degree; *—Close-Up and/or Display*

Geology	M,D
Geophysics	M,D
Horticulture	M,D
Mathematics	M,D
Natural Resources	M,D
Physics	M,D
Plant Sciences	M,D
Statistics	M,D

UNIVERSITY OF MARYLAND, BALTIMORE

Biostatistics	M,D
Environmental Sciences	M,D
Marine Sciences	M,D*

UNIVERSITY OF MARYLAND, BALTIMORE COUNTY

Applied Mathematics	M,D
Applied Physics	M,D
Astrophysics	M,D
Atmospheric Sciences	M,D
Biostatistics	M,D
Chemistry	M,D
Environmental Management and Policy	M,D
Environmental Sciences	M,D
Marine Sciences	M,D*
Optical Sciences	M,D
Physics	M,D
Planetary and Space Sciences	M
Statistics	M,D

UNIVERSITY OF MARYLAND, COLLEGE PARK

Agricultural Sciences—General	P,M,D
Agronomy and Soil Sciences	M,D
Analytical Chemistry	M,D
Animal Sciences	M,D
Applied Mathematics	M,D
Astronomy	M,D
Biostatistics	M,D
Chemical Physics	M,D
Chemistry	M,D
Environmental Sciences	M,D
Food Science and Technology	M,D
Geology	M,D
Horticulture	D
Inorganic Chemistry	M,D
Marine Sciences	M,D*
Mathematics	M,D
Meteorology	M,D
Natural Resources	M,D
Oceanography	M,D
Organic Chemistry	M,D
Physical Chemistry	M,D
Physics	M,D
Statistics	M,D

UNIVERSITY OF MARYLAND EASTERN SHORE

Agricultural Sciences—General	M,D
Environmental Sciences	M,D
Food Science and Technology	M,D
Marine Sciences	M,D*

UNIVERSITY OF MARYLAND UNIVERSITY COLLEGE

Environmental Management and Policy	M,O

UNIVERSITY OF MASSACHUSETTS AMHERST

Agronomy and Soil Sciences	M,D
Animal Sciences	M,D
Applied Mathematics	M
Astronomy	M,D
Biostatistics	M,D
Chemistry	M,D
Fish, Game, and Wildlife Management	M,D
Food Science and Technology	M,D
Forestry	M,D
Geosciences	M,D
Marine Sciences	M,D
Mathematics	M,D
Physics	M,D
Plant Sciences	M,D
Statistics	M,D

UNIVERSITY OF MASSACHUSETTS BOSTON

Applied Physics	M
Chemistry	M
Environmental Sciences	D
Marine Sciences	D

UNIVERSITY OF MASSACHUSETTS DARTMOUTH

Acoustics	M,D,O
Chemistry	M,D
Environmental Management and Policy	M,O
Marine Sciences	M,D
Physics	M

UNIVERSITY OF MASSACHUSETTS LOWELL

Analytical Chemistry	M,D
Applied Mathematics	M,D
Applied Physics	M,D
Atmospheric Sciences	M,D
Chemistry	M,D
Computational Sciences	M,D
Environmental Management and Policy	M,D,O
Environmental Sciences	M,D,O
Inorganic Chemistry	M,D
Mathematics	M,D
Optical Sciences	M,D
Organic Chemistry	M,D
Physics	M,D*

UNIVERSITY OF MEDICINE AND DENTISTRY OF NEW JERSEY

Biostatistics	M,D,O
Environmental Sciences	D

UNIVERSITY OF MEMPHIS

Analytical Chemistry	M,D
Applied Mathematics	M,D
Applied Statistics	M,D
Biostatistics	M
Chemistry	M,D
Geology	M,D,O
Inorganic Chemistry	M,D
Mathematics	M,D
Organic Chemistry	M,D
Physical Chemistry	M,D
Physics	M
Statistics	M,D

UNIVERSITY OF MIAMI

Chemistry	M,D
Environmental Management and Policy	M,D
Fish, Game, and Wildlife Management	M,D
Geophysics	M,D
Inorganic Chemistry	M,D
Marine Affairs	M
Marine Geology	M,D
Marine Sciences	M,D
Mathematics	M,D
Meteorology	M,D
Oceanography	M,D
Organic Chemistry	M,D
Physical Chemistry	M,D
Physics	M,D

UNIVERSITY OF MICHIGAN

Analytical Chemistry	D
Applied Physics	D
Applied Statistics	M,D
Astronomy	D
Astrophysics	D
Atmospheric Sciences	M,D
Biostatistics	M,D
Chemistry	D
Environmental Management and Policy	M,D
Environmental Sciences	M,D
Geology	M,D
Inorganic Chemistry	D
Marine Sciences	M,D
Mathematics	M,D
Natural Resources	M,D
Organic Chemistry	D
Physical Chemistry	D
Physics	M,D
Planetary and Space Sciences	M,D
Statistics	M,D

UNIVERSITY OF MICHIGAN–DEARBORN

Applied Mathematics	M
Computational Sciences	M
Environmental Sciences	M

UNIVERSITY OF MINNESOTA, DULUTH

Applied Mathematics	M*
Chemistry	M
Computational Sciences	M
Geology	M,D
Physics	M

UNIVERSITY OF MINNESOTA, TWIN CITIES CAMPUS

Agricultural Sciences—General	M,D
Agronomy and Soil Sciences	M,D
Animal Sciences	M,D
Astronomy	M,D
Astrophysics	M,D
Biostatistics	M,D
Chemistry	M,D
Computational Sciences	M,D
Environmental Management and Policy	M
Food Science and Technology	M,D
Geology	M,D
Geophysics	M,D
Mathematics	M,D
Natural Resources	M,D
Physics	M,D
Plant Sciences	M,D
Statistics	M,D
Water Resources	M,D

UNIVERSITY OF MISSISSIPPI

Chemistry	M,D
Computational Sciences	M,D
Mathematics	M,D
Physics	M,D

UNIVERSITY OF MISSOURI

Agricultural Sciences—General	M,D,O
Agronomy and Soil Sciences	M,D
Analytical Chemistry	M,D
Animal Sciences	M,D
Applied Mathematics	M
Astronomy	M,D
Atmospheric Sciences	M,D
Chemistry	M,D
Fish, Game, and Wildlife Management	M,D
Food Science and Technology	M,D
Forestry	M,D
Geology	M,D
Horticulture	M,D
Inorganic Chemistry	M,D
Mathematics	M,D
Natural Resources	M
Organic Chemistry	M,D
Physical Chemistry	M,D
Physics	M,D
Plant Sciences	M,D
Statistics	M,D

UNIVERSITY OF MISSOURI–KANSAS CITY

Analytical Chemistry	M,D
Chemistry	M,D
Geology	M,D
Geosciences	M,D
Inorganic Chemistry	M,D
Mathematics	M,D
Organic Chemistry	M,D
Physical Chemistry	M,D
Physics	M,D
Statistics	M,D

UNIVERSITY OF MISSOURI–ST. LOUIS

Applied Mathematics	M,D
Applied Physics	M,D
Astrophysics	M,D
Chemistry	M,D
Environmental Management and Policy	M,D,O
Inorganic Chemistry	M,D
Mathematics	M,D
Organic Chemistry	M,D
Physical Chemistry	M,D
Physics	M,D

THE UNIVERSITY OF MONTANA

Analytical Chemistry	M,D
Chemistry	M,D
Environmental Management and Policy	M
Environmental Sciences	M
Fish, Game, and Wildlife Management	M,D
Forestry	M,D
Geology	M,D
Geosciences	M,D
Inorganic Chemistry	M,D
Mathematics	M,D
Natural Resources	M,D
Organic Chemistry	M,D
Physical Chemistry	M,D

UNIVERSITY OF NEBRASKA AT OMAHA

Mathematics	M

UNIVERSITY OF NEBRASKA–LINCOLN

Agricultural Sciences—General	M,D
Agronomy and Soil Sciences	M,D
Analytical Chemistry	M,D
Animal Sciences	M,D
Astronomy	M,D
Chemistry	M,D
Food Science and Technology	M,D
Geosciences	M,D
Horticulture	M,D
Inorganic Chemistry	M,D
Mathematics	M,D
Natural Resources	M,D
Organic Chemistry	M,D
Physical Chemistry	M,D
Physics	M,D
Statistics	M,D

UNIVERSITY OF NEVADA, LAS VEGAS

Astronomy	M,D
Chemistry	M,D
Environmental Sciences	M,D,O
Geosciences	M,D
Mathematics	M,D
Physics	M,D
Water Resources	M

UNIVERSITY OF NEVADA, RENO

Agricultural Sciences—General	M,D

Animal Sciences	M
Atmospheric Sciences	M,D
Chemical Physics	D
Chemistry	M,D
Environmental Management and Policy	M
Environmental Sciences	M,D
Geochemistry	M,D
Geology	M,D
Geophysics	M,D
Hydrogeology	M,D
Hydrology	M,D
Mathematics	M
Physics	M,D

UNIVERSITY OF NEW BRUNSWICK FREDERICTON

Chemistry	M,D
Environmental Management and Policy	M,D
Forestry	M,D
Geodetic Sciences	M,D,O
Geology	M,D
Hydrology	M,D
Mathematics	M,D
Physics	M,D
Statistics	M,D
Water Resources	M,D

UNIVERSITY OF NEW BRUNSWICK SAINT JOHN

Natural Resources	M

UNIVERSITY OF NEW ENGLAND

Marine Sciences	M

UNIVERSITY OF NEW HAMPSHIRE

Agronomy and Soil Sciences	M
Animal Sciences	M,D
Applied Mathematics	M,D,O
Chemistry	M,D
Environmental Management and Policy	M
Fish, Game, and Wildlife Management	M
Forestry	M
Geochemistry	M
Geology	M
Geosciences	M
Hydrology	M
Mathematics	M,D,O
Natural Resources	M,D
Oceanography	M,D,O
Physics	M,D
Statistics	M,D,O
Water Resources	M

UNIVERSITY OF NEW HAVEN

Computational Sciences	M,O
Environmental Management and Policy	M,O
Environmental Sciences	M,O
Geosciences	M,O

UNIVERSITY OF NEW MEXICO

Chemistry	M,D
Computational Sciences	O
Geosciences	M,D
Mathematics	M,D
Optical Sciences	M,D
Physics	M,D
Planetary and Space Sciences	M,D
Statistics	M,D
Water Resources	M

UNIVERSITY OF NEW ORLEANS

Chemistry	M,D
Environmental Sciences	M
Geosciences	M
Mathematics	M
Physics	M,D

THE UNIVERSITY OF NORTH CAROLINA AT CHAPEL HILL

Astronomy	M,D
Astrophysics	M,D
Atmospheric Sciences	M,D
Biostatistics	M,D
Chemistry	M,D
Environmental Management and Policy	M,D
Environmental Sciences	M,D
Geology	M,D
Marine Sciences	M,D
Mathematics	M,D
Physics	M,D
Statistics	M,D

THE UNIVERSITY OF NORTH CAROLINA AT CHARLOTTE

Applied Mathematics	M,D
Applied Physics	M,D
Chemistry	M
Geosciences	M
Mathematical and Computational Finance	M
Mathematics	M,D
Optical Sciences	M,D

THE UNIVERSITY OF NORTH CAROLINA AT GREENSBORO

Chemistry	M
Mathematics	M,D

THE UNIVERSITY OF NORTH CAROLINA WILMINGTON

Chemistry	M
Environmental Management and Policy	M
Geology	M
Geosciences	M
Marine Sciences	M,D
Mathematics	M

UNIVERSITY OF NORTH DAKOTA

Atmospheric Sciences	M,D
Chemistry	M,D
Fish, Game, and Wildlife Management	M,D
Geology	M,D
Geosciences	M,D
Mathematics	M
Physics	M,D
Planetary and Space Sciences	M

UNIVERSITY OF NORTHERN BRITISH COLUMBIA

Environmental Management and Policy	M,D,O
Mathematics	M,D,O
Natural Resources	M,D,O

UNIVERSITY OF NORTHERN COLORADO

Applied Statistics	M,D
Chemistry	M,D
Geosciences	M
Mathematics	M,D

UNIVERSITY OF NORTHERN IOWA

Chemistry	M
Environmental Sciences	M
Mathematics	M
Physics	M

UNIVERSITY OF NORTH FLORIDA

Mathematics	M
Statistics	M

UNIVERSITY OF NORTH TEXAS

Chemistry	M,D
Environmental Sciences	M,D
Mathematics	M,D
Physics	M,D

UNIVERSITY OF NORTH TEXAS HEALTH SCIENCE CENTER AT FORT WORTH

Biostatistics	M,D

UNIVERSITY OF NOTRE DAME

Applied Mathematics	M,D
Chemistry	M,D
Geosciences	M,D
Inorganic Chemistry	M,D
Mathematics	M,D
Organic Chemistry	M,D
Physical Chemistry	M,D
Physics	M,D

UNIVERSITY OF OKLAHOMA

Astrophysics	M,D
Chemistry	M,D
Environmental Sciences	M,D
Geology	M,D
Geophysics	M
Mathematics	M,D*
Meteorology	M,D
Natural Resources	M,D
Physics	M,D
Water Resources	M,D

UNIVERSITY OF OKLAHOMA HEALTH SCIENCES CENTER

Biostatistics	M,D

UNIVERSITY OF OREGON

Chemistry	M,D
Environmental Management and Policy	M,D
Geology	M,D
Mathematics	M,D
Physics	M,D

UNIVERSITY OF OTTAWA

Chemistry	M,D
Geosciences	M,D
Mathematics	M,D
Physics	M,D
Statistics	M,D

UNIVERSITY OF PENNSYLVANIA

Applied Mathematics	D
Astrophysics	M,D
Biostatistics	M,D
Chemistry	M,D
Computational Sciences	D
Environmental Management and Policy	M
Environmental Sciences	M,D
Geosciences	M,D
Mathematics	M,D
Physics	M,D
Statistics	M,D

UNIVERSITY OF PITTSBURGH

Applied Mathematics	M,D
Applied Statistics	M,D
Biostatistics	M,D
Chemistry	M,D*
Environmental Management and Policy	M,O
Geology	M,D
Mathematics	M,D
Physics	M,D*
Planetary and Space Sciences	M,D
Statistics	M,D

UNIVERSITY OF PRINCE EDWARD ISLAND

Chemistry	M

UNIVERSITY OF PUERTO RICO, MAYAGÜEZ CAMPUS

Agricultural Sciences—General	M
Agronomy and Soil Sciences	M
Animal Sciences	M
Applied Mathematics	M
Chemistry	M,D
Computational Sciences	M
Food Science and Technology	M
Geology	M
Horticulture	M
Marine Sciences	M,D
Mathematics	M
Physics	M
Statistics	M

UNIVERSITY OF PUERTO RICO, MEDICAL SCIENCES CAMPUS

Biostatistics	M

UNIVERSITY OF PUERTO RICO, RÍO PIEDRAS

Chemistry	M,D
Environmental Sciences	M
Mathematics	M,D
Physics	M,D

UNIVERSITY OF REGINA

Analytical Chemistry	M,D
Chemistry	M,D
Geology	M,D
Inorganic Chemistry	M,D
Mathematics	M,D
Organic Chemistry	M,D
Physical Chemistry	M,D
Physics	M,D
Statistics	M,D

UNIVERSITY OF RHODE ISLAND

Animal Sciences	M,D
Applied Mathematics	M,D,O
Aquaculture	M,D
Chemistry	M,D
Environmental Management and Policy	M,D
Environmental Sciences	M,D
Fish, Game, and Wildlife Management	M,D
Food Science and Technology	M,D
Geosciences	M,D
Marine Affairs	M,D
Marine Sciences	M,D
Mathematics	M,D
Natural Resources	M,D
Oceanography	M,D,O
Physics	M,D
Plant Sciences	M,D
Statistics	M,D,O

UNIVERSITY OF ROCHESTER

Astronomy	M,D
Biostatistics	M,D
Chemistry	M,D
Geology	M,D
Geosciences	M,D
Mathematics	M,D
Optical Sciences	M,D,O
Physics	M,D*
Statistics	M,D

UNIVERSITY OF SAN DIEGO

Marine Affairs	M
Marine Sciences	M

UNIVERSITY OF SAN FRANCISCO

Chemistry	M
Natural Resources	M

UNIVERSITY OF SASKATCHEWAN

Agricultural Sciences—General	M,D,O
Agronomy and Soil Sciences	M,D,O
Animal Sciences	M,D
Chemistry	M,D
Environmental Sciences	M

*M—master's degree; P—first professional degree; D—doctorate; O—other advanced degree; *—Close-Up and/or Display*

Food Science and Technology	M,D
Geology	M,D,O
Mathematics	M,D
Physics	M,D
Plant Sciences	M,D
Statistics	M,D

THE UNIVERSITY OF SCRANTON

Chemistry	M

UNIVERSITY OF SOUTH AFRICA

Agricultural Sciences—General	M,D
Environmental Management and Policy	M,D
Environmental Sciences	M,D
Horticulture	M,D
Natural Resources	M,D
Statistics	M,D

UNIVERSITY OF SOUTH ALABAMA

Marine Sciences	M,D
Mathematics	M

UNIVERSITY OF SOUTH CAROLINA

Applied Statistics	M,D,O
Astronomy	M,D
Biostatistics	M,D
Chemistry	M,D
Environmental Management and Policy	M
Geology	M,D
Geosciences	M,D
Marine Sciences	M,D
Mathematics	M,D
Physics	M,D
Statistics	M,D,O

THE UNIVERSITY OF SOUTH DAKOTA

Chemistry	M,D
Computational Sciences	M,D
Mathematics	M
Physics	M,D
Statistics	M,D

UNIVERSITY OF SOUTHERN CALIFORNIA

Applied Mathematics	M,D
Biostatistics	M,D*
Chemical Physics	M,D
Chemistry	M,D
Food Science and Technology	M,D,O
Geosciences	M,D
Marine Sciences	M,D
Mathematical and Computational Finance	M,D
Mathematics	M,D
Oceanography	M,D
Physics	M,D
Statistics	M,D

UNIVERSITY OF SOUTHERN MAINE

Statistics	M

UNIVERSITY OF SOUTHERN MISSISSIPPI

Analytical Chemistry	M,D
Biostatistics	M
Chemistry	M,D
Computational Sciences	M,D
Food Science and Technology	M,D
Geology	M,D
Hydrology	M,D
Inorganic Chemistry	M,D
Marine Sciences	M,D
Mathematics	M,D
Organic Chemistry	M,D
Physical Chemistry	M,D
Physics	M,D

UNIVERSITY OF SOUTH FLORIDA

Analytical Chemistry	M,D
Applied Physics	M,D
Biostatistics	M,D
Chemistry	M,D
Environmental Management and Policy	M
Environmental Sciences	M,D
Geology	M,D
Inorganic Chemistry	M,D
Marine Sciences	M,D
Mathematics	M,D
Oceanography	M,D
Organic Chemistry	M,D
Physical Chemistry	M,D
Physics	M,D
Statistics	M,D

THE UNIVERSITY OF TENNESSEE

Agricultural Sciences—General	M,D
Analytical Chemistry	M,D
Animal Sciences	M,D
Applied Mathematics	M,D
Chemical Physics	M,D
Chemistry	M,D
Environmental Management and Policy	M,D
Fish, Game, and Wildlife Management	M
Food Science and Technology	M,D
Forestry	M
Geology	M,D
Inorganic Chemistry	M,D
Mathematics	M,D
Organic Chemistry	M,D
Physical Chemistry	M,D
Physics	M,D
Plant Sciences	M
Statistics	M,D
Theoretical Chemistry	M,D

THE UNIVERSITY OF TENNESSEE AT CHATTANOOGA

Computational Sciences	M,D
Environmental Sciences	M

THE UNIVERSITY OF TENNESSEE AT MARTIN

Agricultural Sciences—General	M
Food Science and Technology	M

THE UNIVERSITY OF TENNESSEE SPACE INSTITUTE

Applied Mathematics	M
Physics	M,D

THE UNIVERSITY OF TEXAS AT ARLINGTON

Chemistry	M,D
Environmental Sciences	M,D
Geology	M,D
Mathematics	M,D
Physics	M,D

THE UNIVERSITY OF TEXAS AT AUSTIN

Analytical Chemistry	M,D
Applied Mathematics	M,D
Applied Physics	M,D
Astronomy	M,D
Chemistry	M,D
Computational Sciences	M,D
Geology	M,D
Geosciences	M,D
Inorganic Chemistry	M,D
Marine Sciences	M,D
Mathematics	M,D
Natural Resources	M
Organic Chemistry	M,D
Physical Chemistry	M,D
Physics	M,D
Statistics	M

THE UNIVERSITY OF TEXAS AT BROWNSVILLE

Mathematics	M
Physics	M

THE UNIVERSITY OF TEXAS AT DALLAS

Applied Mathematics	M,D
Chemistry	M,D
Geochemistry	M,D
Geophysics	M,D
Geosciences	M,D
Hydrogeology	M,D
Mathematics	M,D*
Paleontology	M,D
Physics	M,D
Statistics	M,D

THE UNIVERSITY OF TEXAS AT EL PASO

Chemistry	M,D
Computational Sciences	M,D
Environmental Sciences	M,D
Geology	M,D
Geophysics	M
Mathematics	M
Physics	M
Statistics	M

THE UNIVERSITY OF TEXAS AT SAN ANTONIO

Applied Mathematics	M
Applied Statistics	M,D
Chemistry	M,D
Environmental Sciences	M,D
Geology	M
Mathematics	M
Physics	M,D
Statistics	M,D

THE UNIVERSITY OF TEXAS AT TYLER

Mathematics	M

THE UNIVERSITY OF TEXAS HEALTH SCIENCE CENTER AT HOUSTON

Biomathematics	M,D
Biostatistics	M,D

THE UNIVERSITY OF TEXAS OF THE PERMIAN BASIN

Geology	M

THE UNIVERSITY OF TEXAS–PAN AMERICAN

Chemistry	M
Mathematics	M

UNIVERSITY OF THE DISTRICT OF COLUMBIA

Applied Statistics	M

UNIVERSITY OF THE INCARNATE WORD

Mathematics	M
Statistics	M

UNIVERSITY OF THE PACIFIC

Water Resources	P,M,D

UNIVERSITY OF THE SCIENCES IN PHILADELPHIA

Chemistry	M,D

UNIVERSITY OF THE VIRGIN ISLANDS

Environmental Sciences	M
Marine Sciences	M

THE UNIVERSITY OF TOLEDO

Analytical Chemistry	M,D
Applied Mathematics	M,D
Biostatistics	M,O
Chemistry	M,D
Environmental Sciences	M,D
Geology	M,D
Geosciences	M,D
Inorganic Chemistry	M,D
Mathematics	M,D
Organic Chemistry	M,D
Physical Chemistry	M,D
Physics	M,D
Statistics	M,D

UNIVERSITY OF TORONTO

Astronomy	M,D
Astrophysics	M,D
Chemistry	M,D
Forestry	M,D
Geology	M,D
Mathematics	M,D
Physics	M,D
Statistics	M,D

UNIVERSITY OF TULSA

Chemistry	M,D
Geosciences	M,D
Mathematics	M
Physics	M

UNIVERSITY OF UTAH

Atmospheric Sciences	M,D
Biostatistics	M,D
Chemical Physics	M,D
Chemistry	M,D
Computational Sciences	M
Environmental Sciences	M
Geology	M,D
Geophysics	M,D
Mathematics	M,D*
Physics	M,D
Statistics	M,D

UNIVERSITY OF VERMONT

Agricultural Sciences—General	M,D
Agronomy and Soil Sciences	M,D
Animal Sciences	M,D
Biostatistics	M
Chemistry	M,D
Food Science and Technology	D
Forestry	M,D
Geology	M
Horticulture	M,D
Mathematics	M,D
Natural Resources	M,D
Physics	M
Plant Sciences	M,D
Statistics	M

UNIVERSITY OF VICTORIA

Astronomy	M,D
Astrophysics	M,D
Chemistry	M,D
Condensed Matter Physics	M,D
Geophysics	M,D
Geosciences	M,D
Mathematics	M,D
Oceanography	M,D
Physics	M,D
Statistics	M,D
Theoretical Physics	M,D

UNIVERSITY OF VIRGINIA

Astronomy	M,D
Chemistry	M,D
Environmental Sciences	M,D
Mathematics	M,D
Physics	M,D
Statistics	M,D

UNIVERSITY OF WASHINGTON

Applied Mathematics	M,D
Applied Physics	M,D
Astronomy	M,D
Atmospheric Sciences	M,D
Biostatistics	M,D

Chemistry	M,D
Computational Sciences	M,D
Environmental Management and Policy	M,D
Fish, Game, and Wildlife Management	M,D
Forestry	M,D
Geology	M,D
Geophysics	M,D
Horticulture	M,D
Hydrology	M,D
Marine Affairs	M,O
Marine Geology	M,D
Mathematics	M,D
Natural Resources	M,D
Oceanography	M,D
Physics	M,D
Statistics	M,D

UNIVERSITY OF WATERLOO

Applied Mathematics	M,D
Biostatistics	M,D
Chemistry	M,D
Environmental Management and Policy	M
Geosciences	M,D
Mathematics	M,D
Physics	M,D
Statistics	M,D

THE UNIVERSITY OF WESTERN ONTARIO

Applied Mathematics	M,D
Astronomy	M,D
Biostatistics	M,D
Chemistry	M,D
Environmental Sciences	M,D
Geology	M,D
Geophysics	M,D
Geosciences	M,D
Mathematics	M,D
Physics	M,D
Plant Sciences	M,D
Statistics	M,D

UNIVERSITY OF WEST FLORIDA

Applied Statistics	M
Environmental Sciences	M
Marine Affairs	M
Mathematics	M

UNIVERSITY OF WEST GEORGIA

Applied Mathematics	M
Mathematics	M

UNIVERSITY OF WINDSOR

Chemistry	M,D
Environmental Sciences	M,D
Geosciences	M,D
Mathematics	M,D
Physics	M,D
Statistics	M,D

UNIVERSITY OF WISCONSIN–GREEN BAY

Environmental Management and Policy	M
Environmental Sciences	M

UNIVERSITY OF WISCONSIN–LA CROSSE

Marine Sciences	M

UNIVERSITY OF WISCONSIN–MADISON

Agricultural Sciences—General	M,D
Agronomy and Soil Sciences	M,D
Animal Sciences	M,D
Astronomy	D
Atmospheric Sciences	M,D
Biometry	M
Chemistry	M,D
Environmental Sciences	M,D
Fish, Game, and Wildlife Management	M,D
Food Science and Technology	M,D
Forestry	M,D
Geology	M,D
Geophysics	M,D
Horticulture	M,D
Limnology	M,D
Marine Sciences	M,D
Mathematics	D
Natural Resources	M,D
Oceanography	M,D
Physics	M,D
Plant Sciences	M,D
Statistics	M,D
Water Resources	M

UNIVERSITY OF WISCONSIN–MILWAUKEE

Chemistry	M,D
Geochemistry	M,D
Geology	M,D
Mathematics	M,D
Physics	M,D

UNIVERSITY OF WISCONSIN–RIVER FALLS

Agricultural Sciences—General	M

UNIVERSITY OF WISCONSIN–STEVENS POINT

Natural Resources	M

UNIVERSITY OF WISCONSIN–STOUT

Food Science and Technology	M

UNIVERSITY OF WYOMING

Agricultural Sciences—General	M,D
Agronomy and Soil Sciences	M,D
Animal Sciences	M,D
Atmospheric Sciences	M,D
Chemistry	M,D
Food Science and Technology	M
Geology	M,D
Geophysics	M,D
Mathematics	M,D
Natural Resources	M,D
Range Science	M,D
Statistics	M,D
Water Resources	M,D

UTAH STATE UNIVERSITY

Agricultural Sciences—General	M,D
Agronomy and Soil Sciences	M,D
Animal Sciences	M,D
Applied Mathematics	M,D
Chemistry	M,D
Environmental Management and Policy	M,D
Fish, Game, and Wildlife Management	M,D
Food Science and Technology	M,D
Forestry	M,D
Geology	M
Mathematics	M,D
Meteorology	M,D
Natural Resources	M
Physics	M,D
Plant Sciences	M,D
Range Science	M,D
Statistics	M,D
Water Resources	M,D

VANDERBILT UNIVERSITY

Analytical Chemistry	M,D
Astronomy	M,D
Chemistry	M,D
Environmental Management and Policy	M,D
Environmental Sciences	M
Inorganic Chemistry	M,D
Mathematics	M,D
Organic Chemistry	M,D
Physical Chemistry	M,D
Physics	M,D
Theoretical Chemistry	M,D

VASSAR COLLEGE

Chemistry	M

VERMONT LAW SCHOOL

Environmental Management and Policy	M,O

VILLANOVA UNIVERSITY

Applied Statistics	M
Chemistry	M*
Mathematics	M*

VIRGINIA COMMONWEALTH UNIVERSITY

Analytical Chemistry	M,D
Applied Mathematics	M,O
Applied Physics	M
Biostatistics	M,D
Chemical Physics	M,D
Chemistry	M,D
Environmental Management and Policy	M
Environmental Sciences	M
Inorganic Chemistry	M,D
Mathematics	M,O
Organic Chemistry	M,D
Physical Chemistry	M,D
Physics	M
Statistics	M,O

VIRGINIA POLYTECHNIC INSTITUTE AND STATE UNIVERSITY

Agricultural Sciences—General	M,D
Agronomy and Soil Sciences	M,D
Animal Sciences	M,D
Applied Mathematics	M,D
Applied Physics	M,D
Chemistry	M,D
Environmental Management and Policy	M,D,O
Environmental Sciences	M,D
Fish, Game, and Wildlife Management	M,D
Food Science and Technology	M,D
Forestry	M,D
Geology	M,D
Geophysics	M,D
Geosciences	M,D
Horticulture	M,D
Mathematical Physics	M,D
Mathematics	M,D
Natural Resources	M,O
Physics	M,D
Statistics	M,D

VIRGINIA STATE UNIVERSITY

Agricultural Sciences—General	M
Mathematics	M
Physics	M
Plant Sciences	M

WAKE FOREST UNIVERSITY

Analytical Chemistry	M,D
Chemistry	M,D
Inorganic Chemistry	M,D
Mathematics	M
Organic Chemistry	M,D
Physical Chemistry	M,D
Physics	M,D

WASHINGTON STATE UNIVERSITY

Agricultural Sciences—General	M
Agronomy and Soil Sciences	M,D
Animal Sciences	M,D
Applied Mathematics	M,D
Applied Statistics	M
Chemistry	M,D
Environmental Sciences	M,D
Food Science and Technology	M,D
Geology	M,D
Geosciences	M,D
Horticulture	M,D
Mathematics	M,D*
Natural Resources	M,D
Physics	M,D
Statistics	M

WASHINGTON STATE UNIVERSITY TRI-CITIES

Chemistry	M,D
Environmental Sciences	M,D

WASHINGTON STATE UNIVERSITY VANCOUVER

Environmental Sciences	M

WASHINGTON UNIVERSITY IN ST. LOUIS

Chemistry	D
Geosciences	M,D
Mathematics	M,D
Physics	D
Planetary and Space Sciences	M,D
Statistics	M,D

WAYNE STATE UNIVERSITY

Applied Mathematics	M,D
Chemistry	M,D
Food Science and Technology	M,D
Geology	M
Mathematics	M,D
Physics	M,D
Statistics	M,D

WEBSTER UNIVERSITY

Environmental Management and Policy	M,D,O

WESLEYAN UNIVERSITY

Astronomy	M
Chemical Physics	M,D
Chemistry	M,D*
Environmental Sciences	M
Geosciences	M
Inorganic Chemistry	M,D
Mathematics	M,D*
Organic Chemistry	M,D
Physics	M,D
Theoretical Chemistry	M,D

WESLEY COLLEGE

Environmental Management and Policy	M

WEST CHESTER UNIVERSITY OF PENNSYLVANIA

Applied Statistics	M,O
Astronomy	M,O
Chemistry	O
Geology	M,O
Geosciences	M,O
Mathematics	M,O
Planetary and Space Sciences	M,O

*M—master's degree; P—first professional degree; D—doctorate; O—other advanced degree; *—Close-Up and/or Display*

WESTERN CAROLINA UNIVERSITY

Chemistry	M
Mathematics	M

WESTERN CONNECTICUT STATE UNIVERSITY

Environmental Sciences	M
Geosciences	M
Mathematics	M
Planetary and Space Sciences	M

WESTERN ILLINOIS UNIVERSITY

Applied Mathematics	M,O
Chemistry	M
Mathematics	M,O
Physics	M

WESTERN KENTUCKY UNIVERSITY

Agricultural Sciences—General	M
Chemistry	M
Geology	M
Mathematics	M

WESTERN MICHIGAN UNIVERSITY

Applied Mathematics	M
Applied Statistics	M,D
Chemistry	M,D
Computational Sciences	M
Geosciences	M,D
Mathematics	M,D
Physics	M,D
Statistics	M,D

WESTERN WASHINGTON UNIVERSITY

Chemistry	M
Environmental Sciences	M
Geology	M
Marine Sciences	M
Mathematics	M

WEST TEXAS A&M UNIVERSITY

Agricultural Sciences—General	M,D
Animal Sciences	M
Chemistry	M
Environmental Sciences	M
Mathematics	M
Plant Sciences	M

WEST VIRGINIA UNIVERSITY

Agricultural Sciences—General	M,D
Agronomy and Soil Sciences	D
Analytical Chemistry	M,D
Animal Sciences	M,D
Applied Mathematics	M,D
Applied Physics	M,D
Chemical Physics	M,D
Chemistry	M,D
Condensed Matter Physics	M,D
Environmental Management and Policy	M,D
Fish, Game, and Wildlife Management	M
Food Science and Technology	M,D
Forestry	M,D
Geology	M,D
Geophysics	M,D
Horticulture	M,D
Hydrogeology	M,D
Inorganic Chemistry	M,D
Mathematics	M,D
Natural Resources	M,D
Organic Chemistry	M,D
Paleontology	M,D
Physical Chemistry	M,D
Physics	M,D
Plant Sciences	D
Plasma Physics	M,D
Statistics	M,D
Theoretical Chemistry	M,D
Theoretical Physics	M,D

WICHITA STATE UNIVERSITY

Applied Mathematics	M,D
Chemistry	M,D
Environmental Sciences	M
Geology	M
Mathematics	M,D

WILFRID LAURIER UNIVERSITY

Chemistry	M
Mathematics	M

WILKES UNIVERSITY

Mathematics	M

WOODS HOLE OCEANOGRAPHIC INSTITUTION

Geochemistry	M,D,O
Geophysics	M,D,O
Marine Geology	M,D,O
Oceanography	M,D,O

WORCESTER POLYTECHNIC INSTITUTE

Applied Mathematics	M,D
Applied Statistics	M,D
Chemistry	M,D
Mathematics	M,D
Physics	M,D

WRIGHT STATE UNIVERSITY

Applied Mathematics	M
Applied Statistics	M
Chemistry	M
Environmental Sciences	M,D
Geology	M
Geophysics	M
Mathematics	M
Physics	M

YALE UNIVERSITY

Applied Mathematics	M,D
Applied Physics	M,D
Astronomy	M,D
Astrophysics	M,D
Atmospheric Sciences	D
Biostatistics	M,D
Chemistry	D
Environmental Management and Policy	M,D
Environmental Sciences	M,D
Forestry	M,D
Geochemistry	D
Geology	D
Geophysics	D
Geosciences	D
Inorganic Chemistry	D
Mathematics	M,D
Meteorology	D
Oceanography	D
Organic Chemistry	D
Paleontology	D
Physical Chemistry	D
Physics	D
Planetary and Space Sciences	M,D
Statistics	M,D
Theoretical Chemistry	D

YORK UNIVERSITY

Applied Mathematics	M,D
Astronomy	M,D
Chemistry	M,D
Environmental Management and Policy	M,D
Geosciences	M,D
Mathematics	M,D
Physics	M,D
Planetary and Space Sciences	M,D
Statistics	M,D

YOUNGSTOWN STATE UNIVERSITY

Analytical Chemistry	M
Applied Mathematics	M
Chemistry	M
Environmental Management and Policy	M,O
Inorganic Chemistry	M
Mathematics	M
Organic Chemistry	M
Physical Chemistry	M
Statistics	M

ACADEMIC AND PROFESSIONAL PROGRAMS IN THE PHYSICAL SCIENCES

Section 1
Astronomy and Astrophysics

This section contains a directory of institutions offering graduate work in astronomy and astrophysics, followed by in-depth entries submitted by institutions that chose to prepare detailed program descriptions. Additional information about programs listed in the directory but not augmented by an in-depth entry may be obtained by writing directly to the dean of a graduate school or chair of a department at the address given in the directory.

For programs offering related work, see also in this book *Geosciences, Meteorology and Atmospheric Sciences,* and *Physics.* In the other guides in this series:

Graduate Programs in the Biological Sciences
See *Biological and Biomedical Sciences and Biophysics*
Graduate Programs in Engineering & Applied Sciences
See *Aerospace/Aeronautical Engineering, Energy and Power Engineering (Nuclear Engineering), Engineering and Applied Sciences,* and *Mechanical Engineering and Mechanics*

CONTENTS

Program Directories

Close-Ups

See:

Astronomy

Boston University, Graduate School of Arts and Sciences, Department of Astronomy, Boston, MA 02215. Offers MA, PhD. *Students:* 38 full-time (20 women); includes 2 minority (1 American Indian/Alaska Native, 1 Hispanic American), 8 international. Average age 26. 64 applicants, 30% accepted, 6 enrolled. In 2009, 8 master's awarded. Terminal master's awarded for partial completion of doctoral program. *Degree requirements:* For master's, one foreign language, comprehensive exam, thesis or alternative; for doctorate, one foreign language, comprehensive exam, thesis/dissertation. *Entrance requirements:* For master's and doctorate, GRE General Test, GRE Subject Test (physics), 3 letters of recommendation. Additional exam requirements/recommendations for international students: Required—TOEFL (minimum score 550 paper-based; 213 computer-based). *Application deadline:* For fall admission, 1/15 for domestic and international students. Application fee: $70. *Expenses:* Tuition: Full-time $37,910; part-time $1184 per credit hour. Required fees: $386; $40 per semester. Part-time tuition and fees vary according to class time, course level, degree level and program. *Financial support:* In 2009–10, 1 fellowship with full tuition reimbursement (averaging $18,900 per year), 31 research assistantships with full tuition reimbursements (averaging $18,400 per year), 9 teaching assistantships with full tuition reimbursements (averaging $18,400 per year) were awarded; Federal Work-Study and unspecified assistantships also available. Support available to part-time students. Financial award application deadline: 1/15; financial award applicants required to submit FAFSA. *Unit head:* James Jackson, Chairman, 617-353-6499, Fax: 617-353-6463, E-mail: jackson@bu.edu. *Application contact:* Laura Wipf, Department Administrator, 617-363-2625, Fax: 617-353-5704, E-mail: lwipf@bu.edu.

Brigham Young University, Graduate Studies, College of Physical and Mathematical Sciences, Department of Physics and Astronomy, Provo, UT 84602-1001. Offers physics (MS, PhD); physics and astronomy (PhD). Part-time programs available. *Faculty:* 27 full-time (2 women). *Students:* 40 full-time (7 women); includes 6 minority (5 Asian Americans or Pacific Islanders, 1 Hispanic American). Average age 29. 14 applicants, 71% accepted, 10 enrolled. In 2009, 5 master's, 3 doctorates awarded. Terminal master's awarded for partial completion of doctoral program. *Degree requirements:* For master's, thesis; for doctorate, thesis/dissertation, qualifying exam. *Entrance requirements:* For master's and doctorate, GRE Subject Test (physics), minimum GPA of 3.0 in last 60 hours, ecclesiastical endorsement. Additional exam requirements/recommendations for international students: Required—TOEFL (minimum score 580 paper-based; 85 iBT), IELTS (minimum score 7). *Application deadline:* For fall admission, 1/15 priority date for domestic and international students. Application fee: $50. Electronic applications accepted. *Expenses:* Tuition: Full-time $5580; part-time $301 per credit hour. Tuition and fees vary according to student's religious affiliation. *Financial support:* In 2009–10, 38 students received support, including 22 research assistantships with full tuition reimbursements available (averaging $19,730 per year), 18 teaching assistantships with full tuition reimbursements available (averaging $18,780 per year); fellowships with full tuition reimbursements available, institutionally sponsored loans and tuition waivers (full) also available. Support available to part-time students. Financial award application deadline: 1/15. *Faculty research:* Acoustics; atomic, molecular, and optical physics; theoretical and mathematical physics; condensed matter; astrophysics and plasma. Total annual research expenditures: $1.8 million. *Unit head:* Dr. Ross L. Spencer, Chair, 801-422-2341, Fax: 801-422-0553, E-mail: ross.spencer@byu.edu. *Application contact:* Dr. J. Ward Moody, Graduate Coordinator, 801-422-4347, Fax: 801-422-0553, E-mail: moody@byu.edu.

California Institute of Technology, Division of Physics, Mathematics and Astronomy, Department of Astronomy, Pasadena, CA 91125-0001. Offers PhD. *Degree requirements:* For doctorate, one foreign language, thesis/dissertation, candidacy and final exams. *Entrance requirements:* For doctorate, GRE General Test, GRE Subject Test. Additional exam requirements/recommendations for international students: Required—TOEFL. *Faculty research:* Observational and theoretical astrophysics, cosmology, radio astronomy, solar physics.

Case Western Reserve University, School of Graduate Studies, Department of Astronomy, Cleveland, OH 44106. Offers MS, PhD. Part-time programs available. *Faculty:* 4 full-time (2 women), 3 part-time/adjunct (1 woman). *Students:* 2 full-time (0 women), 1 international. Average age 25. 13 applicants, 38% accepted, 0 enrolled. *Degree requirements:* For doctorate, thesis/dissertation. *Entrance requirements:* For doctorate, GRE General Test, GRE Subject Test (physics). Additional exam requirements/recommendations for international students: Required—TOEFL (minimum score 550 paper-based; 213 computer-based; 79 iBT). *Application deadline:* For fall admission, 1/15 for domestic students. Applications are processed on a rolling basis. Application fee: $50. Electronic applications accepted. *Financial support:* Fellowships, research assistantships available. Financial award application deadline: 2/15; financial award applicants required to submit FAFSA. *Faculty research:* Ground-based optical astronomy, high- and low-dispersion spectroscopy, theoretical astrophysics, galactic structure. *Unit head:* James Christopher Mihos, Chair, 216-368-3729, Fax: 216-368-5406, E-mail: mihos@case.edu. *Application contact:* Agnes Torontalli, Department Assistant, 216-368-3728, Fax: 216-368-5406, E-mail: agnes@case.edu.

Clemson University, Graduate School, College of Engineering and Science, Department of Physics and Astronomy, Clemson, SC 29634. Offers physics (MS, PhD), including astronomy and astrophysics, atmospheric physics, biophysics. Part-time programs available. *Faculty:* 25 full-time (4 women), 1 part-time/adjunct (0 women). *Students:* 46 full-time (11 women), 3 part-time (0 women); includes 1 minority (African American), 22 international. Average age 27. 71 applicants, 62% accepted, 17 enrolled. In 2009, 8 master's, 5 doctorates awarded. Terminal master's awarded for partial completion of doctoral program. *Degree requirements:* For master's, thesis or alternative; for doctorate, thesis/dissertation. *Entrance requirements:* For master's and doctorate, GRE General Test. Additional exam requirements/recommendations for international students: Required—TOEFL. *Application deadline:* For fall admission, 1/15 priority date for domestic students; for spring admission, 9/15 priority date for domestic students. Applications are processed on a rolling basis. Application fee: $70 ($80 for international students). Electronic applications accepted. *Expenses:* Tuition, state resident: full-time $8684; part-time $528 per credit hour. Tuition, nonresident: full-time $15,330; part-time $1078 per credit hour. Required fees: $736; $37 per semester. Part-time tuition and fees vary according to course load and program. *Financial support:* In 2009–10, 45 students received support, including 1 fellowship with full and partial tuition reimbursement available (averaging $10,000 per year), 13 research assistantships with partial tuition reimbursements available (averaging $21,423 per year), 32 teaching assistantships with partial tuition reimbursements available (averaging $16,490 per year); career-related internships or fieldwork, institutionally sponsored loans, scholarships/grants, health care benefits, and unspecified assistantships also available. Support available to part-time students. Financial award application deadline: 6/1; financial award applicants required to submit FAFSA. *Faculty research:* Radiation physics, solid-state physics, nuclear physics, radar and lidar studies of atmosphere. Total annual research expenditures: $3.1 million. *Unit head:* Dr. Peter Barnes, Chair, 864-656-3419, Fax: 864-656-0805, E-mail: peterb@clemson.edu. *Application contact:* Dr. Murray Daw, Graduate Coordinator, 864-656-6702, Fax: 864-656-0805, E-mail: physgradinfo-l@clemson.edu.

Columbia University, Graduate School of Arts and Sciences, Division of Natural Sciences, Department of Astronomy, New York, NY 10027. Offers M Phil, MA, PhD. Part-time programs available. *Degree requirements:* For doctorate, thesis/dissertation. *Entrance requirements:* For master's and doctorate, GRE General Test, major in astronomy or physics. Additional exam requirements/recommendations for international students: Required—TOEFL. *Faculty research:* Theoretical astrophysics, x-ray astronomy, radio astronomy.

Cornell University, Graduate School, Graduate Fields of Arts and Sciences, Field of Astronomy and Space Sciences, Ithaca, NY 14853-0001. Offers astronomy (PhD); astrophysics (PhD); general space sciences (PhD); infrared astronomy (PhD); planetary studies (PhD); radio astronomy (PhD); radiophysics (PhD); theoretical astrophysics (PhD). *Faculty:* 30 full-time (2 women). *Students:* 31 full-time (12 women); includes 3 minority (2 Asian Americans or Pacific Islanders, 1 Hispanic American), 9 international. Average age 26. 77 applicants, 19% accepted, 3 enrolled. In 2009, 3 doctorates awarded. *Degree requirements:* For doctorate, comprehensive exam, thesis/dissertation. *Entrance requirements:* For doctorate, GRE General Test, GRE Subject Test (physics), 3 letters of recommendation. Additional exam requirements/recommendations for international students: Required—TOEFL (minimum score 600 paper-based; 250 computer-based; 77 iBT). *Application deadline:* For fall admission, 1/15 for domestic students. Application fee: $70. Electronic applications accepted. *Expenses:* Tuition: Full-time $29,500. Required fees: $70. Full-time tuition and fees vary according to degree level, program and student level. *Financial support:* In 2009–10, 31 students received support, including 1 research assistantship with full tuition reimbursement available, 2 teaching assistantships with full tuition reimbursements available; fellowships with full tuition reimbursements available, institutionally sponsored loans, scholarships/grants, health care benefits, tuition waivers (full and partial), and unspecified assistantships also available. Financial award applicants required to submit FAFSA. *Faculty research:* Observational astrophysics, planetary sciences, cosmology, instrumentation, gravitational astrophysics. *Unit head:* Director of Graduate Studies, 607-255-4341. *Application contact:* Graduate Field Assistant, 607-255-4341, E-mail: oconnor@astro.cornell.edu.

Dartmouth College, Arts and Sciences Graduate Programs, Department of Physics and Astronomy, Hanover, NH 03755. Offers MS, PhD. *Faculty:* 17 full-time (4 women), 7 part-time/adjunct (1 woman). *Students:* 51 full-time (16 women); includes 3 minority (1 African American, 1 Asian American or Pacific Islander, 1 Hispanic American), 18 international. Average age 26. 86 applicants, 30% accepted, 15 enrolled. In 2009, 5 doctorates awarded. Terminal master's awarded for partial completion of doctoral program. *Degree requirements:* For master's, thesis; for doctorate, thesis/dissertation. *Entrance requirements:* For master's and doctorate, GRE General Test, GRE Subject Test. Additional exam requirements/recommendations for international students: Required—TOEFL. *Application deadline:* For fall admission, 2/1 priority date for domestic students. Application fee: $15. *Financial support:* In 2009–10, 42 students received support, including fellowships with full tuition reimbursements available (averaging $23,832 per year), research assistantships with full tuition reimbursements available (averaging $23,832 per year), teaching assistantships with full tuition reimbursements available (averaging $23,832 per year); institutionally sponsored loans, scholarships/grants, and tuition waivers (full) also available. *Faculty research:* Matter physics, plasma and beam physics, space physics, astronomy, cosmology. *Unit head:* Walter E. Lawrence, Chair, Graduate Admissions, 603-646-2854, Fax: 603-646-1446. *Application contact:* Judy Lowell, Administrative Assistant, 603-646-2854, Fax: 603-646-1446.

Georgia State University, College of Arts and Sciences, Department of Physics and Astronomy, Program in Astronomy, Atlanta, GA 30302-3083. Offers PhD. *Degree requirements:* For doctorate, 2 foreign languages, thesis/dissertation, exam. *Entrance requirements:* For doctorate, GRE General Test, GRE Subject Test. Additional exam requirements/recommendations for international students: Required—TOEFL. Electronic applications accepted. *Faculty research:* Extragalactic photometry, theoretical astrophysics, young stellar objects.

Harvard University, Graduate School of Arts and Sciences, Department of Astronomy, Cambridge, MA 02138. Offers astronomy (PhD); astrophysics (PhD). *Degree requirements:* For doctorate, thesis/dissertation, paper, research project, 2 semesters of teaching. *Entrance requirements:* For doctorate, GRE General Test, GRE Subject Test (physics). Additional exam requirements/recommendations for international students: Required—TOEFL. Electronic applications accepted. *Expenses:* Tuition: Full-time $33,696. Required fees: $1126. Full-time tuition and fees vary according to program. *Faculty research:* Atomic and molecular physics, electromagnetism, solar physics, nuclear physics, fluid dynamics.

Indiana University Bloomington, University Graduate School, College of Arts and Sciences, Department of Astronomy, Bloomington, IN 47405-7000. Offers astronomy (MA, PhD); astrophysics (PhD). *Faculty:* 9 full-time (5 women), 1 part-time/adjunct (0 women). *Students:* 23 full-time (7 women); includes 2 minority (1 American Indian/Alaska Native, 1 Asian American or Pacific Islander), 1 international. Average age 29. 30 applicants, 27% accepted, 3 enrolled. In 2009, 1 master's awarded. Terminal master's awarded for partial completion of doctoral program. *Degree requirements:* For master's, thesis or alternative, oral exam; for doctorate, comprehensive exam, thesis/dissertation, oral defense. *Entrance requirements:* For master's and doctorate, GRE General Test, GRE Subject Test (physics), BA or BS in science. Additional exam requirements/recommendations for international students: Required—TOEFL. *Application deadline:* For fall admission, 1/15 for domestic students, 12/1 for international students; for spring admission, 9/1 for domestic students. Application fee: $55 ($65 for international students). Electronic applications accepted. *Financial support:* In 2009–10, 21 students received support, including 3 fellowships with full tuition reimbursements available (averaging $15,000 per year), 8 research assistantships with full tuition reimbursements available (averaging $16,667 per year), 10 teaching assistantships with full tuition reimbursements available (averaging $14,008 per year); Federal Work-Study and tuition waivers (full and partial) also available. Support available to part-time students. Financial award application deadline: 1/15. *Faculty research:* Stellar and galaxy dynamics, stellar chemical abundancies, galaxy evolution, observational cosmology, astrophsical disk. *Unit head:* Dr. Catherine Pilachowski, Chair, 812-855-6913, Fax: 812-855-8725, E-mail: catyp@astro.indiana.edu. *Application contact:* Christina Lirot, Department Manager, 812-855-6912, Fax: 812-855-8725, E-mail: clirot@indiana.edu.

Iowa State University of Science and Technology, Graduate College, College of Liberal Arts and Sciences, Department of Physics and Astronomy, Ames, IA 50011. Offers applied physics (MS, PhD); astrophysics (MS, PhD); condensed matter physics (MS, PhD); high energy physics (MS, PhD); nuclear physics (MS, PhD); physics (MS, PhD). Part-time programs available. *Faculty:* 46 full-time (3 women), 4 part-time/adjunct (0 women). *Students:* 94 full-time (21 women), 4 part-time (0 women); includes 3 minority (all Asian Americans or Pacific Islanders), 56 international. 185 applicants, 32% accepted, 15 enrolled. In 2009, 4 master's, 7 doctorates awarded. Terminal master's awarded for partial completion of doctoral program. *Degree requirements:* For master's, thesis (for some programs); for doctorate, thesis/dissertation. *Entrance requirements:* For master's and doctorate, GRE General Test, GRE Subject Test (physics). Additional exam requirements/recommendations for international students: Required—TOEFL (minimum score 550 paper-based; 79 iBT) or IELTS (minimum score 6.5). *Application deadline:* For fall admission, 2/15 priority date for domestic and international students; for spring admission, 10/15 for domestic and international students. Applications are processed on a rolling basis. Application fee: $40 ($90 for international students). Electronic applications accepted. *Expenses:* Tuition, state resident: full-time $6716. Tuition, nonresident: full-time $8908. Tuition and fees vary according to course level, course load, program and student level. *Financial support:* In 2009–10, 58 research assistantships with full and partial tuition reimbursements (averaging $17,000 per year), 33 teaching assistantships with full and partial tuition reimbursements (averaging $16,000 per year) were awarded; fellowships, Federal Work-Study, institutionally sponsored loans, scholarships/grants, health care benefits, and unspecified assistantships also available. Support available to part-time students. Financial award application deadline: 2/15. *Faculty research:* Condensed-matter physics, including superconductivity and new materials; high-energy and nuclear physics; astronomy and astrophysics; atmospheric and environmental physics. Total annual research expenditures: $8.8 million. *Unit head:* Dr. Joseph Shinar, Chair, 515-294-3455, Fax: 515-294-6027, E-mail:

phys_astro@iastate.edu. *Application contact:* Dr. Steven Kawaler, Director of Graduate Education, 515-294-9728, E-mail: phys_astro@iastate.edu.

The Johns Hopkins University, Zanvyl Krieger School of Arts and Sciences, Henry A. Rowland Department of Physics and Astronomy, Baltimore, MD 21218-2699. Offers astronomy (PhD); physics (PhD). *Faculty:* 30 full-time (2 women), 14 part-time/adjunct (3 women). *Students:* 107 full-time (17 women); includes 4 minority (3 Asian Americans or Pacific Islanders, 1 Hispanic American), 47 international. Average age 26. 258 applicants, 19% accepted, 49 enrolled. In 2009, 16 doctorates awarded. Terminal master's awarded for partial completion of doctoral program. *Degree requirements:* For doctorate, comprehensive exam, thesis/dissertation, complete required coursework with minimum B- average. *Entrance requirements:* For doctorate, GRE General Test, GRE Subject Test. Additional exam requirements/recommendations for international students: Required—TOEFL (minimum score 600 paper-based; 250 computer-based; 100 iBT), IELTS. *Application deadline:* For fall admission, 1/14 for domestic and international students. Application fee: $75. Electronic applications accepted. *Financial support:* In 2009–10, 107 students received support, including 4 fellowships with full tuition reimbursements available (averaging $26,000 per year), 55 research assistantships with full tuition reimbursements available (averaging $26,000 per year), 48 teaching assistantships with full tuition reimbursements available (averaging $19,500 per year); career-related internships or fieldwork, Federal Work-Study, institutionally sponsored loans, tuition waivers (partial), and unspecified assistantships also available. Financial award application deadline: 4/15; financial award applicants required to submit FAFSA. *Faculty research:* High-energy physics, condensed-matter, astrophysics, particle and experimental physics, plasma physics. Total annual research expenditures: $24.9 million. *Unit head:* Dr. Daniel H. Reich, Chair, 410-516-7346, Fax: 410-516-7239, E-mail: dhr@pha.jhu.edu. *Application contact:* Carmelita D. King, Academic Affairs Administrator, 410-516-7344, Fax: 410-516-7239, E-mail: jazzy@pha.jhu.edu.

See Close-Up on page 219.

Louisiana State University and Agricultural and Mechanical College, Graduate School, College of Basic Sciences, Department of Physics and Astronomy, Baton Rouge, LA 70803. Offers astronomy (PhD); astrophysics (PhD); medical physics (MS); physics (MS, PhD). *Faculty:* 45 full-time (4 women), 1 part-time/adjunct (0 women). *Students:* 97 full-time (24 women), 5 part-time (1 woman); includes 5 minority (1 African American, 2 Asian Americans or Pacific Islanders, 2 Hispanic Americans), 42 international. Average age 27. 127 applicants, 20% accepted, 21 enrolled. In 2009, 9 master's, 8 doctorates awarded. Terminal master's awarded for partial completion of doctoral program. *Degree requirements:* For master's, thesis or alternative; for doctorate, thesis/dissertation. *Entrance requirements:* For master's and doctorate, GRE General Test, minimum GPA of 3.0. Additional exam requirements/ recommendations for international students: Required—TOEFL (minimum score 550 paper-based; 213 computer-based; 79 iBT) or IELTS (minimum score 6.5). *Application deadline:* For fall admission, 1/25 priority date for domestic students, 5/15 for international students; for spring admission, 10/15 for international students. Applications are processed on a rolling basis. Application fee: $50 ($70 for international students). Electronic applications accepted. *Financial support:* In 2009–10, 16 fellowships with full tuition reimbursements (averaging $24,969 per year), 53 research assistantships with full and partial tuition reimbursements (averaging $20,101 per year), 37 teaching assistantships with full and partial tuition reimbursements (averaging $17,943 per year) were awarded; Federal Work-Study, institutionally sponsored loans, health care benefits, tuition waivers (full and partial), and unspecified assistantships also available. Financial award application deadline: 3/15; financial award applicants required to submit FAFSA. *Faculty research:* Experimentation and numerical relativity, condensed matter astrophysics, quantum computing, medical physics. Total annual research expenditures: $7.5 million. *Unit head:* Dr. Michael Cherry, Chair, 225-578-2261, Fax: 225-578-5855, E-mail: cherry@phys.lsu.edu. *Application contact:* Arnell Dangerfield, Administrative Coordinator, 225-578-1193, Fax: 225-578-5855, E-mail: adanger@lsu.edu.

Michigan State University, The Graduate School, College of Natural Science, Department of Physics and Astronomy, East Lansing, MI 48824. Offers astrophysics and astronomy (MS, PhD); physics (MS, PhD). *Entrance requirements:* Additional exam requirements/ recommendations for international students: Required—TOEFL (minimum score 550 paper-based; 213 computer-based), Michigan State University ELT (85), Michigan ELAB (83). Electronic applications accepted. *Faculty research:* Nuclear and accelerator physics, high energy physics, condensed matter physics, biophysics, astrophysics and astronomy.

Minnesota State University Mankato, College of Graduate Studies, College of Science, Engineering and Technology, Department of Physics and Astronomy, Mankato, MN 56001. Offers MS. *Students:* 4 full-time (1 woman), 3 part-time (1 woman). *Degree requirements:* For master's, one foreign language, comprehensive exam, thesis or alternative. *Entrance requirements:* For master's, minimum GPA of 3.0 during previous 2 years, recommendation letters. Additional exam requirements/recommendations for international students: Required—TOEFL. *Application deadline:* For fall admission, 7/1 priority date for domestic students; for spring admission, 11/1 for domestic students. Applications are processed on a rolling basis. Application fee: $40. Electronic applications accepted. *Expenses:* Tuition, state resident: full-time $5364. Tuition, nonresident: full-time $8314. *Financial support:* Research assistantships, teaching assistantships with full tuition reimbursements, Federal Work-Study and unspecified assistantships available. Support available to part-time students. Financial award application deadline: 3/15; financial award applicants required to submit FAFSA. *Unit head:* Dr. Mark Pickar, Chairperson, 507-389-5743. *Application contact:* 507-389-2321, E-mail: grad@mnsu.edu.

New Mexico State University, Graduate School, College of Arts and Sciences, Department of Astronomy, Las Cruces, NM 88003-8001. Offers MS, PhD. Part-time programs available. *Faculty:* 9 full-time (2 women). *Students:* 30 full-time (11 women), 4 part-time (1 woman); includes 2 minority (1 Asian American or Pacific Islander, 1 Hispanic American), 1 international. Average age 28. 37 applicants, 54% accepted, 7 enrolled. In 2009, 4 master's, 2 doctorates awarded. Terminal master's awarded for partial completion of doctoral program. *Degree requirements:* For master's, thesis (for some programs); for doctorate, thesis/dissertation. *Entrance requirements:* For master's and doctorate, GRE General Test, GRE Subject Test (advanced physics). Additional exam requirements/recommendations for international students: Required—TOEFL. *Application deadline:* For fall admission, 2/15 priority date for domestic and international students. Applications are processed on a rolling basis. Application fee: $30 ($50 for international students). Electronic applications accepted. *Expenses:* Tuition, state resident: full-time $4080; part-time $223 per credit. Tuition, nonresident: full-time $14,256; part-time $647 per credit. Required fees: $1278; $639 per semester. *Financial support:* In 2009–10, 18 research assistantships with tuition reimbursements (averaging $13,943 per year), 7 teaching assistantships with partial tuition reimbursements (averaging $13,600 per year) were awarded; scholarships/grants, health care benefits, and unspecified assistantships also available. Financial award application deadline: 3/1. *Faculty research:* Planetary systems, accreting binary stars, stellar populations, galaxies, interstellar medium. *Unit head:* Dr. James Murphy, Head, 575-646-5333, Fax: 575-646-1602, E-mail: murphy@nmsu.edu. *Application contact:* Dr. James Murphy, Head, 575-646-5333, Fax: 575-646-1602, E-mail: murphy@nmsu.edu.

Northwestern University, The Graduate School, Judd A. and Marjorie Weinberg College of Arts and Sciences, Department of Physics and Astronomy, Evanston, IL 60208. Offers astrophysics (PhD); physics (MS, PhD). Admissions and degrees offered through The Graduate School. *Degree requirements:* For doctorate, thesis/dissertation, qualifying exam. *Entrance requirements:* For doctorate, GRE General Test, GRE Subject Test. Additional exam requirements/recommendations for international students: Required—TOEFL. *Faculty research:* Nuclear and particle physics, condensed-matter physics, nonlinear physics, astrophysics.

The Ohio State University, Graduate School, College of Mathematical and Physical Sciences, Department of Astronomy, Columbus, OH 43210. Offers MS, PhD. *Faculty:* 20. *Students:* 16 full-time (7 women), 13 part-time (5 women); includes 1 minority (Asian American or Pacific Islander), 8 international. Average age 25. In 2009, 3 doctorates awarded. *Degree requirements:* For master's, comprehensive exam, thesis; for doctorate, comprehensive exam, thesis/dissertation. *Entrance requirements:* For master's and doctorate, GRE General Test, GRE Subject Test (physics). Additional exam requirements/recommendations for international students: Required—TOEFL (minimum score 600 paper-based; 250 computer-based). *Application deadline:* For fall admission, 8/15 priority date for domestic students, 7/1 priority date for international students; for winter admission, 12/1 priority date for domestic students, 11/1 priority date for international students; for spring admission, 3/1 priority date for domestic students, 2/1 priority date for international students. Applications are processed on a rolling basis. Application fee: $40 ($50 for international students). Electronic applications accepted. *Expenses:* Tuition, state resident: full-time $10,683. Tuition, nonresident: full-time $25,923. Tuition and fees vary according to course load and program. *Financial support:* Fellowships, research assistantships, teaching assistantships, Federal Work-Study and institutionally sponsored loans available. Support available to part-time students. *Unit head:* B. Scott Gaudi, Graduate Studies Committee Chair, E-mail: gaudi.1@osu.edu. *Application contact:* 614-292-9444, Fax: 614-292-3895, E-mail: domestic.grad@osu.edu.

Ohio University, Graduate College, College of Arts and Sciences, Department of Physics and Astronomy, Athens, OH 45701. Offers astronomy (MS, PhD); physics (MS, PhD). Part-time programs available. *Faculty:* 29 full-time (3 women), 6 part-time/adjunct (0 women). *Students:* 73 full-time (24 women); includes 1 minority (Hispanic American), 57 international. Average age 27. 128 applicants, 30% accepted, 15 enrolled. In 2009, 1 master's, 4 doctorates awarded. Terminal master's awarded for partial completion of doctoral program. *Degree requirements:* For master's, thesis or alternative; for doctorate, comprehensive exam, thesis/dissertation. *Entrance requirements:* For master's and doctorate, minimum GPA of 3.0. Additional exam requirements/recommendations for international students: Required—TOEFL (minimum score 600 paper-based; 250 computer-based; 100 iBT), IELTS (minimum score 7), TWE (minimum score 4). *Application deadline:* For fall admission, 4/1 priority date for domestic and international students. Applications are processed on a rolling basis. Application fee: $55. Electronic applications accepted. *Expenses:* Tuition, state resident: full-time $7839; part-time $323 per quarter hour. Tuition, nonresident: full-time $15,831; part-time $654 per quarter hour. Required fees: $2931. *Financial support:* In 2009–10, 35 research assistantships with full tuition reimbursements (averaging $22,984 per year), 32 teaching assistantships with full tuition reimbursements (averaging $20,886 per year) were awarded; scholarships/grants and unspecified assistantships also available. Financial award application deadline: 4/1. *Faculty research:* Nuclear physics, condensed-matter physics, nonlinear systems, astrophysics, biophysics. Total annual research expenditures: $2.3 million. *Unit head:* Dr. Joseph Shields, Chair, 740-593-0336, Fax: 740-593-0433, E-mail: shields@helios.phy.ohiou.edu. *Application contact:* Dr. Marcus Boettcher, Graduate Admissions Chair, 740-593-1714, Fax: 740-593-0433, E-mail: gradapp@phy.ohiou.edu.

See Close-Up on page 225.

Penn State University Park, Graduate School, Eberly College of Science, Department of Astronomy and Astrophysics, State College, University Park, PA 16802-1503. Offers MS, PhD. *Unit head:* Dr. Eric D. Feigelson, Assistant Department Head, 814-865-0162, Fax: 814-863-3399. *Application contact:* Cynthia E. Nicosia, Director, Graduate Enrollment Services, 814-865-1795, Fax: 814-865-4627, E-mail: cey1@psu.edu.

Princeton University, Graduate School, Department of Astrophysical Sciences, Princeton, NJ 08544-1019. Offers astronomy (PhD); plasma physics (PhD). *Degree requirements:* For doctorate, thesis/dissertation. *Entrance requirements:* For doctorate, GRE General Test, GRE Subject Test (physics). Additional exam requirements/recommendations for international students: Required—TOEFL (minimum score 600 paper-based; 250 computer-based). Electronic applications accepted. *Faculty research:* Theoretical astrophysics, cosmology, galaxy formation, galactic dynamics, interstellar and intergalactic matter.

Rensselaer Polytechnic Institute, Graduate School, School of Science, Department of Physics, Applied Physics and Astronomy, Program in Astronomy, Troy, NY 12180-3590. Offers MS. *Expenses:* Tuition: Full-time $38,100.

Rice University, Graduate Programs, Wiess School of Natural Sciences, Department of Physics and Astronomy, Houston, TX 77251-1892. Offers nanoscale physics (MS); physics and astronomy (PhD); science teaching (MST). Part-time programs available. *Faculty:* 39 full-time (4 women), 9 part-time/adjunct (1 woman). *Students:* 124 full-time (19 women), 12 part-time (7 women); includes 8 minority (5 Asian Americans or Pacific Islanders, 3 Hispanic Americans), 70 international. Average age 28. 192 applicants, 26% accepted, 22 enrolled. In 2009, 16 master's, 21 doctorates awarded. *Degree requirements:* For master's, thesis (for some programs); for doctorate, thesis/dissertation, Maintain at least a B average. *Entrance requirements:* For master's, GRE General Test; for doctorate, General GRE, Subject GRE. Additional exam requirements/recommendations for international students: Required—TOEFL (minimum score 600 paper-based; 250 computer-based; 90 iBT). *Application deadline:* For fall admission, 2/1 priority date for domestic and international students. Application fee: $70. Electronic applications accepted. *Financial support:* In 2009–10, 124 students received support, including 22 fellowships with full tuition reimbursements available (averaging $25,700 per year), 102 research assistantships with full tuition reimbursements available (averaging $25,700 per year). Financial award application deadline: 2/1. *Faculty research:* Optical physics; ultra cold atoms; membrane electr-statics, peptides, proteins and lipids; solar astrophysics; stellar activity; magnetic fields; young stars. *Unit head:* Rose Berridge, Department Administrator, 713-348-4938, Fax: 713-348-4510, E-mail: physics@rice.edu. *Application contact:* Bridgitt G. Ayers, Graduate Program Coordinator, 713-348-6348, Fax: 713-348-4150, E-mail: physgrad@rice.edu.

Rutgers, The State University of New Jersey, New Brunswick, Graduate School-New Brunswick, Department of Physics and Astronomy, Piscataway, NJ 08854-8097. Offers astronomy (MS, PhD); biophysics (PhD); condensed matter physics (MS, PhD); elementary particle physics (MS, PhD); intermediate energy nuclear physics (MS); nuclear physics (MS, PhD); physics (MST); surface science (PhD); theoretical physics (MS, PhD). Part-time programs available. Terminal master's awarded for partial completion of doctoral program. *Degree requirements:* For master's, comprehensive exam, thesis or alternative; for doctorate, comprehensive exam, thesis/dissertation. *Entrance requirements:* For master's and doctorate, GRE General Test, GRE Subject Test. Additional exam requirements/recommendations for international students: Required—TOEFL (minimum score 560 paper-based). Electronic applications accepted. *Faculty research:* Astronomy, high energy, condensed matter, surface, nuclear physics.

Saint Mary's University, Faculty of Science, Department of Astronomy and Physics, Halifax, NS B3H 3C3, Canada. Offers astronomy (M Sc, PhD). Part-time programs available. *Degree requirements:* For master's, thesis optional; for doctorate, comprehensive exam, thesis/dissertation. *Entrance requirements:* For master's, honors degree with minimum GPA of 3.0. Additional exam requirements/recommendations for international students: Required—TOEFL. *Application deadline:* For fall admission, 3/1 priority date for domestic students. Application fee: $35. *Financial support:* Fellowships, research assistantships, teaching assistantships, career-related internships or fieldwork, institutionally sponsored loans, and scholarships/grants available. Support available to part-time students. Financial award application deadline: 5/1. *Faculty research:* Young stellar objects, interstellar medium, star clusters, galactic structure, early-type galaxies. *Unit head:* Ian Short, Chair, 902-420-5828, Fax: 902-496-8218, E-mail:

Astronomy

Saint Mary's University (continued)
ishort@ap.smu.ca. *Application contact:* Ian Short, Chair, 902-420-5828, Fax: 902-496-8218, E-mail: ishort@ap.smu.ca.

San Diego State University, Graduate and Research Affairs, College of Sciences, Department of Astronomy, San Diego, CA 92182. Offers MS. *Degree requirements:* For master's, thesis. *Entrance requirements:* For master's, GRE General Test, letters of reference. Additional exam requirements/recommendations for international students: Required—TOEFL. Electronic applications accepted. *Faculty research:* CCD, classical and dwarf novae, photometry, interactive binaries.

Stony Brook University, State University of New York, Graduate School, College of Arts and Sciences, Department of Physics and Astronomy, Program in Astronomy, Stony Brook, NY 11794. Offers PhD. *Degree requirements:* For doctorate, thesis/dissertation. *Entrance requirements:* For doctorate, GRE General Test, minimum GPA of 3.0. Additional exam requirements/recommendations for international students: Required—TOEFL. *Application deadline:* For fall admission, 1/15 for domestic students. Application fee: $60. *Expenses:* Tuition, state resident: full-time $8370; part-time $349 per credit. Tuition, nonresident: full-time $13,250; part-time $552 per credit. Required fees: $933. *Financial support:* Fellowships, research assistantships, teaching assistantships available. Financial award application deadline: 2/1. *Unit head:* Dr. Peter M. Koch, Chair, 631-632-8100, Fax: 631-632-8176, E-mail: peter.koch@stonybrook.edu. *Application contact:* Dr. Lazlo W. Mihaly, Director, 631-632-8100, Fax: 631-632-8176, E-mail: lazlo.mihaly@stonybrook.edu.

Université de Moncton, Faculty of Science, Department of Physics and Astronomy, Moncton, NB E1A 3E9, Canada. Offers M Sc. Part-time programs available. *Degree requirements:* For master's, thesis. *Entrance requirements:* For master's, proficiency in French. Electronic applications accepted. *Faculty research:* Thin films, optical properties, solar selective surfaces, microgravity and photonic materials.

The University of Arizona, Graduate College, College of Science, Department of Astronomy, Tucson, AZ 85721. Offers MS, PhD. *Faculty:* 20. *Students:* 14 full-time (4 women), 28 part-time (9 women); includes 3 minority (1 American Indian/Alaska Native, 1 Asian American or Pacific Islander, 1 Hispanic American), 11 international. Average age 27. 116 applicants, 12% accepted, 4 enrolled. In 2009, 1 master's, 4 doctorates awarded. *Degree requirements:* For doctorate, thesis/dissertation. *Entrance requirements:* For doctorate, GRE General Test, GRE Subject Test (physics), minimum GPA of 3.5, 3 letters of recommendation. Additional exam requirements/recommendations for international students: Required—TOEFL (minimum score 550 paper-based; 213 computer-based; 79 iBT). *Application deadline:* For fall admission, 1/16 for domestic students, 12/1 for international students. Applications are processed on a rolling basis. Application fee: $75. Electronic applications accepted. *Expenses:* Tuition, state resident: full-time $9028. Tuition, nonresident: full-time $24,890. *Financial support:* In 2009–10, 8 teaching assistantships with full tuition reimbursements (averaging $17,203 per year) were awarded; research assistantships with full tuition reimbursements, scholarships/grants, health care benefits, and unspecified assistantships also available. *Faculty research:* Astrophysics, submillimeter astronomy, infrared astronomy, NICMOS, SIRTF. Total annual research expenditures: $79.3 million. *Unit head:* Dr. Peter A. Strittmatter, Head, 520-621-6524, Fax: 520-621-1532, E-mail: pstrittm@as.arizona.edu. *Application contact:* Erin L. Carlson, Administrative Associate, 520-621-6538, Fax: 520-621-1532, E-mail: ecarlson@as.arizona.edu.

The University of British Columbia, Faculty of Science, Program in Astronomy, Vancouver, BC V6T 1Z1, Canada. Offers M Sc, PhD.

University of Calgary, Faculty of Graduate Studies, Faculty of Science, Department of Physics and Astronomy, Calgary, AB T2N 1N4, Canada. Offers M Sc, PhD. Part-time programs available. *Degree requirements:* For master's, thesis; for doctorate, thesis/dissertation, oral candidacy exam, written qualifying exam. *Entrance requirements:* For master's and doctorate, GRE General Test, GRE Subject Test. Additional exam requirements/recommendations for international students: Required—TOEFL (minimum score 550 paper-based; 213 computer-based). Electronic applications accepted. *Faculty research:* Astronomy and astrophysics, mass spectrometry, atmospheric physics, space physics, medical physics.

University of California, Los Angeles, Graduate Division, College of Letters and Science, Department of Physics and Astronomy, Program in Astronomy, Los Angeles, CA 90095. Offers MAT, MS, PhD. *Students:* 22 full-time (7 women); includes 4 minority (3 Asian Americans or Pacific Islanders, 1 Hispanic American). Average age 27. 60 applicants, 30% accepted, 6 enrolled. In 2009, 2 master's, 7 doctorates awarded. Terminal master's awarded for partial completion of doctoral program. *Degree requirements:* For master's, comprehensive exam; for doctorate, thesis/dissertation, oral and written qualifying exams. *Entrance requirements:* For master's, GRE General Test, GRE Subject Test (physics), minimum GPA of 3.0, statement of purpose, BS in related field; for doctorate, GRE General Test, GRE Subject Test (physics), BS in related field, minimum undergraduate GPA of 3.0. *Application deadline:* For fall admission, 12/15 for domestic and international students. Application fee: $70 ($90 for international students). Electronic applications accepted. *Financial support:* In 2009–10, 10 fellowships with full and partial tuition reimbursements, 20 research assistantships with full and partial tuition reimbursements, 11 teaching assistantships with full and partial tuition reimbursements were awarded; Federal Work-Study, institutionally sponsored loans, scholarships/grants, health care benefits, tuition waivers (full and partial), and unspecified assistantships also available. Financial award application deadline: 3/1; financial award applicants required to submit FAFSA. *Unit head:* Dr. Ferdinand Coroniti, Chair, 310-825-3440. *Application contact:* Carol Finn, Graduate Counselor, 310-825-2307, E-mail: apply@physics.ucla.edu.

University of California, Santa Cruz, Division of Graduate Studies, Division of Physical and Biological Sciences, Department of Astronomy and Astrophysics, Santa Cruz, CA 95064. Offers PhD. *Degree requirements:* For doctorate, one foreign language, thesis/dissertation, qualifying exam. *Entrance requirements:* For doctorate, GRE General Test, GRE Subject Test. Electronic applications accepted. *Faculty research:* Stellar structure and evolution, stellar spectroscopy, the interstellar medium, galactic structure, external galaxies and quasars.

University of Chicago, Division of the Physical Sciences, Department of Astronomy and Astrophysics, Chicago, IL 60637-1513. Offers MS, PhD. Terminal master's awarded for partial completion of doctoral program. *Degree requirements:* For master's, comprehensive exam, thesis optional, candidacy exam; for doctorate, comprehensive exam, thesis/dissertation, dissertation for publication. *Entrance requirements:* For master's, department candidacy examination, minimum GPA of 3.0; for doctorate, GRE General Test, GRE Subject Test, minimum GPA of 3.0. Additional exam requirements/recommendations for international students: Required—TOEFL (minimum score 600 paper-based; 250 computer-based); Recommended—IELTS. Electronic applications accepted. *Faculty research:* Quasi-stellar object absorption lines, fluid dynamics, interstellar matter, particle physics, cosmology.

University of Delaware, College of Arts and Sciences, Department of Physics and Astronomy, Newark, DE 19716. Offers MS, PhD. Part-time programs available. Terminal master's awarded for partial completion of doctoral program. *Degree requirements:* For master's, thesis; for doctorate, thesis/dissertation. *Entrance requirements:* For master's and doctorate, GRE General Test, GRE Subject Test. Additional exam requirements/recommendations for international students: Required—TOEFL (minimum score 600 paper-based; 250 computer-based). Electronic applications accepted. *Faculty research:* Magnetoresistance and magnetic materials, ultrafast optical phenomena, superfluidity, elementary particle physics, stellar atmospheres and interiors.

University of Denver, Faculty of Natural Sciences and Mathematics, Department of Physics and Astronomy, Denver, CO 80208. Offers MS, PhD. Part-time programs available. *Faculty:* 9 full-time (2 women), 1 part-time/adjunct (0 women). *Students:* 4 full-time (2 women), 10 part-time (3 women); includes 1 minority (Hispanic American), 2 international. Average age 28. 23 applicants, 65% accepted, 4 enrolled. In 2009, 1 master's awarded. Terminal master's awarded for partial completion of doctoral program. *Degree requirements:* For master's, thesis optional; for doctorate, thesis/dissertation. *Entrance requirements:* For master's and doctorate, GRE General Test, diagnostic exam. Additional exam requirements/recommendations for international students: Required—TOEFL. *Application deadline:* Applications are processed on a rolling basis. Application fee: $50. Electronic applications accepted. *Expenses:* Tuition: Full-time $34,596; part-time $961 per quarter hour. Required fees: $4 per quarter hour. Tuition and fees vary according to course load, campus/location and program. *Financial support:* In 2009–10, 9 research assistantships with full and partial tuition reimbursements (averaging $18,000 per year), 9 teaching assistantships with full and partial tuition reimbursements (averaging $18,000 per year) were awarded; career-related internships or fieldwork, Federal Work-Study, institutionally sponsored loans, and scholarships/grants also available. Support available to part-time students. Financial award application deadline: 3/1; financial award applicants required to submit FAFSA. *Faculty research:* Atomic and molecular beams and collisions, infrared astronomy, acoustic emission from stressed solids, nano materials. Total annual research expenditures: $1.1 million. *Unit head:* Dr. Davor Balzar, Chair, 303-871-2238. *Application contact:* Information Contact, 303-871-2238, E-mail: bstephen@du.edu.

University of Florida, Graduate School, College of Liberal Arts and Sciences, Department of Astronomy, Gainesville, FL 32611. Offers MS, PhD. Terminal master's awarded for partial completion of doctoral program. *Degree requirements:* For master's, thesis (terminal MS); for doctorate, one foreign language, thesis/dissertation. *Entrance requirements:* For master's and doctorate, GRE General Test, minimum GPA of 3.0. Additional exam requirements/recommendations for international students: Required—TOEFL (minimum score 550 paper-based; 213 computer-based). Electronic applications accepted. *Faculty research:* Cosmology, photometry, variable and binary stars, dynamical solar system astronomy, infrared.

University of Georgia, Graduate School, College of Arts and Sciences, Department of Physics and Astronomy, Athens, GA 30602. Offers physics (MS, PhD). *Faculty:* 22 full-time (2 women). *Students:* 49 full-time (11 women), 3 part-time (2 women); includes 1 minority (African American), 26 international. 110 applicants, 16% accepted, 12 enrolled. In 2009, 9 doctorates awarded. *Degree requirements:* For master's, thesis; for doctorate, one foreign language, thesis/dissertation. *Entrance requirements:* For master's and doctorate, GRE General Test. *Application deadline:* For fall admission, 7/1 priority date for domestic students; for spring admission, 11/15 for domestic students. Application fee: $50. Electronic applications accepted. *Expenses:* Tuition, state resident: full-time $6000; part-time $250 per credit hour. Tuition, nonresident: full-time $20,904; part-time $871 per credit hour. Required fees: $730 per semester. *Financial support:* Fellowships, research assistantships, teaching assistantships, unspecified assistantships available. *Unit head:* Dr. William M. Dennis, Head, 706-542-2485, Fax: 706-542-2492, E-mail: bill@physast.uga.edu. *Application contact:* Dr. Loris Magnani, Graduate Coordinator, 706-542-2876, Fax: 706-542-2492, E-mail: loris@physast.uga.edu.

University of Hawaii at Manoa, Graduate Division, College of Natural Sciences, Department of Physics and Astronomy, Program in Astronomy, Honolulu, HI 96822. Offers MS, PhD. Part-time programs available. *Faculty:* 40 full-time (6 women), 8 part-time/adjunct (0 women). *Students:* 49 full-time (15 women); includes 8 minority (1 American Indian/Alaska Native, 7 Asian Americans or Pacific Islanders), 11 international. Average age 25. 98 applicants, 17% accepted, 5 enrolled. In 2009, 4 master's, 5 doctorates awarded. *Degree requirements:* For master's, thesis optional; for doctorate, comprehensive exam, thesis/dissertation. *Entrance requirements:* For master's and doctorate, GRE General Test. Additional exam requirements/recommendations for international students: Required—TOEFL (minimum score 560 paper-based; 220 computer-based; 83 iBT), IELTS (minimum score 5). *Application deadline:* For fall admission, 12/31 for domestic and international students. Application fee: $60. *Expenses:* Tuition, state resident: full-time $8900; part-time $372 per credit. Tuition, nonresident: full-time $21,400; part-time $898 per credit. Required fees: $207 per semester. *Financial support:* In 2009–10, 40 fellowships (averaging $4,775 per year), 40 research assistantships (averaging $25,510 per year), 5 teaching assistantships (averaging $22,140 per year) were awarded. Total annual research expenditures: $29.3 million. *Application contact:* Joshua Barnes, Graduate Chair, 808-956-8138, Fax: 808-956-4532, E-mail: barnes@hawaii.edu.

University of Illinois at Urbana–Champaign, Graduate College, College of Liberal Arts and Sciences, Department of Astronomy, Champaign, IL 61820. Offers astronomy (PhD). *Faculty:* 12 full-time (1 woman). *Students:* 27 full-time (7 women), 8 part-time (4 women); includes 2 minority (both Asian Americans or Pacific Islanders), 20 international. 53 applicants, 15% accepted, 5 enrolled. In 2009, 3 master's, 4 doctorates awarded. *Entrance requirements:* For master's and doctorate, GRE General Test, minimum GPA of 3.0. Additional exam requirements/recommendations for international students: Required—TOEFL (minimum score 550 paper-based; 213 computer-based). *Application deadline:* Applications are processed on a rolling basis. Application fee: $60 ($75 for international students). Electronic applications accepted. *Financial support:* In 2009–10, 1 fellowship, 24 research assistantships, 14 teaching assistantships were awarded; tuition waivers (full and partial) also available. *Unit head:* You-Hua Chu, Chair, 217-333-5535, Fax: 217-244-7638, E-mail: yhchu@illinois.edu. *Application contact:* Jeri Cochran, Administrative Assistant, 217-333-9784, Fax: 217-244-7638, E-mail: jcochran@illinois.edu.

The University of Iowa, Graduate College, College of Liberal Arts and Sciences, Department of Physics and Astronomy, Program in Astronomy, Iowa City, IA 52242-1316. Offers MS. *Degree requirements:* For master's, thesis optional, exam. *Entrance requirements:* For master's, GRE General Test, minimum GPA of 3.0. Additional exam requirements/recommendations for international students: Required—TOEFL (minimum score 550 paper-based; 213 computer-based; 81 iBT). Electronic applications accepted.

The University of Kansas, Graduate Studies, College of Liberal Arts and Sciences, Department of Physics and Astronomy, Lawrence, KS 66045. Offers computational physics and astronomy (MS); physics (MS, PhD). *Students:* 40 full-time (7 women), 3 part-time (1 woman); includes 3 minority (1 African American, 2 Hispanic Americans), 13 international. Average age 28. 47 applicants, 26% accepted, 6 enrolled. In 2009, 12 master's, 6 doctorates awarded. *Degree requirements:* For master's, thesis (for some programs); for doctorate, comprehensive exam, thesis/dissertation, computer skills, undergraduate certification, communication skills. *Entrance requirements:* For master's and doctorate, GRE Subject Test (physics), undergraduate degree. Additional exam requirements/recommendations for international students: Required—TOEFL. *Application deadline:* For fall admission, 5/1 priority date for domestic and international students; for spring admission, 11/15 for domestic and international students. Applications are processed on a rolling basis. Application fee: $45 ($55 for international students). Electronic applications accepted. *Expenses:* Tuition, state resident: full-time $6492; part-time $270.50 per credit hour. Tuition, nonresident: full-time $15,510; part-time $646.25 per credit hour. Required fees: $847; $70.56 per credit hour. Tuition and fees vary according to course load and program. *Financial support:* Fellowships with full and partial tuition reimbursements, research assistantships with full and partial tuition reimbursements, teaching assistantships with full and partial tuition reimbursements, health care benefits and unspecified assistantships available. Financial award application deadline: 5/1. *Faculty research:* Condensed-matter, cosmology, elementary particles, nuclear physics, space physics, astrophysics, astrobiology, biophysics, high energy. *Unit head:* Dr. Stephen J. Sanders, Chair, 785-864-4626, Fax: 785-864-5262. *Application contact:* Tess Gratton, Graduate Admission Specialist, 785-864-4626, Fax: 785-864-5262, E-mail: physics@ku.edu.

See Close-Up on page 231.

University of Kentucky, Graduate School, College of Arts and Sciences, Program in Physics and Astronomy, Lexington, KY 40506-0032. Offers physics (MS, PhD). *Degree requirements:* For master's, comprehensive exam, thesis optional; for doctorate, comprehensive exam, thesis/dissertation. *Entrance requirements:* For master's, GRE General Test, minimum undergraduate GPA of 2.75; for doctorate, GRE General Test, minimum graduate GPA of 3.0. Additional exam requirements/recommendations for international students: Required—TOEFL (minimum score 550 paper-based; 213 computer-based). Electronic applications accepted. *Faculty research:* Astrophysics, active galactic nuclei, and radio astronomy; Rydbert atoms, and electron scattering; TOF spectroscopy, hyperon interactions and muons; particle theory, lattice gauge theory, quark, and skyrmion models.

University of Maryland, College Park, Academic Affairs, College of Computer, Mathematical and Physical Sciences, Department of Astronomy, College Park, MD 20742. Offers MS, PhD. Part-time and evening/weekend programs available. *Faculty:* 84 full-time (19 women), 14 part-time/adjunct (5 women). *Students:* 33 full-time (15 women), 2 part-time (0 women); includes 4 minority (all Asian Americans or Pacific Islanders), 11 international. 79 applicants, 29% accepted, 6 enrolled. In 2009, 3 doctorates awarded. Terminal master's awarded for partial completion of doctoral program. *Degree requirements:* For master's, thesis or alternative, written exam; for doctorate, thesis/dissertation, research project. *Entrance requirements:* For master's, GRE General Test, GRE Subject Test (physics), minimum GPA of 3.0, 3 letters of recommendation; for doctorate, GRE General Test, GRE Subject Test (physics), 3 letters of recommendation. *Application deadline:* For fall admission, 1/15 for domestic and international students; for spring admission, 6/1 for international students. Applications are processed on a rolling basis. Application fee: $60. Electronic applications accepted. *Expenses:* Tuition, area resident: Part-time $471 per credit hour. Tuition, state resident: part-time $471 per credit hour. Tuition, nonresident: part-time $1016 per credit hour. Required fees: $337.04 per term. *Financial support:* In 2009–10, 1 fellowship with full tuition reimbursement (averaging $19,000 per year), 22 research assistantships with tuition reimbursements (averaging $21,219 per year), 9 teaching assistantships with tuition reimbursements (averaging $18,959 per year) were awarded; career-related internships or fieldwork, Federal Work-Study, and scholarships/grants also available. Support available to part-time students. Financial award applicants required to submit FAFSA. *Faculty research:* Solar radio astronomy, plasma and high-energy astrophysics, galactic and extragalactic astronomy. Total annual research expenditures: $19.4 million. *Unit head:* Stuart N. Vogel, Chair, 301-405-1508, Fax: 301-314-9067, E-mail: svogel@umd.edu. *Application contact:* Dean of Graduate School, 301-405-0358.

University of Massachusetts Amherst, Graduate School, College of Natural Sciences, Department of Astronomy, Amherst, MA 01003. Offers MS, PhD. Part-time programs available. *Faculty:* 17 full-time (3 women). *Students:* 22 full-time (7 women), 2 part-time (0 women); includes 3 minority (1 African American, 1 American Indian/Alaska Native, 1 Hispanic American), 16 international. Average age 28. 45 applicants, 18% accepted, 2 enrolled. In 2009, 5 doctorates awarded. Terminal master's awarded for partial completion of doctoral program. *Degree requirements:* For master's, thesis or alternative; for doctorate, comprehensive exam, thesis/dissertation. *Entrance requirements:* For master's and doctorate, GRE General Test, GRE Subject Test (physics). Additional exam requirements/recommendations for international students: Required—TOEFL (minimum score 550 paper-based; 213 computer-based; 80 iBT), IELTS (minimum score 6.5). *Application deadline:* For fall admission, 2/1 for domestic and international students; for spring admission, 10/1 for domestic and international students. Applications are processed on a rolling basis. Application fee: $50 ($65 for international students). Electronic applications accepted. *Expenses:* Tuition, state resident: full-time $2640; part-time $110 per credit. Tuition, nonresident: full-time $9936; part-time $414 per credit. Tuition and fees vary according to course load. *Financial support:* In 2009–10, 20 research assistantships with full tuition reimbursements (averaging $1,652 per year), 8 teaching assistantships with full tuition reimbursements (averaging $9,950 per year) were awarded; fellowships, career-related internships or fieldwork, Federal Work-Study, scholarships/grants, traineeships, health care benefits, tuition waivers (full), and unspecified assistantships also available. Support available to part-time students. Financial award application deadline: 2/1. *Unit head:* Dr. William M. Irvine, Graduate Program Director, 413-545-2194, Fax: 413-545-4223. *Application contact:* Jean M. Ames, Supervisor of Admissions, 413-545-0722, Fax: 413-577-0010, E-mail: gradadm@grad.umass.edu.

University of Michigan, Horace H. Rackham School of Graduate Studies, College of Literature, Science, and the Arts, Department of Astronomy, Ann Arbor, MI 48109-1042. Offers astronomy and astrophysics (PhD). Terminal master's awarded for partial completion of doctoral program. *Degree requirements:* For doctorate, thesis/dissertation, oral defense of dissertation, preliminary exam. *Entrance requirements:* For doctorate, GRE General Test, GRE Subject Test (physics). Additional exam requirements/recommendations for international students: Required—TOEFL. Electronic applications accepted. *Expenses:* Tuition, state resident: full-time $17,286; part-time $1099 per credit hour. Tuition, nonresident: full-time $34,944; part-time $2080 per credit hour. Required fees: $95 per semester. Tuition and fees vary according to course load, degree level and program. *Faculty research:* Extragalactic and galactic astronomy, cosmology, star and planet formation, high energy astrophysics.

University of Minnesota, Twin Cities Campus, Institute of Technology, School of Physics and Astronomy, Department of Astronomy, Minneapolis, MN 55455-0213. Offers astrophysics (MS, PhD). Terminal master's awarded for partial completion of doctoral program. *Degree requirements:* For master's, thesis optional; for doctorate, thesis/dissertation. *Entrance requirements:* For master's and doctorate, GRE General Test, GRE Subject Test. *Faculty research:* Evolution of stars and galaxies; the interstellar medium; cosmology; observational, optical, infrared, and radio astronomy; computational astrophysics.

University of Missouri, Graduate School, College of Arts and Sciences, Department of Physics and Astronomy, Columbia, MO 65211. Offers MS, PhD. *Faculty:* 34 full-time (9 women), 1 (woman) part-time/adjunct. *Students:* 25 full-time (5 women), 18 part-time (5 women); includes 1 minority (Asian American or Pacific Islander), 25 international. Average age 29. 70 applicants, 14% accepted, 7 enrolled. In 2009, 4 master's, 3 doctorates awarded. Terminal master's awarded for partial completion of doctoral program. *Degree requirements:* For doctorate, one foreign language, comprehensive exam, thesis/dissertation. *Entrance requirements:* For master's and doctorate, GRE General Test, minimum GPA of 3.0. Additional exam requirements/recommendations for international students: Required—TOEFL (minimum score 550 paper-based; 213 computer-based; 80 iBT). *Application deadline:* For fall admission, 3/15 priority date for domestic students. Applications are processed on a rolling basis. Application fee: $45 ($60 for international students). Electronic applications accepted. *Financial support:* In 2009–10, 35 research assistantships with full tuition reimbursements, 10 teaching assistantships with full tuition reimbursements were awarded; institutionally sponsored loans, health care benefits, and unspecified assistantships also available. *Faculty research:* Experimental and theoretical condensed-matter physics, biological physics, astronomy/astrophysics. *Unit head:* Dr. Peter Pfeifer, Department Chair, E-mail: pfeiferp@missouri.edu. *Application contact:* Dr. Carsten Ullrich, Director of Graduate Studies, 573-882-3335, E-mail: ullrichc@missouri.edu.

University of Nebraska–Lincoln, Graduate College, College of Arts and Sciences, Department of Physics and Astronomy, Lincoln, NE 68588. Offers astronomy (MS, PhD); physics (MS, PhD). *Degree requirements:* For master's, thesis optional; for doctorate, comprehensive exam, thesis/dissertation. *Entrance requirements:* For master's and doctorate, GRE General Test. Additional exam requirements/recommendations for international students: Required—TOEFL (minimum score 550 paper-based; 213 computer-based). Electronic applications accepted. *Faculty research:* Electromagnetics of solids and thin films, photoionization, ion collisions with atoms, molecules and surfaces, nanostructures.

University of Nevada, Las Vegas, Graduate College, College of Science, Department of Physics, Las Vegas, NV 89154-4002. Offers astronomy (MS); physics (PhD). Part-time programs available. *Faculty:* 16 full-time (0 women), 6 part-time/adjunct (2 women). *Students:* 21 full-time (4 women), 5 part-time (0 women); includes 3 minority (2 Asian Americans or Pacific Islanders, 1 Hispanic American), 8 international. Average age 31. 19 applicants, 63% accepted, 8 enrolled. In 2009, 3 master's, 1 doctorate awarded. *Degree requirements:* For master's, thesis, oral exam; for doctorate, comprehensive exam, thesis/dissertation. *Entrance requirements:* For master's and doctorate, GRE General Test. Additional exam requirements/recommendations for international students: Required—TOEFL (minimum score 550 paper-based; 213 computer-based; 80 iBT), IELTS (minimum score 7). *Application deadline:* For fall admission, 2/1 priority date for domestic and international students; for spring admission, 10/1 priority date for domestic and international students. Applications are processed on a rolling basis. Application fee: $60 ($95 for international students). Electronic applications accepted. *Financial support:* In 2009–10, 13 research assistantships with partial tuition reimbursements (averaging $16,395 per year), 15 teaching assistantships with partial tuition reimbursements (averaging $12,856 per year) were awarded; institutionally sponsored loans, scholarships/grants, health care benefits, and unspecified assistantships also available. Financial award application deadline: 3/1. *Faculty research:* Gamma-ray bursters, dark matter distribution, experimental high pressure physics, theoretical condensed matter physics, experimental atomic/laser physics. *Unit head:* Dr. Tao Pang, Chair/Professor, 702-895-4454, Fax: 702-895-0804, E-mail: pang@physics.unlv.edu. *Application contact:* Graduate College Admissions Evaluator, 702-895-3320, Fax: 702-895-4180, E-mail: gradcollege@unlv.edu.

The University of North Carolina at Chapel Hill, Graduate School, College of Arts and Sciences, Department of Physics and Astronomy, Chapel Hill, NC 27599. Offers physics (MS, PhD). Terminal master's awarded for partial completion of doctoral program. *Degree requirements:* For master's, comprehensive exam; for doctorate, comprehensive exam, thesis/dissertation. *Entrance requirements:* For master's and doctorate, GRE General Test, minimum GPA of 3.0. Electronic applications accepted. *Faculty research:* Observational astronomy, fullerenes, polarized beams, nanotubes, nucleosynthesis in stars and supernovae, superstring theory, ballistic transport in semiconductors, gravitation.

University of Rochester, The College, Arts and Sciences, Department of Physics and Astronomy, Rochester, NY 14627. Offers physics (MA, MS, PhD); physics and astronomy (PhD). Part-time programs available. Terminal master's awarded for partial completion of doctoral program. *Degree requirements:* For master's, comprehensive exam, thesis (for some programs); for doctorate, comprehensive exam, thesis/dissertation, qualifying exam. *Entrance requirements:* For master's and doctorate, GRE General Test. Additional exam requirements/recommendations for international students: Required—TOEFL.

See Close-Up on page 239.

University of South Carolina, The Graduate School, College of Arts and Sciences, Department of Physics and Astronomy, Columbia, SC 29208. Offers IMA, MAT, MS, PSM, PhD. IMA and MAT offered in cooperation with the College of Education. Part-time programs available. Terminal master's awarded for partial completion of doctoral program. *Degree requirements:* For master's, comprehensive exam, thesis; for doctorate, one foreign language, comprehensive exam, thesis/dissertation. *Entrance requirements:* For master's and doctorate, GRE General Test, GRE Subject Test. Additional exam requirements/recommendations for international students: Required—TOEFL (minimum score 570 paper-based; 230 computer-based; 75 iBT). Electronic applications accepted. *Faculty research:* Condensed matter, intermediate-energy nuclear physics, foundations of quantum mechanics, astronomy/astrophysics.

The University of Texas at Austin, Graduate School, College of Natural Sciences, Department of Astronomy, Austin, TX 78712-1111. Offers MA, PhD. *Entrance requirements:* For master's and doctorate, GRE General Test, GRE Subject Test (physics). Additional exam requirements/recommendations for international students: Required—TOEFL. Electronic applications accepted. *Faculty research:* Stars, interstellar medium, galaxies, planetary astronomy, cosmology.

University of Toronto, School of Graduate Studies, Physical Sciences Division, Department of Astronomy and Astrophysics, Toronto, ON M5S 1A1, Canada. Offers M Sc, PhD. Part-time programs available. *Degree requirements:* For doctorate, thesis/dissertation, qualifying exam, thesis defense. *Entrance requirements:* For master's, minimum B average, bachelor's degree in astronomy or equivalent, 3 letters of reference; for doctorate, GRE General Test, minimum B+ average, master's degree in astronomy or equivalent, demonstrated research competence, 3 letters of reference.

University of Victoria, Faculty of Graduate Studies, Faculty of Science, Department of Physics and Astronomy, Victoria, BC V8W 2Y2, Canada. Offers astronomy and astrophysics (M Sc, PhD); condensed matter physics (M Sc, PhD); experimental particle physics (M Sc, PhD); medical physics (M Sc, PhD); ocean physics (M Sc, PhD); theoretical physics (M Sc, PhD). *Degree requirements:* For master's, thesis; for doctorate, comprehensive exam, thesis/dissertation, candidacy exam. *Entrance requirements:* For master's and doctorate, GRE. Additional exam requirements/recommendations for international students: Required—TOEFL (minimum score 575 paper-based; 233 computer-based), IELTS (minimum score 7). Electronic applications accepted. *Faculty research:* Old stellar populations; observational cosmology and large scale structure; cp violation; atlas.

University of Virginia, College and Graduate School of Arts and Sciences, Department of Astronomy, Charlottesville, VA 22903. Offers MS, PhD. *Faculty:* 18 full-time (2 women), 1 part-time/adjunct (0 women). *Students:* 34 full-time (11 women); includes 1 minority (Asian American or Pacific Islander), 12 international. Average age 26. 79 applicants, 20% accepted, 5 enrolled. In 2009, 6 master's, 2 doctorates awarded. *Degree requirements:* For master's, comprehensive exam, thesis or alternative; for doctorate, comprehensive exam, thesis/dissertation. *Entrance requirements:* For master's and doctorate, GRE General Test, GRE Subject Test. Additional exam requirements/recommendations for international students: Required—TOEFL (minimum score 650 paper-based; 250 computer-based; 90 iBT), IELTS (minimum score 7). *Application deadline:* For fall admission, 12/31 for domestic and international students. Applications are processed on a rolling basis. Application fee: $60. Electronic applications accepted. *Financial support:* Fellowships, research assistantships, teaching assistantships available. Financial award application deadline: 12/3; financial award applicants required to submit FAFSA. *Unit head:* John Hawley, Chair, 434-924-7494, Fax: 434-924-3104, E-mail: jh8h@virginia.edu. *Application contact:* Craig Sarazin, Chair, Graduate Admissions, 434-924-7494, Fax: 434-924-3104, E-mail: gradadm@mail.astro.virginia.edu.

University of Washington, Graduate School, College of Arts and Sciences, Department of Astronomy, Seattle, WA 98195. Offers MS, PhD. Terminal master's awarded for partial completion of doctoral program. *Degree requirements:* For doctorate, thesis/dissertation. *Entrance requirements:* For master's and doctorate, GRE General Test, GRE Subject Test, minimum GPA of 3.0. Additional exam requirements/recommendations for international students: Required—TOEFL. *Faculty research:* Solar system dust, space astronomy, high-energy astrophysics, galactic and extragalactic astronomy, stellar astrophysics.

The University of Western Ontario, Faculty of Graduate Studies, Physical Sciences Division, Department of Physics and Astronomy, Program in Astronomy, London, ON N6A 5B8, Canada. Offers M Sc, PhD. Terminal master's awarded for partial completion of doctoral program. *Degree requirements:* For master's, thesis optional; for doctorate, comprehensive exam, thesis/dissertation. *Entrance requirements:* For master's, GRE Subject Test (physics), honors B Sc degree, minimum B average (Canadian), A—(international); for doctorate, M Sc degree, minimum B average (Canadian), A—(international). Additional exam requirements/recommendations for international students: Required—TOEFL (minimum score 580 paper-

Astronomy

The University of Western Ontario (continued)

based; 237 computer-based). *Faculty research:* Observational and theoretical astrophysics spectroscopy, photometry, spectro-polarimetry, variable stars, cosmology.

University of Wisconsin–Madison, Graduate School, College of Letters and Science, Department of Astronomy, Madison, WI 53706-1380. Offers PhD. *Degree requirements:* For doctorate, comprehensive exam, thesis/dissertation. *Entrance requirements:* For doctorate, GRE General Test, GRE Subject Test (physics), bachelor's degree in related field. Additional exam requirements/recommendations for international students: Required—TOEFL. Electronic applications accepted. *Expenses:* Tuition, state resident: part-time $594 per credit. Tuition, nonresident: part-time $1504 per credit. Required fees: $65 per credit. Tuition and fees vary according to course load, program and reciprocity agreements. *Faculty research:* Kinematics, evolution of galaxies, cosmic distance, scale and large-scale structures, interstellar intergalactic medium, star formation and evolution, solar system chemistry and dynamics.

Vanderbilt University, Graduate School, Department of Physics and Astronomy, Nashville, TN 37240-1001. Offers astronomy (MS); physics (MA, MAT, MS, PhD). *Faculty:* 52 full-time (5 women). *Students:* 66 full-time (16 women), 2 part-time (1 woman); includes 11 minority (5 African Americans, 2 Asian Americans or Pacific Islanders, 4 Hispanic Americans), 16 international. Average age 29. 167 applicants, 21% accepted, 13 enrolled. In 2009, 10 master's, 6 doctorates awarded. *Degree requirements:* For master's, thesis; for doctorate, comprehensive exam, thesis/dissertation, final and qualifying exams. *Entrance requirements:* For master's, GRE General Test; for doctorate, GRE General Test, GRE Subject Test. Additional exam requirements/recommendations for international students: Required—TOEFL (minimum score 570 paper-based; 230 computer-based; 88 iBT). *Application deadline:* For fall admission, 1/15 for domestic and international students. Application fee: $0. Electronic applications accepted. *Financial support:* Fellowships with full and partial tuition reimbursements, research assistantships with full tuition reimbursements, teaching assistantships with full tuition reimbursements, career-related internships or fieldwork, Federal Work-Study, and institutionally sponsored loans available. Financial award application deadline: 1/15; financial award applicants required to submit CSS PROFILE or FAFSA. *Faculty research:* Experimental and theoretical physics, free electron laser, living-state physics, heavy-ion physics, nuclear structure. *Unit head:* Robert J. Scherrer, Chair, 615-322-2828, Fax: 615-343-7263, E-mail: robert.scherrer@vanderbilt.edu. *Application contact:* Richard Haglund, Director of Graduate Studies, 615-322-2828, Fax: 615-343-7263, E-mail: physastro-grad@vanderbilt.edu.

Wesleyan University, Graduate Programs, Department of Astronomy, Middletown, CT 06459. Offers MA. *Faculty:* 3 full-time (0 women). *Students:* 4 full-time (3 women). Average age 24. 16 applicants, 13% accepted, 2 enrolled. In 2009, 3 master's awarded. *Degree requirements:* For master's, thesis. *Entrance requirements:* For master's, GRE General Test, GRE Subject Test. Additional exam requirements/recommendations for international students: Required—TOEFL. *Application deadline:* For fall admission, 3/1 for domestic and international students. Application fee: $0. Electronic applications accepted. *Financial support:* In 2009–10, 4 teaching assistantships with full tuition reimbursements were awarded. Financial award application deadline: 4/15; financial award applicants required to submit FAFSA. *Faculty research:* Observational-theoretical astronomy and astrophysics. *Unit head:* Dr. Edward Moran, Chairman, 860-685-3739, E-mail: emoran@wesleyan.edu. *Application contact:* Linda Shettleworth, Information Contact, 860-685-2130, E-mail: shettleworth@wesleyan.edu.

West Chester University of Pennsylvania, Office of Graduate Studies, College of Arts and Sciences, Department of Geology and Astronomy, West Chester, PA 19383. Offers earth-space science (Teaching Certificate); general science (Teaching Certificate); geoscience (MA). Part-time and evening/weekend programs available. *Students:* 8 full-time (2 women), 24 part-time (16 women). Average age 32. 15 applicants, 100% accepted, 12 enrolled. In 2009, 8 master's awarded. *Degree requirements:* For master's, comprehensive exam (for some programs), thesis optional. *Entrance requirements:* For master's, minimum GPA of 2.5. Additional exam requirements/recommendations for international students: Required—TOEFL (minimum score 550 paper-based; 213 computer-based; 80 iBT). *Application deadline:* For fall admission, 4/15 priority date for domestic students, 3/15 for international students; for spring admission, 10/15 for domestic students, 9/1 for international students. Applications are processed on a rolling basis. Application fee: $35. Electronic applications accepted. *Expenses:* Tuition, state resident: full-time $6666; part-time $370 per credit. Tuition, nonresident: full-time $10,666; part-time $593 per credit. Required fees: $122.56 per credit. *Financial support:* In 2009–10, 1 research assistantship with full and partial tuition reimbursement (averaging $5,000 per year) was awarded; unspecified assistantships also available. Support available to part-time students. Financial award application deadline: 2/15; financial award applicants required to submit FAFSA. *Faculty research:* Developing and using a meteorological data station. *Unit head:* Dr. Marc Gagne, Chair, 610-436-2727, E-mail: mgagne@wcupa.edu. *Application contact:* Dr. Steven Good, Graduate Coordinator, 610-436-2203, E-mail: sgood@wcupa.edu.

Yale University, Graduate School of Arts and Sciences, Department of Astronomy, New Haven, CT 06520. Offers astronomy (PhD); solar and terrestrial physics (PhD). *Degree requirements:* For doctorate, thesis/dissertation. *Entrance requirements:* For doctorate, GRE General Test, GRE Subject Test (physics).

York University, Faculty of Graduate Studies, Faculty of Science and Engineering, Program in Physics and Astronomy, Toronto, ON M3J 1P3, Canada. Offers M Sc, PhD. Part-time and evening/weekend programs available. *Degree requirements:* For master's, thesis or alternative; for doctorate, comprehensive exam, thesis/dissertation. Electronic applications accepted.

Astrophysics

Air Force Institute of Technology, Graduate School of Engineering and Management, Department of Engineering Physics, Dayton, OH 45433-7765. Offers applied physics (MS, PhD); electro-optics (MS, PhD); materials science (PhD); nuclear engineering (MS, PhD); space physics (MS). Part-time programs available. *Degree requirements:* For master's, thesis; for doctorate, thesis/dissertation. *Entrance requirements:* For master's and doctorate, GRE General Test, minimum GPA of 3.0, U.S. citizenship. *Faculty research:* High-energy lasers, space physics, nuclear weapon effects, semiconductor physics.

Arizona State University, Graduate College, College of Liberal Arts and Sciences, Division of Natural Sciences, School of Earth and Space Exploration, Tempe, AZ 85287. Offers astrophysics (MS, PhD); geological sciences (MS, PhD). *Degree requirements:* For master's, thesis or alternative; for doctorate, thesis/dissertation. *Entrance requirements:* For master's and doctorate, GRE.

Clemson University, Graduate School, College of Engineering and Science, Department of Physics and Astronomy, Clemson, SC 29634. Offers physics (MS, PhD), including astronomy and astrophysics, atmospheric physics, biophysics. Part-time programs available. *Faculty:* 25 full-time (4 women), 1 part-time/adjunct (0 women). *Students:* 46 full-time (11 women), 3 part-time (0 women); includes 1 minority (African American), 22 international. Average age 27. 71 applicants, 62% accepted, 17 enrolled. In 2009, 8 master's, 5 doctorates awarded. Terminal master's awarded for partial completion of doctoral program. *Degree requirements:* For master's, thesis or alternative; for doctorate, thesis/dissertation. *Entrance requirements:* For master's and doctorate, GRE General Test. Additional exam requirements/recommendations for international students: Required—TOEFL. *Application deadline:* For fall admission, 1/15 priority date for domestic students; for spring admission, 9/15 priority date for domestic students. Applications are processed on a rolling basis. Application fee: $70 ($80 for international students). Electronic applications accepted. *Expenses:* Tuition, state resident: full-time $8684; part-time $528 per credit hour. Tuition, nonresident: full-time $15,330; part-time $1078 per credit hour. Required fees: $736; $37 per semester. Part-time tuition and fees vary according to course load and program. *Financial support:* In 2009–10, 45 students received support, including 1 fellowship with full and partial tuition reimbursement available (averaging $10,000 per year), 13 research assistantships with partial tuition reimbursements available (averaging $21,423 per year), 32 teaching assistantships with partial tuition reimbursements available (averaging $16,490 per year); career-related internships or fieldwork, institutionally sponsored loans, scholarships/grants, health care benefits, and unspecified assistantships also available. Support available to part-time students. Financial award application deadline: 6/1; financial award applicants required to submit FAFSA. *Faculty research:* Radiation physics, solid-state physics, nuclear physics, radar and lidar studies of atmosphere. Total annual research expenditures: $3.1 million. *Unit head:* Dr. Peter Barnes, Chair, 864-656-3419, Fax: 864-656-0805, E-mail: peterb@clemson.edu. *Application contact:* Dr. Murray Daw, Graduate Coordinator, 864-656-6702, Fax: 864-656-0805, E-mail: physgradinfo-l@clemson.edu.

Cornell University, Graduate School, Graduate Fields of Arts and Sciences, Field of Astronomy and Space Sciences, Ithaca, NY 14853-0001. Offers astronomy (PhD); astrophysics (PhD); general space sciences (PhD); infrared astronomy (PhD); planetary studies (PhD); radio astronomy (PhD); radiophysics (PhD); theoretical astrophysics (PhD). *Faculty:* 30 full-time (2 women). *Students:* 31 full-time (12 women); includes 3 minority (2 Asian Americans or Pacific Islanders, 1 Hispanic American), 9 international. Average age 26. 77 applicants, 19% accepted, 3 enrolled. In 2009, 3 doctorates awarded. *Degree requirements:* For doctorate, comprehensive exam, thesis/dissertation. *Entrance requirements:* For doctorate, GRE General Test, GRE Subject Test (physics), 3 letters of recommendation. Additional exam requirements/recommendations for international students: Required—TOEFL (minimum score 600 paper-based; 250 computer-based; 77 iBT). *Application deadline:* For fall admission, 1/15 for domestic students. Application fee: $70. Electronic applications accepted. *Expenses:* Tuition: Full-time $29,500. Required fees: $70. Full-time tuition and fees vary according to degree level, program and student level. *Financial support:* In 2009–10, 31 students received support, including 1 research assistantship with full tuition reimbursement available, 2 teaching assistantships with full tuition reimbursements available; fellowships with full tuition reimbursements available, institutionally sponsored loans, scholarships/grants, health care benefits, tuition waivers (full and partial), and unspecified assistantships also available. Financial award applicants required to submit FAFSA. *Faculty research:* Observational astrophysics, planetary sciences, cosmology, instrumentation, gravitational astrophysics. *Unit head:* Director of Graduate Studies, 607-255-4341. *Application contact:* Graduate Field Assistant, 607-255-4341, E-mail: oconnor@astro.cornell.edu.

Harvard University, Graduate School of Arts and Sciences, Department of Astronomy, Cambridge, MA 02138. Offers astronomy (PhD); astrophysics (PhD). *Degree requirements:* For doctorate, thesis/dissertation, paper, research project, 2 semesters of teaching. *Entrance requirements:* For doctorate, GRE General Test, GRE Subject Test (physics). Additional exam requirements/recommendations for international students: Required—TOEFL. Electronic applications accepted. *Expenses:* Tuition: Full-time $33,696. Required fees: $1126. Full-time tuition and fees vary according to program. *Faculty research:* Atomic and molecular physics, electromagnetism, solar physics, nuclear physics, fluid dynamics.

ICR Graduate School, Graduate Programs, Santee, CA 92071. Offers astro/geophysics (MS); biology (MS); geology (MS); science education (MS). Part-time programs available. *Degree requirements:* For master's, comprehensive exam (for some programs), thesis (for some programs). *Entrance requirements:* For master's, minimum undergraduate GPA of 3.0, bachelor's degree in science or science education. *Faculty research:* Age of the earth, limits of variation, catastrophe, optimum methods for teaching.

Indiana University Bloomington, University Graduate School, College of Arts and Sciences, Department of Astronomy, Bloomington, IN 47405-7000. Offers astronomy (MA, PhD); astrophysics (PhD). *Faculty:* 9 full-time (5 women), 1 part-time/adjunct (0 women). *Students:* 23 full-time (7 women); includes 2 minority (1 American Indian/Alaska Native, 1 Asian American or Pacific Islander), 1 international. Average age 29. 30 applicants, 27% accepted, 3 enrolled. In 2009, 1 master's awarded. Terminal master's awarded for partial completion of doctoral program. *Degree requirements:* For master's, thesis or alternative, oral exam; for doctorate, comprehensive exam, thesis/dissertation, oral defense. *Entrance requirements:* For master's and doctorate, GRE General Test, GRE Subject Test (physics), BA or BS in science. Additional exam requirements/recommendations for international students: Required—TOEFL. *Application deadline:* For fall admission, 1/15 for domestic students, 12/1 for international students; for spring admission, 9/1 for domestic students. Application fee: $55 ($65 for international students). Electronic applications accepted. *Financial support:* In 2009–10, 21 students received support, including 3 fellowships with full tuition reimbursements available (averaging $15,000 per year), 8 research assistantships with full tuition reimbursements available (averaging $16,667 per year), 10 teaching assistantships with full tuition reimbursements available (averaging $14,008 per year); Federal Work-Study and tuition waivers (full and partial) also available. Support available to part-time students. Financial award application deadline: 1/15. *Faculty research:* Stellar and galaxy dynamics, stellar chemical abundancies, galaxy evolution, observational cosmology, astrophsical disk. *Unit head:* Dr. Catherine Pilachowski, Chair, 812-855-6913, Fax: 812-855-8725, E-mail: catyp@astro.indiana.edu. *Application contact:* Christina Lirot, Department Manager, 812-855-6912, Fax: 812-855-8725, E-mail: clirot@indiana.edu.

Iowa State University of Science and Technology, Graduate College, College of Liberal Arts and Sciences, Department of Physics and Astronomy, Ames, IA 50011. Offers applied physics (MS, PhD); astrophysics (MS, PhD); condensed matter physics (MS, PhD); high energy physics (MS, PhD); nuclear physics (MS, PhD); physics (MS, PhD). Part-time programs available. *Faculty:* 46 full-time (3 women), 4 part-time/adjunct (0 women). *Students:* 94 full-time (21 women), 4 part-time (0 women); includes 3 minority (all Asian Americans or Pacific Islanders), 56 international. 185 applicants, 32% accepted, 15 enrolled. In 2009, 4 master's, 7 doctorates awarded. Terminal master's awarded for partial completion of doctoral program. *Degree requirements:* For master's, thesis (for some programs); for doctorate, thesis/dissertation. *Entrance requirements:* For master's and doctorate, GRE General Test, GRE Subject Test (physics). Additional exam requirements/recommendations for international students: Required—TOEFL (minimum score 550 paper-based; 79 iBT) or IELTS (minimum score 6.5). *Application deadline:* For fall admission, 2/15 priority date for domestic and international students; for spring admission, 10/15 for domestic and international students. Applications are processed on a rolling basis. Application fee: $40 ($90 for international students). Electronic applications accepted. *Expenses:* Tuition, state resident: full-time $6716. Tuition, nonresident: full-time $8908. Tuition and fees vary according to course level, course load, program and student level. *Financial support:* In 2009–10, 58 research assistantships with full and partial tuition reimbursements (averaging $17,000 per year), 33 teaching assistantships with full and partial tuition reimbursements (averaging $16,000 per year) were awarded; fellowships, Federal Work-Study, institutionally sponsored loans, scholarships/grants, health care benefits, and unspecified assistantships also available. Support available to part-time students. Financial award application deadline: 2/15. *Faculty research:* Condensed-matter physics, including superconductivity and new materials; high-energy and nuclear physics; astronomy and astrophysics; atmospheric and environmental physics. Total annual research expenditures: $8.8 million. *Unit head:* Dr. Joseph Shinar, Chair, 515-294-3455, Fax: 515-294-6027, E-mail: phys_astro@iastate.edu. *Application contact:* Dr. Steven Kawaler, Director of Graduate Education, 515-294-9728, E-mail: phys_astro@iastate.edu.

Louisiana State University and Agricultural and Mechanical College, Graduate School, College of Basic Sciences, Department of Physics and Astronomy, Baton Rouge, LA 70803. Offers astronomy (PhD); astrophysics (PhD); medical physics (MS); physics (MS, PhD). *Faculty:* 45 full-time (4 women), 1 part-time/adjunct (0 women). *Students:* 97 full-time (24 women), 5 part-time (1 woman); includes 5 minority (1 African American, 2 Asian Americans or Pacific Islanders, 2 Hispanic Americans), 42 international. Average age 27. 127 applicants, 20% accepted, 21 enrolled. In 2009, 9 master's, 8 doctorates awarded. Terminal master's awarded for partial completion of doctoral program. *Degree requirements:* For master's, thesis or alternative; for doctorate, thesis/dissertation. *Entrance requirements:* For master's and doctorate, GRE General Test, minimum GPA of 3.0. Additional exam requirements/recommendations for international students: Required—TOEFL (minimum score 550 paper-based; 213 computer-based; 79 iBT) or IELTS (minimum score 6.5). *Application deadline:* For fall admission, 1/25 priority date for domestic students, 5/15 for international students; for spring admission, 10/15 for international students. Applications are processed on a rolling basis. Application fee: $50 ($70 for international students). Electronic applications accepted. *Financial support:* In 2009–10, 16 fellowships with full tuition reimbursements (averaging $24,969 per year), 53 research assistantships with full and partial tuition reimbursements (averaging $20,101 per year), 37 teaching assistantships with full and partial tuition reimbursements (averaging $17,943 per year) were awarded; Federal Work-Study, institutionally sponsored loans, health care benefits, tuition waivers (full and partial), and unspecified assistantships also available. Financial award application deadline: 3/15; financial award applicants required to submit FAFSA. *Faculty research:* Experimentation and numerical relativity, condensed matter astrophysics, quantum computing, medical physics. Total annual research expenditures: $7.5 million. *Unit head:* Dr. Michael Cherry, Chair, 225-578-2261, Fax: 225-578-5855, E-mail: cherry@phys.lsu.edu. *Application contact:* Arnell Dangerfield, Administrative Coordinator, 225-578-1193, Fax: 225-578-5855, E-mail: adanger@lsu.edu.

McMaster University, School of Graduate Studies, Faculty of Science, Department of Physics and Astronomy, Hamilton, ON L8S 4M2, Canada. Offers astrophysics (PhD); physics (PhD). Part-time programs available. *Degree requirements:* For doctorate, comprehensive exam, thesis/dissertation. *Entrance requirements:* For doctorate, minimum B+ average. Additional exam requirements/recommendations for international students: Required—TOEFL (minimum score 550 paper-based; 213 computer-based). *Faculty research:* Condensed matter, astrophysics, nuclear, medical, nonlinear dynamics.

Michigan State University, The Graduate School, College of Natural Science, Department of Physics and Astronomy, East Lansing, MI 48824. Offers astrophysics and astronomy (MS, PhD); physics (MS, PhD). *Entrance requirements:* Additional exam requirements/recommendations for international students: Required—TOEFL (minimum score 550 paper-based; 213 computer-based), Michigan State University ELT (85), Michigan ELAB (83). Electronic applications accepted. *Faculty research:* Nuclear and accelerator physics, high energy physics, condensed matter physics, biophysics, astrophysics and astronomy.

New Mexico Institute of Mining and Technology, Graduate Studies, Department of Physics, Socorro, NM 87801. Offers astrophysics (MS, PhD); atmospheric physics (MS, PhD); instrumentation (MS); mathematical physics (PhD). *Degree requirements:* For master's, thesis optional; for doctorate, thesis/dissertation. *Entrance requirements:* For master's, GRE General Test; for doctorate, GRE General Test, GRE Subject Test. Additional exam requirements/recommendations for international students: Required—TOEFL (minimum score 540 paper-based; 207 computer-based). *Faculty research:* Cloud physics, stellar and extragalactic processes.

Northwestern University, The Graduate School, Judd A. and Marjorie Weinberg College of Arts and Sciences, Department of Physics and Astronomy, Evanston, IL 60208. Offers astrophysics (PhD); physics (MS, PhD). Admissions and degrees offered through The Graduate School. *Degree requirements:* For doctorate, thesis/dissertation, qualifying exam. *Entrance requirements:* For doctorate, GRE General Test, GRE Subject Test. Additional exam requirements/recommendations for international students: Required—TOEFL. *Faculty research:* Nuclear and particle physics, condensed-matter physics, nonlinear physics, astrophysics.

Penn State University Park, Graduate School, Eberly College of Science, Department of Astronomy and Astrophysics, State College, University Park, PA 16802-1503. Offers MS, PhD. *Unit head:* Dr. Eric D. Feigelson, Assistant Department Head, 814-865-0162, Fax: 814-863-3399. *Application contact:* Cynthia E. Nicosia, Director, Graduate Enrollment Services, 814-865-1795, Fax: 814-865-4627, E-mail: cey1@psu.edu.

Princeton University, Graduate School, Department of Astrophysical Sciences, Princeton, NJ 08544-1019. Offers astronomy (PhD); plasma physics (PhD). *Degree requirements:* For doctorate, thesis/dissertation. *Entrance requirements:* For doctorate, GRE General Test, GRE Subject Test (physics). Additional exam requirements/recommendations for international students: Required—TOEFL (minimum score 600 paper-based; 250 computer-based). Electronic applications accepted. *Faculty research:* Theoretical astrophysics, cosmology, galaxy formation, galactic dynamics, interstellar and intergalactic matter.

Rensselaer Polytechnic Institute, Graduate School, School of Science, Department of Physics, Applied Physics and Astronomy, Troy, NY 12180-3590. Offers astronomy (MS); physics (MS, PhD). *Faculty:* 24 full-time (4 women), 4 part-time/adjunct (0 women). *Students:* 64 full-time (12 women), 2 part-time (0 women); includes 1 African American, 2 Asian Americans or Pacific Islanders. Average age 25. 146 applicants, 51% accepted, 17 enrolled. In 2009, 5 master's, 13 doctorates awarded. *Degree requirements:* For doctorate, thesis/dissertation. *Entrance requirements:* For master's and doctorate, GRE General Test, GRE Subject Test. Additional exam requirements/recommendations for international students: Required—TOEFL (minimum score 600 paper-based; 250 computer-based). *Application deadline:* For fall admission, 1/1 priority date for domestic and international students; for spring admission, 8/15 priority date for domestic and international students. Applications are processed on a rolling basis. Application fee: $75. Electronic applications accepted. *Expenses:* Tuition: Full-time $38,100. *Financial support:* In 2009–10, 64 students received support, including 4 fellowships with full tuition reimbursements available (averaging $30,000 per year), 37 research assistantships with full tuition reimbursements available (averaging $21,000 per year), 25 teaching assistantships with full tuition reimbursements available (averaging $21,000 per year); career-related internships or fieldwork and institutionally sponsored loans also available. Financial award application deadline: 2/1. *Faculty research:* Astrophysics, condensed matter, nuclear physics, optics, biophysics. Total annual research expenditures: $7.3 million. *Unit head:* Dr. Gwo-Ching Wang, Chair, 518-276-8387, Fax: 518-276-6680, E-mail: wangg@rpi.edu. *Application contact:* Dr. Shengbai Zhang, Chair, Graduate Recruitment Committee, 518-276-8391, Fax: 518-276-6680, E-mail: mcquade@rpi.edu.

Rochester Institute of Technology, Graduate Enrollment Services, College of Science, Department of Astrophysical Sciences and Technology, Rochester, NY 14623-5603. Offers MS, PhD. *Students:* 9 full-time (2 women); includes 1 Hispanic American, 2 international. Average age 31. 14 applicants, 57% accepted, 4 enrolled.Terminal master's awarded for partial completion of doctoral program. *Degree requirements:* For master's, comprehensive exam, thesis. *Entrance requirements:* For master's, GRE. Additional exam requirements/recommendations for international students: Required—TOEFL (minimum score 550 paper-based; 213 computer-based; 79 iBT), or IELTS (minimum score 6.5). *Application deadline:* For fall admission, 1/15 priority date for domestic and international students. Application fee: $50. *Expenses:* Tuition: Full-time $31,533; part-time $876 per credit hour. Required fees: $210. *Financial support:* In 2009–10, 8 students received support; fellowships with full and partial tuition reimbursements available, research assistantships with full and partial tuition reimbursements available, teaching assistantships with full and partial tuition reimbursements available, Federal Work-Study, scholarships/grants, health care benefits, and unspecified assistantships available. *Faculty research:* Supermassive black holes, dark energy, gravitational waves, supernovae, massive stars, the galactic center, star formation, clusters of galaxies, active galactic nuclei, astro-informatics, computational astrophysics, instrument and detector development. *Unit head:* Dr. Christopher O'Dea, Director, 585-475-7493, E-mail: odea@cis.rit.edu. *Application contact:* Diane Ellison, Assistant Vice President, Graduate Enrollment Services, 585-475-2229, Fax: 585-475-7164, E-mail: gradinfo@rit.edu.

Texas Christian University, College of Science and Engineering, Department of Physics and Astronomy, Fort Worth, TX 76129-0002. Offers physics (MA, MS, PhD), including astrophysics (PhD), business (PhD), physics (PhD). Part-time and evening/weekend programs available. *Degree requirements:* For master's, comprehensive exam, thesis; for doctorate, comprehensive exam, thesis/dissertation, paper submitted to a scientific journal. *Entrance requirements:* For master's, GRE; for doctorate, GRE General Test. Additional exam requirements/recommendations for international students: Required—TOEFL (minimum score 600 paper-based). *Application deadline:* For fall admission, 3/1 for domestic students; for spring admission, 12/1 for domestic students. Applications are processed on a rolling basis. Application fee: $50. *Expenses:* Tuition: Full-time $17,640; part-time $980 per credit hour. Tuition and fees vary according to program. *Financial support:* In 2009–10, 10 teaching assistantships (averaging $18,000 per year) were awarded; tuition waivers also available. Financial award application deadline: 3/1. *Unit head:* Dr. T. W. Zerda, Chairperson, 817-257-7375 Ext. 7124, Fax: 817-257-7742, E-mail: t.zerda@tcu.edu. *Application contact:* Dr. William R. M. Graham, Professor, 817-257-7375 Ext. 6383, Fax: 817-257-7742, E-mail: w.graham@tcu.edu.

University of Alaska Fairbanks, College of Natural Sciences and Mathematics, Department of Physics, Fairbanks, AK 99775-5920. Offers computational physics (MS); physics (MAT, MS, PhD); space physics (MS, PhD). Part-time programs available. *Faculty:* 10 full-time (1 woman). *Students:* 23 full-time (3 women), 2 part-time (0 women); includes 1 minority (American Indian/Alaska Native), 8 international. Average age 31. 24 applicants, 25% accepted, 6 enrolled. In 2009, 2 master's awarded. Terminal master's awarded for partial completion of doctoral program. *Degree requirements:* For master's, comprehensive exam, thesis or alternative; for doctorate, comprehensive exam, thesis/dissertation, oral defense. *Entrance requirements:* Additional exam requirements/recommendations for international students: Required—TOEFL (minimum score 550 paper-based; 213 computer-based; 80 iBT). *Application deadline:* For fall admission, 6/1 for domestic students, 3/1 for international students; for spring admission, 10/15 for domestic students, 9/1 for international students. Applications are processed on a rolling basis. Application fee: $60. Electronic applications accepted. *Expenses:* Tuition, state resident: full-time $7584; part-time $316 per credit. Tuition, nonresident: full-time $15,504; part-time $646 per credit. Required fees: $23 per credit. $135 per semester. Tuition and fees vary according to course level, course load and reciprocity agreements. *Financial support:* In 2009–10, 1 fellowship (averaging $16,454 per year), 11 research assistantships (averaging $16,320 per year), 7 teaching assistantships (averaging $15,451 per year) were awarded; Federal Work-Study, scholarships/grants, health care benefits, and unspecified assistantships also available. Support available to part-time students. Financial award application deadline: 2/15; financial award applicants required to submit FAFSA. *Faculty research:* Atmospheric and ionospheric radar studies, space plasma theory, magnetospheric dynamics, space weather and auroral studies, turbulence and complex systems. *Unit head:* John Olson, Chair, 907-474-7339, Fax: 907-474-6130, E-mail: physics@uaf.edu. *Application contact:* John Olson, Chair, 907-474-7339, Fax: 907-474-6130, E-mail: physics@uaf.edu.

University of Alberta, Faculty of Graduate Studies and Research, Department of Physics, Edmonton, AB T6G 2E1, Canada. Offers astrophysics (M Sc, PhD); condensed matter (M Sc, PhD); geophysics (M Sc, PhD); medical physics (M Sc, PhD); subatomic physics (M Sc, PhD). *Faculty:* 36 full-time (3 women), 7 part-time/adjunct (0 women). *Students:* 56 full-time (6 women), 16 part-time (2 women). 85 applicants, 35% accepted. In 2009, 7 master's, 10 doctorates awarded. *Degree requirements:* For master's, thesis; for doctorate, thesis/dissertation. *Entrance requirements:* For master's and doctorate, minimum GPA of 7.0 on a 9.0 scale. Additional exam requirements/recommendations for international students: Required—TOEFL. *Application deadline:* For fall admission, 2/15 priority date for domestic students. Applications are processed on a rolling basis. Tuition and fees charges are reported in Canadian dollars. *Expenses:* Tuition, area resident: Full-time $4626.24 Canadian dollars; part-time $99.72 Canadian dollars per unit. International tuition: $8216 Canadian dollars full-time. Required fees: $3589.92 Canadian dollars; $99.72 Canadian dollars per unit. $215 Canadian dollars per term. *Financial support:* In 2009–10, 6 fellowships with partial tuition reimbursements, 40 teaching assistantships were awarded; research assistantships, career-related internships or fieldwork, institutionally sponsored loans, and scholarships/grants also available. Financial award application deadline: 2/15. *Faculty research:* Cosmology, astroparticle physics, high-intermediate energy, magnetism, superconductivity. Total annual research expenditures: $3.1 million. *Unit head:* Dr. R. Marchand, Associate Chair, 780-492-1072, E-mail: assoc-chair@phys.ualberta.ca. *Application contact:* Lynn Chandler, Program Advisor, 780-492-1072, Fax: 780-492-0714, E-mail: grad.program@phys.ualberta.ca.

University of California, Berkeley, Graduate Division, College of Letters and Science, Department of Astrophysics, Berkeley, CA 94720-1500. Offers PhD. *Faculty:* 17 full-time, 2 part-time/adjunct. *Students:* 32 full-time (11 women). Average age 26. 141 applicants, 3 enrolled. In 2009, 6 doctorates awarded. *Degree requirements:* For doctorate, thesis/dissertation, qualifying exam. *Entrance requirements:* For doctorate, GRE General Test, GRE Subject Test, minimum GPA of 3.0, 3 letters of recommendation. *Application deadline:* For fall admission, 1/5 for domestic students. Application fee: $70 ($90 for international students). *Financial support:* Fellowships with full tuition reimbursements, research assistantships with full tuition reimbursements, teaching assistantships with full tuition reimbursements, scholarships/grants, health care benefits, tuition waivers (full), and unspecified assistantships also available. *Faculty research:* Theory, cosmology, radio astronomy, extra solar planets, infrared instrumentation. *Unit head:* Prof. James Graham, Chair, 510-642-5275, Fax: 510-642-3411, E-mail: ch_astronomy@ls.berkeley.edu. *Application contact:* Dexter G. Stewart, Student Affairs Officer, 510-642-8520, Fax: 510-642-3411, E-mail: gradinfo@astro.berkeley.edu.

University of California, Los Angeles, Graduate Division, College of Letters and Science, Department of Earth and Space Sciences, Program in Geophysics and Space Physics, Los Angeles, CA 90095. Offers MS, PhD. *Students:* 35 full-time (19 women); includes 2 minority (both Asian Americans or Pacific Islanders), 15 international. Average age 27. 50 applicants, 28% accepted, 8 enrolled. In 2009, 8 master's, 6 doctorates awarded. Terminal master's awarded for partial completion of doctoral program. *Degree requirements:* For master's,

Astrophysics

University of California, Los Angeles (continued)
comprehensive exams or thesis; for doctorate, thesis/dissertation, oral and written qualifying exams. *Entrance requirements:* For master's, GRE General Test, minimum GPA of 3.0, bachelor's degree in related field; for doctorate, GRE General Test, minimum undergraduate GPA of 3.0, bachelor's degree in related field. *Application deadline:* For fall admission, 1/15 for domestic and international students. Application fee: $70 ($90 for international students). Electronic applications accepted. *Financial support:* In 2009–10, 27 fellowships with full and partial tuition reimbursements, 30 research assistantships with full and partial tuition reimbursements, 11 teaching assistantships with full and partial tuition reimbursements were awarded; Federal Work-Study, institutionally sponsored loans, scholarships/grants, health care benefits, tuition waivers (full and partial), and unspecified assistantships also available. Financial award application deadline: 3/1; financial award applicants required to submit FAFSA. *Unit head:* Chair, 310-825-3917. *Application contact:* Departmental Office, 888-377-8252, E-mail: holbrook@ess.ucla.edu.

University of California, Santa Cruz, Division of Graduate Studies, Division of Physical and Biological Sciences, Department of Astronomy and Astrophysics, Santa Cruz, CA 95064. Offers PhD. *Degree requirements:* For doctorate, one foreign language, thesis/dissertation, qualifying exam. *Entrance requirements:* For doctorate, GRE General Test, GRE Subject Test. Electronic applications accepted. *Faculty research:* Stellar structure and evolution, stellar spectroscopy, the interstellar medium, galactic structure, external galaxies and quasars.

University of Chicago, Division of the Physical Sciences, Department of Astronomy and Astrophysics, Chicago, IL 60637-1513. Offers MS, PhD. Terminal master's awarded for partial completion of doctoral program. *Degree requirements:* For master's, comprehensive exam, thesis optional, candidacy exam; for doctorate, comprehensive exam, thesis/dissertation, dissertation for publication. *Entrance requirements:* For master's, department candidacy examination, minimum GPA of 3.0; for doctorate, GRE General Test, GRE Subject Test, minimum GPA of 3.0. Additional exam requirements/recommendations for international students: Required—TOEFL (minimum score 600 paper-based; 250 computer-based); Recommended—IELTS. Electronic applications accepted. *Faculty research:* Quasi-stellar object absorption lines, fluid dynamics, interstellar matter, particle physics, cosmology.

University of Colorado at Boulder, Graduate School, College of Arts and Sciences, Department of Astrophysical and Planetary Sciences, Boulder, CO 80309. Offers astrophysics (MS, PhD); planetary science (MS, PhD). *Faculty:* 20 full-time (3 women). *Students:* 27 full-time (6 women), 19 part-time (9 women); includes 3 minority (1 American Indian/Alaska Native, 2 Asian Americans or Pacific Islanders), 4 international. Average age 26. 124 applicants, 23% accepted, 7 enrolled. In 2009, 5 master's, 3 doctorates awarded. Terminal master's awarded for partial completion of doctoral program. *Degree requirements:* For master's, comprehensive exam, thesis or alternative; for doctorate, one foreign language, thesis/dissertation. *Entrance requirements:* For master's, GRE General Test, GRE Subject Test, minimum undergraduate GPA of 3.0; for doctorate, GRE General Test, GRE Subject Test. *Application deadline:* For fall admission, 1/15 priority date for domestic students, 12/1 for international students. Applications are processed on a rolling basis. Application fee: $50 ($60 for international students). *Financial support:* In 2009–10, 13 fellowships (averaging $22,199 per year), 33 research assistantships (averaging $17,541 per year) were awarded; tuition waivers (full) also available. Support available to part-time students. Financial award application deadline: 1/15. *Faculty research:* Stellar and extragalactic astrophysics cosmology, space astronomy, planetary science. Total annual research expenditures: $27.2 million.

University of Maryland, Baltimore County, Graduate School, College of Natural and Mathematical Sciences, Department of Physics, Program in Applied Physics, Baltimore, MD 21250. Offers astrophysics (PhD); optics (MS, PhD); quantum optics (PhD); solid state physics (MS, PhD). Part-time programs available. *Faculty:* 24 full-time (3 women), 18 part-time/adjunct (2 women). *Students:* 31 full-time (10 women), 3 part-time (0 women); includes 3 minority (all African Americans), 15 international. Average age 24. 28 applicants, 43% accepted, 6 enrolled. In 2009, 4 master's, 4 doctorates awarded. Terminal master's awarded for partial completion of doctoral program. *Degree requirements:* For master's, thesis optional; for doctorate, comprehensive exam, thesis/dissertation. *Entrance requirements:* For master's, GRE General Test, minimum GPA of 3.0; for doctorate, GRE General Test, GRE Subject Test, minimum GPA of 3.0. Additional exam requirements/recommendations for international students: Required—TOEFL. *Application deadline:* For fall admission, 5/31 for domestic and international students; for spring admission, 11/30 for domestic students. Applications are processed on a rolling basis. Application fee: $50. Electronic applications accepted. *Financial support:* In 2009–10, 30 students received support, including 4 fellowships with full tuition reimbursements available (averaging $27,000 per year), 14 research assistantships with full tuition reimbursements available (averaging $24,000 per year), 12 teaching assistantships with full tuition reimbursements available (averaging $22,000 per year); career-related internships or fieldwork, scholarships/grants, health care benefits, and unspecified assistantships also available. Support available to part-time students. Financial award application deadline: 5/31. *Faculty research:* Astrophysics, atmospheric physics, nanophysics, optics, quantum optics and quantum information. Total annual research expenditures: $4.8 million. *Unit head:* Dr. Todd Pittman, Graduate Program Director, 410-455-2513, Fax: 410-455-1072, E-mail: todd.pittman@umbc.edu. *Application contact:* Dr. Lazlo L. Takacs, Director, 410-455-2524, Fax: 410-455-1072, E-mail: takacs@umbc.edu.

University of Michigan, Horace H. Rackham School of Graduate Studies, College of Literature, Science, and the Arts, Department of Astronomy, Ann Arbor, MI 48109-1042. Offers astronomy and astrophysics (PhD). Terminal master's awarded for partial completion of doctoral program. *Degree requirements:* For doctorate, thesis/dissertation, oral defense of dissertation, preliminary exam. *Entrance requirements:* For doctorate, GRE General Test, GRE Subject Test (physics). Additional exam requirements/recommendations for international students: Required—TOEFL. Electronic applications accepted. *Expenses:* Tuition, state resident: full-time $17,286; part-time $1099 per credit hour. Tuition, nonresident: full-time $34,944; part-time $2080 per credit hour. Required fees: $95 per semester. Tuition and fees vary according to course load, degree level and program. *Faculty research:* Extragalactic and galactic astronomy, cosmology, star and planet formation, high energy astrophysics.

University of Minnesota, Twin Cities Campus, Institute of Technology, School of Physics and Astronomy, Department of Astronomy, Minneapolis, MN 55455-0213. Offers astrophysics (MS, PhD). Terminal master's awarded for partial completion of doctoral program. *Degree requirements:* For master's, thesis optional; for doctorate, thesis/dissertation. *Entrance requirements:* For master's and doctorate, GRE General Test, GRE Subject Test. *Faculty research:* Evolution of stars and galaxies; the interstellar medium; cosmology; observational, optical, infrared, and radio astronomy; computational astrophysics.

University of Missouri–St. Louis, College of Arts and Sciences, Department of Physics and Astronomy, St. Louis, MO 63121. Offers applied physics (MS); astrophysics (MS); physics (PhD). Part-time and evening/weekend programs available. *Faculty:* 13 full-time (2 women), 3 part-time/adjunct (1 woman). *Students:* 12 full-time (1 woman), 12 part-time (5 women); includes 1 minority (American Indian/Alaska Native), 6 international. Average age 31. 19 applicants, 58% accepted, 8 enrolled. In 2009, 3 master's, 2 doctorates awarded. Terminal master's awarded for partial completion of doctoral program. *Degree requirements:* For master's, thesis optional; for doctorate, thesis/dissertation. *Entrance requirements:* For master's and doctorate, GRE General Test, 2 letters of recommendation. Additional exam requirements/recommendations for international students: Required—TOEFL (minimum score 550 paper-based; 213 computer-based). *Application deadline:* For fall admission, 7/1 for domestic and international students; for spring admission, 12/1 for domestic students, 11/1 for international students. Application fee: $35 ($40 for international students). Electronic applications accepted. *Expenses:* Tuition, state resident: full-time $5377; part-time $297.70 per credit hour. Tuition, nonresident: full-time $13,882; part-time $771.20 per credit hour. Required fees: $220; $12.20 per credit hour. One-time fee: $12. Tuition and fees vary according to course level, campus/location and program. *Financial support:* In 2009–10, 4 research assistantships with full and partial tuition reimbursements (averaging $15,269 per year), 11 teaching assistantships with full and partial tuition reimbursements (averaging $14,926 per year) were awarded; fellowships with full tuition reimbursements, career-related internships or fieldwork also available. Financial award applicants required to submit FAFSA. *Faculty research:* Biophysics, atomic physics, nonlinear dynamics, materials science. *Unit head:* Dr. Phil Fraundorf, Director of Graduate Studies, 314-516-5931, Fax: 314-516-6152, E-mail: fraundorfp@msx.umsl.edu. *Application contact:* 314-516-5458, Fax: 314-516-6996, E-mail: gradadm@umsl.edu.

The University of North Carolina at Chapel Hill, Graduate School, College of Arts and Sciences, Department of Physics and Astronomy, Chapel Hill, NC 27599. Offers physics (MS, PhD). Terminal master's awarded for partial completion of doctoral program. *Degree requirements:* For master's, comprehensive exam; for doctorate, comprehensive exam, thesis/dissertation. *Entrance requirements:* For master's and doctorate, GRE General Test, minimum GPA of 3.0. Electronic applications accepted. *Faculty research:* Observational astronomy, fullerenes, polarized beams, nanotubes, nucleosynthesis in stars and supernovae, superstring theory, ballistic transport in semiconductors, gravitation.

University of Oklahoma, Graduate College, College of Arts and Sciences, Department of Physics and Astronomy, Norman, OK 73019. Offers astrophysics (MS, PhD); physics (MS, PhD). Part-time programs available. *Faculty:* 31 full-time (4 women). *Students:* 57 full-time (15 women), 4 part-time (3 women); includes 2 minority (both Asian Americans or Pacific Islanders), 26 international. 14 applicants, 71% accepted, 10 enrolled. In 2009, 2 master's, 5 doctorates awarded. Terminal master's awarded for partial completion of doctoral program. *Degree requirements:* For master's, thesis or alternative, departmental qualifying exam; for doctorate, thesis/dissertation, comprehensive, departmental qualifying, oral, and written exams. *Entrance requirements:* For master's and doctorate, GRE General Test, GRE Subject Test, 3 letters of recommendation. Additional exam requirements/recommendations for international students: Required—TOEFL (minimum score 600 paper-based; 250 computer-based). *Application deadline:* For fall admission, 3/1 for domestic students, 4/1 for international students; for spring admission, 11/1 for domestic students, 9/1 for international students. Application fee: $40 ($90 for international students). Electronic applications accepted. *Expenses:* Tuition, state resident: full-time $3744; part-time $156 per credit hour. Tuition, nonresident: full-time $13,577; part-time $565.70 per credit hour. Required fees: $2415; $90.10 per credit hour. *Financial support:* In 2009–10, 57 students received support, including 31 research assistantships with partial tuition reimbursements available (averaging $15,751 per year), 29 teaching assistantships with partial tuition reimbursements available (averaging $15,255 per year); Federal Work-Study, scholarships/grants, health care benefits, and unspecified assistantships also available. Financial award application deadline: 3/1; financial award applicants required to submit FAFSA. *Faculty research:* Atomic, molecular, and chemical physics; high energy physics; astrophysics; condensed matter physics. Total annual research expenditures: $4.4 million. *Unit head:* Greg Parker, Chair, 405-325-3961, Fax: 405-325-7557, E-mail: parker@nhn.ou.edu. *Application contact:* Debbie Barnhill, University Student Services Assistant, 405-325-3961 Ext. 36101, Fax: 405-325-7557, E-mail: dbarnhill@ou.edu.

University of Pennsylvania, School of Arts and Sciences, Graduate Group in Physics and Astronomy, Philadelphia, PA 19104. Offers medical physics (MS); physics (PhD). Part-time programs available. *Faculty:* 48 full-time (5 women), 14 part-time/adjunct (1 woman). *Students:* 103 full-time (30 women), 2 part-time (0 women); includes 7 minority (5 Asian Americans or Pacific Islanders, 2 Hispanic Americans), 22 international. 336 applicants, 15% accepted, 21 enrolled. In 2009, 4 master's, 17 doctorates awarded. *Degree requirements:* For doctorate, thesis/dissertation, oral, preliminary, and final exams. *Entrance requirements:* For doctorate, GRE General Test, GRE Subject Test (recommended). Additional exam requirements/recommendations for international students: Required—TOEFL. *Application deadline:* For fall admission, 12/1 priority date for domestic students. Application fee: $70. Electronic applications accepted. *Expenses:* Tuition: Full-time $25,660; part-time $4758 per course. Required fees: $2152; $270 per course. Tuition and fees vary according to course load, degree level and program. *Financial support:* Fellowships, research assistantships, teaching assistantships, institutionally sponsored loans, scholarships/grants, traineeships, health care benefits, and unspecified assistantships available. Financial award application deadline: 12/15. *Faculty research:* Astrophysics, condensed matter experiment, condensed matter theory, particle experiment, particle theory. Total annual research expenditures: $7.3 million.

University of Toronto, School of Graduate Studies, Physical Sciences Division, Department of Astronomy and Astrophysics, Toronto, ON M5S 1A1, Canada. Offers M Sc, PhD. Part-time programs available. *Degree requirements:* For doctorate, thesis/dissertation, qualifying exam, thesis defense. *Entrance requirements:* For master's, minimum B average, bachelor's degree in astronomy or equivalent, 3 letters of reference; for doctorate, GRE General Test, minimum B+ average, master's degree in astronomy or equivalent, demonstrated research competence, 3 letters of reference.

University of Victoria, Faculty of Graduate Studies, Faculty of Science, Department of Physics and Astronomy, Victoria, BC V8W 2Y2, Canada. Offers astronomy and astrophysics (M Sc, PhD); condensed matter physics (M Sc, PhD); experimental particle physics (M Sc, PhD); medical physics (M Sc, PhD); ocean physics (M Sc, PhD); theoretical physics (M Sc, PhD). *Degree requirements:* For master's, thesis; for doctorate, comprehensive exam, thesis/dissertation, candidacy exam. *Entrance requirements:* For master's and doctorate, GRE. Additional exam requirements/recommendations for international students: Required—TOEFL (minimum score 575 paper-based; 233 computer-based), IELTS (minimum score 7). Electronic applications accepted. *Faculty research:* Old stellar populations; observational cosmology and large scale structure; cp violation; atlas.

Yale University, Graduate School of Arts and Sciences, Department of Astronomy, New Haven, CT 06520. Offers astronomy (PhD); solar and terrestrial physics (PhD). *Degree requirements:* For doctorate, thesis/dissertation. *Entrance requirements:* For doctorate, GRE General Test, GRE Subject Test (physics).

Section 2
Chemistry

This section contains a directory of institutions offering graduate work in chemistry, followed by in-depth entries submitted by institutions that chose to prepare detailed program descriptions. Additional information about programs listed in the directory but not augmented by an in-depth entry may be obtained by writing directly to the dean of a graduate school or chair of a department at the address given in the directory.

For programs offering related work, see also in this book *Geosciences* and *Physics*. In the other guides in this series:

Graduate Programs in the Biological Sciences

See *Biological and Biomedical Sciences, Biochemistry, Biophysics, Nutrition,* and *Pharmacology and Toxicology*

Graduate Programs in Engineering & Applied Sciences

See *Engineering and Applied Sciences; Agricultural Engineering; Chemical Engineering; Geological, Mineral/Mining, and Petroleum Engineering; Materials Sciences and Engineering;* and *Pharmaceutical Engineering*

Graduate Programs in Business, Education, Health, Information Studies, Law & Social Work

See *Pharmacy and Pharmaceutical Sciences*

CONTENTS

Program Directories

Close-Ups

Analytical Chemistry

Auburn University, Graduate School, College of Sciences and Mathematics, Department of Chemistry and Biochemistry, Auburn University, AL 36849. Offers analytical chemistry (MS, PhD); biochemistry (MS, PhD); inorganic chemistry (MS, PhD); organic chemistry (MS, PhD); physical chemistry (MS, PhD). Part-time programs available. *Faculty:* 27 full-time (6 women). *Students:* 39 full-time (20 women), 21 part-time (8 women); includes 6 minority (4 African Americans, 1 Asian American or Pacific Islander, 1 Hispanic American), 41 international. Average age 28. 54 applicants, 11% accepted, 3 enrolled. In 2009, 1 master's, 13 doctorates awarded. *Degree requirements:* For master's, thesis (for some programs); for doctorate, thesis/dissertation, oral and written exams. *Entrance requirements:* For master's and doctorate, GRE General Test. *Application deadline:* For fall admission, 7/7 for domestic students; for spring admission, 11/24 for domestic students. Applications are processed on a rolling basis. Application fee: $50 ($60 for international students). Electronic applications accepted. *Expenses:* Tuition, state resident: full-time $6240. Tuition, nonresident: full-time $18,720. International tuition: $18,938 full-time. Required fees: $492. Tuition and fees vary according to course load, program and reciprocity agreements. *Financial support:* Fellowships, research assistantships, teaching assistantships available. Financial award application deadline: 3/15; financial award applicants required to submit FAFSA. *Unit head:* Dr. J. V. Ortiz, Chair, 334-844-4043, Fax: 334-844-4043. *Application contact:* Dr. George Flowers, Dean of the Graduate School, 334-844-2125.

Brigham Young University, Graduate Studies, College of Physical and Mathematical Sciences, Department of Chemistry and Biochemistry, Provo, UT 84602. Offers biochemistry (MS, PhD); chemistry (MS, PhD). *Faculty:* 34 full-time (3 women). *Students:* 95 full-time (33 women); includes 5 minority (4 Asian Americans or Pacific Islanders, 1 Hispanic American), 48 international. Average age 29. 101 applicants, 40% accepted, 18 enrolled. In 2009, 8 master's, 12 doctorates awarded. *Degree requirements:* For master's, thesis; for doctorate, thesis/dissertation, qualifying exam. *Entrance requirements:* For master's and doctorate, GRE General Test, minimum GPA of 3.0 in last 60 hours. Additional exam requirements/recommendations for international students: Required—TOEFL (minimum score 580 paper-based; 237 computer-based; 85 iBT); Recommended—TWE. *Application deadline:* For fall admission, 2/1 priority date for domestic and international students. Applications are processed on a rolling basis. Application fee: $50. Electronic applications accepted. *Expenses:* Tuition: Full-time $5580; part-time $301 per credit hour. Tuition and fees vary according to student's religious affiliation. *Financial support:* In 2009–10, 95 students received support, including 10 fellowships with full tuition reimbursements available (averaging $21,250 per year), 56 research assistantships with full tuition reimbursements available (averaging $21,250 per year), 29 teaching assistantships with full tuition reimbursements available (averaging $21,250 per year); institutionally sponsored loans, scholarships/grants, health care benefits, tuition waivers (full), and unspecified assistantships also available. Financial award application deadline: 2/1. *Faculty research:* Separation science, molecular recognition, organic synthesis and biomedical application, biochemistry and molecular biology, molecular spectroscopy. Total annual research expenditures: $4.4 million. *Unit head:* Dr. Paul B. Farnsworth, Chair, 801-422-6502, Fax: 801-422-0153, E-mail: paul_farnsworth@byu.edu. *Application contact:* Dr. Matthew R. Linford, Graduate Coordinator, 801-422-1699, Fax: 801-422-0153, E-mail: mrlinford@byu.edu.

See Close-Up on page 91.

California State University, Los Angeles, Graduate Studies, College of Natural and Social Sciences, Department of Chemistry and Biochemistry, Los Angeles, CA 90032-8530. Offers analytical chemistry (MS); biochemistry (MS); chemistry (MS); inorganic chemistry (MS); organic chemistry (MS); physical chemistry (MS). Part-time and evening/weekend programs available. *Faculty:* 1 full-time (0 women), 9 part-time/adjunct (4 women). *Students:* 14 full-time (4 women), 31 part-time (15 women); includes 21 minority (5 African Americans, 9 Asian Americans or Pacific Islanders, 7 Hispanic Americans), 10 international. Average age 30. 23 applicants, 91% accepted, 13 enrolled. In 2009, 11 degrees awarded. *Degree requirements:* For master's, one foreign language, comprehensive exam or thesis. *Entrance requirements:* Additional exam requirements/recommendations for international students: Required—TOEFL. *Application deadline:* For fall admission, 5/1 for domestic and international students. Applications are processed on a rolling basis. Application fee: $55. *Financial support:* Federal Work-Study available. Support available to part-time students. Financial award application deadline: 3/1. *Faculty research:* Intercalation of heavy metal, carborane chemistry, conductive polymers and fabrics, titanium reagents, computer modeling and synthesis. *Unit head:* Dr. Scott Grover, Chair, 323-343-2300, Fax: 323-343-6490, E-mail: sgrover@calstatela.edu. *Application contact:* Dr. Cheryl L. Ney, Associate Vice President for Academic Affairs and Dean of Graduate Studies, 323-343-3820 Ext. 3827, Fax: 323-343-5653, E-mail: cney@cslanet.calstatela.edu.

Cleveland State University, College of Graduate Studies, College of Science, Department of Chemistry, Cleveland, OH 44115. Offers analytical chemistry (MS); clinical chemistry (MS); clinical/bioanalytical chemistry (PhD), including clinical chemistry, molecular medicine; environmental chemistry (MS); inorganic chemistry (MS); organic chemistry (MS); physical chemistry (MS). Part-time and evening/weekend programs available. *Degree requirements:* For master's, thesis (for some programs); for doctorate, thesis/dissertation. *Entrance requirements:* For master's and doctorate, GRE General Test. Additional exam requirements/recommendations for international students: Required—TOEFL (minimum score 525 paper-based; 197 computer-based; 65 iBT). Electronic applications accepted. *Faculty research:* MALDI-TOF based DNA sequencing, development of ionic focusing HPLC, synthetic and structural studies of vanadium.

Cornell University, Graduate School, Graduate Fields of Arts and Sciences, Field of Chemistry and Chemical Biology, Ithaca, NY 14853-0001. Offers analytical chemistry (PhD); bio-organic chemistry (PhD); biophysical chemistry (PhD); chemical biology (PhD); chemical physics (PhD); inorganic chemistry (PhD); materials chemistry (PhD); organic chemistry (PhD); organometallic chemistry (PhD); physical chemistry (PhD); polymer chemistry (PhD); theoretical chemistry (PhD). *Faculty:* 48 full-time (3 women). *Students:* 162 full-time (67 women); includes 15 minority (1 African American, 9 Asian Americans or Pacific Islanders, 5 Hispanic Americans), 53 international. Average age 26. 359 applicants, 19% accepted, 39 enrolled. In 2009, 31 doctorates awarded. *Degree requirements:* For doctorate, comprehensive exam, thesis/dissertation. *Entrance requirements:* For doctorate, GRE General Test, GRE Subject Test (chemistry), 3 letters of recommendation. Additional exam requirements/recommendations for international students: Required—TOEFL (minimum score 600 paper-based; 250 computer-based; 77 iBT). *Application deadline:* For fall admission, 1/10 for domestic students. Application fee: $70. Electronic applications accepted. *Expenses:* Tuition: Full-time $29,500. Required fees: $70. Full-time tuition and fees vary according to degree level, program and student level. *Financial support:* In 2009–10, 1 fellowship with full tuition reimbursement, 7 research assistantships with full tuition reimbursements, 29 teaching assistantships with full tuition reimbursements were awarded; institutionally sponsored loans, scholarships/grants, health care benefits, tuition waivers (full and partial), and unspecified assistantships also available. Financial award applicants required to submit FAFSA. *Faculty research:* Analytical, organic, inorganic, physical, materials, chemical biology. *Unit head:* Director of Graduate Studies, 607-255-4139, Fax: 607-255-4137. *Application contact:* Graduate Field Assistant, 607-255-4139, Fax: 607-255-4137, E-mail: chemgrad@cornell.edu.

Florida State University, The Graduate School, College of Arts and Sciences, Department of Chemistry and Biochemistry, Tallahassee, FL 32306-4390. Offers analytical chemistry (MS, PhD); biochemistry (MS, PhD); inorganic chemistry (MS, PhD); materials chemistry (MS, PhD); organic chemistry (MS, PhD); physical chemistry (MS, PhD). *Faculty:* 40 full-time (6 women), 3 part-time/adjunct (0 women). *Students:* 150 full-time (47 women), 9 part-time (6 women); includes 16 minority (5 African Americans, 1 American Indian/Alaska Native, 5 Asian Americans or Pacific Islanders, 5 Hispanic Americans), 68 international. Average age 25. 286 applicants, 21% accepted, 28 enrolled. In 2009, 7 master's, 15 doctorates awarded. Terminal master's awarded for partial completion of doctoral program. *Degree requirements:* For master's, comprehensive exam (for some programs), thesis (for some programs), cumulative and diagnostic exams; for doctorate, comprehensive exam (for some programs), thesis/dissertation, cumulative and diagnostic exams. *Entrance requirements:* For master's and doctorate, GRE General Test, minimum B average in undergraduate course work. Additional exam requirements/recommendations for international students: Required—TOEFL (minimum score 550 paper-based; 213 computer-based; 80 iBT). *Application deadline:* For fall admission, 12/15 for domestic and international students; for spring admission, 9/15 for domestic and international students. Applications are processed on a rolling basis. Application fee: $30. Electronic applications accepted. *Expenses:* Tuition, state resident: full-time $7413.36. Tuition, nonresident: full-time $22,567. *Financial support:* In 2009–10, 150 students received support, including fellowships with full tuition reimbursements available (averaging $19,000 per year), 52 research assistantships with full tuition reimbursements available (averaging $19,000 per year), 100 teaching assistantships with full tuition reimbursements available (averaging $19,000 per year); career-related internships or fieldwork, Federal Work-Study, institutionally sponsored loans, and traineeships also available. Financial award application deadline: 12/15; financial award applicants required to submit FAFSA. *Faculty research:* Materials synthesis including polymers, natural products; catalysis, NMR; mass spectrometry; optical spectroscopy, scattering techniques, computational chemistry, separation technology; nanostructured materials including metallic, semiconducting and magnetic nanocrystals; nanoscience interfaced with biology; supramolecular materials for solar energy conversion. Total annual research expenditures: $5.5 million. *Unit head:* Dr. Joseph Schlenoff, Chairman, 850-644-5195, Fax: 850-644-8281, E-mail: schlen@chem.fsu.edu. *Application contact:* Dr. Tyler McQuade, Chair, Graduate Admissions Committee, 888-525-9286, Fax: 850-644-0465, E-mail: gradinfo@chem.fsu.edu.

Georgetown University, Graduate School of Arts and Sciences, Department of Chemistry, Washington, DC 20057. Offers analytical chemistry (PhD); biochemistry (PhD); computational chemistry (PhD); inorganic chemistry (PhD); materials chemistry (PhD); organic chemistry (PhD); physical chemistry (PhD); theoretical chemistry (PhD). Terminal master's awarded for partial completion of doctoral program. *Degree requirements:* For doctorate, comprehensive exam, thesis/dissertation. *Entrance requirements:* For doctorate, GRE General Test. Additional exam requirements/recommendations for international students: Required—TOEFL.

The George Washington University, Columbian College of Arts and Sciences, Department of Chemistry, Washington, DC 20052. Offers analytical chemistry (MS, PhD); inorganic chemistry (MS, PhD); materials science (MS, PhD); organic chemistry (MS, PhD); physical chemistry (MS, PhD). Part-time and evening/weekend programs available. *Faculty:* 15 full-time (4 women), 7 part-time/adjunct (3 women). *Students:* 19 full-time (12 women), 12 part-time (7 women); includes 4 minority (2 Asian Americans or Pacific Islanders, 2 Hispanic Americans), 12 international. Average age 28. 45 applicants, 49% accepted, 6 enrolled. In 2009, 2 master's, 4 doctorates awarded. Terminal master's awarded for partial completion of doctoral program. *Degree requirements:* For master's, comprehensive exam, thesis or alternative; for doctorate, thesis/dissertation, general exam. *Entrance requirements:* For master's and doctorate, GRE General Test, interview, minimum GPA of 3.0. Additional exam requirements/recommendations for international students: Required—TOEFL (minimum score 550 paper-based; 213 computer-based; 80 iBT). *Application deadline:* For fall admission, 1/15 priority date for domestic and international students; for spring admission, 9/1 priority date for domestic and international students. Applications are processed on a rolling basis. Application fee: $60. Electronic applications accepted. *Financial support:* In 2009–10, 27 students received support; fellowships with tuition reimbursements available, research assistantships, teaching assistantships with tuition reimbursements available, Federal Work-Study and tuition waivers available. Financial award application deadline: 1/15. *Unit head:* Dr. Michael King, Chair, 202-994-6488. *Application contact:* Information Contact, E-mail: gwchem@www.gwu.edu.

Governors State University, College of Arts and Sciences, Program in Analytical Chemistry, University Park, IL 60466-0975. Offers MS. Part-time and evening/weekend programs available. *Degree requirements:* For master's, thesis or alternative. *Faculty research:* Electrochemistry, photochemistry, spectrochemistry, biochemistry.

Howard University, Graduate School, Department of Chemistry, Washington, DC 20059-0002. Offers analytical chemistry (MS, PhD); atmospheric (MS, PhD); biochemistry (MS, PhD); environmental (MS, PhD); inorganic chemistry (MS, PhD); organic chemistry (MS, PhD); physical chemistry (MS, PhD). Terminal master's awarded for partial completion of doctoral program. *Degree requirements:* For master's, comprehensive exam, thesis, teaching experience; for doctorate, comprehensive exam, thesis/dissertation, teaching experience. *Entrance requirements:* For master's, GRE General Test, minimum GPA of 2.7; for doctorate, GRE General Test, minimum GPA of 3.0. Additional exam requirements/recommendations for international students: Required—TOEFL. Electronic applications accepted. *Faculty research:* Synthetic organics, materials, natural products, mass spectrometry.

Illinois Institute of Technology, Graduate College, College of Science and Letters, Department of Biological, Chemical and Physical Sciences, Chemistry Division, Chicago, IL 60616-3793. Offers analytical chemistry (M Ch); chemistry (M Chem, MS, PhD); materials and chemical synthesis (M Ch). Part-time and evening/weekend programs available. Postbaccalaureate distance learning degree programs offered (no on-campus study). Terminal master's awarded for partial completion of doctoral program. *Degree requirements:* For master's, comprehensive exam, thesis (for some programs); for doctorate, comprehensive exam, thesis/dissertation. *Entrance requirements:* For master's and doctorate, GRE General Test, minimum undergraduate GPA of 3.0. Additional exam requirements/recommendations for international students: Required—TOEFL (minimum score 550 paper-based; 213 computer-based; 80 iBT). Electronic applications accepted. *Expenses:* Tuition: Full-time $17,550; part-time $888 per credit hour. Required fees: $850; $7.50 per credit hour. One-time fee: $50 full-time. Full-time tuition and fees vary according to program. *Faculty research:* Organic synthesis for cancer-therapy, nano-materials for environmental/medical applications, single protein/cell functions and dynamics, polymer chemistry.

Indiana University Bloomington, University Graduate School, College of Arts and Sciences, Department of Chemistry, Bloomington, IN 47405-7000. Offers analytical chemistry (PhD); biological chemistry (PhD); chemistry (MAT); inorganic chemistry (PhD); physical chemistry (PhD). *Faculty:* 39 full-time (3 women). *Students:* 190 full-time (67 women), 1 (woman) part-time; includes 13 minority (4 African Americans, 1 American Indian/Alaska Native, 5 Asian Americans or Pacific Islanders, 3 Hispanic Americans), 66 international. Average age 26. 207 applicants, 60% accepted, 49 enrolled. In 2009, 10 master's, 20 doctorates awarded. Terminal master's awarded for partial completion of doctoral program. *Degree requirements:* For master's, thesis; for doctorate, thesis/dissertation. *Entrance requirements:* For master's and doctorate, GRE General Test, GRE Subject Test. Additional exam requirements/recommendations for international students: Required—TOEFL. *Application deadline:* For fall admission, 1/15 priority date for domestic students, 12/15 for international students; for spring admission, 9/1 priority date for domestic students, 9/1 for international students. Applications are processed on a rolling basis. Application fee: $55 ($65 for international students). *Financial support:* Fellowships with full tuition reimbursements, research assistantships with full tuition reimbursements, teaching assistantships with full tuition reimbursements, Federal Work-Study and institutionally sponsored loans available. *Faculty research:* Synthesis of complex natural products, organic reaction mechanisms, organic electrochemistry, transitive-metal chemistry, solid-state and surface chemistry. Total annual research expenditures: $7.7 million. *Unit head:* Jim Reilly, Chairperson, 812-855-6239, E-mail: chemchair@indiana.edu. *Application contact:* Martin Jarrold, Director of Graduate Admissions, 812-855-2069, E-mail: mfj@indiana.edu.

Kansas State University, Graduate School, College of Arts and Sciences, Department of Chemistry, Manhattan, KS 66506. Offers analytical chemistry (MS); biological chemistry (MS); chemistry (PhD); inorganic chemistry (MS); materials chemistry (MS); organic chemistry (MS); physical chemistry (MS). *Faculty:* 16 full-time (2 women), 2 part-time/adjunct (0 women). *Students:* 66 full-time (22 women); includes 2 minority (1 African American, 1 Asian American or Pacific Islander), 54 international. Average age 28. 75 applicants, 23% accepted, 7 enrolled. In 2009, 3 master's, 11 doctorates awarded. Terminal master's awarded for partial completion of doctoral program. *Degree requirements:* For master's, thesis; for doctorate, thesis/dissertation. *Entrance requirements:* For master's and doctorate, GRE, minimum GPA of 3.0. Additional exam requirements/recommendations for international students: Required—TOEFL (minimum score 550 paper-based; 213 computer-based). *Application deadline:* For fall admission, 2/1 priority date for domestic and international students; for spring admission, 8/1 priority date for domestic and international students. Applications are processed on a rolling basis. Application fee: $40 ($55 for international students). Electronic applications accepted. *Financial support:* In 2009–10, 41 research assistantships (averaging $15,040 per year), 22 teaching assistantships with full tuition reimbursements (averaging $15,600 per year) were awarded; institutionally sponsored loans and scholarships/grants also available. Support available to part-time students. Financial award application deadline: 3/1; financial award applicants required to submit FAFSA. *Faculty research:* Inorganic chemistry, organic and biological chemistry, analytical chemistry, physical chemistry, materials chemistry and nanotechnology. Total annual research expenditures: $1.9 million. *Unit head:* Eric Maatta, Head, 785-532-6665, Fax: 785-532-6666, E-mail: eam@ksu.edu. *Application contact:* Christer Aakeroy, Director, 785-532-6096, Fax: 785-532-6666, E-mail: aakeroy@ksu.edu.

Kent State University, College of Arts and Sciences, Department of Chemistry, Kent, OH 44242-0001. Offers analytical chemistry (MS, PhD); biochemistry (MS, PhD); chemistry (MA, MS, PhD); inorganic chemistry (MS, PhD); organic chemistry (MS, PhD); physical chemistry (MS, PhD). Terminal master's awarded for partial completion of doctoral program. *Degree requirements:* For master's, comprehensive exam, thesis; for doctorate, comprehensive exam, thesis/dissertation. *Entrance requirements:* For master's and doctorate, placement exam, GRE General Test, GRE Subject Test (recommended), minimum GPA of 2.75. Additional exam requirements/recommendations for international students: Required—TOEFL (minimum score 575 paper-based; 230 computer-based). Electronic applications accepted. *Faculty research:* Biological chemistry, materials chemistry, molecular spectroscopy.

See Close-Up on page 101.

Laurentian University, School of Graduate Studies and Research, Programme in Chemistry and Biochemistry, Sudbury, ON P3E 2C6, Canada. Offers analytical chemistry (M Sc); biochemistry (M Sc); environmental chemistry (M Sc); organic chemistry (M Sc); physical/theoretical chemistry (M Sc). Part-time programs available. *Degree requirements:* For master's, thesis or alternative. *Entrance requirements:* For master's, honors degree with minimum second class. *Faculty research:* Cell cycle checkpoints, kinetic modeling, toxicology to metal stress, quantum chemistry, biogeochemistry metal speciation.

Marquette University, Graduate School, College of Arts and Sciences, Department of Chemistry, Milwaukee, WI 53201-1881. Offers analytical chemistry (MS, PhD); bioanalytical chemistry (MS, PhD); biophysical chemistry (MS, PhD); chemical physics (MS, PhD); inorganic chemistry (MS, PhD); organic chemistry (MS, PhD); physical chemistry (MS, PhD). Part-time programs available. *Faculty:* 23 full-time (10 women), 1 part-time/adjunct (0 women). *Students:* 34 full-time (9 women), 10 part-time (4 women); includes 4 minority (1 African American, 2 Asian Americans or Pacific Islanders, 1 Hispanic American), 33 international. Average age 29. 23 applicants, 83% accepted, 8 enrolled. In 2009, 4 master's, 5 doctorates awarded. Terminal master's awarded for partial completion of doctoral program. *Degree requirements:* For master's, comprehensive exam; for doctorate, thesis/dissertation, cumulative exams. *Entrance requirements:* For master's and doctorate, GRE Subject Test. Additional exam requirements/recommendations for international students: Required—TOEFL. Application fee: $40. *Financial support:* In 2009–10, 3 research assistantships, 27 teaching assistantships were awarded; fellowships, Federal Work-Study, institutionally sponsored loans, scholarships/grants, and tuition waivers (full and partial) also available. Support available to part-time students. Financial award application deadline: 2/15. *Faculty research:* Inorganic complexes, laser Raman spectroscopy, organic synthesis, chemical dynamics, biophysiology. *Unit head:* Dr. Jeanne Hossenlopp, Chair, 414-288-3537, Fax: 414-288-7066. *Application contact:* Dr. Mark Steinmetz, Director of Graduate Studies, 414-288-7374, Fax: 414-288-7066.

McMaster University, School of Graduate Studies, Faculty of Science, Department of Chemistry, Hamilton, ON L8S 4M2, Canada. Offers analytical chemistry (M Sc, PhD); chemical physics (M Sc, PhD); chemistry (M Sc, PhD); inorganic chemistry (M Sc, PhD); organic chemistry (M Sc, PhD); physical chemistry (M Sc, PhD); polymer chemistry (M Sc, PhD). Part-time programs available. Terminal master's awarded for partial completion of doctoral program. *Degree requirements:* For master's, thesis; for doctorate, comprehensive exam, thesis/dissertation. *Entrance requirements:* For master's, minimum B+ average. Additional exam requirements/recommendations for international students: Required—TOEFL (minimum score 550 paper-based; 213 computer-based).

Northeastern University, College of Science, Department of Chemistry and Chemical Biology, Boston, MA 02115-5096. Offers analytical chemistry (PhD); chemistry (MS, PhD); inorganic chemistry (PhD); organic chemistry (PhD); physical chemistry (PhD). Part-time and evening/weekend programs available. *Faculty:* 24 full-time (5 women), 7 part-time/adjunct (0 women). *Students:* 86 full-time (48 women), 31 part-time (14 women); includes 9 minority (1 African American, 1 American Indian/Alaska Native, 7 Asian Americans or Pacific Islanders), 36 international. 190 applicants, 22% accepted, 15 enrolled. In 2009, 17 master's, 9 doctorates awarded. Terminal master's awarded for partial completion of doctoral program. *Degree requirements:* For master's, thesis (for some programs); for doctorate, thesis/dissertation, qualifying exam in specialty area. *Entrance requirements:* Additional exam requirements/recommendations for international students: Required—TOEFL. *Application deadline:* For fall admission, 2/1 priority date for domestic and international students. Applications are processed on a rolling basis. Application fee: $50. Electronic applications accepted. *Financial support:* In 2009–10, 41 research assistantships with tuition reimbursements (averaging $18,285 per year), 38 teaching assistantships with tuition reimbursements (averaging $18,285 per year) were awarded; fellowships with tuition reimbursements, career-related internships or fieldwork, Federal Work-Study, scholarships/grants, tuition waivers (partial), and unspecified assistantships also available. Financial award application deadline: 3/1; financial award applicants required to submit FAFSA. *Faculty research:* Bioanalysis, biorganic and medicinal chemistry, biophysical chemistry, nanomaterials, proteomics. *Unit head:* Dr. Robert Hanson, Graduate Coordinator, 617-373-3313, Fax: 617-373-8795, E-mail: chemistry-grad-info@neu.edu. *Application contact:* Jo-Anne Dickinson, Admissions Contact, 617-373-5990, Fax: 617-373-7281, E-mail: gsas@neu.edu.

Old Dominion University, College of Sciences, Program in Chemistry, Norfolk, VA 23529. Offers analytical chemistry (MS); biochemistry (MS); chemistry (PhD); environmental chemistry (MS); organic chemistry (MS); physical chemistry (MS). Part-time and evening/weekend programs available. *Faculty:* 14 full-time (5 women), 2 part-time/adjunct (0 women). *Students:* 30 full-time (19 women), 10 part-time (5 women); includes 3 minority (1 African American, 1 Asian American or Pacific Islander, 1 Hispanic American), 17 international. Average age 29. 35 applicants, 60% accepted, 8 enrolled. In 2009, 1 master's awarded. *Degree requirements:* For master's, comprehensive exam, thesis. *Entrance requirements:* For master's, GRE General Test, minimum GPA of 3.0 in major, 2.5 overall; for doctorate, GRE General Test. Additional exam requirements/recommendations for international students: Required—TOEFL. *Application deadline:* For fall admission, 7/1 for domestic students, 1/15 for international students; for spring admission, 11/1 for domestic students, 8/15 for international students. Applications are processed on a rolling basis. Application fee: $30. Electronic applications accepted. *Expenses:* Tuition, state resident: full-time $8112; part-time $338 per credit. Tuition, nonresident: full-time $20,256; part-time $844 per credit. Required fees: $119 per semester. One-time fee: $50. *Financial support:* In 2009–10, 6 students received support, including fellowships (averaging $18,000 per year), research assistantships with tuition reimbursements available (averaging $21,000 per year), teaching assistantships with tuition reimbursements available (averaging $18,000 per year); career-related internships or fieldwork, scholarships/grants, and unspecified assistantships also available. Financial award application deadline: 2/15; financial award applicants required to submit FAFSA. *Faculty research:* Biogeochemistry, materials chemistry, bioanalytical chemistry, computational chemistry, organic chemistry. Total annual research expenditures: $2.6 million. *Unit head:* Dr. Craig A. Bayse, Graduate Program Director, 757-683-4097, Fax: 757-683-4628, E-mail: chemgpd@odu.edu. *Application contact:* Valerie DeCosta, Grants and Graduate Program Assistant, 757-683-6979, Fax: 757-683-4628, E-mail: chemgpd@odu.edu.

Oregon State University, Graduate School, College of Science, Department of Chemistry, Corvallis, OR 97331. Offers analytical chemistry (MS, PhD); chemistry (MA, MAIS); inorganic chemistry (MS, PhD); nuclear and radiation chemistry (MS, PhD); organic chemistry (MS, PhD); physical chemistry (MS, PhD). Part-time programs available. *Faculty:* 24 full-time (3 women), 1 part-time/adjunct (0 women). *Students:* 78 full-time (27 women), 1 part-time (0 women); includes 3 minority (1 African American, 1 Asian American or Pacific Islander, 1 Hispanic American), 50 international. Average age 27. In 2009, 6 master's, 7 doctorates awarded. Terminal master's awarded for partial completion of doctoral program. *Degree requirements:* For master's, one foreign language, thesis; for doctorate, one foreign language, thesis/dissertation. *Entrance requirements:* For master's and doctorate, minimum GPA of 3.0 in last 90 hours of course work. Additional exam requirements/recommendations for international students: Required—TOEFL. *Application deadline:* For fall admission, 3/1 priority date for domestic students. Applications are processed on a rolling basis. Application fee: $50. *Expenses:* Tuition, state resident: full-time $9774; part-time $362 per credit. Tuition, nonresident: full-time $15,849; part-time $587 per credit. Required fees: $1639. Full-time tuition and fees vary according to course load and program. *Financial support:* Fellowships, research assistantships, teaching assistantships, institutionally sponsored loans available. Support available to part-time students. Financial award application deadline: 2/1. *Faculty research:* Solid state chemistry, enzyme reaction mechanisms, structure and dynamics of gas molecules, chemiluminescence, nonlinear optical spectroscopy. *Unit head:* Dr. Kevin P. Gable, Chair, 541-737-6744, Fax: 541-737-2062, E-mail: gablek@chem.orst.edu. *Application contact:* Dr. Kevin P. Gable, Chair, 541-737-6744, Fax: 541-737-2062, E-mail: gablek@chem.orst.edu.

Purdue University, Graduate School, College of Science, Department of Chemistry, West Lafayette, IN 47907. Offers analytical chemistry (MS, PhD); biochemistry (MS, PhD); chemical education (MS, PhD); inorganic chemistry (MS, PhD); organic chemistry (MS, PhD); physical chemistry (MS, PhD). Terminal master's awarded for partial completion of doctoral program. *Degree requirements:* For master's, thesis; for doctorate, thesis/dissertation. *Entrance requirements:* Additional exam requirements/recommendations for international students: Required—TOEFL. Electronic applications accepted.

Rensselaer Polytechnic Institute, Graduate School, School of Science, Department of Chemistry and Chemical Biology, Troy, NY 12180-3590. Offers analytical chemistry (MS, PhD); biochemistry (MS, PhD); inorganic chemistry (MS, PhD); organic chemistry (MS, PhD); physical chemistry (MS, PhD); polymer chemistry (MS, PhD). Part-time and evening/weekend programs available. *Faculty:* 16 full-time (2 women). *Students:* 68 full-time (31 women); includes 1 African American, 6 Asian Americans or Pacific Islanders, 1 Hispanic American, 31 international. Average age 24. 85 applicants, 19% accepted, 5 enrolled. In 2009, 5 master's, 6 doctorates awarded. Terminal master's awarded for partial completion of doctoral program. *Degree requirements:* For master's, thesis (for some programs); for doctorate, comprehensive exam, thesis/dissertation. *Entrance requirements:* For master's, GRE General Test, GRE Subject Test (strongly recommended); for doctorate, GRE General Test, GRE Subject Test (chemistry or biochemistry strongly recommended). Additional exam requirements/recommendations for international students: Required—TOEFL (minimum score 600 paper-based). *Application deadline:* For fall admission, 2/1 priority date for domestic students; for spring admission, 11/15 for domestic students. Applications are processed on a rolling basis. Application fee: $75. Electronic applications accepted. *Expenses:* Tuition: Full-time $38,100. *Financial support:* In 2009–10, 1 fellowship with full tuition reimbursement (averaging $22,500 per year), 18 research assistantships with full tuition reimbursements (averaging $22,500 per year), 24 teaching assistantships with full tuition reimbursements (averaging $22,500 per year) were awarded; institutionally sponsored loans and tuition waivers (full and partial) also available. Financial award application deadline: 2/1. *Faculty research:* Synthetic polymer and biopolymer chemistry, physical chemistry of polymeric systems, bioanalytical chemistry, synthetic and computational drug design, protein folding and protein design. Total annual research expenditures: $1.1 million. *Unit head:* Dr. Curtis M. Breneman, Chair, 518-276-3264, Fax: 518-276-4887, E-mail: brenec@rpi.edu. *Application contact:* Sharon E. Gardner, Graduate Program Administrator, 518-276-2140, Fax: 518-276-4887, E-mail: derris@rpi.edu.

Rutgers, The State University of New Jersey, Newark, Graduate School, Program in Chemistry, Newark, NJ 07102. Offers analytical chemistry (MS, PhD); biochemistry (MS, PhD); inorganic chemistry (MS, PhD); organic chemistry (MS, PhD); physical chemistry (MS, PhD). Part-time and evening/weekend programs available. Terminal master's awarded for partial completion of doctoral program. *Degree requirements:* For master's, thesis optional, cumulative exams; for doctorate, thesis/dissertation, exams, research proposal. *Entrance requirements:* For master's and doctorate, GRE General Test, minimum undergraduate B average. Additional exam requirements/recommendations for international students: Required—TOEFL. Electronic applications accepted. *Faculty research:* Medicinal chemistry, natural products, isotope effects, biophysics and biorganic approaches to enzyme mechanisms, organic and organometallic synthesis.

Seton Hall University, College of Arts and Sciences, Department of Chemistry and Biochemistry, South Orange, NJ 07079-2697. Offers analytical chemistry (MS, PhD); biochemistry (MS, PhD); chemistry (MS); inorganic chemistry (MS, PhD); organic chemistry (MS, PhD); physical chemistry (MS, PhD). Part-time and evening/weekend programs available. *Faculty:* 10 full-time (1 woman). *Students:* 24 full-time (14 women), 47 part-time (15 women); includes 22 minority (10 African Americans, 8 Asian Americans or Pacific Islanders, 4 Hispanic Americans), 11 international. Average age 33. 31 applicants, 68% accepted, 10 enrolled. In 2009, 7 master's, 4 doctorates awarded. Terminal master's awarded for partial completion of doctoral program. *Degree requirements:* For master's, thesis optional; for doctorate, comprehensive exam, thesis/dissertation. *Entrance requirements:* Additional exam requirements/recommendations for international students: Required—TOEFL. *Application deadline:* For fall admission, 7/1 priority date for domestic and international students; for spring admission, 11/1 priority date for domestic and international students. Applications are processed on a rolling basis. Application fee: $50. Electronic applications accepted. *Financial support:* Research assistantships, teaching assistantships with full tuition reimbursements, Federal Work-Study and unspecified assistantships available. Financial award applicants required to submit FAFSA. *Faculty research:* DNA metal reactions; chromatography; bioinorganic, biophysical, organometallic, polymer chemistry; heterogeneous catalyst; synthetic organic and carbohydrate chemistry. *Unit head:* Dr. Nicholas

Analytical Chemistry

Seton Hall University (continued)
Snow, Chair, 973-761-9414, Fax: 973-761-9772, E-mail: snownich@shu.edu. *Application contact:* Dr. Stephen Kelty, Director of Graduate Studies, 973-761-9129, Fax: 973-761-9772, E-mail: keltyste@shu.edu.

Southern University and Agricultural and Mechanical College, Graduate School, College of Sciences, Department of Chemistry, Baton Rouge, LA 70813. Offers analytical chemistry (MS); biochemistry (MS); environmental sciences (MS); inorganic chemistry (MS); organic chemistry (MS); physical chemistry (MS). *Degree requirements:* For master's, thesis. *Entrance requirements:* For master's, GMAT or GRE General Test. Additional exam requirements/recommendations for international students: Required—TOEFL (minimum score 525 paper-based; 193 computer-based). *Faculty research:* Synthesis of macrocyclic ligands, latex accelerators, anticancer drugs, biosensors, absorption isotheums, isolation of specific enzymes from plants.

State University of New York at Binghamton, Graduate School, School of Arts and Sciences, Department of Chemistry, Binghamton, NY 13902-6000. Offers analytical chemistry (PhD); chemistry (MA, MS); inorganic chemistry (PhD); organic chemistry (PhD); physical chemistry (PhD). Part-time programs available. *Faculty:* 14 full-time (3 women), 2 part-time/adjunct (0 women). *Students:* 35 full-time (13 women), 22 part-time (10 women); includes 8 minority (3 African Americans, 4 Asian Americans or Pacific Islanders, 1 Hispanic American), 32 international. Average age 29. 40 applicants, 30% accepted, 6 enrolled. In 2009, 6 master's, 5 doctorates awarded. Terminal master's awarded for partial completion of doctoral program. *Degree requirements:* For master's, thesis or alternative, oral exam, seminar presentation; for doctorate, thesis/dissertation, cumulative exams. *Entrance requirements:* For master's and doctorate, GRE General Test, GRE Subject Test. Additional exam requirements/recommendations for international students: Required—TOEFL (minimum score 550 paper-based; 213 computer-based; 80 iBT). *Application deadline:* For fall admission, 1/15 priority date for domestic and international students; for spring admission, 10/15 priority date for domestic and international students. Applications are processed on a rolling basis. Application fee: $60. Electronic applications accepted. *Financial support:* In 2009–10, 55 students received support, including 4 fellowships with full tuition reimbursements available (averaging $18,000 per year), 8 research assistantships with full tuition reimbursements available (averaging $18,000 per year), 34 teaching assistantships with full tuition reimbursements available (averaging $18,000 per year); career-related internships or fieldwork, Federal Work-Study, institutionally sponsored loans, scholarships/grants, health care benefits, tuition waivers (full), and unspecified assistantships also available. Financial award application deadline: 2/15; financial award applicants required to submit FAFSA. *Unit head:* Dr. Wayne E. Jones, Chairperson, 607-777-2421, E-mail: wjones@binghamton.edu. *Application contact:* Victoria Williams, Recruiting and Admissions Coordinator, 607-777-2151, Fax: 607-777-2501, E-mail: vwilliam@binghamton.edu.

Stevens Institute of Technology, Graduate School, Charles V. Schaefer Jr. School of Engineering, Department of Chemistry, Chemical Biology and Biomedical Engineering, Hoboken, NJ 07030. Offers analytical chemistry (PhD, Certificate); bioinformatics (PhD, Certificate); biomedical chemistry (Certificate); biomedical engineering (M Eng, Certificate); chemical biology (MS, PhD, Certificate); chemical physiology (Certificate); chemistry (MS, PhD); organic chemistry (PhD); physical chemistry (PhD); polymer chemistry (PhD, Certificate). Part-time and evening/weekend programs available. Postbaccalaureate distance learning degree programs offered (no on-campus study). Terminal master's awarded for partial completion of doctoral program. *Degree requirements:* For master's, thesis or alternative; for doctorate, one foreign language, thesis/dissertation; for Certificate, project or thesis. *Entrance requirements:* Additional exam requirements/recommendations for international students: Required—TOEFL. Electronic applications accepted. *Expenses:* Tuition: Full-time $9900; part-time $1100 per credit. Required fees: $286 per semester. *Faculty research:* Biochemical reaction engineering, polymerization engineering, reactor design, biochemical process control and synthesis.

Tufts University, Graduate School of Arts and Sciences, Department of Chemistry, Medford, MA 02155. Offers analytical chemistry (MS, PhD); bioorganic chemistry (MS, PhD); environmental chemistry (MS, PhD); inorganic chemistry (MS, PhD); organic chemistry (MS, PhD); physical chemistry (MS, PhD). *Students:* 61 full-time (29 women); includes 7 minority (1 African American, 1 American Indian/Alaska Native, 4 Asian Americans or Pacific Islanders, 1 Hispanic American), 18 international. 90 applicants, 50% accepted, 14 enrolled. In 2009, 2 master's, 7 doctorates awarded. Terminal master's awarded for partial completion of doctoral program. *Degree requirements:* For master's, thesis optional; for doctorate, thesis/dissertation. *Entrance requirements:* For master's and doctorate, GRE General Test, GRE Subject Test. Additional exam requirements/recommendations for international students: Required—TOEFL (minimum score 600 paper-based; 250 computer-based; 80 iBT). *Application deadline:* For fall admission, 1/15 for domestic students, 12/30 for international students; for spring admission, 10/15 for domestic students, 9/15 for international students. Applications are processed on a rolling basis. Application fee: $75. Electronic applications accepted. *Expenses:* Tuition: Full-time $38,096; part-time $3962 per credit. Required fees: $686; $40 per year. Tuition and fees vary according to course level, course load, degree level, program and student level. *Financial support:* Fellowships, research assistantships with full tuition reimbursements, teaching assistantships with full tuition reimbursements, Federal Work-Study, scholarships/grants, tuition waivers (partial), and unspecified assistantships available. Financial award application deadline: 1/15; financial award applicants required to submit FAFSA. *Unit head:* Arthur Utz, Chair, 617-627-3441. *Application contact:* Samuel Kounaves, Information Contact, 617-627-3441, Fax: 617-627-3443.

University of Calgary, Faculty of Graduate Studies, Faculty of Science, Department of Chemistry, Calgary, AB T2N 1N4, Canada. Offers analytical chemistry (M Sc, PhD); applied chemistry (M Sc, PhD); inorganic chemistry (M Sc, PhD); organic chemistry (M Sc, PhD); physical chemistry (M Sc, PhD); polymer chemistry (M Sc, PhD); theoretical chemistry (M Sc, PhD). *Degree requirements:* For master's, thesis; for doctorate, thesis/dissertation, candidacy exam. *Entrance requirements:* For master's, minimum GPA of 3.0; for doctorate, honors B Sc degree with minimum GPA of 3.7 or M Sc with minimum GPA of 3.3. Additional exam requirements/recommendations for international students: Required—TOEFL (minimum score 580 paper-based; 237 computer-based). Electronic applications accepted. *Faculty research:* Chemical analysis, chemical dynamics, synthesis theory.

University of Cincinnati, Graduate School, McMicken College of Arts and Sciences, Department of Chemistry, Cincinnati, OH 45221. Offers analytical chemistry (MS, PhD); biochemistry (MS, PhD); inorganic chemistry (MS, PhD); organic chemistry (MS, PhD); physical chemistry (MS, PhD); polymer chemistry (MS, PhD); sensors (PhD). Part-time and evening/weekend programs available. Terminal master's awarded for partial completion of doctoral program. *Degree requirements:* For master's, thesis optional; for doctorate, comprehensive exam, thesis/dissertation. *Entrance requirements:* For master's and doctorate, GRE General Test. Additional exam requirements/recommendations for international students: Required—TOEFL (minimum score 580 paper-based; 237 computer-based). Electronic applications accepted. *Faculty research:* Biomedical chemistry, laser chemistry, surface science, chemical sensors, synthesis.

University of Georgia, Graduate School, College of Arts and Sciences, Department of Chemistry, Athens, GA 30602. Offers analytical chemistry (MS, PhD); inorganic chemistry (MS, PhD); organic chemistry (MS, PhD); physical chemistry (MS, PhD). *Faculty:* 25 full-time (1 woman). *Students:* 147 full-time (53 women), 2 part-time (1 woman); includes 14 minority (6 African Americans, 7 Asian Americans or Pacific Islanders, 1 Hispanic American), 61 international. 136 applicants, 55% accepted, 27 enrolled. In 2009, 3 master's, 23 doctorates awarded. Terminal master's awarded for partial completion of doctoral program. *Degree requirements:* For master's, thesis; for doctorate, one foreign language, thesis/dissertation. *Entrance requirements:* For master's and doctorate, GRE General Test. Additional exam requirements/recommendations for international students: Required—TOEFL (minimum score 213 computer-based). *Application deadline:* For fall admission, 7/1 priority date for domestic students; for spring admission, 11/15 for domestic students. Application fee: $50. Electronic applications accepted. *Expenses:* Tuition, state resident: full-time $6000; part-time $250 per credit hour. Tuition, nonresident: full-time $20,904; part-time $871 per credit hour. Required fees: $730 per semester. *Financial support:* Fellowships, research assistantships, teaching assistantships, unspecified assistantships available. *Unit head:* Dr. John L. Stickney, Head, 706-542-2726, Fax: 706-542-9454, E-mail: stickney@chem.uga.edu. *Application contact:* Dr. George F. Majetich, Graduate Coordinator, 706-542-1966, Fax: 706-542-9454, E-mail: majetich@chem.uga.edu.

University of Louisville, Graduate School, College of Arts and Sciences, Department of Chemistry, Louisville, KY 40292-0001. Offers analytical chemistry (MS, PhD); biochemistry (MS, PhD); chemical physics (PhD); inorganic chemistry (MS, PhD); organic chemistry (MS, PhD); physical chemistry (MS, PhD). *Students:* 57 full-time (27 women), 4 part-time (1 woman); includes 2 minority (1 African American, 1 Asian American or Pacific Islander), 43 international. Average age 29. 62 applicants, 31% accepted, 13 enrolled. In 2009, 6 master's, 7 doctorates awarded. *Median time to degree:* Of those who began their doctoral program in fall 2001, 0% received their degree in 8 years or less. *Degree requirements:* For master's, thesis; for doctorate, comprehensive exam, thesis/dissertation. *Entrance requirements:* For master's and doctorate, GRE General Test. Additional exam requirements/recommendations for international students: Required—TOEFL. *Application deadline:* Applications are processed on a rolling basis. Application fee: $50. *Financial support:* Fellowships, research assistantships, teaching assistantships available. *Unit head:* Dr. George R. Pack, Chair, 502-852-6798, Fax: 502-852-8149, E-mail: george.pack@louisville.edu. *Application contact:* Libby Leggett, Director, Graduate Admissions, 502-852-3101, Fax: 502-852-6536, E-mail: gradadm@louisville.edu.

University of Maryland, College Park, Academic Affairs, College of Chemical and Life Sciences, Department of Chemistry and Biochemistry, Chemistry Program, College Park, MD 20742. Offers analytical chemistry (MS, PhD); inorganic chemistry (MS, PhD); organic chemistry (MS, PhD); physical chemistry (MS, PhD). Part-time and evening/weekend programs available. *Students:* 129 full-time (69 women), 5 part-time (3 women); includes 18 minority (13 African Americans, 3 Asian Americans or Pacific Islanders, 2 Hispanic Americans), 70 international. 329 applicants, 22% accepted, 36 enrolled. In 2009, 6 master's, 18 doctorates awarded. Terminal master's awarded for partial completion of doctoral program. *Degree requirements:* For master's, thesis optional; for doctorate, thesis/dissertation, 2 seminar presentations, oral exam. *Entrance requirements:* For master's and doctorate, GRE General Test, GRE Subject Test (recommended), minimum GPA of 3.0, 3 letters of recommendation. Additional exam requirements/recommendations for international students: Required—TOEFL. *Application deadline:* For fall admission, 2/1 for domestic and international students. Applications are processed on a rolling basis. Application fee: $60. Electronic applications accepted. *Expenses:* Tuition, area resident: Part-time $471 per credit hour. Tuition, state resident: part-time $471 per credit hour. Tuition, nonresident: part-time $1016 per credit hour. Required fees: $337.04 per term. *Financial support:* In 2009–10, 7 fellowships with full tuition reimbursements (averaging $27,067 per year), 51 research assistantships (averaging $19,639 per year), 66 teaching assistantships with partial tuition reimbursements (averaging $19,260 per year) were awarded. Financial award applicants required to submit FAFSA. *Faculty research:* Environmental chemistry, nuclear chemistry, lunar and environmental analysis, x-ray crystallography. *Unit head:* Dr. Michael Doyle, Chairperson, 301-405-1795, Fax: 301-314-2779, E-mail: mdoyle3@umd.edu. *Application contact:* Dean of Graduate School, 301-405-0358, Fax: 301-314-9305.

University of Massachusetts Lowell, College of Arts and Sciences, Department of Chemistry, Lowell, MA 01854-2881. Offers analytical chemistry (PhD); biochemistry (PhD); chemistry (MS, PhD); environmental studies (PhD); green chemistry (PhD); inorganic chemistry (PhD); organic chemistry (PhD); polymer science (MS). Terminal master's awarded for partial completion of doctoral program. *Degree requirements:* For master's, thesis; for doctorate, 2 foreign languages, thesis/dissertation. *Entrance requirements:* For master's and doctorate, GRE General Test. Electronic applications accepted.

University of Memphis, Graduate School, College of Arts and Sciences, Department of Chemistry, Memphis, TN 38152. Offers analytical chemistry (PhD); analytical chemsitry (MS); computational chemistry (MS, PhD); inorganic chemistry (MS, PhD); organic chemistry (MS, PhD); physical chemistry (MS, PhD). Part-time programs available. *Faculty:* 6 full-time (1 woman). *Students:* 39 full-time (17 women), 7 part-time (4 women); includes 8 minority (6 African Americans, 1 Asian American or Pacific Islander, 1 Hispanic American), 6 international. Average age 28. 23 applicants, 70% accepted, 14 enrolled. In 2009, 3 master's, 5 doctorates awarded. Terminal master's awarded for partial completion of doctoral program. *Degree requirements:* For master's, comprehensive exam, thesis or alternative; for doctorate, comprehensive exam, thesis/dissertation. *Entrance requirements:* For master's and doctorate, GRE General Test, admission to Graduate School plus 32 undergraduate hours in chemistry. Additional exam requirements/recommendations for international students: Required—TOEFL. *Application deadline:* For fall admission, 7/1 for domestic students, 5/1 for international students; for winter admission, 9/15 for international students; for spring admission, 12/1 for domestic students. Applications are processed on a rolling basis. Application fee: $35 ($60 for international students). Electronic applications accepted. *Expenses:* Tuition, state resident: full-time $6246; part-time $347 per credit hour. Tuition, nonresident: full-time $15,894; part-time $883 per credit hour. Required fees: $1160. Full-time tuition and fees vary according to course load, degree level and program. *Financial support:* In 2009–10, 12 students received support; research assistantships with full tuition reimbursements available, teaching assistantships with full tuition reimbursements available, Federal Work-Study, scholarships/grants, and unspecified assistantships available. Financial award application deadline: 2/15; financial award applicants required to submit FAFSA. *Faculty research:* Computational chemistry, materials chemistry, organic/polymer synthesis, drug design/delivery, water chemistry. *Unit head:* Dr. Abby L. Parrill, Professor and Chair, 901-678-2638, Fax: 901-678-3447, E-mail: aparrill@memphis.edu. *Application contact:* Dr. Gary Emmert, Associate Professor and Graduate Coordinator, 901-678-2636, Fax: 901-678-3447, E-mail: gemmert@memphis.edu.

University of Michigan, Horace H. Rackham School of Graduate Studies, College of Literature, Science, and the Arts, Department of Chemistry, Ann Arbor, MI 48109-1055. Offers analytical chemistry (PhD); chemical biology (PhD); inorganic chemistry (PhD); material chemistry (PhD); organic chemistry (PhD); physical chemistry (PhD). *Faculty:* 42 full-time (10 women). *Students:* 192 full-time (105 women); includes 74 minority (4 African Americans, 64 Asian Americans or Pacific Islanders, 6 Hispanic Americans), 54 international. Average age 26. 558 applicants, 36% accepted, 56 enrolled. In 2009, 28 doctorates awarded. *Degree requirements:* For doctorate, thesis/dissertation, oral defense of dissertation, organic cumulative proficiency exams. *Entrance requirements:* For doctorate, GRE General Test, GRE Subject Test (recommended), 3 letters of recommendation. Additional exam requirements/recommendations for international students: Required—TOEFL (minimum score 560 paper-based; 220 computer-based; 84 iBT). *Application deadline:* For fall admission, 1/15 for domestic students, 12/15 for international students. Applications are processed on a rolling basis. Application fee: $0 ($75 for international students). Electronic applications accepted. *Expenses:* Tuition, state resident: full-time $17,286; part-time $1099 per credit hour. Tuition, nonresident: full-time $34,944; part-time $2080 per credit hour. Required fees: $95 per semester. Tuition and fees vary according to course load, degree level and program. *Financial support:* In 2009–10, 192 students received support, including 20 fellowships with full tuition reimbursements available (averaging $25,000 per year), 75 research assistantships with full tuition reimbursements available (averaging $25,000 per year), 97 teaching assistantships with full tuition reimbursements available (averaging $25,000 per year); career-related internships or fieldwork, scholarships/grants, traineeships, health care benefits, and unspecified assistantships also available. Financial award applicants required to submit FAFSA. *Faculty research:* Biological catalysis, protein engineering, chemical sensors, de novo metalloprotein design, supramolecular architecture. Total annual research expenditures: $15.3 million. *Unit head:* Dr. Carol A. Fierke, Chair, 734-763-9681, Fax: 734-647-4847. *Application contact:* Anna Stryker, Graduate Program Coordinator, 734-764-7278, Fax: 734-647-4865, E-mail: chemadmissions@umich.edu.

University of Missouri, Graduate School, College of Arts and Sciences, Department of Chemistry, Columbia, MO 65211. Offers analytical chemistry (MS, PhD); inorganic chemistry (MS, PhD); organic chemistry (MS, PhD); physical chemistry (MS, PhD). *Faculty:* 30 full-time (6 women), 2 part-time/adjunct (0 women). *Students:* 60 full-time (22 women), 43 part-time (16 women); includes 7 minority (3 African Americans, 1 American Indian/Alaska Native, 3 Asian Americans or Pacific Islanders), 53 international. Average age 27. 93 applicants, 32% accepted, 27 enrolled. In 2009, 4 doctorates awarded. *Degree requirements:* For master's, thesis; for doctorate, one foreign language, comprehensive exam, thesis/dissertation. *Entrance requirements:* For master's, GRE General Test, minimum GPA of 3.0; for doctorate, GRE General Test; V=450, Q=600, A=3.0-4.0, minimum GPA of 3.0. Additional exam requirements/recommendations for international students: Required—TOEFL (minimum score 600 paper-based; 250 computer-based; 100 iBT). *Application deadline:* For fall admission, 4/1 priority date for domestic students; for winter admission, 10/15 for domestic students. Applications are processed on a rolling basis. Application fee: $45 ($60 for international students). *Financial support:* In 2009–10, 9 fellowships with full tuition reimbursements, 15 research assistantships with full tuition reimbursements, 78 teaching assistantships with full tuition reimbursements were awarded; institutionally sponsored loans, traineeships, health care benefits, and unspecified assistantships also available. *Unit head:* Dr. Jerry Atwood, Department Chair, 573-882-8374, E-mail: atwoodj@missouri.edu. *Application contact:* Jerry Brightwell, Administrative Assistant, 573-884-6832, E-mail: brightwellj@missouri.edu.

University of Missouri–Kansas City, College of Arts and Sciences, Department of Chemistry, Kansas City, MO 64110-2499. Offers analytical chemistry (MS, PhD); inorganic chemistry (MS, PhD); organic chemistry (MS, PhD); physical chemistry (MS, PhD); polymer chemistry (MS, PhD). PhD (interdisciplinary) offered through the School of Graduate Studies. Part-time and evening/weekend programs available. *Faculty:* 16 full-time (3 women), 1 part-time/adjunct (0 women). *Students:* 7 part-time (4 women), 2 international. Average age 32. 30 applicants, 67% accepted. In 2009, 1 master's awarded. *Degree requirements:* For master's, thesis (for some programs); for doctorate, thesis/dissertation. *Entrance requirements:* For master's, equivalent of American Chemical Society approved bachelor's degree in chemistry; for doctorate, GRE General Test, equivalent of American Chemical Society approved bachelor's degree in chemistry. Additional exam requirements/recommendations for international students: Required—TOEFL (minimum score 550 paper-based; 213 computer-based; 80 iBT), TWE. *Application deadline:* For fall admission, 4/15 for domestic and international students; for spring admission, 10/15 for domestic and international students. Applications are processed on a rolling basis. Application fee: $45 ($50 for international students). Electronic applications accepted. *Expenses:* Tuition, state resident: full-time $5378; part-time $299 per credit hour. Tuition, nonresident: full-time $13,881; part-time $771 per credit hour. Required fees: $641; $71 per credit hour. Tuition and fees vary according to course load and program. *Financial support:* In 2009–10, 8 research assistantships with partial tuition reimbursements (averaging $17,973 per year), 17 teaching assistantships with partial tuition reimbursements (averaging $17,179 per year) were awarded; Federal Work-Study, institutionally sponsored loans, and scholarships/grants also available. Support available to part-time students. Financial award application deadline: 3/1; financial award applicants required to submit FAFSA. *Faculty research:* Molecular spectroscopy, characterization and synthesis of materials and compounds, computational chemistry, natural products, drug delivery systems and anti-tumor agents. Total annual research expenditures: $1 million. *Unit head:* Dr. Kathleen V. Kilway, Chair, 816-235-2289, Fax: 816-235-5502. *Application contact:* Graduate Recruiting Committee, 816-235-2272, Fax: 816-235-5502, E-mail: umkc-chemdept@umkc.edu.

The University of Montana, Graduate School, College of Arts and Sciences, Department of Chemistry, Missoula, MT 59812-0002. Offers chemistry (MS, PhD), including environmental/analytical chemistry, inorganic chemistry, organic chemistry, physical chemistry. Terminal master's awarded for partial completion of doctoral program. *Degree requirements:* For master's, thesis (for some programs); for doctorate, thesis/dissertation. *Entrance requirements:* For master's and doctorate, GRE General Test. Additional exam requirements/recommendations for international students: Required—TOEFL (minimum score 575 paper-based; 230 computer-based). *Faculty research:* Reaction mechanisms and kinetics, inorganic and organic synthesis, analytical chemistry, natural products.

University of Nebraska–Lincoln, Graduate College, College of Arts and Sciences, Department of Chemistry, Lincoln, NE 68588. Offers analytical chemistry (PhD); biochemistry (PhD); chemistry (MS); inorganic chemistry (PhD); materials chemistry (PhD); organic chemistry (PhD); physical chemistry (PhD). *Degree requirements:* For master's, one foreign language, thesis optional, departmental qualifying exam; for doctorate, one foreign language, comprehensive exam, thesis/dissertation, departmental qualifying exams. *Entrance requirements:* For master's and doctorate, GRE. Additional exam requirements/recommendations for international students: Required—TOEFL (minimum score 550 paper-based; 213 computer-based). Electronic applications accepted. *Faculty research:* Bioorganic and bioinorganic chemistry, biophysical and bioanalytical chemistry, structure-function of DNA and proteins, organometallics, mass spectrometry.

University of Regina, Faculty of Graduate Studies and Research, Faculty of Science, Department of Chemistry and Biochemistry, Regina, SK S4S 0A2, Canada. Offers analytical chemistry (M Sc, PhD); biochemistry (M Sc, PhD); inorganic chemistry (M Sc, PhD); organic chemistry (M Sc, PhD); physical chemistry (M Sc, PhD). Part-time programs available. *Faculty:* 11 full-time (2 women), 3 part-time/adjunct (0 women). *Students:* 20 full-time (8 women). 25 applicants, 28% accepted. In 2009, 2 master's awarded. *Degree requirements:* For master's, thesis, departmental qualifying exam; for doctorate, thesis/dissertation, departmental qualifying exam. *Entrance requirements:* For master's and doctorate, GRE. Additional exam requirements/recommendations for international students: Required—TOEFL (minimum score 580 paper-based; 237 computer-based; 80 iBT). *Application deadline:* For fall admission, 1/1 for domestic students; for winter admission, 7/1 for domestic students. Applications are processed on a rolling basis. Application fee: $90 ($100 for international students). *Financial support:* In 2009–10, 5 fellowships (averaging $19,000 per year), 2 research assistantships (averaging $16,910 per year), 4 teaching assistantships (averaging $6,650 per year) were awarded; scholarships/grants also available. Financial award application deadline: 6/15. *Faculty research:* Organic synthesis, organic oxidations, ionic liquids theoretical/computational chemistry, protein biochemistry/biophysics, environmental analytical, photophysical/photochemistry. *Unit head:* Dr. Tanya Dahms, Head, 306-585-4247, E-mail: tanya.dohms@uregina.ca. *Application contact:* Dr. Scott Murphy, Program Coordinator, 306-585-4247, Fax: 306-585-4894, E-mail: scott.murphy@uregina.ca.

University of Southern Mississippi, Graduate School, College of Science and Technology, Department of Chemistry and Biochemistry, Hattiesburg, MS 39406-0001. Offers analytical chemistry (MS, PhD); biochemistry (MS, PhD); inorganic chemistry (MS, PhD); organic chemistry (MS, PhD); physical chemistry (MS, PhD). *Faculty:* 16 full-time (4 women). *Students:* 14 full-time (0 women), 5 part-time (4 women); includes 1 minority (African American), 12 international. Average age 29. 41 applicants, 17% accepted, 6 enrolled. In 2009, 2 master's, 6 doctorates awarded. *Degree requirements:* For master's, comprehensive exam, thesis; for doctorate, comprehensive exam, thesis/dissertation. *Entrance requirements:* For master's, GRE General Test, minimum GPA of 2.75 in last 60 hours; for doctorate, GRE General Test, minimum GPA of 3.5. Additional exam requirements/recommendations for international students: Required—TOEFL. *Application deadline:* For fall admission, 3/1 priority date for domestic students, 3/1 for international students. Applications are processed on a rolling basis. Application fee: $35. *Expenses:* Tuition, state resident: full-time $5096; part-time $284 per hour. Tuition, nonresident: full-time $13,052; part-time $726 per hour. Required fees: $402. Tuition and fees vary according to course level and course load. *Financial support:* In 2009–10, 3 research assistantships with full tuition reimbursements (averaging $17,000 per year), 19 teaching assistantships with full tuition reimbursements (averaging $20,716 per year) were awarded; fellowships, Federal Work-Study and institutionally sponsored loans also available. Support available to part-time students. Financial award application deadline: 3/15; financial award applicants required to submit FAFSA. *Faculty research:* Plant biochemistry, photo chemistry, polymer chemistry, x-ray analysis, enzyme chemistry. *Unit head:* Dr. Robert Bateman, Chair, 601-266-4701, Fax: 601-266-6075. *Application contact:* Dr. Sabine Heinherst, Graduate Coordinator, 601-266-4702, Fax: 601-266-6075.

University of South Florida, Graduate School, College of Arts and Sciences, Department of Chemistry, Tampa, FL 33620-9951. Offers computational chemistry (PhD); analytical chemistry (MS, PhD); biochemistry (MS, PhD); computational chemistry (MS); environmental chemistry (MS, PhD); inorganic chemistry (MS, PhD); organic chemistry (MS); physical chemistry (MS, PhD); polymer chemistry (PhD). Part-time programs available. *Faculty:* 25 full-time (4 women). *Students:* 113 full-time (36 women), 15 part-time (11 women); includes 19 minority (5 African Americans, 6 Asian Americans or Pacific Islanders, 8 Hispanic Americans), 58 international. Average age 32. 112 applicants, 30% accepted, 21 enrolled. In 2009, 8 master's, 11 doctorates awarded. Terminal master's awarded for partial completion of doctoral program. *Degree requirements:* For master's, comprehensive exam, thesis (for some programs); for doctorate, 2 foreign languages, comprehensive exam, thesis/dissertation. *Entrance requirements:* For master's, GRE General Test or GMAT, minimum GPA of 3.0. Additional exam requirements/recommendations for international students: Required—TOEFL (minimum score 550 paper-based; 213 computer-based). *Application deadline:* For fall admission, 2/15 priority date for domestic students, 1/2 priority date for international students; for spring admission, 10/1 priority date for domestic students, 6/1 priority date for international students. Applications are processed on a rolling basis. Application fee: $30. Electronic applications accepted. *Financial support:* In 2009–10, teaching assistantships with tuition reimbursements (averaging $27,522 per year); unspecified assistantships also available. Financial award application deadline: 6/30. *Faculty research:* Synthesis, bio-organic chemistry, bioinorganic chemistry, environmental chemistry, NMR. Total annual research expenditures: $3.2 million. *Unit head:* Dr. Randy Larsen, Chairperson, 813-974-4129, Fax: 813-974-3203, E-mail: rlarsen@cas.usf.edu. *Application contact:* Patricia Muisener, Director, 813-974-1730, Fax: 813-974-3203, E-mail: muisener@cas.usf.edu.

The University of Tennessee, Graduate School, College of Arts and Sciences, Department of Chemistry, Knoxville, TN 37996. Offers analytical chemistry (MS, PhD); chemical physics (PhD); environmental chemistry (MS, PhD); inorganic chemistry (MS, PhD); organic chemistry (MS, PhD); physical chemistry (MS, PhD); polymer chemistry (MS, PhD); theoretical chemistry (PhD). Part-time programs available. Terminal master's awarded for partial completion of doctoral program. *Degree requirements:* For master's, thesis; for doctorate, thesis/dissertation. *Entrance requirements:* For master's and doctorate, GRE General Test, minimum GPA of 2.7. Additional exam requirements/recommendations for international students: Required—TOEFL. Electronic applications accepted. *Expenses:* Tuition, state resident: full-time $6826; part-time $380 per semester hour. Tuition, nonresident: full-time $21,844; part-time $1147 per semester hour. Tuition and fees vary according to program.

The University of Texas at Austin, Graduate School, College of Natural Sciences, Department of Chemistry and Biochemistry, Austin, TX 78712-1111. Offers analytical chemistry (MA, PhD); biochemistry (MA, PhD); inorganic chemistry (MA, PhD); organic chemistry (MA, PhD); physical chemistry (MA, PhD). *Entrance requirements:* For master's and doctorate, GRE General Test.

The University of Toledo, College of Graduate Studies, College of Arts and Sciences, Department of Chemistry, Toledo, OH 43606-3390. Offers analytical chemistry (MS, PhD); biological chemistry (MS, PhD); inorganic chemistry (MS, PhD); organic chemistry (MS, PhD); physical chemistry (MS, PhD). Part-time programs available. *Degree requirements:* For master's, thesis; for doctorate, thesis/dissertation. *Entrance requirements:* For master's and doctorate, GRE General Test, GRE Subject Test. Additional exam requirements/recommendations for international students: Required—TOEFL. Electronic applications accepted. *Faculty research:* Enzymology, materials chemistry, crystallography, theoretical chemistry.

Vanderbilt University, Graduate School, Department of Chemistry, Nashville, TN 37240-1001. Offers analytical chemistry (MAT, MS, PhD); inorganic chemistry (MAT, MS, PhD); organic chemistry (MAT, MS, PhD); physical chemistry (MAT, MS, PhD); theoretical chemistry (MAT, MS, PhD). *Faculty:* 46 full-time (6 women). *Students:* 106 full-time (38 women); includes 10 minority (5 African Americans, 3 Asian Americans or Pacific Islanders, 2 Hispanic Americans), 21 international. Average age 27. 245 applicants, 27% accepted, 21 enrolled. In 2009, 10 master's, 21 doctorates awarded. Terminal master's awarded for partial completion of doctoral program. *Degree requirements:* For master's, thesis; for doctorate, thesis/dissertation, area, qualifying, and final exams. *Entrance requirements:* For master's and doctorate, GRE General Test, GRE Subject Test (recommended). Additional exam requirements/recommendations for international students: Required—TOEFL (minimum score 570 paper-based; 230 computer-based; 88 iBT). *Application deadline:* For fall admission, 1/15 for domestic and international students. Application fee: $0. Electronic applications accepted. *Financial support:* Fellowships with full and partial tuition reimbursements, research assistantships with full tuition reimbursements, teaching assistantships with full tuition reimbursements, Federal Work-Study, institutionally sponsored loans, scholarships/grants, traineeships, and health care benefits available. Financial award application deadline: 1/15; financial award applicants required to submit CSS PROFILE or FAFSA. *Faculty research:* Chemical synthesis; mechanistic, theoretical, bioorganic, analytical, and spectroscopic chemistry. *Unit head:* Mike P. Stone, Chair, 615-322-2861, Fax: 615-343-1234. *Application contact:* Charles M. Lukehart, Director of Graduate Studies, 615-322-2861, Fax: 615-343-1234, E-mail: charles.m.lukehart@vanderbilt.edu.

Virginia Commonwealth University, Graduate School, College of Humanities and Sciences, Department of Chemistry, Richmond, VA 23284-9005. Offers analytical chemistry (MS, PhD); chemical physics (PhD); inorganic chemistry (MS, PhD); organic chemistry (MS, PhD); physical chemistry (MS, PhD). Part-time programs available. Terminal master's awarded for partial completion of doctoral program. *Degree requirements:* For master's, thesis; for doctorate, thesis/dissertation, comprehensive cumulative exams, research proposal. *Entrance requirements:* For master's, GRE General Test, 30 undergraduate credits in chemistry; for doctorate, GRE General Test. *Faculty research:* Physical, organic, inorganic, analytical, and polymer chemistry; chemical physics.

Wake Forest University, Graduate School of Arts and Sciences, Department of Chemistry, Winston-Salem, NC 27109. Offers analytical chemistry (MS, PhD); inorganic chemistry (MS, PhD); organic chemistry (MS, PhD); physical chemistry (MS, PhD). Part-time programs available. *Degree requirements:* For master's, one foreign language, comprehensive exam, thesis; for doctorate, 2 foreign languages, comprehensive exam, thesis/dissertation. *Entrance requirements:* For master's and doctorate, GRE General Test. Additional exam requirements/recommendations for international students: Required—TOEFL (minimum score 213 computer-based). Electronic applications accepted.

West Virginia University, Eberly College of Arts and Sciences, Department of Chemistry, Morgantown, WV 26506. Offers analytical chemistry (MS, PhD); inorganic chemistry (MS, PhD); organic chemistry (MS, PhD); physical chemistry (MS, PhD); theoretical chemistry (MS,

Analytical Chemistry

West Virginia University (continued)
PhD). Part-time programs available. Postbaccalaureate distance learning degree programs offered (no on-campus study). Terminal master's awarded for partial completion of doctoral program. *Degree requirements:* For master's, thesis; for doctorate, thesis/dissertation. *Entrance requirements:* For master's, GRE General Test, GRE Subject Test (recommended), minimum GPA of 2.5; for doctorate, GRE General Test, GRE Subject Test (recommended), minimum GPA of 2.75. Additional exam requirements/recommendations for international students: Required—TOEFL. Electronic applications accepted. *Faculty research:* Analysis of proteins, drug interactions, solids and effluents by advanced separation methods; new synthetic strategies for complex organic molecules; synthesis and structural characterization of metal complexes for polymerization catalysis, nonlinear science, spectroscopy.

Youngstown State University, Graduate School, College of Science, Technology, Engineering and Mathematics, Department of Chemistry, Youngstown, OH 44555-0001. Offers analytical chemistry (MS); biochemistry (MS); chemistry education (MS); inorganic chemistry (MS); organic chemistry (MS); physical chemistry (MS). Part-time programs available. *Degree requirements:* For master's, thesis. *Entrance requirements:* For master's, bachelor's degree in chemistry, minimum GPA of 2.7. Additional exam requirements/recommendations for international students: Required—TOEFL. *Faculty research:* Analysis of antioxidants, chromatography, defects and disorder in crystalline oxides, hydrogen bonding, novel organic and organometallic materials.

Chemistry

Acadia University, Faculty of Pure and Applied Science, Department of Chemistry, Wolfville, NS B4P 2R6, Canada. Offers M Sc. *Faculty:* 2 full-time (0 women). *Students:* 5 full-time (3 women). Average age 26. 4 applicants, 25% accepted, 1 enrolled. In 2009, 2 master's awarded. *Degree requirements:* For master's, thesis. *Entrance requirements:* For master's, GRE. Additional exam requirements/recommendations for international students: Required—TOEFL (minimum score 580 paper-based; 237 computer-based; 93 iBT), IELTS (minimum score 6.5). *Application deadline:* For fall admission, 2/1 for domestic and international students. Applications are processed on a rolling basis. Application fee: $50. *Financial support:* Research assistantships, teaching assistantships, scholarships/grants and unspecified assistantships available. Financial award application deadline: 2/1. *Faculty research:* Atmospheric chemistry, chemical kinetics, bioelectrochemistry of proteins, self assembling monolayers. *Unit head:* Dr. Jeffrey Banks, Head, 902-585-1242, Fax: 902-585-1114, E-mail: jeffrey.banks@acadiau.ca. *Application contact:* Avril Bird, Secretary, 902-585-1242, Fax: 902-585-1114, E-mail: avril.bird@acadiau.ca.

American University, College of Arts and Sciences, Department of Chemistry, Program in Chemistry, Washington, DC 20016-8014. Offers MS. *Students:* 4 full-time (2 women), 8 part-time (5 women); includes 3 minority (2 African Americans, 1 Asian American or Pacific Islander). Average age 24. 15 applicants, 80% accepted, 7 enrolled. In 2009, 1 master's awarded. *Degree requirements:* For master's, comprehensive exam, thesis, tools of research in foreign language or statistics. *Entrance requirements:* For master's, GRE, minimum GPA of 3.0. Additional exam requirements/recommendations for international students: Required—TOEFL. *Application deadline:* For fall admission, 2/1 priority date for domestic students; for spring admission, 10/1 priority date for domestic students. Applications are processed on a rolling basis. Application fee: $80. *Expenses:* Tuition: Full-time $22,266; part-time $1237 per credit hour. Required fees: $430. Tuition and fees vary according to program. *Financial support:* Fellowships, research assistantships with full and partial tuition reimbursements, teaching assistantships with full and partial tuition reimbursements, career-related internships or fieldwork, Federal Work-Study, scholarships/grants, and traineeships available. Financial award application deadline: 2/1. *Application contact:* Director, Graduate Admissions.

American University of Beirut, Graduate Programs, Faculty of Arts and Sciences, Beirut, Lebanon. Offers anthropology (MA); Arabic language and literature (MA); archaeology (MA); biology (MS); chemistry (MS); computer science (MS); economics (MA); education (MA); English language (MA); English literature (MA); environmental policy planning (MSES); financial economics (MAFE); geology (MS); history (MA); mathematics (MA, MS); Middle Eastern studies (MA); philosophy (MA); physics (MS); political studies (MA); psychology (MA); public administration (MA); sociology (MA); statistics (MA, MS). Part-time programs available. *Degree requirements:* For master's, one foreign language, comprehensive exam, thesis (for some programs). *Entrance requirements:* For master's, GRE, letter of recommendation. Additional exam requirements/recommendations for international students: Required—TOEFL (minimum score 600 paper-based; 250 computer-based; 100 iBT), IELTS (minimum score 7.5). *Faculty research:* String theory and supergravity; computer graphics; algebra and number theory; popular Arabic literature; marine and freshwater biology; integrating science, math and technology.

Arizona State University, Graduate College, College of Liberal Arts and Sciences, Division of Natural Sciences, Department of Chemistry and Biochemistry, Tempe, AZ 85287. Offers MS, PhD. *Degree requirements:* For master's, thesis; for doctorate, one foreign language, thesis/dissertation. *Entrance requirements:* For master's and doctorate, GRE. Additional exam requirements/recommendations for international students: Required—TOEFL.

Arkansas State University—Jonesboro, Graduate School, College of Sciences and Mathematics, Department of Chemistry and Physics, Jonesboro, State University, AR 72467. Offers chemistry (MS); chemistry education (MSE, SCCT). Part-time programs available. *Faculty:* 8 full-time (3 women), 2 part-time/adjunct (1 woman). *Students:* 6 full-time (4 women), 8 part-time (4 women), 11 international. Average age 24. 11 applicants, 55% accepted, 3 enrolled. In 2009, 3 master's awarded. *Degree requirements:* For master's, comprehensive exam, thesis or alternative; for SCCT, comprehensive exam. *Entrance requirements:* For master's, GRE General Test or MAT, appropriate bachelor's degree; for SCCT, GRE General Test or MAT, interview, master's degree, official transcript, immunization records. Additional exam requirements/recommendations for international students: Required—TOEFL (minimum score 550 paper-based; 213 computer-based; 79 iBT), IELTS (minimum score 6). *Application deadline:* For fall admission, 7/1 for domestic and international students; for spring admission, 11/15 for domestic students, 11/13 for international students. Applications are processed on a rolling basis. Application fee: $30 ($40 for international students). Electronic applications accepted. *Expenses:* Tuition, state resident: full-time $3744; part-time $208 per credit hour. Tuition, nonresident: full-time $9540; part-time $530 per credit hour. Required fees: $896; $47 per credit hour. $25 per term. One-time fee: $50. Tuition and fees vary according to course load and program. *Financial support:* In 2009–10, 7 students received support; teaching assistantships, career-related internships or fieldwork, scholarships/grants, and unspecified assistantships available. Financial award application deadline: 7/1; financial award applicants required to submit FAFSA. *Unit head:* Dr. John Pratte, Chair, 870-972-3086, Fax: 870-972-3089, E-mail: jpratte@astate.edu. *Application contact:* Dr. Andrew Sustich, Dean of the Graduate School, 870-972-3029, Fax: 870-972-3857, E-mail: sustich@astate.edu.

Auburn University, Graduate School, College of Sciences and Mathematics, Department of Chemistry and Biochemistry, Auburn University, AL 36849. Offers analytical chemistry (MS, PhD); biochemistry (MS, PhD); inorganic chemistry (MS, PhD); organic chemistry (MS, PhD); physical chemistry (MS, PhD). Part-time programs available. *Faculty:* 27 full-time (6 women). *Students:* 39 full-time (20 women), 21 part-time (8 women); includes 6 minority (4 African Americans, 1 Asian American or Pacific Islander, 1 Hispanic American), 41 international. Average age 28. 54 applicants, 11% accepted, 3 enrolled. In 2009, 1 master's, 13 doctorates awarded. *Degree requirements:* For master's, thesis (for some programs); for doctorate, thesis/dissertation, oral and written exams. *Entrance requirements:* For master's and doctorate, GRE General Test. *Application deadline:* For fall admission, 7/7 for domestic students; for spring admission, 11/24 for domestic students. Applications are processed on a rolling basis. Application fee: $50 ($60 for international students). Electronic applications accepted. *Expenses:* Tuition, state resident: full-time $6240. Tuition, nonresident: full-time $18,720. International tuition: $18,938 full-time. Required fees: $492. Tuition and fees vary according to course load, program and reciprocity agreements. *Financial support:* Fellowships, research assistantships, teaching assistantships available. Financial award application deadline: 3/15; financial award applicants required to submit FAFSA. *Unit head:* Dr. J. V. Ortiz, Chair, 334-844-4043, Fax: 334-844-4043. *Application contact:* Dr. George Flowers, Dean of the Graduate School, 334-844-2125.

Ball State University, Graduate School, College of Sciences and Humanities, Department of Chemistry, Muncie, IN 47306-1099. Offers MA, MS. *Entrance requirements:* For master's, GRE General Test. *Faculty research:* Synthetic and analytical chemistry, biochemistry, theoretical chemistry.

Baylor University, Graduate School, College of Arts and Sciences, Department of Chemistry and Biochemistry, Waco, TX 76798. Offers chemistry (MS, PhD). Part-time programs available. *Faculty:* 14 full-time (2 women). *Students:* 47 full-time (22 women), 1 part-time (0 women); includes 3 minority (1 American Indian/Alaska Native, 1 Asian American or Pacific Islander, 1 Hispanic American), 18 international. In 2009, 2 master's, 6 doctorates awarded. Terminal master's awarded for partial completion of doctoral program. *Degree requirements:* For master's, thesis; for doctorate, comprehensive exam, thesis/dissertation. *Entrance requirements:* For master's and doctorate, GRE General Test, GRE Subject Test. Additional exam requirements/recommendations for international students: Required—TOEFL. *Application deadline:* For fall admission, 8/1 for domestic students. Applications are processed on a rolling basis. Application fee: $25. *Financial support:* In 2009–10, 20 students received support; fellowships, research assistantships, teaching assistantships, Federal Work-Study, institutionally sponsored loans, and tuition waivers (full) available. Support available to part-time students. *Unit head:* Dr. Charles Garner, Graduate Program Director, 254-710-6862, Fax: 254-710-2403, E-mail: charles_garner@baylor.edu. *Application contact:* Nancy Kallas, Administrative Assistant, 254-710-6844, Fax: 254-710-2403, E-mail: nancy_kallas@baylor.edu.

Boston College, Graduate School of Arts and Sciences, Department of Chemistry, Chestnut Hill, MA 02467-3800. Offers biochemistry (PhD); inorganic chemistry (PhD); organic chemistry (PhD); physical chemistry (PhD); science education (MST). Part-time programs available. *Students:* 110 full-time (49 women); includes 8 minority (6 Asian Americans or Pacific Islanders, 2 Hispanic Americans), 49 international. 216 applicants, 34% accepted, 22 enrolled. In 2009, 3 master's, 20 doctorates awarded. *Degree requirements:* For doctorate, thesis/dissertation, qualifying exam. *Entrance requirements:* For doctorate, GRE General Test, GRE Subject Test. Additional exam requirements/recommendations for international students: Required—TOEFL (minimum score 600 paper-based; 250 computer-based; 100 iBT). *Application deadline:* For fall admission, 1/2 for domestic and international students. Application fee: $70. Electronic applications accepted. *Financial support:* In 2009–10, fellowships with full tuition reimbursements (averaging $25,000 per year), research assistantships with full tuition reimbursements (averaging $25,000 per year), teaching assistantships with full tuition reimbursements (averaging $25,000 per year) were awarded; Federal Work-Study also available. Support available to part-time students. Financial award application deadline: 3/1; financial award applicants required to submit FAFSA. *Unit head:* Dr. Amir Hoveyda, Chairperson, 617-552-1735, E-mail: amir.hoveyda@bc.edu. *Application contact:* Dr. Marc Snapper, Graduate Program Director, 617-552-8096, Fax: 617-552-0833, E-mail: marc.snapper@bc.edu.

Boston University, Graduate School of Arts and Sciences, Department of Chemistry, Boston, MA 02215. Offers MA, PhD. *Students:* 96 full-time (45 women), 2 part-time (both women); includes 12 minority (5 African Americans, 2 American Indian/Alaska Native, 5 Asian Americans or Pacific Islanders), 37 international. Average age 26. 193 applicants, 18% accepted, 14 enrolled. In 2009, 21 master's, 15 doctorates awarded. Terminal master's awarded for partial completion of doctoral program. *Degree requirements:* For master's, one foreign language; for doctorate, one foreign language, comprehensive exam, thesis/dissertation. *Entrance requirements:* For master's and doctorate, GRE General Test, GRE Subject Test (recommended), 3 letters of recommendation. Additional exam requirements/recommendations for international students: Required—TOEFL (minimum score 550 paper-based; 213 computer-based). *Application deadline:* For fall admission, 1/1 for domestic and international students; for spring admission, 10/15 for domestic and international students. Application fee: $70. Electronic applications accepted. *Expenses:* Tuition: Full-time $37,910; part-time $1184 per credit hour. Required fees: $386; $40 per semester. Part-time tuition and fees vary according to class time, course level, degree level and program. *Financial support:* In 2009–10, 4 fellowships with full tuition reimbursements (averaging $18,900 per year), 48 research assistantships with full tuition reimbursements (averaging $18,400 per year), 54 teaching assistantships with full tuition reimbursements (averaging $18,400 per year) were awarded; Federal Work-Study, scholarships/grants, and tuition waivers (full) also available. Support available to part-time students. Financial award application deadline: 1/1; financial award applicants required to submit FAFSA. *Unit head:* John Straab, Chairman, 617-353-2498, Fax: 617-353-6466, E-mail: straub@bu.edu. *Application contact:* Sara Coenen, Academic Administrator, 617-353-2503, Fax: 617-353-6466, E-mail: scoenen@bu.edu.

Bowling Green State University, Graduate College, College of Arts and Sciences, Center for Photochemical Sciences, Bowling Green, OH 43403. Offers PhD. *Degree requirements:* For doctorate, comprehensive exam, thesis/dissertation. *Entrance requirements:* For doctorate, GRE General Test. Additional exam requirements/recommendations for international students: Required—TOEFL. Electronic applications accepted. *Faculty research:* Laser-initiated photopolymerization, spectroscopic and kinetic studies, optoelectronics of semiconductor multiple quantum wells, electron transfer processes, carotenoid pigments.

Bowling Green State University, Graduate College, College of Arts and Sciences, Department of Chemistry, Bowling Green, OH 43403. Offers MAT, MS. Part-time programs available. *Degree requirements:* For master's, thesis or alternative. *Entrance requirements:* For master's, GRE General Test. Additional exam requirements/recommendations for international students:

Required—TOEFL. Electronic applications accepted. *Faculty research:* Organic, inorganic, physical, and analytical chemistry; biochemistry; surface science.

Bradley University, Graduate School, College of Liberal Arts and Sciences, Department of Chemistry and Biochemistry, Peoria, IL 61625-0002. Offers chemistry (MS). Part-time and evening/weekend programs available. *Degree requirements:* For master's, comprehensive exam, thesis. *Entrance requirements:* For master's, 2 letters of recommendation. Additional exam requirements/recommendations for international students: Required—TOEFL (minimum score 550 paper-based; 213 computer-based; 79 iBT).

Brandeis University, Graduate School of Arts and Sciences, Department of Chemistry, Waltham, MA 02454. Offers inorganic chemistry (MS, PhD); organic chemistry (MS, PhD); physical chemistry (MS, PhD). *Faculty:* 14 full-time (3 women), 4 part-time/adjunct (3 women). *Students:* 42 full-time (17 women); includes 2 minority (1 African American, 1 Asian American or Pacific Islander), 28 international. 127 applicants, 16% accepted, 8 enrolled. In 2009, 11 master's, 6 doctorates awarded. Terminal master's awarded for partial completion of doctoral program. *Degree requirements:* For master's, thesis, 1 year of residency; for doctorate, one foreign language, thesis/dissertation, 3 years of residency, 2 seminars, qualifying exams. *Entrance requirements:* For master's and doctorate, GRE General Test, resume, letters of recommendation. Additional exam requirements/recommendations for international students: Required—TOEFL (minimum score 600 paper-based; 250 computer-based; 100 iBT); Recommended—IELTS (minimum score 7). *Application deadline:* For fall admission, 1/15 priority date for domestic students. Applications are processed on a rolling basis. Application fee: $75. Electronic applications accepted. *Financial support:* In 2009–10, 23 fellowships with full tuition reimbursements (averaging $24,500 per year), 14 research assistantships with full tuition reimbursements (averaging $24,500 per year), teaching assistantships with partial tuition reimbursements (averaging $3,200 per year) were awarded; scholarships/grants and health care benefits also available. Financial award application deadline: 4/15; financial award applicants required to submit FAFSA. *Faculty research:* Oscillating chemical reactions, molecular recognition systems, protein crystallography, synthesis of natural product spectroscopy and magnetic resonance. *Unit head:* Dr. Judith Herzfeld, Chair, Graduate Program in Chemistry, 781-736-2540, Fax: 781-736-2516, E-mail: herzfeld@brandeis.edu. *Application contact:* Charlotte Haygazian, Graduate Department Coordinator, 781-736-2500, Fax: 781-736-2516, E-mail: chemadm@brandeis.edu.

Brigham Young University, Graduate Studies, College of Physical and Mathematical Sciences, Department of Chemistry and Biochemistry, Provo, UT 84602. Offers biochemistry (MS, PhD); chemistry (MS, PhD). *Faculty:* 34 full-time (3 women). *Students:* 95 full-time (33 women); includes 5 minority (4 Asian Americans or Pacific Islanders, 1 Hispanic American), 48 international. Average age 29. 101 applicants, 40% accepted, 18 enrolled. In 2009, 8 master's, 12 doctorates awarded. *Degree requirements:* For master's, thesis; for doctorate, thesis/dissertation, qualifying exam. *Entrance requirements:* For master's and doctorate, GRE General Test, minimum GPA of 3.0 in last 60 hours. Additional exam requirements/recommendations for international students: Required—TOEFL (minimum score 580 paper-based; 237 computer-based; 85 iBT); Recommended—TWE. *Application deadline:* For fall admission, 2/1 priority date for domestic and international students. Applications are processed on a rolling basis. Application fee: $50. Electronic applications accepted. *Expenses:* Tuition: Full-time $5580; part-time $301 per credit hour. Tuition and fees vary according to student's religious affiliation. *Financial support:* In 2009–10, 95 students received support, including 10 fellowships with full tuition reimbursements available (averaging $21,250 per year), 56 research assistantships with full tuition reimbursements available (averaging $21,250 per year), 29 teaching assistantships with full tuition reimbursements available (averaging $21,250 per year); institutionally sponsored loans, scholarships/grants, health care benefits, tuition waivers (full), and unspecified assistantships also available. Financial award application deadline: 2/1. *Faculty research:* Separation science, molecular recognition, organic synthesis and biomedical application, biochemistry and molecular biology, molecular spectroscopy. Total annual research expenditures: $4.4 million. *Unit head:* Dr. Paul B. Farnsworth, Chair, 801-422-6502, Fax: 801-422-0153, E-mail: paul_farnsworth@byu.edu. *Application contact:* Dr. Matthew R. Linford, Graduate Coordinator, 801-422-1699, Fax: 801-422-0153, E-mail: mrlinford@byu.edu.

See Close-Up on page 91.

Brock University, Faculty of Graduate Studies, Faculty of Mathematics and Science, Program in Chemistry, St. Catharines, ON L2S 3A1, Canada. Offers M Sc, PhD. Part-time programs available. *Degree requirements:* For master's, thesis; for doctorate, thesis/dissertation. *Entrance requirements:* For master's, honors B Sc in chemistry; for doctorate, M Sc. Additional exam requirements/recommendations for international students: Required—TOEFL (minimum score 550 paper-based; 213 computer-based; 80 iBT), IELTS (minimum score 6.5), TWE (minimum score 4). Electronic applications accepted. *Faculty research:* Bioorganic chemistry, trace element analysis, organic synthesis, electrochemistry, structural inorganic chemistry.

Brooklyn College of the City University of New York, Division of Graduate Studies, Department of Chemistry, Brooklyn, NY 11210-2889. Offers MA, PhD. The department offers courses at Brooklyn College that are creditable toward the CUNY doctoral degree. Part-time programs available. *Degree requirements:* For master's, one foreign language, thesis or alternative. *Entrance requirements:* For master's, 2 letters of recommendation. Additional exam requirements/recommendations for international students: Required—TOEFL (minimum score 500 paper-based; 173 computer-based; 61 iBT). Electronic applications accepted.

Brooklyn College of the City University of New York, Division of Graduate Studies, School of Education, Program in Middle Childhood Education (Science), Brooklyn, NY 11210-2889. Offers biology (MA); chemistry (MA); earth science (MA); general science (MA); physics (MA). Part-time and evening/weekend programs available. *Entrance requirements:* For master's, LAST, interview, previous course work in education and mathematics, resume, 2 letters of recommendation. Additional exam requirements/recommendations for international students: Required—TOEFL (minimum score 500 paper-based; 173 computer-based; 61 iBT). Electronic applications accepted. *Faculty research:* Geometric thinking, mastery of basic facts, problem-solving strategies, history of mathematics.

Brown University, Graduate School, Department of Chemistry, Providence, RI 02912. Offers biochemistry (PhD); chemistry (AM, Sc M, PhD). *Degree requirements:* For master's, thesis; for doctorate, one foreign language, thesis/dissertation, cumulative exam.

Bryn Mawr College, Graduate School of Arts and Sciences, Department of Chemistry, Bryn Mawr, PA 19010-2899. Offers MA, PhD. *Degree requirements:* For master's, one foreign language, thesis; for doctorate, 2 foreign languages, comprehensive exam, thesis/dissertation. *Entrance requirements:* For master's and doctorate, GRE General Test, GRE Subject Test. Additional exam requirements/recommendations for international students: Required—TOEFL (minimum score 600 paper-based; 250 computer-based). *Expenses:* Tuition: Full-time $31,340. Required fees: $430.

Bucknell University, Graduate Studies, College of Arts and Sciences, Department of Chemistry, Lewisburg, PA 17837. Offers MA, MS. Part-time programs available. *Degree requirements:* For master's, thesis. *Entrance requirements:* For master's, GRE General Test, GRE Subject Test, minimum GPA of 2.8. Additional exam requirements/recommendations for international students: Required—TOEFL.

Buffalo State College, State University of New York, The Graduate School, Faculty of Natural and Social Sciences, Department of Chemistry, Buffalo, NY 14222-1095. Offers chemistry (MA); secondary education (MS Ed), including chemistry. Part-time and evening/weekend programs available. *Degree requirements:* For master's, thesis (for some programs), project. *Entrance requirements:* For master's, minimum GPA of 2.6, New York teaching certificate (MS Ed). Additional exam requirements/recommendations for international students: Required—TOEFL (minimum score 550 paper-based; 213 computer-based).

California Institute of Technology, Division of Chemistry and Chemical Engineering, Program in Chemistry, Pasadena, CA 91125-0001. Offers MS, PhD. Part-time and evening/weekend programs available. Postbaccalaureate distance learning degree programs offered (minimal on-campus study). *Faculty:* 30 full-time (5 women). *Students:* 211 full-time (80 women). Average age 26. 367 applicants, 25% accepted, 27 enrolled. In 2009, 4 master's, 32 doctorates awarded. Terminal master's awarded for partial completion of doctoral program. *Degree requirements:* For master's, thesis; for doctorate, thesis/dissertation. *Entrance requirements:* Additional exam requirements/recommendations for international students: Required—TOEFL; Recommended—IELTS, TWE. *Application deadline:* For fall admission, 1/1 for domestic and international students. Application fee: $80. Electronic applications accepted. *Financial support:* Fellowships, research assistantships, teaching assistantships, Federal Work-Study, institutionally sponsored loans, scholarships/grants, traineeships, health care benefits, and unspecified assistantships available. Financial award application deadline: 1/1. *Unit head:* Prof. Jacqueline K. Barton, Chair, Chemistry and Chemical Engineering, 626-395-3646, Fax: 626-568-8824, E-mail: jkbarton@caltech.edu. *Application contact:* Agnes Tong, Option Secretary, 626-395-6111, E-mail: agnest@caltech.edu.

California Polytechnic State University, San Luis Obispo, College of Science and Mathematics, Department of Chemistry and Biochemistry, San Luis Obispo, CA 93407. Offers polymers and coating science (MS). Part-time programs available. *Faculty:* 3 full-time (0 women), 1 (woman) part-time/adjunct. *Students:* 2 full-time (1 woman), 2 part-time (1 woman); includes 1 minority (African American). Average age 23. 5 applicants, 80% accepted, 3 enrolled. In 2009, 5 master's awarded. *Degree requirements:* For master's, comprehensive oral exam. *Entrance requirements:* For master's, minimum GPA of 2.5 in last 90 quarter units of course work. Additional exam requirements/recommendations for international students: Required—TOEFL (minimum score 550 paper-based; 213 computer-based), or IELTS (minimum score 6). *Application deadline:* For fall admission, 7/1 for domestic students, 11/30 for international students; for winter admission, 11/1 for domestic students, 6/30 for international students; for spring admission, 2/1 for domestic students. Applications are processed on a rolling basis. Application fee: $55. Electronic applications accepted. *Expenses:* Tuition, nonresident: full-time $11,160; part-time $248 per unit. Required fees: $7134; $1553 per quarter. *Financial support:* Career-related internships or fieldwork, Federal Work-Study, and scholarships/grants available. Support available to part-time students. Financial award application deadline: 3/2; financial award applicants required to submit FAFSA. *Faculty research:* Polymer physical chemistry and analysis, polymer synthesis, coatings formulation. *Unit head:* Dr. Ray Fernando, Graduate Coordinator, 805-756-2395, Fax: 805-756-5500, E-mail: rhfernan@calpoly.edu. *Application contact:* Dr. James Maraviglia, Assistant Vice President for Admissions, Recruitment and Financial Aid, 805-756-2311, Fax: 805-756-5400, E-mail: admissions@calpoly.edu.

California State Polytechnic University, Pomona, Academic Affairs, College of Science, Program in Chemistry, Pomona, CA 91768-2557. Offers MS. Part-time programs available. *Students:* 3 full-time (2 women), 20 part-time (13 women); includes 10 minority (7 Asian Americans or Pacific Islanders, 3 Hispanic Americans), 2 international. Average age 27. 19 applicants, 42% accepted, 4 enrolled. In 2009, 3 master's awarded. *Degree requirements:* For master's, thesis. *Entrance requirements:* For master's, GRE General Test. *Application deadline:* For fall admission, 5/1 priority date for domestic students; for winter admission, 10/15 priority date for domestic students; for spring admission, 1/20 priority date for domestic students. Applications are processed on a rolling basis. Application fee: $55. Electronic applications accepted. *Expenses:* Tuition, nonresident: full-time $6696; part-time $248 per credit. Required fees: $5487; $3237 per term. Tuition and fees vary according to course load, degree level and program. *Financial support:* In 2009–10, 2 students received support. Career-related internships or fieldwork, Federal Work-Study, and institutionally sponsored loans available. Support available to part-time students. Financial award application deadline: 3/2; financial award applicants required to submit FAFSA. *Unit head:* Dr. Sean X. Liu, Assistant Professor, 909-869-3660, Fax: 909-869-4344, E-mail: xcliu@csupomona.edu. *Application contact:* Scott J. Duncan, Director, Admissions, 909-869-3258, Fax: 909-869-4529, E-mail: sjduncan@csupomona.edu.

California State University, East Bay, Academic Programs and Graduate Studies, College of Science, Department of Chemistry, Hayward, CA 94542-3000. Offers biochemistry (MS); chemistry (MS). *Faculty:* 5 full-time (3 women). *Students:* 16 full-time (5 women), 27 part-time (13 women); includes 22 minority (2 African Americans, 17 Asian Americans or Pacific Islanders, 3 Hispanic Americans), 11 international. Average age 28. 37 applicants, 65% accepted, 11 enrolled. In 2009, 12 master's awarded. *Degree requirements:* For master's, comprehensive exam or thesis. *Entrance requirements:* For master's, minimum GPA of 2.5 in field during previous 2 years of course work. Additional exam requirements/recommendations for international students: Required—TOEFL (minimum score 550 paper-based; 213 computer-based). *Application deadline:* For fall admission, 6/30 for domestic and international students. Application fee: $55. Electronic applications accepted. *Financial support:* Fellowships, career-related internships or fieldwork, Federal Work-Study, institutionally sponsored loans, and scholarships/grants available. Support available to part-time students. Financial award application deadline: 3/1; financial award applicants required to submit FAFSA. *Unit head:* Dr. Ann McPartland, Chair, 510-885-3452, Fax: 510-885-4675, E-mail: ann.mcpartland@csueastbay.edu. *Application contact:* Donna Wiley, Interim Associate Director, 510-885-2928, Fax: 510-885-4777, E-mail: donna.wiley@csueastbay.edu.

California State University, Fresno, Division of Graduate Studies, College of Science and Mathematics, Department of Chemistry, Fresno, CA 93740-8027. Offers MS. Part-time programs available. *Degree requirements:* For master's, thesis or alternative. *Entrance requirements:* For master's, GRE General Test, minimum GPA of 2.5. Additional exam requirements/recommendations for international students: Required—TOEFL. Electronic applications accepted. *Faculty research:* Genetics, viticulture, DNA, soils, molecular modeling, analysis of quinone.

California State University, Fullerton, Graduate Studies, College of Natural Science and Mathematics, Department of Chemistry and Biochemistry, Fullerton, CA 92834-9480. Offers chemistry (MS); geochemistry (MS). Part-time programs available. *Students:* 7 full-time (3 women), 29 part-time (17 women); includes 16 minority (1 African American, 14 Asian Americans or Pacific Islanders, 1 Hispanic American), 4 international. Average age 27. 44 applicants, 43% accepted, 9 enrolled. In 2009, 5 master's awarded. *Degree requirements:* For master's, thesis, departmental qualifying exam. *Entrance requirements:* For master's, minimum GPA of 2.5 in last 60 units of course work, major in chemistry or related field. Application fee: $55. *Expenses:* Tuition, nonresident: full-time $11,160; part-time $373 per credit. Required fees: $1440 per term. Tuition and fees vary according to course load, degree level and program. *Financial support:* Research assistantships, teaching assistantships, career-related internships or fieldwork, Federal Work-Study, institutionally sponsored loans, and scholarships/grants available. Support available to part-time students. Financial award application deadline: 3/1; financial award applicants required to submit FAFSA. *Unit head:* Dr. Maria Linder, Chair, 657-278-3621. *Application contact:* Admissions/Applications, 657-278-2371.

California State University, Long Beach, Graduate Studies, College of Natural Sciences and Mathematics, Department of Chemistry and Biochemistry, Long Beach, CA 90840. Offers biochemistry (MS); chemistry (MS). Part-time programs available. *Faculty:* 20 full-time (5 women). *Students:* 10 full-time (5 women), 21 part-time (10 women); includes 8 minority (1 African American, 3 Asian Americans or Pacific Islanders, 4 Hispanic Americans), 9 international. Average age 26. 41 applicants, 44% accepted, 7 enrolled. *Degree requirements:* For master's,

Chemistry

California State University, Long Beach (continued)
thesis, departmental qualifying exam. *Application deadline:* For fall admission, 6/1 for domestic students. Applications are processed on a rolling basis. Application fee: $55. Electronic applications accepted. *Expenses:* Required fees: $1802 per semester. Part-time tuition and fees vary according to course load. *Financial support:* Research assistantships, teaching assistantships, Federal Work-Study, institutionally sponsored loans, scholarships/grants, and unspecified assistantships available. Financial award application deadline: 3/2. *Faculty research:* Enzymology, organic synthesis, molecular modeling, environmental chemistry, reaction kinetics. *Unit head:* Dr. Jeffrey Cohlberg, Chair, 562-985-4944, Fax: 562-985-8557, E-mail: cohlberg@csulb.edu. *Application contact:* Dr. Lijuan Li, Graduate Advisor, 562-985-5068, Fax: 562-985-8557, E-mail: lli@csulb.edu.

California State University, Los Angeles, Graduate Studies, College of Natural and Social Sciences, Department of Chemistry and Biochemistry, Los Angeles, CA 90032-8530. Offers analytical chemistry (MS); biochemistry (MS); chemistry (MS); inorganic chemistry (MS); organic chemistry (MS); physical chemistry (MS). Part-time and evening/weekend programs available. *Faculty:* 1 full-time (0 women), 9 part-time/adjunct (4 women). *Students:* 14 full-time (4 women), 31 part-time (15 women); includes 21 minority (5 African Americans, 9 Asian Americans or Pacific Islanders, 7 Hispanic Americans), 10 international. Average age 30. 23 applicants, 91% accepted, 13 enrolled. In 2009, 11 degrees awarded. *Degree requirements:* For master's, one foreign language, comprehensive exam or thesis. *Entrance requirements:* Additional exam requirements/recommendations for international students: Required—TOEFL. *Application deadline:* For fall admission, 5/1 for domestic and international students. Applications are processed on a rolling basis. Application fee: $55. *Financial support:* Federal Work-Study available. Support available to part-time students. Financial award application deadline: 3/1. *Faculty research:* Intercalation of heavy metal, carborane chemistry, conductive polymers and fabrics, titanium reagents, computer modeling and synthesis. *Unit head:* Dr. Scott Grover, Chair, 323-343-2300, Fax: 323-343-6490, E-mail: sgrover@calstatela.edu. *Application contact:* Dr. Cheryl L. Ney, Associate Vice President for Academic Affairs and Dean of Graduate Studies, 323-343-3820 Ext. 3827, Fax: 323-343-5653, E-mail: cney@cslanet.calstatela.edu.

California State University, Northridge, Graduate Studies, College of Science and Mathematics, Department of Chemistry and Biochemistry, Northridge, CA 91330. Offers biochemistry (MS); chemistry (MS), including chemistry, environmental chemistry. *Faculty:* 14 full-time (4 women), 12 part-time/adjunct (6 women). *Students:* 15 full-time (6 women), 29 part-time (10 women); includes 2 African Americans, 4 Asian Americans or Pacific Islanders, 6 Hispanic Americans, 11 international. Average age 29. 68 applicants, 38% accepted, 12 enrolled. In 2009, 5 master's awarded. *Degree requirements:* For master's, thesis. *Entrance requirements:* For master's, GRE General Test or minimum GPA of 3.0. Additional exam requirements/recommendations for international students: Required—TOEFL. *Application deadline:* For fall admission, 11/30 for domestic students. Application fee: $55. Electronic applications accepted. *Financial support:* Teaching assistantships available. Support available to part-time students. Financial award application deadline: 3/1. *Unit head:* Dr. Taeboem Oh, Chair, 818-677-3381, E-mail: taeboem.oh@csun.edu. *Application contact:* Dr. Taeboem Oh, Chair, 818-677-3381, E-mail: taeboem.oh@csun.edu.

California State University, Sacramento, Graduate Studies, College of Natural Sciences and Mathematics, Department of Chemistry, Sacramento, CA 95819. Offers MS. Part-time programs available. *Degree requirements:* For master's, thesis or alternative, departmental qualifying exam, writing proficiency exam. *Entrance requirements:* For master's, minimum GPA of 2.5 during previous 2 years of course work, BA in chemistry or equivalent. Additional exam requirements/recommendations for international students: Required—TOEFL. Electronic applications accepted.

California State University, San Bernardino, Graduate Studies, College of Social and Behavioral Sciences, Program in Environmental Sciences, San Bernardino, CA 92407-2397. Offers MS. *Faculty:* 3 full-time (1 woman). *Students:* 3 full-time (2 women), 4 part-time (1 woman); includes 1 minority (Hispanic American). Average age 40. 3 applicants, 100% accepted, 1 enrolled. *Unit head:* Dr. Jeff Hackel, Chair, 909-537-5562, E-mail: jhackel@csusb.edu. *Application contact:* Olivia Rosas, Director of Admissions, 909-537-7577, Fax: 909-537-7034, E-mail: orosas@csusb.edu.

Carleton University, Faculty of Graduate Studies, Faculty of Science, Department of Chemistry, Ottawa, ON K1S 5B6, Canada. Offers M Sc, PhD. *Degree requirements:* For master's, thesis; for doctorate, comprehensive exam, thesis/dissertation. *Entrance requirements:* For master's, honors degree; for doctorate, M Sc. Additional exam requirements/recommendations for international students: Required—TOEFL. *Faculty research:* Bioorganic chemistry, analytical toxicology, theoretical and physical chemistry, inorganic chemistry.

Carnegie Mellon University, Mellon College of Science, Department of Chemistry, Pittsburgh, PA 15213-3891. Offers biotechnology and management (MS); chemistry (PhD), including bioinorganic, bioorganic, organic and materials, biophysics and spectroscopy, computational and theoretical, polymer; colloids, polymers and surfaces (MS). Part-time programs available. Terminal master's awarded for partial completion of doctoral program. *Degree requirements:* For doctorate, thesis/dissertation, departmental qualifying and oral exams, teaching experience. *Entrance requirements:* For master's, GRE General Test; for doctorate, GRE General Test, GRE Subject Test. Additional exam requirements/recommendations for international students: Required—TOEFL. Electronic applications accepted. *Faculty research:* Physical and theoretical chemistry, chemical synthesis, biophysical/bioinorganic chemistry.

Case Western Reserve University, School of Graduate Studies, Department of Chemistry, Cleveland, OH 44106. Offers MS, PhD. Part-time programs available. *Faculty:* 20 full-time (4 women). *Students:* 76 full-time (35 women), 18 part-time (5 women); includes 5 minority (2 African Americans, 3 Asian Americans or Pacific Islanders), 63 international. Average age 28. 205 applicants, 26% accepted, 18 enrolled. In 2009, 3 master's, 9 doctorates awarded. Terminal master's awarded for partial completion of doctoral program. *Degree requirements:* For master's, thesis optional; for doctorate, thesis/dissertation. *Entrance requirements:* For master's and doctorate, GRE General Test, GRE Subject Test. Additional exam requirements/recommendations for international students: Required—TOEFL (minimum score 550 paper-based; 213 computer-based; 79 iBT). *Application deadline:* Applications are processed on a rolling basis. Application fee: $8. Electronic applications accepted. *Financial support:* Fellowships, research assistantships, teaching assistantships, unspecified assistantships available. Financial award application deadline: 2/15. *Faculty research:* Electrochemistry, synthetic chemistry, chemistry of life process, spectroscopy, kinetics. *Unit head:* Mary Barkley, Chair, 216-368-3622, Fax: 216-368-3006, E-mail: mary.barkley@case.edu. *Application contact:* Julie Ilhan, Graduate Affairs Coordinator, 216-368-5030, Fax: 216-368-3006, E-mail: julie.ilhan@case.edu.

Central Connecticut State University, School of Graduate Studies, School of Arts and Sciences, Department of Chemistry and Biochemistry, New Britain, CT 06050-4010. Offers natural sciences (MS). Part-time and evening/weekend programs available. *Faculty:* 9 full-time (3 women), 5 part-time/adjunct (1 woman). *Students:* 1 (woman) part-time; minority (Hispanic American). Average age 26. *Degree requirements:* For Certificate, qualifying exam. *Entrance requirements:* Additional exam requirements/recommendations for international students: Required—TOEFL. *Application deadline:* For fall admission, 7/1 for domestic students; for spring admission, 12/1 for domestic students. Applications are processed on a rolling basis. Application fee: $50. Electronic applications accepted. *Expenses:* Tuition, area resident: Full-time $4662; part-time $440 per credit. Tuition, state resident: full-time $6994; part-time $440 per credit. Tuition, nonresident: full-time $12,988; part-time $440 per credit. Required fees: $3606. One-time fee: $62 part-time. *Financial support:* Application deadline: 3/1; *Unit head:* Dr. Thomas Burkholder, Chair, 860-832-2675. *Application contact:* Dr. Thomas Burkholder, Chair, 860-832-2675.

Central Michigan University, College of Graduate Studies, College of Science and Technology, Department of Chemistry, Mount Pleasant, MI 48859. Offers chemistry (MS); teaching chemistry (MA), including teaching college chemistry, teaching high school chemistry. Part-time programs available. *Degree requirements:* For master's, comprehensive exam, thesis or alternative. *Entrance requirements:* For master's, GRE. Electronic applications accepted. *Faculty research:* Analytical and organic-inorganic chemistry, biochemistry, catalysis, dendrimer and polymer studies, nanotechnology.

Central Washington University, Graduate Studies and Research, College of the Sciences, Department of Chemistry, Ellensburg, WA 98926. Offers MS. Part-time programs available. *Faculty:* 12 full-time (4 women). *Students:* 9 full-time (5 women), 1 (woman) part-time; includes 1 minority (Hispanic American). 8 applicants, 88% accepted, 7 enrolled. In 2009, 3 master's awarded. *Degree requirements:* For master's, thesis. *Entrance requirements:* For master's, GRE General Test, minimum GPA of 3.0. Additional exam requirements/recommendations for international students: Required—TOEFL (minimum score 550 paper-based; 213 computer-based; 79 iBT). *Application deadline:* For fall admission, 2/1 for domestic students; for winter admission, 10/1 for domestic students; for spring admission, 1/1 for domestic students. Applications are processed on a rolling basis. Application fee: $50. *Expenses:* Tuition, state resident: full-time $7353; part-time $245 per credit. Tuition, nonresident: full-time $16,383; part-time $546 per credit. Required fees: $882. Tuition and fees vary according to degree level. *Financial support:* In 2009–10, 6 teaching assistantships with full and partial tuition reimbursements (averaging $9,145 per year) were awarded; career-related internships or fieldwork, Federal Work-Study, and health care benefits also available. Financial award application deadline: 3/1; financial award applicants required to submit FAFSA. *Unit head:* Dr. JoAnn Peters, Chair, 509-963-2811, Fax: 509-963-1050. *Application contact:* Justine Eason, Admissions Program Coordinator, 509-963-3103, Fax: 509-963-1799, E-mail: masters@cwu.edu.

City College of the City University of New York, Graduate School, College of Liberal Arts and Science, Division of Science, Department of Chemistry, Program in Chemistry, New York, NY 10031-9198. Offers MA, PhD. Terminal master's awarded for partial completion of doctoral program. *Degree requirements:* For doctorate, one foreign language, thesis/dissertation. *Entrance requirements:* For master's and doctorate, GRE. Additional exam requirements/recommendations for international students: Required—TOEFL (minimum score 500 paper-based; 173 computer-based). *Faculty research:* Laser spectroscopy, bioorganic chemistry, polymer chemistry and crystallography, electroanalytical chemistry, ESR of metal clusters.

Clark Atlanta University, School of Arts and Sciences, Department of Chemistry, Atlanta, GA 30314. Offers MS, PhD. Part-time programs available. *Faculty:* 8 full-time (0 women). *Students:* 10 full-time (9 women), 16 part-time (8 women); includes 21 minority (20 African Americans, 1 American Indian/Alaska Native), 3 international. Average age 30. 8 applicants, 75% accepted, 4 enrolled. In 2009, 4 doctorates awarded. *Degree requirements:* For master's, one foreign language, thesis; for doctorate, 2 foreign languages, thesis/dissertation. *Entrance requirements:* For master's, GRE General Test, minimum GPA of 2.5; for doctorate, GRE General Test, GRE Subject Test, minimum graduate GPA of 3.0. Additional exam requirements/recommendations for international students: Required—TOEFL (minimum score 500 paper-based; 173 computer-based). *Application deadline:* For fall admission, 4/1 for domestic and international students; for spring admission, 11/1 for domestic and international students. Applications are processed on a rolling basis. Application fee: $40 ($55 for international students). *Expenses:* Tuition: Full-time $12,240; part-time $680 per credit hour. Required fees: $710; $355 per semester. *Financial support:* In 2009–10, 4 teaching assistantships were awarded; fellowships, research assistantships, career-related internships or fieldwork, Federal Work-Study, scholarships/grants, traineeships, and unspecified assistantships also available. Support available to part-time students. Financial award application deadline: 4/30; financial award applicants required to submit FAFSA. *Unit head:* Dr. Cass Parker, Chairperson, 404-880-6858, E-mail: cparker@cau.edu. *Application contact:* Michelle Clark-Davis, Graduate Program Admissions, 404-880-6605, E-mail: cauadmissions@cau.edu.

Clarkson University, Graduate School, School of Arts and Sciences, Department of Chemistry and Biomolecular Science, Potsdam, NY 13699. Offers chemistry (MS, PhD). Part-time programs available. *Faculty:* 25 full-time (5 women), 1 (woman) part-time/adjunct. *Students:* 34 full-time (9 women), 24 international. Average age 28. 57 applicants, 53% accepted, 10 enrolled. In 2009, 3 master's, 3 doctorates awarded. *Degree requirements:* For doctorate, comprehensive exam, thesis/dissertation, departmental qualifying exam. *Entrance requirements:* For master's, GRE, 3 letters of recommendation; resume (recommended); for doctorate, GRE, transcripts of all college coursework, three letters of recommendation; resume and personal statement (recommended). Additional exam requirements/recommendations for international students: Required—TOEFL, TSE (recommended). *Application deadline:* For fall admission, 1/30 priority date for domestic and international students; for spring admission, 9/1 priority date for domestic and international students. Applications are processed on a rolling basis. Application fee: $25 ($35 for international students). Electronic applications accepted. *Expenses:* Tuition: Part-time $1074 per credit hour. *Financial support:* In 2009–10, 32 students received support, including 2 fellowships (averaging $30,000 per year), 16 research assistantships (averaging $20,190 per year), 16 teaching assistantships (averaging $20,190 per year); scholarships/grants, tuition waivers (partial), and unspecified assistantships also available. *Faculty research:* Nanomaterial, surface science, polymers chemical biosensing, protein biochemistry drug design/delivery, living radical polymerizations, pharmaceutical synthesis. Total annual research expenditures: $2.2 million. *Unit head:* Dr. Phillip A. Christiansen, Division Head, 315-268-2389, Fax: 315-268-6610, E-mail: pac@clarkson.edu. *Application contact:* Jennifer E. Reed, Graduate School Coordinator for School of Arts and Sciences, 315-268-3802, Fax: 315-268-3989, E-mail: jreed@clarkson.edu.

Clark University, Graduate School, Department of Chemistry, Worcester, MA 01610-1477. Offers MA, PhD. *Faculty:* 9 full-time (2 women), 2 part-time/adjunct (1 woman). *Students:* 19 full-time (10 women), 1 part-time (0 women); includes 1 minority (Asian American or Pacific Islander), 11 international. Average age 26. 38 applicants, 21% accepted, 6 enrolled. Terminal master's awarded for partial completion of doctoral program. *Degree requirements:* For master's, thesis or alternative; for doctorate, one foreign language, thesis/dissertation. *Entrance requirements:* For master's and doctorate, GRE General Test. Additional exam requirements/recommendations for international students: Required—TOEFL. *Application deadline:* For fall admission, 2/15 priority date for domestic students. Applications are processed on a rolling basis. Application fee: $50. *Expenses:* Tuition: Full-time $34,900; part-time $4362.50 per course. *Financial support:* In 2009–10, fellowships with tuition reimbursements (averaging $19,825 per year), 4 research assistantships with full tuition reimbursements (averaging $19,825 per year), 12 teaching assistantships with full tuition reimbursements (averaging $19,825 per year) were awarded; tuition waivers (full) also available. *Faculty research:* Nuclear chemistry, molecular biology simulation, NMR studies, anthrax edema, biochemistry. Total annual research expenditures: $500,000. *Unit head:* Dr. Frederick Greenaway, Chair, 508-793-7116. *Application contact:* Rene Baril, Department Secretary, 528-793-7173, Fax: 528-793-8861, E-mail: chemistry@clarku.edu.

Clemson University, Graduate School, College of Engineering and Science, Department of Chemistry, Clemson, SC 29634. Offers MS, PhD. *Faculty:* 31 full-time (5 women), 5 part-time/adjunct (0 women). *Students:* 92 full-time (31 women), 1 part-time (0 women); includes 9 minority (4 African Americans, 3 Asian Americans or Pacific Islanders, 2 Hispanic Americans), 45 international. Average age 29. 101 applicants, 50% accepted, 21 enrolled. In 2009, 4 master's, 14 doctorates awarded. *Degree requirements:* For master's, one foreign language, thesis; for doctorate, one foreign language, thesis/dissertation. *Entrance requirements:* For master's and doctorate, GRE General Test. Additional exam requirements/recommendations for international students: Required—TOEFL. *Application deadline:* For fall admission, 3/1 for domestic students, 4/15 for international students; for spring admission, 9/15 for international students. Applications are processed on a rolling basis. Application fee: $70 ($80 for international students). Electronic applications accepted. *Expenses:* Tuition, state resident: full-time $8684; part-time $528 per credit hour. Tuition, nonresident: full-time $15,330; part-time $1078 per credit hour. Required fees: $736; $37 per semester. Part-time tuition and fees vary according to course load and program. *Financial support:* In 2009–10, 92 students received support, including 17 research assistantships with partial tuition reimbursements available (averaging $20,794 per year), 75 teaching assistantships with partial tuition reimbursements available (averaging $20,833 per year); fellowships with full and partial tuition reimbursements available, career-related internships or fieldwork, institutionally sponsored loans, scholarships/grants, health care benefits, and unspecified assistantships also available. Support available to part-time students. Financial award applicants required to submit FAFSA. *Faculty research:* Fluorine chemistry, organic synthetic methods and natural products, metal and non-metal clusters, analytical spectroscopies, polymers. Total annual research expenditures: $3.5 million. *Unit head:* Dr. Stephen E. Creager, Chair, 864-656-3065, Fax: 864-656-6613, E-mail: screage@clemson.edu. *Application contact:* Dr. Steve Stuart, Coordinator, 864-656-5013, Fax: 864-656-6613, E-mail: ss@clemson.edu.

Cleveland State University, College of Graduate Studies, College of Science, Department of Chemistry, Cleveland, OH 44115. Offers analytical chemistry (MS); clinical chemistry (MS); clinical/bioanalytical chemistry (PhD), including clinical chemistry, molecular medicine; environmental chemistry (MS); inorganic chemistry (MS); organic chemistry (MS); physical chemistry (MS). Part-time and evening/weekend programs available. *Degree requirements:* For master's, thesis (for some programs); for doctorate, thesis/dissertation. *Entrance requirements:* For master's and doctorate, GRE General Test. Additional exam requirements/recommendations for international students: Required—TOEFL (minimum score 525 paper-based; 197 computer-based; 65 iBT). Electronic applications accepted. *Faculty research:* MALDI-TOF based DNA sequencing, development of ionic focusing HPLC, synthetic and structural studies of vanadium.

The College of William and Mary, Faculty of Arts and Sciences, Department of Chemistry, Williamsburg, VA 23187-8795. Offers MA, MS. *Faculty:* 15 full-time (3 women), 3 part-time/adjunct (0 women). *Students:* 6 full-time (4 women), 2 part-time (both women). Average age 23. 12 applicants, 50% accepted, 5 enrolled. In 2009, 5 master's awarded. *Degree requirements:* For master's, comprehensive exam, thesis (for some programs). *Entrance requirements:* For master's, GRE, minimum GPA of 2.5. Additional exam requirements/recommendations for international students: Required—TOEFL. *Application deadline:* For fall admission, 5/1 priority date for domestic and international students. Applications are processed on a rolling basis. Application fee: $45. Electronic applications accepted. *Expenses:* Tuition, state resident: full-time $6400; part-time $315 per credit hour. Tuition, nonresident: full-time $19,720; part-time $840 per credit hour. Required fees: $4114. *Financial support:* In 2009–10, 7 students received support, including 3 research assistantships (averaging $15,400 per year), 4 teaching assistantships with full tuition reimbursements available (averaging $15,400 per year); health care benefits and unspecified assistantships also available. Financial award application deadline: 5/1; financial award applicants required to submit FAFSA. *Faculty research:* Organic, physical, polymer and analytic chemistry; biochemistry. Total annual research expenditures: $919,246. *Unit head:* Dr. Chris Abelt, Chair, 757-221-2540, Fax: 757-221-2715, E-mail: cjabel@wm.edu. *Application contact:* Dr. Deborah C. Bebout, Graduate Director, 757-221-2558, Fax: 757-221-2715, E-mail: dcbebo@wm.edu.

Colorado School of Mines, Graduate School, Department of Chemistry and Geochemistry, Program in Chemistry, Golden, CO 80401. Offers applied chemistry (PhD); chemistry (MS). Part-time programs available. *Students:* 37 full-time (20 women), 5 part-time (3 women); includes 2 minority (1 Asian American or Pacific Islander, 1 Hispanic American), 12 international. Average age 30. 44 applicants, 48% accepted, 11 enrolled. In 2009, 3 master's, 4 doctorates awarded. *Degree requirements:* For master's, thesis (for some programs); for doctorate, comprehensive exam, thesis/dissertation. *Entrance requirements:* For master's and doctorate, GRE General Test. Additional exam requirements/recommendations for international students: Required—TOEFL (minimum score 550 paper-based; 213 computer-based; 80 iBT). *Application deadline:* For fall admission, 1/15 priority date for domestic and international students; for spring admission, 9/1 priority date for domestic and international students. Application fee: $50 ($70 for international students). Electronic applications accepted. *Expenses:* Tuition, state resident: full-time $10,584; part-time $588 per credit hour. Tuition, nonresident: full-time $24,750; part-time $1375 per credit hour. Required fees: $1654; $827.10 per semester. *Financial support:* In 2009–10, fellowships with full tuition reimbursements (averaging $20,000 per year), research assistantships with full tuition reimbursements (averaging $20,000 per year), teaching assistantships with full tuition reimbursements (averaging $20,000 per year) were awarded; scholarships/grants, health care benefits, and unspecified assistantships also available. Financial award application deadline: 1/15; financial award applicants required to submit FAFSA. *Unit head:* Dr. Dan Knauss, Department Head, 303-273-3625 Ext. 303, Fax: 303-273-3629. *Application contact:* Prof. Tina Voelker, Associate Professor, 303-273-3152, Fax: 303-273-3629, E-mail: tvoelker@mines.edu.

Colorado State University, Graduate School, College of Natural Sciences, Department of Chemistry, Fort Collins, CO 80523-1872. Offers MS, PhD. Postbaccalaureate distance learning degree programs offered (no on-campus study). *Faculty:* 29 full-time (7 women), 1 part-time/adjunct (0 women). *Students:* 46 full-time (15 women), 93 part-time (35 women); includes 15 minority (1 African American, 4 American Indian/Alaska Native, 6 Asian Americans or Pacific Islanders, 4 Hispanic Americans), 15 international. Average age 26. 80 applicants, 25% accepted, 20 enrolled. In 2009, 9 master's, 15 doctorates awarded. Terminal master's awarded for partial completion of doctoral program. *Degree requirements:* For master's, comprehensive exam (for some programs), thesis (for some programs); for doctorate, thesis/dissertation, oral comprehensive exam. *Entrance requirements:* For master's, GRE General Test, minimum GPA of 3.0; 3 letters of recommendation; for doctorate, GRE General Test, minimum GPA of 3.0; 2 transcripts; 3 letters of recommendation; statement of purpose. Additional exam requirements/recommendations for international students: Required—TOEFL (minimum score 550 paper-based; 213 computer-based; 80 iBT). *Application deadline:* For fall admission, 9/15 priority date for domestic and international students; for spring admission, 1/15 priority date for domestic and international students. Applications are processed on a rolling basis. Application fee: $50. Electronic applications accepted. *Expenses:* Tuition, state resident: full-time $6434; part-time $359.10 per credit. Tuition, nonresident: full-time $18,116; part-time $1006.45 per credit. Required fees: $1496; $83 per credit. *Financial support:* In 2009–10, 29 fellowships (averaging $24,110 per year), 78 research assistantships with full tuition reimbursements (averaging $14,566 per year), 71 teaching assistantships with full tuition reimbursements (averaging $13,603 per year) were awarded; health care benefits also available. Financial award application deadline: 1/15; financial award applicants required to submit FAFSA. *Faculty research:* Analytical chemistry, inorganic chemistry, organic chemistry, physical chemistry, materials and biological chemistry. Total annual research expenditures: $7.1 million. *Unit head:* Dr. Ellen R. Fisher, Department Chair, 970-491-6292, Fax: 970-491-1801, E-mail: ellen.fisher@colostate.edu. *Application contact:* Graduate Resources Coordinator, 970-491-0502, E-mail: chemgrad@lamar.colostate.edu.

Colorado State University–Pueblo, College of Science and Mathematics, Pueblo, CO 81001-4901. Offers applied natural science (MS), including biochemistry, biology, chemistry. Part-time and evening/weekend programs available. *Degree requirements:* For master's, comprehensive exam (for some programs), thesis (for some programs), internship report (if non-thesis). *Entrance requirements:* For master's, GRE General Test (minimum score 1000), 2 letters of reference, minimum GPA of 3.0. Additional exam requirements/recommendations for international students: Required—TOEFL (minimum score 500 paper-based; 173 computer-based), IELTS (minimum score 5). *Faculty research:* Fungal cell walls, molecular biology, bioactive materials synthesis, atomic force microscopy-surface chemistry, nanoscience.

Columbia University, Graduate School of Arts and Sciences, Division of Natural Sciences, Department of Chemistry, New York, NY 10027. Offers chemical physics (M Phil, PhD); inorganic chemistry (M Phil, MA, PhD); organic chemistry (M Phil, MA, PhD); MD/PhD. *Degree requirements:* For master's, one foreign language, teaching experience, oral/written exams (M Phil); for doctorate, one foreign language, thesis/dissertation. *Entrance requirements:* For master's and doctorate, GRE General Test, GRE Subject Test. Additional exam requirements/recommendations for international students: Required—TOEFL. *Faculty research:* Biophysics.

Concordia University, School of Graduate Studies, Faculty of Arts and Science, Department of Chemistry and Biochemistry, Montréal, QC H3G 1M8, Canada. Offers chemistry (M Sc, PhD). *Degree requirements:* For master's, thesis; for doctorate, thesis/dissertation. *Entrance requirements:* For master's, honors degree in chemistry; for doctorate, M Sc in biochemistry, biology, or chemistry. *Faculty research:* Bioanalytical, bio-organic, and inorganic chemistry; materials and solid-state chemistry.

Cornell University, Graduate School, Graduate Fields of Arts and Sciences, Field of Chemistry and Chemical Biology, Ithaca, NY 14853-0001. Offers analytical chemistry (PhD); bio-organic chemistry (PhD); biophysical chemistry (PhD); chemical biology (PhD); chemical physics (PhD); inorganic chemistry (PhD); materials chemistry (PhD); organic chemistry (PhD); organometallic chemistry (PhD); physical chemistry (PhD); polymer chemistry (PhD); theoretical chemistry (PhD). *Faculty:* 48 full-time (3 women). *Students:* 162 full-time (67 women); includes 15 minority (1 African American, 9 Asian Americans or Pacific Islanders, 5 Hispanic Americans), 53 international. Average age 26. 359 applicants, 19% accepted, 39 enrolled. In 2009, 31 doctorates awarded. *Degree requirements:* For doctorate, comprehensive exam, thesis/dissertation. *Entrance requirements:* For doctorate, GRE General Test, GRE Subject Test (chemistry), 3 letters of recommendation. Additional exam requirements/recommendations for international students: Required—TOEFL (minimum score 600 paper-based; 250 computer-based; 77 iBT). *Application deadline:* For fall admission, 1/10 for domestic students. Application fee: $70. Electronic applications accepted. *Expenses:* Tuition: Full-time $29,500. Required fees: $70. Full-time tuition and fees vary according to degree level, program and student level. *Financial support:* In 2009–10, 1 fellowship with full tuition reimbursement, 7 research assistantships with full tuition reimbursements, 29 teaching assistantships with full tuition reimbursements were awarded; institutionally sponsored loans, scholarships/grants, health care benefits, tuition waivers (full and partial), and unspecified assistantships also available. Financial award applicants required to submit FAFSA. *Faculty research:* Analytical, organic, inorganic, physical, materials, chemical biology. *Unit head:* Director of Graduate Studies, 607-255-4139, Fax: 607-255-4137. *Application contact:* Graduate Field Assistant, 607-255-4139, Fax: 607-255-4137, E-mail: chemgrad@cornell.edu.

Dalhousie University, Faculty of Science, Department of Chemistry, Halifax, NS B3H 4R2, Canada. Offers M Sc, PhD. Part-time programs available. *Faculty:* 26 full-time (5 women), 15 part-time/adjunct (2 women). *Students:* 69 full-time (29 women); includes 6 minority (1 African American, 3 Asian Americans or Pacific Islanders, 2 Hispanic Americans), 5 international. Average age 25. 65 applicants, 40% accepted, 17 enrolled. In 2009, 4 master's, 9 doctorates awarded. Terminal master's awarded for partial completion of doctoral program. *Degree requirements:* For master's, thesis; for doctorate, thesis/dissertation. *Entrance requirements:* Additional exam requirements/recommendations for international students: Required—TOEFL (minimum score 600 paper-based; 237 computer-based; 92 iBT), IELTS (minimum score 7). *Application deadline:* For fall admission, 6/1 priority date for domestic students, 4/1 priority date for international students; for winter admission, 10/31 priority date for domestic students, 8/31 priority date for international students; for spring admission, 2/28 priority date for domestic students, 12/31 priority date for international students. Applications are processed on a rolling basis. Application fee: $0 ($70 for international students). Electronic applications accepted. *Financial support:* In 2009–10, 70 fellowships with full tuition reimbursements (averaging $10,500 per year), 70 teaching assistantships (averaging $3,620 per year) were awarded; scholarships/grants also available. Financial award application deadline: 4/15. *Faculty research:* Analytical, inorganic, organic, physical, and theoretical chemistry. Total annual research expenditures: $2.5 million. *Unit head:* Dr. Neil Burford, Chair, 902-494-3707, Fax: 902-494-1310, E-mail: neil.burford@dal.ca. *Application contact:* Dr. Mark Stradiotto, Graduate Coordinator, 902-494-3306, Fax: 902-494-1310, E-mail: mark.stradiotto@dal.ca.

Dartmouth College, Arts and Sciences Graduate Programs, Department of Chemistry, Hanover, NH 03755. Offers PhD. *Faculty:* 14 full-time (2 women). *Students:* 29 full-time (13 women), 12 international. Average age 25. 148 applicants, 15% accepted, 9 enrolled. In 2009, 8 doctorates awarded. *Degree requirements:* For doctorate, thesis/dissertation, departmental qualifying exams. *Entrance requirements:* For doctorate, GRE General Test, GRE Subject Test. Additional exam requirements/recommendations for international students: Required—TOEFL. *Application deadline:* For fall admission, 1/15 priority date for domestic students. Application fee: $25. Electronic applications accepted. *Financial support:* In 2009–10, 23 students received support, including fellowships with full tuition reimbursements available (averaging $23,832 per year), research assistantships with full tuition reimbursements available (averaging $23,832 per year), teaching assistantships with full tuition reimbursements available (averaging $23,832 per year); institutionally sponsored loans, scholarships/grants, traineeships, tuition waivers (full), and unspecified assistantships also available. *Faculty research:* Organic and polymer synthesis, bioinorganic chemistry, magnetic resonance parameters. *Unit head:* Dr. David S. Glueck, Chair, 603-646-2501. *Application contact:* Deborah Carr, Administrative Assistant, 603-646-2501, Fax: 603-646-3946, E-mail: deborah.a.carr@dartmouth.edu.

Delaware State University, Graduate Programs, Department of Chemistry, Program in Chemistry, Dover, DE 19901-2277. Offers MS. *Entrance requirements:* For master's, GRE. Additional exam requirements/recommendations for international students: Required—TOEFL (minimum score 550 paper-based). Electronic applications accepted.

DePaul University, College of Liberal Arts and Sciences, Department of Chemistry, Chicago, IL 60614. Offers biochemistry (MS); chemistry (MS); polymer chemistry and coatings technology (MS). Part-time and evening/weekend programs available. *Faculty:* 13 full-time (7 women), 4 part-time/adjunct (1 woman). *Students:* 14 full-time (7 women), 9 part-time (4 women); includes 6 minority (2 African Americans, 3 Asian Americans or Pacific Islanders, 1 Hispanic American), 1 international. Average age 27. 6 applicants, 100% accepted, 4 enrolled. In 2009, 2 master's awarded. *Degree requirements:* For master's, thesis (for some programs), oral exam (for selected programs). *Entrance requirements:* For master's, GRE Subject Test (chemistry), GRE General Test, BS in chemistry or equivalent. Additional exam requirements/recommendations for international students: Required—TOEFL (minimum score 590 paper-based; 243 computer-based). *Application deadline:* For fall admission, 7/15 for domestic students, 5/1 for international students; for winter admission, 11/15 for domestic students, 9/1 for international students; for spring admission, 2/15 for domestic students, 12/1 for international students. Applications are processed on a rolling basis. Application fee: $40. Electronic applications accepted. *Expenses:* Tuition: Full-time $37,525; part-time $620 per credit hour. *Financial support:* In 2009–10, 4 students received support, including 6 teaching assistantships with partial tuition reimbursements available (averaging $9,000 per year). Financial award application deadline: 6/1. *Faculty research:* Computational chemistry, organic synthesis, inorganic synthesis, polymer synthesis, biochemistry. Total annual research expenditures: $30,000. *Unit head:* Dr. Richard F. Niedziela, Chair, 773-325-7307, Fax: 773-325-7421, E-mail: rniedzie@condor.depaul.edu. *Application contact:* Dr. Matthew Dintzner, Director of Graduate Studies, 773-325-4726, Fax: 773-325-7421, E-mail: mdintzne@depaul.edu.

Chemistry

Drew University, Caspersen School of Graduate Studies, Program in Education, Madison, NJ 07940-1493. Offers biology (MAT); chemistry (MAT); English (MAT); French (MAT); Italian (MAT); math (MAT); physics (MAT); social studies (MAT); Spanish (MAT); theatre arts (MAT).

Drexel University, College of Arts and Sciences, Department of Chemistry, Philadelphia, PA 19104-2875. Offers MS, PhD. Part-time programs available. Terminal master's awarded for partial completion of doctoral program. *Degree requirements:* For master's, thesis optional; for doctorate, one foreign language, thesis/dissertation. *Entrance requirements:* For master's and doctorate, GRE. Additional exam requirements/recommendations for international students: Required—TOEFL. Electronic applications accepted. *Faculty research:* Inorganic, analytical, organic, physical, and atmospheric polymer chemistry.

Duke University, Graduate School, Department of Chemistry, Durham, NC 27708. Offers PhD. *Faculty:* 24 full-time. *Students:* 95 full-time (51 women); includes 4 minority (2 African Americans, 2 Hispanic Americans), 25 international. 230 applicants, 23% accepted, 17 enrolled. In 2009, 13 doctorates awarded. *Degree requirements:* For doctorate, one foreign language, thesis/dissertation. *Entrance requirements:* For doctorate, GRE General Test, GRE Subject Test (recommended). Additional exam requirements/recommendations for international students: Required—TOEFL (minimum score 550 paper-based; 213 computer-based; 83 iBT), IELTS (minimum score 7). *Application deadline:* For fall admission, 12/8 priority date for domestic and international students. Application fee: $75. Electronic applications accepted. *Financial support:* Fellowships, research assistantships, teaching assistantships available. Financial award application deadline: 12/31. *Unit head:* Baldwin Steve, Director of Graduate Studies, 919-660-1503, Fax: 919-660-1607. *Application contact:* Cynthia Robertson, Associate Dean for Enrollment Services, 919-684-3913, E-mail: grad-admissions@duke.edu.

Duquesne University, Bayer School of Natural and Environmental Sciences, Department of Chemistry and Biochemistry, Pittsburgh, PA 15282-0001. Offers chemistry (MS, PhD). Part-time programs available. *Faculty:* 14 full-time (4 women), 1 part-time/adjunct (0 women). *Students:* 43 full-time (21 women), 5 part-time (0 women); includes 2 minority (both African Americans), 13 international. Average age 30. 53 applicants, 32% accepted, 8 enrolled. In 2009, 3 doctorates awarded. Terminal master's awarded for partial completion of doctoral program. *Degree requirements:* For master's, comprehensive exam (for some programs), thesis (for some programs); for doctorate, thesis/dissertation. *Entrance requirements:* For master's, GRE General Test, BS in chemistry or related field, 3 letters of recommendation; for doctorate, GRE General Test, BS in chemistry or related field, statement of purpose, official transcripts, 3 letters of recommendation with recommendation forms. Additional exam requirements/recommendations for international students: Required—TOEFL (minimum score 100 iBT). *Application deadline:* For fall admission, 2/15 priority date for domestic students, 2/15 for international students; for spring admission, 10/1 priority date for domestic students, 10/1 for international students. Applications are processed on a rolling basis. Application fee: $0 ($40 for international students). Electronic applications accepted. *Expenses:* Contact institution. *Financial support:* In 2009–10, 42 students received support, including 15 research assistantships with full tuition reimbursements available (averaging $20,800 per year), 27 teaching assistantships with full tuition reimbursements available (averaging $20,800 per year); fellowships with tuition reimbursements available, scholarships/grants and unspecified assistantships also available. Financial award application deadline: 5/31. *Faculty research:* Computational physical chemistry, bioinorganic chemistry, analytical chemistry, biophysics, synthetic organic chemistry. *Unit head:* Dr. Jeffry Madura, Chair, 412-396-6341, Fax: 412-396-5683, E-mail: madura@duq.edu. *Application contact:* Heather Costello, Graduate Academic Advisor, 412-396-6339, Fax: 412-396-4881, E-mail: costelloh@duq.edu.

See Close-Up on page 95.

East Carolina University, Graduate School, Thomas Harriot College of Arts and Sciences, Department of Chemistry, Greenville, NC 27858-4353. Offers MS. Part-time programs available. *Degree requirements:* For master's, one foreign language, comprehensive exam, thesis. *Entrance requirements:* For master's, GRE General Test. Additional exam requirements/recommendations for international students: Required—TOEFL. *Faculty research:* Organometallic, natural-product syntheses; chemometrics; electroanalytical method development; microcomputer adaptations for handicapped students.

Eastern Illinois University, Graduate School, College of Sciences, Department of Chemistry, Charleston, IL 61920-3099. Offers MS. *Faculty:* 13 full-time (2 women). In 2009, 5 master's awarded. *Degree requirements:* For master's, thesis. *Entrance requirements:* For master's, GRE General Test. *Application deadline:* For fall admission, 3/31 priority date for domestic students. Applications are processed on a rolling basis. Application fee: $30. *Expenses:* Tuition, state resident: full-time $9434; part-time $239 per credit hour. Tuition, nonresident: full-time $23,774; part-time $717 per credit hour. Required fees: $802.63. *Financial support:* In 2009–10, 2 research assistantships with tuition reimbursements (averaging $8,100 per year), 2 teaching assistantships with tuition reimbursements (averaging $8,100 per year) were awarded. *Unit head:* Dr. Doug Sheeran, Chairperson, 217-581-6227, E-mail: djsheeran@eiu.edu. *Application contact:* Dr. Barbara Lawrence, Coordinator, 217-581-2720, E-mail: balawrence@eiu.edu.

Eastern Kentucky University, The Graduate School, College of Arts and Sciences, Department of Chemistry, Richmond, KY 40475-3102. Offers MS. Part-time and evening/weekend programs available. *Entrance requirements:* For master's, GRE General Test, minimum GPA of 2.5. *Faculty research:* Organic synthesis, surface chemistry, inorganic chemistry, analytical chemistry.

Eastern Michigan University, Graduate School, College of Arts and Sciences, Department of Chemistry, Ypsilanti, MI 48197. Offers MS. Part-time and evening/weekend programs available. *Faculty:* 21 full-time (8 women). *Students:* 2 full-time (both women), 32 part-time (14 women); includes 2 minority (1 African American, 1 American Indian/Alaska Native), 24 international. Average age 27. 32 applicants, 59% accepted, 10 enrolled. In 2009, 8 master's awarded. *Degree requirements:* For master's, thesis. *Entrance requirements:* For master's, GRE General Test. Additional exam requirements/recommendations for international students: Required—TOEFL. *Application deadline:* For fall admission, 8/1 for domestic students, 5/1 for international students; for winter admission, 12/1 for domestic students, 8/1 for international students; for spring admission, 4/1 for domestic students, 3/1 for international students. Applications are processed on a rolling basis. Application fee: $35. Tuition and fees vary according to course level. *Financial support:* In 2009–10, 2 research assistantships with full tuition reimbursements (averaging $3,000 per year), 16 teaching assistantships with full tuition reimbursements (averaging $6,897 per year) were awarded; fellowships, career-related internships or fieldwork, Federal Work-Study, institutionally sponsored loans, scholarships/grants, tuition waivers (partial), and unspecified assistantships also available. Support available to part-time students. Financial award applicants required to submit FAFSA. *Unit head:* Dr. Ross Nord, Department Head, 734-487-0106, Fax: 734-487-1496, E-mail: ross.nord@emich.edu. *Application contact:* Dr. Timothy Brewer, Coordinator, 734-487-9613, Fax: 734-487-1496, E-mail: tbrewer@emich.edu.

Eastern New Mexico University, Graduate School, College of Liberal Arts and Sciences, Department of Physical Sciences, Portales, NM 88130. Offers chemistry (MS). Part-time programs available. *Faculty:* 7 full-time (0 women). *Students:* 12 part-time (3 women); includes 2 minority (1 Asian American or Pacific Islander, 1 Hispanic American), 6 international. Average age 32. 13 applicants, 46% accepted, 5 enrolled. In 2009, 3 master's awarded. *Degree requirements:* For master's, comprehensive exam, thesis optional. *Entrance requirements:* For master's, ACS placement examination, minimum GPA of 3.0, letters of recommendation. Additional exam requirements/recommendations for international students: Required—TOEFL (minimum score 550 paper-based; 213 computer-based; 79 iBT), IELTS (minimum score 6). *Application deadline:* For fall admission, 7/20 priority date for domestic students, 6/20 priority date for international students. Applications are processed on a rolling basis. Application fee: $10. Electronic applications accepted. *Expenses:* Tuition, state resident: full-time $2922; part-time $121.75 per credit hour. Tuition, nonresident: full-time $8454; part-time $352.25 per credit hour. Required fees: $1038; $43.25 per credit hour. *Financial support:* In 2009–10, 10 teaching assistantships with tuition reimbursements (averaging $4,250 per year) were awarded; fellowships, research assistantships, career-related internships or fieldwork and unspecified assistantships also available. Support available to part-time students. Financial award application deadline: 3/1; financial award applicants required to submit FAFSA. *Faculty research:* Synfuel, electrochemistry, protein chemistry. *Unit head:* Dr. Juacho Yan, Graduate Coordinator, 575-562-2174, E-mail: juacho.yan@enmu.edu. *Application contact:* Dr. Juacho Yan, Graduate Coordinator, 575-562-2174, E-mail: juacho.yan@enmu.edu.

East Tennessee State University, School of Graduate Studies, College of Arts and Sciences, Department of Chemistry, Johnson City, TN 37614. Offers MS. Part-time and evening/weekend programs available. *Degree requirements:* For master's, comprehensive exam, thesis. *Entrance requirements:* For master's, GRE. Additional exam requirements/recommendations for international students: Required—TOEFL (minimum score 550 paper-based; 213 computer-based). *Faculty research:* Development of luminescence techniques for chemical analysis, new functional materials and biosensor technology, synthesis of theoretically significant organic molecules and synthetic metals, synthesis and study of phosphatase enzyme models.

Emory University, Graduate School of Arts and Sciences, Department of Chemistry, Atlanta, GA 30322-1100. Offers PhD. *Degree requirements:* For doctorate, comprehensive exam, thesis/dissertation. *Entrance requirements:* For doctorate, GRE General Test, 3 letters of recommendation, curriculum vitae. Additional exam requirements/recommendations for international students: Required—TOEFL. Electronic applications accepted. *Faculty research:* Organometallic synthesis and catalysis, synthesis of natural products, x-ray crystallography, mass spectrometry, analytical neurochemistry.

Fairleigh Dickinson University, College at Florham, Maxwell Becton College of Arts and Sciences, Department of Chemistry and Geological Sciences, Program in Chemistry, Madison, NJ 07940-1099. Offers MS. *Students:* 76 full-time (25 women), 26 part-time (11 women), 93 international. Average age 24. 137 applicants, 82% accepted, 28 enrolled. In 2009, 24 master's awarded. *Application deadline:* Applications are processed on a rolling basis. Application fee: $40. *Unit head:* Dr. Michael Avaltroni, Chair, 973-443-8500. *Application contact:* Susan Brooman, University Director, Graduate Admissions, 973-443-8905, Fax: 973-443-8088, E-mail: grad@fdu.edu.

Fairleigh Dickinson University, Metropolitan Campus, University College: Arts, Sciences, and Professional Studies, School of Natural Sciences, Program in Chemistry, Teaneck, NJ 07666-1914. Offers MS. *Students:* 48 full-time (20 women), 5 part-time (all women), 51 international. Average age 23. 131 applicants, 44% accepted, 11 enrolled. In 2009, 14 master's awarded. *Application deadline:* Applications are processed on a rolling basis. Application fee: $40. *Application contact:* Susan Brooman, University Director of Graduate Admissions, 201-692-2554, Fax: 201-692-2560, E-mail: globaleducation@fdu.edu.

Fisk University, Division of Graduate Studies, Department of Chemistry, Nashville, TN 37208-3051. Offers MA. Part-time programs available. *Faculty:* 5 full-time (2 women), 2 part-time/adjunct (1 woman). *Students:* 1 (woman) full-time, 1 part-time (0 women); both minorities (both African Americans). Average age 22. 2 applicants, 100% accepted, 2 enrolled. *Degree requirements:* For master's, comprehensive exam, thesis. *Entrance requirements:* For master's, GRE General Test, minimum GPA of 3.0. *Application deadline:* For fall admission, 6/1 priority date for domestic students. Applications are processed on a rolling basis. Application fee: $50. Electronic applications accepted. *Expenses:* Tuition: Full-time $16,848; part-time $936 per credit hour. Required fees: $1510; $465 per semester. *Financial support:* In 2009–10, 2 students received support, including 2 fellowships (averaging $16,852 per year); tuition waivers (full and partial) and unspecified assistantships also available. Financial award applicants required to submit FAFSA. *Faculty research:* Environmental studies, lithium compound synthesis, HIU compound synthesis. Total annual research expenditures: $30,000. *Unit head:* Dr. Princilla Evans-Morris, Chair, 615-329-8624. *Application contact:* Keith Chandler, Dean of Admission, 615-329-8819, Fax: 615-329-8774, E-mail: kchandler@fisk.edu.

Florida Agricultural and Mechanical University, Division of Graduate Studies, Research, and Continuing Education, College of Arts and Sciences, Department of Chemistry, Tallahassee, FL 32307-3200. Offers MS. *Faculty:* 13 full-time (4 women). *Students:* 15 full-time (10 women), 5 part-time (4 women); includes 19 minority (all African Americans), 1 international. In 2009, 7 master's awarded. *Degree requirements:* For master's, comprehensive exam, thesis optional. *Entrance requirements:* For master's, GRE General Test, minimum GPA of 3.0. *Application deadline:* For fall admission, 5/18 for domestic students, 12/18 for international students; for spring admission, 11/12 for domestic students, 5/12 for international students. Application fee: $20. *Unit head:* Dr. Maurice Edington, Chairperson, 850-599-3638, Fax: 740-561-2388. *Application contact:* Dr. Chanta M. Haywood, Dean of Graduate Studies, Research, and Continuing Education, 850-599-3315, Fax: 850-599-3727.

Florida Atlantic University, Charles E. Schmidt College of Science, Department of Chemistry and Biochemistry, Boca Raton, FL 33431-0991. Offers chemistry (MS, MST, PhD). Part-time programs available. *Faculty:* 15 full-time (4 women). *Students:* 31 full-time (18 women), 3 part-time (all women); includes 5 minority (1 African American, 4 Hispanic Americans), 14 international. Average age 29. 32 applicants, 44% accepted, 6 enrolled. In 2009, 15 master's, 5 doctorates awarded. Terminal master's awarded for partial completion of doctoral program. *Degree requirements:* For master's, thesis; for doctorate, comprehensive exam, thesis/dissertation. *Entrance requirements:* For master's, GRE General Test, minimum GPA of 3.0; for doctorate, GRE, minimum GPA of 3.0. Additional exam requirements/recommendations for international students: Required—TOEFL. *Application deadline:* For fall admission, 7/1 priority date for domestic students, 2/15 priority date for international students; for spring admission, 11/1 priority date for domestic students, 7/15 priority date for international students. Applications are processed on a rolling basis. Application fee: $30. *Expenses:* Tuition, state resident: full-time $7055; part-time $293.94 per credit hour. Tuition, nonresident: full-time $22,096; part-time $920.66 per credit hour. *Financial support:* Fellowships, research assistantships with full tuition reimbursements, teaching assistantships with full tuition reimbursements, Federal Work-Study available. *Faculty research:* Polymer synthesis and characterization, spectroscopy, geochemistry, environmental chemistry, biomedical chemistry. *Unit head:* Dr. Ramaswamy Narayanan, Chair, 561-297-2093, Fax: 561-297-2759, E-mail: rnarayan@fau.edu. *Application contact:* Dr. Salvatore D. Lepore, Professor, 561-297-0330, Fax: 561-297-2759, E-mail: slepore@fau.edu.

Florida Institute of Technology, Graduate Programs, College of Science, Department of Chemistry, Melbourne, FL 32901-6975. Offers MS, PhD. Part-time programs available. *Faculty:* 5 full-time (0 women). *Students:* 21 full-time (7 women), 4 part-time (1 woman); includes 2 minority (1 African American, 1 Hispanic American), 14 international. Average age 27. 49 applicants, 69% accepted, 9 enrolled. In 2009, 3 master's, 2 doctorates awarded. *Degree requirements:* For master's, research proposal, thesis and oral examination in defense of the thesis; for doctorate, comprehensive exam, thesis/dissertation, oral defense of dissertation, dissertation research publishable to standards, complete original research study. *Entrance requirements:* For master's, proficiency exams, minimum GPA of 3.0; for doctorate, minimum GPA of 3.3, resume, 3 letters of recommendation, statement of objectives. Additional exam requirements/recommendations for international students: Required—TOEFL (minimum score 550 paper-based; 213 computer-based; 79 iBT). *Application deadline:* For fall admission, 4/1 for international students; for spring admission, 9/30 for international students. Applications are processed on a rolling basis. Application fee: $50. Electronic applications accepted. *Expenses:*

Tuition: Part-time $1015 per credit. Tuition and fees vary according to campus/location and program. *Financial support:* In 2009–10, 17 students received support, including 1 research assistantship with full and partial tuition reimbursement available (averaging $12,800 per year), 16 teaching assistantships with full and partial tuition reimbursements available (averaging $10,788 per year); career-related internships or fieldwork, institutionally sponsored loans, tuition waivers (partial), unspecified assistantships, and tuition remissions also available. Support available to part-time students. Financial award application deadline: 3/1; financial award applicants required to submit FAFSA. *Faculty research:* Energy storage applications, marine and organic chemistry, stereochemistry, medicinal chemistry, environmental chemistry. Total annual research expenditures: $548,807. *Unit head:* Dr. Michael W. Babich, Department Head, 321-674-8046, Fax: 321-674-8951, E-mail: babich@fit.edu. *Application contact:* Thomas M. Shea, Director of Graduate Admissions, 321-674-7577, Fax: 321-723-9468, E-mail: tshea@fit.edu.

Florida International University, College of Arts and Sciences, Department of Chemistry, Chemistry Program, Miami, FL 33199. Offers MS, PhD. *Faculty:* 22 full-time (4 women), 1 part-time/adjunct (0 women). *Students:* 70 full-time (41 women), 16 part-time (10 women); includes 29 minority (9 African Americans, 5 Asian Americans or Pacific Islanders, 15 Hispanic Americans), 41 international. Average age 28. 72 applicants, 22% accepted, 12 enrolled. In 2009, 1 master's, 3 doctorates awarded. *Degree requirements:* For master's, thesis; for doctorate, comprehensive exam, thesis/dissertation. *Entrance requirements:* For master's and doctorate, GRE, minimum GPA of 3.0, 3 letters of recommendation. Additional exam requirements/recommendations for international students: Required—TOEFL (minimum score 550 paper-based; 213 computer-based). *Application deadline:* For fall admission, 6/1 for domestic students, 4/1 for international students; for spring admission, 10/1 for domestic students, 9/1 for international students. Applications are processed on a rolling basis. Application fee: $30. Electronic applications accepted. *Expenses:* Tuition, state resident: full-time $8008; part-time $4004 per year. Tuition, nonresident: full-time $20,104; part-time $10,052 per year. Required fees: $298; $149 per term. *Financial support:* Fellowships, research assistantships, teaching assistantships, Federal Work-Study, institutionally sponsored loans, and scholarships/grants available. Financial award application deadline: 3/1; financial award applicants required to submit FAFSA. *Unit head:* Dr. Kenneth Furton, Dean, 305-348-2864, Fax: 305-348-4172, E-mail: furtonk@fiu.edu. *Application contact:* Nanett Rojas, Coordinator of Graduate Admissions, 305-348-7442, Fax: 305-348-7441, E-mail: gradadm@fiu.edu.

Florida State University, The Graduate School, College of Arts and Sciences, Department of Chemistry and Biochemistry, Tallahassee, FL 32306-4390. Offers analytical chemistry (MS, PhD); biochemistry (MS, PhD); inorganic chemistry (MS, PhD); materials chemistry (MS, PhD); organic chemistry (MS, PhD); physical chemistry (MS, PhD). *Faculty:* 40 full-time (6 women), 3 part-time/adjunct (0 women). *Students:* 150 full-time (47 women), 9 part-time (6 women); includes 16 minority (5 African Americans, 1 American Indian/Alaska Native, 5 Asian Americans or Pacific Islanders, 5 Hispanic Americans), 68 international. Average age 25. 286 applicants, 21% accepted, 28 enrolled. In 2009, 7 master's, 15 doctorates awarded. Terminal master's awarded for partial completion of doctoral program. *Degree requirements:* For master's, comprehensive exam (for some programs), thesis (for some programs), cumulative and diagnostic exams; for doctorate, comprehensive exam (for some programs), thesis/dissertation, cumulative and diagnostic exams. *Entrance requirements:* For master's and doctorate, GRE General Test, minimum B average in undergraduate course work. Additional exam requirements/recommendations for international students: Required—TOEFL (minimum score 550 paper-based; 213 computer-based; 80 iBT). *Application deadline:* For fall admission, 12/15 for domestic and international students; for spring admission, 9/15 for domestic and international students. Applications are processed on a rolling basis. Application fee: $30. Electronic applications accepted. *Expenses:* Tuition, state resident: full-time $7413.36. Tuition, nonresident: full-time $22,567. *Financial support:* In 2009–10, 150 students received support, including fellowships with full tuition reimbursements available (averaging $19,000 per year), 52 research assistantships with full tuition reimbursements available (averaging $19,000 per year), 100 teaching assistantships with full tuition reimbursements available (averaging $19,000 per year); career-related internships or fieldwork, Federal Work-Study, institutionally sponsored loans, and traineeships also available. Financial award application deadline: 12/15; financial award applicants required to submit FAFSA. *Faculty research:* Materials synthesis including polymers, natural products; catalysis, NMR; mass spectrometry; optical spectroscopy, scattering techniques, computational chemistry, separation technology; nanostructured materials including metallic, semiconducting and magnetic nanocrystals; nanoscience interfaced with biology; supramolecular materials for solar energy conversion. Total annual research expenditures: $5.5 million. *Unit head:* Dr. Joseph Schlenoff, Chairman, 850-644-5195, Fax: 850-644-8281, E-mail: schlen@chem.fsu.edu. *Application contact:* Dr. Tyler McQuade, Chair, Graduate Admissions Committee, 888-525-9286, Fax: 850-644-0465, E-mail: gradinfo@chem.fsu.edu.

Furman University, Graduate Division, Department of Chemistry, Greenville, SC 29613. Offers MS. *Faculty:* 9 full-time (3 women). *Students:* 4 full-time (3 women), 1 international. Average age 23. 6 applicants, 100% accepted. In 2009, 1 master's awarded. *Degree requirements:* For master's, comprehensive exam, thesis. *Entrance requirements:* For master's, GRE General Test, GRE Subject Test. *Application deadline:* For fall admission, 8/1 for domestic and international students; for spring admission, 12/10 for domestic and international students. Applications are processed on a rolling basis. Application fee: $50. *Financial support:* In 2009–10, 5 fellowships (averaging $4,350 per year) were awarded; research assistantships, scholarships/grants and unspecified assistantships also available. Financial award application deadline: 7/1; financial award applicants required to submit FAFSA. *Faculty research:* Computer-assisted chemical analysis, DNA-metal interactions, laser-initiated reactions, nucleic acid chemistry and biochemistry. *Unit head:* Dr. Lon B. Knight, Professor, 864-294-3372, Fax: 864-294-3559, E-mail: lon.knight@furman.edu. *Application contact:* Myra Crumley, Information Contact, 864-294-2056, Fax: 864-294-3559, E-mail: myra.crumley@furman.edu.

George Mason University, College of Science, Department of Chemistry and Biochemistry, Fairfax, VA 22030. Offers chemistry (MS). *Degree requirements:* For master's, thesis or alternative. *Entrance requirements:* For master's, GRE General Test, minimum GPA of 3.0 in last 60 hours of course work. Electronic applications accepted. *Expenses:* Tuition, state resident: full-time $7568; part-time $315.33 per credit hour. Tuition, nonresident: full-time $21,704; part-time $904.33 per credit hour. Required fees: $2184; $91 per credit hour.

Georgetown University, Graduate School of Arts and Sciences, Department of Chemistry, Washington, DC 20057. Offers analytical chemistry (PhD); biochemistry (PhD); computational chemistry (PhD); inorganic chemistry (PhD); materials chemistry (PhD); organic chemistry (PhD); physical chemistry (PhD); theoretical chemistry (PhD). Terminal master's awarded for partial completion of doctoral program. *Degree requirements:* For doctorate, comprehensive exam, thesis/dissertation. *Entrance requirements:* For doctorate, GRE General Test. Additional exam requirements/recommendations for international students: Required—TOEFL.

The George Washington University, Columbian College of Arts and Sciences, Department of Chemistry, Washington, DC 20052. Offers analytical chemistry (MS, PhD); inorganic chemistry (MS, PhD); materials science (MS, PhD); organic chemistry (MS, PhD); physical chemistry (MS, PhD). Part-time and evening/weekend programs available. *Faculty:* 15 full-time (4 women), 7 part-time/adjunct (3 women). *Students:* 19 full-time (12 women), 12 part-time (7 women); includes 4 minority (2 Asian Americans or Pacific Islanders, 2 Hispanic Americans), 12 international. Average age 28. 45 applicants, 49% accepted, 6 enrolled. In 2009, 2 master's, 4 doctorates awarded. Terminal master's awarded for partial completion of doctoral program. *Degree requirements:* For master's, comprehensive exam, thesis or alternative; for doctorate, thesis/dissertation, general exam. *Entrance requirements:* For master's and doctorate, GRE General Test, interview, minimum GPA of 3.0. Additional exam requirements/recommendations for international students: Required—TOEFL (minimum score 550 paper-based; 213 computer-based; 80 iBT). *Application deadline:* For fall admission, 1/15 priority date for domestic and international students; for spring admission, 9/1 priority date for domestic and international students. Applications are processed on a rolling basis. Application fee: $60. Electronic applications accepted. *Financial support:* In 2009–10, 27 students received support; fellowships with tuition reimbursements available, research assistantships, teaching assistantships with tuition reimbursements available, Federal Work-Study and tuition waivers available. Financial award application deadline: 1/15. *Unit head:* Dr. Michael King, Chair, 202-994-6488. *Application contact:* Information Contact, E-mail: gwchem@www.gwu.edu.

Georgia Institute of Technology, Graduate Studies and Research, College of Sciences, School of Chemistry and Biochemistry, Atlanta, GA 30332-0001. Offers MS, MS Chem, PhD. Terminal master's awarded for partial completion of doctoral program. *Degree requirements:* For master's, thesis (for some programs); for doctorate, thesis/dissertation. *Entrance requirements:* For master's and doctorate, GRE General Test, GRE Subject Test, minimum GPA of 2.7. Additional exam requirements/recommendations for international students: Required—TOEFL. Electronic applications accepted. *Faculty research:* Inorganic, organic, physical, and analytical chemistry.

Georgia State University, College of Arts and Sciences, Department of Chemistry, Atlanta, GA 30302-3083. Offers MS, PhD. Part-time programs available. Terminal master's awarded for partial completion of doctoral program. *Degree requirements:* For master's, one foreign language, comprehensive exam, thesis or alternative, oral defense or approved non-thesis paper; for doctorate, one foreign language, comprehensive exam, thesis/dissertation, oral defense. *Entrance requirements:* For master's, GRE General Test; for doctorate, GRE General Test, 3 letters of recommendation, departmental supplemental form. Additional exam requirements/recommendations for international students: Required—TOEFL (minimum score 550 paper-based; 213 computer-based; 90 iBT). Electronic applications accepted. *Faculty research:* RNA/DNA, enzymology, drug design/discovery, biochemical-biophysical studies.

Graduate School and University Center of the City University of New York, Graduate Studies, Program in Chemistry, New York, NY 10016-4039. Offers PhD. *Faculty:* 64 full-time (5 women). *Students:* 134 full-time (52 women); includes 14 minority (5 African Americans, 7 Asian Americans or Pacific Islanders, 2 Hispanic Americans), 95 international. Average age 31. 86 applicants, 55% accepted, 25 enrolled. In 2009, 15 doctorates awarded. *Degree requirements:* For doctorate, one foreign language, thesis/dissertation. *Entrance requirements:* For doctorate, GRE General Test. Additional exam requirements/recommendations for international students: Required—TOEFL. *Application deadline:* For fall admission, 2/1 for domestic students. Application fee: $125. Electronic applications accepted. *Financial support:* In 2009–10, 123 students received support, including 114 fellowships, 1 teaching assistantship; research assistantships, career-related internships or fieldwork, Federal Work-Study, institutionally sponsored loans, and tuition waivers (full and partial) also available. Financial award application deadline: 2/1; financial award applicants required to submit FAFSA. *Unit head:* Dr. Mahesh Lakshmani, Executive Officer, 212-817-8136, Fax: 212-817-1507. *Application contact:* Les Gribben, Director of Admissions, 212-817-7470, Fax: 212-817-1624, E-mail: lgribben@gc.cuny.edu.

Hampton University, Graduate College, Department of Chemistry, Hampton, VA 23668. Offers MS. Part-time and evening/weekend programs available. *Degree requirements:* For master's, thesis. *Entrance requirements:* For master's, GRE General Test.

Harvard University, Graduate School of Arts and Sciences, Department of Chemistry and Chemical Biology, Cambridge, MA 02138. Offers biochemical chemistry (PhD); inorganic chemistry (PhD); organic chemistry (PhD); physical chemistry (PhD). *Degree requirements:* For doctorate, thesis/dissertation, cumulative exams. *Entrance requirements:* For doctorate, GRE General Test, GRE Subject Test. Additional exam requirements/recommendations for international students: Required—TOEFL. *Expenses:* Tuition: Full-time $33,696. Required fees: $1126. Full-time tuition and fees vary according to program.

See Close-Up on page 99.

Howard University, Graduate School, Department of Chemistry, Washington, DC 20059-0002. Offers analytical chemistry (MS, PhD); atmospheric (MS, PhD); biochemistry (MS, PhD); environmental (MS, PhD); inorganic chemistry (MS, PhD); organic chemistry (MS, PhD); physical chemistry (MS, PhD). Terminal master's awarded for partial completion of doctoral program. *Degree requirements:* For master's, comprehensive exam, thesis, teaching experience; for doctorate, comprehensive exam, thesis/dissertation, teaching experience. *Entrance requirements:* For master's, GRE General Test, minimum GPA of 2.7; for doctorate, GRE General Test, minimum GPA of 3.0. Additional exam requirements/recommendations for international students: Required—TOEFL. Electronic applications accepted. *Faculty research:* Synthetic organics, materials, natural products, mass spectrometry.

Hunter College of the City University of New York, Graduate School, School of Arts and Sciences, Department of Chemistry, New York, NY 10021-5085. Offers biochemistry (MA, PhD); chemistry (PhD). Part-time programs available. *Faculty:* 4 full-time (3 women). *Students:* 3 full-time (1 woman), 1 part-time (0 women); includes 2 minority (both Asian Americans or Pacific Islanders). Average age 23. 5 applicants, 60% accepted, 2 enrolled. *Degree requirements:* For master's, comprehensive exam or thesis. *Entrance requirements:* For master's, GRE General Test, 1 year of course work in chemistry, quantitative analysis, organic chemistry, physical chemistry, biology, biochemistry lecture and laboratory. Additional exam requirements/recommendations for international students: Required—TOEFL. *Application deadline:* For fall admission, 4/1 for domestic students; for spring admission, 11/1 for domestic students. Application fee: $125. *Expenses:* Tuition, state resident: full-time $7360; part-time $310 per credit. Required fees: $250 per semester. *Financial support:* Teaching assistantships, tuition waivers (partial) available. Support available to part-time students. *Faculty research:* Theoretical chemistry, vibrational optical activity, Raman spectroscopy. *Unit head:* Dr. Gary J. Quigley, Chairperson, 212-772-5330, E-mail: gary.quilgley@hunter.cuny.edu. *Application contact:* William Zlata, Director for Graduate Admissions, 212-772-4482, Fax: 212-650-3336, E-mail: admissions@hunter.cuny.edu.

Idaho State University, Office of Graduate Studies, College of Arts and Sciences, Department of Chemistry, Pocatello, ID 83209-8023. Offers MNS, MS. MS students must enter as undergraduates. Part-time programs available. *Faculty:* 9 full-time (1 woman). *Students:* 7 full-time (0 women), 3 part-time (0 women); includes 2 minority (both Asian Americans or Pacific Islanders), 3 international. Average age 27. In 2009, 3 master's awarded. *Degree requirements:* For master's, comprehensive exam, thesis (for some programs). *Entrance requirements:* For master's, GRE General Test, minimum GPA of 3.0 in all upper-division classes; 1 semester of calculus, inorganic chemistry, and analytical chemistry; 1 year of physics, organic chemistry and physical chemistry. Additional exam requirements/recommendations for international students: Required—TOEFL (minimum score 550 paper-based; 213 computer-based; 80 iBT). *Application deadline:* For fall admission, 7/1 for domestic students, 6/1 for international students; for spring admission, 12/1 for domestic students, 11/1 for international students. Applications are processed on a rolling basis. Application fee: $55. Electronic applications accepted. *Expenses:* Tuition, state resident: full-time $3318; part-time $297 per credit hour. Tuition, nonresident: full-time $13,120; part-time $437 per credit hour. Required fees: $2530. Tuition and fees vary according to program. *Financial support:* In 2009–10, 10 teaching assistantships with full and partial tuition reimbursements (averaging $10,841 per year) were awarded; research assistantships with full and partial tuition reimbursements, Federal Work-Study, institutionally sponsored loans, scholarships/grants, health care benefits, tuition waivers (full and partial), and unspecified assistantships also available. Support

Chemistry

Idaho State University (continued)
available to part-time students. Financial award application deadline: 1/1; financial award applicants required to submit FAFSA. *Faculty research:* Low temperature plasma, organic chemistry, physical chemistry, inorganic chemistry, analytical chemistry. *Unit head:* Dr. Robert Holman, Chair, 208-282-4331, Fax: 208-282-4373, E-mail: holmrobe@isu.edu. *Application contact:* Tami Carson, Graduate School Technical Records Specialist, 208-282-2150, Fax: 208-282-4847, E-mail: carstami@isu.edu.

Illinois Institute of Technology, Graduate College, College of Science and Letters, Department of Biological, Chemical and Physical Sciences, Chemistry Division, Chicago, IL 60616-3793. Offers analytical chemistry (M Ch); chemistry (M Chem, MS, PhD); materials and chemical synthesis (M Ch). Part-time and evening/weekend programs available. Postbaccalaureate distance learning degree programs offered (no on-campus study). Terminal master's awarded for partial completion of doctoral program. *Degree requirements:* For master's, comprehensive exam, thesis (for some programs); for doctorate, comprehensive exam, thesis/dissertation. *Entrance requirements:* For master's and doctorate, GRE General Test, minimum undergraduate GPA of 3.0. Additional exam requirements/recommendations for international students: Required—TOEFL (minimum score 550 paper-based; 213 computer-based; 80 iBT). Electronic applications accepted. *Expenses:* Tuition: Full-time $17,550; part-time $888 per credit hour. Required fees: $850; $7.50 per credit hour. One-time fee: $50 full-time. Full-time tuition and fees vary according to program. *Faculty research:* Organic synthesis for cancer-therapy, nano-materials for environmental/medical applications, single protein/cell functions and dynamics, polymer chemistry.

Illinois State University, Graduate School, College of Arts and Sciences, Department of Chemistry, Normal, IL 61790-2200. Offers MS. *Degree requirements:* For master's, thesis. *Entrance requirements:* For master's, GRE General Test, minimum GPA of 2.6 in last 60 hours of course work. *Faculty research:* Solid-state and solution behavior of lanthanide scorpionates and porphyrinoids; CAREER: Versatile Vanadium: biology, materials science and education through its diverse coordinator carbaporphyrins and other highly modified porphyrinoid systems; oxadiazines: structurally novel templates for catalytic asymmetric synthesis.

Indiana University Bloomington, University Graduate School, College of Arts and Sciences, Department of Chemistry, Bloomington, IN 47405-7000. Offers analytical chemistry (PhD); biological chemistry (PhD); chemistry (MAT); inorganic chemistry (PhD); physical chemistry (PhD). *Faculty:* 39 full-time (3 women). *Students:* 190 full-time (67 women), 1 (woman) part-time; includes 13 minority (4 African Americans, 1 American Indian/Alaska Native, 5 Asian Americans or Pacific Islanders, 3 Hispanic Americans), 66 international. Average age 26. 207 applicants, 60% accepted, 49 enrolled. In 2009, 10 master's, 20 doctorates awarded. Terminal master's awarded for partial completion of doctoral program. *Degree requirements:* For master's, thesis; for doctorate, thesis/dissertation. *Entrance requirements:* For master's and doctorate, GRE General Test, GRE Subject Test. Additional exam requirements/recommendations for international students: Required—TOEFL. *Application deadline:* For fall admission, 1/15 priority date for domestic students, 12/15 for international students; for spring admission, 9/1 priority date for domestic students, 9/1 for international students. Applications are processed on a rolling basis. Application fee: $55 ($65 for international students). *Financial support:* Fellowships with full tuition reimbursements, research assistantships with full tuition reimbursements, teaching assistantships with full tuition reimbursements, Federal Work-Study and institutionally sponsored loans available. *Faculty research:* Synthesis of complex natural products, organic reaction mechanisms, organic electrochemistry, transitive-metal chemistry, solid-state and surface chemistry. Total annual research expenditures: $7.7 million. *Unit head:* Jim Reilly, Chairperson, 812-855-6239, E-mail: chemchair@indiana.edu. *Application contact:* Martin Jarrold, Director of Graduate Admissions, 812-855-2069, E-mail: mfj@indiana.edu.

Indiana University of Pennsylvania, School of Graduate Studies and Research, College of Natural Sciences and Mathematics, Department of Chemistry, Program in Chemistry, Indiana, PA 15705-1087. Offers MA, MS. Part-time programs available. *Faculty:* 7 full-time (1 woman). *Students:* 9 full-time (3 women), 2 part-time (0 women), 5 international. Average age 31. 34 applicants, 32% accepted, 4 enrolled. In 2009, 4 master's awarded. *Degree requirements:* For master's, thesis optional. *Entrance requirements:* For master's, 2 letters of recommendation. Additional exam requirements/recommendations for international students: Required—TOEFL. *Application deadline:* For fall admission, 7/1 priority date for domestic students; for spring admission, 11/1 for domestic students. Applications are processed on a rolling basis. Application fee: $40. *Expenses:* Tuition, state resident: full-time $6666; part-time $370 per credit hour. Tuition, nonresident: full-time $10,666; part-time $593 per credit hour. Required fees: $813 per semester. *Financial support:* In 2009–10, 4 research assistantships with full and partial tuition reimbursements (averaging $6,360 per year) were awarded. Financial award application deadline: 3/15; financial award applicants required to submit FAFSA. *Unit head:* Dr. Keith Kyler, Graduate Coordinator, 724-357-5702, E-mail: keith.kyler@iup.edu. *Application contact:* Dr. Lawrence Kupchella, Graduate Coordinator, 724-357-5702, E-mail: lkup@iup.edu.

Indiana University–Purdue University Indianapolis, School of Science, Department of Chemistry, Indianapolis, IN 46202-2896. Offers MS, PhD, MD/PhD. Part-time and evening/weekend programs available. *Faculty:* 10 full-time (2 women). *Students:* 14 full-time (4 women), 29 part-time (14 women); includes 5 minority (2 African Americans, 3 Asian Americans or Pacific Islanders), 5 international. Average age 29. In 2009, 5 master's awarded. Terminal master's awarded for partial completion of doctoral program. *Degree requirements:* For master's, thesis (for some programs); for doctorate, thesis/dissertation. *Entrance requirements:* For master's and doctorate, minimum GPA of 3.0. Additional exam requirements/recommendations for international students: Required—TOEFL. *Application deadline:* Applications are processed on a rolling basis. Application fee: $50 ($60 for international students). *Financial support:* In 2009–10, 3 fellowships with partial tuition reimbursements (averaging $13,500 per year), 13 teaching assistantships with partial tuition reimbursements (averaging $17,440 per year) were awarded; research assistantships with partial tuition reimbursements, career-related internships or fieldwork, institutionally sponsored loans, tuition waivers (partial), and co-op positions also available. Financial award application deadline: 3/1. *Faculty research:* Analytical, biological, inorganic, organic, and physical chemistry. Total annual research expenditures: $1.6 million. *Application contact:* Eric Long, Information Contact, 317-274-6888, Fax: 317-274-4701, E-mail: long@chem.iupui.edu.

Instituto Tecnológico y de Estudios Superiores de Monterrey, Campus Monterrey, Graduate and Research Division, Program in Natural and Social Sciences, Monterrey, Mexico. Offers biotechnology (MS); chemistry (MS, PhD); communications (MS); education (MA). Part-time programs available. *Degree requirements:* For master's, one foreign language, thesis; for doctorate, one foreign language, thesis/dissertation. *Entrance requirements:* For master's, EXADEP; for doctorate, EXADEP, master's degree in related field. Additional exam requirements/recommendations for international students: Required—TOEFL. *Faculty research:* Cultural industries, mineral substances, bioremediation, food processing, CQ in industrial chemical processing.

Iowa State University of Science and Technology, Graduate College, College of Liberal Arts and Sciences, Department of Chemistry, Ames, IA 50011. Offers MS, PhD. *Faculty:* 32 full-time (6 women), 2 part-time/adjunct (1 woman). *Students:* 162 full-time (59 women), 1 (woman) part-time; includes 6 minority (2 African Americans, 3 Asian Americans or Pacific Islanders, 1 Hispanic American), 86 international. 65 applicants, 48% accepted, 30 enrolled. In 2009, 2 master's, 24 doctorates awarded. *Degree requirements:* For master's, thesis; for doctorate, thesis/dissertation. *Entrance requirements:* Additional exam requirements/recommendations for international students: Required—TOEFL (minimum score 550 paper-based; 80 iBT) or IELTS (minimum score 6.5). *Application deadline:* For fall admission, 2/1 priority date for domestic and international students. Application fee: $40 ($90 for international students). Electronic applications accepted. *Expenses:* Tuition, state resident: full-time $6716. Tuition, nonresident: full-time $8908. Tuition and fees vary according to course level, course load, program and student level. *Financial support:* In 2009–10, 88 research assistantships with full and partial tuition reimbursements (averaging $19,000 per year), 71 teaching assistantships with full and partial tuition reimbursements (averaging $19,000 per year) were awarded; fellowships, scholarships/grants, health care benefits, and unspecified assistantships also available. *Unit head:* Dr. Jacob Petrich, Chair, 515-294-7812, Fax: 515-294-0105, E-mail: chemgrad@iastate.edu. *Application contact:* Dr. Theresa Windus, Director of Graduate Education, 800-521-6134, E-mail: chemgrad@iastate.edu.

Jackson State University, Graduate School, School of Science and Technology, Department of Chemistry, Jackson, MS 39217. Offers MS, PhD. Part-time and evening/weekend programs available. *Degree requirements:* For master's, comprehensive exam, thesis; for doctorate, comprehensive exam, thesis/dissertation. *Entrance requirements:* For master's, GRE General Test; for doctorate, MAT. Additional exam requirements/recommendations for international students: Required—TOEFL. *Faculty research:* Electrochemical and spectroscopic studies on charge transfer and energy transfer processes, spectroscopy of trapped molecular ions, respirable mine dust.

The Johns Hopkins University, Zanvyl Krieger School of Arts and Sciences, Chemistry-Biology Interface Program, Baltimore, MD 21218-2699. Offers PhD. *Faculty:* 32 full-time (6 women). *Students:* 5 full-time (all women); includes 2 minority (1 African American, 1 Hispanic American). Average age 25. 77 applicants, 23% accepted, 3 enrolled. In 2009, 8 doctorates awarded. Terminal master's awarded for partial completion of doctoral program. *Degree requirements:* For doctorate, comprehensive exam, thesis/dissertation, 8 one-semester graduate courses, literature seminar, research proposal. *Entrance requirements:* For doctorate, GRE General Test, GRE Subject Test in biochemistry, cell and molecular biology, biology or chemistry (strongly recommended), 3 letters of recommendation, interview. *Application deadline:* For fall admission, 1/15 for domestic and international students. Applications are processed on a rolling basis. Application fee: $75. Electronic applications accepted. *Financial support:* Fellowships, teaching assistantships, Federal Work-Study, scholarships/grants, health care benefits, and unspecified assistantships available. Financial award application deadline: 4/15; financial award applicants required to submit FAFSA. *Faculty research:* Enzyme mechanisms; inhibitors, and metabolic pathways; DNA replication, damaged, and repair; using small molecules to probe signal transduction, gene regulation, angiogenesis, and other biological processes, synthetic methods and medicinal chemistry; synthetic modeling of metalloenzymes. *Unit head:* Dr. Marc Greenberg, Director, 410-516-8095, Fax: 410-516-7044, E-mail: mgreenberg@jhu.edu. *Application contact:* Lauren Riker, Academic Coordinator, 410-516-7427, Fax: 410-516-8420, E-mail: lriker@jhu.edu.

The Johns Hopkins University, Zanvyl Krieger School of Arts and Sciences, Department of Chemistry, Baltimore, MD 21218-2699. Offers PhD. *Faculty:* 23 full-time (4 women). *Students:* 111 full-time (38 women); includes 7 minority (3 African Americans, 4 Asian Americans or Pacific Islanders), 32 international. Average age 23. 158 applicants, 14% accepted, 22 enrolled. In 2009, 15 doctorates awarded. Terminal master's awarded for partial completion of doctoral program. *Degree requirements:* For doctorate, comprehensive exam, thesis/dissertation, 8 one-semester graduate courses, literature seminar. *Entrance requirements:* For doctorate, GRE General Test, GRE Subject Test. Additional exam requirements/recommendations for international students: Required—TOEFL (minimum score 600 paper-based; 250 computer-based), IELTS. *Application deadline:* For fall admission, 1/5 for domestic and international students. Applications are processed on a rolling basis. Application fee: $60. Electronic applications accepted. *Financial support:* Fellowships, teaching assistantships, Federal Work-Study, scholarships/grants, health care benefits, and unspecified assistantships available. Financial award application deadline: 4/15; financial award applicants required to submit FAFSA. *Faculty research:* Experimental physical, biophysical, inorganic/materials, organic/bioorganic theoretical. Total annual research expenditures: $6.6 million. *Unit head:* Dr. John Toscano, Chair, 410-516-6534, E-mail: jtoscano@jhu.edu. *Application contact:* Jean Goodwin, Academic Program Coordinator, 410-516-7791, Fax: 410-516-8420, E-mail: jeang@jhu.edu.

Kansas State University, Graduate School, College of Arts and Sciences, Department of Chemistry, Manhattan, KS 66506. Offers analytical chemistry (MS); biological chemistry (MS); chemistry (PhD); inorganic chemistry (MS); materials chemistry (MS); organic chemistry (MS); physical chemistry (MS). *Faculty:* 16 full-time (2 women), 2 part-time/adjunct (0 women). *Students:* 66 full-time (22 women); includes 2 minority (1 African American, 1 Asian American or Pacific Islander), 54 international. Average age 28. 75 applicants, 23% accepted, 7 enrolled. In 2009, 3 master's, 11 doctorates awarded. Terminal master's awarded for partial completion of doctoral program. *Degree requirements:* For master's, thesis; for doctorate, thesis/dissertation. *Entrance requirements:* For master's and doctorate, GRE, minimum GPA of 3.0. Additional exam requirements/recommendations for international students: Required—TOEFL (minimum score 550 paper-based; 213 computer-based). *Application deadline:* For fall admission, 2/1 priority date for domestic and international students; for spring admission, 8/1 priority date for domestic and international students. Applications are processed on a rolling basis. Application fee: $40 ($55 for international students). Electronic applications accepted. *Financial support:* In 2009–10, 41 research assistantships (averaging $15,040 per year), 22 teaching assistantships with full tuition reimbursements (averaging $15,600 per year) were awarded; institutionally sponsored loans and scholarships/grants also available. Support available to part-time students. Financial award application deadline: 3/1; financial award applicants required to submit FAFSA. *Faculty research:* Inorganic chemistry, organic and biological chemistry, analytical chemistry, physical chemistry, materials chemistry and nanotechnology. Total annual research expenditures: $1.9 million. *Unit head:* Eric Maatta, Head, 785-532-6665, Fax: 785-532-6666, E-mail: eam@ksu.edu. *Application contact:* Christer Aakeroy, Director, 785-532-6096, Fax: 785-532-6666, E-mail: aakeroy@ksu.edu.

Kent State University, College of Arts and Sciences, Department of Chemistry, Kent, OH 44242-0001. Offers analytical chemistry (MS, PhD); biochemistry (MS, PhD); chemistry (MA, MS, PhD); inorganic chemistry (MS, PhD); organic chemistry (MS, PhD); physical chemistry (MS, PhD). Terminal master's awarded for partial completion of doctoral program. *Degree requirements:* For master's, comprehensive exam, thesis; for doctorate, comprehensive exam, thesis/dissertation. *Entrance requirements:* For master's and doctorate, placement exam, GRE General Test, GRE Subject Test (recommended), minimum GPA of 2.75. Additional exam requirements/recommendations for international students: Required—TOEFL (minimum score 575 paper-based; 230 computer-based). Electronic applications accepted. *Faculty research:* Biological chemistry, materials chemistry, molecular spectroscopy.

See Close-Up on page 101.

Lakehead University, Graduate Studies, Faculty of Social Sciences and Humanities, Department of Chemistry, Thunder Bay, ON P7B 5E1, Canada. Offers M Sc. Part-time and evening/weekend programs available. *Degree requirements:* For master's, thesis, oral examination. *Entrance requirements:* For master's, minimum B+ average. Additional exam requirements/recommendations for international students: Required—TOEFL. *Faculty research:* Physical inorganic chemistry, photochemistry, physical chemistry.

Lamar University, College of Graduate Studies, College of Arts and Sciences, Department of Chemistry and Physics, Beaumont, TX 77710. Offers chemistry (MS). Part-time programs available. *Faculty:* 6 full-time (2 women). *Students:* 27 full-time (16 women), 10 part-time (2 women), 18 international. Average age 24. 41 applicants, 34% accepted, 14 enrolled. In 2009, 5 master's awarded. *Degree requirements:* For master's, thesis, practicum. *Entrance requirements:* For master's, GRE General Test, minimum GPA of 2.5 in last 60 hours of course work. Additional exam requirements/recommendations for international students: Required—TOEFL, TWE. *Application deadline:* For fall admission, 8/1 for domestic students, 7/1 for international students; for spring admission, 12/1 for domestic students, 11/1 for international students. Applications are processed on a rolling basis. Application fee: $25 ($50 for international students). *Financial support:* In 2009–10, 6 students received support, including 5 teaching assistantships with partial tuition reimbursements available (averaging $9,000 per year); tuition waivers (partial) and unspecified assistantships also available. Financial award application deadline: 4/1. *Faculty research:* Environmental chemistry, surface chemistry, polymer chemistry, organic synthesis, computational chemistry. *Unit head:* Dr. Richard S. Lumpkin, Chair, 409-880-8267, Fax: 409-880-8270, E-mail: lumpkines@hal.lamar.edu. *Application contact:* Dr. Paul Bernazzani, Graduate Advisor, 409-880-8272, Fax: 409-880-8270, E-mail: bernazzapx@hal.lamar.edu.

Laurentian University, School of Graduate Studies and Research, Programme in Chemistry and Biochemistry, Sudbury, ON P3E 2C6, Canada. Offers analytical chemistry (M Sc); biochemistry (M Sc); environmental chemistry (M Sc); organic chemistry (M Sc); physical/theoretical chemistry (M Sc). Part-time programs available. *Degree requirements:* For master's, thesis or alternative. *Entrance requirements:* For master's, honors degree with minimum second class. *Faculty research:* Cell cycle checkpoints, kinetic modeling, toxicology to metal stress, quantum chemistry, biogeochemistry metal speciation.

Lehigh University, College of Arts and Sciences, Department of Chemistry, Bethlehem, PA 18015. Offers chemistry (MS, PhD); polymer science and engineering (MS, PhD). Part-time programs available. Postbaccalaureate distance learning degree programs offered (no on-campus study). *Faculty:* 15 full-time (2 women), 1 part-time/adjunct (0 women). *Students:* 36 full-time (17 women), 83 part-time (40 women); includes 15 minority (2 African Americans, 1 American Indian/Alaska Native, 6 Asian Americans or Pacific Islanders, 6 Hispanic Americans), 12 international. Average age 29. 92 applicants, 45% accepted, 35 enrolled. In 2009, 31 master's, 2 doctorates awarded. Terminal master's awarded for partial completion of doctoral program. *Degree requirements:* For master's, comprehensive exam, thesis; for doctorate, comprehensive exam, thesis/dissertation. *Entrance requirements:* Additional exam requirements/recommendations for international students: Required—TOEFL (minimum score 230 computer-based). *Application deadline:* For fall admission, 1/15 priority date for domestic and international students. Applications are processed on a rolling basis. Application fee: $65. Electronic applications accepted. *Financial support:* In 2009–10, 3 fellowships with full tuition reimbursements (averaging $20,000 per year), 8 research assistantships with full tuition reimbursements (averaging $20,000 per year), 19 teaching assistantships with full tuition reimbursements (averaging $20,000 per year) were awarded; career-related internships or fieldwork, Federal Work-Study, institutionally sponsored loans, scholarships/grants, tuition waivers (full and partial), and unspecified assistantships also available. Support available to part-time students. Financial award application deadline: 1/15. *Faculty research:* Materials chemistry, biological chemistry, surface chemistry, nano science. Total annual research expenditures: $3.3 million. *Unit head:* Prof. Robert A. Flowers, Professor/Chair, 610-758-3470, Fax: 610-758-6536, E-mail: rof2@lehigh.edu. *Application contact:* Dr. Rebecca Miller, Graduate Coordinator, 610-758-3471, Fax: 610-758-6536, E-mail: inluchem@lehigh.edu.

Long Island University, Brooklyn Campus, Richard L. Conolly College of Liberal Arts and Sciences, Department of Chemistry, Brooklyn, NY 11201-8423. Offers MS. Part-time and evening/weekend programs available. *Degree requirements:* For master's, thesis or alternative. *Entrance requirements:* For master's, 2 letters of recommendation. Additional exam requirements/recommendations for international students: Required—TOEFL (minimum score 500 paper-based; 173 computer-based). Electronic applications accepted. *Faculty research:* Clinical chemistry, free radicals, heats of hydrogenation.

Louisiana State University and Agricultural and Mechanical College, Graduate School, College of Basic Sciences, Department of Chemistry, Baton Rouge, LA 70803. Offers MS, PhD. Part-time programs available. *Faculty:* 29 full-time (6 women), 1 (woman) part-time/adjunct. *Students:* 158 full-time (64 women), 6 part-time (2 women); includes 33 minority (30 African Americans, 3 Asian Americans or Pacific Islanders), 85 international. Average age 29. 183 applicants, 27% accepted, 28 enrolled. In 2009, 6 master's, 23 doctorates awarded. Terminal master's awarded for partial completion of doctoral program. *Degree requirements:* For master's, thesis (for some programs); for doctorate, thesis/dissertation, general exam. *Entrance requirements:* For master's and doctorate, GRE General Test, minimum GPA of 3.0. Additional exam requirements/recommendations for international students: Required—TOEFL (minimum score 550 paper-based; 213 computer-based; 79 iBT) or IELTS (minimum score 6.5). *Application deadline:* For fall admission, 3/1 priority date for domestic students, 5/15 for international students; for spring admission, 8/1 for domestic students, 10/15 for international students. Applications are processed on a rolling basis. Application fee: $25. Electronic applications accepted. *Financial support:* In 2009–10, 164 students received support, including 32 fellowships with full tuition reimbursements available (averaging $27,536 per year), 66 research assistantships with full and partial tuition reimbursements available (averaging $22,136 per year), 78 teaching assistantships with full and partial tuition reimbursements available (averaging $16,409 per year); career-related internships or fieldwork, Federal Work-Study, scholarships/grants, traineeships, and unspecified assistantships also available. Support available to part-time students. Financial award application deadline: 7/1; financial award applicants required to submit FAFSA. *Faculty research:* Materials, biological, environmental. Total annual research expenditures: $5.7 million. *Unit head:* Dr. Andrew Maverick, Chair, 225-578-3462, Fax: 225-578-3458, E-mail: maverick@lsu.edu. *Application contact:* Dr. John Pojman, Director of Graduate Studies, 225-578-7202, Fax: 225-578-3458, E-mail: japojman@lsu.edu.

Louisiana Tech University, Graduate School, College of Engineering and Science, Department of Chemistry, Ruston, LA 71272. Offers MS. Part-time programs available. *Degree requirements:* For master's, thesis. *Entrance requirements:* For master's, GRE General Test, minimum GPA of 3.0 in last 60 hours. Additional exam requirements/recommendations for international students: Required—TOEFL. *Faculty research:* Vibrational spectroscopy, quantum studies of chemical reactions, enzyme kinetics, synthesis of transition metal compounds, NMR spectrometry.

Loyola University Chicago, Graduate School, Department of Chemistry, Chicago, IL 60660. Offers MS, PhD. Part-time and evening/weekend programs available. *Faculty:* 14 full-time (2 women). *Students:* 28 full-time (16 women), 6 part-time (4 women); includes 6 minority (2 African Americans, 3 Asian Americans or Pacific Islanders, 1 Hispanic American), 3 international. Average age 31. 49 applicants, 51% accepted, 13 enrolled. In 2009, 8 master's, 7 doctorates awarded. Terminal master's awarded for partial completion of doctoral program. *Degree requirements:* For master's, thesis (for some programs); for doctorate, comprehensive exam, thesis/dissertation. *Entrance requirements:* For master's, GRE General Test, GRE Subject Test; for doctorate, GRE General Test, GRE Subject Test, entrance exams. Additional exam requirements/recommendations for international students: Required—TOEFL (minimum score 550 paper-based; 213 computer-based). *Application deadline:* For fall admission, 8/1 priority date for domestic students; for spring admission, 12/1 for domestic students. Applications are processed on a rolling basis. Application fee: $50. Electronic applications accepted. *Expenses:* Tuition: Full-time $14,220; part-time $790 per credit hour. Required fees: $60 per semester hour. Tuition and fees vary according to program. *Financial support:* In 2009–10, 19 students received support, including 3 fellowships with full tuition reimbursements available (averaging $16,000 per year), 16 teaching assistantships with full tuition reimbursements available (averaging $18,000 per year); research assistantships with full and partial tuition reimbursements available, Federal Work-Study, scholarships/grants, traineeships, and unspecified assistantships also available. Financial award application deadline: 2/1; financial award applicants required to submit FAFSA. *Faculty research:* Magnetic resonance of membrane/protein systems, organometallic catalysis, novel synthesis of natural products. Total annual research expenditures: $682,510. *Unit head:* Dr. Richard Holz, Chair, 773-508-7045, Fax: 773-508-3086, E-mail: rholz1@luc.edu. *Application contact:* Stacey N. Lind, Graduate Program Coordinator, 773-508-3104, Fax: 773-508-3086, E-mail: slind@luc.edu.

Marquette University, Graduate School, College of Arts and Sciences, Department of Chemistry, Milwaukee, WI 53201-1881. Offers analytical chemistry (MS, PhD); bioanalytical chemistry (MS, PhD); biophysical chemistry (MS, PhD); chemical physics (MS, PhD); inorganic chemistry (MS, PhD); organic chemistry (MS, PhD); physical chemistry (MS, PhD). Part-time programs available. *Faculty:* 23 full-time (10 women), 1 part-time/adjunct (0 women). *Students:* 34 full-time (9 women), 10 part-time (4 women); includes 4 minority (1 African American, 2 Asian Americans or Pacific Islanders, 1 Hispanic American), 33 international. Average age 29. 23 applicants, 83% accepted, 8 enrolled. In 2009, 4 master's, 5 doctorates awarded. Terminal master's awarded for partial completion of doctoral program. *Degree requirements:* For master's, comprehensive exam; for doctorate, thesis/dissertation, cumulative exams. *Entrance requirements:* For master's and doctorate, GRE Subject Test. Additional exam requirements/recommendations for international students: Required—TOEFL. Application fee: $40. *Financial support:* In 2009–10, 3 research assistantships, 27 teaching assistantships were awarded; fellowships, Federal Work-Study, institutionally sponsored loans, scholarships/grants, and tuition waivers (full and partial) also available. Support available to part-time students. Financial award application deadline: 2/15. *Faculty research:* Inorganic complexes, laser Raman spectroscopy, organic synthesis, chemical dynamics, biophysiology. *Unit head:* Dr. Jeanne Hossenlopp, Chair, 414-288-3537, Fax: 414-288-7066. *Application contact:* Dr. Mark Steinmetz, Director of Graduate Studies, 414-288-7374, Fax: 414-288-7066.

Marshall University, Academic Affairs Division, College of Science, Department of Chemistry, Huntington, WV 25755. Offers MS. *Faculty:* 7 full-time (1 woman). *Students:* 8 full-time (3 women), 3 part-time (2 women), 4 international. Average age 25. In 2009, 2 master's awarded. *Degree requirements:* For master's, thesis. Application fee: $40. *Financial support:* Career-related internships or fieldwork available. *Unit head:* Dr. Michael Castellani, Chairperson, 304-696-6486, E-mail: castella@marshall.edu. *Application contact:* Dr. John Hubbard, Information Contact, 304-696-2430, Fax: 304-746-1902, E-mail: hubbard@marshall.edu.

Massachusetts College of Pharmacy and Health Sciences, Graduate Studies, Program in Medicinal Chemistry, Boston, MA 02115-5896. Offers MS, PhD. *Students:* 1 (woman) full-time, 4 part-time (1 woman); includes 1 minority (Asian American or Pacific Islander), 2 international. Average age 29. 14 applicants, 57% accepted, 1 enrolled. In 2009, 1 doctorate awarded. Terminal master's awarded for partial completion of doctoral program. *Degree requirements:* For master's, thesis, oral defense of thesis; for doctorate, one foreign language, comprehensive exam, thesis/dissertation, oral defense of dissertation, qualifying exam. *Entrance requirements:* For master's and doctorate, GRE General Test, minimum GPA of 3.0. Additional exam requirements/recommendations for international students: Required—TOEFL (minimum score 550 paper-based; 213 computer-based; 79 iBT). *Application deadline:* For fall admission, 2/1 priority date for domestic and international students. Application fee: $70. Electronic applications accepted. *Expenses:* Tuition: Full-time $28,000; part-time $875 per credit hour. Required fees: $750; $190 per semester. Part-time tuition and fees vary according to course load, campus/location, program and student level. *Financial support:* Fellowships with partial tuition reimbursements, research assistantships with partial tuition reimbursements, teaching assistantships with full tuition reimbursements, tuition waivers (partial) and unspecified assistantships available. Financial award application deadline: 3/15. *Faculty research:* Analytical chemistry, medicinal chemistry, organic chemistry, neurochemistry. *Unit head:* Dr. Ahmed Mehanna, Professor, Medicinal Chemistry, 617-732-2955, E-mail: ahmed.mehanna@mcphs.edu. *Application contact:* Tara Hennesey, Coordinator of Graduate Admission, 617-732-2850, E-mail: admissions@mcphs.edu.

Massachusetts Institute of Technology, School of Science, Department of Chemistry, Cambridge, MA 02139-4307. Offers biological chemistry (PhD, Sc D); inorganic chemistry (PhD, Sc D); organic chemistry (PhD, Sc D); physical chemistry (PhD, Sc D). *Faculty:* 29 full-time (7 women). *Students:* 219 full-time (79 women); includes 39 minority (4 African Americans, 27 Asian Americans or Pacific Islanders, 8 Hispanic Americans), 62 international. Average age 26. 548 applicants, 20% accepted, 19 enrolled. In 2009, 43 doctorates awarded. *Degree requirements:* For doctorate, comprehensive exam, thesis/dissertation, 2 terms as a teaching assistant. *Entrance requirements:* For doctorate, GRE General Test. Additional exam requirements/recommendations for international students: Required—IELTS (minimum score 7); Recommended—TOEFL (minimum score 600 paper-based; 250 computer-based). *Application deadline:* For fall admission, 12/15 for domestic and international students. Application fee: $75. Electronic applications accepted. *Financial support:* In 2009–10, 219 students received support, including 57 fellowships with tuition reimbursements available (averaging $34,547 per year), 132 research assistantships with tuition reimbursements available (averaging $29,403 per year), 27 teaching assistantships with tuition reimbursements available (averaging $30,452 per year); Federal Work-Study, institutionally sponsored loans, scholarships/grants, health care benefits, and unspecified assistantships also available. *Faculty research:* Synthetic organic and inorganic chemistry, biomolecular reactions and structure, multidimensional spectroscopy and chemical dynamics, inorganic, organometallic, organic chemical catalysis, materials chemistry including nanoscience and polymers. Total annual research expenditures: $29.1 million. *Unit head:* Prof. Timothy M. Swager, Head, 617-253-1803, Fax: 617-258-7500. *Application contact:* Graduate Administrator, 617-253-1845, Fax: 617-258-0241, E-mail: chemgradeducation@mit.edu.

McGill University, Faculty of Graduate and Postdoctoral Studies, Faculty of Science, Department of Chemistry, Montréal, QC H3A 2T5, Canada. Offers chemical biology (M Sc, PhD); chemistry (M Sc, PhD).

McMaster University, School of Graduate Studies, Faculty of Science, Department of Chemistry, Hamilton, ON L8S 4M2, Canada. Offers analytical chemistry (M Sc, PhD); chemical physics (M Sc, PhD); chemistry (M Sc, PhD); inorganic chemistry (M Sc, PhD); organic chemistry (M Sc, PhD); physical chemistry (M Sc, PhD); polymer chemistry (M Sc, PhD). Part-time programs available. Terminal master's awarded for partial completion of doctoral program. *Degree requirements:* For master's, thesis; for doctorate, comprehensive exam, thesis/dissertation. *Entrance requirements:* For master's, minimum B+ average. Additional exam requirements/recommendations for international students: Required—TOEFL (minimum score 550 paper-based; 213 computer-based).

McNeese State University, Doré School of Graduate Studies, College of Science, Department of Chemistry, Program in Environmental and Chemical Sciences, Lake Charles, LA 70609. Offers chemistry (MS); chemistry education (MS). Evening/weekend programs available. *Degree requirements:* For master's, comprehensive exam, thesis or alternative. *Entrance requirements:* For master's, GRE.

Memorial University of Newfoundland, School of Graduate Studies, Department of Chemistry, St. John's, NL A1C 5S7, Canada. Offers chemistry (M Sc, PhD); instrumental analysis (M Sc). Part-time programs available. *Degree requirements:* For master's, thesis, research seminar, American Chemical Society Exam; for doctorate, comprehensive exam, thesis/dissertation, seminars, oral thesis defense, American Chemical Society Exam. *Entrance requirements:* For master's, B Sc or honors degree in chemistry (preferred); for doctorate, master's degree in chemistry or honors bachelor's degree. Electronic applications accepted. *Faculty research:* Analytical/environmental chemistry; medicinal electrochemistry; inorganic, marine, organic, physical, and theoretical/computational chemistry, environmental science and instrumental analysis.

Chemistry

Miami University, Graduate School, College of Arts and Sciences, Department of Chemistry and Biochemistry, Oxford, OH 45056. Offers MS, PhD. *Students:* 66 full-time (29 women), 2 part-time (0 women); includes 4 minority (2 African Americans, 1 Asian American or Pacific Islander, 1 Hispanic American), 30 international. *Entrance requirements:* For master's, minimum undergraduate GPA of 3.0 during previous 2 years or 2.75 overall; for doctorate, minimum undergraduate GPA of 2.75, 3.0 graduate. Additional exam requirements/recommendations for international students: Required—TOEFL. *Application deadline:* Applications are processed on a rolling basis. Application fee: $50. Electronic applications accepted. *Expenses:* Tuition, state resident: full-time $11,280. Tuition, nonresident: full-time $24,912. Required fees: $516. *Financial support:* Fellowships with full tuition reimbursements, research assistantships with full tuition reimbursements, teaching assistantships with full tuition reimbursements, Federal Work-Study, institutionally sponsored loans, tuition waivers (full), and unspecified assistantships available. Financial award application deadline: 3/1; financial award applicants required to submit FAFSA. *Unit head:* Dr. Chris Makaroff, Chair, 513-529-1659, E-mail: makaroca@muohio.edu. *Application contact:* Dr. Michael Crowder, Chair, Graduate Admissions Committee, 513-529-7274, E-mail: crowdermw@muohio.edu.

Michigan State University, The Graduate School, College of Natural Science, Department of Chemistry, East Lansing, MI 48824. Offers chemical physics (PhD); chemistry (MS, PhD); chemistry-environmental toxicology (PhD); computational chemistry (MS). *Entrance requirements:* Additional exam requirements/recommendations for international students: Required—TOEFL. Electronic applications accepted. *Faculty research:* Analytical chemistry, inorganic and organic chemistry, nuclear chemistry, physical chemistry, theoretical and computational chemistry.

Michigan State University, National Superconducting Cyclotron Laboratory, East Lansing, MI 48824. Offers chemistry (PhD); physics (PhD).

Michigan Technological University, Graduate School, College of Sciences and Arts, Department of Chemistry, Houghton, MI 49931. Offers MS, PhD. Part-time programs available. Terminal master's awarded for partial completion of doctoral program. *Degree requirements:* For master's, thesis; for doctorate, comprehensive exam, thesis/dissertation. *Entrance requirements:* Additional exam requirements/recommendations for international students: Required—TOEFL (minimum score 550 paper-based; 213 computer-based). Electronic applications accepted. *Faculty research:* Inorganic chemistry, physical/theoretical chemistry, bio/organic chemistry, polymer/materials chemistry, analytical/environmental chemistry.

Middle Tennessee State University, College of Graduate Studies, College of Basic and Applied Sciences, Department of Chemistry, Murfreesboro, TN 37132. Offers MS, DA. Part-time and evening/weekend programs available. Postbaccalaureate distance learning degree programs offered. *Faculty:* 21 full-time (8 women). *Students:* 31 part-time (12 women); includes 14 minority (5 African Americans, 9 Asian Americans or Pacific Islanders). Average age 28. 26 applicants, 42% accepted, 11 enrolled. In 2009, 4 master's, 1 doctorate awarded. *Degree requirements:* For master's, one foreign language, comprehensive exam, thesis. *Entrance requirements:* For master's and doctorate, GRE General Test. Additional exam requirements/recommendations for international students: Required—TOEFL (minimum score 525 paper-based; 195 computer-based; 71 iBT) or IELTS (minimum score 6). *Application deadline:* For fall admission, 6/1 for domestic and international students. Applications are processed on a rolling basis. Application fee: $25 ($30 for international students). Electronic applications accepted. *Expenses:* Tuition, state resident: full-time $4404. Tuition, nonresident: full-time $10,956. *Financial support:* In 2009–10, 25 students received support. Institutionally sponsored loans available. Support available to part-time students. Financial award application deadline: 5/1; financial award applicants required to submit FAFSA. *Faculty research:* Chemical education; computational chemistry and visualization; materials science and surface modifications; biochemistry, antibiotics and leukemia; environmental chemistry and toxicology. *Unit head:* Dr. Earl F. Pearson, Chair, 615-898-2958, Fax: 615-898-5182, E-mail: pearson@mtsu.edu. *Application contact:* Dr. Michael Allen, Dean and Vice Provost for Research, 615-898-2840, Fax: 615-904-8020, E-mail: mallen@mtsu.edu.

Mississippi College, Graduate School, College of Arts and Sciences, School of Science and Mathematics, Department of Chemistry and Biochemistry, Clinton, MS 39058. Offers MCS, MS. Part-time programs available. *Faculty:* 2 full-time (0 women), 1 (woman) part-time/adjunct. *Students:* 6 full-time (1 woman), 7 part-time (3 women), 12 international. Average age 23. In 2009, 4 master's awarded. *Degree requirements:* For master's, comprehensive exam, thesis (for some programs). *Entrance requirements:* For master's, GRE. Additional exam requirements/recommendations for international students: Recommended—IELTS. *Application deadline:* For fall admission, 8/15 priority date for domestic students. Applications are processed on a rolling basis. Application fee: $30. Electronic applications accepted. *Expenses:* Tuition: Part-time $452 per credit hour. Required fees: $101 per semester. Tuition and fees vary according to degree level, campus/location, program and student level. *Financial support:* Federal Work-Study and unspecified assistantships available. Support available to part-time students. Financial award applicants required to submit FAFSA. *Unit head:* Dr. Jerry Cannon, Chair, 601-925-3425, E-mail: cannon@mc.edu. *Application contact:* Elnora Lewis, Secretary, 601-925-3225, Fax: 601-925-3889, E-mail: lewis09@mc.edu.

Mississippi State University, College of Arts and Sciences, Department of Chemistry, Mississippi State, MS 39762. Offers chemistry (MS, PhD); interdisciplinary sciences (MA), including biological sciences, chemistry. *Faculty:* 11 full-time (0 women), 1 part-time/adjunct (0 women). *Students:* 46 full-time (13 women), 4 part-time (2 women); includes 5 minority (4 African Americans, 1 Asian American or Pacific Islander), 37 international. Average age 30. 121 applicants, 13% accepted, 15 enrolled. In 2009, 3 doctorates awarded. Terminal master's awarded for partial completion of doctoral program. *Degree requirements:* For master's, thesis, comprehensive oral or written exam; for doctorate, thesis/dissertation, comprehensive oral or written exam. *Entrance requirements:* For master's, minimum GPA of 2.75 on last two years of undergraduate courses; for doctorate, minimum GPA of 2.75. Additional exam requirements/recommendations for international students: Required—TOEFL (minimum score 475 paper-based; 153 computer-based). *Application deadline:* For fall admission, 7/1 for domestic students, 5/1 for international students; for spring admission, 11/1 for domestic students, 9/1 for international students. Applications are processed on a rolling basis. Application fee: $40. Electronic applications accepted. *Expenses:* Tuition, state resident: full-time $2575.50; part-time $286.25 per credit hour. Tuition, nonresident: full-time $6510; part-time $723.50 per credit hour. Tuition and fees vary according to course load. *Financial support:* In 2009–10, 9 research assistantships with full tuition reimbursements (averaging $12,610 per year), 37 teaching assistantships with full tuition reimbursements (averaging $13,900 per year) were awarded; Federal Work-Study, institutionally sponsored loans, scholarships/grants, and unspecified assistantships also available. Financial award applicants required to submit FAFSA. *Faculty research:* Spectroscopy, fluorometry, organic and inorganic synthesis, electrochemistry. Total annual research expenditures: $4.5 million. *Unit head:* Dr. Edwin A. Lewis, Department Head, 662-325-3584, Fax: 662-325-1618, E-mail: elewis@chemistry.msstate.edu. *Application contact:* Dr. Stephen Foster, Graduate Coordinator, 662-325-8854, E-mail: grad@chemistry.msstate.edu.

Missouri State University, Graduate College, College of Natural and Applied Sciences, Department of Chemistry, Springfield, MO 65897. Offers chemistry (MS); natural and applied science (MNAS), including chemistry (MNAS, MS Ed); secondary education (MS Ed), including chemistry (MNAS, MS Ed). Part-time programs available. *Faculty:* 14 full-time (1 woman). *Students:* 7 full-time (4 women), 9 part-time (3 women), 1 international. Average age 28. 10 applicants, 90% accepted, 5 enrolled. In 2009, 3 master's awarded. *Degree requirements:* For master's, comprehensive exam, thesis. *Entrance requirements:* For master's, GRE General Test (MS, MNAS), minimum undergraduate GPA of 3.0 (MS and MNAS), 9-12 teacher certification (MS Ed). Additional exam requirements/recommendations for international students: Required—TOEFL (minimum score 550 paper-based; 213 computer-based; 79 iBT). *Application deadline:* For fall admission, 7/20 priority date for domestic students, 5/1 for international students; for spring admission, 12/20 priority date for domestic students, 9/1 for international students. Applications are processed on a rolling basis. Application fee: $35 ($50 for international students). Electronic applications accepted. *Expenses:* Tuition, state resident: full-time $3852; part-time $214 per credit hour. Tuition, nonresident: full-time $7524; part-time $418 per credit hour. Required fees: $696; $172 per semester. Tuition and fees vary according to course level, course load, degree level and program. *Financial support:* In 2009–10, 1 research assistantship with full tuition reimbursement (averaging $9,730 per year), 9 teaching assistantships with full tuition reimbursements (averaging $9,730 per year) were awarded; Federal Work-Study, institutionally sponsored loans, scholarships/grants, and unspecified assistantships also available. Financial award application deadline: 3/31; financial award applicants required to submit FAFSA. *Faculty research:* Polyethylene glycol derivatives, electrochemiluminescence of environmental systems, enzymology, environmental organic pollutants, DNA repair via NMR. *Unit head:* Dr. Alan Schick, Department Head, 417-836-5506, Fax: 417-836-5507, E-mail: chemistry@missouristate.edu. *Application contact:* Eric Eckert, Coordinator of Admissions and Recruitment, 417-836-5331, Fax: 417-836-6200, E-mail: ericeckert@missouristate.edu.

Missouri University of Science and Technology, Graduate School, Department of Chemistry, Rolla, MO 65409. Offers MS, MST, PhD. Terminal master's awarded for partial completion of doctoral program. *Degree requirements:* For doctorate, one foreign language, thesis/dissertation. *Entrance requirements:* For master's, GRE (minimum score 600 quantitative, 3 writing), minimum GPA of 3.0; for doctorate, GRE (minimum score: quantitative 600, writing 3.5), minimum GPA of 3.0. Additional exam requirements/recommendations for international students: Required—TOEFL (minimum score 550 paper-based; 213 computer-based). Electronic applications accepted. *Faculty research:* Structure and properties of materials; bioanalytical, environmental, and polymer chemistry.

Montana State University, College of Graduate Studies, College of Letters and Science, Department of Chemistry and Biochemistry, Bozeman, MT 59717. Offers biochemistry (MS, PhD); chemistry (MS, PhD). Part-time programs available. *Faculty:* 16 full-time (3 women), 11 part-time/adjunct (6 women). *Students:* 1 full-time (0 women), 68 part-time (22 women); includes 1 minority (Asian American or Pacific Islander), 12 international. Average age 27. 1 applicant, 100% accepted, 0 enrolled. In 2009, 2 master's, 4 doctorates awarded. *Degree requirements:* For master's, comprehensive exam, thesis (for some programs); for doctorate, comprehensive exam, thesis/dissertation. *Entrance requirements:* For master's, GRE General Test, letters of recommendation; for doctorate, GRE General Test, transcripts, letters of recommendation. Additional exam requirements/recommendations for international students: Required—TOEFL (minimum score 550 paper-based; 213 computer-based). *Application deadline:* For fall admission, 7/15 priority date for domestic students, 5/15 priority date for international students; for spring admission, 12/1 priority date for domestic students, 10/1 priority date for international students. Applications are processed on a rolling basis. Application fee: $30. Electronic applications accepted. *Expenses:* Tuition, state resident: full-time $5635; part-time $3492 per year. Tuition, nonresident: full-time $17,212; part-time $7865.10 per year. Required fees: $1441.05; $153.15 per credit. Tuition and fees vary according to course load and program. *Financial support:* In 2009–10, 68 students received support, including 5 fellowships with tuition reimbursements available (averaging $30,000 per year), 28 research assistantships with tuition reimbursements available (averaging $22,000 per year), 35 teaching assistantships with tuition reimbursements available (averaging $22,000 per year). Financial award application deadline: 3/1; financial award applicants required to submit FAFSA. *Faculty research:* Structural biology and proteomics, ultrafast optical spectroscopy and gas-surface dynamics, nanomaterials, natural products chemistry and organic synthesis, metals in biology. Total annual research expenditures: $10 million. *Unit head:* Dr. David Singel, Interim Department Head, 406-994-3960, Fax: 406-994-5407, E-mail: rchds@montana.edu. *Application contact:* Dr. Carl A. Fox, Vice Provost for Graduate Education, 406-994-4145, Fax: 406-994-7433, E-mail: gradstudy@montana.edu.

Montclair State University, The Graduate School, College of Science and Mathematics, Department of Chemistry and Biochemistry, Montclair, NJ 07043-1624. Offers chemical business (MS); chemistry (MS), including biochemistry; MS/MBA. Part-time and evening/weekend programs available. *Faculty:* 14 full-time (3 women), 3 part-time/adjunct (2 women). *Students:* 10 full-time (2 women), 23 part-time (13 women). Average age 28. 16 applicants, 56% accepted, 7 enrolled. In 2009, 8 master's awarded. *Degree requirements:* For master's, comprehensive exam. *Entrance requirements:* For master's, GRE General Test, 24 credits of course work in undergraduate chemistry, 2 letters of recommendation. Additional exam requirements/recommendations for international students: Required—TOEFL (minimum score 83 computer-based), or IELTS. *Application deadline:* For fall admission, 6/1 for international students; for spring admission, 10/1 for international students. Applications are processed on a rolling basis. Application fee: $60. Electronic applications accepted. *Expenses:* Tuition, area resident: Part-time $486.74 per credit. Tuition, state resident: part-time $486.74 per credit. Tuition, nonresident: part-time $751.34 per credit. Tuition and fees vary according to degree level and program. *Financial support:* In 2009–10, 6 research assistantships with full tuition reimbursements (averaging $7,000 per year) were awarded; Federal Work-Study, scholarships/grants, and unspecified assistantships also available. Support available to part-time students. Financial award application deadline: 3/1; financial award applicants required to submit FAFSA. *Faculty research:* Antimicrobial compounds, marine bacteria. *Unit head:* Dr. Marc Kasner, Chair, 973-655-6864. *Application contact:* Amy Aiello, Director of Graduate Admissions and Operations, 973-655-5147, E-mail: graduate.school@montclair.edu.

Morgan State University, School of Graduate Studies, School of Computer, Mathematical, and Natural Sciences, Department of Chemistry, Baltimore, MD 21251. Offers MS. *Degree requirements:* For master's, comprehensive exam, thesis, oral defense of thesis. *Entrance requirements:* For master's, GRE General Test, minimum GPA of 2.5.

Mount Allison University, Department of Chemistry, Sackville, NB E4L 1E4, Canada. Offers M Sc. *Degree requirements:* For master's, thesis. *Entrance requirements:* For master's, honors degree in chemistry. *Faculty research:* Biophysical chemistry of model biomembranes, organic synthesis, fast-reaction kinetics, physical chemistry of micelles.

Murray State University, College of Science, Engineering and Technology, Program in Chemistry, Murray, KY 42071. Offers MS. Part-time programs available. *Degree requirements:* For master's, comprehensive exam (for some programs), thesis (for some programs). *Entrance requirements:* For master's, GRE General Test. Additional exam requirements/recommendations for international students: Required—TOEFL. *Faculty research:* Environmental, organic, biochemistry, analytical.

New Jersey Institute of Technology, Office of Graduate Studies, College of Science and Liberal Arts, Department of Chemistry and Environmental Science, Program in Chemistry, Newark, NJ 07102. Offers MS, PhD. Part-time and evening/weekend programs available. Terminal master's awarded for partial completion of doctoral program. *Degree requirements:* For master's, thesis optional; for doctorate, thesis/dissertation. *Entrance requirements:* For master's, GRE General Test; for doctorate, GRE General Test, minimum graduate GPA of 3.5. Additional exam requirements/recommendations for international students: Required—TOEFL (minimum score 550 paper-based; 213 computer-based; 79 iBT). Electronic applications accepted. *Faculty research:* Medical instrumentation, prosthesis design, biodegradation of hazardous waste, orthopedic biomechanics, image processing.

New Mexico Highlands University, Graduate Studies, College of Arts and Sciences, Department of Natural Sciences, Las Vegas, NM 87701. Offers chemistry (MS); life science

(MS). Part-time programs available. *Degree requirements:* For master's, comprehensive exam, thesis. *Entrance requirements:* For master's, minimum undergraduate GPA of 3.0. Additional exam requirements/recommendations for international students: Required—TOEFL (minimum score 540 paper-based; 207 computer-based). *Faculty research:* Invasive organisms in managed and wildland ecosystems, juniper and pinyon ecology and management, vegetation and community structure, big game management, quantitative forestry.

New Mexico Institute of Mining and Technology, Graduate Studies, Department of Chemistry, Socorro, NM 87801. Offers biochemistry (MS); chemistry (MS); environmental chemistry (PhD); explosives technology and atmospheric chemistry (PhD). Part-time programs available. *Degree requirements:* For master's, thesis; for doctorate, thesis/dissertation. *Entrance requirements:* For master's, GRE General Test; for doctorate, GRE General Test, GRE Subject Test. Additional exam requirements/recommendations for international students: Required—TOEFL (minimum score 540 paper-based; 207 computer-based). Electronic applications accepted. *Faculty research:* Organic, analytical, environmental, and explosives chemistry.

New Mexico State University, Graduate School, College of Arts and Sciences, Department of Chemistry and Biochemistry, Las Cruces, NM 88003-8001. Offers MS, PhD. Part-time programs available. *Faculty:* 16 full-time (3 women), 1 (woman) part-time/adjunct. *Students:* 47 full-time (11 women), 7 part-time (3 women); includes 9 minority (1 African American, 1 American Indian/Alaska Native, 2 Asian Americans or Pacific Islanders, 5 Hispanic Americans), 35 international. Average age 29. 99 applicants, 67% accepted, 20 enrolled. In 2009, 4 master's, 6 doctorates awarded. *Degree requirements:* For master's, comprehensive exam, thesis; for doctorate, comprehensive exam, thesis/dissertation. *Entrance requirements:* For master's and doctorate, GRE, BS in chemistry or biochemistry, minimum GPA of 3.0. Additional exam requirements/recommendations for international students: Required—TOEFL (minimum score 600 paper-based; 250 computer-based). *Application deadline:* For fall admission, 7/1 priority date for domestic students, 3/1 priority date for international students; for spring admission, 11/1 for domestic students. Applications are processed on a rolling basis. Application fee: $30 ($50 for international students). Electronic applications accepted. *Expenses:* Tuition, state resident: full-time $4080; part-time $223 per credit. Tuition, nonresident: full-time $14,256; part-time $647 per credit. Required fees: $1278; $639 per semester. *Financial support:* In 2009–10, 19 research assistantships with tuition reimbursements (averaging $12,356 per year), 27 teaching assistantships with tuition reimbursements (averaging $16,747 per year) were awarded; fellowships with tuition reimbursements, career-related internships or fieldwork, Federal Work-Study, and health care benefits also available. Support available to part-time students. Financial award application deadline: 4/1. *Faculty research:* Clays, surfaces, and water structure; electroanalytical and environmental chemistry; organometallic synthesis and organobiomimetics; molecular genetics, DNA recombination mechanisms, and NMR spectroscopy of protein interactions; spectroscopy and reaction kinetics. *Unit head:* Dr. Glenn D. Kuehn, Head, 575-646-5877, Fax: 575-646-2649, E-mail: gkuehn@nmsu.edu. *Application contact:* Dr. Cynthia Zoski, Associate Professor, Chemistry, 575-646-5292, Fax: 575-646-2649, E-mail: czoski@nmsu.edu.

New York University, Graduate School of Arts and Science, Department of Chemistry, New York, NY 10012-1019. Offers MS, PhD. *Faculty:* 23 full-time (1 woman). *Students:* 101 full-time (49 women), 6 part-time (2 women); includes 9 minority (3 African Americans, 4 Asian Americans or Pacific Islanders, 2 Hispanic Americans), 76 international. Average age 27. 188 applicants, 36% accepted, 27 enrolled. In 2009, 16 master's, 12 doctorates awarded. *Degree requirements:* For master's, thesis or alternative; for doctorate, one foreign language, thesis/dissertation. *Entrance requirements:* For master's and doctorate, GRE General Test, GRE Subject Test. Additional exam requirements/recommendations for international students: Required—TOEFL. *Application deadline:* For fall admission, 12/12 for domestic students. Application fee: $90. *Expenses:* Tuition: Full-time $30,528; part-time $1272 per credit. Required fees: $2177. *Financial support:* Fellowships with tuition reimbursements, research assistantships with tuition reimbursements, teaching assistantships with tuition reimbursements, career-related internships or fieldwork, Federal Work-Study, institutionally sponsored loans, scholarships/grants, health care benefits, and unspecified assistantships available. Financial award application deadline: 12/12; financial award applicants required to submit FAFSA. *Faculty research:* Biomolecular chemistry, theoretical and computational chemistry, physical chemistry, nanotechnology, bio-organic chemistry. *Unit head:* Michael Ward, Chair, 212-998-8400, Fax: 212-260-7905, E-mail: grad.chem@nyu.edu. *Application contact:* Marcus Weck, Director of Graduate Studies, 212-998-8400, Fax: 212-260-7905, E-mail: grad.chem@nyu.edu.

North Carolina Agricultural and Technical State University, Graduate School, College of Arts and Sciences, Department of Chemistry, Greensboro, NC 27411. Offers MS. Part-time and evening/weekend programs available. *Degree requirements:* For master's, comprehensive exam, thesis or alternative, qualifying exam. *Entrance requirements:* For master's, GRE General Test, minimum GPA of 3.0. *Faculty research:* Tobacco pesticides.

North Carolina Central University, Division of Academic Affairs, College of Science and Technology, Department of Chemistry, Durham, NC 27707-3129. Offers MS. *Degree requirements:* For master's, one foreign language, comprehensive exam, thesis. *Entrance requirements:* For master's, GRE, minimum GPA of 3.0 in major, 2.5 overall. Additional exam requirements/recommendations for international students: Required—TOEFL.

North Carolina State University, Graduate School, College of Physical and Mathematical Sciences, Department of Chemistry, Raleigh, NC 27695. Offers MS, PhD. Part-time programs available. Terminal master's awarded for partial completion of doctoral program. *Degree requirements:* For master's, thesis (for some programs); for doctorate, thesis/dissertation. *Entrance requirements:* For master's and doctorate, GRE General Test (recommended). Electronic applications accepted. *Faculty research:* Biological chemistry, electrochemistry, organic/inorganic materials, natural products, organometallics.

North Dakota State University, College of Graduate and Interdisciplinary Studies, College of Science and Mathematics, Department of Biochemistry and Molecular Biology, Program in Chemistry, Fargo, ND 58108. Offers MS, PhD. *Students:* 22 full-time (6 women), 6 part-time (2 women); includes 1 African American, 1 Asian American or Pacific Islander, 11 international. In 2009, 2 master's, 5 doctorates awarded. *Unit head:* Dr. John Hershberger, Chair, 701-231-7678, Fax: 701-231-8831, E-mail: john.hershberger@ndsu.edu. *Application contact:* Dr. Seth Rasmussen, Chair, Graduate Admissions, 701-231-8747, Fax: 701-231-8831, E-mail: seth.rasmussen@ndsu.edu.

Northeastern Illinois University, Graduate College, College of Arts and Sciences, Department of Chemistry, Program in Chemistry, Chicago, IL 60625-4699. Offers MS. Part-time and evening/weekend programs available. *Degree requirements:* For master's, comprehensive exam, final exam or thesis. *Entrance requirements:* For master's, 2 semesters chemistry; 2 semesters calculus, organic chemistry, physical chemistry, and physics; 1 semester analytic chemistry; minimum GPA of 2.75. Additional exam requirements/recommendations for international students: Required—TOEFL (minimum score 550 paper-based; 213 computer-based; 80 iBT). Electronic applications accepted. *Faculty research:* Liquid chromatographic separation of pharmaceuticals, Diels-Alder reaction products, organogermanium chemistry, mass spectroscopy.

Northeastern University, College of Science, Department of Chemistry and Chemical Biology, Boston, MA 02115-5096. Offers analytical chemistry (PhD); chemistry (MS, PhD); inorganic chemistry (PhD); organic chemistry (PhD); physical chemistry (PhD). Part-time and evening/weekend programs available. *Faculty:* 24 full-time (5 women), 7 part-time/adjunct (0 women). *Students:* 86 full-time (48 women), 31 part-time (14 women); includes 9 minority (1 African American, 1 American Indian/Alaska Native, 7 Asian Americans or Pacific Islanders), 36 international. 190 applicants, 22% accepted, 15 enrolled. In 2009, 17 master's, 9 doctorates awarded. Terminal master's awarded for partial completion of doctoral program. *Degree requirements:* For master's, thesis (for some programs); for doctorate, thesis/dissertation, qualifying exam in specialty area. *Entrance requirements:* Additional exam requirements/recommendations for international students: Required—TOEFL. *Application deadline:* For fall admission, 2/1 priority date for domestic and international students. Applications are processed on a rolling basis. Application fee: $50. Electronic applications accepted. *Financial support:* In 2009–10, 41 research assistantships with tuition reimbursements (averaging $18,285 per year), 38 teaching assistantships with tuition reimbursements (averaging $18,285 per year) were awarded; fellowships with tuition reimbursements, career-related internships or fieldwork, Federal Work-Study, scholarships/grants, tuition waivers (partial), and unspecified assistantships also available. Financial award application deadline: 3/1; financial award applicants required to submit FAFSA. *Faculty research:* Bioanalysis, biorganic and medicinal chemistry, biophysical chemistry, nanomaterials, proteomics. *Unit head:* Dr. Robert Hanson, Graduate Coordinator, 617-373-3313, Fax: 617-373-8795, E-mail: chemistry-grad-info@neu.edu. *Application contact:* Jo-Anne Dickinson, Admissions Contact, 617-373-5990, Fax: 617-373-7281, E-mail: gsas@neu.edu.

Northern Arizona University, Graduate College, College of Engineering, Forestry and Natural Sciences, Department of Chemistry and Biochemistry, Flagstaff, AZ 86011. Offers chemistry (MS). Part-time programs available. *Faculty:* 15 full-time (8 women). *Students:* 12 full-time (6 women), 2 part-time (1 woman); includes 4 minority (2 American Indian/Alaska Native, 2 Hispanic Americans), 1 international. Average age 27. 14 applicants, 64% accepted, 7 enrolled. In 2009, 5 master's awarded. *Degree requirements:* For master's, thesis. *Entrance requirements:* For master's, minimum GPA of 3.0. Additional exam requirements/recommendations for international students: Required—TOEFL (minimum score 550 paper-based; 213 computer-based; 80 iBT), IELTS (minimum score 7), or a bachelor's degree from an English-speaking university and demonstrated proficiency. *Application deadline:* For fall admission, 3/1 priority date for domestic students, 9/1 priority date for international students; for spring admission, 10/1 priority date for domestic students. Applications are processed on a rolling basis. Application fee: $65. Electronic applications accepted. *Financial support:* In 2009–10, 1 research assistantship with partial tuition reimbursement (averaging $12,055 per year), 9 teaching assistantships with partial tuition reimbursements (averaging $12,055 per year) were awarded; fellowships, career-related internships or fieldwork, Federal Work-Study, scholarships/grants, traineeships, health care benefits, tuition waivers (full and partial), and unspecified assistantships also available. Support available to part-time students. Financial award application deadline: 3/30; financial award applicants required to submit FAFSA. *Faculty research:* Biochemistry of exercise, organic and inorganic mechanism studies, inhibition of ice mutation, polymer separation. Total annual research expenditures: $261,191. *Unit head:* Dr. Cindy Browder, Chair, 928-523-9062, E-mail: cindy.browder@nau.edu. *Application contact:* Dr. Cindy Browder, Chair, 928-523-9062, E-mail: cindy.browder@nau.edu.

Northern Illinois University, Graduate School, College of Liberal Arts and Sciences, Department of Chemistry and Biochemistry, De Kalb, IL 60115-2854. Offers chemistry (MS, PhD). *Faculty:* 16 full-time (1 woman), 3 part-time/adjunct (1 woman). *Students:* 39 full-time (17 women), 13 part-time (3 women); includes 3 minority (2 Asian Americans or Pacific Islanders, 1 Hispanic American), 17 international. Average age 28. 59 applicants, 39% accepted, 5 enrolled. In 2009, 4 master's, 7 doctorates awarded. Terminal master's awarded for partial completion of doctoral program. *Degree requirements:* For master's, comprehensive exam, thesis optional, research seminar; for doctorate, one foreign language, thesis/dissertation, candidacy exam, dissertation defense, research seminar. *Entrance requirements:* For master's, GRE General Test, bachelor's degree in mathematics or science, minimum GPA of 2.75; for doctorate, GRE General Test, bachelor's degree in mathematics or science; minimum undergraduate GPA of 2.75, 3.2 graduate. Additional exam requirements/recommendations for international students: Required—TOEFL (minimum score 550 paper-based; 213 computer-based). *Application deadline:* For fall admission, 6/1 for domestic students, 5/1 for international students; for spring admission, 11/1 for domestic students, 10/1 for international students. Applications are processed on a rolling basis. Application fee: $30. Electronic applications accepted. *Expenses:* Tuition, state resident: full-time $6576; part-time $274 per credit hour. Tuition, nonresident: full-time $13,152; part-time $548 per credit hour. Required fees: $1813; $75.53 per credit hour. Part-time tuition and fees vary according to course load. *Financial support:* In 2009–10, 7 research assistantships with full tuition reimbursements, 36 teaching assistantships with full tuition reimbursements were awarded; fellowships with full tuition reimbursements, career-related internships or fieldwork, Federal Work-Study, scholarships/grants, tuition waivers (full), and unspecified assistantships also available. Support available to part-time students. Financial award applicants required to submit FAFSA. *Faculty research:* Viscoelastic properties of polymers, lig and buding tocytochrome coxidases, computational inorganic chemistry, chemistry of organosilanes. *Unit head:* Dr. Jon Carnahan, Chair, 815-753-1181, Fax: 815-753-4802, E-mail: carnahan@niu.edu. *Application contact:* Dr. Jon Carnahan, Chair, 815-753-1181, Fax: 815-753-4802, E-mail: carnahan@niu.edu.

Northwestern University, The Graduate School, Judd A. and Marjorie Weinberg College of Arts and Sciences, Department of Chemistry, Evanston, IL 60208. Offers PhD. Admissions and degrees offered through The Graduate School. *Degree requirements:* For doctorate, thesis/dissertation. *Entrance requirements:* For doctorate, GRE General Test, GRE Subject Test (chemistry). Additional exam requirements/recommendations for international students: Required—TOEFL. Electronic applications accepted. *Faculty research:* Inorganic, organic, physical, environmental, materials, and chemistry of life processes.

Oakland University, Graduate Study and Lifelong Learning, College of Arts and Sciences, Department of Chemistry, Rochester, MI 48309-4401. Offers biological sciences: health and environmental chemistry (PhD); chemistry (MS). *Degree requirements:* For master's, thesis; for doctorate, thesis/dissertation. *Entrance requirements:* For master's, minimum GPA of 3.0 for unconditional admission; for doctorate, GRE Subject Test, minimum GPA of 3.0 for unconditional admission. Additional exam requirements/recommendations for international students: Required—TOEFL (minimum score 550 paper-based; 213 computer-based). Electronic applications accepted. *Faculty research:* Chemistry of free radical species generated from biological intermediates; fate of toxic organic compounds in the environment; electroanalytical and surface chemistry at solid/liquid interface; computational modeling of intermolecular interactions and surface phenomena; metabolism and biological activity of modified fatty acids and xenobiotic carboxylic acids; physiologic and pathologic mechanisms that modulate immune responses.

The Ohio State University, Graduate School, College of Mathematical and Physical Sciences, Department of Chemistry, Columbus, OH 43210. Offers MS, PhD. *Faculty:* 39. *Students:* 46 full-time (21 women), 169 part-time (59 women); includes 15 minority (4 African Americans, 1 American Indian/Alaska Native, 7 Asian Americans or Pacific Islanders, 3 Hispanic Americans), 97 international. Average age 26. In 2009, 10 master's, 25 doctorates awarded. *Degree requirements:* For master's, thesis optional; for doctorate, thesis/dissertation. *Entrance requirements:* For master's and doctorate, GRE General Test, GRE Subject Test (chemistry). Additional exam requirements/recommendations for international students: Required—TOEFL (minimum score 600 paper-based; 250 computer-based). *Application deadline:* For fall admission, 8/15 priority date for domestic students, 7/1 priority date for international students; for winter admission, 12/1 priority date for domestic students, 11/1 priority date for international students; for spring admission, 3/1 priority date for domestic students, 2/1 priority date for international students. Applications are processed on a rolling basis. Application fee: $40 ($50 for international students). Electronic applications accepted. *Expenses:* Tuition, state resident: full-time $10,683. Tuition, nonresident: full-time $25,923. Tuition and fees vary according to course load and program. *Financial support:* Fellowships, research assistantships, teaching assistant-

Chemistry

The Ohio State University (continued)

ships, Federal Work-Study and institutionally sponsored loans available. Support available to part-time students. *Unit head:* Robert Coleman, Graduate Studies Committee Chair, 614-292-6723, Fax: 614-292-1685, E-mail: coleman.184@osu.edu. *Application contact:* 614-292-9444, Fax: 614-292-3895, E-mail: domestic.grad@osu.edu.

Oklahoma State University, College of Arts and Sciences, Department of Chemistry, Stillwater, OK 74078. Offers MS, PhD. *Faculty:* 18 full-time (1 woman), 2 part-time/adjunct (1 woman). *Students:* 14 full-time (4 women), 38 part-time (17 women); includes 3 minority (2 African Americans, 1 Hispanic American), 35 international. Average age 29. 103 applicants, 16% accepted, 13 enrolled. In 2009, 3 master's, 6 doctorates awarded. *Degree requirements:* For master's, thesis; for doctorate, comprehensive exam, thesis/dissertation. *Entrance requirements:* For master's and doctorate, GRE or GMAT. Additional exam requirements/recommendations for international students: Required—TOEFL (minimum score 550 paper-based; 79 iBT). *Application deadline:* For fall admission, 3/1 priority date for international students; for spring admission, 8/1 priority date for international students. Applications are processed on a rolling basis. Application fee: $40 ($75 for international students). Electronic applications accepted. *Expenses:* Tuition, state resident: full-time $3716; part-time $154.85 per credit hour. Tuition, nonresident: full-time $14,448; part-time $602 per credit hour. Required fees: $1772; $73.85 per credit hour. One-time fee: $50. Tuition and fees vary according to course load and campus/location. *Financial support:* In 2009–10, 16 research assistantships (averaging $16,939 per year), 33 teaching assistantships (averaging $17,477 per year) were awarded; career-related internships or fieldwork, Federal Work-Study, scholarships/grants, health care benefits, tuition waivers (partial), and unspecified assistantships also available. Support available to part-time students. Financial award application deadline: 3/1; financial award applicants required to submit FAFSA. *Faculty research:* Materials science, surface chemistry, and nanoparticles; theoretical physical chemistry; synthetic and medicinal chemistry; bioanalytical chemistry; electromagnetic (UV, VIS, IR, Raman), mass, and x-ray spectroscopes. *Unit head:* Dr. Jeffery L. White, Interim Head, 405-744-5920, Fax: 405-744-6007. *Application contact:* Dr. Gordon Emslie, Dean, 405-744-6368, Fax: 405-744-0355, E-mail: grad-i@okstate.edu.

Old Dominion University, College of Sciences, Program in Chemistry, Norfolk, VA 23529. Offers analytical chemistry (MS); biochemistry (MS); chemistry (PhD); environmental chemistry (MS); organic chemistry (MS); physical chemistry (MS). Part-time and evening/weekend programs available. *Faculty:* 14 full-time (5 women), 2 part-time/adjunct (0 women). *Students:* 30 full-time (19 women), 10 part-time (5 women); includes 3 minority (1 African American, 1 Asian American or Pacific Islander, 1 Hispanic American), 17 international. Average age 29. 35 applicants, 60% accepted, 8 enrolled. In 2009, 1 master's awarded. *Degree requirements:* For master's, comprehensive exam, thesis. *Entrance requirements:* For master's, GRE General Test, minimum GPA of 3.0 in major, 2.5 overall; for doctorate, GRE General Test. Additional exam requirements/recommendations for international students: Required—TOEFL. *Application deadline:* For fall admission, 7/1 for domestic students, 1/15 for international students; for spring admission, 11/1 for domestic students, 8/15 for international students. Applications are processed on a rolling basis. Application fee: $30. Electronic applications accepted. *Expenses:* Tuition, state resident: full-time $8112; part-time $338 per credit. Tuition, nonresident: full-time $20,256; part-time $844 per credit. Required fees: $119 per semester. One-time fee: $50. *Financial support:* In 2009–10, 6 students received support, including fellowships (averaging $18,000 per year), research assistantships with tuition reimbursements available (averaging $21,000 per year), teaching assistantships with tuition reimbursements available (averaging $18,000 per year); career-related internships or fieldwork, scholarships/grants, and unspecified assistantships also available. Financial award application deadline: 2/15; financial award applicants required to submit FAFSA. *Faculty research:* Biogeochemistry, materials chemistry, bioanalytical chemistry, computational chemistry, organic chemistry. Total annual research expenditures: $2.6 million. *Unit head:* Dr. Craig A. Bayse, Graduate Program Director, 757-683-4097, Fax: 757-683-4628, E-mail: chemgpd@odu.edu. *Application contact:* Valerie DeCosta, Grants and Graduate Program Assistant, 757-683-6979, Fax: 757-683-4628, E-mail: chemgpd@odu.edu.

Old Dominion University, Darden College of Education, Programs in Secondary Education, Norfolk, VA 23529. Offers biology (MS Ed); chemistry (MS Ed); English (MS Ed); instructional technology (MS Ed); library science (MS Ed); secondary education (MS Ed). *Accreditation:* NCATE. Part-time and evening/weekend programs available. Postbaccalaureate distance learning degree programs offered (minimal on-campus study). *Faculty:* 20 full-time (16 women). *Students:* 74 full-time (54 women), 137 part-time (92 women); includes 41 minority (22 African Americans, 1 American Indian/Alaska Native, 11 Asian Americans or Pacific Islanders, 7 Hispanic Americans). Average age 33. 67 applicants, 79% accepted, 53 enrolled. In 2009, 131 master's awarded. *Degree requirements:* For master's, comprehensive exam, thesis. *Entrance requirements:* For master's, GRE General Test or MAT, PRAXIS I (for licensure), minimum GPA of 2.8, teaching certificate. Additional exam requirements/recommendations for international students: Required—TOEFL. *Application deadline:* For fall admission, 6/1 for domestic and international students; for winter admission, 11/1 for domestic and international students; for spring admission, 3/1 for domestic and international students. Applications are processed on a rolling basis. Application fee: $50. Electronic applications accepted. *Expenses:* Tuition, state resident: full-time $8112; part-time $338 per credit. Tuition, nonresident: full-time $20,256; part-time $844 per credit. Required fees: $119 per semester. One-time fee: $50. *Financial support:* In 2009–10, 56 students received support, including fellowships (averaging $15,000 per year), 2 research assistantships with tuition reimbursements available (averaging $9,000 per year), 3 teaching assistantships with tuition reimbursements available (averaging $12,500 per year); career-related internships or fieldwork, Federal Work-Study, institutionally sponsored loans, scholarships/grants, and tuition waivers (partial) also available. Support available to part-time students. Financial award application deadline: 2/15; financial award applicants required to submit FAFSA. *Faculty research:* Use of technology, writing project for teachers, geography teaching, reading. *Unit head:* Dr. Robert Lucking, Graduate Program Director, 757-683-5545, Fax: 757-683-5862, E-mail: rlucking@odu.edu. *Application contact:* Dr. Robert Lucking, Graduate Program Director, 757-683-5545, Fax: 757-683-5862, E-mail: rlucking@odu.edu.

Oregon State University, Graduate School, College of Science, Department of Chemistry, Corvallis, OR 97331. Offers analytical chemistry (MS, PhD); chemistry (MA, MAIS); inorganic chemistry (MS, PhD); nuclear and radiation chemistry (MS, PhD); organic chemistry (MS, PhD); physical chemistry (MS, PhD). Part-time programs available. *Faculty:* 24 full-time (3 women), 1 part-time/adjunct (0 women). *Students:* 78 full-time (27 women), 1 part-time (0 women); includes 3 minority (1 African American, 1 Asian American or Pacific Islander, 1 Hispanic American), 50 international. Average age 27. In 2009, 6 master's, 7 doctorates awarded. Terminal master's awarded for partial completion of doctoral program. *Degree requirements:* For master's, one foreign language, thesis; for doctorate, one foreign language, thesis/dissertation. *Entrance requirements:* For master's and doctorate, minimum GPA of 3.0 in last 90 hours of course work. Additional exam requirements/recommendations for international students: Required—TOEFL. *Application deadline:* For fall admission, 3/1 priority date for domestic students. Applications are processed on a rolling basis. Application fee: $50. *Expenses:* Tuition, state resident: full-time $9774; part-time $362 per credit. Tuition, nonresident: full-time $15,849; part-time $587 per credit. Required fees: $1639. Full-time tuition and fees vary according to course load and program. *Financial support:* Fellowships, research assistantships, teaching assistantships, institutionally sponsored loans available. Support available to part-time students. Financial award application deadline: 2/1. *Faculty research:* Solid state chemistry, enzyme reaction mechanisms, structure and dynamics of gas molecules, chemiluminescence, nonlinear optical spectroscopy. *Unit head:* Dr. Kevin P. Gable, Chair, 541-737-6744, Fax: 541-737-2062, E-mail: gablek@chem.orst.edu. *Application contact:* Dr. Kevin P. Gable, Chair, 541-737-6744, Fax: 541-737-2062, E-mail: gablek@chem.orst.edu.

Penn State University Park, Graduate School, Eberly College of Science, Department of Chemistry, State College, University Park, PA 16802-1503. Offers MS, PhD. *Unit head:* Dr. Ayusman Sen, Head, 814-865-1383, Fax: 814-863-8403, E-mail: axs20@psu.edu. *Application contact:* Dana Coval-Dinant, Graduate Student Recruiting Manager, 814-865-1383, Fax: 814-865-3228, E-mail: dmc6@psu.edu.

Pittsburg State University, Graduate School, College of Arts and Sciences, Department of Chemistry, Pittsburg, KS 66762. Offers MS. *Degree requirements:* For master's, thesis or alternative. *Expenses:* Tuition, state resident: full-time $4212; part-time $176 per credit. Tuition, nonresident: full-time $11,530; part-time $480 per credit. Required fees: $940; $43 per credit. Tuition and fees vary according to course level, course load, degree level, campus/location, reciprocity agreements and student level.

Polytechnic Institute of NYU, Department of Chemical and Biological Sciences, Major in Chemistry, Brooklyn, NY 11201-2990. Offers MS. Part-time and evening/weekend programs available. *Students:* 14 full-time (7 women), 3 part-time (2 women), 15 international. 56 applicants, 45% accepted, 8 enrolled. In 2009, 9 master's awarded. *Degree requirements:* For master's, comprehensive exam (for some programs), thesis (for some programs). *Entrance requirements:* For master's, GRE General Test, GRE Subject Test. Additional exam requirements/recommendations for international students: Required—TOEFL (minimum score 550 paper-based; 213 computer-based; 80 iBT); Recommended—IELTS (minimum score 6.5). *Application deadline:* For fall admission, 7/31 priority date for domestic students, 4/30 priority date for international students; for spring admission, 12/31 priority date for domestic students, 10/30 priority date for international students. Applications are processed on a rolling basis. Application fee: $75. Electronic applications accepted. *Expenses:* Tuition: Full-time $21,492; part-time $1194 per credit hour. Required fees: $1160; $204 per course. *Financial support:* Fellowships, research assistantships, teaching assistantships, institutionally sponsored loans, scholarships/grants, and unspecified assistantships available. Support available to part-time students. Financial award applicants required to submit FAFSA. *Faculty research:* Optical rotation of light by plastic films, supramolecular chemistry, unusual stereochemical opportunities, polyaniline copolymers. *Unit head:* Dr. Bruce Garetz, Department Head, 718-260-3600. *Application contact:* JeanCarlo Bonilla, Dir. Graduate Enrollment Management, 718-260-3182, Fax: 718-260-3624, E-mail: gradinfo@poly.edu.

Polytechnic Institute of NYU, Department of Chemical and Biological Sciences, Major in Materials Chemistry, Brooklyn, NY 11201-2990. Offers PhD. Part-time and evening/weekend programs available. *Students:* 6 full-time (1 woman), 14 part-time (4 women); includes 1 minority (Asian American or Pacific Islander), 18 international. 42 applicants, 24% accepted, 4 enrolled. In 2009, 2 doctorates awarded. *Degree requirements:* For doctorate, comprehensive exam, thesis/dissertation. *Entrance requirements:* Additional exam requirements/recommendations for international students: Required—TOEFL (minimum score 550 paper-based; 213 computer-based; 80 iBT); Recommended—IELTS (minimum score 6.5). *Application deadline:* For fall admission, 7/31 priority date for domestic students, 4/30 priority date for international students; for spring admission, 12/31 priority date for domestic students, 10/30 priority date for international students. Applications are processed on a rolling basis. Application fee: $75. Electronic applications accepted. *Expenses:* Tuition: Full-time $21,492; part-time $1194 per credit hour. Required fees: $1160; $204 per course. *Financial support:* Fellowships, research assistantships, teaching assistantships, institutionally sponsored loans, scholarships/grants, and unspecified assistantships available. Support available to part-time students. Financial award applicants required to submit FAFSA. *Unit head:* Dr. Bruce Garetz, Department Head, 718-260-3600. *Application contact:* JeanCarlo Bonilla, Director of Graduate Enrollment Management, 718-260-3182, Fax: 718-260-3624.

Polytechnic Institute of NYU, Long Island Graduate Center, Graduate Programs, Department of Chemical and Biological Sciences, Major in Chemistry, Melville, NY 11747. Offers MS. *Degree requirements:* For master's, comprehensive exam (for some programs), thesis (for some programs). *Entrance requirements:* Additional exam requirements/recommendations for international students: Required—TOEFL (minimum score 550 paper-based; 213 computer-based; 80 iBT); Recommended—IELTS (minimum score 6.5). *Application deadline:* For fall admission, 7/31 priority date for domestic students, 4/30 priority date for international students; for spring admission, 12/31 priority date for domestic students, 11/30 priority date for international students. Applications are processed on a rolling basis. Application fee: $75. Electronic applications accepted. *Financial support:* Institutionally sponsored loans, scholarships/grants, and unspecified assistantships available. Support available to part-time students. *Unit head:* Prof. Bruce A. Garetz, Department Head, 718-260-3287, E-mail: bgaretz@poly.edu. *Application contact:* JeanCarlo Bonilla, Director of Graduate Enrollment Management, 718-260-3182, Fax: 718-260-3624, E-mail: gradinfo@poly.edu.

Polytechnic Institute of NYU, Westchester Graduate Center, Graduate Programs, Department of Chemical and Biological Sciences, Major in Chemistry, Hawthorne, NY 10532-1507. Offers MS. *Students:* 2 part-time (0 women). Average age 33. In 2009, 3 master's awarded. *Degree requirements:* For master's, comprehensive exam (for some programs), thesis (for some programs). *Entrance requirements:* Additional exam requirements/recommendations for international students: Required—TOEFL (minimum score 550 paper-based; 213 computer-based; 80 iBT); Recommended—IELTS (minimum score 6.5). *Application deadline:* For fall admission, 7/31 priority date for domestic students, 4/30 priority date for international students; for spring admission, 12/31 priority date for domestic students, 11/30 priority date for international students. Applications are processed on a rolling basis. Application fee: $75. Electronic applications accepted. *Financial support:* Institutionally sponsored loans, scholarships/grants, and unspecified assistantships available. Support available to part-time students. *Unit head:* Dr. Bruce A. Garetz, Department Head, 718-260-3287, E-mail: bgaretz@poly.edu. *Application contact:* JeanCarlo Bonilla, Director of Graduate Enrollment Management, 718-260-3182, Fax: 718-260-3624, E-mail: gradinfo@poly.edu.

Pontifical Catholic University of Puerto Rico, College of Sciences, Department of Chemistry, Ponce, PR 00717-0777. Offers MS. Part-time and evening/weekend programs available. *Degree requirements:* For master's, thesis. *Entrance requirements:* For master's, GRE General Test, 2 letters of recommendation, minimum GPA of 3.0, minimum 37 credits in chemistry. Electronic applications accepted.

Portland State University, Graduate Studies, College of Liberal Arts and Sciences, Department of Chemistry, Portland, OR 97207-0751. Offers MA, MS, PhD. Part-time programs available. *Degree requirements:* For master's, one foreign language, thesis; for doctorate, one foreign language, thesis/dissertation, cumulative exams, seminar presentations. *Entrance requirements:* For master's, GRE General Test, GRE Subject Test, minimum GPA of 3.0 in upper-division course work or 2.75 overall, 2 letters of recommendation. Additional exam requirements/recommendations for international students: Required—TOEFL (minimum score 550 paper-based; 213 computer-based). *Faculty research:* Synthetic inorganic chemistry, atmospheric chemistry, organic photochemistry, enzymology, analytical chemistry.

Prairie View A&M University, College of Arts and Sciences, Department of Chemistry, Prairie View, TX 77446-0519. Offers MS. Part-time and evening/weekend programs available. *Faculty:* 3 full-time (0 women). *Students:* 10 full-time (7 women), 1 part-time (0 women); includes 9 African Americans, 2 international. Average age 30. *Degree requirements:* For master's, thesis. *Entrance requirements:* For master's, GRE General Test. *Application deadline:* For fall admission, 4/1 for domestic students; for spring admission, 10/1 for domestic students. Applications are processed on a rolling basis. Application fee: $50. Electronic applications accepted. *Expenses:* Tuition, state resident: full-time $2200. Tuition, nonresident: full-time $5600. Required fees: $1720. Tuition and fees vary according to course load. *Financial support:* In 2009–10, 1 fellowship (averaging $10,000 per year), 2 research assistantships (averaging $7,000 per year), 5 teaching assistantships with partial tuition reimbursements (averaging $9,000 per year) were awarded; career-related internships or fieldwork, Federal Work-Study, institutionally sponsored loans, and tuition waivers (full and partial) also available. Support available to part-time students. Financial award application deadline: 4/1; financial award applicants required to submit FAFSA. *Faculty research:* Material science, environmental characterization (surface phenomena), activation of plasminogens, polymer modifications, organic synthesis. Total annual research expenditures: $114,895. *Unit head:* Dr. Remi R. Oki, Head, 936-261-2616, Fax: 936-261-3105, E-mail: aroki@pvamu.edu. *Application contact:* Dr. Remi R. Oki, Head, 936-261-2616, Fax: 936-261-3105, E-mail: aroki@pvamu.edu.

Princeton University, Graduate School, Department of Chemistry, Princeton, NJ 08544-1019. Offers chemistry (PhD); industrial chemistry (MS). *Degree requirements:* For doctorate, thesis/dissertation, general exams. *Entrance requirements:* For master's, GRE General Test; for doctorate, GRE General Test, GRE Subject Test (recommended). Additional exam requirements/recommendations for international students: Required—TOEFL (minimum score 250 computer-based). Electronic applications accepted. *Faculty research:* Chemistry of interfaces, organic synthesis, organometallic chemistry, inorganic reactions, biostructural chemistry.

See Close-Up on page 105.

Purdue University, Graduate School, College of Science, Department of Chemistry, West Lafayette, IN 47907. Offers analytical chemistry (MS, PhD); biochemistry (MS, PhD); chemical education (MS, PhD); inorganic chemistry (MS, PhD); organic chemistry (MS, PhD); physical chemistry (MS, PhD). Terminal master's awarded for partial completion of doctoral program. *Degree requirements:* For master's, thesis; for doctorate, thesis/dissertation. *Entrance requirements:* Additional exam requirements/recommendations for international students: Required—TOEFL. Electronic applications accepted.

Queens College of the City University of New York, Division of Graduate Studies, Mathematics and Natural Sciences Division, Department of Chemistry and Biochemistry, Flushing, NY 11367-1597. Offers biochemistry (MA); chemistry (MA). Part-time and evening/weekend programs available. *Faculty:* 14 full-time (4 women). *Students:* 8 part-time (6 women). 13 applicants, 38% accepted, 2 enrolled. In 2009, 4 master's awarded. *Degree requirements:* For master's, comprehensive exam. *Entrance requirements:* For master's, GRE, previous course work in calculus and physics, minimum GPA of 3.0. Additional exam requirements/recommendations for international students: Required—TOEFL. *Application deadline:* For fall admission, 4/1 for domestic students; for spring admission, 11/1 for domestic students. Applications are processed on a rolling basis. Application fee: $125. *Expenses:* Tuition, state resident: full-time $7360; part-time $310 per credit. Tuition, nonresident: part-time $575 per credit. One-time fee: $195.25 full-time; $145.25 part-time. *Financial support:* Career-related internships or fieldwork, Federal Work-Study, institutionally sponsored loans, and tuition waivers (partial) available. Support available to part-time students. Financial award application deadline: 4/1; financial award applicants required to submit FAFSA. *Unit head:* Dr. William Hersh, Chairperson, 718-997-4144. *Application contact:* Graduate Adviser, 718-997-4100.

Queen's University at Kingston, School of Graduate Studies and Research, Faculty of Arts and Sciences, Department of Chemistry, Kingston, ON K7L 3N6, Canada. Offers M Sc, PhD. Part-time programs available. *Degree requirements:* For master's, thesis (for some programs); for doctorate, comprehensive exam, thesis/dissertation. *Entrance requirements:* Additional exam requirements/recommendations for international students: Required—TOEFL (minimum score 580 paper-based). *Faculty research:* Medicinal/biological chemistry, materials chemistry, environmental/analytical chemistry, theoretical/computational chemistry.

Rensselaer Polytechnic Institute, Graduate School, School of Science, Department of Chemistry and Chemical Biology, Troy, NY 12180-3590. Offers analytical chemistry (MS, PhD); biochemistry (MS, PhD); inorganic chemistry (MS, PhD); organic chemistry (MS, PhD); physical chemistry (MS, PhD); polymer chemistry (MS, PhD). Part-time and evening/weekend programs available. *Faculty:* 16 full-time (2 women). *Students:* 68 full-time (31 women); includes 1 African American, 6 Asian Americans or Pacific Islanders, 1 Hispanic American, 31 international. Average age 24. 85 applicants, 19% accepted, 5 enrolled. In 2009, 5 master's, 6 doctorates awarded. Terminal master's awarded for partial completion of doctoral program. *Degree requirements:* For master's, thesis (for some programs); for doctorate, comprehensive exam, thesis/dissertation. *Entrance requirements:* For master's, GRE General Test, GRE Subject Test (strongly recommended); for doctorate, GRE General Test, GRE Subject Test (chemistry or biochemistry strongly recommended). Additional exam requirements/recommendations for international students: Required—TOEFL (minimum score 600 paper-based). *Application deadline:* For fall admission, 2/1 priority date for domestic students; for spring admission, 11/15 for domestic students. Applications are processed on a rolling basis. Application fee: $75. Electronic applications accepted. *Expenses:* Tuition: Full-time $38,100. *Financial support:* In 2009–10, 1 fellowship with full tuition reimbursement (averaging $22,500 per year), 18 research assistantships with full tuition reimbursements (averaging $22,500 per year), 24 teaching assistantships with full tuition reimbursements (averaging $22,500 per year) were awarded; institutionally sponsored loans and tuition waivers (full and partial) also available. Financial award application deadline: 2/1. *Faculty research:* Synthetic polymer and biopolymer chemistry, physical chemistry of polymeric systems, bioanalytical chemistry, synthetic and computational drug design, protein folding and protein design. Total annual research expenditures: $1.1 million. *Unit head:* Dr. Curtis M. Breneman, Chair, 518-276-3264, Fax: 518-276-4887, E-mail: brenec@rpi.edu. *Application contact:* Sharon E. Gardner, Graduate Program Administrator, 518-276-2140, Fax: 518-276-4887, E-mail: derris@rpi.edu.

Rice University, Graduate Programs, Wiess School of Natural Sciences, Department of Chemistry, Houston, TX 77251-1892. Offers chemistry (MA); inorganic chemistry (PhD); organic chemistry (PhD); physical chemistry (PhD). Terminal master's awarded for partial completion of doctoral program. *Degree requirements:* For master's, thesis; for doctorate, thesis/dissertation. *Entrance requirements:* For master's and doctorate, GRE General Test, minimum GPA of 3.0. Additional exam requirements/recommendations for international students: Required—TOEFL (minimum score 600 paper-based; 250 computer-based; 90 iBT). Electronic applications accepted. *Faculty research:* Nanoscience, biomaterials, nanobioinformatics, fullerene pharmaceuticals.

Rochester Institute of Technology, Graduate Enrollment Services, College of Science, Department of Chemistry, Rochester, NY 14623-5603. Offers MS. Part-time and evening/weekend programs available. Postbaccalaureate distance learning degree programs offered (minimal on-campus study). *Students:* 10 full-time (6 women), 10 part-time (5 women); includes 2 minority (both Asian Americans or Pacific Islanders), 5 international. Average age 28. 18 applicants, 39% accepted, 7 enrolled. In 2009, 5 master's awarded. *Degree requirements:* For master's, thesis. *Entrance requirements:* For master's, GRE, minimum GPA of 3.0. Additional exam requirements/recommendations for international students: Required—TOEFL (minimum score 550 paper-based; 213 computer-based; 79 iBT), or IELTS (minimum score 6.5). *Application deadline:* For fall admission, 2/15 priority date for domestic and international students; for winter admission, 11/1 for domestic students; for spring admission, 2/1 for domestic students. Applications are processed on a rolling basis. Application fee: $50. Electronic applications accepted. *Expenses:* Tuition: Full-time $31,533; part-time $876 per credit hour. Required fees: $210. *Financial support:* In 2009–10, 13 students received support; fellowships with full and partial tuition reimbursements available, research assistantships with full and partial tuition reimbursements available, teaching assistantships with full and partial tuition reimbursements available, career-related internships or fieldwork, scholarships/grants, and unspecified assistantships available. Support available to part-time students. Financial award applicants required to submit FAFSA. *Faculty research:* Organic polymer chemistry, magnetic resonance and imaging, inorganic coordination polymers, biophysical chemistry, physical polymer chemistry. *Unit head:* Dr. Paul Rosenberg, Department Head, 585-475-2497, Fax: 585-475-7800, E-mail: aemsch@rit.edu. *Application contact:* Diane Ellison, Assistant Vice President, Graduate Enrollment Services, 585-475-2229, Fax: 585-475-7164, E-mail: gradinfo@rit.edu.

Rochester Institute of Technology, Graduate Enrollment Services, College of Science, Department of Medical Sciences, Rochester, NY 14623-5603. Offers clinical chemistry (MS). Part-time programs available. *Students:* 4 full-time (1 woman), 4 part-time (0 women); includes 1 minority (Asian American or Pacific Islander), 6 international. Average age 31. 14 applicants, 43% accepted, 4 enrolled. *Degree requirements:* For master's, thesis. *Entrance requirements:* For master's, minimum GPA of 3.0. Additional exam requirements/recommendations for international students: Required—TOEFL (minimum score 575 paper-based; 233 computer-based; 90 iBT), or IELTS (minimum score 6.5). *Application deadline:* For fall admission, 2/15 priority date for domestic and international students. Applications are processed on a rolling basis. Application fee: $50. *Expenses:* Tuition: Full-time $31,533; part-time $876 per credit hour. Required fees: $210. *Financial support:* In 2009–10, 4 students received support; research assistantships with partial tuition reimbursements available, teaching assistantships with partial tuition reimbursements available, career-related internships or fieldwork, institutionally sponsored loans, scholarships/grants, and unspecified assistantships available. Support available to part-time students. Financial award applicants required to submit FAFSA. *Faculty research:* Pathology, forensic science, clinical chemistry. *Unit head:* James Aumer, Professor and Director of Clinical Chemistry, 585-475-5151, E-mail: llwscl@rit.edu. *Application contact:* Diane Ellison, Assistant Vice President, Graduate Enrollment Services, 585-475-2229, Fax: 585-475-7164, E-mail: gradinfo@rit.edu.

Roosevelt University, Graduate Division, College of Arts and Sciences, Department of Biological, Chemical, and Physical Sciences, Chicago, IL 60605. Offers biotechnology and chemical science (MS). Part-time and evening/weekend programs available. *Degree requirements:* For master's, thesis optional. *Entrance requirements:* For master's, minimum GPA of 2.7, undergraduate course work in science and mathematics. *Faculty research:* Phase-transfer catalysts, bioinorganic chemistry, long chain dicarboxylic acids, organosilicon compounds, spectroscopic studies.

Royal Military College of Canada, Division of Graduate Studies and Research, Science Division, Department of Chemistry and Chemical and Materials Engineering, Kingston, ON K7K 7B4, Canada. Offers chemical engineering (M Eng, MA Sc, PhD); chemistry (M Sc, PhD). *Degree requirements:* For master's, thesis; for doctorate, comprehensive exam, thesis/dissertation. *Entrance requirements:* For master's, honour's degree with second-class standing; for doctorate, master's degree. Electronic applications accepted.

Rutgers, The State University of New Jersey, Camden, Graduate School of Arts and Sciences, Program in Chemistry, Camden, NJ 08102-1401. Offers MS. Part-time and evening/weekend programs available. *Degree requirements:* For master's, comprehensive exam, thesis (for some programs). *Entrance requirements:* For master's, GRE (for assistantships), 3 letters of recommendation. Additional exam requirements/recommendations for international students: Required—TOEFL; Recommended—TWE. Electronic applications accepted. *Faculty research:* Organic and inorganic synthesis, enzyme biochemistry, trace metal analysis, theoretical and molecular modeling.

Rutgers, The State University of New Jersey, Newark, Graduate School, Program in Chemistry, Newark, NJ 07102. Offers analytical chemistry (MS, PhD); biochemistry (MS, PhD); inorganic chemistry (MS, PhD); organic chemistry (MS, PhD); physical chemistry (MS, PhD). Part-time and evening/weekend programs available. Terminal master's awarded for partial completion of doctoral program. *Degree requirements:* For master's, thesis optional, cumulative exams; for doctorate, thesis/dissertation, exams, research proposal. *Entrance requirements:* For master's and doctorate, GRE General Test, minimum undergraduate B average. Additional exam requirements/recommendations for international students: Required—TOEFL. Electronic applications accepted. *Faculty research:* Medicinal chemistry, natural products, isotope effects, biophysics and biorganic approaches to enzyme mechanisms, organic and organometallic synthesis.

Rutgers, The State University of New Jersey, New Brunswick, Graduate School-New Brunswick, Department of Chemistry and Chemical Biology, Piscataway, NJ 08854-8097. Offers biological chemistry (MS, PhD); inorganic chemistry (MS, PhD); organic chemistry (MS, PhD); physical chemistry (MS, PhD). Part-time and evening/weekend programs available. Terminal master's awarded for partial completion of doctoral program. *Degree requirements:* For master's, thesis or alternative, exam; for doctorate, thesis/dissertation, 1 year residency. *Entrance requirements:* For master's and doctorate, GRE General Test, GRE Subject Test. Additional exam requirements/recommendations for international students: Required—TOEFL. Electronic applications accepted. *Faculty research:* Biophysical organic/bioorganic, inorganic/bioinorganic, theoretical, and solid-state/surface chemistry.

Rutgers, The State University of New Jersey, New Brunswick, Graduate School-New Brunswick, Department of Environmental Sciences, Piscataway, NJ 08854-8097. Offers air pollution and resources (MS, PhD); aquatic biology (MS, PhD); aquatic chemistry (MS, PhD); atmospheric science (MS, PhD); chemistry and physics of aerosol and hydrosol systems (MS, PhD); environmental chemistry (MS, PhD); environmental microbiology (MS, PhD); environmental toxicology (PhD); exposure assessment (PhD); fate and effects of pollutants (MS, PhD); pollution prevention and control (MS, PhD); water and wastewater treatment (MS, PhD); water resources (MS, PhD). Terminal master's awarded for partial completion of doctoral program. *Degree requirements:* For master's, comprehensive exam, thesis or alternative, oral final exam; for doctorate, comprehensive exam, thesis/dissertation, thesis defense, qualifying exam. *Entrance requirements:* For master's and doctorate, GRE General Test. Additional exam requirements/recommendations for international students: Required—TOEFL. Electronic applications accepted. *Faculty research:* Biological waste treatment; contaminant fate and transport; air, soil and water quality.

Sacred Heart University, Graduate Programs, College of Arts and Sciences, Department of Chemistry, Fairfield, CT 06825-1000. Offers MS. Part-time and evening/weekend programs available. *Faculty:* 5 full-time (2 women), 15 part-time/adjunct (3 women). *Students:* 36 full-time (11 women), 12 part-time (6 women); includes 5 minority (1 African American, 3 Asian Americans or Pacific Islanders, 1 Hispanic American), 36 international. Average age 28. 39 applicants, 95% accepted, 13 enrolled. In 2009, 6 master's awarded. *Degree requirements:* For master's, thesis optional. *Entrance requirements:* For master's, bachelor's degree in related area, minimum GPA of 2.75. Additional exam requirements/recommendations for international students: Required—TOEFL (minimum score 550 paper-based; 213 computer-based; 75 iBT). *Application deadline:* Applications are processed on a rolling basis. Application fee: $50 ($100 for international students). Electronic applications accepted. *Expenses:* Tuition: Full-time $24,000; part-time $650 per credit. Required fees: $248. *Financial support:* Career-related internships or fieldwork, institutionally sponsored loans, and unspecified assistantships available. Support available to part-time students. Financial award applicants required to submit FAFSA. *Unit head:* Dr. Eid Alkhatib, Chair, 203-365-7546, E-mail: gradstudies@sacredheart.edu. *Application contact:* Alexis Haakonsen, Dean of Graduate Admissions, 203-365-7619, Fax: 203-365-4732, E-mail: haakonsena@sacredheart.edu.

St. Francis Xavier University, Graduate Studies, Department of Chemistry, Antigonish, NS B2G 2W5, Canada. Offers M Sc. *Degree requirements:* For master's, thesis. *Entrance requirements:* Additional exam requirements/recommendations for international students: Required—TOEFL (minimum score 580 paper-based; 236 computer-based). *Faculty research:*

Chemistry

St. Francis Xavier University (continued)

Photoelectron spectroscopy, synthesis and properties of surfactants, nucleic acid synthesis, transition metal chemistry, colloids.

St. John's University, St. John's College of Liberal Arts and Sciences, Department of Chemistry, Queens, NY 11439. Offers MS. Part-time and evening/weekend programs available. *Students:* 13 full-time (9 women), 11 part-time (7 women); includes 14 minority (2 African Americans, 10 Asian Americans or Pacific Islanders, 2 Hispanic Americans), 7 international. Average age 29. 30 applicants, 50% accepted, 10 enrolled. In 2009, 7 master's awarded. *Degree requirements:* For master's, comprehensive exam, thesis optional. *Entrance requirements:* For master's, minimum GPA of 3.0. Additional exam requirements/recommendations for international students: Required—TOEFL (minimum score 500 paper-based; 173 computer-based; 61 iBT), IELTS (minimum score 5.5). *Application deadline:* For fall admission, 5/1 priority date for domestic and international students; for spring admission, 11/1 priority date for domestic and international students. Applications are processed on a rolling basis. Application fee: $70. Electronic applications accepted. *Expenses:* Tuition: Full-time $16,290; part-time $905 per credit. Required fees: $300; $150 per semester. Tuition and fees vary according to program. *Financial support:* Research assistantships, teaching assistantships, scholarships/grants available. Support available to part-time students. Financial award application deadline: 3/1; financial award applicants required to submit FAFSA. *Faculty research:* Synthesis and reactions of a-lactams, NMR spectroscopy or nucleosides, analytical chemistry, environment chemistry and photochemistry of transition metal complexes. *Unit head:* Dr. Richard Rosso, Chair, 718-990-5216, E-mail: rossor@stjohns.edu. *Application contact:* Kathleen Davis, Director of Graduate Admission, 718-990-2790, Fax: 718-990-5686, E-mail: gradhelp@stjohns.edu.

Saint Joseph College, Department of Chemistry, West Hartford, CT 06117-2700. Offers biochemistry (MS); chemistry (MS). Part-time and evening/weekend programs available. Post-baccalaureate distance learning degree programs offered. *Students:* 1 (woman) full-time, 30 part-time (21 women); includes 11 minority (4 African Americans, 4 Asian Americans or Pacific Islanders, 3 Hispanic Americans). *Degree requirements:* For master's, comprehensive exam, thesis optional. *Entrance requirements:* For master's, 2 letters of recommendation. *Application deadline:* Applications are processed on a rolling basis. Application fee: $50. Electronic applications accepted. *Expenses:* Tuition: Part-time $595 per credit. Required fees: $30 per credit. Tuition and fees vary according to program. *Financial support:* Career-related internships or fieldwork and unspecified assistantships available. Support available to part-time students. Financial award applicants required to submit FAFSA. *Application contact:* Graduate Admissions Office, 860-231-5261, E-mail: graduate@sjc.edu.

Saint Louis University, Graduate School, College of Arts and Sciences and Graduate School, Department of Chemistry, St. Louis, MO 63103-2097. Offers MS, MS-R, PhD. Part-time and evening/weekend programs available. *Degree requirements:* For master's, thesis; for doctorate, comprehensive exam, thesis/dissertation. *Entrance requirements:* For master's, letters of recommendation, resume, interview; for doctorate, letters of recommendation, resumé, interview, transcripts, goal statement. Additional exam requirements/recommendations for international students: Required—TOEFL (minimum score 550 paper-based; 213 computer-based; 80 iBT). Electronic applications accepted. *Faculty research:* Photochemistry, energy, materials, biomaterials, nanomaterials.

Sam Houston State University, College of Arts and Sciences, Department of Chemistry, Huntsville, TX 77341. Offers MS. Part-time programs available. *Faculty:* 4 full-time (0 women). *Students:* 3 full-time (2 women), 2 part-time (1 woman), 4 international. Average age 28. 3 applicants, 33% accepted, 0 enrolled. In 2009, 6 master's awarded. *Degree requirements:* For master's, thesis (for some programs). *Entrance requirements:* For master's, GRE General Test. Additional exam requirements/recommendations for international students: Required—TOEFL (minimum score 550 paper-based; 213 computer-based; 79 iBT). *Application deadline:* For fall admission, 8/1 for domestic and international students; for spring admission, 12/1 for domestic and international students. Applications are processed on a rolling basis. Application fee: $20. *Expenses:* Tuition, state resident: full-time $3690; part-time $205 per credit hour. Tuition, nonresident: full-time $8676; part-time $482 per credit hour. Required fees: $1474. Tuition and fees vary according to course load and campus/location. *Financial support:* Research assistantships, teaching assistantships, Federal Work-Study, institutionally sponsored loans, and tuition waivers (partial) available. Support available to part-time students. Financial award application deadline: 5/31; financial award applicants required to submit FAFSA. *Unit head:* Dr. Rick Norman, Chair, 936-294-1527, Fax: 936-294-4996, E-mail: chm_ren@shsu.edu. *Application contact:* Dr. Thomas Chasteen, Advisor, 936-294-1971, E-mail: chm_tgc@shsu.edu.

San Diego State University, Graduate and Research Affairs, College of Sciences, Department of Chemistry, San Diego, CA 92182. Offers MA, MS, PhD. Terminal master's awarded for partial completion of doctoral program. *Degree requirements:* For doctorate, thesis/dissertation. *Entrance requirements:* For master's, GRE General Test, bachelor's degree in related field, 3 letters of reference; for doctorate, GRE General Test, GRE Subject Test. Additional exam requirements/recommendations for international students: Required—TOEFL. Electronic applications accepted. *Faculty research:* Nonlinear, laser, and electrochemistry; surface reaction dynamics; catalysis, synthesis, and organometallics; proteins, enzymology, and gene expression regulation.

San Francisco State University, Division of Graduate Studies, College of Science and Engineering, Department of Chemistry and Biochemistry, San Francisco, CA 94132-1722. Offers chemistry (MS), including biochemistry. Part-time programs available. Electronic applications accepted.

San Jose State University, Graduate Studies and Research, College of Science, Department of Chemistry, San Jose, CA 95192-0001. Offers MA, MS. Part-time and evening/weekend programs available. *Students:* 1 full-time (0 women), 19 part-time (10 women); includes 9 minority (7 Asian Americans or Pacific Islanders, 2 Hispanic Americans), 4 international. Average age 29. 30 applicants, 30% accepted, 3 enrolled. In 2009, 5 master's awarded. *Degree requirements:* For master's, thesis or alternative. *Entrance requirements:* For master's, GRE. *Application deadline:* For fall admission, 6/29 for domestic students; for spring admission, 11/30 for domestic students. Applications are processed on a rolling basis. Application fee: $59. Electronic applications accepted. *Financial support:* Teaching assistantships, career-related internships or fieldwork, Federal Work-Study, and institutionally sponsored loans available. Support available to part-time students. Financial award application deadline: 6/5; financial award applicants required to submit FAFSA. *Faculty research:* Intercalated compounds, organic/biochemical reaction mechanisms, complexing agents in biochemistry, DNA repair, metabolic inhibitors. *Unit head:* Dr. Bradley Stone, Chair, 408-924-5000, Fax: 408-924-4945. *Application contact:* Dr. Bradley Stone, Chair, 408-924-5000, Fax: 408-924-4945.

The Scripps Research Institute, Kellogg School of Science and Technology, La Jolla, CA 92037. Offers chemical and biological sciences (PhD). *Faculty:* 114 full-time (21 women). *Students:* 222 full-time (78 women). 494 applicants, 20% accepted, 32 enrolled. *Degree requirements:* For doctorate, thesis/dissertation. *Entrance requirements:* For doctorate, GRE General Test, GRE Subject Test, 3 letters of recommendation. Additional exam requirements/recommendations for international students: Required—TOEFL. *Application deadline:* For fall admission, 12/1 for domestic and international students. Application fee: $0. Electronic applications accepted. *Expenses:* Tuition: Full-time $5000. *Financial support:* Fellowships, institutionally sponsored loans, tuition waivers (full), and annual stipends available. *Faculty research:* Molecular structure and function, plant biology, immunology, bioorganic chemistry and molecular design, synthetic organic chemistry and natural product synthesis. *Unit head:* Dr. James R. Williamson, Dean, 858-784-8469, Fax: 858-784-2802, E-mail: gradprgm@scripps.edu. *Application contact:* Marylyn Rinaldi, Administrative Director, 858-784-8469, Fax: 858-784-2802, E-mail: mrinaldi@scripps.edu.

Seton Hall University, College of Arts and Sciences, Department of Chemistry and Biochemistry, South Orange, NJ 07079-2697. Offers analytical chemistry (MS, PhD); biochemistry (MS, PhD); chemistry (MS); inorganic chemistry (MS, PhD); organic chemistry (MS, PhD); physical chemistry (MS, PhD). Part-time and evening/weekend programs available. *Faculty:* 10 full-time (1 woman). *Students:* 24 full-time (14 women), 47 part-time (15 women); includes 22 minority (10 African Americans, 8 Asian Americans or Pacific Islanders, 4 Hispanic Americans), 11 international. Average age 33. 31 applicants, 68% accepted, 10 enrolled. In 2009, 7 master's, 4 doctorates awarded. Terminal master's awarded for partial completion of doctoral program. *Degree requirements:* For master's, thesis optional; for doctorate, comprehensive exam, thesis/dissertation. *Entrance requirements:* Additional exam requirements/recommendations for international students: Required—TOEFL. *Application deadline:* For fall admission, 7/1 priority date for domestic and international students; for spring admission, 11/1 priority date for domestic and international students. Applications are processed on a rolling basis. Application fee: $50. Electronic applications accepted. *Financial support:* Research assistantships, teaching assistantships with full tuition reimbursements, Federal Work-Study and unspecified assistantships available. Financial award applicants required to submit FAFSA. *Faculty research:* DNA metal reactions; chromatography; bioinorganic, biophysical, organometallic, polymer chemistry; heterogeneous catalyst; synthetic organic and carbohydrate chemistry. *Unit head:* Dr. Nicholas Snow, Chair, 973-761-9414, Fax: 973-761-9772, E-mail: snownich@shu.edu. *Application contact:* Dr. Stephen Kelty, Director of Graduate Studies, 973-761-9129, Fax: 973-761-9772, E-mail: keltyste@shu.edu.

Simon Fraser University, Graduate Studies, Faculty of Science, Department of Chemistry, Burnaby, BC V5A 1S6, Canada. Offers chemical physics (PhD); chemistry (PhD). *Degree requirements:* For master's, thesis; for doctorate, thesis/dissertation. *Entrance requirements:* For master's, minimum GPA of 3.0. Additional exam requirements/recommendations for international students: Required—TOEFL (minimum score 600 paper-based; 250 computer-based; 100 iBT). Electronic applications accepted. *Faculty research:* Organic chemistry, nuclear chemistry, physical chemistry, inorganic chemistry, theoretical chemistry.

Smith College, Graduate and Special Programs, Department of Chemistry, Northampton, MA 01063. Offers MAT. Part-time programs available. *Faculty:* 9 full-time (6 women). *Entrance requirements:* For master's, GRE General Test, GRE Subject Test. Additional exam requirements/recommendations for international students: Required—TOEFL (minimum score 590 paper-based; 243 computer-based; 97 iBT). *Application deadline:* For fall admission, 4/1 for domestic students, 1/15 for international students; for spring admission, 12/1 for domestic students. Application fee: $60. *Financial support:* Career-related internships or fieldwork and institutionally sponsored loans available. Support available to part-time students. Financial award application deadline: 1/15; financial award applicants required to submit CSS PROFILE or FAFSA. *Unit head:* Kate Queeney, Chair, 413-585-3835, E-mail: kqueeney@smith.edu. *Application contact:* Ruth Morgan, Administrative Assistant, 413-585-3050, Fax: 413-585-3054, E-mail: gradstdy@smith.edu.

South Dakota School of Mines and Technology, Graduate Division, College of Engineering, Master's Program in Materials Engineering and Science, Rapid City, SD 57701-3995. Offers chemistry (MS); metallurgical engineering (MS); physics (MS). *Faculty:* 6 full-time (0 women), 1 part-time/adjunct (0 women). *Students:* 9 full-time (1 woman), 9 part-time (2 women), 8 international. Average age 26. 9 applicants, 56% accepted, 1 enrolled. In 2009, 4 master's awarded. *Entrance requirements:* For master's, GRE General Test. Additional exam requirements/recommendations for international students: Required—TOEFL, TWE. *Application deadline:* For fall admission, 7/1 priority date for domestic students, 4/1 for international students; for spring admission, 11/1 for domestic students, 9/1 for international students. Applications are processed on a rolling basis. Application fee: $35. Electronic applications accepted. *Expenses:* Tuition, state resident: full-time $3340; part-time $139 per credit hour. Tuition, nonresident: full-time $7060; part-time $294 per credit hour. Required fees: $3270. *Financial support:* In 2009–10, 15 research assistantships with partial tuition reimbursements (averaging $11,400 per year), 11 teaching assistantships with partial tuition reimbursements (averaging $4,063 per year) were awarded; fellowships also available. Financial award application deadline: 5/15. *Unit head:* Dr. Jon Kellar, Chair, 605-394-2343, E-mail: jon.kellar@sdsmt.edu. *Application contact:* Jeannette R. Nilson, Administrative Support Coordinator, Graduate Education, 800-454-8162 Ext. 1206, Fax: 605-394-5360, E-mail: graduate_admissions@sdsmt.edu.

South Dakota State University, Graduate School, College of Arts and Science, Department of Chemistry, Brookings, SD 57007. Offers MS, PhD. *Degree requirements:* For master's, thesis, oral exam; for doctorate, thesis/dissertation, preliminary oral and written exams, research tool. *Entrance requirements:* For master's, bachelor's degree in chemistry or closely related discipline; for doctorate, bachelor's degree in chemistry or closely related discipline. Additional exam requirements/recommendations for international students: Required—TOEFL (minimum score 580 paper-based; 237 computer-based; 92 iBT). *Faculty research:* Environmental chemistry, computational chemistry, organic synthesis and photochemistry, novel material development and characterization.

Southeast Missouri State University, School of Graduate Studies, Department of Chemistry, Cape Girardeau, MO 63701-4799. Offers applied chemistry (MNS), including forensic chemistry. Part-time programs available. *Faculty:* 8 full-time (0 women). *Students:* 13 full-time (9 women), 6 part-time (3 women); includes 2 minority (both African Americans), 12 international. Average age 24. 25 applicants, 32% accepted. In 2009, 1 master's awarded. *Degree requirements:* For master's, comprehensive exam (for some programs), thesis (for some programs). *Entrance requirements:* For master's, GRE General Test, minimum GPA of 2.75 for last 30 semester hours of undergraduate science or math courses; 2 letters of recommendation; completed courses with associated labs in organic chemistry, analytical chemistry, chemistry instrumentation or quantitative analysis, and physical chemistry. Additional exam requirements/recommendations for international students: Required—TOEFL (minimum score 550 paper-based; 213 computer-based); Recommended—IELTS (minimum score 6). *Application deadline:* For fall admission, 8/1 for domestic students, 7/1 for international students; for spring admission, 11/21 for domestic students, 11/1 for international students. Applications are processed on a rolling basis. Application fee: $25 ($100 for international students). Electronic applications accepted. *Expenses:* Tuition, state resident: full-time $4266; part-time $237 per credit hour. Tuition, nonresident: full-time $7506; part-time $417 per credit hour. Required fees: $427; $427. *Financial support:* In 2009–10, 8 students received support, including 1 research assistantship with full tuition reimbursement available, 7 teaching assistantships with full tuition reimbursements available (averaging $7,600 per year); unspecified assistantships also available. Financial award applicants required to submit FAFSA. *Faculty research:* Crystallography, trace metal detection, electrochemistry of metalloporphyrins, organic reactions with supported reagents, synthesis of molecules of biological interest. *Unit head:* Dr. Philip W. Crawford, Chairperson and Professor, 573-651-2166, Fax: 573-986-6433, E-mail: pcrawford@semo.edu. *Application contact:* Marsha L. Arant, Senior Administrative Assistant, School of Graduate Studies, 573-651-2192, Fax: 573-651-2001, E-mail: marant@semo.edu.

Southern Connecticut State University, School of Graduate Studies, School of Arts and Sciences, Department of Chemistry, New Haven, CT 06515-1355. Offers MS. Part-time and evening/weekend programs available. *Faculty:* 2 full-time, 3 part-time/adjunct. *Students:* 14 full-time (5 women), 7 part-time (0 women); includes 2 minority (1 Asian American or Pacific Islander, 1 Hispanic American). 6 applicants, 50% accepted, 3 enrolled. In 2009, 3 master's awarded. *Degree requirements:* For master's, thesis or alternative. *Entrance requirements:*

For master's, interview, undergraduate work in chemistry. *Application deadline:* Applications are processed on a rolling basis. Application fee: $50. Electronic applications accepted. Tuition and fees vary according to program. *Financial support:* Teaching assistantships available. Financial award application deadline: 4/15; financial award applicants required to submit FAFSA. *Unit head:* Dr. Gregory Kowalczyk, Chairperson, 203-392-6268, Fax: 203-392-6396, E-mail: kowalczykg1@southernct.edu. *Application contact:* Dr. Robert Snyder, Graduate Coordinator, 203-392-6263, E-mail: snyderr1@southernct.edu.

Southern Illinois University Carbondale, Graduate School, College of Science, Department of Chemistry and Biochemistry, Carbondale, IL 62901-4701. Offers MS, PhD. Part-time programs available. Terminal master's awarded for partial completion of doctoral program. *Degree requirements:* For master's, one foreign language, thesis; for doctorate, variable foreign language requirement, thesis/dissertation. *Entrance requirements:* For master's, minimum GPA of 2.7; for doctorate, GRE General Test, minimum GPA of 3.25. Additional exam requirements/recommendations for international students: Required—TOEFL. *Faculty research:* Materials, separations, computational chemistry, synthetics.

Southern Illinois University Edwardsville, Graduate Studies and Research, College of Arts and Sciences, Department of Chemistry, Edwardsville, IL 62026-0001. Offers MS. Part-time and evening/weekend programs available. *Faculty:* 18 full-time (3 women). *Students:* 16 full-time (4 women), 12 part-time (3 women); includes 4 minority (3 African Americans, 1 Asian American or Pacific Islander), 11 international. Average age 26. 39 applicants, 41% accepted. In 2009, 10 master's awarded. *Degree requirements:* For master's, thesis (for some programs), research paper. *Entrance requirements:* Additional exam requirements/recommendations for international students: Required—TOEFL (minimum score 550 paper-based; 213 computer-based; 79 iBT), IELTS (minimum score 6.5). *Application deadline:* For fall admission, 7/23 for domestic students, 6/1 for international students; for spring admission, 12/11 for domestic students, 10/1 for international students. Applications are processed on a rolling basis. Application fee: $30. Electronic applications accepted. *Expenses:* Tuition, state resident: part-time $1252.50 per semester. Tuition, nonresident: part-time $3131.25 per semester. Required fees: $586.85 per semester. Tuition and fees vary according to course load. *Financial support:* In 2009–10, 1 research assistantship with full tuition reimbursement (averaging $8,064 per year), 30 teaching assistantships with full tuition reimbursements (averaging $8,064 per year) were awarded; fellowships with full tuition reimbursements, career-related internships or fieldwork, Federal Work-Study, institutionally sponsored loans, scholarships/grants, and unspecified assistantships also available. Support available to part-time students. Financial award application deadline: 3/1; financial award applicants required to submit FAFSA. *Unit head:* Dr. Robert P. Dixon, Chair, 618-650-3576, E-mail: rdixon@siue.edu. *Application contact:* Dr. Leah O'Brien, Director, 618-650-3562, E-mail: lobrien@siue.edu.

Southern Methodist University, Dedman College, Department of Chemistry, Dallas, TX 75275-0314. Offers MS, PhD. *Faculty:* 13 full-time (4 women), 1 (woman) part-time/adjunct. *Students:* 9 full-time (3 women), 3 part-time (2 women); includes 1 minority (Hispanic American), 5 international. Average age 28. 15 applicants, 40% accepted, 4 enrolled. In 2009, 1 master's, 3 doctorates awarded. Terminal master's awarded for partial completion of doctoral program. *Degree requirements:* For master's, comprehensive exam (for some programs), thesis; for doctorate, comprehensive exam, thesis/dissertation, presentation. *Entrance requirements:* For master's and doctorate, GRE General Test, bachelor's degree in chemistry, minimum GPA of 3.0. Additional exam requirements/recommendations for international students: Required—TOEFL. *Application deadline:* For fall admission, 2/28 priority date for domestic and international students; for spring admission, 10/1 for domestic students. Applications are processed on a rolling basis. Application fee: $75. Electronic applications accepted. *Financial support:* In 2009–10, 5 research assistantships with full tuition reimbursements (averaging $22,000 per year), 8 teaching assistantships with full tuition reimbursements (averaging $22,000 per year) were awarded; fellowships, institutionally sponsored loans, scholarships/grants, and unspecified assistantships also available. Financial award application deadline: 2/28. *Faculty research:* Organic and inorganic synthesis, theoretical chemistry, organometallic chemistry, inorganic polymer chemistry, fundamental quantum chemistry. Total annual research expenditures: $1 million. *Unit head:* Dr. John A. Maguire, Chairman, 214-768-2480, Fax: 214-768-4089, E-mail: jmaguire@smu.edu. *Application contact:* Dr. Michael Lattman, Graduate Adviser, 214-768-2467, Fax: 214-768-4089, E-mail: mlattman@smu.edu.

Southern University and Agricultural and Mechanical College, Graduate School, College of Sciences, Department of Chemistry, Baton Rouge, LA 70813. Offers analytical chemistry (MS); biochemistry (MS); environmental sciences (MS); inorganic chemistry (MS); organic chemistry (MS); physical chemistry (MS). *Degree requirements:* For master's, thesis. *Entrance requirements:* For master's, GMAT or GRE General Test. Additional exam requirements/recommendations for international students: Required—TOEFL (minimum score 525 paper-based; 193 computer-based). *Faculty research:* Synthesis of macrocyclic ligands, latex accelerators, anticancer drugs, biosensors, absorption isotheums, isolation of specific enzymes from plants.

Stanford University, School of Humanities and Sciences, Department of Chemistry, Stanford, CA 94305-9991. Offers PhD. *Degree requirements:* For doctorate, thesis/dissertation. *Entrance requirements:* For doctorate, GRE General Test, GRE Subject Test. Additional exam requirements/recommendations for international students: Required—TOEFL. Electronic applications accepted. *Expenses:* Tuition: Full-time $37,380; part-time $2760 per quarter. Required fees: $501.

State University of New York at Binghamton, Graduate School, School of Arts and Sciences, Department of Chemistry, Binghamton, NY 13902-6000. Offers analytical chemistry (PhD); chemistry (MA, MS); inorganic chemistry (PhD); organic chemistry (PhD); physical chemistry (PhD). Part-time programs available. *Faculty:* 14 full-time (3 women), 2 part-time/adjunct (0 women). *Students:* 35 full-time (13 women), 22 part-time (10 women); includes 8 minority (3 African Americans, 4 Asian Americans or Pacific Islanders, 1 Hispanic American), 32 international. Average age 29. 40 applicants, 30% accepted, 6 enrolled. In 2009, 6 master's, 5 doctorates awarded. Terminal master's awarded for partial completion of doctoral program. *Degree requirements:* For master's, thesis or alternative, oral exam, seminar presentation; for doctorate, thesis/dissertation, cumulative exams. *Entrance requirements:* For master's and doctorate, GRE General Test, GRE Subject Test. Additional exam requirements/recommendations for international students: Required—TOEFL (minimum score 550 paper-based; 213 computer-based; 80 iBT). *Application deadline:* For fall admission, 1/15 priority date for domestic and international students; for spring admission, 10/15 priority date for domestic and international students. Applications are processed on a rolling basis. Application fee: $60. Electronic applications accepted. *Financial support:* In 2009–10, 55 students received support, including 4 fellowships with full tuition reimbursements available (averaging $18,000 per year), 8 research assistantships with full tuition reimbursements available (averaging $18,000 per year), 34 teaching assistantships with full tuition reimbursements available (averaging $18,000 per year); career-related internships or fieldwork, Federal Work-Study, institutionally sponsored loans, scholarships/grants, health care benefits, tuition waivers (full), and unspecified assistantships also available. Financial award application deadline: 2/15; financial award applicants required to submit FAFSA. *Unit head:* Dr. Wayne E. Jones, Chairperson, 607-777-2421, E-mail: wjones@binghamton.edu. *Application contact:* Victoria Williams, Recruiting and Admissions Coordinator, 607-777-2151, Fax: 607-777-2501, E-mail: vwilliam@binghamton.edu.

State University of New York at Fredonia, Graduate Studies, Department of Chemistry and Biochemistry, Fredonia, NY 14063-1136. Offers chemistry (MS); curriculum and instruction science education (MS Ed). Part-time and evening/weekend programs available. *Degree requirements:* For master's, thesis optional. *Expenses:* Tuition, state resident: full-time $8370; part-time $349 per credit. Tuition, nonresident: full-time $13,250; part-time $552 per credit. Required fees: $1289; $53.55 per credit.

State University of New York at Oswego, Graduate Studies, College of Arts and Sciences, Department of Chemistry, Oswego, NY 13126. Offers MS. Part-time programs available. *Degree requirements:* For master's, comprehensive exam, thesis. *Entrance requirements:* For master's, GRE General Test, GRE Subject Test, BA or BS in chemistry. Additional exam requirements/recommendations for international students: Required—TOEFL (minimum score 560 paper-based; 220 computer-based).

State University of New York College of Environmental Science and Forestry, Department of Chemistry, Syracuse, NY 13210-2779. Offers biochemistry (MPS, MS, PhD); environmental and forest chemistry (MPS, MS, PhD); organic chemistry (MPS); organic chemistry of natural products (MS, PhD); polymer chemistry (MPS, MS, PhD). *Faculty:* 15 full-time (1 woman). *Students:* 40 full-time (23 women), 12 international. Average age 28. 35 applicants, 46% accepted, 5 enrolled. In 2009, 1 master's, 8 doctorates awarded. *Degree requirements:* For master's, thesis; for doctorate, comprehensive exam, thesis/dissertation. *Entrance requirements:* For master's and doctorate, GRE General Test, GRE Subject Test, minimum GPA of 3.0. Additional exam requirements/recommendations for international students: Required—TOEFL (minimum score 550 paper-based; 213 computer-based; 80 iBT), IELTS (minimum score 6). *Application deadline:* For fall admission, 2/1 priority date for domestic and international students; for spring admission, 11/1 priority date for domestic and international students. Applications are processed on a rolling basis. Application fee: $60. Electronic applications accepted. *Financial support:* In 2009–10, 32 students received support, including 2 fellowships with full tuition reimbursements available (averaging $17,500 per year), 7 research assistantships with full tuition reimbursements available (averaging $17,500 per year), 23 teaching assistantships with full tuition reimbursements available (averaging $17,500 per year); Federal Work-Study, institutionally sponsored loans, scholarships/grants, health care benefits, and unspecified assistantships also available. Financial award application deadline: 6/30; financial award applicants required to submit FAFSA. *Faculty research:* Polymer chemistry, biochemistry. Total annual research expenditures: $1.8 million. *Unit head:* Dr. Arthur J. Stipanovic, Chair, 315-470-6855, Fax: 315-470-6856, E-mail: astipano@esf.edu. *Application contact:* Scott S. Shannon, Dean, Instruction and Graduate Studies, 315-470-6599, Fax: 315-470-6978, E-mail: esfgrad@esf.edu.

Stephen F. Austin State University, Graduate School, College of Sciences and Mathematics, Department of Chemistry, Nacogdoches, TX 75962. Offers MS. Part-time programs available. *Degree requirements:* For master's, comprehensive exam. *Entrance requirements:* For master's, GRE General Test, minimum GPA of 2.8 in last 60 hours, 2.5 overall. Additional exam requirements/recommendations for international students: Required—TOEFL. *Faculty research:* Synthesis and chemistry of ferrate ion, properties of fluoroberyllates, polymer chemistry.

Stevens Institute of Technology, Graduate School, Charles V. Schaefer Jr. School of Engineering, Department of Chemistry, Chemical Biology and Biomedical Engineering, Hoboken, NJ 07030. Offers analytical chemistry (PhD, Certificate); bioinformatics (PhD, Certificate); biomedical chemistry (Certificate); biomedical engineering (M Eng, Certificate); chemical biology (MS, PhD, Certificate); chemical physiology (Certificate); chemistry (MS, PhD); organic chemistry (PhD); physical chemistry (PhD); polymer chemistry (PhD, Certificate). Part-time and evening/weekend programs available. Postbaccalaureate distance learning degree programs offered (no on-campus study). Terminal master's awarded for partial completion of doctoral program. *Degree requirements:* For master's, thesis or alternative; for doctorate, one foreign language, thesis/dissertation; for Certificate, project or thesis. *Entrance requirements:* Additional exam requirements/recommendations for international students: Required—TOEFL. Electronic applications accepted. *Expenses:* Tuition: Full-time $9900; part-time $1100 per credit. Required fees: $286 per semester. *Faculty research:* Biochemical reaction engineering, polymerization engineering, reactor design, biochemical process control and synthesis.

Stony Brook University, State University of New York, Graduate School, College of Arts and Sciences, Department of Chemistry, Stony Brook, NY 11794. Offers MS, PhD. *Faculty:* 28 full-time (6 women), 1 part-time/adjunct (0 women). *Students:* 176 full-time (72 women), 4 part-time (3 women); includes 22 minority (4 African Americans, 15 Asian Americans or Pacific Islanders, 3 Hispanic Americans), 110 international. Average age 28. 268 applicants, 41% accepted. In 2009, 9 master's, 15 doctorates awarded. Terminal master's awarded for partial completion of doctoral program. *Degree requirements:* For master's, thesis; for doctorate, one foreign language, thesis/dissertation. *Entrance requirements:* For master's and doctorate, GRE General Test. Additional exam requirements/recommendations for international students: Required—TOEFL. *Application deadline:* For fall admission, 1/15 for domestic students. Application fee: $60. *Expenses:* Tuition, state resident: full-time $8370; part-time $349 per credit. Tuition, nonresident: full-time $13,250; part-time $552 per credit. Required fees: $933. *Financial support:* In 2009–10, 81 research assistantships, 79 teaching assistantships were awarded; fellowships also available. Total annual research expenditures: $70 million. *Unit head:* Prof. Ben Hsiao, Chairman, 631-632-7880, Fax: 631-632-7960. *Application contact:* Prof. Ben Hsiao, Chairman, 631-632-7880, Fax: 631-632-7960.

Syracuse University, College of Arts and Sciences, Program in Chemistry, Syracuse, NY 13244. Offers MS, PhD. *Students:* 74 full-time (29 women), 5 part-time (1 woman); includes 10 minority (1 American Indian/Alaska Native, 7 Asian Americans or Pacific Islanders, 2 Hispanic Americans), 24 international. Average age 26. 105 applicants, 59% accepted, 26 enrolled. In 2009, 2 master's, 10 doctorates awarded. *Degree requirements:* For master's, one foreign language, comprehensive exam, thesis (for some programs); for doctorate, one foreign language, comprehensive exam, thesis/dissertation. *Entrance requirements:* For master's and doctorate, GRE General Test. Additional exam requirements/recommendations for international students: Required—TOEFL (minimum score 100 iBT). *Application deadline:* For fall admission, 3/15 priority date for domestic and international students. Application fee: $75. Electronic applications accepted. *Expenses:* Tuition: Full-time $26,808; part-time $1117 per credit. Required fees: $1024. *Financial support:* Fellowships with full tuition reimbursements, research assistantships with full and partial tuition reimbursements, teaching assistantships with full tuition reimbursements, tuition waivers (full) available. Financial award application deadline: 1/1; financial award applicants required to submit FAFSA. *Faculty research:* Synthetic organic chemistry, biophysical spectroscopy, solid state in organic chemistry, biochemistry, organometallic chemistry. *Unit head:* Dr. Nancy Totah, Graduate Admissions Chair, 315-443-2675, Fax: 315-443-4070. *Application contact:* Joyce Lagoe, Information Contact, 315-443-4109, E-mail: jalagoe@syr.edu.

Temple University, Graduate School, College of Science and Technology, Department of Chemistry, Philadelphia, PA 19122-6096. Offers MA, PhD. Evening/weekend programs available. Terminal master's awarded for partial completion of doctoral program. *Degree requirements:* For master's, thesis (for some programs); for doctorate, thesis/dissertation, teaching experience. *Entrance requirements:* For master's and doctorate, GRE General Test, minimum GPA of 3.0. Additional exam requirements/recommendations for international students: Required—TOEFL (minimum score 550 paper-based; 213 computer-based; 79 iBT). Electronic applications accepted. *Faculty research:* Polymers, nonlinear optics, natural products, materials science, enantioselective synthesis.

Tennessee State University, The School of Graduate Studies and Research, College of Arts and Sciences, Department of Chemistry, Nashville, TN 37209-1561. Offers MS. Part-time programs available. *Degree requirements:* For master's, thesis optional. *Entrance requirements:* For master's, GRE General Test. Electronic applications accepted.

Chemistry

Tennessee Technological University, Graduate School, College of Arts and Sciences, Department of Chemistry, Cookeville, TN 38505. Offers MS. Part-time programs available. *Faculty:* 16 full-time (1 woman). *Students:* 7 full-time (4 women), 5 part-time (1 woman); includes 6 minority (5 Asian Americans or Pacific Islanders, 1 Hispanic American). Average age 28. 16 applicants, 38% accepted, 5 enrolled. In 2009, 7 master's awarded. *Degree requirements:* For master's, thesis. *Entrance requirements:* For master's, GRE. Additional exam requirements/recommendations for international students: Required—TOEFL (minimum score 550 paper-based; 79 iBT), IELTS (minimum score 5.5). *Application deadline:* For fall admission, 8/1 for domestic students, 5/1 for international students; for spring admission, 2/1 for domestic students, 10/1 for international students. Application fee: $25 ($30 for international students). *Expenses:* Tuition, state resident: full-time $7034; part-time $368 per credit hour. *Financial support:* In 2009–10, 1 research assistantship (averaging $10,000 per year), 6 teaching assistantships (averaging $7,500 per year) were awarded; career-related internships or fieldwork also available. Financial award application deadline: 4/1. *Unit head:* Dr. Jeffrey Boles, Interim Chairperson, 931-372-3421, Fax: 931-372-3434, E-mail: jboles@tntech.edu. *Application contact:* Shelia K. Kendrick, Coordinator of Graduate Studies, 931-372-3808, Fax: 931-372-3497, E-mail: skendrick@tntech.edu.

Tennessee Technological University, Graduate School, College of Arts and Sciences, Department of Environmental Sciences, Cookeville, TN 38505. Offers biology (PhD); chemistry (PhD). *Students:* 9 full-time (5 women), 8 part-time (3 women); includes 9 minority (3 African Americans, 3 Asian Americans or Pacific Islanders, 3 Hispanic Americans). 12 applicants, 50% accepted, 3 enrolled. In 2009, 1 doctorate awarded. *Degree requirements:* For doctorate, comprehensive exam, thesis/dissertation. *Entrance requirements:* For doctorate, GRE. Additional exam requirements/recommendations for international students: Required—TOEFL (minimum score 550 paper-based; 79 iBT), IELTS (minimum score 5.5). *Application deadline:* For fall admission, 8/1 for domestic students, 5/1 for international students; for spring admission, 12/1 for domestic students, 10/2 for international students. Application fee: $25 ($30 for international students). Electronic applications accepted. *Expenses:* Tuition, state resident: full-time $7034; part-time $368 per credit hour. *Financial support:* In 2009–10, 5 research assistantships (averaging $10,000 per year), 3 teaching assistantships (averaging $10,000 per year) were awarded; fellowships also available. Financial award application deadline: 4/1. *Unit head:* Dr. Dal Ensor, Director. *Application contact:* Shelia K. Kendrick, Coordinator of Graduate Studies, 931-372-3808, Fax: 931-372-3497, E-mail: skendrick@tntech.edu.

Texas A&M University, College of Science, Department of Chemistry, College Station, TX 77843. Offers MS, PhD. *Faculty:* 47. *Students:* 281 full-time (96 women), 7 part-time (1 woman); includes 39 minority (7 African Americans, 3 American Indian/Alaska Native, 9 Asian Americans or Pacific Islanders, 20 Hispanic Americans), 140 international. Average age 24. In 2009, 4 master's, 40 doctorates awarded. Terminal master's awarded for partial completion of doctoral program. *Degree requirements:* For master's, thesis; for doctorate, thesis/dissertation. *Entrance requirements:* For master's and doctorate, GRE General Test. Additional exam requirements/recommendations for international students: Required—TOEFL. *Application deadline:* For fall admission, 3/1 priority date for domestic students. Applications are processed on a rolling basis. Electronic applications accepted. *Expenses:* Tuition, state resident: full-time $3991.32; part-time $221.74 per credit hour. Tuition, nonresident: full-time $9049; part-time $502.74 per credit hour. *Financial support:* In 2009–10, fellowships with full tuition reimbursements (averaging $21,600 per year), research assistantships with full tuition reimbursements (averaging $18,600 per year), teaching assistantships with full tuition reimbursements (averaging $18,600 per year) were awarded. Financial award application deadline: 3/1; financial award applicants required to submit FAFSA. *Faculty research:* Biological chemistry, spectroscopy, structure and bonding, reactions and mechanisms, theoretical chemistry. *Unit head:* Dr. David Russell, Head, 979-845-3345, E-mail: chemhead@mail.chem.tamu.edu. *Application contact:* Dr. Michael P. Rosynek, Graduate Advisor, 979-845-5345, Fax: 979-854-5211, E-mail: gradmail@mail.chem.tamu.edu.

Texas A&M University–Commerce, Graduate School, College of Arts and Sciences, Department of Chemistry, Commerce, TX 75429-3011. Offers M Ed, MS. Part-time programs available. *Degree requirements:* For master's, comprehensive exam, thesis (for some programs). *Entrance requirements:* For master's, GRE General Test. Electronic applications accepted. *Faculty research:* Analytical organic.

Texas A&M University–Kingsville, College of Graduate Studies, College of Arts and Sciences, Department of Chemistry, Kingsville, TX 78363. Offers MS. Part-time programs available. *Degree requirements:* For master's, comprehensive exam, thesis or alternative. *Entrance requirements:* For master's, GRE General Test, minimum GPA of 3.0. Additional exam requirements/recommendations for international students: Required—TOEFL. *Faculty research:* Organic heterocycles, amino alcohol complexes, rare earth arsine complexes.

Texas Christian University, College of Science and Engineering, Department of Chemistry, Fort Worth, TX 76129-0002. Offers MA, MS, PhD. Part-time and evening/weekend programs available. *Degree requirements:* For master's, one foreign language, thesis optional; for doctorate, one foreign language, thesis/dissertation, cumulative exams. *Entrance requirements:* For master's and doctorate, GRE General Test. Additional exam requirements/recommendations for international students: Required—TOEFL. *Application deadline:* For fall admission, 3/1 for domestic students; for spring admission, 12/1 for domestic students. Applications are processed on a rolling basis. Application fee: $50. *Expenses:* Tuition: Full-time $17,640; part-time $980 per credit hour. Tuition and fees vary according to program. *Financial support:* Fellowships, teaching assistantships, unspecified assistantships available. Financial award application deadline: 3/1. *Unit head:* Dr. Robert Neilson, Chairperson, 817-257-7345, E-mail: r.neilson@tcu.edu. *Application contact:* Dr. Robert Neilson, Chairperson, 817-257-7345, E-mail: r.neilson@tcu.edu.

Texas Southern University, School of Science and Technology, Department of Chemistry, Houston, TX 77004-4584. Offers MS. *Faculty:* 6 full-time (1 woman), 1 part-time/adjunct (0 women). *Students:* 4 full-time (2 women), 2 part-time (both women); includes 5 minority (4 African Americans, 1 Asian American or Pacific Islander), 1 international. Average age 29. 2 applicants, 100% accepted, 2 enrolled. In 2009, 1 master's awarded. *Degree requirements:* For master's, one foreign language, comprehensive exam, thesis. *Entrance requirements:* For master's, GRE General Test, minimum GPA of 2.5. Additional exam requirements/recommendations for international students: Required—TOEFL. *Application deadline:* For fall admission, 7/1 for domestic and international students; for spring admission, 11/1 for domestic and international students. Applications are processed on a rolling basis. Application fee: $50 ($75 for international students). Electronic applications accepted. *Expenses:* Tuition, state resident: full-time $1805; part-time $100 per credit hour. Tuition, nonresident: full-time $6470; part-time $343 per credit hour. Tuition and fees vary according to course level, course load and degree level. *Financial support:* In 2009–10, 1 research assistantship (averaging $8,000 per year), 1 teaching assistantship (averaging $3,400 per year) were awarded; fellowships, scholarships/grants and unspecified assistantships also available. Financial award application deadline: 5/1. *Faculty research:* Analytical and physical chemistry, geochemistry, inorganic chemistry, biochemistry, organic chemistry. *Unit head:* Chair, 713-313-1032, Fax: 713-313-7824, E-mail: sapp_jb@tsu.edu. *Application contact:* Lulueua Nasser, Administrative Secretary, 713-313-7679, E-mail: nasser_la@tsu.edu.

Texas State University–San Marcos, Graduate School, College of Science, Department of Chemistry and Biochemistry, Program in Chemistry, San Marcos, TX 78666. Offers MA, MS. *Faculty:* 6 full-time (1 woman). *Students:* 10 full-time (6 women), 2 part-time (0 women); includes 2 minority (both Hispanic Americans). Average age 29. 9 applicants, 78% accepted, 5 enrolled. In 2009, 2 master's awarded. *Degree requirements:* For master's, comprehensive exam, thesis (for some programs). *Entrance requirements:* For master's, minimum GPA of 2.75 in last 60 hours of course work. Additional exam requirements/recommendations for international students: Required—TOEFL (minimum score 550 paper-based; 213 computer-based). *Application deadline:* For fall admission, 6/15 for domestic students, 6/1 for international students; for spring admission, 10/15 for domestic students, 10/1 for international students. Applications are processed on a rolling basis. Application fee: $40 ($90 for international students). *Expenses:* Tuition, state resident: full-time $5784; part-time $241 per credit hour. Tuition, nonresident: part-time $551 per credit hour. Required fees: $1728; $48 per credit hour. $306. Tuition and fees vary according to course load. *Financial support:* In 2009–10, 8 students received support, including 8 teaching assistantships (averaging $5,865 per year); research assistantships, career-related internships or fieldwork, Federal Work-Study, and institutionally sponsored loans also available. Support available to part-time students. Financial award application deadline: 4/1; financial award applicants required to submit FAFSA. *Faculty research:* Metal ions in biological systems, cancer chemotherapy, absorption of pesticides on solid surfaces, polymer chemistry, biochemistry of nucleic acids. *Unit head:* Dr. Chad Booth, Chair, 512-245-2156, Fax: 512-245-2374, E-mail: chadbooth@txstate.edu. *Application contact:* Dr. J. Michael Willoughby, Dean of Graduate School, 512-245-2581, Fax: 512-245-8365, E-mail: gradcollege@txstate.edu.

Texas Tech University, Graduate School, College of Arts and Sciences, Department of Chemistry and Biochemistry, Lubbock, TX 79409. Offers biotechnology (MS); biotechnology: science and agricultural biotechnology (MS); chemistry (MS, PhD); JD/MS. Part-time programs available. *Faculty:* 21 full-time (2 women), 1 (woman) part-time/adjunct. *Students:* 92 full-time (33 women), 3 part-time (0 women); includes 3 minority (1 African American, 1 Asian American or Pacific Islander, 1 Hispanic American), 69 international. Average age 27. 157 applicants, 31% accepted, 15 enrolled. In 2009, 8 doctorates awarded. *Degree requirements:* For master's, thesis; for doctorate, thesis/dissertation. *Entrance requirements:* For master's and doctorate, GRE General Test. Additional exam requirements/recommendations for international students: Required—TOEFL (minimum score 550 paper-based; 213 computer-based). *Application deadline:* For fall admission, 3/1 priority date for international students; for spring admission, 11/1 priority date for international students. Applications are processed on a rolling basis. Application fee: $50 ($75 for international students). Electronic applications accepted. *Expenses:* Tuition, state resident: full-time $5100; part-time $213 per credit hour. Tuition, nonresident: full-time $11,748; part-time $490 per credit hour. Required fees: $2298; $50 per credit hour. $555 per semester. *Financial support:* In 2009–10, 39 research assistantships with partial tuition reimbursements (averaging $32,533 per year), 56 teaching assistantships with partial tuition reimbursements (averaging $18,612 per year) were awarded; career-related internships or fieldwork, Federal Work-Study, and institutionally sponsored loans also available. Support available to part-time students. Financial award application deadline: 4/15; financial award applicants required to submit FAFSA. *Faculty research:* Theoretical and computational chemistry, plant biochemistry and chemical biology, materials and supramolecular chemistry, nanotechnology, spectroscopic analysis. Total annual research expenditures: $3.7 million. *Unit head:* Dr. Dominick J. Casadonte, Chair, 806-742-3067, Fax: 806-742-1289, E-mail: chemchair@ttu.edu. *Application contact:* Carly Jenkins, Senior Business Assistant, 806-742-3057, Fax: 806-742-4890, E-mail: carly.jenkins@ttu.edu.

Texas Woman's University, Graduate School, College of Arts and Sciences, Department of Chemistry and Physics, Denton, TX 76201. Offers chemistry (MS); chemistry teaching (MS); science teaching (MS). Part-time programs available. *Faculty:* 6 full-time (1 woman), 1 part-time/adjunct (0 women). *Students:* 6 full-time (all women), 2 part-time (both women), 2 international. Average age 28. 6 applicants, 67% accepted, 3 enrolled. In 2009, 3 master's awarded. *Degree requirements:* For master's, comprehensive exam, thesis. *Entrance requirements:* For master's, GRE General Test (minimum score 400 verbal, 550 quantitative), bachelor's degree in chemistry or equivalent, 2 reference contacts. Additional exam requirements/recommendations for international students: Required—TOEFL (minimum score 550 paper-based; 213 computer-based; 79 iBT). *Application deadline:* For fall admission, 7/1 priority date for domestic students, 3/1 for international students; for spring admission, 12/1 priority date for domestic students, 7/1 for international students. Applications are processed on a rolling basis. Application fee: $50. Electronic applications accepted. *Expenses:* Tuition, state resident: full-time $3564; part-time $198 per credit hour. Tuition, nonresident: full-time $8550; part-time $475 per credit hour. Required fees: $69.26 per credit hour. Tuition and fees vary according to course load. *Financial support:* In 2009–10, 4 students received support, including 3 research assistantships (averaging $10,440 per year), 2 teaching assistantships (averaging $10,440 per year); career-related internships or fieldwork, Federal Work-Study, institutionally sponsored loans, scholarships/grants, traineeships, health care benefits, and unspecified assistantships also available. Support available to part-time students. Financial award application deadline: 3/1; financial award applicants required to submit FAFSA. *Faculty research:* Glutathione synthetase, MRI-acquisition of a circular dichroism spectropolarimeter, construction and analysis of aqueous enzyme phase diagrams, development of metallopolymers, basic chemical research. *Unit head:* Dr. Richard Sheardy, Chair, 940-898-2550, Fax: 940-898-2548, E-mail: rsheardy@mail.twu.edu. *Application contact:* Samuel Wheeler, Assistant Director of Admissions, 940-898-3188, Fax: 940-898-3081, E-mail: wheelersr@twu.edu.

Trent University, Graduate Studies, Program in Applications of Modeling in the Natural and Social Sciences, Department of Chemistry, Peterborough, ON K9J 7B8, Canada. Offers M Sc. Part-time programs available. *Degree requirements:* For master's, thesis. *Entrance requirements:* For master's, honours degree. *Faculty research:* Synthetic-organic chemistry, mass spectrometry and ion storage.

Tufts University, Graduate School of Arts and Sciences, Department of Chemistry, Medford, MA 02155. Offers analytical chemistry (MS, PhD); bioorganic chemistry (MS, PhD); environmental chemistry (MS, PhD); inorganic chemistry (MS, PhD); organic chemistry (MS, PhD); physical chemistry (MS, PhD). *Students:* 61 full-time (29 women); includes 7 minority (1 African American, 1 American Indian/Alaska Native, 4 Asian Americans or Pacific Islanders, 1 Hispanic American), 18 international. 90 applicants, 50% accepted, 14 enrolled. In 2009, 2 master's, 7 doctorates awarded. Terminal master's awarded for partial completion of doctoral program. *Degree requirements:* For master's, thesis optional; for doctorate, thesis/dissertation. *Entrance requirements:* For master's and doctorate, GRE General Test, GRE Subject Test. Additional exam requirements/recommendations for international students: Required—TOEFL (minimum score 600 paper-based; 250 computer-based; 80 iBT). *Application deadline:* For fall admission, 1/15 for domestic students, 12/30 for international students; for spring admission, 10/15 for domestic students, 9/15 for international students. Applications are processed on a rolling basis. Application fee: $75. Electronic applications accepted. *Expenses:* Tuition: Full-time $38,096; part-time $3962 per credit. Required fees: $686; $40 per year. Tuition and fees vary according to course level, course load, degree level, program and student level. *Financial support:* Fellowships, research assistantships with full tuition reimbursements, teaching assistantships with full tuition reimbursements, Federal Work-Study, scholarships/grants, tuition waivers (partial), and unspecified assistantships available. Financial award application deadline: 1/15; financial award applicants required to submit FAFSA. *Unit head:* Arthur Utz, Chair, 617-627-3441. *Application contact:* Samuel Kounaves, Information Contact, 617-627-3441, Fax: 617-627-3443.

Tulane University, School of Science and Engineering, Department of Chemistry, New Orleans, LA 70118-5669. Offers MS, PhD. Terminal master's awarded for partial completion of doctoral program. *Degree requirements:* For master's, thesis; for doctorate, thesis/dissertation. *Entrance requirements:* For master's, GRE General Test, minimum B average in undergraduate course work; for doctorate, GRE General Test. Additional exam requirements/recommendations for international students: Required—TOEFL. Electronic applications accepted. *Faculty research:* Enzyme mechanisms, organic synthesis, photochemistry, theory of polymer dynamics.

Tuskegee University, Graduate Programs, College of Agricultural, Environmental and Natural Sciences, Department of Chemistry, Tuskegee, AL 36088. Offers MS. *Faculty:* 6 full-time (1 woman). *Students:* 12 full-time (7 women), 1 part-time (0 women); includes 6 minority (all African Americans), 6 international. Average age 31. In 2009, 1 master's awarded. *Degree requirements:* For master's, thesis. *Entrance requirements:* For master's, GRE General Test. Additional exam requirements/recommendations for international students: Required—TOEFL (minimum score 500 paper-based; 69 computer-based). *Application deadline:* For fall admission, 7/15 for domestic students. Applications are processed on a rolling basis. Application fee: $25 ($35 for international students). *Expenses:* Tuition: Full-time $15,630; part-time $940 per credit hour. Required fees: $650. *Financial support:* Fellowships, teaching assistantships, Federal Work-Study and institutionally sponsored loans available. Support available to part-time students. Financial award application deadline: 4/15. *Unit head:* Dr. Gregory Pritchett, Head, 334-727-8836. *Application contact:* Dr. Robert L. Laney, Vice President/Director of Admissions and Enrollment Management, 334-727-8580, Fax: 334-727-5750, E-mail: planey@tuskegee.edu.

Universidad del Turabo, Graduate Programs, Programs in Science and Technology, Gurabo, PR 00778-3030. Offers environmental analysis (MSE), including environmental chemistry; environmental management (MSE), including pollution management; environmental science (D Sc), including environmental biology. *Students:* 8 full-time (7 women), 110 part-time (76 women); includes 115 Hispanic Americans. Average age 37. 52 applicants, 65% accepted, 30 enrolled. In 2009, 6 master's awarded. *Entrance requirements:* For master's, GRE, EXADEP, interview. *Application deadline:* For fall admission, 8/5 for domestic students. Application fee: $25. *Application contact:* Virginia Gonzalez, Admissions Officer, 787-746-3009.

Université de Moncton, Faculty of Science, Department of Chemistry and Biochemistry, Moncton, NB E1A 3E9, Canada. Offers biochemistry (M Sc); chemistry (M Sc). Part-time programs available. *Degree requirements:* For master's, one foreign language, thesis. *Entrance requirements:* For master's, minimum GPA of 3.0. Electronic applications accepted. *Faculty research:* Environmental contaminants, natural products synthesis, nutraceutical, organic catalysis, molecular biology of cancer.

Université de Montréal, Faculty of Arts and Sciences, Department of Chemistry, Montréal, QC H3C 3J7, Canada. Offers M Sc, PhD. *Degree requirements:* For master's, thesis; for doctorate, thesis/dissertation, general exam. *Entrance requirements:* For master's, B Sc in chemistry or the equivalent; for doctorate, M Sc in chemistry or equivalent. Electronic applications accepted. *Faculty research:* Analytical, inorganic, physical, and organic chemistry.

Université de Sherbrooke, Faculty of Sciences, Department of Chemistry, Sherbrooke, QC J1K 2R1, Canada. Offers M Sc, PhD, Diploma. *Degree requirements:* For master's, thesis; for doctorate, thesis/dissertation. *Entrance requirements:* For doctorate, master's degree. Electronic applications accepted. *Faculty research:* Organic, electro-, theoretical, and physical chemistry.

Université du Québec à Montréal, Graduate Programs, Program in Chemistry, Montréal, QC H3C 3P8, Canada. Offers M Sc, PhD. Part-time programs available. *Degree requirements:* For master's, thesis. *Entrance requirements:* For master's, appropriate bachelor's degree or equivalent and proficiency in French.

Université du Québec à Trois-Rivières, Graduate Programs, Program in Chemistry, Trois-Rivières, QC G9A 5H7, Canada. Offers M Sc. Part-time programs available. *Degree requirements:* For master's, thesis. *Entrance requirements:* For master's, appropriate bachelor's degree, proficiency in French.

Université Laval, Faculty of Sciences and Engineering, Department of Chemistry, Programs in Chemistry, Québec, QC G1K 7P4, Canada. Offers M Sc, PhD. Part-time programs available. Terminal master's awarded for partial completion of doctoral program. *Degree requirements:* For master's, thesis; for doctorate, comprehensive exam, thesis/dissertation. *Entrance requirements:* For master's and doctorate, knowledge of French, comprehension of written English. Electronic applications accepted.

University at Albany, State University of New York, College of Arts and Sciences, Department of Chemistry, Albany, NY 12222-0001. Offers MS, PhD. *Degree requirements:* For master's, one foreign language, thesis, major field exam; for doctorate, 2 foreign languages, thesis/dissertation, cumulative exams, oral proposition. *Entrance requirements:* For doctorate, GRE. Additional exam requirements/recommendations for international students: Required—TOEFL (minimum score 550 paper-based; 213 computer-based). Electronic applications accepted. *Faculty research:* Synthetic, organic, and inorganic chemistry; polymer chemistry; ESR and NMR spectroscopy; theoretical chemistry; physical biochemistry.

University at Albany, State University of New York, School of Public Health, Department of Environmental Health Sciences, Albany, NY 12222-0001. Offers environmental and analytical chemistry (MS, PhD); environmental and occupational health (MS, PhD); toxicology (MS, PhD). *Degree requirements:* For master's, thesis; for doctorate, comprehensive exam, thesis/dissertation. *Entrance requirements:* For master's and doctorate, GRE General Test, GRE Subject Test, 3 letters of reference. Additional exam requirements/recommendations for international students: Required—TOEFL (minimum score 600 paper-based; 213 computer-based). Electronic applications accepted. *Faculty research:* Xenobiotic metabolism, neurotoxicity of halogenated hydrocarbons, pharmac/toxicogenomics, environmental analytical chemistry.

University at Buffalo, the State University of New York, Graduate School, College of Arts and Sciences, Department of Chemistry, Buffalo, NY 14260. Offers chemistry (MA, PhD); medicinal chemistry (MS, PhD). Part-time programs available. *Faculty:* 34 full-time (5 women), 2 part-time/adjunct (1 woman). *Students:* 143 full-time (62 women), 4 part-time (1 woman); includes 21 minority (9 African Americans, 5 Asian Americans or Pacific Islanders, 7 Hispanic Americans), 43 international. Average age 26. 260 applicants, 30% accepted, 34 enrolled. In 2009, 10 master's, 20 doctorates awarded. Terminal master's awarded for partial completion of doctoral program. *Degree requirements:* For master's, thesis or alternative, project; for doctorate, thesis/dissertation, synopsis proposal. *Entrance requirements:* For master's and doctorate, GRE General Test, GRE Subject Test. Additional exam requirements/recommendations for international students: Required—TOEFL (minimum score 550 paper-based; 213 computer-based; 79 iBT). *Application deadline:* For fall admission, 3/1 priority date for domestic students, 3/1 for international students; for spring admission, 11/1 priority date for domestic students. Applications are processed on a rolling basis. Application fee: $50. Electronic applications accepted. *Financial support:* In 2009–10, 10 students received support, including 10 fellowships with full tuition reimbursements available (averaging $21,500 per year), 50 research assistantships with full tuition reimbursements available (averaging $21,500 per year), 75 teaching assistantships with full tuition reimbursements available (averaging $21,500 per year); Federal Work-Study, institutionally sponsored loans, and unspecified assistantships also available. Financial award application deadline: 6/15; financial award applicants required to submit FAFSA. *Faculty research:* Synthesis, measurements, structure theory, translation. Total annual research expenditures: $9.5 million. *Unit head:* Dr. Luis A. Colon, Chairman, 716-645-6824, Fax: 716-645-6963, E-mail: chechair@buffalo.edu. *Application contact:* Dr. Steven T. Diver, Director of Graduate Studies, 716-645-4208, Fax: 716-645-6963, E-mail: diver@buffalo.edu.

The University of Akron, Graduate School, Buchtel College of Arts and Sciences, Department of Chemistry, Akron, OH 44325. Offers MS, PhD. Part-time and evening/weekend programs available. *Faculty:* 19 full-time (2 women), 1 part-time/adjunct (0 women). *Students:* 59 full-time (29 women), 6 part-time (1 woman); includes 2 minority (1 African American, 1 Hispanic American), 33 international. Average age 28. 72 applicants, 32% accepted, 10 enrolled. In 2009, 1 master's, 10 doctorates awarded. Terminal master's awarded for partial completion of doctoral program. *Degree requirements:* For master's, thesis, seminar presentation; for doctorate, comprehensive exam, thesis/dissertation, cumulative exams, oral exam, defense of dissertation. *Entrance requirements:* For master's, GRE (recommended), baccalaureate degree in chemistry, biochemistry, or a related field, minimum GPA of 2.75, 3 letters of recommendation; for doctorate, GRE (recommended), baccalaureate degree in chemistry, biochemistry, or a related field, minimum GPA of 2.75, three letters of recommendation, statement of purpose. Additional exam requirements/recommendations for international students: Required—TOEFL (minimum score 550 paper-based; 213 computer-based; 79 iBT). *Application deadline:* For fall admission, 6/1 for domestic and international students; for spring admission, 11/15 for domestic and international students. Application fee: $30 ($40 for international students). *Expenses:* Tuition, state resident: full-time $6570; part-time $365 per credit hour. Tuition, nonresident: full-time $11,250; part-time $625 per credit hour. *Financial support:* In 2009–10, 17 research assistantships with full tuition reimbursements, 37 teaching assistantships with full tuition reimbursements were awarded; tuition waivers (partial) also available. Support available to part-time students. *Faculty research:* NMR and mass spectrometric characterization of biological and synthetic polymers, synthesis and characterization of new organic and inorganic material, metals in medicine, enzymalogy of gene regulation, high-resolution spectroscopy and ultrafast characterization of organic materials. Total annual research expenditures: $2.1 million. *Unit head:* Dr. Kim Calvo, Chair, 330-972-6135, E-mail: kcalvo@uakron.edu. *Application contact:* Dr. Kim Calvo, Chair, 330-972-6135, E-mail: kcalvo@uakron.edu.

The University of Alabama at Birmingham, College of Arts and Sciences, Program in Chemistry, Birmingham, AL 35294. Offers MS, PhD. *Degree requirements:* For master's, thesis (for some programs); for doctorate, thesis/dissertation. *Entrance requirements:* For master's and doctorate, GRE General Test. Additional exam requirements/recommendations for international students: Required—TOEFL. *Faculty research:* Drug discovery and synthesis, structural biochemistry and physical biochemistry, synthesis and characterization of advanced materials and polymers.

The University of Alabama in Huntsville, School of Graduate Studies, College of Science, Department of Chemistry, Huntsville, AL 35899. Offers MS. Part-time and evening/weekend programs available. *Faculty:* 14 full-time (2 women). *Students:* 9 full-time (4 women), 3 part-time (2 women); includes 3 minority (all African Americans), 3 international. Average age 30. 14 applicants, 64% accepted, 7 enrolled. In 2009, 2 master's awarded. *Degree requirements:* For master's, comprehensive exam, thesis or alternative, oral and written exams. *Entrance requirements:* For master's, GRE General Test, minimum GPA of 3.0. Additional exam requirements/recommendations for international students: Required—TOEFL (minimum score 550 paper-based; 213 computer-based; 62 iBT). *Application deadline:* For fall admission, 7/15 for domestic students, 4/1 for international students; for spring admission, 11/30 for domestic students, 9/1 for international students. Applications are processed on a rolling basis. Application fee: $40 ($50 for international students). Electronic applications accepted. *Expenses:* Tuition, state resident: part-time $355.75 per credit hour. Tuition, nonresident: part-time $847.10 per credit hour. Required fees: $210.80 per semester. Tuition and fees vary according to course load and program. *Financial support:* In 2009–10, 7 students received support, including 7 teaching assistantships with full and partial tuition reimbursements available (averaging $11,116 per year); career-related internships or fieldwork, Federal Work-Study, institutionally sponsored loans, scholarships/grants, health care benefits, and unspecified assistantships also available. Support available to part-time students. Financial award application deadline: 4/1; financial award applicants required to submit FAFSA. *Faculty research:* Kinetics and bonding, organic nonlinear optical materials, x-ray crystallography, crystal growth in space, polymers, Raman spectroscopy. Total annual research expenditures: $2.2 million. *Unit head:* Dr. William Setzer, Chair, 256-824-6153, Fax: 256-824-6349, E-mail: setzerw@uah.edu. *Application contact:* Kathy Biggs, Graduate Studies Admissions Manager, 256-824-6199, Fax: 256-824-6405, E-mail: deangrad@uah.edu.

University of Alaska Fairbanks, College of Natural Sciences and Mathematics, Department of Chemistry and Biochemistry, Fairbanks, AK 99775-6160. Offers biochemistry and molecular biology (MS, PhD); chemistry (MA, MS); environmental chemistry (MS, PhD). Part-time programs available. *Faculty:* 12 full-time (4 women), 2 part-time/adjunct (1 woman). *Students:* 32 full-time (21 women), 9 part-time (5 women); includes 9 minority (2 African Americans, 2 American Indian/Alaska Native, 2 Asian Americans or Pacific Islanders, 3 Hispanic Americans), 5 international. Average age 35. 26 applicants, 38% accepted, 8 enrolled. In 2009, 3 master's, 3 doctorates awarded. *Degree requirements:* For master's, comprehensive exam, thesis or alternative; for doctorate, comprehensive exam, thesis/dissertation, oral defense. *Entrance requirements:* Additional exam requirements/recommendations for international students: Required—TOEFL (minimum score 550 paper-based; 213 computer-based). *Application deadline:* For fall admission, 6/1 for domestic students, 3/1 for international students; for spring admission, 10/15 for domestic students, 9/1 for international students. Applications are processed on a rolling basis. Application fee: $60. Electronic applications accepted. *Expenses:* Tuition, state resident: full-time $7584; part-time $316 per credit. Tuition, nonresident: full-time $15,504; part-time $646 per credit. Required fees: $23 per credit. $135 per semester. Tuition and fees vary according to course level, course load and reciprocity agreements. *Financial support:* In 2009–10, 1 fellowship (averaging $13,500 per year), 15 research assistantships (averaging $14,179 per year), 11 teaching assistantships (averaging $13,937 per year) were awarded; Federal Work-Study, scholarships/grants, health care benefits, and unspecified assistantships also available. Support available to part-time students. Financial award application deadline: 7/1; financial award applicants required to submit FAFSA. *Faculty research:* Atmospheric aerosols, cold adaptation, hibernation and neuroprotection, liganogated ion channels, arctic contaminants. *Unit head:* Dr. John Keller, Department Chair, 907-474-5510, Fax: 907-474-5640, E-mail: fychem@uaf.edu. *Application contact:* Dr. John Keller, Department Chair, 907-474-5510, Fax: 907-474-5640, E-mail: fychem@uaf.edu.

University of Alberta, Faculty of Graduate Studies and Research, Department of Chemistry, Edmonton, AB T6G 2E1, Canada. Offers M Sc, PhD. Part-time programs available. *Faculty:* 29 full-time (1 woman), 1 part-time/adjunct (0 women). *Students:* 137 full-time (39 women), 18 part-time (5 women). 121 applicants, 69% accepted, 29 enrolled. In 2009, 9 master's, 28 doctorates awarded. Terminal master's awarded for partial completion of doctoral program. *Degree requirements:* For master's, thesis; for doctorate, thesis/dissertation. *Entrance requirements:* For master's and doctorate, minimum GPA of 6.5 on 9.0 scale. *Application deadline:* Applications are processed on a rolling basis. *Expenses:* Contact institution. *Financial support:* In 2009–10, 30 fellowships (averaging $21,175 per year), 19 research assistantships (averaging $20,500 per year), 96 teaching assistantships with partial tuition reimbursements (averaging $20,500 per year) were awarded; scholarships/grants also available. *Faculty research:* Synthetic inorganic and organic chemistry, chemical biology and biochemical analysis, materials and surface chemistry, spectroscopy and instrumentation, computational chemistry. Total annual research expenditures: $10 million Canadian dollars. *Unit head:* Dr. Martin Cowie, Chair, 780-492-3249. *Application contact:* Ilona Baker, Department Office, 780-492-4414, Fax: 780-492-8231, E-mail: grad@chem.ualberta.ca.

The University of Arizona, Graduate College, College of Science, Department of Chemistry, Tucson, AZ 85721. Offers MA, MS, PhD. Part-time programs available. *Faculty:* 36. *Students:* 85 full-time (40 women), 105 part-time (42 women); includes 12 minority (2 African Americans, 3 American Indian/Alaska Native, 2 Asian Americans or Pacific Islanders, 5 Hispanic Americans), 80 international. Average age 29. 124 applicants, 31% accepted, 34 enrolled. In 2009, 10 master's, 21 doctorates awarded. Terminal master's awarded for partial completion of doctoral program. *Degree requirements:* For master's, thesis (for some programs); for doctorate, comprehensive exam, thesis/dissertation. *Entrance requirements:* For master's, GRE General Test, 3 letters of recommendation; for doctorate, GRE General Test, 3 letters of recommendation, statement of purpose. Additional exam requirements/recommendations for international students: Required—TOEFL (minimum score 550 paper-based; 213 computer-based;

Chemistry

The University of Arizona (continued)
79 iBT), SPEAK. *Application deadline:* For fall admission, 2/1 for domestic students, 1/1 for international students; for spring admission, 10/15 for domestic and international students. Applications are processed on a rolling basis. Application fee: $75. Electronic applications accepted. *Expenses:* Tuition, state resident: full-time $9028. Tuition, nonresident: full-time $24,890. *Financial support:* In 2009–10, 67 research assistantships with full tuition reimbursements (averaging $18,933 per year), 96 teaching assistantships with full tuition reimbursements (averaging $18,249 per year) were awarded; institutionally sponsored loans, scholarships/grants, health care benefits, tuition waivers (partial), and unspecified assistantships also available. Financial award applicants required to submit FAFSA. *Faculty research:* Analytical, inorganic, organic, physical chemistry, biological chemistry. Total annual research expenditures: $11.6 million. *Unit head:* Mark A. Smith, Head, 520-621-2115, Fax: 520-621-8407, E-mail: msmith@u.arizona.edu. *Application contact:* Lori Boyd, 800-545-5814, Fax: 520-621-8407, E-mail: chemistry@arizona.edu.

University of Arkansas, Graduate School, J. William Fulbright College of Arts and Sciences, Department of Chemistry and Biochemistry, Fayetteville, AR 72701-1201. Offers chemistry (MS, PhD). *Students:* 13 full-time (5 women), 40 part-time (16 women); includes 4 minority (1 American Indian/Alaska Native, 3 Asian Americans or Pacific Islanders), 21 international. In 2009, 2 master's, 9 doctorates awarded. *Degree requirements:* For master's, one foreign language, thesis; for doctorate, one foreign language, thesis/dissertation. Application fee: $40 ($50 for international students). *Expenses:* Tuition, state resident: full-time $7355; part-time $356.58 per hour. Tuition, nonresident: full-time $17,401; part-time $775.17 per hour. Required fees: $1203. *Financial support:* In 2009–10, 9 fellowships with tuition reimbursements, 27 research assistantships, 22 teaching assistantships were awarded; career-related internships or fieldwork and Federal Work-Study also available. Support available to part-time students. Financial award application deadline: 4/1; financial award applicants required to submit FAFSA. *Unit head:* Dr. Bill Durham, Departmental Chairperson, 479-575-4601, Fax: 479-575-4049, E-mail: cehminfo@uark.edu. *Application contact:* Graduate Admissions, 479-575-6246, Fax: 479-575-5908, E-mail: gradinfo@uark.edu.

University of Arkansas at Little Rock, Graduate School, College of Science and Mathematics, Department of Chemistry, Little Rock, AR 72204-1099. Offers MA, MS. Part-time and evening/weekend programs available. *Degree requirements:* For master's, thesis (MS). *Entrance requirements:* For master's, minimum GPA of 2.7.

The University of British Columbia, Faculty of Science, Program in Chemistry, Vancouver, BC V6T 1Z1, Canada. Offers M Sc, PhD. Terminal master's awarded for partial completion of doctoral program. *Degree requirements:* For master's, thesis; for doctorate, comprehensive exam, thesis/dissertation. *Entrance requirements:* For master's and doctorate, GRE General Test, GRE Subject Test. Additional exam requirements/recommendations for international students: Required—TOEFL (minimum score 580 paper-based; 237 computer-based). Electronic applications accepted. *Faculty research:* Organic, physical, analytical, inorganic, and biochemical projects.

University of Calgary, Faculty of Graduate Studies, Faculty of Science, Department of Chemistry, Calgary, AB T2N 1N4, Canada. Offers analytical chemistry (M Sc, PhD); applied chemistry (M Sc, PhD); inorganic chemistry (M Sc, PhD); organic chemistry (M Sc, PhD); physical chemistry (M Sc, PhD); polymer chemistry (M Sc, PhD); theoretical chemistry (M Sc, PhD). *Degree requirements:* For master's, thesis; for doctorate, thesis/dissertation, candidacy exam. *Entrance requirements:* For master's, minimum GPA of 3.0; for doctorate, honors B Sc degree with minimum GPA of 3.7 or M Sc with minimum GPA of 3.3. Additional exam requirements/recommendations for international students: Required—TOEFL (minimum score 580 paper-based; 237 computer-based). Electronic applications accepted. *Faculty research:* Chemical analysis, chemical dynamics, synthesis theory.

University of California, Berkeley, Graduate Division, College of Chemistry, Department of Chemistry, Berkeley, CA 94720-1500. Offers PhD. *Faculty:* 53 full-time, 2 part-time/adjunct. *Students:* 381 full-time (146 women). Average age 26. 663 applicants, 84 enrolled. In 2009, 65 doctorates awarded. *Degree requirements:* For doctorate, thesis/dissertation, qualifying exam. *Entrance requirements:* For doctorate, GRE General Test, GRE Subject Test, minimum GPA of 3.0, 3 letters of recommendation. Additional exam requirements/recommendations for international students: Required—TOEFL. *Application deadline:* For fall admission, 12/21 for domestic students. Applications are processed on a rolling basis. Application fee: $70 ($90 for international students). Electronic applications accepted. *Financial support:* Fellowships, research assistantships with full tuition reimbursements, teaching assistantships with partial tuition reimbursements, unspecified assistantships available. *Faculty research:* Analytical bioinorganic, bio-organic, biophysical environmental, inorganic and organometallic. *Unit head:* Dr. Michael A. Marletta, Chair, 510-643-9057, Fax: 510-642-9675, E-mail: marletta@berkeley.edu. *Application contact:* Aileen Harris, Graduate Student Affairs Officer, 510-642-5882, Fax: 510-642-9675, E-mail: aileenak@berkeley.edu.

University of California, Davis, Graduate Studies, Graduate Group in Agricultural and Environmental Chemistry, Davis, CA 95616. Offers MS, PhD. *Degree requirements:* For master's, thesis; for doctorate, thesis/dissertation. *Entrance requirements:* For master's and doctorate, GRE General Test, minimum GPA of 3.0. Additional exam requirements/recommendations for international students: Required—TOEFL (minimum score 550 paper-based; 213 computer-based). Electronic applications accepted.

University of California, Davis, Graduate Studies, Program in Chemistry, Davis, CA 95616. Offers MS, PhD. Terminal master's awarded for partial completion of doctoral program. *Degree requirements:* For master's, thesis; for doctorate, thesis/dissertation. *Entrance requirements:* For master's, minimum GPA of 3.0; for doctorate, GRE, minimum GPA of 3.0. Additional exam requirements/recommendations for international students: Required—TOEFL (minimum score 550 paper-based; 213 computer-based). Electronic applications accepted. *Faculty research:* Analytical, biological, organic, inorganic, and theoretical chemistry.

University of California, Irvine, Office of Graduate Studies, School of Physical Sciences, Department of Chemistry, Irvine, CA 92697. Offers chemical and material physics (PhD); chemical and materials physics (MS); chemistry (MS, PhD). *Students:* 216 full-time (79 women); includes 40 minority (3 African Americans, 26 Asian Americans or Pacific Islanders, 11 Hispanic Americans), 38 international. Average age 27. 338 applicants, 35% accepted, 36 enrolled. In 2009, 15 master's, 33 doctorates awarded. *Degree requirements:* For doctorate, thesis/dissertation. *Entrance requirements:* For master's and doctorate, GRE General Test, GRE Subject Test, minimum GPA of 3.0. Additional exam requirements/recommendations for international students: Required—TOEFL (minimum score 550 paper-based; 213 computer-based). *Application deadline:* For fall admission, 1/15 priority date for domestic students, 1/15 for international students. Applications are processed on a rolling basis. Application fee: $70 ($90 for international students). Electronic applications accepted. *Financial support:* Fellowships, research assistantships with full tuition reimbursements, teaching assistantships, institutionally sponsored loans, traineeships, health care benefits, and unspecified assistantships available. Financial award application deadline: 3/1; financial award applicants required to submit FAFSA. *Faculty research:* Analytical, organic, inorganic, physical, and atmospheric chemistry; biogeochemistry and climate; synthetic chemistry. *Unit head:* Dr. Kenneth J. Shea, Chair, 949-824-6018, Fax: 949-824-8571, E-mail: kjshea@uci.edu. *Application contact:* Renee Frigo, Graduate Affairs Officer, 949-824-3082, Fax: 949-824-8571, E-mail: rfrigo@uci.edu.

University of California, Los Angeles, Graduate Division, College of Letters and Science, Department of Chemistry and Biochemistry, Program in Chemistry, Los Angeles, CA 90095. Offers MS, PhD. *Students:* 221 full-time (78 women); includes 60 minority (3 African Americans, 1 American Indian/Alaska Native, 39 Asian Americans or Pacific Islanders, 17 Hispanic Americans), 38 international. Average age 26. 316 applicants, 40% accepted, 54 enrolled. In 2009, 12 master's, 39 doctorates awarded. Terminal master's awarded for partial completion of doctoral program. *Degree requirements:* For master's, comprehensive exam or thesis; for doctorate, thesis/dissertation, oral and written exams, 1 year teaching experience. *Entrance requirements:* For master's, GRE General Test, GRE Subject Test, minimum GPA of 3.0; for doctorate, GRE General Test, GRE Subject Test, minimum undergraduate GPA of 3.0. *Application deadline:* For fall admission, 1/15 for domestic and international students. Application fee: $70 ($90 for international students). Electronic applications accepted. *Financial support:* In 2009–10, 185 fellowships with full and partial tuition reimbursements, 122 research assistantships with full and partial tuition reimbursements, 135 teaching assistantships with full and partial tuition reimbursements were awarded; Federal Work-Study, scholarships/grants, health care benefits, tuition waivers (full and partial), and unspecified assistantships also available. Financial award applicants required to submit FAFSA. *Unit head:* Dr. Albert Courey, 310-825-2530. *Application contact:* Departmental Office, 310-825-3150, E-mail: grad@chem.ucla.edu.

University of California, Merced, Division of Graduate Studies, School of Natural Sciences, Merced, CA 95343. Offers applied mathematics (MS, PhD); biological engineering and small-scale technologies (MS, PhD); environmental systems (MS, PhD); mechanical engineering and applied mechanics (MS, PhD); physics and chemistry (PhD); quantitative and systems biology (MS, PhD). *Expenses:* Tuition, nonresident: full-time $15,102. Required fees: $10,919.

University of California, Riverside, Graduate Division, Department of Chemistry, Riverside, CA 92521-0403. Offers MS, PhD. *Faculty:* 27 full-time (5 women). *Students:* 115 full-time (46 women); includes 16 minority (3 African Americans, 4 Asian Americans or Pacific Islanders, 9 Hispanic Americans), 48 international. Average age 27. 334 applicants, 21% accepted, 22 enrolled. In 2009, 11 master's, 11 doctorates awarded. Terminal master's awarded for partial completion of doctoral program. *Degree requirements:* For master's, qualifying exams or thesis; for doctorate, thesis/dissertation, qualifying exams, 3 quarters of teaching experience, research proposition. *Entrance requirements:* For master's and doctorate, GRE General Test, minimum GPA of 3.0. Additional exam requirements/recommendations for international students: Required—TOEFL (minimum score 550 paper-based; 213 computer-based; 80 iBT). *Application deadline:* For fall admission, 5/1 for domestic students, 2/1 for international students; for winter admission, 9/1 for domestic students, 7/1 for international students; for spring admission, 12/1 for domestic students, 10/1 for international students. Applications are processed on a rolling basis. Application fee: $80 ($100 for international students). Electronic applications accepted. *Financial support:* In 2009–10, 111 students received support, including 4 fellowships with full tuition reimbursements available (averaging $23,749 per year), 24 research assistantships with full tuition reimbursements available (averaging $27,820 per year), 85 teaching assistantships with full tuition reimbursements available (averaging $23,012 per year); career-related internships or fieldwork, Federal Work-Study, institutionally sponsored loans, and tuition waivers (full and partial) also available. Financial award application deadline: 2/1; financial award applicants required to submit FAFSA. *Faculty research:* Analytical, inorganic, organic, and physical chemistry; chemical physics. Total annual research expenditures: $4 million. *Unit head:* Prof. Eric L. Chronister, Chair, 951-827-3488, Fax: 951-827-4713, E-mail: chemchr@ucr.edu. *Application contact:* Prof. Ryan R. Julian, Graduate Advisor, 800-445-3153, Fax: 951-827-4713, E-mail: gradchem@ucr.edu.

University of California, San Diego, Office of Graduate Studies, Department of Chemistry and Biochemistry, La Jolla, CA 92093. Offers chemistry (MS, PhD). *Degree requirements:* For doctorate, thesis/dissertation. *Entrance requirements:* For doctorate, GRE General Test, GRE Subject Test. Electronic applications accepted.

See Close-Up on page 109.

University of California, San Francisco, School of Pharmacy and Graduate Division, Chemistry and Chemical Biology Graduate Program, San Francisco, CA 94143. Offers PhD. *Faculty:* 45 full-time (9 women). *Students:* 48 full-time (23 women); includes 18 minority (2 African Americans, 9 Asian Americans or Pacific Islanders, 7 Hispanic Americans), 4 international. Average age 27. 111 applicants, 19% accepted, 9 enrolled. In 2009, 8 doctorates awarded. *Degree requirements:* For doctorate, thesis/dissertation. *Entrance requirements:* For doctorate, GRE General Test, GRE Subject Test, minimum GPA of 3.0. Additional exam requirements/recommendations for international students: Required—TOEFL (minimum score 550 paper-based; 213 computer-based; 80 iBT). *Application deadline:* For fall admission, 12/1 for domestic and international students. Applications are processed on a rolling basis. Application fee: $70 ($90 for international students). Electronic applications accepted. *Financial support:* In 2009–10, 48 students received support, including 41 fellowships with partial tuition reimbursements available (averaging $19,365 per year), 16 research assistantships with full tuition reimbursements available (averaging $27,000 per year), 2 teaching assistantships with partial tuition reimbursements available (averaging $16,000 per year); institutionally sponsored loans, scholarships/grants, traineeships, and tuition waivers (full) also available. Financial award application deadline: 5/15. *Faculty research:* Biochemistry, macromolecular structure, cellular and molecular pharmacology, physical chemistry and computational biology, synthetic chemistry. *Unit head:* Dr. Charles S. Craik, Director, 415-476-8146, E-mail: craik@cgl.ucsf.edu. *Application contact:* Christine Olson, Senior Administrative Analyst, 415-476-1914, Fax: 415-514-1546, E-mail: olson@cmp.ucsf.edu.

University of California, Santa Barbara, Graduate Division, College of Letters and Sciences, Division of Mathematics, Life, and Physical Sciences, Department of Chemistry and Biochemistry, Santa Barbara, CA 93106-9510. Offers chemistry (MA, MS, PhD). *Faculty:* 21 full-time (5 women), 17 part-time/adjunct (2 women). *Students:* 152 full-time (52 women). Average age 27. 206 applicants, 57% accepted, 29 enrolled. In 2009, 7 master's, 18 doctorates awarded. Terminal master's awarded for partial completion of doctoral program. *Degree requirements:* For master's, comprehensive exam, thesis; for doctorate, comprehensive exam, thesis/dissertation. *Entrance requirements:* For master's, GRE, ACS Exams, 3 letters of recommendation, resume/curriculum vitae; for doctorate, GRE, ACS Exams, 3 letters of recommendation, statement of purpose, personal achievements/contributions statement, resume/curriculum vitae, transcripts for post-secondary institutions attended. Additional exam requirements/recommendations for international students: Required—TOEFL (minimum score 550 paper-based; 213 computer-based; 80 iBT) or IELTS (minimum score 7). *Application deadline:* For fall admission, 1/15 priority date for domestic and international students. Applications are processed on a rolling basis. Application fee: $70 ($90 for international students). Electronic applications accepted. *Financial support:* In 2009–10, 149 students received support, including 58 fellowships with full and partial tuition reimbursements available (averaging $7,700 per year), 100 research assistantships with full and partial tuition reimbursements available (averaging $9,500 per year), 92 teaching assistantships with partial tuition reimbursements available (averaging $8,700 per year); career-related internships or fieldwork, Federal Work-Study, institutionally sponsored loans, scholarships/grants, traineeships, health care benefits, tuition waivers (full and partial), and unspecified assistantships also available. Financial award application deadline: 3/2; financial award applicants required to submit FAFSA. *Faculty research:* Organic, inorganic, physical, and materials chemistry, biochemistry. Total annual research expenditures: $4.5 million. *Unit head:* Dr. Alec Wodtke, Chair, 805-893-2056, Fax: 805-893-4120, E-mail: wodtke@chem.ucsb.edu. *Application contact:* Andrea Wells, Student Affairs Manager, 805-893-5675, Fax: 805-893-4120, E-mail: gradprog@chem.ucsb.edu.

University of California, Santa Cruz, Division of Graduate Studies, Division of Physical and Biological Sciences, Department of Chemistry and Biochemistry, Santa Cruz, CA 95064. Offers MS, PhD. *Degree requirements:* For master's, thesis optional; for doctorate, one foreign language, thesis/dissertation, qualifying exam. *Entrance requirements:* For master's and doctorate, GRE General Test, GRE Subject Test. *Faculty research:* Marine chemistry; biochemistry; inorganic, organic, and physical chemistry.

University of Central Florida, College of Sciences, Department of Chemistry, Orlando, FL 32816. Offers chemistry (PhD); computer forensics (Certificate); industrial chemistry (MS). Part-time and evening/weekend programs available. *Faculty:* 24 full-time (1 woman), 4 part-time/adjunct (1 woman). *Students:* 70 full-time (28 women), 12 part-time (4 women); includes 15 minority (2 African Americans, 5 Asian Americans or Pacific Islanders, 8 Hispanic Americans), 35 international. Average age 30. 91 applicants, 30% accepted, 7 enrolled. In 2009, 4 master's, 3 doctorates awarded. *Degree requirements:* For master's, thesis, final exam. *Entrance requirements:* For master's, GRE General Test, minimum GPA of 3.0 in last 60 hours. Additional exam requirements/recommendations for international students: Required—TOEFL. *Application deadline:* For fall admission, 7/15 for domestic students; for spring admission, 12/1 for domestic students. Application fee: $30. Electronic applications accepted. *Expenses:* Tuition, state resident: part-time $306.31 per credit hour. Tuition, nonresident: part-time $1099.01 per credit hour. Part-time tuition and fees vary according to degree level and program. *Financial support:* In 2009–10, 61 students received support, including 12 fellowships with partial tuition reimbursements available (averaging $5,000 per year), 19 research assistantships with partial tuition reimbursements available (averaging $11,600 per year), 39 teaching assistantships with partial tuition reimbursements available (averaging $11,600 per year); career-related internships or fieldwork, Federal Work-Study, institutionally sponsored loans, tuition waivers (partial), and unspecified assistantships also available. Financial award application deadline: 3/1; financial award applicants required to submit FAFSA. *Faculty research:* Physical and synthetic organic chemistry, lasers, polymers, biochemical action of pesticides, environmental analysis. *Unit head:* Dr. Kevin D. Belfield, Chair, 407-823-2246, Fax: 407-823-2252, E-mail: kbelfield@mail.ucf.edu. *Application contact:* Dr. Kevin D. Belfield, Chair, 407-823-2246, Fax: 407-823-2252, E-mail: kbelfield@mail.ucf.edu.

University of Central Oklahoma, College of Graduate Studies and Research, College of Mathematics and Science, Department of Chemistry, Edmond, OK 73034-5209. Offers MS. Part-time programs available. *Entrance requirements:* For master's, GRE General Test. Electronic applications accepted.

University of Chicago, Division of the Physical Sciences, Department of Chemistry, Chicago, IL 60637-1513. Offers PhD. *Faculty:* 25 full-time (2 women). *Students:* 154 full-time (47 women); includes 14 minority (2 African Americans, 7 Asian Americans or Pacific Islanders, 5 Hispanic Americans), 73 international. Average age 24. 308 applicants, 38% accepted, 29 enrolled. In 2009, 28 doctorates awarded. *Degree requirements:* For doctorate, comprehensive exam, thesis/dissertation. *Entrance requirements:* For doctorate, GRE General Test, GRE Subject Test. Additional exam requirements/recommendations for international students: Required—TOEFL (minimum score 600 paper-based; 205 computer-based; 104 iBT), IELTS (minimum score 7). *Application deadline:* For fall admission, 12/31 for domestic and international students. Applications are processed on a rolling basis. Application fee: $55. Electronic applications accepted. *Expenses:* Contact institution. *Financial support:* In 2009–10, 16 fellowships with full tuition reimbursements (averaging $24,410 per year), 117 research assistantships with full tuition reimbursements (averaging $23,831 per year), 26 teaching assistantships with full tuition reimbursements (averaging $25,764 per year) were awarded; institutionally sponsored loans, scholarships/grants, traineeships, health care benefits, and unspecified assistantships also available. Financial award application deadline: 12/31; financial award applicants required to submit FAFSA. *Faculty research:* Organic, inorganic, physical, biological chemistry. Total annual research expenditures: $10.3 million. *Unit head:* Dr. Richard F. Jordan, Chairman, 773-702-8639, Fax: 773-702-6594, E-mail: chem-chair@uchicago.edu. *Application contact:* Dr. Vera Dragisich, Executive Officer, 773-702-7250, Fax: 773-702-6594, E-mail: v-dragisich@uchicago.edu.

University of Cincinnati, Graduate School, McMicken College of Arts and Sciences, Department of Chemistry, Cincinnati, OH 45221. Offers analytical chemistry (MS, PhD); biochemistry (MS, PhD); inorganic chemistry (MS, PhD); organic chemistry (MS, PhD); physical chemistry (MS, PhD); polymer chemistry (MS, PhD); sensors (PhD). Part-time and evening/weekend programs available. Terminal master's awarded for partial completion of doctoral program. *Degree requirements:* For master's, thesis optional; for doctorate, comprehensive exam, thesis/dissertation. *Entrance requirements:* For master's and doctorate, GRE General Test. Additional exam requirements/recommendations for international students: Required—TOEFL (minimum score 580 paper-based; 237 computer-based). Electronic applications accepted. *Faculty research:* Biomedical chemistry, laser chemistry, surface science, chemical sensors, synthesis.

University of Colorado at Boulder, Graduate School, College of Arts and Sciences, Department of Chemistry and Biochemistry, Boulder, CO 80309. Offers biochemistry (PhD); chemistry (MS). *Faculty:* 44 full-time (7 women). *Students:* 127 full-time (49 women), 71 part-time (36 women); includes 20 minority (4 African Americans, 3 American Indian/Alaska Native, 7 Asian Americans or Pacific Islanders, 6 Hispanic Americans), 30 international. Average age 27. 464 applicants, 10% accepted, 47 enrolled. In 2009, 3 master's, 17 doctorates awarded. *Degree requirements:* For master's, comprehensive exam or thesis; for doctorate, comprehensive exam, thesis/dissertation, cumulative exam. *Entrance requirements:* For master's, GRE General Test, GRE Subject Test, minimum undergraduate GPA of 2.75; for doctorate, GRE General Test, GRE Subject Test, minimum GPA of 3.0. *Application deadline:* For fall admission, 1/15 priority date for domestic students, 1/15 for international students. Applications are processed on a rolling basis. Application fee: $50 ($60 for international students). *Financial support:* In 2009–10, 48 fellowships with full tuition reimbursements (averaging $12,195 per year), 110 research assistantships with full tuition reimbursements (averaging $16,014 per year) were awarded; institutionally sponsored loans, traineeships, and tuition waivers (full) also available. Support available to part-time students. *Faculty research:* Analytical, atmospheric, biochemistry, biophysical, chemical physics, environmental, inorganic, organic and physical chemistry. Total annual research expenditures: $18.1 million.

University of Colorado at Colorado Springs, Graduate School, College of Letters, Arts and Sciences, Master of Sciences Program, Colorado Springs, CO 80933-7150. Offers applied science—bioscience (M Sc); applied science—physics (M Sc); biology (M Sc); chemistry (M Sc); physics (M Sc). Part-time programs available. *Faculty:* 39 full-time (14 women), 2 part-time/adjunct (0 women). *Students:* 19 full-time (6 women), 14 part-time (6 women); includes 5 minority (2 Asian Americans or Pacific Islanders, 3 Hispanic Americans). Average age 31. 29 applicants, 52% accepted, 11 enrolled. In 2009, 8 master's awarded. *Degree requirements:* For master's, thesis or alternative. *Entrance requirements:* For master's, minimum GPA of 2.75. *Application deadline:* For fall admission, 7/1 priority date for domestic students; for spring admission, 12/1 for domestic students. Application fee: $60 ($75 for international students). *Expenses:* Contact institution. *Financial support:* Fellowships, research assistantships, teaching assistantships, career-related internships or fieldwork, Federal Work-Study, and scholarships/grants available. Support available to part-time students. Financial award application deadline: 3/1; financial award applicants required to submit FAFSA. *Faculty research:* Biomechanics and physiology of elite athletic training, genetic engineering in yeast and bacteria including phage display and DNA repair, immunology and cell biology, synthetic organic chemistry. *Unit head:* Dr. Sandra Berry-Lowe, Director, 719-255-7552, Fax: 719-255-3047. *Application contact:* Michael Sanderson, Information Contact, 719-255-3417, Fax: 719-255-3037, E-mail: gradschl@uccs.edu.

University of Colorado Denver, College of Liberal Arts and Sciences, Department of Chemistry, Denver, CO 80217-3364. Offers MS. Part-time programs available. *Students:* 7 full-time (4 women), 12 part-time (5 women); includes 4 minority (2 African Americans, 2 Asian Americans or Pacific Islanders), 3 international. 26 applicants, 42% accepted, 3 enrolled. In 2009, 4 master's awarded. *Degree requirements:* For master's, comprehensive exam, thesis or alternative. *Entrance requirements:* For master's, undergraduate degree in chemistry, minimum GPA of 2.75. Additional exam requirements/recommendations for international students: Required—TOEFL (minimum score 525 paper-based; 197 computer-based). *Application deadline:* For fall admission, 1/15 priority date for domestic students; for spring admission, 12/23 priority date for domestic students. Applications are processed on a rolling basis. Application fee: $50 ($75 for international students). Electronic applications accepted. *Financial support:* Research assistantships, teaching assistantships, Federal Work-Study available. Financial award application deadline: 4/1; financial award applicants required to submit FAFSA. *Faculty research:* Protein electrochemistry, indoor air quality, atmospheric carbonul analysis, chemical education. *Unit head:* Dr. Larry Anderson, Chair, 303-556-6711, Fax: 303-556-4776, E-mail: xiaotai.wang@ucdenver.edu. *Application contact:* Laura Cuellar, Program Assistant, 303-556-4885, Fax: 303-556-4776, E-mail: laura.cuellar@ucdenver.edu.

University of Connecticut, Graduate School, College of Liberal Arts and Sciences, Department of Chemistry, Storrs, CT 06269. Offers MS, PhD. *Faculty:* 31 full-time (5 women). *Students:* 129 full-time (48 women), 7 part-time (5 women); includes 14 minority (6 African Americans, 1 American Indian/Alaska Native, 3 Asian Americans or Pacific Islanders, 4 Hispanic Americans), 78 international. Average age 28. 134 applicants, 10% accepted, 8 enrolled. In 2009, 10 master's, 10 doctorates awarded. Terminal master's awarded for partial completion of doctoral program. *Degree requirements:* For master's, comprehensive exam; for doctorate, thesis/dissertation. *Entrance requirements:* For master's and doctorate, GRE General Test, GRE Subject Test. Additional exam requirements/recommendations for international students: Required—TOEFL (minimum score 550 paper-based; 213 computer-based). *Application deadline:* For fall admission, 2/1 priority date for domestic and international students; for spring admission, 11/1 for domestic students, 10/1 for international students. Applications are processed on a rolling basis. Application fee: $55. Electronic applications accepted. *Expenses:* Tuition, state resident: full-time $4725; part-time $525 per credit. Tuition, nonresident: full-time $12,267; part-time $1363 per credit. Required fees: $346 per semester. Tuition and fees vary according to course load. *Financial support:* In 2009–10, 59 research assistantships with full tuition reimbursements, 67 teaching assistantships with full tuition reimbursements were awarded; fellowships, Federal Work-Study, scholarships/grants, health care benefits, and unspecified assistantships also available. Financial award application deadline: 2/1; financial award applicants required to submit FAFSA. *Unit head:* Steven L. Suib, Head, 860-486-2797, Fax: 860-486-2981, E-mail: slsuib@nucleus.chem.uconn.edu. *Application contact:* James F. Rusling, Chairman, 860-486-4909, Fax: 860-480-2981, E-mail: james.rusling@uconn.edu.

University of Dayton, Graduate School, College of Arts and Sciences, Department of Chemistry, Dayton, OH 45469-1300. Offers MS. *Faculty:* 11 full-time (1 woman). *Students:* 6 full-time (3 women), 5 international. Average age 24. 21 applicants, 19% accepted, 3 enrolled. In 2009, 4 master's awarded. *Degree requirements:* For master's, thesis. *Entrance requirements:* For master's, GRE, ACS standardized exams. Additional exam requirements/recommendations for international students: Required—TOEFL (minimum score 550 paper-based; 213 computer-based; 80 iBT), TWE. *Application deadline:* For fall admission, 3/1 priority date for domestic and international students; for winter admission, 7/1 priority date for international students; for spring admission, 1/1 priority date for international students. Applications are processed on a rolling basis. Application fee: $0. Electronic applications accepted. *Expenses:* Tuition: Full-time $8412; part-time $701 per credit hour. Required fees: $325; $65 per course. $25 per semester. Tuition and fees vary according to course load, degree level and program. *Financial support:* In 2009–10, 1 research assistantship with full and partial tuition reimbursement (averaging $11,460 per year), 5 teaching assistantships with full tuition reimbursements (averaging $11,484 per year) were awarded. Financial award applicants required to submit FAFSA. *Faculty research:* Organic synthesis, medicinal chemistry, enzyme purification, physical organic, materials chemistry and nanotechnology. *Unit head:* Dr. Mark Masthay, Chair, Chemistry Department, 937-229-2631, E-mail: mark.masthay@notes.udayton.edu. *Application contact:* Graduate Admissions, 937-229-4411, Fax: 937-229-4729, E-mail: gradadmission@udayton.edu.

University of Delaware, College of Arts and Sciences, Department of Chemistry and Biochemistry, Newark, DE 19716. Offers biochemistry (MA, MS, PhD); chemistry (MA, MS, PhD). Part-time programs available. Terminal master's awarded for partial completion of doctoral program. *Degree requirements:* For master's, one foreign language, thesis (for some programs); for doctorate, one foreign language, thesis/dissertation, cumulative exam. *Entrance requirements:* For master's and doctorate, GRE General Test. Additional exam requirements/recommendations for international students: Required—TOEFL (minimum score 600 paper-based; 260 computer-based). Electronic applications accepted. *Faculty research:* Micro-organisms, bone, cancer metastosis, developmental biology, cell biology, molecular biology.

University of Denver, Faculty of Natural Sciences and Mathematics, Department of Chemistry, Denver, CO 80208. Offers MA, MS, PhD. Part-time programs available. *Faculty:* 14 full-time (3 women). *Students:* 8 full-time (6 women), 9 part-time (4 women); includes 1 minority (American Indian/Alaska Native), 3 international. Average age 25. 44 applicants, 41% accepted, 11 enrolled. In 2009, 5 master's, 2 doctorates awarded. Terminal master's awarded for partial completion of doctoral program. *Degree requirements:* For master's, thesis; for doctorate, thesis/dissertation. *Entrance requirements:* For master's and doctorate, GRE General Test. Additional exam requirements/recommendations for international students: Required—TOEFL. *Application deadline:* Applications are processed on a rolling basis. Application fee: $50. Electronic applications accepted. *Expenses:* Tuition: Full-time $34,596; part-time $961 per quarter hour. Required fees: $4 per quarter hour. Tuition and fees vary according to course load, campus/location and program. *Financial support:* In 2009–10, 7 research assistantships with full and partial tuition reimbursements (averaging $17,000 per year), 12 teaching assistantships with full and partial tuition reimbursements (averaging $17,000 per year) were awarded; career-related internships or fieldwork, Federal Work-Study, institutionally sponsored loans, and scholarships/grants also available. Support available to part-time students. Financial award application deadline: 3/1; financial award applicants required to submit FAFSA. *Faculty research:* Atmospheric chemistry, magnetic resonance, molecular spectroscopy, laser photolysis, biophysical chemistry. Total annual research expenditures: $1.6 million. *Unit head:* Dr. Sandra Eaton, Chairperson, 303-871-3100. *Application contact:* Information Contact, 303-871-2435, E-mail: chem-info@du.edu.

University of Detroit Mercy, College of Engineering and Science, Department of Chemistry and Biochemistry, Detroit, MI 48221. Offers chemistry (MS). Evening/weekend programs available. *Degree requirements:* For master's, thesis. *Entrance requirements:* For master's, GRE General Test, minimum GPA of 3.0. *Faculty research:* Polymer and physical chemistry, industrial aspects of chemistry.

University of Florida, Graduate School, College of Liberal Arts and Sciences, Department of Chemistry, Gainesville, FL 32611. Offers MS, MST, PhD. *Degree requirements:* For master's, thesis; for doctorate, one foreign language, thesis/dissertation. *Entrance requirements:* For master's and doctorate, GRE General Test, minimum GPA of 3.0. Additional exam requirements/recommendations for international students: Required—TOEFL (minimum score 550 paper-based; 213 computer-based). Electronic applications accepted. *Faculty research:* Organic, analytical, physical, inorganic, and biological chemistry.

University of Georgia, Graduate School, College of Arts and Sciences, Department of Chemistry, Athens, GA 30602. Offers analytical chemistry (MS, PhD); inorganic chemistry (MS, PhD); organic chemistry (MS, PhD); physical chemistry (MS, PhD). *Faculty:* 25 full-time (1 woman). *Students:* 147 full-time (53 women), 2 part-time (1 woman); includes 14 minority (6 African Americans, 7 Asian Americans or Pacific Islanders, 1 Hispanic Americans), 61 international. 136 applicants, 55% accepted, 27 enrolled. In 2009, 3 master's, 23 doctorates awarded. Terminal master's awarded for partial completion of doctoral program. *Degree requirements:* For master's, thesis; for doctorate, one foreign language, thesis/dissertation. *Entrance*

Chemistry

University of Georgia (continued)
requirements: For master's and doctorate, GRE General Test. Additional exam requirements/recommendations for international students: Required—TOEFL (minimum score 213 computer-based). *Application deadline:* For fall admission, 7/1 priority date for domestic students; for spring admission, 11/15 for domestic students. Application fee: $50. Electronic applications accepted. *Expenses:* Tuition, state resident: full-time $6000; part-time $250 per credit hour. Tuition, nonresident: full-time $20,904; part-time $871 per credit hour. Required fees: $730 per semester. *Financial support:* Fellowships, research assistantships, teaching assistantships, unspecified assistantships available. *Unit head:* Dr. John L. Stickney, Head, 706-542-2726, Fax: 706-542-9454, E-mail: stickney@chem.uga.edu. *Application contact:* Dr. George F. Majetich, Graduate Coordinator, 706-542-1966, Fax: 706-542-9454, E-mail: majetich@chem.uga.edu.

University of Guelph, Graduate Program Services, College of Physical and Engineering Science, Guelph-Waterloo Centre for Graduate Work in Chemistry and Biochemistry, Guelph, ON N1G 2W1, Canada. Offers M Sc, PhD. Part-time programs available. *Degree requirements:* For master's, thesis; for doctorate, thesis/dissertation. *Faculty research:* Inorganic, analytical, biological, physical/theoretical, polymer, and organic chemistry.

University of Hawaii at Manoa, Graduate Division, College of Natural Sciences, Department of Chemistry, Honolulu, HI 96822. Offers MS, PhD. Part-time programs available. *Faculty:* 12 full-time (2 women), 3 part-time/adjunct (0 women). *Students:* 36 full-time (10 women), 2 part-time (1 woman); includes 10 minority (1 American Indian/Alaska Native, 6 Asian Americans or Pacific Islanders, 3 Hispanic Americans), 11 international. Average age 26. 46 applicants, 48% accepted, 10 enrolled. In 2009, 6 master's, 2 doctorates awarded. *Degree requirements:* For master's, comprehensive exam, thesis; for doctorate, comprehensive exam, thesis/dissertation. *Entrance requirements:* For master's and doctorate, GRE General Test, GRE Subject Test. Additional exam requirements/recommendations for international students: Required—TOEFL (minimum score 500 paper-based; 173 computer-based; 61 iBT), IELTS (minimum score 5). *Application deadline:* For fall admission, 5/1 for domestic students, 3/1 for international students; for spring admission, 9/1 for domestic students, 8/1 for international students. Applications are processed on a rolling basis. Application fee: $60. *Expenses:* Tuition, state resident: full-time $8900; part-time $372 per credit. Tuition, nonresident: full-time $21,400; part-time $898 per credit. Required fees: $207 per semester. *Financial support:* In 2009–10, 1 fellowship (averaging $1,000 per year), 9 research assistantships (averaging $18,079 per year), 26 teaching assistantships (averaging $15,753 per year) were awarded. Support available to part-time students. *Faculty research:* Marine natural products, biophysical spectroscopy, zeolites, organometallic hydrides, new visual pigments, theory of surfaces. Total annual research expenditures: $2.3 million. *Application contact:* Thomas Hemscheidt, Graduate Chair, 808-956-7480, Fax: 808-956-5908, E-mail: hemschei@hawaii.edu.

University of Houston, College of Natural Sciences and Mathematics, Department of Chemistry, Houston, TX 77204. Offers MA, MS, PhD. Part-time programs available. *Faculty:* 22 full-time (1 woman), 4 part-time/adjunct (1 woman). *Students:* 102 full-time (40 women), 4 part-time (1 woman); includes 13 minority (2 African Americans, 7 Asian Americans or Pacific Islanders, 4 Hispanic Americans), 79 international. Average age 29. 32 applicants, 100% accepted, 28 enrolled. In 2009, 8 master's, 16 doctorates awarded. Terminal master's awarded for partial completion of doctoral program. *Degree requirements:* For master's, thesis; for doctorate, thesis/dissertation, oral presentation. *Entrance requirements:* For master's and doctorate, GRE General Test. Additional exam requirements/recommendations for international students: Required—TOEFL. *Application deadline:* Applications are processed on a rolling basis. Application fee: $0 ($75 for international students). Electronic applications accepted. *Expenses:* Tuition, state resident: full-time $7676; part-time $320 per credit hour. Tuition, nonresident: full-time $14,324; part-time $597 per credit hour. Required fees: $3034. *Financial support:* In 2009–10, 70 fellowships with full tuition reimbursements (averaging $13,700 per year), 22 teaching assistantships with full tuition reimbursements (averaging $13,700 per year) were awarded; career-related internships or fieldwork, Federal Work-Study, institutionally sponsored loans, scholarships/grants, health care benefits, and unspecified assistantships also available. Support available to part-time students. Financial award application deadline: 2/1. *Faculty research:* Materials, molecular design, surface science, structural chemistry, synthesis. *Unit head:* Dr. David Hoffman, Chairperson, 713-743-2701, Fax: 713-743-2709, E-mail: hoffman@uh.edu. *Application contact:* Dr. David Hoffman, Chairperson, 713-743-2701, Fax: 713-743-2709, E-mail: hoffman@uh.edu.

University of Houston–Clear Lake, School of Science and Computer Engineering, Program in Chemistry, Houston, TX 77058-1098. Offers MS. Part-time and evening/weekend programs available. *Entrance requirements:* For master's, GRE General Test. Additional exam requirements/recommendations for international students: Required—TOEFL (minimum score 550 paper-based; 213 computer-based).

University of Idaho, College of Graduate Studies, College of Science, Department of Chemistry, Moscow, ID 83844-2282. Offers MS. *Faculty:* 9 full-time, 2 part-time/adjunct. *Students:* 32 full-time, 3 part-time. In 2009, 5 master's awarded. *Degree requirements:* For master's, thesis or alternative. *Entrance requirements:* For master's, minimum GPA of 2.8. *Application deadline:* For fall admission, 8/1 for domestic students; for spring admission, 12/15 for domestic students. Application fee: $55 ($60 for international students). *Expenses:* Tuition, state resident: full-time $6120. Tuition, nonresident: full-time $17,712. *Financial support:* Fellowships, research assistantships, teaching assistantships available. Financial award application deadline: 2/15. *Faculty research:* Analytical chemistry, inorganic chemistry, organic chemistry, physical chemistry. *Unit head:* Dr. Ray von Wandruska, Chair, 208-885-6552. *Application contact:* Dr. Ray von Wandruska, Chair, 208-885-6552.

University of Illinois at Chicago, College of Pharmacy and Graduate College, Graduate Programs in Pharmacy, Chicago, IL 60607-7128. Offers biopharmaceutical sciences (PhD); forensic science (MS); medicinal chemistry (MS, PhD); pharmacognosy (MS, PhD); pharmacy administration (MS, PhD). Terminal master's awarded for partial completion of doctoral program. *Degree requirements:* For master's, variable foreign language requirement, thesis; for doctorate, variable foreign language requirement, thesis/dissertation. *Entrance requirements:* For master's and doctorate, GRE General Test. Additional exam requirements/recommendations for international students: Required—TOEFL. Electronic applications accepted. *Expenses:* Contact institution.

University of Illinois at Chicago, Graduate College, College of Liberal Arts and Sciences, Department of Chemistry, Chicago, IL 60607-7128. Offers MS, PhD. Part-time programs available. Terminal master's awarded for partial completion of doctoral program. *Degree requirements:* For master's, thesis or cumulative exam; for doctorate, one foreign language, thesis/dissertation, cumulative exams. *Entrance requirements:* For master's and doctorate, GRE Subject Test, minimum GPA of 3.0. Additional exam requirements/recommendations for international students: Required—TOEFL. Electronic applications accepted.

University of Illinois at Urbana–Champaign, Graduate College, College of Liberal Arts and Sciences, School of Chemical Sciences, Department of Chemistry, Champaign, IL 61820. Offers astrochemistry (PhD); chemical physics (PhD); chemistry (MA, MS, PhD); teaching of chemistry (MS); MS/JD; MS/MBA. *Faculty:* 34 full-time (6 women). *Students:* 308 full-time (91 women), 4 part-time (1 woman); includes 34 minority (6 African Americans, 3 American Indian/Alaska Native, 18 Asian Americans or Pacific Islanders, 7 Hispanic Americans), 69 international. 502 applicants, 13% accepted, 63 enrolled. In 2009, 14 master's, 51 doctorates awarded. *Entrance requirements:* For master's and doctorate, GRE General Test, GRE Subject Test, minimum GPA of 3.0. Additional exam requirements/recommendations for international students: Required—TOEFL (minimum score 580 paper-based; 237 computer-based). *Application deadline:* Applications are processed on a rolling basis. Application fee: $60 ($75 for international students). Electronic applications accepted. *Financial support:* In 2009–10, 108 fellowships, 186 research assistantships, 164 teaching assistantships were awarded; tuition waivers (full and partial) also available. *Unit head:* Steven C. Zimmerman, Head, 217-333-6655, Fax: 217-244-5943, E-mail: sczimmer@illinois.edu. *Application contact:* Dorothy Ann Gordon, Assistant to the Head, 217-244-0618, Fax: 217-244-5943, E-mail: dorothyh@illinois.edu.

The University of Iowa, Graduate College, College of Liberal Arts and Sciences, Department of Chemistry, Iowa City, IA 52242-1316. Offers MS, PhD. *Degree requirements:* For master's, thesis optional, exam; for doctorate, comprehensive exam, thesis/dissertation. *Entrance requirements:* For master's and doctorate, GRE General Test, minimum GPA of 3.0. Additional exam requirements/recommendations for international students: Required—TOEFL (minimum score 550 paper-based; 213 computer-based; 81 iBT). Electronic applications accepted.

The University of Kansas, Graduate Studies, College of Liberal Arts and Sciences, Department of Chemistry, Lawrence, KS 66045. Offers MS, PhD. *Faculty:* 29. *Students:* 85 full-time (34 women), 7 part-time (4 women); includes 5 minority (2 African Americans, 3 Hispanic Americans), 29 international. Average age 27. 131 applicants, 28% accepted, 11 enrolled. In 2009, 2 master's, 12 doctorates awarded. *Degree requirements:* For master's, thesis; for doctorate, comprehensive exam, thesis/dissertation. *Entrance requirements:* For master's and doctorate, GRE General Test. Additional exam requirements/recommendations for international students: Required—TOEFL. *Application deadline:* For fall admission, 2/1 priority date for domestic and international students; for spring admission, 9/1 priority date for domestic students, 7/1 priority date for international students. Applications are processed on a rolling basis. Application fee: $45 ($55 for international students). Electronic applications accepted. *Expenses:* Tuition, state resident: full-time $6492; part-time $270.50 per credit hour. Tuition, nonresident: full-time $15,510; part-time $646.25 per credit hour. Required fees: $847; $70.56 per credit hour. Tuition and fees vary according to course load and program. *Financial support:* Fellowships with full tuition reimbursements, research assistantships with full and partial tuition reimbursements, teaching assistantships with full and partial tuition reimbursements, scholarships/grants, traineeships, tuition waivers (full), and unspecified assistantships available. Financial award application deadline: 4/15. *Faculty research:* Organometallic and inorganic synthetic methodology, bioanalytical chemistry, computational materials science, proteomics, biophysical chemistry. *Unit head:* Prof. Craig E. Lunte, Chair, 785-864-4670, Fax: 785-864-5396, E-mail: clunte@ku.edu. *Application contact:* Prof. Brian B. Laird, Associate Chair for Graduate Studies, 785-864-4632, Fax: 785-864-5396, E-mail: blaird@ku.edu.

University of Kentucky, Graduate School, College of Arts and Sciences, Program in Chemistry, Lexington, KY 40506-0032. Offers MS, PhD. Part-time programs available. Terminal master's awarded for partial completion of doctoral program. *Degree requirements:* For master's, comprehensive exam, thesis optional; for doctorate, comprehensive exam, thesis/dissertation. *Entrance requirements:* For master's, GRE General Test, minimum undergraduate GPA of 2.75; for doctorate, GRE General Test, minimum graduate GPA of 3.0. Additional exam requirements/recommendations for international students: Required—TOEFL (minimum score 550 paper-based; 213 computer-based). Electronic applications accepted. *Faculty research:* Analytical, inorganic, organic, and physical chemistry; biological chemistry; nuclear chemistry; radiochemistry; materials chemistry.

University of Lethbridge, School of Graduate Studies, Lethbridge, AB T1K 3M4, Canada. Offers accounting (MScM); addictions counseling (M Sc); agricultural biotechnology (M Sc); agricultural studies (M Sc, MA); anthropology (MA); archaeology (MA); art (MA, MFA); biochemistry (M Sc); biological sciences (M Sc); biomolecular science (PhD); biosystems and biodiversity (PhD); Canadian studies (MA); chemistry (M Sc); computer science (M Sc); computer science and geographical information science (M Sc); counseling psychology (M Ed); dramatic arts (MA); earth, space, and physical science (PhD); economics (MA); educational leadership (M Ed); English (MA); environmental science (M Sc); evolution and behavior (PhD); exercise science (M Sc); finance (MScM); French (MA); French/German (MA); French/Spanish (MA); general education (M Ed); general management (MScM); geography (M Sc, MA); German (MA); health science (M Sc); health sciences (MA); history (MA); human resource management and labour relations (MScM); individualized multidisciplinary (M Sc, MA); information systems (MScM); international management (MScM); kinesiology (M Sc, MA); management (M Sc, MA); marketing (MScM); mathematics (M Sc); music (M Mus, MA); Native American studies (MA); neuroscience (M Sc, PhD); new media (MA); nursing (M Sc); philosophy (MA); physics (M Sc); policy and strategy (MScM); political science (MA); psychology (M Sc, MA); religious studies (MA); social sciences (MA); sociology (MA); theatre and dramatic arts (MFA); theoretical and computational science (PhD); urban and regional studies (MA); women's studies (MA). Part-time and evening/weekend programs available. *Degree requirements:* For doctorate, comprehensive exam, thesis/dissertation. *Entrance requirements:* For master's, GMAT (M Sc in management), bachelor's degree in related field, minimum GPA of 3.0 during previous 20 graded semester courses, 2 years teaching or related experience (M Ed); for doctorate, master's degree, minimum graduate GPA of 3.5. Additional exam requirements/recommendations for international students: Required—TOEFL. *Faculty research:* Movement and brain plasticity, gibberellin physiology, photosynthesis, carbon cycling, molecular properties of main-group ring components.

University of Louisville, Graduate School, College of Arts and Sciences, Department of Chemistry, Louisville, KY 40292-0001. Offers analytical chemistry (MS, PhD); biochemistry (MS, PhD); chemical physics (PhD); inorganic chemistry (MS, PhD); organic chemistry (MS, PhD); physical chemistry (MS, PhD). *Students:* 57 full-time (27 women), 4 part-time (1 woman); includes 2 minority (1 African American, 1 Asian American or Pacific Islander), 43 international. Average age 29. 62 applicants, 31% accepted, 13 enrolled. In 2009, 6 master's, 7 doctorates awarded. *Median time to degree:* Of those who began their doctoral program in fall 2001, 0% received their degree in 8 years or less. *Degree requirements:* For master's, thesis; for doctorate, comprehensive exam, thesis/dissertation. *Entrance requirements:* For master's and doctorate, GRE General Test. Additional exam requirements/recommendations for international students: Required—TOEFL. *Application deadline:* Applications are processed on a rolling basis. Application fee: $50. *Financial support:* Fellowships, research assistantships, teaching assistantships available. *Unit head:* Dr. George R. Pack, Chair, 502-852-6798, Fax: 502-852-8149, E-mail: george.pack@louisville.edu. *Application contact:* Libby Leggett, Director, Graduate Admissions, 502-852-3101, Fax: 502-852-6536, E-mail: gradadm@louisville.edu.

University of Maine, Graduate School, College of Liberal Arts and Sciences, Department of Chemistry, Orono, ME 04469. Offers MS, PhD. *Faculty:* 13 full-time (3 women). *Students:* 21 full-time (5 women), 4 part-time (2 women); includes 3 minority (1 American Indian/Alaska Native, 2 Asian Americans or Pacific Islanders), 14 international. Average age 31. 16 applicants, 56% accepted, 3 enrolled. In 2009, 4 doctorates awarded. Terminal master's awarded for partial completion of doctoral program. *Degree requirements:* For master's, thesis; for doctorate, thesis/dissertation, oral exam. *Entrance requirements:* For master's and doctorate, GRE General Test. Additional exam requirements/recommendations for international students: Required—TOEFL. *Application deadline:* For fall admission, 2/1 priority date for domestic students. Applications are processed on a rolling basis. Application fee: $65. Electronic applications accepted. *Financial support:* In 2009–10, 2 research assistantships with tuition reimbursements (averaging $17,550 per year), 15 teaching assistantships with tuition reimbursements (averaging $16,000 per year) were awarded; tuition waivers (full and partial) also available. Financial award application deadline: 3/1. *Faculty research:* Quantum mechanics, insect chemistry, organic synthesis. *Unit head:* Dr. Alice Bruce, Chair, 207-581-1168. *Application contact:* Scott G. Delcourt, Associate Dean of the Graduate School, 207-581-3291, Fax: 207-581-3232, E-mail: graduate@maine.edu.

University of Manitoba, Faculty of Graduate Studies, Faculty of Science, Department of Chemistry, Winnipeg, MB R3T 2N2, Canada. Offers M Sc, PhD. *Degree requirements:* For master's, thesis; for doctorate, one foreign language, thesis/dissertation.

University of Maryland, Baltimore County, Graduate School, College of Arts, Humanities and Social Sciences, Department of Education, Program in Teaching, Baltimore, MD 21250. Offers early childhood education (MAT); elementary education (MAT); secondary education (MAT), including art, biology, chemistry, dance, earth/space science, English, foreign language, mathematics, music, physics, theatre; secondary science (MAT), including social studies. Part-time and evening/weekend programs available. *Faculty:* 24 full-time (18 women), 25 part-time/adjunct (19 women). *Students:* 52 full-time (41 women), 64 part-time (55 women); includes 20 minority (5 African Americans, 1 American Indian/Alaska Native, 10 Asian Americans or Pacific Islanders, 4 Hispanic Americans), 3 international. Average age 31. 88 applicants, 57% accepted, 39 enrolled. In 2009, 106 master's awarded. *Degree requirements:* For master's, comprehensive exam (for some programs), thesis (for some programs). *Entrance requirements:* For master's, PRAXIS I and II, minimum GPA of 3.0. Additional exam requirements/recommendations for international students: Required—TOEFL. *Application deadline:* For fall admission, 6/1 for domestic students; for spring admission, 11/1 for domestic students. Applications are processed on a rolling basis. Application fee: $50. Electronic applications accepted. *Financial support:* In 2009–10, 6 students received support, including research assistantships with full tuition reimbursements available (averaging $12,000 per year); career-related internships or fieldwork, Federal Work-Study, scholarships/grants, tuition waivers, and unspecified assistantships also available. Financial award application deadline: 3/1. *Faculty research:* STEM teacher education, culturally sensitive pedagogy, ESOL/bilingual education, early childhood education, language, literacy and culture. *Unit head:* Dr. Susan M. Blunck, Director, 410-455-2869, Fax: 410-455-3986, E-mail: blunck@umbc.edu. *Application contact:* Dr. Susan M. Blunck, Director, 410-455-2869, Fax: 410-455-3986, E-mail: blunck@umbc.edu.

University of Maryland, Baltimore County, Graduate School, College of Natural and Mathematical Sciences, Department of Chemistry and Biochemistry, Program in Chemistry, Baltimore, MD 21250. Offers MS, PhD. Part-time programs available. *Faculty:* 18 full-time (5 women), 3 part-time/adjunct (0 women). *Students:* 56 full-time (31 women), 2 part-time (1 woman); includes 9 minority (6 African Americans, 3 Asian Americans or Pacific Islanders), 26 international. Average age 27. 73 applicants, 38% accepted, 13 enrolled. In 2009, 1 master's, 7 doctorates awarded. Terminal master's awarded for partial completion of doctoral program. *Degree requirements:* For master's, thesis optional; for doctorate, comprehensive exam, thesis/dissertation. *Entrance requirements:* For master's, GRE General Test, minimum GPA of 3.0; for doctorate, GRE General Test, GRE Subject Test (recommended), minimum GPA of 3.0. Additional exam requirements/recommendations for international students: Required—TOEFL (minimum score 550 paper-based; 213 computer-based; 80 iBT). *Application deadline:* For fall admission, 6/1 for domestic students, 1/1 for international students; for spring admission, 11/1 for domestic students, 5/1 for international students. Applications are processed on a rolling basis. Application fee: $50. Electronic applications accepted. *Financial support:* In 2009–10, 54 students received support, including 5 fellowships with full tuition reimbursements available (averaging $24,000 per year), 22 research assistantships with full tuition reimbursements available (averaging $21,000 per year), 27 teaching assistantships with full tuition reimbursements available (averaging $21,000 per year); health care benefits also available. *Faculty research:* Bio-organic chemistry, enzyme catalysis, protein-nucleic acid interactions. Total annual research expenditures: $4.2 million. *Unit head:* Dr. William R. LaCourse, Director, Graduate Program, 410-455-2491, Fax: 410-455-2608, E-mail: chemgrad@umbc.edu. *Application contact:* Patricia Gagne, Graduate Program Management Specialist, 866-PHD-UMBC, Fax: 410-455-2608, E-mail: pgagne1@umbc.edu.

University of Maryland, College Park, Academic Affairs, College of Chemical and Life Sciences, Department of Chemistry and Biochemistry, Chemistry Program, College Park, MD 20742. Offers analytical chemistry (MS, PhD); inorganic chemistry (MS, PhD); organic chemistry (MS, PhD); physical chemistry (MS, PhD). Part-time and evening/weekend programs available. *Students:* 129 full-time (69 women), 5 part-time (3 women); includes 18 minority (13 African Americans, 3 Asian Americans or Pacific Islanders, 2 Hispanic Americans), 70 international. 329 applicants, 22% accepted, 36 enrolled. In 2009, 6 master's, 18 doctorates awarded. Terminal master's awarded for partial completion of doctoral program. *Degree requirements:* For master's, thesis optional; for doctorate, thesis/dissertation, 2 seminar presentations, oral exam. *Entrance requirements:* For master's and doctorate, GRE General Test, GRE Subject Test (recommended), minimum GPA of 3.0, 3 letters of recommendation. Additional exam requirements/recommendations for international students: Required—TOEFL. *Application deadline:* For fall admission, 2/1 for domestic and international students. Applications are processed on a rolling basis. Application fee: $60. Electronic applications accepted. *Expenses:* Tuition, area resident: Part-time $471 per credit hour. Tuition, state resident: part-time $471 per credit hour. Tuition, nonresident: part-time $1016 per credit hour. Required fees: $337.04 per term. *Financial support:* In 2009–10, 7 fellowships with full tuition reimbursements (averaging $27,067 per year), 51 research assistantships (averaging $19,639 per year), 66 teaching assistantships with partial tuition reimbursements (averaging $19,260 per year) were awarded. Financial award applicants required to submit FAFSA. *Faculty research:* Environmental chemistry, nuclear chemistry, lunar and environmental analysis, x-ray crystallography. *Unit head:* Dr. Michael Doyle, Chairperson, 301-405-1795, Fax: 301-314-2779, E-mail: mdoyle3@umd.edu. *Application contact:* Dean of Graduate School, 301-405-0358, Fax: 301-314-9305.

University of Massachusetts Amherst, Graduate School, College of Natural Sciences, Department of Chemistry, Amherst, MA 01003. Offers MS, PhD. Part-time programs available. *Faculty:* 28 full-time (4 women). *Students:* 132 full-time (55 women); includes 8 minority (3 African Americans, 1 Asian American or Pacific Islander, 4 Hispanic Americans), 86 international. Average age 27. 302 applicants, 27% accepted, 25 enrolled. In 2009, 5 master's, 16 doctorates awarded. Terminal master's awarded for partial completion of doctoral program. *Degree requirements:* For master's, thesis (for some programs); for doctorate, comprehensive exam, thesis/dissertation. *Entrance requirements:* For master's and doctorate, GRE General Test. Additional exam requirements/recommendations for international students: Required—TOEFL (minimum score 550 paper-based; 213 computer-based; 80 iBT), IELTS (minimum score 6.5). *Application deadline:* For fall admission, 1/15 for domestic and international students. Applications are processed on a rolling basis. Application fee: $50 ($65 for international students). Electronic applications accepted. *Expenses:* Tuition, state resident: full-time $2640; part-time $110 per credit. Tuition, nonresident: full-time $9936; part-time $414 per credit. Tuition and fees vary according to course load. *Financial support:* In 2009–10, 6 fellowships with full tuition reimbursements (averaging $5,861 per year), 94 research assistantships with full tuition reimbursements (averaging $15,299 per year), 61 teaching assistantships with full tuition reimbursements (averaging $12,177 per year) were awarded; career-related internships or fieldwork, Federal Work-Study, scholarships/grants, traineeships, health care benefits, tuition waivers (full), and unspecified assistantships also available. Support available to part-time students. Financial award application deadline: 1/15. *Unit head:* Dr. Edward G. Voightman, Graduate Program Director, 413-545-2664, Fax: 413-545-4490. *Application contact:* Jean M. Ames, Supervisor of Admissions, 413-545-0722, Fax: 413-577-0010, E-mail: gradadm@grad.umass.edu.

University of Massachusetts Boston, Office of Graduate Studies, College of Science and Mathematics, Program in Chemistry, Boston, MA 02125-3393. Offers MS. Part-time and evening/weekend programs available. *Degree requirements:* For master's, comprehensive exam, thesis, oral exams. *Entrance requirements:* For master's, GRE General Test, GRE Subject Test, minimum GPA of 2.75. *Faculty research:* Synthesis and mechanisms of organic nitrogen compounds, application of spin resonance in the study of structure and dynamics, chemical education and teacher training, new synthetic reagents, structural study of inorganic solids by infrared and Raman spectroscopy.

University of Massachusetts Dartmouth, Graduate School, College of Arts and Sciences, Department of Chemistry, North Dartmouth, MA 02747-2300. Offers MS, PhD. Part-time programs available. *Faculty:* 17 full-time (3 women), 2 part-time/adjunct (1 woman). *Students:* 16 full-time (5 women), 6 part-time (2 women); includes 1 minority (African American), 18 international. Average age 27. 26 applicants, 73% accepted, 5 enrolled. In 2009, 1 master's awarded. *Degree requirements:* For master's, comprehensive exam (for some programs), thesis or alternative; for doctorate, thesis/dissertation (for some programs). *Entrance requirements:* For master's, GRE (recommended), 2 letters of recommendation; for doctorate, GRE. Additional exam requirements/recommendations for international students: Required—TOEFL (minimum score 550 paper-based). *Application deadline:* For fall admission, 5/1 for domestic students, 3/1 for international students; for spring admission, 11/1 for domestic students, 9/1 for international students. Application fee: $40 ($60 for international students). Electronic applications accepted. *Expenses:* Tuition, state resident: full-time $2071; part-time $86.29 per credit. Tuition, nonresident: full-time $8099; part-time $337.46 per credit. Required fees: $9446. Tuition and fees vary according to class time, course load and reciprocity agreements. *Financial support:* In 2009–10, 6 research assistantships with full tuition reimbursements (averaging $7,969 per year), 10 teaching assistantships with full tuition reimbursements (averaging $13,000 per year) were awarded; Federal Work-Study also available. Support available to part-time students. Financial award application deadline: 3/1; financial award applicants required to submit FAFSA. *Faculty research:* Inorganic chemistry, biochemical kinetics, photochemistry, ion-molecule reactions, atmosphere chemistry. Total annual research expenditures: $2 million. *Unit head:* Dr. Timothy Su, Director, 508-999-8238, Fax: 508-999-9167, E-mail: tsu@umassd.edu. *Application contact:* Elan Turcotte-Shamski, Graduate Admissions Officer, 508-999-8604, Fax: 508-999-8183, E-mail: graduate@umassd.edu.

University of Massachusetts Lowell, College of Arts and Sciences, Department of Chemistry, Lowell, MA 01854-2881. Offers analytical chemistry (PhD); biochemistry (PhD); chemistry (MS, PhD); environmental studies (PhD); green chemistry (PhD); inorganic chemistry (PhD); organic chemistry (PhD); polymer science (MS). Terminal master's awarded for partial completion of doctoral program. *Degree requirements:* For master's, thesis; for doctorate, 2 foreign languages, thesis/dissertation. *Entrance requirements:* For master's and doctorate, GRE General Test. Electronic applications accepted.

University of Memphis, Graduate School, College of Arts and Sciences, Department of Chemistry, Memphis, TN 38152. Offers analytical chemistry (PhD); analytical chemsitry (MS); computational chemistry (MS, PhD); inorganic chemistry (MS, PhD); organic chemistry (MS, PhD); physical chemistry (MS, PhD). Part-time programs available. *Faculty:* 6 full-time (1 woman). *Students:* 39 full-time (17 women), 7 part-time (4 women); includes 8 minority (6 African Americans, 1 Asian American or Pacific Islander, 1 Hispanic American), 6 international. Average age 28. 23 applicants, 70% accepted, 14 enrolled. In 2009, 3 master's, 5 doctorates awarded. Terminal master's awarded for partial completion of doctoral program. *Degree requirements:* For master's, comprehensive exam, thesis or alternative; for doctorate, comprehensive exam, thesis/dissertation. *Entrance requirements:* For master's and doctorate, GRE General Test, admission to Graduate School plus 32 undergraduate hours in chemistry. Additional exam requirements/recommendations for international students: Required—TOEFL. *Application deadline:* For fall admission, 7/1 for domestic students, 5/1 for international students; for winter admission, 9/15 for international students; for spring admission, 12/1 for domestic students. Applications are processed on a rolling basis. Application fee: $35 ($60 for international students). Electronic applications accepted. *Expenses:* Tuition, state resident: full-time $6246; part-time $347 per credit hour. Tuition, nonresident: full-time $15,894; part-time $883 per credit hour. Required fees: $1160. Full-time tuition and fees vary according to course load, degree level and program. *Financial support:* In 2009–10, 12 students received support; research assistantships with full tuition reimbursements available, teaching assistantships with full tuition reimbursements available, Federal Work-Study, scholarships/grants, and unspecified assistantships available. Financial award application deadline: 2/15; financial award applicants required to submit FAFSA. *Faculty research:* Computational chemistry, materials chemistry, organic/polymer synthesis, drug design/delivery, water chemistry. *Unit head:* Dr. Abby L. Parrill, Professor and Chair, 901-678-2638, Fax: 901-678-3447, E-mail: aparrill@memphis.edu. *Application contact:* Dr. Gary Emmert, Associate Professor and Graduate Coordinator, 901-678-2636, Fax: 901-678-3447, E-mail: gemmert@memphis.edu.

University of Miami, Graduate School, College of Arts and Sciences, Department of Chemistry, Coral Gables, FL 33124. Offers chemistry (MS); inorganic chemistry (PhD); organic chemistry (PhD); physical chemistry (PhD). Terminal master's awarded for partial completion of doctoral program. *Degree requirements:* For master's, comprehensive exam; for doctorate, comprehensive exam, thesis/dissertation. *Entrance requirements:* For master's and doctorate, GRE General Test. Additional exam requirements/recommendations for international students: Required—TOEFL (minimum score 550 paper-based; 213 computer-based). Electronic applications accepted. *Faculty research:* Supramolecular chemistry, electrochemistry, surface chemistry, catalysis, organometalic.

University of Michigan, Horace H. Rackham School of Graduate Studies, College of Literature, Science, and the Arts, Department of Chemistry, Ann Arbor, MI 48109-1055. Offers analytical chemistry (PhD); chemical biology (PhD); inorganic chemistry (PhD); material chemistry (PhD); organic chemistry (PhD); physical chemistry (PhD). *Faculty:* 42 full-time (10 women). *Students:* 192 full-time (105 women); includes 74 minority (4 African Americans, 64 Asian Americans or Pacific Islanders, 6 Hispanic Americans), 54 international. Average age 26. 558 applicants, 36% accepted, 56 enrolled. In 2009, 28 doctorates awarded. *Degree requirements:* For doctorate, thesis/dissertation, oral defense of dissertation, organic cumulative proficiency exams. *Entrance requirements:* For doctorate, GRE General Test, GRE Subject Test (recommended), 3 letters of recommendation. Additional exam requirements/recommendations for international students: Required—TOEFL (minimum score 560 paper-based; 220 computer-based; 84 iBT). *Application deadline:* For fall admission, 1/15 for domestic students, 12/15 for international students. Applications are processed on a rolling basis. Application fee: $0 ($75 for international students). Electronic applications accepted. *Expenses:* Tuition, state resident: full-time $17,286; part-time $1099 per credit hour. Tuition, nonresident: full-time $34,944; part-time $2080 per credit hour. Required fees: $95 per semester. Tuition and fees vary according to course load, degree level and program. *Financial support:* In 2009–10, 192 students received support, including 20 fellowships with full tuition reimbursements available (averaging $25,000 per year), 75 research assistantships with full tuition reimbursements available (averaging $25,000 per year), 97 teaching assistantships with full tuition reimbursements available (averaging $25,000 per year); career-related internships or fieldwork, scholarships/grants, traineeships, health care benefits, and unspecified assistantships also available. Financial award applicants required to submit FAFSA. *Faculty research:* Biological catalysis, protein engineering, chemical sensors, de novo metalloprotein design, supramolecular architecture. Total annual research expenditures: $15.3 million. *Unit head:* Dr. Carol A. Fierke, Chair, 734-763-9681, Fax: 734-647-4847. *Application contact:* Anna Stryker, Graduate Program Coordinator, 734-764-7278, Fax: 734-647-4865, E-mail: chemadmissions@umich.edu.

University of Minnesota, Duluth, Graduate School, Swenson College of Science and Engineering, Department of Chemistry and Biochemistry, Duluth, MN 55812-2496. Offers MS. Part-time programs available. *Degree requirements:* For master's, thesis. *Entrance requirements:* For master's, bachelor's degree in chemistry, minimum GPA of 3.0. Additional exam requirements/recommendations for international students: Required—TOEFL (minimum score 550 paper-based; 213 computer-based; 79 iBT), IELTS (minimum score 6.5). *Faculty research:* Physical, inorganic, organic, and analytical chemistry; biochemistry and molecular biology.

Chemistry

University of Minnesota, Twin Cities Campus, Institute of Technology, Department of Chemistry, Minneapolis, MN 55455-0213. Offers MS, PhD. Part-time programs available. Terminal master's awarded for partial completion of doctoral program. *Degree requirements:* For master's, thesis or alternative; for doctorate, thesis/dissertation, preliminary candidacy exams. *Entrance requirements:* For master's and doctorate, GRE General Test. Additional exam requirements/recommendations for international students: Required—TOEFL. *Faculty research:* Analytical, biological, inorganic, organic, and physical chemistry.

University of Minnesota, Twin Cities Campus, School of Public Health, Division of Environmental Health Sciences, Area in Environmental Chemistry, Minneapolis, MN 55455-0213. Offers MS, PhD. *Degree requirements:* For doctorate, thesis/dissertation. *Entrance requirements:* For master's and doctorate, GRE General Test. Electronic applications accepted.

University of Mississippi, Graduate School, College of Liberal Arts, Department of Chemistry and Biochemistry, Oxford, University, MS 38677. Offers MS, DA, PhD. *Faculty:* 19 full-time (2 women). *Students:* 37 full-time (22 women), 3 part-time (1 woman); includes 11 minority (7 African Americans, 2 Asian Americans or Pacific Islanders, 2 Hispanic Americans), 16 international. In 2009, 3 master's, 2 doctorates awarded. *Degree requirements:* For master's, thesis; for doctorate, one foreign language, thesis/dissertation. *Entrance requirements:* For master's, GRE General Test, minimum GPA of 3.0; for doctorate, GRE General Test. Additional exam requirements/recommendations for international students: Required—TOEFL. *Application deadline:* For fall admission, 4/1 for domestic students; for spring admission, 10/1 for domestic students. Applications are processed on a rolling basis. Application fee: $25. Electronic applications accepted. *Financial support:* Scholarships/grants available. Financial award application deadline: 3/1; financial award applicants required to submit FAFSA. *Unit head:* Dr. Charles Hussey, Chairman, 662-915-7301, Fax: 662-915-7300, E-mail: chemistry@olemiss.edu. *Application contact:* Dr. Christy M. Wyandt, Associate Dean, 662-915-7474, Fax: 662-915-7577, E-mail: cwyandt@olemiss.edu.

University of Missouri, Graduate School, College of Arts and Sciences, Department of Chemistry, Columbia, MO 65211. Offers analytical chemistry (MS, PhD); inorganic chemistry (MS, PhD); organic chemistry (MS, PhD); physical chemistry (MS, PhD). *Faculty:* 30 full-time (6 women), 2 part-time/adjunct (0 women). *Students:* 60 full-time (22 women), 43 part-time (16 women); includes 7 minority (3 African Americans, 1 American Indian/Alaska Native, 3 Asian Americans or Pacific Islanders), 53 international. Average age 27. 93 applicants, 32% accepted, 27 enrolled. In 2009, 4 doctorates awarded. *Degree requirements:* For master's, thesis; for doctorate, one foreign language, comprehensive exam, thesis/dissertation. *Entrance requirements:* For master's, GRE General Test, minimum GPA of 3.0; for doctorate, GRE General Test; V=450, Q=600, A=3.0-4.0, minimum GPA of 3.0. Additional exam requirements/recommendations for international students: Required—TOEFL (minimum score 600 paper-based; 250 computer-based; 100 iBT). *Application deadline:* For fall admission, 4/1 priority date for domestic students; for winter admission, 10/15 for domestic students. Applications are processed on a rolling basis. Application fee: $45 ($60 for international students). *Financial support:* In 2009–10, 9 fellowships with full tuition reimbursements, 15 research assistantships with full tuition reimbursements, 78 teaching assistantships with full tuition reimbursements were awarded; institutionally sponsored loans, traineeships, health care benefits, and unspecified assistantships also available. *Unit head:* Dr. Jerry Atwood, Department Chair, 573-882-8374, E-mail: atwoodj@missouri.edu. *Application contact:* Jerry Brightwell, Administrative Assistant, 573-884-6832, E-mail: brightwellj@missouri.edu.

University of Missouri–Kansas City, College of Arts and Sciences, Department of Chemistry, Kansas City, MO 64110-2499. Offers analytical chemistry (MS, PhD); inorganic chemistry (MS, PhD); organic chemistry (MS, PhD); physical chemistry (MS, PhD); polymer chemistry (MS, PhD). PhD (interdisciplinary) offered through the School of Graduate Studies. Part-time and evening/weekend programs available. *Faculty:* 16 full-time (3 women), 1 part-time/adjunct (0 women). *Students:* 7 part-time (4 women), 2 international. Average age 32. 30 applicants, 67% accepted. In 2009, 1 master's awarded. *Degree requirements:* For master's, thesis (for some programs); for doctorate, thesis/dissertation. *Entrance requirements:* For master's, equivalent of American Chemical Society approved bachelor's degree in chemistry; for doctorate, GRE General Test, equivalent of American Chemical Society approved bachelor's degree in chemistry. Additional exam requirements/recommendations for international students: Required—TOEFL (minimum score 550 paper-based; 213 computer-based; 80 iBT), TWE. *Application deadline:* For fall admission, 4/15 for domestic and international students; for spring admission, 10/15 for domestic and international students. Applications are processed on a rolling basis. Application fee: $45 ($50 for international students). Electronic applications accepted. *Expenses:* Tuition, state resident: full-time $5378; part-time $299 per credit hour. Tuition, nonresident: full-time $13,881; part-time $771 per credit hour. Required fees: $641; $71 per credit hour. Tuition and fees vary according to course load and program. *Financial support:* In 2009–10, 8 research assistantships with partial tuition reimbursements (averaging $17,973 per year), 17 teaching assistantships with partial tuition reimbursements (averaging $17,179 per year) were awarded; Federal Work-Study, institutionally sponsored loans, and scholarships/grants also available. Support available to part-time students. Financial award application deadline: 3/1; financial award applicants required to submit FAFSA. *Faculty research:* Molecular spectroscopy, characterization and synthesis of materials and compounds, computational chemistry, natural products, drug delivery systems and anti-tumor agents. Total annual research expenditures: $1 million. *Unit head:* Dr. Kathleen V. Kilway, Chair, 816-235-2289, Fax: 816-235-5502. *Application contact:* Graduate Recruiting Committee, 816-235-2272, Fax: 816-235-5502, E-mail: umkc-chemdept@umkc.edu.

University of Missouri–St. Louis, College of Arts and Sciences, Department of Chemistry and Biochemistry, St. Louis, MO 63121. Offers chemistry (MS, PhD), including biochemistry, inorganic chemistry, organic chemistry, physical chemistry. Part-time and evening/weekend programs available. *Faculty:* 19 full-time (3 women), 6 part-time/adjunct (1 woman). *Students:* 43 full-time (21 women), 19 part-time (8 women); includes 6 minority (4 African Americans, 1 Asian American or Pacific Islander, 1 Hispanic American), 27 international. Average age 29. 81 applicants, 37% accepted, 19 enrolled. In 2009, 9 master's, 6 doctorates awarded. Terminal master's awarded for partial completion of doctoral program. *Degree requirements:* For master's, thesis optional; for doctorate, thesis/dissertation. *Entrance requirements:* For master's, 2 letters of recommendation; for doctorate, GRE General Test, 3 letters of recommendation. Additional exam requirements/recommendations for international students: Required—TOEFL (minimum score 550 paper-based; 213 computer-based). *Application deadline:* For fall admission, 7/1 priority date for domestic and international students; for spring admission, 12/1 priority date for domestic and international students. Applications are processed on a rolling basis. Application fee: $35 ($40 for international students). Electronic applications accepted. *Expenses:* Tuition, state resident: full-time $5377; part-time $297.70 per credit hour. Tuition, nonresident: full-time $13,882; part-time $771.20 per credit hour. Required fees: $220; $12.20 per credit hour. One-time fee: $12. Tuition and fees vary according to course level, campus/location and program. *Financial support:* In 2009–10, 25 research assistantships with full and partial tuition reimbursements (averaging $17,840 per year), 13 teaching assistantships with full and partial tuition reimbursements (averaging $13,300 per year) were awarded; fellowships with full and partial tuition reimbursements also available. *Faculty research:* Metallaborane chemistry, serum transferrin chemistry, natural products chemistry, organic synthesis. *Unit head:* Dr. Cynthia Dupureur, Director of Graduate Studies, 314-516-5311, Fax: 314-516-5342, E-mail: gradchem@umsl.edu. *Application contact:* 314-516-5458, Fax: 314-516-6996, E-mail: gradadm@umsl.edu.

The University of Montana, Graduate School, College of Arts and Sciences, Department of Chemistry, Missoula, MT 59812-0002. Offers chemistry (MS, PhD), including environmental/analytical chemistry, inorganic chemistry, organic chemistry, physical chemistry. Terminal master's awarded for partial completion of doctoral program. *Degree requirements:* For master's, thesis (for some programs); for doctorate, thesis/dissertation. *Entrance requirements:* For master's and doctorate, GRE General Test. Additional exam requirements/recommendations for international students: Required—TOEFL (minimum score 575 paper-based; 230 computer-based). *Faculty research:* Reaction mechanisms and kinetics, inorganic and organic synthesis, analytical chemistry, natural products.

University of Nebraska–Lincoln, Graduate College, College of Arts and Sciences, Department of Chemistry, Lincoln, NE 68588. Offers analytical chemistry (PhD); biochemistry (PhD); chemistry (MS); inorganic chemistry (PhD); materials chemistry (PhD); organic chemistry (PhD); physical chemistry (PhD). *Degree requirements:* For master's, one foreign language, thesis optional, departmental qualifying exam; for doctorate, one foreign language, comprehensive exam, thesis/dissertation, departmental qualifying exams. *Entrance requirements:* For master's and doctorate, GRE. Additional exam requirements/recommendations for international students: Required—TOEFL (minimum score 550 paper-based; 213 computer-based). Electronic applications accepted. *Faculty research:* Bioorganic and bioinorganic chemistry, biophysical and bioanalytical chemistry, structure-function of DNA and proteins, organometallics, mass spectrometry.

University of Nevada, Las Vegas, Graduate College, College of Science, Department of Chemistry, Las Vegas, NV 89154-4003. Offers biochemistry (MS); chemistry (MS, PhD); radiochemistry (PhD). Part-time programs available. *Faculty:* 18 full-time (3 women), 1 part-time/adjunct (0 women). *Students:* 40 full-time (16 women), 18 part-time (9 women); includes 11 minority (2 African Americans, 7 Asian Americans or Pacific Islanders, 2 Hispanic Americans), 17 international. Average age 32. 29 applicants, 55% accepted, 10 enrolled. In 2009, 7 master's, 6 doctorates awarded. *Degree requirements:* For master's, thesis. *Entrance requirements:* For master's and doctorate, GRE General Test. Additional exam requirements/recommendations for international students: Required—TOEFL (minimum score 550 paper-based; 213 computer-based; 80 iBT), IELTS (minimum score 7). *Application deadline:* For fall admission, 2/1 priority date for domestic and international students; for spring admission, 10/1 priority date for domestic and international students. Applications are processed on a rolling basis. Application fee: $60 ($95 for international students). Electronic applications accepted. *Financial support:* In 2009–10, 23 students received support, including 7 research assistantships with partial tuition reimbursements available (averaging $17,957 per year), 16 teaching assistantships with partial tuition reimbursements available (averaging $11,250 per year); institutionally sponsored loans, scholarships/grants, health care benefits, and unspecified assistantships also available. Financial award application deadline: 3/1. *Faculty research:* Inorganic and organic chemistry, physical chemistry, radio-chemistry, materials science, biochemistry. *Unit head:* Dr. Dennis Lindle, Chair/ Professor, 702-895-4426, Fax: 702-895-4072, E-mail: lindle@unlv.nevada.edu. *Application contact:* Graduate Coordinator, 702-895-3320, Fax: 702-895-4180, E-mail: gradcollege@unlv.edu.

University of Nevada, Reno, Graduate School, College of Science, Department of Chemistry, Reno, NV 89557. Offers MS, PhD. Terminal master's awarded for partial completion of doctoral program. *Degree requirements:* For master's, thesis; for doctorate, one foreign language, thesis/dissertation. *Entrance requirements:* For master's, GRE, minimum GPA of 2.75; for doctorate, GRE, minimum GPA of 3.0. Additional exam requirements/recommendations for international students: Required—TOEFL (minimum score 500 paper-based; 173 computer-based; 61 iBT), IELTS (minimum score 6). Electronic applications accepted. *Faculty research:* Organic/inorganic chemistry, physical chemistry, chemical chemistry, physics, organometallic chemistry.

University of New Brunswick Fredericton, School of Graduate Studies, Faculty of Science, Department of Chemistry, Fredericton, NB E3B 5A3, Canada. Offers M Sc, PhD. *Faculty:* 18 full-time (3 women). *Students:* 31 full-time (12 women); includes 10 minority (1 African American, 9 Asian Americans or Pacific Islanders). In 2009, 1 master's, 2 doctorates awarded. Terminal master's awarded for partial completion of doctoral program. *Degree requirements:* For master's, thesis; for doctorate, comprehensive exam, thesis/dissertation, Courses. *Entrance requirements:* For master's and doctorate, minimum GPA of 3.0; Each accepted on the individual's merit. Additional exam requirements/recommendations for international students: Required—TOEFL, IELTS. *Application deadline:* For fall admission, 3/1 priority date for domestic students. Application fee: $50 Canadian dollars. Tuition and fees charges are reported in Canadian dollars. *Expenses:* Tuition, area resident: Full-time $5562 Canadian dollars; part-time $2781 Canadian dollars per year. Required fees: $49.75 Canadian dollars per term. *Financial support:* In 2009–10, 4 fellowships (averaging $18,000 per year), 28 research assistantships (averaging $1,595 per year), 27 teaching assistantships (averaging $3,800 per year) were awarded; scholarships/grants also available. *Faculty research:* Electrochemistry, synthetic inorganic and organic chemistry; molecular spectroscopy; computational and theoretical chemistry; catalytic processes. Total annual research expenditures: $1.1 million. *Unit head:* Dr. Sean McGrady, Director of Graduate Studies, 506-452-6340, Fax: 506-453-4981, E-mail: smcgrady@unb.ca. *Application contact:* Krista Coy, Graduate Secretary, 506-453-4781, Fax: 506-453-4981, E-mail: coyy@unb.ca.

University of New Hampshire, Graduate School, College of Engineering and Physical Sciences, Department of Chemistry, Durham, NH 03824. Offers chemistry (MS, MST, PhD); chemistry education (PhD). *Faculty:* 28 full-time (17 women). *Students:* 35 full-time (13 women), 18 part-time (7 women); includes 2 minority (1 African American, 1 Hispanic American), 15 international. Average age 31. 55 applicants, 45% accepted, 12 enrolled. In 2009, 7 master's, 3 doctorates awarded. Terminal master's awarded for partial completion of doctoral program. *Degree requirements:* For master's, thesis; for doctorate, one foreign language, thesis/dissertation. *Entrance requirements:* Additional exam requirements/recommendations for international students: Required—TOEFL (minimum score 550 paper-based; 213 computer-based; 80 iBT). *Application deadline:* For fall admission, 4/1 priority date for domestic students, 4/1 for international students; for spring admission, 12/1 for domestic students. Applications are processed on a rolling basis. Application fee: $65. *Expenses:* Tuition, state resident: full-time $10,380; part-time $577 per credit hour. Tuition, nonresident: full-time $24,350; part-time $1002 per credit hour. Required fees: $1550; $387.50 per semester. Tuition and fees vary according to course load and program. *Financial support:* In 2009–10, 44 students received support, including 1 fellowship, 6 research assistantships, 36 teaching assistantships; Federal Work-Study, scholarships/grants, and tuition waivers (full and partial) also available. Support available to part-time students. Financial award application deadline: 2/15. *Faculty research:* Analytical, physical, organic, and inorganic chemistry. *Unit head:* Dr. Chris Bauer, Chairperson, 603-862-1550. *Application contact:* Cindi Rohwer, Coordinator, 603-862-1550, E-mail: chem.dept@unh.edu.

University of New Mexico, Graduate School, College of Arts and Sciences, Department of Chemistry and Chemical Biology, Albuquerque, NM 87131-2039. Offers MS, PhD. *Faculty:* 21 full-time (7 women), 3 part-time/adjunct (1 woman). *Students:* 48 full-time (12 women), 10 part-time (5 women); includes 7 minority (2 African Americans, 2 American Indian/Alaska Native, 3 Hispanic Americans), 34 international. Average age 31. 39 applicants, 41% accepted, 13 enrolled. In 2009, 2 master's, 7 doctorates awarded. Terminal master's awarded for partial completion of doctoral program. *Degree requirements:* For master's, comprehensive exam, thesis (for some programs); for doctorate, comprehensive exam, thesis/dissertation. *Entrance requirements:* For master's and doctorate, Department Entrance Exams. Additional exam requirements/recommendations for international students: Required—TOEFL (minimum score 550 paper-based; 213 computer-based). *Application deadline:* For fall admission, 2/1 for domestic and international students. Application fee: $50. Electronic applications accepted. *Expenses:* Tuition, state resident: full-time $2098.80; part-time $233.20 per credit hour. Tuition, nonresident: full-time $6650. Required fees: $25 per semester. Tuition and fees vary according to course load, program and reciprocity agreements. *Financial support:* In 2009–10, 10 students received support, including 5 fellowships (averaging $4,000 per year), 24 research assistantships with tuition reimbursements available (averaging $11,919 per year), 42 teaching assistantships (averaging $13,891 per year); scholarships/grants, health care benefits, and unspecified assistantships also available. Financial award application deadline: 2/1; financial award applicants required to submit FAFSA. *Faculty research:* Analytical, inorganic, organic, and physical chemistry; biological chemistry. Total annual research expenditures: $1.8 million. *Unit head:* Dr. David G. Bear, Chair, 505-277-6655, Fax: 505-277-2609, E-mail: dbear@salud.unm.edu. *Application contact:* Karen McElveny, Coordinator, Program Advisement, 505-277-1779, Fax: 505-277-2609, E-mail: kamc@unm.edu.

University of New Orleans, Graduate School, College of Sciences, Department of Chemistry, New Orleans, LA 70148. Offers MS, PhD. *Degree requirements:* For master's, variable foreign language requirement, thesis, departmental qualifying exam; for doctorate, variable foreign language requirement, thesis/dissertation, departmental qualifying exam. *Entrance requirements:* For master's and doctorate, GRE General Test. Additional exam requirements/recommendations for international students: Required—TOEFL (minimum score 550 paper-based; 213 computer-based; 79 iBT). Electronic applications accepted. *Faculty research:* Synthesis and reactions of novel compounds, high-temperature kinetics, calculations of molecular electrostatic potentials, structures and reactions of metal complexes.

The University of North Carolina at Chapel Hill, Graduate School, College of Arts and Sciences, Department of Chemistry, Chapel Hill, NC 27599. Offers MA, MS, PhD. *Degree requirements:* For master's, comprehensive exam, thesis (for some programs); for doctorate, comprehensive exam, thesis/dissertation. *Entrance requirements:* For master's and doctorate, GRE General Test, GRE Subject Test, minimum GPA of 3.0.

The University of North Carolina at Charlotte, Graduate School, College of Arts and Sciences, Department of Chemistry, Charlotte, NC 28223-0001. Offers MS. Part-time programs available. *Faculty:* 14 full-time (3 women). *Students:* 1 (woman) full-time, 23 part-time (11 women); includes 3 minority (2 African Americans, 1 Asian American or Pacific Islander), 5 international. Average age 26. 32 applicants, 38% accepted, 10 enrolled. In 2009, 8 master's awarded. Terminal master's awarded for partial completion of doctoral program. *Degree requirements:* For master's, thesis. *Entrance requirements:* For master's, GRE General Test or MAT, minimum GPA of 3.0 in undergraduate major, 2.75 overall. Additional exam requirements/recommendations for international students: Required—TOEFL (minimum score 557 paper-based; 220 computer-based; 83 iBT). *Application deadline:* For fall admission, 7/1 for domestic students, 5/1 for international students; for spring admission, 11/1 for domestic students, 10/1 for international students. Applications are processed on a rolling basis. Application fee: $55. Electronic applications accepted. *Financial support:* In 2009–10, 3 fellowships (averaging $35,871 per year), 5 research assistantships (averaging $20,400 per year), 26 teaching assistantships (averaging $14,324 per year) were awarded; career-related internships or fieldwork, Federal Work-Study, institutionally sponsored loans, scholarships/grants, and unspecified assistantships also available. Support available to part-time students. Financial award application deadline: 4/1; financial award applicants required to submit FAFSA. *Faculty research:* Biophysical organic chemistry and biochemistry; polymers, biomaterials and nanostructures; materials chemistry; synthetic organic and inorganic chemistry; bioanalytical chemistry. Total annual research expenditures: $504,212. *Unit head:* Dr. Bernadette T. Donovan-Merkert, Chair, 704-687-4436, Fax: 704-687-3151, E-mail: bdonovan@uncc.edu. *Application contact:* Kathy B. Giddings, Director of Graduate Admissions, 704-687-5503, Fax: 704-687-3279, E-mail: gradadm@uncc.edu.

The University of North Carolina at Greensboro, Graduate School, College of Arts and Sciences, Department of Chemistry and Biochemistry, Greensboro, NC 27412-5001. Offers biochemistry (MS); chemistry (MS). *Degree requirements:* For master's, one foreign language, thesis. *Entrance requirements:* For master's, GRE General Test. Additional exam requirements/recommendations for international students: Required—TOEFL. Electronic applications accepted. *Faculty research:* Synthesis of novel cyclopentadienes, molybdenum hydroxylase-cata ladder polymers, vinyl silicones.

The University of North Carolina Wilmington, College of Arts and Sciences, Department of Chemistry and Biochemistry, Wilmington, NC 28403-3297. Offers MS. Part-time programs available. *Degree requirements:* For master's, comprehensive exam, thesis. *Entrance requirements:* For master's, GRE General Test, minimum B average in undergraduate major. Additional exam requirements/recommendations for international students: Required—TOEFL (minimum score 550 paper-based; 217 computer-based; 79 iBT), IELTS (minimum score 6.5).

University of North Dakota, Graduate School, College of Arts and Sciences, Department of Chemistry, Grand Forks, ND 58202. Offers MS, PhD. Terminal master's awarded for partial completion of doctoral program. *Degree requirements:* For master's, thesis, final exam; for doctorate, comprehensive exam, thesis/dissertation, final exam. *Entrance requirements:* For master's and doctorate, GRE General Test, GRE Subject Test, minimum GPA of 3.0. Additional exam requirements/recommendations for international students: Required—TOEFL (minimum score 550 paper-based; 213 computer-based; 79 iBT), IELTS (minimum score 6.5). Electronic applications accepted. *Faculty research:* Synthetic and structural organometallic chemistry, photochemistry, theoretical chemistry, chromatographic chemistry, x-ray crystallography.

University of Northern Colorado, Graduate School, College of Natural and Health Sciences, School of Chemistry, Earth Sciences and Physics, Program in Chemistry, Greeley, CO 80639. Offers chemistry education (PhD); chemistry: education (MS); chemistry: research (MS). Part-time programs available. *Faculty:* 9 full-time (3 women). *Students:* 12 full-time (5 women), 3 part-time (2 women), 1 international. Average age 31. 15 applicants, 53% accepted, 4 enrolled. In 2009, 2 master's, 3 doctorates awarded. *Degree requirements:* For master's, comprehensive exam, thesis or alternative; for doctorate, comprehensive exam, thesis/dissertation. *Entrance requirements:* For master's, 3 letters of reference; for doctorate, GRE General Test, 3 letters of reference. *Application deadline:* Applications are processed on a rolling basis. Application fee: $50 ($60 for international students). Electronic applications accepted. *Expenses:* Tuition, state resident: full-time $5770; part-time $320.55 per credit hour. Tuition, nonresident: full-time $13,847; part-time $769.27 per credit hour. Required fees: $948.78; $52.72 per credit. *Financial support:* In 2009–10, 6 research assistantships (averaging $4,950 per year), 4 teaching assistantships (averaging $11,019 per year) were awarded; fellowships, unspecified assistantships also available. Financial award application deadline: 3/1; financial award applicants required to submit FAFSA. *Unit head:* Dr. Richard Hyslop, Program Coordinator, 970-351-2559. *Application contact:* Linda Sisson, Graduate Student Admission Coordinator, 970-351-1807, Fax: 970-351-2371, E-mail: linda.sisson@unco.edu.

University of Northern Iowa, Graduate College, College of Natural Sciences, Department of Chemistry, Cedar Falls, IA 50614. Offers MA, MS, PSM. Part-time programs available. *Students:* 9 full-time (6 women), 2 part-time (0 women), 7 international. 11 applicants, 45% accepted, 5 enrolled. In 2009, 4 master's awarded. *Degree requirements:* For master's, comprehensive exam (for some programs), thesis (for some programs). *Entrance requirements:* For master's, minimum GPA of 3.0, 3 letters of recommendation. Additional exam requirements/recommendations for international students: Required—TOEFL (minimum score 500 paper-based; 180 computer-based; 61 iBT). *Application deadline:* For fall admission, 8/1 priority date for domestic students. Applications are processed on a rolling basis. Application fee: $30 ($50 for international students). Electronic applications accepted. *Financial support:* Career-related internships or fieldwork, Federal Work-Study, scholarships/grants, and tuition waivers (full and partial) available. Support available to part-time students. Financial award application deadline: 2/1. *Unit head:* Dr. William S. Harwood, Head, 319-273-2437, Fax: 319-273-7127, E-mail: bill.harwood@uni.edu. *Application contact:* Laurie S. Russell, Record Analyst, 319-273-2623, Fax: 319-273-6792, E-mail: laurie.russell@uni.edu.

University of North Texas, Robert B. Toulouse School of Graduate Studies, College of Arts and Sciences, Department of Chemistry, Denton, TX 76203. Offers MS, PhD. Part-time and evening/weekend programs available. *Faculty:* 21 full-time (6 women). *Students:* 62 applicants, 55% accepted, 23 enrolled. In 2009, 3 master's, 1 doctorate awarded. Terminal master's awarded for partial completion of doctoral program. *Degree requirements:* For master's, comprehensive exam, thesis (for some programs); for doctorate, one foreign language, comprehensive exam, thesis/dissertation. *Entrance requirements:* For master's, GRE General Test, 2 letters of recommendation; for doctorate, GRE General Test, 2 letters of recommendation, transcripts, statement of purpose. Additional exam requirements/recommendations for international students: Required—proof of English language proficiency required for non-native English speakers; Recommended—TOEFL (minimum score 550 paper-based; 213 computer-based). *Application deadline:* For fall admission, 7/15 for domestic students; for spring admission, 11/15 for domestic students. Application fee: $50 ($75 for international students). *Expenses:* Tuition, state resident: full-time $4298; part-time $239 per contact hour. Tuition, nonresident: full-time $9878; part-time $549 per contact hour. Required fees: $265 per contact hour. *Financial support:* Fellowships with full tuition reimbursements, research assistantships with partial tuition reimbursements, teaching assistantships with partial tuition reimbursements, career-related internships or fieldwork, Federal Work-Study, and institutionally sponsored loans available. Financial award application deadline: 4/1. *Faculty research:* Analytical, inorganic, physical, and organic chemistry and materials. *Application contact:* Graduate Coordinator, 940-565-3554, Fax: 940-565-4318.

University of Notre Dame, Graduate School, College of Science, Department of Chemistry and Biochemistry, Notre Dame, IN 46556. Offers biochemistry (MS, PhD); inorganic chemistry (MS, PhD); organic chemistry (MS, PhD); physical chemistry (MS, PhD). Terminal master's awarded for partial completion of doctoral program. *Degree requirements:* For master's, comprehensive exam, thesis; for doctorate, thesis/dissertation, qualifying exam. *Entrance requirements:* For master's and doctorate, GRE General Test, GRE Subject Test (strongly recommended). Additional exam requirements/recommendations for international students: Required—TOEFL (minimum score 600 paper-based; 250 computer-based; 80 iBT). Electronic applications accepted. *Faculty research:* Reaction design and mechanistic studies; reactive intermediates; synthesis, structure and reactivity of organometallic cluster complexes and biologically active natural products; bioorganic chemistry; enzymology.

University of Oklahoma, Graduate College, College of Arts and Sciences, Department of Chemistry and Biochemistry, Norman, OK 73019. Offers MS, PhD. *Faculty:* 29 full-time (6 women). *Students:* 85 full-time (37 women), 11 part-time (6 women); includes 12 minority (5 African Americans, 2 American Indian/Alaska Native, 4 Asian Americans or Pacific Islanders, 1 Hispanic American), 48 international. 32 applicants, 56% accepted, 18 enrolled. In 2009, 12 master's, 18 doctorates awarded. Terminal master's awarded for partial completion of doctoral program. *Degree requirements:* For master's, thesis optional; for doctorate, thesis/dissertation. *Entrance requirements:* For master's, GRE, BS in chemistry; for doctorate, GRE. Additional exam requirements/recommendations for international students: Required—TOEFL (minimum score 550 paper-based; 213 computer-based). *Application deadline:* For fall admission, 4/1 priority date for domestic students, 4/1 for international students; for spring admission, 9/1 priority date for domestic students, 9/1 for international students. Applications are processed on a rolling basis. Application fee: $40 ($90 for international students). Electronic applications accepted. *Expenses:* Tuition, state resident: full-time $3744; part-time $156 per credit hour. Tuition, nonresident: full-time $13,577; part-time $565.70 per credit hour. Required fees: $2415; $90.10 per credit hour. *Financial support:* In 2009–10, 73 students received support, including 3 fellowships with full tuition reimbursements available (averaging $5,000 per year), 21 research assistantships with partial tuition reimbursements available (averaging $15,232 per year), 71 teaching assistantships with partial tuition reimbursements available (averaging $15,776 per year); scholarships/grants, health care benefits, and unspecified assistantships also available. Financial award application deadline: 4/1; financial award applicants required to submit FAFSA. *Faculty research:* Catalysis, metals in biology, materials science, nucleic acid structure and function, natural products drug discovery. Total annual research expenditures: $4.4 million. *Unit head:* Dr. George Richter-Addo, Chair, 405-325-4811, Fax: 405-325-6111, E-mail: grichteraddo@ou.edu. *Application contact:* Carol Jones, Graduate Program Assistant, 405-325-2946, Fax: 405-325-6111, E-mail: chemadmit@ou.edu.

University of Oregon, Graduate School, College of Arts and Sciences, Department of Chemistry, Eugene, OR 97403. Offers biochemistry (MA, MS, PhD); chemistry (MA, MS, PhD). Terminal master's awarded for partial completion of doctoral program. *Degree requirements:* For doctorate, thesis/dissertation. *Entrance requirements:* For master's and doctorate, GRE General Test, minimum GPA of 3.0. Additional exam requirements/recommendations for international students: Required—TOEFL. *Faculty research:* Organic chemistry, organometallic chemistry, inorganic chemistry, physical chemistry, materials science, biochemistry, chemical physics, molecular or cell biology.

University of Ottawa, Faculty of Graduate and Postdoctoral Studies, Faculty of Science, Ottawa-Carleton Chemistry Institute, Ottawa, ON K1N 6N5, Canada. Offers M Sc, PhD. *Degree requirements:* For master's, thesis, seminar; for doctorate, comprehensive exam, thesis/dissertation, 2 seminars. *Entrance requirements:* For master's, honors B Sc degree or equivalent, minimum B average; for doctorate, honors B Sc with minimum B average or M Sc in chemistry with minimum B+ average. Electronic applications accepted. *Faculty research:* Organic chemistry, physical chemistry, inorganic chemistry.

University of Pennsylvania, School of Arts and Sciences, Graduate Group in Chemistry, Philadelphia, PA 19104. Offers MS, PhD. *Faculty:* 29 full-time (4 women), 9 part-time/adjunct (1 woman). *Students:* 193 full-time (87 women); includes 15 minority (2 African Americans, 7 Asian Americans or Pacific Islanders, 6 Hispanic Americans), 87 international. 465 applicants, 26% accepted, 37 enrolled. In 2009, 19 master's, 37 doctorates awarded. *Degree requirements:* For doctorate, thesis/dissertation. *Entrance requirements:* For doctorate, GRE General Test, GRE Subject Test, previous graduate course work in organic, inorganic, and physical chemistry each with a lab, differential and integral calculus, and general physics with a lab. Additional exam requirements/recommendations for international students: Required—TOEFL. *Application deadline:* For fall admission, 12/1 priority date for domestic students. Application fee: $70. Electronic applications accepted. *Expenses:* Tuition: Full-time $25,660; part-time $4758 per course. Required fees: $2152; $270 per course. Tuition and fees vary according to course load, degree level and program. *Financial support:* Fellowships, research assistantships, teaching assistantships, institutionally sponsored loans, scholarships/grants, traineeships, health care benefits, and unspecified assistantships available. Financial award application deadline: 12/15.

University of Pittsburgh, School of Arts and Sciences, Department of Chemistry, Pittsburgh, PA 15260. Offers MS, PhD. Part-time and evening/weekend programs available. *Faculty:* 31 full-time (4 women), 15 part-time/adjunct (3 women). *Students:* 198 full-time (66 women), 1 (woman) part-time; includes 6 minority (2 African Americans, 3 Asian Americans or Pacific Islanders, 1 Hispanic American), 98 international. Average age 24. 330 applicants, 42% accepted, 41 enrolled. In 2009, 8 master's, 22 doctorates awarded. Terminal master's awarded for partial completion of doctoral program. *Degree requirements:* For master's, comprehensive exam, thesis; for doctorate, comprehensive exam, thesis/dissertation. *Entrance requirements:* For master's and doctorate, GRE General Test, GRE Subject Test. Additional exam requirements/recommendations for international students: Required—TOEFL (minimum score 600 paper-based; 250 computer-based; 100 iBT). *Application deadline:* For fall admission, 2/1 priority date for domestic and international students. Applications are processed on a rolling basis. Application fee: $50. Electronic applications accepted. *Expenses:* Tuition, state resident: full-time $16,402; part-time $665 per credit. Tuition, nonresident: full-time $28,694; part-time

Chemistry

University of Pittsburgh (continued)

$1175 per credit. Required fees: $690; $175 per term. Tuition and fees vary according to program. *Financial support:* In 2009–10, 198 students received support, including 9 fellowships with tuition reimbursements available (averaging $24,034 per year), 119 research assistantships with tuition reimbursements available (averaging $22,140 per year), 70 teaching assistantships with tuition reimbursements available (averaging $22,597 per year); Federal Work-Study, scholarships/grants, health care benefits, and unspecified assistantships also available. Financial award application deadline: 2/1. *Faculty research:* Analytical, biological, inorganic and materials including nanostructured materials, organic, physical and theoretical. Total annual research expenditures: $10.1 million. *Unit head:* Dr. David H. Waldeck, Chairman, 412-624-0415, Fax: 412-624-1649, E-mail: chemchr@pitt.edu. *Application contact:* Fran Nagy, Graduate Program Administrator, 412-624-8501, Fax: 412-624-8611, E-mail: fnagy@pitt.edu.

See Close-Up on page 111.

University of Prince Edward Island, Faculty of Science, Charlottetown, PE C1A 4P3, Canada. Offers biology (M Sc); chemistry (M Sc). *Degree requirements:* For master's, thesis. *Entrance requirements:* Additional exam requirements/recommendations for international students: Required—TOEFL (minimum score 550 paper-based; 213 computer-based; 80 iBT), Canadian Academic English Language Assessment, Michigan English Language Assessment Battery, Canadian Test of English for Scholars and Trainees. *Faculty research:* Ecology and wildlife biology, molecular, genetics and biotechnology, organametallic, bio-organic, supramolecular and synthetic organic chemistry, neurobiology and stoke materials science.

University of Puerto Rico, Mayagüez Campus, Graduate Studies, College of Arts and Sciences, Department of Chemistry, Mayagüez, PR 00681-9000. Offers chemistry (MS, PhD). Part-time programs available. *Degree requirements:* For master's, one foreign language, comprehensive exam, thesis; for doctorate, comprehensive exam, thesis/dissertation. *Entrance requirements:* For master's, GRE, BS in chemistry or the equivalent. *Faculty research:* Biochemistry, spectroscopy, food chemistry, physical chemistry, electrochemistry.

University of Puerto Rico, Río Piedras, College of Natural Sciences, Department of Chemistry, San Juan, PR 00931-3300. Offers MS, PhD. Part-time programs available. *Degree requirements:* For master's, one foreign language, comprehensive exam, thesis; for doctorate, one foreign language, comprehensive exam, thesis/dissertation. *Entrance requirements:* For master's, GRE General Test, GRE Subject Test, interview, minimum GPA of 3.0, letter of recommendation; for doctorate, GRE General Test, GRE Subject Test, minimum GPA of 3.0, letter of recommendation. Additional exam requirements/recommendations for international students: Required—TOEFL.

University of Regina, Faculty of Graduate Studies and Research, Faculty of Science, Department of Chemistry and Biochemistry, Regina, SK S4S 0A2, Canada. Offers analytical chemistry (M Sc, PhD); biochemistry (M Sc, PhD); inorganic chemistry (M Sc, PhD); organic chemistry (M Sc, PhD); physical chemistry (M Sc, PhD). Part-time programs available. *Faculty:* 11 full-time (2 women), 3 part-time/adjunct (0 women). *Students:* 20 full-time (8 women). 25 applicants, 28% accepted. In 2009, 2 master's awarded. *Degree requirements:* For master's, thesis, departmental qualifying exam; for doctorate, thesis/dissertation, departmental qualifying exam. *Entrance requirements:* For master's and doctorate, GRE. Additional exam requirements/recommendations for international students: Required—TOEFL (minimum score 580 paper-based; 237 computer-based; 80 iBT). *Application deadline:* For fall admission, 1/1 for domestic students; for winter admission, 7/1 for domestic students. Applications are processed on a rolling basis. Application fee: $90 ($100 for international students). *Financial support:* In 2009–10, 5 fellowships (averaging $19,000 per year), 2 research assistantships (averaging $16,910 per year), 4 teaching assistantships (averaging $6,650 per year) were awarded; scholarships/grants also available. Financial award application deadline: 6/15. *Faculty research:* Organic synthesis, organic oxidations, ionic liquids theoretical/computational chemistry, protein biochemistry/biophysics, environmental analytical, photophysical/photochemistry. *Unit head:* Dr. Tanya Dahms, Head, 306-585-4247, E-mail: tanya.dohms@uregina.ca. *Application contact:* Dr. Scott Murphy, Program Coordinator, 306-585-4247, Fax: 306-585-4894, E-mail: scott.murphy@uregina.ca.

University of Rhode Island, Graduate School, College of Arts and Sciences, Department of Chemistry, Kingston, RI 02881. Offers MS, PhD. Part-time and evening/weekend programs available. *Faculty:* 15 full-time (4 women), 2 part-time/adjunct (0 women). *Students:* 41 full-time (14 women), 11 part-time (5 women); includes 6 minority (2 African Americans, 4 Asian Americans or Pacific Islanders), 20 international. In 2009, 7 master's, 3 doctorates awarded. *Degree requirements:* For master's, comprehensive exam (for some programs), thesis optional; for doctorate, comprehensive exam, thesis/dissertation. *Entrance requirements:* For master's, GRE (for graduates of non-US universities), 2 letters of recommendation; for doctorate, GRE (for graduates of non-U. S. universities), 2 letters of recommendation. Additional exam requirements/recommendations for international students: Required—TOEFL (minimum score 550 paper-based; 213 computer-based). *Application deadline:* For fall admission, 7/15 for domestic students, 1/15 for international students; for spring admission, 11/15 for domestic students, 9/15 for international students. Application fee: $65. Electronic applications accepted. *Expenses:* Tuition, state resident: full-time $8828; part-time $490 per credit hour. Tuition, nonresident: full-time $22,100; part-time $1228 per credit hour. Required fees: $1118; $57 per semester. Tuition and fees vary according to program. *Financial support:* In 2009–10, 4 research assistantships with full and partial tuition reimbursements (averaging $8,265 per year), 33 teaching assistantships with full and partial tuition reimbursements (averaging $12,575 per year) were awarded. Financial award applicants required to submit FAFSA. *Faculty research:* Analytical chemistry, biochemistry, analytical/nanoscience, materials/analytical, theoretical chemistry. Total annual research expenditures: $1.4 million. *Unit head:* Dr. William Euler, Chairperson, 401-874-5090, Fax: 401-874-5072, E-mail: weuler@chm.uri.edu. *Application contact:* Dr. William Euler, Chairperson, 401-874-5090, Fax: 401-874-5072, E-mail: weuler@chm.uri.edu.

University of Rochester, The College, Arts and Sciences, Department of Chemistry, Rochester, NY 14627. Offers MS, PhD. Terminal master's awarded for partial completion of doctoral program. *Degree requirements:* For doctorate, thesis/dissertation, qualifying exam. *Entrance requirements:* For master's and doctorate, GRE General Test. Additional exam requirements/recommendations for international students: Required—TOEFL.

University of San Francisco, College of Arts and Sciences, Department of Chemistry, San Francisco, CA 94117-1080. Offers MS. Part-time and evening/weekend programs available. *Faculty:* 2 full-time (0 women). *Students:* 11 full-time (6 women); includes 2 minority (both Asian Americans or Pacific Islanders), 6 international. Average age 25. 47 applicants, 19% accepted, 6 enrolled. In 2009, 2 master's awarded. *Degree requirements:* For master's, thesis. *Entrance requirements:* For master's, GRE General Test, GRE Subject Test, BS in chemistry or related field. *Application deadline:* Applications are processed on a rolling basis. Application fee: $55 ($65 for international students). *Expenses:* Tuition: Full-time $19,710; part-time $1095 per unit. Part-time tuition and fees vary according to degree level, campus/location and program. *Financial support:* In 2009–10, 11 students received support; fellowships, research assistantships, teaching assistantships, career-related internships or fieldwork, Federal Work-Study, institutionally sponsored loans, and tuition waivers (partial) available. Support available to part-time students. Financial award application deadline: 3/2; financial award applicants required to submit FAFSA. *Faculty research:* Organic photochemistry, genetics of chromatic adaptation, electron transfer processes in solution, metabolism of protein hormones. Total annual research expenditures: $75,000. *Unit head:* Dr. Jeff Curtis, Chair, 415-422-6157, Fax: 415-422-5157. *Application contact:* Information Contact, 415-422-5135, Fax: 415-422-2217, E-mail: asgraduate@usfca.edu.

University of Saskatchewan, College of Graduate Studies and Research, College of Arts and Sciences, Department of Chemistry, Saskatoon, SK S7N 5A2, Canada. Offers M Sc, PhD. *Faculty:* 29. *Students:* 67. In 2009, 5 master's, 9 doctorates awarded. *Degree requirements:* For master's, thesis; for doctorate, comprehensive exam (for some programs), thesis/dissertation. *Entrance requirements:* Additional exam requirements/recommendations for international students: Required—TOEFL (minimum score 80 iBT); Recommended—IELTS (minimum score 6.5). *Application deadline:* For fall admission, 7/1 priority date for domestic students. Applications are processed on a rolling basis. Application fee: $75. Electronic applications accepted. Tuition and fees charges are reported in Canadian dollars. *Expenses:* Tuition, area resident: Full-time $3000 Canadian dollars; part-time $500 Canadian dollars per term. Required fees: $700 Canadian dollars; $100 Canadian dollars per term. *Financial support:* Fellowships, research assistantships, teaching assistantships available. Financial award application deadline: 1/31. *Unit head:* Dr. Marek Majewski, Head, 306-966-4655, Fax: 306-966-4730, E-mail: marek.majewski@usask.ca. *Application contact:* Dr. Dale Ward, Graduate Chair, 306-966-4655, Fax: 306-966-4730, E-mail: dale.ward@usask.ca.

The University of Scranton, College of Graduate and Continuing Education, Department of Chemistry, Program in Chemistry, Scranton, PA 18510. Offers MA, MS. Part-time and evening/weekend programs available. *Faculty:* 10 full-time (3 women), 1 part-time/adjunct (0 women). *Students:* 10 full-time (3 women), 3 part-time (2 women), 6 international. Average age 27. 14 applicants, 93% accepted. In 2009, 1 master's awarded. *Degree requirements:* For master's, comprehensive exam (for some programs), thesis (for some programs), capstone experience. *Entrance requirements:* For master's, minimum GPA of 2.75. Additional exam requirements/recommendations for international students: Required—TOEFL (minimum score 500 paper-based; 173 computer-based), IELTS (minimum score 5.5). *Application deadline:* Applications are processed on a rolling basis. Application fee: $0. *Financial support:* Fellowships, teaching assistantships, career-related internships or fieldwork, Federal Work-Study, and unspecified assistantships available. Support available to part-time students. Financial award application deadline: 3/1. *Unit head:* Dr. Christopher A. Baumann, Director, 570-941-6389, Fax: 570-941-7510, E-mail: cab@scranton.edu. *Application contact:* Dr. Christopher A. Baumann, Director, 570-941-6389, Fax: 570-941-7510, E-mail: cab@scranton.edu.

The University of Scranton, College of Graduate and Continuing Education, Department of Chemistry, Program in Clinical Chemistry, Scranton, PA 18510. Offers MA, MS. Part-time and evening/weekend programs available. *Faculty:* 10 full-time (3 women), 1 part-time/adjunct (0 women). *Students:* 6 full-time (5 women), 1 (woman) part-time; includes 1 minority (Hispanic American), 2 international. Average age 24. 12 applicants, 92% accepted. *Degree requirements:* For master's, comprehensive exam (for some programs), thesis (for some programs), capstone experience. *Entrance requirements:* For master's, minimum GPA of 2.75. Additional exam requirements/recommendations for international students: Required—TOEFL (minimum score 500 paper-based; 173 computer-based), IELTS (minimum score 5.5). *Application deadline:* Applications are processed on a rolling basis. Application fee: $0. *Financial support:* Fellowships, teaching assistantships, career-related internships or fieldwork, Federal Work-Study, and unspecified assistantships available. Support available to part-time students. Financial award application deadline: 3/1. *Unit head:* Dr. Christopher A. Baumann, Director, 570-941-6389, Fax: 570-941-7510, E-mail: cab@scranton.edu. *Application contact:* Dr. Christopher A. Baumann, Director, 570-941-6389, Fax: 570-941-7510, E-mail: cab@scranton.edu.

University of South Carolina, The Graduate School, College of Arts and Sciences, Department of Chemistry and Biochemistry, Columbia, SC 29208. Offers IMA, MAT, MS, PhD. IMA and MAT offered in cooperation with the College of Education. Part-time programs available. Terminal master's awarded for partial completion of doctoral program. *Degree requirements:* For master's, comprehensive exam, thesis; for doctorate, comprehensive exam, thesis/dissertation. *Entrance requirements:* For master's and doctorate, GRE General Test. Additional exam requirements/recommendations for international students: Required—TOEFL. Electronic applications accepted. *Faculty research:* Spectroscopy, crystallography, organic and organometallic synthesis, analytical chemistry, materials.

The University of South Dakota, Graduate School, College of Arts and Sciences, Department of Chemistry, Vermillion, SD 57069-2390. Offers MNS, MS, PhD. *Degree requirements:* For master's, comprehensive exam, thesis. *Entrance requirements:* For master's, minimum GPA of 2.7; for doctorate, GRE, minimum GPA of 2.7. Additional exam requirements/recommendations for international students: Required—TOEFL (minimum score 550 paper-based; 213 computer-based; 79 iBT), GRE. Electronic applications accepted. *Faculty research:* Electrochemistry, photochemistry, inorganic synthesis, environmental and solid-state chemistry.

University of Southern California, Graduate School, College of Letters, Arts and Sciences, Department of Chemistry, Los Angeles, CA 90089. Offers chemical physics (PhD); chemistry (MA, MS, PhD). *Faculty:* 30 full-time (3 women). *Students:* 126 full-time (42 women); includes 5 minority (3 Asian Americans or Pacific Islanders, 2 Hispanic Americans), 66 international. Average age 26. 125 applicants, 53% accepted, 25 enrolled. In 2009, 3 master's, 16 doctorates awarded. Terminal master's awarded for partial completion of doctoral program. *Degree requirements:* For master's, comprehensive exam (for some programs), thesis optional; for doctorate, thesis/dissertation, qualifying exam. *Entrance requirements:* For master's and doctorate, GRE General Test. Additional exam requirements/recommendations for international students: Required—TOEFL (minimum score 600 paper-based; 250 computer-based; 100 iBT). *Application deadline:* For fall admission, 2/1 priority date for domestic and international students; for winter admission, 11/1 for domestic and international students. Applications are processed on a rolling basis. Application fee: $0. Electronic applications accepted. *Expenses:* Tuition: Full-time $25,980; part-time $1315 per unit. Required fees: $554. One-time fee: $35 full-time. Full-time tuition and fees vary according to degree level and program. *Financial support:* In 2009–10, 126 students received support, including fellowships with full tuition reimbursements available (averaging $30,332 per year), research assistantships with full tuition reimbursements available (averaging $25,332 per year), teaching assistantships with full tuition reimbursements available (averaging $25,332 per year); institutionally sponsored loans, scholarships/grants, health care benefits, and unspecified assistantships also available. Financial award application deadline: 3/1. *Faculty research:* Biological chemistry, inorganic chemistry, organic chemistry, physical chemistry, theoretical chemistry. Total annual research expenditures: $7.2 million. *Unit head:* Dr. Charles McKenna, Chair, 213-740-6857, Fax: 213-740-2701, E-mail: chemmail@chem1.usc.edu. *Application contact:* Katie McKissick, Graduate Advisor, 213-740-6855, Fax: 213-740-2701, E-mail: mckissic@usc.edu.

University of Southern Mississippi, Graduate School, College of Science and Technology, Department of Chemistry and Biochemistry, Hattiesburg, MS 39406-0001. Offers analytical chemistry (MS, PhD); biochemistry (MS, PhD); inorganic chemistry (MS, PhD); organic chemistry (MS, PhD); physical chemistry (MS, PhD). *Faculty:* 16 full-time (4 women). *Students:* 14 full-time (0 women), 5 part-time (4 women); includes 1 minority (African American), 12 international. Average age 29. 41 applicants, 17% accepted, 6 enrolled. In 2009, 2 master's, 6 doctorates awarded. *Degree requirements:* For master's, comprehensive exam, thesis; for doctorate, comprehensive exam, thesis/dissertation. *Entrance requirements:* For master's, GRE General Test, minimum GPA of 2.75 in last 60 hours; for doctorate, GRE General Test, minimum GPA of 3.5. Additional exam requirements/recommendations for international students: Required—TOEFL. *Application deadline:* For fall admission, 3/1 priority date for domestic students, 3/1 for international students. Applications are processed on a rolling basis. Application fee: $35. *Expenses:* Tuition, state resident: full-time $5096; part-time $284 per hour. Tuition, nonresident: full-time $13,052; part-time $726 per hour. Required fees: $402. Tuition and fees vary according to course level and course load. *Financial support:* In 2009–10, 3 research assistantships with full tuition reimbursements (averaging $17,000 per year), 19 teaching assistantships with full tuition reimbursements (averaging $20,716 per year) were awarded;

fellowships, Federal Work-Study and institutionally sponsored loans also available. Support available to part-time students. Financial award application deadline: 3/15; financial award applicants required to submit FAFSA. *Faculty research:* Plant biochemistry, photo chemistry, polymer chemistry, x-ray analysis, enzyme chemistry. *Unit head:* Dr. Robert Bateman, Chair, 601-266-4701, Fax: 601-266-6075. *Application contact:* Dr. Sabine Heinhorst, Graduate Coordinator, 601-266-4702, Fax: 601-266-6075.

University of South Florida, Graduate School, College of Arts and Sciences, Department of Chemistry, Tampa, FL 33620-9951. Offers computational chemistry (PhD); analytical chemistry (MS, PhD); biochemistry (MS, PhD); computational chemistry (MS); environmental chemistry (MS, PhD); inorganic chemistry (MS, PhD); organic chemistry (MS); physical chemistry (MS, PhD); polymer chemistry (PhD). Part-time programs available. *Faculty:* 25 full-time (4 women). *Students:* 113 full-time (36 women), 15 part-time (11 women); includes 19 minority (5 African Americans, 6 Asian Americans or Pacific Islanders, 8 Hispanic Americans), 58 international. Average age 32. 112 applicants, 30% accepted, 21 enrolled. In 2009, 8 master's, 11 doctorates awarded. Terminal master's awarded for partial completion of doctoral program. *Degree requirements:* For master's, comprehensive exam, thesis (for some programs); for doctorate, 2 foreign languages, comprehensive exam, thesis/dissertation. *Entrance requirements:* For master's, GRE General Test or GMAT, minimum GPA of 3.0. Additional exam requirements/recommendations for international students: Required—TOEFL (minimum score 550 paper-based; 213 computer-based). *Application deadline:* For fall admission, 2/15 priority date for domestic students, 1/2 priority date for international students; for spring admission, 10/1 priority date for domestic students, 6/1 priority date for international students. Applications are processed on a rolling basis. Application fee: $30. Electronic applications accepted. *Financial support:* In 2009–10, teaching assistantships with tuition reimbursements (averaging $27,522 per year); unspecified assistantships also available. Financial award application deadline: 6/30. *Faculty research:* Synthesis, bio-organic chemistry, bioinorganic chemistry, environmental chemistry, NMR. Total annual research expenditures: $3.2 million. *Unit head:* Dr. Randy Larsen, Chairperson, 813-974-4129, Fax: 813-974-3203, E-mail: rlarsen@cas.usf.edu. *Application contact:* Patricia Muisener, Director, 813-974-1730, Fax: 813-974-3203, E-mail: muisener@cas.usf.edu.

The University of Tennessee, Graduate School, College of Arts and Sciences, Department of Chemistry, Knoxville, TN 37996. Offers analytical chemistry (MS, PhD); chemical physics (PhD); environmental chemistry (MS, PhD); inorganic chemistry (MS, PhD); organic chemistry (MS, PhD); physical chemistry (MS, PhD); polymer chemistry (MS, PhD); theoretical chemistry (PhD). Part-time programs available. Terminal master's awarded for partial completion of doctoral program. *Degree requirements:* For master's, thesis; for doctorate, thesis/dissertation. *Entrance requirements:* For master's and doctorate, GRE General Test, minimum GPA of 2.7. Additional exam requirements/recommendations for international students: Required—TOEFL. Electronic applications accepted. *Expenses:* Tuition, state resident: full-time $6826; part-time $380 per semester hour. Tuition, nonresident: full-time $21,844; part-time $1147 per semester hour. Tuition and fees vary according to program.

The University of Texas at Arlington, Graduate School, College of Science, Department of Chemistry and Biochemistry, Arlington, TX 76019. Offers chemistry (MS, PhD). Part-time programs available. *Faculty:* 15 full-time (0 women), 4 part-time/adjunct (0 women). *Students:* 69 full-time (28 women), 8 part-time (4 women); includes 8 minority (7 Asian Americans or Pacific Islanders, 1 Hispanic American), 48 international. 48 applicants, 100% accepted, 21 enrolled. In 2009, 5 master's, 7 doctorates awarded. Terminal master's awarded for partial completion of doctoral program. *Degree requirements:* For master's, comprehensive exam (for some programs), thesis optional; for doctorate, comprehensive exam, thesis/dissertation, internship, oral defense of dissertation. *Entrance requirements:* For master's, GRE General Test, minimum GPA of 3.0 in last 60 hours of course work; for doctorate, GRE General Test, minimum GPA of 3.0 in last 60 hours of coursework. Additional exam requirements/recommendations for international students: Required—TOEFL (minimum score 550 paper-based; 213 computer-based; 80 iBT). *Application deadline:* For fall admission, 6/16 for domestic students, 4/4 for international students; for spring admission, 10/19 for domestic students, 9/7 for international students. Applications are processed on a rolling basis. Application fee: $40 ($70 for international students). Electronic applications accepted. *Financial support:* In 2009–10, 4 fellowships (averaging $1,000 per year), 36 research assistantships with partial tuition reimbursements (averaging $21,000 per year), 28 teaching assistantships with partial tuition reimbursements (averaging $20,000 per year) were awarded; career-related internships or fieldwork, Federal Work-Study, institutionally sponsored loans, scholarships/grants, health care benefits, tuition waivers (partial), and unspecified assistantships also available. Financial award application deadline: 6/1; financial award applicants required to submit FAFSA. *Unit head:* Dr. Purnendu Dasgupta, Chairman, 817-272-3171, Fax: 817-272-3808, E-mail: dasgupta@uta.edu. *Application contact:* Dr. Zoltan Schelly, Graduate Adviser, 817-272-3803, Fax: 817-272-3808, E-mail: schelly@uta.edu.

The University of Texas at Austin, Graduate School, College of Natural Sciences, Department of Chemistry and Biochemistry, Austin, TX 78712-1111. Offers analytical chemistry (MA, PhD); biochemistry (MA, PhD); inorganic chemistry (MA, PhD); organic chemistry (MA, PhD); physical chemistry (MA, PhD). *Entrance requirements:* For master's and doctorate, GRE General Test.

The University of Texas at Dallas, School of Natural Sciences and Mathematics, Programs in Chemistry, Richardson, TX 75080. Offers MS, PhD. Part-time and evening/weekend programs available. *Faculty:* 17 full-time (2 women). *Students:* 48 full-time (25 women), 5 part-time (4 women); includes 10 minority (7 Asian Americans or Pacific Islanders, 3 Hispanic Americans), 35 international. Average age 28. 92 applicants, 30% accepted, 15 enrolled. In 2009, 7 master's, 6 doctorates awarded. *Degree requirements:* For master's, thesis or internship; for doctorate, research practica. *Entrance requirements:* For master's and doctorate, GRE General Test, minimum GPA of 3.0 in upper-level course work in field. Additional exam requirements/recommendations for international students: Required—TOEFL (minimum score 550 paper-based; 213 computer-based). *Application deadline:* For fall admission, 7/15 for domestic students, 5/1 priority date for international students; for spring admission, 11/15 for domestic students, 9/1 priority date for international students. Applications are processed on a rolling basis. Application fee: $50 ($100 for international students). Electronic applications accepted. *Expenses:* Tuition, state resident: full-time $11,068; part-time $461 per credit hour. Tuition, nonresident: full-time $21,178; part-time $882 per credit hour. Tuition and fees vary according to course load. *Financial support:* In 2009–10, 20 research assistantships with full tuition reimbursements (averaging $14,530 per year), 25 teaching assistantships with full tuition reimbursements (averaging $13,500 per year) were awarded; fellowships, career-related internships or fieldwork, Federal Work-Study, institutionally sponsored loans, scholarships/grants, and unspecified assistantships also available. Support available to part-time students. Financial award application deadline: 4/30; financial award applicants required to submit FAFSA. *Faculty research:* Organic photochemistry, bioinorganic chemistry, organic solid-state and polymer chemistry, environmental chemistry, scanning probe microscopy. *Unit head:* Dr. John P. Ferraris, Department Head, 972-883-2901, Fax: 972-883-2925, E-mail: chemistry@utdallas.edu. *Application contact:* Dr. Inga H. Musselman, Associate Department Head, 972-883-2706, Fax: 972-883-2925, E-mail: imusselm@utdallas.edu.

The University of Texas at El Paso, Graduate School, College of Science, Department of Chemistry, El Paso, TX 79968-0001. Offers MS, PhD. Part-time and evening/weekend programs available. *Students:* 42 (15 women); includes 23 minority (1 Asian American or Pacific Islander, 22 Hispanic Americans), 16 international. Average age 34. In 2009, 8 master's, 1 doctorate awarded. *Degree requirements:* For master's, thesis; for doctorate, thesis/dissertation. *Entrance requirements:* For master's, GRE, minimum GPA of 3.0; for doctorate, GRE, Letters of Recommendation. Additional exam requirements/recommendations for international students: Required—TOEFL; Recommended—IELTS. *Application deadline:* For fall admission, 8/1 priority date for domestic students, 3/1 for international students; for spring admission, 11/1 priority date for domestic students, 9/1 for international students. Applications are processed on a rolling basis. Application fee: $45 ($80 for international students). Electronic applications accepted. *Financial support:* In 2009–10, research assistantships with partial tuition reimbursements (averaging $20,250 per year), teaching assistantships with partial tuition reimbursements (averaging $16,200 per year) were awarded; fellowships with partial tuition reimbursements, institutionally sponsored loans, scholarships/grants, health care benefits, tuition waivers (partial), and unspecified assistantships also available. Support available to part-time students. Financial award application deadline: 3/15; financial award applicants required to submit FAFSA. *Unit head:* Dr. Jorge Gardea-Torresdey, Chairperson, 915-747-5359, Fax: 915-747-5748, E-mail: jgardea@utep.edu. *Application contact:* Dr. Patricia D. Witherspoon, Dean of the Graduate School, 915-747-5491, Fax: 915-747-5788, E-mail: withersp@utep.edu.

The University of Texas at San Antonio, College of Sciences, Department of Chemistry, San Antonio, TX 78249-0617. Offers MS, PhD. Part-time programs available. *Faculty:* 10 full-time (1 woman), 2 part-time/adjunct (0 women). *Students:* 25 full-time (9 women), 10 part-time (4 women); includes 10 minority (2 African Americans, 3 Asian Americans or Pacific Islanders, 5 Hispanic Americans), 10 international. Average age 30. 42 applicants, 52% accepted, 13 enrolled. In 2009, 4 master's, 3 doctorates awarded. *Degree requirements:* For master's, comprehensive exam (for some programs), thesis (for some programs). *Entrance requirements:* For master's, GRE General Test, minimum GPA of 3.0 in all undergraduate chemistry courses, 2 letters of recommendation. Additional exam requirements/recommendations for international students: Required—TOEFL (minimum score 500 paper-based; 173 computer-based; 61 iBT), IELTS (minimum score 5). *Application deadline:* For fall admission, 7/1 for domestic students, 4/1 for international students; for spring admission, 11/1 for domestic students, 9/1 for international students. Applications are processed on a rolling basis. Application fee: $45 ($80 for international students). Electronic applications accepted. *Expenses:* Tuition, state resident: full-time $3975; part-time $221 per contact hour. Tuition, nonresident: full-time $13,947; part-time $775 per contact hour. Required fees: $1853. *Financial support:* In 2009–10, 27 students received support, including 27 fellowships (averaging $27,532 per year), 9 research assistantships (averaging $22,294 per year), 27 teaching assistantships (averaging $13,167 per year); career-related internships or fieldwork, scholarships/grants, tuition waivers, and unspecified assistantships also available. Support available to part-time students. *Faculty research:* Sensors and micro fluidics; signal transduction and transcription factor purification; metals in medicine and nanomaterials; asymmetric and catalytic synthesis; experimental, theoretical and computational techniques. Total annual research expenditures: $1 million. *Unit head:* Dr. Waldemar Gorski, Interim Chair, 210-458-4961, Fax: 210-458-7428, E-mail: waldemar.gorski@utsa.edu. *Application contact:* Edward Tiekink, Graduate Advisor, 210-458-5774, E-mail: edward.tiekink@utsa.edu.

The University of Texas–Pan American, College of Science and Engineering, Department of Chemistry, Edinburg, TX 78539. Offers MS. *Expenses:* Tuition, state resident: full-time $3630.60; part-time $201.70 per credit hour. Tuition, nonresident: full-time $8617; part-time $478.70 per credit hour. Required fees: $806.50.

University of the Sciences in Philadelphia, College of Graduate Studies, Program in Chemistry, Biochemistry and Pharmacognosy, Philadelphia, PA 19104-4495. Offers biochemistry (MS, PhD); chemistry (MS, PhD); pharmacognosy (MS, PhD). Part-time programs available. *Degree requirements:* For master's, thesis, qualifying exams; for doctorate, comprehensive exam, thesis/dissertation, qualifying exams. *Entrance requirements:* For master's and doctorate, GRE General Test, GRE Subject Test. Additional exam requirements/recommendations for international students: Required—TOEFL, TWE. *Expenses:* Contact institution. *Faculty research:* Organic and medicinal synthesis, mass spectroscopy use in protein analysis, study of analogues of taxol, cholesteryl esters.

The University of Toledo, College of Graduate Studies, College of Arts and Sciences, Department of Chemistry, Toledo, OH 43606-3390. Offers analytical chemistry (MS, PhD); biological chemistry (MS, PhD); inorganic chemistry (MS, PhD); organic chemistry (MS, PhD); physical chemistry (MS, PhD). Part-time programs available. *Degree requirements:* For master's, thesis; for doctorate, thesis/dissertation. *Entrance requirements:* For master's and doctorate, GRE General Test, GRE Subject Test. Additional exam requirements/recommendations for international students: Required—TOEFL. Electronic applications accepted. *Faculty research:* Enzymology, materials chemistry, crystallography, theoretical chemistry.

University of Toronto, School of Graduate Studies, Physical Sciences Division, Department of Chemistry, Toronto, ON M5S 1A1, Canada. Offers M Sc, PhD. *Degree requirements:* For master's, thesis; for doctorate, thesis/dissertation, oral exam, thesis defense. *Entrance requirements:* For master's, bachelor's degree in chemistry or a related field; for doctorate, master's degree in chemistry or a related field.

University of Tulsa, Graduate School, College of Engineering and Natural Sciences, Department of Chemistry and Biochemistry, Program in Chemistry, Tulsa, OK 74104-3189. Offers MS, PhD. Part-time programs available. *Faculty:* 9 full-time (0 women). *Students:* 13 full-time (10 women), 4 international. Average age 29. 18 applicants, 61% accepted, 6 enrolled. In 2009, 1 master's awarded. *Degree requirements:* For master's, thesis (for some programs). *Entrance requirements:* For master's, GRE General Test. Additional exam requirements/recommendations for international students: Required—TOEFL (minimum score 550 paper-based; 213 computer-based; 80 iBT), IELTS (minimum score 6). *Application deadline:* Applications are processed on a rolling basis. Application fee: $40. Electronic applications accepted. *Expenses:* Tuition: Full-time $16,182; part-time $899 per credit hour. Required fees: $4 per credit hour. Tuition and fees vary according to course load. *Financial support:* In 2009–10, 11 students received support, including 4 fellowships (averaging $826 per year), 3 research assistantships with full tuition reimbursements available (averaging $16,760 per year), 8 teaching assistantships with full tuition reimbursements available (averaging $11,860 per year); career-related internships or fieldwork, Federal Work-Study, scholarships/grants, health care benefits, tuition waivers (full and partial), and unspecified assistantships also available. Support available to part-time students. Financial award application deadline: 2/1; financial award applicants required to submit FAFSA. *Faculty research:* Analytical, organic, inorganic, and physical chemistry; specialty courses in materials chemistry, polymer chemistry, nanotechnology, medicinal chemistry, environmental chemistry, biochemistry of disease, chemical kinetics, surface chemistry, and spectroscopy. *Unit head:* Dr. Dale C. Teeters, Chairperson, 918-631-2515, Fax: 918-631-3404, E-mail: dale-teeters@utulsa.edu. *Application contact:* Dr. Kenneth Roberts, Advisor, 918-631-3090, Fax: 918-631-3404, E-mail: kproberts@utulsa.edu.

University of Utah, The Graduate School, College of Science, Department of Chemistry, Salt Lake City, UT 84112-0850. Offers chemical physics (PhD); chemistry (M Phil, MA, MS, PhD); science teacher education (MS). Part-time programs available. Postbaccalaureate distance learning degree programs offered. *Faculty:* 30 full-time (4 women), 4 part-time/adjunct (1 woman). *Students:* 145 full-time (47 women), 27 part-time (12 women); includes 10 minority (1 African American, 5 Asian Americans or Pacific Islanders, 4 Hispanic Americans), 68 international. Average age 28. 352 applicants, 24% accepted, 31 enrolled. In 2009, 9 master's, 29 doctorates awarded. Terminal master's awarded for partial completion of doctoral program. *Degree requirements:* For master's, thesis optional, 20 hours course work, 10 hours research; for doctorate, thesis/dissertation, 18 hours course work, 14 hours research. *Entrance requirements:* For master's and doctorate, GRE General Test, minimum GPA of 3.0. Additional exam requirements/recommendations for international students: Required—TOEFL (minimum score 620 paper-based; 260 computer-based; 105 iBT). *Application deadline:* For fall admission, 4/1 for domestic and international students; for spring admission, 11/1 for domestic and international students. Application fee: $55 ($65 for international students). Electronic applications

Chemistry

University of Utah (continued)

accepted. *Expenses:* Tuition, state resident: full-time $4004; part-time $1674 per semester. Tuition, nonresident: full-time $14,134; part-time $5915 per semester. Required fees: $324 per semester. Tuition and fees vary according to course load, degree level and program. *Financial support:* In 2009–10, 1 fellowship with tuition reimbursement (averaging $22,000 per year), 116 research assistantships with tuition reimbursements (averaging $22,500 per year), 50 teaching assistantships with tuition reimbursements (averaging $22,000 per year) were awarded; scholarships/grants and tuition waivers (full) also available. Financial award application deadline: 4/1; financial award applicants required to submit FAFSA. *Faculty research:* Biological, theoretical, inorganic, organic, and physical-analytical chemistry. Total annual research expenditures: $14.2 million. *Unit head:* Dr. Henry S. White, Chair, 801-585-6256, Fax: 801-581-8433, E-mail: chair@chemistry.utah.edu. *Application contact:* Jo Hoovey, Graduate Coordinator, 801-581-4393, Fax: 801-581-5408, E-mail: jhoovey@chem.utah.edu.

University of Vermont, Graduate College, College of Arts and Sciences, Department of Chemistry, Burlington, VT 05405. Offers chemistry (MS, PhD). *Students:* 41 (17 women); includes 3 minority (2 African Americans, 1 Hispanic American), 17 international. 48 applicants, 48% accepted, 12 enrolled. In 2009, 2 master's, 5 doctorates awarded. *Degree requirements:* For master's, one foreign language, thesis; for doctorate, 2 foreign languages, thesis/dissertation. *Entrance requirements:* For master's and doctorate, GRE General Test. Additional exam requirements/recommendations for international students: Required—TOEFL (minimum score 550 paper-based; 213 computer-based; 80 iBT). *Application deadline:* For fall admission, 4/1 priority date for domestic students. Applications are processed on a rolling basis. Application fee: $40. Electronic applications accepted. *Expenses:* Tuition, area resident: Part-time $508 per credit hour. Tuition, state resident: part-time $508 per credit hour. Tuition, nonresident: part-time $1281 per credit hour. *Financial support:* Fellowships, research assistantships, teaching assistantships available. Financial award application deadline: 3/1. *Unit head:* Dr. D. Matthews, Chairperson, 802-656-2594. *Application contact:* Dr. Rory Waterman, Coordinator, 802-656-2594.

University of Victoria, Faculty of Graduate Studies, Faculty of Science, Department of Chemistry, Victoria, BC V8W 2Y2, Canada. Offers M Sc, PhD. *Degree requirements:* For master's, thesis; for doctorate, thesis/dissertation, candidacy exam. *Entrance requirements:* For master's and doctorate, GRE Subject Test. Additional exam requirements/recommendations for international students: Required—TOEFL (minimum score 575 paper-based; 233 computer-based), IELTS (minimum score 7). Electronic applications accepted. *Faculty research:* Laser spectroscopy and dynamics; inorganic, organic, and organometallic synthesis; electro and surface chemistry.

University of Virginia, College and Graduate School of Arts and Sciences, Department of Chemistry, Charlottesville, VA 22903. Offers MA, MS, PhD. *Faculty:* 27 full-time (3 women), 1 part-time/adjunct (0 women). *Students:* 105 full-time (42 women); includes 7 minority (1 African American, 4 Asian Americans or Pacific Islanders, 2 Hispanic Americans), 24 international. Average age 25. 149 applicants, 46% accepted, 29 enrolled. In 2009, 4 master's, 15 doctorates awarded. *Degree requirements:* For master's, comprehensive exam, thesis; for doctorate, comprehensive exam, thesis/dissertation. *Entrance requirements:* For master's and doctorate, GRE General Test; GRE Subject Test (recommended). Additional exam requirements/recommendations for international students: Required—TOEFL (minimum score 600 paper-based; 250 computer-based; 90 iBT), IELTS (minimum score 7). *Application deadline:* For fall admission, 2/1 for domestic and international students. Application fee: $60. Electronic applications accepted. *Financial support:* Fellowships, teaching assistantships available. Financial award applicants required to submit FAFSA. *Unit head:* David Cafiso, Chairman, 434-924-3344, Fax: 434-924-3710, E-mail: chem@virginia.edu. *Application contact:* David Cafiso, Chairman, 434-924-3344, Fax: 434-924-3710, E-mail: chem@virginia.edu.

University of Washington, Graduate School, College of Arts and Sciences, Department of Chemistry, Seattle, WA 98195. Offers MS, PhD. Terminal master's awarded for partial completion of doctoral program. *Degree requirements:* For master's, thesis (for some programs); for doctorate, thesis/dissertation. *Entrance requirements:* For master's and doctorate, GRE Subject Test, minimum GPA of 3.0. Additional exam requirements/recommendations for international students: Required—TOEFL. *Faculty research:* Biopolymers, material science and nanotechnology, organometallic chemistry, analytical chemistry, bioorganic chemistry.

University of Waterloo, Graduate Studies, Faculty of Science, Guelph-Waterloo Centre for Graduate Work in Chemistry and Biochemistry, Waterloo, ON N2L 3G1, Canada. Offers M Sc, PhD. Part-time programs available. *Degree requirements:* For master's and doctorate, project or thesis. *Entrance requirements:* For master's, GRE, honors degree, minimum B average; for doctorate, GRE, master's degree, minimum B average. Additional exam requirements/recommendations for international students: Required—TOEFL, TWE. Electronic applications accepted. *Faculty research:* Polymer, physical, inorganic, organic, and theoretical chemistry.

The University of Western Ontario, Faculty of Graduate Studies, Physical Sciences Division, Department of Chemistry, London, ON N6A 5B8, Canada. Offers M Sc, PhD. *Degree requirements:* For master's, thesis; for doctorate, thesis/dissertation. *Entrance requirements:* For master's, minimum B+ average, honors B Sc in chemistry; for doctorate, M Sc or equivalent in chemistry. Additional exam requirements/recommendations for international students: Required—TOEFL (paper-based 570; computer-based 230) or IELTS (paper-based 6). *Faculty research:* Materials, inorganic, organic, physical and theoretical chemistry.

University of Windsor, Faculty of Graduate Studies, Faculty of Science, Department of Chemistry and Biochemistry, Windsor, ON N9B 3P4, Canada. Offers M Sc, PhD. Part-time programs available. *Degree requirements:* For master's, thesis; for doctorate, comprehensive exam, thesis/dissertation. *Entrance requirements:* For master's and doctorate, minimum B average. Additional exam requirements/recommendations for international students: Required—TOEFL (minimum score 560 paper-based; 220 computer-based), GRE. Electronic applications accepted. *Faculty research:* Molecular biology/recombinant DNA techniques (PCR, cloning mutagenesis), No/02 detectors, western immunoblotting and detection, CD/NMR protein/peptide structure determination, confocal/electron microscopes.

University of Wisconsin–Madison, Graduate School, College of Engineering, Program in Environmental Chemistry and Technology, Madison, WI 53706. Offers MS, PhD. Part-time programs available. Terminal master's awarded for partial completion of doctoral program. *Degree requirements:* For master's, thesis or alternative; for doctorate, thesis/dissertation. *Entrance requirements:* For master's and doctorate, GRE General Test. Additional exam requirements/recommendations for international students: Required—TOEFL. Electronic applications accepted. *Expenses:* Tuition, state resident: part-time $594 per credit. Tuition, nonresident: part-time $1504 per credit. Required fees: $65 per credit. Tuition and fees vary according to course load, program and reciprocity agreements. *Faculty research:* Chemical limnology, chemical remediation, geochemistry, photocatalysis, water quality.

University of Wisconsin–Madison, Graduate School, College of Letters and Science, Department of Chemistry, Madison, WI 53706-1380. Offers MS, PhD. Part-time programs available. Terminal master's awarded for partial completion of doctoral program. *Degree requirements:* For master's, thesis (for some programs); for doctorate, thesis/dissertation, cumulative exams, research proposal, seminar. *Entrance requirements:* For master's and doctorate, GRE, minimum GPA of 3.0. Additional exam requirements/recommendations for international students: Required—TOEFL. Electronic applications accepted. *Expenses:* Tuition, state resident: part-time $594 per credit. Tuition, nonresident: part-time $1504 per credit. Required fees: $65 per credit. Tuition and fees vary according to course load, program and reciprocity agreements. *Faculty research:* Analytical, inorganic, organic, physical, and macromolecular chemistry.

University of Wisconsin–Milwaukee, Graduate School, College of Letters and Sciences, Department of Chemistry, Milwaukee, WI 53201-0413. Offers biogeochemistry (PhD); chemistry (MS, PhD). *Faculty:* 22 full-time (3 women). *Students:* 68 full-time (22 women), 8 part-time (5 women); includes 9 minority (3 African Americans, 6 Asian Americans or Pacific Islanders), 27 international. Average age 30. 55 applicants, 45% accepted, 17 enrolled. In 2009, 4 master's, 16 doctorates awarded. *Degree requirements:* For master's, thesis or alternative; for doctorate, thesis/dissertation. *Entrance requirements:* For doctorate, GRE General Test. Additional exam requirements/recommendations for international students: Required—TOEFL (minimum score 600 paper-based; 79 iBT), IELTS (minimum score 6.5). *Application deadline:* For fall admission, 1/1 priority date for domestic students; for spring admission, 9/1 for domestic students. Applications are processed on a rolling basis. Application fee: $45 ($75 for international students). *Expenses:* Tuition, state resident: full-time $8800. Tuition, nonresident: full-time $20,760. Tuition and fees vary according to program and reciprocity agreements. *Financial support:* In 2009–10, 22 research assistantships, 48 teaching assistantships were awarded; career-related internships or fieldwork and unspecified assistantships also available. Support available to part-time students. Financial award application deadline: 4/15. *Faculty research:* Analytical chemistry, biochemistry, inorganic chemistry, organic chemistry, physical chemistry. Total annual research expenditures: $2.4 million. *Unit head:* Peter Geissinger, Representative, 414-229-5230, Fax: 414-229-5530, E-mail: geissing@uwm.edu. *Application contact:* Joseph Aldstadt, General Information Contact, 414-229-5605, Fax: 414-229-6967, E-mail: aldstadt@uwm.edu.

University of Wyoming, College of Arts and Sciences, Department of Chemistry, Laramie, WY 82070. Offers MS, PhD. *Degree requirements:* For master's, thesis; for doctorate, thesis/dissertation. *Entrance requirements:* For master's and doctorate, GRE General Test, minimum GPA of 3.0. Additional exam requirements/recommendations for international students: Required—TOEFL (minimum score 600 paper-based). Electronic applications accepted. *Faculty research:* Organic chemistry, inorganic chemistry, analytical chemistry, physical chemistry.

Utah State University, School of Graduate Studies, College of Science, Department of Chemistry and Biochemistry, Logan, UT 84322. Offers biochemistry (MS, PhD); chemistry (MS, PhD). Part-time programs available. Terminal master's awarded for partial completion of doctoral program. *Degree requirements:* For master's, thesis, oral and written exams; for doctorate, thesis/dissertation, oral and written exams. *Entrance requirements:* For master's and doctorate, GRE General Test, minimum GPA of 3.0. Additional exam requirements/recommendations for international students: Required—TOEFL. *Faculty research:* Analytical, inorganic, organic, and physical chemistry; iron in asbestos chemistry and carcinogenicity; dicopper complexes; photothermal spectrometry; metal molecule clusters.

Vanderbilt University, Graduate School, Department of Chemistry, Nashville, TN 37240-1001. Offers analytical chemistry (MAT, MS, PhD); inorganic chemistry (MAT, MS, PhD); organic chemistry (MAT, MS, PhD); physical chemistry (MAT, MS, PhD); theoretical chemistry (MAT, MS, PhD). *Faculty:* 46 full-time (6 women). *Students:* 106 full-time (38 women); includes 10 minority (5 African Americans, 3 Asian Americans or Pacific Islanders, 2 Hispanic Americans), 21 international. Average age 27. 245 applicants, 27% accepted, 21 enrolled. In 2009, 10 master's, 21 doctorates awarded. Terminal master's awarded for partial completion of doctoral program. *Degree requirements:* For master's, thesis; for doctorate, thesis/dissertation, area, qualifying, and final exams. *Entrance requirements:* For master's and doctorate, GRE General Test, GRE Subject Test (recommended). Additional exam requirements/recommendations for international students: Required—TOEFL (minimum score 570 paper-based; 230 computer-based; 88 iBT). *Application deadline:* For fall admission, 1/15 for domestic and international students. Application fee: $0. Electronic applications accepted. *Financial support:* Fellowships with full and partial tuition reimbursements, research assistantships with full tuition reimbursements, teaching assistantships with full tuition reimbursements, Federal Work-Study, institutionally sponsored loans, scholarships/grants, traineeships, and health care benefits available. Financial award application deadline: 1/15; financial award applicants required to submit CSS PROFILE or FAFSA. *Faculty research:* Chemical synthesis; mechanistic, theoretical, bioorganic, analytical, and spectroscopic chemistry. *Unit head:* Mike P. Stone, Chair, 615-322-2861, Fax: 615-343-1234. *Application contact:* Charles M. Lukehart, Director of Graduate Studies, 615-322-2861, Fax: 615-343-1234, E-mail: charles.m.lukehart@vanderbilt.edu.

Vassar College, Graduate Programs, Poughkeepsie, NY 12604. Offers biology (MA, MS); chemistry (MA, MS). Applicants accepted only if enrolled in undergraduate programs at Vassar College. Part-time programs available. *Students:* 1 (woman) part-time. *Degree requirements:* For master's, thesis. *Entrance requirements:* For master's, GRE General Test, bachelor's degree in related field. *Application deadline:* Applications are processed on a rolling basis. Application fee: $60. *Expenses:* Tuition: Full-time $41,335; part-time $4890 per course. *Financial support:* Career-related internships or fieldwork available. *Unit head:* Joanne Long, Dean of Studies, 914-437-5257, E-mail: long@vassar.edu. *Application contact:* Joanne Long, Dean of Studies, 914-437-5257, E-mail: long@vassar.edu.

Villanova University, Graduate School of Liberal Arts and Sciences, Department of Chemistry, Villanova, PA 19085-1699. Offers MS. Part-time and evening/weekend programs available. *Faculty:* 5 full-time (0 women), 1 part-time/adjunct (0 women). *Students:* 25 full-time (17 women), 17 part-time (9 women); includes 8 minority (2 African Americans, 4 Asian Americans or Pacific Islanders, 2 Hispanic Americans), 5 international. Average age 26. 33 applicants, 52% accepted, 10 enrolled. In 2009, 10 master's awarded. *Degree requirements:* For master's, thesis (for some programs). *Entrance requirements:* For master's, GRE General Test, minimum GPA of 2.5. Additional exam requirements/recommendations for international students: Required—TOEFL. *Application deadline:* For fall admission, 3/1 priority date for domestic and international students; for spring admission, 11/15 priority date for domestic and international students. Applications are processed on a rolling basis. Application fee: $50. Electronic applications accepted. *Expenses:* Contact institution. *Financial support:* Research assistantships, Federal Work-Study and unspecified assistantships available. Financial award applicants required to submit FAFSA. *Unit head:* Dr. Barry Selinsky, Chair, 610-519-4840. *Application contact:* Dr. Barry Selinsky, Chair, 610-519-4840.

See Close-Up on page 113.

Virginia Commonwealth University, Graduate School, College of Humanities and Sciences, Department of Chemistry, Richmond, VA 23284-9005. Offers analytical chemistry (MS, PhD); chemical physics (PhD); inorganic chemistry (MS, PhD); organic chemistry (MS, PhD); physical chemistry (MS, PhD). Part-time programs available. Terminal master's awarded for partial completion of doctoral program. *Degree requirements:* For master's, thesis; for doctorate, thesis/dissertation, comprehensive cumulative exams, research proposal. *Entrance requirements:* For master's, GRE General Test, 30 undergraduate credits in chemistry; for doctorate, GRE General Test. *Faculty research:* Physical, organic, inorganic, analytical, and polymer chemistry; chemical physics.

Virginia Polytechnic Institute and State University, Graduate School, College of Science, Department of Chemistry, Blacksburg, VA 24061. Offers MS, PhD. *Entrance requirements:* Additional exam requirements/recommendations for international students: Required—TOEFL (minimum score 600 paper-based; 250 computer-based), GRE. Electronic applications accepted. *Faculty research:* Analytical, inorganic, organic, physical, and polymer chemistry.

Wake Forest University, Graduate School of Arts and Sciences, Department of Chemistry, Winston-Salem, NC 27109. Offers analytical chemistry (MS, PhD); inorganic chemistry (MS, PhD); organic chemistry (MS, PhD); physical chemistry (MS, PhD). Part-time programs available.

Degree requirements: For master's, one foreign language, comprehensive exam, thesis; for doctorate, 2 foreign languages, comprehensive exam, thesis/dissertation. *Entrance requirements:* For master's and doctorate, GRE General Test. Additional exam requirements/recommendations for international students: Required—TOEFL (minimum score 213 computer-based). Electronic applications accepted.

Washington State University, Graduate School, College of Sciences, Department of Chemistry, Pullman, WA 99164. Offers MS, PhD. *Faculty:* 25. *Students:* 74 full-time (27 women), 12 part-time (5 women); includes 8 minority (1 African American, 5 Asian Americans or Pacific Islanders, 2 Hispanic Americans), 19 international. Average age 29. 186 applicants, 20% accepted, 18 enrolled. In 2009, 6 master's, 4 doctorates awarded. Terminal master's awarded for partial completion of doctoral program. *Degree requirements:* For master's, comprehensive exam (for some programs), thesis (for some programs), oral exam, teaching experience; for doctorate, comprehensive exam, thesis/dissertation, oral exam, written exam. *Entrance requirements:* For master's and doctorate, GRE General Test, 1. Transcripts from each post-secondary school attended (photocopies are acceptable) 2. Names and email addresses of three people who are willing to write letters of recommendation for you 3. GRE Scores (General Test Required; Subject recommended) 4. TOEFL scores (International Students Only) . Additional exam requirements/recommendations for international students: Required—TOEFL. *Application deadline:* For fall admission, 3/1 priority date for domestic students, 3/1 for international students; for spring admission, 10/1 priority date for domestic students, 7/1 for international students. Applications are processed on a rolling basis. Application fee: $50. *Financial support:* In 2009–10, 3 fellowships (averaging $8,977 per year), 12 research assistantships with full and partial tuition reimbursements (averaging $13,917 per year), 23 teaching assistantships with full and partial tuition reimbursements (averaging $13,056 per year) were awarded; career-related internships or fieldwork, Federal Work-Study, institutionally sponsored loans, scholarships/grants, health care benefits, and unspecified assistantships also available. Financial award application deadline: 2/15; financial award applicants required to submit FAFSA. *Faculty research:* Environmental chemistry, materials chemistry, radio chemistry, bio-organic, computational chemistry. *Unit head:* Kerry W. Hipps, Chair, 509-335-8866, Fax: 509-335-8867, E-mail: chemistry@wsu.edu. *Application contact:* Graduate School Admissions, 800-GRADWSU, Fax: 509-335-1949, E-mail: gradsch@wsu.edu.

Washington State University Tri-Cities, Graduate Programs, Program in Chemistry, Richland, WA 99354. Offers MS, PhD. *Faculty:* 25. *Students:* 2 full-time (0 women), 8 part-time (3 women). Average age 35. 186 applicants, 20% accepted.Terminal master's awarded for partial completion of doctoral program. *Degree requirements:* For master's, comprehensive exam (for some programs), thesis; for doctorate, comprehensive exam, thesis/dissertation. *Entrance requirements:* For master's and doctorate, GRE, minimum GPA of 3.0, 3 letters of recommendation. Additional exam requirements/recommendations for international students: Required—TOEFL. *Application deadline:* For fall admission, 3/1 priority date for domestic students, 3/1 for international students; for spring admission, 10/1 priority date for domestic students, 7/1 for international students. Applications are processed on a rolling basis. Application fee: $50. *Expenses:* Tuition, state resident: part-time $423 per credit. Tuition, nonresident: part-time $1032 per credit. *Financial support:* In 2009–10, 1 student received support. Career-related internships or fieldwork, Federal Work-Study, institutionally sponsored loans, scholarships/grants, health care benefits, and unspecified assistantships available. Financial award application deadline: 2/15; financial award applicants required to submit FAFSA. *Unit head:* Dr. Kerry Hipps, Chair, 509-335-3442. *Application contact:* Bonnie Bates, Academic Coordinator, 509-372-7171, Fax: 509-335-1949, E-mail: bbates@tricity.wsu.edu.

Washington University in St. Louis, Graduate School of Arts and Sciences, Department of Chemistry, St. Louis, MO 63130-4899. Offers PhD. Terminal master's awarded for partial completion of doctoral program. *Degree requirements:* For doctorate, thesis/dissertation. *Entrance requirements:* For doctorate, GRE General Test, GRE Subject Test. Electronic applications accepted.

Wayne State University, College of Liberal Arts and Sciences, Department of Chemistry, Detroit, MI 48202. Offers MA, MS, PhD. *Degree requirements:* For master's, thesis (for some programs); for doctorate, thesis/dissertation. *Entrance requirements:* For master's, BA with minimum GPA of 3.0, letters of recommendation. Additional exam requirements/recommendations for international students: Required—TOEFL (minimum score 550 paper-based; 213 computer-based); Recommended—TWE (minimum score 6). Electronic applications accepted. *Faculty research:* Natural products synthesis, molecular biology, molecular mechanics calculations, organometallic chemistry, experimental physical chemistry.

Wesleyan University, Graduate Programs, Department of Chemistry, Middletown, CT 06459. Offers biochemistry (MA, PhD); chemical physics (MA, PhD); inorganic chemistry (MA, PhD); organic chemistry (MA, PhD); physical chemistry (MA, PhD); theoretical chemistry (MA, PhD). *Faculty:* 14 full-time (2 women), 2 part-time/adjunct (1 woman). *Students:* 19 full-time (8 women), 2 part-time (0 women), 9 international. Average age 26. 40 applicants, 63% accepted, 4 enrolled. In 2009, 3 master's, 5 doctorates awarded. Terminal master's awarded for partial completion of doctoral program. *Degree requirements:* For master's, thesis, proposal; for doctorate, thesis/dissertation, proposal. *Entrance requirements:* For doctorate, GRE General Test, 3 recommendations. Additional exam requirements/recommendations for international students: Required—TOEFL. *Application deadline:* Applications are processed on a rolling basis. Application fee: $0. Electronic applications accepted. *Financial support:* In 2009–10, 4 research assistantships with full tuition reimbursements, 12 teaching assistantships with full tuition reimbursements were awarded; institutionally sponsored loans also available. Financial award application deadline: 4/15; financial award applicants required to submit FAFSA. *Unit head:* Dr. Joseph Knee, Chair, 860-685-2210. *Application contact:* Cait Zinser, Information Contact, 860-685-2573, Fax: 860-685-2211, E-mail: czinser@wesleyan.edu.

See Close-Up on page 115.

West Chester University of Pennsylvania, Office of Graduate Studies, College of Arts and Sciences, Department of Chemistry, West Chester, PA 19383. Offers Teaching Certificate. Part-time and evening/weekend programs available. *Students:* 1 full-time (0 women), 1 (woman) part-time. Average age 29. 4 applicants, 100% accepted, 2 enrolled. *Entrance requirements:* For degree, GRE General Test (recommended). Additional exam requirements/recommendations for international students: Required—TOEFL (minimum score 550 paper-based; 213 computer-based; 80 iBT). *Application deadline:* For fall admission, 4/15 priority date for domestic students, 3/15 for international students; for spring admission, 10/15 for domestic students, 9/1 for international students. Applications are processed on a rolling basis. Application fee: $35. Electronic applications accepted. *Expenses:* Tuition, state resident: full-time $6666; part-time $370 per credit. Tuition, nonresident: full-time $10,666; part-time $593 per credit. Required fees: $122.56 per credit. *Financial support:* In 2009–10, research assistantships with full and partial tuition reimbursements (averaging $5,000 per year); unspecified assistantships also available. Support available to part-time students. Financial award application deadline: 2/15; financial award applicants required to submit FAFSA. *Faculty research:* Solid phase rates into monodisperse polymers and palladium-mediated rates into novel materials. *Unit head:* Dr. Blaise Frost, Chair, 610-436-2526, E-mail: bfrost@wcupa.edu. *Application contact:* Dr. John Townsend, Secondary Education Advisor, 610-436-1063, E-mail: jtownsend@wcupa.edu.

Western Carolina University, Graduate School, College of Arts and Sciences, Department of Chemistry and Physics, Cullowhee, NC 28723. Offers chemistry (MS). *Students:* 13 full-time (5 women), 5 part-time (2 women). Average age 27. 12 applicants, 83% accepted, 7 enrolled. In 2009, 4 master's awarded. *Degree requirements:* For master's, thesis. *Entrance requirements:* For master's, GRE General Test, undergraduate science degree with minimum GPA of 3.0, 3 letters of recommendation. Additional exam requirements/recommendations for international students: Required—TOEFL (minimum score 550 paper-based; 270 computer-based; 79 iBT). *Application deadline:* For fall admission, 5/1 priority date for domestic students; for spring admission, 9/1 priority date for domestic students. Applications are processed on a rolling basis. Application fee: $45. *Financial support:* In 2009–10, 11 students received support, including 11 teaching assistantships with full and partial tuition reimbursements available (averaging $10,500 per year); fellowships, research assistantships with full and partial tuition reimbursements available, career-related internships or fieldwork, institutionally sponsored loans, scholarships/grants, and unspecified assistantships also available. Financial award application deadline: 3/31; financial award applicants required to submit FAFSA. *Faculty research:* Trace metal analysis, metal waste reduction, supramolecular chemistry, free radical biophysical chemistry. *Unit head:* Dr. Cynthia Atterholt, Head, 828-227-7260, Fax: 828-227-7393, E-mail: atterholt@email.wcu.edu. *Application contact:* Admissions Specialist for Chemistry, 828-227-7398, Fax: 828-227-7480, E-mail: gradsch@email.wcu.edu.

Western Illinois University, School of Graduate Studies, College of Arts and Sciences, Department of Chemistry, Macomb, IL 61455-1390. Offers MS. Part-time programs available. *Students:* 33 full-time (17 women), 4 part-time (3 women); includes 1 minority (Asian American or Pacific Islander), 30 international. Average age 24. 59 applicants, 54% accepted. In 2009, 10 master's awarded. *Degree requirements:* For master's, thesis or alternative. *Entrance requirements:* Additional exam requirements/recommendations for international students: Required—TOEFL (minimum score 530 paper-based; 71 iBT). *Application deadline:* Applications are processed on a rolling basis. Application fee: $30. Electronic applications accepted. *Expenses:* Tuition, state resident: full-time $4486; part-time $249.21 per credit hour. Tuition, nonresident: full-time $8972; part-time $498.42 per credit hour. Required fees: $72.62 per credit hour. *Financial support:* In 2009–10, 27 students received support, including 23 research assistantships with full tuition reimbursements available (averaging $7,280 per year), 4 teaching assistantships with full tuition reimbursements available (averaging $8,400 per year). Financial award applicants required to submit FAFSA. *Unit head:* Dr. Rose McConnell, Chairperson, 309-298-1538. *Application contact:* Evelyn Hoing, Assistant Director of Graduate Studies, 309-298-1806, Fax: 309-298-2345, E-mail: grad-office@wiu.edu.

Western Kentucky University, Graduate Studies, Ogden College of Science and Engineering, Department of Chemistry, Bowling Green, KY 42101. Offers chemistry (MA Ed, MS). *Degree requirements:* For master's, comprehensive exam, thesis. *Entrance requirements:* For master's, GRE General Test, minimum GPA of 2.75. Additional exam requirements/recommendations for international students: Required—TOEFL (minimum score 555 paper-based; 213 computer-based). *Expenses:* Tuition, state resident: full-time $4160; part-time $416 per credit hour. Tuition, nonresident: full-time $9550; part-time $506 per credit hour. Tuition and fees vary according to campus/location and reciprocity agreements. *Faculty research:* Catatonic surfactants, directed orthometalation reactions, thermal stability and degradation mechanisms, co-firing refused derived fuels, laser fluorescence.

Western Michigan University, Graduate College, College of Arts and Sciences, Department of Chemistry, Kalamazoo, MI 49008. Offers MA, PhD. *Degree requirements:* For master's, thesis, departmental qualifying and oral exams; for doctorate, thesis/dissertation.

Western Washington University, Graduate School, College of Sciences and Technology, Department of Chemistry, Bellingham, WA 98225-5996. Offers MS. Part-time programs available. *Degree requirements:* For master's, thesis (for some programs). *Entrance requirements:* For master's, GRE General Test, minimum GPA of 3.0 in last 60 semester hours or last 90 quarter hours. Additional exam requirements/recommendations for international students: Required—TOEFL (minimum score 567 paper-based; 227 computer-based). Electronic applications accepted. *Faculty research:* Bio-, organic, inorganic, physical, analytical chemistry.

West Texas A&M University, College of Agriculture, Nursing, and Natural Sciences, Department of Mathematics, Physical Sciences and Engineering Technology, Program in Chemistry, Canyon, TX 79016-0001. Offers MS. Part-time programs available. *Degree requirements:* For master's, comprehensive exam, thesis optional. *Entrance requirements:* For master's, GRE General Test. Additional exam requirements/recommendations for international students: Required—TOEFL (minimum score 550 paper-based). Electronic applications accepted. *Faculty research:* Biochemistry; inorganic, organic, and physical chemistry; vibrational spectroscopy; magnetic susceptibilities; carbene chemistry.

West Virginia University, Eberly College of Arts and Sciences, Department of Chemistry, Morgantown, WV 26506. Offers analytical chemistry (MS, PhD); inorganic chemistry (MS, PhD); organic chemistry (MS, PhD); physical chemistry (MS, PhD); theoretical chemistry (MS, PhD). Part-time programs available. Postbaccalaureate distance learning degree programs offered (no on-campus study). Terminal master's awarded for partial completion of doctoral program. *Degree requirements:* For master's, thesis; for doctorate, thesis/dissertation. *Entrance requirements:* For master's, GRE General Test, GRE Subject Test (recommended), minimum GPA of 2.5; for doctorate, GRE General Test, GRE Subject Test (recommended), minimum GPA of 2.75. Additional exam requirements/recommendations for international students: Required—TOEFL. Electronic applications accepted. *Faculty research:* Analysis of proteins, drug interactions, solids and effluents by advanced separation methods; new synthetic strategies for complex organic molecules; synthesis and structural characterization of metal complexes for polymerization catalysis, nonlinear science, spectroscopy.

Wichita State University, Graduate School, Fairmount College of Liberal Arts and Sciences, Department of Chemistry, Wichita, KS 67260. Offers MS, PhD. *Expenses:* Tuition, state resident: full-time $4247; part-time $235.95 per credit hour. Tuition, nonresident: full-time $11,171; part-time $620.60 per credit hour. Required fees: $34; $3.60 per credit hour. $17 per term. Tuition and fees vary according to campus/location and program. *Unit head:* Dr. David Eichhorn, Chair, 316-978-3120, Fax: 316-978-3431, E-mail: david.eichhorn@wichita.edu. *Application contact:* Dr. David Eichhorn, Chair, 316-978-3120, Fax: 316-978-3431, E-mail: david.eichhorn@wichita.edu.

Wilfrid Laurier University, Faculty of Graduate Studies, Faculty of Science, Department of Chemistry, Waterloo, ON N2L 3C5, Canada. Offers M Sc. *Entrance requirements:* For master's, honors degree or equivalent in chemistry, biochemistry or a related discipline; minimum B average in last two full-time undergraduate years. Additional exam requirements/recommendations for international students: Required—TOEFL.

Worcester Polytechnic Institute, Graduate Studies and Research, Department of Chemistry and Biochemistry, Worcester, MA 01609-2280. Offers biochemistry (MS, PhD); chemistry (MS, PhD). Evening/weekend programs available. *Faculty:* 5 full-time (0 women), 4 part-time/adjunct (1 woman). *Students:* 11 full-time (7 women), 9 part-time (1 woman). 55 applicants, 33% accepted, 10 enrolled. In 2009, 6 master's, 2 doctorates awarded. *Degree requirements:* For master's, thesis; for doctorate, comprehensive exam, thesis/dissertation. *Entrance requirements:* For master's, GRE General Test, 3 letters of recommendation; for doctorate, GRE General Test, 3 letters of recommendation, statement of purpose. Additional exam requirements/recommendations for international students: Required—TOEFL (minimum score 550 paper-based; 213 computer-based; 79 iBT), IELTS (minimum score 6.5). *Application deadline:* For fall admission, 1/15 priority date for domestic and international students; for spring admission, 10/15 priority date for domestic and international students. Applications are processed on a rolling basis. Application fee: $70. Electronic applications accepted. *Financial support:* Career-related internships or fieldwork, institutionally sponsored loans, scholarships/grants, and unspecified assistantships available. Financial award application deadline: 1/15. *Faculty research:* Photochemistry, organic and materials synthesis, surface chemistry, ion transport. *Unit head:* Dr. Kristin K. Wobbe, Interim Head, 508-831-5371, Fax: 508-831-5933,

Chemistry

Worcester Polytechnic Institute (continued)
E-mail: kwobbe@wpi.edu. *Application contact:* Dr. James Dittami, Graduate Coordinator, 508-831-5371, Fax: 508-831-5933, E-mail: jdittami@wpi.edu.

Wright State University, School of Graduate Studies, College of Science and Mathematics, Department of Chemistry, Dayton, OH 45435. Offers chemistry (MS); environmental sciences (MS). Part-time and evening/weekend programs available. *Degree requirements:* For master's, oral defense of thesis, seminar. *Entrance requirements:* Additional exam requirements/recommendations for international students: Required—TOEFL. *Faculty research:* Polymer synthesis and characterization, laser kinetics, organic and inorganic synthesis, analytical and environmental chemistry.

Yale University, Graduate School of Arts and Sciences, Department of Chemistry, New Haven, CT 06520. Offers biophysical chemistry (PhD); inorganic chemistry (PhD); organic chemistry (PhD); physical and theoretical chemistry (PhD). *Degree requirements:* For doctorate, thesis/dissertation. *Entrance requirements:* For doctorate, GRE General Test, GRE Subject Test. Additional exam requirements/recommendations for international students: Required—TOEFL.

York University, Faculty of Graduate Studies, Faculty of Science and Engineering, Program in Chemistry, Toronto, ON M3J 1P3, Canada. Offers M Sc, PhD. Part-time and evening/weekend programs available. *Degree requirements:* For master's, thesis or alternative; for doctorate, thesis/dissertation. Electronic applications accepted.

Youngstown State University, Graduate School, College of Science, Technology, Engineering and Mathematics, Department of Chemistry, Youngstown, OH 44555-0001. Offers analytical chemistry (MS); biochemistry (MS); chemistry education (MS); inorganic chemistry (MS); organic chemistry (MS); physical chemistry (MS). Part-time programs available. *Degree requirements:* For master's, thesis. *Entrance requirements:* For master's, bachelor's degree in chemistry, minimum GPA of 2.7. Additional exam requirements/recommendations for international students: Required—TOEFL. *Faculty research:* Analysis of antioxidants, chromatography, defects and disorder in crystalline oxides, hydrogen bonding, novel organic and organometallic materials.

Inorganic Chemistry

Auburn University, Graduate School, College of Sciences and Mathematics, Department of Chemistry and Biochemistry, Auburn University, AL 36849. Offers analytical chemistry (MS, PhD); biochemistry (MS, PhD); inorganic chemistry (MS, PhD); organic chemistry (MS, PhD); physical chemistry (MS, PhD). Part-time programs available. *Faculty:* 27 full-time (6 women). *Students:* 39 full-time (20 women), 21 part-time (8 women); includes 6 minority (4 African Americans, 1 Asian American or Pacific Islander, 1 Hispanic American), 41 international. Average age 28. 54 applicants, 11% accepted, 3 enrolled. In 2009, 1 master's, 13 doctorates awarded. *Degree requirements:* For master's, thesis (for some programs); for doctorate, thesis/dissertation, oral and written exams. *Entrance requirements:* For master's and doctorate, GRE General Test. *Application deadline:* For fall admission, 7/7 for domestic students; for spring admission, 11/24 for domestic students. Applications are processed on a rolling basis. Application fee: $50 ($60 for international students). Electronic applications accepted. *Expenses:* Tuition, state resident: full-time $6240. Tuition, nonresident: full-time $18,720. International tuition: $18,938 full-time. Required fees: $492. Tuition and fees vary according to course load, program and reciprocity agreements. *Financial support:* Fellowships, research assistantships, teaching assistantships available. Financial award application deadline: 3/15; financial award applicants required to submit FAFSA. *Unit head:* Dr. J. V. Ortiz, Chair, 334-844-4043, Fax: 334-844-4043. *Application contact:* Dr. George Flowers, Dean of the Graduate School, 334-844-2125.

Boston College, Graduate School of Arts and Sciences, Department of Chemistry, Chestnut Hill, MA 02467-3800. Offers biochemistry (PhD); inorganic chemistry (PhD); organic chemistry (PhD); physical chemistry (PhD); science education (MST). Part-time programs available. *Students:* 110 full-time (49 women); includes 8 minority (6 Asian Americans or Pacific Islanders, 2 Hispanic Americans), 49 international. 216 applicants, 34% accepted, 22 enrolled. In 2009, 3 master's, 20 doctorates awarded. *Degree requirements:* For doctorate, thesis/dissertation, qualifying exam. *Entrance requirements:* For doctorate, GRE General Test, GRE Subject Test. Additional exam requirements/recommendations for international students: Required—TOEFL (minimum score 600 paper-based; 250 computer-based; 100 iBT). *Application deadline:* For fall admission, 1/2 for domestic and international students. Application fee: $70. Electronic applications accepted. *Financial support:* In 2009–10, fellowships with full tuition reimbursements (averaging $25,000 per year), research assistantships with full tuition reimbursements (averaging $25,000 per year), teaching assistantships with full tuition reimbursements (averaging $25,000 per year) were awarded; Federal Work-Study also available. Support available to part-time students. Financial award application deadline: 3/1; financial award applicants required to submit FAFSA. *Unit head:* Dr. Amir Hoveyda, Chairperson, 617-552-1735, E-mail: amir.hoveyda@bc.edu. *Application contact:* Dr. Marc Snapper, Graduate Program Director, 617-552-8096, Fax: 617-552-0833, E-mail: marc.snapper@bc.edu.

Brandeis University, Graduate School of Arts and Sciences, Department of Chemistry, Waltham, MA 02454. Offers inorganic chemistry (MS, PhD); organic chemistry (MS, PhD); physical chemistry (MS, PhD). *Faculty:* 14 full-time (3 women), 4 part-time/adjunct (3 women). *Students:* 42 full-time (17 women); includes 2 minority (1 African American, 1 Asian American or Pacific Islander), 28 international. 127 applicants, 16% accepted, 8 enrolled. In 2009, 11 master's, 6 doctorates awarded. Terminal master's awarded for partial completion of doctoral program. *Degree requirements:* For master's, thesis, 1 year of residency; for doctorate, one foreign language, thesis/dissertation, 3 years of residency, 2 seminars, qualifying exams. *Entrance requirements:* For master's and doctorate, GRE General Test, resume, letters of recommendation. Additional exam requirements/recommendations for international students: Required—TOEFL (minimum score 600 paper-based; 250 computer-based; 100 iBT); Recommended—IELTS (minimum score 7). *Application deadline:* For fall admission, 1/15 priority date for domestic students. Applications are processed on a rolling basis. Application fee: $75. Electronic applications accepted. *Financial support:* In 2009–10, 23 fellowships with full tuition reimbursements (averaging $24,500 per year), 14 research assistantships with full tuition reimbursements (averaging $24,500 per year), teaching assistantships with partial tuition reimbursements (averaging $3,200 per year) were awarded; scholarships/grants and health care benefits also available. Financial award application deadline: 4/15; financial award applicants required to submit FAFSA. *Faculty research:* Oscillating chemical reactions, molecular recognition systems, protein crystallography, synthesis of natural product spectroscopy and magnetic resonance. *Unit head:* Dr. Judith Herzfeld, Chair, Graduate Program in Chemistry, 781-736-2540, Fax: 781-736-2516, E-mail: herzfeld@brandeis.edu. *Application contact:* Charlotte Haygazian, Graduate Department Coordinator, 781-736-2500, Fax: 781-736-2516, E-mail: chemadm@brandeis.edu.

California State University, Los Angeles, Graduate Studies, College of Natural and Social Sciences, Department of Chemistry and Biochemistry, Los Angeles, CA 90032-8530. Offers analytical chemistry (MS); biochemistry (MS); chemistry (MS); inorganic chemistry (MS); organic chemistry (MS); physical chemistry (MS). Part-time and evening/weekend programs available. *Faculty:* 1 full-time (0 women), 9 part-time/adjunct (4 women). *Students:* 14 full-time (4 women), 31 part-time (15 women); includes 21 minority (5 African Americans, 9 Asian Americans or Pacific Islanders, 7 Hispanic Americans), 10 international. Average age 30. 23 applicants, 91% accepted, 13 enrolled. In 2009, 11 degrees awarded. *Degree requirements:* For master's, one foreign language, comprehensive exam or thesis. *Entrance requirements:* Additional exam requirements/recommendations for international students: Required—TOEFL. *Application deadline:* For fall admission, 5/1 for domestic and international students. Applications are processed on a rolling basis. Application fee: $55. *Financial support:* Federal Work-Study available. Support available to part-time students. Financial award application deadline: 3/1. *Faculty research:* Intercalation of heavy metal, carborane chemistry, conductive polymers and fabrics, titanium reagents, computer modeling and synthesis. *Unit head:* Dr. Scott Grover, Chair, 323-343-2300, Fax: 323-343-6490, E-mail: sgrover@calstatela.edu. *Application contact:* Dr. Cheryl L. Ney, Associate Vice President for Academic Affairs and Dean of Graduate Studies, 323-343-3820 Ext. 3827, Fax: 323-343-5653, E-mail: cney@cslanet.calstatela.edu.

Carnegie Mellon University, Mellon College of Science, Department of Chemistry, Pittsburgh, PA 15213-3891. Offers biotechnology and management (MS); chemistry (PhD), including bioinorganic, bioorganic, organic and materials, biophysics and spectroscopy, computational and theoretical, polymer; colloids, polymers and surfaces (MS). Part-time programs available. Terminal master's awarded for partial completion of doctoral program. *Degree requirements:* For doctorate, thesis/dissertation, departmental qualifying and oral exams, teaching experience. *Entrance requirements:* For master's, GRE General Test; for doctorate, GRE General Test, GRE Subject Test. Additional exam requirements/recommendations for international students: Required—TOEFL. Electronic applications accepted. *Faculty research:* Physical and theoretical chemistry, chemical synthesis, biophysical/bioinorganic chemistry.

Cleveland State University, College of Graduate Studies, College of Science, Department of Chemistry, Cleveland, OH 44115. Offers analytical chemistry (MS); clinical chemistry (MS); clinical/bioanalytical chemistry (PhD), including clinical chemistry, molecular medicine; environmental chemistry (MS); inorganic chemistry (MS); organic chemistry (MS); physical chemistry (MS). Part-time and evening/weekend programs available. *Degree requirements:* For master's, thesis (for some programs); for doctorate, thesis/dissertation. *Entrance requirements:* For master's and doctorate, GRE General Test. Additional exam requirements/recommendations for international students: Required—TOEFL (minimum score 525 paper-based; 197 computer-based; 65 iBT). Electronic applications accepted. *Faculty research:* MALDI-TOF based DNA sequencing, development of ionic focusing HPLC, synthetic and structural studies of vanadium.

Columbia University, Graduate School of Arts and Sciences, Division of Natural Sciences, Department of Chemistry, New York, NY 10027. Offers chemical physics (M Phil, PhD); inorganic chemistry (M Phil, MA, PhD); organic chemistry (M Phil, MA, PhD); MD/PhD. *Degree requirements:* For master's, one foreign language, teaching experience, oral/written exams (M Phil); for doctorate, one foreign language, thesis/dissertation. *Entrance requirements:* For master's and doctorate, GRE General Test, GRE Subject Test. Additional exam requirements/recommendations for international students: Required—TOEFL. *Faculty research:* Biophysics.

Cornell University, Graduate School, Graduate Fields of Arts and Sciences, Field of Chemistry and Chemical Biology, Ithaca, NY 14853-0001. Offers analytical chemistry (PhD); bio-organic chemistry (PhD); biophysical chemistry (PhD); chemical biology (PhD); chemical physics (PhD); inorganic chemistry (PhD); materials chemistry (PhD); organic chemistry (PhD); organometallic chemistry (PhD); physical chemistry (PhD); polymer chemistry (PhD); theoretical chemistry (PhD). *Faculty:* 48 full-time (3 women). *Students:* 162 full-time (67 women); includes 15 minority (1 African American, 9 Asian Americans or Pacific Islanders, 5 Hispanic Americans), 53 international. Average age 26. 359 applicants, 19% accepted, 39 enrolled. In 2009, 31 doctorates awarded. *Degree requirements:* For doctorate, comprehensive exam, thesis/dissertation. *Entrance requirements:* For doctorate, GRE General Test, GRE Subject Test (chemistry), 3 letters of recommendation. Additional exam requirements/recommendations for international students: Required—TOEFL (minimum score 600 paper-based; 250 computer-based; 77 iBT). *Application deadline:* For fall admission, 1/10 for domestic students. Application fee: $70. Electronic applications accepted. *Expenses:* Tuition: Full-time $29,500. Required fees: $70. Full-time tuition and fees vary according to degree level, program and student level. *Financial support:* In 2009–10, 1 fellowship with full tuition reimbursement, 7 research assistantships with full tuition reimbursements, 29 teaching assistantships with full tuition reimbursements were awarded; institutionally sponsored loans, scholarships/grants, health care benefits, tuition waivers (full and partial), and unspecified assistantships also available. Financial award applicants required to submit FAFSA. *Faculty research:* Analytical, organic, inorganic, physical, materials, chemical biology. *Unit head:* Director of Graduate Studies, 607-255-4139, Fax: 607-255-4137. *Application contact:* Graduate Field Assistant, 607-255-4139, Fax: 607-255-4137, E-mail: chemgrad@cornell.edu.

Florida State University, The Graduate School, College of Arts and Sciences, Department of Chemistry and Biochemistry, Tallahassee, FL 32306-4390. Offers analytical chemistry (MS, PhD); biochemistry (MS, PhD); inorganic chemistry (MS, PhD); materials chemistry (MS, PhD); organic chemistry (MS, PhD); physical chemistry (MS, PhD). *Faculty:* 40 full-time (6 women), 3 part-time/adjunct (0 women). *Students:* 150 full-time (47 women), 9 part-time (6 women); includes 16 minority (5 African Americans, 1 American Indian/Alaska Native, 5 Asian Americans or Pacific Islanders, 5 Hispanic Americans), 68 international. Average age 25. 286 applicants, 21% accepted, 28 enrolled. In 2009, 7 master's, 15 doctorates awarded. Terminal master's awarded for partial completion of doctoral program. *Degree requirements:* For master's, comprehensive exam (for some programs), thesis (for some programs), cumulative and diagnostic exams; for doctorate, comprehensive exam (for some programs), thesis/dissertation, cumulative and diagnostic exams. *Entrance requirements:* For master's and doctorate, GRE General Test, minimum B average in undergraduate course work. Additional exam requirements/recommendations for international students: Required—TOEFL (minimum score 550 paper-based; 213 computer-based; 80 iBT). *Application deadline:* For fall admission, 12/15 for domestic and international students; for spring admission, 9/15 for domestic and international students. Applications are processed on a rolling basis. Application fee: $30. Electronic applications accepted. *Expenses:* Tuition, state resident: full-time $7413.36. Tuition, nonresident: full-time $22,567. *Financial support:* In 2009–10, 150 students received support, including fellowships with full tuition reimbursements available (averaging $19,000 per year), 52 research assistantships with full tuition reimbursements available (averaging $19,000 per year), 100 teaching assistantships with full tuition reimbursements available (averaging $19,000 per year); career-related internships or fieldwork, Federal Work-Study, institutionally sponsored loans, and traineeships also available. Financial award application deadline: 12/15; financial award applicants required to submit FAFSA. *Faculty research:* Materials synthesis including polymers, natural products; catalysis, NMR; mass spectrometry; optical spectroscopy, scattering techniques, computational chemistry, separation technology; nanostructured materials including metallic, semiconducting and magnetic nanocrystals; nanoscience interfaced with biology; supramolecular materials for solar energy conversion. Total annual research expenditures: $5.5 million. *Unit head:* Dr. Joseph Schlenoff, Chairman, 850-644-5195, Fax: 850-644-8281, E-mail: schlen@chem.fsu.edu. *Application contact:* Dr. Tyler McQuade, Chair, Graduate Admissions Committee, 888-525-9286, Fax: 850-644-0465, E-mail: gradinfo@chem.fsu.edu.

Georgetown University, Graduate School of Arts and Sciences, Department of Chemistry, Washington, DC 20057. Offers analytical chemistry (PhD); biochemistry (PhD); computational chemistry (PhD); inorganic chemistry (PhD); materials chemistry (PhD); organic chemistry (PhD); physical chemistry (PhD); theoretical chemistry (PhD). Terminal master's awarded for partial completion of doctoral program. *Degree requirements:* For doctorate, comprehensive exam, thesis/dissertation. *Entrance requirements:* For doctorate, GRE General Test. Additional exam requirements/recommendations for international students: Required—TOEFL.

The George Washington University, Columbian College of Arts and Sciences, Department of Chemistry, Washington, DC 20052. Offers analytical chemistry (MS, PhD); inorganic chemistry (MS, PhD); materials science (MS, PhD); organic chemistry (MS, PhD); physical chemistry (MS, PhD). Part-time and evening/weekend programs available. *Faculty:* 15 full-time (4 women), 7 part-time/adjunct (3 women). *Students:* 19 full-time (12 women), 12 part-time (7 women); includes 4 minority (2 Asian Americans or Pacific Islanders, 2 Hispanic Americans), 12 international. Average age 28. 45 applicants, 49% accepted, 6 enrolled. In 2009, 2 master's, 4 doctorates awarded. Terminal master's awarded for partial completion of doctoral program. *Degree requirements:* For master's, comprehensive exam, thesis or alternative; for doctorate, thesis/dissertation, general exam. *Entrance requirements:* For master's and doctorate, GRE General Test, interview, minimum GPA of 3.0. Additional exam requirements/recommendations for international students: Required—TOEFL (minimum score 550 paper-based; 213 computer-based; 80 iBT). *Application deadline:* For fall admission, 1/15 priority date for domestic and international students; for spring admission, 9/1 priority date for domestic and international students. Applications are processed on a rolling basis. Application fee: $60. Electronic applications accepted. *Financial support:* In 2009–10, 27 students received support; fellowships with tuition reimbursements available, research assistantships, teaching assistantships with tuition reimbursements available, Federal Work-Study and tuition waivers available. Financial award application deadline: 1/15. *Unit head:* Dr. Michael King, Chair, 202-994-6488. *Application contact:* Information Contact, E-mail: gwchem@www.gwu.edu.

Harvard University, Graduate School of Arts and Sciences, Department of Chemistry and Chemical Biology, Cambridge, MA 02138. Offers biochemical chemistry (PhD); inorganic chemistry (PhD); organic chemistry (PhD); physical chemistry (PhD). *Degree requirements:* For doctorate, thesis/dissertation, cumulative exams. *Entrance requirements:* For doctorate, GRE General Test, GRE Subject Test. Additional exam requirements/recommendations for international students: Required—TOEFL. *Expenses:* Tuition: Full-time $33,696. Required fees: $1126. Full-time tuition and fees vary according to program.

See Close-Up on page 99.

Howard University, Graduate School, Department of Chemistry, Washington, DC 20059-0002. Offers analytical chemistry (MS, PhD); atmospheric (MS, PhD); biochemistry (MS, PhD); environmental (MS, PhD); inorganic chemistry (MS, PhD); organic chemistry (MS, PhD); physical chemistry (MS, PhD). Terminal master's awarded for partial completion of doctoral program. *Degree requirements:* For master's, comprehensive exam, thesis, teaching experience; for doctorate, comprehensive exam, thesis/dissertation, teaching experience. *Entrance requirements:* For master's, GRE General Test, minimum GPA of 2.7; for doctorate, GRE General Test, minimum GPA of 3.0. Additional exam requirements/recommendations for international students: Required—TOEFL. Electronic applications accepted. *Faculty research:* Synthetic organics, materials, natural products, mass spectrometry.

Indiana University Bloomington, University Graduate School, College of Arts and Sciences, Department of Chemistry, Bloomington, IN 47405-7000. Offers analytical chemistry (PhD); biological chemistry (PhD); chemistry (MAT); inorganic chemistry (PhD); physical chemistry (PhD). *Faculty:* 39 full-time (3 women). *Students:* 190 full-time (67 women), 1 (woman) part-time; includes 13 minority (4 African Americans, 1 American Indian/Alaska Native, 5 Asian Americans or Pacific Islanders, 3 Hispanic Americans), 66 international. Average age 26. 207 applicants, 60% accepted, 49 enrolled. In 2009, 10 master's, 20 doctorates awarded. Terminal master's awarded for partial completion of doctoral program. *Degree requirements:* For master's, thesis; for doctorate, thesis/dissertation. *Entrance requirements:* For master's and doctorate, GRE General Test, GRE Subject Test. Additional exam requirements/recommendations for international students: Required—TOEFL. *Application deadline:* For fall admission, 1/15 priority date for domestic students, 12/15 for international students; for spring admission, 9/1 priority date for domestic students, 9/1 for international students. Applications are processed on a rolling basis. Application fee: $55 ($65 for international students). *Financial support:* Fellowships with full tuition reimbursements, research assistantships with full tuition reimbursements, teaching assistantships with full tuition reimbursements, Federal Work-Study and institutionally sponsored loans available. *Faculty research:* Synthesis of complex natural products, organic reaction mechanisms, organic electrochemistry, transitive-metal chemistry, solid-state and surface chemistry. Total annual research expenditures: $7.7 million. *Unit head:* Jim Reilly, Chairperson, 812-855-6239, E-mail: chemchair@indiana.edu. *Application contact:* Martin Jarrold, Director of Graduate Admissions, 812-855-2069, E-mail: mfj@indiana.edu.

Kansas State University, Graduate School, College of Arts and Sciences, Department of Chemistry, Manhattan, KS 66506. Offers analytical chemistry (MS); biological chemistry (MS); chemistry (PhD); inorganic chemistry (MS); materials chemistry (MS); organic chemistry (MS); physical chemistry (MS). *Faculty:* 16 full-time (2 women), 2 part-time/adjunct (0 women). *Students:* 66 full-time (22 women); includes 2 minority (1 African American, 1 Asian American or Pacific Islander), 54 international. Average age 28. 75 applicants, 23% accepted, 7 enrolled. In 2009, 3 master's, 11 doctorates awarded. Terminal master's awarded for partial completion of doctoral program. *Degree requirements:* For master's, thesis; for doctorate, thesis/dissertation. *Entrance requirements:* For master's and doctorate, GRE, minimum GPA of 3.0. Additional exam requirements/recommendations for international students: Required—TOEFL (minimum score 550 paper-based; 213 computer-based). *Application deadline:* For fall admission, 2/1 priority date for domestic and international students; for spring admission, 8/1 priority date for domestic and international students. Applications are processed on a rolling basis. Application fee: $40 ($55 for international students). Electronic applications accepted. *Financial support:* In 2009–10, 41 research assistantships (averaging $15,040 per year), 22 teaching assistantships with full tuition reimbursements (averaging $15,600 per year) were awarded; institutionally sponsored loans and scholarships/grants also available. Support available to part-time students. Financial award application deadline: 3/1; financial award applicants required to submit FAFSA. *Faculty research:* Inorganic chemistry, organic and biological chemistry, analytical chemistry, physical chemistry, materials chemistry and nanotechnology. Total annual research expenditures: $1.9 million. *Unit head:* Eric Maatta, Head, 785-532-6665, Fax: 785-532-6666, E-mail: eam@ksu.edu. *Application contact:* Christer Aakeroy, Director, 785-532-6096, Fax: 785-532-6666, E-mail: aakeroy@ksu.edu.

Kent State University, College of Arts and Sciences, Department of Chemistry, Kent, OH 44242-0001. Offers analytical chemistry (MS, PhD); biochemistry (MS, PhD); chemistry (MA, MS, PhD); inorganic chemistry (MS, PhD); organic chemistry (MS, PhD); physical chemistry (MS, PhD). Terminal master's awarded for partial completion of doctoral program. *Degree requirements:* For master's, comprehensive exam, thesis; for doctorate, comprehensive exam, thesis/dissertation. *Entrance requirements:* For master's and doctorate, placement exam, GRE General Test, GRE Subject Test (recommended), minimum GPA of 2.75. Additional exam requirements/recommendations for international students: Required—TOEFL (minimum score 575 paper-based; 230 computer-based). Electronic applications accepted. *Faculty research:* Biological chemistry, materials chemistry, molecular spectroscopy.

See Close-Up on page 101.

Marquette University, Graduate School, College of Arts and Sciences, Department of Chemistry, Milwaukee, WI 53201-1881. Offers analytical chemistry (MS, PhD); bioanalytical chemistry (MS, PhD); biophysical chemistry (MS, PhD); chemical physics (MS, PhD); inorganic chemistry (MS, PhD); organic chemistry (MS, PhD); physical chemistry (MS, PhD). Part-time programs available. *Faculty:* 23 full-time (10 women), 1 part-time/adjunct (0 women). *Students:* 34 full-time (9 women), 10 part-time (4 women); includes 4 minority (1 African American, 2 Asian Americans or Pacific Islanders, 1 Hispanic American), 33 international. Average age 29. 23 applicants, 83% accepted, 8 enrolled. In 2009, 4 master's, 5 doctorates awarded. Terminal master's awarded for partial completion of doctoral program. *Degree requirements:* For master's, comprehensive exam; for doctorate, thesis/dissertation, cumulative exams. *Entrance requirements:* For master's and doctorate, GRE Subject Test. Additional exam requirements/recommendations for international students: Required—TOEFL. Application fee: $40. *Financial support:* In 2009–10, 3 research assistantships, 27 teaching assistantships were awarded; fellowships, Federal Work-Study, institutionally sponsored loans, scholarships/grants, and tuition waivers (full and partial) also available. Support available to part-time students. Financial award application deadline: 2/15. *Faculty research:* Inorganic complexes, laser Raman spectroscopy, organic synthesis, chemical dynamics, biophysiology. *Unit head:* Dr. Jeanne Hossenlopp, Chair, 414-288-3537, Fax: 414-288-7066. *Application contact:* Dr. Mark Steinmetz, Director of Graduate Studies, 414-288-7374, Fax: 414-288-7066.

Massachusetts Institute of Technology, School of Science, Department of Chemistry, Cambridge, MA 02139-4307. Offers biological chemistry (PhD, Sc D); inorganic chemistry (PhD, Sc D); organic chemistry (PhD, Sc D); physical chemistry (PhD, Sc D). *Faculty:* 29 full-time (7 women). *Students:* 219 full-time (79 women); includes 39 minority (4 African Americans, 27 Asian Americans or Pacific Islanders, 8 Hispanic Americans), 62 international. Average age 26. 548 applicants, 20% accepted, 19 enrolled. In 2009, 43 doctorates awarded. *Degree requirements:* For doctorate, comprehensive exam, thesis/dissertation, 2 terms as a teaching assistant. *Entrance requirements:* For doctorate, GRE General Test. Additional exam requirements/recommendations for international students: Required—IELTS (minimum score 7); Recommended—TOEFL (minimum score 600 paper-based; 250 computer-based). *Application deadline:* For fall admission, 12/15 for domestic and international students. Application fee: $75. Electronic applications accepted. *Financial support:* In 2009–10, 219 students received support, including 57 fellowships with tuition reimbursements available (averaging $34,547 per year), 132 research assistantships with tuition reimbursements available (averaging $29,403 per year), 27 teaching assistantships with tuition reimbursements available (averaging $30,452 per year); Federal Work-Study, institutionally sponsored loans, scholarships/grants, health care benefits, and unspecified assistantships also available. *Faculty research:* Synthetic organic and inorganic chemistry, biomolecular reactions and structure, multidimensional spectroscopy and chemical dynamics, inorganic, organometallic, organic chemical catalysis, materials chemistry including nanoscience and polymers. Total annual research expenditures: $29.1 million. *Unit head:* Prof. Timothy M. Swager, Head, 617-253-1803, Fax: 617-258-7500. *Application contact:* Graduate Administrator, 617-253-1845, Fax: 617-258-0241, E-mail: chemgradeducation@mit.edu.

McMaster University, School of Graduate Studies, Faculty of Science, Department of Chemistry, Hamilton, ON L8S 4M2, Canada. Offers analytical chemistry (M Sc, PhD); chemical physics (M Sc, PhD); chemistry (M Sc, PhD); inorganic chemistry (M Sc, PhD); organic chemistry (M Sc, PhD); physical chemistry (M Sc, PhD); polymer chemistry (M Sc, PhD). Part-time programs available. Terminal master's awarded for partial completion of doctoral program. *Degree requirements:* For master's, thesis; for doctorate, comprehensive exam, thesis/dissertation. *Entrance requirements:* For master's, minimum B+ average. Additional exam requirements/recommendations for international students: Required—TOEFL (minimum score 550 paper-based; 213 computer-based).

Northeastern University, College of Science, Department of Chemistry and Chemical Biology, Boston, MA 02115-5096. Offers analytical chemistry (PhD); chemistry (MS, PhD); inorganic chemistry (PhD); organic chemistry (PhD); physical chemistry (PhD). Part-time and evening/weekend programs available. *Faculty:* 24 full-time (5 women), 7 part-time/adjunct (0 women). *Students:* 86 full-time (48 women), 31 part-time (14 women); includes 9 minority (1 African American, 1 American Indian/Alaska Native, 7 Asian Americans or Pacific Islanders), 36 international. 190 applicants, 22% accepted, 15 enrolled. In 2009, 17 master's, 9 doctorates awarded. Terminal master's awarded for partial completion of doctoral program. *Degree requirements:* For master's, thesis (for some programs); for doctorate, thesis/dissertation, qualifying exam in specialty area. *Entrance requirements:* Additional exam requirements/recommendations for international students: Required—TOEFL. *Application deadline:* For fall admission, 2/1 priority date for domestic and international students. Applications are processed on a rolling basis. Application fee: $50. Electronic applications accepted. *Financial support:* In 2009–10, 41 research assistantships with tuition reimbursements (averaging $18,285 per year), 38 teaching assistantships with tuition reimbursements (averaging $18,285 per year) were awarded; fellowships with tuition reimbursements, career-related internships or fieldwork, Federal Work-Study, scholarships/grants, tuition waivers (partial), and unspecified assistantships also available. Financial award application deadline: 3/1; financial award applicants required to submit FAFSA. *Faculty research:* Bioanalysis, biorganic and medicinal chemistry, biophysical chemistry, nanomaterials, proteonics. *Unit head:* Dr. Robert Hanson, Graduate Coordinator, 617-373-3313, Fax: 617-373-8795, E-mail: chemistry-grad-info@neu.edu. *Application contact:* Jo-Anne Dickinson, Admissions Contact, 617-373-5990, Fax: 617-373-7281, E-mail: gsas@neu.edu.

Oregon State University, Graduate School, College of Science, Department of Chemistry, Corvallis, OR 97331. Offers analytical chemistry (MS, PhD); chemistry (MA, MAIS); inorganic chemistry (MS, PhD); nuclear and radiation chemistry (MS, PhD); organic chemistry (MS, PhD); physical chemistry (MS, PhD). Part-time programs available. *Faculty:* 24 full-time (3 women), 1 part-time/adjunct (0 women). *Students:* 78 full-time (27 women), 1 part-time (0 women); includes 3 minority (1 African American, 1 Asian American or Pacific Islander, 1 Hispanic American), 50 international. Average age 27. In 2009, 6 master's, 7 doctorates awarded. Terminal master's awarded for partial completion of doctoral program. *Degree requirements:* For master's, one foreign language, thesis; for doctorate, one foreign language, thesis/dissertation. *Entrance requirements:* For master's and doctorate, minimum GPA of 3.0 in last 90 hours of course work. Additional exam requirements/recommendations for international students: Required—TOEFL. *Application deadline:* For fall admission, 3/1 priority date for domestic students. Applications are processed on a rolling basis. Application fee: $50. *Expenses:* Tuition, state resident: full-time $9774; part-time $362 per credit. Tuition, nonresident: full-time $15,849; part-time $587 per credit. Required fees: $1639. Full-time tuition and fees vary according to course load and program. *Financial support:* Fellowships, research assistantships, teaching assistantships, institutionally sponsored loans available. Support available to part-time students. Financial award application deadline: 2/1. *Faculty research:* Solid state chemistry, enzyme reaction mechanisms, structure and dynamics of gas molecules, chemiluminescence, nonlinear optical spectroscopy. *Unit head:* Dr. Kevin P. Gable, Chair, 541-737-6744, Fax: 541-737-2062, E-mail: gablek@chem.orst.edu. *Application contact:* Dr. Kevin P. Gable, Chair, 541-737-6744, Fax: 541-737-2062, E-mail: gablek@chem.orst.edu.

Purdue University, Graduate School, College of Science, Department of Chemistry, West Lafayette, IN 47907. Offers analytical chemistry (MS, PhD); biochemistry (MS, PhD); chemical education (MS, PhD); inorganic chemistry (MS, PhD); organic chemistry (MS, PhD); physical

Inorganic Chemistry

Purdue University (continued)
chemistry (MS, PhD). Terminal master's awarded for partial completion of doctoral program. *Degree requirements:* For master's, thesis; for doctorate, thesis/dissertation. *Entrance requirements:* Additional exam requirements/recommendations for international students: Required—TOEFL. Electronic applications accepted.

Rensselaer Polytechnic Institute, Graduate School, School of Science, Department of Chemistry and Chemical Biology, Troy, NY 12180-3590. Offers analytical chemistry (MS, PhD); biochemistry (MS, PhD); inorganic chemistry (MS, PhD); organic chemistry (MS, PhD); physical chemistry (MS, PhD); polymer chemistry (MS, PhD). Part-time and evening/weekend programs available. *Faculty:* 16 full-time (2 women). *Students:* 68 full-time (31 women); includes 1 African American, 6 Asian Americans or Pacific Islanders, 1 Hispanic American, 31 international. Average age 24. 85 applicants, 19% accepted, 5 enrolled. In 2009, 5 master's, 6 doctorates awarded. Terminal master's awarded for partial completion of doctoral program. *Degree requirements:* For master's, thesis (for some programs); for doctorate, comprehensive exam, thesis/dissertation. *Entrance requirements:* For master's, GRE General Test, GRE Subject Test (strongly recommended); for doctorate, GRE General Test, GRE Subject Test (chemistry or biochemistry strongly recommended). Additional exam requirements/recommendations for international students: Required—TOEFL (minimum score 600 paper-based). *Application deadline:* For fall admission, 2/1 priority date for domestic students; for spring admission, 11/15 for domestic students. Applications are processed on a rolling basis. Application fee: $75. Electronic applications accepted. *Expenses:* Tuition: Full-time $38,100. *Financial support:* In 2009–10, 1 fellowship with full tuition reimbursement (averaging $22,500 per year), 18 research assistantships with full tuition reimbursements (averaging $22,500 per year), 24 teaching assistantships with full tuition reimbursements (averaging $22,500 per year) were awarded; institutionally sponsored loans and tuition waivers (full and partial) also available. Financial award application deadline: 2/1. *Faculty research:* Synthetic polymer and biopolymer chemistry, physical chemistry of polymeric systems, bioanalytical chemistry, synthetic and computational drug design, protein folding and protein design. Total annual research expenditures: $1.1 million. *Unit head:* Dr. Curtis M. Breneman, Chair, 518-276-3264, Fax: 518-276-4887, E-mail: brenec@rpi.edu. *Application contact:* Sharon E. Gardner, Graduate Program Administrator, 518-276-2140, Fax: 518-276-4887, E-mail: derris@rpi.edu.

Rice University, Graduate Programs, Wiess School of Natural Sciences, Department of Chemistry, Houston, TX 77251-1892. Offers chemistry (MA); inorganic chemistry (PhD); organic chemistry (PhD); physical chemistry (PhD). Terminal master's awarded for partial completion of doctoral program. *Degree requirements:* For master's, thesis; for doctorate, thesis/dissertation. *Entrance requirements:* For master's and doctorate, GRE General Test, minimum GPA of 3.0. Additional exam requirements/recommendations for international students: Required—TOEFL (minimum score 600 paper-based; 250 computer-based; 90 iBT). Electronic applications accepted. *Faculty research:* Nanoscience, biomaterials, nanobioinformatics, fullerene pharmaceuticals.

Rutgers, The State University of New Jersey, Newark, Graduate School, Program in Chemistry, Newark, NJ 07102. Offers analytical chemistry (MS, PhD); biochemistry (MS, PhD); inorganic chemistry (MS, PhD); organic chemistry (MS, PhD); physical chemistry (MS, PhD). Part-time and evening/weekend programs available. Terminal master's awarded for partial completion of doctoral program. *Degree requirements:* For master's, thesis optional, cumulative exams; for doctorate, thesis/dissertation, exams, research proposal. *Entrance requirements:* For master's and doctorate, GRE General Test, minimum undergraduate B average. Additional exam requirements/recommendations for international students: Required—TOEFL. Electronic applications accepted. *Faculty research:* Medicinal chemistry, natural products, isotope effects, biophysics and biorganic approaches to enzyme mechanisms, organic and organometallic synthesis.

Rutgers, The State University of New Jersey, New Brunswick, Graduate School-New Brunswick, Department of Chemistry and Chemical Biology, Piscataway, NJ 08854-8097. Offers biological chemistry (MS, PhD); inorganic chemistry (MS, PhD); organic chemistry (MS, PhD); physical chemistry (MS, PhD). Part-time and evening/weekend programs available. Terminal master's awarded for partial completion of doctoral program. *Degree requirements:* For master's, thesis or alternative, exam; for doctorate, thesis/dissertation, 1 year residency. *Entrance requirements:* For master's and doctorate, GRE General Test, GRE Subject Test. Additional exam requirements/recommendations for international students: Required—TOEFL. Electronic applications accepted. *Faculty research:* Biophysical organic/bioorganic, inorganic/bioinorganic, theoretical, and solid-state/surface chemistry.

Seton Hall University, College of Arts and Sciences, Department of Chemistry and Biochemistry, South Orange, NJ 07079-2697. Offers analytical chemistry (MS, PhD); biochemistry (MS, PhD); chemistry (MS); inorganic chemistry (MS, PhD); organic chemistry (MS, PhD); physical chemistry (MS, PhD). Part-time and evening/weekend programs available. *Faculty:* 10 full-time (1 woman). *Students:* 24 full-time (14 women), 47 part-time (15 women); includes 22 minority (10 African Americans, 8 Asian Americans or Pacific Islanders, 4 Hispanic Americans), 11 international. Average age 33. 31 applicants, 68% accepted, 10 enrolled. In 2009, 7 master's, 4 doctorates awarded. Terminal master's awarded for partial completion of doctoral program. *Degree requirements:* For master's, thesis optional; for doctorate, comprehensive exam, thesis/dissertation. *Entrance requirements:* Additional exam requirements/recommendations for international students: Required—TOEFL. *Application deadline:* For fall admission, 7/1 priority date for domestic and international students; for spring admission, 11/1 priority date for domestic and international students. Applications are processed on a rolling basis. Application fee: $50. Electronic applications accepted. *Financial support:* Research assistantships, teaching assistantships with full tuition reimbursements, Federal Work-Study and unspecified assistantships available. Financial award applicants required to submit FAFSA. *Faculty research:* DNA metal reactions; chromatography; bioinorganic, biophysical, organometallic, polymer chemistry; heterogeneous catalyst; synthetic organic and carbohydrate chemistry. *Unit head:* Dr. Nicholas Snow, Chair, 973-761-9414, Fax: 973-761-9772, E-mail: snownich@shu.edu. *Application contact:* Dr. Stephen Kelty, Director of Graduate Studies, 973-761-9129, Fax: 973-761-9772, E-mail: keltyste@shu.edu.

Southern University and Agricultural and Mechanical College, Graduate School, College of Sciences, Department of Chemistry, Baton Rouge, LA 70813. Offers analytical chemistry (MS); biochemistry (MS); environmental sciences (MS); inorganic chemistry (MS); organic chemistry (MS); physical chemistry (MS). *Degree requirements:* For master's, thesis. *Entrance requirements:* For master's, GMAT or GRE General Test. Additional exam requirements/recommendations for international students: Required—TOEFL (minimum score 525 paper-based; 193 computer-based). *Faculty research:* Synthesis of macrocyclic ligands, latex accelerators, anticancer drugs, biosensors, absorption isotheums, isolation of specific enzymes from plants.

State University of New York at Binghamton, Graduate School, School of Arts and Sciences, Department of Chemistry, Binghamton, NY 13902-6000. Offers analytical chemistry (PhD); chemistry (MA, MS); inorganic chemistry (PhD); organic chemistry (PhD); physical chemistry (PhD). Part-time programs available. *Faculty:* 14 full-time (3 women), 2 part-time/adjunct (0 women). *Students:* 35 full-time (13 women), 22 part-time (10 women); includes 8 minority (3 African Americans, 4 Asian Americans or Pacific Islanders, 1 Hispanic American), 32 international. Average age 29. 40 applicants, 30% accepted, 6 enrolled. In 2009, 6 master's, 5 doctorates awarded. Terminal master's awarded for partial completion of doctoral program. *Degree requirements:* For master's, thesis or alternative, oral exam, seminar presentation; for doctorate, thesis/dissertation, cumulative exams. *Entrance requirements:* For master's and doctorate, GRE General Test, GRE Subject Test. Additional exam requirements/recommendations for international students: Required—TOEFL (minimum score 550 paper-based; 213 computer-based; 80 iBT). *Application deadline:* For fall admission, 1/15 priority date for domestic and international students; for spring admission, 10/15 priority date for domestic and international students. Applications are processed on a rolling basis. Application fee: $60. Electronic applications accepted. *Financial support:* In 2009–10, 55 students received support, including 4 fellowships with full tuition reimbursements available (averaging $18,000 per year), 8 research assistantships with full tuition reimbursements available (averaging $18,000 per year), 34 teaching assistantships with full tuition reimbursements available (averaging $18,000 per year); career-related internships or fieldwork, Federal Work-Study, institutionally sponsored loans, scholarships/grants, health care benefits, tuition waivers (full), and unspecified assistantships also available. Financial award application deadline: 2/15; financial award applicants required to submit FAFSA. *Unit head:* Dr. Wayne E. Jones, Chairperson, 607-777-2421, E-mail: wjones@binghamton.edu. *Application contact:* Victoria Williams, Recruiting and Admissions Coordinator, 607-777-2151, Fax: 607-777-2501, E-mail: vwilliam@binghamton.edu.

Tufts University, Graduate School of Arts and Sciences, Department of Chemistry, Medford, MA 02155. Offers analytical chemistry (MS, PhD); bioorganic chemistry (MS, PhD); environmental chemistry (MS, PhD); inorganic chemistry (MS, PhD); organic chemistry (MS, PhD); physical chemistry (MS, PhD). *Students:* 61 full-time (29 women); includes 7 minority (1 African American, 1 American Indian/Alaska Native, 4 Asian Americans or Pacific Islanders, 1 Hispanic American), 18 international. 90 applicants, 50% accepted, 14 enrolled. In 2009, 2 master's, 7 doctorates awarded. Terminal master's awarded for partial completion of doctoral program. *Degree requirements:* For master's, thesis optional; for doctorate, thesis/dissertation. *Entrance requirements:* For master's and doctorate, GRE General Test, GRE Subject Test. Additional exam requirements/recommendations for international students: Required—TOEFL (minimum score 600 paper-based; 250 computer-based; 80 iBT). *Application deadline:* For fall admission, 1/15 for domestic students, 12/30 for international students; for spring admission, 10/15 for domestic students, 9/15 for international students. Applications are processed on a rolling basis. Application fee: $75. Electronic applications accepted. *Expenses:* Tuition: Full-time $38,096; part-time $3962 per credit. Required fees: $686; $40 per year. Tuition and fees vary according to course level, course load, degree level, program and student level. *Financial support:* Fellowships, research assistantships with full tuition reimbursements, teaching assistantships with full tuition reimbursements, Federal Work-Study, scholarships/grants, tuition waivers (partial), and unspecified assistantships available. Financial award application deadline: 1/15; financial award applicants required to submit FAFSA. *Unit head:* Arthur Utz, Chair, 617-627-3441. *Application contact:* Samuel Kounaves, Information Contact, 617-627-3441, Fax: 617-627-3443.

University of Calgary, Faculty of Graduate Studies, Faculty of Science, Department of Chemistry, Calgary, AB T2N 1N4, Canada. Offers analytical chemistry (M Sc, PhD); applied chemistry (M Sc, PhD); inorganic chemistry (M Sc, PhD); organic chemistry (M Sc, PhD); physical chemistry (M Sc, PhD); polymer chemistry (M Sc, PhD); theoretical chemistry (M Sc, PhD). *Degree requirements:* For master's, thesis; for doctorate, thesis/dissertation, candidacy exam. *Entrance requirements:* For master's, minimum GPA of 3.0; for doctorate, honors B Sc degree with minimum GPA of 3.7 or M Sc with minimum GPA of 3.3. Additional exam requirements/recommendations for international students: Required—TOEFL (minimum score 580 paper-based; 237 computer-based). Electronic applications accepted. *Faculty research:* Chemical analysis, chemical dynamics, synthesis theory.

University of Cincinnati, Graduate School, McMicken College of Arts and Sciences, Department of Chemistry, Cincinnati, OH 45221. Offers analytical chemistry (MS, PhD); biochemistry (MS, PhD); inorganic chemistry (MS, PhD); organic chemistry (MS, PhD); physical chemistry (MS, PhD); polymer chemistry (MS, PhD); sensors (PhD). Part-time and evening/weekend programs available. Terminal master's awarded for partial completion of doctoral program. *Degree requirements:* For master's, thesis optional; for doctorate, comprehensive exam, thesis/dissertation. *Entrance requirements:* For master's and doctorate, GRE General Test. Additional exam requirements/recommendations for international students: Required—TOEFL (minimum score 580 paper-based; 237 computer-based). Electronic applications accepted. *Faculty research:* Biomedical chemistry, laser chemistry, surface science, chemical sensors, synthesis.

University of Georgia, Graduate School, College of Arts and Sciences, Department of Chemistry, Athens, GA 30602. Offers analytical chemistry (MS, PhD); inorganic chemistry (MS, PhD); organic chemistry (MS, PhD); physical chemistry (MS, PhD). *Faculty:* 25 full-time (1 woman). *Students:* 147 full-time (53 women), 2 part-time (1 woman); includes 14 minority (6 African Americans, 7 Asian Americans or Pacific Islanders, 1 Hispanic American), 61 international. 136 applicants, 55% accepted, 27 enrolled. In 2009, 3 master's, 23 doctorates awarded. Terminal master's awarded for partial completion of doctoral program. *Degree requirements:* For master's, thesis; for doctorate, one foreign language, thesis/dissertation. *Entrance requirements:* For master's and doctorate, GRE General Test. Additional exam requirements/recommendations for international students: Required—TOEFL (minimum score 213 computer-based). *Application deadline:* For fall admission, 7/1 priority date for domestic students; for spring admission, 11/15 for domestic students. Application fee: $50. Electronic applications accepted. *Expenses:* Tuition, state resident: full-time $6000; part-time $250 per credit hour. Tuition, nonresident: full-time $20,904; part-time $871 per credit hour. Required fees: $730 per semester. *Financial support:* Fellowships, research assistantships, teaching assistantships, unspecified assistantships available. *Unit head:* Dr. John L. Stickney, Head, 706-542-2726, Fax: 706-542-9454, E-mail: stickney@chem.uga.edu. *Application contact:* Dr. George F. Majetich, Graduate Coordinator, 706-542-1966, Fax: 706-542-9454, E-mail: majetich@chem.uga.edu.

University of Louisville, Graduate School, College of Arts and Sciences, Department of Chemistry, Louisville, KY 40292-0001. Offers analytical chemistry (MS, PhD); biochemistry (MS, PhD); chemical physics (PhD); inorganic chemistry (MS, PhD); organic chemistry (MS, PhD); physical chemistry (MS, PhD). *Students:* 57 full-time (27 women), 4 part-time (1 woman); includes 2 minority (1 African American, 1 Asian American or Pacific Islander), 43 international. Average age 29. 62 applicants, 31% accepted, 13 enrolled. In 2009, 6 master's, 7 doctorates awarded. *Median time to degree:* Of those who began their doctoral program in fall 2001, 0% received their degree in 8 years or less. *Degree requirements:* For master's, thesis; for doctorate, comprehensive exam, thesis/dissertation. *Entrance requirements:* For master's and doctorate, GRE General Test. Additional exam requirements/recommendations for international students: Required—TOEFL. *Application deadline:* Applications are processed on a rolling basis. Application fee: $50. *Financial support:* Fellowships, research assistantships, teaching assistantships available. *Unit head:* Dr. George R. Pack, Chair, 502-852-6798, Fax: 502-852-8149, E-mail: george.pack@louisville.edu. *Application contact:* Libby Leggett, Director, Graduate Admissions, 502-852-3101, Fax: 502-852-6536, E-mail: gradadm@louisville.edu.

University of Maryland, College Park, Academic Affairs, College of Chemical and Life Sciences, Department of Chemistry and Biochemistry, Chemistry Program, College Park, MD 20742. Offers analytical chemistry (MS, PhD); inorganic chemistry (MS, PhD); organic chemistry (MS, PhD); physical chemistry (MS, PhD). Part-time and evening/weekend programs available. *Students:* 129 full-time (69 women), 5 part-time (3 women); includes 18 minority (13 African Americans, 3 Asian Americans or Pacific Islanders, 2 Hispanic Americans), 70 international. 329 applicants, 22% accepted, 36 enrolled. In 2009, 6 master's, 18 doctorates awarded. Terminal master's awarded for partial completion of doctoral program. *Degree requirements:* For master's, thesis optional; for doctorate, thesis/dissertation, 2 seminar presentations, oral exam. *Entrance requirements:* For master's and doctorate, GRE General Test, GRE Subject Test (recommended), minimum GPA of 3.0, 3 letters of recommendation. Additional exam requirements/recommendations for international students: Required—TOEFL. *Application deadline:* For fall admission, 2/1 for domestic and international students. Applications are processed on a rolling basis. Application fee: $60. Electronic applications accepted. *Expenses:* Tuition, area resident: Part-time $471 per credit hour. Tuition, state resident: part-time $471 per credit hour. Tuition, nonresident: part-time $1016 per credit hour. Required fees: $337.04 per term. *Financial support:* In 2009–10, 7 fellowships with full tuition reimbursements (averaging $27,067 per year), 51 research assistantships (averaging $19,639 per year), 66 teaching assistantships with partial tuition reimbursements (averaging $19,260 per year) were awarded. Financial award applicants required to submit FAFSA. *Faculty research:* Environmental chemistry, nuclear chemistry, lunar and environmental analysis, x-ray crystallography. *Unit head:* Dr. Michael Doyle, Chairperson, 301-405-1795, Fax: 301-314-2779, E-mail: mdoyle3@umd.edu. *Application contact:* Dean of Graduate School, 301-405-0358, Fax: 301-314-9305.

University of Massachusetts Lowell, College of Arts and Sciences, Department of Chemistry, Lowell, MA 01854-2881. Offers analytical chemistry (PhD); biochemistry (PhD); chemistry (MS, PhD); environmental studies (PhD); green chemistry (PhD); inorganic chemistry (PhD); organic chemistry (PhD); polymer science (MS). Terminal master's awarded for partial completion of doctoral program. *Degree requirements:* For master's, thesis; for doctorate, 2 foreign languages, thesis/dissertation. *Entrance requirements:* For master's and doctorate, GRE General Test. Electronic applications accepted.

University of Memphis, Graduate School, College of Arts and Sciences, Department of Chemistry, Memphis, TN 38152. Offers analytical chemistry (PhD); analytical chemsitry (MS); computational chemistry (MS, PhD); inorganic chemistry (MS, PhD); organic chemistry (MS, PhD); physical chemistry (MS, PhD). Part-time programs available. *Faculty:* 6 full-time (1 woman). *Students:* 39 full-time (17 women), 7 part-time (4 women); includes 8 minority (6 African Americans, 1 Asian American or Pacific Islander, 1 Hispanic American), 6 international. Average age 28. 23 applicants, 70% accepted, 14 enrolled. In 2009, 3 master's, 5 doctorates awarded. Terminal master's awarded for partial completion of doctoral program. *Degree requirements:* For master's, comprehensive exam, thesis or alternative; for doctorate, comprehensive exam, thesis/dissertation. *Entrance requirements:* For master's and doctorate, GRE General Test, admission to Graduate School plus 32 undergraduate hours in chemistry. Additional exam requirements/recommendations for international students: Required—TOEFL. *Application deadline:* For fall admission, 7/1 for domestic students, 5/1 for international students; for winter admission, 9/15 for international students; for spring admission, 12/1 for domestic students. Applications are processed on a rolling basis. Application fee: $35 ($60 for international students). Electronic applications accepted. *Expenses:* Tuition, state resident: full-time $6246; part-time $347 per credit hour. Tuition, nonresident: full-time $15,894; part-time $883 per credit hour. Required fees: $1160. Full-time tuition and fees vary according to course load, degree level and program. *Financial support:* In 2009–10, 12 students received support; research assistantships with full tuition reimbursements available, teaching assistantships with full tuition reimbursements available, Federal Work-Study, scholarships/grants, and unspecified assistantships available. Financial award application deadline: 2/15; financial award applicants required to submit FAFSA. *Faculty research:* Computational chemistry, materials chemistry, organic/polymer synthesis, drug design/delivery, water chemistry. *Unit head:* Dr. Abby L. Parrill, Professor and Chair, 901-678-2638, Fax: 901-678-3447, E-mail: aparrill@memphis.edu. *Application contact:* Dr. Gary Emmert, Associate Professor and Graduate Coordinator, 901-678-2636, Fax: 901-678-3447, E-mail: gemmert@memphis.edu.

University of Miami, Graduate School, College of Arts and Sciences, Department of Chemistry, Coral Gables, FL 33124. Offers chemistry (MS); inorganic chemistry (PhD); organic chemistry (PhD); physical chemistry (PhD). Terminal master's awarded for partial completion of doctoral program. *Degree requirements:* For master's, comprehensive exam; for doctorate, comprehensive exam, thesis/dissertation. *Entrance requirements:* For master's and doctorate, GRE General Test. Additional exam requirements/recommendations for international students: Required—TOEFL (minimum score 550 paper-based; 213 computer-based). Electronic applications accepted. *Faculty research:* Supramolecular chemistry, electrochemistry, surface chemistry, catalysis, organometalic.

University of Michigan, Horace H. Rackham School of Graduate Studies, College of Literature, Science, and the Arts, Department of Chemistry, Ann Arbor, MI 48109-1055. Offers analytical chemistry (PhD); chemical biology (PhD); inorganic chemistry (PhD); material chemistry (PhD); organic chemistry (PhD); physical chemistry (PhD). *Faculty:* 42 full-time (10 women). *Students:* 192 full-time (105 women); includes 74 minority (4 African Americans, 64 Asian Americans or Pacific Islanders, 6 Hispanic Americans), 54 international. Average age 26. 558 applicants, 36% accepted, 56 enrolled. In 2009, 28 doctorates awarded. *Degree requirements:* For doctorate, thesis/dissertation, oral defense of dissertation, organic cumulative proficiency exams. *Entrance requirements:* For doctorate, GRE General Test, GRE Subject Test (recommended), 3 letters of recommendation. Additional exam requirements/recommendations for international students: Required—TOEFL (minimum score 560 paper-based; 220 computer-based; 84 iBT). *Application deadline:* For fall admission, 1/15 for domestic students, 12/15 for international students. Applications are processed on a rolling basis. Application fee: $0 ($75 for international students). Electronic applications accepted. *Expenses:* Tuition, state resident: full-time $17,286; part-time $1099 per credit hour. Tuition, nonresident: full-time $34,944; part-time $2080 per credit hour. Required fees: $95 per semester. Tuition and fees vary according to course load, degree level and program. *Financial support:* In 2009–10, 192 students received support, including 20 fellowships with full tuition reimbursements available (averaging $25,000 per year), 75 research assistantships with full tuition reimbursements available (averaging $25,000 per year), 97 teaching assistantships with full tuition reimbursements available (averaging $25,000 per year); career-related internships or fieldwork, scholarships/grants, traineeships, health care benefits, and unspecified assistantships also available. Financial award applicants required to submit FAFSA. *Faculty research:* Biological catalysis, protein engineering, chemical sensors, de novo metalloprotein design, supramolecular architecture. Total annual research expenditures: $15.3 million. *Unit head:* Dr. Carol A. Fierke, Chair, 734-763-9681, Fax: 734-647-4847. *Application contact:* Anna Stryker, Graduate Program Coordinator, 734-764-7278, Fax: 734-647-4865, E-mail: chemadmissions@umich.edu.

University of Missouri, Graduate School, College of Arts and Sciences, Department of Chemistry, Columbia, MO 65211. Offers analytical chemistry (MS, PhD); inorganic chemistry (MS, PhD); organic chemistry (MS, PhD); physical chemistry (MS, PhD). *Faculty:* 30 full-time (6 women), 2 part-time/adjunct (0 women). *Students:* 60 full-time (22 women), 43 part-time (16 women); includes 7 minority (3 African Americans, 1 American Indian/Alaska Native, 3 Asian Americans or Pacific Islanders), 53 international. Average age 27. 93 applicants, 32% accepted, 27 enrolled. In 2009, 4 doctorates awarded. *Degree requirements:* For master's, thesis; for doctorate, one foreign language, comprehensive exam, thesis/dissertation. *Entrance requirements:* For master's, GRE General Test, minimum GPA of 3.0; for doctorate, GRE General Test; V=450, Q=600, A=3.0-4.0, minimum GPA of 3.0. Additional exam requirements/recommendations for international students: Required—TOEFL (minimum score 600 paper-based; 250 computer-based; 100 iBT). *Application deadline:* For fall admission, 4/1 priority date for domestic students; for winter admission, 10/15 for domestic students. Applications are processed on a rolling basis. Application fee: $45 ($60 for international students). *Financial support:* In 2009–10, 9 fellowships with full tuition reimbursements, 15 research assistantships with full tuition reimbursements, 78 teaching assistantships with full tuition reimbursements were awarded; institutionally sponsored loans, traineeships, health care benefits, and unspecified assistantships also available. *Unit head:* Dr. Jerry Atwood, Department Chair, 573-882-8374, E-mail: atwoodj@missouri.edu. *Application contact:* Jerry Brightwell, Administrative Assistant, 573-884-6832, E-mail: brightwellj@missouri.edu.

University of Missouri–Kansas City, College of Arts and Sciences, Department of Chemistry, Kansas City, MO 64110-2499. Offers analytical chemistry (MS, PhD); inorganic chemistry (MS, PhD); organic chemistry (MS, PhD); physical chemistry (MS, PhD); polymer chemistry (MS, PhD). PhD (interdisciplinary) offered through the School of Graduate Studies. Part-time and evening/weekend programs available. *Faculty:* 16 full-time (3 women), 1 part-time/adjunct (0 women). *Students:* 7 part-time (4 women), 2 international. Average age 32. 30 applicants, 67% accepted. In 2009, 1 master's awarded. *Degree requirements:* For master's, thesis (for some programs); for doctorate, thesis/dissertation. *Entrance requirements:* For master's, equivalent of American Chemical Society approved bachelor's degree in chemistry; for doctorate, GRE General Test, equivalent of American Chemical Society approved bachelor's degree in chemistry. Additional exam requirements/recommendations for international students: Required—TOEFL (minimum score 550 paper-based; 213 computer-based; 80 iBT), TWE. *Application deadline:* For fall admission, 4/15 for domestic and international students; for spring admission, 10/15 for domestic and international students. Applications are processed on a rolling basis. Application fee: $45 ($50 for international students). Electronic applications accepted. *Expenses:* Tuition, state resident: full-time $5378; part-time $299 per credit hour. Tuition, nonresident: full-time $13,881; part-time $771 per credit hour. Required fees: $641; $71 per credit hour. Tuition and fees vary according to course load and program. *Financial support:* In 2009–10, 8 research assistantships with partial tuition reimbursements (averaging $17,973 per year), 17 teaching assistantships with partial tuition reimbursements (averaging $17,179 per year) were awarded; Federal Work-Study, institutionally sponsored loans, and scholarships/grants also available. Support available to part-time students. Financial award application deadline: 3/1; financial award applicants required to submit FAFSA. *Faculty research:* Molecular spectroscopy, characterization and synthesis of materials and compounds, computational chemistry, natural products, drug delivery systems and anti-tumor agents. Total annual research expenditures: $1 million. *Unit head:* Dr. Kathleen V. Kilway, Chair, 816-235-2289, Fax: 816-235-5502. *Application contact:* Graduate Recruiting Committee, 816-235-2272, Fax: 816-235-5502, E-mail: umkc-chemdept@umkc.edu.

University of Missouri–St. Louis, College of Arts and Sciences, Department of Chemistry and Biochemistry, St. Louis, MO 63121. Offers chemistry (MS, PhD), including biochemistry, inorganic chemistry, organic chemistry, physical chemistry. Part-time and evening/weekend programs available. *Faculty:* 19 full-time (3 women), 6 part-time/adjunct (1 woman). *Students:* 43 full-time (21 women), 19 part-time (8 women); includes 6 minority (4 African Americans, 1 Asian American or Pacific Islander, 1 Hispanic American), 27 international. Average age 29. 81 applicants, 37% accepted, 19 enrolled. In 2009, 9 master's, 6 doctorates awarded. Terminal master's awarded for partial completion of doctoral program. *Degree requirements:* For master's, thesis optional; for doctorate, thesis/dissertation. *Entrance requirements:* For master's, 2 letters of recommendation; for doctorate, GRE General Test, 3 letters of recommendation. Additional exam requirements/recommendations for international students: Required—TOEFL (minimum score 550 paper-based; 213 computer-based). *Application deadline:* For fall admission, 7/1 priority date for domestic and international students; for spring admission, 12/1 priority date for domestic and international students. Applications are processed on a rolling basis. Application fee: $35 ($40 for international students). Electronic applications accepted. *Expenses:* Tuition, state resident: full-time $5377; part-time $297.70 per credit hour. Tuition, nonresident: full-time $13,882; part-time $771.20 per credit hour. Required fees: $220; $12.20 per credit hour. One-time fee: $12. Tuition and fees vary according to course level, campus/location and program. *Financial support:* In 2009–10, 25 research assistantships with full and partial tuition reimbursements (averaging $17,840 per year), 13 teaching assistantships with full and partial tuition reimbursements (averaging $13,300 per year) were awarded; fellowships with full and partial tuition reimbursements also available. *Faculty research:* Metallaborane chemistry, serum transferrin chemistry, natural products chemistry, organic synthesis. *Unit head:* Dr. Cynthia Dupureur, Director of Graduate Studies, 314-516-5311, Fax: 314-516-5342, E-mail: gradchem@umsl.edu. *Application contact:* 314-516-5458, Fax: 314-516-6996, E-mail: gradadm@umsl.edu.

The University of Montana, Graduate School, College of Arts and Sciences, Department of Chemistry, Missoula, MT 59812-0002. Offers chemistry (MS, PhD), including environmental/analytical chemistry, inorganic chemistry, organic chemistry, physical chemistry. Terminal master's awarded for partial completion of doctoral program. *Degree requirements:* For master's, thesis (for some programs); for doctorate, thesis/dissertation. *Entrance requirements:* For master's and doctorate, GRE General Test. Additional exam requirements/recommendations for international students: Required—TOEFL (minimum score 575 paper-based; 230 computer-based). *Faculty research:* Reaction mechanisms and kinetics, inorganic and organic synthesis, analytical chemistry, natural products.

University of Nebraska–Lincoln, Graduate College, College of Arts and Sciences, Department of Chemistry, Lincoln, NE 68588. Offers analytical chemistry (PhD); biochemistry (PhD); chemistry (MS); inorganic chemistry (PhD); materials chemistry (PhD); organic chemistry (PhD); physical chemistry (PhD). *Degree requirements:* For master's, one foreign language, thesis optional, departmental qualifying exam; for doctorate, one foreign language, comprehensive exam, thesis/dissertation, departmental qualifying exams. *Entrance requirements:* For master's and doctorate, GRE. Additional exam requirements/recommendations for international students: Required—TOEFL (minimum score 550 paper-based; 213 computer-based). Electronic applications accepted. *Faculty research:* Bioorganic and bioinorganic chemistry, biophysical and bioanalytical chemistry, structure-function of DNA and proteins, organometallics, mass spectrometry.

University of Notre Dame, Graduate School, College of Science, Department of Chemistry and Biochemistry, Notre Dame, IN 46556. Offers biochemistry (MS, PhD); inorganic chemistry (MS, PhD); organic chemistry (MS, PhD); physical chemistry (MS, PhD). Terminal master's awarded for partial completion of doctoral program. *Degree requirements:* For master's, comprehensive exam, thesis; for doctorate, thesis/dissertation, qualifying exam. *Entrance requirements:* For master's and doctorate, GRE General Test, GRE Subject Test (strongly recommended). Additional exam requirements/recommendations for international students: Required—TOEFL (minimum score 600 paper-based; 250 computer-based; 80 iBT). Electronic applications accepted. *Faculty research:* Reaction design and mechanistic studies; reactive intermediates; synthesis, structure and reactivity of organometallic cluster complexes and biologically active natural products; bioorganic chemistry; enzymology.

University of Regina, Faculty of Graduate Studies and Research, Faculty of Science, Department of Chemistry and Biochemistry, Regina, SK S4S 0A2, Canada. Offers analytical chemistry (M Sc, PhD); biochemistry (M Sc, PhD); inorganic chemistry (M Sc, PhD); organic chemistry (M Sc, PhD); physical chemistry (M Sc, PhD). Part-time programs available. *Faculty:* 11 full-time (2 women), 3 part-time/adjunct (0 women). *Students:* 20 full-time (8 women). 25 applicants, 28% accepted. In 2009, 2 master's awarded. *Degree requirements:* For master's, thesis, departmental qualifying exam; for doctorate, thesis/dissertation, departmental qualifying exam. *Entrance requirements:* For master's and doctorate, GRE. Additional exam requirements/recommendations for international students: Required—TOEFL (minimum score 580 paper-based; 237 computer-based; 80 iBT). *Application deadline:* For fall admission, 1/1 for domestic students; for winter admission, 7/1 for domestic students. Applications are processed on a rolling basis. Application fee: $90 ($100 for international students). *Financial support:* In 2009–10, 5 fellowships (averaging $19,000 per year), 2 research assistantships (averaging $16,910 per year), 4 teaching assistantships (averaging $6,650 per year) were awarded; scholarships/grants also available. Financial award application deadline: 6/15. *Faculty research:* Organic synthesis, organic oxidations, ionic liquids theoretical/computational chemistry, protein biochemistry/biophysics, environmental analytical, photophysical/photochemistry. *Unit head:* Dr. Tanya Dahms, Head, 306-585-4247, E-mail: tanya.dohms@uregina.ca. *Application contact:* Dr. Scott Murphy, Program Coordinator, 306-585-4247, Fax: 306-585-4894, E-mail: scott.murphy@uregina.ca.

University of Southern Mississippi, Graduate School, College of Science and Technology, Department of Chemistry and Biochemistry, Hattiesburg, MS 39406-0001. Offers analytical

Inorganic Chemistry

University of Southern Mississippi (continued)
chemistry (MS, PhD); biochemistry (MS, PhD); inorganic chemistry (MS, PhD); organic chemistry (MS, PhD); physical chemistry (MS, PhD). *Faculty:* 16 full-time (4 women). *Students:* 14 full-time (0 women), 5 part-time (4 women); includes 1 minority (African American), 12 international. Average age 29. 41 applicants, 17% accepted, 6 enrolled. In 2009, 2 master's, 6 doctorates awarded. *Degree requirements:* For master's, comprehensive exam, thesis; for doctorate, comprehensive exam, thesis/dissertation. *Entrance requirements:* For master's, GRE General Test, minimum GPA of 2.75 in last 60 hours; for doctorate, GRE General Test, minimum GPA of 3.5. Additional exam requirements/recommendations for international students: Required—TOEFL. *Application deadline:* For fall admission, 3/1 priority date for domestic students, 3/1 for international students. Applications are processed on a rolling basis. Application fee: $35. *Expenses:* Tuition, state resident: full-time $5096; part-time $284 per hour. Tuition, nonresident: full-time $13,052; part-time $726 per hour. Required fees: $402. Tuition and fees vary according to course level and course load. *Financial support:* In 2009–10, 3 research assistantships with full tuition reimbursements (averaging $17,000 per year), 19 teaching assistantships with full tuition reimbursements (averaging $20,716 per year) were awarded; fellowships, Federal Work-Study and institutionally sponsored loans also available. Support available to part-time students. Financial award application deadline: 3/15; financial award applicants required to submit FAFSA. *Faculty research:* Plant biochemistry, photo chemistry, polymer chemistry, x-ray analysis, enzyme chemistry. *Unit head:* Dr. Robert Bateman, Chair, 601-266-4701, Fax: 601-266-6075. *Application contact:* Dr. Sabine Heinherst, Graduate Coordinator, 601-266-4702, Fax: 601-266-6075.

University of South Florida, Graduate School, College of Arts and Sciences, Department of Chemistry, Tampa, FL 33620-9951. Offers computational chemistry (PhD); analytical chemistry (MS, PhD); biochemistry (MS, PhD); computational chemistry (MS); environmental chemistry (MS, PhD); inorganic chemistry (MS, PhD); organic chemistry (MS); physical chemistry (MS, PhD); polymer chemistry (PhD). Part-time programs available. *Faculty:* 25 full-time (4 women). *Students:* 113 full-time (36 women), 15 part-time (11 women); includes 19 minority (5 African Americans, 6 Asian Americans or Pacific Islanders, 8 Hispanic Americans), 58 international. Average age 32. 112 applicants, 30% accepted, 21 enrolled. In 2009, 8 master's, 11 doctorates awarded. Terminal master's awarded for partial completion of doctoral program. *Degree requirements:* For master's, comprehensive exam, thesis (for some programs); for doctorate, 2 foreign languages, comprehensive exam, thesis/dissertation. *Entrance requirements:* For master's, GRE General Test or GMAT, minimum GPA of 3.0. Additional exam requirements/recommendations for international students: Required—TOEFL (minimum score 550 paper-based; 213 computer-based). *Application deadline:* For fall admission, 2/15 priority date for domestic students, 1/2 priority date for international students; for spring admission, 10/1 priority date for domestic students, 6/1 priority date for international students. Applications are processed on a rolling basis. Application fee: $30. Electronic applications accepted. *Financial support:* In 2009–10, teaching assistantships with tuition reimbursements (averaging $27,522 per year); unspecified assistantships also available. Financial award application deadline: 6/30. *Faculty research:* Synthesis, bio-organic chemistry, bioinorganic chemistry, environmental chemistry, NMR. Total annual research expenditures: $3.2 million. *Unit head:* Dr. Randy Larsen, Chairperson, 813-974-4129, Fax: 813-974-3203, E-mail: rlarsen@cas.usf.edu. *Application contact:* Patricia Muisener, Director, 813-974-1730, Fax: 813-974-3203, E-mail: muisener@cas.usf.edu.

The University of Tennessee, Graduate School, College of Arts and Sciences, Department of Chemistry, Knoxville, TN 37996. Offers analytical chemistry (MS, PhD); chemical physics (PhD); environmental chemistry (MS, PhD); inorganic chemistry (MS, PhD); organic chemistry (MS, PhD); physical chemistry (MS, PhD); polymer chemistry (MS, PhD); theoretical chemistry (PhD). Part-time programs available. Terminal master's awarded for partial completion of doctoral program. *Degree requirements:* For master's, thesis; for doctorate, thesis/dissertation. *Entrance requirements:* For master's and doctorate, GRE General Test, minimum GPA of 2.7. Additional exam requirements/recommendations for international students: Required—TOEFL. Electronic applications accepted. *Expenses:* Tuition, state resident: full-time $6826; part-time $380 per semester hour. Tuition, nonresident: full-time $21,844; part-time $1147 per semester hour. Tuition and fees vary according to program.

The University of Texas at Austin, Graduate School, College of Natural Sciences, Department of Chemistry and Biochemistry, Austin, TX 78712-1111. Offers analytical chemistry (MA, PhD); biochemistry (MA, PhD); inorganic chemistry (MA, PhD); organic chemistry (MA, PhD); physical chemistry (MA, PhD). *Entrance requirements:* For master's and doctorate, GRE General Test.

The University of Toledo, College of Graduate Studies, College of Arts and Sciences, Department of Chemistry, Toledo, OH 43606-3390. Offers analytical chemistry (MS, PhD); biological chemistry (MS, PhD); inorganic chemistry (MS, PhD); organic chemistry (MS, PhD); physical chemistry (MS, PhD). Part-time programs available. *Degree requirements:* For master's, thesis; for doctorate, thesis/dissertation. *Entrance requirements:* For master's and doctorate, GRE General Test, GRE Subject Test. Additional exam requirements/recommendations for international students: Required—TOEFL. Electronic applications accepted. *Faculty research:* Enzymology, materials chemistry, crystallography, theoretical chemistry.

Vanderbilt University, Graduate School, Department of Chemistry, Nashville, TN 37240-1001. Offers analytical chemistry (MAT, MS, PhD); inorganic chemistry (MAT, MS, PhD); organic chemistry (MAT, MS, PhD); physical chemistry (MAT, MS, PhD); theoretical chemistry (MAT, MS, PhD). *Faculty:* 46 full-time (6 women). *Students:* 106 full-time (38 women); includes 10 minority (5 African Americans, 3 Asian Americans or Pacific Islanders, 2 Hispanic Americans), 21 international. Average age 27. 245 applicants, 27% accepted, 21 enrolled. In 2009, 10 master's, 21 doctorates awarded. Terminal master's awarded for partial completion of doctoral program. *Degree requirements:* For master's, thesis; for doctorate, thesis/dissertation, area, qualifying, and final exams. *Entrance requirements:* For master's and doctorate, GRE General Test, GRE Subject Test (recommended). Additional exam requirements/recommendations for international students: Required—TOEFL (minimum score 570 paper-based; 230 computer-based; 88 iBT). *Application deadline:* For fall admission, 1/15 for domestic and international students. Application fee: $0. Electronic applications accepted. *Financial support:* Fellowships with full and partial tuition reimbursements, research assistantships with full tuition reimbursements, teaching assistantships with full tuition reimbursements, Federal Work-Study, institutionally sponsored loans, scholarships/grants, traineeships, and health care benefits available. Financial award application deadline: 1/15; financial award applicants required to submit CSS PROFILE or FAFSA. *Faculty research:* Chemical synthesis; mechanistic, theoretical, bioorganic, analytical, and spectroscopic chemistry. *Unit head:* Mike P. Stone, Chair, 615-322-2861, Fax: 615-343-1234. *Application contact:* Charles M. Lukehart, Director of Graduate Studies, 615-322-2861, Fax: 615-343-1234, E-mail: charles.m.lukehart@vanderbilt.edu.

Virginia Commonwealth University, Graduate School, College of Humanities and Sciences, Department of Chemistry, Richmond, VA 23284-9005. Offers analytical chemistry (MS, PhD); chemical physics (PhD); inorganic chemistry (MS, PhD); organic chemistry (MS, PhD); physical chemistry (MS, PhD). Part-time programs available. Terminal master's awarded for partial completion of doctoral program. *Degree requirements:* For master's, thesis; for doctorate, thesis/dissertation, comprehensive cumulative exams, research proposal. *Entrance requirements:* For master's, GRE General Test, 30 undergraduate credits in chemistry; for doctorate, GRE General Test. *Faculty research:* Physical, organic, inorganic, analytical, and polymer chemistry; chemical physics.

Wake Forest University, Graduate School of Arts and Sciences, Department of Chemistry, Winston-Salem, NC 27109. Offers analytical chemistry (MS, PhD); inorganic chemistry (MS, PhD); organic chemistry (MS, PhD); physical chemistry (MS, PhD). Part-time programs available. *Degree requirements:* For master's, one foreign language, comprehensive exam, thesis; for doctorate, 2 foreign languages, comprehensive exam, thesis/dissertation. *Entrance requirements:* For master's and doctorate, GRE General Test. Additional exam requirements/recommendations for international students: Required—TOEFL (minimum score 213 computer-based). Electronic applications accepted.

Wesleyan University, Graduate Programs, Department of Chemistry, Middletown, CT 06459. Offers biochemistry (MA, PhD); chemical physics (MA, PhD); inorganic chemistry (MA, PhD); organic chemistry (MA, PhD); physical chemistry (MA, PhD); theoretical chemistry (MA, PhD). *Faculty:* 14 full-time (2 women), 2 part-time/adjunct (1 woman). *Students:* 19 full-time (8 women), 2 part-time (0 women), 9 international. Average age 26. 40 applicants, 63% accepted, 4 enrolled. In 2009, 3 master's, 5 doctorates awarded. Terminal master's awarded for partial completion of doctoral program. *Degree requirements:* For master's, thesis, proposal; for doctorate, thesis/dissertation, proposal. *Entrance requirements:* For doctorate, GRE General Test, 3 recommendations. Additional exam requirements/recommendations for international students: Required—TOEFL. *Application deadline:* Applications are processed on a rolling basis. Application fee: $0. Electronic applications accepted. *Financial support:* In 2009–10, 4 research assistantships with full tuition reimbursements, 12 teaching assistantships with full tuition reimbursements were awarded; institutionally sponsored loans also available. Financial award application deadline: 4/15; financial award applicants required to submit FAFSA. *Unit head:* Dr. Joseph Knee, Chair, 860-685-2210. *Application contact:* Cait Zinser, Information Contact, 860-685-2573, Fax: 860-685-2211, E-mail: czinser@wesleyan.edu.

See Close-Up on page 115.

West Virginia University, Eberly College of Arts and Sciences, Department of Chemistry, Morgantown, WV 26506. Offers analytical chemistry (MS, PhD); inorganic chemistry (MS, PhD); organic chemistry (MS, PhD); physical chemistry (MS, PhD); theoretical chemistry (MS, PhD). Part-time programs available. Postbaccalaureate distance learning degree programs offered (no on-campus study). Terminal master's awarded for partial completion of doctoral program. *Degree requirements:* For master's, thesis; for doctorate, thesis/dissertation. *Entrance requirements:* For master's, GRE General Test, GRE Subject Test (recommended), minimum GPA of 2.5; for doctorate, GRE General Test, GRE Subject Test (recommended), minimum GPA of 2.75. Additional exam requirements/recommendations for international students: Required—TOEFL. Electronic applications accepted. *Faculty research:* Analysis of proteins, drug interactions, solids and effluents by advanced separation methods; new synthetic strategies for complex organic molecules; synthesis and structural characterization of metal complexes for polymerization catalysis, nonlinear science, spectroscopy.

Yale University, Graduate School of Arts and Sciences, Department of Chemistry, New Haven, CT 06520. Offers biophysical chemistry (PhD); inorganic chemistry (PhD); organic chemistry (PhD); physical and theoretical chemistry (PhD). *Degree requirements:* For doctorate, thesis/dissertation. *Entrance requirements:* For doctorate, GRE General Test, GRE Subject Test. Additional exam requirements/recommendations for international students: Required—TOEFL.

Youngstown State University, Graduate School, College of Science, Technology, Engineering and Mathematics, Department of Chemistry, Youngstown, OH 44555-0001. Offers analytical chemistry (MS); biochemistry (MS); chemistry education (MS); inorganic chemistry (MS); organic chemistry (MS); physical chemistry (MS). Part-time programs available. *Degree requirements:* For master's, thesis. *Entrance requirements:* For master's, bachelor's degree in chemistry, minimum GPA of 2.7. Additional exam requirements/recommendations for international students: Required—TOEFL. *Faculty research:* Analysis of antioxidants, chromatography, defects and disorder in crystalline oxides, hydrogen bonding, novel organic and organometallic materials.

Organic Chemistry

Auburn University, Graduate School, College of Sciences and Mathematics, Department of Chemistry and Biochemistry, Auburn University, AL 36849. Offers analytical chemistry (MS, PhD); biochemistry (MS, PhD); inorganic chemistry (MS, PhD); organic chemistry (MS, PhD); physical chemistry (MS, PhD). Part-time programs available. *Faculty:* 27 full-time (6 women). *Students:* 39 full-time (20 women), 21 part-time (8 women); includes 6 minority (4 African Americans, 1 Asian American or Pacific Islander, 1 Hispanic American), 41 international. Average age 28. 54 applicants, 11% accepted, 3 enrolled. In 2009, 1 master's, 13 doctorates awarded. *Degree requirements:* For master's, thesis (for some programs); for doctorate, thesis/dissertation, oral and written exams. *Entrance requirements:* For master's and doctorate, GRE General Test. *Application deadline:* For fall admission, 7/7 for domestic students; for spring admission, 11/24 for domestic students. Applications are processed on a rolling basis. Application fee: $50 ($60 for international students). Electronic applications accepted. *Expenses:* Tuition, state resident: full-time $6240. Tuition, nonresident: full-time $18,720. International tuition: $18,938 full-time. Required fees: $492. Tuition and fees vary according to course load, program and reciprocity agreements. *Financial support:* Fellowships, research assistantships, teaching assistantships available. Financial award application deadline: 3/15; financial award applicants required to submit FAFSA. *Unit head:* Dr. J. V. Ortiz, Chair, 334-844-4043, Fax: 334-844-4043. *Application contact:* Dr. George Flowers, Dean of the Graduate School, 334-844-2125.

Boston College, Graduate School of Arts and Sciences, Department of Chemistry, Chestnut Hill, MA 02467-3800. Offers biochemistry (PhD); inorganic chemistry (PhD); organic chemistry (PhD); physical chemistry (PhD); science education (MST). Part-time programs available. *Students:* 110 full-time (49 women); includes 8 minority (6 Asian Americans or Pacific Islanders, 2 Hispanic Americans), 49 international. 216 applicants, 34% accepted, 22 enrolled. In 2009, 3 master's, 20 doctorates awarded. *Degree requirements:* For doctorate, thesis/dissertation, qualifying exam. *Entrance requirements:* For doctorate, GRE General Test, GRE Subject Test. Additional exam requirements/recommendations for international students: Required—TOEFL (minimum score 600 paper-based; 250 computer-based; 100 iBT). *Application deadline:* For fall admission, 1/2 for domestic and international students. Application fee: $70. Electronic applications accepted. *Financial support:* In 2009–10, fellowships with full tuition reimbursements (averaging $25,000 per year), research assistantships with full tuition reimbursements (averaging $25,000 per year), teaching assistantships with full tuition reimbursements (averaging $25,000 per year) were awarded; Federal Work-Study also available. Support available to part-time students. Financial award application deadline: 3/1; financial award applicants required to submit FAFSA. *Unit head:* Dr. Amir Hoveyda, Chairperson, 617-552-1735, E-mail: amir.hoveyda@bc.edu. *Application contact:* Dr. Marc Snapper, Graduate Program Director, 617-552-8096, Fax: 617-552-0833, E-mail: marc.snapper@bc.edu.

Brandeis University, Graduate School of Arts and Sciences, Department of Chemistry, Waltham, MA 02454. Offers inorganic chemistry (MS, PhD); organic chemistry (MS, PhD); physical chemistry (MS, PhD). *Faculty:* 14 full-time (3 women), 4 part-time/adjunct (3 women). *Students:* 42 full-time (17 women); includes 2 minority (1 African American, 1 Asian American or Pacific Islander), 28 international. 127 applicants, 16% accepted, 8 enrolled. In 2009, 11 master's, 6 doctorates awarded. Terminal master's awarded for partial completion of doctoral program. *Degree requirements:* For master's, thesis, 1 year of residency; for doctorate, one foreign language, thesis/dissertation, 3 years of residency, 2 seminars, qualifying exams. *Entrance requirements:* For master's and doctorate, GRE General Test, resume, letters of recommendation. Additional exam requirements/recommendations for international students: Required—TOEFL (minimum score 600 paper-based; 250 computer-based; 100 iBT); Recommended—IELTS (minimum score 7). *Application deadline:* For fall admission, 1/15 priority date for domestic students. Applications are processed on a rolling basis. Application fee: $75. Electronic applications accepted. *Financial support:* In 2009–10, 23 fellowships with full tuition reimbursements (averaging $24,500 per year), 14 research assistantships with full tuition reimbursements (averaging $24,500 per year), teaching assistantships with partial tuition reimbursements (averaging $3,200 per year) were awarded; scholarships/grants and health care benefits also available. Financial award application deadline: 4/15; financial award applicants required to submit FAFSA. *Faculty research:* Oscillating chemical reactions, molecular recognition systems, protein crystallography, synthesis of natural product spectroscopy and magnetic resonance. *Unit head:* Dr. Judith Herzfeld, Chair, Graduate Program in Chemistry, 781-736-2540, Fax: 781-736-2516, E-mail: herzfeld@brandeis.edu. *Application contact:* Charlotte Haygazian, Graduate Department Coordinator, 781-736-2500, Fax: 781-736-2516, E-mail: chemadm@brandeis.edu.

California State University, Los Angeles, Graduate Studies, College of Natural and Social Sciences, Department of Chemistry and Biochemistry, Los Angeles, CA 90032-8530. Offers analytical chemistry (MS); biochemistry (MS); chemistry (MS); inorganic chemistry (MS); organic chemistry (MS); physical chemistry (MS). Part-time and evening/weekend programs available. *Faculty:* 1 full-time (0 women), 9 part-time/adjunct (4 women). *Students:* 14 full-time (4 women), 31 part-time (15 women); includes 21 minority (5 African Americans, 9 Asian Americans or Pacific Islanders, 7 Hispanic Americans), 10 international. Average age 30. 23 applicants, 91% accepted, 13 enrolled. In 2009, 11 degrees awarded. *Degree requirements:* For master's, one foreign language, comprehensive exam or thesis. *Entrance requirements:* Additional exam requirements/recommendations for international students: Required—TOEFL. *Application deadline:* For fall admission, 5/1 for domestic and international students. Applications are processed on a rolling basis. Application fee: $55. *Financial support:* Federal Work-Study available. Support available to part-time students. Financial award application deadline: 3/1. *Faculty research:* Intercalation of heavy metal, carborane chemistry, conductive polymers and fabrics, titanium reagents, computer modeling and synthesis. *Unit head:* Dr. Scott Grover, Chair, 323-343-2300, Fax: 323-343-6490, E-mail: sgrover@calstatela.edu. *Application contact:* Dr. Cheryl L. Ney, Associate Vice President for Academic Affairs and Dean of Graduate Studies, 323-343-3820 Ext. 3827, Fax: 323-343-5653, E-mail: cney@cslanet.calstatela.edu.

Carnegie Mellon University, Mellon College of Science, Department of Chemistry, Pittsburgh, PA 15213-3891. Offers biotechnology and management (MS); chemistry (PhD), including bioinorganic, bioorganic, organic and materials, biophysics and spectroscopy, computational and theoretical, polymer; colloids, polymers and surfaces (MS). Part-time programs available. Terminal master's awarded for partial completion of doctoral program. *Degree requirements:* For doctorate, thesis/dissertation, departmental qualifying and oral exams, teaching experience. *Entrance requirements:* For master's, GRE General Test; for doctorate, GRE General Test, GRE Subject Test. Additional exam requirements/recommendations for international students: Required—TOEFL. Electronic applications accepted. *Faculty research:* Physical and theoretical chemistry, chemical synthesis, biophysical/bioinorganic chemistry.

Cleveland State University, College of Graduate Studies, College of Science, Department of Chemistry, Cleveland, OH 44115. Offers analytical chemistry (MS); clinical chemistry (MS); clinical/bioanalytical chemistry (PhD), including clinical chemistry, molecular medicine; environmental chemistry (MS); inorganic chemistry (MS); organic chemistry (MS); physical chemistry (MS). Part-time and evening/weekend programs available. *Degree requirements:* For master's, thesis (for some programs); for doctorate, thesis/dissertation. *Entrance requirements:* For master's and doctorate, GRE General Test. Additional exam requirements/recommendations for international students: Required—TOEFL (minimum score 525 paper-based; 197 computer-based; 65 iBT). Electronic applications accepted. *Faculty research:* MALDI-TOF based DNA sequencing, development of ionic focusing HPLC, synthetic and structural studies of vanadium.

Columbia University, Graduate School of Arts and Sciences, Division of Natural Sciences, Department of Chemistry, New York, NY 10027. Offers chemical physics (M Phil, PhD); inorganic chemistry (M Phil, MA, PhD); organic chemistry (M Phil, MA, PhD); MD/PhD. *Degree requirements:* For master's, one foreign language, teaching experience, oral/written exams (M Phil); for doctorate, one foreign language, thesis/dissertation. *Entrance requirements:* For master's and doctorate, GRE General Test, GRE Subject Test. Additional exam requirements/recommendations for international students: Required—TOEFL. *Faculty research:* Biophysics.

Cornell University, Graduate School, Graduate Fields of Arts and Sciences, Field of Chemistry and Chemical Biology, Ithaca, NY 14853-0001. Offers analytical chemistry (PhD); bio-organic chemistry (PhD); biophysical chemistry (PhD); chemical biology (PhD); chemical physics (PhD); inorganic chemistry (PhD); materials chemistry (PhD); organic chemistry (PhD); organometallic chemistry (PhD); physical chemistry (PhD); polymer chemistry (PhD); theoretical chemistry (PhD). *Faculty:* 48 full-time (3 women). *Students:* 162 full-time (67 women); includes 15 minority (1 African American, 9 Asian Americans or Pacific Islanders, 5 Hispanic Americans), 53 international. Average age 26. 359 applicants, 19% accepted, 39 enrolled. In 2009, 31 doctorates awarded. *Degree requirements:* For doctorate, comprehensive exam, thesis/dissertation. *Entrance requirements:* For doctorate, GRE General Test, GRE Subject Test (chemistry), 3 letters of recommendation. Additional exam requirements/recommendations for international students: Required—TOEFL (minimum score 600 paper-based; 250 computer-based; 77 iBT). *Application deadline:* For fall admission, 1/10 for domestic students. Application fee: $70. Electronic applications accepted. *Expenses:* Tuition: Full-time $29,500. Required fees: $70. Full-time tuition and fees vary according to degree level, program and student level. *Financial support:* In 2009–10, 1 fellowship with full tuition reimbursement, 7 research assistantships with full tuition reimbursements, 29 teaching assistantships with full tuition reimbursements were awarded; institutionally sponsored loans, scholarships/grants, health care benefits, tuition waivers (full and partial), and unspecified assistantships also available. Financial award applicants required to submit FAFSA. *Faculty research:* Analytical, organic, inorganic, physical, materials, chemical biology. *Unit head:* Director of Graduate Studies, 607-255-4139, Fax: 607-255-4137. *Application contact:* Graduate Field Assistant, 607-255-4139, Fax: 607-255-4137, E-mail: chemgrad@cornell.edu.

Florida State University, The Graduate School, College of Arts and Sciences, Department of Chemistry and Biochemistry, Tallahassee, FL 32306-4390. Offers analytical chemistry (MS, PhD); biochemistry (MS, PhD); inorganic chemistry (MS, PhD); materials chemistry (MS, PhD); organic chemistry (MS, PhD); physical chemistry (MS, PhD). *Faculty:* 40 full-time (6 women), 3 part-time/adjunct (0 women). *Students:* 150 full-time (47 women), 9 part-time (6 women); includes 16 minority (5 African Americans, 1 American Indian/Alaska Native, 5 Asian Americans or Pacific Islanders, 5 Hispanic Americans), 68 international. Average age 25. 286 applicants, 21% accepted, 28 enrolled. In 2009, 7 master's, 15 doctorates awarded. Terminal master's awarded for partial completion of doctoral program. *Degree requirements:* For master's, comprehensive exam (for some programs), thesis (for some programs), cumulative and diagnostic exams; for doctorate, comprehensive exam (for some programs), thesis/dissertation, cumulative and diagnostic exams. *Entrance requirements:* For master's and doctorate, GRE General Test, minimum B average in undergraduate course work. Additional exam requirements/recommendations for international students: Required—TOEFL (minimum score 550 paper-based; 213 computer-based; 80 iBT). *Application deadline:* For fall admission, 12/15 for domestic and international students; for spring admission, 9/15 for domestic and international students. Applications are processed on a rolling basis. Application fee: $30. Electronic applications accepted. *Expenses:* Tuition, state resident: full-time $7413.36. Tuition, nonresident: full-time $22,567. *Financial support:* In 2009–10, 150 students received support, including fellowships with full tuition reimbursements available (averaging $19,000 per year), 52 research assistantships with full tuition reimbursements available (averaging $19,000 per year), 100 teaching assistantships with full tuition reimbursements available (averaging $19,000 per year); career-related internships or fieldwork, Federal Work-Study, institutionally sponsored loans, and traineeships also available. Financial award application deadline: 12/15; financial award applicants required to submit FAFSA. *Faculty research:* Materials synthesis including polymers, natural products; catalysis, NMR; mass spectrometry; optical spectroscopy, scattering techniques, computational chemistry, separation technology; nanostructured materials including metallic, semiconducting and magnetic nanocrystals; nanoscience interfaced with biology; supramolecular materials for solar energy conversion. Total annual research expenditures: $5.5 million. *Unit head:* Dr. Joseph Schlenoff, Chairman, 850-644-5195, Fax: 850-644-8281, E-mail: schlen@chem.fsu.edu. *Application contact:* Dr. Tyler McQuade, Chair, Graduate Admissions Committee, 888-525-9286, Fax: 850-644-0465, E-mail: gradinfo@chem.fsu.edu.

Georgetown University, Graduate School of Arts and Sciences, Department of Chemistry, Washington, DC 20057. Offers analytical chemistry (PhD); biochemistry (PhD); computational chemistry (PhD); inorganic chemistry (PhD); materials chemistry (PhD); organic chemistry (PhD); physical chemistry (PhD); theoretical chemistry (PhD). Terminal master's awarded for partial completion of doctoral program. *Degree requirements:* For doctorate, comprehensive exam, thesis/dissertation. *Entrance requirements:* For doctorate, GRE General Test. Additional exam requirements/recommendations for international students: Required—TOEFL.

The George Washington University, Columbian College of Arts and Sciences, Department of Chemistry, Washington, DC 20052. Offers analytical chemistry (MS, PhD); inorganic chemistry (MS, PhD); materials science (MS, PhD); organic chemistry (MS, PhD); physical chemistry (MS, PhD). Part-time and evening/weekend programs available. *Faculty:* 15 full-time (4 women), 7 part-time/adjunct (3 women). *Students:* 19 full-time (12 women), 12 part-time (7 women); includes 4 minority (2 Asian Americans or Pacific Islanders, 2 Hispanic Americans), 12 international. Average age 28. 45 applicants, 49% accepted, 6 enrolled. In 2009, 2 master's, 4 doctorates awarded. Terminal master's awarded for partial completion of doctoral program. *Degree requirements:* For master's, comprehensive exam, thesis or alternative; for doctorate, thesis/dissertation, general exam. *Entrance requirements:* For master's and doctorate, GRE General Test, interview, minimum GPA of 3.0. Additional exam requirements/recommendations for international students: Required—TOEFL (minimum score 550 paper-based; 213 computer-based; 80 iBT). *Application deadline:* For fall admission, 1/15 priority date for domestic and international students; for spring admission, 9/1 priority date for domestic and international students. Applications are processed on a rolling basis. Application fee: $60. Electronic applications accepted. *Financial support:* In 2009–10, 27 students received support; fellowships with tuition reimbursements available, research assistantships, teaching assistantships with tuition reimbursements available, Federal Work-Study and tuition waivers available. Financial award application deadline: 1/15. *Unit head:* Dr. Michael King, Chair, 202-994-6488. *Application contact:* Information Contact, E-mail: gwchem@www.gwu.edu.

Harvard University, Graduate School of Arts and Sciences, Department of Chemistry and Chemical Biology, Cambridge, MA 02138. Offers biochemical chemistry (PhD); inorganic chemistry (PhD); organic chemistry (PhD); physical chemistry (PhD). *Degree requirements:* For doctorate, thesis/dissertation, cumulative exams. *Entrance requirements:* For doctorate, GRE General Test, GRE Subject Test. Additional exam requirements/recommendations for international students: Required—TOEFL. *Expenses:* Tuition: Full-time $33,696. Required fees: $1126. Full-time tuition and fees vary according to program.

See Close-Up on page 99.

Howard University, Graduate School, Department of Chemistry, Washington, DC 20059-0002. Offers analytical chemistry (MS, PhD); atmospheric (MS, PhD); biochemistry (MS, PhD); environmental (MS, PhD); inorganic chemistry (MS, PhD); organic chemistry (MS, PhD); physical chemistry (MS, PhD). Terminal master's awarded for partial completion of doctoral program. *Degree requirements:* For master's, comprehensive exam, thesis, teaching experience; for doctorate, comprehensive exam, thesis/dissertation, teaching experience. *Entrance requirements:* For master's, GRE General Test, minimum GPA of 2.7; for doctorate, GRE General Test, minimum GPA of 3.0. Additional exam requirements/recommendations for international students: Required—TOEFL. Electronic applications accepted. *Faculty research:* Synthetic organics, materials, natural products, mass spectrometry.

Instituto Tecnológico y de Estudios Superiores de Monterrey, Campus Monterrey, Graduate and Research Division, Program in Natural and Social Sciences, Monterrey, Mexico. Offers biotechnology (MS); chemistry (MS, PhD); communications (MS); education (MA). Part-time programs available. *Degree requirements:* For master's, one foreign language, thesis; for doctorate, one foreign language, thesis/dissertation. *Entrance requirements:* For master's, EXADEP; for doctorate, EXADEP, master's degree in related field. Additional exam requirements/recommendations for international students: Required—TOEFL. *Faculty research:* Cultural industries, mineral substances, bioremediation, food processing, CQ in industrial chemical processing.

Kansas State University, Graduate School, College of Arts and Sciences, Department of Chemistry, Manhattan, KS 66506. Offers analytical chemistry (MS); biological chemistry (MS); chemistry (PhD); inorganic chemistry (MS); materials chemistry (MS); organic chemistry (MS); physical chemistry (MS). *Faculty:* 16 full-time (2 women), 2 part-time/adjunct (0 women). *Students:* 66 full-time (22 women); includes 2 minority (1 African American, 1 Asian American or Pacific Islander), 54 international. Average age 28. 75 applicants, 23% accepted, 7 enrolled. In 2009, 3 master's, 11 doctorates awarded. Terminal master's awarded for partial completion of doctoral program. *Degree requirements:* For master's, thesis; for doctorate, thesis/dissertation. *Entrance requirements:* For master's and doctorate, GRE, minimum GPA of 3.0. Additional exam requirements/recommendations for international students: Required—TOEFL (minimum score 550 paper-based; 213 computer-based). *Application deadline:* For fall admission, 2/1 priority date for domestic and international students; for spring admission, 8/1 priority date for domestic and international students. Applications are processed on a rolling basis. Application fee: $40 ($55 for international students). Electronic applications accepted. *Financial support:* In 2009–10, 41 research assistantships (averaging $15,040 per year), 22 teaching assistantships with full tuition reimbursements (averaging $15,600 per year) were awarded; institutionally sponsored loans and scholarships/grants also available. Support available to part-time students. Financial award application deadline: 3/1; financial award applicants required to submit FAFSA. *Faculty research:* Inorganic chemistry, organic and biological chemistry, analytical chemistry, physical chemistry, materials chemistry and nanotechnology. Total annual research expenditures: $1.9 million. *Unit head:* Eric Maatta, Head, 785-532-6665, Fax: 785-532-6666, E-mail: eam@ksu.edu. *Application contact:* Christer Aakeroy, Director, 785-532-6096, Fax: 785-532-6666, E-mail: aakeroy@ksu.edu.

Organic Chemistry

Kent State University, College of Arts and Sciences, Department of Chemistry, Kent, OH 44242-0001. Offers analytical chemistry (MS, PhD); biochemistry (MS, PhD); chemistry (MA, MS, PhD); inorganic chemistry (MS, PhD); organic chemistry (MS, PhD); physical chemistry (MS, PhD). Terminal master's awarded for partial completion of doctoral program. *Degree requirements:* For master's, comprehensive exam, thesis; for doctorate, comprehensive exam, thesis/dissertation. *Entrance requirements:* For master's and doctorate, placement exam, GRE General Test, GRE Subject Test (recommended), minimum GPA of 2.75. Additional exam requirements/recommendations for international students: Required—TOEFL (minimum score 575 paper-based; 230 computer-based). Electronic applications accepted. *Faculty research:* Biological chemistry, materials chemistry, molecular spectroscopy.

See Close-Up on page 101.

Laurentian University, School of Graduate Studies and Research, Programme in Chemistry and Biochemistry, Sudbury, ON P3E 2C6, Canada. Offers analytical chemistry (M Sc); biochemistry (M Sc); environmental chemistry (M Sc); organic chemistry (M Sc); physical/theoretical chemistry (M Sc). Part-time programs available. *Degree requirements:* For master's, thesis or alternative. *Entrance requirements:* For master's, honors degree with minimum second class. *Faculty research:* Cell cycle checkpoints, kinetic modeling, toxicology to metal stress, quantum chemistry, biogeochemistry metal speciation.

Marquette University, Graduate School, College of Arts and Sciences, Department of Chemistry, Milwaukee, WI 53201-1881. Offers analytical chemistry (MS, PhD); bioanalytical chemistry (MS, PhD); biophysical chemistry (MS, PhD); chemical physics (MS, PhD); inorganic chemistry (MS, PhD); organic chemistry (MS, PhD); physical chemistry (MS, PhD). Part-time programs available. *Faculty:* 23 full-time (10 women), 1 part-time/adjunct (0 women). *Students:* 34 full-time (9 women), 10 part-time (4 women); includes 4 minority (1 African American, 2 Asian Americans or Pacific Islanders, 1 Hispanic American), 33 international. Average age 29. 23 applicants, 83% accepted, 8 enrolled. In 2009, 4 master's, 5 doctorates awarded. Terminal master's awarded for partial completion of doctoral program. *Degree requirements:* For master's, comprehensive exam; for doctorate, thesis/dissertation, cumulative exams. *Entrance requirements:* For master's and doctorate, GRE Subject Test. Additional exam requirements/recommendations for international students: Required—TOEFL. Application fee: $40. *Financial support:* In 2009–10, 3 research assistantships, 27 teaching assistantships were awarded; fellowships, Federal Work-Study, institutionally sponsored loans, scholarships/grants, and tuition waivers (full and partial) also available. Support available to part-time students. Financial award application deadline: 2/15. *Faculty research:* Inorganic complexes, laser Raman spectroscopy, organic synthesis, chemical dynamics, biophysiology. *Unit head:* Dr. Jeanne Hossenlopp, Chair, 414-288-3537, Fax: 414-288-7066. *Application contact:* Dr. Mark Steinmetz, Director of Graduate Studies, 414-288-7374, Fax: 414-288-7066.

Massachusetts College of Pharmacy and Health Sciences, Graduate Studies, Program in Applied Natural Products, Boston, MA 02115-5896. Offers MANP. *Students:* 1 (woman) full-time, 12 part-time (10 women); includes 2 minority (both Asian Americans or Pacific Islanders), 1 international. Average age 40. 5 applicants, 80% accepted, 4 enrolled. *Application deadline:* For fall admission, 7/1 priority date for domestic students, 7/1 for international students. Application fee: $70. *Expenses:* Tuition: Full-time $28,000; part-time $875 per credit hour. Required fees: $750; $190 per semester. Part-time tuition and fees vary according to course load, campus/location, program and student level. *Financial support:* Application deadline: 3/15. *Unit head:* Lana Dvorkin-Camiel, Director of Master of Applied Natural Products Program, 617-732-2939, E-mail: lana.dvorkin-camiel@mcphs.edu. *Application contact:* Tara Hennesey, Coordinator of Graduate Admission, 617-732-2850, E-mail: admissions@mcphs.edu.

Massachusetts Institute of Technology, School of Engineering, Department of Civil and Environmental Engineering, Cambridge, MA 02139-4307. Offers biological oceanography (PhD, Sc D); chemical oceanography (PhD, Sc D); civil and environmental engineering (M Eng, SM, PhD, Sc D); civil and environmental systems (PhD, Sc D); civil engineering (PhD, Sc D, CE); coastal engineering (PhD, Sc D); construction engineering and management (PhD, Sc D); environmental biology (PhD, Sc D); environmental chemistry (PhD, Sc D); environmental engineering (PhD, Sc D); environmental fluid mechanics (PhD, Sc D); geotechnical and geoenvironmental engineering (PhD, Sc D); hydrology (PhD, Sc D); information technology (PhD, Sc D); oceanographic engineering (PhD, Sc D); structures and materials (PhD, Sc D); transportation (PhD, Sc D); SM/MBA. *Faculty:* 36 full-time (5 women). *Students:* 190 full-time (59 women); includes 22 minority (2 African Americans, 14 Asian Americans or Pacific Islanders, 6 Hispanic Americans), 103 international. Average age 26. 478 applicants, 25% accepted, 76 enrolled. In 2009, 72 master's, 14 doctorates awarded. *Degree requirements:* For master's and CE, thesis; for doctorate, comprehensive exam, thesis/dissertation. *Entrance requirements:* For master's and doctorate, GRE General Test. Additional exam requirements/recommendations for international students: Required—TOEFL (minimum score 577 paper-based; 233 computer-based; 90 iBT), IELTS (minimum score 7). *Application deadline:* For fall admission, 1/2 for domestic and international students. Application fee: $75. Electronic applications accepted. *Financial support:* In 2009–10, 185 students received support, including 40 fellowships with tuition reimbursements available (averaging $27,725 per year), 97 research assistantships with tuition reimbursements available (averaging $28,035 per year), 21 teaching assistantships with tuition reimbursements available (averaging $24,802 per year); career-related internships or fieldwork, Federal Work-Study, institutionally sponsored loans, scholarships/grants, health care benefits, and unspecified assistantships also available. *Faculty research:* Environmental chemistry, environmental microbiology, environmental fluid mechanics and coastal engineering, geotechnical engineering and geomechanics, hydrology and hydroclimatology, mechanics of materials and structures, operations research/supply chain, transportation. Total annual research expenditures: $16.6 million. *Unit head:* Prof. Andrew Whittle, Department Head, 617-253-7101. *Application contact:* Patricia Glidden, Graduate Admissions Coordinator, 617-253-7119, Fax: 617-258-6775, E-mail: cee-admissions@mit.edu.

Massachusetts Institute of Technology, School of Science, Department of Chemistry, Cambridge, MA 02139-4307. Offers biological chemistry (PhD, Sc D); inorganic chemistry (PhD, Sc D); organic chemistry (PhD, Sc D); physical chemistry (PhD, Sc D). *Faculty:* 29 full-time (7 women). *Students:* 219 full-time (79 women); includes 39 minority (4 African Americans, 27 Asian Americans or Pacific Islanders, 8 Hispanic Americans), 62 international. Average age 26. 548 applicants, 20% accepted, 19 enrolled. In 2009, 43 doctorates awarded. *Degree requirements:* For doctorate, comprehensive exam, thesis/dissertation, 2 terms as a teaching assistant. *Entrance requirements:* For doctorate, GRE General Test. Additional exam requirements/recommendations for international students: Required—IELTS (minimum score 7); Recommended—TOEFL (minimum score 600 paper-based; 250 computer-based). *Application deadline:* For fall admission, 12/15 for domestic and international students. Application fee: $75. Electronic applications accepted. *Financial support:* In 2009–10, 219 students received support, including 57 fellowships with tuition reimbursements available (averaging $34,547 per year), 132 research assistantships with tuition reimbursements available (averaging $29,403 per year), 27 teaching assistantships with tuition reimbursements available (averaging $30,452 per year); Federal Work-Study, institutionally sponsored loans, scholarships/grants, health care benefits, and unspecified assistantships also available. *Faculty research:* Synthetic organic and inorganic chemistry, biomolecular reactions and structure, multidimensional spectroscopy and chemical dynamics, inorganic, organometallic, organic chemical catalysis, materials chemistry including nanoscience and polymers. Total annual research expenditures: $29.1 million. *Unit head:* Prof. Timothy M. Swager, Head, 617-253-1803, Fax: 617-258-7500. *Application contact:* Graduate Administrator, 617-253-1845, Fax: 617-258-0241, E-mail: chemgradeducation@mit.edu.

McMaster University, School of Graduate Studies, Faculty of Science, Department of Chemistry, Hamilton, ON L8S 4M2, Canada. Offers analytical chemistry (M Sc, PhD); chemical physics (M Sc, PhD); chemistry (M Sc, PhD); inorganic chemistry (M Sc, PhD); organic chemistry (M Sc, PhD); physical chemistry (M Sc, PhD); polymer chemistry (M Sc, PhD). Part-time programs available. Terminal master's awarded for partial completion of doctoral program. *Degree requirements:* For master's, thesis; for doctorate, comprehensive exam, thesis/dissertation. *Entrance requirements:* For master's, minimum B+ average. Additional exam requirements/recommendations for international students: Required—TOEFL (minimum score 550 paper-based; 213 computer-based).

Northeastern University, College of Science, Department of Chemistry and Chemical Biology, Boston, MA 02115-5096. Offers analytical chemistry (PhD); chemistry (MS, PhD); inorganic chemistry (PhD); organic chemistry (PhD); physical chemistry (PhD). Part-time and evening/weekend programs available. *Faculty:* 24 full-time (5 women), 7 part-time/adjunct (0 women). *Students:* 86 full-time (48 women), 31 part-time (14 women); includes 9 minority (1 African American, 1 American Indian/Alaska Native, 7 Asian Americans or Pacific Islanders), 36 international. 190 applicants, 22% accepted, 15 enrolled. In 2009, 17 master's, 9 doctorates awarded. Terminal master's awarded for partial completion of doctoral program. *Degree requirements:* For master's, thesis (for some programs); for doctorate, thesis/dissertation, qualifying exam in specialty area. *Entrance requirements:* Additional exam requirements/recommendations for international students: Required—TOEFL. *Application deadline:* For fall admission, 2/1 priority date for domestic and international students. Applications are processed on a rolling basis. Application fee: $50. Electronic applications accepted. *Financial support:* In 2009–10, 41 research assistantships with tuition reimbursements (averaging $18,285 per year), 38 teaching assistantships with tuition reimbursements (averaging $18,285 per year) were awarded; fellowships with tuition reimbursements, career-related internships or fieldwork, Federal Work-Study, scholarships/grants, tuition waivers (partial), and unspecified assistantships also available. Financial award application deadline: 3/1; financial award applicants required to submit FAFSA. *Faculty research:* Bioanalysis, biorganic and medicinal chemistry, biophysical chemistry, nanomaterials, proteonics. *Unit head:* Dr. Robert Hanson, Graduate Coordinator, 617-373-3313, Fax: 617-373-8795, E-mail: chemistry-grad-info@neu.edu. *Application contact:* Jo-Anne Dickinson, Admissions Contact, 617-373-5990, Fax: 617-373-7281, E-mail: gsas@neu.edu.

Old Dominion University, College of Sciences, Program in Chemistry, Norfolk, VA 23529. Offers analytical chemistry (MS); biochemistry (MS); chemistry (PhD); environmental chemistry (MS); organic chemistry (MS); physical chemistry (MS). Part-time and evening/weekend programs available. *Faculty:* 14 full-time (5 women), 2 part-time/adjunct (0 women). *Students:* 30 full-time (19 women), 10 part-time (5 women); includes 3 minority (1 African American, 1 Asian American or Pacific Islander, 1 Hispanic American), 17 international. Average age 29. 35 applicants, 60% accepted, 8 enrolled. In 2009, 1 master's awarded. *Degree requirements:* For master's, comprehensive exam, thesis. *Entrance requirements:* For master's, GRE General Test, minimum GPA of 3.0 in major, 2.5 overall; for doctorate, GRE General Test. Additional exam requirements/recommendations for international students: Required—TOEFL. *Application deadline:* For fall admission, 7/1 for domestic students, 1/15 for international students; for spring admission, 11/1 for domestic students, 8/15 for international students. Applications are processed on a rolling basis. Application fee: $30. Electronic applications accepted. *Expenses:* Tuition, state resident: full-time $8112; part-time $338 per credit. Tuition, nonresident: full-time $20,256; part-time $844 per credit. Required fees: $119 per semester. One-time fee: $50. *Financial support:* In 2009–10, 6 students received support, including fellowships (averaging $18,000 per year), research assistantships with tuition reimbursements available (averaging $21,000 per year), teaching assistantships with tuition reimbursements available (averaging $18,000 per year); career-related internships or fieldwork, scholarships/grants, and unspecified assistantships also available. Financial award application deadline: 2/15; financial award applicants required to submit FAFSA. *Faculty research:* Biogeochemistry, materials chemistry, bioanalytical chemistry, computational chemistry, organic chemistry. Total annual research expenditures: $2.6 million. *Unit head:* Dr. Craig A. Bayse, Graduate Program Director, 757-683-4097, Fax: 757-683-4628, E-mail: chemgpd@odu.edu. *Application contact:* Valerie DeCosta, Grants and Graduate Program Assistant, 757-683-6979, Fax: 757-683-4628, E-mail: chemgpd@odu.edu.

Oregon State University, Graduate School, College of Science, Department of Chemistry, Corvallis, OR 97331. Offers analytical chemistry (MS, PhD); chemistry (MA, MAIS); inorganic chemistry (MS, PhD); nuclear and radiation chemistry (MS, PhD); organic chemistry (MS, PhD); physical chemistry (MS, PhD). Part-time programs available. *Faculty:* 24 full-time (3 women), 1 part-time/adjunct (0 women). *Students:* 78 full-time (27 women), 1 part-time (0 women); includes 3 minority (1 African American, 1 Asian American or Pacific Islander, 1 Hispanic American), 50 international. Average age 27. In 2009, 6 master's, 7 doctorates awarded. Terminal master's awarded for partial completion of doctoral program. *Degree requirements:* For master's, one foreign language, thesis; for doctorate, one foreign language, thesis/dissertation. *Entrance requirements:* For master's and doctorate, minimum GPA of 3.0 in last 90 hours of course work. Additional exam requirements/recommendations for international students: Required—TOEFL. *Application deadline:* For fall admission, 3/1 priority date for domestic students. Applications are processed on a rolling basis. Application fee: $50. *Expenses:* Tuition, state resident: full-time $9774; part-time $362 per credit. Tuition, nonresident: full-time $15,849; part-time $587 per credit. Required fees: $1639. Full-time tuition and fees vary according to course load and program. *Financial support:* Fellowships, research assistantships, teaching assistantships, institutionally sponsored loans available. Support available to part-time students. Financial award application deadline: 2/1. *Faculty research:* Solid state chemistry, enzyme reaction mechanisms, structure and dynamics of gas molecules, chemiluminescence, nonlinear optical spectroscopy. *Unit head:* Dr. Kevin P. Gable, Chair, 541-737-6744, Fax: 541-737-2062, E-mail: gablek@chem.orst.edu. *Application contact:* Dr. Kevin P. Gable, Chair, 541-737-6744, Fax: 541-737-2062, E-mail: gablek@chem.orst.edu.

Purdue University, Graduate School, College of Science, Department of Chemistry, West Lafayette, IN 47907. Offers analytical chemistry (MS, PhD); biochemistry (MS, PhD); chemical education (MS, PhD); inorganic chemistry (MS, PhD); organic chemistry (MS, PhD); physical chemistry (MS, PhD). Terminal master's awarded for partial completion of doctoral program. *Degree requirements:* For master's, thesis; for doctorate, thesis/dissertation. *Entrance requirements:* Additional exam requirements/recommendations for international students: Required—TOEFL. Electronic applications accepted.

Rensselaer Polytechnic Institute, Graduate School, School of Science, Department of Chemistry and Chemical Biology, Troy, NY 12180-3590. Offers analytical chemistry (MS, PhD); biochemistry (MS, PhD); inorganic chemistry (MS, PhD); organic chemistry (MS, PhD); physical chemistry (MS, PhD); polymer chemistry (MS, PhD). Part-time and evening/weekend programs available. *Faculty:* 16 full-time (2 women). *Students:* 68 full-time (31 women); includes 1 African American, 6 Asian Americans or Pacific Islanders, 1 Hispanic American, 31 international. Average age 24. 85 applicants, 19% accepted, 5 enrolled. In 2009, 5 master's, 6 doctorates awarded. Terminal master's awarded for partial completion of doctoral program. *Degree requirements:* For master's, thesis (for some programs); for doctorate, comprehensive exam, thesis/dissertation. *Entrance requirements:* For master's, GRE General Test, GRE Subject Test (strongly recommended); for doctorate, GRE General Test, GRE Subject Test (chemistry or biochemistry strongly recommended). Additional exam requirements/recommendations for international students: Required—TOEFL (minimum score 600 paper-based). *Application deadline:* For fall admission, 2/1 priority date for domestic students; for spring admission, 11/15 for domestic students. Applications are processed on a rolling basis. Application fee: $75. Electronic applications accepted. *Expenses:* Tuition: Full-time $38,100. *Financial support:* In 2009–10, 1 fellowship with full tuition reimbursement (averaging $22,500 per year), 18 research assistantships with full tuition reimbursements (averaging $22,500 per year), 24 teaching assistantships with full tuition reimbursements (averaging $22,500 per year) were awarded; institutionally sponsored loans and tuition waivers (full and partial) also available. Financial award application deadline: 2/1. *Faculty research:* Synthetic polymer and biopolymer chemistry, physical chemistry of polymeric systems, bioanalytical chemistry, synthetic and computational drug design, protein folding and protein design. Total annual research expenditures: $1.1 million. *Unit head:* Dr. Curtis M. Breneman, Chair, 518-276-3264, Fax: 518-276-4887, E-mail: brenec@rpi.edu. *Application contact:* Sharon E. Gardner, Graduate Program Administrator, 518-276-2140, Fax: 518-276-4887, E-mail: derris@rpi.edu.

Rice University, Graduate Programs, Wiess School of Natural Sciences, Department of Chemistry, Houston, TX 77251-1892. Offers chemistry (MA); inorganic chemistry (PhD); organic chemistry (PhD); physical chemistry (PhD). Terminal master's awarded for partial completion of doctoral program. *Degree requirements:* For master's, thesis; for doctorate, thesis/dissertation. *Entrance requirements:* For master's and doctorate, GRE General Test, minimum GPA of 3.0. Additional exam requirements/recommendations for international students: Required—TOEFL (minimum score 600 paper-based; 250 computer-based; 90 iBT). Electronic applications accepted. *Faculty research:* Nanoscience, biomaterials, nanobioinformatics, fullerene pharmaceuticals.

Rutgers, The State University of New Jersey, Newark, Graduate School, Program in Chemistry, Newark, NJ 07102. Offers analytical chemistry (MS, PhD); biochemistry (MS, PhD); inorganic chemistry (MS, PhD); organic chemistry (MS, PhD); physical chemistry (MS, PhD). Part-time and evening/weekend programs available. Terminal master's awarded for partial completion of doctoral program. *Degree requirements:* For master's, thesis optional, cumulative exams; for doctorate, thesis/dissertation, exams, research proposal. *Entrance requirements:* For master's and doctorate, GRE General Test, minimum undergraduate B average. Additional exam requirements/recommendations for international students: Required—TOEFL. Electronic applications accepted. *Faculty research:* Medicinal chemistry, natural products, isotope effects, biophysics and biorganic approaches to enzyme mechanisms, organic and organometallic synthesis.

Rutgers, The State University of New Jersey, New Brunswick, Graduate School-New Brunswick, Department of Chemistry and Chemical Biology, Piscataway, NJ 08854-8097. Offers biological chemistry (MS, PhD); inorganic chemistry (MS, PhD); organic chemistry (MS, PhD); physical chemistry (MS, PhD). Part-time and evening/weekend programs available. Terminal master's awarded for partial completion of doctoral program. *Degree requirements:* For master's, thesis or alternative, exam; for doctorate, thesis/dissertation, 1 year residency. *Entrance requirements:* For master's and doctorate, GRE General Test, GRE Subject Test. Additional exam requirements/recommendations for international students: Required—TOEFL. Electronic applications accepted. *Faculty research:* Biophysical organic/bioorganic, inorganic/bioinorganic, theoretical, and solid-state/surface chemistry.

Seton Hall University, College of Arts and Sciences, Department of Chemistry and Biochemistry, South Orange, NJ 07079-2697. Offers analytical chemistry (MS, PhD); biochemistry (MS, PhD); chemistry (MS); inorganic chemistry (MS, PhD); organic chemistry (MS, PhD); physical chemistry (MS, PhD). Part-time and evening/weekend programs available. *Faculty:* 10 full-time (1 woman). *Students:* 24 full-time (14 women), 47 part-time (15 women); includes 22 minority (10 African Americans, 8 Asian Americans or Pacific Islanders, 4 Hispanic Americans), 11 international. Average age 33. 31 applicants, 68% accepted, 10 enrolled. In 2009, 7 master's, 4 doctorates awarded. Terminal master's awarded for partial completion of doctoral program. *Degree requirements:* For master's, thesis optional; for doctorate, comprehensive exam, thesis/dissertation. *Entrance requirements:* Additional exam requirements/recommendations for international students: Required—TOEFL. *Application deadline:* For fall admission, 7/1 priority date for domestic and international students; for spring admission, 11/1 priority date for domestic and international students. Applications are processed on a rolling basis. Application fee: $50. Electronic applications accepted. *Financial support:* Research assistantships, teaching assistantships with full tuition reimbursements, Federal Work-Study and unspecified assistantships available. Financial award applicants required to submit FAFSA. *Faculty research:* DNA metal reactions; chromatography; bioinorganic, biophysical, organometallic, polymer chemistry; heterogeneous catalyst; synthetic organic and carbohydrate chemistry. *Unit head:* Dr. Nicholas Snow, Chair, 973-761-9414, Fax: 973-761-9772, E-mail: snownich@shu.edu. *Application contact:* Dr. Stephen Kelty, Director of Graduate Studies, 973-761-9129, Fax: 973-761-9772, E-mail: keltyste@shu.edu.

Southern University and Agricultural and Mechanical College, Graduate School, College of Sciences, Department of Chemistry, Baton Rouge, LA 70813. Offers analytical chemistry (MS); biochemistry (MS); environmental sciences (MS); inorganic chemistry (MS); organic chemistry (MS); physical chemistry (MS). *Degree requirements:* For master's, thesis. *Entrance requirements:* For master's, GMAT or GRE General Test. Additional exam requirements/recommendations for international students: Required—TOEFL (minimum score 525 paper-based; 193 computer-based). *Faculty research:* Synthesis of macrocyclic ligands, latex accelerators, anticancer drugs, biosensors, absorption isotheums, isolation of specific enzymes from plants.

State University of New York at Binghamton, Graduate School, School of Arts and Sciences, Department of Chemistry, Binghamton, NY 13902-6000. Offers analytical chemistry (PhD); chemistry (MA, MS); inorganic chemistry (PhD); organic chemistry (PhD); physical chemistry (PhD). Part-time programs available. *Faculty:* 14 full-time (3 women), 2 part-time/adjunct (0 women). *Students:* 35 full-time (13 women), 22 part-time (10 women); includes 8 minority (3 African Americans, 4 Asian Americans or Pacific Islanders, 1 Hispanic American), 32 international. Average age 29. 40 applicants, 30% accepted, 6 enrolled. In 2009, 6 master's, 5 doctorates awarded. Terminal master's awarded for partial completion of doctoral program. *Degree requirements:* For master's, thesis or alternative, oral exam, seminar presentation; for doctorate, thesis/dissertation, cumulative exams. *Entrance requirements:* For master's and doctorate, GRE General Test, GRE Subject Test. Additional exam requirements/recommendations for international students: Required—TOEFL (minimum score 550 paper-based; 213 computer-based; 80 iBT). *Application deadline:* For fall admission, 1/15 priority date for domestic and international students; for spring admission, 10/15 priority date for domestic and international students. Applications are processed on a rolling basis. Application fee: $60. Electronic applications accepted. *Financial support:* In 2009–10, 55 students received support, including 4 fellowships with full tuition reimbursements available (averaging $18,000 per year), 8 research assistantships with full tuition reimbursements available (averaging $18,000 per year), 34 teaching assistantships with full tuition reimbursements available (averaging $18,000 per year); career-related internships or fieldwork, Federal Work-Study, institutionally sponsored loans, scholarships/grants, health care benefits, tuition waivers (full), and unspecified assistantships also available. Financial award application deadline: 2/15; financial award applicants required to submit FAFSA. *Unit head:* Dr. Wayne E. Jones, Chairperson, 607-777-2421, E-mail: wjones@binghamton.edu. *Application contact:* Victoria Williams, Recruiting and Admissions Coordinator, 607-777-2151, Fax: 607-777-2501, E-mail: vwilliam@binghamton.edu.

State University of New York College of Environmental Science and Forestry, Department of Chemistry, Syracuse, NY 13210-2779. Offers biochemistry (MPS, MS, PhD); environmental and forest chemistry (MPS, MS, PhD); organic chemistry (MPS); organic chemistry of natural products (MS, PhD); polymer chemistry (MPS, MS, PhD). *Faculty:* 15 full-time (1 woman). *Students:* 40 full-time (23 women), 12 international. Average age 28. 35 applicants, 46% accepted, 5 enrolled. In 2009, 1 master's, 8 doctorates awarded. *Degree requirements:* For master's, thesis; for doctorate, comprehensive exam, thesis/dissertation. *Entrance requirements:* For master's and doctorate, GRE General Test, GRE Subject Test, minimum GPA of 3.0. Additional exam requirements/recommendations for international students: Required—TOEFL (minimum score 550 paper-based; 213 computer-based; 80 iBT), IELTS (minimum score 6). *Application deadline:* For fall admission, 2/1 priority date for domestic and international students; for spring admission, 11/1 priority date for domestic and international students. Applications are processed on a rolling basis. Application fee: $60. Electronic applications accepted. *Financial support:* In 2009–10, 32 students received support, including 2 fellowships with full tuition reimbursements available (averaging $17,500 per year), 7 research assistantships with full tuition reimbursements available (averaging $17,500 per year), 23 teaching assistantships with full tuition reimbursements available (averaging $17,500 per year); Federal Work-Study, institutionally sponsored loans, scholarships/grants, health care benefits, and unspecified assistantships also available. Financial award application deadline: 6/30; financial award applicants required to submit FAFSA. *Faculty research:* Polymer chemistry, biochemistry. Total annual research expenditures: $1.8 million. *Unit head:* Dr. Arthur J. Stipanovic, Chair, 315-470-6855, Fax: 315-470-6856, E-mail: astipano@esf.edu. *Application contact:* Scott S. Shannon, Dean, Instruction and Graduate Studies, 315-470-6599, Fax: 315-470-6978, E-mail: esfgrad@esf.edu.

Stevens Institute of Technology, Graduate School, Charles V. Schaefer Jr. School of Engineering, Department of Chemistry, Chemical Biology and Biomedical Engineering, Hoboken, NJ 07030. Offers analytical chemistry (PhD, Certificate); bioinformatics (PhD, Certificate); biomedical chemistry (Certificate); biomedical engineering (M Eng, Certificate); chemical biology (MS, PhD, Certificate); chemical physiology (Certificate); chemistry (MS, PhD); organic chemistry (PhD); physical chemistry (PhD); polymer chemistry (PhD, Certificate). Part-time and evening/weekend programs available. Postbaccalaureate distance learning degree programs offered (no on-campus study). Terminal master's awarded for partial completion of doctoral program. *Degree requirements:* For master's, thesis or alternative; for doctorate, one foreign language, thesis/dissertation; for Certificate, project or thesis. *Entrance requirements:* Additional exam requirements/recommendations for international students: Required—TOEFL. Electronic applications accepted. *Expenses:* Tuition: Full-time $9900; part-time $1100 per credit. Required fees: $286 per semester. *Faculty research:* Biochemical reaction engineering, polymerization engineering, reactor design, biochemical process control and synthesis.

Tufts University, Graduate School of Arts and Sciences, Department of Chemistry, Medford, MA 02155. Offers analytical chemistry (MS, PhD); bioorganic chemistry (MS, PhD); environmental chemistry (MS, PhD); inorganic chemistry (MS, PhD); organic chemistry (MS, PhD); physical chemistry (MS, PhD). *Students:* 61 full-time (29 women); includes 7 minority (1 African American, 1 American Indian/Alaska Native, 4 Asian Americans or Pacific Islanders, 1 Hispanic American), 18 international. 90 applicants, 50% accepted, 14 enrolled. In 2009, 2 master's, 7 doctorates awarded. Terminal master's awarded for partial completion of doctoral program. *Degree requirements:* For master's, thesis optional; for doctorate, thesis/dissertation. *Entrance requirements:* For master's and doctorate, GRE General Test, GRE Subject Test. Additional exam requirements/recommendations for international students: Required—TOEFL (minimum score 600 paper-based; 250 computer-based; 80 iBT). *Application deadline:* For fall admission, 1/15 for domestic students, 12/30 for international students; for spring admission, 10/15 for domestic students, 9/15 for international students. Applications are processed on a rolling basis. Application fee: $75. Electronic applications accepted. *Expenses:* Tuition: Full-time $38,096; part-time $3962 per credit. Required fees: $686; $40 per year. Tuition and fees vary according to course level, course load, degree level, program and student level. *Financial support:* Fellowships, research assistantships with full tuition reimbursements, teaching assistantships with full tuition reimbursements, Federal Work-Study, scholarships/grants, tuition waivers (partial), and unspecified assistantships available. Financial award application deadline: 1/15; financial award applicants required to submit FAFSA. *Unit head:* Arthur Utz, Chair, 617-627-3441. *Application contact:* Samuel Kounaves, Information Contact, 617-627-3441, Fax: 617-627-3443.

University of Calgary, Faculty of Graduate Studies, Faculty of Science, Department of Chemistry, Calgary, AB T2N 1N4, Canada. Offers analytical chemistry (M Sc, PhD); applied chemistry (M Sc, PhD); inorganic chemistry (M Sc, PhD); organic chemistry (M Sc, PhD); physical chemistry (M Sc, PhD); polymer chemistry (M Sc, PhD); theoretical chemistry (M Sc, PhD). *Degree requirements:* For master's, thesis; for doctorate, thesis/dissertation, candidacy exam. *Entrance requirements:* For master's, minimum GPA of 3.0; for doctorate, honors B Sc degree with minimum GPA of 3.7 or M Sc with minimum GPA of 3.3. Additional exam requirements/recommendations for international students: Required—TOEFL (minimum score 580 paper-based; 237 computer-based). Electronic applications accepted. *Faculty research:* Chemical analysis, chemical dynamics, synthesis theory.

University of Cincinnati, Graduate School, McMicken College of Arts and Sciences, Department of Chemistry, Cincinnati, OH 45221. Offers analytical chemistry (MS, PhD); biochemistry (MS, PhD); inorganic chemistry (MS, PhD); organic chemistry (MS, PhD); physical chemistry (MS, PhD); polymer chemistry (MS, PhD); sensors (PhD). Part-time and evening/weekend programs available. Terminal master's awarded for partial completion of doctoral program. *Degree requirements:* For master's, thesis optional; for doctorate, comprehensive exam, thesis/dissertation. *Entrance requirements:* For master's and doctorate, GRE General Test. Additional exam requirements/recommendations for international students: Required—TOEFL (minimum score 580 paper-based; 237 computer-based). Electronic applications accepted. *Faculty research:* Biomedical chemistry, laser chemistry, surface science, chemical sensors, synthesis.

University of Georgia, Graduate School, College of Arts and Sciences, Department of Chemistry, Athens, GA 30602. Offers analytical chemistry (MS, PhD); inorganic chemistry (MS, PhD); organic chemistry (MS, PhD); physical chemistry (MS, PhD). *Faculty:* 25 full-time (1 woman). *Students:* 147 full-time (53 women), 2 part-time (1 woman); includes 14 minority (6 African Americans, 7 Asian Americans or Pacific Islanders, 1 Hispanic American), 61 international. 136 applicants, 55% accepted, 27 enrolled. In 2009, 3 master's, 23 doctorates awarded. Terminal master's awarded for partial completion of doctoral program. *Degree requirements:* For master's, thesis; for doctorate, one foreign language, thesis/dissertation. *Entrance requirements:* For master's and doctorate, GRE General Test. Additional exam requirements/recommendations for international students: Required—TOEFL (minimum score 213 computer-based). *Application deadline:* For fall admission, 7/1 priority date for domestic students; for spring admission, 11/15 for domestic students. Application fee: $50. Electronic applications accepted. *Expenses:* Tuition, state resident: full-time $6000; part-time $250 per credit hour. Tuition, nonresident: full-time $20,904; part-time $871 per credit hour. Required fees: $730 per semester. *Financial support:* Fellowships, research assistantships, teaching assistantships, unspecified assistantships also available. *Unit head:* Dr. John L. Stickney, Head, 706-542-2726, Fax: 706-542-9454, E-mail: stickney@chem.uga.edu. *Application contact:* Dr. George F. Majetich, Graduate Coordinator, 706-542-1966, Fax: 706-542-9454, E-mail: majetich@chem.uga.edu.

University of Louisville, Graduate School, College of Arts and Sciences, Department of Chemistry, Louisville, KY 40292-0001. Offers analytical chemistry (MS, PhD); biochemistry (MS, PhD); chemical physics (PhD); inorganic chemistry (MS, PhD); organic chemistry (MS, PhD); physical chemistry (MS, PhD). *Students:* 57 full-time (27 women), 4 part-time (1 woman); includes 2 minority (1 African American, 1 Asian American or Pacific Islander), 43 international. Average age 29. 62 applicants, 31% accepted, 13 enrolled. In 2009, 6 master's, 7 doctorates awarded. *Median time to degree:* Of those who began their doctoral program in fall 2001, 0% received their degree in 8 years or less. *Degree requirements:* For master's, thesis; for doctorate, comprehensive exam, thesis/dissertation. *Entrance requirements:* For master's and doctorate, GRE General Test. Additional exam requirements/recommendations for international students: Required—TOEFL. *Application deadline:* Applications are processed on a rolling basis. Application fee: $50. *Financial support:* Fellowships, research assistantships, teaching assistantships available. *Unit head:* Dr. George R. Pack, Chair, 502-852-6798, Fax: 502-852-8149, E-mail: george.pack@louisville.edu. *Application contact:* Libby Leggett, Director, Graduate Admissions, 502-852-3101, Fax: 502-852-6536, E-mail: gradadm@louisville.edu.

Organic Chemistry

University of Maryland, College Park, Academic Affairs, College of Chemical and Life Sciences, Department of Chemistry and Biochemistry, Chemistry Program, College Park, MD 20742. Offers analytical chemistry (MS, PhD); inorganic chemistry (MS, PhD); organic chemistry (MS, PhD); physical chemistry (MS, PhD). Part-time and evening/weekend programs available. *Students:* 129 full-time (69 women), 5 part-time (3 women); includes 18 minority (13 African Americans, 3 Asian Americans or Pacific Islanders, 2 Hispanic Americans), 70 international. 329 applicants, 22% accepted, 36 enrolled. In 2009, 6 master's, 18 doctorates awarded. Terminal master's awarded for partial completion of doctoral program. *Degree requirements:* For master's, thesis optional; for doctorate, thesis/dissertation, 2 seminar presentations, oral exam. *Entrance requirements:* For master's and doctorate, GRE General Test, GRE Subject Test (recommended), minimum GPA of 3.0, 3 letters of recommendation. Additional exam requirements/recommendations for international students: Required—TOEFL. *Application deadline:* For fall admission, 2/1 for domestic and international students. Applications are processed on a rolling basis. Application fee: $60. Electronic applications accepted. *Expenses:* Tuition, area resident: Part-time $471 per credit hour. Tuition, state resident: part-time $471 per credit hour. Tuition, nonresident: part-time $1016 per credit hour. Required fees: $337.04 per term. *Financial support:* In 2009–10, 7 fellowships with full tuition reimbursements (averaging $27,067 per year), 51 research assistantships (averaging $19,639 per year), 66 teaching assistantships with partial tuition reimbursements (averaging $19,260 per year) were awarded. Financial award applicants required to submit FAFSA. *Faculty research:* Environmental chemistry, nuclear chemistry, lunar and environmental analysis, x-ray crystallography. *Unit head:* Dr. Michael Doyle, Chairperson, 301-405-1795, Fax: 301-314-2779, E-mail: mdoyle3@umd.edu. *Application contact:* Dean of Graduate School, 301-405-0358, Fax: 301-314-9305.

University of Massachusetts Lowell, College of Arts and Sciences, Department of Chemistry, Lowell, MA 01854-2881. Offers analytical chemistry (PhD); biochemistry (PhD); chemistry (MS, PhD); environmental studies (PhD); green chemistry (PhD); inorganic chemistry (PhD); organic chemistry (PhD); polymer science (MS). Terminal master's awarded for partial completion of doctoral program. *Degree requirements:* For master's, thesis; for doctorate, 2 foreign languages, thesis/dissertation. *Entrance requirements:* For master's and doctorate, GRE General Test. Electronic applications accepted.

University of Memphis, Graduate School, College of Arts and Sciences, Department of Chemistry, Memphis, TN 38152. Offers analytical chemistry (PhD); analytical chemsitry (MS); computational chemistry (MS, PhD); inorganic chemistry (MS, PhD); organic chemistry (MS, PhD); physical chemistry (MS, PhD). Part-time programs available. *Faculty:* 6 full-time (1 woman). *Students:* 39 full-time (17 women), 7 part-time (4 women); includes 8 minority (6 African Americans, 1 Asian American or Pacific Islander, 1 Hispanic American), 6 international. Average age 28. 23 applicants, 70% accepted, 14 enrolled. In 2009, 3 master's, 5 doctorates awarded. Terminal master's awarded for partial completion of doctoral program. *Degree requirements:* For master's, comprehensive exam, thesis or alternative; for doctorate, comprehensive exam, thesis/dissertation. *Entrance requirements:* For master's and doctorate, GRE General Test, admission to Graduate School plus 32 undergraduate hours in chemistry. Additional exam requirements/recommendations for international students: Required—TOEFL. *Application deadline:* For fall admission, 7/1 for domestic students, 5/1 for international students; for winter admission, 9/15 for international students; for spring admission, 12/1 for domestic students. Applications are processed on a rolling basis. Application fee: $35 ($60 for international students). Electronic applications accepted. *Expenses:* Tuition, state resident: full-time $6246; part-time $347 per credit hour. Tuition, nonresident: full-time $15,894; part-time $883 per credit hour. Required fees: $1160. Full-time tuition and fees vary according to course load, degree level and program. *Financial support:* In 2009–10, 12 students received support; research assistantships with full tuition reimbursements available, teaching assistantships with full tuition reimbursements available, Federal Work-Study, scholarships/grants, and unspecified assistantships available. Financial award application deadline: 2/15; financial award applicants required to submit FAFSA. *Faculty research:* Computational chemistry, materials chemistry, organic/polymer synthesis, drug design/delivery, water chemistry. *Unit head:* Dr. Abby L. Parrill, Professor and Chair, 901-678-2638, Fax: 901-678-3447, E-mail: aparrill@memphis.edu. *Application contact:* Dr. Gary Emmert, Associate Professor and Graduate Coordinator, 901-678-2636, Fax: 901-678-3447, E-mail: gemmert@memphis.edu.

University of Miami, Graduate School, College of Arts and Sciences, Department of Chemistry, Coral Gables, FL 33124. Offers chemistry (MS); inorganic chemistry (PhD); organic chemistry (PhD); physical chemistry (PhD). Terminal master's awarded for partial completion of doctoral program. *Degree requirements:* For master's, comprehensive exam; for doctorate, comprehensive exam, thesis/dissertation. *Entrance requirements:* For master's and doctorate, GRE General Test. Additional exam requirements/recommendations for international students: Required—TOEFL (minimum score 550 paper-based; 213 computer-based). Electronic applications accepted. *Faculty research:* Supramolecular chemistry, electrochemistry, surface chemistry, catalysis, organometalic.

University of Michigan, Horace H. Rackham School of Graduate Studies, College of Literature, Science, and the Arts, Department of Chemistry, Ann Arbor, MI 48109-1055. Offers analytical chemistry (PhD); chemical biology (PhD); inorganic chemistry (PhD); material chemistry (PhD); organic chemistry (PhD); physical chemistry (PhD). *Faculty:* 42 full-time (10 women). *Students:* 192 full-time (105 women); includes 74 minority (4 African Americans, 64 Asian Americans or Pacific Islanders, 6 Hispanic Americans), 54 international. Average age 26. 558 applicants, 36% accepted, 56 enrolled. In 2009, 28 doctorates awarded. *Degree requirements:* For doctorate, thesis/dissertation, oral defense of dissertation, organic cumulative proficiency exams. *Entrance requirements:* For doctorate, GRE General Test, GRE Subject Test (recommended), 3 letters of recommendation. Additional exam requirements/recommendations for international students: Required—TOEFL (minimum score 560 paper-based; 220 computer-based; 84 iBT). *Application deadline:* For fall admission, 1/15 for domestic students, 12/15 for international students. Applications are processed on a rolling basis. Application fee: $0 ($75 for international students). Electronic applications accepted. *Expenses:* Tuition, state resident: full-time $17,286; part-time $1099 per credit hour. Tuition, nonresident: full-time $34,944; part-time $2080 per credit hour. Required fees: $95 per semester. Tuition and fees vary according to course load, degree level and program. *Financial support:* In 2009–10, 192 students received support, including 20 fellowships with full tuition reimbursements available (averaging $25,000 per year), 75 research assistantships with full tuition reimbursements available (averaging $25,000 per year), 97 teaching assistantships with full tuition reimbursements available (averaging $25,000 per year); career-related internships or fieldwork, scholarships/grants, traineeships, health care benefits, and unspecified assistantships also available. Financial award applicants required to submit FAFSA. *Faculty research:* Biological catalysis, protein engineering, chemical sensors, de novo metalloprotein design, supramolecular architecture. Total annual research expenditures: $15.3 million. *Unit head:* Dr. Carol A. Fierke, Chair, 734-763-9681, Fax: 734-647-4847. *Application contact:* Anna Stryker, Graduate Program Coordinator, 734-764-7278, Fax: 734-647-4865, E-mail: chemadmissions@umich.edu.

University of Missouri, Graduate School, College of Arts and Sciences, Department of Chemistry, Columbia, MO 65211. Offers analytical chemistry (MS, PhD); inorganic chemistry (MS, PhD); organic chemistry (MS, PhD); physical chemistry (MS, PhD). *Faculty:* 30 full-time (6 women), 2 part-time/adjunct (0 women). *Students:* 60 full-time (22 women), 43 part-time (16 women); includes 7 minority (3 African Americans, 1 American Indian/Alaska Native, 3 Asian Americans or Pacific Islanders), 53 international. Average age 27. 93 applicants, 32% accepted, 27 enrolled. In 2009, 4 doctorates awarded. *Degree requirements:* For master's, thesis; for doctorate, one foreign language, comprehensive exam, thesis/dissertation. *Entrance requirements:* For master's, GRE General Test, minimum GPA of 3.0; for doctorate, GRE General Test; V=450, Q=600, A=3.0-4.0, minimum GPA of 3.0. Additional exam requirements/recommendations for international students: Required—TOEFL (minimum score 600 paper-based; 250 computer-based; 100 iBT). *Application deadline:* For fall admission, 4/1 priority date for domestic students; for winter admission, 10/15 for domestic students. Applications are processed on a rolling basis. Application fee: $45 ($60 for international students). *Financial support:* In 2009–10, 0 fellowships with full tuition reimbursements, 15 research assistantships with full tuition reimbursements, 78 teaching assistantships with full tuition reimbursements were awarded; institutionally sponsored loans, traineeships, health care benefits, and unspecified assistantships also available. *Unit head:* Dr. Jerry Atwood, Department Chair, 573-882-8374, E-mail: atwoodj@missouri.edu. *Application contact:* Jerry Brightwell, Administrative Assistant, 573-884-6832, E-mail: brightwellj@missouri.edu.

University of Missouri–Kansas City, College of Arts and Sciences, Department of Chemistry, Kansas City, MO 64110-2499. Offers analytical chemistry (MS, PhD); inorganic chemistry (MS, PhD); organic chemistry (MS, PhD); physical chemistry (MS, PhD); polymer chemistry (MS, PhD). PhD (interdisciplinary) offered through the School of Graduate Studies. Part-time and evening/weekend programs available. *Faculty:* 16 full-time (3 women), 1 part-time/adjunct (0 women). *Students:* 7 part-time (4 women), 2 international. Average age 32. 30 applicants, 67% accepted. In 2009, 1 master's awarded. *Degree requirements:* For master's, thesis (for some programs); for doctorate, thesis/dissertation. *Entrance requirements:* For master's, equivalent of American Chemical Society approved bachelor's degree in chemistry; for doctorate, GRE General Test, equivalent of American Chemical Society approved bachelor's degree in chemistry. Additional exam requirements/recommendations for international students: Required—TOEFL (minimum score 550 paper-based; 213 computer-based; 80 iBT), TWE. *Application deadline:* For fall admission, 4/15 for domestic and international students; for spring admission, 10/15 for domestic and international students. Applications are processed on a rolling basis. Application fee: $45 ($50 for international students). Electronic applications accepted. *Expenses:* Tuition, state resident: full-time $5378; part-time $299 per credit hour. Tuition, nonresident: full-time $13,881; part-time $771 per credit hour. Required fees: $641; $71 per credit hour. Tuition and fees vary according to course load and program. *Financial support:* In 2009–10, 8 research assistantships with partial tuition reimbursements (averaging $17,973 per year), 17 teaching assistantships with partial tuition reimbursements (averaging $17,179 per year) were awarded; Federal Work-Study, institutionally sponsored loans, and scholarships/grants also available. Support available to part-time students. Financial award application deadline: 3/1; financial award applicants required to submit FAFSA. *Faculty research:* Molecular spectroscopy, characterization and synthesis of materials and compounds, computational chemistry, natural products, drug delivery systems and anti-tumor agents. Total annual research expenditures: $1 million. *Unit head:* Dr. Kathleen V. Kilway, Chair, 816-235-2289, Fax: 816-235-5502. *Application contact:* Graduate Recruiting Committee, 816-235-2272, Fax: 816-235-5502, E-mail: umkc-chemdept@umkc.edu.

University of Missouri–St. Louis, College of Arts and Sciences, Department of Chemistry and Biochemistry, St. Louis, MO 63121. Offers chemistry (MS, PhD), including biochemistry, inorganic chemistry, organic chemistry, physical chemistry. Part-time and evening/weekend programs available. *Faculty:* 19 full-time (3 women), 6 part-time/adjunct (1 woman). *Students:* 43 full-time (21 women), 19 part-time (8 women); includes 6 minority (4 African Americans, 1 Asian American or Pacific Islander, 1 Hispanic American), 27 international. Average age 29. 81 applicants, 37% accepted, 19 enrolled. In 2009, 9 master's, 6 doctorates awarded. Terminal master's awarded for partial completion of doctoral program. *Degree requirements:* For master's, thesis optional; for doctorate, thesis/dissertation. *Entrance requirements:* For master's, 2 letters of recommendation; for doctorate, GRE General Test, 3 letters of recommendation. Additional exam requirements/recommendations for international students: Required—TOEFL (minimum score 550 paper-based; 213 computer-based). *Application deadline:* For fall admission, 7/1 priority date for domestic and international students; for spring admission, 12/1 priority date for domestic and international students. Applications are processed on a rolling basis. Application fee: $35 ($40 for international students). Electronic applications accepted. *Expenses:* Tuition, state resident: full-time $5377; part-time $297.70 per credit hour. Tuition, nonresident: full-time $13,882; part-time $771.20 per credit hour. Required fees: $220; $12.20 per credit hour. One-time fee: $12. Tuition and fees vary according to course level, campus/location and program. *Financial support:* In 2009–10, 25 research assistantships with full and partial tuition reimbursements (averaging $17,840 per year), 13 teaching assistantships with full and partial tuition reimbursements (averaging $13,300 per year) were awarded; fellowships with full and partial tuition reimbursements also available. *Faculty research:* Metallaborane chemistry, serum transferrin chemistry, natural products chemistry, organic synthesis. *Unit head:* Dr. Cynthia Dupureur, Director of Graduate Studies, 314-516-5311, Fax: 314-516-5342, E-mail: gradchem@umsl.edu. *Application contact:* 314-516-5458, Fax: 314-516-6996, E-mail: gradadm@umsl.edu.

The University of Montana, Graduate School, College of Arts and Sciences, Department of Chemistry, Missoula, MT 59812-0002. Offers chemistry (MS, PhD), including environmental/analytical chemistry, inorganic chemistry, organic chemistry, physical chemistry. Terminal master's awarded for partial completion of doctoral program. *Degree requirements:* For master's, thesis (for some programs); for doctorate, thesis/dissertation. *Entrance requirements:* For master's and doctorate, GRE General Test. Additional exam requirements/recommendations for international students: Required—TOEFL (minimum score 575 paper-based; 230 computer-based). *Faculty research:* Reaction mechanisms and kinetics, inorganic and organic synthesis, analytical chemistry, natural products.

University of Nebraska–Lincoln, Graduate College, College of Arts and Sciences, Department of Chemistry, Lincoln, NE 68588. Offers analytical chemistry (PhD); biochemistry (PhD); chemistry (MS); inorganic chemistry (PhD); materials chemistry (PhD); organic chemistry (PhD); physical chemistry (PhD). *Degree requirements:* For master's, one foreign language, thesis optional, departmental qualifying exam; for doctorate, one foreign language, comprehensive exam, thesis/dissertation, departmental qualifying exams. *Entrance requirements:* For master's and doctorate, GRE. Additional exam requirements/recommendations for international students: Required—TOEFL (minimum score 550 paper-based; 213 computer-based). Electronic applications accepted. *Faculty research:* Bioorganic and bioinorganic chemistry, biophysical and bioanalytical chemistry, structure-function of DNA and proteins, organometallics, mass spectrometry.

University of Notre Dame, Graduate School, College of Science, Department of Chemistry and Biochemistry, Notre Dame, IN 46556. Offers biochemistry (MS, PhD); inorganic chemistry (MS, PhD); organic chemistry (MS, PhD); physical chemistry (MS, PhD). Terminal master's awarded for partial completion of doctoral program. *Degree requirements:* For master's, comprehensive exam, thesis; for doctorate, thesis/dissertation, qualifying exam. *Entrance requirements:* For master's and doctorate, GRE General Test, GRE Subject Test (strongly recommended). Additional exam requirements/recommendations for international students: Required—TOEFL (minimum score 600 paper-based; 250 computer-based; 80 iBT). Electronic applications accepted. *Faculty research:* Reaction design and mechanistic studies; reactive intermediates; synthesis, structure and reactivity of organometallic cluster complexes and biologically active natural products; bioorganic chemistry; enzymology.

University of Regina, Faculty of Graduate Studies and Research, Faculty of Science, Department of Chemistry and Biochemistry, Regina, SK S4S 0A2, Canada. Offers analytical chemistry (M Sc, PhD); biochemistry (M Sc, PhD); inorganic chemistry (M Sc, PhD); organic chemistry (M Sc, PhD); physical chemistry (M Sc, PhD). Part-time programs available. *Faculty:* 11 full-time (2 women), 3 part-time/adjunct (0 women). *Students:* 20 full-time (8 women). 25 applicants, 28% accepted. In 2009, 2 master's awarded. *Degree requirements:* For master's, thesis, departmental qualifying exam; for doctorate, thesis/dissertation, departmental qualifying exam. *Entrance requirements:* For master's and doctorate, GRE. Additional exam requirements/recommendations for international students: Required—TOEFL (minimum score 580 paper-based; 237 computer-based; 80 iBT). *Application deadline:* For fall admission, 1/1 for domestic students; for winter admission, 7/1 for domestic students. Applications are processed on a rolling basis. Application fee: $90 ($100 for international students). *Financial support:* In 2009–10, 5 fellowships (averaging $19,000 per year), 2 research assistantships (averaging $16,910 per year), 4 teaching assistantships (averaging $6,650 per year) were awarded; scholarships/grants also available. Financial award application deadline: 6/15. *Faculty research:* Organic synthesis, organic oxidations, ionic liquids theoretical/computational chemistry, protein biochemistry/biophysics, environmental analytical, photophysical/photochemistry. *Unit head:* Dr. Tanya Dahms, Head, 306-585-4247, E-mail: tanya.dohms@uregina.ca. *Application contact:* Dr. Scott Murphy, Program Coordinator, 306-585-4247, Fax: 306-585-4894, E-mail: scott.murphy@uregina.ca.

University of Southern Mississippi, Graduate School, College of Science and Technology, Department of Chemistry and Biochemistry, Hattiesburg, MS 39406-0001. Offers analytical chemistry (MS, PhD); biochemistry (MS, PhD); inorganic chemistry (MS, PhD); organic chemistry (MS, PhD); physical chemistry (MS, PhD). *Faculty:* 16 full-time (4 women). *Students:* 14 full-time (0 women), 5 part-time (4 women); includes 1 minority (African American), 12 international. Average age 29. 41 applicants, 17% accepted, 6 enrolled. In 2009, 2 master's, 6 doctorates awarded. *Degree requirements:* For master's, comprehensive exam, thesis; for doctorate, comprehensive exam, thesis/dissertation. *Entrance requirements:* For master's, GRE General Test, minimum GPA of 2.75 in last 60 hours; for doctorate, GRE General Test, minimum GPA of 3.5. Additional exam requirements/recommendations for international students: Required—TOEFL. *Application deadline:* For fall admission, 3/1 priority date for domestic students, 3/1 for international students. Applications are processed on a rolling basis. Application fee: $35. *Expenses:* Tuition, state resident: full-time $5096; part-time $284 per hour. Tuition, nonresident: full-time $13,052; part-time $726 per hour. Required fees: $402. Tuition and fees vary according to course level and course load. *Financial support:* In 2009–10, 3 research assistantships with full tuition reimbursements (averaging $17,000 per year), 19 teaching assistantships with full tuition reimbursements (averaging $20,716 per year) were awarded; fellowships, Federal Work-Study and institutionally sponsored loans also available. Support available to part-time students. Financial award application deadline: 3/15; financial award applicants required to submit FAFSA. *Faculty research:* Plant biochemistry, photo chemistry, polymer chemistry, x-ray analysis, enzyme chemistry. *Unit head:* Dr. Robert Bateman, Chair, 601-266-4701, Fax: 601-266-6075. *Application contact:* Dr. Sabine Heinherst, Graduate Coordinator, 601-266-4702, Fax: 601-266-6075.

University of South Florida, Graduate School, College of Arts and Sciences, Department of Chemistry, Tampa, FL 33620-9951. Offers computational chemistry (PhD); analytical chemistry (MS, PhD); biochemistry (MS, PhD); computational chemistry (MS); environmental chemistry (MS, PhD); inorganic chemistry (MS, PhD); organic chemistry (MS); physical chemistry (MS, PhD); polymer chemistry (PhD). Part-time programs available. *Faculty:* 25 full-time (4 women). *Students:* 113 full-time (36 women), 15 part-time (11 women); includes 19 minority (5 African Americans, 6 Asian Americans or Pacific Islanders, 8 Hispanic Americans), 58 international. Average age 32. 112 applicants, 30% accepted, 21 enrolled. In 2009, 8 master's, 11 doctorates awarded. Terminal master's awarded for partial completion of doctoral program. *Degree requirements:* For master's, comprehensive exam, thesis (for some programs); for doctorate, 2 foreign languages, comprehensive exam, thesis/dissertation. *Entrance requirements:* For master's, GRE General Test or GMAT, minimum GPA of 3.0. Additional exam requirements/recommendations for international students: Required—TOEFL (minimum score 550 paper-based; 213 computer-based). *Application deadline:* For fall admission, 2/15 priority date for domestic students, 1/2 priority date for international students; for spring admission, 10/1 priority date for domestic students, 6/1 priority date for international students. Applications are processed on a rolling basis. Application fee: $30. Electronic applications accepted. *Financial support:* In 2009–10, teaching assistantships with tuition reimbursements (averaging $27,522 per year); unspecified assistantships also available. Financial award application deadline: 6/30. *Faculty research:* Synthesis, bio-organic chemistry, bioinorganic chemistry, environmental chemistry, NMR. Total annual research expenditures: $3.2 million. *Unit head:* Dr. Randy Larsen, Chairperson, 813-974-4129, Fax: 813-974-3203, E-mail: rlarsen@cas.usf.edu. *Application contact:* Patricia Muisener, Director, 813-974-1730, Fax: 813-974-3203, E-mail: muisener@cas.usf.edu.

The University of Tennessee, Graduate School, College of Arts and Sciences, Department of Chemistry, Knoxville, TN 37996. Offers analytical chemistry (MS, PhD); chemical physics (PhD); environmental chemistry (MS, PhD); inorganic chemistry (MS, PhD); organic chemistry (MS, PhD); physical chemistry (MS, PhD); polymer chemistry (MS, PhD); theoretical chemistry (PhD). Part-time programs available. Terminal master's awarded for partial completion of doctoral program. *Degree requirements:* For master's, thesis; for doctorate, thesis/dissertation. *Entrance requirements:* For master's and doctorate, GRE General Test, minimum GPA of 2.7. Additional exam requirements/recommendations for international students: Required—TOEFL. Electronic applications accepted. *Expenses:* Tuition, state resident: full-time $6826; part-time $380 per semester hour. Tuition, nonresident: full-time $21,844; part-time $1147 per semester hour. Tuition and fees vary according to program.

The University of Texas at Austin, Graduate School, College of Natural Sciences, Department of Chemistry and Biochemistry, Austin, TX 78712-1111. Offers analytical chemistry (MA, PhD); biochemistry (MA, PhD); inorganic chemistry (MA, PhD); organic chemistry (MA, PhD); physical chemistry (MA, PhD). *Entrance requirements:* For master's and doctorate, GRE General Test.

The University of Toledo, College of Graduate Studies, College of Arts and Sciences, Department of Chemistry, Toledo, OH 43606-3390. Offers analytical chemistry (MS, PhD); biological chemistry (MS, PhD); inorganic chemistry (MS, PhD); organic chemistry (MS, PhD); physical chemistry (MS, PhD). Part-time programs available. *Degree requirements:* For master's, thesis; for doctorate, thesis/dissertation. *Entrance requirements:* For master's and doctorate, GRE General Test, GRE Subject Test. Additional exam requirements/recommendations for international students: Required—TOEFL. Electronic applications accepted. *Faculty research:* Enzymology, materials chemistry, crystallography, theoretical chemistry.

Vanderbilt University, Graduate School, Department of Chemistry, Nashville, TN 37240-1001. Offers analytical chemistry (MAT, MS, PhD); inorganic chemistry (MAT, MS, PhD); organic chemistry (MAT, MS, PhD); physical chemistry (MAT, MS, PhD); theoretical chemistry (MAT, MS, PhD). *Faculty:* 46 full-time (6 women). *Students:* 106 full-time (38 women); includes 10 minority (5 African Americans, 3 Asian Americans or Pacific Islanders, 2 Hispanic Americans), 21 international. Average age 27. 245 applicants, 27% accepted, 21 enrolled. In 2009, 10 master's, 21 doctorates awarded. Terminal master's awarded for partial completion of doctoral program. *Degree requirements:* For master's, thesis; for doctorate, thesis/dissertation, area, qualifying, and final exams. *Entrance requirements:* For master's and doctorate, GRE General Test, GRE Subject Test (recommended). Additional exam requirements/recommendations for international students: Required—TOEFL (minimum score 570 paper-based; 230 computer-based; 88 iBT). *Application deadline:* For fall admission, 1/15 for domestic and international students. Application fee: $0. Electronic applications accepted. *Financial support:* Fellowships with full and partial tuition reimbursements, research assistantships with full tuition reimbursements, teaching assistantships with full tuition reimbursements, Federal Work-Study, institutionally sponsored loans, scholarships/grants, traineeships, and health care benefits available. Financial award application deadline: 1/15; financial award applicants required to submit CSS PROFILE or FAFSA. *Faculty research:* Chemical synthesis; mechanistic, theoretical, bioorganic, analytical, and spectroscopic chemistry. *Unit head:* Mike P. Stone, Chair, 615-322-2861, Fax: 615-343-1234. *Application contact:* Charles M. Lukehart, Director of Graduate Studies, 615-322-2861, Fax: 615-343-1234, E-mail: charles.m.lukehart@vanderbilt.edu.

Virginia Commonwealth University, Graduate School, College of Humanities and Sciences, Department of Chemistry, Richmond, VA 23284-9005. Offers analytical chemistry (MS, PhD); chemical physics (PhD); inorganic chemistry (MS, PhD); organic chemistry (MS, PhD); physical chemistry (MS, PhD). Part-time programs available. Terminal master's awarded for partial completion of doctoral program. *Degree requirements:* For master's, thesis; for doctorate, thesis/dissertation, comprehensive cumulative exams, research proposal. *Entrance requirements:* For master's, GRE General Test, 30 undergraduate credits in chemistry; for doctorate, GRE General Test. *Faculty research:* Physical, organic, inorganic, analytical, and polymer chemistry; chemical physics.

Wake Forest University, Graduate School of Arts and Sciences, Department of Chemistry, Winston-Salem, NC 27109. Offers analytical chemistry (MS, PhD); inorganic chemistry (MS, PhD); organic chemistry (MS, PhD); physical chemistry (MS, PhD). Part-time programs available. *Degree requirements:* For master's, one foreign language, comprehensive exam, thesis; for doctorate, 2 foreign languages, comprehensive exam, thesis/dissertation. *Entrance requirements:* For master's and doctorate, GRE General Test. Additional exam requirements/recommendations for international students: Required—TOEFL (minimum score 213 computer-based). Electronic applications accepted.

Wesleyan University, Graduate Programs, Department of Chemistry, Middletown, CT 06459. Offers biochemistry (MA, PhD); chemical physics (MA, PhD); inorganic chemistry (MA, PhD); organic chemistry (MA, PhD); physical chemistry (MA, PhD); theoretical chemistry (MA, PhD). *Faculty:* 14 full-time (2 women), 2 part-time/adjunct (1 woman). *Students:* 19 full-time (8 women), 2 part-time (0 women), 9 international. Average age 26. 40 applicants, 63% accepted, 4 enrolled. In 2009, 3 master's, 5 doctorates awarded. Terminal master's awarded for partial completion of doctoral program. *Degree requirements:* For master's, thesis, proposal; for doctorate, thesis/dissertation, proposal. *Entrance requirements:* For doctorate, GRE General Test, 3 recommendations. Additional exam requirements/recommendations for international students: Required—TOEFL. *Application deadline:* Applications are processed on a rolling basis. Application fee: $0. Electronic applications accepted. *Financial support:* In 2009–10, 4 research assistantships with full tuition reimbursements, 12 teaching assistantships with full tuition reimbursements were awarded; institutionally sponsored loans also available. Financial award application deadline: 4/15; financial award applicants required to submit FAFSA. *Unit head:* Dr. Joseph Knee, Chair, 860-685-2210. *Application contact:* Cait Zinser, Information Contact, 860-685-2573, Fax: 860-685-2211, E-mail: czinser@wesleyan.edu.

See Close-Up on page 115.

West Virginia University, Eberly College of Arts and Sciences, Department of Chemistry, Morgantown, WV 26506. Offers analytical chemistry (MS, PhD); inorganic chemistry (MS, PhD); organic chemistry (MS, PhD); physical chemistry (MS, PhD); theoretical chemistry (MS, PhD). Part-time programs available. Postbaccalaureate distance learning degree programs offered (no on-campus study). Terminal master's awarded for partial completion of doctoral program. *Degree requirements:* For master's, thesis; for doctorate, thesis/dissertation. *Entrance requirements:* For master's, GRE General Test, GRE Subject Test (recommended), minimum GPA of 2.5; for doctorate, GRE General Test, GRE Subject Test (recommended), minimum GPA of 2.75. Additional exam requirements/recommendations for international students: Required—TOEFL. Electronic applications accepted. *Faculty research:* Analysis of proteins, drug interactions, solids and effluents by advanced separation methods; new synthetic strategies for complex organic molecules; synthesis and structural characterization of metal complexes for polymerization catalysis, nonlinear science, spectroscopy.

Yale University, Graduate School of Arts and Sciences, Department of Chemistry, New Haven, CT 06520. Offers biophysical chemistry (PhD); inorganic chemistry (PhD); organic chemistry (PhD); physical and theoretical chemistry (PhD). *Degree requirements:* For doctorate, thesis/dissertation. *Entrance requirements:* For doctorate, GRE General Test, GRE Subject Test. Additional exam requirements/recommendations for international students: Required—TOEFL.

Youngstown State University, Graduate School, College of Science, Technology, Engineering and Mathematics, Department of Chemistry, Youngstown, OH 44555-0001. Offers analytical chemistry (MS); biochemistry (MS); chemistry education (MS); inorganic chemistry (MS); organic chemistry (MS); physical chemistry (MS). Part-time programs available. *Degree requirements:* For master's, thesis. *Entrance requirements:* For master's, bachelor's degree in chemistry, minimum GPA of 2.7. Additional exam requirements/recommendations for international students: Required—TOEFL. *Faculty research:* Analysis of antioxidants, chromatography, defects and disorder in crystalline oxides, hydrogen bonding, novel organic and organometallic materials.

Physical Chemistry

Auburn University, Graduate School, College of Sciences and Mathematics, Department of Chemistry and Biochemistry, Auburn University, AL 36849. Offers analytical chemistry (MS, PhD); biochemistry (MS, PhD); inorganic chemistry (MS, PhD); organic chemistry (MS, PhD); physical chemistry (MS, PhD). Part-time programs available. *Faculty:* 27 full-time (6 women). *Students:* 39 full-time (20 women), 21 part-time (8 women); includes 6 minority (4 African Americans, 1 Asian American or Pacific Islander, 1 Hispanic American), 41 international. Average age 28. 54 applicants, 11% accepted, 3 enrolled. In 2009, 1 master's, 13 doctorates awarded. *Degree requirements:* For master's, thesis (for some programs); for doctorate, thesis/dissertation, oral and written exams. *Entrance requirements:* For master's and doctorate, GRE General Test. *Application deadline:* For fall admission, 7/7 for domestic students; for spring admission, 11/24 for domestic students. Applications are processed on a rolling basis. Application fee: $50 ($60 for international students). Electronic applications accepted. *Expenses:* Tuition, state resident: full-time $6240. Tuition, nonresident: full-time $18,720. International tuition: $18,938 full-time. Required fees: $492. Tuition and fees vary according to course load, program and reciprocity agreements. *Financial support:* Fellowships, research assistantships, teaching assistantships available. Financial award application deadline: 3/15; financial award applicants required to submit FAFSA. *Unit head:* Dr. J. V. Ortiz, Chair, 334-844-4043, Fax: 334-844-4043. *Application contact:* Dr. George Flowers, Dean of the Graduate School, 334-844-2125.

Boston College, Graduate School of Arts and Sciences, Department of Chemistry, Chestnut Hill, MA 02467-3800. Offers biochemistry (PhD); inorganic chemistry (PhD); organic chemistry (PhD); physical chemistry (PhD); science education (MST). Part-time programs available.

Physical Chemistry

Boston College (continued)

Students: 110 full-time (49 women); includes 8 minority (6 Asian Americans or Pacific Islanders, 2 Hispanic Americans), 49 international. 216 applicants, 34% accepted, 22 enrolled. In 2009, 3 master's, 20 doctorates awarded. *Degree requirements:* For doctorate, thesis/dissertation, qualifying exam. *Entrance requirements:* For doctorate, GRE General Test, GRE Subject Test. Additional exam requirements/recommendations for international students: Required—TOEFL (minimum score 600 paper-based; 250 computer-based; 100 iBT). *Application deadline:* For fall admission, 1/2 for domestic and international students. Application fee: $70. Electronic applications accepted. *Financial support:* In 2009–10, fellowships with full tuition reimbursements (averaging $25,000 per year), research assistantships with full tuition reimbursements (averaging $25,000 per year), teaching assistantships with full tuition reimbursements (averaging $25,000 per year) were awarded; Federal Work-Study also available. Support available to part-time students. Financial award application deadline: 3/1; financial award applicants required to submit FAFSA. *Unit head:* Dr. Amir Hoveyda, Chairperson, 617-552-1735, E-mail: amir.hoveyda@bc.edu. *Application contact:* Dr. Marc Snapper, Graduate Program Director, 617-552-8096, Fax: 617-552-0833, E-mail: marc.snapper@bc.edu.

Brandeis University, Graduate School of Arts and Sciences, Department of Chemistry, Waltham, MA 02454. Offers inorganic chemistry (MS, PhD); organic chemistry (MS, PhD); physical chemistry (MS, PhD). *Faculty:* 14 full-time (3 women), 4 part-time/adjunct (3 women). *Students:* 42 full-time (17 women); includes 2 minority (1 African American, 1 Asian American or Pacific Islander), 28 international. 127 applicants, 16% accepted, 8 enrolled. In 2009, 11 master's, 6 doctorates awarded. Terminal master's awarded for partial completion of doctoral program. *Degree requirements:* For master's, thesis, 1 year of residency; for doctorate, one foreign language, thesis/dissertation, 3 years of residency, 2 seminars, qualifying exams. *Entrance requirements:* For master's and doctorate, GRE General Test, resume, letters of recommendation. Additional exam requirements/recommendations for international students: Required—TOEFL (minimum score 600 paper-based; 250 computer-based; 100 iBT); Recommended—IELTS (minimum score 7). *Application deadline:* For fall admission, 1/15 priority date for domestic students. Applications are processed on a rolling basis. Application fee: $75. Electronic applications accepted. *Financial support:* In 2009–10, 23 fellowships with full tuition reimbursements (averaging $24,500 per year), 14 research assistantships with full tuition reimbursements (averaging $24,500 per year), teaching assistantships with partial tuition reimbursements (averaging $3,200 per year) were awarded; scholarships/grants and health care benefits also available. Financial award application deadline: 4/15; financial award applicants required to submit FAFSA. *Faculty research:* Oscillating chemical reactions, molecular recognition systems, protein crystallography, synthesis of natural product spectroscopy and magnetic resonance. *Unit head:* Dr. Judith Herzfeld, Chair, Graduate Program in Chemistry, 781-736-2540, Fax: 781-736-2516, E-mail: herzfeld@brandeis.edu. *Application contact:* Charlotte Haygazian, Graduate Department Coordinator, 781-736-2500, Fax: 781-736-2516, E-mail: chemadm@brandeis.edu.

California State University, Los Angeles, Graduate Studies, College of Natural and Social Sciences, Department of Chemistry and Biochemistry, Los Angeles, CA 90032-8530. Offers analytical chemistry (MS); biochemistry (MS); chemistry (MS); inorganic chemistry (MS); organic chemistry (MS); physical chemistry (MS). Part-time and evening/weekend programs available. *Faculty:* 1 full-time (0 women), 9 part-time/adjunct (4 women). *Students:* 14 full-time (4 women), 31 part-time (15 women); includes 21 minority (5 African Americans, 9 Asian Americans or Pacific Islanders, 7 Hispanic Americans), 10 international. Average age 30. 23 applicants, 91% accepted, 13 enrolled. In 2009, 11 degrees awarded. *Degree requirements:* For master's, one foreign language, comprehensive exam or thesis. *Entrance requirements:* Additional exam requirements/recommendations for international students: Required—TOEFL. *Application deadline:* For fall admission, 5/1 for domestic and international students. Applications are processed on a rolling basis. Application fee: $55. *Financial support:* Federal Work-Study available. Support available to part-time students. Financial award application deadline: 3/1. *Faculty research:* Intercalation of heavy metal, carborane chemistry, conductive polymers and fabrics, titanium reagents, computer modeling and synthesis. *Unit head:* Dr. Scott Grover, Chair, 323-343-2300, Fax: 323-343-6490, E-mail: sgrover@calstatela.edu. *Application contact:* Dr. Cheryl L. Ney, Associate Vice President for Academic Affairs and Dean of Graduate Studies, 323-343-3820 Ext. 3827, Fax: 323-343-5653, E-mail: cney@cslanet.calstatela.edu.

Cleveland State University, College of Graduate Studies, College of Science, Department of Chemistry, Cleveland, OH 44115. Offers analytical chemistry (MS); clinical chemistry (MS); clinical/bioanalytical chemistry (PhD), including clinical chemistry, molecular medicine; environmental chemistry (MS); inorganic chemistry (MS); organic chemistry (MS); physical chemistry (MS). Part-time and evening/weekend programs available. *Degree requirements:* For master's, thesis (for some programs); for doctorate, thesis/dissertation. *Entrance requirements:* For master's and doctorate, GRE General Test. Additional exam requirements/recommendations for international students: Required—TOEFL (minimum score 525 paper-based; 197 computer-based; 65 iBT). Electronic applications accepted. *Faculty research:* MALDI-TOF based DNA sequencing, development of ionic focusing HPLC, synthetic and structural studies of vanadium.

Cornell University, Graduate School, Graduate Fields of Arts and Sciences, Field of Chemistry and Chemical Biology, Ithaca, NY 14853-0001. Offers analytical chemistry (PhD); bio-organic chemistry (PhD); biophysical chemistry (PhD); chemical biology (PhD); chemical physics (PhD); inorganic chemistry (PhD); materials chemistry (PhD); organic chemistry (PhD); organometallic chemistry (PhD); physical chemistry (PhD); polymer chemistry (PhD); theoretical chemistry (PhD). *Faculty:* 48 full-time (3 women). *Students:* 162 full-time (67 women); includes 15 minority (1 African American, 9 Asian Americans or Pacific Islanders, 5 Hispanic Americans), 53 international. Average age 26. 359 applicants, 19% accepted, 39 enrolled. In 2009, 31 doctorates awarded. *Degree requirements:* For doctorate, comprehensive exam, thesis/dissertation. *Entrance requirements:* For doctorate, GRE General Test, GRE Subject Test (chemistry), 3 letters of recommendation. Additional exam requirements/recommendations for international students: Required—TOEFL (minimum score 600 paper-based; 250 computer-based; 77 iBT). *Application deadline:* For fall admission, 1/10 for domestic students. Application fee: $70. Electronic applications accepted. *Expenses:* Tuition: Full-time $29,500. Required fees: $70. Full-time tuition and fees vary according to degree level, program and student level. *Financial support:* In 2009–10, 1 fellowship with full tuition reimbursement, 7 research assistantships with full tuition reimbursements, 29 teaching assistantships with full tuition reimbursements were awarded; institutionally sponsored loans, scholarships/grants, health care benefits, tuition waivers (full and partial), and unspecified assistantships also available. Financial award applicants required to submit FAFSA. *Faculty research:* Analytical, organic, inorganic, physical, materials, chemical biology. *Unit head:* Director of Graduate Studies, 607-255-4139, Fax: 607-255-4137. *Application contact:* Graduate Field Assistant, 607-255-4139, Fax: 607-255-4137, E-mail: chemgrad@cornell.edu.

Florida State University, The Graduate School, College of Arts and Sciences, Department of Chemistry and Biochemistry, Tallahassee, FL 32306-4390. Offers analytical chemistry (MS, PhD); biochemistry (MS, PhD); inorganic chemistry (MS, PhD); materials chemistry (MS, PhD); organic chemistry (MS, PhD); physical chemistry (MS, PhD). *Faculty:* 40 full-time (6 women), 3 part-time/adjunct (0 women). *Students:* 150 full-time (47 women), 9 part-time (6 women); includes 16 minority (5 African Americans, 1 American Indian/Alaska Native, 5 Asian Americans or Pacific Islanders, 5 Hispanic Americans), 68 international. Average age 25. 286 applicants, 21% accepted, 28 enrolled. In 2009, 7 master's, 15 doctorates awarded. Terminal master's awarded for partial completion of doctoral program. *Degree requirements:* For master's, comprehensive exam (for some programs), thesis (for some programs), cumulative and diagnostic exams; for doctorate, comprehensive exam (for some programs), thesis/dissertation, cumulative and diagnostic exams. *Entrance requirements:* For master's and doctorate, GRE General Test, minimum B average in undergraduate course work. Additional exam requirements/recommendations for international students: Required—TOEFL (minimum score 550 paper-based; 213 computer-based; 80 iBT). *Application deadline:* For fall admission, 12/15 for domestic and international students; for spring admission, 9/15 for domestic and international students. Applications are processed on a rolling basis. Application fee: $30. Electronic applications accepted. *Expenses:* Tuition, state resident: full-time $7413.36. Tuition, nonresident: full-time $22,567. *Financial support:* In 2009–10, 150 students received support, including fellowships with full tuition reimbursements available (averaging $19,000 per year), 52 research assistantships with full tuition reimbursements available (averaging $19,000 per year), 100 teaching assistantships with full tuition reimbursements available (averaging $19,000 per year); career-related internships or fieldwork, Federal Work-Study, institutionally sponsored loans, and traineeships also available. Financial award application deadline: 12/15; financial award applicants required to submit FAFSA. *Faculty research:* Materials synthesis including polymers, natural products; catalysis, NMR; mass spectrometry; optical spectroscopy, scattering techniques, computational chemistry, separation technology; nanostructured materials including metallic, semiconducting and magnetic nanocrystals; nanoscience interfaced with biology; supramolecular materials for solar energy conversion. Total annual research expenditures: $5.5 million. *Unit head:* Dr. Joseph Schlenoff, Chairman, 850-644-5195, Fax: 850-644-8281, E-mail: schlen@chem.fsu.edu. *Application contact:* Dr. Tyler McQuade, Chair, Graduate Admissions Committee, 888-525-9286, Fax: 850-644-0465, E-mail: gradinfo@chem.fsu.edu.

Georgetown University, Graduate School of Arts and Sciences, Department of Chemistry, Washington, DC 20057. Offers analytical chemistry (PhD); biochemistry (PhD); computational chemistry (PhD); inorganic chemistry (PhD); materials chemistry (PhD); organic chemistry (PhD); physical chemistry (PhD); theoretical chemistry (PhD). Terminal master's awarded for partial completion of doctoral program. *Degree requirements:* For doctorate, comprehensive exam, thesis/dissertation. *Entrance requirements:* For doctorate, GRE General Test. Additional exam requirements/recommendations for international students: Required—TOEFL.

The George Washington University, Columbian College of Arts and Sciences, Department of Chemistry, Washington, DC 20052. Offers analytical chemistry (MS, PhD); inorganic chemistry (MS, PhD); materials science (MS, PhD); organic chemistry (MS, PhD); physical chemistry (MS, PhD). Part-time and evening/weekend programs available. *Faculty:* 15 full-time (4 women), 7 part-time/adjunct (3 women). *Students:* 19 full-time (12 women), 12 part-time (7 women); includes 4 minority (2 Asian Americans or Pacific Islanders, 2 Hispanic Americans), 12 international. Average age 28. 45 applicants, 49% accepted, 6 enrolled. In 2009, 2 master's, 4 doctorates awarded. Terminal master's awarded for partial completion of doctoral program. *Degree requirements:* For master's, comprehensive exam, thesis or alternative; for doctorate, thesis/dissertation, general exam. *Entrance requirements:* For master's and doctorate, GRE General Test, interview, minimum GPA of 3.0. Additional exam requirements/recommendations for international students: Required—TOEFL (minimum score 550 paper-based; 213 computer-based; 80 iBT). *Application deadline:* For fall admission, 1/15 priority date for domestic and international students; for spring admission, 9/1 priority date for domestic and international students. Applications are processed on a rolling basis. Application fee: $60. Electronic applications accepted. *Financial support:* In 2009–10, 27 students received support; fellowships with tuition reimbursements available, research assistantships, teaching assistantships with tuition reimbursements available, Federal Work-Study and tuition waivers available. Financial award application deadline: 1/15. *Unit head:* Dr. Michael King, Chair, 202-994-6488. *Application contact:* Information Contact, E-mail: gwchem@www.gwu.edu.

Harvard University, Graduate School of Arts and Sciences, Department of Chemistry and Chemical Biology, Cambridge, MA 02138. Offers biochemical chemistry (PhD); inorganic chemistry (PhD); organic chemistry (PhD); physical chemistry (PhD). *Degree requirements:* For doctorate, thesis/dissertation, cumulative exams. *Entrance requirements:* For doctorate, GRE General Test, GRE Subject Test. Additional exam requirements/recommendations for international students: Required—TOEFL. *Expenses:* Tuition: Full-time $33,696. Required fees: $1126. Full-time tuition and fees vary according to program.

See Close-Up on page 99.

Howard University, Graduate School, Department of Chemistry, Washington, DC 20059-0002. Offers analytical chemistry (MS, PhD); atmospheric (MS, PhD); biochemistry (MS, PhD); environmental (MS, PhD); inorganic chemistry (MS, PhD); organic chemistry (MS, PhD); physical chemistry (MS, PhD). Terminal master's awarded for partial completion of doctoral program. *Degree requirements:* For master's, comprehensive exam, thesis, teaching experience; for doctorate, comprehensive exam, thesis/dissertation, teaching experience. *Entrance requirements:* For master's, GRE General Test, minimum GPA of 2.7; for doctorate, GRE General Test, minimum GPA of 3.0. Additional exam requirements/recommendations for international students: Required—TOEFL. Electronic applications accepted. *Faculty research:* Synthetic organics, materials, natural products, mass spectrometry.

Indiana University Bloomington, University Graduate School, College of Arts and Sciences, Department of Chemistry, Bloomington, IN 47405-7000. Offers analytical chemistry (PhD); biological chemistry (PhD); chemistry (MAT); inorganic chemistry (PhD); physical chemistry (PhD). *Faculty:* 39 full-time (3 women). *Students:* 190 full-time (67 women), 1 (woman) part-time; includes 13 minority (4 African Americans, 1 American Indian/Alaska Native, 5 Asian Americans or Pacific Islanders, 3 Hispanic Americans), 66 international. Average age 26. 207 applicants, 60% accepted, 49 enrolled. In 2009, 10 master's, 20 doctorates awarded. Terminal master's awarded for partial completion of doctoral program. *Degree requirements:* For master's, thesis; for doctorate, thesis/dissertation. *Entrance requirements:* For master's and doctorate, GRE General Test, GRE Subject Test. Additional exam requirements/recommendations for international students: Required—TOEFL. *Application deadline:* For fall admission, 1/15 priority date for domestic students, 12/15 for international students; for spring admission, 9/1 priority date for domestic students, 9/1 for international students. Applications are processed on a rolling basis. Application fee: $55 ($65 for international students). *Financial support:* Fellowships with full tuition reimbursements, research assistantships with full tuition reimbursements, teaching assistantships with full tuition reimbursements, Federal Work-Study and institutionally sponsored loans available. *Faculty research:* Synthesis of complex natural products, organic reaction mechanisms, organic electrochemistry, transitive-metal chemistry, solid-state and surface chemistry. Total annual research expenditures: $7.7 million. *Unit head:* Jim Reilly, Chairperson, 812-855-6239, E-mail: chemchair@indiana.edu. *Application contact:* Martin Jarrold, Director of Graduate Admissions, 812-855-2069, E-mail: mfj@indiana.edu.

Kansas State University, Graduate School, College of Arts and Sciences, Department of Chemistry, Manhattan, KS 66506. Offers analytical chemistry (MS); biological chemistry (MS); chemistry (PhD); inorganic chemistry (MS); materials chemistry (MS); organic chemistry (MS); physical chemistry (MS). *Faculty:* 16 full-time (2 women), 2 part-time/adjunct (0 women). *Students:* 66 full-time (22 women); includes 2 minority (1 African American, 1 Asian American or Pacific Islander), 54 international. Average age 28. 75 applicants, 23% accepted, 7 enrolled. In 2009, 3 master's, 11 doctorates awarded. Terminal master's awarded for partial completion of doctoral program. *Degree requirements:* For master's, thesis; for doctorate, thesis/dissertation. *Entrance requirements:* For master's and doctorate, GRE, minimum GPA of 3.0. Additional exam requirements/recommendations for international students: Required—TOEFL (minimum score 550 paper-based; 213 computer-based). *Application deadline:* For fall admission, 2/1 priority date for domestic and international students; for spring admission, 8/1 priority date for domestic and international students. Applications are processed on a rolling basis. Application fee: $40 ($55 for international students). Electronic applications accepted. *Financial support:* In 2009–10, 41 research assistantships (averaging $15,040 per year), 22 teaching assistantships with full tuition reimbursements (averaging $15,600 per year) were awarded; institutionally sponsored loans and scholarships/grants also available. Support available to part-time students.

Financial award application deadline: 3/1; financial award applicants required to submit FAFSA. *Faculty research:* Inorganic chemistry, organic and biological chemistry, analytical chemistry, physical chemistry, materials chemistry and nanotechnology. Total annual research expenditures: $1.9 million. *Unit head:* Eric Maatta, Head, 785-532-6665, Fax: 785-532-6666, E-mail: eam@ksu.edu. *Application contact:* Christer Aakeroy, Director, 785-532-6096, Fax: 785-532-6666, E-mail: aakeroy@ksu.edu.

Kent State University, College of Arts and Sciences, Department of Chemistry, Kent, OH 44242-0001. Offers analytical chemistry (MS, PhD); biochemistry (MS, PhD); chemistry (MA, MS, PhD); inorganic chemistry (MS, PhD); organic chemistry (MS, PhD); physical chemistry (MS, PhD). Terminal master's awarded for partial completion of doctoral program. *Degree requirements:* For master's, comprehensive exam, thesis; for doctorate, comprehensive exam, thesis/dissertation. *Entrance requirements:* For master's and doctorate, placement exam, GRE General Test, GRE Subject Test (recommended), minimum GPA of 2.75. Additional exam requirements/recommendations for international students: Required—TOEFL (minimum score 575 paper-based; 230 computer-based). Electronic applications accepted. *Faculty research:* Biological chemistry, materials chemistry, molecular spectroscopy.

See Close-Up on page 101.

Laurentian University, School of Graduate Studies and Research, Programme in Chemistry and Biochemistry, Sudbury, ON P3E 2C6, Canada. Offers analytical chemistry (M Sc); biochemistry (M Sc); environmental chemistry (M Sc); organic chemistry (M Sc); physical/theoretical chemistry (M Sc). Part-time programs available. *Degree requirements:* For master's, thesis or alternative. *Entrance requirements:* For master's, honors degree with minimum second class. *Faculty research:* Cell cycle checkpoints, kinetic modeling, toxicology to metal stress, quantum chemistry, biogeochemistry metal speciation.

Marquette University, Graduate School, College of Arts and Sciences, Department of Chemistry, Milwaukee, WI 53201-1881. Offers analytical chemistry (MS, PhD); bioanalytical chemistry (MS, PhD); biophysical chemistry (MS, PhD); chemical physics (MS, PhD); inorganic chemistry (MS, PhD); organic chemistry (MS, PhD); physical chemistry (MS, PhD). Part-time programs available. *Faculty:* 23 full-time (10 women), 1 part-time/adjunct (0 women). *Students:* 34 full-time (9 women), 10 part-time (4 women); includes 4 minority (1 African American, 2 Asian Americans or Pacific Islanders, 1 Hispanic American), 33 international. Average age 29. 23 applicants, 83% accepted, 8 enrolled. In 2009, 4 master's, 5 doctorates awarded. Terminal master's awarded for partial completion of doctoral program. *Degree requirements:* For master's, comprehensive exam; for doctorate, thesis/dissertation, cumulative exams. *Entrance requirements:* For master's and doctorate, GRE Subject Test. Additional exam requirements/recommendations for international students: Required—TOEFL. Application fee: $40. *Financial support:* In 2009–10, 3 research assistantships, 27 teaching assistantships were awarded; fellowships, Federal Work-Study, institutionally sponsored loans, scholarships/grants, and tuition waivers (full and partial) also available. Support available to part-time students. Financial award application deadline: 2/15. *Faculty research:* Inorganic complexes, laser Raman spectroscopy, organic synthesis, chemical dynamics, biophysiology. *Unit head:* Dr. Jeanne Hossenlopp, Chair, 414-288-3537, Fax: 414-288-7066. *Application contact:* Dr. Mark Steinmetz, Director of Graduate Studies, 414-288-7374, Fax: 414-288-7066.

Massachusetts Institute of Technology, School of Science, Department of Chemistry, Cambridge, MA 02139-4307. Offers biological chemistry (PhD, Sc D); inorganic chemistry (PhD, Sc D); organic chemistry (PhD, Sc D); physical chemistry (PhD, Sc D). *Faculty:* 29 full-time (7 women). *Students:* 219 full-time (79 women); includes 39 minority (4 African Americans, 27 Asian Americans or Pacific Islanders, 8 Hispanic Americans), 62 international. Average age 26. 548 applicants, 20% accepted, 19 enrolled. In 2009, 43 doctorates awarded. *Degree requirements:* For doctorate, comprehensive exam, thesis/dissertation, 2 terms as a teaching assistant. *Entrance requirements:* For doctorate, GRE General Test. Additional exam requirements/recommendations for international students: Required—IELTS (minimum score 7); Recommended—TOEFL (minimum score 600 paper-based; 250 computer-based). *Application deadline:* For fall admission, 12/15 for domestic and international students. Application fee: $75. Electronic applications accepted. *Financial support:* In 2009–10, 219 students received support, including 57 fellowships with tuition reimbursements available (averaging $34,547 per year), 132 research assistantships with tuition reimbursements available (averaging $29,403 per year), 27 teaching assistantships with tuition reimbursements available (averaging $30,452 per year); Federal Work-Study, institutionally sponsored loans, scholarships/grants, health care benefits, and unspecified assistantships also available. *Faculty research:* Synthetic organic and inorganic chemistry, biomolecular reactions and structure, multidimensional spectroscopy and chemical dynamics, inorganic, organometallic, organic chemical catalysis, materials chemistry including nanoscience and polymers. Total annual research expenditures: $29.1 million. *Unit head:* Prof. Timothy M. Swager, Head, 617-253-1803, Fax: 617-258-7500. *Application contact:* Graduate Administrator, 617-253-1845, Fax: 617-258-0241, E-mail: chemgradeducation@mit.edu.

McMaster University, School of Graduate Studies, Faculty of Science, Department of Chemistry, Hamilton, ON L8S 4M2, Canada. Offers analytical chemistry (M Sc, PhD); chemical physics (M Sc, PhD); chemistry (M Sc, PhD); inorganic chemistry (M Sc, PhD); organic chemistry (M Sc, PhD); physical chemistry (M Sc, PhD); polymer chemistry (M Sc, PhD). Part-time programs available. Terminal master's awarded for partial completion of doctoral program. *Degree requirements:* For master's, thesis; for doctorate, comprehensive exam, thesis/dissertation. *Entrance requirements:* For master's, minimum B+ average. Additional exam requirements/recommendations for international students: Required—TOEFL (minimum score 550 paper-based; 213 computer-based).

Northeastern University, College of Science, Department of Chemistry and Chemical Biology, Boston, MA 02115-5096. Offers analytical chemistry (PhD); chemistry (MS, PhD); inorganic chemistry (PhD); organic chemistry (PhD); physical chemistry (PhD). Part-time and evening/weekend programs available. *Faculty:* 24 full-time (5 women), 7 part-time/adjunct (0 women). *Students:* 86 full-time (48 women), 31 part-time (14 women); includes 9 minority (1 African American, 1 American Indian/Alaska Native, 7 Asian Americans or Pacific Islanders), 36 international. 190 applicants, 22% accepted, 15 enrolled. In 2009, 17 master's, 9 doctorates awarded. Terminal master's awarded for partial completion of doctoral program. *Degree requirements:* For master's, thesis (for some programs); for doctorate, thesis/dissertation, qualifying exam in specialty area. *Entrance requirements:* Additional exam requirements/recommendations for international students: Required—TOEFL. *Application deadline:* For fall admission, 2/1 priority date for domestic and international students. Applications are processed on a rolling basis. Application fee: $50. Electronic applications accepted. *Financial support:* In 2009–10, 41 research assistantships with tuition reimbursements (averaging $18,285 per year), 38 teaching assistantships with tuition reimbursements (averaging $18,285 per year) were awarded; fellowships with tuition reimbursements, career-related internships or fieldwork, Federal Work-Study, scholarships/grants, tuition waivers (partial), and unspecified assistantships also available. Financial award application deadline: 3/1; financial award applicants required to submit FAFSA. *Faculty research:* Bioanalysis, biorganic and medicinal chemistry, biophysical chemistry, nanomaterials, proteonics. *Unit head:* Dr. Robert Hanson, Graduate Coordinator, 617-373-3313, Fax: 617-373-8795, E-mail: chemistry-grad-info@neu.edu. *Application contact:* Jo-Anne Dickinson, Admissions Contact, 617-373-5990, Fax: 617-373-7281, E-mail: gsas@neu.edu.

Old Dominion University, College of Sciences, Program in Chemistry, Norfolk, VA 23529. Offers analytical chemistry (MS); biochemistry (MS); chemistry (PhD); environmental chemistry (MS); organic chemistry (MS); physical chemistry (MS). Part-time and evening/weekend programs available. *Faculty:* 14 full-time (5 women), 2 part-time/adjunct (0 women). *Students:* 30 full-time (19 women), 10 part-time (5 women); includes 3 minority (1 African American, 1 Asian American or Pacific Islander, 1 Hispanic American), 17 international. Average age 29. 35 applicants, 60% accepted, 8 enrolled. In 2009, 1 master's awarded. *Degree requirements:* For master's, comprehensive exam, thesis. *Entrance requirements:* For master's, GRE General Test, minimum GPA of 3.0 in major, 2.5 overall; for doctorate, GRE General Test. Additional exam requirements/recommendations for international students: Required—TOEFL. *Application deadline:* For fall admission, 7/1 for domestic students, 1/15 for international students; for spring admission, 11/1 for domestic students, 8/15 for international students. Applications are processed on a rolling basis. Application fee: $30. Electronic applications accepted. *Expenses:* Tuition, state resident: full-time $8112; part-time $338 per credit. Tuition, nonresident: full-time $20,256; part-time $844 per credit. Required fees: $119 per semester. One-time fee: $50. *Financial support:* In 2009–10, 6 students received support, including fellowships (averaging $18,000 per year), research assistantships with tuition reimbursements available (averaging $21,000 per year), teaching assistantships with tuition reimbursements available (averaging $18,000 per year); career-related internships or fieldwork, scholarships/grants, and unspecified assistantships also available. Financial award application deadline: 2/15; financial award applicants required to submit FAFSA. *Faculty research:* Biogeochemistry, materials chemistry, bioanalytical chemistry, computational chemistry, organic chemistry. Total annual research expenditures: $2.6 million. *Unit head:* Dr. Craig A. Bayse, Graduate Program Director, 757-683-4097, Fax: 757-683-4628, E-mail: chemgpd@odu.edu. *Application contact:* Valerie DeCosta, Grants and Graduate Program Assistant, 757-683-6979, Fax: 757-683-4628, E-mail: chemgpd@odu.edu.

Oregon State University, Graduate School, College of Science, Department of Chemistry, Corvallis, OR 97331. Offers analytical chemistry (MS, PhD); chemistry (MA, MAIS); inorganic chemistry (MS, PhD); nuclear and radiation chemistry (MS, PhD); organic chemistry (MS, PhD); physical chemistry (MS, PhD). Part-time programs available. *Faculty:* 24 full-time (3 women), 1 part-time/adjunct (0 women). *Students:* 78 full-time (27 women), 1 part-time (0 women); includes 3 minority (1 African American, 1 Asian American or Pacific Islander, 1 Hispanic American), 50 international. Average age 27. In 2009, 6 master's, 7 doctorates awarded. Terminal master's awarded for partial completion of doctoral program. *Degree requirements:* For master's, one foreign language, thesis; for doctorate, one foreign language, thesis/dissertation. *Entrance requirements:* For master's and doctorate, minimum GPA of 3.0 in last 90 hours of course work. Additional exam requirements/recommendations for international students: Required—TOEFL. *Application deadline:* For fall admission, 3/1 priority date for domestic students. Applications are processed on a rolling basis. Application fee: $50. *Expenses:* Tuition, state resident: full-time $9774; part-time $362 per credit. Tuition, nonresident: full-time $15,849; part-time $587 per credit. Required fees: $1639. Full-time tuition and fees vary according to course load and program. *Financial support:* Fellowships, research assistantships, teaching assistantships, institutionally sponsored loans available. Support available to part-time students. Financial award application deadline: 2/1. *Faculty research:* Solid state chemistry, enzyme reaction mechanisms, structure and dynamics of gas molecules, chemiluminescence, nonlinear optical spectroscopy. *Unit head:* Dr. Kevin P. Gable, Chair, 541-737-6744, Fax: 541-737-2062, E-mail: gablek@chem.orst.edu. *Application contact:* Dr. Kevin P. Gable, Chair, 541-737-6744, Fax: 541-737-2062, E-mail: gablek@chem.orst.edu.

Purdue University, Graduate School, College of Science, Department of Chemistry, West Lafayette, IN 47907. Offers analytical chemistry (MS, PhD); biochemistry (MS, PhD); chemical education (MS, PhD); inorganic chemistry (MS, PhD); organic chemistry (MS, PhD); physical chemistry (MS, PhD). Terminal master's awarded for partial completion of doctoral program. *Degree requirements:* For master's, thesis; for doctorate, thesis/dissertation. *Entrance requirements:* Additional exam requirements/recommendations for international students: Required—TOEFL. Electronic applications accepted.

Rensselaer Polytechnic Institute, Graduate School, School of Science, Department of Chemistry and Chemical Biology, Troy, NY 12180-3590. Offers analytical chemistry (MS, PhD); biochemistry (MS, PhD); inorganic chemistry (MS, PhD); organic chemistry (MS, PhD); physical chemistry (MS, PhD); polymer chemistry (MS, PhD). Part-time and evening/weekend programs available. *Faculty:* 16 full-time (2 women). *Students:* 68 full-time (31 women); includes 1 African American, 6 Asian Americans or Pacific Islanders, 1 Hispanic American, 31 international. Average age 24. 85 applicants, 19% accepted, 5 enrolled. In 2009, 5 master's, 6 doctorates awarded. Terminal master's awarded for partial completion of doctoral program. *Degree requirements:* For master's, thesis (for some programs); for doctorate, comprehensive exam, thesis/dissertation. *Entrance requirements:* For master's, GRE General Test, GRE Subject Test (strongly recommended); for doctorate, GRE General Test, GRE Subject Test (chemistry or biochemistry strongly recommended). Additional exam requirements/recommendations for international students: Required—TOEFL (minimum score 600 paper-based). *Application deadline:* For fall admission, 2/1 priority date for domestic students; for spring admission, 11/15 for domestic students. Applications are processed on a rolling basis. Application fee: $75. Electronic applications accepted. *Expenses:* Tuition: Full-time $38,100. *Financial support:* In 2009–10, 1 fellowship with full tuition reimbursement (averaging $22,500 per year), 18 research assistantships with full tuition reimbursements (averaging $22,500 per year), 24 teaching assistantships with full tuition reimbursements (averaging $22,500 per year) were awarded; institutionally sponsored loans and tuition waivers (full and partial) also available. Financial award application deadline: 2/1. *Faculty research:* Synthetic polymer and biopolymer chemistry, physical chemistry of polymeric systems, bioanalytical chemistry, synthetic and computational drug design, protein folding and protein design. Total annual research expenditures: $1.1 million. *Unit head:* Dr. Curtis M. Breneman, Chair, 518-276-3264, Fax: 518-276-4887, E-mail: brenec@rpi.edu. *Application contact:* Sharon E. Gardner, Graduate Program Administrator, 518-276-2140, Fax: 518-276-4887, E-mail: derris@rpi.edu.

Rice University, Graduate Programs, Wiess School of Natural Sciences, Department of Chemistry, Houston, TX 77251-1892. Offers chemistry (MA); inorganic chemistry (PhD); organic chemistry (PhD); physical chemistry (PhD). Terminal master's awarded for partial completion of doctoral program. *Degree requirements:* For master's, thesis; for doctorate, thesis/dissertation. *Entrance requirements:* For master's and doctorate, GRE General Test, minimum GPA of 3.0. Additional exam requirements/recommendations for international students: Required—TOEFL (minimum score 600 paper-based; 250 computer-based; 90 iBT). Electronic applications accepted. *Faculty research:* Nanoscience, biomaterials, nanobioinformatics, fullerene pharmaceuticals.

Rutgers, The State University of New Jersey, Newark, Graduate School, Program in Chemistry, Newark, NJ 07102. Offers analytical chemistry (MS, PhD); biochemistry (MS, PhD); inorganic chemistry (MS, PhD); organic chemistry (MS, PhD); physical chemistry (MS, PhD). Part-time and evening/weekend programs available. Terminal master's awarded for partial completion of doctoral program. *Degree requirements:* For master's, thesis optional, cumulative exams; for doctorate, thesis/dissertation, exams, research proposal. *Entrance requirements:* For master's and doctorate, GRE General Test, minimum undergraduate B average. Additional exam requirements/recommendations for international students: Required—TOEFL. Electronic applications accepted. *Faculty research:* Medicinal chemistry, natural products, isotope effects, biophysics and biorganic approaches to enzyme mechanisms, organic and organometallic synthesis.

Rutgers, The State University of New Jersey, New Brunswick, Graduate School-New Brunswick, Department of Chemistry and Chemical Biology, Piscataway, NJ 08854-8097. Offers biological chemistry (MS, PhD); inorganic chemistry (MS, PhD); organic chemistry (MS, PhD); physical chemistry (MS, PhD). Part-time and evening/weekend programs available. Terminal master's awarded for partial completion of doctoral program. *Degree requirements:* For master's, thesis or alternative, exam; for doctorate, thesis/dissertation, 1 year residency.

Physical Chemistry

Rutgers, The State University of New Jersey, New Brunswick (continued)
Entrance requirements: For master's and doctorate, GRE General Test, GRE Subject Test. Additional exam requirements/recommendations for international students: Required—TOEFL. Electronic applications accepted. *Faculty research:* Biophysical organic/bioorganic, inorganic/bioinorganic, theoretical, and solid-state/surface chemistry.

Seton Hall University, College of Arts and Sciences, Department of Chemistry and Biochemistry, South Orange, NJ 07079-2697. Offers analytical chemistry (MS, PhD); biochemistry (MS, PhD); chemistry (MS); inorganic chemistry (MS, PhD); organic chemistry (MS, PhD); physical chemistry (MS, PhD). Part-time and evening/weekend programs available. *Faculty:* 10 full-time (1 woman). *Students:* 24 full-time (14 women), 47 part-time (15 women); includes 22 minority (10 African Americans, 8 Asian Americans or Pacific Islanders, 4 Hispanic Americans), 11 international. Average age 33. 31 applicants, 68% accepted, 10 enrolled. In 2009, 7 master's, 4 doctorates awarded. Terminal master's awarded for partial completion of doctoral program. *Degree requirements:* For master's, thesis optional; for doctorate, comprehensive exam, thesis/dissertation. *Entrance requirements:* Additional exam requirements/recommendations for international students: Required—TOEFL. *Application deadline:* For fall admission, 7/1 priority date for domestic and international students; for spring admission, 11/1 priority date for domestic and international students. Applications are processed on a rolling basis. Application fee: $50. Electronic applications accepted. *Financial support:* Research assistantships, teaching assistantships with full tuition reimbursements, Federal Work-Study and unspecified assistantships available. Financial award applicants required to submit FAFSA. *Faculty research:* DNA metal reactions; chromatography; bioinorganic, biophysical, organometallic, polymer chemistry; heterogeneous catalyst; synthetic organic and carbohydrate chemistry. *Unit head:* Dr. Nicholas Snow, Chair, 973-761-9414, Fax: 973-761-9772, E-mail: snownich@shu.edu. *Application contact:* Dr. Stephen Kelty, Director of Graduate Studies, 973-761-9129, Fax: 973-761-9772, E-mail: keltyste@shu.edu.

Southern University and Agricultural and Mechanical College, Graduate School, College of Sciences, Department of Chemistry, Baton Rouge, LA 70813. Offers analytical chemistry (MS); biochemistry (MS); environmental sciences (MS); inorganic chemistry (MS); organic chemistry (MS); physical chemistry (MS). *Degree requirements:* For master's, thesis. *Entrance requirements:* For master's, GMAT or GRE General Test. Additional exam requirements/recommendations for international students: Required—TOEFL (minimum score 525 paper-based; 193 computer-based). *Faculty research:* Synthesis of macrocyclic ligands, latex accelerators, anticancer drugs, biosensors, absorption isotheums, isolation of specific enzymes from plants.

State University of New York at Binghamton, Graduate School, School of Arts and Sciences, Department of Chemistry, Binghamton, NY 13902-6000. Offers analytical chemistry (PhD); chemistry (MA, MS); inorganic chemistry (PhD); organic chemistry (PhD); physical chemistry (PhD). Part-time programs available. *Faculty:* 14 full-time (3 women), 2 part-time/adjunct (0 women). *Students:* 35 full-time (13 women), 22 part-time (10 women); includes 8 minority (3 African Americans, 4 Asian Americans or Pacific Islanders, 1 Hispanic American), 32 international. Average age 29. 40 applicants, 30% accepted, 6 enrolled. In 2009, 6 master's, 5 doctorates awarded. Terminal master's awarded for partial completion of doctoral program. *Degree requirements:* For master's, thesis or alternative, oral exam, seminar presentation; for doctorate, thesis/dissertation, cumulative exams. *Entrance requirements:* For master's and doctorate, GRE General Test, GRE Subject Test. Additional exam requirements/recommendations for international students: Required—TOEFL (minimum score 550 paper-based; 213 computer-based; 80 iBT). *Application deadline:* For fall admission, 1/15 priority date for domestic and international students; for spring admission, 10/15 priority date for domestic and international students. Applications are processed on a rolling basis. Application fee: $60. Electronic applications accepted. *Financial support:* In 2009–10, 55 students received support, including 4 fellowships with full tuition reimbursements available (averaging $18,000 per year), 8 research assistantships with full tuition reimbursements available (averaging $18,000 per year), 34 teaching assistantships with full tuition reimbursements available (averaging $18,000 per year); career-related internships or fieldwork, Federal Work-Study, institutionally sponsored loans, scholarships/grants, health care benefits, tuition waivers (full), and unspecified assistantships also available. Financial award application deadline: 2/15; financial award applicants required to submit FAFSA. *Unit head:* Dr. Wayne E. Jones, Chairperson, 607-777-2421, E-mail: wjones@binghamton.edu. *Application contact:* Victoria Williams, Recruiting and Admissions Coordinator, 607-777-2151, Fax: 607-777-2501, E-mail: vwilliam@binghamton.edu.

Stevens Institute of Technology, Graduate School, Charles V. Schaefer Jr. School of Engineering, Department of Chemistry, Chemical Biology and Biomedical Engineering, Hoboken, NJ 07030. Offers analytical chemistry (PhD, Certificate); bioinformatics (PhD, Certificate); biomedical chemistry (Certificate); biomedical engineering (M Eng, Certificate); chemical biology (MS, PhD, Certificate); chemical physiology (Certificate); chemistry (MS, PhD); organic chemistry (PhD); physical chemistry (PhD); polymer chemistry (PhD, Certificate). Part-time and evening/weekend programs available. Postbaccalaureate distance learning degree programs offered (no on-campus study). Terminal master's awarded for partial completion of doctoral program. *Degree requirements:* For master's, thesis or alternative; for doctorate, one foreign language, thesis/dissertation; for Certificate, project or thesis. *Entrance requirements:* Additional exam requirements/recommendations for international students: Required—TOEFL. Electronic applications accepted. *Expenses:* Tuition: Full-time $9900; part-time $1100 per credit. Required fees: $286 per semester. *Faculty research:* Biochemical reaction engineering, polymerization engineering, reactor design, biochemical process control and synthesis.

Tufts University, Graduate School of Arts and Sciences, Department of Chemistry, Medford, MA 02155. Offers analytical chemistry (MS, PhD); bioorganic chemistry (MS, PhD); environmental chemistry (MS, PhD); inorganic chemistry (MS, PhD); organic chemistry (MS, PhD); physical chemistry (MS, PhD). *Students:* 61 full-time (29 women); includes 7 minority (1 African American, 1 American Indian/Alaska Native, 4 Asian Americans or Pacific Islanders, 1 Hispanic American), 18 international. 90 applicants, 50% accepted, 14 enrolled. In 2009, 2 master's, 7 doctorates awarded. Terminal master's awarded for partial completion of doctoral program. *Degree requirements:* For master's, thesis optional; for doctorate, thesis/dissertation. *Entrance requirements:* For master's and doctorate, GRE General Test, GRE Subject Test. Additional exam requirements/recommendations for international students: Required—TOEFL (minimum score 600 paper-based; 250 computer-based; 80 iBT). *Application deadline:* For fall admission, 1/15 for domestic students, 12/30 for international students; for spring admission, 10/15 for domestic students, 9/15 for international students. Applications are processed on a rolling basis. Application fee: $75. Electronic applications accepted. *Expenses:* Tuition: Full-time $38,096; part-time $3962 per credit. Required fees: $686; $40 per year. Tuition and fees vary according to course level, course load, degree level, program and student level. *Financial support:* Fellowships, research assistantships with full tuition reimbursements, teaching assistantships with full tuition reimbursements, Federal Work-Study, scholarships/grants, tuition waivers (partial), and unspecified assistantships available. Financial award application deadline: 1/15; financial award applicants required to submit FAFSA. *Unit head:* Arthur Utz, Chair, 617-627-3441. *Application contact:* Samuel Kounaves, Information Contact, 617-627-3441, Fax: 617-627-3443.

University of Calgary, Faculty of Graduate Studies, Faculty of Science, Department of Chemistry, Calgary, AB T2N 1N4, Canada. Offers analytical chemistry (M Sc, PhD); applied chemistry (M Sc, PhD); inorganic chemistry (M Sc, PhD); organic chemistry (M Sc, PhD); physical chemistry (M Sc, PhD); polymer chemistry (M Sc, PhD); theoretical chemistry (M Sc, PhD). *Degree requirements:* For master's, thesis; for doctorate, thesis/dissertation, candidacy exam. *Entrance requirements:* For master's, minimum GPA of 3.0; for doctorate, honors B Sc degree with minimum GPA of 3.7 or M Sc with minimum GPA of 3.3. Additional exam requirements/recommendations for international students: Required—TOEFL (minimum score 580 paper-based; 237 computer-based). Electronic applications accepted. *Faculty research:* Chemical analysis, chemical dynamics, synthesis theory.

University of Cincinnati, Graduate School, McMicken College of Arts and Sciences, Department of Chemistry, Cincinnati, OH 45221. Offers analytical chemistry (MS, PhD); biochemistry (MS, PhD); inorganic chemistry (MS, PhD); organic chemistry (MS, PhD); physical chemistry (MS, PhD); polymer chemistry (MS, PhD); sensors (PhD). Part-time and evening/weekend programs available. Terminal master's awarded for partial completion of doctoral program. *Degree requirements:* For master's, thesis optional; for doctorate, comprehensive exam, thesis/dissertation. *Entrance requirements:* For master's and doctorate, GRE General Test. Additional exam requirements/recommendations for international students: Required—TOEFL (minimum score 580 paper-based; 237 computer-based). Electronic applications accepted. *Faculty research:* Biomedical chemistry, laser chemistry, surface science, chemical sensors, synthesis.

University of Georgia, Graduate School, College of Arts and Sciences, Department of Chemistry, Athens, GA 30602. Offers analytical chemistry (MS, PhD); inorganic chemistry (MS, PhD); organic chemistry (MS, PhD); physical chemistry (MS, PhD). *Faculty:* 25 full-time (1 woman). *Students:* 147 full-time (53 women), 2 part-time (1 woman); includes 14 minority (6 African Americans, 7 Asian Americans or Pacific Islanders, 1 Hispanic American), 61 international. 136 applicants, 55% accepted, 27 enrolled. In 2009, 3 master's, 23 doctorates awarded. Terminal master's awarded for partial completion of doctoral program. *Degree requirements:* For master's, thesis; for doctorate, one foreign language, thesis/dissertation. *Entrance requirements:* For master's and doctorate, GRE General Test. Additional exam requirements/recommendations for international students: Required—TOEFL (minimum score 213 computer-based). *Application deadline:* For fall admission, 7/1 priority date for domestic students; for spring admission, 11/15 for domestic students. Application fee: $50. Electronic applications accepted. *Expenses:* Tuition, state resident: full-time $6000; part-time $250 per credit hour. Tuition, nonresident: full-time $20,904; part-time $871 per credit hour. Required fees: $730 per semester. *Financial support:* Fellowships, research assistantships, teaching assistantships, unspecified assistantships available. *Unit head:* Dr. John L. Stickney, Head, 706-542-2726, Fax: 706-542-9454, E-mail: stickney@chem.uga.edu. *Application contact:* Dr. George F. Majetich, Graduate Coordinator, 706-542-1966, Fax: 706-542-9454, E-mail: majetich@chem.uga.edu.

University of Louisville, Graduate School, College of Arts and Sciences, Department of Chemistry, Louisville, KY 40292-0001. Offers analytical chemistry (MS, PhD); biochemistry (MS, PhD); chemical physics (PhD); inorganic chemistry (MS, PhD); organic chemistry (MS, PhD); physical chemistry (MS, PhD). *Students:* 57 full-time (27 women), 4 part-time (1 woman); includes 2 minority (1 African American, 1 Asian American or Pacific Islander), 43 international. Average age 29. 62 applicants, 31% accepted, 13 enrolled. In 2009, 6 master's, 7 doctorates awarded. *Median time to degree:* Of those who began their doctoral program in fall 2001, 0% received their degree in 8 years or less. *Degree requirements:* For master's, thesis; for doctorate, comprehensive exam, thesis/dissertation. *Entrance requirements:* For master's and doctorate, GRE General Test. Additional exam requirements/recommendations for international students: Required—TOEFL. *Application deadline:* Applications are processed on a rolling basis. Application fee: $50. *Financial support:* Fellowships, research assistantships, teaching assistantships available. *Unit head:* Dr. George R. Pack, Chair, 502-852-6798, Fax: 502-852-8149, E-mail: george.pack@louisville.edu. *Application contact:* Libby Leggett, Director, Graduate Admissions, 502-852-3101, Fax: 502-852-6536, E-mail: gradadm@louisville.edu.

University of Maryland, College Park, Academic Affairs, College of Chemical and Life Sciences, Department of Chemistry and Biochemistry, Chemistry Program, College Park, MD 20742. Offers analytical chemistry (MS, PhD); inorganic chemistry (MS, PhD); organic chemistry (MS, PhD); physical chemistry (MS, PhD). Part-time and evening/weekend programs available. *Students:* 129 full-time (69 women), 5 part-time (3 women); includes 18 minority (13 African Americans, 3 Asian Americans or Pacific Islanders, 2 Hispanic Americans), 70 international. 329 applicants, 22% accepted, 36 enrolled. In 2009, 6 master's, 18 doctorates awarded. Terminal master's awarded for partial completion of doctoral program. *Degree requirements:* For master's, thesis optional; for doctorate, thesis/dissertation, 2 seminar presentations, oral exam. *Entrance requirements:* For master's and doctorate, GRE General Test, GRE Subject Test (recommended), minimum GPA of 3.0, 3 letters of recommendation. Additional exam requirements/recommendations for international students: Required—TOEFL. *Application deadline:* For fall admission, 2/1 for domestic and international students. Applications are processed on a rolling basis. Application fee: $60. Electronic applications accepted. *Expenses:* Tuition, area resident: Part-time $471 per credit hour. Tuition, state resident: part-time $471 per credit hour. Tuition, nonresident: part-time $1016 per credit hour. Required fees: $337.04 per term. *Financial support:* In 2009–10, 7 fellowships with full tuition reimbursements (averaging $27,067 per year), 51 research assistantships (averaging $19,639 per year), 66 teaching assistantships with partial tuition reimbursements (averaging $19,260 per year) were awarded. Financial award applicants required to submit FAFSA. *Faculty research:* Environmental chemistry, nuclear chemistry, lunar and environmental analysis, x-ray crystallography. *Unit head:* Dr. Michael Doyle, Chairperson, 301-405-1795, Fax: 301-314-2779, E-mail: mdoyle3@umd.edu. *Application contact:* Dean of Graduate School, 301-405-0358, Fax: 301-314-9305.

University of Memphis, Graduate School, College of Arts and Sciences, Department of Chemistry, Memphis, TN 38152. Offers analytical chemistry (PhD); analytical chemsitry (MS); computational chemistry (MS, PhD); inorganic chemistry (MS, PhD); organic chemistry (MS, PhD); physical chemistry (MS, PhD). Part-time programs available. *Faculty:* 6 full-time (1 woman). *Students:* 39 full-time (17 women), 7 part-time (4 women); includes 8 minority (6 African Americans, 1 Asian American or Pacific Islander, 1 Hispanic American), 6 international. Average age 28. 23 applicants, 70% accepted, 14 enrolled. In 2009, 3 master's, 5 doctorates awarded. Terminal master's awarded for partial completion of doctoral program. *Degree requirements:* For master's, comprehensive exam, thesis or alternative; for doctorate, comprehensive exam, thesis/dissertation. *Entrance requirements:* For master's and doctorate, GRE General Test, admission to Graduate School plus 32 undergraduate hours in chemistry. Additional exam requirements/recommendations for international students: Required—TOEFL. *Application deadline:* For fall admission, 7/1 for domestic students, 5/1 for international students; for winter admission, 9/15 for international students; for spring admission, 12/1 for domestic students. Applications are processed on a rolling basis. Application fee: $35 ($60 for international students). Electronic applications accepted. *Expenses:* Tuition, state resident: full-time $6246; part-time $347 per credit hour. Tuition, nonresident: full-time $15,894; part-time $883 per credit hour. Required fees: $1160. Full-time tuition and fees vary according to course load, degree level and program. *Financial support:* In 2009–10, 12 students received support; research assistantships with full tuition reimbursements available, teaching assistantships with full tuition reimbursements available, Federal Work-Study, scholarships/grants, and unspecified assistantships available. Financial award application deadline: 2/15; financial award applicants required to submit FAFSA. *Faculty research:* Computational chemistry, materials chemistry, organic/polymer synthesis, drug design/delivery, water chemistry. *Unit head:* Dr. Abby L. Parrill, Professor and Chair, 901-678-2638, Fax: 901-678-3447, E-mail: aparrill@memphis.edu. *Application contact:* Dr. Gary Emmert, Associate Professor and Graduate Coordinator, 901-678-2636, Fax: 901-678-3447, E-mail: gemmert@memphis.edu.

University of Miami, Graduate School, College of Arts and Sciences, Department of Chemistry, Coral Gables, FL 33124. Offers chemistry (MS); inorganic chemistry (PhD); organic chemistry (PhD); physical chemistry (PhD). Terminal master's awarded for partial completion of doctoral program. *Degree requirements:* For master's, comprehensive exam; for doctorate, comprehensive exam, thesis/dissertation. *Entrance requirements:* For master's and doctorate, GRE General Test. Additional exam requirements/recommendations for international students: Required—

TOEFL (minimum score 550 paper-based; 213 computer-based). Electronic applications accepted. *Faculty research:* Supramolecular chemistry, electrochemistry, surface chemistry, catalysis, organometalic.

University of Michigan, Horace H. Rackham School of Graduate Studies, College of Literature, Science, and the Arts, Department of Chemistry, Ann Arbor, MI 48109-1055. Offers analytical chemistry (PhD); chemical biology (PhD); inorganic chemistry (PhD); material chemistry (PhD); organic chemistry (PhD); physical chemistry (PhD). *Faculty:* 42 full-time (10 women). *Students:* 192 full-time (105 women); includes 74 minority (4 African Americans, 64 Asian Americans or Pacific Islanders, 6 Hispanic Americans), 54 international. Average age 26. 558 applicants, 36% accepted, 56 enrolled. In 2009, 28 doctorates awarded. *Degree requirements:* For doctorate, thesis/dissertation, oral defense of dissertation, organic cumulative proficiency exams. *Entrance requirements:* For doctorate, GRE General Test, GRE Subject Test (recommended), 3 letters of recommendation. Additional exam requirements/recommendations for international students: Required—TOEFL (minimum score 560 paper-based; 220 computer-based; 84 iBT). *Application deadline:* For fall admission, 1/15 for domestic students, 12/15 for international students. Applications are processed on a rolling basis. Application fee: $0 ($75 for international students). Electronic applications accepted. *Expenses:* Tuition, state resident: full-time $17,286; part-time $1099 per credit hour. Tuition, nonresident: full-time $34,944; part-time $2080 per credit hour. Required fees: $95 per semester. Tuition and fees vary according to course load, degree level and program. *Financial support:* In 2009–10, 192 students received support, including 20 fellowships with full tuition reimbursements available (averaging $25,000 per year), 75 research assistantships with full tuition reimbursements available (averaging $25,000 per year), 97 teaching assistantships with full tuition reimbursements available (averaging $25,000 per year); career-related internships or fieldwork, scholarships/grants, traineeships, health care benefits, and unspecified assistantships also available. Financial award applicants required to submit FAFSA. *Faculty research:* Biological catalysis, protein engineering, chemical sensors, de novo metalloprotein design, supramolecular architecture. Total annual research expenditures: $15.3 million. *Unit head:* Dr. Carol A. Fierke, Chair, 734-763-9681, Fax: 734-647-4847. *Application contact:* Anna Stryker, Graduate Program Coordinator, 734-764-7278, Fax: 734-647-4865, E-mail: chemadmissions@umich.edu.

University of Missouri, Graduate School, College of Arts and Sciences, Department of Chemistry, Columbia, MO 65211. Offers analytical chemistry (MS, PhD); inorganic chemistry (MS, PhD); organic chemistry (MS, PhD); physical chemistry (MS, PhD). *Faculty:* 30 full-time (6 women), 2 part-time/adjunct (0 women). *Students:* 60 full-time (22 women), 43 part-time (16 women); includes 7 minority (3 African Americans, 1 American Indian/Alaska Native, 3 Asian Americans or Pacific Islanders), 53 international. Average age 27. 93 applicants, 32% accepted, 27 enrolled. In 2009, 4 doctorates awarded. *Degree requirements:* For master's, thesis; for doctorate, one foreign language, comprehensive exam, thesis/dissertation. *Entrance requirements:* For master's, GRE General Test, minimum GPA of 3.0; for doctorate, GRE General Test; V=450, Q=600, A=3.0-4.0, minimum GPA of 3.0. Additional exam requirements/recommendations for international students: Required—TOEFL (minimum score 600 paper-based; 250 computer-based; 100 iBT). *Application deadline:* For fall admission, 4/1 priority date for domestic students; for winter admission, 10/15 for domestic students. Applications are processed on a rolling basis. Application fee: $45 ($60 for international students). *Financial support:* In 2009–10, 9 fellowships with full tuition reimbursements, 15 research assistantships with full tuition reimbursements, 78 teaching assistantships with full tuition reimbursements were awarded; institutionally sponsored loans, traineeships, health care benefits, and unspecified assistantships also available. *Unit head:* Dr. Jerry Atwood, Department Chair, 573-882-8374, E-mail: atwoodj@missouri.edu. *Application contact:* Jerry Brightwell, Administrative Assistant, 573-884-6832, E-mail: brightwellj@missouri.edu.

University of Missouri–Kansas City, College of Arts and Sciences, Department of Chemistry, Kansas City, MO 64110-2499. Offers analytical chemistry (MS, PhD); inorganic chemistry (MS, PhD); organic chemistry (MS, PhD); physical chemistry (MS, PhD); polymer chemistry (MS, PhD). PhD (interdisciplinary) offered through the School of Graduate Studies. Part-time and evening/weekend programs available. *Faculty:* 16 full-time (3 women), 1 part-time/adjunct (0 women). *Students:* 7 part-time (4 women), 2 international. Average age 32. 30 applicants, 67% accepted. In 2009, 1 master's awarded. *Degree requirements:* For master's, thesis (for some programs); for doctorate, thesis/dissertation. *Entrance requirements:* For master's, equivalent of American Chemical Society approved bachelor's degree in chemistry; for doctorate, GRE General Test, equivalent of American Chemical Society approved bachelor's degree in chemistry. Additional exam requirements/recommendations for international students: Required—TOEFL (minimum score 550 paper-based; 213 computer-based; 80 iBT), TWE. *Application deadline:* For fall admission, 4/15 for domestic and international students; for spring admission, 10/15 for domestic and international students. Applications are processed on a rolling basis. Application fee: $45 ($50 for international students). Electronic applications accepted. *Expenses:* Tuition, state resident: full-time $5378; part-time $299 per credit hour. Tuition, nonresident: full-time $13,881; part-time $771 per credit hour. Required fees: $641; $71 per credit hour. Tuition and fees vary according to course load and program. *Financial support:* In 2009–10, 8 research assistantships with partial tuition reimbursements (averaging $17,973 per year), 17 teaching assistantships with partial tuition reimbursements (averaging $17,179 per year) were awarded; Federal Work-Study, institutionally sponsored loans, and scholarships/grants also available. Support available to part-time students. Financial award application deadline: 3/1; financial award applicants required to submit FAFSA. *Faculty research:* Molecular spectroscopy, characterization and synthesis of materials and compounds, computational chemistry, natural products, drug delivery systems and anti-tumor agents. Total annual research expenditures: $1 million. *Unit head:* Dr. Kathleen V. Kilway, Chair, 816-235-2289, Fax: 816-235-5502. *Application contact:* Graduate Recruiting Committee, 816-235-2272, Fax: 816-235-5502, E-mail: umkc-chemdept@umkc.edu.

University of Missouri–St. Louis, College of Arts and Sciences, Department of Chemistry and Biochemistry, St. Louis, MO 63121. Offers chemistry (MS, PhD), including biochemistry, inorganic chemistry, organic chemistry, physical chemistry. Part-time and evening/weekend programs available. *Faculty:* 19 full-time (3 women), 6 part-time/adjunct (1 woman). *Students:* 43 full-time (21 women), 19 part-time (8 women); includes 6 minority (4 African Americans, 1 Asian American or Pacific Islander, 1 Hispanic American), 27 international. Average age 29. 81 applicants, 37% accepted, 19 enrolled. In 2009, 9 master's, 6 doctorates awarded. Terminal master's awarded for partial completion of doctoral program. *Degree requirements:* For master's, thesis optional; for doctorate, thesis/dissertation. *Entrance requirements:* For master's, 2 letters of recommendation; for doctorate, GRE General Test, 3 letters of recommendation. Additional exam requirements/recommendations for international students: Required—TOEFL (minimum score 550 paper-based; 213 computer-based). *Application deadline:* For fall admission, 7/1 priority date for domestic and international students; for spring admission, 12/1 priority date for domestic and international students. Applications are processed on a rolling basis. Application fee: $35 ($40 for international students). Electronic applications accepted. *Expenses:* Tuition, state resident: full-time $5377; part-time $297.70 per credit hour. Tuition, nonresident: full-time $13,882; part-time $771.20 per credit hour. Required fees: $220; $12.20 per credit hour. One-time fee: $12. Tuition and fees vary according to course level, campus/location and program. *Financial support:* In 2009–10, 25 research assistantships with full and partial tuition reimbursements (averaging $17,840 per year), 13 teaching assistantships with full and partial tuition reimbursements (averaging $13,300 per year) were awarded; fellowships with full and partial tuition reimbursements also available. *Faculty research:* Metallaborane chemistry, serum transferrin chemistry, natural products chemistry, organic synthesis. *Unit head:* Dr. Cynthia Dupureur, Director of Graduate Studies, 314-516-5311, Fax: 314-516-5342, E-mail: gradchem@umsl.edu. *Application contact:* 314-516-5458, Fax: 314-516-6996, E-mail: gradadm@umsl.edu.

The University of Montana, Graduate School, College of Arts and Sciences, Department of Chemistry, Missoula, MT 59812-0002. Offers chemistry (MS, PhD), including environmental/analytical chemistry, inorganic chemistry, organic chemistry, physical chemistry. Terminal master's awarded for partial completion of doctoral program. *Degree requirements:* For master's, thesis (for some programs); for doctorate, thesis/dissertation. *Entrance requirements:* For master's and doctorate, GRE General Test. Additional exam requirements/recommendations for international students: Required—TOEFL (minimum score 575 paper-based; 230 computer-based). *Faculty research:* Reaction mechanisms and kinetics, inorganic and organic synthesis, analytical chemistry, natural products.

University of Nebraska–Lincoln, Graduate College, College of Arts and Sciences, Department of Chemistry, Lincoln, NE 68588. Offers analytical chemistry (PhD); biochemistry (PhD); chemistry (MS); inorganic chemistry (PhD); materials chemistry (PhD); organic chemistry (PhD); physical chemistry (PhD). *Degree requirements:* For master's, one foreign language, thesis optional, departmental qualifying exam; for doctorate, one foreign language, comprehensive exam, thesis/dissertation, departmental qualifying exams. *Entrance requirements:* For master's and doctorate, GRE. Additional exam requirements/recommendations for international students: Required—TOEFL (minimum score 550 paper-based; 213 computer-based). Electronic applications accepted. *Faculty research:* Bioorganic and bioinorganic chemistry, biophysical and bioanalytical chemistry, structure-function of DNA and proteins, organometallics, mass spectrometry.

University of Notre Dame, Graduate School, College of Science, Department of Chemistry and Biochemistry, Notre Dame, IN 46556. Offers biochemistry (MS, PhD); inorganic chemistry (MS, PhD); organic chemistry (MS, PhD); physical chemistry (MS, PhD). Terminal master's awarded for partial completion of doctoral program. *Degree requirements:* For master's, comprehensive exam, thesis; for doctorate, thesis/dissertation, qualifying exam. *Entrance requirements:* For master's and doctorate, GRE General Test, GRE Subject Test (strongly recommended). Additional exam requirements/recommendations for international students: Required—TOEFL (minimum score 600 paper-based; 250 computer-based; 80 iBT). Electronic applications accepted. *Faculty research:* Reaction design and mechanistic studies; reactive intermediates; synthesis, structure and reactivity of organometallic cluster complexes and biologically active natural products; bioorganic chemistry; enzymology.

University of Regina, Faculty of Graduate Studies and Research, Faculty of Science, Department of Chemistry and Biochemistry, Regina, SK S4S 0A2, Canada. Offers analytical chemistry (M Sc, PhD); biochemistry (M Sc, PhD); inorganic chemistry (M Sc, PhD); organic chemistry (M Sc, PhD); physical chemistry (M Sc, PhD). Part-time programs available. *Faculty:* 11 full-time (2 women), 3 part-time/adjunct (0 women). *Students:* 20 full-time (8 women). 25 applicants, 28% accepted. In 2009, 2 master's awarded. *Degree requirements:* For master's, thesis, departmental qualifying exam; for doctorate, thesis/dissertation, departmental qualifying exam. *Entrance requirements:* For master's and doctorate, GRE. Additional exam requirements/recommendations for international students: Required—TOEFL (minimum score 580 paper-based; 237 computer-based; 80 iBT). *Application deadline:* For fall admission, 1/1 for domestic students; for winter admission, 7/1 for domestic students. Applications are processed on a rolling basis. Application fee: $90 ($100 for international students). *Financial support:* In 2009–10, 5 fellowships (averaging $19,000 per year), 2 research assistantships (averaging $16,910 per year), 4 teaching assistantships (averaging $6,650 per year) were awarded; scholarships/grants also available. Financial award application deadline: 6/15. *Faculty research:* Organic synthesis, organic oxidations, ionic liquids theoretical/computational chemistry, protein biochemistry/biophysics, environmental analytical, photophysical/photochemistry. *Unit head:* Dr. Tanya Dahms, Head, 306-585-4247, E-mail: tanya.dohms@uregina.ca. *Application contact:* Dr. Scott Murphy, Program Coordinator, 306-585-4247, Fax: 306-585-4894, E-mail: scott.murphy@uregina.ca.

University of Southern Mississippi, Graduate School, College of Science and Technology, Department of Chemistry and Biochemistry, Hattiesburg, MS 39406-0001. Offers analytical chemistry (MS, PhD); biochemistry (MS, PhD); inorganic chemistry (MS, PhD); organic chemistry (MS, PhD); physical chemistry (MS, PhD). *Faculty:* 16 full-time (4 women). *Students:* 14 full-time (0 women), 5 part-time (4 women); includes 1 minority (African American), 12 international. Average age 29. 41 applicants, 17% accepted, 6 enrolled. In 2009, 2 master's, 6 doctorates awarded. *Degree requirements:* For master's, comprehensive exam, thesis; for doctorate, comprehensive exam, thesis/dissertation. *Entrance requirements:* For master's, GRE General Test, minimum GPA of 2.75 in last 60 hours; for doctorate, GRE General Test, minimum GPA of 3.5. Additional exam requirements/recommendations for international students: Required—TOEFL. *Application deadline:* For fall admission, 3/1 priority date for domestic students, 3/1 for international students. Applications are processed on a rolling basis. Application fee: $35. *Expenses:* Tuition, state resident: full-time $5096; part-time $284 per hour. Tuition, nonresident: full-time $13,052; part-time $726 per hour. Required fees: $402. Tuition and fees vary according to course level and course load. *Financial support:* In 2009–10, 3 research assistantships with full tuition reimbursements (averaging $17,000 per year), 19 teaching assistantships with full tuition reimbursements (averaging $20,716 per year) were awarded; fellowships, Federal Work-Study and institutionally sponsored loans also available. Support available to part-time students. Financial award application deadline: 3/15; financial award applicants required to submit FAFSA. *Faculty research:* Plant biochemistry, photo chemistry, polymer chemistry, x-ray analysis, enzyme chemistry. *Unit head:* Dr. Robert Bateman, Chair, 601-266-4701, Fax: 601-266-6075. *Application contact:* Dr. Sabine Heinhorst, Graduate Coordinator, 601-266-4702, Fax: 601-266-6075.

University of South Florida, Graduate School, College of Arts and Sciences, Department of Chemistry, Tampa, FL 33620-9951. Offers computational chemistry (PhD); analytical chemistry (MS, PhD); biochemistry (MS, PhD); computational chemistry (MS); environmental chemistry (MS, PhD); inorganic chemistry (MS, PhD); organic chemistry (MS); physical chemistry (MS, PhD); polymer chemistry (PhD). Part-time programs available. *Faculty:* 25 full-time (4 women). *Students:* 113 full-time (36 women), 15 part-time (11 women); includes 19 minority (5 African Americans, 6 Asian Americans or Pacific Islanders, 8 Hispanic Americans), 58 international. Average age 32. 112 applicants, 30% accepted, 21 enrolled. In 2009, 8 master's, 11 doctorates awarded. Terminal master's awarded for partial completion of doctoral program. *Degree requirements:* For master's, comprehensive exam, thesis (for some programs); for doctorate, 2 foreign languages, comprehensive exam, thesis/dissertation. *Entrance requirements:* For master's, GRE General Test or GMAT, minimum GPA of 3.0. Additional exam requirements/recommendations for international students: Required—TOEFL (minimum score 550 paper-based; 213 computer-based). *Application deadline:* For fall admission, 2/15 priority date for domestic students, 1/2 priority date for international students; for spring admission, 10/1 priority date for domestic students, 6/1 priority date for international students. Applications are processed on a rolling basis. Application fee: $30. Electronic applications accepted. *Financial support:* In 2009–10, teaching assistantships with tuition reimbursements (averaging $27,522 per year); unspecified assistantships also available. Financial award application deadline: 6/30. *Faculty research:* Synthesis, bio-organic chemistry, bioinorganic chemistry, environmental chemistry, NMR. Total annual research expenditures: $3.2 million. *Unit head:* Dr. Randy Larsen, Chairperson, 813-974-4129, Fax: 813-974-3203, E-mail: rlarsen@cas.usf.edu. *Application contact:* Patricia Muisener, Director, 813-974-1730, Fax: 813-974-3203, E-mail: muisener@cas.usf.edu.

The University of Tennessee, Graduate School, College of Arts and Sciences, Department of Chemistry, Knoxville, TN 37996. Offers analytical chemistry (MS, PhD); chemical physics (PhD); environmental chemistry (MS, PhD); inorganic chemistry (MS, PhD); organic chemistry (MS, PhD); physical chemistry (MS, PhD); polymer chemistry (MS, PhD); theoretical chemistry (PhD). Part-time programs available. Terminal master's awarded for partial completion of doctoral program. *Degree requirements:* For master's, thesis; for doctorate, thesis/dissertation. *Entrance requirements:* For master's and doctorate, GRE General Test, minimum GPA of 2.7.

Physical Chemistry

The University of Tennessee (continued)

Additional exam requirements/recommendations for international students: Required—TOEFL. Electronic applications accepted. *Expenses:* Tuition, state resident: full-time $6826; part-time $380 per semester hour. Tuition, nonresident: full-time $21,844; part-time $1147 per semester hour. Tuition and fees vary according to program.

The University of Texas at Austin, Graduate School, College of Natural Sciences, Department of Chemistry and Biochemistry, Austin, TX 78712-1111. Offers analytical chemistry (MA, PhD); biochemistry (MA, PhD); inorganic chemistry (MA, PhD); organic chemistry (MA, PhD); physical chemistry (MA, PhD). *Entrance requirements:* For master's and doctorate, GRE General Test.

The University of Toledo, College of Graduate Studies, College of Arts and Sciences, Department of Chemistry, Toledo, OH 43606-3390. Offers analytical chemistry (MS, PhD); biological chemistry (MS, PhD); inorganic chemistry (MS, PhD); organic chemistry (MS, PhD); physical chemistry (MS, PhD). Part-time programs available. *Degree requirements:* For master's, thesis; for doctorate, thesis/dissertation. *Entrance requirements:* For master's and doctorate, GRE General Test, GRE Subject Test. Additional exam requirements/recommendations for international students: Required—TOEFL. Electronic applications accepted. *Faculty research:* Enzymology, materials chemistry, crystallography, theoretical chemistry.

Vanderbilt University, Graduate School, Department of Chemistry, Nashville, TN 37240-1001. Offers analytical chemistry (MAT, MS, PhD); inorganic chemistry (MAT, MS, PhD); organic chemistry (MAT, MS, PhD); physical chemistry (MAT, MS, PhD); theoretical chemistry (MAT, MS, PhD). *Faculty:* 46 full-time (6 women). *Students:* 106 full-time (38 women); includes 10 minority (5 African Americans, 3 Asian Americans or Pacific Islanders, 2 Hispanic Americans), 21 international. Average age 27. 245 applicants, 27% accepted, 21 enrolled. In 2009, 10 master's, 21 doctorates awarded. Terminal master's awarded for partial completion of doctoral program. *Degree requirements:* For master's, thesis; for doctorate, thesis/dissertation, area, qualifying, and final exams. *Entrance requirements:* For master's and doctorate, GRE General Test, GRE Subject Test (recommended). Additional exam requirements/recommendations for international students: Required—TOEFL (minimum score 570 paper-based; 230 computer-based; 88 iBT). *Application deadline:* For fall admission, 1/15 for domestic and international students. Application fee: $0. Electronic applications accepted. *Financial support:* Fellowships with full and partial tuition reimbursements, research assistantships with full tuition reimbursements, teaching assistantships with full tuition reimbursements, Federal Work-Study, institutionally sponsored loans, scholarships/grants, traineeships, and health care benefits available. Financial award application deadline: 1/15; financial award applicants required to submit CSS PROFILE or FAFSA. *Faculty research:* Chemical synthesis; mechanistic, theoretical, bioorganic, analytical, and spectroscopic chemistry. *Unit head:* Mike P. Stone, Chair, 615-322-2861, Fax: 615-343-1234. *Application contact:* Charles M. Lukehart, Director of Graduate Studies, 615-322-2861, Fax: 615-343-1234, E-mail: charles.m.lukehart@vanderbilt.edu.

Virginia Commonwealth University, Graduate School, College of Humanities and Sciences, Department of Chemistry, Richmond, VA 23284-9005. Offers analytical chemistry (MS, PhD); chemical physics (PhD); inorganic chemistry (MS, PhD); organic chemistry (MS, PhD); physical chemistry (MS, PhD). Part-time programs available. Terminal master's awarded for partial completion of doctoral program. *Degree requirements:* For master's, thesis; for doctorate, thesis/dissertation, comprehensive cumulative exams, research proposal. *Entrance requirements:* For master's, GRE General Test, 30 undergraduate credits in chemistry; for doctorate, GRE General Test. *Faculty research:* Physical, organic, inorganic, analytical, and polymer chemistry; chemical physics.

Wake Forest University, Graduate School of Arts and Sciences, Department of Chemistry, Winston-Salem, NC 27109. Offers analytical chemistry (MS, PhD); inorganic chemistry (MS, PhD); organic chemistry (MS, PhD); physical chemistry (MS, PhD). Part-time programs available. *Degree requirements:* For master's, one foreign language, comprehensive exam, thesis; for doctorate, 2 foreign languages, comprehensive exam, thesis/dissertation. *Entrance requirements:* For master's and doctorate, GRE General Test. Additional exam requirements/recommendations for international students: Required—TOEFL (minimum score 213 computer-based). Electronic applications accepted.

West Virginia University, Eberly College of Arts and Sciences, Department of Chemistry, Morgantown, WV 26506. Offers analytical chemistry (MS, PhD); inorganic chemistry (MS, PhD); organic chemistry (MS, PhD); physical chemistry (MS, PhD); theoretical chemistry (MS, PhD). Part-time programs available. Postbaccalaureate distance learning degree programs offered (no on-campus study). Terminal master's awarded for partial completion of doctoral program. *Degree requirements:* For master's, thesis; for doctorate, thesis/dissertation. *Entrance requirements:* For master's, GRE General Test, GRE Subject Test (recommended), minimum GPA of 2.5; for doctorate, GRE General Test, GRE Subject Test (recommended), minimum GPA of 2.75. Additional exam requirements/recommendations for international students: Required—TOEFL. Electronic applications accepted. *Faculty research:* Analysis of proteins, drug interactions, solids and effluents by advanced separation methods; new synthetic strategies for complex organic molecules; synthesis and structural characterization of metal complexes for polymerization catalysis, nonlinear science, spectroscopy.

Yale University, Graduate School of Arts and Sciences, Department of Chemistry, New Haven, CT 06520. Offers biophysical chemistry (PhD); inorganic chemistry (PhD); organic chemistry (PhD); physical and theoretical chemistry (PhD). *Degree requirements:* For doctorate, thesis/dissertation. *Entrance requirements:* For doctorate, GRE General Test, GRE Subject Test. Additional exam requirements/recommendations for international students: Required—TOEFL.

Youngstown State University, Graduate School, College of Science, Technology, Engineering and Mathematics, Department of Chemistry, Youngstown, OH 44555-0001. Offers analytical chemistry (MS); biochemistry (MS); chemistry education (MS); inorganic chemistry (MS); organic chemistry (MS); physical chemistry (MS). Part-time programs available. *Degree requirements:* For master's, thesis. *Entrance requirements:* For master's, bachelor's degree in chemistry, minimum GPA of 2.7. Additional exam requirements/recommendations for international students: Required—TOEFL. *Faculty research:* Analysis of antioxidants, chromatography, defects and disorder in crystalline oxides, hydrogen bonding, novel organic and organometallic materials.

Theoretical Chemistry

Carnegie Mellon University, Mellon College of Science, Department of Chemistry, Pittsburgh, PA 15213-3891. Offers biotechnology and management (MS); chemistry (PhD), including bioinorganic, bioorganic, organic and materials, biophysics and spectroscopy, computational and theoretical, polymer; colloids, polymers and surfaces (MS). Part-time programs available. Terminal master's awarded for partial completion of doctoral program. *Degree requirements:* For doctorate, thesis/dissertation, departmental qualifying and oral exams, teaching experience. *Entrance requirements:* For master's, GRE General Test; for doctorate, GRE General Test, GRE Subject Test. Additional exam requirements/recommendations for international students: Required—TOEFL. Electronic applications accepted. *Faculty research:* Physical and theoretical chemistry, chemical synthesis, biophysical/bioinorganic chemistry.

Cornell University, Graduate School, Graduate Fields of Arts and Sciences, Field of Chemistry and Chemical Biology, Ithaca, NY 14853-0001. Offers analytical chemistry (PhD); bio-organic chemistry (PhD); biophysical chemistry (PhD); chemical biology (PhD); chemical physics (PhD); inorganic chemistry (PhD); materials chemistry (PhD); organic chemistry (PhD); organometallic chemistry (PhD); physical chemistry (PhD); polymer chemistry (PhD); theoretical chemistry (PhD). *Faculty:* 48 full-time (3 women). *Students:* 162 full-time (67 women); includes 15 minority (1 African American, 9 Asian Americans or Pacific Islanders, 5 Hispanic Americans), 53 international. Average age 26. 359 applicants, 19% accepted, 39 enrolled. In 2009, 31 doctorates awarded. *Degree requirements:* For doctorate, comprehensive exam, thesis/dissertation. *Entrance requirements:* For doctorate, GRE General Test, GRE Subject Test (chemistry), 3 letters of recommendation. Additional exam requirements/recommendations for international students: Required—TOEFL (minimum score 600 paper-based; 250 computer-based; 77 iBT). *Application deadline:* For fall admission, 1/10 for domestic students. Application fee: $70. Electronic applications accepted. *Expenses:* Tuition: Full-time $29,500. Required fees: $70. Full-time tuition and fees vary according to degree level, program and student level. *Financial support:* In 2009–10, 1 fellowship with full tuition reimbursement, 7 research assistantships with full tuition reimbursements, 29 teaching assistantships with full tuition reimbursements were awarded; institutionally sponsored loans, scholarships/grants, health care benefits, tuition waivers (full and partial), and unspecified assistantships also available. Financial award applicants required to submit FAFSA. *Faculty research:* Analytical, organic, inorganic, physical, materials, chemical biology. *Unit head:* Director of Graduate Studies, 607-255-4139, Fax: 607-255-4137. *Application contact:* Graduate Field Assistant, 607-255-4139, Fax: 607-255-4137, E-mail: chemgrad@cornell.edu.

Georgetown University, Graduate School of Arts and Sciences, Department of Chemistry, Washington, DC 20057. Offers analytical chemistry (PhD); biochemistry (PhD); computational chemistry (PhD); inorganic chemistry (PhD); materials chemistry (PhD); organic chemistry (PhD); physical chemistry (PhD); theoretical chemistry (PhD). Terminal master's awarded for partial completion of doctoral program. *Degree requirements:* For doctorate, comprehensive exam, thesis/dissertation. *Entrance requirements:* For doctorate, GRE General Test. Additional exam requirements/recommendations for international students: Required—TOEFL.

Laurentian University, School of Graduate Studies and Research, Programme in Chemistry and Biochemistry, Sudbury, ON P3E 2C6, Canada. Offers analytical chemistry (M Sc); biochemistry (M Sc); environmental chemistry (M Sc); organic chemistry (M Sc); physical/theoretical chemistry (M Sc). Part-time programs available. *Degree requirements:* For master's, thesis or alternative. *Entrance requirements:* For master's, honors degree with minimum second class. *Faculty research:* Cell cycle checkpoints, kinetic modeling, toxicology to metal stress, quantum chemistry, biogeochemistry metal speciation.

University of Calgary, Faculty of Graduate Studies, Faculty of Science, Department of Chemistry, Calgary, AB T2N 1N4, Canada. Offers analytical chemistry (M Sc, PhD); applied chemistry (M Sc, PhD); inorganic chemistry (M Sc, PhD); organic chemistry (M Sc, PhD); physical chemistry (M Sc, PhD); polymer chemistry (M Sc, PhD); theoretical chemistry (M Sc, PhD). *Degree requirements:* For master's, thesis; for doctorate, thesis/dissertation, candidacy exam. *Entrance requirements:* For master's, minimum GPA of 3.0; for doctorate, honors B Sc degree with minimum GPA of 3.7 or M Sc with minimum GPA of 3.3. Additional exam requirements/recommendations for international students: Required—TOEFL (minimum score 580 paper-based; 237 computer-based). Electronic applications accepted. *Faculty research:* Chemical analysis, chemical dynamics, synthesis theory.

The University of Tennessee, Graduate School, College of Arts and Sciences, Department of Chemistry, Knoxville, TN 37996. Offers analytical chemistry (MS, PhD); chemical physics (PhD); environmental chemistry (MS, PhD); inorganic chemistry (MS, PhD); organic chemistry (MS, PhD); physical chemistry (MS, PhD); polymer chemistry (MS, PhD); theoretical chemistry (PhD). Part-time programs available. Terminal master's awarded for partial completion of doctoral program. *Degree requirements:* For master's, thesis; for doctorate, thesis/dissertation. *Entrance requirements:* For master's and doctorate, GRE General Test, minimum GPA of 2.7. Additional exam requirements/recommendations for international students: Required—TOEFL. Electronic applications accepted. *Expenses:* Tuition, state resident: full-time $6826; part-time $380 per semester hour. Tuition, nonresident: full-time $21,844; part-time $1147 per semester hour. Tuition and fees vary according to program.

Vanderbilt University, Graduate School, Department of Chemistry, Nashville, TN 37240-1001. Offers analytical chemistry (MAT, MS, PhD); inorganic chemistry (MAT, MS, PhD); organic chemistry (MAT, MS, PhD); physical chemistry (MAT, MS, PhD); theoretical chemistry (MAT, MS, PhD). *Faculty:* 46 full-time (6 women). *Students:* 106 full-time (38 women); includes 10 minority (5 African Americans, 3 Asian Americans or Pacific Islanders, 2 Hispanic Americans), 21 international. Average age 27. 245 applicants, 27% accepted, 21 enrolled. In 2009, 10 master's, 21 doctorates awarded. Terminal master's awarded for partial completion of doctoral program. *Degree requirements:* For master's, thesis; for doctorate, thesis/dissertation, area, qualifying, and final exams. *Entrance requirements:* For master's and doctorate, GRE General Test, GRE Subject Test (recommended). Additional exam requirements/recommendations for international students: Required—TOEFL (minimum score 570 paper-based; 230 computer-based; 88 iBT). *Application deadline:* For fall admission, 1/15 for domestic and international students. Application fee: $0. Electronic applications accepted. *Financial support:* Fellowships with full and partial tuition reimbursements, research assistantships with full tuition reimbursements, teaching assistantships with full tuition reimbursements, Federal Work-Study, institutionally sponsored loans, scholarships/grants, traineeships, and health care benefits available. Financial award application deadline: 1/15; financial award applicants required to submit CSS PROFILE or FAFSA. *Faculty research:* Chemical synthesis; mechanistic, theoretical, bioorganic, analytical, and spectroscopic chemistry. *Unit head:* Mike P. Stone, Chair, 615-322-2861, Fax: 615-343-1234. *Application contact:* Charles M. Lukehart, Director of Graduate Studies, 615-322-2861, Fax: 615-343-1234, E-mail: charles.m.lukehart@vanderbilt.edu.

Wesleyan University, Graduate Programs, Department of Chemistry, Middletown, CT 06459. Offers biochemistry (MA, PhD); chemical physics (MA, PhD); inorganic chemistry (MA, PhD); organic chemistry (MA, PhD); physical chemistry (MA, PhD); theoretical chemistry (MA, PhD). *Faculty:* 14 full-time (2 women), 2 part-time/adjunct (1 woman). *Students:* 19 full-time (8 women), 2 part-time (0 women), 9 international. Average age 26. 40 applicants, 63% accepted, 4 enrolled. In 2009, 3 master's, 5 doctorates awarded. Terminal master's awarded for partial completion of doctoral program. *Degree requirements:* For master's, thesis, proposal; for doctorate, thesis/dissertation, proposal. *Entrance requirements:* For doctorate, GRE General Test, 3 recommendations. Additional exam requirements/recommendations for international students: Required—TOEFL. *Application deadline:* Applications are processed on a rolling basis. Application fee: $0. Electronic applications accepted. *Financial support:* In 2009–10, 4 research assistantships with full tuition reimbursements, 12 teaching assistantships with full tuition reimbursements were awarded; institutionally sponsored loans also available. Financial award application deadline: 4/15; financial award applicants required to submit FAFSA. *Unit head:* Dr. Joseph Knee, Chair, 860-685-2210. *Application contact:* Cait Zinser, Information Contact, 860-685-2573, Fax: 860-685-2211, E-mail: czinser@wesleyan.edu.

See Close-Up on page 115.

West Virginia University, Eberly College of Arts and Sciences, Department of Chemistry, Morgantown, WV 26506. Offers analytical chemistry (MS, PhD); inorganic chemistry (MS, PhD); organic chemistry (MS, PhD); physical chemistry (MS, PhD); theoretical chemistry (MS, PhD). Part-time programs available. Postbaccalaureate distance learning degree programs offered (no on-campus study). Terminal master's awarded for partial completion of doctoral program. *Degree requirements:* For master's, thesis; for doctorate, thesis/dissertation. *Entrance requirements:* For master's, GRE General Test, GRE Subject Test (recommended), minimum GPA of 2.5; for doctorate, GRE General Test, GRE Subject Test (recommended), minimum GPA of 2.75. Additional exam requirements/recommendations for international students: Required—TOEFL. Electronic applications accepted. *Faculty research:* Analysis of proteins, drug interactions, solids and effluents by advanced separation methods; new synthetic strategies for complex organic molecules; synthesis and structural characterization of metal complexes for polymerization catalysis, nonlinear science, spectroscopy.

Yale University, Graduate School of Arts and Sciences, Department of Chemistry, New Haven, CT 06520. Offers biophysical chemistry (PhD); inorganic chemistry (PhD); organic chemistry (PhD); physical and theoretical chemistry (PhD). *Degree requirements:* For doctorate, thesis/dissertation. *Entrance requirements:* For doctorate, GRE General Test, GRE Subject Test. Additional exam requirements/recommendations for international students: Required—TOEFL.

BRIGHAM YOUNG UNIVERSITY

Department of Chemistry and Biochemistry

Programs of Study

The Department of Chemistry and Biochemistry at Brigham Young University (BYU) offers courses of study leading to Ph.D. and M.S. degrees in the areas of analytical, inorganic, organic, physical chemistry, and biochemistry. The research experience is the major element of the graduate programs. Most students complete their Ph.D. research in four to five years. Research groups often include cross-disciplinary collaboration with faculty members and students in biology, engineering, and physics as well as with other areas within chemistry and biochemistry. Department faculty members are highly involved in each student's progress and foster a strong tradition of mentoring. All chemistry students must pass proficiency exams demonstrating competence at the undergraduate level in at least four subject areas by the end of their first year; biochemistry students must prove proficiency in biochemistry. An individualized schedule of graduate courses is established for each student based on their needs and interests. Most of this course work is taken during the first year, with the remainder in the second year. Depending on the area of study chosen by the student, either a form of comprehensive examination or several periodic cumulative examinations are required. Students present annual reviews and a research proposal to their faculty advisory committee. An active seminar schedule provides exposure to recent developments worldwide. Successful defense of a dissertation or thesis completes a student's training.

Research Facilities

Research activities occupy more than 50 percent of a 192,000-square-foot building. The University library, where the science collection includes more than 500,000 volumes and about 9,000 journal subscriptions, is located about 150 yards away. Major equipment available in the Department includes NMR (300 and two 500 MHz); mass spectrometry (ICR MS, ToF-SIMS, MALDI MS, Orbitrap MS, GC-MS, and LC-MS); X-ray diffraction (powder and single crystal); spectrophotometry (IR, visible, and UV); lasers (YAG, gas, excimer, Ti:sapphire, and dye); separations, including GC, LC, IC, GC-MS, LC-MS, CE, and microchip CE; particle size analyzers; environmental chambers; ICP; thermodynamics (calorimeters of all types, including temperature and pressure scanning, titration, flow, heat conduction, power compensation, combustion, and metabolic); and molecular biology (DNA synthesizer and sequencer, phosphorimager, tissue culture facility, recombinant DNA facility, fluorescence-activated cell sorter, and ultracentrifuges). All computing facilities are fully networked, including computational chemistry and laboratory workstations as well as office personal computers, with convenient connection to supercomputing facilities and the Internet.

The Department staffs a state-of-the-art electronics shop and small machine shop. The University maintains a precision machining facility with a full complement of state-of-the-art tools, including computer numerically controlled (CNC) lathe, mill, EDM drill, and wire EDM machine, as well as precision grinders and welders.

The College of Engineering and Technology supports an integrated microelectronics laboratory which provides a hands-on environment for fabricating microelectromechanical systems and optics. The laboratory is located in a 2,500-square-foot, class 10 cleanroom facility on campus. All necessary equipment for photolithography, etching, oxidation, thin film deposition, device testing, and device packaging is located in the cleanroom. A full-time engineer supervises all activities in the cleanroom.

Financial Aid

The Department provides full financial assistance to all students through teaching and research assistantships, fellowships, and tuition scholarships. The twelve-month stipend for beginning students for the 2010–11 year was $21,250 (taxable). The amount of the stipend is adjusted annually.

Cost of Study

Full-tuition scholarships are provided to all graduate students making satisfactory progress. Books average about $200 per semester.

Living and Housing Costs

The University Housing Office assists students in locating accommodation for on- and off-campus housing. Monthly rent and utilities range from $220 to $350 for a single student and from $450 to $800 for families. Other monthly expenses typically range from $150 to $300 for single students and from $250 to $500 for families.

Student Group

BYU has about 35,000 full-time students, with about 3,000 full-time graduate students. Students come from various academic and ethnic backgrounds and many geographic areas. The Department averages 95 graduate students. Currently, 39 percent are women and 51 percent are international students from sixteen countries.

Student Outcomes

BYU graduate degrees lead to a wide range of independent careers, with former students serving in academia, government, and industrial positions. About half of the Department's recent Ph.D.'s have continued their training in postdoctoral positions at leading research institutions, with the remainder finding employment directly with regional or national firms, in academia, or at government labs.

Location

BYU's beautiful 560-acre campus, with all the cultural and sports programs of a major university, is located in Provo, Utah (population 110,500), a semiurban area at the foot of Utah Valley's Wasatch Mountains. Outdoor recreational areas for skiing (snow and water), hiking, and camping are nearby, including nine spectacular national parks, six beautiful national monuments, fourteen major ski resorts, and forty-five diverse state parks. The Utah Symphony, Ballet West, Pioneer Theater Company, and the Utah Jazz basketball team are located in Salt Lake City, 45 miles to the north.

The University

Brigham Young University is one of the largest privately owned universities in the United States. Established in 1875 as Brigham Young Academy and sponsored by the Church of Jesus Christ of Latter-day Saints, BYU has a tradition of high standards in moral integrity and academic scholarship. Along with extensive undergraduate programs, BYU offers graduate degrees in a variety of disciplines through fifty-two graduate departments, including the Marriott School of Management and the J. Reuben Clark Law School. The Department of Chemistry and Biochemistry is one of the leading research departments at BYU.

Applying

Applicants should apply online at http://www.byu.edu/gradstudies. They must submit transcripts, letters of recommendation, and a $50 application fee. International students must pass the Test of English as a Foreign Language (TOEFL) or the International English Language Testing System (IELTS). The minimum TOEFL iBT score requirement is 85, with a minimum score of 22 required on the speaking section and 21 on the other sections. The IELTS requirement is an overall band score of 7.0, with a minimum band score of 6.0 in each module. The GRE General Test is required; GRE Subject Tests in chemistry or biochemistry are highly recommended. All application materials should be received by Graduate Studies no later than February 1 to be considered for admission the following fall. Applicants are not discriminated against on the basis of race, color, national origin, religion, gender, or handicap.

Correspondence and Information

Dr. Matthew R. Linford
Coordinator, Graduate Admissions
C101 BNSN (Benson Science Building)
Brigham Young University
Provo, Utah 84602

Phone: 801-422-4845
Fax: 801-422-0153
E-mail: chemguide@byu.edu
Web site: http://www.chem.byu.edu

Brigham Young University

THE FACULTY AND THEIR RESEARCH

Merritt B. Andrus, Professor; Ph.D., Utah, 1991; postdoctoral study at Harvard. Organic chemistry: synthetic methodology, asymmetric catalysis, natural products, and drug design.

Matthew C. Asplund, Associate Professor; Ph.D., Berkeley, 1998; postdoctoral study at Pennsylvania. Physical chemistry: ultrafast time-resolved vibrational and electronic spectroscopy of chemical reactions in solution; organometallic catalysis; salvation and charge transfer in solution; laser surface modification.

Daniel E. Austin, Assistant Professor; Ph.D., Caltech, 2002. Staff Scientist, Sandia National Labs, 2002–05. Analytical chemistry: mass spectrometry instrument development, microfabricated ion traps, microparticle acceleration and impact processes; portable instrumentation.

Emily A. Bates, Assistant Professor; Ph.D., Harvard, 2005. Biochemistry: genetics; molecular mechanisms of genetic human disorders: migraine and Anderson-Tawil syndrome.

David M. Belnap, Assistant Professor; Ph.D., Purdue, 1995; postdoctoral study at National Institutes of Health. Biochemistry: three-dimensional electron microscopy; structural studies of viruses and other macromolecular complexes; structural characterization of poliovirus cell-entry; development of 3DEM techniques.

Juliana Boerio-Goates, Professor; Ph.D., Michigan, 1979; postdoctoral study at Michigan. Physical chemistry: synthesis, energetics, and phase stabilities of nanoparticles and the dynamics of molecules absorbed on nanoparticle surfaces; thermodynamics of small biological molecules in the condensed phase.

Gregory F. Burton, Professor; Ph.D., Virginia Commonwealth, 1989; postdoctoral study at Virginia Commonwealth, 1989–91. Immunology/biochemistry; HIV/AIDS: contributions of follicular dendritic cells to HIV immunopathogenesis.

Allen R. Buskirk, Associate Professor; Ph.D., Harvard, 2004. Biochemistry and molecular biology: directed molecular evolution; ribosome stalling; bacterial ribosome rescue by tmRNA.

Steven L. Castle, Associate Professor; Ph.D., Scripps Research Institute, 2000. NIH Fellowship, 2000–02, California, Irvine. Organic chemistry: new synthetic methodology; total synthesis of complex natural products; synthesis of medicinally important compounds.

David V. Dearden, Professor; Ph.D., Caltech, 1989. NRC Fellowship, 1989, U.S. National Institute of Standards and Technology. Analytical/physical chemistry: host-guest molecular recognition in ion-molecule reactions, Fourier transform ion cyclotron resonance mass spectrometry with electrospray and laser ionization.

Daniel H. Ess, Assistant Professor; Ph.D., UCLA, 2007; postdoctoral research at Caltech and Scripps Research Institute, 2007–09 and North Carolina at Chapel Hill, 2009–10. Computational chemistry: quantum chemistry of organic and organometallic catalytic processes and reactive intermediates; hydrocarbon and small molecule activation and functionalization; reactivity and selectivity in organic and organometallic reactions.

Paul B. Farnsworth, Professor; Ph.D., Wisconsin, 1981; postdoctoral study at Indiana. Analytical chemistry: fundamental and applied measurements on inductively coupled plasmas; elemental mass spectrometry; laser spectrometry; ambient ionization for mass spectrometry.

Steven R. Goates, Professor; Ph.D., Michigan, 1981; postdoctoral study at Columbia. Analytical/physical chemistry: analysis of complex samples by optical and especially laser-based methods; supersonic jet spectroscopy; spectroscopy of interfaces; investigation of chromatographic processes.

Steven W. Graves, Professor; Ph.D., Yale, 1978; postdoctoral fellow, Tufts University School of Medicine, 1978–81; clinical chemistry fellow, Washington University School of Medicine, 1981–83. Biochemistry/bioanalytical chemistry: endogenous sodium pump inhibitors in hypertension and hypertensive pregnancy, especially preeclampsia; protein and mRNA expression of sodium pump isoforms in human pregnancy, parturition, and pregnancy complications; serum proteomics of human disease, especially complications of pregnancy, e.g., preeclampsia and preterm birth.

Young Wan Ham, Assistant Professor; Ph.D., Purdue, 2002; postdoctoral study at The Scripps Research Institute. Organic chemistry: design and synthesis of small RNA binding molecules for sequence/site-specific recognition of RNAs; nanoparticular drug delivery systems.

Jaron C. Hansen, Assistant Professor; Ph.D., Purdue, 2002; postdoctoral study at Caltech Jet Propulsion Laboratory. Analytical/physical chemistry: kinetics and spectroscopy of atmospherically important molecules; development of novel kinetic techniques and instrumentation.

Roger G. Harrison, Associate Professor; Ph.D., Utah, 1993; postdoctoral study at Minnesota. Inorganic chemistry: supramolecular chemistry; metal-assembled cage complexes; porous metal-organic materials; removal of organic compounds from water; metal-promoted catalysis; CdSe and ZnO nanocrystals.

Steven R. Herron, Assistant Research Professor; Ph.D., California, Irvine, 2001. Staff Scientist, 2001–04, California State, Fullerton. Biochemistry: protein and small molecule crystallography; protein structure-function studies.

John D. Lamb, Eliot A. Butler Professor; Ph.D., Brigham Young, 1978. Program Manager, Separations and Analysis, Office of Basic Energy Sciences, U.S. D.O.E., 1982–84; Associate Dean, Undergraduate Education, BYU. Inorganic chemistry: macrocyclic ligand chemistry, liquid membrane separations, ion chromatography, calorimetry.

Milton L. Lee, H. Tracy Hall Professor; Ph.D., Indiana, 1975; postdoctoral study at MIT. Analytical chemistry: microcolumn separations; microfluidic separations; microseparations-mass spectrometry.

Matthew R. Linford, Associate Professor; Ph.D., Stanford, 1996; postdoctoral study at the Max Planck Institute for Surface and Colloid Science. Analytical chemistry: surface and particle functionalization, patterning and characterization with thin organic films; new, high stability materials for chromatography, optical data storage, and silane deposition by CVD.

James E. Patterson, Assistant Professor; Ph.D., Illinois at Urbana-Champaign, 2004; Institute for Shock Physics, Washington State University, 2004–07. Physical chemistry: nonlinear vibrational spectroscopy of buried interfaces, links between structure and function in bonded materials, molecular basis for chromatographic retention.

Matt A. Peterson, Associate Professor; Ph.D., Arizona, 1992. NIH Fellowship, 1993–94, Colorado State. Organic chemistry: synthetic methods, synthesis of modified nucleosides and oligonucleotides, synthesis of medicinally important compounds.

Paul B. Savage, Professor; Ph.D., Wisconsin, 1993. NIH Fellowship, 1994–95, Ohio State. Organic chemistry: discovery of structural requirements of glycolipids for stimulation of natural killer T cells; development of new amphiphilic antibiotics.

Eric T. Sevy, Associate Professor; Ph.D., Columbia, 1999; postdoctoral study at MIT. Physical chemistry: chemical and molecular dynamics of collisional relaxation, energy transfer processes, and unimolecular reactions.

Randall B. Shirts, Associate Professor; Ph.D., Harvard, 1979; postdoctoral study at Joint Institute for Laboratory Astrophysics and University of Colorado. Theoretical chemistry: semiclassical quantization, quantum-classical correspondence, and statistical mechanics of nanoscale systems.

Daniel L. Simmons, Professor; Ph.D., Wisconsin, 1986. NIH and Leukemia Society Fellowships, 1986–89, Harvard. Biochemistry: cyclooxygenase-2 (COX-2), its biochemistry and molecular regulation.

Heidi R. Vollmer-Snarr, Assistant Professor; D.Phil., Oxford, 2000. NIH Fellowships, 2001–02, Sloan-Kettering Cancer Center and Columbia. Organic chemistry: synthetic, organic, bioorganic, and natural products chemistry, applicable to cancer and macular degeneration.

Richard K. Watt, Assistant Professor; Ph.D., Wisconsin–Madison, 1998; postdoctoral study at Princeton. Bioinorganic chemistry/biochemistry: synthesis of bionanomaterials, photocatalysis with bionanoparticles; role of metal ions in oxidative damage diseases; studies on anemia.

Barry M. Willardson, Professor; Ph.D., Purdue, 1990; postdoctoral study at Los Alamos National Laboratory. Biochemistry: molecular aspects of G-protein–medicated cellular signal transduction and chaperone-assisted assembly of the G-protein heterotrimeric complex.

Brian F. Woodfield, Professor; Ph.D., Berkeley, 1994; postdoctoral study at Naval Research Laboratory, Material Physics Branch, Washington, D.C. Physical chemistry: magnetic materials, superconductivity, and other technologically important solids using specific-heat measurements from 0.5 K to 400 K.

Adam T. Woolley, Professor; Ph.D., Berkeley, 1997. Runyon-Winchell Cancer Research Fund Fellowship, 1998–2000, Harvard. Analytical/physical chemistry: micro- and nano-fluidic devices for chemical and biochemical analysis, biotemplated lithography and nanofabrication, microcantilever-based biomarker sensing.

Brigham Young University

SELECTED PUBLICATIONS

Ma, Y., C. Song, J. We, and **M. B. Andrus.** Asymmetric, arylboronic acid addition to enones using novel dicyclophane imidazolium carbene-rhodium catalysts. *Angew. Chem. Int. Ed.* 42:5871–4, 2003.

Andrus, M. B., et al. Total synthesis of (+)-geldanamycin and (-)-ortho-quino-geldanamycin, asymmetric glycolate aldol reactions and biological evaluation. *J. Org. Chem.* 68:8162–9, 2003.

Andrus, M. B., J. Liu, E. L. Meredith, and E. Nartey. Synthesis of resveratrol using a direct decarbonylative heck approach from resorcylic acid. *Tetrahedron Lett.* 44:4819–22, 2003.

Pan, T., et al. **(M. C. Asplund).** Fabrication of calcium fluoride capillary electrophoresis microdevices for on-chip infrared detection. *J. Chromatogr. A* 1027(1–2):231–5, 2004.

Husseini, G. A., et al. **(M. C. Asplund, E. T. Sevy,** and **M. R. Linford).** Photochemical lithography: Creation of patterned, acid chloride functionalized surfaces using UV light and gas-phase oxalyl chloride. *Langmuir* 19(11):4856–8, 2003.

Lua, Y.-Y., et al. **(M. C. Asplund, S. A. Fleming,** and **M. R. Linford).** Amine-reactive monolayers on scribed silicon with controlled levels of functionality: The reaction of scribed silicon with mono- and diepoxides. *Angew. Chem. Int. Ed.* 42:4046–9, 2003.

Asplund, M. C., M. T. Zanni, and R. M. Hochstrasser. Two-dimensional infrared spectroscopy of peptides by phase-controlled femtosecond vibrational photon echoes. *Proc. Natl. Acad. Sci. U.S.A.* 97:8219–24, 2000.

Austin, D. E., B. K. Hansen, Y. Peng, and Z. Zhang. Multipole expansion in quadrupolar devices comprised of planar electrode arrays. *Int. J. Mass Spectrom.*, 2010. doi:10.1016/j.ijms.2010.05.009.

Austin, D. E., et al. Novel ion traps using planar resistive electrodes: Implications for miniaturized mass analyzers. *J. Am. Soc. Mass. Spectrom.* 19(10):1435–41, 2008.

Austin, D. E., et al. **(M. L. Lee).** Halo ion trap mass spectrometer. *Anal. Chem.* 79(7):2927–32, 2007.

Blain, M. G., et al. **(D. E. Austin).** Towards the hand-held mass spectrometer: design considerations, simulation, and fabrication of micrometer-scaled cylindrical ion traps. *Int. J. Mass Spectrom.* 236(1–3):91–104, 2004.

Bates, E. A., et al. Sumatriptan alleviates nitroglycerin-induced mechanical and thermal allodynia in mice. *Cephalalgia* 30(2):170–8, 2009.

Voisine, C., H., et al. **(E. A. Bates).** Identification of potential therapeutic drugs for Huntington's disease using *Caenorhabditis elegans*. *PLoS ONE.* 2(6):e504, 2007.

Bates, E. A., et al. Differential contributions of *Caenorhabditis elegans* histone deacetylases to huntingtin polyglutamine toxicity. *J. Neurosci.* 26(10):2830–8, 2006.

Faber, P. W., et al. **(E. A. Bates).** Glutamine/proline-rich PQE-1 proteins protect *Caenorhabditis elegans* neurons from huntingtin polyglutamine neurotoxicity. *Proc. Natl. Acad. Sci. U.S.A.* 99(26):17131–6, 2002.

Sanz-Garcia, E., A. B. Stewart, and **D. M. Belnap.** The random-model method enables ab initio three-dimensional reconstruction of asymmetric particles and determination of particle symmetry. *J. Struct. Biol.*, in press.

Hamblin, M. N., et al. **(D. M. Belnap, A. T. Woolley,** and **M. L. Lee).** Selective trapping and concentration of nanoparticles and viruses in dual-height nanofluidic channels. *Lab on a Chip* 10(2):173–8, 2010.

Budzinski, K. L., et al. **(D. M. Belnap).** Large structural change in isolated synaptic vesicles upon loading with neurotransmitter. *Biophys. J.* 97(9):2577–84, 2009.

Bubeck, D., et al. **(D. M. Belnap).** The structure of the poliovirus 135S cell entry intermediate at 10-Angstrom resolution reveals the location of an externalized polypeptide that binds to membranes. *J. Virol.* 79:7745–55, 2005.

Heymann, J. B., M. Chagoyen, and **D. M. Belnap.** Common conventions for interchange and archiving of three-dimensional electron microscopy information in structural biology. *J. Struct. Biol.* 151:196–207, 2005.

Ams, B. E., et al. **(J. Boerio-Goates).** Thermochemistry of a synthetic Na-Mg-rich triple-chain silicate: Determination of thermodynamic variables. *Am. Mineral.* 94(8–9):1242–54, 2009.

Navrotsky, A., et al. **(J. Boerio-Goates** and **B. F. Woodfield).** Application of calorimetry on a chip to high-pressure materials. *Proc. Natl. Acad. Sci. U.S.A.* 104(22):9187–91, 2007.

Liu, S., Q. Liu, **J. Boerio-Goates,** and **B. F. Woodfield.** Preparation of a wide array of ultra-high purity metals, metal oxides and mixed metal oxides with uniform particle sizes from 1 nm to bulk. *J. Advan. Mat.* 39(2):18–23, 2007.

Boerio-Goates, J., et al. **(B. F. Woodfield).** Surface water and the origin of the positive excess specific heat for 7 nm rutile and anatase nanoparticles. *Nano Lett.* 6(4):750–4, 2006.

Levchenko, A. A., et al. **(J. Boerio-Goates** and **B. F. Woodfield).** TiO_2 stability landscape: Polymorphism, surface energy, and bound water energetics. *Chem. Mater.* 18:6324–32, 2006.

Thacker, T. C., et al. **(G. F. Burton).** Follicular dendritic cells and human immunodeficiency virus type 1 transcription in CD4+ T cells. *J. Virol.* 83:150–8, 2009.

El Shikh, M. E., R. M. El Sayed, J. G. Tew, and **G. F. Burton.** Follicular dendritic cells (B lymphocyte stimulating). In *Encyclopedia of Life Sciences* Hoboken, New Jersey: John Wiley and Sons, 2009.

Keele, B., et al. **(G. F. Burton).** Characterization of the follicular dendritic cell reservoir of human immunodeficiency virus Type 1. *J. Virol.* 82:5548–61, 2008.

Estes, J. D., et al. **(G. F. Burton).** Follicular dendritic cell regulation of CXCR4-mediated germinal center CD4 T cell migration. *J. Immunol.* 173:6169–78, 2004.

Heath, S. L., et al. **G. F. Burton.** Follicular dendritic cells and human immunodeficiency virus infectivity. *Nature* 377:740–4, 1995.

Crandall, J., et al. **(A. R. Buskirk).** rRNA mutations that inhibit transfer-messenger RNA activity on stalled ribosomes. *J. Bacteriol.* 192(2):553–9, 2010.

Tanner, D. R., et al. **(A. R. Buskirk).** Genetic identification of nascent peptides that induce ribosome stalling. *J. Biol. Chem.* 284(50):34809–18, 2009.

Watts, T., D. Cazier, D. Healey, and **A. R. Buskirk.** SmpB contributes to reading frame selection in the translation of transfer-messenger RNA. *J. Mol. Biol.* 391(2):275–81, 2009.

Tanner, D. R., J. D. Dewey, M. R. Miller, and **A. R. Buskirk.** Genetic analysis of the structure and function of transfer messenger RNA pseudoknot 1. *J. Biol. Chem.* 281(15):10561–6, 2006.

Ma, B., et al. **(S. L. Castle).** Total synthesis of the antimitotic bicyclic peptide celogentin C. *J. Am. Chem. Soc.* 132(3):1159–71, 2010.

Nielsen, D. K., et al. **(S. L. Castle).** Synthesis of isohasubanan alkaloids via enantioselective ketone allylation and discovery of an unexpected rearrangement. *J. Org. Chem.* 74:1187–99, 2009.

Li, F., and **S. L. Castle.** Synthesis of the acutumine spirocycle via a radical-polar crossover reaction. *Org. Lett.* 9(20):4033–6, 2007.

Jones, S. B., et al. **(S. L. Castle).** Total synthesis of (±)–hasubanonine. *Org. Lett.* 8:3757–60, 2006.

He, L., et al. **(S. L. Castle).** Synthesis of the celogentin C. right-hand ring. *Org. Lett.* 8:1165–8, 2006.

Rockwood, A. L., J. R. Van Orman, and **D. V. Dearden.** Isotopic compositions and exact masses of single isotopic peaks. *J. Am. Soc. Mass Spectrom.* 15:12–21, 2004.

Zhang, H., et al. **(D. V. Dearden).** Cucurbit[6]uril pseudorotaxanes: Distinctive gas phase dissociation and reactivity. *J. Am. Chem. Soc.* 125:9284–5, 2003.

Zhou, L., et al. **(D. V. Dearden** and **M. L. Lee).** Incorporation of a venturi device in electrospray ionization. *Anal. Chem.* 75:5978, 2003.

Ess, D. H. Distortion, interaction, and conceptual DFT perspectives of MO4-alkene (M = Os, Re, Tc, Mn) cycloadditions. *J. Org. Chem.* 74(4):1498–508, 2009.

Ess, D. H., R. J. Nielsen, W. A. Goddard III, and R. A. Periana. Transition-state charge transfer reveals electrophilic, ambiphilic, and nucelophilic carbon-hydrogen bond activation. *J. Am. Chem. Soc.* 131(33):11686–8, 2009.

Ess, D. H., J. Kister, M. Chen, and W. R. Roush. Origin of thermodynamic versus kinetic control of allene hydroboration with 9-borabicyclo[3.3.1]nonane and 10(R)-trimethylsilyl-9-borabicyclo[3.3.2]decane. *Org. Lett.* 11(23):5538–41, 2009.

Ess, D. H., J. Kister, M. Chen, and W. R. Roush. Quantum-mechanical study of 10-R-9-borabicyclo[3.3.2]decane alkene hydroboration. *J. Org. Chem.* 74(22):8626–37, 2009.

Ess, D. H., and K. N. Houk. Distortion/interaction energy control of 1,3-dipolar cycloaddition reactivity. *J. Am. Chem. Soc.* 130(31):10187–98, 2008.

Farnsworth, P. B., et al. A comparison of ion and atom behavior in the first stage of an inductively coupled plasma mass spectrometer vacuum interface: Evidence of the effect of an ambipolar electric field. *Spectrochim. Acta B Atom. Spectros.* 64(9):905–10, 2009.

Spencer, R. L., N. Taylor, and **P. B. Farnsworth.** Comparison of calculated and experimental flow velocities upstream from the sampling cone of an inductively coupled plasma mass spectrometer. *Spectrochim. Acta B Atom. Spectros.* 64(9):921–4, 2009.

Wood, M. C., D. K. Busby, and **P. B. Farmsworth.** Microscopic imaging of glass surfaces under the effects of desorption electrospray ionization. *Anal. Chem.* 81(15):6407–15, 2009.

Ma, H., N. Taylor, and **P. B. Farnsworth.** The effect of the sampling interface on spatial distributions of barium ions and atoms in an inductively coupled plasma ion source. *Spectrochim. Acta B Atom. Spectros.* 64(5)384–91, 2009.

Radicic, W. N., et al. **(P B. Farnsworth).** Characterization of the supersonic expansion in the vacuum interface of an inductively coupled plasma mass spectrometer by high-resolution diode laser spectroscopy. *Spectrochim. Acta* 61B:686–95, 2006.

Olsen, J. B., J. H. Macedone, and **P. B. Farnsworth.** Source gas kinetic temperatures in an ICP-MS determined by measurements of the gas velocities in the first vacuum stage. *J. Anal. At. Spectrom.* 21:856–60, 2006.

Baker, L. R., et al. **(S. R. Goates).** Density gradients in packed columns part I: Effects of density gradients on analyte retention and separation speed. *J. Chrom. A,* 1216:5588–93, 2009.

Baker, L. R., et al. **(S. R. Goates).** Density gradients in packed columns part II: Effects of density gradients on separation efficiency. *J. Chrom. A,* 1216:5594–9, 2009.

Baker, L. R., A. W. Orton, **S. R. Goates,** and B. A. Horn. Characterization of carbon dioxide mobile phase density profiles in packed capillary columns by Raman microscopy. *Appl. Spectros.* 63(1):108–11, 2009.

Ahmed, S. B., et al. **(S. W. Graves).** A comparison of prediction equations for estimating glomerular filtration rate in pregnancy. *Hypertens. Pregnancy* 28(3):243–55, 2009.

Merrell, K., et al. **(S. W. Graves).** An integrated serum proteomic approach capable of monitoring the low molecular weight proteome with sequencing of intermediate to large peptides. *Rapid Comm. Mass Spectrom.* 23(17):2685–96, 2009.

Bently-Lewis, R., **S. W. Graves,** and E. W. Seely. The renin-aldosterone response to stimulation and suppression during normal pregnancy. *Hypertens. Pregnancy* 24:1–16, 2005.

Merrell, K., et al. **(S. W. Graves).** Analysis of low-abundance, low-molecular-weight serum proteins using mass spectrometry. *J. Biomol. Tech.* 14:235–44, 2004.

Esplin, M. S., M. B. Fausett, D. S. Faux, and **S. W. Graves.** Changes in the isoforms of the sodium pump in the placenta and myometrium of women in labor. *Am. J. Obstet. Gynecol.* 188:759–64, 2003.

Shultz, M. D., et al. **(Y. W. Ham).** Small molecule dimerization inhibitors of wild type and mutant HIV protease: A focused library approach. *J. Am. Chem. Soc.* 126:9886–7, 2004.

Ham, Y. W., and D. L. Boger. A powerful selection assay for mixture libraries of DNA alkylating agents. *J. Am. Chem. Soc.* 126:9194–5, 2004.

Ham, Y. W., W. Tse, and D. L. Boger. High-resolution assessment of protein DNA binding affinity and selectivity utilizing a fluorescent intercalator displacement (FID) assay. *Bioorg. Med. Chem. Lett.* 13:3805–7, 2003.

Brigham Young University

Wang, J., **R. G. Harrison,** and **J. D. Lamb.** Anion separation and preconcentration with cyclen-resorcinarene derivatives. *J. Chromatogr. Sci.* 47(7):510–5, 2009.

Harrison, R. G., A. L. Washburn, A. T. Pickett, and D. M. Call. Assembly of CdSe nanoparticles into microspheres by a liquid droplet emulsion process. *J. Mater. Chem.* 18:3718–22, 2008.

Bair, J. S., and **R. G. Harrison.** Synthesis and optical properties of bifunctional thiophene molecules coordinated to ruthenium. *J. Org. Chem.* 72(18):6653–61, 2007.

Liu, R., **S. R. Herron,** and **S. A. Fleming.** Copper catalyzed aziridination of tethered alkenes. *J. Org. Chem.* 72:5587–91, 2007.

Reinheimer, E. W., et al. **(S. R. Herron).** Crystal structures of diphosphinated group 6 Fischer alkoxy carbenes. *J. Chem. Crystallogr.* 33:503–14, 2003.

Herron, S. R., et al. Characterization and implications of Ca^{2+} binding to pectate lyase C. *J. Biol. Chem.* 278:12271–7, 2003.

Herron, S. R., et al. Structure and function of pectic enzymes: Virulence factors of plant pathogens. *Proc. Natl. Acad. Sci. U.S.A.* 97:8762–9, 2000.

Wang, J., **J. D. Lamb,** L. D. Hansen, and **R. G. Harrison.** Multiple anion binding by a zinc-containing tetratopic cyclen-resorcinarene. *Journal of Inclusion Phenomena* 67(1–2):55–61, 2010.

Lamb, J. D. *Let's Start Chemistry* (text and CD). Tokyo: Sankyo Shuppan, 2009.

Lamb, J. D., et al. **(R. G. Harrison).** Cation effect on anion separations by aza-crown ligands in liquid membranes. *J. Membr. Sci.* 321(1):15–21, 2008.

Lamb, J. D., et al. Determination of perchlorate in drinking water by ion chromatography using macrocycle-based concentration and separation methods. *J. Chromatogr. A* 1118:100–5, 2006.

Chen, X., H. D.Tolley, and **M. L. Lee.** Polymeric cation-exchange monolithic columns containing phosphoric acid functional groups for capillary liquid chromatography of peptides and proteins. *J. Chrom.* 1217(24):3844–54, 2010.

Zhang, Z., et al. **(M. L. Lee** and **D. E. Austin).** Paul trap mass analyzer consisting of opposing microfabricated electrode plates. *Anal. Chem.* 81(13):5241–8, 2009.

Li, Y., H. D. Tolley, and **M. L. Lee.** Poly[hydroxyethyl acrylate-co-poly(ethylene glycol) diacrylate] monolithic column for efficient hydrophobic interaction chromatography of proteins. *Anal. Chem.* 81(22):9416–24, 2009.

Sun, X., D. Li, and **M. L. Lee.** Poly(ethylene glycol)-functionalized polymeric microchips for capillary electrophoresis. *Anal. Chem.* 81(15):6278–84, 2009.

Truong, T. V., et al. **(M. L. Lee).** Sample introduction in gas chromatography using a coiled wire filament. *J. Chrom.* 1216(40):6852–7, 2009.

Li, Y., H. D.Tolley, and **M. L. Lee.** Preparation of polymer monoliths that exhibit size exclusion properties for proteins and peptides. *Anal. Chem.* 81(11):4406–13, 2009.

Hill, J. P., et al. **(M. R. Linford).** Macroporous poly(aromatic amine): Synthesis and film fabrication. *Colloid. Surface. Physicochem. Eng. Aspect.* 354:156–61, 2010.

Lunt, B. M., and **M. R. Linford.** Long-term digital data storage. U.S. Patent number 7613869, awarded 2009.

Shirahata, N., et al. **(M. R. Linford** and **M. C. Asplund).** Laser-derived one-pot synthesis of silicon nanocrystals terminated with organic monolayers. *Chem. Commun.* (31):4684–6, 2009.

Lunt, B. M., and **M. R. Linford.** Predicting the reliability of data on DVD-R discs. Proceedings of ODS 2009 (Optical Data Storage), May 10–13, 2009.

Lunt, B. M., and **M. R. Linford.** Towards a true archival-quality optical disc. Proceedings of International Symposium on Optical Memory (ISOM), October 4–8, 2009.

Blake, R. B., et al. **(M. R. Linford).** One-step growth of ca. 2-15 nm polymer thin films on hydrogen-terminated silicon. *Macromol. Rapid Comm.* 29(8):638–44, 2008.

Patterson, J. E., Z. A. Dreger, and Y. M. Gupta. Shock wave induced phase transition in RDX single crystals. *J. Phys. Chem. B* 111(37):10897–904, 2007.

Pang, Y., et al. **(J. E. Patterson).** Vibrational energy in molecules probed with high time and space resolution. *Int. Rev. Phys. Chem.* 26(1):223–48, 2006.

Huang, W., **J. E. Patterson,** A. Lagutchev, and D. D. Dlott. Shock compression spectroscopy with high time and space resolution. In *Shock Compression of Condensed Matter–2005,* American Institute of Physics Conference Proceedings, vol. 845, pp. 1265–70, eds. M. D. Furnish, M. Elert, T. P. Russell, and C. T. White, 2006.

Patterson, J. E., et al. Time- and space-resolved studies of shock compression molecular dynamics. *Shock Waves* 14(5/6):391–402, 2005.

Peterson, M. A., M. Oliveira, and M. C. Christiansen. Antiproliferative and protein kinase binding activities of some N6,5'-bis-ureido 5'-amino-5'-deoxyadenosine derivatives. *Nucleos. Nucleot. Nucleic Acids* 28:394–407, 2009.

Robins, M. J., et al. **(M. A. Peterson).** Synthesis and biological evaluation of 3,3-difluoropyridine-2,4(1H,3H)-dione and 3-deaza-3-fluorouracil base and nucleoside derivatives. *J. Med. Chem.* 52:3018–27, 2009.

Peterson, M. A., M. Oliveira, M. A. Christiansen, and C. E. Cutler. Preliminary SAR analysis of novel antiproliferative n6,5'-bis-ureidoadenosine derivatives. *Bioorg. Med. Chem. Lett.* 19(23):6775–9, 2009.

Morshed, S. R., et al. **(P. B. Savage).** B-galactosylceramide alters invariant natural killer T cell function and is effective treatment for lupus. *Clin. Immunol.* 132(3):321–33, 2009.

Yin, N., et al. **(P. B. Savage).** Alpha anomers of iGb3 and Gb3 stimulate cytokine production by natural killer T cells. *ACS Chemical Biology* 4(3):199–208, 2009

Kim, H. Y., et al. **(P. B. Savage).** The development of airway hyperreactivity in T-bet-deficient mice requires CD1 d-restricted NKT cells. *J. Immunol.* 182(5):3252–61, 2009.

Monine, M. I., et al. **(P. B. Savage).** Modeling multivalent ligand-receptor interactions with steric constraints on configurations of cell-surface receptor aggregates. *Biophys. J.* 98(1):48–56, 2010.

Lai, X.-Z., et al. **(P. B. Savage).** Ceragenins: cholic acid-based mimics of antimicrobial peptides. *Accounts Chem. Res.* 41(10):1233–40, 2008.

Mattner, J., and **P. B. Savage** et al. Liver autoimmunity triggered by microbial activation of natural killer T cells. *Cell Host & Microbe* 3(5):304–15, 2008.

Johnson, J. A., et al. **(E. T. Sevy).** Rotationally resolved IR-diode laser studies of ground state CO_2 excited by collisions with vibrationally excited pyridine. *J. Phys. Chem. A* 112(12):2543–52, 2008.

Johnson, J. A., et al. **(E. T. Sevy).** Quenching of highly vibrationally excited pyrimidine by collisions with CO_2. *J. Chem. Phys.* 128(5):054304, 2008.

Mitchell, D. G., et al. **(E. T. Sevy).** Collisional relaxation of the three vibrationally excited difluorobenzene isomers by collisions with CO_2: Effect of donor vibrational mode. *J. Phys. Chem. A* 112(6):1157–67, 2008.

Duffin, A. M., J. A. Johnson, M. A. Muyskens, and **E. T. Sevy.** Competition between photochemistry and energy transfer in UV-excited diazabenzenes. 4. UV photodissociation of 2,3- ,2,5-, and 2,6- dimethylpyrazine. *J. Phys. Chem. A* 111(51):13330–38, 2007.

Shirts, R. B. Correcting two long-standing errors in point group symmetry character tables. *J. Chem. Educ.* 84(11):1882, 2007.

Shirts, R. B., S. R. Burt, and A. M. Johnson. Periodic boundary condition induced breakdown of the equipartition principle and other kenetic effects of finite sample size in classical hard-sphere molecular dynamics simulation. *J. Chem. Phys.* 124:164102, 2006.

Shirts, R. B., and M. R. Shirts. Deviations from the Boltzmann distribution in small microcanonical quantum systems: Two approximate one-particle energy distributions. *J. Chem. Phys.* 117:5564–75, 2002.

Ballif, B. A., et al. **(D. L. Simmons).** Interaction of cyclooxygenases with an apoptosis- and autoimmunity-associated protein. *Proc. Natl. Acad. Sci. U.S.A.* 93:5544–9, 1996.

Lu, X., et al. **(D. L. Simmons).** Nonsteroidal anti-inflammatory drugs cause apoptosis and induce cyclooxygenases in chicken embryo fibroblasts. *Proc. Natl. Acad. Sci. U.S.A.* 92:7961–5, 1995.

Xie, W., et al. **(D. L. Simmons).** Expression of a mitogen-responsive gene encoding prostaglandin synthase is regulated by mRNA splicing. *Proc. Natl. Acad. Sci. U.S.A.* 88:2692–6, 1991.

Cristofol, V.-B., et al. **(H. R. Vollmer-Snarr).** The age lipid A2E and mitochondrial dysfunction synergistically impair phagocytosis by retinal pigment epithelial cells. *J. Biol. Chem.* 283(36):24770–80, 2008.

Vollmer-Snarr, H. R., et al. Amino-retinoid compounds in the human retinal pigment epithelium. In *Retinal Degenerations,* eds. Hollyfield, J. G., R. E. Anderson, and M. M. LaVail. New York: Springer, 2006.

Karan, G., et al. **(H. R. Vollmer-Snarr).** Lipofuscin accumulation, abnormal electrophysiology, and photoreceptor degeneration in mutant *ELOVL4* transgenic mice: A model for macular degeneration. *Proc. Natl. Acad. Sci. U.S.A.* 102(11):4164–9, 2005.

Mazzola, R. D., Jr.; T. D. White, **H. R. Vollmer-Snarr,** and F. G. West. Stereoselective Nazarov cyclizations of bridged bicyclic dienones. *Org. Lett.* 7(13):2799–801, 2005.

Jockusch, S., et al. **(H. R. Vollmer-Snarr).** Photochemistry of A1E, a retinoid with a conjugated pyridinium moiety: Competition between pericyclic photooxygenation and pericyclization. *J. Am. Chem. Soc.* 126(14):4646–52, 2004.

Hilton, R. J., J. D. Keyes, and **R. K. Watt.** Photoreduction of Au(III) to form Au(0) nanoparticles using ferritin as a photocatalyst. *Proceedings of SPIE* 7646:764607, 2010.

Hilton, R. J., J. D. Keyes, and **R. K. Watt.** Maximizing the photocatalytic properties of ferritin as a photocatalyst in an artificial photosynthesis system. *Proceedings of SPIE* 7646:76460J, 2010.

Watt, R. K., R. J. Hilton, and D. M. Graff. Oxido-reduction is not the only mechanism allowing ions to traverse the ferritin protein shell. *Biochim. Biophys. Acta,* 2010. doi: 10.1016/j.bbagen.2010.03.001.

Zhang, B., et al. **(R. K. Watt).** Rate of iron transfer through the horse spleen ferritin shell determined by the rate of formation of Prussian Blue and Fe-desferrioxamine within the ferritin cavity. *Biophys. Chem.* 120(2):96–105, 2006.

Cutler, C., et al. **(R. K. Watt).** Iron loading into ferritin can be stimulated or inhibited by the presence of cations and anions: A specific role for phosphate. *J. Inorg. Biochem.* 99(12):2270–5, 2005.

Smrcka, A. V., et al. **(B. M. Willardson).** NMR analysis of G protein beta/gamma subunit complexes reveals a dynamic Ga-Gbg subunit interface and multiple protein recognition modes. *Proc. Nat'l. Acad. Sci. U.S.A.* 107:639–44, 2010.

Lukov, G. L., et al. **(B. M. Willardson).** Mechanism of assembly of G protein bg subunits by protein kinase CK2-phosphorylated phosducin-like protein and the cytosolic chaperonin complex: *J. Biol. Chem.* 281:22261–74, 2006.

Becerril, H. A., P. J. Ludtke, **B. M. Willardson,** and **A. T. Woolley.** DNA-templated nickel nanostructures and protein assemblies. *Langmuir* 22:10140–4, 2006.

Lukov, G. L., et al. **(B. M. Willardson).** Phosducin-like protein acts as a molecular chaperone for G protein bg dimer assembly. *EMBO J.* 24:1965–75, 2005.

Martin-Benito, J., et al. **(B. M. Willardson).** Structure of the complex between phosduin-like protein and the cytosolic chaperonin complex. *Proc. Natl. Acad. Sci. U.S.A.* 101:17410–15, 2004.

Ming, Y., W. Hsiang-Yu, and **A. T. Woolley.** Polymer microchip CE of proteins either off- or on-chip labeled with chameleon dye for simplified analysis. *Electrophoresis* 30(24):4230–6, 2009.

Yang, W., X. Sun, H. Wang, and **A. T. Woolley.** Integrated microfluidic device for serum biomarker quantitation using either standard addition or a calibration curve. *Anal. Chem.* 81(19):8230–5, 2009.

Becerril, H. A., and **A. T. Woolley.** DNA-templated nanofabrication. *Chem. Soc. Rev.* 38(2):329–37, 2009.

Pound, E., J. R. Ashton, H. A. Becerril, and **A. T. Woolley.** PCR-based scaffold preparation for the production of thin, branched DNA origami nanostructures of arbitrary sizes. *Nano Lett.* 9(12):4302–5, 2009

DUQUESNE UNIVERSITY

School of Natural and Environmental Sciences
Department of Chemistry and Biochemistry

Program of Study

The Department of Chemistry and Biochemistry offers a program of graduate study in chemistry and biochemistry leading to the Ph.D. and M.S. degrees.

Graduate students begin laboratory research during their first semester in residence and participate in two semester-long research experiences in the laboratories of 2 different investigators during their first year. First-year students enroll in several short, intensive courses that emphasize applied research skills. Students typically do not enroll in any other courses during the first year, allowing complete focus upon research during this period. At the end of the first year, students are advanced to Ph.D. candidacy based upon successful completion and defense of their research projects. Academic requirements during the second and subsequent years are determined by the student's dissertation committee and are designed on an individual basis. Candidates for the Ph.D. degree are required to submit and defend an original research proposal in an area unrelated to their dissertation research. The Department sponsors a weekly research colloquium series that features speakers from academia, industry, and government.

For the M.S. degree, a minimum of 30 semester hours of combined course and research credits are required.

Research Facilities

The Department of Chemistry and Biochemistry is housed in the Richard King Mellon Hall of Science, an award-winning laboratory designed by Mies van der Rohe. Spectroscopic capability within the Department includes multinuclear 500- and 300-MHz NMRs, GC/MS, three LC/MS (Bruker micrOTOF, Agilent TOF, and Waters Z-spray), laser Raman, FT-IR, UV/visible, fluorescence, and atomic absorption spectroscopies. Separations instrumentation includes ultra-high-speed and high-speed centrifuges, gas chromatographs, an ion chromatographic system, capillary electrophoresis, nanoelectrospray systems, two ICP-MS systems, and HPLCs. An electrochemical instrumentation laboratory, a robotics and automation facility, a computer-controlled chemical microwave system, two clean-laboratory facilities and a single-crystal X-ray diffraction facility, and ICP-MS capabilities are available for research. Modeling and computing have SGI supercomputers available within the Center for Computational Sciences.

Financial Aid

A number of teaching and research assistantships are available for Ph.D. students. For 2010–11, annual stipends are $20,800, plus tuition remission. Several prestigious fellowships for graduate studies are offered by the Bayer School.

Cost of Study

Tuition in 2010–11 is $907 per credit. Scholarships provide tuition remission for teaching and research assistants, as described above.

Living and Housing Costs

Off-campus housing is available within easy walking or commuting distance of the University. Living costs for off-campus housing are very reasonable compared with those in other urban areas of the United States.

Student Group

Duquesne University has a total enrollment of more than 10,000 students in its ten schools. With 150 graduate students and 43 full-time faculty members in the graduate programs in the Bayer School of Natural and Environmental Sciences, the University offers students a highly personalized learning and advisement environment.

Location

Duquesne University is located on a bluff overlooking the city of Pittsburgh. This location offers ready access to the many cultural, social, and entertainment attractions of the city. Within walking distance of the campus are Heinz Hall for the Performing Arts (home of the symphony, opera, ballet, theater, and other musical and cultural institutions), the Mellon Arena (center for indoor sporting events and various exhibitions, concerts, and conventions), Heinz Field and PNC Park (for outdoor sporting events), and Market Square (entertainment and nightlife center). The libraries, museums, art galleries, and music hall of the Carnegie Institute in the Oakland area are easily accessible by public transportation (routes pass immediately adjacent to the campus) or by private automobile. As the third-largest center for corporate headquarters and one of the twenty largest metropolitan areas in the United States, Pittsburgh also offers many professional career opportunities for its residents.

The University

Founded in 1878 by the Fathers and Brothers of the Congregation of the Holy Ghost, Duquesne University has provided the opportunity for an education to students from many backgrounds, without regard to sex, race, creed, color, or national or ethnic origins. In the past twenty-five years, the University has undergone a dramatic physical transformation, from a makeshift physical plant occupying approximately 12 acres to a modern, highly functional educational facility that is located on its own 40-acre hilltop overlooking downtown Pittsburgh.

Applying

Applications for admission to graduate study with financial aid should be submitted no later than February 15 for the academic year beginning in the following September. Applications for admission without financial aid may be made up to one month prior to the beginning of the term in which the student desires to begin graduate work. All applications require official transcripts of previous undergraduate and graduate work and three letters of recommendation from faculty members who are familiar with the applicant's past academic progress. Application forms are available online at http://www.duq.edu/chemistry/grad-admissions.cfm or by writing to or calling the Office of the Dean, Bayer School of Natural and Environmental Sciences, Department of Chemistry and Biochemistry.

Correspondence and Information

Graduate Programs
Bayer School of Natural and Environmental Sciences
100 Mellon Hall
Duquesne University
Pittsburgh, Pennsylvania 15282

Phone: 412-396-4900
Fax: 412-396-4881
E-mail: gradinfo@duq.edu
Web site: http://www.science.duq.edu

Duquesne University

THE FACULTY

Jennifer Aitken, Associate Professor; Ph.D., Michigan State. Solid-state inorganic materials chemistry: elucidation of new crystal structures, synthesis and study of novel solid-state materials with potential use in optical and electronic technologies, crystal growth.
Partha Basu, Professor; Ph.D., Jadavpur (India), 1991. Inorganic/bioinorganic/biochemistry: structure-function relation in arsenic and nitrate metabolism, signaling.
Bruce D. Beaver, Professor; Ph.D., Massachusetts, 1984. Organic chemistry: oxygenation of organic molecules, development of new antioxidants, oxidative degradation of petroleum products, chemistry of wine making.
Michael Cascio, Associate Professor; Ph.D., Columbia, 1988. Structure-function studies of ion channels, membrane biophysics, proteomic studies of neurodegenerative disorders.
Jeffrey D. Evanseck, Professor; Ph.D., UCLA, 1990. Theoretical and computational chemistry: quantum and classical simulations coupled with experiment, energy landscapes of biomolecules, novel ionic liquids for catalysis, influence of solvent on organic reaction mechanism, supramolecular complexation for nanotechnology.
Fraser F. Fleming, Professor; Ph.D., British Columbia, 1990. Organic chemistry: developing new reactions of nitriles, synthesis of anti-AIDS and anticancer drugs, synthesis of natural products.
Ellen Gawalt, Associate Professor; Ph.D., Princeton. Bioorganic and materials chemistry: chemical modification of metal oxide surfaces used in biomaterials and reaction mechanisms of interfacial reactions.
Mitchell E. Johnson, Associate Professor; Ph.D., Massachusetts Amherst, 1993. Analytical chemistry: trace analysis of lipids, high-efficiency separations, laser-induced fluorescence, multidimensional chromatography, microfluidics, bioanalytical chemistry.
Paul G. Johnson, Director of Departmental Affairs; Ph.D., Duquesne, 1971.
Shahed Khan, Associate Professor; Ph.D., Flinders (Australia), 1977. Physical chemistry: electrochemistry, photoelectrochemistry, solar energy conversion by thin-film organic and inorganic semiconductors, electrocatalytic biosensors, electrosynthesis of conducting polymers, electrochemical surface modification, theory of electron transfer reactions in condensed medium, effect of solvent dynamics on electrochemical electron transfer reactions.
H. M. Kingston, Professor; Ph.D., American, 1978. Analytical and environmental chemistry: microwave chemistry application, environmental methods and instrument development, speciated analysis, ICP-MS clean-room chemistry, chromatography, laboratory automation.
Jeffry D. Madura, Professor and Chair; Ph.D., Purdue, 1985. Theoretical physical chemistry: computational chemistry and biophysics, classical simulations of biomolecules, Poisson-Boltzmann electrostatics coupled to molecular dynamics, simulation of proteins at ice/water interface, simulation of biomolecular diffusion-controlled rate constants, quantum mechanical calculation of small molecules.
Mihaela Rita Mihailescu, Associate Professor; Ph.D., Wesleyan, 2001. Molecular biology and biochemistry: protein–nucleic acid interactions studied by NMR, fluorescence spectroscopy, and other biophysical techniques.
Tomislav Pintauer, Assistant Professor; Ph.D., Carnegie Mellon, 2002. Chemistry: inorganic, organometallic, and polymer chemistry, with emphasis on homogeneous and heterogeneous catalysis.
David W. Seybert, Professor and Dean; Ph.D., Cornell, 1976. Biochemistry: lipid peroxidation in biomembranes and lipoproteins, antioxidants and inhibition of LDL oxidation, mechanism and regulation of cytochrome P450 catalyzed steroid hydroxylations.
Omar W. Steward, Professor Emeritus; Ph.D., Penn State, 1957. Inorganic chemistry, crystal engineering: synthesis and structural studies of homonuclear and heteronuclear coordination polymers and supramolecular polymer matrices containing molecular and ionic species—how are the metals arranged?
Stephanie Wetzel, Assistant Professor; Ph.D., American, 2001. Analytical chemistry, instrumental methods, forensic chemistry, synthetic polymer characterization by mass spectrometry.

Richard King Mellon Hall of Science, which houses the Department of Chemistry and Biochemistry.

Research laboratory in Mellon Hall.

A student at work at Duquesne University.

SELECTED PUBLICATIONS

Yao, J., et al. **(J. A. Aitken).** Site preference of manganese on the copper site in Mn-substituted $CuInSe_2$ chalcopyrites revealed by a combined neutron and X-ray powder diffraction study. *Chem. Mater.* 22:1647–55, 2010.

Yao, J., et al. **(J. A. Aitken).** Effects of Mn substitution on the structure and properties of chalcopyrite-type $CuInSe_2$. *J. Solid State Chem.* 182:2579–86, 2009.

Lekse, J. W., et al. **(J. A. Aitken).** Second harmonic generation and crystal structure of the diamond-like semiconductors Li_2CdGeS_4 and Li_2CdSnS_4. *Inorg. Chem.* 48:7516–8, 2009.

Aitken, J. A., J. W. Lekse, and R. Quinones. Synthesis, structure, and physicochemical characterization of a noncentrosymmetric, quaternary thiostannate: $EuCu_2SnS_4$. *J. Solid State Chem.* 182:141–6, 2009.

Lekse, J. W., B. M. Leverette, C. H. Lake, and **J. A. Aitken.** Synthesis, physicochemical characterization, and crystallographic twinning of Li_2ZnSnS_4. *J. Solid State Chem.* 81:3217–22, 2008.

Takas, N. J., et al. **(J. A. Aitken).** A simple aqueous metathesis reaction yields new lanthanide monothiophosphates. *J. Solid State Chem.* 181:3044–50, 2008.

Mastrovito, C., J. W. Lekse, and **J. A. Aitken.** Rapid solid-state synthesis of binary group 15 chalcogenides using microwave irradiation. *J. Solid State Chem.* 180:3262–70, 2007.

Takas, N. J., and **J. A. Aitken.** An in situ time-of-flight neutron powder diffraction study of the humidity-induced phase transition in sodium monothiophosphate. *J. Solid State Chem.* 180:2034–43, 2007.

Lekse, J. W., T. S. Stagger, and **J. A. Aitken.** Microwave metallurgy: Synthesis of intermetallic compounds via microwave irradiation. *Chem. Mater.* 19:3601–3, 2007.

Lekse, J. W., A. M. Pischera, and **J. A. Aitken.** Understanding solid-state microwave synthesis using the diamond-like semiconductor, $AgInSe_2$, as a case study. *Mater. Res. Bull.* 42:395–403, 2007.

Basu, P., and **M. E. Johnson,** eds. *The Integrated Approach to Chemistry Laboratory*. Lancaster, Pa.: DEStech Publications, 2009.

Stolz, J. F., et al. **(P. Basu).** Biotransformation of 3-nitro-4-hydroxbenzene arsonic acid (roxarsone) and release of inorganic arsenic by *Clostridium* species. *Environ. Sci. Tech.* 41:818–23, 2007.

Kail, B. W., and **P. Basu.** Solvent effects in the geometric reorganization of an oxomolybdenum(V) system. *J. Chem. Soc., Dalton Trans.* 1419–23, 2006.

Kail, B. W., et al. **(P. Basu).** Mechanistic investigation of the oxygen atom transfer reactivity of dioxomolybdenum(VI) complexes. *Chem. Eur. J.* 12:7501–9, 2006.

Stolz, J. F., **P. Basu,** J. M. Santini, and R. S. Oremland. Arsenic and selenium in microbial metabolism. *Annu. Rev. Microbiol.* 60:107–30, 2006.

Nemykin, V. N., J. G. Olsen, E. Perera, and **P. Basu.** Synthesis, characterization, and crystal structure of the $(Me^2Pipdt)Mo(CO)^4$ complex (Me^2Pipdt = N,N'-dimethylpiperazine-2,3-dithione). A DFT, TDDFT, and TDDFT-PCM study on its electronic structure, excited states, and solvatochromism. *Inorg. Chem.* 45:7494–502, 2006.

Rogers, W. J., and **P. Basu.** Factor regulating macrophage endocytosis of nanoparticles: Implications for targeted magnetic resonance plaque imaging. *Atherosclerosis* 178:67–73, 2005.

Millar, A. J., et al. **(P. Basu).** Oxygen atom transfer in models for molybdenum enzymes: Isolation and spectroscopic and structural characterization of intermediates in the transfer of oxygen from Mo(VI) to P(III). *Chem. Eur. J.* 11:3255–67, 2005.

Nemykin, V. N., and **P. Basu.** Energy dependent electrospray ionisation mass spectrometric studies of mononuclear metal carbonyls. *Inorg. Chim. Acta* 358:2876–82, 2005.

Nemykin, V. N., and **P. Basu.** Oxygen atom transfer reactivity from a dioxo-Mo(VI) complex to tertiary phosphine: Synthesis, characterization and structure of phosphoryl intermediate complexes. *Inorg. Chem.* 44:7494–502, 2005.

McNaughton, R. L., et al. **(P. Basu).** Oxomolybdenum tetrathiolates with sterically encumbering ligands: Modeling the effect of a protein matrix on electronic structure and reduction potentials. *Inorg. Chem.* 44:8216–22, 2005.

Basu, P., et al. Donor atom dependent geometric isomers in mononuclear oxo-molybdenum^V complexes: Implications for coordinated endogenous ligation in molybdoenzymes. *Inorg. Chem.* 42:5999–6007, 2003.

Afkar, E., and **P. Basu** et al. The respiratory arsenate reductase from a haloalkaliphilic bacterium *Bacillus selenitireducens* strain MLS10. *FEMS Microbiol. Lett.* 226:107–12, 2003.

Basu, P., V. N. Nemykin, and R. S. Sengar. Electronic properties of para-substituted thiophenols and disulfides from ^{13}C NMR spectroscopy and ab initio calculations: Relations to the Hammett parameters and atomic charges. *New J. Chem.* 27:1115–23, 2003.

Basu, P., and V. N. Nemykin. Comparative theoretical investigation of the vertical excitation energies and the electronic structure of $[Mo^VOCl_4]^-$: Influence of basis set and geometry. *Inorg. Chem.* 42:4046–56, 2003.

Basu, P., J. F. Stolz, and M. T. Smith. A coordination chemist's view of the active sites of mononuclear molybdenum enzymes. *Curr. Sci.* 84:1412–8, 2003.

Beaver, B., et al. High heat sink jet fuels, part 1: Development of potential oxidative and pyrolytic additives for JP-8. *Energy Fuels* 20(4):1639–46, 2006.

Beaver, B., L. Gao, C. Burgess-Clifford, and M. Sobkowiak. On the mechanisms of formation of thermal oxidative deposits in jet fuels. Is a unified mechanism possible for both storage and thermal oxidative deposit formation for middle distillate fuels? *Energy Fuels* 19:1574–9, 2005.

Beaver, B., et al. Development of oxygen scavenger additives for future jet fuels. A role for electron-transfer-initiated oxygenation (ETIO) of 1,2,5-trimethylpyrrole? *Energy Fuels* 14:441–7, 2000.

Van Laar, V. S., A. J. Mishizen, **M. Cascio,** and T. G. Hastings. Proteomic identification of dopamine-conjugated proteins from isolate rat brain mitochondria and SH-SY5Y cells. *Neurobiol. Dis.* 34:467–500, 2009.

Liu, Z., et al. **(M. Cascio).** Overexpression and functional characterization of a mutated form of the extracellular domain of human homomeric a1 glycine receptor. *Biochemistry* 47:9803–10, 2008.

Cheng, M. H., R. D. Coalson, and **M. Cascio.** Molecular dynamics simulations of ethanol binding to the transmembrane domain of the glycine receptor: Implications for the channel potentiation mechanism. *Protein. Struct. Funct. Genet.* 71:972–81, 2008.

Srinivasan, R., et al. **(M. Cascio).** An HSV vector system for selection of ligand-gated ion channel modulators. *Nature Methods* 4:733–9, 2007.

Cascio, M. Structure and function of the glycine receptor and related nicontinicoid receptors. *J. Biol. Chem.* 279:19383–6, 2004.

Evanseck, J. D., and J. A. Plumley. Periodic trends and index of boron Lewis acidity. *J. Phys. Chem.,* 113(2):5985–92, 2009.

Evanseck, J. D., et al. **(E.S. Gawalt, J. D. Madura,** and **D. W. Seybert).** Broadening participation in undergraduate research: Fostering excellence and enhancing the impact. In *Optimizing Research Productivity While Maintaining Educational Excellence: A Collaborative Endeavor,* eds. Mary K. Boyd and Jodi L. Wesemann. Washington D.C.: Council on Undergradate Research, 2009.

Ricardo, C., L. M. Matosziuk, **J. D. Evanseck,** and **T. Pintauer.** Strong coordination of tetraphenylborate anion to copper(I) bipyridine and phenanthroline-based complexes and its effect on catalytic activity in the cyclopropanation of styrene. *Inorg. Chem.* 48(1):16–8, 2009.

Plumley, J. A., and **J. D. Evanseck.** Hybrid meta-generalized gradient functional modeling of boron-nitrogen coordinate covalent bonds. *J. Chem. Theor. Comput.* 4:1249–53, 2008.

Ruben, E. A., J. A. Plumley, M. S. Chapman, and **J. D. Evanseck.** Anomeric effect in 'high energy' phosphate bonds. Selective destabilitation of the scissile bond and modulation of the exothermicity of hydrolysis. *J. Am. Chem. Soc.* 130(111):3349–58, 2008.

Ruben, E. A., M. S. Chapman, and **J. D. Evanseck.** Hydrogen bonding mediated by key orbital interactions determines hydration enthalpy differences of phosphate water clusters. *J. Phys. Chem.* 111(42):10804–14, 2007.

Plumley, J. A., and **J. D. Evanseck.** Covalent and ionic nature of the dative bond and account of accurate ammonia borane binding enthalpies. *J. Phys. Chem.* 111(51):13472–83, 2007.

Acevedo, O., W. L. Jorgensen, and **J. D. Evanseck.** Elucidation of rate variations for a Diels-Alder reaction in ionic liquids from WM/MM simulations. *J. Chem. Theor. Comput.* 3:132–8, 2007.

Mueller Stein, S. A., et al. **(J. D. Evanseck).** Principal components analysis: A review of its application on molecular dynamics data. *Ann. Rep. Comp. Chem.* 2:233–61, 2006.

Henriksen, B. S., et al. **(J. D. Evanseck).** Computational and conformational evaluation of FTase alternative substrates: Insight into a novel enzyme-binding pocket. *J. Chem. Inf. Model.* 45(4):1047–52, 2005.

Zhou, Z., M. Madrid, **J. D. Evanseck,** and **J. D. Madura.** Effect of a bound non-nucleoside RT inhibitor on the dynamics of wild type and mutant HIV-1 reverse transcriptase. *J. Am. Chem. Soc.* 127:17253–60, 2005.

Ruben, E. A., M. S. Chapman, and **J. D. Evanseck.** Generalized anomeric interpretation of the high energy N-P bond in N-methyl-N'-phosphorylguanidine: Breakdown of opposing resonance theory. *J. Am. Chem. Soc.* 127:17789–98, 2005.

Fleming, F. F., Y. Wei, W. Liu, and Z. Zhang. Metalated nitriles: Stereodivergent cation-controlled cyclizations. *Tetrahedron* 64:7477–88, 2008.

Fleming, F. F., G. Wei and **O. W. Steward.** Cyclic nitriles: Stereodivergent addition-alkylation-cyclization to *cis-* and *trans-* abietanes. *J. Org. Chem.* 73:3674–9, 2008.

Fleming, F. F., W. Liu, S. Ghosh, and **O. W. Steward.** Metalated nitriles: Internal 1,2-asymmetric induction. *J. Org. Chem.* 73:2803–10, 2008.

Rauhut, C. G., V. A. Vu, **F. F. Fleming,** and P. Knochel. Preparation of functionalized alkylmagnesium derivatives using an I/Mg-exchange. *Org. Lett.* 10:1187–9, 2008.

Fleming, F. F., and S. Gudipati. Cyclic metalated nitriles: Stereoselective cyclizations to *cis*-and *trans-* hydrindanes, decalins, and bicyclo[4.3.0]undecanes. *Eur. J. Org. Chem.* 5365–74, 2008.

Fleming, F. F., and B. C. Shook. 1-Oxo-2-cyclohexenyl-2-carbonitrile. *Org. Syn.* 77:254–60, 2001.

Fleming, F. F., Q. Wang, and **O. W. Steward.** Hydroxylated α,β-unsaturated nitriles: Stereoselective synthesis. *J. Org. Chem.* 66:2171–4, 2001.

Fleming, F. F., and P. Iyer. Flood prevention by recirculating condenser-cooling water. *J. Chem. Educ.* 78:946, 2001.

Fleming, F. F., and B. C. Shook. α,β-unsaturated nitriles: Preparative MgO elimination. *Tetrahedron Lett.* 41:8847–51, 2000.

Fleming, F. F., Q. Wang, and **O. W. Steward.** γ-hydroxy unsaturated nitriles: Chelation-controlled conjugate additions. *Org. Lett.* 2:1477–9, 2000.

Raman, A., M. Dubey, I. Gouzman, and **E. S. Gawalt.** Formation of self-assembled monolayers of alkylphosphonic acid on native oxide surface of SS316L. *Langmuir* 22(15):6469–72, 2006.

Gawalt, E. S., et al. Bonding organics to Ti alloys: Facilitating human osteoblast attachment and spreading on surgical implant materials. *Langmuir* 19:200–4, 2003.

Houseman, B. T., **E. S. Gawalt,** and M. Mrksich. Maleimide-functionalized self-assembled monolayers for the preparation of peptide and carbohydrate biochips. *Langmuir* 19:1522–31, 2003.

Schwartz, J., et al. **(E. S. Gawalt).** Cell attachment and spreading on metal implant materials. *Mater. Sci. Eng., C* 23:395–400, 2003.

Gawalt, E. S., et al. Enhanced bonding of organometallics to titanium via a titanium (III) phosphate interface. *Langmuir* 17:6743–5, 2001.

Gawalt, E. S., M. J. Avaltroni, N. Koch, and J. Schwartz. Self-assembly and bonding of alkanephosphonic acids on the native oxide surface of titanium. *Langmuir* 17:5736–8, 2001.

Sultana, T., and **M. E. Johnson.** Sample preparation and gas chromatography of primary fatty acid amides. *J. Chromatogr. B* 1101:278–85, 2006.

Kail, B., C. G. Young, **M. E. Johnson,** and **P. Basu.** Understanding oxotransferase reactivity in a model system using singular value decomposition analysis. In *Bioinorganic Chemistry: Cellular Systems and Synthetic Models*, eds. E. C. Long, and M. J. Baldwin. Washington D.C.: American Chemical Society, 2009.

Johnson, M. E., et al. Chapter 11: Solid phase extraction of lipids from a cellular lysate on a microfluidic device. In *The Integrated Approach to Chemistry Laboratory*, eds. **P. Basu** and **M. E. Johnson.** Lancaster, Pa.: DEStech Publishers, 2009.

Johnson, M. E., et al. Chapter 6: Protein unfolding kinetics. In *The Integrated Approach to Chemistry Laboratory*, eds. **P. Basu** and **M. E. Johnson.** Lancaster, Pa.: DEStech Publishers, 2009.

Johnson, M. E., and T. S. Carpenter. The use of solid phase supports for derivatization in chromatography and spectroscopy. *Appl. Spectrosc. Rev.* 40:1–22, 2005.

Johnson, M. E., and J. P. Landers. Fundamentals and practice for ultrasensitive laser-induced fluorescence detection in microanalytical systems. *Electrophoresis* 25:3513–27, 2004.

Duquesne University

Merkler, D. J., et al. **(M. E. Johnson).** Oleic acid derived metabolites in mouse neuroblastoma N18TG2 cells. *Biochemistry* 43:12667–74, 2004.

Carpenter, T., et al. **(M. E. Johnson).** Liquid chromatographic separation of fatty acid amides and N-acyl glycines for biological assays. *J. Chromatogr. B Biomed. Appl.* 809:15–21, 2004.

Shah, J. M., and **S. U. M. Khan.** Detection of glucose by electroreduction at a semiconductor electrode: An implantable non-enzymatic glucose sensor. In *Chemical and Biological Sensors and Analytical Methods II,* vol. 2001–18, pp. 259–71, eds. M. Butler, P. Vanysek, and Y. Yamazoe. Pennington: Electrochemical Society, 2001.

Sultana, T., and **S. U. M. Khan.** Photoelectrichemical splitting of water on nanocrystalline n-TiO_2 thin film and quantum wire electrodes. In *Quantum Confinement VI: Nanostructured Materials and Devices,* vol. 2001–19, pp. 9–19, eds. M. Cahay et al. Pennington: Electrochemical Society, 2001.

Reyes, L. J., et al. **(H. M. Kingston).** Simultaneous determination of arsenic and selenium species in fish tissues by microwave-assisted enzymatic extraction and ion chromatography-inductively coupled plasma mass spectrometry. *Talanta,* in press.

Faber, S., et al. **(H. M. Kingston).** The relationship between serum copper and plasma zinc in children with autism spectrum disorders. *Pediatr. Neurol.,* in press.

Reyes, L. H., G. M. Mizanur Rahman, and **H. M. (Skip) Kingston.** Robust microwave-assisted extraction protocol for determination of total mercury and methylmercury in fish tissues. *Anal. Chim. Acta,* 2008. doi:10/1016/j.aca.2008.10.044.

Rahman, G. M. M., T. Fahrenholz, and **H. M. (Skip) Kingston.** Application of speciated isotope dilution mass spectrometry to evaluate some literature methods with respect to efficiencies, recoveries, and quantification of mercury species transformations in human hair. *JAAS,* 2008. doi: 10/1039/b805249b.

Reyes, L. H., et al. **(H. M. Kingston).** Evaluation of extraction methods and bias correction by EPA Method 6800 protocol for mercury species in tuna fish tissue using an ion chromatograph coupled to an ICP-MS. *LC-GC North America,* (Suppl.)26–9, 2008.

Reyes, L. H., et al. **(H. M. Kingston).** Comparison of methods with respect to efficiencies, recoveries, and quantitation of mercury species interconversion in food demonstrated using tuna fish. *Analytical and Bioanalytical Chemistry* 390:2123–32, 2008.

Kingston, H. M., H. Dengwei, and M. Rahman. RCRA Method 6800: Elemental and speciated isotope dilution mass spectrometry. *SW-846: Test Methods for Evaluating Solid Waste, Physical/Chemical Methods, Update IV.* Washington, DC: U.S. Government Printing Office, 2008.

Kingston, H. M., and H. Boylan. RCRA Method 7473: Mercury in solids and solutions by thermal decomposition, amalgamation, and atomic absorption. *SW-846: Test Methods for Evaluating Solid Waste, Physical/Chemical Methods, Update IV.* Washington, DC: U.S. Government Printing Office, 2008.

Kingston, H. M., P. Walter, and D. Link. RCRA Method 3015A: Microwave assisted acid digestion of sediments, sludges, soils, and oils. *SW-846: Test Methods for Evaluating Solid Waste, Physical/Chemical Methods, Update IV.* Washington, DC: U.S. Government Printing Office, 2008.

Kingston, H. M., P. Walter, and D. Link. RCRA Method 3015A: Microwave assisted acid digestion of aqueous samples and extracts. *SW-846: Test Methods for Evaluating Solid Waste, Physical/Chemical Methods, Update IV.* Washington, DC: U.S. Government Printing Office, 2008.

Kingston, H. M., and J. Para. RCRA Method 3546: Microwave extraction. *SW-846: Test Methods for Evaluating Solid Waste, Physical/Chemical Methods, Update IV.* Washington, DC: U.S. Government Printing Office, 2008.

Kingston, H. M. Chapter Three: Inorganic analytes. *SW-846: Test Methods for Evaluating Solid Waste, Physical/Chemical Methods, Update IV.* Washington, DC: U.S. Government Printing Office, 2008.

Boylan, H. M., R. D. Cain, and **H. M. Kingston.** A new method to assess mercury emissions: A study of three coal-fired electric generating power stations. *Air Waste Manage. Assoc.* 53:1318–25, 2003.

Bhandari, S., **H. M. Kingston,** and G. M. M. Rahman. Synthesis and characterization of isotopically enriched methylmercury ($CH_3{}^{201}Hg^+$). *Appl. Organometal. Chem.* 17:913–20, 2003.

Gazmuri, R. J., et al. **(H. M. Kingston).** Myocardial protection during ventricular fibrillation by interventions that limit proton-driven sarcolemmal sodium influx, American Heart Association. *J. Lab. Clin. Med.* 137(1):43–55, 2001.

Han, Y., **H. M. Kingston,** R. C. Richter, and C. Pirola. Dual-vessel integrated microwave sample decomposition and digest evaporation for trace element analysis of silicon material by ICP-MS: Design and application. *Anal. Chem.* 73(6):1106–11, 2001.

Richter, R. C., L. Dirk, and **H. M. Kingston.** Microwave enhanced chemistry: Standardizing sample preparation. *Anal. Chem.* 73(1):30A–7A, 2001.

Huo, D., and **H. M. Kingston.** Correction of species transformations in the analysis of Cr(VI) in solid environmental samples using speciated isotope dilution mass spectrometry. *Anal. Chem.* 72(20):5047–54, 2000.

Boylan, H. M., T. A. Ronning, R. L. DeGroot, and **H. M. Kingston.** Field analysis using Method 7473: Minimizing the cost of mercury cleanup. *Environ. Test. Anal.,* 2000.

Link, D. D., and **H. M. Kingston.** Use of microwave-assisted evaporation for the complete recovery of volatile species of inorganic trace analytes. *Anal. Chem.* 72(13):2908–13, 2000.

Richter, R. C., D. D. Link, and **H. M. Kingston.** On demand production of high-purity acids in the analytical laboratory. *Spectroscopy,* 2000.

Asciutto, E., K. Myer, and **J. D. Madura.** Sodium perchlorate effects on the helical stability of a mainly alanine peptide. *Biophys. J.* 98(2):186–96, 2010.

Gedeon, P. G., M. Indarte, C. K. Surratt, and **J. D. Madura.** Molecular dynamics of leucine and dopamine transporter proteins in a model cell membrane lipid bilayer. *Protein. Struct. Funct. Bioinf.* 78(4):797–811, 2010.

Xiong, Kan, E. K. Asciutto, **J. D. Madura,** and S. A. Asher. Salt dependence of α-helical peptide folding energy landscapes. *Biochemistry* 48(45):10818–26, 2009.

Dick, T. J., A. Wierzbicki, and **J. D. Madura.** Chapter 17: CO2(aq) parameterization through free energy perturbation/Monte Carlo simulations for use in CO2 sequestration. In *Practical Aspects of Computational Chemistry.* eds. J. Leszyzynski and M. J. Shukla. Amsterdam: Springer Netherlands, 2009.

Dick, T. J., A. Wierzbicki, and **J. D. Madura.** Chapter 18: Free energy perturbation of Monte Carlo simulations of salt influences on aqueous freezing point depression. In *Practical Aspects of Computational Chemistry,* eds. J. Leszyzynsky and M. K. Shukla. Amsterdam: Springer Netherlands, 2009.

Asciutto, E. K., and **(J. D. Madura)** et al. Structural and dynamic implications of an effector-induced backbone amide cis-trans isomerization in cytochrome $P450_{cam}$. *J. Mol. Biol.* 388:801–14, 2009.

Shetty, S., et al. **(M. R. Mihailescu).** Hepatitis C virus genomic RNA dimerization is mediated via a kissing complex intermediate. *RNA* 16(5):913–25, 2010.

Lipay, J. M., and **M. R. Mihailescu.** NMR spectroscopy and kinetic studies of the quadruplex forming RNA (rUGGAGGU). *Molecular BioSystems* 5(11):1347–55, 2009.

Bole, M., L. Menon, and **M. R. Mihailescu.** Fragile X mental retardation protein recognition of G quadruplex structure per se is sufficient for high affinity binding to RNA. *Molecular BioSystems* 4(12):1212–9, 2008.

Menon, L., S. A. Mader, and **M. R. Mihailescu.** Fragile X mental retardation protein interactions with the microtubule associated protein 1B. *RNA* 14:1644–55, 2008. doi 10.1261/rna.1100708.

Menon, L., and **M. R. Mihailescu.** Interactions of the G quartet forming semaphorin 3F RNA with the RGG box domain of the fragile X protein family. *Nucleic Acids Res.* 36(16):5379–92, 2007.

Zanotti, K. J., P. E. Lackey, G. L. Evans, and **M. R. Mihailescu.** Thermodynamics of the fragile X mental retardation protein RGG box interactions with G quartet forming RNA. *Biochemistry* 45(27):8319–30, 2006.

Mihailescu, M. R., and J. P. Marino. A proton-coupled dynamic conformational switch in the HIV-1 dimerization initiation site-kissing complex. *Proc. Natl. Acad. Sci. Unit. States Am.* 101(5):1189–94, 2004.

Mihailescu, M. R., C. Fronticelli, and I. M. Russu. Allosteric free energy changes at the alpha 1 beta 2 interface of human hemoglobin probed by proton exchange of Trp beta 37. *Proteins* 44(2):73–8, 2001.

Mihailescu, M. R., and I. M. Russu. A signature of the TR transition in human hemoglobin. *Proc. Natl. Acad. Sci. Unit.States Am.,* 98(7):3773–7, 2001.

Eckenhoff, W. T., and **T. Pintauer.** Copper catalyzed atom transfer radical addition (ATRA) and cyclization (ATRC) reactions in the presence of reducing agents. *Catal. Rev.,* 51:1–59, 2010.

Cohen, N. A., et al. **(T. Pintauer).** Effect of the ligand in atom transfer radical polymerization reactions initiated by photodimers of 9-bromoanthracene. *Macromol. Chem. Phys.* 210:263, 2009.

Pintauer, T. 'Greening' of copper catalyzed atom transfer radical addition (ATRA) and cyclization (ATRC) reactions. *ACS Symposium Series* 1023:63–85, 2009.

Balili, M. N. C., and **T. Pintauer.** Persistent radical effect in action: Kinetic studies of copper catalyzed atom transfer radical addition (ATRA) in the presence of free-radical diazo initiators as reducing agents. *Inorg. Chem.* 48(18):9018–26, 2009.

Pintauer, T., and K. Matyjaszewski. Structural and mechanistic aspects of copper catalyzed atom transfer radical polymerization. *Top. Organomet. Chem.* 26:221–51, 2009.

Pintauer, T., et al. Highly efficient ambient-temperature copper-catalyzed atom-transfer radical addition (ATRA) in the presence of free-radical initiator (V-70) as a reducing agent. *Chem. Eur. J.* 15(1):38–41, 2008.

Seybert, D. S., J. D. Evanseck, and J. S. Doctor. Integrated biological and chemical laboratory experiences for enhanced education, research opportunities, and career development. *CUR Q.* 26:104–8, 2006.

Owens, J. W., M. B. Perry, and **D. W. Seybert.** Reactions of nitric oxide with cobaltous tetraphenylporphyrin and phthalocyanines. *Inorg. Chim. Acta* 277:1–7, 1998.

Hanlon, M. C., and **D. W. Seybert.** The pH dependence of lipid peroxidation using water-soluble azo initiators. *Free Radical Biol. Med.* 23:712–9, 1997.

Warburton, R. J., and **D. W. Seybert.** Structural and functional characterization of bovine adrenodoxin reductase by limited proteolysis. *Biochim. Biophys. Acta* 1246:39–46, 1995.

Wetzel, S. J., C. M. Guttman, K. M. Flynn, and J. J. Filliban. A statistical analysis of the optimization of the MALDI-TOF-MS. *J. Am. Soc. Mass Spectrom.* 17:246–52, 2006.

Guttman, C. M., and **S. J. Wetzel** et al. Matrix-assisted laser desorption/ionization time-of-flight mass spectrometry interlaboratory comparison of mixtures of polystyrene with different end groups: Statistical analysis of mass fractions and mass moments. *Anal. Chem.* 77:4539–48, 2005.

Wetzel, S. J., C. M. Guttman, and K. M. Flynn. The influence of electrospray deposition in MALDI-MS sample preparation for synthetic polymers. *Rapid Commun. Mass Spectrom.* 18:1139–46, 2004.

Lin-Gibson, S., et al. **(S. J. Wetzel).** Synthesis and characterization of PEG dimethacrylates and their hydrogels. *Biomacromolecules* 5(4):1280–7, 2004.

Wetzel, S. J., C. M. Guttman, and J. E. Girard. Influence of laser power and matrix on the molecular mass distribution of synthetic polymers obtained by MALDI-TOF-MS. *Int. J. Mass Spectrom.* 238(3):215–25, 2004.

Wallace, W. E., C. M. Guttman, **S. J. Wetzel,** and S. D. Hanton. Mass spectrometry of synthetic-polymer mixtures workshop. *Rapid Commun. Mass Spectrom.* 18:518–21, 2004.

HARVARD UNIVERSITY

Department of Chemistry and Chemical Biology

Programs of Study

The Department of Chemistry and Chemical Biology offers a program of study that leads to the degree of Doctor of Philosophy (Ph.D.) in chemistry in the special fields of biological, inorganic, organic, and physical chemistry. An interdepartmental Ph.D. program in chemical physics is also available. Upon entering the program, students formulate a plan of study in consultation with a Curriculum Advising Committee. Students must obtain honor grades in four advanced half courses (five for chemical physics). The course work is usually expected to be completed by the end of the second term of residence. All students must present and defend a research proposal in their second year of residence. Although the curriculum for the Ph.D. degree includes the course, research proposal, and oral defense requirements, the majority of the graduate student's time and energy is devoted to original investigations in a chosen field of research. Students are expected to join a research group in their second term of residence, but no later than the third. The Ph.D. dissertation is based on independent scholarly research, which, upon conclusion, is defended in an oral examination before a Ph.D. committee. The preparation of a satisfactory thesis normally requires at least four years of full-time research.

Research Facilities

The facilities of the Department of Chemistry and Chemical Biology are housed in five buildings in the Cabot Science Complex, with the adjacent Science Center providing major undergraduate lecture and laboratory areas. Three centers of research provide a central location for the following research instruments: for NMR research, one Bruker Avance 700-MHz NMR, one Varian 600-MHz NMR, three Varian 500-MHz NMRs, two Varian 400-MHz NMRs, one Varian 300-MHz NMR, and one Bruker ESP 300 EPR spectrometer; for mass spectroscopy, a JEOL-SX102A mass spectrometer, a Micromass LCT Platform II mass spectrometer equipped with APCI ionization, a Waters Q-Tof micro MS/MS mass spectrometer equipped with both electrospray and APCI ionization, an Agilent 6890/5973 GC-MS (gas chromatography–mass spectrometer), and an Applied Biosystems MALDI (matrix-assisted laser desorption ionization time-of-flight mass spectrometer); and for X-ray crystallography, two Bruker X-ray diffractometers, both with area-detection systems using Apex detectors. Computing in the Department is done mostly on workstations in individual research groups, with more than 1,200 devices linked by a Department-wide network. The Department, along with the Materials Research Laboratories at Harvard and MIT, operates and manages a Surface Sciences Center.

Financial Aid

The Department of Chemistry and Chemical Biology meets the financial needs of its graduate students through Departmental scholarships, Departmental fellowships, teaching fellowships, research assistantships, and independent outside fellowships. Financial support is awarded on a twelve-month basis, enabling students to pursue their research throughout the year. Tuition is afforded to all graduate students in good standing for the tenure of the Ph.D. program.

Cost of Study

As stated in the Financial Aid section, tuition is waived for all Ph.D. students in good standing.

Living and Housing Costs

Dormitory rooms for single students are available, with costs (excluding meals) that ranged from $5482 for a single room to $8608 for a two-room suite in 2009–10. Married and single students may apply for apartments managed by Harvard Planning and Real Estate. The monthly costs are studio apartment, $929–$1659; one-bedroom apartment, $1335–$2091; two-bedroom apartment, $1560–$2862; and three-bedroom apartment, $1890–$3183. There are also many privately owned apartments nearby and within commuting distance.

Student Group

The Graduate School of Arts and Sciences (GSAS) has an enrollment of about 3,700 graduate students. There are approximately 175 students in the Department of Chemistry and Chemical Biology, 35 percent of whom are international students.

Student Outcomes

In 2009, 11 percent of the Ph.D. recipients entered positions in academia, 7 percent accepted permanent positions in industry, 71 percent conducted postdoctoral research before accepting permanent positions in academia or industry, and 11 percent pursued other directions.

Location

Cambridge, a city of 101,355, is just minutes from Boston. It is a scientific and intellectual center, teeming with activities in all areas of creativity and study. The Cambridge/Boston area is a major cultural center, with its many public and university museums, theaters, symphony, and numerous private, special interest, and historical collections and performances. New England abounds in possibilities for recreational pursuits, from camping, hiking, and skiing in the mountains of New Hampshire and Vermont to swimming and sailing on the seashores of Cape Cod and Maine.

The University

Harvard College was established in 1636, and its charter, which still guides the University, was granted in 1650. An early brochure, published in 1643, justified the College's existence: "To advance Learning and perpetuate it to Posterity...." Today, Harvard University, with its network of graduate and professional schools, occupies a noteworthy position in the academic world, and the Department of Chemistry and Chemical Biology offers an educational program in keeping with the University's long-standing record of achievement.

Applying

Applications for admission to study for the Ph.D. degree in chemistry may be accessed at the GSAS Web site at http://www.gsas.harvard.edu/apply/apply.php. Applications are accepted from students who have received a bachelor's degree or equivalent. Online submission of the admission application is encouraged. If a paper application is utilized, the application and all supporting documents must be enclosed in the admission envelope to ensure full consideration.

The application process should begin during the summer or fall of the year preceding desired entrance. Completed online applications and any paper supporting materials should be returned to the GSAS Admissions Office by December 8, though this date may vary slightly from year to year.

Correspondence and Information

Graduate Admissions Office
Department of Chemistry and Chemical Biology
Harvard University
12 Oxford Street
Cambridge, Massachusetts 02138

Phone: 617-496-3208
E-mail: admissions@chemistry.harvard.edu
Web site: http://www.chem.harvard.edu

Harvard University

THE FACULTY AND THEIR RESEARCH

Joanna Aizenberg, Gordon McKay Professor of Materials Science, Susan S. and Kenneth L. Wallach Professor at the Radcliffe Institute for Advanced Study, and Professor of Chemistry and Chemical Biology; Ph.D., Weizmann (Israel). Biomimetic inorganic materials synthesis, self-assembly, crystal engineering, surface chemistry, nanofabrication, biomaterials, biomechanics, biooptics.

James G. Anderson, Professor; Ph.D. (physical chemistry), Colorado, 1970. Chemical reactivity of radical-molecule systems; molecular orbital analysis of barrier height control; coupling of chemistry, radiation, and climate in the earth system; photochemistry of planetary atmospheres; in situ detection of radicals in troposphere and stratosphere.

Alan Aspuru-Guzik, Assistant Professor; Ph.D. (physical chemistry), Berkeley, 2004. Theoretical physical chemistry, quantum computation and its application to chemistry problems, development of electronic structure methods for atoms and molecules: density functional theory and quantum Monte Carlo, theoretical understanding and design of renewable energy materials.

Theodore A. Betley, Assistant Professor; Ph.D. (inorganic chemistry), Caltech, 2005. Synthetic inorganic chemistry targeting chemical energy conversion, structure and reactivity of polymetallic and organometallic compounds.

Adam E. Cohen, Assistant Professor; Ph.D. (physics), Cambridge, 2003, and Stanford, 2006. Single-molecule spectroscopy and biophysics; Brownian motion and feedback control; electrokinetics, polymer physics, fluctuation-induced forces; nonequilibrium van der Waals/Cashmir forces; instrumentation.

Cynthia M. Friend, Professor; Ph.D. (physical chemistry), Berkeley, 1981. Physical chemistry of surface phenomena, materials chemistry and catalysis, electron spectroscopies and chemical techniques applied to the understanding of complex surface reactions, relating chemical processes to electronic structure on surfaces.

Roy Gerald Gordon, Professor; Ph.D. (physical chemistry), Harvard, 1964. Intermolecular forces, transport processes and molecular motion, theory of crystal structures and phase transitions, kinetics of crystal growth, solar energy, chemical vapor deposition, synthesis of inorganic precursors to new materials, thin films and their applications to microelectronics and solar cells.

Eric J. Heller, Professor; Ph.D. (chemical physics), Harvard, 1973. Few-body quantum mechanics, scattering theory, and quantum chaos; physics of semiconductor devices, ultracold molecular collisions, and nonadiabatic I interactions in molecules and gases.

Eric N. Jacobsen, Professor; Ph.D. (organic chemistry), Berkeley, 1986. Mechanistic and synthetic organic chemistry; development of new synthetic methods, with emphasis on asymmetric catalysis; physical-organic studies of reactivity and recognition phenomena in homogeneous catalysis; stereoselective synthesis of natural products.

Daniel Kahne, Professor; Ph.D. (organic chemistry), Columbia, 1986. Synthetic organic chemistry and its applications to problems in chemistry and biology.

Charles M. Lieber, Professor; Ph.D. (physical chemistry), Stanford, 1985. Chemistry and physics of materials, with an emphasis on nanoscale systems; rational synthesis of new nanoscale building blocks and nanostructured solids; development of methodologies for hierarchical assembly of nanoscale building blocks into complex and functional systems; investigation of fundamental electronic, optical, and optoelectronic properties of nanoscale materials; design and development of nanoelectronics and nanophotonic systems, with emphasis on electrically based biological detection, digital and quantum computing, and photonic systems.

David Liu, Professor; Ph.D. (organic chemistry and chemical biology), Berkeley, 1999. Organic chemistry and chemical biology of molecular evolution, nucleic acid–templated organic synthesis, reaction discovery, protein and nucleic acid evolution and engineering, synthetic polymer evolution; generally, effective molarity-based approaches to controlling reactivity and evolution-based approaches to the discovery of functional synthetic and biological molecules.

Andrew G. Myers, Professor; Ph.D. (organic chemistry), Harvard, 1985. Synthesis and study of complex organic molecules of importance in biology and human medicine.

Erin O'Shea, Professor of Molecular and Cellular Biology and of Chemistry and Chemical Biology, Howard Hughes Medical Institute Investigator, and Director of the Center for Systems Biology; Ph.D., MIT, 1992. Systems-level and molecular analysis of signaling pathways; transcriptional regulatory network architecture, function, and evolution; regulation and mechanism of oscillation of a circadian clock.

Hongkun Park, Professor; Ph.D. (physical chemistry and chemical physics), Stanford, 1996. Physics and chemistry of nanostructured materials; electron transport in individual molecules, inorganic clusters, nanowires, and nanotubes; single-molecule optoelectronics; synthesis and characterization of transition-metal-oxide and chalcogenide nanostructures with novel electronic and magnetic properties.

Tobias Ritter, Assistant Professor; Ph.D. (organic chemistry), Swiss Federal Institute of Technology, 2004. Synthetic organic and organometallic chemistry, development of new synthetic methods based on transition-metal catalysis, stereoselective synthesis of biologically active natural and unnatural products.

Alan Saghatelian, Assistant Professor; Ph.D. (organic chemistry), California, San Diego (Scripps), 2002. Development and application of global metabolite profiling (metabolomics) as a general discovery tool for chemical biology.

Stuart L. Schreiber, Professor; Ph.D. (organic synthesis), Harvard, 1981. Development and application of diversity-oriented organic synthesis to cell circuitry and genomic medicine.

Matthew D. Shair, Professor; Ph.D. (synthetic chemistry and chemical biology), Columbia, 1995. Synthesis of small molecules that have interesting biological functions and elucidation of their cellular mechanisms, development of organic synthesis.

Eugene I. Shakhnovich, Professor; Ph.D. (physical chemistry), Moscow, 1984. Theoretical biomolecular science, including protein folding, theory of molecular evolution, structural bioinformatics, rational drug design, populational genomics, and other systems, including complex polymers, spin glasses, etc.

Gregory L. Verdine, Professor; Ph.D. (organic chemistry, chemical biology, structural biology), Columbia, 1986. DNA repair, transcriptional control, chemistry for the conversion of peptides to ligands having cellular activity.

George M. Whitesides, Professor; Ph.D. (organic chemistry), Caltech, 1964. Physical organic chemistry, materials science, biophysics, complexity, surface science, microfluidics, self-assembly, microtechnology and nanotechnology, cell-surface biochemistry.

X. Sunney Xie, Professor; Ph.D. (physical chemistry), California, San Diego, 1990. Biophysical chemistry, single-molecule spectroscopy and dynamics, developments of new approaches for molecular and cellular imaging.

Xiaowei Zhuang, Professor; Ph.D. (physics), Berkeley, 1996. Biophysical chemistry, single-molecule biophysics, fluorescence microscopy and spectroscopy, microscopic and nanoscopic imaging of biomolecular and cellular systems.

Affiliate Members of the Department of Chemistry and Chemical Biology

Jon Clardy, Professor of Biological Chemistry and Molecular Pharmacology (Medical School); Ph.D., Harvard, 1969. Discovery of biologically active small molecules using DNA-based approaches or high-throughput screening and chemical analysis, protein structure and enzymology, functioning of small molecules as carriers of biological information, new biosynthetic pathways, new microbial biology.

Efthimios Kaxiras, Gordon McKay Professor of Applied Physics and Professor of Physics (SEAS); Ph.D., MIT, 1987. Development of computational methodologies for coupling spatial and temporal scales; optical and electronic properties for nucleic acids, melanin, and flavonoids; structure and properties of carbon and other nanotubes, surface nanowires and nanodots, and graphene nanoflakes; effect of chemical impurities on the large-scale mechanical behavior of solids.

Suzanne Walker, Professor of Microbiology and Molecular Genetics. Chemical biology: synthetic organic chemistry applied to the study of biochemical molecules, enzymology, mechanism of action of antibiotics.

Christopher Walsh, Hamilton Kuhn Professor of Biological Chemistry and Molecular Pharmacology (Medical School); Ph.D., Rockefeller, 1970. Molecular basis of biological catalysis, with focus on the structure and function of enzymes; biosynthesis and mechanism of action of antibiotics and bacterial siderophores.

KENT STATE UNIVERSITY

KENT STATE UNIVERSITY

Department of Chemistry and Biochemistry

Programs of Study

The Department of Chemistry and Biochemistry offers programs leading to the Master of Science (M.S.) and Doctor of Philosophy (Ph.D.) degrees in the traditional divisions of analytical, inorganic, organic, and physical chemistry and biochemistry. A variety of interdisciplinary areas are covered in bioanalytical chemistry, bioinorganic chemistry, biophysics, and molecular/cell biology. Faculty members also have research interests in the specialty areas of liquid crystals, photonic materials, spectroscopy, nanomaterials, separations, and surface science.

Graduate students are required to complete a program of core courses in their area of specialization and at least one (for M.S. candidates) or two (for Ph.D. candidates) elective courses in other areas of chemistry. The extraordinary breadth of the program gives students considerable flexibility in curriculum design, ensuring a modern and dynamic graduate education. At the end of the second year, doctoral students must pass a written examination in their field of specialization and defend an original research proposal for their dissertation. Students typically complete their doctoral program with their thesis defense after 4.5 years.

Research Facilities

Kent State University is home to excellent research facilities. The chemistry department has advanced NMR, X-ray, mass spectrometry, and proteomics core facilities. Research laboratories are located primarily in Williams Hall and the attached Science Research Laboratory. In addition, excellent materials' characterization facilities and one of the largest academic clean room facilities in the nation are housed in the nearby Liquid Crystal Institute. A confocal microscopy core facility located in the biology department is also available to chemistry students. Williams Hall houses two large lecture halls, classrooms, undergraduate and research laboratories, the Chemistry-Physics Library, chemical stockrooms, and glass and electronics shops. A machine shop, which is jointly operated with the physics department, is located in adjoining Smith Hall. Spectrometers include 500-MHz, 400-MHz (solids), and 300-MHz high-resolution NMR instruments; electrospray, MALDI-TOF, LC/ESI, protein chip SELDI mass spectrometers; various high-end FT-IR spectrometers, including a focal plane array FT-IR microscope for spectroscopic imaging; photon-counting fluorometer; circular dichroism; ESR, FPLC, UV/visible spectrometers; AA/AE equipment; and an EDX-700 energy dispersive X-ray spectrometer. An X-ray facility includes a Siemens D5000 Powder diffractometer and a Bruker AXS CCD instrument for single-crystal structural elucidation. Equipment available in specialty areas includes a microwave spectrometer, an LCQ electrospray mass spectrometer with MS/MS capability, a phosphorimager, Microcal VP DSC and ITC calorimeters, Bruker Vector 33 FTIR-NIR, Jobin Yvon Raman spectrometer with inverted microscope, laser tweezer instrumentation, particle sizer, Cary Eclipse fluorescence spectrophotometer, MF^2 Jobin Yvon fluorescence lifetime spectrometer, fluorescence correlation spectrometer, ThermoFinnigan Polaris Q115W GC-MS, a BAS electrochemical analyzer, various preparative centrifuges, a molecular dynamic Typhoon 8600 imaging system, and PCR and DNA sequencing and cell culture facilities. Individual research groups in the Department of Chemistry and Biochemistry maintain a variety of computer systems, including PCs and workstations. High-performance computing is made possible with access to the Ohio Supercomputer Center, which maintains Cray T94, Cray T3E, IBM SP2, and SGI Origin 2000 supercomputers. The Department has advanced molecular modeling facilities, including Cerius, Felix, Hyperchem, InsightII/Discover, Macromodel, and Spartan packages for modeling surfaces and interfaces, polymers, proteins, and nucleic acids, as well as facilities for performing ab initio calculations of molecular properties and molecular dynamics. A 3-D immersive classroom equipped with a rear projection system that generates 6' x 7' three-dimensional images when viewed with shutter glasses is available in Williams Hall and is frequently used for a variety of graduate classes. The chemistry/physics library in Williams Hall provides online access to virtually all chemical/biochemical journals as well as a broad variety of chemical databases, including the Chemical Abstracts SciFinder Service.

Financial Aid

Graduate students are generously supported through teaching and research assistantships as well as University fellowships. Students in good academic standing are guaranteed appointments for periods of at least 4½ years (Ph.D. candidates) or 2½ years (M.S. candidates). Stipends for 2009–10 range from $18,000 (M.S.) to $20,000 (Ph.D.) for a twelve-month appointment. A $1010 credit is made toward the University's health insurance plan. First-year bonuses and renewable merit fellowships providing an additional $2500 per year are available to outstanding doctoral applicants. In addition, first-year bonuses of $1250 are available for highly talented students pursuing their Ph.D. in physical chemistry. Advanced Ph.D. students are typically funded through research assistantships ($20,000 or higher) provided by their respective advisors.

Cost of Study

Graduate tuition and fees for the 2010–11 academic year are $6528, for which a tuition scholarship is provided.

Living and Housing Costs

Rooms in the graduate hall of residence are $2515 to $3360 per semester; married students' apartments may be rented for $669 to $699 per month (all utilities included). Information concerning off-campus housing may be obtained from the University housing office. Costs vary widely, but apartments typically rent for $500 to $600 per month.

Student Group

The ethnically diverse and highly talented chemistry graduate student population currently numbers about 50. There are approximately 23,000 students enrolled at the main campus of Kent State University; 12,000 additional students attend the seven regional campuses.

Location

Kent, a college town of about 28,000, is located 35 miles southeast of Cleveland and 12 miles east of Akron in a peaceful suburban setting. Kent offers the cultural advantages of a major metropolitan complex as well as the relaxed pace of semirural living. There are a number of music (e.g., Kent State's folk festival and free chamber music concerts in the summer), theater, and visual art groups at the University and in the community. Blossom Music Center, the summer home of the Cleveland Orchestra and the site of Kent State's cooperative programs in art, music, and theater, is only 15 miles from the main campus. This beautiful outdoor concert venue is also the site for many critically acclaimed rock concerts throughout the summer months. The newly expanded Akron and Cleveland art museums are within easy reach of the campus. Cleveland is also the home of the world-renowned Rock and Roll Hall of Fame and several professional sport teams. There are a wide variety of recreational facilities available on the campus and within the local area, including West Branch State Park and the Cuyahoga Valley National Park. Nearby Lake Erie and its beaches offer a broad range of water recreational activities. Winter activities include ice skating as well as downhill and cross-country skiing. Kent State's state-of-the-art recreation and wellness center is available for graduate students free of charge.

The University

Established in 1910, Kent State University is one of Ohio's largest and oldest state universities. The campus contains 820 acres of wooded hillsides plus an airport and an eighteen-hole golf course. There are approximately 100 buildings on the main campus. Bachelor's, master's, and doctoral degrees are offered in more than thirty subject areas. The full-time faculty numbers approximately 1,200.

Applying

The online application system for the graduate program is located at: http://www.kent.edu/admissions/apply/. To ensure full consideration, candidates for admission for the upcoming fall semester should make certain that all their application material is received by the University no later than January 10. However, applications will be accepted until all positions are filled. In the case that late applications cannot be considered for fall admission, they will be automatically considered for admission the following spring semester. A limited number of positions are available for spring admission. Candidates should ensure that their application package is complete no later than September 1.

Application material must include all pertinent transcripts, general GRE exam, personal statement, three letters of recommendation, and a CV/resume. Domestic applicants can send all application materials to: Research and Graduate Studies, Office of Graduate Services, 16 Cartwright Hall, Kent State University, P. O. Box 5190, Kent, Ohio 44242-0001.

Foreign students must also provide TOEFL or IELTS exam scores. The minimum cutoff for the TOEFL is 525 on the paper-based exam, and 71 on the Internet-based test. The minimum cutoff for the IELTS is a score of six. Although the subject GRE is not required, candidates are encouraged to provide a subject GRE to strengthen their file. International applicants can send all application materials to: Office of International Affairs, Kent State University, 106 Van Campen Hall, 21 Loop Road, Kent, Ohio 44242, U.S.A.

Correspondence and Information

General Correspondence:

Graduate Coordinator
Department of Chemistry and Biochemistry
Kent State University
Kent, Ohio 44242

Phone: 330-672-2032
Fax: 330-672-3816
E-mail: chemgc@kent.edu
Web site: http://www.kent.edu/chemistry

Kent State University

THE FACULTY AND THEIR RESEARCH

Research groups are supported through grants awarded by the National Science Foundation, the National Institutes of Health, the Department of Energy, the Department of Defense, and other federal and state funding agencies.

Soumitra Basu, Assistant Professor; Ph.D., Thomas Jefferson, 1996. Biochemistry: molecular modulation of RNA function, anticancer therapeutics using RNAi, alternative translation modes with implications for tumor angiogenesis, chemical modification of RNA, toxicoribonomics.

Nicola E. Brasch, Associate Professor; Ph.D., Otago (New Zealand), 1994. Bioinorganic and medicinal chemistry; vitamin B_{12} and the B_{12}-dependent enzyme reactions; vanadium chemistry; inorganic drug delivery systems; synthesis, kinetics, and mechanism.

Scott D. Bunge, Assistant Professor; Ph.D., Georgia Tech, 2001. Inorganic chemistry: molecular design, organometallics, coordination chemistry, air-sensitive synthesis, catalysis, X-ray crystallography, thin films, nanomaterials.

Bansidhar Datta, Associate Professor; Ph.D., Nebraska–Lincoln, 1989. Biochemistry and molecular biology: mechanism of protein synthesis initiation in mammals; studies of posttranslational modifications, such as O-glycosylation and phosphorylation of translational regulator, p67; molecular cloning of translational regulatory proteins; studies of the evolutionary origins of the regulatory/structural domains in p67.

Arne Gericke, Associate Professor; Dr.rer.nat., Hamburg (Germany), 1994. Biophysical chemistry: lipid mediated protein functions, membrane trafficking (phosphoinositide mediated signaling pathways, tumor suppressor protein PTEN, sphingolipids); IR spectroscopy, surface enhanced Raman spectroscopy, calorimetry (ITC/DSC); advanced fluorescence techniques, including fluorescence correlation spectroscopy, fluorescence lifetime measurements, and confocal and single molecule microscopy; infrared and Raman spectroscopic imaging of pathological tissue (e.g., heart tissue damage and multiple sclerosis).

Edwin S. Gould, University Professor; Ph.D., UCLA, 1950. Inorganic chemistry: mechanisms of inorganic redox reactions; catalysis of redox reactions by organic species; electron-transfer reactions of flavin-related systems; reactions of cobalt, chromium, vanadium, titanium, europium, uranium, ruthenium, indium, peroxynitrous acid, and trioxodinitrate; reactions of water-soluble radical species.

Roger B. Gregory, Professor; Ph.D., Sheffield (England), 1980. Biochemistry: protein conformational dynamics; the characterization of dynamic substructures in proteins; protein hydration and glass transition behavior; proteomics: development and application of high-sensitivity methods for protein characterization, including protein-protein interactions and protein chemical modifications.

Songping D. Huang, Associate Professor; Ph.D., Michigan State, 1993. Inorganic chemistry: molecule-based magnetic and nonlinear optical materials, organic conductors and superconductors, novel microporous and mesoporous materials, synthesis and crystal growth of metal oxides and chalcogenides.

Mietek Jaroniec, Professor; Ph.D., Lublin (Poland), 1976. Physical/analytical/materials chemistry: adsorption and chromatography at the gas/solid and liquid/solid interface; synthesis and modification of adsorbents, catalysts, and chromatographic packings with tailored surface and structural properties; self-assembled organic-inorganic nanomaterials; ordered mesoporous carbons synthesized via templating and imprinting methods; characterization of nanoporous materials.

Anatoly K. Khitrin, Associate Professor; Ph.D., Institute of Chemical Physics, Russian Academy of Sciences, 1985. Physical chemistry: NMR techniques, theory of magnetic resonance, material science, quantum computing and microimaging.

Shanhu Lee, Associate Professor; Ph.D., Tokyo, 1997. Analytical chemistry: atmospheric chemistry, laboratory studies of atmospheric aerosol particles, field measurements of aerosol sizes, atmospheric sulfuric acid (a major aerosol precursor).

Hanbin Mao, Assistant Professor; Ph.D., Texas A&M, 2003. Bioanalytical and biophysical chemistry: micro total analysis systems ("lab-on-a-chip"), laser and magnetic tweezers, single-molecule DNA and DNA-protein interactions, drug-screening.

Paul Sampson, Professor; Ph.D., Birmingham (England), 1983. Synthetic organic chemistry: development of new synthetic methods; synthetic (stereoselective) organofluorine chemistry, with applications to the synthesis of fluorinated liquid crystals and carbohydrate analogs; development of new organometallic synthons as building blocks for organic synthesis.

Alexander J. Seed, Associate Professor; Ph.D., Hull (England), 1995. Organic chemistry, design, synthesis, and physical characterization of liquid crystals; ferroelectric, antiferroelectric, and high-twisting power materials for optical applications; new heterocyclic synthetic methodology.

Diane Stroup, Associate Professor; Ph.D., Ohio State, 1992. Biochemistry: control of mammalian gene expression by regulation of transcriptional and posttranscriptional processes, study of nuclear hormone receptors and signal transduction events.

Chun-che Tsai, Professor; Ph.D., Indiana, 1968. Biochemistry: interaction of drugs with nucleic acids; structure and activity of anticancer drugs, antiviral agents, antibiotic drugs, and interferon inducers; structure and biological function relationships; X-ray diffraction; quantitative structure-activity relationships (QSAR); molecular and drug design.

Michael J. Tubergen, Associate Professor; Ph.D., Chicago, 1991. Physical chemistry: high-resolution microwave spectroscopy for molecular structure determination of hydrogen-bonded complexes and biological molecules.

Robert J. Twieg, Distinguished Professor; Ph.D., Berkeley, 1976. Organic chemistry and materials science: development of organic and polymeric materials with novel electronic and optoelectronic properties, including nonlinear optical chromophores, photorefractive chromophores, organic semiconductors, fluorescent tags, and liquid crystals, with emphasis on applications and durability issues.

John L. West, Professor; Vice President of Research and Dean of Graduate Studies; Ph.D., Carnegie Mellon, 1980. Physical chemistry: materials science; liquid crystal polymer formulations for display applications, basic studies of liquid crystal alignment.

SELECTED PUBLICATIONS

Basu, S., and S. A. Strobel. Identification of specific monovalent metal ion binding sites within RNA. *Methods* 122:264–75, 2001.

Basu, S., A. Szewczak, M. Cocco, and S. A. Strobel. Direct detection of specific monovalent metal ion binding to a DNA G-quartet by ^{205}T1 NMR. *J. Am. Chem. Soc.* 122:3240–1, 2000.

Basu, S., and S. A. Strobel. Thiophilic metal ion rescue of phosphorothioate interference within the Tetrahymena ribozyme P4-P6 domain. *RNA* 5:1399–407, 1999.

Hannibal, L., C. A. Smith, D. W. Jacobsen, and **N. E. Brasch.** Nitroxylcob(III)alamin: Synthesis and X-ray structural characterization. *Angew. Chem.* 46:5140, 2007.

Hannibal, L., et al. **(N. E. Brasch).** X-ray structural characterization of imidazolylcobalamin and histidinylcobalamin: Cobalamin models for aquacobalamin bound to the B_{12} transporter protein transcobalamin. *Inorg. Chem.* 46:3613, 2007.

Mukherjee, R., et al. **(N. E. Brasch).** Structural and spectroscopic evidence for the formation of trinuclear and tetranuclear V(III)/carboxylate complexes of acetate and related derivatives in aqueous solution. *Inorg. Chem.* 46:1575, 2007.

Bunge, S. D., J. A. Bertke, and T. L. Cleland. Synthesis, structure, and reactivity of low-coordinate 1,1,3,3-tetraethylguanidinate complexes. *Inorg. Chem.* 48(16):8037–43, 2009.

Bunge, S. D., J. A. Ocana, T. L. Cleland, and J. L. Steele. Synthetic, structural, and theoretical investigation of guanidinate complexes containing planar Cu_6 cores. *Inorg. Chem.* 48(11):4619–21, 2009.

Monegan, J. D., and **S. D. Bunge.** Structurally characterized 1,1,3,3-tetramethylguanidine solvated magnesium aryloxide complexes: $[Mg(\mu\text{-OEt})(DBP)(H\text{-TMG})]_2$, $[Mg(\mu\text{-OBc})(DBP)(H\text{-TMG})]_2$, $[Mg(\mu\text{-TMBA})(DBP)(H\text{-TMG})]_2$, $[Mg(\mu\text{-DPP})(DBP)(H\text{-TMG})]_2$, $[Mg(BMP)_2(H\text{-TMG})_2]$, $[Mg(O\text{-}2,6\text{-}Ph_2C_6H_3)_2(H\text{-TMG})_2]$. Inorg. Chem. 48(7):3248–56, 2009.

Datta, B., et al. Autoproteolysis of rat p67 generates several peptide fragments: The N-terminal fragment, p26, is required for the protection of eIF2 alpha from phosphorylation. *Biochemistry* 46(11):3465, 2007.

Ghosh A., et al. **(B. Datta).** The N-terminal lysine residue-rich domain II and the 340-430 amino acid segment of eukaryotic initiation factor 2-associated glycoprotein p67 are the binding sites for the gamma subunit of eIF2. *Exp. Cell Res.* 312(16):3184, 2006.

Datta, B., et al. The binding between p67 and eukaryotic initiation factor 2 plays important roles in the protection of eIF2 alpha from phosphorylation by kinases. *Arch. Biochem. Biophys.* 452(2):138, 2006.

Ross, A. H. and **A. Gericke.** Phosphorylation keeps PTEN phosphatase closed for business. *Proc. Natl. Acad. Sci., U.S.A.* 106:1297–8, 2009.

Redfern, R. E., et al. **(A. Gericke).** PTEN phosphatase selectively binds phosphoinositides and undergoes structural changes. *Biochemistry* 47:2162–71, 2008.

Gericke, A., M. Munson, and A. H. Ross. Regulation of the PTEN phosphatase. *Gene* 374:1, 2006.

Mukherjee, R., Z. Y. Yang, and **E. S. Gould.** Reductions by titanium(II) as catalyzed by titanium(IV). *Dalton Trans.* 6:772, 2006.

Yang, Z. Y., and **E. S. Gould.** Reactions of molybdenum(VI) with metal ion reductants. *Dalt. Trans.* 28:3427, 2006.

Yang, Z., and **E. S. Gould.** Electron transfer. 160. Reductions by aquatitanium(II). *Dalton Trans.* 1781, 2005.

Roh, J. H., et al. **(R. B. Gregory).** Influence of hydration on the dynamics of lysozyme. *Biophys. J.* 91(7):2573, 2006.

Roh, J. H., et al. **(R. B. Gregory).** Onsets of anharmonicity in protein dynamics. *Phys. Rev. Lett.* 95(3): Art. No. 038101, 2005.

Gregory, R. B. Protein hydration and glass transitions. In *The Properties of Water in Foods,* pp. 55–99, ed. D. Reid. New York: Chapman-Hall, 1997.

Fu, D. W., et al. **(S. D. Huang).** Dielectric anisotropy of a homochiral trinuclear nickel(II) complex. *J. Am. Chem. Soc.* 129(17):5346, 2007.

Ye, Q., et al. **(S. D. Huang).** Ferroelectric metal-organic framework with a high dielectric constant. *J. Am. Chem. Soc.* 128(20):6554, 2006.

Vanchura, B. A., et al. **(S. D. Huang).** Direct synthesis of mesostructured lamellar molybdenum disulfides using a molten neutral n-alkylamine as the solvent and template. *J. Am. Chem. Soc.* 124(41):12090, 2002.

Celer, E. B., and **M. Jaroniec.** Temperature-programmed microwave-assisted synthesis of SBA-15 ordered mesoporous silica. *J. Am. Chem. Soc.* 128(44):14408, 2006.

Gierszal, K. P., and **M. Jaroniec.** Carbons with extremely large volume of uniform mesopores synthesized by carbonization of phenolic resin film formed on colloidal silica template. *J. Am. Chem. Soc.* 128(31):10026, 2006.

Jaroniec, M. Materials science: Organosilica the conciliator. *Nature* 442(7103):638, 2006.

Lee, J. S., T. Adams, and **A. K. Khitrin.** Experimental demonstration of a stimulated polarization wave in a chain of nuclear spins. *New J. Phys.* 9: Art. No. 83, 2007.

Lee, J. S., and **A. K. Khitrin.** Constant-time method for measuring inter-nuclear distances in static powders. *J. Magn. Reson.* 186:327, 2007.

Lee, J. S., and **A. K. Khitrin.** NMR quantum toys. *Concepts Magn. Reson.* 30A:194, 2007.

Young, L.-H., et al. **S.-H. Lee.** Laboratory studies of sulfuric acid and water binary homogenous nucleation: Evaluation of laboratory setup and preliminary results. *Atmos. Chem. Phys.* 8:1–20, 2008.

Benson, D. R., L.-H. Young, F. R. Kameel, and S.-H. Lee. Laboratory-measured sulfuric acid and water homogenous nucleation rates from the SO_2 + OH reaction. *Geophys. Res. Lett.* 35:L11801. doi:2008GL033387.

Benson, D. R., et al. S.-H. Lee. When does new particle formation not occur in the upper troposphere? *Atmos. Chem. Phys.* 7:14209–32, 2007.

Lee, S.-H., et al. Particle formation by ion nucleation in the upper troposphere and lower stratosphere. *Science* 301:1886, 2003.

Lee, S.-H., D. M. Murphy, D. S. Thomson, and A. M. Middlebrook. Nitrate and oxidized organics in single particle mass particle mass spectra during the 1999 Atlanta Supersites project. *J. Geophys. Res.* 108, 2003, doi:10.1029/2001JD001455.

Luchette, P., N. Abiy, and **H. Mao.** Microanalysis of clouding process at the single droplet level. *Sensor. Actuator. B Chem.* 128:154–60, 2007.

Mao, H., et al. Temperature control methods in a laser-tweezers system. *Biophys. J.* 89:1308, 2005.

Mao, H., P. Cremer, and M. Manson. A versatile, sensitive microfluidic assay for bacterial chemotaxis. *Proc. Natl. Acad. Sci. U.S.A.* 100:5449, 2003.

Chumachenko, N., and **P. Sampson.** Synthesis of beta-hydroxy sulfones via opening of hydrophilic epoxides with zinc sulfinates in aqueous media. *Tetrahedron* 62(18):4540, 2006.

Novikov, Y. Y., and **P. Sampson.** 1-bromo-1-lithioethene: A practical reagent in organic synthesis. *J. Org. Chem.* 70(25):10247, 2005.

Chumachenko, N., **P. Sampson,** A. D. Hunter, and M. Zeller. β-acyloxysulfonyl tethers for intramolecular Diels-Alder cycloaddition reactions. *Org. Lett.* 7:3203, 2005.

Sybo, B., et al. **(P. Sampson** and **A. J. Seed).** 1,3,4-Thiadiazole-2-carboxylate esters: New synthetic methodology for the preparation of an elusive family of self-organizing materials. *J. Mater. Chem.* 17(32):3406–11, 2007.

Seed, A. J. Synthesis of self-organizing mesogenic materials containing a sulfur-based five-membered heterocyclic core. *Chem. Soc. Rev.* 36(12):2046–69, 2007.

McCoy, B. K., et al. **(A. J. Seed).** Smectic-C^*_α phase with two coexistent helical pitch values and a first-order smectic-C^*_α to smectic-C^* transition. *Phys. Rev. E* 75(5-1), article no. 051706, 2007.

Docherty, J., et al. **(C. C. Tsai).** In vivo anti-herpes simplex virus activity of resveratrol, a cyclin dependent kinase gene inhibitor. *Antivir. Res.* 57(3):86, 2003.

Tsai, C. C., et al. In vivo and in vitro antiherpetic effects of hydroxytolans. *Antivir. Res.* 57(3):87, 2003.

Nassiri, M. R., et al. **(C. C. Tsai).** The activity of Mg2+ and poly r(A-U) against HIV-I. *Antivir. Res.* 46(1):32, 2000.

Kent State University

Tubergen, M. J., et al. Rotational spectra and conformational structures of 1-phenyl-2-propanol, methamphetamine, and 1-phenyl-2-propanone. *J. Phys. Chem. A* 110(49):13188, 2006.

Tubergen, M. J., et al. Rotational spectra, nuclear quadrupole hyperfine tensors, and conformational structures of the mustard gas simulent 2-chloroethyl ethyl sulfide. *J. Mol. Spectros.* 233(2):180, 2005.

Tubergen, M. J., C. R. Torok, and R. J. Lavrich. Effect of solvent on molecular conformation: Microwave spectra and structures of 2-aminoethanol van der Waals complexes. *J. Chem. Phys.* 119:8397–403, 2003.

Wang, H., et al. **(R. J. Twieg).** The influence of tetrahydroquinoline rings in dicyanomethylenedihydrofuran (DCDHF) single-molecule fluorophores. *Tetrahedron* 63(1):103, 2007.

Lu, Z. K., et al. **(R. J. Twieg).** Long-wavelength analogue of PRODAN: Synthesis and properties of Anthradan, a fluorophore with a 2,6-donor-acceptor anthracene structure. *J. Org. Chem.* 71(26):9651, 2006.

Ellman, B., et al. **(R. J. Twieg).** High mobility, low dispersion hole transport in 1,4-diiodobenzene. *Adv. Mater.* 18(17):2284, 2006.

Li, F. H., et al. **(J. West).** Orientational coupling amplification in ferroelectric nematic colloids. *Phys. Rev. Lett.* 97(14): Art. No. 147801, 2006.

Buyuktanir, E. A., et al. **(J. L. West).** Field-induced polymer wall formation in a bistable smectic—A liquid crystal display. *Appl. Phys. Lett.* 89(3): Art. No. 031101, 2006.

West, J. L., et al. Colloidal particles at a nematic-isotropic interface: Effects of confinement. *Eur. Phys. J. E* 20(2):237, 2006.

PRINCETON UNIVERSITY

Department of Chemistry

Programs of Study

The Department of Chemistry offers a program of study leading to the degree of Doctor of Philosophy. The graduate program emphasizes research, and students enter a research group by the end of the first semester. Students are required to take six graduate courses in chemistry and allied areas, satisfying at least four of ten areas of distribution, and are expected to participate in the active lecture and seminar programs throughout their graduate careers.

Early in the second year, students take a general examination that consists of an oral defense of a thesis-related subject. Upon satisfactory performance in the general examination, students advance to candidacy for the degree of Doctor of Philosophy in chemistry. The degree is awarded primarily on the basis of a thesis describing original research in one of the areas of chemistry. The normal length of the entire Ph.D. program is four to five years.

Programs of graduate study in materials and neuroscience are also offered, in cooperation with other science departments at Princeton University.

Research Facilities

In fall 2010, the department is scheduled to move to a new, state-of-the-art chemistry building designed by Hopkins Architects, a London-based firm that has earned numerous awards for its work in the United Kingdom. The new building is adjacent to the physics, molecular biology, and mathematics departments as well as the Lewis-Siegler Genomics Institute. A wide variety of research instrumentation is available, both in the departmental instrument facility and in individual faculty members' laboratories. This instrumentation includes NMR; ESR; mass spectrometry (high-resolution and gas chromatograph integrated); and visible, ultraviolet, and infrared spectrometers. Recent instrument acquisitions include three 500 MHz NMRs with cryoprobes and autosamplers, a high resolution ESI-TOF mass spectrometer, an LC-interfaced Q-TOF mass spectrometer for proteomics studies, a fast LC-triple quadrupole mass spectrometer, and a suite of bench-top FT-IR spectrometers for routine analysis. There is research equipment for ultrahigh vacuum surface studies, including electron diffraction and electron spectroscopy equipment. Tunable and fixed wavelength laser sources, gas and liquid chromatographic equipment, X-ray diffraction facilities, and controlled atmosphere dry boxes also are available to students.

Financial Aid

All admitted students receive funding during the normal period of study, usually five years. This funding covers tuition, health insurance, and a maintenance allowance, typically in the form of assistantships in instruction or research. In 2010–11, students earn $22,250 to $25,750 during the ten-month academic year, plus a summer stipend of $5000. First-year graduate students are not required to teach, as they receive fellowship funds that allow them to concentrate on course work.

Cost of Study

See the Financial Aid section.

Living and Housing Costs

Rooms at the Graduate College cost from $4092 to $7135 for the 2010–11 academic year of thirty-five weeks. Several meal plans are available, priced from $3305 to $5498. University apartments for both single and married students currently rent for $684 to $2000 per month. Accommodations are also available in the surrounding community.

Student Group

The total number of graduate students in chemistry is currently about 140. Postdoctoral students number about 70. A wide variety of academic, ethnic, and national backgrounds is represented among these students.

Location

Princeton University and the surrounding community together provide an ideal environment for learning and research. From the point of view of a chemist at the University, the engineering, physics, mathematics, and molecular biology departments, as well as the plasma physics lab on the Forrestal campus, provide valuable associates, supplementary facilities, and sources of special knowledge. Many corporations have located their research laboratories near Princeton, leading to fruitful collaborations, seminars and lecture series, and employment opportunities after graduation.

Because of the nature of the institutions located here, the small community of Princeton has a very high proportion of professional people. To satisfy the needs of this unusual community, the intellectual and cultural activities approach the number and variety ordinarily found only in large cities, but with the advantage that everything is within walking distance. There are many film series, a resident repertory theater, orchestras, ballet, and chamber music and choral groups. Scientific seminars and other symposia bring prominent visitors from every field of endeavor.

Princeton's picturesque countryside provides a pleasant area for work and recreation, yet New York City and Philadelphia are each only about an hour away.

The University

Princeton University was founded in 1746 as the College of New Jersey. At its 150th anniversary in 1896, the trustees changed the name to Princeton University. The Graduate School was organized in 1901 and has since won international recognition in mathematics, the natural sciences, philosophy, and the humanities.

Applying

Application instructions, including an online application, are available at http://gso.princeton.edu/admission/. The application deadline for the Department of Chemistry is December 15 for all applicants. All applications must be accompanied by an application fee, which is discounted for online applications submitted prior to December 1.

Admission consideration is given to all candidates without regard to race, color, national origin, religion, sex, or handicap.

Correspondence and Information

Sallie Dunner
Graduate Administrator
Department of Chemistry
Princeton University
Princeton, New Jersey 08544

Phone: 609-258-4116
E-mail: sdunner@princeton.edu
Web site: http://www.princeton.edu/~chemdept

Princeton University

THE FACULTY AND THEIR RESEARCH

Although the faculty members represent all major areas of chemistry, the Department is small, which allows for the development of fruitful collaborations. The following list briefly indicates the areas of interest of each professor.

S. L. Bernasek. Chemical physics of surfaces: basic studies of chemisorption on well-characterized transition-metal surfaces using electron diffraction and electron spectroscopy, surface reaction dynamics, heterogeneous catalysis.
A. B. Bocarsly. Inorganic materials chemistry, chemistry of alternate energy systems, chemical mitigation of carbon dioxide, electrochemistry, photochemistry, semiconductor photoelectrochemistry, coordination chemistry.
R. Car. Chemical physics and materials science; electronic structure theory and ab initio molecular dynamics; computer modeling and simulation of solids, liquids, disordered systems, and molecular structures; structural phase transitions and chemical reactions.
J. Carey. Biophysical chemistry: protein and nucleic acid structure, function, and interactions; protein folding and stability.
R. J. Cava. Materials chemistry; synthesis of new oxide, intermetallic, pnictide, and chalcogenide compounds, and characterization of their crystal structures and electronic and magnetic properties.
P. J. Chirik. (joining January 2011). Organic and inorganic chemistry: discovery of energy-efficient chemical transformations.
A. G. Doyle. Organic and organometallic chemistry: discovery and development of new catalytic routes to chiral building blocks of importance in the enantioselective synthesis of natural products, pharmaceuticals, materials.
D. Fiedler. Chemical biology, bioinorganic chemistry: signaling functions of small molecule second messengers.
J. T. Groves. Bioorganic and bioinorganic chemistry, synthetic and mechanistic studies of reactions of biological interest, transition metal redox catalysis, models and mimics of metalloenzymes, biochemical mechanisms of protein nitration, the chemical biology of iron acquisition by siderophores and models of biological membranes.
M. Hecht. Biochemistry and chemical biology, protein folding and misfolding, protein design, synthetic biology, Alzheimer's disease.
D. W. C. MacMillan. Organic synthesis and catalysis: new concepts in synthetic organic chemistry involving organocatalysis, organo-cascade catalysis, metal-mediated catalysis, and total synthesis of natural products and pharmaceuticals.
T. W. Muir. (Joining January 2011). Organic chemistry, biochemistry, and cell biology: the physicochemical basis of protein function in complex systems of biomedical interest.
J. Rabinowitz. Biochemical kinetics, cellular metabolism, chemical basis of complex biological processes.
H. Rabitz. Physical chemistry, biomolecular modeling, laser control of molecular processes, molecular collisions, theory of chemical reactions, time- and space-dependent molecular manipulation.
C. E. Schutt. Structural biology, structure and function of proteins and cellular organelles, X-ray crystallography.
J. Schwartz. Organometallic chemistry, surface and interface organic and inorganic chemistry and their applications to biomaterials and electronic materials.
A. Selloni. Computational physics and chemistry and modeling of materials; structural, electronic, and dynamic properties of semiconductor and oxide surfaces; chemisorption and surface reactions.
M. F. Semmelhack. Organometallic and electrogenerated intermediates in organic synthesis, synthesis of unusual ring systems in natural and unnatural molecules.
Z. G. Soos. Chemical physics, electronic states of conjugated polymers and ion-radical solids, paramagnetic and charge transfer excitons, one-dimensional models.
E. J. Sorensen. Organic chemistry: chemical synthesis of bioactive natural products and molecular probes for biological research, bioinspired strategies for chemical synthesis, architectural self-constructions and novel methods for synthesis.
S. Torquato. Statistical mechanics and materials science; theory and computer simulations of disordered heterogeneous materials, liquids, amorphous solids, and biological materials; optimization in materials science; simulations of peptide binding; modeling the growth of tumors.
H. Yang. Physical chemistry, reaction dynamics in complex systems, development and application of single-molecule spectroscopy and methods to elucidate functional consequences in protein conformational dynamics in vitro and in living cells, self assembly of biological macromolecules and nanostructures, biofuels and basic sciences in sustainable energy solutions.

Associated Faculty

E. A. Carter, Department of Mechanical and Aerospace Engineering and of Applied and Computational Mathematics. Development of quantum mechanics-based methods to predict behavior of molecules and materials, with applications to combustion chemistry, nanoscale physics, and materials science, with a new emphasis on alternative energy research.
B. Garcia. Department of Molecular Biology. Quantitative biochemistry applied to the analysis of chromatin and nuclear signaling proteins.
F. M. Hughson, Department of Molecular Biology. Biochemical and X-ray crystallographic studies of intracellular trafficking and bacterial quorum sensing.
M. Llanas, Department of Molecular Biology. Cellular metabolism, biochemistry, genomics, microbiology, parasitology.
M. C. McAlpine. Department of Mechanical and Aerospace Engineering. Materials science: nanotechnology and biomaterials-enabled approaches to addressing fundamental problems in medicine, energy, and flexible electronics.
F. M. M. Morel, Department of Geosciences. Environmental chemistry, trace metal geochemistry, metals-biota interactions.
S. M. Myneni, Department of Geosciences. Environmental chemistry, ion hydration and complexation, interfacial chemistry, X-ray spectroscopy.
J. Stock, Department of Molecular Biology. Protein chemistry, cell biology, pharmacology.

Rendering of new chemistry building, Princeton University.

SELECTED PUBLICATIONS

Tao, F., G.-Q. Xu, and **(S. L. Bernasek).** Electronic and structural factors in modification and functionalization of clean and passivated semiconductor surfaces with aromatic systems. *Chem. Rev.* 109(9):3991–4024, 2009.

Peng, T. L., and **S. L. Bernasek.** The internal energy of CO_2 produced by the catalytic oxidation of CH_3OH by O_2 on polycrystalline platinum. *J. Chem. Phys.* 131(15):154701–10, 2009.

Oncel, N. and **S. L. Bernasek.** Ni(II)- and vanadyloctaethylporphyrin self-assembled layers formed on bare and 5-(octadecyloxy)isophthalic acid covered graphite. *Langmuir* 25(16):9290–5, 2009.

Bhargava, G., T. A. Ramanarayanan, and **S. L. Bernasek.** Imidazole-Fe interaction in an aqueous chloride medium: Effect of cathodic reduction of the native oxide. *Langmuir* 26(1):215–9, 2009.

McDermott, J. E., et al. **(S. L. Bernasek** and **J. Schwartz).** Organophosphonate self-assembled monolayers for gate dielectric surface modification of pentacene-based organic thin-film transistors: A comparative study. *J. Phys. Chem.* 111(49):12333–8, 2007.

Burgess, C. M., N. Yao, and **A. B. Bocarsly.** Stabilizing cyanosols: Amorphous cyanide bridged transition metal polymer nanoparticles. *J. Mat. Chem.* 19(46):8846–55, 2009.

Barton, E. E., D. M. Rampulla, and **A. B. Bocarsly.** Selective solar-driven reduction of CO_2 to methanol using a catalyzed p-GaP based photoelectrochemical cell. *J. Am. Chem. Soc.* 130(20):6342–4, 2008.

Majsztrik, P., **A. B. Bocarsly,** and J. Benziger. Water permeation through nafion membranes: The role of water activity. *J. Phys. Chem. B* 112(51):16280–9, 2008.

Vondrova, M., et al. **(A. B. Bocarsly).** Autoreduction of Pd-Co and Pt-Co cyanogels: Exploration of cyanometalate coordination chemistry at elevated temperatures. *J. Am. Chem. Soc.* 130(16):5563–72, 2008.

Melichercik, S. R., et al. **(J. Carey).** Symmetric allosteric mechanism of hexameric *Escherichia coli* arginine repressor exploits competition between L-arginine ligands and resident arginine residues. *PLoS Computational Biology* 6(6):e1000801, 2010.

Lapkouski, M., et al. **(J. Carey).** Structure of the motor subunit of type I restriction-modification complex EcoR124I. *Nat. Struct. Mol. Biol.* 16:94–5, 2008.

Carey, J., et al. WrbA bridges bacterial flavodoxins and eukaryotic NAD(P)H:quinone oxidoreductases. *Protein Sci.* 16(10):2301–5, 2007.

Chwee, T. S., and **E. A. Carter.** Cholesky decomposition within local multireference singles and doubles configuration interaction. *J. Chem. Phys.* 132(7):074104–14, 2010.

Huang, C., and **E. A. Carter.** Nonlocal orbital-free kinetic energy density functional for semiconductors. *Phys. Rev. B* 81(4):045206–21, 2010.

Sharifzadeh, S., P. Huang, and **E. A. Carter.** Origin of tunneling lineshape trends for Kondo states of Co adatoms on coinage metal surfaces. J. *Phys. Condens. Matter* 21(35):355501, 2009.

McQueen, T.M., et. al. **(R. J. Cava).** Tetragonal-to-orthorhombic structural phase transition at 90K in the superconductor $Fe_{1.01}Se$. *Phys. Rev. Lett.* 103(5):057002, 2009.

McQueen, T. M., et al. **(R. J. Cava, R. A. Pascal, Jr.,** and **Z. G. Soos).** Realization of the bond order wave (BOW) phase of extended Hubbard models in Rb-TCNQ(II). *Chem. Phys. Lett.* 475(1–3):44–8, 2009.

West, D.V. et. al. **(R. J. Cava).** The $A^{2+}Mn_5(SO_4)_6$ family of triangular lattice, ferrimagnetic sulfates. *J. Solid State Chem.* 182(6):1343–50, 2009.

Klimczuk, T., et. al. **(R. J. Cava).** Superconductivity at 2.2 K in the layered oxypnictide $La_3Ni_4P_4O_2$. *Phys. Rev. B* 79(1):012505, 2009.

Kalow, J. A., and **Doyle, A. G.** Enantioselective ring opening of epoxides by fluoride anion promoted by a cooperative dual-catalyst system. *J. Am. Chem. Soc.* 132(10):3268–9, 2010.

Zee, B. M., et al. **(B. A. Garcia).** In vivo residue-specific histone methylation dynamics. *J. Biol. Chem.* 285(5):3341–50, 2010.

Zee, B. M., and **B. A. Garcia.** Electron transfer dissociation facilitates sequencing of adenosine diphosphate-ribosylated peptides. *Anal. Chem.* 82(1):28–31, 2010.

Young, N. L., et al. **(B. A. Garcia).** High throughput characterization of combinatorial histone codes. *Mol. Cell. Proteomics* 8(10):2266–84, 2009.

LeRoy, G., et al. **(B. A. Garcia).** Heterochromatin protein 1 is extensively decorated with histone code-like post-translational modifications. *Mol. Cell. Proteomics* 8(11):2432–42, 2009.

Bell, S. R., and **J. T. Groves.** A highly reactive P450 model compound I. *J. Am. Chem. Soc.* 131(28):9640–1, 2009.

Su, J., and **J. T. Groves.** Direct detection of the oxygen rebound intermediates, ferryl Mb and NO_2, in the reaction of metMyoglobin with peroxynitrite. *J. Am. Chem. Soc.* 131(36):12979–88, 2009.

Austin, R. N., et al. **(J. T. Groves).** Cage escape competes with geminate recombination during alkane hydroxylation by the diiron oxygenase AlkB. *Angew. Chem.* 47(28):5232–4, 2008, doi:10.1002/anie.200801184.

Jin, N., M. Ibrahim, T. G. Spiro, and **J. T. Groves.** Trans-dioxo manganese(V) porphyrins. *J. Am. Chem. Soc.* 129(41):12416–7, 2007.

Patel, S., L. H. Bradley, S. Jinadasa, and **M. H. Hecht.** Cofactor binding and enzymatic activity in an unevolved superfamily of de novo designed 4-helix bundle proteins. *Protein Sci.* 18(7):1388–1400, 2009.

Kim, W., and **M. H. Hecht.** Mutations enhance the aggregation propensity of the Alzheimer's Aβ peptide. *J. Mol. Biol.* 377(2):565–74, 2008.

Go, A., S. Kim, J. Baum, and **M. H. Hecht.** Structure and dynamics of de novo proteins from a designed superfamily of 4-helix bundles. *Protein Sci.* 17(5):821–32, 2008.

Kim, W., et al. **(M. H. Hecht.)** A high throughput screen for compounds that inhibit aggregation of the Alzheimer's peptide. *ACS Chemical Biology* 1(7):461–9, 2006.

Hecht, M. H., et al. De novo proteins from designed combinatorial libraries. *Protein Sci.* 13(7):1711–23, 2004.

Richardson, B. C., et al. **(F. M. Hughson).** Structural basis for a human glycosylation disorder caused by mutation of the COG_4 gene. *Proc. Natl. Acad. Sci. Unit. States Am.* 106(32):13329–34, 2009.

Ren, Y., et al. **(F. M. Hughson).** A structure-based mechanism for vesicle capture by the multisubunit tethering complex Dsl1. *Cell* 139(6):1119–29, 2009.

Boer, V. M., et al. **(J. D. Rabinowitz).** Growth-limiting intracellular metabolites in yeast growing under diverse nutrient limitations. *Mol. Biol. Cell* 21(1):198–211, 2010.

Princeton University

Lu, W., et al. **(J. D.Rabinowitz).** Metabolomic analysis via reversed-phase ion-pairing liquid chromatography coupled to a stand alone orbitrap mass spectrometer. *Anal. Chem.* 82(8):3212–21, 2010.

DiMaggio Jr., P. A., et al. **(J. D. Rabinowitz** and **H. A. Rabitz).** Enhancing molecular discovery using descriptor-free rearrangement clustering techniques for sparse data sets. *AIChE Journal* 56(2):405–18, 2010.

Kelly, R. C., et al. **(J. D. Rabinowitz, M. F. Semmelhack,** and **F. M. Hughson).** The *Vibrio cholerae* quorum-sensing autoinducer CAI-1: Analysis of the biosynthetic enzyme CqsA. *Nat. Chem. Biol.* 5:891–5, 2009.

Dang, L., et al. **(J. D. Rabinowitz).** Cancer-associated IDH1 mutations produce 2-hydroxyglutarate. *Nature* 462:739–44, 2009.

Bennett, B. D., et al. **(J. D. Rabinowitz).** Absolute metabolite concentrations and implied enzyme active site occupancy in *Escherichia coli. Nat. Chem. Biol.*5:593–9, 2009.

Roth, M., et al. **(H. Rabitz).** Quantum control of tightly competitive product channels. *Phys. Rev. Lett.* 102(25):253001, 2009.

Yuan, J., et al. **(H. Rabitz** and **J. Rabinowitz).** Metabolomics-driven quantitative analysis of ammonia assimilation in *E. coli. Mol. Syst. Biol.* 5:302, 2009.

Hillberg, L., et al. **(C. E. Schutt).** Tropomyosins are present in lamellipodia of motile cells. *Eur. J. Cell Biol.* 85:399–409, 2006.

Schuler, H., R. Karlsson, **C. E. Schutt,** and U. Lindberg. The connection between actin ATPase and polymerization. *Adv. Mol. Cell Biol.* 37:49–66, 2006.

Traina, C. A., T. J. Dennes, and **J. Schwartz.** A modular monolayer coating enables cell targeting by luminescent yttria nanoparticles. *Bioconjugate Chem.* 20(3):437–9, 2009.

Dennes, T. J., and **J. Schwartz.** A nanoscale adhesion layer to promote cell attachment on PEEK. *J. Am. Chem. Soc.* 131(10):3456–7, 2009.

Liang, J., Q. Sun, **A. Selloni,** and **G. Scoles.** Side-by-side characterization of electron tunneling through monolayers of isomeric molecules: A combined experimental and theoretical study. *J. Phys. Chem. B* 110:24797, 2006.

Sun, Q., and **A. Selloni.** Interface and molecular electronic structure vs tunneling characteristics of CH3- and CF3-terminated thiol monolayers on Au(111). *J. Phys. Chem. A* 110:11396–400, 2006.

Gong, X., **A. Selloni,** M. Batzill, and U. Diebold. Steps on anatase TiO2(101). *Nat. Mater.* 5:665–70, 2006.

Miller, S. T., et al. **(M. F. Semmelhack** and **F. M. Hughson).** Salmonella typhimurium recognizes a chemically distinct form of the bacterial quorum sensing signal AI-2. *Mol. Cell* 15:677–87, 2004.

Semmelhack, M. F., and R. J. Hooley. Palladium-catalyzed hydrostannylations of highly hindered acetyolenes in hexane. *Tetrahedron Lett.* 44:5737–9, 2003.

Semmelhack, M. F., L. Wu, **R. A. Pascal Jr.,** and D. M. Ho. Conformational control in activation of an enediyne. *J. Am. Chem. Soc.* 125:10496–7, 2003.

D'Avino, G., et al. **(Z. G. Soos).** Anomalous dispersion of optical phonons at the neutral-ionic transition: Evidence from diffuse X-ray scattering. *Phys. Rev. Lett.* 99(15):156407, 2007.

Bewick, S. A., and **Z. G. Soos.** Peierls transitions in ionic organic charge-transfer crystals with spin and charge degrees of freedom. *J. Phys. Chem. B* 110(38):18748–57, 2006.

Anderson, E. A., E. J. Alexanian, and **E. J. Sorensen.** A synthesis of the furanosteroidal antibiotic viridian. *Angew. Chem. Int. Ed.* 43:1998–2001, 2004.

Adam, G. C., C. D. Vanderwal, **E. J. Sorensen,** and B. F. Cravatt. (-)-FR182877 is a potent and selective inhibitor of carboxylesterase-1. *Angew. Chem. Int. Ed.* 42:5480–4, 2003.

Vosburg, D. A., S. Weiler, and **E. J. Sorensen.** Concise stereocontrolled routes to fumagillol, fumagillin, and TNP-470. *Chirality* 15:156–66, 2003.

Vanderwal, C. D., D. A. Vosburg, S. Weiler, and **E. J. Sorensen.** An enantioselective synthesis of FR182877 provides a chemical rationalization of its structure and affords multigram quantities of its direct precursor. *J. Am. Chem. Soc.* 125:5393–407, 2003.

Li, Z., and **J. B. Stock.** Protein carboxyl methylation and the biochemistry of memory. *Biol. Chem.* 390(11):1087–96, 2009.

Xing, Y., et al. **(J. B. Stock).** .Structural mechanism of demethylation and inactivation of protein phosphatase 2A. *Cell* 133(1):154–63, 2008.

Gordon, J. S., et al. **(J. B. Stock).** Topical N-acetyl-S-farnesyl-L-cysteine inhibits mouse skin inflammation, and unlike dexamethasone, its effects are restricted to the application site. *J. Invest. Dermatol.* 128(3):643–54, 2008.

Torquato, S., and Y. Jiao. Dense packings of the Platonic and Archimedean solids. *Nature* 460:876–9, 2009.

Batten, R. D., F. H. Stillinger, and **S. Torquato.** Interactions leading to disordered ground states and unusual low-temperature behavior. *Phys. Rev. E* 80(3):031105–29, 2009.

Torquato, S., and Y. Jiao. Dense packings of polyhedra: Platonic and Archimedean solids. *Phys. Rev. E* 80:041104–35, 2009.

Florescu, M., **S. Torquato,** and P. J. Steinhardt. Complete band gaps in two-dimensional photonic quasicrystals. *Phys. Rev. B* 80(15):155112–9, 2009.

Y. Jiaoa, F. H. Stillinger, and **S. Torquato.** A superior descriptor of random textures and its predictive capacity. *Proc. Natl. Acad. Sci. Unit. States Am.* 106(42):17634–9, 2009.

UNIVERSITY OF CALIFORNIA, SAN DIEGO

Department of Chemistry and Biochemistry

Program of Study

The goal of the program is to prepare students for careers in science as researchers and educators by expanding their knowledge of chemistry while developing their ability for critical analysis, creativity, and independent study. Research opportunities are comprehensive and interdisciplinary, spanning biochemistry; bioinformatics; biophysics; inorganic, organic, physical, analytical, computational, and theoretical chemistry; surface and materials chemistry; and atmospheric and environmental chemistry. During the first year, students take courses, begin their teaching apprenticeships, choose a research adviser, and embark on their thesis research; students whose native language is not English must pass an English proficiency examination. In the second year, there is an oral examination, which includes critical discussion of a recent research article. In the third year, students advance to candidacy for the doctorate by defending the topic, preliminary findings, and future research plans for their dissertation. Subsequent years focus on thesis research and writing the dissertation. Most students graduate during their fifth year.

At the University of California, San Diego (UCSD), chemists and biochemists are part of a thriving community that stretches across the campus and out into research institutions throughout the San Diego area, uniting researchers in substantive interactions and collaborations. Seminars are presented weekly in biochemistry and inorganic, organic, and physical chemistry. Interdisciplinary programs in nonlinear science, materials science, biophysics, bioinformatics, and atmospheric and planetary chemistry also hold regular seminars.

Research Facilities

State-of-the-art facilities include a national laboratory for protein crystal structure determination; high-field nuclear magnetic resonance (NMR) instruments; the Natural Sciences Graphics Laboratory, which provides high-end graphics workstation resources; and laser spectroscopic equipment. Buildings specially designed for chemical research, a computational center, a laboratory fabrication and construction facility, and machine, glass, and electronic shops are part of the high-quality research support system.

The UCSD library collection is one of the largest in the country, with superior computerized reference and research services. Access to the facilities at the Scripps Institute of Oceanography, the San Diego Supercomputer Center, the Salk Institute, the Scripps Research Institute, and a thriving technological park, all within blocks of the campus, make the overall scope of available research facilities among the best in the world.

Financial Aid

All students who remain in good academic standing are provided year-round support packages of a stipend plus fees and tuition. Support comes from a variety of sources, including teaching assistantships, research assistantships, fellowships, and awards. Special fellowships/awards, such as the Urey, Kamen/Kaplan, Zimm, Cota Robles, and San Diego fellowships, are available to outstanding students. Students are strongly encouraged to apply for outside fellowships, and the Department supplements such awards. The twelve-month stipend is adjusted annually; for 2010–11 it is $24,500, and entering students receive $600 in relocation allowance. Emergency short-term as well as long-term loan programs are administered by the UCSD Student Financial Services office.

Cost of Study

Registration fees and tuition (paid by the Department) are $10,933 for residents and $25,969 for nonresidents per year. Premiums for a primary health-care program, which covers most major medical expenses and a portion of dental fees, are covered by registration fees. The Student Health Center treats minor illnesses and injuries. Optional health and dental coverage for dependents is at the student's expense.

Living and Housing Costs

The University's Affiliated Housing (http://hds.ucsd.edu/hsgaffil/index.html) operates apartments for families, couples, and single graduate students. There are several apartment complexes near the campus at higher rents; rental sharing is a common way to reduce the expense. The Off Campus Student Housing Office (http://offcampushousing.ucsd.edu/) maintains extensive current rental and rental-share opportunities.

Student Group

Students are drawn from the top ranks of U.S. and international colleges and universities. There are 4,000 graduate students on the general campus and at the Scripps Institute of Oceanography and 700 in the School of Medicine and School of Pharmacy and Pharmaceutical Sciences. Within the Department, there are 300 graduate students and 1,200 undergraduate majors. The graduate student population reflects diversity in culture, gender, and ethnicity.

Student Outcomes

Graduates typically obtain jobs in academia (65 percent) or in the chemical industry (35 percent). Many take postdoctoral research positions in academic institutions or national laboratories that lead to future academic or industrial careers.

Location

The campus sits on 1,200 acres of eucalyptus groves near the Pacific Ocean. Surrounding the campus is La Jolla, a picturesque community of boutiques, bistros, and businesses. Seven miles south of the campus is San Diego, with its world-acclaimed zoo, aquariums, museums, and theaters. The Laguna Mountains and the Anza-Borrego Desert are within a 2-hour drive east of the campus.

The University

UCSD, a comparatively young university, has already achieved widespread recognition, ranking in the top 7 in federal funding for research and development and in the top 10 of all doctoral degree–granting institutions in a study conducted by the National Research Council. Recently, the Institute for Scientific Information ranked UCSD's Department of Chemistry and Biochemistry as third in the nation for "High Impact U.S. Universities, 2001–05." Programs span the arts and humanities, engineering, international studies, and the social, natural, and physical sciences. The intellectual climate is enhanced by a variety of social, educational, professional, political, religious, and recreational opportunities and services.

Applying

Application packets include a completed UCSD application form, a statement of purpose, official transcripts from previous colleges, three letters of recommendation, GRE scores (general and advanced chemistry or biochemistry), and a TOEFL score (for noncitizens only; a minimum score of 550 on the paper-based test or 220 on the computer-based test is required). Research experience should be described. Copies of or references to any publications should be included with the application. Complete applications received by January 15 receive the highest priority.

Correspondence and Information

Graduate Admissions Coordinator
Department of Chemistry and Biochemistry 0303
University of California, San Diego
9500 Gilman Drive
La Jolla, California 92093-0303

Phone: 858-534-9728
Fax: 858-534-7687
E-mail: chemgradinfo@ucsd.edu
Web site: http://www-chem.ucsd.edu/

University of California, San Diego

THE FACULTY AND THEIR RESEARCH

Timothy S. Baker, Ph.D., UCLA. Macromolecular, cryoelectron microscopy, and three-dimensional image reconstruction techniques.
Timothy Bertram, Ph.D., Berkeley. Environmental/atmospheric chemistry: heterogenous reactions on aerosol particles, atmosphere-ocean interactions, chemical ionization mass spectrometry.
Stacey Brydges, Ph.D., McMaster. Chemical Education.
Michael D. Burkart, Ph.D., Scripps Research Institute. Natural product synthesis/biosynthesis, biological chemistry and enzymology, metabolic engineering.
Seth Cohen, Ph.D., Berkeley. Bioinorganic and coordination chemistry, metalloprotein inhibitors, supramolecular materials.
Robert E. Continetti, Ph.D., Berkeley. Dissociation dynamics of transient species, three-body reaction dynamics, novel mass-spectrometric methods.
John E. Crowell, Ph.D., Berkeley. Materials chemistry, surface kinetics of metals/semiconductors, CVD, photo-induced deposition, thin-film spectroscopy.
John Czworkowski, Ph.D., Yale. Science and Math Initiative/California Teach program, problem-based learning, use of computer multimedia for science instruction.
Edward A. Dennis, Ph.D., Harvard. Biochemistry: phospholipase A2, signal transduction in macrophages, mechanism, prostaglandin regulation, mass spectrometry of lipids and proteins.
Jack Dixon, Ph.D., California, Santa Barbara. Protein tyrosine phosphatase, dual-specific phosphatase, PTEN.
Daniel J. Donoghue, Ph.D., MIT. Signal transduction, human cancer, receptor tyrosine kinase, cell cycle, tumor suppressor, oncogenesis.
Pieter Dorrestein, Ph.D., Cornell. Biochemistry, chemical biology, mass spectrometry, harvesting genomic information for therapeutics.
Arthur Ellis, Ph.D., MIT. Inorganic chemistry, nanoscale materials, smart materials.
Joshua Figueroa, Ph.D., MIT. Inorganic and organometallic chemistry: synthesis, small-molecule activation, new transformations.
Marye Anne Fox, Chancellor; Ph.D., Dartmouth. Organic chemistry: physical organic chemistry, photochemistry, nanoscience of organized arrays.
Michael Galperin, Ph.D., Tel Aviv. Physical/analytical: Computational and theoretical, transport in molecular junctions, molecular spectroscopy at non-equilibrium.
Gourisankar Ghosh, Ph.D., Yeshiva (Einstein). Biochemistry and biophysics: transcription; signaling; pre-mRNA splicing; mRNA transport; protein-protein, protein-DNA, and protein-RNA interactions.
Partho Ghosh, Ph.D., California, San Francisco. Mechanisms of bacterial and protozoan pathogenesis, host response against infectious microbes.
Nathan Gianneschi, Ph.D., Northwestern. Organic chemistry: Bioorganicmaterials, bioorganic chemistry, supramolecular chemistry, bionanotechnology, materials, synthesis.
David N. Hendrickson, Ph.D., Berkeley. Inorganic chemistry, materials chemistry, single-molecule magnets, dynamics of transition-metal complexes.
Thomas C. Hermann, Ph.D., Ludwig Maximilians (Germany). Drug design and discovery, RNA molecular recognition, antibiotics, antivirals.
Alexander Hoffman, Ph.D., Rockefeller. Biochemistry: signaling, transcription, computational network, stress and immune responses, apoptosis, proliferation.
Patricia A. Jennings, Ph.D., Penn State. Biophysical chemistry: protein structure, dynamics, and folding; 2-, 3-, and 4-D NMR; equilibrium/kinetic fluorescence; circular dichroism spectroscopies.
Simpson Joseph, Ph.D., Vermont. Biochemistry and biophysics: ribosome structure, function, and dynamics; discovery of novel antibiotics.
Judy E. Kim, Ph.D., Berkeley. Biophysical chemistry: spectroscopic studies of membrane protein folding and dynamics.
Yoshihisa Kobayashi, Ph.D., Tokyo. Natural product synthesis, new reaction and catalyst, heterocycles synthesis, elucidation of stereostructure.
Elizabeth A. Komives, Ph.D., California, San Francisco. Structure, function, dynamics, and thermodynamics of protein-protein interactions: NMR, mass spectrometry, and kinetics.
Clifford P. Kubiak, Chair; Ph.D., Rochester. Inorganic chemistry: electron transfer, organometallic chemistry; nanoscience: molecular electronics, nanosensors.
Andrew C. Kummel, Ph.D., Stanford. STM/STS of gate oxides on compound semiconductors and adsorbates on organic semiconductors.
Katja Lindenberg, Ph.D., Cornell. Theoretical chemical physics: nonequilibrium statistical mechanics, stochastic processes, nonlinear phenomena, complex systems, condensed matter.
Douglas Magde, Ph.D., Cornell. Experimental physical chemistry: photochemistry and photobiophysics, picosecond and femtosecond lasers.
J. Andrew McCammon, Ph.D., Harvard. Statistical mechanics and computational chemistry, with applications to biological systems.
Mario J. Molina, Ph.D., Berkeley. Physical chemistry: gas-phase chemical kinetics and photochemistry, chemistry of atmospheric aerosols, air pollution in megacities of the developing world.
Tadeusz Molinski, Ph.D., Australian National. Organic chemistry of marine natural products, synthesis, NMR, and biomedical applications.
Ulrich Muller, Ph.D., Munich. Biochemistry: catalytic RNA, origin of life, therapeutic RNA splicing.
Terunaga Nakagawa, Ph.D., Tokyo. Biochemistry: function and structural changes of protein complexes involved in synaptic plasticity.
K. C. Nicolaou, Ph.D., University College, London. Total synthesis and chemical biology of natural and designed molecules.
Joseph M. O'Connor, Ph.D., Wisconsin–Madison. Organotransition metal; organic, bioorganometallic, and inorganic chemistry.
Stanley Opella, Ph.D., Stanford. NMR structural studies of proteins in membranes and other supramolecular assemblies.
Francesco Paesani, Ph.D., Rome. Theoretical chemical physics of complex interfaces of relevance to the environment.
Charles L. Perrin, Ph.D., Harvard. Physical-organic chemistry: stereoelectronic effects, hydrogen bonding, isotope effects, ionic solvation.
Robert Pomeroy, Ph.D., Arizona. Application of analytical chemistry to forensic, environmental, and industrial chemistry, bridging these experiences into the classroom; the role technology and instrumentation play in discovery and problem solving.
Kimberly A. Prather, Ph.D., California, Davis. Environmental, analytical chemistry: gas/particle processes of tropospheric significance, mass spectrometry, laser-based techniques.
Arnold Rheingold, Ph.D., Maryland. Inorganic chemistry: small-molecule crystallography, synthesis of transition-metal/p-block clusters.
Michael J. Sailor, Ph.D., Northwestern. Nanomaterials: porous silicon, chemical and biological sensors, biomaterials, electrochemistry.
Barbara A. Sawrey, Ph.D., California, San Diego, and San Diego State. Chemical education: development of computer-based multimedia to assist student learning of complex scientific processes and concepts.
Amitabha Sinha, Ph.D., MIT. Experimental physical chemistry: photochemistry, laser spectroscopy, reaction dynamics of vibrationally excited molecules.
Michael Tauber, Ph.D., Berkeley. Physical chemistry, optical and magnetic spectroscopy, fundamental studies of charge transport and solvation, applications to energy conversion and energy storage.
Susan S. Taylor, Ph.D., Johns Hopkins. Protein kinases/signal transduction: structure/function and localization, biophysics, crystallography, NMR, fluorescence/FRET.
F. Akif Tezcan, Ph.D., Caltech. Bioinorganic and biophysical chemistry: metalloprotein structure, function, and biosynthesis.
Emmanuel A. Theodorakis, Ph.D., Paris XI (South). Synthetic, medicinal, bioorganic, and biological chemistry; methods and strategies in natural products chemistry.
Mark H. Thiemens, Ph.D., Florida State. Atmospheric chemistry: physical chemistry of isotope effects, solar system formation.
Navtej Toor, Ph.D., Calgary. Structure and function of introns and retroelements.
Yitzhak Tor, Ph.D., Weizmann (Israel). Ligand–nucleic acid interactions, antiviral and antibacterial agents, fluorescent nucleosides and nucleotides, cellular delivery vehicles.
William C. Trogler, Ph.D., Caltech. Inorganic chemistry: polymer chemistry, nanotechnology applied to chemical and environmental sensing.
Roger Y. Tsien, Ph.D., Cambridge. Chemical biology; design, synthesis, and application of molecular probes of biological function.
Robert H. Tukey, Ph.D., Iowa. Environmental toxicology: role of environmental and chemical toxicants on gene expression.
Hector Viadiu, Ph.D., Columbia. Biochemistry: X-ray crystallography and cryoelectron microscopy (electron crystallography and single-particle reconstruction), DNA binding proteins, membrane proteins.
Wei Wang, Ph.D., California, San Francisco. Inference of gene regulatory networks and determination of protein specificity.
John H. Weare, Ph.D., Johns Hopkins. Physical chemistry: calculations of the dynamics of complex systems, theoretical geochemistry.
Leor Weinberger, Ph.D., Berkeley. Dynamical systems biology, transcriptional feedback and stochastic noise in gene circuits (specifically HIV and herpes), live single-cell imaging and spectroscopy, coupling theory and experiment.
Haim Weizman, Ph.D., Weizmann (Israel). Chemical education, bioorganic chemistry.
James K. Whitesell, Ph.D., Harvard. Organic chemistry: studies of stereochemistry both in a molecular and a supramolecular sense.
Peter Wolynes, Ph.D., Harvard. Theoretical chemical physics, protein folding and function, glasses and stochastic cell biology.
Jerry Yang, Ph.D., Columbia. Bioorganic chemistry: molecular self-assembly, materials chemistry, bionanotechnology.

Adjunct Faculty
Kim Baldridge, Ph.D., North Dakota State; Jack E. Johnson, Ph.D., Iowa State; John Newsam; Joseph P. Noel, Ph.D., Ohio State; Shankar Subramaniam, Ph.D., Indian Institute of Technology (Kanpur); Lei Wang, Ph.D., Berkeley; John Wooley, Ph.D., Chicago.

UNIVERSITY OF PITTSBURGH

Department of Chemistry

Programs of Study

The Department offers programs of study leading to the M.S. and Ph.D. degrees in analytical, biological, inorganic, organic, and physical chemistry and in chemical physics. Interdisciplinary research is currently conducted in the areas of surface science, natural product synthesis, biological chemistry, bioanalytical chemistry, combinatorial chemistry, laser spectroscopy, materials science, electrochemistry, nanoscience, organometallic chemistry, and computational and theoretical chemistry. Both advanced degree programs involve original research and course work. Other requirements include a comprehensive examination, a thesis, a seminar, and, for the Ph.D. candidate, a proposal. For the typical Ph.D. candidate, this process takes four to five years. Representative of current research activities in the Department in analytical chemistry are techniques in electroanalytical chemistry, in vivo electrochemistry, UV resonance Raman spectroscopy, microseparations and nanoseparations, sensors and selective extraction, NMR, EPR, mass spectrometry, and vibrational circular dichroism. Fields of research in biological chemistry include structural dynamics of biological systems, design of soluble membrane proteins, neurochemistry, and molecular design and recognition. In inorganic chemistry, studies are being conducted on organo–transition-metal complexes, redox reactions, complexes of biological interest, transition-metal polymers, and optoelectronic materials; in organic chemistry, on reaction mechanisms, ion transport, total synthesis, drug design, natural products synthesis, bioorganic chemistry, synthetic methodology, organometallics, enzyme mechanisms, and physical-organic chemistry. Research areas in physical chemistry include Raman, photoelectron, Auger, NMR, EPR, infrared, and mass spectroscopy; electron-stimulated desorption ion angular distribution (ESDIAD); condensed-phase spectroscopy; high-resolution laser spectroscopy; molecular spectroscopy; electron and molecular beam scattering; electronic emission spectroscopy; and catalysis. Theoretical fields of research include electronic structure, reaction mechanisms, electron transfer theory, quantum mechanics, and new material design. Research on computer applications to chemistry is under way in a variety of areas.

Research Facilities

The Department of Chemistry is housed in two buildings, a fifteen-story and a three-story complex, containing a vast array of modern research instruments and in-house machine, electronics, and glassblowing shops. The Chemistry Library is a spacious 4,000-square-foot facility that contains more than 30,000 monographs and bound periodicals and more than 200 maintained journal subscriptions. These and many related journals, as well as search capabilities, are available online for free. Three other chemistry libraries are nearby. In 2002, the Department of Chemistry received a five-year, $9.6-million grant from the National Institute of General Medical Sciences (NIGMS, a subdivision of NIH) to build one of the nation's first Centers for Excellence in Chemical Methods and Library Development. Shared Departmental instrumentation includes four 300-MHz NMRs, one 500-MHz NMR, and one 600-MHz NMR with LC-NMR and MAS capabilities; three high-resolution mass spectrometers; an LC/MS, a triple quadrupole MS, and four low-resolution mass spectrometers; a light-scattering instrument; a circular dichroism spectrophotometer; a spectropolarimeter; X-ray systems—single crystal, powder, small-angle scattering, and fluorescence; a scanning electron microscope; a vibrating sample magnetometer; several FT-IR and UV-VIS spectrophotometers; and computer and workstation clusters.

Financial Aid

Seventy teaching assistantships and teaching fellowships are available. The former provided $22,596 in 2009–10 for the three trimesters of the year; the fellowships (awarded to superior students after their first year) carried an annual stipend of $23,513. Most advanced students are supported by research assistantships and fellowships, which paid up to $2153 per month. All teaching assistantships, fellowships, and research assistantships include a full scholarship that covers all tuition, fees, and medical insurance. Special Kaufman Arts and Sciences Fellowships are offered to qualified entering students to assist them in career development throughout their graduate studies. These fellowships consist of the following: (1) a stipend (approximately $25,500) for the first year, during which the student receives two semesters of fellowship support and teaching experience through a one-semester TA appointment; (2) an academic spending account totaling $1500 for the purchase of books, software, or other items intended to advance the student's research endeavors; and funding for travel (up to $500) to a scientific meeting of the student's choosing; (3) up to $2000 for the purchase of a personal computer (Mac or PC, desktop or portable, including software); upon successful completion of the Ph.D. program at Pitt, the title of the computer will be transferred from the University to the student; and (4) a stipend of $1450 per month (up to $5800) for the summer term prior to enrollment in classes, allowing the student to conduct research in any Chemistry Department faculty member's laboratory (with mutual consent). Partial support for these fellowships is provided through funds from Bayer BMS, Sunoco, and the Ashe Fund (University of Pittsburgh).

Cost of Study

All graduate assistants and fellows receive full-tuition scholarships. Tuition and fees for full-time study in 2009 were $14,672 per term for out-of-state students and $8526 for state residents.

Living and Housing Costs

Most graduate students prefer private housing, which is available in a wide range of apartments and rooms in areas of Pittsburgh near the campus. The University maintains a housing office to assist students seeking off-campus housing. Living costs compare favorably with other urban areas.

Student Group

The University enrolls about 17,000 students, including about 9,500 graduate and professional school students. Most parts of the United States and many other countries are represented. Almost 200 full-time graduate chemistry students are supported by the various sources listed under Financial Aid. The University is coeducational in all schools and divisions; more than one third of the graduate chemistry students are women. An honorary chemistry society promotes a social program for all faculty members and graduate students in the Department.

Location

Deservedly, Pittsburgh is currently ranked "among the most livable cities in the United States" by Rand McNally. It is recognized for its outstanding blend of cultural, educational, and technological resources. Pittsburgh's famous Golden Triangle is enclosed by the Allegheny and Monongahela Rivers, which meet at the Point in downtown Pittsburgh to form the Ohio River. Pittsburgh has enjoyed a dynamic renaissance in the last few years. The city's cultural resources include the Pittsburgh Ballet, Opera Company, Symphony Orchestra, Civic Light Opera, and Public Theatre and the Three Rivers Shakespeare Festival. Many outdoor activities, such as rock climbing, rafting, sailing, skiing, and hunting, are also available within a 50-mile radius.

The University

The University of Pittsburgh, founded in 1787, is the oldest school west of the Allegheny Mountains. Although privately endowed and controlled, the University is state related to permit lower tuition rates for Pennsylvania residents and to provide a steady source of funds for all of its programs. Attracting more than $310 million in sponsored research annually, the University has continued to increase in stature.

Applying

Applications for September admission and assistantships should be made prior to February 1. However, special cases may be considered throughout the year. A background that includes a B.S. degree in chemistry, with courses in mathematics through integral calculus, is preferred. GRE scores, including the chemistry Subject Test, are required for fellowship consideration (see the Financial Aid section). For admission, the General Test of the GRE is required, and the Subject Test in chemistry is suggested. International applicants must submit TOEFL, GRE Subject, and GRE test scores.

Correspondence and Information

Graduate Admissions
Department of Chemistry
University of Pittsburgh
Pittsburgh, Pennsylvania 15260

Phone: 412-624-8501
E-mail: gradadm@pitt.edu
Web site: http://www.chem.pitt.edu

University of Pittsburgh

THE FACULTY AND THEIR RESEARCH

S. Amemiya, Associate Professor; Ph.D., Tokyo, 1998. Analytical chemistry: electrochemical sensors, scanning electrochemical microscopy, chemical imaging, nanostructures, ion and electron transfer at interfaces, liquid-liquid interfaces, biomembranes, molecular recognition, ion channel.
S. A. Asher, Professor; Ph.D., Berkeley, 1977. Analytical and physical chemistry: resonance Raman spectroscopy, biophysical chemistry, material science, protein folding, nanoscale and mesoscale smart materials, heme proteins, photonic crystals.
K. Brummond, Professor; Ph.D., Penn State, 1991. Organic chemistry: organometallic chemistry, synthesis of natural products, diversity-oriented synthesis.
T. M. Chapman, Associate Professor; Ph.D., Polytechnic of Brooklyn, 1965. Organic chemistry: new polymers of uncommon architecture, dendritic polymers, polymer surfactants and emulsifiers, tissue engineering, controlled drug delivery, gene transfer, electron transfer in dendritic polymers, polymers for CO_2 sequestration.
L. T. Chong, Assistant Professor; Ph.D., California, San Francisco, 2002. Computational chemistry: protein folding, binding, and catalysis; unstructured proteins; molecular dynamics simulations.
R. D. Coalson, Professor of Chemistry and Physics; Ph.D., Harvard, 1984. Physical chemistry: quantum theory of rate processes, optical spectroscopy, computational techniques for quantum dynamics, structure and energetics of macroions in solution; design of optical waveguides and photonic bandgap structures; laser control of condensed-phase electron transfer; theoretical/computational approaches to the transport of ions and polymers through biological (protein) pores.
T. Cohen, Professor Emeritus; Ph.D., USC, 1955. Organic chemistry: new synthetic methods, particularly those involving organometallics, most often of main group elements; synthesis of natural products using the new synthetic methods; mechanistic studies.
N. J. Cooper, Bettye J. and Ralph E. Bailey Dean of Arts and Sciences and Dean of the College of General Studies; D.Phil., Oxford, 1976. Inorganic chemistry: synthetic and mechanistic inorganic and organometallic chemistry.
D. P. Curran, Bayer Professor and Distinguished Service Professor; Ph.D., Rochester, 1979. Organic chemistry: natural products total synthesis and new synthetic methodology, synthesis via free-radical reactions, fluorous chemistry, combinatorial chemistry.
D. J. Earl, Assistant Professor; Ph.D., Durham (England), 2003. Theoretical and computational chemistry: computer-aided design of nanostructured and nanoporous materials, phase behavior of complex molecules, immune system modeling and infectious diseases.
P. Floreancig, Associate Professor; Ph.D., Stanford, 1997. Organic chemistry: total synthesis of natural products and bioactive analogs, methodology development, electron transfer chemistry.
M. F. Golde, Associate Professor; Ph.D., Cambridge, 1972. Physical chemistry: kinetic and spectroscopic studies of mechanisms of formation and removal of electronically excited atoms and small molecules, ion-electron recombination and similar species.
J. J. Grabowski, Associate Professor; Ph.D., Colorado, 1983. Physical-organic chemistry: reactive intermediates; reaction mechanisms; novel uses of mass spectrometry and photochemistry for organic, analytical, or environmental chemistry; novel uses of modern technology for chemical education.
W. S. Horne, Assistant Professor; Ph.D., Scripps Research Institute, 2005. Bioorganic chemistry: design, synthesis, and study of synthetic analogues of polypeptides and proteins for biomedical and materials applications.
G. R. Hutchison, Assistant Professor; Ph.D., Northwestern, 2004. Molecular materials: design and characterization of electronic materials, computational and theoretical modeling, charge transport, mechanical dynamics of smart materials, reversible self-assembly, organic photovoltaics.
K. D. Jordan, Professor; Ph.D., MIT, 1974. Physical chemistry: theoretical studies of the electronic structure of molecules, electron-induced chemistry, computer simulations, hydrogen-bonded clusters, chemical reactions at semiconductor and carbon nanotube surfaces, properties of hydrates, parallel computational methods.
K. Koide, Associate Professor; Ph.D., California, San Diego, 1997. Organic chemistry and chemical biology: natural product synthesis, automated synthesis, fluorescent sensors for RNA and ion imaging, synthetic methodology.
T. Y. Meyer, Associate Professor; Ph.D., Iowa, 1991. Polymer and inorganic chemistry: polymer synthesis, structure-function correlations in repeating sequence copolymers, nanoscience, preparation of materials for biomedical applications, sensors, organometallic chemistry.
A. C. Michael, Professor; Ph.D., Emory, 1987. Analytical chemistry: new microsensor technologies for neurochemical monitoring in the central nervous system; investigations of the chemical aspects of brain disorders such as Parkinson's disease, schizophrenia, and substance abuse; quantitative aspects of in vivo chemical measurements.
S. G. Nelson, Associate Professor; Ph.D., Rochester, 1991. Organic chemistry: natural products total synthesis, new synthetic methods, asymmetric catalysis and organometallic chemistry.
D. W. Pratt, Professor; Ph.D., Berkeley, 1967. Physical chemistry: molecular structure and dynamics as revealed by high-resolution laser, microwave, and magnetic resonance spectroscopy in the gas phase and in the condensed phase, especially of biological molecules; optical trapping, nucleation, and imaging using focused laser beams; science education, especially for nonscience students.
R. A. S. Robinson, Assistant Professor; Ph.D., Indiana Bloomington, 2007. Analytical and biological chemistry: proteomics of aging, immunosenescence, and neurodegenerative diseases; multidimensional separations involving liquid chromatography, mass spectrometry, and ion mobility spectrometry; instrumentation development; bioinformatics.
N. L. Rosi, Assistant Professor; Ph.D., Michigan, 2003. Materials chemistry: hybrid organic and inorganic solid-state materials; biomaterials; bioinspired design and assembly of new materials; nanoparticle synthesis and assembly; porous materials; gas storage (hydrogen, methane); drug delivery.
S. K. Saxena, Assistant Professor; Ph.D., Cornell, 1997. Analytical, biophysical, and physical chemistry: spectroscopy; pulsed electron spin resonance; structure, folding, and dynamics of nanostructured materials; protein-DNA complexes and membrane proteins; metals in biology.
M. M. Spence, Assistant Professor; Ph.D., Berkeley, 2002. Physical chemistry: membrane proteins, antimicrobial peptides, peptide neurotoxins, lipid structure and dynamics, liquid- and solid-state NMR.
A. Star, Assistant Professor; Ph.D., Tel Aviv, 2000. Analytical and materials chemistry; nanotechnology-enabled chemical sensing and energy conversion.
M. A. Trakselis, Assistant Professor; Ph.D., Penn State, 2002. Biological chemistry: enzymatic mechanisms of proteins alone and in complexes involved in DNA replication and repair, biophysical and biochemical characterization of enzyme complexes, and the design of novel biohybrid polymeric catalysts.
D. H. Waldeck, Professor and Department Chair; Ph.D., Chicago, 1983. Analytical and physical chemistry: bioelectrochemistry; biophysics; electrochemistry, electron tunneling; homogenous and heterogenous electron transfer, nanoscience; molecular electronics; plasmonics; solar energy conversion; solvation; ultrafast spectroscopy.
S. G. Weber, Professor; Ph.D., McGill, 1979. Analytical chemistry: capillary separations and sensitive detection for bioanalysis; sampling, sensors and selective extraction; microreactors; electrochemistry.
C. S. Wilcox, Professor; Ph.D., Caltech, 1979. Organic chemistry: diffusion-reaction processes, precipitons and separation methods for parallel synthesis and combinatorial chemistry, chemical synthesis, molecular recognition and the molecular torsion balance, self-assembling materials.
P. Wipf, Distinguished University Professor of Chemistry, Professor of Pharmaceutical Sciences, and Director, Center for Chemical Methodologies and Library Development; Ph.D., Zurich, 1987. Organic chemistry: total synthesis of natural products; organometallic, heterocyclic, and medicinal chemistry.

VILLANOVA UNIVERSITY

College of Liberal Arts and Sciences
Department of Chemistry

Programs of Study

The Department of Chemistry at Villanova offers the Master of Science (M.S.) degree in all traditional areas of chemistry. The degree can be earned full-time or part-time. The thesis option requires the successful completion of six courses and a research project culminated by a written thesis. The nonthesis option requires the completion of ten courses and a seminar course based on work experience. All students are required to take three core courses in either analytical, biological, inorganic, organic, or physical chemistry, followed by elective courses. Comprehensive exams are also required for the Master of Science degree.

Research Facilities

In 1999, Villanova completed a $35-million expansion renovation to Mendel Science Center, resulting in a state-of-the-art teaching and research facility. The Department is well equipped with instrumentation. Two FT-NMR spectrometers (both 300 MHz), including a Varian Mercury instrument with an MAS probe for solids analysis, are available. Other instrumentation includes an HP GC–mass spectrometer, a Siemens single-crystal diffractometer, DSC, TG, ultracentrifugation, and polarimeter. Spectroscopy is performed with several FT-IRs and UV-visible, CE, and fluorescence spectrophotometers. Chromatographs include several GC and LC instruments. The Department's Computational Chemistry Lab holds an IBM RISC station along with a Linux cluster and a Silicon Graphics O2 workstation.

Financial Aid

Most full-time graduate students in the Department hold teaching or research assistantships of $15,603 for nine months plus full tuition remission. Limited research and teaching fellowships are available for summer months.

Cost of Study

The tuition for graduate chemistry at Villanova is $700 per credit hour in 2010–11, with a general fee of $30 per semester.

Living and Housing Costs

Although on-campus housing is not available, ample apartments/rooms are available in the suburban neighborhoods surrounding Villanova. The Office of Residence Life offers assistance by providing rental lists to students. Living expenses for a single student are estimated at $13,000 per year.

Student Group

There are 40 graduate students (18 full-time) and 15 tenure-track faculty members in the Department. About 40 percent of the students are women and 10 percent are international.

Student Outcomes

Some graduates are employed by the nine major pharmaceutical firms in the Philadelphia area. Others choose employment at smaller companies, and some continue their studies in doctoral programs in chemistry and related areas.

Location

Located in a safe, suburban community 12 miles west of Philadelphia, the picturesque 254-acre campus features sixty buildings. Bryn Mawr and Haverford Colleges are nearby, and major Universities in Philadelphia (Penn, Temple, Drexel, and others) are easily accessible by public transportation. Philadelphia supports many cultural opportunities including theater, opera, symphony concerts, and ballet, as well as professional sports teams of every variety.

The University

Founded in 1842 by the priests and brothers of the Order of St. Augustine, Villanova University is the oldest and largest Catholic university in the Commonwealth of Pennsylvania. The University's commitment to love and service is reflected in the Latin words of its seal, which translate into truth, unity, and love.

Applying

An application form, with full instructions, is available on the Web at http://www.gradartsci.villanova.edu. The application fee is $50. Application deadlines are August 1 (fall), December 1 (spring), and May 1 (summer). Applicants who wish to be considered for assistantships should submit their application by March 1 (fall) and October 1 (spring) for priority evaluation. The GRE General Test is required of all students; the TOEFL is required of international applicants whose native language is not English. The most important criterion for admission is a sincere desire to study chemistry. Applications from second-career, older, and other nontraditional chemistry students are encouraged.

Correspondence and Information

Graduate Chairperson
Department of Chemistry
Villanova University
800 Lancaster Avenue
Villanova, Pennsylvania 19085-1699

Phone: 610-519-4840
Fax: 610-519-7167
E-mail: chemistrygrad@villanova.edu
Web site: http://www.chemistry.villanova.edu

Villanova University

THE FACULTY AND THEIR RESEARCH

Temer S. Ahmadi, Ph.D., UCLA. Materials/physical chemistry: synthesis and optical properties of metal-polymer, metal-semiconductor, and luminescent semiconductor nanomaterials.

Joseph W. Bausch, Ph.D., USC. Organic and computational chemistry: synthetic and computational studies of electron-deficient clusters, carborane synthesis, structure prediction.

Eduard G. Casillas, Ph.D., Johns Hopkins. Organic chemistry: natural product synthesis, synthesis of antagonists for plant/fungal secondary metabolic pathways, terpene biomimetic synthesis.

Timothy J. Dudley, Ph.D., North Dakota. Computational/theoretical chemistry: characterization of transition-metal–hydrocarbon complexes, biological and atmospheric photochemistry, *ab initio* method development.

Robert M. Giuliano, Ph.D., Virginia. Organic chemistry: carbohydrate chemistry, synthesis of vinyl glycosides and carbohydrate vinyl ethers, branched-chain carbohydrates, nitrosugars.

Amanda M. Grannas, Ph.D., Purdue. Analytical/environmental chemistry: Photochemical degradation of environmental pollutants in surface waters, photo chemistry of organics in snow and ice, redox chemistry of soil and sediments, Arctic climate change.

W. Scott Kassel, Ph.D., Florida. Inorganic chemistry: solid-base catalysis, X-ray diffraction, synthesis of chiral pyrrolidine transition-metal complexes as enantioselective catalysts.

Anthony F. Lagalante, Ph.D., Colorado. Analytical/environmental chemistry: environmental/food/agricultural applications of solid phase microextraction (SPME), high-pressure spectroscopy in supercritical fluids used as "green" solvents.

Christine A. Martey-Ochola, Ph.D., Lehigh. Biochemistry: effect of cigarette smoke and airborne nanoparticles on normal human lung cells, synthesis and characterization of novel drug-polymer conjugates.

Brian K. Ohta, Ph.D., California, San Diego. Organic chemistry: NMR spectroscopy, intermediate characterization in photosensitized oxidation reactions, hydrogen bond asymmetry.

Jennifer B. Palenchar, Ph.D., Delaware. Biochemistry: enzymology of bacterial aspartate kinase, transcriptional initiation complexes in *Trypanosoma brucei.*

Jared Paul, Ph.D., North Carolina at Chapel Hill. Inorganic chemistry: study of proton-coupled electron-transfer reactions of small organic molecules and metal complexes in biological and chemical systems.

Barry S. Selinsky, Ph.D., SUNY at Buffalo. Biochemistry: membrane biophysics, structural analysis of membrane proteins, membrane-active antibiotics, anticoagulants.

Deanna L. Zubris, Ph.D., Caltech. Inorganic chemistry: synthesis of organometallic complexes as polymerization catalysts, mechanistic studies.

WESLEYAN UNIVERSITY

Department of Chemistry

Program of Study

The Department of Chemistry offers a program of study leading to the Ph.D. degree. Students are awarded this degree upon demonstration of creativity and scholarly achievement. This demands intensive specialization in one field of chemistry as well as broad knowledge of related areas. The Department provides coverage of physical, organic, inorganic, bioorganic, and biophysical chemistry. The first year of graduate study contains much of the required course work, although most students also choose a research adviser and begin a research program at the beginning of the second semester. Students are expected to demonstrate knowledge of five core areas of chemistry, either by taking the appropriate course or by passing a placement examination. In addition, students take advanced courses in their area of specialization. Classes are small (5–10 students) and emphasize interaction and discussion. Student seminar presentations are also emphasized. Election of interdisciplinary programs in chemical physics and molecular biophysics in conjunction with the Departments of Physics and Molecular Biology and Biochemistry, respectively, is also possible. Students are admitted to Ph.D. candidacy, generally in the second year, by demonstrating proficiency in the core course curriculum, passing a specified number of regularly scheduled progress exams, demonstrating an aptitude for original research, and defending a research proposal in the second and fourth year of the Ph.D. program. The progress and development of a student is monitored throughout by a 3-member faculty advisory committee. The Ph.D. program, culminating in the completion of a Ph.D. thesis, is normally completed within four to five years. Two semesters of teaching in undergraduate courses is required, where the load is, on average, about 5 hours per week during the academic year. This requirement is normally met in the first year.

Research Facilities

The Department of Chemistry is housed in an air-conditioned building, sharing space with the Departments of Biology and Molecular Biology and Biochemistry. Major items of equipment include a Hewlett-Packard GC (5890) mass spectrometer; Perkin-Elmer M1600 FT-IR, Spectrum BX FTIR; Fluoromax-2 spectrofluorimeter, a stop-flow reactions kinetics system; picosecond CW mode-locked Nd:YAG laser with cavity-dumped dye laser; JASCO J810 spectropolarimeter equipped with a Peltier temperature controller, a Beckman DU650 spectrophotometer equipped with a Peltier temperature controller; Johnson-Matthey magnetic susceptibility balance; a variety of gas and liquid chromatographs; Perkin-Elmer LS-50 spectrofluorimeter; Hitachi F2900 UV/VIS; three HP diode array UV/VIS, Shimadz4 UV 2401 PC UV-VIS spectrophotometer; Perkin-Elmer 241 polarimeter, a Hewlett-Packard 5973 GC mass spectrometer; Photon Technologies LS-100 luminescence lifetime apparatus; Jobin Yvon 1500 high-resolution optical spectrometer; two high-throughput molecular jet machines; pulsed-jet Fabry-Perot Fourier-transform microwave spectrometer; Innovative Technology Glove Box with oxygen analyzer and VAC He493/M05 Glove Box; Storm 840 ImageQuant gel; blot analysis system, and a Wallac 1409DSA liquid scintillation counter. The NMR facilities consist of a Varian Gemini two-channel, broadband Mercury Vx with gradients; a two-channel Unity Plus 400 with gradients and a three-channel Unity Inova 500 with gradients; and a Bruker MQ20 Mini Spec, NMR relaxometer. The Chemistry Department depends heavily on computers. Among other systems, the Department has a SUN IPX workstation, SUN Ultraspark workstation, IBM RISK6000 3CT workstation, Silicon Graphics Octane2 workstation, Silicon Graphics Indigo 2 10000 workstation, and two IBM RD6000 workstations. Ethernet connects all Department computers to the University computer and to the Internet.

Recent equipment acquisitions include: LC-mass spectrometer, gel permeation chromatograph, YAG dye laser, scanning electron microscope, 128 node cluster and facility, microplate reader, isothermal titration calorimeter, META confocal microscope system, and 600 MHz NMR.

Financial Aid

All students receive a twelve-month stipend, which, for 2010–11, is $23,005. In the first year, this stipend derives from a teaching assistantship. In later academic years, students may be supported by research assistantships where funds are available or by further teaching assistantships.

Cost of Study

Tuition for 2010–11 is $4795.50 per course credit, but remission of this is granted to all holders of teaching and research assistantships.

Living and Housing Costs

Most graduate students, both single and married, live in houses administered and maintained by the University, with rents ranging between $500 and $800 per month.

Student Group

The student body at Wesleyan is composed of some 2,750 undergraduates and 170 graduate students. Of the latter, most are in the sciences, with 40 divided between men and women in the Department of Chemistry. Most graduates obtain industrial positions, although some choose academic careers, normally after postdoctoral experience in each case.

Student Outcomes

All Ph.D. graduates in the last two years have gone on to postdoctoral fellowships at major universities such as Harvard, Yale, and California Institute of Technology. Earlier graduates are now on college faculties or have research positions in the chemical industry.

Location

Middletown is a small city on the west bank of the Connecticut River, 15 miles south of Hartford, the state capital. New Haven is 24 miles to the southwest; New York City and Boston are 2 hours away by automobile. Middletown's population of 50,000 is spread over an area of 43 square miles, much of which is rural. Although Wesleyan is the primary source of cultural activity in Middletown, the city is not a "college town" but serves as a busy commercial center for the region between Hartford and the coast. Water sports, skiing, hiking, and other outdoor activities can be enjoyed in the hills, lakes, and river nearby.

The University

For more than 150 years, Wesleyan University has been identified with the highest aspirations and achievements of private liberal arts higher education. Wesleyan's commitment to the sciences dates from the founding of the University, when natural sciences and modern languages were placed on an equal footing with traditional classical studies. In order to maintain and strengthen this commitment, graduate programs leading to the Ph.D. degree in the sciences were established in the late 1960s. The program in chemistry was designed to be small, distinctive, and personal, emphasizing research, acquisition of a broad knowledge of advanced chemistry, and creative thinking.

Applying

By and large, a rolling admissions policy is in place, although applicants seeking admission in September are advised to submit applications (no application fee) as early as possible in the calendar year. Three letters of recommendation are required, and applicants are required to take the Graduate Record Examinations. Students whose native language is not English should take the TOEFL. Applicants are strongly encouraged to visit the University after arrangements are made with the Department.

To apply to the Wesleyan University Department of Chemistry graduate program go to http://www.wesleyan.edu/chem/chem_grad/overview.html.

Correspondence and Information

Chemistry Graduate Coordinator
Department of Chemistry
Hall-Atwater Laboratories
Wesleyan University
Middletown, Connecticut 06459-0001

Phone: 860-685-2210
Fax: 860-685-2211
E-mail: chemistry@wesleyan.edu
Web site: http://www.wesleyan.edu/chem/

Wesleyan University

THE FACULTY AND THEIR RESEARCH

David L. Beveridge, Professor; Ph.D., Cincinnati, 1965. Theoretical physical chemistry and molecular biophysics: statistical thermodynamics and computer simulation studies of hydrated biological molecules, structure and motions of nucleic acid, environmental effects on conformational stability, organization of water in crystal hydrates.

Philip H. Bolton, Professor; Ph.D., California, San Diego, 1976. Biochemistry and physical chemistry: NMR and modeling studies of duplex DNA; the structure of DNA containing abasic sites and other damaged DNA; studies on aptamer, telomere, and triplet repeat DNA; development of NMR methodology.

Joseph W. Bruno, Professor; Ph.D., Northwestern, 1983. Inorganic and organometallic chemistry: synthetic and mechanistic studies of transition-metal compounds, organometallic photochemistry, metal-mediated reactions of unsaturated organics.

Michael A. Calter, Associate Professor; Ph.D., Harvard, 1993. Synthetic organic chemistry, particularly in the area of asymmetric catalysis.

Michael J. Frisch, Visiting Scholar; Ph.D., Carnegie-Mellon, 1983. Theoretical chemistry: method development and applications to problems of current interest.

Albert J. Fry, Professor; Ph.D., Wisconsin, 1963. Organic chemistry: mechanisms of organic electrode processes, development of synthetically useful organic electrochemical reactions.

Joseph L. Knee, Professor; Ph.D., SUNY at Stony Brook, 1983. Chemical physics: investigation of ultrafast energy redistribution in molecules using picosecond laser techniques, emphasis on isolated molecule processes, including unimolecular photodissociation reaction rates.

Brian H. Northrop, Assistant Professor; Ph.D., UCLA, 2006. Organic chemistry. materials science in chemistry: the design and synthesis of new organic materials together with experimental and theoretical analysis of their formation and properties.

Stewart E. Novick, Professor; Ph.D., Harvard, 1973. Physical chemistry: pulsed-jet Fabry-Perot Fourier-transform microwave spectroscopy, structure and dynamics of weakly bound complexes, high-resolution spectroscopy of radicals important in the interstellar medium.

George A. Petersson, Professor; Ph.D., Caltech, 1970. Theoretical chemistry: development of improved methods for electronic structure calculations, with applications to small molecular systems and chemical reactions.

Herbert McWilliams Pickett, Visiting Scholar; Ph.D., Berkeley, 1969. Physical chemistry.

Rex F. Pratt, Professor; Ph.D., Melbourne (Australia), 1969. Bioorganic chemistry: enzyme mechanisms and inhibitor design, beta-lactam antibiotics and beta-lactamases, protein chemistry.

Wallace C. Pringle, Professor; Ph.D., MIT, 1966. Physical chemistry: spectroscopic studies of internal interactions in small molecules, collision-induced spectra, environmental chemistry.

Irina M. Russu, Professor; Ph.D., Pittsburgh, 1979. Biochemistry and molecular biophysics: structure and dynamics of nucleic acids, allosteric mechanisms in human hemoglobin, nuclear magnetic resonance spectroscopy.

Erika A. Taylor, Assistant Professor; Ph.D., Illinois at Urbana-Champaign, 2004. Biological chemistry: antibiotic development targeting gram-negative lipopolysaccharide biosynthesis, enzyme discovery, and directed evolution with biomass to biofuel applications.

T. David Westmoreland, Associate Professor; Ph.D., North Carolina, 1985. Inorganic and bioinorganic chemistry: electronic structure and mechanism in molybdenum-containing enzymes, fundamental aspects of atom transfer reactions in solution.

The Hall-Atwater Laboratory, which houses the Department of Chemistry.

SELECTED PUBLICATIONS

David L. Beveridge

A systematic molecular dynamics study of nearest-neighbor effects on base pair and base pair step conformations and fluctuations in B-DNA. *Nucleic Acids Res.* 38(1):299–313, 2010.

Dynamics of water and ions near DNA: Comparison of simulation to time-resolved stokes-shift experiments. *J. Am. Chem. Soc.* 131(5):1724–35, 2009.

Characterization of the dynamics of an essential helix in the U1A protein by time-resolved fluorescence measurements. *J. Phys. Chem. B* 112(19):6122–30, 2008.

Spectroscopic and molecular dynamics evidence for a sequential mechanism for the A-to-B transition in DNA. *Biophys. J.* 95:257–72, 2008.

Characterization of the dynamics of an essential helix in the U1A protein by time-resolved fluorescence measurements. *J. Phys. Chem. B* 112:6122–30, 2008.

Identification of an amnioacridine derivative that binds to RNA tetraloops. *J. Med. Chem.* 50:4096–104, 2007.

Affinity and specificity of protein U1A-RNA complex formation based on an additive component free energy model. *J. Mol. Biol.* 371:1405–19, 2007.

A study of collective atomic fluctuations and cooperativity in the U1A-RNA complex based on molecular dynamics simulations. *J. Struc. Biol.* 157:500–13, 2007.

Do collective atomic fluctuations account for cooperative effects? Molecular dynamic studies of U1A-RNA complex. *J. Am. Chem. Soc.* 128:8992–3, 2006.

Structural bioinformatics of DNA: A web-based tool for the analysis of molecular dynamics results and structure prediction. *Bioinformatics Appl. Notes* 22(8):1007–9, 2006.

Root mean square deviation probability analysis of molecular dynamics trajectories on DNA. *J. Chem. Inform. Model.* 46:1084–93, 2006.

Molecular dynamics simulation studies of a protein-RNA complex with a selectively modified binding interface. *Biopolymers* 81(4):256–69, 2006.

Philip H. Bolton

Mix and measure fluorescence screening for selective quadruplex binders. *Nucleic Acids Res.* 36(17): e106, 2008.

Selective recognition in RNA helices containing dangling ends by a Quinoline derivative. *ChemBioChem* 8:1658–61, 2007.

Molecular beacon-equilibrium cyclization detection of DNA-protein complexes. *Biophys. J.* 93:3210–17, 2007.

Circular dichroism of quadruplex DNAs: Applications to structure, cation effects and ligand binding. *Methods* 43(4):324–31, 2007.

Vertebrate telomere repeat DNAs favor external loop propeller quadruplex structures in the presence of high concentrations of potassium. *Nucleic Acids Res.* 33:2022–31, 2005.

Joseph W. Bruno

Hydricities of BzNADH, C5H5Mo(PMe3)(CO)2H, and C5Me5Mo(PMe3)(CO)2H in acetonitrile. *J. Am. Chem. Soc.* 126:2738–43, 2004.

Sterically-congested bisphosphite ligands for the catalytic hydrosilation of ketones. *Phosphorus, Sulfur Silicon Relat. Elem.* 177:479–85, 2002.

Supercritical methanol drying as a convenient route to phenolic-furfural aerogels. *J. Non-Cryst. Solids* 296:1, 2001.

Chelating aryloxide ligands in the synthesis of titanium, niobium, and tantalum compounds: Electrochemical studies and styrene polymerization activities. *Organometallics* 20:5547, 2001.

Thermodynamic studies of hydride transfer for a series of niobium and tantalum compounds. *Organometallics* 20:51, 2001.

Michael A. Calter

Catalytic, asymmetric Michael reactions of cyclic diketones with β,γ-unsaturated-α-ketoesters. *Org. Lett.* 11(10): 2205–8, 2009.

Catalytic, asymmetric synthesis of α-phenoxy-β-aryl-β-lactams. *Tetrahedron Lett.* 48(9):1657–9, 2007.

Formation of disubstituted β-lactones using bifunctional catalysis. *Org. Lett.* 7:1809–12, 2005.

Synthesis of the C_1-C_{27} portion of the aplyronines. *Tetrahedron Lett.* 45:4847–50, 2004.

Catalytic, asymmetric synthesis and diastereoselective aldol reactions of dipropionate equivalents. *J. Org. Chem.* 69:1270–5, 2004.

Michael J. Frisch

Automatically generated Coulomb-fitting basis sets: Design and accuracy for systems containing H to Kr. *J. Chem. Phys.* 127:074102, 2007.

Toward effective and reliable fluorescence energies in solution by a new state-specific polarizable continuum model time dependent DFT approach. *J. Chem. Phys.* 127:074504, 2007.

Energy-represented direct inversion in the iterative subspace within a hybrid geometry optimization method. *J. Chem. Theor. Comput.* 2(3):835–9, 2006.

Combining quantum mechanics methods with molecular mechanics methods in ONIOM. *J. Chem. Theor. Comput.* 2(3):815–26, 2006.

Calculation of nuclear spin-spin coupling constants of molecules with first and second row atoms in study of basis set dependence. *J. Chem. Theor. Comput.* 2(4):1028–37, 2006.

Efficient evaluation of short-range Hartree-Fock exchange in large molecules and periodic systems. *J. Chem. Phys.* 125(10):104103, 2006.

A state-specific PCM TD-DFT method for equilibrium and non-equilibrium excited state calculations in solution. *J. Chem. Phys.* 125:054103, 2006.

Modeling proton transfer in zeolites: Convergence behavior of embedded and constrained cluster calculations. *J. Theor. Comput. Chem.* 1:(6)1232–9, 2005.

Determination of absolute configurations of chiral molecules using ab initio time-dependent density functional theory calculations of optical rotation: How reliable are absolute configurations obtained for molecules with small rotations? *Chirality* 17:S52–S64, 2005.

Albert J. Fry

Stanley Wawzonek and the introduction of polar aprotic solvents into organic electrochemistry. *Interface* 19(1):55–8, 2010.

Tetraalkylammonium ions are surrounded by an inner solvation shell in strong electron pair donor solvents. *Electrochem. Comm.* 11:309–12, 2009.

Substituents on the redox properties and structure of substituted triphenylamines: An experimental and computational study. *Tetrahedron* 65:208–14, 2009.

A computational examination of substituent effects on the interconversion of 1.3.5-cyclooctatriene and bicyclo[4.2.0]-2.4-octadiene. *Tetrahedron* 64:2102, 2008.

Electrocatalytic cleavage of electronegatively substituted stilbenes employing a new high potential electrocatalyst. An electrochemical equivalent of ozonolysis. *Org. Lett.* 9:5633, 2007.

Experimental/computational study of the electrochemical oxidation of cyclooctatetraene in protic media. Solvent effects. *Org. Lett.* 9:1671, 2007.

Construction of electrocatalytic electrodes bearing the triphenylamine nucleus covalently bound to carbon. A halogen dance in protonated aminotriphenylamines. *Org. Lett.* 8:411, 2006.

Effects of strong ion-pairing on the electrochemical reduction of cyclooctatetraene in tetrahydrofuran in the presence of lithium ion. Peak coalescence does not imply potential inversion. *Electroanalysis* 18:379, 2006.

Electrophilic nitration of triphenylamines as a route to high oxidation potential electrocatalysts. Polynitration, nitrodebromination, and bromine dance. *Tetrahedron Lett.* 47(44) 7667–9, 2006.

A computational study of solution effects on the disproportionation of electrochemically generated polycyclic aromatic hydrocarbon radical anions. Thermodynamics and structures. *Tetrahedron* 62:6558, 2006.

Further studies on the reduction of benzylic alcohols by hypophosphorous acid/iodine. *ARKIVOC* 6:393, 2005.

Disproportionation of arene radical anions is driven overwhelmingly by solvation, not ion pairing. *Electrochem. Commun.* 7:602, 2005.

Joseph L. Knee

ZEKE spectroscopy of tryptamine and the dissociation pathway of the singly hydrated cation cluster. Invited paper, submitted 2010.

Photoionization spectroscopy of even-parity autoionizing Rydberg states of argon: Experimental and theoretical investigation of Fano profiles and resonance widths. *Phys. Rev. A.* 77:062512, 2008.

Cation spectroscopy and binding energy determination for 1,4-benzodioxan –Ar_1 and Ar_2 complexes. *J. Phys. Chem.* 112(30):6823–8, 2008.

Binding energies and dissociation pathways in the aniline- Ar_2cation complex. *J. Chem. Phys.* 128(6):064311–8, 2008.

Characterization of the dynamics of an essential helix in the U1A protein by time-resolved fluorescence measurements. *J. Phys. Chem. B.* 112(19):6122–30, 2008.

Tryptophol cation conformations studied with ZEKE spectroscopy. *J. Phys. Chem. A.* 111:808, 2007.

Vibrational dynamics of 9-fluorenemethanol using infrared-ultraviolet double resonance spectroscopy. *J. Chem. Phys.* 120:5631, 2004.

Brian H. Northrop

Photophysical properties of coordination-driven self-assembled metallosupramolecular rhomboids: Experimental and theoretical investigations. *J. Phys. Chem. A* 114(10):3418–22, 2010.

Ultrafast optical excitations in supramolecular metallacycles with charge transfer properties. *J. Am. Chem. Soc.* 132(4):1348–58, 2010.

2D assembly of metallacycles on HOPG by shape-persistent macrocycle templates. *J. Am. Chem. Soc.* 132(4):1328–33, 2010.

Synthesis and X-ray structural analysis of platinum and ethynyl-platinum corannulenes: Supramolecular tectons. *Org. Biomol. Chem.* 7(23):4881–85, 2009.

Self-organization in coordination-driven self-assembly. *Accounts Chem. Res.* 42(10):1554–63, 2009.

Facile self-assembly of neutral dendritic metallocycles via oxygen-to-platinum coordination. *J. Org. Chem.* 74(18):7067–74, 2009.

Geometry directed self-selection in the coordination-driven self-assembly of irregular supramolecular polygons. *J. Org. Chem.* 74(9):3554–57, 2009.

Introduction of heterofunctional groups onto molecular hexagons via coordination-driven self-assembly. *J. Org. Chem.* 74(13):4828–33, 2009.

Synthesis of six-component metallodendrimers via [3+3] coordination-driven self-assembly. *J. Org. Chem.* 74(9):3524–27, 2009.

Surface confined metallosupramolecular architectures: Formation and STM characterization. *Accounts Chem. Res.* 42(2):249–59, 2009.

Photostability of pentacene and 6,13-disubstituted pentacene derivatives: A theoretical and experimental mechanistic study. *Photochemical and Photobiological Sciences* 7:1463–8, 2008.

Exploring the limits of self-organization in the self-assembly of supramolecular metallacycles. *Inorg. Chem.* 47:11257–8, 2008.

Coordination-driven self-assembly of functionalized supramolecular metallacycles. *Chem. Comm.* 5896–908, 2008.

Synthesis of a new family of hexakisferrocenyl hexagons and their electrochemical behavior *J. Org. Chem.* 73:8553–7, 2008.

Self-assembly of carbon-rich supramolecular metallacycles and metallacages. *Tetrahedron* 64:11495–503, 2008.

Nanopatterning of donor/acceptor hybrid supramolecular architectures on HOPG: An STM study. *J. Am. Chem. Soc.* 130:13433–41, 2008.

Supramolecule-to-supramolecule transformations of coordination-driven self-assembled polygons. *J. Am. Chm. Soc.* 130:11886–8, 2008.

Self-selection in the self-assembly of isomeric supramolecular squares from usymmetrical bis(4-pyridyl)acetylene ligands. *J. Org. Chem.* 73:6580–6, 2008.

An STM investigation of a supramolecular self-assembled 3-dimensional chiral prism on a Au(111) surface. *J. Am. Chem. Soc.* 130:8878–9, 2008.

Size selective self-sorting in coordination-driven self-assembly of finite ensembles. *Inorg. Chem.* 47:4706–11, 2008.

Coordination-driven self-assembly of cavity-cored multiple crown ether derivatives and poly[2]pseudorotaxanes. *J. Am. Chem. Soc.* 130:5320–34, 2008.

A new family of multiferrocene complexes with enhanced control of structure and stoichiometry via coordination-driven self-assembly and their electrochemistry. *J. Am. Chem. Soc.* 130:839–41, 2008.

Functionalized hydrophobic and hydrophilic self-assembled supramolecular rectangles. *J. Org. Chem.* 73:1787–94, 2008.

A highly efficient approach to the self-assembly of hexagonal cavity-cored tris[2]pseudorotaxanes from several components via multiple noncovalent interactions. *J. Am. Chem Soc.* 129:14187–9, 2007.

The control of supramolecular rectangle self-assembly with a molecular template. *J. Am. Chem. Soc.* 129:9268–9, 2007.

Self-recognition in the coordination-driven self-assembly of three-dimensional M_3L_2 polyhedra. *Org. Lett.* 9:1561–4, 2007.

Efficient routes to novel molecular architectures: Template-directed self-assembly of mechanically interlocked suitanes. *Chimica Oggi/Chemistry Today* 25:38–41, 2007.

On the mechanism of peripentacene formation from pentacene: Computational studies of a prototype for graphene formation from smaller acenes. *J. Am. Chem Soc.* 129:6536–46, 2007.

A molecular plug-socket connector. *J. Am. Chem. Soc.* 129:4633–42, 2007.

In *CRC Handbook of Nanoscience, Engineering, and Technology, second edition,* 11/1–48, eds. Iafrate, Brenner, Goddard, and Lyshevski. Boca Raton, Florida: CRC Press, 2007.

Why 6-methylpentacene deconjugates but avoids the thermally allowed unimolecular mechanism. *Org. Lett.* 8:4915–8, 2006.

Suitanes. *Angew. Chem. Int. Ed.* 45:6665–9, 2006.

Template-directed synthesis of mechanically interlocked molecular bundles using dynamic covalent chemistry. *Org. Lett.* 8:3899–902, 2006.

Wesleyan University

Supramolecular self-assembly of dendronized polymers: Reversible control of the polymer architectures through acid-base reactions. *J. Am. Chem. Soc.* 128:10707–15, 2006.

Evaluation of synthetic linear motor-molecule actuation energetics. *Proc. Natl. Acad. Sci. USA* 103:8583–8, 2006.

The mechanism of the vinylcyclobutane rearrangements of sceptrin to ageliferin and nagelamide E. *Angew. Chem. Int. Ed.* 45:4126–30, 2006.

Kinetically controlled self-assembly of pseudorotaxanes on crystallization. *Org. Lett.* 8:2159–62, 2006.

Structural control at the organic-solid interface. *J. Mater. Chem.* 16:32–44, 2006.

Theoretical exploration of mechanism and relationship to the Diels-Alder potential surface. *J. Org. Chem.* 71:3–13, 2006.

Molecular muscles. *J. Am. Chem. Soc.* 127:9745–59, 2006.

The three corrugated surfaces of 1,4-divinyltetramethylene diradical intermediates and their connections to 1,2-divinylcyclobutane, 4-vinylcyclohexene, 1,5-cyclooctadiene, and two butadienes. *J. Org. Chem.* 70:2994–3008, 2005.

The influence of constitutional isomerism and change on molecular recognition processes. *Chem. Eur. J.* 10:5406–21, 2004.

Stewart E. Novick

Determination of the structure of cyclopentene oxide and the argon–cyclopentene oxide van der Waals complex. *J. Phys. Chem. A* 114(3):1427–31, 2010.

Microwave spectrum of the argon-tropolone van der Waals complex. *J. Phys. Chem. A* 113(47):13076–80, 2009.

Microwave spectra and structural parameters of equatorial-trans cyclobutanol. *J. Mol. Struct.* 922:83–7, 2009.

Fourier transform microwave spectroscopy of monobromogermylene (HGeBr and DGeBr), a heavy atom carbene analog. *J. Chem. Phys.* 130:124317, 2009.

Microwave spectrum and structure of the polar N2O dimer. *J. Mol. Spectros.* 251:153–8, 2008.

Determination of the structure of methylene cyclobutane confirming a non-planar ethene and the structure of the argon-methylene cyclobutane van der Waals complex. *J. Mol. Spectros.* 251:210–6, 2008.

Microwave spectra and ab initio studies of Ar-propane and Ne-propane complexes: Structure and dynamics. *J. Chem. Phys.* 127:184306, 2007.

Microwave observation of the 'recently found' polar OCS dimer. *J. Chem. Phys.* 126:101101, 2007.

Rotational spectra of gauche perfluoro-n-butane, C4F10; perfluoro-iso-butane, (CF3)3CF; and tris[trifluoromethyl]-methane, (CF3)3CH. *J. Mol. Spectrosc.* 242:129–38, 2007.

The microwave spectrum and structure of the argon trifluoroacetonitrile complex. *J. Mol. Spectrosc.* 243:32–6, 2007.

Microwave spectra and ab initio studies of Ar-propane and Ne-propane complexes: Structure and dynamics. *J. Chem. Phys.* 127:184306, 2007.

High resolution studies of tropolone in the S0 and S1 electronic states: Isotope driven dynamics in the zero-point energy levels. *J. Chem. Phys.* 124:074309, 2006.

The microwave spectrum of the 1,1-difluoroprop-2-ynyl radical, F2CCCH. *J. Chem. Phys.* 125:054309, 2006.

The microwave spectrum of phosphaacetylnitrile, H2PCCCN. *J. Mol. Spectrosc.* 240:255–9, 2006.

The microwave spectrum of HGeCl. *J. Mol. Spectrosc.* 230:93–8, 2005.

George A. Petersson

MP2/CBS atomic and molecular benchmarks for H through Ar. *J. Chem. Phys.* 132(11), 11411, 2010.

Unrestricted coupled cluster and Brueckner doubles variations of W1 theory. *J. Chem. Theor. Comput.* 5(10):2687–93, 2009.

Intramolecular nonbonded attractive interactions: 1-substituted propenes. *J. Chem. Theor. Comput.* 5(4):1033–37, 2009.

The CCSD(T) complete basis set limit for Ne revisited. *J. Chem. Phys.* 129, 194115, 2008.

Uniformly convergent n-tuple-z augmented polarized (nZaP) basis sets for complete basis set extrapolations. I. Self-consistent field energies. *J. Chem. Phys.* 129, 184116, 2008.

The convergence of CASSCF-CISD energies to the complete basis set limit. *J. Chem. Phys.* 125:44107, 2006.

A restricted-open-shell complete-basis-set model chemistry. *J. Chem. Phys.* 125:94106, 2006.

The convergence of CASSCF energies to the complete basis set limit. *J. Chem. Phys.* 123:74111, 2005.

Rex F. Pratt

Substituted aryl malonamates as new serine ß-lactamase substrates: Structure-activity studies. *Bioorg. Med. Chem.* 18(1):282–91, 2010.

Structural basis of the inhibition of class A ß-lactamases and penicillin-binding proteins by 6 ß-iodopenicillanate. *J. Am. Chem. Soc.* 131(42):15262–9, 2009.

Intramolecular cooperativity in the reaction of diacyl phosphates with serine ß-lactamases. *Biochemistry* 48(35):8293–8, 2009.

Inhibition of class A and C ß-lactamases by diaroyl phosphates. *Biochemistry* 48(35):8285–92, 2009.

Approaches to the simultaneous inactivation of metallo and serine- ßeta-lactamases. *Bioorg. Med. Chem. Lett.* 19:1618, 2009.

Kinetics and mechanism of inhibition of a serine ß-lactamase by O-aryloxycarbonyl hydroxamates. *Biochemistry* 47:12037, 2008.

ß-Ketophosphonates as ß-lactamases inhibitors: Intramolecular cooperativity between the hydrophobic subsites of class D-ß-lactamase. *Bioorg. Med. Chem.* 16:6987–94, 2008.

Crystal structures of complexes of bacterial DD-peptidases with peptidoglycan-mimetic ligands: The substrate specificity puzzle. *J. Mol. Biol.* 381:383–93, 2008.

Substrate specificity of bacterial DD-peptidases (penicillin-binding proteins). *Cell. Mol. Life Sci.* 65:2138, 2008.

Inhibition of serine ß-lactamases by vanadate–catechol complexes. *Biochemistry* 47:9467–74, 2008.

Inhibition of chymotrypsin by a complex of ortho-vanadate and benzohydroxamic acid: Structure of the inert complex and its mechanistic interpretation. *Biochemistry* 46:5982, 2007.

Crystal structure of the *Bacillus subtilis* penicillin-binding protein 4a, and its complex with the peptidoglycan mimetic peptide. *J. Mol. Biol.* 371:528, 2007.

O-aryloxycarbonyl hydroxamates: New β-lactamase inhibitors that cross-link the active site. *J. Amer. Chem Soc.* 10:1021/ja072370u, 2007.

Reactions of peptidoglycan-mimetic β-lactams with penicillin-binding proteins in vivo and in membranes. *ACS Chemical Biology* 2(9):620–4, 2007.

Synthesis and reactivity with β-lactamases of a monobactam bearing a retro-amide side chain. *Bioorg. Med. Chem.* 16:869–71, 2006.

Synthesis and β-lactamases reactivity of a-substituted phenaceturates. *Bioorg. Med. Chem.* 14:7023–33, 2006.

Synthesis and evaluation of ketophosph(on)ates as β-lactamase inhibitors. *J. Org. Chem.* 71:4778–85, 2006.

Deacylation transition states of a bacterial DD-peptidase. *Biochemistry* 45:13074–82, 2006.

Inhibition of class D β-lactamase by acyl phosphates and phosphonates. *Antimicrob. Agents Chemother.* 49:4410–2, 2005.

Inhibition of class D β-lactamases by diaroyl phosphates. *Biochemistry* 44:16121–9, 2005.

Transpeptidation reactions of a specific substrate catalyzed by the streptomyces R61 DD-peptidase: Characterization of a chromogenic substrate and acyl acceptor. *Biochemistry* 44:9971–9, 2005.

Transpeptidation reactions of a specific substrate catalyzed by the streptomyces R61 DD-peptidase: The structural basis of acyl acceptor specificity. *Biochemistry* 44(30):9961–70, 2005.

Ketophosph(on)ates—A new lead to inhibitors of beta-lactamases. *FASEB J.* 19:A862, 2005.

The D-methyl group in ß-lactamase evolution: Evidence from the Y221G and GC1 mutants of the class C ß-lactamase of *Enterobacter cloacae* P99. *Biochemistry* 44:7543, 2005.

Crystal structures of complexes between the R61 DD-peptidase and peptidoglycan-mimetic ß-lactams: A non-covalent complex with a "perfect Penicillin." *J. Mol. Biol.* 345:521, 2005.

Wallace C. Pringle

Microwave spectrum of the argon-tropolone van der Waals complex. *J. Phys. Chem. A* 113(47):13076–80, 2009.

Microwave spectra and structural parameters of equatorial-trans cyclobutanol. *J. Mol. Struct.* 922(1-3):83–7, 2009.

Determination of the structures of methylene cyclobutane and the argon methylene cyclobutane van der Waals complex. *J. Mol. Spectros.* 251:210–6, 2008.

High resolution studies of tropolone in the S0 and S1 electronic states: Isotope driven dynamics in the zero-point energy levels. *J. Chem. Phys.* 124:074309, 2006.

Rotational spectrum, nuclear quadrupole coupling constants, and structure of six isotopomers of the argon-chlorocyclobutane van der Waals complex. *J. Mol. Struct.* 742:165–72, 2005.

Irina M. Russu

Structural energetics of the adenine tract from an intrinsic transcription terminator. *J. Mol. Biol.* 397(3):677–88, 2010.

Dynamics and stability of individual base pairs in two homologous RNA-DNA hybrids. *Biochemistry* 48:3988–97, 2009.

Influence of magnesium ions on spontaneous opening of DNA base pairs. *J. Phys. Chem. B* 112:7689, 2008.

Probing the role of hydrogen bonds in the stability of base pairs in double-helical DNA. *Biopolymers* 87:165–73, 2007.

Structural energetics and base-pair opening dynamics in sarcin-ricin domain RNA. *Biochemistry* 45:13606–13, 2006.

Base pair opening in three DNA-unwinding elements. *J. Biol. Chem.* 280:20216, 2005.

Probing site-specific energetics in proteins and nucleic acids by hydrogen exchange and NMR spectroscopy. *Methods Enzymol.* 379:152–75, 2004.

Site-resolved stabilization a DNA triple helix by magnesium ions. *Nucleic Acids Res.* 32:878–83, 2004.

Sequence-dependence of the energetics of opening of AT base pairs in DNA. *Biophys. J.* 87:2545–51, 2004.

Erika A. Taylor

Blocking transmission of malaria: In vivo studies with immucillin-H. *PLoS Pathogens,* in press.

Second-sphere amino acids contribute to transition-state structure in bovine purine nucleoside phosphorylase. *Biochemistry* 47:2577–83, 2008.

Anopheles gambiae purine nucleoside phosphorylase: Catalysis, structure and inhibition. *Biochemistry* 46:12405–15, 2007.

Transition state structures of human, bovine and *Plasmodium falciparum* adenosine deaminases. *J. Am. Chem. Soc.* 129:8008–17, 2007.

Acyclic ribooxacarbenium ion mimics as transition state analogues of human and malarial purine nucleoside phosphorylases. *J. Am. Chem. Soc.* 129:6984–5, 2007.

Synthesis of 5′-methylthio coformycins: Specific inhibitors for malarial adenosine deaminase. *J. Am. Chem. Soc.* 129:6872–9, 2007.

Neighboring group participation in the transition state of human purine nucleoside phosphorylase. *Biochemistry* 46:5038–49, 2007.

Transition state analogue discrimination by related purine nucleoside phosphorylases. *J. Am. Chem. Soc.* 128:7126–7, 2006.

Syntheses and bio-activities of the L-enantiomers of two potent transition state analogue inhibitors of purine nucleoside phosphorylases. *Org. Biomol. Chem.* 4:1131–9, 2006.

Transition states and inhibitors of the purine nucleoside phosphorylase family. *Curr. Top. Med. Chem.* 5:1237–58, 2005.

Energetic mapping of transition state analogue interactions with human and *Plasmodium falciparum* purine nucleoside phosphorylases. *J. Biol. Chem.* 280:30320–8, 2005.

Targeting a novel Plasmodium falciparum purine recycling pathway with specific immucillins. *J. Biol. Chem.* 280:9547–54, 2005.

T. David Westmoreland

Correlation of relaxivity with coordination number in six-, seven-, and eight-coordinate Mn(II) complexes of pendant-arm cyclen derivatives. *Inorg. Chem.* 48(2):719–27, 2009.

Symmetry control of chemical reactions: Applications to the berry pseudorotation of five-coordinate transition metal complexes. *Inorg. Chem. Acta* 361:1187–91, 2008.

Electronic effects on the rates of coupled two-electron/halide self-exchange reactions of substituted ruthenocenes. *Inorg. Chem.* 39:1573, 2000.

Section 3
Geosciences

This section contains a directory of institutions offering graduate work in geosciences, followed by in-depth entries submitted by institutions that chose to prepare detailed program descriptions. Additional information about programs listed in the directory but not augmented by an in-depth entry may be obtained by writing directly to the dean of a graduate school or chair of a department at the address given in the directory.

For programs offering related work, see all other areas in this book. In the other guides in this series:

Graduate Programs in the Humanities, Arts & Social Sciences
See *Geography*

Graduate Programs in the Biological Sciences
See *Biological and Biomedical Sciences, Biophysics,* and *Botany and Plant Biology*

Graduate Programs in Engineering & Applied Sciences
See *Aerospace/Aeronautical Engineering; Agricultural Engineering and Bioengineering; Civil and Environmental Engineering; Energy and Power Engineering (Nuclear Engineering); Engineering and Applied Sciences; Geological, Mineral/Mining, and Petroleum Engineering;* and *Mechanical Engineering and Mechanics*

CONTENTS

Program Directories

Geochemistry

California Institute of Technology, Division of Geological and Planetary Sciences, Pasadena, CA 91125-0001. Offers geobiology (MS, PhD); geochemistry (MS, PhD); geology (MS, PhD); geophysics (MS, PhD); planetary science (MS, PhD). *Faculty:* 38 full-time (6 women). *Students:* 75 full-time (38 women); includes 21 minority (1 African American, 18 Asian Americans or Pacific Islanders, 2 Hispanic Americans). Average age 26. 102 applicants, 28% accepted, 9 enrolled. In 2009, 13 master's, 13 doctorates awarded. *Degree requirements:* For doctorate, thesis/dissertation. *Entrance requirements:* For doctorate, GRE General Test. Additional exam requirements/recommendations for international students: Required—TOEFL; Recommended—IELTS, TWE. *Application deadline:* For fall admission, 1/1 for domestic and international students. Application fee: $80. Electronic applications accepted. *Financial support:* In 2009–10, 75 students received support, including 15 fellowships with full tuition reimbursements available (averaging $27,000 per year), 60 research assistantships with full tuition reimbursements available (averaging $27,000 per year); teaching assistantships with full tuition reimbursements available, institutionally sponsored loans, scholarships/grants, health care benefits, and unspecified assistantships also available. Financial award applicants required to submit FAFSA. *Faculty research:* Astronomy, evolution of anaerobic respiratory processes, structural geology and tectonics, theoretical and numerical seismology, global biogeochemical cycles. *Unit head:* Dr. Kenneth A. Farley, Chairman, 626-395-6111, Fax: 626-795-6028, E-mail: dianb@gps.caltech.edu. *Application contact:* Dr. Robert W. Clayton, Academic Officer, 626-395-6909, Fax: 626-795-6028, E-mail: dianb@gps.caltech.edu.

California State University, Fullerton, Graduate Studies, College of Natural Science and Mathematics, Department of Chemistry and Biochemistry, Fullerton, CA 92834-9480. Offers chemistry (MS); geochemistry (MS). Part-time programs available. *Students:* 7 full-time (3 women), 29 part-time (17 women); includes 16 minority (1 African American, 14 Asian Americans or Pacific Islanders, 1 Hispanic American), 4 international. Average age 27. 44 applicants, 43% accepted, 9 enrolled. In 2009, 5 master's awarded. *Degree requirements:* For master's, thesis, departmental qualifying exam. *Entrance requirements:* For master's, minimum GPA of 2.5 in last 60 units of course work, major in chemistry or related field. Application fee: $55. *Expenses:* Tuition, nonresident: full-time $11,160; part-time $373 per credit. Required fees: $1440 per term. Tuition and fees vary according to course load, degree level and program. *Financial support:* Research assistantships, teaching assistantships, career-related internships or fieldwork, Federal Work-Study, institutionally sponsored loans, and scholarships/grants available. Support available to part-time students. Financial award application deadline: 3/1; financial award applicants required to submit FAFSA. *Unit head:* Dr. Maria Linder, Chair, 657-278-3621. *Application contact:* Admissions/Applications, 657-278-2371.

Colorado School of Mines, Graduate School, Department of Chemistry and Geochemistry and Department of Geology and Geological Engineering, Program in Geochemistry, Golden, CO 80401. Offers MS, PhD. Part-time programs available. *Students:* 2 full-time (1 woman), 1 (woman) part-time. Average age 22. 14 applicants, 36% accepted, 2 enrolled. In 2009, 1 doctorate awarded. *Degree requirements:* For master's, thesis (for some programs); for doctorate, comprehensive exam, thesis/dissertation. *Entrance requirements:* For master's and doctorate, GRE General Test. Additional exam requirements/recommendations for international students: Required—TOEFL (minimum score 550 paper-based; 213 computer-based; 80 iBT). *Application deadline:* For fall admission, 1/15 for domestic students, 1/15 priority date for international students; for spring admission, 9/1 priority date for domestic and international students. Application fee: $50 ($70 for international students). Electronic applications accepted. *Expenses:* Tuition, state resident: full-time $10,584; part-time $588 per credit hour. Tuition, nonresident: full-time $24,750; part-time $1375 per credit hour. Required fees: $1654; $827.10 per semester. *Financial support:* In 2009–10, fellowships with full tuition reimbursements (averaging $20,000 per year), research assistantships with full tuition reimbursements (averaging $20,000 per year), teaching assistantships with full tuition reimbursements (averaging $20,000 per year) were awarded; scholarships/grants, health care benefits, and unspecified assistantships also available. Financial award application deadline: 1/15; financial award applicants required to submit FAFSA. *Faculty research:* Geochemical analysis, organic geochemistry, hydrochemical systems, environmental microbiology, process control programming. *Unit head:* Dr. Dan Knauss, Department Head, 303-273-3625, Fax: 303-273-3629, E-mail: dknauss@mines.edu. *Application contact:* Tina Voelker, Associate Professor, 303-273-3152, Fax: 303-273-3629, E-mail: tvoelker@mines.edu.

Colorado School of Mines, Graduate School, Department of Geology and Geological Engineering, Golden, CO 80401. Offers geochemistry (MS, PMS, PhD); geological engineering (ME, MS, PhD); geology (MS, PhD). Part-time programs available. *Faculty:* 26 full-time (7 women), 4 part-time/adjunct (2 women). *Students:* 101 full-time (38 women), 24 part-time (10 women); includes 8 minority (1 African American, 2 American Indian/Alaska Native, 2 Asian Americans or Pacific Islanders, 3 Hispanic Americans), 19 international. Average age 29. 175 applicants, 65% accepted, 40 enrolled. In 2009, 28 master's, 3 doctorates awarded. *Degree requirements:* For master's, thesis (for some programs); for doctorate, comprehensive exam, thesis/dissertation. *Entrance requirements:* For master's and doctorate, GRE General Test. Additional exam requirements/recommendations for international students: Required—TOEFL (minimum score 550 paper-based; 213 computer-based; 80 iBT). *Application deadline:* For fall admission, 1/15 for domestic and international students; for spring admission, 9/1 for domestic and international students. Application fee: $50 ($70 for international students). Electronic applications accepted. *Expenses:* Tuition, state resident: full-time $10,584; part-time $588 per credit hour. Tuition, nonresident: full-time $24,750; part-time $1375 per credit hour. Required fees: $1654; $827.10 per semester. *Financial support:* In 2009–10, 65 students received support, including 7 fellowships with full tuition reimbursements available (averaging $20,000 per year), 40 research assistantships with full tuition reimbursements available (averaging $20,000 per year), 18 teaching assistantships with full tuition reimbursements available (averaging $20,000 per year); scholarships/grants, health care benefits, and unspecified assistantships also available. Financial award application deadline: 1/15; financial award applicants required to submit FAFSA. *Faculty research:* Predictive sediment modeling, petrophysics, aquifer-contaminant flow modeling, water-rock interactions, geotechnical engineering. Total annual research expenditures: $2.6 million. *Unit head:* Dr. John Humphrey, Department Head, 303-273-3819, Fax: 303-273-3859, E-mail: jhumphre@mines.edu. *Application contact:* Marilyn Schwinger, Administrative Assistant, 303-273-3800, Fax: 303-273-3859, E-mail: mschwing@mines.edu.

Columbia University, Graduate School of Arts and Sciences, Division of Natural Sciences, Department of Earth and Environmental Sciences, New York, NY 10027. Offers geochemistry (M Phil, MA, PhD); geodetic sciences (M Phil, MA, PhD); geophysics (M Phil, MA, PhD); oceanography (M Phil, MA, PhD). *Degree requirements:* For master's, thesis or alternative, fieldwork, written exam; for doctorate, one foreign language, thesis/dissertation. *Entrance requirements:* For master's and doctorate, GRE General Test, GRE Subject Test, major in natural or physical science. Additional exam requirements/recommendations for international students: Required—TOEFL. *Faculty research:* Structural geology and stratigraphy, petrology, paleontology, rare gas, isotope and aqueous geochemistry.

Cornell University, Graduate School, Graduate Fields of Engineering, Field of Geological Sciences, Ithaca, NY 14853-0001. Offers economic geology (M Eng, MS, PhD); engineering geology (M Eng, MS, PhD); environmental geophysics (M Eng, MS, PhD); general geology (M Eng, MS, PhD); geobiology (M Eng, MS, PhD); geochemistry and isotope geology (M Eng, MS, PhD); geohydrology (M Eng, MS, PhD); geomorphology (M Eng, MS, PhD); geophysics (M Eng, MS, PhD); geotectonics (M Eng, MS, PhD); marine geology (MS, PhD); mineralogy (M Eng, MS, PhD); paleontology (M Eng, MS, PhD); petroleum geology (M Eng, MS, PhD); petrology (M Eng, MS, PhD); planetary geology (M Eng, MS, PhD); Precambrian geology (M Eng, MS, PhD); Quaternary geology (M Eng, MS, PhD); rock mechanics (M Eng, MS, PhD); sedimentology (M Eng, MS, PhD); seismology (M Eng, MS, PhD); stratigraphy (M Eng, MS, PhD); structural geology (M Eng, MS, PhD). *Faculty:* 38 full-time (6 women). *Students:* 32 full-time (14 women); includes 2 minority (1 African American, 1 Asian American or Pacific Islander), 9 international. Average age 29. 61 applicants, 23% accepted, 8 enrolled. In 2009, 3 doctorates awarded. *Degree requirements:* For master's, thesis (MS); for doctorate, comprehensive exam, thesis/dissertation. *Entrance requirements:* For master's and doctorate, GRE General Test, 3 letters of recommendation. Additional exam requirements/recommendations for international students: Required—TOEFL (minimum score 550 paper-based; 213 computer-based; 77 iBT). *Application deadline:* For fall admission, 1/15 priority date for domestic students. Applications are processed on a rolling basis. Application fee: $70. Electronic applications accepted. *Expenses:* Tuition: Full-time $29,500. Required fees: $70. Full-time tuition and fees vary according to degree level, program and student level. *Financial support:* In 2009–10, 25 students received support, including 2 fellowships with full tuition reimbursements available, 3 research assistantships with full tuition reimbursements available, 1 teaching assistantship with full tuition reimbursement available; institutionally sponsored loans, scholarships/grants, health care benefits, tuition waivers (full and partial), and unspecified assistantships also available. Financial award applicants required to submit FAFSA. *Faculty research:* Geophysics, structural geology, petrology, geochemistry, geodynamics. *Unit head:* Director of Graduate Studies, 607-255-5466, Fax: 607-254-4780. *Application contact:* Graduate Field Assistant, 607-255-5466, Fax: 607-254-4780, E-mail: gradprog@geology.cornell.edu.

Georgia Institute of Technology, Graduate Studies and Research, College of Sciences, School of Earth and Atmospheric Sciences, Atlanta, GA 30332-0340. Offers atmospheric chemistry, aerosols and clouds (MS, PhD); dynamics of weather and climate (MS, PhD); geochemistry (MS, PhD); geophysics (MS, PhD); oceanography (MS, PhD); paleoclimate (MS, PhD); planetary science (MS, PhD); remote sensing (MS, PhD). Part-time programs available. Terminal master's awarded for partial completion of doctoral program. *Degree requirements:* For master's, thesis or alternative; for doctorate, comprehensive exam, thesis/dissertation. *Entrance requirements:* For master's, GRE, letters of recommendation; for doctorate, GRE, academic transcripts, letters of recommendation, personal statement. Additional exam requirements/recommendations for international students: Required—TOEFL (minimum score 550 paper-based; 213 computer-based; 79 iBT). *Faculty research:* Geophysics; atmospheric chemistry, aerosols and clouds; dynamics of weather and climate; geochemistry; oceanography; paleoclimate; planetary science; remote sensing.

Indiana University Bloomington, University Graduate School, College of Arts and Sciences, Department of Geological Sciences, Bloomington, IN 47405-7000. Offers biogeochemistry (MS, PhD); economic geology (MS, PhD); geobiology (MS, PhD); geophysics, structural geology and tectonics (MS, PhD); hydrogeology (MS, PhD); mineralogy (MS, PhD); stratigraphy and sedimentology (MS, PhD). *Faculty:* 17 full-time (1 woman). *Students:* 52 full-time (24 women), 3 part-time (0 women); includes 4 minority (2 African Americans, 1 Asian American or Pacific Islander, 1 Hispanic American), 24 international. Average age 30. 46 applicants, 65% accepted, 11 enrolled. In 2009, 9 master's, 1 doctorate awarded. Terminal master's awarded for partial completion of doctoral program. *Degree requirements:* For master's, thesis or alternative; for doctorate, comprehensive exam, thesis/dissertation. *Entrance requirements:* For master's and doctorate, GRE General Test. Additional exam requirements/recommendations for international students: Required—TOEFL. *Application deadline:* For fall admission, 1/15 priority date for domestic students, 12/15 for international students; for spring admission, 9/1 priority date for domestic students, 9/1 for international students. Applications are processed on a rolling basis. Application fee: $55 ($65 for international students). *Financial support:* In 2009–10, 11 fellowships with full tuition reimbursements (averaging $15,000 per year), 14 research assistantships with full tuition reimbursements (averaging $15,000 per year), 21 teaching assistantships with full tuition reimbursements (averaging $14,073 per year) were awarded; career-related internships or fieldwork, Federal Work-Study, and institutionally sponsored loans also available. *Faculty research:* Geophysics, geochemistry, hydrogeology, geobiology, planetary science. Total annual research expenditures: $644,299. *Unit head:* Simon Brassell, Chair, 812-855-5581, Fax: 812-855-7899, E-mail: geochair@indiana.edu. *Application contact:* Mary Iverson, Graduate Secretary, 812-855-7214, Fax: 812-855-7899, E-mail: miverson@indiana.edu.

Massachusetts Institute of Technology, School of Science, Department of Earth, Atmospheric, and Planetary Sciences, Cambridge, MA 02139-4307. Offers atmospheric chemistry (PhD, Sc D); atmospheric science (SM, PhD, Sc D); chemical oceanography (SM, PhD, Sc D); climate physics and chemistry (SM, PhD, Sc D); earth and planetary sciences (SM); geochemistry (PhD, Sc D); geology (PhD, Sc D); geophysics (PhD, Sc D); marine geology and geophysics (SM, PhD, Sc D); physical oceanography (SM, PhD, Sc D); planetary sciences (PhD, Sc D). *Faculty:* 37 full-time (7 women). *Students:* 158 full-time (74 women); includes 14 minority (1 African American, 1 American Indian/Alaska Native, 6 Asian Americans or Pacific Islanders, 6 Hispanic Americans), 58 international. Average age 27. 205 applicants, 30% accepted, 18 enrolled. In 2009, 10 master's, 25 doctorates awarded. Terminal master's awarded for partial completion of doctoral program. *Degree requirements:* For master's, thesis; for doctorate, comprehensive exam, thesis/dissertation. *Entrance requirements:* For master's, GRE General Test; for doctorate, GRE General Test, GRE Subject Test (chemistry or physics for planetary science area). Additional exam requirements/recommendations for international students: Required—IELTS (minimum score 6); Recommended—TOEFL (minimum score 577 paper-based; 233 computer-based; 91 iBT). *Application deadline:* For fall admission, 1/5 for domestic and international students; for spring admission, 11/1 for domestic and international students. Application fee: $75. Electronic applications accepted. *Financial support:* In 2009–10, 112 students received support, including 31 fellowships with tuition reimbursements available (averaging $30,513 per year), 89 research assistantships with tuition reimbursements available (averaging $21,168 per year), 17 teaching assistantships with tuition reimbursements available (averaging $28,372 per year); Federal Work-Study, institutionally sponsored loans, scholarships/grants, health care benefits, and unspecified assistantships also available. *Faculty research:* Formation, dynamics and evolution of planetary systems, origin, evolution and interaction of the physical, characterization of past, interplay of energy and the environment, present and potential future climates and the causes and consequences of climate change, chemical, geological and biological components of the Earth system, composition, structure and dynamics of the atmospheres, oceans, surfaces and interiors of the Earth and other planets. Total annual research expenditures: $19.5 million. *Unit head:* Prof. Maria Zuber, Head, 617-253-2127, Fax: 617-253-8298, E-mail: eapsinfo@mit.edu. *Application contact:* EAPS Education Office, 617-253-3381, Fax: 617-253-8298, E-mail: eapsinfo@mit.edu.

McMaster University, School of Graduate Studies, Faculty of Science, School of Geography and Earth Sciences, Hamilton, ON L8S 4M2, Canada. Offers geochemistry (PhD); geology (M Sc, PhD); human geography (MA, PhD); physical geography (M Sc, PhD). Part-time programs available. Terminal master's awarded for partial completion of doctoral program. *Degree requirements:* For master's, thesis; for doctorate, comprehensive exam, thesis/dissertation. *Entrance requirements:* For master's, minimum B+ average. Additional exam requirements/recommendations for international students: Required—TOEFL (minimum score 550 paper-based; 213 computer-based).

Missouri University of Science and Technology, Graduate School, Department of Geological Sciences and Engineering, Rolla, MO 65409. Offers geological engineering (MS, DE, PhD); geology and geophysics (MS, PhD), including geochemistry, geology, geophysics, groundwater and environmental geology; petroleum engineering (MS, DE, PhD). Part-time programs available. *Degree requirements:* For master's, thesis optional; for doctorate, comprehensive exam, thesis/dissertation. *Entrance requirements:* For master's, GRE General Test (minimum score 600 quantitative, writing 3.5), minimum GPA of 3.0 in last 4 semesters; for doctorate, GRE General Test (minimum: Q 600, GRE WR 3.5). Additional exam requirements/recommendations for international students: Required—TOEFL. Electronic applications accepted. *Faculty research:* Digital image processing and geographic information systems, mineralogy, igneous and sedimentary petrology-geochemistry, sedimentology groundwater hydrology and contaminant transport.

Montana Tech of The University of Montana, Graduate School, Geosciences Programs, Butte, MT 59701-8997. Offers geochemistry (MS); geological engineering (MS); geology (MS); geophysical engineering (MS); hydrogeological engineering (MS); hydrogeology (MS). Part-time programs available. *Faculty:* 18 full-time (4 women), 3 part-time/adjunct (2 women). *Students:* 16 full-time (8 women), 6 part-time (4 women); includes 1 minority (African American), 1 international. 6 applicants, 67% accepted, 4 enrolled. In 2009, 7 degrees awarded. *Degree requirements:* For master's, comprehensive exam (for some programs), thesis (for some programs). *Entrance requirements:* For master's, GRE General Test, minimum GPA of 3.0. Additional exam requirements/recommendations for international students: Required—TOEFL (minimum score 525 paper-based; 195 computer-based; 71 iBT). *Application deadline:* For fall admission, 4/1 priority date for domestic students, 3/1 priority date for international students; for spring admission, 10/1 priority date for domestic students, 7/1 priority date for international students. Applications are processed on a rolling basis. Application fee: $30. Electronic applications accepted. *Expenses:* Tuition, state resident: full-time $5068; part-time $319 per credit. Tuition, nonresident: full-time $14,815; part-time $875 per credit. Tuition and fees vary according to course load and campus/location. *Financial support:* In 2009–10, 11 students received support, including 5 teaching assistantships with partial tuition reimbursements available (averaging $8,000 per year); research assistantships with partial tuition reimbursements available, career-related internships or fieldwork, tuition waivers (full and partial), and unspecified assistantships also available. Financial award application deadline: 4/1; financial award applicants required to submit FAFSA. *Faculty research:* Water resource development, seismic processing, petroleum reservoir characterization, environmental geochemistry, geologic mapping. *Unit head:* Dr. Diane Wolfgram, Department Head, 406-496-4353, Fax: 406-496-4260, E-mail: dwolfgram@mtech.edu. *Application contact:* Cindy Dunstan, Administrator, Graduate School, 406-496-4304, Fax: 406-496-4710, E-mail: cdunstan@mtech.edu.

New Mexico Institute of Mining and Technology, Graduate Studies, Department of Earth and Environmental Science, Program in Geology and Geochemistry, Socorro, NM 87801. Offers geochemistry (MS, PhD); geology (MS, PhD). *Degree requirements:* For master's, thesis optional; for doctorate, thesis/dissertation. *Entrance requirements:* For master's, GRE General Test; for doctorate, GRE General Test, GRE Subject Test. Additional exam requirements/recommendations for international students: Required—TOEFL (minimum score 540 paper-based; 207 computer-based). Electronic applications accepted. *Faculty research:* Care and karst topography, soil/water chemistry and properties, geochemistry of ore deposits.

Ohio University, Graduate College, College of Arts and Sciences, Department of Geological Sciences, Athens, OH 45701-2979. Offers environmental geochemistry (MS); environmental geology (MS); environmental/hydrology (MS); geology (MS); geology education (MS); geomorphology/surficial processes (MS); geophysics (MS); hydrogeology (MS); sedimentology (MS); structure/tectonics (MS). Part-time programs available. *Faculty:* 10 full-time (4 women), 4 part-time/adjunct (1 woman). *Students:* 18 full-time (13 women), 1 part-time (0 women), 9 international. 15 applicants, 67% accepted, 6 enrolled. In 2009, 5 master's awarded. *Degree requirements:* For master's, thesis. *Entrance requirements:* Additional exam requirements/recommendations for international students: Required—TOEFL (minimum score 550 paper-based; 80 iBT) or IELTS Academic (minimum score 6.5). *Application deadline:* For fall admission, 2/1 priority date for domestic and international students. Application fee: $50 ($55 for international students). Electronic applications accepted. *Expenses:* Tuition, state resident: full-time $7839; part-time $323 per quarter hour. Tuition, nonresident: full-time $15,831; part-time $654 per quarter hour. Required fees: $2931. *Financial support:* Research assistantships with full tuition reimbursements, teaching assistantships with full tuition reimbursements, Federal Work-Study, institutionally sponsored loans, scholarships/grants, tuition waivers (partial), and unspecified assistantships available. Financial award application deadline: 2/1. *Faculty research:* Geoscience education, tectonics, fluvial geomorphology, invertebrate paleontology, mine/hydrology. Total annual research expenditures: $649,020. *Unit head:* Dr. Gregory Nadon, Chair, 740-593-4212, Fax: 740-593-0486, E-mail: nadon@ohio.edu. *Application contact:* Dr. Douglas Green, Graduate Chair, 740-593-1843, Fax: 740-593-0486, E-mail: green@ohio.edu.

Penn State University Park, Graduate School, Intercollege Graduate Programs, State College, University Park, PA 16802-1503. Offers acoustics (M Eng, MS, PhD); bioengineering (MS, PhD); biogeochemistry (dual) (PhD); business administration (MBA); cell and developmental biology (PhD); demography (dual) (MA); ecology (MS, PhD); environmental pollution control (MEPC, MS); genetics (MS, PhD); human dimensions of natural resources and the environment (dual) (MA, MS, PhD); immunology and infectious diseases (MS); integrative biosciences (MS, PhD), including integrative biosciences; materials science and engineering (PhD); operations research (dual) (M Eng, MA, MS, PhD); physiology (MS, PhD); plant physiology (MS, PhD); quality and manufacturing management (MMM). *Students:* 371 full-time (157 women), 22 part-time (7 women). Average age 27. 1,074 applicants, 18% accepted, 130 enrolled. *Entrance requirements:* Additional exam requirements/recommendations for international students: Required—TOEFL (minimum score 550 paper-based; 213 computer-based; 80 iBT). *Application deadline:* Applications are processed on a rolling basis. Application fee: $45. Electronic applications accepted. *Financial support:* Fellowships, research assistantships, teaching assistantships available. Financial award applicants required to submit FAFSA. *Unit head:* Dr. Regina Vasilatos-Younken, Senior Associate Dean, 814-865-2516, Fax: 814-863-4627, E-mail: rxv@psu.edu. *Application contact:* Cynthia E. Nicosia, Director, Graduate Enrollment Services, 814-865-1795, Fax: 814-865-4627, E-mail: cey1@psu.edu.

Rensselaer Polytechnic Institute, Graduate School, School of Science, Department of Earth and Environmental Sciences, Troy, NY 12180-3590. Offers geochemistry (MS, PhD); geology (MS, PhD); geophysics (MS, PhD); petrology (MS, PhD). Part-time programs available. *Faculty:* 8 full-time (1 woman), 1 part-time/adjunct (0 women). *Students:* 8 full-time (5 women), 1 (woman) part-time; includes 1 minority (Asian American or Pacific Islander). Average age 24. 48 applicants, 15% accepted. In 2009, 2 master's, 3 doctorates awarded. Terminal master's awarded for partial completion of doctoral program. *Degree requirements:* For master's, comprehensive exam, thesis (for some programs); for doctorate, comprehensive exam, thesis/dissertation. *Entrance requirements:* For master's and doctorate, GRE General Test. Additional exam requirements/recommendations for international students: Required—TOEFL. *Application deadline:* For fall admission, 1/15 priority date for domestic students. Applications are processed on a rolling basis. Application fee: $75. Electronic applications accepted. *Expenses:* Tuition: Full-time $38,100. *Financial support:* In 2009–10, 7 research assistantships with full tuition reimbursements (averaging $23,000 per year), 4 teaching assistantships with full tuition reimbursements (averaging $23,000 per year) were awarded; fellowships with full tuition reimbursements, career-related internships or fieldwork, institutionally sponsored loans, and scholarships/grants also available. Financial award application deadline: 2/1; financial award applicants required to submit FAFSA. *Faculty research:* Mantel geochemistry, contaminant geochemistry, seismology, GPS geodesy, remote sensing petrology. Total annual research expenditures: $2.3 million. *Unit head:* Dr. Frank Spear, Chair, 518-276-6474, Fax: 518-276-2012, E-mail: ees@rpi.edu. *Application contact:* Dr. Steven Roecker, Professor, 518-276-6773, Fax: 518-276-2012, E-mail: ees@rpi.edu.

University of California, Los Angeles, Graduate Division, College of Letters and Science, Department of Earth and Space Sciences, Program in Geochemistry, Los Angeles, CA 90095. Offers MS, PhD. *Students:* 13 full-time (7 women); includes 2 minority (1 African American, 1 Asian American or Pacific Islander). Average age 32. 8 applicants, 25% accepted, 1 enrolled. In 2009, 2 master's, 2 doctorates awarded. Terminal master's awarded for partial completion of doctoral program. *Degree requirements:* For master's, comprehensive exams or thesis; for doctorate, thesis/dissertation, oral and written qualifying exams. *Entrance requirements:* For master's, GRE General Test, minimum GPA of 3.0, bachelor's degree in related field; for doctorate, GRE General Test, minimum undergraduate GPA of 3.0, bachelor's degree in related field. *Application deadline:* For fall admission, 1/15 for domestic and international students. Application fee: $70 ($90 for international students). Electronic applications accepted. *Financial support:* In 2009–10, 12 fellowships with full and partial tuition reimbursements, 14 research assistantships with full and partial tuition reimbursements, 11 teaching assistantships with full and partial tuition reimbursements were awarded; Federal Work-Study, institutionally sponsored loans, scholarships/grants, health care benefits, tuition waivers (full and partial), and unspecified assistantships also available. Financial award application deadline: 3/1; financial award applicants required to submit FAFSA. *Unit head:* Dr. Craig Manning, 310-825-1475. *Application contact:* Departmental Office, 888-377-8252, E-mail: holbrook@ess.ucla.edu.

University of Hawaii at Manoa, Graduate Division, School of Ocean and Earth Science and Technology, Department of Geology and Geophysics, Honolulu, HI 96822. Offers high-pressure geophysics and geochemistry (MS, PhD); hydrogeology and engineering geology (MS, PhD); marine geology and geophysics (MS, PhD); planetary geosciences and remote sensing (MS, PhD); seismology and solid-earth geophysics (MS, PhD); volcanology, petrology, and geochemistry (MS, PhD). Part-time programs available. *Faculty:* 73 full-time (16 women), 15 part-time/adjunct (3 women). *Students:* 42 full-time (20 women), 8 part-time (5 women); includes 7 minority (1 African American, 4 Asian Americans or Pacific Islanders, 2 Hispanic Americans), 6 international. Average age 29. 56 applicants, 25% accepted, 6 enrolled. In 2009, 4 master's, 7 doctorates awarded. Terminal master's awarded for partial completion of doctoral program. *Degree requirements:* For master's, thesis optional; for doctorate, comprehensive exam, thesis/dissertation. *Entrance requirements:* For master's and doctorate, GRE General Test, minimum GPA of 3.0. Additional exam requirements/recommendations for international students: Required—TOEFL (minimum score 580 paper-based; 237 computer-based; 92 iBT), IELTS (minimum score 5). *Application deadline:* For fall admission, 1/15 for domestic students, 1/1 for international students; for spring admission, 9/1 for domestic students, 8/15 for international students. Application fee: $60. *Expenses:* Tuition, state resident: full-time $8900; part-time $372 per credit. Tuition, nonresident: full-time $21,400; part-time $898 per credit. Required fees: $207 per semester. *Financial support:* In 2009–10, 1 student received support, including 4 fellowships (averaging $9,338 per year), 31 research assistantships (averaging $23,877 per year), 5 teaching assistantships (averaging $20,466 per year). Total annual research expenditures: $3.8 million. *Application contact:* Dr. Charles Fletcher, Chair, 808-956-7640, Fax: 808-956-5512, E-mail: gg-grad-chair@hawaii.edu.

University of Nevada, Reno, Graduate School, College of Science, Mackay School of Earth Sciences and Engineering, Department of Geological Sciences, Program in Geochemistry, Reno, NV 89557. Offers MS, PhD. Terminal master's awarded for partial completion of doctoral program. *Degree requirements:* For master's, thesis optional; for doctorate, thesis/dissertation. *Entrance requirements:* For master's, GRE General Test, minimum GPA of 2.75; for doctorate, GRE General Test, minimum GPA of 3.0. Additional exam requirements/recommendations for international students: Required—TOEFL (minimum score 500 paper-based; 173 computer-based; 61 iBT), IELTS (minimum score 6). Electronic applications accepted.

University of New Hampshire, Graduate School, College of Engineering and Physical Sciences, Department of Earth Sciences, Durham, NH 03824. Offers earth sciences (MS), including geochemical systems, geology, ocean mapping, oceanography; hydrology (MS). *Faculty:* 17 full-time (5 women). *Students:* 7 full-time (5 women), 15 part-time (7 women), 1 international. Average age 27. 27 applicants, 56% accepted, 5 enrolled. In 2009, 18 master's awarded. *Degree requirements:* For master's, thesis. *Entrance requirements:* For master's, GRE General Test. Additional exam requirements/recommendations for international students: Required—TOEFL (minimum score 550 paper-based; 213 computer-based; 80 iBT). *Application deadline:* For fall admission, 4/1 priority date for domestic students, 4/1 for international students; for spring admission, 12/1 for domestic students. Applications are processed on a rolling basis. Application fee: $65. Electronic applications accepted. *Expenses:* Tuition, state resident: full-time $10,380; part-time $577 per credit hour. Tuition, nonresident: full-time $24,350; part-time $1002 per credit hour. Required fees: $1550; $387.50 per semester. Tuition and fees vary according to course load and program. *Financial support:* In 2009–10, 17 students received support, including 1 fellowship, 6 research assistantships, 8 teaching assistantships; career-related internships or fieldwork, Federal Work-Study, scholarships/grants, and tuition waivers (full and partial) also available. Support available to part-time students. Financial award application deadline: 2/15. *Unit head:* Dr. Will Clyde, Chairperson, 603-862-1718, E-mail: earth.sciences@unh.edu. *Application contact:* Sue Clark, Administrative Assistant, 603-862-1718, E-mail: earth.sciences@unh.edu.

The University of Texas at Dallas, School of Natural Sciences and Mathematics, Program in Geosciences, Richardson, TX 75080. Offers geochemistry (MS, PhD); geophysics (MS); geospatial information sciences (MS, PhD); hydrogeology (MS, PhD); sedimentary, stratigraphy, paleontology (PhD); stratigraphy, paleontology (MS); structural geology and tectonics (MS, PhD). Part-time and evening/weekend programs available. *Faculty:* 9 full-time (1 woman). *Students:* 30 full-time (10 women), 11 part-time (4 women); includes 7 minority (1 African American, 4 Asian Americans or Pacific Islanders, 2 Hispanic Americans), 21 international. Average age 32. 42 applicants, 43% accepted, 14 enrolled. In 2009, 4 master's, 4 doctorates awarded. *Degree requirements:* For master's, thesis optional; for doctorate, thesis/dissertation. *Entrance requirements:* For master's and doctorate, GRE General Test, minimum GPA of 3.0 in upper-level course work in field. Additional exam requirements/recommendations for international students: Required—TOEFL (minimum score 550 paper-based; 213 computer-based). *Application deadline:* For fall admission, 7/15 for domestic students, 5/1 priority date for international students; for spring admission, 11/15 for domestic students, 9/1 priority date for international students. Applications are processed on a rolling basis. Application fee: $50 ($100 for international students). Electronic applications accepted. *Expenses:* Tuition, state resident: full-time $11,068; part-time $461 per credit hour. Tuition, nonresident: full-time $21,178; part-time $882 per credit hour. Tuition and fees vary according to course load. *Financial support:* In 2009–10, 10 research assistantships with full tuition reimbursements (averaging $13,500 per year), 11 teaching assistantships with full tuition reimbursements (averaging $13,500 per year) were awarded; fellowships, career-related internships or fieldwork, Federal Work-Study, institutionally sponsored loans, scholarships/grants, and unspecified assistantships also available. Support available to part-time students. Financial award application deadline: 4/30; financial award applicants required to submit FAFSA. *Faculty research:* Hydrology, organic geochemistry, tectonic structures, seismic characteristics, digital geologic mapping. *Unit head:* Dr. John Oldow, Department Head, 972-883-2401, Fax: 972-883-2537, E-mail: geosciences@utdallas.edu. *Application contact:* Dr. Robert J. Stern, Graduate Advisor, 972-883-2442, Fax: 972-883-2537, E-mail: rjstern@utdallas.edu.

University of Wisconsin–Milwaukee, Graduate School, College of Letters and Sciences, Department of Chemistry, Milwaukee, WI 53201-0413. Offers biogeochemistry (PhD); chemistry (MS, PhD). *Faculty:* 22 full-time (3 women). *Students:* 68 full-time (22 women), 8 part-time (5 women); includes 9 minority (3 African Americans, 6 Asian Americans or Pacific Islanders), 27 international. Average age 30. 55 applicants, 45% accepted, 17 enrolled. In 2009, 4 master's, 16 doctorates awarded. *Degree requirements:* For master's, thesis or alternative; for doctorate, thesis/dissertation. *Entrance requirements:* For doctorate, GRE General Test. Additional exam

University of Wisconsin–Milwaukee (continued)
requirements/recommendations for international students: Required—TOEFL (minimum score 600 paper-based; 79 iBT), IELTS (minimum score 6.5). *Application deadline:* For fall admission, 1/1 priority date for domestic students; for spring admission, 9/1 for domestic students. Applications are processed on a rolling basis. Application fee: $45 ($75 for international students). *Expenses:* Tuition, state resident: full-time $8800. Tuition, nonresident: full-time $20,760. Tuition and fees vary according to program and reciprocity agreements. *Financial support:* In 2009–10, 22 research assistantships, 48 teaching assistantships were awarded; career-related internships or fieldwork and unspecified assistantships also available. Support available to part-time students. Financial award application deadline: 4/15. *Faculty research:* Analytical chemistry, biochemistry, inorganic chemistry, organic chemistry, physical chemistry. Total annual research expenditures: $2.4 million. *Unit head:* Peter Geissinger, Representative, 414-229-5230, Fax: 414-229-5530, E-mail: geissing@uwm.edu. *Application contact:* Joseph Aldstadt, General Information Contact, 414-229-5605, Fax: 414-229-6967, E-mail: aldstadt@uwm.edu.

Woods Hole Oceanographic Institution, MIT/WHOI Joint Program in Oceanography/Applied Ocean Science and Engineering, Woods Hole, MA 02543-1541. Offers applied ocean sciences (PhD); biological oceanography (PhD, Sc D); chemical oceanography (PhD, Sc D); civil and environmental and oceanographic engineering (PhD); electrical and oceanographic engineering (PhD); geochemistry (PhD); geophysics (PhD); marine biology (PhD); marine geochemistry (PhD, Sc D); marine geology (PhD, Sc D); marine geophysics (PhD); mechanical and oceanographic engineering (PhD); ocean engineering (PhD); oceanographic engineering (M Eng, MS, PhD, Sc D, Eng); paleoceanography (PhD); physical oceanography (PhD, Sc D). Terminal master's awarded for partial completion of doctoral program. *Degree requirements:* For master's and Eng, thesis (for some programs); for doctorate, thesis/dissertation. *Entrance requirements:* For master's, GRE General Test; for doctorate, GRE General Test, GRE Subject Test. Additional exam requirements/recommendations for international students: Required—TOEFL. Electronic applications accepted.

Yale University, Graduate School of Arts and Sciences, Department of Geology and Geophysics, New Haven, CT 06520. Offers biogeochemistry (PhD); climate dynamics (PhD); geochemistry (PhD); geophysics (PhD); meteorology (PhD); oceanography (PhD); paleontology (PhD); paleooceanography (PhD); petrology (PhD); tectonics (PhD). *Degree requirements:* For doctorate, thesis/dissertation. *Entrance requirements:* For doctorate, GRE General Test. Additional exam requirements/recommendations for international students: Required—TOEFL.

Geodetic Sciences

Columbia University, Graduate School of Arts and Sciences, Division of Natural Sciences, Department of Earth and Environmental Sciences, New York, NY 10027. Offers geochemistry (M Phil, MA, PhD); geodetic sciences (M Phil, MA, PhD); geophysics (M Phil, MA, PhD); oceanography (M Phil, MA, PhD). *Degree requirements:* For master's, thesis or alternative, fieldwork, written exam; for doctorate, one foreign language, thesis/dissertation. *Entrance requirements:* For master's and doctorate, GRE General Test, GRE Subject Test, major in natural or physical science. Additional exam requirements/recommendations for international students: Required—TOEFL. *Faculty research:* Structural geology and stratigraphy, petrology, paleontology, rare gas, isotope and aqueous geochemistry.

George Mason University, College of Science, Fairfax, VA 22030. Offers biodefense (MS, PhD); bioinformatics and computational biology (MS, PhD, Certificate); biology (MS, PhD), including bioinformatics (MS), ecology, systematics and evolution (MS), interpretive biology (MS), molecular and cellular biology (MS), molecular and microbiology (PhD), organismal biology (MS); chemistry and biochemistry (MS), including chemistry; climate dynamics (PhD); computational and data sciences (MS, PhD, Certificate); computational social science (PhD); computational techniques and applications (Certificate); earth systems and geoinformation sciences (MS, PhD, Certificate); environmental science and policy (MS, PhD); geography (MS), including geographic and cartographic sciences; mathematical sciences (MS, PhD), including mathematics; nanotechnology and nanoscience (Certificate); neuroscience (PhD); physical sciences (PhD); physics and astronomy (MS), including applied and engineering physics; remote sensing and earth image processing (Certificate). Part-time and evening/weekend programs available. *Degree requirements:* For doctorate, comprehensive exam, thesis/dissertation. *Entrance requirements:* For master's and doctorate, GRE General Test, minimum GPA of 3.0 in last 60 hours. Additional exam requirements/recommendations for international students: Required—TOEFL. Electronic applications accepted. *Expenses:* Tuition, state resident: full-time $7568; part-time $315.33 per credit hour. Tuition, nonresident: full-time $21,704; part-time $904.33 per credit hour. Required fees: $2184; $91 per credit hour. *Faculty research:* Space sciences and astrophysics, fluid dynamics, materials modeling and simulation, bioinformatics, global changes and statistics.

The Ohio State University, Graduate School, College of Engineering, Program in Geodetic Science and Surveying, Columbus, OH 43210. Offers MS, PhD. *Faculty:* 12. *Students:* 15 full-time (2 women), 1 (woman) part-time; includes 1 minority (African American), 12 international. Average age 28. In 2009, 1 doctorate awarded. *Degree requirements:* For master's, thesis optional; for doctorate, thesis/dissertation. *Entrance requirements:* For master's, GRE General Test (if overall GPA less than 3.0); for doctorate, GRE General Test (if GPA is below 3.0 overall). Additional exam requirements/recommendations for international students: Recommended—TOEFL (minimum score 600 paper-based; 250 computer-based). *Application deadline:* For fall admission, 8/15 priority date for domestic students, 7/1 priority date for international students; for winter admission, 12/1 priority date for domestic students, 11/1 priority date for international students; for spring admission, 3/1 priority date for domestic students, 2/1 priority date for international students. Applications are processed on a rolling basis. Application fee: $40 ($50 for international students). Electronic applications accepted. *Expenses:* Tuition, state resident: full-time $10,683. Tuition, nonresident: full-time $25,923. Tuition and fees vary according to course load and program. *Financial support:* Fellowships, research assistantships, teaching assistantships, Federal Work-Study and institutionally sponsored loans available. Support available to part-time students. *Faculty research:* Photogrammetry, cartography, geodesy, land information systems. *Unit head:* Alan S. Saalfeld, Graduate Studies Committee Chair, 614-292-8787, Fax: 614-292-3780, E-mail: soalfeld.1@osu.edu. *Application contact:* 614-292-944, Fax: 614-292-3895, E-mail: domestic.grad@osu.edu.

The Ohio State University, Graduate School, College of Mathematical and Physical Sciences, Program in Geodetic Science, Columbus, OH 43210. Offers MS. *Students:* 19 full-time (1 woman), 16 part-time (5 women); includes 1 minority (African American), 30 international. Average age 32. In 2009, 5 master's awarded. *Application deadline:* Applications are processed on a rolling basis. Application fee: $40 ($50 for international students). Electronic applications accepted. *Expenses:* Tuition, state resident: full-time $10,683. Tuition, nonresident: full-time $25,923. Tuition and fees vary according to course load and program.

Université Laval, Faculty of Forestry and Geomatics, Department of Geomatics Sciences, Programs in Geomatics Sciences, Québec, QC G1K 7P4, Canada. Offers M Sc, PhD. Terminal master's awarded for partial completion of doctoral program. *Degree requirements:* For master's, thesis (for some programs); for doctorate, comprehensive exam, thesis/dissertation. *Entrance requirements:* For master's and doctorate, knowledge of French and English. Electronic applications accepted.

University of New Brunswick Fredericton, School of Graduate Studies, Faculty of Engineering, Department of Geodesy and Geomatics, Fredericton, NB E3B 5A3, Canada. Offers land information management (Diploma); mapping, charting and geodesy (Diploma); surveying engineering (M Eng, M Sc E, PhD). *Faculty:* 10 full-time (2 women). *Students:* 37 full-time (7 women), 4 part-time (1 woman). In 2009, 10 master's, 3 doctorates awarded. *Degree requirements:* For master's, thesis; for doctorate, comprehensive exam, thesis/dissertation, qualifying exam. *Entrance requirements:* For master's and doctorate, minimum GPA of 3.0. Additional exam requirements/recommendations for international students: Required—TOEFL (minimum score 580 paper-based), TWE (minimum score 4). *Application deadline:* For fall admission, 3/1 priority date for domestic students. Applications are processed on a rolling basis. Application fee: $50 Canadian dollars. Tuition and fees charges are reported in Canadian dollars. *Expenses:* Tuition, area resident: Full-time $5562 Canadian dollars; part-time $2781 Canadian dollars per year. Required fees: $49.75 Canadian dollars per term. *Financial support:* In 2009–10, 2 fellowships, 46 research assistantships, 23 teaching assistantships were awarded. *Faculty research:* Remote sensing, ocean mapping, land administration. *Unit head:* Dr. Sue Nichols, Director of Graduate Studies, 506-453-5141, Fax: 506-453-4943, E-mail: nichols@unb.ca. *Application contact:* Sylvia Whitaker, Graduate Secretary, 506-458-7085, Fax: 506-453-4943, E-mail: swhitake@unb.ca.

Geology

Acadia University, Faculty of Pure and Applied Science, Department of Earth and Environmental Science, Wolfville, NS B4P 2R6, Canada. Offers M Sc. *Faculty:* 5 full-time (1 woman). *Students:* 7 full-time (0 women), 3 part-time (2 women). Average age 24. 6 applicants, 83% accepted, 3 enrolled. In 2009, 2 master's awarded. *Degree requirements:* For master's, thesis. *Entrance requirements:* For master's, BSC (honours) in geology or equivalent. Additional exam requirements/recommendations for international students: Required—TOEFL (minimum score 580 paper-based; 237 computer-based; 93 iBT), IELTS (minimum score 6.5). *Application deadline:* For fall admission, 2/1 priority date for domestic and international students. Applications are processed on a rolling basis. Application fee: $50. *Financial support:* Research assistantships, teaching assistantships, scholarships/grants and unspecified assistantships available. Financial award application deadline: 2/1. *Faculty research:* Igneous, metamorphic, and Quaternary geology; stratigraphy; remote sensing; tectonics, carbonate sedimentology. *Unit head:* Dr. Robert Raeside, Head, 902-585-1323, Fax: 902-585-1816, E-mail: rob.raeside@acadiau.ca. *Application contact:* Dr. Robert Raeside, Head, 902-585-1323, Fax: 902-585-1816, E-mail: rob.raeside@acadiau.ca.

American University of Beirut, Graduate Programs, Faculty of Arts and Sciences, Beirut, Lebanon. Offers anthropology (MA); Arabic language and literature (MA); archaeology (MA); biology (MS); chemistry (MS); computer science (MS); economics (MA); education (MA); English language (MA); English literature (MA); environmental policy planning (MSES); financial economics (MAFE); geology (MS); history (MA); mathematics (MA, MS); Middle Eastern studies (MA); philosophy (MA); physics (MS); political studies (MA); psychology (MA); public administration (MA); sociology (MA); statistics (MA, MS). Part-time programs available. *Degree requirements:* For master's, one foreign language, comprehensive exam, thesis (for some programs). *Entrance requirements:* For master's, GRE, letter of recommendation. Additional exam requirements/recommendations for international students: Required—TOEFL (minimum score 600 paper-based; 250 computer-based; 100 iBT), IELTS (minimum score 7.5). *Faculty research:* String theory and supergravity; computer graphics; algebra and number theory; popular Arabic literature; marine and freshwater biology; integrating science, math and technology.

Arizona State University, Graduate College, College of Liberal Arts and Sciences, Division of Natural Sciences, School of Earth and Space Exploration, Tempe, AZ 85287. Offers astrophysics (MS, PhD); geological sciences (MS, PhD). *Degree requirements:* For master's, thesis or alternative; for doctorate, thesis/dissertation. *Entrance requirements:* For master's and doctorate, GRE.

Auburn University, Graduate School, College of Sciences and Mathematics, Department of Geology and Geography, Auburn University, AL 36849. Offers geography (MS); geology (MS). Part-time programs available. *Faculty:* 14 full-time (2 women), 1 part-time/adjunct (0 women). *Students:* 13 full-time (3 women), 8 part-time (3 women), 4 international. Average age 28. 25 applicants, 56% accepted, 7 enrolled. In 2009, 5 master's awarded. *Degree requirements:* For master's, computer language or geographic information systems, field camp. *Entrance requirements:* For master's, GRE General Test. *Application deadline:* For fall admission, 7/7 for domestic students; for spring admission, 11/24 for domestic students. Applications are processed on a rolling basis. Application fee: $50 ($60 for international students). Electronic applications accepted. *Expenses:* Tuition, state resident: full-time $6240. Tuition, nonresident: full-time $18,720. International tuition: $18,938 full-time. Required fees: $492. Tuition and fees vary according to course load, program and reciprocity agreements. *Financial support:* Research assistantships, teaching assistantships, Federal Work-Study available. Support available to part-time students. Financial award application deadline: 3/15; financial award applicants required to submit FAFSA. *Faculty research:* Empirical magma dynamics and melt migration, ore mineralogy, role of terrestrial plant biomass in deposition, metamorphic petrology and isotope geochemistry, reef development, crinoid topology. *Unit head:* Dr. Charles E. Savrda,

Chair, 334-844-4282. *Application contact:* Dr. George Flowers, Dean of the Graduate School, 334-844-2125.

See Display on this page.

Ball State University, Graduate School, College of Sciences and Humanities, Department of Geology, Muncie, IN 47306-1099. Offers MA, MS. *Degree requirements:* For master's, thesis (for some programs). *Entrance requirements:* For master's, GRE General Test. *Faculty research:* Environmental geology, geophysics, stratigraphy.

Baylor University, Graduate School, College of Arts and Sciences, Department of Geology, Waco, TX 76798. Offers earth science (MA); geology (MS, PhD). *Faculty:* 12 full-time (1 woman). *Students:* 16 full-time (7 women), 9 part-time (3 women); includes 1 minority (American Indian/Alaska Native), 4 international. In 2009, 6 master's, 1 doctorate awarded. *Degree requirements:* For master's, thesis; for doctorate, thesis/dissertation. *Entrance requirements:* For master's and doctorate, GRE General Test. *Application deadline:* For fall admission, 3/15 priority date for domestic students. Applications are processed on a rolling basis. Application fee: $25. *Financial support:* In 2009–10, 18 teaching assistantships were awarded; Federal Work-Study and institutionally sponsored loans also available. *Faculty research:* Petroleum geology, geophysics, engineering geology, hydrogeology. *Unit head:* Dr. Steve Dworkin, Graduate Program Director, 254-710-2186, Fax: 254-710-2673, E-mail: steve_dworkin@baylor.edu. *Application contact:* Paulette Penney, Administrative Assistant, 254-710-2361, Fax: 254-710-3870, E-mail: paulette_penney@baylor.edu.

Boise State University, Graduate College, College of Arts and Sciences, Department of Geosciences, Program in Geology, Boise, ID 83725-0399. Offers MS, PhD. Part-time programs available. *Degree requirements:* For master's, thesis. *Entrance requirements:* For master's, GRE General Test, BS in related field, minimum GPA of 3.0. Electronic applications accepted. *Expenses:* Tuition, state resident: full-time $3106; part-time $209 per credit. Tuition, nonresident: part-time $284 per credit.

Boston College, Graduate School of Arts and Sciences, Department of Geology and Geophysics, Chestnut Hill, MA 02467-3800. Offers MS, MBA/MS. *Students:* 25 full-time (10 women), 1 (woman) part-time; includes 2 minority (1 Asian American or Pacific Islander, 1 Hispanic American), 2 international. 22 applicants, 82% accepted, 8 enrolled. In 2009, 6 master's awarded. *Degree requirements:* For master's, thesis. *Entrance requirements:* For master's, GRE General Test, GRE Subject Test. Additional exam requirements/recommendations for international students: Required—TOEFL (minimum score 600 paper-based; 250 computer-based; 100 iBT). *Application deadline:* For fall admission, 2/1 priority date for domestic students, 2/1 for international students. Application fee: $70. Electronic applications accepted. *Financial support:* Research assistantships with full tuition reimbursements, teaching assistantships with full tuition reimbursements, Federal Work-Study available. Support available to part-time students. Financial award application deadline: 3/1; financial award applicants required to submit FAFSA. *Faculty research:* Coastal and marine geology, experimental sedimentology, geomagnetism, igneous petrology, paleontology. *Unit head:* Dr. Gail Kineke, Chairperson, 617-552-3640. *Application contact:* Dr. John Ebel, Graduate Program Director, 617-552-3640, E-mail: john.ebel@bc.edu.

Bowling Green State University, Graduate College, College of Arts and Sciences, Department of Geology, Bowling Green, OH 43403. Offers MS. Part-time programs available. *Degree requirements:* For master's, thesis. *Entrance requirements:* For master's, GRE General Test. Additional exam requirements/recommendations for international students: Required—TOEFL. Electronic applications accepted. *Faculty research:* Remote sensing, environmental geology, geological information systems, structural geology, geochemistry.

Brigham Young University, Graduate Studies, College of Physical and Mathematical Sciences, Department of Geological Sciences, Provo, UT 84602-1001. Offers MS. *Faculty:* 16 full-time (2 women), 2 part-time/adjunct (0 women). *Students:* 25 full-time (7 women); includes 2 minority (1 American Indian/Alaska Native, 1 Asian American or Pacific Islander). Average age 23. 15 applicants, 87% accepted, 7 enrolled. In 2009, 5 master's awarded. *Degree requirements:* For master's, thesis. *Entrance requirements:* For master's, GRE General Test, minimum GPA of 3.0 in last 60 hours of course work. Additional exam requirements/recommendations for international students: Required—TOEFL. *Application deadline:* For fall admission, 2/1 priority date for domestic students, 2/1 for international students; for winter admission, 9/15 priority date for domestic students, 9/15 for international students. Applications are processed on a rolling basis. Application fee: $50. *Expenses:* Tuition: Full-time $5580; part-time $301 per credit hour. Tuition and fees vary according to student's religious affiliation. *Financial support:* In 2009–10, 25 students received support, including 2 research assistantships with partial tuition reimbursements available (averaging $11,534 per year), 17 teaching assistantships with full and partial tuition reimbursements available (averaging $11,743 per year); career-related internships or fieldwork, institutionally sponsored loans, scholarships/grants, and tuition waivers (partial) also available. Financial award application deadline: 2/1. *Faculty research:* Regional tectonics, hydrogeochemistry, crystal chemistry and crystallography, stratigraphy, environmental geophysics, petrology. Total annual research expenditures: $112,000. *Unit head:* Dr. Scott Ritter, Chairman, 801-422-4239, Fax: 801-422-0267, E-mail: scott_ritter@byu.edu. *Application contact:* Dr. Michael J. Dorais, Graduate Coordinator, 801-422-1347, Fax: 801-422-0267, E-mail: michael_dorais@byu.edu.

Brooklyn College of the City University of New York, Division of Graduate Studies, Department of Geology, Brooklyn, NY 11210-2889. Offers MA, PhD. The department offers courses at Brooklyn College that are creditable toward the CUNY doctoral degree (with permission of the executive officer of the doctoral program). Evening/weekend programs available. Terminal master's awarded for partial completion of doctoral program. *Degree requirements:* For master's, comprehensive exam, thesis or alternative, qualifying exams. *Entrance requirements:* For master's, bachelor's degree in geology or equivalent, fieldwork, 2 letters of recommendation; for doctorate, GRE. Additional exam requirements/recommendations for international students: Required—TOEFL. Electronic applications accepted. *Faculty research:* Geochemistry, petrology, tectonophysics, hydrogeology, sedimentary geology, environmental geology.

California Institute of Technology, Division of Geological and Planetary Sciences, Pasadena, CA 91125-0001. Offers geobiology (MS, PhD); geochemistry (MS, PhD); geology (MS, PhD); geophysics (MS, PhD); planetary science (MS, PhD). *Faculty:* 38 full-time (6 women). *Students:* 75 full-time (38 women); includes 21 minority (1 African American, 18 Asian Americans or Pacific Islanders, 2 Hispanic Americans). Average age 26. 102 applicants, 28% accepted, 9 enrolled. In 2009, 13 master's, 13 doctorates awarded. *Degree requirements:* For doctorate, thesis/dissertation. *Entrance requirements:* For doctorate, GRE General Test. Additional exam requirements/recommendations for international students: Required—TOEFL; Recommended—IELTS, TWE. *Application deadline:* For fall admission, 1/1 for domestic and international students. Application fee: $80. Electronic applications accepted. *Financial support:* In 2009–10, 75 students received support, including 15 fellowships with full tuition reimbursements available (averaging $27,000 per year), 60 research assistantships with full tuition reimbursements available (averaging $27,000 per year); teaching assistantships with full tuition reimbursements available, institutionally sponsored loans, scholarships/grants, health care benefits, and unspecified assistantships also available. Financial award applicants required to submit FAFSA. *Faculty research:* Astronomy, evolution of anaerobic respiratory processes, structural geology and tectonics, theoretical and numerical seismology, global biogeochemical cycles. *Unit head:* Dr. Kenneth A. Farley, Chairman, 626-395-6111, Fax: 626-795-6028, E-mail: dianb@gps.caltech.edu. *Application contact:* Dr. Robert W. Clayton, Academic Officer, 626-395-6909, Fax: 626-795-6028, E-mail: dianb@gps.caltech.edu.

Geology

California State University, Bakersfield, Division of Graduate Studies, School of Natural Sciences and Mathematics, Program in Geology, Bakersfield, CA 93311. Offers geology (MS); hydrogeology (MS); petroleum geology (MS). Part-time and evening/weekend programs available. *Degree requirements:* For master's, thesis. *Entrance requirements:* For master's, GRE General Test, BS in geology.

California State University, Chico, Graduate School, College of Natural Sciences, Department of Geological and Environmental Sciences, Chico, CA 95929-0722. Offers environmental science (MS); geosciences (MS), including hydrology/hydrogeology. Part-time programs available. *Students:* 19 full-time (6 women), 8 part-time (5 women); includes 1 Asian American or Pacific Islander, 2 international. Average age 30. 20 applicants, 95% accepted, 10 enrolled. In 2009, 3 master's awarded. *Entrance requirements:* For master's, GRE General Test. Additional exam requirements/recommendations for international students: Required—TOEFL (minimum score 550 paper-based; 213 computer-based; 80 iBT), IELTS (minimum score 6.5). *Application deadline:* For fall admission, 3/1 priority date for domestic students, 3/1 for international students; for spring admission, 9/15 priority date for domestic students, 9/15 for international students. Applications are processed on a rolling basis. Application fee: $55. Electronic applications accepted. *Financial support:* Fellowships, teaching assistantships available. *Unit head:* Dr. Karolyn Johnston, Chair, 530-898-5262. *Application contact:* Dr. Karolyn Johnston, Chair, 530-898-5262.

California State University, East Bay, Academic Programs and Graduate Studies, College of Science, Department of Earth and Environmental Sciences, Hayward, CA 94542-3000. Offers geology (MS). Evening/weekend programs available. *Faculty:* 3 full-time (0 women), 2 part-time/adjunct (1 woman). *Students:* 6 full-time (3 women), 8 part-time (3 women); includes 1 minority (African American), 1 international. Average age 32. 12 applicants, 100% accepted, 10 enrolled. *Degree requirements:* For master's, thesis. *Entrance requirements:* For master's, GRE, minimum GPA of 2.75 in field, 2.5 overall. Additional exam requirements/recommendations for international students: Required—TOEFL (minimum score 550 paper-based; 213 computer-based). *Application deadline:* For fall admission, 6/30 for domestic and international students. Application fee: $55. Electronic applications accepted. *Financial support:* Career-related internships or fieldwork, Federal Work-Study, and institutionally sponsored loans available. Support available to part-time students. Financial award application deadline: 3/1; financial award applicants required to submit FAFSA. *Unit head:* Dr. Jeffrey Seitz, Chair/Graduate Coordinator, 510-885-3486, Fax: 510-885-2526, E-mail: jeffrey.seitz@csueastbay.edu. *Application contact:* Donna Wiley, Interim Associate Director, 510-885-2928, Fax: 510-885-4777, E-mail: donna.wiley@csueastbay.edu.

California State University, Fresno, Division of Graduate Studies, College of Science and Mathematics, Department of Earth and Environmental Sciences, Fresno, CA 93740-8027. Offers geology (MS). Part-time programs available. *Degree requirements:* For master's, thesis. *Entrance requirements:* For master's, GRE General Test, undergraduate geology degree, minimum GPA of 2.7. Additional exam requirements/recommendations for international students: Required—TOEFL. Electronic applications accepted. *Faculty research:* Water drainage, pollution, cartography, creek restoration, nitrate contamination.

California State University, Fullerton, Graduate Studies, College of Natural Science and Mathematics, Department of Geological Sciences, Fullerton, CA 92834-9480. Offers MS. Part-time programs available. *Students:* 7 full-time (6 women), 13 part-time (8 women); includes 3 minority (1 Asian American or Pacific Islander, 2 Hispanic Americans), 1 international. Average age 30. 10 applicants, 50% accepted, 4 enrolled. In 2009, 1 master's awarded. *Degree requirements:* For master's, thesis. *Entrance requirements:* For master's, bachelor's degree in geology, minimum GPA of 3.0 in geology courses. Application fee: $55. *Expenses:* Tuition, nonresident: full-time $11,160; part-time $373 per credit. Required fees: $1440 per term. Tuition and fees vary according to course load, degree level and program. *Financial support:* Research assistantships, teaching assistantships, career-related internships or fieldwork, Federal Work-Study, institutionally sponsored loans, and scholarships/grants available. Support available to part-time students. Financial award application deadline: 3/1; financial award applicants required to submit FAFSA. *Unit head:* Dr. David Bowman, Chair, 657-278-3882. *Application contact:* Admissions/Applications, 657-278-2371.

California State University, Long Beach, Graduate Studies, College of Natural Sciences and Mathematics, Department of Geological Sciences, Long Beach, CA 90840. Offers geology (MS); geophysics (MS). Part-time programs available. *Faculty:* 6 full-time (0 women). *Students:* 9 full-time (4 women), 20 part-time (11 women); includes 7 minority (1 African American, 2 Asian Americans or Pacific Islanders, 4 Hispanic Americans). Average age 35. 21 applicants, 52% accepted, 7 enrolled. *Degree requirements:* For master's, thesis. *Entrance requirements:* For master's, GRE General Test. *Application deadline:* For fall admission, 7/1 for domestic students. Applications are processed on a rolling basis. Application fee: $55. Electronic applications accepted. *Expenses:* Required fees: $1802 per semester. Part-time tuition and fees vary according to course load. *Financial support:* Research assistantships, teaching assistantships, Federal Work-Study, institutionally sponsored loans, and scholarships/grants available. Financial award application deadline: 3/2. *Faculty research:* Paleontology, geophysics, structural geology, organic geochemistry, sedimentary geology. *Unit head:* Robert D. Francis, Chair, 562-985-4929, Fax: 562-985-8638, E-mail: rfrancis@csulb.edu. *Application contact:* Gregory Holk, Graduate Advisor, 562-985-5006, Fax: 562-985-8638, E-mail: gholk@csulb.edu.

California State University, Los Angeles, Graduate Studies, College of Natural and Social Sciences, Department of Geological Sciences, Los Angeles, CA 90032-8530. Offers MS. Part-time and evening/weekend programs available. *Faculty:* 3 full-time (1 woman). *Students:* 19 full-time (14 women), 18 part-time (7 women); includes 17 minority (1 African American, 11 Asian Americans or Pacific Islanders, 5 Hispanic Americans), 2 international. Average age 30. 19 applicants, 100% accepted, 11 enrolled. In 2009, 4 master's awarded. *Degree requirements:* For master's, comprehensive exam or thesis. *Entrance requirements:* Additional exam requirements/recommendations for international students: Required—TOEFL (minimum score 500 paper-based; 173 computer-based). *Application deadline:* For fall admission, 5/1 for domestic and international students. Applications are processed on a rolling basis. Application fee: $55. Electronic applications accepted. *Financial support:* Federal Work-Study available. Support available to part-time students. Financial award application deadline: 3/1. *Unit head:* Dr. Kim Bishop, Chair, 323-343-2435, Fax: 323-343-5609, E-mail: kbishop@calstatela.edu. *Application contact:* Dr. Cheryl L. Ney, Associate Vice President for Academic Affairs and Dean of Graduate Studies, 323-343-3820, Fax: 323-343-5653, E-mail: cney@cslanet.calstatela.edu.

California State University, Northridge, Graduate Studies, College of Science and Mathematics, Department of Geological Sciences, Northridge, CA 91330. Offers geology (MS). Part-time and evening/weekend programs available. *Faculty:* 11 full-time (4 women), 4 part-time/adjunct (2 women). *Students:* 6 full-time (4 women), 12 part-time (3 women); includes 2 Hispanic Americans, 2 international. Average age 33. 20 applicants, 80% accepted, 7 enrolled. In 2009, 2 master's awarded. *Degree requirements:* For master's, thesis. *Entrance requirements:* For master's, GRE General Test, minimum GPA of 2.75. Additional exam requirements/recommendations for international students: Required—TOEFL. *Application deadline:* For fall admission, 11/30 for domestic students. Application fee: $55. *Financial support:* Research assistantships, teaching assistantships, Federal Work-Study and scholarships/grants available. Financial award application deadline: 3/1. *Faculty research:* Petrology of California Miocene volcanics, sedimentology of California Miocene formations, Eocene gastropods, structure of White/Inyo Mountains, seismology of Californian and Mexican earthquakes. *Unit head:* Dr. Vicki Pedone, Chair, 818-677-3541, E-mail: vicki.pedone@csun.edu. *Application contact:* Dr. Vicki Pedone, Chair, 818-677-3541, E-mail: vicki.pedone@csun.edu.

Case Western Reserve University, School of Graduate Studies, Department of Geological Sciences, Cleveland, OH 44106. Offers MS, PhD. Part-time programs available. *Faculty:* 7 full-time (1 woman), 7 part-time/adjunct (1 woman). *Students:* 7 full-time (3 women), 4 international. Average age 29. 7 applicants, 43% accepted, 2 enrolled. In 2009, 1 master's awarded. Terminal master's awarded for partial completion of doctoral program. *Degree requirements:* For master's, thesis or alternative; for doctorate, thesis/dissertation. *Entrance requirements:* For master's and doctorate, GRE General Test, GRE Subject Test. Additional exam requirements/recommendations for international students: Required—TOEFL (minimum score 550 paper-based; 213 computer-based; 79 iBT). *Application deadline:* For fall admission, 2/1 priority date for domestic students; for spring admission, 11/15 for domestic students. Applications are processed on a rolling basis. Application fee: $50. Electronic applications accepted. *Financial support:* Research assistantships, teaching assistantships, Federal Work-Study and tuition waivers (partial) available. Support available to part-time students. Financial award application deadline: 2/1; financial award applicants required to submit FAFSA. *Faculty research:* Geochemistry, hydrology, geochronology, paleoclimates, geomorphology. *Unit head:* Gerald Matisoff, Chairman, 216-368-3677, Fax: 216-368-3691, E-mail: gerald.matisoff@case.edu. *Application contact:* James Van Orman, Chair, Graduate Admission Committee, 216-368-3690, Fax: 216-368-3691, E-mail: james.vanorman@case.edu.

Central Washington University, Graduate Studies and Research, College of the Sciences, Department of Geological Sciences, Ellensburg, WA 98926. Offers MS. Part-time programs available. *Faculty:* 15 full-time (7 women). *Students:* 14 full-time (9 women), 7 part-time (2 women). 27 applicants, 56% accepted, 15 enrolled. In 2009, 4 master's awarded. *Degree requirements:* For master's, thesis. *Entrance requirements:* For master's, GRE General Test, minimum GPA of 3.0. Additional exam requirements/recommendations for international students: Required—TOEFL (minimum score 550 paper-based; 213 computer-based; 79 iBT). *Application deadline:* For fall admission, 2/1 priority date for domestic students; for winter admission, 10/1 for domestic students; for spring admission, 1/1 for domestic students. Applications are processed on a rolling basis. Application fee: $50. *Expenses:* Tuition, state resident: full-time $7353; part-time $245 per credit. Tuition, nonresident: full-time $16,383; part-time $546 per credit. Required fees: $882. Tuition and fees vary according to degree level. *Financial support:* In 2009–10, 8 fellowships with full and partial tuition reimbursements (averaging $31,000 per year), 7 research assistantships with full and partial tuition reimbursements (averaging $9,145 per year), 6 teaching assistantships with full and partial tuition reimbursements (averaging $9,145 per year) were awarded; career-related internships or fieldwork, Federal Work-Study, health care benefits, and unspecified assistantships also available. Financial award application deadline: 3/1; financial award applicants required to submit FAFSA. *Unit head:* Dr. Wendy Bohrson, Chair, 509-963-2701. *Application contact:* Justine Eason, Admissions Program Coordinator, 509-963-3103, Fax: 509-963-1799, E-mail: masters@cwu.edu.

Colorado School of Mines, Graduate School, Department of Geology and Geological Engineering, Golden, CO 80401. Offers geochemistry (MS, PMS, PhD); geological engineering (ME, MS, PhD); geology (MS, PhD). Part-time programs available. *Faculty:* 26 full-time (7 women), 4 part-time/adjunct (2 women). *Students:* 101 full-time (38 women), 24 part-time (10 women); includes 8 minority (1 African American, 2 American Indian/Alaska Native, 2 Asian Americans or Pacific Islanders, 3 Hispanic Americans), 19 international. Average age 29. 175 applicants, 65% accepted, 40 enrolled. In 2009, 28 master's, 3 doctorates awarded. *Degree requirements:* For master's, thesis (for some programs); for doctorate, comprehensive exam, thesis/dissertation. *Entrance requirements:* For master's and doctorate, GRE General Test. Additional exam requirements/recommendations for international students: Required—TOEFL (minimum score 550 paper-based; 213 computer-based; 80 iBT). *Application deadline:* For fall admission, 1/15 for domestic and international students; for spring admission, 9/1 for domestic and international students. Application fee: $50 ($70 for international students). Electronic applications accepted. *Expenses:* Tuition, state resident: full-time $10,584; part-time $588 per credit hour. Tuition, nonresident: full-time $24,750; part-time $1375 per credit hour. Required fees: $1654; $827.10 per semester. *Financial support:* In 2009–10, 65 students received support, including 7 fellowships with full tuition reimbursements available (averaging $20,000 per year), 40 research assistantships with full tuition reimbursements available (averaging $20,000 per year), 18 teaching assistantships with full tuition reimbursements available (averaging $20,000 per year); scholarships/grants, health care benefits, and unspecified assistantships also available. Financial award application deadline: 1/15; financial award applicants required to submit FAFSA. *Faculty research:* Predictive sediment modeling, petrophysics, aquifer-contaminant flow modeling, water-rock interactions, geotechnical engineering. Total annual research expenditures: $2.6 million. *Unit head:* Dr. John Humphrey, Department Head, 303-273-3819, Fax: 303-273-3859, E-mail: jhumphre@mines.edu. *Application contact:* Marilyn Schwinger, Administrative Assistant, 303-273-3800, Fax: 303-273-3859, E-mail: mschwing@mines.edu.

Cornell University, Graduate School, Graduate Fields of Engineering, Field of Geological Sciences, Ithaca, NY 14853-0001. Offers economic geology (M Eng, MS, PhD); engineering geology (M Eng, MS, PhD); environmental geophysics (M Eng, MS, PhD); general geology (M Eng, MS, PhD); geobiology (M Eng, MS, PhD); geochemistry and isotope geology (M Eng, MS, PhD); geohydrology (M Eng, MS, PhD); geomorphology (M Eng, MS, PhD); geophysics (M Eng, MS, PhD); geotectonics (M Eng, MS, PhD); marine geology (MS, PhD); mineralogy (M Eng, MS, PhD); paleontology (M Eng, MS, PhD); petroleum geology (M Eng, MS, PhD); petrology (M Eng, MS, PhD); planetary geology (M Eng, MS, PhD); Precambrian geology (M Eng, MS, PhD); Quaternary geology (M Eng, MS, PhD); rock mechanics (M Eng, MS, PhD); sedimentology (M Eng, MS, PhD); seismology (M Eng, MS, PhD); stratigraphy (M Eng, MS, PhD); structural geology (M Eng, MS, PhD). *Faculty:* 38 full-time (6 women). *Students:* 32 full-time (14 women); includes 2 minority (1 African American, 1 Asian American or Pacific Islander), 9 international. Average age 29. 61 applicants, 23% accepted, 8 enrolled. In 2009, 3 doctorates awarded. *Degree requirements:* For master's, thesis (MS); for doctorate, comprehensive exam, thesis/dissertation. *Entrance requirements:* For master's and doctorate, GRE General Test, 3 letters of recommendation. Additional exam requirements/recommendations for international students: Required—TOEFL (minimum score 550 paper-based; 213 computer-based; 77 iBT). *Application deadline:* For fall admission, 1/15 priority date for domestic students. Applications are processed on a rolling basis. Application fee: $70. Electronic applications accepted. *Expenses:* Tuition: Full-time $29,500. Required fees: $70. Full-time tuition and fees vary according to degree level, program and student level. *Financial support:* In 2009–10, 25 students received support, including 2 fellowships with full tuition reimbursements available, 3 research assistantships with full tuition reimbursements available, 1 teaching assistantship with full tuition reimbursement available; institutionally sponsored loans, scholarships/grants, health care benefits, tuition waivers (full and partial), and unspecified assistantships also available. Financial award applicants required to submit FAFSA. *Faculty research:* Geophysics, structural geology, petrology, geochemistry, geodynamics. *Unit head:* Director of Graduate Studies, 607-255-5466, Fax: 607-254-4780. *Application contact:* Graduate Field Assistant, 607-255-5466, Fax: 607-254-4780, E-mail: gradprog@geology.cornell.edu.

Duke University, Graduate School, Division of Earth and Ocean Sciences, Durham, NC 27708-0586. Offers MS, PhD. Part-time programs available. *Faculty:* 11 full-time. *Students:* 19 full-time (8 women); includes 1 minority (Asian American or Pacific Islander), 4 international. 35 applicants, 17% accepted, 4 enrolled. In 2009, 2 master's, 2 doctorates awarded. Terminal master's awarded for partial completion of doctoral program. *Degree requirements:* For master's, thesis; for doctorate, thesis/dissertation. *Entrance requirements:* For master's and doctorate, GRE General Test. Additional exam requirements/recommendations for international students: Required—TOEFL (minimum score 550 paper-based; 213 computer-based; 83 iBT), IELTS (minimum score 7). *Application deadline:* For fall admission, 12/8 priority date for domestic and international students; for spring admission, 11/1 for domestic students. Application fee: $75. Electronic applications accepted. *Financial support:* Fellowships, research assistantships, teaching assistantships, Federal Work-Study available. Financial award application deadline: 12/31. *Unit head:* Alan Boudreau, Director of Graduate Studies, 919-684-5847, Fax: 919-681-4426, E-mail: cabrera@duke.edu. *Application contact:* Cynthia Robertson, Associate Dean for Enrollment Services, 919-684-3913, E-mail: grad-admissions@duke.edu.

East Carolina University, Graduate School, Thomas Harriot College of Arts and Sciences, Department of Geology, Greenville, NC 27858-4353. Offers MS. Part-time programs available. *Degree requirements:* For master's, one foreign language, comprehensive exam, thesis. *Entrance requirements:* For master's, GRE General Test. Additional exam requirements/recommendations for international students: Required—TOEFL.

Eastern Kentucky University, The Graduate School, College of Arts and Sciences, Department of Earth Sciences, Richmond, KY 40475-3102. Offers geology (MS, PhD). Part-time programs available. *Degree requirements:* For master's, thesis. *Entrance requirements:* For master's, GRE General Test, minimum GPA of 2.5. *Faculty research:* Hydrogeology, sedimentary geology, geochemistry, environmental geology, tectonics.

Florida Atlantic University, Charles E. Schmidt College of Science, Department of Geosciences, Program in Geology, Boca Raton, FL 33431-0991. Offers MS. Part-time programs available. *Students:* 16 full-time (9 women), 7 part-time (3 women); includes 4 minority (1 Asian American or Pacific Islander, 3 Hispanic Americans), 1 international. Average age 34. 21 applicants, 57% accepted, 10 enrolled. In 2009, 7 master's awarded. *Degree requirements:* For master's, thesis (for some programs). *Entrance requirements:* For master's, GRE General Test, minimum GPA of 3.0. *Application deadline:* For fall admission, 3/15 for domestic and international students; for spring admission, 10/15 for domestic and international students. Applications are processed on a rolling basis. Application fee: $30. Electronic applications accepted. *Expenses:* Tuition, state resident: full-time $7055; part-time $293.94 per credit hour. Tuition, nonresident: full-time $22,096; part-time $920.66 per credit hour. *Financial support:* Research assistantships with partial tuition reimbursements, teaching assistantships with partial tuition reimbursements, Federal Work-Study available. *Faculty research:* Paleontology, beach erosion, stratigraphy, hydrogeology, environmental geology. *Unit head:* Dr. Russell Ivy, Chair, 561-297-3295, Fax: 561-297-2745, E-mail: ivy@fau.edu. *Application contact:* Dr. David Warburton, Graduate Coordinator, 561-297-3312, Fax: 561-297-2745, E-mail: warburto@fau.edu.

Florida State University, The Graduate School, College of Arts and Sciences, Department of Geological Sciences, Tallahassee, FL 32306. Offers MS, PhD. *Faculty:* 14 full-time (1 woman), 1 part-time/adjunct (0 women). *Students:* 36 full-time (21 women), 7 part-time (4 women). Average age 27. *Degree requirements:* For master's, thesis; for doctorate, thesis/dissertation. *Entrance requirements:* For master's and doctorate, GRE General Test, minimum GPA of 3.0. Additional exam requirements/recommendations for international students: Required—TOEFL (minimum score 550 paper-based; 213 computer-based; 80 iBT). *Application deadline:* For fall admission, 3/1 priority date for domestic students; for spring admission, 8/1 priority date for domestic students. Applications are processed on a rolling basis. Application fee: $30. Electronic applications accepted. *Expenses:* Tuition, state resident: full-time $7413.36. Tuition, nonresident: full-time $22,567. *Financial support:* In 2009–10, 18 students received support; fellowships, research assistantships, teaching assistantships, career-related internships or fieldwork and Federal Work-Study available. Financial award application deadline: 2/7; financial award applicants required to submit FAFSA. *Faculty research:* Appalachian and collisional tectonics, surface and groundwater hydrogeology, micropaleontology, isotope and trace element geochemistry, coastal and estuarine studies. Total annual research expenditures: $2.3 million. *Unit head:* Dr. A. Leroy Odom, Chairman, 850-644-6706, Fax: 850-644-4214, E-mail: odom@magnet.fsu.edu. *Application contact:* Sharon R. Wynn, Student Coordinator, 850-644-5861, Fax: 850-644-4214, E-mail: srwynn@fsu.edu.

Fort Hays State University, Graduate School, College of Arts and Sciences, Department of Geosciences, Program in Geosciences, Hays, KS 67601-4099. Offers geography (MS); geology (MS). *Degree requirements:* For master's, comprehensive exam, thesis. *Entrance requirements:* For master's, GRE General Test. Additional exam requirements/recommendations for international students: Required—TOEFL (minimum score 550 paper-based; 213 computer-based). Electronic applications accepted. *Faculty research:* Cretaceous and late Cenozoic stratigraphy, sedimentation, paleontology.

Georgia State University, College of Arts and Sciences, Department of Geosciences, Program in Geology, Atlanta, GA 30302-3083. Offers MA. *Degree requirements:* For master's, one foreign language, comprehensive exam (for some programs), thesis or alternative. *Entrance requirements:* For master's, GRE General Test, minimum GPA of 2.75. Additional exam requirements/recommendations for international students: Required—TOEFL.

Humboldt State University, Graduate Studies, College of Natural Resources and Sciences, Programs in Environmental Systems, Arcata, CA 95521-8299. Offers environmental systems (MS), including energy, environment and society, environmental resources engineering, geology, math modeling. *Students:* 31 full-time (11 women), 7 part-time (1 woman); includes 4 minority (2 Asian Americans or Pacific Islanders, 2 Hispanic Americans), 1 international. Average age 30. 54 applicants, 57% accepted, 17 enrolled. In 2009, 13 master's awarded. *Degree requirements:* For master's, thesis. *Entrance requirements:* For master's, GRE, appropriate bachelor's degree, minimum GPA of 2.5, 3 letters of recommendation. Additional exam requirements/recommendations for international students: Required—TOEFL. *Application deadline:* For fall admission, 3/15 for domestic students; for spring admission, 10/15 for domestic students. Applications are processed on a rolling basis. Application fee: $55. *Expenses:* Tuition, nonresident: full-time $8928. Required fees: $6102. Tuition and fees vary according to program. *Financial support:* Application deadline: 3/1; *Faculty research:* Mathematical modeling, international development technology, geology, environmental resources engineering. *Unit head:* Dr. Chris Dugaw, Chair, 707-826-4251, Fax: 707-826-4145, E-mail: dugaw@humboldt.edu. *Application contact:* Julie Tucker, Administrative Support, 707-826-3256, Fax: 707-826-3140, E-mail: jlt7002@humboldt.edu.

ICR Graduate School, Graduate Programs, Santee, CA 92071. Offers astro/geophysics (MS); biology (MS); geology (MS); science education (MS). Part-time programs available. *Degree requirements:* For master's, comprehensive exam (for some programs), thesis (for some programs). *Entrance requirements:* For master's, minimum undergraduate GPA of 3.0, bachelor's degree in science or science education. *Faculty research:* Age of the earth, limits of variation, catastrophe, optimum methods for teaching.

Idaho State University, Office of Graduate Studies, College of Arts and Sciences, Department of Geosciences, Pocatello, ID 83209-8072. Offers geographic information science (MS); geology (MNS, MS); geology emphasis environmental geoscience (MS); geophysics/hydrology/geology (MS); geotechnology (Postbaccalaureate Certificate). Part-time programs available. *Faculty:* 8 full-time (1 woman). *Students:* 25 full-time (12 women), 20 part-time (6 women); includes 1 minority (Asian American or Pacific Islander), 4 international. Average age 33. In 2009, 7 master's, 2 other advanced degrees awarded. *Degree requirements:* For master's, comprehensive exam, thesis, oral colloquium; for Postbaccalaureate Certificate, thesis optional, minimum 19 credits. *Entrance requirements:* For master's, GRE General Test (minimum 50th percentile in 2 sections), 3 letters of recommendation; for Postbaccalaureate Certificate, GRE General Test, 3 letters of recommendation, bachelor's degree, statement of goals. Additional exam requirements/recommendations for international students: Required—TOEFL (minimum score 550 paper-based; 213 computer-based; 80 iBT). *Application deadline:* For fall admission, 7/1 for domestic students, 6/1 for international students; for spring admission, 12/1 for domestic students, 11/1 for international students. Applications are processed on a rolling basis. Application fee: $55. Electronic applications accepted. *Expenses:* Tuition, state resident: full-time $3318; part-time $297 per credit hour. Tuition, nonresident: full-time $13,120; part-time $437 per credit hour. Required fees: $2530. Tuition and fees vary according to program. *Financial support:* In 2009–10, 20 research assistantships with full and partial tuition reimbursements (averaging $9,713 per year), 7 teaching assistantships with full and partial tuition reimbursements (averaging $10,841 per year) were awarded; career-related internships or fieldwork, Federal Work-Study, institutionally sponsored loans, scholarships/grants, health care benefits, tuition waivers (full and partial), and unspecified assistantships also available. Support available to part-time students. Financial award application deadline: 1/1; financial award applicants required to submit FAFSA. *Faculty research:* Quantitative field mapping and sampling: microscopic, geochemical, and isotopic analysis of rocks, minerals and water; remote sensing, geographic information systems, and global positioning systems: environmental and watershed management; surficial and fluvial processes: landscape change; regional tectonics, structural geology; planetary geology. *Unit head:* Dr. David Rodgers, Chairman, 208-282-3365, Fax: 208-282-4414, E-mail: rodgdavi@isu.edu. *Application contact:* Tami Carson, Graduate School Technical Records Specialist, 208-282-2150, Fax: 208-282-4847, E-mail: carstami@isu.edu.

Indiana University Bloomington, University Graduate School, College of Arts and Sciences, Department of Geological Sciences, Bloomington, IN 47405-7000. Offers biogeochemistry (MS, PhD); economic geology (MS, PhD); geobiology (MS, PhD); geophysics, structural geology and tectonics (MS, PhD); hydrogeology (MS, PhD); mineralogy (MS, PhD); stratigraphy and sedimentology (MS, PhD). *Faculty:* 17 full-time (1 woman). *Students:* 52 full-time (24 women), 3 part-time (0 women); includes 4 minority (2 African Americans, 1 Asian American or Pacific Islander, 1 Hispanic American), 24 international. Average age 30. 46 applicants, 65% accepted, 11 enrolled. In 2009, 9 master's, 1 doctorate awarded. Terminal master's awarded for partial completion of doctoral program. *Degree requirements:* For master's, thesis or alternative; for doctorate, comprehensive exam, thesis/dissertation. *Entrance requirements:* For master's and doctorate, GRE General Test. Additional exam requirements/recommendations for international students: Required—TOEFL. *Application deadline:* For fall admission, 1/15 priority date for domestic students, 12/15 for international students; for spring admission, 9/1 priority date for domestic students, 9/1 for international students. Applications are processed on a rolling basis. Application fee: $55 ($65 for international students). *Financial support:* In 2009–10, 11 fellowships with full tuition reimbursements (averaging $15,000 per year), 14 research assistantships with full tuition reimbursements (averaging $15,000 per year), 21 teaching assistantships with full tuition reimbursements (averaging $14,073 per year) were awarded; career-related internships or fieldwork, Federal Work-Study, and institutionally sponsored loans also available. *Faculty research:* Geophysics, geochemistry, hydrogeology, geobiology, planetary science. Total annual research expenditures: $644,299. *Unit head:* Simon Brassell, Chair, 812-855-5581, Fax: 812-855-7899, E-mail: geochair@indiana.edu. *Application contact:* Mary Iverson, Graduate Secretary, 812-855-7214, Fax: 812-855-7899, E-mail: miverson@indiana.edu.

Indiana University–Purdue University Indianapolis, School of Science, Department of Geology, Indianapolis, IN 46202-3272. Offers MS. Part-time and evening/weekend programs available. *Faculty:* 8 full-time (2 women). *Students:* 11 full-time (7 women), 11 part-time (6 women), 6 international. Average age 29. *Degree requirements:* For master's, thesis (for some programs). *Entrance requirements:* For master's, GRE General Test, minimum GPA of 3.0. Application fee: $50 ($60 for international students). *Financial support:* In 2009–10, 2 fellowships with full tuition reimbursements (averaging $12,000 per year), 7 teaching assistantships with full tuition reimbursements (averaging $12,103 per year) were awarded; research assistantships with full tuition reimbursements, scholarships/grants also available. Financial award application deadline: 3/1. *Faculty research:* Wetland hydrology, groundwater contamination, soils, sedimentology, sediment chemistry. *Unit head:* Gabriel Filippelli, Chair, 317-274-7484, Fax: 317-274-7966. *Application contact:* Lenore P. Tedesco, Associate Professor, 317-274-7484, Fax: 317-274-7966, E-mail: ltedesco@iupui.edu.

Iowa State University of Science and Technology, Graduate College, College of Liberal Arts and Sciences, Department of Geological and Atmospheric Sciences, Ames, IA 50011. Offers earth science (MS, PhD); environmental science (MS, PhD); geology (MS, PhD); meteorology (MS, PhD). *Faculty:* 15 full-time (2 women), 1 part-time/adjunct (0 women). *Students:* 31 full-time (6 women), 3 part-time (0 women); includes 1 minority (Asian American or Pacific Islander), 8 international. 33 applicants, 55% accepted, 9 enrolled. In 2009, 3 master's, 2 doctorates awarded. *Degree requirements:* For master's, thesis (for some programs); for doctorate, thesis/dissertation. *Entrance requirements:* For master's and doctorate, GRE General Test. Additional exam requirements/recommendations for international students: Required—TOEFL (minimum score 550 paper-based; 79 iBT) or IELTS (minimum score 6.5). *Application deadline:* For fall admission, 1/1 priority date for domestic students. Applications are processed on a rolling basis. Application fee: $40 ($90 for international students). Electronic applications accepted. *Expenses:* Tuition, state resident: full-time $6716. Tuition, nonresident: full-time $8908. Tuition and fees vary according to course level, course load, program and student level. *Financial support:* In 2009–10, 21 research assistantships with full and partial tuition reimbursements (averaging $14,610 per year), 7 teaching assistantships with full and partial tuition reimbursements (averaging $14,610 per year) were awarded; fellowships, scholarships/grants, health care benefits, and unspecified assistantships also available. *Unit head:* Dr. Carl E. Jacobson, Chair, 515-294-4477. *Application contact:* Dr. Carl E. Jacobson, Chair, 515-294-4477.

Kansas State University, Graduate School, College of Arts and Sciences, Department of Geology, Manhattan, KS 66506. Offers MS. *Faculty:* 10 full-time (1 woman), 4 part-time/adjunct (0 women). *Students:* 10 full-time (3 women); includes 1 minority (African American). Average age 27. 8 applicants, 100% accepted, 6 enrolled. In 2009, 8 master's awarded. *Degree requirements:* For master's, thesis. *Entrance requirements:* For master's, GRE General Test, GRE Subject Test. Additional exam requirements/recommendations for international students: Required—TOEFL. *Application deadline:* For fall admission, 2/1 priority date for domestic and international students; for spring admission, 8/1 priority date for domestic and international students. Applications are processed on a rolling basis. Application fee: $40 ($55 for international students). Electronic applications accepted. *Financial support:* In 2009–10, 1 research assistantship (averaging $18,827 per year), 7 teaching assistantships with full tuition reimbursements (averaging $10,472 per year) were awarded; career-related internships or fieldwork, Federal Work-Study, institutionally sponsored loans, and scholarships/grants also available. Support available to part-time students. Financial award application deadline: 3/1; financial award applicants required to submit FAFSA. *Faculty research:* Seismology/tectonics, sedimentology and paleobiology, quaternary geology, orogenesis, earth science education, igneous petrology. Total annual research expenditures: $123,924. *Unit head:* George Clark, Head, 785-532-2242, Fax: 785-532-5159, E-mail: grc@ksu.edu. *Application contact:* Matthew Brueseke, Domestic Director, 785-532-1908, Fax: 785-532-5159, E-mail: brueseke@ksu.edu.

Kent State University, College of Arts and Sciences, Department of Geology, Kent, OH 44242-0001. Offers applied geology (PhD); geology (MS). *Degree requirements:* For master's, thesis; for doctorate, one foreign language, thesis/dissertation. *Entrance requirements:* For master's, minimum GPA of 2.75; for doctorate, GRE General Test, GRE Subject Test, minimum GPA of 3.0. Additional exam requirements/recommendations for international students: Required—TOEFL (minimum score 575 paper-based; 232 computer-based). Electronic applications accepted. *Faculty research:* Groundwater, surface water, engineering geology, paleontology, structural geology.

Lakehead University, Graduate Studies, Department of Geology, Thunder Bay, ON P7B 5E1, Canada. Offers M Sc. Part-time and evening/weekend programs available. *Degree requirements:* For master's, thesis, department seminar, oral exam. *Entrance requirements:* For master's, minimum B average, honours bachelors degree in geology. Additional exam requirements/

Geology

Lakehead University (continued)

recommendations for international students: Required—TOEFL. *Faculty research:* Rock physics, sedimentology, mineralogy and economic geology, geochemistry, petrology of alkaline rocks.

Laurentian University, School of Graduate Studies and Research, Programme in Geology (Earth Sciences), Sudbury, ON P3E 2C6, Canada. Offers geology (M Sc); mineral deposits and precambrian geology (PhD); mineral exploration (M Sc). Part-time programs available. *Degree requirements:* For master's, thesis. *Entrance requirements:* For master's, honors degree with second class or better. *Faculty research:* Localization and metallogenesis of Ni-Cu-(PGE) sulfide mineralization in the Thompson Nickel Belt, mapping lithology and ore-grade and monitoring dissolved organic carbon in lakes using remote sensing, global reefs, volcanic effects on VMS deposits.

Lehigh University, College of Arts and Sciences, Department of Earth and Environmental Sciences, Bethlehem, PA 18015. Offers MS, PhD. *Faculty:* 14 full-time (1 woman), 1 (woman) part-time/adjunct. *Students:* 25 full-time (12 women), 4 international. Average age 26. 55 applicants, 42% accepted, 7 enrolled. In 2009, 8 master's, 3 doctorates awarded. *Degree requirements:* For doctorate, comprehensive exam, thesis/dissertation. *Entrance requirements:* For master's and doctorate, GRE General Test. Additional exam requirements/recommendations for international students: Required—TOEFL. *Application deadline:* For fall admission, 1/15 for domestic and international students. Applications are processed on a rolling basis. Application fee: $65. Electronic applications accepted. *Financial support:* In 2009–10, 13 students received support, including 3 fellowships with full tuition reimbursements available (averaging $15,400 per year), 12 research assistantships with full tuition reimbursements available (averaging $15,400 per year), 10 teaching assistantships with full tuition reimbursements available (averaging $15,400 per year); career-related internships or fieldwork, Federal Work-Study, institutionally sponsored loans, scholarships/grants, tuition waivers (full and partial), and unspecified assistantships also available. Support available to part-time students. Financial award application deadline: 1/15. *Faculty research:* Tectonics, surficial processes, aquatic ecology. Total annual research expenditures: $866,594. *Unit head:* Dr. Frank J. Pazzaglia, Chairman, 610-758-3671, Fax: 610-758-3677, E-mail: fjp3@lehigh.edu. *Application contact:* Dr. Zicheng Yu, Graduate Coordinator, 610-758-3660 Ext. 6751, Fax: 610-758-3677, E-mail: ziy2@lehigh.edu.

Louisiana State University and Agricultural and Mechanical College, Graduate School, College of Basic Sciences, Department of Geology and Geophysics, Baton Rouge, LA 70803. Offers MS, PhD. *Faculty:* 16 full-time (6 women), 1 (woman) part-time/adjunct. *Students:* 43 full-time (12 women), 7 part-time (1 woman); includes 3 African Americans, 1 Asian American or Pacific Islander, 2 Hispanic Americans, 8 international. Average age 26. 50 applicants, 44% accepted, 13 enrolled. In 2009, 5 master's, 2 doctorates awarded. Terminal master's awarded for partial completion of doctoral program. *Degree requirements:* For master's, thesis; for doctorate, thesis/dissertation. *Entrance requirements:* For master's and doctorate, GRE General Test, minimum GPA of 3.0. Additional exam requirements/recommendations for international students: Required—TOEFL (minimum score 550 paper-based; 213 computer-based; 79 iBT) or IELTS (minimum score 6.5). *Application deadline:* For fall admission, 1/25 priority date for domestic students, 5/15 for international students; for spring admission, 10/15 for international students. Applications are processed on a rolling basis. Application fee: $50 ($70 for international students). Electronic applications accepted. *Financial support:* In 2009–10, 37 students received support, including 3 fellowships with full tuition reimbursements available (averaging $24,897 per year), 25 research assistantships with full and partial tuition reimbursements available (averaging $18,660 per year), 13 teaching assistantships with full and partial tuition reimbursements available (averaging $15,230 per year); career-related internships or fieldwork, Federal Work-Study, institutionally sponsored loans, health care benefits, tuition waivers (full and partial), and unspecified assistantships also available. Financial award application deadline: 3/15; financial award applicants required to submit FAFSA. *Faculty research:* Geophysics, sedimentology, geochemistry, geomicrobiology, tectonics. Total annual research expenditures: $863,173. *Unit head:* Dr. Carol Wicks, Chair, 225-578-3353, Fax: 225-578-2302, E-mail: glande@lsu.edu. *Application contact:* Jeffrey Nunn, Graduate Coordinator, 225-578-6657, E-mail: gljeff@lsu.edu.

Massachusetts Institute of Technology, School of Science, Department of Earth, Atmospheric, and Planetary Sciences, Cambridge, MA 02139-4307. Offers atmospheric chemistry (PhD, Sc D); atmospheric science (SM, PhD, Sc D); chemical oceanography (SM, PhD, Sc D); climate physics and chemistry (SM, PhD, Sc D); earth and planetary sciences (SM); geochemistry (PhD, Sc D); geology (PhD, Sc D); geophysics (PhD, Sc D); marine geology and geophysics (SM, PhD, Sc D); physical oceanography (SM, PhD, Sc D); planetary sciences (PhD, Sc D). *Faculty:* 37 full-time (7 women). *Students:* 158 full-time (74 women); includes 14 minority (1 African American, 1 American Indian/Alaska Native, 6 Asian Americans or Pacific Islanders, 6 Hispanic Americans), 58 international. Average age 27. 205 applicants, 30% accepted, 18 enrolled. In 2009, 10 master's, 25 doctorates awarded. Terminal master's awarded for partial completion of doctoral program. *Degree requirements:* For master's, thesis; for doctorate, comprehensive exam, thesis/dissertation. *Entrance requirements:* For master's, GRE General Test; for doctorate, GRE General Test, GRE Subject Test (chemistry or physics for planetary science area). Additional exam requirements/recommendations for international students: Required—IELTS (minimum score 6); Recommended—TOEFL (minimum score 577 paper-based; 233 computer-based; 91 iBT). *Application deadline:* For fall admission, 1/5 for domestic and international students; for spring admission, 11/1 for domestic and international students. Application fee: $75. Electronic applications accepted. *Financial support:* In 2009–10, 112 students received support, including 31 fellowships with tuition reimbursements available (averaging $30,513 per year), 89 research assistantships with tuition reimbursements available (averaging $21,168 per year), 17 teaching assistantships with tuition reimbursements available (averaging $28,372 per year); Federal Work-Study, institutionally sponsored loans, scholarships/grants, health care benefits, and unspecified assistantships also available. *Faculty research:* Formation, dynamics and evolution of planetary systems, origin, evolution and interaction of the physical, characterization of past, interplay of energy and the environment, present and potential future climates and the causes and consequences of climate change, chemical, geological and biological components of the Earth system, composition, structure and dynamics of the atmospheres, oceans, surfaces and interiors of the Earth and other planets. Total annual research expenditures: $19.5 million. *Unit head:* Prof. Maria Zuber, Head, 617-253-2127, Fax: 617-253-8298, E-mail: eapsinfo@mit.edu. *Application contact:* EAPS Education Office, 617-253-3381, Fax: 617-253-8298, E-mail: eapsinfo@mit.edu.

McMaster University, School of Graduate Studies, Faculty of Science, School of Geography and Earth Sciences, Hamilton, ON L8S 4M2, Canada. Offers geochemistry (PhD); geology (M Sc, PhD); human geography (MA, PhD); physical geography (M Sc, PhD). Part-time programs available. Terminal master's awarded for partial completion of doctoral program. *Degree requirements:* For master's, thesis; for doctorate, comprehensive exam, thesis/dissertation. *Entrance requirements:* For master's, minimum B+ average. Additional exam requirements/recommendations for international students: Required—TOEFL (minimum score 550 paper-based; 213 computer-based).

Memorial University of Newfoundland, School of Graduate Studies, Department of Earth Sciences, St. John's, NL A1C 5S7, Canada. Offers geology (M Sc, PhD); geophysics (M Sc, PhD). Part-time programs available. *Degree requirements:* For master's, thesis; for doctorate, comprehensive exam, thesis/dissertation, oral thesis defense, entry evaluation. *Entrance requirements:* For master's, honors B Sc; for doctorate, M Sc. Electronic applications accepted. *Faculty research:* Geochemistry, sedimentology, paleoceanography and global change, mineral deposits, petroleum geology, hydrology.

Miami University, Graduate School, College of Arts and Sciences, Department of Geology, Oxford, OH 45056. Offers MA, MS, PhD. Part-time programs available. *Students:* 26 full-time (13 women), 1 (woman) part-time; includes 3 minority (1 African American, 2 Asian Americans or Pacific Islanders), 13 international. *Entrance requirements:* For master's, GRE General Test, GRE Subject Test, minimum undergraduate GPA of 3.0 during previous 2 years or 2.75 overall; for doctorate, GRE General Test, GRE Subject Test, minimum GPA of 2.75 (undergraduate) or 3.0 (graduate). Additional exam requirements/recommendations for international students: Required—TOEFL. *Application deadline:* For fall admission, 2/1 for domestic and international students. Application fee: $35. *Expenses:* Tuition, state resident: full-time $11,280. Tuition, nonresident: full-time $24,912. Required fees: $516. *Financial support:* Fellowships with full tuition reimbursements, research assistantships with full tuition reimbursements, teaching assistantships with full tuition reimbursements, Federal Work-Study, institutionally sponsored loans, health care benefits, tuition waivers (full), and unspecified assistantships available. Financial award application deadline: 3/1; financial award applicants required to submit FAFSA. *Unit head:* Dr. William Hart, Chair, 513-529-3216, Fax: 513-529-1542, E-mail: hartwk@muohio.edu. *Application contact:* Dr. Elisabeth Widom, Director of Graduate Studies, 513-529-5048, E-mail: widome@muohio.edu.

Michigan Technological University, Graduate School, College of Engineering, Department of Geological and Mining Engineering and Sciences, Program in Geology, Houghton, MI 49931. Offers MS, PhD. Part-time programs available. Terminal master's awarded for partial completion of doctoral program. *Degree requirements:* For master's, comprehensive exam; for doctorate, comprehensive exam, thesis/dissertation. *Entrance requirements:* Additional exam requirements/recommendations for international students: Required—TOEFL (minimum score 550 paper-based; 213 computer-based). Electronic applications accepted.

Missouri State University, Graduate College, College of Natural and Applied Sciences, Department of Geography, Geology, and Planning, Springfield, MO 65897. Offers geospatial sciences (MS); natural and applied science (MNAS), including geography, geology and planning; secondary education (MS Ed), including earth science, geography. *Accreditation:* ACSP. Part-time and evening/weekend programs available. *Faculty:* 20 full-time (4 women). *Students:* 19 full-time (10 women), 12 part-time (5 women); includes 1 minority (American Indian/Alaska Native), 1 international. Average age 29. 19 applicants, 100% accepted, 13 enrolled. In 2009, 4 master's awarded. *Degree requirements:* For master's, comprehensive exam, thesis (for some programs). *Entrance requirements:* For master's, GRE General Test (MS, MNAS), minimum undergraduate GPA of 3.0 (MS, MNAS), 9-12 teacher certification (MS Ed). Additional exam requirements/recommendations for international students: Required—TOEFL (minimum score 550 paper-based; 213 computer-based; 79 iBT). *Application deadline:* For fall admission, 7/20 priority date for domestic students, 5/1 for international students; for spring admission, 12/20 priority date for domestic students, 9/1 for international students. Applications are processed on a rolling basis. Application fee: $35 ($50 for international students). Electronic applications accepted. *Expenses:* Tuition, state resident: full-time $3852; part-time $214 per credit hour. Tuition, nonresident: full-time $7524; part-time $418 per credit hour. Required fees: $696; $172 per semester. Tuition and fees vary according to course level, course load, degree level and program. *Financial support:* In 2009–10, 7 research assistantships with full tuition reimbursements (averaging $8,933 per year), 8 teaching assistantships with full tuition reimbursements (averaging $8,236 per year) were awarded; career-related internships or fieldwork, Federal Work-Study, institutionally sponsored loans, scholarships/grants, and unspecified assistantships also available. Financial award application deadline: 3/31; financial award applicants required to submit FAFSA. *Faculty research:* Stratigraphy and ancient meteorite impacts, environmental geochemistry of karst, hyperspectral image processing, water quality, small town planning. *Unit head:* Dr. Thomas Plymate, Head, 417-836-5800, Fax: 417-836-6934, E-mail: tomplymate@missouristate.edu. *Application contact:* Eric Eckert, Coordinator of Graduate Admissions and Recruitment, 417-836-5331, Fax: 417-836-6200, E-mail: ericeckert@missouristate.edu.

Missouri University of Science and Technology, Graduate School, Department of Geological Sciences and Engineering, Rolla, MO 65409. Offers geological engineering (MS, DE, PhD); geology and geophysics (MS, PhD), including geochemistry, geology, geophysics, groundwater and environmental geology; petroleum engineering (MS, DE, PhD). Part-time programs available. *Degree requirements:* For master's, thesis optional; for doctorate, comprehensive exam, thesis/dissertation. *Entrance requirements:* For master's, GRE General Test (minimum score 600 quantitative, writing 3.5), minimum GPA of 3.0 in last 4 semesters; for doctorate, GRE General Test (minimum: Q 600, GRE WR 3.5). Additional exam requirements/recommendations for international students: Required—TOEFL. Electronic applications accepted. *Faculty research:* Digital image processing and geographic information systems, mineralogy, igneous and sedimentary petrology-geochemistry, sedimentology groundwater hydrology and contaminant transport.

Montana Tech of The University of Montana, Graduate School, Geosciences Programs, Butte, MT 59701-8997. Offers geochemistry (MS); geological engineering (MS); geology (MS); geophysical engineering (MS); hydrogeological engineering (MS); hydrogeology (MS). Part-time programs available. *Faculty:* 18 full-time (4 women), 3 part-time/adjunct (2 women). *Students:* 16 full-time (8 women), 6 part-time (4 women); includes 1 minority (African American), 1 international. 6 applicants, 67% accepted, 4 enrolled. In 2009, 7 degrees awarded. *Degree requirements:* For master's, comprehensive exam (for some programs), thesis (for some programs). *Entrance requirements:* For master's, GRE General Test, minimum GPA of 3.0. Additional exam requirements/recommendations for international students: Required—TOEFL (minimum score 525 paper-based; 195 computer-based; 71 iBT). *Application deadline:* For fall admission, 4/1 priority date for domestic students, 3/1 priority date for international students; for spring admission, 10/1 priority date for domestic students, 7/1 priority date for international students. Applications are processed on a rolling basis. Application fee: $30. Electronic applications accepted. *Expenses:* Tuition, state resident: full-time $5068; part-time $319 per credit. Tuition, nonresident: full-time $14,815; part-time $875 per credit. Tuition and fees vary according to course load and campus/location. *Financial support:* In 2009–10, 11 students received support, including 5 teaching assistantships with partial tuition reimbursements available (averaging $8,000 per year); research assistantships with partial tuition reimbursements available, career-related internships or fieldwork, tuition waivers (full and partial), and unspecified assistantships also available. Financial award application deadline: 4/1; financial award applicants required to submit FAFSA. *Faculty research:* Water resource development, seismic processing, petroleum reservoir characterization, environmental geochemistry, geologic mapping. *Unit head:* Dr. Diane Wolfgram, Department Head, 406-496-4353, Fax: 406-496-4260, E-mail: dwolfgram@mtech.edu. *Application contact:* Cindy Dunstan, Administrator, Graduate School, 406-496-4304, Fax: 406-496-4710, E-mail: cdunstan@mtech.edu.

New Mexico Institute of Mining and Technology, Graduate Studies, Department of Earth and Environmental Science, Program in Geology and Geochemistry, Socorro, NM 87801. Offers geochemistry (MS, PhD); geology (MS, PhD). *Degree requirements:* For master's, thesis optional; for doctorate, thesis/dissertation. *Entrance requirements:* For master's, GRE General Test; for doctorate, GRE General Test, GRE Subject Test. Additional exam requirements/recommendations for international students: Required—TOEFL (minimum score 540 paper-based; 207 computer-based). Electronic applications accepted. *Faculty research:* Care and karst topography, soil/water chemistry and properties, geochemistry of ore deposits.

New Mexico State University, Graduate School, College of Arts and Sciences, Department of Geological Sciences, Las Cruces, NM 88003-8001. Offers MS. Part-time programs available. *Faculty:* 7 full-time (2 women). *Students:* 14 full-time (3 women), 5 part-time (1 woman); includes 1 minority (Hispanic American). Average age 26. 22 applicants, 91% accepted, 8 enrolled. In 2009, 9 master's awarded. *Degree requirements:* For master's, thesis. *Entrance* *requirements:* For master's, GRE General Test, BS in geology or the equivalent. Additional exam requirements/recommendations for international students: Required—TOEFL. *Application deadline:* For fall admission, 7/1 priority date for domestic and international students; for spring admission, 11/1 priority date for domestic and international students. Applications are processed on a rolling basis. Application fee: $30 ($50 for international students). Electronic applications accepted. *Expenses:* Tuition, state resident: full-time $4080; part-time $223 per credit. Tuition, nonresident: full-time $14,256; part-time $647 per credit. Required fees: $1278; $639 per semester. *Financial support:* In 2009–10, 1 research assistantship with full tuition reimbursement (averaging $8,616 per year), 12 teaching assistantships with partial tuition reimbursements (averaging $17,223 per year) were awarded; career-related internships or fieldwork, Federal Work-Study, institutionally sponsored loans, scholarships/grants, health care benefits, and unspecified assistantships also available. Support available to part-time students. Financial award application deadline: 2/15; financial award applicants required to submit FAFSA. *Faculty research:* Geochemistry, tectonics, sedimentology, stratigraphy, igneous petrology. *Unit head:* Dr. Nancy J. McMillan, Head, 575-646-2708, Fax: 575-646-1056, E-mail: nmcmille@nmsu.edu. *Application contact:* Dr. Katherine A. Giles, Professor, 575-646-2033, Fax: 575-646-1056, E-mail: kgiles@nmsu.edu.

Northern Arizona University, Graduate College, College of Engineering, Forestry and Natural Sciences, Program in Quaternary Sciences, Flagstaff, AZ 86011. Offers MS. *Students:* 1 full-time (0 women), 1 part-time (0 women). Average age 34. 2 applicants, 0% accepted, 0 enrolled. In 2009, 3 master's awarded. *Degree requirements:* For master's, thesis. *Entrance requirements:* For master's, GRE General Test. Additional exam requirements/recommendations for international students: Required—TOEFL (minimum score 550 paper-based; 213 computer-based; 80 iBT), IELTS (minimum score 7), or a bachelor's degree from an English-speaking university and demonstrated proficiency. *Application deadline:* For fall admission, 2/15 priority date for domestic students, 9/1 priority date for international students. Applications are processed on a rolling basis. Application fee: $65. Electronic applications accepted. *Financial support:* In 2009–10, 5 research assistantships were awarded; career-related internships or fieldwork, Federal Work-Study, tuition waivers (full and partial), and unspecified assistantships also available. Financial award application deadline: 3/30. *Faculty research:* Sandbar stability in the Grand Canyon; Stone Age site excavation in South Africa; neogene reptile and mammal evolution; mammoths of Hot Springs, South Dakota; quaternary science of national parks on Colorado Plateau. *Unit head:* Dr. Jim Mead, Director, 928-523-1829, Fax: 928-523-7423, E-mail: jim.i.mead@nau.edu. *Application contact:* Dr. Jim Mead, Director, 928-523-1829, Fax: 928-523-7423, E-mail: jim.i.mead@nau.edu.

Northern Arizona University, Graduate College, College of Engineering, Forestry and Natural Sciences, School of Earth Sciences and Environmental Sustainability, Program in Geology, Flagstaff, AZ 86011. Offers MS. *Faculty:* 22 full-time (5 women). *Students:* 20 full-time (8 women), 11 part-time (5 women); includes 1 minority (American Indian/Alaska Native), 1 international. Average age 27. 48 applicants, 35% accepted, 11 enrolled. In 2009, 12 master's awarded. *Degree requirements:* For master's, thesis. *Entrance requirements:* For master's, GRE General Test. Additional exam requirements/recommendations for international students: Required—TOEFL (minimum score 550 paper-based; 213 computer-based; 80 iBT), IELTS (minimum score 7), or a bachelor's degree from an English-speaking university and demonstrated proficiency. *Application deadline:* For fall admission, 2/1 priority date for domestic students, 9/1 priority date for international students. Application fee: $65. Electronic applications accepted. *Financial support:* In 2009–10, 2 research assistantships with partial tuition reimbursements (averaging $12,821 per year), 18 teaching assistantships with partial tuition reimbursements (averaging $12,821 per year) were awarded; career-related internships or fieldwork, Federal Work-Study, scholarships/grants, health care benefits, tuition waivers (full and partial), and unspecified assistantships also available. Support available to part-time students. Financial award application deadline: 3/30; financial award applicants required to submit FAFSA. Total annual research expenditures: $499,385. *Unit head:* Dr. Mary Ried, Chair, 928-523-7200, Fax: 928-523-9220, E-mail: mary.ried@nau.edu. *Application contact:* Dr. Paul Umhoefer, Coordinator, 928-523-6464, Fax: 928-523-9220, E-mail: cefnsacademic@nau.edu.

Northern Illinois University, Graduate School, College of Liberal Arts and Sciences, Department of Geology and Environmental Geosciences, De Kalb, IL 60115-2854. Offers geology (MS, PhD). Part-time programs available. *Faculty:* 11 full-time (1 woman), 1 (woman) part-time/adjunct. *Students:* 25 full-time (10 women), 21 part-time (6 women); includes 3 minority (1 African American, 2 Asian Americans or Pacific Islanders), 5 international. Average age 28. 25 applicants, 72% accepted, 12 enrolled. In 2009, 3 master's, 2 doctorates awarded. Terminal master's awarded for partial completion of doctoral program. *Degree requirements:* For master's, comprehensive exam, thesis optional, research seminar; for doctorate, thesis/dissertation, candidacy exam, dissertation defense, internship, research seminar. *Entrance requirements:* For master's, GRE General Test, bachelor's degree in engineering or science, minimum GPA of 2.75; for doctorate, GRE General Test, bachelor's or master's degree in engineering or science, minimum graduate GPA of 3.2. Additional exam requirements/recommendations for international students: Required—TOEFL (minimum score 550 paper-based; 213 computer-based). *Application deadline:* For fall admission, 6/1 for domestic students, 5/1 for international students; for spring admission, 11/1 for domestic students, 10/1 for international students. Applications are processed on a rolling basis. Application fee: $30. Electronic applications accepted. *Expenses:* Tuition, state resident: full-time $6576; part-time $274 per credit hour. Tuition, nonresident: full-time $13,152; part-time $548 per credit hour. Required fees: $1813; $75.53 per credit hour. Part-time tuition and fees vary according to course load. *Financial support:* In 2009–10, 6 research assistantships with full tuition reimbursements, 26 teaching assistantships with full tuition reimbursements were awarded; fellowships with full tuition reimbursements, career-related internships or fieldwork, Federal Work-Study, scholarships/grants, tuition waivers (full), and unspecified assistantships also available. Support available to part-time students. Financial award applicants required to submit FAFSA. *Faculty research:* Micropaleontology, environmental geochemistry, glacial geology, igneous petrology, statistical analyses of fracture networks. *Unit head:* Dr. Colin Booth, Chair, 815-753-0523, Fax: 815-753-1945, E-mail: cbooth@niu.edu. *Application contact:* Dr. James Walker, Director of Graduate Studies, 815-753-7936, E-mail: jim@geol.niu.edu.

Northwestern University, The Graduate School, Judd A. and Marjorie Weinberg College of Arts and Sciences, Department of Geological Sciences, Evanston, IL 60208. Offers MS, PhD. Admissions and degrees offered through The Graduate School. Part-time programs available. *Degree requirements:* For doctorate, thesis/dissertation. *Entrance requirements:* For master's and doctorate, GRE General Test. Additional exam requirements/recommendations for international students: Required—TOEFL. Electronic applications accepted.

The Ohio State University, Graduate School, College of Mathematical and Physical Sciences, School of Earth Sciences, Department of Geological Sciences, Columbus, OH 43210. Offers MS, PhD. *Faculty:* 44. *Students:* 32 full-time (15 women), 12 part-time (5 women); includes 3 minority (1 African American, 2 Hispanic Americans), 7 international. Average age 28. In 2009, 12 master's, 4 doctorates awarded. *Degree requirements:* For master's, thesis; for doctorate, one foreign language, thesis/dissertation. *Entrance requirements:* For master's and doctorate, GRE General Test. Additional exam requirements/recommendations for international students: Required—TOEFL (minimum score 600 paper-based; 250 computer-based). *Application deadline:* For fall admission, 8/15 priority date for domestic students, 7/1 priority date for international students; for winter admission, 12/1 priority date for domestic students, 11/1 priority date for international students; for spring admission, 3/1 priority date for domestic students, 2/1 priority date for international students. Applications are processed on a rolling basis. Application fee: $40 ($50 for international students). Electronic applications accepted. *Expenses:* Tuition, state resident: full-time $10,683. Tuition, nonresident: full-time $25,923. Tuition and fees vary according to course load and program. *Financial support:* Fellowships, research assistantships, teaching assistantships, Federal Work-Study and institutionally sponsored loans available. Support available to part-time students. *Unit head:* W. Berry Lyons, Graduate Studies Committee Chair, 614-292-0069, Fax: 614-292-7688, E-mail: lyons.142@osu.edu. *Application contact:* 614-292-9444, Fax: 614-292-3895, E-mail: domestic.grad@geology.ohio-state.edu.

Ohio University, Graduate College, College of Arts and Sciences, Department of Geological Sciences, Athens, OH 45701-2979. Offers environmental geochemistry (MS); environmental geology (MS); environmental/hydrology (MS); geology (MS); geology education (MS); geomorphology/surficial processes (MS); geophysics (MS); hydrogeology (MS); sedimentology (MS); structure/tectonics (MS). Part-time programs available. *Faculty:* 10 full-time (4 women), 4 part-time/adjunct (1 woman). *Students:* 18 full-time (13 women), 1 part-time (0 women), 9 international. 15 applicants, 67% accepted, 6 enrolled. In 2009, 5 master's awarded. *Degree requirements:* For master's, thesis. *Entrance requirements:* Additional exam requirements/recommendations for international students: Required—TOEFL (minimum score 550 paper-based; 80 iBT) or IELTS Academic (minimum score 6.5). *Application deadline:* For fall admission, 2/1 priority date for domestic and international students. Application fee: $50 ($55 for international students). Electronic applications accepted. *Expenses:* Tuition, state resident: full-time $7839; part-time $323 per quarter hour. Tuition, nonresident: full-time $15,831; part-time $654 per quarter hour. Required fees: $2931. *Financial support:* Research assistantships with full tuition reimbursements, teaching assistantships with full tuition reimbursements, Federal Work-Study, institutionally sponsored loans, scholarships/grants, tuition waivers (partial), and unspecified assistantships available. Financial award application deadline: 2/1. *Faculty research:* Geoscience education, tectonics, fluvial geomorphology, invertebrate paleontology, mine/hydrology. Total annual research expenditures: $649,020. *Unit head:* Dr. Gregory Nadon, Chair, 740-593-4212, Fax: 740-593-0486, E-mail: nadon@ohio.edu. *Application contact:* Dr. Douglas Green, Graduate Chair, 740-593-1843, Fax: 740-593-0486, E-mail: green@ohio.edu.

Oklahoma State University, College of Arts and Sciences, School of Geology, Stillwater, OK 74078. Offers MS, PhD. *Faculty:* 12 full-time (3 women), 1 (woman) part-time/adjunct. *Students:* 32 full-time (11 women), 23 part-time (7 women); includes 8 minority (3 African Americans, 2 American Indian/Alaska Native, 1 Asian American or Pacific Islander, 2 Hispanic Americans), 7 international. Average age 29. 64 applicants, 45% accepted, 17 enrolled. In 2009, 16 master's awarded. *Degree requirements:* For master's, thesis; for doctorate, comprehensive exam, thesis/dissertation. *Entrance requirements:* For master's, GRE; for doctorate, GRE. Additional exam requirements/recommendations for international students: Required—TOEFL (minimum score 550 paper-based; 79 iBT). *Application deadline:* For fall admission, 3/1 priority date for international students; for spring admission, 8/1 priority date for international students. Applications are processed on a rolling basis. Application fee: $40 ($75 for international students). Electronic applications accepted. *Expenses:* Tuition, state resident: full-time $3716; part-time $154.85 per credit hour. Tuition, nonresident: full-time $14,448; part-time $602 per credit hour. Required fees: $1772; $73.85 per credit hour. One-time fee: $50. Tuition and fees vary according to course load and campus/location. *Financial support:* In 2009–10, 7 research assistantships (averaging $10,103 per year), 24 teaching assistantships (averaging $7,963 per year) were awarded; career-related internships or fieldwork, Federal Work-Study, scholarships/grants, health care benefits, tuition waivers (partial), and unspecified assistantships also available. Support available to part-time students. Financial award application deadline: 3/1; financial award applicants required to submit FAFSA. *Faculty research:* Groundwater hydrology, petroleum geology. *Unit head:* Dr. Jay Gregg, Head, 405-744-6358, Fax: 405-744-7841. *Application contact:* Dr. Gordon Emslie, Dean, 405-744-6368, Fax: 405-744-0355, E-mail: grad-i@okstate.edu.

Oregon State University, Graduate School, College of Science, Department of Geosciences, Program in Geology, Corvallis, OR 97331. Offers MA, MAIS, MS, PhD. Part-time programs available. *Students:* 29 full-time (12 women), 1 part-time (0 women); includes 1 minority (Asian American or Pacific Islander), 1 international. Average age 28. In 2009, 2 master's, 2 doctorates awarded. Terminal master's awarded for partial completion of doctoral program. *Degree requirements:* For master's, variable foreign language requirement, thesis; for doctorate, one foreign language, thesis/dissertation. *Entrance requirements:* For master's and doctorate, GRE General Test, GRE Subject Test, minimum GPA of 3.0 in last 90 hours. Additional exam requirements/recommendations for international students: Required—TOEFL. *Application deadline:* For fall admission, 2/1 for domestic students. Applications are processed on a rolling basis. Application fee: $50. *Expenses:* Tuition, state resident: full-time $9774; part-time $362 per credit. Tuition, nonresident: full-time $15,849; part-time $587 per credit. Required fees: $1639. Full-time tuition and fees vary according to course load and program. *Financial support:* Fellowships, research assistantships, teaching assistantships, Federal Work-Study and institutionally sponsored loans available. Support available to part-time students. Financial award application deadline: 2/1. *Faculty research:* Hydrogeology, geomorphology, ocean geology, geochemistry, earthquake geology. *Unit head:* Dr. Peter U. Clark, Director, 541-737-1247, Fax: 541-737-1200, E-mail: clarkp@geo.oregonstate.edu. *Application contact:* Stacey Schulte, Office Specialist 2, 541-737-1221, Fax: 541-737-1200, E-mail: schultes@gco.oregonstate.edu.

Portland State University, Graduate Studies, College of Liberal Arts and Sciences, Department of Geology, Portland, OR 97207-0751. Offers environmental sciences and resources (PhD); geology (MA, MS); science/geology (MAT, MST). Part-time programs available. *Degree requirements:* For master's, comprehensive exam, thesis, field comprehensive; for doctorate, thesis/dissertation, 2 years of residency. *Entrance requirements:* For master's, GRE General Test, GRE Subject Test, BA/BS in geology, minimum GPA of 3.0 in upper-division course work or 2.75 overall. Additional exam requirements/recommendations for international students: Required—TOEFL (minimum score 550 paper-based; 213 computer-based). *Faculty research:* Sediment transport, volcanic environmental geology, coastal and fluvial processes.

Queens College of the City University of New York, Division of Graduate Studies, Mathematics and Natural Sciences Division, School of Earth and Environmental Sciences, Flushing, NY 11367-1597. Offers MA. Part-time and evening/weekend programs available. *Faculty:* 14 full-time (4 women). *Students:* 2 full-time (both women), 10 part-time (5 women). 13 applicants, 38% accepted, 3 enrolled. In 2009, 3 master's awarded. *Degree requirements:* For master's, comprehensive exam, thesis. *Entrance requirements:* For master's, GRE, previous course work in calculus, physics, and chemistry; minimum GPA of 3.0. Additional exam requirements/recommendations for international students: Required—TOEFL. *Application deadline:* For fall admission, 4/1 for domestic students; for spring admission, 11/1 for domestic students. Applications are processed on a rolling basis. Application fee: $125. *Expenses:* Tuition, state resident: full-time $7360; part-time $310 per credit. Tuition, nonresident: part-time $575 per credit. One-time fee: $195.25 full-time; $145.25 part-time. *Financial support:* Career-related internships or fieldwork, Federal Work-Study, institutionally sponsored loans, tuition waivers (partial), and unspecified assistantships available. Support available to part-time students. Financial award application deadline: 4/1; financial award applicants required to submit FAFSA. *Faculty research:* Sedimentology/stratigraphy, paleontology, field petrology. *Unit head:* Dr. Yan Zheng, Chairperson, 718-997-3300. *Application contact:* Dr. Hannes Brueckner, Graduate Adviser, 718-997-3300, E-mail: hannes_brueckner@qc.edu.

Queen's University at Kingston, School of Graduate Studies and Research, Faculty of Arts and Sciences, Department of Geological Sciences and Geological Engineering, Kingston, ON K7L 3N6, Canada. Offers M Sc, M Sc Eng, PhD. Part-time programs available. *Degree requirements:* For master's, thesis (for some programs); for doctorate, comprehensive exam, thesis/dissertation. *Entrance requirements:* Additional exam requirements/recommendations for international students: Required—TOEFL. *Faculty research:* Geochemistry, sedimentology, geophysics, economic geology, structural geology.

Geology

Rensselaer Polytechnic Institute, Graduate School, School of Science, Department of Earth and Environmental Sciences, Program in Geology, Troy, NY 12180-3590. Offers MS, PhD. Part-time programs available. *Faculty:* 8 full-time (1 woman), 1 part-time/adjunct (0 women). *Students:* 8 full-time (5 women), 1 (woman) part-time; includes 1 minority (Asian American or Pacific Islander). Average age 26. 48 applicants, 15% accepted. In 2009, 2 master's, 3 doctorates awarded. Terminal master's awarded for partial completion of doctoral program. *Degree requirements:* For master's, comprehensive exam, thesis (for some programs); for doctorate, comprehensive exam, thesis/dissertation. *Entrance requirements:* For master's and doctorate, GRE General Test. Additional exam requirements/recommendations for international students: Required—TOEFL. *Application deadline:* For fall admission, 1/15 priority date for domestic students. Applications are processed on a rolling basis. Application fee: $75. Electronic applications accepted. *Expenses:* Tuition: Full-time $38,100. *Financial support:* In 2009–10, 7 research assistantships with full tuition reimbursements (averaging $23,000 per year), 4 teaching assistantships with full tuition reimbursements (averaging $23,000 per year) were awarded; fellowships with full tuition reimbursements, career-related internships or fieldwork and scholarships/grants also available. Financial award application deadline: 2/1; financial award applicants required to submit FAFSA. *Faculty research:* Geochemistry, petrology, geophysics, environmental geochemistry, planetary geology. Total annual research expenditures: $2.3 million. *Unit head:* Dr. Frank Spear, Chair, 518-276-6474, Fax: 518-276-2012, E-mail: ees@rpi.edu. *Application contact:* Dr. Steven Roecker, Professor, 518-276-6773, Fax: 518-276-2012, E-mail: ees@rpi.edu.

Rutgers, The State University of New Jersey, Newark, Graduate School, Program in Environmental Geology, Newark, NJ 07102. Offers MS. Part-time and evening/weekend programs available. *Degree requirements:* For master's, comprehensive exam, thesis optional. *Entrance requirements:* For master's, GRE General Test, minimum B average. Electronic applications accepted. *Faculty research:* Environmental geology, plate tectonics, geoarchaeology, geophysics, mineralogy-petrology.

Rutgers, The State University of New Jersey, New Brunswick, Graduate School-New Brunswick, Department of Earth and Planetary Sciences, Piscataway, NJ 08854-8097. Offers geological sciences (MS, PhD). Part-time programs available. *Degree requirements:* For master's, thesis; for doctorate, comprehensive exam, thesis/dissertation. *Entrance requirements:* For master's and doctorate, GRE General Test, GRE Subject Test (recommended). Electronic applications accepted. *Faculty research:* Basin analysis, volcanology, quaternary studies, engineering geophysics, marine geology, biogeochemistry and paleoceanography.

St. Francis Xavier University, Graduate Studies, Department of Earth Sciences, Antigonish, NS B2G 2W5, Canada. Offers M Sc. *Degree requirements:* For master's, thesis. *Entrance requirements:* Additional exam requirements/recommendations for international students: Required—TOEFL (minimum score 580 paper-based; 236 computer-based). *Faculty research:* Environmental earth sciences, global change tectonics, paleoclimatology, crustal fluids.

San Diego State University, Graduate and Research Affairs, College of Sciences, Department of Geological Sciences, San Diego, CA 92182. Offers MS. Part-time programs available. *Degree requirements:* For master's, thesis. *Entrance requirements:* For master's, GRE General Test, bachelor's degree in related field, 2 letters of reference. Additional exam requirements/recommendations for international students: Required—TOEFL. Electronic applications accepted. *Faculty research:* Earthquakes, hydrology, meteorological analysis and tomography studies.

San Jose State University, Graduate Studies and Research, College of Science, Department of Geology, San Jose, CA 95192-0001. Offers MS. *Students:* 12 full-time (8 women), 6 part-time (4 women); includes 4 minority (all Hispanic Americans), 2 international. Average age 33. 13 applicants, 54% accepted, 6 enrolled. In 2009, 4 master's awarded. *Degree requirements:* For master's, thesis. *Entrance requirements:* For master's, GRE. *Application deadline:* For fall admission, 6/29 for domestic students; for spring admission, 11/30 for domestic students. Applications are processed on a rolling basis. Application fee: $59. Electronic applications accepted. *Financial support:* Teaching assistantships, Federal Work-Study available. Financial award applicants required to submit FAFSA. *Unit head:* Dr. Richard Sedlock, Chair, 408-924-5050, Fax: 408-924-5053. *Application contact:* Dave Andersen, Graduate Adviser, 408-924-5014.

South Dakota School of Mines and Technology, Graduate Division, College of Engineering, Department of Geology and Geological Engineering, Rapid City, SD 57701-3995. Offers geology and geological engineering (MS, PhD); paleontology (MS). Part-time programs available. *Faculty:* 7 full-time (0 women). *Students:* 19 full-time (2 women), 10 part-time (3 women); includes 2 minority (1 African American, 1 American Indian/Alaska Native), 6 international. Average age 31. 23 applicants, 70% accepted, 6 enrolled. In 2009, 10 master's awarded. *Degree requirements:* For master's, thesis; for doctorate, thesis/dissertation. *Entrance requirements:* For master's and doctorate, GRE General Test, GRE Subject Test. Additional exam requirements/recommendations for international students: Required—TOEFL, TWE. *Application deadline:* For fall admission, 7/1 priority date for domestic students, 4/1 for international students; for spring admission, 11/1 for domestic students, 9/1 for international students. Applications are processed on a rolling basis. Application fee: $35. Electronic applications accepted. *Expenses:* Tuition, state resident: full-time $3340; part-time $139 per credit hour. Tuition, nonresident: full-time $7060; part-time $294 per credit hour. Required fees: $3270. *Financial support:* In 2009–10, 4 fellowships (averaging $1,800 per year), 4 research assistantships with partial tuition reimbursements (averaging $7,047 per year), 8 teaching assistantships with partial tuition reimbursements (averaging $5,286 per year) were awarded; Federal Work-Study and institutionally sponsored loans also available. Support available to part-time students. Financial award application deadline: 5/15. *Faculty research:* Contaminants in soil, nitrate leaching, environmental changes, fracture formations, greenhouse effect. Total annual research expenditures: $18,865. *Unit head:* Dr. Maribeth Price, Chair, 605-394-1290, E-mail: maribeth.price@sdsmt.edu. *Application contact:* Jeannette R. Nilson, Administrative Support Coordinator, Graduate Education, 800-454-8162 Ext. 1206, Fax: 605-394-5360, E-mail: graduate_admissions@sdsmt.edu.

Southern Illinois University Carbondale, Graduate School, College of Science, Department of Geology, Carbondale, IL 62901-4701. Offers environmental resources and policy (PhD); geology (MS, PhD). *Degree requirements:* For master's, thesis; for doctorate, one foreign language, thesis/dissertation. *Entrance requirements:* For master's, GRE, minimum GPA of 2.7; for doctorate, GRE General Test, minimum GPA of 3.25. Additional exam requirements/recommendations for international students: Required—TOEFL.

Southern Methodist University, Dedman College, Department of Earth Sciences, Program in Geology, Dallas, TX 75275. Offers MS, PhD. Part-time programs available. *Faculty:* 7 full-time (0 women), 6 part-time/adjunct (2 women). *Students:* 25 applicants, 16% accepted. In 2009, 3 master's, 3 doctorates awarded. *Degree requirements:* For master's, thesis, qualifying exam; for doctorate, thesis/dissertation, qualifying exam. *Entrance requirements:* For master's and doctorate, GRE General Test, minimum GPA of 3.0, letters of recommendation. Additional exam requirements/recommendations for international students: Required—TOEFL. *Application deadline:* For fall admission, 2/1 priority date for domestic and international students; for spring admission, 11/30 for domestic students. Applications are processed on a rolling basis. Application fee: $50. *Financial support:* In 2009–10, fellowships with full tuition reimbursements (averaging $15,000 per year), research assistantships with full tuition reimbursements (averaging $15,000 per year), teaching assistantships with full tuition reimbursements (averaging $15,000 per year) were awarded; scholarships/grants and unspecified assistantships also available. Financial award application deadline: 2/1; financial award applicants required to submit FAFSA. *Faculty research:* Geothermal, paleontology, environmental, stable isotope geochemistry. Total annual research expenditures: $400,000. *Unit head:* Dr. Robert T. Gregory, Chair, 214-768-3075, Fax: 214-768-2701, E-mail: bgregory@smu.edu. *Application contact:* Dr. John V. Walther, Graduate Advisor, 214-768-3174, Fax: 214-768-2701, E-mail: walther@smu.edu.

State University of New York at Binghamton, Graduate School, School of Arts and Sciences, Department of Geological Sciences, Binghamton, NY 13902-6000. Offers MA, PhD. Part-time programs available. *Faculty:* 12 full-time (1 woman), 1 part-time/adjunct (0 women). *Students:* 15 full-time (4 women), 21 part-time (13 women); includes 4 minority (1 Asian American or Pacific Islander, 3 Hispanic Americans), 4 international. Average age 30. 12 applicants, 67% accepted, 6 enrolled. In 2009, 5 master's, 1 doctorate awarded. Terminal master's awarded for partial completion of doctoral program. *Degree requirements:* For master's, thesis or alternative; for doctorate, variable foreign language requirement, thesis/dissertation, departmental qualifying exam. *Entrance requirements:* For master's and doctorate, GRE General Test, GRE Subject Test. Additional exam requirements/recommendations for international students: Required—TOEFL (minimum score 550 paper-based; 213 computer-based; 80 iBT). *Application deadline:* For fall admission, 2/15 priority date for domestic and international students; for spring admission, 9/15 priority date for domestic and international students. Applications are processed on a rolling basis. Application fee: $60. Electronic applications accepted. *Financial support:* In 2009–10, 14 students received support, including 4 research assistantships with full tuition reimbursements available (averaging $10,000 per year), 11 teaching assistantships with full tuition reimbursements available (averaging $15,500 per year); career-related internships or fieldwork, Federal Work-Study, institutionally sponsored loans, scholarships/grants, health care benefits, and unspecified assistantships also available. Financial award application deadline: 2/15; financial award applicants required to submit FAFSA. *Unit head:* Dr. Robert Demicco, Chairperson, 607-777-2604, E-mail: demicco@binghamton.edu. *Application contact:* Victoria Williams, Recruiting and Admissions Coordinator, 607-777-2151, Fax: 607-777-2501, E-mail: vwilliam@binghamton.edu.

Stephen F. Austin State University, Graduate School, College of Sciences and Mathematics, Department of Geology, Nacogdoches, TX 75962. Offers MS, MSNS. *Degree requirements:* For master's, comprehensive exam. *Entrance requirements:* For master's, GRE General Test, minimum GPA of 2.8 in last 60 hours, 2.5 overall. Additional exam requirements/recommendations for international students: Required—TOEFL. *Faculty research:* Stratigraphy of Kaibab limestone, Utah; structure of Ouachita Mountains, Arkansas; groundwater chemistry of Carrizo Sand, Texas.

Sul Ross State University, School of Arts and Sciences, Department of Earth and Physical Sciences, Alpine, TX 79832. Offers MS. Part-time programs available. *Degree requirements:* For master's, thesis optional. *Entrance requirements:* For master's, GRE General Test, minimum GPA of 2.5 in last 60 hours of undergraduate work.

See Display on page 129.

Syracuse University, College of Arts and Sciences, Program in Earth Sciences, Syracuse, NY 13244. Offers MA, MS, PhD. Part-time programs available. *Students:* 23 full-time (7 women), 4 part-time (2 women); includes 2 minority (1 African American, 1 Asian American or Pacific Islander), 5 international. Average age 27. 33 applicants, 39% accepted, 11 enrolled. In 2009, 4 master's, 1 doctorate awarded. *Degree requirements:* For master's, thesis (for some programs), research tool; for doctorate, thesis/dissertation, 2 research tools. *Entrance requirements:* For master's and doctorate, GRE General Test, GRE Subject Test. Additional exam requirements/recommendations for international students: Required—TOEFL (minimum score 100 iBT). *Application deadline:* For fall admission, 1/15 priority date for domestic and international students. Application fee: $75. Electronic applications accepted. *Expenses:* Tuition: Full-time $26,808; part-time $1117 per credit. Required fees: $1024. *Financial support:* Fellowships with full tuition reimbursements, research assistantships with full tuition reimbursements, teaching assistantships with full and partial tuition reimbursements, tuition waivers (partial) available. Financial award application deadline: 1/1; financial award applicants required to submit FAFSA. *Unit head:* Dr. Jeff Karson, Chair, 315-443-7976, Fax: 315-443-3363, E-mail: jakarson@syr.edu. *Application contact:* Jolene Fitch, Information Contact, 315-4443-2672, E-mail: jofitch@syr.edu.

Temple University, Graduate School, College of Science and Technology, Department of Geology, Philadelphia, PA 19122-6096. Offers MS. *Degree requirements:* For master's, thesis, qualifying exam. *Entrance requirements:* For master's, GRE General Test, minimum GPA of 3.0. Additional exam requirements/recommendations for international students: Required—TOEFL (minimum score 550 paper-based; 213 computer-based; 79 iBT). Electronic applications accepted. *Faculty research:* Hydraulic modeling, environmental geochemistry and geophysics, paleosas, cyclic stratigraphy, materials research.

Texas A&M University, College of Geosciences, Department of Geology and Geophysics, College Station, TX 77843. Offers geology (MS, PhD); geophysics (MS, PhD). *Faculty:* 30. *Students:* 101 full-time (39 women), 17 part-time (4 women); includes 11 minority (1 American Indian/Alaska Native, 6 Asian Americans or Pacific Islanders, 4 Hispanic Americans), 51 international. Average age 31. In 2009, 10 master's, 4 doctorates awarded. *Degree requirements:* For master's, thesis; for doctorate, thesis/dissertation. *Entrance requirements:* For master's and doctorate, GRE General Test. Additional exam requirements/recommendations for international students: Required—TOEFL. *Application deadline:* For fall admission, 3/1 priority date for domestic students, 1/15 for international students; for spring admission, 10/1 priority date for domestic students, 8/15 for international students. Applications are processed on a rolling basis. Application fee: $50 ($75 for international students). Electronic applications accepted. *Expenses:* Tuition, state resident: full-time $3991.32; part-time $221.74 per credit hour. Tuition, nonresident: full-time $9049; part-time $502.74 per credit hour. *Financial support:* In 2009–10, fellowships with partial tuition reimbursements (averaging $1,000 per year), research assistantships with partial tuition reimbursements (averaging $11,925 per year), teaching assistantships with partial tuition reimbursements (averaging $11,925 per year) were awarded; Federal Work-Study, institutionally sponsored loans, scholarships/grants, tuition waivers (partial), and unspecified assistantships also available. Financial award application deadline: 3/1; financial award applicants required to submit FAFSA. *Faculty research:* Environmental and engineering geology and geophysics, petroleum geology, tectonophysics, geochemistry. *Unit head:* Head, 979-845-0132, E-mail: geoaggie@geo.tamu.edu. *Application contact:* Graduate Adviser, 979-845-2451, Fax: 979-845-6162, E-mail: geoaggie@geo.tamu.edu.

Texas A&M University–Kingsville, College of Graduate Studies, College of Arts and Sciences, Department of Geosciences, Kingsville, TX 78363. Offers applied geology (MS). Part-time and evening/weekend programs available. *Degree requirements:* For master's, comprehensive exam, thesis. *Entrance requirements:* For master's, GRE General Test, minimum GPA of 3.0. Additional exam requirements/recommendations for international students: Required—TOEFL. *Faculty research:* Stratigraphy and sedimentology of modern coastal sediments, sandstone diagnosis, vertebrate paleontology, structural geology.

Texas Christian University, College of Science and Engineering, Department of Geology, Fort Worth, TX 76129-0002. Offers MS. Part-time and evening/weekend programs available. *Degree requirements:* For master's, thesis, preliminary exam. *Entrance requirements:* For master's, GRE General Test. Additional exam requirements/recommendations for international students: Required—TOEFL. *Application deadline:* For fall admission, 3/1 for domestic students; for spring admission, 12/1 for domestic students. Applications are processed on a rolling basis. Application fee: $0. *Expenses:* Tuition: Full-time $17,640; part-time $980 per credit hour. Tuition and fees vary according to program. *Financial support:* Teaching assistantships, unspecified assistantships available. Financial award application deadline: 3/1. *Unit head:* Dr. Richard Hanson, Chairperson, 817-257-7270, E-mail: r.hanson@tcu.edu. *Application contact:* Dr. Richard Hanson, Chairperson, 817-257-7270, E-mail: r.hanson@tcu.edu.

Tulane University, School of Science and Engineering, Department of Earth and Environmental Sciences, New Orleans, LA 70118-5669. Offers MS, PhD. *Degree requirements:* For master's, one foreign language, thesis or alternative; for doctorate, one foreign language, thesis/dissertation. *Entrance requirements:* For master's, GRE General Test, minimum B average in undergraduate course work; for doctorate, GRE General Test. Additional exam requirements/recommendations for international students: Required—TOEFL. Electronic applications accepted. *Faculty research:* Sedimentation, isotopes, biogeochemistry, marine geology, structural geology.

Université du Québec à Montréal, Graduate Programs, Program in Earth Sciences, Montreal, QC H3C 3P8, Canada. Offers earth sciences (M Sc); mineral resources (PhD); non-renewable resources (DESS). Part-time programs available. Terminal master's awarded for partial completion of doctoral program. *Degree requirements:* For master's, thesis (for some programs); for doctorate, thesis/dissertation. *Entrance requirements:* For master's, appropriate bachelor's degree or equivalent, proficiency in French. *Faculty research:* Economic geology, structural geology, geochemistry, Quaternary geology, isotopic geochemistry.

Université Laval, Faculty of Sciences and Engineering, Department of Geology and Geological Engineering, Québec, QC G1K 7P4, Canada. Offers earth sciences (M Sc, PhD), including earth sciences, environmental technologies (M Sc); geology (M Sc, PhD). Terminal master's awarded for partial completion of doctoral program. *Degree requirements:* For master's, thesis (for some programs); for doctorate, comprehensive exam, thesis/dissertation. *Entrance requirements:* For master's and doctorate, knowledge of French. Electronic applications accepted. *Faculty research:* Engineering, economics, regional geology.

University at Albany, State University of New York, College of Arts and Sciences, Department of Earth and Atmospheric Sciences, Albany, NY 12222-0001. Offers atmospheric science (MS, PhD); geology (MS, PhD). *Degree requirements:* For master's, one foreign language, comprehensive exam, thesis; for doctorate, 2 foreign languages, comprehensive exam, thesis/dissertation, oral exams. *Entrance requirements:* For master's and doctorate, GRE General Test. Additional exam requirements/recommendations for international students: Required—TOEFL (minimum score 550 paper-based; 213 computer-based). Electronic applications accepted. *Faculty research:* Environmental geochemistry, tectonics, mesoscale meteorology, atmospheric chemistry.

University at Buffalo, the State University of New York, Graduate School, College of Arts and Sciences, Department of Geology, Buffalo, NY 14260. Offers MA, MS, PhD. Part-time programs available. *Faculty:* 13 full-time (6 women), 3 part-time/adjunct (1 woman). *Students:* 47 full-time (22 women), 2 part-time (both women); includes 4 minority (2 African Americans, 2 Hispanic Americans), 2 international. Average age 28. 45 applicants, 78% accepted, 16 enrolled. In 2009, 10 master's, 2 doctorates awarded. *Degree requirements:* For master's, project or thesis; for doctorate, thesis/dissertation, dissertation defense. *Entrance requirements:* For master's and doctorate, GRE General Test. Additional exam requirements/recommendations for international students: Required—TOEFL (minimum score 550 paper-based; 213 computer-based; 79 iBT). *Application deadline:* For fall admission, 2/1 priority date for domestic and international students; for spring admission, 10/1 priority date for domestic and international students. Applications are processed on a rolling basis. Application fee: $75. Electronic applications accepted. *Financial support:* In 2009–10, 34 students received support, including 4 fellowships with full tuition reimbursements available (averaging $6,000 per year), 16 research assistantships with full tuition reimbursements available (averaging $15,000 per year), 14 teaching assistantships with full tuition reimbursements available (averaging $15,000 per year); Federal Work-Study, scholarships/grants, health care benefits, and unspecified assistantships also available. Financial award application deadline: 2/1; financial award applicants required to submit FAFSA. *Faculty research:* Environmental geophysics, hydrogeology, geochemistry, fractured rocks, volcanology. Total annual research expenditures: $1.9 million. *Unit head:* Dr. Richelle M. Allen-King, Professor and Chair, 716-645-3489, Fax: 716-645-3999, E-mail: geology@buffalo.edu. *Application contact:* Dr. Charles E. Mitchell, Director of Graduate Studies, 716-645-4290, Fax: 716-645-3999, E-mail: cem@buffalo.edu.

The University of Akron, Graduate School, Buchtel College of Arts and Sciences, Department of Geology, Akron, OH 44325. Offers earth science (MS); environmental geology (MS); geology (MS); geophysics (MS). Part-time programs available. *Faculty:* 9 full-time (2 women), 1 part-time/adjunct (0 women). *Students:* 14 full-time (2 women), 3 part-time (2 women), 3 international. Average age 30. 16 applicants, 81% accepted, 6 enrolled. In 2009, 4 master's awarded. *Degree requirements:* For master's, comprehensive exam, thesis, seminar, proficiency exam. *Entrance requirements:* For master's, minimum GPA of 2.75, 3 letters of recommendation. Additional exam requirements/recommendations for international students: Required—TOEFL (minimum score 550 paper-based; 213 computer-based; 79 iBT). *Application deadline:* Applications are processed on a rolling basis. Application fee: $30 ($40 for international students). Electronic applications accepted. *Expenses:* Tuition, state resident: full-time $6570; part-time $365 per credit hour. Tuition, nonresident: full-time $11,250; part-time $625 per credit hour. *Financial support:* In 2009–10, 12 teaching assistantships with full tuition reimbursements were awarded; research assistantships with full tuition reimbursements. *Faculty research:* Terrestrial environmental change, Karst hydrogeology, lacustrine paleoenvironments, environmental magnetism and geophysics. Total annual research expenditures: $443,929. *Unit head:* Dr. John Szabo, Chair, 330-972-8039, E-mail: jszabo@uakron.edu. *Application contact:* Dr. LaVerne Friberg, Director of Graduate Studies, 330-972-8046, E-mail: lfribe1@uakron.edu.

The University of Alabama, Graduate School, College of Arts and Sciences, Department of Geological Sciences, Tuscaloosa, AL 35487. Offers MS, PhD. *Faculty:* 14 full-time (3 women). *Students:* 33 full-time (10 women), 15 part-time (5 women); includes 1 minority (American Indian/Alaska Native), 15 international. Average age 29. 42 applicants, 62% accepted, 14 enrolled. In 2009, 2 master's, 1 doctorate awarded. Terminal master's awarded for partial completion of doctoral program. *Degree requirements:* For master's, comprehensive exam, thesis; for doctorate, comprehensive exam, thesis/dissertation. *Entrance requirements:* For master's and doctorate, GRE. Additional exam requirements/recommendations for international students: Required—TOEFL (minimum score 550 paper-based; 213 computer-based; 79 iBT). *Application deadline:* For fall admission, 3/1 priority date for domestic and international students; for spring admission, 10/1 priority date for domestic and international students. Applications are processed on a rolling basis. Application fee: $50 ($60 for international students). Electronic applications accepted. *Expenses:* Tuition, state resident: full-time $7000. Tuition, nonresident: full-time $19,200. *Financial support:* In 2009–10, 11 research assistantships with full tuition reimbursements (averaging $13,595 per year), 29 teaching assistantships with full tuition reimbursements (averaging $13,365 per year) were awarded; career-related internships or fieldwork, Federal Work-Study, and institutionally sponsored loans also available. *Faculty research:* Structure, petrology, stratigraphy, geochemistry, hydrogeology, geophysics. Total annual research expenditures: $744,826. *Unit head:* Dr. Harold H. Stowell, Chairperson and Professor, 205-348-5095, E-mail: hstowell@wgs.geo.ua.edu. *Application contact:* Dr. Andrew Mark Goodliffe, Graduate Program Director, 205-348-7167, E-mail: amg@ua.edu.

University of Alaska Fairbanks, College of Natural Sciences and Mathematics, Department of Geology and Geophysics, Fairbanks, AK 99775-5780. Offers geology (MS, PhD), including economic geology (PhD), petroleum geology (MS), quaternary geology (PhD), remote sensing, volcanology (PhD); geophysics (MS, PhD), including remote sensing, snow, ice, and permafrost geophysics (MS), solid-earth geophysics (MS). Part-time programs available. *Faculty:* 16 full-time (4 women), 3 part-time/adjunct (0 women). *Students:* 56 full-time (24 women), 18 part-time (10 women); includes 3 minority (1 African American, 1 Asian American or Pacific Islander, 1 Hispanic American), 12 international. Average age 30. 57 applicants, 30% accepted, 16 enrolled. In 2009, 6 master's, 4 doctorates awarded. Terminal master's awarded for partial

Geology

University of Alaska Fairbanks (continued)

completion of doctoral program. *Degree requirements:* For master's, comprehensive exam, thesis, oral exam, oral defense; for doctorate, comprehensive exam, thesis/dissertation, oral exam, oral defense. *Entrance requirements:* For master's and doctorate, GRE General Test. Additional exam requirements/recommendations for international students: Required—TOEFL (minimum score 550 paper-based; 213 computer-based). *Application deadline:* For fall admission, 6/1 for domestic students, 3/1 for international students; for spring admission, 10/15 for domestic students, 9/1 for international students. Applications are processed on a rolling basis. Application fee: $60. Electronic applications accepted. *Expenses:* Tuition, state resident: full-time $7584; part-time $316 per credit. Tuition, nonresident: full-time $15,504; part-time $646 per credit. Required fees: $23 per credit. $135 per semester. Tuition and fees vary according to course level, course load and reciprocity agreements. *Financial support:* In 2009–10, 1 fellowship (averaging $16,454 per year), 32 research assistantships (averaging $15,811 per year), 7 teaching assistantships (averaging $14,143 per year) were awarded; Federal Work-Study, scholarships/grants, health care benefits, and unspecified assistantships also available. Support available to part-time students. Financial award application deadline: 2/15; financial award applicants required to submit FAFSA. *Faculty research:* Glacial surging, volcanology, geochronology, impact cratering, permafrost geophysics. *Unit head:* Dr. Benard Coakley, Co-Chair, 907-474-7565, Fax: 907-474-5163, E-mail: geology@uaf.edu. *Application contact:* Dr. Benard Coakley, Co-Chair, 907-474-7565, Fax: 907-474-5163, E-mail: geology@uaf.edu.

University of Arkansas, Graduate School, J. William Fulbright College of Arts and Sciences, Department of Geosciences, Program in Geology, Fayetteville, AR 72701-1201. Offers MS. Part-time programs available. *Students:* 11 full-time (5 women), 11 part-time (3 women), 1 international. In 2009, 6 master's awarded. *Degree requirements:* For master's, thesis. Application fee: $40 ($50 for international students). *Expenses:* Tuition, state resident: full-time $7355; part-time $356.58 per hour. Tuition, nonresident: full-time $17,401; part-time $775.17 per hour. Required fees: $1203. *Financial support:* In 2009–10, 11 teaching assistantships were awarded; fellowships, research assistantships, career-related internships or fieldwork and Federal Work-Study also available. Support available to part-time students. Financial award application deadline: 4/1; financial award applicants required to submit FAFSA. *Unit head:* Dr. Ralph Davis, Graduate Coordinator, 479-575-3355, Fax: 479-575-3469, E-mail: ralphd@uark.edu. *Application contact:* Dr. Doy Zachry, Graduate Admissions, 479-575-2785, E-mail: dzachry@uark.edu.

The University of British Columbia, Faculty of Science, Department of Earth and Ocean Sciences, Vancouver, BC V6T 1Z4, Canada. Offers atmospheric science (M Sc, PhD); geological engineering (M Eng, MA Sc, PhD); geological sciences (M Sc, PhD); geophysics (M Sc, MA Sc, PhD); oceanography (M Sc, PhD). *Degree requirements:* For master's, thesis (for some programs); for doctorate, comprehensive exam, thesis/dissertation. *Entrance requirements:* Additional exam requirements/recommendations for international students: Required—TOEFL (minimum score 600 paper-based; 250 computer-based; 100 iBT). Electronic applications accepted. *Faculty research:* Oceans and atmosphere, environmental earth science, hydro geology, mineral deposits, geophysics.

University of Calgary, Faculty of Graduate Studies, Faculty of Science, Department of Geology and Geophysics, Calgary, AB T2N 1N4, Canada. Offers geology (M Sc, PhD); geophysics (M Sc, PhD). Part-time programs available. Terminal master's awarded for partial completion of doctoral program. *Degree requirements:* For master's, thesis; for doctorate, thesis/dissertation, candidacy exam. *Entrance requirements:* For master's, B Sc; for doctorate, honors B Sc or M Sc. Additional exam requirements/recommendations for international students: Required—TOEFL. Electronic applications accepted. *Faculty research:* Geochemistry, petrology, paleontology, stratigraphy, exploration and solid-earth geophysics.

University of California, Berkeley, Graduate Division, College of Letters and Science, Department of Earth and Planetary Science, Berkeley, CA 94720-1500. Offers geology (MA, MS, PhD); geophysics (MA, MS, PhD). *Students:* 64 full-time (30 women). Average age 29. 166 applicants, 17 enrolled. In 2009, 1 master's, 11 doctorates awarded. Terminal master's awarded for partial completion of doctoral program. *Degree requirements:* For master's, oral exam (MA), thesis (MS); for doctorate, comprehensive exam, thesis/dissertation, candidacy exams. *Entrance requirements:* For master's and doctorate, GRE General Test, minimum GPA of 3.0, 3 letters of recommendation. Additional exam requirements/recommendations for international students: Required—TOEFL. *Application deadline:* For fall admission, 12/28 for domestic students. Application fee: $70 ($90 for international students). *Financial support:* Fellowships, research assistantships, teaching assistantships, Federal Work-Study and unspecified assistantships available. *Faculty research:* Tectonics, environmental geology, high-pressure geophysics and seismology, economic geology, geochemistry. *Unit head:* Prof. Roland Burgmann, Chair, 510-642-3993, Fax: 510-643-9980, E-mail: ch_eps@ls.berkeley.edu. *Application contact:* Margie Winn, Student Affairs Officer, 510-642-5574, Fax: 510-643-9980, E-mail: gradadm@eps.berkeley.edu.

University of California, Davis, Graduate Studies, Program in Geology, Davis, CA 95616. Offers MS, PhD. Terminal master's awarded for partial completion of doctoral program. *Degree requirements:* For master's, thesis; for doctorate, thesis/dissertation. *Entrance requirements:* For master's and doctorate, GRE General Test, GRE Subject Test, minimum GPA of 3.0. Additional exam requirements/recommendations for international students: Required—TOEFL (minimum score 550 paper-based; 213 computer-based). Electronic applications accepted. *Faculty research:* Petrology, paleontology, geophysics, sedimentology, structure/tectonics.

University of California, Los Angeles, Graduate Division, College of Letters and Science, Department of Earth and Space Sciences, Program in Geology, Los Angeles, CA 90095. Offers MS, PhD. *Students:* 12 full-time (4 women); includes 1 minority (Asian American or Pacific Islander). Average age 27. 25 applicants, 40% accepted, 4 enrolled. In 2009, 2 master's, 1 doctorate awarded. Terminal master's awarded for partial completion of doctoral program. *Degree requirements:* For master's, comprehensive exams or thesis; for doctorate, thesis/dissertation, oral and written qualifying exams. *Entrance requirements:* For master's, GRE General Test, minimum GPA of 3.0, bachelor's degree in related field; for doctorate, GRE General Test, minimum undergraduate GPA of 3.0, bachelor's degree in related field. *Application deadline:* For fall admission, 1/15 for domestic and international students. Application fee: $70 ($90 for international students). Electronic applications accepted. *Financial support:* In 2009–10, 10 fellowships with full and partial tuition reimbursements, 6 research assistantships with full and partial tuition reimbursements, 10 teaching assistantships with full and partial tuition reimbursements were awarded; Federal Work-Study, institutionally sponsored loans, scholarships/grants, health care benefits, tuition waivers (full and partial), and unspecified assistantships also available. Financial award application deadline: 3/1; financial award applicants required to submit FAFSA. *Application contact:* Departmental Office, 888-377-8252, E-mail: holbrook@ess.ucla.edu.

University of California, Riverside, Graduate Division, Department of Earth Sciences, Riverside, CA 92521-0102. Offers geological sciences (MS, PhD). *Faculty:* 13 full-time (1 woman). *Students:* 31 full-time (10 women); includes 2 minority (both Hispanic Americans), 2 international. Average age 30. In 2009, 2 doctorates awarded. Terminal master's awarded for partial completion of doctoral program. *Degree requirements:* For master's, thesis, final oral exam; for doctorate, thesis/dissertation, qualifying exams, final oral exam. *Entrance requirements:* For master's and doctorate, GRE General Test, minimum GPA of 3.2. Additional exam requirements/recommendations for international students: Required—TOEFL (minimum score 550 paper-based; 213 computer-based; 80 iBT). *Application deadline:* For fall admission, 5/1 for domestic students, 2/1 for international students; for winter admission, 9/1 for domestic students, 7/1 for international students; for spring admission, 12/1 for domestic students, 10/1 for international students. Applications are processed on a rolling basis. Application fee: $60 ($75 for international students). Electronic applications accepted. *Financial support:* In 2009–10, fellowships with full and partial tuition reimbursements (averaging $12,000 per year), research assistantships with full and partial tuition reimbursements (averaging $16,000 per year), teaching assistantships with full and partial tuition reimbursements (averaging $16,500 per year) were awarded; career-related internships or fieldwork, Federal Work-Study, institutionally sponsored loans, health care benefits, tuition waivers (full and partial), and unspecified assistantships also available. Financial award application deadline: 1/5; financial award applicants required to submit FAFSA. *Faculty research:* Applied and solid earth geophysics, tectonic geomorphology, fluid-rock interaction, paleobiology-ecology, sedimentary-geochemistry. *Unit head:* Dr. Mary Droser, Chair, 951-827-3797, Fax: 951-827-4324, E-mail: mary.droser@ucr.edu. *Application contact:* John Herring, Graduate Program Assistant, 951-827-3435, Fax: 951-827-4324, E-mail: geology@ucr.edu.

See Display on page 130.

University of California, Santa Barbara, Graduate Division, College of Letters and Sciences, Division of Mathematics, Life, and Physical Sciences, Department of Earth Science, Santa Barbara, CA 93106-9620. Offers geological sciences (MS, PhD), including computational science and engineering (MS), geological sciences; geophysics (MS), including computational science and engineering, geophysics. *Faculty:* 20 full-time (4 women). *Students:* 35 full-time (15 women). Average age 27. 90 applicants, 27% accepted, 9 enrolled. In 2009, 3 master's, 4 doctorates awarded. *Degree requirements:* For master's, comprehensive exam, thesis; for doctorate, comprehensive exam, thesis/dissertation. *Entrance requirements:* For master's, GRE General Test, 3 letters of recommendation, resume/curriculum vitae; for doctorate, GRE General Test, 3 letters of recommendation, statement of purpose, personal achievements/contributions statement, resume/curriculum vitae, transcripts for post-secondary institutions attended. Additional exam requirements/recommendations for international students: Required—TOEFL (minimum score 550 paper-based; 213 computer-based; 80 iBT) or IELTS (minimum score 7). *Application deadline:* For fall admission, 2/1 for domestic students, 1/1 for international students. Application fee: $70 ($90 for international students). Electronic applications accepted. *Financial support:* In 2009–10, 35 students received support, including 21 fellowships with full and partial tuition reimbursements available (averaging $6,200 per year), 17 research assistantships with full and partial tuition reimbursements available (averaging $6,000 per year), 28 teaching assistantships with partial tuition reimbursements available (averaging $7,600 per year); career-related internships or fieldwork, Federal Work-Study, institutionally sponsored loans, scholarships/grants, traineeships, health care benefits, and unspecified assistantships also available. Financial award applicants required to submit FAFSA. *Faculty research:* Tectonics, geochronology, paleontology, volcanology, geomorphology. *Unit head:* Dr. Ralph Archuleta, Chair, 805-893-8441, E-mail: ralph@crustal.ucsb.edu. *Application contact:* Samuel C. Rifkin, Graduate Program Assistant, 805-893-3329, Fax: 805-893-2314, E-mail: rifkin@geol.ucsb.edu.

University of Cincinnati, Graduate School, McMicken College of Arts and Sciences, Department of Geology, Cincinnati, OH 45221. Offers MS, PhD. Part-time programs available. *Degree requirements:* For master's, thesis; for doctorate, comprehensive exam, thesis/dissertation. *Entrance requirements:* For master's and doctorate, GRE General Test, 1 year of course work in physics, chemistry, and calculus. Additional exam requirements/recommendations for international students: Required—TOEFL. Electronic applications accepted. *Faculty research:* Paleobiology, sequence stratigraphy, earth systems history, quaternary, groundwater.

University of Colorado at Boulder, Graduate School, College of Arts and Sciences, Department of Geological Sciences, Boulder, CO 80309. Offers geology (MS, PhD); geophysics (PhD). *Faculty:* 28 full-time (8 women). *Students:* 60 full-time (31 women), 31 part-time (16 women); includes 7 minority (2 American Indian/Alaska Native, 2 Asian Americans or Pacific Islanders, 3 Hispanic Americans), 9 international. Average age 29. 176 applicants, 13% accepted, 23 enrolled. In 2009, 4 master's, 12 doctorates awarded. Terminal master's awarded for partial completion of doctoral program. *Degree requirements:* For master's, comprehensive exam, thesis; for doctorate, comprehensive exam, thesis/dissertation. *Entrance requirements:* For master's, GRE General Test, minimum undergraduate GPA of 3.0; for doctorate, GRE General Test, minimum GPA of 2.75. *Application deadline:* For fall admission, 12/15 priority date for domestic students, 12/1 for international students. Application fee: $50 ($60 for international students). *Financial support:* In 2009–10, 28 fellowships with full tuition reimbursements (averaging $13,580 per year), 45 research assistantships with full tuition reimbursements (averaging $15,474 per year) were awarded; Federal Work-Study, institutionally sponsored loans, scholarships/grants, and tuition waivers (full) also available. Financial award application deadline: 1/15. *Faculty research:* Sedimentology, stratigraphy, economic geology of mineral deposits, fossil fuels, hydrogeology and water resources, geophysics, isotope geology, paleobiology, mineralogy, remote sensing. Total annual research expenditures: $6 million.

University of Connecticut, Graduate School, College of Liberal Arts and Sciences, Center for Integrative Geosciences, Storrs, CT 06269. Offers geological sciences (MS, PhD). *Faculty:* 19 full-time (4 women). *Students:* 13 full-time (6 women), 6 part-time (2 women), 8 international. Average age 33. 11 applicants, 36% accepted, 1 enrolled. In 2009, 4 master's awarded. *Degree requirements:* For doctorate, thesis/dissertation. *Entrance requirements:* For master's and doctorate, GRE General Test. Additional exam requirements/recommendations for international students: Required—TOEFL (minimum score 550 paper-based; 213 computer-based). *Application deadline:* For fall admission, 2/1 priority date for domestic and international students; for spring admission, 11/1 for domestic students, 10/1 for international students. Applications are processed on a rolling basis. Application fee: $55. Electronic applications accepted. *Expenses:* Tuition, state resident: full-time $4725; part-time $525 per credit. Tuition, nonresident: full-time $12,267; part-time $1363 per credit. Required fees: $346 per semester. Tuition and fees vary according to course load. *Financial support:* In 2009–10, 7 research assistantships with full tuition reimbursements, 4 teaching assistantships with full tuition reimbursements were awarded; fellowships, Federal Work-Study, scholarships/grants, health care benefits, and unspecified assistantships also available. Financial award application deadline: 2/1. *Unit head:* Pieter Visscher, Director, 860-486-4434, Fax: 860-486-1383, E-mail: pieter.visscher@uconn.edu. *Application contact:* Pieter Visscher, Director, 860-486-4434, Fax: 860-486-1383, E-mail: pieter.visscher@uconn.edu.

University of Delaware, College of Marine and Earth Studies, Department of Geological Sciences, Newark, DE 19716. Offers MA, PhD.

University of Florida, Graduate School, College of Liberal Arts and Sciences, Department of Geological Sciences, Gainesville, FL 32611. Offers geology (MS, MST, PhD). Terminal master's awarded for partial completion of doctoral program. *Degree requirements:* For master's, thesis (for some programs); for doctorate, one foreign language, thesis/dissertation. *Entrance requirements:* For master's and doctorate, GRE General Test, GRE Subject Test, minimum GPA of 3.0. Additional exam requirements/recommendations for international students: Required—TOEFL (minimum score 550 paper-based; 213 computer-based). Electronic applications accepted. *Faculty research:* Paleoclimatology, tectonophysics, petrochemistry, marine geology, geochemistry, hydrology.

University of Georgia, Graduate School, College of Arts and Sciences, Department of Geology, Athens, GA 30602. Offers MS, PhD. *Faculty:* 14 full-time (3 women), 1 part-time/adjunct (0 women). *Students:* 26 full-time (10 women), 10 part-time (4 women); includes 1 minority (African American). 40 applicants, 50% accepted, 13 enrolled. In 2009, 7 master's, 2 doctorates awarded. *Degree requirements:* For master's, thesis; for doctorate, one foreign language, thesis/dissertation. *Entrance requirements:* For master's and doctorate, GRE General Test. *Application deadline:* For fall admission, 7/1 priority date for domestic students; for spring admission, 11/15 for domestic students. Application fee: $50. Electronic applications accepted. *Expenses:* Tuition, state resident: full-time $6000; part-time $250 per credit hour. Tuition, nonresident: full-time $20,904; part-time $871 per credit hour. Required fees: $730 per semester. *Financial support:* Fellowships, research assistantships, teaching assistantships, unspecified assistantships available. *Unit head:* Dr. Michael F. Roden, Head, 706-542-2416, Fax: 706-542-2425, E-mail: mroden@uga.edu. *Application contact:* Dr. Steven M. Holland, Graduate Coordinator, 706-542-0424, Fax: 706-542-2425, E-mail: stratum@uga.edu.

University of Hawaii at Manoa, Graduate Division, School of Ocean and Earth Science and Technology, Department of Geology and Geophysics, Honolulu, HI 96822. Offers high-pressure geophysics and geochemistry (MS, PhD); hydrogeology and engineering geology (MS, PhD); marine geology and geophysics (MS, PhD); planetary geosciences and remote sensing (MS, PhD); seismology and solid-earth geophysics (MS, PhD); volcanology, petrology, and geochemistry (MS, PhD). Part-time programs available. *Faculty:* 73 full-time (16 women), 15 part-time/adjunct (3 women). *Students:* 42 full-time (20 women), 8 part-time (5 women); includes 7 minority (1 African American, 4 Asian Americans or Pacific Islanders, 2 Hispanic Americans), 6 international. Average age 29. 56 applicants, 25% accepted, 6 enrolled. In 2009, 4 master's, 7 doctorates awarded. Terminal master's awarded for partial completion of doctoral program. *Degree requirements:* For master's, thesis optional; for doctorate, comprehensive exam, thesis/dissertation. *Entrance requirements:* For master's and doctorate, GRE General Test, minimum GPA of 3.0. Additional exam requirements/recommendations for international students: Required—TOEFL (minimum score 580 paper-based; 237 computer-based; 92 iBT), IELTS (minimum score 5). *Application deadline:* For fall admission, 1/15 for domestic students, 1/1 for international students; for spring admission, 9/1 for domestic students, 8/15 for international students. Application fee: $60. *Expenses:* Tuition, state resident: full-time $8900; part-time $372 per credit. Tuition, nonresident: full-time $21,400; part-time $898 per credit. Required fees: $207 per semester. *Financial support:* In 2009–10, 1 student received support, including 4 fellowships (averaging $9,338 per year), 31 research assistantships (averaging $23,877 per year), 5 teaching assistantships (averaging $20,466 per year). Total annual research expenditures: $3.8 million. *Application contact:* Dr. Charles Fletcher, Chair, 808-956-7640, Fax: 808-956-5512, E-mail: gg-grad-chair@hawaii.edu.

University of Houston, College of Natural Sciences and Mathematics, Department of Earth and Atmospheric Sciences, Houston, TX 77204. Offers MA, MS, PhD. Part-time and evening/weekend programs available. *Faculty:* 23 full-time (5 women), 4 part-time/adjunct (0 women). *Students:* 118 full-time (42 women), 69 part-time (15 women); includes 26 minority (8 African Americans, 7 Asian Americans or Pacific Islanders, 11 Hispanic Americans), 72 international. Average age 31. 110 applicants, 77% accepted, 42 enrolled. In 2009, 25 master's, 11 doctorates awarded. *Degree requirements:* For master's, comprehensive exam; for doctorate, comprehensive exam, thesis/dissertation. *Entrance requirements:* For master's, GRE, letter of recommendation; for doctorate, GRE, Transcript, letter of recommendations. Additional exam requirements/recommendations for international students: Required—TOEFL (minimum score 550 paper-based; 213 computer-based; 79 iBT), IELTS (minimum score 6). *Application deadline:* For fall admission, 7/1 for domestic students, 4/1 for international students; for spring admission, 12/1 for domestic students, 10/1 for international students. Applications are processed on a rolling basis. Application fee: $0 ($75 for international students). Electronic applications accepted. *Expenses:* Tuition, state resident: full-time $7676; part-time $320 per credit hour. Tuition, nonresident: full-time $14,324; part-time $597 per credit hour. Required fees: $3034. *Financial support:* In 2009–10, 34 research assistantships with full tuition reimbursements (averaging $17,200 per year), 26 teaching assistantships with full tuition reimbursements (averaging $17,200 per year) were awarded; career-related internships or fieldwork, Federal Work-Study, institutionally sponsored loans, scholarships/grants, health care benefits, and unspecified assistantships also available. Support available to part-time students. Financial award application deadline: 2/1. *Faculty research:* Atmospheric sciences, seismic and solid earth geophysics, tectonics, environmental hydrochemistry, carbonates, micropaleontology, structure and tectonics, petroleum geology. *Unit head:* Dr. John Casey, Chairman, 713-743-3399, Fax: 713-748-7906, E-mail: jfcasey@uh.edu. *Application contact:* Sylvia Marshall, Advising Assistant, 713-743-3401, Fax: 713-748-7906, E-mail: smarshall@uh.edu.

University of Idaho, College of Graduate Studies, College of Science, Department of Geological Sciences, Program in Geology, Moscow, ID 83844-2282. Offers MS, PhD. *Students:* 20 full-time, 6 part-time. In 2009, 6 master's awarded. *Entrance requirements:* For master's, minimum GPA of 2.8. *Application deadline:* For fall admission, 8/1 for domestic students; for spring admission, 12/15 for domestic students. Application fee: $55 ($60 for international students). *Expenses:* Tuition, state resident: full-time $6120. Tuition, nonresident: full-time $17,712. *Financial support:* Application deadline: 2/15. *Unit head:* Dr. Mickey Gunter, Head, 208-885-6491. *Application contact:* Dr. Mickey Gunter, Head, 208-885-6491.

University of Illinois at Chicago, Graduate College, College of Liberal Arts and Sciences, Department of Earth and Environmental Sciences, Chicago, IL 60607-7128. Offers MS, PhD. *Degree requirements:* For master's, thesis; for doctorate, thesis/dissertation. *Entrance requirements:* For master's and doctorate, GRE General Test, minimum GPA of 2.75. Additional exam requirements/recommendations for international students: Required—TOEFL. Electronic applications accepted.

University of Illinois at Urbana–Champaign, Graduate College, College of Liberal Arts and Sciences, School of Earth, Society and Environment, Department of Geology, Champaign, IL 61820. Offers geology (MS, PhD); teaching of earth sciences (MS). *Faculty:* 14 full-time (4 women). *Students:* 30 full-time (16 women), 2 part-time (1 woman); includes 2 minority (both Asian Americans or Pacific Islanders), 11 international. 53 applicants, 36% accepted, 8 enrolled. In 2009, 8 master's, 4 doctorates awarded. Terminal master's awarded for partial completion of doctoral program. *Entrance requirements:* For master's and doctorate, GRE General Test, minimum GPA of 3.0. Additional exam requirements/recommendations for international students: Required—TOEFL. *Application deadline:* Applications are processed on a rolling basis. Application fee: $60 ($75 for international students). Electronic applications accepted. *Financial support:* In 2009–10, 3 fellowships, 16 research assistantships, 16 teaching assistantships were awarded; Federal Work-Study and tuition waivers (full and partial) also available. *Faculty research:* Hydrogeology, structure/tectonics, mineral science. *Unit head:* Wang-Ping Chen, Head, 217-333-2744, Fax: 217-244-4996, E-mail: wpchen@illinois.edu. *Application contact:* Marilyn K. Whalen, Office Administrator, 217-333-3542, Fax: 217-244-4996, E-mail: mkt@illinois.edu.

The University of Kansas, Graduate Studies, College of Liberal Arts and Sciences, Department of Geology, Lawrence, KS 66045. Offers MS, PhD. *Faculty:* 18. *Students:* 73 full-time (26 women), 17 part-time (8 women); includes 11 minority (2 American Indian/Alaska Native, 1 Asian American or Pacific Islander, 8 Hispanic Americans), 14 international. Average age 27. 83 applicants, 47% accepted, 23 enrolled. In 2009, 5 master's, 1 doctorate awarded. *Degree requirements:* For master's, thesis or alternative; for doctorate, comprehensive exam, thesis/dissertation. *Entrance requirements:* For master's and doctorate, GRE General Test, 3 letters of recommendation. Additional exam requirements/recommendations for international students: Required—TOEFL. *Application deadline:* For fall admission, 2/1 priority date for domestic and international students; for spring admission, 10/31 priority date for domestic and international students. Applications are processed on a rolling basis. Application fee: $45 ($55 for international students). Electronic applications accepted. *Expenses:* Tuition, state resident: full-time $6492; part-time $270.50 per credit hour. Tuition, nonresident: full-time $15,510; part-time $646.25 per credit hour. Required fees: $847; $70.56 per credit hour. Tuition and fees vary according to course load and program. *Financial support:* Fellowships with full and partial tuition reimbursements, research assistantships with full and partial tuition reimbursements, teaching assistantships with full and partial tuition reimbursements, unspecified assistantships available. Financial award application deadline: 2/1. *Faculty research:* Sedimentology, paleontology, tectonics, geophysics, hyrdogeology. *Unit head:* Robert H. Goldstein, Chair, 785-864-4974, Fax: 785-864-5276, E-mail: gold@ku.edu. *Application contact:* Yolanda G. Davis, Graduate Coordinator, 785-864-4975, Fax: 785-864-5276, E-mail: yolanda@ku.edu.

Geology

University of Kentucky, Graduate School, College of Arts and Sciences, Program in Geology, Lexington, KY 40506-0032. Offers MS, PhD. *Degree requirements:* For master's, comprehensive exam, thesis; for doctorate, comprehensive exam, thesis/dissertation. *Entrance requirements:* For master's, GRE General Test, minimum undergraduate GPA of 2.75; for doctorate, GRE General Test, minimum graduate GPA of 3.0. Additional exam requirements/recommendations for international students: Required—TOEFL (minimum score 550 paper-based; 213 computer-based). Electronic applications accepted. *Faculty research:* Structure tectonics, geophysics, stratigraphy, hydrogeology, coal geology.

University of Louisiana at Lafayette, College of Sciences, Department of Geology, Lafayette, LA 70504. Offers MS. Part-time programs available. *Degree requirements:* For master's, comprehensive exam, thesis. *Entrance requirements:* For master's, GRE General Test, minimum GPA of 2.75. Additional exam requirements/recommendations for international students: Required—TOEFL (minimum score 550 paper-based; 213 computer-based). Electronic applications accepted. *Faculty research:* Aquifer contamination, coastal erosion, geochemistry of peat, petroleum geology and geophysics, remote sensing and geographic information systems applications.

University of Maine, Graduate School, Climate Change Institute, Orono, ME 04469. Offers MS. Part-time programs available. *Faculty:* 2 full-time (both women), 2 part-time/adjunct (both women). *Students:* 8 full-time (5 women), 2 part-time (1 woman), 1 international. Average age 27. 21 applicants, 38% accepted, 3 enrolled. *Degree requirements:* For master's, thesis. *Entrance requirements:* For master's, GRE General Test. Additional exam requirements/recommendations for international students: Required—TOEFL. *Application deadline:* For fall admission, 2/1 priority date for domestic students. Applications are processed on a rolling basis. Application fee: $65. Electronic applications accepted. *Financial support:* In 2009–10, 8 research assistantships with tuition reimbursements (averaging $17,425 per year), 2 teaching assistantships (averaging $12,790 per year) were awarded. Financial award application deadline: 3/1. *Faculty research:* Geology, glacial geology, anthropology. *Unit head:* Dr. Paul Mayewski, Director, 207-581-3019, Fax: 207-581-1203. *Application contact:* Scott G. Delcourt, Associate Dean of the Graduate School, 207-581-3291, Fax: 207-581-3232, E-mail: graduate@maine.edu.

University of Maine, Graduate School, College of Natural Sciences, Forestry, and Agriculture, Department of Earth Sciences, Orono, ME 04469. Offers MS, PhD. Part-time programs available. *Faculty:* 9 full-time (2 women), 1 part-time/adjunct (0 women). *Students:* 16 full-time (8 women), 11 part-time (4 women), 5 international. Average age 27. 23 applicants, 70% accepted, 6 enrolled. In 2009, 4 master's, 1 doctorate awarded. *Degree requirements:* For master's, thesis; for doctorate, one foreign language, thesis/dissertation. *Entrance requirements:* For master's and doctorate, GRE General Test. Additional exam requirements/recommendations for international students: Required—TOEFL. *Application deadline:* For fall admission, 2/1 priority date for domestic students. Applications are processed on a rolling basis. Application fee: $65. Electronic applications accepted. *Financial support:* In 2009–10, 5 research assistantships with tuition reimbursements (averaging $16,130 per year), 6 teaching assistantships with tuition reimbursements (averaging $12,790 per year) were awarded; Federal Work-Study, institutionally sponsored loans, and tuition waivers (full and partial) also available. Financial award application deadline: 3/1. *Faculty research:* Appalachian bedrock geology, Quaternary studies, marine geology. *Unit head:* Dr. Joseph Kelley, Chair, 207-581-2162, Fax: 207-581-2202. *Application contact:* Scott G. Delcourt, Associate Dean of the Graduate School, 207-581-3291, Fax: 207-581-3232, E-mail: graduate@maine.edu.

University of Manitoba, Faculty of Graduate Studies, Clayton H. Riddell Faculty of Environment, Earth, and Resources, Department of Geological Sciences, Winnipeg, MB R3T 2N2, Canada. Offers geology (M Sc, PhD); geophysics (M Sc, PhD). *Degree requirements:* For master's, thesis; for doctorate, thesis/dissertation. *Entrance requirements:* For master's and doctorate, GRE General Test, GRE Subject Test (geology), minimum GPA of 3.0. Additional exam requirements/recommendations for international students: Required—TOEFL.

University of Maryland, College Park, Academic Affairs, College of Computer, Mathematical and Physical Sciences, Department of Geology, College Park, MD 20742. Offers MS, PhD. *Faculty:* 32 full-time (8 women), 2 part-time/adjunct (1 woman). *Students:* 29 full-time (11 women), 3 part-time (1 woman); includes 4 minority (1 African American, 3 Hispanic Americans), 5 international. 56 applicants, 34% accepted, 14 enrolled. In 2009, 5 master's, 2 doctorates awarded. *Degree requirements:* For master's, thesis, oral defense; for doctorate, thesis/dissertation. *Entrance requirements:* For master's, GRE General Test, minimum GPA of 3.0, 3 letters of recommendation; for doctorate, GRE General Test, 3 letters of recommendation. Additional exam requirements/recommendations for international students: Required—TOEFL. *Application deadline:* For fall admission, 3/15 for domestic students, 2/1 for international students; for spring admission, 10/1 for domestic students, 6/1 for international students. Applications are processed on a rolling basis. Application fee: $60. Electronic applications accepted. *Expenses:* Tuition, area resident: Part-time $471 per credit hour. Tuition, state resident: part-time $471 per credit hour. Tuition, nonresident: part-time $1016 per credit hour. Required fees: $337.04 per term. *Financial support:* In 2009–10, 4 fellowships with full and partial tuition reimbursements (averaging $18,837 per year), 2 research assistantships with tuition reimbursements (averaging $19,920 per year), 25 teaching assistantships with tuition reimbursements (averaging $19,931 per year) were awarded; Federal Work-Study and scholarships/grants also available. Support available to part-time students. Financial award application deadline: 2/15; financial award applicants required to submit FAFSA. Total annual research expenditures: $1.9 million. *Unit head:* Dr. Michael Brown, Chairman, 301-405-4065, Fax: 301-314-9661, E-mail: mbrown@umd.edu. *Application contact:* Dean of Graduate School, 301-405-0358, Fax: 301-314-9305.

University of Memphis, Graduate School, College of Arts and Sciences, Department of Earth Sciences, Memphis, TN 38152. Offers MA, MS, PhD, Graduate Certificate. Part-time programs available. *Faculty:* 15 full-time (3 women), 6 part-time/adjunct (2 women). *Students:* 28 full-time (6 women), 18 part-time (9 women); includes 4 African Americans, 2 Asian Americans or Pacific Islanders, 12 international. Average age 33. 28 applicants, 82% accepted, 12 enrolled. In 2009, 2 master's, 2 doctorates, 1 other advanced degree awarded. Terminal master's awarded for partial completion of doctoral program. *Degree requirements:* For master's, comprehensive exam, thesis, seminar presentation; for doctorate, thesis/dissertation. *Entrance requirements:* For master's and doctorate, GRE General Test. Additional exam requirements/recommendations for international students: Required—TOEFL. *Application deadline:* For fall admission, 8/1 for domestic students; for spring admission, 12/1 for domestic students. Applications are processed on a rolling basis. Application fee: $35 ($60 for international students). Electronic applications accepted. *Expenses:* Tuition, state resident: full-time $6246; part-time $347 per credit hour. Tuition, nonresident: full-time $15,894; part-time $883 per credit hour. Required fees: $1160. Full-time tuition and fees vary according to course load, degree level and program. *Financial support:* In 2009–10, 18 students received support; fellowships with full tuition reimbursements available, research assistantships with full tuition reimbursements available, teaching assistantships with full tuition reimbursements available, Federal Work-Study, scholarships/grants, and unspecified assistantships available. Financial award application deadline: 2/15; financial award applicants required to submit FAFSA. *Faculty research:* Hazards, active tectonics, geophysics, hydrology and water resources, spatial analysis. *Unit head:* Dr. M. Jerry Bartholomew, Chair, 901-678-4536, Fax: 901-678-4467, E-mail: jbrthlm1@memphis.edu. *Application contact:* Dr. Daniel Larsen, Coordinator of Graduate Studies, 901-678-4358, Fax: 901-678-2178, E-mail: dlarsen@memphis.edu.

University of Michigan, Horace H. Rackham School of Graduate Studies, College of Literature, Science, and the Arts, Department of Geological Sciences, Ann Arbor, MI 48109-1005. Offers geology (MS, PhD). *Faculty:* 29 full-time (6 women), 5 part-time/adjunct (2 women). *Students:* 53 full-time (26 women), 1 part-time (0 women); includes 4 minority (2 Asian Americans or Pacific Islanders, 2 Hispanic Americans), 18 international. Average age 28. 65 applicants, 46% accepted, 18 enrolled. In 2009, 4 master's, 9 doctorates awarded. Terminal master's awarded for partial completion of doctoral program. *Degree requirements:* For master's, thesis; for doctorate, thesis/dissertation, oral defense of dissertation, preliminary exam. *Entrance requirements:* For master's and doctorate, GRE General Test. Additional exam requirements/recommendations for international students: Required—TOEFL (minimum score 560 paper-based; 220 computer-based; 84 iBT). *Application deadline:* For fall admission, 1/5 for domestic and international students; for winter admission, 11/1 for domestic and international students. Applications are processed on a rolling basis. Application fee: $60 ($75 for international students). Electronic applications accepted. *Expenses:* Tuition, state resident: full-time $17,286; part-time $1099 per credit hour. Tuition, nonresident: full-time $34,944; part-time $2080 per credit hour. Required fees: $95 per semester. Tuition and fees vary according to course load, degree level and program. *Financial support:* In 2009–10, 45 students received support, including 9 fellowships with full tuition reimbursements available (averaging $25,041 per year), 17 research assistantships with full tuition reimbursements available (averaging $25,041 per year), 19 teaching assistantships with full tuition reimbursements available (averaging $25,041 per year); career-related internships or fieldwork, Federal Work-Study, scholarships/grants, health care benefits, and unspecified assistantships also available. Financial award application deadline: 1/5; financial award applicants required to submit FAFSA. *Faculty research:* Isotope geochemistry, paleoclimatology, mineral physics, tectonics, paleontology. Total annual research expenditures: $3 million. *Unit head:* Dr. Samuel B. Mukasa, Chair, 734-764-1435, Fax: 734-763-4690. *Application contact:* Anne Hudon, Graduate Program Coordinator, 734-615-3034, Fax: 734-763-4690, E-mail: ahudon@umich.edu.

University of Minnesota, Duluth, Graduate School, Swenson College of Science and Engineering, Department of Geological Sciences, Duluth, MN 55812-2496. Offers MS, PhD. Part-time programs available. *Faculty:* 9 full-time (4 women), 5 part-time/adjunct (0 women). *Students:* 22 full-time (12 women), 15 part-time (7 women), 2 international. Average age 24. 33 applicants, 61% accepted, 11 enrolled. In 2009, 7 master's, 1 doctorate awarded. *Degree requirements:* For master's, thesis, final oral exam, written and oral research proposal. *Entrance requirements:* For master's, GRE General Test, minimum GPA of 3.0. Additional exam requirements/recommendations for international students: Required—TOEFL (minimum score 550 paper-based; 213 computer-based). *Application deadline:* For fall admission, 1/15 for domestic and international students; for spring admission, 10/15 for domestic and international students. Applications are processed on a rolling basis. Application fee: $75 ($95 for international students). Electronic applications accepted. *Financial support:* In 2009–10, 22 students received support, including 6 fellowships with full and partial tuition reimbursements available (averaging $25,000 per year), 4 research assistantships with full tuition reimbursements available (averaging $15,500 per year), 12 teaching assistantships with full tuition reimbursements available (averaging $13,300 per year); career-related internships or fieldwork, health care benefits, and unspecified assistantships also available. Support available to part-time students. Financial award application deadline: 1/5. *Faculty research:* Surface processes, tectonics, planetary geology, paleoclimate, petrology. Total annual research expenditures: $842,926. *Unit head:* Dr. Penelope Morton, Director of Graduate Studies, 218-726-7962, Fax: 218-726-8275, E-mail: pmorton@d.umn.edu. *Application contact:* M. J. Leone, Executive Administrative Specialist, 218-726-7523, Fax: 218-726-6970, E-mail: grad@d.umn.edu.

University of Minnesota, Twin Cities Campus, Institute of Technology, Department of Geology and Geophysics, Minneapolis, MN 55455-0213. Offers geology (MS, PhD); geophysics (MS, PhD). Terminal master's awarded for partial completion of doctoral program. *Degree requirements:* For master's, thesis; for doctorate, thesis/dissertation. *Entrance requirements:* For master's and doctorate, GRE General Test, 3 letters of recommendation. Additional exam requirements/recommendations for international students: Required—TOEFL (minimum score 550 paper-based; 213 computer-based). Electronic applications accepted. *Faculty research:* Geochemistry, paleoclimate studies, structure/tectonics, geofluids.

University of Missouri, Graduate School, College of Arts and Sciences, Department of Geological Sciences, Columbia, MO 65211. Offers MS, PhD. *Faculty:* 13 full-time (4 women), 2 part-time/adjunct (0 women). *Students:* 25 full-time (11 women), 7 part-time (1 women), 10 international. Average age 27. 38 applicants, 47% accepted, 9 enrolled. In 2009, 1 master's awarded. *Degree requirements:* For master's, thesis; for doctorate, variable foreign language requirement, thesis/dissertation. *Entrance requirements:* For master's and doctorate, GRE General Test, minimum GPA of 3.0. Additional exam requirements/recommendations for international students: Required—TOEFL (minimum score 530 paper-based; 197 computer-based; 71 iBT). *Application deadline:* For fall admission, 2/15 priority date for domestic students. Applications are processed on a rolling basis. Application fee: $45 ($60 for international students). Electronic applications accepted. *Financial support:* In 2009–10, 2 fellowships with full tuition reimbursements, 17 research assistantships with full tuition reimbursements, 13 teaching assistantships with full tuition reimbursements were awarded; institutionally sponsored loans, health care benefits, and unspecified assistantships also available. *Unit head:* Dr. Kevin Shelton, Department Chair, E-mail: sheltonkl@missouri.edu. *Application contact:* Alice Thompson, Administrative Assistant, 573-882-6785, E-mail: thompsonae@missouri.edu.

University of Missouri–Kansas City, College of Arts and Sciences, Department of Geosciences, Kansas City, MO 64110-2499. Offers environmental and urban geosciences (MS); geosciences (PhD). PhD (interdisciplinary) offered through the School of Graduate Studies. Part-time programs available. *Faculty:* 11 full-time (3 women), 1 part-time/adjunct (0 women). *Students:* 6 full-time (3 women), 14 part-time (6 women); includes 2 minority (both Hispanic Americans), 2 international. Average age 34. 16 applicants, 56% accepted, 6 enrolled. In 2009, 1 degree awarded. *Degree requirements:* For master's, thesis; for doctorate, thesis/dissertation. *Entrance requirements:* For master's, GRE General Test, minimum GPA of 3.0; for doctorate, qualifying exam. Additional exam requirements/recommendations for international students: Required—TOEFL (minimum score 550 paper-based; 213 computer-based; 80 iBT). *Application deadline:* For fall admission, 3/15 priority date for domestic and international students. Applications are processed on a rolling basis. Application fee: $45 ($50 for international students). Electronic applications accepted. *Expenses:* Tuition, state resident: full-time $5378; part-time $299 per credit hour. Tuition, nonresident: full-time $13,881; part-time $771 per credit hour. Required fees: $641; $71 per credit hour. Tuition and fees vary according to course load and program. *Financial support:* In 2009–10, 2 research assistantships with partial tuition reimbursements (averaging $10,200 per year), 10 teaching assistantships with partial tuition reimbursements (averaging $10,550 per year) were awarded; Federal Work-Study, institutionally sponsored loans, and tuition waivers (full and partial) also available. Support available to part-time students. Financial award application deadline: 3/1; financial award applicants required to submit FAFSA. *Faculty research:* Neotectonics and applied geophysics, environmental geosciences, urban geoscience, geoinformatics–remote sensing, atmospheric research. Total annual research expenditures: $481,906. *Unit head:* Dr. Jimmy Adegoke, Chair, 816-235-1334, Fax: 816-235-5535, E-mail: adegokej@umkc.edu. *Application contact:* Dr. Ray Coveney, Associate Professor, 816-235-1334, Fax: 816-235-5535, E-mail: coveneyr@umkc.edu.

The University of Montana, Graduate School, College of Arts and Sciences, Department of Geology, Missoula, MT 59812-0002. Offers applied geoscience (PhD); geology (MS, PhD). *Degree requirements:* For doctorate, thesis/dissertation. *Entrance requirements:* For master's and doctorate, GRE General Test. Additional exam requirements/recommendations for international students: Required—TOEFL (minimum score 525 paper-based; 197 computer-based). *Faculty research:* Environmental geoscience, regional structure and tectonics, groundwater geology, petrology, mineral deposits.

University of Nevada, Reno, Graduate School, College of Science, Mackay School of Earth Sciences and Engineering, Department of Geological Sciences, Program in Geology, Reno,

NV 89557. Offers MS, PhD. Terminal master's awarded for partial completion of doctoral program. *Degree requirements:* For master's, thesis optional; for doctorate, thesis/dissertation. *Entrance requirements:* For master's, GRE General Test, minimum GPA of 2.75; for doctorate, GRE General Test, minimum GPA of 3.0. Additional exam requirements/recommendations for international students: Required—TOEFL (minimum score 500 paper-based; 173 computer-based; 61 iBT), IELTS (minimum score 6). Electronic applications accepted. *Faculty research:* Mineral exploration, geochemistry, hydrology.

University of New Brunswick Fredericton, School of Graduate Studies, Faculty of Science, Department of Geology, Fredericton, NB E3B 5A3, Canada. Offers M Sc, PhD. Part-time programs available. *Faculty:* 11 full-time (0 women), 5 part-time/adjunct (0 women). *Students:* 30 full-time (14 women), 2 part-time (0 women). In 2009, 4 master's, 2 doctorates awarded. *Degree requirements:* For master's, thesis; for doctorate, thesis/dissertation. *Entrance requirements:* For master's, minimum GPA of 3.0, BSc in Earth Sciences of related subject.; for doctorate, minimum GPA of 3.0; MSc in Earth Science or related subject; Case by case. Additional exam requirements/recommendations for international students: Required—TOEFL, IELTS, TWE. *Application deadline:* For fall admission, 3/1 priority date for domestic students. Applications are processed on a rolling basis. Application fee: $50 Canadian dollars. Tuition and fees charges are reported in Canadian dollars. *Expenses:* Tuition, area resident: Full-time $5562 Canadian dollars; part-time $2781 Canadian dollars per year. Required fees: $49.75 Canadian dollars per term. *Financial support:* In 2009–10, 38 research assistantships (averaging $1,160 per year), 26 teaching assistantships (averaging $2,016 per year) were awarded. *Faculty research:* Hydrogeology, glacial geology, petrology, paleontology, aqueous and hydrothermal geochemistry. Total annual research expenditures: $133,936. *Unit head:* Dr. David Keighley, Director of Graduate Studies, 506-453-5196, Fax: 506-453-5055, E-mail: keig@unb.ca. *Application contact:* Christine Lodge, 506-453-4803, Fax: 506-453-5055, E-mail: lodge@unb.ca.

University of New Hampshire, Graduate School, College of Engineering and Physical Sciences, Department of Earth Sciences, Durham, NH 03824. Offers earth sciences (MS), including geochemical systems, geology, ocean mapping, oceanography; hydrology (MS). *Faculty:* 17 full-time (5 women). *Students:* 7 full-time (5 women), 15 part-time (7 women), 1 international. Average age 27. 27 applicants, 56% accepted, 5 enrolled. In 2009, 18 master's awarded. *Degree requirements:* For master's, thesis. *Entrance requirements:* For master's, GRE General Test. Additional exam requirements/recommendations for international students: Required—TOEFL (minimum score 550 paper-based; 213 computer-based; 80 iBT). *Application deadline:* For fall admission, 4/1 priority date for domestic students, 4/1 for international students; for spring admission, 12/1 for domestic students. Applications are processed on a rolling basis. Application fee: $65. Electronic applications accepted. *Expenses:* Tuition, state resident: full-time $10,380; part-time $577 per credit hour. Tuition, nonresident: full-time $24,350; part-time $1002 per credit hour. Required fees: $1550; $387.50 per semester. Tuition and fees vary according to course load and program. *Financial support:* In 2009–10, 17 students received support, including 1 fellowship, 6 research assistantships, 8 teaching assistantships; career-related internships or fieldwork, Federal Work-Study, scholarships/grants, and tuition waivers (full and partial) also available. Support available to part-time students. Financial award application deadline: 2/15. *Unit head:* Dr. Will Clyde, Chairperson, 603-862-1718, E-mail: earth.sciences@unh.edu. *Application contact:* Sue Clark, Administrative Assistant, 603-862-1718, E-mail: earth.sciences@unh.edu.

The University of North Carolina at Chapel Hill, Graduate School, College of Arts and Sciences, Department of Geological Sciences, Chapel Hill, NC 27599. Offers MS, PhD. *Degree requirements:* For master's, comprehensive exam, thesis; for doctorate, one foreign language, comprehensive exam, thesis/dissertation. *Entrance requirements:* For master's and doctorate, GRE General Test, minimum GPA of 3.0. Electronic applications accepted. *Faculty research:* Paleoceanography, igneous petrology, paleontology, geophysics, structural geology.

The University of North Carolina Wilmington, College of Arts and Sciences, Department of Geography and Geology, Wilmington, NC 28403-3297. Offers geology (MS); marine science (MS). *Degree requirements:* For master's, comprehensive exam, thesis. *Entrance requirements:* For master's, GRE General Test, GRE Subject Test, minimum B average in undergraduate major and basic courses for prerequisite to geology.

University of North Dakota, Graduate School, School of Engineering and Mines, Department of Geology, Grand Forks, ND 58202. Offers MA, MS, PhD. *Degree requirements:* For master's, thesis, final exam; for doctorate, one foreign language, comprehensive exam, thesis/dissertation, final exam. *Entrance requirements:* For master's and doctorate, GRE General Test, minimum GPA of 3.0. Additional exam requirements/recommendations for international students: Required—TOEFL (minimum score 550 paper-based; 213 computer-based; 79 iBT), IELTS (minimum score 6.5). Electronic applications accepted. *Faculty research:* Hydrogeology, environmental geology, geological engineering, sedimentology, geomorphology.

University of Oklahoma, Graduate College, College of Earth and Energy, Conoco Phillips School of Geology and Geophysics, Program in Geology, Norman, OK 73019. Offers MS, PhD. *Students:* 54 full-time (14 women), 14 part-time (5 women); includes 5 minority (1 American Indian/Alaska Native, 2 Asian Americans or Pacific Islanders, 2 Hispanic Americans), 24 international. 65 applicants, 42% accepted, 17 enrolled. In 2009, 9 master's, 9 doctorates awarded. *Degree requirements:* For master's, comprehensive exam, thesis; for doctorate, one foreign language, thesis/dissertation, general exam. *Entrance requirements:* For master's, GRE General Test, bachelor's degree in geology; for doctorate, GRE General Test. Additional exam requirements/recommendations for international students: Required—TOEFL (minimum score 550 paper-based; 213 computer-based). *Application deadline:* For fall admission, 2/1 priority date for domestic students, 4/1 for international students; for spring admission, 9/1 for domestic and international students. Applications are processed on a rolling basis. Application fee: $40 ($90 for international students). Electronic applications accepted. *Expenses:* Tuition, state resident: full-time $3744; part-time $156 per credit hour. Tuition, nonresident: full-time $13,577; part-time $565.70 per credit hour. Required fees: $2415; $90.10 per credit hour. *Financial support:* In 2009–10, 57 students received support. Career-related internships or fieldwork, scholarships/grants, health care benefits, and unspecified assistantships available. Financial award application deadline: 2/1; financial award applicants required to submit FAFSA. *Faculty research:* Energy, geochemistry, sedimentary geology, earth systems, lithopheric dynamics, paleontology. *Unit head:* Dr. Douglas Elmore, Director and Associate Provost, 405-325-3253, Fax: 405-325-3140, E-mail: delmore@ou.edu. *Application contact:* Donna S. Mullins, Coordinator for Administrative Student Services and Corporate Recruiting, 405-325-3255, Fax: 405-325-3140, E-mail: dsmullins@ou.edu.

University of Oregon, Graduate School, College of Arts and Sciences, Department of Geological Sciences, Eugene, OR 97403. Offers MA, MS, PhD. *Degree requirements:* For master's, foreign language (MA). *Entrance requirements:* For master's and doctorate, GRE General Test, GRE Subject Test.

University of Pittsburgh, School of Arts and Sciences, Department of Geology and Planetary Science, Pittsburgh, PA 15260-3332. Offers geographical information systems (PM Sc); geology and planetary science (MS, PhD). Part-time programs available. *Faculty:* 9 full-time (1 woman), 4 part-time/adjunct (1 woman). *Students:* 27 full-time (15 women), 7 part-time (4 women), 1 international. Average age 30. 38 applicants, 24% accepted, 6 enrolled. In 2009, 1 doctorate awarded. *Degree requirements:* For master's, thesis, oral thesis defense; for doctorate, comprehensive exam, thesis/dissertation, oral dissertation defense. *Entrance requirements:* For master's and doctorate, GRE General Test. Additional exam requirements/recommendations for international students: Required—TOEFL (minimum score 550 paper-based; 213 computer-based; 80 iBT). *Application deadline:* For fall admission, 2/1 priority date for domestic students, 2/1 for international students. Application fee: $50. Electronic applications accepted. *Expenses:* Tuition, state resident: full-time $16,402; part-time $665 per credit. Tuition, nonresident: full-time $28,694; part-time $1175 per credit. Required fees: $690; $175 per term. Tuition and fees vary according to program. *Financial support:* In 2009–10, 25 students received support, including 2 fellowships with full tuition reimbursements available (averaging $14,400 per year), 13 research assistantships with full and partial tuition reimbursements available (averaging $14,400 per year), 10 teaching assistantships with full and partial tuition reimbursements available (averaging $15,065 per year); career-related internships or fieldwork, Federal Work-Study, institutionally sponsored loans, scholarships/grants, and tuition waivers (full and partial) also available. Support available to part-time students. Financial award application deadline: 2/1; financial award applicants required to submit FAFSA. *Faculty research:* Geographical information systems, hydrology, low temperature geochemistry, volcanology, paleoclimatology. Total annual research expenditures: $1.2 million. *Unit head:* Dr. Thomas Anderson, Chair, 412-624-8783, Fax: 412-624-3914, E-mail: bstewart@pitt.edu. *Application contact:* Dr. Brian W. Stewart, Graduate Adviser, 412-624-8883, Fax: 412-624-3914, E-mail: taco@pitt.edu.

University of Puerto Rico, Mayagüez Campus, Graduate Studies, College of Arts and Sciences, Department of Geology, Mayagüez, PR 00681-9000. Offers MS. Part-time programs available. *Degree requirements:* For master's, comprehensive exam, thesis. *Entrance requirements:* For master's, GRE General Test, BS degree in geology or the equivalent; minimum GPA of 2.8. *Faculty research:* Seismology, applied geophysics, geographic information systems, environmental remote sensing, petrology.

University of Regina, Faculty of Graduate Studies and Research, Faculty of Science, Department of Geology, Regina, SK S4S 0A2, Canada. Offers M Sc, PhD. PhD program offered on a special case basis. *Faculty:* 7 full-time (3 women), 6 part-time/adjunct (0 women). *Students:* 5 full-time (2 women), 7 part-time (3 women). 11 applicants, 64% accepted. In 2009, 1 master's awarded. *Degree requirements:* For master's, thesis; for doctorate, thesis/dissertation. *Entrance requirements:* Additional exam requirements/recommendations for international students: Required—TOEFL (minimum score 580 paper-based; 237 computer-based; 80 iBT). *Application deadline:* Applications are processed on a rolling basis. Application fee: $90 ($100 for international students). *Financial support:* In 2009–10, 3 fellowships (averaging $19,000 per year), 2 teaching assistantships (averaging $6,650 per year) were awarded; research assistantships, scholarships/grants also available. Financial award application deadline: 6/15. *Faculty research:* Geological and planetary science, petrology, mineralogy and economic geology. *Unit head:* Dr. Janis Dale, Head, 306-585-4840, Fax: 306-585-5433, E-mail: janis.dale@uregina.ca. *Application contact:* Dr. Hairuo Qing, Graduate Program Coordinator, 306-585-4677, E-mail: hairuo.qing@uregina.ca.

University of Rochester, The College, Arts and Sciences, Department of Earth and Environmental Sciences, Rochester, NY 14627. Offers geological sciences (MS, PhD). *Degree requirements:* For doctorate, thesis/dissertation, qualifying exam. *Entrance requirements:* For master's and doctorate, GRE General Test. Additional exam requirements/recommendations for international students: Required—TOEFL.

University of Saskatchewan, College of Graduate Studies and Research, College of Arts and Sciences and College of Engineering, Department of Geological Sciences, Saskatoon, SK S7N 5A2, Canada. Offers M Sc, PhD, Diploma. *Faculty:* 31. *Students:* 32. In 2009, 7 master's, 5 doctorates awarded. *Degree requirements:* For master's, thesis; for doctorate, comprehensive exam (for some programs), thesis/dissertation. *Entrance requirements:* Additional exam requirements/recommendations for international students: Required—TOEFL (minimum score 80 iBT); Recommended—IELTS (minimum score 6.5). *Application deadline:* For fall admission, 7/1 priority date for domestic students. Applications are processed on a rolling basis. Application fee: $75. Electronic applications accepted. Tuition and fees charges are reported in Canadian dollars. *Expenses:* Tuition, area resident: Full-time $3000 Canadian dollars; part-time $500 Canadian dollars per term. Required fees: $700 Canadian dollars; $100 Canadian dollars per term. *Financial support:* Fellowships, research assistantships, teaching assistantships available. Financial award application deadline: 1/31. *Unit head:* Dr. Kevin Ansdell, Head, 306-966-5698, Fax: 306-966-8593, E-mail: kevin.ansdell@usask.ca. *Application contact:* Dr. Yuanming Pan, Graduate Chair, 306-966-5699, Fax: 306-966-8593, E-mail: yuanming.pan@usask.ca.

University of South Carolina, The Graduate School, College of Arts and Sciences, Department of Geological Sciences, Columbia, SC 29208. Offers MS, PhD. Terminal master's awarded for partial completion of doctoral program. *Degree requirements:* For master's, thesis; for doctorate, comprehensive exam, thesis/dissertation, published paper. *Entrance requirements:* For master's and doctorate, GRE General Test. Additional exam requirements/recommendations for international students: Required—TOEFL (minimum score 570 paper-based; 230 computer-based; 75 iBT). Electronic applications accepted. *Faculty research:* Environmental geology, tectonics, petrology, coastal processes, paleoclimatology.

University of Southern Mississippi, Graduate School, College of Science and Technology, Department of Geography and Geology, Hattiesburg, MS 39406-0001. Offers geography (MS, PhD); geology (MS). Part-time programs available. *Faculty:* 11 full-time (2 women), 1 part-time/adjunct (0 women). *Students:* 16 full-time (7 women), 15 part-time (3 women); includes 1 minority (African American). Average age 34. 9 applicants, 89% accepted, 7 enrolled. In 2009, 2 master's awarded. *Degree requirements:* For master's, comprehensive exam, thesis (for some programs), internships; for doctorate, comprehensive exam, thesis/dissertation. *Entrance requirements:* For master's, GMAT, GRE General Test, minimum GPA of 3.0. Additional exam requirements/recommendations for international students: Required—TOEFL. *Application deadline:* For fall admission, 3/15 for domestic and international students; for spring admission, 1/3 for domestic students. Applications are processed on a rolling basis. Application fee: $35. Electronic applications accepted. *Expenses:* Tuition, state resident: full-time $5096; part-time $284 per hour. Tuition, nonresident: full-time $13,052; part-time $726 per hour. Required fees: $402. Tuition and fees vary according to course level and course load. *Financial support:* In 2009–10, 1 research assistantship with tuition reimbursement (averaging $18,000 per year), 8 teaching assistantships with full tuition reimbursements (averaging $8,632 per year) were awarded; fellowships with full tuition reimbursements, career-related internships or fieldwork, Federal Work-Study, and institutionally sponsored loans also available. Financial award application deadline: 3/15; financial award applicants required to submit FAFSA. *Faculty research:* City and regional planning, geographic techniques, physical geography, human geography. *Unit head:* Dr. Clifton Dixon, Chair, 601-266-4729, Fax: 601-266-6219, E-mail: c.dixon@usm.edu. *Application contact:* Dr. Gail Russell, Graduate Coordinator, 601-266-6519, Fax: 601-266-6219.

University of South Florida, Graduate School, College of Arts and Sciences, Department of Geology, Tampa, FL 33620-9951. Offers MS, PhD. Part-time programs available. *Faculty:* 14 full-time (2 women). *Students:* 40 full-time (16 women), 16 part-time (4 women); includes 2 minority (1 African American, 1 Asian American or Pacific Islander), 13 international. Average age 32. 37 applicants, 43% accepted, 13 enrolled. In 2009, 8 master's, 3 doctorates awarded. *Degree requirements:* For master's, comprehensive exam, thesis (for some programs); for doctorate, comprehensive exam, thesis/dissertation. *Entrance requirements:* For master's, GRE General Test, minimum GPA of 3.0 in last 60 hours of course work; for doctorate, GRE General Test. Additional exam requirements/recommendations for international students: Required—TOEFL (minimum score 550 paper-based; 213 computer-based). *Application deadline:* For fall admission, 2/15 for domestic students, 1/2 for international students; for spring admission, 10/15 for domestic students, 6/1 for international students. Application fee: $30. Electronic applications accepted. *Financial support:* In 2009–10, teaching assistantships with tuition reimbursements (averaging $26,659 per year); unspecified assistantships also available. Financial award application deadline: 6/30; financial award applicants required to submit FAFSA. Total annual research expenditures: $1.2 million. *Unit head:* Chuck Connor,

Geology

University of South Florida (continued)
Chairperson, 813-974-0325, Fax: 813-974-2654, E-mail: cconnor@cas.usf.edu. *Application contact:* Ping Wang, Director, 813-974-9170, Fax: 813-974-2654, E-mail: pwang@cas.usf.edu.

The University of Tennessee, Graduate School, College of Arts and Sciences, Department of Geological Sciences, Knoxville, TN 37996. Offers geology (MS, PhD). Part-time programs available. *Degree requirements:* For master's, thesis; for doctorate, one foreign language, thesis/dissertation. *Entrance requirements:* For master's and doctorate, GRE General Test, minimum GPA of 2.7. Additional exam requirements/recommendations for international students: Required—TOEFL. Electronic applications accepted. *Expenses:* Tuition, state resident: full-time $6826; part-time $380 per semester hour. Tuition, nonresident: full-time $21,844; part-time $1147 per semester hour. Tuition and fees vary according to program.

The University of Texas at Arlington, Graduate School, College of Science, Department of Earth and Environmental Sciences, Program in Environmental and Earth Sciences, Arlington, TX 76019. Offers environmental science (MS, PhD); geology (MS, PhD). Part-time and evening/weekend programs available. *Faculty:* 7 full-time (0 women), 5 part-time/adjunct (0 women). *Students:* 22 full-time (13 women), 25 part-time (12 women); includes 9 minority (2 African Americans, 1 American Indian/Alaska Native, 2 Asian Americans or Pacific Islanders, 4 Hispanic Americans), 11 international. 23 applicants, 74% accepted, 10 enrolled. In 2009, 11 master's, 1 doctorate awarded. Terminal master's awarded for partial completion of doctoral program. *Degree requirements:* For master's, thesis optional; for doctorate, comprehensive exam, thesis/dissertation. *Entrance requirements:* For master's, GRE General Test. Additional exam requirements/recommendations for international students: Required—TOEFL (minimum score 550 paper-based; 213 computer-based). *Financial support:* In 2009–10, 4 fellowships (averaging $1,000 per year), 7 teaching assistantships (averaging $14,700 per year) were awarded; career-related internships or fieldwork, Federal Work-Study, institutionally sponsored loans, scholarships/grants, health care benefits, and unspecified assistantships also available. *Unit head:* Dr. John S. Wickham, Chair, 817-272-2987, Fax: 817-272-2628, E-mail: wickham@uta.edu. *Application contact:* Dr. Andrew Hunt, Graduate Advisor, 817-272-2987, Fax: 817-272-2628, E-mail: hunt@uta.edu.

The University of Texas at Austin, Graduate School, Jackson School of Geosciences, Austin, TX 78712-1111. Offers MA, MS, PhD. Part-time programs available. *Degree requirements:* For master's, report (MA), thesis (MS); for doctorate, thesis/dissertation. *Entrance requirements:* For master's and doctorate, GRE General Test. Electronic applications accepted. *Faculty research:* Sedimentary geology, geophysics, hydrogeology, structure/tectonics, vertebrate paleontology.

The University of Texas at El Paso, Graduate School, College of Science, Department of Geological Sciences, El Paso, TX 79968-0001. Offers geological sciences (MS, PhD); geophysics (MS). Part-time and evening/weekend programs available. *Degree requirements:* For master's, thesis; for doctorate, one foreign language, thesis/dissertation. *Entrance requirements:* For master's, GRE, minimum GPA of 3.0, BS in geology or equivalent; for doctorate, GRE, minimum GPA of 3.0, MS in geology or equivalent. Additional exam requirements/recommendations for international students: Required—TOEFL. Electronic applications accepted.

The University of Texas at San Antonio, College of Sciences, Department of Geological Sciences, San Antonio, TX 78249-0617. Offers MS. Part-time programs available. *Faculty:* 9 full-time (2 women). *Students:* 11 full-time (3 women), 5 part-time (2 women); includes 3 minority (1 Asian American or Pacific Islander, 2 Hispanic Americans), 2 international. Average age 28. 13 applicants, 77% accepted, 6 enrolled. In 2009, 4 master's awarded. *Degree requirements:* For master's, comprehensive exam (for some programs), thesis (for some programs). *Entrance requirements:* For master's, GRE General Test, minimum GPA of 3.0 in last 60 hours. Additional exam requirements/recommendations for international students: Required—TOEFL (minimum score 500 paper-based; 173 computer-based; 61 iBT), IELTS (minimum score 5). *Application deadline:* For fall admission, 7/1 for domestic students, 4/1 for international students; for spring admission, 11/1 for domestic students, 9/1 for international students. Applications are processed on a rolling basis. Application fee: $45 ($80 for international students). Electronic applications accepted. *Expenses:* Tuition, state resident: full-time $3975; part-time $221 per contact hour. Tuition, nonresident: full-time $13,947; part-time $775 per contact hour. Required fees: $1853. *Financial support:* In 2009–10, 7 students received support, including 2 fellowships (averaging $31,999 per year), 10 teaching assistantships (averaging $9,463 per year); scholarships/grants, tuition waivers, and unspecified assistantships also available. Support available to part-time students. *Faculty research:* Water resources/hydrogeology, low-temperature geochemistry, petrology and tectonics, energy resources, paleoclimatology, landscape dynamics. Total annual research expenditures: $396,687. *Unit head:* Dr. Allan R. Dutton, Interim Chair, 210-458-5746, E-mail: allan.dutton@utsa.edu. *Application contact:* Dorothy A. Flannagan, Dean of the Graduate School, 210-458-4330, Fax: 210-458-4332, E-mail: dorothy.flannagan@utsa.edu.

The University of Texas of the Permian Basin, Office of Graduate Studies, College of Arts and Sciences, Department of Physical Sciences, Program in Geology, Odessa, TX 79762-0001. Offers MS. *Degree requirements:* For master's, comprehensive exam, thesis or alternative. *Entrance requirements:* For master's, GRE General Test. Additional exam requirements/recommendations for international students: Required—TOEFL (minimum score 550 paper-based; 213 computer-based).

The University of Toledo, College of Graduate Studies, College of Arts and Sciences, Department of Environmental Sciences, Toledo, OH 43606-3390. Offers biology (ecology track) (MS, PhD); geology (MS), including earth surface processes, general geology. Part-time programs available. *Degree requirements:* For master's, thesis. *Entrance requirements:* For master's, GRE General Test. Additional exam requirements/recommendations for international students: Required—TOEFL. Electronic applications accepted. *Faculty research:* Environmental geochemistry, geophysics, petrology and mineralogy, paleontology, geohydrology.

University of Toronto, School of Graduate Studies, Physical Sciences Division, Department of Geology, Toronto, ON M5S 1A1, Canada. Offers M Sc, MA Sc, PhD. Part-time programs available. *Degree requirements:* For master's, thesis (for some programs); for doctorate, thesis/dissertation. *Entrance requirements:* For master's, B Sc or BA Sc, or equivalent; letters of reference; for doctorate, M Sc or equivalent, minimum B+ average, letters of reference.

University of Utah, The Graduate School, College of Mines and Earth Sciences, Department of Geology and Geophysics, Salt Lake City, UT 84112. Offers environmental engineering (ME, MS, PhD); geological engineering (ME, MS, PhD); geology (MS, PhD); geophysics (MS, PhD). *Faculty:* 20 full-time (3 women), 5 part-time/adjunct (1 woman). *Students:* 40 full-time (16 women), 27 part-time (9 women); includes 1 minority (Hispanic American), 17 international. Average age 32. 109 applicants, 23% accepted, 17 enrolled. In 2009, 18 master's, 5 doctorates awarded. Terminal master's awarded for partial completion of doctoral program. *Degree requirements:* For master's, comprehensive exam, thesis; for doctorate, thesis/dissertation, qualifying exam (written and oral). *Entrance requirements:* For master's and doctorate, GRE General Test, minimum GPA of 3.25. Additional exam requirements/recommendations for international students: Required—TOEFL (minimum score 500 paper-based; 173 computer-based). *Application deadline:* For fall admission, 1/15 priority date for domestic and international students. Applications are processed on a rolling basis. Application fee: $55 ($65 for international students). Electronic applications accepted. *Expenses:* Tuition, state resident: full-time $4004; part-time $1674 per semester. Tuition, nonresident: full-time $14,134; part-time $5915 per semester. Required fees: $324 per semester. Tuition and fees vary according to course load, degree level and program. *Financial support:* In 2009–10, 22 students received support, including 11 fellowships with full tuition reimbursements available (averaging $13,450 per year), 45 research assistantships with full tuition reimbursements available (averaging $21,858 per year), 11 teaching assistantships with full tuition reimbursements available (averaging $13,450 per year); career-related internships or fieldwork, institutionally sponsored loans, scholarships/grants, unspecified assistantships, and stipends also available. Financial award application deadline: 1/15; financial award applicants required to submit FAFSA. *Faculty research:* Igneous, metamorphic, and sedimentary petrology; ore deposits; aqueous geochemistry; isotope geochemistry; heat flow. Total annual research expenditures: $2.2 million. *Unit head:* Dr. Marjorie A. Chan, Chair, 801-581-7162, Fax: 801-581-7065, E-mail: marjorie.chan@utah.edu. *Application contact:* Dr. Allan A. Ekdale, Director of Graduate Studies, 801-581-7266, Fax: 801-581-7065, E-mail: a.ekdale@utah.edu.

University of Vermont, Graduate College, College of Arts and Sciences, Department of Geology, Burlington, VT 05405. Offers MS. *Students:* 10 (5 women). 25 applicants, 20% accepted, 4 enrolled. In 2009, 4 master's awarded. *Degree requirements:* For master's, thesis. *Entrance requirements:* For master's, GRE General Test. Additional exam requirements/recommendations for international students: Required—TOEFL (minimum score 550 paper-based; 213 computer-based; 80 iBT). *Application deadline:* For fall admission, 2/15 priority date for domestic students. Applications are processed on a rolling basis. Application fee: $40. Electronic applications accepted. *Expenses:* Tuition, area resident: Part-time $508 per credit hour. Tuition, state resident: part-time $508 per credit hour. Tuition, nonresident: part-time $1281 per credit hour. *Financial support:* Research assistantships, teaching assistantships available. Financial award application deadline: 3/1. *Faculty research:* Mineralogy, lake sediments, structural geology. *Unit head:* Dr. Char Mehrtens, Chairperson, 802-656-3396. *Application contact:* Dr. A. Lini, Coordinator, 802-656-3396.

University of Washington, Graduate School, College of Arts and Sciences, Department of Earth and Space Sciences, Seattle, WA 98195. Offers geology (MS, PhD); geophysics (MS, PhD). *Degree requirements:* For master's, thesis or alternative, departmental qualifying exam, final exam; for doctorate, thesis/dissertation, departmental qualifying exam, general and final exams. *Entrance requirements:* For master's and doctorate, GRE General Test, minimum GPA of 3.0. Additional exam requirements/recommendations for international students: Required—TOEFL (minimum score 580 paper-based). Electronic applications accepted.

The University of Western Ontario, Faculty of Graduate Studies, Physical Sciences Division, Department of Earth Sciences, London, ON N6A 5B8, Canada. Offers environment and sustainability (MES); geology (M Sc, PhD); geology and environmental science (M Sc, PhD); geophysics (M Sc, PhD); geophysics and environmental science (M Sc, PhD). *Degree requirements:* For master's, thesis; for doctorate, thesis/dissertation, qualifying exam. *Entrance requirements:* For master's, honors in B Sc; for doctorate, M Sc. Additional exam requirements/recommendations for international students: Required—TOEFL. *Faculty research:* Geophysics, geochemistry, paleontology, sedimentology/stratigraphy, glaciology/quaternary.

University of Wisconsin–Madison, Graduate School, College of Letters and Science, Department of Geology and Geophysics, Program in Geology, Madison, WI 53706-1380. Offers MS, PhD. *Degree requirements:* For master's, thesis; for doctorate, one foreign language, thesis/dissertation. *Entrance requirements:* For master's and doctorate, GRE General Test. *Expenses:* Tuition, state resident: part-time $594 per credit. Tuition, nonresident: part-time $1504 per credit. Required fees: $65 per credit. Tuition and fees vary according to course load, program and reciprocity agreements.

University of Wisconsin–Milwaukee, Graduate School, College of Letters and Sciences, Department of Geosciences, Milwaukee, WI 53201-0413. Offers geological sciences (MS, PhD). *Faculty:* 12 full-time (3 women). *Students:* 13 full-time (10 women), 9 part-time (5 women), 2 international. Average age 32. 23 applicants, 74% accepted, 5 enrolled. In 2009, 2 master's awarded. *Degree requirements:* For master's, thesis; for doctorate, one foreign language, thesis/dissertation. *Entrance requirements:* For master's, GRE General Test, minimum GPA of 3.0; for doctorate, GRE General Test, master's degree. Additional exam requirements/recommendations for international students: Required—TOEFL (minimum score 550 paper-based; 79 iBT), IELTS (minimum score 6.5). *Application deadline:* For fall admission, 1/1 priority date for domestic students; for spring admission, 9/1 for domestic students. Applications are processed on a rolling basis. Application fee: $45 ($75 for international students). *Expenses:* Tuition, state resident: full-time $8800. Tuition, nonresident: full-time $20,760. Tuition and fees vary according to program and reciprocity agreements. *Financial support:* In 2009–10, 4 research assistantships, 11 teaching assistantships were awarded; career-related internships or fieldwork and unspecified assistantships also available. Support available to part-time students. Financial award application deadline: 4/15. *Faculty research:* Geology, geosciences, geophysics, hydrogeology, paleontology. Total annual research expenditures: $180,956. *Unit head:* Barry Cameron, Representative, 414-229-3136, Fax: 414-229-5452, E-mail: bcameron@uwm.edu. *Application contact:* General Information Contact, 414-229-4982, Fax: 414-229-6967, E-mail: gradschool@uwm.edu.

University of Wyoming, College of Arts and Sciences, Department of Geology and Geophysics, Laramie, WY 82070. Offers geology (MS, PhD); geophysics (MS, PhD). Part-time programs available. *Degree requirements:* For master's, comprehensive exam, thesis; for doctorate, comprehensive exam, thesis/dissertation. *Entrance requirements:* For master's and doctorate, GRE General Test, minimum GPA of 3.0. *Faculty research:* Low-temp geochemistry, geohydrology, paleontology, structure/tectonics, sedimentation and petroleum geology, petrology, geophysics/seismology.

Utah State University, School of Graduate Studies, College of Science, Department of Geology, Logan, UT 84322. Offers MS. *Degree requirements:* For master's, thesis. *Entrance requirements:* For master's, GRE General Test, minimum GPA of 3.0. Additional exam requirements/recommendations for international students: Required—TOEFL. *Faculty research:* Sedimentary geology, structural geology, regional tectonics, hydrogeology petrology.

Virginia Polytechnic Institute and State University, Graduate School, College of Science, Department of Geosciences, Blacksburg, VA 24061. Offers geological sciences (MS, PhD); geophysics (MS, PhD). *Entrance requirements:* For master's and doctorate, GRE General Test. Additional exam requirements/recommendations for international students: Required—TOEFL (minimum score 550 paper-based; 213 computer-based). Electronic applications accepted. *Faculty research:* Paleontology/geobiology, active tectonics, geomorphology, mineralogy/crystallography, mineral physics.

Washington State University, Graduate School, College of Sciences, School of Earth and Environmental Sciences, Department of Geology, Pullman, WA 99164. Offers MS, PhD. *Faculty:* 9. *Students:* 20 full-time (7 women), 5 part-time (2 women); includes 1 American Indian/Alaska Native. Average age 29. 31 applicants, 19% accepted, 6 enrolled. In 2009, 3 master's, 1 doctorate awarded. *Degree requirements:* For master's, comprehensive exam (for some programs), thesis, oral exam; for doctorate, one foreign language, comprehensive exam, thesis/dissertation, oral exam, written exam. *Entrance requirements:* For master's and doctorate, GRE General Test, Submit a letter of application stating qualification, personal goals, and objectives of graduate study; official GRE scores; official copies of college transcripts; and three letters of recommendation from academic advisors and/or faculty you have taken classes from. Minimum GPA of 3.0, 3 letters of recommendation. Additional exam requirements/recommendations for international students: Required—TOEFL (minimum score 560 paper-based; 220 computer-based). *Application deadline:* For fall admission, 1/10 priority date for domestic students, 1/10 for international students; for spring admission, 7/1 priority date for domestic students, 7/1 for international students. Applications are processed on a rolling basis. Application fee: $50. Electronic applications accepted. *Financial support:* In 2009–10, 4 fellowships (averaging $2,700 per year), 5 research assistantships with full and partial tuition reimbursements (averaging $13,917 per year), 18 teaching assistantships with full and partial tuition reimbursements (averaging $13,056 per year) were awarded; career-related internships or fieldwork, Federal Work-Study, institutionally sponsored loans, and scholarships/grants also available. Financial award application deadline: 2/1; financial award applicants required to submit FAFSA. *Faculty research:* Genesis of ore deposits, geohydrology of the Pacific Northwest, geochemistry and petrology of plateau basalts. Total annual research expenditures: $358,000. *Unit head:* Dr. John A. Wolff, Acting Director, 509-335-2825, Fax: 509-335-7816, E-mail: jawolff@mail.wsu.edu. *Application contact:* Graduate School Admissions, 800-GRADWSU, Fax: 509-335-1949, E-mail: gradsch@wsu.edu.

Wayne State University, College of Liberal Arts and Sciences, Department of Geology, Detroit, MI 48202. Offers MA, MS. *Degree requirements:* For master's, thesis. *Entrance requirements:* For master's, GRE General Test. Additional exam requirements/recommendations for international students: Required—TOEFL (minimum score 550 paper-based; 213 computer-based); Recommended—TWE (minimum score 6). Electronic applications accepted. *Faculty research:* Glacial geology of Southeastern Michigan; applications of U-Th-series, cosmogenic and anthrogenic radionuclides as tracers and chronometers in the environment; geochemical exploration of ore deposits using trace-elemental and stable isotopic (light-elemental) analytical tools; fate and transport of groundwater contaminants in glacial sediments; environmental radioactivity and geochronology.

West Chester University of Pennsylvania, Office of Graduate Studies, College of Arts and Sciences, Department of Geology and Astronomy, West Chester, PA 19383. Offers earth-space science (Teaching Certificate); general science (Teaching Certificate); geoscience (MA). Part-time and evening/weekend programs available. *Students:* 8 full-time (2 women), 24 part-time (16 women). Average age 32. 15 applicants, 100% accepted, 12 enrolled. In 2009, 8 master's awarded. *Degree requirements:* For master's, comprehensive exam (for some programs), thesis optional. *Entrance requirements:* For master's, minimum GPA of 2.5. Additional exam requirements/recommendations for international students: Required—TOEFL (minimum score 550 paper-based; 213 computer-based; 80 iBT). *Application deadline:* For fall admission, 4/15 priority date for domestic students, 3/15 for international students; for spring admission, 10/15 for domestic students, 9/1 for international students. Applications are processed on a rolling basis. Application fee: $35. Electronic applications accepted. *Expenses:* Tuition, state resident: full-time $6666; part-time $370 per credit. Tuition, nonresident: full-time $10,666; part-time $593 per credit. Required fees: $122.56 per credit. *Financial support:* In 2009–10, 1 research assistantship with full and partial tuition reimbursement (averaging $5,000 per year) was awarded; unspecified assistantships also available. Support available to part-time students. Financial award application deadline: 2/15; financial award applicants required to submit FAFSA. *Faculty research:* Developing and using a meteorological data station. *Unit head:* Dr. Marc Gagne, Chair, 610-436-2727, E-mail: mgagne@wcupa.edu. *Application contact:* Dr. Steven Good, Graduate Coordinator, 610-436-2203, E-mail: sgood@wcupa.edu.

Western Kentucky University, Graduate Studies, Ogden College of Science and Engineering, Department of Geography and Geology, Bowling Green, KY 42101. Offers MAE, MS. *Degree requirements:* For master's, comprehensive exam, thesis or alternative. *Entrance requirements:* For master's, GRE General Test, minimum GPA of 2.75. Additional exam requirements/recommendations for international students: Required—TOEFL (minimum score 555 paper-based; 213 computer-based; 79 iBT). *Expenses:* Tuition, state resident: full-time $4160; part-time $416 per credit hour. Tuition, nonresident: full-time $9550; part-time $506 per credit hour. Tuition and fees vary according to campus/location and reciprocity agreements. *Faculty research:* Hydroclimatology, electronic data sets, groundwater, sinkhole liquification potential, meteorological analysis.

Western Washington University, Graduate School, College of Sciences and Technology, Department of Geology, Bellingham, WA 98225-5996. Offers MS. Part-time programs available. *Degree requirements:* For master's, thesis. *Entrance requirements:* For master's, GRE General Test, minimum GPA of 3.0 in last 60 semester hours or last 90 quarter hours. Additional exam requirements/recommendations for international students: Required—TOEFL (minimum score 567 paper-based; 227 computer-based). Electronic applications accepted. *Faculty research:* Structure/tectonics; sedimentary, glacial and quaternary geomorphology; igneous and metamorphic petrology; hydrology, geophysics.

West Virginia University, Eberly College of Arts and Sciences, Department of Geology and Geography, Program in Geology, Morgantown, WV 26506. Offers geomorphology (MS, PhD); geophysics (MS, PhD); hydrogeology (MS, PhD); paleontology (MS, PhD); petroleum geology (PhD); petrology (MS, PhD); stratigraphy (MS, PhD); structure (MS, PhD). Part-time programs available. Terminal master's awarded for partial completion of doctoral program. *Degree requirements:* For master's, thesis (for some programs); for doctorate, comprehensive exam, thesis/dissertation. *Entrance requirements:* For master's, GRE General Test, minimum GPA of 2.5; for doctorate, GRE General Test, minimum GPA of 3.3. Additional exam requirements/recommendations for international students: Required—TOEFL.

Wichita State University, Graduate School, Fairmount College of Liberal Arts and Sciences, Department of Geology, Wichita, KS 67260. Offers earth, environmental, and physical sciences (MS). Part-time programs available. *Expenses:* Tuition, state resident: full-time $4247; part-time $235.95 per credit hour. Tuition, nonresident: full-time $11,171; part-time $620.60 per credit hour. Required fees: $34; $3.60 per credit hour. $17 per term. Tuition and fees vary according to campus/location and program. *Unit head:* Dr. William Parcell, Chair, 316-978-3140, E-mail: william.parcell@wichita.edu. *Application contact:* Dr. William Parcell, Chair, 316-978-3140, E-mail: william.parcell@wichita.edu.

Wright State University, School of Graduate Studies, College of Science and Mathematics, Department of Earth and Environmental Sciences, Program in Geological Sciences, Dayton, OH 45435. Offers MS. Part-time programs available. *Degree requirements:* For master's, thesis. *Entrance requirements:* Additional exam requirements/recommendations for international students: Required—TOEFL.

Yale University, Graduate School of Arts and Sciences, Department of Geology and Geophysics, New Haven, CT 06520. Offers biogeochemistry (PhD); climate dynamics (PhD); geochemistry (PhD); geophysics (PhD); meteorology (PhD); oceanography (PhD); paleontology (PhD); paleooceanography (PhD); petrology (PhD); tectonics (PhD). *Degree requirements:* For doctorate, thesis/dissertation. *Entrance requirements:* For doctorate, GRE General Test. Additional exam requirements/recommendations for international students: Required—TOEFL.

Geophysics

Boise State University, Graduate College, College of Arts and Sciences, Department of Geosciences, Master's Program in Geophysics, Boise, ID 83725-0399. Offers MS. Part-time programs available. *Degree requirements:* For master's, thesis. *Entrance requirements:* For master's, GRE General Test, minimum GPA of 3.0, BS in related field. Additional exam requirements/recommendations for international students: Required—TOEFL. Electronic applications accepted. *Expenses:* Tuition, state resident: full-time $3106; part-time $209 per credit. Tuition, nonresident: part-time $284 per credit. *Faculty research:* Shallow seismic profile, seismic hazard, tectonics, hazardous waste disposal.

Boise State University, Graduate College, College of Arts and Sciences, Department of Geosciences, Program in Geophysics, Boise, ID 83725-0399. Offers PhD. Part-time programs available. *Degree requirements:* For doctorate, comprehensive exam, thesis/dissertation. *Entrance requirements:* For doctorate, GRE General Test. Electronic applications accepted. *Expenses:* Tuition, state resident: full-time $3106; part-time $209 per credit. Tuition, nonresident: part-time $284 per credit.

Boston College, Graduate School of Arts and Sciences, Department of Geology and Geophysics, Chestnut Hill, MA 02467-3800. Offers MS, MBA/MS. *Students:* 25 full-time (10 women), 1 (woman) part-time; includes 2 minority (1 Asian American or Pacific Islander, 1 Hispanic American), 2 international. 22 applicants, 82% accepted, 8 enrolled. In 2009, 6 master's awarded. *Degree requirements:* For master's, thesis. *Entrance requirements:* For master's, GRE General Test, GRE Subject Test. Additional exam requirements/recommendations for international students: Required—TOEFL (minimum score 600 paper-based; 250 computer-based; 100 iBT). *Application deadline:* For fall admission, 2/1 priority date for domestic students, 2/1 for international students. Application fee: $70. Electronic applications accepted. *Financial support:* Research assistantships with full tuition reimbursements, teaching assistantships with full tuition reimbursements, Federal Work-Study available. Support available to part-time students. Financial award application deadline: 3/1; financial award applicants required to submit FAFSA. *Faculty research:* Coastal and marine geology, experimental sedimentology, geomagnetism, igneous petrology, paleontology. *Unit head:* Dr. Gail Kineke, Chairperson, 617-552-3640. *Application contact:* Dr. John Ebel, Graduate Program Director, 617-552-3640, E-mail: john.ebel@bc.edu.

Bowling Green State University, Graduate College, College of Arts and Sciences, Department of Physics and Astronomy, Bowling Green, OH 43403. Offers geophysics (MS); physics (MAT, MS). *Degree requirements:* For master's, thesis or alternative. *Entrance requirements:* For master's, GRE General Test. Additional exam requirements/recommendations for international students: Required—TOEFL. Electronic applications accepted. *Faculty research:* Computational physics, solid-state physics, materials science, theoretical physics.

California Institute of Technology, Division of Geological and Planetary Sciences, Pasadena, CA 91125-0001. Offers geobiology (MS, PhD); geochemistry (MS, PhD); geology (MS, PhD); geophysics (MS, PhD); planetary science (MS, PhD). *Faculty:* 38 full-time (6 women). *Students:* 75 full-time (38 women); includes 21 minority (1 African American, 18 Asian Americans or Pacific Islanders, 2 Hispanic Americans). Average age 26. 102 applicants, 28% accepted, 9 enrolled. In 2009, 13 master's, 13 doctorates awarded. *Degree requirements:* For doctorate, thesis/dissertation. *Entrance requirements:* For doctorate, GRE General Test. Additional exam requirements/recommendations for international students: Required—TOEFL; Recommended—IELTS, TWE. *Application deadline:* For fall admission, 1/1 for domestic and international students. Application fee: $80. Electronic applications accepted. *Financial support:* In 2009–10, 75 students received support, including 15 fellowships with full tuition reimbursements available (averaging $27,000 per year), 60 research assistantships with full tuition reimbursements available (averaging $27,000 per year); teaching assistantships with full tuition reimbursements available, institutionally sponsored loans, scholarships/grants, health care benefits, and unspecified assistantships also available. Financial award applicants required to submit FAFSA. *Faculty research:* Astronomy, evolution of anaerobic respiratory processes, structural geology and tectonics, theoretical and numerical seismology, global biogeochemical cycles. *Unit head:* Dr. Kenneth A. Farley, Chairman, 626-395-6111, Fax: 626-795-6028, E-mail: dianb@gps.caltech.edu. *Application contact:* Dr. Robert W. Clayton, Academic Officer, 626-395-6909, Fax: 626-795-6028, E-mail: dianb@gps.caltech.edu.

California State University, Long Beach, Graduate Studies, College of Natural Sciences and Mathematics, Department of Geological Sciences, Long Beach, CA 90840. Offers geology (MS); geophysics (MS). Part-time programs available. *Faculty:* 6 full-time (0 women). *Students:* 9 full-time (4 women), 20 part-time (11 women); includes 7 minority (1 African American, 2 Asian Americans or Pacific Islanders, 4 Hispanic Americans). Average age 35. 21 applicants, 52% accepted, 7 enrolled. *Degree requirements:* For master's, thesis. *Entrance requirements:* For master's, GRE General Test. *Application deadline:* For fall admission, 7/1 for domestic students. Applications are processed on a rolling basis. Application fee: $55. Electronic applications accepted. *Expenses:* Required fees: $1802 per semester. Part-time tuition and fees vary according to course load. *Financial support:* Research assistantships, teaching assistantships, Federal Work-Study, institutionally sponsored loans, and scholarships/grants available. Financial award application deadline: 3/2. *Faculty research:* Paleontology, geophysics, structural geology, organic geochemistry, sedimentary geology. *Unit head:* Robert D. Francis, Chair, 562-985-4929, Fax: 562-985-8638, E-mail: rfrancis@csulb.edu. *Application contact:* Gregory Holk, Graduate Advisor, 562-985-5006, Fax: 562-985-8638, E-mail: gholk@csulb.edu.

Colorado School of Mines, Graduate School, Department of Geophysics, Golden, CO 80401. Offers geophysical engineering (ME, MS, PhD); geophysics (MS, PhD); mineral exploration and mining geosciences (PMS). Part-time programs available. *Faculty:* 15 full-time (1 woman), 4 part-time/adjunct (0 women). *Students:* 67 full-time (15 women), 6 part-time (1 woman); includes 5 minority (1 American Indian/Alaska Native, 2 Asian Americans or Pacific Islanders, 2 Hispanic Americans), 40 international. Average age 30. 130 applicants, 40% accepted, 20 enrolled. In 2009, 9 master's, 6 doctorates awarded. *Degree requirements:* For master's, thesis (for some programs); for doctorate, one foreign language, comprehensive exam, thesis/dissertation, oral exams. *Entrance requirements:* For master's and doctorate, GRE General Test. Additional exam requirements/recommendations for international students: Required—TOEFL (minimum score 550 paper-based; 213 computer-based; 80 iBT). *Application deadline:* For fall admission, 1/15 for domestic and international students; for spring admission, 9/1 for domestic and international students. Application fee: $50 ($70 for international students). Electronic applications accepted. *Expenses:* Tuition, state resident: full-time $10,584; part-time $588 per credit hour. Tuition, nonresident: full-time $24,750; part-time $1375 per credit hour. Required fees: $1654; $827.10 per semester. *Financial support:* In 2009–10, 58 students received support, including 6 fellowships with full tuition reimbursements available (averaging $20,000 per year), 47 research assistantships with full tuition reimbursements available (averaging $20,000 per year), 5 teaching assistantships with full tuition reimbursements available (averaging $20,000 per year); scholarships/grants, health care benefits, and unspecified assistantships also available. Financial award application deadline: 1/15; financial award applicants required to submit FAFSA. *Faculty research:* Seismic exploration, gravity and geomagnetic fields, electrical mapping and sounding, bore hole measurements, environmental physics. Total annual research expenditures: $3.8 million. *Unit head:* Dr. Terence K. Young, Department Head, 303-273-3454, Fax: 303-273-3478, E-mail: tkyoung@mines.edu. *Application contact:* Michelle Szobody, Office Manager, 303-273-3935, Fax: 303-273-3478, E-mail: mszobody@mines.edu.

Columbia University, Graduate School of Arts and Sciences, Division of Natural Sciences, Department of Earth and Environmental Sciences, New York, NY 10027. Offers geochemistry

Geophysics

Columbia University (continued)
(M Phil, MA, PhD); geodetic sciences (M Phil, MA, PhD); geophysics (M Phil, MA, PhD); oceanography (M Phil, MA, PhD). *Degree requirements:* For master's, thesis or alternative, fieldwork, written exam; for doctorate, one foreign language, thesis/dissertation. *Entrance requirements:* For master's and doctorate, GRE General Test, GRE Subject Test, major in natural or physical science. Additional exam requirements/recommendations for international students: Required—TOEFL. *Faculty research:* Structural geology and stratigraphy, petrology, paleontology, rare gas, isotope and aqueous geochemistry.

Cornell University, Graduate School, Graduate Fields of Engineering, Field of Geological Sciences, Ithaca, NY 14853-0001. Offers economic geology (M Eng, MS, PhD); engineering geology (M Eng, MS, PhD); environmental geophysics (M Eng, MS, PhD); general geology (M Eng, MS, PhD); geobiology (M Eng, MS, PhD); geochemistry and isotope geology (M Eng, MS, PhD); geohydrology (M Eng, MS, PhD); geomorphology (M Eng, MS, PhD); geophysics (M Eng, MS, PhD); geotectonics (M Eng, MS, PhD); marine geology (MS, PhD); mineralogy (M Eng, MS, PhD); paleontology (M Eng, MS, PhD); petroleum geology (M Eng, MS, PhD); petrology (M Eng, MS, PhD); planetary geology (M Eng, MS, PhD); Precambrian geology (M Eng, MS, PhD); Quaternary geology (M Eng, MS, PhD); rock mechanics (M Eng, MS, PhD); sedimentology (M Eng, MS, PhD); seismology (M Eng, MS, PhD); stratigraphy (M Eng, MS, PhD); structural geology (M Eng, MS, PhD). *Faculty:* 38 full-time (6 women). *Students:* 32 full-time (14 women); includes 2 minority (1 African American, 1 Asian American or Pacific Islander), 9 international. Average age 29. 61 applicants, 23% accepted, 8 enrolled. In 2009, 3 doctorates awarded. *Degree requirements:* For master's, thesis (MS); for doctorate, comprehensive exam, thesis/dissertation. *Entrance requirements:* For master's and doctorate, GRE General Test, 3 letters of recommendation. Additional exam requirements/recommendations for international students: Required—TOEFL (minimum score 550 paper-based; 213 computer-based; 77 iBT). *Application deadline:* For fall admission, 1/15 priority date for domestic students. Applications are processed on a rolling basis. Application fee: $70. Electronic applications accepted. *Expenses:* Tuition: Full-time $29,500. Required fees: $70. Full-time tuition and fees vary according to degree level, program and student level. *Financial support:* In 2009–10, 25 students received support, including 2 fellowships with full tuition reimbursements available, 3 research assistantships with full tuition reimbursements available, 1 teaching assistantship with full tuition reimbursement available; institutionally sponsored loans, scholarships/grants, health care benefits, tuition waivers (full and partial), and unspecified assistantships also available. Financial award applicants required to submit FAFSA. *Faculty research:* Geophysics, structural geology, petrology, geochemistry, geodynamics. *Unit head:* Director of Graduate Studies, 607-255-5466, Fax: 607-254-4780. *Application contact:* Graduate Field Assistant, 607-255-5466, Fax: 607-254-4780, E-mail: gradprog@geology.cornell.edu.

Florida State University, The Graduate School, College of Arts and Sciences, Interdisciplinary Program in Geophysical Fluid Dynamics, Tallahassee, FL 32306. Offers PhD. *Faculty:* 18 full-time (2 women). *Students:* 2 full-time (0 women), 1 part-time (0 women), 1 international. Average age 30. 4 applicants, 0% accepted, 0 enrolled. In 2009, 2 doctorates awarded. *Degree requirements:* For doctorate, thesis/dissertation, departmental qualifying exam. *Entrance requirements:* For doctorate, GRE General Test, GRE Subject Test, minimum GPA of 3.0. Additional exam requirements/recommendations for international students: Required—TOEFL (minimum score 550 paper-based; 80 iBT). *Application deadline:* For fall admission, 3/30 for domestic and international students. Application fee: $30. Electronic applications accepted. *Expenses:* Tuition, state resident: full-time $7413.36. Tuition, nonresident: full-time $22,567. *Financial support:* In 2009–10, 1 research assistantship (averaging $18,500 per year) was awarded; fellowships, unspecified assistantships also available. Financial award applicants required to submit FAFSA. *Faculty research:* Hurricane dynamics, convection, air-sea interaction, wave-mean flow interaction, numerical models. Total annual research expenditures: $369,802. *Unit head:* Dr. Carol A. Clayson, Director, 850-644-2488, Fax: 850-644-8972, E-mail: clayson@met.fsu.edu. *Application contact:* Vijaya Challa, Academic Coordinator, 850-644-5594, Fax: 850-644-8972, E-mail: vijaya@gfdi.fsu.edu.

Georgia Institute of Technology, Graduate Studies and Research, College of Sciences, School of Earth and Atmospheric Sciences, Atlanta, GA 30332-0340. Offers atmospheric chemistry, aerosols and clouds (MS, PhD); dynamics of weather and climate (MS, PhD); geochemistry (MS, PhD); geophysics (MS, PhD); oceanography (MS, PhD); paleoclimate (MS, PhD); planetary science (MS, PhD); remote sensing (MS, PhD). Part-time programs available. Terminal master's awarded for partial completion of doctoral program. *Degree requirements:* For master's, thesis or alternative; for doctorate, comprehensive exam, thesis/dissertation. *Entrance requirements:* For master's, GRE, letters of recommendation; for doctorate, GRE, academic transcripts, letters of recommendation, personal statement. Additional exam requirements/recommendations for international students: Required—TOEFL (minimum score 550 paper-based; 213 computer-based; 79 iBT). *Faculty research:* Geophysics; atmospheric chemistry, aerosols and clouds; dynamics of weather and climate; geochemistry; oceanography; paleoclimate; planetary science; remote sensing.

ICR Graduate School, Graduate Programs, Santee, CA 92071. Offers astro/geophysics (MS); biology (MS); geology (MS); science education (MS). Part-time programs available. *Degree requirements:* For master's, comprehensive exam (for some programs), thesis (for some programs). *Entrance requirements:* For master's, minimum undergraduate GPA of 3.0, bachelor's degree in science or science education. *Faculty research:* Age of the earth, limits of variation, catastrophe, optimum methods for teaching.

Idaho State University, Office of Graduate Studies, College of Arts and Sciences, Department of Geosciences, Pocatello, ID 83209-8072. Offers geographic information science (MS); geology (MNS, MS); geology emphasis environmental geoscience (MS); geophysics/hydrology/geology (MS); geotechnology (Postbaccalaureate Certificate). Part-time programs available. *Faculty:* 8 full-time (1 woman). *Students:* 25 full-time (12 women), 20 part-time (6 women); includes 1 minority (Asian American or Pacific Islander), 4 international. Average age 33. In 2009, 7 master's, 2 other advanced degrees awarded. *Degree requirements:* For master's, comprehensive exam, thesis, oral colloquium; for Postbaccalaureate Certificate, thesis optional, minimum 19 credits. *Entrance requirements:* For master's, GRE General Test (minimum 50th percentile in 2 sections), 3 letters of recommendation; for Postbaccalaureate Certificate, GRE General Test, 3 letters of recommendation, bachelor's degree, statement of goals. Additional exam requirements/recommendations for international students: Required—TOEFL (minimum score 550 paper-based; 213 computer-based; 80 iBT). *Application deadline:* For fall admission, 7/1 for domestic students, 6/1 for international students; for spring admission, 12/1 for domestic students, 11/1 for international students. Applications are processed on a rolling basis. Application fee: $55. Electronic applications accepted. *Expenses:* Tuition, state resident: full-time $3318; part-time $297 per credit hour. Tuition, nonresident: full-time $13,120; part-time $437 per credit hour. Required fees: $2530. Tuition and fees vary according to program. *Financial support:* In 2009–10, 20 research assistantships with full and partial tuition reimbursements (averaging $9,713 per year), 7 teaching assistantships with full and partial tuition reimbursements (averaging $10,841 per year) were awarded; career-related internships or fieldwork, Federal Work-Study, institutionally sponsored loans, scholarships/grants, health care benefits, tuition waivers (full and partial), and unspecified assistantships also available. Support available to part-time students. Financial award application deadline: 1/1; financial award applicants required to submit FAFSA. *Faculty research:* Quantitative field mapping and sampling: microscopic, geochemical, and isotopic analysis of rocks, minerals and water; remote sensing, geographic information systems, and global positioning systems: environmental and watershed management; surficial and fluvial processes: landscape change; regional tectonics, structural geology; planetary geology. *Unit head:* Dr. David Rodgers, Chairman, 208-282-3365, Fax: 208-282-4414, E-mail: rodgdavi@isu.edu. *Application contact:* Tami Carson, Graduate School Technical Records Specialist, 208-282-2150, Fax: 208-282-4847, E-mail: carstami@isu.edu.

Indiana University Bloomington, University Graduate School, College of Arts and Sciences, Department of Geological Sciences, Bloomington, IN 47405-7000. Offers biogeochemistry (MS, PhD); economic geology (MS, PhD); geobiology (MS, PhD); geophysics, structural geology and tectonics (MS, PhD); hydrogeology (MS, PhD); mineralogy (MS, PhD); stratigraphy and sedimentology (MS, PhD). *Faculty:* 17 full-time (1 woman). *Students:* 52 full-time (24 women), 3 part-time (0 women); includes 4 minority (2 African Americans, 1 Asian American or Pacific Islander, 1 Hispanic American), 24 international. Average age 30. 46 applicants, 65% accepted, 11 enrolled. In 2009, 9 master's, 1 doctorate awarded. Terminal master's awarded for partial completion of doctoral program. *Degree requirements:* For master's, thesis or alternative; for doctorate, comprehensive exam, thesis/dissertation. *Entrance requirements:* For master's and doctorate, GRE General Test. Additional exam requirements/recommendations for international students: Required—TOEFL. *Application deadline:* For fall admission, 1/15 priority date for domestic students, 12/15 for international students; for spring admission, 9/1 priority date for domestic students, 9/1 for international students. Applications are processed on a rolling basis. Application fee: $55 ($65 for international students). *Financial support:* In 2009–10, 11 fellowships with full tuition reimbursements (averaging $15,000 per year), 14 research assistantships with full tuition reimbursements (averaging $15,000 per year), 21 teaching assistantships with full tuition reimbursements (averaging $14,073 per year) were awarded; career-related internships or fieldwork, Federal Work-Study, and institutionally sponsored loans also available. *Faculty research:* Geophysics, geochemistry, hydrogeology, geobiology, planetary science. Total annual research expenditures: $644,299. *Unit head:* Simon Brassell, Chair, 812-855-5581, Fax: 812-855-7899, E-mail: geochair@indiana.edu. *Application contact:* Mary Iverson, Graduate Secretary, 812-855-7214, Fax: 812-855-7899, E-mail: miverson@indiana.edu.

Louisiana State University and Agricultural and Mechanical College, Graduate School, College of Basic Sciences, Department of Geology and Geophysics, Baton Rouge, LA 70803. Offers MS, PhD. *Faculty:* 16 full-time (6 women), 1 (woman) part-time/adjunct. *Students:* 43 full-time (12 women), 7 part-time (1 woman); includes 3 African Americans, 1 Asian American or Pacific Islander, 2 Hispanic Americans, 8 international. Average age 26. 50 applicants, 44% accepted, 13 enrolled. In 2009, 5 master's, 2 doctorates awarded. Terminal master's awarded for partial completion of doctoral program. *Degree requirements:* For master's, thesis; for doctorate, thesis/dissertation. *Entrance requirements:* For master's and doctorate, GRE General Test, minimum GPA of 3.0. Additional exam requirements/recommendations for international students: Required—TOEFL (minimum score 550 paper-based; 213 computer-based; 79 iBT) or IELTS (minimum score 6.5). *Application deadline:* For fall admission, 1/25 priority date for domestic students, 5/15 for international students; for spring admission, 10/15 for international students. Applications are processed on a rolling basis. Application fee: $50 ($70 for international students). Electronic applications accepted. *Financial support:* In 2009–10, 37 students received support, including 3 fellowships with full tuition reimbursements available (averaging $24,897 per year), 25 research assistantships with full and partial tuition reimbursements available (averaging $18,660 per year), 13 teaching assistantships with full and partial tuition reimbursements available (averaging $15,230 per year); career-related internships or fieldwork, Federal Work-Study, institutionally sponsored loans, health care benefits, tuition waivers (full and partial), and unspecified assistantships also available. Financial award application deadline: 3/15; financial award applicants required to submit FAFSA. *Faculty research:* Geophysics, sedimentology, geochemistry, geomicrobiology, tectonics. Total annual research expenditures: $863,173. *Unit head:* Dr. Carol Wicks, Chair, 225-578-3353, Fax: 225-578-2302, E-mail: glande@lsu.edu. *Application contact:* Jeffrey Nunn, Graduate Coordinator, 225-578-6657, E-mail: gljeff@lsu.edu.

Massachusetts Institute of Technology, School of Science, Department of Earth, Atmospheric, and Planetary Sciences, Cambridge, MA 02139-4307. Offers atmospheric chemistry (PhD, Sc D); atmospheric science (SM, PhD, Sc D); chemical oceanography (SM, PhD, Sc D); climate physics and chemistry (SM, PhD, Sc D); earth and planetary sciences (SM); geochemistry (PhD, Sc D); geology (PhD, Sc D); geophysics (PhD, Sc D); marine geology and geophysics (SM, PhD, Sc D); physical oceanography (SM, PhD, Sc D); planetary sciences (PhD, Sc D). *Faculty:* 37 full-time (7 women). *Students:* 158 full-time (74 women); includes 14 minority (1 African American, 1 American Indian/Alaska Native, 6 Asian Americans or Pacific Islanders, 6 Hispanic Americans), 58 international. Average age 27. 205 applicants, 30% accepted, 18 enrolled. In 2009, 10 master's, 25 doctorates awarded. Terminal master's awarded for partial completion of doctoral program. *Degree requirements:* For master's, thesis; for doctorate, comprehensive exam, thesis/dissertation. *Entrance requirements:* For master's, GRE General Test; for doctorate, GRE General Test, GRE Subject Test (chemistry or physics for planetary science area). Additional exam requirements/recommendations for international students: Required—IELTS (minimum score 6); Recommended—TOEFL (minimum score 577 paper-based; 233 computer-based; 91 iBT). *Application deadline:* For fall admission, 1/5 for domestic and international students; for spring admission, 11/1 for domestic and international students. Application fee: $75. Electronic applications accepted. *Financial support:* In 2009–10, 112 students received support, including 31 fellowships with tuition reimbursements available (averaging $30,513 per year), 89 research assistantships with tuition reimbursements available (averaging $21,168 per year), 17 teaching assistantships with tuition reimbursements available (averaging $28,372 per year); Federal Work-Study, institutionally sponsored loans, scholarships/grants, health care benefits, and unspecified assistantships also available. *Faculty research:* Formation, dynamics and evolution of planetary systems, origin, evolution and interaction of the physical, characterization of past, interplay of energy and the environment, present and potential future climates and the causes and consequences of climate change, chemical, geological and biological components of the Earth system, composition, structure and dynamics of the atmospheres, oceans, surfaces and interiors of the Earth and other planets. Total annual research expenditures: $19.5 million. *Unit head:* Prof. Maria Zuber, Head, 617-253-2127, Fax: 617-253-8298, E-mail: eapsinfo@mit.edu. *Application contact:* EAPS Education Office, 617-253-3381, Fax: 617-253-8298, E-mail: eapsinfo@mit.edu.

Memorial University of Newfoundland, School of Graduate Studies, Department of Earth Sciences, St. John's, NL A1C 5S7, Canada. Offers geology (M Sc, PhD); geophysics (M Sc, PhD). Part-time programs available. *Degree requirements:* For master's, thesis; for doctorate, comprehensive exam, thesis/dissertation, oral thesis defense, entry evaluation. *Entrance requirements:* For master's, honors B Sc; for doctorate, M Sc. Electronic applications accepted. *Faculty research:* Geochemistry, sedimentology, paleoceanography and global change, mineral deposits, petroleum geology, hydrology.

Michigan Technological University, Graduate School, College of Engineering, Department of Geological and Mining Engineering and Sciences, Program in Geophysics, Houghton, MI 49931. Offers MS. Part-time programs available. *Degree requirements:* For master's, comprehensive exam. *Entrance requirements:* Additional exam requirements/recommendations for international students: Required—TOEFL (minimum score 550 paper-based; 213 computer-based). Electronic applications accepted.

Missouri University of Science and Technology, Graduate School, Department of Geological Sciences and Engineering, Rolla, MO 65409. Offers geological engineering (MS, DE, PhD); geology and geophysics (MS, PhD), including geochemistry, geology, geophysics, groundwater and environmental geology; petroleum engineering (MS, DE, PhD). Part-time programs available. *Degree requirements:* For master's, thesis optional; for doctorate, comprehensive exam, thesis/dissertation. *Entrance requirements:* For master's, GRE General Test (minimum score 600 quantitative, writing 3.5), minimum GPA of 3.0 in last 4 semesters; for doctorate, GRE General Test (minimum: Q 600, GRE WR 3.5). Additional exam requirements/recommendations for international students: Required—TOEFL. Electronic applications accepted. *Faculty research:* Digital image processing and geographic information systems, mineralogy, igneous and sedimentary petrology-geochemistry, sedimentology groundwater hydrology and contaminant transport.

New Mexico Institute of Mining and Technology, Graduate Studies, Department of Earth and Environmental Science, Program in Geophysics, Socorro, NM 87801. Offers MS, PhD. *Degree requirements:* For master's, thesis optional; for doctorate, thesis/dissertation. *Entrance requirements:* For master's, GRE General Test; for doctorate, GRE General Test, GRE Subject Test. Additional exam requirements/recommendations for international students: Required—TOEFL (minimum score 540 paper-based; 207 computer-based). *Faculty research:* Earthquake and volcanic seismology, subduction zone tectonics, network seismology, physical properties of sediments in fault zones.

Ohio University, Graduate College, College of Arts and Sciences, Department of Geological Sciences, Athens, OH 45701-2979. Offers environmental geochemistry (MS); environmental geology (MS); environmental/hydrology (MS); geology (MS); geology education (MS); geomorphology/surficial processes (MS); geophysics (MS); hydrogeology (MS); sedimentology (MS); structure/tectonics (MS). Part-time programs available. *Faculty:* 10 full-time (4 women), 4 part-time/adjunct (1 woman). *Students:* 18 full-time (13 women), 1 part-time (0 women), 9 international. 15 applicants, 67% accepted, 6 enrolled. In 2009, 5 master's awarded. *Degree requirements:* For master's, thesis. *Entrance requirements:* Additional exam requirements/recommendations for international students: Required—TOEFL (minimum score 550 paper-based; 80 iBT) or IELTS Academic (minimum score 6.5). *Application deadline:* For fall admission, 2/1 priority date for domestic and international students. Application fee: $50 ($55 for international students). Electronic applications accepted. *Expenses:* Tuition, state resident: full-time $7839; part-time $323 per quarter hour. Tuition, nonresident: full-time $15,831; part-time $654 per quarter hour. Required fees: $2931. *Financial support:* Research assistantships with full tuition reimbursements, teaching assistantships with full tuition reimbursements, Federal Work-Study, institutionally sponsored loans, scholarships/grants, tuition waivers (partial), and unspecified assistantships available. Financial award application deadline: 2/1. *Faculty research:* Geoscience education, tectonics, fluvial geomorphology, invertebrate paleontology, mine/hydrology. Total annual research expenditures: $649,020. *Unit head:* Dr. Gregory Nadon, Chair, 740-593-4212, Fax: 740-593-0486, E-mail: nadon@ohio.edu. *Application contact:* Dr. Douglas Green, Graduate Chair, 740-593-1843, Fax: 740-593-0486, E-mail: green@ohio.edu.

Oregon State University, Graduate School, College of Oceanic and Atmospheric Sciences, Program in Geophysics, Corvallis, OR 97331. Offers MA, MS, PhD. *Students:* 4 full-time (0 women), 1 part-time (0 women). Average age 28.Terminal master's awarded for partial completion of doctoral program. *Degree requirements:* For master's, thesis optional; for doctorate, thesis/dissertation. *Entrance requirements:* For master's and doctorate, GRE General Test, minimum GPA of 3.0 in last 90 hours. Additional exam requirements/recommendations for international students: Required—TOEFL. *Application deadline:* For fall admission, 2/1 for domestic students. Applications are processed on a rolling basis. Application fee: $50. *Expenses:* Tuition, state resident: full-time $9774; part-time $362 per credit. Tuition, nonresident: full-time $15,849; part-time $587 per credit. Required fees: $1639. Full-time tuition and fees vary according to course load and program. *Financial support:* Fellowships, research assistantships, teaching assistantships, career-related internships or fieldwork, Federal Work-Study, and institutionally sponsored loans available. Support available to part-time students. Financial award application deadline: 2/1. *Faculty research:* Seismic waves; gravitational, geothermal, and electromagnetic fields; rock magnetism; paleomagnetism. *Unit head:* Dr. Robert A. Duncan, Associate Dean for Student Programs, 541-737-5189, Fax: 541-737-2540, E-mail: rduncan@coas.oregonstate.edu. *Application contact:* Dr. Robert S. Allan, Assistant Director, Student Programs, 541-737-1340, Fax: 541-737-2064, E-mail: rallan@coas.oregonstate.edu.

Rensselaer Polytechnic Institute, Graduate School, School of Science, Department of Earth and Environmental Sciences, Troy, NY 12180-3590. Offers geochemistry (MS, PhD); geology (MS, PhD); geophysics (MS, PhD); petrology (MS, PhD). Part-time programs available. *Faculty:* 8 full-time (1 woman), 1 part-time/adjunct (0 women). *Students:* 8 full-time (5 women), 1 (woman) part-time; includes 1 minority (Asian American or Pacific Islander). Average age 24. 48 applicants, 15% accepted. In 2009, 2 master's, 3 doctorates awarded. Terminal master's awarded for partial completion of doctoral program. *Degree requirements:* For master's, comprehensive exam, thesis (for some programs); for doctorate, comprehensive exam, thesis/dissertation. *Entrance requirements:* For master's and doctorate, GRE General Test. Additional exam requirements/recommendations for international students: Required—TOEFL. *Application deadline:* For fall admission, 1/15 priority date for domestic students. Applications are processed on a rolling basis. Application fee: $75. Electronic applications accepted. *Expenses:* Tuition: Full-time $38,100. *Financial support:* In 2009–10, 7 research assistantships with full tuition reimbursements (averaging $23,000 per year), 4 teaching assistantships with full tuition reimbursements (averaging $23,000 per year) were awarded; fellowships with full tuition reimbursements, career-related internships or fieldwork, institutionally sponsored loans, and scholarships/grants also available. Financial award application deadline: 2/1; financial award applicants required to submit FAFSA. *Faculty research:* Mantel geochemistry, contaminant geochemistry, seismology, GPS geodesy, remote sensing petrology. Total annual research expenditures: $2.3 million. *Unit head:* Dr. Frank Spear, Chair, 518-276-6474, Fax: 518-276-2012, E-mail: ees@rpi.edu. *Application contact:* Dr. Steven Roecker, Professor, 518-276-6773, Fax: 518-276-2012, E-mail: ees@rpi.edu.

Rice University, Graduate Programs, Wiess School–Professional Science Master's Programs, Professional Master's Program in Subsurface Geosciences, Houston, TX 77251-1892. Offers geophysics (MS). Part-time programs available. *Degree requirements:* For master's, internship. *Entrance requirements:* For master's, GRE, letters of recommendation (4). Additional exam requirements/recommendations for international students: Required—TOEFL (minimum score 600 paper-based; 250 computer-based; 90 iBT). Electronic applications accepted. *Faculty research:* Seismology, geodynamics, wave propagation, bio-geochemistry, remote sensing.

Saint Louis University, Graduate School, College of Arts and Sciences and Graduate School, Department of Earth and Atmospheric Sciences, St. Louis, MO 63103-2097. Offers geophysics (PhD); geoscience (MS); meteorology (M Pr Met, MS-R, PhD). Part-time programs available. *Degree requirements:* For master's, thesis (for some programs), comprehensive oral exam; for doctorate, thesis/dissertation, preliminary exams. *Entrance requirements:* For master's, GRE General Test, letters of recommendation, resume; for doctorate, GRE General Test, letters of recommendation, resumé, goal statement, transcripts. Additional exam requirements/recommendations for international students: Required—TOEFL (minimum score 525 paper-based; 194 computer-based). Electronic applications accepted. *Faculty research:* Structural geology, mesoscale meteorology and severe storms, weather and climate change prediction.

Southern Methodist University, Dedman College, Department of Earth Sciences, Program in Applied Geophysics, Dallas, TX 75275. Offers MS. Part-time programs available. *Faculty:* 3 full-time (0 women), 2 part-time/adjunct (0 women). *Degree requirements:* For master's, thesis optional, qualifying exam. *Entrance requirements:* For master's, GRE General Test, minimum GPA of 3.0, letters of recommendation. Additional exam requirements/recommendations for international students: Required—TOEFL. *Application deadline:* For fall admission, 2/1 priority date for domestic and international students; for spring admission, 11/30 for domestic students. Applications are processed on a rolling basis. Application fee: $50. *Financial support:* Tuition waivers (full and partial) available. Financial award application deadline: 2/1; financial award applicants required to submit FAFSA. *Faculty research:* Geothermal energy, seismology. Total annual research expenditures: $800,000. *Unit head:* Dr. Robert T. Gregory, Chair, 214-768-3075, Fax: 214-768-2701, E-mail: bgregory@smu.edu. *Application contact:* Dr. John V. Walther, Graduate Advisor, 214-768-3174, Fax: 214-768-2701, E-mail: walther@smu.edu.

Southern Methodist University, Dedman College, Department of Earth Sciences, Program in Geophysics, Dallas, TX 75275. Offers MS, PhD. Part-time programs available. *Faculty:* 3 full-time (0 women), 2 part-time/adjunct (0 women). *Students:* 12 applicants, 42% accepted. In 2009, 2 master's, 2 doctorates awarded. *Degree requirements:* For master's, thesis (for some programs), qualifying exam; for doctorate, thesis/dissertation, qualifying exam. *Entrance requirements:* For master's and doctorate, GRE General Test, minimum GPA of 3.0, letters of recommendation. Additional exam requirements/recommendations for international students: Required—TOEFL. *Application deadline:* For fall admission, 2/1 priority date for domestic and international students; for spring admission, 11/30 for domestic students. Applications are processed on a rolling basis. Application fee: $50. *Financial support:* In 2009–10, fellowships with full tuition reimbursements (averaging $15,000 per year), research assistantships with full tuition reimbursements (averaging $15,000 per year), teaching assistantships with full tuition reimbursements (averaging $15,000 per year) were awarded; scholarships/grants, tuition waivers (full and partial), and unspecified assistantships also available. Financial award application deadline: 2/1; financial award applicants required to submit FAFSA. *Faculty research:* Seismology, heat flow, tectonics. Total annual research expenditures: $800,000. *Unit head:* Dr. Robert T. Gregory, Chair, 214-768-3075, Fax: 214-768-2701, E-mail: bgregory@smu.edu. *Application contact:* Dr. John V. Walther, Graduate Advisor, 214-768-3174, Fax: 214-768-2701, E-mail: walther@smu.edu.

Stanford University, School of Earth Sciences, Department of Geophysics, Stanford, CA 94305-9991. Offers MS, PhD. Terminal master's awarded for partial completion of doctoral program. *Degree requirements:* For master's, thesis; for doctorate, thesis/dissertation. *Entrance requirements:* For master's and doctorate, GRE General Test. Additional exam requirements/recommendations for international students: Required—TOEFL. Electronic applications accepted. *Expenses:* Tuition: Full-time $37,380; part-time $2760 per quarter. Required fees: $501.

Texas A&M University, College of Geosciences, Department of Geology and Geophysics, College Station, TX 77843. Offers geology (MS, PhD); geophysics (MS, PhD). *Faculty:* 30. *Students:* 101 full-time (39 women), 17 part-time (4 women); includes 11 minority (1 American Indian/Alaska Native, 6 Asian Americans or Pacific Islanders, 4 Hispanic Americans), 51 international. Average age 31. In 2009, 10 master's, 4 doctorates awarded. *Degree requirements:* For master's, thesis; for doctorate, thesis/dissertation. *Entrance requirements:* For master's and doctorate, GRE General Test. Additional exam requirements/recommendations for international students: Required—TOEFL. *Application deadline:* For fall admission, 3/1 priority date for domestic students, 1/15 for international students; for spring admission, 10/1 priority date for domestic students, 8/15 for international students. Applications are processed on a rolling basis. Application fee: $50 ($75 for international students). Electronic applications accepted. *Expenses:* Tuition, state resident: full-time $3991.32; part-time $221.74 per credit hour. Tuition, nonresident: full-time $9049; part-time $502.74 per credit hour. *Financial support:* In 2009–10, fellowships with partial tuition reimbursements (averaging $1,000 per year), research assistantships with partial tuition reimbursements (averaging $11,925 per year), teaching assistantships with partial tuition reimbursements (averaging $11,925 per year) were awarded; Federal Work-Study, institutionally sponsored loans, scholarships/grants, tuition waivers (partial), and unspecified assistantships also available. Financial award application deadline: 3/1; financial award applicants required to submit FAFSA. *Faculty research:* Environmental and engineering geology and geophysics, petroleum geology, tectonophysics, geochemistry. *Unit head:* Head, 979-845-0132, E-mail: geoaggie@geo.tamu.edu. *Application contact:* Graduate Adviser, 979-845-2451, Fax: 979-845-6162, E-mail: geoaggie@geo.tamu.edu.

The University of Akron, Graduate School, Buchtel College of Arts and Sciences, Department of Geology, Program in Geophysics, Akron, OH 44325. Offers MS. *Students:* 1 full-time (0 women), all international. Average age 28. 1 applicant, 100% accepted, 1 enrolled. *Degree requirements:* For master's, comprehensive exam, thesis, seminar, proficiency exam. *Entrance requirements:* For master's, minimum GPA of 2.75, letters of recommendation. Additional exam requirements/recommendations for international students: Required—TOEFL (minimum score 550 paper-based; 213 computer-based; 79 iBT). *Application deadline:* Applications are processed on a rolling basis. Application fee: $30 ($40 for international students). Electronic applications accepted. *Expenses:* Tuition, state resident: full-time $6570; part-time $365 per credit hour. Tuition, nonresident: full-time $11,250; part-time $625 per credit hour. *Unit head:* Dr. LaVerne Friberg, Director of Graduate Studies, 330-972-8046, E-mail: lfribe1@uakron.edu. *Application contact:* Dr. LaVerne Friberg, Director of Graduate Studies, 330-972-8046, E-mail: lfribe1@uakron.edu.

University of Alaska Fairbanks, College of Natural Sciences and Mathematics, Department of Geology and Geophysics, Fairbanks, AK 99775-5780. Offers geology (MS, PhD), including economic geology (PhD), petroleum geology (MS), quaternary geology (PhD), remote sensing, volcanology (PhD); geophysics (MS, PhD), including remote sensing, snow, ice, and permafrost geophysics (MS), solid-earth geophysics (MS). Part-time programs available. *Faculty:* 16 full-time (4 women), 3 part-time/adjunct (0 women). *Students:* 56 full-time (24 women), 18 part-time (10 women); includes 3 minority (1 African American, 1 Asian American or Pacific Islander, 1 Hispanic American), 12 international. Average age 30. 57 applicants, 30% accepted, 16 enrolled. In 2009, 6 master's, 4 doctorates awarded. Terminal master's awarded for partial completion of doctoral program. *Degree requirements:* For master's, comprehensive exam, thesis, oral exam, oral defense; for doctorate, comprehensive exam, thesis/dissertation, oral exam, oral defense. *Entrance requirements:* For master's and doctorate, GRE General Test. Additional exam requirements/recommendations for international students: Required—TOEFL (minimum score 550 paper-based; 213 computer-based). *Application deadline:* For fall admission, 6/1 for domestic students, 3/1 for international students; for spring admission, 10/15 for domestic students, 9/1 for international students. Applications are processed on a rolling basis. Application fee: $60. Electronic applications accepted. *Expenses:* Tuition, state resident: full-time $7584; part-time $316 per credit. Tuition, nonresident: full-time $15,504; part-time $646 per credit. Required fees: $23 per credit. $135 per semester. Tuition and fees vary according to course level, course load and reciprocity agreements. *Financial support:* In 2009–10, 1 fellowship (averaging $16,454 per year), 32 research assistantships (averaging $15,811 per year), 7 teaching assistantships (averaging $14,143 per year) were awarded; Federal Work-Study, scholarships/grants, health care benefits, and unspecified assistantships also available. Support available to part-time students. Financial award application deadline: 2/15; financial award applicants required to submit FAFSA. *Faculty research:* Glacial surging, volcanology, geochronology, impact cratering, permafrost geophysics. *Unit head:* Dr. Benard Coakley, Co-Chair, 907-474-7565, Fax: 907-474-5163, E-mail: geology@uaf.edu. *Application contact:* Dr. Benard Coakley, Co-Chair, 907-474-7565, Fax: 907-474-5163, E-mail: geology@uaf.edu.

University of Alberta, Faculty of Graduate Studies and Research, Department of Physics, Edmonton, AB T6G 2E1, Canada. Offers astrophysics (M Sc, PhD); condensed matter (M Sc, PhD); geophysics (M Sc, PhD); medical physics (M Sc, PhD); subatomic physics (M Sc, PhD). *Faculty:* 36 full-time (3 women), 7 part-time/adjunct (0 women). *Students:* 56 full-time (6 women), 16 part-time (2 women). 85 applicants, 35% accepted. In 2009, 7 master's, 10 doctorates awarded. *Degree requirements:* For master's, thesis; for doctorate, thesis/dissertation. *Entrance requirements:* For master's and doctorate, minimum GPA of 7.0 on a 9.0 scale. Additional exam requirements/recommendations for international students: Required—TOEFL. *Application deadline:* For fall admission, 2/15 priority date for domestic students. Applications are processed on a rolling basis. Tuition and fees charges are reported in Canadian dollars. *Expenses:* Tuition, area resident: Full-time $4626.24 Canadian dollars; part-time $99.72 Canadian dollars per unit. International tuition: $8216 Canadian dollars full-time. Required fees: $3589.92 Canadian dollars; $99.72 Canadian dollars per unit. $215 Canadian dollars per term. *Financial support:* In 2009–10, 6 fellowships with partial tuition reimbursements, 40 teaching assistantships were awarded; research assistantships, career-related internships or fieldwork, institutionally sponsored loans, and scholarships/grants also available. Financial award application deadline: 2/15. *Faculty research:* Cosmology, astroparticle physics, high-intermediate energy, magnetism, superconductivity. Total annual research expenditures: $3.1 million. *Unit head:* Dr. R. Marchand, Associate Chair, 780-492-1072, E-mail: assoc-chair@

Geophysics

University of Alberta (continued)

phys.ualberta.ca. *Application contact:* Lynn Chandler, Program Advisor, 780-492-1072, Fax: 780-492-0714, E-mail: grad.program@phys.ualberta.ca.

The University of British Columbia, Faculty of Science, Department of Earth and Ocean Sciences, Vancouver, BC V6T 1Z4, Canada. Offers atmospheric science (M Sc, PhD); geological engineering (M Eng, MA Sc, PhD); geological sciences (M Sc, PhD); geophysics (M Sc, MA Sc, PhD); oceanography (M Sc, PhD). *Degree requirements:* For master's, thesis (for some programs); for doctorate, comprehensive exam, thesis/dissertation. *Entrance requirements:* Additional exam requirements/recommendations for international students: Required—TOEFL (minimum score 600 paper-based; 250 computer-based; 100 iBT). Electronic applications accepted. *Faculty research:* Oceans and atmosphere, environmental earth science, hydro geology, mineral deposits, geophysics.

University of Calgary, Faculty of Graduate Studies, Faculty of Science, Department of Geology and Geophysics, Calgary, AB T2N 1N4, Canada. Offers geology (M Sc, PhD); geophysics (M Sc, PhD). Part-time programs available. Terminal master's awarded for partial completion of doctoral program. *Degree requirements:* For master's, thesis; for doctorate, thesis/dissertation, candidacy exam. *Entrance requirements:* For master's, B Sc; for doctorate, honors B Sc or M Sc. Additional exam requirements/recommendations for international students: Required—TOEFL. Electronic applications accepted. *Faculty research:* Geochemistry, petrology, paleontology, stratigraphy, exploration and solid-earth geophysics.

University of California, Berkeley, Graduate Division, College of Letters and Science, Department of Earth and Planetary Science, Berkeley, CA 94720-1500. Offers geology (MA, MS, PhD); geophysics (MA, MS, PhD). *Students:* 64 full-time (30 women). Average age 29. 166 applicants, 17 enrolled. In 2009, 1 master's, 11 doctorates awarded. Terminal master's awarded for partial completion of doctoral program. *Degree requirements:* For master's, oral exam (MA), thesis (MS); for doctorate, comprehensive exam, thesis/dissertation, candidacy exams. *Entrance requirements:* For master's and doctorate, GRE General Test, minimum GPA of 3.0, 3 letters of recommendation. Additional exam requirements/recommendations for international students: Required—TOEFL. *Application deadline:* For fall admission, 12/28 for domestic students. Application fee: $70 ($90 for international students). *Financial support:* Fellowships, research assistantships, teaching assistantships, Federal Work-Study and unspecified assistantships available. *Faculty research:* Tectonics, environmental geology, high-pressure geophysics and seismology, economic geology, geochemistry. *Unit head:* Prof. Roland Burgmann, Chair, 510-642-3993, Fax: 510-643-9980, E-mail: ch_eps@ls.berkeley.edu. *Application contact:* Margie Winn, Student Affairs Officer, 510-642-5574, Fax: 510-643-9980, E-mail: gradadm@eps.berkeley.edu.

University of California, Los Angeles, Graduate Division, College of Letters and Science, Department of Earth and Space Sciences, Program in Geophysics and Space Physics, Los Angeles, CA 90095. Offers MS, PhD. *Students:* 35 full-time (19 women); includes 2 minority (both Asian Americans or Pacific Islanders), 15 international. Average age 27. 50 applicants, 28% accepted, 8 enrolled. In 2009, 8 master's, 6 doctorates awarded. Terminal master's awarded for partial completion of doctoral program. *Degree requirements:* For master's, comprehensive exams or thesis; for doctorate, thesis/dissertation, oral and written qualifying exams. *Entrance requirements:* For master's, GRE General Test, minimum GPA of 3.0, bachelor's degree in related field; for doctorate, GRE General Test, minimum undergraduate GPA of 3.0, bachelor's degree in related field. *Application deadline:* For fall admission, 1/15 for domestic and international students. Application fee: $70 ($90 for international students). Electronic applications accepted. *Financial support:* In 2009–10, 27 fellowships with full and partial tuition reimbursements, 30 research assistantships with full and partial tuition reimbursements, 11 teaching assistantships with full and partial tuition reimbursements were awarded; Federal Work-Study, institutionally sponsored loans, scholarships/grants, health care benefits, tuition waivers (full and partial), and unspecified assistantships also available. Financial award application deadline: 3/1; financial award applicants required to submit FAFSA. *Unit head:* Chair, 310-825-3917. *Application contact:* Departmental Office, 888-377-8252, E-mail: holbrook@ess.ucla.edu.

University of California, Santa Barbara, Graduate Division, College of Letters and Sciences, Division of Mathematics, Life, and Physical Sciences, Department of Earth Science, Santa Barbara, CA 93106-9620. Offers geological sciences (MS, PhD), including computational science and engineering (MS), geological sciences; geophysics (MS), including computational science and engineering, geophysics. *Faculty:* 20 full-time (4 women). *Students:* 35 full-time (15 women). Average age 27. 90 applicants, 27% accepted, 9 enrolled. In 2009, 3 master's, 4 doctorates awarded. *Degree requirements:* For master's, comprehensive exam, thesis; for doctorate, comprehensive exam, thesis/dissertation. *Entrance requirements:* For master's, GRE General Test, 3 letters of recommendation, resume/curriculum vitae; for doctorate, GRE General Test, 3 letters of recommendation, statement of purpose, personal achievements/contributions statement, resume/curriculum vitae, transcripts for post-secondary institutions attended. Additional exam requirements/recommendations for international students: Required—TOEFL (minimum score 550 paper-based; 213 computer-based; 80 iBT) or IELTS (minimum score 7). *Application deadline:* For fall admission, 2/1 for domestic students, 1/1 for international students. Application fee: $70 ($90 for international students). Electronic applications accepted. *Financial support:* In 2009–10, 35 students received support, including 21 fellowships with full and partial tuition reimbursements available (averaging $6,200 per year), 17 research assistantships with full and partial tuition reimbursements available (averaging $6,000 per year), 28 teaching assistantships with partial tuition reimbursements available (averaging $7,600 per year); career-related internships or fieldwork, Federal Work-Study, institutionally sponsored loans, scholarships/grants, traineeships, health care benefits, and unspecified assistantships also available. Financial award applicants required to submit FAFSA. *Faculty research:* Tectonics, geochronology, paleontology, volcanology, geomorphology. *Unit head:* Dr. Ralph Archuleta, Chair, 805-893-8441, E-mail: ralph@crustal.ucsb.edu. *Application contact:* Samuel C. Rifkin, Graduate Program Assistant, 805-893-3329, Fax: 805-893-2314, E-mail: rifkin@geol.ucsb.edu.

University of Chicago, Division of the Physical Sciences, Department of the Geophysical Sciences, Chicago, IL 60637-1513. Offers atmospheric sciences (SM, PhD); earth sciences (SM, PhD); paleobiology (PhD); planetary and space sciences (SM, PhD). *Faculty:* 21 full-time (3 women). *Students:* 37 full-time (23 women); includes 1 minority (Hispanic American), 14 international. Average age 27. 63 applicants, 35% accepted, 9 enrolled. In 2009, 1 doctorate awarded. Terminal master's awarded for partial completion of doctoral program. *Degree requirements:* For master's, thesis, seminar; for doctorate, variable foreign language requirement, comprehensive exam, thesis/dissertation. *Entrance requirements:* For doctorate, GRE General Test. Additional exam requirements/recommendations for international students: Required—TOEFL (minimum score 600 paper-based; 250 computer-based; 96 iBT), IELTS (minimum score 7). *Application deadline:* For fall admission, 1/10 for domestic and international students. Application fee: $55. Electronic applications accepted. *Financial support:* In 2009–10, research assistantships with full tuition reimbursements (averaging $20,511 per year), teaching assistantships with full tuition reimbursements (averaging $21,915 per year) were awarded; fellowships, Federal Work-Study, institutionally sponsored loans, scholarships/grants, tuition waivers (partial), and unspecified assistantships also available. Financial award application deadline: 1/15. *Faculty research:* Climatology, evolutionary paleontology, petrology, geochemistry, oceanic sciences. *Unit head:* Dr. Michael Foote, Chairman, 773-702-8102, Fax: 773-702-9505. *Application contact:* David J. Taylor, Graduate Student Services Coordinator, 773-702-8180, Fax: 773-702-9505, E-mail: info@geosci.uchicago.edu.

University of Colorado at Boulder, Graduate School, College of Arts and Sciences, Department of Geological Sciences, Boulder, CO 80309. Offers geology (MS, PhD); geophysics (PhD). *Faculty:* 28 full-time (8 women). *Students:* 60 full-time (31 women), 31 part-time (16 women); includes 7 minority (2 American Indian/Alaska Native, 2 Asian Americans or Pacific Islanders, 3 Hispanic Americans), 9 international. Average age 29. 176 applicants, 13% accepted, 23 enrolled. In 2009, 4 master's, 12 doctorates awarded. Terminal master's awarded for partial completion of doctoral program. *Degree requirements:* For master's, comprehensive exam, thesis; for doctorate, comprehensive exam, thesis/dissertation. *Entrance requirements:* For master's, GRE General Test, minimum undergraduate GPA of 3.0; for doctorate, GRE General Test, minimum GPA of 2.75. *Application deadline:* For fall admission, 12/15 priority date for domestic students, 12/1 for international students. Application fee: $50 ($60 for international students). *Financial support:* In 2009–10, 28 fellowships with full tuition reimbursements (averaging $13,580 per year), 45 research assistantships with full tuition reimbursements (averaging $15,474 per year) were awarded; Federal Work-Study, institutionally sponsored loans, scholarships/grants, and tuition waivers (full) also available. Financial award application deadline: 1/15. *Faculty research:* Sedimentology, stratigraphy, economic geology of mineral deposits, fossil fuels, hydrogeology and water resources, geophysics, isotope geology, paleobiology, mineralogy, remote sensing. Total annual research expenditures: $6 million.

University of Colorado at Boulder, Graduate School, College of Arts and Sciences, Department of Physics, Boulder, CO 80309. Offers chemical physics (PhD); geophysics (PhD); liquid crystal science and technology (PhD); mathematical physics (PhD); medical physics (PhD); optical sciences and engineering (PhD); physics (MS, PhD). *Faculty:* 48 full-time (6 women). *Students:* 160 full-time (24 women), 47 part-time (8 women); includes 9 minority (6 Asian Americans or Pacific Islanders, 3 Hispanic Americans), 65 international. Average age 27. 548 applicants, 5% accepted, 27 enrolled. In 2009, 17 master's, 23 doctorates awarded. Terminal master's awarded for partial completion of doctoral program. *Degree requirements:* For master's, comprehensive exam, thesis or alternative; for doctorate, comprehensive exam, thesis/dissertation. *Entrance requirements:* For master's and doctorate, GRE General Test, GRE Subject Test, minimum undergraduate GPA of 3.0. Additional exam requirements/recommendations for international students: Required—TOEFL. *Application deadline:* For fall admission, 1/15 priority date for domestic students, 1/15 for international students. Applications are processed on a rolling basis. Application fee: $50 ($60 for international students). Electronic applications accepted. *Financial support:* In 2009–10, 21 fellowships with full tuition reimbursements (averaging $15,999 per year), 146 research assistantships with full tuition reimbursements (averaging $16,586 per year) were awarded; scholarships/grants also available. Financial award application deadline: 1/15. *Faculty research:* Atomic and molecular physics, nuclear physics, condensed matter, elementary particle physics, laser or optical physics, plasma physics, geophysics, astrophysics and chemical physics. Total annual research expenditures: $14.2 million.

University of Hawaii at Manoa, Graduate Division, School of Ocean and Earth Science and Technology, Department of Geology and Geophysics, Honolulu, HI 96822. Offers high-pressure geophysics and geochemistry (MS, PhD); hydrogeology and engineering geology (MS, PhD); marine geology and geophysics (MS, PhD); planetary geosciences and remote sensing (MS, PhD); seismology and solid-earth geophysics (MS, PhD); volcanology, petrology, and geochemistry (MS, PhD). Part-time programs available. *Faculty:* 73 full-time (16 women), 15 part-time/adjunct (3 women). *Students:* 42 full-time (20 women), 8 part-time (5 women); includes 7 minority (1 African American, 4 Asian Americans or Pacific Islanders, 2 Hispanic Americans), 6 international. Average age 29. 56 applicants, 25% accepted, 6 enrolled. In 2009, 4 master's, 7 doctorates awarded. Terminal master's awarded for partial completion of doctoral program. *Degree requirements:* For master's, thesis optional; for doctorate, comprehensive exam, thesis/dissertation. *Entrance requirements:* For master's and doctorate, GRE General Test, minimum GPA of 3.0. Additional exam requirements/recommendations for international students: Required—TOEFL (minimum score 580 paper-based; 237 computer-based; 92 iBT), IELTS (minimum score 5). *Application deadline:* For fall admission, 1/15 for domestic students, 1/1 for international students; for spring admission, 9/1 for domestic students, 8/15 for international students. Application fee: $60. *Expenses:* Tuition, state resident: full-time $8900; part-time $372 per credit. Tuition, nonresident: full-time $21,400; part-time $898 per credit. Required fees: $207 per semester. *Financial support:* In 2009–10, 1 student received support, including 4 fellowships (averaging $9,338 per year), 31 research assistantships (averaging $23,877 per year), 5 teaching assistantships (averaging $20,466 per year). Total annual research expenditures: $3.8 million. *Application contact:* Dr. Charles Fletcher, Chair, 808-956-7640, Fax: 808-956-5512, E-mail: gg-grad-chair@hawaii.edu.

University of Houston, College of Natural Sciences and Mathematics, Department of Earth and Atmospheric Sciences, Houston, TX 77204. Offers MA, MS, PhD. Part-time and evening/weekend programs available. *Faculty:* 23 full-time (5 women), 4 part-time/adjunct (0 women). *Students:* 118 full-time (42 women), 69 part-time (15 women); includes 26 minority (8 African Americans, 7 Asian Americans or Pacific Islanders, 11 Hispanic Americans), 72 international. Average age 31. 110 applicants, 77% accepted, 42 enrolled. In 2009, 25 master's, 11 doctorates awarded. *Degree requirements:* For master's, comprehensive exam; for doctorate, comprehensive exam, thesis/dissertation. *Entrance requirements:* For master's, GRE, letter of recommendation; for doctorate, GRE, Transcript, letter of recommendations. Additional exam requirements/recommendations for international students: Required—TOEFL (minimum score 550 paper-based; 213 computer-based; 79 iBT), IELTS (minimum score 6). *Application deadline:* For fall admission, 7/1 for domestic students, 4/1 for international students; for spring admission, 12/1 for domestic students, 10/1 for international students. Applications are processed on a rolling basis. Application fee: $0 ($75 for international students). Electronic applications accepted. *Expenses:* Tuition, state resident: full-time $7676; part-time $320 per credit hour. Tuition, nonresident: full-time $14,324; part-time $597 per credit hour. Required fees: $3034. *Financial support:* In 2009–10, 34 research assistantships with full tuition reimbursements (averaging $17,200 per year), 26 teaching assistantships with full tuition reimbursements (averaging $17,200 per year) were awarded; career-related internships or fieldwork, Federal Work-Study, institutionally sponsored loans, scholarships/grants, health care benefits, and unspecified assistantships also available. Support available to part-time students. Financial award application deadline: 2/1. *Faculty research:* Atmospherics sciences, seismic and solid earth geophysics, tectonics, environmental hydrochemistry, carbonates, micropaleontology, structure and tectonics, petroleum geology. *Unit head:* Dr. John Casey, Chairman, 713-743-3399, Fax: 713-748-7906, E-mail: jfcasey@uh.edu. *Application contact:* Sylvia Marshall, Advising Assistant, 713-743-3401, Fax: 713-748-7906, E-mail: smarshall@uh.edu.

University of Manitoba, Faculty of Graduate Studies, Clayton H. Riddell Faculty of Environment, Earth, and Resources, Department of Geological Sciences, Winnipeg, MB R3T 2N2, Canada. Offers geology (M Sc, PhD); geophysics (M Sc, PhD). *Degree requirements:* For master's, thesis; for doctorate, thesis/dissertation. *Entrance requirements:* For master's and doctorate, GRE General Test, GRE Subject Test (geology), minimum GPA of 3.0. Additional exam requirements/recommendations for international students: Required—TOEFL.

University of Miami, Graduate School, Rosenstiel School of Marine and Atmospheric Science, Division of Marine Geology and Geophysics, Coral Gables, FL 33124. Offers MS, PhD. Terminal master's awarded for partial completion of doctoral program. *Degree requirements:* For master's, comprehensive exam, thesis; for doctorate, comprehensive exam, thesis/dissertation. *Entrance requirements:* For master's and doctorate, GRE General Test. Additional exam requirements/recommendations for international students: Required—TOEFL (minimum score 550 paper-based; 213 computer-based). Electronic applications accepted. *Faculty research:* Carbonate sedimentology, low-temperature geochemistry, paleoceanography, geodesy and tectonics.

University of Minnesota, Twin Cities Campus, Institute of Technology, Department of Geology and Geophysics, Minneapolis, MN 55455-0213. Offers geology (MS, PhD); geophysics (MS,

PhD). Terminal master's awarded for partial completion of doctoral program. *Degree requirements:* For master's, thesis; for doctorate, thesis/dissertation. *Entrance requirements:* For master's and doctorate, GRE General Test, 3 letters of recommendation. Additional exam requirements/recommendations for international students: Required—TOEFL (minimum score 550 paper-based; 213 computer-based). Electronic applications accepted. *Faculty research:* Geochemistry, paleoclimate studies, structure/tectonics, geofluids.

University of Nevada, Reno, Graduate School, College of Science, Mackay School of Earth Sciences and Engineering, Department of Geological Sciences, Program in Geophysics, Reno, NV 89557. Offers MS, PhD. Terminal master's awarded for partial completion of doctoral program. *Degree requirements:* For master's, thesis optional; for doctorate, thesis/dissertation. *Entrance requirements:* For master's, GRE General Test, minimum GPA of 2.75; for doctorate, GRE General Test, minimum GPA of 3.0. Additional exam requirements/recommendations for international students: Required—TOEFL (minimum score 500 paper-based; 173 computer-based; 61 iBT), IELTS (minimum score 6). Electronic applications accepted. *Faculty research:* Geophysics exploration, seismology, remote sensing.

University of Oklahoma, Graduate College, College of Earth and Energy, Conoco Phillips School of Geology and Geophysics, Program in Geophysics, Norman, OK 73019. Offers MS. Part-time programs available. *Students:* 29 full-time (8 women), 2 part-time (0 women); includes 3 minority (1 American Indian/Alaska Native, 1 Asian American or Pacific Islander, 1 Hispanic American), 18 international. 17 applicants, 65% accepted, 9 enrolled. In 2009, 3 master's awarded. *Degree requirements:* For master's, comprehensive exam, thesis. *Entrance requirements:* For master's, GRE General Test. Additional exam requirements/recommendations for international students: Required—TOEFL (minimum score 550 paper-based; 213 computer-based). *Application deadline:* For fall admission, 2/1 priority date for domestic students, 4/1 for international students; for spring admission, 9/1 for domestic and international students. Applications are processed on a rolling basis. Application fee: $40 ($90 for international students). Electronic applications accepted. *Expenses:* Tuition, state resident: full-time $3744; part-time $156 per credit hour. Tuition, nonresident: full-time $13,577; part-time $565.70 per credit hour. Required fees: $2415; $90.10 per credit hour. *Financial support:* In 2009–10, 23 students received support. Career-related internships or fieldwork, scholarships/grants, health care benefits, and unspecified assistantships available. Financial award application deadline: 2/1; financial award applicants required to submit FAFSA. *Faculty research:* Basin studies, lithospheric structure and evolution, paleomagnetism, exploration geophysics, solid-earth. *Unit head:* Doug Elmore, Associate Provost/Director, 405-325-3253, Fax: 405-325-3140, E-mail: delmore@ou.edu. *Application contact:* Donna S. Mullins, Coordinator of Administrative Student Services and Corporate Recruiting, 405-325-3255, Fax: 405-325-3140, E-mail: dsmullins@ou.edu.

The University of Texas at Dallas, School of Natural Sciences and Mathematics, Program in Geosciences, Richardson, TX 75080. Offers geochemistry (MS, PhD); geophysics (MS); geospatial information sciences (MS, PhD); hydrogeology (MS, PhD); sedimentary, stratigraphy, paleontology (PhD); stratigraphy, paleontology (MS); structural geology and tectonics (MS, PhD). Part-time and evening/weekend programs available. *Faculty:* 9 full-time (1 woman). *Students:* 30 full-time (10 women), 11 part-time (4 women); includes 7 minority (1 African American, 4 Asian Americans or Pacific Islanders, 2 Hispanic Americans), 21 international. Average age 32. 42 applicants, 43% accepted, 14 enrolled. In 2009, 4 master's, 4 doctorates awarded. *Degree requirements:* For master's, thesis optional; for doctorate, thesis/dissertation. *Entrance requirements:* For master's and doctorate, GRE General Test, minimum GPA of 3.0 in upper-level course work in field. Additional exam requirements/recommendations for international students: Required—TOEFL (minimum score 550 paper-based; 213 computer-based). *Application deadline:* For fall admission, 7/15 for domestic students, 5/1 priority date for international students; for spring admission, 11/15 for domestic students, 9/1 priority date for international students. Applications are processed on a rolling basis. Application fee: $50 ($100 for international students). Electronic applications accepted. *Expenses:* Tuition, state resident: full-time $11,068; part-time $461 per credit hour. Tuition, nonresident: full-time $21,178; part-time $882 per credit hour. Tuition and fees vary according to course load. *Financial support:* In 2009–10, 10 research assistantships with full tuition reimbursements (averaging $13,500 per year), 11 teaching assistantships with full tuition reimbursements (averaging $13,500 per year) were awarded; fellowships, career-related internships or fieldwork, Federal Work-Study, institutionally sponsored loans, scholarships/grants, and unspecified assistantships also available. Support available to part-time students. Financial award application deadline: 4/30; financial award applicants required to submit FAFSA. *Faculty research:* Hydrology, organic geochemistry, tectonic structures, seismic characteristics, digital geologic mapping. *Unit head:* Dr. John Oldow, Department Head, 972-883-2401, Fax: 972-883-2537, E-mail: geosciences@utdallas.edu. *Application contact:* Dr. Robert J. Stem, Graduate Advisor, 972-883-2442, Fax: 972-883-2537, E-mail: rjstern@utdallas.edu.

The University of Texas at El Paso, Graduate School, College of Science, Department of Geological Sciences, Program in Geophysics, El Paso, TX 79968-0001. Offers MS. Part-time and evening/weekend programs available. *Students:* 8 (2 women); includes 5 minority (1 African American, 4 Hispanic Americans), 1 international. Average age 34. In 2009, 3 master's awarded. *Degree requirements:* For master's, thesis. *Entrance requirements:* For master's, minimum GPA of 3.0, letters of recommendation. Additional exam requirements/recommendations for international students: Required—TOEFL; Recommended—IELTS. *Application deadline:* For fall admission, 8/1 priority date for domestic students, 3/1 for international students; for spring admission, 11/1 priority date for domestic students, 9/1 for international students. Applications are processed on a rolling basis. Application fee: $45 ($80 for international students). Electronic applications accepted. *Financial support:* In 2009–10, research assistantships with partial tuition reimbursements (averaging $21,812 per year), teaching assistantships with partial tuition reimbursements (averaging $17,450 per year) were awarded; fellowships with partial tuition reimbursements, institutionally sponsored loans, scholarships/grants, health care benefits, tuition waivers (partial), and unspecified assistantships also available. Support available to part-time students. Financial award application deadline: 3/15; financial award applicants required to submit FAFSA. *Unit head:* Dr. Diane Doser, Coordinator, 915-747-5501, Fax: 915-747-5073, E-mail: doser@utep.edu. *Application contact:* Dr. Patricia D. Witherspoon, Dean of the Graduate School, 915-747-5491, Fax: 915-747-5788, E-mail: withersp@utep.edu.

University of Utah, The Graduate School, College of Mines and Earth Sciences, Department of Geology and Geophysics, Salt Lake City, UT 84112. Offers environmental engineering (ME, MS, PhD); geological engineering (ME, MS, PhD); geology (MS, PhD); geophysics (MS, PhD). *Faculty:* 20 full-time (3 women), 5 part-time/adjunct (1 woman). *Students:* 40 full-time (16 women), 27 part-time (9 women); includes 1 minority (Hispanic American), 17 international. Average age 32. 109 applicants, 23% accepted, 17 enrolled. In 2009, 18 master's, 5 doctorates awarded. Terminal master's awarded for partial completion of doctoral program. *Degree requirements:* For master's, comprehensive exam, thesis; for doctorate, thesis/dissertation, qualifying exam (written and oral). *Entrance requirements:* For master's and doctorate, GRE General Test, minimum GPA of 3.25. Additional exam requirements/recommendations for international students: Required—TOEFL (minimum score 500 paper-based; 173 computer-based). *Application deadline:* For fall admission, 1/15 priority date for domestic and international students. Applications are processed on a rolling basis. Application fee: $55 ($65 for international students). Electronic applications accepted. *Expenses:* Tuition, state resident: full-time $4004; part-time $1674 per semester. Tuition, nonresident: full-time $14,134; part-time $5915 per semester. Required fees: $324 per semester. Tuition and fees vary according to course load, degree level and program. *Financial support:* In 2009–10, 22 students received support, including 11 fellowships with full tuition reimbursements available (averaging $13,450 per year), 45 research assistantships with full tuition reimbursements available (averaging $21,858 per year), 11 teaching assistantships with full tuition reimbursements available (averaging $13,450 per year); career-related internships or fieldwork, institutionally sponsored loans, scholarships/grants, unspecified assistantships, and stipends also available. Financial award application deadline: 1/15; financial award applicants required to submit FAFSA. *Faculty research:* Igneous, metamorphic, and sedimentary petrology; ore deposits; aqueous geochemistry; isotope geochemistry; heat flow. Total annual research expenditures: $2.2 million. *Unit head:* Dr. Marjorie A. Chan, Chair, 801-581-7162, Fax: 801-581-7065, E-mail: marjorie.chan@utah.edu. *Application contact:* Dr. Allan A. Ekdale, Director of Graduate Studies, 801-581-7266, Fax: 801-581-7065, E-mail: a.ekdale@utah.edu.

University of Victoria, Faculty of Graduate Studies, Faculty of Science, Department of Physics and Astronomy, Victoria, BC V8W 2Y2, Canada. Offers astronomy and astrophysics (M Sc, PhD); condensed matter physics (M Sc, PhD); experimental particle physics (M Sc, PhD); medical physics (M Sc, PhD); ocean physics (M Sc, PhD); theoretical physics (M Sc, PhD). *Degree requirements:* For master's, thesis; for doctorate, comprehensive exam, thesis/dissertation, candidacy exam. *Entrance requirements:* For master's and doctorate, GRE. Additional exam requirements/recommendations for international students: Required—TOEFL (minimum score 575 paper-based; 233 computer-based), IELTS (minimum score 7). Electronic applications accepted. *Faculty research:* Old stellar populations; observational cosmology and large scale structure; cp violation; atlas.

University of Washington, Graduate School, College of Arts and Sciences, Department of Earth and Space Sciences, Seattle, WA 98195. Offers geology (MS, PhD); geophysics (MS, PhD). *Degree requirements:* For master's, thesis or alternative, departmental qualifying exam, final exam; for doctorate, thesis/dissertation, departmental qualifying exam, general and final exams. *Entrance requirements:* For master's and doctorate, GRE General Test, minimum GPA of 3.0. Additional exam requirements/recommendations for international students: Required—TOEFL (minimum score 580 paper-based). Electronic applications accepted.

The University of Western Ontario, Faculty of Graduate Studies, Physical Sciences Division, Department of Earth Sciences, London, ON N6A 5B8, Canada. Offers environment and sustainability (MES); geology (M Sc, PhD); geology and environmental science (M Sc, PhD); geophysics (M Sc, PhD); geophysics and environmental science (M Sc, PhD). *Degree requirements:* For master's, thesis; for doctorate, thesis/dissertation, qualifying exam. *Entrance requirements:* For master's, honors in B Sc; for doctorate, M Sc. Additional exam requirements/recommendations for international students: Required—TOEFL. *Faculty research:* Geophysics, geochemistry, paleontology, sedimentology/stratigraphy, glaciology/quaternary.

University of Wisconsin–Madison, Graduate School, College of Letters and Science, Department of Geology and Geophysics, Program in Geophysics, Madison, WI 53706-1380. Offers MS, PhD. *Degree requirements:* For master's, thesis; for doctorate, one foreign language, thesis/dissertation. *Entrance requirements:* For master's and doctorate, GRE General Test. *Expenses:* Tuition, state resident: part-time $594 per credit. Tuition, nonresident: part-time $1504 per credit. Required fees: $65 per credit. Tuition and fees vary according to course load, program and reciprocity agreements.

University of Wyoming, College of Arts and Sciences, Department of Geology and Geophysics, Laramie, WY 82070. Offers geology (MS, PhD); geophysics (MS, PhD). Part-time programs available. *Degree requirements:* For master's, comprehensive exam, thesis; for doctorate, comprehensive exam, thesis/dissertation. *Entrance requirements:* For master's and doctorate, GRE General Test, minimum GPA of 3.0. *Faculty research:* Low-temp geochemistry, geohydrology, paleontology, structure/tectonics, sedimentation and petroleum geology, petrology, geophysics/seismology.

Virginia Polytechnic Institute and State University, Graduate School, College of Science, Department of Geosciences, Blacksburg, VA 24061. Offers geological sciences (MS, PhD); geophysics (MS, PhD). *Entrance requirements:* For master's and doctorate, GRE General Test. Additional exam requirements/recommendations for international students: Required—TOEFL (minimum score 550 paper-based; 213 computer-based). Electronic applications accepted. *Faculty research:* Paleontology/geobiology, active tectonics, geomorphology, mineralogy/crystallography, mineral physics.

West Virginia University, Eberly College of Arts and Sciences, Department of Geology and Geography, Program in Geology, Morgantown, WV 26506. Offers geomorphology (MS, PhD); geophysics (MS, PhD); hydrogeology (MS, PhD); paleontology (MS, PhD); petroleum geology (PhD); petrology (MS, PhD); stratigraphy (MS, PhD); structure (MS, PhD). Part-time programs available. Terminal master's awarded for partial completion of doctoral program. *Degree requirements:* For master's, thesis (for some programs); for doctorate, comprehensive exam, thesis/dissertation. *Entrance requirements:* For master's, GRE General Test, minimum GPA of 2.5; for doctorate, GRE General Test, minimum GPA of 3.3. Additional exam requirements/recommendations for international students: Required—TOEFL.

Woods Hole Oceanographic Institution, MIT/WHOI Joint Program in Oceanography/Applied Ocean Science and Engineering, Woods Hole, MA 02543-1541. Offers applied ocean sciences (PhD); biological oceanography (PhD, Sc D); chemical oceanography (PhD, Sc D); civil and environmental and oceanographic engineering (PhD); electrical and oceanographic engineering (PhD); geochemistry (PhD); geophysics (PhD); marine biology (PhD); marine geochemistry (PhD, Sc D); marine geology (PhD, Sc D); marine geophysics (PhD); mechanical and oceanographic engineering (PhD); ocean engineering (PhD); oceanographic engineering (M Eng, MS, PhD, Sc D, Eng); paleoceanography (PhD); physical oceanography (PhD, Sc D). Terminal master's awarded for partial completion of doctoral program. *Degree requirements:* For master's and Eng, thesis (for some programs); for doctorate, thesis/dissertation. *Entrance requirements:* For master's, GRE General Test; for doctorate, GRE General Test, GRE Subject Test. Additional exam requirements/recommendations for international students: Required—TOEFL. Electronic applications accepted.

Wright State University, School of Graduate Studies, College of Science and Mathematics, Department of Physics, Program in Physics, Dayton, OH 45435. Offers geophysics (MS); medical physics (MS). Part-time and evening/weekend programs available. *Degree requirements:* For master's, thesis. *Entrance requirements:* Additional exam requirements/recommendations for international students: Required—TOEFL. *Faculty research:* Solid-state physics, optics, geophysics.

Yale University, Graduate School of Arts and Sciences, Department of Geology and Geophysics, New Haven, CT 06520. Offers biogeochemistry (PhD); climate dynamics (PhD); geochemistry (PhD); geophysics (PhD); meteorology (PhD); oceanography (PhD); paleontology (PhD); paleooceanography (PhD); petrology (PhD); tectonics (PhD). *Degree requirements:* For doctorate, thesis/dissertation. *Entrance requirements:* For doctorate, GRE General Test. Additional exam requirements/recommendations for international students: Required—TOEFL.

Geosciences

Arizona State University, Graduate College, College of Liberal Arts and Sciences, Division of Natural Sciences, School of Earth and Space Exploration, Tempe, AZ 85287. Offers astrophysics (MS, PhD); geological sciences (MS, PhD). *Degree requirements:* For master's, thesis or alternative; for doctorate, thesis/dissertation. *Entrance requirements:* For master's and doctorate, GRE.

Ball State University, Graduate School, College of Sciences and Humanities, Department of Geography, Muncie, IN 47306-1099. Offers earth sciences (MA). *Faculty research:* Remote sensing, tourism and recreation, Latin American urbanization.

Baylor University, Graduate School, College of Arts and Sciences, Department of Geology, Waco, TX 76798. Offers earth science (MA); geology (MS, PhD). *Faculty:* 12 full-time (1 woman). *Students:* 16 full-time (7 women), 9 part-time (3 women); includes 1 minority (American Indian/Alaska Native), 4 international. In 2009, 6 master's, 1 doctorate awarded. *Degree requirements:* For master's, thesis; for doctorate, thesis/dissertation. *Entrance requirements:* For master's and doctorate, GRE General Test. *Application deadline:* For fall admission, 3/15 priority date for domestic students. Applications are processed on a rolling basis. Application fee: $25. *Financial support:* In 2009–10, 18 teaching assistantships were awarded; Federal Work-Study and institutionally sponsored loans also available. *Faculty research:* Petroleum geology, geophysics, engineering geology, hydrogeology. *Unit head:* Dr. Steve Dworkin, Graduate Program Director, 254-710-2186, Fax: 254-710-2673, E-mail: steve_dworkin@baylor.edu. *Application contact:* Paulette Penney, Administrative Assistant, 254-710-2361, Fax: 254-710-3870, E-mail: paulette_penney@baylor.edu.

Baylor University, Graduate School, College of Arts and Sciences, The Institute of Ecological, Earth and Environmental Sciences, Waco, TX 76798. Offers PhD. *Students:* 5 full-time (2 women), 3 international. *Unit head:* Dr. Joseph D. White, Director, 254-710-2911, E-mail: joseph_d_white@baylor.edu. *Application contact:* Suzanne Keener, Administrative Assistant, 254-710-3588, Fax: 254-710-3870.

Boise State University, Graduate College, College of Arts and Sciences, Department of Geosciences, Program in Earth Science, Boise, ID 83725-0399. Offers MS. Part-time programs available. *Degree requirements:* For master's, thesis. *Entrance requirements:* For master's, GRE General Test, minimum GPA of 3.0, BS in related field. Electronic applications accepted. *Expenses:* Tuition, state resident: full-time $3106; part-time $209 per credit. Tuition, nonresident: part-time $284 per credit.

Boston University, Graduate School of Arts and Sciences, Department of Earth Sciences, Boston, MA 02215. Offers MA, PhD. *Students:* 17 full-time (7 women), 3 international. Average age 28. 58 applicants, 31% accepted, 6 enrolled. In 2009, 3 master's, 6 doctorates awarded. Terminal master's awarded for partial completion of doctoral program. *Degree requirements:* For master's, one foreign language, comprehensive exam, thesis; for doctorate, one foreign language, comprehensive exam, thesis/dissertation. *Entrance requirements:* For master's and doctorate, GRE General Test, 3 letters of recommendation. Additional exam requirements/recommendations for international students: Required—TOEFL (minimum score 550 paper-based; 213 computer-based). *Application deadline:* For fall admission, 1/15 for domestic and international students; for spring admission, 10/15 for domestic and international students. Application fee: $70. Electronic applications accepted. *Expenses:* Tuition: Full-time $37,910; part-time $1184 per credit hour. Required fees: $386; $40 per semester. Part-time tuition and fees vary according to class time, course level, degree level and program. *Financial support:* In 2009–10, 1 fellowship with full tuition reimbursement (averaging $18,900 per year), 8 research assistantships with tuition reimbursements (averaging $18,400 per year), 8 teaching assistantships with full tuition reimbursements (averaging $18,400 per year) were awarded; Federal Work-Study and unspecified assistantships also available. Support available to part-time students. Financial award application deadline: 1/15; financial award applicants required to submit FAFSA. *Unit head:* Dr. Guido Salvucci, Chairman, 617-353-4213, Fax: 617-353-3290, E-mail: gdsalvuc@bu.edu. *Application contact:* Eric Jones, Department Administrator, 617-353-2529, Fax: 617-353-3290, E-mail: epjones@bu.edu.

Brock University, Faculty of Graduate Studies, Faculty of Mathematics and Science, Program in Earth Sciences, St. Catharines, ON L2S 3A1, Canada. Offers M Sc. Part-time programs available. *Degree requirements:* For master's, thesis. *Entrance requirements:* For master's, honors B Sc in earth sciences. Additional exam requirements/recommendations for international students: Required—TOEFL (minimum score 550 paper-based; 213 computer-based; 80 iBT), IELTS (minimum score 6.5), TWE (minimum score 4). Electronic applications accepted. *Faculty research:* Clastic sedimentology, environmental geology, geochemistry, micropaleontology, structural geology.

Brooklyn College of the City University of New York, Division of Graduate Studies, School of Education, Program in Middle Childhood Education (Science), Brooklyn, NY 11210-2889. Offers biology (MA); chemistry (MA); earth science (MA); general science (MA); physics (MA). Part-time and evening/weekend programs available. *Entrance requirements:* For master's, LAST, interview, previous course work in education and mathematics, resume, 2 letters of recommendation. Additional exam requirements/recommendations for international students: Required—TOEFL (minimum score 500 paper-based; 173 computer-based; 61 iBT). Electronic applications accepted. *Faculty research:* Geometric thinking, mastery of basic facts, problem-solving strategies, history of mathematics.

Brown University, Graduate School, Department of Geological Sciences, Providence, RI 02912. Offers MA, Sc M, PhD. *Degree requirements:* For doctorate, thesis/dissertation, 1 semester of teaching experience, preliminary exam. *Faculty research:* Geochemistry, mineral kinetics, igneous and metamorphic petrology, tectonophysics including geophysics and structural geology, paleoclimatology, paleoceanography, sedimentation, planetary geology.

California State University, Chico, Graduate School, College of Natural Sciences, Department of Geological and Environmental Sciences, Program in Geosciences, Chico, CA 95929-0722. Offers hydrology/hydrogeology (MS). Part-time programs available. *Students:* 9 full-time (2 women), 4 part-time (2 women). Average age 34. 8 applicants, 100% accepted, 4 enrolled. In 2009, 2 master's awarded. *Degree requirements:* For master's, thesis, oral exam. *Entrance requirements:* For master's, GRE General Test. Additional exam requirements/recommendations for international students: Required—TOEFL (minimum score 550 paper-based; 213 computer-based; 80 iBT), IELTS (minimum score 6.5). *Application deadline:* For fall admission, 3/1 priority date for domestic students, 3/1 for international students; for spring admission, 9/15 priority date for domestic students, 9/15 for international students. Applications are processed on a rolling basis. Application fee: $55. Electronic applications accepted. *Financial support:* Fellowships available. *Unit head:* Dr. William Murphy, Graduate Coordinator, 530-898-5163. *Application contact:* Dr. William Murphy, Graduate Coordinator, 530-898-5163.

Carleton University, Faculty of Graduate Studies, Faculty of Science, Department of Earth Sciences, Ottawa, ON K1S 5B6, Canada. Offers M Sc, PhD. *Degree requirements:* For master's, thesis, seminar; for doctorate, comprehensive exam, thesis/dissertation, seminar. *Entrance requirements:* For master's, honors degree in science; for doctorate, M Sc. Additional exam requirements/recommendations for international students: Required—TOEFL. *Faculty research:* Resource geology, geophysics, basin analysis, lithosphere dynamics.

Case Western Reserve University, School of Graduate Studies, Department of Geological Sciences, Cleveland, OH 44106. Offers MS, PhD. Part-time programs available. *Faculty:* 7 full-time (1 woman), 7 part-time/adjunct (1 woman). *Students:* 7 full-time (3 women), 4 international. Average age 29. 7 applicants, 43% accepted, 2 enrolled. In 2009, 1 master's awarded. Terminal master's awarded for partial completion of doctoral program. *Degree requirements:* For master's, thesis or alternative; for doctorate, thesis/dissertation. *Entrance requirements:* For master's and doctorate, GRE General Test, GRE Subject Test. Additional exam requirements/recommendations for international students: Required—TOEFL (minimum score 550 paper-based; 213 computer-based; 79 iBT). *Application deadline:* For fall admission, 2/1 priority date for domestic students; for spring admission, 11/15 for domestic students. Applications are processed on a rolling basis. Application fee: $50. Electronic applications accepted. *Financial support:* Research assistantships, teaching assistantships, Federal Work-Study and tuition waivers (partial) available. Support available to part-time students. Financial award application deadline: 2/1; financial award applicants required to submit FAFSA. *Faculty research:* Geochemistry, hydrology, geochronology, paleoclimates, geomorphology. *Unit head:* Gerald Matisoff, Chairman, 216-368-3677, Fax: 216-368-3691, E-mail: gerald.matisoff@case.edu. *Application contact:* James Van Orman, Chair, Graduate Admission Committee, 216-368-3690, Fax: 216-368-3691, E-mail: james.vanorman@case.edu.

Central Connecticut State University, School of Graduate Studies, School of Arts and Sciences, Department of Physics and Earth Science, New Britain, CT 06050-4010. Offers natural sciences (MS); science education (Certificate). Part-time and evening/weekend programs available. *Faculty:* 12 full-time (4 women), 15 part-time/adjunct (4 women). *Students:* 22 part-time (11 women); includes 2 minority (1 African American, 1 Asian American or Pacific Islander). Average age 37. 14 applicants, 79% accepted, 7 enrolled. In 2009, 10 master's, 1 other advanced degree awarded. *Degree requirements:* For master's, comprehensive exam, thesis or alternative; for Certificate, qualifying exam. *Entrance requirements:* For master's, minimum undergraduate GPA of 2.7. Additional exam requirements/recommendations for international students: Required—TOEFL. *Application deadline:* For fall admission, 7/1 for domestic students; for spring admission, 12/1 for domestic students. Applications are processed on a rolling basis. Application fee: $50. Electronic applications accepted. *Expenses:* Tuition, area resident: Full-time $4662; part-time $440 per credit. Tuition, state resident: full-time $6994; part-time $440 per credit. Tuition, nonresident: full-time $12,988; part-time $440 per credit. Required fees: $3606. One-time fee: $62 part-time. *Financial support:* In 2009–10, 1 student received support. Career-related internships or fieldwork, Federal Work-Study, scholarships/grants, and unspecified assistantships available. Support available to part-time students. Financial award application deadline: 3/1; financial award applicants required to submit FAFSA. *Faculty research:* Elementary/secondary science education, particle and solid states, weather patterns, planetary studies. *Unit head:* Dr. Ali Antar, Chair, 860-832-2930. *Application contact:* Dr. Ali Antar, Chair, 860-832-2930.

City College of the City University of New York, Graduate School, College of Liberal Arts and Science, Division of Science, Department of Earth and Atmospheric Sciences, New York, NY 10031-9198. Offers earth and environmental science (PhD); earth systems science (MA). *Degree requirements:* For master's, comprehensive exam, thesis. *Entrance requirements:* Additional exam requirements/recommendations for international students: Required—TOEFL (minimum score 500 paper-based; 61 iBT). Electronic applications accepted. *Faculty research:* Water resources, high-temperature geochemistry, sedimentary basin analysis, tectonics.

Colorado State University, Graduate School, Warner College of Natural Resources, Department of Geosciences, Fort Collins, CO 80523-1482. Offers earth sciences (PhD); geosciences (MS). Part-time programs available. *Faculty:* 10 full-time (3 women). *Students:* 21 full-time (7 women), 27 part-time (11 women); includes 2 minority (both Hispanic Americans), 2 international. Average age 31. 44 applicants, 45% accepted, 8 enrolled. In 2009, 8 master's, 2 doctorates awarded. *Degree requirements:* For master's, thesis; for doctorate, comprehensive exam, thesis/dissertation. *Entrance requirements:* For master's and doctorate, GRE General Test, minimum GPA of 3.0, letters of recommendation. Additional exam requirements/recommendations for international students: Required—TOEFL (minimum score 550 paper-based; 213 computer-based; 80 iBT); Recommended—IELTS (minimum score 6). *Application deadline:* For fall admission, 2/15 priority date for domestic and international students; for spring admission, 7/15 priority date for domestic and international students. Applications are processed on a rolling basis. Application fee: $50. Electronic applications accepted. *Expenses:* Tuition, state resident: full-time $6434; part-time $359.10 per credit. Tuition, nonresident: full-time $18,116; part-time $1006.45 per credit. Required fees: $1496; $83 per credit. *Financial support:* In 2009–10, 20 students received support, including 1 fellowship (averaging $44,500 per year), 16 research assistantships with partial tuition reimbursements available (averaging $11,078 per year), 3 teaching assistantships with full tuition reimbursements available (averaging $9,807 per year); scholarships/grants also available. Financial award application deadline: 2/15; financial award applicants required to submit FAFSA. *Faculty research:* Snow, surface, and groundwater hydrology; fluvial geomorphology; geographic information systems; geochemistry; chemical weathering. Total annual research expenditures: $1.5 million. *Unit head:* Dr. Sally J. Sutton, Head, 970-491-5995, Fax: 970-491-6307, E-mail: sally.sutton@colostate.edu. *Application contact:* Sharyl Pierson, Administrative Assistant, 970-491-5661, Fax: 970-491-6307, E-mail: sharyl@cnr.colostate.edu.

Columbia University, Graduate School of Arts and Sciences, Division of Natural Sciences, Department of Earth and Environmental Sciences, New York, NY 10027. Offers geochemistry (M Phil, MA, PhD); geodetic sciences (M Phil, MA, PhD); geophysics (M Phil, MA, PhD); oceanography (M Phil, MA, PhD). *Degree requirements:* For master's, thesis or alternative, fieldwork, written exam; for doctorate, one foreign language, thesis/dissertation. *Entrance requirements:* For master's and doctorate, GRE General Test, GRE Subject Test, major in natural or physical science. Additional exam requirements/recommendations for international students: Required—TOEFL. *Faculty research:* Structural geology and stratigraphy, petrology, paleontology, rare gas, isotope and aqueous geochemistry.

Cornell University, Graduate School, Graduate Fields of Engineering, Field of Geological Sciences, Ithaca, NY 14853-0001. Offers economic geology (M Eng, MS, PhD); engineering geology (M Eng, MS, PhD); environmental geophysics (M Eng, MS, PhD); general geology (M Eng, MS, PhD); geobiology (M Eng, MS, PhD); geochemistry and isotope geology (M Eng, MS, PhD); geohydrology (M Eng, MS, PhD); geomorphology (M Eng, MS, PhD); geophysics (M Eng, MS, PhD); geotectonics (M Eng, MS, PhD); marine geology (MS, PhD); mineralogy (M Eng, MS, PhD); paleontology (M Eng, MS, PhD); petroleum geology (M Eng, MS, PhD); petrology (M Eng, MS, PhD); planetary geology (M Eng, MS, PhD); Precambrian geology (M Eng, MS, PhD); Quaternary geology (M Eng, MS, PhD); rock mechanics (M Eng, MS, PhD); sedimentology (M Eng, MS, PhD); seismology (M Eng, MS, PhD); stratigraphy (M Eng, MS, PhD); structural geology (M Eng, MS, PhD). *Faculty:* 38 full-time (6 women). *Students:* 32 full-time (14 women); includes 2 minority (1 African American, 1 Asian American or Pacific Islander), 9 international. Average age 29. 61 applicants, 23% accepted, 8 enrolled. In 2009, 3 doctorates awarded. *Degree requirements:* For master's, thesis (MS); for doctorate, comprehensive exam, thesis/dissertation. *Entrance requirements:* For master's and doctorate, GRE General Test, 3 letters of recommendation. Additional exam requirements/recommendations for international students: Required—TOEFL (minimum score 550 paper-based; 213 computer-based; 77 iBT). *Application deadline:* For fall admission, 1/15 priority date for domestic students. Applications are processed on a rolling basis. Application fee: $70. Electronic applications accepted. *Expenses:* Tuition: Full-time $29,500. Required fees: $70. Full-time tuition and fees vary according to degree level, program and student level. *Financial support:* In 2009–10, 25 students received support, including 2 fellowships with full tuition reimbursements available, 3 research assistantships with full tuition reimbursements available, 1 teaching assistantship with full tuition reimbursement available; institutionally sponsored loans, scholarships/grants, health care benefits, tuition waivers (full and partial), and unspecified assistantships also available. Financial award applicants required to submit FAFSA. *Faculty research:* Geophysics, structural geology, petrology, geochemistry, geodynamics. *Unit head:* Director of Graduate Studies, 607-255-5466, Fax: 607-254-4780. *Application contact:* Graduate Field Assistant, 607-255-5466, Fax: 607-254-4780, E-mail: gradprog@geology.cornell.edu.

Dalhousie University, Faculty of Science, Department of Earth Sciences, Halifax, NS B3H 4R2, Canada. Offers M Sc, PhD. *Faculty:* 11 full-time (2 women), 20 part-time/adjunct (5 women). *Students:* 22 full-time (14 women), 6 international. *Degree requirements:* For master's, one foreign language, thesis; for doctorate, one foreign language, thesis/dissertation. *Entrance requirements:* Additional exam requirements/recommendations for international students: Required—TOEFL, IELTS, CANTEST, CAEL, or Michigan English Language Assessment Battery. *Application deadline:* For fall admission, 6/1 for domestic students, 4/1 for international students; for winter admission, 11/15 for domestic students, 8/31 for international students; for spring admission, 2/28 for domestic students, 12/31 for international students. Applications are processed on a rolling basis. Application fee: $70. *Financial support:* Fellowships, career-related internships or fieldwork, institutionally sponsored loans, and health care benefits available. *Faculty research:* Marine geology and geophysics, Appalachian and Grenville geology, micropaleontology, geodynamics and structural geology, geochronology. *Unit head:* Dr. Nicholas Culshaw, Graduate Coordinator, 902-494-3501, Fax: 902-494-6889, E-mail: nicholas.culshaw@dal.ca. *Application contact:* Jane Barrett, Graduate Secretary, 902-494-2358, Fax: 902-494-6889, E-mail: earth.sciences@dal.ca.

Dartmouth College, Arts and Sciences Graduate Programs, Department of Earth Sciences, Hanover, NH 03755. Offers MS, PhD. *Faculty:* 11 full-time (2 women), 3 part-time/adjunct (1 woman). *Students:* 18 full-time (7 women); includes 1 minority (Asian American or Pacific Islander), 3 international. Average age 26. 38 applicants, 47% accepted, 8 enrolled. In 2009, 4 master's, 4 doctorates awarded. Terminal master's awarded for partial completion of doctoral program. *Degree requirements:* For master's, thesis; for doctorate, thesis/dissertation. *Entrance requirements:* For master's and doctorate, GRE General Test, GRE Subject Test. Additional exam requirements/recommendations for international students: Required—TOEFL. *Application deadline:* For fall admission, 1/15 for domestic students. Application fee: $15. *Financial support:* In 2009–10, 13 students received support, including fellowships with full tuition reimbursements available (averaging $23,832 per year), research assistantships with full tuition reimbursements available (averaging $23,832 per year), teaching assistantships with full tuition reimbursements available (averaging $23,832 per year); career-related internships or fieldwork, institutionally sponsored loans, scholarships/grants, tuition waivers (full), and unspecified assistantships also available. *Faculty research:* Geochemistry, remote sensing, geophysics, hydrology, economic geology. *Unit head:* Dr. Carl E. Renshaw, Chair, 603-646-2373. *Application contact:* Suzanne Auerbach, Departmental Administration, 603-646-2373, Fax: 603-646-3922.

Eastern Michigan University, Graduate School, College of Arts and Sciences, Department of Geography and Geology, Program in Earth Science Education, Ypsilanti, MI 48197. Offers MS. *Students:* 2 full-time (both women), 9 part-time (4 women). Average age 35. In 2009, 1 master's awarded. Application fee: $35. Tuition and fees vary according to course level. *Application contact:* Dr. Sandra Rutherford, Program Advisor, 734-487-8588, Fax: 734-487-6979, E-mail: srutherf@emich.edu.

Emporia State University, School of Graduate Studies, College of Liberal Arts and Sciences, Department of Physical Sciences, Emporia, KS 66801-5087. Offers earth science (MS); geospatial analysis (Postbaccalaureate Certificate); physical science (MS). Part-time programs available. Postbaccalaureate distance learning degree programs offered (minimal on-campus study). *Faculty:* 15 full-time (2 women), 2 part-time/adjunct (1 woman). *Students:* 9 full-time (3 women), 23 part-time (7 women); includes 4 minority (1 American Indian/Alaska Native, 2 Asian Americans or Pacific Islanders, 1 Hispanic American), 6 international. 10 applicants, 80% accepted, 8 enrolled. In 2009, 7 master's, 2 other advanced degrees awarded. *Degree requirements:* For master's, comprehensive exam or thesis. *Entrance requirements:* For master's, physical science qualifying exam, appropriate undergraduate degree. Additional exam requirements/recommendations for international students: Required—TOEFL (minimum score 520 paper-based; 133 computer-based; 68 iBT). *Application deadline:* For fall admission, 8/15 priority date for domestic students. Applications are processed on a rolling basis. Application fee: $30 ($75 for international students). Electronic applications accepted. *Expenses:* Tuition, state resident: full-time $4154; part-time $173 per credit hour. Tuition, nonresident: full-time $12,864; part-time $536 per credit hour. Required fees: $948; $58 per credit hour. Tuition and fees vary according to campus/location. *Financial support:* In 2009–10, 7 teaching assistantships with full tuition reimbursements (averaging $6,177 per year) were awarded; Federal Work-Study, institutionally sponsored loans, health care benefits, and unspecified assistantships also available. Financial award application deadline: 3/15; financial award applicants required to submit FAFSA. *Faculty research:* Bredigite, larnite, and dicalcium silicates–Marble Canyon. *Unit head:* Dr. DeWayne Backhus, Chair, 620-341-5330, Fax: 620-341-6055, E-mail: dbackhus@emporia.edu. *Application contact:* Dr. DeWayne Backhus, Chair, 620-341-5330, Fax: 620-341-6055, E-mail: dbackhus@emporia.edu.

Florida Atlantic University, Charles E. Schmidt College of Science, Department of Geosciences, Boca Raton, FL 33431-0991. Offers geography (MA); geology (MS); geosciences (PhD). Part-time programs available. *Faculty:* 12 full-time (3 women), 3 part-time/adjunct (1 woman). *Students:* 20 full-time (10 women), 12 part-time (5 women); includes 6 minority (1 Asian American or Pacific Islander, 5 Hispanic Americans), 2 international. Average age 35. 24 applicants, 58% accepted, 11 enrolled. In 2009, 12 master's awarded. *Degree requirements:* For master's, thesis (for some programs). *Entrance requirements:* For master's, GRE General Test, minimum GPA of 3.0. *Application deadline:* For fall admission, 3/15 for domestic and international students; for spring admission, 10/15 for domestic and international students. Applications are processed on a rolling basis. Application fee: $30. Electronic applications accepted. *Expenses:* Tuition, state resident: full-time $7055; part-time $293.94 per credit hour. Tuition, nonresident: full-time $22,096; part-time $920.66 per credit hour. *Financial support:* Research assistantships with partial tuition reimbursements, teaching assistantships with partial tuition reimbursements, career-related internships or fieldwork, Federal Work-Study, institutionally sponsored loans, and unspecified assistantships available. *Faculty research:* GIS applications, paleontology, hydrogeology, economic development. *Unit head:* Dr. Russell Ivy, Chair, 561-297-3295, Fax: 561-297-2745, E-mail: ivy@fau.edu. *Application contact:* Dr. David Warburton, Graduate Coordinator, 561-297-3312, Fax: 561-297-2745, E-mail: warburto@fau.edu.

Florida International University, College of Arts and Sciences, Department of Earth and Environment, Program in Geosciences, Miami, FL 33199. Offers MS, PhD. Part-time and evening/weekend programs available. *Students:* 26 full-time (10 women), 5 part-time (2 women); includes 9 minority (3 African Americans, 6 Hispanic Americans), 12 international. Average age 28. 22 applicants, 27% accepted, 6 enrolled. In 2009, 5 master's, 5 doctorates awarded. *Degree requirements:* For master's, thesis optional; for doctorate, comprehensive exam, thesis/dissertation. *Entrance requirements:* For master's, GRE (1000 or higher), 3.0 GPA during the last two years of undergraduate study; Letter of intent, 3 letters of recommendation, resume; for doctorate, GRE (1120 or higher), 3.0 GPA during the last two years of undergraduate study; Letter of intent, 3 letters of recommendation, resume. Additional exam requirements/recommendations for international students: Required—TOEFL (minimum score 550 paper-based; 80 iBT). *Application deadline:* For fall admission, 2/15 for domestic and international students; for spring admission, 9/1 for domestic and international students. Application fee: $30. Electronic applications accepted. *Expenses:* Tuition, state resident: full-time $8008; part-time $4004 per year. Tuition, nonresident: full-time $20,104; part-time $10,052 per year. Required fees: $298; $149 per term. *Financial support:* Institutionally sponsored loans and scholarships/grants available. Financial award application deadline: 3/1; financial award applicants required to submit FAFSA. *Unit head:* Dr. Rosemary Hickey-Vargas, Chair, Earth and Environment Department, 305-348-2365, Fax: 305-348-3877. *Application contact:* Dr. Andrew Macfarlane, Earth Sciences, Graduate Program Director, 305-348-2365, Fax: 305-348-3877, E-mail: macfarla@fiu.edu.

Fort Hays State University, Graduate School, College of Arts and Sciences, Department of Geosciences, Program in Geosciences, Hays, KS 67601-4099. Offers geography (MS); geology (MS). *Degree requirements:* For master's, comprehensive exam, thesis. *Entrance requirements:* For master's, GRE General Test. Additional exam requirements/recommendations for international students: Required—TOEFL (minimum score 550 paper-based; 213 computer-based). Electronic applications accepted. *Faculty research:* Cretaceous and late Cenozoic stratigraphy, sedimentation, paleontology.

Georgia Institute of Technology, Graduate Studies and Research, College of Sciences, School of Earth and Atmospheric Sciences, Atlanta, GA 30332-0340. Offers atmospheric chemistry, aerosols and clouds (MS, PhD); dynamics of weather and climate (MS, PhD); geochemistry (MS, PhD); geophysics (MS, PhD); oceanography (MS, PhD); paleoclimate (MS, PhD); planetary science (MS, PhD); remote sensing (MS, PhD). Part-time programs available. Terminal master's awarded for partial completion of doctoral program. *Degree requirements:* For master's, thesis or alternative; for doctorate, comprehensive exam, thesis/dissertation. *Entrance requirements:* For master's, GRE, letters of recommendation; for doctorate, GRE, academic transcripts, letters of recommendation, personal statement. Additional exam requirements/recommendations for international students: Required—TOEFL (minimum score 550 paper-based; 213 computer-based; 79 iBT). *Faculty research:* Geophysics; atmospheric chemistry, aerosols and clouds; dynamics of weather and climate; geochemistry; oceanography; paleoclimate; planetary science; remote sensing.

Georgia State University, College of Arts and Sciences, Department of Geosciences, Atlanta, GA 30302-3083. Offers geographic information systems (Certificate); geography (MA); geology (MA); hydrogeology (Certificate). Part-time and evening/weekend programs available. *Degree requirements:* For master's, one foreign language, comprehensive exam (for some programs), thesis or alternative. *Entrance requirements:* For master's, GRE General Test, minimum GPA of 2.75. Additional exam requirements/recommendations for international students: Required—TOEFL. Electronic applications accepted. *Faculty research:* Clay mineralogy, geoinformatics, fracture analysis, sedimentology, groundwater.

Graduate School and University Center of the City University of New York, Graduate Studies, Program in Earth and Environmental Sciences, New York, NY 10016-4039. Offers PhD. *Faculty:* 36 full-time (5 women). *Students:* 76 full-time (35 women), 5 part-time (3 women); includes 11 minority (2 African Americans, 5 Asian Americans or Pacific Islanders, 4 Hispanic Americans), 18 international. Average age 36. 49 applicants, 55% accepted, 14 enrolled. In 2009, 5 doctorates awarded. *Degree requirements:* For doctorate, one foreign language, comprehensive exam, thesis/dissertation. *Entrance requirements:* For doctorate, GRE General Test. Additional exam requirements/recommendations for international students: Required—TOEFL. *Application deadline:* For fall admission, 1/15 priority date for domestic students. Application fee: $125. Electronic applications accepted. *Financial support:* In 2009–10, 52 students received support, including 51 fellowships, 2 research assistantships, 1 teaching assistantship; career-related internships or fieldwork, Federal Work-Study, institutionally sponsored loans, and tuition waivers (full and partial) also available. Financial award application deadline: 2/1; financial award applicants required to submit FAFSA. *Unit head:* Dr. Yehuda Klein, Executive Officer, 212-817-8241, Fax: 212-817-1513. *Application contact:* Les Gribben, Director of Admissions, 212-817-7470, Fax: 212-817-1624, E-mail: lgribben@gc.cuny.edu.

Harvard University, Graduate School of Arts and Sciences, Department of Earth and Planetary Sciences, Cambridge, MA 02138. Offers AM, PhD. Terminal master's awarded for partial completion of doctoral program. *Degree requirements:* For doctorate, comprehensive exam, thesis/dissertation. *Entrance requirements:* For doctorate, GRE General Test. Additional exam requirements/recommendations for international students: Required—TOEFL. Electronic applications accepted. *Expenses:* Tuition: Full-time $33,696. Required fees: $1126. Full-time tuition and fees vary according to program. *Faculty research:* Economic geography, geochemistry, geophysics, mineralogy, crystallography.

Hunter College of the City University of New York, Graduate School, School of Arts and Sciences, Department of Geography, New York, NY 10021-5085. Offers analytical geography (MA); earth system science (MA); environmental and social issues (MA); geographic information science (Certificate); geographic information systems (MA); teaching earth science (MA). Part-time and evening/weekend programs available. *Faculty:* 12 full-time (5 women), 4 part-time/adjunct (0 women). *Students:* 17 full-time (16 women), 20 part-time (19 women); includes 9 minority (1 African American, 1 American Indian/Alaska Native, 4 Asian Americans or Pacific Islanders, 3 Hispanic Americans). Average age 31. 13 applicants, 92% accepted, 9 enrolled. In 2009, 10 master's, 3 other advanced degrees awarded. *Degree requirements:* For master's, comprehensive exam or thesis. *Entrance requirements:* For master's, GRE General Test, minimum B average in major, B- overall; 18 credits of course work in geography; 2 letters of recommendation; for Certificate, minimum B average in major, B- overall. Additional exam requirements/recommendations for international students: Required—TOEFL. *Application deadline:* For fall admission, 4/1 for domestic students; for spring admission, 11/1 for domestic students. Applications are processed on a rolling basis. Application fee: $125. *Expenses:* Tuition, state resident: full-time $7360; part-time $310 per credit. Required fees: $250 per semester. *Financial support:* In 2009–10, 1 fellowship (averaging $3,000 per year), 2 research assistantships (averaging $10,000 per year), 10 teaching assistantships (averaging $6,000 per year) were awarded; career-related internships or fieldwork, Federal Work-Study, institutionally sponsored loans, and unspecified assistantships also available. Financial award application deadline: 3/1. *Faculty research:* Urban geography, economic geography, geographic information science, demographic methods, climate change. *Unit head:* Prof. William Solecki, Chair, 212-772-4536, Fax: 212-772-5268, E-mail: wsolecki@hunter.cuny.edu. *Application contact:* Prof. Marianna Pavlovskaya, Graduate Adviser, 212-772-5320, Fax: 212-772-5268, E-mail: mpavlov@geo.hunter.cuny.edu.

Hunter College of the City University of New York, Graduate School, School of Education, Programs in Secondary Education, New York, NY 10021-5085. Offers biology education (MA); chemistry education (MA); earth science (MA); English education (MA); French education (MA); Italian education (MA); mathematics education (MA); physics education (MA); social studies education (MA); Spanish education (MA). *Accreditation:* NCATE. *Faculty:* 12 full-time (6 women), 57 part-time/adjunct (42 women). *Students:* 33 full-time (22 women), 312 part-time (183 women); includes 79 minority (18 African Americans, 1 American Indian/Alaska Native, 18 Asian Americans or Pacific Islanders, 42 Hispanic Americans). Average age 32. 659 applicants, 56% accepted, 226 enrolled. In 2009, 159 master's awarded. *Degree requirements:* For master's, thesis. *Entrance requirements:* Additional exam requirements/recommendations for international students: Required—TOEFL. *Application deadline:* For fall admission, 4/1 for domestic students, 2/1 for international students; for spring admission, 11/1 for domestic students, 9/1 for international students. Applications are processed on a rolling basis. Application fee: $125. *Expenses:* Tuition, state resident: full-time $7360; part-time $310 per credit. Required fees: $250 per semester. *Financial support:* Fellowships, tuition waivers (full and partial) available. Support available to part-time students. *Unit head:* Dr. Kate Garret, Coordinator, 212-772-4700, E-mail: kgarret@hunter.cuny.edu. *Application contact:* Milena Solo, Director for Graduate Admissions, 212-772-4482, Fax: 212-650-3336, E-mail: milena.solo@hunter.cuny.edu.

Idaho State University, Office of Graduate Studies, College of Arts and Sciences, Department of Geosciences, Pocatello, ID 83209-8072. Offers geographic information science (MS); geology

Geosciences

Idaho State University (continued)
(MNS, MS); geology emphasis environmental geoscience (MS); geophysics/hydrology/geology (MS); geotechnology (Postbaccalaureate Certificate). Part-time programs available. *Faculty:* 8 full-time (1 woman). *Students:* 25 full-time (12 women), 20 part-time (6 women); includes 1 minority (Asian American or Pacific Islander), 4 international. Average age 33. In 2009, 7 master's, 2 other advanced degrees awarded. *Degree requirements:* For master's, comprehensive exam, thesis, oral colloquium; for Postbaccalaureate Certificate, thesis optional, minimum 19 credits. *Entrance requirements:* For master's, GRE General Test (minimum 50th percentile in 2 sections), 3 letters of recommendation; for Postbaccalaureate Certificate, GRE General Test, 3 letters of recommendation, bachelor's degree, statement of goals. Additional exam requirements/recommendations for international students: Required—TOEFL (minimum score 550 paper-based; 213 computer-based; 80 iBT). *Application deadline:* For fall admission, 7/1 for domestic students, 6/1 for international students; for spring admission, 12/1 for domestic students, 11/1 for international students. Applications are processed on a rolling basis. Application fee: $55. Electronic applications accepted. *Expenses:* Tuition, state resident: full-time $3318; part-time $297 per credit hour. Tuition, nonresident: full-time $13,120; part-time $437 per credit hour. Required fees: $2530. Tuition and fees vary according to program. *Financial support:* In 2009–10, 20 research assistantships with full and partial tuition reimbursements (averaging $9,713 per year), 7 teaching assistantships with full and partial tuition reimbursements (averaging $10,841 per year) were awarded; career-related internships or fieldwork, Federal Work-Study, institutionally sponsored loans, scholarships/grants, health care benefits, tuition waivers (full and partial), and unspecified assistantships also available. Support available to part-time students. Financial award application deadline: 1/1; financial award applicants required to submit FAFSA. *Faculty research:* Quantitative field mapping and sampling: microscopic, geochemical, and isotopic analysis of rocks, minerals and water; remote sensing, geographic information systems, and global positioning systems: environmental and watershed management; surficial and fluvial processes: landscape change; regional tectonics, structural geology; planetary geology. *Unit head:* Dr. David Rodgers, Chairman, 208-282-3365, Fax: 208-282-4414, E-mail: rodgdavi@isu.edu. *Application contact:* Tami Carson, Graduate School Technical Records Specialist, 208-282-2150, Fax: 208-282-4847, E-mail: carstami@isu.edu.

Indiana University Bloomington, University Graduate School, College of Arts and Sciences, Department of Geological Sciences, Bloomington, IN 47405-7000. Offers biogeochemistry (MS, PhD); economic geology (MS, PhD); geobiology (MS, PhD); geophysics, structural geology and tectonics (MS, PhD); hydrogeology (MS, PhD); mineralogy (MS, PhD); stratigraphy and sedimentology (MS, PhD). *Faculty:* 17 full-time (1 woman). *Students:* 52 full-time (24 women), 3 part-time (0 women); includes 4 minority (2 African Americans, 1 Asian American or Pacific Islander, 1 Hispanic American), 24 international. Average age 30. 46 applicants, 65% accepted, 11 enrolled. In 2009, 9 master's, 1 doctorate awarded. Terminal master's awarded for partial completion of doctoral program. *Degree requirements:* For master's, thesis or alternative; for doctorate, comprehensive exam, thesis/dissertation. *Entrance requirements:* For master's and doctorate, GRE General Test. Additional exam requirements/recommendations for international students: Required—TOEFL. *Application deadline:* For fall admission, 1/15 priority date for domestic students, 12/15 for international students; for spring admission, 9/1 priority date for domestic students, 9/1 for international students. Applications are processed on a rolling basis. Application fee: $55 ($65 for international students). *Financial support:* In 2009–10, 11 fellowships with full tuition reimbursements (averaging $15,000 per year), 14 research assistantships with full tuition reimbursements (averaging $15,000 per year), 21 teaching assistantships with full tuition reimbursements (averaging $14,073 per year) were awarded; career-related internships or fieldwork, Federal Work-Study, and institutionally sponsored loans also available. *Faculty research:* Geophysics, geochemistry, hydrogeology, geobiology, planetary science. Total annual research expenditures: $644,299. *Unit head:* Simon Brassell, Chair, 812-855-5581, Fax: 812-855-7899, E-mail: geochair@indiana.edu. *Application contact:* Mary Iverson, Graduate Secretary, 812-855-7214, Fax: 812-855-7899, E-mail: miverson@indiana.edu.

Iowa State University of Science and Technology, Graduate College, College of Liberal Arts and Sciences, Department of Geological and Atmospheric Sciences, Ames, IA 50011. Offers earth science (MS, PhD); environmental science (MS, PhD); geology (MS, PhD); meteorology (MS, PhD). *Faculty:* 15 full-time (2 women), 1 part-time/adjunct (0 women). *Students:* 31 full-time (6 women), 3 part-time (0 women); includes 1 minority (Asian American or Pacific Islander), 8 international. 33 applicants, 55% accepted, 9 enrolled. In 2009, 3 master's, 2 doctorates awarded. *Degree requirements:* For master's, thesis (for some programs); for doctorate, thesis/dissertation. *Entrance requirements:* For master's and doctorate, GRE General Test. Additional exam requirements/recommendations for international students: Required—TOEFL (minimum score 550 paper-based; 79 iBT) or IELTS (minimum score 6.5). *Application deadline:* For fall admission, 1/1 priority date for domestic students. Applications are processed on a rolling basis. Application fee: $40 ($90 for international students). Electronic applications accepted. *Expenses:* Tuition, state resident: full-time $6716. Tuition, nonresident: full-time $8908. Tuition and fees vary according to course level, course load, program and student level. *Financial support:* In 2009–10, 21 research assistantships with full and partial tuition reimbursements (averaging $14,610 per year), 7 teaching assistantships with full and partial tuition reimbursements (averaging $14,610 per year) were awarded; fellowships, scholarships/grants, health care benefits, and unspecified assistantships also available. *Unit head:* Dr. Carl E. Jacobson, Chair, 515-294-4477. *Application contact:* Dr. Carl E. Jacobson, Chair, 515-294-4477.

The Johns Hopkins University, Zanvyl Krieger School of Arts and Sciences, The Morton K. Blaustein Department of Earth and Planetary Sciences, Baltimore, MD 21218-2699. Offers MA, PhD. *Faculty:* 11 full-time (1 woman), 5 part-time/adjunct (4 women). *Students:* 25 full-time (11 women); includes 1 minority (Hispanic American), 7 international. Average age 27. 32 applicants, 44% accepted, 12 enrolled. In 2009, 3 master's, 4 doctorates awarded. *Degree requirements:* For doctorate, comprehensive exam, thesis/dissertation. *Entrance requirements:* For master's and doctorate, GRE General Test. Additional exam requirements/recommendations for international students: Required—TOEFL (minimum score 600 paper-based; 250 computer-based; 100 iBT), IELTS. *Application deadline:* For fall admission, 1/17 for domestic and international students. Application fee: $75. Electronic applications accepted. *Financial support:* In 2009–10, 23 students received support, including 14 fellowships with full tuition reimbursements available (averaging $24,666 per year), 7 research assistantships with full tuition reimbursements available (averaging $24,666 per year), 5 teaching assistantships with full tuition reimbursements available (averaging $24,666 per year); institutionally sponsored loans, scholarships/grants, traineeships, health care benefits, tuition waivers (full), and unspecified assistantships also available. Financial award application deadline: 4/15; financial award applicants required to submit FAFSA. *Faculty research:* Oceanography, atmospheric sciences, geophysics, geology, geochemistry. Total annual research expenditures: $2.2 million. *Unit head:* Dr. Darryn Waugh, Chair, 410-516-8344, Fax: 410-516-7933, E-mail: waugh@jhu.edu. *Application contact:* Kristen L. Gaines, Academic Program Coordinator, 410-516-7034, Fax: 410-516-7933, E-mail: kgaines@jhu.edu.

Lehigh University, College of Arts and Sciences, Department of Earth and Environmental Sciences, Bethlehem, PA 18015. Offers MS, PhD. *Faculty:* 14 full-time (1 woman), 1 (woman) part-time/adjunct. *Students:* 25 full-time (12 women), 4 international. Average age 26. 55 applicants, 42% accepted, 7 enrolled. In 2009, 8 master's, 3 doctorates awarded. *Degree requirements:* For doctorate, comprehensive exam, thesis/dissertation. *Entrance requirements:* For master's and doctorate, GRE General Test. Additional exam requirements/recommendations for international students: Required—TOEFL. *Application deadline:* For fall admission, 1/15 for domestic and international students. Applications are processed on a rolling basis. Application fee: $65. Electronic applications accepted. *Financial support:* In 2009–10, 13 students received support, including 3 fellowships with full tuition reimbursements available (averaging $15,400 per year), 12 research assistantships with full tuition reimbursements available (averaging $15,400 per year), 10 teaching assistantships with full tuition reimbursements available (averaging $15,400 per year); career-related internships or fieldwork, Federal Work-Study, institutionally sponsored loans, scholarships/grants, tuition waivers (full and partial), and unspecified assistantships also available. Support available to part-time students. Financial award application deadline: 1/15. *Faculty research:* Tectonics, surficial processes, aquatic ecology. Total annual research expenditures: $866,594. *Unit head:* Dr. Frank J. Pazzaglia, Chairman, 610-758-3671, Fax: 610-758-3677, E-mail: fjp3@lehigh.edu. *Application contact:* Dr. Zicheng Yu, Graduate Coordinator, 610-758-3660 Ext. 6751, Fax: 610-758-3677, E-mail: ziy2@lehigh.edu.

Loma Linda University, School of Science and Technology, Department of Biological and Earth Sciences, Loma Linda, CA 92350. Offers MS, PhD. *Degree requirements:* For master's, comprehensive exam, thesis; for doctorate, comprehensive exam, thesis/dissertation. *Entrance requirements:* For master's, minimum GPA of 3.0. Additional exam requirements/recommendations for international students: Required—TOEFL (minimum score 550 paper-based; 213 computer-based).

Long Island University, C.W. Post Campus, College of Liberal Arts and Sciences, Department of Earth and Environmental Science, Brookville, NY 11548-1300. Offers earth science (MS); earth science education (MS); environmental studies (MS).

Massachusetts Institute of Technology, School of Science, Department of Earth, Atmospheric, and Planetary Sciences, Cambridge, MA 02139-4307. Offers atmospheric chemistry (PhD, Sc D); atmospheric science (SM, PhD, Sc D); chemical oceanography (SM, PhD, Sc D); climate physics and chemistry (SM, PhD, Sc D); earth and planetary sciences (SM); geochemistry (PhD, Sc D); geology (PhD, Sc D); geophysics (PhD, Sc D); marine geology and geophysics (SM, PhD, Sc D); physical oceanography (SM, PhD, Sc D); planetary sciences (PhD, Sc D). *Faculty:* 37 full-time (7 women). *Students:* 158 full-time (74 women); includes 14 minority (1 African American, 1 American Indian/Alaska Native, 6 Asian Americans or Pacific Islanders, 6 Hispanic Americans), 58 international. Average age 27. 205 applicants, 30% accepted, 18 enrolled. In 2009, 10 master's, 25 doctorates awarded. Terminal master's awarded for partial completion of doctoral program. *Degree requirements:* For master's, thesis; for doctorate, comprehensive exam, thesis/dissertation. *Entrance requirements:* For master's, GRE General Test; for doctorate, GRE General Test, GRE Subject Test (chemistry or physics for planetary science area). Additional exam requirements/recommendations for international students: Required—IELTS (minimum score 6); Recommended—TOEFL (minimum score 577 paper-based; 233 computer-based; 91 iBT). *Application deadline:* For fall admission, 1/5 for domestic and international students; for spring admission, 11/1 for domestic and international students. Application fee: $75. Electronic applications accepted. *Financial support:* In 2009–10, 112 students received support, including 31 fellowships with tuition reimbursements available (averaging $30,513 per year), 89 research assistantships with tuition reimbursements available (averaging $21,168 per year), 17 teaching assistantships with tuition reimbursements available (averaging $28,372 per year); Federal Work-Study, institutionally sponsored loans, scholarships/grants, health care benefits, and unspecified assistantships also available. *Faculty research:* Formation, dynamics and evolution of planetary systems, origin, evolution and interaction of the physical, characterization of past, interplay of energy and the environment, present and potential future climates and the causes and consequences of climate change, chemical, geological and biological components of the Earth system, composition, structure and dynamics of the atmospheres, oceans, surfaces and interiors of the Earth and other planets. Total annual research expenditures: $19.5 million. *Unit head:* Prof. Maria Zuber, Head, 617-253-2127, Fax: 617-253-8298, E-mail: eapsinfo@mit.edu. *Application contact:* EAPS Education Office, 617-253-3381, Fax: 617-253-8298, E-mail: eapsinfo@mit.edu.

McGill University, Faculty of Graduate and Postdoctoral Studies, Faculty of Science, Department of Earth and Planetary Sciences, Montréal, QC H3A 2T5, Canada. Offers M Sc, PhD.

McMaster University, School of Graduate Studies, Faculty of Science, School of Geography and Earth Sciences, Hamilton, ON L8S 4M2, Canada. Offers geochemistry (PhD); geology (M Sc, PhD); human geography (MA, PhD); physical geography (M Sc, PhD). Part-time programs available. Terminal master's awarded for partial completion of doctoral program. *Degree requirements:* For master's, thesis; for doctorate, comprehensive exam, thesis/dissertation. *Entrance requirements:* For master's, minimum B+ average. Additional exam requirements/recommendations for international students: Required—TOEFL (minimum score 550 paper-based; 213 computer-based).

Memorial University of Newfoundland, School of Graduate Studies, Department of Earth Sciences, St. John's, NL A1C 5S7, Canada. Offers geology (M Sc, PhD); geophysics (M Sc, PhD). Part-time programs available. *Degree requirements:* For master's, thesis; for doctorate, comprehensive exam, thesis/dissertation, oral thesis defense, entry evaluation. *Entrance requirements:* For master's, honors B Sc; for doctorate, M Sc. Electronic applications accepted. *Faculty research:* Geochemistry, sedimentology, paleoceanography and global change, mineral deposits, petroleum geology, hydrology.

Michigan State University, The Graduate School, College of Natural Science, Department of Geological Sciences, East Lansing, MI 48824. Offers environmental geosciences (MS, PhD); environmental geosciences-environmental toxicology (PhD); geological sciences (MS, PhD). *Degree requirements:* For master's, thesis (for those without prior thesis work); for doctorate, thesis/dissertation. *Entrance requirements:* For master's, GRE General Test, minimum GPA of 3.0, course work in geoscience, 3 letters of recommendation; for doctorate, GRE General Test, 3 letters of recommendation. Additional exam requirements/recommendations for international students: Required—TOEFL (minimum score 550 paper-based; 213 computer-based), Michigan State University ELT (85), Michigan English Language Assessment Battery (83). Electronic applications accepted. *Faculty research:* Water in the environment, global and biological change, crystal dynamics.

Middle Tennessee State University, College of Graduate Studies, College of Liberal Arts, Department of Geosciences, Murfreesboro, TN 37132. Offers Graduate Certificate. Part-time and evening/weekend programs available. Postbaccalaureate distance learning degree programs offered. *Entrance requirements:* Additional exam requirements/recommendations for international students: Required—TOEFL (minimum score 525 paper-based; 195 computer-based; 71 iBT) or IELTS (minimum score 6). *Expenses:* Tuition, state resident: full-time $4404. Tuition, nonresident: full-time $10,956. *Financial support:* Application deadline: 5/1. *Unit head:* Dr. Ronald L. Zawislak, Chair, 615-898-2726. *Application contact:* Dr. Michael Allen, Dean and Vice Provost for Research, 615-898-2840, Fax: 615-904-8020, E-mail: mallen@mtsu.edu.

Mississippi State University, College of Arts and Sciences, Department of Geosciences, Mississippi State, MS 39762. Offers earth and atmospheric science (PhD); geoscience (MS). Postbaccalaureate distance learning degree programs offered (no on-campus study). *Faculty:* 17 full-time (3 women), 2 part-time/adjunct (0 women). *Students:* 45 full-time (15 women), 260 part-time (127 women); includes 23 minority (8 African Americans, 3 American Indian/Alaska Native, 4 Asian Americans or Pacific Islanders, 8 Hispanic Americans), 6 international. Average age 37. 171 applicants, 81% accepted, 117 enrolled. In 2009, 88 master's awarded. *Degree requirements:* For master's, thesis (for some programs), comprehensive oral or written exam. *Entrance requirements:* For master's, GRE (for on-campus applicants), minimum undergraduate GPA of 2.75. Additional exam requirements/recommendations for international students: Required—TOEFL (minimum score 475 paper-based; 153 computer-based; 53 iBT); Recommended—IELTS (minimum score 4.5). *Application deadline:* For fall admission, 7/1 for domestic students, 5/1 for international students; for spring admission, 11/1 for domestic students, 9/1 for international students. Applications are processed on a rolling basis. Application fee: $40. Electronic applications accepted. *Expenses:* Tuition, state resident: full-time $2575.50; part-time $286.25 per credit hour. Tuition, nonresident: full-time $6510; part-time $723.50 per credit hour. Tuition and fees vary according to course load. *Financial support:* In 2009–10, 6 research assistantships with full tuition reimbursements (averaging $13,000 per year), 19 teaching assistantships with full tuition reimbursements (averaging $12,116 per year) were awarded; Federal Work-Study, institutionally sponsored loans, scholarships/grants, tuition waivers (partial), and unspecified assistantships also available. Financial award application deadline: 4/1; financial award applicants required to submit FAFSA. *Faculty research:* Climatology, hydrogeology, sedimentology, meteorology. Total annual research expenditures: $2.8 million. *Unit head:* Dr. Darrel Schmitz, Professor and Head, 662-325-3915, Fax: 662-325-9423, E-mail: schmitz@geosci.msstate.edu. *Application contact:* Dr. Christopher P. Dewey, Associate Professor/Graduate Coordinator, 662-325-2909, Fax: 662-325-9423, E-mail: cpd4@msstate.edu.

Missouri State University, Graduate College, College of Natural and Applied Sciences, Department of Geography, Geology, and Planning, Springfield, MO 65897. Offers geospatial sciences (MS); natural and applied science (MNAS), including geography, geology and planning; secondary education (MS Ed), including earth science, geography. *Accreditation:* ACSP. Part-time and evening/weekend programs available. *Faculty:* 20 full-time (4 women). *Students:* 19 full-time (10 women), 12 part-time (5 women); includes 1 minority (American Indian/Alaska Native), 1 international. Average age 29. 19 applicants, 100% accepted, 13 enrolled. In 2009, 4 master's awarded. *Degree requirements:* For master's, comprehensive exam, thesis (for some programs). *Entrance requirements:* For master's, GRE General Test (MS, MNAS), minimum undergraduate GPA of 3.0 (MS, MNAS), 9-12 teacher certification (MS Ed). Additional exam requirements/recommendations for international students: Required—TOEFL (minimum score 550 paper-based; 213 computer-based; 79 iBT). *Application deadline:* For fall admission, 7/20 priority date for domestic students, 5/1 for international students; for spring admission, 12/20 priority date for domestic students, 9/1 for international students. Applications are processed on a rolling basis. Application fee: $35 ($50 for international students). Electronic applications accepted. *Expenses:* Tuition, state resident: full-time $3852; part-time $214 per credit hour. Tuition, nonresident: full-time $7524; part-time $418 per credit hour. Required fees: $696; $172 per semester. Tuition and fees vary according to course level, course load, degree level and program. *Financial support:* In 2009–10, 7 research assistantships with full tuition reimbursements (averaging $8,933 per year), 8 teaching assistantships with full tuition reimbursements (averaging $8,236 per year) were awarded; career-related internships or fieldwork, Federal Work-Study, institutionally sponsored loans, scholarships/grants, and unspecified assistantships also available. Financial award application deadline: 3/31; financial award applicants required to submit FAFSA. *Faculty research:* Stratigraphy and ancient meteorite impacts, environmental geochemistry of karst, hyperspectral image processing, water quality, small town planning. *Unit head:* Dr. Thomas Plymate, Head, 417-836-5800, Fax: 417-836-6934, E-mail: tomplymate@missouristate.edu. *Application contact:* Eric Eckert, Coordinator of Graduate Admissions and Recruitment, 417-836-5331, Fax: 417-836-6200, E-mail: ericeckert@missouristate.edu.

Montana State University, College of Graduate Studies, College of Letters and Science, Department of Earth Sciences, Bozeman, MT 59717. Offers MS, PhD. Part-time programs available. *Faculty:* 12 full-time (1 woman), 2 part-time/adjunct (0 women). *Students:* 17 full-time (9 women), 35 part-time (16 women); includes 2 minority (1 African American, 1 Hispanic American), 8 international. Average age 28. 51 applicants, 33% accepted, 8 enrolled. In 2009, 14 master's, 1 doctorate awarded. *Degree requirements:* For master's, comprehensive exam, thesis (for some programs); for doctorate, comprehensive exam, thesis/dissertation. *Entrance requirements:* For master's and doctorate, GRE General Test, minimum GPA of 3.0. Additional exam requirements/recommendations for international students: Required—TOEFL (minimum score 550 paper-based; 213 computer-based). *Application deadline:* For fall admission, 7/15 priority date for domestic students, 5/15 priority date for international students; for spring admission, 12/1 priority date for domestic students, 10/1 priority date for international students. Applications are processed on a rolling basis. Application fee: $30. Electronic applications accepted. *Expenses:* Tuition, state resident: full-time $5635; part-time $3492 per year. Tuition, nonresident: full-time $17,212; part-time $7865.10 per year. Required fees: $1441.05; $153.15 per credit. Tuition and fees vary according to course load and program. *Financial support:* In 2009–10, 27 students received support, including 7 research assistantships with full tuition reimbursements available (averaging $17,450 per year), 15 teaching assistantships with full tuition reimbursements available (averaging $10,485 per year); career-related internships or fieldwork, scholarships/grants, traineeships, tuition waivers (full and partial), and unspecified assistantships also available. Financial award application deadline: 3/1; financial award applicants required to submit FAFSA. *Faculty research:* Sedimentology/stratigraphy/basin analysis; structural geology snow science, vertebrate paleontology, quaternary studies, paleoclimatology, geography of the Northern Rockies (historical geography), economic/urban geography. Total annual research expenditures: $738,774. *Unit head:* Dr. Stephan Custer, Head, 406-994-6906, Fax: 406-994-6923, E-mail: scuster@montana.edu. *Application contact:* Dr. Carl A. Fox, Vice Provost for Graduate Education, 406-994-4145, Fax: 406-994-7433, E-mail: gradstudy@montana.edu.

Montana Tech of The University of Montana, Graduate School, Geosciences Programs, Butte, MT 59701-8997. Offers geochemistry (MS); geological engineering (MS); geology (MS); geophysical engineering (MS); hydrogeological engineering (MS); hydrogeology (MS). Part-time programs available. *Faculty:* 18 full-time (4 women), 3 part-time/adjunct (2 women). *Students:* 16 full-time (8 women), 6 part-time (4 women); includes 1 minority (African American), 1 international. 6 applicants, 67% accepted, 4 enrolled. In 2009, 7 degrees awarded. *Degree requirements:* For master's, comprehensive exam (for some programs), thesis (for some programs). *Entrance requirements:* For master's, GRE General Test, minimum GPA of 3.0. Additional exam requirements/recommendations for international students: Required—TOEFL (minimum score 525 paper-based; 195 computer-based; 71 iBT). *Application deadline:* For fall admission, 4/1 priority date for domestic students, 3/1 priority date for international students; for spring admission, 10/1 priority date for domestic students, 7/1 priority date for international students. Applications are processed on a rolling basis. Application fee: $30. Electronic applications accepted. *Expenses:* Tuition, state resident: full-time $5068; part-time $319 per credit. Tuition, nonresident: full-time $14,815; part-time $875 per credit. Tuition and fees vary according to course load and campus/location. *Financial support:* In 2009–10, 11 students received support, including 5 teaching assistantships with partial tuition reimbursements available (averaging $8,000 per year); research assistantships with partial tuition reimbursements available, career-related internships or fieldwork, tuition waivers (full and partial), and unspecified assistantships also available. Financial award application deadline: 4/1; financial award applicants required to submit FAFSA. *Faculty research:* Water resource development, seismic processing, petroleum reservoir characterization, environmental geochemistry, geologic mapping. *Unit head:* Dr. Diane Wolfgram, Department Head, 406-496-4353, Fax: 406-496-4260, E-mail: dwolfgram@mtech.edu. *Application contact:* Cindy Dunstan, Administrator, Graduate School, 406-496-4304, Fax: 406-496-4710, E-mail: cdunstan@mtech.edu.

Montclair State University, The Graduate School, College of Science and Mathematics, Department of Earth and Environmental Studies, Montclair, NJ 07043-1624. Offers earth science (Certificate); environmental management (MA, D Env M); environmental studies (MS), including environmental education, environmental health, environmental management, environmental science; geographic information science (Certificate); geoscience (MS, Certificate), including geoscience (MS), water resource management (Certificate). Part-time and evening/weekend programs available. *Faculty:* 16 full-time (2 women), 13 part-time/adjunct (4 women). *Students:* 36 full-time (17 women), 60 part-time (26 women). Average age 34. 42 applicants, 60% accepted, 17 enrolled. In 2009, 11 degrees awarded. *Degree requirements:* For master's, comprehensive exam, thesis or alternative; for doctorate, thesis/dissertation. *Entrance requirements:* For master's, GRE General Test, 2 letters of recommendation; for doctorate, GRE General Test, 3 letters of recommendation. Additional exam requirements/recommendations for international students: Required—TOEFL (minimum score 83 computer-based), or IELTS. *Application deadline:* For fall admission, 6/1 for international students; for spring admission, 10/1 for international students. Applications are processed on a rolling basis. Application fee: $60. Electronic applications accepted. *Expenses:* Tuition, area resident: Part-time $486.74 per credit. Tuition, state resident: part-time $486.74 per credit. Tuition, nonresident: part-time $751.34 per credit. Tuition and fees vary according to degree level and program. *Financial support:* In 2009–10, 3 fellowships (averaging $15,000 per year), 12 research assistantships with full tuition reimbursements (averaging $8,500 per year), 11 teaching assistantships with full tuition reimbursements (averaging $15,000 per year) were awarded; Federal Work-Study, scholarships/grants, and unspecified assistantships also available. Support available to part-time students. Financial award application deadline: 3/1; financial award applicants required to submit FAFSA. *Faculty research:* Antarctica, carbon pools, contaminated sediments, wetlands. *Unit head:* Dr. Duke Ophori, Chairperson, 973-655-7558. *Application contact:* Amy Aiello, Director of Graduate Admissions and Operations, 973-655-5147, Fax: 973-655-7869, E-mail: graduate.school@montclair.edu.

Murray State University, College of Science, Engineering and Technology, Program in Geosciences, Murray, KY 42071. Offers MS. Part-time programs available. *Degree requirements:* For master's, comprehensive exam, thesis optional. *Entrance requirements:* Additional exam requirements/recommendations for international students: Required—TOEFL, IELTS.

New Mexico Institute of Mining and Technology, Graduate Studies, Department of Earth and Environmental Science, Socorro, NM 87801. Offers geology and geochemistry (MS, PhD), including geochemistry, geology; geophysics (MS, PhD); hydrology (MS, PhD). *Degree requirements:* For master's, thesis optional; for doctorate, thesis/dissertation. *Entrance requirements:* For master's, GRE General Test; for doctorate, GRE General Test, GRE Subject Test. Additional exam requirements/recommendations for international students: Required—TOEFL. *Faculty research:* Seismology, geochemistry, caves and karst topography, hydrology, volcanology.

North Carolina Central University, Division of Academic Affairs, College of Science and Technology, Department of Environmental, Earth and Geospatial Sciences, Durham, NC 27707-3129. Offers earth sciences (MS). *Degree requirements:* For master's, one foreign language, comprehensive exam. *Entrance requirements:* For master's, GRE, minimum GPA of 3.0 in major, 2.5 overall. Additional exam requirements/recommendations for international students: Required—TOEFL.

North Carolina State University, Graduate School, College of Physical and Mathematical Sciences, Department of Marine, Earth, and Atmospheric Sciences, Raleigh, NC 27695. Offers marine, earth, and atmospheric sciences (MS, PhD); meteorology (MS, PhD); oceanography (MS, PhD). Terminal master's awarded for partial completion of doctoral program. *Degree requirements:* For master's, thesis (for some programs), final oral exam; for doctorate, comprehensive exam, thesis/dissertation, final oral exam, preliminary oral and written exams. *Entrance requirements:* For master's, GRE General Test, minimum GPA of 3.0; for doctorate, GRE General Test, GRE Subject Test (for disciplines in biological oceanography and geology), minimum GPA of 3.0. Additional exam requirements/recommendations for international students: Required—TOEFL (minimum score 550 paper-based). Electronic applications accepted. *Faculty research:* Boundary layer and air quality meteorology; climate and mesoscale dynamics; biological, chemical, geological, and physical oceanography; hard rock, soft rock, environmental, and paleo-geology.

Northeastern Illinois University, Graduate College, College of Arts and Sciences, Department of Earth Science, Program in Earth Science, Chicago, IL 60625-4699. Offers MS. Part-time and evening/weekend programs available. *Degree requirements:* For master's, thesis optional, oral presentation. *Entrance requirements:* For master's, 15 undergraduate hours in earth science, 8 undergraduate hours in chemistry and physics, minimum GPA of 2.75. Additional exam requirements/recommendations for international students: Required—TOEFL (minimum score 550 paper-based; 213 computer-based; 80 iBT). Electronic applications accepted. *Faculty research:* Coastal engineering, Paleozoic and Precambrian tectonics and volcanology, ravine erosion control, well head protection delineation, genesis and evolution of basaltic magma.

Northwestern University, The Graduate School, Judd A. and Marjorie Weinberg College of Arts and Sciences, Department of Geological Sciences, Evanston, IL 60208. Offers MS, PhD. Admissions and degrees offered through The Graduate School. Part-time programs available. *Degree requirements:* For doctorate, thesis/dissertation. *Entrance requirements:* For master's and doctorate, GRE General Test. Additional exam requirements/recommendations for international students: Required—TOEFL. Electronic applications accepted.

Oregon State University, Graduate School, College of Science, Department of Geosciences, Corvallis, OR 97331. Offers geography (MA, MAIS, MS, PhD); geology (MA, MAIS, MS, PhD). Part-time programs available. *Faculty:* 18 full-time (4 women), 4 part-time/adjunct (1 woman). *Students:* 51 full-time (21 women), 8 part-time (3 women); includes 4 minority (1 Asian American or Pacific Islander, 3 Hispanic Americans), 3 international. Average age 31. In 2009, 12 master's, 2 doctorates awarded. Terminal master's awarded for partial completion of doctoral program. *Degree requirements:* For doctorate, one foreign language, thesis/dissertation. *Entrance requirements:* For master's and doctorate, GRE General Test, GRE Subject Test, minimum GPA of 3.0 in last 90 hours. Additional exam requirements/recommendations for international students: Required—TOEFL. *Application deadline:* For fall admission, 2/1 for domestic students. Applications are processed on a rolling basis. Application fee: $50. *Expenses:* Tuition, state resident: full-time $9774; part-time $362 per credit. Tuition, nonresident: full-time $15,849; part-time $587 per credit. Required fees: $1639. Full-time tuition and fees vary according to course load and program. *Financial support:* Fellowships, research assistantships, teaching assistantships, career-related internships or fieldwork, Federal Work-Study, and institutionally sponsored loans available. Support available to part-time students. Financial award application deadline: 2/1. *Unit head:* Dr. Roger L. Nielsen, Department Chair, 541-737-1235, Fax: 541-737-1200, E-mail: nielsenr@oregonstate.edu. *Application contact:* Stacey Schulte, Office Specialist 2, 541-737-1221, Fax: 541-737-1200, E-mail: schultes@gco.oregonstate.edu.

Penn State University Park, Graduate School, College of Earth and Mineral Sciences, Department of Geosciences, State College, University Park, PA 16802-1503. Offers MS, PhD.

Princeton University, Graduate School, Department of Geosciences, Princeton, NJ 08544-1019. Offers atmospheric and oceanic sciences (PhD); geosciences (PhD); ocean sciences and marine biology (PhD). *Degree requirements:* For doctorate, one foreign language, thesis/dissertation. *Entrance requirements:* For doctorate, GRE General Test. Additional exam requirements/recommendations for international students: Required—TOEFL (minimum score 600 paper-based; 250 computer-based). Electronic applications accepted. *Faculty research:* Biogeochemistry, climate science, earth history, regional geology and tectonics, solid–earth geophysics.

Purdue University, Graduate School, College of Science, Department of Earth and Atmospheric Sciences, West Lafayette, IN 47907. Offers MS, PhD. *Degree requirements:* For master's, thesis; for doctorate, one foreign language, thesis/dissertation. *Entrance requirements:* For master's and doctorate, GRE General Test. Additional exam requirements/recommendations for international students: Required—TOEFL. Electronic applications accepted. *Faculty research:* Geology, geophysics, hydrogeology, paleoclimatology, environmental science.

Geosciences

Rensselaer Polytechnic Institute, Graduate School, School of Science, Department of Earth and Environmental Sciences, Troy, NY 12180-3590. Offers geochemistry (MS, PhD); geology (MS, PhD); geophysics (MS, PhD); petrology (MS, PhD). Part-time programs available. *Faculty:* 8 full-time (1 woman), 1 part-time/adjunct (0 women). *Students:* 8 full-time (5 women), 1 (woman) part-time; includes 1 minority (Asian American or Pacific Islander). Average age 24. 48 applicants, 15% accepted. In 2009, 2 master's, 3 doctorates awarded. Terminal master's awarded for partial completion of doctoral program. *Degree requirements:* For master's, comprehensive exam, thesis (for some programs); for doctorate, comprehensive exam, thesis/dissertation. *Entrance requirements:* For master's and doctorate, GRE General Test. Additional exam requirements/recommendations for international students: Required—TOEFL. *Application deadline:* For fall admission, 1/15 priority date for domestic students. Applications are processed on a rolling basis. Application fee: $75. Electronic applications accepted. *Expenses:* Tuition: Full-time $38,100. *Financial support:* In 2009–10, 7 research assistantships with full tuition reimbursements (averaging $23,000 per year), 4 teaching assistantships with full tuition reimbursements (averaging $23,000 per year) were awarded; fellowships with full tuition reimbursements, career-related internships or fieldwork, institutionally sponsored loans, and scholarships/grants also available. Financial award application deadline: 2/1; financial award applicants required to submit FAFSA. *Faculty research:* Mantel geochemistry, contaminant geochemistry, seismology, GPS geodesy, remote sensing petrology. Total annual research expenditures: $2.3 million. *Unit head:* Dr. Frank Spear, Chair, 518-276-6474, Fax: 518-276-2012, E-mail: ees@rpi.edu. *Application contact:* Dr. Steven Roecker, Professor, 518-276-6773, Fax: 518-276-2012, E-mail: ees@rpi.edu.

Rice University, Graduate Programs, Wiess School of Natural Sciences, Department of Earth Science, Houston, TX 77251-1892. Offers MS, PhD. *Faculty:* 17 full-time (2 women), 15 part-time/adjunct (2 women). *Students:* 34 full-time (20 women); includes 3 minority (1 Asian American or Pacific Islander, 2 Hispanic Americans), 17 international. Average age 26. Terminal master's awarded for partial completion of doctoral program. *Degree requirements:* For master's, comprehensive exam, thesis, annual department report and presentation, qualifying exam, orals, 2 publications; for doctorate, comprehensive exam, thesis/dissertation, annual report and presentation; qualifying exam, orals, 3 publications. *Entrance requirements:* For master's and doctorate, GRE. Additional exam requirements/recommendations for international students: Required—TOEFL (minimum score 600 paper-based; 90 iBT), IELTS. *Application deadline:* For fall admission, 1/1 for domestic students; for spring admission, 11/1 for domestic students. Applications are processed on a rolling basis. Application fee: $40. Electronic applications accepted. *Financial support:* In 2009–10, 31 fellowships (averaging $22,800 per year), 14 research assistantships (averaging $22,800 per year), 19 teaching assistantships (averaging $22,800 per year) were awarded. *Faculty research:* Seismology, structural geology, tectonics and paleomagnetism, geodynamics, high temperature geochemistry, volcanic processes. *Unit head:* Lee Willson, Department Administrator, 713-348-6219, Fax: 713-348-5214, E-mail: shiree@rice.edu. *Application contact:* Mary Ann Lebar, Graduate Student Coordinator, 713-348-6068, Fax: 713-348-5214, E-mail: ml15@rice.edu.

Rice University, Graduate Programs, Wiess School–Professional Science Master's Programs, Professional Master's Program in Subsurface Geosciences, Houston, TX 77251-1892. Offers geophysics (MS). Part-time programs available. *Degree requirements:* For master's, internship. *Entrance requirements:* For master's, GRE, letters of recommendation (4). Additional exam requirements/recommendations for international students: Required—TOEFL (minimum score 600 paper-based; 250 computer-based; 90 iBT). Electronic applications accepted. *Faculty research:* Seismology, geodynamics, wave propagation, bio-geochemistry, remote sensing.

St. Francis Xavier University, Graduate Studies, Department of Earth Sciences, Antigonish, NS B2G 2W5, Canada. Offers M Sc. *Degree requirements:* For master's, thesis. *Entrance requirements:* Additional exam requirements/recommendations for international students: Required—TOEFL (minimum score 580 paper-based; 236 computer-based). *Faculty research:* Environmental earth sciences, global change tectonics, paleoclimatology, crustal fluids.

Saint Louis University, Graduate School, College of Arts and Sciences and Graduate School, Department of Earth and Atmospheric Sciences, St. Louis, MO 63103-2097. Offers geophysics (PhD); geoscience (MS); meteorology (M Pr Met, MS-R, PhD). Part-time programs available. *Degree requirements:* For master's, thesis (for some programs), comprehensive oral exam; for doctorate, thesis/dissertation, preliminary exams. *Entrance requirements:* For master's, GRE General Test, letters of recommendation, resume; for doctorate, GRE General Test, letters of recommendation, resumé, goal statement, transcripts. Additional exam requirements/recommendations for international students: Required—TOEFL (minimum score 525 paper-based; 194 computer-based). Electronic applications accepted. *Faculty research:* Structural geology, mesoscale meteorology and severe storms, weather and climate change prediction.

St. Thomas University, School of Leadership Studies, Institute for Education, Miami Gardens, FL 33054-6459. Offers earth/space science (Certificate); educational administration (MS, Certificate); educational leadership (Ed D); elementary education (MS); ESOL (Certificate); gifted education (Certificate); instructional technology (MS, Certificate); professional/studies (Certificate); reading (MS, Certificate); special education (MS). Part-time and evening/weekend programs available. *Degree requirements:* For master's, comprehensive exam; for doctorate, comprehensive exam, thesis/dissertation. *Entrance requirements:* For master's, interview, minimum GPA of 3.0 or GRE; for doctorate, GRE or MAT. Additional exam requirements/recommendations for international students: Required—TOEFL (minimum score 550 paper-based; 213 computer-based; 79 iBT). Electronic applications accepted.

San Francisco State University, Division of Graduate Studies, College of Science and Engineering, Department of Geosciences, San Francisco, CA 94132-1722. Offers applied geosciences (MS).

Simon Fraser University, Graduate Studies, Faculty of Science, Department of Earth Sciences, Burnaby, BC V5A 1S6, Canada. Offers M Sc, PhD. Part-time programs available. *Degree requirements:* For master's, thesis. *Entrance requirements:* For master's, minimum GPA of 3.0. Additional exam requirements/recommendations for international students: Required—TOEFL or IELTS. Electronic applications accepted. *Faculty research:* Earth surface processes, environmental geoscience, surficial and Quaternary geology, sedimentology.

South Dakota State University, Graduate School, College of Engineering, Department of Mathematics and Statistics, Brookings, SD 57007. Offers computational science and statistics (PhD); geospatial science and engineering (PhD); mathematics (MS). Part-time programs available. *Degree requirements:* For master's, thesis (for some programs), oral exam; for doctorate, comprehensive exam, thesis/dissertation, oral and written exams. *Entrance requirements:* Additional exam requirements/recommendations for international students: Required—TOEFL (minimum score 550 paper-based; 213 computer-based; 80 iBT); Recommended—IELTS. *Faculty research:* Mathematics, biostatistics, computational science, numerical linear algebra, statistics, applied quality number theory, abstract algebra.

South Dakota State University, Graduate School, College of Engineering, Geospatial Science and Engineering Program, Brookings, SD 57007. Offers PhD. Part-time programs available. *Degree requirements:* For doctorate, comprehensive exam, thesis/dissertation. *Entrance requirements:* For doctorate, GRE. Additional exam requirements/recommendations for international students: Required—TOEFL (minimum score 525 paper-based; 197 computer-based; 71 iBT). *Faculty research:* Deforestation, land use/cover change, GIS spatial modeling.

Stanford University, School of Earth Sciences, Department of Geological and Environmental Sciences, Stanford, CA 94305-9991. Offers MS, PhD, Eng. Terminal master's awarded for partial completion of doctoral program. *Degree requirements:* For master's and Eng, thesis; for doctorate, thesis/dissertation. *Entrance requirements:* For master's, doctorate, and Eng, GRE General Test. Additional exam requirements/recommendations for international students: Required—TOEFL. Electronic applications accepted. *Expenses:* Tuition: Full-time $37,380; part-time $2760 per quarter. Required fees: $501.

Stanford University, School of Earth Sciences, Earth Systems Program, Stanford, CA 94305-9991. Offers MS. Students admitted at the undergraduate level. Electronic applications accepted. *Expenses:* Tuition: Full-time $37,380; part-time $2760 per quarter. Required fees: $501.

State University of New York College at Oneonta, Graduate Education, Department of Earth Sciences, Oneonta, NY 13820-4015. Offers MA. Part-time and evening/weekend programs available. *Students:* 2 full-time (1 woman). *Degree requirements:* For master's, thesis. *Entrance requirements:* For master's, GRE General Test. *Application deadline:* For fall admission, 3/25 priority date for domestic students; for spring admission, 10/1 priority date for domestic students. Applications are processed on a rolling basis. Application fee: $50. *Expenses:* Tuition, state resident: part-time $349 per credit hour. Tuition, nonresident: full-time $12,870; part-time $552 per credit hour. Required fees: $1280; $15.85 per credit hour. *Financial support:* Fellowships available. *Unit head:* Dr. James Ebert, Chair, 607-436-3707, E-mail: ebertjr@oneonta.edu. *Application contact:* Dean, 607-436-2523, Fax: 607-436-3084, E-mail: gradoffice@oneonta.edu.

Stony Brook University, State University of New York, Graduate School, College of Arts and Sciences, Department of Geosciences, Stony Brook, NY 11794. Offers earth science (MAT); geosciences (MS, PhD). MAT offered through the School of Professional Development. *Faculty:* 18 full-time (2 women). *Students:* 33 full-time (19 women), 6 part-time (2 women); includes 3 minority (1 African American, 1 American Indian/Alaska Native, 1 Hispanic American), 10 international. Average age 29. 34 applicants, 56% accepted. In 2009, 6 master's, 7 doctorates awarded. Terminal master's awarded for partial completion of doctoral program. *Degree requirements:* For master's, thesis or alternative; for doctorate, thesis/dissertation. *Entrance requirements:* For master's and doctorate, GRE General Test, minimum GPA of 3.0. Additional exam requirements/recommendations for international students: Required—TOEFL. *Application deadline:* For fall admission, 1/15 for domestic students. Application fee: $60. *Expenses:* Tuition, state resident: full-time $8370; part-time $349 per credit. Tuition, nonresident: full-time $13,250; part-time $552 per credit. Required fees: $933. *Financial support:* In 2009–10, 18 research assistantships, 9 teaching assistantships were awarded; fellowships also available. *Faculty research:* Astronomy, theoretical and observational astrophysics, paleontology, petrology, crystallography. Total annual research expenditures: $2.5 million. *Unit head:* Dr. Richard Reeder, Chair, 631-632-8139, Fax: 631-632-8240, E-mail: rjreeder@stonybrook.edu. *Application contact:* Dr. Daniel Davis, Director, 631-632-8200, Fax: 631-632-8240, E-mail: daniel.davis@notes.cc.sunysb.edu.

Texas A&M University–Commerce, Graduate School, College of Arts and Sciences, Department of Biological and Earth Sciences, Commerce, TX 75429-3011. Offers M Ed, MS. *Degree requirements:* For master's, comprehensive exam, thesis (for some programs). *Entrance requirements:* For master's, GRE General Test. Electronic applications accepted. *Faculty research:* Microbiology, botany, environmental science, birds.

Texas Tech University, Graduate School, College of Arts and Sciences, Department of Geosciences, Lubbock, TX 79409. Offers atmospheric sciences (MS); geoscience (MS, PhD). Part-time programs available. *Faculty:* 16 full-time (2 women), 1 part-time/adjunct (0 women). *Students:* 42 full-time (14 women), 15 part-time (3 women); includes 5 minority (1 African American, 4 Hispanic Americans), 10 international. Average age 28. 70 applicants, 30% accepted, 15 enrolled. In 2009, 4 master's, 2 doctorates awarded. *Degree requirements:* For master's, thesis or alternative; for doctorate, thesis/dissertation. *Entrance requirements:* For master's and doctorate, GRE General Test. Additional exam requirements/recommendations for international students: Required—TOEFL (minimum score 550 paper-based; 213 computer-based). *Application deadline:* For fall admission, 3/1 priority date for international students; for spring admission, 11/1 priority date for international students. Applications are processed on a rolling basis. Application fee: $50 ($75 for international students). Electronic applications accepted. *Expenses:* Tuition, state resident: full-time $5100; part-time $213 per credit hour. Tuition, nonresident: full-time $11,748; part-time $490 per credit hour. Required fees: $2298; $50 per credit hour. $555 per semester. *Financial support:* In 2009–10, 3 research assistantships with partial tuition reimbursements (averaging $25,886 per year), 14 teaching assistantships with partial tuition reimbursements (averaging $17,545 per year) were awarded; Federal Work-Study and institutionally sponsored loans also available. Support available to part-time students. Financial award application deadline: 4/15; financial award applicants required to submit FAFSA. *Faculty research:* Petroleum geology and geophysics, tectonics and arc magnetism, aqueous and environmental geochemistry, hurricanes and severe storms, wind power. Total annual research expenditures: $686,238. *Unit head:* Dr. Calvin Barnes, Chairman, 806-742-3102, Fax: 806-742-0100, E-mail: cal.barnes@ttu.edu. *Application contact:* Dr. Aaron Yoshinobu, Graduate Adviser, 806-742-3102, Fax: 806-724-0100, E-mail: aaron.yoshinobu@ttu.edu.

Tulane University, School of Science and Engineering, Department of Earth and Environmental Sciences, New Orleans, LA 70118-5669. Offers MS, PhD. *Degree requirements:* For master's, one foreign language, thesis or alternative; for doctorate, one foreign language, thesis/dissertation. *Entrance requirements:* For master's, GRE General Test, minimum B average in undergraduate course work; for doctorate, GRE General Test. Additional exam requirements/recommendations for international students: Required—TOEFL. Electronic applications accepted. *Faculty research:* Sedimentation, isotopes, biogeochemistry, marine geology, structural geology.

Université du Québec à Chicoutimi, Graduate Programs, Program in Earth Sciences, Chicoutimi, QC G7H 2B1, Canada. Offers M Sc A. Part-time programs available. *Degree requirements:* For master's, thesis. *Entrance requirements:* For master's, appropriate bachelor's degree, proficiency in French.

Université du Québec à Montréal, Graduate Programs, Program in Earth and Atmospheric Sciences, Montréal, QC H3C 3P8, Canada. Offers atmospheric sciences (M Sc); Earth and atmospheric sciences (PhD); Earth science (M Sc); meteorology (PhD, Diploma). Part-time programs available. *Degree requirements:* For master's, thesis. *Entrance requirements:* For master's and Diploma, appropriate bachelor's degree or equivalent, proficiency in French; for doctorate, appropriate master's degree or equivalent, proficiency in French.

Université du Québec à Montréal, Graduate Programs, Program in Earth Sciences, Montreal, QC H3C 3P8, Canada. Offers earth sciences (M Sc); mineral resources (PhD); non-renewable resources (DESS). Part-time programs available. Terminal master's awarded for partial completion of doctoral program. *Degree requirements:* For master's, thesis (for some programs); for doctorate, thesis/dissertation. *Entrance requirements:* For master's, appropriate bachelor's degree or equivalent, proficiency in French. *Faculty research:* Economic geology, structural geology, geochemistry, Quaternary geology, isotopic geochemistry.

Université du Québec, Institut National de la Recherche Scientifique, Graduate Programs, Research Center—Water, Earth and Environment, Québec, QC G1K 9A9, Canada. Offers earth sciences (M Sc, PhD); earth sciences-environmental technologies (M Sc); water sciences (M Sc, PhD). Part-time programs available. *Faculty:* 42. *Students:* 181 full-time (70 women), 9 part-time (1 woman), 74 international. Average age 30. In 2009, 19 master's, 10 doctorates awarded. *Degree requirements:* For master's, thesis optional; for doctorate, thesis/dissertation. *Entrance requirements:* For master's, appropriate bachelor's degree, proficiency in French; for doctorate, appropriate master's degree, proficiency in French. *Application deadline:* For fall admission, 3/30 for domestic and international students; for winter admission, 11/1 for domestic and international students. Application fee: $30. *Financial support:* Fellowships, research assistantships, teaching assistantships available. *Faculty research:* Land use, impacts of climate change, adaptation to climate change, integrated management of resources (mineral and water). *Unit head:* Yves Begin, Director, 418-654-2524, Fax: 418-654-2600, E-mail: info@ete.inrs.ca. *Application contact:* Yvonne Boisvert, Registrar, 418-654-3861, Fax: 418-654-3858, E-mail: registrariat@adm.inrs.ca.

Université Laval, Faculty of Sciences and Engineering, Department of Geology and Geological Engineering, Programs in Earth Sciences, Québec, QC G1K 7P4, Canada. Offers earth sciences (M Sc, PhD); environmental technologies (M Sc). Offered jointly with INRS-Géressources. Terminal master's awarded for partial completion of doctoral program. *Degree requirements:* For master's, thesis (for some programs); for doctorate, comprehensive exam, thesis/dissertation. *Entrance requirements:* For master's and doctorate, knowledge of French. Electronic applications accepted.

University at Albany, State University of New York, College of Arts and Sciences, Department of Earth and Atmospheric Sciences, Albany, NY 12222-0001. Offers atmospheric science (MS, PhD); geology (MS, PhD). *Degree requirements:* For master's, one foreign language, comprehensive exam, thesis; for doctorate, 2 foreign languages, comprehensive exam, thesis/dissertation, oral exams. *Entrance requirements:* For master's and doctorate, GRE General Test. Additional exam requirements/recommendations for international students: Required—TOEFL (minimum score 550 paper-based; 213 computer-based). Electronic applications accepted. *Faculty research:* Environmental geochemistry, tectonics, mesoscale meteorology, atmospheric chemistry.

University at Buffalo, the State University of New York, Graduate School, College of Arts and Sciences, Department of Geography, Buffalo, NY 14260. Offers earth systems science (MA); economic geography and international business and world trade (MA); environmental and earth systems science (MS); environmental modeling and analysis (MA); geographic information science (MA, Certificate); geographic information systems and science (MS); geography (MA, PhD); urban and regional geography (MA); MA/MBA. *Faculty:* 14 full-time (6 women), 2 part-time/adjunct (0 women). *Students:* 63 full-time (16 women), 32 part-time (8 women); includes 31 minority (3 African Americans, 26 Asian Americans or Pacific Islanders, 2 Hispanic Americans), 3 international. Average age 29. 154 applicants, 42% accepted, 24 enrolled. In 2009, 18 master's, 6 doctorates awarded. *Degree requirements:* For master's, thesis (for some programs), project; for doctorate, thesis/dissertation. *Entrance requirements:* For master's, GRE General Test, minimum GPA of 2.9; for doctorate, GRE General Test, minimum GPA of 3.0. Additional exam requirements/recommendations for international students: Required—TOEFL (minimum score 550 paper-based; 213 computer-based; 79 iBT). *Application deadline:* For fall admission, 7/1 priority date for domestic students, 1/10 priority date for international students; for spring admission, 12/1 priority date for domestic students, 10/1 priority date for international students. Applications are processed on a rolling basis. Application fee: $75. Electronic applications accepted. *Financial support:* In 2009–10, 19 students received support, including 6 fellowships with full tuition reimbursements available (averaging $4,333 per year), 14 teaching assistantships with full tuition reimbursements available (averaging $13,361 per year); research assistantships with full tuition reimbursements available, career-related internships or fieldwork, Federal Work-Study, institutionally sponsored loans, traineeships, health care benefits, and unspecified assistantships also available. Financial award application deadline: 1/10. *Faculty research:* International business and world trade, geographic information systems and cartography, transportation, urban and regional analysis, physical and environmental geography. Total annual research expenditures: $944,614. *Unit head:* Dr. Peter Rogerson, Chairman, 716-645-0473, Fax: 716-645-2329, E-mail: rogerson@buffalo.edu. *Application contact:* Betsy Abraham, Graduate Secretary, 716-645-0471, Fax: 716-645-2329, E-mail: babraham@buffalo.edu.

The University of Akron, Graduate School, Buchtel College of Arts and Sciences, Department of Geology, Program in Earth Science, Akron, OH 44325. Offers MS. *Students:* 4 full-time (2 women). Average age 26. 2 applicants, 50% accepted, 1 enrolled. In 2009, 2 master's awarded. *Degree requirements:* For master's, comprehensive exam, thesis, seminar, proficiency exam. *Entrance requirements:* For master's, minimum GPA of 2.75, letters of recommendation. Additional exam requirements/recommendations for international students: Required—TOEFL (minimum score 550 paper-based; 213 computer-based; 79 iBT). *Application deadline:* Applications are processed on a rolling basis. Application fee: $30 ($40 for international students). Electronic applications accepted. *Expenses:* Tuition, state resident: full-time $6570; part-time $365 per credit hour. Tuition, nonresident: full-time $11,250; part-time $625 per credit hour. *Unit head:* Dr. LaVerne Friberg, Director of Graduate Studies, 330-972-8046, E-mail: lfribe1@uakron.edu. *Application contact:* Dr. LaVerne Friberg, Director of Graduate Studies, 330-972-8046, E-mail: lfribe1@uakron.edu.

University of Alberta, Faculty of Graduate Studies and Research, Department of Earth and Atmospheric Sciences, Edmonton, AB T6G 2E1, Canada. Offers M Sc, MA, PhD. *Faculty:* 38 full-time (4 women), 15 part-time/adjunct (0 women). *Students:* 19 full-time (6 women). Average age 30. 88 applicants, 43% accepted. In 2009, 14 master's, 7 doctorates awarded. *Degree requirements:* For master's, thesis, residency; for doctorate, thesis/dissertation, residency. *Entrance requirements:* For master's, B Sc, minimum GPA of 6.5 on a 9.0 scale; for doctorate, M Sc. Additional exam requirements/recommendations for international students: Required—TOEFL or Michigan English Language Assessment Battery. *Application deadline:* Applications are processed on a rolling basis. Electronic applications accepted. Tuition and fees charges are reported in Canadian dollars. *Expenses:* Tuition, area resident: Full-time $4626.24 Canadian dollars; part-time $99.72 Canadian dollars per unit. International tuition: $8216 Canadian dollars full-time. Required fees: $3589.92 Canadian dollars; $99.72 Canadian dollars per unit. $215 Canadian dollars per term. *Financial support:* In 2009–10, 10 fellowships, 15 research assistantships were awarded; teaching assistantships, scholarships/grants and unspecified assistantships also available. *Faculty research:* Geology, human geography, physical geography, meteorology. Total annual research expenditures: $10 million. *Unit head:* Dr. Martin J. Sharp, Chair, 403-492-3329, Fax: 403-492-7598, E-mail: eas.inquiries@ualberta.ca. *Application contact:* Dr. Martin J. Sharp, Chair, 403-492-3329, Fax: 403-492-7598, E-mail: eas.inquiries@ualberta.ca.

The University of Arizona, Graduate College, College of Science, Department of Geosciences, Tucson, AZ 85721. Offers MS, PhD. Part-time programs available. *Faculty:* 23. *Students:* 65 full-time (23 women), 11 part-time (6 women); includes 2 minority (both Hispanic Americans), 15 international. Average age 29. 171 applicants, 15% accepted, 13 enrolled. In 2009, 14 master's, 12 doctorates awarded. Terminal master's awarded for partial completion of doctoral program. *Degree requirements:* For master's, thesis or prepublication; for doctorate, comprehensive exam, thesis/dissertation. *Entrance requirements:* For master's, GRE General Test, 3 letters of recommendation, curriculum vitae; for doctorate, GRE General Test, statement of purpose, 3 letters of recommendation, curriculum vitae. Additional exam requirements/recommendations for international students: Required—TOEFL (minimum score 550 paper-based; 213 computer-based; 79 iBT). *Application deadline:* For fall admission, 1/15 for domestic and international students. Applications are processed on a rolling basis. Application fee: $75. Electronic applications accepted. *Expenses:* Tuition, state resident: full-time $9028. Tuition, nonresident: full-time $24,890. *Financial support:* In 2009–10, 26 research assistantships with full tuition reimbursements (averaging $18,070 per year), 26 teaching assistantships with full tuition reimbursements (averaging $17,703 per year) were awarded; career-related internships or fieldwork, institutionally sponsored loans, scholarships/grants, health care benefits, tuition waivers (partial), and unspecified assistantships also available. Financial award application deadline: 1/15. *Faculty research:* Tectonics, geophysics, geochemistry/petrology, economic geology, Quaternary studies, stratigraphy/paleontology. Total annual research expenditures: $4.9 million. *Unit head:* Dr. Karl Flessa, Head, 520-621-7336, Fax: 520-621-2672, E-mail: kflessa@geo.arizona.edu. *Application contact:* Anne Chase, Graduate Program Office, 520-621-6004, Fax: 520-621-2672, E-mail: gradapps@geo.arizona.edu.

University of Arkansas at Little Rock, Graduate School, College of Science and Mathematics, Program in Geospatial Technology, Little Rock, AR 72204-1099. Offers Graduate Certificate.

University of California, Irvine, Office of Graduate Studies, School of Physical Sciences, Department of Earth System Science, Irvine, CA 92697. Offers MS, PhD. *Students:* 39 full-time (25 women); includes 3 minority (1 African American, 1 Asian American or Pacific Islander, 1 Hispanic American); 15 international. Average age 30. 38 applicants, 42% accepted, 9 enrolled. In 2009, 13 master's, 5 doctorates awarded. *Degree requirements:* For doctorate, thesis/dissertation. *Entrance requirements:* For master's and doctorate, GRE General Test, GRE Subject Test, minimum GPA of 3.0. Additional exam requirements/recommendations for international students: Required—TOEFL (minimum score 550 paper-based; 213 computer-based). *Application deadline:* For fall admission, 1/15 priority date for domestic students, 1/15 for international students. Applications are processed on a rolling basis. Application fee: $70 ($90 for international students). Electronic applications accepted. *Financial support:* Fellowships, research assistantships with full tuition reimbursements, teaching assistantships, career-related internships or fieldwork, institutionally sponsored loans, traineeships, health care benefits, and unspecified assistantships available. Financial award application deadline: 3/1; financial award applicants required to submit FAFSA. *Faculty research:* Atmospheric chemistry, climate change, isotope biogeochemistry, global environmental chemistry. *Unit head:* Eric Saltzman, Chair, 949-824-3936, Fax: 949-824-3256, E-mail: esaltzma@uci.edu. *Application contact:* Kathy Vonk, Department Assistant, 949-824-3876, Fax: 949-824-3256, E-mail: kvonk@uci.edu.

University of California, Los Angeles, Graduate Division, College of Letters and Science, Department of Earth and Space Sciences, Los Angeles, CA 90095. Offers geochemistry (MS, PhD); geology (MS, PhD); geophysics and space physics (MS, PhD). *Students:* 60 full-time (30 women); includes 5 minority (1 African American, 4 Asian Americans or Pacific Islanders), 15 international. Average age 28. 83 applicants, 31% accepted, 13 enrolled. In 2009, 6 master's, 7 doctorates awarded. Terminal master's awarded for partial completion of doctoral program. *Degree requirements:* For master's, comprehensive exams or thesis; for doctorate, thesis/dissertation, oral and written qualifying exams. *Entrance requirements:* For master's, GRE General Test, minimum GPA of 3.0; for doctorate, GRE General Test, minimum undergraduate GPA of 3.0. *Application deadline:* For fall admission, 1/15 for domestic and international students. Application fee: $70 ($90 for international students). Electronic applications accepted. *Financial support:* In 2009–10, 49 fellowships with full and partial tuition reimbursements, 50 research assistantships with full and partial tuition reimbursements, 32 teaching assistantships with full and partial tuition reimbursements were awarded; Federal Work-Study, institutionally sponsored loans, scholarships/grants, traineeships, health care benefits, tuition waivers (full and partial), and unspecified assistantships also available. Financial award application deadline: 3/1; financial award applicants required to submit FAFSA. *Unit head:* Craig Manning, Chair, 310-825-1475. *Application contact:* Departmental Office, 888-377-8252, E-mail: holbrook@ess.ucla.edu.

University of California, San Diego, Office of Graduate Studies, Scripps Institution of Oceanography, La Jolla, CA 92093. Offers earth sciences (PhD); marine biodiversity and conservation (MAS); marine biology (PhD); oceanography (PhD). *Entrance requirements:* For doctorate, GRE General Test, GRE Subject Test. Additional exam requirements/recommendations for international students: Required—TOEFL (minimum score 550 paper-based; 213 computer-based). Electronic applications accepted.

University of California, Santa Barbara, Graduate Division, College of Letters and Sciences, Division of Mathematics, Life, and Physical Sciences, Department of Earth Science, Santa Barbara, CA 93106-9620. Offers geological sciences (MS, PhD), including computational science and engineering (MS), geological sciences; geophysics (MS), including computational science and engineering, geophysics. *Faculty:* 20 full-time (4 women). *Students:* 35 full-time (15 women). Average age 27. 90 applicants, 27% accepted, 9 enrolled. In 2009, 3 master's, 4 doctorates awarded. *Degree requirements:* For master's, comprehensive exam, thesis; for doctorate, comprehensive exam, thesis/dissertation. *Entrance requirements:* For master's, GRE General Test, 3 letters of recommendation, resume/curriculum vitae; for doctorate, GRE General Test, 3 letters of recommendation, statement of purpose, personal achievements/contributions statement, resume/curriculum vitae, transcripts for post-secondary institutions attended. Additional exam requirements/recommendations for international students: Required—TOEFL (minimum score 550 paper-based; 213 computer-based; 80 iBT) or IELTS (minimum score 7). *Application deadline:* For fall admission, 2/1 for domestic students, 1/1 for international students. Application fee: $70 ($90 for international students). Electronic applications accepted. *Financial support:* In 2009–10, 35 students received support, including 21 fellowships with full and partial tuition reimbursements available (averaging $6,200 per year), 17 research assistantships with full and partial tuition reimbursements available (averaging $6,000 per year), 28 teaching assistantships with partial tuition reimbursements available (averaging $7,600 per year); career-related internships or fieldwork, Federal Work-Study, institutionally sponsored loans, scholarships/grants, traineeships, health care benefits, and unspecified assistantships also available. Financial award applicants required to submit FAFSA. *Faculty research:* Tectonics, geochronology, paleontology, volcanology, geomorphology. *Unit head:* Dr. Ralph Archuleta, Chair, 805-893-8441, E-mail: ralph@crustal.ucsb.edu. *Application contact:* Samuel C. Rifkin, Graduate Program Assistant, 805-893-3329, Fax: 805-893-2314, E-mail: rifkin@geol.ucsb.edu.

University of California, Santa Cruz, Division of Graduate Studies, Division of Physical and Biological Sciences, Department of Earth and Planetary Sciences, Santa Cruz, CA 95064. Offers MS, PhD. *Degree requirements:* For master's, thesis; for doctorate, one foreign language, thesis/dissertation, qualifying exam. *Entrance requirements:* For master's and doctorate, GRE General Test. Additional exam requirements/recommendations for international students: Required—TOEFL (minimum score 550 paper-based; 220 computer-based). *Faculty research:* Evolution of continental margins and orogenic belts, geologic processes occurring at plate boundaries, deep-sea sediment diagenesis, paleoecology, hydrogeology.

University of Chicago, Division of the Physical Sciences, Department of the Geophysical Sciences, Chicago, IL 60637-1513. Offers atmospheric sciences (SM, PhD); earth sciences (SM, PhD); paleobiology (PhD); planetary and space sciences (SM, PhD). *Faculty:* 21 full-time (3 women). *Students:* 37 full-time (23 women); includes 1 minority (Hispanic American), 14 international. Average age 27. 63 applicants, 35% accepted, 9 enrolled. In 2009, 1 doctorate awarded. Terminal master's awarded for partial completion of doctoral program. *Degree requirements:* For master's, thesis, seminar; for doctorate, variable foreign language requirement, comprehensive exam, thesis/dissertation. *Entrance requirements:* For doctorate, GRE General Test. Additional exam requirements/recommendations for international students: Required—TOEFL (minimum score 600 paper-based; 250 computer-based; 96 iBT), IELTS (minimum score 7). *Application deadline:* For fall admission, 1/10 for domestic and international students. Application fee: $55. Electronic applications accepted. *Financial support:* In 2009–10, research assistantships with full tuition reimbursements (averaging $20,511 per year), teaching assistantships with full tuition reimbursements (averaging $21,915 per year) were awarded; fellowships, Federal Work-Study, institutionally sponsored loans, scholarships/grants, tuition waivers (partial), and unspecified assistantships also available. Financial award application deadline: 1/15. *Faculty research:* Climatology, evolutionary paleontology, petrology, geochemistry, oceanic sciences. *Unit head:* Dr. Michael Foote, Chairman, 773-702-8102, Fax: 773-702-9505. *Application contact:* David J. Taylor, Graduate Student Services Coordinator, 773-702-8180, Fax: 773-702-9505, E-mail: info@geosci.uchicago.edu.

Geosciences

University of Florida, Graduate School, College of Liberal Arts and Sciences, Department of Geological Sciences, Gainesville, FL 32611. Offers geology (MS, MST, PhD). Terminal master's awarded for partial completion of doctoral program. *Degree requirements:* For master's, thesis (for some programs); for doctorate, one foreign language, thesis/dissertation. *Entrance requirements:* For master's and doctorate, GRE General Test, GRE Subject Test, minimum GPA of 3.0. Additional exam requirements/recommendations for international students: Required—TOEFL (minimum score 550 paper-based; 213 computer-based). Electronic applications accepted. *Faculty research:* Paleoclimatology, tectonophysics, petrochemistry, marine geology, geochemistry, hydrology.

University of Illinois at Chicago, Graduate College, College of Liberal Arts and Sciences, Department of Earth and Environmental Sciences, Chicago, IL 60607-7128. Offers MS, PhD. *Degree requirements:* For master's, thesis; for doctorate, thesis/dissertation. *Entrance requirements:* For master's and doctorate, GRE General Test, minimum GPA of 2.75. Additional exam requirements/recommendations for international students: Required—TOEFL. Electronic applications accepted.

University of Illinois at Urbana–Champaign, Graduate College, College of Liberal Arts and Sciences, School of Earth, Society and Environment, Department of Geology, Champaign, IL 61820. Offers geology (MS, PhD); teaching of earth sciences (MS). *Faculty:* 14 full-time (4 women). *Students:* 30 full-time (16 women), 2 part-time (1 woman); includes 2 minority (both Asian Americans or Pacific Islanders), 11 international. 53 applicants, 36% accepted, 8 enrolled. In 2009, 8 master's, 4 doctorates awarded. Terminal master's awarded for partial completion of doctoral program. *Entrance requirements:* For master's and doctorate, GRE General Test, minimum GPA of 3.0. Additional exam requirements/recommendations for international students: Required—TOEFL. *Application deadline:* Applications are processed on a rolling basis. Application fee: $60 ($75 for international students). Electronic applications accepted. *Financial support:* In 2009–10, 3 fellowships, 16 research assistantships, 16 teaching assistantships were awarded; Federal Work-Study and tuition waivers (full and partial) also available. *Faculty research:* Hydrogeology, structure/tectonics, mineral science. *Unit head:* Wang-Ping Chen, Head, 217-333-2744, Fax: 217-244-4996, E-mail: wpchen@illinois.edu. *Application contact:* Marilyn K. Whalen, Office Administrator, 217-333-3542, Fax: 217-244-4996, E-mail: mkt@illinois.edu.

The University of Iowa, Graduate College, College of Liberal Arts and Sciences, Department of Geoscience, Iowa City, IA 52242-1316. Offers MS, PhD. *Degree requirements:* For master's, thesis optional, exam; for doctorate, comprehensive exam, thesis/dissertation. *Entrance requirements:* For master's and doctorate, GRE General Test, minimum GPA of 3.0. Additional exam requirements/recommendations for international students: Required—TOEFL (minimum score 550 paper-based; 213 computer-based; 81 iBT). Electronic applications accepted.

University of Maine, Graduate School, College of Natural Sciences, Forestry, and Agriculture, Department of Earth Sciences, Orono, ME 04469. Offers MS, PhD. Part-time programs available. *Faculty:* 9 full-time (2 women), 1 part-time/adjunct (0 women). *Students:* 16 full-time (8 women), 11 part-time (4 women), 5 international. Average age 27. 23 applicants, 70% accepted, 6 enrolled. In 2009, 4 master's, 1 doctorate awarded. *Degree requirements:* For master's, thesis; for doctorate, one foreign language, thesis/dissertation. *Entrance requirements:* For master's and doctorate, GRE General Test. Additional exam requirements/recommendations for international students: Required—TOEFL. *Application deadline:* For fall admission, 2/1 priority date for domestic students. Applications are processed on a rolling basis. Application fee: $65. Electronic applications accepted. *Financial support:* In 2009–10, 5 research assistantships with tuition reimbursements (averaging $16,130 per year), 6 teaching assistantships with tuition reimbursements (averaging $12,790 per year) were awarded; Federal Work-Study, institutionally sponsored loans, and tuition waivers (full and partial) also available. Financial award application deadline: 3/1. *Faculty research:* Appalachian bedrock geology, Quaternary studies, marine geology. *Unit head:* Dr. Joseph Kelley, Chair, 207-581-2162, Fax: 207-581-2202. *Application contact:* Scott G. Delcourt, Associate Dean of the Graduate School, 207-581-3291, Fax: 207-581-3232, E-mail: graduate@maine.edu.

University of Massachusetts Amherst, Graduate School, College of Natural Sciences, Department of Geosciences, Program in Geosciences, Amherst, MA 01003. Offers MS, PhD. Part-time programs available. *Students:* 30 full-time (15 women), 25 part-time (14 women); includes 1 minority (Asian American or Pacific Islander), 8 international. Average age 34. 60 applicants, 43% accepted, 12 enrolled. In 2009, 12 master's, 5 doctorates awarded. Terminal master's awarded for partial completion of doctoral program. *Degree requirements:* For master's, thesis or alternative; for doctorate, one foreign language, comprehensive exam, thesis/dissertation. *Entrance requirements:* For master's and doctorate, GRE General Test. Additional exam requirements/recommendations for international students: Required—TOEFL (minimum score 550 paper-based; 213 computer-based; 80 iBT), IELTS (minimum score 6.5). *Application deadline:* For fall admission, 1/15 for domestic and international students; for spring admission, 10/1 for domestic and international students. Applications are processed on a rolling basis. Application fee: $50 ($65 for international students). Electronic applications accepted. *Expenses:* Tuition, state resident: full-time $2640; part-time $110 per credit. Tuition, nonresident: full-time $9936; part-time $414 per credit. Tuition and fees vary according to course load. *Financial support:* Fellowships, research assistantships, teaching assistantships, career-related internships or fieldwork, Federal Work-Study, scholarships/grants, traineeships, health care benefits, tuition waivers (full), and unspecified assistantships available. Support available to part-time students. Financial award application deadline: 1/15. *Unit head:* Dr. Sheila J. Seaman, Graduate Program Director, 413-545-2286, Fax: 413-545-1200. *Application contact:* Jean M. Ames, Supervisor of Admissions, 413-545-0722, Fax: 413-577-0010, E-mail: gradadm@grad.umass.edu.

University of Missouri–Kansas City, College of Arts and Sciences, Department of Geosciences, Kansas City, MO 64110-2499. Offers environmental and urban geosciences (MS); geosciences (PhD). PhD (interdisciplinary) offered through the School of Graduate Studies. Part-time programs available. *Faculty:* 11 full-time (3 women), 1 part-time/adjunct (0 women). *Students:* 6 full-time (3 women), 14 part-time (6 women); includes 2 minority (both Hispanic Americans), 2 international. Average age 34. 16 applicants, 56% accepted, 6 enrolled. In 2009, 1 degree awarded. *Degree requirements:* For master's, thesis; for doctorate, thesis/dissertation. *Entrance requirements:* For master's, GRE General Test, minimum GPA of 3.0; for doctorate, qualifying exam. Additional exam requirements/recommendations for international students: Required—TOEFL (minimum score 550 paper-based; 213 computer-based; 80 iBT). *Application deadline:* For fall admission, 3/15 priority date for domestic and international students. Applications are processed on a rolling basis. Application fee: $45 ($50 for international students). Electronic applications accepted. *Expenses:* Tuition, state resident: full-time $5378; part-time $299 per credit hour. Tuition, nonresident: full-time $13,881; part-time $771 per credit hour. Required fees: $641; $71 per credit hour. Tuition and fees vary according to course load and program. *Financial support:* In 2009–10, 2 research assistantships with partial tuition reimbursements (averaging $10,200 per year), 10 teaching assistantships with partial tuition reimbursements (averaging $10,550 per year) were awarded; Federal Work-Study, institutionally sponsored loans, and tuition waivers (full and partial) also available. Support available to part-time students. Financial award application deadline: 3/1; financial award applicants required to submit FAFSA. *Faculty research:* Neotectonics and applied geophysics, environmental geosciences, urban geoscience, geoinformatics–remote sensing, atmospheric research. Total annual research expenditures: $481,906. *Unit head:* Dr. Jimmy Adegoke, Chair, 816-235-1334, Fax: 816-235-5535, E-mail: adegokej@umkc.edu. *Application contact:* Dr. Ray Coveney, Associate Professor, 816-235-1334, Fax: 816-235-5535, E-mail: coveneyr@umkc.edu.

The University of Montana, Graduate School, College of Arts and Sciences, Department of Geology, Missoula, MT 59812-0002. Offers applied geoscience (PhD); geology (MS, PhD). *Degree requirements:* For doctorate, thesis/dissertation. *Entrance requirements:* For master's and doctorate, GRE General Test. Additional exam requirements/recommendations for international students: Required—TOEFL (minimum score 525 paper-based; 197 computer-based). *Faculty research:* Environmental geoscience, regional structure and tectonics, groundwater geology, petrology, mineral deposits.

University of Nebraska–Lincoln, Graduate College, College of Arts and Sciences, Department of Geosciences, Lincoln, NE 68588. Offers MS, PhD. *Degree requirements:* For master's, thesis optional, departmental qualifying exam; for doctorate, comprehensive exam, thesis/dissertation, departmental qualifying exams. *Entrance requirements:* For master's and doctorate, GRE General Test. Additional exam requirements/recommendations for international students: Required—TOEFL (minimum score 550 paper-based; 213 computer-based). Electronic applications accepted. *Faculty research:* Hydrogeology, sedimentology, environmental geology, vertebrate paleontology.

University of Nevada, Las Vegas, Graduate College, College of Science, Department of Geoscience, Las Vegas, NV 89154-4010. Offers MS, PhD. Part-time programs available. *Faculty:* 16 full-time (3 women), 1 (woman) part-time/adjunct. *Students:* 36 full-time (15 women), 13 part-time (6 women); includes 5 minority (2 African Americans, 1 American Indian/Alaska Native, 1 Asian American or Pacific Islander, 1 Hispanic American), 6 international. Average age 31. 32 applicants, 66% accepted, 9 enrolled. In 2009, 6 master's, 2 doctorates awarded. *Degree requirements:* For master's, comprehensive exam, thesis; for doctorate, comprehensive exam, thesis/dissertation. *Entrance requirements:* For master's and doctorate, GRE General Test. Additional exam requirements/recommendations for international students: Required—TOEFL (minimum score 550 paper-based; 213 computer-based; 80 iBT), IELTS (minimum score 7). *Application deadline:* For fall admission, 2/1 priority date for domestic and international students; for spring admission, 10/1 priority date for domestic and international students. Applications are processed on a rolling basis. Application fee: $60 ($95 for international students). Electronic applications accepted. *Financial support:* In 2009–10, 37 students received support, including 1 fellowship with full tuition reimbursement available (averaging $20,000 per year), 14 research assistantships with partial tuition reimbursements available (averaging $16,706 per year), 22 teaching assistantships with partial tuition reimbursements available (averaging $12,318 per year); institutionally sponsored loans, scholarships/grants, health care benefits, and unspecified assistantships also available. Financial award application deadline: 3/1. *Faculty research:* Geochemistry, hydrogeology, paleontology, environmental geology, volcanology. *Unit head:* Dr. Michael Wells, Chair/ Professor, 702-895-0828, Fax: 702-895-4064, E-mail: michael.wells@unlv.edu. *Application contact:* Graduate College Admissions Evaluator, 702-895-3320, Fax: 702-895-4180, E-mail: gradcollege@unlv.edu.

University of New Hampshire, Graduate School, College of Engineering and Physical Sciences, Department of Earth Sciences, Durham, NH 03824. Offers earth sciences (MS), including geochemical systems, geology, ocean mapping, oceanography; hydrology (MS). *Faculty:* 17 full-time (5 women). *Students:* 7 full-time (5 women), 15 part-time (7 women), 1 international. Average age 27. 27 applicants, 56% accepted, 5 enrolled. In 2009, 18 master's awarded. *Degree requirements:* For master's, thesis. *Entrance requirements:* For master's, GRE General Test. Additional exam requirements/recommendations for international students: Required—TOEFL (minimum score 550 paper-based; 213 computer-based; 80 iBT). *Application deadline:* For fall admission, 4/1 priority date for domestic students, 4/1 for international students; for spring admission, 12/1 for domestic students. Applications are processed on a rolling basis. Application fee: $65. Electronic applications accepted. *Expenses:* Tuition, state resident: full-time $10,380; part-time $577 per credit hour. Tuition, nonresident: full-time $24,350; part-time $1002 per credit hour. Required fees: $1550; $387.50 per semester. Tuition and fees vary according to course load and program. *Financial support:* In 2009–10, 17 students received support, including 1 fellowship, 6 research assistantships, 8 teaching assistantships; career-related internships or fieldwork, Federal Work-Study, scholarships/grants, and tuition waivers (full and partial) also available. Support available to part-time students. Financial award application deadline: 2/15. *Unit head:* Dr. Will Clyde, Chairperson, 603-862-1718, E-mail: earth.sciences@unh.edu. *Application contact:* Sue Clark, Administrative Assistant, 603-862-1718, E-mail: earth.sciences@unh.edu.

University of New Haven, Graduate School, College of Arts and Sciences, Program in Environmental Sciences, West Haven, CT 06516-1916. Offers environmental ecology (Certificate); environmental geoscience (MS); environmental health and management (MS); environmental science (MS); geographical information systems (Certificate). Part-time and evening/weekend programs available. *Faculty:* 6 full-time (3 women), 8 part-time/adjunct (2 women). *Students:* 8 full-time (5 women), 21 part-time (9 women); includes 2 minority (both African Americans), 4 international. Average age 27. 28 applicants, 79% accepted, 4 enrolled. In 2009, 7 master's, 5 other advanced degrees awarded. *Degree requirements:* For master's, thesis or alternative. *Entrance requirements:* Additional exam requirements/recommendations for international students: Required—TOEFL (minimum score 520 paper-based; 190 computer-based; 70 iBT); Recommended—IELTS (minimum score 5.5). *Application deadline:* For fall admission, 5/31 for international students; for winter admission, 10/15 for international students; for spring admission, 1/15 for international students. Applications are processed on a rolling basis. Application fee: $50. Electronic applications accepted. *Expenses:* Tuition: Part-time $700 per credit. Required fees: $45 per term. One-time fee: $390 part-time. *Financial support:* Research assistantships with partial tuition reimbursements, teaching assistantships with partial tuition reimbursements, career-related internships or fieldwork, Federal Work-Study, scholarships/grants, tuition waivers, and unspecified assistantships available. Support available to part-time students. Financial award applicants required to submit FAFSA. *Faculty research:* Mapping and assessing geological and living resources in Long Island Sound, geology, San Salvador Island, Bahamas. *Unit head:* Dr. Roman Zajac, Coordinator, 203-932-7108. *Application contact:* Eloise Gormley, Director of Graduate Admissions, 203-932-7449, Fax: 203-932-7137, E-mail: gradinfo@newhaven.edu.

University of New Mexico, Graduate School, College of Arts and Sciences, Department of Earth and Planetary Sciences, Albuquerque, NM 87131-2039. Offers MS, PhD. Part-time programs available. *Faculty:* 26 full-time (7 women), 4 part-time/adjunct (1 woman). *Students:* 48 full-time (30 women), 7 part-time (6 women); includes 3 minority (1 American Indian/Alaska Native, 2 Hispanic Americans), 6 international. Average age 30. 40 applicants, 18% accepted, 7 enrolled. In 2009, 6 master's, 2 doctorates awarded. Terminal master's awarded for partial completion of doctoral program. *Degree requirements:* For master's, comprehensive exam, thesis; for doctorate, comprehensive exam, thesis/dissertation. *Entrance requirements:* For master's and doctorate, GRE General Test. Additional exam requirements/recommendations for international students: Required—TOEFL. *Application deadline:* For fall admission, 1/31 priority date for domestic students, 1/31 for international students; for spring admission, 11/1 priority date for domestic and international students. Application fee: $50. Electronic applications accepted. *Expenses:* Tuition, state resident: full-time $2098.80; part-time $233.20 per credit hour. Tuition, nonresident: full-time $6650. Required fees: $25 per semester. Tuition and fees vary according to course load, program and reciprocity agreements. *Financial support:* In 2009–10, 17 students received support, including 2 fellowships with full tuition reimbursements available (averaging $22,500 per year), 24 research assistantships with full tuition reimbursements available (averaging $17,000 per year), 15 teaching assistantships with full tuition reimbursements available (averaging $16,900 per year); scholarships/grants and health care benefits also available. Financial award application deadline: 1/31; financial award applicants required to submit FAFSA. *Faculty research:* Climatology, experimental petrology, geochemistry, geographic information technologies, geomorphology, geophysics, hydrogeology, ingeneous petrology, metamorphic petrology, meteoritics, meteorology, micrometeorites, mineralogy, paleoclimatology, paleonology, pedology, petrology, physical volcanology, planetary sciences, precambrian geology, quantenary geology, sedimentary geochemistry, sedimentology, stable isotope geochemistry, stratigraphy, structural geology, tectonics, volcanology. Total annual research expenditures: $2.5 million. *Unit head:* Dr. John W. Geissman, Chair, 505-277-4204, Fax: 505-277-8843, E-mail: jgeiss@unm.edu. *Application contact:* Cindy Jaramillo, Administrative Assistant II, 505-277-1635, Fax: 505-277-8843, E-mail: epsdept@unm.edu.

University of New Orleans, Graduate School, College of Sciences, Department of Earth and Environmental Sciences, New Orleans, LA 70148. Offers MS. Evening/weekend programs available. *Degree requirements:* For master's, thesis. *Entrance requirements:* For master's, GRE General Test. Additional exam requirements/recommendations for international students: Required—TOEFL (minimum score 550 paper-based; 213 computer-based; 79 iBT). Electronic applications accepted. *Faculty research:* Continental margin structure and seismology, burial diagenesis of siliclastic sediments, tectonics at convergent plate margins, continental shelf sediment stability, early diagenesis of carbonates.

The University of North Carolina at Charlotte, Graduate School, College of Arts and Sciences, Department of Geography and Earth Sciences, Program in Earth Sciences, Charlotte, NC 28223-0001. Offers MS. Part-time and evening/weekend programs available. *Faculty:* 25 full-time (8 women), 1 part-time/adjunct (0 women). *Students:* 14 full-time (3 women), 20 part-time (7 women), 2 international. Average age 28. 21 applicants, 71% accepted, 14 enrolled. In 2009, 3 master's awarded. *Degree requirements:* For master's, thesis optional. *Entrance requirements:* For master's, GRE General Test, minimum GPA of 3.0 in science major. Additional exam requirements/recommendations for international students: Required—TOEFL (minimum score 557 paper-based; 220 computer-based; 83 iBT). *Application deadline:* For fall admission, 7/1 for domestic students, 5/1 for international students; for spring admission, 11/1 for domestic students, 10/1 for international students. Applications are processed on a rolling basis. Application fee: $55. Electronic applications accepted. *Financial support:* In 2009–10, 9 students received support, including 9 teaching assistantships (averaging $7,748 per year). Financial award application deadline: 4/1; financial award applicants required to submit FAFSA. *Faculty research:* Environmental geology, trace element geochemistry, geomorphology, hydrogeology, mineralogy and petrology. *Unit head:* Dr. Andy Bobyarchick, Graduate Coordinator, 704-687-5998, Fax: 704-687-3182, E-mail: arbobyar@uncc.edu. *Application contact:* Kathy B. Giddings, Director of Graduate Admissions, 704-687-5503, Fax: 704-687-3279, E-mail: gradadm@uncc.edu.

The University of North Carolina Wilmington, College of Arts and Sciences, Department of Geography and Geology, Wilmington, NC 28403-3297. Offers geology (MS); marine science (MS). *Degree requirements:* For master's, comprehensive exam, thesis. *Entrance requirements:* For master's, GRE General Test, GRE Subject Test, minimum B average in undergraduate major and basic courses for prerequisite to geology.

University of North Dakota, Graduate School, Program in Earth System Science and Policy, Grand Forks, ND 58202. Offers MEM, MS, PhD. Part-time programs available. *Degree requirements:* For master's, thesis (for some programs); for doctorate, thesis/dissertation (for some programs). *Entrance requirements:* For master's and doctorate, GRE General Test, minimum GPA of 3.0. Additional exam requirements/recommendations for international students: Required—TOEFL (minimum score 550 paper-based; 213 computer-based; 79 iBT); IELTS (minimum score 6.5). Electronic applications accepted.

University of Northern Colorado, Graduate School, College of Natural and Health Sciences, School of Chemistry, Earth Sciences and Physics, Program in Earth Sciences, Greeley, CO 80639. Offers MA. Part-time programs available. *Faculty:* 8 full-time (2 women). *Students:* 9 full-time (5 women), 4 part-time (1 woman), 1 international. Average age 35. 7 applicants, 71% accepted, 4 enrolled. *Degree requirements:* For master's, comprehensive exam. *Entrance requirements:* For master's, GRE General Test, 3 letters of recommendation. *Application deadline:* Applications are processed on a rolling basis. Application fee: $50 ($60 for international students). Electronic applications accepted. *Expenses:* Tuition, state resident: full-time $5770; part-time $320.55 per credit hour. Tuition, nonresident: full-time $13,847; part-time $769.27 per credit hour. Required fees: $948.78; $52.72 per credit. *Financial support:* In 2009–10, 1 research assistantship (averaging $3,011 per year), 4 teaching assistantships (averaging $7,622 per year) were awarded; fellowships, unspecified assistantships also available. Financial award application deadline: 3/1; financial award applicants required to submit FAFSA. *Unit head:* Dr. Emmett Evanoff, Program Coordinator, 970-351-2647. *Application contact:* Linda Sisson, Graduate Student Admission Coordinator, 970-351-1807, Fax: 970-351-2371, E-mail: linda.sisson@unco.edu.

University of Notre Dame, Graduate School, College of Engineering, Department of Civil Engineering and Geological Sciences, Notre Dame, IN 46556. Offers bioengineering (MS Bio E); civil engineering (MSCE); civil engineering and geological sciences (PhD); environmental engineering (MS Env E); geological sciences (MS). Terminal master's awarded for partial completion of doctoral program. *Degree requirements:* For master's, comprehensive exam; for doctorate, thesis/dissertation, candidacy exam. *Entrance requirements:* For master's and doctorate, GRE General Test. Additional exam requirements/recommendations for international students: Required—TOEFL (minimum score 600 paper-based; 250 computer-based; 80 iBT). Electronic applications accepted. *Faculty research:* Environmental modeling, biological-waste treatment, petrology, environmental geology, geochemistry.

University of Ottawa, Faculty of Graduate and Postdoctoral Studies, Faculty of Science, Ottawa-Carleton Geoscience Centre, Ottawa, ON K1N 6N5, Canada. Offers earth sciences (M Sc, PhD). *Degree requirements:* For master's, thesis, seminar; for doctorate, comprehensive exam, thesis/dissertation, seminar. *Entrance requirements:* For master's, honors B Sc degree or equivalent, minimum B average; for doctorate, honors B Sc with minimum B average or M Sc with minimum B+ average. Electronic applications accepted. *Faculty research:* Environmental geoscience, geochemistry/petrology, geomatics/geomathematics, mineral resource studies.

University of Pennsylvania, School of Arts and Sciences, Graduate Group in Earth and Environmental Science, Philadelphia, PA 19104. Offers MS, PhD. Part-time programs available. *Faculty:* 8 full-time (0 women), 3 part-time/adjunct (0 women). *Students:* 17 full-time (9 women), 6 international. 27 applicants, 22% accepted, 6 enrolled. In 2009, 5 doctorates awarded. *Degree requirements:* For master's, one foreign language, thesis; for doctorate, one foreign language, thesis/dissertation. *Entrance requirements:* For master's and doctorate, GRE General Test. Additional exam requirements/recommendations for international students: Required—TOEFL. *Application deadline:* For fall admission, 12/1 priority date for domestic students. Application fee: $70. Electronic applications accepted. *Expenses:* Tuition: Full-time $25,660; part-time $4758 per course. Required fees: $2152; $270 per course. Tuition and fees vary according to course load, degree level and program. *Financial support:* Fellowships, research assistantships, teaching assistantships, institutionally sponsored loans, scholarships/grants, traineeships, health care benefits, and unspecified assistantships available. Financial award application deadline: 12/15. *Faculty research:* Isotope geochemistry, regional tectonics, environmental geology, metamorphic and igneous petrology, paleontology.

University of Rhode Island, Graduate School, College of the Environment and Life Sciences, Department of Geosciences, Kingston, RI 02881. Offers environmental science and management (MESM); environmental sciences (MS, PhD). Part-time programs available. *Faculty:* 5 full-time (1 woman), 2 part-time/adjunct (0 women). *Students:* 7 full-time (2 women), 6 part-time (4 women). In 2009, 2 doctorates awarded. *Degree requirements:* For master's, comprehensive exam (for some programs), thesis optional; for doctorate, comprehensive exam, thesis/dissertation. *Entrance requirements:* For master's and doctorate, GRE, 2 letters of recommendation. Additional exam requirements/recommendations for international students: Required—TOEFL (minimum score 550 paper-based; 213 computer-based). *Application deadline:* For fall admission, 7/15 for domestic students, 2/1 for international students; for spring admission, 11/15 for domestic students, 7/15 for international students. Application fee: $65. Electronic applications accepted. *Expenses:* Tuition, state resident: full-time $8828; part-time $490 per credit hour. Tuition, nonresident: full-time $22,100; part-time $1228 per credit hour. Required fees: $1118; $57 per semester. Tuition and fees vary according to program. *Financial support:* In 2009–10, 1 research assistantship with partial tuition reimbursement (averaging $7,403 per year), 5 teaching assistantships with full tuition reimbursements (averaging $13,894 per year) were awarded. Financial award application deadline: 7/15; financial award applicants required to submit FAFSA. *Faculty research:* Hydrology and water resources, interior of the earth, quaternary and modern depositional environments, geobiology of Mesozoic terrestrial ecosystems. Total annual research expenditures: $1.7 million. *Unit head:* Dr. Anne Veeger, Chair, 401-874-2187, Fax: 401-874-2190, E-mail: veeger@uri.edu. *Application contact:* Dr. Thomas Boving, Director of Graduate Studies, 401-874-7053, Fax: 401-874-2190, E-mail: boving@uri.edu.

University of Rochester, The College, Arts and Sciences, Department of Earth and Environmental Sciences, Rochester, NY 14627. Offers geological sciences (MS, PhD). *Degree requirements:* For doctorate, thesis/dissertation, qualifying exam. *Entrance requirements:* For master's and doctorate, GRE General Test. Additional exam requirements/recommendations for international students: Required—TOEFL.

University of South Carolina, The Graduate School, College of Arts and Sciences, Department of Geological Sciences, Columbia, SC 29208. Offers MS, PhD. Terminal master's awarded for partial completion of doctoral program. *Degree requirements:* For master's, thesis; for doctorate, comprehensive exam, thesis/dissertation, published paper. *Entrance requirements:* For master's and doctorate, GRE General Test. Additional exam requirements/recommendations for international students: Required—TOEFL (minimum score 570 paper-based; 230 computer-based; 75 iBT). Electronic applications accepted. *Faculty research:* Environmental geology, tectonics, petrology, coastal processes, paleoclimatology.

University of Southern California, Graduate School, College of Letters, Arts and Sciences, Department of Earth Sciences, Los Angeles, CA 90089. Offers geological sciences (MS, PhD). MS is incidental for PhD or self-funded students. Part-time programs available. *Faculty:* 20 full-time (2 women), 3 part-time/adjunct (1 woman). *Students:* 54 full-time (24 women), 2 part-time (1 woman); includes 9 minority (1 African American, 5 Asian Americans or Pacific Islanders, 3 Hispanic Americans), 17 international. 55 applicants, 44% accepted, 18 enrolled. In 2009, 12 doctorates awarded. Terminal master's awarded for partial completion of doctoral program. *Degree requirements:* For master's, thesis; for doctorate, comprehensive exam, thesis/dissertation. *Entrance requirements:* For master's and doctorate, GRE. *Application deadline:* For fall admission, 1/1 priority date for domestic and international students; for spring admission, 10/15 priority date for domestic students, 9/1 priority date for international students. Applications are processed on a rolling basis. Application fee: $85. Electronic applications accepted. *Expenses:* Tuition: Full-time $25,980; part-time $1315 per unit. Required fees: $554. One-time fee: $35 full-time. Full-time tuition and fees vary according to degree level and program. *Financial support:* In 2009–10, 49 students received support, including 12 fellowships with full tuition reimbursements available (averaging $21,000 per year), 14 research assistantships with full tuition reimbursements available (averaging $19,300 per year), 25 teaching assistantships with full tuition reimbursements available (averaging $19,300 per year); health care benefits also available. *Faculty research:* Geophysics, paleoceanography, geochemistry, geobiology, structure, tectonics. Total annual research expenditures: $13 million. *Unit head:* Prof. David J. Bottjer, Chair, 213-740-6601, Fax: 213-740-8801, E-mail: dbottjer@usc.edu. *Application contact:* Cynthia Waite, Academic Advisor, 213-740-6109, Fax: 213-740-8801, E-mail: waite@usc.edu.

The University of Texas at Austin, Graduate School, Jackson School of Geosciences, Austin, TX 78712-1111. Offers MA, MS, PhD. Part-time programs available. *Degree requirements:* For master's, report (MA), thesis (MS); for doctorate, thesis/dissertation. *Entrance requirements:* For master's and doctorate, GRE General Test. Electronic applications accepted. *Faculty research:* Sedimentary geology, geophysics, hydrogeology, structure/tectonics, vertebrate paleontology.

The University of Texas at Dallas, School of Natural Sciences and Mathematics, Program in Geosciences, Richardson, TX 75080. Offers geochemistry (MS, PhD); geophysics (MS); geospatial information sciences (MS, PhD); hydrogeology (MS, PhD); sedimentary, stratigraphy, paleontology (PhD); stratigraphy, paleontology (MS); structural geology and tectonics (MS, PhD). Part-time and evening/weekend programs available. *Faculty:* 9 full-time (1 woman). *Students:* 30 full-time (10 women), 11 part-time (4 women); includes 7 minority (1 African American, 4 Asian Americans or Pacific Islanders, 2 Hispanic Americans), 21 international. Average age 32. 42 applicants, 43% accepted, 14 enrolled. In 2009, 4 master's, 4 doctorates awarded. *Degree requirements:* For master's, thesis optional; for doctorate, thesis/dissertation. *Entrance requirements:* For master's and doctorate, GRE General Test, minimum GPA of 3.0 in upper-level course work in field. Additional exam requirements/recommendations for international students: Required—TOEFL (minimum score 550 paper-based; 213 computer-based). *Application deadline:* For fall admission, 7/15 for domestic students, 5/1 priority date for international students; for spring admission, 11/15 for domestic students, 9/1 priority date for international students. Applications are processed on a rolling basis. Application fee: $50 ($100 for international students). Electronic applications accepted. *Expenses:* Tuition, state resident: full-time $11,068; part-time $461 per credit hour. Tuition, nonresident: full-time $21,178; part-time $882 per credit hour. Tuition and fees vary according to course load. *Financial support:* In 2009–10, 10 research assistantships with full tuition reimbursements (averaging $13,500 per year), 11 teaching assistantships with full tuition reimbursements (averaging $13,500 per year) were awarded; fellowships, career-related internships or fieldwork, Federal Work-Study, institutionally sponsored loans, scholarships/grants, and unspecified assistantships also available. Support available to part-time students. Financial award application deadline: 4/30; financial award applicants required to submit FAFSA. *Faculty research:* Hydrology, organic geochemistry, tectonic structures, seismic characteristics, digital geologic mapping. *Unit head:* Dr. John Oldow, Department Head, 972-883-2401, Fax: 972-883-2537, E-mail: geosciences@utdallas.edu. *Application contact:* Dr. Robert J. Stem, Graduate Advisor, 972-883-2442, Fax: 972-883-2537, E-mail: rjstern@utdallas.edu.

The University of Toledo, College of Graduate Studies, College of Arts and Sciences, Department of Environmental Sciences, Toledo, OH 43606-3390. Offers biology (ecology track) (MS, PhD); geology (MS), including earth surface processes, general geology. Part-time programs available. *Degree requirements:* For master's, thesis. *Entrance requirements:* For master's, GRE General Test. Additional exam requirements/recommendations for international students: Required—TOEFL. Electronic applications accepted. *Faculty research:* Environmental geochemistry, geophysics, petrology and mineralogy, paleontology, geohydrology.

University of Tulsa, Graduate School, College of Engineering and Natural Sciences, Department of Geosciences, Tulsa, OK 74104-3189. Offers MS, PhD, JD/MS. Part-time programs available. *Faculty:* 9 full-time (1 woman), 1 (woman) part-time/adjunct. *Students:* 12 full-time (7 women), 9 part-time (5 women); includes 2 minority (1 African American, 1 American Indian/Alaska Native), 6 international. Average age 28. 35 applicants, 57% accepted, 9 enrolled. In 2009, 2 master's awarded. *Degree requirements:* For master's, thesis (for some programs); for doctorate, comprehensive exam, thesis/dissertation. *Entrance requirements:* For master's and doctorate, GRE General Test. Additional exam requirements/recommendations for international students: Required—TOEFL (minimum score 550 paper-based; 213 computer-based; 80 iBT), IELTS (minimum score 6). *Application deadline:* Applications are processed on a rolling basis.

Geosciences

University of Tulsa (continued)

Application fee: $40. Electronic applications accepted. *Expenses:* Tuition: Full-time $16,182; part-time $899 per credit hour. Required fees: $4 per credit hour. Tuition and fees vary according to course load. *Financial support:* In 2009–10, 9 students received support, including 1 fellowship with full and partial tuition reimbursement available (averaging $3,950 per year), 3 research assistantships with full and partial tuition reimbursements available (averaging $8,036 per year), 6 teaching assistantships with full and partial tuition reimbursements available (averaging $11,665 per year); career-related internships or fieldwork, scholarships/grants, health care benefits, tuition waivers (full and partial), and unspecified assistantships also available. Support available to part-time students. Financial award application deadline: 2/1; financial award applicants required to submit FAFSA. *Faculty research:* Petroleum exploration/production and environmental science, including clastic sedimentology, petroleum seismology, seismic stratigraphy, structural geology, geochemistry, and biogeoscience. Total annual research expenditures: $969,189. *Unit head:* Dr. Bryan Tapp, Chairperson, 918-631-3018, Fax: 918-631-2091, E-mail: jbt@utulsa.edu. *Application contact:* Dr. Peter J. Michael, Adviser, 918-631-3017, Fax: 918-631-2156, E-mail: pjm@utulsa.edu.

University of Victoria, Faculty of Graduate Studies, Faculty of Science, School of Earth and Ocean Sciences, Victoria, BC V8W 2Y2, Canada. Offers M Sc, PhD. Part-time programs available. *Degree requirements:* For master's, thesis; for doctorate, thesis/dissertation, candidacy exam. *Entrance requirements:* For master's and doctorate, GRE. Additional exam requirements/recommendations for international students: Required—TOEFL (minimum score 575 paper-based; 233 computer-based), IELTS (minimum score 7). Electronic applications accepted. *Faculty research:* Climate modeling, geology.

University of Waterloo, Graduate Studies, Faculty of Science, Department of Earth Sciences, Waterloo, ON N2L 3G1, Canada. Offers M Sc, PhD. Part-time programs available. *Degree requirements:* For master's, research paper or thesis; for doctorate, comprehensive exam, thesis/dissertation. *Entrance requirements:* For master's, GRE, honors degree, minimum B average; for doctorate, GRE, master's degree, minimum B average. Additional exam requirements/recommendations for international students: Required—TOEFL, TWE. Electronic applications accepted. *Faculty research:* Environmental geology, soil physics.

The University of Western Ontario, Faculty of Graduate Studies, Physical Sciences Division, Department of Earth Sciences, London, ON N6A 5B8, Canada. Offers environment and sustainability (MES); geology (M Sc, PhD); geology and environmental science (M Sc, PhD); geophysics (M Sc, PhD); geophysics and environmental science (M Sc, PhD). *Degree requirements:* For master's, thesis; for doctorate, thesis/dissertation, qualifying exam. *Entrance requirements:* For master's, honors in B Sc; for doctorate, M Sc. Additional exam requirements/recommendations for international students: Required—TOEFL. *Faculty research:* Geophysics, geochemistry, paleontology, sedimentology/stratigraphy, glaciology/quaternary.

University of Windsor, Faculty of Graduate Studies, Faculty of Science, Department of Earth Sciences, Windsor, ON N9B 3P4, Canada. Offers M Sc, PhD. Part-time programs available. *Degree requirements:* For master's, thesis; for doctorate, comprehensive exam, thesis/dissertation. *Entrance requirements:* For master's, minimum B average; for doctorate, minimum B average, copies of publication abstract. Additional exam requirements/recommendations for international students: Required—TOEFL (minimum score 560 paper-based; 220 computer-based). *Faculty research:* Aqueous geochemistry and hydrothermal processes, igneous petrochemistry, radiogenic isotopes, radiometric age-dating, diagenetic and sedimentary geochemistry.

Virginia Polytechnic Institute and State University, Graduate School, College of Science, Department of Geosciences, Blacksburg, VA 24061. Offers geological sciences (MS, PhD); geophysics (MS, PhD). *Entrance requirements:* For master's and doctorate, GRE General Test. Additional exam requirements/recommendations for international students: Required—TOEFL (minimum score 550 paper-based; 213 computer-based). Electronic applications accepted. *Faculty research:* Paleontology/geobiology, active tectonics, geomorphology, mineralogy/crystallography, mineral physics.

Washington State University, Graduate School, College of Sciences, School of Earth and Environmental Sciences, Pullman, WA 99164. Offers MS, PhD.

Washington University in St. Louis, Graduate School of Arts and Sciences, Department of Earth and Planetary Sciences, St. Louis, MO 63130-4899. Offers earth and planetary sciences (MA); planetary sciences (PhD). Terminal master's awarded for partial completion of doctoral program. *Degree requirements:* For master's, thesis; for doctorate, thesis/dissertation. *Entrance requirements:* For master's and doctorate, GRE General Test. Electronic applications accepted.

Wesleyan University, Graduate Programs, Department of Earth and Environmental Sciences, Middletown, CT 06459. Offers MA. *Faculty:* 10 full-time (3 women). *Students:* 4 full-time (2 women). Average age 25. 6 applicants, 50% accepted, 1 enrolled. In 2009, 1 master's awarded. *Degree requirements:* For master's, thesis. *Entrance requirements:* For master's, GRE General Test, GRE Subject Test. Additional exam requirements/recommendations for international students: Required—TOEFL. *Application deadline:* For fall admission, 1/15 for domestic and international students. Applications are processed on a rolling basis. Application fee: $0. Electronic applications accepted. *Financial support:* In 2009–10, 3 teaching assistantships with full tuition reimbursements were awarded; tuition waivers (full and partial) also available. Financial award application deadline: 4/15; financial award applicants required to submit FAFSA. *Faculty research:* Tectonics, volcanology, stratigraphy, coastal processes, geochemistry. *Unit head:* Dr. Peter Patton, Chair, 860-685-2268, E-mail: ppatton@wesleyan.edu. *Application contact:* Ginny Harris, Administrative Assistant, 860-685-2244, E-mail: vharris@wesleyan.edu.

West Chester University of Pennsylvania, Office of Graduate Studies, College of Arts and Sciences, Department of Geology and Astronomy, West Chester, PA 19383. Offers earth-space science (Teaching Certificate); general science (Teaching Certificate); geoscience (MA). Part-time and evening/weekend programs available. *Students:* 8 full-time (2 women), 24 part-time (16 women). Average age 32. 15 applicants, 100% accepted, 12 enrolled. In 2009, 8 master's awarded. *Degree requirements:* For master's, comprehensive exam (for some programs), thesis optional. *Entrance requirements:* For master's, minimum GPA of 2.5. Additional exam requirements/recommendations for international students: Required—TOEFL (minimum score 550 paper-based; 213 computer-based; 80 iBT). *Application deadline:* For fall admission, 4/15 priority date for domestic students, 3/15 for international students; for spring admission, 10/15 for domestic students, 9/1 for international students. Applications are processed on a rolling basis. Application fee: $35. Electronic applications accepted. *Expenses:* Tuition, state resident: full-time $6666; part-time $370 per credit. Tuition, nonresident: full-time $10,666; part-time $593 per credit. Required fees: $122.56 per credit. *Financial support:* In 2009–10, 1 research assistantship with full and partial tuition reimbursement (averaging $5,000 per year) was awarded; unspecified assistantships also available. Support available to part-time students. Financial award application deadline: 2/15; financial award applicants required to submit FAFSA. *Faculty research:* Developing and using a meteorological data station. *Unit head:* Dr. Marc Gagne, Chair, 610-436-2727, E-mail: mgagne@wcupa.edu. *Application contact:* Dr. Steven Good, Graduate Coordinator, 610-436-2203, E-mail: sgood@wcupa.edu.

Western Connecticut State University, Division of Graduate Studies, School of Arts and Sciences, Department of Physics, Astronomy and Meteorology, Danbury, CT 06810-6885. Offers earth and planetary sciences (MA). Part-time programs available. *Faculty:* 1 full-time (0 women). *Students:* 1 full-time (0 women), 5 part-time (1 woman); includes 1 minority (Hispanic American). Average age 32. 7 applicants, 71% accepted, 2 enrolled. *Degree requirements:* For master's, thesis, completion of program in 6 years. *Entrance requirements:* For master's, minimum GPA of 2.5 or GRE; one year of calculus-based physics, one year of calculus, and semester course in differential equations. Additional exam requirements/recommendations for international students: Recommended—TOEFL (minimum score 550 paper-based; 213 computer-based; 79 iBT), IELTS (minimum score 6). *Application deadline:* For fall admission, 8/5 priority date for domestic students; for spring admission, 1/5 priority date for domestic students. Applications are processed on a rolling basis. Application fee: $50. *Expenses:* Tuition, state resident: full-time $5012; part-time $278 per credit hour. Tuition, nonresident: full-time $13,962; part-time $284 per credit hour. Required fees: $3886; $139 per credit hour. Full-time tuition and fees vary according to course load and program. Part-time tuition and fees vary according to course level, degree level and program. *Financial support:* Application deadline: 5/1; *Unit head:* Dr. Alice Chance, Chairperson, 203-837-8667. *Application contact:* Chris Shankle, Associate Director of Graduate Admissions, 203-837-9005, Fax: 203-837-8326, E-mail: shanklec@wcsu.edu.

Western Michigan University, Graduate College, College of Arts and Sciences, Department of Geosciences, Program in Earth Science, Kalamazoo, MI 49008. Offers MA, MS. *Degree requirements:* For master's, thesis or alternative, oral exam. *Entrance requirements:* For master's, GRE General Test.

Western Michigan University, Graduate College, College of Arts and Sciences, Department of Geosciences, Program in Geosciences, Kalamazoo, MI 49008. Offers MS, PhD. *Degree requirements:* For master's, oral exam; for doctorate, thesis/dissertation, oral exam. *Entrance requirements:* For master's and doctorate, GRE General Test.

Yale University, Graduate School of Arts and Sciences, Department of Geology and Geophysics, New Haven, CT 06520. Offers biogeochemistry (PhD); climate dynamics (PhD); geochemistry (PhD); geophysics (PhD); meteorology (PhD); oceanography (PhD); paleontology (PhD); paleooceanography (PhD); petrology (PhD); tectonics (PhD). *Degree requirements:* For doctorate, thesis/dissertation. *Entrance requirements:* For doctorate, GRE General Test. Additional exam requirements/recommendations for international students: Required—TOEFL.

York University, Faculty of Graduate Studies, Faculty of Science and Engineering, Program in Earth and Space Science, Toronto, ON M3J 1P3, Canada. Offers M Sc, PhD. Part-time and evening/weekend programs available. *Degree requirements:* For master's, thesis or alternative; for doctorate, thesis/dissertation. Electronic applications accepted.

Hydrogeology

California State University, Chico, Graduate School, College of Natural Sciences, Department of Geological and Environmental Sciences, Program in Geosciences, Chico, CA 95929-0722. Offers hydrology/hydrogeology (MS). Part-time programs available. *Students:* 9 full-time (2 women), 4 part-time (2 women). Average age 34. 8 applicants, 100% accepted, 4 enrolled. In 2009, 2 master's awarded. *Degree requirements:* For master's, thesis, oral exam. *Entrance requirements:* For master's, GRE General Test. Additional exam requirements/recommendations for international students: Required—TOEFL (minimum score 550 paper-based; 213 computer-based; 80 iBT), IELTS (minimum score 6.5). *Application deadline:* For fall admission, 3/1 priority date for domestic students, 3/1 for international students; for spring admission, 9/15 priority date for domestic students, 9/15 for international students. Applications are processed on a rolling basis. Application fee: $55. Electronic applications accepted. *Financial support:* Fellowships available. *Unit head:* Dr. William Murphy, Graduate Coordinator, 530-898-5163. *Application contact:* Dr. William Murphy, Graduate Coordinator, 530-898-5163.

Clemson University, Graduate School, College of Engineering and Science, Department of Environmental Engineering and Earth Sciences, Program in Hydrogeology, Clemson, SC 29634. Offers MS. *Students:* 13 full-time (5 women), 6 part-time (2 women), 2 international. Average age 25. 16 applicants, 75% accepted, 5 enrolled. In 2009, 2 master's awarded. *Degree requirements:* For master's, thesis optional. *Entrance requirements:* For master's, GRE General Test, minimum GPA of 3.0 during previous 2 years. Additional exam requirements/recommendations for international students: Required—TOEFL. *Application deadline:* Applications are processed on a rolling basis. Application fee: $70 ($80 for international students). Electronic applications accepted. *Expenses:* Tuition, state resident: full-time $8684; part-time $528 per credit hour. Tuition, nonresident: full-time $15,330; part-time $1078 per credit hour. Required fees: $736; $37 per semester. Part-time tuition and fees vary according to course load and program. *Financial support:* In 2009–10, 12 students received support, including 5 research assistantships with partial tuition reimbursements available (averaging $17,784 per year), 4 teaching assistantships with partial tuition reimbursements available (averaging $17,784 per year); fellowships, career-related internships or fieldwork, institutionally sponsored loans, scholarships/grants, health care benefits, and unspecified assistantships also available. Support available to part-time students. Financial award application deadline: 6/1; financial award applicants required to submit FAFSA. *Faculty research:* Groundwater, geology, environmental geology, geochemistry, remediation, stratigraphy. Total annual research expenditures: $670,000. *Unit head:* Dr. Tanju Karanfil, Chair, 864-653-1005, Fax: 864-656-5973, E-mail: tkaranf@clemson.edu. *Application contact:* Dr. James W. Castle, Graduate Program Coordinator, 864-656-5015, Fax: 864-656-5973, E-mail: jcastle@clemson.edu.

Georgia State University, College of Arts and Sciences, Department of Geosciences, Atlanta, GA 30302-3083. Offers geographic information systems (Certificate); geography (MA); geology (MA); hydrogeology (Certificate). Part-time and evening/weekend programs available. *Degree requirements:* For master's, one foreign language, comprehensive exam (for some programs), thesis or alternative. *Entrance requirements:* For master's, GRE General Test, minimum GPA of 2.75. Additional exam requirements/recommendations for international students: Required—TOEFL. Electronic applications accepted. *Faculty research:* Clay mineralogy, geoinformatics, fracture analysis, sedimentology, groundwater.

Illinois State University, Graduate School, College of Arts and Sciences, Department of Geography-Geology, Normal, IL 61790-2200. Offers hydrogeology (MS). *Degree requirements:* For master's, thesis optional. *Entrance requirements:* For master's, GRE General Test. *Faculty research:* Thermal transport within the hyporheic zone, nutrient cycling in watersheds, water quality in karst systems, ground water dating using dissolved helium.

Indiana University Bloomington, University Graduate School, College of Arts and Sciences, Department of Geological Sciences, Bloomington, IN 47405-7000. Offers biogeochemistry

(MS, PhD); economic geology (MS, PhD); geobiology (MS, PhD); geophysics, structural geology and tectonics (MS, PhD); hydrogeology (MS, PhD); mineralogy (MS, PhD); stratigraphy and sedimentology (MS, PhD). *Faculty:* 17 full-time (1 woman). *Students:* 52 full-time (24 women), 3 part-time (0 women); includes 4 minority (2 African Americans, 1 Asian American or Pacific Islander, 1 Hispanic American), 24 international. Average age 30. 46 applicants, 65% accepted, 11 enrolled. In 2009, 9 master's, 1 doctorate awarded. Terminal master's awarded for partial completion of doctoral program. *Degree requirements:* For master's, thesis or alternative; for doctorate, comprehensive exam, thesis/dissertation. *Entrance requirements:* For master's and doctorate, GRE General Test. Additional exam requirements/recommendations for international students: Required—TOEFL. *Application deadline:* For fall admission, 1/15 priority date for domestic students, 12/15 for international students; for spring admission, 9/1 priority date for domestic students, 9/1 for international students. Applications are processed on a rolling basis. Application fee: $55 ($65 for international students). *Financial support:* In 2009–10, 11 fellowships with full tuition reimbursements (averaging $15,000 per year), 14 research assistantships with full tuition reimbursements (averaging $15,000 per year), 21 teaching assistantships with full tuition reimbursements (averaging $14,073 per year) were awarded; career-related internships or fieldwork, Federal Work-Study, and institutionally sponsored loans also available. *Faculty research:* Geophysics, geochemistry, hydrogeology, geobiology, planetary science. Total annual research expenditures: $644,299. *Unit head:* Simon Brassell, Chair, 812-855-5581, Fax: 812-855-7899, E-mail: geochair@indiana.edu. *Application contact:* Mary Iverson, Graduate Secretary, 812-855-7214, Fax: 812-855-7899, E-mail: miverson@indiana.edu.

Montana Tech of The University of Montana, Graduate School, Geosciences Programs, Butte, MT 59701-8997. Offers geochemistry (MS); geological engineering (MS); geology (MS); geophysical engineering (MS); hydrogeological engineering (MS); hydrogeology (MS). Part-time programs available. *Faculty:* 18 full-time (4 women), 3 part-time/adjunct (2 women). *Students:* 16 full-time (8 women), 6 part-time (4 women); includes 1 minority (African American), 1 international. 6 applicants, 67% accepted, 4 enrolled. In 2009, 7 degrees awarded. *Degree requirements:* For master's, comprehensive exam (for some programs), thesis (for some programs). *Entrance requirements:* For master's, GRE General Test, minimum GPA of 3.0. Additional exam requirements/recommendations for international students: Required—TOEFL (minimum score 525 paper-based; 195 computer-based; 71 iBT). *Application deadline:* For fall admission, 4/1 priority date for domestic students, 3/1 priority date for international students; for spring admission, 10/1 priority date for domestic students, 7/1 priority date for international students. Applications are processed on a rolling basis. Application fee: $30. Electronic applications accepted. *Expenses:* Tuition, state resident: full-time $5068; part-time $319 per credit. Tuition, nonresident: full-time $14,815; part-time $875 per credit. Tuition and fees vary according to course load and campus/location. *Financial support:* In 2009–10, 11 students received support, including 5 teaching assistantships with partial tuition reimbursements available (averaging $8,000 per year); research assistantships with partial tuition reimbursements available, career-related internships or fieldwork, tuition waivers (full and partial), and unspecified assistantships also available. Financial award application deadline: 4/1; financial award applicants required to submit FAFSA. *Faculty research:* Water resource development, seismic processing, petroleum reservoir characterization, environmental geochemistry, geologic mapping. *Unit head:* Dr. Diane Wolfgram, Department Head, 406-496-4353, Fax: 406-496-4260, E-mail: dwolfgram@mtech.edu. *Application contact:* Cindy Dunstan, Administrator, Graduate School, 406-496-4304, Fax: 406-496-4710, E-mail: cdunstan@mtech.edu.

Ohio University, Graduate College, College of Arts and Sciences, Department of Geological Sciences, Athens, OH 45701-2979. Offers environmental geochemistry (MS); environmental geology (MS); environmental/hydrology (MS); geology (MS); geology education (MS); geomorphology/surficial processes (MS); geophysics (MS); hydrogeology (MS); sedimentology (MS); structure/tectonics (MS). Part-time programs available. *Faculty:* 10 full-time (4 women), 4 part-time/adjunct (1 woman). *Students:* 18 full-time (13 women), 1 part-time (0 women), 9 international. 15 applicants, 67% accepted, 6 enrolled. In 2009, 5 master's awarded. *Degree requirements:* For master's, thesis. *Entrance requirements:* Additional exam requirements/recommendations for international students: Required—TOEFL (minimum score 550 paper-based; 80 iBT) or IELTS Academic (minimum score 6.5). *Application deadline:* For fall admission, 2/1 priority date for domestic and international students. Application fee: $50 ($55 for international students). Electronic applications accepted. *Expenses:* Tuition, state resident: full-time $7839; part-time $323 per quarter hour. Tuition, nonresident: full-time $15,831; part-time $654 per quarter hour. Required fees: $2931. *Financial support:* Research assistantships with full tuition reimbursements, teaching assistantships with full tuition reimbursements, Federal Work-Study, institutionally sponsored loans, scholarships/grants, tuition waivers (partial), and unspecified assistantships available. Financial award application deadline: 2/1. *Faculty research:* Geoscience education, tectonics, fluvial geomorphology, invertebrate paleontology, mine/hydrology. Total annual research expenditures: $649,020. *Unit head:* Dr. Gregory Nadon, Chair, 740-593-4212, Fax: 740-593-0486, E-mail: nadon@ohio.edu. *Application contact:* Dr. Douglas Green, Graduate Chair, 740-593-1843, Fax: 740-593-0486, E-mail: green@ohio.edu.

University of Hawaii at Manoa, Graduate Division, School of Ocean and Earth Science and Technology, Department of Geology and Geophysics, Honolulu, HI 96822. Offers high-pressure geophysics and geochemistry (MS, PhD); hydrogeology and engineering geology (MS, PhD); marine geology and geophysics (MS, PhD); planetary geosciences and remote sensing (MS, PhD); seismology and solid-earth geophysics (MS, PhD); volcanology, petrology, and geochemistry (MS, PhD). Part-time programs available. *Faculty:* 73 full-time (16 women), 15 part-time/adjunct (3 women). *Students:* 42 full-time (20 women), 8 part-time (5 women); includes 7 minority (1 African American, 4 Asian Americans or Pacific Islanders, 2 Hispanic Americans), 6 international. Average age 29. 56 applicants, 25% accepted, 6 enrolled. In 2009, 4 master's, 7 doctorates awarded. Terminal master's awarded for partial completion of doctoral program. *Degree requirements:* For master's, thesis optional; for doctorate, comprehensive exam, thesis/dissertation. *Entrance requirements:* For master's and doctorate, GRE General Test, minimum GPA of 3.0. Additional exam requirements/recommendations for international students: Required—TOEFL (minimum score 580 paper-based; 237 computer-based; 92 iBT), IELTS (minimum score 5). *Application deadline:* For fall admission, 1/15 for domestic students, 1/1 for international students; for spring admission, 9/1 for domestic students, 8/15 for international students. Application fee: $60. *Expenses:* Tuition, state resident: full-time $8900; part-time $372 per credit. Tuition, nonresident: full-time $21,400; part-time $898 per credit. Required fees: $207 per semester. *Financial support:* In 2009–10, 1 student received support, including 4 fellowships (averaging $9,338 per year), 31 research assistantships (averaging $23,877 per year), 5 teaching assistantships (averaging $20,466 per year). Total annual research expenditures: $3.8 million. *Application contact:* Dr. Charles Fletcher, Chair, 808-956-7640, Fax: 808-956-5512, E-mail: gg-grad-chair@hawaii.edu.

University of Nevada, Reno, Graduate School, Interdisciplinary Program in Hydrologic Sciences, Reno, NV 89557. Offers hydrogeology (MS, PhD); hydrology (MS, PhD). Offered through the M. C. Fleischmann College of Agriculture, the College of Engineering, the Mackay School of Mines, and the Desert Research Institute. Terminal master's awarded for partial completion of doctoral program. *Degree requirements:* For master's, thesis optional; for doctorate, thesis/dissertation. *Entrance requirements:* For master's and doctorate, GRE General Test, minimum GPA of 3.0. Additional exam requirements/recommendations for international students: Required—TOEFL (minimum score 500 paper-based; 173 computer-based; 61 iBT), IELTS (minimum score 6). Electronic applications accepted. *Faculty research:* Groundwater, water resources, surface water, soil science.

The University of Texas at Dallas, School of Natural Sciences and Mathematics, Program in Geosciences, Richardson, TX 75080. Offers geochemistry (MS, PhD); geophysics (MS); geospatial information sciences (MS, PhD); hydrogeology (MS, PhD); sedimentary, stratigraphy, paleontology (PhD); stratigraphy, paleontology (MS); structural geology and tectonics (MS, PhD). Part-time and evening/weekend programs available. *Faculty:* 9 full-time (1 woman). *Students:* 30 full-time (10 women), 11 part-time (4 women); includes 7 minority (1 African American, 4 Asian Americans or Pacific Islanders, 2 Hispanic Americans), 21 international. Average age 32. 42 applicants, 43% accepted, 14 enrolled. In 2009, 4 master's, 4 doctorates awarded. *Degree requirements:* For master's, thesis optional; for doctorate, thesis/dissertation. *Entrance requirements:* For master's and doctorate, GRE General Test, minimum GPA of 3.0 in upper-level course work in field. Additional exam requirements/recommendations for international students: Required—TOEFL (minimum score 550 paper-based; 213 computer-based). *Application deadline:* For fall admission, 7/15 for domestic students, 5/1 priority date for international students; for spring admission, 11/15 for domestic students, 9/1 priority date for international students. Applications are processed on a rolling basis. Application fee: $50 ($100 for international students). Electronic applications accepted. *Expenses:* Tuition, state resident: full-time $11,068; part-time $461 per credit hour. Tuition, nonresident: full-time $21,178; part-time $882 per credit hour. Tuition and fees vary according to course load. *Financial support:* In 2009–10, 10 research assistantships with full tuition reimbursements (averaging $13,500 per year), 11 teaching assistantships with full tuition reimbursements (averaging $13,500 per year) were awarded; fellowships, career-related internships or fieldwork, Federal Work-Study, institutionally sponsored loans, scholarships/grants, and unspecified assistantships also available. Support available to part-time students. Financial award application deadline: 4/30; financial award applicants required to submit FAFSA. *Faculty research:* Hydrology, organic geochemistry, tectonic structures, seismic characteristics, digital geologic mapping. *Unit head:* Dr. John Oldow, Department Head, 972-883-2401, Fax: 972-883-2537, E-mail: geosciences@utdallas.edu. *Application contact:* Dr. Robert J. Stem, Graduate Advisor, 972-883-2442, Fax: 972-883-2537, E-mail: rjstern@utdallas.edu.

West Virginia University, Eberly College of Arts and Sciences, Department of Geology and Geography, Program in Geology, Morgantown, WV 26506. Offers geomorphology (MS, PhD); geophysics (MS, PhD); hydrogeology (MS, PhD); paleontology (MS, PhD); petroleum geology (PhD); petrology (MS, PhD); stratigraphy (MS, PhD); structure (MS, PhD). Part-time programs available. Terminal master's awarded for partial completion of doctoral program. *Degree requirements:* For master's, thesis (for some programs); for doctorate, comprehensive exam, thesis/dissertation. *Entrance requirements:* For master's, GRE General Test, minimum GPA of 2.5; for doctorate, GRE General Test, minimum GPA of 3.3. Additional exam requirements/recommendations for international students: Required—TOEFL.

Hydrology

Auburn University, Graduate School, Ginn College of Engineering, Department of Civil Engineering, Auburn University, AL 36849. Offers construction engineering and management (MCE, MS, PhD); environmental engineering (MCE, MS, PhD); geotechnical/materials engineering (MCE, MS, PhD); hydraulics/hydrology (MCE, MS, PhD); structural engineering (MCE, MS, PhD); transportation engineering (MCE, MS, PhD). Part-time programs available. *Faculty:* 21 full-time (1 woman), 3 part-time/adjunct (1 woman). *Students:* 46 full-time (15 women), 39 part-time (5 women); includes 4 minority (3 African Americans, 1 Asian American or Pacific Islander), 29 international. Average age 26. 136 applicants, 43% accepted, 26 enrolled. In 2009, 19 master's, 4 doctorates awarded. *Degree requirements:* For master's, project (MCE), thesis (MS); for doctorate, comprehensive exam, thesis/dissertation. *Entrance requirements:* For master's and doctorate, GRE General Test. *Application deadline:* For fall admission, 7/7 for domestic students; for spring admission, 11/24 for domestic students. Applications are processed on a rolling basis. Application fee: $50 ($60 for international students). Electronic applications accepted. *Expenses:* Tuition, state resident: full-time $6240. Tuition, nonresident: full-time $18,720. International tuition: $18,938 full-time. Required fees: $492. Tuition and fees vary according to course load, program and reciprocity agreements. *Financial support:* Fellowships, research assistantships, teaching assistantships, Federal Work-Study available. Support available to part-time students. Financial award application deadline: 3/15; financial award applicants required to submit FAFSA. *Unit head:* Dr. J. Michael Stallings, Head, 334-844-4320. *Application contact:* Dr. George Flowers, Dean of the Graduate School, 334-844-2125.

California State University, Bakersfield, Division of Graduate Studies, School of Natural Sciences and Mathematics, Program in Geology, Bakersfield, CA 93311. Offers geology (MS); hydrogeology (MS); petroleum geology (MS). Part-time and evening/weekend programs available. *Degree requirements:* For master's, thesis. *Entrance requirements:* For master's, GRE General Test, BS in geology.

California State University, Chico, Graduate School, College of Natural Sciences, Department of Geological and Environmental Sciences, Program in Geosciences, Chico, CA 95929-0722. Offers hydrology/hydrogeology (MS). Part-time programs available. *Students:* 9 full-time (2 women), 4 part-time (2 women). Average age 34. 8 applicants, 100% accepted, 4 enrolled. In 2009, 2 master's awarded. *Degree requirements:* For master's, thesis, oral exam. *Entrance requirements:* For master's, GRE General Test. Additional exam requirements/recommendations for international students: Required—TOEFL (minimum score 550 paper-based; 213 computer-based; 80 iBT), IELTS (minimum score 6.5). *Application deadline:* For fall admission, 3/1 priority date for domestic students, 3/1 for international students; for spring admission, 9/15 priority date for domestic students, 9/15 for international students. Applications are processed on a rolling basis. Application fee: $55. Electronic applications accepted. *Financial support:* Fellowships available. *Unit head:* Dr. William Murphy, Graduate Coordinator, 530-898-5163. *Application contact:* Dr. William Murphy, Graduate Coordinator, 530-898-5163.

Colorado State University, Graduate School, Warner College of Natural Resources, Department of Forest, Rangeland, and Watershed Stewardship, Fort Collins, CO 80523-1472. Offers forest sciences (MS, PhD); natural resources stewardship (MNRS); rangeland ecosystem science (MS, PhD); watershed science (MS). Part-time programs available. Postbaccalaureate distance learning degree programs offered (no on-campus study). *Faculty:* 21 full-time (5 women), 1 part-time/adjunct (0 women). *Students:* 47 full-time (23 women), 76 part-time (21 women); includes 9 minority (3 American Indian/Alaska Native, 1 Asian American or Pacific Islander, 5 Hispanic Americans), 7 international. Average age 33. 53 applicants, 81% accepted, 33 enrolled. In 2009, 26 master's, 7 doctorates awarded. *Degree requirements:* For master's, thesis (for some programs); for doctorate, comprehensive exam, thesis/dissertation. *Entrance*

Hydrology

Colorado State University (continued)

requirements: For master's, GRE General Test (minimum score 1000 verbal and quantitative), minimum GPA of 3.0, 3 letters of recommendation; for doctorate, GRE General Test (combined minimum score of 1100 on the Verbal and Quantitative sections), minimum GPA of 3.0, 3 letters of recommendation, statement of research interest. Additional exam requirements/recommendations for international students: Required—TOEFL (minimum score 550 paper-based; 213 computer-based; 80 iBT), IELTS (minimum score 6). *Application deadline:* For fall admission, 8/1 priority date for domestic students, 6/25 priority date for international students; for spring admission, 12/1 priority date for domestic students, 11/25 priority date for international students. Applications are processed on a rolling basis. Application fee: $50. Electronic applications accepted. *Expenses:* Tuition, state resident: full-time $6434; part-time $359.10 per credit. Tuition, nonresident: full-time $18,116; part-time $1006.45 per credit. Required fees: $1496; $83 per credit. *Financial support:* In 2009–10, 43 students received support, including 3 fellowships (averaging $40,417 per year), 33 research assistantships with full and partial tuition reimbursements available (averaging $15,898 per year), 7 teaching assistantships with full and partial tuition reimbursements available (averaging $6,506 per year); Federal Work-Study, scholarships/grants, and unspecified assistantships also available. Financial award applicants required to submit FAFSA. *Faculty research:* Ecology, natural resource management, hydrology, restoration, human dimensions. Total annual research expenditures: $3.7 million. *Unit head:* Dr. N. Thompson Hobbs, Head, 970-491-6911, Fax: 970-491-6754, E-mail: nthobbs@warnercnr@colostate.edu. *Application contact:* Sonya LeFebre, Coordinator, 970-491-1907, Fax: 970-491-6754, E-mail: sonya.lefebre@colostate.edu.

Cornell University, Graduate School, Graduate Fields of Engineering, Field of Civil and Environmental Engineering, Ithaca, NY 14853-0001. Offers engineering management (M Eng, MS, PhD); environmental engineering (M Eng, MS, PhD); environmental fluid mechanics and hydrology (M Eng, MS, PhD); environmental systems engineering (M Eng, MS, PhD); geotechnical engineering (M Eng, MS, PhD); remote sensing (M Eng, MS, PhD); structural engineering (M Eng, MS, PhD); structural mechanics (M Eng, MS); transportation engineering (MS, PhD); transportation systems engineering (M Eng); water resource systems (M Eng, MS, PhD). *Faculty:* 40 full-time (7 women). *Students:* 144 full-time (48 women); includes 12 minority (2 African Americans, 1 American Indian/Alaska Native, 5 Asian Americans or Pacific Islanders, 4 Hispanic Americans), 58 international. Average age 25. 454 applicants, 57% accepted, 86 enrolled. In 2009, 69 master's, 5 doctorates awarded. Terminal master's awarded for partial completion of doctoral program. *Degree requirements:* For master's, thesis (MS); for doctorate, comprehensive exam, thesis/dissertation. *Entrance requirements:* For master's and doctorate, GRE General Test (recommended), 2 letters of recommendation. Additional exam requirements/recommendations for international students: Required—TOEFL (minimum score 600 paper-based; 250 computer-based; 77 iBT). *Application deadline:* For fall admission, 1/15 priority date for domestic students; for spring admission, 10/15 for domestic students. Application fee: $70. Electronic applications accepted. *Expenses:* Tuition: Full-time $29,500. Required fees: $70. Full-time tuition and fees vary according to degree level, program and student level. *Financial support:* In 2009–10, 50 students received support, including 6 fellowships with full tuition reimbursements available, 5 research assistantships with full tuition reimbursements available, 1 teaching assistantship with full tuition reimbursement available; institutionally sponsored loans, scholarships/grants, health care benefits, tuition waivers (full and partial), and unspecified assistantships also available. Financial award applicants required to submit FAFSA. *Faculty research:* Environmental engineering, geotechnical engineering remote sensing, environmental fluid mechanics and hydrology, structural engineering. *Unit head:* Director of Graduate Studies, 607-255-7560, Fax: 607-255-9004. *Application contact:* Graduate Field Assistant, 607-255-7560, Fax: 607-255-9004, E-mail: cee_grad@cornell.edu.

Cornell University, Graduate School, Graduate Fields of Engineering, Field of Geological Sciences, Ithaca, NY 14853-0001. Offers economic geology (M Eng, MS, PhD); engineering geology (M Eng, MS, PhD); environmental geophysics (M Eng, MS, PhD); general geology (M Eng, MS, PhD); geobiology (M Eng, MS, PhD); geochemistry and isotope geology (M Eng, MS, PhD); geohydrology (M Eng, MS, PhD); geomorphology (M Eng, MS, PhD); geophysics (M Eng, MS, PhD); geotectonics (M Eng, MS, PhD); marine geology (MS, PhD); mineralogy (M Eng, MS, PhD); paleontology (M Eng, MS, PhD); petroleum geology (M Eng, MS, PhD); petrology (M Eng, MS, PhD); planetary geology (M Eng, MS, PhD); Precambrian geology (M Eng, MS, PhD); Quaternary geology (M Eng, MS, PhD); rock mechanics (M Eng, MS, PhD); sedimentology (M Eng, MS, PhD); seismology (M Eng, MS, PhD); stratigraphy (M Eng, MS, PhD); structural geology (M Eng, MS, PhD). *Faculty:* 38 full-time (6 women). *Students:* 32 full-time (14 women); includes 2 minority (1 African American, 1 Asian American or Pacific Islander), 9 international. Average age 29. 61 applicants, 23% accepted, 8 enrolled. In 2009, 3 doctorates awarded. *Degree requirements:* For master's, thesis (MS); for doctorate, comprehensive exam, thesis/dissertation. *Entrance requirements:* For master's and doctorate, GRE General Test, 3 letters of recommendation. Additional exam requirements/recommendations for international students: Required—TOEFL (minimum score 550 paper-based; 213 computer-based; 77 iBT). *Application deadline:* For fall admission, 1/15 priority date for domestic students. Applications are processed on a rolling basis. Application fee: $70. Electronic applications accepted. *Expenses:* Tuition: Full-time $29,500. Required fees: $70. Full-time tuition and fees vary according to degree level, program and student level. *Financial support:* In 2009–10, 25 students received support, including 2 fellowships with full tuition reimbursements available, 3 research assistantships with full tuition reimbursements available, 1 teaching assistantship with full tuition reimbursement available; institutionally sponsored loans, scholarships/grants, health care benefits, tuition waivers (full and partial), and unspecified assistantships also available. Financial award applicants required to submit FAFSA. *Faculty research:* Geophysics, structural geology, petrology, geochemistry, geodynamics. *Unit head:* Director of Graduate Studies, 607-255-5466, Fax: 607-254-4780. *Application contact:* Graduate Field Assistant, 607-255-5466, Fax: 607-254-4780, E-mail: gradprog@geology.cornell.edu.

Drexel University, College of Engineering, Department of Civil, Architectural, and Environmental Engineering, Philadelphia, PA 19104-2875. Offers architectural / building systems engineering (MS, PhD); civil engineering (MS, PhD); environmental engineering (MS, PhD); geotechnical, geoenvironmental and geosynthetics engineering (MS, PhD); hydraulics, hydrology and water resources engineering (MS, PhD); structures (MS). Part-time and evening/weekend programs available. *Degree requirements:* For master's, thesis optional; for doctorate, thesis/dissertation. *Entrance requirements:* For master's, minimum GPA of 3.0; for doctorate, minimum GPA of 3.5, MS in civil engineering. Additional exam requirements/recommendations for international students: Required—TOEFL. Electronic applications accepted. *Faculty research:* Structural dynamics, hazardous wastes, water resources, pavement materials, groundwater.

Idaho State University, Office of Graduate Studies, College of Arts and Sciences, Department of Geosciences, Pocatello, ID 83209-8072. Offers geographic information science (MS); geology (MNS, MS); geology emphasis environmental geoscience (MS); geophysics/hydrology/geology (MS); geotechnology (Postbaccalaureate Certificate). Part-time programs available. *Faculty:* 8 full-time (1 woman). *Students:* 25 full-time (12 women), 20 part-time (6 women); includes 1 minority (Asian American or Pacific Islander), 4 international. Average age 33. In 2009, 7 master's, 2 other advanced degrees awarded. *Degree requirements:* For master's, comprehensive exam, thesis, oral colloquium; for Postbaccalaureate Certificate, thesis optional, minimum 19 credits. *Entrance requirements:* For master's, GRE General Test (minimum 50th percentile in 2 sections), 3 letters of recommendation; for Postbaccalaureate Certificate, GRE General Test, 3 letters of recommendation, bachelor's degree, statement of goals. Additional exam requirements/recommendations for international students: Required—TOEFL (minimum score 550 paper-based; 213 computer-based; 80 iBT). *Application deadline:* For fall admission, 7/1 for domestic students, 6/1 for international students; for spring admission, 12/1 for domestic students, 11/1 for international students. Applications are processed on a rolling basis. Application fee: $55. Electronic applications accepted. *Expenses:* Tuition, state resident: full-time $3318; part-time $297 per credit hour. Tuition, nonresident: full-time $13,120; part-time $437 per credit hour. Required fees: $2530. Tuition and fees vary according to program. *Financial support:* In 2009–10, 20 research assistantships with full and partial tuition reimbursements (averaging $9,713 per year), 7 teaching assistantships with full and partial tuition reimbursements (averaging $10,841 per year) were awarded; career-related internships or fieldwork, Federal Work-Study, institutionally sponsored loans, scholarships/grants, health care benefits, tuition waivers (full and partial), and unspecified assistantships also available. Support available to part-time students. Financial award application deadline: 1/1; financial award applicants required to submit FAFSA. *Faculty research:* Quantitative field mapping and sampling: microscopic, geochemical, and isotopic analysis of rocks, minerals and water; remote sensing, geographic information systems, and global positioning systems: environmental and watershed management; surficial and fluvial processes: landscape change; regional tectonics, structural geology; planetary geology. *Unit head:* Dr. David Rodgers, Chairman, 208-282-3365, Fax: 208-282-4414, E-mail: rodgdavi@isu.edu. *Application contact:* Tami Carson, Graduate School Technical Records Specialist, 208-282-2150, Fax: 208-282-4847, E-mail: carstami@isu.edu.

Illinois State University, Graduate School, College of Arts and Sciences, Department of Geography-Geology, Normal, IL 61790-2200. Offers hydrogeology (MS). *Degree requirements:* For master's, thesis optional. *Entrance requirements:* For master's, GRE General Test. *Faculty research:* Thermal transport within the hyporheic zone, nutrient cycling in watersheds, water quality in karst systems, ground water dating using dissolved helium.

Massachusetts Institute of Technology, School of Engineering, Department of Civil and Environmental Engineering, Cambridge, MA 02139-4307. Offers biological oceanography (PhD, Sc D); chemical oceanography (PhD, Sc D); civil and environmental engineering (M Eng, SM, PhD, Sc D); civil and environmental systems (PhD, Sc D); civil engineering (PhD, Sc D, CE); coastal engineering (PhD, Sc D); construction engineering and management (PhD, Sc D); environmental biology (PhD, Sc D); environmental chemistry (PhD, Sc D); environmental engineering (PhD, Sc D); environmental fluid mechanics (PhD, Sc D); geotechnical and geoenvironmental engineering (PhD, Sc D); hydrology (PhD, Sc D); information technology (PhD, Sc D); oceanographic engineering (PhD, Sc D); structures and materials (PhD, Sc D); transportation (PhD, Sc D); SM/MBA. *Faculty:* 36 full-time (5 women). *Students:* 190 full-time (59 women); includes 22 minority (2 African Americans, 14 Asian Americans or Pacific Islanders, 6 Hispanic Americans), 103 international. Average age 26. 478 applicants, 25% accepted, 76 enrolled. In 2009, 72 master's, 14 doctorates awarded. *Degree requirements:* For master's and CE, thesis; for doctorate, comprehensive exam, thesis/dissertation. *Entrance requirements:* For master's and doctorate, GRE General Test. Additional exam requirements/recommendations for international students: Required—TOEFL (minimum score 577 paper-based; 233 computer-based; 90 iBT), IELTS (minimum score 7). *Application deadline:* For fall admission, 1/2 for domestic and international students. Application fee: $75. Electronic applications accepted. *Financial support:* In 2009–10, 185 students received support, including 40 fellowships with tuition reimbursements available (averaging $27,725 per year), 97 research assistantships with tuition reimbursements available (averaging $28,035 per year), 21 teaching assistantships with tuition reimbursements available (averaging $24,802 per year); career-related internships or fieldwork, Federal Work-Study, institutionally sponsored loans, scholarships/grants, health care benefits, and unspecified assistantships also available. *Faculty research:* Environmental chemistry, environmental microbiology, environmental fluid mechanics and coastal engineering, geotechnical engineering and geomechanics, hydrology and hydroclimatology, mechanics of materials and structures, operations research/supply chain, transportation. Total annual research expenditures: $16.6 million. *Unit head:* Prof. Andrew Whittle, Department Head, 617-253-7101. *Application contact:* Patricia Glidden, Graduate Admissions Coordinator, 617-253-7119, Fax: 617-258-6775, E-mail: cee-admissions@mit.edu.

Missouri University of Science and Technology, Graduate School, Department of Civil, Architectural, and Environmental Engineering, Rolla, MO 65409. Offers civil engineering (MS, DE, PhD); construction engineering (MS, DE, PhD); environmental engineering (MS); fluid mechanics (MS, DE, PhD); geotechnical engineering (MS, DE, PhD); hydrology and hydraulic engineering (MS, DE, PhD). Part-time and evening/weekend programs available. Terminal master's awarded for partial completion of doctoral program. *Degree requirements:* For master's, thesis optional; for doctorate, comprehensive exam, thesis/dissertation. *Entrance requirements:* For master's, GRE General Test (minimum combined score 1100), minimum GPA of 3.0; for doctorate, GRE General Test (minimum score: verbal and quantitative 400, writing 3.5), minimum GPA of 3.0. Additional exam requirements/recommendations for international students: Required—TOEFL. Electronic applications accepted. *Faculty research:* Earthquake engineering, structural optimization and control systems, structural health monitoring/damage detection, soil-structure interaction, soil mechanics and foundation engineering.

Murray State University, College of Science, Engineering and Technology, Program in Water Science, Murray, KY 42071. Offers MS. Part-time programs available. *Degree requirements:* For master's, comprehensive exam, thesis. *Entrance requirements:* For master's, GRE General Test. Electronic applications accepted. *Faculty research:* Water chemistry, GIS, amphibian biology, nutrient chemistry, limnology.

New Mexico Institute of Mining and Technology, Graduate Studies, Department of Earth and Environmental Science, Program in Hydrology, Socorro, NM 87801. Offers MS, PhD. *Degree requirements:* For master's, thesis; for doctorate, thesis/dissertation. *Entrance requirements:* For master's, GRE General Test; for doctorate, GRE General Test, GRE Subject Test. Additional exam requirements/recommendations for international students: Required—TOEFL (minimum score 540 paper-based; 207 computer-based). *Faculty research:* Surface and subsurface hydrology, numerical simulation, stochastic hydrology, water quality, modeling.

State University of New York College of Environmental Science and Forestry, Department of Forest and Natural Resources Management, Syracuse, NY 13210-2779. Offers environmental and natural resource policy (MS, PhD); environmental and natural resources policy (MPS); forest management and operations (MF); forestry ecosystems science and applications (MPS, MS, PhD); natural resources management (MPS, MS, PhD); quantitative methods and management in forest science (MPS, MS, PhD); recreation and resource management (MPS, MS, PhD); watershed management and forest hydrology (MPS, MS, PhD). *Degree requirements:* For master's, thesis (for some programs); for doctorate, comprehensive exam, thesis/dissertation. *Entrance requirements:* For master's and doctorate, GRE General Test, minimum GPA of 3.0. Additional exam requirements/recommendations for international students: Required—TOEFL (minimum score 550 paper-based; 213 computer-based; 80 iBT), IELTS (minimum score 6). *Faculty research:* Silviculture recreation management, tree improvement, operations management, economics.

Stevens Institute of Technology, Graduate School, Charles V. Schaefer Jr. School of Engineering, Department of Civil, Environmental, and Ocean Engineering, Program in Civil Engineering, Hoboken, NJ 07030. Offers civil engineering (PhD); geotechnical engineering (Certificate); geotechnical/geoenvironmental engineering (M Eng, Engr); hydrologic modeling (M Eng); stormwater management (M Eng); structural engineering (M Eng, Engr); water resources engineering (M Eng). *Degree requirements:* For master's, thesis optional; for doctorate, variable foreign language requirement, thesis/dissertation; for other advanced degree, project or thesis. *Entrance requirements:* For doctorate, GRE. Additional exam requirements/recommendations for international students: Required—TOEFL. Electronic applications accepted. *Expenses:* Tuition: Full-time $9900; part-time $1100 per credit. Required fees: $286 per semester.

Université du Québec, Institut National de la Recherche Scientifique, Graduate Programs, Research Center—Water, Earth and Environment, Québec, QC G1K 9A9, Canada. Offers earth sciences (M Sc, PhD); earth sciences-environmental technologies (M Sc); water sciences (M Sc, PhD). Part-time programs available. *Faculty:* 42. *Students:* 181 full-time (70 women), 9 part-time (1 woman), 74 international. Average age 30. In 2009, 19 master's, 10 doctorates awarded. *Degree requirements:* For master's, thesis optional; for doctorate, thesis/dissertation. *Entrance requirements:* For master's, appropriate bachelor's degree, proficiency in French; for doctorate, appropriate master's degree, proficiency in French. *Application deadline:* For fall admission, 3/30 for domestic and international students; for winter admission, 11/1 for domestic and international students. Application fee: $30. *Financial support:* Fellowships, research assistantships, teaching assistantships available. *Faculty research:* Land use, impacts of climate change, adaptation to climate change, integrated management of resources (mineral and water). *Unit head:* Yves Begin, Director, 418-654-2524, Fax: 418-654-2600, E-mail: info@ete.inrs.ca. *Application contact:* Yvonne Boisvert, Registrar, 418-654-3861, Fax: 418-654-3858, E-mail: registrariat@adm.inrs.ca.

The University of Arizona, Graduate College, College of Science, Department of Hydrology and Water Resources, Tucson, AZ 85721. Offers MS, PhD. Part-time programs available. *Faculty:* 14. *Students:* 44 full-time (16 women), 8 part-time (4 women); includes 4 minority (all Hispanic Americans), 17 international. Average age 32. 66 applicants, 14% accepted, 9 enrolled. In 2009, 6 master's, 4 doctorates awarded. *Degree requirements:* For master's, thesis; for doctorate, thesis/dissertation. *Entrance requirements:* For master's, GRE General Test, 3 letters of recommendation, bachelor's degree in related field; for doctorate, GRE General Test, minimum undergraduate GPA of 3.2, graduate 3.4; 3 letters of recommendation; master's degree in related field; master's thesis abstract. Additional exam requirements/recommendations for international students: Required—TOEFL (minimum score 550 paper-based; 213 computer-based; 79 iBT). *Application deadline:* For fall admission, 5/1 for domestic students, 12/1 for international students; for spring admission, 10/1 for domestic students, 6/1 for international students. Applications are processed on a rolling basis. Application fee: $75. Electronic applications accepted. *Expenses:* Tuition, state resident: full-time $9028. Tuition, nonresident: full-time $24,890. *Financial support:* In 2009–10, 25 research assistantships with full tuition reimbursements (averaging $18,532 per year), 4 teaching assistantships with full tuition reimbursements (averaging $18,074 per year) were awarded; institutionally sponsored loans, scholarships/grants, health care benefits, and unspecified assistantships also available. Financial award application deadline: 1/31. *Faculty research:* Subsurface and surface hydrology, hydrometeorology/climatology, applied remote sensing, water resource systems, environmental hydrology and water quality. Total annual research expenditures: $5.5 million. *Unit head:* Thomas Maddock, Department Head, 520-621-7120, E-mail: maddock@hwr.arizona.edu. *Application contact:* Terrie Thompson, Academic Advising Coordinator, 520-621-3131, Fax: 520-621-1422, E-mail: programs@hwr.arizona.edu.

University of California, Davis, Graduate Studies, Graduate Group in Hydrologic Sciences, Davis, CA 95616. Offers MS, PhD. Terminal master's awarded for partial completion of doctoral program. *Degree requirements:* For master's, comprehensive exam (for some programs), thesis (for some programs); for doctorate, thesis/dissertation. *Entrance requirements:* For master's, GRE General Test, minimum GPA of 3.0; for doctorate, GRE. Additional exam requirements/recommendations for international students: Required—TOEFL (minimum score 550 paper-based; 213 computer-based). Electronic applications accepted. *Faculty research:* Pollutant transport in surface and subsurface waters, subsurface heterogeneity, micrometeorology evaporation, biodegradation.

University of Colorado at Boulder, Graduate School, College of Engineering and Applied Science, Department of Civil, Environmental, and Architectural Engineering, Boulder, CO 80309. Offers building systems (MS, PhD); construction engineering management (MS, PhD); environmental engineering (MS, PhD); geotechnical engineering and geomechanics (MS, PhD); hydrology, water resources and environmental fluid mechanics (MS, PhD); structural engineering and structural mechanics (MS, PhD). *Faculty:* 39 full-time (5 women). *Students:* 202 full-time (62 women), 29 part-time (6 women); includes 34 minority (3 African Americans, 3 American Indian/Alaska Native, 12 Asian Americans or Pacific Islanders, 16 Hispanic Americans), 53 international. Average age 29. 384 applicants, 44% accepted, 80 enrolled. In 2009, 60 master's, 7 doctorates awarded. *Degree requirements:* For master's, comprehensive exam, thesis or alternative; for doctorate, thesis/dissertation. *Entrance requirements:* For master's, GRE General Test, minimum undergraduate GPA of 3.0. *Application deadline:* For fall admission, 3/1 for domestic students, 12/1 for international students; for spring admission, 10/31 for domestic students, 10/1 for international students. Application fee: $50 ($60 for international students). *Financial support:* In 2009–10, 45 fellowships (averaging $7,876 per year), 68 research assistantships (averaging $15,204 per year) were awarded. Financial award application deadline: 1/15. *Faculty research:* Building systems engineering, construction engineering and management, environmental engineering, geoenvironmental engineering, geotechnical engineering, materials and mechanics, structural engineering, water resources engineering, life-cycle engineering. Total annual research expenditures: $6.1 million.

University of Idaho, College of Graduate Studies, College of Science, Department of Geological Sciences, Program in Hydrology, Moscow, ID 83844-2282. Offers MS. *Students:* 2 full-time, 2 part-time. In 2009, 4 master's awarded. *Entrance requirements:* For master's, minimum GPA of 2.8. *Application deadline:* For fall admission, 8/1 for domestic students; for spring admission, 12/15 for domestic students. Application fee: $55 ($60 for international students). *Expenses:* Tuition, state resident: full-time $6120. Tuition, nonresident: full-time $17,712. *Financial support:* Application deadline: 2/15. *Unit head:* Dr. Mickey Gunter, Head, 208-885-6491. *Application contact:* Dr. Mickey Gunter, Head, 208-885-6491.

University of Nevada, Reno, Graduate School, Interdisciplinary Program in Hydrologic Sciences, Reno, NV 89557. Offers hydrogeology (MS, PhD); hydrology (MS, PhD). Offered through the M. C. Fleischmann College of Agriculture, the College of Engineering, the Mackay School of Mines, and the Desert Research Institute. Terminal master's awarded for partial completion of doctoral program. *Degree requirements:* For master's, thesis optional; for doctorate, thesis/dissertation. *Entrance requirements:* For master's and doctorate, GRE General Test, minimum GPA of 3.0. Additional exam requirements/recommendations for international students: Required—TOEFL (minimum score 500 paper-based; 173 computer-based; 61 iBT), IELTS (minimum score 6). Electronic applications accepted. *Faculty research:* Groundwater, water resources, surface water, soil science.

University of New Brunswick Fredericton, School of Graduate Studies, Faculty of Engineering, Department of Civil Engineering, Fredericton, NB E3B 5A3, Canada. Offers construction engineering and management (M Eng, M Sc E, PhD); environmental engineering (M Eng, M Sc E, PhD); environmental studies (M Eng); geotechnical engineering (M Eng, M Sc E, PhD); groundwater/hydrology (M Eng, M Sc E, PhD); materials (M Eng, M Sc E, PhD); pavements (M Eng, M Sc E, PhD); structures (M Eng, M Sc E, PhD); transportation (M Eng, M Sc E, PhD). Part-time programs available. *Faculty:* 18 full-time (1 woman), 1 (woman) part-time/adjunct. *Students:* 42 full-time (9 women), 18 part-time (2 women). In 2009, 11 master's, 4 doctorates awarded. *Degree requirements:* For master's, thesis, proposal; for doctorate, comprehensive exam, thesis/dissertation, Qualifying exam; Proposal; 27 credit hours of courses. *Entrance requirements:* For master's, Minimum GPA of 3.0; BScE in Civil Engineering or related engineering degree.; for doctorate, Minimum GPA of 3.0; Candidates are normally required to have a graduate degree in engineering or applied science. Additional exam requirements/recommendations for international students: Required—TOEFL (minimum score 580 paper-based; 237 computer-based), TWE (minimum score 4), or IELTS (minimum score 7.5). *Application deadline:* For fall admission, 5/1 priority date for domestic students; for winter admission, 11/1 priority date for domestic students. Applications are processed on a rolling basis. Application fee: $50 Canadian dollars. Tuition and fees charges are reported in Canadian dollars. *Expenses:* Tuition, area resident: Full-time $5562 Canadian dollars; part-time $2781 Canadian dollars per year. Required fees: $49.75 Canadian dollars per term. *Financial support:* In 2009–10, 51 research assistantships (averaging $7,000 per year), 43 teaching assistantships (averaging $2,000 per year) were awarded; career-related internships or fieldwork and scholarships/grants also available. *Faculty research:* Construction engineering and management, concrete materials and structural engineering, transportation and asset management, geotechnical engineering, water and environmental engineering. *Unit head:* Dr. Eric Hildebrand, Director of Graduate Studies, 506-453-5113, Fax: 506-453-3568, E-mail: ktm@unb.ca. *Application contact:* Joyce Moore, Graduate Secretary, 506-452-6127, Fax: 506-453-3568, E-mail: civil-grad@unb.ca.

University of New Hampshire, Graduate School, College of Engineering and Physical Sciences, Department of Earth Sciences, Durham, NH 03824. Offers earth sciences (MS), including geochemical systems, geology, ocean mapping, oceanography; hydrology (MS). *Faculty:* 17 full-time (5 women). *Students:* 7 full-time (5 women), 15 part-time (7 women), 1 international. Average age 27. 27 applicants, 56% accepted, 5 enrolled. In 2009, 18 master's awarded. *Degree requirements:* For master's, thesis. *Entrance requirements:* For master's, GRE General Test. Additional exam requirements/recommendations for international students: Required—TOEFL (minimum score 550 paper-based; 213 computer-based; 80 iBT). *Application deadline:* For fall admission, 4/1 priority date for domestic students, 4/1 for international students; for spring admission, 12/1 for domestic students. Applications are processed on a rolling basis. Application fee: $65. Electronic applications accepted. *Expenses:* Tuition, state resident: full-time $10,380; part-time $577 per credit hour. Tuition, nonresident: full-time $24,350; part-time $1002 per credit hour. Required fees: $1550; $387.50 per semester. Tuition and fees vary according to course load and program. *Financial support:* In 2009–10, 17 students received support, including 1 fellowship, 6 research assistantships, 8 teaching assistantships; career-related internships or fieldwork, Federal Work-Study, scholarships/grants, and tuition waivers (full and partial) also available. Support available to part-time students. Financial award application deadline: 2/15. *Unit head:* Dr. Will Clyde, Chairperson, 603-862-1718, E-mail: earth.sciences@unh.edu. *Application contact:* Sue Clark, Administrative Assistant, 603-862-1718, E-mail: earth.sciences@unh.edu.

University of Southern Mississippi, Graduate School, College of Science and Technology, Department of Marine Science, Stennis Space Center, MS 39529. Offers hydrographic science (MS); marine science (MS, PhD). Part-time programs available. *Faculty:* 17 full-time (2 women), 2 part-time/adjunct (0 women). *Students:* 27 full-time (11 women), 13 part-time (6 women); includes 15 minority (12 Asian Americans or Pacific Islanders, 3 Hispanic Americans). Average age 30. 12 applicants, 58% accepted, 4 enrolled. In 2009, 10 master's, 2 doctorates awarded. *Degree requirements:* For master's, comprehensive exam, thesis, oral qualifying exam (marine science); for doctorate, 2 foreign languages, comprehensive exam, thesis/dissertation, oral qualifying exam. *Entrance requirements:* For master's, GRE General Test, minimum GPA of 3.0; for doctorate, GRE General Test, minimum GPA of 3.0 (undergraduate), 3.5 (graduate). Additional exam requirements/recommendations for international students: Required—TOEFL. *Application deadline:* For fall admission, 3/1 priority date for domestic and international students. Applications are processed on a rolling basis. Application fee: $35. Electronic applications accepted. *Expenses:* Tuition, state resident: full-time $5096; part-time $284 per hour. Tuition, nonresident: full-time $13,052; part-time $726 per hour. Required fees: $402. Tuition and fees vary according to course level and course load. *Financial support:* In 2009–10, 4 students received support, including 28 research assistantships with full tuition reimbursements available (averaging $20,400 per year), 4 teaching assistantships with full tuition reimbursements available (averaging $20,400 per year); Federal Work-Study and institutionally sponsored loans also available. Financial award application deadline: 3/15. *Faculty research:* Chemical, biological, physical, and geological marine science; remote sensing; bio-optics; numerical modeling; hydrography. Total annual research expenditures: $5.8 million. *Unit head:* Dr. Steven E. Lohrenz, Chair, 228-688-3177, Fax: 228-688-1121, E-mail: marine.science@usm.edu. *Application contact:* Adm. Linda J. Downs, Academic and Recruitment Coordinator, 228-688-3177, Fax: 228-688-1121, E-mail: linda.downs@usm.edu.

University of Washington, Graduate School, College of Engineering, Department of Civil and Environmental Engineering, Seattle, WA 98195-2700. Offers construction engineering (MSCE); environmental engineering (MS, MSCE, MSE, PhD); hydrology, water resources, and environmental fluid mechanics (MS, MSCE, MSE, PhD); structural and geotechnical engineering and mechanics (MS, MSCE, MSE, PhD); transportation and construction engineering (MS, MSE, PhD); transportation engineering (MSCE). Part-time programs available. Postbaccalaureate distance learning degree programs offered (no on-campus study). *Faculty:* 36 full-time (9 women), 16 part-time/adjunct (6 women). *Students:* 186 full-time (62 women), 57 part-time (10 women); includes 35 minority (24 Asian Americans or Pacific Islanders, 11 Hispanic Americans), 58 international. 360 applicants, 68% accepted, 98 enrolled. In 2009, 74 master's, 8 doctorates awarded. Terminal master's awarded for partial completion of doctoral program. *Degree requirements:* For master's, thesis (for some programs); for doctorate, comprehensive exam, thesis/dissertation. *Entrance requirements:* For master's, GRE General Test, minimum GPA of 3.0; for doctorate, GRE, minimum GPA of 3.5. Additional exam requirements/recommendations for international students: Required—TOEFL (minimum score 580 paper-based; 237 computer-based; 70 iBT). *Application deadline:* For fall admission, 1/15 priority date for domestic and international students. Applications are processed on a rolling basis. Application fee: $65. Electronic applications accepted. *Financial support:* In 2009–10, 5 students received support, including 13 fellowships with full and partial tuition reimbursements available (averaging $16,173 per year), 68 research assistantships with full tuition reimbursements available (averaging $16,173 per year), 12 teaching assistantships with full tuition reimbursements available (averaging $16,173 per year); scholarships/grants also available. Financial award application deadline: 1/15. *Faculty research:* Environmental/water resources, hydrology; construction/transportation; structures/ geotechnical. Total annual research expenditures: $11.4 million. *Unit head:* Dr. Gregory R. Miller, Professor and Chair, 206-543-0350, Fax: 206-543-1543, E-mail: gmiller@uw.edu. *Application contact:* Lorna Latal, Graduate Adviser, 206-543-2574, Fax: 206-543-1543, E-mail: llatal@u.washington.edu.

Limnology

Baylor University, Graduate School, College of Arts and Sciences, Department of Biology, Waco, TX 76798. Offers biology (MA, MS, PhD); environmental biology (MS); limnology (MS). Part-time programs available. *Faculty:* 13 full-time (3 women). *Students:* 34 full-time (15 women); includes 1 minority (Asian American or Pacific Islander), 10 international. In 2009, 8 master's, 4 doctorates awarded. *Degree requirements:* For master's, thesis (for some programs); for doctorate, thesis/dissertation. *Entrance requirements:* For master's and doctorate, GRE General Test. *Application deadline:* For fall admission, 1/31 priority date for domestic students. Applications are processed on a rolling basis. Application fee: $25. *Financial support:* Teaching assistantships, career-related internships or fieldwork, Federal Work-Study, institutionally sponsored loans, and tuition waivers (full and partial) available. Support available to part-time students. Financial award application deadline: 2/28. *Faculty research:* Terrestrial ecology, aquatic ecology, genetics. *Unit head:* Dr. Myeongwoo Lee, Graduate Program Director, 254-710-2141, Fax: 254-710-2969, E-mail: myeongwoo_lee@baylor.edu. *Application contact:* Tamara Lehmann, Administrative Assistant, 254-710-2911, Fax: 254-710-2969, E-mail: tamara_lehmann@baylor.edu.

Cornell University, Graduate School, Graduate Fields of Agriculture and Life Sciences, Field of Ecology and Evolutionary Biology, Ithaca, NY 14853-0001. Offers ecology (PhD), including animal ecology, applied ecology, biogeochemistry, community and ecosystem ecology, limnology, oceanography, physiological ecology, plant ecology, population ecology, theoretical ecology, vertebrate zoology; evolutionary biology (PhD), including ecological genetics, paleobiology, population biology, systematics. *Faculty:* 53 full-time (14 women). *Students:* 57 full-time (43 women); includes 4 minority (2 Asian Americans or Pacific Islanders, 2 Hispanic Americans), 8 international. Average age 29. 99 applicants, 11% accepted, 8 enrolled. In 2009, 12 doctorates awarded. *Degree requirements:* For doctorate, comprehensive exam, thesis/dissertation, 2 semesters of teaching experience. *Entrance requirements:* For doctorate, GRE General Test, GRE Subject Test (biology), 2 letters of recommendation. Additional exam requirements/recommendations for international students: Required—TOEFL (minimum score 550 paper-based; 213 computer-based; 77 iBT). *Application deadline:* For fall admission, 12/15 for domestic students. Application fee: $70. Electronic applications accepted. *Expenses:* Tuition: Full-time $29,500. Required fees: $70. Full-time tuition and fees vary according to degree level, program and student level. *Financial support:* In 2009–10, 56 students received support, including 7 fellowships with full tuition reimbursements available, 1 teaching assistantship with full tuition reimbursement available; research assistantships with full tuition reimbursements available, institutionally sponsored loans, scholarships/grants, health care benefits, tuition waivers (full and partial), and unspecified assistantships also available. Financial award applicants required to submit FAFSA. *Faculty research:* Population and organismal biology, population and evolutionary genetics, systematics and macroevolution, biochemistry, conservation biology. *Unit head:* Director of Graduate Studies, 607-254-4230. *Application contact:* Graduate Field Assistant, 607-254-4230, E-mail: eeb_grad_req@cornell.edu.

University of Alaska Fairbanks, School of Fisheries and Ocean Sciences, Program in Marine Sciences and Limnology, Fairbanks, AK 99775-7220. Offers marine biology (MS, PhD); oceanography (PhD), including biological oceanography, chemical oceanography, fisheries, geological oceanography, physical oceanography. Part-time programs available. *Faculty:* 12 full-time (5 women), 2 part-time/adjunct (0 women). *Students:* 29 full-time (17 women), 14 part-time (9 women); includes 4 minority (2 Asian Americans or Pacific Islanders, 2 Hispanic Americans), 2 international. Average age 33. 45 applicants, 18% accepted, 8 enrolled. In 2009, 8 master's, 2 doctorates awarded. *Degree requirements:* For master's, comprehensive exam, thesis, oral defense; for doctorate, comprehensive exam, thesis/dissertation, oral defense. *Entrance requirements:* For master's and doctorate, GRE General Test. Additional exam requirements/recommendations for international students: Required—TOEFL (minimum score 550 paper-based; 213 computer-based; 80 iBT). *Application deadline:* For fall admission, 6/1 for domestic students, 3/1 for international students; for spring admission, 10/15 for domestic students, 8/1 for international students. Applications are processed on a rolling basis. Application fee: $60. Electronic applications accepted. *Expenses:* Tuition, state resident: full-time $7584; part-time $316 per credit. Tuition, nonresident: full-time $15,504; part-time $646 per credit. Required fees: $23 per credit. $135 per semester. Tuition and fees vary according to course level, course load and reciprocity agreements. *Financial support:* In 2009–10, 3 fellowships (averaging $10,865 per year), 18 research assistantships (averaging $10,454 per year), 6 teaching assistantships (averaging $10,748 per year) were awarded; career-related internships or fieldwork, Federal Work-Study, scholarships/grants, health care benefits, and unspecified assistantships also available. Support available to part-time students. Financial award application deadline: 7/1; financial award applicants required to submit FAFSA. *Unit head:* Dr. Denis Wiesenberg, Dean, 907-474-7824, Fax: 907-474-7204, E-mail: info@sfos.uaf.edu. *Application contact:* Katie Straub, Recruitment and Retention Coordinator, 907-474-6786, Fax: 907-474-5863, E-mail: kmstraub@alaska.edu.

University of Florida, Graduate School, College of Agricultural and Life Sciences, Department of Fisheries and Aquatic Sciences, Gainesville, FL 32611. Offers MFAS, MS, PhD. *Degree requirements:* For master's, thesis optional; for doctorate, thesis/dissertation. *Entrance requirements:* For master's and doctorate, GRE General Test, minimum GPA of 3.0. Additional exam requirements/recommendations for international students: Required—TOEFL. Electronic applications accepted.

University of Wisconsin–Madison, Graduate School, College of Engineering, Program in Limnology and Marine Science, Madison, WI 53706. Offers MS, PhD. Terminal master's awarded for partial completion of doctoral program. *Degree requirements:* For master's, thesis; for doctorate, thesis/dissertation. *Entrance requirements:* For master's and doctorate, GRE General Test. Additional exam requirements/recommendations for international students: Required—TOEFL. Electronic applications accepted. *Expenses:* Tuition, state resident: part-time $594 per credit. Tuition, nonresident: part-time $1504 per credit. Required fees: $65 per credit. Tuition and fees vary according to course load, program and reciprocity agreements. *Faculty research:* Lake ecosystems, ecosystem modeling, geochemistry, physiological ecology, chemical limnology.

Marine Geology

Cornell University, Graduate School, Graduate Fields of Engineering, Field of Geological Sciences, Ithaca, NY 14853-0001. Offers economic geology (M Eng, MS, PhD); engineering geology (M Eng, MS, PhD); environmental geophysics (M Eng, MS, PhD); general geology (M Eng, MS, PhD); geobiology (M Eng, MS, PhD); geochemistry and isotope geology (M Eng, MS, PhD); geohydrology (M Eng, MS, PhD); geomorphology (M Eng, MS, PhD); geophysics (M Eng, MS, PhD); geotectonics (M Eng, MS, PhD); marine geology (MS, PhD); mineralogy (M Eng, MS, PhD); paleontology (M Eng, MS, PhD); petroleum geology (M Eng, MS, PhD); petrology (M Eng, MS, PhD); planetary geology (M Eng, MS, PhD); Precambrian geology (M Eng, MS, PhD); Quaternary geology (M Eng, MS, PhD); rock mechanics (M Eng, MS, PhD); sedimentology (M Eng, MS, PhD); seismology (M Eng, MS, PhD); stratigraphy (M Eng, MS, PhD); structural geology (M Eng, MS, PhD). *Faculty:* 38 full-time (6 women). *Students:* 32 full-time (14 women); includes 2 minority (1 African American, 1 Asian American or Pacific Islander), 9 international. Average age 29. 61 applicants, 23% accepted, 8 enrolled. In 2009, 3 doctorates awarded. *Degree requirements:* For master's, thesis (MS); for doctorate, comprehensive exam, thesis/dissertation. *Entrance requirements:* For master's and doctorate, GRE General Test, 3 letters of recommendation. Additional exam requirements/recommendations for international students: Required—TOEFL (minimum score 550 paper-based; 213 computer-based; 77 iBT). *Application deadline:* For fall admission, 1/15 priority date for domestic students. Applications are processed on a rolling basis. Application fee: $70. Electronic applications accepted. *Expenses:* Tuition: Full-time $29,500. Required fees: $70. Full-time tuition and fees vary according to degree level, program and student level. *Financial support:* In 2009–10, 25 students received support, including 2 fellowships with full tuition reimbursements available, 3 research assistantships with full tuition reimbursements available, 1 teaching assistantship with full tuition reimbursement available; institutionally sponsored loans, scholarships/grants, health care benefits, tuition waivers (full and partial), and unspecified assistantships also available. Financial award applicants required to submit FAFSA. *Faculty research:* Geophysics, structural geology, petrology, geochemistry, geodynamics. *Unit head:* Director of Graduate Studies, 607-255-5466, Fax: 607-254-4780. *Application contact:* Graduate Field Assistant, 607-255-5466, Fax: 607-254-4780, E-mail: gradprog@geology.cornell.edu.

Massachusetts Institute of Technology, School of Science, Department of Earth, Atmospheric, and Planetary Sciences, Cambridge, MA 02139-4307. Offers atmospheric chemistry (PhD, Sc D); atmospheric science (SM, PhD, Sc D); chemical oceanography (SM, PhD, Sc D); climate physics and chemistry (SM, PhD, Sc D); earth and planetary sciences (SM); geochemistry (PhD, Sc D); geology (PhD, Sc D); geophysics (PhD, Sc D); marine geology and geophysics (SM, PhD, Sc D); physical oceanography (SM, PhD, Sc D); planetary sciences (PhD, Sc D). *Faculty:* 37 full-time (7 women). *Students:* 158 full-time (74 women); includes 14 minority (1 African American, 1 American Indian/Alaska Native, 6 Asian Americans or Pacific Islanders, 6 Hispanic Americans), 58 international. Average age 27. 205 applicants, 30% accepted, 18 enrolled. In 2009, 10 master's, 25 doctorates awarded. Terminal master's awarded for partial completion of doctoral program. *Degree requirements:* For master's, thesis; for doctorate, comprehensive exam, thesis/dissertation. *Entrance requirements:* For master's, GRE General Test; for doctorate, GRE General Test, GRE Subject Test (chemistry or physics for planetary science area). Additional exam requirements/recommendations for international students: Required—IELTS (minimum score 6); Recommended—TOEFL (minimum score 577 paper-based; 233 computer-based; 91 iBT). *Application deadline:* For fall admission, 1/5 for domestic and international students; for spring admission, 11/1 for domestic and international students. Application fee: $75. Electronic applications accepted. *Financial support:* In 2009–10, 112 students received support, including 31 fellowships with tuition reimbursements available (averaging $30,513 per year), 89 research assistantships with tuition reimbursements available (averaging $21,168 per year), 17 teaching assistantships with tuition reimbursements available (averaging $28,372 per year); Federal Work-Study, institutionally sponsored loans, scholarships/grants, health care benefits, and unspecified assistantships also available. *Faculty research:* Formation, dynamics and evolution of planetary systems, origin, evolution and interaction of the physical, characterization of past, interplay of energy and the environment, present and potential future climates and the causes and consequences of climate change, chemical, geological and biological components of the Earth system, composition, structure and dynamics of the atmospheres, oceans, surfaces and interiors of the Earth and other planets. Total annual research expenditures: $19.5 million. *Unit head:* Prof. Maria Zuber, Head, 617-253-2127, Fax: 617-253-8298, E-mail: eapsinfo@mit.edu. *Application contact:* EAPS Education Office, 617-253-3381, Fax: 617-253-8298, E-mail: eapsinfo@mit.edu.

University of Delaware, College of Marine and Earth Studies, Newark, DE 19716. Offers geology (MS, PhD); marine policy (MS); marine studies (MMP, MS, PhD); oceanography (MS, PhD). *Degree requirements:* For master's, thesis; for doctorate, thesis/dissertation. *Entrance requirements:* For master's and doctorate, GRE General Test. Additional exam requirements/recommendations for international students: Required—TOEFL. Electronic applications accepted. *Faculty research:* Marine biology and biochemistry, oceanography, marine policy, physical ocean science and engineering, ocean engineering.

University of Hawaii at Manoa, Graduate Division, School of Ocean and Earth Science and Technology, Department of Geology and Geophysics, Honolulu, HI 96822. Offers high-pressure geophysics and geochemistry (MS, PhD); hydrogeology and engineering geology (MS, PhD); marine geology and geophysics (MS, PhD); planetary geosciences and remote sensing (MS, PhD); seismology and solid-earth geophysics (MS, PhD); volcanology, petrology, and geochemistry (MS, PhD). Part-time programs available. *Faculty:* 73 full-time (16 women), 15 part-time/adjunct (3 women). *Students:* 42 full-time (20 women), 8 part-time (5 women); includes 7 minority (1 African American, 4 Asian Americans or Pacific Islanders, 2 Hispanic Americans), 6 international. Average age 29. 56 applicants, 25% accepted, 6 enrolled. In 2009, 4 master's, 7 doctorates awarded. Terminal master's awarded for partial completion of doctoral program. *Degree requirements:* For master's, thesis optional; for doctorate, comprehensive exam, thesis/dissertation. *Entrance requirements:* For master's and doctorate, GRE General Test, minimum GPA of 3.0. Additional exam requirements/recommendations for international students: Required—TOEFL (minimum score 580 paper-based; 237 computer-based; 92 iBT), IELTS (minimum score 5). *Application deadline:* For fall admission, 1/15 for domestic students, 1/1 for international students; for spring admission, 9/1 for domestic students, 8/15 for international students. Application fee: $60. *Expenses:* Tuition, state resident: full-time $8900; part-time $372 per credit. Tuition, nonresident: full-time $21,400; part-time $898 per credit. Required fees: $207 per semester. *Financial support:* In 2009–10, 1 student received support, including 4 fellowships (averaging $9,338 per year), 31 research assistantships (averaging $23,877 per year), 5 teaching assistantships (averaging $20,466 per year). Total annual research expenditures: $3.8 million. *Application contact:* Dr. Charles Fletcher, Chair, 808-956-7640, Fax: 808-956-5512, E-mail: gg-grad-chair@hawaii.edu.

University of Miami, Graduate School, Rosenstiel School of Marine and Atmospheric Science, Division of Marine Geology and Geophysics, Coral Gables, FL 33124. Offers MS, PhD. Terminal master's awarded for partial completion of doctoral program. *Degree requirements:* For master's, comprehensive exam, thesis; for doctorate, comprehensive exam, thesis/dissertation. *Entrance requirements:* For master's and doctorate, GRE General Test. Additional exam requirements/recommendations for international students: Required—TOEFL (minimum score 550 paper-based; 213 computer-based). Electronic applications accepted. *Faculty research:* Carbonate sedimentology, low-temperature geochemistry, paleoceanography, geodesy and tectonics.

University of Washington, Graduate School, College of Ocean and Fishery Sciences, School of Oceanography, Seattle, WA 98195. Offers biological oceanography (MS, PhD); chemical oceanography (MS, PhD); marine geology and geophysics (MS, PhD); physical oceanography (MS, PhD). Terminal master's awarded for partial completion of doctoral program. *Degree requirements:* For master's, research project; for doctorate, thesis/dissertation. *Entrance requirements:* For master's and doctorate, GRE General Test, minimum GPA of 3.0. Additional exam requirements/recommendations for international students: Required—TOEFL. Electronic applications accepted. *Faculty research:* Global climate change, hydrothermal vent systems, marine microbiology, marine and freshwater biogeochemistry, biological-physical interactions.

Woods Hole Oceanographic Institution, MIT/WHOI Joint Program in Oceanography/Applied Ocean Science and Engineering, Woods Hole, MA 02543-1541. Offers applied ocean sciences (PhD); biological oceanography (PhD, Sc D); chemical oceanography (PhD, Sc D); civil and environmental and oceanographic engineering (PhD); electrical and oceanographic engineering (PhD); geochemistry (PhD); geophysics (PhD); marine biology (PhD); marine geochemistry (PhD, Sc D); marine geology (PhD, Sc D); marine geophysics (PhD); mechanical and oceanographic engineering (PhD); ocean engineering (PhD); oceanographic engineering (M Eng, MS, PhD, Sc D, Eng); paleoceanography (PhD); physical oceanography (PhD, Sc D). Terminal master's awarded for partial completion of doctoral program. *Degree requirements:* For master's and Eng, thesis (for some programs); for doctorate, thesis/dissertation. *Entrance requirements:* For master's, GRE General Test; for doctorate, GRE General Test, GRE Subject Test. Additional exam requirements/recommendations for international students: Required—TOEFL. Electronic applications accepted.

Mineralogy

Cornell University, Graduate School, Graduate Fields of Engineering, Field of Geological Sciences, Ithaca, NY 14853-0001. Offers economic geology (M Eng, MS, PhD); engineering geology (M Eng, MS, PhD); environmental geophysics (M Eng, MS, PhD); general geology (M Eng, MS, PhD); geobiology (M Eng, MS, PhD); geochemistry and isotope geology (M Eng, MS, PhD); geohydrology (M Eng, MS, PhD); geomorphology (M Eng, MS, PhD); geophysics (M Eng, MS, PhD); geotectonics (M Eng, MS, PhD); marine geology (MS, PhD); mineralogy (M Eng, MS, PhD); paleontology (M Eng, MS, PhD); petroleum geology (M Eng, MS, PhD); petrology (M Eng, MS, PhD); planetary geology (M Eng, MS, PhD); Precambrian geology (M Eng, MS, PhD); Quaternary geology (M Eng, MS, PhD); rock mechanics (M Eng, MS, PhD); sedimentology (M Eng, MS, PhD); seismology (M Eng, MS, PhD); stratigraphy (M Eng, MS, PhD); structural geology (M Eng, MS, PhD). *Faculty:* 38 full-time (6 women). *Students:* 32 full-time (14 women); includes 2 minority (1 African American, 1 Asian American or Pacific Islander), 9 international. Average age 29. 61 applicants, 23% accepted, 8 enrolled. In 2009, 3 doctorates awarded. *Degree requirements:* For master's, thesis (MS); for doctorate, comprehensive exam, thesis/dissertation. *Entrance requirements:* For master's and doctorate, GRE General Test, 3 letters of recommendation. Additional exam requirements/recommendations for international students: Required—TOEFL (minimum score 550 paper-based; 213 computer-based; 77 iBT). *Application deadline:* For fall admission, 1/15 priority date for domestic students. Applications are processed on a rolling basis. Application fee: $70. Electronic applications accepted. *Expenses:* Tuition: Full-time $29,500. Required fees: $70. Full-time tuition and fees vary according to degree level, program and student level. *Financial support:* In 2009–10, 25 students received support, including 2 fellowships with full tuition reimbursements available, 3 research assistantships with full tuition reimbursements available, 1 teaching assistantship with full tuition reimbursement available; institutionally sponsored loans, scholarships/grants, health care benefits, tuition waivers (full and partial), and unspecified assistantships also available. Financial award applicants required to submit FAFSA. *Faculty research:* Geophysics, structural geology, petrology, geochemistry, geodynamics. *Unit head:* Director of Graduate Studies, 607-255-5466, Fax: 607-254-4780. *Application contact:* Graduate Field Assistant, 607-255-5466, Fax: 607-254-4780, E-mail: gradprog@geology.cornell.edu.

Indiana University Bloomington, University Graduate School, College of Arts and Sciences, Department of Geological Sciences, Bloomington, IN 47405-7000. Offers biogeochemistry (MS, PhD); economic geology (MS, PhD); geobiology (MS, PhD); geophysics, structural geology and tectonics (MS, PhD); hydrogeology (MS, PhD); mineralogy (MS, PhD); stratigraphy and sedimentology (MS, PhD). *Faculty:* 17 full-time (1 woman). *Students:* 52 full-time (24 women), 3 part-time (0 women); includes 4 minority (2 African Americans, 1 Asian American or Pacific Islander, 1 Hispanic American), 24 international. Average age 30. 46 applicants, 65% accepted, 11 enrolled. In 2009, 9 master's, 1 doctorate awarded. Terminal master's awarded for partial completion of doctoral program. *Degree requirements:* For master's, thesis or alternative; for doctorate, comprehensive exam, thesis/dissertation. *Entrance requirements:* For master's and doctorate, GRE General Test. Additional exam requirements/recommendations for international students: Required—TOEFL. *Application deadline:* For fall admission, 1/15 priority date for domestic students, 12/15 for international students; for spring admission, 9/1 priority date for domestic students, 9/1 for international students. Applications are processed on a rolling basis. Application fee: $55 ($65 for international students). *Financial support:* In 2009–10, 11 fellowships with full tuition reimbursements (averaging $15,000 per year), 14 research assistantships with full tuition reimbursements (averaging $15,000 per year), 21 teaching assistantships with full tuition reimbursements (averaging $14,073 per year) were awarded; career-related internships or fieldwork, Federal Work-Study, and institutionally sponsored loans also available. *Faculty research:* Geophysics, geochemistry, hydrogeology, geobiology, planetary science. Total annual research expenditures: $644,299. *Unit head:* Simon Brassell, Chair, 812-855-5581, Fax: 812-855-7899, E-mail: geochair@indiana.edu. *Application contact:* Mary Iverson, Graduate Secretary, 812-855-7214, Fax: 812-855-7899, E-mail: miverson@indiana.edu.

Université du Québec à Chicoutimi, Graduate Programs, Program in Mineral Resources, Chicoutimi, QC G7H 2B1, Canada. Offers PhD. Part-time programs available. *Degree requirements:* For doctorate, thesis/dissertation. *Entrance requirements:* For doctorate, appropriate master's degree, proficiency in French.

Université du Québec à Montréal, Graduate Programs, Program in Earth Sciences, Montreal, QC H3C 3P8, Canada. Offers earth sciences (M Sc); mineral resources (PhD); non-renewable resources (DESS). Part-time programs available. Terminal master's awarded for partial completion of doctoral program. *Degree requirements:* For master's, thesis (for some programs); for doctorate, thesis/dissertation. *Entrance requirements:* For master's, appropriate bachelor's degree or equivalent, proficiency in French. *Faculty research:* Economic geology, structural geology, geochemistry, Quaternary geology, isotopic geochemistry.

Université du Québec à Montréal, Graduate Programs, Program in Mineral Resources, Montréal, QC H3C 3P8, Canada. Offers PhD. Part-time programs available. *Degree requirements:* For doctorate, thesis/dissertation. *Entrance requirements:* For doctorate, appropriate master's degree or equivalent, proficiency in French.

Paleontology

Cornell University, Graduate School, Graduate Fields of Engineering, Field of Geological Sciences, Ithaca, NY 14853-0001. Offers economic geology (M Eng, MS, PhD); engineering geology (M Eng, MS, PhD); environmental geophysics (M Eng, MS, PhD); general geology (M Eng, MS, PhD); geobiology (M Eng, MS, PhD); geochemistry and isotope geology (M Eng, MS, PhD); geohydrology (M Eng, MS, PhD); geomorphology (M Eng, MS, PhD); geophysics (M Eng, MS, PhD); geotectonics (M Eng, MS, PhD); marine geology (MS, PhD); mineralogy (M Eng, MS, PhD); paleontology (M Eng, MS, PhD); petroleum geology (M Eng, MS, PhD); petrology (M Eng, MS, PhD); planetary geology (M Eng, MS, PhD); Precambrian geology (M Eng, MS, PhD); Quaternary geology (M Eng, MS, PhD); rock mechanics (M Eng, MS, PhD); sedimentology (M Eng, MS, PhD); seismology (M Eng, MS, PhD); stratigraphy (M Eng, MS, PhD); structural geology (M Eng, MS, PhD). *Faculty:* 38 full-time (6 women). *Students:* 32 full-time (14 women); includes 2 minority (1 African American, 1 Asian American or Pacific Islander), 9 international. Average age 29. 61 applicants, 23% accepted, 8 enrolled. In 2009, 3 doctorates awarded. *Degree requirements:* For master's, thesis (MS); for doctorate, comprehensive exam, thesis/dissertation. *Entrance requirements:* For master's and doctorate, GRE General Test, 3 letters of recommendation. Additional exam requirements/recommendations for international students: Required—TOEFL (minimum score 550 paper-based; 213 computer-based; 77 iBT). *Application deadline:* For fall admission, 1/15 priority date for domestic students. Applications are processed on a rolling basis. Application fee: $70. Electronic applications accepted. *Expenses:* Tuition: Full-time $29,500. Required fees: $70. Full-time tuition and fees vary according to degree level, program and student level. *Financial support:* In 2009–10, 25 students received support, including 2 fellowships with full tuition reimbursements available, 3 research assistantships with full tuition reimbursements available, 1 teaching assistantship with full tuition reimbursement available; institutionally sponsored loans, scholarships/grants, health care benefits, tuition waivers (full and partial), and unspecified assistantships also available. Financial award applicants required to submit FAFSA. *Faculty research:* Geophysics, structural geology, petrology, geochemistry, geodynamics. *Unit head:* Director of Graduate Studies, 607-255-5466, Fax: 607-254-4780. *Application contact:* Graduate Field Assistant, 607-255-5466, Fax: 607-254-4780, E-mail: gradprog@geology.cornell.edu.

Duke University, Graduate School, Department of Biological Anthropology and Anatomy, Durham, NC 27710. Offers cellular and molecular biology (PhD); gross anatomy and physical anthropology (PhD), including comparative morphology of human and non-human primates, primate social behavior, vertebrate paleontology; neuroanatomy (PhD). *Faculty:* 8 full-time. *Students:* 14 full-time (9 women); includes 2 minority (1 African American, 1 Hispanic American), 1 international. 39 applicants, 15% accepted, 4 enrolled. In 2009, 4 doctorates awarded. *Degree requirements:* For doctorate, one foreign language, thesis/dissertation. *Entrance requirements:* For doctorate, GRE General Test. Additional exam requirements/recommendations for international students: Required—TOEFL (minimum score 550 paper-based; 213 computer-based; 83 iBT), IELTS (minimum score 7). *Application deadline:* For fall admission, 12/8 priority date for domestic and international students. Application fee: $75. Electronic applications accepted. *Financial support:* Fellowships, teaching assistantships, Federal Work-Study available. Financial award application deadline: 12/31. *Unit head:* Daniel Schmitt, Director of Graduate Studies, 919-684-5664, Fax: 919-684-4124, E-mail: mlsquire@duke.edu. *Application contact:* Cynthia Robertson, Associate Dean for Enrollment Services, 919-684-3913, E-mail: grad-admissions@duke.edu.

South Dakota School of Mines and Technology, Graduate Division, College of Engineering, Department of Geology and Geological Engineering, Program in Paleontology, Rapid City, SD 57701-3995. Offers MS. Part-time programs available. *Faculty:* 3 part-time/adjunct (1 woman). *Students:* 7 full-time (5 women), 8 part-time (2 women). Average age 27. 10 applicants, 60% accepted, 2 enrolled. In 2009, 3 master's awarded. *Degree requirements:* For master's, thesis. *Entrance requirements:* For master's, GRE General Test, GRE Subject Test. Additional exam requirements/recommendations for international students: Required—TOEFL, TWE. *Application deadline:* For fall admission, 7/1 priority date for domestic students, 4/1 for international students; for spring admission, 11/1 for domestic students, 9/1 for international students. Applications are processed on a rolling basis. Application fee: $35. Electronic applications accepted. *Expenses:* Tuition, state resident: full-time $3340; part-time $139 per credit hour. Tuition, nonresident: full-time $7060; part-time $294 per credit hour. Required fees: $3270. *Financial support:* In 2009–10, 1 fellowship (averaging $2,000 per year), 3 research assistantships with partial tuition reimbursements (averaging $12,349 per year), 4 teaching assistantships with partial tuition reimbursements (averaging $2,940 per year) were awarded; Federal Work-Study and institutionally sponsored loans also available. Support available to part-time students. Financial award application deadline: 5/15. *Faculty research:* Cretaceous vertebrates, Miocene vertebrates, Oligocene vertebrates. *Unit head:* Dr. James Martin, Assistant Professor, 605-394-2427, E-mail: james.martin@sdsmt.edu. *Application contact:* Jeannette R. Nilson, Administrative Support Coordinator, Graduate Education, 800-454-8162 Ext. 1206, Fax: 605-394-5360, E-mail: graduate_admissions@sdsmt.edu.

University of Chicago, Division of the Physical Sciences, Department of the Geophysical Sciences, Chicago, IL 60637-1513. Offers atmospheric sciences (SM, PhD); earth sciences (SM, PhD); paleobiology (PhD); planetary and space sciences (SM, PhD). *Faculty:* 21 full-time (3 women). *Students:* 37 full-time (23 women); includes 1 minority (Hispanic American), 14 international. Average age 27. 63 applicants, 35% accepted, 9 enrolled. In 2009, 1 doctorate awarded. Terminal master's awarded for partial completion of doctoral program. *Degree requirements:* For master's, thesis, seminar; for doctorate, variable foreign language requirement, comprehensive exam, thesis/dissertation. *Entrance requirements:* For doctorate, GRE General Test. Additional exam requirements/recommendations for international students: Required—TOEFL (minimum score 600 paper-based; 250 computer-based; 96 iBT), IELTS (minimum score 7). *Application deadline:* For fall admission, 1/10 for domestic and international students. Application fee: $55. Electronic applications accepted. *Financial support:* In 2009–10, research assistantships with full tuition reimbursements (averaging $20,511 per year), teaching assistant-

Paleontology

University of Chicago (continued)
ships with full tuition reimbursements (averaging $21,915 per year) were awarded; fellowships, Federal Work-Study, institutionally sponsored loans, scholarships/grants, tuition waivers (partial), and unspecified assistantships also available. Financial award application deadline: 1/15. *Faculty research:* Climatology, evolutionary paleontology, petrology, geochemistry, oceanic sciences. *Unit head:* Dr. Michael Foote, Chairman, 773-702-8102, Fax: 773-702-9505. *Application contact:* David J. Taylor, Graduate Student Services Coordinator, 773-702-8180, Fax: 773-702-9505, E-mail: info@geosci.uchicago.edu.

The University of Texas at Dallas, School of Natural Sciences and Mathematics, Program in Geosciences, Richardson, TX 75080. Offers geochemistry (MS, PhD); geophysics (MS); geospatial information sciences (MS, PhD); hydrogeology (MS, PhD); sedimentary, stratigraphy, paleontology (PhD); stratigraphy, paleontology (MS); structural geology and tectonics (MS, PhD). Part-time and evening/weekend programs available. *Faculty:* 9 full-time (1 woman). *Students:* 30 full-time (10 women), 11 part-time (4 women); includes 7 minority (1 African American, 4 Asian Americans or Pacific Islanders, 2 Hispanic Americans), 21 international. Average age 32. 42 applicants, 43% accepted, 14 enrolled. In 2009, 4 master's, 4 doctorates awarded. *Degree requirements:* For master's, thesis optional; for doctorate, thesis/dissertation. *Entrance requirements:* For master's and doctorate, GRE General Test, minimum GPA of 3.0 in upper-level course work in field. Additional exam requirements/recommendations for international students: Required—TOEFL (minimum score 550 paper-based; 213 computer-based). *Application deadline:* For fall admission, 7/15 for domestic students, 5/1 priority date for international students; for spring admission, 11/15 for domestic students, 9/1 priority date for international students. Applications are processed on a rolling basis. Application fee: $50 ($100 for international students). Electronic applications accepted. *Expenses:* Tuition, state resident: full-time $11,068; part-time $461 per credit hour. Tuition, nonresident: full-time $21,178; part-time $882 per credit hour. Tuition and fees vary according to course load. *Financial support:* In 2009–10, 10 research assistantships with full tuition reimbursements (averaging $13,500 per year), 11 teaching assistantships with full tuition reimbursements (averaging $13,500 per year) were awarded; fellowships, career-related internships or fieldwork, Federal Work-Study, institutionally sponsored loans, scholarships/grants, and unspecified assistantships also available. Support available to part-time students. Financial award application deadline: 4/30; financial award applicants required to submit FAFSA. *Faculty research:* Hydrology, organic geochemistry, tectonic structures, seismic characteristics, digital geologic mapping. *Unit head:* Dr. John Oldow, Department Head, 972-883-2401, Fax: 972-883-2537, E-mail: geosciences@utdallas.edu. *Application contact:* Dr. Robert J. Stern, Graduate Advisor, 972-883-2442, Fax: 972-883-2537, E-mail: rjstern@utdallas.edu.

West Virginia University, Eberly College of Arts and Sciences, Department of Geology and Geography, Program in Geology, Morgantown, WV 26506. Offers geomorphology (MS, PhD); geophysics (MS, PhD); hydrogeology (MS, PhD); paleontology (MS, PhD); petroleum geology (PhD); petrology (MS, PhD); stratigraphy (MS, PhD); structure (MS, PhD). Part-time programs available. Terminal master's awarded for partial completion of doctoral program. *Degree requirements:* For master's, thesis (for some programs); for doctorate, comprehensive exam, thesis/dissertation. *Entrance requirements:* For master's, GRE General Test, minimum GPA of 2.5; for doctorate, GRE General Test, minimum GPA of 3.3. Additional exam requirements/recommendations for international students: Required—TOEFL.

Yale University, Graduate School of Arts and Sciences, Department of Geology and Geophysics, New Haven, CT 06520. Offers biogeochemistry (PhD); climate dynamics (PhD); geochemistry (PhD); geophysics (PhD); meteorology (PhD); oceanography (PhD); paleontology (PhD); paleooceanography (PhD); petrology (PhD); tectonics (PhD). *Degree requirements:* For doctorate, thesis/dissertation. *Entrance requirements:* For doctorate, GRE General Test. Additional exam requirements/recommendations for international students: Required—TOEFL.

Planetary and Space Sciences

Air Force Institute of Technology, Graduate School of Engineering and Management, Department of Operational Sciences, Dayton, OH 45433-7765. Offers logistics management (MS); operations research (MS, PhD); space operations (MS). Part-time programs available. *Degree requirements:* For master's, thesis; for doctorate, thesis/dissertation. *Entrance requirements:* For doctorate, GRE General Test, minimum GPA of 3.0, U.S. citizenship. *Faculty research:* Optimization, simulation, combat modeling and analysis, reliability and maintainability, resource scheduling.

California Institute of Technology, Division of Geological and Planetary Sciences, Pasadena, CA 91125-0001. Offers geobiology (MS, PhD); geochemistry (MS, PhD); geology (MS, PhD); geophysics (MS, PhD); planetary science (MS, PhD). *Faculty:* 38 full-time (6 women). *Students:* 75 full-time (38 women); includes 21 minority (1 African American, 18 Asian Americans or Pacific Islanders, 2 Hispanic Americans). Average age 26. 102 applicants, 28% accepted, 9 enrolled. In 2009, 13 master's, 13 doctorates awarded. *Degree requirements:* For doctorate, thesis/dissertation. *Entrance requirements:* For doctorate, GRE General Test. Additional exam requirements/recommendations for international students: Required—TOEFL; Recommended—IELTS, TWE. *Application deadline:* For fall admission, 1/1 for domestic and international students. Application fee: $80. Electronic applications accepted. *Financial support:* In 2009–10, 75 students received support, including 15 fellowships with full tuition reimbursements available (averaging $27,000 per year), 60 research assistantships with full tuition reimbursements available (averaging $27,000 per year); teaching assistantships with full tuition reimbursements available, institutionally sponsored loans, scholarships/grants, health care benefits, and unspecified assistantships also available. Financial award applicants required to submit FAFSA. *Faculty research:* Astronomy, evolution of anaerobic respiratory processes, structural geology and tectonics, theoretical and numerical seismology, global biogeochemical cycles. *Unit head:* Dr. Kenneth A. Farley, Chairman, 626-395-6111, Fax: 626-795-6028, E-mail: dianb@gps.caltech.edu. *Application contact:* Dr. Robert W. Clayton, Academic Officer, 626-395-6909, Fax: 626-795-6028, E-mail: dianb@gps.caltech.edu.

Columbia University, Graduate School of Arts and Sciences, Division of Natural Sciences, Program in Atmospheric and Planetary Science, New York, NY 10027. Offers M Phil, PhD. Offered jointly through the Departments of Geological Sciences, Astronomy, and Physics and in cooperation with NASA Goddard Space Flight Center's Institute for Space Studies. *Degree requirements:* For doctorate, variable foreign language requirement, thesis/dissertation. *Entrance requirements:* For doctorate, GRE General Test, GRE Subject Test, previous course work in mathematics and physics. Additional exam requirements/recommendations for international students: Required—TOEFL. *Faculty research:* Climate, weather prediction.

Cornell University, Graduate School, Graduate Fields of Arts and Sciences, Field of Astronomy and Space Sciences, Ithaca, NY 14853-0001. Offers astronomy (PhD); astrophysics (PhD); general space sciences (PhD); infrared astronomy (PhD); planetary studies (PhD); radio astronomy (PhD); radiophysics (PhD); theoretical astrophysics (PhD). *Faculty:* 30 full-time (2 women). *Students:* 31 full-time (12 women); includes 3 minority (2 Asian Americans or Pacific Islanders, 1 Hispanic American), 9 international. Average age 26. 77 applicants, 19% accepted, 3 enrolled. In 2009, 3 doctorates awarded. *Degree requirements:* For doctorate, comprehensive exam, thesis/dissertation. *Entrance requirements:* For doctorate, GRE General Test, GRE Subject Test (physics), 3 letters of recommendation. Additional exam requirements/recommendations for international students: Required—TOEFL (minimum score 600 paper-based; 250 computer-based; 77 iBT). *Application deadline:* For fall admission, 1/15 for domestic students. Application fee: $70. Electronic applications accepted. *Expenses:* Tuition: Full-time $29,500. Required fees: $70. Full-time tuition and fees vary according to degree level, program and student level. *Financial support:* In 2009–10, 31 students received support, including 1 research assistantship with full tuition reimbursement available, 2 teaching assistantships with full tuition reimbursements available; fellowships with full tuition reimbursements available, institutionally sponsored loans, scholarships/grants, health care benefits, tuition waivers (full and partial), and unspecified assistantships also available. Financial award applicants required to submit FAFSA. *Faculty research:* Observational astrophysics, planetary sciences, cosmology, instrumentation, gravitational astrophysics. *Unit head:* Director of Graduate Studies, 607-255-4341. *Application contact:* Graduate Field Assistant, 607-255-4341, E-mail: oconnor@astro.cornell.edu.

Florida Institute of Technology, Graduate Programs, College of Science, Department of Physics and Space Sciences, Melbourne, FL 32901-6975. Offers physics (MS, PhD); space sciences (MS, PhD). Part-time programs available. *Faculty:* 13 full-time (1 woman), 1 part-time/adjunct (0 women). *Students:* 35 full-time (9 women), 8 part-time (4 women); includes 2 minority (both Hispanic Americans), 13 international. Average age 28. 52 applicants, 42% accepted, 7 enrolled. In 2009, 2 master's, 3 doctorates awarded. *Degree requirements:* For master's, comprehensive exam (for some programs), thesis optional, oral exam; for doctorate, one foreign language, comprehensive exam, thesis/dissertation, publication in referred journal, seminar on dissertation research, dissertation published in a major journal. *Entrance requirements:* For master's, minimum GPA of 3.0, resume, 3 letters of recommendation, vector analysis; for doctorate, GRE General and Subject Tests (recommended), minimum GPA of 3.2, resume, 3 letters of recommendation, statement of objectives. Additional exam requirements/recommendations for international students: Required—TOEFL (minimum score 550 paper-based; 213 computer-based; 79 iBT). *Application deadline:* For fall admission, 4/1 for international students; for spring admission, 9/30 for international students. Applications are processed on a rolling basis. Application fee: $50. Electronic applications accepted. *Expenses:* Tuition: Part-time $1015 per credit. Tuition and fees vary according to campus/location and program. *Financial support:* In 2009–10, 29 students received support, including 14 research assistantships with full and partial tuition reimbursements available (averaging $12,926 per year), 15 teaching assistantships with full and partial tuition reimbursements available (averaging $13,462 per year); career-related internships or fieldwork, institutionally sponsored loans, tuition waivers (partial), unspecified assistantships, and tuition remissions also available. Support available to part-time students. Financial award application deadline: 3/1; financial award applicants required to submit FAFSA. *Faculty research:* Lasers, semiconductors, magnetism, quantum devices, high energy physics. Total annual research expenditures: $2.9 million. *Unit head:* Dr. Terry D. Oswalt, Department Head, 321-674-7325, Fax: 321-674-7482, E-mail: toswalt@fit.edu. *Application contact:* Thomas M. Shea, Director of Graduate Admissions, 321-674-7577, Fax: 321-723-9468, E-mail: tshea@fit.edu.

Georgia Institute of Technology, Graduate Studies and Research, College of Sciences, School of Earth and Atmospheric Sciences, Atlanta, GA 30332-0340. Offers atmospheric chemistry, aerosols and clouds (MS, PhD); dynamics of weather and climate (MS, PhD); geochemistry (MS, PhD); geophysics (MS, PhD); oceanography (MS, PhD); paleoclimate (MS, PhD); planetary science (MS, PhD); remote sensing (MS, PhD). Part-time programs available. Terminal master's awarded for partial completion of doctoral program. *Degree requirements:* For master's, thesis or alternative; for doctorate, comprehensive exam, thesis/dissertation. *Entrance requirements:* For master's, GRE, letters of recommendation; for doctorate, GRE, academic transcripts, letters of recommendation, personal statement. Additional exam requirements/recommendations for international students: Required—TOEFL (minimum score 550 paper-based; 213 computer-based; 79 iBT). *Faculty research:* Geophysics; atmospheric chemistry, aerosols and clouds; dynamics of weather and climate; geochemistry; oceanography; paleoclimate; planetary science; remote sensing.

Harvard University, Graduate School of Arts and Sciences, Department of Earth and Planetary Sciences, Cambridge, MA 02138. Offers AM, PhD. Terminal master's awarded for partial completion of doctoral program. *Degree requirements:* For doctorate, comprehensive exam, thesis/dissertation. *Entrance requirements:* For doctorate, GRE General Test. Additional exam requirements/recommendations for international students: Required—TOEFL. Electronic applications accepted. *Expenses:* Tuition: Full-time $33,696. Required fees: $1126. Full-time tuition and fees vary according to program. *Faculty research:* Economic geography, geochemistry, geophysics, mineralogy, crystallography.

Massachusetts Institute of Technology, School of Science, Department of Earth, Atmospheric, and Planetary Sciences, Cambridge, MA 02139-4307. Offers atmospheric chemistry (PhD, Sc D); atmospheric science (SM, PhD, Sc D); chemical oceanography (SM, PhD, Sc D); climate physics and chemistry (SM, PhD, Sc D); earth and planetary sciences (SM); geochemistry (PhD, Sc D); geology (PhD, Sc D); geophysics (PhD, Sc D); marine geology and geophysics (SM, PhD, Sc D); physical oceanography (SM, PhD, Sc D); planetary sciences (PhD, Sc D). *Faculty:* 37 full-time (7 women). *Students:* 158 full-time (74 women); includes 14 minority (1 African American, 1 American Indian/Alaska Native, 6 Asian Americans or Pacific Islanders, 6 Hispanic Americans), 58 international. Average age 27. 205 applicants, 30% accepted, 18 enrolled. In 2009, 10 master's, 25 doctorates awarded. Terminal master's awarded for partial completion of doctoral program. *Degree requirements:* For master's, thesis; for doctorate, comprehensive exam, thesis/dissertation. *Entrance requirements:* For master's, GRE General Test; for doctorate, GRE General Test, GRE Subject Test (chemistry or physics for planetary science area). Additional exam requirements/recommendations for international students: Required—IELTS (minimum score 6); Recommended—TOEFL (minimum score 577 paper-based; 233 computer-based; 91 iBT). *Application deadline:* For fall admission, 1/5 for domestic and international students; for spring admission, 11/1 for domestic and international students. Application fee: $75. Electronic applications accepted. *Financial support:* In 2009–10, 112 students received support, including 31 fellowships with tuition reimbursements available (averaging $30,513 per year), 89 research assistantships with tuition reimbursements available (averaging $21,168 per year), 17 teaching assistantships with tuition reimbursements available (averaging $28,372 per year); Federal Work-Study, institutionally sponsored loans, scholarships/grants, health care benefits, and unspecified assistantships also available. *Faculty research:*

Formation, dynamics and evolution of planetary systems, origin, evolution and interaction of the physical, characterization of past, interplay of energy and the environment, present and potential future climates and the causes and consequences of climate change, chemical, geological and biological components of the Earth system, composition, structure and dynamics of the atmospheres, oceans, surfaces and interiors of the Earth and other planets. Total annual research expenditures: $19.5 million. *Unit head:* Prof. Maria Zuber, Head, 617-253-2127, Fax: 617-253-8298, E-mail: eapsinfo@mit.edu. *Application contact:* EAPS Education Office, 617-253-3381, Fax: 617-253-8298, E-mail: eapsinfo@mit.edu.

McGill University, Faculty of Graduate and Postdoctoral Studies, Faculty of Science, Department of Earth and Planetary Sciences, Montréal, QC H3A 2T5, Canada. Offers M Sc, PhD.

St. Thomas University, School of Leadership Studies, Institute for Education, Miami Gardens, FL 33054-6459. Offers earth/space science (Certificate); educational administration (MS, Certificate); educational leadership (Ed D); elementary education (MS); ESOL (Certificate); gifted education (Certificate); instructional technology (MS, Certificate); professional/studies (Certificate); reading (MS, Certificate); special education (MS). Part-time and evening/weekend programs available. *Degree requirements:* For master's, comprehensive exam; for doctorate, comprehensive exam, thesis/dissertation. *Entrance requirements:* For master's, interview, minimum GPA of 3.0 or GRE; for doctorate, GRE or MAT. Additional exam requirements/recommendations for international students: Required—TOEFL (minimum score 550 paper-based; 213 computer-based; 79 iBT). Electronic applications accepted.

The University of Arizona, Graduate College, College of Science, Department of Planetary Sciences, Tucson, AZ 85721. Offers MS, PhD. *Faculty:* 17. *Students:* 12 full-time (5 women), 16 part-time (9 women); includes 1 minority (Asian American or Pacific Islander), 8 international. Average age 28. 51 applicants, 14% accepted, 7 enrolled. In 2009, 9 doctorates awarded. *Degree requirements:* For master's, thesis (for some programs); for doctorate, one foreign language, thesis/dissertation. *Entrance requirements:* For master's and doctorate, 3 letters of recommendation. Additional exam requirements/recommendations for international students: Required—TOEFL (minimum score 550 paper-based; 213 computer-based; 79 iBT). *Application deadline:* For fall admission, 1/15 for domestic and international students. Applications are processed on a rolling basis. Application fee: $75. Electronic applications accepted. *Expenses:* Tuition, state resident: full-time $9028. Tuition, nonresident: full-time $24,890. *Financial support:* In 2009–10, 17 teaching assistantships with full tuition reimbursements (averaging $15,724 per year) were awarded; scholarships/grants, health care benefits, tuition waivers (partial), and unspecified assistantships also available. Financial award application deadline: 2/15. *Faculty research:* Cosmochemistry, planetary geology, astronomy, space physics, planetary physics. Total annual research expenditures: $20.6 million. *Unit head:* Dr. Michael Drake, Regents Professor, Head and Director, 520-621-6962, Fax: 520-621-4933, E-mail: drake@lpl.arizona.edu. *Application contact:* Pam Streett, Information Contact, 520-621-6954, Fax: 520-621-4933, E-mail: admissions@lpl.arizona.edu.

University of Arkansas, Graduate School, Interdisciplinary Program in Space and Planetary Sciences, Fayetteville, AR 72701-1201. Offers MS, PhD. *Students:* 10 full-time (5 women), 11 part-time (2 women); includes 2 minority (1 African American, 1 Hispanic American), 3 international. In 2009, 1 doctorate awarded. Application fee: $40 ($50 for international students). *Expenses:* Tuition, state resident: full-time $7355; part-time $356.58 per hour. Tuition, nonresident: full-time $17,401; part-time $775.17 per hour. Required fees: $1203. *Financial support:* In 2009–10, 5 fellowships, 6 research assistantships, 7 teaching assistantships were awarded. *Unit head:* Dr. Larry Roe, Director, 479-575-7625, Fax: 479-575-7778, E-mail: lar@uark.edu. *Application contact:* Graduate Admissions, 479-575-6246, Fax: 479-575-5908, E-mail: gradinfo@uark.edu.

University of California, Los Angeles, Graduate Division, College of Letters and Science, Department of Earth and Space Sciences, Los Angeles, CA 90095. Offers geochemistry (MS, PhD); geology (MS, PhD); geophysics and space physics (MS, PhD). *Students:* 60 full-time (30 women); includes 5 minority (1 African American, 4 Asian Americans or Pacific Islanders), 15 international. Average age 28. 83 applicants, 31% accepted, 13 enrolled. In 2009, 6 master's, 7 doctorates awarded. Terminal master's awarded for partial completion of doctoral program. *Degree requirements:* For master's, comprehensive exams or thesis; for doctorate, thesis/dissertation, oral and written qualifying exams. *Entrance requirements:* For master's, GRE General Test, minimum GPA of 3.0; for doctorate, GRE General Test, minimum undergraduate GPA of 3.0. *Application deadline:* For fall admission, 1/15 for domestic and international students. Application fee: $70 ($90 for international students). Electronic applications accepted. *Financial support:* In 2009–10, 49 fellowships with full and partial tuition reimbursements, 50 research assistantships with full and partial tuition reimbursements, 32 teaching assistantships with full and partial tuition reimbursements were awarded; Federal Work-Study, institutionally sponsored loans, scholarships/grants, traineeships, health care benefits, tuition waivers (full and partial), and unspecified assistantships also available. Financial award application deadline: 3/1; financial award applicants required to submit FAFSA. *Unit head:* Craig Manning, Chair, 310-825-1475. *Application contact:* Departmental Office, 888-377-8252, E-mail: holbrook@ess.ucla.edu.

University of California, Santa Cruz, Division of Graduate Studies, Division of Physical and Biological Sciences, Department of Earth and Planetary Sciences, Santa Cruz, CA 95064. Offers MS, PhD. *Degree requirements:* For master's, thesis; for doctorate, one foreign language, thesis/dissertation, qualifying exam. *Entrance requirements:* For master's and doctorate, GRE General Test. Additional exam requirements/recommendations for international students: Required—TOEFL (minimum score 550 paper-based; 220 computer-based). *Faculty research:* Evolution of continental margins and orogenic belts, geologic processes occurring at plate boundaries, deep-sea sediment diagenesis, paleoecology, hydrogeology.

University of Chicago, Division of the Physical Sciences, Department of the Geophysical Sciences, Chicago, IL 60637-1513. Offers atmospheric sciences (SM, PhD); earth sciences (SM, PhD); paleobiology (PhD); planetary and space sciences (SM, PhD). *Faculty:* 21 full-time (3 women). *Students:* 37 full-time (23 women); includes 1 minority (Hispanic American), 14 international. Average age 27. 63 applicants, 35% accepted, 9 enrolled. In 2009, 1 doctorate awarded. Terminal master's awarded for partial completion of doctoral program. *Degree requirements:* For master's, thesis, seminar; for doctorate, variable foreign language requirement, comprehensive exam, thesis/dissertation. *Entrance requirements:* For doctorate, GRE General Test. Additional exam requirements/recommendations for international students: Required—TOEFL (minimum score 600 paper-based; 250 computer-based; 96 iBT), IELTS (minimum score 7). *Application deadline:* For fall admission, 1/10 for domestic and international students. Application fee: $55. Electronic applications accepted. *Financial support:* In 2009–10, research assistantships with full tuition reimbursements (averaging $20,511 per year), teaching assistantships with full tuition reimbursements (averaging $21,915 per year) were awarded; fellowships, Federal Work-Study, institutionally sponsored loans, scholarships/grants, tuition waivers (partial), and unspecified assistantships also available. Financial award application deadline: 1/15. *Faculty research:* Climatology, evolutionary paleontology, petrology, geochemistry, oceanic sciences. *Unit head:* Dr. Michael Foote, Chairman, 773-702-8102, Fax: 773-702-9505. *Application contact:* David J. Taylor, Graduate Student Services Coordinator, 773-702-8180, Fax: 773-702-9505, E-mail: info@geosci.uchicago.edu.

University of Hawaii at Manoa, Graduate Division, School of Ocean and Earth Science and Technology, Department of Geology and Geophysics, Honolulu, HI 96822. Offers high-pressure geophysics and geochemistry (MS, PhD); hydrogeology and engineering geology (MS, PhD); marine geology and geophysics (MS, PhD); planetary geosciences and remote sensing (MS, PhD); seismology and solid-earth geophysics (MS, PhD); volcanology, petrology, and geochemistry (MS, PhD). Part-time programs available. *Faculty:* 73 full-time (16 women), 15 part-time/adjunct (3 women). *Students:* 42 full-time (20 women), 8 part-time (5 women); includes 7 minority (1 African American, 4 Asian Americans or Pacific Islanders, 2 Hispanic Americans), 6 international. Average age 29. 56 applicants, 25% accepted, 6 enrolled. In 2009, 4 master's, 7 doctorates awarded. Terminal master's awarded for partial completion of doctoral program. *Degree requirements:* For master's, thesis optional; for doctorate, comprehensive exam, thesis/dissertation. *Entrance requirements:* For master's and doctorate, GRE General Test, minimum GPA of 3.0. Additional exam requirements/recommendations for international students: Required—TOEFL (minimum score 580 paper-based; 237 computer-based; 92 iBT), IELTS (minimum score 5). *Application deadline:* For fall admission, 1/15 for domestic students, 1/1 for international students; for spring admission, 9/1 for domestic students, 8/15 for international students. Application fee: $60. *Expenses:* Tuition, state resident: full-time $8900; part-time $372 per credit. Tuition, nonresident: full-time $21,400; part-time $898 per credit. Required fees: $207 per semester. *Financial support:* In 2009–10, 1 student received support, including 4 fellowships (averaging $9,338 per year), 31 research assistantships (averaging $23,877 per year), 5 teaching assistantships (averaging $20,466 per year). Total annual research expenditures: $3.8 million. *Application contact:* Dr. Charles Fletcher, Chair, 808-956-7640, Fax: 808-956-5512, E-mail: gg-grad-chair@hawaii.edu.

University of Houston, College of Education, Department of Health and Human Performance, Houston, TX 77204. Offers allied health education and administration (M Ed, Ed D); exercise science (MS); health education (M Ed); human nutrition (MS); human space exploration sciences (MS); kinesiology (PhD); physical education (M Ed). *Accreditation:* NCATE (one or more programs are accredited). Part-time and evening/weekend programs available. *Faculty:* 12 full-time (4 women), 4 part-time/adjunct (3 women). *Students:* 53 full-time (26 women), 39 part-time (25 women); includes 21 minority (12 African Americans, 6 Asian Americans or Pacific Islanders, 3 Hispanic Americans), 14 international. Average age 29. 78 applicants, 64% accepted, 26 enrolled. In 2009, 20 master's, 2 doctorates awarded. *Degree requirements:* For master's, comprehensive exam, thesis (for some programs); for doctorate, comprehensive exam, thesis/dissertation, qualifying exam, candidacy paper. *Entrance requirements:* For master's, GRE (minimum 35th percentile on each section), minimum cumulative GPA of 3.0; for doctorate, GRE >35th percentile on each section, GPA>3.3 cumulative. Additional exam requirements/recommendations for international students: Required—TOEFL (minimum score 550 paper-based; 79 iBT). *Application deadline:* For fall admission, 5/1 for domestic students, 4/1 for international students; for spring admission, 10/1 for domestic and international students. Applications are processed on a rolling basis. Application fee: $45 ($75 for international students). Electronic applications accepted. *Expenses:* Tuition, state resident: full-time $7676; part-time $320 per credit hour. Tuition, nonresident: full-time $14,324; part-time $597 per credit hour. Required fees: $3034. *Financial support:* In 2009–10, 7 fellowships with full tuition reimbursements (averaging $9,500 per year), 8 research assistantships with full tuition reimbursements (averaging $9,850 per year), 12 teaching assistantships with full tuition reimbursements (averaging $9,850 per year) were awarded; career-related internships or fieldwork, Federal Work-Study, institutionally sponsored loans, scholarships/grants, health care benefits, and unspecified assistantships also available. Support available to part-time students. Financial award application deadline: 2/1. *Faculty research:* Biomechanics, exercise physiology, obesity, nutrition, space exploration science. *Unit head:* Dr. Charles Layne, Chairperson, 713-743-9868, Fax: 713-743-9860, E-mail: clayne2@uh.edu. *Application contact:* Todd Boutte, Graduate Admission Counselor, 713-743-0571, Fax: 713-743-0123, E-mail: tboutte@mail.coe.uh.edu.

University of Maryland, Baltimore County, Graduate School, College of Arts, Humanities and Social Sciences, Department of Education, Program in Teaching, Baltimore, MD 21250. Offers early childhood education (MAT); elementary education (MAT); secondary education (MAT), including art, biology, chemistry, dance, earth/space science, English, foreign language, mathematics, music, physics, theatre; secondary science (MAT), including social studies. Part-time and evening/weekend programs available. *Faculty:* 24 full-time (18 women), 25 part-time/adjunct (19 women). *Students:* 52 full-time (41 women), 64 part-time (55 women); includes 20 minority (5 African Americans, 1 American Indian/Alaska Native, 10 Asian Americans or Pacific Islanders, 4 Hispanic Americans), 3 international. Average age 31. 88 applicants, 57% accepted, 39 enrolled. In 2009, 106 master's awarded. *Degree requirements:* For master's, comprehensive exam (for some programs), thesis (for some programs). *Entrance requirements:* For master's, PRAXIS I and II, minimum GPA of 3.0. Additional exam requirements/recommendations for international students: Required—TOEFL. *Application deadline:* For fall admission, 6/1 for domestic students; for spring admission, 11/1 for domestic students. Applications are processed on a rolling basis. Application fee: $50. Electronic applications accepted. *Financial support:* In 2009–10, 6 students received support, including research assistantships with full tuition reimbursements available (averaging $12,000 per year); career-related internships or fieldwork, Federal Work-Study, scholarships/grants, tuition waivers, and unspecified assistantships also available. Financial award application deadline: 3/1. *Faculty research:* STEM teacher education, culturally sensitive pedagogy, ESOL/bilingual education, early childhood education, language, literacy and culture. *Unit head:* Dr. Susan M. Blunck, Director, 410-455-2869, Fax: 410-455-3986, E-mail: blunck@umbc.edu. *Application contact:* Dr. Susan M. Blunck, Director, 410-455-2869, Fax: 410-455-3986, E-mail: blunck@umbc.edu.

University of Michigan, Horace H. Rackham School of Graduate Studies, College of Engineering, Department of Atmospheric, Oceanic, and Space Sciences, Ann Arbor, MI 48109. Offers atmospheric (MS); atmospheric and space sciences (PhD); geoscience and remote sensing (PhD); space and planetary sciences (PhD); space engineering (M Eng); space sciences (MS). Part-time programs available. *Faculty:* 22 full-time (4 women). *Students:* 74 full-time (30 women), 1 part-time (0 women); includes 4 minority (1 African American, 2 Asian Americans or Pacific Islanders, 1 Hispanic American), 29 international. 62 applicants, 48% accepted, 17 enrolled. In 2009, 38 master's, 4 doctorates awarded. Terminal master's awarded for partial completion of doctoral program. *Degree requirements:* For master's, thesis (for some programs); for doctorate, thesis/dissertation, oral defense of dissertation, preliminary exams. *Entrance requirements:* For master's and doctorate, GRE General Test. Additional exam requirements/recommendations for international students: Required—TOEFL. *Application deadline:* Applications are processed on a rolling basis. Application fee: $60 ($75 for international students). Electronic applications accepted. *Expenses:* Tuition, state resident: full-time $17,286; part-time $1099 per credit hour. Tuition, nonresident: full-time $34,944; part-time $2080 per credit hour. Required fees: $95 per semester. Tuition and fees vary according to course load, degree level and program. *Financial support:* Fellowships, research assistantships, teaching assistantships, career-related internships or fieldwork, Federal Work-Study, institutionally sponsored loans, and health care benefits available. Support available to part-time students. Financial award applicants required to submit FAFSA. *Faculty research:* Planetary environments, space instrumentation, air pollution meteorology, global climate change, sun-earth connection, space weather. *Unit head:* Tamas Gombosi, Chair, 734-764-7222, Fax: 734-615-4645, E-mail: tamas@umich.edu. *Application contact:* Margaret Reid, Student Services Associate, 734-936-0482, Fax: 734-763-0437, E-mail: aoss.um@umich.edu.

Planetary and Space Sciences

University of New Mexico, Graduate School, College of Arts and Sciences, Department of Earth and Planetary Sciences, Albuquerque, NM 87131-2039. Offers MS, PhD. Part-time programs available. *Faculty:* 26 full-time (7 women), 4 part-time/adjunct (1 woman). *Students:* 48 full-time (30 women), 7 part-time (6 women); includes 3 minority (1 American Indian/Alaska Native, 2 Hispanic Americans), 6 international. Average age 30. 40 applicants, 18% accepted, 7 enrolled. In 2009, 6 master's, 2 doctorates awarded. Terminal master's awarded for partial completion of doctoral program. *Degree requirements:* For master's, comprehensive exam, thesis; for doctorate, comprehensive exam, thesis/dissertation. *Entrance requirements:* For master's and doctorate, GRE General Test. Additional exam requirements/recommendations for international students: Required—TOEFL. *Application deadline:* For fall admission, 1/31 priority date for domestic students, 1/31 for international students; for spring admission, 11/1 priority date for domestic and international students. Application fee: $50. Electronic applications accepted. *Expenses:* Tuition, state resident: full-time $2098.80; part-time $233.20 per credit hour. Tuition, nonresident: full-time $6650. Required fees: $25 per semester. Tuition and fees vary according to course load, program and reciprocity agreements. *Financial support:* In 2009–10, 17 students received support, including 2 fellowships with full tuition reimbursements available (averaging $22,500 per year), 24 research assistantships with full tuition reimbursements available (averaging $17,000 per year), 15 teaching assistantships with full tuition reimbursements available (averaging $16,900 per year); scholarships/grants and health care benefits also available. Financial award application deadline: 1/31; financial award applicants required to submit FAFSA. *Faculty research:* Climatology, experimental petrology, geochemistry, geographic information technologies, geomorphology, geophysics, hydrogeology, ingeneous petrology, metamorphic petrology, meteoritics, meteorology, micrometeorites, mineralogy, paleoclimatology, paleonology, pedology, petrology, physical volcanology, planetary sciences, precambrian geology, quantenary geology, sedimentary geochemistry, sedimentology, stable isotope geochemistry, stratigraphy, structural geology, tectonics, volcanology. Total annual research expenditures: $2.5 million. *Unit head:* Dr. John W. Geissman, Chair, 505-277-4204, Fax: 505-277-8843, E-mail: jgeiss@unm.edu. *Application contact:* Cindy Jaramillo, Administrative Assistant II, 505-277-1635, Fax: 505-277-8843, E-mail: epsdept@unm.edu.

University of North Dakota, Graduate School, John D. Odegard School of Aerospace Sciences, Space Studies Program, Grand Forks, ND 58202. Offers MS. Part-time programs available. Postbaccalaureate distance learning degree programs offered (minimal on-campus study). *Degree requirements:* For master's, comprehensive exam, thesis or alternative. *Entrance requirements:* For master's, minimum GPA of 3.0. Additional exam requirements/recommendations for international students: Required—TOEFL (minimum score 550 paper-based; 213 computer-based; 79 iBT), IELTS (minimum score 6.5). Electronic applications accepted. *Faculty research:* Earth-approaching asteroids, international remote sensing statutes, Mercury fly-by design, origin of meteorites, craters on Venus.

University of Pittsburgh, School of Arts and Sciences, Department of Geology and Planetary Science, Pittsburgh, PA 15260-3332. Offers geographical information systems (PM Sc); geology and planetary science (MS, PhD). Part-time programs available. *Faculty:* 9 full-time (1 woman), 4 part-time/adjunct (1 woman). *Students:* 27 full-time (15 women), 7 part-time (4 women), 1 international. Average age 30. 38 applicants, 24% accepted, 6 enrolled. In 2009, 1 doctorate awarded. *Degree requirements:* For master's, thesis, oral thesis defense; for doctorate, comprehensive exam, thesis/dissertation, oral dissertation defense. *Entrance requirements:* For master's and doctorate, GRE General Test. Additional exam requirements/recommendations for international students: Required—TOEFL (minimum score 550 paper-based; 213 computer-based; 80 iBT). *Application deadline:* For fall admission, 2/1 priority date for domestic students, 2/1 for international students. Application fee: $50. Electronic applications accepted. *Expenses:* Tuition, state resident: full-time $16,402; part-time $665 per credit. Tuition, nonresident: full-time $28,694; part-time $1175 per credit. Required fees: $690; $175 per term. Tuition and fees vary according to program. *Financial support:* In 2009–10, 25 students received support, including 2 fellowships with full tuition reimbursements available (averaging $14,400 per year), 13 research assistantships with full and partial tuition reimbursements available (averaging $14,400 per year), 10 teaching assistantships with full and partial tuition reimbursements available (averaging $15,065 per year); career-related internships or fieldwork, Federal Work-Study, institutionally sponsored loans, scholarships/grants, and tuition waivers (full and partial) also available. Support available to part-time students. Financial award application deadline: 2/1; financial award applicants required to submit FAFSA. *Faculty research:* Geographical information systems, hydrology, low temperature geochemistry, volcanology, paleoclimatology. Total annual research expenditures: $1.2 million. *Unit head:* Dr. Thomas Anderson, Chair, 412-624-8783, Fax: 412-624-3914, E-mail: bstewart@pitt.edu. *Application contact:* Dr. Brian W. Stewart, Graduate Adviser, 412-624-8883, Fax: 412-624-3914, E-mail: taco@pitt.edu.

Washington University in St. Louis, Graduate School of Arts and Sciences, Department of Earth and Planetary Sciences, St. Louis, MO 63130-4899. Offers earth and planetary sciences (MA); planetary sciences (PhD). Terminal master's awarded for partial completion of doctoral program. *Degree requirements:* For master's, thesis; for doctorate, thesis/dissertation. *Entrance requirements:* For master's and doctorate, GRE General Test. Electronic applications accepted.

West Chester University of Pennsylvania, Office of Graduate Studies, College of Arts and Sciences, Department of Geology and Astronomy, West Chester, PA 19383. Offers earth-space science (Teaching Certificate); general science (Teaching Certificate); geoscience (MA). Part-time and evening/weekend programs available. *Students:* 8 full-time (2 women), 24 part-time (16 women). Average age 32. 15 applicants, 100% accepted, 12 enrolled. In 2009, 8 master's awarded. *Degree requirements:* For master's, comprehensive exam (for some programs), thesis optional. *Entrance requirements:* For master's, minimum GPA of 2.5. Additional exam requirements/recommendations for international students: Required—TOEFL (minimum score 550 paper-based; 213 computer-based; 80 iBT). *Application deadline:* For fall admission, 4/15 priority date for domestic students, 3/15 for international students; for spring admission, 10/15 for domestic students, 9/1 for international students. Applications are processed on a rolling basis. Application fee: $35. Electronic applications accepted. *Expenses:* Tuition, state resident: full-time $6666; part-time $370 per credit. Tuition, nonresident: full-time $10,666; part-time $593 per credit. Required fees: $122.56 per credit. *Financial support:* In 2009–10, 1 research assistantship with full and partial tuition reimbursement (averaging $5,000 per year) was awarded; unspecified assistantships also available. Support available to part-time students. Financial award application deadline: 2/15; financial award applicants required to submit FAFSA. *Faculty research:* Developing and using a meteorological data station. *Unit head:* Dr. Marc Gagne, Chair, 610-436-2727, E-mail: mgagne@wcupa.edu. *Application contact:* Dr. Steven Good, Graduate Coordinator, 610-436-2203, E-mail: sgood@wcupa.edu.

Western Connecticut State University, Division of Graduate Studies, School of Arts and Sciences, Department of Physics, Astronomy and Meteorology, Danbury, CT 06810-6885. Offers earth and planetary sciences (MA). Part-time programs available. *Faculty:* 1 full-time (0 women). *Students:* 1 full-time (0 women), 5 part-time (1 woman); includes 1 minority (Hispanic American). Average age 32. 7 applicants, 71% accepted, 2 enrolled. *Degree requirements:* For master's, thesis, completion of program in 6 years. *Entrance requirements:* For master's, minimum GPA of 2.5 or GRE; one year of calculus-based physics, one year of calculus, and semester course in differential equations. Additional exam requirements/recommendations for international students: Recommended—TOEFL (minimum score 550 paper-based; 213 computer-based; 79 iBT), IELTS (minimum score 6). *Application deadline:* For fall admission, 8/5 priority date for domestic students; for spring admission, 1/5 priority date for domestic students. Applications are processed on a rolling basis. Application fee: $50. *Expenses:* Tuition, state resident: full-time $5012; part-time $278 per credit hour. Tuition, nonresident: full-time $13,962; part-time $284 per credit hour. Required fees: $3886; $139 per credit hour. Full-time tuition and fees vary according to course load and program. Part-time tuition and fees vary according to course level, degree level and program. *Financial support:* Application deadline: 5/1; *Unit head:* Dr. Alice Chance, Chairperson, 203-837-8667. *Application contact:* Chris Shankle, Associate Director of Graduate Admissions, 203-837-9005, Fax: 203-837-8326, E-mail: shanklec@wcsu.edu.

Yale University, Graduate School of Arts and Sciences, Department of Astronomy, New Haven, CT 06520. Offers astronomy (PhD); solar and terrestrial physics (PhD). *Degree requirements:* For doctorate, thesis/dissertation. *Entrance requirements:* For doctorate, GRE General Test, GRE Subject Test (physics).

York University, Faculty of Graduate Studies, Faculty of Science and Engineering, Program in Earth and Space Science, Toronto, ON M3J 1P3, Canada. Offers M Sc, PhD. Part-time and evening/weekend programs available. *Degree requirements:* For master's, thesis or alternative; for doctorate, thesis/dissertation. Electronic applications accepted.

Section 4
Marine Sciences and Oceanography

This section contains a directory of institutions offering graduate work in marine sciences and oceanography, followed by in-depth entries submitted by institutions that chose to prepare detailed program descriptions. Additional information about programs listed in the directory but not augmented by an in-depth entry may be obtained by writing directly to the dean of a graduate school or chair of a department at the address given in the directory.

For programs offering related work, see also in this book *Chemistry, Geosciences, Meteorology and Atmospheric Sciences,* and *Physics.* In the other guides in this series:

Graduate Programs in the Biological Sciences

See *Biological and Biomedical Sciences; Ecology, Environmental Biology, and Evolutionary Biology;* and *Marine Biology*

Graduate Programs in Engineering & Applied Sciences

See *Civil and Environmental Engineering, Engineering and Applied Sciences,* and *Ocean Engineering*

CONTENTS

Program Directories

Close-Ups

See also:

Marine Sciences

American University, College of Arts and Sciences, Department of Biology, Washington, DC 20016-8007. Offers applied science (MS); biology (MA, MS); environmental science (MS), including environmental science, marine science. Part-time programs available. *Faculty:* 7 full-time (3 women), 3 part-time/adjunct (1 woman). *Students:* 20 full-time (11 women), 17 part-time (15 women); includes 4 minority (2 African Americans, 2 Asian Americans or Pacific Islanders), 6 international. Average age 27. 55 applicants, 60% accepted, 15 enrolled. In 2009, 12 master's awarded. *Degree requirements:* For master's, comprehensive exam, thesis (for some programs). *Entrance requirements:* For master's, GRE General Test, GRE Subject Test. Additional exam requirements/recommendations for international students: Required—TOEFL. *Application deadline:* For fall admission, 2/1 for domestic students; for spring admission, 10/1 for domestic students. Application fee: $80. *Expenses:* Tuition: Full-time $22,266; part-time $1237 per credit hour. Required fees: $430. Tuition and fees vary according to program. *Financial support:* Fellowships, research assistantships with tuition reimbursements, teaching assistantships with tuition reimbursements, career-related internships or fieldwork, Federal Work-Study, and institutionally sponsored loans available. Financial award application deadline: 2/1. *Faculty research:* Neurobiology, cave biology, population genetics, vertebrate physiology. *Unit head:* Victoria Connaughton, Chair, 202-885-2194, Fax: 202-885-2182, E-mail: vconn@american.edu. *Application contact:* Kathleen Clowery, Director, Graduate Admissions, 202-885-3621, Fax: 202-885-1505.

California State University, East Bay, Academic Programs and Graduate Studies, College of Science, Department of Biological Sciences, Marine Science Program, Moss Landing, CA 95039. Offers MS. *Degree requirements:* For master's, thesis. *Entrance requirements:* For master's, GRE Subject Test, minimum GPA of 3.0 in field, 2.75 overall. Additional exam requirements/recommendations for international students: Required—TOEFL. *Application deadline:* For fall admission, 3/15 for domestic students; for spring admission, 10/15 for domestic students. Application fee: $55. *Financial support:* Federal Work-Study, institutionally sponsored loans, and scholarships/grants available. Support available to part-time students. Financial award application deadline: 3/1; financial award applicants required to submit FAFSA. *Unit head:* Dr. Kenneth H. Coale, Director, 831-771-4400, Fax: 831-632-4403, E-mail: coale@mlml.calstate.edu. *Application contact:* Donna Wiley, Administrative Support Coordinator, 510-885-2928, Fax: 510-885-4777, E-mail: donna.wiley@csueastbay.edu.

California State University, Fresno, Division of Graduate Studies, College of Science and Mathematics, Program in Marine Sciences, Fresno, CA 93740-8027. Offers MS. Part-time programs available. Postbaccalaureate distance learning degree programs offered. *Degree requirements:* For master's, thesis. *Entrance requirements:* For master's, GRE General Test, minimum GPA of 3.0. Additional exam requirements/recommendations for international students: Required—TOEFL. Electronic applications accepted. *Faculty research:* Wetlands ecology, land/water conservation, water irrigation.

California State University, Monterey Bay, College of Science, Media Arts and Technology, Moss Landing Marine Laboratories, Seaside, CA 93955-8001. Offers MS. Part-time programs available. *Degree requirements:* For master's, thesis, thesis defense. *Entrance requirements:* For master's, selected MLML faculty member to serve as potential thesis advisor and selected consortium institution to serve as home campus. Additional exam requirements/recommendations for international students: Required—TOEFL (minimum score 525 paper-based; 213 computer-based; 71 iBT). Electronic applications accepted. *Faculty research:* Remote sensing micro-biology trace elements, chemistry ecology of birds, mammals, turtles and fish, invasive species, marine phycology.

California State University, Sacramento, Graduate Studies, College of Natural Sciences and Mathematics, Department of Biological Sciences, Sacramento, CA 95819. Offers biological sciences (MA, MS); immunohematology (MS); marine science (MS). Part-time programs available. *Degree requirements:* For master's, thesis, writing proficiency exam. *Entrance requirements:* For master's, bachelor's degree in biology or equivalent, minimum GPA of 3.0 in biology, minimum overall GPA of 2.75 during last 2 years of course work. Additional exam requirements/recommendations for international students: Required—TOEFL. Electronic applications accepted.

California State University, Stanislaus, College of Natural Sciences, Department of Biological Sciences, Turlock, CA 95382. Offers ecology and sustainability (MS); genetic counseling (MS); marine sciences (MS). Part-time programs available. *Degree requirements:* For master's, thesis. *Entrance requirements:* For master's, GRE General Test, GRE Subject Test, minimum GPA of 3.0, 3 letters of reference. Additional exam requirements/recommendations for international students: Required—TOEFL (minimum score 550 paper-based; 213 computer-based). Electronic applications accepted. *Faculty research:* Long-term smoking and pregnancy rate, vertebrate paleobiology, terrestrial animals, benthic invertebrates of central California coastline.

Coastal Carolina University, College of Natural and Applied Sciences, Conway, SC 29528-6054. Offers coastal marine and wetland studies (MS). Part-time and evening/weekend programs available. *Faculty:* 19 full-time (2 women), 2 part-time/adjunct (0 women). *Students:* 14 full-time (10 women), 23 part-time (13 women). Average age 25. 37 applicants, 51% accepted, 14 enrolled. In 2009, 10 master's awarded. *Degree requirements:* For master's, thesis. *Entrance requirements:* For master's, GRE, 2 letters of recommendation, resume. Additional exam requirements/recommendations for international students: Required—TOEFL (minimum score 550 paper-based; 213 computer-based; 79 iBT). *Application deadline:* For fall admission, 3/1 priority date for domestic and international students; for spring admission, 11/1 priority date for domestic and international students. Applications are processed on a rolling basis. Application fee: $45. Electronic applications accepted. *Expenses:* Tuition, state resident: full-time $9600; part-time $400 per credit hour. Tuition, nonresident: full-time $11,880; part-time $495 per credit hour. Required fees: $80; $40 per term. *Financial support:* Fellowships, research assistantships, unspecified assistantships available. Support available to part-time students. Financial award application deadline: 3/1; financial award applicants required to submit FAFSA. *Unit head:* Dr. Michael H. Roberts, Dean, 843-349-2282, Fax: 843-349-2545, E-mail: mroberts@coastal.edu. *Application contact:* Dr. Richard L. Johnson, Director of Graduate Studies, 843-349-2192, Fax: 843-349-6444, E-mail: rjohnson@coastal.edu.

College of Charleston, Graduate School, School of Sciences and Mathematics, Program in Marine Biology, Charleston, SC 29412. Offers MS. *Faculty:* 100. *Students:* 52 full-time (31 women); includes 1 minority (Hispanic American). Average age 26. 88 applicants, 25% accepted, 16 enrolled. In 2009, 14 master's awarded. *Degree requirements:* For master's, comprehensive exam, thesis. *Entrance requirements:* For master's, GRE General Test, 3 letters of recommendation. Additional exam requirements/recommendations for international students: Required—TOEFL. *Application deadline:* For fall admission, 2/1 for domestic and international students; for spring admission, 11/1 for domestic and international students. Application fee: $45. Electronic applications accepted. *Financial support:* In 2009–10, 4 fellowships (averaging $22,000 per year), 22 research assistantships, 19 teaching assistantships were awarded; career-related internships or fieldwork, Federal Work-Study, institutionally sponsored loans, scholarships/grants, and unspecified assistantships also available. Support available to part-time students. Financial award application deadline: 4/1; financial award applicants required to submit FAFSA. *Faculty research:* Ecology, environmental physiology, marine genomics, bioinformatics, toxicology, cell biology, population biology, fisheries science, animal physiology, biodiversity, estuarine ecology, evolution and systematics, microbial processes, plant physiology, immunology. *Unit head:* Dr. Craig J. Plante, Director, 843-953-9187, Fax: 843-953-9199, E-mail: plantec@cofc.edu. *Application contact:* Susan Hallatt, Director of Graduate Admissions, 843-953-5614, Fax: 843-953-1434, E-mail: hallatts@cofc.edu.

The College of William and Mary, Virginia Institute of Marine Science, Gloucester Point, VA 23062. Offers MS, PhD. *Faculty:* 54 full-time (13 women), 9 part-time/adjunct (1 woman). *Students:* 93 full-time (65 women), 3 part-time (1 woman); includes 9 minority (3 African Americans, 1 American Indian/Alaska Native, 2 Asian Americans or Pacific Islanders, 3 Hispanic Americans), 11 international. Average age 28. 132 applicants, 23% accepted, 25 enrolled. In 2009, 9 master's, 11 doctorates awarded. *Degree requirements:* For master's, thesis, qualifying exam; for doctorate, comprehensive exam, thesis/dissertation, qualifying exam. *Entrance requirements:* For master's, GRE, appropriate bachelor's degree; for doctorate, GRE, appropriate bachelor's and master's degrees. Additional exam requirements/recommendations for international students: Required—TOEFL. *Application deadline:* For fall admission, 1/15 for domestic and international students. Application fee: $50. Electronic applications accepted. *Expenses:* Tuition, state resident: full-time $6400; part-time $315 per credit hour. Tuition, nonresident: full-time $19,720; part-time $840 per credit hour. Required fees: $4114. *Financial support:* In 2009–10, 93 students received support, including 15 fellowships with full tuition reimbursements available (averaging $19,005 per year), 70 research assistantships with full tuition reimbursements available (averaging $19,005 per year), 8 teaching assistantships with full tuition reimbursements available (averaging $6,500 per year); career-related internships or fieldwork, Federal Work-Study, scholarships/grants, health care benefits, and unspecified assistantships also available. Support available to part-time students. Financial award application deadline: 6/15; financial award applicants required to submit FAFSA. Total annual research expenditures: $19.4 million. *Unit head:* Dr. John T. Wells, Dean/Director, 804-684-7102, Fax: 804-684-7009, E-mail: wells@vims.edu. *Application contact:* Fonda J. Powell, Admissions Coordinator, 804-684-7105, Fax: 804-684-7881, E-mail: fonda@vims.edu.

Cornell University, Graduate School, Graduate Fields of Agriculture and Life Sciences, Field of Natural Resources, Ithaca, NY 14853-0001. Offers aquatic science (MPS, MS, PhD); environmental management (MPS); fishery science (MPS, MS, PhD); forest science (MPS, MS, PhD); resource policy and management (MPS, MS, PhD); wildlife science (MPS, MS, PhD). *Faculty:* 39 full-time (7 women). *Students:* 60 full-time (28 women); includes 4 minority (2 American Indian/Alaska Native, 1 Asian American or Pacific Islander, 1 Hispanic American), 13 international. Average age 31. 63 applicants, 32% accepted, 19 enrolled. In 2009, 6 master's, 7 doctorates awarded. *Degree requirements:* For master's, thesis (MS), project paper (MPS); for doctorate, comprehensive exam, thesis/dissertation. *Entrance requirements:* For master's and doctorate, GRE General Test, 2 letters of recommendation. Additional exam requirements/recommendations for international students: Required—TOEFL (minimum score 550 paper-based; 213 computer-based; 77 iBT). *Application deadline:* For spring admission, 10/30 for domestic students. Applications are processed on a rolling basis. Application fee: $70. Electronic applications accepted. *Expenses:* Tuition: Full-time $29,500. Required fees: $70. Full-time tuition and fees vary according to degree level, program and student level. *Financial support:* In 2009–10, 39 students received support, including 12 research assistantships with full tuition reimbursements available, 5 teaching assistantships with full tuition reimbursements available; fellowships with full tuition reimbursements available, institutionally sponsored loans, scholarships/grants, health care benefits, tuition waivers (full and partial), and unspecified assistantships also available. Financial award applicants required to submit FAFSA. *Faculty research:* Ecosystem-level dynamics, systems modeling, conservation biology/management, resource management's human dimensions, biogeochemistry. *Unit head:* Director of Graduate Studies, 607-255-2807, Fax: 607-255-0349. *Application contact:* Graduate Field Assistant, 607-255-2807, Fax: 607-255-0349, E-mail: nrgrad@cornell.edu.

Duke University, Nicholas School of the Environment, Durham, NC 27708-0328. Offers coastal environmental management (MEM); DEL-environmental leadership (MEM); energy and environment (MEM); environmental economics and policy (MEM); environmental health and security (MEM); forest resource management (MF); global environmental change (MEM); resource ecology (MEM); water and air resources (MEM); JD/AM; JD/MEM; JD/MF; MAT/MEM; MBA/MEM; MBA/MF; MEM/MPP; MF/MPP. *Accreditation:* SAF (one or more programs are accredited). Part-time programs available. *Degree requirements:* For master's, thesis. *Entrance requirements:* For master's, GRE General Test, previous course work in biology or ecology, calculus, statistics, and microeconomics; computer familiarity with word processing and data analysis. Additional exam requirements/recommendations for international students: Required—TOEFL (minimum score 550 paper-based; 213 computer-based). Electronic applications accepted. *Expenses:* Contact institution. *Faculty research:* Ecosystem management, conservation ecology, earth systems, risk assessment.

Florida Institute of Technology, Graduate Programs, College of Engineering, Department of Marine and Environmental Systems, Program in Oceanography, Melbourne, FL 32901-6975. Offers biological oceanography (MS); chemical oceanography (MS); coastal zone management (MS); geological oceanography (MS); oceanography (PhD); physical oceanography (MS). Part-time programs available. *Students:* Average age 30. Terminal master's awarded for partial completion of doctoral program. *Degree requirements:* For master's, thesis (for some programs); for doctorate, one foreign language, comprehensive exam, thesis/dissertation, departmental qualifying exams. *Entrance requirements:* For master's, GRE General Test, minimum GPA of 3.0; for doctorate, GRE General Test, minimum GPA of 3.3, resume. *Application deadline:* Applications are processed on a rolling basis. Electronic applications accepted. *Expenses:* Tuition: Part-time $1015 per credit. Tuition and fees vary according to campus/location and program. *Financial support:* Research assistantships with full and partial tuition reimbursements, teaching assistantships with full and partial tuition reimbursements, career-related internships or fieldwork and tuition remissions available. Financial award application deadline: 3/1; financial award applicants required to submit FAFSA. *Faculty research:* Marine geochemistry, ecosystem dynamics, coastal processes, marine pollution, environmental modeling. Total annual research expenditures: $938,395. *Unit head:* Dr. Dean R. Norris, Chair, 321-674-7377, Fax: 321-674-7212, E-mail: norris@fit.edu. *Application contact:* Carolyn P. Shea.

See Close-Ups on pages 167 and 411.

Georgia Institute of Technology, Graduate Studies and Research, College of Sciences, School of Earth and Atmospheric Sciences, Atlanta, GA 30332-0340. Offers atmospheric chemistry, aerosols and clouds (MS, PhD); dynamics of weather and climate (MS, PhD); geochemistry (MS, PhD); geophysics (MS, PhD); oceanography (MS, PhD); paleoclimate (MS, PhD); planetary science (MS, PhD); remote sensing (MS, PhD). Part-time programs available. Terminal master's awarded for partial completion of doctoral program. *Degree requirements:* For master's, thesis or alternative; for doctorate, comprehensive exam, thesis/dissertation. *Entrance requirements:* For master's, GRE, letters of recommendation; for doctorate, GRE, academic transcripts, letters of recommendation, personal statement. Additional exam requirements/recommendations for international students: Required—TOEFL (minimum score 550 paper-based; 213 computer-based; 79 iBT). *Faculty research:* Geophysics; atmospheric chemistry, aerosols and clouds; dynamics of weather and climate; geochemistry; oceanography; paleoclimate; planetary science; remote sensing.

Hawai'i Pacific University, College of Natural and Computational Sciences, Honolulu, HI 96813. Offers global leadership and sustainable development (MA); marine science (MS). *Faculty:* 15 full-time (5 women), 5 part-time/adjunct (1 woman). *Students:* 23 full-time (14 women), 8 part-time (7 women); includes 4 minority (all Asian Americans or Pacific Islanders), 2 international. Average age 25. 38 applicants, 71% accepted, 15 enrolled. In 2009, 3 master's awarded. *Degree requirements:* For master's, thesis. *Entrance requirements:* For master's,

GRE, bachelor's degree in science or marine science, minimum GPA of 3.0. Additional exam requirements/recommendations for international students: Recommended—TOEFL (minimum score 550 paper-based; 213 computer-based; 80 iBT), TWE (minimum score 5). *Application deadline:* For fall admission, 2/15 priority date for domestic students; for spring admission, 10/15 priority date for domestic students. Applications are processed on a rolling basis. Application fee: $50. Electronic applications accepted. *Expenses:* Tuition: Full-time $12,600; part-time $700 per credit hour. Tuition and fees vary according to program. *Financial support:* In 2009–10, 21 students received support. Federal Work-Study, scholarships/grants, and unspecified assistantships available. Support available to part-time students. *Unit head:* Dr. Andrew Brittain, Vice President, Research/Dean, 808-236-3553, Fax: 808-236-5880, E-mail: abrittain@hpu.edu. *Application contact:* Danny Lam, Assistant Director of Graduate Admissions, 808-544-1135, Fax: 808-544-0280, E-mail: graduate@hpu.edu.

Medical University of South Carolina, College of Graduate Studies, Program in Molecular and Cellular Biology and Pathobiology, Charleston, SC 29425. Offers cancer biology (PhD); cardiovascular biology (PhD); cardiovascular imaging (PhD); cell regulation (PhD); craniofacial biology (PhD); genetics and development (PhD); marine biomedicine (PhD); DMD/PhD; MD/PhD. *Faculty:* 137 full-time (33 women). *Students:* 39 full-time (25 women); includes 6 minority (4 African Americans, 1 Asian American or Pacific Islander, 1 Hispanic American), 9 international. Average age 28. In 2009, 16 doctorates awarded. *Degree requirements:* For doctorate, thesis/dissertation, oral and written exams. *Entrance requirements:* For doctorate, GRE General Test, interview, minimum GPA of 3.0. Additional exam requirements/recommendations for international students: Required—TOEFL (minimum score 600 paper-based; 250 computer-based; 100 iBT). *Application deadline:* For fall admission, 1/15 priority date for domestic and international students. Applications are processed on a rolling basis. Application fee: $0 ($85 for international students). Electronic applications accepted. *Financial support:* In 2009–10, 39 students received support, including 39 research assistantships with partial tuition reimbursements available (averaging $23,000 per year); Federal Work-Study and scholarships/grants also available. Support available to part-time students. Financial award application deadline: 3/10; financial award applicants required to submit FAFSA. *Unit head:* Dr. Donald R. Menick, Director, 843-876-5045, Fax: 843-792-6590, E-mail: menickd@musc.edu. *Application contact:* Dr. Cynthia F. Wright, Associate Dean for Admissions and Career Development, 843-792-2564, Fax: 843-792-6590, E-mail: wrightcf@musc.edu.

Memorial University of Newfoundland, School of Graduate Studies, Interdisciplinary Program in Marine Studies, St. John's, NL A1C 5S7, Canada. Offers fisheries resource management (MMS, Advanced Diploma). Part-time programs available. *Degree requirements:* For master's, report. *Entrance requirements:* For master's and Advanced Diploma, high 2nd class degree from a recognized university. *Faculty research:* Biological, ecological and oceanographic aspects of world fisheries; economics; political science; sociology.

North Carolina State University, Graduate School, College of Physical and Mathematical Sciences, Department of Marine, Earth, and Atmospheric Sciences, Raleigh, NC 27695. Offers marine, earth, and atmospheric sciences (MS, PhD); meteorology (MS, PhD); oceanography (MS, PhD). Terminal master's awarded for partial completion of doctoral program. *Degree requirements:* For master's, thesis (for some programs), final oral exam; for doctorate, comprehensive exam, thesis/dissertation, final oral exam, preliminary oral and written exams. *Entrance requirements:* For master's, GRE General Test, minimum GPA of 3.0; for doctorate, GRE General Test, GRE Subject Test (for disciplines in biological oceanography and geology), minimum GPA of 3.0. Additional exam requirements/recommendations for international students: Required—TOEFL (minimum score 550 paper-based). Electronic applications accepted. *Faculty research:* Boundary layer and air quality meteorology; climate and mesoscale dynamics; biological, chemical, geological, and physical oceanography; hard rock, soft rock, environmental, and paleo-geology.

Nova Southeastern University, Oceanographic Center, Program in Coastal Zone Management, Dania Beach, FL 33004. Offers MS. *Faculty:* 15 full-time (1 woman), 5 part-time/adjunct (0 women). *Students:* 16 full-time (11 women), 50 part-time (34 women); includes 10 minority (6 African Americans, 1 Asian American or Pacific Islander, 3 Hispanic Americans). Average age 28. 35 applicants, 86% accepted, 20 enrolled. In 2009, 5 master's awarded. *Entrance requirements:* For master's, GRE. Additional exam requirements/recommendations for international students: Required—TOEFL (minimum score 550 paper-based). *Application deadline:* Applications are processed on a rolling basis. Application fee: $50. *Financial support:* Career-related internships or fieldwork, Federal Work-Study, scholarships/grants, and unspecified assistantships available. Financial award applicants required to submit FAFSA. *Unit head:* Dr. Richard Spieler, Director of Academic Programs, 954-262-3600, Fax: 954-262-4020, E-mail: spieler@nova.edu. *Application contact:* Dr. Richard Spieler, Director of Academic Programs, 954-262-3600, Fax: 954-262-4020, E-mail: spieler@nova.edu.

Nova Southeastern University, Oceanographic Center, Program in Marine Environmental Science, Fort Lauderdale, FL 33314-7796. Offers MS. *Faculty:* 15 full-time (1 woman), 5 part-time/adjunct (0 women). *Students:* 4 full-time (3 women), 4 part-time (3 women). 10 applicants, 100% accepted, 3 enrolled. In 2009, 1 master's awarded. *Degree requirements:* For master's, thesis. *Entrance requirements:* For master's, GRE. Additional exam requirements/recommendations for international students: Required—TOEFL (minimum score 550 paper-based). *Application deadline:* Applications are processed on a rolling basis. Application fee: $50. *Unit head:* Dr. Richard Dodge, Dean, 954-262-3600, Fax: 954-262-4020, E-mail: dodge@nsu.nova.edu. *Application contact:* Dr. Richard Spieler, Director of Academic Programs, 954-262-3600, Fax: 954-262-4020, E-mail: spieler@nova.edu.

Oregon State University, Graduate School, College of Oceanic and Atmospheric Sciences, Program in Marine Resource Management, Corvallis, OR 97331. Offers MA, MS. *Students:* 26 full-time (15 women), 3 part-time (all women); includes 3 minority (2 Asian Americans or Pacific Islanders, 1 Hispanic American), 2 international. Average age 30. In 2009, 9 master's awarded. *Degree requirements:* For master's, thesis optional. *Entrance requirements:* For master's, GRE General Test, minimum GPA of 3.0 in last 90 hours of course work. Additional exam requirements/recommendations for international students: Required—TOEFL. *Application deadline:* For fall admission, 2/1 priority date for domestic students. Applications are processed on a rolling basis. Application fee: $50. *Expenses:* Tuition, state resident: full-time $9774; part-time $362 per credit. Tuition, nonresident: full-time $15,849; part-time $587 per credit. Required fees: $1639. Full-time tuition and fees vary according to course load and program. *Financial support:* Fellowships, research assistantships, teaching assistantships, career-related internships or fieldwork, Federal Work-Study, and institutionally sponsored loans available. Support available to part-time students. Financial award application deadline: 2/1. *Faculty research:* Ocean and coastal resources, fisheries resources, marine pollution, marine recreation and tourism. *Unit head:* Dr. Robert S. Allan, Assistant Director, Student Programs, 541-737-1340, Fax: 541-737-2064, E-mail: rallan@coas.oregonstate.edu. *Application contact:* Dr. Robert S. Allan, Assistant Director, Student Programs, 541-737-1340, Fax: 541-737-2064, E-mail: rallan@coas.oregonstate.edu.

San Francisco State University, Division of Graduate Studies, College of Science and Engineering, Department of Biology, Program in Marine Science, San Francisco, CA 94132-1722. Offers MS.

San Jose State University, Graduate Studies and Research, College of Science, Moss Landing Marine Laboratories, San Jose, CA 95192-0001. Offers MS. *Students:* 1 (woman) full-time, 29 part-time (21 women); includes 6 minority (5 Asian Americans or Pacific Islanders, 1 Hispanic American). Average age 30. 19 applicants, 21% accepted, 4 enrolled. In 2009, 2 master's awarded. *Degree requirements:* For master's, thesis, qualifying exam. *Entrance requirements:* For master's, GRE. *Application deadline:* For fall admission, 6/29 for domestic students; for spring admission, 11/30 for domestic students. Applications are processed on a rolling basis. Application fee: $59. Electronic applications accepted. *Financial support:* Teaching assistantships, career-related internships or fieldwork available. Support available to part-time students. Financial award applicants required to submit FAFSA. *Faculty research:* Physical oceanography, marine geology, ecology, ichthyology, invertebrate zoology. *Unit head:* Dr. Kenneth H. Coale, Director, 831-771-4400, Fax: 831-632-4403. *Application contact:* Dr. Kenneth H. Coale, Director, 831-771-4400, Fax: 831-632-4403.

Savannah State University, Master of Science in Marine Sciences Program, Savannah, GA 31404. Offers MS. Part-time programs available. *Students:* 8 full-time (6 women), 9 part-time (7 women); includes 3 African Americans, 1 Asian American or Pacific Islander. In 2009, 5 master's awarded. *Entrance requirements:* For master's, GRE General Test. Additional exam requirements/recommendations for international students: Required—TOEFL. *Application deadline:* For fall admission, 7/1 for domestic students, 5/15 for international students; for spring admission, 10/31 for domestic students, 10/1 for international students. Applications are processed on a rolling basis. Application fee: $20. Electronic applications accepted. *Expenses:* Tuition, state resident: full-time $3662; part-time $153 per credit hour. Tuition, nonresident: full-time $14,648. Required fees: $450 per term. *Financial support:* Career-related internships or fieldwork, Federal Work-Study, institutionally sponsored loans, scholarships/grants, and unspecified assistantships available. Financial award applicants required to submit FAFSA. *Unit head:* Dr. Matthew Gilligan, Coordinator, 912-356-2808, E-mail: gilliganm@savannahstate.edu. *Application contact:* Emily Crawford, Interim Dean of Graduate Studies, 912-356-2244, Fax: 912-356-2299, E-mail: crawford@savnnahstate.edu.

Stony Brook University, State University of New York, Graduate School, School of Marine and Atmospheric Sciences, Institute for Terrestrial and Planetary Atmospheres, Program in Marine Sciences, Stony Brook, NY 11794. Offers MS, PhD. Evening/weekend programs available. *Degree requirements:* For doctorate, one foreign language, comprehensive exam, thesis/dissertation. *Entrance requirements:* For master's, GRE General Test, official transcripts, minimum GPA of 3.0, 3 letters of recommendation; for doctorate, GRE General Test, minimum GPA of 3.0, 3 letters of recommendation. Additional exam requirements/recommendations for international students: Required—TOEFL (minimum score 600 paper-based; 213 computer-based). *Application deadline:* For fall admission, 1/15 priority date for domestic students; for spring admission, 10/1 priority date for domestic students. Application fee: $60. Electronic applications accepted. *Expenses:* Tuition, state resident: full-time $8370; part-time $349 per credit. Tuition, nonresident: full-time $13,250; part-time $552 per credit. Required fees: $933. *Financial support:* Fellowships, research assistantships, teaching assistantships, career-related internships or fieldworks available. *Unit head:* Minghua Zhang, Director, 631-632-8318. *Application contact:* Dr. Glenn R. Lopez, Assistant Director, 631-632-8660, Fax: 631-632-8200, E-mail: glopez@notes.cc.sunysb.edu.

Texas A&M University at Galveston, Department of Marine Sciences, Galveston, TX 77553-1675. Offers marine resources management (MMRM). *Faculty:* 33 full-time (7 women). *Students:* 18 full-time (15 women), 13 part-time (8 women); includes 2 minority (both African Americans). Average age 23. 11 applicants, 64% accepted, 7 enrolled. In 2009, 5 master's awarded. *Entrance requirements:* For master's, GRE, course work in economics. Additional exam requirements/recommendations for international students: Required—TOEFL (minimum score 550 paper-based; 213 computer-based). *Application deadline:* Applications are processed on a rolling basis. Application fee: $50 ($75 for international students). Electronic applications accepted. *Financial support:* In 2009–10, 14 students received support; research assistantships, teaching assistantships, scholarships/grants, health care benefits, and unspecified assistantships available. Financial award application deadline: 4/1; financial award applicants required to submit FAFSA. *Faculty research:* Biogeochemistry, physical oceanography, theoretical chemistry, marine policy. Total annual research expenditures: $3.8 million. *Unit head:* Dr. Ernest Estes, Head, 409-710-4599. *Application contact:* Dr. Frederick C. Schlemmer, Associate Professor/Graduate Advisor, 409-740-4518, Fax: 409-740-4429, E-mail: schlemme@tamug.edu.

Texas A&M University–Corpus Christi, Graduate Studies and Research, College of Science and Technology, Program in Coastal and Marine System Science, Corpus Christi, TX 78412-5503. Offers PhD.

University of Alaska Fairbanks, School of Fisheries and Ocean Sciences, Program in Marine Sciences and Limnology, Fairbanks, AK 99775-7220. Offers marine biology (MS, PhD); oceanography (PhD), including biological oceanography, chemical oceanography, fisheries, geological oceanography, physical oceanography. Part-time programs available. *Faculty:* 12 full-time (5 women), 2 part-time/adjunct (0 women). *Students:* 29 full-time (17 women), 14 part-time (9 women); includes 4 minority (2 Asian Americans or Pacific Islanders, 2 Hispanic Americans), 2 international. Average age 33. 45 applicants, 18% accepted, 8 enrolled. In 2009, 8 master's, 2 doctorates awarded. *Degree requirements:* For master's, comprehensive exam, thesis, oral defense; for doctorate, comprehensive exam, thesis/dissertation, oral defense. *Entrance requirements:* For master's and doctorate, GRE General Test. Additional exam requirements/recommendations for international students: Required—TOEFL (minimum score 550 paper-based; 213 computer-based; 80 iBT). *Application deadline:* For fall admission, 6/1 for domestic students, 3/1 for international students; for spring admission, 10/15 for domestic students, 8/1 for international students. Applications are processed on a rolling basis. Application fee: $60. Electronic applications accepted. *Expenses:* Tuition, state resident: full-time $7584; part-time $316 per credit. Tuition, nonresident: full-time $15,504; part-time $646 per credit. Required fees: $23 per credit. $135 per semester. Tuition and fees vary according to course level, course load and reciprocity agreements. *Financial support:* In 2009–10, 3 fellowships (averaging $10,865 per year), 18 research assistantships (averaging $10,454 per year), 6 teaching assistantships (averaging $10,748 per year) were awarded; career-related internships or fieldwork, Federal Work-Study, scholarships/grants, health care benefits, and unspecified assistantships also available. Support available to part-time students. Financial award application deadline: 7/1; financial award applicants required to submit FAFSA. *Unit head:* Dr. Denis Wiesenberg, Dean, 907-474-7824, Fax: 907-474-7204, E-mail: info@sfos.uaf.edu. *Application contact:* Katie Straub, Recruitment and Retention Coordinator, 907-474-6786, Fax: 907-474-5863, E-mail: kmstraub@alaska.edu.

The University of British Columbia, Faculty of Science, Department of Earth and Ocean Sciences, Vancouver, BC V6T 1Z4, Canada. Offers atmospheric science (M Sc, PhD); geological engineering (M Eng, MA Sc, PhD); geological sciences (M Sc, PhD); geophysics (M Sc, MA Sc, PhD); oceanography (M Sc, PhD). *Degree requirements:* For master's, thesis (for some programs); for doctorate, comprehensive exam, thesis/dissertation. *Entrance requirements:* Additional exam requirements/recommendations for international students: Required—TOEFL (minimum score 600 paper-based; 250 computer-based; 100 iBT). Electronic applications accepted. *Faculty research:* Oceans and atmosphere, environmental earth science, hydro geology, mineral deposits, geophysics.

University of California, San Diego, Office of Graduate Studies, Scripps Institution of Oceanography, Program in Marine Biodiversity and Conservation, La Jolla, CA 92093. Offers MAS. *Entrance requirements:* For master's, minimum 3 years post-baccalaureate work experience. Additional exam requirements/recommendations for international students: Required—TOEFL. Electronic applications accepted.

University of California, Santa Barbara, Graduate Division, College of Letters and Sciences, Division of Mathematics, Life, and Physical Sciences, Interdepartmental Program in Marine Science, Santa Barbara, CA 93106-9620. Offers MS, PhD. *Faculty:* 47 full-time (11 women). *Students:* 34 full-time (18 women). Average age 29. 44 applicants, 23% accepted, 6 enrolled. In 2009, 1 master's, 9 doctorates awarded. *Degree requirements:* For master's, thesis; for doctorate, comprehensive exam, thesis/dissertation, 31 units. *Entrance requirements:* For

Marine Sciences

University of California, Santa Barbara (continued)
master's, GRE, 3 letters of recommendation, resume/curriculum vitae; for doctorate, GRE, 3 letters of recommendation, statement of purpose, personal achievements/contributions statement, resume/curriculum vitae, transcripts for post-secondary institutions attended. Additional exam requirements/recommendations for international students: Required—TOEFL (minimum score 550 paper-based; 213 computer-based; 80 iBT) or IELTS (minimum score 7). *Application deadline:* For fall admission, 12/15 for domestic and international students. Application fee: $70 ($90 for international students). Electronic applications accepted. *Financial support:* In 2009–10, 32 students received support, including 18 fellowships with full and partial tuition reimbursements available (averaging $14,200 per year), 19 research assistantships with full and partial tuition reimbursements available (averaging $6,900 per year), 14 teaching assistantships with partial tuition reimbursements available (averaging $8,200 per year); career-related internships or fieldwork, Federal Work-Study, institutionally sponsored loans, scholarships/grants, health care benefits, tuition waivers (full and partial), and unspecified assistantships also available. Financial award application deadline: 12/15; financial award applicants required to submit FAFSA. *Faculty research:* Ocean carbon cycling, paleooceanography, physiology of marine organisms, bio-optical oceanography, biological oceanography. *Unit head:* Prof. Libe Washburn, Chair, 805-893-7367, Fax: 805-893-2578, E-mail: washburn@icess.ucsb.edu. *Application contact:* Melanie Fujii, Graduate Program Assistant, 805-893-8162, Fax: 805-893-5885, E-mail: fujii@lifesci.ucsb.edu.

University of California, Santa Cruz, Division of Graduate Studies, Division of Physical and Biological Sciences, Department of Ocean Sciences, Santa Cruz, CA 95064. Offers MS, PhD. *Degree requirements:* For doctorate, one foreign language, thesis/dissertation. *Entrance requirements:* For doctorate, GRE General Test, GRE Subject Test. Electronic applications accepted.

University of Connecticut, Graduate School, College of Liberal Arts and Sciences, Department of Marine Sciences, Storrs, CT 06269. Offers MS, PhD. *Faculty:* 25 full-time (6 women). *Students:* 28 full-time (17 women), 10 part-time (5 women); includes 3 minority (2 African Americans, 1 Hispanic American), 8 international. Average age 33. 24 applicants, 4% accepted, 1 enrolled. In 2009, 5 master's, 1 doctorate awarded. Terminal master's awarded for partial completion of doctoral program. *Degree requirements:* For master's, comprehensive exam; for doctorate, thesis/dissertation. *Entrance requirements:* Additional exam requirements/recommendations for international students: Required—TOEFL (minimum score 550 paper-based; 213 computer-based). *Application deadline:* For fall admission, 2/1 for domestic and international students; for spring admission, 11/1 for domestic students, 10/1 for international students. Applications are processed on a rolling basis. Application fee: $55. Electronic applications accepted. *Expenses:* Tuition, state resident: full-time $4725; part-time $525 per credit. Tuition, nonresident: full-time $12,267; part-time $1363 per credit. Required fees: $346 per semester. Tuition and fees vary according to course load. *Financial support:* In 2009–10, 17 research assistantships with full tuition reimbursements, 11 teaching assistantships with full tuition reimbursements were awarded; fellowships, Federal Work-Study, scholarships/grants, health care benefits, and unspecified assistantships also available. Financial award application deadline: 2/1; financial award applicants required to submit FAFSA. *Unit head:* Ann Bucklin, Director, 860-405-9208, Fax: 860-405-9153, E-mail: ann.bucklin@uconn.edu. *Application contact:* Pieter Visscher, Chairperson, 860-405-9159, Fax: 860-405-9153, E-mail: visscher@uconnvm.uconn.edu.

University of Delaware, College of Marine and Earth Studies, Newark, DE 19716. Offers geology (MS, PhD); marine policy (MS); marine studies (MMP, MS, PhD); oceanography (MS, PhD). *Degree requirements:* For master's, thesis; for doctorate, thesis/dissertation. *Entrance requirements:* For master's and doctorate, GRE General Test. Additional exam requirements/recommendations for international students: Required—TOEFL. Electronic applications accepted. *Faculty research:* Marine biology and biochemistry, oceanography, marine policy, physical ocean science and engineering, ocean engineering.

University of Florida, Graduate School, College of Agricultural and Life Sciences, Department of Fisheries and Aquatic Sciences, Gainesville, FL 32611. Offers MFAS, MS, PhD. *Degree requirements:* For master's, thesis optional; for doctorate, thesis/dissertation. *Entrance requirements:* For master's and doctorate, GRE General Test, minimum GPA of 3.0. Additional exam requirements/recommendations for international students: Required—TOEFL. Electronic applications accepted.

University of Georgia, Graduate School, College of Arts and Sciences, Department of Marine Sciences, Athens, GA 30602. Offers MS, PhD. *Faculty:* 16 full-time (5 women), 1 part-time/adjunct (0 women). *Students:* 28 full-time (14 women), 1 (woman) part-time; includes 2 minority (both Hispanic Americans), 7 international. Average age 28. 45 applicants, 31% accepted, 9 enrolled. In 2009, 1 master's, 1 doctorate awarded. *Degree requirements:* For master's, thesis; for doctorate, comprehensive exam, thesis/dissertation, teaching experience, field research experience. *Entrance requirements:* For master's and doctorate, GRE General Test. Additional exam requirements/recommendations for international students: Required—TOEFL. *Application deadline:* For fall admission, 2/1 priority date for domestic and international students; for spring admission, 10/15 priority date for domestic students, 9/1 priority date for international students. Applications are processed on a rolling basis. Application fee: $50. Electronic applications accepted. *Expenses:* Tuition, state resident: full-time $6000; part-time $250 per credit hour. Tuition, nonresident: full-time $20,904; part-time $871 per credit hour. Required fees: $730 per semester. *Financial support:* In 2009–10, 9 fellowships with full tuition reimbursements (averaging $20,000 per year), 21 research assistantships with full tuition reimbursements (averaging $18,000 per year), 11 teaching assistantships with full tuition reimbursements (averaging $18,000 per year) were awarded. *Faculty research:* Microbial ecology, biogeochemistry, polar biology, coastal ecology, coastal circulation. *Unit head:* Dr. James T. Hollibaugh, Director, 706-542-7671, Fax: 706-542-5888, E-mail: aquadoc@uga.edu. *Application contact:* Dr. Wei-Jun Cai, Graduate Coordinator, 706-542-1285, E-mail: gradmar@uga.edu.

University of Hawaii at Manoa, Graduate Division, College of Social Sciences, Department of Geography, Graduate Ocean Policy Certificate Program, Honolulu, HI 96822. Offers Graduate Certificate. Part-time programs available. *Students:* 4 full-time (2 women), 2 part-time (1 woman). 4 applicants, 100% accepted, 2 enrolled. In 2009, 2 Graduate Certificates awarded. *Entrance requirements:* Additional exam requirements/recommendations for international students: Required—TOEFL (minimum score 500 paper-based; 173 computer-based; 61 iBT), IELTS (minimum score 5). *Application deadline:* For fall admission, 3/1 for domestic students, 2/1 for international students; for spring admission, 9/1 for domestic students, 8/1 for international students. Application fee: $60. *Expenses:* Tuition, state resident: full-time $8900; part-time $372 per credit. Tuition, nonresident: full-time $21,400; part-time $898 per credit. Required fees: $207 per semester. *Financial support:* In 2009–10, 1 student received support, including 2 fellowships (averaging $936 per year), 1 research assistantship (averaging $25,902 per year), 1 teaching assistantship (averaging $15,558 per year). Total annual research expenditures: $21.4 million. *Application contact:* Alison Rieser, Program Director, 808-956-8467, Fax: 808-956-3512, E-mail: rieser@hawaii.edu.

University of Maine, Graduate School, College of Natural Sciences, Forestry, and Agriculture, School of Marine Sciences, Orono, ME 04469. Offers marine biology (MS, PhD); marine policy (MS); oceanography (MS, PhD). Part-time programs available. *Faculty:* 27 full-time (9 women), 3 part-time/adjunct (1 woman). *Students:* 33 full-time (17 women), 20 part-time (9 women); includes 1 minority (Hispanic American), 7 international. Average age 29. 77 applicants, 18% accepted, 10 enrolled. In 2009, 12 master's, 3 doctorates awarded. *Degree requirements:* For master's, thesis; for doctorate, thesis/dissertation. *Entrance requirements:* For master's and doctorate, GRE General Test. Additional exam requirements/recommendations for international students: Required—TOEFL. *Application deadline:* For fall admission, 2/1 priority date for domestic students. Applications are processed on a rolling basis. Application fee: $65. Electronic applications accepted. *Financial support:* In 2009–10, 1 fellowship with tuition reimbursement (averaging $20,000 per year), 42 research assistantships with tuition reimbursements (averaging $19,170 per year), 3 teaching assistantships with tuition reimbursements (averaging $12,790 per year) were awarded; career-related internships or fieldwork, Federal Work-Study, and tuition waivers (full and partial) also available. Support available to part-time students. Financial award application deadline: 3/1. *Faculty research:* Coastal processes, microbial ecology, crustacean systematics. *Unit head:* Dr. Peter Jumars, Director, 207-581-3321, Fax: 207-581-4388. *Application contact:* Scott G. Delcourt, Associate Dean of the Graduate School, 207-581-3291, Fax: 207-581-3232, E-mail: graduate@maine.edu.

University of Maryland, Baltimore, Graduate School, Program in Marine-Estuarine-Environmental Sciences, Baltimore, MD 21201. Offers MS, PhD. Part-time programs available. *Faculty:* 8. Terminal master's awarded for partial completion of doctoral program. *Degree requirements:* For master's, thesis, oral defense; for doctorate, comprehensive exam, thesis/dissertation, proposal defense, oral defense. *Entrance requirements:* For master's and doctorate, GRE General Test, minimum GPA of 3.0. Additional exam requirements/recommendations for international students: Required—TOEFL. *Application deadline:* For fall admission, 2/1 for domestic students, 1/1 for international students; for spring admission, 9/1 for domestic students. Applications are processed on a rolling basis. Application fee: $50. Electronic applications accepted. *Expenses:* Tuition, state resident: full-time $7290; part-time $405 per credit hour. Tuition, nonresident: full-time $12,780; part-time $710 per credit hour. Required fees: $774; $10 per credit hour. $297 per semester. Tuition and fees vary according to course load, degree level and program. *Financial support:* Fellowships with tuition reimbursements, research assistantships with tuition reimbursements, teaching assistantships with tuition reimbursements, scholarships/grants and unspecified assistantships available. *Unit head:* Dr. Kennedy T. Paynter, Director, 301-405-6938, Fax: 301-314-4139, E-mail: mees@umd.edu. *Application contact:* Dr. Kennedy T. Paynter, Director, 301-405-6938, Fax: 301-314-4139, E-mail: mees@umd.edu.

See Close-Up on page 169 and Display on page 161.

University of Maryland, Baltimore County, Graduate School, Program in Marine-Estuarine-Environmental Sciences, Baltimore, MD 21250. Offers MS, PhD. Part-time programs available. *Faculty:* 16. *Students:* 7 full-time (4 women), 1 part-time (0 women); includes 2 minority (1 African American, 1 Hispanic American), 1 international. 12 applicants, 8% accepted, 1 enrolled. In 2009, 1 doctorate awarded. *Degree requirements:* For master's, thesis, oral defense; for doctorate, comprehensive exam, thesis/dissertation, proposal defense, oral defense. *Entrance requirements:* For master's and doctorate, GRE General Test, minimum GPA of 3.0. Additional exam requirements/recommendations for international students: Required—TOEFL. *Application deadline:* For fall admission, 2/1 for domestic students, 1/1 for international students; for spring admission, 9/1 for domestic students. Applications are processed on a rolling basis. Application fee: $50. Electronic applications accepted. *Financial support:* In 2009–10, 3 fellowships with tuition reimbursements (averaging $22,500 per year), 2 research assistantships with tuition reimbursements (averaging $21,000 per year), 2 teaching assistantships with tuition reimbursements (averaging $20,000 per year) were awarded; career-related internships or fieldwork, scholarships/grants, and unspecified assistantships also available. Financial award application deadline: 12/1. *Unit head:* Dr. Kennedy T. Paynter, Director, 301-405-6938, Fax: 301-314-4139, E-mail: mees@umd.edu. *Application contact:* Dr. Kennedy T. Paynter, Director, 301-405-6938, Fax: 301-314-4139, E-mail: mees@umd.edu.

See Close-Up on page 169 and Display on page 161.

University of Maryland, College Park, Academic Affairs, College of Chemical and Life Sciences, Program in Marine-Estuarine-Environmental Sciences, College Park, MD 20742. Offers MS, PhD. Intercampus, interdisciplinary program. Part-time programs available. *Faculty:* 133. *Students:* 114 (69 women); includes 9 minority (4 African Americans, 2 Asian Americans or Pacific Islanders, 3 Hispanic Americans), 24 international. 99 applicants, 33% accepted, 24 enrolled. In 2009, 21 master's, 11 doctorates awarded. Terminal master's awarded for partial completion of doctoral program. *Degree requirements:* For master's, thesis, oral defense; for doctorate, comprehensive exam, thesis/dissertation, proposal defense, oral defense. *Entrance requirements:* For master's and doctorate, GRE General Test, minimum GPA of 3.0. Additional exam requirements/recommendations for international students: Required—TOEFL. *Application deadline:* For fall admission, 2/1 for domestic and international students; for spring admission, 9/1 for domestic students, 6/1 for international students. Applications are processed on a rolling basis. Application fee: $60. Electronic applications accepted. *Expenses:* Tuition, area resident: Part-time $471 per credit hour. Tuition, state resident: part-time $471 per credit hour. Tuition, nonresident: part-time $1016 per credit hour. Required fees: $337.04 per term. *Financial support:* In 2009–10, 9 teaching assistantships with full tuition reimbursements were awarded; fellowships with full tuition reimbursements, research assistantships with full tuition reimbursements, Federal Work-Study, scholarships/grants, traineeships, health care benefits, and unspecified assistantships also available. Financial award application deadline: 1/1; financial award applicants required to submit FAFSA. *Faculty research:* Marine and estuarine organisms, terrestrial and freshwater ecology, remote environmental sensing. *Unit head:* Dr. Kennedy T. Paynter, Director, 301-405-6938, Fax: 301-314-4139, E-mail: mees@umd.edu. *Application contact:* Dean of Graduate School, 301-405-0376, Fax: 301-314-9305.

See Close-Up on page 169 and Display on page 161.

University of Maryland Eastern Shore, Graduate Programs, Department of Natural Sciences, Program in Marine-Estuarine-Environmental Sciences, Princess Anne, MD 21853-1299. Offers MS, PhD. Part-time programs available. *Faculty:* 28. *Students:* 30 (19 women); includes 15 minority (all African Americans), 8 international. 15 applicants, 47% accepted, 6 enrolled. In 2009, 3 master's, 1 doctorate awarded. *Degree requirements:* For master's, thesis; for doctorate, comprehensive exam, thesis/dissertation, proposal defense. *Entrance requirements:* For master's and doctorate, GRE General Test, minimum GPA of 3.0. Additional exam requirements/recommendations for international students: Required—TOEFL. *Application deadline:* For fall admission, 2/1 for domestic and international students; for spring admission, 9/1 for domestic students, 8/1 for international students. Applications are processed on a rolling basis. Application fee: $30. Electronic applications accepted. *Financial support:* In 2009–10, 30 students received support; fellowships with tuition reimbursements available, research assistantships with tuition reimbursements available, teaching assistantships with tuition reimbursements available, career-related internships or fieldwork, scholarships/grants, and unspecified assistantships available. Support available to part-time students. Financial award application deadline: 1/1. *Unit head:* Dr. Kennedy T. Paynter, Director, 301-405-6938, Fax: 301-314-4139, E-mail: mees@umd.edu. *Application contact:* Dr. Kennedy T. Paynter, Director, 301-405-6938, Fax: 301-314-4139, E-mail: mees@umd.edu.

See Close-Up on page 169 and Display on page 161.

University of Massachusetts Amherst, Graduate School, Interdisciplinary Programs, Program in Marine Science and Technology, Amherst, MA 01003. Offers MS, PhD. Part-time programs available. *Students:* 2 full-time (both women), 1 (woman) part-time. Average age 29. Terminal master's awarded for partial completion of doctoral program. *Degree requirements:* For master's, thesis optional; for doctorate, comprehensive exam, thesis/dissertation. *Entrance requirements:* For master's and doctorate, GRE General Test, 3 letters of recommendation. Additional exam requirements/recommendations for international students: Required—TOEFL (minimum score 550 paper-based; 213 computer-based; 80 iBT), IELTS (minimum score 6.5). *Application deadline:* For fall admission, 12/15 for domestic and international students; for spring admission,

10/1 for domestic and international students. Applications are processed on a rolling basis. Application fee: $50 ($65 for international students). Electronic applications accepted. *Expenses:* Tuition, state resident: full-time $2640; part-time $110 per credit. Tuition, nonresident: full-time $9936; part-time $414 per credit. Tuition and fees vary according to course load. *Financial support:* Fellowships, research assistantships, teaching assistantships, career-related internships or fieldwork, Federal Work-Study, scholarships/grants, traineeships, health care benefits, tuition waivers (full), and unspecified assistantships available. Support available to part-time students. *Unit head:* Dr. Kevin McGarigal, Graduate Program Director, 413-545-2666, Fax: 413-545-4358. *Application contact:* Jean M. Ames, Supervisor of Admissions, 413-545-0722, Fax: 413-577-0010, E-mail: gradadm@grad.umass.edu.

University of Massachusetts Boston, Office of Graduate Studies, College of Science and Mathematics, Department of Environmental, Earth and Ocean Sciences, Track in Environmental, Earth and Ocean Sciences, Boston, MA 02125-3393. Offers PhD. Part-time and evening/weekend programs available. *Degree requirements:* For doctorate, comprehensive exam, thesis/dissertation, oral exams. *Entrance requirements:* For doctorate, GRE General Test, minimum GPA of 2.75. *Faculty research:* Conservation genetics, anthropogenic and natural influences on community structures of coral reef factors, geographical variation in mitochondrial DNA, protein chemistry and enzymology pertaining to insect cuticle.

University of Massachusetts Dartmouth, Graduate School, School of Marine Science and Technology, Program in Marine Science and Technology, North Dartmouth, MA 02747-2300. Offers MS, PhD. *Faculty:* 11 full-time (1 woman), 1 part-time/adjunct (0 women). *Students:* 33 full-time (11 women), 22 part-time (11 women); includes 1 minority (African American), 15 international. Average age 30. 39 applicants, 64% accepted, 15 enrolled. In 2009, 2 master's, 3 doctorates awarded. Terminal master's awarded for partial completion of doctoral program. *Degree requirements:* For master's, thesis or alternative; for doctorate, comprehensive exam, thesis/dissertation. *Entrance requirements:* For master's and doctorate, GRE, minimum GPA of 3.0, 3 letters of recommendation. Additional exam requirements/recommendations for international students: Required—TOEFL (minimum score 600 paper-based; 213 computer-based). *Application deadline:* For fall admission, 4/20 priority date for domestic students, 2/20 priority date for international students. Applications are processed on a rolling basis. Application fee: $40 ($60 for international students). Electronic applications accepted. *Expenses:* Tuition, state resident: full-time $2071; part-time $86.29 per credit. Tuition, nonresident: full-time $8099; part-time $337.46 per credit. Required fees: $9446. Tuition and fees vary according to class time, course load and reciprocity agreements. *Financial support:* In 2009–10, 2 fellowships with full tuition reimbursements (averaging $15,307 per year), 31 research assistantships with full tuition reimbursements (averaging $13,121 per year), 2 teaching assistantships with full tuition reimbursements (averaging $12,000 per year) were awarded. Financial award application deadline: 3/1; financial award applicants required to submit FAFSA. *Faculty research:* Storm-forced and internal wave dynamics, estuarine circulation, marine biogeochemical cycles, spatial distributions of marine fishes and invertebrates, plankton communities. Total annual research expenditures: $8.4 million. *Unit head:* Dr. Avijit Gangopadhyay, Associate Dean, 508-910-6330, Fax: 508-999-8197, E-mail: agangopadhya@umassd.edu. *Application contact:* Elan Turcotte-Shamski, Graduate Admissions Officer, 508-999-8604, Fax: 508-999-8183, E-mail: graduate@umassd.edu.

University of Miami, Graduate School, Rosenstiel School of Marine and Atmospheric Science, Division of Applied Marine Physics, Coral Gables, FL 33124. Offers applied marine physics (MS, PhD), including coastal ocean dynamics, underwater acoustics and geoacoustics (PhD), wave surface dynamics and air-sea interaction (PhD). Part-time programs available. Terminal master's awarded for partial completion of doctoral program. *Degree requirements:* For master's, comprehensive exam, thesis; for doctorate, comprehensive exam, thesis/dissertation. *Entrance requirements:* For master's and doctorate, GRE General Test. Additional exam requirements/recommendations for international students: Required—TOEFL (minimum score 550 paper-based; 213 computer-based). Electronic applications accepted.

University of Miami, Graduate School, Rosenstiel School of Marine and Atmospheric Science, Division of Marine and Atmospheric Chemistry, Coral Gables, FL 33124. Offers MS, PhD. Terminal master's awarded for partial completion of doctoral program. *Degree requirements:* For master's, comprehensive exam, thesis; for doctorate, comprehensive exam, thesis/dissertation. *Entrance requirements:* For master's and doctorate, GRE General Test. Additional exam requirements/recommendations for international students: Required—TOEFL (minimum score 550 paper-based; 213 computer-based). Electronic applications accepted. *Faculty research:* Global change issues, chemistry of marine waters and marine atmosphere.

University of Michigan, School of Natural Resources and Environment, Program in Natural Resources and Environment, Ann Arbor, MI 48109. Offers aquatic sciences: research and management (MS); behavior, education and communication (MS); conservation biology (MS); environmental informatics (MS); environmental justice (MS); environmental policy and planning (MS); natural resources and environment (PhD); sustainable systems (MS); terrestrial ecosystems (MS); MS/AM; MS/JD; MS/MBA. *Students:* Average age 27. In 2009, 87 master's, 14 doctorates awarded. Terminal master's awarded for partial completion of doctoral program. *Degree requirements:* For master's, practicum or group project; for doctorate, comprehensive exam, thesis/dissertation, oral defense of dissertation, preliminary exam. *Entrance requirements:* For master's, GRE General Test; for doctorate, GRE General Test, master's degree. Additional exam requirements/recommendations for international students: Required—TOEFL (minimum score 560 paper-based; 220 computer-based; 84 iBT). *Application deadline:* For fall admission, 1/5 priority date for domestic and international students. Applications are processed on a rolling basis. Application fee: $60 ($75 for international students). Electronic applications accepted. *Expenses:* Tuition, state resident: full-time $17,286; part-time $1099 per credit hour. Tuition, nonresident: full-time $34,944; part-time $2080 per credit hour. Required fees: $95 per semester. Tuition and fees vary according to course load, degree level and program. *Financial support:* Fellowships with tuition reimbursements, research assistantships with tuition reimbursements, teaching assistantships with tuition reimbursements, career-related internships or fieldwork, Federal Work-Study, institutionally sponsored loans, scholarships/grants, health care benefits, and unspecified assistantships available. Support available to part-time students. Financial award application deadline: 1/5; financial award applicants required to submit FAFSA. *Faculty research:* Stream ecology, plant-insect interactions, fish biology, resource control and reproductive success, remote sensing. *Application contact:* Graduate Admissions Team, 734-764-6453, Fax: 734-936-2195, E-mail: snre.admissions@umich.edu.

University of New England, College of Arts and Sciences, Program in Marine Sciences, Biddeford, ME 04005-9526. Offers MS. *Faculty:* 7 full-time (2 women). *Students:* 10 full-time (8 women), 3 part-time (2 women). *Degree requirements:* For master's, thesis. *Application deadline:* For fall admission, 2/15 for domestic students. *Unit head:* Stephan I. Zeeman, Chair, Department of Marine Sciences, 207-602-2410, E-mail: szeeman@une.edu. *Application contact:* Stacy Gato, Assistant Director of Graduate Admissions, 207-221-4225, Fax: 207-221-4898, E-mail: gradadmissions@une.edu.

The University of North Carolina at Chapel Hill, Graduate School, College of Arts and Sciences, Department of Marine Sciences, Chapel Hill, NC 27599. Offers MS, PhD. *Degree requirements:* For master's, comprehensive exam, thesis; for doctorate, comprehensive exam, thesis/dissertation. *Entrance requirements:* For master's and doctorate, GRE General Test, GRE Subject Test, minimum GPA of 3.0.

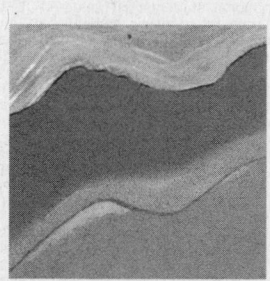

The University of North Carolina at Chapel Hill, Graduate School, School of Public Health, Department of Environmental Sciences and Engineering, Chapel Hill, NC 27599. Offers air, radiation and industrial hygiene (MPH, MS, MSEE, MSPH, PhD); aquatic and atmospheric sciences (MPH, MS, MSPH, PhD); environmental engineering (MPH, MS, MSEE, MSPH, PhD); environmental health sciences (MPH, MS, MSPH, PhD); environmental management and policy (MPH, MS, MSPH, PhD). Terminal master's awarded for partial completion of doctoral program. *Degree requirements:* For master's, comprehensive exam, thesis (for some programs), research paper; for doctorate, comprehensive exam, thesis/dissertation. *Entrance*

Marine Sciences

The University of North Carolina at Chapel Hill (continued)
requirements: For master's and doctorate, GRE General Test, minimum GPA of 3.0. Additional exam requirements/recommendations for international students: Required—TOEFL. Electronic applications accepted. *Faculty research:* Air, radiation and industrial hygiene, aquatic and atmospheric sciences, environmental health sciences, environmental management and policy, water resources engineering.

The University of North Carolina Wilmington, College of Arts and Sciences, Department of Biology and Marine Biology, Wilmington, NC 28403-3297. Offers biology (MS); marine biology (MS, PhD). Part-time programs available. *Degree requirements:* For master's, comprehensive exam, thesis; for doctorate, comprehensive exam, thesis/dissertation. *Entrance requirements:* For master's, GRE General Test, GRE Subject Test, minimum B average in undergraduate major; for doctorate, GRE General Test, minimum B average in undergraduate major and graduate courses. Additional exam requirements/recommendations for international students: Required—TOEFL (minimum score 550 paper-based; 217 computer-based; 79 iBT), IELTS (minimum score 6.5). Electronic applications accepted. *Faculty research:* Ecology, physiology, cell and molecular biology, systematics, biomechanics.

University of Puerto Rico, Mayagüez Campus, Graduate Studies, College of Arts and Sciences, Department of Marine Sciences, Mayagüez, PR 00681-9000. Offers MS, PhD. Part-time programs available. *Degree requirements:* For master's, one foreign language, thesis, departmental and comprehensive final exams; for doctorate, one foreign language, thesis/dissertation, qualifying, comprehensive, and final exams. *Faculty research:* Marine botany, ecology, chemistry, and parasitology; fisheries; ichthyology; aquaculture.

University of Rhode Island, Graduate School, College of the Environment and Life Sciences, Department of Fisheries, Animal and Veterinary Science, Kingston, RI 02881. Offers animal health and disease (MS); animal science (MS); aquaculture (MS); aquatic pathology (MS); environmental sciences (PhD), including animal science, aquacultural science, aquatic pathology, fisheries science; fisheries (MS). *Faculty:* 10 full-time (4 women). *Students:* 14 full-time (7 women), 12 part-time (7 women); includes 5 minority (2 African Americans, 3 Hispanic Americans), 3 international. In 2009, 3 master's, 2 doctorates awarded. *Degree requirements:* For master's, comprehensive exam (for some programs), thesis optional; for doctorate, comprehensive exam, thesis/dissertation. *Entrance requirements:* For master's and doctorate, GRE, 2 letters of recommendation. Additional exam requirements/recommendations for international students: Required—TOEFL (minimum score 550 paper-based; 213 computer-based). *Application deadline:* For fall admission, 7/15 for domestic students, 2/1 for international students; for spring admission, 11/15 for domestic students, 7/15 for international students. Application fee: $65. Electronic applications accepted. *Expenses:* Tuition, state resident: full-time $8828; part-time $490 per credit hour. Tuition, nonresident: full-time $22,100; part-time $1228 per credit hour. Required fees: $1118; $57 per semester. Tuition and fees vary according to program. *Financial support:* In 2009–10, 4 research assistantships with full and partial tuition reimbursements (averaging $11,386 per year), 7 teaching assistantships with full and partial tuition reimbursements (averaging $10,940 per year) were awarded. Financial award application deadline: 7/15; financial award applicants required to submit FAFSA. Total annual research expenditures: $2.1 million. *Unit head:* Dr. David Bengtson, Chair, 401-874-2668, Fax: 401-874-7575, E-mail: bengtson@uri.edu. *Application contact:* Dr. Marta Gomez-Chiarra, Director of Graduate Studies, 401-874-2917, Fax: 401-874-7575, E-mail: gomezchi@uri.edu.

University of San Diego, College of Arts and Sciences, Department of Marine Science and Environmental Studies, San Diego, CA 92110-2492. Offers marine science (MS). Part-time programs available. *Faculty:* 3 full-time (2 women). *Students:* 5 full-time (4 women), 14 part-time (7 women); includes 1 minority (Hispanic American). Average age 27. 14 applicants, 64% accepted, 4 enrolled. In 2009, 3 master's awarded. *Degree requirements:* For master's, thesis. *Entrance requirements:* For master's, GRE General Test, minimum GPA of 3.0, undergraduate major in science. Additional exam requirements/recommendations for international students: Required—TOEFL (minimum score 580 paper-based; 237 computer-based; 83 iBT), TWE. *Application deadline:* For fall admission, 4/1 for domestic and international students. Applications are processed on a rolling basis. Application fee: $45. Electronic applications accepted. *Expenses:* Tuition: Full-time $21,042; part-time $1169 per unit. Required fees: $224. Full-time tuition and fees vary according to course load and degree level. *Financial support:* In 2009–10, 9 students received support. Career-related internships or fieldwork, Federal Work-Study, institutionally sponsored loans, and unspecified assistantships available. Support available to part-time students. Financial award application deadline: 4/1; financial award applicants required to submit FAFSA. *Faculty research:* Bioacoustics, aquaculture, molecular genetics, ecology, physiology. *Unit head:* Dr. Ronald S. Kaufmann, Director, 619-260-5904, Fax: 619-260-6874, E-mail: kaufmann@sandiego.edu. *Application contact:* Dr. John Mosby, Associate Director of Graduate Admissions, 619-260-4524, Fax: 619-260-4158, E-mail: grads@sandiego.edu.

University of South Alabama, Graduate School, College of Arts and Sciences, Department of Marine Sciences, Mobile, AL 36688-0002. Offers MS, PhD. *Degree requirements:* For master's, comprehensive exam, thesis optional; for doctorate, one foreign language, comprehensive exam, thesis/dissertation, research project. *Entrance requirements:* For master's, GRE, minimum GPA of 3.0, BS in marine sciences or related discipline; for doctorate, GRE, BS or MS in marine sciences or related discipline; minimum undergraduate GPA of 3.0, graduate 3.25. *Expenses:* Tuition, state resident: part-time $218 per contact hour. Required fees: $1102 per year.

University of South Carolina, The Graduate School, College of Arts and Sciences, Marine Science Program, Columbia, SC 29208. Offers MS, PhD. *Degree requirements:* For master's, thesis; for doctorate, comprehensive exam, thesis/dissertation. *Entrance requirements:* For master's and doctorate, GRE General Test. Additional exam requirements/recommendations for international students: Required—TOEFL (minimum score 570 paper-based; 230 computer-based). Electronic applications accepted. *Faculty research:* Biological, chemical, geological, and physical oceanography; policy.

University of Southern California, Graduate School, College of Letters, Arts and Sciences, Graduate Program in Ocean Sciences, Los Angeles, CA 90089. Offers MS, PhD. Part-time programs available. *Faculty:* 20 full-time (6 women), 1 (woman) part-time/adjunct. *Students:* 5 full-time (2 women), 3 international. 4 applicants, 75% accepted, 2 enrolled. In 2009, 1 doctorate awarded. Terminal master's awarded for partial completion of doctoral program. *Degree requirements:* For master's, thesis; for doctorate, comprehensive exam, thesis/dissertation. *Entrance requirements:* For master's, GRE. *Application deadline:* For fall admission, 1/1 for domestic and international students; for spring admission, 10/15 for domestic students, 9/1 for international students. Application fee: $85. Electronic applications accepted. *Expenses:* Tuition: Full-time $25,980; part-time $1315 per unit. Required fees: $554. One-time fee: $35 full-time. Full-time tuition and fees vary according to degree level and program. *Financial support:* In 2009–10, 5 students received support, including 2 fellowships with full tuition reimbursements available (averaging $20,500 per year), 1 research assistantship with full tuition reimbursement available (averaging $19,300 per year), 2 teaching assistantships with full tuition reimbursements available (averaging $19,300 per year); health care benefits and unspecified assistantships also available. *Faculty research:* Microbial ecology, biogeochemical cycles, marine chemistry, marine biology, global change. *Unit head:* Prof. Douglas E. Hammond, Program Director, 213-740-5837, Fax: 213-740-8801, E-mail: dhammond@usc.edu. *Application contact:* Cynthia Waite, Academic Advisor, 213-740-6109, Fax: 213-740-8801, E-mail: waite@usc.edu.

University of Southern Mississippi, Graduate School, College of Science and Technology, Department of Coastal Sciences, Ocean Springs, MS 39566-7000. Offers MS, PhD. Part-time programs available. *Faculty:* 17 full-time (4 women), 2 part-time/adjunct (0 women). *Students:* 36 full-time (20 women), 12 part-time (5 women); includes 2 minority (1 Asian American or Pacific Islander, 1 Hispanic American), 6 international. Average age 31. 18 applicants, 56% accepted, 10 enrolled. In 2009, 8 master's, 4 doctorates awarded. *Degree requirements:* For master's, comprehensive exam, thesis; for doctorate, comprehensive exam, thesis/dissertation. *Entrance requirements:* For master's, GRE General Test, minimum GPA of 3.0; for doctorate, GRE General Test, minimum undergraduate GPA of 3.0, graduate 3.5. Additional exam requirements/recommendations for international students: Required—TOEFL. *Application deadline:* For fall admission, 3/1 priority date for domestic students, 3/1 for international students. Applications are processed on a rolling basis. Application fee: $35. Electronic applications accepted. *Expenses:* Tuition, state resident: full-time $5096; part-time $284 per hour. Tuition, nonresident: full-time $13,052; part-time $726 per hour. Required fees: $402. Tuition and fees vary according to course level and course load. *Financial support:* In 2009–10, 1 fellowship with full tuition reimbursement (averaging $10,000 per year), 34 research assistantships with full tuition reimbursements (averaging $16,232 per year) were awarded; teaching assistantships with full tuition reimbursements, Federal Work-Study and institutionally sponsored loans also available. Financial award application deadline: 3/15; financial award applicants required to submit FAFSA. *Unit head:* Dr. Jeffrey Lotz, Chair, 228-872-4215, Fax: 228-872-4295. *Application contact:* Kalin Buttrich, Administrative Assistant, 228-872-4201, Fax: 228-872-4295.

University of Southern Mississippi, Graduate School, College of Science and Technology, Department of Marine Science, Stennis Space Center, MS 39529. Offers hydrographic science (MS); marine science (MS, PhD). Part-time programs available. *Faculty:* 17 full-time (2 women), 2 part-time/adjunct (0 women). *Students:* 27 full-time (11 women), 13 part-time (6 women); includes 15 minority (12 Asian Americans or Pacific Islanders, 3 Hispanic Americans). Average age 30. 12 applicants, 58% accepted, 4 enrolled. In 2009, 10 master's, 2 doctorates awarded. *Degree requirements:* For master's, comprehensive exam, thesis, oral qualifying exam (marine science); for doctorate, 2 foreign languages, comprehensive exam, thesis/dissertation, oral qualifying exam. *Entrance requirements:* For master's, GRE General Test, minimum GPA of 3.0; for doctorate, GRE General Test, minimum GPA of 3.0 (undergraduate), 3.5 (graduate). Additional exam requirements/recommendations for international students: Required—TOEFL. *Application deadline:* For fall admission, 3/1 priority date for domestic and international students. Applications are processed on a rolling basis. Application fee: $35. Electronic applications accepted. *Expenses:* Tuition, state resident: full-time $5096; part-time $284 per hour. Tuition, nonresident: full-time $13,052; part-time $726 per hour. Required fees: $402. Tuition and fees vary according to course level and course load. *Financial support:* In 2009–10, 4 students received support, including 28 research assistantships with full tuition reimbursements available (averaging $20,400 per year), 4 teaching assistantships with full tuition reimbursements available (averaging $20,400 per year); Federal Work-Study and institutionally sponsored loans also available. Financial award application deadline: 3/15. *Faculty research:* Chemical, biological, physical, and geological marine science; remote sensing; bio-optics; numerical modeling; hydrography. Total annual research expenditures: $5.8 million. *Unit head:* Dr. Steven E. Lohrenz, Chair, 228-688-3177, Fax: 228-688-1121, E-mail: marine.science@usm.edu. *Application contact:* Adm. Linda J. Downs, Academic and Recruitment Coordinator, 228-688-3177, Fax: 228-688-1121, E-mail: linda.downs@usm.edu.

University of South Florida, Graduate School, College of Marine Science, St. Petersburg, FL 33701. Offers biological oceanography (MS, PhD); chemical oceanography (MS, PhD); geological oceanography (MS, PhD); interdisciplinary (MS, PhD); marine resource assessment (MS, PhD); physical oceanography (MS, PhD). Part-time programs available. *Faculty:* 24 full-time (4 women). *Students:* 73 full-time (44 women), 26 part-time (18 women); includes 16 minority (7 African Americans, 9 Hispanic Americans), 10 international. Average age 32. 80 applicants, 34% accepted, 19 enrolled. In 2009, 14 master's, 10 doctorates awarded. Terminal master's awarded for partial completion of doctoral program. *Degree requirements:* For master's, thesis, successful oral defense; for doctorate, comprehensive exam, thesis/dissertation, successful oral defense. *Entrance requirements:* For master's, GRE General Test; for doctorate, GRE General Test, ??? Bachelor???s degree or equivalent from a regionally accredited university ??????B??? (3.0 on a 4.0 scale) average or better in all work attempted while registered as an upper division student working for a baccalaureate degree ??? Completed coursework listed on our website: http://www.marine.usf.edu/prospective-students/undergraduate-preparat. Additional exam requirements/recommendations for international students: Required—TOEFL (minimum score 550 paper-based; 213 computer-based; 79 iBT). *Application deadline:* For fall admission, 1/15 for domestic students, 1/2 for international students; for spring admission, 10/1 for domestic students, 7/1 for international students. Applications are processed on a rolling basis. Application fee: $30. *Financial support:* In 2009–10, 73 students received support, including 19 fellowships with partial tuition reimbursements available (averaging $13,972 per year), 36 research assistantships with partial tuition reimbursements available (averaging $13,972 per year), 7 teaching assistantships with partial tuition reimbursements available (averaging $13,972 per year); health care benefits and unspecified assistantships also available. Financial award application deadline: 1/15. *Faculty research:* Trace metal chemistry, water quality, organic and isotopic geochemistry, physical chemistry, nutrient chemistry. Total annual research expenditures: $11.9 million. *Unit head:* Dr. Edward S. Van Vleet, Professor and Director of Academic Programs and Student Affairs, 727-553-1165, Fax: 727-553-1189, E-mail: vanvleet@marine.usf.edu. *Application contact:* Dawna L. Ishler, Academic Services Administrator, 727-553-3944, Fax: 727-553-1189, E-mail: dishler@usf.edu.

The University of Texas at Austin, Graduate School, College of Natural Sciences, Department of Marine Science, Austin, TX 78712-1111. Offers MS, PhD. *Degree requirements:* For master's, thesis; for doctorate, thesis/dissertation. *Entrance requirements:* For master's and doctorate, GRE General Test. Additional exam requirements/recommendations for international students: Required—TOEFL.

University of the Virgin Islands, Graduate Programs, Division of Science and Mathematics, Program in Environmental and Marine Science, Saint Thomas, VI 00802-9990. Offers MS. *Entrance requirements:* For master's, GRE. Additional exam requirements/recommendations for international students: Required—TOEFL (minimum score 550 paper-based; 213 computer-based).

University of Wisconsin–La Crosse, Office of University Graduate Studies, College of Science and Health, Department of Biology, La Crosse, WI 54601-3742. Offers aquatic sciences (MS); biology (MS); cellular and molecular biology (MS); clinical microbiology (MS); microbiology (MS); nurse anesthesia (MS); physiology (MS). Part-time programs available. *Faculty:* 27 full-time (7 women). *Students:* 19 full-time (8 women), 35 part-time (20 women); includes 1 minority (Asian American or Pacific Islander), 2 international. Average age 28. 87 applicants, 32% accepted, 21 enrolled. In 2009, 18 master's awarded. *Degree requirements:* For master's, comprehensive exam, thesis. *Entrance requirements:* For master's, GRE General Test, minimum GPA of 2.85. Additional exam requirements/recommendations for international students: Required—TOEFL (minimum score 550 paper-based; 213 computer-based; 79 iBT). Application fee: $56. Electronic applications accepted. *Financial support:* In 2009–10, 19 research assistantships with partial tuition reimbursements (averaging $10,021 per year) were awarded; career-related internships or fieldwork, Federal Work-Study, health care benefits, unspecified assistantships, and grant-funded positions also available. Support available to part-time students. Financial award application deadline: 3/15; financial award applicants required to submit FAFSA. *Unit head:* Dr. David Howard, Chair, 608-785-6455, E-mail: howard.davi@uwlax.edu. *Application contact:* Kathryn Kiefer, Director of Admissions, 608-785-8939, E-mail: admissions@uwlax.edu.

University of Wisconsin–Madison, Graduate School, College of Letters and Science, Department of Atmospheric and Oceanic Sciences, Madison, WI 53706-1380. Offers MS,

PhD. Part-time programs available. *Degree requirements:* For master's, thesis (for some programs); for doctorate, thesis/dissertation. *Entrance requirements:* For master's and doctorate, GRE General Test, minimum GPA of 3.0; previous course work in chemistry, mathematics, and physics. Electronic applications accepted. *Expenses:* Tuition, state resident: part-time $594 per credit. Tuition, nonresident: part-time $1504 per credit. Required fees: $65 per credit. Tuition and fees vary according to course load, program and reciprocity agreements. *Faculty research:* Satellite meteorology, weather systems, global climate change, numerical modeling, atmosphere-ocean interaction.

Western Washington University, Graduate School, Huxley College of the Environment, Department of Environmental Sciences, Bellingham, WA 98225-5996. Offers environmental science (MS); marine and estuarine science (MS). Part-time programs available. *Degree requirements:* For master's, thesis. *Entrance requirements:* For master's, GRE General Test, minimum GPA of 3.0 in last 60 semester hours or last 90 quarter hours. Additional exam requirements/recommendations for international students: Required—TOEFL (minimum score 567 paper-based; 227 computer-based). Electronic applications accepted. *Faculty research:* Landscape ecology, climate change, watershed studies, environmental toxicology and risk assessment, aquatic toxicology, toxic algae, invasive species.

Oceanography

Columbia University, Graduate School of Arts and Sciences, Division of Natural Sciences, Department of Earth and Environmental Sciences, New York, NY 10027. Offers geochemistry (M Phil, MA, PhD); geodetic sciences (M Phil, MA, PhD); geophysics (M Phil, MA, PhD); oceanography (M Phil, MA, PhD). *Degree requirements:* For master's, thesis or alternative, fieldwork, written exam; for doctorate, one foreign language, thesis/dissertation. *Entrance requirements:* For master's and doctorate, GRE General Test, GRE Subject Test, major in natural or physical science. Additional exam requirements/recommendations for international students: Required—TOEFL. *Faculty research:* Structural geology and stratigraphy, petrology, paleontology, rare gas, isotope and aqueous geochemistry.

Cornell University, Graduate School, Graduate Fields of Agriculture and Life Sciences, Field of Ecology and Evolutionary Biology, Ithaca, NY 14853-0001. Offers ecology (PhD), including animal ecology, applied ecology, biogeochemistry, community and ecosystem ecology, limnology, oceanography, physiological ecology, plant ecology, population ecology, theoretical ecology, vertebrate zoology; evolutionary biology (PhD), including ecological genetics, paleobiology, population biology, systematics. *Faculty:* 53 full-time (14 women). *Students:* 57 full-time (43 women); includes 4 minority (2 Asian Americans or Pacific Islanders, 2 Hispanic Americans), 8 international. Average age 29. 99 applicants, 11% accepted, 8 enrolled. In 2009, 12 doctorates awarded. *Degree requirements:* For doctorate, comprehensive exam, thesis/dissertation, 2 semesters of teaching experience. *Entrance requirements:* For doctorate, GRE General Test, GRE Subject Test (biology), 2 letters of recommendation. Additional exam requirements/recommendations for international students: Required—TOEFL (minimum score 550 paper-based; 213 computer-based; 77 iBT). *Application deadline:* For fall admission, 12/15 for domestic students. Application fee: $70. Electronic applications accepted. *Expenses:* Tuition: Full-time $29,500. Required fees: $70. Full-time tuition and fees vary according to degree level, program and student level. *Financial support:* In 2009–10, 56 students received support, including 7 fellowships with full tuition reimbursements available, 1 teaching assistantship with full tuition reimbursement available; research assistantships with full tuition reimbursements available, institutionally sponsored loans, scholarships/grants, health care benefits, tuition waivers (full and partial), and unspecified assistantships also available. Financial award applicants required to submit FAFSA. *Faculty research:* Population and organismal biology, population and evolutionary genetics, systematics and macroevolution, biochemistry, conservation biology. *Unit head:* Director of Graduate Studies, 607-254-4230. *Application contact:* Graduate Field Assistant, 607-254-4230, E-mail: eeb_grad_req@cornell.edu.

Dalhousie University, Faculty of Science, Department of Oceanography, Halifax, NS B3H 4R2, Canada. Offers M Sc, PhD. *Faculty:* 22 full-time (2 women), 16 part-time/adjunct (2 women). *Students:* 40 full-time (18 women), 14 international. Average age 27. 69 applicants, 25% accepted. In 2009, 6 master's, 5 doctorates awarded. *Degree requirements:* For master's, thesis; for doctorate, thesis/dissertation. *Entrance requirements:* Additional exam requirements/recommendations for international students: Required—TOEFL, IELTS, CANTEST, CAEL, or Michigan English Language Assessment Battery. Application fee: $70. Electronic applications accepted. *Financial support:* In 2009–10, 37 fellowships, 10 teaching assistantships were awarded; career-related internships or fieldwork, scholarships/grants, and health care benefits also available. *Faculty research:* Biological and physical oceanography, chemical and geological oceanography, atmospheric sciences. *Unit head:* Dr. Daniel Kelly, Graduate Coordinator, 902-494-1694, Fax: 902-494-3877, E-mail: dan.kelley@dal.ca. *Application contact:* Tamara Cantrill, Graduate Secretary, 902-494-3558, Fax: 902-494-3877, E-mail: graduate.ocean@dal.ca.

Florida Institute of Technology, Graduate Programs, College of Engineering, Department of Marine and Environmental Systems, Program in Oceanography, Melbourne, FL 32901-6975. Offers biological oceanography (MS); chemical oceanography (MS); coastal zone management (MS); geological oceanography (MS); oceanography (PhD); physical oceanography (MS). Part-time programs available. *Students:* Average age 30.Terminal master's awarded for partial completion of doctoral program. *Degree requirements:* For master's, thesis (for some programs); for doctorate, one foreign language, comprehensive exam, thesis/dissertation, departmental qualifying exams. *Entrance requirements:* For master's, GRE General Test, minimum GPA of 3.0; for doctorate, GRE General Test, minimum GPA of 3.3, resume. *Application deadline:* Applications are processed on a rolling basis. Electronic applications accepted. *Expenses:* Tuition: Part-time $1015 per credit. Tuition and fees vary according to campus/location and program. *Financial support:* Research assistantships with full and partial tuition reimbursements, teaching assistantships with full and partial tuition reimbursements, career-related internships or fieldwork and tuition remissions available. Financial award application deadline: 3/1; financial award applicants required to submit FAFSA. *Faculty research:* Marine geochemistry, ecosystem dynamics, coastal processes, marine pollution, environmental modeling. Total annual research expenditures: $938,395. *Unit head:* Dr. Dean R. Norris, Chair, 321-674-7377, Fax: 321-674-7212, E-mail: norris@fit.edu. *Application contact:* Carolyn P. Shea.

See Close-Ups on pages 167 and 411.

Florida State University, The Graduate School, College of Arts and Sciences, Department of Earth, Ocean and Atmospheric Science, Tallahassee, FL 32306-4320. Offers aquatic environmental science (MS); oceanography (MS, PhD). *Faculty:* 17 full-time (1 woman). *Students:* 49 full-time (26 women); includes 4 minority (1 African American, 3 Asian Americans or Pacific Islanders), 10 international. Average age 28. 60 applicants, 33% accepted, 15 enrolled. In 2009, 7 master's, 4 doctorates awarded. *Degree requirements:* For master's, thesis; for doctorate, comprehensive exam, thesis/dissertation. *Entrance requirements:* For master's and doctorate, GRE General Test. Additional exam requirements/recommendations for international students: Required—TOEFL (minimum score 550 paper-based; 213 computer-based; 80 iBT). *Application deadline:* For fall admission, 2/15 priority date for domestic and international students; for spring admission, 7/15 priority date for domestic and international students. Applications are processed on a rolling basis. Application fee: $35. Electronic applications accepted. *Expenses:* Tuition, state resident: full-time $7413.36. Tuition, nonresident: full-time $22,567. *Financial support:* In 2009–10, 40 students received support, including 1 fellowship with full tuition reimbursement available, 36 research assistantships with full tuition reimbursements available, 8 teaching assistantships with full tuition reimbursements available. Financial award application deadline: 2/15; financial award applicants required to submit FAFSA. *Faculty research:* Trace metals in seawater, currents and waves, modeling, benthic ecology, marine biogeochemistry. Total annual research expenditures: $3.8 million. *Unit head:* Dr. William K. Dewar, Chair, 850-644-6700, Fax: 850-644-2581, E-mail: dewar@ocean.fsu.edu. *Application contact:* Michaela Lupiani, Academic Coordinator, 850-644-6700, Fax: 850-644-2581, E-mail: admissions@ocean.fsu.edu.

Georgia Institute of Technology, Graduate Studies and Research, College of Sciences, School of Earth and Atmospheric Sciences, Atlanta, GA 30332-0340. Offers atmospheric chemistry, aerosols and clouds (MS, PhD); dynamics of weather and climate (MS, PhD); geochemistry (MS, PhD); geophysics (MS, PhD); oceanography (MS, PhD); paleoclimate (MS, PhD); planetary science (MS, PhD); remote sensing (MS, PhD). Part-time programs available. Terminal master's awarded for partial completion of doctoral program. *Degree requirements:* For master's, thesis or alternative; for doctorate, comprehensive exam, thesis/dissertation. *Entrance requirements:* For master's, GRE, letters of recommendation; for doctorate, GRE, academic transcripts, letters of recommendation, personal statement. Additional exam requirements/recommendations for international students: Required—TOEFL (minimum score 550 paper-based; 213 computer-based; 79 iBT). *Faculty research:* Geophysics; atmospheric chemistry, aerosols and clouds; dynamics of weather and climate; geochemistry; oceanography; paleoclimate; planetary science; remote sensing.

Louisiana State University and Agricultural and Mechanical College, Graduate School, School of the Coast and Environment, Department of Oceanography and Coastal Sciences, Baton Rouge, LA 70803. Offers MS, PhD. *Faculty:* 29 full-time (4 women), 2 part-time/adjunct (0 women). *Students:* 53 full-time (32 women), 8 part-time (3 women); includes 2 Hispanic Americans, 15 international. Average age 30. 33 applicants, 42% accepted, 9 enrolled. In 2009, 9 master's, 11 doctorates awarded. *Degree requirements:* For master's, thesis (for some programs); for doctorate, one foreign language, thesis/dissertation. *Entrance requirements:* For master's, GRE General Test, minimum GPA of 3.0; for doctorate, GRE General Test, MA or MS, minimum GPA of 3.0. Additional exam requirements/recommendations for international students: Required—TOEFL (minimum score 550 paper-based; 213 computer-based; 79 iBT) or IELTS (minimum score 6.5). *Application deadline:* For fall admission, 1/25 priority date for domestic students, 5/15 for international students; for spring admission, 10/15 for international students. Applications are processed on a rolling basis. Application fee: $50 ($70 for international students). *Financial support:* In 2009–10, 55 students received support, including 8 fellowships (averaging $24,370 per year), 42 research assistantships with full and partial tuition reimbursements available (averaging $19,799 per year), 5 teaching assistantships with full and partial tuition reimbursements available (averaging $15,533 per year); Federal Work-Study, institutionally sponsored loans, scholarships/grants, health care benefits, tuition waivers (full and partial), and unspecified assistantships also available. Support available to part-time students. Financial award applicants required to submit FAFSA. *Faculty research:* Physical and geological oceanography, wetland sustainability and restoration fisheries, coastal ecology and biogeochemistry. Total annual research expenditures: $8.9 million. *Unit head:* Dr. Donald Baltz, Chair, 225-578-6308, Fax: 225-578-6307, E-mail: dbaltz@lsu.edu. *Application contact:* Dr. Charles Lindau, Graduate Adviser, 225-578-8766, Fax: 225-578-6423, E-mail: clinda1@lsu.edu.

Massachusetts Institute of Technology, School of Engineering, Department of Civil and Environmental Engineering, Cambridge, MA 02139-4307. Offers biological oceanography (PhD, Sc D); chemical oceanography (PhD, Sc D); civil and environmental engineering (M Eng, SM, PhD, Sc D); civil and environmental systems (PhD, Sc D); civil engineering (PhD, Sc D, CE); coastal engineering (PhD, Sc D); construction engineering and management (PhD, Sc D); environmental biology (PhD, Sc D); environmental chemistry (PhD, Sc D); environmental engineering (PhD, Sc D); environmental fluid mechanics (PhD, Sc D); geotechnical and geoenvironmental engineering (PhD, Sc D); hydrology (PhD, Sc D); information technology (PhD, Sc D); oceanographic engineering (PhD, Sc D); structures and materials (PhD, Sc D); transportation (PhD, Sc D); SM/MBA. *Faculty:* 36 full-time (5 women). *Students:* 190 full-time (59 women); includes 22 minority (2 African Americans, 14 Asian Americans or Pacific Islanders, 6 Hispanic Americans), 103 international. Average age 26. 478 applicants, 25% accepted, 76 enrolled. In 2009, 72 master's, 14 doctorates awarded. *Degree requirements:* For master's and CE, thesis; for doctorate, comprehensive exam, thesis/dissertation. *Entrance requirements:* For master's and doctorate, GRE General Test. Additional exam requirements/recommendations for international students: Required—TOEFL (minimum score 577 paper-based; 233 computer-based; 90 iBT), IELTS (minimum score 7). *Application deadline:* For fall admission, 1/2 for domestic and international students. Application fee: $75. Electronic applications accepted. *Financial support:* In 2009–10, 185 students received support, including 40 fellowships with tuition reimbursements available (averaging $27,725 per year), 97 research assistantships with tuition reimbursements available (averaging $28,035 per year), 21 teaching assistantships with tuition reimbursements available (averaging $24,802 per year); career-related internships or fieldwork, Federal Work-Study, institutionally sponsored loans, scholarships/grants, health care benefits, and unspecified assistantships also available. *Faculty research:* Environmental chemistry, environmental microbiology, environmental fluid mechanics and coastal engineering, geotechnical engineering and geomechanics, hydrology and hydroclimatology, mechanics of materials and structures, operations research/supply chain, transportation. Total annual research expenditures: $16.6 million. *Unit head:* Prof. Andrew Whittle, Department Head, 617-253-7101. *Application contact:* Patricia Glidden, Graduate Admissions Coordinator, 617-253-7119, Fax: 617-258-6775, E-mail: cee-admissions@mit.edu.

Massachusetts Institute of Technology, School of Science, Department of Biology, Cambridge, MA 02139-4307. Offers biochemistry (PhD); biological oceanography (PhD); biology (PhD); biophysical chemistry and molecular structure (PhD); cell biology (PhD); computational and systems biology (PhD); developmental biology (PhD); genetics (PhD); immunology (PhD); microbiology (PhD); molecular biology (PhD); neurobiology (PhD). *Faculty:* 54 full-time (14 women). *Students:* 237 full-time (128 women); includes 65 minority (4 African Americans, 2 American Indian/Alaska Native, 33 Asian Americans or Pacific Islanders, 26 Hispanic Americans), 25 international. Average age 26. 645 applicants, 18% accepted, 49 enrolled. In 2009, 41 doctorates awarded. *Degree requirements:* For doctorate, comprehensive exam, thesis/dissertation. *Entrance requirements:* For doctorate, GRE General Test. Additional exam requirements/recommendations for international students: Required—TOEFL (minimum score 577 paper-based; 233 computer-based), IELTS (minimum score 6.5). *Application deadline:* For fall admission, 12/1 for domestic and international students. Application fee: $75. Electronic applications accepted. *Financial support:* In 2009–10, 218 students received support, including

Oceanography

Massachusetts Institute of Technology (continued)
113 fellowships with tuition reimbursements available (averaging $31,816 per year), 109 research assistantships with tuition reimbursements available (averaging $29,254 per year); teaching assistantships with tuition reimbursements available, Federal Work-Study, institutionally sponsored loans, scholarships/grants, traineeships, health care benefits, and unspecified assistantships also available. *Faculty research:* DNA recombination, transcription and gene regulation, signal transduction, cell cycle, neuronal cell fate, replication and repair. Total annual research expenditures: $114 million. *Unit head:* Prof. Chris Kaiser, Department Head, 617-253-4701, E-mail: mitbio@mit.edu. *Application contact:* Biology Education Office, 617-253-3717, Fax: 617-258-9329, E-mail: gradbio@mit.edu.

Massachusetts Institute of Technology, School of Science, Department of Earth, Atmospheric, and Planetary Sciences, Cambridge, MA 02139-4307. Offers atmospheric chemistry (PhD, Sc D); atmospheric science (SM, PhD, Sc D); chemical oceanography (SM, PhD, Sc D); climate physics and chemistry (SM, PhD, Sc D); earth and planetary sciences (SM); geochemistry (PhD, Sc D); geology (PhD, Sc D); geophysics (PhD, Sc D); marine geology and geophysics (SM, PhD, Sc D); physical oceanography (SM, PhD, Sc D); planetary sciences (PhD, Sc D). *Faculty:* 37 full-time (7 women). *Students:* 158 full-time (74 women); includes 14 minority (1 African American, 1 American Indian/Alaska Native, 6 Asian Americans or Pacific Islanders, 6 Hispanic Americans), 58 international. Average age 27. 205 applicants, 30% accepted, 18 enrolled. In 2009, 10 master's, 25 doctorates awarded. Terminal master's awarded for partial completion of doctoral program. *Degree requirements:* For master's, thesis; for doctorate, comprehensive exam, thesis/dissertation. *Entrance requirements:* For master's, GRE General Test; for doctorate, GRE General Test, GRE Subject Test (chemistry or physics for planetary science area). Additional exam requirements/recommendations for international students: Required—IELTS (minimum score 6); Recommended—TOEFL (minimum score 577 paper-based; 233 computer-based; 91 iBT). *Application deadline:* For fall admission, 1/5 for domestic and international students; for spring admission, 11/1 for domestic and international students. Application fee: $75. Electronic applications accepted. *Financial support:* In 2009–10, 112 students received support, including 31 fellowships with tuition reimbursements available (averaging $30,513 per year), 89 research assistantships with tuition reimbursements available (averaging $21,168 per year), 17 teaching assistantships with tuition reimbursements available (averaging $28,372 per year); Federal Work-Study, institutionally sponsored loans, scholarships/grants, health care benefits, and unspecified assistantships also available. *Faculty research:* Formation, dynamics and evolution of planetary systems, origin, evolution and interaction of the physical, characterization of past, interplay of energy and the environment, present and potential future climates and the causes and consequences of climate change, chemical, geological and biological components of the Earth system, composition, structure and dynamics of the atmospheres, oceans, surfaces and interiors of the Earth and other planets. Total annual research expenditures: $19.5 million. *Unit head:* Prof. Maria Zuber, Head, 617-253-2127, Fax: 617-253-8298, E-mail: eapsinfo@mit.edu. *Application contact:* EAPS Education Office, 617-253-3381, Fax: 617-253-8298, E-mail: eapsinfo@mit.edu.

McGill University, Faculty of Graduate and Postdoctoral Studies, Faculty of Science, Department of Atmospheric and Oceanic Sciences, Montréal, QC H3A 2T5, Canada. Offers atmospheric science (M Sc, PhD); physical oceanography (M Sc, PhD).

Memorial University of Newfoundland, School of Graduate Studies, Department of Physics and Physical Oceanography, St. John's, NL A1C 5S7, Canada. Offers atomic and molecular physics (M Sc, PhD); condensed matter physics (M Sc, PhD); physical oceanography (M Sc, PhD); physics (M Sc). Part-time programs available. *Degree requirements:* For master's, thesis, seminar presentation on thesis topic; for doctorate, comprehensive exam, thesis/dissertation, oral defense of thesis. *Entrance requirements:* For master's, honors B Sc or equivalent; for doctorate, M Sc or equivalent. Electronic applications accepted. *Faculty research:* Experiment and theory in atomic and molecular physics, condensed matter physics, physical oceanography, theoretical geophysics and applied nuclear physics.

Naval Postgraduate School, Graduate Programs, Department of Oceanography, Monterey, CA 93943. Offers MS, PhD. Program only open to commissioned officers of the United States and friendly nations and selected United States federal civilian employees. Part-time programs available. *Degree requirements:* For master's, thesis; for doctorate, one foreign language, thesis/dissertation.

Naval Postgraduate School, Graduate Programs, Program in Undersea Warfare, Monterey, CA 93943. Offers applied science (MS); electrical engineering (MS); engineering acoustics (MS); operations research (MS); physical oceanography (MS). Program only open to commissioned officers of the United States and friendly nations and selected United States federal civilian employees. Part-time programs available. *Degree requirements:* For master's, thesis.

North Carolina State University, Graduate School, College of Physical and Mathematical Sciences, Department of Marine, Earth, and Atmospheric Sciences, Raleigh, NC 27695. Offers marine, earth, and atmospheric sciences (MS, PhD); meteorology (MS, PhD); oceanography (MS, PhD). Terminal master's awarded for partial completion of doctoral program. *Degree requirements:* For master's, thesis (for some programs), final oral exam; for doctorate, comprehensive exam, thesis/dissertation, final oral exam, preliminary oral and written exams. *Entrance requirements:* For master's, GRE General Test, minimum GPA of 3.0; for doctorate, GRE General Test, GRE Subject Test (for disciplines in biological oceanography and geology), minimum GPA of 3.0. Additional exam requirements/recommendations for international students: Required—TOEFL (minimum score 550 paper-based). Electronic applications accepted. *Faculty research:* Boundary layer and air quality meteorology; climate and mesoscale dynamics; biological, chemical, geological, and physical oceanography; hard rock, soft rock, environmental, and paleo-geology.

Nova Southeastern University, Oceanographic Center, Program in Marine Biology and Oceanography, Fort Lauderdale, FL 33314-7796. Offers marine biology (PhD); oceanography (PhD). *Faculty:* 15 full-time (1 woman), 5 part-time/adjunct (0 women). *Students:* 10 full-time (4 women), 5 part-time (4 women); includes 1 minority (African American), 1 international. 5 applicants, 80% accepted, 3 enrolled. In 2009, 1 doctorate awarded. *Degree requirements:* For doctorate, comprehensive exam, thesis/dissertation. *Entrance requirements:* For doctorate, GRE, master's degree. Application fee: $50. *Financial support:* In 2009–10, research assistantships (averaging $18,000 per year); Federal Work-Study, scholarships/grants, and unspecified assistantships also available. Support available to part-time students. *Unit head:* Dr. Richard Dodge, Dean, 954-262-3600, Fax: 954-262-4020, E-mail: dodge@nsu.nova.edu. *Application contact:* Dr. Richard Spieler, Director of Academic Programs, 954-262-3600, Fax: 954-262-4020, E-mail: spieler@nova.edu.

Nova Southeastern University, Oceanographic Center, Program in Physical Oceanography, Fort Lauderdale, FL 33314-7796. Offers MS. *Faculty:* 15 full-time (1 woman), 5 part-time/adjunct (0 women). *Students:* 7 applicants, 14% accepted, 0 enrolled. *Degree requirements:* For master's, thesis. *Entrance requirements:* For master's, GRE, 1 year course work in calculus. Additional exam requirements/recommendations for international students: Required—TOEFL (minimum score 550 paper-based). *Application deadline:* Applications are processed on a rolling basis. Application fee: $50. *Unit head:* Dr. Richard Dodge, Dean, 954-262-3600, Fax: 954-262-4020, E-mail: dodge@nsu.nova.edu. *Application contact:* Dr. Richard Spieler, Director of Academic Programs, 954-262-3600, Fax: 954-262-4020, E-mail: spieler@nova.edu.

Old Dominion University, College of Sciences, Department of Ocean, Earth and Atmospheric Sciences, Norfolk, VA 23529. Offers ocean and earth sciences (MS); oceanography (PhD). Part-time programs available. *Faculty:* 27 full-time (8 women). *Students:* 33 full-time (18 women), 9 part-time (4 women); includes 2 minority (both African Americans), 10 international. Average age 31. 19 applicants, 68% accepted, 10 enrolled. In 2009, 6 master's, 4 doctorates awarded. Terminal master's awarded for partial completion of doctoral program. *Degree requirements:* For master's, comprehensive exam (for some programs), thesis (for some programs), 10 days of ship time or fieldwork; for doctorate, comprehensive exam, thesis/dissertation, 10 days of ship time or fieldwork. *Entrance requirements:* For master's, GRE General Test, minimum GPA of 3.0 in major, 2.8 overall; for doctorate, GRE General Test. Additional exam requirements/recommendations for international students: Required—TOEFL (minimum score 550 paper-based; 213 computer-based). *Application deadline:* For fall admission, 2/1 priority date for domestic and international students. Applications are processed on a rolling basis. Application fee: $40. Electronic applications accepted. *Expenses:* Tuition, state resident: full-time $8112; part-time $338 per credit. Tuition, nonresident: full-time $20,256; part-time $844 per credit. Required fees: $119 per semester. One-time fee: $50. *Financial support:* In 2009–10, 42 students received support, including 3 fellowships with full tuition reimbursements available (averaging $22,000 per year), 28 research assistantships with full tuition reimbursements available, 14 teaching assistantships with full tuition reimbursements available (averaging $15,500 per year); career-related internships or fieldwork, scholarships/grants, and unspecified assistantships also available. Support available to part-time students. Financial award application deadline: 2/1; financial award applicants required to submit FAFSA. *Faculty research:* Biological, chemical, geological and physical oceanography. Total annual research expenditures: $4 million. *Unit head:* Dr. Fred Dobbs, Graduate Program Director, 757-683-5329, Fax: 757-683-5303, E-mail: oceangpd@odu.edu. *Application contact:* Dr. Fred Dobbs, Graduate Program Director, 757-683-5329, Fax: 757-683-5303, E-mail: oceangpd@odu.edu.

Oregon State University, Graduate School, College of Oceanic and Atmospheric Sciences, Program in Oceanography, Corvallis, OR 97331. Offers MA, MS, PhD. *Students:* 61 full-time (26 women), 3 part-time (2 women); includes 7 minority (1 American Indian/Alaska Native, 2 Asian Americans or Pacific Islanders, 4 Hispanic Americans), 10 international. Average age 31. In 2009, 3 master's, 6 doctorates awarded. Terminal master's awarded for partial completion of doctoral program. *Degree requirements:* For master's, thesis optional; for doctorate, thesis/dissertation. *Entrance requirements:* For master's and doctorate, GRE General Test, minimum GPA of 3.0 in last 90 hours of course work. Additional exam requirements/recommendations for international students: Required—TOEFL. *Application deadline:* For fall admission, 2/1 priority date for domestic students. Applications are processed on a rolling basis. Application fee: $50. *Expenses:* Tuition, state resident: full-time $9774; part-time $362 per credit. Tuition, nonresident: full-time $15,849; part-time $587 per credit. Required fees: $1639. Full-time tuition and fees vary according to course load and program. *Financial support:* Fellowships, research assistantships, teaching assistantships, career-related internships or fieldwork, Federal Work-Study, and institutionally sponsored loans available. Support available to part-time students. Financial award application deadline: 2/1. *Faculty research:* Biological, chemical, geological, and physical oceanography. *Unit head:* Dr. Robert A. Duncan, Associate Dean for Student Programs, 541-737-5189, Fax: 541-737-2540, E-mail: rduncan@coas.oregonstate.edu. *Application contact:* Dr. Robert A. Duncan, Associate Dean for Student Programs, 541-737-5189, Fax: 541-737-2540, E-mail: rduncan@coas.oregonstate.edu.

Princeton University, Graduate School, Department of Geosciences, Program in Atmospheric and Oceanic Sciences, Princeton, NJ 08544-1019. Offers PhD. *Degree requirements:* For doctorate, one foreign language, thesis/dissertation. *Entrance requirements:* For doctorate, GRE General Test, GRE Subject Test. Additional exam requirements/recommendations for international students: Required—TOEFL (minimum score 600 paper-based; 250 computer-based). Electronic applications accepted. *Faculty research:* Climate dynamics, middle atmosphere dynamics and chemistry, oceanic circulation, marine geochemistry, numerical modeling.

Rutgers, The State University of New Jersey, New Brunswick, Graduate School-New Brunswick, Program in Oceanography, Piscataway, NJ 08854-8097. Offers MS, PhD. Terminal master's awarded for partial completion of doctoral program. *Degree requirements:* For master's, thesis; for doctorate, comprehensive exam, thesis/dissertation. *Entrance requirements:* For master's and doctorate, GRE General Test, 1 year course work in calculus, physics, chemistry. Additional exam requirements/recommendations for international students: Required—TOEFL. Electronic applications accepted. *Faculty research:* Coastal observations and modeling, estuarine ecology/fish/benthos, geochemistry, deep sea ecology/hydrothermal vents, molecular biology applications.

Texas A&M University, College of Geosciences, Department of Oceanography, College Station, TX 77843. Offers MS, PhD. *Faculty:* 27. *Students:* 64 full-time (38 women), 12 part-time (4 women); includes 5 minority (3 Asian Americans or Pacific Islanders, 2 Hispanic Americans), 28 international. Average age 28. In 2009, 4 master's, 6 doctorates awarded. *Degree requirements:* For master's, thesis; for doctorate, thesis/dissertation. *Entrance requirements:* For master's and doctorate, GRE General Test. Additional exam requirements/recommendations for international students: Required—TOEFL. *Application deadline:* For fall admission, 1/15 priority date for domestic students; for spring admission, 10/1 for domestic students. Applications are processed on a rolling basis. Application fee: $50 ($75 for international students). Electronic applications accepted. *Expenses:* Tuition, state resident: full-time $3991.32; part-time $221.74 per credit hour. Tuition, nonresident: full-time $9049; part-time $502.74 per credit hour. *Financial support:* In 2009–10, fellowships with partial tuition reimbursements (averaging $18,000 per year), research assistantships with partial tuition reimbursements (averaging $18,000 per year), teaching assistantships with partial tuition reimbursements (averaging $18,000 per year) were awarded; Federal Work-Study, scholarships/grants, and tuition waivers (partial) also available. Financial award application deadline: 1/15. *Faculty research:* Ocean circulation, climate studies, coastal and shelf dynamics, marine phytoplankton, stable isotope geochemistry. *Unit head:* Head, 979-845-7211, Fax: 979-845-6331. *Application contact:* Academic Advisor, 979-845-7412, Fax: 979-845-6331, E-mail: b-giese@tamu.edu.

Université du Québec à Rimouski, Graduate Programs, Program in Oceanography, Rimouski, QC G5L 3A1, Canada. Offers M Sc, PhD. Part-time programs available. *Degree requirements:* For master's, thesis; for doctorate, thesis/dissertation. *Entrance requirements:* For master's, appropriate bachelor's degree, proficiency in French; for doctorate, appropriate master's degree, proficiency in French.

Université Laval, Faculty of Sciences and Engineering, Program in Oceanography, Québec, QC G1K 7P4, Canada. Offers PhD. *Degree requirements:* For doctorate, comprehensive exam, thesis/dissertation. *Entrance requirements:* For doctorate, knowledge of French, knowledge of English. Additional exam requirements/recommendations for international students: Required—TOEFL. Electronic applications accepted.

University of Alaska Fairbanks, School of Fisheries and Ocean Sciences, Program in Marine Sciences and Limnology, Fairbanks, AK 99775-7220. Offers marine biology (MS, PhD); oceanography (PhD), including biological oceanography, chemical oceanography, fisheries, geological oceanography, physical oceanography. Part-time programs available. *Faculty:* 12 full-time (5 women), 2 part-time/adjunct (0 women). *Students:* 29 full-time (17 women), 14 part-time (9 women); includes 4 minority (2 Asian Americans or Pacific Islanders, 2 Hispanic Americans), 2 international. Average age 33. 45 applicants, 18% accepted, 8 enrolled. In 2009, 8 master's, 2 doctorates awarded. *Degree requirements:* For master's, comprehensive exam, thesis, oral defense; for doctorate, comprehensive exam, thesis/dissertation, oral defense. *Entrance requirements:* For master's and doctorate, GRE General Test. Additional exam requirements/recommendations for international students: Required—TOEFL (minimum score 550 paper-based; 213 computer-based; 80 iBT). *Application deadline:* For fall admission, 6/1 for domestic students, 3/1 for international students; for spring admission, 10/15 for domestic students, 8/1 for international students. Applications are processed on a rolling basis. Application fee: $60. Electronic applications accepted. *Expenses:* Tuition, state resident: full-time $7584; part-time $316 per credit. Tuition, nonresident: full-time $15,504; part-time $646 per credit. Required fees: $23 per credit. $135 per semester. Tuition and fees vary according to course level, course load and reciprocity agreements. *Financial support:* In 2009–10, 3 fellowships (averaging $10,865 per year), 18 research assistantships (averaging $10,454 per year), 6 teaching assistantships (averaging $10,748 per year) were awarded; career-related internships or fieldwork, Federal Work-Study, scholarships/grants, health care benefits, and unspecified assistantships also available. Support available to part-time students. Financial award application deadline: 7/1; financial award applicants required to submit FAFSA. *Unit head:* Dr. Denis Wiesenberg, Dean, 907-474-7824, Fax: 907-474-7204, E-mail: info@sfos.uaf.edu. *Application contact:* Katie Straub, Recruitment and Retention Coordinator, 907-474-6786, Fax: 907-474-5863, E-mail: kmstraub@alaska.edu.

The University of British Columbia, Faculty of Science, Department of Earth and Ocean Sciences, Vancouver, BC V6T 1Z4, Canada. Offers atmospheric science (M Sc, PhD); geological engineering (M Eng, MA Sc, PhD); geological sciences (M Sc, PhD); geophysics (M Sc, MA Sc, PhD); oceanography (M Sc, PhD). *Degree requirements:* For master's, thesis (for some programs); for doctorate, comprehensive exam, thesis/dissertation. *Entrance requirements:* Additional exam requirements/recommendations for international students: Required—TOEFL (minimum score 600 paper-based; 250 computer-based; 100 iBT). Electronic applications accepted. *Faculty research:* Oceans and atmosphere, environmental earth science, hydro geology, mineral deposits, geophysics.

University of California, San Diego, Office of Graduate Studies, Scripps Institution of Oceanography, La Jolla, CA 92093. Offers earth sciences (PhD); marine biodiversity and conservation (MAS); marine biology (PhD); oceanography (PhD). *Entrance requirements:* For doctorate, GRE General Test, GRE Subject Test. Additional exam requirements/recommendations for international students: Required—TOEFL (minimum score 550 paper-based; 213 computer-based). Electronic applications accepted.

University of Colorado at Boulder, Graduate School, College of Arts and Sciences, Department of Atmospheric and Oceanic Sciences, Boulder, CO 80309. Offers MS, PhD. *Faculty:* 11 full-time (4 women). *Students:* 43 full-time (23 women), 22 part-time (9 women); includes 7 minority (1 African American, 3 Asian Americans or Pacific Islanders, 3 Hispanic Americans), 11 international. Average age 30. 85 applicants, 15% accepted, 9 enrolled. In 2009, 4 master's, 5 doctorates awarded. *Entrance requirements:* For master's, minimum undergraduate GPA of 3.0. *Application deadline:* For fall admission, 2/1 for domestic students, 12/1 for international students; for spring admission, 10/1 for domestic and international students. *Financial support:* In 2009–10, 11 fellowships (averaging $2,321 per year), 40 research assistantships (averaging $16,795 per year) were awarded. *Faculty research:* Large-scale dynamics of the ocean and the atmosphere, air-sea interaction, radiative transfer and remote sensing of the ocean and the atmosphere, sea ice and its role in climate. Total annual research expenditures: $6.7 million.

University of Connecticut, Graduate School, College of Liberal Arts and Sciences, Department of Marine Sciences, Storrs, CT 06269. Offers MS, PhD. *Faculty:* 25 full-time (6 women). *Students:* 28 full-time (17 women), 10 part-time (5 women); includes 3 minority (2 African Americans, 1 Hispanic American), 8 international. Average age 33. 24 applicants, 4% accepted, 1 enrolled. In 2009, 5 master's, 1 doctorate awarded. Terminal master's awarded for partial completion of doctoral program. *Degree requirements:* For master's, comprehensive exam; for doctorate, thesis/dissertation. *Entrance requirements:* Additional exam requirements/recommendations for international students: Required—TOEFL (minimum score 550 paper-based; 213 computer-based). *Application deadline:* For fall admission, 2/1 for domestic and international students; for spring admission, 11/1 for domestic students, 10/1 for international students. Applications are processed on a rolling basis. Application fee: $55. Electronic applications accepted. *Expenses:* Tuition, state resident: full-time $4725; part-time $525 per credit. Tuition, nonresident: full-time $12,267; part-time $1363 per credit. Required fees: $346 per semester. Tuition and fees vary according to course load. *Financial support:* In 2009–10, 17 research assistantships with full tuition reimbursements, 11 teaching assistantships with full tuition reimbursements were awarded; fellowships, Federal Work-Study, scholarships/grants, health care benefits, and unspecified assistantships also available. Financial award application deadline: 2/1; financial award applicants required to submit FAFSA. *Unit head:* Ann Bucklin, Director, 860-405-9208, Fax: 860-405-9153, E-mail: ann.bucklin@uconn.edu. *Application contact:* Pieter Visscher, Chairperson, 860-405-9159, Fax: 860-405-9153, E-mail: visscher@uconnvm.uconn.edu.

University of Delaware, College of Marine and Earth Studies, Newark, DE 19716. Offers geology (MS, PhD); marine policy (MS); marine studies (MMP, MS, PhD); oceanography (MS, PhD). *Degree requirements:* For master's, thesis; for doctorate, thesis/dissertation. *Entrance requirements:* For master's and doctorate, GRE General Test. Additional exam requirements/recommendations for international students: Required—TOEFL. Electronic applications accepted. *Faculty research:* Marine biology and biochemistry, oceanography, marine policy, physical ocean science and engineering, ocean engineering.

University of Georgia, Graduate School, College of Arts and Sciences, Department of Marine Sciences, Athens, GA 30602. Offers MS, PhD. *Faculty:* 16 full-time (5 women), 1 part-time/adjunct (0 women). *Students:* 28 full-time (14 women), 1 (woman) part-time; includes 2 minority (both Hispanic Americans), 7 international. Average age 28. 45 applicants, 31% accepted, 9 enrolled. In 2009, 1 master's, 1 doctorate awarded. *Degree requirements:* For master's, thesis; for doctorate, comprehensive exam, thesis/dissertation, teaching experience, field research experience. *Entrance requirements:* For master's and doctorate, GRE General Test. Additional exam requirements/recommendations for international students: Required—TOEFL. *Application deadline:* For fall admission, 2/1 priority date for domestic and international students; for spring admission, 10/15 priority date for domestic students, 9/1 priority date for international students. Applications are processed on a rolling basis. Application fee: $50. Electronic applications accepted. *Expenses:* Tuition, state resident: full-time $6000; part-time $250 per credit hour. Tuition, nonresident: full-time $20,904; part-time $871 per credit hour. Required fees: $730 per semester. *Financial support:* In 2009–10, 9 fellowships with full tuition reimbursements (averaging $20,000 per year), 21 research assistantships with full tuition reimbursements (averaging $18,000 per year), 11 teaching assistantships with full tuition reimbursements (averaging $18,000 per year) were awarded. *Faculty research:* Microbial ecology, biogeochemistry, polar biology, coastal ecology, coastal circulation. *Unit head:* Dr. James T. Hollibaugh, Director, 706-542-7671, Fax: 706-542-5888, E-mail: aquadoc@uga.edu. *Application contact:* Dr. Wei-Jun Cai, Graduate Coordinator, 706-542-1285, E-mail: gradmar@uga.edu.

University of Hawaii at Manoa, Graduate Division, School of Ocean and Earth Science and Technology, Department of Oceanography, Honolulu, HI 96822. Offers MS, PhD. Part-time programs available. *Faculty:* 54 full-time (7 women), 15 part-time/adjunct (2 women). *Students:* 77 full-time (42 women), 2 part-time (1 woman); includes 16 minority (1 African American, 12 Asian Americans or Pacific Islanders, 3 Hispanic Americans), 21 international. Average age 27. 96 applicants, 18% accepted, 16 enrolled. In 2009, 10 master's, 7 doctorates awarded. Terminal master's awarded for partial completion of doctoral program. *Degree requirements:* For master's, one foreign language, comprehensive exam, thesis, field experience; for doctorate, one foreign language, comprehensive exam, thesis/dissertation, field experience. *Entrance requirements:* For master's and doctorate, GRE General Test. Additional exam requirements/recommendations for international students: Required—TOEFL (minimum score 560 paper-based; 220 computer-based; 83 iBT), IELTS (minimum score 5). *Application deadline:* For fall admission, 1/15 for domestic and international students; for spring admission, 9/1 for domestic students, 8/15 for international students. Application fee: $60. *Expenses:* Tuition, state resident: full-time $8900; part-time $372 per credit. Tuition, nonresident: full-time $21,400; part-time $898 per credit. Required fees: $207 per semester. *Financial support:* In 2009–10, 4 students received support, including 2 fellowships (averaging $3,075 per year), 60 research assistantships (averaging $23,114 per year), 13 teaching assistantships (averaging $22,140 per year); career-related internships or fieldwork, institutionally sponsored loans, and tuition waivers (full and partial) also available. Financial award applicants required to submit FAFSA. *Faculty research:* Physical oceanography, marine chemistry, biological oceanography, atmospheric chemistry, marine geology. *Application contact:* Francis Sansone, Graduate Chair, 808-956-2913, Fax: 808-956-9225, E-mail: sansone@hawaii.edu.

University of Maine, Graduate School, College of Natural Sciences, Forestry, and Agriculture, School of Marine Sciences, Program in Oceanography, Orono, ME 04469. Offers MS, PhD. Part-time programs available. *Students:* 11 full-time (4 women), 8 part-time (2 women), 4 international. Average age 29. 15 applicants, 40% accepted, 6 enrolled. In 2009, 3 doctorates awarded. *Degree requirements:* For master's, thesis; for doctorate, thesis/dissertation. *Entrance requirements:* For master's and doctorate, GRE General Test. Additional exam requirements/recommendations for international students: Required—TOEFL. *Application deadline:* For fall admission, 2/1 priority date for domestic students. Applications are processed on a rolling basis. Application fee: $65. Electronic applications accepted. *Financial support:* Fellowships with tuition reimbursements, research assistantships with tuition reimbursements, teaching assistantships with tuition reimbursements, career-related internships or fieldwork, Federal Work-Study, and tuition waivers (full and partial) available. Support available to part-time students. Financial award application deadline: 3/1. *Faculty research:* Coastal processes, microbial ecology, crustacean systematics. *Unit head:* Dr. Larry Mayer, Coordinator, 207-581-3321. *Application contact:* Scott G. Delcourt, Associate Dean of the Graduate School, 207-581-3291, Fax: 207-581-3232, E-mail: graduate@maine.edu.

University of Maryland, College Park, Academic Affairs, College of Computer, Mathematical and Physical Sciences, Department of Atmospheric and Oceanic Science, College Park, MD 20742. Offers MS, PhD. Part-time and evening/weekend programs available. Postbaccalaureate distance learning degree programs offered. *Faculty:* 31 full-time (8 women), 7 part-time/adjunct (1 woman). *Students:* 50 full-time (21 women), 11 part-time (6 women); includes 3 minority (all Asian Americans or Pacific Islanders), 23 international. 82 applicants, 30% accepted, 16 enrolled. In 2009, 6 master's, 10 doctorates awarded. Terminal master's awarded for partial completion of doctoral program. *Degree requirements:* For master's, comprehensive exam, scholarly paper, written and oral exams; for doctorate, thesis/dissertation, exam. *Entrance requirements:* For master's, GRE General Test, background in mathematics, experience in scientific computer languages, 3 letters of recommendation; for doctorate, GRE General Test. *Application deadline:* For fall admission, 1/15 for domestic and international students; for spring admission, 11/1 for domestic students, 6/1 for international students. Applications are processed on a rolling basis. Application fee: $60. Electronic applications accepted. *Expenses:* Tuition, area resident: Part-time $471 per credit hour. Tuition, state resident: part-time $471 per credit hour. Tuition, nonresident: part-time $1016 per credit hour. Required fees: $337.04 per term. *Financial support:* In 2009–10, 3 fellowships with full and partial tuition reimbursements (averaging $13,629 per year), 28 research assistantships with tuition reimbursements (averaging $20,600 per year), 11 teaching assistantships with tuition reimbursements (averaging $20,611 per year) were awarded; Federal Work-Study and scholarships/grants also available. Support available to part-time students. Financial award applicants required to submit FAFSA. *Faculty research:* Weather, atmospheric chemistry, air pollution, global change, radiation. Total annual research expenditures: $4 million. *Unit head:* James A. Carton, Chair, 301-405-5365, Fax: 301-314-9482, E-mail: carton@atmos.umd.edu. *Application contact:* Dean of Graduate School, 301-405-0358.

University of Miami, Graduate School, Rosenstiel School of Marine and Atmospheric Science, Division of Meteorology and Physical Oceanography, Coral Gables, FL 33124. Offers meteorology (MS, PhD); physical oceanography (MS, PhD). Terminal master's awarded for partial completion of doctoral program. *Degree requirements:* For master's, comprehensive exam, thesis; for doctorate, comprehensive exam, thesis/dissertation. *Entrance requirements:* For master's and doctorate, GRE General Test. Additional exam requirements/recommendations for international students: Required—TOEFL (minimum score 550 paper-based; 213 computer-based). Electronic applications accepted.

University of New Hampshire, Graduate School, College of Engineering and Physical Sciences, Department of Earth Sciences, Durham, NH 03824. Offers earth sciences (MS), including geochemical systems, geology, ocean mapping, oceanography; hydrology (MS). *Faculty:* 17 full-time (5 women). *Students:* 7 full-time (5 women), 15 part-time (7 women), 1 international. Average age 27. 27 applicants, 56% accepted, 5 enrolled. In 2009, 18 master's awarded. *Degree requirements:* For master's, thesis. *Entrance requirements:* For master's, GRE General Test. Additional exam requirements/recommendations for international students: Required—TOEFL (minimum score 550 paper-based; 213 computer-based; 80 iBT). *Application deadline:* For fall admission, 4/1 priority date for domestic students, 4/1 for international students; for spring admission, 12/1 for domestic students. Applications are processed on a rolling basis. Application fee: $65. Electronic applications accepted. *Expenses:* Tuition, state resident: full-time $10,380; part-time $577 per credit hour. Tuition, nonresident: full-time $24,350; part-time $1002 per credit hour. Required fees: $1550; $387.50 per semester. Tuition and fees vary according to course load and program. *Financial support:* In 2009–10, 17 students received support, including 1 fellowship, 6 research assistantships, 8 teaching assistantships; career-related internships or fieldwork, Federal Work-Study, scholarships/grants, and tuition waivers (full and partial) also available. Support available to part-time students. Financial award application deadline: 2/15. *Unit head:* Dr. Will Clyde, Chairperson, 603-862-1718, E-mail: earth.sciences@unh.edu. *Application contact:* Sue Clark, Administrative Assistant, 603-862-1718, E-mail: earth.sciences@unh.edu.

University of New Hampshire, Graduate School, College of Engineering and Physical Sciences, Program in Ocean Engineering, Durham, NH 03824. Offers ocean engineering (MS, PhD); ocean mapping (MS, Postbaccalaureate Certificate). *Faculty:* 13 full-time (1 woman). *Students:* 12 full-time (5 women), 4 part-time (0 women); includes 1 minority (Hispanic American), 10 international. Average age 30. 17 applicants, 76% accepted, 8 enrolled. In 2009, 2 master's, 1 doctorate, 4 other advanced degrees awarded. *Degree requirements:* For master's, thesis. *Entrance requirements:* Additional exam requirements/recommendations for international students: Required—TOEFL (minimum score 550 paper-based; 213 computer-based; 80 iBT). *Application deadline:* For fall admission, 4/1 priority date for domestic students; for spring admission, 12/1 for domestic students. Applications are processed on a rolling basis. Application fee: $65. Electronic applications accepted. *Expenses:* Tuition, state resident: full-time $10,380; part-time $577 per credit hour. Tuition, nonresident: full-time $24,350; part-time $1002 per credit hour. Required fees: $1550; $387.50 per semester. Tuition and fees vary according to course load and program. *Financial support:* In 2009–10, 11 students received support, including 10 research assistantships, 1 teaching assistantship; fellowships, Federal Work-Study, scholarships/grants, and tuition waivers (full and partial) also available. Support available to part-time students. Financial award application deadline: 2/15. *Unit head:* Dr. Kenneth Baldwin, Chairperson, 603-862-1898. *Application contact:* Jennifer Bedsole, Information Contact, 603-862-0672, E-mail: ocean.engineering@unh.edu.

University of Rhode Island, Graduate School, Graduate School of Oceanography, Narragansett, RI 02882. Offers MO, MS, PhD, MBA/MO, PhD/MMA, PhD/MA. Part-time programs available. *Faculty:* 28 full-time (8 women), 1 part-time/adjunct (0 women). *Students:* 61 full-time (38 women), 27 part-time (15 women); includes 2 minority (both Asian Americans or Pacific Islanders), 7 international. In 2009, 6 master's, 6 doctorates awarded. *Degree requirements:* For master's, comprehensive exam (for some programs), thesis optional; for doctorate,

Oceanography

University of Rhode Island (continued)

comprehensive exam, thesis/dissertation. *Entrance requirements:* For master's, GRE, 2 letters of recommendation; for doctorate, GRE, 3 letters of recommendation. Additional exam requirements/recommendations for international students: Required—TOEFL (minimum score 600 paper-based; 250 computer-based; 100 iBT). *Application deadline:* For fall admission, 1/15 for domestic and international students; for spring admission, 11/15 for domestic students, 7/15 for international students. Application fee: $65. Electronic applications accepted. *Expenses:* Tuition, state resident: full-time $8828; part-time $490 per credit hour. Tuition, nonresident: full-time $22,100; part-time $1228 per credit hour. Required fees: $1118; $57 per semester. Tuition and fees vary according to program. *Financial support:* In 2009–10, 33 research assistantships with full and partial tuition reimbursements (averaging $10,345 per year), 11 teaching assistantships with full and partial tuition reimbursements (averaging $10,982 per year) were awarded. Financial award application deadline: 1/15; financial award applicants required to submit FAFSA. *Faculty research:* The Subduction Factory, life in extreme environments, the marine nitrogen cycle, hurricane prediction, Antarctic ocean circulation. Total annual research expenditures: $22.1 million. *Unit head:* Dr. David M. Farmer, Dean, 401-874-6222, Fax: 401-874-6889, E-mail: thedean@gso.uri.edu. *Application contact:* Dr. David M. Farmer, Dean, 401-874-6222, Fax: 401-874-6889, E-mail: thedean@gso.uri.edu.

University of Southern California, Graduate School, College of Letters, Arts and Sciences, Department of Biological Sciences, Program in Marine Biology and Biological Oceanography, Los Angeles, CA 90089. Offers marine and environmental biology (MS); marine biology and biological oceanography (PhD). *Faculty:* 27 full-time (8 women), 7 part-time/adjunct (2 women). *Students:* 2 full-time (1 woman), 1 international. 36 applicants, 50% accepted. In 2009, 1 master's awarded. Terminal master's awarded for partial completion of doctoral program. *Degree requirements:* For master's, comprehensive exam (for some programs), research paper; for doctorate, thesis/dissertation, course work, qualifying examination, dissertation defense. *Entrance requirements:* For master's and doctorate, General Record Exam, 3 letters of recommendation, personal statement, resume?, GPA >3.0. Additional exam requirements/recommendations for international students: Required—TOEFL (minimum score 600 paper-based; 250 computer-based; 100 iBT). *Application deadline:* For fall admission, 12/1 priority date for domestic and international students. Application fee: $85. Electronic applications accepted. *Expenses:* Tuition: Full-time $25,980; part-time $1315 per unit. Required fees: $554. One-time fee: $35 full-time. Full-time tuition and fees vary according to degree level and program. *Financial support:* In 2009–10, 10 fellowships with full tuition reimbursements (averaging $25,333 per year), 14 research assistantships with full tuition reimbursements (averaging $25,333 per year), 14 teaching assistantships with full tuition reimbursements (averaging $25,333 per year) were awarded; scholarships/grants, traineeships, health care benefits, and tuition waivers also available. *Faculty research:* Adaptation, evolution, and population dynamics; marine microbiology; global biogeochemical cycles; coastal water quality; marine environmental genomics. *Unit head:* Dr. David A. Caron, Professor of Biological Sciences, Director of the MBBO Graduate Program, 213-740-0203, E-mail: dcaron@usc.edu. *Application contact:* Adolfo dela Rosa, Student Services Advisor I, 213-821-3164, Fax: 213-740-1380, E-mail: adolfode@usc.edu.

University of South Florida, Graduate School, College of Marine Science, St. Petersburg, FL 33701. Offers biological oceanography (MS, PhD); chemical oceanography (MS, PhD); geological oceanography (MS, PhD); interdisciplinary (MS, PhD); marine resource assessment (MS, PhD); physical oceanography (MS, PhD). Part-time programs available. *Faculty:* 24 full-time (4 women). *Students:* 73 full-time (44 women), 26 part-time (18 women); includes 16 minority (7 African Americans, 9 Hispanic Americans), 10 international. Average age 32. 80 applicants, 34% accepted, 19 enrolled. In 2009, 14 master's, 10 doctorates awarded. Terminal master's awarded for partial completion of doctoral program. *Degree requirements:* For master's, thesis, successful oral defense; for doctorate, comprehensive exam, thesis/dissertation, successful oral defense. *Entrance requirements:* For master's, GRE General Test; for doctorate, GRE General Test, ??? Bachelor???s degree or equivalent from a regionally accredited university ??????B??? (3.0 on a 4.0 scale) average or better in all work attempted while registered as an upper division student working for a baccalaureate degree ??? Completed coursework listed on our website: http://www.marine.usf.edu/prospective-students/undergraduate-preparat. Additional exam requirements/recommendations for international students: Required—TOEFL (minimum score 550 paper-based; 213 computer-based; 79 iBT). *Application deadline:* For fall admission, 1/15 for domestic students, 1/2 for international students; for spring admission, 10/1 for domestic students, 7/1 for international students. Applications are processed on a rolling basis. Application fee: $30. *Financial support:* In 2009–10, 73 students received support, including 19 fellowships with partial tuition reimbursements available (averaging $13,972 per year), 36 research assistantships with partial tuition reimbursements available (averaging $13,972 per year), 7 teaching assistantships with partial tuition reimbursements available (averaging $13,972 per year); health care benefits and unspecified assistantships also available. Financial award application deadline: 1/15. *Faculty research:* Trace metal chemistry, water quality, organic and isotopic geochemistry, physical chemistry, nutrient chemistry. Total annual research expenditures: $11.9 million. *Unit head:* Dr. Edward S. Van Vleet, Professor and Director of Academic Programs and Student Affairs, 727-553-1165, Fax: 727-553-1189, E-mail: vanvleet@marine.usf.edu. *Application contact:* Dawna L. Ishler, Academic Services Administrator, 727-553-3944, Fax: 727-553-1189, E-mail: dishler@usf.edu.

University of Victoria, Faculty of Graduate Studies, Faculty of Science, School of Earth and Ocean Sciences, Victoria, BC V8W 2Y2, Canada. Offers M Sc, PhD. Part-time programs available. *Degree requirements:* For master's, thesis; for doctorate, thesis/dissertation, candidacy exam. *Entrance requirements:* For master's and doctorate, GRE. Additional exam requirements/recommendations for international students: Required—TOEFL (minimum score 575 paper-based; 233 computer-based), IELTS (minimum score 7). Electronic applications accepted. *Faculty research:* Climate modeling, geology.

University of Washington, Graduate School, College of Ocean and Fishery Sciences, School of Oceanography, Seattle, WA 98195. Offers biological oceanography (MS, PhD); chemical oceanography (MS, PhD); marine geology and geophysics (MS, PhD); physical oceanography (MS, PhD). Terminal master's awarded for partial completion of doctoral program. *Degree requirements:* For master's, research project; for doctorate, thesis/dissertation. *Entrance requirements:* For master's and doctorate, GRE General Test, minimum GPA of 3.0. Additional exam requirements/recommendations for international students: Required—TOEFL. Electronic applications accepted. *Faculty research:* Global climate change, hydrothermal vent systems, marine microbiology, marine and freshwater biogeochemistry, biological-physical interactions.

University of Wisconsin–Madison, Graduate School, College of Engineering, Program in Limnology and Marine Science, Madison, WI 53706. Offers MS, PhD. Terminal master's awarded for partial completion of doctoral program. *Degree requirements:* For master's, thesis; for doctorate, thesis/dissertation. *Entrance requirements:* For master's and doctorate, GRE General Test. Additional exam requirements/recommendations for international students: Required—TOEFL. Electronic applications accepted. *Expenses:* Tuition, state resident: part-time $594 per credit. Tuition, nonresident: part-time $1504 per credit. Required fees: $65 per credit. Tuition and fees vary according to course load, program and reciprocity agreements. *Faculty research:* Lake ecosystems, ecosystem modeling, geochemistry, physiological ecology, chemical limnology.

University of Wisconsin–Madison, Graduate School, College of Letters and Science, Department of Atmospheric and Oceanic Sciences, Madison, WI 53706-1380. Offers MS, PhD. Part-time programs available. *Degree requirements:* For master's, thesis (for some programs); for doctorate, thesis/dissertation. *Entrance requirements:* For master's and doctorate, GRE General Test, minimum GPA of 3.0; previous course work in chemistry, mathematics, and physics. Electronic applications accepted. *Expenses:* Tuition, state resident: part-time $594 per credit. Tuition, nonresident: part-time $1504 per credit. Required fees: $65 per credit. Tuition and fees vary according to course load, program and reciprocity agreements. *Faculty research:* Satellite meteorology, weather systems, global climate change, numerical modeling, atmosphere-ocean interaction.

Woods Hole Oceanographic Institution, MIT/WHOI Joint Program in Oceanography/Applied Ocean Science and Engineering, Woods Hole, MA 02543-1541. Offers applied ocean sciences (PhD); biological oceanography (PhD, Sc D); chemical oceanography (PhD, Sc D); civil and environmental and oceanographic engineering (PhD); electrical and oceanographic engineering (PhD); geochemistry (PhD); geophysics (PhD); marine biology (PhD); marine geochemistry (PhD, Sc D); marine geology (PhD, Sc D); marine geophysics (PhD); mechanical and oceanographic engineering (PhD); ocean engineering (PhD); oceanographic engineering (M Eng, MS, PhD, Sc D, Eng); paleoceanography (PhD); physical oceanography (PhD, Sc D). Terminal master's awarded for partial completion of doctoral program. *Degree requirements:* For master's and Eng, thesis (for some programs); for doctorate, thesis/dissertation. *Entrance requirements:* For master's, GRE General Test; for doctorate, GRE General Test, GRE Subject Test. Additional exam requirements/recommendations for international students: Required—TOEFL. Electronic applications accepted.

Yale University, Graduate School of Arts and Sciences, Department of Geology and Geophysics, New Haven, CT 06520. Offers biogeochemistry (PhD); climate dynamics (PhD); geochemistry (PhD); geophysics (PhD); meteorology (PhD); oceanography (PhD); paleontology (PhD); paleooceanography (PhD); petrology (PhD); tectonics (PhD). *Degree requirements:* For doctorate, thesis/dissertation. *Entrance requirements:* For doctorate, GRE General Test. Additional exam requirements/recommendations for international students: Required—TOEFL.

FLORIDA INSTITUTE OF TECHNOLOGY

Department of Marine and Environmental Systems
Programs in Oceanography and Coastal Zone Management

Programs of Study

Florida Institute of Technology offers programs of research and study options in the fields of biological, chemical, geological, and physical oceanography; marine meteorology; and environmental and marine chemistry that lead to M.S. and Ph.D. degrees in oceanography. An M.S. in oceanography with an option in coastal zone management is also offered. Those students interested in the graduate program in ocean engineering should consult the program description at http://coe.fit.edu/dmes/ocean.php.

Research Facilities

Florida Institute of Technology is conveniently located on the Indian River Lagoon, a major east-central Florida estuarine system recently designated an Estuary of National Significance. Marine and environmental laboratories and field research stations are located on the lagoon and at an oceanfront marine research facility. Marine operations, located just 5 minutes from the campus, house a fleet of small outboard-powered craft and medium-sized work boats. These boats are available to students and faculty members for teaching and research in the freshwater tributaries and the Indian River Lagoon.

Florida Tech's oceanfront marine research facility, the Vero Beach Marine Laboratory, just 40 minutes from the campus, provides facilities, including flowing seawater from the Atlantic Ocean, to support research in such areas as aquaculture, biofouling, and corrosion. On the Melbourne campus, the Departmental teaching and research facilities include separate laboratories for biological, chemical, physical, geological, and instrumentation investigations. In addition, high-pressure, hydroacoustics, fluid dynamics, and GIS/remote sensing facilities are available.

About an hour from campus is the Harbor Branch Oceanographic Institute of Florida Atlantic University; scientists and engineers there pursue their own research and development activities and interact with Florida Tech students and faculty members on projects of mutual interest.

The Biological Oceanography Laboratory is fully equipped for research on plankton, benthos, and fishes of coastal and estuarine ecosystems. Collection gear; analytical equipment, including a flow-through fluorometer; and a controlled environment room are available for student and research use. Areas of research have included toxic algal blooms, sea grass ecology, and artificial and natural reef communities.

The Marine and Environmental Chemistry Laboratories are equipped to do both routine and research-level operations on open-ocean and coastal lagoonal waters. Major and minor nutrients, heavy-metal contaminants, and biological pollutants can be quantitatively determined. Analytical methods available include liquid chromatography, infrared and visible light spectrophotometry, and atomic absorption spectrometry.

The Physical Oceanography Laboratory and the Surf Mechanics Laboratory support graduate research in ocean waves, coastal processes, circulation, and pollutant transport. In addition, CTD and XBT systems, ADCP and other current meters, tide and wind recorders, salinometers, wave-height gauges, side-scan sonar, and other oceanographic instruments are available for field work. An Environmental and Optics Laboratory provides capabilities for analyzing ocean color data and collecting in situ hydrologic optics data.

The Marine Geology Laboratory is used to study nearshore sedimentation and stratigraphy. The lab equipment includes a state-of-the-art computerized rapid sediment analyzer, a magnetic heavy-mineral separator, and computer-assisted sieve systems.

Financial Aid

Graduate teaching, research assistantships, and endowed fellowships are available to qualified students. For 2010–11, financial support ranges from approximately $9000 to $16,000, including stipend and tuition, per academic year for approximately half-time duties. Stipend-only assistantships are sometimes awarded for less time commitment. Most coastal zone management students receive support through internship appointments.

Cost of Study

In 2010–11, tuition is $1040 per graduate semester credit hour.

Living and Housing Costs

Room and board on campus cost approximately $4500 per semester in 2010–11. On-campus housing (dormitories and apartments) is available for full-time single and married graduate students, but priority for dormitory rooms is given to undergraduate students. Many apartment complexes and rental houses are available near the campus.

Student Group

The College of Engineering has 450 graduate students. Oceanography currently has approximately 25 graduate and 40 undergraduate students.

Student Outcomes

Graduates have gone on to careers with such institutions as NOAA, EPA, Florida Water Management Districts, Western Geophysical, Naval Oceanographic Office, Digicon, county and state agencies, consulting firms, and other universities.

Location

The campus is located in Melbourne, on Florida's east coast. It is an area, located 4 miles from the Atlantic Ocean beaches, with a year-round subtropical climate. The area's economy is supported by a well-balanced mix of industries in electronics, aviation, light manufacturing, optics, communications, agriculture, and tourism. Many industries support activities at the Kennedy Space Center.

The Institute

Florida Institute of Technology is a distinctive, independent university, founded in 1958 by a group of scientists and engineers to fulfill a need for specialized advanced educational opportunities on the Space Coast of Florida. Florida Tech is the only independent technological university in the Southeast. Supported by both industry and the community, Florida Tech is the recipient of many research grants and contracts, a number of which provide financial support for graduate students.

Applying

Forms and instructions for applying for admission and assistantships are sent on request. Admission is possible at the beginning of any semester, but admission in the fall semester is recommended. It is advantageous to apply early.

Correspondence and Information

Dr. John G. Windsor Jr., Program Chairman
Oceanography Program
Florida Institute of Technology
Melbourne, Florida 32901-6975
Phone: 321-674-8096
Fax: 321-674-7212
E-mail: dmes@fit.edu
Web site: http://www.fit.edu/AcadRes/dmes

Office of Graduate Admissions
Florida Institute of Technology
Melbourne, Florida 32901-6975
Phone: 321-674-8027
800-944-4348 (toll-free in the U.S.)
Fax: 321-723-9468
E-mail: grad-admissions@fit.edu
Web site: http://www.fit.edu

Florida Institute of Technology

THE FACULTY AND THEIR RESEARCH

(For additional details, please see http://www.fit.edu/faculty/profiles/)

Charles R. Bostater Jr., Associate Professor; Ph.D., Delaware. Remote sensing, hydrologic optics, particle dynamics in estuaries, modeling of toxic substances, physical oceanography of coastal waters, environmental modeling.

Iver W. Duedall, Professor Emeritus; Ph.D., Dalhousie. Chemical oceanography, physical chemistry of seawater, geochemistry, marine pollution, ocean management.

Lee E. Harris, Associate Professor; Ph.D., Florida Atlantic; PE. Coastal engineering, coastal structures, beach erosion and control, physical oceanography.

Elizabeth A. Irlandi, Associate Professor; Ph.D., North Carolina. Landscape ecology in aquatic environments, sea grass ecosystems, coastal zone management.

Kevin B. Johnson, Associate Professor; Ph.D., Oregon. Zooplankton ecology, predator-prey interactions, metamorphosis, larval transport and settlement, larval behavior, invasive species.

George A. Maul, Professor; Ph.D., Miami (Florida). Physical oceanography, marine meteorology, climate and sea-level change, satellite oceanography, earth system science, tsunamis and other coastal hazards.

Dean R. Norris, Professor Emeritus; Ph.D., Texas A&M. Taxonomy and ecology of marine phytoplankton, particularly dinoflagellates; ecology and life cycles of toxic dinoflagellates.

Geoffrey W. J. Swain, Professor; Ph.D., Southampton. Materials corrosion, biofouling, offshore technology, ship operations.

John H. Trefry, Professor; Ph.D., Texas A&M. Trace metal geochemistry and pollution, geochemistry of rivers, global chemical cycles, deep-sea hydrothermal systems.

John G. Windsor Jr., Professor; Ph.D., William and Mary. Trace organic analysis, organic chemistry, sediment-sea interaction, air-sea interaction, coastal management, environmental education.

Gary Zarillo, Professor; Ph.D., Georgia; PG. Sediment transport and morphodynamics, tidal inlet–barrier dynamics, numerical modeling of inlet hydrodynamics.

Adjunct Faculty

Eric D. Thosteson, Ph.D., Florida; PE. Coastal processes, wave mechanics.
Robert W. Virnstein, Ph.D., William and Mary. Limnology.
Christopher Combs, M.S., Texas A&M. Descriptive oceanography.

UNIVERSITY OF MARYLAND

Graduate Program in Marine-Estuarine-Environmental Sciences

Program of Study

The specific objective of the all-University Graduate Program in Marine-Estuarine-Environmental Sciences (MEES) is the training of qualified graduate students who are working toward the M.S. or Ph.D. degree and have research interests in fields of study that involve interactions between biological systems and physical or chemical systems in the marine, estuarine, or terrestrial environments. The program comprises six Areas of Specialization (AOS): Oceanography, Environmental Chemistry (and toxicology), Ecology, Environmental Molecular Biology/Biotechnology, Fisheries Science, and Environmental Science. Students work with their advisory committee to develop a customized course of study based on research interests and previous experience.

All students must demonstrate competence in statistics. Each student is required to complete a thesis or dissertation reporting the results of an original investigation. The research problem is selected and pursued under the guidance of the student's adviser and advisory committee.

Research Facilities

Students may conduct their research either in the laboratories and facilities of the College Park (UMCP), Baltimore (UMB), Baltimore County (UMBC), or Eastern Shore (UMES) campuses; in one of the laboratories of the University of Maryland Center for Environmental Science (UMCES): Chesapeake Biological Laboratory (CBL) at Solomons, Maryland; the Horn Point Laboratory (HPL) in Cambridge, Maryland; and the Appalachian Laboratory (AL) in Frostburg, Maryland; or at the Center of Marine Biotechnology (COMB) in Baltimore, Maryland. CBL and HPL are located on the Chesapeake Bay. They include excellent facilities for the culture of estuarine organisms. The laboratories are provided with running salt water, which may be heated or cooled and may be filtered. Berthed at CBL are the University's research vessels. At HPL, there are extensive marshes, intertidal areas, oyster reefs, tidal creeks, and rock jetties. AL, which is located in the mountains of western Maryland, specializes in terrestrial and freshwater ecology.

Specialized laboratory facilities for environmental research are located on the campuses. These facilities provide space for microbiology, biotechnology, water chemistry, and cellular, molecular, and organismal biology. There are also specialized facilities for the rearing and maintenance of both terrestrial and aquatic organisms of all kinds. There are extensive facilities for remote sensing of the environment. Extensive field sites for environmental research are available through the University's agricultural programs and through cooperation with many other organizations in the state.

Financial Aid

University fellowships, research assistantships and traineeships, and teaching assistantships are available. In general, aid provides for full living and educational expenses. Some partial assistance may also be available. Research support from federal, state, and private sources often provides opportunities for additional student support through either research assistantships or part-time employment on research projects.

Cost of Study

In 2009–10, tuition for graduate students was $444 for Maryland residents and $958 for nonresidents for each credit hour. In addition, stipulated fees ranged from $327 to $569 per semester for each student. However, financial aid typically covers most of these expenses.

Living and Housing Costs

Commercial housing is plentiful in the area around the campuses. For students who are working at HPL or CBL, limited dormitory-type housing is available on site. Minimum living expenses for a year's study at College Park or in the Baltimore area are about $19,000, exclusive of tuition and fees. Costs may be lower at the UMES campus.

Student Group

About 185 students are enrolled in the program. They come from a variety of academic backgrounds. There are a number of international students. About 50 percent of the students are in the doctoral program, and 50 percent are working toward the M.S. Some of the master's students expect to continue toward the doctorate. While most of the students are biologists, some come with undergraduate majors in chemistry, biochemistry, geology, economics, political science, or engineering. The program encourages and accommodates such diversity in its students.

Location

The MEES program is offered on the campuses of the University at College Park, Baltimore, Baltimore County, and Eastern Shore and at the UMCES laboratories and COMB. Students normally enroll on the campus where their adviser is located. Of particular relevance for the MEES program is the University's location near Chesapeake Bay, one of the world's most important estuarine systems, which in many aspects serves as the program's principal laboratory resource.

The University

The University of Maryland is the state's land grant and sea grant university. It has comprehensive programs at both the undergraduate and graduate levels on the campuses at College Park, Baltimore County, and Eastern Shore. Programs in the health sciences and the professions are located in Baltimore. There are approximately 8,400 graduate students at College Park, 800 at Baltimore, 300 at Baltimore County, and 75 at Eastern Shore.

Applying

Applications for admission in the fall semester must be completed by February 1; however, to be considered for financial support, it is better to apply by December 1. Some students are admitted for the semester starting in January, for which the deadline is September 1. Applicants must submit an official application to the University of Maryland Graduate School, along with official transcripts of all previous collegiate work, three letters of recommendation, and scores on the General Test (aptitude) of the Graduate Record Examinations. It is particularly important that a student articulate clearly in the application a statement of goals and objectives pertaining to their future work in the field. Because of the interdisciplinary and interdepartmental nature of the program, only students for whom a specific adviser is identified in advance can be admitted. Prior communication with individual members of the faculty is encouraged.

Correspondence and Information

Graduate Program in Marine-Estuarine-Environmental Sciences
0105 Cole
University of Maryland
College Park, Maryland 20742
Phone: 301-405-6938
Fax: 301-314-4139
E-mail: mees@umd.edu
Web site: http://www.mees.umd.edu

University of Maryland

THE FACULTY AND THEIR RESEARCH

Baltimore Campus. Da-Wei Gong: molecular and cell biology of energy metabolism. Raymond T. Jones: pathophysiology of elasmobranch and teleost fishes. Silvia A. Pineiro: genomics, functional genomics, taxonomy, and ecology of the *Bdellovibrio* and like organisms. Henry N. Williams: ecology of the bacterial predator, *Bdellovibrio*, in the Chesapeake Bay.

Baltimore County Campus. C. Allen Bush: environmental molecular biology, molecular structure determination. Erle C. Ellis: landscape ecology, biogeochemistry, sustainable resource management. Upal Ghosh: experimental investigation, design, and modeling of physiochemical and biological processes that affect water quality. Raymond Hoff: optical properties of aerosols and gases in the atmosphere, pathways and fates of toxic organic and elemental chemicals in the environment. Jeffrey Leips: evolution of life history traits, specifically focused on understanding how the genetic architecture underlying these traits guides and constrains their evolutionary responses to natural selection. Laura Lewis: Biogeography of crop species; domestication and radiation of agricultural species; agro-ecology, germplasm management, genetic resources conservation; applied urban ethnobotany/ethnobiolgoy. Andrew J. Miller: surface-water hydrology and fluvial geomorphology, effects of human activities on watershed hydrology and river channels. Robert R. Provine: fish and waterfowl behavioral ecology. Brian E. Reed: sorption of organics/inorganics, surface chemistry, water and wastewater treatment, soil and site remediation. Youngsinn Sohn: applications of GIS and digital image analysis for addressing environmental problems, monitoring, and mapping. Philip G. Sokolove: endogenous rhythms and neuroendocrinology. Lynn C. Sparling: understanding the dynamical, chemical, and transport processes in the atmosphere and ocean that contribute to the observed spatiotemporal variability in chemical tracers and dynamical fields. Christopher Swan: benthic evolution and ecology, community ecology, limnology, systems, biostatistics. Claire Welty: fundamental understanding of transport processes in aquifers, mathematical modeling of groundwater flow.

College Park Campus. Lowell W. Adams: wildlife biology, ecology, and management. Andrew H. Baldwin: wetland ecology, plant community ecology of coastal marshes and mangroves. Jennifer Becker: microbial communities that biodegrade xenobiotics, bioremediation of contaminated groundwater systems, anaerobic biological treatment processes for waste streams. Neil V. Blough: methods for detecting and identifying free radicals in condensed phases, impact of (photo) oxidative reactions on the transformation and fate of organic and inorganic compounds. Amy Brown: toxicology, epidemiology, effects of pesticides on human health. Kaye L. Brubaker: physical hydrology, numerical modeling, stream and estuary water-quality modeling. James Carton: physical oceanography, ocean modeling, atmosphere-ocean interactions. James Dietz: mammalian ecology and conservation. William Fagan: meshing field research with theoretical models to address critical questions in community ecology and conservation biology, ecological "edge effects" and spatial dynamics, ecoinformatics. Irwin Forseth: plant ecology and physiology. Oliver J. Hao: waste management and environmental engineering. Robert L. Hill: soil runoff, nonpoint source pollution in soil systems. Anwarul Huq: isolation, identification, and characterization of enteric bacterial agents using conventional, immunological, and genetic methods; mode of transmission of medically important pathogens; measures for prevention of disease. David W. Inouye: terrestrial ecology, especially plant-animal interactions. Patrick Kangas: modeling and measuring of whole ecosystems, with emphasis on management and ecology. Thomas Kocher: evolution of cichlid fish: evolution and development of the jaw and feeding behaviors and speciation. William O. Lamp: crop protection from arthropods through integration of crop management practices with arthropod-plant interactions, development of non-pesticide management tactics. Stephanie Lansing: anaerobic digestion, ecological waste treatment, treatment wetlands, nutrient cycling, energy analysis, ecological modeling. Paul Leisnham: ecology of native and invasive mosquitoes in water-filled containers, wetlands, and drainage systems; species that are affected both by human disruption and that present social, economic, and health risks. Marla McIntosh: sludge utilization in woodlands, genetic diversity of food crops. Bahram Momen: applied statistics, plant ecophysiology, environmental stress on plants. Judd O. Nelson: environmental toxicology of pesticides. Mary Ann Ottinger: effect of toxic substances on avian reproduction. Michael Paolisso: applied anthropology, environment and pollution, international and rural development. Kennedy T. Paynter Jr.: physiology and biochemistry of estuarine organisms, oyster reef restoration. Karen Prestegaard: watershed and wetland hydrology. Marjorie Reaka-Kudla: zoogeography, symbiosis, and behavior of marine crustaceans. Adel Shirmohammadi: impact of agricultural pest management practices on water quality. Frank Siewerdt: quantitative genetics theory, selection strategies, population genetics of *Tribolium castaneum.* Joseph Sullivan: responses of plants to various forms of environmental stress, both natural and anthropogenic; physiological mechanisms that enable plants to exist in a wide range of environmental conditions; how human activities such as stratospheric ozone depletion, global climate change, or urbanization may impact plant, agricultural, or ecosystem productivity or ecosystem structure and functioning. Daniel E. Terlizzi: plant aquaculture, phycology. David Tilley: ecological engineering, industrial ecology, ecological decision making for sustainable development. Alba Torrents: organic pollutants, soil/water interface. Ray R. Weil: disturbed-land revegetation, land application of organic wastes. L. Curry Woods: aquaculture, problems related to the domestication of striped bass, cryopreservation of sperm, physiological responsiveness to stress, selective breeding.

Eastern Shore Campus. Isoken Aighewi: soil-water pollution, environmental soil chemistry. Eugene L. Bass: algal toxins, acclimatization of animals to environmental variables. Paulinus Chigbu: fisheries ecology, influence of variations in climatic factors on water quality and biota, culture of rotifers and copepods for use in rearing marine fish larvae, trophic dynamics in marine and freshwater environments, zooplankton ecology. Robert B. Dadson: soybean breeding, insect resistance, biological nitrogen fixation. Joseph Dodoo: coal technology, kinetic studies of coal pyrolysis. Thomas Handwerker: small-scale alternative crops. Jeannine M. Harter-Dennis: roasters chicken nutrition, reduction of fat. George E. Heath: food safety and drug residues, pharmokinetics. Ali B. Ishaque: marine ecotoxicology; behavior, transport, distribution, and fate of chemical stressors in marine environments. Andrea K. Johnson: assessing the health of Atlantic menhaden using several biomarkers of fish health: indicators of tissue damage, nutritional status, and exposure to environmental stressors. Gerald E. Kananen: analytical instrumentation, environmental pollutants. Joseph Love: ichthyology, advanced ecological methods. Eric P. May: responses of fish to injurious agents, markers of population health. Madhumi Mitra: paleontology, paleoecology, and paleoenvironmental studies of cretaceous-quaternary sediments of Atlantic coastal plain. Abhijit Naghaudhuri: integration of advanced technologies of mechatronics in the fields of precision agriculture, environmental and marine sciences, and geosciences. Anthony K. Nyame. Joseph Okoh: carbon reaction chemistry. Salina Parveen: genotypic and phenotypic methods for detecting sources of fecal pollution in aquatic environments. Joseph Pitula: molecular biology of protozoan parasites. Douglas E. Ruby: population ecology and behavior of reptiles. Jeurel Singleton: aquatic and terrestrial invertebrate community ecology and population dynamics; population dynamics of phytoplankton and zooplankton communities in reservoirs, lakes, and fish-rearing facilities. Yan Waguespeck: spectroscopic studies of temperature- and gas pressure–induced chemical changes.

Appalachian Laboratory. Mark S. Castro: atmosphere-biosphere interactions. Andrew Elmore: land use and land cover change, ecohydrology, biogeochemistry, remote sensing and spatial analysis. Katharina Engelhardt: effects of species richness on wetland ecosystem functioning and services, community and ecosystem ecology. Keith N. Eshleman: watershed and wetlands hydrology and hydrobiogeochemistry. Robert H. Gardner: landscape ecology, ecosystem modeling. J. Edward Gates: behavioral ecology of vertebrates, habitat analysis and evaluation. Robert H. Hilderbrand: ecology and conservation biology of running waters, watershed and stream habitat restoration, linking landscapes and populations, dynamic modeling of watersheds. John L. Hoogland: vertebrate behavioral ecology, evolutionary biology of mammals. Cathlyn D. Stylinski: environmental science education and scientific inquiry in precollege classrooms.

Chesapeake Biological Laboratory. Robert Anderson: biochemical toxicology, effects of stress on marine invertebrate immunology. Walter R. Boynton: nutrient cycling in estuarine systems, food-web studies. Lee Cooper: interdisciplinary aspects of biogeochemistry and ecology including stable radioisotope composition of organic materials and natural waters, aquatic plant physiology, high latitude oceanography hydrology. Lora Harris: systems ecology, theoretical ecology, primary producers from phytoplankton to macrophytes, ecosystem modeling. H. Rodger Harvey: sources and fates of organic compounds in aquatic environments. Edward D. Houde: fishery science, population dynamics, ecology of the larval stage. Sujay S. Kaushal: fate and transport of pollutants, biochemistry, limnology, organic geochemistry, environmental history. Roberta L. Marinelli: benthic ecology, animal-sediment interaction, benthic larval recruitment, modeling benthic processes. Thomas J. Miller: fish ecology, population dynamics. Carys L. Mitchelmore: molecular, biochemical, and cellular responses of aquatic organisms to inorganic and organic pollutants. Margaret Palmer: stream and estuarine ecology and hydrodynamics. Kennedy T. Paynter Jr.: physiology and biochemistry of estuarine organisms, oyster reef restoration. Christopher L. Rowe: physiological, population, and community responses to sublethal levels of pollutants. Johan Schijf: chemical oceanography, physical chemistry, aqueous geochemistry of trace metals, geochemistry of marine anoxic basins. David H. Secor: fisheries ecology, demographics, migration. Marcelino Suzuki: marine microbial ecology, application of molecular approaches to the study of aquatic microbes. Mario Tamburri: coastal sensor development, ecosystem monitoring. Robert E. Ulanowicz: estuarine food-chain dynamics, hydrological-biological modeling. Lisa Wainger: risk analysis and decision-support tools for prioritizing natural resource management options, invasive species risk assessment, wetland restoration prioritization. Michael Wilberg: stock assessment, dynamics of exploited populations, harvest policy development and application, statistical model selection and averaging. David A. Wright: comparative physiology of marine and estuarine animals, inorganic pollutants.

Horn Point Laboratory. William Boicourt: physical oceanography, continental shelf and estuarine circulation. Shenn-yu Chao: physical oceanography, continental shelf and slope circulation, western boundary currents. Louis A. Codispoti: chemical oceanography, oceanic nitrogen cycle. Victoria J. Coles: observation and modeling of seasonal to climate-scale variability in ocean circulation. Jeffrey C. Cornwell: nutrient, metal, and sulfur cycling in estuaries and wetlands. Byron C. Crump: microbial ecology, bacterial and Achaeal diversity, organic matter and nutrient cycling. William C. Dennison: coastal ecosystem ecology, ecophysiology of marine plants. Thomas R. Fisher Jr.: nitrogen cycles in Atlantic coastal plain estuaries, nutrient cycling in tropical lakes. Patricia M. Glibert: phytoplankton and microplankton ecology, nitrogen cycling, photosynthesis. Lawrence W. Harding: biological oceanography, phytoplankton physiology and ecology. Raleigh R. Hood: phytoplankton production and light response, modeling of primary production. Todd M. Kana: phytoplankton physiology. W. Michael Kemp: systems ecology, watershed nutrient budgets, submerged aquatic vegetation. Victor S. Kennedy: ecology and dynamics of benthic communities, particularly bivalves. Evamaria W. Koch: ecology of submerged aquatic vegetation and coastal seagrass ecosystems. Andrew Lazur: food and baitfish culture, integration of aquaculture with agriculture for nutrient reduction. Ming Li: geophysical fluid dynamics, ocean mixing processes, numerical modeling, biological/physical interactions, marine pollution. Thomas Malone: phytoplankton ecology and nutrient cycling. Donald W. Meritt: oyster aquaculture and restoration. Laura Murray: wetlands, seagrass ecology. Roger I. E. Newell: physiological and behavioral adaptations of invertebrates, especially bivalve mollusks. Elizabeth W. North: biological-physical interactions, hydrodynamics and particle trajectory modeling, ichthyoplankton and zooplankton ecology. Judith O'Neil: cyanobacteria ecophysiology, plankton trophodynamics. Cindy Palinkas: continental margin sedimentation, formation and preservation of sedimentary strata in the geological record, deposition and accumulation of fluvial sediment in the coastal ocean. Michael R. Roman: zooplankton ecology, plankton food-chain energetics, detrital food chains. Lawrence P. Sanford: physical oceanography, geophysical boundary layers, turbulence and mixing processes. J. Court Stevenson: marsh ecology, nutrient loading in coastal watersheds. Diane Stoecker: role of heterotrophic and mixotrophic protists in food webs.

Center of Marine Biotechnology. Hafiz Ahmed: biological roles of galectins in early embryo development and immune function, structure-function studies of galectins. Robert M. Belas Jr.: sensory transduction and genetic regulation of gram-negative bacteria. Feng Chen: bacterio- and phytoplankton production; biomass and growth in aquatic environments; ecological interaction among marine viruses, bacteria, and phytoplankton; phylogenetic relationship and coevolution among marine microorganisms. J. Sook Chung: response of crustaceans to the neurotransmitters, neurohormones, hormone, and pheromones that regulate critical life-cycle events. Shiladitya DasSarma: halophilic archael genomes; structure, function, and evolution of genomes. Shao-Jun (Jim) Du: cellular and molecular mechanisms controlling differentiation of muscle and nerve cells during embryogenesis. Russell T. Hill: natural products from marine microorganisms, actinomycete molecular biology and ecology, use in bioremediation. Rosemary Jagus: developmental regulation of gene expression in sea urchin embryos. Zvi Kelman: biochemistry and molecular interactions, biochemical characterization of DNA replication, DNA replication of Archaea. Zeev Pancer: vertebrate adaptive immunity, antigen receptors of jawless vertebrates. Allen Place: biochemical adaptations in marine organisms. Frank T. Robb: genetics of thermophilic marine bacteria. Eric Schott: parasites and pathogens of estuarine invertebrates, evolutionary adaptations of protistan parasites to the host and environment. Harold J. Schreier: adaptation of microorganisms to extreme environments, biochemistry and molecular biology of Archaea. Kevin R. Sowers: molecular genetics and adaptation of anaerobic archaebacteria. John M. Trant: reproductive physiology, molecular endocrinology. Gerardo Vasta: cellular nonself recognition and cell-cell interactions. Yonathan Zohar: physiology and endocrinology of fish reproduction.

Section 5
Meteorology and Atmospheric Sciences

This section contains a directory of institutions offering graduate work in meteorology and atmospheric sciences, followed by in-depth entries submitted by institutions that chose to prepare detailed program descriptions. Additional information about programs listed in the directory but not augmented by an in-depth entry may be obtained by writing directly to the dean of a graduate school or chair of a department at the address given in the directory.

For programs offering related work, see also in this book *Astronomy and Astrophysics, Geosciences, Marine Sciences and Oceanography,* and *Physics.* In the other guides in this series:

Graduate Programs in the Biological Sciences

See *Biological and Biomedical Sciences* and *Biophysics*

Graduate Programs in Engineering & Applied Sciences

See *Aerospace/Aeronautical Engineering, Civil and Environmental Engineering, Engineering and Applied Sciences,* and *Mechanical Engineering and Mechanics*

CONTENTS

Program Directories

Close-Up

See:

Atmospheric Sciences

City College of the City University of New York, Graduate School, College of Liberal Arts and Science, Division of Science, Department of Earth and Atmospheric Sciences, New York, NY 10031-9198. Offers earth and environmental science (PhD); earth systems science (MA). *Degree requirements:* For master's, comprehensive exam, thesis. *Entrance requirements:* Additional exam requirements/recommendations for international students: Required—TOEFL (minimum score 500 paper-based; 61 iBT). Electronic applications accepted. *Faculty research:* Water resources, high-temperature geochemistry, sedimentary basin analysis, tectonics.

Clemson University, Graduate School, College of Engineering and Science, Department of Physics and Astronomy, Clemson, SC 29634. Offers physics (MS, PhD), including astronomy and astrophysics, atmospheric physics, biophysics. Part-time programs available. *Faculty:* 25 full-time (4 women), 1 part-time/adjunct (0 women). *Students:* 46 full-time (11 women), 3 part-time (0 women); includes 1 minority (African American), 22 international. Average age 27. 71 applicants, 62% accepted, 17 enrolled. In 2009, 8 master's, 5 doctorates awarded. Terminal master's awarded for partial completion of doctoral program. *Degree requirements:* For master's, thesis or alternative; for doctorate, thesis/dissertation. *Entrance requirements:* For master's and doctorate, GRE General Test. Additional exam requirements/recommendations for international students: Required—TOEFL. *Application deadline:* For fall admission, 1/15 priority date for domestic students; for spring admission, 9/15 priority date for domestic students. Applications are processed on a rolling basis. Application fee: $70 ($80 for international students). Electronic applications accepted. *Expenses:* Tuition, state resident: full-time $8684; part-time $528 per credit hour. Tuition, nonresident: full-time $15,330; part-time $1078 per credit hour. Required fees: $736; $37 per semester. Part-time tuition and fees vary according to course load and program. *Financial support:* In 2009–10, 45 students received support, including 1 fellowship with full and partial tuition reimbursement available (averaging $10,000 per year), 13 research assistantships with partial tuition reimbursements available (averaging $21,423 per year), 32 teaching assistantships with partial tuition reimbursements available (averaging $16,490 per year); career-related internships or fieldwork, institutionally sponsored loans, scholarships/grants, health care benefits, and unspecified assistantships also available. Support available to part-time students. Financial award application deadline: 6/1; financial award applicants required to submit FAFSA. *Faculty research:* Radiation physics, solid-state physics, nuclear physics, radar and lidar studies of atmosphere. Total annual research expenditures: $3.1 million. *Unit head:* Dr. Peter Barnes, Chair, 864-656-3419, Fax: 864-656-0805, E-mail: peterb@clemson.edu. *Application contact:* Dr. Murray Daw, Graduate Coordinator, 864-656-6702, Fax: 864-656-0805, E-mail: physgradinfo-l@clemson.edu.

Colorado State University, Graduate School, College of Engineering, Department of Atmospheric Science, Fort Collins, CO 80523-1371. Offers MS, PhD. Part-time programs available. *Faculty:* 16 full-time (3 women), 1 part-time/adjunct (0 women). *Students:* 63 full-time (26 women), 22 part-time (10 women); includes 8 minority (1 African American, 2 American Indian/Alaska Native, 1 Asian American or Pacific Islander, 4 Hispanic Americans), 7 international. Average age 28. 92 applicants, 37% accepted, 13 enrolled. In 2009, 20 master's, 14 doctorates awarded. *Degree requirements:* For master's, thesis or alternative, defense; for doctorate, comprehensive exam, thesis/dissertation. *Entrance requirements:* For master's, GRE General Test, minimum GPA of 3.0; BS in physics, math, atmospheric science, engineering, chemistry or related major; calculus-based math and differential equations; calculus-based physics; letters of recommendation; for doctorate, GRE General Test, minimum GPA of 3.0; MS with thesis in atmospheric science or related field; statement with interests; curriculum vitae; letters of recommendation. Additional exam requirements/recommendations for international students: Required—TOEFL (minimum score 550 paper-based; 213 computer-based; 80 iBT), IELTS (minimum score 6). *Application deadline:* For fall admission, 1/15 priority date for domestic and international students; for spring admission, 9/15 priority date for domestic and international students. Applications are processed on a rolling basis. Application fee: $50. Electronic applications accepted. *Expenses:* Tuition, state resident: full-time $6434; part-time $359.10 per credit. Tuition, nonresident: full-time $18,116; part-time $1006.45 per credit. Required fees: $1496; $83 per credit. *Financial support:* In 2009–10, 66 students received support, including 8 fellowships with full tuition reimbursements available (averaging $33,123 per year), 57 research assistantships with full tuition reimbursements available (averaging $24,866 per year), 1 teaching assistantship with partial tuition reimbursement available (averaging $1,817 per year); unspecified assistantships also available. Financial award application deadline: 2/15; financial award applicants required to submit FAFSA. *Faculty research:* Global circulation and climate, atmospheric chemistry, radiation and remote sensing, marine meteorology, mesoscale meteorology. Total annual research expenditures: $15.5 million. *Unit head:* Dr. Richard Johnson, Head, 970-491-8321, Fax: 970-491-8449, E-mail: richard.johnson@colostate.edu. *Application contact:* Dr. Sonia Kreidenweis, Student Counselor, 970-491-8350, Fax: 970-491-8483, E-mail: sonia@atmos.colostate.edu.

Columbia University, Graduate School of Arts and Sciences, Division of Natural Sciences, Program in Atmospheric and Planetary Science, New York, NY 10027. Offers M Phil, PhD. Offered jointly through the Departments of Geological Sciences, Astronomy, and Physics and in cooperation with NASA Goddard Space Flight Center's Institute for Space Studies. *Degree requirements:* For doctorate, variable foreign language requirement, thesis/dissertation. *Entrance requirements:* For doctorate, GRE General Test, GRE Subject Test, previous course work in mathematics and physics. Additional exam requirements/recommendations for international students: Required—TOEFL. *Faculty research:* Climate, weather prediction.

Columbia University, Graduate School of Arts and Sciences, Program in Climate and Society, New York, NY 10027. Offers MA.

Cornell University, Graduate School, Graduate Fields of Agriculture and Life Sciences, Field of Atmospheric Science, Ithaca, NY 14853-0001. Offers MS, PhD. *Faculty:* 18 full-time (2 women). *Students:* 8 full-time (4 women); includes 1 minority (African American), 1 international. Average age 27. 21 applicants, 14% accepted, 1 enrolled. In 2009, 1 master's awarded. *Degree requirements:* For master's, thesis; for doctorate, comprehensive exam, thesis/dissertation. *Entrance requirements:* For master's and doctorate, GRE General Test, 2 letters of recommendation. Additional exam requirements/recommendations for international students: Required—TOEFL (minimum score 550 paper-based; 213 computer-based; 77 iBT). *Application deadline:* For fall admission, 2/1 for domestic students; for spring admission, 8/1 priority date for domestic students. Application fee: $70. Electronic applications accepted. *Expenses:* Tuition: Full-time $29,500. Required fees: $70. Full-time tuition and fees vary according to degree level, program and student level. *Financial support:* In 2009–10, 8 students received support, including 1 fellowship with full tuition reimbursement available; research assistantships with full tuition reimbursements available, teaching assistantships with full tuition reimbursements available, institutionally sponsored loans, traineeships, health care benefits, tuition waivers (full and partial), and unspecified assistantships also available. Financial award applicants required to submit FAFSA. *Faculty research:* Applied climatology, climate dynamics, statistical meteorology/climatology, synoptic meteorology, upper atmospheric science. *Unit head:* Director of Graduate Studies, 607-255-3034, Fax: 607-255-2106, E-mail: atmscigradfield@cornell.edu. *Application contact:* Graduate Field Assistant, 607-255-3034, Fax: 607-255-2106, E-mail: pmv2@cornell.edu.

Creighton University, Graduate School, College of Arts and Sciences, Program in Atmospheric Sciences, Omaha, NE 68178-0001. Offers MS. Part-time programs available. *Faculty:* 10 full-time (3 women). *Students:* 5 full-time (1 woman), 1 part-time (0 women). Average age 27. 7 applicants, 86% accepted, 2 enrolled. In 2009, 3 master's awarded. *Degree requirements:* For master's, thesis optional. *Entrance requirements:* For master's, GRE General Test, 3 letters of recommendation. Additional exam requirements/recommendations for international students: Required—TOEFL (minimum score 550 paper-based; 213 computer-based; 80 iBT). *Application deadline:* For fall admission, 3/1 for domestic and international students. Application fee: $50. Electronic applications accepted. *Expenses:* Tuition: Full-time $11,700; part-time $650 per credit hour. Required fees: $126 per semester. *Financial support:* In 2009–10, 3 fellowships (averaging $10,438 per year) were awarded. Support available to part-time students. Financial award applicants required to submit FAFSA. *Unit head:* Dr. Joseph Zehnder, Chair, 402-280-2448, E-mail: zehnder@creighton.edu. *Application contact:* Taunya Plater, Senior Program Coordinator, 402-280-2870, Fax: 402-280-2899, E-mail: taunyaplater@creighton.edu.

George Mason University, College of Science, Department of Climate Dynamics, Fairfax, VA 22030. Offers PhD. *Expenses:* Tuition, state resident: full-time $7568; part-time $315.33 per credit hour. Tuition, nonresident: full-time $21,704; part-time $904.33 per credit hour. Required fees: $2184; $91 per credit hour.

Georgia Institute of Technology, Graduate Studies and Research, College of Sciences, School of Earth and Atmospheric Sciences, Atlanta, GA 30332-0340. Offers atmospheric chemistry, aerosols and clouds (MS, PhD); dynamics of weather and climate (MS, PhD); geochemistry (MS, PhD); geophysics (MS, PhD); oceanography (MS, PhD); paleoclimate (MS, PhD); planetary science (MS, PhD); remote sensing (MS, PhD). Part-time programs available. Terminal master's awarded for partial completion of doctoral program. *Degree requirements:* For master's, thesis or alternative; for doctorate, comprehensive exam, thesis/dissertation. *Entrance requirements:* For master's, GRE, letters of recommendation; for doctorate, GRE, academic transcripts, letters of recommendation, personal statement. Additional exam requirements/recommendations for international students: Required—TOEFL (minimum score 550 paper-based; 213 computer-based; 79 iBT). *Faculty research:* Geophysics; atmospheric chemistry, aerosols and clouds; dynamics of weather and climate; geochemistry; oceanography; paleoclimate; planetary science; remote sensing.

Hampton University, Graduate College, Department of Physics, Hampton, VA 23668. Offers atmospheric physics (MS, PhD); medical physics (MS, PhD); nuclear physics (MS, PhD); optical physics (MS, PhD). Part-time and evening/weekend programs available. Terminal master's awarded for partial completion of doctoral program. *Degree requirements:* For master's, thesis optional; for doctorate, thesis/dissertation, oral defense, qualifying exam. *Entrance requirements:* For master's, GRE General Test; for doctorate, GRE General Test, minimum GPA of 3.0 or master's degree in physics or related field. *Faculty research:* Laser optics, remote sensing.

Howard University, Graduate School and School of Engineering and Computer Science, Department of Atmospheric Sciences, Washington, DC 20059-0002. Offers MS, PhD. Part-time programs available. Terminal master's awarded for partial completion of doctoral program. *Degree requirements:* For master's, thesis; for doctorate, one foreign language, comprehensive exam, thesis/dissertation. *Entrance requirements:* For master's, GRE General Test, minimum GPA of 3.0; for doctorate, GRE General Test, minimum GPA of 3.2. Additional exam requirements/recommendations for international students: Required—TOEFL (minimum score 550 paper-based; 213 computer-based). *Faculty research:* Atmospheric chemistry, climate, atmospheric radiation, gravity waves, aerosols, extraterrestrial atmospheres, turbulence.

Howard University, Graduate School, Department of Chemistry, Washington, DC 20059-0002. Offers analytical chemistry (MS, PhD); atmospheric (MS, PhD); biochemistry (MS, PhD); environmental (MS, PhD); inorganic chemistry (MS, PhD); organic chemistry (MS, PhD); physical chemistry (MS, PhD). Terminal master's awarded for partial completion of doctoral program. *Degree requirements:* For master's, comprehensive exam, thesis, teaching experience; for doctorate, comprehensive exam, thesis/dissertation, teaching experience. *Entrance requirements:* For master's, GRE General Test, minimum GPA of 2.7; for doctorate, GRE General Test, minimum GPA of 3.0. Additional exam requirements/recommendations for international students: Required—TOEFL. Electronic applications accepted. *Faculty research:* Synthetic organics, materials, natural products, mass spectrometry.

Massachusetts Institute of Technology, School of Science, Department of Earth, Atmospheric, and Planetary Sciences, Cambridge, MA 02139-4307. Offers atmospheric chemistry (PhD, Sc D); atmospheric science (SM, PhD, Sc D); chemical oceanography (SM, PhD, Sc D); climate physics and chemistry (SM, PhD, Sc D); earth and planetary sciences (SM); geochemistry (PhD, Sc D); geology (PhD, Sc D); geophysics (PhD, Sc D); marine geology and geophysics (SM, PhD, Sc D); physical oceanography (SM, PhD, Sc D); planetary sciences (PhD, Sc D). *Faculty:* 37 full-time (7 women). *Students:* 158 full-time (74 women); includes 14 minority (1 African American, 1 American Indian/Alaska Native, 6 Asian Americans or Pacific Islanders, 6 Hispanic Americans), 58 international. Average age 27. 205 applicants, 30% accepted, 18 enrolled. In 2009, 10 master's, 25 doctorates awarded. Terminal master's awarded for partial completion of doctoral program. *Degree requirements:* For master's, thesis; for doctorate, comprehensive exam, thesis/dissertation. *Entrance requirements:* For master's, GRE General Test; for doctorate, GRE General Test, GRE Subject Test (chemistry or physics for planetary science area). Additional exam requirements/recommendations for international students: Required—IELTS (minimum score 6); Recommended—TOEFL (minimum score 577 paper-based; 233 computer-based; 91 iBT). *Application deadline:* For fall admission, 1/5 for domestic and international students; for spring admission, 11/1 for domestic and international students. Application fee: $75. Electronic applications accepted. *Financial support:* In 2009–10, 112 students received support, including 31 fellowships with tuition reimbursements available (averaging $30,513 per year), 89 research assistantships with tuition reimbursements available (averaging $21,168 per year), 17 teaching assistantships with tuition reimbursements available (averaging $28,372 per year); Federal Work-Study, institutionally sponsored loans, scholarships/grants, health care benefits, and unspecified assistantships also available. *Faculty research:* Formation, dynamics and evolution of planetary systems, origin, evolution and interaction of the physical, characterization of past, interplay of energy and the environment, present and potential future climates and the causes and consequences of climate change, chemical, geological and biological components of the Earth system, composition, structure and dynamics of the atmospheres, oceans, surfaces and interiors of the Earth and other planets. Total annual research expenditures: $19.5 million. *Unit head:* Prof. Maria Zuber, Head, 617-253-2127, Fax: 617-253-8298, E-mail: eapsinfo@mit.edu. *Application contact:* EAPS Education Office, 617-253-3381, Fax: 617-253-8298, E-mail: eapsinfo@mit.edu.

McGill University, Faculty of Graduate and Postdoctoral Studies, Faculty of Science, Department of Atmospheric and Oceanic Sciences, Montréal, QC H3A 2T5, Canada. Offers atmospheric science (M Sc, PhD); physical oceanography (M Sc, PhD).

Michigan Technological University, Graduate School, College of Sciences and Arts, Atmospheric Sciences Program, Houghton, MI 49931. Offers PhD. *Degree requirements:* For doctorate, comprehensive exam, thesis/dissertation. *Entrance requirements:* For doctorate, GRE, minimum GPA of 3.0. Additional exam requirements/recommendations for international students: Required—TOEFL (minimum score 600 paper-based). *Faculty research:* Volcano/atmospheric interactions, atmospheric chemistry, atmospheric physics, atmosphere-biosphere interactions.

Mississippi State University, College of Arts and Sciences, Department of Geosciences, Mississippi State, MS 39762. Offers earth and atmospheric science (PhD); geoscience (MS). Postbaccalaureate distance learning degree programs offered (no on-campus study). *Faculty:* 17 full-time (3 women), 2 part-time/adjunct (0 women). *Students:* 45 full-time (15 women), 260 part-time (127 women); includes 23 minority (8 African Americans, 3 American Indian/Alaska Native, 4 Asian Americans or Pacific Islanders, 8 Hispanic Americans), 6 international. Average

age 37. 171 applicants, 81% accepted, 117 enrolled. In 2009, 88 master's awarded. *Degree requirements:* For master's, thesis (for some programs), comprehensive oral or written exam. *Entrance requirements:* For master's, GRE (for on-campus applicants), minimum undergraduate GPA of 2.75. Additional exam requirements/recommendations for international students: Required—TOEFL (minimum score 475 paper-based; 153 computer-based; 53 iBT); Recommended—IELTS (minimum score 4.5). *Application deadline:* For fall admission, 7/1 for domestic students, 5/1 for international students; for spring admission, 11/1 for domestic students, 9/1 for international students. Applications are processed on a rolling basis. Application fee: $40. Electronic applications accepted. *Expenses:* Tuition, state resident: full-time $2575.50; part-time $286.25 per credit hour. Tuition, nonresident: full-time $6510; part-time $723.50 per credit hour. Tuition and fees vary according to course load. *Financial support:* In 2009–10, 6 research assistantships with full tuition reimbursements (averaging $13,000 per year), 19 teaching assistantships with full tuition reimbursements (averaging $12,116 per year) were awarded; Federal Work-Study, institutionally sponsored loans, scholarships/grants, tuition waivers (partial), and unspecified assistantships also available. Financial award application deadline: 4/1; financial award applicants required to submit FAFSA. *Faculty research:* Climatology, hydrogeology, sedimentology, meteorology. Total annual research expenditures: $2.8 million. *Unit head:* Dr. Darrel Schmitz, Professor and Head, 662-325-3915, Fax: 662-325-9423, E-mail: schmitz@geosci.msstate.edu. *Application contact:* Dr. Christopher P. Dewey, Associate Professor/Graduate Coordinator, 662-325-2909, Fax: 662-325-9423, E-mail: cpd4@msstate.edu.

New Mexico Institute of Mining and Technology, Graduate Studies, Department of Physics, Socorro, NM 87801. Offers astrophysics (MS, PhD); atmospheric physics (MS, PhD); instrumentation (MS); mathematical physics (PhD). *Degree requirements:* For master's, thesis optional; for doctorate, thesis/dissertation. *Entrance requirements:* For master's, GRE General Test; for doctorate, GRE General Test, GRE Subject Test. Additional exam requirements/recommendations for international students: Required—TOEFL (minimum score 540 paper-based; 207 computer-based). *Faculty research:* Cloud physics, stellar and extragalactic processes.

North Carolina State University, Graduate School, College of Physical and Mathematical Sciences, Department of Marine, Earth, and Atmospheric Sciences, Raleigh, NC 27695. Offers marine, earth, and atmospheric sciences (MS, PhD); meteorology (MS, PhD); oceanography (MS, PhD). Terminal master's awarded for partial completion of doctoral program. *Degree requirements:* For master's, thesis (for some programs), final oral exam; for doctorate, comprehensive exam, thesis/dissertation, final oral exam, preliminary oral and written exams. *Entrance requirements:* For master's, GRE General Test, minimum GPA of 3.0; for doctorate, GRE General Test, GRE Subject Test (for disciplines in biological oceanography and geology), minimum GPA of 3.0. Additional exam requirements/recommendations for international students: Required—TOEFL (minimum score 550 paper-based). Electronic applications accepted. *Faculty research:* Boundary layer and air quality meteorology; climate and mesoscale dynamics; biological, chemical, geological, and physical oceanography; hard rock, soft rock, environmental, and paleo-geology.

Northern Arizona University, Graduate College, College of Engineering, Forestry and Natural Sciences, School of Earth Sciences and Environmental Sustainability, Flagstaff, AZ 86011. Offers climate science and solutions (MS); environmental sciences and policy (MS); geology (MS). *Faculty:* 22 full-time (5 women). *Students:* 28 full-time (17 women), 25 part-time (21 women); includes 6 minority (2 American Indian/Alaska Native, 1 Asian American or Pacific Islander, 3 Hispanic Americans). 70 applicants, 36% accepted, 17 enrolled. In 2009, 19 master's awarded. *Entrance requirements:* Additional exam requirements/recommendations for international students: Required—TOEFL (minimum score 550 paper-based; 213 computer-based; 80 iBT), IELTS (minimum score 7), or a bachelor's degree from an English-speaking university and demonstrated proficiency. *Application deadline:* For fall admission, 2/15 for domestic and international students. Application fee: $65. *Financial support:* In 2009–10, 32 students received support, including 7 research assistantships with partial tuition reimbursements available, 26 teaching assistantships with partial tuition reimbursements available; Federal Work-Study, scholarships/grants, health care benefits, and unspecified assistantships also available. Support available to part-time students. Financial award applicants required to submit FAFSA. *Unit head:* Dr. Abe Springer, Director, 928-523-7198. *Application contact:* Dr. Abe Springer, Director, 928-523-7198.

The Ohio State University, Graduate School, College of Social and Behavioral Sciences, School of Social and Behavioral Science, Department of Geography, Program in Atmospheric Sciences, Columbus, OH 43210. Offers MS, PhD. *Faculty:* 11. *Students:* 12 full-time (3 women), 1 international. Average age 26. In 2009, 5 master's, 1 doctorate awarded. *Degree requirements:* For master's, thesis; for doctorate, thesis/dissertation. *Entrance requirements:* For master's and doctorate, GRE General Test. Additional exam requirements/recommendations for international students: Required—TOEFL (minimum score 600 paper-based; 250 computer-based). *Application deadline:* For fall admission, 8/15 priority date for domestic students, 7/1 priority date for international students; for winter admission, 12/1 priority date for domestic students, 11/1 priority date for international students; for spring admission, 3/1 priority date for domestic students, 2/1 priority date for international students. Applications are processed on a rolling basis. Application fee: $40 ($50 for international students). Electronic applications accepted. *Expenses:* Tuition, state resident: full-time $10,683. Tuition, nonresident: full-time $25,923. Tuition and fees vary according to course load and program. *Financial support:* Fellowships, research assistantships, teaching assistantships, Federal Work-Study and institutionally sponsored loans available. Support available to part-time students. *Faculty research:* Climatology, aeronomy, solar-terrestrial physics, air environment. *Unit head:* Jeffrey C. Rogers, Graduate Studies Committee Chair, 614-292-3999, Fax: 614-292-6213, E-mail: rogers.21@osu.edu. *Application contact:* 614-292-9444, Fax: 614-292-3895, E-mail: domestic.grad@osu.edu.

Oregon State University, Graduate School, College of Oceanic and Atmospheric Sciences, Program in Atmospheric Sciences, Corvallis, OR 97331. Offers MA, MS, PhD. *Students:* 7 full-time (2 women), 1 international. Average age 28. In 2009, 1 master's awarded. Terminal master's awarded for partial completion of doctoral program. *Degree requirements:* For master's, variable foreign language requirement, thesis, qualifying exams; for doctorate, thesis/dissertation, qualifying exams. *Entrance requirements:* For master's and doctorate, GRE General Test, minimum GPA of 3.0 in last 90 hours of course work. Additional exam requirements/recommendations for international students: Required—TOEFL. *Application deadline:* For fall admission, 2/1 priority date for domestic students. Applications are processed on a rolling basis. Application fee: $50. *Expenses:* Tuition, state resident: full-time $9774; part-time $362 per credit. Tuition, nonresident: full-time $15,849; part-time $587 per credit. Required fees: $1639. Full-time tuition and fees vary according to course load and program. *Financial support:* Fellowships, research assistantships, teaching assistantships, career-related internships or fieldwork, Federal Work-Study, and institutionally sponsored loans available. Support available to part-time students. Financial award application deadline: 2/1. *Faculty research:* Planetary atmospheres, boundary layer dynamics, climate, statistical meteorology, satellite meteorology, atmospheric chemistry. *Unit head:* Dr. Robert A. Duncan, Associate Dean for Student Programs, 541-737-5189, Fax: 541-737-2540, E-mail: rduncan@coas.oregonstate.edu. *Application contact:* Dr. Robert S. Allan, Assistant Director, Student Programs, 541-737-1340, Fax: 541-737-2064, E-mail: rallan@coas.oregonstate.edu.

Princeton University, Graduate School, Department of Geosciences, Program in Atmospheric and Oceanic Sciences, Princeton, NJ 08544-1019. Offers PhD. *Degree requirements:* For doctorate, one foreign language, thesis/dissertation. *Entrance requirements:* For doctorate, GRE General Test, GRE Subject Test. Additional exam requirements/recommendations for international students: Required—TOEFL (minimum score 600 paper-based; 250 computer-based). Electronic applications accepted. *Faculty research:* Climate dynamics, middle atmosphere dynamics and chemistry, oceanic circulation, marine geochemistry, numerical modeling.

Purdue University, Graduate School, College of Science, Department of Earth and Atmospheric Sciences, West Lafayette, IN 47907. Offers MS, PhD. *Degree requirements:* For master's, thesis; for doctorate, one foreign language, thesis/dissertation. *Entrance requirements:* For master's and doctorate, GRE General Test. Additional exam requirements/recommendations for international students: Required—TOEFL. Electronic applications accepted. *Faculty research:* Geology, geophysics, hydrogeology, paleoclimatology, environmental science.

Rutgers, The State University of New Jersey, New Brunswick, Graduate School-New Brunswick, Department of Environmental Sciences, Piscataway, NJ 08854-8097. Offers air pollution and resources (MS, PhD); aquatic biology (MS, PhD); aquatic chemistry (MS, PhD); atmospheric science (MS, PhD); chemistry and physics of aerosol and hydrosol systems (MS, PhD); environmental chemistry (MS, PhD); environmental microbiology (MS, PhD); environmental toxicology (PhD); exposure assessment (PhD); fate and effects of pollutants (MS, PhD); pollution prevention and control (MS, PhD); water and wastewater treatment (MS, PhD); water resources (MS, PhD). Terminal master's awarded for partial completion of doctoral program. *Degree requirements:* For master's, comprehensive exam, thesis or alternative, oral final exam; for doctorate, comprehensive exam, thesis/dissertation, thesis defense, qualifying exam. *Entrance requirements:* For master's and doctorate, GRE General Test. Additional exam requirements/recommendations for international students: Required—TOEFL. Electronic applications accepted. *Faculty research:* Biological waste treatment; contaminant fate and transport; air, soil and water quality.

South Dakota School of Mines and Technology, Graduate Division, College of Science and Letters, Department of Atmospheric Sciences, Rapid City, SD 57701-3995. Offers atmospheric and environmental sciences (PhD); atmospheric sciences (MS). Part-time programs available. *Faculty:* 6 part-time/adjunct (0 women). *Students:* 7 full-time (2 women), 2 part-time (1 woman); includes 1 minority (American Indian/Alaska Native), 1 international. Average age 27. 7 applicants, 71% accepted, 2 enrolled. In 2009, 2 master's, 2 doctorates awarded. *Degree requirements:* For master's, thesis; for doctorate, thesis/dissertation. *Entrance requirements:* Additional exam requirements/recommendations for international students: Required—TOEFL, TWE. *Application deadline:* For fall admission, 7/1 priority date for domestic students, 4/1 for international students; for spring admission, 11/1 for domestic students, 9/1 for international students. Applications are processed on a rolling basis. Application fee: $35. Electronic applications accepted. *Expenses:* Tuition, state resident: full-time $3340; part-time $139 per credit hour. Tuition, nonresident: full-time $7060; part-time $294 per credit hour. Required fees: $3270. *Financial support:* In 2009–10, 1 fellowship (averaging $2,500 per year), 10 research assistantships with partial tuition reimbursements (averaging $15,919 per year) were awarded; teaching assistantships with partial tuition reimbursements, Federal Work-Study and institutionally sponsored loans also available. Support available to part-time students. Financial award application deadline: 5/15. *Faculty research:* Hailstorm observations and numerical modeling, microbursts and lightning, radiative transfer, remote sensing. Total annual research expenditures: $1.3 million. *Unit head:* Dr. Mark Hjelmfelt, Chair, 605-394-1991, E-mail: mark.hjelmfelt@sdsmt.edu. *Application contact:* Jeannette R. Nilson, Administrative Support Coordinator, Graduate Education, 800-454-8162 Ext. 1206, Fax: 605-394-5360, E-mail: graduate_admissions@sdsmt.edu.

Stony Brook University, State University of New York, Graduate School, School of Marine and Atmospheric Sciences, Institute for Terrestrial and Planetary Atmospheres, Program in Atmospheric Sciences, Stony Brook, NY 11794. Offers MS, PhD. Evening/weekend programs available. *Students:* 112 full-time (65 women), 6 part-time (2 women); includes 10 minority (1 African American, 3 Asian Americans or Pacific Islanders, 6 Hispanic Americans), 38 international. *Degree requirements:* For doctorate, one foreign language, comprehensive exam, thesis/dissertation. *Entrance requirements:* For master's, GRE, minimum GPA of 3.0, 3 letters of recommendation; for doctorate, GRE, official transcripts, minimum GPA of 3.0, 3 letters of recommendation. Additional exam requirements/recommendations for international students: Required—TOEFL (minimum score 600 paper-based; 213 computer-based). *Application deadline:* For fall admission, 1/15 priority date for domestic students; for spring admission, 10/1 priority date for domestic students. Application fee: $60. Electronic applications accepted. *Expenses:* Tuition, state resident: full-time $8370; part-time $349 per credit. Tuition, nonresident: full-time $13,250; part-time $552 per credit. Required fees: $933. *Financial support:* Fellowships, research assistantships, teaching assistantships, career-related internships or fieldwork available. *Unit head:* Minghua Zhang, Director, 631-632-8318. *Application contact:* Dr. Glenn R. Lopez, Assistant Director, 631-632-8660, Fax: 631-632-8200, E-mail: glopez@notes.cc.sunysb.edu.

Texas Tech University, Graduate School, College of Arts and Sciences, Department of Geosciences, Lubbock, TX 79409. Offers atmospheric sciences (MS); geoscience (MS, PhD). Part-time programs available. *Faculty:* 16 full-time (2 women), 1 part-time/adjunct (0 women). *Students:* 42 full-time (14 women), 15 part-time (3 women); includes 5 minority (1 African American, 4 Hispanic Americans), 10 international. Average age 28. 70 applicants, 30% accepted, 15 enrolled. In 2009, 4 master's, 2 doctorates awarded. *Degree requirements:* For master's, thesis or alternative; for doctorate, thesis/dissertation. *Entrance requirements:* For master's and doctorate, GRE General Test. Additional exam requirements/recommendations for international students: Required—TOEFL (minimum score 550 paper-based; 213 computer-based). *Application deadline:* For fall admission, 3/1 priority date for international students; for spring admission, 11/1 priority date for international students. Applications are processed on a rolling basis. Application fee: $50 ($75 for international students). Electronic applications accepted. *Expenses:* Tuition, state resident: full-time $5100; part-time $213 per credit hour. Tuition, nonresident: full-time $11,748; part-time $490 per credit hour. Required fees: $2298; $50 per credit hour. $555 per semester. *Financial support:* In 2009–10, 3 research assistantships with partial tuition reimbursements (averaging $25,886 per year), 14 teaching assistantships with partial tuition reimbursements (averaging $17,545 per year) were awarded; Federal Work-Study and institutionally sponsored loans also available. Support available to part-time students. Financial award application deadline: 4/15; financial award applicants required to submit FAFSA. *Faculty research:* Petroleum geology and geophysics, tectonics and arc magnetism, aqueous and environmental geochemistry, hurricanes and severe storms, wind power. Total annual research expenditures: $686,238. *Unit head:* Dr. Calvin Barnes, Chairman, 806-742-3102, Fax: 806-742-0100, E-mail: cal.barnes@ttu.edu. *Application contact:* Dr. Aaron Yoshinobu, Graduate Adviser, 806-742-3102, Fax: 806-724-0100, E-mail: aaron.yoshinobu@ttu.edu.

Université du Québec à Montréal, Graduate Programs, Program in Earth and Atmospheric Sciences, Montréal, QC H3C 3P8, Canada. Offers atmospheric sciences (M Sc); Earth and atmospheric sciences (PhD); Earth science (M Sc); meteorology (PhD, Diploma). Part-time programs available. *Degree requirements:* For master's, thesis. *Entrance requirements:* For master's and Diploma, appropriate bachelor's degree or equivalent, proficiency in French; for doctorate, appropriate master's degree or equivalent, proficiency in French.

University at Albany, State University of New York, College of Arts and Sciences, Department of Earth and Atmospheric Sciences, Albany, NY 12222-0001. Offers atmospheric science (MS, PhD); geology (MS, PhD). *Degree requirements:* For master's, one foreign language, comprehensive exam, thesis; for doctorate, 2 foreign languages, comprehensive exam, thesis/dissertation, oral exams. *Entrance requirements:* For master's and doctorate, GRE General Test. Additional exam requirements/recommendations for international students: Required—TOEFL (minimum score 550 paper-based; 213 computer-based). Electronic applications

Atmospheric Sciences

University at Albany, State University of New York (continued)
accepted. *Faculty research:* Environmental geochemistry, tectonics, mesoscale meteorology, atmospheric chemistry.

The University of Alabama in Huntsville, School of Graduate Studies, College of Science, Department of Atmospheric and Environmental Science, Huntsville, AL 35899. Offers MS, PhD. Part-time and evening/weekend programs available. *Faculty:* 8 full-time (0 women), 1 part-time/adjunct (0 women). *Students:* 31 full-time (14 women), 12 part-time (4 women); includes 3 minority (2 African Americans, 1 Hispanic American), 9 international. Average age 28. 25 applicants, 80% accepted, 8 enrolled. In 2009, 15 master's, 3 doctorates awarded. *Degree requirements:* For master's, comprehensive exam, thesis or alternative, oral and written exams; for doctorate, comprehensive exam, thesis/dissertation, oral and written exams. *Entrance requirements:* For master's, GRE General Test, minimum GPA of 3.0; sequence of courses in calculus (including the calculus of vector-valued functions); course in linear algebra; course in ordinary differential equations; two semesters of chemistry; two semesters of calculus-based physics; proficiency in at least one high-level computer programming language; for doctorate, GRE General Test, minimum GPA of 3.0. Additional exam requirements/recommendations for international students: Required—TOEFL (minimum score 550 paper-based; 213 computer-based; 62 iBT). *Application deadline:* For fall admission, 7/15 for domestic students, 4/1 for international students; for spring admission, 11/30 for domestic students, 9/1 for international students. Applications are processed on a rolling basis. Application fee: $40 ($50 for international students). Electronic applications accepted. *Expenses:* Tuition, state resident: part-time $355.75 per credit hour. Tuition, nonresident: part-time $847.10 per credit hour. Required fees: $210.80 per semester. Tuition and fees vary according to course load and program. *Financial support:* In 2009–10, 34 students received support, including 32 research assistantships with full and partial tuition reimbursements available (averaging $1,480 per year), 1 teaching assistantship with full and partial tuition reimbursement available (averaging $13,500 per year); career-related internships or fieldwork, Federal Work-Study, institutionally sponsored loans, scholarships/grants, health care benefits, tuition waivers, and unspecified assistantships also available. Support available to part-time students. Financial award application deadline: 4/1; financial award applicants required to submit FAFSA. *Faculty research:* Satellite remote sensing, severe weather, mesoscale modeling, atmospheric chemistry, data assimilation. Total annual research expenditures: $10.7 million. *Unit head:* Dr. John Christy, Chair, 256-922-7789, Fax: 256-922-7755, E-mail: christy@nsstc.uah.edu. *Application contact:* Kathy Biggs, Graduate Studies Admissions Manager, 256-824-6199, Fax: 256-824-6405, E-mail: deangrad@uah.edu.

University of Alaska Fairbanks, College of Natural Sciences and Mathematics, Program in Atmospheric Science, Fairbanks, AK 99775-7320. Offers MS, PhD. Part-time programs available. *Faculty:* 6 full-time (3 women). *Students:* 17 full-time (7 women), 5 part-time (2 women); includes 1 minority (Asian American or Pacific Islander), 4 international. Average age 29. 18 applicants, 39% accepted, 5 enrolled. In 2009, 5 master's, 5 doctorates awarded. Terminal master's awarded for partial completion of doctoral program. *Degree requirements:* For master's, comprehensive exam, thesis, oral defense; for doctorate, comprehensive exam, thesis/dissertation, oral defense. *Entrance requirements:* Additional exam requirements/recommendations for international students: Required—TOEFL (minimum score 550 paper-based; 213 computer-based; 80 iBT). *Application deadline:* For fall admission, 6/1 for domestic students, 3/1 for international students; for spring admission, 10/15 for domestic students, 9/1 for international students. Applications are processed on a rolling basis. Application fee: $60. Electronic applications accepted. *Expenses:* Tuition, state resident: full-time $7584; part-time $316 per credit. Tuition, nonresident: full-time $15,504; part-time $646 per credit. Required fees: $23 per credit. $135 per semester. Tuition and fees vary according to course level, course load and reciprocity agreements. *Financial support:* In 2009–10, 1 fellowship (averaging $18,346 per year), 8 research assistantships (averaging $15,085 per year) were awarded; teaching assistantships, Federal Work-Study, scholarships/grants, health care benefits, and unspecified assistantships also available. Support available to part-time students. Financial award application deadline: 2/15; financial award applicants required to submit FAFSA. *Faculty research:* Sea ice, climate modeling, atmospheric chemistry, global change, cloud and aerosol physics. *Unit head:* Dr. Nicole Moelders, Program Chair, 907-474-7368, Fax: 907-474-7379, E-mail: atmos@gi.alaska.edu. *Application contact:* Dr. Nicole Moelders, Program Chair, 907-474-7368, Fax: 907-474-7379, E-mail: atmos@gi.alaska.edu.

The University of Arizona, Graduate College, College of Science, Department of Atmospheric Sciences, Tucson, AZ 85721. Offers MS, PhD. *Faculty:* 7. *Students:* 14 full-time (5 women), 12 part-time (8 women); includes 1 minority (Hispanic American), 4 international. Average age 28. 34 applicants, 18% accepted, 6 enrolled. In 2009, 5 master's, 1 doctorate awarded. *Degree requirements:* For master's, thesis or alternative; for doctorate, comprehensive exam, thesis/dissertation. *Entrance requirements:* For master's, GRE General Test, 3 letters of recommendation; for doctorate, GRE General Test, 3 letters of recommendation, statement of purpose. Additional exam requirements/recommendations for international students: Required—TOEFL (minimum score 550 paper-based; 213 computer-based; 79 iBT). *Application deadline:* For fall admission, 2/1 for domestic students, 12/1 for international students. Applications are processed on a rolling basis. Application fee: $75. Electronic applications accepted. *Expenses:* Tuition, state resident: full-time $9028. Tuition, nonresident: full-time $24,890. *Financial support:* In 2009–10, 2 research assistantships with full tuition reimbursements (averaging $16,076 per year), 7 teaching assistantships with full tuition reimbursements (averaging $16,086 per year) were awarded; scholarships/grants, health care benefits, tuition waivers (full), and unspecified assistantships also available. *Faculty research:* Climate dynamics, radiative transfer and remote sensing, atmospheric chemistry, atmosphere dynamics, atmospheric electricity. Total annual research expenditures: $2.4 million. *Unit head:* Eric A. Betterton, Head, 520-621-6831, E-mail: betterton@atmo.arizona.edu. *Application contact:* Sonya Flores-Basurto, Information Contact, 520-621-6831, Fax: 520-621-6833, E-mail: sfloresb@email.arizona.edu.

The University of British Columbia, Faculty of Science, Department of Earth and Ocean Sciences, Vancouver, BC V6T 1Z4, Canada. Offers atmospheric science (M Sc, PhD); geological engineering (M Eng, MA Sc, PhD); geological sciences (M Sc, PhD); geophysics (M Sc, MA Sc, PhD); oceanography (M Sc, PhD). *Degree requirements:* For master's, thesis (for some programs); for doctorate, comprehensive exam, thesis/dissertation. *Entrance requirements:* Additional exam requirements/recommendations for international students: Required—TOEFL (minimum score 600 paper-based; 250 computer-based; 100 iBT). Electronic applications accepted. *Faculty research:* Oceans and atmosphere, environmental earth science, hydro geology, mineral deposits, geophysics.

University of California, Davis, Graduate Studies, Graduate Group in Atmospheric Sciences, Davis, CA 95616. Offers MS, PhD. *Degree requirements:* For master's, comprehensive exam or thesis; for doctorate, thesis/dissertation, 3 part qualifying exam. *Entrance requirements:* For master's and doctorate, GRE General Test, minimum GPA of 3.0. Additional exam requirements/recommendations for international students: Required—TOEFL (minimum score 550 paper-based; 213 computer-based). Electronic applications accepted. *Faculty research:* Air quality, biometeorology, climate dynamics, boundary layer large-scale dynamics.

University of California, Los Angeles, Graduate Division, College of Letters and Science, Department of Atmospheric Sciences, Los Angeles, CA 90095. Offers MS, PhD. *Students:* 39 full-time (19 women); includes 5 minority (4 Asian Americans or Pacific Islanders, 1 Hispanic American), 18 international. Average age 26. 61 applicants, 36% accepted, 7 enrolled. In 2009, 10 master's, 5 doctorates awarded. Terminal master's awarded for partial completion of doctoral program. *Degree requirements:* For master's, comprehensive exam or thesis; for doctorate, thesis/dissertation, oral and written qualifying exams. *Entrance requirements:* For master's, GRE General Test, minimum GPA of 3.0; for doctorate, GRE General Test, minimum undergraduate GPA of 3.0. *Application deadline:* For fall admission, 12/15 for domestic and international students. Application fee: $60 ($80 for international students). Electronic applications accepted. *Financial support:* In 2009–10, 28 fellowships with full and partial tuition reimbursements, 29 research assistantships with full and partial tuition reimbursements, 15 teaching assistantships with full and partial tuition reimbursements were awarded; Federal Work-Study, institutionally sponsored loans, scholarships/grants, health care benefits, tuition waivers (full and partial), and unspecified assistantships also available. Financial award application deadline: 3/1; financial award applicants required to submit FAFSA. *Unit head:* Dr. James C. McWilliams, Chair, 310-825-1217. *Application contact:* Departmental Office, 310-825-1217, E-mail: studentinfo@atmos.ucla.edu.

University of Chicago, Division of the Physical Sciences, Department of the Geophysical Sciences, Chicago, IL 60637-1513. Offers atmospheric sciences (SM, PhD); earth sciences (SM, PhD); paleobiology (PhD); planetary and space sciences (SM, PhD). *Faculty:* 21 full-time (3 women). *Students:* 37 full-time (23 women); includes 1 minority (Hispanic American), 14 international. Average age 27. 63 applicants, 35% accepted, 9 enrolled. In 2009, 1 doctorate awarded. Terminal master's awarded for partial completion of doctoral program. *Degree requirements:* For master's, thesis, seminar; for doctorate, variable foreign language requirement, comprehensive exam, thesis/dissertation. *Entrance requirements:* For doctorate, GRE General Test. Additional exam requirements/recommendations for international students: Required—TOEFL (minimum score 600 paper-based; 250 computer-based; 96 iBT), IELTS (minimum score 7). *Application deadline:* For fall admission, 1/10 for domestic and international students. Application fee: $55. Electronic applications accepted. *Financial support:* In 2009–10, research assistantships with full tuition reimbursements (averaging $20,511 per year), teaching assistantships with full tuition reimbursements (averaging $21,915 per year) were awarded; fellowships, Federal Work-Study, institutionally sponsored loans, scholarships/grants, tuition waivers (partial), and unspecified assistantships also available. Financial award application deadline: 1/15. *Faculty research:* Climatology, evolutionary paleontology, petrology, geochemistry, oceanic sciences. *Unit head:* Dr. Michael Foote, Chairman, 773-702-8102, Fax: 773-702-9505. *Application contact:* David J. Taylor, Graduate Student Services Coordinator, 773-702-8180, Fax: 773-702-9505, E-mail: info@geosci.uchicago.edu.

University of Colorado at Boulder, Graduate School, College of Arts and Sciences, Department of Atmospheric and Oceanic Sciences, Boulder, CO 80309. Offers MS, PhD. *Faculty:* 11 full-time (4 women). *Students:* 43 full-time (23 women), 22 part-time (9 women); includes 7 minority (1 African American, 3 Asian Americans or Pacific Islanders, 3 Hispanic Americans), 11 international. Average age 30. 85 applicants, 15% accepted, 9 enrolled. In 2009, 4 master's, 5 doctorates awarded. *Entrance requirements:* For master's, minimum undergraduate GPA of 3.0. *Application deadline:* For fall admission, 2/1 for domestic students, 12/1 for international students; for spring admission, 10/1 for domestic and international students. *Financial support:* In 2009–10, 11 fellowships (averaging $2,321 per year), 40 research assistantships (averaging $16,795 per year) were awarded. *Faculty research:* Large-scale dynamics of the ocean and the atmosphere, air-sea interaction, radiative transfer and remote sensing of the ocean and the atmosphere, sea ice and its role in climate. Total annual research expenditures: $6.7 million.

University of Delaware, College of Arts and Sciences, Department of Geography, Newark, DE 19716. Offers climatology (PhD); geography (MA, MS). *Degree requirements:* For master's, thesis; for doctorate, thesis/dissertation. *Entrance requirements:* For master's and doctorate, GRE General Test. Additional exam requirements/recommendations for international students: Required—TOEFL. Electronic applications accepted. *Faculty research:* Permafrost, Glaciers, Climatology, Physical Geography, Human Geography.

University of Guelph, Graduate Program Services, Ontario Agricultural College, Department of Land Resource Science, Guelph, ON N1G 2W1, Canada. Offers atmospheric science (M Sc, PhD); environmental and agricultural earth sciences (M Sc, PhD); land resources management (M Sc, PhD); soil science (M Sc, PhD). Part-time programs available. *Degree requirements:* For master's, thesis (for some programs), research project (non-thesis track); for doctorate, comprehensive exam, thesis/dissertation. *Entrance requirements:* For master's, minimum B- average during previous 2 years of course work; for doctorate, minimum B average during previous 2 years of course work. Additional exam requirements/recommendations for international students: Required—TOEFL (minimum score 550 paper-based; 213 computer-based). Electronic applications accepted. *Faculty research:* Soil science, environmental earth science, land resource management.

University of Illinois at Urbana–Champaign, Graduate College, College of Liberal Arts and Sciences, School of Earth, Society and Environment, Department of Atmospheric Sciences, Champaign, IL 61820. Offers MS, PhD. *Faculty:* 10 full-time (2 women). *Students:* 45 full-time (23 women), 8 part-time (4 women); includes 4 minority (1 African American, 1 Asian American or Pacific Islander, 2 Hispanic Americans), 17 international. 62 applicants, 31% accepted, 13 enrolled. In 2009, 7 master's, 1 doctorate awarded. *Entrance requirements:* For master's and doctorate, GRE General Test, minimum GPA of 3.0. Additional exam requirements/recommendations for international students: Required—TOEFL. *Application deadline:* Applications are processed on a rolling basis. Application fee: $60 ($75 for international students). Electronic applications accepted. *Financial support:* In 2009–10, 3 fellowships, 38 research assistantships, 16 teaching assistantships were awarded; tuition waivers (full and partial) also available. *Unit head:* Robert Rauber, Head, 217-333-2835, Fax: 217-244-4393, E-mail: r-rauber@illinois.edu. *Application contact:* Nena L. Richards, Office Administrator, 217-333-2046, Fax: 217-244-4393, E-mail: nenar@illinois.edu.

The University of Kansas, Graduate Studies, College of Liberal Arts and Sciences, Department of Geography, Lawrence, KS 66045-7613. Offers atmospheric science (MS); geography (MA, PhD); MUP/MA. Part-time programs available. *Students:* 74 full-time (27 women), 16 part-time (2 women); includes 4 minority (1 African American, 3 American Indian/Alaska Native), 13 international. Average age 32. 58 applicants, 59% accepted, 15 enrolled. In 2009, 10 master's, 6 doctorates awarded. *Degree requirements:* For master's, comprehensive exam, thesis, thesis defense; for doctorate, one foreign language, comprehensive exam, thesis/dissertation, dissertation defense. *Entrance requirements:* For master's, GRE General Test, 3 letters of reference; for doctorate, GRE General Test, 3 letters of reference, transcripts, statement of interests. Additional exam requirements/recommendations for international students: Required—TOEFL. *Application deadline:* For fall admission, 1/15 for domestic students, 1/15 priority date for international students; for spring admission, 11/1 for domestic students, 10/1 for international students. Applications are processed on a rolling basis. Application fee: $45 ($55 for international students). Electronic applications accepted. *Expenses:* Tuition, state resident: full-time $6492; part-time $270.50 per credit hour. Tuition, nonresident: full-time $15,510; part-time $646.25 per credit hour. Required fees: $847; $70.56 per credit hour. Tuition and fees vary according to course load and program. *Financial support:* Fellowships with full tuition reimbursements, research assistantships with full tuition reimbursements, teaching assistantships with full and partial tuition reimbursements, unspecified assistantships available. Financial award application deadline: 1/15. *Faculty research:* Physical geography, techniques (cartography, GIS, remote sensing), cultural/regional geography, atmospheric science. *Unit head:* Terry Slocum, Chair, 785-864-5146, Fax: 785-864-5378, E-mail: t-slocum@ku.edu. *Application contact:* Stephen Egbert, Graduate Director, 785-864-4252, Fax: 785-864-5378, E-mail: s-egbert@ku.edu.

University of Maryland, Baltimore County, Graduate School, College of Natural and Mathematical Sciences, Department of Physics, Program in Atmospheric Physics, Baltimore, MD 21250. Offers MS, PhD. *Faculty:* 25 full-time (4 women), 20 part-time/adjunct (1 woman). *Students:* 13 full-time (5 women), 8 international. Average age 25. 5 applicants, 80% accepted, 3 enrolled. In 2009, 1 doctorate awarded. *Degree requirements:* For master's, thesis optional;

for doctorate, comprehensive exam, thesis/dissertation. *Entrance requirements:* For master's and doctorate, GRE General Test, minimum GPA of 3.0. Additional exam requirements/recommendations for international students: Required—TOEFL (minimum score 587 paper-based; 240 computer-based; 95 iBT). *Application deadline:* For fall admission, 6/1 for domestic students, 5/1 for international students; for spring admission, 1/1 for domestic students, 11/1 for international students. Applications are processed on a rolling basis. Application fee: $50. Electronic applications accepted. *Financial support:* In 2009–10, 11 students received support, including 1 fellowship with full tuition reimbursement available (averaging $30,000 per year), 7 research assistantships with full tuition reimbursements available (averaging $25,000 per year), 4 teaching assistantships with full tuition reimbursements available (averaging $22,000 per year); career-related internships or fieldwork, scholarships/grants, health care benefits, unspecified assistantships, and NASA Student Fellowship also available. Support available to part-time students. Financial award application deadline: 5/31. *Faculty research:* Lidar, remote sensing, aerosols, satellite remote sensing. Total annual research expenditures: $2.7 million. *Unit head:* Dr. Vanderlei Martins, Graduate Program Director, 410-455-2513, Fax: 410-455-1072, E-mail: martins@umbc.edu. *Application contact:* Dr. Vanderlei Martins, 410-455-2513, Fax: 410-455-1072, E-mail: martins@umbc.edu.

University of Massachusetts Lowell, College of Arts and Sciences, Department of Environmental, Earth and Atmospheric Sciences, Lowell, MA 01854-2881. Offers atmospheric science (MS, PhD).

University of Michigan, Horace H. Rackham School of Graduate Studies, College of Engineering, Department of Atmospheric, Oceanic, and Space Sciences, Ann Arbor, MI 48109. Offers atmospheric (MS); atmospheric and space sciences (PhD); geoscience and remote sensing (PhD); space and planetary sciences (PhD); space engineering (M Eng); space sciences (MS). Part-time programs available. *Faculty:* 22 full-time (4 women). *Students:* 74 full-time (30 women), 1 part-time (0 women); includes 4 minority (1 African American, 2 Asian Americans or Pacific Islanders, 1 Hispanic American), 29 international. 62 applicants, 48% accepted, 17 enrolled. In 2009, 38 master's, 4 doctorates awarded. Terminal master's awarded for partial completion of doctoral program. *Degree requirements:* For master's, thesis (for some programs); for doctorate, thesis/dissertation, oral defense of dissertation, preliminary exams. *Entrance requirements:* For master's and doctorate, GRE General Test. Additional exam requirements/recommendations for international students: Required—TOEFL. *Application deadline:* Applications are processed on a rolling basis. Application fee: $60 ($75 for international students). Electronic applications accepted. *Expenses:* Tuition, state resident: full-time $17,286; part-time $1099 per credit hour. Tuition, nonresident: full-time $34,944; part-time $2080 per credit hour. Required fees: $95 per semester. Tuition and fees vary according to course load, degree level and program. *Financial support:* Fellowships, research assistantships, teaching assistantships, career-related internships or fieldwork, Federal Work-Study, institutionally sponsored loans, and health care benefits available. Support available to part-time students. Financial award applicants required to submit FAFSA. *Faculty research:* Planetary environments, space instrumentation, air pollution meteorology, global climate change, sun-earth connection, space weather. *Unit head:* Tamas Gombosi, Chair, 734-764-7222, Fax: 734-615-4645, E-mail: tamas@umich.edu. *Application contact:* Margaret Reid, Student Services Associate, 734-936-0482, Fax: 734-763-0437, E-mail: aoss.um@umich.edu.

University of Missouri, Graduate School, School of Natural Resources, Department of Soil, Environmental, and Atmospheric Sciences, Columbia, MO 65211. Offers atmospheric science (MS, PhD); soil science (MS, PhD). *Degree requirements:* For doctorate, thesis/dissertation. *Entrance requirements:* For master's and doctorate, GRE General Test, minimum GPA of 3.0. Additional exam requirements/recommendations for international students: Required—TOEFL (minimum score 530 paper-based; 197 computer-based; 71 iBT).

University of Nevada, Reno, Graduate School, Interdisciplinary Program in Atmospheric Sciences, Reno, NV 89557. Offers MS, PhD. Terminal master's awarded for partial completion of doctoral program. *Degree requirements:* For master's, thesis optional; for doctorate, thesis/dissertation. *Entrance requirements:* For master's, GRE (recommended), minimum GPA of 2.75; for doctorate, GRE (recommended), minimum GPA of 3.0. Additional exam requirements/recommendations for international students: Required—TOEFL (minimum score 500 paper-based; 173 computer-based; 61 iBT), IELTS (minimum score 6). Electronic applications accepted. *Faculty research:* Atmospheric chemistry, cloud and aerosol physics, atmospheric optics, mesoscale meterology.

The University of North Carolina at Chapel Hill, Graduate School, School of Public Health, Department of Environmental Sciences and Engineering, Chapel Hill, NC 27599. Offers air, radiation and industrial hygiene (MPH, MS, MSEE, MSPH, PhD); aquatic and atmospheric sciences (MPH, MS, MSPH, PhD); environmental engineering (MPH, MS, MSEE, MSPH, PhD); environmental health sciences (MPH, MS, MSPH, PhD); environmental management and policy (MPH, MS, MSPH, PhD). Terminal master's awarded for partial completion of doctoral program. *Degree requirements:* For master's, comprehensive exam, thesis (for some programs), research paper; for doctorate, comprehensive exam, thesis/dissertation. *Entrance requirements:* For master's and doctorate, GRE General Test, minimum GPA of 3.0. Additional exam requirements/recommendations for international students: Required—TOEFL. Electronic applications accepted. *Faculty research:* Air, radiation and industrial hygiene, aquatic and atmospheric sciences, environmental health sciences, environmental management and policy, water resources engineering.

University of North Dakota, Graduate School, John D. Odegard School of Aerospace Sciences, Department of Atmospheric Sciences, Grand Forks, ND 58202. Offers MS, PhD. Part-time programs available. *Degree requirements:* For master's, comprehensive exam, thesis or alternative. *Entrance requirements:* For master's and doctorate, GRE General Test, minimum GPA of 3.0. Additional exam requirements/recommendations for international students: Required—TOEFL (minimum score 550 paper-based; 213 computer-based; 79 iBT), IELTS (minimum score 6.5). Electronic applications accepted.

University of Utah, The Graduate School, College of Mines and Earth Sciences, Department of Atmospheric Sciences, Salt Lake City, UT 84112. Offers MS, PhD. Part-time programs available. *Faculty:* 11 full-time (2 women), 1 part-time/adjunct (0 women). *Students:* 28 full-time (10 women), 16 part-time (2 women); includes 3 minority (all Hispanic Americans), 7 international. Average age 27. 46 applicants, 37% accepted, 14 enrolled. In 2009, 7 master's, 2 doctorates awarded. Terminal master's awarded for partial completion of doctoral program. *Degree requirements:* For master's, comprehensive exam, thesis optional; for doctorate, comprehensive exam, thesis/dissertation. *Entrance requirements:* For master's and doctorate, GRE General Test, minimum GPA of 3.0, 3 letters of reference. Additional exam requirements/recommendations for international students: Required—TOEFL (minimum score 500 paper-based; 173 computer-based; 61 iBT). *Application deadline:* For fall admission, 1/7 priority date for domestic and international students. Applications are processed on a rolling basis. Application fee: $55 ($65 for international students). Electronic applications accepted. *Expenses:* Tuition, state resident: full-time $4004; part-time $1674 per semester. Tuition, nonresident: full-time $14,134; part-time $5915 per semester. Required fees: $324 per semester. Tuition and fees vary according to course load, degree level and program. *Financial support:* In 2009–10, 31 students received support, including 3 fellowships (averaging $30,000 per year), 34 research assistantships (averaging $21,000 per year), 2 teaching assistantships (averaging $5,500 per year); unspecified assistantships also available. Financial award application deadline: 2/15; financial award applicants required to submit FAFSA. *Faculty research:* Clouds, aerosols, and climate; numerical weather prediction; mountain weather and climate; tropical convection and storms; climate variability and change. Total annual research expenditures: $3.3 million. *Unit head:* Dr. W. James Steenburgh, Chair, 801-585-9482, Fax: 801-585-3681, E-mail: jim.steenburg@utah.edu. *Application contact:* Kathy Roberts, Executive Secretary, 801-581-6136, Fax: 801-585-3681, E-mail: kathy.roberts@utah.edu.

University of Washington, Graduate School, College of Arts and Sciences, Department of Atmospheric Sciences, Seattle, WA 98195. Offers MS, PhD. *Degree requirements:* For master's, thesis; for doctorate, thesis/dissertation, qualifying exam. *Entrance requirements:* For master's and doctorate, GRE General Test, minimum GPA of 3.0. Additional exam requirements/recommendations for international students: Required—TOEFL. *Faculty research:* Climate change, synoptic and mesoscale meteorology, atmospheric chemistry, cloud physics, dynamics of the atmosphere.

University of Wisconsin–Madison, Graduate School, College of Letters and Science, Department of Atmospheric and Oceanic Sciences, Madison, WI 53706-1380. Offers MS, PhD. Part-time programs available. *Degree requirements:* For master's, thesis (for some programs); for doctorate, thesis/dissertation. *Entrance requirements:* For master's and doctorate, GRE General Test, minimum GPA of 3.0; previous course work in chemistry, mathematics, and physics. Electronic applications accepted. *Expenses:* Tuition, state resident: part-time $594 per credit. Tuition, nonresident: part-time $1504 per credit. Required fees: $65 per credit. Tuition and fees vary according to course load, program and reciprocity agreements. *Faculty research:* Satellite meteorology, weather systems, global climate change, numerical modeling, atmosphere-ocean interaction.

University of Wyoming, College of Engineering and Applied Sciences, Department of Atmospheric Science, Laramie, WY 82070. Offers MS, PhD. Postbaccalaureate distance learning degree programs offered (minimal on-campus study). Terminal master's awarded for partial completion of doctoral program. *Degree requirements:* For master's, thesis; for doctorate, comprehensive exam, thesis/dissertation. *Entrance requirements:* For master's and doctorate, GRE General Test, minimum GPA of 3.0. Additional exam requirements/recommendations for international students: Required—TOEFL (minimum score 525 paper-based; 250 computer-based). Electronic applications accepted. *Expenses:* Contact institution. *Faculty research:* Cloud physics; aerosols, boundary layer processes; airborne observations; stratospheric aerosols and gases.

Yale University, Graduate School of Arts and Sciences, Department of Geology and Geophysics, New Haven, CT 06520. Offers biogeochemistry (PhD); climate dynamics (PhD); geochemistry (PhD); geophysics (PhD); meteorology (PhD); oceanography (PhD); paleontology (PhD); paleooceanography (PhD); petrology (PhD); tectonics (PhD). *Degree requirements:* For doctorate, thesis/dissertation. *Entrance requirements:* For doctorate, GRE General Test. Additional exam requirements/recommendations for international students: Required—TOEFL.

Meteorology

Columbia University, Graduate School of Arts and Sciences, Program in Climate and Society, New York, NY 10027. Offers MA.

Florida Institute of Technology, Graduate Programs, College of Engineering, Department of Marine and Environmental Systems, Melbourne, FL 32901-6975. Offers earth remote sensing (MS); environmental resource management (MS); environmental science (MS, PhD); meteorology (MS); ocean engineering (MS, PhD); oceanography (MS, PhD), including biological oceanography (MS), chemical oceanography (MS), coastal zone management (MS), geological oceanography (MS), oceanography (PhD), physical oceanography (MS). Part-time programs available. *Faculty:* 12 full-time (1 woman), 1 part-time/adjunct (0 women). *Students:* 42 full-time (18 women), 23 part-time (9 women); includes 2 minority (1 African American, 1 Asian American or Pacific Islander), 11 international. Average age 28. 103 applicants, 50% accepted, 16 enrolled. In 2009, 22 master's, 1 doctorate awarded. *Degree requirements:* For master's, comprehensive exam (for some programs), thesis (for some programs), seminar, field project, written final exam, internship, technical paper, oral presentation or internship; for doctorate, comprehensive exam, thesis/dissertation, seminar, internships (oceanography and environmental science), publications. *Entrance requirements:* For master's, GRE General Test (environmental science, oceanography, environmental resource management, meteorology, earth remote sensing), 3 letters of recommendation, minimum GPA of 3.0, resume; for doctorate, GRE General Test (oceanography, environmental science), resume, 3 letters of recommendation, minimum GPA of 3.3, statement of objectives, on campus interview (highly recommended). Additional exam requirements/recommendations for international students: Required—TOEFL (minimum score 550 paper-based; 213 computer-based; 79 iBT). *Application deadline:* For fall admission, 4/1 for international students; for spring admission, 9/30 for international students. Applications are processed on a rolling basis. Application fee: $50. Electronic applications accepted. *Expenses:* Tuition: Part-time $1015 per credit. Tuition and fees vary according to campus/location and program. *Financial support:* In 2009–10, 19 students received support, including 5 fellowships with full and partial tuition reimbursements available (averaging $7,240 per year), 9 research assistantships with full and partial tuition reimbursements available (averaging $5,542 per year), 10 teaching assistantships with full and partial tuition reimbursements available (averaging $5,411 per year); career-related internships or fieldwork, institutionally sponsored loans, tuition waivers (partial), unspecified assistantships, and tuition remissions also available. Support available to part-time students. Financial award application deadline: 3/1; financial award applicants required to submit FAFSA. Total annual research expenditures: $1.7 million. *Unit head:* Dr. George Maul, Department Head, 321-674-7453, Fax: 321-674-7212, E-mail: gmaul@fit.edu. *Application contact:* Thomas M. Shea, Director of Graduate Admissions, 321-674-7577, Fax: 321-723-9468, E-mail: tshea@fit.edu.

See Close-Up on page 411.

Florida State University, The Graduate School, College of Arts and Sciences, Department of Meteorology, Tallahassee, FL 32306-4520. Offers MS, PhD. *Faculty:* 15 full-time (3 women). *Students:* 62 full-time (17 women), 16 part-time (5 women); includes 11 minority (4 African Americans, 1 American Indian/Alaska Native, 1 Asian American or Pacific Islander, 5 Hispanic Americans), 7 international. Average age 25. 68 applicants, 56% accepted, 18 enrolled. In 2009, 13 master's, 4 doctorates awarded. Terminal master's awarded for partial completion of doctoral program. *Degree requirements:* For master's, thesis optional; for doctorate, comprehensive exam, thesis/dissertation. *Entrance requirements:* For master's, GRE General Test (minimum score 1100 verbal and quantitative), minimum GPA of 3.0 in upper-division work; for doctorate, GRE General Test (minimum combined Verbal and Quantitative score: 1100), minimum GPA of 3.0, faculty sponsor. Additional exam requirements/recommendations

Meteorology

Florida State University (continued)
for international students: Required—TOEFL (minimum score 550 paper-based; 213 computer-based; 80 iBT). *Application deadline:* For fall admission, 2/15 priority date for domestic students, 2/1 for international students; for spring admission, 11/1 for domestic students, 6/30 for international students. Applications are processed on a rolling basis. Application fee: $30. *Expenses:* Tuition, state resident: full-time $7413.36. Tuition, nonresident: full-time $22,567. *Financial support:* In 2009–10, 56 students received support, including 2 fellowships with partial tuition reimbursements available (averaging $19,000 per year), 34 research assistantships with partial tuition reimbursements available (averaging $21,500 per year), 20 teaching assistantships with partial tuition reimbursements available (averaging $21,500 per year); career-related internships or fieldwork, scholarships/grants, and unspecified assistantships also available. *Faculty research:* Physical, dynamic, and synoptic meteorology; climatology. Total annual research expenditures: $600,000. *Unit head:* Dr. Robert G. Ellingson, Chairman, 850-644-6205, Fax: 850-644-9642, E-mail: bobe@met.fsu.edu. *Application contact:* Marc Unger, Academic Program Specialist, 850-644-8580, Fax: 850-644-9642, E-mail: ungerm@met.fsu.edu.

Georgia Institute of Technology, Graduate Studies and Research, College of Sciences, School of Earth and Atmospheric Sciences, Atlanta, GA 30332-0340. Offers atmospheric chemistry, aerosols and clouds (MS, PhD); dynamics of weather and climate (MS, PhD); geochemistry (MS, PhD); geophysics (MS, PhD); oceanography (MS, PhD); paleoclimate (MS, PhD); planetary science (MS, PhD); remote sensing (MS, PhD). Part-time programs available. Terminal master's awarded for partial completion of doctoral program. *Degree requirements:* For master's, thesis or alternative; for doctorate, comprehensive exam, thesis/dissertation. *Entrance requirements:* For master's, GRE, letters of recommendation; for doctorate, GRE, academic transcripts, letters of recommendation, personal statement. Additional exam requirements/recommendations for international students: Required—TOEFL (minimum score 550 paper-based; 213 computer-based; 79 iBT). *Faculty research:* Geophysics; atmospheric chemistry, aerosols and clouds; dynamics of weather and climate; geochemistry; oceanography; paleoclimate; planetary science; remote sensing.

Iowa State University of Science and Technology, Graduate College, College of Liberal Arts and Sciences, Department of Geological and Atmospheric Sciences, Ames, IA 50011. Offers earth science (MS, PhD); environmental science (MS, PhD); geology (MS, PhD); meteorology (MS, PhD). *Faculty:* 15 full-time (2 women), 1 part-time/adjunct (0 women). *Students:* 31 full-time (6 women), 3 part-time (0 women); includes 1 minority (Asian American or Pacific Islander), 8 international. 33 applicants, 55% accepted, 9 enrolled. In 2009, 3 master's, 2 doctorates awarded. *Degree requirements:* For master's, thesis (for some programs); for doctorate, thesis/dissertation. *Entrance requirements:* For master's and doctorate, GRE General Test. Additional exam requirements/recommendations for international students: Required—TOEFL (minimum score 550 paper-based; 79 iBT) or IELTS (minimum score 6.5). *Application deadline:* For fall admission, 1/1 priority date for domestic students. Applications are processed on a rolling basis. Application fee: $40 ($90 for international students). Electronic applications accepted. *Expenses:* Tuition, state resident: full-time $6716. Tuition, nonresident: full-time $8908. Tuition and fees vary according to course level, course load, program and student level. *Financial support:* In 2009–10, 21 research assistantships with full and partial tuition reimbursements (averaging $14,610 per year), 7 teaching assistantships with full and partial tuition reimbursements (averaging $14,610 per year) were awarded; fellowships, scholarships/grants, health care benefits, and unspecified assistantships also available. *Unit head:* Dr. Carl E. Jacobson, Chair, 515-294-4477. *Application contact:* Dr. Carl E. Jacobson, Chair, 515-294-4477.

McGill University, Faculty of Graduate and Postdoctoral Studies, Faculty of Agricultural and Environmental Sciences, Department of Natural Resource Sciences, Montréal, QC H3A 2T5, Canada. Offers entomology (M Sc, PhD); environmental assessment (M Sc); forest science (M Sc, PhD); microbiology (M Sc, PhD); micrometeorology (M Sc, PhD); neotropical environment (M Sc, PhD); soil science (M Sc, PhD); wildlife biology (M Sc, PhD).

Naval Postgraduate School, Graduate Programs, Department of Meteorology, Monterey, CA 93943. Offers MS, PhD. Program only open to commissioned officers of the United States and friendly nations and selected United States federal civilian employees. Part-time programs available. *Degree requirements:* For master's, thesis; for doctorate, one foreign language, thesis/dissertation.

North Carolina State University, Graduate School, College of Physical and Mathematical Sciences, Department of Marine, Earth, and Atmospheric Sciences, Raleigh, NC 27695. Offers marine, earth, and atmospheric sciences (MS, PhD); meteorology (MS, PhD); oceanography (MS, PhD). Terminal master's awarded for partial completion of doctoral program. *Degree requirements:* For master's, thesis (for some programs), final oral exam; for doctorate, comprehensive exam, thesis/dissertation, final oral exam, preliminary oral and written exams. *Entrance requirements:* For master's, GRE General Test, minimum GPA of 3.0; for doctorate, GRE General Test, GRE Subject Test (for disciplines in biological oceanography and geology), minimum GPA of 3.0. Additional exam requirements/recommendations for international students: Required—TOEFL (minimum score 550 paper-based). Electronic applications accepted. *Faculty research:* Boundary layer and air quality meteorology; climate and mesoscale dynamics; biological, chemical, geological, and physical oceanography; hard rock, soft rock, environmental, and paleo-geology.

Northern Arizona University, Graduate College, College of Engineering, Forestry and Natural Sciences, School of Earth Sciences and Environmental Sustainability, Flagstaff, AZ 86011. Offers climate science and solutions (MS); environmental sciences and policy (MS); geology (MS). *Faculty:* 22 full-time (5 women). *Students:* 28 full-time (17 women), 25 part-time (21 women); includes 6 minority (2 American Indian/Alaska Native, 1 Asian American or Pacific Islander, 3 Hispanic Americans). 70 applicants, 36% accepted, 17 enrolled. In 2009, 19 master's awarded. *Entrance requirements:* Additional exam requirements/recommendations for international students: Required—TOEFL (minimum score 550 paper-based; 213 computer-based; 80 iBT), IELTS (minimum score 7), or a bachelor's degree from an English-speaking university and demonstrated proficiency. *Application deadline:* For fall admission, 2/15 for domestic and international students. Application fee: $65. *Financial support:* In 2009–10, 32 students received support, including 7 research assistantships with partial tuition reimbursements available, 26 teaching assistantships with partial tuition reimbursements available; Federal Work-Study, scholarships/grants, health care benefits, and unspecified assistantships also available. Support available to part-time students. Financial award applicants required to submit FAFSA. *Unit head:* Dr. Abe Springer, Director, 928-523-7198. *Application contact:* Dr. Abe Springer, Director, 928-523-7198.

Penn State University Park, Graduate School, College of Earth and Mineral Sciences, Department of Meteorology, State College, University Park, PA 16802-1503. Offers MS, PhD.

Plymouth State University, College of Graduate Studies, Graduate Studies in Education, Program in Science, Plymouth, NH 03264-1595. Offers applied meteorology (MS); environmental science and policy (MS); science education (MS).

Saint Louis University, Graduate School, College of Arts and Sciences and Graduate School, Department of Earth and Atmospheric Sciences, St. Louis, MO 63103-2097. Offers geophysics (PhD); geoscience (MS); meteorology (M Pr Met, MS-R, PhD). Part-time programs available. *Degree requirements:* For master's, thesis (for some programs), comprehensive oral exam; for doctorate, thesis/dissertation, preliminary exams. *Entrance requirements:* For master's, GRE General Test, letters of recommendation, resume; for doctorate, GRE General Test, letters of recommendation, resumé, goal statement, transcripts. Additional exam requirements/recommendations for international students: Required—TOEFL (minimum score 525 paper-based; 194 computer-based). Electronic applications accepted. *Faculty research:* Structural geology, mesoscale meteorology and severe storms, weather and climate change prediction.

San Jose State University, Graduate Studies and Research, College of Science, Department of Meteorology and Climate Science, San Jose, CA 95192-0001. Offers meteorology (MS). *Students:* 5 full-time (1 woman), 2 part-time (1 woman); includes 1 minority (Asian American or Pacific Islander), 1 international. Average age 26. 15 applicants, 67% accepted, 3 enrolled. In 2009, 2 master's awarded. *Degree requirements:* For master's, thesis or alternative. *Entrance requirements:* For master's, GRE. *Application deadline:* For fall admission, 6/29 for domestic students; for spring admission, 11/30 for domestic students. Applications are processed on a rolling basis. Application fee: $59. Electronic applications accepted. *Financial support:* Applicants required to submit FAFSA. *Unit head:* Dr. Alison Bridger, Chair, 408-924-5200, Fax: 408-924-5191. *Application contact:* Dr. Alison Bridger, Chair, 408-924-5200, Fax: 408-924-5191.

Texas A&M University, College of Geosciences, Department of Atmospheric Sciences, College Station, TX 77843. Offers MS, PhD. *Faculty:* 18. *Students:* 48 full-time (15 women), 6 part-time (0 women), 27 international. Average age 28. In 2009, 9 master's, 3 doctorates awarded. *Degree requirements:* For master's, thesis; for doctorate, thesis/dissertation. *Entrance requirements:* For master's and doctorate, GRE General Test. Additional exam requirements/recommendations for international students: Required—TOEFL. *Application deadline:* For fall admission, 3/1 for domestic students; for spring admission, 10/1 for domestic students. Applications are processed on a rolling basis. Application fee: $50 ($75 for international students). Electronic applications accepted. *Expenses:* Tuition, state resident: full-time $3991.32; part-time $221.74 per credit hour. Tuition, nonresident: full-time $9049; part-time $502.74 per credit hour. *Financial support:* In 2009–10, fellowships (averaging $16,500 per year), research assistantships with tuition reimbursements (averaging $15,000 per year), teaching assistantships (averaging $15,000 per year) were awarded; career-related internships or fieldwork, institutionally sponsored loans, scholarships/grants, and tuition waivers (partial) also available. Financial award application deadline: 3/1; financial award applicants required to submit FAFSA. *Faculty research:* Radar and satellite rainfall relationships, mesoscale dynamics and numerical modeling, climatology. *Unit head:* Head, 979-862-4060, E-mail: info@ariel.tamu.edu. *Application contact:* Patricia Price, Academic Advisor, 979-845-7688, Fax: 979-862-4466, E-mail: info@ariel.tamu.edu.

Université du Québec à Montréal, Graduate Programs, Program in Earth and Atmospheric Sciences, Montréal, QC H3C 3P8, Canada. Offers atmospheric sciences (M Sc); Earth and atmospheric sciences (PhD); Earth science (M Sc); meteorology (PhD, Diploma). Part-time programs available. *Degree requirements:* For master's, thesis. *Entrance requirements:* For master's and Diploma, appropriate bachelor's degree or equivalent, proficiency in French; for doctorate, appropriate master's degree or equivalent, proficiency in French.

University of Hawaii at Manoa, Graduate Division, School of Ocean and Earth Science and Technology, Department of Meteorology, Honolulu, HI 96822. Offers MS, PhD. Part-time programs available. *Faculty:* 20 full-time (2 women), 4 part-time/adjunct (0 women). *Students:* 27 full-time (10 women), 3 part-time (1 woman); includes 3 minority (2 Asian Americans or Pacific Islanders, 1 Hispanic American), 12 international. Average age 28. 35 applicants, 54% accepted, 8 enrolled. In 2009, 3 master's, 5 doctorates awarded. *Degree requirements:* For master's, comprehensive exam, thesis; for doctorate, comprehensive exam, thesis/dissertation. *Entrance requirements:* For master's and doctorate, GRE General Test. Additional exam requirements/recommendations for international students: Required—TOEFL (minimum score 560 paper-based; 220 computer-based; 83 iBT), IELTS (minimum score 5). *Application deadline:* For fall admission, 3/1 for domestic students, 1/15 for international students; for spring admission, 9/1 for domestic students, 8/1 for international students. Application fee: $60. *Expenses:* Tuition, state resident: full-time $8900; part-time $372 per credit. Tuition, nonresident: full-time $21,400; part-time $898 per credit. Required fees: $207 per semester. *Financial support:* In 2009–10, 1 fellowship (averaging $2,750 per year), 19 research assistantships (averaging $20,250 per year), 3 teaching assistantships (averaging $19,428 per year) were awarded; Federal Work-Study and tuition waivers (full) also available. *Faculty research:* Tropical cyclones, air-sea interactions, mesoscale meteorology, intraseasonal oscillations, tropical climate. Total annual research expenditures: $6 million. *Application contact:* Pao-Shin Chu, Graduate Chairperson, 808-956-8775, Fax: 808-956-2877, E-mail: chu@hawaii.edu.

University of Maryland, College Park, Academic Affairs, College of Computer, Mathematical and Physical Sciences, Department of Atmospheric and Oceanic Science, College Park, MD 20742. Offers MS, PhD. Part-time and evening/weekend programs available. Postbaccalaureate distance learning degree programs offered. *Faculty:* 31 full-time (8 women), 7 part-time/adjunct (1 woman). *Students:* 50 full-time (21 women), 11 part-time (6 women); includes 3 minority (all Asian Americans or Pacific Islanders), 23 international. 82 applicants, 30% accepted, 16 enrolled. In 2009, 6 master's, 10 doctorates awarded. Terminal master's awarded for partial completion of doctoral program. *Degree requirements:* For master's, comprehensive exam, scholarly paper, written and oral exams; for doctorate, thesis/dissertation, exam. *Entrance requirements:* For master's, GRE General Test, background in mathematics, experience in scientific computer languages, 3 letters of recommendation; for doctorate, GRE General Test. *Application deadline:* For fall admission, 1/15 for domestic and international students; for spring admission, 11/1 for domestic students, 6/1 for international students. Applications are processed on a rolling basis. Application fee: $60. Electronic applications accepted. *Expenses:* Tuition, area resident: Part-time $471 per credit hour. Tuition, state resident: part-time $471 per credit hour. Tuition, nonresident: part-time $1016 per credit hour. Required fees: $337.04 per term. *Financial support:* In 2009–10, 3 fellowships with full and partial tuition reimbursements (averaging $13,629 per year), 28 research assistantships with tuition reimbursements (averaging $20,600 per year), 11 teaching assistantships with tuition reimbursements (averaging $20,611 per year) were awarded; Federal Work-Study and scholarships/grants also available. Support available to part-time students. Financial award applicants required to submit FAFSA. *Faculty research:* Weather, atmospheric chemistry, air pollution, global change, radiation. Total annual research expenditures: $4 million. *Unit head:* James A. Carton, Chair, 301-405-5365, Fax: 301-314-9482, E-mail: carton@atmos.umd.edu. *Application contact:* Dean of Graduate School, 301-405-0358.

University of Miami, Graduate School, Rosenstiel School of Marine and Atmospheric Science, Division of Meteorology and Physical Oceanography, Coral Gables, FL 33124. Offers meteorology (MS, PhD); physical oceanography (MS, PhD). Terminal master's awarded for partial completion of doctoral program. *Degree requirements:* For master's, comprehensive exam, thesis; for doctorate, comprehensive exam, thesis/dissertation. *Entrance requirements:* For master's and doctorate, GRE General Test. Additional exam requirements/recommendations for international students: Required—TOEFL (minimum score 550 paper-based; 213 computer-based). Electronic applications accepted.

University of Oklahoma, Graduate College, College of Atmospheric and Geographic Sciences, School of Meteorology, Norman, OK 73072. Offers M Pr Met, MS Metr, PhD. Part-time programs available. *Faculty:* 44 full-time (6 women), 6 part-time/adjunct (1 woman). *Students:* 86 full-time (27 women), 16 part-time (5 women); includes 9 minority (1 African American, 1 American Indian/Alaska Native, 6 Asian Americans or Pacific Islanders, 1 Hispanic American), 15 international. 68 applicants, 32% accepted, 20 enrolled. In 2009, 18 master's, 7 doctorates awarded. Terminal master's awarded for partial completion of doctoral program. *Degree requirements:* For master's, comprehensive exam, thesis or alternative; for doctorate, one foreign language, thesis/dissertation, departmental qualifying exam. *Entrance requirements:* For master's, GRE, bachelor's degree in related area; for doctorate, GRE. Additional exam requirements/recommendations for international students: Required—TOEFL (minimum score 600 paper-based). *Application deadline:* For fall admission, 2/1 priority date for domestic students, 4/1 for international students; for spring admission, 11/1 for domestic students, 9/1 for international students. Applications are processed on a rolling basis. Application fee: $40 ($90 for international students). Electronic applications accepted. *Expenses:* Tuition, state resident: full-time $3744; part-time $156 per credit hour. Tuition, nonresident: full-time $13,577; part-time $565.70 per credit hour. Required fees: $2415; $90.10 per credit hour. *Financial support:* In 2009–10, 100 students received support, including 8 fellowships with full tuition reimbursements available (averaging $5,000 per year), 91 research assistantships (averaging $16,785 per year), 20 teaching assistantships with partial tuition reimbursements available (averaging $16,173 per year); career-related internships or fieldwork, institutionally sponsored loans, scholarships/grants, health care benefits, tuition waivers (partial), and unspecified assistantships also available. Financial award application deadline: 2/1; financial award applicants required to submit FAFSA. *Faculty research:* Radar meteorology, mesoscale meteorology, numerical weather prediction and data assimilation, regional climate change and climate variability, surface and boundary layer meteorology. Total annual research expenditures: $8.5 million. *Unit head:* Dr. Frederick H. Carr, Director, 405-325-6561, Fax: 405-325-7689, E-mail: fcarr@ou.edu. *Application contact:* Celia Jones, Coordinator, Academic Student Services, 405-325-6571, Fax: 405-325-7689, E-mail: cjones@ou.edu.

Utah State University, School of Graduate Studies, College of Agriculture, Department of Plants, Soils, and Biometeorology, Logan, UT 84322. Offers biometeorology (MS, PhD); ecology (MS, PhD); plant science (MS, PhD); soil science (MS, PhD). Part-time programs available. Terminal master's awarded for partial completion of doctoral program. *Degree requirements:* For master's, thesis; for doctorate, thesis/dissertation. *Entrance requirements:* For master's, GRE General Test, BS in plant, soil, atmospheric science, or related field; minimum GPA of 3.0; for doctorate, GRE General Test, minimum GPA of 3.0. Additional exam requirements/recommendations for international students: Required—TOEFL. Electronic applications accepted. *Faculty research:* Biotechnology and genomics, plant physiology and biology, nutrient and water efficient landscapes, physical-chemical-biological processes in soil, environmental biophysics and climate.

Yale University, Graduate School of Arts and Sciences, Department of Geology and Geophysics, New Haven, CT 06520. Offers biogeochemistry (PhD); climate dynamics (PhD); geochemistry (PhD); geophysics (PhD); meteorology (PhD); oceanography (PhD); paleontology (PhD); paleooceanography (PhD); petrology (PhD); tectonics (PhD). *Degree requirements:* For doctorate, thesis/dissertation. *Entrance requirements:* For doctorate, GRE General Test. Additional exam requirements/recommendations for international students: Required—TOEFL.

Section 6
Physics

This section contains a directory of institutions offering graduate work in physics, followed by in-depth entries submitted by institutions that chose to prepare detailed program descriptions. Additional information about programs listed in the directory but not augmented by an in-depth entry may be obtained by writing directly to the dean of a graduate school or chair of a department at the address given in the directory.

For programs offering related work, see all other areas in this book. In the other guides in this series:

Graduate Programs in the Biological Sciences
See *Biological and Biomedical Sciences* and *Biophysics*

Graduate Programs in Engineering & Applied Sciences
See *Aerospace/Aeronautical Engineering, Electrical and Computer Engineering, Energy and Power Engineering (Nuclear Engineering), Engineering and Applied Sciences, Engineering Physics, Materials Sciences and Engineering,* and *Mechanical Engineering and Mechanics*

Graduate Programs in Business, Education, Health, Information Studies, Law & Social Work
See *Allied Health* and *Optometry and Vision Sciences*

CONTENTS

Program Directories

Close-Ups

Acoustics

Penn State University Park, Graduate School, Intercollege Graduate Programs and College of Engineering, Intercollege Graduate Program in Acoustics, State College, University Park, PA 16802-1503. Offers M Eng, MS, PhD. *Unit head:* Dr. Anthony Atchley, Project Chair, 814-865-6364, Fax: 814-865-7595, E-mail: atchley@psu.edu. *Application contact:* Cynthia E. Nicosia, Director, Graduate Enrollment Services, 814-865-1795, Fax: 814-865-4627, E-mail: cey1@psu.edu.

Rensselaer Polytechnic Institute, Graduate School, School of Architecture, MS Program in Architectural Sciences, Troy, NY 12180-3590. Offers acoustics (MS); built ecologies (MS); lighting (MS). *Faculty:* 15 full-time (4 women), 8 part-time/adjunct (1 woman). *Students:* 20 full-time (2 women), 1 part-time (0 women); includes 1 Asian American or Pacific Islander, 1 Hispanic American, 4 international. Average age 21. 46 applicants, 54% accepted, 11 enrolled. In 2009, 22 master's awarded. *Degree requirements:* For master's, thesis. *Entrance requirements:* For master's, GRE General Test. Additional exam requirements/recommendations for international students: Required—TOEFL (minimum score 570 paper-based; 230 computer-based; 89 iBT), IELTS (minimum score 6.5). *Application deadline:* For fall admission, 1/1 priority date for domestic and international students. Applications are processed on a rolling basis. Application fee: $75. Electronic applications accepted. *Expenses:* Tuition: Full-time $38,100. *Financial support:* In 2009–10, 5 students received support, including 4 research assistantships with tuition reimbursements available (averaging $16,500 per year), 1 teaching assistantship with tuition reimbursement available (averaging $16,500 per year); institutionally sponsored loans and unspecified assistantships also available. Financial award application deadline: 1/1. *Faculty research:* Acoustics: modeling, auralization, signal processing; built ecologies: emerging materials and technologies, sustainable built environments; lighting: energy-efficient lighting, product development, daylighting, transportation, lighting, light and health, solid state lighting. *Unit head:* Prof. Ted Krueger, Head, Graduate Programs, 518-276-6466, E-mail: krueger@rpi.edu. *Application contact:* Erin Bermingham, Senior Program Administrator, 518-276-3986, Fax: 518-276-3034, E-mail: bermie@rpi.edu.

University of Massachusetts Dartmouth, Graduate School, College of Engineering, Department of Electrical and Computer Engineering, North Dartmouth, MA 02747-2300. Offers acoustics (Postbaccalaureate Certificate); communications (Postbaccalaureate Certificate); computer engineering (MS, PhD); computer systems engineering (Postbaccalaureate Certificate); digital signal processing (Postbaccalaureate Certificate); electrical engineering (MS, PhD); electrical engineering systems (Postbaccalaureate Certificate). Part-time programs available. *Faculty:* 18 full-time (3 women), 4 part-time/adjunct (0 women). *Students:* 39 full-time (11 women), 42 part-time (8 women); includes 8 minority (2 African Americans, 5 Asian Americans or Pacific Islanders, 1 Hispanic American), 46 international. Average age 28. 99 applicants, 80% accepted, 26 enrolled. In 2009, 34 master's, 1 doctorate, 3 other advanced degrees awarded. *Degree requirements:* For master's, culminating project or thesis; for doctorate, comprehensive exam, thesis/dissertation. *Entrance requirements:* For master's, GRE General Test, minimum undergraduate GPA of 3.0, 3 letters or recommendation; for doctorate, GRE. Additional exam requirements/recommendations for international students: Required—TOEFL (minimum score 550 paper-based; 213 computer-based). *Application deadline:* For fall admission, 2/1 priority date for domestic students, 12/1 for international students; for spring admission, 11/1 priority date for domestic students, 9/1 for international students. Applications are processed on a rolling basis. Application fee: $40 ($60 for international students). Electronic applications accepted. *Expenses:* Tuition, state resident: full-time $2071; part-time $86.29 per credit. Tuition, nonresident: full-time $8099; part-time $337.46 per credit. Required fees: $9446. Tuition and fees vary according to class time, course load and reciprocity agreements. *Financial support:* In 2009–10, 2 fellowships with full tuition reimbursements (averaging $16,000 per year), 14 research assistantships with full tuition reimbursements (averaging $11,096 per year), 9 teaching assistantships with full tuition reimbursements (averaging $12,500 per year) were awarded; Federal Work-Study and unspecified assistantships also available. Support available to part-time students. Financial award application deadline: 3/1; financial award applicants required to submit FAFSA. *Faculty research:* Speech acoustics, marine applications, signals and systems, applies electromagnetics, intelligent agency. Total annual research expenditures: $935,000. *Unit head:* Dr. Karen Payton, Director, 508-999-8434, Fax: 508-999-8489, E-mail: kpayton@umassd.edu. *Application contact:* Elan Turcotte-Shamski, Graduate Admissions Officer, 508-999-8604, Fax: 508-999-8183, E-mail: graduate@umassd.edu.

Applied Physics

Air Force Institute of Technology, Graduate School of Engineering and Management, Department of Engineering Physics, Dayton, OH 45433-7765. Offers applied physics (MS, PhD); electro-optics (MS, PhD); materials science (PhD); nuclear engineering (MS, PhD); space physics (MS). Part-time programs available. *Degree requirements:* For master's, thesis; for doctorate, thesis/dissertation. *Entrance requirements:* For master's and doctorate, GRE General Test, minimum GPA of 3.0, U.S. citizenship. *Faculty research:* High-energy lasers, space physics, nuclear weapon effects, semiconductor physics.

Alabama Agricultural and Mechanical University, School of Graduate Studies, School of Arts and Sciences, Department of Physics, Huntsville, AL 35811. Offers physics (MS, PhD), including applied physics (PhD), materials science (PhD), optics/lasers (PhD). Part-time and evening/weekend programs available. *Degree requirements:* For doctorate, thesis/dissertation. *Entrance requirements:* For master's and doctorate, GRE General Test. Additional exam requirements/recommendations for international students: Required—TOEFL (minimum score 500 paper-based; 173 computer-based; 61 iBT). Electronic applications accepted.

Brooklyn College of the City University of New York, Division of Graduate Studies, Department of Physics, Brooklyn, NY 11210-2889. Offers applied physics (MA); physics (MA, PhD). The department is a full participant in the PhD program; it offers a complete sequence of courses that are creditable toward the CUNY doctoral degree and a wide range of research opportunities in fulfillment of the doctoral dissertation requirements for that degree. Part-time programs available. Terminal master's awarded for partial completion of doctoral program. *Degree requirements:* For master's, comprehensive exam, thesis or alternative. *Entrance requirements:* For master's, 2 letters of recommendation, 12 credits in advanced physics; for doctorate, GRE. Additional exam requirements/recommendations for international students: Required—TOEFL. Electronic applications accepted.

California Institute of Technology, Division of Engineering and Applied Science, Option in Applied Physics, Pasadena, CA 91125-0001. Offers MS, PhD. *Faculty:* 10 full-time (1 woman). *Students:* 42 full-time (7 women). 149 applicants, 17% accepted, 7 enrolled. In 2009, 1 master's, 13 doctorates awarded. *Degree requirements:* For doctorate, thesis/dissertation. *Application deadline:* For fall admission, 1/1 for domestic students. Application fee: $0. Electronic applications accepted. *Financial support:* In 2009–10, 6 fellowships, 19 research assistantships, 11 teaching assistantships were awarded. *Faculty research:* Solid-state electronics, quantum electronics, plasmas, linear and nonlinear laser optics, electromagnetic theory. *Unit head:* Dr. Sandra M. Troian, Option Representative, 626-395-3362, E-mail: stroian@caltech.edu. *Application contact:* Natalie Gilmore, Assistant Dean of Graduate Studies, 626-395-3812, Fax: 626-577-9246, E-mail: ngilmore@caltech.edu.

Carnegie Mellon University, Mellon College of Science, Department of Physics, Pittsburgh, PA 15213-3891. Offers applied physics (PhD); physics (MS, PhD). *Degree requirements:* For doctorate, thesis/dissertation, qualifying exam. *Entrance requirements:* For doctorate, GRE General Test, GRE Subject Test. Additional exam requirements/recommendations for international students: Required—TOEFL. Electronic applications accepted. *Faculty research:* Astrophysics, condensed matter physics, biological physics, medium energy and nuclear physics, high-energy physics.

Christopher Newport University, Graduate Studies, Department of Physics, Computer Science, and Engineering, Newport News, VA 23606-2998. Offers applied physics and computer science (MS). Part-time and evening/weekend programs available. *Faculty:* 6 full-time (0 women), 3 part-time/adjunct (2 women). *Students:* 6 full-time (1 woman), 23 part-time (2 women); includes 2 minority (both African Americans). Average age 29. 10 applicants, 100% accepted, 7 enrolled. In 2009, 7 master's awarded. *Degree requirements:* For master's, comprehensive exam (for some programs), thesis optional. *Entrance requirements:* For master's, GRE General Test, minimum GPA of 3.0. Additional exam requirements/recommendations for international students: Required—TOEFL (minimum score 580 paper-based; 237 computer-based; 92 iBT). *Application deadline:* For fall admission, 8/15 priority date for domestic students, 4/1 for international students; for spring admission, 10/15 for domestic students, 10/1 for international students. Applications are processed on a rolling basis. Application fee: $45. Electronic applications accepted. *Expenses:* Tuition, area resident: Part-time $384 per credit hour. Tuition, state resident: part-time $384 per credit hour. Tuition, nonresident: part-time $701 per credit hour. *Financial support:* In 2009–10, 3 research assistantships with full and partial tuition reimbursements (averaging $2,000 per year) were awarded; fellowships with full tuition reimbursements, career-related internships or fieldwork, Federal Work-Study, and unspecified assistantships also available. Support available to part-time students. Financial award application deadline: 2/1; financial award applicants required to submit FAFSA. *Faculty research:* Advanced programming methodologies, experimental nuclear physics, computer architecture, semiconductor nanophysics, laser and optical fiber sensors. *Unit head:* Dr. Antonio Siochi, Coordinator, 757-594-7569, Fax: 757-594-7919, E-mail: siochi@cnu.edu. *Application contact:* Lyn Sawyer, Associate Director, Graduate Admissions and Records, 757-594-7544, Fax: 757-594-7649, E-mail: gradstdy@cnu.edu.

Colorado School of Mines, Graduate School, Department of Physics, Golden, CO 80401. Offers applied physics (MS, PhD). Part-time programs available. *Faculty:* 26 full-time (1 woman), 7 part-time/adjunct (0 women). *Students:* 47 full-time (5 women), 4 part-time (0 women); includes 5 minority (2 Asian Americans or Pacific Islanders, 3 Hispanic Americans), 7 international. Average age 30. 57 applicants, 44% accepted, 19 enrolled. In 2009, 6 master's, 4 doctorates awarded. *Degree requirements:* For master's, thesis (for some programs); for doctorate, comprehensive exam, thesis/dissertation. *Entrance requirements:* For master's and doctorate, GRE General Test, GRE Subject Test. Additional exam requirements/recommendations for international students: Required—TOEFL (minimum score 550 paper-based; 213 computer-based; 80 iBT). *Application deadline:* For fall admission, 1/15 priority date for domestic and international students; for spring admission, 9/1 priority date for domestic and international students. Application fee: $50 ($70 for international students). Electronic applications accepted. *Expenses:* Tuition, state resident: full-time $10,584; part-time $588 per credit hour. Tuition, nonresident: full-time $24,750; part-time $1375 per credit hour. Required fees: $1654; $827.10 per semester. *Financial support:* In 2009–10, 49 students received support, including 1 fellowship with full tuition reimbursement available (averaging $20,000 per year), 32 research assistantships with full tuition reimbursements available (averaging $20,000 per year), 16 teaching assistantships with full tuition reimbursements available (averaging $20,000 per year); scholarships/grants, health care benefits, and unspecified assistantships also available. Financial award application deadline: 1/15; financial award applicants required to submit FAFSA. *Faculty research:* Light scattering, low-energy nuclear physics, high fusion plasma diagnostics, laser operations, mathematical physics. Total annual research expenditures: $2.9 million. *Unit head:* Dr. Thomas Furtak, Department Head, 303-273-3843, Fax: 303-273-3919, E-mail: tfurtak@mines.edu. *Application contact:* Dr. Tim Ohno, Professor, 303-273-3847, Fax: 303-273-3919, E-mail: tohno@mines.edu.

Columbia University, Fu Foundation School of Engineering and Applied Science, Department of Applied Physics and Applied Mathematics, New York, NY 10027. Offers applied physics (Eng Sc D); applied physics and applied mathematics (MS, PhD, Engr); materials science and engineering (MS, Eng Sc D, PhD); medical physics (MS). Part-time programs available. Post-baccalaureate distance learning degree programs offered (no on-campus study). *Faculty:* 19 full-time (1 woman), 3 part-time/adjunct (1 woman). *Students:* 127 full-time (24 women), 44 part-time (7 women); includes 12 minority (2 African Americans, 1 American Indian/Alaska Native, 8 Asian Americans or Pacific Islanders, 1 Hispanic American), 73 international. Average age 27. 300 applicants, 35% accepted, 45 enrolled. In 2009, 31 master's, 10 doctorates awarded. Terminal master's awarded for partial completion of doctoral program. *Degree requirements:* For master's, comprehensive exam; for doctorate, thesis/dissertation, qualifying exam. *Entrance requirements:* For master's, GRE General Test, GRE Subject Test (strongly recommended); for doctorate, GRE General Test, GRE Subject Test (physics); for Engr, GRE General Test. Additional exam requirements/recommendations for international students: Required—TOEFL. *Application deadline:* For fall admission, 12/1 priority date for domestic and international students; for spring admission, 10/1 priority date for domestic and international students. Application fee: $70. Electronic applications accepted. *Financial support:* In 2009–10, 70 students received support, including 4 fellowships with full and partial tuition reimbursements available, 50 research assistantships with full tuition reimbursements available (averaging $30,000 per year), 18 teaching assistantships with full tuition reimbursements available (averaging $30,000 per year); health care benefits and unspecified assistantships also available. Financial award application deadline: 12/1; financial award applicants required to submit FAFSA. *Faculty research:* Plasma, solid state, optical and laser physics; atmospheric, oceanic and earth physics; computational math and applied mathematics; materials science and engineering. *Unit head:* Dr. Irving P. Herman, Professor and Chair, 212-854-4457, E-mail: seasinfo.apam@columbia.edu. *Application contact:* Montserrat Fernandez-Pinkley, Student Services Coordinator, 212-854-4457, Fax: 212-854-8257, E-mail: mf2157@columbia.edu.

See Close-Up on page 215.

Cornell University, Graduate School, Graduate Fields of Engineering, Field of Applied Physics, Ithaca, NY 14853-0001. Offers applied physics (PhD); engineering physics (M Eng). *Faculty:* 48 full-time (5 women). *Students:* 72 full-time (10 women); includes 10 minority (8 Asian Americans or Pacific Islanders, 2 Hispanic Americans), 30 international. Average age 26. 153

applicants, 37% accepted, 18 enrolled. In 2009, 15 master's, 16 doctorates awarded. *Degree requirements:* For doctorate, comprehensive exam, thesis/dissertation, written exams. *Entrance requirements:* For master's, GRE General Test, 3 letters of recommendation; for doctorate, GRE General Test, GRE Subject Test (physics), GRE Writing Assessment, 3 letters of recommendation. Additional exam requirements/recommendations for international students: Required—TOEFL (minimum score 600 paper-based; 250 computer-based; 77 iBT). *Application deadline:* For fall admission, 1/15 for domestic students. Application fee: $70. Electronic applications accepted. *Expenses:* Tuition: Full-time $29,500. Required fees: $70. Full-time tuition and fees vary according to degree level, program and student level. *Financial support:* In 2009–10, 70 students received support, including 1 fellowship with full tuition reimbursement available, 3 research assistantships with full tuition reimbursements available, 8 teaching assistantships with full tuition reimbursements available; institutionally sponsored loans, scholarships/grants, health care benefits, tuition waivers (full and partial), and unspecified assistantships also available. *Faculty research:* Quantum and nonlinear optics, plasma physics, solid state physics, condensed matter physics and nanotechnology, electron and x-ray spectroscopy. *Unit head:* Graduate Faculty Representative, 607-255-0638. *Application contact:* Graduate Field Assistant, 607-255-0638, E-mail: aep_info@cornell.edu.

DePaul University, College of Liberal Arts and Sciences, Department of Physics, Chicago, IL 60604-2287. Offers applied physics (MS). Part-time and evening/weekend programs available. *Faculty:* 6 full-time (2 women), 3 part-time/adjunct (0 women). *Students:* 10 full-time (5 women), 3 part-time (1 woman); includes 2 minority (1 African American, 1 Hispanic American), 1 international. Average age 23. 12 applicants, 42% accepted, 3 enrolled. In 2009, 3 master's awarded. *Degree requirements:* For master's, thesis, oral exams. *Entrance requirements:* For master's, 2 letters of recommendation, BA in physics or closely related field. Additional exam requirements/recommendations for international students: Required—TOEFL. *Application deadline:* For fall admission, 5/1 priority date for domestic students, 4/1 priority date for international students. Applications are processed on a rolling basis. Application fee: $25. Electronic applications accepted. *Expenses:* Tuition: Full-time $37,525; part-time $620 per credit hour. *Financial support:* In 2009–10, teaching assistantships with full tuition reimbursements (averaging $9,000 per year); tuition waivers (full) also available. *Faculty research:* Optics, solid-state physics, cosmology, atomic physics, nuclear physics. Total annual research expenditures: $54,000. *Unit head:* Dr. Christopher G. Goedde, Chairman, 773-325-7330, Fax: 773-325-7334, E-mail: egoedde@condor.depaul.edu. *Application contact:* Dr. Jesus Pando, Associate Professor, 773-325-7330, Fax: 773-325-7334.

George Mason University, College of Science, Department of Physics and Astronomy, Fairfax, VA 22030. Offers applied and engineering physics (MS). *Degree requirements:* For master's, thesis optional. *Entrance requirements:* For master's, minimum GPA of 2.75 in last 60 hours of course work. Electronic applications accepted. *Expenses:* Tuition, state resident: full-time $7568; part-time $315.33 per credit hour. Tuition, nonresident: full-time $21,704; part-time $904.33 per credit hour. Required fees: $2184; $91 per credit hour.

Harvard University, Graduate School of Arts and Sciences, Department of Physics, Cambridge, MA 02138. Offers experimental physics (PhD); medical engineering/medical physics (PhD), including applied physics, engineering sciences, physics; theoretical physics (PhD). *Degree requirements:* For doctorate, thesis/dissertation, final exams, laboratory experience. *Entrance requirements:* For doctorate, GRE General Test, GRE Subject Test. Additional exam requirements/recommendations for international students: Required—TOEFL. *Expenses:* Tuition: Full-time $33,696. Required fees: $1126. Full-time tuition and fees vary according to program. *Faculty research:* Particle physics, condensed matter physics, atomic physics.

Harvard University, Graduate School of Arts and Sciences, School of Engineering and Applied Sciences, Cambridge, MA 02138. Offers applied mathematics (ME, SM, PhD); applied physics (ME, SM, PhD); computer science (ME, SM, PhD); engineering science (ME); engineering sciences (SM, PhD). Part-time programs available. *Faculty:* 57 full-time (9 women), 9 part-time/adjunct (1 woman). *Students:* 355 full-time (89 women), 3 part-time (0 women); includes 50 minority (4 African Americans, 40 Asian Americans or Pacific Islanders, 6 Hispanic Americans), 166 international. 1,617 applicants, 11% accepted, 88 enrolled. In 2009, 67 master's, 53 doctorates awarded. Terminal master's awarded for partial completion of doctoral program. *Degree requirements:* For master's, thesis optional; for doctorate, comprehensive exam, thesis/dissertation. *Entrance requirements:* For master's and doctorate, GRE General Test, GRE Subject Test (recommended), 3 letters of recommendation. Additional exam requirements/recommendations for international students: Required—TOEFL (minimum score 80 iBT). *Application deadline:* For fall admission, 12/31 priority date for domestic and international students. Application fee: $105. Electronic applications accepted. *Expenses:* Tuition: Full-time $33,696. Required fees: $1126. Full-time tuition and fees vary according to program. *Financial support:* In 2009–10, 115 fellowships with full tuition reimbursements (averaging $21,375 per year), 184 research assistantships with full and partial tuition reimbursements (averaging $28,500 per year), 76 teaching assistantships with full and partial tuition reimbursements (averaging $5,563 per year) were awarded; Federal Work-Study, institutionally sponsored loans, traineeships, and health care benefits also available. *Faculty research:* Applied mathematics, applied physics, computer science and electrical engineering, environmental engineering, mechanical and biomedical engineering. Total annual research expenditures: $43.8 million. *Unit head:* Cherry Murray, Dean, 617-495-5829, Fax: 617-495-5264, E-mail: dean@seas.harvard.edu. *Application contact:* Office of Admissions and Financial Aid, 617-495-5315, E-mail: admissions@seas.harvard.edu.

Idaho State University, Office of Graduate Studies, College of Arts and Sciences, Department of Physics, Pocatello, ID 83209-8106. Offers applied physics (PhD); health physics (MS); physics (MNS). Part-time programs available. *Faculty:* 7 full-time (1 woman), 1 part-time/adjunct (0 women). *Students:* 43 full-time (8 women), 28 part-time (5 women); includes 3 minority (1 African American, 2 Hispanic Americans), 27 international. Average age 32. In 2009, 2 doctorates awarded. *Degree requirements:* For master's, comprehensive exam, thesis (for some programs), oral exam (for some programs); for doctorate, comprehensive exam, thesis/dissertation (for some programs), oral exam, written qualifying exam in physics or health physics after 1st year. *Entrance requirements:* For master's, GRE General Test, 3 letters of recommendation, BS or BA in physics, teaching certificate (MNS); for doctorate, GRE General Test (minimum 50th percentile), 3 letters of recommendation, statement of career goals. Additional exam requirements/recommendations for international students: Required—TOEFL (minimum score 550 paper-based; 213 computer-based; 80 iBT). *Application deadline:* For fall admission, 7/1 for domestic students, 6/1 for international students; for spring admission, 12/1 for domestic students, 11/1 for international students. Applications are processed on a rolling basis. Application fee: $55. Electronic applications accepted. *Expenses:* Tuition, state resident: full-time $3318; part-time $297 per credit hour. Tuition, nonresident: full-time $13,120; part-time $437 per credit hour. Required fees: $2530. Tuition and fees vary according to program. *Financial support:* In 2009–10, 38 research assistantships with full and partial tuition reimbursements (averaging $13,169 per year), 7 teaching assistantships with full and partial tuition reimbursements (averaging $10,841 per year) were awarded; fellowships with full and partial tuition reimbursements, career-related internships or fieldwork, Federal Work-Study, institutionally sponsored loans, scholarships/grants, health care benefits, tuition waivers (full), and unspecified assistantships also available. Support available to part-time students. Financial award application deadline: 1/1; financial award applicants required to submit FAFSA. *Faculty research:* Ion beam applications, low-energy nuclear physics, relativity and cosmology, observational astronomy. *Unit head:* Dr. Richard Brey, Interim Chair, 208-282-3467, Fax: 208-282-4649, E-mail: brey@physics.isu.edu. *Application contact:* Tami Carson, Graduate School Technical Records Specialist, 208-282-2150, Fax: 208-282-4847, E-mail: carstami@isu.edu.

Iowa State University of Science and Technology, Graduate College, College of Liberal Arts and Sciences, Department of Physics and Astronomy, Ames, IA 50011. Offers applied physics (MS, PhD); astrophysics (MS, PhD); condensed matter physics (MS, PhD); high energy physics (MS, PhD); nuclear physics (MS, PhD); physics (MS, PhD). Part-time programs available. *Faculty:* 46 full-time (3 women), 4 part-time/adjunct (0 women). *Students:* 94 full-time (21 women), 4 part-time (0 women); includes 3 minority (all Asian Americans or Pacific Islanders), 56 international. 185 applicants, 32% accepted, 15 enrolled. In 2009, 4 master's, 7 doctorates awarded. Terminal master's awarded for partial completion of doctoral program. *Degree requirements:* For master's, thesis (for some programs); for doctorate, thesis/dissertation. *Entrance requirements:* For master's and doctorate, GRE General Test, GRE Subject Test (physics). Additional exam requirements/recommendations for international students: Required—TOEFL (minimum score 550 paper-based; 79 iBT) or IELTS (minimum score 6.5). *Application deadline:* For fall admission, 2/15 priority date for domestic and international students; for spring admission, 10/15 for domestic and international students. Applications are processed on a rolling basis. Application fee: $40 ($90 for international students). Electronic applications accepted. *Expenses:* Tuition, state resident: full-time $6716. Tuition, nonresident: full-time $8908. Tuition and fees vary according to course level, course load, program and student level. *Financial support:* In 2009–10, 58 research assistantships with full and partial tuition reimbursements (averaging $17,000 per year), 33 teaching assistantships with full and partial tuition reimbursements (averaging $16,000 per year) were awarded; fellowships, Federal Work-Study, institutionally sponsored loans, scholarships/grants, health care benefits, and unspecified assistantships also available. Support available to part-time students. Financial award application deadline: 2/15. *Faculty research:* Condensed-matter physics, including superconductivity and new materials; high-energy and nuclear physics; astronomy and astrophysics; atmospheric and environmental physics. Total annual research expenditures: $8.8 million. *Unit head:* Dr. Joseph Shinar, Chair, 515-294-3455, Fax: 515-294-6027, E-mail: phys_astro@iastate.edu. *Application contact:* Dr. Steven Kawaler, Director of Graduate Education, 515-294-9728, E-mail: phys_astro@iastate.edu.

The Johns Hopkins University, Engineering for Professionals, Part-time Program in Applied Physics, Baltimore, MD 21218-2699. Offers MS, Post-Master's Certificate. Part-time and evening/weekend programs available. *Faculty:* 10 part-time/adjunct (0 women). *Students:* 3 full-time (1 woman), 59 part-time (15 women); includes 11 minority (5 African Americans, 3 Asian Americans or Pacific Islanders, 3 Hispanic Americans). Average age 30. In 2009, 19 master's awarded. *Application deadline:* Applications are processed on a rolling basis. Application fee: $75. Electronic applications accepted. *Financial support:* Institutionally sponsored loans available. *Unit head:* Dr. Harry K. Charles, Chair, 443-778-8050, E-mail: harry.charles@jhuapl.edu. *Application contact:* Priyanka Dwivedi, Admissions Manager, 410-516-2300, Fax: 410-579-8049, E-mail: pdwived1@jhu.edu.

Laurentian University, School of Graduate Studies and Research, Programme in Physics, Sudbury, ON P3E 2C6, Canada. Offers M Sc. Part-time programs available. *Degree requirements:* For master's, thesis or alternative. *Entrance requirements:* For master's, honors degree with second class or better. *Faculty research:* Solar neutrino physics and astrophysics, applied acoustics and ultrasonics, powder science and technology, solid state physics, theoretical physics.

Mississippi State University, College of Arts and Sciences, Department of Physics and Astronomy, Mississippi State, MS 39762. Offers engineering (PhD), including applied physics; physics (MS). Part-time programs available. *Faculty:* 13 full-time (0 women). *Students:* 25 full-time (5 women); includes 2 minority (1 African American, 1 Hispanic American), 20 international. Average age 26. 45 applicants, 24% accepted, 9 enrolled. In 2009, 7 master's awarded. *Degree requirements:* For master's, thesis optional, comprehensive oral or written exam; for doctorate, thesis/dissertation, comprehensive oral or written exam. *Entrance requirements:* For master's, GRE, minimum GPA of 2.75 on last two year's of undergraduate courses; for doctorate, GRE. Additional exam requirements/recommendations for international students: Required—TOEFL (minimum score 475 paper-based; 153 computer-based; 53 iBT); Recommended—IELTS (minimum score 4.5). *Application deadline:* For fall admission, 7/1 priority date for domestic students, 5/1 for international students; for spring admission, 11/1 priority date for domestic students, 9/1 for international students. Applications are processed on a rolling basis. Application fee: $40. Electronic applications accepted. *Expenses:* Tuition, state resident: full-time $2575.50; part-time $286.25 per credit hour. Tuition, nonresident: full-time $6510; part-time $723.50 per credit hour. Tuition and fees vary according to course load. *Financial support:* In 2009–10, 22 research assistantships with full tuition reimbursements (averaging $12,719 per year), 16 teaching assistantships with full tuition reimbursements (averaging $12,139 per year) were awarded; Federal Work-Study, institutionally sponsored loans, and unspecified assistantships also available. Financial award application deadline: 3/15; financial award applicants required to submit FAFSA. *Faculty research:* Atomic/molecular spectroscopy, theoretical optics, gamma-ray astronomy, experimental nuclear physics, computational physics. Total annual research expenditures: $2.3 million. *Unit head:* Dr. Mark A. Novotny, Department Head and Professor, 662-325-2806, Fax: 662-325-8898, E-mail: man40@ra.msstate.edu. *Application contact:* Dr. David Monts, Professor and Graduate Coordinator, 662-325-2931, Fax: 662-325-8898, E-mail: physics@msstate.edu.

Naval Postgraduate School, Graduate Programs, Department of Physics, Monterey, CA 93943. Offers applied physics (MS); engineering acoustics (MS); physics (MS, PhD). Program only open to commissioned officers of the United States and friendly nations and selected United States federal civilian employees. Part-time programs available. *Degree requirements:* For master's, thesis; for doctorate, one foreign language, thesis/dissertation.

New Jersey Institute of Technology, Office of Graduate Studies, College of Science and Liberal Arts, Department of Physics, Program in Applied Physics, Newark, NJ 07102. Offers MS, PhD. Part-time and evening/weekend programs available. Terminal master's awarded for partial completion of doctoral program. *Degree requirements:* For master's, thesis optional; for doctorate, thesis/dissertation, residency. *Entrance requirements:* For master's, GRE General Test; for doctorate, GRE General Test, minimum graduate GPA of 3.5. Additional exam requirements/recommendations for international students: Required—TOEFL (minimum score 550 paper-based; 213 computer-based; 79 iBT). Electronic applications accepted.

Northern Arizona University, Graduate College, College of Engineering, Forestry and Natural Sciences, Department of Physics and Astronomy, Flagstaff, AZ 86011. Offers applied physics (MS); science education (MAT). Part-time programs available. *Faculty:* 13 full-time (2 women). *Students:* 13 full-time (5 women), 4 part-time (2 women); includes 2 minority (1 American Indian/Alaska Native, 1 Asian American or Pacific Islander), 1 international. Average age 37. 14 applicants, 71% accepted, 7 enrolled. In 2009, 7 master's awarded. *Degree requirements:* For master's, thesis optional. *Entrance requirements:* For master's, GRE. Additional exam requirements/recommendations for international students: Required—TOEFL (minimum score 550 paper-based; 213 computer-based; 80 iBT), IELTS (minimum score 7), or a bachelor's degree from an English-speaking university and demonstrated proficiency. *Application deadline:* For fall admission, 3/15 priority date for domestic students, 9/1 for international students; for spring admission, 10/15 priority date for domestic students. Applications are processed on a rolling basis. Application fee: $65. Electronic applications accepted. *Financial support:* In 2009–10, 1 research assistantship with partial tuition reimbursement (averaging $12,390 per year), 9 teaching assistantships with partial tuition reimbursements (averaging $12,390 per year) were awarded; career-related internships or fieldwork, Federal Work-Study, health care benefits, tuition waivers (full and partial), and unspecified assistantships also available. Support available to part-time students. Financial award application deadline: 3/30; financial award applicants required to submit FAFSA. *Unit head:* Dr. Nadine Barlow, Chair, 928-523-5452, Fax: 928-523-1371, E-mail: nadine.barlow@nau.edu. *Application contact:* Dr. Gary Bowman, Graduate Coordinator, 928-523-1114, Fax: 928-523-1371, E-mail: gary.bowman@nau.edu.

Applied Physics

Oregon State University, Graduate School, College of Science, Department of Physics, Corvallis, OR 97331. Offers applied physics (MS); physics (MA, MS, PhD). Part-time programs available. *Faculty:* 15 full-time (4 women). *Students:* 30 full-time (7 women), 4 part-time (0 women); includes 2 minority (1 Asian American or Pacific Islander, 1 Hispanic American), 8 international. Average age 29. In 2009, 2 master's, 3 doctorates awarded. Terminal master's awarded for partial completion of doctoral program. *Degree requirements:* For master's, thesis optional, qualifying exam; for doctorate, thesis/dissertation, qualifying exam. *Entrance requirements:* For master's and doctorate, minimum GPA of 3.0 in last 90 hours. Additional exam requirements/recommendations for international students: Required—TOEFL. *Application deadline:* For fall admission, 3/1 for domestic students. Application fee: $50. *Expenses:* Tuition, state resident: full-time $9774; part-time $362 per credit. Tuition, nonresident: full-time $15,849; part-time $587 per credit. Required fees: $1639. Full-time tuition and fees vary according to course load and program. *Financial support:* Fellowships, research assistantships, teaching assistantships, Federal Work-Study and institutionally sponsored loans available. Support available to part-time students. Financial award application deadline: 2/1. *Unit head:* Dr. Henri J. F. Jansen, Chair, 541-737-1668, Fax: 541-737-1683, E-mail: physics.chair@science.oregonstate.edu. *Application contact:* Dr. Henri J. F. Jansen, Chair, 541-737-1668, Fax: 541-737-1683, E-mail: physics.chair@science.oregonstate.edu.

Pittsburg State University, Graduate School, College of Arts and Sciences, Department of Physics, Pittsburg, KS 66762. Offers applied physics (MS); physics (MS); professional physics (MS). *Degree requirements:* For master's, thesis or alternative. *Expenses:* Tuition, state resident: full-time $4212; part-time $176 per credit. Tuition, nonresident: full-time $11,530; part-time $480 per credit. Required fees: $940; $43 per credit. Tuition and fees vary according to course level, course load, degree level, campus/location, reciprocity agreements and student level.

Rensselaer Polytechnic Institute, Graduate School, School of Science, Department of Physics, Applied Physics and Astronomy, Troy, NY 12180-3590. Offers astronomy (MS); physics (MS, PhD). *Faculty:* 24 full-time (4 women), 4 part-time/adjunct (0 women). *Students:* 64 full-time (12 women), 2 part-time (0 women); includes 1 African American, 2 Asian Americans or Pacific Islanders. Average age 25. 140 applicants, 51% accepted, 17 enrolled. In 2009, 5 master's, 13 doctorates awarded. *Degree requirements:* For doctorate, thesis/dissertation. *Entrance requirements:* For master's and doctorate, GRE General Test, GRE Subject Test. Additional exam requirements/recommendations for international students: Required—TOEFL (minimum score 600 paper-based; 250 computer-based). *Application deadline:* For fall admission, 1/1 priority date for domestic and international students; for spring admission, 8/15 priority date for domestic and international students. Applications are processed on a rolling basis. Application fee: $75. Electronic applications accepted. *Expenses:* Tuition: Full-time $38,100. *Financial support:* In 2009–10, 64 students received support, including 4 fellowships with full tuition reimbursements available (averaging $30,000 per year), 37 research assistantships with full tuition reimbursements available (averaging $21,000 per year), 25 teaching assistantships with full tuition reimbursements available (averaging $21,000 per year); career-related internships or fieldwork and institutionally sponsored loans also available. Financial award application deadline: 2/1. *Faculty research:* Astrophysics, condensed matter, nuclear physics, optics, biophysics. Total annual research expenditures: $7.3 million. *Unit head:* Dr. Gwo-Ching Wang, Chair, 518-276-8387, Fax: 518-276-6680, E-mail: wangg@rpi.edu. *Application contact:* Dr. Shengbai Zhang, Chair, Graduate Recruitment Committee, 518-276-8391, Fax: 518-276-6680, E-mail: mcquade@rpi.edu.

Rice University, Rice Quantum Institute, Houston, TX 77251-1892. Offers MS, PhD. *Degree requirements:* For master's, thesis; for doctorate, thesis/dissertation. *Entrance requirements:* For master's and doctorate, GRE General Test, GRE Subject Test (physics), minimum GPA of 3.0. Additional exam requirements/recommendations for international students: Required—TOEFL (minimum score 600 paper-based; 250 computer-based; 90 iBT). Electronic applications accepted. *Faculty research:* Nanotechnology, solid state materials, atomic physics, thin films.

Rutgers, The State University of New Jersey, Newark, Graduate School, Program in Applied Physics, Newark, NJ 07102. Offers MS, PhD. *Entrance requirements:* For master's and doctorate, GRE. Additional exam requirements/recommendations for international students: Required—TOEFL.

Southern Illinois University Carbondale, Graduate School, College of Science, Department of Physics, Carbondale, IL 62901-4701. Offers MS, PhD. *Degree requirements:* For master's, one foreign language, thesis. *Entrance requirements:* For master's, minimum GPA of 2.7. Additional exam requirements/recommendations for international students: Required—TOEFL. *Faculty research:* Atomic, molecular, nuclear, and mathematical physics; statistical mechanics; solid-state and low-temperature physics; rheology; material science.

Stanford University, School of Humanities and Sciences, Department of Applied Physics, Stanford, CA 94305-9991. Offers MS, PhD. Terminal master's awarded for partial completion of doctoral program. *Degree requirements:* For doctorate, thesis/dissertation. *Entrance requirements:* For master's and doctorate, GRE General Test, GRE Subject Test. Additional exam requirements/recommendations for international students: Required—TOEFL. Electronic applications accepted. *Expenses:* Tuition: Full-time $37,380; part-time $2760 per quarter. Required fees: $501.

State University of New York at Binghamton, Graduate School, School of Arts and Sciences, Department of Physics, Applied Physics, and Astronomy, Binghamton, NY 13902-6000. Offers applied physics (MS); physics (MA, MS). *Faculty:* 9 full-time (0 women), 4 part-time/adjunct (1 woman). *Students:* 9 full-time (1 woman), 1 part-time (0 women), 2 international. Average age 26. 14 applicants, 71% accepted, 4 enrolled. In 2009, 3 master's awarded. *Degree requirements:* For master's, thesis or alternative. *Entrance requirements:* For master's, GRE General Test, GRE Subject Test. Additional exam requirements/recommendations for international students: Required—TOEFL (minimum score 550 paper-based; 213 computer-based; 80 iBT). *Application deadline:* For fall admission, 2/15 priority date for domestic and international students; for spring admission, 10/15 priority date for domestic and international students. Applications are processed on a rolling basis. Application fee: $60. Electronic applications accepted. *Financial support:* In 2009–10, fellowships (averaging $11,000 per year), 13 teaching assistantships with full tuition reimbursements (averaging $11,000 per year) were awarded; career-related internships or fieldwork, Federal Work-Study, institutionally sponsored loans, scholarships/grants, health care benefits, and unspecified assistantships also available. Financial award application deadline: 2/15; financial award applicants required to submit FAFSA. *Unit head:* Dr. Eric Cotts, Chairperson, 607-777-4371, E-mail: ecotts@binghamton.edu. *Application contact:* Victoria Williams, Recruiting and Admissions Coordinator, 607-777-2151, Fax: 607-777-2501, E-mail: vwilliam@binghamton.edu.

Texas A&M University, College of Science, Department of Physics, College Station, TX 77843. Offers applied physics (PhD); physics (MS, PhD). *Faculty:* 48. *Students:* 146 full-time (24 women), 7 part-time (1 woman); includes 23 minority (2 African Americans, 2 American Indian/Alaska Native, 7 Asian Americans or Pacific Islanders, 12 Hispanic Americans), 79 international. In 2009, 5 master's, 16 doctorates awarded. Terminal master's awarded for partial completion of doctoral program. *Degree requirements:* For master's, thesis (for some programs); for doctorate, thesis/dissertation. *Entrance requirements:* For master's and doctorate, GRE General Test, GRE Subject Test. Additional exam requirements/recommendations for international students: Required—TOEFL. *Application deadline:* For fall admission, 3/1 priority date for domestic students; for spring admission, 8/1 for domestic students. Application fee: $50 ($75 for international students). Electronic applications accepted. *Expenses:* Tuition, state resident: full-time $3991.32; part-time $221.74 per credit hour. Tuition, nonresident: full-time $9049; part-time $502.74 per credit hour. *Financial support:* In 2009–10, research assistantships (averaging $16,200 per year), teaching assistantships (averaging $16,200 per year) were awarded; fellowships also available. Financial award application deadline: 3/1; financial award applicants required to submit FAFSA. *Faculty research:* Condensed-matter, atomic/molecular, high-energy, and nuclear physics; quantum optics. *Unit head:* Dr. Edward S. Fry, Head, 979-845-1910, E-mail: fry@physics.tamu.edu. *Application contact:* Dr. George W. Kattawar, Professor, 979-845-1180, Fax: 979-845-2590, E-mail: kattawar@physics.tamu.edu.

Texas Tech University, Graduate School, College of Arts and Sciences, Department of Physics, Lubbock, TX 79409. Offers applied physics (MS); physics (MS, PhD). Part-time programs available. *Faculty:* 14 full-time (1 woman), 1 part-time/adjunct (0 women). *Students:* 46 full-time (11 women), 2 part-time (0 women); includes 5 minority (1 African American, 2 Asian Americans or Pacific Islanders, 2 Hispanic Americans), 30 international. Average age 32. 72 applicants, 35% accepted, 15 enrolled. In 2009, 5 master's, 1 doctorate awarded. *Degree requirements:* For master's, variable foreign language requirement, thesis or alternative; for doctorate, variable foreign language requirement, thesis/dissertation. *Entrance requirements:* For master's and doctorate, GRE General Test. Additional exam requirements/recommendations for international students: Required—TOEFL (minimum score 550 paper-based; 213 computer-based). *Application deadline:* For fall admission, 3/1 priority date for international students; for spring admission, 11/1 priority date for international students. Applications are processed on a rolling basis. Application fee: $50 ($75 for international students). Electronic applications accepted. *Expenses:* Tuition, state resident: full-time $5100; part-time $213 per credit hour. Tuition, nonresident: full-time $11,748; part-time $490 per credit hour. Required fees: $2298; $50 per credit hour. $555 per semester. *Financial support:* In 2009–10, 12 teaching assistantships with partial tuition reimbursements (averaging $23,158 per year) were awarded; research assistantships with partial tuition reimbursements, career-related internships or fieldwork, Federal Work-Study, and institutionally sponsored loans also available. Support available to part-time students. Financial award application deadline: 4/15; financial award applicants required to submit FAFSA. *Faculty research:* Biophysics, high energy and nuclear physics, condensed matter physics, atomic and molecular physics, physics education. Total annual research expenditures: $1 million. *Unit head:* Dr. Roger Lichti, Chair, 806-742-3767, Fax: 806-742-1182, E-mail: roger.lichti@ttu.edu. *Application contact:* Dr. Mahdi Sanati, Graduate Recruiter, 806-742-3767, Fax: 806-742-1182, E-mail: m.sanati@ttu.edu.

The University of Arizona, Graduate College, College of Science, Department of Physics, Program in Applied and Industrial Physics, Tucson, AZ 85721. Offers PMS. Part-time programs available. *Students:* 5 full-time (1 woman), 1 part-time (0 women), 2 international. Average age 30. 13 applicants, 38% accepted, 5 enrolled. In 2009, 4 master's awarded. *Degree requirements:* For master's, thesis or alternative, internship, colloquium, business courses. *Entrance requirements:* Additional exam requirements/recommendations for international students: Required—TOEFL (minimum score 550 paper-based; 213 computer-based; 79 iBT). Application fee: $75. Electronic applications accepted. *Expenses:* Tuition, state resident: full-time $9028. Tuition, nonresident: full-time $24,890. *Financial support:* Career-related internships or fieldwork, Federal Work-Study, and scholarships/grants available. *Faculty research:* Nanotechnology, optics, medical imaging, high energy physics, biophysics. *Unit head:* Dr. Michael Shupe, Department Head, 520-621-2679, E-mail: shupe@physics.arizona.edu. *Application contact:* Lisa Shapouri, Graduate Coordinator, 520-621-2290, Fax: 520-621-4721, E-mail: lisas@physics.arizona.edu.

University of Arkansas, Graduate School, J. William Fulbright College of Arts and Sciences, Department of Physics, Fayetteville, AR 72701-1201. Offers applied physics (MS); physics (MS, PhD); physics education (MA). *Students:* 4 full-time (1 woman), 39 part-time (7 women); includes 2 minority (1 African American, 1 Asian American or Pacific Islander), 23 international. In 2009, 6 master's awarded. *Degree requirements:* For master's, thesis; for doctorate, thesis/dissertation. Application fee: $40 ($50 for international students). *Expenses:* Tuition, state resident: full-time $7355; part-time $356.58 per hour. Tuition, nonresident: full-time $17,401; part-time $775.17 per hour. Required fees: $1203. *Financial support:* In 2009–10, 7 fellowships with tuition reimbursements, 20 research assistantships, 16 teaching assistantships were awarded; career-related internships or fieldwork and Federal Work-Study also available. Support available to part-time students. Financial award application deadline: 4/1; financial award applicants required to submit FAFSA. *Unit head:* Dr. Surendra Singh, Departmental Chairperson, 479-575-2506, Fax: 479-575-4580, E-mail: ssingh@uark.edu. *Application contact:* Dr. Huaxiang Fu, Graduate Coordinator, 479-575-8606, E-mail: hfu@uark.edu.

University of California, San Diego, Office of Graduate Studies, Department of Electrical and Computer Engineering, La Jolla, CA 92093. Offers applied ocean science (MS, PhD); applied physics (MS, PhD); communication theory and systems (MS, PhD); computer engineering (MS, PhD); electrical engineering (M Eng); electronic circuits and systems (MS, PhD); intelligent systems, robotics and control (MS, PhD); photonics (MS, PhD); signal and image processing (MS, PhD). MS only offered to students who have been admitted to the PhD program. *Entrance requirements:* For master's and doctorate, GRE General Test. Electronic applications accepted.

University of Denver, Faculty of Natural Sciences and Mathematics, Department of Physics and Astronomy, Denver, CO 80208. Offers MS, PhD. Part-time programs available. *Faculty:* 9 full-time (2 women), 1 part-time/adjunct (0 women). *Students:* 4 full-time (2 women), 10 part-time (3 women); includes 1 minority (Hispanic American), 2 international. Average age 28. 23 applicants, 65% accepted, 4 enrolled. In 2009, 1 master's awarded. Terminal master's awarded for partial completion of doctoral program. *Degree requirements:* For master's, thesis optional; for doctorate, thesis/dissertation. *Entrance requirements:* For master's and doctorate, GRE General Test, diagnostic exam. Additional exam requirements/recommendations for international students: Required—TOEFL. *Application deadline:* Applications are processed on a rolling basis. Application fee: $50. Electronic applications accepted. *Expenses:* Tuition: Full-time $34,596; part-time $961 per quarter hour. Required fees: $4 per quarter hour. Tuition and fees vary according to course load, campus/location and program. *Financial support:* In 2009–10, 9 research assistantships with full and partial tuition reimbursements (averaging $18,000 per year), 9 teaching assistantships with full and partial tuition reimbursements (averaging $18,000 per year) were awarded; career-related internships or fieldwork, Federal Work-Study, institutionally sponsored loans, and scholarships/grants also available. Support available to part-time students. Financial award application deadline: 3/1; financial award applicants required to submit FAFSA. *Faculty research:* Atomic and molecular beams and collisions, infrared astronomy, acoustic emission from stressed solids, nano materials. Total annual research expenditures: $1.1 million. *Unit head:* Dr. Davor Balzar, Chair, 303-871-2238. *Application contact:* Information Contact, 303-871-2238, E-mail: bstephen@du.edu.

University of Maryland, Baltimore County, Graduate School, College of Natural and Mathematical Sciences, Department of Physics, Program in Applied Physics, Baltimore, MD 21250. Offers astrophysics (PhD); optics (MS, PhD); quantum optics (PhD); solid state physics (MS, PhD). Part-time programs available. *Faculty:* 24 full-time (3 women), 18 part-time/adjunct (2 women). *Students:* 31 full-time (10 women), 3 part-time (0 women); includes 3 minority (all African Americans), 15 international. Average age 24. 28 applicants, 43% accepted, 6 enrolled. In 2009, 4 master's, 4 doctorates awarded. Terminal master's awarded for partial completion of doctoral program. *Degree requirements:* For master's, thesis optional; for doctorate, comprehensive exam, thesis/dissertation. *Entrance requirements:* For master's, GRE General Test, minimum GPA of 3.0; for doctorate, GRE General Test, GRE Subject Test, minimum GPA of 3.0. Additional exam requirements/recommendations for international students: Required—TOEFL. *Application deadline:* For fall admission, 5/31 for domestic and international students; for spring admission, 11/30 for domestic students. Applications are processed on a rolling basis. Application fee: $50. Electronic applications accepted. *Financial support:* In 2009–10,

30 students received support, including 4 fellowships with full tuition reimbursements available (averaging $27,000 per year), 14 research assistantships with full tuition reimbursements available (averaging $24,000 per year), 12 teaching assistantships with full tuition reimbursements available (averaging $22,000 per year); career-related internships or fieldwork, scholarships/grants, health care benefits, and unspecified assistantships also available. Support available to part-time students. Financial award application deadline: 5/31. *Faculty research:* Astrophysics, atmospheric physics, nanophysics, optics, quantum optics and quantum information. Total annual research expenditures: $4.8 million. *Unit head:* Dr. Todd Pittman, Graduate Program Director, 410-455-2513, Fax: 410-455-1072, E-mail: todd.pittman@umbc.edu. *Application contact:* Dr. Lazlo L. Takacs, Director, 410-455-2524, Fax: 410-455-1072, E-mail: takacs@umbc.edu.

University of Massachusetts Boston, Office of Graduate Studies, College of Science and Mathematics, Program in Applied Physics, Boston, MA 02125-3393. Offers MS. Part-time and evening/weekend programs available. *Degree requirements:* For master's, thesis optional. *Entrance requirements:* For master's, minimum GPA of 2.75. *Faculty research:* Experimental laser research, nonlinear optics, experimental and theoretical solid state physics, semiconductor devices, opto-electronics.

University of Massachusetts Lowell, College of Arts and Sciences, Department of Physics and Applied Physics, Program in Applied Physics, Lowell, MA 01854-2881. Offers applied mechanics (PhD); applied physics (MS, PhD), including optical sciences (MS). Terminal master's awarded for partial completion of doctoral program. *Degree requirements:* For master's, thesis; for doctorate, 2 foreign languages, thesis/dissertation. *Entrance requirements:* For master's, GRE General Test, 3 letters of reference; for doctorate, GRE General Test, transcripts, 3 letters of reference. Additional exam requirements/recommendations for international students: Required—TOEFL.

University of Michigan, Horace H. Rackham School of Graduate Studies, College of Literature, Science, and the Arts and College of Literature, Science, and the Arts, Applied Physics Program, Ann Arbor, MI 48198. Offers PhD. *Faculty:* 98 full-time (15 women). *Students:* 75 full-time (16 women); includes 17 minority (12 African Americans, 1 American Indian/Alaska Native, 2 Asian Americans or Pacific Islanders, 2 Hispanic Americans), 10 international. Average age 23. 102 applicants, 21% accepted, 10 enrolled. In 2009, 19 doctorates awarded. *Degree requirements:* For doctorate, oral defense of dissertation, preliminary and qualifying exams. *Entrance requirements:* For doctorate, GRE General Test. Additional exam requirements/recommendations for international students: Required—TOEFL. *Application deadline:* For fall admission, 1/15 for domestic and international students. Applications are processed on a rolling basis. Application fee: $60 ($75 for international students). Electronic applications accepted. *Expenses:* Tuition, state resident: full-time $17,286; part-time $1099 per credit hour. Tuition, nonresident: full-time $34,944; part-time $2080 per credit hour. Required fees: $95 per semester. Tuition and fees vary according to course load, degree level and program. *Financial support:* In 2009–10, 23 students received support, including 38 fellowships with full tuition reimbursements available (averaging $26,000 per year), 33 research assistantships with full tuition reimbursements available (averaging $26,000 per year), 4 teaching assistantships with full tuition reimbursements available; traineeships, health care benefits, and unspecified assistantships also available. Financial award application deadline: 1/15; financial award applicants required to submit FAFSA. *Faculty research:* Optical sciences, materials research, quantum structures, medical imaging, environment and science policy. Total annual research expenditures: $1.1 million. *Unit head:* Bradford G. Orr, Director, 734-936-0653, Fax: 734-764-2193, E-mail: orr@umich.edu. *Application contact:* Charles N. Sutton, Program Assistant, 734-764-4595, Fax: 734-764-2193, E-mail: csutton@umich.edu.

University of Missouri–St. Louis, College of Arts and Sciences, Department of Physics and Astronomy, St. Louis, MO 63121. Offers applied physics (MS); astrophysics (MS); physics (PhD). Part-time and evening/weekend programs available. *Faculty:* 13 full-time (2 women), 3 part-time/adjunct (1 woman). *Students:* 12 full-time (1 woman), 12 part-time (5 women); includes 1 minority (American Indian/Alaska Native), 6 international. Average age 31. 19 applicants, 58% accepted, 8 enrolled. In 2009, 3 master's, 2 doctorates awarded. Terminal master's awarded for partial completion of doctoral program. *Degree requirements:* For master's, thesis optional; for doctorate, thesis/dissertation. *Entrance requirements:* For master's and doctorate, GRE General Test, 2 letters of recommendation. Additional exam requirements/recommendations for international students: Required—TOEFL (minimum score 550 paper-based; 213 computer-based). *Application deadline:* For fall admission, 7/1 for domestic and international students; for spring admission, 12/1 for domestic students, 11/1 for international students. Application fee: $35 ($40 for international students). Electronic applications accepted. *Expenses:* Tuition, state resident: full-time $5377; part-time $297.70 per credit hour. Tuition, nonresident: full-time $13,882; part-time $771.20 per credit hour. Required fees: $220; $12.20 per credit hour. One-time fee: $12. Tuition and fees vary according to course level, campus/location and program. *Financial support:* In 2009–10, 4 research assistantships with full and partial tuition reimbursements (averaging $15,269 per year), 11 teaching assistantships with full and partial tuition reimbursements (averaging $14,926 per year) were awarded; fellowships with full tuition reimbursements, career-related internships or fieldwork also available. Financial award applicants required to submit FAFSA. *Faculty research:* Biophysics, atomic physics, nonlinear dynamics, materials science. *Unit head:* Dr. Phil Fraundorf, Director of Graduate Studies, 314-516-5931, Fax: 314-516-6152, E-mail: fraundorfp@msx.umsl.edu. *Application contact:* 314-516-5458, Fax: 314-516-6996, E-mail: gradadm@umsl.edu.

The University of North Carolina at Charlotte, Graduate School, College of Arts and Sciences, Department of Physics and Optical Science, Charlotte, NC 28223-0001. Offers applied physics (MS); optical science and engineering (MS, PhD). *Faculty:* 18 full-time (3 women), 1 part-time/adjunct (0 women). *Students:* 32 full-time (4 women), 17 part-time (4 women); includes 1 African American, 1 Asian American or Pacific Islander, 21 international. Average age 30. 37 applicants, 46% accepted, 11 enrolled. In 2009, 3 master's, 2 doctorates awarded. Terminal master's awarded for partial completion of doctoral program. *Degree requirements:* For master's, thesis optional; for doctorate, thesis/dissertation optional. *Entrance requirements:* For master's, GRE General Test, minimum GPA of 3.0 during previous 2 years, 2.75 overall. Additional exam requirements/recommendations for international students: Required—TOEFL (minimum score 557 paper-based; 220 computer-based; 83 iBT). *Application deadline:* For fall admission, 7/15 for domestic students, 5/1 for international students; for spring admission, 11/15 for domestic students, 10/1 for international students. Applications are processed on a rolling basis. Application fee: $55. Electronic applications accepted. *Financial support:* In 2009–10, 33 students received support, including 6 fellowships (averaging $39,477 per year), 6 research assistantships (averaging $10,611 per year), 21 teaching assistantships (averaging $12,455 per year); career-related internships or fieldwork, institutionally sponsored loans, scholarships/grants, and unspecified assistantships also available. Support available to part-time students. Financial award application deadline: 4/1; financial award applicants required to submit FAFSA. *Faculty research:* Optics, lasers, microscopy, fibers, astrophysics. Total annual research expenditures: $1.1 million. *Unit head:* Dr. Patrick Moyer, Interim Chair, 704-687-8148, Fax: 704-687-3160, E-mail: pjmoyer@uncc.edu. *Application contact:* Kathy B. Giddings, Director of Graduate Admissions, 704-687-5503, Fax: 704-687-3279, E-mail: gradadm@uncc.edu.

University of South Florida, Graduate School, College of Arts and Sciences, Department of Physics, Tampa, FL 33620-9951. Offers applied physics (PhD); physics (MS). Part-time programs available. *Faculty:* 23 full-time (3 women). *Students:* 60 full-time (11 women), 7 part-time (1 woman); includes 7 minority (2 African Americans, 2 Asian Americans or Pacific Islanders, 3 Hispanic Americans), 30 international. Average age 32. 81 applicants, 49% accepted, 17 enrolled. In 2009, 9 master's, 4 doctorates awarded. *Degree requirements:* For master's, comprehensive exam, thesis optional; for doctorate, 2 foreign languages, comprehensive exam, thesis/dissertation. *Entrance requirements:* For master's, GRE General Test, minimum GPA of 3.0 in last 60 hours of course work; for doctorate, GRE General Test, minimum graduate GPA of 3.2. Additional exam requirements/recommendations for international students: Required—TOEFL (minimum score 550 paper-based). *Application deadline:* For fall admission, 2/15 priority date for domestic students, 1/2 for international students; for spring admission, 9/1 for domestic students, 7/1 for international students. Applications are processed on a rolling basis. Application fee: $30. Electronic applications accepted. *Financial support:* In 2009–10, teaching assistantships with tuition reimbursements (averaging $13,739 per year); unspecified assistantships also available. *Faculty research:* Biophysics and biomedical physics, atomic molecular and optical physics, solid state and materials physics, physics education. Total annual research expenditures: $2.2 million. *Unit head:* Dr. Pritish Mukherjee, Director of Graduate Studies, 813-974-2871, Fax: 813-974-5813, E-mail: pritish@cas.usf.edu. *Application contact:* Dale Johnson, Program Director, 813-974-5125, Fax: 813-974-5813, E-mail: dejohnso@cas.usf.edu.

The University of Texas at Austin, Graduate School, College of Natural Sciences, Department of Physics, Austin, TX 78712-1111. Offers MA, MS, PhD. *Degree requirements:* For master's, thesis; for doctorate, thesis/dissertation. *Entrance requirements:* For master's and doctorate, GRE General Test, GRE Subject Test (physics). Electronic applications accepted.

University of Washington, Graduate School, College of Arts and Sciences, Department of Physics, Seattle, WA 98195. Offers MS, PhD. Part-time and evening/weekend programs available. Terminal master's awarded for partial completion of doctoral program. *Degree requirements:* For doctorate, thesis/dissertation. *Entrance requirements:* For master's, GRE; for doctorate, GRE General Test, GRE Subject Test. Additional exam requirements/recommendations for international students: Required—TOEFL. Electronic applications accepted. *Faculty research:* Astro-, atomic, condensed-matter, nuclear, and particle physics; physics education.

Virginia Commonwealth University, Graduate School, College of Humanities and Sciences, Department of Physics, Program in Physics and Applied Physics, Richmond, VA 23284-9005. Offers MS.

Virginia Polytechnic Institute and State University, Graduate School, College of Science, Department of Physics, Blacksburg, VA 24061. Offers applied physics (MS, PhD); physics (MS, PhD). *Entrance requirements:* For master's and doctorate, GRE Subject Test. Additional exam requirements/recommendations for international students: Required—TOEFL (minimum score 550 paper-based; 213 computer-based). Electronic applications accepted. *Faculty research:* Condensed matter, particle physics, theoretical and experimental astrophysics, biophysics, mathematical physics.

West Virginia University, Eberly College of Arts and Sciences, Department of Physics, Morgantown, WV 26506. Offers applied physics (MS, PhD); astrophysics (MS, PhD); chemical physics (MS, PhD); condensed matter physics (MS, PhD); elementary particle physics (MS, PhD); materials physics (MS, PhD); plasma physics (MS, PhD); solid state physics (MS, PhD); statistical physics (MS, PhD); theoretical physics (MS, PhD). Terminal master's awarded for partial completion of doctoral program. *Degree requirements:* For master's, thesis or alternative, qualifying exam; for doctorate, thesis/dissertation, qualifying exam. *Entrance requirements:* For master's and doctorate, GRE General Test, minimum GPA of 3.0. Additional exam requirements/recommendations for international students: Required—TOEFL. *Faculty research:* Experimental and theoretical condensed-matter, plasma, high-energy theory, nonlinear dynamics, space physics.

Yale University, Graduate School of Arts and Sciences, School of Engineering and Applied Science, Department of Applied Physics, New Haven, CT 06520. Offers MS, PhD. Terminal master's awarded for partial completion of doctoral program. *Degree requirements:* For doctorate, thesis/dissertation, area exam. *Entrance requirements:* For master's and doctorate, GRE General Test. Additional exam requirements/recommendations for international students: Required—TOEFL. *Faculty research:* Condensed-matter physics, optical physics, materials science.

Chemical Physics

Columbia University, Graduate School of Arts and Sciences, Division of Natural Sciences, Department of Chemistry, Program in Chemical Physics, New York, NY 10027. Offers M Phil, PhD. *Entrance requirements:* For master's, GRE General Test, GRE Subject Test. Additional exam requirements/recommendations for international students: Required—TOEFL.

Cornell University, Graduate School, Graduate Fields of Arts and Sciences, Field of Chemistry and Chemical Biology, Ithaca, NY 14853-0001. Offers analytical chemistry (PhD); bio-organic chemistry (PhD); biophysical chemistry (PhD); chemical biology (PhD); chemical physics (PhD); inorganic chemistry (PhD); materials chemistry (PhD); organic chemistry (PhD); organometallic chemistry (PhD); physical chemistry (PhD); polymer chemistry (PhD); theoretical chemistry (PhD). *Faculty:* 48 full-time (3 women). *Students:* 162 full-time (67 women); includes 15 minority (1 African American, 9 Asian Americans or Pacific Islanders, 5 Hispanic Americans), 53 international. Average age 26. 359 applicants, 19% accepted, 39 enrolled. In 2009, 31 doctorates awarded. *Degree requirements:* For doctorate, comprehensive exam, thesis/dissertation. *Entrance requirements:* For doctorate, GRE General Test, GRE Subject Test (chemistry), 3 letters of recommendation. Additional exam requirements/recommendations for international students: Required—TOEFL (minimum score 600 paper-based; 250 computer-based; 77 iBT). *Application deadline:* For fall admission, 1/10 for domestic students. Application fee: $70. Electronic applications accepted. *Expenses:* Tuition: Full-time $29,500. Required fees: $70. Full-time tuition and fees vary according to degree level, program and student level. *Financial support:* In 2009–10, 1 fellowship with full tuition reimbursement, 7 research assistantships with full tuition reimbursements, 29 teaching assistantships with full tuition reimbursements were awarded; institutionally sponsored loans, scholarships/grants, health care benefits, tuition waivers (full and partial), and unspecified assistantships also available. Financial award applicants required to submit FAFSA. *Faculty research:* Analytical, organic, inorganic, physical, materials, chemical biology. *Unit head:* Director of Graduate Studies, 607-255-4139, Fax: 607-255-4137. *Application contact:* Graduate Field Assistant, 607-255-4139, Fax: 607-255-4137, E-mail: chemgrad@cornell.edu.

Chemical Physics

Harvard University, Graduate School of Arts and Sciences, Committee on Chemical Physics, Cambridge, MA 02138. Offers PhD. *Degree requirements:* For doctorate, one foreign language, thesis/dissertation, cumulative exams. *Entrance requirements:* For doctorate, GRE General Test, GRE Subject Test. Additional exam requirements/recommendations for international students: Required—TOEFL. *Expenses:* Tuition: Full-time $33,696. Required fees: $1126. Full-time tuition and fees vary according to program.

Kent State University, College of Arts and Sciences, Chemical Physics Interdisciplinary Program, Kent, OH 44242-0001. Offers MS, PhD. Offered in cooperation with the Departments of Chemistry, Mathematics and Computer Science, and Physics and the Liquid Crystal Institute. Terminal master's awarded for partial completion of doctoral program. *Degree requirements:* For master's, thesis; for doctorate, thesis/dissertation, candidacy exam. *Entrance requirements:* For master's and doctorate, GRE. Additional exam requirements/recommendations for international students: Required—TOEFL (minimum score 525 paper-based; 197 computer-based). Electronic applications accepted.

Marquette University, Graduate School, College of Arts and Sciences, Department of Chemistry, Milwaukee, WI 53201-1881. Offers analytical chemistry (MS, PhD); bioanalytical chemistry (MS, PhD); biophysical chemistry (MS, PhD); chemical physics (MS, PhD); inorganic chemistry (MS, PhD); organic chemistry (MS, PhD); physical chemistry (MS, PhD). Part-time programs available. *Faculty:* 23 full-time (10 women), 1 part-time/adjunct (0 women). *Students:* 34 full-time (9 women), 10 part-time (4 women); includes 4 minority (1 African American, 2 Asian Americans or Pacific Islanders, 1 Hispanic American), 33 international. Average age 29. 23 applicants, 83% accepted, 8 enrolled. In 2009, 4 master's, 5 doctorates awarded. Terminal master's awarded for partial completion of doctoral program. *Degree requirements:* For master's, comprehensive exam; for doctorate, thesis/dissertation, cumulative exams. *Entrance requirements:* For master's and doctorate, GRE Subject Test. Additional exam requirements/recommendations for international students: Required—TOEFL. Application fee: $40. *Financial support:* In 2009–10, 3 research assistantships, 27 teaching assistantships were awarded; fellowships, Federal Work-Study, institutionally sponsored loans, scholarships/grants, and tuition waivers (full and partial) also available. Support available to part-time students. Financial award application deadline: 2/15. *Faculty research:* Inorganic complexes, laser Raman spectroscopy, organic synthesis, chemical dynamics, biophysiology. *Unit head:* Dr. Jeanne Hossenlopp, Chair, 414-288-3537, Fax: 414-288-7066. *Application contact:* Dr. Mark Steinmetz, Director of Graduate Studies, 414-288-7374, Fax: 414-288-7066.

McMaster University, School of Graduate Studies, Faculty of Science, Department of Chemistry, Hamilton, ON L8S 4M2, Canada. Offers analytical chemistry (M Sc, PhD); chemical physics (M Sc, PhD); chemistry (M Sc, PhD); inorganic chemistry (M Sc, PhD); organic chemistry (M Sc, PhD); physical chemistry (M Sc, PhD); polymer chemistry (M Sc, PhD). Part-time programs available. Terminal master's awarded for partial completion of doctoral program. *Degree requirements:* For master's, thesis; for doctorate, comprehensive exam, thesis/dissertation. *Entrance requirements:* For master's, minimum B+ average. Additional exam requirements/recommendations for international students: Required—TOEFL (minimum score 550 paper-based; 213 computer-based).

Michigan State University, The Graduate School, College of Natural Science, Department of Chemistry, East Lansing, MI 48824. Offers chemical physics (PhD); chemistry (MS, PhD); chemistry-environmental toxicology (PhD); computational chemistry (MS). *Entrance requirements:* Additional exam requirements/recommendations for international students: Required—TOEFL. Electronic applications accepted. *Faculty research:* Analytical chemistry, inorganic and organic chemistry, nuclear chemistry, physical chemistry, theoretical and computational chemistry.

The Ohio State University, Graduate School, College of Mathematical and Physical Sciences, Program in Chemical Physics, Columbus, OH 43210. Offers MS, PhD. *Faculty:* 34. *Students:* 1 (woman) full-time, 14 part-time (5 women), 8 international. Average age 30. *Degree requirements:* For master's, thesis optional; for doctorate, thesis/dissertation. *Entrance requirements:* For master's and doctorate, GRE General Test, GRE Subject Test (chemistry or physics). Additional exam requirements/recommendations for international students: Recommended—TOEFL (minimum score 600 paper-based; 250 computer-based). *Application deadline:* For fall admission, 8/15 priority date for domestic students, 7/1 priority date for international students; for winter admission, 12/1 priority date for domestic students, 11/1 priority date for international students; for spring admission, 3/1 priority date for domestic students, 2/1 priority date for international students. Applications are processed on a rolling basis. Application fee: $40 ($50 for international students). Electronic applications accepted. *Expenses:* Tuition, state resident: full-time $10,683. Tuition, nonresident: full-time $25,923. Tuition and fees vary according to course load and program. *Financial support:* Fellowships, research assistantships, teaching assistantships, Federal Work-Study and institutionally sponsored loans available. Support available to part-time students. *Unit head:* Dr. Terry A. Miller, Director, 614-292-2569, Fax: 614-292-1948, E-mail: miller.104@osu.edu. *Application contact:* 614-292-9444, Fax: 614-292-3895, E-mail: domestic.grad@osu.edu.

Simon Fraser University, Graduate Studies, Faculty of Science, Department of Chemistry, Burnaby, BC V5A 1S6, Canada. Offers chemical physics (PhD); chemistry (PhD). *Degree requirements:* For master's, thesis; for doctorate, thesis/dissertation. *Entrance requirements:* For master's, minimum GPA of 3.0. Additional exam requirements/recommendations for international students: Required—TOEFL (minimum score 600 paper-based; 250 computer-based; 100 iBT). Electronic applications accepted. *Faculty research:* Organic chemistry, nuclear chemistry, physical chemistry, inorganic chemistry, theoretical chemistry.

Simon Fraser University, Graduate Studies, Faculty of Science, Department of Physics, Burnaby, BC V5A 1S6, Canada. Offers biophysics (M Sc, PhD); chemical physics (M Sc, PhD); physics (M Sc, PhD). *Degree requirements:* For master's, thesis; for doctorate, thesis/dissertation. *Entrance requirements:* For master's, minimum GPA of 3.0; for doctorate, minimum GPA of 3.5. Additional exam requirements/recommendations for international students: Required—TOEFL or IELTS. *Faculty research:* Solid-state physics, magnetism, energy research, superconductivity, nuclear physics.

University of Colorado at Boulder, Graduate School, College of Arts and Sciences, Department of Physics, Boulder, CO 80309. Offers chemical physics (PhD); geophysics (PhD); liquid crystal science and technology (PhD); mathematical physics (PhD); medical physics (PhD); optical sciences and engineering (PhD); physics (MS, PhD). *Faculty:* 48 full-time (6 women). *Students:* 160 full-time (24 women), 47 part-time (8 women); includes 9 minority (6 Asian Americans or Pacific Islanders, 3 Hispanic Americans), 65 international. Average age 27. 548 applicants, 5% accepted, 27 enrolled. In 2009, 17 master's, 23 doctorates awarded. Terminal master's awarded for partial completion of doctoral program. *Degree requirements:* For master's, comprehensive exam, thesis or alternative; for doctorate, comprehensive exam, thesis/dissertation. *Entrance requirements:* For master's and doctorate, GRE General Test, GRE Subject Test, minimum undergraduate GPA of 3.0. Additional exam requirements/recommendations for international students: Required—TOEFL. *Application deadline:* For fall admission, 1/15 priority date for domestic students, 1/15 for international students. Applications are processed on a rolling basis. Application fee: $50 ($60 for international students). Electronic applications accepted. *Financial support:* In 2009–10, 21 fellowships with full tuition reimbursements (averaging $15,999 per year), 146 research assistantships with full tuition reimbursements (averaging $16,586 per year) were awarded; scholarships/grants also available. Financial award application deadline: 1/15. *Faculty research:* Atomic and molecular physics, nuclear physics, condensed matter, elementary particle physics, laser or optical physics, plasma physics, geophysics, astrophysics and chemical physics. Total annual research expenditures: $14.2 million.

University of Illinois at Urbana–Champaign, Graduate College, College of Liberal Arts and Sciences, School of Chemical Sciences, Department of Chemistry, Champaign, IL 61820. Offers astrochemistry (PhD); chemical physics (PhD); chemistry (MA, MS, PhD); teaching of chemistry (MS); MS/JD; MS/MBA. *Faculty:* 34 full-time (6 women). *Students:* 308 full-time (91 women), 4 part-time (1 woman); includes 34 minority (6 African Americans, 3 American Indian/Alaska Native, 18 Asian Americans or Pacific Islanders, 7 Hispanic Americans), 69 international. 502 applicants, 13% accepted, 63 enrolled. In 2009, 14 master's, 51 doctorates awarded. *Entrance requirements:* For master's and doctorate, GRE General Test, GRE Subject Test, minimum GPA of 3.0. Additional exam requirements/recommendations for international students: Required—TOEFL (minimum score 580 paper-based; 237 computer-based). *Application deadline:* Applications are processed on a rolling basis. Application fee: $60 ($75 for international students). Electronic applications accepted. *Financial support:* In 2009–10, 108 fellowships, 186 research assistantships, 164 teaching assistantships were awarded; tuition waivers (full and partial) also available. *Unit head:* Steven C. Zimmerman, Head, 217-333-6655, Fax: 217-244-5943, E-mail: sczimmer@illinois.edu. *Application contact:* Dorothy Ann Gordon, Assistant to the Head, 217-244-0618, Fax: 217-244-5943, E-mail: dorothyh@illinois.edu.

University of Louisville, Graduate School, College of Arts and Sciences, Department of Chemistry, Louisville, KY 40292-0001. Offers analytical chemistry (MS, PhD); biochemistry (MS, PhD); chemical physics (PhD); inorganic chemistry (MS, PhD); organic chemistry (MS, PhD); physical chemistry (MS, PhD). *Students:* 57 full-time (27 women), 4 part-time (1 woman); includes 2 minority (1 African American, 1 Asian American or Pacific Islander), 43 international. Average age 29. 62 applicants, 31% accepted, 13 enrolled. In 2009, 6 master's, 7 doctorates awarded. *Median time to degree:* Of those who began their doctoral program in fall 2001, 0% received their degree in 8 years or less. *Degree requirements:* For master's, thesis; for doctorate, comprehensive exam, thesis/dissertation. *Entrance requirements:* For master's and doctorate, GRE General Test. Additional exam requirements/recommendations for international students: Required—TOEFL. *Application deadline:* Applications are processed on a rolling basis. Application fee: $50. *Financial support:* Fellowships, research assistantships, teaching assistantships available. *Unit head:* Dr. George R. Pack, Chair, 502-852-6798, Fax: 502-852-8149, E-mail: george.pack@louisville.edu. *Application contact:* Libby Leggett, Director, Graduate Admissions, 502-852-3101, Fax: 502-852-6536, E-mail: gradadm@louisville.edu.

University of Maryland, College Park, Academic Affairs, College of Computer, Mathematical and Physical Sciences, Institute for Physical Science and Technology, Program in Chemical Physics, College Park, MD 20742. Offers MS, PhD. Part-time and evening/weekend programs available. *Students:* 35 full-time (12 women), 2 part-time (1 woman); includes 3 minority (all Asian Americans or Pacific Islanders), 19 international. 29 applicants, 31% accepted, 4 enrolled. In 2009, 3 master's, 7 doctorates awarded. Terminal master's awarded for partial completion of doctoral program. *Degree requirements:* For master's, thesis optional, paper, qualifying exam; for doctorate, thesis/dissertation, seminars. *Entrance requirements:* For master's, GRE General Test, GRE Subject Test (chemistry, math or physics), minimum GPA of 3.3, 3 letters of recommendation; for doctorate, GRE Subject Test (chemistry, math, or physics), GRE General Test, minimum GPA of 3.3, 3 letters of recommendation. *Application deadline:* For fall admission, 2/1 for domestic and international students. Applications are processed on a rolling basis. Application fee: $60. Electronic applications accepted. *Expenses:* Tuition, area resident: Part-time $471 per credit hour. Tuition, state resident: part-time $471 per credit hour. Tuition, nonresident: part-time $1016 per credit hour. Required fees: $337.04 per term. *Financial support:* In 2009–10, 1 fellowship with partial tuition reimbursement (averaging $9,500 per year), 28 research assistantships (averaging $19,960 per year), 4 teaching assistantships (averaging $17,633 per year) were awarded; Federal Work-Study and scholarships/grants also available. Financial award applicants required to submit FAFSA. *Faculty research:* Discrete molecules and gases; dynamic phenomena; thermodynamics, statistical mechanical theory and quantum mechanical theory; atmospheric physics; biophysics. *Unit head:* Dr. Michael A. Coplan, Director, 301-405-4858, Fax: 301-314-9396, E-mail: coplan@umd.edu. *Application contact:* Dean of Graduate School, 301-405-0358, Fax: 301-314-9305.

University of Nevada, Reno, Graduate School, Interdisciplinary Program in Chemical Physics, Reno, NV 89557. Offers PhD. *Degree requirements:* For doctorate, thesis/dissertation. *Entrance requirements:* For doctorate, GRE, minimum GPA of 3.0. Additional exam requirements/recommendations for international students: Required—TOEFL (minimum score 500 paper-based; 173 computer-based; 61 iBT). Electronic applications accepted. *Faculty research:* Atomic and molecular physics, physical chemistry.

University of Southern California, Graduate School, College of Letters, Arts and Sciences, Department of Chemistry, Los Angeles, CA 90089. Offers chemical physics (PhD); chemistry (MA, MS, PhD). *Faculty:* 30 full-time (3 women). *Students:* 126 full-time (42 women); includes 5 minority (3 Asian Americans or Pacific Islanders, 2 Hispanic Americans), 66 international. Average age 26. 125 applicants, 53% accepted, 25 enrolled. In 2009, 3 master's, 16 doctorates awarded. Terminal master's awarded for partial completion of doctoral program. *Degree requirements:* For master's, comprehensive exam (for some programs), thesis optional; for doctorate, thesis/dissertation, qualifying exam. *Entrance requirements:* For master's and doctorate, GRE General Test. Additional exam requirements/recommendations for international students: Required—TOEFL (minimum score 600 paper-based; 250 computer-based; 100 iBT). *Application deadline:* For fall admission, 2/1 priority date for domestic and international students; for winter admission, 11/1 for domestic and international students. Applications are processed on a rolling basis. Application fee: $0. Electronic applications accepted. *Expenses:* Tuition: Full-time $25,980; part-time $1315 per unit. Required fees: $554. One-time fee: $35 full-time. Full-time tuition and fees vary according to degree level and program. *Financial support:* In 2009–10, 126 students received support, including fellowships with full tuition reimbursements available (averaging $30,332 per year), research assistantships with full tuition reimbursements available (averaging $25,332 per year), teaching assistantships with full tuition reimbursements available (averaging $25,332 per year); institutionally sponsored loans, scholarships/grants, health care benefits, and unspecified assistantships also available. Financial award application deadline: 3/1. *Faculty research:* Biological chemistry, inorganic chemistry, organic chemistry, physical chemistry, theoretical chemistry. Total annual research expenditures: $7.2 million. *Unit head:* Dr. Charles McKenna, Chair, 213-740-6857, Fax: 213-740-2701, E-mail: chemmail@chem1.usc.edu. *Application contact:* Katie McKissick, Graduate Advisor, 213-740-6855, Fax: 213-740-2701, E-mail: mckissic@usc.edu.

The University of Tennessee, Graduate School, College of Arts and Sciences, Department of Chemistry, Knoxville, TN 37996. Offers analytical chemistry (MS, PhD); chemical physics (PhD); environmental chemistry (MS, PhD); inorganic chemistry (MS, PhD); organic chemistry (MS, PhD); physical chemistry (MS, PhD); polymer chemistry (MS, PhD); theoretical chemistry (PhD). Part-time programs available. Terminal master's awarded for partial completion of doctoral program. *Degree requirements:* For master's, thesis; for doctorate, thesis/dissertation. *Entrance requirements:* For master's and doctorate, GRE General Test, minimum GPA of 2.7. Additional exam requirements/recommendations for international students: Required—TOEFL. Electronic applications accepted. *Expenses:* Tuition, state resident: full-time $6826; part-time $380 per semester hour. Tuition, nonresident: full-time $21,844; part-time $1147 per semester hour. Tuition and fees vary according to program.

University of Utah, The Graduate School, College of Science, Department of Chemistry, Salt Lake City, UT 84112-0850. Offers chemical physics (PhD); chemistry (M Phil, MA, MS, PhD); science teacher education (MS). Part-time programs available. Postbaccalaureate distance learning degree programs offered. *Faculty:* 30 full-time (4 women), 4 part-time/adjunct (1 woman). *Students:* 145 full-time (47 women), 27 part-time (12 women); includes 10 minority (1 African American, 5 Asian Americans or Pacific Islanders, 4 Hispanic Americans), 68 international.

Average age 28. 352 applicants, 24% accepted, 31 enrolled. In 2009, 9 master's, 29 doctorates awarded. Terminal master's awarded for partial completion of doctoral program. *Degree requirements:* For master's, thesis optional, 20 hours course work, 10 hours research; for doctorate, thesis/dissertation, 18 hours course work, 14 hours research. *Entrance requirements:* For master's and doctorate, GRE General Test, minimum GPA of 3.0. Additional exam requirements/recommendations for international students: Required—TOEFL (minimum score 620 paper-based; 260 computer-based; 105 iBT). *Application deadline:* For fall admission, 4/1 for domestic and international students; for spring admission, 11/1 for domestic and international students. Application fee: $55 ($65 for international students). Electronic applications accepted. *Expenses:* Tuition, state resident: full-time $4004; part-time $1674 per semester. Tuition, nonresident: full-time $14,134; part-time $5915 per semester. Required fees: $324 per semester. Tuition and fees vary according to course load, degree level and program. *Financial support:* In 2009–10, 1 fellowship with tuition reimbursement (averaging $22,000 per year), 116 research assistantships with tuition reimbursements (averaging $22,500 per year), 50 teaching assistantships with tuition reimbursements (averaging $22,000 per year) were awarded; scholarships/grants and tuition waivers (full) also available. Financial award application deadline: 4/1; financial award applicants required to submit FAFSA. *Faculty research:* Biological, theoretical, inorganic, organic, and physical-analytical chemistry. Total annual research expenditures: $14.2 million. *Unit head:* Dr. Henry S. White, Chair, 801-585-6256, Fax: 801-581-8433, E-mail: chair@chemistry.utah.edu. *Application contact:* Jo Hoovey, Graduate Coordinator, 801-581-4393, Fax: 801-581-5408, E-mail: jhoovey@chem.utah.edu.

University of Utah, The Graduate School, College of Science, Department of Physics and Astronomy, Salt Lake City, UT 84112. Offers chemical physics (PhD); medical physics (MS, PhD); physics (MA, MS, PhD); physics teaching (PhD). Part-time programs available. *Faculty:* 32 full-time (1 woman), 2 part-time/adjunct (0 women). *Students:* 76 full-time (16 women), 25 part-time (6 women); includes 3 minority (1 Asian American or Pacific Islander, 2 Hispanic Americans), 48 international. Average age 30. 135 applicants, 25% accepted, 17 enrolled. In 2009, 5 master's, 14 doctorates awarded. Terminal master's awarded for partial completion of doctoral program. *Degree requirements:* For master's, comprehensive exam (for some programs), thesis or alternative, teaching experience, departmental exam; for doctorate, comprehensive exam, thesis/dissertation, departmental qualifying exam. *Entrance requirements:* For master's and doctorate, GRE General Test, GRE Subject Test, minimum GPA of 3.0. Additional exam requirements/recommendations for international students: Required—TOEFL (minimum score 500 paper-based; 173 computer-based; 69 iBT). *Application deadline:* For fall admission, 2/1 priority date for domestic students, 2/1 for international students. Applications are processed on a rolling basis. Application fee: $55 ($65 for international students). Electronic applications accepted. *Expenses:* Tuition, state resident: full-time $4004; part-time $1674 per semester. Tuition, nonresident: full-time $14,134; part-time $5915 per semester. Required fees: $324 per semester. Tuition and fees vary according to course load, degree level and program. *Financial support:* In 2009–10, 3 fellowships with full tuition reimbursements (averaging $19,000 per year), 27 research assistantships with full and partial tuition reimbursements (averaging $19,420 per year), 45 teaching assistantships with full and partial tuition reimbursements (averaging $14,626 per year) were awarded; Federal Work-Study, institutionally sponsored loans, and scholarships/grants also available. Financial award application deadline: 2/15; financial award applicants required to submit FAFSA. *Faculty research:* High-energy, cosmic-ray, astrophysics, medical physics, condensed matter, relativity applied physics. Total annual research expenditures: $4.7 million. *Unit head:* Dr. David Kieda, Chair, 801-581-6901, Fax: 801-581-4801, E-mail: kieda@physics.utah.edu. *Application contact:* Jackie Hadley, Graduate Secretary, 801-581-6861, Fax: 801-581-4801, E-mail: jackie@physics.utah.edu.

University of Utah, The Graduate School, College of Science, Interdepartmental Program in Chemical Physics, Salt Lake City, UT 84112-1107. Offers PhD. *Students:* 1 applicant, 100% accepted, 0 enrolled. *Degree requirements:* For doctorate, comprehensive exam, thesis/dissertation. *Entrance requirements:* For doctorate, GRE General Test, GRE Subject Test (physics), minimum undergraduate GPA of 3.0. Additional exam requirements/recommendations for international students: Required—TOEFL (minimum score 500 paper-based; 173 computer-based). *Application deadline:* For fall admission, 4/1 for domestic and international students; for spring admission, 11/1 for domestic and international students. Application fee: $55 ($65 for international students). *Expenses:* Tuition, state resident: full-time $4004; part-time $1674 per semester. Tuition, nonresident: full-time $14,134; part-time $5915 per semester. Required fees: $324 per semester. Tuition and fees vary according to course load, degree level and program. *Financial support:* Applicants required to submit FAFSA. *Unit head:* Dr. Charles A. Wight, Coordinator of Medical Physics, E-mail: wight@chemistry.utah.edu. *Application contact:* Information Contact, 801-581-6958, E-mail: office@science.utah.edu.

Virginia Commonwealth University, Graduate School, College of Humanities and Sciences, Department of Chemistry, Richmond, VA 23284-9005. Offers analytical chemistry (MS, PhD); chemical physics (PhD); inorganic chemistry (MS, PhD); organic chemistry (MS, PhD); physical chemistry (MS, PhD). Part-time programs available. Terminal master's awarded for partial completion of doctoral program. *Degree requirements:* For master's, thesis; for doctorate, thesis/dissertation, comprehensive cumulative exams, research proposal. *Entrance requirements:* For master's, GRE General Test, 30 undergraduate credits in chemistry; for doctorate, GRE General Test. *Faculty research:* Physical, organic, inorganic, analytical, and polymer chemistry; chemical physics.

Wesleyan University, Graduate Programs, Department of Chemistry and Department of Physics, Program in Chemical Physics, Middletown, CT 06459. Offers MA, PhD. Terminal master's awarded for partial completion of doctoral program. *Degree requirements:* For master's, one foreign language, thesis; for doctorate, one foreign language, thesis/dissertation. *Entrance requirements:* For master's, GRE General Test, GRE Subject Test; for doctorate, GRE Subject Test, BA or BS in chemistry or physics. Additional exam requirements/recommendations for international students: Required—TOEFL. *Application deadline:* Applications are processed on a rolling basis. Application fee: $0. Electronic applications accepted. *Financial support:* Application deadline: 4/15; *Faculty research:* Spectroscopy, photochemistry, reactive collisions, surface physics, quantum theory. *Unit head:* Dr. Joseph Knee, Chair, 860-685-2727, E-mail: jknee@wesleyan.edu. *Application contact:* Dr. Joseph Knee, Chair, 860-685-2727, E-mail: jknee@wesleyan.edu.

See Close-Up on page 115.

West Virginia University, Eberly College of Arts and Sciences, Department of Physics, Morgantown, WV 26506. Offers applied physics (MS, PhD); astrophysics (MS, PhD); chemical physics (MS, PhD); condensed matter physics (MS, PhD); elementary particle physics (MS, PhD); materials physics (MS, PhD); plasma physics (MS, PhD); solid state physics (MS, PhD); statistical physics (MS, PhD); theoretical physics (MS, PhD). Terminal master's awarded for partial completion of doctoral program. *Degree requirements:* For master's, thesis or alternative, qualifying exam; for doctorate, thesis/dissertation, qualifying exam. *Entrance requirements:* For master's and doctorate, GRE General Test, minimum GPA of 3.0. Additional exam requirements/recommendations for international students: Required—TOEFL. *Faculty research:* Experimental and theoretical condensed-matter, plasma, high-energy theory, nonlinear dynamics, space physics.

Condensed Matter Physics

Cleveland State University, College of Graduate Studies, College of Science, Department of Physics, Cleveland, OH 44115. Offers applied optics (MS); condensed matter physics (MS); medical physics (MS); optics and materials (MS); optics and medical imaging (MS). Part-time and evening/weekend programs available. *Entrance requirements:* For master's, undergraduate degree in engineering, physics, chemistry or mathematics. Additional exam requirements/recommendations for international students: Required—TOEFL (minimum score 525 paper-based; 197 computer-based), GRE. Electronic applications accepted. *Faculty research:* Statistical physics, experimental solid-state physics, theoretical optics, experimental biological physics (macromolecular crystallography), experimental optics.

Emory University, Graduate School of Arts and Sciences, Department of Physics, Atlanta, GA 30322-1100. Offers biophysics (PhD); condensed matter physics (PhD); non-linear physics (PhD); radiological physics (PhD); soft condensed matter physics (PhD); solid-state physics (PhD); statistical physics (PhD); MS/PhD. *Degree requirements:* For doctorate, thesis/dissertation, qualifier proposal (PhD). *Entrance requirements:* For doctorate, GRE General Test, minimum GPA of 3.0. Additional exam requirements/recommendations for international students: Required—TOEFL (minimum score 600 paper-based). Electronic applications accepted. *Faculty research:* Experimental studies of the structure and function of metalloproteins, soft condensed matter, granular materials, biophotonics and fluorescence correlation spectroscopy, single molecule studies of DNA-protein systems.

Iowa State University of Science and Technology, Graduate College, College of Liberal Arts and Sciences, Department of Physics and Astronomy, Ames, IA 50011. Offers applied physics (MS, PhD); astrophysics (MS, PhD); condensed matter physics (MS, PhD); high energy physics (MS, PhD); nuclear physics (MS, PhD); physics (MS, PhD). Part-time programs available. *Faculty:* 46 full-time (3 women), 4 part-time/adjunct (0 women). *Students:* 94 full-time (21 women), 4 part-time (0 women); includes 3 minority (all Asian Americans or Pacific Islanders), 56 international. 185 applicants, 32% accepted, 15 enrolled. In 2009, 4 master's, 7 doctorates awarded. Terminal master's awarded for partial completion of doctoral program. *Degree requirements:* For master's, thesis (for some programs); for doctorate, thesis/dissertation. *Entrance requirements:* For master's and doctorate, GRE General Test, GRE Subject Test (physics). Additional exam requirements/recommendations for international students: Required—TOEFL (minimum score 550 paper-based; 79 iBT) or IELTS (minimum score 6.5). *Application deadline:* For fall admission, 2/15 priority date for domestic and international students; for spring admission, 10/15 for domestic and international students. Applications are processed on a rolling basis. Application fee: $40 ($90 for international students). Electronic applications accepted. *Expenses:* Tuition, state resident: full-time $6716. Tuition, nonresident: full-time $8908. Tuition and fees vary according to course level, course load, program and student level. *Financial support:* In 2009–10, 58 research assistantships with full and partial tuition reimbursements (averaging $17,000 per year), 33 teaching assistantships with full and partial tuition reimbursements (averaging $16,000 per year) were awarded; fellowships, Federal Work-Study, institutionally sponsored loans, scholarships/grants, health care benefits, and unspecified assistantships also available. Support available to part-time students. Financial award application deadline: 2/15. *Faculty research:* Condensed-matter physics, including superconductivity and new materials; high-energy and nuclear physics; astronomy and astrophysics; atmospheric and environmental physics. Total annual research expenditures: $8.8 million. *Unit head:* Dr. Joseph Shinar, Chair, 515-294-3455, Fax: 515-294-6027, E-mail: phys_astro@iastate.edu. *Application contact:* Dr. Steven Kawaler, Director of Graduate Education, 515-294-9728, E-mail: phys_astro@iastate.edu.

Memorial University of Newfoundland, School of Graduate Studies, Department of Physics and Physical Oceanography, St. John's, NL A1C 5S7, Canada. Offers atomic and molecular physics (M Sc, PhD); condensed matter physics (M Sc, PhD); physical oceanography (M Sc, PhD); physics (M Sc). Part-time programs available. *Degree requirements:* For master's, thesis, seminar presentation on thesis topic; for doctorate, comprehensive exam, thesis/dissertation, oral defense of thesis. *Entrance requirements:* For master's, honors B Sc or equivalent; for doctorate, M Sc or equivalent. Electronic applications accepted. *Faculty research:* Experiment and theory in atomic and molecular physics, condensed matter physics, physical oceanography, theoretical geophysics and applied nuclear physics.

Rutgers, The State University of New Jersey, New Brunswick, Graduate School-New Brunswick, Department of Physics and Astronomy, Piscataway, NJ 08854-8097. Offers astronomy (MS, PhD); biophysics (PhD); condensed matter physics (MS, PhD); elementary particle physics (MS, PhD); intermediate energy nuclear physics (MS); nuclear physics (MS, PhD); physics (MST); surface science (PhD); theoretical physics (MS, PhD). Part-time programs available. Terminal master's awarded for partial completion of doctoral program. *Degree requirements:* For master's, comprehensive exam, thesis or alternative; for doctorate, comprehensive exam, thesis/dissertation. *Entrance requirements:* For master's and doctorate, GRE General Test, GRE Subject Test. Additional exam requirements/recommendations for international students: Required—TOEFL (minimum score 560 paper-based). Electronic applications accepted. *Faculty research:* Astronomy, high energy, condensed matter, surface, nuclear physics.

University of Alberta, Faculty of Graduate Studies and Research, Department of Physics, Edmonton, AB T6G 2E1, Canada. Offers astrophysics (M Sc, PhD); condensed matter (M Sc, PhD); geophysics (M Sc, PhD); medical physics (M Sc, PhD); subatomic physics (M Sc, PhD). *Faculty:* 36 full-time (3 women), 7 part-time/adjunct (0 women). *Students:* 56 full-time (6 women), 16 part-time (2 women). 85 applicants, 35% accepted. In 2009, 7 master's, 10 doctorates awarded. *Degree requirements:* For master's, thesis; for doctorate, thesis/dissertation. *Entrance requirements:* For master's and doctorate, minimum GPA of 7.0 on a 9.0 scale. Additional exam requirements/recommendations for international students: Required—TOEFL. *Application deadline:* For fall admission, 2/15 priority date for domestic students. Applications are processed on a rolling basis. Tuition and fees charges are reported in Canadian dollars. *Expenses:* Tuition, area resident: Full-time $4626.24 Canadian dollars; part-time $99.72 Canadian dollars per unit. International tuition: $8216 Canadian dollars full-time. Required fees: $3589.92 Canadian dollars; $99.72 Canadian dollars per unit. $215 Canadian dollars per term. *Financial support:* In 2009–10, 6 fellowships with partial tuition reimbursements, 40 teaching assistantships were awarded; research assistantships, career-related internships or fieldwork, institutionally sponsored loans, and scholarships/grants also available. Financial award application deadline: 2/15. *Faculty research:* Cosmology, astroparticle physics, high-intermediate energy, magnetism, superconductivity. Total annual research expenditures: $3.1 million. *Unit head:* Dr. R. Marchand, Associate Chair, 780-492-1072, E-mail: assoc-chair@phys.ualberta.ca. *Application contact:* Lynn Chandler, Program Advisor, 780-492-1072, Fax: 780-492-0714, E-mail: grad.program@phys.ualberta.ca.

University of Victoria, Faculty of Graduate Studies, Faculty of Science, Department of Physics and Astronomy, Victoria, BC V8W 2Y2, Canada. Offers astronomy and astrophysics

University of Victoria (continued)
(M Sc, PhD); condensed matter physics (M Sc, PhD); experimental particle physics (M Sc, PhD); medical physics (M Sc, PhD); ocean physics (M Sc, PhD); theoretical physics (M Sc, PhD). *Degree requirements:* For master's, thesis; for doctorate, comprehensive exam, thesis/dissertation, candidacy exam. *Entrance requirements:* For master's and doctorate, GRE. Additional exam requirements/recommendations for international students: Required—TOEFL (minimum score 575 paper-based; 233 computer-based), IELTS (minimum score 7). Electronic applications accepted. *Faculty research:* Old stellar populations; observational cosmology and large scale structure; cp violation; atlas.

West Virginia University, Eberly College of Arts and Sciences, Department of Physics, Morgantown, WV 26506. Offers applied physics (MS, PhD); astrophysics (MS, PhD); chemical physics (MS, PhD); condensed matter physics (MS, PhD); elementary particle physics (MS, PhD); materials physics (MS, PhD); plasma physics (MS, PhD); solid state physics (MS, PhD); statistical physics (MS, PhD); theoretical physics (MS, PhD). Terminal master's awarded for partial completion of doctoral program. *Degree requirements:* For master's, thesis or alternative, qualifying exam; for doctorate, thesis/dissertation, qualifying exam. *Entrance requirements:* For master's and doctorate, GRE General Test, minimum GPA of 3.0. Additional exam requirements/recommendations for international students: Required—TOEFL. *Faculty research:* Experimental and theoretical condensed-matter, plasma, high-energy theory, nonlinear dynamics, space physics.

Mathematical Physics

New Mexico Institute of Mining and Technology, Graduate Studies, Department of Physics, Socorro, NM 87801. Offers astrophysics (MS, PhD); atmospheric physics (MS, PhD); instrumentation (MS); mathematical physics (PhD). *Degree requirements:* For master's, thesis optional; for doctorate, thesis/dissertation. *Entrance requirements:* For master's, GRE General Test; for doctorate, GRE General Test, GRE Subject Test. Additional exam requirements/recommendations for international students: Required—TOEFL (minimum score 540 paper-based; 207 computer-based). *Faculty research:* Cloud physics, stellar and extragalactic processes.

University of Alberta, Faculty of Graduate Studies and Research, Department of Mathematical and Statistical Sciences, Edmonton, AB T6G 2E1, Canada. Offers applied mathematics (M Sc, PhD); biostatistics (M Sc); mathematical finance (M Sc, PhD); mathematical physics (M Sc, PhD); mathematics (M Sc, PhD); statistics (M Sc, PhD, Postgraduate Diploma). Part-time programs available. *Faculty:* 48 full-time (4 women). *Students:* 112 full-time (41 women), 5 part-time (0 women). Average age 24. 776 applicants, 5% accepted, 34 enrolled. In 2009, 12 master's, 10 doctorates awarded. Terminal master's awarded for partial completion of doctoral program. *Degree requirements:* For master's, thesis (for some programs); for doctorate, comprehensive exam, thesis/dissertation. *Entrance requirements:* Additional exam requirements/recommendations for international students: Required—TOEFL (minimum score 580 paper-based; 237 computer-based). *Application deadline:* For fall admission, 3/1 for domestic students, 2/1 for international students. Applications are processed on a rolling basis. Application fee: $0. Electronic applications accepted. Tuition and fees charges are reported in Canadian dollars. *Expenses:* Tuition, area resident: Full-time $4626.24 Canadian dollars; part-time $99.72 Canadian dollars per unit. International tuition: $8216 Canadian dollars full-time. Required fees: $3589.92 Canadian dollars; $99.72 Canadian dollars per unit. $215 Canadian dollars per term. *Financial support:* In 2009–10, 51 research assistantships, 88 teaching assistantships with full and partial tuition reimbursements were awarded; scholarships/grants also available. Financial award application deadline: 5/1. *Faculty research:* Classical and functional analysis, algebra, differential equations, geometry. *Unit head:* Dr. Anthony To-Ming Lau, Chair, 403-492-5141, E-mail: tlau@math.ualberta.ca. *Application contact:* Dr. Yau Shu Wong, Associate Chair, Graduate Studies, 403-492-5799, Fax: 403-492-6828, E-mail: gradmail@math.ualberta.ca.

University of Colorado at Boulder, Graduate School, College of Arts and Sciences, Department of Physics, Boulder, CO 80309. Offers chemical physics (PhD); geophysics (PhD); liquid crystal science and technology (PhD); mathematical physics (PhD); medical physics (PhD); optical sciences and engineering (PhD); physics (MS, PhD). *Faculty:* 48 full-time (6 women). *Students:* 160 full-time (24 women), 47 part-time (8 women); includes 9 minority (6 Asian Americans or Pacific Islanders, 3 Hispanic Americans), 65 international. Average age 27. 548 applicants, 5% accepted, 27 enrolled. In 2009, 17 master's, 23 doctorates awarded. Terminal master's awarded for partial completion of doctoral program. *Degree requirements:* For master's, comprehensive exam, thesis or alternative; for doctorate, comprehensive exam, thesis/dissertation. *Entrance requirements:* For master's and doctorate, GRE General Test, GRE Subject Test, minimum undergraduate GPA of 3.0. Additional exam requirements/recommendations for international students: Required—TOEFL. *Application deadline:* For fall admission, 1/15 priority date for domestic students, 1/15 for international students. Applications are processed on a rolling basis. Application fee: $50 ($60 for international students). Electronic applications accepted. *Financial support:* In 2009–10, 21 fellowships with full tuition reimbursements (averaging $15,999 per year), 146 research assistantships with full tuition reimbursements (averaging $16,586 per year) were awarded; scholarships/grants also available. Financial award application deadline: 1/15. *Faculty research:* Atomic and molecular physics, nuclear physics, condensed matter, elementary particle physics, laser or optical physics, plasma physics, geophysics, astrophysics and chemical physics. Total annual research expenditures: $14.2 million.

Virginia Polytechnic Institute and State University, Graduate School, College of Science, Department of Mathematics, Blacksburg, VA 24061. Offers applied mathematics (MS, PhD); mathematical physics (MS, PhD); pure mathematics (MS, PhD). *Entrance requirements:* For master's and doctorate, GRE. Additional exam requirements/recommendations for international students: Required—TOEFL (minimum score 550 paper-based; 213 computer-based). Electronic applications accepted. *Faculty research:* Differential equations, operator theory, numerical analysis, algebra, control theory.

Optical Sciences

Air Force Institute of Technology, Graduate School of Engineering and Management, Department of Electrical and Computer Engineering, Dayton, OH 45433-7765. Offers computer engineering (MS, PhD); computer systems/science (MS); electrical engineering (MS, PhD); electro-optics (MS, PhD). *Accreditation:* ABET (one or more programs are accredited). Part-time programs available. *Degree requirements:* For master's, thesis; for doctorate, thesis/dissertation. *Entrance requirements:* For master's and doctorate, GRE General Test, minimum GPA of 3.0, U.S. citizenship. *Faculty research:* Remote sensing, information survivability, microelectronics, computer networks, artificial intelligence.

Air Force Institute of Technology, Graduate School of Engineering and Management, Department of Engineering Physics, Dayton, OH 45433-7765. Offers applied physics (MS, PhD); electro-optics (MS, PhD); materials science (PhD); nuclear engineering (MS, PhD); space physics (MS). Part-time programs available. *Degree requirements:* For master's, thesis; for doctorate, thesis/dissertation. *Entrance requirements:* For master's and doctorate, GRE General Test, minimum GPA of 3.0, U.S. citizenship. *Faculty research:* High-energy lasers, space physics, nuclear weapon effects, semiconductor physics.

Alabama Agricultural and Mechanical University, School of Graduate Studies, School of Arts and Sciences, Department of Physics, Huntsville, AL 35811. Offers physics (MS, PhD), including applied physics (PhD), materials science (PhD), optics/lasers (PhD). Part-time and evening/weekend programs available. *Degree requirements:* For doctorate, thesis/dissertation. *Entrance requirements:* For master's and doctorate, GRE General Test. Additional exam requirements/recommendations for international students: Required—TOEFL (minimum score 500 paper-based; 173 computer-based; 61 iBT). Electronic applications accepted.

The Catholic University of America, School of Engineering, Department of Electrical Engineering and Computer Science, Washington, DC 20064. Offers antennas and electromagnetic propagation (MEE, MSCS, D Engr); bioimaging (MEE, MSCS, PhD); bioinformatics and intelligent information systems (MEE, D Engr, PhD); distributed and real-time systems (MEE, MSCS, D Engr, PhD); high speed communications and networking (MSCS, D Engr, PhD); information security (MEE, MSCS, PhD); micro-optics (MEE, MSCS, D Engr, PhD); signal and image processing (MEE, MSCS, D Engr). Part-time programs available. *Faculty:* 7 full-time (2 women), 6 part-time/adjunct (0 women). *Students:* 10 full-time (4 women), 50 part-time (7 women); includes 10 minority (3 African Americans, 4 Asian Americans or Pacific Islanders, 3 Hispanic Americans), 12 international. Average age 34. 50 applicants, 54% accepted, 11 enrolled. In 2009, 10 master's awarded. *Degree requirements:* For master's, thesis or alternative; for doctorate, comprehensive exam, thesis/dissertation, qualifying exam, oral exams. *Entrance requirements:* For master's, statement of purpose, official copies of academic transcripts, three letters of recommendation; for doctorate, 3 letters of recommendation. Additional exam requirements/recommendations for international students: Required—TOEFL (minimum score 580 paper-based; 237 computer-based). *Application deadline:* For fall admission, 8/1 priority date for domestic students, 7/15 for international students; for spring admission, 12/1 priority date for domestic students, 10/15 for international students. Applications are processed on a rolling basis. Application fee: $55. Electronic applications accepted. *Expenses:* Contact institution. *Financial support:* Fellowships, research assistantships, teaching assistantships, Federal Work-Study, scholarships/grants, tuition waivers (full and partial), and unspecified assistantships available. Financial award application deadline: 2/1; financial award applicants required to submit FAFSA. *Faculty research:* Signal and image processing, computer communications, robotics, intelligent controls, bioelectromagnetics. Total annual research expenditures: $1.2 million. *Unit head:* Dr. Phillip Regalia, Chair, 202-319-5879, Fax: 202-319-5195, E-mail: regalia@cua.edu. *Application contact:* Julie Schwing, Director of Graduate Admissions, 202-319-5057, Fax: 202-319-6533, E-mail: cua-admissions@cua.edu.

Cleveland State University, College of Graduate Studies, College of Science, Department of Physics, Cleveland, OH 44115. Offers applied optics (MS); condensed matter physics (MS); medical physics (MS); optics and materials (MS); optics and medical imaging (MS). Part-time and evening/weekend programs available. *Entrance requirements:* For master's, undergraduate degree in engineering, physics, chemistry or mathematics. Additional exam requirements/recommendations for international students: Required—TOEFL (minimum score 525 paper-based; 197 computer-based), GRE. Electronic applications accepted. *Faculty research:* Statistical physics, experimental solid-state physics, theoretical optics, experimental biological physics (macromolecular crystallography), experimental optics.

Delaware State University, Graduate Programs, Department of Physics, Dover, DE 19901-2277. Offers applied optics (MS); optics (PhD); physics (MS); physics teaching (MS). Part-time and evening/weekend programs available. *Entrance requirements:* For master's, minimum GPA of 3.0 in major, 2.75 overall. Additional exam requirements/recommendations for international students: Required—TOEFL. Electronic applications accepted. *Faculty research:* Thermal properties of solids, nuclear physics, radiation damage in solids.

École Polytechnique de Montréal, Graduate Programs, Department of Engineering Physics, Montréal, QC H3C 3A7, Canada. Offers optical engineering (M Eng, M Sc A, PhD); solid-state physics and engineering (M Eng, M Sc A, PhD). Part-time programs available. *Degree requirements:* For master's, one foreign language, thesis; for doctorate, one foreign language, thesis/dissertation. *Entrance requirements:* For master's, minimum GPA of 2.75; for doctorate, minimum GPA of 3.0. *Faculty research:* Optics, thin-film physics, laser spectroscopy, plasmas, photonic devices.

Norfolk State University, School of Graduate Studies, School of Science and Technology, Program in Optical Engineering, Norfolk, VA 23504. Offers MS.

North Carolina Agricultural and Technical State University, Graduate School, College of Engineering, Department of Electrical and Computer Engineering, Greensboro, NC 27411. Offers electrical engineering (MSEE, PhD), including communications and signal processing (MSEE), computer engineering (MSEE), electronic and optical materials and devices (MSEE), power systems and controls (MSEE). Part-time programs available. *Degree requirements:* For master's, project, thesis defense; for doctorate, thesis/dissertation. *Entrance requirements:* For master's, GRE General Test, GRE Subject Test, minimum GPA of 2.8; for doctorate, GRE General Test, minimum GPA of 3.0. *Faculty research:* Semiconductor compounds, VLSI design, image processing, optical systems and devices, fault-tolerant computing.

The Ohio State University, College of Optometry and Graduate School, Program in Vision Science, Columbus, OH 43210. Offers MS, PhD, OD/MS. *Faculty:* 19 full-time (6 women), 3 part-time/adjunct (0 women). *Students:* 3 full-time (2 women), 7 part-time (4 women), 2 international. Average age 33. In 2009, 12 master's, 1 doctorate awarded. *Degree requirements:* For master's, thesis; for doctorate, thesis/dissertation. *Entrance requirements:* For master's and doctorate, GRE General Test. Additional exam requirements/recommendations for international students: Required—TOEFL. *Application deadline:* Applications are processed on a rolling basis. Application fee: $40 ($50 for international students). Electronic applications accepted. *Expenses:* Tuition, state resident: full-time $10,683. Tuition, nonresident: full-time $25,923. Tuition and fees vary according to course load and program. *Financial support:* In 2009–10, fellowships with tuition reimbursements (averaging $42,000 per year), research assistantships with full tuition reimbursements (averaging $12,000 per year), teaching assistantships with full tuition reimbursements (averaging $22,000 per year) were awarded; Federal Work-Study, scholarships/grants, traineeships, and unspecified assistantships also available. Financial award application deadline: 2/1; financial award applicants required to submit FAFSA. *Faculty research:* Ocular development, myopia, cornea, refractive error, quality of life. Total annual research expenditures: $9 million. *Unit head:* Dr. Karla Zadnik, Graduate Studies Committee Chair, 614-292-6606, Fax: 614-292-7493, E-mail: zadnik.4@osu.edu. *Application contact:* Graduate Admissions, 614-292-9444, Fax: 614-292-3895, E-mail: domestic.grad@osu.edu.

Rochester Institute of Technology, Graduate Enrollment Services, College of Science, Center for Imaging Science, Rochester, NY 14623-5603. Offers MS, PhD. Part-time programs available. Postbaccalaureate distance learning degree programs offered (no on-campus study). *Students:* 63 full-time (18 women), 36 part-time (6 women); includes 8 minority (3 African Americans, 3 Asian Americans or Pacific Islanders, 2 Hispanic Americans), 35 international. Average age 31. 69 applicants, 61% accepted, 29 enrolled. In 2009, 19 master's, 9 doctorates awarded. Terminal master's awarded for partial completion of doctoral program. *Degree requirements:* For master's, thesis; for doctorate, thesis/dissertation. *Entrance requirements:* For master's, GRE, minimum GPA of 3.0. Additional exam requirements/recommendations for international students: Required—TOEFL (minimum score 600 paper-based; 250 computer-based; 100 iBT), or IELTS (minimum score 6.5). *Application deadline:* For fall admission, 1/15 priority date for domestic and international students. Applications are processed on a rolling basis. Application fee: $50. Electronic applications accepted. *Expenses:* Tuition: Full-time $31,533; part-time $876 per credit hour. Required fees: $210. *Financial support:* In 2009–10, 70 students received support; fellowships with full and partial tuition reimbursements available, research assistantships with full and partial tuition reimbursements available, teaching assistantships with full and partial tuition reimbursements available, career-related internships or fieldwork, scholarships/grants, and unspecified assistantships available. Support available to part-time students. Financial award applicants required to submit FAFSA. *Faculty research:* Algorithms, astrophysics, biomedical, color science, nanoimaging and materials, printing materials and processes, remote sensing, sensors and imaging systems, vision. *Unit head:* Dr. Stefi Baum, Director, 585-475-6220, Fax: 585-475-5988, E-mail: baum@cis.rit.edu. *Application contact:* Diane Ellison, Assistant Vice President, Graduate Enrollment Services, 585-475-2229, Fax: 585-475-7164, E-mail: gradinfo@rit.edu.

Rose-Hulman Institute of Technology, Faculty of Engineering and Applied Sciences, Department of Physics and Optical Engineering, Terre Haute, IN 47803-3999. Offers optical engineering (MS). Part-time programs available. *Faculty:* 16 full-time (3 women), 1 part-time/adjunct (0 women). *Students:* 8 full-time (2 women), 2 part-time (0 women), 2 international. Average age 24. 12 applicants, 92% accepted, 7 enrolled. In 2009, 2 master's awarded. *Degree requirements:* For master's, thesis. *Entrance requirements:* For master's, GRE, minimum GPA of 3.0. Additional exam requirements/recommendations for international students: Required—TOEFL (minimum score 580 paper-based; 237 computer-based; 92 iBT). *Application deadline:* For fall admission, 2/1 priority date for domestic students. Applications are processed on a rolling basis. Application fee: $0. *Expenses:* Tuition: Full-time $33,900; part-time $987 per credit hour. *Financial support:* In 2009–10, 6 students received support; fellowships with full and partial tuition reimbursements available, research assistantships with full and partial tuition reimbursements available, teaching assistantships, institutionally sponsored loans, scholarships/grants, and tuition waivers (full and partial) available. Financial award application deadline: 2/1. *Faculty research:* Optical design, laser systems, non-linear optics, metrology, optical MEMs, bio-photonics. Total annual research expenditures: $430,205. *Unit head:* Dr. Charles Joenathan, Chairman, 812-877-8494, Fax: 812-877-8023, E-mail: charles.joenathan@rose-hulman.edu. *Application contact:* Dr. Daniel J. Moore, Associate Dean of the Faculty, 812-877-8110, Fax: 812-877-8061, E-mail: daniel.j.moore@rose-hulman.edu.

The University of Alabama in Huntsville, School of Graduate Studies, College of Engineering, Department of Electrical and Computer Engineering, Huntsville, AL 35899. Offers computer engineering (MSE, PhD); electrical engineering (MSE, PhD); optical science and engineering (PhD); optics and photonics (MSE); software engineering (MSSE). Part-time and evening/weekend programs available. *Faculty:* 22 full-time (2 women), 3 part-time/adjunct (0 women). *Students:* 42 full-time (10 women), 147 part-time (18 women); includes 16 minority (7 African Americans, 6 Asian Americans or Pacific Islanders, 3 Hispanic Americans), 28 international. Average age 31. 205 applicants, 53% accepted, 58 enrolled. In 2009, 53 master's, 4 doctorates awarded. *Degree requirements:* For master's, comprehensive exam, thesis or alternative, oral and written exams; for doctorate, comprehensive exam, thesis/dissertation, oral and written exams. *Entrance requirements:* For master's, GRE General Test, appropriate bachelor's degree, minimum GPA of 3.0; for doctorate, GRE General Test, minimum GPA of 3.0. Additional exam requirements/recommendations for international students: Required—TOEFL (minimum score 500 paper-based; 173 computer-based; 62 iBT). *Application deadline:* For fall admission, 7/15 for domestic students, 4/1 for international students; for spring admission, 11/30 for domestic students, 9/1 for international students. Applications are processed on a rolling basis. Application fee: $40 ($50 for international students). Electronic applications accepted. *Expenses:* Tuition, state resident: part-time $355.75 per credit hour. Tuition, nonresident: part-time $847.10 per credit hour. Required fees: $210.80 per semester. Tuition and fees vary according to course load and program. *Financial support:* In 2009–10, 28 students received support, including 11 research assistantships with full and partial tuition reimbursements available (averaging $11,113 per year), 16 teaching assistantships with full and partial tuition reimbursements available (averaging $10,479 per year); career-related internships or fieldwork, Federal Work-Study, institutionally sponsored loans, scholarships/grants, health care benefits, tuition waivers, and unspecified assistantships also available. Support available to part-time students. Financial award application deadline: 4/1; financial award applicants required to submit FAFSA. *Faculty research:* Optical signal processing, electromagnetics, photonics, nonlinear waves, computer architecture. Total annual research expenditures: $3.4 million. *Unit head:* Dr. Reza Adhami, Chair, 256-824-6316, Fax: 256-824-6803, E-mail: adhami@ece.uah.edu. *Application contact:* Kathy Biggs, Graduate Studies Admissions Manager, 256-824-6199, Fax: 256-824-6405, E-mail: deangrad@uah.edu.

The University of Alabama in Huntsville, School of Graduate Studies, Interdisciplinary Studies, Interdisciplinary Program in Optical Science and Engineering, Huntsville, AL 35899. Offers PhD. Part-time and evening/weekend programs available. *Faculty:* 17 full-time (0 women). *Students:* 7 full-time (1 woman), 7 part-time (0 women); includes 1 minority (African American), 6 international. Average age 30. 15 applicants, 27% accepted, 0 enrolled. *Degree requirements:* For doctorate, comprehensive exam, thesis/dissertation, written and oral exams. *Entrance requirements:* For doctorate, GRE General Test, minimum GPA of 3.0, BS in physical science or engineering. Additional exam requirements/recommendations for international students: Required—TOEFL (minimum score 550 paper-based; 213 computer-based; 62 iBT). *Application deadline:* For fall admission, 7/15 for domestic students, 4/1 for international students; for spring admission, 11/30 for domestic students, 9/1 for international students. Applications are processed on a rolling basis. Application fee: $40 ($50 for international students). Electronic applications accepted. *Expenses:* Tuition, state resident: part-time $355.75 per credit hour. Tuition, nonresident: part-time $847.10 per credit hour. Required fees: $210.80 per semester. Tuition and fees vary according to course load and program. *Financial support:* In 2009–10, 6 students received support, including 5 research assistantships with full and partial tuition reimbursements available (averaging $11,987 per year), 1 teaching assistantship with full and partial tuition reimbursement available (averaging $12,600 per year); career-related internships or fieldwork, Federal Work-Study, institutionally sponsored loans, scholarships/grants, health care benefits, and unspecified assistantships also available. Support available to part-time students. Financial award application deadline: 4/1; financial award applicants required to submit FAFSA. *Faculty research:* Laser technology, holography, optical communications, medical image processing, computer design. Total annual research expenditures: $1.3 million. *Unit head:* Dr. Robert G. Lindquist, Program Director, 256-824-2882, Fax: 256-824-6618, E-mail: lindquist@ece.uah.edu. *Application contact:* Kathy Biggs, Graduate Studies Admissions Manager, 256-824-6199, Fax: 256-824-6405, E-mail: deangrad@uah.edu.

The University of Arizona, College of Optical Sciences, Tucson, AZ 85721. Offers MS, PhD. Part-time programs available. *Faculty:* 28. *Students:* 87 full-time (24 women), 189 part-time (31 women); includes 5 minority (1 African American, 2 Asian Americans or Pacific Islanders, 2 Hispanic Americans), 86 international. Average age 31. 214 applicants, 29% accepted, 57 enrolled. In 2009, 45 master's, 23 doctorates awarded. *Degree requirements:* For master's, thesis (for some programs), exam; for doctorate, thesis/dissertation, oral and written exams. *Entrance requirements:* For master's, GRE General Test, GRE Subject Test (recommended), minimum GPA of 3.0, 2 letters of recommendation, resume; for doctorate, GRE General Test, GRE Subject Test (recommended), minimum GPA of 3.0, 2 letters of recommendation, statement of purpose, resume. Additional exam requirements/recommendations for international students: Required—TOEFL. *Application deadline:* For fall admission, 1/1 for domestic students, 12/1 for international students. Applications are processed on a rolling basis. Application fee: $75. Electronic applications accepted. *Expenses:* Tuition, state resident: full-time $9028. Tuition, nonresident: full-time $24,890. *Financial support:* In 2009–10, 98 research assistantships with full tuition reimbursements (averaging $17,153 per year), 25 teaching assistantships with full tuition reimbursements (averaging $16,159 per year) were awarded; fellowships, scholarships/grants also available. Financial award application deadline: 1/1. *Faculty research:* Medical optics, medical imaging, optical data storage, optical bistability, nonlinear optical effects. Total annual research expenditures: $17.8 million. *Unit head:* Dr. James Wyant, Dean, 520-621-6997, Fax: 520-621-9613, E-mail: jcwyant@optics.arizona.edu. *Application contact:* Gail Varin, Coordinator, Graduate Academic Progress, 520-626-0888, E-mail: gail@optics.arizona.edu.

University of Central Florida, College of Optics and Photonics, Orlando, FL 32816. Offers optics (MS, PhD). Part-time and evening/weekend programs available. *Faculty:* 20 full-time (0 women). *Students:* 116 full-time (22 women), 14 part-time (0 women); includes 10 minority (4 African Americans, 2 Asian Americans or Pacific Islanders, 4 Hispanic Americans), 71 international. Average age 28. 155 applicants, 32% accepted, 24 enrolled. In 2009, 27 master's, 12 doctorates awarded. *Degree requirements:* For master's, thesis or alternative; for doctorate, thesis/dissertation, departmental qualifying exam, candidacy exam. *Entrance requirements:* For master's, GRE General Test, minimum GPA of 3.0 in last 60 hours; for doctorate, GRE General Test, minimum GPA of 3.5 in last 60 hours. Additional exam requirements/recommendations for international students: Required—TOEFL. *Application deadline:* For fall admission, 2/1 priority date for domestic students; for spring admission, 12/1 for domestic students. Application fee: $30. Electronic applications accepted. *Expenses:* Tuition, state resident: part-time $306.31 per credit hour. Tuition, nonresident: part-time $1099.01 per credit hour. Part-time tuition and fees vary according to degree level and program. *Financial support:* In 2009–10, 93 students received support, including 17 fellowships with partial tuition reimbursements available (averaging $4,800 per year), 118 research assistantships with partial tuition reimbursements available (averaging $11,100 per year); teaching assistantships with partial tuition reimbursements available, career-related internships or fieldwork, Federal Work-Study, institutionally sponsored loans, tuition waivers (partial), and unspecified assistantships also available. Financial award application deadline: 3/1; financial award applicants required to submit FAFSA. *Unit head:* Dr. Bahaa E. Saleh, Dean and Director, 407-882-3326, E-mail: besaleh@creol.ucf.edu. *Application contact:* Dr. Bahaa E. Saleh, Dean and Director, 407-882-3326, E-mail: besaleh@creol.ucf.edu.

University of Colorado at Boulder, Graduate School, College of Arts and Sciences, Department of Physics, Boulder, CO 80309. Offers chemical physics (PhD); geophysics (PhD); liquid crystal science and technology (PhD); mathematical physics (PhD); medical physics (PhD); optical sciences and engineering (PhD); physics (MS, PhD). *Faculty:* 48 full-time (6 women). *Students:* 160 full-time (24 women), 47 part-time (8 women); includes 9 minority (6 Asian Americans or Pacific Islanders, 3 Hispanic Americans), 65 international. Average age 27. 548 applicants, 5% accepted, 27 enrolled. In 2009, 17 master's, 23 doctorates awarded. Terminal master's awarded for partial completion of doctoral program. *Degree requirements:* For master's, comprehensive exam, thesis or alternative; for doctorate, comprehensive exam, thesis/dissertation. *Entrance requirements:* For master's and doctorate, GRE General Test, GRE Subject Test, minimum undergraduate GPA of 3.0. Additional exam requirements/recommendations for international students: Required—TOEFL. *Application deadline:* For fall admission, 1/15 priority date for domestic students, 1/15 for international students. Applications are processed on a rolling basis. Application fee: $50 ($60 for international students). Electronic applications accepted. *Financial support:* In 2009–10, 21 fellowships with full tuition reimbursements (averaging $15,999 per year), 146 research assistantships with full tuition reimbursements (averaging $16,586 per year) were awarded; scholarships/grants also available. Financial award application deadline: 1/15. *Faculty research:* Atomic and molecular physics, nuclear physics, condensed matter, elementary particle physics, laser or optical physics, plasma physics, geophysics, astrophysics and chemical physics. Total annual research expenditures: $14.2 million.

University of Dayton, Graduate School, School of Engineering, Program in Electro-Optics, Dayton, OH 45469-1300. Offers MSEO, PhD. Part-time and evening/weekend programs available. *Faculty:* 6 full-time (0 women), 2 part-time/adjunct (0 women). *Students:* 30 full-time (6 women), 6 part-time (0 women); includes 1 minority (Asian American or Pacific Islander), 14 international. Average age 27. 72 applicants, 44% accepted, 13 enrolled. In 2009, 6 master's, 5 doctorates awarded. *Degree requirements:* For master's, thesis optional; for doctorate, thesis/dissertation, departmental qualifying exam. *Entrance requirements:* For doctorate, MS. Additional exam requirements/recommendations for international students: Required—TOEFL (minimum score 550 paper-based; 213 computer-based; 80 iBT). *Application deadline:* For fall admission, 8/1 for domestic students, 3/1 priority date for international students; for winter admission, 7/1 priority date for international students; for spring admission, 1/1 priority date for international students. Applications are processed on a rolling basis. Application fee: $0 ($50 for international students). Electronic applications accepted. *Expenses:* Tuition: Full-time $8412; part-time $701 per credit hour. Required fees: $325; $65 per course. $25 per semester. Tuition and fees vary according to course load, degree level and program. *Financial support:* In 2009–10, 3 fellowships with full tuition reimbursements (averaging $30,000 per year), 15 research assistantships with full tuition reimbursements (averaging $15,000 per year), 3 teaching assistantships with full tuition reimbursements (averaging $9,000 per year) were awarded. Financial award applicants required to submit FAFSA. *Faculty research:* Spatial and spatiotemporal solitary waves and their stabilization in nonlinear negative index materials, stimulated photorefractive backscatter leading to six-wave mixing and phase conjugation in iron doped lithium niobate, modeling and characterization of PLZT adaptive microlenses, experimental investigation of self-starting operation in a F8L based on a symmetrical NOLM, negative refraction and sub-wavelength focusing in the visible range using transparent metallo-dielectric stacks. Total annual research expenditures: $1.8 million. *Unit head:* Dr. Joseph W.

Optical Sciences

University of Dayton (continued)
Haus, Director, 937-229-2797, Fax: 937-229-2097, E-mail: jhaus@notes.udayton.edu. *Application contact:* Graduate Admissions, 937-229-4411, Fax: 937-229-4729, E-mail: gradadmission@udayton.edu.

University of Maryland, Baltimore County, Graduate School, College of Natural and Mathematical Sciences, Department of Physics, Program in Applied Physics, Baltimore, MD 21250. Offers astrophysics (PhD); optics (MS, PhD); quantum optics (PhD); solid state physics (MS, PhD). Part-time programs available. *Faculty:* 24 full-time (3 women), 18 part-time/adjunct (2 women). *Students:* 31 full-time (10 women), 3 part-time (0 women); includes 3 minority (all African Americans), 15 international. Average age 24. 28 applicants, 43% accepted, 6 enrolled. In 2009, 4 master's, 4 doctorates awarded. Terminal master's awarded for partial completion of doctoral program. *Degree requirements:* For master's, thesis optional; for doctorate, comprehensive exam, thesis/dissertation. *Entrance requirements:* For master's, GRE General Test, minimum GPA of 3.0; for doctorate, GRE General Test, GRE Subject Test, minimum GPA of 3.0. Additional exam requirements/recommendations for international students: Required—TOEFL. *Application deadline:* For fall admission, 5/31 for domestic and international students; for spring admission, 11/30 for domestic students. Applications are processed on a rolling basis. Application fee: $50. Electronic applications accepted. *Financial support:* In 2009–10, 30 students received support, including 4 fellowships with full tuition reimbursements available (averaging $27,000 per year), 14 research assistantships with full tuition reimbursements available (averaging $24,000 per year), 12 teaching assistantships with full tuition reimbursements available (averaging $22,000 per year); career-related internships or fieldwork, scholarships/grants, health care benefits, and unspecified assistantships also available. Support available to part-time students. Financial award application deadline: 5/31. *Faculty research:* Astrophysics, atmospheric physics, nanophysics, optics, quantum optics and quantum information. Total annual research expenditures: $4.8 million. *Unit head:* Dr. Todd Pittman, Graduate Program Director, 410-455-2513, Fax: 410-455-1072, E-mail: todd.pittman@umbc.edu. *Application contact:* Dr. Lazlo L. Takacs, Director, 410-455-2524, Fax: 410-455-1072, E-mail: takacs@umbc.edu.

University of Massachusetts Lowell, College of Arts and Sciences, Department of Physics and Applied Physics, Program in Applied Physics, Lowell, MA 01854-2881. Offers applied mechanics (PhD); applied physics (MS, PhD), including optical sciences (MS). Terminal master's awarded for partial completion of doctoral program. *Degree requirements:* For master's, thesis; for doctorate, 2 foreign languages, thesis/dissertation. *Entrance requirements:* For master's, GRE General Test, 3 letters of reference; for doctorate, GRE General Test, transcripts, 3 letters of reference. Additional exam requirements/recommendations for international students: Required—TOEFL.

University of New Mexico, Graduate School, College of Arts and Sciences, Program in Optical Science and Engineering, Albuquerque, NM 87131-2039. Offers MS, PhD. Part-time programs available. *Students:* 36 full-time (10 women), 22 part-time (1 woman); includes 1 minority (Asian American or Pacific Islander), 35 international. Average age 29. 79 applicants, 43% accepted, 16 enrolled. In 2009, 7 master's, 5 doctorates awarded. Terminal master's awarded for partial completion of doctoral program. *Degree requirements:* For master's, comprehensive exam (for some programs), thesis (for some programs); for doctorate, comprehensive exam, thesis/dissertation. *Entrance requirements:* For master's, GRE, relevant undergraduate coursework, GPA, CV and letters of recommendation; for doctorate, GRE, relevant undergraduate coursework, GPA, CV, letters of recommendation. Additional exam requirements/recommendations for international students: Required—TOEFL (minimum score 575 paper-based; 213 computer-based; 79 iBT). *Application deadline:* For fall admission, 1/15 for domestic students; for spring admission, 8/1 for domestic students. Application fee: $50. Electronic applications accepted. *Expenses:* Tuition, state resident: full-time $2098.80; part-time $233.20 per credit hour. Tuition, nonresident: full-time $6650. Required fees: $25 per semester. Tuition and fees vary according to course load, program and reciprocity agreements. *Financial support:* In 2009–10, 24 research assistantships with full tuition reimbursements (averaging $15,000 per year), 6 teaching assistantships with full tuition reimbursements (averaging $15,000 per year) were awarded; fellowships with full tuition reimbursements, career-related internships or fieldwork, scholarships/grants, health care benefits, and unspecified assistantships also available. Support available to part-time students. Financial award application deadline: 2/1. *Faculty research:* Advanced materials, atom optics, biomedical optics, fiber optics, laser cooling, high intensity interactions, lithography, nano photonics, nonlinear optics, optical imaging, optical sensors, optoelectronics, quantum optics, spectroscopy, ultrafast phenomena. *Unit head:* Dr. Luke Lester, General Chair, 505-277-7805, Fax: 505-277-7801, E-mail: luke@chtm.unm.edu. *Application contact:* Doris Williams, Program Advisor, 505-277-7764, Fax: 505-277-7801, E-mail: dorisw@chtm.unm.edu.

The University of North Carolina at Charlotte, Graduate School, College of Arts and Sciences, Department of Physics and Optical Science, Program in Optical Science and Engineering, Charlotte, NC 28223-0001. Offers MS, PhD. Part-time programs available. *Faculty:* 23 full-time (3 women), 4 part-time/adjunct (0 women). *Students:* 27 full-time (2 women), 14 part-time (4 women); includes 1 Asian American or Pacific Islander, 21 international. Average age 30. 33 applicants, 48% accepted, 11 enrolled. In 2009, 1 master's, 2 doctorates awarded. *Degree requirements:* For master's, thesis; for doctorate, thesis/dissertation. *Entrance requirements:* For master's, GRE, minimum GPA of 3.0; for doctorate, GRE, minimum GPA of 3.2 in major, 3.0 overall. Additional exam requirements/recommendations for international students: Required—TOEFL (minimum score 557 paper-based; 220 computer-based; 83 iBT). *Application deadline:* For fall admission, 7/15 for domestic students, 5/1 for international students; for spring admission, 11/15 for domestic students, 10/1 for international students. Applications are processed on a rolling basis. Application fee: $55. Electronic applications accepted. *Financial support:* In 2009–10, 33 students received support, including 6 fellowships (averaging $39,477 per year), 6 research assistantships (averaging $10,611 per year), 21 teaching assistantships (averaging $12,455 per year); career-related internships or fieldwork, institutionally sponsored loans, scholarships/grants, and administrative assistantship also available. Support available to part-time students. Financial award application deadline: 4/1; financial award applicants required to submit FAFSA. Total annual research expenditures: $1.1 million. *Unit head:* Dr. Angela Davies, Graduate Coordinator, 704-687-8135, Fax: 704-687-3160, E-mail: adavies@uncc.edu. *Application contact:* Kathy B. Giddings, Director of Graduate Admissions, 704-687-5503, Fax: 704-687-3279, E-mail: gradadm@uncc.edu.

University of Rochester, The College, School of Engineering and Applied Sciences, Institute of Optics, Rochester, NY 14627. Offers MS, PhD. Terminal master's awarded for partial completion of doctoral program. *Degree requirements:* For master's, comprehensive exam; for doctorate, thesis/dissertation, preliminary and qualifying exams. *Entrance requirements:* For master's and doctorate, GRE. Additional exam requirements/recommendations for international students: Required—TOEFL.

University of Rochester, School of Nursing, Rochester, NY 14642. Offers acute care nurse practitioner (MS); adult nurse practitioner (MS); adult psychiatric mental health nurse practitioner (MS); adult/geriatric nurse practitioner (MS); care of children and families/pediatric nurse practitioner (MS); care of children and families/pediatric nurse practitioner with pediatric behavioral health (MS); care of children and families/pediatric nurse practitioner/neonatal nurse practitioner (MS); child and adolescent psychiatric mental health nurse practitioner (MS); clinical nurse leader (MS); disaster response and emergency preparedness (MS); family nurse practitioner (MS); health care organization management and leadership (MS); health practice research (PhD); health promotion, education and technology (MS); nursing (Certificate). *Accreditation:* AACN; NLN (one or more programs are accredited). Part-time programs available. Postbaccalaureate distance learning degree programs offered (minimal on-campus study). *Faculty:* 26 full-time (24 women), 20 part-time/adjunct (15 women). *Students:* 50 full-time (45 women), 178 part-time (165 women); includes 33 minority (17 African Americans, 2 American Indian/Alaska Native, 10 Asian Americans or Pacific Islanders, 4 Hispanic Americans), 11 international. Average age 35. 56 applicants, 80% accepted, 35 enrolled. In 2009, 53 master's, 5 doctorates awarded. Terminal master's awarded for partial completion of doctoral program. *Degree requirements:* For master's, comprehensive exam or thesis; for doctorate, thesis/dissertation. *Entrance requirements:* For master's, BS in nursing, minimum GPA of 3.0, course work in statistics; for doctorate, GRE General Test, MS in nursing, minimum GPA of 3.5; for Certificate, MS in nursing. Additional exam requirements/recommendations for international students: Recommended—TOEFL (minimum score 560 paper-based; 230 computer-based; 88 iBT). *Application deadline:* For fall admission, 11/1 priority date for domestic and international students. Application fee: $50. *Financial support:* In 2009–10, 53 students received support, including 14 fellowships with full and partial tuition reimbursements available (averaging $17,497 per year); scholarships/grants, traineeships, health care benefits, tuition waivers (partial), and unspecified assistantships also available. Support available to part-time students. Financial award application deadline: 6/30. *Faculty research:* Clinical research in aging, managing asthma in children, interventions to improve outcomes in critically ill children and their mothers, nurse home visitation studies, medical device evaluation, critical care clinical studies, high risk behavior and prevention, palliative care, pregnancy-related weight gain. Total annual research expenditures: $4.8 million. *Unit head:* Dr. Kathy P. Parker, Dean, 585-273-5639, Fax: 585-273-1268, E-mail: kathy_parker@urmc.rochester.edu. *Application contact:* Elaine Andolina, Director of Admissions, 585-275-2375, Fax: 585-756-8299, E-mail: elaine_andolina@urmc.rochester.edu.

Photonics

Boston University, College of Engineering, Department of Electrical and Computer Engineering, Boston, MA 02215. Offers computer engineering (MS, PhD); electrical engineering (MS, PhD); photonics (MS). Part-time programs available. *Faculty:* 41 full-time (3 women). *Students:* 182 full-time (40 women), 16 part-time (2 women); includes 21 minority (4 African Americans, 15 Asian Americans or Pacific Islanders, 2 Hispanic Americans), 118 international. Average age 24. 592 applicants, 30% accepted, 66 enrolled. In 2009, 62 master's, 19 doctorates awarded. Terminal master's awarded for partial completion of doctoral program. *Degree requirements:* For master's, thesis optional; for doctorate, comprehensive exam, thesis/dissertation. *Entrance requirements:* For master's and doctorate, GRE General Test. Additional exam requirements/recommendations for international students: Required—TOEFL (minimum score 550 paper-based; 213 computer-based; 84 iBT), IELTS (minimum score 6). *Application deadline:* For fall admission, 4/1 for domestic and international students; for spring admission, 10/1 for domestic and international students. Applications are processed on a rolling basis. Application fee: $70. Electronic applications accepted. *Expenses:* Tuition: Full-time $37,910; part-time $1184 per credit hour. Required fees: $386; $40 per semester. Part-time tuition and fees vary according to class time, course level, degree level and program. *Financial support:* In 2009–10, 134 students received support, including 11 fellowships with full tuition reimbursements available (averaging $27,600 per year), 88 research assistantships with full tuition reimbursements available (averaging $18,400 per year), 18 teaching assistantships with full tuition reimbursements available (averaging $18,400 per year); career-related internships or fieldwork, Federal Work-Study, institutionally sponsored loans, scholarships/grants, traineeships, and health care benefits also available. Financial award application deadline: 1/15; financial award applicants required to submit FAFSA. *Faculty research:* Communications and computer networks; signal, image, video, and multimedia processing; solid-state materials, devices, and photonics; systems, control, and reliable computing; VLSI, computer engineering and high-performance computing. *Unit head:* Dr. Francesco Cerrina, Chairman, 617-353-7175, Fax: 617-353-6440, E-mail: fcerrina@bu.edu. *Application contact:* Cheryl Kelley, Director of Graduate Programs, 617-353-9760, Fax: 617-353-0259, E-mail: enggrad@bu.edu.

Lehigh University, College of Arts and Sciences, Department of Physics, Bethlehem, PA 18015. Offers photonics (MS); physics (MS, PhD); polymer science (MS, PhD). Part-time programs available. *Faculty:* 17 full-time (1 woman), 1 part-time/adjunct (0 women). *Students:* 48 full-time (13 women), 1 part-time (0 women); includes 1 minority (African American), 19 international. Average age 26. 100 applicants, 13% accepted, 9 enrolled. In 2009, 6 doctorates awarded. *Degree requirements:* For doctorate, comprehensive exam, thesis/dissertation. *Entrance requirements:* Additional exam requirements/recommendations for international students: Required—TOEFL (minimum score 213 computer-based; 85 iBT). *Application deadline:* For fall admission, 2/15 priority date for domestic and international students. Applications are processed on a rolling basis. Application fee: $65. Electronic applications accepted. *Financial support:* In 2009–10, 47 students received support, including 4 fellowships with full tuition reimbursements available (averaging $23,000 per year), 23 research assistantships with full tuition reimbursements available (averaging $22,180 per year), 20 teaching assistantships with full tuition reimbursements available (averaging $22,180 per year); career-related internships or fieldwork, Federal Work-Study, institutionally sponsored loans, scholarships/grants, tuition waivers (full and partial), and unspecified assistantships also available. Support available to part-time students. Financial award application deadline: 1/15. *Faculty research:* Condensed matter physics; atomic, molecular and optical physics; plasma physics; nonlinear optics and photonics; astronomy and astrophysics. Total annual research expenditures: $2.9 million. *Unit head:* Dr. Volkmar Dierolf, Chair, 610-758-3915, Fax: 610-758-5730, E-mail: vod2@lehigh.edu. *Application contact:* Dr. Ivan Biaggio, Graduate Admissions Officer, 610-758-4916, Fax: 610-758-5730, E-mail: ivb2@lehigh.edu.

Lehigh University, P.C. Rossin College of Engineering and Applied Science, Department of Electrical and Computer Engineering, Bethlehem, PA 18015. Offers electrical engineering (M Eng, MS, PhD); photonics (MS); wireless network engineering (MS). Part-time programs available. *Faculty:* 19 full-time (3 women). *Students:* 68 full-time (15 women), 16 part-time (5 women), 66 international. Average age 27. 215 applicants, 23% accepted, 22 enrolled. In 2009, 13 master's, 6 doctorates awarded. Terminal master's awarded for partial completion of doctoral program. *Degree requirements:* For master's, thesis optional; for doctorate, thesis/dissertation, qualifying or comprehensive exam for all 1st year PhD's; general exam 7 months or more prior to completion/dissertation defense. *Entrance requirements:* For master's and doctorate, GRE General Test, BS in field or related field. Additional exam requirements/recommendations for international students: Required—TOEFL (minimum score 79 iBT). *Application deadline:* For fall admission, 1/15 priority date for domestic and international students; for spring admission, 11/1 for domestic and international students. Application fee: $70. Electronic applications accepted. *Financial support:* In 2009–10, 67 students received support, including 4 fellowships with full tuition reimbursements available (averaging $15,300 per year), 42 research assistantships with full tuition reimbursements available (averaging $20,000 per year), 6 teaching assistantships with full tuition reimbursements available (averaging $15,300 per year); career-related internships or fieldwork, Federal Work-Study, institutionally sponsored loans, scholarships/grants, tuition waivers (full and partial), and unspecified assistantships also available. Support available to part-time students. Financial award application deadline: 1/15. *Faculty research:* Nanostructures/nanodevices, Terahertz generation, analog devices, mixed mode design and signal circuits, optoelectronic sensors, micro-fabrication technology and design, packaging/reliability of microsensors, coding and networking information theory, radio frequency, wireless and optical wireless communication, wireless networks. Total annual research expenditures: $3.6 million. *Unit head:* Dr. Filbert J. Bartoli, Chair, 610-758-4069, Fax: 610-758-6279, E-mail: dmb4@lehigh.edu. *Application contact:* Tammy Shellock, Graduate Coordinator, 610-758-4072, Fax: 610-758-6279, E-mail: tjs7@lehigh.edu.

Lehigh University, P.C. Rossin College of Engineering and Applied Science, Department of Materials Science and Engineering, Bethlehem, PA 18015. Offers materials science and engineering (M Eng, MS, PhD); photonics (MS); polymer science/engineering (M Eng, MS, PhD); MBA/E. Part-time programs available. *Faculty:* 13 full-time (3 women). *Students:* 26 full-time (3 women), 4 part-time (2 women), 15 international. Average age 26. 163 applicants, 4% accepted, 2 enrolled. In 2009, 2 master's, 4 doctorates awarded. *Degree requirements:* For master's, thesis; for doctorate, comprehensive exam, thesis/dissertation. *Entrance requirements:* For master's and doctorate, GRE General Test, minimum GPA of 3.0. Additional exam requirements/recommendations for international students: Required—TOEFL. *Application deadline:* For fall admission, 1/15 priority date for domestic students, 1/15 for international students; for spring admission, 12/1 priority date for domestic students, 12/1 for international students. Applications are processed on a rolling basis. Application fee: $65. Electronic applications accepted. *Financial support:* In 2009–10, 27 students received support, including 5 fellowships with full and partial tuition reimbursements available (averaging $22,400 per year), 21 research assistantships with full tuition reimbursements available (averaging $22,449 per year), 6 teaching assistantships with partial tuition reimbursements available (averaging $17,512 per year); career-related internships or fieldwork, Federal Work-Study, institutionally sponsored loans, scholarships/grants, and unspecified assistantships also available. Support available to part-time students. Financial award application deadline: 1/15. *Faculty research:* Metals, ceramics, crystals, polymers, fatigue crack propagation. Total annual research expenditures: $4 million. *Unit head:* Dr. Helen Chan, Chairperson, 610-758-5554, Fax: 610-758-4244, E-mail: hmc0@lehigh.edu. *Application contact:* Anne Marie Lobley, Graduate Administrative Coordinator, 610-758-4222, Fax: 610-758-4244, E-mail: amme@lehigh.edu.

Oklahoma State University, College of Arts and Sciences, Department of Physics, Stillwater, OK 74078. Offers photonics (MS, PhD); physics (MS, PhD). *Faculty:* 30 full-time (8 women), 1 part-time/adjunct (0 women). *Students:* 1 full-time (0 women), 45 part-time (9 women); includes 3 minority (all Hispanic Americans), 31 international. Average age 29. 54 applicants, 31% accepted, 6 enrolled. In 2009, 2 master's, 2 doctorates awarded. *Degree requirements:* For master's, thesis; for doctorate, comprehensive exam, thesis/dissertation, oral defense of dissertation, preliminary exam, qualifying exam. *Entrance requirements:* For master's and doctorate, GRE. Additional exam requirements/recommendations for international students: Required—TOEFL (minimum score 550 paper-based; 79 iBT). *Application deadline:* For fall admission, 3/1 priority date for international students; for spring admission, 8/1 priority date for international students. Applications are processed on a rolling basis. Application fee: $40 ($75 for international students). Electronic applications accepted. *Expenses:* Tuition, state resident: full-time $3716; part-time $154.85 per credit hour. Tuition, nonresident: full-time $14,448; part-time $602 per credit hour. Required fees: $1772; $73.85 per credit hour. One-time fee: $50. Tuition and fees vary according to course load and campus/location. *Financial support:* In 2009–10, 24 research assistantships (averaging $18,130 per year), 35 teaching assistantships (averaging $17,127 per year) were awarded; career-related internships or fieldwork, Federal Work-Study, scholarships/grants, health care benefits, tuition waivers (partial), and unspecified assistantships also available. Support available to part-time students. Financial award application deadline: 3/1; financial award applicants required to submit FAFSA. *Faculty research:* Lasers and photonics, non-linear optical materials, turbulence, structure and function of biological membranes, particle theory. *Unit head:* Dr. James Wicksted, Head, 405-744-5796, Fax: 405-744-6811. *Application contact:* Dr. Gordon Emslie, Dean, 405-744-6368, Fax: 405-744-0355, E-mail: grad-i@okstate.edu.

Oklahoma State University, Graduate College, Stillwater, OK 74078. Offers environmental science (MS); international studies (MS); natural and applied science (MS); photonics (PhD); plant science (PhD). Programs are interdisciplinary. *Faculty:* 2 full-time (0 women). *Students:* 82 full-time (47 women), 156 part-time (75 women); includes 49 minority (15 African Americans, 17 American Indian/Alaska Native, 10 Asian Americans or Pacific Islanders, 7 Hispanic Americans), 68 international. Average age 32. 779 applicants, 68% accepted, 87 enrolled. In 2009, 77 master's, 8 doctorates awarded. *Degree requirements:* For master's, thesis (for some programs); for doctorate, comprehensive exam, thesis/dissertation. *Entrance requirements:* For master's and doctorate, GRE or GMAT. Additional exam requirements/recommendations for international students: Required—TOEFL (minimum score 550 paper-based; 79 iBT). *Application deadline:* For fall admission, 3/1 priority date for international students; for spring admission, 8/1 priority date for international students. Applications are processed on a rolling basis. Application fee: $40 ($75 for international students). Electronic applications accepted. *Expenses:* Tuition, state resident: full-time $3716; part-time $154.85 per credit hour. Tuition, nonresident: full-time $14,448; part-time $602 per credit hour. Required fees: $1772; $73.85 per credit hour. One-time fee: $50. Tuition and fees vary according to course load and campus/location. *Financial support:* In 2009–10, 2 research assistantships (averaging $10,200 per year) were awarded; career-related internships or fieldwork, Federal Work-Study, scholarships/grants, health care benefits, tuition waivers (partial), and unspecified assistantships also available. Support available to part-time students. Financial award application deadline: 3/1; financial award applicants required to submit FAFSA. *Unit head:* Dr. Gordon Emslie, Dean, 405-744-6368, Fax: 405-744-0355, E-mail: grad-i@okstate.edu. *Application contact:* Dr. Susan Mathew, Coordinator of Admissions, 405-744-6368, Fax: 405-744-0355, E-mail: grad-i@okstate.edu.

Princeton University, Princeton Institute for the Science and Technology of Materials (PRISM), Princeton, NJ 08544-1019. Offers materials (PhD).

Stevens Institute of Technology, Graduate School, Charles V. Schaefer Jr. School of Engineering, Department of Electrical and Computer Engineering, Program in Electrical Engineering, Hoboken, NJ 07030. Offers computer architecture and digital system design (M Eng); electrical engineering (PhD); microelectronics and photonics science and technology (M Eng); signal processing for communications (M Eng); telecommunications systems engineering (M Eng); wireless communications (M Eng, Certificate). *Degree requirements:* For master's, thesis optional; for doctorate, variable foreign language requirement, thesis/dissertation. *Entrance requirements:* For master's, doctorate, and Certificate, GRE. Additional exam requirements/recommendations for international students: Required—TOEFL. Electronic applications accepted. *Expenses:* Tuition: Full-time $9900; part-time $1100 per credit. Required fees: $286 per semester.

Stevens Institute of Technology, Graduate School, Charles V. Schaefer Jr. School of Engineering, Interdisciplinary Program in Microelectronics and Photonics, Hoboken, NJ 07030. Offers Certificate. *Expenses:* Tuition: Full-time $9900; part-time $1100 per credit. Required fees: $286 per semester.

The University of Alabama in Huntsville, School of Graduate Studies, College of Engineering, Department of Electrical and Computer Engineering, Huntsville, AL 35899. Offers computer engineering (MSE, PhD); electrical engineering (MSE, PhD); optical science and engineering (PhD); optics and photonics (MSE); software engineering (MSSE). Part-time and evening/weekend programs available. *Faculty:* 22 full-time (2 women), 3 part-time/adjunct (0 women). *Students:* 42 full-time (10 women), 147 part-time (18 women); includes 16 minority (7 African Americans, 6 Asian Americans or Pacific Islanders, 3 Hispanic Americans), 28 international. Average age 31. 205 applicants, 53% accepted, 58 enrolled. In 2009, 53 master's, 4 doctorates awarded. *Degree requirements:* For master's, comprehensive exam, thesis or alternative, oral and written exams; for doctorate, comprehensive exam, thesis/dissertation, oral and written exams. *Entrance requirements:* For master's, GRE General Test, appropriate bachelor's degree, minimum GPA of 3.0; for doctorate, GRE General Test, minimum GPA of 3.0. Additional exam requirements/recommendations for international students: Required—TOEFL (minimum score 500 paper-based; 173 computer-based; 62 iBT). *Application deadline:* For fall admission, 7/15 for domestic students, 4/1 for international students; for spring admission, 11/30 for domestic students, 9/1 for international students. Applications are processed on a rolling basis. Application fee: $40 ($50 for international students). Electronic applications accepted. *Expenses:* Tuition, state resident: part-time $355.75 per credit hour. Tuition, nonresident: part-time $847.10 per credit hour. Required fees: $210.80 per semester. Tuition and fees vary according to course load and program. *Financial support:* In 2009–10, 28 students received support, including 11 research assistantships with full and partial tuition reimbursements available (averaging $11,113 per year), 16 teaching assistantships with full and partial tuition reimbursements available (averaging $10,479 per year); career-related internships or fieldwork, Federal Work-Study, institutionally sponsored loans, scholarships/grants, health care benefits, tuition waivers, and unspecified assistantships also available. Support available to part-time students. Financial award application deadline: 4/1; financial award applicants required to submit FAFSA. *Faculty research:* Optical signal processing, electromagnetics, photonics, nonlinear waves, computer architecture. Total annual research expenditures: $3.4 million. *Unit head:* Dr. Reza Adhami, Chair, 256-824-6316, Fax: 256-824-6803, E-mail: adhami@ece.uah.edu. *Application contact:* Kathy Biggs, Graduate Studies Admissions Manager, 256-824-6199, Fax: 256-824-6405, E-mail: deangrad@uah.edu.

The University of Alabama in Huntsville, School of Graduate Studies, College of Science, Department of Physics, Huntsville, AL 35899. Offers optics and photonics technology (MS); physics (MS, PhD). Part-time and evening/weekend programs available. *Faculty:* 19 full-time (0 women), 2 part-time/adjunct (0 women). *Students:* 33 full-time (12 women), 15 part-time (5 women); includes 2 minority (both Asian Americans or Pacific Islanders), 10 international. Average age 29. 51 applicants, 59% accepted, 19 enrolled. In 2009, 9 master's, 3 doctorates awarded. *Degree requirements:* For master's, comprehensive exam, thesis or alternative, oral and written exams; for doctorate, comprehensive exam, thesis/dissertation, oral and written exams. *Entrance requirements:* For master's and doctorate, GRE General Test, minimum GPA of 3.0. Additional exam requirements/recommendations for international students: Required—TOEFL (minimum score 550 paper-based; 213 computer-based; 62 iBT). *Application deadline:* For fall admission, 7/15 for domestic students, 4/1 for international students; for spring admission, 11/30 for domestic students, 9/1 for international students. Applications are processed on a rolling basis. Application fee: $40 ($50 for international students). Electronic applications accepted. *Expenses:* Tuition, state resident: part-time $355.75 per credit hour. Tuition, nonresident: part-time $847.10 per credit hour. Required fees: $210.80 per semester. Tuition and fees vary according to course load and program. *Financial support:* In 2009–10, 26 students received support, including 16 research assistantships with full and partial tuition reimbursements available (averaging $13,242 per year), 10 teaching assistantships with full and partial tuition reimbursements available (averaging $12,600 per year); career-related internships or fieldwork, Federal Work-Study, institutionally sponsored loans, scholarships/grants, health care benefits, and unspecified assistantships also available. Support available to part-time students. Financial award application deadline: 4/1; financial award applicants required to submit FAFSA. *Faculty research:* Space physics, cosmology/general relativity, optics/quantum optics, astrophysics/gamma-ray astronomy, strophysical instrumentation. Total annual research expenditures: $4.1 million. *Unit head:* Dr. James Miller, Chair, 256-824-2481, Fax: 256-824-6873, E-mail: millerj@cspan.uah.edu. *Application contact:* Kathy Biggs, Graduate Studies Admissions Manager, 256-824-6199, Fax: 256-824-6405, E-mail: deangrad@uah.edu.

University of Arkansas, Graduate School, Interdisciplinary Program in Microelectronics and Photonics, Fayetteville, AR 72701-1201. Offers MS, PhD. *Students:* 12 full-time (0 women), 35 part-time (4 women); includes 5 minority (4 African Americans, 1 Hispanic American), 20 international. 29 applicants, 59% accepted. In 2009, 11 master's, 7 doctorates awarded. *Degree requirements:* For doctorate, thesis/dissertation. Application fee: $40 ($50 for international students). *Expenses:* Tuition, state resident: full-time $7355; part-time $356.58 per hour. Tuition, nonresident: full-time $17,401; part-time $775.17 per hour. Required fees: $1203. *Financial support:* In 2009–10, 8 fellowships with tuition reimbursements, 9 research assistantships, 4 teaching assistantships were awarded. Financial award application deadline: 4/1; financial award applicants required to submit FAFSA. *Unit head:* Dr. Ken Vickers, Head, 479-575-2875, Fax: 479-575-4580, E-mail: vickers@uark.edu. *Application contact:* Graduate Admissions, 479-575-6246, Fax: 479-575-5908, E-mail: gradinfo@uark.edu.

University of California, San Diego, Office of Graduate Studies, Department of Electrical and Computer Engineering, La Jolla, CA 92093. Offers applied ocean science (MS, PhD); applied physics (MS, PhD); communication theory and systems (MS, PhD); computer engineering (MS, PhD); electrical engineering (M Eng); electronic circuits and systems (MS, PhD); intelligent systems, robotics and control (MS, PhD); photonics (MS, PhD); signal and image processing (MS, PhD). MS only offered to students who have been admitted to the PhD program. *Entrance requirements:* For master's and doctorate, GRE General Test. Electronic applications accepted.

University of Central Florida, College of Optics and Photonics, Orlando, FL 32816. Offers optics (MS, PhD). Part-time and evening/weekend programs available. *Faculty:* 20 full-time (0 women). *Students:* 116 full-time (22 women), 14 part-time (0 women); includes 10 minority (4 African Americans, 2 Asian Americans or Pacific Islanders, 4 Hispanic Americans), 71 international. Average age 28. 155 applicants, 32% accepted, 24 enrolled. In 2009, 27 master's, 12 doctorates awarded. *Degree requirements:* For master's, thesis or alternative; for doctorate, thesis/dissertation, departmental qualifying exam, candidacy exam. *Entrance requirements:* For master's, GRE General Test, minimum GPA of 3.0 in last 60 hours; for doctorate, GRE General Test, minimum GPA of 3.5 in last 60 hours. Additional exam requirements/recommendations for international students: Required—TOEFL. *Application deadline:* For fall admission, 2/1 priority date for domestic students; for spring admission, 12/1 for domestic students. Application fee: $30. Electronic applications accepted. *Expenses:* Tuition, state resident: part-time $306.31 per credit hour. Tuition, nonresident: part-time $1099.01 per credit hour. Part-time tuition and fees vary according to degree level and program. *Financial support:* In 2009–10, 93 students received support, including 17 fellowships with partial tuition reimbursements available (averaging $4,800 per year), 118 research assistantships with partial tuition reimbursements available (averaging $11,100 per year); teaching assistantships with partial tuition reimbursements available, career-related internships or fieldwork, Federal Work-Study, institutionally sponsored loans, tuition waivers (partial), and unspecified assistantships also available. Financial award application deadline: 3/1; financial award applicants required to submit FAFSA. *Unit head:* Dr. Bahaa E. Saleh, Dean and Director, 407-882-3326, E-mail: besaleh@creol.ucf.edu. *Application contact:* Dr. Bahaa E. Saleh, Dean and Director, 407-882-3326, E-mail: besaleh@creol.ucf.edu.

Physics

Adelphi University, Graduate School of Arts and Sciences, Department of Physics, Garden City, NY 11530-0701. Offers MS. *Degree requirements:* For master's, thesis optional. *Entrance requirements:* Additional exam requirements/recommendations for international students: Required—TOEFL (minimum score 550 paper-based; 213 computer-based; 80 iBT). *Application deadline:* For fall admission, 5/1 for international students; for spring admission, 12/1 for international students. Applications are processed on a rolling basis. Application fee: $50. Electronic applications accepted. *Expenses:* Tuition: Full-time $28,340; part-time $830 per credit. Required fees: $600; $250 per credit. Full-time tuition and fees vary according to course load and program. *Unit head:* Dr. Gottipaty Rao, Chair, 516-877-4877, E-mail: rao@adelphi.edu. *Application contact:* Dr. Gottipaty Rao, Chair, 516-877-4877, E-mail: rao@adelphi.edu.

Alabama Agricultural and Mechanical University, School of Graduate Studies, School of Arts and Sciences, Department of Physics, Huntsville, AL 35811. Offers physics (MS, PhD), including applied physics (PhD), materials science (PhD), optics/lasers (PhD). Part-time and evening/weekend programs available. *Degree requirements:* For doctorate, thesis/dissertation. *Entrance requirements:* For master's and doctorate, GRE General Test. Additional exam requirements/recommendations for international students: Required—TOEFL (minimum score 500 paper-based; 173 computer-based; 61 iBT). Electronic applications accepted.

American University of Beirut, Graduate Programs, Faculty of Arts and Sciences, Beirut, Lebanon. Offers anthropology (MA); Arabic language and literature (MA); archaeology (MA); biology (MS); chemistry (MS); computer science (MS); economics (MA); education (MA); English language (MA); English literature (MA); environmental policy planning (MSES); financial economics (MAFE); geology (MS); history (MA); mathematics (MA, MS); Middle Eastern studies (MA); philosophy (MA); physics (MS); political studies (MA); psychology (MA); public administration (MA); sociology (MA); statistics (MA, MS). Part-time programs available. *Degree requirements:* For master's, one foreign language, comprehensive exam, thesis (for some programs). *Entrance requirements:* For master's, GRE, letter of recommendation. Additional exam requirements/recommendations for international students: Required—TOEFL (minimum score 600 paper-based; 250 computer-based; 100 iBT), IELTS (minimum score 7.5). *Faculty research:* String theory and supergravity; computer graphics; algebra and number theory; popular Arabic literature; marine and freshwater biology; integrating science, math and technology.

Arizona State University, Graduate College, College of Liberal Arts and Sciences, Division of Natural Sciences, Department of Physics, Tempe, AZ 85287. Offers nanoscience (PSM); physics (MNS, MS, PhD). *Degree requirements:* For master's, thesis, oral and written exams; for doctorate, thesis/dissertation. *Entrance requirements:* For master's and doctorate, GRE.

Auburn University, Graduate School, College of Sciences and Mathematics, Department of Physics, Auburn University, AL 36849. Offers MS, PhD. Part-time programs available. *Faculty:* 23 full-time (1 woman). *Students:* 21 full-time (3 women), 25 part-time (6 women); includes 4 minority (1 Asian American or Pacific Islander, 3 Hispanic Americans), 16 international. Average age 28. 32 applicants, 31% accepted, 9 enrolled. In 2009, 5 master's, 4 doctorates awarded. *Degree requirements:* For doctorate, thesis/dissertation, oral and written exams. *Entrance requirements:* For master's and doctorate, GRE General Test. *Application deadline:* For fall admission, 7/7 for domestic students; for spring admission, 11/24 for domestic students. Applications are processed on a rolling basis. Application fee: $50 ($60 for international students). Electronic applications accepted. *Expenses:* Tuition, state resident: full-time $6240. Tuition, nonresident: full-time $18,720. International tuition: $18,938 full-time. Required fees: $492. Tuition and fees vary according to course load, program and reciprocity agreements. *Financial support:* Research assistantships, teaching assistantships, career-related internships or fieldwork and Federal Work-Study available. Support available to part-time students. Financial award application deadline: 3/15; financial award applicants required to submit FAFSA. *Faculty research:* Atomic/radiative physics, plasma physics, condensed matter physics, space physics, nonlinear dynamics. *Unit head:* Dr. Joe D. Perez, Head, 334-844-4264. *Application contact:* Dr. George Flowers, Dean of the Graduate School, 334-844-2125.

Ball State University, Graduate School, College of Sciences and Humanities, Department of Physics and Astronomy, Program in Physics, Muncie, IN 47306-1099. Offers MA, MS. *Entrance requirements:* For master's, GRE General Test. *Faculty research:* Solar energy, particle physics, atomic spectroscopy.

Baylor University, Graduate School, College of Arts and Sciences, Department of Physics, Waco, TX 76798. Offers MA, MS, PhD. *Students:* 24 full-time (4 women); includes 1 minority (Hispanic American), 9 international. In 2009, 1 master's, 4 doctorates awarded. *Degree requirements:* For master's, thesis or alternative; for doctorate, one foreign language, thesis/dissertation. *Entrance requirements:* For master's and doctorate, GRE General Test. *Application deadline:* Applications are processed on a rolling basis. Application fee: $25. *Financial support:* Fellowships, teaching assistantships, Federal Work-Study and institutionally sponsored loans available. *Unit head:* Dr. Walter Wilcox, Graduate Program Director, 254-710-2510, Fax: 254-710-5083, E-mail: walter_wilcox@baylor.edu. *Application contact:* Marian Nunn-Graves, Administrative Assistant, 254-710-2511, Fax: 254-710-3870, E-mail: marian_nunn-graves@baylor.edu.

Boston College, Graduate School of Arts and Sciences, Department of Physics, Chestnut Hill, MA 02467-3800. Offers MS, PhD. *Students:* 49 full-time (7 women), 30 international. 110 applicants, 10% accepted, 8 enrolled. In 2009, 1 doctorate awarded. Terminal master's awarded for partial completion of doctoral program. *Degree requirements:* For master's, thesis (for some programs); for doctorate, thesis/dissertation. *Entrance requirements:* For master's and doctorate, GRE General Test, GRE Subject Test. Additional exam requirements/recommendations for international students: Required—TOEFL (minimum score 600 paper-based; 250 computer-based; 100 iBT). *Application deadline:* For fall admission, 1/2 for domestic and international students. Application fee: $70. Electronic applications accepted. *Financial support:* Fellowships with full tuition reimbursements, research assistantships with full tuition reimbursements, teaching assistantships with full tuition reimbursements, Federal Work-Study and scholarships/grants available. Support available to part-time students. Financial award application deadline: 3/1; financial award applicants required to submit FAFSA. *Faculty research:* Atmospheric/space physics, astrophysics, atomic and molecular physics, fusion and plasmas, solid-state physics. *Unit head:* Dr. Michael Naughton, Chairperson, 617-552-3576, E-mail: michael.naughton@bc.edu. *Application contact:* Dr. Rein Uritam, Graduate Program Director, 617-552-3576, E-mail: rein.uritam@bc.edu.

Boston University, Graduate School of Arts and Sciences, Department of Physics, Boston, MA 02215. Offers MA, PhD. *Students:* 101 full-time (16 women); includes 4 minority (1 Asian American or Pacific Islander, 3 Hispanic Americans), 44 international. Average age 26. 318 applicants, 20% accepted, 17 enrolled. In 2009, 14 master's, 16 doctorates awarded. Terminal master's awarded for partial completion of doctoral program. *Degree requirements:* For master's, one foreign language, comprehensive exam, thesis or alternative; for doctorate, one foreign language, comprehensive exam, thesis/dissertation. *Entrance requirements:* For master's and doctorate, GRE General Test, GRE Subject Test. Additional exam requirements/recommendations for international students: Required—TOEFL (minimum score 600 paper-based; 250 computer-based). *Application deadline:* For fall admission, 1/15 for domestic and international students. Application fee: $70. Electronic applications accepted. *Expenses:* Tuition: Full-time $37,910; part-time $1184 per credit hour. Required fees: $386; $40 per semester. Part-time tuition and fees vary according to class time, course level, degree level and program. *Financial support:* In 2009–10, 2 fellowships with full tuition reimbursements (averaging $18,900 per year), 63 research assistantships (averaging $18,400 per year), 29 teaching assistantships with full tuition reimbursements (averaging $18,400 per year) were awarded; Federal Work-Study and scholarships/grants also available. Support available to part-time students. Financial award application deadline: 1/15; financial award applicants required to submit FAFSA. *Unit head:* Dr. Bennett Goldberg, Acting Chairman, 617-353-5789, Fax: 617-353-9393, E-mail: goldberg@bu.edu. *Application contact:* Mirtha M. Cabello, Administrative Coordinator, 617-353-2623, Fax: 617-353-9393, E-mail: cabello@bu.edu.

See Close-Up on page 211.

Bowling Green State University, Graduate College, College of Arts and Sciences, Department of Physics and Astronomy, Bowling Green, OH 43403. Offers geophysics (MS); physics (MAT, MS). *Degree requirements:* For master's, thesis or alternative. *Entrance requirements:* For master's, GRE General Test. Additional exam requirements/recommendations for international students: Required—TOEFL. Electronic applications accepted. *Faculty research:* Computational physics, solid-state physics, materials science, theoretical physics.

Brandeis University, Graduate School of Arts and Sciences, Department of Physics, Waltham, MA 02454-9110. Offers MS, PhD. Part-time programs available. *Faculty:* 18 full-time (2 women). *Students:* 41 full-time (5 women); includes 1 minority (Hispanic American), 17 international. Average age 23. 107 applicants, 21% accepted, 8 enrolled. In 2009, 6 master's, 3 doctorates awarded. Terminal master's awarded for partial completion of doctoral program. *Degree requirements:* For master's, qualifying exam, 1 year residency; for doctorate, thesis/dissertation, advanced exam. *Entrance requirements:* For master's, GRE General Test, GRE Subject Test, resume, letters of recommendation; for doctorate, GRE General Test, GRE Subject Test, resume, 2 letters of recommendation (3rd suggested). Additional exam requirements/recommendations for international students: Required—TOEFL (minimum score 600 paper-based; 250 computer-based; 100 iBT); Recommended—IELTS (minimum score 7). *Application deadline:* For fall admission, 1/15 priority date for domestic students. Application fee: $75. Electronic applications accepted. *Financial support:* In 2009–10, 16 fellowships with full tuition reimbursements (averaging $23,100 per year), 26 research assistantships with full tuition reimbursements (averaging $23,100 per year), 10 teaching assistantships with partial tuition reimbursements (averaging $1,250 per year) were awarded; scholarships/grants, health care benefits, and tuition waivers (full) also available. Financial award application deadline: 1/15; financial award applicants required to submit FAFSA. *Faculty research:* Theoretical physics, experimental physics, astrophysics, computational neuroscience, condensed matter, high energy physics. *Unit head:* Dr. Howard Schnitzer, Chair, 781-736-2882, Fax: 781-736-2915, E-mail: schnitzr@brandeis.edu. *Application contact:* Catherine Broderick, Department Administrator, 781-736-2802, Fax: 781-736-3412, E-mail: cbroderi@brandeis.edu.

Brigham Young University, Graduate Studies, College of Physical and Mathematical Sciences, Department of Physics and Astronomy, Provo, UT 84602-1001. Offers physics (MS, PhD); physics and astronomy (PhD). Part-time programs available. *Faculty:* 27 full-time (2 women). *Students:* 40 full-time (7 women); includes 6 minority (5 Asian Americans or Pacific Islanders, 1 Hispanic American). Average age 29. 14 applicants, 71% accepted, 10 enrolled. In 2009, 5 master's, 3 doctorates awarded. Terminal master's awarded for partial completion of doctoral program. *Degree requirements:* For master's, thesis; for doctorate, thesis/dissertation, qualifying exam. *Entrance requirements:* For master's and doctorate, GRE Subject Test (physics), minimum GPA of 3.0 in last 60 hours, ecclesiastical endorsement. Additional exam requirements/recommendations for international students: Required—TOEFL (minimum score 580 paper-based; 85 iBT), IELTS (minimum score 7). *Application deadline:* For fall admission, 1/15 priority date for domestic and international students. Application fee: $50. Electronic applications accepted. *Expenses:* Tuition: Full-time $5580; part-time $301 per credit hour. Tuition and fees vary according to student's religious affiliation. *Financial support:* In 2009–10, 38 students received support, including 22 research assistantships with full tuition reimbursements available (averaging $19,730 per year), 18 teaching assistantships with full tuition reimbursements available (averaging $18,780 per year); fellowships with full tuition reimbursements available, institutionally sponsored loans and tuition waivers (full) also available. Support available to part-time students. Financial award application deadline: 1/15. *Faculty research:* Acoustics; atomic, molecular, and optical physics; theoretical and mathematical physics; condensed matter; astrophysics and plasma. Total annual research expenditures: $1.8 million. *Unit head:* Dr. Ross L. Spencer, Chair, 801-422-2341, Fax: 801-422-0553, E-mail: ross.spencer@byu.edu. *Application contact:* Dr. J. Ward Moody, Graduate Coordinator, 801-422-4347, Fax: 801-422-0553, E-mail: moody@byu.edu.

Brock University, Faculty of Graduate Studies, Faculty of Mathematics and Science, Program in Physics, St. Catharines, ON L2S 3A1, Canada. Offers M Sc. Part-time programs available. *Degree requirements:* For master's, thesis. *Entrance requirements:* For master's, honors B Sc in physics. Additional exam requirements/recommendations for international students: Required—TOEFL (minimum score 550 paper-based; 213 computer-based; 80 iBT), IELTS (minimum score 6.5), TWE (minimum score 4). Electronic applications accepted. *Faculty research:* Quantum physics, optical properties, non-crystalline materials, condensed matter physics, biophysics.

Brooklyn College of the City University of New York, Division of Graduate Studies, Department of Physics, Brooklyn, NY 11210-2889. Offers applied physics (MA); physics (MA, PhD). The department is a full participant in the PhD program; it offers a complete sequence of courses that are creditable toward the CUNY doctoral degree and a wide range of research opportunities in fulfillment of the doctoral dissertation requirements for that degree. Part-time programs available. Terminal master's awarded for partial completion of doctoral program. *Degree requirements:* For master's, comprehensive exam, thesis or alternative. *Entrance requirements:* For master's, 2 letters of recommendation, 12 credits in advanced physics; for doctorate, GRE. Additional exam requirements/recommendations for international students: Required—TOEFL. Electronic applications accepted.

Brooklyn College of the City University of New York, Division of Graduate Studies, School of Education, Program in Middle Childhood Education (Science), Brooklyn, NY 11210-2889. Offers biology (MA); chemistry (MA); earth science (MA); general science (MA); physics (MA). Part-time and evening/weekend programs available. *Entrance requirements:* For master's, LAST, interview, previous course work in education and mathematics, resume, 2 letters of recommendation. Additional exam requirements/recommendations for international students: Required—TOEFL (minimum score 500 paper-based; 173 computer-based; 61 iBT). Electronic applications accepted. *Faculty research:* Geometric thinking, mastery of basic facts, problem-solving strategies, history of mathematics.

Brown University, Graduate School, Department of Physics, Providence, RI 02912. Offers Sc M, PhD. *Degree requirements:* For doctorate, thesis/dissertation, qualifying and oral exams.

Bryn Mawr College, Graduate School of Arts and Sciences, Department of Physics, Bryn Mawr, PA 19010-2899. Offers MA, PhD. *Degree requirements:* For master's, one foreign language, thesis; for doctorate, one foreign language, thesis/dissertation. *Entrance requirements:* For master's and doctorate, GRE General Test, GRE Subject Test. Additional exam requirements/recommendations for international students: Required—TOEFL (minimum score 600 paper-based; 250 computer-based). *Expenses:* Tuition: Full-time $31,340. Required fees: $430.

California Institute of Technology, Division of Physics, Mathematics and Astronomy, Department of Physics, Pasadena, CA 91125-0001. Offers PhD. *Degree requirements:* For doctorate, thesis/dissertation, candidacy and final exams. *Entrance requirements:* For doctorate,

GRE General Test, GRE Subject Test. Additional exam requirements/recommendations for international students: Required—TOEFL. *Faculty research:* High-energy physics, nuclear physics, condensed-matter physics, theoretical physics and astrophysics, gravity physics.

California State University, Fresno, Division of Graduate Studies, College of Science and Mathematics, Department of Physics, Fresno, CA 93740-8027. Offers MS. Part-time programs available. *Degree requirements:* For master's, thesis or alternative. *Entrance requirements:* For master's, GRE General Test, minimum GPA of 2.5. Additional exam requirements/ recommendations for international students: Required—TOEFL. Electronic applications accepted. *Faculty research:* Energy, astronomy, silicon vertex detector, neuroimaging, particle physics.

California State University, Fullerton, Graduate Studies, College of Natural Science and Mathematics, Department of Physics, Fullerton, CA 92834-9480. Offers MA. Part-time programs available. *Students:* 10 full-time (3 women), 2 part-time (0 women); includes 3 minority (all Asian Americans or Pacific Islanders), 2 international. Average age 27. 14 applicants, 71% accepted, 5 enrolled. In 2009, 4 master's awarded. Application fee: $55. *Expenses:* Tuition, nonresident: full-time $11,160; part-time $373 per credit. Required fees: $1440 per term. Tuition and fees vary according to course load, degree level and program. *Financial support:* Research assistantships, teaching assistantships, career-related internships or fieldwork, Federal Work-Study, institutionally sponsored loans, and scholarships/grants available. Support available to part-time students. Financial award application deadline: 3/1; financial award applicants required to submit FAFSA. *Unit head:* Dr. Morty Khakoo, Chair, 657-278-3366. *Application contact:* Admissions/Applications, 657-278-2371.

California State University, Long Beach, Graduate Studies, College of Natural Sciences and Mathematics, Department of Physics and Astronomy, Long Beach, CA 90840. Offers physics (MS). Part-time programs available. *Faculty:* 13 full-time (3 women). *Students:* 13 full-time (4 women), 22 part-time (4 women); includes 11 minority (1 African American, 7 Asian Americans or Pacific Islanders, 3 Hispanic Americans), 1 international. Average age 34. 25 applicants, 64% accepted, 8 enrolled. *Degree requirements:* For master's, comprehensive exam or thesis. *Application deadline:* For fall admission, 7/1 for domestic students. Applications are processed on a rolling basis. Application fee: $55. Electronic applications accepted. *Expenses:* Required fees: $1802 per semester. Part-time tuition and fees vary according to course load. *Financial support:* Federal Work-Study, institutionally sponsored loans, and scholarships/grants available. Financial award application deadline: 3/2. *Faculty research:* Musical acoustics, modern optics, neutrino physics, quantum gravity, atomic physics. *Unit head:* Dr. Patrick Kenealy, Chair, 562-985-8745, Fax: 562-985-7924, E-mail: kenealyp@csulb.edu. *Application contact:* Dr. Chuhee Kwon, Graduate Advisor, 562-985-4855, Fax: 562-985-7924, E-mail: ckwon@csulb.edu.

California State University, Los Angeles, Graduate Studies, College of Natural and Social Sciences, Department of Physics and Astronomy, Los Angeles, CA 90032-8530. Offers physics (MS). Part-time and evening/weekend programs available. *Faculty:* 4 full-time (0 women), 4 part-time/adjunct (1 woman). *Students:* 8 full-time (3 women), 10 part-time (1 woman); includes 10 minority (1 African American, 5 Asian Americans or Pacific Islanders, 4 Hispanic Americans), 2 international. Average age 31. 8 applicants, 100% accepted, 2 enrolled. In 2009, 3 master's awarded. *Degree requirements:* For master's, comprehensive exam or thesis. *Entrance requirements:* Additional exam requirements/recommendations for international students: Required—TOEFL (minimum score 500 paper-based; 173 computer-based). *Application deadline:* For fall admission, 5/1 for domestic and international students. Applications are processed on a rolling basis. Application fee: $55. Electronic applications accepted. *Financial support:* Federal Work-Study available. Support available to part-time students. Financial award application deadline: 3/1. *Faculty research:* Intermediate energy, nuclear physics, condensed-matter physics, biophysics. *Unit head:* Dr. Edward Rezayi, Chair, 323-343-2100, Fax: 323-343-2497, E-mail: erizayi@calstatela.edu. *Application contact:* Dr. Cheryl L. Ney, Associate Vice President for Academic Affairs and Dean of Graduate Studies, 323-343-3820, Fax: 323-343-5653, E-mail: cney@cslanet.calstatela.edu.

California State University, Northridge, Graduate Studies, College of Science and Mathematics, Department of Physics and Astronomy, Northridge, CA 91330. Offers physics (MS). Part-time and evening/weekend programs available. *Faculty:* 14 full-time (3 women), 9 part-time/adjunct (2 women). *Students:* 10 full-time (3 women), 30 part-time (6 women); includes 4 Asian Americans or Pacific Islanders, 5 Hispanic Americans, 5 international. Average age 33. 41 applicants, 76% accepted, 19 enrolled. In 2009, 6 master's awarded. *Degree requirements:* For master's, thesis or comprehensive exam. *Entrance requirements:* For master's, GRE General Test or minimum GPA of 3.0. Additional exam requirements/recommendations for international students: Required—TOEFL. *Application deadline:* For fall admission, 11/30 for domestic students. Application fee: $55. *Financial support:* Teaching assistantships available. Financial award application deadline: 3/1. *Unit head:* Dr. Ana Cristina Cadavid, Chair, 818-677-2171, E-mail: ana.cadavid@csun.edu. *Application contact:* Dr. Ana Cristina Cadavid, Chair, 818-677-2171, E-mail: ana.cadavid@csun.edu.

Carleton University, Faculty of Graduate Studies, Faculty of Science, Department of Physics, Ottawa, ON K1S 5B6, Canada. Offers M Sc, PhD. *Degree requirements:* For master's, thesis optional, seminar; for doctorate, comprehensive exam, thesis/dissertation, seminar. *Entrance requirements:* For master's, honors degree in science; for doctorate, M Sc. Additional exam requirements/recommendations for international students: Required—TOEFL. *Faculty research:* Experimental and theoretical elementary particle physics, medical physics.

Carnegie Mellon University, Mellon College of Science, Department of Physics, Pittsburgh, PA 15213-3891. Offers applied physics (PhD); physics (MS, PhD). *Degree requirements:* For doctorate, thesis/dissertation, qualifying exam. *Entrance requirements:* For doctorate, GRE General Test, GRE Subject Test. Additional exam requirements/recommendations for international students: Required—TOEFL. Electronic applications accepted. *Faculty research:* Astrophysics, condensed matter physics, biological physics, medium energy and nuclear physics, high-energy physics.

Case Western Reserve University, School of Graduate Studies, Department of Physics, Cleveland, OH 44106. Offers MS, PhD. Part-time programs available. *Faculty:* 19 full-time (3 women), 4 part-time/adjunct (0 women). *Students:* 49 full-time (8 women); includes 1 minority (Hispanic American), 23 international. Average age 26. 191 applicants, 24% accepted, 13 enrolled. In 2009, 4 master's, 8 doctorates awarded. Terminal master's awarded for partial completion of doctoral program. *Degree requirements:* For master's, exam; for doctorate, thesis/dissertation, qualifying exam, topical exam. *Entrance requirements:* For master's and doctorate, GRE General Test, GRE Subject Test (physics). Additional exam requirements/ recommendations for international students: Required—TOEFL (minimum score 550 paper-based; 213 computer-based; 79 iBT). *Application deadline:* For fall admission, 1/15 priority date for domestic students. Applications are processed on a rolling basis. Application fee: $8. Electronic applications accepted. *Financial support:* Fellowships, research assistantships, teaching assistantships available. Financial award application deadline: 2/15. *Faculty research:* Condensed-matter physics, imaging physics, nonlinear optics, high-energy physics, cosmology and astrophysics. *Unit head:* Daniel Akerib, Chairman, 216-368-4000, E-mail: daniel.akerib@case.edu. *Application contact:* Patricia Bacevice, Admissions, 216-368-4000, Fax: 216-368-4671, E-mail: pab6@case.edu.

The Catholic University of America, School of Arts and Sciences, Department of Physics, Washington, DC 20064. Offers MS, PhD. Part-time programs available. *Faculty:* 12 full-time (2 women), 1 part-time/adjunct (0 women). *Students:* 8 full-time (2 women), 17 part-time (6 women); includes 3 minority (1 African American, 1 Asian American or Pacific Islander, 1 Hispanic American), 4 international. Average age 31. 20 applicants, 75% accepted, 6 enrolled. In 2009, 5 master's, 4 doctorates awarded. *Degree requirements:* For master's, comprehensive exam, thesis or alternative; for doctorate, comprehensive exam, thesis/dissertation, oral exam. *Entrance requirements:* For master's and doctorate, GRE General Test, statement of purpose, official copies of academic transcripts, three letters of recommendation. Additional exam requirements/recommendations for international students: Required—TOEFL (minimum score 580 paper-based; 237 computer-based). *Application deadline:* For fall admission, 8/1 priority date for domestic students, 7/15 for international students; for spring admission, 12/1 priority date for domestic students, 10/15 for international students. Applications are processed on a rolling basis. Application fee: $55. Electronic applications accepted. *Expenses:* Tuition: Full-time $31,740; part-time $1245 per credit hour. Required fees: $50; $25 per semester hour. One-time fee: $425. *Financial support:* Fellowships, research assistantships, teaching assistantships, Federal Work-Study, scholarships/grants, tuition waivers (full and partial), and unspecified assistantships available. Financial award application deadline: 2/1; financial award applicants required to submit FAFSA. *Faculty research:* Glass and ceramics technologies, astrophysics and computational sciences, the role of evolution in galaxy properties, nuclear physics, biophysics. Total annual research expenditures: $11.6 million. *Unit head:* Dr. Daniel I. Sober, Chair, 202-319-5347, Fax: 202-319-4448, E-mail: sober@cua.edu. *Application contact:* Julie Schwing, Director of Graduate Admissions, 202-319-5057, Fax: 202-319-6533, E-mail: cua-admissions@cua.edu.

Central Connecticut State University, School of Graduate Studies, School of Arts and Sciences, Department of Physics and Earth Science, New Britain, CT 06050-4010. Offers natural sciences (MS); science education (Certificate). Part-time and evening/weekend programs available. *Faculty:* 12 full-time (4 women), 15 part-time/adjunct (4 women). *Students:* 22 part-time (11 women); includes 2 minority (1 African American, 1 Asian American or Pacific Islander). Average age 37. 14 applicants, 79% accepted, 7 enrolled. In 2009, 10 master's, 1 other advanced degree awarded. *Degree requirements:* For master's, comprehensive exam, thesis or alternative; for Certificate, qualifying exam. *Entrance requirements:* For master's, minimum undergraduate GPA of 2.7. Additional exam requirements/recommendations for international students: Required—TOEFL. *Application deadline:* For fall admission, 7/1 for domestic students; for spring admission, 12/1 for domestic students. Applications are processed on a rolling basis. Application fee: $50. Electronic applications accepted. *Expenses:* Tuition, area resident: Full-time $4662; part-time $440 per credit. Tuition, state resident: full-time $6994; part-time $440 per credit. Tuition, nonresident: full-time $12,988; part-time $440 per credit. Required fees: $3606. One-time fee: $62 part-time. *Financial support:* In 2009–10, 1 student received support. Career-related internships or fieldwork, Federal Work-Study, scholarships/grants, and unspecified assistantships available. Support available to part-time students. Financial award application deadline: 3/1; financial award applicants required to submit FAFSA. *Faculty research:* Elementary/secondary science education, particle and solid states, weather patterns, planetary studies. *Unit head:* Dr. Ali Antar, Chair, 860-832-2930. *Application contact:* Dr. Ali Antar, Chair, 860-832-2930.

Central Michigan University, College of Graduate Studies, College of Science and Technology, Department of Physics, Mount Pleasant, MI 48859. Offers physics (MS); science of advanced materials (PhD). PhD is an interdisciplinary program. Part-time programs available. *Degree requirements:* For master's, thesis or alternative; for doctorate, comprehensive exam, thesis/ dissertation. *Entrance requirements:* For doctorate, GRE, bachelor's degree in physics, chemistry, biochemistry, biology, geology, engineering, mathematics, or other relevant area. Electronic applications accepted. *Faculty research:* Science of advanced materials, polymer physics, laser spectroscopy, observational astronomy, nuclear physics.

Christopher Newport University, Graduate Studies, Department of Physics, Computer Science, and Engineering, Newport News, VA 23606-2998. Offers applied physics and computer science (MS). Part-time and evening/weekend programs available. *Faculty:* 6 full-time (0 women), 3 part-time/adjunct (2 women). *Students:* 6 full-time (1 woman), 23 part-time (2 women); includes 2 minority (both African Americans). Average age 29. 10 applicants, 100% accepted, 7 enrolled. In 2009, 7 master's awarded. *Degree requirements:* For master's, comprehensive exam (for some programs), thesis optional. *Entrance requirements:* For master's, GRE General Test, minimum GPA of 3.0. Additional exam requirements/recommendations for international students: Required—TOEFL (minimum score 580 paper-based; 237 computer-based; 92 iBT). *Application deadline:* For fall admission, 8/15 priority date for domestic students, 4/1 for international students; for spring admission, 10/15 for domestic students, 10/1 for international students. Applications are processed on a rolling basis. Application fee: $45. Electronic applications accepted. *Expenses:* Tuition, area resident: Part-time $384 per credit hour. Tuition, state resident: part-time $384 per credit hour. Tuition, nonresident: part-time $701 per credit hour. *Financial support:* In 2009–10, 3 research assistantships with full and partial tuition reimbursements (averaging $2,000 per year) were awarded; fellowships with full tuition reimbursements, career-related internships or fieldwork, Federal Work-Study, and unspecified assistantships also available. Support available to part-time students. Financial award application deadline: 2/1; financial award applicants required to submit FAFSA. *Faculty research:* Advanced programming methodologies, experimental nuclear physics, computer architecture, semiconductor nanophysics, laser and optical fiber sensors. *Unit head:* Dr. Antonio Siochi, Coordinator, 757-594-7569, Fax: 757-594-7919, E-mail: siochi@cnu.edu. *Application contact:* Lyn Sawyer, Associate Director, Graduate Admissions and Records, 757-594-7544, Fax: 757-594-7649, E-mail: gradstdy@cnu.edu.

City College of the City University of New York, Graduate School, College of Liberal Arts and Science, Division of Science, Department of Physics, New York, NY 10031-9198. Offers MA, PhD. Terminal master's awarded for partial completion of doctoral program. *Degree requirements:* For master's, comprehensive exam; for doctorate, thesis/dissertation. *Entrance requirements:* For doctorate, GRE. Additional exam requirements/recommendations for international students: Required—TOEFL (minimum score 500 paper-based; 61 iBT). Electronic applications accepted.

See Close-Up on page 213.

Clark Atlanta University, School of Arts and Sciences, Department of Physics, Atlanta, GA 30314. Offers MS. Part-time programs available. *Faculty:* 4 full-time (0 women), 1 part-time/ adjunct (0 women). *Students:* 1 full-time (0 women), 2 part-time (0 women); includes 1 minority (African American), 2 international. Average age 32. 4 applicants, 100% accepted, 1 enrolled. In 2009, 1 master's awarded. *Degree requirements:* For master's, one foreign language, comprehensive exam, thesis optional. *Entrance requirements:* For master's, GRE General Test, minimum GPA of 2.5. Additional exam requirements/recommendations for international students: Required—TOEFL (minimum score 500 paper-based; 173 computer-based). *Application deadline:* For fall admission, 4/1 for domestic and international students; for spring admission, 11/1 for domestic and international students. Applications are processed on a rolling basis. Application fee: $40 ($55 for international students). *Expenses:* Tuition: Full-time $12,240; part-time $680 per credit hour. Required fees: $710; $355 per semester. *Financial support:* In 2009–10, 2 research assistantships were awarded; scholarships/grants and unspecified assistantships also available. Financial award application deadline: 4/30; financial award applicants required to submit FAFSA. *Faculty research:* Fusion energy, investigations of nonlinear differential equations, difference schemes, collisions in dense plasma. *Unit head:* Dr. Swaraj Tayal, Chairperson, 404-880-6877, E-mail: stayal@cau.edu. *Application contact:* Michelle Clark-Davis, Graduate Program Admissions, 404-880-6605, E-mail: cauadmissions@cau.edu.

Clarkson University, Graduate School, School of Arts and Sciences, Department of Physics, Potsdam, NY 13699. Offers MS, PhD. Part-time programs available. *Faculty:* 10 full-time (2 women), 1 part-time/adjunct (0 women). *Students:* 13 full-time (1 woman), 7 international. Average age 27. 19 applicants, 32% accepted, 1 enrolled. In 2009, 3 master's, 3 doctorates awarded. Terminal master's awarded for partial completion of doctoral program. *Degree*

Physics

Clarkson University (continued)

requirements: For doctorate, thesis/dissertation, departmental qualifying exam. *Entrance requirements:* For master's, GRE, 3 letters of recommendation; resume (recommended); for doctorate, GRE, transcripts of all college coursework, three letters of recommendation; resume and personal statement (recommended). Additional exam requirements/recommendations for international students: Required—TOEFL, TSE (recommended). *Application deadline:* For fall admission, 1/30 priority date for domestic and international students; for spring admission, 9/1 priority date for domestic and international students. Applications are processed on a rolling basis. Application fee: $25 ($35 for international students). Electronic applications accepted. *Expenses:* Tuition: Part-time $1074 per credit hour. *Financial support:* In 2009–10, 12 students received support, including 3 fellowships (averaging $30,000 per year), 2 research assistantships (averaging $20,190 per year), 6 teaching assistantships (averaging $20,190 per year); scholarships/grants, tuition waivers (partial), and unspecified assistantships also available. *Faculty research:* Surface science optics, computational bionanotechnology, chemical mechanical planarization, quantum computing, colloids, biophysics. Total annual research expenditures: $770,369. *Unit head:* Dr. Phillip A. Christiansen, Division Head, 315-268-2389, Fax: 315-268-6610, E-mail: pac@clarkson.edu. *Application contact:* Jennifer E. Reed, Graduate School Coordinator for School of Arts and Sciences, 315-268-3802, Fax: 315-268-3989, E-mail: jreed@clarkson.edu.

Clark University, Graduate School, Department of Physics, Worcester, MA 01610-1477. Offers MA, PhD. Part-time programs available. *Faculty:* 6 full-time (0 women). *Students:* 10 full-time (4 women), 1 (woman) part-time, 4 international. Average age 28. 23 applicants, 17% accepted, 3 enrolled. In 2009, 1 master's awarded. Terminal master's awarded for partial completion of doctoral program. *Degree requirements:* For master's, thesis or alternative; for doctorate, one foreign language, thesis/dissertation. *Entrance requirements:* Additional exam requirements/recommendations for international students: Required—TOEFL. *Application deadline:* For fall admission, 2/1 for domestic students. Application fee: $50. *Expenses:* Tuition: Full-time $34,900; part-time $4362.50 per course. *Financial support:* In 2009–10, fellowships with full and partial tuition reimbursements (averaging $18,280 per year), 8 research assistantships with full tuition reimbursements (averaging $18,280 per year), 5 teaching assistantships with full tuition reimbursements (averaging $18,280 per year) were awarded; Federal Work-Study and tuition waivers (full and partial) also available. Financial award application deadline: 4/1. *Faculty research:* Statistical and thermal physics, magnetic properties of materials, computer simulation, particle diffusion. Total annual research expenditures: $740,000. *Unit head:* Dr. Clark Agosta, Chair, 508-793-7169. *Application contact:* Sujata Davis, Department Secretary, 508-793-7169, Fax: 508-793-8861, E-mail: sdavis1@clarku.edu.

Clemson University, Graduate School, College of Engineering and Science, Department of Physics and Astronomy, Clemson, SC 29634. Offers physics (MS, PhD), including astronomy and astrophysics, atmospheric physics, biophysics. Part-time programs available. *Faculty:* 25 full-time (4 women), 1 part-time/adjunct (0 women). *Students:* 46 full-time (11 women), 3 part-time (0 women); includes 1 minority (African American), 22 international. Average age 27. 71 applicants, 62% accepted, 17 enrolled. In 2009, 8 master's, 5 doctorates awarded. Terminal master's awarded for partial completion of doctoral program. *Degree requirements:* For master's, thesis or alternative; for doctorate, thesis/dissertation. *Entrance requirements:* For master's and doctorate, GRE General Test. Additional exam requirements/recommendations for international students: Required—TOEFL. *Application deadline:* For fall admission, 1/15 priority date for domestic students; for spring admission, 9/15 priority date for domestic students. Applications are processed on a rolling basis. Application fee: $70 ($80 for international students). Electronic applications accepted. *Expenses:* Tuition, state resident: full-time $8684; part-time $528 per credit hour. Tuition, nonresident: full-time $15,330; part-time $1078 per credit hour. Required fees: $736; $37 per semester. Part-time tuition and fees vary according to course load and program. *Financial support:* In 2009–10, 45 students received support, including 1 fellowship with full and partial tuition reimbursement available (averaging $10,000 per year), 13 research assistantships with partial tuition reimbursements available (averaging $21,423 per year), 32 teaching assistantships with partial tuition reimbursements available (averaging $16,490 per year); career-related internships or fieldwork, institutionally sponsored loans, scholarships/grants, health care benefits, and unspecified assistantships also available. Support available to part-time students. Financial award application deadline: 6/1; financial award applicants required to submit FAFSA. *Faculty research:* Radiation physics, solid-state physics, nuclear physics, radar and lidar studies of atmosphere. Total annual research expenditures: $3.1 million. *Unit head:* Dr. Peter Barnes, Chair, 864-656-3419, Fax: 864-656-0805, E-mail: peterb@clemson.edu. *Application contact:* Dr. Murray Daw, Graduate Coordinator, 864-656-6702, Fax: 864-656-0805, E-mail: physgradinfo-l@clemson.edu.

Cleveland State University, College of Graduate Studies, College of Science, Department of Physics, Cleveland, OH 44115. Offers applied optics (MS); condensed matter physics (MS); medical physics (MS); optics and materials (MS); optics and medical imaging (MS). Part-time and evening/weekend programs available. *Entrance requirements:* For master's, undergraduate degree in engineering, physics, chemistry or mathematics. Additional exam requirements/recommendations for international students: Required—TOEFL (minimum score 525 paper-based; 197 computer-based), GRE. Electronic applications accepted. *Faculty research:* Statistical physics, experimental solid-state physics, theoretical optics, experimental biological physics (macromolecular crystallography), experimental optics.

The College of William and Mary, Faculty of Arts and Sciences, Department of Physics, Williamsburg, VA 23187-8795. Offers MS, PhD. *Faculty:* 26 full-time (4 women), 13 part-time/adjunct (3 women). *Students:* 63 full-time (19 women), 1 (woman) part-time; includes 2 minority (1 American Indian/Alaska Native, 1 Hispanic American), 24 international. Average age 26. 102 applicants, 26% accepted, 14 enrolled. In 2009, 23 master's, 8 doctorates awarded. Terminal master's awarded for partial completion of doctoral program. *Degree requirements:* For master's, minimum GPA of 3.0, 32 credit hours; for doctorate, comprehensive exam, thesis/dissertation, 1 year residency, 2 semesters of physics teaching. *Entrance requirements:* For doctorate, GRE General Test, GRE Subject Test, minimum GPA of 2.5. Additional exam requirements/recommendations for international students: Required—TOEFL. *Application deadline:* For fall admission, 2/1 priority date for domestic and international students. Applications are processed on a rolling basis. Application fee: $45. Electronic applications accepted. *Expenses:* Tuition, state resident: full-time $6400; part-time $315 per credit hour. Tuition, nonresident: full-time $19,720; part-time $840 per credit hour. Required fees: $4114. *Financial support:* In 2009–10, 64 students received support, including research assistantships with full tuition reimbursements available (averaging $22,000 per year), teaching assistantships with full tuition reimbursements available (averaging $22,000 per year); career-related internships or fieldwork, health care benefits, tuition waivers (full), and unspecified assistantships also available. *Faculty research:* Nuclear/particle, condensed-matter, atomic, and plasma physics; accelerator physics; molecular/optical physics; computational/nonlinear physics. Total annual research expenditures: $4.2 million. *Unit head:* Dr. Keith Griffioen, Chair, 757-221-3500, Fax: 757-221-3540, E-mail: chair@physics.wm.edu. *Application contact:* Dr. Marc Sher, Chair of Admissions, 757-221-3538, Fax: 757-221-3540, E-mail: grad@physics.wm.edu.

Colorado School of Mines, Graduate School, Department of Physics, Golden, CO 80401. Offers applied physics (MS, PhD). Part-time programs available. *Faculty:* 26 full-time (1 woman), 7 part-time/adjunct (0 women). *Students:* 47 full-time (5 women), 4 part-time (0 women); includes 5 minority (2 Asian Americans or Pacific Islanders, 3 Hispanic Americans), 7 international. Average age 30. 57 applicants, 44% accepted, 19 enrolled. In 2009, 6 master's, 4 doctorates awarded. *Degree requirements:* For master's, thesis (for some programs); for doctorate, comprehensive exam, thesis/dissertation. *Entrance requirements:* For master's and doctorate, GRE General Test, GRE Subject Test. Additional exam requirements/recommendations for international students: Required—TOEFL (minimum score 550 paper-based; 213 computer-based; 80 iBT). *Application deadline:* For fall admission, 1/15 priority date for domestic and international students; for spring admission, 9/1 priority date for domestic and international students. Application fee: $50 ($70 for international students). Electronic applications accepted. *Expenses:* Tuition, state resident: full-time $10,584; part-time $588 per credit hour. Tuition, nonresident: full-time $24,750; part-time $1375 per credit hour. Required fees: $1654; $827.10 per semester. *Financial support:* In 2009–10, 49 students received support, including 1 fellowship with full tuition reimbursement available (averaging $20,000 per year), 32 research assistantships with full tuition reimbursements available (averaging $20,000 per year), 16 teaching assistantships with full tuition reimbursements available (averaging $20,000 per year); scholarships/grants, health care benefits, and unspecified assistantships also available. Financial award application deadline: 1/15; financial award applicants required to submit FAFSA. *Faculty research:* Light scattering, low-energy nuclear physics, high fusion plasma diagnostics, laser operations, mathematical physics. Total annual research expenditures: $2.9 million. *Unit head:* Dr. Thomas Furtak, Department Head, 303-273-3843, Fax: 303-273-3919, E-mail: tfurtak@mines.edu. *Application contact:* Dr. Tim Ohno, Professor, 303-273-3847, Fax: 303-273-3919, E-mail: tohno@mines.edu.

Colorado State University, Graduate School, College of Natural Sciences, Department of Physics, Fort Collins, CO 80523-1875. Offers MS, PhD. Postbaccalaureate distance learning degree programs offered (no on-campus study). *Faculty:* 20 full-time (2 women), 2 part-time/adjunct (0 women). *Students:* 30 full-time (6 women), 23 part-time (3 women); includes 5 minority (1 African American, 1 American Indian/Alaska Native, 3 Asian Americans or Pacific Islanders), 13 international. Average age 27. 101 applicants, 32% accepted, 11 enrolled. In 2009, 7 master's, 2 doctorates awarded. Terminal master's awarded for partial completion of doctoral program. *Degree requirements:* For master's, comprehensive exam (for some programs), thesis (for some programs); for doctorate, comprehensive exam, thesis/dissertation. *Entrance requirements:* For master's, GRE General Test or GRE Subject Test (physics), minimum GPA of 3.0; 3 letters of recommendation; for doctorate, GRE General Test or GRE Subject Test (physics), minimum GPA of 3.0; transcripts; 3 letters of recommendation; BA (for domestic students); statement of purpose. Additional exam requirements/recommendations for international students: Required—TOEFL (minimum score 550 paper-based; 213 computer-based; 80 iBT). *Application deadline:* For fall admission, 9/15 priority date for domestic and international students; for spring admission, 1/15 priority date for domestic and international students. Applications are processed on a rolling basis. Application fee: $50. Electronic applications accepted. *Expenses:* Tuition, state resident: full-time $6434; part-time $359.10 per credit. Tuition, nonresident: full-time $18,116; part-time $1006.45 per credit. Required fees: $1496; $83 per credit. *Financial support:* In 2009–10, 52 students received support, including 7 fellowships (averaging $28,655 per year), 21 research assistantships with full tuition reimbursements available (averaging $14,605 per year), 24 teaching assistantships with full tuition reimbursements available (averaging $13,809 per year); health care benefits also available. Financial award application deadline: 1/15; financial award applicants required to submit FAFSA. *Faculty research:* Experimental condensed-matter physics, laser spectroscopy, optics, theoretical condensed-matter physics, particle physics. Total annual research expenditures: $3 million. *Unit head:* Dr. Hans Dieter Hochheimer, Chair, 970-491-6246, Fax: 970-491-7947, E-mail: dieter@lamar.colostate.edu. *Application contact:* Wendy Gleason, Secretary, Graduate Admissions Committee, 970-491-6207, Fax: 970-491-7947, E-mail: wendy.gleason@colostate.edu.

Columbia University, Graduate School of Arts and Sciences, Division of Natural Sciences, Department of Physics, New York, NY 10027. Offers philosophical foundations of physics (MA); physics (M Phil, PhD). *Degree requirements:* For doctorate, thesis/dissertation. *Entrance requirements:* For master's and doctorate, GRE General Test, GRE Subject Test, 3 years of course work in physics. Additional exam requirements/recommendations for international students: Required—TOEFL. *Faculty research:* Theoretical physics; astrophysics; low-, medium-, and high-energy physics.

Concordia University, School of Graduate Studies, Faculty of Arts and Science, Department of Physics, Montréal, QC H3G 1M8, Canada. Offers M Sc, PhD.

Cornell University, Graduate School, Graduate Fields of Arts and Sciences, Field of Physics, Ithaca, NY 14853-0001. Offers experimental physics (MS, PhD); physics (MS, PhD); theoretical physics (MS, PhD). *Faculty:* 70 full-time (5 women). *Students:* 148 full-time (24 women); includes 8 minority (1 African American, 5 Asian Americans or Pacific Islanders, 2 Hispanic Americans), 73 international. Average age 26. 358 applicants, 23% accepted, 23 enrolled. In 2009, 22 master's, 33 doctorates awarded. *Degree requirements:* For doctorate, comprehensive exam, thesis/dissertation. *Entrance requirements:* For doctorate, GRE General Test, GRE Subject Test (physics), 3 letters of recommendation. Additional exam requirements/recommendations for international students: Required—TOEFL (minimum score 620 paper-based; 260 computer-based; 105 iBT). *Application deadline:* For fall admission, 1/3 for domestic students. Application fee: $70. Electronic applications accepted. *Expenses:* Tuition: Full-time $29,500. Required fees: $70. Full-time tuition and fees vary according to degree level, program and student level. *Financial support:* In 2009–10, 4 fellowships with full tuition reimbursements, 1 research assistantship with full tuition reimbursement, 17 teaching assistantships with full tuition reimbursements were awarded; institutionally sponsored loans, scholarships/grants, health care benefits, tuition waivers (full and partial), and unspecified assistantships also available. Financial award applicants required to submit FAFSA. *Faculty research:* Experimental condensed matter physics, theoretical condensed matter physics, experimental high energy particle physics, theoretical particle physics and field theory, theoretical astrophysics. *Unit head:* Director of Graduate Studies, 607-255-7561. *Application contact:* Graduate Field Assistant, 607-255-7561, E-mail: physics-grad-adm@cornell.edu.

Creighton University, Graduate School, College of Arts and Sciences, Program in Physics, Omaha, NE 68178-0001. Offers MS. Part-time programs available. *Faculty:* 11 full-time (1 woman). *Students:* 7 full-time (0 women), 1 part-time (0 women); includes 1 minority (Hispanic American), 3 international. Average age 25. 13 applicants, 77% accepted, 7 enrolled. In 2009, 6 master's awarded. *Degree requirements:* For master's, thesis (for some programs). *Entrance requirements:* For master's, GRE General Test, 3 letters of recommendation. Additional exam requirements/recommendations for international students: Required—TOEFL (minimum score 550 paper-based; 213 computer-based; 80 iBT). *Application deadline:* For fall admission, 3/1 for domestic and international students. Applications are processed on a rolling basis. Application fee: $50. Electronic applications accepted. *Expenses:* Tuition: Full-time $11,700; part-time $650 per credit hour. Required fees: $126 per semester. *Financial support:* In 2009–10, 8 students received support, including 4 research assistantships with full tuition reimbursements available (averaging $10,803 per year), 3 teaching assistantships with full tuition reimbursements available (averaging $10,803 per year). Financial award applicants required to submit FAFSA. *Unit head:* Dr. Sam Cipolla, Chair, 402-280-2133, E-mail: samcip@creighton.edu. *Application contact:* Taunya Plater, Senior Program Coordinator, 402-280-2870, Fax: 402-280-2899, E-mail: taunyaplater@creighton.edu.

Dalhousie University, Faculty of Science, Department of Physics and Atmospheric Science, Halifax, NS B3H 3J5, Canada. Offers M Sc, PhD. *Faculty:* 13 full-time (1 woman), 18 part-time/adjunct (1 woman). *Students:* 20 full-time (3 women), 1 part-time (0 women); includes 6 minority (all Asian Americans or Pacific Islanders), 2 international. Average age 26. In 2009, 2 master's, 3 doctorates awarded. *Degree requirements:* For master's, thesis; for doctorate, thesis/dissertation. *Entrance requirements:* Additional exam requirements/recommendations for international students: Required—TOEFL, IELTS, CANTEST, CAEL, or Michigan English Language Assessment Battery. *Application deadline:* For fall admission, 6/1 for domestic students, 4/1 for international students; for winter admission, 11/15 for domestic students, 8/31 for international students; for spring admission, 2/28 for domestic students, 12/30 for international students. Application fee: $70. Electronic applications accepted. *Financial support:* Fellowships, teaching assistantships, career-related internships or fieldwork, scholarships/grants, and health care benefits available. Financial award application deadline: 3/1. *Faculty research:* Applied, experimental, and solid-state physics. Total annual research expenditures: $1.4 million. *Unit head:* Dr. Ted Monchesky, Graduate Coordinator, 902-494-3582, Fax: 902-494-5191, E-mail: physics@dal.ca. *Application contact:* Krista Culluymore, Graduate Secretary, 902-494-6835, Fax: 902-494-5191, E-mail: gradc@fizz.phys.dal.ca.

Dartmouth College, Arts and Sciences Graduate Programs, Department of Physics and Astronomy, Hanover, NH 03755. Offers MS, PhD. *Faculty:* 17 full-time (4 women), 7 part-time/adjunct (1 woman). *Students:* 51 full-time (16 women); includes 3 minority (1 African American, 1 Asian American or Pacific Islander, 1 Hispanic American), 18 international. Average age 26. 86 applicants, 30% accepted, 15 enrolled. In 2009, 5 doctorates awarded. Terminal master's awarded for partial completion of doctoral program. *Degree requirements:* For master's, thesis; for doctorate, thesis/dissertation. *Entrance requirements:* For master's and doctorate, GRE General Test, GRE Subject Test. Additional exam requirements/recommendations for international students: Required—TOEFL. *Application deadline:* For fall admission, 2/1 priority date for domestic students. Application fee: $15. *Financial support:* In 2009–10, 42 students received support, including fellowships with full tuition reimbursements available (averaging $23,832 per year), research assistantships with full tuition reimbursements available (averaging $23,832 per year), teaching assistantships with full tuition reimbursements available (averaging $23,832 per year); institutionally sponsored loans, scholarships/grants, and tuition waivers (full) also available. *Faculty research:* Matter physics, plasma and beam physics, space physics, astronomy, cosmology. *Unit head:* Walter E. Lawrence, Chair, Graduate Admissions, 603-646-2854, Fax: 603-646-1446. *Application contact:* Judy Lowell, Administrative Assistant, 603-646-2854, Fax: 603-646-1446.

Delaware State University, Graduate Programs, Department of Physics, Dover, DE 19901-2277. Offers applied optics (MS); optics (PhD); physics (MS); physics teaching (MS). Part-time and evening/weekend programs available. *Entrance requirements:* For master's, minimum GPA of 3.0 in major, 2.75 overall. Additional exam requirements/recommendations for international students: Required—TOEFL. Electronic applications accepted. *Faculty research:* Thermal properties of solids, nuclear physics, radiation damage in solids.

DePaul University, College of Liberal Arts and Sciences, Department of Physics, Chicago, IL 60604-2287. Offers applied physics (MS). Part-time and evening/weekend programs available. *Faculty:* 6 full-time (2 women), 3 part-time/adjunct (0 women). *Students:* 10 full-time (5 women), 3 part-time (1 woman); includes 2 minority (1 African American, 1 Hispanic American), 1 international. Average age 23. 12 applicants, 42% accepted, 3 enrolled. In 2009, 3 master's awarded. *Degree requirements:* For master's, thesis, oral exams. *Entrance requirements:* For master's, 2 letters of recommendation, BA in physics or closely related field. Additional exam requirements/recommendations for international students: Required—TOEFL. *Application deadline:* For fall admission, 5/1 priority date for domestic students, 4/1 priority date for international students. Applications are processed on a rolling basis. Application fee: $25. Electronic applications accepted. *Expenses:* Tuition: Full-time $37,525; part-time $620 per credit hour. *Financial support:* In 2009–10, teaching assistantships with full tuition reimbursements (averaging $9,000 per year); tuition waivers (full) also available. *Faculty research:* Optics, solid-state physics, cosmology, atomic physics, nuclear physics. Total annual research expenditures: $54,000. *Unit head:* Dr. Christopher G. Goedde, Chairman, 773-325-7330, Fax: 773-325-7334, E-mail: egoedde@condor.depaul.edu. *Application contact:* Dr. Jesus Pando, Associate Professor, 773-325-7330, Fax: 773-325-7334.

Drew University, Casperson School of Graduate Studies, Program in Education, Madison, NJ 07940-1493. Offers biology (MAT); chemistry (MAT); English (MAT); French (MAT); Italian (MAT); math (MAT); physics (MAT); social studies (MAT); Spanish (MAT); theatre arts (MAT).

Drexel University, College of Arts and Sciences, Department of Physics, Philadelphia, PA 19104-2875. Offers MS, PhD. Terminal master's awarded for partial completion of doctoral program. *Degree requirements:* For doctorate, thesis/dissertation. *Entrance requirements:* For master's and doctorate, GRE. Additional exam requirements/recommendations for international students: Required—TOEFL. Electronic applications accepted. *Faculty research:* Nuclear structure, mesoscale meteorology, numerical astrophysics, numerical weather prediction, earth energy radiation budget.

Duke University, Graduate School, Department of Medical Physics, Durham, NC 27708-0586. Offers MS, PhD. *Faculty:* 50 full-time. *Students:* 44 full-time (13 women); includes 7 minority (1 African American, 5 Asian Americans or Pacific Islanders, 1 Hispanic American), 10 international. 152 applicants, 31% accepted, 13 enrolled. In 2009, 15 master's awarded. *Entrance requirements:* Additional exam requirements/recommendations for international students: Required—TOEFL (minimum score 550 paper-based; 213 computer-based; 83 iBT), IELTS (minimum score 7). *Application deadline:* For fall admission, 12/8 priority date for domestic and international students. Application fee: $75. Electronic applications accepted. *Financial support:* Application deadline: 12/15. *Unit head:* Ehsan Samei, Director, 919-684-1400, Fax: 919-684-1490, E-mail: olga.baranova@duke.edu. *Application contact:* Cynthia Robertson, Associate Dean for Enrollment Services, 919-684-3913, E-mail: grad-admissions@duke.edu.

Duke University, Graduate School, Department of Physics, Durham, NC 27708-0586. Offers PhD. Part-time programs available. *Faculty:* 33 full-time. *Students:* 70 full-time (13 women); includes 4 minority (all Asian Americans or Pacific Islanders), 43 international. 210 applicants, 28% accepted, 13 enrolled. In 2009, 1 doctorate awarded. *Degree requirements:* For doctorate, thesis/dissertation. *Entrance requirements:* For doctorate, GRE General Test, GRE Subject Test. Additional exam requirements/recommendations for international students: Required—TOEFL (minimum score 550 paper-based; 213 computer-based; 83 iBT), IELTS (minimum score 7). *Application deadline:* For fall admission, 12/8 priority date for domestic and international students. Application fee: $75. *Financial support:* Fellowships, research assistantships, teaching assistantships, Federal Work-Study available. Financial award application deadline: 12/31. *Unit head:* Dr. Richard G. Palmer, Director of Graduate Studies, 919-660-2502, Fax: 919-606-2525, E-mail: donna@phy.duke.edu. *Application contact:* Cynthia Robertson, Associate Dean for Enrollment Services, 919-684-3913, E-mail: grad-admissions@duke.edu.

East Carolina University, Graduate School, Thomas Harriot College of Arts and Sciences, Department of Physics, Greenville, NC 27858-4353. Offers applied and biomedical physics (MS); medical physics (MS); physics (PhD). Part-time programs available. *Degree requirements:* For master's, one foreign language, comprehensive exam. *Entrance requirements:* For master's, GRE General Test. Additional exam requirements/recommendations for international students: Required—TOEFL.

Eastern Michigan University, Graduate School, College of Arts and Sciences, Department of Physics and Astronomy, Ypsilanti, MI 48197. Offers general science (MS); physics (MS); physics education (MS). Part-time and evening/weekend programs available. Postbaccalaureate distance learning degree programs offered (minimal on-campus study). *Faculty:* 10 full-time (4 women). *Students:* 2 full-time (0 women), 14 part-time (7 women); includes 3 minority (2 African Americans, 1 Asian American or Pacific Islander), 1 international. Average age 29. 16 applicants, 88% accepted, 8 enrolled. In 2009, 6 master's awarded. *Entrance requirements:* Additional exam requirements/recommendations for international students: Required—TOEFL. *Application deadline:* Applications are processed on a rolling basis. Application fee: $35. Tuition and fees vary according to course level. *Financial support:* In 2009–10, 8 teaching assistantships with full tuition reimbursements (averaging $8,562 per year) were awarded; fellowships, research assistantships with full tuition reimbursements, career-related internships or fieldwork, Federal Work-Study, institutionally sponsored loans, scholarships/grants, tuition waivers, and unspecified assistantships also available. Support available to part-time students. Financial award applicants required to submit FAFSA. *Unit head:* James Carroll, Interim Department Head, 734-487-4144, Fax: 734-487-0989, E-mail: jcarroll@emich.edu. *Application contact:* Graduate Admissions, 734-487-3400, Fax: 734-487-6559, E-mail: graduate.admissions@emich.edu.

Emory University, Graduate School of Arts and Sciences, Department of Physics, Atlanta, GA 30322-1100. Offers biophysics (PhD); condensed matter physics (PhD); non-linear physics (PhD); radiological physics (PhD); soft condensed matter physics (PhD); solid-state physics (PhD); statistical physics (PhD); MS/PhD. *Degree requirements:* For doctorate, thesis/dissertation, qualifier proposal (PhD). *Entrance requirements:* For doctorate, GRE General Test, minimum GPA of 3.0. Additional exam requirements/recommendations for international students: Required—TOEFL (minimum score 600 paper-based). Electronic applications accepted. *Faculty research:* Experimental studies of the structure and function of metalloproteins, soft condensed matter, granular materials, biophotonics and fluorescence correlation spectroscopy, single molecule studies of DNA-protein systems.

Fisk University, Division of Graduate Studies, Department of Physics, Nashville, TN 37208-3051. Offers MA. *Faculty:* 5 full-time (0 women), 1 (woman) part-time/adjunct. *Students:* 16 full-time (7 women), 4 part-time (1 woman); includes 15 minority (13 African Americans, 1 Asian American or Pacific Islander, 1 Hispanic American), 2 international. Average age 28. 20 applicants, 55% accepted, 8 enrolled. In 2009, 3 master's awarded. *Degree requirements:* For master's, thesis. *Entrance requirements:* For master's, GRE General Test, GRE Subject Test, minimum GPA of 3.0. *Application deadline:* For fall admission, 6/1 priority date for domestic students. Applications are processed on a rolling basis. Application fee: $50. Electronic applications accepted. *Expenses:* Tuition: Full-time $16,848; part-time $936 per credit hour. Required fees: $1510; $465 per semester. *Financial support:* In 2009–10, 1 student received support, including 1 research assistantship with full tuition reimbursement available (averaging $12,224 per year); fellowships, teaching assistantships, tuition waivers (full) and unspecified assistantships also available. Financial award applicants required to submit FAFSA. *Faculty research:* Molecular physics, astrophysics, surface physics, nanobase materials, optical processing. Total annual research expenditures: $3.1 million. *Unit head:* Dr. Steve Morgan, Chair, 615-329-8605. *Application contact:* Keith Chandler, Director of Admissions, 615-329-8819, Fax: 615-329-8774, E-mail: kchandler@fisk.edu.

Florida Agricultural and Mechanical University, Division of Graduate Studies, Research, and Continuing Education, College of Arts and Sciences, Department of Physics, Tallahassee, FL 32307-3200. Offers MS, PhD. *Faculty:* 21 full-time (4 women). *Students:* 18 full-time (4 women); includes 15 minority (14 African Americans, 1 Hispanic American), 2 international. In 2009, 2 master's awarded. *Degree requirements:* For master's, comprehensive exam, thesis optional; for doctorate, comprehensive exam, thesis/dissertation. *Entrance requirements:* For master's, GRE General Test, minimum GPA of 3.0; for doctorate, GRE General Test, minimum GPA of 3.0, letters of recommendation (2). Additional exam requirements/recommendations for international students: Required—TOEFL (minimum score 550 paper-based). *Application deadline:* For fall admission, 5/18 for domestic students, 12/18 for international students; for spring admission, 11/12 for domestic students, 5/12 for international students. Application fee: $30. *Faculty research:* Plasma physics, quantum mechanics, condensed matter physics, astrophysics, laser ablation. *Unit head:* Dr. Mogus Mochena, Chairperson, 850-599-3470, Fax: 850-599-3577. *Application contact:* Dr. Chanta M. Haywood, Dean of Graduate Studies, Research, and Continuing Education, 850-599-3315, Fax: 850-599-3727.

Florida Atlantic University, Charles E. Schmidt College of Science, Department of Physics, Boca Raton, FL 33431-0991. Offers MS, PhD. Part-time programs available. *Faculty:* 13 full-time (2 women), 1 part-time/adjunct (0 women). *Students:* 24 full-time (5 women), 4 part-time (3 women), 19 international. Average age 32. 16 applicants, 44% accepted, 0 enrolled. In 2009, 1 master's, 2 doctorates awarded. *Degree requirements:* For master's, thesis; for doctorate, thesis/dissertation. *Entrance requirements:* For master's, GRE General Test, minimum GPA of 3.0; for doctorate, GRE General Test. Additional exam requirements/recommendations for international students: Required—TOEFL (minimum score 500 paper-based; 173 computer-based). *Application deadline:* For fall admission, 7/1 for domestic students, 2/15 for international students; for spring admission, 11/1 for domestic students, 7/15 for international students. Applications are processed on a rolling basis. Application fee: $30. *Expenses:* Tuition, state resident: full-time $7055; part-time $293.94 per credit hour. Tuition, nonresident: full-time $22,096; part-time $920.66 per credit hour. *Financial support:* Fellowships, research assistantships with tuition reimbursements, teaching assistantships with tuition reimbursements, Federal Work-Study and unspecified assistantships available. *Faculty research:* Astrophysics, spectroscopy, mathematical physics, theory of metals, superconductivity. *Unit head:* Dr. Warner A. Miller, Chair, 561-297-3382, Fax: 561-297-2662, E-mail: wam@physics.fau.edu. *Application contact:* Dr. Warner A. Miller, Chair, 561-297-3382, Fax: 561-297-2662, E-mail: wam@physics.fau.edu.

Florida Institute of Technology, Graduate Programs, College of Science, Department of Physics and Space Sciences, Melbourne, FL 32901-6975. Offers physics (MS, PhD); space sciences (MS, PhD). Part-time programs available. *Faculty:* 13 full-time (1 woman), 1 part-time/adjunct (0 women). *Students:* 35 full-time (9 women), 8 part-time (4 women); includes 2 minority (both Hispanic Americans), 13 international. Average age 28. 52 applicants, 42% accepted, 7 enrolled. In 2009, 2 master's, 3 doctorates awarded. *Degree requirements:* For master's, comprehensive exam (for some programs), thesis optional, oral exam; for doctorate, one foreign language, comprehensive exam, thesis/dissertation, publication in referred journal, seminar on dissertation research, dissertation published in a major journal. *Entrance requirements:* For master's, minimum GPA of 3.0, resume, 3 letters of recommendation, vector analysis; for doctorate, GRE General and Subject Tests (recommended), minimum GPA of 3.2, resume, 3 letters of recommendation, statement of objectives. Additional exam requirements/recommendations for international students: Required—TOEFL (minimum score 550 paper-based; 213 computer-based; 79 iBT). *Application deadline:* For fall admission, 4/1 for international students; for spring admission, 9/30 for international students. Applications are processed on a rolling basis. Application fee: $50. Electronic applications accepted. *Expenses:* Tuition: Part-time $1015 per credit. Tuition and fees vary according to campus/location and program. *Financial support:* In 2009–10, 29 students received support, including 14 research assistantships with full and partial tuition reimbursements available (averaging $12,926 per year), 15 teaching assistantships with full and partial tuition reimbursements available (averaging $13,462 per year); career-related internships or fieldwork, institutionally sponsored loans, tuition waivers (partial), unspecified assistantships, and tuition remissions also available. Support available to part-time students. Financial award application deadline: 3/1; financial award applicants required to submit FAFSA. *Faculty research:* Lasers, semiconductors, magnetism, quantum devices, high energy physics. Total annual research expenditures: $2.9 million. *Unit head:* Dr. Terry D. Oswalt, Department Head, 321-674-7325, Fax: 321-674-7482, E-mail: toswalt@fit.edu. *Application contact:* Thomas M. Shea, Director of Graduate Admissions, 321-674-7577, Fax: 321-723-9468, E-mail: tshea@fit.edu.

Florida International University, College of Arts and Sciences, Department of Physics, Miami, FL 33199. Offers MS, PhD. Part-time and evening/weekend programs available. *Faculty:* 18 full-time (2 women), 1 part-time/adjunct (0 women). *Students:* 30 full-time (7 women), 6 part-time (2 women); includes 14 minority (1 Asian American or Pacific Islander, 13 Hispanic Americans), 15 international. Average age 27. 43 applicants, 19% accepted, 8 enrolled. In 2009, 4 master's, 3 doctorates awarded. *Degree requirements:* For master's, one foreign language, thesis; for doctorate, one foreign language, comprehensive exam, thesis/dissertation. *Entrance requirements:* For master's and doctorate, GRE General Test, 2 letters of

Physics

Florida International University (continued)

recommendation. Additional exam requirements/recommendations for international students: Required—TOEFL (minimum score 550 paper-based; 80 iBT). *Application deadline:* For fall admission, 6/1 for domestic students, 4/1 for international students; for spring admission, 10/1 for domestic students, 9/1 for international students. Applications are processed on a rolling basis. Application fee: $30. Electronic applications accepted. *Expenses:* Tuition, state resident: full-time $8008; part-time $4004 per year. Tuition, nonresident: full-time $20,104; part-time $10,052 per year. Required fees: $298; $149 per term. *Financial support:* Institutionally sponsored loans and scholarships/grants available. Financial award application deadline: 3/1; financial award applicants required to submit FAFSA. *Faculty research:* Molecular collision processes (molecular beams), biophysical optics. *Unit head:* Dr. Walter Van Hamme, Chair, Physics Department, 305-348-2605, Fax: 305-348-3053, E-mail: walter.vanhamme@fiu.edu. *Application contact:* Dr. Brain Raue, Graduate Program Director, 305-348-3958, Fax: 305-348-3053, E-mail: brian.raue@fiu.edu.

Florida State University, The Graduate School, College of Arts and Sciences, Department of Physics, Tallahassee, FL 32306. Offers MS, PhD. *Faculty:* 45 full-time (2 women), 4 part-time/adjunct (2 women). *Students:* 112 full-time (18 women); includes 55 minority (1 African American, 1 American Indian/Alaska Native, 49 Asian Americans or Pacific Islanders, 4 Hispanic Americans). Average age 28. 221 applicants, 33% accepted, 29 enrolled. In 2009, 19 master's, 18 doctorates awarded. *Degree requirements:* For doctorate, comprehensive exam, thesis/dissertation. *Entrance requirements:* For master's and doctorate, GRE General Test, minimum GPA of 3.0. Additional exam requirements/recommendations for international students: Required—TOEFL (minimum score 550 paper-based; 213 computer-based; 80 iBT). *Application deadline:* For fall admission, 4/15 for domestic and international students. Application fee: $30. Electronic applications accepted. *Expenses:* Tuition, state resident: full-time $7413.36. Tuition, nonresident: full-time $22,567. *Financial support:* In 2009–10, 112 students received support, including 82 research assistantships with full tuition reimbursements available (averaging $18,000 per year), 30 teaching assistantships with full tuition reimbursements available (averaging $18,000 per year); fellowships, career-related internships or fieldwork and Federal Work-Study also available. Financial award application deadline: 2/15; financial award applicants required to submit FAFSA. *Faculty research:* High energy physics, computational physics, biophysics, condensed matter physics, nuclear physics, astrophysics. Total annual research expenditures: $3.2 million. *Unit head:* Dr. Mark A. Riley, Chairman, 850-644-2867, Fax: 850-644-8630, E-mail: mriley@nucmar.physics.fsu.edu. *Application contact:* Sherry Ann Tointigh, Academic Support Assistant, 850-644-4473, Fax: 850-644-8630, E-mail: graduate@phy.fsu.edu.

George Mason University, College of Science, Department of Physics and Astronomy, Fairfax, VA 22030. Offers applied and engineering physics (MS). *Degree requirements:* For master's, thesis optional. *Entrance requirements:* For master's, minimum GPA of 2.75 in last 60 hours of course work. Electronic applications accepted. *Expenses:* Tuition, state resident: full-time $7568; part-time $315.33 per credit hour. Tuition, nonresident: full-time $21,704; part-time $904.33 per credit hour. Required fees: $2184; $91 per credit hour.

The George Washington University, Columbian College of Arts and Sciences, Department of Physics, Washington, DC 20052. Offers MA, PhD. Part-time and evening/weekend programs available. *Faculty:* 20 full-time (2 women), 9 part-time/adjunct (3 women). *Students:* 18 full-time (6 women), 12 part-time (4 women); includes 4 minority (all Asian Americans or Pacific Islanders), 20 international. Average age 29. 43 applicants, 67% accepted, 5 enrolled. In 2009, 2 master's, 1 doctorate awarded. *Degree requirements:* For doctorate, thesis/dissertation, general exam. *Entrance requirements:* For master's and doctorate, GRE General Test, minimum GPA of 3.0. Additional exam requirements/recommendations for international students: Required—TOEFL (minimum score 550 paper-based; 213 computer-based; 80 iBT). *Application deadline:* For fall admission, 1/15 priority date for domestic and international students; for spring admission, 10/1 priority date for domestic students, 9/1 priority date for international students. Applications are processed on a rolling basis. Application fee: $60. Electronic applications accepted. *Financial support:* In 2009–10, 24 students received support; fellowships with full tuition reimbursements available, research assistantships, teaching assistantships with tuition reimbursements available, Federal Work-Study and tuition waivers available. Financial award application deadline: 1/15. *Unit head:* Dr. Cornelius Bennhold, Chair, 202-994-6274. *Application contact:* Dr. Mark Reeves, Director, 202-994-6279, Fax: 202-994-3001, E-mail: reevesme@gwu.edu.

Georgia Institute of Technology, Graduate Studies and Research, College of Sciences, School of Physics, Atlanta, GA 30332-0001. Offers MS, PhD. Part-time programs available. Terminal master's awarded for partial completion of doctoral program. *Degree requirements:* For doctorate, comprehensive exam, thesis/dissertation. *Entrance requirements:* For master's, GRE General Test, GRE Subject Test, minimum GPA of 3.0; for doctorate, GRE General Test, GRE Subject Test, minimum GPA of 3.4. Additional exam requirements/recommendations for international students: Required—TOEFL. Electronic applications accepted. *Faculty research:* Atomic and molecular physics, chemical physics, condensed matter, optics, nonlinear physics and chaos.

Georgia State University, College of Arts and Sciences, Department of Physics and Astronomy, Program in Physics, Atlanta, GA 30302-3083. Offers MS, PhD. Part-time and evening/weekend programs available. Terminal master's awarded for partial completion of doctoral program. *Degree requirements:* For master's, one foreign language, thesis or alternative, exam; for doctorate, 2 foreign languages, thesis/dissertation, exam. *Entrance requirements:* For master's, GRE General Test; for doctorate, GRE General Test, GRE Subject Test. Additional exam requirements/recommendations for international students: Required—TOEFL. Electronic applications accepted. *Faculty research:* Biophysics; nuclear, condensed-matter, and atomic physics; astrophysics.

Graduate School and University Center of the City University of New York, Graduate Studies, Program in Physics, New York, NY 10016-4039. Offers PhD. *Faculty:* 105 full-time (3 women). *Students:* 99 full-time (25 women); includes 7 minority (1 African American, 2 Asian Americans or Pacific Islanders, 4 Hispanic Americans), 67 international. Average age 28. 71 applicants, 42% accepted, 16 enrolled. In 2009, 13 doctorates awarded. *Degree requirements:* For doctorate, thesis/dissertation. *Entrance requirements:* For doctorate, GRE General Test. Additional exam requirements/recommendations for international students: Required—TOEFL. *Application deadline:* For fall admission, 1/15 for domestic students. Application fee: $125. Electronic applications accepted. *Financial support:* In 2009–10, 84 students received support, including 84 fellowships, 1 teaching assistantship; research assistantships, career-related internships or fieldwork, Federal Work-Study, institutionally sponsored loans, and tuition waivers (full and partial) also available. Financial award application deadline: 2/1; financial award applicants required to submit FAFSA. *Faculty research:* Condensed-matter, particle, nuclear, and atomic physics. *Unit head:* Dr. Steven Greenbaum, Executive Officer, 212-817-8651, Fax: 212-817-1531. *Application contact:* Les Gribben, Director of Admissions, 212-817-7470, Fax: 212-817-1624, E-mail: lgribben@gc.cuny.edu.

Hampton University, Graduate College, Department of Physics, Hampton, VA 23668. Offers atmospheric physics (MS, PhD); medical physics (MS, PhD); nuclear physics (MS, PhD); optical physics (MS, PhD). Part-time and evening/weekend programs available. Terminal master's awarded for partial completion of doctoral program. *Degree requirements:* For master's, thesis optional; for doctorate, thesis/dissertation, oral defense, qualifying exam. *Entrance requirements:* For master's, GRE General Test; for doctorate, GRE General Test, minimum GPA of 3.0 or master's degree in physics or related field. *Faculty research:* Laser optics, remote sensing.

Harvard University, Graduate School of Arts and Sciences, Department of Physics, Cambridge, MA 02138. Offers experimental physics (PhD); medical engineering/medical physics (PhD), including applied physics, engineering sciences, physics; theoretical physics (PhD). *Degree requirements:* For doctorate, thesis/dissertation, final exams, laboratory experience. *Entrance requirements:* For doctorate, GRE General Test, GRE Subject Test. Additional exam requirements/recommendations for international students: Required—TOEFL. *Expenses:* Tuition: Full-time $33,696. Required fees: $1126. Full-time tuition and fees vary according to program. *Faculty research:* Particle physics, condensed matter physics, atomic physics.

Howard University, Graduate School, Department of Physics and Astronomy, Washington, DC 20059-0002. Offers physics (MS, PhD). *Degree requirements:* For master's, comprehensive exam (for some programs), thesis (for some programs); for doctorate, comprehensive exam, thesis/dissertation, departmental qualifying exam. *Entrance requirements:* For master's, GRE General Test, bachelor's degree in physics or related field, minimum GPA of 3.0; for doctorate, GRE General Test, bachelor's or master's degree in physics or related field, minimum GPA of 3.0. Additional exam requirements/recommendations for international students: Required—TOEFL (minimum score 550 paper-based; 213 computer-based). Electronic applications accepted. *Faculty research:* Atmospheric physics, spectroscopy and optical physics, high energy physics, condensed matter.

Hunter College of the City University of New York, Graduate School, School of Arts and Sciences, Department of Physics, New York, NY 10021-5085. Offers MA, PhD. Part-time programs available. *Faculty:* 3 full-time (1 woman). *Students:* 6 full-time (2 women), 4 part-time (2 women); includes 3 minority (2 African Americans, 1 Hispanic American). Average age 25. 10 applicants, 60% accepted, 3 enrolled. In 2009, 3 master's awarded. Terminal master's awarded for partial completion of doctoral program. *Degree requirements:* For master's, comprehensive exam or thesis. *Entrance requirements:* For master's, minimum 36 credits of course work in mathematics and physics. Additional exam requirements/recommendations for international students: Required—TOEFL. *Application deadline:* For fall admission, 4/1 for domestic students, 2/1 for international students; for spring admission, 11/1 for domestic students, 9/1 for international students. Application fee: $125. *Expenses:* Tuition, state resident: full-time $7360; part-time $310 per credit. Required fees: $250 per semester. *Financial support:* In 2009–10, research assistantships (averaging $20,000 per year), teaching assistantships (averaging $9,000 per year) were awarded; Federal Work-Study, scholarships/grants, and tuition waivers (partial) also available. Support available to part-time students. *Faculty research:* Experimental and theoretical quantum optics, experimental and theoretical condensed matter, mathematical physics. *Unit head:* Ying-Chin Chen, Chairperson, 212-772-5248, Fax: 212-772-5390, E-mail: y.c.chen@hunter.cuny.edu. *Application contact:* William Zlata, Director for Graduate Admissions, 212-772-4482, Fax: 212-650-3336, E-mail: admissions@hunter.cuny.edu.

Idaho State University, Office of Graduate Studies, College of Arts and Sciences, Department of Physics, Pocatello, ID 83209-8106. Offers applied physics (PhD); health physics (MS); physics (MNS). Part-time programs available. *Faculty:* 7 full-time (1 woman), 1 part-time/adjunct (0 women). *Students:* 43 full-time (8 women), 28 part-time (5 women); includes 3 minority (1 African American, 2 Hispanic Americans), 27 international. Average age 32. In 2009, 2 doctorates awarded. *Degree requirements:* For master's, comprehensive exam, thesis (for some programs), oral exam (for some programs); for doctorate, comprehensive exam, thesis/dissertation (for some programs), oral exam, written qualifying exam in physics or health physics after 1st year. *Entrance requirements:* For master's, GRE General Test, 3 letters of recommendation, BS or BA in physics, teaching certificate (MNS); for doctorate, GRE General Test (minimum 50th percentile), 3 letters of recommendation, statement of career goals. Additional exam requirements/recommendations for international students: Required—TOEFL (minimum score 550 paper-based; 213 computer-based; 80 iBT). *Application deadline:* For fall admission, 7/1 for domestic students, 6/1 for international students; for spring admission, 12/1 for domestic students, 11/1 for international students. Applications are processed on a rolling basis. Application fee: $55. Electronic applications accepted. *Expenses:* Tuition, state resident: full-time $3318; part-time $297 per credit hour. Tuition, nonresident: full-time $13,120; part-time $437 per credit hour. Required fees: $2530. Tuition and fees vary according to program. *Financial support:* In 2009–10, 38 research assistantships with full and partial tuition reimbursements (averaging $13,169 per year), 7 teaching assistantships with full and partial tuition reimbursements (averaging $10,841 per year) were awarded; fellowships with full and partial tuition reimbursements, career-related internships or fieldwork, Federal Work-Study, institutionally sponsored loans, scholarships/grants, health care benefits, tuition waivers (full), and unspecified assistantships also available. Support available to part-time students. Financial award application deadline: 1/1; financial award applicants required to submit FAFSA. *Faculty research:* Ion beam applications, low-energy nuclear physics, relativity and cosmology, observational astronomy. *Unit head:* Dr. Richard Brey, Interim Chair, 208-282-3467, Fax: 208-282-4649, E-mail: brey@physics.isu.edu. *Application contact:* Tami Carson, Graduate School Technical Records Specialist, 208-282-2150, Fax: 208-282-4847, E-mail: carstami@isu.edu.

Illinois Institute of Technology, Graduate College, College of Science and Letters, Department of Biological, Chemical and Physical Sciences, Physics Division, Chicago, IL 60616-3793. Offers health physics (MHP); physics (MS, PhD). Part-time programs available. Postbaccalaureate distance learning degree programs offered. Terminal master's awarded for partial completion of doctoral program. *Degree requirements:* For master's, comprehensive exam, thesis (for some programs); for doctorate, comprehensive exam, thesis/dissertation. *Entrance requirements:* For master's and doctorate, GRE General Test, minimum undergraduate GPA of 3.0. Additional exam requirements/recommendations for international students: Required—TOEFL (minimum score 550 paper-based; 213 computer-based; 80 iBT). Electronic applications accepted. *Expenses:* Tuition: Full-time $17,550; part-time $888 per credit hour. Required fees: $850; $7.50 per credit hour. One-time fee: $50 full-time. Full-time tuition and fees vary according to program. *Faculty research:* Elementary particle physics, accelerator physics, synchrotron radiation, research on materials and biological systems, XANES and XAFS, computational simulation of membranes.

Indiana University Bloomington, University Graduate School, College of Arts and Sciences, Department of Physics, Bloomington, IN 47405-7000. Offers MAT, MS, PhD. Part-time programs available. Postbaccalaureate distance learning degree programs offered (no on-campus study). *Faculty:* 36 full-time (5 women), 11 part-time/adjunct (0 women). *Students:* 79 full-time (17 women), 1 part-time (0 women); includes 7 minority (2 African Americans, 3 Asian Americans or Pacific Islanders, 2 Hispanic Americans), 42 international. Average age 27. 175 applicants, 36% accepted, 12 enrolled. In 2009, 13 master's, 17 doctorates awarded. Terminal master's awarded for partial completion of doctoral program. *Degree requirements:* For master's, comprehensive exam (for some programs), thesis (for some programs), qualifying exam; for doctorate, comprehensive exam, thesis/dissertation, qualifying exam. *Entrance requirements:* For master's and doctorate, GRE General Test, GRE Subject Test (physics), minimum GPA of 3.0. Additional exam requirements/recommendations for international students: Required—TOEFL (minimum score 550 paper-based; 213 computer-based; 80 iBT). *Application deadline:* For fall admission, 1/15 priority date for domestic students, 12/1 priority date for international students; for spring admission, 10/1 priority date for domestic students, 9/1 priority date for international students. Applications are processed on a rolling basis. Application fee: $55 ($65 for international students). Electronic applications accepted. *Financial support:* In 2009–10, 74 students received support, including 6 fellowships with full and partial tuition reimbursements available (averaging $21,700 per year), 38 research assistantships with partial tuition reimbursements available (averaging $20,000 per year), 27 teaching assistantships with partial tuition reimbursements available (averaging $15,700 per year); health care benefits also available. *Unit head:* Dr. Rick Van Kooten, Chair, 812-855-1247, Fax: 812-855-5533, E-mail: gradphys@indiana.edu. *Application contact:* Tracey McGookey, Student Services Assistant, 812-856-7059, E-mail: tmcgooke@indiana.edu.

Indiana University of Pennsylvania, School of Graduate Studies and Research, College of Natural Sciences and Mathematics, Department of Physics, Program in Physics, Indiana, PA 15705-1087. Offers MA, MS. Part-time programs available. *Faculty:* 7 full-time (0 women). *Students:* 8 full-time (1 woman), 1 (woman) part-time; includes 1 minority (African American), 2 international. Average age 26. 13 applicants, 46% accepted, 4 enrolled. In 2009, 5 master's awarded. *Degree requirements:* For master's, comprehensive exam (for some programs), thesis (for some programs). *Application deadline:* For fall admission, 7/1 priority date for domestic students; for spring admission, 11/1 for domestic students. Applications are processed on a rolling basis. Application fee: $40. *Expenses:* Tuition, state resident: full-time $6666; part-time $370 per credit hour. Tuition, nonresident: full-time $10,666; part-time $593 per credit hour. Required fees: $813 per semester. *Financial support:* In 2009–10, 6 research assistantships with full and partial tuition reimbursements (averaging $5,830 per year) were awarded; Federal Work-Study also available. Support available to part-time students. Financial award application deadline: 3/15; financial award applicants required to submit FAFSA. *Unit head:* Dr. Greg Kenning, Graduate Coordinator, 724-357-2318, E-mail: greg.kenning@iup.edu. *Application contact:* Dr. Muhammad Numan, Graduate Coordinator, 724-357-2318, E-mail: mznuman@iup.edu.

Indiana University–Purdue University Indianapolis, School of Science, Department of Physics, Indianapolis, IN 46202-2896. Offers MS, PhD. Part-time programs available. *Faculty:* 4 full-time (0 women). *Students:* 21 full-time (1 woman), 5 part-time (2 women); includes 3 minority (2 African Americans, 1 Hispanic American), 10 international. Average age 31. 20 applicants, 60% accepted, 8 enrolled. In 2009, 2 master's awarded. Terminal master's awarded for partial completion of doctoral program. *Degree requirements:* For master's, thesis optional; for doctorate, thesis/dissertation. *Entrance requirements:* Additional exam requirements/recommendations for international students: Required—TOEFL. *Application deadline:* For fall admission, 3/1 priority date for domestic students. Applications are processed on a rolling basis. Application fee: $55 ($65 for international students). *Financial support:* In 2009–10, 6 fellowships with full tuition reimbursements (averaging $14,204 per year), 6 teaching assistantships with full tuition reimbursements (averaging $6,245 per year) were awarded; research assistantships with full tuition reimbursements, Federal Work-Study, institutionally sponsored loans, and tuition waivers (full and partial) also available. Support available to part-time students. Financial award application deadline: 3/1. *Faculty research:* Magnetic resonance, photosynthesis, optical physics, biophysics, physics of materials. *Unit head:* Guantam Vemuri, Chair, 317-274-6900, E-mail: gvemuri@iupui.edu. *Application contact:* Guantam Vemuri, Chair, 317-274-6900, E-mail: gvemuri@iupui.edu.

Iowa State University of Science and Technology, Graduate College, College of Liberal Arts and Sciences, Department of Physics and Astronomy, Ames, IA 50011. Offers applied physics (MS, PhD); astrophysics (MS, PhD); condensed matter physics (MS, PhD); high energy physics (MS, PhD); nuclear physics (MS, PhD); physics (MS, PhD). Part-time programs available. *Faculty:* 46 full-time (3 women), 4 part-time/adjunct (0 women). *Students:* 94 full-time (21 women), 4 part-time (0 women); includes 3 minority (all Asian Americans or Pacific Islanders), 56 international. 185 applicants, 32% accepted, 15 enrolled. In 2009, 4 master's, 7 doctorates awarded. Terminal master's awarded for partial completion of doctoral program. *Degree requirements:* For master's, thesis (for some programs); for doctorate, thesis/dissertation. *Entrance requirements:* For master's and doctorate, GRE General Test, GRE Subject Test (physics). Additional exam requirements/recommendations for international students: Required—TOEFL (minimum score 550 paper-based; 79 iBT) or IELTS (minimum score 6.5). *Application deadline:* For fall admission, 2/15 priority date for domestic and international students; for spring admission, 10/15 for domestic and international students. Applications are processed on a rolling basis. Application fee: $40 ($90 for international students). Electronic applications accepted. *Expenses:* Tuition, state resident: full-time $6716. Tuition, nonresident: full-time $8908. Tuition and fees vary according to course level, course load, program and student level. *Financial support:* In 2009–10, 58 research assistantships with full and partial tuition reimbursements (averaging $17,000 per year), 33 teaching assistantships with full and partial tuition reimbursements (averaging $16,000 per year) were awarded; fellowships, Federal Work-Study, institutionally sponsored loans, scholarships/grants, health care benefits, and unspecified assistantships also available. Support available to part-time students. Financial award application deadline: 2/15. *Faculty research:* Condensed-matter physics, including superconductivity and new materials; high-energy and nuclear physics; astronomy and astrophysics; atmospheric and environmental physics. Total annual research expenditures: $8.8 million. *Unit head:* Dr. Joseph Shinar, Chair, 515-294-3455, Fax: 515-294-6027, E-mail: phys_astro@iastate.edu. *Application contact:* Dr. Steven Kawaler, Director of Graduate Education, 515-294-9728, E-mail: phys_astro@iastate.edu.

The Johns Hopkins University, Zanvyl Krieger School of Arts and Sciences, Henry A. Rowland Department of Physics and Astronomy, Baltimore, MD 21218-2699. Offers astronomy (PhD); physics (PhD). *Faculty:* 30 full-time (2 women), 14 part-time/adjunct (3 women). *Students:* 107 full-time (17 women); includes 4 minority (3 Asian Americans or Pacific Islanders, 1 Hispanic American), 47 international. Average age 26. 258 applicants, 19% accepted, 49 enrolled. In 2009, 16 doctorates awarded. Terminal master's awarded for partial completion of doctoral program. *Degree requirements:* For doctorate, comprehensive exam, thesis/dissertation, complete required coursework with minimum B- average. *Entrance requirements:* For doctorate, GRE General Test, GRE Subject Test. Additional exam requirements/recommendations for international students: Required—TOEFL (minimum score 600 paper-based; 250 computer-based; 100 iBT), IELTS. *Application deadline:* For fall admission, 1/14 for domestic and international students. Application fee: $75. Electronic applications accepted. *Financial support:* In 2009–10, 107 students received support, including 4 fellowships with full tuition reimbursements available (averaging $26,000 per year), 55 research assistantships with full tuition reimbursements available (averaging $26,000 per year), 48 teaching assistantships with full tuition reimbursements available (averaging $19,500 per year); career-related internships or fieldwork, Federal Work-Study, institutionally sponsored loans, tuition waivers (partial), and unspecified assistantships also available. Financial award application deadline: 4/15; financial award applicants required to submit FAFSA. *Faculty research:* High-energy physics, condensed-matter, astrophysics, particle and experimental physics, plasma physics. Total annual research expenditures: $24.9 million. *Unit head:* Dr. Daniel H. Reich, Chair, 410-516-7346, Fax: 410-516-7239, E-mail: dhr@pha.jhu.edu. *Application contact:* Carmelita D. King, Academic Affairs Administrator, 410-516-7344, Fax: 410-516-7239, E-mail: jazzy@pha.jhu.edu.

See Close-Up on page 219.

Kent State University, College of Arts and Sciences, Department of Physics, Kent, OH 44242-0001. Offers MA, MS, PhD. Terminal master's awarded for partial completion of doctoral program. *Degree requirements:* For master's, thesis; for doctorate, comprehensive exam, thesis/dissertation. *Entrance requirements:* For master's and doctorate, GRE, minimum GPA of 3.0. Additional exam requirements/recommendations for international students: Required—TOEFL. Electronic applications accepted. *Faculty research:* Correlated electron materials physics, liquid crystals, complex fluids, computational biophysics, QCD-Hadranphysics.

Lakehead University, Graduate Studies, Department of Physics, Thunder Bay, ON P7B 5E1, Canada. Offers M Sc. *Degree requirements:* For master's, thesis or alternative. *Entrance requirements:* For master's, minimum B average. Additional exam requirements/recommendations for international students: Required—TOEFL. *Faculty research:* Absorbed water, radiation reaction, superlattices and quantum well structures, polaron interactions.

Lehigh University, College of Arts and Sciences, Department of Physics, Bethlehem, PA 18015. Offers photonics (MS); physics (MS, PhD); polymer science (MS, PhD). Part-time programs available. *Faculty:* 17 full-time (1 woman), 1 part-time/adjunct (0 women). *Students:* 48 full-time (13 women), 1 part-time (0 women); includes 1 minority (African American), 19 international. Average age 26. 100 applicants, 13% accepted, 9 enrolled. In 2009, 6 doctorates awarded. *Degree requirements:* For doctorate, comprehensive exam, thesis/dissertation. *Entrance requirements:* Additional exam requirements/recommendations for international students: Required—TOEFL (minimum score 213 computer-based; 85 iBT). *Application deadline:* For fall admission, 2/15 priority date for domestic and international students. Applications are processed on a rolling basis. Application fee: $65. Electronic applications accepted. *Financial support:* In 2009–10, 47 students received support, including 4 fellowships with full tuition reimbursements available (averaging $23,000 per year), 23 research assistantships with full tuition reimbursements available (averaging $22,180 per year), 20 teaching assistantships with full tuition reimbursements available (averaging $22,180 per year); career-related internships or fieldwork, Federal Work-Study, institutionally sponsored loans, scholarships/grants, tuition waivers (full and partial), and unspecified assistantships also available. Support available to part-time students. Financial award application deadline: 1/15. *Faculty research:* Condensed matter physics; atomic, molecular and optical physics; plasma physics; nonlinear optics and photonics; astronomy and astrophysics. Total annual research expenditures: $2.9 million. *Unit head:* Dr. Volkmar Dierolf, Chair, 610-758-3915, Fax: 610-758-5730, E-mail: vod2@lehigh.edu. *Application contact:* Dr. Ivan Biaggio, Graduate Admissions Officer, 610-758-4916, Fax: 610-758-5730, E-mail: ivb2@lehigh.edu.

Louisiana State University and Agricultural and Mechanical College, Graduate School, College of Basic Sciences, Department of Physics and Astronomy, Baton Rouge, LA 70803. Offers astronomy (PhD); astrophysics (PhD); medical physics (MS); physics (MS, PhD). *Faculty:* 45 full-time (4 women), 1 part-time/adjunct (0 women). *Students:* 97 full-time (24 women), 5 part-time (1 woman); includes 5 minority (1 African American, 2 Asian Americans or Pacific Islanders, 2 Hispanic Americans), 42 international. Average age 27. 127 applicants, 20% accepted, 21 enrolled. In 2009, 9 master's, 8 doctorates awarded. Terminal master's awarded for partial completion of doctoral program. *Degree requirements:* For master's, thesis or alternative; for doctorate, thesis/dissertation. *Entrance requirements:* For master's and doctorate, GRE General Test, minimum GPA of 3.0. Additional exam requirements/recommendations for international students: Required—TOEFL (minimum score 550 paper-based; 213 computer-based; 79 iBT) or IELTS (minimum score 6.5). *Application deadline:* For fall admission, 1/25 priority date for domestic students, 5/15 for international students; for spring admission, 10/15 for international students. Applications are processed on a rolling basis. Application fee: $50 ($70 for international students). Electronic applications accepted. *Financial support:* In 2009–10, 16 fellowships with full tuition reimbursements (averaging $24,969 per year), 53 research assistantships with full and partial tuition reimbursements (averaging $20,101 per year), 37 teaching assistantships with full and partial tuition reimbursements (averaging $17,943 per year) were awarded; Federal Work-Study, institutionally sponsored loans, health care benefits, tuition waivers (full and partial), and unspecified assistantships also available. Financial award application deadline: 3/15; financial award applicants required to submit FAFSA. *Faculty research:* Experimentation and numerical relativity, condensed matter astrophysics, quantum computing, medical physics. Total annual research expenditures: $7.5 million. *Unit head:* Dr. Michael Cherry, Chair, 225-578-2261, Fax: 225-578-5855, E-mail: cherry@phys.lsu.edu. *Application contact:* Arnell Dangerfield, Administrative Coordinator, 225-578-1193, Fax: 225-578-5855, E-mail: adanger@lsu.edu.

Louisiana Tech University, Graduate School, College of Engineering and Science, Department of Physics, Ruston, LA 71272. Offers applied computational analysis and modeling (PhD); physics (MS). Part-time programs available. *Degree requirements:* For master's, thesis or alternative; for doctorate, thesis/dissertation. *Entrance requirements:* For master's, GRE General Test, minimum GPA of 3.0 in last 60 hours. Additional exam requirements/recommendations for international students: Required—TOEFL. *Faculty research:* Experimental high energy physics, laser/optics, computational physics, quantum gravity.

Marshall University, Academic Affairs Division, College of Science, Department of Physical Science and Physics, Huntington, WV 25755. Offers physical science (MS). *Faculty:* 5 full-time (2 women), 6 part-time/adjunct (1 woman). *Students:* 15 full-time (6 women), 4 part-time (2 women); includes 4 minority (2 African Americans, 2 American Indian/Alaska Native), 5 international. Average age 30. In 2009, 13 master's awarded. *Degree requirements:* For master's, thesis optional. *Entrance requirements:* For master's, GRE General Test. Application fee: $40. *Unit head:* Dr. Nicola Orsini, Chairperson, 304-696-2756, E-mail: orsini@marshall.edu. *Application contact:* Information Contact, 304-746-1900, Fax: 304-746-1902, E-mail: services@marshall.edu.

Massachusetts Institute of Technology, School of Science, Department of Physics, Cambridge, MA 02139-4307. Offers SM, PhD. *Faculty:* 73 full-time (6 women). *Students:* 235 full-time (40 women); includes 24 minority (4 African Americans, 11 Asian Americans or Pacific Islanders, 9 Hispanic Americans), 118 international. Average age 26. 535 applicants, 17% accepted, 40 enrolled. In 2009, 4 master's, 37 doctorates awarded. Terminal master's awarded for partial completion of doctoral program. *Degree requirements:* For master's, thesis; for doctorate, comprehensive exam, thesis/dissertation. *Entrance requirements:* For master's and doctorate, GRE General Test, GRE Subject Test (physics). Additional exam requirements/recommendations for international students: Required—IELTS (minimum score 6.5). *Application deadline:* For fall admission, 12/15 for domestic and international students; for spring admission, 11/1 for domestic and international students. Application fee: $75. Electronic applications accepted. *Financial support:* In 2009–10, 234 students received support, including 52 fellowships with tuition reimbursements available (averaging $30,454 per year), 143 research assistantships with tuition reimbursements available (averaging $30,609 per year), 31 teaching assistantships with tuition reimbursements available (averaging $30,829 per year); career-related internships or fieldwork, Federal Work-Study, institutionally sponsored loans, scholarships/grants, health care benefits, and unspecified assistantships also available. *Faculty research:* High-energy and nuclear physics, condensed matter physics, astrophysics, atomic physics, biophysics, plasma physics. Total annual research expenditures: $95.1 million. *Unit head:* Prof. Edmund Bertschinger, Head, 617-253-4800, Fax: 617-253-8554, E-mail: physics@mit.edu. *Application contact:* Graduate Admissions, 617-253-4841, Fax: 617-258-8319, E-mail: physics-grad@mit.edu.

McGill University, Faculty of Graduate and Postdoctoral Studies, Faculty of Science, Department of Physics, Montréal, QC H3A 2T5, Canada. Offers M Sc, PhD.

McMaster University, School of Graduate Studies, Faculty of Science, Department of Physics and Astronomy, Hamilton, ON L8S 4M2, Canada. Offers astrophysics (PhD); physics (PhD). Part-time programs available. *Degree requirements:* For doctorate, comprehensive exam, thesis/dissertation. *Entrance requirements:* For doctorate, minimum B+ average. Additional exam requirements/recommendations for international students: Required—TOEFL (minimum score 550 paper-based; 213 computer-based). *Faculty research:* Condensed matter, astrophysics, nuclear, medical, nonlinear dynamics.

Memorial University of Newfoundland, School of Graduate Studies, Department of Physics and Physical Oceanography, St. John's, NL A1C 5S7, Canada. Offers atomic and molecular physics (M Sc, PhD); condensed matter physics (M Sc, PhD); physical oceanography (M Sc, PhD); physics (M Sc). Part-time programs available. *Degree requirements:* For master's, thesis, seminar presentation on thesis topic; for doctorate, comprehensive exam, thesis/dissertation, oral defense of thesis. *Entrance requirements:* For master's, honors B Sc or equivalent; for doctorate, M Sc or equivalent. Electronic applications accepted. *Faculty research:* Experiment and theory in atomic and molecular physics, condensed matter physics, physical oceanography, theoretical geophysics and applied nuclear physics.

Miami University, Graduate School, College of Arts and Sciences, Department of Physics, Oxford, OH 45056. Offers MAT. Part-time programs available. *Students:* 15 full-time (1 woman),

Physics

Miami University (continued)

1 (woman) part-time; includes 1 minority (Asian American or Pacific Islander), 5 international. *Entrance requirements:* For master's, GRE (recommended), minimum undergraduate cumulative GPA of 2.75. Additional exam requirements/recommendations for international students: Required—TOEFL. Application fee: $50. *Expenses:* Tuition, state resident: full-time $11,280. Tuition, nonresident: full-time $24,912. Required fees: $516. *Financial support:* Fellowships with full tuition reimbursements, research assistantships, teaching assistantships, Federal Work-Study, institutionally sponsored loans, health care benefits, tuition waivers (full), and unspecified assistantships available. Financial award application deadline: 3/1; financial award applicants required to submit FAFSA. *Unit head:* Dr. Michael Pechan, Chair, 513-529-4518, Fax: 513-529-5629, E-mail: pechanmj@muohio.edu. *Application contact:* Dr. Samir Bali, Graduate Director, 513-529-5635, E-mail: balis@muohio.edu.

Michigan State University, The Graduate School, College of Natural Science, Department of Physics and Astronomy, East Lansing, MI 48824. Offers astrophysics and astronomy (MS, PhD); physics (MS, PhD). *Entrance requirements:* Additional exam requirements/ recommendations for international students: Required—TOEFL (minimum score 550 paper-based; 213 computer-based), Michigan State University ELT (85), Michigan ELAB (83). Electronic applications accepted. *Faculty research:* Nuclear and accelerator physics, high energy physics, condensed matter physics, biophysics, astrophysics and astronomy.

Michigan State University, National Superconducting Cyclotron Laboratory, East Lansing, MI 48824. Offers chemistry (PhD); physics (PhD).

Michigan Technological University, Graduate School, College of Sciences and Arts, Department of Physics, Program in Physics, Houghton, MI 49931. Offers MS, PhD. Part-time programs available. Terminal master's awarded for partial completion of doctoral program. *Degree requirements:* For master's, comprehensive exam (for some programs), thesis (for some programs); for doctorate, comprehensive exam, thesis/dissertation. *Entrance requirements:* For master's and doctorate, GRE, BS in physics or related discipline. Additional exam requirements/recommendations for international students: Required—TOEFL (minimum score 570 paper-based; 230 computer-based). Electronic applications accepted.

Minnesota State University Mankato, College of Graduate Studies, College of Science, Engineering and Technology, Department of Physics and Astronomy, Mankato, MN 56001. Offers MS. *Students:* 4 full-time (1 woman), 3 part-time (1 woman). *Degree requirements:* For master's, one foreign language, comprehensive exam, thesis or alternative. *Entrance requirements:* For master's, minimum GPA of 3.0 during previous 2 years, recommendation letters. Additional exam requirements/recommendations for international students: Required—TOEFL. *Application deadline:* For fall admission, 7/1 priority date for domestic students; for spring admission, 11/1 for domestic students. Applications are processed on a rolling basis. Application fee: $40. Electronic applications accepted. *Expenses:* Tuition, state resident: full-time $5364. Tuition, nonresident: full-time $8314. *Financial support:* Research assistantships, teaching assistantships with full tuition reimbursements, Federal Work-Study and unspecified assistantships available. Support available to part-time students. Financial award application deadline: 3/15; financial award applicants required to submit FAFSA. *Unit head:* Dr. Mark Pickar, Chairperson, 507-389-5743. *Application contact:* 507-389-2321, E-mail: grad@mnsu.edu.

Mississippi State University, College of Arts and Sciences, Department of Physics and Astronomy, Mississippi State, MS 39762. Offers engineering (PhD), including applied physics; physics (MS). Part-time programs available. *Faculty:* 13 full-time (0 women). *Students:* 25 full-time (5 women); includes 2 minority (1 African American, 1 Hispanic American), 20 international. Average age 26. 45 applicants, 24% accepted, 9 enrolled. In 2009, 7 master's awarded. *Degree requirements:* For master's, thesis optional, comprehensive oral or written exam; for doctorate, thesis/dissertation, comprehensive oral or written exam. *Entrance requirements:* For master's, GRE, minimum GPA of 2.75 on last two year's of undergraduate courses; for doctorate, GRE. Additional exam requirements/recommendations for international students: Required—TOEFL (minimum score 475 paper-based; 153 computer-based; 53 iBT); Recommended—IELTS (minimum score 4.5). *Application deadline:* For fall admission, 7/1 priority date for domestic students, 5/1 for international students; for spring admission, 11/1 priority date for domestic students, 9/1 for international students. Applications are processed on a rolling basis. Application fee: $40. Electronic applications accepted. *Expenses:* Tuition, state resident: full-time $2575.50; part-time $286.25 per credit hour. Tuition, nonresident: full-time $6510; part-time $723.50 per credit hour. Tuition and fees vary according to course load. *Financial support:* In 2009–10, 22 research assistantships with full tuition reimbursements (averaging $12,719 per year), 16 teaching assistantships with full tuition reimbursements (averaging $12,139 per year) were awarded; Federal Work-Study, institutionally sponsored loans, and unspecified assistantships also available. Financial award application deadline: 3/15; financial award applicants required to submit FAFSA. *Faculty research:* Atomic/ molecular spectroscopy, theoretical optics, gamma-ray astronomy, experimental nuclear physics, computational physics. Total annual research expenditures: $2.3 million. *Unit head:* Dr. Mark A. Novotny, Department Head and Professor, 662-325-2806, Fax: 662-325-8898, E-mail: man40@ra.msstate.edu. *Application contact:* Dr. David Monts, Professor and Graduate Coordinator, 662-325-2931, Fax: 662-325-8898, E-mail: physics@msstate.edu.

Missouri University of Science and Technology, Graduate School, Department of Physics, Rolla, MO 65409. Offers MS, MST, PhD. *Entrance requirements:* For master's, GRE (minimum score 600 quantitative, 3 writing); for doctorate, GRE (minimum score: 600 quantitative, 3.5 writing). Additional exam requirements/recommendations for international students: Required—TOEFL (minimum score 550 paper-based; 213 computer-based).

Montana State University, College of Graduate Studies, College of Letters and Science, Department of Physics, Bozeman, MT 59717. Offers MS, PhD. Part-time programs available. *Faculty:* 16 full-time (3 women), 2 part-time/adjunct (both women). *Students:* 54 full-time (12 women), 6 part-time (1 woman); includes 1 minority (African American), 12 international. Average age 28. 55 applicants, 22% accepted, 9 enrolled. In 2009, 8 master's, 5 doctorates awarded. *Degree requirements:* For master's, comprehensive exam, thesis (for some programs); for doctorate, comprehensive exam, thesis/dissertation. *Entrance requirements:* For master's and doctorate, GRE General Test, GRE Subject Test (physics). Additional exam requirements/ recommendations for international students: Required—TOEFL (minimum score 550 paper-based; 213 computer-based). *Application deadline:* For fall admission, 7/15 priority date for domestic students, 5/15 priority date for international students; for spring admission, 12/1 priority date for domestic students, 10/1 priority date for international students. Applications are processed on a rolling basis. Application fee: $30. Electronic applications accepted. *Expenses:* Tuition, state resident: full-time $5635; part-time $3492 per year. Tuition, nonresident: full-time $17,212; part-time $7865.10 per year. Required fees: $1441.05; $153.15 per credit. Tuition and fees vary according to course load and program. *Financial support:* In 2009–10, 60 students received support, including 36 research assistantships with full tuition reimbursements available (averaging $18,960 per year), 24 teaching assistantships with full tuition reimbursements available (averaging $17,380 per year); career-related internships or fieldwork, health care benefits, and unspecified assistantships also available. Financial award application deadline: 3/1; financial award applicants required to submit FAFSA. *Faculty research:* Nanotechnology, gravitational wave, astronomy, photodynamic theory, diode laser development, solar radiation transfer. Total annual research expenditures: $6 million. *Unit head:* Dr. Richard Smith, Head, 406-994-6152, Fax: 406-994-4452, E-mail: smith@physics.montana.edu. *Application contact:* Dr. Carl A. Fox, Vice Provost for Graduate Education, 406-994-4145, Fax: 406-994-7433, E-mail: gradstudy@montana.edu.

Naval Postgraduate School, Graduate Programs, Department of Physics, Monterey, CA 93943. Offers applied physics (MS); engineering acoustics (MS); physics (MS, PhD). Program only open to commissioned officers of the United States and friendly nations and selected United States federal civilian employees. Part-time programs available. *Degree requirements:* For master's, thesis; for doctorate, one foreign language, thesis/dissertation.

New Mexico Institute of Mining and Technology, Graduate Studies, Department of Physics, Socorro, NM 87801. Offers astrophysics (MS, PhD); atmospheric physics (MS, PhD); instrumentation (MS); mathematical physics (PhD). *Degree requirements:* For master's, thesis optional; for doctorate, thesis/dissertation. *Entrance requirements:* For master's, GRE General Test; for doctorate, GRE General Test, GRE Subject Test. Additional exam requirements/ recommendations for international students: Required—TOEFL (minimum score 540 paper-based; 207 computer-based). *Faculty research:* Cloud physics, stellar and extragalactic processes.

New Mexico State University, Graduate School, College of Arts and Sciences, Department of Physics, Las Cruces, NM 88003-8001. Offers MS, PhD. Part-time programs available. *Faculty:* 14 full-time (1 woman), 1 part-time/adjunct (0 women). *Students:* 35 full-time (6 women), 1 (woman) part-time; includes 4 minority (1 African American, 1 American Indian/Alaska Native, 2 Hispanic Americans), 26 international. Average age 32. 30 applicants, 87% accepted, 5 enrolled. In 2009, 3 master's, 2 doctorates awarded. Terminal master's awarded for partial completion of doctoral program. *Degree requirements:* For master's, thesis optional; for doctorate, comprehensive exam, thesis/dissertation. *Entrance requirements:* For master's and doctorate, GRE General Test, GRE Subject Test. Additional exam requirements/recommendations for international students: Required—TOEFL. *Application deadline:* For fall admission, 3/1 priority date for domestic and international students; for spring admission, 10/1 priority date for domestic and international students. Applications are processed on a rolling basis. Application fee: $30 ($50 for international students). Electronic applications accepted. *Expenses:* Tuition, state resident: full-time $4080; part-time $223 per credit. Tuition, nonresident: full-time $14,256; part-time $647 per credit. Required fees: $1278; $639 per semester. *Financial support:* In 2009–10, 19 research assistantships (averaging $12,692 per year), 15 teaching assistantships (averaging $7,407 per year) were awarded; fellowships, health care benefits also available. Financial award application deadline: 3/15. *Faculty research:* Nuclear and particle physics, optics, materials science, geophysics, physics education, atmospheric physics. *Unit head:* Dr. William Gibbs, Head, 575-646-5076, Fax: 575-646-1934, E-mail: gibbs@nmsu.edu. *Application contact:* Dr. Matthias Burkhardt, 575-646-1928, Fax: 575-646-1934.

New York University, Graduate School of Arts and Science, Department of Physics, New York, NY 10012-1019. Offers MS, PhD. Part-time programs available. *Faculty:* 25 full-time (1 woman), 5 part-time/adjunct (0 women). *Students:* 70 full-time (9 women), 6 part-time (0 women); includes 1 minority (Hispanic American), 48 international. Average age 27. 225 applicants, 27% accepted, 23 enrolled. In 2009, 1 master's, 5 doctorates awarded. Terminal master's awarded for partial completion of doctoral program. *Degree requirements:* For master's, thesis (for some programs); for doctorate, one foreign language, thesis/dissertation, research seminar, teaching experience. *Entrance requirements:* For master's, GRE General Test, GRE Subject Test, bachelor's degree in physics; for doctorate, GRE General Test, GRE Subject Test. Additional exam requirements/recommendations for international students: Required—TOEFL. *Application deadline:* For fall admission, 12/12 for domestic students. Application fee: $90. *Expenses:* Tuition: Full-time $30,528; part-time $1272 per credit. Required fees: $2177. *Financial support:* Fellowships with tuition reimbursements, research assistantships with tuition reimbursements, teaching assistantships with tuition reimbursements, Federal Work-Study, institutionally sponsored loans, scholarships/grants, health care benefits, and unspecified assistantships available. Financial award application deadline: 12/12; financial award applicants required to submit FAFSA. *Faculty research:* Atomic physics, elementary particles and fields, astrophysics, condensed-matter physics, neuromagnetism. *Unit head:* David Grier, Chairman, 212-998-7700, Fax: 212-995-4016, E-mail: dgphys@nyu.edu. *Application contact:* Andrew Kent, Director of Graduate Studies, 212-998-7700, Fax: 212-995-4016, E-mail: dgsphys@nyu.edu.

North Carolina Central University, Division of Academic Affairs, College of Science and Technology, Department of Physics, Durham, NC 27707-3129. Offers MS.

North Carolina State University, Graduate School, College of Physical and Mathematical Sciences, Department of Physics, Raleigh, NC 27695. Offers MS, PhD. Part-time programs available. Terminal master's awarded for partial completion of doctoral program. *Degree requirements:* For master's, thesis (for some programs); for doctorate, thesis/dissertation. *Entrance requirements:* For master's and doctorate, GRE General Test, GRE Subject Test. Electronic applications accepted. *Faculty research:* Astrophysics, optics, physics education, biophysics, geophysics.

North Dakota State University, College of Graduate and Interdisciplinary Studies, College of Science and Mathematics, Department of Physics, Fargo, ND 58108. Offers MS, PhD. Part-time programs available. *Faculty:* 4 full-time. *Students:* 5 full-time (0 women); includes 2 minority (both Asian Americans or Pacific Islanders). Average age 25. 14 applicants, 21% accepted. Terminal master's awarded for partial completion of doctoral program. *Degree requirements:* For master's, thesis; for doctorate, comprehensive exam, thesis/dissertation. *Entrance requirements:* Additional exam requirements/recommendations for international students: Required—TOEFL (minimum score 550 paper-based; 215 computer-based; 79 iBT). *Application deadline:* For fall admission, 3/1 priority date for domestic students, 5/1 priority date for international students; for spring admission, 9/1 priority date for domestic and international students. Applications are processed on a rolling basis. Application fee: $45 ($60 for international students). *Financial support:* In 2009–10, 2 students received support, including 2 research assistantships with tuition reimbursements available (averaging $16,000 per year), teaching assistantships with tuition reimbursements available (averaging $12,000 per year); career-related internships or fieldwork, scholarships/grants, and unspecified assistantships also available. Support available to part-time students. Financial award application deadline: 4/15; financial award applicants required to submit FAFSA. *Faculty research:* Biophysics; condensed matter; surface physics; general relativity, gravitation, and space physics; nonlinear physics. Total annual research expenditures: $105,500. *Unit head:* Dr. Daniel Kroll, Director, 701-231-8968, Fax: 701-231-7088, E-mail: daniel.kroll@ndsu.edu. *Application contact:* Dr. Alexander Wagner, Graduate Advisory Committee Chair, 701-231-9582, Fax: 701-231-7088, E-mail: alexander.wagner@ndsu.edu.

Northeastern University, College of Science, Department of Physics, Boston, MA 02115-5096. Offers MS, PhD. Part-time programs available. *Faculty:* 27 full-time (3 women), 9 part-time/adjunct (4 women). *Students:* 52 full-time (9 women); includes 1 Hispanic American, 35 international. Average age 30. 198 applicants, 22% accepted, 15 enrolled. In 2009, 11 master's, 8 doctorates awarded. Terminal master's awarded for partial completion of doctoral program. *Degree requirements:* For master's, thesis optional; for doctorate, thesis/dissertation, qualifying exam. *Entrance requirements:* For master's and doctorate, GRE General Test, GRE Subject Test. *Application deadline:* For fall admission, 2/1 priority date for domestic and international students. Application fee: $50. *Financial support:* In 2009–10, 20 research assistantships with tuition reimbursements (averaging $18,285 per year), 34 teaching assistantships with tuition reimbursements (averaging $18,285 per year) were awarded; Federal Work-Study, tuition waivers (full and partial), and unspecified assistantships also available. Financial award application deadline: 3/1; financial award applicants required to submit FAFSA. *Faculty research:* Elementary particles and astroparticle physics, nanophysics and condensed matter physics, biological and biomedical physics. *Unit head:* Dr. George Alverson, Graduate Coordinator,

617-373-2938, Fax: 617-373-2943, E-mail: gradphysics@neu.edu. *Application contact:* Jo-Anne Dickinson, Admissions Contact, 617-363-5990, Fax: 617-373-7281, E-mail: gsas@neu.edu.

See Close-Up on page 221.

Northern Arizona University, Graduate College, College of Engineering, Forestry and Natural Sciences, Department of Physics and Astronomy, Flagstaff, AZ 86011. Offers applied physics (MS); science education (MAT). Part-time programs available. *Faculty:* 13 full-time (2 women). *Students:* 13 full-time (5 women), 4 part-time (2 women); includes 2 minority (1 American Indian/Alaska Native, 1 Asian American or Pacific Islander), 1 international. Average age 37. 14 applicants, 71% accepted, 7 enrolled. In 2009, 7 master's awarded. *Degree requirements:* For master's, thesis optional. *Entrance requirements:* For master's, GRE. Additional exam requirements/recommendations for international students: Required—TOEFL (minimum score 550 paper-based; 213 computer-based; 80 iBT), IELTS (minimum score 7), or a bachelor's degree from an English-speaking university and demonstrated proficiency. *Application deadline:* For fall admission, 3/15 priority date for domestic students, 9/1 for international students; for spring admission, 10/15 priority date for domestic students. Applications are processed on a rolling basis. Application fee: $65. Electronic applications accepted. *Financial support:* In 2009–10, 1 research assistantship with partial tuition reimbursement (averaging $12,390 per year), 9 teaching assistantships with partial tuition reimbursements (averaging $12,390 per year) were awarded; career-related internships or fieldwork, Federal Work-Study, health care benefits, tuition waivers (full and partial), and unspecified assistantships also available. Support available to part-time students. Financial award application deadline: 3/30; financial award applicants required to submit FAFSA. *Unit head:* Dr. Nadine Barlow, Chair, 928-523-5452, Fax: 928-523-1371, E-mail: nadine.barlow@nau.edu. *Application contact:* Dr. Gary Bowman, Graduate Coordinator, 928-523-1114, Fax: 928-523-1371, E-mail: gary.bowman@nau.edu.

Northern Illinois University, Graduate School, College of Liberal Arts and Sciences, Department of Physics, De Kalb, IL 60115-2854. Offers MS, PhD. Part-time programs available. *Faculty:* 18 full-time (3 women), 3 part-time/adjunct (0 women). *Students:* 37 full-time (5 women), 17 part-time (1 woman); includes 5 minority (1 African American, 2 Asian Americans or Pacific Islanders, 2 Hispanic Americans), 15 international. Average age 30. 51 applicants, 63% accepted, 12 enrolled. In 2009, 3 master's, 2 doctorates awarded. Terminal master's awarded for partial completion of doctoral program. *Degree requirements:* For master's, comprehensive exam, thesis or alternative, research seminar; for doctorate, thesis/dissertation, candidacy exam, dissertation defense, research seminar. *Entrance requirements:* For master's, GRE General Test, minimum GPA of 2.75; for doctorate, GRE General Test, GRE Subject Test (physics), bachelor's degree in physics or related field; minimum undergraduate GPA of 2.75, graduate 3.2. Additional exam requirements/recommendations for international students: Required—TOEFL (minimum score 550 paper-based; 213 computer-based). *Application deadline:* For fall admission, 6/1 for domestic students, 5/1 for international students; for spring admission, 11/1 for domestic students, 10/1 for international students. Applications are processed on a rolling basis. Application fee: $30. Electronic applications accepted. *Expenses:* Tuition, state resident: full-time $6576; part-time $274 per credit hour. Tuition, nonresident: full-time $13,152; part-time $548 per credit hour. Required fees: $1813; $75.53 per credit hour. Part-time tuition and fees vary according to course load. *Financial support:* In 2009–10, 1 research assistantship with full tuition reimbursement, 23 teaching assistantships with full tuition reimbursements were awarded; fellowships with full tuition reimbursements, career-related internships or fieldwork, Federal Work-Study, scholarships/grants, and unspecified assistantships also available. Support available to part-time students. Financial award applicants required to submit FAFSA. *Faculty research:* Band-structure interpolation schemes, nonlinear procession beams, Mossbauer spectrascopy, beam physics. *Unit head:* Dr. Suzanne Willis, Chair, 815-753-6470, Fax: 815-753-8565, E-mail: swillis@niu.edu. *Application contact:* Dr. David Hedin, Director of Graduate Studies, 815-753-6483, E-mail: hedin@niu.edu.

Northwestern University, The Graduate School, Judd A. and Marjorie Weinberg College of Arts and Sciences, Department of Physics and Astronomy, Evanston, IL 60208. Offers astrophysics (PhD); physics (MS, PhD). Admissions and degrees offered through The Graduate School. *Degree requirements:* For doctorate, thesis/dissertation, qualifying exam. *Entrance requirements:* For doctorate, GRE General Test, GRE Subject Test. Additional exam requirements/recommendations for international students: Required—TOEFL. *Faculty research:* Nuclear and particle physics, condensed-matter physics, nonlinear physics, astrophysics.

Oakland University, Graduate Study and Lifelong Learning, College of Arts and Sciences, Department of Physics, Rochester, MI 48309-4401. Offers medical physics (PhD); physics (MS). *Degree requirements:* For doctorate, thesis/dissertation. *Entrance requirements:* For master's, minimum GPA of 3.0 for unconditional admission; for doctorate, GRE Subject Test, GRE General Test, minimum GPA of 3.0 for unconditional admission. Additional exam requirements/recommendations for international students: Required—TOEFL (minimum score 550 paper-based; 213 computer-based). Electronic applications accepted. *Expenses:* Contact institution. *Faculty research:* Quantitative molecular imagings of articular cartilage, multifunctional ferrite-ferroelectric layered structures for microwave and millimeter wave devices, magnoelectric materials for antenna structures.

The Ohio State University, Graduate School, College of Mathematical and Physical Sciences, Department of Physics, Columbus, OH 43210. Offers MS, PhD. *Faculty:* 61. *Students:* 75 full-time (16 women), 102 part-time (12 women); includes 9 minority (1 African American, 1 American Indian/Alaska Native, 4 Asian Americans or Pacific Islanders, 3 Hispanic Americans), 40 international. Average age 26. In 2009, 18 master's, 20 doctorates awarded. *Degree requirements:* For master's, thesis optional; for doctorate, thesis/dissertation. *Entrance requirements:* For master's and doctorate, GRE General Test, GRE Subject Test in physics. Additional exam requirements/recommendations for international students: Required—TOEFL (minimum score 600 paper-based; 250 computer-based). *Application deadline:* For fall admission, 8/15 priority date for domestic students, 7/1 priority date for international students; for winter admission, 12/1 priority date for domestic students, 11/1 priority date for international students; for spring admission, 3/1 priority date for domestic students, 2/1 priority date for international students. Applications are processed on a rolling basis. Application fee: $40 ($50 for international students). Electronic applications accepted. *Expenses:* Tuition, state resident: full-time $10,683. Tuition, nonresident: full-time $25,923. Tuition and fees vary according to course load and program. *Financial support:* Fellowships, research assistantships, teaching assistantships, Federal Work-Study and institutionally sponsored loans available. Support available to part-time students. *Unit head:* Jonathan Pelz, Graduate Studies Committee Chair, E-mail: pelz.2@osu.edu. *Application contact:* 614-292-9444, Fax: 614-292-3895, E-mail: domestic.grad@osu.edu.

Ohio University, Graduate College, College of Arts and Sciences, Department of Physics and Astronomy, Athens, OH 45701. Offers astronomy (MS, PhD); physics (MS, PhD). Part-time programs available. *Faculty:* 29 full-time (3 women), 6 part-time/adjunct (0 women). *Students:* 73 full-time (24 women); includes 1 minority (Hispanic American), 57 international. Average age 27. 128 applicants, 30% accepted, 15 enrolled. In 2009, 1 master's, 4 doctorates awarded. Terminal master's awarded for partial completion of doctoral program. *Degree requirements:* For master's, thesis or alternative; for doctorate, comprehensive exam, thesis/dissertation. *Entrance requirements:* For master's and doctorate, minimum GPA of 3.0. Additional exam requirements/recommendations for international students: Required—TOEFL (minimum score 600 paper-based; 250 computer-based; 100 iBT), IELTS (minimum score 7), TWE (minimum score 4). *Application deadline:* For fall admission, 4/1 priority date for domestic and international students. Applications are processed on a rolling basis. Application fee: $55. Electronic applications accepted. *Expenses:* Tuition, state resident: full-time $7839; part-time $323 per quarter hour. Tuition, nonresident: full-time $15,831; part-time $654 per quarter hour. Required fees: $2931. *Financial support:* In 2009–10, 35 research assistantships with full tuition reimbursements (averaging $22,984 per year), 32 teaching assistantships with full tuition reimbursements (averaging $20,886 per year) were awarded; scholarships/grants and unspecified assistantships also available. Financial award application deadline: 4/1. *Faculty research:* Nuclear physics, condensed-matter physics, nonlinear systems, astrophysics, biophysics. Total annual research expenditures: $2.3 million. *Unit head:* Dr. Joseph Shields, Chair, 740-593-0336, Fax: 740-593-0433, E-mail: shields@helios.phy.ohiou.edu. *Application contact:* Dr. Marcus Boettcher, Graduate Admissions Chair, 740-593-1714, Fax: 740-593-0433, E-mail: gradapp@phy.ohiou.edu.

See Close-Up on page 225.

Oklahoma State University, College of Arts and Sciences, Department of Physics, Stillwater, OK 74078. Offers photonics (MS, PhD); physics (MS, PhD). *Faculty:* 30 full-time (8 women), 1 part-time/adjunct (0 women). *Students:* 1 full-time (0 women), 45 part-time (9 women); includes 3 minority (all Hispanic Americans), 31 international. Average age 29. 54 applicants, 31% accepted, 6 enrolled. In 2009, 2 master's, 2 doctorates awarded. *Degree requirements:* For master's, thesis; for doctorate, comprehensive exam, thesis/dissertation, oral defense of dissertation, preliminary exam, qualifying exam. *Entrance requirements:* For master's and doctorate, GRE. Additional exam requirements/recommendations for international students: Required—TOEFL (minimum score 550 paper-based; 79 iBT). *Application deadline:* For fall admission, 3/1 priority date for international students; for spring admission, 8/1 priority date for international students. Applications are processed on a rolling basis. Application fee: $40 ($75 for international students). Electronic applications accepted. *Expenses:* Tuition, state resident: full-time $3716; part-time $154.85 per credit hour. Tuition, nonresident: full-time $14,448; part-time $602 per credit hour. Required fees: $1772; $73.85 per credit hour. One-time fee: $50. Tuition and fees vary according to course load and campus/location. *Financial support:* In 2009–10, 24 research assistantships (averaging $18,130 per year), 35 teaching assistantships (averaging $17,127 per year) were awarded; career-related internships or fieldwork, Federal Work-Study, scholarships/grants, health care benefits, tuition waivers (partial), and unspecified assistantships also available. Support available to part-time students. Financial award application deadline: 3/1; financial award applicants required to submit FAFSA. *Faculty research:* Lasers and photonics, non-linear optical materials, turbulence, structure and function of biological membranes, particle theory. *Unit head:* Dr. James Wicksted, Head, 405-744-5796, Fax: 405-744-6811. *Application contact:* Dr. Gordon Emslie, Dean, 405-744-6368, Fax: 405-744-0355, E-mail: grad-i@okstate.edu.

Old Dominion University, College of Sciences, Program in Physics, Norfolk, VA 23529. Offers MS, PhD. *Faculty:* 21 full-time (2 women), 14 part-time/adjunct (1 woman). *Students:* 48 full-time (16 women), 4 part-time (2 women), 33 international. Average age 31. 53 applicants, 38% accepted, 10 enrolled. In 2009, 8 master's, 6 doctorates awarded. Terminal master's awarded for partial completion of doctoral program. *Degree requirements:* For master's, comprehensive exam, thesis optional; for doctorate, comprehensive exam, thesis/dissertation. *Entrance requirements:* For master's, BS in physics or related field, minimum GPA of 3.0 in major; for doctorate, GRE General Test; GRE Subject Test (strongly recommended), minimum GPA of 3.0; two reference letters. Additional exam requirements/recommendations for international students: Required—TOEFL (minimum score 550 paper-based; 213 computer-based; 79 iBT). *Application deadline:* For fall admission, 2/15 for domestic and international students. Applications are processed on a rolling basis. Application fee: $40. Electronic applications accepted. *Expenses:* Tuition, state resident: full-time $8112; part-time $338 per credit. Tuition, nonresident: full-time $20,256; part-time $844 per credit. Required fees: $119 per semester. One-time fee: $50. *Financial support:* In 2009–10, 48 students received support, including 2 fellowships (averaging $15,000 per year), 32 research assistantships with full and partial tuition reimbursements available (averaging $23,500 per year), 14 teaching assistantships with full tuition reimbursements available (averaging $21,500 per year); career-related internships or fieldwork, scholarships/grants, tuition waivers (full), and unspecified assistantships also available. Support available to part-time students. Financial award application deadline: 2/15; financial award applicants required to submit FAFSA. *Faculty research:* Nuclear and particle physics, atomic physics, condensed-matter physics, plasma physics, accelerator physics. Total annual research expenditures: $1.9 million. *Unit head:* Dr. Lepsha Vuskovic, Graduate Program Director, 757-683-4611, Fax: 757-683-3038, E-mail: vuskovic@odu.edu. *Application contact:* Dr. Mark Havey, Graduate Recruitment and Admissions Director, 757-683-4612, Fax: 757-683-3038, E-mail: mhavey@odu.edu.

Oregon State University, Graduate School, College of Science, Department of Physics, Corvallis, OR 97331. Offers applied physics (MS); physics (MA, MS, PhD). Part-time programs available. *Faculty:* 15 full-time (4 women). *Students:* 30 full-time (7 women), 4 part-time (0 women); includes 2 minority (1 Asian American or Pacific Islander, 1 Hispanic American), 8 international. Average age 29. In 2009, 2 master's, 3 doctorates awarded. Terminal master's awarded for partial completion of doctoral program. *Degree requirements:* For master's, thesis optional, qualifying exam; for doctorate, thesis/dissertation, qualifying exam. *Entrance requirements:* For master's and doctorate, minimum GPA of 3.0 in last 90 hours. Additional exam requirements/recommendations for international students: Required—TOEFL. *Application deadline:* For fall admission, 3/1 for domestic students. Application fee: $50. *Expenses:* Tuition, state resident: full-time $9774; part-time $362 per credit. Tuition, nonresident: full-time $15,849; part-time $587 per credit. Required fees: $1639. Full-time tuition and fees vary according to course load and program. *Financial support:* Fellowships, research assistantships, teaching assistantships, Federal Work-Study and institutionally sponsored loans available. Support available to part-time students. Financial award application deadline: 2/1. *Unit head:* Dr. Henri J. F. Jansen, Chair, 541-737-1668, Fax: 541-737-1683, E-mail: physics.chair@science.oregonstate.edu. *Application contact:* Dr. Henri J. F. Jansen, Chair, 541-737-1668, Fax: 541-737-1683, E-mail: physics.chair@science.oregonstate.edu.

Penn State University Park, Graduate School, Eberly College of Science, Department of Physics, State College, University Park, PA 16802-1503. Offers M Ed, MS, D Ed, PhD. *Unit head:* Dr. Jayanth R. Banavar, Head, 814-865-7533, Fax: 814-865-0978, E-mail: jrb16@psu.edu. *Application contact:* Rick Robinett, Director of Graduate Studies, 814-863-0965, E-mail: rq9@psu.edu.

Pittsburg State University, Graduate School, College of Arts and Sciences, Department of Physics, Pittsburg, KS 66762. Offers applied physics (MS); physics (MS); professional physics (MS). *Degree requirements:* For master's, thesis or alternative. *Expenses:* Tuition, state resident: full-time $4212; part-time $176 per credit. Tuition, nonresident: full-time $11,530; part-time $480 per credit. Required fees: $940; $43 per credit. Tuition and fees vary according to course level, course load, degree level, campus/location, reciprocity agreements and student level.

Polytechnic Institute of NYU, Department of Physics, Brooklyn, NY 11201-2990. Offers MS, PhD. Part-time and evening/weekend programs available. *Degree requirements:* For master's, comprehensive exam (for some programs), thesis (for some programs); for doctorate, comprehensive exam, thesis/dissertation. *Entrance requirements:* For master's, BA in physics; for doctorate, departmental qualifying exam, BS in physics. Additional exam requirements/recommendations for international students: Required—TOEFL (minimum score 550 paper-based; 213 computer-based; 80 iBT); Recommended—IELTS (minimum score 6.5). *Application deadline:* For fall admission, 7/31 priority date for domestic students, 4/30 priority date for international students; for spring admission, 12/31 priority date for domestic students, 11/30 priority date for international students. Applications are processed on a rolling basis. Application fee: $75. Electronic applications accepted. *Expenses:* Tuition: Full-time $21,492; part-time $1194 per credit hour. Required fees: $1160; $204 per course. *Financial support:* Fellowships, research assistantships, teaching assistantships, institutionally sponsored loans available. Support available to part-time students. Financial award applicants required to submit FAFSA.

Physics

Polytechnic Institute of NYU (continued)
Faculty research: Combining microdroplets, UHV cryogenic scanning, tunneling, surface spectroscopy of a single aerosol particle. Total annual research expenditures: $184,514. *Unit head:* Dr. Lorcan M. Folan, Head, 718-260-3072, E-mail: lfolan@poly.edu. *Application contact:* JeanCarlo Bonilla, Director of Graduate Enrollment Management, 718-260-3182, Fax: 718-260-3624, E-mail: gradinfo@poly.edu.

Portland State University, Graduate Studies, College of Liberal Arts and Sciences, Department of Physics, Portland, OR 97207-0751. Offers MA, MS, PhD. Part-time programs available. *Degree requirements:* For master's, variable foreign language requirement, thesis, oral exam, written report; for doctorate, thesis/dissertation. *Entrance requirements:* For master's, GRE General Test, minimum GPA of 3.0 in upper-division course work or 2.75 overall, 2 letters of recommendation. Additional exam requirements/recommendations for international students: Required—TOEFL (minimum score 550 paper-based; 213 computer-based). *Faculty research:* Statistical physics, membrane biophysics, low-temperature physics, electron microscopy, atmospheric physics.

Princeton University, Graduate School, Department of Physics, Princeton, NJ 08544-1019. Offers PhD. *Degree requirements:* For doctorate, thesis/dissertation, qualifying exam. *Entrance requirements:* For doctorate, GRE General Test, GRE Subject Test. Additional exam requirements/recommendations for international students: Required—TOEFL (minimum score 600 paper-based; 250 computer-based). Electronic applications accepted.

Purdue University, Graduate School, College of Science, Department of Physics, West Lafayette, IN 47907. Offers MS, PhD. Part-time programs available. Terminal master's awarded for partial completion of doctoral program. *Degree requirements:* For master's, qualifying exam; for doctorate, thesis/dissertation, qualifying exam. *Entrance requirements:* For master's and doctorate, GRE General Test, GRE Subject Test (physics). Additional exam requirements/recommendations for international students: Required—TOEFL. Electronic applications accepted. *Faculty research:* Solid-state, elementary particle, and nuclear physics; biological physics; acoustics; astrophysics.

Queens College of the City University of New York, Division of Graduate Studies, Mathematics and Natural Sciences Division, Department of Physics, Flushing, NY 11367-1597. Offers MA, PhD. Part-time and evening/weekend programs available. *Faculty:* 11 full-time (1 woman). *Students:* 4 part-time (3 women). 11 applicants, 36% accepted, 2 enrolled. In 2009, 2 master's awarded. *Degree requirements:* For master's, comprehensive exam. *Entrance requirements:* For master's, previous course work in calculus, minimum GPA of 3.0. Additional exam requirements/recommendations for international students: Required—TOEFL. *Application deadline:* For fall admission, 4/1 for domestic students; for spring admission, 11/1 for domestic students. Applications are processed on a rolling basis. Application fee: $125. *Expenses:* Tuition, state resident: full-time $7360; part-time $310 per credit. Tuition, nonresident: part-time $575 per credit. One-time fee: $195.25 full-time; $145.25 part-time. *Financial support:* Career-related internships or fieldwork, Federal Work-Study, institutionally sponsored loans, and tuition waivers (partial) available. Support available to part-time students. Financial award application deadline: 4/1; financial award applicants required to submit FAFSA. *Faculty research:* Solid-state physics, low temperature physics, elementary particles and fields. *Unit head:* Dr. Alexander Lisyansky, Chairperson, 718-997-3350, E-mail: alexander_lisyansky@qc.edu. *Application contact:* Dr. J. Marion Dickey, Graduate Adviser, 718-997-3350.

Queen's University at Kingston, School of Graduate Studies and Research, Faculty of Arts and Sciences, Department of Physics, Kingston, ON K7L 3N6, Canada. Offers M Sc, M Sc Eng, PhD. Part-time programs available. *Degree requirements:* For master's, thesis; for doctorate, comprehensive exam, thesis/dissertation. *Entrance requirements:* For master's, first or upper second class honours in Physics; for doctorate, M Sc or M Sc Eng. Additional exam requirements/recommendations for international students: Required—TOEFL (minimum score 550 paper-based; 213 computer-based). *Faculty research:* Theoretical physics, astronomy and astrophysics, subatomic, condensed matter, applied and engineering.

Rensselaer Polytechnic Institute, Graduate School, School of Science, Department of Physics, Applied Physics and Astronomy, Program in Physics, Troy, NY 12180-3590. Offers MS, PhD. *Expenses:* Tuition: Full-time $38,100.

Rice University, Graduate Programs, Wiess School of Natural Sciences, Department of Physics and Astronomy, Houston, TX 77251-1892. Offers nanoscale physics (MS); physics and astronomy (PhD); science teaching (MST). Part-time programs available. *Faculty:* 39 full-time (4 women), 9 part-time/adjunct (1 woman). *Students:* 124 full-time (19 women), 12 part-time (7 women); includes 8 minority (5 Asian Americans or Pacific Islanders, 3 Hispanic Americans), 70 international. Average age 28. 192 applicants, 26% accepted, 22 enrolled. In 2009, 16 master's, 21 doctorates awarded. *Degree requirements:* For master's, thesis (for some programs); for doctorate, thesis/dissertation, Maintain at least a B average. *Entrance requirements:* For master's, GRE General Test; for doctorate, General GRE, Subject GRE. Additional exam requirements/recommendations for international students: Required—TOEFL (minimum score 600 paper-based; 250 computer-based; 90 iBT). *Application deadline:* For fall admission, 2/1 priority date for domestic and international students. Application fee: $70. Electronic applications accepted. *Financial support:* In 2009–10, 124 students received support, including 22 fellowships with full tuition reimbursements available (averaging $25,700 per year), 102 research assistantships with full tuition reimbursements available (averaging $25,700 per year). Financial award application deadline: 2/1. *Faculty research:* Optical physics; ultra cold atoms; membrane electr-statics, peptides, proteins and lipids; solar astrophysics; stellar activity; magnetic fields; young stars. *Unit head:* Rose Berridge, Department Administrator, 713-348-4938, Fax: 713-348-4510, E-mail: physics@rice.edu. *Application contact:* Bridgitt G. Ayers, Graduate Program Coordinator, 713-348-6348, Fax: 713-348-4150, E-mail: physgrad@rice.edu.

Rice University, Graduate Programs, Wiess School–Professional Science Master's Programs, Professional Master's Program in Nanoscale Physics, Houston, TX 77251-1892. Offers MS. *Degree requirements:* For master's, internship. *Entrance requirements:* For master's, GRE General Test, bachelor's degree in physics and related field, 4 letters of recommendation. Additional exam requirements/recommendations for international students: Required—TOEFL (minimum score 600 paper-based; 250 computer-based; 90 iBT). Electronic applications accepted. *Faculty research:* Atomic, molecular, and applied physics, surface and condensed matter physics.

Royal Military College of Canada, Division of Graduate Studies and Research, Science Division, Department of Physics, Kingston, ON K7K 7B4, Canada. Offers M Sc. *Degree requirements:* For master's, thesis. *Entrance requirements:* For master's, honour's degree wtih second-class standing. Electronic applications accepted.

Rutgers, The State University of New Jersey, New Brunswick, Graduate School-New Brunswick, Department of Physics and Astronomy, Piscataway, NJ 08854-8097. Offers astronomy (MS, PhD); biophysics (PhD); condensed matter physics (MS, PhD); elementary particle physics (MS, PhD); intermediate energy nuclear physics (MS); nuclear physics (MS, PhD); physics (MST); surface science (PhD); theoretical physics (MS, PhD). Part-time programs available. Terminal master's awarded for partial completion of doctoral program. *Degree requirements:* For master's, comprehensive exam, thesis or alternative; for doctorate, comprehensive exam, thesis/dissertation. *Entrance requirements:* For master's and doctorate, GRE General Test, GRE Subject Test. Additional exam requirements/recommendations for international students: Required—TOEFL (minimum score 560 paper-based). Electronic applications accepted. *Faculty research:* Astronomy, high energy, condensed matter, surface, nuclear physics.

St. Francis Xavier University, Graduate Studies, Department of Physics, Antigonish, NS B2G 2W5, Canada. Offers M Sc. *Degree requirements:* For master's, thesis. *Entrance requirements:* For master's, minimum B average in undergraduate course work, honors degree in physics or related area. Additional exam requirements/recommendations for international students: Required—TOEFL (minimum score 580 paper-based; 236 computer-based). *Faculty research:* Atomic and molecular spectroscopy, quantum theory, many body theory, mathematical physics, phase transitions.

San Diego State University, Graduate and Research Affairs, College of Sciences, Department of Physics, Program in Physics, San Diego, CA 92182. Offers MA, MS. Part-time programs available. *Degree requirements:* For master's, thesis, oral exam. *Entrance requirements:* For master's, GRE General Test, GRE Subject Test (physics), 2 letters of recommendation. Additional exam requirements/recommendations for international students: Required—TOEFL. Electronic applications accepted.

San Francisco State University, Division of Graduate Studies, College of Science and Engineering, Department of Physics and Astronomy, San Francisco, CA 94132-1722. Offers physics (MS). Part-time programs available. Electronic applications accepted.

San Jose State University, Graduate Studies and Research, College of Science, Department of Physics and Astronomy, San Jose, CA 95192-0001. Offers computational physics (MS); physics (MS). Part-time and evening/weekend programs available. *Students:* 7 full-time (1 woman), 19 part-time (6 women); includes 9 minority (1 African American, 5 Asian Americans or Pacific Islanders, 3 Hispanic Americans), 2 international. Average age 31. 28 applicants, 50% accepted, 11 enrolled. In 2009, 9 master's awarded. *Degree requirements:* For master's, thesis optional. *Entrance requirements:* For master's, GRE. *Application deadline:* For fall admission, 6/29 for domestic students; for spring admission, 11/30 for domestic students. Applications are processed on a rolling basis. Application fee: $59. Electronic applications accepted. *Financial support:* Teaching assistantships, career-related internships or fieldwork, Federal Work-Study, and institutionally sponsored loans available. Support available to part-time students. Financial award application deadline: 3/1; financial award applicants required to submit FAFSA. *Faculty research:* Astrophysics, atmospheric physics, elementary particles, dislocation theory, general relativity. *Unit head:* Dr. Kiumars Parvin, Chair, 408-924-5210, Fax: 408-924-2917. *Application contact:* Dr. Kiumars Parvin, Chair, 408-924-5210, Fax: 408-924-2917.

Simon Fraser University, Graduate Studies, Faculty of Science, Department of Physics, Burnaby, BC V5A 1S6, Canada. Offers biophysics (M Sc, PhD); chemical physics (M Sc, PhD); physics (M Sc, PhD). *Degree requirements:* For master's, thesis; for doctorate, thesis/dissertation. *Entrance requirements:* For master's, minimum GPA of 3.0; for doctorate, minimum GPA of 3.5. Additional exam requirements/recommendations for international students: Required—TOEFL or IELTS. *Faculty research:* Solid-state physics, magnetism, energy research, superconductivity, nuclear physics.

South Dakota School of Mines and Technology, Graduate Division, College of Engineering, Master's Program in Materials Engineering and Science, Rapid City, SD 57701-3995. Offers chemistry (MS); metallurgical engineering (MS); physics (MS). *Faculty:* 6 full-time (0 women), 1 part-time/adjunct (0 women). *Students:* 9 full-time (1 woman), 9 part-time (2 women), 8 international. Average age 26. 9 applicants, 56% accepted, 1 enrolled. In 2009, 4 master's awarded. *Entrance requirements:* For master's, GRE General Test. Additional exam requirements/recommendations for international students: Required—TOEFL, TWE. *Application deadline:* For fall admission, 7/1 priority date for domestic students, 4/1 for international students; for spring admission, 11/1 for domestic students, 9/1 for international students. Applications are processed on a rolling basis. Application fee: $35. Electronic applications accepted. *Expenses:* Tuition, state resident: full-time $3340; part-time $139 per credit hour. Tuition, nonresident: full-time $7060; part-time $294 per credit hour. Required fees: $3270. *Financial support:* In 2009–10, 15 research assistantships with partial tuition reimbursements (averaging $11,400 per year), 11 teaching assistantships with partial tuition reimbursements (averaging $4,063 per year) were awarded; fellowships also available. Financial award application deadline: 5/15. *Unit head:* Dr. Jon Kellar, Chair, 605-394-2343, E-mail: jon.kellar@sdsmt.edu. *Application contact:* Jeannette R. Nilson, Administrative Support Coordinator, Graduate Education, 800-454-8162 Ext. 1206, Fax: 605-394-5360, E-mail: graduate_admissions@sdsmt.edu.

South Dakota State University, Graduate School, College of Engineering, Department of Physics, Brookings, SD 57007. Offers engineering (MS). Part-time programs available. *Degree requirements:* For master's, comprehensive exam (for some programs), thesis (for some programs), oral exam. *Entrance requirements:* Additional exam requirements/recommendations for international students: Required—TOEFL (minimum score 580 paper-based; 237 computer-based). *Faculty research:* Materials science, astrophysics, remote sensing and atmospheric corrections, theoretical and computational physics, applied physics.

Southern Illinois University Carbondale, Graduate School, College of Science, Department of Physics, Carbondale, IL 62901-4701. Offers MS, PhD. *Degree requirements:* For master's, one foreign language, thesis. *Entrance requirements:* For master's, minimum GPA of 2.7. Additional exam requirements/recommendations for international students: Required—TOEFL. *Faculty research:* Atomic, molecular, nuclear, and mathematical physics; statistical mechanics; solid-state and low-temperature physics; rheology; material science.

Southern Methodist University, Dedman College, Department of Physics, Dallas, TX 75275. Offers MS, PhD. Part-time programs available. *Faculty:* 13 full-time (1 woman), 2 part-time/adjunct (0 women). *Students:* 15 full-time (6 women), 1 part-time (0 women); includes 1 minority (Hispanic American), 13 international. Average age 26. 30 applicants, 27% accepted, 6 enrolled. In 2009, 2 doctorates awarded. Terminal master's awarded for partial completion of doctoral program. *Degree requirements:* For master's, thesis optional, oral exam; for doctorate, thesis/dissertation, written exam. *Entrance requirements:* For master's and doctorate, GRE General Test, GRE Subject Test (physics), minimum GPA of 3.0. Additional exam requirements/recommendations for international students: Required—TOEFL. *Application deadline:* For fall admission, 2/1 priority date for domestic and international students. Application fee: $60. Electronic applications accepted. *Financial support:* In 2009–10, 4 research assistantships with full tuition reimbursements (averaging $21,000 per year), 6 teaching assistantships with full tuition reimbursements (averaging $19,500 per year) were awarded; health care benefits and tuition waivers (partial) also available. Financial award application deadline: 2/1; financial award applicants required to submit FAFSA. *Faculty research:* Particle physics, cosmology, astrophysics, mathematics physics, computational physics. Total annual research expenditures: $1 million. *Unit head:* Prof. Fredrick Olness, Head, 214-768-2495, Fax: 214-768-4095, E-mail: olness@smu.edu. *Application contact:* Prof. Jingbo Ye, Director of Graduate Recruitment, Fax: 214-768-4095.

Southern University and Agricultural and Mechanical College, Graduate School, College of Sciences, Department of Physics, Baton Rouge, LA 70813. Offers MS. *Degree requirements:* For master's, thesis. *Entrance requirements:* For master's, GMAT or GRE General Test. Additional exam requirements/recommendations for international students: Required—TOEFL (minimum score 525 paper-based; 193 computer-based). *Faculty research:* Piezoelectric materials and devices, predictive ab-instio calculations, high energy physics, surface growth studies, semiconductor and intermetallics.

Stanford University, School of Humanities and Sciences, Department of Physics, Stanford, CA 94305-9991. Offers PhD. *Degree requirements:* For doctorate, thesis/dissertation, oral exam, qualifying exam. *Entrance requirements:* For doctorate, GRE General Test, GRE Subject Test. Additional exam requirements/recommendations for international students: Required—TOEFL. Electronic applications accepted. *Expenses:* Tuition: Full-time $37,380; part-time $2760 per quarter. Required fees: $501.

State University of New York at Binghamton, Graduate School, School of Arts and Sciences, Department of Physics, Applied Physics, and Astronomy, Binghamton, NY 13902-6000. Offers applied physics (MS); physics (MA, MS). *Faculty:* 9 full-time (0 women), 4 part-time/adjunct (1 woman). *Students:* 9 full-time (1 woman), 1 part-time (0 women), 2 international. Average age 26. 14 applicants, 71% accepted, 4 enrolled. In 2009, 3 master's awarded. *Degree requirements:* For master's, thesis or alternative. *Entrance requirements:* For master's, GRE General Test, GRE Subject Test. Additional exam requirements/recommendations for international students: Required—TOEFL (minimum score 550 paper-based; 213 computer-based; 80 iBT). *Application deadline:* For fall admission, 2/15 priority date for domestic and international students; for spring admission, 10/15 priority date for domestic and international students. Applications are processed on a rolling basis. Application fee: $60. Electronic applications accepted. *Financial support:* In 2009–10, fellowships (averaging $11,000 per year), 13 teaching assistantships with full tuition reimbursements (averaging $11,000 per year) were awarded; career-related internships or fieldwork, Federal Work-Study, institutionally sponsored loans, scholarships/grants, health care benefits, and unspecified assistantships also available. Financial award application deadline: 2/15; financial award applicants required to submit FAFSA. *Unit head:* Dr. Eric Cotts, Chairperson, 607-777-4371, E-mail: ecotts@binghamton.edu. *Application contact:* Victoria Williams, Recruiting and Admissions Coordinator, 607-777-2151, Fax: 607-777-2501, E-mail: vwilliam@binghamton.edu.

Stephen F. Austin State University, Graduate School, College of Sciences and Mathematics, Department of Physics and Astronomy, Nacogdoches, TX 75962. Offers physics (MS). Part-time programs available. *Degree requirements:* For master's, comprehensive exam. *Entrance requirements:* For master's, GRE General Test, minimum GPA of 2.8 in last 60 hours, 2.5 overall. Additional exam requirements/recommendations for international students: Required—TOEFL. *Faculty research:* Low-temperature physics, x-ray spectroscopy and metallic glasses, infrared spectroscopy.

Stevens Institute of Technology, Graduate School, Charles V. Schaefer Jr. School of Engineering, Department of Physics and Engineering Physics, Hoboken, NJ 07030. Offers applied optics (Certificate); engineering physics (M Eng); microdevices and microsystems (Certificate); physics (MS, PhD); plasma and surface physics (Certificate). Part-time and evening/weekend programs available. Terminal master's awarded for partial completion of doctoral program. *Degree requirements:* For master's, thesis optional; for doctorate, thesis/dissertation. *Entrance requirements:* For master's and doctorate, GRE. Additional exam requirements/recommendations for international students: Required—TOEFL. Electronic applications accepted. *Expenses:* Tuition: Full-time $9900; part-time $1100 per credit. Required fees: $286 per semester. *Faculty research:* Laser spectroscopy, physical kinetics, semiconductor-device physics, condensed-matter theory.

Stony Brook University, State University of New York, Graduate School, College of Arts and Sciences, Department of Physics and Astronomy, Program in Physics, Stony Brook, NY 11794. Offers modern research instrumentation (MS); physics (MA, PhD); physics education (MAT). *Students:* 183 full-time (34 women), 2 part-time (0 women); includes 12 minority (1 African American, 3 Asian Americans or Pacific Islanders, 8 Hispanic Americans), 100 international. *Degree requirements:* For doctorate, one foreign language, thesis/dissertation. *Entrance requirements:* For master's and doctorate, GRE General Test. Additional exam requirements/recommendations for international students: Required—TOEFL. *Application deadline:* For fall admission, 1/15 for domestic students. Application fee: $60. *Expenses:* Tuition, state resident: full-time $8370; part-time $349 per credit. Tuition, nonresident: full-time $13,250; part-time $552 per credit. Required fees: $933. *Financial support:* Fellowships, research assistantships, teaching assistantships available. Financial award application deadline: 2/1. *Unit head:* Dr. Peter M. Koch, Chair, 631-632-8100, Fax: 631-632-8176, E-mail: peter.koch@stonybrook.edu. *Application contact:* Dr. Lazlo W. Mihaly, Director, 631-632-8279, Fax: 631-632-8176, E-mail: lazlo.mihaly@stonybrook.edu.

Syracuse University, College of Arts and Sciences, Program in Physics, Syracuse, NY 13244. Offers MS, PhD. Part-time programs available. *Students:* 59 full-time (9 women), 7 part-time (1 woman); includes 1 minority (Hispanic American), 45 international. Average age 28. 133 applicants, 42% accepted, 18 enrolled. In 2009, 5 master's, 8 doctorates awarded. Terminal master's awarded for partial completion of doctoral program. *Degree requirements:* For master's, thesis or alternative; for doctorate, thesis/dissertation. *Entrance requirements:* For master's and doctorate, GRE General Test, GRE Subject Test. Additional exam requirements/recommendations for international students: Required—TOEFL (minimum score 100 iBT). *Application deadline:* For fall admission, 2/1 priority date for domestic and international students. Application fee: $75. Electronic applications accepted. *Expenses:* Tuition: Full-time $26,808; part-time $1117 per credit. Required fees: $1024. *Financial support:* Fellowships with full tuition reimbursements, research assistantships with full and partial tuition reimbursements, teaching assistantships with full and partial tuition reimbursements, tuition waivers (partial) available. Financial award application deadline: 1/1; financial award applicants required to submit FAFSA. *Unit head:* Dr. Mark Bowick, Director of Graduate Studies, 315-443-5979, E-mail: bowick@phy.syr.edu.

Temple University, Graduate School, College of Science and Technology, Department of Physics, Philadelphia, PA 19122-6096. Offers MA, PhD. Terminal master's awarded for partial completion of doctoral program. *Degree requirements:* For master's, comprehensive exam, thesis or alternative; for doctorate, thesis/dissertation, 2 comprehensive exams. *Entrance requirements:* For master's and doctorate, GRE General Test, minimum GPA of 3.0. Additional exam requirements/recommendations for international students: Required—TOEFL (minimum score 550 paper-based; 213 computer-based; 79 iBT). Electronic applications accepted. *Faculty research:* Laser-based molecular spectroscopy, elementary particle physics, statistical mechanics, solid-state physics.

See Close-Up on page 229.

Texas A&M International University, Office of Graduate Studies and Research, College of Arts and Sciences, Department of Mathematical and Physical Science, Laredo, TX 78041-1900. Offers MA. *Faculty:* 3 full-time (0 women). *Students:* 2 full-time (0 women), 9 part-time (2 women); includes 9 minority (all Hispanic Americans), 1 international. Average age 31. 9 applicants, 56% accepted, 4 enrolled. In 2009, 1 master's awarded. *Entrance requirements:* For master's, GRE General Test. Additional exam requirements/recommendations for international students: Required—TOEFL (minimum score 550 paper-based; 213 computer-based). *Application deadline:* For fall admission, 4/30 priority date for domestic students; for spring admission, 11/30 for domestic students. Applications are processed on a rolling basis. Application fee: $25. *Financial support:* In 2009–10, 1 student received support. Application deadline: 11/1. *Unit head:* Dr. Hoonandara Goonatilake, Interim Chair, 956-326-2588, E-mail: rbachnak@tamiu.edu. *Application contact:* Rosie Espinoza-Dickinson, Director of Admissions, 956-326-2200, Fax: 956-326-2199, E-mail: enroll@tamiu.edu.

Texas A&M University, College of Science, Department of Physics, College Station, TX 77843. Offers applied physics (PhD); physics (MS, PhD). *Faculty:* 48. *Students:* 146 full-time (24 women), 7 part-time (1 woman); includes 23 minority (2 African Americans, 2 American Indian/Alaska Native, 7 Asian Americans or Pacific Islanders, 12 Hispanic Americans), 79 international. In 2009, 5 master's, 16 doctorates awarded. Terminal master's awarded for partial completion of doctoral program. *Degree requirements:* For master's, thesis (for some programs); for doctorate, thesis/dissertation. *Entrance requirements:* For master's and doctorate, GRE General Test, GRE Subject Test. Additional exam requirements/recommendations for international students: Required—TOEFL. *Application deadline:* For fall admission, 3/1 priority date for domestic students; for spring admission, 8/1 for domestic students. Application fee: $50 ($75 for international students). Electronic applications accepted. *Expenses:* Tuition, state resident: full-time $3991.32; part-time $221.74 per credit hour. Tuition, nonresident: full-time $9049; part-time $502.74 per credit hour. *Financial support:* In 2009–10, research assistantships (averaging $16,200 per year), teaching assistantships (averaging $16,200 per year) were awarded; fellowships also available. Financial award application deadline: 3/1; financial award applicants required to submit FAFSA. *Faculty research:* Condensed-matter, atomic/molecular, high-energy, and nuclear physics; quantum optics. *Unit head:* Dr. Edward S. Fry, Head, 979-845-1910, E-mail: fry@physics.tamu.edu. *Application contact:* Dr. George W. Kattawar, Professor, 979-845-1180, Fax: 979-845-2590, E-mail: kattawar@physics.tamu.edu.

Texas A&M University–Commerce, Graduate School, College of Arts and Sciences, Department of Physics, Commerce, TX 75429-3011. Offers M Ed, MS. Part-time programs available. *Degree requirements:* For master's, comprehensive exam, thesis (for some programs). *Entrance requirements:* For master's, GRE General Test. Electronic applications accepted.

Texas Christian University, College of Science and Engineering, Department of Physics and Astronomy, Fort Worth, TX 76129-0002. Offers physics (MA, MS, PhD), including astrophysics (PhD), business (PhD), physics (PhD). Part-time and evening/weekend programs available. *Degree requirements:* For master's, comprehensive exam, thesis; for doctorate, comprehensive exam, thesis/dissertation, paper submitted to a scientific journal. *Entrance requirements:* For master's, GRE; for doctorate, GRE General Test. Additional exam requirements/recommendations for international students: Required—TOEFL (minimum score 600 paper-based). *Application deadline:* For fall admission, 3/1 for domestic students; for spring admission, 12/1 for domestic students. Applications are processed on a rolling basis. Application fee: $50. *Expenses:* Tuition: Full-time $17,640; part-time $980 per credit hour. Tuition and fees vary according to program. *Financial support:* In 2009–10, 10 teaching assistantships (averaging $18,000 per year) were awarded; tuition waivers also available. Financial award application deadline: 3/1. *Unit head:* Dr. T. W. Zerda, Chairperson, 817-257-7375 Ext. 7124, Fax: 817-257-7742, E-mail: t.zerda@tcu.edu. *Application contact:* Dr. William R. M. Graham, Professor, 817-257-7375 Ext. 6383, Fax: 817-257-7742, E-mail: w.graham@tcu.edu.

Texas State University–San Marcos, Graduate School, College of Science, Department of Physics, San Marcos, TX 78666. Offers material physics (MS); physics (MS). Part-time programs available. *Faculty:* 6 full-time (1 woman). *Students:* 10 full-time (2 women), 9 part-time (1 woman); includes 4 minority (2 African Americans, 2 Hispanic Americans). Average age 28. 10 applicants, 90% accepted, 4 enrolled. In 2009, 7 master's awarded. *Degree requirements:* For master's, comprehensive exam, thesis (for some programs). *Entrance requirements:* For master's, minimum GPA of 2.75 in junior and senior level physics courses, or 2.5 to 2.75 GPA with a GRE of 900 (v&q). Additional exam requirements/recommendations for international students: Required—TOEFL (minimum score 550 paper-based; 213 computer-based). *Application deadline:* For fall admission, 6/15 priority date for domestic students, 6/1 priority date for international students; for spring admission, 10/15 priority date for domestic students, 10/1 priority date for international students. Applications are processed on a rolling basis. Application fee: $40 ($90 for international students). Electronic applications accepted. *Expenses:* Tuition, state resident: full-time $5784; part-time $241 per credit hour. Tuition, nonresident: part-time $551 per credit hour. Required fees: $1728; $48 per credit hour. $306. Tuition and fees vary according to course load. *Financial support:* In 2009–10, 14 students received support, including 2 research assistantships (averaging $4,087 per year), 9 teaching assistantships (averaging $5,076 per year); career-related internships or fieldwork, Federal Work-Study, and institutionally sponsored loans also available. Support available to part-time students. Financial award application deadline: 4/1; financial award applicants required to submit FAFSA. *Faculty research:* High-temperature superconductors, historical astronomy, general relativity. Total annual research expenditures: $1.4 million. *Unit head:* Dr. David Donnelly, Chair, 512-245-2131, Fax: 512-245-2131, E-mail: dd14@txstate.edu. *Application contact:* Dr. J. Michael Willoughby, Dean of Graduate School, 512-245-2581, Fax: 512-245-8365, E-mail: gradcollege@txstate.edu.

Texas Tech University, Graduate School, College of Arts and Sciences, Department of Physics, Lubbock, TX 79409. Offers applied physics (MS); physics (MS, PhD). Part-time programs available. *Faculty:* 14 full-time (1 woman), 1 part-time/adjunct (0 women). *Students:* 46 full-time (11 women), 2 part-time (0 women); includes 5 minority (1 African American, 2 Asian Americans or Pacific Islanders, 2 Hispanic Americans), 30 international. Average age 32. 72 applicants, 35% accepted, 15 enrolled. In 2009, 5 master's, 1 doctorate awarded. *Degree requirements:* For master's, variable foreign language requirement, thesis or alternative; for doctorate, variable foreign language requirement, thesis/dissertation. *Entrance requirements:* For master's and doctorate, GRE General Test. Additional exam requirements/recommendations for international students: Required—TOEFL (minimum score 550 paper-based; 213 computer-based). *Application deadline:* For fall admission, 3/1 priority date for international students; for spring admission, 11/1 priority date for international students. Applications are processed on a rolling basis. Application fee: $50 ($75 for international students). Electronic applications accepted. *Expenses:* Tuition, state resident: full-time $5100; part-time $213 per credit hour. Tuition, nonresident: full-time $11,748; part-time $490 per credit hour. Required fees: $2298; $50 per credit hour. $555 per semester. *Financial support:* In 2009–10, 12 teaching assistantships with partial tuition reimbursements (averaging $23,158 per year) were awarded; research assistantships with partial tuition reimbursements, career-related internships or fieldwork, Federal Work-Study, and institutionally sponsored loans also available. Support available to part-time students. Financial award application deadline: 4/15; financial award applicants required to submit FAFSA. *Faculty research:* Biophysics, high energy and nuclear physics, condensed matter physics, atomic and molecular physics, physics education. Total annual research expenditures: $1 million. *Unit head:* Dr. Roger Lichti, Chair, 806-742-3767, Fax: 806-742-1182, E-mail: roger.lichti@ttu.edu. *Application contact:* Dr. Mahdi Sanati, Graduate Recruiter, 806-742-3767, Fax: 806-742-1182, E-mail: m.sanati@ttu.edu.

Trent University, Graduate Studies, Program in Applications of Modeling in the Natural and Social Sciences, Department of Physics, Peterborough, ON K9J 7B8, Canada. Offers M Sc. Part-time programs available. *Degree requirements:* For master's, thesis. *Entrance requirements:* For master's, honours degree. *Faculty research:* Radiation physics, chemical physics.

Tufts University, Graduate School of Arts and Sciences, Department of Physics and Astronomy, Medford, MA 02155. Offers physics (MS, PhD). *Faculty:* 17 full-time, 2 part-time/adjunct. *Students:* 26 full-time (7 women); includes 1 minority (Hispanic American), 9 international. Average age 27. 89 applicants, 19% accepted, 4 enrolled. In 2009, 3 master's, 5 doctorates awarded. Terminal master's awarded for partial completion of doctoral program. *Degree requirements:* For master's, thesis optional; for doctorate, thesis/dissertation. *Entrance requirements:* For master's and doctorate, GRE General Test. Additional exam requirements/recommendations for international students: Required—TOEFL (minimum score 550 paper-based; 213 computer-based; 80 iBT). *Application deadline:* For fall admission, 2/15 for domestic students, 12/15 for international students; for spring admission, 10/15 for domestic students, 9/15 for international students. Applications are processed on a rolling basis. Application fee: $75. Electronic applications accepted. *Expenses:* Tuition: Full-time $38,096; part-time $3962 per credit. Required fees: $686; $40 per year. Tuition and fees vary according to course level, course load, degree level, program and student level. *Financial support:* Fellowships, research assistantships with full tuition reimbursements, teaching assistantships with full tuition reimbursements, Federal Work-Study, scholarships/grants, tuition waivers (partial), and unspecified

Physics

Tufts University (continued)
assistantships available. Financial award application deadline: 1/15; financial award applicants required to submit FAFSA. *Unit head:* Roger Tobin, Chair, 617-627-3029. *Application contact:* Dr. Krzysztof Sliwa, Graduate Advisor, 617-627-3029.

Tulane University, School of Science and Engineering, Department of Physics and Engineering Physics, New Orleans, LA 70118-5669. Offers physics (PhD). *Degree requirements:* For doctorate, thesis/dissertation. *Entrance requirements:* For doctorate, GRE General Test. Additional exam requirements/recommendations for international students: Required—TOEFL. Electronic applications accepted. *Faculty research:* Surface physics, condensed-matter experiment, condensed-matter theory, nuclear theory, polymers.

Université de Moncton, Faculty of Science, Department of Physics and Astronomy, Moncton, NB E1A 3E9, Canada. Offers M Sc. Part-time programs available. *Degree requirements:* For master's, thesis. *Entrance requirements:* For master's, proficiency in French. Electronic applications accepted. *Faculty research:* Thin films, optical properties, solar selective surfaces, microgravity and photonic materials.

Université de Montréal, Faculty of Arts and Sciences, Department of Physics, Montréal, QC H3C 3J7, Canada. Offers M Sc, PhD. *Degree requirements:* For doctorate, thesis/dissertation, general exam. Electronic applications accepted. *Faculty research:* Astronomy; biophysics; solid-state, plasma, and nuclear physics.

Université de Sherbrooke, Faculty of Sciences, Department of Physics, Sherbrooke, QC J1K 2R1, Canada. Offers M Sc, PhD. *Degree requirements:* For master's, thesis; for doctorate, comprehensive exam, thesis/dissertation. *Entrance requirements:* For doctorate, master's degree. Electronic applications accepted. *Faculty research:* Solid-state physics, quantum computing.

Université du Québec à Trois-Rivières, Graduate Programs, Program in Physics, Trois-Rivières, QC G9A 5H7, Canada. Offers matter and energy (MS, PhD).

Université Laval, Faculty of Sciences and Engineering, Department of Physics, Physical Engineering, and Optics, Programs in Physics, Québec, QC G1K 7P4, Canada. Offers M Sc, PhD. Terminal master's awarded for partial completion of doctoral program. *Degree requirements:* For master's, thesis; for doctorate, comprehensive exam, thesis/dissertation. *Entrance requirements:* For master's and doctorate, knowledge of French, comprehension of written English. Electronic applications accepted.

University at Albany, State University of New York, College of Arts and Sciences, Department of Physics, Albany, NY 12222-0001. Offers MS, PhD. *Degree requirements:* For master's, one foreign language; for doctorate, one foreign language, thesis/dissertation. *Entrance requirements:* Additional exam requirements/recommendations for international students: Required—TOEFL (minimum score 550 paper-based; 213 computer-based). Electronic applications accepted. *Faculty research:* Condensed-matter physics, high-energy physics, applied physics, electronic materials, theoretical particle physics.

University at Buffalo, the State University of New York, Graduate School, College of Arts and Sciences, Department of Physics, Buffalo, NY 14260. Offers MS, PhD. Part-time programs available. Terminal master's awarded for partial completion of doctoral program. *Degree requirements:* For master's, thesis, qualifying exam; for doctorate, thesis/dissertation, qualifying exams. *Entrance requirements:* For master's and doctorate, GRE General Test, letters of recommendation. Additional exam requirements/recommendations for international students: Required—TOEFL (minimum score 550 paper-based; 213 computer-based; 79 iBT). Electronic applications accepted. *Faculty research:* Condensed-matter physics (experimental and theoretical), cosmology (theoretical), high energy and particle physics (experimental and theoretical), computational physics, biophysics (experimental and theoretical) medical physics, materials physics.

The University of Akron, Graduate School, Buchtel College of Arts and Sciences, Department of Physics, Akron, OH 44325. Offers MS. Part-time and evening/weekend programs available. *Faculty:* 9 full-time (1 woman), 1 part-time/adjunct (0 women). *Students:* 13 full-time (6 women), 2 part-time (0 women), 13 international. Average age 27. 21 applicants, 38% accepted, 4 enrolled. In 2009, 3 master's awarded. *Degree requirements:* For master's, thesis, written exam or formal report. *Entrance requirements:* For master's, minimum GPA of 2.75, letters of recommendation, resume. Additional exam requirements/recommendations for international students: Required—TOEFL (minimum score 550 paper-based; 213 computer-based; 79 iBT). *Application deadline:* For fall admission, 3/15 for domestic students. Applications are processed on a rolling basis. Application fee: $30 ($40 for international students). Electronic applications accepted. *Expenses:* Tuition, state resident: full-time $6570; part-time $365 per credit hour. Tuition, nonresident: full-time $11,250; part-time $625 per credit hour. *Financial support:* In 2009–10, 16 teaching assistantships with full tuition reimbursements were awarded. *Faculty research:* Materials physics, surface physics, nanotechnology, polymer physics, condensed matter physics. Total annual research expenditures: $94,214. *Unit head:* Dr. Robert Mallik, Chair, 330-972-7145, E-mail: rmallik@uakron.edu. *Application contact:* Dr. Ben Hu, Graduate Director, 330-972-8093, E-mail: byhu@uakron.edu.

The University of Alabama, Graduate School, College of Arts and Sciences, Department of Physics and Astronomy, Tuscaloosa, AL 35487-0324. Offers physics (MS, PhD). *Faculty:* 18 full-time (0 women), 1 (woman) part-time/adjunct. *Students:* 38 full-time (9 women), 2 part-time (0 women), 22 international. Average age 27. 40 applicants, 28% accepted, 7 enrolled. In 2009, 5 master's, 7 doctorates awarded. Terminal master's awarded for partial completion of doctoral program. *Median time to degree:* Of those who began their doctoral program in fall 2001, 60% received their degree in 8 years or less. *Degree requirements:* For master's, thesis optional, oral exam; for doctorate, thesis/dissertation, oral and written exams. *Entrance requirements:* For master's and doctorate, GRE General or Subject Test, minimum GPA of 3.0. Additional exam requirements/recommendations for international students: Required—TOEFL (minimum score 550 paper-based; 213 computer-based; 79 iBT). *Application deadline:* For fall admission, 7/6 priority date for domestic students, 2/1 for international students; for spring admission, 11/22 for domestic students. Applications are processed on a rolling basis. Application fee: $50 ($60 for international students). Electronic applications accepted. *Expenses:* Tuition, state resident: full-time $7000. Tuition, nonresident: full-time $19,200. *Financial support:* In 2009–10, 39 students received support, including 1 fellowship with full tuition reimbursement available (averaging $18,000 per year), 13 research assistantships with full tuition reimbursements available (averaging $14,000 per year), 25 teaching assistantships with full tuition reimbursements available (averaging $13,900 per year); career-related internships or fieldwork and institutionally sponsored loans also available. Financial award application deadline: 4/1. *Faculty research:* Condensed-matter, high-energy physics; molecular spectroscopy; astrophysics; particle astrophysics. Total annual research expenditures: $1.6 million. *Unit head:* Dr. Raymond E. White, Chairman and Professor, 205-348-5050, Fax: 205-348-5051, E-mail: rwhite@ua.edu. *Application contact:* Louise F. Labosier, Admissions Officer, 205-348-5921, Fax: 205-348-0400, E-mail: labosier@aalan.ua.edu.

The University of Alabama at Birmingham, College of Arts and Sciences, Program in Physics, Birmingham, AL 35294. Offers MS, PhD. Terminal master's awarded for partial completion of doctoral program. *Degree requirements:* For master's, thesis optional; for doctorate, thesis/dissertation. *Entrance requirements:* For master's and doctorate, GRE General Test, minimum GPA of 3.0. Additional exam requirements/recommendations for international students: Required—TOEFL. Electronic applications accepted. *Faculty research:* Laser physics, space physics, optics, biophysics, material physics.

The University of Alabama in Huntsville, School of Graduate Studies, College of Science, Department of Physics, Huntsville, AL 35899. Offers optics and photonics technology (MS); physics (MS, PhD). Part-time and evening/weekend programs available. *Faculty:* 19 full-time (0 women), 2 part-time/adjunct (0 women). *Students:* 33 full-time (12 women), 15 part-time (5 women); includes 2 minority (both Asian Americans or Pacific Islanders), 10 international. Average age 29. 51 applicants, 59% accepted, 19 enrolled. In 2009, 9 master's, 3 doctorates awarded. *Degree requirements:* For master's, comprehensive exam, thesis or alternative, oral and written exams; for doctorate, comprehensive exam, thesis/dissertation, oral and written exams. *Entrance requirements:* For master's and doctorate, GRE General Test, minimum GPA of 3.0. Additional exam requirements/recommendations for international students: Required—TOEFL (minimum score 550 paper-based; 213 computer-based; 62 iBT). *Application deadline:* For fall admission, 7/15 for domestic students, 4/1 for international students; for spring admission, 11/30 for domestic students, 9/1 for international students. Applications are processed on a rolling basis. Application fee: $40 ($50 for international students). Electronic applications accepted. *Expenses:* Tuition, state resident: part-time $355.75 per credit hour. Tuition, nonresident: part-time $847.10 per credit hour. Required fees: $210.80 per semester. Tuition and fees vary according to course load and program. *Financial support:* In 2009–10, 26 students received support, including 16 research assistantships with full and partial tuition reimbursements available (averaging $13,242 per year), 10 teaching assistantships with full and partial tuition reimbursements available (averaging $12,600 per year); career-related internships or fieldwork, Federal Work-Study, institutionally sponsored loans, scholarships/grants, health care benefits, and unspecified assistantships also available. Support available to part-time students. Financial award application deadline: 4/1; financial award applicants required to submit FAFSA. *Faculty research:* Space physics, cosmology/general relativity, optics/quantum optics, astrophysics/gamma-ray astronomy, strophysical instrumentation. Total annual research expenditures: $4.1 million. *Unit head:* Dr. James Miller, Chair, 256-824-2481, Fax: 256-824-6873, E-mail: millerj@cspan.uah.edu. *Application contact:* Kathy Biggs, Graduate Studies Admissions Manager, 256-824-6199, Fax: 256-824-6405, E-mail: deangrad@uah.edu.

University of Alaska Fairbanks, College of Natural Sciences and Mathematics, Department of Physics, Fairbanks, AK 99775-5920. Offers computational physics (MS); physics (MAT, MS, PhD); space physics (MS, PhD). Part-time programs available. *Faculty:* 10 full-time (1 woman). *Students:* 23 full-time (3 women), 2 part-time (0 women); includes 1 minority (American Indian/Alaska Native), 8 international. Average age 31. 24 applicants, 25% accepted, 6 enrolled. In 2009, 2 master's awarded. Terminal master's awarded for partial completion of doctoral program. *Degree requirements:* For master's, comprehensive exam, thesis or alternative; for doctorate, comprehensive exam, thesis/dissertation, oral defense. *Entrance requirements:* Additional exam requirements/recommendations for international students: Required—TOEFL (minimum score 550 paper-based; 213 computer-based; 80 iBT). *Application deadline:* For fall admission, 6/1 for domestic students, 3/1 for international students; for spring admission, 10/15 for domestic students, 9/1 for international students. Applications are processed on a rolling basis. Application fee: $60. Electronic applications accepted. *Expenses:* Tuition, state resident: full-time $7584; part-time $316 per credit. Tuition, nonresident: full-time $15,504; part-time $646 per credit. Required fees: $23 per credit. $135 per semester. Tuition and fees vary according to course level, course load and reciprocity agreements. *Financial support:* In 2009–10, 1 fellowship (averaging $16,454 per year), 11 research assistantships (averaging $16,320 per year), 7 teaching assistantships (averaging $15,451 per year) were awarded; Federal Work-Study, scholarships/grants, health care benefits, and unspecified assistantships also available. Support available to part-time students. Financial award application deadline: 2/15; financial award applicants required to submit FAFSA. *Faculty research:* Atmospheric and ionospheric radar studies, space plasma theory, magnetospheric dynamics, space weather and auroral studies, turbulence and complex systems. *Unit head:* John Olson, Chair, 907-474-7339, Fax: 907-474-6130, E-mail: physics@uaf.edu. *Application contact:* John Olson, Chair, 907-474-7339, Fax: 907-474-6130, E-mail: physics@uaf.edu.

University of Alberta, Faculty of Graduate Studies and Research, Department of Physics, Edmonton, AB T6G 2E1, Canada. Offers astrophysics (M Sc, PhD); condensed matter (M Sc, PhD); geophysics (M Sc, PhD); medical physics (M Sc, PhD); subatomic physics (M Sc, PhD). *Faculty:* 36 full-time (3 women), 7 part-time/adjunct (0 women). *Students:* 56 full-time (6 women), 16 part-time (2 women). 85 applicants, 35% accepted. In 2009, 7 master's, 10 doctorates awarded. *Degree requirements:* For master's, thesis; for doctorate, thesis/dissertation. *Entrance requirements:* For master's and doctorate, minimum GPA of 7.0 on a 9.0 scale. Additional exam requirements/recommendations for international students: Required—TOEFL. *Application deadline:* For fall admission, 2/15 priority date for domestic students. Applications are processed on a rolling basis. Tuition and fees charges are reported in Canadian dollars. *Expenses:* Tuition, area resident: Full-time $4626.24 Canadian dollars; part-time $99.72 Canadian dollars per unit. International tuition: $8216 Canadian dollars full-time. Required fees: $3589.92 Canadian dollars; $99.72 Canadian dollars per unit. $215 Canadian dollars per term. *Financial support:* In 2009–10, 6 fellowships with partial tuition reimbursements, 40 teaching assistantships were awarded; research assistantships, career-related internships or fieldwork, institutionally sponsored loans, and scholarships/grants also available. Financial award application deadline: 2/15. *Faculty research:* Cosmology, astroparticle physics, high-intermediate energy, magnetism, superconductivity. Total annual research expenditures: $3.1 million. *Unit head:* Dr. R. Marchand, Associate Chair, 780-492-1072, E-mail: assoc-chair@phys.ualberta.ca. *Application contact:* Lynn Chandler, Program Advisor, 780-492-1072, Fax: 780-492-0714, E-mail: grad.program@phys.ualberta.ca.

The University of Arizona, Graduate College, College of Science, Department of Physics, Tucson, AZ 85721. Offers applied and industrial physics (PMS); physics (MS, PhD). Part-time programs available. *Faculty:* 27. *Students:* 42 full-time (5 women), 36 part-time (6 women), 37 international. Average age 29. 154 applicants. In 2009, 1 master's, 8 doctorates awarded. Terminal master's awarded for partial completion of doctoral program. *Degree requirements:* For master's, comprehensive exam (for some programs), thesis optional; for doctorate, comprehensive exam, thesis/dissertation. *Entrance requirements:* For master's and doctorate, GRE General Test, GRE Subject Test, minimum GPA of 3.2, 3 letters of recommendation. Additional exam requirements/recommendations for international students: Required—TOEFL (minimum score 550 paper-based; 213 computer-based; 79 iBT). *Application deadline:* For fall admission, 2/1 for domestic students, 12/1 for international students. Applications are processed on a rolling basis. Application fee: $75. Electronic applications accepted. *Expenses:* Tuition, state resident: full-time $9028. Tuition, nonresident: full-time $24,890. *Financial support:* In 2009–10, 19 research assistantships with full tuition reimbursements (averaging $16,221 per year), 40 teaching assistantships with full tuition reimbursements (averaging $15,471 per year) were awarded; career-related internships or fieldwork, scholarships/grants, health care benefits, tuition waivers (full and partial), and unspecified assistantships also available. Financial award application deadline: 5/1. *Faculty research:* Astrophysics; high-energy, condensed-matter, atomic and molecular physics; optics. Total annual research expenditures: $3.8 million. *Unit head:* Dr. Michael Shupe, Head, 520-621-2679, E-mail: shupe@physics.arizona.edu. *Application contact:* Lisa Shapouri, Graduate Coordinator, 520-621-2290, Fax: 520-621-4721, E-mail: lisas@physics.arizona.edu.

University of Arkansas, Graduate School, J. William Fulbright College of Arts and Sciences, Department of Physics, Fayetteville, AR 72701-1201. Offers applied physics (MS); physics (MS, PhD); physics education (MA). *Students:* 4 full-time (1 woman), 39 part-time (7 women); includes 2 minority (1 African American, 1 Asian American or Pacific Islander), 23 international. In 2009, 6 master's awarded. *Degree requirements:* For master's, thesis; for doctorate, thesis/dissertation. Application fee: $40 ($50 for international students). *Expenses:* Tuition, state resident: full-time $7355; part-time $356.58 per hour. Tuition, nonresident: full-time $17,401; part-time $775.17 per hour. Required fees: $1203. *Financial support:* In 2009–10, 7 fellowships with tuition reimbursements, 20 research assistantships, 16 teaching assistantships were awarded; career-related internships or fieldwork and Federal Work-Study also available. Support available to part-time students. Financial award application deadline: 4/1; financial award applicants required to submit FAFSA. *Unit head:* Dr. Surendra Singh, Departmental Chairperson, 479-575-2506, Fax: 479-575-4580, E-mail: ssingh@uark.edu. *Application contact:* Dr. Huaxiang Fu, Graduate Coordinator, 479-575-8606, E-mail: hfu@uark.edu.

The University of British Columbia, Faculty of Science, Program in Physics, Vancouver, BC V6T 1Z1, Canada. Offers engineering physics (MA Sc); physics (M Sc, PhD). *Degree requirements:* For master's, thesis; for doctorate, comprehensive exam, thesis/dissertation. *Entrance requirements:* For master's, GRE General Test, honors degree; for doctorate, GRE General Test, master's degree. Additional exam requirements/recommendations for international students: Required—TOEFL. *Faculty research:* Applied physics, astrophysics, condensed matter, plasma physics, subatomic physics, astronomy.

University of Calgary, Faculty of Graduate Studies, Faculty of Science, Department of Physics and Astronomy, Calgary, AB T2N 1N4, Canada. Offers M Sc, PhD. Part-time programs available. *Degree requirements:* For master's, thesis; for doctorate, thesis/dissertation, oral candidacy exam, written qualifying exam. *Entrance requirements:* For master's and doctorate, GRE General Test, GRE Subject Test. Additional exam requirements/recommendations for international students: Required—TOEFL (minimum score 550 paper-based; 213 computer-based). Electronic applications accepted. *Faculty research:* Astronomy and astrophysics, mass spectrometry, atmospheric physics, space physics, medical physics.

University of California, Berkeley, Graduate Division, College of Letters and Science, Department of Physics, Berkeley, CA 94720-1500. Offers PhD. *Students:* 244 full-time (38 women). Average age 27. 677 applicants, 48 enrolled. In 2009, 33 doctorates awarded. *Degree requirements:* For doctorate, thesis/dissertation, qualifying exam. *Entrance requirements:* For doctorate, GRE General Test, GRE Subject Test, minimum GPA of 3.0, 3 letters of recommendation. Additional exam requirements/recommendations for international students: Required—TOEFL (minimum score 570 paper-based; 230 computer-based). *Application deadline:* For fall admission, 12/15 for domestic students. Application fee: $70 ($90 for international students). *Financial support:* Fellowships with full tuition reimbursements, research assistantships with full tuition reimbursements, teaching assistantships with full tuition reimbursements, institutionally sponsored loans, health care benefits, and unspecified assistantships available. Financial award applicants required to submit FAFSA. *Faculty research:* Astrophysics (experimental and theoretical), condensed matter physics (experimental and theoretical), particle physics (experimental and theoretical), atomic/molecular physics, biophysics and complex systems. *Unit head:* Prof. Frances Hellman, Chair, 510-642-7166, Fax: 510-643-8497, E-mail: chair@physics.berkeley.edu. *Application contact:* Donna K. Sakima, Student Affairs Officer, 510-642-0596, Fax: 510-643-8497, E-mail: sakima@physics.berkeley.edu.

University of California, Davis, Graduate Studies, Program in Physics, Davis, CA 95616. Offers MS, PhD. Terminal master's awarded for partial completion of doctoral program. *Degree requirements:* For master's, comprehensive exam (for some programs), thesis (for some programs); for doctorate, thesis/dissertation. *Entrance requirements:* For master's and doctorate, GRE General Test, GRE Subject Test, minimum GPA of 3.0. Additional exam requirements/recommendations for international students: Required—TOEFL (minimum score 550 paper-based; 213 computer-based). Electronic applications accepted. *Faculty research:* Astrophysics, condensed-matter physics, nuclear physics, particle physics, quantum optics.

University of California, Irvine, Office of Graduate Studies, School of Physical Sciences, Department of Physics and Astronomy, Irvine, CA 92697. Offers physics (MS, PhD); MD/PhD. *Students:* 133 full-time (22 women); includes 20 minority (1 African American, 15 Asian Americans or Pacific Islanders, 4 Hispanic Americans), 31 international. Average age 27. 354 applicants, 20% accepted, 24 enrolled. In 2009, 24 master's, 20 doctorates awarded. Terminal master's awarded for partial completion of doctoral program. *Degree requirements:* For doctorate, thesis/dissertation. *Entrance requirements:* For master's and doctorate, GRE General Test, GRE Subject Test, minimum GPA of 3.0. Additional exam requirements/recommendations for international students: Required—TOEFL (minimum score 550 paper-based; 213 computer-based). *Application deadline:* For fall admission, 1/15 priority date for domestic and international students. Application fee: $70 ($90 for international students). Electronic applications accepted. *Financial support:* In 2009–10, fellowships with full tuition reimbursements (averaging $7,500 per year), research assistantships with full tuition reimbursements (averaging $18,300 per year), teaching assistantships with partial tuition reimbursements (averaging $13,595 per year) were awarded; institutionally sponsored loans, traineeships, health care benefits, and unspecified assistantships also available. Financial award application deadline: 3/1; financial award applicants required to submit FAFSA. *Faculty research:* Condensed-matter physics, plasma physics, astrophysics, particle physics, chemical and materials physics, biophysics. *Unit head:* Jaycee Chu, Student Affairs Officer, 949-824-3496, Fax: 949-824-7988, E-mail: physgrad@uci.edu. *Application contact:* Jaycee Chu, Student Affairs Officer, 949-824-3496, Fax: 949-824-7988, E-mail: physgrad@uci.edu.

University of California, Los Angeles, Graduate Division, College of Letters and Science, Department of Physics and Astronomy, Program in Physics, Los Angeles, CA 90095. Offers physics (MS, PhD); physics education (MAT). MAT admits only applicants whose objective is PhD. *Students:* 143 full-time (19 women); includes 19 minority (3 African Americans, 14 Asian Americans or Pacific Islanders, 2 Hispanic Americans), 30 international. Average age 26. 287 applicants, 20% accepted, 23 enrolled. In 2009, 15 master's, 30 doctorates awarded. Terminal master's awarded for partial completion of doctoral program. *Degree requirements:* For master's, comprehensive exam; for doctorate, thesis/dissertation, oral and written qualifying exams. *Entrance requirements:* For master's, GRE General Test, GRE Subject Test (physics), minimum GPA of 3.0, BS in related field; for doctorate, GRE General Test, GRE Subject Test (physics), minimum undergraduate GPA of 3.0, BS in related field. *Application deadline:* For fall admission, 12/15 for domestic and international students. Application fee: $70 ($90 for international students). Electronic applications accepted. *Financial support:* In 2009–10, 94 fellowships with full and partial tuition reimbursements, 103 research assistantships with full and partial tuition reimbursements, 94 teaching assistantships with full and partial tuition reimbursements were awarded; Federal Work-Study, institutionally sponsored loans, scholarships/grants, health care benefits, tuition waivers (full and partial), and unspecified assistantships also available. Financial award application deadline: 3/1; financial award applicants required to submit FAFSA. *Unit head:* Dr. Ferdinand Coroniti, Chair, 310-825-3440. *Application contact:* Carol Finn, Graduate Counselor, 310-825-2307, E-mail: apply@physics.ucla.edu.

University of California, Merced, Division of Graduate Studies, School of Natural Sciences, Merced, CA 95343. Offers applied mathematics (MS, PhD); biological engineering and small-scale technologies (MS, PhD); environmental systems (MS, PhD); mechanical engineering and applied mechanics (MS, PhD); physics and chemistry (PhD); quantitative and systems biology (MS, PhD). *Expenses:* Tuition, nonresident: full-time $15,102. Required fees: $10,919.

University of California, Riverside, Graduate Division, Department of Physics and Astronomy, Riverside, CA 92521-0102. Offers physics (MS, PhD). Part-time programs available. Terminal master's awarded for partial completion of doctoral program. *Degree requirements:* For master's, comprehensive exams or thesis; for doctorate, thesis/dissertation, qualifying exams. *Entrance requirements:* For master's and doctorate, GRE General Test, GRE Subject Test, minimum GPA of 3.2. Additional exam requirements/recommendations for international students: Required—TOEFL (minimum score 550 paper-based; 213 computer-based; 80 iBT). Electronic applications accepted. *Faculty research:* Laser physics and surface science, elementary particle and heavy ion physics, plasma physics, optical physics, astrophysics.

University of California, San Diego, Office of Graduate Studies, Department of Physics, La Jolla, CA 92093. Offers biophysics (MS, PhD); physics (MS, PhD); physics/materials physics (MS). *Degree requirements:* For doctorate, thesis/dissertation. *Entrance requirements:* For master's and doctorate, GRE General Test, GRE Subject Test. Additional exam requirements/recommendations for international students: Required—TOEFL. Electronic applications accepted.

University of California, Santa Barbara, Graduate Division, College of Letters and Sciences, Division of Mathematics, Life, and Physical Sciences, Department of Physics, Santa Barbara, CA 93106-9530. Offers PhD, MA/PhD. *Faculty:* 73 full-time (5 women), 1 part-time/adjunct (0 women). *Students:* 135 full-time (20 women). Average age 26. 513 applicants, 20% accepted, 25 enrolled. In 2009, 14 doctorates awarded. *Degree requirements:* For doctorate, comprehensive exam, thesis/dissertation. *Entrance requirements:* For doctorate, GRE General Test, GRE Subject Test (physics), 3 letters of recommendation, resume/curriculum vitae. Additional exam requirements/recommendations for international students: Required—TOEFL (minimum score 550 paper-based; 213 computer-based; 80 iBT) or IELTS (minimum score 7). *Application deadline:* For fall admission, 12/15 priority date for domestic and international students. Application fee: $70 ($90 for international students). Electronic applications accepted. *Financial support:* In 2009–10, 129 students received support, including 37 fellowships with full and partial tuition reimbursements available (averaging $14,300 per year), 81 research assistantships with full and partial tuition reimbursements available (averaging $10,500 per year), 69 teaching assistantships with partial tuition reimbursements available (averaging $8,000 per year); career-related internships or fieldwork, Federal Work-Study, institutionally sponsored loans, scholarships/grants, health care benefits, tuition waivers (full and partial), and unspecified assistantships also available. Financial award application deadline: 12/15; financial award applicants required to submit FAFSA. *Faculty research:* High energy theory/experimental physics, condensed matter theory/experimental physics, astrophysics, biophysics, gravity and relativity. Total annual research expenditures: $6.9 million. *Unit head:* Prof. Mark Srednicki, Chair, 805-893-2165, Fax: 805-893-3307, E-mail: mark@physics.ucsb.edu. *Application contact:* Prof. John Martinis, Admissions Chair, 805-893-3910, Fax: 805-893-3307, E-mail: martinis@physics.ucsb.edu.

University of California, Santa Cruz, Division of Graduate Studies, Division of Physical and Biological Sciences, Department of Physics, Santa Cruz, CA 95064. Offers MS, PhD. *Degree requirements:* For master's, thesis; for doctorate, one foreign language, thesis/dissertation, qualifying exam. *Entrance requirements:* For master's and doctorate, GRE General Test, GRE Subject Test. Electronic applications accepted. *Faculty research:* Theoretical and experimental high-energy physics, theoretical and experimental solid-state physics, critical phenomena, theoretical fluid dynamics, experimental biophysics.

University of Central Florida, College of Sciences, Department of Physics, Orlando, FL 32816. Offers MS, PhD. Part-time and evening/weekend programs available. *Faculty:* 32 full-time (6 women). *Students:* 71 full-time (12 women), 5 part-time (2 women); includes 5 minority (1 Asian American or Pacific Islander, 4 Hispanic Americans), 49 international. Average age 30. 79 applicants, 66% accepted, 18 enrolled. In 2009, 4 master's, 1 doctorate awarded. *Degree requirements:* For master's, thesis or alternative; for doctorate, thesis/dissertation, candidacy and qualifying exams. *Entrance requirements:* For master's, GRE General Test, minimum GPA of 3.0 in last 60 hours of course work; for doctorate, GRE General Test, GRE Subject Test, minimum GPA of 3.0 in last 60 hours or master's qualifying exam. Additional exam requirements/recommendations for international students: Required—TOEFL. *Application deadline:* For fall admission, 2/15 priority date for domestic students. Application fee: $30. Electronic applications accepted. *Expenses:* Tuition, state resident: part-time $306.31 per credit hour. Tuition, nonresident: part-time $1099.01 per credit hour. Part-time tuition and fees vary according to degree level and program. *Financial support:* In 2009–10, 58 students received support, including 9 fellowships with partial tuition reimbursements available (averaging $2,900 per year), 40 research assistantships with partial tuition reimbursements available (averaging $11,800 per year), 29 teaching assistantships with partial tuition reimbursements available (averaging $12,500 per year); career-related internships or fieldwork, Federal Work-Study, institutionally sponsored loans, tuition waivers (partial), and unspecified assistantships also available. Financial award application deadline: 3/1; financial award applicants required to submit FAFSA. *Faculty research:* Atomic-molecular physics, condensed-matter physics, biophysics of proteins, laser physics. *Unit head:* Dr. Talat Rahman, Chair, 407-823-5785, E-mail: trahman@mail.ucf.edu. *Application contact:* Dr. Talat Rahman, Chair, 407-823-5785, E-mail: trahman@mail.ucf.edu.

University of Central Oklahoma, College of Graduate Studies and Research, College of Mathematics and Science, Department of Physics and Engineering, Edmond, OK 73034-5209. Offers MS. Part-time programs available. *Degree requirements:* For master's, thesis optional. *Entrance requirements:* For master's, 24 hours of course work in physics. Additional exam requirements/recommendations for international students: Required—TOEFL (minimum score 550 paper-based; 213 computer-based). Electronic applications accepted. *Faculty research:* Acoustics, solid-state physics/optical properties, molecular dynamics, nuclear physics, crystallography.

University of Chicago, Division of the Physical Sciences, Department of Physics, Chicago, IL 60637-1513. Offers PhD. *Faculty:* 43 full-time (5 women), 5 part-time/adjunct (1 woman). *Students:* 127 full-time (19 women); includes 7 minority (1 African American, 5 Asian Americans or Pacific Islanders, 1 Hispanic American), 51 international. 476 applicants, 20% accepted, 24 enrolled. In 2009, 20 doctorates awarded. *Degree requirements:* For doctorate, comprehensive exam, thesis/dissertation. *Entrance requirements:* For doctorate, bachelor's degree in physics or related area. Additional exam requirements/recommendations for international students: Required—TOEFL (minimum score 102 iBT). *Application deadline:* For fall admission, 12/28 for domestic and international students. Applications are processed on a rolling basis. Application fee: $55. *Financial support:* In 2009–10, 30 fellowships with tuition reimbursements (averaging $27,000 per year), 34 research assistantships with tuition reimbursements (averaging $29,000 per year), 33 teaching assistantships with tuition reimbursements (averaging $22,000 per year) were awarded; health care benefits and unspecified assistantships also available. Financial award application deadline: 12/28. *Unit head:* Nobuko McNeill, Assistant to the Chairman for Graduate Affairs, 773-702-7007, Fax: 773-702-2045, E-mail: n-mcneill@uchicago.edu. *Application contact:* Nobuko McNeill, Assistant to the Chairman for Graduate Affairs, 773-702-7007, Fax: 773-702-2045, E-mail: n-mcneill@uchicago.edu.

University of Chicago, Division of the Physical Sciences, Program in the Physical Sciences, Chicago, IL 60637-1513. Offers MS. Part-time programs available. *Degree requirements:* For master's, thesis. *Entrance requirements:* For master's, GRE. Additional exam requirements/recommendations for international students: Required—TOEFL.

University of Cincinnati, Graduate School, McMicken College of Arts and Sciences, Department of Physics, Cincinnati, OH 45221. Offers MS, PhD. Terminal master's awarded for partial completion of doctoral program. *Degree requirements:* For master's, thesis optional; for doctorate, thesis/dissertation. *Entrance requirements:* For master's and doctorate, GRE General Test, GRE Subject Test. Additional exam requirements/recommendations for international students: Required—TOEFL (minimum score 540 paper-based; 207 computer-based). Electronic applications accepted. *Faculty research:* Condensed matter physics, experimental particle physics, theoretical high energy physics, astronomy and astrophysics, computational physics.

University of Colorado at Boulder, Graduate School, College of Arts and Sciences, Department of Physics, Boulder, CO 80309. Offers chemical physics (PhD); geophysics (PhD); liquid crystal science and technology (PhD); mathematical physics (PhD); medical physics (PhD); optical sciences and engineering (PhD); physics (MS, PhD). *Faculty:* 48 full-time (6 women). *Students:* 160 full-time (24 women), 47 part-time (8 women); includes 9 minority (6 Asian

Physics

University of Colorado at Boulder (continued)
Americans or Pacific Islanders, 3 Hispanic Americans), 65 international. Average age 27. 548 applicants, 5% accepted, 27 enrolled. In 2009, 17 master's, 23 doctorates awarded. Terminal master's awarded for partial completion of doctoral program. *Degree requirements:* For master's, comprehensive exam, thesis or alternative; for doctorate, comprehensive exam, thesis/dissertation. *Entrance requirements:* For master's and doctorate, GRE General Test, GRE Subject Test, minimum undergraduate GPA of 3.0. Additional exam requirements/recommendations for international students: Required—TOEFL. *Application deadline:* For fall admission, 1/15 priority date for domestic students, 1/15 for international students. Applications are processed on a rolling basis. Application fee: $50 ($60 for international students). Electronic applications accepted. *Financial support:* In 2009–10, 21 fellowships with full tuition reimbursements (averaging $15,999 per year), 146 research assistantships with full tuition reimbursements (averaging $16,586 per year) were awarded; scholarships/grants also available. Financial award application deadline: 1/15. *Faculty research:* Atomic and molecular physics, nuclear physics, condensed matter, elementary particle physics, laser or optical physics, plasma physics, geophysics, astrophysics and chemical physics. Total annual research expenditures: $14.2 million.

University of Colorado at Colorado Springs, Graduate School, College of Letters, Arts and Sciences, Master of Sciences Program, Colorado Springs, CO 80933-7150. Offers applied science—bioscience (M Sc); applied science—physics (M Sc); biology (M Sc); chemistry (M Sc); physics (M Sc). Part-time programs available. *Faculty:* 39 full-time (14 women), 2 part-time/adjunct (0 women). *Students:* 19 full-time (6 women), 14 part-time (6 women); includes 5 minority (2 Asian Americans or Pacific Islanders, 3 Hispanic Americans). Average age 31. 29 applicants, 52% accepted, 11 enrolled. In 2009, 8 master's awarded. *Degree requirements:* For master's, thesis or alternative. *Entrance requirements:* For master's, minimum GPA of 2.75. *Application deadline:* For fall admission, 7/1 priority date for domestic students; for spring admission, 12/1 for domestic students. Application fee: $60 ($75 for international students). *Expenses:* Contact institution. *Financial support:* Fellowships, research assistantships, teaching assistantships, career-related internships or fieldwork, Federal Work-Study, and scholarships/grants available. Support available to part-time students. Financial award application deadline: 3/1; financial award applicants required to submit FAFSA. *Faculty research:* Biomechanics and physiology of elite athletic training, genetic engineering in yeast and bacteria including phage display and DNA repair, immunology and cell biology, synthetic organic chemistry. *Unit head:* Dr. Sandra Berry-Lowe, Director, 719-255-7552, Fax: 719-255-3047. *Application contact:* Michael Sanderson, Information Contact, 719-255-3417, Fax: 719-255-3037, E-mail: gradschl@uccs.edu.

University of Connecticut, Graduate School, College of Liberal Arts and Sciences, Department of Physics, Storrs, CT 06269. Offers MS, PhD. *Faculty:* 41 full-time (3 women). *Students:* 80 full-time (10 women), 3 part-time (0 women); includes 5 minority (1 African American, 2 Asian Americans or Pacific Islanders, 2 Hispanic Americans), 36 international. Average age 29. 109 applicants, 10% accepted, 10 enrolled. In 2009, 16 master's, 4 doctorates awarded. *Degree requirements:* For master's, comprehensive exam; for doctorate, thesis/dissertation. *Entrance requirements:* For master's and doctorate, GRE General Test, GRE Subject Test. Additional exam requirements/recommendations for international students: Required—TOEFL (minimum score 550 paper-based; 213 computer-based). *Application deadline:* For fall admission, 2/1 priority date for domestic and international students; for spring admission, 11/1 for domestic students, 10/1 for international students. Applications are processed on a rolling basis. Application fee: $55. Electronic applications accepted. *Expenses:* Tuition, state resident: full-time $4725; part-time $525 per credit. Tuition, nonresident: full-time $12,267; part-time $1363 per credit. Required fees: $346 per semester. Tuition and fees vary according to course load. *Financial support:* In 2009–10, 47 research assistantships with full tuition reimbursements, 32 teaching assistantships with full tuition reimbursements were awarded; fellowships, Federal Work-Study, scholarships/grants, health care benefits, and unspecified assistantships also available. Financial award application deadline: 2/1; financial award applicants required to submit FAFSA. *Unit head:* William C. Stwalley, Head, 860-486-4924, Fax: 860-486-3346, E-mail: w.stwalley@uconn.edu. *Application contact:* Gerald Dunne, Chairperson, 860-486-4978, E-mail: gerald.dunne@uconn.edu.

University of Delaware, College of Arts and Sciences, Department of Physics and Astronomy, Newark, DE 19716. Offers MS, PhD. Part-time programs available. Terminal master's awarded for partial completion of doctoral program. *Degree requirements:* For master's, thesis; for doctorate, thesis/dissertation. *Entrance requirements:* For master's and doctorate, GRE General Test, GRE Subject Test. Additional exam requirements/recommendations for international students: Required—TOEFL (minimum score 600 paper-based; 250 computer-based). Electronic applications accepted. *Faculty research:* Magnetoresistance and magnetic materials, ultrafast optical phenomena, superfluidity, elementary particle physics, stellar atmospheres and interiors.

University of Denver, Faculty of Natural Sciences and Mathematics, Department of Physics and Astronomy, Denver, CO 80208. Offers MS, PhD. Part-time programs available. *Faculty:* 9 full-time (2 women), 1 part-time/adjunct (0 women). *Students:* 4 full-time (2 women), 10 part-time (3 women); includes 1 minority (Hispanic American), 2 international. Average age 28. 23 applicants, 65% accepted, 4 enrolled. In 2009, 1 master's awarded. Terminal master's awarded for partial completion of doctoral program. *Degree requirements:* For master's, thesis optional; for doctorate, thesis/dissertation. *Entrance requirements:* For master's and doctorate, GRE General Test, diagnostic exam. Additional exam requirements/recommendations for international students: Required—TOEFL. *Application deadline:* Applications are processed on a rolling basis. Application fee: $50. Electronic applications accepted. *Expenses:* Tuition: Full-time $34,596; part-time $961 per quarter hour. Required fees: $4 per quarter hour. Tuition and fees vary according to course load, campus/location and program. *Financial support:* In 2009–10, 9 research assistantships with full and partial tuition reimbursements (averaging $18,000 per year), 9 teaching assistantships with full and partial tuition reimbursements (averaging $18,000 per year) were awarded; career-related internships or fieldwork, Federal Work-Study, institutionally sponsored loans, and scholarships/grants also available. Support available to part-time students. Financial award application deadline: 3/1; financial award applicants required to submit FAFSA. *Faculty research:* Atomic and molecular beams and collisions, infrared astronomy, acoustic emission from stressed solids, nano materials. Total annual research expenditures: $1.1 million. *Unit head:* Dr. Davor Balzar, Chair, 303-871-2238. *Application contact:* Information Contact, 303-871-2238, E-mail: bstephen@du.edu.

University of Florida, Graduate School, College of Liberal Arts and Sciences, Department of Physics, Gainesville, FL 32611. Offers MS, MST, PhD. *Degree requirements:* For master's, variable foreign language requirement, thesis (for some programs); for doctorate, one foreign language, thesis/dissertation. *Entrance requirements:* For master's and doctorate, GRE General Test, minimum GPA of 3.0. Additional exam requirements/recommendations for international students: Required—TOEFL (minimum score 550 paper-based; 213 computer-based). Electronic applications accepted. *Faculty research:* Astrophysics, condensed-matter physics, elementary particle physics, statistical mechanics, quantum theory.

University of Georgia, Graduate School, College of Arts and Sciences, Department of Physics and Astronomy, Athens, GA 30602. Offers physics (MS, PhD). *Faculty:* 22 full-time (2 women). *Students:* 49 full-time (11 women), 3 part-time (2 women); includes 1 minority (African American), 26 international. 110 applicants, 16% accepted, 12 enrolled. In 2009, 9 doctorates awarded. *Degree requirements:* For master's, thesis; for doctorate, one foreign language, thesis/dissertation. *Entrance requirements:* For master's and doctorate, GRE General Test. *Application deadline:* For fall admission, 7/1 priority date for domestic students; for spring admission, 11/15 for domestic students. Application fee: $50. Electronic applications accepted. *Expenses:* Tuition, state resident: full-time $6000; part-time $250 per credit hour. Tuition, nonresident: full-time $20,904; part-time $871 per credit hour. Required fees: $730 per semester. *Financial support:* Fellowships, research assistantships, teaching assistantships, unspecified assistantships available. *Unit head:* Dr. William M. Dennis, Head, 706-542-2485, Fax: 706-542-2492, E-mail: bill@physast.uga.edu. *Application contact:* Dr. Loris Magnani, Graduate Coordinator, 706-542-2876, Fax: 706-542-2492, E-mail: loris@physast.uga.edu.

University of Guelph, Graduate Program Services, College of Physical and Engineering Science, Guelph-Waterloo Physics Institute, Guelph, ON N1G 2W1, Canada. Offers M Sc, PhD. Part-time programs available. *Degree requirements:* For master's, project or thesis; for doctorate, comprehensive exam, thesis/dissertation. *Entrance requirements:* For master's, GRE Subject Test, minimum B average for honors degree; for doctorate, GRE Subject Test, minimum B average. Additional exam requirements/recommendations for international students: Required—TOEFL (minimum score 550 paper-based; 213 computer-based), TWE (minimum score 4). *Faculty research:* Condensed matter and material physics, quantum computing, astrophysics and gravitation, industrial and applied physics, subatomic physics.

University of Hawaii at Manoa, Graduate Division, College of Natural Sciences, Department of Physics and Astronomy, Program in Physics, Honolulu, HI 96822. Offers MS, PhD. Part-time programs available. *Faculty:* 24 full-time (1 woman), 4 part-time/adjunct (0 women). *Students:* 23 full-time (2 women), 2 part-time (0 women); includes 5 minority (1 African American, 2 Asian Americans or Pacific Islanders, 2 Hispanic Americans), 4 international. Average age 28. 40 applicants, 45% accepted, 3 enrolled. In 2009, 4 master's awarded. *Degree requirements:* For master's, thesis optional; for doctorate, comprehensive exam, thesis/dissertation. *Entrance requirements:* For master's and doctorate, GRE General Test. Additional exam requirements/recommendations for international students: Required—TOEFL (minimum score 560 paper-based; 220 computer-based; 83 iBT), IELTS (minimum score 5). *Application deadline:* For fall admission, 1/15 for domestic and international students; for spring admission, 8/1 for domestic and international students. Application fee: $60. *Expenses:* Tuition, state resident: full-time $8900; part-time $372 per credit. Tuition, nonresident: full-time $21,400; part-time $898 per credit. Required fees: $207 per semester. *Financial support:* In 2009–10, 1 student received support, including 4 fellowships (averaging $1,413 per year), 12 research assistantships (averaging $19,416 per year), 12 teaching assistantships (averaging $16,303 per year). Total annual research expenditures: $2.5 million. *Application contact:* Pui K Lam, Graduate Chairperson, 808-956-7087, Fax: 808-956-7107, E-mail: plam@hawaii.edu.

University of Houston, College of Natural Sciences and Mathematics, Department of Physics, Houston, TX 77204. Offers MA, MS, PhD. Part-time programs available. *Faculty:* 21 full-time (2 women), 6 part-time/adjunct (1 woman). *Students:* 82 full-time (27 women), 16 part-time (7 women); includes 5 minority (4 Asian Americans or Pacific Islanders, 1 Hispanic American), 70 international. Average age 29. 27 applicants, 100% accepted, 24 enrolled. In 2009, 8 master's, 6 doctorates awarded. Terminal master's awarded for partial completion of doctoral program. *Degree requirements:* For doctorate, thesis/dissertation. *Entrance requirements:* For master's and doctorate, GRE General Test. Additional exam requirements/recommendations for international students: Required—TOEFL. *Application deadline:* For fall admission, 7/1 for domestic students; for spring admission, 11/1 for domestic students. Applications are processed on a rolling basis. Application fee: $0 ($75 for international students). Electronic applications accepted. *Expenses:* Tuition, state resident: full-time $7676; part-time $320 per credit hour. Tuition, nonresident: full-time $14,324; part-time $597 per credit hour. Required fees: $3034. *Financial support:* In 2009–10, 2 fellowships with full tuition reimbursements (averaging $14,300 per year), 32 research assistantships with full tuition reimbursements (averaging $14,300 per year), 28 teaching assistantships with full tuition reimbursements (averaging $15,300 per year) were awarded; career-related internships or fieldwork, Federal Work-Study, institutionally sponsored loans, scholarships/grants, health care benefits, and unspecified assistantships also available. Support available to part-time students. Financial award application deadline: 2/1. *Faculty research:* Condensed-matter, particle physics; high-temperature superconductivity; material/space physics; chaos. *Unit head:* Dr. Lawrence Pinsky, Chairman, 713-743-3552, Fax: 713-743-3589, E-mail: pinsky@uh.edu. *Application contact:* Dr. Lawrence Pinsky, Chairman, 713-743-3552, Fax: 713-743-3589, E-mail: pinsky@uh.edu.

University of Houston–Clear Lake, School of Science and Computer Engineering, Program in Physics, Houston, TX 77058-1098. Offers MS. Part-time and evening/weekend programs available. *Entrance requirements:* For master's, GRE General Test. Additional exam requirements/recommendations for international students: Required—TOEFL (minimum score 550 paper-based; 213 computer-based).

University of Idaho, College of Graduate Studies, College of Science, Department of Physics, Moscow, ID 83844-2282. Offers MS, PhD. *Faculty:* 7 full-time, 1 part-time/adjunct. *Students:* 27 full-time, 3 part-time. In 2009, 5 master's, 1 doctorate awarded. *Degree requirements:* For master's, thesis; for doctorate, thesis/dissertation. *Entrance requirements:* For master's, GRE, minimum GPA of 2.8; for doctorate, GRE, minimum undergraduate GPA of 2.8, 3.0 graduate. *Application deadline:* For fall admission, 8/1 for domestic students; for spring admission, 12/15 for domestic students. Application fee: $55 ($60 for international students). *Expenses:* Tuition, state resident: full-time $6120. Tuition, nonresident: full-time $17,712. *Financial support:* Research assistantships, teaching assistantships available. Financial award application deadline: 2/15. *Faculty research:* Condensed matter physics, nuclear physics, biological physics, astronomy/planetary science. *Unit head:* Dr. Wei Jiang Yeh, Chair, 208-885-6380. *Application contact:* Dr. Wei Jiang Yeh, Chair, 208-885-6380.

University of Illinois at Chicago, Graduate College, College of Liberal Arts and Sciences, Department of Physics, Chicago, IL 60607-7128. Offers MS, PhD. Terminal master's awarded for partial completion of doctoral program. *Degree requirements:* For doctorate, thesis/dissertation. *Entrance requirements:* For master's and doctorate, GRE General Test, minimum GPA of 3.0. Additional exam requirements/recommendations for international students: Required—TOEFL. Electronic applications accepted. *Faculty research:* High-energy, laser, and solid-state physics.

University of Illinois at Urbana–Champaign, Graduate College, College of Engineering, Department of Physics, Champaign, IL 61820. Offers physics (MS, PhD); teaching of physics (MS). *Faculty:* 56 full-time (6 women), 1 part-time/adjunct (0 women). *Students:* 195 full-time (25 women), 80 part-time (12 women); includes 21 minority (2 African Americans, 15 Asian Americans or Pacific Islanders, 4 Hispanic Americans), 136 international. 582 applicants, 5% accepted, 27 enrolled. In 2009, 16 master's, 33 doctorates awarded. *Entrance requirements:* For master's, GRE, minimum GPA of 3.0; for doctorate, GRE, minimum GPA of 3.5. Additional exam requirements/recommendations for international students: Required—TOEFL (minimum score 550 paper-based; 213 computer-based; 79 iBT), or IELTS (minimum score 6.5). *Application deadline:* Applications are processed on a rolling basis. Application fee: $60 ($75 for international students). Electronic applications accepted. *Financial support:* In 2009–10, 18 fellowships, 185 research assistantships, 133 teaching assistantships were awarded; tuition waivers (full and partial) also available. *Unit head:* Dale J. VanHarlingen, Head, 217-333-3760, Fax: 217-244-4293, E-mail: dvh@illinois.edu. *Application contact:* Melodee Jo Schweighart, Office Manager, 217-333-3645, Fax: 217-244-5073, E-mail: mschweig@illinois.edu.

The University of Iowa, Graduate College, College of Liberal Arts and Sciences, Department of Physics and Astronomy, Program in Physics, Iowa City, IA 52242-1316. Offers MS, PhD. *Degree requirements:* For master's, thesis optional, exam; for doctorate, comprehensive exam, thesis/dissertation. *Entrance requirements:* For master's and doctorate, GRE General Test, minimum GPA of 3.0. Additional exam requirements/recommendations for international students: Required—TOEFL (minimum score 550 paper-based; 213 computer-based; 81 iBT). Electronic applications accepted.

The University of Kansas, Graduate Studies, College of Liberal Arts and Sciences, Department of Physics and Astronomy, Lawrence, KS 66045. Offers computational physics and astronomy (MS); physics (MS, PhD). *Students:* 40 full-time (7 women), 3 part-time (1 woman); includes 3 minority (1 African American, 2 Hispanic Americans), 13 international. Average age 28. 47 applicants, 26% accepted, 6 enrolled. In 2009, 12 master's, 6 doctorates awarded. *Degree requirements:* For master's, thesis (for some programs); for doctorate, comprehensive exam, thesis/dissertation, computer skills, undergraduate certification, communication skills. *Entrance requirements:* For master's and doctorate, GRE Subject Test (physics), undergraduate degree. Additional exam requirements/recommendations for international students: Required—TOEFL. *Application deadline:* For fall admission, 5/1 priority date for domestic and international students; for spring admission, 11/15 for domestic and international students. Applications are processed on a rolling basis. Application fee: $45 ($55 for international students). Electronic applications accepted. *Expenses:* Tuition, state resident: full-time $6492; part-time $270.50 per credit hour. Tuition, nonresident: full-time $15,510; part-time $646.25 per credit hour. Required fees: $847; $70.56 per credit hour. Tuition and fees vary according to course load and program. *Financial support:* Fellowships with full and partial tuition reimbursements, research assistantships with full and partial tuition reimbursements, teaching assistantships with full and partial tuition reimbursements, health care benefits and unspecified assistantships available. Financial award application deadline: 5/1. *Faculty research:* Condensed-matter, cosmology, elementary particles, nuclear physics, space physics, astrophysics, astrobiology, biophysics, high energy. *Unit head:* Dr. Stephen J. Sanders, Chair, 785-864-4626, Fax: 785-864-5262. *Application contact:* Tess Gratton, Graduate Admission Specialist, 785-864-4626, Fax: 785-864-5262, E-mail: physics@ku.edu.

See Close-Up on page 231 and Display on this page.

University of Kentucky, Graduate School, College of Arts and Sciences, Program in Physics and Astronomy, Lexington, KY 40506-0032. Offers physics (MS, PhD). *Degree requirements:* For master's, comprehensive exam, thesis optional; for doctorate, comprehensive exam, thesis/dissertation. *Entrance requirements:* For master's, GRE General Test, minimum undergraduate GPA of 2.75; for doctorate, GRE General Test, minimum graduate GPA of 3.0. Additional exam requirements/recommendations for international students: Required—TOEFL (minimum score 550 paper-based; 213 computer-based). Electronic applications accepted. *Faculty research:* Astrophysics, active galactic nuclei, and radio astronomy; Rydbert atoms, and electron scattering; TOF spectroscopy, hyperon interactions and muons; particle theory, lattice gauge theory, quark, and skyrmion models.

University of Lethbridge, School of Graduate Studies, Lethbridge, AB T1K 3M4, Canada. Offers accounting (MScM); addictions counseling (M Sc), agricultural biotechnology (M Sc); agricultural studies (M Sc, MA); anthropology (MA); archaeology (MA); art (MA, MFA); biochemistry (M Sc); biological sciences (M Sc); biomolecular science (PhD); biosystems and biodiversity (PhD); Canadian studies (MA); chemistry (M Sc); computer science (M Sc); computer science and geographical information science (M Sc); counseling psychology (M Ed); dramatic arts (MA); earth, space, and physical science (PhD); economics (MA); educational leadership (M Ed); English (MA); environmental science (M Sc); evolution and behavior (PhD); exercise science (M Sc); finance (MScM); French (MA); French/German (MA); French/Spanish (MA); general education (M Ed); general management (MScM); geography (M Sc, MA); German (MA); health science (M Sc); health sciences (MA); history (MA); human resource management and labour relations (MScM); individualized multidisciplinary (M Sc, MA); information systems (MScM); international management (MScM); kinesiology (M Sc, MA); management (M Sc, MA); marketing (MScM); mathematics (M Sc); music (M Mus, MA); Native American studies (MA); neuroscience (M Sc, PhD); new media (MA); nursing (M Sc); philosophy (MA); physics (M Sc); policy and strategy (MScM); political science (MA); psychology (M Sc, MA); religious studies (MA); social sciences (MA); sociology (MA); theatre and dramatic arts (MFA); theoretical and computational science (PhD); urban and regional studies (MA); women's studies (MA). Part-time and evening/weekend programs available. *Degree requirements:* For doctorate, comprehensive exam, thesis/dissertation. *Entrance requirements:* For master's, GMAT (M Sc in management), bachelor's degree in related field, minimum GPA of 3.0 during previous 20 graded semester courses, 2 years teaching or related experience (M Ed); for doctorate, master's degree, minimum graduate GPA of 3.5. Additional exam requirements/recommendations for international students: Required—TOEFL. *Faculty research:* Movement and brain plasticity, gibberellin physiology, photosynthesis, carbon cycling, molecular properties of main-group ring components.

University of Louisiana at Lafayette, College of Sciences, Department of Physics, Lafayette, LA 70504. Offers MS. Part-time programs available. *Degree requirements:* For master's, thesis. *Entrance requirements:* For master's, GRE General Test, minimum GPA of 2.75. Additional exam requirements/recommendations for international students: Required—TOEFL (minimum score 550 paper-based; 213 computer-based). Electronic applications accepted. *Faculty research:* Environmental physics, geophysics, astrophysics, acoustics, atomic physics.

University of Louisville, Graduate School, College of Arts and Sciences, Department of Physics and Astronomy, Louisville, KY 40292. Offers physics (MS, PhD). Part-time programs available. *Faculty:* 17 full-time (2 women), 8 part-time/adjunct (0 women). *Students:* 19 full-time (4 women), 2 part-time (0 women), 6 international. Average age 32. 32 applicants, 41% accepted, 10 enrolled. In 2009, 4 master's awarded. Terminal master's awarded for partial completion of doctoral program. *Degree requirements:* For master's, thesis optional; for doctorate, comprehensive exam, thesis/dissertation. *Entrance requirements:* For master's, GRE General Test. Additional exam requirements/recommendations for international students: Required—TOEFL (minimum score 550 paper-based; 213 computer-based; 80 iBT). *Application deadline:* For fall admission, 3/1 priority date for domestic and international students. Applications are processed on a rolling basis. Application fee: $50. Electronic applications accepted. *Financial support:* In 2009–10, 19 students received support; fellowships, research assistantships, teaching assistantships available. *Faculty research:* Condensed matter physics; atmospheric science; high energy physics; astrophysics; atomic, molecular, and optical physics. *Unit head:* Dr. David N. Brown, Professor/Chair, 502-852-6790, Fax: 502-852-0742, E-mail: d.n.brown@louisville.edu. *Application contact:* Dr. Chris L. Davis, Professor of Physics, 502-852-0852, Fax: 502-852-0742, E-mail: c.l.davis@louisville.edu.

University of Maine, Graduate School, College of Liberal Arts and Sciences, Department of Physics and Astronomy, Orono, ME 04469. Offers engineering physics (M Eng); physics (MS, PhD). *Faculty:* 13 full-time (1 woman), 4 part-time/adjunct (2 women). *Students:* 19 full-time (2 women), 18 part-time (4 women); includes 2 minority (1 Asian American or Pacific Islander, 1 Hispanic American), 6 international. Average age 29. 18 applicants, 39% accepted, 4 enrolled. In 2009, 2 doctorates awarded. Terminal master's awarded for partial completion of doctoral program. *Degree requirements:* For doctorate, thesis/dissertation. *Entrance requirements:* For master's, GRE General Test, GRE Subject Test; for doctorate, GRE General Test. Additional exam requirements/recommendations for international students: Required—TOEFL. *Application deadline:* For fall admission, 2/1 priority date for domestic students. Applications are processed on a rolling basis. Application fee: $65. Electronic applications accepted. *Financial support:* In 2009–10, 5 research assistantships with tuition reimbursements (averaging $14,842 per year), 15 teaching assistantships with tuition reimbursements (averaging $13,815 per year) were awarded; tuition waivers (full and partial) also available. Financial award application deadline: 3/1. *Faculty research:* Solid-state physics, fluids, biophysics, plasma physics, surface physics. *Unit head:* Dr. Susan McKay, Chair, 207-581-1015, Fax: 207-581-3410. *Application contact:* Scott G. Delcourt, Associate Dean of the Graduate School, 207-581-3291, Fax: 207-581-3232, E-mail: graduate@maine.edu.

University of Manitoba, Faculty of Graduate Studies, Faculty of Science, Department of Physics and Astronomy, Winnipeg, MB R3T 2N2, Canada. Offers M Sc, PhD. *Degree requirements:* For master's, thesis; for doctorate, one foreign language, thesis/dissertation.

Physics

University of Maryland, Baltimore County, Graduate School, College of Arts, Humanities and Social Sciences, Department of Education, Program in Teaching, Baltimore, MD 21250. Offers early childhood education (MAT); elementary education (MAT); secondary education (MAT), including art, biology, chemistry, dance, earth/space science, English, foreign language, mathematics, music, physics, theatre; secondary science (MAT), including social studies. Part-time and evening/weekend programs available. *Faculty:* 24 full-time (18 women), 25 part-time/adjunct (19 women). *Students:* 52 full-time (41 women), 64 part-time (55 women); includes 20 minority (5 African Americans, 1 American Indian/Alaska Native, 10 Asian Americans or Pacific Islanders, 4 Hispanic Americans), 3 international. Average age 31. 88 applicants, 57% accepted, 39 enrolled. In 2009, 106 master's awarded. *Degree requirements:* For master's, comprehensive exam (for some programs), thesis (for some programs). *Entrance requirements:* For master's, PRAXIS I and II, minimum GPA of 3.0. Additional exam requirements/recommendations for international students: Required—TOEFL. *Application deadline:* For fall admission, 6/1 for domestic students; for spring admission, 11/1 for domestic students. Applications are processed on a rolling basis. Application fee: $50. Electronic applications accepted. *Financial support:* In 2009–10, 6 students received support, including research assistantships with full tuition reimbursements available (averaging $12,000 per year); career-related internships or fieldwork, Federal Work-Study, scholarships/grants, tuition waivers, and unspecified assistantships also available. Financial award application deadline: 3/1. *Faculty research:* STEM teacher education, culturally sensitive pedagogy, ESOL/bilingual education, early childhood education, language, literacy and culture. *Unit head:* Dr. Susan M. Blunck, Director, 410-455-2869, Fax: 410-455-3986, E-mail: blunck@umbc.edu. *Application contact:* Dr. Susan M. Blunck, Director, 410-455-2869, Fax: 410-455-3986, E-mail: blunck@umbc.edu.

University of Maryland, Baltimore County, Graduate School, College of Natural and Mathematical Sciences, Department of Physics, Baltimore, MD 21250. Offers applied physics (MS, PhD), including astrophysics (PhD), optics, quantum optics (PhD), solid state physics; atmospheric physics (MS, PhD). Part-time programs available. *Faculty:* 24 full-time (3 women), 18 part-time/adjunct (2 women). *Students:* 43 full-time (14 women), 3 part-time (0 women); includes 4 minority (all African Americans), 26 international. Average age 24. 33 applicants, 48% accepted, 10 enrolled. In 2009, 6 master's, 5 doctorates awarded. Terminal master's awarded for partial completion of doctoral program. *Degree requirements:* For master's, thesis optional; for doctorate, comprehensive exam, thesis/dissertation. *Entrance requirements:* For master's and doctorate, GRE General Test, GRE Subject Test, minimum GPA of 3.0. Additional exam requirements/recommendations for international students: Required—TOEFL. *Application deadline:* For fall admission, 5/31 for domestic and international students; for spring admission, 11/30 for domestic students. Applications are processed on a rolling basis. Application fee: $50. Electronic applications accepted. *Financial support:* In 2009–10, 42 students received support, including 5 fellowships with full tuition reimbursements available (averaging $30,000 per year), 21 research assistantships with full tuition reimbursements available (averaging $26,000 per year), 16 teaching assistantships with full tuition reimbursements available (averaging $22,000 per year); career-related internships or fieldwork, scholarships/grants, health care benefits, and unspecified assistantships also available. Support available to part-time students. Financial award application deadline: 5/31. *Faculty research:* Quantum optics and computing, optics, astrophysics, atmospheric physics, nanophysics. Total annual research expenditures: $7.5 million. *Unit head:* Dr. L. Michael Hayden, Chairman, 410-455-2513, Fax: 410-455-1072, E-mail: hayden@umbc.edu. *Application contact:* Dr. Lazlo Takacs, Graduate Admissions Director, 410-455-2524, Fax: 410-455-1072, E-mail: takacs@umbc.edu.

University of Maryland, College Park, Academic Affairs, College of Computer, Mathematical and Physical Sciences, Department of Physics, College Park, MD 20742. Offers MS, PhD. Part-time and evening/weekend programs available. *Faculty:* 130 full-time (14 women), 24 part-time/adjunct (4 women). *Students:* 225 full-time (29 women), 6 part-time (2 women); includes 12 minority (3 African Americans, 8 Asian Americans or Pacific Islanders, 1 Hispanic American), 86 international. 640 applicants, 19% accepted, 32 enrolled. In 2009, 5 master's, 25 doctorates awarded. Terminal master's awarded for partial completion of doctoral program. *Degree requirements:* For master's, thesis optional; for doctorate, thesis/dissertation. *Entrance requirements:* For master's, GRE General Test, GRE Subject Test (physics), minimum GPA of 3.0, 3 letters of recommendation; for doctorate, GRE General Test, GRE Subject Test (physics), 3 letters of recommendation. *Application deadline:* For fall admission, 1/15 for domestic and international students. Applications are processed on a rolling basis. Application fee: $60. Electronic applications accepted. *Expenses:* Tuition, area resident: Part-time $471 per credit hour. Tuition, state resident: part-time $471 per credit hour. Tuition, nonresident: part-time $1016 per credit hour. Required fees: $337.04 per term. *Financial support:* In 2009–10, 11 fellowships with full and partial tuition reimbursements (averaging $13,458 per year), 170 research assistantships with tuition reimbursements (averaging $19,475 per year), 57 teaching assistantships with tuition reimbursements (averaging $17,644 per year) were awarded; Federal Work-Study and scholarships/grants also available. Support available to part-time students. Financial award applicants required to submit FAFSA. *Faculty research:* Astrometeorology, superconductivity, particle astrophysics, plasma physics, elementary particle theory. Total annual research expenditures: $22.6 million. *Unit head:* Dr. Drew Baden, Chair, 301-405-5946, Fax: 301-405-0327, E-mail: drew@umd.edu. *Application contact:* Dean of the Graduate School, 301-401-0358.

University of Massachusetts Amherst, Graduate School, College of Natural Sciences, Department of Physics, Amherst, MA 01003. Offers MS, PhD. Part-time programs available. *Faculty:* 39 full-time (4 women). *Students:* 83 full-time (18 women), 1 (woman) part-time; includes 4 minority (1 American Indian/Alaska Native, 3 Hispanic Americans), 54 international. Average age 27. 166 applicants, 30% accepted, 17 enrolled. In 2009, 7 master's, 4 doctorates awarded. Terminal master's awarded for partial completion of doctoral program. *Degree requirements:* For master's, thesis or alternative; for doctorate, comprehensive exam, thesis/dissertation. *Entrance requirements:* For master's and doctorate, GRE General Test, GRE Subject Test (physics). Additional exam requirements/recommendations for international students: Required—TOEFL (minimum score 550 paper-based; 213 computer-based; 80 iBT), IELTS (minimum score 6.5). *Application deadline:* For fall admission, 2/1 for domestic and international students. Applications are processed on a rolling basis. Application fee: $50 ($65 for international students). Electronic applications accepted. *Expenses:* Tuition, state resident: full-time $2640; part-time $110 per credit. Tuition, nonresident: full-time $9936; part-time $414 per credit. Tuition and fees vary according to course load. *Financial support:* In 2009–10, 1 fellowship with full tuition reimbursement (averaging $1,840 per year), 48 research assistantships with full tuition reimbursements (averaging $15,412 per year), 40 teaching assistantships with full tuition reimbursements (averaging $10,070 per year) were awarded; career-related internships or fieldwork, Federal Work-Study, scholarships/grants, traineeships, health care benefits, tuition waivers (full), and unspecified assistantships also available. Support available to part-time students. Financial award application deadline: 2/1. *Unit head:* Dr. Krishna S. Kumar, Graduate Program Director, 413-545-2548, Fax: 413-545-0648. *Application contact:* Jean M. Ames, Supervisor of Admissions, 413-545-0722, Fax: 413-577-0010, E-mail: gradadm@grad.umass.edu.

University of Massachusetts Dartmouth, Graduate School, College of Engineering, Department of Physics, North Dartmouth, MA 02747-2300. Offers MS. Part-time programs available. *Faculty:* 11 full-time (1 woman), 1 part-time/adjunct (0 women). *Students:* 16 full-time (5 women), 4 part-time (0 women); includes 1 minority (Asian American or Pacific Islander), 11 international. Average age 26. 27 applicants, 85% accepted, 9 enrolled. In 2009, 4 master's awarded. *Degree requirements:* For master's, thesis or alternative. *Entrance requirements:* For master's, GRE (for financial consideration), 3 letters of recommendation. Additional exam requirements/recommendations for international students: Required—TOEFL (minimum score 500 paper-based). *Application deadline:* For fall admission, 4/20 priority date for domestic students, 2/20 priority date for international students; for spring admission, 11/15 priority date for domestic students, 9/15 priority date for international students. Applications are processed on a rolling basis. Application fee: $40 ($60 for international students). Electronic applications accepted. *Expenses:* Tuition, state resident: full-time $2071; part-time $86.29 per credit. Tuition, nonresident: full-time $8099; part-time $337.46 per credit. Required fees: $9446. Tuition and fees vary according to class time, course load and reciprocity agreements. *Financial support:* In 2009–10, 7 research assistantships with full tuition reimbursements (averaging $8,154 per year), 8 teaching assistantships with full tuition reimbursements (averaging $12,500 per year) were awarded; Federal Work-Study also available. Support available to part-time students. Financial award application deadline: 3/1; financial award applicants required to submit FAFSA. *Faculty research:* AMO physics, ocean physics, experimental nuclear physics, theoretical particle physics, astrophysics. Total annual research expenditures: $405,000. *Unit head:* Dr. Gaurav Khanna, Director, 508-910-6605, Fax: 508-999-9115, E-mail: gkhanna@umassd.edu. *Application contact:* Elan Turcotte-Shamski, Graduate Admissions Officer, 508-999-8604, Fax: 508-999-8183, E-mail: graduate@umassd.edu.

University of Massachusetts Lowell, College of Arts and Sciences, Department of Physics and Applied Physics, Program in Physics, Lowell, MA 01854-2881. Offers MS, PhD. *Degree requirements:* For master's, thesis; for doctorate, 2 foreign languages, thesis/dissertation. *Entrance requirements:* For master's, GRE General Test, 3 letters of reference; for doctorate, GRE General Test, transcripts, 3 letters of reference. Additional exam requirements/recommendations for international students: Required—TOEFL.

See Close-Up on page 233 and Display on page 205.

University of Memphis, Graduate School, College of Arts and Sciences, Department of Physics, Memphis, TN 38152. Offers MS. Part-time programs available. *Faculty:* 4 full-time (0 women). *Students:* 8 full-time (2 women), 2 part-time (1 woman), 2 international. Average age 32. 9 applicants, 78% accepted, 2 enrolled. In 2009, 6 master's awarded. *Degree requirements:* For master's, comprehensive exam, thesis or alternative. *Entrance requirements:* For master's, GRE General Test or MAT, 20 undergraduate hours of course work in physics. *Application deadline:* For fall admission, 8/1 for domestic students; for spring admission, 12/1 for domestic students. Applications are processed on a rolling basis. Application fee: $35 ($60 for international students). Electronic applications accepted. *Expenses:* Tuition, state resident: full-time $6246; part-time $347 per credit hour. Tuition, nonresident: full-time $15,894; part-time $883 per credit hour. Required fees: $1160. Full-time tuition and fees vary according to course load, degree level and program. *Financial support:* In 2009–10, 5 students received support; research assistantships with full tuition reimbursements available, teaching assistantships with full tuition reimbursements available, Federal Work-Study, institutionally sponsored loans, scholarships/grants, and unspecified assistantships available. Financial award application deadline: 2/15; financial award applicants required to submit FAFSA. *Faculty research:* Solid-state physics, materials science, biophysics, astrophysics, physics education. *Unit head:* Dr. M. Shah Jahan, Chair, 901-678-2620, Fax: 901-678-4733, E-mail: mjahan@memphis.edu. *Application contact:* Dr. Sanjay Mishra, Coordinator of Graduate Studies, 901-678-3115, Fax: 901-678-4733, E-mail: srmishra@memphis.edu.

University of Miami, Graduate School, College of Arts and Sciences, Department of Physics, Coral Gables, FL 33124. Offers MS, PhD. Terminal master's awarded for partial completion of doctoral program. *Degree requirements:* For master's, comprehensive exam; for doctorate, comprehensive exam, thesis/dissertation. *Entrance requirements:* For master's and doctorate, GRE General Test, GRE Subject Test. Additional exam requirements/recommendations for international students: Required—TOEFL (minimum score 550 paper-based; 213 computer-based; 80 iBT). Electronic applications accepted. *Faculty research:* High-energy theory, marine and atmospheric optics, plasma physics, solid-state physics.

University of Michigan, Horace H. Rackham School of Graduate Studies, College of Literature, Science, and the Arts, Department of Physics, Ann Arbor, MI 48109. Offers MS, PhD. *Faculty:* 60 full-time (8 women). *Students:* 110 full-time (24 women); includes 11 minority (4 African Americans, 1 American Indian/Alaska Native, 2 Asian Americans or Pacific Islanders, 4 Hispanic Americans), 42 international. Average age 28. 402 applicants, 21% accepted, 21 enrolled. In 2009, 11 master's, 15 doctorates awarded. Terminal master's awarded for partial completion of doctoral program. *Degree requirements:* For doctorate, thesis/dissertation, oral defense of dissertation, preliminary exam. *Entrance requirements:* For master's and doctorate, GRE General Test. Additional exam requirements/recommendations for international students: Required—TOEFL (minimum score 600 paper-based; 250 computer-based; 100 iBT). *Application deadline:* For fall admission, 1/15 for domestic students, 12/8 for international students. Application fee: $60 ($75 for international students). Electronic applications accepted. *Expenses:* Tuition, state resident: full-time $17,286; part-time $1099 per credit hour. Tuition, nonresident: full-time $34,944; part-time $2080 per credit hour. Required fees: $95 per semester. Tuition and fees vary according to course load, degree level and program. *Financial support:* In 2009–10, 25,041 fellowships with full tuition reimbursements (averaging $24,600 per year), research assistantships with full tuition reimbursements (averaging $22,797 per year), 20,867 teaching assistantships with full tuition reimbursements (averaging $22,797 per year) were awarded. *Faculty research:* Elementary particle, solid-state, atomic, and molecular physics (theoretical and experimental). Total annual research expenditures: $12 million. *Unit head:* Dr. Bradford Orr, Chair, 734-764-4437. *Application contact:* Christina A. Zigulis, Graduate Coordinator, 734-936-0658, Fax: 734-763-9694, E-mail: physics.inquiries@umich.edu.

University of Minnesota, Duluth, Graduate School, Swenson College of Science and Engineering, Department of Physics, Duluth, MN 55812-2496. Offers MS. Part-time programs available. *Faculty:* 7 full-time (0 women), 1 part-time/adjunct (0 women). *Students:* 10 full-time (0 women); includes 1 minority (African American), 7 international. Average age 27. 15 applicants, 53% accepted, 7 enrolled. In 2009, 3 master's awarded. *Degree requirements:* For master's, thesis optional, final oral exam. *Entrance requirements:* For master's, GPA of 3.0 or better preferred. Additional exam requirements/recommendations for international students: Required—TOEFL (minimum score 550 paper-based; 213 computer-based; 79 iBT), IELTS (minimum score 6.5), TOEFL, IELTS, or MELAB (minimum score 80). *Application deadline:* For fall admission, 7/15 for domestic and international students; for spring admission, 11/1 for domestic and international students. Applications are processed on a rolling basis. Application fee: $75 ($95 for international students). Electronic applications accepted. *Financial support:* In 2009–10, 10 students received support, including 2 fellowships (averaging $3,000 per year), 1 research assistantship with full tuition reimbursement available (averaging $13,100 per year), 9 teaching assistantships with full tuition reimbursements available (averaging $13,100 per year); Federal Work-Study, institutionally sponsored loans, scholarships/grants, health care benefits, and unspecified assistantships also available. Support available to part-time students. Financial award application deadline: 3/15. *Faculty research:* Computational physics, neutrino physics, oceanography, computational particle physics, optics, condensed matter. Total annual research expenditures: $111,000. *Unit head:* Dr. Jonathan Maps, Head, 218-726-8125, Fax: 218-726-6942, E-mail: jmaps@d.umn.edu. *Application contact:* Dr. Alec Habig, Director of Graduate Studies, 218-726-7214, Fax: 218-726-6942, E-mail: ahabig@d.umn.edu.

University of Minnesota, Twin Cities Campus, Institute of Technology, School of Physics and Astronomy, Department of Physics, Minneapolis, MN 55455-0213. Offers MS, PhD. Part-time programs available. *Degree requirements:* For master's, thesis; for doctorate, thesis/dissertation. *Entrance requirements:* For master's and doctorate, GRE General Test, GRE Subject Test. *Faculty research:* Condensed matter, elementary particle, space, nuclear and atomic physics.

University of Mississippi, Graduate School, College of Liberal Arts, Department of Physics and Astronomy, Oxford, University, MS 38677. Offers physics (MA, MS, PhD). *Faculty:* 18 full-time (1 woman), 1 (woman) part-time/adjunct. *Students:* 28 full-time (5 women), 1 (woman) part-time; includes 2 minority (both Asian Americans or Pacific Islanders), 15 international. In 2009, 3 master's, 2 doctorates awarded. *Degree requirements:* For master's, thesis (for some programs); for doctorate, thesis/dissertation. *Entrance requirements:* For master's, GRE General Test, minimum GPA of 3.0; for doctorate, GRE General Test. Additional exam requirements/recommendations for international students: Required—TOEFL. *Application deadline:* For fall admission, 4/1 for domestic students; for spring admission, 10/1 for domestic students. Applications are processed on a rolling basis. Application fee: $25. Electronic applications accepted. *Financial support:* Scholarships/grants available. Financial award application deadline: 3/1; financial award applicants required to submit FAFSA. *Unit head:* Thomas C. Marshall, Chairman, 662-915-5325, Fax: 662-915-5045, E-mail: physics@phy.olemiss.edu. *Application contact:* Dr. Christy M. Wyandt, Associate Dean, 662-915-7474, Fax: 662-915-7577, E-mail: cwyandt@olemiss.edu.

University of Missouri, Graduate School, College of Arts and Sciences, Department of Physics and Astronomy, Columbia, MO 65211. Offers MS, PhD. *Faculty:* 34 full-time (9 women), 1 (woman) part-time/adjunct. *Students:* 25 full-time (5 women), 18 part-time (5 women); includes 1 minority (Asian American or Pacific Islander), 25 international. Average age 29. 70 applicants, 14% accepted, 7 enrolled. In 2009, 4 master's, 3 doctorates awarded. Terminal master's awarded for partial completion of doctoral program. *Degree requirements:* For doctorate, one foreign language, comprehensive exam, thesis/dissertation. *Entrance requirements:* For master's and doctorate, GRE General Test, minimum GPA of 3.0. Additional exam requirements/recommendations for international students: Required—TOEFL (minimum score 550 paper-based; 213 computer-based; 80 iBT). *Application deadline:* For fall admission, 3/15 priority date for domestic students. Applications are processed on a rolling basis. Application fee: $45 ($60 for international students). Electronic applications accepted. *Financial support:* In 2009–10, 35 research assistantships with full tuition reimbursements, 10 teaching assistantships with full tuition reimbursements were awarded; institutionally sponsored loans, health care benefits, and unspecified assistantships also available. *Faculty research:* Experimental and theoretical condensed-matter physics, biological physics, astronomy/astrophysics. *Unit head:* Dr. Peter Pfeifer, Department Chair, E-mail: pfeiferp@missouri.edu. *Application contact:* Dr. Carsten Ullrich, Director of Graduate Studies, 573-882-3335, E-mail: ullrichc@missouri.edu.

University of Missouri–Kansas City, College of Arts and Sciences, Department of Physics, Kansas City, MO 64110-2499. Offers MS, PhD. PhD (interdisciplinary) offered through the School of Graduate Studies. Part-time and evening/weekend programs available. *Faculty:* 12 full-time (1 woman). *Students:* 5 full-time (2 women), 13 part-time (1 woman), 8 international. Average age 29. 4 applicants, 100% accepted, 2 enrolled. In 2009, 4 master's awarded. Terminal master's awarded for partial completion of doctoral program. *Degree requirements:* For master's, comprehensive exam, thesis optional; for doctorate, comprehensive exam, thesis/dissertation. *Entrance requirements:* For master's and doctorate, GRE General Test. Additional exam requirements/recommendations for international students: Required—TOEFL (minimum score 550 paper-based; 213 computer-based; 80 iBT). *Application deadline:* For fall admission, 4/1 priority date for domestic and international students; for spring admission, 11/1 priority date for domestic and international students. Applications are processed on a rolling basis. Application fee: $45 ($50 for international students). Electronic applications accepted. *Expenses:* Tuition, state resident: full-time $5378; part-time $299 per credit hour. Tuition, nonresident: full-time $13,881; part-time $771 per credit hour. Required fees: $641; $71 per credit hour. Tuition and fees vary according to course load and program. *Financial support:* In 2009–10, 4 research assistantships with full and partial tuition reimbursements (averaging $13,425 per year), 13 teaching assistantships with full and partial tuition reimbursements (averaging $13,259 per year) were awarded; Federal Work-Study, institutionally sponsored loans, and tuition waivers (full and partial) also available. Support available to part-time students. Financial award application deadline: 3/1; financial award applicants required to submit FAFSA. *Faculty research:* Surface physics, material science, statistical mechanics, computational physics, relativity and quantum theory. Total annual research expenditures: $1.2 million. *Unit head:* Dr. Michael Kruger, Chair, 816-235-5441, E-mail: krugerm@umkc.edu. *Application contact:* Dr. Da Ming Zhu, Principal Graduate Advisor, 816-235-5326, Fax: 816-235-5221, E-mail: zhud@umkc.edu.

University of Missouri–St. Louis, College of Arts and Sciences, Department of Physics and Astronomy, St. Louis, MO 63121. Offers applied physics (MS); astrophysics (MS); physics (PhD). Part-time and evening/weekend programs available. *Faculty:* 13 full-time (2 women), 3 part-time/adjunct (1 woman). *Students:* 12 full-time (1 woman), 12 part-time (5 women); includes 1 minority (American Indian/Alaska Native), 6 international. Average age 31. 19 applicants, 58% accepted, 8 enrolled. In 2009, 3 master's, 2 doctorates awarded. Terminal master's awarded for partial completion of doctoral program. *Degree requirements:* For master's, thesis optional; for doctorate, thesis/dissertation. *Entrance requirements:* For master's and doctorate, GRE General Test, 2 letters of recommendation. Additional exam requirements/recommendations for international students: Required—TOEFL (minimum score 550 paper-based; 213 computer-based). *Application deadline:* For fall admission, 7/1 for domestic and international students; for spring admission, 12/1 for domestic students, 11/1 for international students. Application fee: $35 ($40 for international students). Electronic applications accepted. *Expenses:* Tuition, state resident: full-time $5377; part-time $297.70 per credit hour. Tuition, nonresident: full-time $13,882; part-time $771.20 per credit hour. Required fees: $220; $12.20 per credit hour. One-time fee: $12. Tuition and fees vary according to course level, campus/location and program. *Financial support:* In 2009–10, 4 research assistantships with full and partial tuition reimbursements (averaging $15,269 per year), 11 teaching assistantships with full and partial tuition reimbursements (averaging $14,926 per year) were awarded; fellowships with full tuition reimbursements, career-related internships or fieldwork also available. Financial award applicants required to submit FAFSA. *Faculty research:* Biophysics, atomic physics, nonlinear dynamics, materials science. *Unit head:* Dr. Phil Fraundorf, Director of Graduate Studies, 314-516-5931, Fax: 314-516-6152, E-mail: fraundorfp@msx.umsl.edu. *Application contact:* 314-516-5458, Fax: 314-516-6996, E-mail: gradadm@umsl.edu.

University of Nebraska–Lincoln, Graduate College, College of Arts and Sciences, Department of Physics and Astronomy, Lincoln, NE 68588. Offers astronomy (MS, PhD); physics (MS, PhD). *Degree requirements:* For master's, thesis optional; for doctorate, comprehensive exam, thesis/dissertation. *Entrance requirements:* For master's and doctorate, GRE General Test. Additional exam requirements/recommendations for international students: Required—TOEFL (minimum score 550 paper-based; 213 computer-based). Electronic applications accepted. *Faculty research:* Electromagnetics of solids and thin films, photoionization, ion collisions with atoms, molecules and surfaces, nanostructures.

University of Nevada, Las Vegas, Graduate College, College of Science, Department of Physics, Las Vegas, NV 89154-4002. Offers astronomy (MS); physics (PhD). Part-time programs available. *Faculty:* 16 full-time (0 women), 6 part-time/adjunct (2 women). *Students:* 21 full-time (4 women), 5 part-time (0 women); includes 3 minority (2 Asian Americans or Pacific Islanders, 1 Hispanic American), 8 international. Average age 31. 19 applicants, 63% accepted, 8 enrolled. In 2009, 3 master's, 1 doctorate awarded. *Degree requirements:* For master's, thesis, oral exam; for doctorate, comprehensive exam, thesis/dissertation. *Entrance requirements:* For master's and doctorate, GRE General Test. Additional exam requirements/recommendations for international students: Required—TOEFL (minimum score 550 paper-based; 213 computer-based; 80 iBT), IELTS (minimum score 7). *Application deadline:* For fall admission, 2/1 priority date for domestic and international students; for spring admission, 10/1 priority date for domestic and international students. Applications are processed on a rolling basis. Application fee: $60 ($95 for international students). Electronic applications accepted. *Financial support:* In 2009–10, 13 research assistantships with partial tuition reimbursements (averaging $16,395 per year), 15 teaching assistantships with partial tuition reimbursements (averaging $12,856 per year) were awarded; institutionally sponsored loans, scholarships/grants, health care

Physics

University of Nevada, Las Vegas (continued)

benefits, and unspecified assistantships also available. Financial award application deadline: 3/1. *Faculty research:* Gamma-ray bursters, dark matter distribution, experimental high pressure physics, theoretical condensed matter physics, experimental atomic/laser physics. *Unit head:* Dr. Tao Pang, Chair/Professor, 702-895-4454, Fax: 702-895-0804, E-mail: pang@physics.unlv.edu. *Application contact:* Graduate College Admissions Evaluator, 702-895-3320, Fax: 702-895-4180, E-mail: gradcollege@unlv.edu.

University of Nevada, Reno, Graduate School, College of Science, Department of Physics, Reno, NV 89557. Offers MS, PhD. Terminal master's awarded for partial completion of doctoral program. *Degree requirements:* For master's, thesis optional; for doctorate, thesis/dissertation. *Entrance requirements:* For master's, GRE General Test, GRE Subject Test, minimum GPA of 2.75; for doctorate, GRE General Test, GRE Subject Test, minimum GPA of 3.0. Additional exam requirements/recommendations for international students: Required—TOEFL (minimum score 500 paper-based; 173 computer-based; 61 iBT), IELTS (minimum score 6). Electronic applications accepted. *Faculty research:* Atomic and molecular physics.

University of New Brunswick Fredericton, School of Graduate Studies, Faculty of Science, Department of Physics, Fredericton, NB E3B 5A3, Canada. Offers M Sc, PhD. Part-time programs available. *Faculty:* 15 full-time (2 women). *Students:* 18 full-time (2 women). In 2009, 1 master's awarded. *Degree requirements:* For master's, thesis; for doctorate, comprehensive exam, thesis/dissertation. *Entrance requirements:* For master's, BSc with a B average; for doctorate, MSc; minimum GPA of 3.0. Additional exam requirements/recommendations for international students: Required—TOEFL, TWE. *Application deadline:* For fall admission, 3/1 priority date for domestic students. Applications are processed on a rolling basis. Application fee: $50 Canadian dollars. Electronic applications accepted. Tuition and fees charges are reported in Canadian dollars. *Expenses:* Tuition, area resident: Full-time $5562 Canadian dollars; part-time $2781 Canadian dollars per year. Required fees: $49.75 Canadian dollars per term. *Financial support:* In 2009–10, 2 fellowships with tuition reimbursements (averaging $17,500 per year), 15 research assistantships (averaging $12,000 per year), 29 teaching assistantships (averaging $4,200 per year) were awarded. *Faculty research:* Laser spectroscopy, infrared and microwave spectroscopy, magnetic resonance imaging, space and atmospheric physics, theoretical studies-molecular systems, space plasma and high-precision calculations. *Unit head:* Dr. Zong-Chao Yan, Director of Graduate Studies, 506-458-7936, Fax: 506-453-4581, E-mail: zyan@unb.ca. *Application contact:* Elinor MacFarlane, Graduate Secretary, 506-453-4723, Fax: 506-453-4581, E-mail: elinor@unb.ca.

University of New Hampshire, Graduate School, College of Engineering and Physical Sciences, Department of Physics, Durham, NH 03824. Offers MS, PhD. *Faculty:* 32 full-time (4 women). *Students:* 32 full-time (7 women), 22 part-time (8 women); includes 3 minority (1 American Indian/Alaska Native, 2 Asian Americans or Pacific Islanders), 25 international. Average age 28. 91 applicants, 42% accepted, 13 enrolled. In 2009, 3 master's, 2 doctorates awarded. Terminal master's awarded for partial completion of doctoral program. *Degree requirements:* For master's, thesis or alternative; for doctorate, thesis/dissertation. *Entrance requirements:* For master's and doctorate, GRE General Test. Additional exam requirements/recommendations for international students: Required—TOEFL (minimum score 550 paper-based; 213 computer-based; 80 iBT). *Application deadline:* For fall admission, 4/1 priority date for domestic students, 4/1 for international students; for spring admission, 12/1 for domestic students. Applications are processed on a rolling basis. Application fee: $65. Electronic applications accepted. *Expenses:* Tuition, state resident: full-time $10,380; part-time $577 per credit hour. Tuition, nonresident: full-time $24,350; part-time $1002 per credit hour. Required fees: $1550; $387.50 per semester. Tuition and fees vary according to course load and program. *Financial support:* In 2009–10, 53 students received support, including 2 fellowships, 34 research assistantships, 17 teaching assistantships; Federal Work-Study, scholarships/grants, and tuition waivers (full and partial) also available. Support available to part-time students. Financial award application deadline: 2/15. *Faculty research:* Astrophysics and space physics, nuclear physics, atomic and molecular physics, nonlinear dynamical systems. *Unit head:* Dr. Eberhard Moebius, Chairperson, 603-862-1951. *Application contact:* Katie Makem-Boucher, Administrative Assistant, 603-862-2669, E-mail: physics.grad.info@unh.edu.

University of New Mexico, Graduate School, College of Arts and Sciences, Department of Physics and Astronomy, Albuquerque, NM 87131-2039. Offers biomedical physics (MS, PhD); physics (MS, PhD). Part-time programs available. *Faculty:* 39 full-time (4 women), 2 part-time/adjunct (0 women). *Students:* 71 full-time (19 women), 10 part-time (0 women); includes 7 minority (4 Asian Americans or Pacific Islanders, 3 Hispanic Americans), 30 international. Average age 28. 110 applicants, 35% accepted, 16 enrolled. In 2009, 7 master's, 11 doctorates awarded. Terminal master's awarded for partial completion of doctoral program. *Degree requirements:* For master's, comprehensive exam (for some programs), thesis optional; for doctorate, comprehensive exam, thesis/dissertation. *Entrance requirements:* For master's, GRE, Relevant undergraduate coursework, GPA; for doctorate, GRE, physics subject is recommended, Relevant undergraduate coursework, GPA. Additional exam requirements/recommendations for international students: Required—TOEFL (minimum score 550 paper-based; 213 computer-based; 80 iBT). *Application deadline:* For fall admission, 1/15 for domestic and international students; for spring admission, 8/1 for domestic and international students. Application fee: $50. Electronic applications accepted. *Expenses:* Tuition, state resident: full-time $2098.80; part-time $233.20 per credit hour. Tuition, nonresident: full-time $6650. Required fees: $25 per semester. Tuition and fees vary according to course load, program and reciprocity agreements. *Financial support:* In 2009–10, 15 students received support, including 3 fellowships with full tuition reimbursements available (averaging $30,000 per year), 54 research assistantships with full tuition reimbursements available (averaging $15,550 per year), 37 teaching assistantships with full tuition reimbursements available (averaging $13,814 per year); career-related internships or fieldwork, scholarships/grants, traineeships, health care benefits, and unspecified assistantships also available. Support available to part-time students. Financial award application deadline: 2/1; financial award applicants required to submit FAFSA. *Faculty research:* Astronomy and astrophysics, biological physics, condensed-matter physics, nonlinear science and complexity, optics and photonics, quantum information, subatomic physics. Total annual research expenditures: $6 million. *Unit head:* Dr. Bernd Bassalleck, Chair, 505-277-1517, Fax: 505-277-1520, E-mail: bossek@unm.edu. *Application contact:* Alisia Gibson, Program Advisement Coordinator, 505-277-1514, Fax: 505-277-1514, E-mail: agibson@unm.edu.

University of New Orleans, Graduate School, College of Sciences, Department of Physics, New Orleans, LA 70148. Offers MS, PhD. Part-time and evening/weekend programs available. *Degree requirements:* For master's, thesis (for some programs). *Entrance requirements:* For master's, GRE General Test. Additional exam requirements/recommendations for international students: Required—TOEFL (minimum score 550 paper-based; 213 computer-based; 79 iBT). Electronic applications accepted. *Faculty research:* Underwater acoustics, applied electromagnetics, experimental atomic beams, digital signal processing, astrophysics.

The University of North Carolina at Chapel Hill, Graduate School, College of Arts and Sciences, Department of Physics and Astronomy, Chapel Hill, NC 27599. Offers physics (MS, PhD). Terminal master's awarded for partial completion of doctoral program. *Degree requirements:* For master's, comprehensive exam; for doctorate, comprehensive exam, thesis/dissertation. *Entrance requirements:* For master's and doctorate, GRE General Test, minimum GPA of 3.0. Electronic applications accepted. *Faculty research:* Observational astronomy, fullerenes, polarized beams, nanotubes, nucleosynthesis in stars and supernovae, superstring theory, ballistic transport in semiconductors, gravitation.

University of North Dakota, Graduate School, College of Arts and Sciences, Department of Physics, Grand Forks, ND 58202. Offers MS, PhD. *Degree requirements:* For master's, thesis, final exam; for doctorate, comprehensive exam, thesis/dissertation, final exam. *Entrance requirements:* For master's, minimum GPA of 3.0; for doctorate, minimum GPA of 3.5. Additional exam requirements/recommendations for international students: Required—TOEFL (minimum score 550 paper-based; 213 computer-based; 79 iBT), IELTS (minimum score 6.5). Electronic applications accepted. *Faculty research:* Solid state physics, atomic and molecular physics, astrophysics, health physics.

University of Northern Iowa, Graduate College, College of Natural Sciences, Department of Physics, Cedar Falls, IA 50614. Offers MA, PSM. *Students:* 5 full-time (1 woman), 3 part-time (1 woman), 2 international. 10 applicants, 80% accepted, 4 enrolled. In 2009, 3 master's awarded. *Degree requirements:* For master's, comprehensive exam (for some programs), thesis or alternative. *Entrance requirements:* For master's, minimum GPA of 3.0. Additional exam requirements/recommendations for international students: Required—TOEFL (minimum score 500 paper-based; 180 computer-based; 61 iBT). *Application deadline:* For fall admission, 8/1 priority date for domestic students. Applications are processed on a rolling basis. Application fee: $30 ($50 for international students). Electronic applications accepted. *Financial support:* Career-related internships or fieldwork, Federal Work-Study, scholarships/grants, and tuition waivers (full and partial) available. Support available to part-time students. Financial award application deadline: 2/1. *Unit head:* Dr. C. Clifton Chancey, Head, 319-273-2420, E-mail: c.chancey@uni.edu. *Application contact:* Laurie S. Russell, Record Analyst, 319-273-2623, Fax: 319-273-6792, E-mail: laurie.russell@uni.edu.

University of North Texas, Robert B. Toulouse School of Graduate Studies, College of Arts and Sciences, Department of Physics, Denton, TX 76203. Offers MA, MS, PhD. Terminal master's awarded for partial completion of doctoral program. *Degree requirements:* For master's, comprehensive exam (for some programs), thesis or problems; for doctorate, one foreign language, comprehensive exam (for some programs), thesis/dissertation. *Entrance requirements:* For master's and doctorate, GRE General Test, two letters of recommendation. Additional exam requirements/recommendations for international students: Required—proof of English language proficiency; Recommended—TOEFL (minimum score 550 paper-based; 213 computer-based; 79 iBT). *Application deadline:* Applications are processed on a rolling basis. Application fee: $50 ($75 for international students). Electronic applications accepted. *Expenses:* Tuition, state resident: full-time $4298; part-time $239 per contact hour. Tuition, nonresident: full-time $9878; part-time $549 per contact hour. Required fees: $265 per contact hour. *Financial support:* Fellowships with tuition reimbursements, research assistantships with tuition reimbursements, teaching assistantships, scholarships/grants, health care benefits, and unspecified assistantships available. Financial award applicants required to submit FAFSA. *Faculty research:* Atomic, molecular optical; condensed matter, experimental microwave, theoretical, semiconductor. *Application contact:* Graduate Adviser, 940-565-2630, Fax: 940-565-2515.

University of Notre Dame, Graduate School, College of Science, Department of Physics, Notre Dame, IN 46556. Offers MS, PhD. *Degree requirements:* For doctorate, thesis/dissertation, candidacy exam. *Entrance requirements:* For doctorate, GRE General Test, GRE Subject Test. Additional exam requirements/recommendations for international students: Required—TOEFL (minimum score 600 paper-based; 250 computer-based; 80 iBT). Electronic applications accepted. *Faculty research:* High energy, nuclear, atomic, condensed-matter physics; astrophysics; biophysics.

University of Oklahoma, Graduate College, College of Arts and Sciences, Department of Physics and Astronomy, Norman, OK 73019. Offers astrophysics (MS, PhD); physics (MS, PhD). Part-time programs available. *Faculty:* 31 full-time (4 women). *Students:* 37 full-time (15 women), 4 part-time (3 women); includes 2 minority (both Asian Americans or Pacific Islanders), 26 international. 14 applicants, 71% accepted, 10 enrolled. In 2009, 2 master's, 5 doctorates awarded. Terminal master's awarded for partial completion of doctoral program. *Degree requirements:* For master's, thesis or alternative, departmental qualifying exam; for doctorate, thesis/dissertation, comprehensive, departmental qualifying, oral, and written exams. *Entrance requirements:* For master's and doctorate, GRE General Test, GRE Subject Test, 3 letters of recommendation. Additional exam requirements/recommendations for international students: Required—TOEFL (minimum score 600 paper-based; 250 computer-based). *Application deadline:* For fall admission, 3/1 for domestic students, 4/1 for international students; for spring admission, 11/1 for domestic students, 9/1 for international students. Application fee: $40 ($90 for international students). Electronic applications accepted. *Expenses:* Tuition, state resident: full-time $3744; part-time $156 per credit hour. Tuition, nonresident: full-time $13,577; part-time $565.70 per credit hour. Required fees: $2415; $90.10 per credit hour. *Financial support:* In 2009–10, 57 students received support, including 31 research assistantships with partial tuition reimbursements available (averaging $15,751 per year), 29 teaching assistantships with partial tuition reimbursements available (averaging $15,255 per year); Federal Work-Study, scholarships/grants, health care benefits, and unspecified assistantships also available. Financial award application deadline: 3/1; financial award applicants required to submit FAFSA. *Faculty research:* Atomic, molecular, and chemical physics; high energy physics; astrophysics; condensed matter physics. Total annual research expenditures: $4.4 million. *Unit head:* Greg Parker, Chair, 405-325-3961, Fax: 405-325-7557, E-mail: parker@nhn.ou.edu. *Application contact:* Debbie Barnhill, University Student Services Assistant, 405-325-3961 Ext. 36101, Fax: 405-325-7557, E-mail: dbarnhill@ou.edu.

University of Oregon, Graduate School, College of Arts and Sciences, Department of Physics, Eugene, OR 97403. Offers MA, MS, PhD. Terminal master's awarded for partial completion of doctoral program. *Degree requirements:* For doctorate, thesis/dissertation. *Entrance requirements:* For master's and doctorate, GRE General Test, GRE Subject Test, minimum GPA of 3.0. Additional exam requirements/recommendations for international students: Required—TOEFL. *Faculty research:* Solid-state and chemical physics, optical physics, elementary particle physics, astrophysics, atomic and molecular physics.

University of Ottawa, Faculty of Graduate and Postdoctoral Studies, Faculty of Science, Ottawa-Carleton Institute for Physics, Ottawa, ON K1N 6N5, Canada. Offers M Sc, PhD. *Degree requirements:* For master's, thesis or alternative; for doctorate, comprehensive exam, thesis/dissertation, seminar. *Entrance requirements:* For master's, honors B Sc degree or equivalent, minimum B average; for doctorate, M Sc, minimum B+ average. Electronic applications accepted. *Faculty research:* Condensed matter physics and statistical physics (CMS), subatomic physics (SAP), medical physics (Med).

University of Pennsylvania, School of Arts and Sciences, Graduate Group in Physics and Astronomy, Philadelphia, PA 19104. Offers medical physics (MS); physics (PhD). Part-time programs available. *Faculty:* 48 full-time (5 women), 14 part-time/adjunct (1 woman). *Students:* 103 full-time (30 women), 2 part-time (0 women); includes 7 minority (5 Asian Americans or Pacific Islanders, 2 Hispanic Americans), 22 international. 336 applicants, 15% accepted, 21 enrolled. In 2009, 4 master's, 17 doctorates awarded. *Degree requirements:* For doctorate, thesis/dissertation, oral, preliminary, and final exams. *Entrance requirements:* For doctorate, GRE General Test, GRE Subject Test (recommended). Additional exam requirements/recommendations for international students: Required—TOEFL. *Application deadline:* For fall admission, 12/1 priority date for domestic students. Application fee: $70. Electronic applications accepted. *Expenses:* Tuition: Full-time $25,660; part-time $4758 per course. Required fees: $2152; $270 per course. Tuition and fees vary according to course load, degree level and program. *Financial support:* Fellowships, research assistantships, teaching assistantships, institutionally sponsored loans, scholarships/grants, traineeships, health care benefits, and unspecified assistantships available. Financial award application deadline: 12/15. *Faculty research:* Astrophysics, condensed matter experiment, condensed matter theory, particle experiment, particle theory. Total annual research expenditures: $7.3 million.

University of Pittsburgh, School of Arts and Sciences, Department of Physics and Astronomy, Pittsburgh, PA 15260. Offers physics (MS, PhD). *Faculty:* 38 full-time (6 women). *Students:* 78 full-time (21 women); includes 1 minority (Asian American or Pacific Islander), 51 international. Average age 25. 299 applicants, 28% accepted, 17 enrolled. In 2009, 6 master's, 10 doctorates awarded. Terminal master's awarded for partial completion of doctoral program. *Degree requirements:* For master's, comprehensive exam, thesis optional; for doctorate, comprehensive exam, thesis/dissertation, preliminary and comprehensive exams, 2 terms of student teaching, seminar and/or professional talk presentations, annual committee review meeting, oral/written dissertation. *Entrance requirements:* For master's and doctorate, GRE General Test, GRE Subject Test, minimum QPA of 3.0. Additional exam requirements/recommendations for international students: Required—TOEFL (minimum score 577 paper-based; 233 computer-based; 90 iBT), IELTS, TOEFL (minimum score 577 paper-based; 233 computer-based; 90 iBT) or IELTS (minimum score 6.5). *Application deadline:* For fall admission, 1/31 priority date for domestic and international students. Applications are processed on a rolling basis. Application fee: $0 ($50 for international students). Electronic applications accepted. *Expenses:* Tuition, state resident: full-time $16,402; part-time $665 per credit. Tuition, nonresident: full-time $28,694; part-time $1175 per credit. Required fees: $690; $175 per term. Tuition and fees vary according to program. *Financial support:* In 2009–10, 5 fellowships with full tuition reimbursements (averaging $18,500 per year), 41 research assistantships with full tuition reimbursements (averaging $22,597 per year), 29 teaching assistantships with full tuition reimbursements (averaging $22,597 per year) were awarded; scholarships/grants, health care benefits, tuition waivers, and unspecified assistantships also available. Financial award application deadline: 1/31. *Faculty research:* Astrophysics and cosmology, particle and astroparticle physics, condensed matter and solid-state physics, quantum information, biological physics, nanoscience. Total annual research expenditures: $5.5 million. *Unit head:* Dr. David Turnshek, Chairman, 412-624-6381, Fax: 412-624-9163, E-mail: davidt@pitt.edu. *Application contact:* Dr. Andrew Zentner, Admissions, 412-624-9000, Fax: 412-624-9163, E-mail: zentner@pitt.edu.

See Close-Up on page 237.

University of Puerto Rico, Mayagüez Campus, Graduate Studies, College of Arts and Sciences, Department of Physics, Mayagüez, PR 00681-9000. Offers MS. Part-time programs available. *Degree requirements:* For master's, comprehensive exam, thesis. *Entrance requirements:* For master's, bachelor's degree in physics or its equivalent. *Faculty research:* Atomic and molecular physics, nuclear physics, nonlinear thermostatics, fluid dynamics, molecular spectroscopy.

University of Puerto Rico, Río Piedras, College of Natural Sciences, Department of Physics, San Juan, PR 00931-3300. Offers chemical physics (PhD); physics (MS). Part-time programs available. *Degree requirements:* For master's, comprehensive exam, thesis; for doctorate, comprehensive exam, thesis/dissertation. *Entrance requirements:* For master's, GRE General Test, GRE Subject Test, interview, minimum GPA of 3.0, letter of recommendation (3); for doctorate, GRE, master's degree, minimum GPA of 3.0, letter of recommendation (3). Additional exam requirements/recommendations for international students: Required—TOEFL. *Faculty research:* Energy transfer process through Van der Vacqs interactions, study of the photodissociation of ketene.

University of Regina, Faculty of Graduate Studies and Research, Faculty of Science, Department of Physics, Regina, SK S4S 0A2, Canada. Offers M Sc, PhD. *Faculty:* 9 full-time (0 women), 3 part-time/adjunct (0 women). *Students:* 7 full-time (1 woman), 2 part-time (0 women). 7 applicants, 86% accepted. In 2009, 1 master's awarded. Terminal master's awarded for partial completion of doctoral program. *Degree requirements:* For master's, thesis; for doctorate, thesis/dissertation. *Entrance requirements:* For master's, honors degree in physics or engineering physics; for doctorate, M Sc or equivalent. Additional exam requirements/recommendations for international students: Required—TOEFL (minimum score 580 paper-based; 237 computer-based; 80 iBT). *Application deadline:* For fall admission, 5/15 for domestic students; for winter admission, 8/15 for domestic students. Applications are processed on a rolling basis. Application fee: $90 ($100 for international students). *Financial support:* In 2009–10, 3 fellowships (averaging $19,000 per year), 1 teaching assistantship (averaging $6,650 per year) were awarded; research assistantships, career-related internships or fieldwork and scholarships/grants also available. Financial award application deadline: 6/15. *Faculty research:* Experimental and theoretical subatomic physics. Total annual research expenditures: $2.1 million. *Unit head:* Dr. Neil Ashton, Head, 306-585-4252, Fax: 306-585-5659, E-mail: neil.ashton@uregina.ca. *Application contact:* Dr. Zisis Papandreaou, Graduate Program Coordinator, 306-585-5379, Fax: 306-585-5659, E-mail: zisis@uregina.ca.

University of Rhode Island, Graduate School, College of Arts and Sciences, Department of Physics, Kingston, RI 02881. Offers MS, PhD. Part-time and evening/weekend programs available. *Faculty:* 16 full-time (2 women). *Students:* 14 full-time (5 women), 2 part-time (0 women); includes 1 minority (Asian American or Pacific Islander), 9 international. In 2009, 5 doctorates awarded. *Degree requirements:* For master's, comprehensive exam (for some programs), thesis optional; for doctorate, comprehensive exam, thesis/dissertation. *Entrance requirements:* For master's and doctorate, 2 letters of recommendation. Additional exam requirements/recommendations for international students: Required—TOEFL (minimum score 550 paper-based; 213 computer-based). *Application deadline:* For fall admission, 4/15 for domestic students, 2/1 for international students. Application fee: $65. Electronic applications accepted. *Expenses:* Tuition, state resident: full-time $8828; part-time $490 per credit hour. Tuition, nonresident: full-time $22,100; part-time $1228 per credit hour. Required fees: $1118; $57 per semester. Tuition and fees vary according to program. *Financial support:* In 2009–10, 2 research assistantships with full tuition reimbursements (averaging $13,894 per year), 14 teaching assistantships with full and partial tuition reimbursements (averaging $13,745 per year) were awarded. Financial award application deadline: 3/1; financial award applicants required to submit FAFSA. Total annual research expenditures: $637,368. *Unit head:* Dr. Jan Northby, Chair, 401-874-2042, Fax: 401-874-2380, E-mail: jnorthby@uri.edu. *Application contact:* Dr. Jan Northby, Chair, 401-874-2042, Fax: 401-874-2380, E-mail: jnorthby@uri.edu.

University of Rochester, The College, Arts and Sciences, Department of Physics and Astronomy, Rochester, NY 14627. Offers physics (MA, MS, PhD); physics and astronomy (PhD). Part-time programs available. Terminal master's awarded for partial completion of doctoral program. *Degree requirements:* For master's, comprehensive exam, thesis (for some programs); for doctorate, comprehensive exam, thesis/dissertation, qualifying exam. *Entrance requirements:* For master's and doctorate, GRE General Test. Additional exam requirements/recommendations for international students: Required—TOEFL.

See Close-Up on page 239.

University of Saskatchewan, College of Graduate Studies and Research, College of Arts and Sciences, Department of Physics and Engineering Physics, Saskatoon, SK S7N 5A2, Canada. Offers M Sc, PhD. *Faculty:* 40. *Students:* 46. In 2009, 6 master's, 3 doctorates awarded. *Degree requirements:* For master's, thesis; for doctorate, comprehensive exam (for some programs), thesis/dissertation. *Entrance requirements:* Additional exam requirements/recommendations for international students: Required—TOEFL (minimum score 80 iBT); Recommended—IELTS (minimum score 6.5). *Application deadline:* For fall admission, 7/1 priority date for domestic students. Applications are processed on a rolling basis. Application fee: $75. Electronic applications accepted. Tuition and fees charges are reported in Canadian dollars. *Expenses:* Tuition, area resident: Full-time $3000 Canadian dollars; part-time $500 Canadian dollars per term. Required fees: $700 Canadian dollars; $100 Canadian dollars per term. *Financial support:* Fellowships, research assistantships, teaching assistantships available. Financial award application deadline: 1/31. *Unit head:* Dr. Cary Rangacharyulu, Head, 306-966-6393, Fax: 306-966-6400, E-mail: cary@sask.usask.ca. *Application contact:* Dr. Chijin Xiao, Graduate Chair, 306-966-6409, Fax: 306-966-6400, E-mail: chijin.xiao@usask.ca.

University of South Carolina, The Graduate School, College of Arts and Sciences, Department of Physics and Astronomy, Columbia, SC 29208. Offers IMA, MAT, MS, PSM, PhD. IMA and MAT offered in cooperation with the College of Education. Part-time programs available. Terminal master's awarded for partial completion of doctoral program. *Degree requirements:* For master's, comprehensive exam, thesis; for doctorate, one foreign language, comprehensive exam, thesis/dissertation. *Entrance requirements:* For master's and doctorate, GRE General Test, GRE Subject Test. Additional exam requirements/recommendations for international students: Required—TOEFL (minimum score 570 paper-based; 230 computer-based; 75 iBT). Electronic applications accepted. *Faculty research:* Condensed matter, intermediate-energy nuclear physics, foundations of quantum mechanics, astronomy/astrophysics.

The University of South Dakota, Graduate School, College of Arts and Sciences, Department of Earth Sciences and Physics, Vermillion, SD 57069-2390. Offers physics (MS, PhD). *Entrance requirements:* For master's and doctorate, GRE.

University of Southern California, Graduate School, College of Letters, Arts and Sciences, Department of Physics and Astronomy, Los Angeles, CA 90089. Offers physics (MA, MS, PhD). Part-time programs available. *Faculty:* 20 full-time (2 women). *Students:* 68 full-time (9 women); includes 6 minority (4 Asian Americans or Pacific Islanders, 2 Hispanic Americans), 46 international. 130 applicants, 17% accepted, 8 enrolled. In 2009, 9 doctorates awarded. Terminal master's awarded for partial completion of doctoral program. *Degree requirements:* For master's, comprehensive exam, thesis (for some programs); for doctorate, comprehensive exam, thesis/dissertation. *Entrance requirements:* For master's, No admits to Master's must be admitted to Ph.D; for doctorate, GRE General Test, GRE Subject Test (physics), 3 letters of recommendation. Additional exam requirements/recommendations for international students: Required—TOEFL (minimum score 550 paper-based; 213 computer-based; 80 iBT). *Application deadline:* For fall admission, 12/1 priority date for domestic and international students. Application fee: $85. Electronic applications accepted. *Expenses:* Tuition: Full-time $25,980; part-time $1315 per unit. Required fees: $554. One-time fee: $35 full-time. Full-time tuition and fees vary according to degree level and program. *Financial support:* In 2009–10, 64 students received support, including 4 fellowships with full tuition reimbursements available (averaging $28,000 per year), 6 research assistantships with full tuition reimbursements available (averaging $19,000 per year), 45 teaching assistantships with full tuition reimbursements available (averaging $19,000 per year). Financial award application deadline: 12/1. *Faculty research:* High-energy particle theory, condensed matter physics, astrophysics, solar and cosmology, biophysics, computational physics. Total annual research expenditures: $4 million. *Unit head:* Dr. Werner Dappen, Chair, 213-740-0848, Fax: 213-740-8094, E-mail: physics@college.usc.edu. *Application contact:* Dr. Elena Pierpaoli, Graduate Student Advisor, 213-740-1117, Fax: 213-740-8094, E-mail: pierpaol@usc.edu.

University of Southern Mississippi, Graduate School, College of Science and Technology, Department of Physics and Astronomy, Hattiesburg, MS 39406-0001. Offers computational science (PhD); physics (MS). *Faculty:* 10 full-time (1 woman). *Students:* 7 full-time (3 women), 1 part-time (0 women), 4 international. Average age 31. 17 applicants, 29% accepted, 3 enrolled. In 2009, 6 master's awarded. *Degree requirements:* For master's, comprehensive exam, thesis. *Entrance requirements:* For master's, GRE General Test, minimum GPA of 2.75 in last 60 hours. Additional exam requirements/recommendations for international students: Required—TOEFL. *Application deadline:* For fall admission, 3/1 priority date for domestic students, 3/1 for international students. Applications are processed on a rolling basis. Application fee: $35. *Expenses:* Tuition, state resident: full-time $5096; part-time $284 per hour. Tuition, nonresident: full-time $13,052; part-time $726 per hour. Required fees: $402. Tuition and fees vary according to course level and course load. *Financial support:* In 2009–10, 15 teaching assistantships with full tuition reimbursements (averaging $11,745 per year) were awarded; research assistantships, Federal Work-Study also available. Financial award application deadline: 3/15; financial award applicants required to submit FAFSA. *Faculty research:* Polymers, atomic physics, fluid mechanics, liquid crystals, refractory materials. *Unit head:* Dr. Khin Maung, Chair, 601-266-4934, Fax: 601-266-5149. *Application contact:* Shonna Breland, Manager of Graduate Admissions, 601-266-6563, Fax: 601-266-5138.

University of South Florida, Graduate School, College of Arts and Sciences, Department of Physics, Tampa, FL 33620-9951. Offers applied physics (PhD); physics (MS). Part-time programs available. *Faculty:* 23 full-time (3 women). *Students:* 60 full-time (11 women), 7 part-time (1 woman); includes 7 minority (2 African Americans, 2 Asian Americans or Pacific Islanders, 3 Hispanic Americans), 30 international. Average age 32. 81 applicants, 49% accepted, 17 enrolled. In 2009, 9 master's, 4 doctorates awarded. *Degree requirements:* For master's, comprehensive exam, thesis optional; for doctorate, 2 foreign languages, comprehensive exam, thesis/dissertation. *Entrance requirements:* For master's, GRE General Test, minimum GPA of 3.0 in last 60 hours of course work; for doctorate, GRE General Test, minimum graduate GPA of 3.2. Additional exam requirements/recommendations for international students: Required—TOEFL (minimum score 550 paper-based). *Application deadline:* For fall admission, 2/15 priority date for domestic students, 1/2 for international students; for spring admission, 9/1 for domestic students, 7/1 for international students. Applications are processed on a rolling basis. Application fee: $30. Electronic applications accepted. *Financial support:* In 2009–10, teaching assistantships with tuition reimbursements (averaging $13,739 per year); unspecified assistantships also available. *Faculty research:* Biophysics and biomedical physics, atomic molecular and optical physics, solid state and materials physics, physics education. Total annual research expenditures: $2.2 million. *Unit head:* Dr. Pritish Mukherjee, Director of Graduate Studies, 813-974-2871, Fax: 813-974-5813, E-mail: pritish@cas.usf.edu. *Application contact:* Dale Johnson, Program Director, 813-974-5125, Fax: 813-974-5813, E-mail: dejohnso@cas.usf.edu.

The University of Tennessee, Graduate School, College of Arts and Sciences, Department of Physics and Astronomy, Knoxville, TN 37996. Offers physics (MS, PhD). Part-time programs available. *Degree requirements:* For master's, thesis or alternative; for doctorate, thesis/dissertation. *Entrance requirements:* For master's and doctorate, minimum GPA of 2.7. Additional exam requirements/recommendations for international students: Required—TOEFL. Electronic applications accepted. *Expenses:* Tuition, state resident: full-time $6826; part-time $380 per semester hour. Tuition, nonresident: full-time $21,844; part-time $1147 per semester hour. Tuition and fees vary according to program.

The University of Tennessee Space Institute, Graduate Programs, Program in Physics, Tullahoma, TN 37388-9700. Offers MS, PhD. *Faculty:* 4 full-time (1 woman), 2 part-time/adjunct (0 women). *Students:* 6 full-time (0 women), 4 part-time (1 woman); includes 1 minority (Asian American or Pacific Islander), 1 international. 4 applicants, 50% accepted, 0 enrolled. In 2009, 2 master's, 1 doctorate awarded. *Degree requirements:* For master's, thesis (for some programs); for doctorate, one foreign language, thesis/dissertation. *Entrance requirements:* For master's and doctorate, GRE General Test, GRE Subject Test. Additional exam requirements/recommendations for international students: Required—TOEFL (minimum score 550 paper-based; 213 computer-based; 80 iBT), IELTS (minimum score 6.5). *Application deadline:* For fall admission, 2/1 for international students; for spring admission, 6/15 for international students. Applications are processed on a rolling basis. Application fee: $35. Electronic applications accepted. *Expenses:* Tuition, state resident: full-time $6826; part-time $380 per hour. Tuition, nonresident: full-time $20,622; part-time $1147 per hour. Required fees: $10 per hour. One-time fee: $90 full-time. *Financial support:* In 2009–10, 2 fellowships, 6 research assistantships with full tuition reimbursements (averaging $17,791 per year) were awarded; career-related internships or fieldwork, Federal Work-Study, institutionally sponsored loans, health care benefits, tuition waivers (full and partial), and unspecified assistantships also available. Financial award applicants required to submit FAFSA. *Unit head:* Dr. Horace Crater, Degree

Physics

The University of Tennessee Space Institute (continued)
Program Chairman, 931-393-7469, Fax: 931-393-7444, E-mail: hcrater@utsi.edu. *Application contact:* Dee Merriman, Coordinator III, 931-393-7293, Fax: 931-393-7201, E-mail: dmerrima@utsi.edu.

The University of Texas at Arlington, Graduate School, College of Science, Department of Physics, Arlington, TX 76019. Offers physics (MS); physics and applied physics (PhD). Part-time programs available. *Faculty:* 17 full-time (1 woman), 4 part-time/adjunct (0 women). *Students:* 44 full-time (14 women), 4 part-time (0 women); includes 9 minority (1 African American, 5 Asian Americans or Pacific Islanders, 3 Hispanic Americans), 24 international. 22 applicants, 100% accepted, 11 enrolled. In 2009, 8 master's, 4 doctorates awarded. Terminal master's awarded for partial completion of doctoral program. *Degree requirements:* For master's, thesis optional; for doctorate, comprehensive exam, thesis/dissertation, internship or substitute. *Entrance requirements:* For master's, GRE General Test, minimum GPA of 3.0 in last 60 hours of course work; for doctorate, GRE General Test, minimum GPA of 3.0 in last 60 hours of course work, 30 hours graduate course work in physics. Additional exam requirements/recommendations for international students: Required—TOEFL (minimum score 550 paper-based; 213 computer-based). *Application deadline:* For fall admission, 6/16 for domestic students. Applications are processed on a rolling basis. Application fee: $35 ($50 for international students). *Financial support:* In 2009–10, 21 students received support, including 4 fellowships with partial tuition reimbursements available (averaging $1,000 per year), research assistantships (averaging $20,280 per year), 11 teaching assistantships (averaging $20,280 per year); career-related internships or fieldwork, Federal Work-Study, institutionally sponsored loans, scholarships/grants, health care benefits, tuition waivers, and unspecified assistantships also available. Support available to part-time students. Financial award application deadline: 6/1; financial award applicants required to submit FAFSA. *Faculty research:* Particle physics, astrophysics, condensed matter theory and experiment. Total annual research expenditures: $1.5 million. *Unit head:* Dr. Alex Weiss, Chair, 807-272-2266, Fax: 817-272-3637, E-mail: weiss@uta.edu. *Application contact:* Dr. Qiming Zhang, Graduate Advisor, 817-272-2266, Fax: 817-272-3637, E-mail: zhang@uta.edu.

The University of Texas at Austin, Graduate School, College of Natural Sciences, Department of Physics, Austin, TX 78712-1111. Offers MA, MS, PhD. *Degree requirements:* For master's, thesis; for doctorate, thesis/dissertation. *Entrance requirements:* For master's and doctorate, GRE General Test, GRE Subject Test (physics). Electronic applications accepted.

The University of Texas at Brownsville, Graduate Studies, College of Science, Mathematics and Technology, Brownsville, TX 78520-4991. Offers biological sciences (MS, MSIS); mathematics (MS); physics (MS). Part-time and evening/weekend programs available. *Degree requirements:* For master's, comprehensive exam, thesis optional. *Entrance requirements:* For master's, GRE General Test. Additional exam requirements/recommendations for international students: Required—TOEFL. *Faculty research:* Fish, insects, barrier islands, algae, curlits.

The University of Texas at Dallas, School of Natural Sciences and Mathematics, Program in Physics, Richardson, TX 75080. Offers applied physics (MS); physics (MS, PhD). Part-time and evening/weekend programs available. *Faculty:* 18 full-time (1 woman). *Students:* 48 full-time (6 women), 15 part-time (4 women); includes 6 minority (1 African American, 3 Asian Americans or Pacific Islanders, 2 Hispanic Americans), 27 international. Average age 31. 62 applicants, 34% accepted, 16 enrolled. In 2009, 8 master's, 7 doctorates awarded. *Degree requirements:* For master's, thesis optional, industrial internship; for doctorate, thesis/dissertation, publishable paper. *Entrance requirements:* For master's and doctorate, GRE General Test, minimum GPA of 3.0 in upper-level coursework in field. Additional exam requirements/recommendations for international students: Required—TOEFL (minimum score 550 paper-based; 213 computer-based). *Application deadline:* For fall admission, 7/15 for domestic students, 5/1 priority date for international students; for spring admission, 11/15 for domestic students, 9/1 priority date for international students. Applications are processed on a rolling basis. Application fee: $50 ($100 for international students). Electronic applications accepted. *Expenses:* Tuition, state resident: full-time $11,068; part-time $461 per credit hour. Tuition, nonresident: full-time $21,178; part-time $882 per credit hour. Tuition and fees vary according to course load. *Financial support:* In 2009–10, 18 research assistantships with full tuition reimbursements (averaging $14,388 per year), 23 teaching assistantships with full tuition reimbursements (averaging $13,500 per year) were awarded; fellowships, career-related internships or fieldwork, Federal Work-Study, institutionally sponsored loans, scholarships/grants, and unspecified assistantships also available. Support available to part-time students. Financial award application deadline: 4/30; financial award applicants required to submit FAFSA. *Faculty research:* Atomic, molecular, atmospheric, chemical, solid-state, and space physics; optics and quantum electronics; relativity and astrophysics; high-energy particles. *Unit head:* Dr. Robert Glosser, Department Head, 972-883-2884, Fax: 972-883-2848, E-mail: physweb@utdallas.edu. *Application contact:* Dr. Gregory D. Earle, Graduate Advisor, 972-883-6828, Fax: 972-883-2848, E-mail: physweb@utdallas.edu.

The University of Texas at El Paso, Graduate School, College of Science, Department of Physics, El Paso, TX 79968-0001. Offers MS. Part-time and evening/weekend programs available. *Students:* 14 (4 women); includes 4 minority (all Hispanic Americans), 10 international. Average age 34. In 2009, 8 master's awarded. *Degree requirements:* For master's, thesis optional. *Entrance requirements:* For master's, GRE, minimum GPA of 3.0. Additional exam requirements/recommendations for international students: Required—TOEFL; Recommended—IELTS. *Application deadline:* For fall admission, 8/1 priority date for domestic students, 3/1 for international students; for spring admission, 11/1 priority date for domestic students, 9/1 for international students. Applications are processed on a rolling basis. Application fee: $45 ($80 for international students). Electronic applications accepted. *Financial support:* In 2009–10, research assistantships with partial tuition reimbursements (averaging $20,250 per year), teaching assistantships (averaging $16,200 per year) were awarded; fellowships with partial tuition reimbursements, institutionally sponsored loans, scholarships/grants, health care benefits, tuition waivers (partial), and unspecified assistantships also available. Support available to part-time students. Financial award application deadline: 3/15; financial award applicants required to submit FAFSA. *Unit head:* Dr. Vivian Incera, Chair, 915-747-5715, Fax: 915-747-5447, E-mail: vincera@utep.edu. *Application contact:* Dr. Patricia D. Witherspoon, Dean of the Graduate School, 915-747-5491, Fax: 915-747-5788, E-mail: withersp@utep.edu.

The University of Texas at San Antonio, College of Sciences, Department of Physics and Astronomy, San Antonio, TX 78249-0617. Offers physics (MS, PhD). *Faculty:* 11 full-time (0 women), 4 part-time/adjunct (0 women). *Students:* 31 full-time (2 women), 9 part-time (2 women); includes 10 minority (1 African American, 3 Asian Americans or Pacific Islanders, 6 Hispanic Americans), 6 international. Average age 29. 20 applicants, 85% accepted, 11 enrolled. In 2009, 2 master's, 1 doctorate awarded. *Degree requirements:* For master's, comprehensive exam (for some programs), thesis (for some programs); for doctorate, comprehensive exam, thesis/dissertation (for some programs). *Entrance requirements:* For master's and doctorate, GRE, minimum GPA of 3.0. Additional exam requirements/recommendations for international students: Required—TOEFL (minimum score 500 paper-based; 173 computer-based; 61 iBT), IELTS (minimum score 5). *Application deadline:* For fall admission, 7/1 for domestic students, 4/1 for international students; for spring admission, 11/1 for domestic students, 9/1 for international students. Applications are processed on a rolling basis. Application fee: $45 ($80 for international students). Electronic applications accepted. *Expenses:* Tuition, state resident: full-time $3975; part-time $221 per contact hour. Tuition, nonresident: full-time $13,947; part-time $775 per contact hour. Required fees: $1853. *Financial support:* In 2009–10, 25 students received support, including 3 fellowships (averaging $29,206 per year), 6 research assistantships (averaging $25,000 per year), 18 teaching assistantships (averaging $7,875 per year); career-related internships or fieldwork, scholarships/grants, tuition waivers, and unspecified assistantships also available. Support available to part-time students. *Faculty research:* Nanotechnology, experimental physics, astrophysics, theoretical physics. Total annual research expenditures: $1.8 million. *Unit head:* Dr. Miguel Yacaman, Chair, 210-458-6954, Fax: 210-458-4919, E-mail: miguel.yacaman@utsa.edu. *Application contact:* Lorenzo Brancaleon, Graduate Advisor, 210-458-5462, E-mail: lorenzo.brancaleon@utsa.edu.

The University of Toledo, College of Graduate Studies, College of Arts and Sciences, Department of Physics and Astronomy, Toledo, OH 43606-3390. Offers physics (MS, PhD). *Degree requirements:* For master's, thesis; for doctorate, thesis/dissertation, departmental qualifying exam. *Entrance requirements:* For master's and doctorate, GRE General Test, GRE Subject Test. Additional exam requirements/recommendations for international students: Required—TOEFL. Electronic applications accepted. *Faculty research:* Atomic physics, solid-state physics, materials science, astrophysics.

University of Toronto, School of Graduate Studies, Physical Sciences Division, Department of Physics, Toronto, ON M5S 1A1, Canada. Offers M Sc, PhD. *Degree requirements:* For master's, thesis optional; for doctorate, thesis/dissertation. *Entrance requirements:* For master's, minimum B+ average in an honors physics program or equivalent, 2 letters of reference; for doctorate, M Sc degree in physics or a related field, 2 letters of reference.

University of Tulsa, Graduate School, College of Engineering and Natural Sciences, Department of Physics and Engineering Physics, Program in Physics, Tulsa, OK 74104-3189. Offers MS. Part-time programs available. *Faculty:* 10 full-time (0 women). *Students:* 5 full-time (2 women), all international. Average age 25. 18 applicants, 22% accepted, 3 enrolled. *Degree requirements:* For master's, thesis. *Entrance requirements:* For master's, GRE General Test. Additional exam requirements/recommendations for international students: Required—TOEFL (minimum score 550 paper-based; 213 computer-based; 80 iBT), IELTS (minimum score 6). *Application deadline:* Applications are processed on a rolling basis. Application fee: $40. Electronic applications accepted. *Expenses:* Tuition: Full-time $16,182; part-time $899 per credit hour. Required fees: $4 per credit hour. Tuition and fees vary according to course load. *Financial support:* In 2009–10, 5 students received support, including 2 research assistantships (averaging $8,500 per year), 4 teaching assistantships (averaging $11,594 per year); fellowships, career-related internships or fieldwork, Federal Work-Study, scholarships/grants, health care benefits, tuition waivers, and unspecified assistantships also available. Support available to part-time students. Financial award application deadline: 2/1. *Faculty research:* Nanotechnology, theoretical plasma physics, theoretical and experimental condensed matter, optics, applications of laser spectroscopy to environmental applications. *Unit head:* Dr. George Miller, Advisor and Program Chair, 918-631-3021, Fax: 918-631-2995, E-mail: george-miller@utulsa.edu. *Application contact:* Dr. George Miller, Advisor and Program Chair, 918-631-3021, Fax: 918-631-2995, E-mail: george-miller@utulsa.edu.

University of Utah, The Graduate School, College of Science, Department of Physics and Astronomy, Salt Lake City, UT 84112. Offers chemical physics (PhD); medical physics (MS, PhD); physics (MA, MS, PhD); physics teaching (PhD). Part-time programs available. *Faculty:* 32 full-time (1 woman), 2 part-time/adjunct (0 women). *Students:* 76 full-time (16 women), 25 part-time (6 women); includes 3 minority (1 Asian American or Pacific Islander, 2 Hispanic Americans), 48 international. Average age 30. 135 applicants, 25% accepted, 17 enrolled. In 2009, 5 master's, 14 doctorates awarded. Terminal master's awarded for partial completion of doctoral program. *Degree requirements:* For master's, comprehensive exam (for some programs), thesis or alternative, teaching experience, departmental exam; for doctorate, comprehensive exam, thesis/dissertation, departmental qualifying exam. *Entrance requirements:* For master's and doctorate, GRE General Test, GRE Subject Test, minimum GPA of 3.0. Additional exam requirements/recommendations for international students: Required—TOEFL (minimum score 500 paper-based; 173 computer-based; 69 iBT). *Application deadline:* For fall admission, 2/1 priority date for domestic students, 2/1 for international students. Applications are processed on a rolling basis. Application fee: $55 ($65 for international students). Electronic applications accepted. *Expenses:* Tuition, state resident: full-time $4004; part-time $1674 per semester. Tuition, nonresident: full-time $14,134; part-time $5915 per semester. Required fees: $324 per semester. Tuition and fees vary according to course load, degree level and program. *Financial support:* In 2009–10, 3 fellowships with full tuition reimbursements (averaging $19,000 per year), 27 research assistantships with full and partial tuition reimbursements (averaging $19,420 per year), 45 teaching assistantships with full and partial tuition reimbursements (averaging $14,626 per year) were awarded; Federal Work-Study, institutionally sponsored loans, and scholarships/grants also available. Financial award application deadline: 2/15; financial award applicants required to submit FAFSA. *Faculty research:* High-energy, cosmic-ray, astrophysics, medical physics, condensed matter, relativity applied physics. Total annual research expenditures: $4.7 million. *Unit head:* Dr. David Kieda, Chair, 801-581-6901, Fax: 801-581-4801, E-mail: kieda@physics.utah.edu. *Application contact:* Jackie Hadley, Graduate Secretary, 801-581-6861, Fax: 801-581-4801, E-mail: jackie@physics.utah.edu.

University of Vermont, Graduate College, College of Arts and Sciences, Department of Physics, Burlington, VT 05405. Offers MS. *Students:* 3 (1 woman). 3 applicants, 67% accepted, 0 enrolled. *Entrance requirements:* For master's, GRE General Test. Additional exam requirements/recommendations for international students: Required—TOEFL (minimum score 550 paper-based; 213 computer-based; 80 iBT). *Application deadline:* For fall admission, 4/1 priority date for domestic students. Applications are processed on a rolling basis. Application fee: $40. Electronic applications accepted. *Expenses:* Tuition, area resident: Part-time $508 per credit hour. Tuition, state resident: part-time $508 per credit hour. Tuition, nonresident: part-time $1281 per credit hour. *Financial support:* Fellowships, research assistantships, teaching assistantships available. Financial award application deadline: 3/1. *Unit head:* Dr. D. Clougherty, Chairperson, 802-656-2644. *Application contact:* Prof. Kevork Spartalian, Coordinator, 802-656-2644.

University of Victoria, Faculty of Graduate Studies, Faculty of Science, Department of Physics and Astronomy, Victoria, BC V8W 2Y2, Canada. Offers astronomy and astrophysics (M Sc, PhD); condensed matter physics (M Sc, PhD); experimental particle physics (M Sc, PhD); medical physics (M Sc, PhD); ocean physics (M Sc, PhD); theoretical physics (M Sc, PhD). *Degree requirements:* For master's, thesis; for doctorate, comprehensive exam, thesis/dissertation, candidacy exam. *Entrance requirements:* For master's and doctorate, GRE. Additional exam requirements/recommendations for international students: Required—TOEFL (minimum score 575 paper-based; 233 computer-based), IELTS (minimum score 7). Electronic applications accepted. *Faculty research:* Old stellar populations; observational cosmology and large scale structure; cp violation; atlas.

University of Virginia, College and Graduate School of Arts and Sciences, Department of Physics, Charlottesville, VA 22903. Offers physics (MA, MS, PhD); physics education (MA). *Faculty:* 38 full-time (4 women). *Students:* 96 full-time (24 women), 1 part-time (0 women); includes 1 minority (Asian American or Pacific Islander), 59 international. Average age 26. 201 applicants, 33% accepted, 24 enrolled. In 2009, 15 master's, 9 doctorates awarded. *Degree requirements:* For master's, thesis (for some programs); for doctorate, comprehensive exam, thesis/dissertation. *Entrance requirements:* For master's and doctorate, GRE General Test, GRE Subject Test, 2 or more letters of recommendation. Additional exam requirements/recommendations for international students: Required—TOEFL (minimum score 600 paper-based; 250 computer-based; 90 iBT), IELTS. *Application deadline:* For fall admission, 1/7 for domestic and international students. Applications are processed on a rolling basis. Application fee: $60. Electronic applications accepted. *Financial support:* Fellowships, research assistantships, teaching assistantships available. Financial award applicants required to submit FAFSA. *Unit head:* Dinko Pocanic, Chair, 434-924-3781, Fax: 434-924-4576, E-mail: phys-chair@physics.virginia.edu. *Application contact:* Charles Sackett, Associate Chair for Graduate Studies, 434-924-3781, Fax: 434-924-4576, E-mail: grad-info-request@physics.virginia.edu.

University of Washington, Graduate School, College of Arts and Sciences, Department of Physics, Seattle, WA 98195. Offers MS, PhD. Part-time and evening/weekend programs available. Terminal master's awarded for partial completion of doctoral program. *Degree requirements:* For doctorate, thesis/dissertation. *Entrance requirements:* For master's, GRE; for doctorate, GRE General Test, GRE Subject Test. Additional exam requirements/recommendations for international students: Required—TOEFL. Electronic applications accepted. *Faculty research:* Astro-, atomic, condensed-matter, nuclear, and particle physics; physics education.

University of Waterloo, Graduate Studies, Faculty of Science, Guelph-Waterloo Physics Institute, Waterloo, ON N2L 3G1, Canada. Offers M Sc, PhD. Part-time programs available. *Degree requirements:* For master's, project or thesis; for doctorate, thesis/dissertation. *Entrance requirements:* For master's, GRE Subject Test, honors degree, minimum B average; for doctorate, GRE Subject Test, master's degree, minimum B average. Additional exam requirements/recommendations for international students: Required—TOEFL, TWE. Electronic applications accepted. *Faculty research:* Condensed-matter and materials physics; industrial and applied physics; subatomic physics; astrophysics and gravitation; atomic, molecular, and optical physics.

The University of Western Ontario, Faculty of Graduate Studies, Physical Sciences Division, Department of Applied Mathematics, London, ON N6A 5B8, Canada. Offers applied mathematics (M Sc, PhD); theoretical physics (PhD). *Degree requirements:* For master's, thesis or alternative; for doctorate, comprehensive exam, thesis/dissertation. *Entrance requirements:* For master's and doctorate, minimum B average. Additional exam requirements/recommendations for international students: Required—TOEFL. *Faculty research:* Fluid dynamics, mathematical and computational methods, theoretical physics.

The University of Western Ontario, Faculty of Graduate Studies, Physical Sciences Division, Department of Physics and Astronomy, Program in Physics, London, ON N6A 5B8, Canada. Offers M Sc, PhD. Terminal master's awarded for partial completion of doctoral program. *Degree requirements:* For master's, thesis; for doctorate, comprehensive exam, thesis/dissertation. *Entrance requirements:* For master's, GRE Subject Test (physics), honors B Sc degree, minimum B average (Canadian), A- (international); for doctorate, minimum B average (Canadian), A- (international). Additional exam requirements/recommendations for international students: Required—TOEFL (minimum score 580 paper-based; 237 computer-based). *Faculty research:* Condensed-matter and surface science, space and atmospheric physics, atomic and molecular physics, medical physics, theoretical physics.

University of Windsor, Faculty of Graduate Studies, Faculty of Science, Department of Physics, Windsor, ON N9B 3P4, Canada. Offers M Sc, PhD. Part-time programs available. *Degree requirements:* For master's, thesis or alternative; for doctorate, thesis/dissertation. *Entrance requirements:* For master's, GRE General Test, minimum B average; for doctorate, GRE General Test, master's degree. Additional exam requirements/recommendations for international students: Required—TOEFL (minimum score 560 paper-based; 220 computer-based), GRE Subject Test in physics. Electronic applications accepted. *Faculty research:* Electrodynamics, plasma physics, atomic structure/particles, spectroscopy, quantum mechanics.

University of Wisconsin–Madison, Graduate School, College of Letters and Science, Department of Physics, Madison, WI 53706-1380. Offers MA, MS, PhD. Terminal master's awarded for partial completion of doctoral program. *Degree requirements:* For master's, qualifying exam, thesis (MS); for doctorate, thesis/dissertation, preliminary and qualifying exams. *Entrance requirements:* For master's and doctorate, GRE, minimum GPA of 3.0. Additional exam requirements/recommendations for international students: Required—TOEFL. Electronic applications accepted. *Expenses:* Tuition, state resident: part-time $594 per credit. Tuition, nonresident: part-time $1504 per credit. Required fees: $65 per credit. Tuition and fees vary according to course load, program and reciprocity agreements. *Faculty research:* Atomic, physics, condensed matter, astrophysics, particles and fields.

University of Wisconsin–Milwaukee, Graduate School, College of Letters and Sciences, Department of Physics, Milwaukee, WI 53201-0413. Offers MS, PhD. *Faculty:* 20 full-time (3 women). *Students:* 28 full-time (5 women), 10 part-time (5 women); includes 1 Asian American or Pacific Islander, 26 international. Average age 29. 46 applicants, 30% accepted, 5 enrolled. In 2009, 5 master's, 2 doctorates awarded. *Degree requirements:* For master's, thesis or alternative; for doctorate, one foreign language, thesis/dissertation. *Entrance requirements:* For master's, GRE General Test, curriculum vitae; for doctorate, GRE General Test. Additional exam requirements/recommendations for international students: Required—TOEFL (minimum score 550 paper-based; 79 iBT), IELTS (minimum score 6.5). *Application deadline:* For fall admission, 1/1 priority date for domestic students; for spring admission, 9/1 for domestic students. Applications are processed on a rolling basis. Application fee: $45 ($75 for international students). *Expenses:* Tuition, state resident: full-time $8800. Tuition, nonresident: full-time $20,760. Tuition and fees vary according to program and reciprocity agreements. *Financial support:* In 2009–10, 1 fellowship, 14 research assistantships, 20 teaching assistantships were awarded; career-related internships or fieldwork and unspecified assistantships also available. Support available to part-time students. Financial award application deadline: 4/15. *Faculty research:* Gravitation, biophysics, condensed matter, optics, medical. Total annual research expenditures: $3.4 million. *Unit head:* Paul Lyman, Representative, 414-229-4626, Fax: 414-229-4474, E-mail: plyman@uwm.edu. *Application contact:* General Information Contact, 414-229-4982, Fax: 414-229-6967, E-mail: gradschool@uwm.edu.

Utah State University, School of Graduate Studies, College of Science, Department of Physics, Logan, UT 84322. Offers MS, PhD. Part-time programs available. Terminal master's awarded for partial completion of doctoral program. *Degree requirements:* For master's, thesis; for doctorate, comprehensive exam, thesis/dissertation. *Entrance requirements:* For master's and doctorate, GRE General Test, minimum GPA of 3.0. Additional exam requirements/recommendations for international students: Required—TOEFL (minimum score 550 paper-based; 213 computer-based). Electronic applications accepted. *Faculty research:* Upper-atmosphere physics, relativity, gravitational magnetism, particle physics, nanotechnology.

Vanderbilt University, Graduate School, Department of Physics and Astronomy, Nashville, TN 37240-1001. Offers astronomy (MS); physics (MA, MAT, MS, PhD). *Faculty:* 52 full-time (5 women). *Students:* 66 full-time (16 women), 2 part-time (1 woman); includes 11 minority (5 African Americans, 2 Asian Americans or Pacific Islanders, 4 Hispanic Americans), 16 international. Average age 29. 167 applicants, 21% accepted, 13 enrolled. In 2009, 10 master's, 6 doctorates awarded. *Degree requirements:* For master's, thesis; for doctorate, comprehensive exam, thesis/dissertation, final and qualifying exams. *Entrance requirements:* For master's, GRE General Test; for doctorate, GRE General Test, GRE Subject Test. Additional exam requirements/recommendations for international students: Required—TOEFL (minimum score 570 paper-based; 230 computer-based; 88 iBT). *Application deadline:* For fall admission, 1/15 for domestic and international students. Application fee: $0. Electronic applications accepted. *Financial support:* Fellowships with full and partial tuition reimbursements, research assistantships with full tuition reimbursements, teaching assistantships with full tuition reimbursements, career-related internships or fieldwork, Federal Work-Study, and institutionally sponsored loans available. Financial award application deadline: 1/15; financial award applicants required to submit CSS PROFILE or FAFSA. *Faculty research:* Experimental and theoretical physics, free electron laser, living-state physics, heavy-ion physics, nuclear structure. *Unit head:* Robert J. Scherrer, Chair, 615-322-2828, Fax: 615-343-7263, E-mail: robert.scherrer@vanderbilt.edu. *Application contact:* Richard Haglund, Director of Graduate Studies, 615-322-2828, Fax: 615-343-7263, E-mail: physastro-grad@vanderbilt.edu.

Virginia Commonwealth University, Graduate School, College of Humanities and Sciences, Department of Physics, Program in Physics and Applied Physics, Richmond, VA 23284-9005. Offers MS.

Virginia Polytechnic Institute and State University, Graduate School, College of Science, Department of Physics, Blacksburg, VA 24061. Offers applied physics (MS, PhD); physics (MS, PhD). *Entrance requirements:* For master's and doctorate, GRE Subject Test. Additional exam requirements/recommendations for international students: Required—TOEFL (minimum score 550 paper-based; 213 computer-based). Electronic applications accepted. *Faculty research:* Condensed matter, particle physics, theoretical and experimental astrophysics, biophysics, mathematical physics.

Virginia State University, School of Graduate Studies, Research, and Outreach, School of Engineering, Science and Technology, Department of Chemistry and Physics, Petersburg, VA 23806-0001. Offers physics (MS). *Degree requirements:* For master's, one foreign language, thesis. *Entrance requirements:* For master's, GRE General Test.

Wake Forest University, Graduate School of Arts and Sciences, Department of Physics, Winston-Salem, NC 27109. Offers MS, PhD. Part-time programs available. *Degree requirements:* For master's, thesis; for doctorate, comprehensive exam, thesis/dissertation. *Entrance requirements:* For master's and doctorate, GRE General Test. Additional exam requirements/recommendations for international students: Required—TOEFL (minimum score 213 computer-based; 79 iBT). Electronic applications accepted.

Washington State University, Graduate School, College of Sciences, Department of Physics and Astronomy, Pullman, WA 99164. Offers physics (MS, PhD). *Faculty:* 20. *Students:* 64 full-time (12 women); includes 1 minority (Hispanic American), 34 international. Average age 28. 127 applicants, 39% accepted, 12 enrolled. In 2009, 6 master's, 2 doctorates awarded. Terminal master's awarded for partial completion of doctoral program. *Degree requirements:* For master's, comprehensive exam (for some programs), thesis (for some programs), oral exam; for doctorate, comprehensive exam, thesis/dissertation, oral exam, written exam. *Entrance requirements:* For master's and doctorate, GRE General Test, GRE Subject Test, Minimum GPA of 3.0 in last half of the undergraduate work completed. No minimum acceptable scores specified. Students from non-English speaking countries recommended to demonstrate proficiency in English via the TOEFL exam. acceptable score for admission is 550 (paper based), 214 (computer based), or 80 Internet based (IBT). Additional exam requirements/recommendations for international students: Required—TOEFL (minimum score 550 paper-based; 214 computer-based), IELTS. *Application deadline:* For fall admission, 1/10 priority date for domestic students, 1/10 for international students; for spring admission, 7/1 priority date for domestic students, 7/1 for international students. Applications are processed on a rolling basis. Application fee: $50. Electronic applications accepted. *Financial support:* In 2009–10, 41 students received support, including 1 fellowship with full and partial tuition reimbursement available (averaging $5,000 per year), 15 research assistantships with full and partial tuition reimbursements available (averaging $13,917 per year), 25 teaching assistantships with full and partial tuition reimbursements available (averaging $13,056 per year); Federal Work-Study and institutionally sponsored loans also available. Financial award application deadline: 3/1; financial award applicants required to submit FAFSA. *Faculty research:* Linear and nonlinear acoustics and optics, shock wave dynamics, solid-state physics, surface physics, high-pressure and semiconductor physics. Total annual research expenditures: $2.5 million. *Unit head:* Steve L. Tomsovic, Chair, 509-335-7207, Fax: 509-335-7816, E-mail: tomsovic@wsu.edu. *Application contact:* Graduate School Admissions, 800-GRADWSU, Fax: 509-335-1949, E-mail: gradsch@wsu.edu.

Washington University in St. Louis, Graduate School of Arts and Sciences, Department of Physics, St. Louis, MO 63130-4899. Offers PhD. Terminal master's awarded for partial completion of doctoral program. *Degree requirements:* For doctorate, thesis/dissertation. *Entrance requirements:* For doctorate, GRE General Test. Electronic applications accepted.

Wayne State University, College of Liberal Arts and Sciences, Department of Physics and Astronomy, Detroit, MI 48202. Offers physics (MA, MS, PhD). *Degree requirements:* For doctorate, thesis/dissertation. *Entrance requirements:* For master's, GRE, 3 letters of recommendation; for doctorate, GRE, 3 letters of recommendation; personal statement. Additional exam requirements/recommendations for international students: Required—TOEFL (minimum score 550 paper-based; 213 computer-based); Recommended—TWE (minimum score 6). Electronic applications accepted. *Faculty research:* High energy particle physics, relativistic heavy ion physics, theoretical physics, positron and atomic physics, condensed matter and nano-scale physics.

Wesleyan University, Graduate Programs, Department of Physics, Middletown, CT 06459. Offers MA, PhD. *Faculty:* 9 full-time (1 woman), 2 part-time/adjunct (1 woman). *Students:* 15 full-time (4 women), 10 international. Average age 25. 60 applicants, 7% accepted, 1 enrolled. In 2009, 1 master's awarded. Terminal master's awarded for partial completion of doctoral program. *Degree requirements:* For master's, thesis; for doctorate, thesis/dissertation. *Entrance requirements:* For master's, GRE General Test, GRE Subject Test; for doctorate, GRE Subject Test. Additional exam requirements/recommendations for international students: Required—TOEFL. *Application deadline:* Applications are processed on a rolling basis. Application fee: $0. Electronic applications accepted. *Financial support:* In 2009–10, 2 research assistantships with full tuition reimbursements, 11 teaching assistantships with full tuition reimbursements were awarded; institutionally sponsored loans and tuition waivers (full) also available. Financial award application deadline: 4/15; financial award applicants required to submit FAFSA. *Faculty research:* Biophysics, computational soft matter physics, mesoscopic transport, semiclassical methods and quantum chaos, disordered systems, theoretical atomic physics, low-temperature physics, magnetic resonance, atomic collisions, laser spectroscopy, surface physics, turbulence, granular media. *Unit head:* Dr. Reinhold Blumel, Chairman, 860-685-2032, E-mail: rblumel@wesleyan.edu. *Application contact:* Erinn Savage, Information Contact, 860-685-2030, Fax: 860-685-2031, E-mail: esavage@wesleyan.edu.

Western Illinois University, School of Graduate Studies, College of Arts and Sciences, Department of Physics, Macomb, IL 61455-1390. Offers MS. Part-time programs available. *Students:* 11 full-time (3 women), 2 part-time (both women), 9 international. Average age 27. 10 applicants, 80% accepted. In 2009, 11 master's awarded. *Degree requirements:* For master's, thesis or alternative. *Entrance requirements:* Additional exam requirements/recommendations for international students: Required—TOEFL (minimum score 550 paper-based; 213 computer-based; 80 iBT). *Application deadline:* Applications are processed on a rolling basis. Application fee: $30. Electronic applications accepted. *Expenses:* Tuition, state resident: full-time $4486; part-time $249.21 per credit hour. Tuition, nonresident: full-time $8972; part-time $498.42 per credit hour. Required fees: $72.62 per credit hour. *Financial support:* In 2009–10, 7 students received support, including 7 research assistantships with full tuition reimbursements available (averaging $7,280 per year); health care benefits also available. Financial award applicants required to submit FAFSA. *Unit head:* Dr. Mark Boley, Interim Chairperson, 309-298-1538. *Application contact:* Evelyn Hoing, Assistant Director of Graduate Studies, 309-298-1806, Fax: 309-298-2345, E-mail: grad-office@wiu.edu.

Western Michigan University, Graduate College, College of Arts and Sciences, Department of Physics, Kalamazoo, MI 49008. Offers MA, PhD. *Degree requirements:* For master's, thesis; for doctorate, thesis/dissertation, oral exam. *Entrance requirements:* For doctorate, GRE General Test.

West Virginia University, Eberly College of Arts and Sciences, Department of Physics, Morgantown, WV 26506. Offers applied physics (MS, PhD); astrophysics (MS, PhD); chemical physics (MS, PhD); condensed matter physics (MS, PhD); elementary particle physics (MS,

Physics

West Virginia University (continued)

PhD); materials physics (MS, PhD); plasma physics (MS, PhD); solid state physics (MS, PhD); statistical physics (MS, PhD); theoretical physics (MS, PhD). Terminal master's awarded for partial completion of doctoral program. *Degree requirements:* For master's, thesis or alternative, qualifying exam; for doctorate, thesis/dissertation, qualifying exam. *Entrance requirements:* For master's and doctorate, GRE General Test, minimum GPA of 3.0. Additional exam requirements/recommendations for international students: Required—TOEFL. *Faculty research:* Experimental and theoretical condensed-matter, plasma, high-energy theory, nonlinear dynamics, space physics.

Worcester Polytechnic Institute, Graduate Studies and Research, Department of Physics, Worcester, MA 01609-2280. Offers MS, PhD. *Faculty:* 8 full-time (1 woman), 1 (woman) part-time/adjunct. *Students:* 11 full-time (2 women), 3 part-time (1 woman). 26 applicants, 15% accepted, 2 enrolled. In 2009, 1 master's, 1 doctorate awarded. *Degree requirements:* For master's, thesis; for doctorate, comprehensive exam, thesis/dissertation. *Entrance requirements:* For master's, GRE (recommended), 3 letters of recommendation; for doctorate, GRE (recommended), 3 letters of recommendation, statement of purpose (recommended). Additional exam requirements/recommendations for international students: Required—TOEFL (minimum score 550 paper-based; 213 computer-based; 79 iBT), IELTS (minimum score 6.5). *Application deadline:* For fall admission, 1/15 priority date for domestic students, 1/15 for international students; for spring admission, 10/15 priority date for domestic students, 10/15 for international students. Applications are processed on a rolling basis. Application fee: $70. Electronic applications accepted. *Financial support:* Career-related internships or fieldwork, institutionally sponsored loans, scholarships/grants, and unspecified assistantships available. Financial award application deadline: 1/15. *Faculty research:* Soft-condensed matter, complex fluids, biophysics, quantum and atom optics, wave function engineering. *Unit head:* Dr. Germano S. Iannacchione, Head, 508-831-5258, Fax: 508-831-5886, E-mail: gsiannac@wpi.edu. *Application contact:* Dr. L. R. Ram-Mohan, Graduate Coordinator, 508-831-5258, Fax: 508-831-5886, E-mail: lram@wpi.edu.

Wright State University, School of Graduate Studies, College of Science and Mathematics, Department of Physics, Program in Physics, Dayton, OH 45435. Offers geophysics (MS); medical physics (MS). Part-time and evening/weekend programs available. *Degree requirements:* For master's, thesis. *Entrance requirements:* Additional exam requirements/recommendations for international students: Required—TOEFL. *Faculty research:* Solid-state physics, optics, geophysics.

Yale University, Graduate School of Arts and Sciences, Department of Physics, New Haven, CT 06520. Offers PhD. *Degree requirements:* For doctorate, thesis/dissertation. *Entrance requirements:* For doctorate, GRE General Test, GRE Subject Test.

York University, Faculty of Graduate Studies, Faculty of Science and Engineering, Program in Physics and Astronomy, Toronto, ON M3J 1P3, Canada. Offers M Sc, PhD. Part-time and evening/weekend programs available. *Degree requirements:* For master's, thesis or alternative; for doctorate, comprehensive exam, thesis/dissertation. Electronic applications accepted.

Plasma Physics

Princeton University, Graduate School, Department of Astrophysical Sciences, Program in Plasma Physics, Princeton, NJ 08544-1019. Offers PhD. *Degree requirements:* For doctorate, thesis/dissertation. *Entrance requirements:* For doctorate, GRE General Test, GRE Subject Test. Additional exam requirements/recommendations for international students: Required—TOEFL (minimum score 600 paper-based; 250 computer-based). *Faculty research:* Magnetic fusion energy research, plasma physics, x-ray laser studies.

University of Colorado at Boulder, Graduate School, College of Arts and Sciences, Department of Astrophysical and Planetary Sciences, Boulder, CO 80309. Offers astrophysics (MS, PhD); planetary science (MS, PhD). *Faculty:* 20 full-time (3 women). *Students:* 27 full-time (6 women), 19 part-time (9 women); includes 3 minority (1 American Indian/Alaska Native, 2 Asian Americans or Pacific Islanders), 4 international. Average age 26. 124 applicants, 23% accepted, 7 enrolled. In 2009, 5 master's, 3 doctorates awarded. Terminal master's awarded for partial completion of doctoral program. *Degree requirements:* For master's, comprehensive exam, thesis or alternative; for doctorate, one foreign language, thesis/dissertation. *Entrance requirements:* For master's, GRE General Test, GRE Subject Test, minimum undergraduate GPA of 3.0; for doctorate, GRE General Test, GRE Subject Test. *Application deadline:* For fall admission, 1/15 priority date for domestic students, 12/1 for international students. Applications are processed on a rolling basis. Application fee: $50 ($60 for international students). *Financial support:* In 2009–10, 13 fellowships (averaging $22,199 per year), 33 research assistantships (averaging $17,541 per year) were awarded; tuition waivers (full) also available. Support available to part-time students. Financial award application deadline: 1/15. *Faculty research:* Stellar and extragalactic astrophysics cosmology, space astronomy, planetary science. Total annual research expenditures: $27.2 million.

West Virginia University, Eberly College of Arts and Sciences, Department of Physics, Morgantown, WV 26506. Offers applied physics (MS, PhD); astrophysics (MS, PhD); chemical physics (MS, PhD); condensed matter physics (MS, PhD); elementary particle physics (MS, PhD); materials physics (MS, PhD); plasma physics (MS, PhD); solid state physics (MS, PhD); statistical physics (MS, PhD); theoretical physics (MS, PhD). Terminal master's awarded for partial completion of doctoral program. *Degree requirements:* For master's, thesis or alternative, qualifying exam; for doctorate, thesis/dissertation, qualifying exam. *Entrance requirements:* For master's and doctorate, GRE General Test, minimum GPA of 3.0. Additional exam requirements/recommendations for international students: Required—TOEFL. *Faculty research:* Experimental and theoretical condensed-matter, plasma, high-energy theory, nonlinear dynamics, space physics.

Theoretical Physics

Cornell University, Graduate School, Graduate Fields of Arts and Sciences, Field of Physics, Ithaca, NY 14853-0001. Offers experimental physics (MS, PhD); physics (MS, PhD); theoretical physics (MS, PhD). *Faculty:* 70 full-time (5 women). *Students:* 148 full-time (24 women); includes 8 minority (1 African American, 5 Asian Americans or Pacific Islanders, 2 Hispanic Americans), 73 international. Average age 26. 358 applicants, 23% accepted, 23 enrolled. In 2009, 22 master's, 33 doctorates awarded. *Degree requirements:* For doctorate, comprehensive exam, thesis/dissertation. *Entrance requirements:* For doctorate, GRE General Test, GRE Subject Test (physics), 3 letters of recommendation. Additional exam requirements/recommendations for international students: Required—TOEFL (minimum score 620 paper-based; 260 computer-based; 105 iBT). *Application deadline:* For fall admission, 1/3 for domestic students. Application fee: $70. Electronic applications accepted. *Expenses:* Tuition: Full-time $29,500. Required fees: $70. Full-time tuition and fees vary according to degree level, program and student level. *Financial support:* In 2009–10, 4 fellowships with full tuition reimbursements, 1 research assistantship with full tuition reimbursement, 17 teaching assistantships with full tuition reimbursements were awarded; institutionally sponsored loans, scholarships/grants, health care benefits, tuition waivers (full and partial), and unspecified assistantships also available. Financial award applicants required to submit FAFSA. *Faculty research:* Experimental condensed matter physics, theoretical condensed matter physics, experimental high energy particle physics, theoretical particle physics and field theory, theoretical astrophysics. *Unit head:* Director of Graduate Studies, 607-255-7561. *Application contact:* Graduate Field Assistant, 607-255-7561, E-mail: physics-grad-adm@cornell.edu.

Delaware State University, Graduate Programs, Department of Applied Mathematics and Theoretical Physics, Interdisciplinary Program in Applied Mathematics and Theoretical Physics, Dover, DE 19901-2277. Offers PhD. *Degree requirements:* For doctorate, one foreign language, thesis defense. *Entrance requirements:* For doctorate, GRE General Test, MS degree in physics or mathematics. Additional exam requirements/recommendations for international students: Required—TOEFL (minimum score 550 paper-based).

Harvard University, Graduate School of Arts and Sciences, Department of Physics, Cambridge, MA 02138. Offers experimental physics (PhD); medical engineering/medical physics (PhD), including applied physics, engineering sciences, physics; theoretical physics (PhD). *Degree requirements:* For doctorate, thesis/dissertation, final exams, laboratory experience. *Entrance requirements:* For doctorate, GRE General Test, GRE Subject Test. Additional exam requirements/recommendations for international students: Required—TOEFL. *Expenses:* Tuition: Full-time $33,696. Required fees: $1126. Full-time tuition and fees vary according to program. *Faculty research:* Particle physics, condensed matter physics, atomic physics.

Rutgers, The State University of New Jersey, New Brunswick, Graduate School-New Brunswick, Department of Physics and Astronomy, Piscataway, NJ 08854-8097. Offers astronomy (MS, PhD); biophysics (PhD); condensed matter physics (MS, PhD); elementary particle physics (MS, PhD); intermediate energy nuclear physics (MS); nuclear physics (MS, PhD); physics (MST); surface science (PhD); theoretical physics (MS, PhD). Part-time programs available. Terminal master's awarded for partial completion of doctoral program. *Degree requirements:* For master's, comprehensive exam, thesis or alternative; for doctorate, comprehensive exam, thesis/dissertation. *Entrance requirements:* For master's and doctorate, GRE General Test, GRE Subject Test. Additional exam requirements/recommendations for international students: Required—TOEFL (minimum score 560 paper-based). Electronic applications accepted. *Faculty research:* Astronomy, high energy, condensed matter, surface, nuclear physics.

University of Victoria, Faculty of Graduate Studies, Faculty of Science, Department of Physics and Astronomy, Victoria, BC V8W 2Y2, Canada. Offers astronomy and astrophysics (M Sc, PhD); condensed matter physics (M Sc, PhD); experimental particle physics (M Sc, PhD); medical physics (M Sc, PhD); ocean physics (M Sc, PhD); theoretical physics (M Sc, PhD). *Degree requirements:* For master's, thesis; for doctorate, comprehensive exam, thesis/dissertation, candidacy exam. *Entrance requirements:* For master's and doctorate, GRE. Additional exam requirements/recommendations for international students: Required—TOEFL (minimum score 575 paper-based; 233 computer-based), IELTS (minimum score 7). Electronic applications accepted. *Faculty research:* Old stellar populations; observational cosmology and large scale structure; cp violation; atlas.

West Virginia University, Eberly College of Arts and Sciences, Department of Physics, Morgantown, WV 26506. Offers applied physics (MS, PhD); astrophysics (MS, PhD); chemical physics (MS, PhD); condensed matter physics (MS, PhD); elementary particle physics (MS, PhD); materials physics (MS, PhD); plasma physics (MS, PhD); solid state physics (MS, PhD); statistical physics (MS, PhD); theoretical physics (MS, PhD). Terminal master's awarded for partial completion of doctoral program. *Degree requirements:* For master's, thesis or alternative, qualifying exam; for doctorate, thesis/dissertation, qualifying exam. *Entrance requirements:* For master's and doctorate, GRE General Test, minimum GPA of 3.0. Additional exam requirements/recommendations for international students: Required—TOEFL. *Faculty research:* Experimental and theoretical condensed-matter, plasma, high-energy theory, nonlinear dynamics, space physics.

BOSTON UNIVERSITY

BOSTON UNIVERSITY

Department of Physics

Programs of Study

The Department of Physics offers multiple programs leading to the Ph.D. in physics with an optional M.A. degree. Research opportunities are offered in experimental high-energy particle physics, particle astrophysics, theoretical particle physics and cosmology, biological physics, experimental and theoretical condensed-matter physics, polymer physics, econophysics, and statistical physics.

The Ph.D. degree requires the completion of 64 credit hours (equivalent to sixteen semester courses), an honors grade on the written comprehensive exam, an oral comprehensive exam, a departmental seminar, completion of a dissertation, and a dissertation oral defense. The dissertation must exhibit an original contribution to the field. Each student must satisfy a residency requirement of a minimum of two consecutive semesters of full-time graduate study at Boston University. The average time to complete a Ph.D. degree is about 5½ years.

The M.A. degree requires the completion of 32 credit hours (equivalent to eight semester courses) and a passing grade on the written comprehensive exam or the completion of a master's thesis. The requirements for a master's degree may be satisfied as part of the Ph.D. degree program. Each student must satisfy a residency requirement of a minimum of two consecutive semesters of full-time graduate study at Boston University.

Research Facilities

The Department of Physics is part of Boston University's Science and Engineering Complex, centrally located on the main Charles River Campus. Condensed-matter physics facilities include electronic and mechanical nanostructure fabrication and measurement, metastable-helium-atom probes of surface spin order and dynamics, photoemission and soft X-ray fluorescence probes of electronic structure in novel materials, X-ray diffractometers, and the optics and transport of electrons at high fields and low temperatures. Biological physics and polymer physics labs include dynamical light scattering, Raman and Brillouin scattering, and infrared and far-infrared absorption spectroscopy as well as modern facilities for genetically manipulating biomolecules. Physicists at the Center for Photonics develop and use near-field scanning optical and infrared microscopy, ultrafast infrared spectroscopy, entangled photons for quantum information processing and entangled photon microscopy, and a full complement of molecular beam epitaxy and device processing facilities, the latter primarily with InGaAl-nitride wide-band-gap semiconductor materials and devices. The high-energy physics labs include facilities for the design, production, and testing of key components of various particle detectors. Collaborations include the D0 experiment at Fermilab; the ATLAS and CMS experiments at the CERN Large Hadron Collider; the MuLan experiment at PSI, Switzerland; the Super-Kamiokande experiment in Kamioka, Japan, including the KEK/K2K and T2K/JPARC neutrino accelerator projects; the CLEAN/DEAP dark matter experiments; and the neutron EDM experiment at ORNL. For computation, workstations are networked to two major Departmental SGI servers as well as computer clusters provided by the University for student use. In addition, students have access to the University's high-end computational resources, which include IBM p690 servers with 112 processors (580 Gflops), an IBM p655 system with forty-eight processors (210 Gflops), an IBM Linux cluster with fifty-two dual-processor compute nodes and twenty-four display nodes, and advanced visualization facilities.

Financial Aid

Through a combination of teaching fellowships, research assistantships, and University fellowships, physics graduate students are supported full-time and receive full-tuition scholarships for the duration of their studies. The standard stipend for teaching fellows and research assistants is currently $28,200 per calendar year plus student medical insurance.

Cost of Study

Tuition and fees are provided for as described above. Books and supplies are estimated to cost an additional $400 per year.

Living and Housing Costs

A limited amount of graduate student housing is available on the Boston University campus at approximately $12,000 per year for room and board. However, most graduate students generally rent apartments, which are widely available from private sources in the Boston area.

Student Group

Currently, the Department has 116 graduate students engaged in work toward the Ph.D. and M.A. degrees, and it prides itself on the close contact maintained between students and faculty members.

Student Outcomes

Recent Ph.D. recipients from the Department of Physics have been awarded the Wigner Fellowship at Oak Ridge, National Research Council Postdoctoral Fellowships, and the IBM Supercomputer Research Award, among others. Other graduates have gone on to permanent positions at Bell Laboratories, NEC Corporation, NASA, and NIST and to tenure-track faculty positions at major research universities.

Location

Boston University is located in Boston, Massachusetts, which is a major metropolitan center of cultural, scholarly, scientific, and technological activity. Besides Boston University, there are many major academic institutions in the area. Seminars and colloquia are announced in a Boston Area Physics Calendar.

The University and The Department

Boston University is a private urban university with a faculty of 3,859 members and a student population of 32,557. The University consists of fifteen schools and colleges. The Department of Physics is part of the College of Arts and Sciences and the Graduate School. The Department has a young and active faculty of 38 full-time members and has experienced significant growth in recent years.

Applying

The application deadlines are December 15 for admission in September for the fall semester. Spring semester admission is possible but is uncommon; interested applicants should send an inquiry to the Department of Physics Director of Graduate Studies before applying. Application information and forms are available online at http://physics.bu.edu/grad.html. For admission to the graduate programs, a bachelor's degree in physics or astronomy is required. Exceptional candidates from other fields are considered. Official test results of the Graduate Record Examinations (GRE) (General Test and Subject Test in physics) are required. The minimum acceptable score for admission is dependent on the applicant's overall record. Official results of the Test of English as a Foreign Language (TOEFL) are required of all applicants whose native language is not English. The minimum score requirement is 250 (computer-based test), 84 (Internet-based test), or 600 (paper-based test).

Correspondence and Information

Chair, Graduate Admissions Committee
Department of Physics
Boston University
590 Commonwealth Avenue
Boston, Massachusetts 02215

Phone: 617-353-2623
E-mail: cabello@physics.bu.edu
Web site: http://physics.bu.edu/

Boston University

THE FACULTY AND THEIR RESEARCH

Steven Ahlen, Ph.D., Berkeley, 1976. Experimental particle physics and astrophysics, ATLAS.
Richard Averitt, Ph.D., Rice, 1998. Experimental condensed-matter physics.
Rama Bansil, Ph.D., Rochester, 1974. Biological physics, polymers.
Irving Bigio, joint appointment with the College of Engineering; Ph.D., Michigan, 1974. Biomedical and biological physics.
Ed Booth, Emeritus; Ph.D., Johns Hopkins, 1955. Biological physics.
Tulika Bose, Ph.D., Columbia, 2006. High-energy physics.
Kenneth Brecher, joint appointment with the Department of Astronomy; Ph.D., MIT, 1969. Theoretical astrophysics, relativity, cosmology.
Richard Brower, joint appointment with the College of Engineering; Ph.D., Berkeley, 1969. Theoretical particle physics.
John Butler, Ph.D., Stanford, 1986. Experimental high-energy physics, D0.
David Campbell, joint appointment with the College of Engineering; Ph.D., Cambridge, 1970. Theoretical physics and applied mathematics.
Robert Carey, Ph.D., Harvard, 1989. Experimental high-energy physics, muon g-2.
Antonio H. Castro Neto, Ph.D., Illinois, 1994. Condensed-matter theory.
Claudio Chamon, Ph.D., MIT, 1996. Condensed-matter theory.
Bernard Chasan, Emeritus; Ph.D., Cornell, 1961. Biological physics.
Andrew G. Cohen, Ph.D., Harvard, 1986. Elementary particle physics.
Robert Cohen, Director Emeritus; Ph.D., Yale, 1948.
Ernesto Corinaldesi, Emeritus; Ph.D., Manchester, 1951. Quantum mechanics.
Charles Delisi, joint appointment with the College of Engineering; Ph.D., NYU, 1969. Elementary particle theory.
Alvaro DeRújula, joint appointment with CERN; Ph.D., Madrid, 1968. Theoretical particle physics, phenomenology.
Andrew G. Duffy, Ph.D., Queen's at Kingston, 1995. Physics education research.
Dean S. Edmonds Jr., Emeritus; Ph.D., MIT, 1958. Electronics and instrumentation.
Maged El-Batanouny, Ph.D., California, Davis, 1978. Surface physics, solitons.
Shyamsunder Erramilli, Ph.D., Illinois, 1986. Biological physics.
Evan Evans, joint appointment with the College of Engineering; Ph.D., California, San Diego, 1970. Biological physics.
Wolfgang Franzen, Emeritus; Ph.D., Pennsylvania, 1949. Atomic physics, surface physics.
Roscoe Giles, joint appointment with the College of Engineering; Ph.D., Stanford. Theoretical condensed matter.
Sheldon Glashow, Ph.D., Harvard, 1958. Theoretical particle physics.
Bennett B. Goldberg, Ph.D., Brown, 1987. Condensed-matter physics.
Bill Hellman, Emeritus; Ph.D., Syracuse, 1961. Elementary particle theory.
Emanuel Katz, Ph.D., MIT, 2001. High-energy theory.
Edward Kearns, Ph.D., Harvard, 1990. Neutrino physics and particle astrophysics, Super-Kamiokande.
William Klein, Ph.D., Temple, 1972. Condensed-matter theory.
Dirk Kreimer, joint appointment with the Department of Math and Statistics; Ph.D., Johannes Gutenberg, 1992. Quantum field theory.
Kenneth D. Lane, Ph.D., Johns Hopkins, 1970. Theoretical high-energy physics.
Karl Ludwig, Ph.D., Stanford, 1986. Experimental condensed-matter physics.
Amit Meller, Ph.D., Weizmann Institute of Science, 1998. Biological physics.
Jerome Mertz, joint appointment with the College of Engineering; Ph.D., Paris VI (joint with California, Santa Barbara), 1991. Biological physics.
James Miller, Ph.D., Carnegie Mellon, 1974. Intermediate- and high-energy experimental physics, muon g-2.
Pritiraj Mohanty, Ph.D., Maryland, College Park, 1998. Experimental condensed-matter physics.
Theodore Moustakas, joint appointment with the College of Engineering; Ph.D., Columbia, 1974. Synthetic novel materials.
So-Young Pi, Ph.D., SUNY at Stony Brook, 1974. Field theory, theoretical elementary particle physics.
Anatoli Polkovnikov, Ph.D., Yale, 2003. Condensed-matter theory.
Claudio Rebbi, Ph.D., Turin (Italy), 1967. Theoretical physics, lattice quantum chromodynamics, computational physics.
Sidney Redner, Ph.D., MIT, 1977. Statistical physics, condensed-matter theory.
B. Lee Roberts, Ph.D., William and Mary, 1974. Intermediate- and high-energy experimental physics, muon g-2, CP violation.
James Rohlf, Ph.D., Caltech, 1980. Experimental particle physics, hadron collider physics, CMS.
Kenneth Rothschild, Ph.D., MIT, 1973. Biophysics, molecular electronics, physics of vision.
Anders Sandvik, Ph.D., California, Santa Barbara, 1993. Condensed-matter computational physics.
Martin Schmaltz, Ph.D., California, San Diego, 1995. Theoretical particle physics.
Alexander Sergienko, joint appointment with the College of Engineering; Ph.D., Moscow, 1987. Correlation spectroscopy, field optical microscopy.
Abner Shimony, Emeritus; Ph.D. Princeton, 1962. Foundations of physics.
William J. Skocpol, Ph.D., Harvard, 1974. Experimental condensed-matter physics.
Kevin E. Smith, Ph.D., Yale, 1988. Experimental condensed-matter physics.
John Stachel, Emeritus, Curator of Einstein papers in the United States; Ph.D., Stevens, 1952. General relativity, foundations of relativistic space-time theories.
H. Eugene Stanley, Ph.D., Harvard, 1967. Phase transitions, scaling, polymer physics, fractals and chaos.
James L. Stone, Ph.D., Michigan, 1976. Experimental particle physics and astrophysics, neutrinos, proton decay, Super-Kamiokande.
Lawrence R. Sulak, Ph.D., Princeton, 1970. Experimental particle physics, proton decay, monopoles, muon g-2, neutrinos.
Anna Swan, joint appointment with the College of Engineering; Ph.D., 1993, Boston University. Experimental condensed-matter physics.
Malvin Teich, joint appointment with the College of Engineering; Ph.D., Cornell, 1966. Quantum optics and imaging.
Ophelia Tsui, Ph.D., Princeton, 1996. Soft condensed-matter physics.
M. Selim Unlu, joint appointment with the College of Engineering; Ph.D., Illinois, 1997. Nearfield optical microscopy and spectroscopy, nanoscale imaging.
J. Scott Whitaker, Ph.D., Berkeley, 1976. Experimental colliding-beam physics, supersymmetric particle searches.
Charles R. Willis, Emeritus; Ph.D., Syracuse, 1957. Biophysics, nonlinear physics, statistical physics.
George O. Zimmerman, Emeritus; Ph.D., Yale, 1963. Low-temperature physics, magnetism.

Research Faculty and Staff
Mi Kyung Hong, Ph.D., Illinois, 1988. Experimental biophysics.
Plamen Ivanov, Ph.D., Boston University, 1998. Polymer physics.
Paul Krapivsky, Ph.D., Moscow Physical Technical Institute, 1991. Theoretical condensed-matter physics.
James Shank, Ph.D., Berkeley, 1998. High-energy physics.
Saul Youseff, Ph.D., Carnegie Mellon, 1992. High-energy physics.

the
City College
of New York

CITY COLLEGE OF THE CITY UNIVERSITY OF NEW YORK

Department of Physics

Programs of Study

The Department of Physics offers students the opportunity for study and research leading to the degrees of Doctor of Philosophy (Ph.D.) and Master of Arts (M.A.).

Students in the Ph.D. program usually take a year of graduate courses before the first qualifying examination, although some advanced students take the examination after half a year of course work. The examination tests classical mechanics and electromagnetism, quantum theory, and general undergraduate physics. Students entering the biophysics subspecialty are allowed to substitute a biophysics examination for classical mechanics. Sixty credits of course work are normally required for the Ph.D. degree program; advanced students with an M.A. degree can usually transfer 30 credits of previous graduate work. In addition, arrangements are always made so that advanced students meet course requirements by working at their appropriate level in connection with their anticipated thesis research. After passing the qualifying examination, students choose faculty mentors for their thesis research. When student and mentor feel confident of the area of thesis research, the student takes an oral second examination before an appropriately chosen thesis committee. During this examination, the student describes the proposed research and demonstrates familiarity with the physics in the area of research. When students complete their original research, they defend a written thesis before their thesis committee at a final thesis defense.

Students in the M.A. program normally take the qualifying examination after 1 or 1½ years, when they have completed the necessary course work. Students who pass the qualifying examination are often admitted to the Ph.D. program. Students who do not pass the qualifying examination but show satisfactory performance at the master's level are awarded a master's degree when they have completed 30 credits of course work. The M.A. program normally requires 1½ years to complete.

Research Facilities

The physics department is housed on three floors (about 70,000 square feet) of the thirteen-story Marshak Science Building, which also houses the other CCNY science departments. FT-IR, X-ray diffraction, UV-visible spectrometers, ultrafast laser instrumentation in picosecond and femtosecond regimes, and departmental computers are available to students. In addition, high-resolution FT-NMR spectrometers and mass spectrometers are run by operators for any research group. A wide variety of equipment is used by individual research groups, including lasers of many kinds, molecular beam instrumentation, a microwave spectrometer, computers, ultrahigh-vacuum systems for surface studies, two He3-He4 dilution refrigerators, a SQUID-based magnetometer, e-beam evaporators, crystal growing equipment, Raman spectrometers, ultrafast time-resolving instrumentation, and atomic beam systems. The department has an electronics shop, a machine shop, a student machine shop, and a glassblower available for designing and building equipment. The Institute for Ultrafast Spectroscopy and Lasers has eight laboratories in the Science Building and the Engineering Building. The New York State Center for Advanced Technology in Ultrafast Photonic Materials and Applications focuses on photonics research with commercial applications.

Financial Aid

Students accepted into the Ph.D. program are normally offered financial support by the Department of Physics. The support is in the form of fellowships and/or research assistantships, for a total stipend of $24,000 (taxable) per year, plus tuition waiver and medical insurance. The exact amount depends on the student's progress in the program, tuition costs, and need. Some New York State residents are also eligible for other stipends or awards. More advanced students are generally awarded research assistantships.

Cost of Study

Tuition for fall 2009 was $7730 for an entering student ($3290 for New York residents), $4576 for an intermediate-level student ($2060 for New York residents), and $1633 for an advanced student ($815 for New York residents).

Living and Housing Costs

There is new but very limited on-campus housing available at City College. For more information, students should visit http://www.ccnytowers.com/.

Graduate student housing is available for some students and is run by the City University of New York in midtown Manhattan. Many students live in rooms and apartments throughout New York City, paying $550–$750 per person per month.

Student Group

The total number of graduate students in the physics department is currently about 35. There are 8 postdoctoral assistants. A wide variety of academic, ethnic, and national backgrounds are represented among these students.

Location

The City College is located in an urban setting in the upper part of Manhattan. The College is part of the City University of New York, which includes eighteen campuses—among them Brooklyn, Hunter, and Queens colleges. Physics research at these other branches of the City University complements that at City College. The College is near many other institutions in the New York metropolitan area, including Columbia University, Rockefeller University, and New York University, and has cooperative arrangements with Brookhaven National Laboratory on Long Island. A number of world-famous industrial research laboratories are near New York City, including AT&T Bell Laboratories, IBM's Thomas J. Watson Laboratory, RCA's David Sarnoff Laboratory, and the Exxon Research Center.

New York City is a major cultural, artistic, communications, medical, and scientific center with numerous resources and opportunities. The city is also a focus of international travel, and visiting scientists often come to City College as part of their itinerary in the United States.

The College

The City College of the City University of New York is the lineal descendant of the Free Academy of New York City, founded in 1847. City College is the oldest and best-known component of the City University of New York.

Applying

Information and application forms can be obtained online. An application fee of $125 must accompany the application, with the exception of international students with financial difficulties, for whom the fee can be deferred until registration.

For the Ph.D. program, students may apply online at http://www.gc.cuny.edu/admin_offices/admissions/index.htm or http://www.gc.cuny.edu/admin_offices/admissions/online_app.htm. Information about admission to the master's program in physics is available at http://www1.ccny.cuny.edu/prospective/admissions/grad/index.cfm. Master's degree applicants may apply online at https://app.applyyourself.com/?id=CUNYCCNYG. Additional master's program information is available at http://www1.ccny.cuny.edu/prospective/admissions/applications.cfm.

Correspondence and Information

Doctoral Program in Physics
The City University of New York
Graduate School and University Center
365 Fifth Avenue
New York, New York 10016
Phone: 212-817-8860
E-mail: physics@gc.cuny.edu
Web site: http://web.gc.cuny.edu/Science

Master's Program in Physics
The City College of the City University of New York
Admissions Office, Room A101
160 Convent Avenue
New York, New York
Phone: 212-650-6891

City College of the City University of New York

THE FACULTY AND THEIR RESEARCH

Robert R. Alfano, Distinguished Professor; Ph.D., NYU. Ultrafast picosecond and femtosecond laser spectroscopy applied to physical and biological systems: nonlinear optics, optical imaging, medical applications of photonics, laser development.

Joseph L. Birman, Distinguished Professor; Ph.D., Columbia. Theoretical physics: condensed-matter theory; symmetry and symmetry breaking and restoration; optical response of matter, including nonlinear response and response of strongly correlated electronic systems (quantum Hall systems); microscopic theory of high-Tc superconductors; many-body theory, including use of quantum deformed algebras.

Timothy Boyer, Professor; Ph.D., Harvard. Connections between classical and quantum theories: zero-point radiation, stochastic electrodynamics, van der Waals forces, classical electromagnetism.

Ngee-Pong Chang, Professor; Ph.D., Columbia. Unification and dynamical symmetry breaking: origin of mass and chirality, quark-gluon plasma and handedness of the early universe, neutrino mass oscillations.

Morton Denn, Professor; Ph.D., Minnesota. Polymeric materials, complex fluids, rheology.

Harold Falk, Professor; Ph.D., Washington (Seattle). Statistical mechanics, especially exact results for spin-systems: discrete-time, nonlinear, and stochastic models.

Swapan K. Gayen, Professor; Ph.D., Connecticut. Photonics, ultrafast laser spectroscopy, optical imaging of biological and turbid media, spectroscopy and microscopy of nanoscale systems, turnable solid state lasers.

Joel Gersten, Professor; Ph.D., Columbia. Solid-state theory: interactions involving small solid-state particles or solid-state surfaces, sonoluminescence.

Daniel M. Greenberger, Professor; Ph.D., Illinois. Fundamental problems in quantum mechanics: the neutron interferometer, coherence in and interpretation of quantum theory, relativistic considerations.

Marilyn Gunner, Professor; Ph.D., Pennsylvania. Experimental and theoretical biophysics: proteins in electron and proton transfer reactions, time-resolved spectroscopic measurements in photosynthesis.

Michio Kaku, Professor; Ph.D., Berkeley. Superstring theory, supersymmetry, supergravity, string field theory, quantum gravity, quantum chromodynamics.

Ronald Koder, Assistant Professor; Ph.D., Johns Hopkins. Computational protein design and nuclear magnetic resonance to test understanding of the fundamental interactions underlying protein folding as well as create new proteins for use in cancer therapies, explosives biosensing and the bioremediation of hazardous wastes.

Joel Koplik, Professor; Ph.D., Berkeley. Molecular dynamics of microscopic fluid flow: transport in disordered systems, superfluid vortex dynamics, pattern selection in nonequilibrium growth processes.

Matthias Lenzner, Associate Professor; Ph.D., Schiller (Germany). Application of ultrafast lasers in biomedical optics, machining, and imaging; femtosecond UV solid-state lasers; quantum cryptography.

Michael S. Lubell, Professor; Ph.D., Yale. Photon-atom interactions, synchrotron radiation studies, polarized electron physics, two-electron systems, science and technology policy.

Hernan Makse, Professor; Ph.D., Boston University. Condensed-matter physics, granular materials, nonlinear elasticity, Edwards thermodynamics and jamming, discrete element modeling, interface roughening, porous media, dynamics of urban populations.

Carlos A. Meriles, Associate Professor; Ph.D., Córdoba (Argentina). Nobel magnetic resonance methods and instruments, hyperpolarization and ultrasensitive detection, optical NMR, low/zero field spectroscopy and imaging, applications to semiconductors and spintronics.

V. Parameswaran Nair, Professor and Chair; Ph.D., Syracuse. Mathematical and topological aspects of quantum field theory: skyrmions, quantum breaking of classical symmetries, conformal field theory, black holes, quantum chromodynamics, interaction of anyons.

Vladimir Petricevic, Professor; Ph.D., CUNY. Growth of solid-state laser materials, laser development, photonics, spectroscopy of ions in solids, ultrafast phenomena.

Alexios Polychronakos, Professor; Ph.D., Caltech. Quantum field theory, mathematical physics.

Alexander Punnoose, Associate Professor; Ph.D., Indian Institute of Science (Bangalore). Theoretical condensed matter physics.

Myriam P. Sarachik, Distinguished Professor; Ph.D., Columbia. Physics of solids at low temperatures, MI transitions, magnetic materials, molecular magnetism.

David Schmeltzer, Professor; D.Sc., Technion (Israel). Many-body physics of strongly correlated fermions: Fermi and non-Fermi liquids, Luttinger liquids, fractional quantum Hall effect, renormalization group, bosonization; metal-insulator transition, persistent currents; high-Tc superconductivity.

Mark Shattuck, Associate Professor; Ph.D., Duke. Soft condensed matter, granular media, pattern formation, nonlinear dynamics.

Frederick W. Smith, Professor; Ph.D., Brown. Deposition and characterization of semiconducting and dielectric thin films; modeling of local atomic bonding in amorphous films; chemical vapor deposition of diamond.

Richard N. Steinberg, Professor; Ph.D., Yale. Physics education research.

Jiufeng, J. Tu, Associate Professor; Ph.D., Cornell. Optical studies of correlated systems and nanosystems, infrared and Raman studies of superconductors and nanosystems.

Sergey A. Vitkalov, Associate Professor; Ph.D., Russian Academy of Sciences. Experimental condensed-matter physics, dynamical properties of low-dimensional quantum systems.

Professors Emeriti

Adolf Abrahamson, Michael E. Arons, Alvin Bachman, Robert Callender, Victor Chung, Erich Erlbach, Paul Harris, Hiram Hart, Martin Kramer, Robert M. Lea, Harry Lustig, William Miller, Marvin Mittleman, Leonard Roellig, David Shelupsky, Martin Tiersten.

COLUMBIA UNIVERSITY

Department of Applied Physics and Applied Mathematics

Programs of Study

The Department of Applied Physics and Applied Mathematics offers graduate study leading to the degrees of Master of Science (M.S.), Doctor of Engineering Science (Eng.Sc.D.), and Doctor of Philosophy (Ph.D.).

The following fields of research (topics of emphasis in parentheses) are available for doctoral study: theoretical and experimental plasma physics (fusion and space plasmas), applied mathematics (analysis of partial differential equations, large-scale scientific computing, nonlinear dynamics, inverse problems, medical imaging, geophysical/geological fluid dynamics, and biomathematics), solid-state physics (semiconductor, surface, low-dimensional physics, and molecular electronics), optical and laser physics (laser interactions with matter and quantum optics), nuclear science (medical applications), earth science (atmosphere, ocean, and climate science and geophysics), and materials science and engineering (thin films; nanomaterials; electronic, optical, and magnetic materials; and mechanical response of materials). Successful completion of 30 points (semester hours) or more of approved graduate course work beyond the master's degree is required for the doctoral degree. In addition, all doctoral candidates must pass written and oral qualifying exams and successfully defend an approved dissertation based on original research. For the M.S. degree, candidates must successfully complete a minimum of 30 points of credit of approved graduate course work at Columbia. A 36-point CAMPEP-approved M.S. degree in medical physics is offered in collaboration with faculty members from the College of Physicians and Surgeons and the Mailman School of Public Health. It prepares students for professional careers in medical physics and provides preparation for the ABR certification exam.

Research Facilities

Research equipment in the Plasma Physics Laboratory includes a toroidal high-beta tokamak for basic and applied research, a steady-state plasma experiment using a linear magnetic mirror, a large laboratory collisionless terrella used to investigate space plasma physics, and the CNT stellarator for nonneutral and antimatter plasma research. The plasma physics group is jointly operating a plasma confinement experiment, LDX, with MIT, incorporating a levitated superconducting ring. The plasma physics group is also actively involved in the NSTX experiment at the Princeton Plasma Physics Laboratory and on the DIII-D Tokamak at General Atomics in San Diego and is part of the U.S. national effort on the ITER project. Research equipment in the solid-state physics and laser physics laboratories includes extensive laser and spectroscopy facilities, a clean room that includes photolithography and thin-film fabrication systems, ultrahigh-vacuum surface preparation and analysis chambers, direct laser writing stations, a molecular-beam epitaxy machine, picosecond and femtosecond lasers, and diamond anvil cells. Research is also conducted in the shared characterization laboratories operated by the NSF Materials Research Science and Engineering Center, the NSF Nanoscale Science and Engineering Center, and the DOE Energy Frontier Research Center, which focuses on conversion of sunlight into electricity in nanometer-sized thin films. Materials science and engineering facilities include transmission and scanning electron microscopes, scanning tunneling microscopes and atomic-force microscopes, X-ray diffractometers, an ellipsometer, an X-ray photoelectron spectrometer, laser processing equipment, and mechanical testing equipment. Magnetic and electrical measurement characterization equipment is also available.

There are research opportunities in medical physics at the Columbia–Presbyterian Medical Center, as well as at other medical institutes, employing state-of-the-art medical diagnostic imaging and treatment equipment.

The Applied Mathematics Division is closely linked with the Lamont Doherty Earth Observatory (LDEO), with 5 faculty members sharing appointments in the Department of Earth and Environmental Sciences and with the NASA Goddard Institute for Space Studies (GISS). There are also close ties with Columbia's Center for Computational Biology and Bioinformatics (C2B2) and Columbia's Center for the Multiscale Analysis of Genomic and Cellular Networks (MAGNet).

The Department maintains an extensive network of workstations and desktop computers. It has recently acquired a SiCortex supercomputer with 1458 cores which is used for a wide range of departmental computational activities. The research of the plasma physics group is supported by a dedicated data acquisition/data analysis system. Computational researchers have local access to Columbia's 256-processor Linux cluster and to supercomputer systems at the National Center for Atmospheric Research and the Lawrence Berkeley, Brookhaven, and Oak Ridge National Laboratories.

Financial Aid

Financial support is awarded to doctoral candidates only on a competitive basis in the form of assistantships that provide a stipend, a tuition allowance, and medical fees. For 2010–11, the stipend for teaching assistants is $23,000 for nine months; for research assistants, the stipend is $30,660 for twelve months.

Cost of Study

For 2010–11, full-time tuition (RU) for the academic year is $36,458; for master's degree and for part-time study, the cost is $1370 per credit. In addition to medical fees (approximately $2350), annual fees range from $698–$1000.

Living and Housing Costs

The cost of on-campus, single-student housing (dormitories, suites, and apartments) ranges from $3000 to $6700 per term; married student accommodations range from $1300 to $2250 per month. For the single student, a minimum of $23,000 should be allowed for board, room, and personal expenses for the academic year.

Student Group

Approximately 26,400 students attend the fifteen schools and colleges of Columbia University; more than half are graduate students. On average, the Department has 120 graduate and 110 undergraduate students. The student population has a diverse and international character. Admission is highly competitive; in 2009–10, 45 master's- and Ph.D.-track students matriculated out of 308 applicants, with all doctoral program students being fully supported.

Student Outcomes

Recent Ph.D. recipients have found employment as postdoctoral research scientists at universities in the United States and abroad and as staff members in advanced technology industries and at national laboratories. Some have secured college-level faculty positions. Most M.S. graduates continue studying for the doctorate; a few go on to medical school or law school. M.S. graduates from the program in medical physics have secured positions in hospital departments of radiology and nuclear medicine or have entered doctoral programs.

Location

The 32-acre campus is situated in Morningside Heights on the Upper West Side of Manhattan. This location, 15 minutes from the heart of New York City, allows Columbia to be an integral part of the city while maintaining the character of a unique neighborhood. Cultural, recreational, and athletic opportunities abound at city museums, libraries, concert halls, theaters, restaurants, stadiums, parks, and beaches.

The University and The Department

With extensive resources and an outstanding faculty, Columbia University has played an eminent role in American education since its founding in 1754. The Department of Applied Physics and Applied Mathematics, a department at the forefront of interdisciplinary research and teaching, was established in 1978 as part of the Graduate School of Arts and Sciences and the Fu Foundation School of Engineering and Applied Sciences. The Graduate Program in Materials Science and Engineering joined the Department in fall 2000.

Applying

For fall admission, applications should be submitted online as follows: December 1 for doctoral, doctoral-track, and all financial aid applicants; applications for Master of Science, part-time, and nondegree candidates are reviewed on a rolling basis. Scores from the GRE General Test are required. The GRE Subject Test is required for applicants to the applied physics doctoral program. The GRE Subject Test is strongly urged for doctoral applicants in applied mathematics and materials science and engineering. TOEFL scores are required for students from non-English-speaking countries.

Admissions information and application forms can be found online at http://www.engineering.columbia.edu/graduate-2.

Correspondence and Information

Chairman, Graduate Admissions Committee
Department of Applied Physics and Applied Mathematics
200 S. W. Mudd Building, MC 4701
Columbia University
New York, New York 10027

Phone: 212-854-4457
E-mail: seasinfo.apam@columbia.edu
Web site: http://www.apam.columbia.edu

Columbia University

THE FACULTY AND THEIR RESEARCH

In the Department of Applied Physics and Applied Mathematics, theoretical and experimental research is conducted by 34 full-time faculty members, 18 adjunct professors, and 53 research scientists. Areas of research include applied mathematics, earth/atmosphere/ocean/climate science, biomathematics, biophysics, numerical analysis, inverse problems, medical imaging, space physics, surface physics, condensed-matter physics, electromagnetism, materials science, nanoscience, medical physics, optical and laser physics, plasma physics, and fusion energy science.

William E. Bailey, Associate Professor; Ph.D., Stanford, 1999. Nanoscale magnetic films and heterostructures, materials issues in spin-polarized transport, materials engineering of magnetic dynamics.

Guillaume Bal, Professor; Ph.D., Paris, 1997. Applied mathematics, partial differential equations with random coefficients, high-frequency waves in random media and application to time reversal, inverse problems and imaging with applications to medical imaging and geophysical imaging.

Daniel Bienstock, Professor (joint with Industrial Engineering and Operations Research); Ph.D., MIT, 1985. Applied mathematics, methodology and high-performance implementation of optimization algorithms, applications of optimization: preventing national-scale blackouts, emergency management, approximate solution of massively large optimization problems, higher-dimensional reformulation techniques for integer programming, robust optimization.

Simon J. L. Billinge, Professor; Ph.D., Pennsylvania, 1992. Nanoscale structure-property relationships in functional nanomaterials studied using novel X-ray and neutron scattering techniques coupled with advanced computing, solving the nanostructure problem.

Allen H. Boozer, Professor; Ph.D., Cornell, 1970. Plasma theory, theory of magnetic confinement for fusion energy, nonlinear dynamics.

Mark A. Cane, Professor (joint with Earth and Environmental Sciences); Ph.D., MIT, 1975. Climate dynamics, impacts of climate on society, climate forecasting, physical oceanography, geophysical fluid dynamics, computational fluid dynamics.

Siu-Wai Chan, Professor; Sc.D., MIT, 1985. Nanoparticles, electronic ceramics, grain boundaries and interfaces, oxide thin films.

C. K. Chu, Professor Emeritus; Ph.D., NYU (Courant), 1959. Applied mathematics.

Dirk R. Englund, Assistant Professor (joint with Electrical Engineering); Ph.D., Stanford, 2008. Quantum optics in photonic nanostructures, photonic crystal optoelectronic devices and networks, quantum information and metrology, nonlinear optics, electron and nuclear spin-dynamics in solid state systems.

Morton B. Friedman, Professor (joint with Civil Engineering); D.Sc., NYU, 1953. Applied mathematics and mechanics, numerical analysis, parallel computing.

Pierre Gentine, Assistant Professor; Ph.D., MIT, 2009. Applied mathematics, land-atmosphere interactions, soil-vegetation-transfer-atmosphere models, applications of stochastic processes to hydrology and atmospheric boundary-layer, stochastic rainfall and soil moisture, data-assimilation (filtering) of remote sensing measurements to estimate land-surface variables.

Irving P. Herman, Professor; Ph.D., MIT, 1977. Nanocrystals, optical spectroscopy of nanostructured materials, laser diagnostics of thin-film processing, mechanical properties of nanomaterials.

James Im, Professor; Ph.D., MIT, 1985. Laser-induced crystallization of thin films, phase transformations and nucleation in condensed systems.

David E. Keyes, Professor; Ph.D., Harvard, 1984. Applied and computational mathematics for PDEs, computational science, parallel numerical algorithms, parallel performance analysis, PDE-constrained optimization.

Philip Kim, Professor (joint with Physics); Harvard, 1999. Experimental condensed matter physics, physical properties and applications of nanoscale low-dimensional materials, quantum thermal transport phenomena in 1-dimensional nanoscaled materials, mesoscopic thermoelectricity and thermoelectric applications of nanoscale materials, quantum transport in novel 2-dimensional materials, mesoscopic electron transport, thermodynamic processes for sensors and electric devices.

Chris A. Marianetti, Assistant Professor; Ph.D., MIT, 2004. Predicting materials properties from first-principles computations, density-functional theory, dynamical mean-field theory, transition-metal oxides, actinides, energy storage and conversion materials.

Thomas C. Marshall, Professor Emeritus; Ph.D., Illinois, 1960. Accelerator concepts, relativistic beams and radiation, free-electron lasers.

Michael E. Mauel, Professor; Sc.D., MIT, 1983. Plasma physics, waves and instabilities, fusion and equilibrium control, space physics, plasma processing, international energy policy.

Gerald A. Navratil, Professor; Ph.D., Wisconsin–Madison, 1976. Plasma physics, plasma diagnostics, fusion energy science.

Gertrude F. Neumark, Professor; Ph.D., Columbia, 1951. Materials science and physics of semiconductors, with emphasis on optical and electrical properties of wide-bandgap semiconductors and their light-emitting devices.

I. Cevdet Noyan, Professor; Ph.D., Northwestern, 1984. Characterization and modeling of mechanical and micromechanical deformation, residual stress analysis and nondestructive testing, X-ray and neutron diffraction, microdiffrication analysis.

Richard M. Osgood, Professor (joint with Electrical Engineering); Ph.D., MIT, 1973. Nanoscale optical and electronic phenomena (experimental and computational), femtosecond lasers and laser probing, low-dimensional physics, integrated optics, nanofabrication and materials growth.

Thomas S. Pedersen, Associate Professor; Ph.D., MIT, 2000. Plasma physics, magnetic confinement, fusion energy, nonneutral plasmas, positron-electron plasmas, plasma turbulence.

Aron Pinczuk, Professor; Ph.D., Pennsylvania, 1969. Spectroscopy of semiconductors and insulators, quantum structures, systems of reduced dimensions, atomic layers of graphene, electron quantum fluids.

Lorenzo M. Polvani, Professor; Ph.D., MIT, 1988. Atmospheric and climate dynamics, geophysical fluid dynamics, numerical methods for weather and climate modeling, planetary atmospheres.

Malvin A. Ruderman, Professor (joint with Physics); Ph.D., Caltech, 1951. Theoretical astrophysics, neutron stars, pulsars, early universe, cosmic gamma rays.

Christopher H. Scholz, Professor (joint with Earth and Environmental Sciences); Ph.D., MIT, 1967. Experimental and theoretical rock mechanics, especially friction, fracture, and hydraulic transport properties; nonlinear systems; mechanics of earthquakes and faulting.

Amiya K. Sen, Professor (joint with Electrical Engineering); Ph.D., Columbia, 1963. Plasma physics, fluctuations and anomalous transport in plasmas, control of plasma instabilities, plasma transport.

Adam H. Sobel, Professor; Ph.D., MIT, 1998. Atmospheric science, geophysical fluid dynamics, tropical meteorology, climate dynamics.

Marc W. Spiegelman, Professor; Ph.D., Cambridge, 1989. Coupled fluid/solid mechanics, reactive fluid flow, solid earth and magma dynamics, scientific computation/modeling.

Horst L. Stormer, Professor; Ph.D., Stuttgart, 1977. Semiconductors, electronic transport, lower-dimensional physics, transport in nanostructures.

Latha Venkataraman, Assistant Professor; Ph.D., Harvard, 1999. Single-molecule transport, single-molecule-force spectroscopy, electron transport in nanowires, scanning tunneling microscopy and spectroscopy.

Wen I. Wang, Professor (joint with Electrical Engineering); Ph.D., Cornell, 1981. Heterostructure devices and physics, materials properties, molecular-beam epitaxy.

Michael I. Weinstein, Professor; Ph.D., NYU (Courant), 1982. Applied mathematics; partial differential equations and analysis; waves in nonlinear, inhomogeneous, and random media; dynamical systems; multiscale phenomena; applications to nonlinear optics; mathematical physics; fluid dynamics; geosciences.

Chris H. Wiggins, Associate Professor; Ph.D., Princeton, 1998. Applied mathematics, mathematical biology, biopolymer dynamics, soft condensed matter, genetic networks and network inference, machine learning.

Cheng-Shie Wuu, Professor (Public Health, Environmental Health Sciences, and Applied Physics); Ph.D., Kansas, 1985. Microdosimetry, biophysical modeling, dosimetry of brachytherapy, gel dosimetry, second cancers induced by radiotherapy, medical physics.

The Schapiro Center for Engineering and Physical Science Research; to the right, the Seeley W. Mudd Building, home of the Fu Foundation School of Engineering and Applied Science.

Faculty and research staff members and students of the Plasma Physics Laboratory in front of the Tokamak, HBT-EP.

Low Memorial Library and grounds.

SELECTED PUBLICATIONS

William E. Bailey

Interface-related damping in polycrystalline Ni81Fe19/Cu/Co93Zr7 tri-layers. *J. Appl. Phys.* 105:07D309, 2009.

Weakly coupled motion of individual layers in ferromagnetic resonance. *Phys. Rev. B: Condens. Matter* 74(6):064409, 2006.

Low relaxation rate in epitaxial vanadium-doped ultrathin iron films. *Phys. Rev. Lett.* 98(11):117601, 2007.

Dopants for independent control of precessional frequency and damping in Ni0.8Fe 0.2(50 nm) thin films. *Appl. Phys. Lett.* 77(6), 2006.

Guillaume Bal

Inverse of transport theory and applications. *Inverse Probl.* 25:053001, 2009.

Convergence to SPDEs Stratonovich form. *Comm. Math. Phys.* 292(2):457–77, 2009.

Time reversal and refocusing in random media. *SIAM J. Appl. Math.* 63(5):1475–98, 2003.

Radiative transport limit for the random Schroedinger equation. *Nonlinearity* 15:513–29, 2002.

Daniel Bienstock

The N – k problem in power grids: New models, formulations and computation. *SIAM J. Optim.* 20(5):2352–80.

Faster approximation algorithms for covering and packing problems. *SIAM J. Comput.* 35:825–54, 2006.

Subset algebra lift operators for 0-1 integer programming. *SIAM J. Optim.* 15:63–95, 2004.

Potential function methods for approximately solving linear programming problems, theory and practice. *Kluwer Academic Publishers.* Boston, 2002.

Simon J. L. Billinge

The problem with determining atomic structure at the nanoscale. *Science* 316:561–5, 2007.

Ab initio determination of solid-state nanostructure. *Nature* 440:655–8, 2006.

Underneath the Bragg Peaks: Structural Analysis of Complex Materials. Elsevier Science: Oxford, 2004.

Beyond crystallography: The study of disorder nanocrystallinity and crystallographically challenged materials. *Chem. Commun.* 7:749–60, 2004.

Allen H. Boozer

Use of non-axisymmetric shaping in magnetic fusion. *Phys. Plasmas* 16:058102, 2009.

Stellarators and the path from ITER to DEMO. *Plasma Phys. Contr. Fusion* 50:124005, 2008.

Control of asymmetric magnetic perturbations in tokamaks. *Phys. Rev. Lett.* 99:195003, 2007.

Physics of magnetically confined plasmas. *Rev. Modern Phys.* 76:1071–141, 2004.

Mark A. Cane

The El Niño–Southern Oscillation Phenomenon. London: Cambridge University Press, 2010.

The evolution of El Niño, past and future. *Earth Planet. Sci. Lett.* 104:1–10, 2005.

Mapping tropical Pacific sea level: Data assimilation via a reduced state space Kalman filter. *J. Geophys. Res.* 101:22,599–617, 1996.

Experimental forecasts of El Niño. *Nature* 322:827–32, 1986.

Siu-Wai Chan

Controlled synthesis of Co_3O_4 nanopolyhedrons and nanosheets at low temperature. *Chem. Comm.* 48:7569–71, 2009.

In situ ultra-small-angle X-ray scattering study of solution-mediated formation and growth of nanocrystalline ceria. *J. Appl. Crystallogr.* 41(5):918–29, 2008.

Cubic phase stabilization in nanoparticles of hafnia-zirconia oxides: Particle-size and annealing environment effects. *J. Appl. Phys.* 103(12):124303–7, 2008.

Synthesis and redox behavior of nanocrystalline hausmannite. *Chem. Mater.* 19:5609–16, 2007.

C. K. Chu

Domain decomposition for shallow water equations. In *Contemporary Mathematics, Proceedings of the 7th International Conference on Domain Decomposition Methods in Science and Engineering,* October 1993.

Equilibrium response of ocean deep-water circulation to variations in Ekman pumping and deep-water sources. *J. Phys. Oceanogr.* 22:1129, 1992.

Lagrangian turbulence in Stokes flow. *Phys. Fluids* 30:687, 1987.

Solitary waves generated by boundary motion. *Comm. Pure Appl. Math.* 36:495, 1983.

Dirk R. Englund

Resonant excitation of a quantum dot strongly coupled to a photonic crystal nanocavity. *Phys. Rev. Lett.* 104(7):073904, 2010.

Controlled phase shifts with a single quantum dot. *Science* 320(5877):769–72, 2008.

Controlling cavity reflectivity with a single quantum dot. *Nature* 450(7171):857–61, 2007.

Controlling the spontaneous emission rate of single quantum dots in a 2D photonic crystal. *Phys. Rev. Lett.* 95(1):013904, 2005.

Pierre Gentine

Harmonic propagation of variability in surface energy 2 balance within a coupled soil-atmosphere system. *Water Resour. Res.,* in press.

Spectral behaviour of a coupled land and boundary-layer system. *Boundary-Layer Meterorology.* 134(1):157–80, 2010.

Analysis of evaporative fraction diurnal behaviour. *Agr. Forest Meteorol.* 143(1-2):13–29, 2007.

Monitoring water stress using time series of observed to unstressed surface temperature difference. *Agr. Forest Meteorol.* 146(3-4):159–72, 2007.

Irving P. Herman

Formation of thick, large-area nanoparticle superlattices in lithographically defined geometries. *Nano Lett.* 10(4):1517–21, 2010.

Viscoplastic and granular behavior in films of colloidal nanocrystals. *Phys. Rev. Lett.* 98:026103, 2007.

Physics of the Human Body. Berlin/Heidelberg/New York: Springer, 2007.

Raman microprobe analysis of elastic strain and fracture in electrophoretically deposited CdSe nanocrystal films. *Nano Lett.* 6:175–80, 2006.

James Im

Stochastic modeling of solid nucleation in supercooled liquids. *Appl. Phys. Lett.* 78:3454–6, 2001.

On determining the relevance of athermal nucleation in rapidly quenched liquids. *Appl. Phys. Lett.* 72:662, 1998.

Sequential lateral solidification of thin silicon films on SiO_2. *Appl. Phys. Lett.* 69:2864, 1996.

Phase transformation mechanisms involved in excimer laser crystallization of amorphous silicon films. *Appl. Phys. Lett.* 63:1969–71, 1993.

David E. Keyes

Fusion simulation project workshop report. *J. Fusion Energ.* 28:1–59, 2009.

Reconstructing parameters of the Fitzhugh-Nagumo System from boundary potential measurements. *J. Comput. Neurosci.* 23:251–64, 2007.

Jacobian-free Newton-Krylov methods: A survey of approaches and application. *J. Comp. Phys.* 193:357, 2004.

Nonlinear preconditioned inexact newton algorithms. *SIAM J. Sci. Comput.* 24:183–200, 2002.

Philip Kim

Symmetry breaking of the zero energy Landau level in bilayer graphene. *Phys. Rev. Lett.* 104(6):066801, 2010.

Observation of the fractional quantum hall effect in graphene. *Nature* 462(7270):196–9, 2009.

Thermoelectric and magnetothermoelectric transport measurements of graphene. *Phys. Rev. Lett.* 102(9):096807, 2009.

Quantum interference and carrier collimation in grapheneheterojunctions. *Nat. Phys.* 5:222–6, 2009.

Chris A. Marianetti

Electronic coherence in delta-Pu: A DMFT study. *Phys. Rev. Lett.* 101:056403, 2008.

Quasiparticle dispersion and heat capacity of Na0.3CoO2: A DMFT study. *Phys. Rev. Lett.* 99:246404, 2007.

Na induced correlations in the cobaltates. *Phys. Rev. Lett.* 98:176405, 2007.

Electronic structure calculations with dynamical mean-field theory. *Rev. Mod. Phys.* 78:865, 2006.

Thomas C. Marshall

Experimental observation of constructive superposition of wake fields generated by electron bunches in a dielectric-lined waveguide. *Phys. Rev. Sci. Tech.* 9:011301, 2006.

Rectangular dielectric-lined two-beam accelerator structure. In *Particle Accelerator Conference Proceedings,* May 2005.

Nondestructive diagnostic for electron bunch length in accelerators using the wake field radiation spectrum. *Phys. Rev. Sci. Tech.* 8:062801, 2005.

Strong wake fields generated by a train of femtosecond bunches in a planar dielectric microstructure. *Phys. Rev. Special Top.–Accelerators Beams* 7:05130, 2004.

Michael E. Mauel

Turbulent inward pinch of plasma confined by a levitated dipole magnet. *Nat. Phys.* 6:207–12, 2010.

Global and local characterization of turbulent and chaotic structures in a dipole-confined plasma. *Phys. Plasmas* 16:055902, 2009.

Confinement improvement with magnetic levitation of a superconducting dipole. *Nucl. Fusion* 49:055023, 2009.

A Kalman filter for feedback control of rotating external kink instabilities in the presence of noise. *Phys. Plasmas* 16:056112, 2009.

Helium-catalyzed D-D fusion in a levitated dipole. *Nucl. Fusion* 44:193–203, 2004.

Gerald A. Navratil

Measurement of resistive wall mode stability in rotating high-beta DIII-D plasmas. *Nucl. Fusion* 45:368, 2005.

Scaling of the critical plasma rotation for stabilization of the n+1 RWM in DIII-D. *Nucl. Fusion* 44:1197, 2004.

Sustained rotational stabilization of DIII-D plasmas above the no-wall beta limit. *Phys. Plasmas* 9:1997, 2002.

Modeling of active control of external MHD instabilities. *Phys. Plasmas* 8:2170, 2001.

Gertrude F. Neumark

Doping aspects of wide bandgap zinc compounds. In *Handbook of Electronic and Photonic Materials.* Springer, 2006.

Decay dynamics in disordered systems: Application to heavily doped semiconductors. *Phys. Rev. Lett.* 80:2413, 1998.

Defects In wide-bandgap II-VI crystals. *Mater. Sci. Eng. Rep. R* 21(1), 1997.

Wide-bandgap light-emitting device materials and doping problems. *Mater. Lett.* 30:131, 1997 (published as materials update).

I. Cevdet Noyan.

Columbia University

Measurement of strain/load transfer in parallel seven-wire strands with neutron diffraction. *Exp. Mech.* 50(2):265–72, 2010.

A rigorous comparison of X-ray diffraction thickness measurement techniques using silicon-on-insulator thin films. *J. Appl. Cryst.* 42(3):401–10, 2009.

Strain measured in a silicon-on-insulator, complementary metal-oxide-semiconductor device channel induced by embedded silicon-carbon source/drain regions. *Appl. Phys. Lett.* 94(6):063502, 2009.

Applicability of real-space methods to diffraction strain measurements in single crystals. *J. Appl. Cryst.* 41(5):944–9, 2008.

Richard M. Osgood Jr.

Spectro-microscopy of single- and multi-layer graphene supported by a weakly interacting substrate. *Phys. Rev. B (Rapid Comms)* 78:201408.

Engineering nonlinearities in nanoscale optical systems: physics and applications in dispersion-engineered Si nanophotonic wires. *Adv. Opt. Photon.* 1:162–235, 2009.

Experimental demonstration of near-infrared negative-index metamaterials. *Phys. Rev. Lett.* 95:137404, 2005.

Image-state electron scattering on flat Ag/Pt(111) and stepped Ag/Pt(997) surfaces. *Phys. Rev. B* 71:165424, 2004.

Thomas S. Pedersen

Observations of an ion-driven instability in nonneutral plasmas confined on magnetic surfaces. *Phys. Rev. Lett.* 100:065002, 2008.

Experimental confirmation of stable, small-Debye-length, pure electron-plasma equilibria in a stellarator. *Phys. Rev. Lett.* 97:095003, 2006.

Prospects for the creation of positron-electron plasmas in a nonneutral stellarator. *J. Phys. B* 36:1029, 2003.

Confinement of nonneutral plasmas on magnetic surfaces. *Phys. Rev. Lett.* 88:205002, 2002.

Aron Pinczuk

Electric field effect tuning of electron-phonon coupling in graphene. *Phys. Rev. Lett.* 98(16):166802, 2007.

Transition from free to interacting composite fermions away from nu=1/3. *Phys. Rev. Lett.* 97:036804, 2006.

Extrinsic optical recombination in pentacene single crystals: Evidence of gap states. *Appl. Phys. Lett.* 87(21):211117, 2005.

Splitting of long-wavelength modes of the fractional quantum hall liquid at nu=1/3. *Phys. Rev. Lett.* 95(6):066803, 2005.

Lorenzo M. Polvani

The impact of stratospheric ozone recovery on the Southern Hemisphere westerly jet. *Science* 320(5882):1486–9, 2008.

Transport and mixing of chemical airmasses in idealized baroclinic life cycles. *J. Geophys. Res. Atmos.* 112:D23102, 2007.

Numerically converged solutions of the global primitive equations for testing the dynamical core of atmospheric GCMs. *Monthly Weather Rev.* 11:2539–52, 2004.

Tropospheric response to stratospheric perturbations in a relatively simple general circulation model. *Geophys. Res. Lett.* 29(7):1114, 2002.

The morphogenesis of bands and zonal winds with the atmospheres of the giant outer planets. *Science* 273:335–7, 1996.

Malvin A. Ruderman

A central engine for cosmic gamma-ray burst sources. *Astrophys. J.* 542:243, 2000.

Millisecond pulsar alignment: PSR 0437–47. *Astrophys. J.* 493:397, 1998.

Neutron star magnetic field evolution, crust movement and glitches. *Astrophys. J.* 492:267, 1998.

Models for X-ray emission from isolated pulsars. *Astrophys. J.* 498:373, 1998.

Christopher H. Scholz.

Transition regimes for growing crack populations. *Phys. Rev. E* 65:056105, 2002.

Slip-length scaling for earthquakes: Observations and theory and implications for earthquake physics. *Geophys. Res. Lett.* 28:2995–8, 2001.

Evidence of a strong San Andreas fault. *Geology* 28:163–6, 2000.

Experimental evidence for different strain regimes of crack populations in a clay model. *Geophys. Res. Lett.* 26:1081–4, 1999.

Amiya K. Sen

Radial plasma transport in axisymmetricmagneticfields. *Trans.Fusion& Technology* 48:51111, 2006.

Observation and identification of zonal flows in a basic experiment. *Plasma Phys. Controlled Fusion* 48:51111, 2006.

A new paradigm of plasma transport. *Phys. Plasmas* 13, 2006.

Adaptive optimal stochastic state feedback control of resistive wall modes in tokamaks. *Phys. Plasmas* 13:012512, 2006.

Adam H. Sobel

Poleward-propagating intraseasonal monsoon disturbances in an intermediate-complexity axisymmetric model. *J. Atmos. Sci.* 65:470–89, 2008.

Instability of the axisymmetric monsoon flow and intraseasonal oscillation. *J. Geophys. Res.* 113: D07108, 2008. doi:10.1029/2007JD009291

On the wavelength of the Rossby waves radiated by tropical cyclones. *J. Atmos. Sci.* 65:644–54, 2008.

The role of surface fluxes in tropical intraseasonal oscillations. *Nature Geoscience* 1:653–7, 2008.

Marc W. Spiegelman

A semi-Lagrangian Crank-Nicolson algorithm for the numerical solution of advection-diffusion problems. *Geochem. Geophys. Geosyst.* 7(4):Q04014, 2006.

Linear analysis of melt band formation by simple shear. *Geochem. Geophys. Geosyst.* 4(9):8615, 2003.

Extreme chemical variability as a consequence of channelized melt transport. *Geochem. Geophys. Geosyst.* 4(7):1055, 2003.

Causes and consequences of flow organization during melt transport: The reaction infiltration instability in compactible media. *J. Geophys. Res.* 106(B2):2061–77, 2001.

Horst L. Stormer

High frequency magneto oscillations in GaAs/AlGaAs quantum wells. *Phys. Rev. Lett.* 98:036804, 2007.

Experimental observation of the quantum Hall effect and Berry's phase in graphene. *Nature* 438:201, 2005.

Quantization of the diagonal resistance: Density gradients and the empirical resistance rule in a 2D system. *Phys. Rev. Lett.* 95:066808, 2005.

Evidence for skyrmion crystallization from NMR relaxation experiments. *Phys. Rev. Lett.* 94:196803, 2005.

Latha Venkataraman

Mechanically-controlled binary conductance switching of a single-molecule junction. *Nature Nanotechnology* 4:230, 2009.

Formation and evolution of single molecule junctions. *Phys. Rev. Lett.* 102:126803, 2009.

Single molecule conductance and link chemistry: A comparison of phosphines, methyl thiols and amines. *J. Am. Chem. Soc.* 129:15768–9, 2007.

Single molecule conductance and link chemistry: A comparison of phosphines, methyl thiols and amines. *J. Am. Chem. Soc.* 129:15768–9, 2007.

Electronics and chemistry: Varying single molecule junction conductance with chemical substituent. *Nano Letters* 7:502–6, 2007.

Dependence of single molecule junction conductance on molecular conformation. *Nature* 442:904–7, 2006.

Single-molecule circuits with well-defined molecular conductance. *Nano Letters* 6:458–62, 2006.

Wen I. Wang

Normal incidence intervalence subband absorption in GaSb quantum well enhanced by coupling to InAs conduction band. *Appl. Phys. Lett.* 62:609–11, 1993.

Normal incidence infrared absorption in AlAs/AlGaAs x-valley multiquantum wells. *Appl. Phys. Lett.* 61:1697–9, 1992.

High breakdown voltage AlSbAs/InAs n-channel field effect transistors. *IEEE Electron Device Lett.* 13:192–4, 1992.

Michael I. Weinstein

Cloaking via change of variables for the Helmholtz equation. *Comm. Pure Appl. Math.* 63(8):973–1016, 2010.

A multiscale model of partial melts: 1. Effective equations. *J. Geophys. Res.* 115:B04410, 2010.

A multiscale model of partial melts: 2. Computational studies. *J. Geophys. Res.* 115:B04411, 2010.

Band-edge solitons, nonlinear Schrodinger/Gross–Pitaevskii equations, and effective media. *SIAM J. Multiscale Modeling and Simulation* 8(4):1055–101, 2010.

Chris H. Wiggins

A stochastic spectral analysis of transcriptional regulatory cascades. *Proc. Natl. Acad. Sci. U.S.A.* 106:6529–34, 2009. http://www.ncbi.nlm.nih.gov/pubmed/19351901?dopt=Abstract

A Bayesian approach to network modularity. *Phys. Rev. Lett.* 100:258701, 2008. http://link.aps.org/doi/10.1103/PhysRevLett.100.258701

Multiple events on single molecules: Unbiased estimation in single-molecule biophysics. *Proc. Natl. Acad. Sci. U.S.A.* 104:1750–5, 2006.

Information-theoretic approach to network modularity. *Physical Review E* 71:046117, 2005.

Inferring network mechanisms: The *Drosophila melanogaster* protein interaction network. *Proc. Natl. Acad. Sci. U.S.A.* 102(9):3192–7, 2005.

Cheng-Shie Wuu

3-D dose verification for IMRT using optical CT based polymer gel dosimetry. *Med. Phys.* 33(5):1412–9, 2006.

Radiation-induced second cancers: The impact of 3D-CRT and IMRT. *Int. J. Radiat. Oncol. Biol. Phys.* 56(1):83–8, 2003.

Dosimetry study of Re-188 liquid balloon for intravascular brachytherapy using polymer gel dosimeters and laser-beam optical CT scanner. *Med. Phys.* 30(2):132–7, 2003.

Dosimetric and volumetric criteria for selecting a source activity and/or a source type (I-125 or Pd-103) in the presence of irregular seed placement in permanent prostate implants. *Int. J. Radiat. Oncol. Biol. Phys.* 47:815–20, 2000.

THE JOHNS HOPKINS UNIVERSITY

Henry A. Rowland Department of Physics and Astronomy

Program of Study

The Department offers a broad program for graduate and postdoctoral study in physics and astronomy in which intermediate, advanced, and specialized courses are offered. These courses and student research, begun as soon as possible, form the basis of the Ph.D. program. Considerable flexibility is available in each student's program, which is shaped to individual needs by recommendation from faculty and staff advisers. Students may choose to specialize in either physics or astrophysics, with a full curriculum of graduate courses available in both areas. In addition to required courses, candidates take written and oral preliminary examinations. Written examinations, covering intermediate-level material, must be passed by the end of the third semester. These exams are followed by an intermediate-level oral examination in the second year. A comprehensive oral examination is taken at the beginning of full-time research (usually in the third year). After completion of the student's research, an oral defense of the thesis is required. During residence, some teaching is usually required. Only those students who expect to complete the Ph.D. are admitted.

Research Facilities

The high-energy physics group has facilities for constructing the electronics and detectors needed in experiments as well as independent computing capabilities that allow full analyses of data. Nuclear physics equipment includes facilities for relativistic heavy-ion collision studies. Facilities for condensed-matter physics include systems for molecular beam epitaxy, He^3-He^4 dilution refrigeration, high-rate sputtering, ultrahigh-vacuum thin-film deposition, automatic X-ray diffraction, scanning electron microscopy, X-ray fluorescence, LEED/Auger spectroscopy, SQUID and vibrating-sample magnetometry, ferromagnetic resonance, magnetooptics, neutron scattering, four-circle X-ray diffractometry, optical and electron-beam lithography, and dielectric susceptibility. For atomic, molecular, and plasma physics, facilities include high-resolution and very sensitive spectrometers for measurements of infrared to ultraviolet wavelengths, a high-precision X-ray spectrometer, extensive spectroscopic facilities, and lasers. The astrophysics group maintains a calibration and test facility for testing instrumentation for rocket and space flights. Computer facilities in the Department include a large number of Sun, DEC, SGI, HP, and Intel-based workstations. These machines support a wide range of functions, including data reduction, image processing, and simulation of physical processes. All are networked to universities, national laboratories, and supercomputer facilities throughout the world, and Hopkins is part of Internet2 and VBNS. The Johns Hopkins University is the home of the Space Telescope Science Institute, is a partner in the Sloan Digital Sky Survey, and owns a share of the ARC 3.5-meter optical/infrared telescope. The Materials Research Science and Engineering Center (MRSEC) at Hopkins is one of twenty-four centers funded by the National Science Foundation to confront major challenges in the field of materials research. Facilities at the following laboratories and observatories are also frequently used: Brookhaven National Laboratory, Stanford Linear Accelerator Center, Fermi National Accelerator Laboratory, CERN, the University's own Applied Physics Laboratory, National Institute of Standards and Technology, Lawrence Berkeley Laboratory, Francis Bitter National Magnet Laboratory, Lawrence Livermore National Laboratory, the White Sands Missile Range, Kitt Peak National Observatory, Cerro Tololo Interamerican Observatory, the Very Large Array of the National Radio Astronomy Observatory, the Las Campanas Observatory, NASA's Goddard Space Flight Center and Space Telescope Science Institute, Anglo-Australian Observatory, Gemini Observatories, Chandra and XMM-Neutron X-ray Observatories, Argonne National Laboratory, NIST Center for Neutron Research, ISIS Facility, and Rutherford Appleton Laboratory.

Financial Aid

Various tuition fellowships are usually awarded to all full-time Ph.D. candidates. Nonservice University fellowships and teaching assistantships offer a minimum of $19,500 (plus full tuition remission) for the nine-month academic year in 2010–11. Summer research assistantships may be available at $6500. Holders of teaching assistantships must assist in teaching general physics and introductory courses. This experience is useful for students interested in a college teaching career. In addition to teaching assistantships, research assistantships that pay $26,000 annually (plus full tuition remission) are also available for graduate students. These assistantships are awarded on the basis of experience, merit, and academic performance. (These awards are not usually given to first-year students unless they have special experience.)

Cost of Study

Tuition is $40,680 for the 2010–11 academic year; however, full tuition support is given to all Ph.D. candidates as part of the financial package, which also includes either a full teaching or research assistantship. A one-time matriculation fee of $500 is required at registration.

Living and Housing Costs

In general, graduate students live in apartments or rent private homes in residential areas near the University. In 2009–10, rates for unfurnished and furnished apartments varied from $500 to $1000 per month. A campus housing office assists students in finding rooms and apartments in the surrounding residential area.

Student Group

The University's Homewood Campus (the Schools of Arts and Sciences and of Engineering) had 4,744 undergraduates and 1,693 graduate students in 2009–10. There were 110 graduate students in physics and astronomy; all received financial support of some kind. Admission to graduate study in the Department is highly competitive. An average of 20 new students are admitted each year; the majority enroll directly from college.

Location

Located in the northern section of Baltimore, the University is adjacent to one of the finest residential areas of the city, while most of the cultural activities of the large metropolitan area are but minutes away.

The University

The concept of graduate study came into being in America with the founding of the Johns Hopkins University in 1876. From the beginning, the hallmark of the University has been one of creative scholarship.

Applying

Requirements for admission after completion of the bachelor's or master's degree are transcripts of previous academic work, letters of recommendation, and GRE scores, including the General Test and the Subject Test in physics. International students whose native language is not English must submit their scores on the Test of English as a Foreign Language (TOEFL) or the International English Language Testing System (IELTS). Students are admitted only in September. Applications and all supporting materials must be received by January 14. The application fee is $75, but it is temporarily waived for students with either financial need or foreign exchange problems. Application materials may be obtained from the Department's Web site.

Correspondence and Information

Graduate Admissions
Henry A. Rowland Department of Physics and Astronomy
Bloomberg Center, Room 366
The Johns Hopkins University
3400 North Charles Street
Baltimore, Maryland 21218-2686
Phone: 410-516-7344
Fax: 410-516-7239
E-mail: admissions@pha.jhu.edu
Web site: http://www.pha.jhu.edu

The Johns Hopkins University

THE FACULTY AND THEIR RESEARCH

N. Peter Armitage, Assistant Professor. Experimental condensed-matter physics.
Jonathan A. Bagger, Krieger Eisenhower Professor and Vice Provost for Graduate and Postdoctoral Programs and Special Projects. Theoretical high-energy physics.
Bruce A. Barnett, Professor. Experimental particle physics.
Charles L. Bennett, Professor. Experimental cosmology.
Luciana Bianchi, Research Professor. Astronomy.
William P. Blair, Research Professor. Astrophysics, shockwaves, spectroscopy of plasmas.
Barry J. Blumenfeld, Professor. Experimental particle physics.
Collin Broholm, Gerhard H. Dieke Professor. Experimental condensed-matter physics.
Chia-Ling Chien, Jacob L. Hain Professor and Director, Materials Research Science and Engineering Center. Condensed-matter physics, artificially structured solids.
Chih-Yung Chien, Professor. Experimental high-energy physics.
Gabor Domokos, Professor Emeritus. Theoretical high-energy physics, astroparticle physics.
Gordon Feldman, Professor Emeritus. Quantum field theory, theory of elementary particles.
Paul D. Feldman, Professor. Astrophysics, spectroscopy, space physics, planetary and cometary atmospheres.
Michael Finkenthal, Research Professor. Plasma physics.
Holland Ford, Professor. Stellar dynamics, evolution of galaxies, active galactic nuclei, astronomical instrumentation.
Thomas Fulton, Professor Emeritus. Quantum electrodynamics, high-energy particle physics, atomic theory.
Riccardo Giacconi, University Professor. Astrophysics.
Andrei Gritsan, Assistant Professor. Experimental high-energy physics.
Timothy Heckman, Professor and Director, Center for Astrophysical Sciences. Galaxy evolution, starburst galaxies, active galactic nuclei.
Richard C. Henry, Professor and Director, Maryland Space Grant Consortium. Astronomy, astrophysics.
Brian R. Judd, Gerhard H. Dieke Professor Emeritus. Theoretical atomic and molecular physics, group theory, solid-state theory.
David Kaplan, Associate Professor. Theoretical particle physics.
Chung W. Kim, Professor Emeritus. Theory of elementary particles, nuclear theory, cosmology.
Susan Kövesi-Domokos, Professor Emeritus. Theoretical high-energy physics, astroparticle physics.
Julian H. Krolik, Professor. Theoretical astrophysics.
Yung Keun Lee, Professor Emeritus. Nuclear physics.
Robert Leheny, Associate Professor. Experimental condensed-matter physics.
Petar Maksimovic, Associate Professor. Experimental high-energy physics.
Nina Markovic, Assistant Professor. Experimental condensed-matter physics.
Kirill Melnikov, Associate Professor. Theoretical particle physics.
H. Warren Moos, Research Professor. Astrophysics, plasma physics.
Charles Mattias Mountain, Professor and Director, Space Telescope Science Institute. Star formation in galaxies, capabilities of "second-generation telescope."
David A. Neufeld, Professor. Theoretical astrophysics, interstellar medium, astrophysical masers, submillimeter astronomy.
Colin A. Norman, Professor. Theoretical astrophysics.
Aihud Pevsner, Jacob L. Hain Professor Emeritus. High-energy physics.
Daniel H. Reich, Professor and Chair. Experimental condensed-matter physics.
Adam Riess, Professor. Astrophysics.
Mark O. Robbins, Professor. Theoretical condensed-matter physics.
Raman Sundrum, Alumni Centennial Professor and Director, Theoretical Interdisciplinary Physics and Astrophysics Center. Theoretical particle physics, including the physics of extra space-time dimensions, supersymmetry, and non-perturbative phenomena.
Morris Swartz, Professor. Experimental high-energy physics.
Alexander S. Szalay, Alumni Centennial Professor. Theoretical astrophysics, galaxy formation.
Oleg Tchernyshyov, Associate Professor. Theoretical condensed-matter physics, frustrated and quantum magnets, superconducting cuprates.
Zlatko Tesanovic, Professor. Theoretical condensed-matter physics.
J. C. Walker, Professor Emeritus. Condensed-matter physics, thin films and surfaces, nuclear physics.
Rosemary F. G. Wyse, Professor. Astrophysics, galaxy formation and evolution.

Adjunct and Visiting Appointments
Ronald J. Allen, Adjunct Professor, Space Telescope Science Institute. Spiral structure of galaxies, interstellar medium, radio and optical imaging.
Michael Fall, Adjunct Professor, Space Telescope Science Institute. Astrophysics.
Henry Ferguson, Adjunct Professor, Space Telescope Science Institute. Observational cosmology, galaxy evolution, dwarf galaxies, space astronomy instrumentation.
Michael G. Hauser, Adjunct Professor, Space Telescope Science Institute. Cosmology, especially infrared background radiation.
Ann Hornschemeier, Adjunct Assistant Professor, NASA Goddard. Astronomy and astrophysics.
Gerard A. Kriss, Adjunct Professor, Space Telescope Science Institute. Astrophysics, observations of active galactic nuclei and clusters of galaxies.
Mario Livio, Adjunct Professor, Space Telescope Science Institute. Theoretical astrophysics, accretion onto white dwarfs, neutron stars and black holes, novae and supernovae.
Antonella Nota, Adjunct Professor, Space Telescope Science Institute. Astronomy.
Cedomir Petrovic, Adjunct Assistant Professor, Brookhaven National Laboratory. Condensed-matter physics.
Ethan Schreier, Adjunct Professor and President, AUI. Astrophysics, active galaxies and jets.
Mark Stiles, Adjunct Professor, NIST. Condensed-matter experiment.
Roeland van der Marel, Adjunct Associate Professor, Space Telescope Science Institute. Black holes, cluster of galaxies, dark halos, galaxy structure and dynamics.
Kimberly Weaver, Adjunct Professor, NASA Goddard Space Flight Center. High-energy astrophysics.
Robert Williams, Adjunct Professor, Space Telescope Science Institute. Novae, emission line analysis.

Joint Appointments
Shiyi Chen, Professor, Mechanical Engineering. Statistical theory, computation of fluid turbulence.
Gregory Eyink, Professor, Applied Mathematics and Statistics. Mathematical physics, fluid mechanics, turbulence.
Michael Falk, Associate Professor, Materials Science and Engineering. Theoretical and computational research.
Tyrel McQueen, Assistant Professor, Chemistry. Solid-state chemistry, condensed-matter physics.
Jack Morava, Professor, Mathematics. Algebraic topology, mathematical physics.
Peter Searson, Professor, Materials Science and Engineering. Electronic, nanophase, semiconductor materials.
Darrell F. Strobel, Professor, Earth and Planetary Sciences. Planetary atmospheres, astrophysics.

RESEARCH ACTIVITIES

Astrophysics. Observational programs include the use of ground-based optical and radio telescopes, analysis of archival data from previous space experiments, new research with existing satellites and sounding rockets, and space experiments. There is extensive laboratory work on detectors and instrument development for ultraviolet and optical astronomy. Research is concentrated in the following areas of astrophysics: cosmology, active galactic nuclei and quasars, galaxies and galaxy dynamics, stellar populations, the interstellar medium, comets and planetary atmospheres, and diffuse ultraviolet background studies.

Atomic Physics. Research in this area includes theoretical work on the electronic structure of atoms and molecules.

Condensed-Matter Physics. Research programs involve studies of very thin magnetic films; interfaces and surfaces; amorphous materials; conducting, superconducting, and magnetic properties of artificially structured materials; nanocrystals of metals and alloys; low-dimensional quantum magnets; highly correlated electron systems; high-T_c superconductors; complex fluids; glass-forming systems; and nonequilibrium phenomena. Techniques involve SQUID magnetometry, X-ray diffraction, atomic-force and magnetic-force microscopy, neutron scattering, various cryogenic techniques, DC and AC conductivity, LEED and Auger spectroscopies, ferromagnetic resonance, and vibrating-sample magnetometry and dielectric susceptibility.

High-Energy Physics. Current programs involve the study of strong, electromagnetic, and weak interactions. Experiments currently in progress are being performed at the Tevatron pp^- collider at Fermilab, at LEP and SPS, in CERN in Switzerland, and an experiment CMS at LHC in CERN. Data analysis is in progress at these facilities and at the Homewood Campus. Facilities for the construction and testing of particle detectors and associated electronics are available.

Plasma Spectroscopy. Extreme ultraviolet/soft X-ray diagnostic instrumentation is used to study high-temperature plasma devices in controlled thermonuclear research.

Relativistic Heavy-Ion and Medium-Energy Nuclear Physics. The heavy-ion physics program includes the study of quark gluon plasma at the RHIC collider with the STAR and the BRAMS detectors at the Brookhaven National Laboratory.

Theoretical Physics. Areas of current research include particle physics, condensed-matter physics, molecular and atomic structure, quantum optics, and astrophysics. The particle theory group currently conducts research in supersymmetric theories, heavy-quark theory, and astroparticle physics. The condensed-matter theory group studies superconductivity, quantum Hall effect, magnetism, quantum critical phenomena, and various forms of nonequilibrium and growth phenomena. Members of the theory group specializing in different areas maintain close contact with each other and with the experimental groups.

Northeastern
UNIVERSITY

NORTHEASTERN UNIVERSITY

Department of Physics

Programs of Study

The Department offers a full-time program leading to the Ph.D. and full-time and part-time programs leading to the M.S. Requirements for the Ph.D. include 42 semester hours of course work, a written qualifying examination, a thesis describing the results of independent research, and a final oral examination. Students may pursue basic research in elementary particle physics, condensed-matter physics, and molecular biophysics or in interdisciplinary areas such as materials science, surface sciences, chemical physics, biophysics, and applied engineering physics. They also may carry out cooperative research at technologically advanced industrial, governmental, and national and international laboratories and at medical research institutions in the Boston area. Requirements for the M.S. are 32 semester hours of credit, up to 8 of which may be transfer credit, if approved. There is no language requirement for any of the degrees.

Research Facilities

The Department is housed in the Dana Research Center, with optics and condensed-matter labs in the Egan Research Center. There are ample modern research laboratories, Department and student machine shops, an electronics shop, conference and seminar rooms, and faculty and graduate student offices. The Egan Center provides a direct interface with materials researchers in chemistry and engineering and includes extensive meeting space in the Technology Transfer Center. In 1999, the Department received a $1.2-million NSF grant to establish the Advanced Scientific Computing Center (ASCC) in the Dana Research Center, which has been expanded and upgraded since. In addition to the research they do at campus facilities, faculty members and graduate students also work at research centers located in the United States and Europe. High-energy physics experiments are under way at Fermilab in Batavia, Illinois, and at CERN, Geneva, Switzerland. High-magnetic-field experiments are in progress at the National High-Field Magnet Laboratory in Tallahassee, Florida, and Los Alamos National Laboratory, New Mexico. Several groups use the synchrotron facilities at Brookhaven National Laboratory, Long Island, New York, and Argonne National Laboratory, Argonne, Illinois, and many faculty members have flourishing collaborations with scientists in Europe, Asia, and South America.

Financial Aid

Northeastern awards financial aid through the Federal Perkins Loan, Federal Work-Study, and Federal Stafford Student Loan Programs and through minority fellowships, including G. E. Fellowships and Martin Luther King Jr. Scholarships. The Graduate School offers teaching and research assistantships that include tuition remission and a stipend (currently $18,285 for two semesters) and require 20 hours of work per week. The Department's Lawrence Award Program honors students with Excellence in Teaching Awards, Academic Excellence Awards, and a Speaker's Prize.

Cost of Study

Tuition for the 2009–10 academic year was $1065 per semester hour. Books and supplies cost about $875 per year. Tuition charges are made for Ph.D. thesis and continuation. Other charges include the Student Center fee and University Health and Counseling Services fee, which are required of all full-time students.

Living and Housing Costs

On-campus housing for graduate students is limited and granted on a space-available basis. For more information about on- and off-campus housing options, students may visit http://www.housing.neu.edu. A public transportation system serves the greater Boston area, and there are subway and bus services that are convenient to the University.

Student Group

In fall 2009, 22,091 students were enrolled at the University, representing a wide variety of academic, professional, geographic, and cultural backgrounds. The Department enrolled 51 full-time students, of whom 100 percent received some form of financial support. The Department awards roughly seven Ph.D. degrees and five M.S. degrees per year. Most graduates have continued to pursue research careers, either in academic institutions as postdoctoral fellows or in industrial, medical, or government laboratories.

Location

Boston, Massachusetts, offers a rich cultural and intellectual history and is the premier educational center of the country, with more than thirty-five colleges in the city region. Cultural offerings, including several world-class museums, a bevy of art galleries, and the Boston Symphony, are diverse, and the city is home to people of every race, ethnicity, political persuasion, and religion. Boston also offers world-class restaurants and a range of outdoor activities and is steeped in New England tradition.

The University and The Department

Founded in 1898, Northeastern University is a privately endowed, nonsectarian institution of higher learning. Located in heart of Boston, Massachusetts, Northeastern is a world leader in cooperative education and recognized for its expert faculty and first-rate academic and research facilities. It offers a variety of curricula through six undergraduate colleges, eight graduate and professional schools, two part-time undergraduate divisions, a number of continuing education programs, an extensive research division, and several institutes. The Department offers opportunities for students to work on a wide range of groundbreaking research programs with an internationally recognized faculty whose goal is to provide an effective education to students with varied backgrounds.

Applying

Although there is no absolute deadline for applying, completed applications should be received by February 1 to secure priority consideration for September acceptance, especially if financial assistance is sought. Scores on the GRE General Test and the Subject Test in physics are required. The latter is given considerable weight in the admissions and assistantship awarding process. For international students, a TOEFL or IELTS score is required for admission.

Correspondence and Information

Graduate Secretary
Department of Physics
111 Dana Research Center
Northeastern University
360 Huntington Avenue
Boston, Massachusetts 02115
Phone: 617-373-4240
Fax: 617-373-2943
E-mail: gradphysics@neu.edu
Web site: http://www.physics.neu.edu

Northeastern University

THE FACULTY AND THEIR RESEARCH

Professors

Arun Bansil, Ph.D., Harvard, 1974. Condensed-matter theory.
Albert-Laszlo Barabasi, Ph.D., Boston University, 1994. Condensed-matter/biological and medical physics.
Paul M. Champion, Ph.D., Illinois at Urbana-Champaign, 1975. Biological and medical physics.
Haim Goldberg, Ph.D., MIT, 1963. Particle theory.
Donald Heiman, Ph.D., California, Irvine, 1975. Condensed-matter experimental physics.
Alain Karma, Ph.D., California, Santa Barbara, 1986. Condensed-matter theory.
Sergy Kravchenko, Ph.D., Institute of Solid State Physics (Chernogolovka), 1988. Condensed-matter experimental physics.
Robert P. Lowndes, Ph.D., London, 1966. Condensed-matter experimental physics.
Robert S. Markiewicz, Ph.D., Berkeley, 1975. Condensed-matter experimental physics.
Pran Nath, Ph.D., Stanford, 1964. Particle theory.
Jeffrey B. Sokoloff, Ph.D., MIT, 1967. Condensed-matter theory.
Srinivas Sridhar, Chairman of the Physics Department, Ph.D., Caltech, 1983. Condensed-matter experimental physics.
Tomasz Taylor, Ph.D., Warsaw, 1981. Particle theory.
Allan Widom, Ph.D., Cornell, 1967. Condensed-matter theory.
Mark C. Williams, Ph.D., Minnesota, 1998. Molecular biophysics.
Darien Wood, Ph.D., Berkeley, 1987. High-energy experimental physics.

Associate Professors

George Alverson, Graduate Coordinator; Ph.D., Illinois at Urbana-Champaign, 1979. High-energy experimental physics.
Emanuela Barberis, Ph.D., California, Santa Cruz, 1996. High energy experimental physics.
Nathan Israeloff, Ph.D., Illinois at Urbana-Champaign, 1990. Condensed-matter experimental physics.
Latika Menon, Ph.D., Tata Institute of Fundamental Research (Mumbai), 1998. Nanoscaled materials.
J. Timothy Sage, Ph.D., Illinois at Urbana-Champaign, 1986. Molecular biophysics.
Armen Stepanyants, Ph.D., Rhode Island, 1999. Condensed-matter theory.
John D. Swain, Ph.D., Toronto, 1990. High-energy experimental physics.

Assistant Professors

Ginestra Bianconi, Ph.D., Notre Dame, 2002. Theoretical condensed-matter physics.
Swastik Kar, Ph.D., Indian Institute of Science, 2004. Condensed-matter experiment.
Brent Nelson, Ph.D., Berkeley, 2001. Theoretical elementary astroparticle physics.

Emeritus Professors

Ronald Aaron, Ph.D., Pennsylvania, 1961. Medical physics.
Petros Argyres, Ph.D., Berkeley, 1954. Condensed-matter theory.
David A. Garelick, Ph.D., MIT, 1963. Medical physics.
Michael J. Glaubman, Ph.D., Illinois, 1953. High-energy experimental physics.
Jorge V. José, D.Sc., National of Mexico, 1976. Condensed-matter theory.
Bertram J. Malenka, Ph.D., Harvard, 1951. Particle theory.
Clive H. Perry, Ph.D., London, 1960. Condensed-matter experimental physics.
Stephen Reucroft, Ph.D., Liverpool, 1969. High-energy experimental physics.
Eugene J. Saletan, Ph.D., Princeton, 1962. High-energy experimental physics.
Carl A. Shiffman, D.Phil., Oxford, 1956. Medical physics.
Yogendra N. Srivastava, Ph.D., Indiana, 1964. Particle theory.
Michael T. Vaughn, Ph.D., Purdue, 1960. Particle theory.
Eberhard von Goeler, Ph.D., Illinois, 1961. High-energy experimental physics.
Fa-Yueh Wu, Ph.D., Washington (St. Louis), 1963. Condensed-matter theory.

Research Associates

Alex Barabanschikov, Ph.D., Northeastern, 2005: biological physics. Bernardo Barbiellini, Ph.D., Geneva, 1991: condensed-matter theory. Abdelkrim Benabbas, Ph.D., Louis Pasteur (France), 2004: biological physics. Gavin Hesketh, Ph.D., Manchester (England), 2003: high-energy experimental physics. Stanislaw Kaprzyk, Ph.D., Academy of Metallurgy (Krakow), 1981: condensed-matter theory. Matti Lindroos, Ph.D., Tampere (Finland), 1979: condensed-matter theory. Wentao Lu, Ph.D., Northeastern, 2001: condensed-matter theory. Micah McCauley, Ph.D., Colorado State, 2001: laser physics, biophysics. Dattatri Nagesha, Ph.D., Oklahoma State, 2002: condensed matter. Pantanjali V. Parimi, Ph.D., Hyderabad (India), 1998: condensed-matter physics. Thomas Paul, Ph.D., Johns Hopkins, 1994: high-energy experimental physics.

Adjunct Professors

Luis Anchordoqui, Ph.D., Universidad Nacional de La Plata (Argentina), 1998: particle and astroparticle physics. George Tze Yung Chen, Ph.D., Brown, 1972: biomedical physics. Maria-Theresa Dova, Ph.D., Universidad Nacional de La Plata (Argentina), 1988: high-energy physics. Graham Farmelo, Ph.D., Liverpool, 1977: high-energy experimental physics. Howard Fenker, Ph.D., Vanderbilt, 1978: high-energy experimental physics. Maria Araceli Gongora-Trevino, Ph.D., Oxford (UK), 1984: theoretical physics. Wolfhard Kern, Ph.D., Bonn (Germany), 1958: high-energy experimental physics and education. Peter Mijnarends, Ph.D., Delft University of Technology, 1969: condensed-matter theory. C. Robert Morgan, Ph.D., MIT, 1969: condensed-matter theory. Fabio Sauli, Ph.D., Trieste (Italy), 1963: high-energy experimental physics.

RESEARCH ACTIVITIES

Biological and Medical Physics. The group performs research on multiple levels from molecules (DNA and proteins) to cells (regulatory and metabolic protein networks) to tissue (cell-to-cell signaling in heart muscle and brain). Eight faculty members have externally funded research programs in specific research areas, including single-molecule DNA-protein interactions, vibrational dynamics of biomolecules, femtosecond protein dynamics, biological networks (signaling, metabolic, and transcription-regulatory networks), cardiac nonlinear dynamics, and theoretical/computational neuroscience.

Experimental Nanophysics. The faculty members are actively pursuing research at the frontiers of nanoscience. The thrust areas in nanophysics include left-handed metamaterials for photonic crystals, nanomedicine, spintronics, mesoscopic physics, low-dimensional electronic systems, nanomagnetism, and quantum chaos. Research is aimed at the synthesis of nanoscale materials and devices, as well as fundamental materials issues.

Experimental Particle/Astroparticle Physics. The Experimental Elementary Particle and Astroparticle Physics group concentrates its efforts on the following three activities: DØ, CMS, and the Pierre Auger Observatory. The DØ detector at the Tevatron collider at Fermi National Accelerator Laboratory in Illinois measures the products of 2 TeV head-on collisions of protons and antiprotons. Fermilab is unique because nowhere else in the world are such high energies, essential for the study of such massive particles as the top quark, available. Northeastern is participating in improving the muon detector system, in event and data visualization, in the upgrade of the trigger system, the analysis of top-quark properties, and electroweak physics of Ws and Zs. The CMS detector at the Large Hadron Collider at CERN is presently nearing completion. Designed to operate at an energy of 14 TeV, well beyond that available at Fermilab, it will search for signals of new physics such as the elusive Higgs particle and supersymmetric particles. The group is working on the APD-based electromagnetic calorimeter readout, the muon endcap chambers, data visualization, and grid-based computing. The Astroparticle physics group has an active program at the Pierre Auger Cosmic Ray Observatory, nearing completion in Argentina. This project aims to elucidate the origin and nature of the highest-energy cosmic rays. Northeastern takes a leading role in development of software for data analysis at Auger.

Theoretical Condensed-Matter Physics. The group performs research on diverse topics that span forefront areas of hard/soft condensed-matter physics and emerging areas at the intersection of physics and other disciplines. Specific research areas include the electronic structure and spectroscopy of high-temperature superconductors and other complex materials; nanotribology (atomic-scale friction) in crystalline and polymeric materials; network science with applications to technological, biological, and social networks; theoretical/computational materials science; cardiac nonlinear dynamics; and theoretical/computational neuroscience.

Theoretical Elementary Particle Physics. The faculty and students in the Elementary Particle Theory group are actively exploring questions concerning supersymmetry (SUSY) and, more specifically, its local extension to supergravity (SUGRA), with a view to understanding the connection between the universe at very large and very small. This leads to the study of supersymmetry and supergravity, possible extra dimensions beyond the usual four, and related exotic phenomena such as mini–black holes, which may be produced at accelerators or by ultrahigh energy cosmic rays. The group's formal investigations in superstring theory and M-theory are also conducted with the purpose of making connection between fundamental theory and experiment. The elementary particle theory group at NU initiated the PASCOS and SUSY series of conferences, which have become major conferences in high energy physics. Further, to mark twenty years since the formulation of supergravity (sugra) models at NU, the Physics Department held an international conference (SUGRA20) at NU during the period March 17–20, 2003.

SELECTED PUBLICATIONS

George Alverson

Measurement of the W boson helicity in top quark decay at D0. *Phys. Rev. D* 75:031102, 2007.

Measurement of B_d mixing using opposite-side flavor tagging. *Phys. Rev. D* 74:112002, 2006.

Measurement of the top quark mass in the lepton+jets final state with the matrix element method. *Phys. Rev. D* 74:092005, 2006.

Measurement of the CP-violation parameter of B^0 mixing and decay with p anti-p $\rightarrow \mu \mu$ X data. *Phys. Rev. D* 74:092001, 2006.

Search for the standard model Higgs boson in the p anti-p $\rightarrow$ ZH $\rightarrow$ ν anti-ν b anti-b channel. *Phys. Rev. Lett.* 97:161803, 2006.

Arun Bansil

Nodeless d-wave superconducting pairing due to residual antiferromagnetism in underdoped $Pr_{2-x}Ce_xCuO_{4-\delta}$. *Phys. Rev. Lett.* 98:197004, 2007.

Anomalous electronic correlations in the ground-state momentum density of $Al_{97}Li_3$. *Phys. Rev. Lett.* 96:186403, 2006.

Collapse of the magnetic gap of cuprate superconductors within a three-band model of resonant inelastic X-ray scattering. *Phys. Rev. Lett.* 96:107005, 2006.

Study of colloidal quantum dot surfaces using an innovative thin-film positron 2D-ACAR method. *Nat. Mater.* 5:23, 2006; *Nano Today* 14, 2006.

Raising Bi-O bands above the fermi energy level of hole-doped $Bi_2Sr_2CaCu_2O_{8+\delta}$ and other cuprate superconductors. *Phys. Rev. Lett.* 96:097001, 2006.

Emanuela Barberis

Evidence for production of single top quarks and first direct measurement of $|Vt_b|$. 98:181902, 2007.

Measurement of the ttbar cross section in ppbar collisions at sqrt(s)=1.96 TeV using secondary vertex b tagging. *Phys. Rev. D* 74:12004, 2006.

Measurement of the top quark mass in the lepton+jets final state with the matrix element method. *Phys. Rev. D* 74:092005, 2006.

Direct limits on B_s^0 oscillation frequency. *Phys. Rev. Lett.* 97:021802, 2006.

The upgraded D0 detector. *Nucl. Instr. Meth. A* 565:463, 2006.

Paul M. Champion

Optical scanning instrument for ultrafast pump-probe spectroscopy of biomolecules at cryogenic temperatures. *Rev. Sci. Instrum.* 77:064303, 2006.

Dynamics of nitric oxide rebinding and escape in horseradish peroxide. *J. Am. Chem. Soc.* 128:1444, 2006.

Two-color pump-probe laser spectroscopy instrument with picosecond time-resolved electronic delay and extended time range. *Rev. Sci. Instrum.* 76:114301, 2005.

Temperature dependent studies of no recombination to heme and heme proteins. *J. Am. Chem. Soc.* 127:16921, 2005.

Following the flow of energy in biomolecules. *Science* 310:980, 2005.

Haim Goldberg

TeV gamma-rays and neutrinos from photo-disintegration of nuclei in Cygnus OB2. *Phys. Rev. D* 75:063001, 2007.

TeV gamma-rays from photo-disintegration of cosmic-ray nuclei. *Phys. Rev. Lett.* 98:121101, 2007.

Particle physics on ice: Constraints on neutrino interactions far above the weak scale. *Phys. Rev. Lett.* 96:021101, 2006.

Mini Z' burst from relic supernova neutrinos and late neutrino masses. *J. High Energ. Phys.* 0611:023, 2006.

Probing leptoquark production at IceCube. *Phys. Rev. D* 74:125021, 2006.

Donald Heiman

Generation and detection of spin current in GaAs with MgO tunnel barriers. *Phys. Rev. Lett.*, in press.

Room temperature magnetism in semiconducting films of ZnO doped with ferric ions. *J. Appl. Phys.* 99:1, 2006.

Enhanced ferromagnetic phase diagram of epitaxial (Co,Mn) alloys on GaAs(001). *J. Appl. Phys.* 98:106101, 2005.

Coexistence of ferromagnetism and superconductivity in Ni/Bi bilayers. *Phys. Rev. Lett.* 94:037006, 2005.

Heusler half-metals on GaAs for spin injection, compound semiconductors. *Inst. Phys. Conf. Ser.* 184:153–60, 2005.

Nathan Israeloff

Imaging nanoscale spatio-temporal thermal fluctuations. *Nano Lett.* 6:887–9, 2006.

Local polarization fluctuations in an aging glass. *Phys. Rev. Lett.* 95:067205, 2005.

Direct observation of molecular cooperativity near the glass transition. *Nature* 408:695–8, 2000.

Observation of fluctuation-dissipation-theorem violations in a structural glass. *Phys. Rev. Lett.* 83:5038–41, 1999.

Scale delectric fluctuations at the glass transition. *Phys. Rev. Lett.* 81:1461–4, 1998

Alain Karma

Orientation selection in dendritic evolution. *Nat. Mater.* 5:660–64, 2006.

Interface mobility from interface random walk. *Science* 314:632–5, 2006.

Turing instability mediated by voltage and calcium diffusion in paced cardiac cells. *Proc. Nat. Acad. Sci. U.S.A.* 103:5670–5, 2006.

Control of electrical alternans in canine cardiac Purkinje fibers. *Phys. Rev. Lett.* 96:104101, 2006.

Spatially discordant alternans in cardiac tissue: Role of calcium cycling. *Circ. Res.* 99:520–7, 2006.

Robert S. Markiewicz

Dispersion anomalies induced by the low-energy plasmon in the cuprates. *Phys. Rev. B* 75:020508, 2007.

Nodeless d-wave superconducting pairing due to residual antiferromagnetism in underdoped $Pr_{2-x}Ce_xCuO_{4-\delta}$. *Phys. Rev. Lett.* 98:197004, 2007.

Raising Bi-O bands above the fermi energy level of hole-doped $Bi_2Sr_2CaCu_2O_{8+\delta}$ and other cuprate superconductors. *Phys. Rev. Lett.* 96:097001, 2006.

Collapse of the magnetic gap of cuprate superconductors within a three-band model of resonant inelastic X-ray scattering. *Phys. Rev. Lett.* 96:107005, 2006.

Evolution of mid-gap states and residual three dimensionality in $La_{2-x}Sr_xCuO_4$. *Phys. Rev. Lett.* 95:157601, 2005.

Latika Menon

Ultra-high aspect ratio titania nanotubes. *Adv. Mater.* 19:946, 2007.

Dendritic-pattern formation in anodic aluminum oxide templates. *J. Appl. Phys.* 101:084310, 2007.

High-throughput assembly of nanoelements in nanoporous alumina templates. *Appl. Phys. Lett.* 90:163119, 2007.

Diffusion process and formation of super-spin-glass state in soft magnetic Fe/Pt system. *Appl. Phys. Lett.* 89:092501, 2006.

Nanoarrays fabricated from nanoporous alumina. In *Encyclopedia of Nanoscience and Nanotechnology*. Marcel-Dekker Publications, 2004.

Pran Nath

Proton stability in grand unified theories, in strings, and in branes. *Phys. Rep.* 441:191, 2007.

CP violation from standard model to strings. *Rev. Mod. Phys.*, 2007. (arXiv:0705.2008 [hep-ph])

Extra-weakly interacting dark matter. *Phys. Rev. D* 75:023503, 2007.

Couplings of vector-spinor representation for SO(10) model building. *J. High Energ. Phys.* 0602:022, 2006.

The Stueckelberg Z prime at the LHC: Discovery potential, signature spaces and model discrimination. *J. High Energ. Phys.* 0611:007, 2006.

Brent Nelson

Kahler stabilized, modular invariant heterotic string models. *Int J. Mod. Phys. A* 22:145, 2007.

Exploring the vaccum geometry of N=1 gauge theories. *Nucl. Phys. B* 750:1, 2006. (hep-th/0604208).

The geometry of particle physics. *Phys. Lett. B* 638:253, 2006. (hep-th/0511062v2).

On quadratic divergences in supergravity, vacuum energy and the supersymmetric flavor problem. *Nucl. Phys. B* 751:75, 2006. (hep-ph/0511234v1).

Twenty-five questions for string theorists. *J. Phys. G* 32:129, 2006. (hep-th/0509157)

Stephen Reucroft

A new way to detect the Higgs. Presented at 2nd Workshop on TeV Particle Astrophysics, Madison, Wisconsin, 28–31, August, 2006. *J. Phys.: Conf. Ser. 60* 187–90, 2007.

Anisotropy studies around the galactic centre at EeV energies with the Auger Observatory. *Astropart. Phys.*27:244-253, 2007.

Search for a Higgs boson produced in association with a Z boson in p anti-p collisions. (arXiv:0704.2000 [hep-ex])

Northeastern University

Probing the Higgs field using massive particles as sources and detectors. *Eur. Phys. J. C* 48:781–6, 2006.

Results of the first performance tests of the CMS electromagnetic calorimeter. *Eur. Phys. J. C* 44S1:1–10, 2006.

J. Timothy Sage

Quantitative vibrational dynamics of iron in carbonyl porphyrins. *Biophys. J.* 92:3764–83, 2007.

Charge transfer in green fluorescent protein. *Photochem. Photobiol. Sci.* 5:597–602, 2006.

Ultrafast and low barrier motions in the photoreactions of the green fluorescent protein. *J. Biol. Chem.* 280:33652–9, 2005.

Direct probe of iron vibrations elucidates NO activation of heme proteins. *J. Am. Chem. Soc.* 127:11200–1, 2005.

Nuclear resonance vibrational spectroscopy–NRVS. *J. Inorg. Biochem.* 99:60–71, 2005.

Jeffrey B. Sokoloff

Theory of friction between neutral polymer brushes. *Macromolecules,* 40(11):4053–8, 2007.

Superlubricity for incommensurate, crystalline and disordered interfaces. In *Superlubricity*, eds. A. Erdemir and J.-M. Martin. Boston: Elsevier, 2007.

Theory of the effects of multiscale surface roughness and stiffness on static friction. *Phys. Rev. E* 73:016104, 2006.

Srinivas Sridhar

Duality between classical and quantum dynamics for integrable billiards. *Phys. Rev. E* 73:046201, 2006.

Negative refraction and plano-concave lens focusing in one-dimensional photonic crystals. *Appl. Phys. Lett.* 89:084104, 2006.

Hetero-bifunctional poly(ethylene glycol) modified gold nanoparticles as an intracellular tracking and delivery agent. In. *Technical Proceedings of the 2005 NTSI Nanotechnology Conference and Trade Show* 1(6):324–7, 2005.

Yogendra Srivastava

Gauge invariant formulations of Dicke-Preparata super-radiant models. *Phys. A* 301:241, 2001.

Super-radiance and the unstable photon oscillator. *Int. J. Mod. Phys. B* 15:537, 2001.

Hadronic equipartition of quark and glue momenta. *Phys. Rev. D* 63:077502, 2001.

The inverse problem extracting time-like form factor from space-like data, 2001. (eConf C010430:T20)

Dispersive techniques for α_s and R_{had} and the instability of the QCD vacuum, 2001. (eConf CO10430:T19)

Armen Stepanyants

Local potential connectivity in cat primary visual cortex. *Cerebr. Cortex,* 2007. (doi: 10.1093/cercor/bhm027)

Neurogeometry and potential synaptic connectivity. *Trends Neurosci.* 28(7):387–94, 2005.

Geometric and functional organization of cortical circuits. *Nat. Neurosci.* 8(6):782–90, 2005.

Class-specific features of neuronal wiring. *Neuron* 43:251–9, 2004.

Geometry and structural plasticity of synaptic connectivity. *Neuron* 34:275–88, 2002.

John D. Swain

Study of the W+ W- gamma process and limits on anomalous quartic gauge boson couplings at LEP. *Phys. Lett. B* 527:29–38, 2002.

An Introduction to Science, 2nd ed. McGraw-Hill/Primis, 2000.

Anomalous electroweak couplings of the tau and tau neutrino. In *Proceedings of the Sixth International Workshop on Tau LEPton Physics (TAU2000),* Victoria, B.C., Canada, September 18–21, 2000. *Nucl. Phys. Proc. Suppl.* 98:351, 2001.

Tomasz Taylor

Multi-gluon scattering in open superstring theory. *Phys. Rev. D* 74:126007, 2006.

Amplitude for N-gluon superstring scattering. *Phys. Rev. Lett.* 97:211601, 2006.

Note on mediation of supersymmetry breaking from closed to open strings. *Nucl. Phys. B* 731:164–70, 2005.

Open string topological amplitudes and gaugino masses. *Nucl. Phys. B* 729:235–77, 2005.

Topological masses from broken supersymmetry. *Nucl. Phys. B* 695:103–31, 2004.

Michael T. Vaughn

Introduction to Mathematical Physics. Wiley–VCH, 2007.

Stripe disordering transition. In *University of Miami Conference on High Temperature Superconductivity–HTS99,* Miami, Florida, Jan. 7–13, 1999. (cond-mat/9903422)

SO(6)-generalized pseudogap model of the cuprates. In *University of Miami Conference on High Temperature Superconductivity–HTS99,* Miami, Florida, Jan. 7–13, 1999. (cond-mat/9903421)

Tunneling and photoemission in an SO(6) superconductor. (cond-mat/9807067)

Higher symmetries in condensed-matter physics. In *Particles, Strings and Cosmology–PASCOS98.* Singapore: World Scientific, 1999. (cond-mat/9809119)

Allan Widom

Quantum dissipation induced noncommutative geometry. *Phys. Lett. A,* 311(2–3):97–105, 2003.

Equivalent circuit and simulations for the Landau-Khalatnikov model of ferroelectric hysteresis. *IEEE (UFFC),* 50(8):950–7, 2003.

Microscopic basis of thermal superradiance. *J. Phys.: Condens. Mater.* 15:1109, 2003.

Hadronic equipartition of quark and glue momenta. *Phys. Rev. D* 63:077502, 2001.

Dispersive techniques for α_s and R_{had} and the instability of the QCD vacuum, 2001. (eConf CO10430:T19)

Mark C. Williams

Quantifying force-dependent and zero-force DNA intercalation by single-molecule stretching. *Nat. Meth.,* 4:517–22, 2007.

Quantifying DNA-protein interactions by single molecule stretching. In *Biophysical Tools for the Biologist,* vol. 1 of the *Methods in Cell Biology* series, eds. John J. Correia and H. William Dietrich. New York: Elsevier, 2007.

Mechanisms of DNA binding determined in optical tweezers experiments. *Biopolymers* 85:154–68, 2007.

Single molecule force spectroscopy of salt-dependent bacteriophage T7 gene 2.5 protein binding to single-stranded DNA. *J. Biol. Chem.* 281:38689–96, 2006.

Single DNA molecule stretching measures the activity of chemicals that target the HIV-1 nucleocapsid protein. *Anal. Biochem.* 358:159–70, 2006.

Darien Wood

Evidence for production of single top quarks and first direct measurement of |Vtb|. *Phys. Rev. Lett.* 98:181902, 2007. (http://arxiv.org/hep-ex/0612052)

Search for the W' decay in the top quark channel. *Phys. Lett. B* 641:423, 2006. (http://arxiv.org/hep-ex/0607032)

The upgraded D0 detector. *Nucl. Instr. Meth. A* 565:463, 2006. (http://arxiv.org/physics/0507191)

Search for the standard model Higgs boson in the ppbar->ZH-> ν ν bar b bbar channel. *Phys. Rev. Lett.* 97:161803, 2006. (http://arxiv.org/hep-ex/0607022)

The Run IIb trigger upgrade for the D0 experiment. *IEEE Trans. of Nucl. Sci.* 51:340, 2004. (http://www-d0.fnal.gov/trigger/runIIb/documents/docs.html)

OHIO UNIVERSITY

Department of Physics and Astronomy

Programs of Study

The Department of Physics and Astronomy offers graduate study and research programs leading to the Master of Arts, Master of Science, and Doctor of Philosophy degrees. The program of study emphasizes individual needs and interests in addition to essential general requirements of the discipline. Major areas of current research are experimental and theoretical condensed-matter and surface physics, nanoscience, mathematical and computational physics, biological physics, astronomy and astrophysics.

At the end of a student's first year of graduate study, his or her suitability to continue toward the Ph.D. is evaluated by the full faculty. This evaluation is based primarily on the student's GPA in the core courses. The courses in the second year cover more advanced topics. Master's degrees require completion of 45 graduate credits in physics and have both thesis and nonthesis options.

Research Facilities

The physics department occupies two wings of Clippinger Laboratories, a modern, well-equipped research building; the Edwards Accelerator Building, which contains Ohio University's 4.5-MV high-intensity tandem Van de Graaff accelerator; and the Surface Science Research Laboratory, which is isolated from mechanical and electrical disturbances. Specialized facilities for measuring structural, thermal, transport, optical, and magnetic properties of condensed matter are available. In addition to research computers in laboratories, students have access to a Beowulf cluster and the Ohio Supercomputer Center, where massively parallel systems are located. Ohio University is a partner in the MDM Observatory at Kitt Peak, Arizona, which provides guaranteed access to major research telescopes.

Financial Aid

Financial aid is available in the form of teaching assistantships (TAs) and research assistantships (RAs). All cover the full cost of tuition plus a stipend from which a quarterly fee of $338 must be paid by the student. The current stipend level for TAs and RAs is $21,511 per year. TAs require approximately 15 to 20 hours per week of laboratory and/or teaching duties.

Cost of Study

Tuition and fees are $3126 per quarter for Ohio residents and $5790 per quarter for out-of-state students. Tuition and fees for part-time students are prorated.

Living and Housing Costs

On-campus rooms for single students are $1265 per quarter, while married student apartments cost from $650 to $950 per month. A number of off-campus apartments and rooms are available at various costs.

Student Group

About 20,042 students study on the main campus of the University, and 3,353 of these are graduate students. The graduate student enrollment in the physics department ranges from 70 to 80.

Location

Athens is a city of about 25,000, situated in the rolling Appalachian foothills of southeastern Ohio. The surrounding landscape consists of wooded hills rising about the Hocking River valley, and the area offers many outdoor recreational opportunities. Eight state parks lie within easy driving distance of the campus and are popular spots for relaxation. The outstanding intellectual and cultural activities sponsored by this diverse university community are pleasantly blended in Athens with a vibrant tradition in the visual and performing arts.

The University and The Department

Ohio University, founded in 1804 and the oldest institution of higher education in the Northwest Territory, is a comprehensive university with a wide range of graduate and undergraduate programs. The Ph.D. program in physics began in 1959, and more than 250 doctoral degrees have been awarded. Currently, the Department has 27 regular faculty members and additional part-time faculty and postdoctoral fellows. Sponsored research in the Department amounts to approximately $4.1 million per year and comes from NSF, DOE, DOD, NASA, and the state of Ohio. Further information can be found at the Department's home page (http://www.phy.ohiou.edu).

Applying

Online application procedures and downloadable forms can be found at http://www.ohio.edu/graduate/apply.cfm. Information can also be obtained by writing to the Department of Physics and Astronomy.

Correspondence and Information

Graduate Admissions Chair
Department of Physics and Astronomy
Ohio University
Athens, Ohio 45701
Phone: 740-593-1718
Web site: http://www.phy.ohiou.edu

Ohio University

THE FACULTY AND THEIR RESEARCH

Professors
Carl R. Brune, Ph.D., Caltech, 1994. Experimental nuclear astrophysics.
David A. Drabold, Distinguished Professor; Ph.D., Washington (St. Louis), 1989. Theoretical condensed matter, computational methodology for electronic structure, theory of topologically disordered materials.
Charlotte Elster, Dr.rer.nat., Bonn, 1986. Nuclear and intermediate-energy theory.
Alexander O. Govorov, Ph.D., Novosibirsk (Russia), 1991. Theoretical condensed-matter physics, nanoscience.
Steven M. Grimes, Distinguished Professor, Emeritus; Ph.D., Wisconsin–Madison, 1968. Nuclear physics.
Kenneth H. Hicks, Ph.D., Colorado, 1984. Nuclear and intermediate-energy physics.
David C. Ingram, Ph.D., Salford (England), 1980. Atomic collisions in solids, thin films, deposition and analysis, surface physics.
Peter Jung, Distinguished Professor; Ph.D., Ulm (Germany), 1985. Nonequilibrium statistical physics, nonlinear stochastic processes, pattern formation, biophysics.
Martin E. Kordesch, Ph.D., Case Western Reserve, 1984. Surface physics, wide-gap materials.
Daniel Phillips, Ph.D., Flinders (Australia), 1995. Theoretical nuclear and particle physics.
Prakash Madappa, Ph.D., Bombay, 1979. Theoretical nuclear and particle astrophysics.
Joseph C. Shields, Chair of the Department; Ph.D., Berkeley, 1991. Astrophysics, interstellar medium, active galactic nuclei.
Arthur Smith, Ph.D., Texas at Austin, 1995. Experimental semiconductors, thin film.
Thomas S. Statler, Ph.D., Princeton, 1986. Astrophysics, galactic structure and dynamics.
Sergio E. Ulloa, Ph.D., SUNY at Buffalo, 1984. Theoretical condensed-matter physics.

Associate Professors
Markus Böttcher, Ph.D., Bonn, 1997. High-energy astrophysics.
Ido Braslavsky, Ph.D., Israel Institute of Technology, 1998. Biophysics.
Horacio E. Castillo, Ph.D., Illinois, 1998. Theoretical condensed-matter physics.
Saw-Wai Hla, Ph.D., Ljubljana, 1997. Experimental condensed-matter and surface physics, nanoscience.
Mark Lucas, Ph.D., Illinois, 1994. Experimental nuclear physics., physics education.
Alexander Neiman, Ph.D., Saratov State (Russia), 1991. Biophysics, nonlinear dynamics, stochastic processes.
David F. J. Tees, Ph.D., McGill, 1996. Experimental biophysics, nanoscience.

Assistant Professors
Gang Chen, Ph.D., Lehigh, 2004. Experimental condensed-matter physics.
Douglas Clowe, Ph.D., Hawaii, 1998. Observation astrophysics.
Justin Frantz, Ph.D., Columbia, 2004. Experimental Nuclear Physics.
Julie Roche, Ph.D., Un. B. Pascal (France), 1998. Nuclear and intermediate-energy physics.
Nancy Sandler, Ph.D., Illinois, 1998. Theoretical condensed-matter physics.
Andreas Schiller, Ph.D., Oslo, 2000. Experimental nuclear physics.
Eric Stinaff, Ph.D., Iowa State, 2002. Experimental nanoscience.

THEORETICAL RESEARCH ACTIVITIES

Astrophysics. Studies of galaxies and galaxy clusters, with emphasis on galaxy structure, dynamics, and interactions; dark matter and dark energy; quasars and supermassive black holes in galaxy nuclei; high-energy astrophysics related to accretion onto compact objects, relativistic jets, and gamma-ray bursts; asteroids and solar system dynamics. Investigations into these topics employ multiwavelength observations with major facilities (Hubble Space Telescope, Chandra X-ray Observatory, MDM Observatory at Kitt Peak, Arizona) as well as theoretical efforts, including analytic calculations and large-scale numerical simulations.

Biophysics. Computational modeling of complex cellular signaling networks, especially intracellular and intercellular calcium signaling, modeling of neural and glial functions in healthy and epileptic tissue, stochastic modeling of electroreceptors in paddle fish, modeling of the neuronal circuitry of the cat's retina, stochastic and coherence resonance in excitable biologic systems, nanoscale ion channel and receptor clusters, and modeling slow axonal transport.

Condensed-Matter Theory. Statistical mechanics and nonequilibrium dynamics of disordered systems and glassy materials. Some areas of interest include nanoscale-sized dynamical heterogeneities in glassy materials, slow activation-controlled motion of topological defects (e.g., vortices, dislocations), and disordered electronic systems; methodology of first principles simulation: development of local basis density functional methods, time-dependent density functional theory and efficient computation of Wannier functions, and the single-particle-density matrix; theory of disordered insulators: Anderson transition, photo-structural response, novel schemes for structural modeling of glasses, and studies of pressure-induced polyamorphism; and optical and transport phenomena in nanoscale systems, including quantum dots, rings, and channels. Recent activity covers excitons in quantum rings, spin transport in nanocrystals, and quantum acoustoelectric interactions on nanoscale. Other nanoscience problems of interest include electronic transport in complex molecule systems, the role of controlled disorder on the metallic or insulating nature of one- and two-dimensional systems, and the role of collective effects on the optical and transport properties of quantum dot arrays and studies of low-dimensional strongly correlated electron systems, disordered electronic systems, and quantum-Hall-effect physics.

Mathematical and Computational Physics. Quantum simulation, ab initio calculations, and visualization of many-body and few-body systems in condensed-matter and nuclear physics; numerical methods and algorithmic development for high-performance vector and parallel computers; analytical and algorithmic studies in differential and integral equations, probability theory, and series expansions.

Nuclear and Intermediate-Energy Physics. Research in theoretical nuclear and particle physics at Ohio University has as its major component the modeling of processes involving atomic nuclei with mass numbers 1, 2, 3, and 4 in an attempt to reveal aspects of the forces that are at work inside the nucleus by examining data obtained when targets made of hydrogen and helium isotopes are bombarded with photons, electrons, neutrons, and pions. In order to understand the dynamics of the nucleus, theoretical descriptions of these reactions are built and the group's predictions are compared to the experimental results. "Light nuclei" (nuclei containing up to four nucleons) are particularly useful in this regard because once the nuclear dynamics are specified, the Schrodinger equation for these systems can be solved exactly. A recent focus of the group has been the application of effective field theory techniques to such reactions. Using these, and other, theoretical techniques, nucleon-nucleon scattering; nucleon-deuteron scattering at intermediate energies; meson-production in nucleon-nucleon collisions at intermediate energies; relativistic effects in nuclear physics; electron-deuteron scattering; Compton scattering from the proton, deuteron, and Helium-3; pion photo- and electro-production on the proton; and charge-symmetry breaking in nuclear physics have been worked on. Charge-symmetry breaking is of particular current interest, since here nuclear reactions such as the production of neutral pions in deuterium-deuterium collisions reveal aspects of quantum chromodynamics associated with the difference between up and down quarks. Lastly, providing reliable predictions for processes of relevance to astrophysics and cosmology are being worked on (e.g., neutron interactions that contribute to supernova and neutron-star cooling). Such projects are relevant to the Ohio University's newly-established research priority on "Structure of the Universe: From Quarks to Superclusters."

EXPERIMENTAL RESEARCH ACTIVITIES

Astrophysics. Spectroscopic observations of stellar motions and stellar populations in elliptical galaxies and evidence for dark matter, ionized gas in galaxies, gravitational lensing studies of galaxy clusters, nuclear physics applied to astrophysics.

Biological Physics. Stochastic resonance in psychophysics and animal behavior, studies of stochastic nonlinear dynamics in paddlefish electroreceptors, experimental determination of the response of single-cell-adhesion molecules to applied forces using a microcantilever device, lipid bilayer tether pulling on leukocytes and platelets using micropipette aspiration, studies of cell adhesion in pressure gradients in micropipettes, determination of cell membrane mechanical properties, optical studies of biomolecules at the single-molecule level using total internal reflection fluorescence microscopy and fluorescence resonance energy transfer, biomineralization, studies of ice-modifying antifreeze proteins, studies of DNA-protein interactions using optical methods.

Condensed-Matter and Surface Science. Current projects encompass various areas in nanoscale science; scanning-probe techniques; and synthesis and characterization of photonic, composite, and electronic materials. Relevant projects are illustrated by the following list: thin-film growth (by molecular-beam epitaxy) and characterization (using scanning-probe microscopy techniques, including spin-polarized) of the structural, electronic, and magnetic properties of transition-metal nitride layers and magnetic-doped nitride semiconductors; single-atom/molecule manipulation using ultrahigh-vacuum, low-temperature scanning-tunneling microscopy; development of single-molecule electronics; molecular and metal thin films; surface science; electron microscopy of nanoscale structures; amorphous semiconductors and their photonics and electronic properties; MeV ion-beam analysis of materials and measurement of relevant cross-sections; ion-beam and plasma deposition of materials and their characterization; effect of hydrogen and nitrogen to the properties of amorphous carbon; optical spectroscopy and ultrafast laser studies of semiconductor nanostructures and nanostructure-based devices; optical spin manipulation and nanophotonics of individual and coupled nanostructures; growth of semiconducting chalcogenide nanowires for nonvolatile electric memory; synthesis of periodic mesoporous materials through a self-assembly approach; atomic and nanoscale structure characterization by X-ray absorption, fine structure, and small/wide angle X-ray scattering; and study of transparent conductive oxides, low work function surfaces, and thermionic cathodes.

Nuclear and Intermediate-Energy Physics. Contemporary research in experimental nuclear physics involves collaboration with scientists from many different institutions and heavy use of specialized accelerator facilities around the world. Ohio University nuclear physicists are recognized leaders in a variety of experimental programs spanning a broad energy domain. At higher energies, Ohio University's faculty members are leading research programs at Jefferson Laboratory in Virginia. These include the study of electromagnetic production of strange baryons and the search for new exotic baryons in Hall B, precision measurements of the weak charge of the proton in Hall C, and the study of the nature of the gluonic flux tube in Hall D; an active program studying the photoexcitation of the nucleon is also ongoing at the SPring-8 experiment in Japan. At lower energies, faculty members are directing research programs in several distinct areas, including fundamental symmetries in nuclear reactions via precision tests of charge symmetry breaking at TRIUMF in Canada, exotic nuclei far from the line of stability at GANIL and the Hahn-Meitner Institute in Europe, measurements of neutron cross sections at Los Alamos in New Mexico, studies of nuclear level densities at the Holifield Radioactive Ion Beam Facility in Tennessee, and studies of pion photoproduction and QCD sum rules with the LEGS facility at Brookhaven National Laboratory in New York. The Department also operates the high-intensity Ohio University Tandem Van de Graaff accelerator with its unique beam swinger magnet and long flight path for high-precision measurements of various nuclear cross sections and projects in medical physics. The research program is supported by the Ohio University Institute for Nuclear and Particle Physics. Grants are provided by the U.S. National Science Foundation and the U.S. Department of Energy.

SELECTED PUBLICATIONS

Böttcher, M., and D. Principe. The optical variability of the quasar 3C279: The signature of a decelerating jet? *Astrophys. J.* 692:1374, 2009.

Böttcher, M., K. Fultz, et al. The WEBT campaign on the intermediate BL lac object 3C66A in 2007–08. *Astrophys. J.* 694:174, 2009.

Böttcher, M., C. D. Dermer, and J. D. Finke. The hard VHE gamma-ray emission in high-redshift TeV blazars: Comptonization of cosmic microwave background radiation in an extended jet? *Astrophys. J.* 679:L9, 2008.

Matei, C., and **C. R. Brune.** Measurement of the cascade transition via the first excited state of 16O in the 12C(alpha,gamma)16O reaction, and its S factor in stellar helium burning. *Phys. Rev. Lett.* 97:242503, 2006.

Kozub, R. L., and **C. R. Brune.** New constraints on the 18F(p,alpha)15O rate in novae from the (d,p) reaction. *Phys. Rev. C* 71:032801(R), 2005.

Brune, C. R. Alternative parametrization of R-matrix theory. *Phys. Rev. C* 66:044611, 2002.

Castillo, H. E., and A. Parsaeian. Local fluctuations in the ageing of a simple structural glass. *Nat. Phys.* 3:26–28, 2007.

Castillo, H. E., C. Chamon, L. F. Cugliandolo, and M. P. Kennett. Heterogeneous aging in spin glasses. *Phys. Rev. Lett.* 88(23):237201, 2002.

Goldbart, P. M., **H. E. Castillo,** and A. Zippelius. Randomly crosslinked macromolecular systems: Vulcanization transition to and properties of the amorphous solid state. *Adv. Phys.* 45(5):393–468, 1996.

Drabold, D. A. Colloquium: Topics in the theory of amorphous materials. *Eur. Phys. J. B* 68:1, 2009.

Biswas, P., et al. **(D. A. Drabold).** Materials modeling by design: application to amorphous solids. *J. Phys. Condens. Matter* 21:084207, 2009.

Pan, Y., F. Inam, M. Zhang, and **D. A. Drabold.** Atomistic origin of Urbach tails in amorphous silicon. *Phys. Rev. Lett.* 100:206403, 2008.

Elster, Ch., W. Glöckle, and H. Witala. A new approach to the 3D Faddeev equation for three-body scattering. *Few Body Syst.* 45:1, 2009.

Elster, Ch., T. Lin, W. Glöckle, and S. Jeschonnek. Faddeev and Glauber calculations at intermediate energies in a model for n+d scattering. *Phys. Rev. C* 78:034002, 2008.

T. Lin, et al. **(Ch. Elster).** Poincaré invariant three-body scattering at intermediate energies. *Phys. Rev. C* 78:024002, 2008.

Govorov, A. O., and J. J. Heremans. Hydrodynamic effects in interacting Fermi electron jets. *Phys. Rev. Lett.* 92:26803, 2004.

Govorov, A. O., et al. Self-induced acoustic transparency in semiconductor quantum films. *Phys. Rev. Lett.* 87:226803, 2001.

Rotter, M., et al. **(A. O. Govorov).** Charge conveyance and nonlinear acoustoelectric phenomena for intense surface acoustic waves on a semiconductor quantum well. *Phys. Rev. Lett.* 82:2171–4, 1999.

Nakano, T., and **K. Hicks.** Discovery of the strangeness S=+1 pentaquark. *Mod. Phys. Lett. A* 19:645–57, 2004.

Thomas, A. W., **K. Hicks,** and A. Hosaka. A method to unambiguously determine the parity of the theta+ pentaquark. *Prog. Theor. Phys.* 111:291–3, 2004.

Hla, S.-W., and K.-H. Rieder. STM control of chemical reactions: Single molecule synthesis. *Ann. Rev. Phys. Chem.* 54:307–30, 2003.

Hla, S.-W., K.-F. Braun, and K.-H. Rieder. Single-atom manipulation mechanisms during a quantum corral construction. *Phys. Rev. B* 67:201402(R), 2003.

Kang, Y., and **D. C. Ingram.** Properties of amorphous GaNx prepared by ion beam assisted deposition at room temperature. *J. Appl. Phys.* 93:3954, 2003.

Haider, M. B., et al. **(D. C. Ingram** and **A. R. Smith).** Ga/N flux ratio influence on Mn incorporation, surface morphology, and lattice polarity during radio frequency molecular beam epitaxy of (Ga,Mn)N. *J. Appl. Phys.* 93:5274, 2003.

Nadkarni, S., and **P. Jung.** Modeling synaptic transmission of the tripartite synapse. *Phys. Biol.* 4:1–9, 2007.

Ullah, G., **P. Jung,** and A. H. Cornell-Bell. Antiphase calcium oscillations in astrocytes via inositol (1,4,5)-triphosphate regeneration. *Cell Calcium* 39:197, 2006.

Brown, A., L. Wang, and **P. Jung.** Stochastic simulation of neurofilament transport in axons: The "stop and go" hypothesis. *Mol. Biol. Cell* 16:4243–55, 2005.

Vaughn, J. M., K. D. Jamison, and **M. E. Kordesch.** In situ emission microscopy of scandium/scandium-oxide and barium/barium-oxide thin films on tungsten. *IEEE Trans. Electron. Dev.* 56(5):794–8, 2009.

Khoshman, J. M., W. D. Jennings, and **M. E. Kordesch.** Ellipsometric study of a-Be3N2 thin films prepared by radio frequency magnetron sputtering. *Appl. Surf. Sci.* 255:12, 6190–4, 2009.

Blanpied, G., et al. **(M. Lucas).** The N $\rightarrow$ Δ transition from simultaneous measurements of $p(\gamma,\pi^{+})$ and $p(\gamma,\gamma)$. *Phys. Rev. Lett.* 79:4337, 1997.

Feldman, G., et al. **(M. Lucas).** Compton scattering, meson-exchange, and the polarizabilities of bound nucleons. *Phys. Rev. C: Nucl. Phys.* 54:2124, 1996.

Fuwape, I., and **A. B. Neiman.** Spontaneous firing statistics and information transfer in electroreceptors of paddlefish. *Phys. Rev. E.* 78:051922, 2008.

Neiman, A., T.A. Yakusheva, and D. F. Russell. Noise-induced transition to bursting in responses of paddlefish electroreceptor afferents. *J. Neurophysiol.* 98:2795–806, 2007.

Lindner, B., J. Garcia Ojalvo, A. Neiman, and L. Schimansky-Geier. Effects of noise in excitable systems. *Phys. Rep.* 392:321–424, 2004.

Hammer, H-W., L. Platter, and **D. R. Phillips.** Pion-mass dependence of three-nucleon observables. *Eur. Phys. J.* A32:335–47, 2007.

Choudhury, D., A. Nogga, and **D. R. Phillips.** Investigating neutron polarizabilities through Compton scattering on helium-3. *Phys. Rev. Lett.* 98:232303, 2007.

Gardestig, A., and **D. R. Phillips.** How low-energy weak reactions can constrain three-nucleon forces and the neutron-neutron scattering length. *Phys. Rev. Lett.* 96:232301, 2006.

Armstrong, D. S., et al. **(J. Roche)** (G0 Collaboration). Strange quark contributions to parity-violating asymmetries in the forward G0 electron proton scattering experiment. *Phys. Rev. Lett.* 95:092001, 2005.

Zarea, M., and **N. Sandler.** Rashba spin-orbit interaction in graphene and zigzag nanoribbons. *Phys. Rev. B* 79:165442, 2009.

Ohio University

Dias da Silva, L. G. G. V., et al. **(N. Sandler** and **S. E. Ulloa).** Tunable pseudogap Kondo effect and quantum phase transitions in Aharonov-Bohm interferometers. *Phys. Rev. Lett.* 102:166806, 2009.

Zarea, M., Carlos Büsser, and **N. Sandler.** Unscreened Coulomb interactions and the quantum spin hall phase in neutral zigzag graphene ribbons *Phys. Rev. Lett.* 101:196802, 2008.

Schiller, A., et al. Selective population and neutron decay of an excited state of $_{23}$O. *Phys. Rev. Lett.* 99:112501, 2007.

Schiller, A., and M. Thoennessen. Compilation of giant electric dipole resonances built on excited states. *At. Data Nucl. Data Tables* 93:549, 2007.

Schiller, A., et al. Low-energy M1 excitation mode in $_{172}$Yb. *Phys. Lett. B* 633:225, 2006.

Ghosh, H., et al. **(J. C. Shields).** Chandra observations of candidate "true" Seyfert 2 nuclei. *Astrophys. J.* 656:105, 2007.

Pidopryhora, Y., F. J. Lockman, and **J. C. Shields.** The Ophiuchus Superbubble: A gigantic eruption from the inner disk of the Milky Way. *Astrophys. J.* 656:928, 2007.

Shields, J. C., et al. The survey of nearby nuclei with the space telescope imaging spectrograph: Emission-line nuclei at Hubble Space Telescope resolution. *Astrophys. J.* 654:125, 2007.

Smith, A. R., R. Yang, H. Yang, and W. R. L. Lambrecht. Aspects of spin-polarized scanning tunneling microscopy at the atomic scale: Experiment, theory, and simulation. *Surf. Sci.* 561(2–3):154, 2004.

Yang, H., **A. R. Smith,** M. Prikhodko, and W. R. L. Lambrecht. Atomic-scale spin-polarized scanning tunneling microscopy applied to Mn3N2 (010). *Phys. Rev. Lett.* 89:226101, 2002.

Smith, A. R., et al. Reconstructions of the GaN(000-1) surface. *Phys. Rev. Lett.* 79:3934, 1997.

Diehl, S., and **T. S. Statler.** The hot interstellar medium in normal elliptical galaxies. I. A Chandra gas gallery and comparison of X-ray and optical morphology. *Astrophys. J.* 668:150, 2007.

Diehl, S., and **T. S. Statler.** Adaptive binning of X-ray data with weighted Voronoi tesselations. *Mon. Not. R. Astron. Soc.* 36:497, 2006.

Statler, T. S., E. Emsellem, R. F. Peletier, and R. Bacon. Long-lived triaxiality in the dynamically old elliptical galaxy NGC 4365: Limits on chaos and black hole mass. *Mon. Not. R. Astron. Soc.* 353:1, 2004.

Stinaff, E. A., et al. Optical signatures of coupled quantum dots. *Science* 311:636, 2006.

Ware, M. E., and **E. A. Stinaff** et al. Polarized fine structure in the photoluminescence excitation spectrum of a negatively charged quantum dot. *Phys. Rev. Lett.* 95:177403, 2005.

Bracker, A. S., and **E. A. Stinaff** et al. Optical pumping of the electronic and nuclear spin of single charge-tunable quantum dots. *Phys. Rev. Lett.* 94:047402, 2005.

Pai, A., Prithu Sundd, and D. F. J. Tees. In situ microrheological determination of neutrophil stiffening following adhesion in a model capillary. *Ann. Biomed. Eng.* 36:596–603, 2008.

Sundd, P., X. Zou, D.J. Goetz, and D. F. J. Tees. Leukocyte adhesion in capillary-sized, P-selectin-coated micropipettes. *Microcirculation* 15:109–22, 2008.

Tees, D. F. J., R. E. Waugh, and D. A. Hammer. A microcantilever device to assess the effect of force on the lifetime of selectin-carbohydrate bonds. *Biophys. J.* 80:668–82, 2001.

Ngo, A. T., J. M. Villas-Boas, and **S. E. Ulloa.** Spin polarization control via magnetic barriers and spin-orbit effects. *Phys. Rev. B* 78:245310, 2008.

Rolon, J. E., and **S. E. Ulloa,** Forster signatures and qubits in optically driven quantum dot molecules. *Physica E* 40:1481–83, 2008.

TEMPLE UNIVERSITY

of the Commonwealth System of Higher Education

Department of Physics

Programs of Study

The Department of Physics at the Temple University offers the M.A. and Ph.D. degrees. The M.A. program requires 24 semester hours of credit. Normally, required courses for the M.A. degree encompass 18 hours; the other 6 semester hours are used for thesis research or for additional courses. The student must also pass the M.A. comprehensive examination in physics. No specific number of graduate credits is required for the Ph.D. degree, but an approved program of graduate courses must be satisfactorily completed. A dissertation and dissertation examination are required. An M.A. degree is not necessary for the Ph.D. degree. The Ph.D. qualifying examination in physics is taken after completion of two years of graduate study. There is a one-year residence requirement for the Ph.D. degree. Students whose native language is not English must pass an examination in spoken and written English. There is no other language requirement for either the M.A. or the Ph.D. degree. Each full-time graduate student is given a desk in one of the several student offices. Lecturers from other institutions describe their research activities at a weekly colloquium. Informal discussions with members of the faculty are frequent.

Research Facilities

The Department is housed in Barton Hall, which has "smart" lecture theaters, offices, classrooms, and laboratories. Temple's library provides online access to frequently used journals, and contains several thousand volumes of books. A student shop and a materials preparation facility are available. The University computer facilities are based on a UNIX-cluster-composed Digital Equipment Corporation Alphas, including a high-performance numerical compute-server. The Departmental computer facilities include a local area network (LAN) of five Windows XP workstations, and eight host LAN of Linux workstations. The Departmental local area networks are connected to a fiber-optic campus backbone through which all University mainframe computer facilities can be reached. High-speed access to the Internet is readily available from all Departmental computers. Electronic information retrieval is provided by the Temple University library's Scholars Information System, which subscribes to a wide range of online databases. The research laboratories are conducting a variety of studies on optical hole-burning and multiple quantum well structures; laser-based molecular spectroscopy; low-temperature properties of alloys and intermetallics, including valence fluctuations and heavy fermion behavior; high-temperature superconductivity; Mössbauer spectroscopy; nucleon structure; dark-matter detection; and electrorheology and magnetorheology. The Department also uses outside facilities, including the Los Alamos Meson Physics Facility, the Brookhaven National Laboratory, the Stanford Linear Accelerator Center, the Thomas Jefferson National Accelerator Facility, and the National High Magnetic Laboratory. Theoretical work is being conducted in such areas as elementary particles and their interactions, statistical mechanics, biophysics, general relativity, and condensed-matter theory.

Financial Aid

Aid is available to qualified full-time students in the form of assistantships and fellowships funded by the University and various extramural agencies. All forms of financial aid include a stipend plus tuition. The specific type of aid offered to a particular student depends on the student's qualifications and program of study. Summer support for qualified students is also normally available. Currently, the minimum stipend for the academic year is $16,204, but it can be supplemented up to $18,535. In addition, academic year stipends can be supplemented by summer stipends. For students with grant-supported research assistantships, the stipend is much higher.

Cost of Study

The annual tuition for full-time graduate study in 2010–11 is $894 per credit hour for residents of Pennsylvania and $925 per credit hour for nonresidents. Minimal fees are charged for various services, such as microfilming theses.

Living and Housing Costs

Room and board costs for students living on campus are $9500 per year in 2010–11. University-sponsored apartments, both furnished and unfurnished, are available.

Student Group

The Department has 30 full-time graduate students; nearly all are supported by assistantships or fellowships.

Location

Philadelphia is the fifth-largest city in the country, with a metropolitan population of more than 2 million. The city has a world-renowned symphony orchestra, a ballet company, two professional opera companies, and a chamber music society. Besides attracting touring plays, Philadelphia has a professional repertory theater, and many amateur troupes. All sports and forms of recreation are easily accessible. The city is world famous for its historic sites and parks, and for the eighteenth-century charm that is carefully maintained in the oldest section. The climate is temperate, with an average winter temperature of 33 degrees, and an average summer temperature of 75 degrees.

The University

The development of Temple University has been in line with the ideal of "educational opportunity for the able and deserving student of limited means." With a rich heritage of social purpose, Temple seeks to provide the opportunity for high-quality education without regard to a student's race, creed, or station in life. Affiliation with the Commonwealth System of Higher Education underpins Temple's character as a public institution.

Applying

All application material, both for admission and for financial awards, should be received by early March for admission in the fall semester. Notification regarding admission and the awarding of an assistantship is made as soon as the application has been screened.

Correspondence and Information

For program information and all applications:
Graduate Chairman
Department of Physics 009-00
Barton Hall
Temple University
Philadelphia, Pennsylvania 19122-6052
Phone: 215-204-7736
Fax: 215-204-5652
E-mail: physics@temple.edu
Web site: http://www.temple.edu/physics

For general information on graduate programs:
Dean
Graduate School
Temple University
Philadelphia, Pennsylvania 19122

Temple University

THE FACULTY AND THEIR RESEARCH

Atomic, Molecular and Optical Physics

Z. Hasan, Professor; Ph.D., Australian National, 1979. Laser materials, laser spectroscopy of solids.
R. L. Intemann, Professor Emeritus; Ph.D., Stevens, 1964. Theoretical atomic physics, inner-shell processes.
S. Kotochigova, Research Associate Professor; Ph.D., St. Petersburg. Relativistic quantum theory: atomic and molecular applications.
M. Lyyra, Professor; Ph.D., Stockholm, 1984. Laser spectroscopy, molecular coherence effects, laser-atom interactions.
M. Mackie, Research Assistant Professor; Ph.D., Connecticut, 1999. Bose-Einstein condensates.
R. Tao, Professor and Chairman; Ph.D., Columbia, 1982. Photonic crystals, nonlinear optics.

Condensed-Matter Physics

K. Chen, Professor; Ph.D., Chinese Academy of Sciences, 2001. Superconductivity, thin film.
Z. Hasan, Professor; Ph.D., Australian National, 1979. Optical and magnetooptical properties of solids.
M. Ivarone, Associate Professor; Ph.D., Napoli (Italy), 1996. Experimental condensed-matter physics.
C. L. Lin, Associate Professor; Ph.D., Temple, 1985. Heavy fermions, crystal fields, valence fluctuations, the Kondo effect, high-temperature superconductivity.
T. Mihalisin, Professor; Ph.D., Rochester, 1967. Crystal fields, valence fluctuations and the Kondo effect in magnetic systems.
P. S. Riseborough, Professor; Ph.D., Imperial College (London), 1977. Theoretical condensed-matter physics and statistical mechanics.
D. Santamore, Assistant Professor; Ph.D., Caltech, 2003. Theoretical condensed-matter physics and atomic physics, solid-state implantations of a quantum computer exploration of many-body physics in ultracold atom systems.
R. Tahir-Kheli, Professor; D.Phil., Oxford, 1962. Theory of magnetism, randomly disordered systems.
R. Tao, Professor and Chairman; Ph.D., Columbia, 1982. Electrorheological and magnetorheological fluids, self-aggregation of superconducting particles.
X. Xi, Professor, Ph.D. Beijing University, 1987. Materials physics of oxide and boride thin films at the nanoscale level.
T. Yuen, Associate Professor; Ph.D., Temple, 1990. Experimental condensed-matter physics, Mössbauer spectroscopy.

Educational Development Physics

L. Dubeck, Professor; Ph.D., Rutgers, 1965. Development, publication, and testing of precollege science materials.
Z. Dziembowski, Associate Professor; Ph.D., Warsaw, 1975. In-service elementary and secondary teacher training, inquiry-based instruction.
R. B. Weinberg, Professor Emeritus; Ph.D., Columbia, 1963. Teaching physicist.

Elementary Particle Physics and Cosmology

Z. Dziembowski, Associate Professor; Ph.D., Warsaw, 1975. Theoretical particle physics.
J. Franklin, Professor Emeritus; Ph.D., Illinois, 1956. Theoretical particle physics, quark and parton theory, S-matrix theory.
C. J. Martoff, Professor; Ph.D., Berkeley, 1980. Experimental particle physics: investigation of weak interactions and development of particle detectors for the study of dark matter, using negative ion drift.
A. Metz, Assistant Professor; Ph.D., Mainz, 1997. Theoretical nuclear and particle physics: investigation of the quark and gluon structure of strongly interacting particles (most notably the nucleon) through the electroweak and strong interaction.
Z. E. Meziani, Professor; Ph.D., Paris, 1984. Experimental high-energy nuclear physics: investigation of the flavor and spin structure of the nucleon at the Stanford Linear Accelerator Center, search for transition region between nucleon-meson to quark-gluon description of few-body nuclear systems at the Continuous Electron Beam Accelerator Facility.
D. E. Neville, Professor Emeritus; Ph.D., Chicago, 1962. Theoretical particle physics, symmetries and quark models, quantum gravity.

Statistical Physics

T. Burkhardt, Professor; Ph.D., Stanford, 1967. Statistical mechanics and many-body theory.
E. Gawlinski, Associate Professor; Ph.D., Boston University, 1983. Statistical mechanics and computational physics.
P. S. Riseborough, Professor; Ph.D., Imperial College (London), 1977. Theoretical condensed-matter physics and statistical mechanics.

Barton Hall, the physics building.

The Elementary Particle Physics Laboratory.

THE UNIVERSITY OF KANSAS

Department of Physics and Astronomy

Programs of Study

The Department of Physics and Astronomy offers programs of study leading to the Ph.D. in physics and the M.S. in physics and computational physics and astronomy.

The master's degree in physics requires 30 hours of advanced courses (up to 6 of which may be transferred from another accredited university) and at least 2 hours of master's research with satisfactory progress. A minimum average of B is required, as is a general examination in physics. The various master's programs differ in their detailed requirements.

The Ph.D. program begins with formal course work (which typically extends through two years for a well-prepared student) and, after admission to candidacy, is followed by Ph.D. research. The required courses include those needed for the M.S. in physics, so it is possible to obtain the M.S. on the way to the Ph.D. degree. Course work should average better than a B. There is no language requirement, but a demonstrated skill in computer programming related to the student's field of study is required. Certification of knowledge of undergraduate physics by the Graduate Advisor and Graduate Director and an oral comprehensive exam are required for admission to candidacy. Following the comprehensive exam, the student may choose a research project from the broad spectrum of experimental and theoretical research areas represented within the Department. These include high-energy particle physics, astrophysics and cosmology, biophysics, astrobiology, space physics, plasma physics, solid-state and condensed-matter physics, nonlinear dynamics, and nuclear physics. After carrying out the research project under the guidance of a faculty member, the student must submit a dissertation showing the results of original research and must defend it in a final oral examination. A minimum of three full academic years of residency is required; the actual time taken to complete the Ph.D. varies considerably.

Research Facilities

Extensive computing facilities exist both in the Department and at the University. Condensed-matter physics facilities include an advanced materials research lab, a quantum electronics lab, and an ultrafast laser lab. These labs are well equipped with thin-film deposition systems, a scanning electron microscope, a unique UHV multiprobe scanning microscopy system, an X-ray diffractometer, SQUID magnetometers, a 6-mK dilution refrigerator, microwave synthesizers, a vector network analyzer, a femtosecond laser system, and self-build optical setups. A clean room with photo- and electron-beam lithography as well as wafer processing tools is also available for microfabrication and nanofabrication of solid-state devices and circuits. The high-energy physics and nuclear physics groups utilize experimental facilities at various universities and international laboratories as part of collaborative experiments. The Astrobiology Working Group collaborates with the Biodiversity Research Institute, the Department of Geology, and the Department of Ecology and Evolutionary Biology.

Financial Aid

The principal form of financial aid is the graduate teaching assistantship; most first-year graduate students in the Department have this type of support. A half-time teaching assistantship, which is the usual appointment, carries a nine-month stipend of at least $17,000 plus a 100 percent tuition fee waiver. Summer support is also available. Beginning graduate students may also be considered for graduate school fellowships in a University-wide competition. A few research assistantships are available for qualified first-year students, although the tendency is to award such assistantships to more advanced students.

Cost of Study

Full-time students with private support or with fellowships from sources outside the University paid tuition of $271 per credit hour for graduate-level courses in 2009–10 if they were Kansas residents and $646 per credit hour if they were nonresidents. Typical enrollment is about 9 hours per semester during the first year. University fees are set by the Board of Regents and are subject to change at any time.

Living and Housing Costs

Room and board are available in University dormitories. The cost starts at $3642 for a nine-month contract. There are a limited number of one- and two-bedroom University apartments for married students and their families with the cost for a twelve-month lease ranging from $3852 to $7728. Many rooms and apartments, both furnished and unfurnished, are available off campus.

Student Group

The University of Kansas has an enrollment of nearly 30,000 students, including about 6,400 graduate students. The Department enrolls approximately 50 graduate students drawn from throughout the United States and abroad. Most of these students are supported as either teaching assistants or research assistants.

Location

The University's main campus occupies 1,000 acres on and around Mount Oread in the city of Lawrence, a growing community of 75,000 located among the forested, rolling hills of eastern Kansas. Near Lawrence are four lake resort areas for boating, fishing, and swimming. Metropolitan Kansas City lies about 40 miles east of Lawrence via interstate highway and offers a variety of cultural and recreational activities.

The University

The University of Kansas is a state-supported school founded in 1866. Long known for its commitment to academic excellence, the University considers research an important part of the educational process. In addition to the College of Liberal Arts and Sciences and the Graduate School, the University houses a number of professional schools and programs, which include Engineering, Medicine, Law, Business, Journalism, and many others.

Applying

Online applications for the fall semester should be completed by April 1; paper applications should be completed by May 1. Assistantships are offered on a first-come, first-served basis, and the Department begins evaluating applications in January. For consideration of University fellowships, completed applications must be received by December 31. For spring semester admission, all application materials must be received by November 15. The GRE and the GRE Advanced Physics are strongly recommended. Students from non-English speaking countries are required to demonstrate proficiency in English by either the TOEFL or TOEFL iBT exams. The TSE exam is recommended for those applying for a teaching assistantship and who have not taken the TOEFL iBT exam.

Correspondence and Information

For application forms and admission:

Graduate Admissions Officer
Department of Physics and Astronomy
1251 Wescoe Hall Drive, Room 1082
The University of Kansas
Lawrence, Kansas 66045-7572

Phone: 785-864-1222
E-mail: physics@ku.edu
Web site: http://www.physics.ku.edu

The University of Kansas

THE FACULTY AND THEIR RESEARCH

Barbara J. Anthony-Twarog, Professor; Ph.D., Yale, 1981. Observational astronomy, stellar evolution in open star clusters, CCD and photoelectric photometry, globular clusters.
Matthew Antonik, Assistant Professor; Ph.D., Maine, Orono, 1994. Biophysics.
Philip S. Baringer, Professor and Associate Chairman; Ph.D., Indiana, 1985. Experimental high-energy physics.
Alice L. Bean, Professor; Ph.D., Carnegie Mellon, 1987. Experimental high-energy physics.
David Z. Besson, Professor; Ph.D., Rutgers, 1986. Experimental high-energy physics.
Thomas E. Cravens, Professor and Director of Graduate Studies; Ph.D., Harvard, 1975. Space physics, plasma physics.
Hume A. Feldman, Associate Professor; Ph.D., SUNY at Stony Brook, 1989. Astrophysics and cosmology.
Christopher J. Fischer, Assistant Professor; Ph.D., Michigan, 2000. Biophysics.
Siyuan Han, Professor; Ph.D., Iowa State, 1986. Experimental condensed-matter physics.
Steven A. Hawley, Professor; Ph.D., California, Santa Cruz, 1977. Astronomy.
Kyoungchul Kong, Ph.D., Florida, 2006. Theoretical physics, elementary particle physics.
Danny Marfatia, Associate Professor; Ph.D., Wisconsin, 2001. Theoretical elementary particle physics and particle astrophysics.
Mikhail V. Medvedev, Associate Professor; Ph.D., California, San Diego, 1996. Theoretical astrophysics, space physics, plasma physics, astrobiophysics.
Adrian L. Melott, Professor; Ph.D., Texas, 1981. Astrobiophysics, computational physical cosmology.
Michael J. Murray, Associate Professor; Ph.D., Pittsburgh, 1989. Experimental nuclear physics.
John P. Ralston, Professor; Ph.D., Oregon, 1980. Theoretical elementary particle physics and particle astrophysics.
Gregory H. Rudnick, Assistant Professor; Ph.D., Arizona, 2001. Astronomy.
Stephen J. Sanders, Professor and Department Chairman; Ph.D., Yale, 1977. Experimental nuclear physics.
Sergei F. Shandarin, Professor; Ph.D., Moscow Physical Technical Institute, 1971. Astrophysics and cosmology, large-scale structure, nonlinear dynamics, computational physics.
Jicong Shi, Associate Professor; Ph.D., Houston, 1991. Theoretical physics, nonlinear dynamics, beam dynamics, accelerator physics.
Bruce A. Twarog, Professor; Ph.D., Yale, 1980. Observational astronomy, stellar nucleosynthesis, chemical evolution of galaxies, stellar photometry.
Graham W. Wilson, Associate Professor; Ph.D., Lancaster, 1989. Experimental high-energy physics.
Judy Z. Wu, Distinguished Professor; Ph.D., Houston, 1993. Experimental condensed-matter physics, low-temperature physics.
Hui Zhao, Assistant Professor; Ph.D., Northern Jiaotong (Beijing), 2000. Experimental condensed-matter physics.

University of Massachusetts Lowell

UNIVERSITY OF MASSACHUSETTS LOWELL

Department of Physics and Applied Physics

Programs of Study

The Department of Physics and Applied Physics offers programs leading to the degrees of Master of Science and Doctor of Philosophy.

The M.S. degree may be taken in physics or radiological science and protection (health physics) or in the applied physics option in optical sciences. Course requirements for the M.S. program consist of 30 credits, including work on a thesis or project. The M.S. may serve as a basis for further study toward a Ph.D. degree. Students are expected to complete the M.S. program in two years.

The Ph.D. program requires 60 credits beyond the bachelor's degree, including dissertation research. Candidates for the degree must pass a written and oral comprehensive examination and a doctoral research admission examination (taken after successfully completing two semesters of an advanced research project or successfully defending a master's thesis) and demonstrate proficiency in computer programming. Areas of research include materials physics, optics, photonics, experimental nuclear physics and applications of nuclear technology, experimental and theoretical solid-state physics, laser physics and far-infrared spectroscopy including terahertz applications, biophotonics and its medical applications, nanoscale physics, atmospheric and space physics, energy applications, aerosol science, and radiological sciences, which includes radiological health physics and medical physics.

Research Facilities

Numerous research programs and facilities are available to students in the Department. The Center for Advanced Materials investigates polymeric materials for innovative applications. The Photonics Center, with three molecular beam epitaxy machines, designs and fabricates semiconductor-based photonic devices for defense, medical, and commercial applications. The Submillimeter-wave Technology Laboratory designs and fabricates terahertz transmitter/receiver systems, ultrastable optically pumped lasers, laser/microwave hybrid systems, and high-resolution imaging systems for industrial, defense, and medical applications. The Radiation Laboratory houses a 1-megawatt nuclear reactor, an intense cobalt-60 gamma source, and a 5.5-megavolt Van de Graaff accelerator for materials studies and basic/applied nuclear physics. The Advanced Biophotonics Laboratory is involved in structural and functional characterization of pathology for exploratory efforts in medical and bioengineering applications.

The Computational Nano Materials Group conducts theoretical/experimental investigations in solid nanomaterials. The Femtosecond Laser Group employs a regenerative amplified femtosecond Ti:sapphire laser to study effects of femtosecond laser light on material structures and chemical reactions at the molecular level. The Center for Atmospheric Research maintains a 1,400-square-meter facility for automated data acquisition from ground-based and spaceborne atmospheric observatories.

Financial Aid

In 2010–11, financial aid is available in the form of teaching and research assistantships at $14,780 plus a full-tuition and fee waiver. Summer research stipends are available for qualified students at $1600 per month.

Cost of Study

In 2009–10, tuition and fees for full-time students were $10,000 for Massachusetts residents and $18,730 for nonresidents. Health insurance is $952 per year. The international student fee is $150. As explained in the Financial Aid section, tuition and fees are waived for teaching and research assistants. Health insurance is approximately $1000 for the academic year.

Living and Housing Costs

The Lowell area offers a great variety of living accommodations. There is a limited amount of on-campus housing available for graduate students, including single student accommodations with cooking facilities. Early application for these is essential. Residence hall costs are approximately $8675 per academic year.

Student Group

In September 2009, the total University enrollment was 11,087, including 2,517 graduate students. There are about 78 graduate students in physics. Fifty of these students receive financial support as teaching or research assistants. Approximately 25 percent of the physics graduate students are women, and about 50 percent are international students.

Student Outcomes

Advanced degree recipients currently hold positions in academia, government laboratories, major medical facilities, and industry. Recent graduates have been successful in gaining employment in areas dealing with properties of materials, optics, photonics, computer modeling, data analysis software development, radiation safety and protection, and medical physics. Others have obtained postdoctoral appointments at major research universities, national laboratories, and teaching hospitals.

Location

The University is located in Lowell, population 110,000, on the Merrimack River, 30 miles northwest of Boston. The cultural, educational, and recreational activities of the Greater Boston area are within an hour's drive. The lake and mountain regions of New Hampshire and the Atlantic beaches are easily accessible for outdoor activities, including hiking and skiing.

The University and The Department

The University of Massachusetts Lowell was formerly the University of Lowell and in 1991 became one of the five campuses of the University of Massachusetts. The Department of Physics and Applied Physics has offered the Ph.D. since 1967; the total number of students who have received graduate degrees from the Department is about 600. The Department's external research funding totals over $10 million per year.

Applying

To be considered for a teaching assistantship for the fall semester applications must be submitted no later than March 15. The General Test of the GRE, the TOEFL for international students whose native language is not English, transcripts, and three letters of reference are required. The physics GRE subject test is strongly recommended for Ph.D. applicants. There is an application fee of $50. All application materials must be sent to the Office of Graduate Admissions. See http://www.uml.edu/grad/ for further information.

Correspondence and Information

Prof. James J. Egan
Coordinator of Graduate Programs
Department of Physics and Applied Physics
University of Massachusetts Lowell
1 University Avenue
Lowell, Massachusetts 01854-5043
Phone: 978-934-3774
E-mail: james_egan@uml.edu

University of Massachusetts Lowell

THE FACULTY AND THEIR RESEARCH

Professors

A. Altman (Emeritus), Ph.D., Maryland. Theoretical atomic physics.
P. Chowdhury, Ph.D., SUNY at Stony Brook. Experimental nuclear physics, materials.
J. J. Egan, Graduate Coordinator; Ph.D., Kentucky. Experimental nuclear physics, accelerator applications.
C. S. French, Ph.D., Massachusetts Lowell. Radiological science and protection, medical physics.
R. Giles, Department Chair; Ph.D., Massachusetts Lowell. Submillimeter-wave technology and terahertz physics, optics.
W. Goodhue, Ph.D., Massachusetts Lowell. Photonics, submicron devices.
A. S. Karakashian (Emeritus), Ph.D., Maryland. Theoretical solid-state physics, optics.
G. H. R. Kegel, Ph.D., MIT. Experimental nuclear physics, radiation effects in materials.
J. Kumar, Ph.D., Rutgers. Materials physics, optics.
A. Mittler, Ph.D., Kentucky. Experimental nuclear physics, physics education.
V. Podolskiy, Ph.D., New Mexico State. Photonics, plasmonics, materials science.
D. J. Pullen (Emeritus), D.Phil., Oxford. Experimental nuclear physics, physics education.
E. Sajo, Ph.D., Massachusetts Lowell. Medical physics, health physics, aerosol science.
W. A. Schier, Ph.D., Notre Dame. Experimental nuclear physics.
K. J. Sebastian, Ph.D., Maryland. Particle physics theory, atomic physics.
P. Song, Ph.D., UCLA. Space physics.
R. W. Stimets, Ph.D., MIT. Experimental laser physics, astronomy, image processing.
J. Waldman (Emeritus), Ph.D., MIT. Experimental laser physics, infrared spectroscopy.

Associate Professors

R. D. McLeod, M.S., Lowell Technological Institute. Theory of vision.
M. Shen, Ph.D., China. Nanotechnology, femtosecond lasers, materials.
M. Tries, Ph.D., Massachusetts Lowell. Radiological sciences, health physics, medical physics.
A. Yaroslavsky, Ph.D., Saratov State (Russia). Medical imaging, biophysics.

Assistant Professor

D. Wasserman, Ph.D., Princeton. Photonics.

Adjunct Faculty

J. J. Antal, Ph.D., Saint Louis. Neutron radiography.
C. S. Baird, Ph.D. Massachusetts Lowell. Electromagnetic theory, radar scattering.
D. F. Bliss, Ph.D., Stony Brook, SUNY. Material science, substrate engineering, crystal growth.
L. Bobek, M.S., Massachusetts Lowell. UML reactor supervisor, radiological sciences.
M. Coulombe, B.S., Massachusetts Lowell. Radar systems designer, UML Submillimeter Technology lab.
H. Fox, Ph.D., Massachusetts Lowell. Physics education.
A. Gatesman, Ph.D., Massachusetts Lowell. Radar signatures, submillimeter- and millimeter-wave optical systems.
T. M. Goyette, Ph.D., Duke. Laser systems, terahertz spectroscopy.
L. Li, Ph.D., Massachusetts Lowell. Nonlinear optics.
D. C. Medich, Ph.D., Massachusetts Lowell. Radiological health physics, medical physics, radiation safety.
M. Montesalvo, M.S., M.B.A., Massachusetts Lowell. Radiological science.
C. Narayan, Ph.D., Massachusetts Lowell. Physics education.
T. Regan, M.S., Massachusetts Lowell. Nuclear engineering, neutron radiography, gamma-ray spectroscopy.
M. Rivard, Ph.D., Wayne State (Michigan). Medical physics.
E. T. Salesky, Ph.D., Massachusetts Lowell. Theoretical applied physics.
M. R. Squillante, Ph.D., Tufts. Nuclear detectors.
N. L. B. Sullivan, Ph.D., Massachusetts Lowell. Physics education.
S. Vangala, Ph.D., Massachusetts Lowell. Photonics.
K. Yang, Ph.D., Massachusetts Lowell. Optics, materials science.

RESEARCH ACTIVITIES AND PARTICIPATING FACULTY

Experimental Physics

Optics and solid-state physics: materials, tunable visible-infrared and far-infrared lasers, optoelectronic materials and devices, photonics and optoelectronics, molecular-beam epitaxy, image processing, surface plasmons, polymers and biological materials, biophotonics, radiation damage in optical and electronic materials and devices. (Goodhue, Giles, Kumar, Podolskiy, Stimets, Waldman, Wasserman, Yaroslavsky)

Applied and basic experimental nuclear physics: radiation effects in materials, Rutherford back-scattering, PIXE, materials characterization, nuclear instrumentation, detector development, neutron cross-section measurements, fission reaction studies, inelastic neutron scattering, in-beam gamma-ray spectroscopy, high-spin nuclear structure, heavy-ion fusion reactions. (Chowdhury, Egan, Kegel, Mittler, Schier, Tries, Regan)

Nanoscale physics and femtosecond laser interactions with materials. (Shen)

Space physics studies: three-fluid Ohm's Law and solar wind–magnetosphere-ionosphere-thermosphere coupling, radiation belt remediation, physics of the magnetosheath, physics of the magnetopause, magnetospheric global modeling, space weather, space physics data analysis methodology, space and earth physics. (Song)

Radiological Sciences

Internal and external radiation dosimetry, biological effects of radiation, radioactive aerosol studies, environmental sampling and analysis. (French, Medich, Sajo, Tries)

Medical physics: radiation therapy, diagnostics, CT and MRI imaging, biophotonics. (French, Medich, Sajo, Tries, Yaroslavsky)

Theoretical Physics

Elementary particles and quantum field theory: (Sebastian)

Optics and solid-state physics: quantum optics, dielectric waveguides, surface plasmons, ultraviolet and far-infrared spectra, electronic and vibrational cluster calculations, optical and electronic properties of semiconductors and multiple-quantum-well structures. (Baird, Goyette, Podolskiy)

University of Massachusetts Lowell

SELECTED PUBLICATIONS

Tandel, U. S., et al. **(P. Chowdhury).** Collective oblate rotation at high spins in neutron-rich ^{180}Hf. *Phys. Rev. Lett.* 101(18):182503, 2008.

Tandel, S. K., et al. **(P. Chowdhury).** K Isomers in ^{254}No: probing single-particle energies and pairing strengths in the heaviest nuclei. *Phys. Rev. Lett.* 97(8):082502, 2006.

Tandel, S. K., et al. **(P. Chowdhury).** High-*K* isomers and rotational structures in *174*W. *Phys. Rev. C.* 73(4):044306, 2006.

Chowdhury, P. Microscopy of femtoscale structures. *Pramana - Journal of Physics* 57(1):31–40, 2001.

D'Alarcao, R., et al. **(P. Chowdhury).** High-K isomers in neutron-rich hafnium nuclei at and beyond the stability line. *Phys. Rev. C.* 59(3):R1227–31, 1999.

Chowdhury, P., et al. K-isomers at gammasphere. In *Proceedings of the Workshop on Gammasphere Physics,* p. 212, eds. M. A. Deleplanque, I. Y. Lee, and A. O. Machiavelli. Singapore: World Scientific, 1996.

Crowell, B., et al. **(P. Chowdhury).** Novel decay modes of high-*K* isomers: Tunneling in a triaxial landscape. *Phys. Rev. Lett.* 72:1164, 1994.

Chowdhury, P., et al. Large B(M1) staggering at high spins in ^{86}Zr: Broken boson pairs in the four-quasiparticle regime. *Phys. Rev. Lett.* 67(21):2950–3, 1991.

Seo, P.-N., **J. J. Egan,** and **G. H. R. Kegel** et al. Neutron inelastic scattering cross sections from ^{159}Tb(n,n'γ). *J. Nucl. Sci. Tech.,* Supplement 2, 307, 2002.

Ko, Y. J., **J. J. Egan,** and **G. H. R. Kegel** et al. Thulium-169 neutron inelastic scattering cross section measurements via the ^{169}Tn(n,n'γ) reaction. *Nucl. Phys. A* 679:147–62, 2000.

Staples, P., **J. J. Egan, G. H. R. Kegel,** and **A. Mittler.** The ^{14}N (n,n'g) cross section of the 2,313-MeV first excited state. *Nucl. Sci. Eng.* 126:168–75, 1997.

Yue, G., M. O'Connor, **J. J. Egan,** and **G. H. R. Kegel.** Neutron scattering angular distributions in ^{239}Pu at 570 keV and 700 keV. *Nucl. Sci. Eng.* 122:366, 1996.

Staples, P., et al. **(J. J. Egan, G. H. R. Kegel,** and **A. Mittler).** Prompt fission neutron energy spectra induced by fast neutrons. *Nucl. Phys. A* 591:41, 1995.

Wu, C., et al. **(A. J. Gatesman** and **R. H. Giles).** Terahertz backscattering behavior of various absorbing materials. *Proceedings of SPIE* 7311:73110M, 2009.

Mathur, V., et al. **(W. D. Goodhue).** An all optically driven integrated deformable mirror device. *Appl. Phys. Lett.* 96(21):211103, 2010.

Miao, X., et al. **(W. D. Goodhue).** Doping tunable resonance: Toward electrically tunable mid-infrared metamaterials. *Appl. Phys. Lett.* 96:101111, 2010.

Passmore, B. S., et al. **(W. D. Goodhue** and **D. Wasserman).** Mid-infrared doping tunable transmission through subwavelength metal hole arrays on InSb. *Optic. Express* 17(12):10223–30, 2009.

Ehasz, E. J., **T. M. Goyette, R. H. Giles,** and W. E. Nixon. High-resolution frequency measurements of far-infrared laser lines. *IEEE J. Quant. Electron.* 46(4):474–7, April 2010.

Danylov, A. A., et al. **(T. M. Goyette, J. Waldman, A. J. Gatesman, R. H. Giles,** and **W. D. Goodhue).** Coherent imaging at 2.4 THz with a CW quantum cascade laser transmitter. *Proceedings of SPIE* 7601:760105–8, 2010.

Danylov, A. A., et al. **(T. M. Goyette, J. Waldman, A. J. Gatesman,** and **W. D. Goodhue).** Frequency stabilization of a single mode terahertz quantum cascade laser to the kilohertz level. *Optic. Express* 17(9):7525–32, 2009.

Erickson, N. R., and **T. M. Goyette.** Terahertz Schottky-diode balanced mixers. *Proceedings of SPIE* 7215:721508, 2009.

Goyette, T. M., et al. **(J. Waldman** and **R. H. Giles).** 1.56 terahertz 2-frames per second standoff imaging. *Proceedings of SPIE* 6893:6893J–11, 2008.

Chuncheng, J., **G. H. R. Kegel,** and **J. J. Egan** et al. Measurement of U-235 fission neutron spectra using a multiple gamma coincidence technique. *Proc. Int. Conf. Nucl. Data Sci. Tech.*, Santa Fe, NM, 26 Sept 26–Oct. 1, 2004, eds. R. C. Haight, M. B. Chadwick, T. Kawano, and P. Talou. Melville, New York: American Institute of Physics, AIP Conference Proceedings 769:1051, 2005.

Afrim Alimeti, **G. H. R. Kegel,** and **J. J. Egan** et al. Neutron scattering cross section measurements for ^{169}Tm via the (n,n') Technique. *Proc. Int. Conf. Nucl. Data Sci. Tech.*, Santa Fe, NM, 26 Sept 26–Oct. 1, 2004, eds. R. C. Haight, M. B. Chadwick, T. Kawano, and P. Talou. Melville, New York: American Institute of Physics, AIP Conference Proceedings 769:1054, 2005.

Kumar, A., et al. **(J. Kumar).** Sensory response of pegylated and siloxanated 4,8-dimethylcoumarins: A fluorescence quenching study by nitro aromatics. *Sensor. Actuator. B Chem.* 147(1):105–10, 2010.

Kim, M., et al. **(J. Kumar).** Facile patterning of period arrays of metal oxides. *Adv. Mater.* 18:1622, 2006.

Trakhtenberg, S., et al. **(J. Kumar).** Spectroscopic and microscopic analysis of photo-cross-linked vinylbenzylthymine copolymers for photoresist applications. *Chem. Mater.* 18(12):2873–8, 2006.

Kim, S., et al. **(J. Kumar).** Self-doped polyaniline/poly(diallydimethyl ammonium chloride) complex: N-type doping with high stability. *Chem. Mater.* 18(9):2201–4, 2006.

Kumar, A., et al. **(J. Kumar).** Temperature and electric-field dependences of hole mobility in light-emitting diodes based on poly [2-methoxy-5-(2-ethylhexoxy)-1,4-phenylene vinylene]. *J. Appl. Phys.* 98(2):0245021–3, 2005.

Trakhtenberg, S., et al. **(J. Kumar).** Photo-cross-linked immobilization of polyelectrolytes for enzymatic construction of conductive nanocomposites. *J. Am. Chem. Soc.* 127(25):9100–4, 2005.

Huh, P., et al. **(L. Li** and **J. Kumar).** Simple fabrication of zinc oxide nanostructures. *J. Mater. Chem.* 18:637–9, 2008.

Adams, D. C. et al. **(V. A. Podolskiy** and **D. Wasserman).** Plasmonic mid-infrared beam steering. *Appl. Phys. Lett.* 96(20):201112, 2010.

Thongrattanasiri, S., J. Elser, and **V. A. Podolskiy.** Quasi-planar optics: Computing light propagation and scattering in planar waveguide arrays. *J. Opt. Soc. Am.* B 26(12):B102–10, 2009.

Kabashin, A., et al. **(V. Podolskiy).** Plasmonic nanorod metamaterials for biosensing. *Nat. Mater.* 8:867–71, 2009.

Pollard, R. J., et al. **(V. Podolskiy).** Optical nonlocalities and additional waves in epsilon-near-zero metamaterials. *Phys. Rev. Lett.* 102(12):127405, 2009.

Thongrattanasiri, S., and **(V. A. Podolskiy).** Hyper-gratings: Nanophotonics in planar anisotropic metamaterials. *Optic. Lett.* 34(7):890–2, 2009.

Noginov, M. A., et al. **(V. A. Podolskiy).** Stimulated emission of surface plasmon polaritons. *Phys. Rev. Lett.* 101(22):226806, 2008.

Elser, J., and **V. A. Podolskiy.** Scattering-free plasmonic optics with anisotropic metamaterials. *Phys. Rev. Lett.* 100(6):066402, 2008.

Tipnis, S. V., et al. **(W. A. Schier** and **D. J. Pullen).** Yields of short-lived fission products produced following ^{235}U (n_{th},f). *Phys. Rev. C* 58:905, 1998.

Schier, W. A., et al. (D. J. Pullen). Beta particle spectrometer for measuring aggregate beta spectra following fission. *Nucl. Instrum. Methods Phys. Res., Sect. A* 404:173, 1998.

Mok, A. W. K., and **K. J. Sebastian.** Polarized angular distributions in the decays of the triplet $^3D_2$ state of charmonium directly produced in unpolarized proton-antiproton collisions. *European Physical Journal C* 67:125–141, 2010.

Mok, A. W. K., and **K. J. Sebastian.** Angular distributions in the decays of the singlet D2 state of charmonium directly produced in unpolarized proton-antiproton collisions. *European Physical Journal C* 63:101–14, 2009.

Mok, A. W. K., and **K. J. Sebastian.** Polarized angular distributions in the decays of the ψ' charmonium state directly produced in unpolarized proton-antiproton collisions. *European Physical Journal C* 56(2):189–202, 2008.

Mok, A. W. K. and **K. J. Sebastian.** Angular distributions in the decays of the psi prime charmonium state directly produced in polarized proton-antiproton collisions. *Il Nuovo Cimento* 110:429–45, 1998.

Savin, S., et al. **(P. Song).** Magnetosheath interaction with the high latitude magnetopause. *Surv. Geophys.* 26:95–133, 2005.

University of Massachusetts Lowell

Song, P., V. M. Vasyliunas, and L. Ma. A three-fluid model of solar wind-magnetosphere-ionosphere-thermosphere coupling. In *Multiscale Coupling of Sun-Earth Processes,* pp. 447–56, eds. A. T. Y. Lui, Y. Kamide, and G. Consolini. Elsevier, 2005.

Song, P., et al. Comment on "Steady state slow shock inside the Earth's magnetosheath: To be or not to be. 1. The original observation revisited" by Hubert and Samsonov. *J. Geophys. Res.* 110(A11):A11210, doi: 10.1029/2005JA011161, 2005.

Song, P., V. M. Vasyliunas, and L. Ma. Solar-wind-magnetosphere-ionosphere coupling: Neutral atmosphere effects on signal propagation. *J. Geophys. Res.* 110(A9):A09309, doi: 10.1029/2005JA011139, 2005.

Tu, J.-N., and **P. Song** et al. Electron density images of the middle and high latitude magnetosphere in response to the solar wind. *J. Geophys. Res.* 110(A12):A12210, doi: 10.1029/2005JA011328, 2005.

Song, P., B. W. Reinisch, X. Huang, and J. L. Green. Magnetospheric active wave experiments. *Frontiers of Magnetospheric Plasma Physics,* COSPAR Colloquia Series, 16:235–46, 2004.

Song, P., and C. T. Russell. Time series data analyses in space physics. *Space Sci. Rev.* 87:387–463, 1999.

Song, P., et al. Properties of the ELF emissions in the dayside magnetopause. *J. Geophys. Res.* 103:26495, 1998.

Zhu, Z., and **P. Song** et al. The relationship between ELF-VLF waves and magnetic shear at the dayside magnetopause. *Geophys. Res. Lett.* 23:773, 1996.

Vorotnikova, E., et al. **(M. Tries).** Novel synthetic SOD/catalase mimetics can mitigate capillary endothelial cell apoptosis caused by ionizing radiation. *Radiation Research* 173(6):748–59, 2010.

Waldman, J., et al **(T. M. Goyette, R. H. Giles, A. J. Gatesman,** and **W. D. Goodhue).** Prospects for quantum cascade lasers as transmitters and local oscillators in coherent terahertz transmitter/receiver systems. *Proceedings of SPIE* 7215:72150C, 2009.

Danylov, A. A., et al. **(J. Waldman, T. M. Goyette, A. J. Gatesman, R. H. Giles,** and **W. D. Goodhue).** Terahertz sideband-tuned quantum cascade laser radiation. *Optic. Express* 16(8):5171–80, 2008.

Qian, X., et al. **(D. Wasserman,** and **W. D. Goodhue).** High-optical-quality nanosphere lithographically formed InGaAs quantum dots using molecular beam epitaxy assisted GaAs mass transport and overgrowth. *Journal of Vacuum Science and Technology B* 28(3):C3C9–14, 2010.

Ribaudo, T., et al. **(D. Wasserman).** Active control and spatial mapping of mid-infrared propagating surface plasmons. *Optic. Express,* 17(9):7019–24, 2009.

Ribaudo, T., et al. **(D. Wasserman).** Spectral and spatial investigation of midinfrared surface waves on a plasmonic grating. *Appl. Phys. Lett.* 94(20):201109, 2009.

Wasserman, D., et al. Room temperature midinfrared electroluminescence from InAs quantum dots. *Appl. Phys. Lett.* 94(6):061101, 2009.

Ribaudo, T., et al. **(D. Wasserman).** Loss mechanisms in mid-infrared extraordinary optical transmission gratings. *Optic. Express* 17(2):666–75, 2009.

Ribaudo, T., et al. **(D. Wasserman).** Active control of propagating waves on plasmonic surfaces. *Proceedings of SPIE* 7221:722110P, 2009.

Franz, K. J., et al. **(D. Wasserman).** High *k*-space lasing in a dual-wavelength quantum cascade laser. *Nature Photonics* 3:50–4, 2009.

Wasserman, D., E. A. Shaner, and J. G. Cederberg. Midinfrared doping tunable extraordinary transmission from sub-wavelength gratings. *Appl. Phys. Lett.* 90(19):191102–3, 2007.

Qian, X., J. Li, **D. Wasserman,** and **W. D. Goodhue.** Uniform InGaAs quantum dot arrays fabricated using nanosphere lithography. *Appl. Phys. Lett.* 93(23):231907, 2008.

Howard, S. S., et al. **(D. Wasserman).** High-performance quantum cascade lasers: Optimized design through waveguide and thermal modeling. *IEEE J. Sel. Top. Quant. Elect.* 13(5):1054–64, 2007.

Shaner, E. A., J. Cederberg, and **D. Wasserman.** Electrically tunable extraordinary optical transmission gratings. *Appl. Phys. Lett.* 91:181110, 2007.

Hoffman, A. J., et al. **(D. Wasserman** and **V. A. Podolskiy).** Negative refraction in semiconductor metamaterials. *Nat. Mater.* 6:946–50, 2007.

Yang, K., S. Yang, and **J. Kumar.** Formation mechanism of surface relief structures on amorphous azopolymer films. *Phys. Rev. B* 73(16):1652041–2, 2006.

Yang, K., et al. **(J. Kumar).** Study of a poly-1,6-dicarbazolyl-2,4-hexadiyne nanocrystal film by the fifth-order electroabsorption spectroscopy. *J. Opt. Soc. Am.* 22(3):623–32, 2005.

Yang, K., et al. **(J. Kumar).** Determining the dispersions of the fifth- and seventh-order nonlinear optical susceptibilities of a poly(4-BCMU) film through electroabsorption spectroscopy. *Optic. Lett.* 25(16):1186–8, 2000.

Joseph, C. S., et al. **(A. N. Yaroslavsky, T. M. Goyette,** and **R. H. Giles).** Dual-frequency continuous-wave terahertz transmission imaging of nonmelanoma skin cancers. *Proceedings of SPIE* 7601:760104–8, 2010.

Park, J., P. Mroz, M. R. Hamblin, and **A. N. Yaroslavsky.** Dye-enhanced multimodal confocal microscopy for noninvasive detection of skin cancers in mouse models. *J. Biomed. Optic.* 15(2):026023, 2010.

Joseph, C. S., et al. **(A. N. Yaroslavsky, T. M. Goyette, A. J. Gatesman,** and **R. H. Giles).** Terahertz spectroscopy of intrinsic biomarkers for nonmelanoma skin cancer. *Proceedings of SPIE* 7215:72150I, 2009.

Salomatina, E., A. Muzikansky, V. Neel, and **A. N. Yaroslavsky.** Multimodal optical imaging and spectroscopy for the intraoperative mapping of nonmelanoma skin cancer. *J. Appl. Phys.* 105(10):102010–7, 2009.

Yang, M. F., V. V. Tuchin, and **A. N. Yaroslavsky.** Principles of light-skin interactions, ed. E. Baron. In *Light-Based Therapies for Skin of Color,* ed. E. Baron. London: Springer, 2009.

Tannous, Z., M. Al-Arashi, S. Shah, and **A. N. Yaroslavsky.** Delineating melanoma using multimodal polarized light imaging. *Laser. Surg. Med.* 41(1):10–6, 2009.

Al-Arashi, M., E. Salomatina, and **A. N. Yaroslavsky.** Multimodal confocal microscopy for diagnosing nonmelanoma skin cancers. *Laser. Surg. Med.* 39(9):696–705, 2007.

Yaroslavsky, A. N., et al. Fluorescence polarization of tetracycline derivatives as a technique for mapping nonmelanoma skin cancers. *J. Biomed. Optic.* 12(1):014005, (2007).

Chan, B. P., et al. **(A. N. Yaroslavsky).** Photochemical cross-linking for collagen-based scaffolds: A study on optical properties, mechanical properties, stability, and hematocompatibility. *Tissue Eng.* 13(1): (2007).

Salomatina, E., B. Jiang, J. Novak, and **A. N. Yaroslavsky.** Optical properties of normal and cancerous human skin in the visible and near infrared spectral range. *J. Biomed. Optic.* 11(6):064026, 2006.

Yaroslavsky A. N., et al. Combining multi-spectral polarized-light imaging and confocal microscopy for localization of nonmelanoma skin cancer. *J. Biomed. Optic.* 10(1):014011, 2005.

Yaroslavsky, A. N., V. Neel, and R. R. Anderson. Fluorescence polarization imaging for delineating nonmelanoma skin cancers. *Optic. Lett.* 29(17):2010–12, 2004.

Yaroslavsky, A. N., V. Neel, and R. R. Anderson. Demarcation of nonmelanoma skin cancer margins using multi-spectral polarized-light imaging. *J. Investig. Dermatol.* 121:259–66, 2003.

Yaroslavsky, A. N., et al. Optical properties of selected native and coagulated human brain tissues in vitro in the visible and near infrared spectral range. *Phys. Med. Biol.* 47(12):2059–73, 2002

Yaroslavsky, A. N., et al. Optics of blood. In *Handbook of Optical Biomedical Diagnostics,* pp. 169–216, ed. V. V. Tuchin. Bellingham, Wash.:SPIE Publications, 2002.

UNIVERSITY OF PITTSBURGH

Department of Physics and Astronomy

Programs of Study

The graduate programs in the Department of Physics and Astronomy are designed primarily for students who wish to obtain the Ph.D. degree, although the M.S. degree is also offered. The Ph.D. program provides high-quality training for students without needlessly emphasizing formal requirements. Upon arrival, each graduate student is appointed a faculty adviser to provide personalized guidance through the core curriculum. A set of basic courses is to be taken by all graduate students unless the equivalent material has been demonstrably mastered in other ways. These basic courses include mathematical methods, dynamical systems, quantum mechanics, electromagnetic theory, and statistical physics and thermodynamics. More advanced and special-topics courses are offered in a range of areas, including, but not limited to, condensed-matter, statistical, solid-state, and biological physics; high-energy and particle physics; nanoscience; astrophysics; cosmology; particle astrophysics; relativity; and astronomical techniques.

Students have a wide variety of programs from which to choose a thesis topic. University faculty members have active research programs in astrophysics/cosmology, condensed matter physics, particle physics, and physics education research. Topics in astrophysics/cosmology include: observational, numerical, and theoretical cosmology; dark matter and dark energy; galaxies; active galactic nuclei and quasars; galactic and intergalactic medium; stellar atmospheres and massive stars; supernovae; and physics of the early universe. Topics in condensed matter physics include: biological physics; nanoscience; quantum information; quantum kinetics; quantum optics; quantum states of matter; semiconductor physics; soft condensed matter physics; statistical physics; superconductivity and superfluidity; and ultrafast optics. Topics in particle physics include: the origin of mass and flavor; the search for new symmetries of nature; neutrino physics; CP violation; heavy quarks; leptoquarks; supersymmetry; extra dimensions; baryogenesis; effective field theory; and strongly interacting field theory. Topics in physics education research include: cognitive issues in learning physics; and development and evaluation of research-based curricula for introductory and advanced physics courses. Multidisciplinary thesis research may also be carried out in, for example, particle astrophysics, biophysics, chemical physics, laser physics, materials science, nanoscience, and surface science. This research may be done in cooperation with faculty from other departments of the University.

Interdisciplinary research programs may be arranged on a case-by-case basis. There have been physics doctorates awarded for work done in collaboration with faculty members in the Department of Biological Sciences, the Department of Chemistry, the Department of Mathematics, the Department of Materials Science, the Departments of Electrical and Chemical Engineering, the Department of Computational Biology, the Department of Radiological Sciences, and the Department of Radiology in the School of Medicine, among others.

Research Facilities

The Department's facilities include professionally staffed machine, electronics, and glassblowing shops; a large stockroom; and specialized clean rooms for electronics assembly, as well as extensive Departmental and University computer resources. Departmental students have easy access to the facilities and expertise available at the Peterson Institute of NanoScience and Engineering (PINSE) and the Pittsburgh Supercomputing Center (PSC), which are both on the University campus. Other local facilities include Allegheny Observatory. Experiments in particle physics are carried out at national and international facilities such as Fermi National Accelerator Laboratory in Illinois, J-PARC in Japan, and CERN in Switzerland. Similarly, astrophysics/cosmology ground-based programs are conducted at national and international observatories at such locations as Kitt Peak and Mount Hopkins in Arizona; Cerro Tololo, Las Campanas, and La Silla in Chile; Mauna Kea in Hawaii; and Apache Point in New Mexico. Pitt faculty members make use of space-based telescopes, including the Hubble Space Telescope, the Chandra X-ray Observatory, and the GALEX UV Telescope. They also belong to several current and/or future large-telescope consortia: the Sloan Digital Sky Survey (SDSS), the Atacama Cosmology Telescope (ACT), the Panoramic Survey Telescope and Rapid Response System (Pan-STARRS), and the Large Synoptic Survey Telescope (LSST).

Financial Aid

Financial aid is normally provided through teaching assistantships during the first year and through research assistantships thereafter. These awards carry automatic tuition scholarships and benefits. The University provides individual health insurance under the Graduate Student Plan. The Department has several fellowships, including the Arts and Sciences Graduate Fellowships, the A&S Summer Fellowship, established for entering graduate students. They are awarded on a competitive basis, with all qualified applicants automatically considered. Some University fellowships are also available and are awarded in a University-wide competition. Students are generally supported throughout their entire graduate career, provided they maintain good academic standing, make progress toward their degree, and are in residence in the Department, or at an appropriate research facility. Teaching and research assistantship appointments carried a stipend of $7532.50 per term in 2009–10, plus a tuition scholarship, bringing the annual stipend to $22,597.50 for students supported throughout the year, plus a tuition scholarship and benefits. Similar research assistantship appointments may be held in connection with most of the Department's research programs.

Cost of Study

For full-time students who are not Pennsylvania residents, tuition and fees per term in 2009–10 were $14,347. Part-time students paid $1175 per credit plus fees. Full-time students who are Pennsylvania residents paid $8201 per term, including fees, and part-time students who are Pennsylvania residents paid $665 per credit plus fees.

Living and Housing Costs

Most University of Pittsburgh students live in rooms or apartments in the Oakland area. The typical cost of rooms or apartments ranges from $400 to $600 per month for housing. Meals range from $350 to $450 per month. Further information may be found online at http://www.ocl.pitt.edu.

Student Group

The Department's graduate student body in 2009–10 consisted of 77 students, all of whom received financial support. These figures are typical of the Department's graduate enrollment.

Student Outcomes

Many Ph.D. graduates accept postdoctoral positions at major research universities, often leading to teaching and research positions at outstanding universities in the United States and around the world. Other recent graduates have entered research careers in the private sector. One former graduate received the American Physical Society's Nicholas Metropolis Award for Outstanding Doctoral Thesis Work in Computational Physics.

Location

Pittsburgh is situated in a hilly and wooded region of western Pennsylvania, where the Allegheny and Monongahela Rivers join to form the Ohio. The region has a natural beauty. The terrain of western Pennsylvania and nearby West Virginia is excellent for outdoor activities, including cycling, hiking, downhill and cross-country skiing, white-water rafting and kayaking, rock climbing, hunting, and fishing. The University is located about 3 miles east of downtown Pittsburgh in the city's cultural center. Adjacent to the campus are Carnegie Mellon University and the Carnegie, comprising the Museum of Art, the Museum of Natural History, the Carnegie Library, and the Carnegie Music Hall. Schenley Park adjoins the campus; it has picnic areas, playing fields, jogging trails, and an excellent botanical conservatory. The Pittsburgh area has several professional sports teams; for detailed information, students should visit http://www.pitt.edu/about.html.

The Department

The Department has long been active in research; guided by faculty mentors, it has trained more than 600 recipients for the Ph.D. degree. Close cooperation exists between this Department and the physics department of Carnegie Mellon University; all seminars, colloquiums, and courses are shared. The graduate students of both institutions benefit from belonging to one of the largest communities of active physicists in the country. Furthermore, basic research, conducted at the University of Pittsburgh Medical Center and the School of Medicine, provides additional opportunities for research with multidisciplinary perspectives.

Applying

Students who wish to apply for admission or financial aid should apply online and take the GRE, including the Subject Test in physics. Applicants should request that the registrars of their undergraduate and graduate schools send transcripts of their records to the Department. Three letters of recommendation are required for admission with aid. Unless English is the applicant's native language, the TOEFL (IBT) or IELTS exam is required, except in cases in which an international applicant has received an advanced degree from a U.S. institution. Acceptable minimum scores are listed in the application instructions. The application deadline is January 31. Late applications are accepted on the basis of space availability.

Correspondence and Information

Professor Andrew Zentner
Admissions Committee
Department of Physics and Astronomy
University of Pittsburgh
Pittsburgh,, Pennsylvania 15260

Phone: 412-624-9066
Web site: http://www.physicsandastronomy.pitt.edu/

University of Pittsburgh

THE FACULTY AND THEIR RESEARCH

Joseph Boudreau, Associate Professor; Ph.D., Wisconsin. Experimental particle physics.
Daniel Boyanovsky, Professor; Ph.D., California, Santa Barbara. Theoretical condensed-matter physics, particle astrophysics, astrophysics and cosmology.
Wolfgang J. Choyke, Research Professor; Ph.D., Ohio State. Experimental solid-state physics, defect states in semiconductors, large-bandgap spectroscopy.
Russell Clark, Lecturer/Lab Supervisor; Ph.D., LSU. Physics education research, neutrino physics.
Rob Coalson, Professor; Ph.D., Harvard. Chemical physics.
Andrew Daley, Assistant Professor; Ph.D., Innsbruck (Austria). Theoretical condensed matter.
Robert P. Devaty, Associate Professor; Ph.D., Cornell. Experimental solid-state physics.
H. E. Anthony Duncan, Professor; Ph.D., MIT. Theoretical particle physics.
Brian D'Urso, Assistant Professor; Ph.D., Harvard. Experimental condensed-matter physics, nanoscience.
Gurudev Dutt, Assistant Professor; Ph.D., Michigan. Experimental condensed matter/AMO, nanoscience, quantum information.
Steven A. Dytman, Professor; Ph.D., Carnegie Mellon. Experimental particle physics, neutrino physics.
Min Feng, Research Assistant Professor; Ph.D., Chinese Academy of Sciences (Beijing). Experimental condensed matter.
Ayres Freitas, Assistant Professor; Ph.D., Hamburg. Theoretical particle physics.
D. John Hillier, Professor; Ph.D., Australian National. Theoretical and observational astrophysics, computational physics.
David M. Jasnow, Professor; Ph.D., Illinois. Theory of phase transitions, statistical physics, biological physics.
Arthur Kosowsky, Associate Professor; Ph.D., Chicago. Theoretical and experimental cosmology and astrophysics.
Adam Leibovich, Associate Professor and Graduate Program Director; Ph.D., Caltech. Theoretical particle physics.
Jeremy Levy, Professor; Ph.D., California, Santa Barbara. Experimental condensed matter, quantum information.
W. Vincent Liu, Associate Professor; Ph.D., Texas at Austin. Theoretical condensed matter.
James V. Maher, Professor; Ph.D., Yale. Experimental statistical physics, critical phenomena, physics of fluids.
James Mueller, Associate Professor and Undergraduate Program Director; Ph.D., Cornell. Experimental particle physics.
Donna Naples, Associate Professor; Ph.D., Maryland. Experimental neutrino physics.
Jeffrey Newman, Assistant Professor; Ph.D., Berkeley. Astrophysics, extragalactic astronomy, observational cosmology.
Vittorio Paolone, Associate Professor; Ph.D., California, Davis. Experimental particle physics, neutrino physics.
Hrvoje Petek, Professor; Ph.D., Berkeley. Experimental condensed matter/AMO, nanoscience, solid-state physics.
Richard H. Pratt, Research Professor; Ph.D., Chicago. Theoretical atomic and low-energy particle physics, bremsstrahlung, hot plasma processes, photon scattering.
Sandhya Rao, Research Associate Professor; Ph.D., Pittsburgh. Astrophysics, extragalactic astronomy, observational cosmology.
Ralph Z. Roskies, Professor and Co-Director of the Pittsburgh Supercomputing Center; Ph.D., Princeton. Theoretical particle physics, use of computers in theoretical physics.
Hanna Salman, Assistant Professor; Ph.D., Weizmann Institute (Israel). Experimental biological physics.
Vladimir Savinov, Associate Professor; Ph.D., Minnesota. Experimental particle physics.
Regina E. Schulte-Ladbeck, Professor; Ph.D., Heidelberg. Astrophysics.
Paul F. Shepard, Professor; Ph.D., Princeton. Experimental particle physics.
Chandralekha Singh, Associate Professor; Ph.D., California, Santa Barbara. Physics education research, polymer physics.
David Snoke, Professor; Ph.D., Illinois at Urbana-Champaign. Experimental condensed-matter and solid-state physics.
Eric Swanson, Associate Professor; Ph.D., Toronto. Theoretical particle physics.
David A. Turnshek, Professor and Department Chair; Ph.D., Arizona. Astrophysics, extragalactic astronomy, observational cosmology.
Jon Weisheit, Research Professor; Ph.D., Rice. Theoretical atomic physics, astrophysics.
Jeffrey Winicour, Research Professor; Ph.D., Syracuse. General relativity, numerical relativity.
Michael Wood-Vasey, Assistant Professor; Ph.D., Berkeley. Astrophysics, extragalactic astronomy, observational cosmology.
Xiao-Lun Wu, Professor; Ph.D., Cornell. Experimental condensed-matter physics, biological physics.
Judith Yang, Adjunct Professor; Ph.D., Cornell. Materials science and engineering.
Andrew Zentner, Assistant Professor and Chairperson of the Admissions Committee; Ph.D., Ohio State. Theoretical cosmology.
Jin Zhao, Research Assistant Professor; Ph.D., University of Sciences and Technology of China. Theoretical condensed matter.

EMERITUS FACULTY
Elizabeth U. Baranger, Professor; Ph.D., Cornell. Theoretical nuclear physics.
Wilfred W. Cleland, Professor; Ph.D., Yale. Experimental particle physics.
Bernard L. Cohen, Professor; Ph.D., Carnegie Mellon. Energy and environment, nuclear physics.
Eugene Engels Jr., Professor; Ph.D., Princeton. Experimental particle physics.
Edward Gerjuoy, Professor; Ph.D., Berkeley. Theoretical atomic physics.
Walter I. Goldburg, Professor; Ph.D., Duke. Experimental solid-state physics, phase transitions, light scattering, turbulence.
Allen I. Janis, Professor; Ph.D., Syracuse. General relativity, philosophy of science.
Rainer Johnsen, Professor; Ph.D., Kiel (Germany). Experimental atomic and plasma physics.
Peter F. M. Koehler, Professor and Graduate Program Director; Ph.D., Rochester. Experimental high-energy physics, physics education research.
Ezra T. Newman, Professor; Ph.D., Syracuse. General relativity, gravitational lensing.
Juerg X. Saladin, Professor; Ph.D., Swiss Federal Institute of Technology. Experimental nuclear physics.
C. Martin Vincent, Professor; Ph.D., Witwatersrand (South Africa). Theoretical intermediate-energy physics.

Allen Hall, home to the Department.

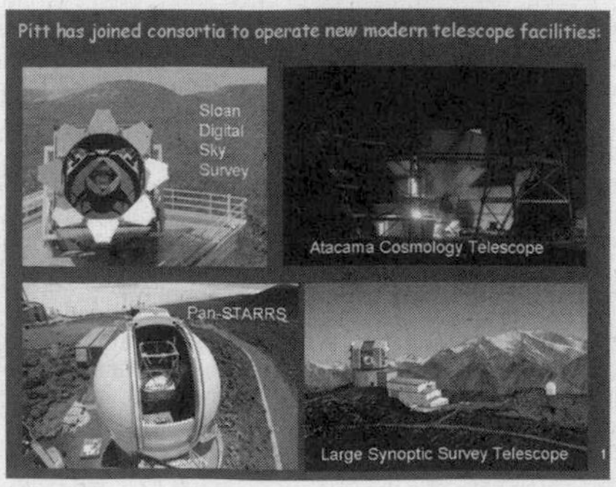

ATLAS is a new detector at the Large Hadron Collider, Geneva, Switzerland.

UNIVERSITY OF ROCHESTER

Department of Physics and Astronomy

Programs of Study

The Department offers programs of study leading to the Ph.D. degree in physics or physics and astronomy. Students normally earn the M.A. or M.S. degree in physics en route to the Ph.D. The M.A. is awarded after the completion of 30 semester hours of course work and a comprehensive examination; the M.S. degree in physics requires a thesis in addition to the course work. Students are not usually admitted to work toward a terminal master's degree (exceptions include students in the 3-2 programs in physics for undergraduates).

Most candidates for the Ph.D. degree take two years of course work and a written preliminary examination during their second year. Requirements for the Ph.D. include demonstrating (via a comprehensive written exam) competence in graduate-level quantum mechanics, mathematical methods, electromagnetic theory, and statistical physics. Students must also demonstrate (via an oral qualifying exam) competence in an advanced area of research specialization. A doctoral thesis, based on significant original research, and a final oral thesis defense are required of all Ph.D. candidates. A typical program of study takes five or six years to complete. A minor is not required, although students are encouraged to broaden their understanding of other subfields of physics or astronomy beyond the area of their thesis research. There is no foreign language requirement.

The Department provides opportunities for research in observational, theoretical, and laboratory astrophysics; biological and medical physics; and experimental and theoretical areas of condensed-matter physics; chemical physics; cross-disciplinary physics; elementary particle physics; nuclear physics; plasma physics; quantum optics; and atomic, molecular, and optical physics.

Research Facilities

The astronomy/astrophysics group has extensive programs in the development of advanced detector arrays, electronics, and instrumentation for astronomy. The results are in use on several ground-based observatories in Arizona and Hawaii and in space on the NASA Spitzer Space Telescope. There are also diverse research programs in both computational and analytic theory covering a range of solar, stellar, galactic, and extragalactic phenomena, often linking to fundamental plasma, fluid, and gravitational dynamics. Development of computational tools as well as application of those tools is ongoing. The high energy densities that can be produced by the Omega laser at the Laboratory for Laser Energetics offer unique opportunities for the laboratory study of matter under conditions ordinarily associated with high-energy astrophysical phenomena such as supernova blasts.

The atomic molecular and optical physics group offers extensive facilities, including a broad range of ultraviolet, visible, and infrared lasers; ultrahigh-stability CW dye, solid-state, and diode laser systems; ultrafast lasers (femtosecond); and an ultrahigh-power (psec, chirped-pulse, regeneratively amplified) pulsed solid-state laser system. The group's capabilities include sophisticated photon counting, laser cooling and trapping, atomic beam, and laser physics experimentation.

For research in condensed matter, the Department offers a unique magnetooptical spectroscopy lab and an advanced surface science research lab that is equipped with X-ray, ultraviolet, and inverse photoemission spectroscopy; scanning-tunneling, atomic-force, and near-field microscopy; low-energy electron and photoelectron diffraction facilities; and advanced thin-film deposition systems.

Research in high-energy and nuclear physics includes projects to develop state-of-the-art detectors for application in high-energy and nuclear physics, which are designed and tested on campus and then assembled and operated at international and national laboratories, including CERN (CMS), Fermilab (Dzero, CDF, NuTeV, and MINERvA), Brookhaven (PHOBOS/RHIC), the Stanford Linear Accelerator Center, Jefferson Laboratory, Lawrence Berkeley Laboratory, Argonne, KEK/JPARC (Japan), the Boulby Mine (UK), and Wilson Lab at Ithaca, New York. The facilities of the University's Laboratory for Laser Energetics, the Institute of Optics, and the Center for Optoelectronics and Imaging are also available for collaborative efforts.

Financial Aid

In 2010–11, graduate teaching and research assistantships, which require 16 hours of work per week during the academic year, carry stipends of $18,000 for nine months. Additional support is available for participation in summer research. A graduate assistant who also takes part in full-time summer research receives a total of $24,000 for the calendar year. A few special University and Departmental fellowships provide stipends of up to $26,000 for the calendar year. In addition, the Department of Education's GAANN program, Robert E. Marshak Fellowships, Provost Fellowships, and Sproull Fellowships for academic excellence are available to supplement teaching or research assistantships for outstanding students.

Cost of Study

For students with fewer than 90 semester hours of accumulated graduate course work, tuition for the 2010–11 academic year is $39,488. Tuition for more advanced students is $1900 per academic year. (Currently, all graduate students in the Department receive special awards to cover tuition.) All full-time graduate students are required to have health insurance. The $2112 fee is paid by the department. The cost of books and supplies is about $2100 per year.

Living and Housing Costs

The cost of living in Rochester is among the lowest for metropolitan areas. Supermarkets with moderate prices are located near the University, or meals can be obtained on campus. University-operated housing for either single or married graduate students is available within easy walking distance of the campus. Free shuttle-bus service is available within the University complex. Additional privately owned rooms and apartments are available in the residential areas near the University.

Student Group

There are approximately 120 graduate students in physics and astronomy; about 18 percent are women, and about 28 percent of the students are married. All full-time students receive some form of financial aid. Admission to graduate study is highly competitive, with only about 20 new students admitted each year; about 50 percent have undergraduate degrees from institutions outside the United States.

Location

The Rochester metropolitan area is the third largest in the state. A city with its economy based on high-technology industries, it is located on the southern shore of Lake Ontario. Niagara Falls, the scenic Finger Lakes district, and the rugged Adirondack Mountains are all within a few hours' drive. The Rochester Philharmonic Orchestra and the Rochester Americans ice-hockey team provide two examples of the range of experiences available. Rochester is readily accessible both by air and by car.

The University and The Department

The University of Rochester is a private institution with 5,374 undergraduates, 4,057 graduate students, and 1,331 faculty members. The Department of Physics and Astronomy, one of the largest and strongest departments within the University, has a reputation for excellence in graduate education and research spanning more than fifty years. Many faculty members of the Department have been awarded major fellowships and prizes in recognition of their research accomplishments.

Applying

Application information can be obtained from the Department's Web site. Students are admitted only in September, and completed applications should be received by January 15 in order for applicants to be considered for financial aid. Applicants should take the GRE General Test and physics Subject Test in time for scores to arrive by January 15. TOEFL scores are required of international students whose native language is not English.

Correspondence and Information

Graduate Program Coordinator
Department of Physics and Astronomy
University of Rochester
Rochester, New York 14627

Phone: 585-275-4356
Web site: http://www.pas.rochester.edu

University of Rochester

THE FACULTY AND THEIR RESEARCH

G. P. Agrawal, Professor; Ph.D., Indian Institute of Technology (New Delhi), 1974. Fiber optics, lasers, optical communications.
Antonio Badolato, Assistant Professor; Ph.D., California, Santa Barbara, 2005. Semiconductor quantum heterostructures with emphasis on solid-state cavity quantum electrodynamics.
R. Betti, Professor; Ph.D., MIT, 1992. Theoretical plasma physics, nuclear and mechanical engineering, computational and plasma physics.
N. P. Bigelow, Lee A. DuBridge Professor; Ph.D., Cornell, 1989. Experimental and theoretical quantum optics and quantum physics, Bose-Einstein condensate, laser-cooled and trapped atoms.
Eric G. Blackman, Professor; Ph.D., Harvard, 1995. Theoretical astrophysics, astrophysical plasmas and magnetic fields; accretion and ejection phenomena; relativistic and high-energy astrophysics.
M. F. Bocko, Professor; Ph.D., Rochester, 1984. Superconducting electronics, quantum computing, musical acoustics, digital audio technology, sensors.
A. Bodek, George E. Pake Professor; Ph.D., MIT, 1972. Experimental elementary particle physics, proton-antiproton collisions, QCD and structure functions, neutrino physics, electron scattering, tile-fiber calorimetric detectors.
R. W. Boyd, M. Parker Givens Professor; Ph.D., Berkeley, 1977. Nonlinear optics.
T. G. Castner, Professor Emeritus; Ph.D., Illinois, 1958. Experimental condensed-matter physics, metal insulator transition.
D. Cline, Professor; Ph.D., Manchester (England), 1963. Extreme states of nuclei pairing and shape correlations in nuclei.
E. Conwell, Professor; Ph.D., Chicago, 1948. Theoretical chemical physics, condensed-matter physics, biological physics.
A. Das, Professor; Ph.D., SUNY at Stony Brook, 1977. Theoretical particle physics, finite temperature field theory, integrable systems, phenomenology, noncommutative field theory, string/M theory.
R. Demina, Associate Professor; Ph.D., Northeastern, 1994. Experimental particle physics, proton-antiproton collisions, top and electroweak physics.
H. Dery, Assistant Professor; Ph.D., Technion (Israel), 2004. Theory of semiconductor spin electronics.
D. H. Douglass, Professor; Ph.D., MIT, 1959. Experimental condensed-matter physics, climate change and pollution.
Charles B. Duke, Professor; Ph.D., Princeton, 1963. Theoretical condensed-matter physics, geophysics, climate.
J. H. Eberly, Andrew Carnegie Professor; Ph.D., Stanford, 1962. Theoretical quantum optics, quantum entanglement, cavity QED, atoms in strong laser fields, dark-state optical control theory.
P. M. Fauchet, Professor; Ph.D., Stanford, 1984. Semiconductor materials and device physics, materials sciences, biomedical engineering, optics.
T. Ferbel, Professor; Ph.D., Yale, 1963. Experimental elementary particle physics, studies of the top quark in hadronic collisions.
W. J. Forrest, Professor Emeritus; Ph.D., California, San Diego, 1974. Observational astrophysics, infrared astronomy, stellar and planetary formation, low-mass stars and brown dwarfs, development of infrared detector arrays and instrumentation.
T. H. Foster, Professor; Ph.D., Rochester, 1990. Biological and medical physics.
A. Frank, Professor; Ph.D., Washington (Seattle), 1992. Theoretical astrophysics, astrophysical plasmas, numerical hydrodynamics and magnetohydrodynamics.
Y. Gao, Professor; Ph.D., Purdue, 1986. Experimental condensed-matter physics, surface physics.
Aran Garcia-Bellido, Assistant Professor; Ph.D., Royal Holloway, London, 2002. Experimental particle physics, with interests in supersymmetry and physics of the top quark and in particular electroweak production of single top quarks.
C. R. Hagen, Professor; Ph.D., MIT, 1962. Theoretical elementary particle physics, quantum field theory and particularly 2+1 dimensional theories.
H. L. Helfer, Professor Emeritus; Ph.D., Chicago, 1953. Theoretical astrophysics and plasma physics, high-energy astrophysics, dark matter in galactic haloes.
John Howell, Assistant Professor; Ph.D., Penn State, 2000. Experimental quantum optics and quantum physics, quantum cryptography and quantum computation.
J. R. Huizenga, Professor Emeritus; Ph.D., Illinois 1949. Nuclear chemistry, nuclear physics.
E. H. Jacobsen, Professor Emeritus; Ph.D., MIT, 1954. Electron optics.
Andrew N. Jordan, Assistant Professor; Ph.D., California, Santa Barbara, 2002. Theoretical quantum optics, condensed-matter physics.
R. S. Knox, Professor Emeritus; Ph.D., Rochester, 1958. Theoretical biological physics, condensed-matter physics, energy-balance models of climate.
W. H. Knox, Professor; Ph.D., Rochester, 1984. Ultrafast sciences and technology, telecommunications, ultrafast biomedical optics, optics education.
D. S. Koltun, Professor Emeritus; Ph.D., Princeton, 1961. Theoretical nuclear physics, meson interactions with nuclei, many-body theory, electron scattering.
Eric E. Mamajek, Assistant Professor; Ph.D., Arizona, 2004. Observational astronomy, stellar evolution, young stellar clusters, protoplanetary disks, stellar and planetary-system formation.
S. L. Manly, Professor; Ph.D., Columbia, 1989. Experimental relativistic heavy-ion physics, experimental elementary particle physics.
Robert L. McCrory, Professor and Director, Laboratory for Laser Energetics; Ph.D., MIT, 1973. Nuclear and mechanical engineering, computational hydrodynamics.
K. S. McFarland, Professor; Ph.D., Chicago, 1994. Experimental elementary particle physics: properties of top quarks, neutrino physics, electroweak unification.
A. C. Melissinos, Professor; Ph.D., MIT, 1958. Experimental particle physics, high-intensity laser-particle interactions, free-electron lasers, searches for relic gravitational radiation.
D. D. Meyerhofer, Professor; Ph.D., Princeton, 1987. Experimental plasma and laser physics, high-energy-density physics and inertial confinement fusion, high-intensity laser-matter interaction experiments, quantum optics.
Lukas Novotny, Professor; D.Sc.Tech., Swiss Federal Institute of Technology, 1996. Nanooptics, nanoscale phenomena, biophysics.
S. Okubo, Professor Emeritus; Ph.D., Rochester, 1958. Theoretical particle physics and mathematical physics, Lie and nonassociative algebras.
L. Orr, Professor; Ph.D., Chicago, 1991. Theoretical elementary particle physics, phenomenology, quantum chromodynamics and electroweak physics.
J. L. Pipher, Professor Emeritus; Ph.D., Cornell, 1971. Observational astrophysics, infrared astronomy, galactic and extragalactic star formation, low-mass stars and brown dwarfs, development of infrared detector arrays and instrumentation.
Alice Quillen, Associate Professor; Ph.D., Caltech, 1993. Observational astrophysics, galactic structure and dynamics, active galactic nuclei, dynamics of planetary and protoplanetary systems.
S. G. Rajeev, Professor; Ph.D., Syracuse, 1984. Theoretical particle physics, nonperturbative quantum field theory applied to strong interactions.
Chuang Ren, Assistant Professor; Ph.D., Wisconsin–Madison, 1998. Theoretical and computational plasma physics, controlled fusion.
L. Rothberg, Professor; Ph.D., Harvard, 1983. Experimental chemical physics, organic electronics and biomolecular sensing.
M. P. Savedoff, Professor Emeritus; Ph.D., Princeton, 1957. Theoretical astrophysics, stellar interiors, interstellar matter, high-energy astrophysics.
Wold-Udo Schröder, Professor; Ph.D., Darmstadt (Germany), 1971. Experimental nuclear physics, dynamics of complex nuclear reactions, fundamental properties of nuclear matter, nuclear transmutation, nuclear technology applications.
Y. Shapir, Professor; Ph.D., Tel Aviv, 1981. Theoretical condensed-matter physics, statistical mechanics, critical phenomena in ordered and disordered systems, fractal growth.
S. L. Sharpless, Professor Emeritus; Ph.D., Chicago, 1952. Observational astrophysics.
A. Simon, Professor Emeritus; Ph.D., Rochester, 1950. Theoretical plasma physics, controlled thermonuclear fusion.
P. F. Slattery, Professor; Ph.D., Yale, 1967. Experimental elementary particle physics, investigation of QCD via direct photon production, top quark studies and searches for new phenomena using high-energy colliders.
R. Sobolewski, Professor; Ph.D., Polish Academy of Sciences (Warsaw), 1983. Applied superconductivity, ultrafast electronics and optoelectronics.
R. L. Sproull, Professor Emeritus; Ph.D., Cornell, 1943. Experimental condensed-matter physics.
Carlos R. Stroud Jr., Professor; Ph.D., Washington (St. Louis), 1969. Quantum optics, short-pulse excitation of atoms and molecules, quantum information.
Ching W. Tang, Doris Johns Cherry Professor; Ph.D., Cornell, 1975. Chemical and condensed-matter physics, organic electronics.
J. A. Tarduno, Professor; Ph.D., Stanford, 1987. Geophysics, geomagnetism and geodynamics, plate tectonics and polar wander, geomagnetic reversals, fine-particle magnetism, planetary astrophysics.
S. L. Teitel, Professor; Ph.D., Cornell, 1981. Statistical and condensed-matter physics.
J. H. Thomas, Professor; Ph.D., Purdue, 1966. Theoretical astrophysics, astrophysical plasmas, astrophysical fluid dynamics and magnetohydrodynamics, solar physics.
E. H. Thorndike, Professor; Ph.D., Harvard, 1960. Experimental elementary particle physics, weak decays of bottom and charm quarks.
H. M. Van Horn, Professor Emeritus; Ph.D., Cornell, 1965. Theoretical astrophysics, degenerate stars.
D. M. Watson, Professor; Ph.D., Berkeley, 1983. Observational astrophysics, infrared astronomy, stellar and planetary formation, low-mass stars and brown dwarfs, development of infrared detector arrays and instrumentation.
E. Wolf, Wilson Professor; Ph.D., Bristol (England), 1948. Theoretical optics, statistical optics, theory of coherence and polarization, inverse scattering, diffraction tomography.
F. L. H. Wolfs, Professor; Ph.D., Chicago, 1987. Experimental high-energy/nuclear physics, relativistic heavy-ion physics, dark-matter searches.
Jianhui Zhong, Professor; Ph.D., Brown, 1988. Biological and medical physics, advanced medical imaging, novel MRI techniques, physiological properties, biological tissues.

RECENT FACULTY PUBLICATIONS

Badolato, A., et al. Cavity QED effects with single quantum dots. *Compt. Rendus. Phys.* 9(8):850–6, 2008.
Nordhaus, J. and **E. G. Blackman.** Dynamos and chemical mixing in evolved stars. *Am. Inst. Phys. Conf. Proc.* 1001:306–12, 2008.
Bodek, A. (CDF collaboration) First observation of vector boson pairs in a hadronic final state at the tevatron collider. *Phys. Rev. Lett.* 103(9):091803, 2009.
Boersma, J. and A. Whitbeck. Decays of the littlest Higgs Z_H and the onset of strong dynamics. *Phys. Rev. D* 77(5):55012–8, 2008.
Schumaker, M. A., et al. **(D. Cline).** First Results with Tigress and accelerated radioactive ion beams from ISACII: Coulomb excitation of ^{20,21,29}Na. *Am. Inst. Phys. Conf. Proc.* 1099:754, 2009.
Das, A., H. Falomir, J. Gamboa, and F. Méndez. Non-commutative supersymmetric quantum mechanics. *Phys. Lett. B* 670(4–5):407–15, 2009.
Abazov V. M., et al. (R. Demina). Determination of the strong coupling constant from the inclusive jet cross section in pp collisions at $\sqrt{s}$ = 1.96 TeV. *Phys. Rev. D.* 80(11):111107–14, 2009.
Groves, E., B. D. Clauder, and **J. H. Eberly.** Multipulse quantum control: Exact solutions. *Optic. Lett.* 34(16):2539–41, 2009.
Bellan, P. M., et al. (A. Frank). Astrophysical jets: Observations, numerical simulations, and laboratory experiments. *Phys. Plasma.* 16(4):041005–13, 2009.
Ding, H. and **Y. Gao.** Electronic structure at rubrene metal interfaces. *Appl. Phys. Mater. Sci. Process.* 95(1):89–94, 2009.
Aaltonen, T., et al. (A. Garcia-Bellido). (CDF and D0 collaborations). Combination of Tevatron searches for the standard model Higgs boson in the $^{W+W-}$ decay mode. *Phys. Rev. Lett.* 104(6):061802–13, 2010.
Starling, D. J., P. B. Dixon, A. N. Jordan, and **J. C. Howell.** Optimizing the signal-to-noise ratio of a beam-deflection measurement with interferometric weak values. *Phys. Rev. A* 80(4):041803–7, 2009.
Dressel, J., S. Agarwal, and **A. N. Jordan.** Contextual values of observables in quantum measurements. *arXiv.org*, 2010, http://arxiv.org/abs/0911.4474v2.
Douglass, D. H. and **R. S. Knox.** Ocean heat content and earth's radiation imbalance. *Phys. Lett. A* 373(36):3296–300, 2009.
Kun, M., et al. (E. E. Mamajek). Pre-main-sequence stars in the Cepheus flare region. *Astrophys. J. Suppl.* 185(2):451, 2009.
T. Aaltonen, et al. **(K. S. McFarland).** (CDF collaboration). Measurement of the inclusive isolated prompt photon cross section in ppbar collisions at sqrt{s} = 1.96 TeV using the CDF detector. *Phys. Rev. D* 80:111106, 2009.
Alver, B., et al. **(S. Manly** and **F. Wolfs)** High transverse momentum triggered correlations over a large pseudorapidity acceptance in Au+Au collisions at $\sqrt{s_{NN}}$=200 GeV. *Phys. Rev. Lett.* 104(6):062301, 2010.
Melissinos, A. C. Proposal for a search for cosmic axions using an optical cavity. *Phys. Rev. Lett.* 102(20):202001–5, 2009.
Baur, U., and L. H. Orr. Searching for tt resonances at the CERN Large Hadron Collider. *Phys. Rev. D* 77(11):114001, 2008.
Quillen, A. C., I. Minchev, J. Bland-Hawthorn, and M. Haywood. Radial mixing in the outer Milky Way disk caused by an orbiting satellite. *Mon. Not. Roy. Astron. Soc.* 397(3):1599–1606, 2009.
Rajeev, S. G. The Langevin equation on Lie algebras: Maxwell-Boltzmann is not always the equilibrium. *Ann. Phys.* 324(12):2586–98, 2009.
Chen, C.-L., Y. Shapir, and E. H. Chimowitz. Diffusion scaling through structural templates given by the 3d dynamic Ising model. *Chem. Phys. Lett.* 469(1–3):210–13, 2009.
Olsson, P., and S. Teitel. Unified phase diagram for the three-dimensional XY model of a point-disordered type-II superconductor. *Phys. Rev. B* 79(21):214503–18, 2009.
Yelton, J., et al. (E. H. Thorndike). Absolute branching fraction measurements for exclusive D_s semileptonic decays. *Phys. Rev D* 80(5):052007, 2009.
Najita, J. R., et al. **(D. M. Watson).** Spitzer spectroscopy of the transition object TW Hya. *Astrophys. J.* 712(1):274–86, 2010.

ACADEMIC AND PROFESSIONAL PROGRAMS IN MATHEMATICS

Section 7
Mathematical Sciences

This section contains a directory of institutions offering graduate work in mathematical sciences, followed by in-depth entries submitted by institutions that chose to prepare detailed program descriptions. Additional information about programs listed in the directory but not augmented by an in-depth entry may be obtained by writing directly to the dean of a graduate school or chair of a department at the address given in the directory.

For programs offering work in related fields, see all other areas in this book. In the other guides in this series:

Graduate Programs in the Humanities, Arts & Social Sciences
See *Economics* and *Psychology and Counseling*

Graduate Programs in the Biological Sciences
See *Biological and Biomedical Sciences; Biophysics; Genetics, Developmental Biology, and Reproductive Biology;* and *Pharmacology and Toxicology*

Graduate Programs in Engineering & Applied Sciences
See *Biomedical Engineering and Biotechnology; Chemical Engineering (Biochemical Engineering); Computer Science and Information Technology; Electrical and Computer Engineering; Engineering and Applied Sciences;* and *Industrial Engineering*

Graduate Programs in Business, Education, Health, Information Studies, Law & Social Work
See *Business Administration and Management, Library and Information Studies,* and *Public Health*

CONTENTS

Program Directories

Close-Ups

See also:

Applied Mathematics

Acadia University, Faculty of Pure and Applied Science, Department of Mathematics and Statistics, Wolfville, NS B4P 2R6, Canada. Offers applied mathematics and statistics (M Sc). *Faculty:* 13 full-time (2 women). *Students:* 3 full-time (1 woman), 1 part-time (0 women). 6 applicants, 17% accepted, 1 enrolled. In 2009, 6 master's awarded. *Degree requirements:* For master's, thesis. *Entrance requirements:* For master's, honors degree in mathematics, statistics or equivalent. Additional exam requirements/recommendations for international students: Required—TOEFL (minimum score 580 paper-based; 237 computer-based; 93 iBT), IELTS (minimum score 6.5). *Application deadline:* For fall admission, 2/1 priority date for domestic and international students. Applications are processed on a rolling basis. Application fee: $50. *Financial support:* Research assistantships, teaching assistantships, career-related internships or fieldwork and unspecified assistantships available. Financial award application deadline: 2/1. *Faculty research:* Geophysical fluid dynamics, machine scheduling problems, control theory, stochastic optimization, survival analysis. *Unit head:* Dr. Jeff Hooper, Head, 902-585-1382, Fax: 902-585-1074, E-mail: jeff.hooper@acadiau.ca. *Application contact:* Dr. Richard Karsten, Professor, 902-585-1608, Fax: 902-585-1074, E-mail: richard.karsten@acadiau.ca.

Air Force Institute of Technology, Graduate School of Engineering and Management, Department of Mathematics and Statistics, Dayton, OH 45433-7765. Offers applied mathematics (MS, PhD). Part-time programs available. *Degree requirements:* For master's, thesis; for doctorate, thesis/dissertation. *Entrance requirements:* For master's, GRE General Test, minimum GPA of 3.0, U.S. citizenship or permanent U.S. residency; for doctorate, GRE General Test, minimum GPA of 3.5, U.S. citizenship or permanent U.S. residency. *Faculty research:* Electromagnetics, groundwater modeling, nonlinear diffusion, goodness of fit, finite element analysis.

Arizona State University, Graduate College, College of Liberal Arts and Sciences, Division of Social Sciences, School of Human Evolution and Social Change, Tempe, AZ 85287. Offers anthropology (PhD); applied mathematics for the life and social sciences (PhD); environmental social science (PhD); museum studies in anthropology (MA); social science and health (PhD). *Degree requirements:* For master's, thesis or alternative; for doctorate, thesis/dissertation. *Entrance requirements:* For master's and doctorate, GRE.

Auburn University, Graduate School, College of Sciences and Mathematics, Department of Mathematics and Statistics, Auburn University, AL 36849. Offers applied mathematics (MAM, MS); mathematics (MS, PhD); probability and statistics (M Prob S); statistics (MS). *Faculty:* 54 full-time (8 women), 4 part-time/adjunct (1 woman). *Students:* 50 full-time (8 women), 44 part-time (17 women); includes 4 minority (2 African Americans, 1 Asian American or Pacific Islander, 1 Hispanic American), 46 international. Average age 28. 212 applicants, 52% accepted, 20 enrolled. In 2009, 16 master's, 10 doctorates awarded. *Degree requirements:* For doctorate, thesis/dissertation. *Entrance requirements:* For master's, GRE General Test, undergraduate mathematics background; for doctorate, GRE General Test, GRE Subject Test. *Application deadline:* For fall admission, 7/7 priority date for domestic students; for spring admission, 11/24 for domestic students. Applications are processed on a rolling basis. Application fee: $50 ($60 for international students). Electronic applications accepted. *Expenses:* Tuition, state resident: full-time $6240. Tuition, nonresident: full-time $18,720. International tuition: $18,938 full-time. Required fees: $492. Tuition and fees vary according to course load, program and reciprocity agreements. *Financial support:* Fellowships, teaching assistantships, special tuition awards available. Financial award applicants required to submit FAFSA. *Faculty research:* Pure and applied mathematics. *Unit head:* Dr. Michel Smith, Chair, 334-844-4290, Fax: 334-844-6655. *Application contact:* Dr. George Flowers, Dean of the Graduate School, 334-844-2125.

Bowie State University, Graduate Programs, Program in Applied and Computational Mathematics, Bowie, MD 20715-9465. Offers MS. Part-time and evening/weekend programs available. *Degree requirements:* For master's, comprehensive exam. *Entrance requirements:* For master's, calculus sequence, differential equations, linear algebra, CORTT, mathematical probability and statistics. Electronic applications accepted.

Brown University, Graduate School, Division of Applied Mathematics, Providence, RI 02912. Offers Sc M, PhD. *Degree requirements:* For master's, thesis or alternative; for doctorate, one foreign language, thesis/dissertation, oral exam. *Entrance requirements:* For master's and doctorate, GRE General Test.

California Institute of Technology, Division of Engineering and Applied Science, Option in Applied and Computational Mathematics, Pasadena, CA 91125-0001. Offers MS, PhD. *Faculty:* 5 full-time (0 women). *Students:* 23 full-time (3 women). 92 applicants, 3% accepted, 3 enrolled. In 2009, 2 master's, 4 doctorates awarded. *Degree requirements:* For doctorate, thesis/dissertation. *Entrance requirements:* For doctorate, GRE Subject Test. *Application deadline:* For fall admission, 1/1 for domestic students. Application fee: $0. Electronic applications accepted. *Financial support:* In 2009–10, 6 fellowships, 10 research assistantships, 14 teaching assistantships were awarded. *Faculty research:* Theoretical and computational fluid mechanics, numerical analysis, ordinary and partial differential equations, linear and nonlinear wave propagation, perturbation and asymptotic methods. *Unit head:* Dr. Thomas Y. Hou, Option Representative, 626-395-4546, E-mail: hou@acm.caltech.edu. *Application contact:* Natalie Gilmore, Assistant Dean of Graduate Studies, 626-395-3812, Fax: 626-577-9246, E-mail: ngilmore@caltech.edu.

California State Polytechnic University, Pomona, Academic Affairs, College of Science, Program in Mathematics, Pomona, CA 91768-2557. Offers applied mathematics (MS); pure mathematics (MS). Part-time programs available. *Students:* 27 full-time (16 women), 31 part-time (14 women); includes 30 minority (18 Asian Americans or Pacific Islanders, 12 Hispanic Americans), 5 international. Average age 32. 55 applicants, 69% accepted, 26 enrolled. In 2009, 11 master's awarded. *Degree requirements:* For master's, thesis or alternative. *Entrance requirements:* For master's, GRE General Test. *Application deadline:* For fall admission, 5/1 priority date for domestic students; for winter admission, 10/15 priority date for domestic students; for spring admission, 1/20 priority date for domestic students. Applications are processed on a rolling basis. Application fee: $55. Electronic applications accepted. *Expenses:* Tuition, nonresident: full-time $6696; part-time $248 per credit. Required fees: $5487; $3237 per term. Tuition and fees vary according to course load, degree level and program. *Financial support:* Career-related internships or fieldwork, Federal Work-Study, and institutionally sponsored loans available. Support available to part-time students. Financial award application deadline: 3/2; financial award applicants required to submit FAFSA. *Unit head:* Dr. Amber Rosin, Assistant Professor, 909-869-2426, Fax: 909-869-4904, E-mail: arrosin@csupomona.edu. *Application contact:* Scott J. Duncan, Director, Admissions, 909-869-3258, Fax: 909-869-4529, E-mail: sjduncan@csupomona.edu.

California State University, Fullerton, Graduate Studies, College of Natural Science and Mathematics, Department of Mathematics, Fullerton, CA 92834-9480. Offers applied mathematics (MA); mathematics (MA); mathematics for secondary school teachers (MA). Part-time programs available. *Students:* 15 full-time (8 women), 58 part-time (31 women); includes 30 minority (25 Asian Americans or Pacific Islanders, 5 Hispanic Americans), 3 international. Average age 30. 62 applicants, 76% accepted, 31 enrolled. In 2009, 25 master's awarded. *Degree requirements:* For master's, comprehensive exam or project. *Entrance requirements:* For master's, minimum GPA of 2.5 in last 60 units of course work, major in mathematics or related field. Application fee: $55. *Expenses:* Tuition, nonresident: full-time $11,160; part-time $373 per credit. Required fees: $1440 per term. Tuition and fees vary according to course load, degree level and program. *Financial support:* Research assistantships, teaching assistantships, career-related internships or fieldwork, Federal Work-Study, institutionally sponsored loans, and scholarships/grants available. Support available to part-time students. Financial award application deadline: 3/1; financial award applicants required to submit FAFSA. *Unit head:* Dr. Paul Deland, Chair, 657-278-3631. *Application contact:* Admissions/Applications, 657-278-2371.

California State University, Long Beach, Graduate Studies, College of Engineering, Department of Mechanical and Aerospace Engineering, Long Beach, CA 90840. Offers aerospace engineering (MSAE); engineering and industrial applied mathematics (PhD); interdisciplinary engineering (MSE); management engineering (MSE); mechanical engineering (MSME). Part-time programs available. *Faculty:* 16 full-time (2 women), 3 part-time/adjunct (0 women). *Students:* 47 full-time (6 women), 75 part-time (9 women); includes 51 minority (5 African Americans, 30 Asian Americans or Pacific Islanders, 16 Hispanic Americans), 28 international. Average age 28. 162 applicants, 63% accepted, 44 enrolled. *Entrance requirements:* Additional exam requirements/recommendations for international students: Required—TOEFL. *Application deadline:* For fall admission, 7/1 for domestic students. Application fee: $55. Electronic applications accepted. *Expenses:* Required fees: $1802 per semester. Part-time tuition and fees vary according to course load. *Financial support:* Career-related internships or fieldwork, Federal Work-Study, institutionally sponsored loans, scholarships/grants, and unspecified assistantships available. Financial award application deadline: 3/2. *Faculty research:* Unsteady turbulent flows, solar energy, energy conversion, CAD/CAM, computer-assisted instruction. *Unit head:* Dr. Hamid Hefazi, Chair, 562-985-1502, Fax: 562-985-1564, E-mail: hefazi@csulb.edu. *Application contact:* Dr. Hamid Rahai, Graduate Advisor, 562-985-5132, Fax: 562-985-4408, E-mail: rahai@csulb.edu.

California State University, Long Beach, Graduate Studies, College of Natural Sciences and Mathematics, Department of Mathematics and Statistics, Long Beach, CA 90840. Offers mathematics (MS), including applied mathematics, applied statistics, mathematics education for secondary school teachers. Part-time programs available. *Faculty:* 11 full-time (5 women). *Students:* 73 full-time (30 women), 90 part-time (36 women); includes 75 minority (6 African Americans, 47 Asian Americans or Pacific Islanders, 22 Hispanic Americans), 15 international. Average age 30. 123 applicants, 69% accepted, 44 enrolled. *Degree requirements:* For master's, comprehensive exam or thesis. *Application deadline:* For fall admission, 7/1 for domestic students; for spring admission, 12/1 for domestic students. Applications are processed on a rolling basis. Application fee: $55. Electronic applications accepted. *Expenses:* Required fees: $1802 per semester. Part-time tuition and fees vary according to course load. *Financial support:* Teaching assistantships, Federal Work-Study, institutionally sponsored loans, scholarships/grants, and traineeships available. Financial award application deadline: 3/2. *Faculty research:* Algebra, functional analysis, partial differential equations, operator theory, numerical analysis. *Unit head:* Dr. Robert Mena, Chair, 562-985-4721, Fax: 562-985-8227, E-mail: rmena@csulb.edu. *Application contact:* Dr. Ngo Viet, Graduate Associate Chair, 562-985-4721, Fax: 562-985-8227, E-mail: viet@csulb.edu.

California State University, Los Angeles, Graduate Studies, College of Natural and Social Sciences, Department of Mathematics, Los Angeles, CA 90032-8530. Offers mathematics (MS), including applied mathematics, mathematics. Part-time and evening/weekend programs available. *Faculty:* 8 full-time (1 woman), 2 part-time/adjunct (1 woman). *Students:* 26 full-time (12 women), 34 part-time (14 women); includes 29 minority (3 African Americans, 17 Asian Americans or Pacific Islanders, 9 Hispanic Americans), 11 international. Average age 34. 32 applicants, 100% accepted, 13 enrolled. In 2009, 18 master's awarded. *Degree requirements:* For master's, comprehensive exam or thesis. *Entrance requirements:* For master's, previous course work in mathematics. Additional exam requirements/recommendations for international students: Required—TOEFL (minimum score 500 paper-based; 173 computer-based). *Application deadline:* For fall admission, 5/1 for domestic and international students. Applications are processed on a rolling basis. Application fee: $55. Electronic applications accepted. *Financial support:* Teaching assistantships, Federal Work-Study available. Support available to part-time students. Financial award application deadline: 3/1. *Faculty research:* Group theory, functional analysis, convexity theory, ordered geometry. *Unit head:* Dr. Silva Heubach, Chair, 323-343-2150, Fax: 323-343-5071, E-mail: sheubac@calstatela.edu. *Application contact:* Dr. Cheryl L. Ney, Associate Vice President for Academic Affairs and Dean of Graduate Studies, 323-343-3820, Fax: 323-343-5653, E-mail: cney@cslanet.calstatela.edu.

California State University, Northridge, Graduate Studies, College of Science and Mathematics, Department of Mathematics, Northridge, CA 91330. Offers applied mathematics (MS); mathematics (MS); mathematics for educational careers (MS). Part-time and evening/weekend programs available. *Faculty:* 34 full-time (9 women), 36 part-time/adjunct (17 women). *Students:* 19 full-time (11 women), 34 part-time (12 women); includes 1 African American, 4 Asian Americans or Pacific Islanders, 9 Hispanic Americans, 2 international. Average age 31. 86 applicants, 49% accepted, 27 enrolled. In 2009, 16 master's awarded. *Degree requirements:* For master's, thesis (for some programs). *Entrance requirements:* For master's, GRE (if cumulative undergraduate GPA less than 3.0). Additional exam requirements/recommendations for international students: Required—TOEFL. *Application deadline:* For fall admission, 4/15 priority date for domestic students. Application fee: $55. *Financial support:* Teaching assistantships, Federal Work-Study and institutionally sponsored loans available. Support available to part-time students. Financial award application deadline: 3/1. *Unit head:* Dr. Werner Horn, Graduate Coordinator, 818-677-7794, E-mail: werner.horn@csun.edu. *Application contact:* Dr. Werner Horn, Graduate Coordinator, 818-677-7794, E-mail: werner.horn@csun.edu.

Carnegie Mellon University, Mellon College of Science, Department of Mathematical Sciences, Pittsburgh, PA 15213-3891. Offers algorithms, combinatorics, and optimization (PhD); applied mathematics (PhD); computational finance (MS); mathematical finance (PhD); mathematical sciences (MS, DA, PhD); pure and applied logic (PhD). Part-time programs available. Terminal master's awarded for partial completion of doctoral program. *Degree requirements:* For doctorate, thesis/dissertation. *Entrance requirements:* For master's and doctorate, GRE General Test, GRE Subject Test. Additional exam requirements/recommendations for international students: Required—TOEFL. Electronic applications accepted. *Faculty research:* Continuum mechanics, discrete mathematics, applied and computational mathematics.

Case Western Reserve University, School of Graduate Studies, Department of Mathematics, Cleveland, OH 44106. Offers applied mathematics (MS, PhD); mathematics (MS, PhD). Part-time programs available. *Faculty:* 18 full-time (5 women), 2 part-time/adjunct (1 woman). *Students:* 19 full-time (10 women), 1 part-time (0 women), 7 international. Average age 25. 55 applicants, 38% accepted, 8 enrolled. In 2009, 5 master's, 1 doctorate awarded. Terminal master's awarded for partial completion of doctoral program. *Degree requirements:* For master's, thesis or alternative, thesis (applied mathematics); for doctorate, thesis/dissertation. *Entrance requirements:* For master's and doctorate, GRE General Test. Additional exam requirements/recommendations for international students: Required—TOEFL (minimum score 550 paper-based; 213 computer-based; 79 iBT). *Application deadline:* For fall admission, 2/15 priority date for domestic students; for spring admission, 11/12 for domestic students. Applications are processed on a rolling basis. Application fee: $50. Electronic applications accepted. *Financial support:* Research assistantships, teaching assistantships available. Financial award application deadline: 2/15. *Faculty research:* Probability theory, differential equations and control theory, differential geometry and topology, Lie groups, functional and harmonic analysis. *Unit head:* Daniela Calvetti, Chair, 216-368-2880, Fax: 216-368-5163, E-mail: daniela.calvetti@case.edu. *Application contact:* Gaythresa Lewis, Admissions, 216-368-5014, Fax: 216-368-5163, E-mail: gxl34@case.edu.

Central European University, Graduate Studies, School of Social Sciences and Humanities, Budapest, Hungary. Offers economics (MA, PhD); gender studies (MA, PhD); international relations and European studies (MA, PhD); mathematics and its applications (MS, PhD); medieval studies (MA, PhD); nationalism studies (MA, PhD); philosophy (MA, PhD); political science (MA, PhD); public policy (MA, PhD); sociology and social anthropology (MA, PhD). Terminal master's awarded for partial completion of doctoral program. *Degree requirements:* For master's, one foreign language, thesis; for doctorate, one foreign language, comprehensive exam, thesis/dissertation. *Entrance requirements:* For master's, interview; for doctorate, GRE, CEU subject test, interview. Additional exam requirements/recommendations for international students: Required—TOEFL (minimum score 570 paper-based; 230 computer-based). Electronic applications accepted. *Faculty research:* Civil society, fiscal decentralization, party politics, political philosophy (especially Liberalism, theory of Democracy).

Claremont Graduate University, Graduate Programs, School of Mathematical Sciences, Claremont, CA 91711-6160. Offers computational and systems biology (PhD); computational mathematics and numerical analysis (MA, MS); computational science (PhD); engineering and industrial applied mathematics (PhD); mathematics (PhD); operations research and statistics (MA, MS); physical applied mathematics (MA, MS); pure mathematics (MA, MS); scientific computing (MA, MS); systems and control theory (MA, MS). Part-time programs available. *Faculty:* 5 full-time (0 women), 2 part-time/adjunct (0 women). *Students:* 56 full-time (20 women), 12 part-time (3 women); includes 13 minority (2 African Americans, 6 Asian Americans or Pacific Islanders, 5 Hispanic Americans), 25 international. Average age 33. In 2009, 7 master's, 7 doctorates awarded. Terminal master's awarded for partial completion of doctoral program. *Entrance requirements:* For master's and doctorate, GRE General Test. Additional exam requirements/recommendations for international students: Required—TOEFL (minimum score 550 paper-based; 213 computer-based; 80 iBT). *Application deadline:* For fall admission, 2/1 priority date for domestic students. Applications are processed on a rolling basis. Application fee: $60. Electronic applications accepted. *Expenses:* Tuition: Full-time $35,046; part-time $1524 per credit. Required fees: $161 per semester. *Financial support:* Fellowships, research assistantships, Federal Work-Study, institutionally sponsored loans, scholarships/grants, and tuition waivers (full and partial) available. Support available to part-time students. Financial award application deadline: 2/15; financial award applicants required to submit FAFSA. *Unit head:* John Angus, Dean, 909-621-8080, Fax: 909-607-8261, E-mail: john.angus@cgu.edu. *Application contact:* Susan Townzen, Program Coordinator, 909-621-8080, Fax: 909-607-8261, E-mail: susan.n.townzen@cgu.edu.

Clemson University, Graduate School, College of Engineering and Science, Department of Mathematical Sciences, Clemson, SC 29634. Offers applied and pure mathematics (MS, PhD); computational mathematics (MS, PhD); operations research (MS, PhD); statistics (MS, PhD). Part-time programs available. *Faculty:* 51 full-time (14 women), 9 part-time/adjunct (2 women). *Students:* 92 full-time (39 women), 1 part-time (0 women); includes 3 minority (2 African Americans, 1 American Indian/Alaska Native), 31 international. Average age 26. 134 applicants, 76% accepted, 20 enrolled. In 2009, 36 master's, 13 doctorates awarded. *Degree requirements:* For master's, thesis optional, final project; for doctorate, thesis/dissertation, qualifying exams. *Entrance requirements:* For master's and doctorate, GRE General Test. Additional exam requirements/recommendations for international students: Required—TOEFL. *Application deadline:* For fall admission, 1/15 priority date for domestic students, 2/15 priority date for international students; for spring admission, 10/1 priority date for domestic students, 9/15 priority date for international students. Applications are processed on a rolling basis. Application fee: $70 ($80 for international students). Electronic applications accepted. *Expenses:* Tuition, state resident: full-time $8684; part-time $528 per credit hour. Tuition, nonresident: full-time $15,330; part-time $1078 per credit hour. Required fees: $736; $37 per semester. Part-time tuition and fees vary according to course load and program. *Financial support:* In 2009–10, 85 students received support, including 1 fellowship with full and partial tuition reimbursement available (averaging $10,000 per year), 7 research assistantships with partial tuition reimbursements available (averaging $17,591 per year), 66 teaching assistantships with partial tuition reimbursements available (averaging $18,593 per year); career-related internships or fieldwork, institutionally sponsored loans, scholarships/grants, health care benefits, and unspecified assistantships also available. Support available to part-time students. Financial award application deadline: 4/15. *Faculty research:* Applied and computational analysis, cryptography, discrete mathematics, optimization, statistics. Total annual research expenditures: $535,985. *Unit head:* Dr. Robert L. Taylor, Chair, 864-656-5240, Fax: 864-656-5230, E-mail: rtaylo2@clemson.edu. *Application contact:* Dr. K. B. Kulasekera, Graduate Coordinator, 864-656-5231, Fax: 864-656-5230, E-mail: kk@clemson.edu.

Columbia University, Fu Foundation School of Engineering and Applied Science, Department of Applied Physics and Applied Mathematics, New York, NY 10027. Offers applied physics (Eng Sc D); applied physics and applied mathematics (MS, PhD, Engr); materials science and engineering (MS, Eng Sc D, PhD); medical physics (MS). Part-time programs available. Post-baccalaureate distance learning degree programs offered (no on-campus study). *Faculty:* 19 full-time (1 woman), 3 part-time/adjunct (1 woman). *Students:* 127 full-time (24 women), 44 part-time (7 women); includes 12 minority (2 African Americans, 1 American Indian/Alaska Native, 8 Asian Americans or Pacific Islanders, 1 Hispanic American), 73 international. Average age 27. 300 applicants, 35% accepted, 45 enrolled. In 2009, 31 master's, 10 doctorates awarded. Terminal master's awarded for partial completion of doctoral program. *Degree requirements:* For master's, comprehensive exam; for doctorate, thesis/dissertation, qualifying exam. *Entrance requirements:* For master's, GRE General Test, GRE Subject Test (strongly recommended); for doctorate, GRE General Test, GRE Subject Test (physics); for Engr, GRE General Test. Additional exam requirements/recommendations for international students: Required—TOEFL. *Application deadline:* For fall admission, 12/1 priority date for domestic and international students; for spring admission, 10/1 priority date for domestic and international students. Application fee: $70. Electronic applications accepted. *Financial support:* In 2009–10, 70 students received support, including 4 fellowships with full and partial tuition reimbursements available, 50 research assistantships with full tuition reimbursements available (averaging $30,000 per year), 18 teaching assistantships with full tuition reimbursements available (averaging $30,000 per year); health care benefits and unspecified assistantships also available. Financial award application deadline: 12/1; financial award applicants required to submit FAFSA. *Faculty research:* Plasma, solid state, optical and laser physics; atmospheric, oceanic and earth physics; computational math and applied mathematics; materials science and engineering. *Unit head:* Dr. Irving P. Herman, Professor and Chair, 212-854-4457, E-mail: seasinfo.apam@columbia.edu. *Application contact:* Montserrat Fernandez-Pinkley, Student Services Coordinator, 212-854-4457, Fax: 212-854-8257, E-mail: mf2157@columbia.edu.

See Close-Up on page 215.

Cornell University, Graduate School, Graduate Fields of Arts and Sciences, Center for Applied Mathematics, Ithaca, NY 14853-0001. Offers PhD. *Faculty:* 106 full-time (7 women). *Students:* 41 full-time (14 women); includes 6 minority (2 Asian Americans or Pacific Islanders, 4 Hispanic Americans), 8 international. Average age 26. 144 applicants, 11% accepted, 5 enrolled. In 2009, 5 doctorates awarded. *Degree requirements:* For doctorate, one foreign language, comprehensive exam, thesis/dissertation. *Entrance requirements:* For doctorate, GRE General Test, GRE Subject Test (mathematics recommended), 3 letters of recommendation. Additional exam requirements/recommendations for international students: Required—TOEFL (minimum score 550 paper-based; 213 computer-based; 77 iBT). *Application deadline:* For fall admission, 1/15 for domestic students. Application fee: $70. Electronic applications accepted. *Expenses:* Tuition: Full-time $29,500. Required fees: $70. Full-time tuition and fees vary according to degree level, program and student level. *Financial support:* In 2009–10, 34 students received support, including 2 fellowships with full tuition reimbursements available, 2 teaching assistantships with full tuition reimbursements available; research assistantships with full tuition reimbursements available, institutionally sponsored loans, scholarships/grants, health care benefits, tuition waivers (full and partial), and unspecified assistantships also available. Financial award applicants required to submit FAFSA. *Faculty research:* Nonlinear systems and PDE's, numerical methods, signal and image processing, mathematical biology, discrete mathematics and optimization. *Unit head:* Director of Graduate Studies, 607-255-4756, Fax: 607-255-9860. *Application contact:* Graduate Field Assistant, 607-255-4756, Fax: 607-255-9860, E-mail: appliedmath@cornell.edu.

Cornell University, Graduate School, Graduate Fields of Engineering, Field of Chemical Engineering, Ithaca, NY 14853-0001. Offers advanced materials processing (M Eng, MS, PhD); applied mathematics and computational methods (M Eng, MS, PhD); biochemical engineering (M Eng, MS, PhD); chemical reaction engineering (M Eng, MS, PhD); classical and statistical thermodynamics (M Eng, MS, PhD); fluid dynamics, rheology and biorheology (M Eng, MS, PhD); heat and mass transfer (M Eng, MS, PhD); kinetics and catalysis (M Eng, MS, PhD); polymers (M Eng, MS, PhD); surface science (M Eng, MS, PhD). *Faculty:* 29 full-time (2 women). *Students:* 95 full-time (30 women); includes 9 minority (1 African American, 5 Asian Americans or Pacific Islanders, 3 Hispanic Americans), 41 international. Average age 25. 317 applicants, 38% accepted, 46 enrolled. In 2009, 22 master's, 17 doctorates awarded. *Degree requirements:* For master's, thesis (MS); for doctorate, comprehensive exam, thesis/dissertation. *Entrance requirements:* For master's and doctorate, GRE General Test, 2 letters of recommendation. Additional exam requirements/recommendations for international students: Required—TOEFL (minimum score 600 paper-based; 237 computer-based; 77 iBT). *Application deadline:* For fall admission, 1/15 priority date for domestic students. Application fee: $70. Electronic applications accepted. *Expenses:* Tuition: Full-time $29,500. Required fees: $70. Full-time tuition and fees vary according to degree level, program and student level. *Financial support:* In 2009–10, 67 students received support, including 3 fellowships with full tuition reimbursements available, 3 research assistantships with full tuition reimbursements available; teaching assistantships with full tuition reimbursements available, institutionally sponsored loans, scholarships/grants, health care benefits, tuition waivers (full and partial), and unspecified assistantships also available. Financial award applicants required to submit FAFSA. *Faculty research:* Biochemical, biomedical and metabolic engineering; fluid and polymer dynamics; surface science and chemical kinetics; electronics materials; microchemical systems and nanotechnology. *Unit head:* Director of Graduate Studies, 607-255-4550. *Application contact:* Graduate Field Assistant, 607-255-4550, E-mail: dgs@cheme.cornell.edu.

Cornell University, Graduate School, Graduate Fields of Engineering, Field of Operations Research and Information Engineering, Ithaca, NY 14853-0001. Offers applied probability and statistics (PhD); manufacturing systems engineering (PhD); mathematical programming (PhD); operations research and industrial engineering (M Eng). *Faculty:* 46 full-time (9 women). *Students:* 163 full-time (46 women); includes 20 minority (2 African Americans, 12 Asian Americans or Pacific Islanders, 6 Hispanic Americans), 103 international. Average age 25. 774 applicants, 29% accepted, 91 enrolled. In 2009, 85 master's, 6 doctorates awarded. *Degree requirements:* For doctorate, comprehensive exam, thesis/dissertation. *Entrance requirements:* For master's and doctorate, GRE General Test, 3 letters of recommendation. Additional exam requirements/recommendations for international students: Required—TOEFL (minimum score 600 paper-based; 250 computer-based; 77 iBT). *Application deadline:* For fall admission, 1/15 for domestic students. Application fee: $70. Electronic applications accepted. *Expenses:* Tuition: Full-time $29,500. Required fees: $70. Full-time tuition and fees vary according to degree level, program and student level. *Financial support:* In 2009–10, 44 students received support, including 6 fellowships with full tuition reimbursements available, 5 teaching assistantships with full tuition reimbursements available; research assistantships with full tuition reimbursements available, institutionally sponsored loans, scholarships/grants, health care benefits, tuition waivers (full and partial), and unspecified assistantships also available. Financial award applicants required to submit FAFSA. *Faculty research:* Mathematical programming and combinatorial optimization, statistics, stochastic processes, mathematical finance, simulation, manufacturing, e-commerce. *Unit head:* Director of Graduate Studies, 607-255-9128, Fax: 607-255-9129. *Application contact:* Graduate Field Assistant, 607-255-9128, Fax: 607-255-9129, E-mail: orie@cornell.edu.

Dalhousie University, Faculty of Engineering, Department of Engineering Mathematics, Halifax, NS B3J 2X4, Canada. Offers M Sc, PhD. *Faculty:* 6 full-time (1 woman), 2 part-time/adjunct (0 women). *Students:* 7 full-time (1 woman), 1 part-time (0 women). Average age 28. 7 applicants, 43% accepted. In 2009, 1 master's awarded. *Degree requirements:* For master's, thesis; for doctorate, thesis/dissertation. *Entrance requirements:* Additional exam requirements/recommendations for international students: Required—TOEFL, IELTS, CANTEST, CAEL, or Michigan English Language Assessment Battery. *Application deadline:* For fall admission, 6/1 for domestic students, 4/1 for international students; for winter admission, 11/15 for domestic students, 8/31 for international students; for spring admission, 2/28 for domestic students, 12/31 for international students. Applications are processed on a rolling basis. Application fee: $70. Electronic applications accepted. *Financial support:* In 2009–10, 1 fellowship (averaging $12,000 per year), 1 research assistantship (averaging $3,600 per year), 3 teaching assistantships (averaging $4,800 per year) were awarded; scholarships/grants also available. *Faculty research:* Piecewise regression and robust statistics, random field theory, dynamical systems, wave loads on offshore structures, digital signal processing. *Unit head:* Dr. W. J. Phillips, Head, 902-494-6085, Fax: 902-423-1801, E-mail: engineering.mathematics@dal.ca. *Application contact:* Dr. Guy Kember, Graduate Coordinator, 902-494-3262, Fax: 902-423-1801, E-mail: guy.kember@dal.ca.

Delaware State University, Graduate Programs, Department of Applied Mathematics and Theoretical Physics, Interdisciplinary Program in Applied Mathematics and Theoretical Physics, Dover, DE 19901-2277. Offers PhD. *Degree requirements:* For doctorate, one foreign language, thesis defense. *Entrance requirements:* For doctorate, GRE General Test, MS degree in physics or mathematics. Additional exam requirements/recommendations for international students: Required—TOEFL (minimum score 550 paper-based).

Delaware State University, Graduate Programs, Department of Mathematics, Program in Applied Mathematics, Dover, DE 19901-2277. Offers MS. *Entrance requirements:* Additional exam requirements/recommendations for international students: Required—TOEFL (minimum score 550 paper-based). Electronic applications accepted.

DePaul University, College of Liberal Arts and Sciences, Department of Mathematical Sciences, Chicago, IL 60614. Offers applied mathematics (MS), including actuarial science or statistics; applied statistics (MS, Certificate); mathematics education (MA). Part-time and evening/weekend programs available. *Faculty:* 23 full-time (6 women), 18 part-time/adjunct (5 women). *Students:* 117 full-time (64 women), 67 part-time (37 women); includes 47 minority (22 African Americans, 15 Asian Americans or Pacific Islanders, 10 Hispanic Americans), 13 international. Average age 30. 40 applicants, 100% accepted. In 2009, 30 master's awarded. *Degree requirements:* For master's, comprehensive exam. *Entrance requirements:* Additional exam requirements/recommendations for international students: Required—TOEFL. *Application deadline:* For fall admission, 7/30 for domestic students, 6/30 for international students; for winter admission, 11/30 for domestic students, 10/31 for international students; for spring admission, 2/15 for domestic students. Applications are processed on a rolling basis. Application fee: $25. *Expenses:* Tuition: Full-time $37,525; part-time $620 per credit hour. *Financial support:* In 2009–10, 12 students received support, including research assistantships with partial tuition reimbursements available (averaging $6,000 per year); teaching assistantships, tuition waivers (full) also available. Financial award application deadline: 4/30. *Faculty research:* Verbally prime algebras, enveloping algebras of Lie, superalgebras and related rings, harmonic analysis, estimation theory. *Unit head:* Dr. Ahmed I. Zayed, Chairperson, 773-325-7806, Fax:

Applied Mathematics

DePaul University (continued)

773-325-7807, E-mail: azayed@depaul.edu. *Application contact:* Ann Spittle, Director of Graduate Admissions, 312-362-8300, Fax: 312-362-5749, E-mail: admitdpu@depaul.edu.

East Carolina University, Graduate School, Thomas Harriot College of Arts and Sciences, Department of Mathematics, Greenville, NC 27858-4353. Offers applied mathematics (MA); mathematics (MA). Part-time and evening/weekend programs available. *Degree requirements:* For master's, comprehensive exam. *Entrance requirements:* For master's, GRE General Test, MAT. Additional exam requirements/recommendations for international students: Required—TOEFL.

École Polytechnique de Montréal, Graduate Programs, Department of Mathematics and Industrial Engineering, Montréal, QC H3C 3A7, Canada. Offers ergonomy (M Eng, M Sc A, DESS); mathematical method in CA engineering (M Eng, M Sc A, PhD); operational research (M Eng, M Sc A, PhD); production (M Eng, M Sc A); technology management (M Eng, M Sc A). Part-time programs available. *Degree requirements:* For master's, one foreign language, thesis. *Entrance requirements:* For master's, minimum GPA of 2.75. *Faculty research:* Use of computers in organizations.

Florida Atlantic University, Charles E. Schmidt College of Science, Department of Mathematical Sciences, Boca Raton, FL 33431-0991. Offers applied mathematics and statistics (MS); mathematical sciences (MS, MST, PhD). Part-time programs available. *Faculty:* 36 full-time (5 women), 5 part-time/adjunct (1 woman). *Students:* 52 full-time (14 women), 31 part-time (19 women); includes 13 minority (5 African Americans, 5 Asian Americans or Pacific Islanders, 3 Hispanic Americans), 29 international. Average age 32. 62 applicants, 58% accepted, 18 enrolled. In 2009, 23 master's, 4 doctorates awarded. Terminal master's awarded for partial completion of doctoral program. *Degree requirements:* For master's, comprehensive exam (for some programs), thesis (for some programs); for doctorate, comprehensive exam, thesis/dissertation. *Entrance requirements:* For master's and doctorate, GRE General Test, minimum GPA of 3.0. Additional exam requirements/recommendations for international students: Required—TOEFL (minimum score 500 paper-based; 173 computer-based). *Application deadline:* For fall admission, 7/1 priority date for domestic students, 2/15 priority date for international students; for spring admission, 11/1 priority date for domestic students, 7/15 priority date for international students. Applications are processed on a rolling basis. Application fee: $30. Electronic applications accepted. *Expenses:* Tuition, state resident: full-time $7055; part-time $293.94 per credit hour. Tuition, nonresident: full-time $22,096; part-time $920.66 per credit hour. *Financial support:* In 2009–10, fellowships with partial tuition reimbursements (averaging $20,000 per year), teaching assistantships with partial tuition reimbursements (averaging $20,000 per year) were awarded; Federal Work-Study also available. Financial award application deadline: 4/1. *Faculty research:* Cryptography, statistics, algebra, analysis, combinatorics. *Unit head:* Dr. Lee Klingler, Chair, 561-297-0274, Fax: 561-297-2436, E-mail: klingler@fau.edu. *Application contact:* Dr. Heinrich Niederhausen, Graduate Director, 561-297-3237, Fax: 561-297-2436, E-mail: niederha@fau.edu.

Florida Institute of Technology, Graduate Programs, College of Science, Department of Mathematical Sciences, Melbourne, FL 32901-6975. Offers applied mathematics (MS, PhD); operations research (MS, PhD). Part-time and evening/weekend programs available. *Faculty:* 11 full-time (1 woman). *Students:* 33 full-time (9 women), 30 part-time (14 women); includes 15 minority (9 African Americans, 3 Asian Americans or Pacific Islanders, 3 Hispanic Americans), 17 international. Average age 34. 75 applicants, 57% accepted, 20 enrolled. In 2009, 19 master's, 3 doctorates awarded. *Degree requirements:* For master's, comprehensive exam (for some programs), thesis optional; for doctorate, comprehensive exam, thesis/dissertation. *Entrance requirements:* For master's, minimum GPA of 3.0, computer literacy; for doctorate, minimum GPA of 3.2, resume, 3 letters of recommendation, statement of objectives. Additional exam requirements/recommendations for international students: Required—TOEFL (minimum score 550 paper-based; 213 computer-based; 79 iBT). *Application deadline:* For fall admission, 4/1 for international students; for spring admission, 9/30 for international students. Applications are processed on a rolling basis. Application fee: $50. Electronic applications accepted. *Expenses:* Tuition: Part-time $1015 per credit. Tuition and fees vary according to campus/location and program. *Financial support:* In 2009–10, 12 students received support, including 1 research assistantship (averaging $8,960 per year), 11 teaching assistantships with full and partial tuition reimbursements available (averaging $9,478 per year); career-related internships or fieldwork, institutionally sponsored loans, tuition waivers (partial), unspecified assistantships, and tuition remissions also available. Support available to part-time students. Financial award application deadline: 3/1; financial award applicants required to submit FAFSA. *Faculty research:* Real analysis, numerical analysis, statistics, data analysis, combinatorics, artificial intelligence, simulation. Total annual research expenditures: $99,058. *Unit head:* Dr. Semem Koksal, Department Head, 321-674-8765, Fax: 321-674-7412, E-mail: skokal@fit.edu. *Application contact:* Thomas M. Shea, Director of Graduate Admissions, 321-674-7577, Fax: 321-723-9468, E-mail: tshea@fit.edu.

Florida State University, The Graduate School, College of Arts and Sciences, Department of Mathematics, Tallahassee, FL 32306-4510. Offers applied computational mathematics (MS, PhD); biomedical mathematics (MS, PhD); financial mathematics (MS, PhD); pure mathematics (MS, PhD). Part-time programs available. *Faculty:* 57 full-time (14 women). *Students:* 140 full-time (35 women), 9 part-time (2 women); includes 8 minority (2 African Americans, 2 Asian Americans or Pacific Islanders, 4 Hispanic Americans), 84 international. Average age 26. 273 applicants, 38% accepted, 34 enrolled. In 2009, 36 master's, 6 doctorates awarded. Terminal master's awarded for partial completion of doctoral program. *Degree requirements:* For master's, comprehensive exam (for some programs), thesis optional; for doctorate, comprehensive exam (for some programs), thesis/dissertation, candidacy exam. *Entrance requirements:* For master's and doctorate, GRE General Test, minimum upper-division GPA of 3.0, 4-year bachelor's degree. Additional exam requirements/recommendations for international students: Required—TOEFL (minimum score 550 paper-based; 213 computer-based; 80 iBT), or IELTS. *Application deadline:* For fall admission, 1/10 priority date for domestic students, 12/15 priority date for international students; for spring admission, 11/1 for domestic and international students. Applications are processed on a rolling basis. Application fee: $30. Electronic applications accepted. *Expenses:* Tuition, state resident: full-time $7413.36. Tuition, nonresident: full-time $22,567. *Financial support:* In 2009–10, 102 students received support, including 4 fellowships with full tuition reimbursements available (averaging $19,000 per year), 12 research assistantships with full tuition reimbursements available (averaging $20,000 per year), 84 teaching assistantships with full tuition reimbursements available (averaging $17,000 per year); career-related internships or fieldwork, scholarships/grants, and unspecified assistantships also available. Financial award application deadline: 4/1. *Faculty research:* Geometric topology, algebraic geometry, fluid dynamics, financial mathematics, biomedical mathematics. *Unit head:* Dr. Philip L. Bowers, Chairperson, 850-645-3338, Fax: 850-644-4053, E-mail: bowers@math.fsu.edu. *Application contact:* Dr. Bettye Anne Case, Associate Chair for Graduate Studies, 850-644-1586, Fax: 850-644-4053, E-mail: case@math.fsu.edu.

The George Washington University, Columbian College of Arts and Sciences, Department of Mathematics, Washington, DC 20052. Offers applied mathematics (MA, MS, PhD); pure mathematics (MA, MS, PhD). Part-time and evening/weekend programs available. *Faculty:* 18 full-time (3 women), 5 part-time/adjunct (1 woman). *Students:* 16 full-time (4 women), 11 part-time (6 women); includes 4 minority (all Asian Americans or Pacific Islanders), 10 international. Average age 27. 62 applicants, 81% accepted, 9 enrolled. In 2009, 2 master's, 2 doctorates awarded. Terminal master's awarded for partial completion of doctoral program. *Degree requirements:* For master's, comprehensive exam; for doctorate, one foreign language, thesis/dissertation, general exam. *Entrance requirements:* For master's and doctorate, GRE General Test, minimum GPA of 3.0, interview. Additional exam requirements/recommendations for international students: Required—TOEFL (minimum score 550 paper-based; 213 computer-based; 80 iBT). *Application deadline:* For fall admission, 1/15 priority date for domestic and international students; for spring admission, 10/1 priority date for domestic students, 9/1 priority date for international students. Applications are processed on a rolling basis. Application fee: $60. Electronic applications accepted. *Financial support:* In 2009–10, 17 students received support; fellowships with full tuition reimbursements available, teaching assistantships with tuition reimbursements available, Federal Work-Study and tuition waivers available. Financial award application deadline: 1/15. *Unit head:* John B. Conway, Chair, 202-994-0553, E-mail: conway@gwu.edu. *Application contact:* John B. Conway, Chair, 202-994-0553, E-mail: conway@gwu.edu.

Georgia Institute of Technology, Graduate Studies and Research, College of Sciences, School of Mathematics, Atlanta, GA 30332-0001. Offers algorithms, combinatorics, and optimization (PhD); applied mathematics (MS); bioinformatics (PhD); mathematics (PhD); quantitative and computational finance (MS); statistics (MS Stat). Terminal master's awarded for partial completion of doctoral program. *Degree requirements:* For master's, thesis or alternative; for doctorate, one foreign language, thesis/dissertation. *Entrance requirements:* For master's, GRE General Test, minimum GPA of 3.0; for doctorate, GRE General Test, GRE Subject Test, minimum GPA of 3.0. Additional exam requirements/recommendations for international students: Required—TOEFL. Electronic applications accepted. *Faculty research:* Dynamical systems, discrete mathematics, probability and statistics, mathematical physics.

Hampton University, Graduate College, Program in Applied Mathematics, Hampton, VA 23668. Offers computational mathematics (MS); nonlinear science (MS); statistics and probability (MS). *Degree requirements:* For master's, thesis optional. *Entrance requirements:* For master's, GRE General Test.

Harvard University, Graduate School of Arts and Sciences, School of Engineering and Applied Sciences, Cambridge, MA 02138. Offers applied mathematics (ME, SM, PhD); applied physics (ME, SM, PhD); computer science (ME, SM, PhD); engineering science (ME); engineering sciences (SM, PhD). Part-time programs available. *Faculty:* 57 full-time (9 women), 9 part-time/adjunct (1 woman). *Students:* 355 full-time (89 women), 3 part-time (0 women); includes 50 minority (4 African Americans, 40 Asian Americans or Pacific Islanders, 6 Hispanic Americans), 166 international. 1,617 applicants, 11% accepted, 88 enrolled. In 2009, 67 master's, 53 doctorates awarded. Terminal master's awarded for partial completion of doctoral program. *Degree requirements:* For master's, thesis optional; for doctorate, comprehensive exam, thesis/dissertation. *Entrance requirements:* For master's and doctorate, GRE General Test, GRE Subject Test (recommended), 3 letters of recommendation. Additional exam requirements/recommendations for international students: Required—TOEFL (minimum score 80 iBT). *Application deadline:* For fall admission, 12/31 priority date for domestic and international students. Application fee: $105. Electronic applications accepted. *Expenses:* Tuition: Full-time $33,696. Required fees: $1126. Full-time tuition and fees vary according to program. *Financial support:* In 2009–10, 115 fellowships with full tuition reimbursements (averaging $21,375 per year), 184 research assistantships with full and partial tuition reimbursements (averaging $28,500 per year), 76 teaching assistantships with full and partial tuition reimbursements (averaging $5,563 per year) were awarded; Federal Work-Study, institutionally sponsored loans, traineeships, and health care benefits also available. *Faculty research:* Applied mathematics, applied physics, computer science and electrical engineering, environmental engineering, mechanical and biomedical engineering. Total annual research expenditures: $43.8 million. *Unit head:* Cherry Murray, Dean, 617-495-5829, Fax: 617-495-5264, E-mail: dean@seas.harvard.edu. *Application contact:* Office of Admissions and Financial Aid, 617-495-5315, E-mail: admissions@seas.harvard.edu.

Hofstra University, College of Liberal Arts and Sciences, Department of Mathematics, Hempstead, NY 11549. Offers applied mathematics (MS); mathematics (MA). Part-time and evening/weekend programs available. *Faculty:* 3 full-time (2 women). *Students:* 7 full-time (3 women), 6 part-time (3 women); includes 1 minority (Asian American or Pacific Islander), 1 international. Average age 28. 11 applicants, 100% accepted, 6 enrolled. In 2009, 4 master's awarded. *Degree requirements:* For master's, thesis or alternative. *Entrance requirements:* For master's, bachelor's degree with strong background in math. Additional exam requirements/recommendations for international students: Required—TOEFL (minimum score 550 paper-based; 213 computer-based; 80 iBT). *Application deadline:* Applications are processed on a rolling basis. Application fee: $60. Electronic applications accepted. *Expenses:* Tuition: Full-time $16,200; part-time $900 per credit hour. Required fees: $970; $145 per term. Tuition and fees vary according to program. *Financial support:* In 2009–10, 9 students received support; fellowships with full and partial tuition reimbursements available, research assistantships with full and partial tuition reimbursements available, Federal Work-Study, institutionally sponsored loans, scholarships/grants, and tuition waivers (full and partial) available. Support available to part-time students. Financial award applicants required to submit FAFSA. *Faculty research:* Number theory; topology; discrete geometry, combinatorics; functional analysis, real analysis; set theory, logic. *Unit head:* Dr. Sylvia Silberger, Chairperson, 516-463-5580, Fax: 516-463-6596, E-mail: matsbs@hofstra.edu. *Application contact:* Carol Drummer, Dean of Graduate Admissions, 516-463-4876, Fax: 516-463-4664, E-mail: gradstudent@hofstra.edu.

Howard University, Graduate School, Department of Mathematics, Washington, DC 20059-0002. Offers applied mathematics (MS, PhD); mathematics (MS, PhD). Part-time programs available. Terminal master's awarded for partial completion of doctoral program. *Degree requirements:* For master's, comprehensive exam, thesis or alternative, qualifying exam; for doctorate, 2 foreign languages, comprehensive exam, thesis/dissertation, qualifying exams. *Entrance requirements:* For master's, GRE General Test, minimum GPA of 3.0; for doctorate, GRE General Test. Additional exam requirements/recommendations for international students: Required—TOEFL. Electronic applications accepted.

Hunter College of the City University of New York, Graduate School, School of Arts and Sciences, Department of Mathematics and Statistics, New York, NY 10021-5085. Offers applied mathematics (MA); mathematics for secondary education (MA); pure mathematics (MA). Part-time and evening/weekend programs available. *Faculty:* 7 full-time (1 woman). *Students:* 19 full-time (7 women), 56 part-time (26 women); includes 24 minority (3 African Americans, 18 Asian Americans or Pacific Islanders, 3 Hispanic Americans). Average age 31. 43 applicants, 77% accepted, 21 enrolled. In 2009, 35 master's awarded. *Degree requirements:* For master's, one foreign language, comprehensive exam, thesis (for some programs). *Entrance requirements:* For master's, GRE General Test, 24 credits in mathematics. Additional exam requirements/recommendations for international students: Required—TOEFL. *Application deadline:* For fall admission, 4/1 for domestic students, 2/1 for international students; for spring admission, 11/1 for domestic students, 9/1 for international students. Application fee: $125. *Expenses:* Tuition, state resident: full-time $7360; part-time $310 per credit. Required fees: $250 per semester. *Financial support:* Federal Work-Study, institutionally sponsored loans, scholarships/grants, and tuition waivers (partial) available. Support available to part-time students. *Faculty research:* Data analysis, dynamical systems, computer graphics, topology, statistical decision theory. *Unit head:* Ada Peluso, Chairperson, 212-772-5300, Fax: 212-772-4858, E-mail: peluso@math.hunter.cuny.edu. *Application contact:* William Zlata, Director for Graduate Admissions, 212-772-4482, Fax: 212-650-3336, E-mail: admissions@hunter.cuny.edu.

Illinois Institute of Technology, Graduate College, College of Science and Letters, Department of Applied Mathematics, Chicago, IL 60616-3793. Offers applied mathematics (MS, PhD); mathematical finance (MMF). Terminal master's awarded for partial completion of doctoral program. *Degree requirements:* For master's, comprehensive exam; for doctorate, comprehensive exam, thesis/dissertation. *Entrance requirements:* For master's, GRE General Test, minimum undergraduate GPA of 3.0; for doctorate, GRE General Test, minimum undergraduate GPA of 3.5. Additional exam requirements/recommendations for international students: Required—

TOEFL (minimum score 550 paper-based; 213 computer-based; 80 iBT). Electronic applications accepted. *Expenses:* Tuition: Full-time $17,550; part-time $888 per credit hour. Required fees: $850; $7.50 per credit hour. One-time fee: $50 full-time. Full-time tuition and fees vary according to program. *Faculty research:* Applied analysis, computational mathematics, discrete applied mathematics, stochastics, mathematical finance.

Indiana University Bloomington, University Graduate School, College of Arts and Sciences, Department of Mathematics, Bloomington, IN 47405-7000. Offers applied mathematics–numerical analysis (MA, PhD); mathematics education (MAT); probability-statistics (MA, PhD); pure mathematics (MA). *Faculty:* 46 full-time (4 women). *Students:* 131 full-time (26 women); includes 10 minority (1 African American, 1 American Indian/Alaska Native, 7 Asian Americans or Pacific Islanders, 1 Hispanic American), 67 international. Average age 28. 211 applicants, 29% accepted, 26 enrolled. In 2009, 13 master's, 18 doctorates awarded. Terminal master's awarded for partial completion of doctoral program. *Degree requirements:* For doctorate, one foreign language, thesis/dissertation. *Entrance requirements:* For master's and doctorate, GRE General Test, GRE Subject Test. Additional exam requirements/recommendations for international students: Required—TOEFL. *Application deadline:* For fall admission, 1/15 priority date for domestic and international students. Applications are processed on a rolling basis. Application fee: $55 ($65 for international students). Electronic applications accepted. *Financial support:* In 2009–10, 9 fellowships with full tuition reimbursements (averaging $20,000 per year), 5 research assistantships with full tuition reimbursements (averaging $16,440 per year), 106 teaching assistantships with full tuition reimbursements (averaging $15,940 per year) were awarded; scholarships/grants, health care benefits, and unspecified assistantships also available. Financial award application deadline: 1/15. *Faculty research:* Topology, geometry, algebra. *Unit head:* James F. Davis, Chair, 812-855-2200. *Application contact:* Kate Bowman, Graduate Secretary, 812-855-2645, Fax: 812-855-0046, E-mail: gradmath@indiana.edu.

Indiana University of Pennsylvania, School of Graduate Studies and Research, College of Natural Sciences and Mathematics, Department of Mathematics, Program in Applied Mathematics, Indiana, PA 15705-1087. Offers MS. *Faculty:* 10 full-time (3 women). *Students:* 17 full-time (3 women), 4 part-time (0 women); includes 3 minority (2 African Americans, 1 Asian American or Pacific Islander), 7 international. Average age 28. 30 applicants, 53% accepted, 8 enrolled. In 2009, 4 master's awarded. *Degree requirements:* For master's, thesis optional. *Entrance requirements:* For master's, 2 letters of recommendation. Additional exam requirements/recommendations for international students: Required—TOEFL. *Application deadline:* For fall admission, 7/1 priority date for domestic students; for spring admission, 11/1 for domestic students. Applications are processed on a rolling basis. Application fee: $40. *Expenses:* Tuition, state resident: full-time $6666; part-time $370 per credit hour. Tuition, nonresident: full-time $10,666; part-time $593 per credit hour. Required fees: $813 per semester. *Financial support:* In 2009–10, 9 research assistantships with full and partial tuition reimbursements (averaging $3,887 per year) were awarded; Federal Work-Study also available. Support available to part-time students. Financial award application deadline: 3/15; financial award applicants required to submit FAFSA. *Unit head:* Dr. Yu-Ju Kuo, Graduate Coordinator, 724-357-4765, E-mail: yuJu.kuo@iup.edu. *Application contact:* Dr. Jacqueline Gorman, Dean's Associate, 724-357-2609, E-mail: jgorman@iup.edu.

Indiana University–Purdue University Fort Wayne, College of Arts and Sciences, Department of Mathematical Sciences, Fort Wayne, IN 46805-1499. Offers applied mathematics (MS); applied statistics (Certificate); mathematics (MS); operations research (MS); teaching (MAT). Part-time and evening/weekend programs available. *Faculty:* 17 full-time (4 women), 2 part-time/adjunct (1 woman). *Students:* 2 full-time (0 women), 15 part-time (6 women); includes 2 minority (1 American Indian/Alaska Native, 1 Asian American or Pacific Islander), 1 international. Average age 35. 5 applicants, 60% accepted, 3 enrolled. In 2009, 2 master's, 2 other advanced degrees awarded. *Entrance requirements:* For master's, minimum GPA of 3.0, major or minor in mathematics, three letters of recommendation. Additional exam requirements/recommendations for international students: Required—TOEFL (minimum score 550 paper-based; 213 computer-based; 77 iBT); Recommended—TWE. *Application deadline:* For fall admission, 8/1 priority date for domestic students, 7/1 priority date for international students; for spring admission, 12/1 for domestic students, 10/1 for international students. Applications are processed on a rolling basis. Application fee: $55 ($60 for international students). Electronic applications accepted. *Expenses:* Tuition, state resident: full-time $4595; part-time $255 per credit. Tuition, nonresident: full-time $10,963; part-time $609 per credit. Required fees: $528; $29.35 per credit. Tuition and fees vary according to course load. *Financial support:* In 2009–10, 1 research assistantship with partial tuition reimbursement (averaging $12,740 per year), 6 teaching assistantships with partial tuition reimbursements (averaging $12,740 per year) were awarded; scholarships/grants and unspecified assistantships also available. Support available to part-time students. Financial award application deadline: 3/1; financial award applicants required to submit FAFSA. *Faculty research:* Target value, toroidal queen's graph, holomorphic maps. *Unit head:* Dr. David A. Legg, Chair, 260-481-6222, Fax: 260-481-0155, E-mail: legg@ipfw.edu. *Application contact:* Dr. W. Douglas Weakley, Director of Graduate Studies, 260-481-6233, Fax: 260-481-0155, E-mail: weakley@ipfw.edu.

Indiana University–Purdue University Indianapolis, School of Science, Department of Mathematical Sciences, Doctoral Program in Mathematics, Indianapolis, IN 46202-2896. Offers applied mathematics (PhD); mathematics (PhD). Application fee: $50 ($60 for international students). *Unit head:* Slawomir Klimek, Director of Graduate Programs, 317-274-6918, E-mail: grad-program@math.iupui.edu. *Application contact:* Slawomir Klimek, Director of Graduate Programs, 317-274-6918, E-mail: grad-program@math.iupui.edu.

Indiana University–Purdue University Indianapolis, School of Science, Department of Mathematical Sciences, Master's Program in Mathematics, Indianapolis, IN 46202-2896. Offers applied mathematics (MS); applied statistics (MS); mathematics (MS). Application fee: $50 ($60 for international students). *Unit head:* Slawomir Klimek, Director of Graduate Programs, 317-274-6918, E-mail: grad-program@math.iupui.edu. *Application contact:* Slawomir Klimek, Director of Graduate Programs, 317-274-6918, E-mail: grad-program@math.iupui.edu.

Indiana University South Bend, College of Liberal Arts and Sciences, South Bend, IN 46634-7111. Offers applied mathematics and computer science (MS); applied psychology (MA); English (MA); liberal studies (MLS). Part-time and evening/weekend programs available. *Faculty:* 79 full-time (33 women). *Students:* 27 full-time (10 women), 83 part-time (55 women); includes 17 minority (10 African Americans, 2 American Indian/Alaska Native, 2 Asian Americans or Pacific Islanders, 3 Hispanic Americans), 10 international. Average age 36. In 2009, 24 master's awarded. *Degree requirements:* For master's, thesis (for some programs). *Entrance requirements:* For master's, minimum GPA of 3.0. Additional exam requirements/recommendations for international students: Required—TOEFL. *Application deadline:* For fall admission, 7/31 priority date for domestic students, 7/1 priority date for international students; for spring admission, 3/31 priority date for domestic students, 11/1 priority date for international students. Applications are processed on a rolling basis. Application fee: $46 ($58 for international students). *Financial support:* In 2009–10, 5 students received support, including 5 teaching assistantships; Federal Work-Study also available. Support available to part-time students. *Faculty research:* Artificial intelligence, bioinformatics, English language and literature, creative writing, computer networks. Total annual research expenditures: $127,000. *Unit head:* Dr. Lynn R. Williams, Dean, 574-520-4322, Fax: 574-520-4528, E-mail: lwilliam@iusb.edu. *Application contact:* Dr. Lynn R. Williams, Dean, 574-520-4322, Fax: 574-520-4528, E-mail: lwilliam@iusb.edu.

Inter American University of Puerto Rico, San Germán Campus, Graduate Studies Center, Program in Applied Mathematics, San Germán, PR 00683-5008. Offers MA. Part-time and evening/weekend programs available. *Degree requirements:* For master's, comprehensive exam. *Entrance requirements:* For master's, EXADEP or GRE General Test, minimum GPA of 3.0.

Iowa State University of Science and Technology, Graduate College, College of Liberal Arts and Sciences, Department of Mathematics, Ames, IA 50011. Offers applied mathematics (MS, PhD); mathematics (MS, PhD); school mathematics (MSM). *Faculty:* 44 full-time (5 women), 2 part-time/adjunct (1 woman). *Students:* 76 full-time (18 women), 10 part-time (2 women); includes 4 minority (1 African American, 2 Asian Americans or Pacific Islanders, 1 Hispanic American), 38 international. 133 applicants, 25% accepted, 24 enrolled. In 2009, 12 master's, 10 doctorates awarded. *Degree requirements:* For master's, thesis or alternative; for doctorate, thesis/dissertation. *Entrance requirements:* For master's and doctorate, GRE General Test. Additional exam requirements/recommendations for international students: Required—TOEFL (minimum score 550 paper-based; 79 iBT) or IELTS (minimum score 6.5). *Application deadline:* For fall admission, 2/1 priority date for domestic and international students; for spring admission, 10/1 priority date for domestic and international students. Application fee: $40 ($90 for international students). Electronic applications accepted. *Expenses:* Tuition, state resident: full-time $6716. Tuition, nonresident: full-time $8908. Tuition and fees vary according to course level, course load, program and student level. *Financial support:* In 2009–10, 15 research assistantships with full and partial tuition reimbursements (averaging $13,500 per year), 66 teaching assistantships with full and partial tuition reimbursements (averaging $16,400 per year) were awarded; fellowships, scholarships/grants, health care benefits, and unspecified assistantships also available. *Unit head:* Dr. Wolfgang Kliemann, Chair, 515-294-1752, Fax: 515-294-5454, E-mail: gradmath@iastate.edu. *Application contact:* Dr. Paul Sacks, Director of Graduate Education, 515-294-0393, E-mail: gradmath@iastate.edu.

The Johns Hopkins University, Engineering for Professionals, Part-time Program in Applied and Computational Mathematics, Baltimore, MD 21218-2699. Offers MS, Post-Master's Certificate. Part-time and evening/weekend programs available. *Faculty:* 13 part-time/adjunct (2 women). *Students:* 6 full-time (1 woman), 101 part-time (31 women); includes 15 minority (4 African Americans, 7 Asian Americans or Pacific Islanders, 4 Hispanic Americans), 4 international. Average age 29. In 2009, 23 master's awarded. *Application deadline:* Applications are processed on a rolling basis. Application fee: $75. Electronic applications accepted. *Financial support:* Institutionally sponsored loans available. Financial award applicants required to submit FAFSA. Total annual research expenditures: $606,210. *Unit head:* Dr. Jim Spall, Program Chair, 443-778-4960, E-mail: james.spall@jhuapl.edu. *Application contact:* Priyanka Dwivedi, Admissions Manager, 410-516-2300, Fax: 410-579-8049, E-mail: pdwived1@jhu.edu.

The Johns Hopkins University, G. W. C. Whiting School of Engineering, Department of Applied Mathematics and Statistics, Baltimore, MD 21218-2699. Offers computational medicine (PhD); discrete mathematics (MA, MSE, PhD); financial mathematics (MSE); operations research/optimization/decision science (MA, MSE, PhD); statistics/probability/stochastic processes (MA, MSE, PhD). *Faculty:* 17 full-time (3 women), 4 part-time/adjunct (0 women). *Students:* 56 full-time (19 women), 5 part-time (2 women); includes 7 minority (1 African American, 6 Asian Americans or Pacific Islanders), 37 international. Average age 27. 213 applicants, 51% accepted, 16 enrolled. In 2009, 24 master's, 4 doctorates awarded. Terminal master's awarded for partial completion of doctoral program. *Degree requirements:* For master's, thesis (for some programs); for doctorate, thesis/dissertation, oral exam, introductory exam. *Entrance requirements:* For master's and doctorate, GRE General Test, GRE Subject Test. Additional exam requirements/recommendations for international students: Required—TOEFL (minimum score 600 paper-based; 250 computer-based; 100 iBT). *Application deadline:* For fall admission, 1/15 for domestic and international students; for spring admission, 9/15 for domestic and international students. Application fee: $75. Electronic applications accepted. *Financial support:* In 2009–10, 40 students received support, including 3 fellowships with full tuition reimbursements available (averaging $3,000 per year), 13 research assistantships with full tuition reimbursements available (averaging $22,333 per year), 15 teaching assistantships with full tuition reimbursements available (averaging $16,750 per year); Federal Work-Study, institutionally sponsored loans, scholarships/grants, health care benefits, tuition waivers (partial), and unspecified assistantships also available. Financial award application deadline: 1/15. *Faculty research:* Discrete mathematics, probability, statistics, optimization and operations research, scientific computation, financial mathematics. Total annual research expenditures: $1.1 million. *Unit head:* Dr. Daniel Q. Naiman, Chair, 410-516-7203, Fax: 410-516-7459, E-mail: daniel.naiman@jhu.edu. *Application contact:* Kristin Bechtel, Academic Program Coordinator, 410-516-7198, Fax: 410-516-7459, E-mail: kbechtel@jhu.edu.

Kent State University, College of Arts and Sciences, Department of Mathematical Sciences, Kent, OH 44242-0001. Offers applied mathematics (MA, MS, PhD); pure mathematics (MA, MS, PhD). Part-time programs available. *Degree requirements:* For master's, thesis optional; for doctorate, one foreign language, thesis/dissertation. Electronic applications accepted. *Faculty research:* Approximation theory, measure theory, ring theory, functional analysis, complex analysis.

Lehigh University, College of Arts and Sciences, Department of Mathematics, Bethlehem, PA 18015. Offers applied mathematics (MS, PhD); mathematics (MS, PhD); statistics (MS). Part-time programs available. *Faculty:* 21 full-time (1 woman), 1 part-time/adjunct (0 women). *Students:* 35 full-time (18 women), 5 part-time (1 woman); includes 3 minority (1 African American, 1 Asian American or Pacific Islander, 1 Hispanic American), 15 international. Average age 28. 85 applicants, 42% accepted, 10 enrolled. In 2009, 12 master's, 3 doctorates awarded. Terminal master's awarded for partial completion of doctoral program. *Degree requirements:* For master's, comprehensive exam, thesis optional; for doctorate, comprehensive exam, thesis/dissertation, qualifying exams, general exam. *Entrance requirements:* For master's and doctorate, minimum undergraduate GPA of 2.75, 3.0 for last two semesters; adequate background in math. Additional exam requirements/recommendations for international students: Required—TOEFL (minimum score 550 paper-based; 213 computer-based; 85 iBT). *Application deadline:* For fall admission, 1/15 priority date for domestic and international students; for spring admission, 12/1 priority date for domestic and international students. Applications are processed on a rolling basis. Application fee: $75. Electronic applications accepted. *Financial support:* In 2009–10, 28 students received support, including 2 fellowships with full tuition reimbursements available (averaging $22,000 per year), 23 teaching assistantships with full tuition reimbursements available (averaging $16,900 per year); research assistantships with full tuition reimbursements available, scholarships/grants and tuition waivers (partial) also available. Financial award application deadline: 1/15. *Faculty research:* Probability and statistics, geometry and topology, number theory, algebra, differential equations. Total annual research expenditures: $196,010. *Unit head:* Dr. Wei-Min Huang, Chairman, 610-758-3730, Fax: 610-758-3767, E-mail: wh02@lehigh.edu. *Application contact:* Dr. Terry Napier, Graduate Coordinator, 610-758-3755, E-mail: mathgrad@lehigh.edu.

Lehigh University, P.C. Rossin College of Engineering and Applied Science, Department of Mechanical Engineering and Mechanics, Bethlehem, PA 18015. Offers applied mathematics (MS, PhD); computational engineering and mechanics (MS, PhD); mechanical engineering (M Eng, MS, PhD, MBA/E); polymer science/engineering (M Eng, MS, PhD, MBA/E); MBA/E. Part-time and evening/weekend programs available. Postbaccalaureate distance learning degree programs offered. *Faculty:* 20 full-time (0 women). *Students:* 85 full-time (12 women), 32 part-time (3 women); includes 4 minority (1 African American, 2 Asian Americans or Pacific Islanders, 1 Hispanic American), 51 international. Average age 27. 320 applicants, 29% accepted, 45 enrolled. In 2009, 23 master's, 6 doctorates awarded. Terminal master's awarded for partial completion of doctoral program. *Degree requirements:* For master's, thesis; for doctorate, thesis/dissertation, general exam. *Entrance requirements:* Additional exam requirements/recommendations for international students: Required—TOEFL (minimum score

Applied Mathematics

Lehigh University (continued)
550 paper-based; 213 computer-based; 79 iBT). *Application deadline:* For fall admission, 7/15 for domestic and international students; for spring admission, 12/1 for domestic and international students. Applications are processed on a rolling basis. Application fee: $75. Electronic applications accepted. *Financial support:* In 2009–10, 30 students received support, including 8 fellowships with full and partial tuition reimbursements available (averaging $21,060 per year), 24 research assistantships with full and partial tuition reimbursements available (averaging $20,700 per year), 18 teaching assistantships with full and partial tuition reimbursements available (averaging $21,060 per year); unspecified assistantships also available. Financial award application deadline: 1/15. *Faculty research:* Thermofluids, dynamic systems, CAD/CAM, computational mechanics, solid mechanics. Total annual research expenditures: $3.1 million. *Unit head:* Dr. D. Gary Harlow, Chairman, 610-758-4102, Fax: 610-758-6224, E-mail: dgh0@lehigh.edu. *Application contact:* Jo Ann M. Casciano, Graduate Coordinator, 610-758-4107, Fax: 610-758-6224, E-mail: jmc4@lehigh.edu.

Long Island University, C.W. Post Campus, College of Liberal Arts and Sciences, Department of Mathematics, Brookville, NY 11548-1300. Offers applied mathematics (MS); mathematics education (MS); mathematics for secondary school teachers (MS). Part-time and evening/weekend programs available. *Degree requirements:* For master's, thesis or alternative, oral presentation. *Entrance requirements:* Additional exam requirements/recommendations for international students: Required—TOEFL. Electronic applications accepted. *Faculty research:* Differential geometry, topological groups, general topology, number theory, analysis and statistics, numerical analysis.

McGill University, Faculty of Graduate and Postdoctoral Studies, Faculty of Science, Department of Mathematics and Statistics, Montréal, QC H3A 2T5, Canada. Offers computational science and engineering (M Sc); mathematics and statistics (M Sc, MA, PhD), including applied mathematics (M Sc, MA), pure mathematics (M Sc, MA), statistics (M Sc, MA).

Michigan State University, The Graduate School, College of Natural Science, Department of Mathematics, East Lansing, MI 48824. Offers applied mathematics (MS, PhD); industrial mathematics (MS); mathematics (MAT, MS, PhD). *Entrance requirements:* Additional exam requirements/recommendations for international students: Required—TOEFL. Electronic applications accepted.

Missouri University of Science and Technology, Graduate School, Department of Mathematics and Statistics, Rolla, MO 65409. Offers applied mathematics (MS); mathematics (MST, PhD), including mathematics (PhD), mathematics education (MST), statistics (PhD). Terminal master's awarded for partial completion of doctoral program. *Degree requirements:* For master's, thesis or alternative; for doctorate, one foreign language, thesis/dissertation. *Entrance requirements:* For master's and doctorate, GRE General Test, GRE Subject Test. Electronic applications accepted. *Faculty research:* Analysis, differential equations, topology, statistics.

Montclair State University, The Graduate School, College of Science and Mathematics, Department of Computer Science, Montclair, NJ 07043-1624. Offers applied mathematics (MS); applied statistics (MS); CISCO (Certificate); informatics (MS); object oriented computing (Certificate). Part-time and evening/weekend programs available. *Faculty:* 14 full-time (3 women), 16 part-time/adjunct (6 women). *Students:* 10 full-time (6 women), 21 part-time (6 women). Average age 31. 15 applicants, 67% accepted, 6 enrolled. In 2009, 11 master's awarded. *Degree requirements:* For master's, comprehensive exam, thesis or alternative. *Entrance requirements:* For master's, GRE General Test, 2 letters of recommendation. Additional exam requirements/recommendations for international students: Required—TOEFL (minimum score 83 computer-based), or IELTS. *Application deadline:* For fall admission, 6/1 for international students; for spring admission, 10/1 for international students. Applications are processed on a rolling basis. Application fee: $60. Electronic applications accepted. *Expenses:* Tuition, area resident: Part-time $486.74 per credit. Tuition, state resident: part-time $486.74 per credit. Tuition, nonresident: part-time $751.34 per credit. Tuition and fees vary according to degree level and program. *Financial support:* In 2009–10, 4 research assistantships with full tuition reimbursements (averaging $7,000 per year) were awarded; Federal Work-Study, scholarships/grants, and unspecified assistantships also available. Support available to part-time students. Financial award application deadline: 3/1; financial award applicants required to submit FAFSA. *Unit head:* Dr. Dorothy Deremer, Chairperson, 973-655-4166. *Application contact:* Amy Aiello, Director of Graduate Admissions and Operations, 973-655-5147, Fax: 973-655-7869, E-mail: graduate.school@montclair.edu.

Montclair State University, The Graduate School, College of Science and Mathematics, Department of Mathematics, Montclair, NJ 07043-1624. Offers math pedagogy (Ed D); mathematics (MS), including computer science, mathematics education, pure and applied mathematics, statistics; physical science (Certificate); teaching middle grades math (MS, Certificate). Part-time and evening/weekend programs available. *Faculty:* 30 full-time (10 women), 39 part-time/adjunct (19 women). *Students:* 15 full-time (7 women), 101 part-time (75 women). Average age 32. 55 applicants, 76% accepted, 31 enrolled. In 2009, 32 master's, 2 doctorates, 9 other advanced degrees awarded. *Degree requirements:* For master's, comprehensive exam. *Entrance requirements:* For master's, GRE General Test, 2 letters of recommendation. Additional exam requirements/recommendations for international students: Required—TOEFL (minimum score 83 computer-based), or IELTS. *Application deadline:* For fall admission, 6/1 for international students; for spring admission, 10/1 for international students. Applications are processed on a rolling basis. Application fee: $60. *Expenses:* Tuition, area resident: Part-time $486.74 per credit. Tuition, state resident: part-time $486.74 per credit. Tuition, nonresident: part-time $751.34 per credit. Tuition and fees vary according to degree level and program. *Financial support:* In 2009–10, 9 research assistantships with full tuition reimbursements (averaging $7,000 per year), 1 teaching assistantship with full tuition reimbursement (averaging $15,000 per year) were awarded; Federal Work-Study, scholarships/grants, and unspecified assistantships also available. Support available to part-time students. Financial award application deadline: 3/1; financial award applicants required to submit FAFSA. *Faculty research:* Infectious disease. *Unit head:* Dr. Helen Roberts, Chairperson, 973-655-5132. *Application contact:* Amy Aiello, Director of Graduate Admissions and Operations, 973-655-5147, Fax: 973-655-7869, E-mail: graduate.school@montclair.edu.

Naval Postgraduate School, Graduate Programs, Department of Mathematics, Monterey, CA 93943. Offers applied mathematics (MS, PhD). Program only open to commissioned officers of the United States and friendly nations and selected United States federal civilian employees. Part-time programs available. *Degree requirements:* For master's, thesis; for doctorate, one foreign language, thesis/dissertation.

New Jersey Institute of Technology, Office of Graduate Studies, College of Science and Liberal Arts, Department of Mathematical Science, Program in Applied Mathematics, Newark, NJ 07102. Offers MS. Part-time and evening/weekend programs available. *Entrance requirements:* For master's, GRE General Test. Additional exam requirements/recommendations for international students: Required—TOEFL (minimum score 550 paper-based; 213 computer-based; 79 iBT). Electronic applications accepted.

New Mexico Institute of Mining and Technology, Graduate Studies, Department of Mathematics, Socorro, NM 87801. Offers applied math (PhD); mathematics (MS); operations research (MS). *Degree requirements:* For master's, thesis optional; for doctorate, thesis/dissertation. *Entrance requirements:* For master's, GRE General Test. Additional exam requirements/recommendations for international students: Required—TOEFL (minimum score 540 paper-based; 207 computer-based). *Faculty research:* Applied mathematics, differential equations, industrial mathematics, numerical analysis, stochastic processes.

North Carolina Central University, Division of Academic Affairs, College of Science and Technology, Department of Mathematics and Computer Science, Durham, NC 27707-3129. Offers applied mathematics (MS); mathematics education (MS); pure mathematics (MS). Part-time and evening/weekend programs available. *Degree requirements:* For master's, one foreign language, comprehensive exam, thesis. *Entrance requirements:* For master's, minimum GPA of 3.0 in major, 2.5 overall. Additional exam requirements/recommendations for international students: Required—TOEFL. *Faculty research:* Structure theorems for Lie algebra, Kleene monoids and semi-groups, theoretical computer science, mathematics education.

North Carolina State University, Graduate School, College of Physical and Mathematical Sciences, Department of Mathematics, Program in Applied Mathematics, Raleigh, NC 27695. Offers MS, PhD. *Degree requirements:* For master's, thesis (for some programs); for doctorate, thesis/dissertation. *Entrance requirements:* For master's and doctorate, GRE, GRE Subject Test. Electronic applications accepted. *Faculty research:* Biological and physical modeling, numerical analysis, control, stochastic processes, industrial mathematics.

North Dakota State University, College of Graduate and Interdisciplinary Studies, College of Science and Mathematics, Department of Mathematics, Fargo, ND 58108. Offers applied mathematics (MS, PhD); mathematics (MS, PhD). *Faculty:* 15 full-time, 4 part-time/adjunct. *Students:* 22 full-time (6 women), 7 part-time (4 women), 7 international. Average age 28. 7 applicants, 100% accepted, 5 enrolled. In 2009, 1 master's, 2 doctorates awarded. *Degree requirements:* For master's, comprehensive exam, thesis; for doctorate, one foreign language, comprehensive exam, thesis/dissertation, computer proficiency. *Entrance requirements:* For master's and doctorate, GRE General Test. Additional exam requirements/recommendations for international students: Required—TOEFL (minimum score 525 paper-based; 197 computer-based; 71 iBT), IELTS. *Application deadline:* For fall admission, 5/1 priority date for domestic and international students; for spring admission, 8/1 for domestic students, 8/1 priority date for international students. Applications are processed on a rolling basis. Application fee: $45 ($60 for international students). Electronic applications accepted. *Financial support:* In 2009–10, 5 fellowships with full tuition reimbursements (averaging $18,000 per year), 1 research assistantship with tuition reimbursement (averaging $14,000 per year), 17 teaching assistantships with full tuition reimbursements (averaging $9,300 per year) were awarded; Federal Work-Study, institutionally sponsored loans, and tuition waivers (full) also available. Support available to part-time students. Financial award application deadline: 3/31. *Faculty research:* Discrete mathematics, number theory, analysis theory, algebra, applied math. Total annual research expenditures: $33,227. *Unit head:* Dr. Warren Shreve, Chair, 701-231-8171, Fax: 701-231-7598, E-mail: warren.shreve@ndsu.edu. *Application contact:* Dr. Jim Coykendall, Graduate Program Director, 701-231-8079, Fax: 701-231-7598, E-mail: jim.coykendall@ndsu.edu.

Northeastern University, College of Science, Department of Mathematics, Boston, MA 02115-5096. Offers applied mathematics (MS); mathematics (MS, PhD); operations research (MSOR). Part-time and evening/weekend programs available. *Faculty:* 39 full-time (5 women), 15 part-time/adjunct (7 women). *Students:* 52 full-time (17 women), 4 part-time (1 woman); includes 2 Asian Americans or Pacific Islanders, 1 Hispanic American, 28 international. 146 applicants, 76% accepted, 23 enrolled. In 2009, 8 master's, 6 doctorates awarded. *Degree requirements:* For master's, thesis (for some programs); for doctorate, thesis/dissertation, qualifying exams. *Entrance requirements:* For master's and doctorate, GRE Subject Test, GRE General Test. Additional exam requirements/recommendations for international students: Required—TOEFL. *Application deadline:* For fall admission, 2/1 priority date for domestic and international students. Applications are processed on a rolling basis. Application fee: $50. Electronic applications accepted. *Financial support:* In 2009–10, 26 teaching assistantships with tuition reimbursements (averaging $17,345 per year) were awarded; research assistantships with tuition reimbursements, Federal Work-Study, institutionally sponsored loans, tuition waivers (full and partial), and unspecified assistantships also available. Financial award application deadline: 3/1; financial award applicants required to submit FAFSA. *Faculty research:* Algebra and singularities, combinatorics, topology, probability and statistics, geometric analysis and partial differential equations. *Unit head:* Dr. Jerzy Weyman, Graduate Coordinator, 617-373-5513, Fax: 617-373-5658, E-mail: j.weyman@neu.edu. *Application contact:* Jo-Anne Dickinson, Admissions Contact, 617-373-5990, Fax: 617-373-7281, E-mail: gsas@neu.edu.

Northwestern University, The Graduate School, Interdepartmental Programs, Program in Mathematical Methods in Social Science, Evanston, IL 60208. Offers MS.

Northwestern University, McCormick School of Engineering and Applied Science, Program in Applied Mathematics, Evanston, IL 60208. Offers MS, PhD. Admissions and degrees offered through The Graduate School. Part-time programs available. Terminal master's awarded for partial completion of doctoral program. *Degree requirements:* For master's, comprehensive exam, thesis or alternative; for doctorate, comprehensive exam, thesis/dissertation. *Entrance requirements:* For master's and doctorate, GRE. Additional exam requirements/recommendations for international students: Required—TOEFL. Electronic applications accepted. *Faculty research:* Combustion, interfacial phenomena, nonlinear optics, dynamical systems, scientific computation.

Oakland University, Graduate Study and Lifelong Learning, College of Arts and Sciences, Department of Mathematics and Statistics, Program in Applied Mathematical Sciences, Rochester, MI 48309-4401. Offers PhD.

Oakland University, Graduate Study and Lifelong Learning, College of Arts and Sciences, Department of Mathematics and Statistics, Program in Industrial Applied Mathematics, Rochester, MI 48309-4401. Offers MS. Part-time and evening/weekend programs available. *Entrance requirements:* For master's, minimum GPA of 3.0 for unconditional admission. Additional exam requirements/recommendations for international students: Required—TOEFL (minimum score 550 paper-based; 213 computer-based). Electronic applications accepted. *Expenses:* Contact institution.

Penn State University Park, Graduate School, Eberly College of Science, Department of Mathematics, State College, University Park, PA 16802-1503. Offers mathematics (MA), including applied mathematics. *Unit head:* Dr. John Roe, Head, 814-865-7527, Fax: 814-865-3735, E-mail: roe@math.psu.edu. *Application contact:* Dr. Dimitri Burago, Associate Head of Graduate Studies, 814-865-7741, E-mail: burago@math.psu.edu.

Princeton University, Graduate School, Program in Applied and Computational Mathematics, Princeton, NJ 08544-1019. Offers PhD. *Degree requirements:* For doctorate, thesis/dissertation. *Entrance requirements:* For doctorate, GRE General Test, GRE Subject Test. Additional exam requirements/recommendations for international students: Required—TOEFL (minimum score 600 paper-based; 250 computer-based). Electronic applications accepted.

Rensselaer Polytechnic Institute, Graduate School, School of Science, Department of Mathematical Sciences, Program in Applied Mathematics, Troy, NY 12180-3590. Offers MS. Part-time programs available. *Faculty:* 23 full-time (3 women), 4 part-time/adjunct (1 woman). *Students:* 45 full-time (18 women), 3 part-time (2 women); includes 3 African Americans, 5 Asian Americans or Pacific Islanders, 1 Hispanic American. Average age 22. 87 applicants, 52% accepted, 15 enrolled. In 2009, 9 master's awarded. *Entrance requirements:* For master's, GRE General Test. Additional exam requirements/recommendations for international students: Required—TOEFL. *Application deadline:* For fall admission, 1/15 priority date for domestic students. Applications are processed on a rolling basis. Application fee: $75. Electronic applications accepted. *Expenses:* Tuition: Full-time $38,100. *Financial support:* In 2009–10, 3 students received support. Career-related internships or fieldwork and institutionally sponsored loans available. Financial award application deadline: 1/15. *Faculty research:* Mathematical modeling, differential equations, applications of mathematics in science and engineering, operations research, analysis. Total annual research expenditures: $3.2 million. *Application contact:* Dawnmarie Robens, Graduate Student Coordinator, 518-276-6414, Fax: 518-276-4824, E-mail: robensd@rpi.edu.

Rice University, Graduate Programs, George R. Brown School of Engineering, Department of Computational and Applied Mathematics, Houston, TX 77251-1892. Offers computational and applied mathematics (MA, MCAM, PhD); computational science and engineering (MCSE, PhD). *Degree requirements:* For master's, comprehensive exam (for some programs), thesis (for some programs); for doctorate, comprehensive exam, thesis/dissertation. *Entrance requirements:* For master's and doctorate, GRE General Test, minimum GPA of 3.0. Additional exam requirements/recommendations for international students: Required—TOEFL (minimum score 600 paper-based; 250 computer-based). Electronic applications accepted. *Faculty research:* Inverse problems, partial differential equations, computer algorithms, computational modeling, optimization theory.

Rochester Institute of Technology, Graduate Enrollment Services, College of Science, School of Mathematical Sciences, Rochester, NY 14623-5603. Offers industrial and applied mathematics (MS). Part-time and evening/weekend programs available. *Students:* 14 full-time (6 women), 4 part-time (2 women); includes 2 minority (1 African American, 1 Hispanic American), 5 international. Average age 25. 24 applicants, 79% accepted, 7 enrolled. In 2009, 5 master's awarded. *Degree requirements:* For master's, thesis. *Entrance requirements:* For master's, GRE General Test (recommended), minimum GPA of 3.0. Additional exam requirements/recommendations for international students: Required—TOEFL (minimum score 550 paper-based; 213 computer-based; 79 iBT), or IELTS (minimum score 6.5). *Application deadline:* For fall admission, 2/15 priority date for domestic and international students. Applications are processed on a rolling basis. Application fee: $50. Electronic applications accepted. *Expenses:* Tuition: Full-time $31,533; part-time $876 per credit hour. Required fees: $210. *Financial support:* In 2009–10, 13 students received support; research assistantships with partial tuition reimbursements available, teaching assistantships with partial tuition reimbursements available, career-related internships or fieldwork, scholarships/grants, and unspecified assistantships available. Support available to part-time students. Financial award applicants required to submit FAFSA. *Faculty research:* Abstract algebra, bioinformatics, combinatorics and graph theory, complex variables, cryptography, dynamical systems and chaos, statistics, topology. *Unit head:* Dr. Hossein Shahmohamad, Graduate Program Coordinator, 585-475-7564, E-mail: hxssma@rit.edu. *Application contact:* Diane Ellison, Assistant Vice President, Graduate Enrollment Services, 585-475-2229, Fax: 585-475-7164, E-mail: gradinfo@rit.edu.

Rutgers, The State University of New Jersey, New Brunswick, Graduate School-New Brunswick, Department of Mathematics, Piscataway, NJ 08854-8097. Offers applied mathematics (MS, PhD); mathematics (MS, PhD). Part-time programs available. *Degree requirements:* For doctorate, one foreign language, comprehensive exam, thesis/dissertation. *Entrance requirements:* For master's and doctorate, GRE General Test, GRE Subject Test. Additional exam requirements/recommendations for international students: Required—TOEFL. *Faculty research:* Logic and set theory, number theory, mathematical physics, control theory, partial differential equations.

St. John's University, St. John's College of Liberal Arts and Sciences, Department of Mathematics and Computer Science, Queens, NY 11439. Offers algebra (MA); analysis (MA); applied mathematics (MA); computer science (MA); geometry-topology (MA); logic and foundations (MA); probability and statistics (MA). Part-time and evening/weekend programs available. *Students:* 3 full-time (0 women), 2 part-time (1 woman); includes 1 minority (Hispanic American), 1 international. Average age 25. 21 applicants, 67% accepted, 3 enrolled. In 2009, 2 master's awarded. *Degree requirements:* For master's, comprehensive exam, thesis optional. *Entrance requirements:* For master's, minimum GPA of 3.0. Additional exam requirements/recommendations for international students: Required—TOEFL (minimum score 500 paper-based; 173 computer-based; 61 iBT), IELTS (minimum score 5.5). *Application deadline:* For fall admission, 5/1 priority date for domestic and international students; for spring admission, 11/1 priority date for domestic and international students. Applications are processed on a rolling basis. Application fee: $70. Electronic applications accepted. *Expenses:* Tuition: Full-time $16,290; part-time $905 per credit. Required fees: $300; $150 per semester. Tuition and fees vary according to program. *Financial support:* Research assistantships, scholarships/grants available. Support available to part-time students. Financial award application deadline: 3/1; financial award applicants required to submit FAFSA. *Faculty research:* Functional analysis and operator theory, algebraic K-theory, applied mathematics, measure theory, differential geometry and mathematics education. *Unit head:* Dr. Charles Traina, Chair, 718-990-6166, E-mail: trainac@stjohns.edu. *Application contact:* Kathleen Davis, Director of Graduate Admission, 718-990-2790, Fax: 718-990-5686, E-mail: gradhelp@stjohns.edu.

San Diego State University, Graduate and Research Affairs, College of Sciences, Department of Mathematics and Statistics, Program in Applied Mathematics, San Diego, CA 92182. Offers MS. Part-time programs available. *Degree requirements:* For master's, comprehensive exam. *Entrance requirements:* For master's, GRE General Test. Additional exam requirements/recommendations for international students: Required—TOEFL. Electronic applications accepted. *Faculty research:* Modeling, computational fluid dynamics, biomathematics, thermodynamics.

San Jose State University, Graduate Studies and Research, College of Science, Department of Mathematics, San Jose, CA 95192-0001. Offers applied mathematics (MS); mathematics (MA, MS); mathematics education (MA); statistics (MA). Part-time and evening/weekend programs available. *Students:* 13 full-time (7 women), 22 part-time (8 women); includes 17 minority (1 African American, 12 Asian Americans or Pacific Islanders, 4 Hispanic Americans), 5 international. Average age 34. 50 applicants, 30% accepted, 10 enrolled. In 2009, 7 master's awarded. *Degree requirements:* For master's, comprehensive exam, thesis (for some programs). *Entrance requirements:* For master's, GRE Subject Test. *Application deadline:* For fall admission, 6/29 for domestic students; for spring admission, 11/30 for domestic students. Applications are processed on a rolling basis. Application fee: $59. Electronic applications accepted. *Financial support:* Teaching assistantships, career-related internships or fieldwork and Federal Work-Study available. Support available to part-time students. Financial award applicants required to submit FAFSA. *Faculty research:* Artificial intelligence, algorithms, numerical analysis, software database, number theory. *Unit head:* Dr. Bradley Jackson, Chair, 408-924-5100, Fax: 408-924-5080. *Application contact:* Prof. Richard Kubelka, Graduate Coordinator, 408-924-5132, E-mail: kubelka@math.sjsu.edu.

Santa Clara University, School of Engineering, Department of Applied Mathematics, Santa Clara, CA 95053. Offers MS. Part-time and evening/weekend programs available. *Students:* 2 full-time (1 woman), 9 part-time (4 women); includes 3 minority (all Asian Americans or Pacific Islanders), 1 international. Average age 29. *Degree requirements:* For master's, thesis (for some programs). *Entrance requirements:* For master's, GRE (waiver may be available). Additional exam requirements/recommendations for international students: Required—TOEFL (minimum score 550 paper-based; 213 computer-based; 79 iBT). *Application deadline:* For fall admission, 8/13 for domestic students, 7/16 for international students; for winter admission, 10/29 for domestic students, 9/24 for international students; for spring admission, 2/25 for domestic students, 1/21 for international students. Applications are processed on a rolling basis. Application fee: $60. *Expenses:* Contact institution. *Financial support:* Research assistantships, teaching assistantships available. Financial award application deadline: 3/2; financial award applicants required to submit FAFSA. *Unit head:* Dr. Alex Zecevic, Associate Dean for Graduate Studies, 408-554-2394, E-mail: azecevic@scu.edu. *Application contact:* Stacey Tinker, Director of Enrollment Management, 408-554-4748, Fax: 408-554-4323, E-mail: stinker@scu.edu.

Simon Fraser University, Graduate Studies, Faculty of Science, Department of Mathematics, Burnaby, BC V5A 1S6, Canada. Offers applied and computational mathematics (M Sc, PhD); mathematics (M Sc, PhD). *Degree requirements:* For master's, thesis; for doctorate, thesis/dissertation. *Entrance requirements:* For master's, GRE General Test, minimum GPA of 3.0, 3 letters of reference; for doctorate, GRE General Test, minimum GPA of 3.5, 3 letters of reference. Additional exam requirements/recommendations for international students: Required—TWE or IELTS. Electronic applications accepted. *Faculty research:* Semi-groups, number theory, optimization, combinations.

Southern Methodist University, Dedman College, Department of Mathematics, Dallas, TX 75275. Offers computational and applied mathematics (MS, PhD). *Faculty:* 17 full-time (2 women). *Students:* 18 full-time (6 women); includes 9 minority (5 Asian Americans or Pacific Islanders, 4 Hispanic Americans). Average age 26. 18 applicants, 44% accepted, 7 enrolled. In 2009, 3 master's, 4 doctorates awarded. *Degree requirements:* For master's, oral and written exams; for doctorate, thesis/dissertation, oral and written exams. *Entrance requirements:* For master's and doctorate, GRE General Test, minimum GPA of 3.0, 18 undergraduate hours in mathematics beyond first and second year calculus. Additional exam requirements/recommendations for international students: Required—TOEFL. *Application deadline:* For fall admission, 2/1 priority date for domestic students, 2/1 for international students; for spring admission, 11/30 for domestic students. Applications are processed on a rolling basis. Application fee: $75. Electronic applications accepted. *Financial support:* In 2009–10, 18 students received support, including 6 research assistantships with full tuition reimbursements available (averaging $16,500 per year), 12 teaching assistantships with full tuition reimbursements available (averaging $16,500 per year); career-related internships or fieldwork, scholarships/grants, health care benefits, tuition waivers, and unspecified assistantships also available. Support available to part-time students. Financial award application deadline: 2/1; financial award applicants required to submit FAFSA. *Faculty research:* Numerical analysis, scientific computation, fluid dynamics, software development, differential equations. Total annual research expenditures: $92,000. *Unit head:* Dr. Douglas A. Reinelt, Chairman, 214-768-2506, Fax: 214-768-2355, E-mail: mathchair@mail.smu.edu. *Application contact:* Dr. Thomas W. Carr, Director of Graduate Studies, 214-768-3460, E-mail: math@mail.smu.edu.

Stevens Institute of Technology, Graduate School, Charles V. Schaefer Jr. School of Engineering, Department of Mathematical Sciences, Program in Applied Mathematics, Hoboken, NJ 07030. Offers MS. *Degree requirements:* For master's, thesis optional. *Entrance requirements:* For master's, GRE. Additional exam requirements/recommendations for international students: Required—TOEFL. Electronic applications accepted. *Expenses:* Tuition: Full-time $9900; part-time $1100 per credit. Required fees: $286 per semester.

Stony Brook University, State University of New York, Graduate School, College of Engineering and Applied Sciences, Department of Applied Mathematics and Statistics, Stony Brook, NY 11794. Offers MS, PhD. *Faculty:* 19 full-time (3 women), 1 part-time/adjunct (0 women). *Students:* 179 full-time (60 women), 20 part-time (9 women); includes 28 minority (6 African Americans, 18 Asian Americans or Pacific Islanders, 4 Hispanic Americans), 132 international. Average age 28. 275 applicants, 41% accepted. In 2009, 35 master's, 21 doctorates awarded. *Degree requirements:* For master's, thesis or alternative; for doctorate, one foreign language, comprehensive exam, thesis/dissertation. *Entrance requirements:* For master's and doctorate, GRE General Test. Additional exam requirements/recommendations for international students: Required—TOEFL. *Application deadline:* For fall admission, 1/15 for domestic students. Application fee: $60. *Expenses:* Tuition, state resident: full-time $8370; part-time $349 per credit. Tuition, nonresident: full-time $13,250; part-time $552 per credit. Required fees: $933. *Financial support:* In 2009–10, 32 research assistantships, 42 teaching assistantships were awarded; fellowships also available. *Faculty research:* Biostatistics, combinatorial analysis, differential equations, modeling. Total annual research expenditures: $2.7 million. *Unit head:* Dr. Jim Glimm, Chairman, 631-632-8360. *Application contact:* Dr. Xiaolin Li, Graduate Director, 631-632-8354, Fax: 631-632-8490, E-mail: linli@ams.sunysb.edu.

Temple University, Graduate School, College of Science and Technology, Department of Mathematics, Philadelphia, PA 19122-6096. Offers applied mathematics (MA); mathematics (PhD); pure mathematics (MA). Part-time and evening/weekend programs available. Terminal master's awarded for partial completion of doctoral program. *Degree requirements:* For master's, thesis optional, written exam; for doctorate, 2 foreign languages, thesis/dissertation, oral and written exams. *Entrance requirements:* For master's, GRE General Test, minimum GPA of 3.0; for doctorate, GRE General Test, GRE Subject Test, minimum GPA of 3.0. Additional exam requirements/recommendations for international students: Required—TOEFL (minimum score 550 paper-based; 213 computer-based; 79 iBT). Electronic applications accepted. *Faculty research:* Differential geometry, numerical analysis.

Texas A&M University–Corpus Christi, Graduate Studies and Research, College of Science and Technology, Program in Mathematics, Corpus Christi, TX 78412-5503. Offers applied and computational mathematics (MS); curriculum content (MS). Part-time programs available. *Degree requirements:* For master's, thesis (for some programs). *Entrance requirements:* For master's, 2 letters of recommendation.

Texas State University–San Marcos, Graduate School, College of Science, Department of Mathematics, Program in Industrial Mathematics, San Marcos, TX 78666. Offers MS. Part-time programs available. *Students:* 1 (woman) full-time. Average age 29. 2 applicants, 100% accepted, 1 enrolled. *Degree requirements:* For master's, comprehensive exam, thesis. *Entrance requirements:* For master's, GRE, minimum GPA of 2.75 in last 60 hours of undergraduate work. Additional exam requirements/recommendations for international students: Required—TOEFL (minimum score 550 paper-based; 213 computer-based). *Application deadline:* For fall admission, 6/15 priority date for domestic students, 6/1 priority date for international students; for spring admission, 10/15 priority date for domestic students, 10/1 priority date for international students. Applications are processed on a rolling basis. Application fee: $40 ($90 for international students). Electronic applications accepted. *Expenses:* Tuition, state resident: full-time $5784; part-time $241 per credit hour. Tuition, nonresident: part-time $551 per credit hour. Required fees: $1728; $48 per credit hour. $306. Tuition and fees vary according to course load. *Financial support:* In 2009–10, 1 student received support, including 1 research assistantship (averaging $4,928 per year); teaching assistantships, Federal Work-Study and institutionally sponsored loans also available. Support available to part-time students. Financial award application deadline: 4/1; financial award applicants required to submit FAFSA. *Unit head:* Dr. Stanley Wayment, Graduate Advisor, 512-245-2551, Fax: 512-245-3425, E-mail: sw05@txstate.edu. *Application contact:* Dr. Gregory Passty, Graduate Adviser, 512-245-3446, Fax: 512-245-3425, E-mail: gp02@txstate.edu.

Texas State University–San Marcos, Graduate School, College of Science, Department of Mathematics, Program in Mathematics, San Marcos, TX 78666. Offers MS. *Faculty:* 18 full-time (6 women). *Students:* 13 full-time (7 women), 14 part-time (6 women); includes 8 minority (3 African Americans, 2 Asian Americans or Pacific Islanders, 3 Hispanic Americans). Average age 32. 12 applicants, 83% accepted, 8 enrolled. In 2009, 5 master's awarded. *Degree requirements:* For master's, comprehensive exam, thesis (for some programs). *Entrance requirements:* For master's, GRE, minimum GPA of 2.75 in last 60 hours of undergraduate course work. Additional exam requirements/recommendations for international students: Required—TOEFL (minimum score 550 paper-based; 213 computer-based). *Application deadline:* For fall admission, 6/15 priority date for domestic students, 6/1 priority date for international students; for spring admission, 10/15 priority date for domestic students, 10/1 priority date for international students. Applications are processed on a rolling basis. Application fee: $40 ($90 for international students). Electronic applications accepted. *Expenses:* Tuition, state resident: full-time $5784; part-time $241 per credit hour. Tuition, nonresident: part-time $551 per credit hour. Required fees: $1728; $48 per credit hour. $306. Tuition and fees vary according to course load. *Financial support:* In 2009–10, 25 students received support, including 5 teaching assistantships (averaging $6,257 per year). Financial award application deadline:

Applied Mathematics

Texas State University–San Marcos (continued)
4/1; financial award applicants required to submit FAFSA. *Unit head:* Dr. Stanley Wayment, Graduate Advisor, 512-245-3555, Fax: 512-245-3425, E-mail: sw05@txstate.edu. *Application contact:* Dr. Gregory Passty, Graduate Adviser, 512-245-3446, Fax: 512-245-3425, E-mail: gp02@txstate.edu.

Towson University, College of Graduate Studies and Research, Program in Applied and Industrial Mathematics, Towson, MD 21252-0001. Offers MS. Part-time and evening/weekend programs available. *Degree requirements:* For master's, internships. *Entrance requirements:* For master's, bachelor's degree in mathematics or related field, minimum GPA of 3.0, including (3) terms of calculus, (1) differential equivalent one in linear algebra. Additional exam requirements/recommendations for international students: Required—TOEFL (minimum score 550 paper-based). Electronic applications accepted. *Faculty research:* Partial differential equations, numerical computations, statistics, probability, game theory.

Tulane University, School of Science and Engineering, Department of Mathematics, New Orleans, LA 70118-5669. Offers applied mathematics (MS); mathematics (MS, PhD); statistics (MS). *Degree requirements:* For master's, thesis (for some programs); for doctorate, thesis/dissertation. *Entrance requirements:* For master's, GRE General Test, minimum B average in undergraduate course work; for doctorate, GRE General Test. Additional exam requirements/recommendations for international students: Required—TOEFL. Electronic applications accepted.

The University of Akron, Graduate School, Buchtel College of Arts and Sciences, Department of Theoretical and Applied Mathematics, Program in Applied Mathematics, Akron, OH 44325. Offers MS. *Students:* 13 full-time (6 women); includes 2 minority (1 Asian American or Pacific Islander, 1 Hispanic American), 2 international. Average age 24. 7 applicants, 100% accepted, 3 enrolled. In 2009, 7 master's awarded. *Degree requirements:* For master's, seminar and comprehensive exam or thesis. *Entrance requirements:* For master's, minimum GPA of 2.75, letters of recommendation. Additional exam requirements/recommendations for international students: Required—TOEFL (minimum score 550 paper-based; 213 computer-based; 79 iBT). *Application deadline:* Applications are processed on a rolling basis. Application fee: $30 ($40 for international students). Electronic applications accepted. *Expenses:* Tuition, state resident: full-time $6570; part-time $365 per credit hour. Tuition, nonresident: full-time $11,250; part-time $625 per credit hour. *Faculty research:* Analysis of nonlinear partial differential equations, finite groups and character theory, mathematics education, modeling and simulation of continuum and nanoscale systems, numerical analysis and scientific computation. *Unit head:* Dr. Gerald Young, Coordinator, 330-972-5731, Fax: 330-972-8630, E-mail: gwyoung1@uakron.edu. *Application contact:* Dr. Gerald Young, Coordinator, 330-972-5731, Fax: 330-972-8630, E-mail: gwyoung1@uakron.edu.

The University of Akron, Graduate School, College of Engineering, Program in Engineering Applied Mathematics, Akron, OH 44325. Offers PhD. *Students:* 6 full-time (3 women), 2 part-time (0 women); includes 1 minority (African American), 4 international. Average age 31. 2 applicants, 100% accepted, 1 enrolled. In 2009, 1 doctorate awarded. *Degree requirements:* For doctorate, one foreign language, thesis/dissertation, candidacy exam, qualifying exam. *Entrance requirements:* For doctorate, GRE, minimum GPA of 3.0 with bachelor's degree, 3.5 with master's degree; letters of recommendation. Additional exam requirements/recommendations for international students: Required—TOEFL (minimum score 550 paper-based; 213 computer-based; 79 iBT). *Application deadline:* Applications are processed on a rolling basis. Application fee: $30 ($40 for international students). Electronic applications accepted. *Expenses:* Tuition, state resident: full-time $6570; part-time $365 per credit hour. Tuition, nonresident: full-time $11,250; part-time $625 per credit hour. *Unit head:* Dr. Gerald Young, Coordinator, 330-972-5731, E-mail: jerry@math.uakron.edu. *Application contact:* Dr. Craig Menzemer, Director of Graduate Studies, College of Engineering, 330-972-5536, E-mail: ccmenze@uakron.edu.

The University of Alabama, Graduate School, College of Arts and Sciences, Department of Mathematics, Tuscaloosa, AL 35487. Offers applied mathematics (PhD); mathematics (MA, PhD); pure mathematics (PhD). *Faculty:* 23 full-time (1 woman). *Students:* 32 full-time (11 women), 10 part-time (2 women); includes 2 minority (both African Americans), 27 international. Average age 29. 34 applicants, 47% accepted, 12 enrolled. In 2009, 8 master's, 7 doctorates awarded. Terminal master's awarded for partial completion of doctoral program. *Median time to degree:* Of those who began their doctoral program in fall 2001, 85% received their degree in 8 years or less. *Degree requirements:* For master's, thesis or alternative; for doctorate, thesis/dissertation. *Entrance requirements:* For master's and doctorate, GRE General Test, minimum GPA of 3.0. Additional exam requirements/recommendations for international students: Required—TOEFL (minimum score 550 paper-based; 79 iBT). *Application deadline:* For fall admission, 7/1 for domestic students, 5/31 for international students; for spring admission, 11/30 for domestic students, 10/31 for international students. Applications are processed on a rolling basis. Application fee: $50 ($60 for international students). Electronic applications accepted. *Expenses:* Tuition, state resident: full-time $7000. Tuition, nonresident: full-time $19,200. *Financial support:* In 2009–10, 1 fellowship with full tuition reimbursement (averaging $30,000 per year), 35 teaching assistantships with full tuition reimbursements (averaging $12,258 per year) were awarded; research assistantships with full tuition reimbursements, Federal Work-Study, institutionally sponsored loans, scholarships/grants, and unspecified assistantships also available. Support available to part-time students. Financial award application deadline: 7/1. *Faculty research:* Analysis, topology, algebra, fluid mechanics and system control theory, optimization, stochastic processes, numerical analysis. Total annual research expenditures: $25,303. *Unit head:* Dr. Zhijian Wu, Chairperson and Professor, 205-348-5080, Fax: 205-348-7067, E-mail: zwu@as.ua.edu. *Application contact:* Dr. Vo Liem, Director, 205-348-4898, Fax: 205-348-7067, E-mail: vliem@as.ua.edu.

The University of Alabama in Huntsville, School of Graduate Studies, College of Science, Department of Mathematical Sciences, Huntsville, AL 35899. Offers applied mathematics (PhD); mathematics (MA, MS). Part-time and evening/weekend programs available. *Faculty:* 13 full-time (0 women). *Students:* 19 full-time (9 women), 15 part-time (6 women); includes 6 minority (4 African Americans, 2 Asian Americans or Pacific Islanders), 6 international. Average age 30. 38 applicants, 55% accepted, 12 enrolled. In 2009, 4 master's, 2 doctorates awarded. *Degree requirements:* For master's, comprehensive exam, thesis or alternative, oral and written exams; for doctorate, comprehensive exam, thesis/dissertation, oral and written exams. *Entrance requirements:* For master's and doctorate, GRE General Test, minimum GPA of 3.0. Additional exam requirements/recommendations for international students: Required—TOEFL (minimum score 550 paper-based; 213 computer-based; 62 iBT). *Application deadline:* For fall admission, 7/15 for domestic students, 4/1 for international students; for spring admission, 11/30 for domestic students, 9/1 for international students. Applications are processed on a rolling basis. Application fee: $40 ($50 for international students). Electronic applications accepted. *Expenses:* Tuition, state resident: part-time $355.75 per credit hour. Tuition, nonresident: part-time $847.10 per credit hour. Required fees: $210.80 per semester. Tuition and fees vary according to course load and program. *Financial support:* In 2009–10, 16 students received support, including 16 teaching assistantships with full and partial tuition reimbursements available (averaging $10,793 per year); career-related internships or fieldwork, Federal Work-Study, institutionally sponsored loans, scholarships/grants, health care benefits, and unspecified assistantships also available. Support available to part-time students. Financial award application deadline: 4/1; financial award applicants required to submit FAFSA. *Faculty research:* Dynamical systems, mathematical biology, stochastic processes, numerical analysis, combinatorics. Total annual research expenditures: $290,027. *Unit head:* Dr. Jia Li, Chair, 256-824-6470, Fax: 256-824-6173, E-mail: li@math.uah.edu. *Application contact:* Kathy Biggs, Graduate Studies Admissions Manager, 256-824-6199, Fax: 256-824-6405, E-mail: deangrad@uah.edu.

University of Alberta, Faculty of Graduate Studies and Research, Department of Mathematical and Statistical Sciences, Edmonton, AB T6G 2E1, Canada. Offers applied mathematics (M Sc, PhD); biostatistics (M Sc); mathematical finance (M Sc, PhD); mathematical physics (M Sc, PhD); mathematics (M Sc, PhD); statistics (M Sc, PhD, Postgraduate Diploma). Part-time programs available. *Faculty:* 48 full-time (4 women). *Students:* 112 full-time (41 women), 5 part-time (0 women). Average age 24. 776 applicants, 5% accepted, 34 enrolled. In 2009, 12 master's, 10 doctorates awarded. Terminal master's awarded for partial completion of doctoral program. *Degree requirements:* For master's, thesis (for some programs); for doctorate, comprehensive exam, thesis/dissertation. *Entrance requirements:* Additional exam requirements/recommendations for international students: Required—TOEFL (minimum score 580 paper-based; 237 computer-based). *Application deadline:* For fall admission, 3/1 for domestic students, 2/1 for international students. Applications are processed on a rolling basis. Application fee: $0. Electronic applications accepted. Tuition and fees charges are reported in Canadian dollars. *Expenses:* Tuition, area resident: Full-time $4626.24 Canadian dollars; part-time $99.72 Canadian dollars per unit. International tuition: $8216 Canadian dollars full-time. Required fees: $3589.92 Canadian dollars; $99.72 Canadian dollars per unit. $215 Canadian dollars per term. *Financial support:* In 2009–10, 51 research assistantships, 88 teaching assistantships with full and partial tuition reimbursements were awarded; scholarships/grants also available. Financial award application deadline: 5/1. *Faculty research:* Classical and functional analysis, algebra, differential equations, geometry. *Unit head:* Dr. Anthony To-Ming Lau, Chair, 403-492-5141, E-mail: tlau@math.ualberta.ca. *Application contact:* Dr. Yau Shu Wong, Associate Chair, Graduate Studies, 403-492-5799, Fax: 403-492-6828, E-mail: gradmail@math.ualberta.ca.

The University of Arizona, Graduate College, College of Science, Department of Mathematics, Program in Mathematical Sciences, Tucson, AZ 85721. Offers applied science and business (PMS). Part-time programs available. *Students:* 51 full-time (13 women), 46 part-time (31 women); includes 7 minority (2 African Americans, 1 American Indian/Alaska Native, 2 Asian Americans or Pacific Islanders, 2 Hispanic Americans), 15 international. Average age 33. *Degree requirements:* For master's, thesis, internships, colloquium, business courses. *Entrance requirements:* For master's, GRE, minimum GPA of 3.0, statement of purpose. Additional exam requirements/recommendations for international students: Required—TOEFL (minimum score 550 paper-based). Application fee: $75. *Expenses:* Tuition, state resident: full-time $9028. Tuition, nonresident: full-time $24,890. *Financial support:* Research assistantships, teaching assistantships, career-related internships or fieldwork, Federal Work-Study, scholarships/grants, health care benefits, and unspecified assistantships available. *Faculty research:* Algebra, coding theory, graph theory, combinatorics, probability. *Unit head:* Dr. Michael Tabor, Head, 520-621-4664, Fax: 520-626-5048, E-mail: tabor@math.arizona.edu. *Application contact:* Alaina G. Levine, Director of Special Projects, College of Science, 520-621-3374, Fax: 520-621-8389, E-mail: alaina@u.arizona.edu.

The University of Arizona, Graduate College, Graduate Interdisciplinary Programs, Graduate Interdisciplinary Program in Applied Mathematics, Tucson, AZ 85721. Offers applied mathematics (MS, PhD); mathematical sciences (PMS). *Faculty:* 1. *Students:* 35 full-time (4 women), 12 part-time (6 women); includes 9 minority (3 Asian Americans or Pacific Islanders, 6 Hispanic Americans), 8 international. Average age 28. 108 applicants, 10% accepted, 11 enrolled. In 2009, 9 master's, 7 doctorates awarded. Terminal master's awarded for partial completion of doctoral program. *Degree requirements:* For master's, thesis (for some programs); for doctorate, comprehensive exam, thesis/dissertation. *Entrance requirements:* For master's, GRE, 3 letters of recommendation; for doctorate, GRE, 3 letters of recommendation, statement of purpose. Additional exam requirements/recommendations for international students: Required—TOEFL (minimum score 575 paper-based; 230 computer-based; 80 iBT). *Application deadline:* For fall admission, 1/23 for domestic students, 1/30 for international students. Applications are processed on a rolling basis. Application fee: $65. Electronic applications accepted. *Expenses:* Tuition, state resident: full-time $9028. Tuition, nonresident: full-time $24,890. *Financial support:* In 2009–10, 1 research assistantship with full tuition reimbursement (averaging $17,120 per year) was awarded; institutionally sponsored loans, scholarships/grants, health care benefits, tuition waivers (full), and unspecified assistantships also available. Financial award application deadline: 3/1; financial award applicants required to submit FAFSA. *Faculty research:* Dynamical systems and chaos, partial differential equations, pattern formation, fluid dynamics and turbulence, scientific computation, mathematical physics, mathematical biology, medical imaging, applied probability and stochastic processes. Total annual research expenditures: $22,526. *Unit head:* Dr. Michael Tabor, Head, 520-621-4664, Fax: 520-626-5048, E-mail: tabor@math.arizona.edu. *Application contact:* Graduate Coordinator, 520-621-2016, Fax: 520-626-5048, E-mail: applmath@u.arizona.edu.

University of Arkansas at Little Rock, Graduate School, College of Science and Mathematics, Department of Mathematics and Statistics, Little Rock, AR 72204-1099. Offers applied statistics (Graduate Certificate); mathematical sciences (MS). Part-time and evening/weekend programs available. *Degree requirements:* For master's, comprehensive exam. *Entrance requirements:* For master's, GRE General Test, GRE Subject Test, minimum GPA of 2.7, previous course work in advanced mathematics.

The University of British Columbia, Institute of Applied Mathematics, Vancouver, BC V6T 1Z1, Canada. Offers M Sc, PhD. *Degree requirements:* For master's, thesis (for some programs); for doctorate, comprehensive exam, thesis/dissertation. *Entrance requirements:* For doctorate, master's degree. Additional exam requirements/recommendations for international students: Required—TOEFL. *Faculty research:* Applied analysis, optimization, mathematical biology, numerical analysis, fluid mechanics.

University of California, Berkeley, Graduate Division, College of Letters and Science, Department of Mathematics, Program in Applied Mathematics, Berkeley, CA 94720-1500. Offers PhD. *Students:* 9 full-time (3 women). Average age 26. 66 applicants, 0 enrolled. *Degree requirements:* For doctorate, 2 foreign languages, thesis/dissertation, qualifying exam. *Entrance requirements:* For doctorate, GRE General Test, GRE Subject Test, minimum GPA of 3.0, 3 letters of recommendation. *Application deadline:* For fall admission, 12/10 for domestic students. Application fee: $70 ($90 for international students). *Financial support:* Fellowships, research assistantships, teaching assistantships, unspecified assistantships available. *Unit head:* Prof. Theodore A. Slaman, Chair, 510-642-6550, E-mail: ch_math@ls.berkeley.edu. *Application contact:* Barbara F. Waller, Student Affairs Officer, 510-642-0665, E-mail: barb@math.berkeley.edu.

University of California, Davis, Graduate Studies, Graduate Group in Applied Mathematics, Davis, CA 95616. Offers MS, PhD. Terminal master's awarded for partial completion of doctoral program. *Degree requirements:* For master's, thesis; for doctorate, one foreign language, thesis/dissertation. *Entrance requirements:* For master's, GRE General Test, GRE Subject Test, minimum GPA of 3.0; for doctorate, GRE General Test, GRE Subject Test, master's degree, minimum GPA of 3.0. Additional exam requirements/recommendations for international students: Required—TOEFL (minimum score 550 paper-based; 213 computer-based). Electronic applications accepted. *Faculty research:* Mathematical biology, control and optimization, atmospheric sciences, theoretical chemistry, mathematical physics.

University of California, Merced, Division of Graduate Studies, School of Natural Sciences, Merced, CA 95343. Offers applied mathematics (MS, PhD); biological engineering and small-scale technologies (MS, PhD); environmental systems (MS, PhD); mechanical engineering and applied mechanics (MS, PhD); physics and chemistry (PhD); quantitative and systems biology (MS, PhD). *Expenses:* Tuition, nonresident: full-time $15,102. Required fees: $10,919.

University of California, San Diego, Office of Graduate Studies, Department of Mathematics, La Jolla, CA 92093. Offers applied mathematics (MA); mathematics (MA, PhD); statistics (MS).

Degree requirements: For doctorate, thesis/dissertation. *Entrance requirements:* For master's and doctorate, GRE General Test, GRE Subject Test. Electronic applications accepted.

University of California, Santa Barbara, Graduate Division, College of Letters and Sciences, Division of Mathematics, Life, and Physical Sciences, Department of Mathematics, Santa Barbara, CA 93106-3080. Offers applied mathematics (MA); computational science and engineering (PhD); mathematics (MA, PhD); MA/PhD. *Faculty:* 31 full-time (3 women). *Students:* 54 full-time (14 women). Average age 26. 151 applicants, 26% accepted, 14 enrolled. In 2009, 5 master's, 14 doctorates awarded. Terminal master's awarded for partial completion of doctoral program. *Degree requirements:* For master's, comprehensive exam (for some programs), thesis (for some programs); for doctorate, comprehensive exam, thesis/dissertation. *Entrance requirements:* For master's, GRE General Test, GRE Subject Test (mathematics), 3 letters of recommendation, resume/curriculum vitae; for doctorate, GRE General Test, GRE Subject Test (math), 3 letters of recommendation, statement of purpose, personal achievements/contributions statement, resume/curriculum vitae, transcripts for post-secondary institutions attended. Additional exam requirements/recommendations for international students: Required—TOEFL (minimum score 575 paper-based; 231 computer-based; 80 iBT) or IELTS (7). *Application deadline:* For fall admission, 1/1 for domestic and international students. Application fee: $70 ($90 for international students). Electronic applications accepted. *Financial support:* In 2009–10, 54 students received support, including 13 fellowships with full and partial tuition reimbursements available (averaging $13,200 per year), 13 research assistantships with full and partial tuition reimbursements available (averaging $6,500 per year), 48 teaching assistantships with partial tuition reimbursements available (averaging $10,600 per year); Federal Work-Study, institutionally sponsored loans, scholarships/grants, health care benefits, and unspecified assistantships also available. Financial award applicants required to submit FAFSA. *Faculty research:* Topology, differential geometry, algebra, applied mathematics, partial differential equations. Total annual research expenditures: $204,214. *Unit head:* Prof. Jeffrey Stopple, Chair, 805-893-8330, Fax: 805-893-2385, E-mail: stopple@math.ucsb.edu. *Application contact:* Medina Price, Graduate Advisor, 805-893-8192, Fax: 805-893-2385, E-mail: price@math.ucsb.edu.

University of California, Santa Cruz, Division of Graduate Studies, Jack Baskin School of Engineering, Program in Statistics and Applied Mathematics, Santa Cruz, CA 95064. Offers MS, PhD. *Degree requirements:* For master's, seminar, qualifying exam, capstone project; for doctorate, thesis/dissertation, seminar, qualifying exam.

University of Central Arkansas, Graduate School, College of Natural Sciences and Math, Department of Mathematics, Conway, AR 72035-0001. Offers applied mathematics (MS); math education (MA). Part-time programs available. *Faculty:* 16 full-time (4 women). *Students:* 17 full-time (10 women), 8 part-time (6 women); includes 2 minority (1 African American, 1 Asian American or Pacific Islander), 2 international. Average age 28. 8 applicants, 100% accepted, 4 enrolled. In 2009, 5 master's awarded. *Degree requirements:* For master's, comprehensive exam, thesis optional. *Entrance requirements:* For master's, GRE General Test, minimum GPA of 2.7. Additional exam requirements/recommendations for international students: Required—TOEFL (minimum score 550 paper-based; 213 computer-based). *Application deadline:* For fall admission, 3/1 priority date for domestic students; for spring admission, 10/1 priority date for domestic students. Applications are processed on a rolling basis. Application fee: $25 ($50 for international students). *Expenses:* Tuition, state resident: full-time $5136; part-time $214 per credit hour. Required fees: $379.50; $127 per term. Tuition and fees vary according to course level, course load and campus/location. *Financial support:* In 2009–10, 11 teaching assistantships with partial tuition reimbursements (averaging $8,500 per year) were awarded; Federal Work-Study, scholarships/grants, and unspecified assistantships also available. Financial award application deadline: 2/15; financial award applicants required to submit FAFSA. *Unit head:* Dr. Ramesh Garimella, Chair, 501-450-3147, Fax: 501-450-5662, E-mail: rameshg@uca.edu. *Application contact:* Brenda Herring, Admissions Assistant, 501-450-5065, Fax: 501-450-5678, E-mail: bherring@uca.edu.

University of Central Florida, College of Sciences, Department of Mathematics, Orlando, FL 32816. Offers applied mathematics (Certificate); mathematical science (MS); mathematics (PhD). Part-time and evening/weekend programs available. *Faculty:* 31 full-time (10 women), 10 part-time/adjunct (0 women). *Students:* 36 full-time (10 women), 14 part-time (7 women); includes 9 minority (1 African American, 3 Asian Americans or Pacific Islanders, 5 Hispanic Americans), 12 international. Average age 32. 55 applicants, 53% accepted, 16 enrolled. In 2009, 8 master's, 8 doctorates awarded. *Degree requirements:* For master's, thesis or alternative; for doctorate, thesis/dissertation, candidacy exam. *Entrance requirements:* For master's, GRE General Test, minimum GPA of 3.0 in last 60 hours; for doctorate, GRE Subject Test, minimum GPA of 3.0 in last 60 hours or master's qualifying exam. Additional exam requirements/recommendations for international students: Required—TOEFL. *Application deadline:* For fall admission, 7/15 for domestic students; for spring admission, 12/1 for domestic students. Application fee: $30. Electronic applications accepted. *Expenses:* Tuition, state resident: part-time $306.31 per credit hour. Tuition, nonresident: part-time $1099.01 per credit hour. Part-time tuition and fees vary according to degree level and program. *Financial support:* In 2009–10, 27 students received support, including 1 fellowship with partial tuition reimbursement available (averaging $18,000 per year), 3 research assistantships with partial tuition reimbursements available (averaging $13,000 per year), 23 teaching assistantships with partial tuition reimbursements available (averaging $14,400 per year); career-related internships or fieldwork, Federal Work-Study, institutionally sponsored loans, tuition waivers (partial), and unspecified assistantships also available. Financial award application deadline: 3/1; financial award applicants required to submit FAFSA. *Faculty research:* Applied mathematics, analysis, approximation theory, graph theory, mathematical statistics. *Unit head:* Dr. Piotr Mikusinski, Chair, 407-823-0445, Fax: 407-823-6253, E-mail: piotrm@mail.ucf.edu. *Application contact:* Dr. Piotr Mikusinski, Chair, 407-823-0445, Fax: 407-823-6253, E-mail: piotrm@mail.ucf.edu.

University of Central Missouri, The Graduate School, College of Science and Technology, Warrensburg, MO 64093. Offers applied mathematics (MS); aviation safety (MS); biology (MS); computer science (MS); environmental studies (MA); industrial management (MS); mathematics (MS); technology (MS); technology management (PhD). Part-time programs available. Postbaccalaureate distance learning degree programs offered. *Faculty:* 59. *Students:* 99 full-time (31 women), 85 part-time (37 women). Average age 33. 45 applicants, 96% accepted, 42 enrolled. In 2009, 68 master's awarded. *Entrance requirements:* Additional exam requirements/recommendations for international students: Required—TOEFL (minimum score 550 paper-based; 79 computer-based). *Application deadline:* For fall admission, 6/1 priority date for domestic students, 5/1 for international students; for spring admission, 10/1 priority date for domestic students, 10/1 for international students. Applications are processed on a rolling basis. Application fee: $30 ($75 for international students). Electronic applications accepted. *Expenses:* Tuition, area resident: Part-time $245.80 per credit hour. Tuition, nonresident: part-time $491.60 per credit hour. Required fees: $24.20 per credit hour. Full-time tuition and fees vary according to course load, degree level, campus/location and reciprocity agreements. *Financial support:* In 2009–10, 15 students received support; fellowships with full and partial tuition reimbursements available, research assistantships with full and partial tuition reimbursements available, teaching assistantships with full and partial tuition reimbursements available, career-related internships or fieldwork, Federal Work-Study, scholarships/grants, and administrative and laboratory assistantships available. Support available to part-time students. Financial award application deadline: 3/1; financial award applicants required to submit FAFSA. *Unit head:* Dr. Alice Greife, Dean, 660-543-4450, Fax: 660-543-8031, E-mail: greife@ucmo.edu. *Application contact:* Laurie Delap, Admissions Coordinator, 660-543-4621, Fax: 660-543-4778, E-mail: gradinfo@ucmo.edu.

University of Central Oklahoma, College of Graduate Studies and Research, College of Mathematics and Science, Department of Mathematics and Statistics, Edmond, OK 73034-5209. Offers applied mathematical sciences (MS), including computer science, mathematics, mathematics/computer science teaching, statistics. Part-time programs available. *Degree requirements:* For master's, thesis. *Entrance requirements:* Additional exam requirements/recommendations for international students: Required—TOEFL (minimum score 550 paper-based; 213 computer-based). Electronic applications accepted. *Faculty research:* Curvaturo, FAA, math education.

University of Chicago, Division of the Physical Sciences, Department of Mathematics, Program in Applied Mathematics, Chicago, IL 60637-1513. Offers SM, PhD. *Degree requirements:* For master's, one foreign language, oral exams; for doctorate, one foreign language, thesis/dissertation, 2 qualifying exams. *Entrance requirements:* For master's and doctorate, GRE General Test, GRE Subject Test. Additional exam requirements/recommendations for international students: Required—TOEFL (minimum score 600 paper-based; 250 computer-based). Electronic applications accepted. *Faculty research:* Applied analysis, dynamical systems, theoretical biology, math-physics.

University of Cincinnati, Graduate School, McMicken College of Arts and Sciences, Department of Mathematical Sciences, Cincinnati, OH 45221. Offers applied mathematics (MS, PhD); mathematics education (MAT); pure mathematics (MS, PhD); statistics (MS, PhD). Part-time programs available. Terminal master's awarded for partial completion of doctoral program. *Degree requirements:* For master's, comprehensive exam, thesis or alternative; for doctorate, one foreign language, comprehensive exam, thesis/dissertation. *Entrance requirements:* For master's, GRE, teacher certification (MAT); for doctorate, GRE. Additional exam requirements/recommendations for international students: Required—TOEFL. Electronic applications accepted. *Faculty research:* Algebra, analysis, differential equations, numerical analysis, statistics.

University of Colorado at Boulder, Graduate School, College of Arts and Sciences, Department of Applied Mathematics, Boulder, CO 80309. Offers MS, PhD. Part-time programs available. *Faculty:* 16 full-time (1 woman). *Students:* 62 full-time (13 women), 12 part-time (4 women); includes 11 minority (2 African Americans, 5 Asian Americans or Pacific Islanders, 4 Hispanic Americans), 11 international. Average age 27. 79 applicants, 28% accepted, 20 enrolled. In 2009, 13 master's, 7 doctorates awarded. Terminal master's awarded for partial completion of doctoral program. *Degree requirements:* For master's, comprehensive exam, thesis or alternative; for doctorate, one foreign language, comprehensive exam, thesis/dissertation. *Entrance requirements:* For master's, GRE General Test, minimum undergraduate GPA of 2.75; for doctorate, GRE General Test. Additional exam requirements/recommendations for international students: Required—TOEFL. *Application deadline:* For fall admission, 2/1 priority date for domestic students, 12/1 for international students. Applications are processed on a rolling basis. Application fee: $50 ($60 for international students). *Financial support:* In 2009–10, 24 fellowships (averaging $7,649 per year), 25 research assistantships (averaging $14,920 per year) were awarded; scholarships/grants and traineeships also available. Support available to part-time students. *Faculty research:* Non-linear phenomena, computational mathematics, physical applied mathematics, statistics. Total annual research expenditures: $1.9 million.

University of Colorado at Colorado Springs, Graduate School, College of Letters, Arts and Sciences, Department of Mathematics, Colorado Springs, CO 80933-7150. Offers applied mathematics (MS); mathematics (M Sc). Part-time and evening/weekend programs available. *Faculty:* 12 full-time (2 women). *Students:* 12 full-time (7 women), 16 part-time (8 women); includes 3 minority (1 Asian American or Pacific Islander, 2 Hispanic Americans). Average age 38. 12 applicants, 75% accepted, 6 enrolled. In 2009, 7 master's awarded. *Degree requirements:* For master's, thesis, qualifying exam. *Entrance requirements:* For master's, GRE General Test, minimum GPA of 3.0. Additional exam requirements/recommendations for international students: Required—TOEFL. *Application deadline:* For fall admission, 6/15 for domestic students. Application fee: $60 ($75 for international students). *Expenses:* Tuition, state resident: full-time $8922; part-time $639 per credit hour. Tuition, nonresident: full-time $19,372; part-time $1154 per credit hour. Tuition and fees vary according to course level, course load, degree level, program, reciprocity agreements and student level. *Financial support:* Teaching assistantships, Federal Work-Study and scholarships/grants available. Support available to part-time students. Financial award application deadline: 3/1; financial award applicants required to submit FAFSA. *Faculty research:* Abelian groups and noncommutative rings, hormone analysis and computer vision, probability and mathematical physics, stochastic dynamics, probability models. *Unit head:* Dr. Rinaldo Schinazi, Chair, 719-255-3920, Fax: 719-255-3605. *Application contact:* Dr. James Daly, Director of Graduate Studies, 719-255-3428, Fax: 719-255-3605, E-mail: jdaly@uccs.edu.

University of Colorado Denver, College of Liberal Arts and Sciences, Department of Mathematical Sciences, Denver, CO 80217-3364. Offers applied mathematics (MS, PhD). Part-time and evening/weekend programs available. *Students:* 21 full-time (9 women), 38 part-time (11 women); includes 5 minority (all Asian Americans or Pacific Islanders), 10 international. 47 applicants, 66% accepted, 15 enrolled. In 2009, 18 master's, 4 doctorates awarded. *Degree requirements:* For master's, comprehensive exam, thesis optional; for doctorate, comprehensive exam, thesis/dissertation. *Entrance requirements:* For master's, GRE, 30 hours of course work in mathematics, 24 hours of course work in upper division mathematics, minimum GPA of 2.75; for doctorate, GRE, 24 hours of course work in upper division mathematics. Additional exam requirements/recommendations for international students: Required—TOEFL (minimum score 525 paper-based; 197 computer-based). *Application deadline:* For fall admission, 4/1 for domestic students; for spring admission, 11/1 for domestic students. Applications are processed on a rolling basis. Application fee: $50 ($75 for international students). Electronic applications accepted. *Financial support:* Fellowships with partial tuition reimbursements, research assistantships with full tuition reimbursements, teaching assistantships with full tuition reimbursements, Federal Work-Study available. Financial award application deadline: 4/1; financial award applicants required to submit FAFSA. *Faculty research:* Computational mathematics, computational biology, discrete mathematics and geometry probability and statistics, optimization. *Unit head:* Prof. Stephen Billups, Graduate Program Director, 303-556-8442, Fax: 303-556-8550, E-mail: stephen.billups@ucdenver.edu. *Application contact:* Dawn Arge, Program Assistant, 303-556-8442, Fax: 303-556-8550, E-mail: dawn.arge@ucdenver.edu.

University of Connecticut, Graduate School, College of Liberal Arts and Sciences, Department of Mathematics, Field of Applied Financial Mathematics, Storrs, CT 06269. Offers MS. *Faculty:* 49 full-time (10 women). *Students:* 18 full-time (3 women), 3 part-time (0 women); includes 1 minority (African American), 14 international. Average age 29. 105 applicants, 7% accepted, 5 enrolled. In 2009, 6 master's awarded. *Degree requirements:* For master's, comprehensive exam. *Entrance requirements:* Additional exam requirements/recommendations for international students: Required—TOEFL (minimum score 550 paper-based; 213 computer-based). *Application deadline:* For fall admission, 2/1 priority date for domestic and international students; for spring admission, 11/1 for domestic students, 10/1 for international students. Applications are processed on a rolling basis. Application fee: $55. Electronic applications accepted. *Expenses:* Tuition, state resident: full-time $4725; part-time $525 per credit. Tuition, nonresident: full-time $12,267; part-time $1363 per credit. Required fees: $346 per semester. Tuition and fees vary according to course load. *Financial support:* In 2009–10, 6 research assistantships with full tuition reimbursements, 6 teaching assistantships with full tuition reimbursements were awarded; Federal Work-Study and scholarships/grants also available. Financial award application deadline: 2/1; financial award applicants required to submit FAFSA. *Unit head:* James Bridgeman, Program Director, 860-486-8382, Fax: 860-486-4283, E-mail: james.bridgeman@uconn.edu. *Application contact:* Sharon McDermott, Administrative Assistant, 860-486-6452, Fax: 860-486-4283, E-mail: gradadm@math.uconn.edu.

University of Dayton, Graduate School, College of Arts and Sciences, Department of Mathematics, Dayton, OH 45469-1300. Offers applied mathematics (MAS); financial mathematics

Applied Mathematics

University of Dayton (continued)
(MFM); mathematics (MME). Part-time and evening/weekend programs available. *Faculty:* 15 full-time (5 women). *Students:* 15 full-time (5 women), 5 part-time (2 women), 10 international. Average age 31. 51 applicants, 57% accepted, 8 enrolled. In 2009, 4 master's awarded. *Entrance requirements:* For master's, minimum undergraduate GPA of 2.8 (MAS), 3.0 (MFM, MME). Additional exam requirements/recommendations for international students: Required—TOEFL (minimum score 550 paper-based; 213 computer-based; 80 iBT). *Application deadline:* For fall admission, 3/1 priority date for domestic students, 7/1 priority date for international students; for winter admission, 7/1 priority date for international students; for spring admission, 1/1 priority date for international students. Application fee: $0 ($50 for international students). Electronic applications accepted. *Expenses:* Tuition: Full-time $8412; part-time $701 per credit hour. Required fees: $325; $65 per course. $25 per semester. Tuition and fees vary according to course load, degree level and program. *Financial support:* In 2009–10, 7 teaching assistantships with full tuition reimbursements (averaging $12,755 per year) were awarded; institutionally sponsored loans, health care benefits, and unspecified assistantships also available. Financial award applicants required to submit FAFSA. *Faculty research:* Differential equations, integral equations, general topology, measure theory, graph theory, financial math, math education, numerical analysis. *Unit head:* Dr. Joe D. Mashburn, Chair, 937-229-2511, Fax: 937-229-2566, E-mail: joe.mashburn@notes.udayton.edu. *Application contact:* Associate Director of Graduate Admissions, 937-229-4411, Fax: 937-229-4729, E-mail: gradadmission@udayton.edu.

University of Delaware, College of Arts and Sciences, Department of Mathematical Sciences, Newark, DE 19716. Offers applied mathematics (MS, PhD); mathematics (MS, PhD). Part-time programs available. Terminal master's awarded for partial completion of doctoral program. *Degree requirements:* For master's, thesis (for some programs); for doctorate, one foreign language, thesis/dissertation, qualifying exam. *Entrance requirements:* For master's and doctorate, GRE General Test. Additional exam requirements/recommendations for international students: Required—TOEFL. Electronic applications accepted. *Faculty research:* Scattering theory, inverse problems, fluid dynamics, numerical analysis, combinatorics.

See Close-Up on page 323.

University of Denver, Faculty of Natural Sciences and Mathematics, Department of Mathematics, Denver, CO 80208. Offers applied mathematics (MA, MS); computer science (MS); mathematics (PhD). Part-time programs available. *Faculty:* 14 full-time (5 women), 1 part-time/adjunct (0 women). *Students:* 4 full-time (1 woman), 9 part-time (4 women); includes 2 minority (both Hispanic Americans), 4 international. Average age 27. 33 applicants, 82% accepted, 8 enrolled. In 2009, 4 master's awarded. Terminal master's awarded for partial completion of doctoral program. *Degree requirements:* For master's, computer language, foreign language, or laboratory experience; for doctorate, one foreign language, thesis/dissertation, oral and written exams. *Entrance requirements:* For master's and doctorate, GRE General Test. Additional exam requirements/recommendations for international students: Required—TOEFL. *Application deadline:* Applications are processed on a rolling basis. Application fee: $50. Electronic applications accepted. *Expenses:* Tuition: Full-time $34,596; part-time $961 per quarter hour. Required fees: $4 per quarter hour. Tuition and fees vary according to course load, campus/location and program. *Financial support:* In 2009–10, 1 research assistantship with full and partial tuition reimbursement (averaging $17,000 per year), 11 teaching assistantships with full and partial tuition reimbursements (averaging $17,000 per year) were awarded; career-related internships or fieldwork, Federal Work-Study, institutionally sponsored loans, and scholarships/grants also available. Support available to part-time students. Financial award application deadline: 3/1; financial award applicants required to submit FAFSA. *Faculty research:* Real-time software, convex bodies, multidimensional data, parallel computer clusters. *Unit head:* Dr. Alvaro Arias, Chairperson, 303-871-3559. *Application contact:* Information Contact, 303-871-2911, E-mail: info@math.du.edu.

University of Georgia, Graduate School, College of Arts and Sciences, Department of Mathematics, Athens, GA 30602. Offers applied mathematical science (MAMS); mathematics (MA, PhD). *Faculty:* 32 full-time (4 women). *Students:* 43 full-time (14 women), 1 part-time (0 women); includes 2 minority (both Hispanic Americans), 13 international. 119 applicants, 18% accepted, 9 enrolled. In 2009, 9 master's, 6 doctorates awarded. *Degree requirements:* For master's, one foreign language, thesis (for some programs); for doctorate, 2 foreign languages, thesis/dissertation. *Entrance requirements:* For master's and doctorate, GRE General Test. *Application deadline:* For fall admission, 7/1 priority date for domestic students; for spring admission, 11/15 for domestic students. Application fee: $50. Electronic applications accepted. *Expenses:* Tuition, state resident: full-time $6000; part-time $250 per credit hour. Tuition, nonresident: full-time $20,904; part-time $871 per credit hour. Required fees: $730 per semester. *Financial support:* Fellowships, research assistantships, teaching assistantships, unspecified assistantships available. *Unit head:* Dr. Joseph H. G. Fu, Head, 706-542-2564, Fax: 706-542-2573, E-mail: fu@math.uga.edu. *Application contact:* Dr. Brian D. Boe, Graduate Coordinator, 706-542-2547, Fax: 706-542-2573, E-mail: grad@math.uga.edu.

University of Guelph, Graduate Program Services, College of Physical and Engineering Science, Department of Mathematics and Statistics, Guelph, ON N1G 2W1, Canada. Offers applied mathematics (PhD); applied statistics (PhD); mathematics and statistics (M Sc). Part-time programs available. *Degree requirements:* For master's, thesis (for some programs); for doctorate, thesis/dissertation. *Entrance requirements:* For master's, minimum B- average during previous 2 years of course work; for doctorate, minimum B average. Additional exam requirements/recommendations for international students: Required—TOEFL (minimum score 550 paper-based; 213 computer-based; 89 iBT), IELTS (minimum score 6.5). *Faculty research:* Dynamical systems, mathematical biology, numerical analysis, linear and nonlinear models, reliability and bioassay.

University of Illinois at Chicago, Graduate College, College of Liberal Arts and Sciences, Department of Mathematics, Statistics, and Computer Science, Chicago, IL 60607-7128. Offers applied mathematics (MS, PhD); computational finance (MS, PhD); computer science (MS, PhD); mathematics (DA); mathematics and information sciences for industry (MS); probability and statistics (PhD); pure mathematics (MS, PhD); statistics (MS); teaching of mathematics (MST), including elementary, secondary. Part-time programs available. *Degree requirements:* For master's, comprehensive exam; for doctorate, one foreign language, thesis/dissertation. *Entrance requirements:* For master's and doctorate, GRE General Test, minimum GPA of 2.75. Additional exam requirements/recommendations for international students: Required—TOEFL. Electronic applications accepted.

University of Illinois at Urbana–Champaign, Graduate College, College of Liberal Arts and Sciences, Department of Mathematics, Champaign, IL 61820. Offers applied mathematics (MS); applied mathematics: actuarial science (MS); mathematics (MA, MS, PhD); teaching of mathematics (MS). *Faculty:* 67 full-time (5 women), 3 part-time/adjunct (0 women). *Students:* 161 full-time (40 women), 25 part-time (8 women); includes 13 minority (1 African American, 10 Asian Americans or Pacific Islanders, 2 Hispanic Americans), 107 international. 361 applicants, 25% accepted, 37 enrolled. In 2009, 41 master's, 23 doctorates awarded. *Entrance requirements:* For master's, GRE General Test, GRE Subject Test (mathematics), minimum GPA of 3.0; for doctorate, GRE General Test, GRE Subject Test (math), minimum GPA of 3.0. Additional exam requirements/recommendations for international students: Required—TOEFL (minimum score 550 paper-based; 213 computer-based). *Application deadline:* Applications are processed on a rolling basis. Application fee: $60 ($75 for international students). Electronic applications accepted. *Financial support:* In 2009–10, 22 fellowships, 44 research assistantships, 148 teaching assistantships were awarded; tuition waivers (full and partial) also available. *Unit head:* Sheldon Katz, Chair, 217-265-6258, Fax: 217-333-9576, E-mail: katzs@illinois.edu. *Application contact:* Marci Blocher, Office Support Specialist, 217-333-3350, Fax: 217-333-9576, E-mail: mblocher@illinois.edu.

The University of Iowa, Graduate College, Program in Applied Mathematical and Computational Sciences, Iowa City, IA 52242-1316. Offers PhD. *Degree requirements:* For doctorate, comprehensive exam, thesis/dissertation. *Entrance requirements:* For doctorate, GRE General Test, minimum GPA of 3.0. Additional exam requirements/recommendations for international students: Required—TOEFL (minimum score 620 paper-based; 260 computer-based; 105 iBT). Electronic applications accepted.

University of Kentucky, Graduate School, College of Arts and Sciences, Program in Mathematics, Lexington, KY 40506-0032. Offers applied mathematics (MS); mathematics (MA, MS, PhD). *Degree requirements:* For master's, comprehensive exam, thesis optional; for doctorate, one foreign language, comprehensive exam, thesis/dissertation. *Entrance requirements:* For master's, GRE General Test, minimum undergraduate GPA of 2.75; for doctorate, GRE General Test, minimum graduate GPA of 3.0. Additional exam requirements/recommendations for international students: Required—TOEFL (minimum score 550 paper-based; 213 computer-based). Electronic applications accepted. *Faculty research:* Numerical analysis, combinatorics, partial differential equations, algebra and number theory, real and complex analysis.

University of Louisville, Graduate School, College of Arts and Sciences, Department of Mathematics, Louisville, KY 40292. Offers applied and industrial mathematics (PhD); mathematics (MA). Part-time programs available. *Faculty:* 30 full-time (8 women), 3 part-time/adjunct (1 woman). *Students:* 28 full-time (12 women), 6 part-time (2 women); includes 2 minority (both African Americans), 7 international. Average age 29. 29 applicants, 52% accepted, 12 enrolled. In 2009, 6 master's, 3 doctorates awarded. Terminal master's awarded for partial completion of doctoral program. *Degree requirements:* For master's, comprehensive exam (for some programs), thesis optional; for doctorate, comprehensive exam, thesis/dissertation, internship, project. *Entrance requirements:* For master's and doctorate, GRE General Test. Additional exam requirements/recommendations for international students: Required—TOEFL (minimum score 550 paper-based; 215 computer-based; 79 iBT). *Application deadline:* For fall admission, 3/15 priority date for domestic students, 3/31 priority date for international students; for winter admission, 8/15 priority date for domestic students, 8/31 priority date for international students. Applications are processed on a rolling basis. Application fee: $50. Electronic applications accepted. *Financial support:* In 2009–10, 2 fellowships with tuition reimbursements (averaging $20,000 per year), 1 research assistantship (averaging $20,000 per year), 25 teaching assistantships with tuition reimbursements (averaging $20,000 per year) were awarded; health care benefits and unspecified assistantships also available. *Faculty research:* Algebra, analysis, biomathematics, combinatorics, math financial. *Unit head:* Dr. Thomas Riedel, Chair, 502-852-6826, Fax: 502-852-7132, E-mail: thomas.riedel@louisville.edu. *Application contact:* Dr. Bingtuan Li, Graduate Studies Director, 502-852-6826, Fax: 502-852-7132, E-mail: bing.li@louisville.edu.

University of Maryland, Baltimore County, Graduate School, College of Natural and Mathematical Sciences, Department of Mathematics and Statistics, Program in Applied Mathematics, Baltimore, MD 21250. Offers MS, PhD. Part-time and evening/weekend programs available. *Faculty:* 21 full-time (2 women). *Students:* 15 full-time (6 women), 17 part-time (7 women); includes 10 minority (1 African American, 8 Asian Americans or Pacific Islanders, 1 Hispanic American), 10 international. Average age 29. 32 applicants, 47% accepted, 8 enrolled. In 2009, 6 master's, 3 doctorates awarded. Terminal master's awarded for partial completion of doctoral program. *Degree requirements:* For master's, comprehensive exam (for some programs), thesis (for some programs); for doctorate, comprehensive exam, thesis/dissertation. *Entrance requirements:* For master's and doctorate, GRE General Test, minimum GPA of 3.0. Additional exam requirements/recommendations for international students: Required—TOEFL (minimum score 600 paper-based; 250 computer-based; 100 iBT). *Application deadline:* For fall admission, 2/15 priority date for domestic students, 1/1 priority date for international students; for spring admission, 10/15 priority date for domestic students, 5/1 priority date for international students. Applications are processed on a rolling basis. Application fee: $50. Electronic applications accepted. *Financial support:* In 2009–10, 15 students received support, including 3 research assistantships with full tuition reimbursements available (averaging $15,500 per year), 12 teaching assistantships with full tuition reimbursements available (averaging $15,500 per year); fellowships with full tuition reimbursements available, career-related internships or fieldwork, scholarships/grants, health care benefits, tuition waivers (full and partial), and unspecified assistantships also available. Support available to part-time students. Financial award application deadline: 2/15. *Faculty research:* Numerical analysis and scientific computation, optimization theory and algorithms, differential equations and mathematical modeling, mathematical biology and bioinformatics. Total annual research expenditures: $101,659. *Unit head:* Dr. Kathleen Hoffman, Director, 410-455-2434, Fax: 410-455-1066, E-mail: khoffman@math.umbc.edu. *Application contact:* Dr. Kathleen Hoffman, Director, 410-455-2434, Fax: 410-455-1066, E-mail: khoffman@math.umbc.edu.

University of Maryland, College Park, Academic Affairs, College of Computer, Mathematical and Physical Sciences, Department of Mathematics, Applied Mathematics Program, College Park, MD 20742. Offers MS, PhD. Part-time and evening/weekend programs available. *Students:* 78 full-time (26 women), 16 part-time (6 women); includes 14 minority (5 African Americans, 1 American Indian/Alaska Native, 6 Asian Americans or Pacific Islanders, 2 Hispanic Americans), 33 international. 185 applicants, 17% accepted, 22 enrolled. In 2009, 9 master's, 14 doctorates awarded. Terminal master's awarded for partial completion of doctoral program. *Degree requirements:* For master's, thesis optional, seminar, scholarly paper; for doctorate, comprehensive exam, thesis/dissertation, exams, seminars. *Entrance requirements:* For master's and doctorate, GRE General Test, GRE Subject Test, minimum GPA of 3.0, 3 letters of recommendation. *Application deadline:* For fall admission, 1/10 for domestic and international students; for spring admission, 9/15 for domestic students, 6/1 for international students. Applications are processed on a rolling basis. Application fee: $60. Electronic applications accepted. *Expenses:* Tuition, area resident: Part-time $471 per credit hour. Tuition, state resident: part-time $471 per credit hour. Tuition, nonresident: part-time $1016 per credit hour. Required fees: $337.04 per term. *Financial support:* In 2009–10, 6 fellowships with full and partial tuition reimbursements (averaging $18,939 per year), 20 research assistantships (averaging $19,459 per year), 42 teaching assistantships (averaging $17,121 per year) were awarded. Financial award applicants required to submit FAFSA. *Unit head:* Konstantina Travisa, Director, 301-405-4489, Fax: 301-314-8027, E-mail: trivisa@umd.edu. *Application contact:* Dean of Graduate School, 301-405-0376, Fax: 301-314-9305.

University of Massachusetts Amherst, Graduate School, College of Natural Sciences, Department of Mathematics and Statistics, Program in Applied Mathematics, Amherst, MA 01003. Offers MS. *Students:* 7 full-time (1 woman), 2 international. Average age 25. 37 applicants, 27% accepted, 5 enrolled. In 2009, 6 master's awarded. *Degree requirements:* For master's, thesis or alternative. *Entrance requirements:* Additional exam requirements/recommendations for international students: Required—TOEFL (minimum score 550 paper-based; 213 computer-based; 80 iBT), IELTS (minimum score 6.5). *Application deadline:* For fall admission, 2/1 for domestic and international students. Applications are processed on a rolling basis. Application fee: $50 ($65 for international students). Electronic applications accepted. *Expenses:* Tuition, state resident: full-time $2640; part-time $110 per credit. Tuition, nonresident: full-time $9936; part-time $414 per credit. Tuition and fees vary according to course load. *Financial support:* Fellowships, research assistantships, teaching assistantships, career-related internships or fieldwork, Federal Work-Study, scholarships/grants, traineeships, health care benefits, tuition waivers (full), and unspecified assistantships available. Support available to part-time students. Financial award application deadline: 2/1. *Unit head:* Dr. Siman Wong, Graduate Program Director, 413-545-2282, Fax: 413-545-1801. *Application contact:* Jean M. Ames, Chair, Admissions Committee, 413-545-0722, Fax: 413-577-0010, E-mail: gradadm@grad.umass.edu.

University of Massachusetts Lowell, College of Arts and Sciences, Department of Mathematical Sciences, Lowell, MA 01854-2881. Offers applied mathematics (MS); computational mathematics (PhD); mathematics (MS). Part-time programs available. *Entrance requirements:* For master's, GRE General Test.

University of Memphis, Graduate School, College of Arts and Sciences, Department of Mathematical Sciences, Memphis, TN 38152. Offers applied mathematics (MS); applied statistics (PhD); bioinformatics (MS); computer science (PhD); computer sciences (MS); mathematics (MS, PhD); statistics (MS, PhD). Part-time programs available. *Faculty:* 19 full-time (4 women), 3 part-time/adjunct (0 women). *Students:* 38 full-time (19 women), 25 part-time (9 women); includes 4 minority (2 African Americans, 2 Asian Americans or Pacific Islanders), 29 international. Average age 34. 26 applicants, 96% accepted, 11 enrolled. In 2009, 6 master's, 5 doctorates awarded. Terminal master's awarded for partial completion of doctoral program. *Degree requirements:* For master's, comprehensive exam; for doctorate, one foreign language, thesis/dissertation, oral exams. *Entrance requirements:* For master's and doctorate, GRE General Test, minimum GPA of 2.5. Additional exam requirements/recommendations for international students: Required—TOEFL (minimum score 550 paper-based; 210 computer-based). *Application deadline:* For fall admission, 8/1 for domestic students, 5/1 priority date for international students; for spring admission, 12/1 for domestic students, 9/1 priority date for international students. Applications are processed on a rolling basis. Application fee: $35 ($60 for international students). Electronic applications accepted. *Expenses:* Tuition, state resident: full-time $6246; part-time $347 per credit hour. Tuition, nonresident: full-time $15,894; part-time $883 per credit hour. Required fees: $1160. Full-time tuition and fees vary according to course load, degree level and program. *Financial support:* In 2009–10, 22 students received support; fellowships with full tuition reimbursements available, research assistantships with full tuition reimbursements available, teaching assistantships with full tuition reimbursements available, career-related internships or fieldwork, Federal Work-Study, scholarships/grants, and unspecified assistantships available. Financial award application deadline: 2/15; financial award applicants required to submit FAFSA. *Faculty research:* Combinatorics, ergodic theory, graph theory, Ramsey theory, applied statistics. *Unit head:* Dr. James E. Jamison, Chairman, 901-678-2482, Fax: 901-678-2480, E-mail: jjamison@memphis.edu. *Application contact:* Dr. Anna Kaminska, Coordinator of Graduate Studies, 901-678-2494, Fax: 901-678-2480.

University of Michigan–Dearborn, College of Arts, Sciences, and Letters, Master of Science in Applied and Computational Mathematics Program, Dearborn, MI 48128. Offers MS. Part-time and evening/weekend programs available. *Faculty:* 9 full-time (3 women). *Students:* 17 part-time (8 women); includes 2 minority (1 African American, 1 Asian American or Pacific Islander). Average age 38. 4 applicants, 50% accepted, 2 enrolled. In 2009, 3 master's awarded. *Degree requirements:* For master's, thesis or alternative, project. *Entrance requirements:* For master's, 3 letters of recommendation, minimum GPA of 3.0, 2 years course work in math. Additional exam requirements/recommendations for international students: Required—TOEFL (minimum score 560 paper-based; 220 computer-based). *Application deadline:* For fall admission, 8/1 priority date for domestic students, 4/1 for international students; for winter admission, 12/1 priority date for domestic students, 11/1 for international students; for spring admission, 4/1 for domestic students, 3/1 for international students. Applications are processed on a rolling basis. Application fee: $60 ($75 for international students). Electronic applications accepted. *Expenses:* Tuition, area resident: Part-time $504.10 per credit hour. Tuition, state resident: part-time $504.10 per credit hour. Tuition, nonresident: part-time $957.90 per credit hour. *Financial support:* Federal Work-Study and scholarships/grants available. Support available to part-time students. Financial award application deadline: 4/1; financial award applicants required to submit FAFSA. *Faculty research:* Partial differential equations, statistics, discrete optimization, approximation theory, stochastic processes. *Unit head:* Dr. Joan Remski, Director, 313-593-4994, E-mail: remski@umd.umich.edu. *Application contact:* Carol Ligienza, Graduate Program Coordinator, CASL Graduate Programs, 313-593-1183, Fax: 313-583-6700, E-mail: caslgrad@umd.umich.edu.

University of Minnesota, Duluth, Graduate School, Swenson College of Science and Engineering, Department of Mathematics and Statistics, Duluth, MN 55812-2496. Offers applied and computational mathematics (MS). Part-time programs available. *Faculty:* 17 full-time (3 women). *Students:* 30 full-time (14 women); includes 13 minority (all Asian Americans or Pacific Islanders), 15 international. Average age 24. 22 applicants, 95% accepted, 11 enrolled. In 2009, 15 master's awarded. *Degree requirements:* For master's, thesis or alternative. *Entrance requirements:* For master's, GRE General Test, minimum GPA of 3.0. Additional exam requirements/recommendations for international students: Required—TOEFL (minimum score 550 paper-based; 213 computer-based; 79 iBT); Recommended—TWE. *Application deadline:* For fall admission, 2/15 priority date for domestic and international students; for spring admission, 11/1 for domestic and international students. Applications are processed on a rolling basis. Application fee: $75 ($95 for international students). Electronic applications accepted. *Financial support:* In 2009–10, 24 students received support, including 1 research assistantship with full tuition reimbursement available (averaging $13,120 per year), 22 teaching assistantships with full tuition reimbursements available (averaging $13,120 per year); fellowships, scholarships/grants, health care benefits, and unspecified assistantships also available. Financial award application deadline: 2/15. *Faculty research:* Discrete mathematics, diagnostic markers, combinatorics, biostatistics, mathematical modeling and scientific computation. Total annual research expenditures: $680,763. *Unit head:* Dr. Dalibor Froncek, Director of Graduate Studies, 218-726-7598, Fax: 218-726-8399, E-mail: dfroncek@d.umn.edu. *Application contact:* Jenny Kroft, Principal Office Administrative Specialist, 218-726-8747, Fax: 218-726-8399, E-mail: mkroft@d.umn.edu.

See Display on this page.

University of Missouri, Graduate School, College of Arts and Sciences, Department of Mathematics, Program in Applied Mathematics, Columbia, MO 65211. Offers MS. *Degree requirements:* For master's, thesis. *Entrance requirements:* For master's, GRE General Test, minimum GPA of 3.0. Additional exam requirements/recommendations for international students: Required—TOEFL (minimum score 500 paper-based; 173 computer-based; 61 iBT).

University of Missouri–St. Louis, College of Arts and Sciences, Department of Mathematics and Computer Science, St. Louis, MO 63121. Offers applied mathematics (PhD), including computer science; computer science (MS); mathematics (MA). Part-time and evening/weekend programs available. *Faculty:* 16 full-time (2 women), 1 part-time/adjunct (0 women). *Students:* 24 full-time (11 women), 47 part-time (11 women); includes 7 minority (5 African Americans, 1 American Indian/Alaska Native, 1 Asian American or Pacific Islander), 27 international. Average age 30. 88 applicants, 53% accepted, 20 enrolled. In 2009, 23 master's, 1 doctorate awarded. *Degree requirements:* For master's, thesis optional; for doctorate, thesis/dissertation. *Entrance requirements:* For master's, 2 letters of recommendation; for doctorate, GRE General Test, 3 letters of recommendation. Additional exam requirements/recommendations for international students: Required—TOEFL (minimum score 550 paper-based; 213 computer-based). *Application deadline:* For fall admission, 7/1 priority date for domestic and international students; for spring admission, 12/1 priority date for domestic and international students. Applications are processed on a rolling basis. Application fee: $35 ($40 for international students). Electronic applications accepted. *Expenses:* Tuition, state resident: full-time $5377; part-time $297.70 per credit hour. Tuition, nonresident: full-time $13,882; part-time $771.20 per credit hour. Required fees: $220; $12.20 per credit hour. One-time fee: $12. Tuition and fees vary according to course level, campus/location and program. *Financial support:* In 2009–10, 3 research assistantships with full and partial tuition reimbursements (averaging $9,563 per year), 5 teaching assistantships with full and partial tuition reimbursements (averaging $13,500 per year) were awarded; fellowships with full tuition reimbursements also available. Financial award applicants required to submit FAFSA. *Faculty research:* Statistics, algebra, analysis. *Unit head:* Dr. Shiying Zhao, Director of Graduate Studies, 314-516-5741, Fax: 314-516-5400, E-mail: zhao@arch.cs.umsl.edu. *Application contact:* 314-516-5458, Fax: 314-516-6996, E-mail: gradadm@umsl.edu.

University of New Hampshire, Graduate School, College of Engineering and Physical Sciences, Department of Mathematics and Statistics, Durham, NH 03824. Offers applied mathematics (MS); industrial statistics (Postbaccalaureate Certificate); mathematics (MS, MST, PhD); mathematics education (PhD); statistics (MS). *Faculty:* 21 full-time (5 women). *Students:* 34 full-time (21 women), 24 part-time (8 women); includes 4 minority (1 Asian American or

Applied Mathematics

University of New Hampshire (continued)
Pacific Islander, 3 Hispanic Americans), 20 international. Average age 29. 76 applicants, 50% accepted, 17 enrolled. In 2009, 17 master's, 7 doctorates, 1 other advanced degree awarded. Terminal master's awarded for partial completion of doctoral program. *Degree requirements:* For doctorate, 2 foreign languages, thesis/dissertation. *Entrance requirements:* Additional exam requirements/recommendations for international students: Required—TOEFL (minimum score 550 paper-based; 213 computer-based; 80 iBT). *Application deadline:* For fall admission, 4/1 priority date for domestic students, 4/1 for international students; for spring admission, 12/1 for domestic students. Applications are processed on a rolling basis. Application fee: $65. Electronic applications accepted. *Expenses:* Tuition, state resident: full-time $10,380; part-time $577 per credit hour. Tuition, nonresident: full-time $24,350; part-time $1002 per credit hour. Required fees: $1550; $387.50 per semester. Tuition and fees vary according to course load and program. *Financial support:* In 2009–10, 35 students received support, including 2 fellowships, 1 research assistantship, 32 teaching assistantships; Federal Work-Study, scholarships/grants, and tuition waivers (full and partial) also available. Support available to part-time students. Financial award application deadline: 2/15. *Faculty research:* Operator theory, complex analysis, algebra, nonlinear dynamics, statistics. *Unit head:* Dr. Eric Grinberg, Chairperson, 603-862-5772. *Application contact:* Jan Jankowski, Administrative Assistant, 603-862-2320, E-mail: jan.jankowski@unh.edu.

The University of North Carolina at Charlotte, Graduate School, College of Arts and Sciences, Department of Mathematics and Statistics, Charlotte, NC 28223-0001. Offers applied mathematics (MS, PhD); mathematics (MS); mathematics education (MA). Part-time and evening/weekend programs available. *Faculty:* 43 full-time (5 women). *Students:* 48 full-time (19 women), 35 part-time (16 women); includes 7 African Americans, 4 Asian Americans or Pacific Islanders, 35 international. Average age 29. 45 applicants, 96% accepted, 16 enrolled. In 2009, 13 master's, 5 doctorates awarded. *Degree requirements:* For master's, comprehensive exam; for doctorate, thesis/dissertation. *Entrance requirements:* For master's, GRE General Test, minimum GPA of 3.0 in undergraduate major, 2.75 overall; for doctorate, GRE General Test, minimum overall GPA of 3.0. Additional exam requirements/recommendations for international students: Required—TOEFL (minimum score 557 paper-based; 220 computer-based; or 83 iBT), Michigan English Language Assessment Battery (minimum score 78), IELTS (minimum 6.5), or post-secondary degree earned in a country or province where English is the primary spoken language. *Application deadline:* For fall admission, 7/1 for domestic students, 5/1 for international students; for spring admission, 11/1 for domestic students, 10/1 for international students. Applications are processed on a rolling basis. Application fee: $55. Electronic applications accepted. *Financial support:* In 2009–10, 41 students received support, including 5 fellowships (averaging $26,412 per year), 4 research assistantships (averaging $14,075 per year), 32 teaching assistantships (averaging $14,680 per year); career-related internships or fieldwork, Federal Work-Study, institutionally sponsored loans, scholarships/grants, and unspecified assistantships also available. Support available to part-time students. Financial award application deadline: 4/1; financial award applicants required to submit FAFSA. *Faculty research:* Numerical analysis, differential equations, probability, algebra, analysis, mathematics education, statistics. Total annual research expenditures: $997,165. *Unit head:* Dr. Alan S. Dow, Chair, 704-687-4560, Fax: 704-687-6415, E-mail: adow@uncc.edu. *Application contact:* Kathy B. Giddings, Director of Graduate Admissions, 704-687-5503, Fax: 704-687-3279, E-mail: gradadm@uncc.edu.

University of Notre Dame, Graduate School, College of Science, Department of Mathematics, Notre Dame, IN 46556. Offers algebra (PhD); algebraic geometry (PhD); applied mathematics (MSAM); complex analysis (PhD); differential geometry (PhD); logic (PhD); partial differential equations (PhD); topology (PhD). Terminal master's awarded for partial completion of doctoral program. *Degree requirements:* For doctorate, one foreign language, thesis/dissertation, qualifying exam. *Entrance requirements:* For master's and doctorate, GRE General Test, GRE Subject Test. Additional exam requirements/recommendations for international students: Required—TOEFL (minimum score 600 paper-based; 250 computer-based; 80 iBT). Electronic applications accepted. *Faculty research:* Algebra, analysis, geometry/topology, logic, applied math.

University of Pennsylvania, School of Arts and Sciences, Graduate Group in Applied Mathematics and Computational Science, Philadelphia, PA 19104. Offers PhD. *Faculty:* 46 full-time (3 women), 1 part-time/adjunct (0 women). *Students:* 14 full-time (8 women), 13 international. 92 applicants, 15% accepted, 7 enrolled. *Application deadline:* For fall admission, 1/15 for domestic students. *Expenses:* Tuition: Full-time $25,660; part-time $4758 per course. Required fees: $2152; $270 per course. Tuition and fees vary according to course load, degree level and program. *Financial support:* Institutionally sponsored loans, scholarships/grants, traineeships, health care benefits, and unspecified assistantships available.

University of Pittsburgh, School of Arts and Sciences, Department of Mathematics, Pittsburgh, PA 15260. Offers applied mathematics (MA, MS); mathematics (MA, MS, PhD). Part-time programs available. *Faculty:* 33 full-time (5 women), 16 part-time/adjunct (2 women). *Students:* 83 full-time (23 women), 7 part-time (4 women); includes 3 minority (2 African Americans, 1 Asian American or Pacific Islander), 40 international. 250 applicants, 31% accepted, 14 enrolled. In 2009, 13 master's, 3 doctorates awarded. Terminal master's awarded for partial completion of doctoral program. *Degree requirements:* For master's, comprehensive exam, thesis (for some programs); for doctorate, comprehensive exam, thesis/dissertation, preliminary exams, defense of dissertation. *Entrance requirements:* For master's, GRE General Test, GRE Subject Test (recommended), minimum GPA of 3.0; for doctorate, GRE General Test, GRE Subject Test (recommended), minimum GPA of 3.0, minimum QPA of 3.25 in math curriculum. Additional exam requirements/recommendations for international students: Required—TOEFL (minimum score 550 paper-based; 213 computer-based; 80 iBT), IELTS (minimum score 6.5). *Application deadline:* For fall admission, 1/4 priority date for domestic and international students; for spring admission, 9/1 priority date for domestic students, 9/1 for international students. Applications are processed on a rolling basis. Application fee: $50. Electronic applications accepted. *Expenses:* Tuition, state resident: full-time $16,402; part-time $665 per credit. Tuition, nonresident: full-time $28,694; part-time $1175 per credit. Required fees: $690; $175 per term. Tuition and fees vary according to program. *Financial support:* In 2009–10, 84 students received support, including 8 fellowships with full and partial tuition reimbursements available (averaging $18,200 per year), 14 research assistantships with full and partial tuition reimbursements available (averaging $16,000 per year), 50 teaching assistantships with full and partial tuition reimbursements available (averaging $15,300 per year); institutionally sponsored loans, scholarships/grants, traineeships, health care benefits, tuition waivers (partial), and unspecified assistantships also available. Financial award application deadline: 1/4. *Faculty research:* Algebra, analysis, computational math, geometry/topology, math biology. Total annual research expenditures: $1 million. *Unit head:* Ivan Yotov, Chair, 412-624-8361, Fax: 412-624-8397, E-mail: yotov@math.pitt.edu. *Application contact:* Molly Williams, Administrator, 412-624-1175, Fax: 412-624-8397, E-mail: mollyw@pitt.edu.

University of Puerto Rico, Mayagüez Campus, Graduate Studies, College of Arts and Sciences, Department of Mathematics, Mayagüez, PR 00681-9000. Offers applied mathematics (MS); computational sciences (MS); pure mathematics (MS); statistics (MS). Part-time programs available. *Degree requirements:* For master's, one foreign language, comprehensive exam, thesis optional. *Entrance requirements:* For master's, undergraduate degree in mathematics or its equivalent. *Faculty research:* Automata theory, linear algebra, logic.

University of Rhode Island, Graduate School, College of Arts and Sciences, Department of Computer Science and Statistics, Kingston, RI 02881. Offers applied mathematics (PhD), including computer science, statistics; computer science (MS, PhD); digital forensics (Graduate Certificate); statistics (MS). Part-time programs available. *Faculty:* 10 full-time (3 women), 3 part-time/adjunct (1 woman). *Students:* 18 full-time (5 women), 20 part-time (6 women); includes 4 minority (2 Asian Americans or Pacific Islanders, 2 Hispanic Americans), 7 international. In 2009, 7 master's awarded. *Degree requirements:* For master's, comprehensive exam (for some programs), thesis optional; for doctorate, comprehensive exam, thesis/dissertation. *Entrance requirements:* For master's and doctorate, GRE, 2 letters of recommendation. Additional exam requirements/recommendations for international students: Required—TOEFL (minimum score 550 paper-based; 213 computer-based). *Application deadline:* For fall admission, 7/15 for domestic students, 2/1 for international students; for spring admission, 11/15 for domestic students, 7/15 for international students. Application fee: $65. Electronic applications accepted. *Expenses:* Tuition, state resident: full-time $8828; part-time $490 per credit hour. Tuition, nonresident: full-time $22,100; part-time $1228 per credit hour. Required fees: $1118; $57 per semester. Tuition and fees vary according to program. *Financial support:* In 2009–10, 10 teaching assistantships with full and partial tuition reimbursements (averaging $11,094 per year) were awarded. Financial award application deadline: 2/1; financial award applicants required to submit FAFSA. *Faculty research:* Bioinformatics, computer and digital forensics, behavioral model of pedestrian dynamics, real-time distributed object computing, cryptography. Total annual research expenditures: $694,026. *Unit head:* Dr. James G. Kowalski, Chair, 401-874-2510, Fax: 401-874-4617, E-mail: kowalski@cs.uri.edu. *Application contact:* Dr. Victor Fay-Wolfe, Director of Graduate Studies, 401-874-2701, Fax: 401-874-4617, E-mail: wolfe@cs.uri.edu.

University of Rhode Island, Graduate School, College of Arts and Sciences, Department of Mathematics, Kingston, RI 02881. Offers applied mathematical sciences (MS, PhD); mathematics (MS, PhD). Part-time programs available. *Faculty:* 19 full-time (4 women). *Students:* 24 full-time (5 women), 10 part-time (5 women), 4 international. In 2009, 4 master's, 2 doctorates awarded. *Degree requirements:* For master's, comprehensive exam (for some programs), thesis optional; for doctorate, one foreign language, comprehensive exam, thesis/dissertation optional. *Entrance requirements:* For master's and doctorate, 2 letters of recommendation. Additional exam requirements/recommendations for international students: Required—TOEFL (minimum score 550 paper-based; 213 computer-based). *Application deadline:* For fall admission, 7/15 for domestic students, 2/1 for international students; for spring admission, 11/15 for domestic students, 7/15 for international students. Application fee: $65. Electronic applications accepted. *Expenses:* Tuition, state resident: full-time $8828; part-time $490 per credit hour. Tuition, nonresident: full-time $22,100; part-time $1228 per credit hour. Required fees: $1118; $57 per semester. Tuition and fees vary according to program. *Financial support:* In 2009–10, 2 research assistantships with full tuition reimbursements (averaging $13,894 per year), 13 teaching assistantships with full and partial tuition reimbursements (averaging $13,560 per year) were awarded. Financial award application deadline: 7/15; financial award applicants required to submit FAFSA. *Unit head:* Dr. Nancy Eaton, Chairman, 401-874-2709, Fax: 401-874-4454, E-mail: eaton@math.uri.edu. *Application contact:* Dr. Woong Kook, Director of Graduate Studies, 401-874-4421, Fax: 401-874-4454, E-mail: andrewk@math.uri.edu.

University of Southern California, Graduate School, College of Letters, Arts and Sciences, Department of Mathematics, Los Angeles, CA 90089. Offers applied mathematics (MA, MS, PhD); mathematical finance (MS); mathematics (MA, PhD); statistics (MS). Part-time programs available. *Faculty:* 50 full-time (5 women). *Students:* 102 full-time (33 women), 16 part-time (8 women); includes 10 minority (9 Asian Americans or Pacific Islanders, 1 Hispanic American), 87 international. 500 applicants, 20% accepted, 28 enrolled. In 2009, 37 master's, 7 doctorates awarded. Terminal master's awarded for partial completion of doctoral program. *Degree requirements:* For master's, comprehensive exam (for some programs), thesis (for some programs); for doctorate, 2 foreign languages, comprehensive exam, thesis/dissertation. *Entrance requirements:* For master's, GRE General Test, GMAT; for doctorate, GRE General Test. Additional exam requirements/recommendations for international students: Recommended—TOEFL (minimum score 100 iBT). *Application deadline:* For fall admission, 12/1 for domestic students, 2/15 for international students; for spring admission, 9/1 for domestic and international students. Applications are processed on a rolling basis. Application fee: $85. Electronic applications accepted. *Expenses:* Tuition: Full-time $25,980; part-time $1315 per unit. Required fees: $554. One-time fee: $35 full-time. Full-time tuition and fees vary according to degree level and program. *Financial support:* In 2009–10, 67 students received support, including 5 fellowships with full tuition reimbursements available (averaging $19,000 per year), 9 research assistantships with full tuition reimbursements available (averaging $19,000 per year), 53 teaching assistantships with full tuition reimbursements available (averaging $19,000 per year). Financial award application deadline: 12/1. *Faculty research:* Algebra, algebraic geometry and number theory, analysis/partial differential equations, applied mathematics, financial mathematics, probability, combinatorics and statistics. Total annual research expenditures: $2 million. *Unit head:* Prof. Gary Rosen, Chair, 213-740-1717, Fax: 213-740-2424, E-mail: grosen@usc.edu. *Application contact:* Amy Yung, Department Coordinator, 213-740-8168, Fax: 213-740-2424, E-mail: amy@usc.edu.

The University of Tennessee, Graduate School, College of Arts and Sciences, Department of Mathematics, Knoxville, TN 37996. Offers applied mathematics (MS); mathematical ecology (PhD); mathematics (M Math, MS, PhD). Part-time programs available. *Degree requirements:* For master's, thesis or alternative; for doctorate, one foreign language, thesis/dissertation. *Entrance requirements:* For master's and doctorate, minimum GPA of 2.7. Additional exam requirements/recommendations for international students: Required—TOEFL. Electronic applications accepted. *Expenses:* Tuition, state resident: full-time $6826; part-time $380 per semester hour. Tuition, nonresident: full-time $21,844; part-time $1147 per semester hour. Tuition and fees vary according to program.

The University of Tennessee Space Institute, Graduate Programs, Program in Applied Mathematics, Tullahoma, TN 37388-9700. Offers MS. Part-time programs available. *Faculty:* 1 full-time (0 women), 3 part-time/adjunct (1 woman). *Students:* 1 (woman) full-time, all international. 2 applicants, 100% accepted, 0 enrolled. *Degree requirements:* For master's, thesis (for some programs). *Entrance requirements:* Additional exam requirements/recommendations for international students: Required—TOEFL (minimum score 550 paper-based; 213 computer-based; 80 iBT), IELTS (minimum score 6.5). *Application deadline:* For fall admission, 2/1 for international students; for spring admission, 6/15 for international students. Applications are processed on a rolling basis. Application fee: $35. *Expenses:* Tuition, state resident: full-time $6826; part-time $380 per hour. Tuition, nonresident: full-time $20,622; part-time $1147 per hour. Required fees: $10 per hour. One-time fee: $90 full-time. *Financial support:* In 2009–10, 1 research assistantship with full tuition reimbursement (averaging $17,791 per year) was awarded; fellowships, career-related internships or fieldwork, Federal Work-Study, institutionally sponsored loans, health care benefits, tuition waivers (partial), and unspecified assistantships also available. Financial award applicants required to submit FAFSA. *Unit head:* Dr. Boris Kuperschmidt, Degree Program Chairman, 931-393-7465, Fax: 931-393-7444, E-mail: bkupersc@utsi.edu. *Application contact:* Dee Merriman, Coordinator III, 931-393-7293, Fax: 931-393-7201, E-mail: dmerrima@utsi.edu.

The University of Texas at Austin, Graduate School, Program in Computational and Applied Mathematics, Austin, TX 78712-1111. Offers MA, PhD. Terminal master's awarded for partial completion of doctoral program. *Degree requirements:* For master's, thesis optional; for doctorate, thesis/dissertation, 3 area qualifying exams. Electronic applications accepted.

The University of Texas at Dallas, School of Natural Sciences and Mathematics, Programs in Mathematical Sciences, Richardson, TX 75080. Offers applied mathematics (MS, PhD); engineering mathematics (MS); mathematical science (MS); statistics (MS, PhD). Part-time and evening/weekend programs available. *Faculty:* 13 full-time (1 woman), 1 (woman) part-time/adjunct. *Students:* 35 full-time (14 women), 25 part-time (6 women); includes 20 minority (4 African Americans, 15 Asian Americans or Pacific Islanders, 1 Hispanic American), 22 international. Average age 32. 79 applicants, 44% accepted, 13 enrolled. In 2009, 17 master's, 1 doctorate awarded. *Degree requirements:* For master's, thesis optional; for doctorate, thesis/dissertation. *Entrance requirements:* For master's, GRE General Test, minimum GPA of 3.0 in upper-level course work in field; for doctorate, GRE General Test, minimum GPA of 3.5 in upper-level course work in field. Additional exam requirements/recommendations for international students: Required—TOEFL (minimum score 550 paper-based; 213 computer-based). *Application deadline:* For fall admission, 7/15 for domestic students, 5/1 priority date for international students; for spring admission, 11/15 for domestic students, 9/1 priority date for international students. Applications are processed on a rolling basis. Application fee: $50 ($100 for international students). Electronic applications accepted. *Expenses:* Tuition, state resident: full-time $11,068; part-time $461 per credit hour. Tuition, nonresident: full-time $21,178; part-time $882 per credit hour. Tuition and fees vary according to course load. *Financial support:* In 2009–10, 30 teaching assistantships with full tuition reimbursements (averaging $13,500 per year) were awarded; fellowships, research assistantships, career-related internships or fieldwork, Federal Work-Study, institutionally sponsored loans, scholarships/grants, and unspecified assistantships also available. Support available to part-time students. Financial award application deadline: 4/30; financial award applicants required to submit FAFSA. *Faculty research:* Statistical methods, control theory, mathematical modeling and analyses of biological and physical systems. *Unit head:* Dr. Wieslaw Z. Krawcewicz, Department Head, 972-883-2161, Fax: 972-883-6622, E-mail: utdmath@utdallas.edu. *Application contact:* Dr. Michael Baron, Graduate Advisor, 972-883-6874, Fax: 972-883-6622, E-mail: mbaron@utdallas.edu.

See Close-Up on page 327.

The University of Texas at San Antonio, College of Sciences, Department of Mathematics, San Antonio, TX 78249-0617. Offers applied/industrial mathematics (MS); mathematics (MS). Part-time and evening/weekend programs available. *Faculty:* 10 full-time (2 women). *Students:* 15 full-time (6 women), 36 part-time (17 women); includes 22 minority (4 African Americans, 1 Asian American or Pacific Islander, 17 Hispanic Americans), 7 international. Average age 31. 34 applicants, 79% accepted, 16 enrolled. In 2009, 13 master's awarded. *Degree requirements:* For master's, comprehensive exam (for some programs), thesis (for some programs). *Entrance requirements:* For master's, GRE General Test, minimum GPA of 3.0 in last 60 hours. Additional exam requirements/recommendations for international students: Required—TOEFL (minimum score 500 paper-based; 173 computer-based; 61 iBT), IELTS (minimum score 5). *Application deadline:* For fall admission, 7/1 for domestic students, 4/1 for international students; for spring admission, 11/1 for domestic students, 9/1 for international students. Applications are processed on a rolling basis. Application fee: $45 ($80 for international students). Electronic applications accepted. *Expenses:* Tuition, state resident: full-time $3975; part-time $221 per contact hour. Tuition, nonresident: full-time $13,947; part-time $775 per contact hour. Required fees: $1853. *Financial support:* In 2009–10, 9 students received support, including 22 teaching assistantships (averaging $12,682 per year); research assistantships, scholarships/grants, tuition waivers, and unspecified assistantships also available. Support available to part-time students. *Faculty research:* Computational statistics, deterministic and stochastic differential equations, applications of mathematics to architecture and urbanism, mathematical biology, numerical analysis. Total annual research expenditures: $117,596. *Unit head:* Dr. Francis A. Norman, Interim Chair, 210-458-4494, Fax: 210-458-4439, E-mail: sandy.norman@utsa.edu. *Application contact:* Dr. Dorothy A. Flannagan, Dean of the Graduate School, 210-458-4330, Fax: 210-458-4332, E-mail: dorothy.flannagan@utsa.edu.

The University of Toledo, College of Graduate Studies, College of Arts and Sciences, Department of Mathematics, Toledo, OH 43606-3390. Offers applied mathematics (MS, PhD); mathematics (MA, PhD); statistics (MS, PhD). Part-time programs available. *Degree requirements:* For doctorate, 2 foreign languages, thesis/dissertation. *Entrance requirements:* For master's and doctorate, GRE General Test, GRE Subject Test. Electronic applications accepted. *Faculty research:* Topology.

University of Washington, Graduate School, College of Arts and Sciences, Department of Applied Mathematics, Seattle, WA 98195. Offers MS, PhD. Terminal master's awarded for partial completion of doctoral program. *Degree requirements:* For master's, thesis optional; for doctorate, thesis/dissertation. *Entrance requirements:* For master's and doctorate, GRE, minimum GPA of 3.0. Additional exam requirements/recommendations for international students: Required—TOEFL. Electronic applications accepted. *Faculty research:* Mathematical modeling for physical, biological, social, and engineering sciences; development of mathematical methods for analysis, including perturbation, asymptotic, transform, vocational, and numerical methods.

University of Washington, Graduate School, College of Arts and Sciences, Department of Mathematics, Seattle, WA 98195. Offers mathematics (MA, MS, PhD); numerical analysis (MS); optimization (MS). Part-time programs available. Terminal master's awarded for partial completion of doctoral program. *Degree requirements:* For master's, thesis optional; for doctorate, 2 foreign languages, thesis/dissertation. *Entrance requirements:* For master's, GRE, minimum GPA of 3.0; for doctorate, GRE General Test, GRE Subject Test (mathematics), minimum GPA of 3.0. Additional exam requirements/recommendations for international students: Required—TOEFL. Electronic applications accepted. *Faculty research:* Algebra, analysis, probability, combinatorics and geometry.

University of Waterloo, Graduate Studies, Faculty of Mathematics, Department of Applied Mathematics, Waterloo, ON N2L 3G1, Canada. Offers M Math, PhD. Part-time programs available. *Degree requirements:* For master's, research paper or thesis; for doctorate, thesis/dissertation. *Entrance requirements:* For master's, honors degree in field, minimum B+ average; for doctorate, master's degree, minimum B+ average. Additional exam requirements/recommendations for international students: Required—TOEFL (minimum score 600 paper-based; 250 computer-based; 100 iBT), TWE (minimum score 4). Electronic applications accepted. *Faculty research:* Differential equations, quantum theory, statistical mechanics, fluid mechanics, relativity, control theory.

The University of Western Ontario, Faculty of Graduate Studies, Physical Sciences Division, Department of Applied Mathematics, London, ON N6A 5B8, Canada. Offers applied mathematics (M Sc, PhD); theoretical physics (PhD). *Degree requirements:* For master's, thesis or alternative; for doctorate, comprehensive exam, thesis/dissertation. *Entrance requirements:* For master's and doctorate, minimum B average. Additional exam requirements/recommendations for international students: Required—TOEFL. *Faculty research:* Fluid dynamics, mathematical and computational methods, theoretical physics.

University of West Georgia, Graduate School, College of Arts and Sciences, Department of Mathematics, Carrollton, GA 30118. Offers mathematics (MSM); teaching and applied mathematics (MS). *Faculty:* 13 full-time (2 women). *Students:* 3 full-time (1 woman), 3 part-time (1 woman); includes 1 minority (African American), 1 international. Average age 25. 6 applicants, 50% accepted, 1 enrolled. *Application deadline:* For fall admission, 7/17 for domestic students; for spring admission, 11/20 for domestic students. Applications are processed on a rolling basis. Application fee: $30. Electronic applications accepted. *Expenses:* Tuition, state resident: full-time $2952; part-time $164 per semester hour. Tuition, nonresident: full-time $11,808; part-time $656 per semester hour. Required fees: $42.90 per semester hour. $307 per semester. Tuition and fees vary according to course load. *Unit head:* Dr. Bruce Landman, Chair, 678-839-6489, E-mail: landman@westga.edu. *Application contact:* Dr. Charles W. Clark, Dean, 678-839-6508, E-mail: cclark@westga.edu.

Utah State University, School of Graduate Studies, College of Science, Department of Mathematics and Statistics, Logan, UT 84322. Offers industrial mathematics (MS); mathematical sciences (PhD); mathematics (M Math, MS); statistics (MS). Part-time programs available. Terminal master's awarded for partial completion of doctoral program. *Degree requirements:* For master's, thesis optional, qualifying exam; for doctorate, one foreign language, comprehensive exam, thesis/dissertation. *Entrance requirements:* For master's and doctorate, GRE General Test, minimum GPA of 3.0. Additional exam requirements/recommendations for international students: Required—TOEFL. *Faculty research:* Differential equations, computational mathematics, dynamical systems, probability and statistics, pure mathematics.

Virginia Commonwealth University, Graduate School, College of Humanities and Sciences, Department of Mathematics and Applied Mathematics, Richmond, VA 23284-9005. Offers applied mathematics (MS); mathematics (MS); operations research (MS); statistical sciences and operations research (MS, Certificate). *Degree requirements:* For master's, thesis optional. *Entrance requirements:* For master's, GRE General Test, GRE Subject Test. Additional exam requirements/recommendations for international students: Required—TOEFL.

Virginia Polytechnic Institute and State University, Graduate School, College of Science, Department of Mathematics, Blacksburg, VA 24061. Offers applied mathematics (MS, PhD); mathematical physics (MS, PhD); pure mathematics (MS, PhD). *Entrance requirements:* For master's and doctorate, GRE. Additional exam requirements/recommendations for international students: Required—TOEFL (minimum score 550 paper-based; 213 computer-based). Electronic applications accepted. *Faculty research:* Differential equations, operator theory, numerical analysis, algebra, control theory.

Washington State University, Graduate School, College of Sciences, Department of Mathematics, Pullman, WA 99164. Offers applied mathematics (MS, PhD); mathematics teaching (MS, PhD). Part-time programs available. *Faculty:* 26. *Students:* 33 full-time (11 women), 5 part-time (3 women); includes 3 minority (1 African American, 2 Asian Americans or Pacific Islanders), 10 international. Average age 29. 84 applicants, 29% accepted, 9 enrolled. In 2009, 7 master's, 1 doctorate awarded. *Degree requirements:* For master's, comprehensive exam (for some programs), thesis (for some programs), oral exam, project; for doctorate, 2 foreign languages, comprehensive exam, thesis/dissertation, oral exam, written exam. *Entrance requirements:* For master's and doctorate, minimum GPA of 3.0, 3 letters of recommendation. Additional exam requirements/recommendations for international students: Required—TOEFL (minimum score 600 paper-based; 250 computer-based), IELTS. *Application deadline:* For fall admission, 1/10 for domestic and international students; for spring admission, 7/1 for domestic and international students. Applications are processed on a rolling basis. Application fee: $50. Electronic applications accepted. *Financial support:* In 2009–10, 33 students received support, including 2 fellowships with tuition reimbursements available (averaging $2,500 per year), 3 research assistantships with full and partial tuition reimbursements available (averaging $14,634 per year), 27 teaching assistantships with full and partial tuition reimbursements available (averaging $13,383 per year); career-related internships or fieldwork, Federal Work-Study, institutionally sponsored loans, health care benefits, and tuition waivers (partial) also available. Financial award application deadline: 2/15; financial award applicants required to submit FAFSA. *Faculty research:* Computational mathematics, operations research, modeling in the natural sciences, applied statistics. *Unit head:* Dr. K. A. Ariyawansa, Chair, 509-335-4918, Fax: 509-335-1188, E-mail: ari@wsu.edu. *Application contact:* Graduate School Admissions, 800-GRADWSU, Fax: 509-335-1949, E-mail: gradsch@wsu.edu.

See Close-Up on page 333.

Wayne State University, College of Liberal Arts and Sciences, Department of Mathematics, Program in Applied Mathematics, Detroit, MI 48202. Offers MA, PhD. *Degree requirements:* For doctorate, thesis/dissertation. *Entrance requirements:* Additional exam requirements/recommendations for international students: Required—TOEFL (minimum score 550 paper-based; 213 computer-based); Recommended—TWE (minimum score 6). Electronic applications accepted.

Western Illinois University, School of Graduate Studies, College of Arts and Sciences, Department of Mathematics, Macomb, IL 61455-1390. Offers applied math (Certificate); mathematics (MS). Part-time programs available. *Students:* 13 full-time (5 women), 3 part-time (2 women), 5 international. Average age 31. 11 applicants, 91% accepted. In 2009, 3 master's awarded. *Degree requirements:* For master's, thesis or alternative. *Entrance requirements:* Additional exam requirements/recommendations for international students: Required—TOEFL (minimum score 500 paper-based; 173 computer-based; 61 iBT). *Application deadline:* Applications are processed on a rolling basis. Application fee: $30. Electronic applications accepted. *Expenses:* Tuition, state resident: full-time $4486; part-time $249.21 per credit hour. Tuition, nonresident: full-time $8972; part-time $498.42 per credit hour. Required fees: $72.62 per credit hour. *Financial support:* In 2009–10, 12 students received support, including 9 research assistantships with full tuition reimbursements available (averaging $7,280 per year), 3 teaching assistantships with full tuition reimbursements available (averaging $8,400 per year). Financial award applicants required to submit FAFSA. *Unit head:* Dr. Iraj Kalantari, Chairperson, 309-298-1054. *Application contact:* Evelyn Hoing, Assistant Director of Graduate Studies, 309-298-1806, Fax: 309-298-2345, E-mail: grad-office@wiu.edu.

Western Michigan University, Graduate College, College of Arts and Sciences, Department of Mathematics, Program in Applied and Computational Mathematics, Kalamazoo, MI 49008. Offers MS.

West Virginia University, Eberly College of Arts and Sciences, Department of Mathematics, Morgantown, WV 26506. Offers applied mathematics (MS, PhD); discrete mathematics (PhD); interdisciplinary mathematics (MS); mathematics for secondary education (MS); pure mathematics (MS). Part-time programs available. Terminal master's awarded for partial completion of doctoral program. *Degree requirements:* For master's, comprehensive exam (for some programs), thesis optional; for doctorate, one foreign language, comprehensive exam, thesis/dissertation. *Entrance requirements:* For master's, GRE Subject Test (recommended), minimum GPA of 2.5; for doctorate, GRE Subject Test (recommended), master's degree in mathematics. Additional exam requirements/recommendations for international students: Required—TOEFL (paper-based 550; computer-based 213) or IELTS (paper-based 6). *Faculty research:* Combinatorics and graph theory, differential equations, applied and computational mathematics.

Wichita State University, Graduate School, Fairmount College of Liberal Arts and Sciences, Department of Mathematics and Statistics, Wichita, KS 67260. Offers applied mathematics (PhD); mathematics (MS). Part-time programs available. *Expenses:* Tuition, state resident: full-time $4247; part-time $235.95 per credit hour. Tuition, nonresident: full-time $11,171; part-time $620.60 per credit hour. Required fees: $34; $3.60 per credit hour. $17 per term. Tuition and fees vary according to campus/location and program. *Unit head:* Dr. Buma Fridman, Chair, 316-978-3160, Fax: 316-978-3748, E-mail: buma.fridman@wichita.edu. *Application contact:* Dr. Buma Fridman, Chair, 316-978-3160, Fax: 316-978-3748, E-mail: buma.fridman@wichita.edu.

Worcester Polytechnic Institute, Graduate Studies and Research, Department of Mathematical Sciences, Worcester, MA 01609-2280. Offers applied mathematics (MS); applied statistics (MS); financial mathematics (MS); industrial mathematics (MS); mathematical sciences (PhD); mathematics (MME). Part-time and evening/weekend programs available. *Faculty:* 15 full-time (2 women), 7 part-time/adjunct (1 woman). *Students:* 28 full-time (13 women), 36 part-time (17 women). 172 applicants, 77% accepted, 32 enrolled. In 2009, 29 master's, 1 doctorate awarded. *Degree requirements:* For master's, thesis (for some programs); for doctorate, comprehensive exam, thesis/dissertation. *Entrance requirements:* For master's and doctorate, GRE General Test, GRE Subject Test in math (recommended), 3 letters of recommendation. Additional exam requirements/recommendations for international students: Required—TOEFL (minimum score 550 paper-based; 213 computer-based; 79 iBT), IELTS (minimum score 6.5). *Application deadline:* For fall admission, 1/15 priority date for domestic students, 1/15 for international students; for spring admission, 10/15 priority date for domestic students, 10/15 for

Applied Mathematics

Worcester Polytechnic Institute (continued)
international students. Applications are processed on a rolling basis. Application fee: $70. Electronic applications accepted. *Financial support:* Career-related internships or fieldwork, institutionally sponsored loans, scholarships/grants, and unspecified assistantships available. Financial award application deadline: 1/15. *Faculty research:* Applied analysis and differential equations, computational mathematics, discrete mathematics, applied and computational statistics, industrial and financial mathematics. *Unit head:* Dr. Bogdan Vernescu, Head, 508-831-5241, Fax: 508-831-5824, E-mail: vernescu@wpi.edu. *Application contact:* Dr. Joseph Petruccelli, Graduate Coordinator, 508-831-5241, Fax: 508-831-5824, E-mail: jdp@wpi.edu.

Wright State University, School of Graduate Studies, College of Science and Mathematics, Department of Mathematics and Statistics, Program in Applied Mathematics, Dayton, OH 45435. Offers MS. *Degree requirements:* For master's, comprehensive exam. *Entrance requirements:* For master's, bachelor's degree in mathematics or related field. Additional exam requirements/recommendations for international students: Required—TOEFL. *Faculty research:* Control theory, ordinary differential equations, partial differential equations, numerical analysis, mathematical modeling.

Yale University, Graduate School of Arts and Sciences, Program in Applied Mathematics, New Haven, CT 06520. Offers M Phil, MS, PhD. *Entrance requirements:* For doctorate, GRE General Test.

York University, Faculty of Graduate Studies, Faculty of Science and Engineering, Program in Mathematics and Statistics, Toronto, ON M3J 1P3, Canada. Offers industrial and applied mathematics (M Sc); mathematics and statistics (MA, PhD). Part-time programs available. *Degree requirements:* For master's, thesis optional; for doctorate, one foreign language, comprehensive exam, thesis/dissertation. Electronic applications accepted.

Youngstown State University, Graduate School, College of Science, Technology, Engineering and Mathematics, Department of Mathematics and Statistics, Youngstown, OH 44555-0001. Offers applied mathematics (MS); computer science (MS); secondary mathematics (MS); statistics (MS). Part-time programs available. *Degree requirements:* For master's, comprehensive exam, thesis optional. *Entrance requirements:* For master's, minimum GPA of 2.7 in computer science and mathematics. Additional exam requirements/recommendations for international students: Required—TOEFL. *Faculty research:* Regression analysis, numerical analysis, statistics, Markov chain, topology and fuzzy sets.

Applied Statistics

American University, College of Arts and Sciences, Department of Mathematics and Statistics, Program in Statistics, Washington, DC 22016-8050. Offers applied statistics (Certificate); statistics (MS). Part-time and evening/weekend programs available. *Students:* 6 full-time (2 women), 7 part-time (6 women); includes 1 minority (Asian American or Pacific Islander), 6 international. Average age 27. 26 applicants, 46% accepted, 5 enrolled. In 2009, 4 master's awarded. *Degree requirements:* For master's, comprehensive exam, thesis or alternative, tools of research; foreign language, computer language, or analytic skill. *Entrance requirements:* For master's, GRE; for Certificate, bachelor's degree. Additional exam requirements/recommendations for international students: Required—TOEFL. *Application deadline:* For fall admission, 2/1 for domestic students; for spring admission, 10/1 for domestic students. Application fee: $80. *Expenses:* Tuition: Full-time $22,266; part-time $1237 per credit hour. Required fees: $430. Tuition and fees vary according to program. *Financial support:* Fellowships, teaching assistantships, career-related internships or fieldwork, Federal Work-Study, and institutionally sponsored loans available. Support available to part-time students. Financial award application deadline: 2/1. *Faculty research:* Statistical computing; data analysis; random processes; environmental, meteorological, and biological applications. *Unit head:* Dr. Jeffrey Hakim, Chair, 202-885-3131, Fax: 202-885-3155. *Application contact:* Dr. Jeffrey Hakim, Chair, 202-885-3131, Fax: 202-885-3155.

Bowling Green State University, Graduate College, College of Arts and Sciences, Department of Mathematics and Statistics, Bowling Green, OH 43403. Offers applied statistics (MS); mathematics (MA, MAT, PhD); statistics (PhD). Part-time programs available. *Degree requirements:* For master's, thesis or alternative; for doctorate, comprehensive exam, thesis/dissertation. *Entrance requirements:* For master's and doctorate, GRE General Test. Additional exam requirements/recommendations for international students: Required—TOEFL. Electronic applications accepted. *Faculty research:* Statistics and probability, algebra, analysis.

Bowling Green State University, Graduate College, College of Business Administration, Department of Applied Statistics and Operations Research, Bowling Green, OH 43403. Offers applied statistics (MS). Part-time programs available. *Degree requirements:* For master's, thesis or alternative. *Entrance requirements:* For master's, GRE General Test. Additional exam requirements/recommendations for international students: Required—TOEFL. Electronic applications accepted. *Faculty research:* Reliability, linear models, time series, statistical quality control.

Brigham Young University, Graduate Studies, College of Physical and Mathematical Sciences, Department of Statistics, Provo, UT 84602-1001. Offers applied statistics (MS). *Faculty:* 15 full-time (2 women). *Students:* 20 full-time (9 women); includes 1 minority (Asian American or Pacific Islander). Average age 26. 25 applicants, 68% accepted, 13 enrolled. In 2009, 9 master's awarded. *Degree requirements:* For master's, comprehensive exam, thesis (for some programs). *Entrance requirements:* For master's, GRE General Test, minimum undergraduate GPA of 3.3; course work in statistical methods, theory, multivariable calculus and linear algebra with minimum B- average. Additional exam requirements/recommendations for international students: Required—TOEFL (minimum score 580 paper-based; 237 computer-based; 85 iBT). *Application deadline:* For fall admission, 2/1 for domestic and international students. Application fee: $50. Electronic applications accepted. *Expenses:* Tuition: Full-time $5580; part-time $301 per credit hour. Tuition and fees vary according to student's religious affiliation. *Financial support:* In 2009–10, 20 students received support, including 2 research assistantships with full and partial tuition reimbursements available (averaging $10,000 per year), 18 teaching assistantships with full and partial tuition reimbursements available (averaging $10,000 per year); scholarships/grants and unspecified assistantships also available. Financial award application deadline: 2/1. *Faculty research:* Statistical genetics, reliability and pollution monitoring, Bayesian methods. Total annual research expenditures: $50,000. *Unit head:* Dr. Del T. Scott, Chair, 801-422-7054, Fax: 801-422-0635, E-mail: scottd@byu.edu. *Application contact:* Dr. Scott D. Grimshaw, Graduate Coordinator, 801-422-6251, Fax: 801-422-0635, E-mail: grimshaw@byu.edu.

California State University, Long Beach, Graduate Studies, College of Natural Sciences and Mathematics, Department of Mathematics and Statistics, Long Beach, CA 90840. Offers mathematics (MS), including applied mathematics, applied statistics, mathematics education for secondary school teachers. Part-time programs available. *Faculty:* 11 full-time (5 women). *Students:* 73 full-time (30 women), 90 part-time (36 women); includes 75 minority (6 African Americans, 47 Asian Americans or Pacific Islanders, 22 Hispanic Americans), 15 international. Average age 30. 123 applicants, 69% accepted, 44 enrolled. *Degree requirements:* For master's, comprehensive exam or thesis. *Application deadline:* For fall admission, 7/1 for domestic students; for spring admission, 12/1 for domestic students. Applications are processed on a rolling basis. Application fee: $55. Electronic applications accepted. *Expenses:* Required fees: $1802 per semester. Part-time tuition and fees vary according to course load. *Financial support:* Teaching assistantships, Federal Work-Study, institutionally sponsored loans, scholarships/grants, and traineeships available. Financial award application deadline: 3/2. *Faculty research:* Algebra, functional analysis, partial differential equations, operator theory, numerical analysis. *Unit head:* Dr. Robert Mena, Chair, 562-985-4721, Fax: 562-985-8227, E-mail: rmena@csulb.edu. *Application contact:* Dr. Ngo Viet, Graduate Associate Chair, 562-985-4721, Fax: 562-985-8227, E-mail: viet@csulb.edu.

Cornell University, Graduate School, Graduate Fields of Engineering, Field of Statistics, Ithaca, NY 14853-0001. Offers applied statistics (MPS); biometry (MS, PhD); decision theory (MS, PhD); economic and social statistics (MS, PhD); engineering statistics (MS, PhD); experimental design (MS, PhD); mathematical statistics (MS, PhD); probability (MS, PhD); sampling (MS, PhD); statistical computing (MS, PhD); stochastic processes (MS, PhD). *Faculty:* 33 full-time (4 women). *Students:* 62 full-time (22 women); includes 5 minority (4 Asian Americans or Pacific Islanders, 1 Hispanic American), 37 international. Average age 27. 306 applicants, 24% accepted, 31 enrolled. In 2009, 36 master's, 3 doctorates awarded. Terminal master's awarded for partial completion of doctoral program. *Degree requirements:* For master's, project (MPS), thesis (MS); for doctorate, one foreign language, thesis/dissertation. *Entrance requirements:* For master's, GRE General Test (MS), 2 letters of recommendation (MS, MPS); for doctorate, GRE General Test, 2 letters of recommendation. Additional exam requirements/recommendations for international students: Required—TOEFL (minimum score 550 paper-based; 213 computer-based; 77 iBT). *Application deadline:* For fall admission, 1/15 for domestic students. Applications are processed on a rolling basis. Application fee: $70. Electronic applications accepted. *Expenses:* Tuition: Full-time $29,500. Required fees: $70. Full-time tuition and fees vary according to degree level, program and student level. *Financial support:* In 2009–10, 26 students received support, including 1 fellowship with full tuition reimbursement available, 3 teaching assistantships with full tuition reimbursements available; research assistantships with full tuition reimbursements available, institutionally sponsored loans, scholarships/grants, tuition waivers (full and partial), and unspecified assistantships also available. Financial award applicants required to submit FAFSA. *Faculty research:* Bayesian analysis, survival analysis, nonparametric statistics, stochastic processes, mathematical statistics. *Unit head:* Director of Graduate Studies, 607-255-8066. *Application contact:* Graduate Field Assistant, 607-255-8066, E-mail: csc@cornell.edu.

DePaul University, College of Liberal Arts and Sciences, Department of Mathematical Sciences, Chicago, IL 60614. Offers applied mathematics (MS), including actuarial science or statistics; applied statistics (MS, Certificate); mathematics education (MA). Part-time and evening/weekend programs available. *Faculty:* 23 full-time (6 women), 18 part-time/adjunct (5 women). *Students:* 117 full-time (64 women), 67 part-time (37 women); includes 47 minority (22 African Americans, 15 Asian Americans or Pacific Islanders, 10 Hispanic Americans), 13 international. Average age 30. 40 applicants, 100% accepted. In 2009, 30 master's awarded. *Degree requirements:* For master's, comprehensive exam. *Entrance requirements:* Additional exam requirements/recommendations for international students: Required—TOEFL. *Application deadline:* For fall admission, 7/30 for domestic students, 6/30 for international students; for winter admission, 11/30 for domestic students, 10/31 for international students; for spring admission, 2/15 for domestic students. Applications are processed on a rolling basis. Application fee: $25. *Expenses:* Tuition: Full-time $37,525; part-time $620 per credit hour. *Financial support:* In 2009–10, 12 students received support, including research assistantships with partial tuition reimbursements available (averaging $6,000 per year); teaching assistantships, tuition waivers (full) also available. Financial award application deadline: 4/30. *Faculty research:* Verbally prime algebras, enveloping algebras of Lie, superalgebras and related rings, harmonic analysis, estimation theory. *Unit head:* Dr. Ahmed I. Zayed, Chairperson, 773-325-7806, Fax: 773-325-7807, E-mail: azayed@depaul.edu. *Application contact:* Ann Spittle, Director of Graduate Admissions, 312-362-8300, Fax: 312-362-5749, E-mail: admitdpu@depaul.edu.

Eastern Michigan University, Graduate School, College of Arts and Sciences, Department of Mathematics, Ypsilanti, MI 48197. Offers applied statistics (MA); computer science (MA); mathematics (MA); mathematics education (MA). Part-time and evening/weekend programs available. Postbaccalaureate distance learning degree programs offered (minimal on-campus study). *Faculty:* 25 full-time (10 women). *Students:* 11 full-time (7 women), 39 part-time (17 women); includes 2 minority (1 African American, 1 Asian American or Pacific Islander), 11 international. Average age 35. 28 applicants, 75% accepted, 14 enrolled. In 2009, 15 master's awarded. *Degree requirements:* For master's, thesis optional. *Entrance requirements:* Additional exam requirements/recommendations for international students: Required—TOEFL. *Application deadline:* Applications are processed on a rolling basis. Application fee: $35. Tuition and fees vary according to course level. *Financial support:* Fellowships, research assistantships with full tuition reimbursements, teaching assistantships with full tuition reimbursements, career-related internships or fieldwork, Federal Work-Study, institutionally sponsored loans, scholarships/grants, tuition waivers (partial), and unspecified assistantships available. Support available to part-time students. Financial award applicants required to submit FAFSA. *Unit head:* Dr. Christopher Gardiner, Interim Department Head, 734-487-1444, Fax: 734-487-2489, E-mail: cgardiner@emich.edu. *Application contact:* Dr. Bingwu Wang, Graduate Coordinator, 734-487-5044, Fax: 734-487-2489, E-mail: bwang@emich.edu.

Florida State University, The Graduate School, College of Arts and Sciences, Department of Statistics, Tallahassee, FL 32306-4330. Offers applied statistics (MS); biostatistics (MS, PhD); mathematical statistics (MS, PhD). Part-time programs available. *Faculty:* 15 full-time (2 women). *Students:* 51 full-time (22 women), 6 part-time (1 woman); includes 18 minority (8 African Americans, 5 Asian Americans or Pacific Islanders, 5 Hispanic Americans), 23 international. Average age 31. 139 applicants, 19% accepted, 14 enrolled. In 2009, 12 master's, 10 doctorates awarded. Terminal master's awarded for partial completion of doctoral program. *Degree requirements:* For doctorate, thesis/dissertation, departmental qualifying exam. *Entrance requirements:* For master's, GRE General Test, previous course work in calculus, minimum GPA of 3.0; for doctorate, GRE General Test, minimum GPA of 3.0, 1 course in linear algebra (preferred), Calculus I-III, Real Analysis. Additional exam requirements/recommendations for international students: Required—TOEFL (minimum score 600 paper-based; 250 computer-based; 100 iBT). *Application deadline:* For fall admission, 7/1 for domestic and international students; for spring admission, 11/1 for domestic and international students. Applications are processed on a rolling basis. Application fee: $30. Electronic applications accepted. *Expenses:* Tuition, state resident: full-time $7413.36. Tuition, nonresident: full-time $22,567. *Financial support:* In 2009–10, 48 students received support, including 7 research assistantships with full tuition reimbursements available (averaging $19,575 per year), 41 teaching assistantships with full tuition reimbursements available (averaging $19,575 per year); fellowships with full tuition reimbursements available, Federal Work-Study, institutionally sponsored loans, scholarships/grants, health care benefits, and unspecified assistantships also available. Support available to part-time students. Financial award application deadline: 2/15; financial award applicants required to submit FAFSA. *Faculty research:* Statistical inference, probability theory, biostatistics, nonparametric estimation, automatic target recognition. Total annual research expenditures: $747,131. *Unit head:* Dr. Dan McGee, Chairman, 850-644-3218, Fax: 850-644-5271, E-mail: info@stat.fsu.edu. *Application contact:* Chauncey Richburg, Academic Support Assistant, 850-644-3514, Fax: 850-644-5271, E-mail: richburg@stat.fsu.edu.

Indiana University–Purdue University Fort Wayne, College of Arts and Sciences, Department of Mathematical Sciences, Fort Wayne, IN 46805-1499. Offers applied mathematics (MS); applied statistics (Certificate); mathematics (MS); operations research (MS); teaching (MAT). Part-time and evening/weekend programs available. *Faculty:* 17 full-time (4 women), 2 part-time/adjunct (1 woman). *Students:* 2 full-time (0 women), 15 part-time (6 women); includes 2 minority (1 American Indian/Alaska Native, 1 Asian American or Pacific Islander), 1 international. Average age 35. 5 applicants, 60% accepted, 3 enrolled. In 2009, 2 master's, 2 other advanced degrees awarded. *Entrance requirements:* For master's, minimum GPA of 3.0, major or minor in mathematics, three letters of recommendation. Additional exam requirements/recommendations for international students: Required—TOEFL (minimum score 550 paper-based; 213 computer-based; 77 iBT); Recommended—TWE. *Application deadline:* For fall admission, 8/1 priority date for domestic students, 7/1 priority date for international students; for spring admission, 12/1 for domestic students, 10/1 for international students. Applications are processed on a rolling basis. Application fee: $55 ($60 for international students). Electronic applications accepted. *Expenses:* Tuition, state resident: full-time $4595; part-time $255 per credit. Tuition, nonresident: full-time $10,963; part-time $609 per credit. Required fees: $528; $29.35 per credit. Tuition and fees vary according to course load. *Financial support:* In 2009–10, 1 research assistantship with partial tuition reimbursement (averaging $12,740 per year), 6 teaching assistantships with partial tuition reimbursements (averaging $12,740 per year) were awarded; scholarships/grants and unspecified assistantships also available. Support available to part-time students. Financial award application deadline: 3/1; financial award applicants required to submit FAFSA. *Faculty research:* Target value, toroidal queen's graph, holomorphic maps. *Unit head:* Dr. David A. Legg, Chair, 260-481-6222, Fax: 260-481-0155, E-mail: legg@ipfw.edu. *Application contact:* Dr. W. Douglas Weakley, Director of Graduate Studies, 260-481-6233, Fax: 260-481-0155, E-mail: weakley@ipfw.edu.

Indiana University–Purdue University Indianapolis, School of Science, Department of Mathematical Sciences, Master's Program in Mathematics, Indianapolis, IN 46202-2896. Offers applied mathematics (MS); applied statistics (MS); mathematics (MS). Application fee: $50 ($60 for international students). *Unit head:* Slawomir Klimek, Director of Graduate Programs, 317-274-6918, E-mail: grad-program@math.iupui.edu. *Application contact:* Slawomir Klimek, Director of Graduate Programs, 317-274-6918, E-mail: grad-program@math.iupui.edu.

Instituto Tecnológico y de Estudios Superiores de Monterrey, Campus Monterrey, Graduate and Research Division, Programs in Engineering, Monterrey, Mexico. Offers applied statistics (M Eng); artificial intelligence (PhD); automation engineering (M Eng); chemical engineering (M Eng); civil engineering (M Eng); electrical engineering (M Eng); electronic engineering (M Eng); environmental engineering (M Eng); industrial engineering (M Eng, PhD); manufacturing engineering (M Eng); mechanical engineering (M Eng); systems and quality engineering (M Eng). Part-time and evening/weekend programs available. Terminal master's awarded for partial completion of doctoral program. *Degree requirements:* For master's, one foreign language, thesis; for doctorate, one foreign language, thesis/dissertation. *Entrance requirements:* For master's, EXADEP; for doctorate, GRE, master's degree in related field. Additional exam requirements/recommendations for international students: Required—TOEFL. *Faculty research:* Flexible manufacturing cells, materials, statistical methods, environmental prevention, control and evaluation.

Kennesaw State University, College of Science and Mathematics, Program in Applied Statistics, Kennesaw, GA 30144-5591. Offers MSAS. Part-time and evening/weekend programs available. *Students:* 14 full-time (7 women), 47 part-time (17 women); includes 17 minority (13 African Americans, 1 American Indian/Alaska Native, 2 Asian Americans or Pacific Islanders, 1 Hispanic American), 6 international. Average age 33. 31 applicants, 71% accepted, 14 enrolled. In 2009, 20 master's awarded. *Entrance requirements:* For master's, GRE, minimum GPA of 2.75, resume. Additional exam requirements/recommendations for international students: Required—TOEFL (minimum score 550 paper-based; 213 computer-based; 80 iBT), IELTS (minimum score 6). *Application deadline:* For fall admission, 6/1 for domestic and international students; for spring admission, 11/1 for domestic and international students. Applications are processed on a rolling basis. Application fee: $60. Electronic applications accepted. *Expenses:* Tuition, state resident: full-time $2341; part-time $196 per credit hour. Tuition, nonresident: full-time $9396; part-time $783 per credit hour. Required fees: $573 per semester. *Financial support:* In 2009–10, 2 research assistantships (averaging $4,000 per year) were awarded; unspecified assistantships also available. Financial award application deadline: 6/15; financial award applicants required to submit FAFSA. *Unit head:* Dr. Lewis Van Brackle, Director, 678-797-2409, E-mail: lvanbrac@kennesaw.edu. *Application contact:* Vilma Marquez, Admissions Counselor, 770-420-4377, Fax: 770-423-6885, E-mail: vmarquez@kennesaw.edu.

Louisiana State University and Agricultural and Mechanical College, Graduate School, College of Agriculture, Department of Experimental Statistics, Baton Rouge, LA 70803. Offers applied statistics (M App St). Part-time programs available. *Faculty:* 9 full-time (1 woman). *Students:* 13 full-time (11 women), 3 part-time (1 woman); includes 1 Asian American or Pacific Islander, 9 international. Average age 29. 13 applicants, 38% accepted, 3 enrolled. In 2009, 10 master's awarded. *Degree requirements:* For master's, project. *Entrance requirements:* For master's, GRE General Test, minimum GPA of 3.0. Additional exam requirements/recommendations for international students: Required—TOEFL (minimum score 550 paper-based; 213 computer-based; 79 iBT) or IELTS (minimum score 6.5). *Application deadline:* For fall admission, 1/25 priority date for domestic students, 5/15 for international students; for spring admission, 10/15 priority date for domestic students, 10/15 for international students. Applications are processed on a rolling basis. Application fee: $50 ($70 for international students). Electronic applications accepted. *Financial support:* In 2009–10, 14 students received support, including 1 research assistantship with partial tuition reimbursement available (averaging $12,000 per year), 11 teaching assistantships with partial tuition reimbursements available (averaging $10,800 per year); fellowships, career-related internships or fieldwork, Federal Work-Study, institutionally sponsored loans, tuition waivers (full and partial), and unspecified assistantships also available. Financial award application deadline: 4/1; financial award applicants required to submit FAFSA. *Faculty research:* Linear models, statistical computing, ecological statistics. Total annual research expenditures: $1,511. *Unit head:* Dr. James Geaghan, Head, 225-578-8303, Fax: 225-578-8344, E-mail: head@stat.lsu.edu. *Application contact:* Dr. James Geaghan, Graduate Adviser, 225-578-8303, E-mail: jgeaghan@lsu.edu.

Loyola University Chicago, Graduate School, Department of Mathematical Sciences and Statistics, Chicago, IL 60660. Offers applied statistics (MS); mathematics and statistics (MS), including pure mathematics. Part-time programs available. *Faculty:* 19 full-time (4 women). *Students:* 24 full-time (16 women), 8 part-time (3 women); includes 7 minority (3 African Americans, 4 Asian Americans or Pacific Islanders), 8 international. Average age 28. 49 applicants, 63% accepted, 16 enrolled. In 2009, 11 master's awarded. *Entrance requirements:* For master's, GRE General Test. Additional exam requirements/recommendations for international students: Required—TOEFL. *Application deadline:* For fall admission, 8/1 for domestic students; for spring admission, 12/1 for domestic students. Applications are processed on a rolling basis. Application fee: $0. Electronic applications accepted. *Expenses:* Tuition: Full-time $14,220; part-time $790 per credit hour. Required fees: $60 per semester hour. Tuition and fees vary according to program. *Financial support:* In 2009–10, 13 students received support, including 6 teaching assistantships with tuition reimbursements available (averaging $10,000 per year); career-related internships or fieldwork, Federal Work-Study, institutionally sponsored loans, and tuition waivers (partial) also available. Financial award application deadline: 3/15. *Faculty research:* Probability and statistics, differential equations, algebra, combinations. Total annual research expenditures: $10,000. *Unit head:* Dr. Robert Jensen, Chair, 773-508-3578, Fax: 773-508-2123, E-mail: rjensen@luc.edu. *Application contact:* Dr. Joseph Mayne, Director, 773-508-3574, Fax: 773-508-2123, E-mail: jmayne@luc.edu.

McMaster University, School of Graduate Studies, Faculty of Science, Department of Mathematics and Statistics, Program in Statistics, Hamilton, ON L8S 4M2, Canada. Offers applied statistics (M Sc); medical statistics (M Sc); statistical theory (M Sc). *Degree requirements:* For master's, thesis or alternative. *Entrance requirements:* For master's, honors degree background in mathematics and statistics. Additional exam requirements/recommendations for international students: Required—TOEFL (minimum score 550 paper-based; 213 computer-based). *Faculty research:* Development of polymer production technology, quality of life in patients who use pharmaceutical agents, mathematical modeling, order statistics from progressively censored samples, nonlinear stochastic model in genetics.

Michigan State University, The Graduate School, College of Natural Science, Department of Statistics and Probability, East Lansing, MI 48824. Offers applied statistics (MS); statistics (MS, PhD). *Entrance requirements:* Additional exam requirements/recommendations for international students: Required—TOEFL. Electronic applications accepted.

Montclair State University, The Graduate School, College of Science and Mathematics, Department of Computer Science, Montclair, NJ 07043-1624. Offers applied mathematics (MS); applied statistics (MS); CISCO (Certificate); informatics (MS); object oriented computing (Certificate). Part-time and evening/weekend programs available. *Faculty:* 14 full-time (3 women), 16 part-time/adjunct (6 women). *Students:* 10 full-time (6 women), 21 part-time (6 women). Average age 31. 15 applicants, 67% accepted, 6 enrolled. In 2009, 11 master's awarded. *Degree requirements:* For master's, comprehensive exam, thesis or alternative. *Entrance requirements:* For master's, GRE General Test, 2 letters of recommendation. Additional exam requirements/recommendations for international students: Required—TOEFL (minimum score 83 computer-based), or IELTS. *Application deadline:* For fall admission, 6/1 for international students; for spring admission, 10/1 for international students. Applications are processed on a rolling basis. Application fee: $60. Electronic applications accepted. *Expenses:* Tuition, area resident: Part-time $486.74 per credit. Tuition, state resident: part-time $486.74 per credit. Tuition, nonresident: part-time $751.34 per credit. Tuition and fees vary according to degree level and program. *Financial support:* In 2009–10, 4 research assistantships with full tuition reimbursements (averaging $7,000 per year) were awarded; Federal Work-Study, scholarships/grants, and unspecified assistantships also available. Support available to part-time students. Financial award application deadline: 3/1; financial award applicants required to submit FAFSA. *Unit head:* Dr. Dorothy Deremer, Chairperson, 973-655-4166. *Application contact:* Amy Aiello, Director of Graduate Admissions and Operations, 973-655-5147, Fax: 973-655-7869, E-mail: graduate.school@montclair.edu.

New Jersey Institute of Technology, Office of Graduate Studies, College of Science and Liberal Arts, Department of Mathematical Science, Program in Applied Statistics, Newark, NJ 07102. Offers MS. Part-time and evening/weekend programs available. *Entrance requirements:* For master's, GRE General Test. Additional exam requirements/recommendations for international students: Required—TOEFL (minimum score 550 paper-based; 213 computer-based; 79 iBT). Electronic applications accepted.

New Mexico State University, Graduate School, College of Business, Department of Economics and International Business, Las Cruces, NM 88003-8001. Offers applied statistics (MS); economic development (DED); economics (MA). Part-time programs available. *Faculty:* 13 full-time (3 women), 1 part-time/adjunct (0 women). *Students:* 54 full-time (22 women), 15 part-time (4 women); includes 21 minority (4 African Americans, 1 Asian American or Pacific Islander, 16 Hispanic Americans), 29 international. Average age 31. 74 applicants, 85% accepted, 38 enrolled. In 2009, 23 master's awarded. *Degree requirements:* For master's, comprehensive exam, thesis or alternative; for doctorate, comprehensive exam, thesis/dissertation or alternative. *Entrance requirements:* For master's, minimum GPA of 3.0; for doctorate, appropriate master's degree. Additional exam requirements/recommendations for international students: Required—TOEFL. *Application deadline:* Applications are processed on a rolling basis. Application fee: $30 ($50 for international students). Electronic applications accepted. *Expenses:* Tuition, state resident: full-time $4080; part-time $223 per credit. Tuition, nonresident: full-time $14,256; part-time $647 per credit. Required fees: $1278; $639 per semester. *Financial support:* In 2009–10, 34 students received support, including 19 research assistantships (averaging $13,031 per year), 19 teaching assistantships (averaging $7,939 per year); fellowships, career-related internships or fieldwork, Federal Work-Study, and health care benefits also available. Support available to part-time students. Financial award application deadline: 3/1. *Faculty research:* Public utilities, environment, linear models, biological sampling, public policy, economics development. Total annual research expenditures: $400,000. *Unit head:* Dr. Anthony Popp, Graduate Adviser, 575-646-5198, Fax: 575-646-1915, E-mail: apopp@nmsu.edu. *Application contact:* Dr. Anthony Popp, Graduate Adviser, 575-646-5198, Fax: 575-646-1915, E-mail: apopp@nmsu.edu.

North Dakota State University, College of Graduate and Interdisciplinary Studies, College of Science and Mathematics, Department of Statistics, Fargo, ND 58108. Offers applied statistics (MS, Certificate); statistics (PhD); MS/MS. *Faculty:* 4 full-time (2 women), 1 part-time/adjunct (0 women). *Students:* 24 full-time (10 women), 1 (woman) part-time; includes 1 minority (African American), 16 international. Average age 24. 14 applicants, 79% accepted, 5 enrolled. In 2009, 7 master's awarded. *Degree requirements:* For master's, comprehensive exam, thesis; for doctorate, comprehensive exam, thesis/dissertation. *Entrance requirements:* For master's and doctorate, minimum GPA of 3.0. Additional exam requirements/recommendations for international students: Required—TOEFL (minimum score 550 paper-based; 213 computer-based; 79 iBT). *Application deadline:* Applications are processed on a rolling basis. Application fee: $45 ($60 for international students). *Financial support:* In 2009–10, 2 fellowships with full tuition reimbursements, 7 research assistantships with full tuition reimbursements, 9 teaching assistantships with full tuition reimbursements were awarded; career-related internships or fieldwork, Federal Work-Study, institutionally sponsored loans, and tuition waivers (full) also available. Financial award application deadline: 4/15. *Faculty research:* Nonparametric statistics, survival analysis, multivariate analysis, distribution theory, inference modeling, biostatistics. *Unit head:* Dr. Rhonda Magel, Chair, 701-231-7532, Fax: 701-231-8734, E-mail: ndsu.stats@ndsu.edu. *Application contact:* Judy Normann, Academic Assistant, 701-231-7532, Fax: 702-231-8734, E-mail: ndsu.stats@ndsu.edu.

Oakland University, Graduate Study and Lifelong Learning, College of Arts and Sciences, Department of Mathematics and Statistics, Program in Applied Statistics, Rochester, MI 48309-4401. Offers MS. Part-time and evening/weekend programs available. *Entrance requirements:* For master's, minimum GPA of 3.0 for unconditional admission. Additional exam requirements/recommendations for international students: Required—TOEFL (minimum score 550 paper-based; 213 computer-based). Electronic applications accepted. *Expenses:* Contact institution.

Rochester Institute of Technology, Graduate Enrollment Services, Kate Gleason College of Engineering, Center of Quality and Applied Statistics, Rochester, NY 14623-5603. Offers applied statistics (MS); statistical quality (AC). Part-time and evening/weekend programs available. Postbaccalaureate distance learning degree programs offered (no on-campus study). *Students:* 17 full-time (11 women), 31 part-time (10 women); includes 9 minority (2 African Americans, 4 Asian Americans or Pacific Islanders, 3 Hispanic Americans), 11 international. Average age 32. 46 applicants, 67% accepted, 21 enrolled. In 2009, 21 master's, 3 other

Applied Statistics

Rochester Institute of Technology (continued)
advanced degrees awarded. *Degree requirements:* For master's, oral exam. *Entrance requirements:* For master's, course work in calculus, minimum GPA of 3.0. Additional exam requirements/recommendations for international students: Required—TOEFL (minimum score 570 paper-based; 230 computer-based; 88 iBT), or IELTS (minimum score 6.5). *Application deadline:* For fall admission, 2/15 priority date for domestic and international students; for winter admission, 10/15 for domestic students; for spring admission, 2/1 for domestic students. Applications are processed on a rolling basis. Application fee: $50. *Expenses:* Tuition: Full-time $31,533; part-time $876 per credit hour. Required fees: $210. *Financial support:* In 2009–10, 33 students received support; research assistantships with partial tuition reimbursements available, career-related internships or fieldwork, institutionally sponsored loans, scholarships/grants, and unspecified assistantships available. Support available to part-time students. Financial award applicants required to submit FAFSA. *Faculty research:* Industrial statistics, quality control. *Unit head:* Dr. Donald Baker, Director, 585-475-6990, Fax: 585-475-5959, E-mail: cqas@rit.edu. *Application contact:* Diane Ellison, Assistant Vice President, Graduate Enrollment Services, 585-475-2229, Fax: 585-475-7164, E-mail: gradinfo@rit.edu.

Rutgers, The State University of New Jersey, New Brunswick, Graduate School-New Brunswick, Program in Statistics, Piscataway, NJ 08854-8097. Offers applied statistics (MS); biostatistics (MS); data mining (MS); quality and productivity management (MS); statistics (MS, PhD). Part-time programs available. Terminal master's awarded for partial completion of doctoral program. *Degree requirements:* For master's, comprehensive exam, essay, exam, non-thesis essay paper; for doctorate, one foreign language, thesis/dissertation, qualifying oral and written exams. *Entrance requirements:* For master's, GRE General Test; for doctorate, GRE General Test, GRE Subject Test (recommended). Additional exam requirements/recommendations for international students: Required—TOEFL (minimum score 550 paper-based; 213 computer-based). Electronic applications accepted. *Faculty research:* Probability, decision theory, linear models, multivariate statistics, statistical computing.

St. Cloud State University, School of Graduate Studies, College of Science and Engineering, Program in Applied Statistics, St. Cloud, MN 56301-4498. Offers MS. *Faculty:* 10 full-time (3 women). *Students:* 10 full-time (3 women), 1 part-time (0 women); includes 1 minority (Hispanic American), 6 international. 8 applicants, 100% accepted. *Unit head:* Dr. Leonard Onyiah, Coordinator, 320-308-2278, E-mail: lconyiah@stcloudstate.edu. *Application contact:* Linda Lou Krueger, School of Graduate Studies, 320-308-2113, Fax: 320-308-5371, E-mail: lekrueger@stcloudstate.edu.

Stevens Institute of Technology, Graduate School, Charles V. Schaefer Jr. School of Engineering, Department of Mathematical Sciences, Program in Applied Statistics, Hoboken, NJ 07030. Offers Certificate. *Entrance requirements:* Additional exam requirements/recommendations for international students: Required—TOEFL. Electronic applications accepted. *Expenses:* Tuition: Full-time $9900; part-time $1100 per credit. Required fees: $286 per semester.

Syracuse University, College of Arts and Sciences, Program in Applied Statistics, Syracuse, NY 13244. Offers MS. Part-time programs available. *Students:* 4 full-time (all women), all international. Average age 24. 22 applicants, 59% accepted, 3 enrolled. In 2009, 8 master's awarded. *Entrance requirements:* For master's, GRE General Test. Additional exam requirements/recommendations for international students: Required—TOEFL (minimum score 100 iBT). *Application deadline:* For fall admission, 2/1 priority date for domestic and international students. Application fee: $75. Electronic applications accepted. *Expenses:* Tuition: Full-time $26,808; part-time $1117 per credit. Required fees: $1024. *Financial support:* Fellowships with tuition reimbursements, teaching assistantships with tuition reimbursements, tuition waivers available. Financial award application deadline: 1/1; financial award applicants required to submit FAFSA. *Unit head:* Dr. Pinyuen Chen, Graduate Contact, 315-443-1577, E-mail: pinchen@syr.edu. *Application contact:* Dr. Pinyuen Chen, Graduate Contact, 315-443-1577, E-mail: pinchen@syr.edu.

Teachers College, Columbia University, Graduate Faculty of Education, Department of Human Development, Program in Applied Statistics, New York, NY 10027-6696. Offers MS.

The University of Alabama, Graduate School, Manderson Graduate School of Business, Department of Information Systems, Statistics, and Management Science, Program of Information Systems, Statistics, and Management Science—Applied Statistics, Tuscaloosa, AL 35487. Offers applied statistics (MS, PhD). *Faculty:* 23 full-time (3 women). *Students:* 22 full-time (8 women), 4 part-time (0 women); includes 1 minority (Asian American or Pacific Islander), 11 international. Average age 29. 28 applicants, 25% accepted, 5 enrolled. In 2009, 11 degrees awarded. Terminal master's awarded for partial completion of doctoral program. *Degree requirements:* For master's, comprehensive exam; for doctorate, comprehensive exam, thesis/dissertation. *Entrance requirements:* For master's and doctorate, GMAT or GRE, 3 semesters of calculus and linear algebra. Additional exam requirements/recommendations for international students: Required—TOEFL (minimum score 550 paper-based; 213 computer-based), IELTS (minimum score 6.5). *Application deadline:* For spring admission, 3/1 priority date for domestic and international students. Applications are processed on a rolling basis. Application fee: $50 ($60 for international students). Electronic applications accepted. *Expenses:* Tuition, state resident: full-time $7000. Tuition, nonresident: full-time $19,200. *Financial support:* In 2009–10, 9 students received support, including 7 teaching assistantships with tuition reimbursements available (averaging $13,500 per year); scholarships/grants and health care benefits also available. Financial award application deadline: 3/1. *Faculty research:* Data mining, regression analysis, statistical quality control, nonparametric statistics, design of experiments. *Unit head:* Dr. Michael D. Conerly, Professor and Department Head, 205-348-8902, E-mail: mconerly@cba.ua.edu. *Application contact:* Dana Merchant, Administrative Secretary, 205-348-8904, E-mail: dmerchan@cba.ua.edu.

University of Arkansas at Little Rock, Graduate School, College of Science and Mathematics, Department of Mathematics and Statistics, Little Rock, AR 72204-1099. Offers applied statistics (Graduate Certificate); mathematical sciences (MS). Part-time and evening/weekend programs available. *Degree requirements:* For master's, comprehensive exam. *Entrance requirements:* For master's, GRE General Test, GRE Subject Test, minimum GPA of 2.7, previous course work in advanced mathematics.

University of California, Riverside, Graduate Division, Department of Statistics, Riverside, CA 92521-0102. Offers applied statistics (PhD); statistics (MS). *Faculty:* 10 full-time (4 women), 1 (woman) part-time/adjunct. *Students:* 47 full-time (18 women); includes 32 minority (30 Asian Americans or Pacific Islanders, 2 Hispanic Americans), 5 international. Average age 26. 141 applicants, 20% accepted, 10 enrolled. In 2009, 18 master's, 7 doctorates awarded. Terminal master's awarded for partial completion of doctoral program. *Degree requirements:* For master's, comprehensive exam; for doctorate, comprehensive exam, thesis/dissertation. *Entrance requirements:* For master's and doctorate, GRE General Test. Additional exam requirements/recommendations for international students: Required—TOEFL (minimum score 550 paper-based; 213 computer-based; 80 iBT). *Application deadline:* For fall admission, 5/1 priority date for domestic and international students; for winter admission, 9/1 for domestic students, 7/1 for international students; for spring admission, 12/1 for domestic students, 10/1 for international students. Applications are processed on a rolling basis. Application fee: $80 ($100 for international students). Electronic applications accepted. *Financial support:* In 2009–10, 5 students received support, including 5 fellowships with full tuition reimbursements available (averaging $23,150 per year), 4 research assistantships with partial tuition reimbursements available (averaging $16,405 per year), 24 teaching assistantships with partial tuition reimbursements available (averaging $16,637 per year); tuition waivers also available. Financial award application deadline: 1/5; financial award applicants required to submit FAFSA. *Faculty research:* Design and analysis of gene expression experiments using DNA microarrays, statistical design and analysis of experiments, linear models, probability models and statistical inference, SNP/SFP discovery using DNA microarray, genetic mapping. *Unit head:* Dr. Subir Ghosh, Graduate Advisor for Admissions and Recruitment, 951-827-3781, Fax: 951-827-3286. *Application contact:* Perla Fabelo, Graduate Student Affairs Assistant, 951-827-4716, Fax: 951-827-5517, E-mail: fabelo@ucr.edu.

University of California, Santa Barbara, Graduate Division, College of Letters and Sciences, Division of Mathematics, Life, and Physical Sciences, Department of Statistics and Applied Probability, Santa Barbara, CA 93106-3110. Offers financial mathematics and statistics (PhD); quantitative methods in the social sciences (PhD); statistics (MA), including applied statistics, mathematical statistics; statistics and applied probability (PhD); MA/PhD. *Faculty:* 12 full-time (3 women), 4 part-time/adjunct (1 woman). *Students:* 42 full-time (12 women). Average age 28. 218 applicants, 39% accepted, 14 enrolled. In 2009, 20 master's, 1 doctorate awarded. Terminal master's awarded for partial completion of doctoral program. *Degree requirements:* For master's, comprehensive exam, thesis or alternative; for doctorate, comprehensive exam, thesis/dissertation. *Entrance requirements:* For master's, GRE General Test, 3 letters of recommendation, resume/curriculum vitae; for doctorate, GRE General Test, 3 letters of recommendation, statement of purpose, personal achievements/contributions statement, resume/curriculum vitae, transcripts for post-secondary institutions attended. Additional exam requirements/recommendations for international students: Required—TOEFL (minimum score 550 paper-based; 213 computer-based; 80 iBT), or IELTS (minimum score 7). *Application deadline:* For fall admission, 1/1 for domestic and international students; for winter admission, 11/1 for domestic and international students; for spring admission, 2/1 for domestic and international students. Application fee: $70 ($90 for international students). Electronic applications accepted. *Financial support:* In 2009–10, 29 students received support, including 5 fellowships with full and partial tuition reimbursements available (averaging $7,400 per year), 28 teaching assistantships with partial tuition reimbursements available (averaging $10,300 per year); Federal Work-Study, institutionally sponsored loans, scholarships/grants, health care benefits, and unspecified assistantships also available. Financial award application deadline: 1/1; financial award applicants required to submit FAFSA. *Faculty research:* Bayesian inference, financial mathematics, stochastic processes, environmental statistics, biostatistical modeling. *Unit head:* Dr. Yuedong Wang, Chair, 805-893-4870, Fax: 805-893-2334, E-mail: yeudong@pstat.ucsb.edu. *Application contact:* Rickie R. Lazzerini, Graduate Program Assistant, 805-893-4857, Fax: 805-893-2334, E-mail: gradinfo@pstat.ucsb.edu.

University of Guelph, Graduate Program Services, College of Physical and Engineering Science, Department of Mathematics and Statistics, Guelph, ON N1G 2W1, Canada. Offers applied mathematics (PhD); applied statistics (PhD); mathematics and statistics (M Sc). Part-time programs available. *Degree requirements:* For master's, thesis (for some programs); for doctorate, thesis/dissertation. *Entrance requirements:* For master's, minimum B- average during previous 2 years of course work; for doctorate, minimum B average. Additional exam requirements/recommendations for international students: Required—TOEFL (minimum score 550 paper-based; 213 computer-based; 89 iBT), IELTS (minimum score 6.5). *Faculty research:* Dynamical systems, mathematical biology, numerical analysis, linear and nonlinear models, reliability and bioassay.

University of Illinois at Urbana–Champaign, Graduate College, College of Liberal Arts and Sciences, Department of Statistics, Champaign, IL 61820. Offers applied statistics (MS); statistics (PhD). *Faculty:* 12 full-time (4 women). *Students:* 50 full-time (29 women), 11 part-time (3 women); includes 3 minority (1 African American, 2 Asian Americans or Pacific Islanders), 45 international. 230 applicants, 11% accepted, 17 enrolled. In 2009, 38 master's, 2 doctorates awarded. *Entrance requirements:* For master's and doctorate, GRE, minimum GPA of 3.0. Additional exam requirements/recommendations for international students: Required—TOEFL (minimum score 590 paper-based; 243 computer-based). *Application deadline:* Applications are processed on a rolling basis. Application fee: $60 ($75 for international students). Electronic applications accepted. *Financial support:* In 2009–10, 1 fellowship, 24 research assistantships, 38 teaching assistantships were awarded; tuition waivers (full and partial) also available. *Faculty research:* Statistical decision theory, sequential analysis, computer-aided stochastic modeling. *Unit head:* Douglas G. Simpson, Chair, 217-244-0885, Fax: 217-244-7190, E-mail: dgs@illinois.edu. *Application contact:* Melissa Banks, Office Support Specialist, 217-333-2167, Fax: 217-244-7190, E-mail: mdbanks@illinois.edu.

University of Memphis, Graduate School, College of Arts and Sciences, Department of Mathematical Sciences, Memphis, TN 38152. Offers applied mathematics (MS); applied statistics (PhD); bioinformatics (MS); computer science (PhD); computer sciences (MS); mathematics (MS, PhD); statistics (MS, PhD). Part-time programs available. *Faculty:* 19 full-time (4 women), 3 part-time/adjunct (0 women). *Students:* 38 full-time (19 women), 25 part-time (9 women); includes 4 minority (2 African Americans, 2 Asian Americans or Pacific Islanders), 29 international. Average age 34. 26 applicants, 96% accepted, 11 enrolled. In 2009, 6 master's, 5 doctorates awarded. Terminal master's awarded for partial completion of doctoral program. *Degree requirements:* For master's, comprehensive exam; for doctorate, one foreign language, thesis/dissertation, oral exams. *Entrance requirements:* For master's and doctorate, GRE General Test, minimum GPA of 2.5. Additional exam requirements/recommendations for international students: Required—TOEFL (minimum score 550 paper-based; 210 computer-based). *Application deadline:* For fall admission, 8/1 for domestic students, 5/1 priority date for international students; for spring admission, 12/1 for domestic students, 9/1 priority date for international students. Applications are processed on a rolling basis. Application fee: $35 ($60 for international students). Electronic applications accepted. *Expenses:* Tuition, state resident: full-time $6246; part-time $347 per credit hour. Tuition, nonresident: full-time $15,894; part-time $883 per credit hour. Required fees: $1160. Full-time tuition and fees vary according to course load, degree level and program. *Financial support:* In 2009–10, 22 students received support; fellowships with full tuition reimbursements available, research assistantships with full tuition reimbursements available, teaching assistantships with full tuition reimbursements available, career-related internships or fieldwork, Federal Work-Study, scholarships/grants, and unspecified assistantships available. Financial award application deadline: 2/15; financial award applicants required to submit FAFSA. *Faculty research:* Combinatorics, ergodic theory, graph theory, Ramsey theory, applied statistics. *Unit head:* Dr. James E. Jamison, Chairman, 901-678-2482, Fax: 901-678-2480, E-mail: jjamison@memphis.edu. *Application contact:* Dr. Anna Kaminska, Coordinator of Graduate Studies, 901-678-2494, Fax: 901-678-2480.

University of Michigan, Horace H. Rackham School of Graduate Studies, College of Literature, Science, and the Arts, Department of Statistics, Ann Arbor, MI 48109. Offers applied statistics (AM); statistics (AM, PhD). *Faculty:* 32 full-time (8 women), 1 part-time/adjunct (0 women). *Students:* 92 full-time (44 women); includes 5 minority (1 African American, 1 American Indian/Alaska Native, 2 Asian Americans or Pacific Islanders, 1 Hispanic American), 54 international. Average age 24. 327 applicants, 17% accepted, 20 enrolled. In 2009, 23 master's, 11 doctorates awarded. Terminal master's awarded for partial completion of doctoral program. *Degree requirements:* For master's, thesis; for doctorate, thesis/dissertation, oral defense of dissertation, preliminary exam. *Entrance requirements:* For master's and doctorate, GRE General Test. Additional exam requirements/recommendations for international students: Required—TOEFL (minimum score 560 paper-based; 220 computer-based; 84 iBT), IELTS (minimum score 6.5). *Application deadline:* For fall admission, 1/31 priority date for domestic students, 1/15 priority date for international students. Applications are processed on a rolling basis. Application fee: $60 ($75 for international students). Electronic applications accepted. *Expenses:* Tuition, state resident: full-time $17,286; part-time $1099 per credit hour. Tuition, nonresident: full-time $34,944; part-time $2080 per credit hour. Required fees: $95 per semester. Tuition and fees vary according to course load, degree level and program. *Financial support:* In 2009–10, 62 students received support, including 4 fellowships with full and partial tuition reimbursements available (averaging $23,000 per year), 15 research assistantships with full and partial tuition reimbursements available (averaging $16,694 per year), 43 teaching assistantships with full and partial tuition reimbursements available (averaging $16,694 per year); career-related internships or fieldwork, Federal Work-Study, institutionally sponsored loans, scholarships/grants, health care benefits, and unspecified assistantships also available. Financial award application deadline: 1/31. *Faculty research:* Reliability and degradation modeling, biological and legal applications, bioinformatics, statistical computing, covariance estimation. *Unit head:* Prof. Vijay Nair, Chair, 734-763-3520, Fax: 734-763-4676, E-mail: statchair@umich.edu. *Application contact:* Lu Ann Custer, Graduate Secretary, 734-763-3520, Fax: 734-763-4676, E-mail: stat-admiss-ques@umich.edu.

University of Northern Colorado, Graduate School, College of Education and Behavioral Sciences, School of Educational Research, Leadership and Technology, Program in Applied Statistics and Research Methods, Greeley, CO 80639. Offers MS, PhD. Part-time programs available. *Faculty:* 8 full-time (4 women). *Students:* 26 full-time (11 women), 21 part-time (10 women); includes 4 minority (1 African American, 1 Asian American or Pacific Islander, 2 Hispanic Americans), 9 international. Average age 37. 25 applicants, 80% accepted, 12 enrolled. In 2009, 4 master's, 9 doctorates awarded. *Degree requirements:* For master's, comprehensive exam; for doctorate, comprehensive exam, thesis/dissertation. *Entrance requirements:* For master's, 3 letters of reference; for doctorate, GRE General Test, 3 letters of reference. *Application deadline:* Applications are processed on a rolling basis. Application fee: $50 ($60 for international students). Electronic applications accepted. *Expenses:* Tuition, state resident: full-time $5770; part-time $320.55 per credit hour. Tuition, nonresident: full-time $13,847; part-time $769.27 per credit hour. Required fees: $948.78; $52.72 per credit. *Financial support:* In 2009–10, 7 research assistantships (averaging $2,908 per year), 5 teaching assistantships (averaging $3,419 per year) were awarded; fellowships also available. Financial award application deadline: 3/1. *Unit head:* Dr. Susan Hutchinson, Program Coordinator, 970-351-2807, Fax: 970-351-1669. *Application contact:* Linda Sisson, Graduate Student Admission Coordinator, 970-351-1807, Fax: 970-351-2371, E-mail: linda.sisson@unco.edu.

University of Pittsburgh, School of Arts and Sciences, Department of Statistics, Pittsburgh, PA 15260. Offers applied statistics (MA, MS); statistics (MA, MS, PhD). Part-time programs available. *Faculty:* 8 full-time (1 woman). *Students:* 29 full-time (14 women), 6 part-time (2 women); includes 1 African American, 26 international. Average age 23. 219 applicants, 18% accepted, 3 enrolled. In 2009, 7 master's, 2 doctorates awarded. Terminal master's awarded for partial completion of doctoral program. *Degree requirements:* For master's, comprehensive exam, thesis (for some programs); for doctorate, comprehensive exam, thesis/dissertation. *Entrance requirements:* For master's, 3 semesters of calculus, 1 semester of linear algebra, 1 year of mathematical statistics; for doctorate, 3 semesters of calculus, 1 semester of linear algebra, 1 year of mathematical statistics, 1 semester of advanced calculus. Additional exam requirements/recommendations for international students: Required—TOEFL (minimum score 550 paper-based; 213 computer-based; 80 iBT). *Application deadline:* For fall admission, 1/15 priority date for domestic and international students; for spring admission, 10/1 priority date for domestic students, 9/1 priority date for international students. Applications are processed on a rolling basis. Application fee: $50. Electronic applications accepted. *Expenses:* Tuition, state resident: full-time $16,402; part-time $665 per credit. Tuition, nonresident: full-time $28,694; part-time $1175 per credit. Required fees: $690; $175 per term. Tuition and fees vary according to program. *Financial support:* In 2009–10, 1 fellowship with full tuition reimbursement (averaging $17,822 per year), 7 research assistantships with full tuition reimbursements (averaging $15,675 per year), 13 teaching assistantships with full tuition reimbursements (averaging $15,065 per year) were awarded; career-related internships or fieldwork, Federal Work-Study, institutionally sponsored loans, scholarships/grants, health care benefits, and unspecified assistantships also available. Financial award application deadline: 1/15. *Faculty research:* Multivariate statistics, time series, reliability, meta-analysis, linear and nonlinear regression modeling. *Unit head:* Henry Block, Chairman, 412-624-8369, Fax: 412-648-8814, E-mail: hwb@pitt.edu. *Application contact:* Leon J. Gleser, Director of Graduate Studies, 412-624-3925, Fax: 412-648-8814, E-mail: gleser@pitt.edu.

University of South Carolina, The Graduate School, College of Arts and Sciences, Department of Statistics, Columbia, SC 29208. Offers applied statistics (CAS); industrial statistics (MIS); statistics (MS, PhD). Part-time and evening/weekend programs available. Postbaccalaureate distance learning degree programs offered (minimal on-campus study). Terminal master's awarded for partial completion of doctoral program. *Degree requirements:* For master's, thesis; for doctorate, comprehensive exam, thesis/dissertation. *Entrance requirements:* For master's, GRE General Test or GMAT, 2 years of work experience (MIS); for doctorate, GRE General Test; for CAS, GRE General Test or GMAT. Additional exam requirements/recommendations for international students: Required—TOEFL (minimum score 600 paper-based; 250 computer-based; 100 iBT). Electronic applications accepted. *Expenses:* Contact institution. *Faculty research:* Reliability, environmentrics, statistics computing, psychometrics, bioinformatics.

The University of Texas at San Antonio, College of Business, Department of Management Science and Statistics, San Antonio, TX 78249-0617. Offers applied statistics (PhD); management science (MBA); statistics (MS). *Accreditation:* AACSB. Part-time and evening/weekend programs available. *Faculty:* 14 full-time (4 women), 1 part-time/adjunct (0 women). *Students:* 16 full-time (5 women), 88 part-time (22 women); includes 33 minority (4 African Americans, 1 American Indian/Alaska Native, 6 Asian Americans or Pacific Islanders, 22 Hispanic Americans), 8 international. Average age 34. 29 applicants, 59% accepted, 14 enrolled. In 2009, 14 master's awarded. *Degree requirements:* For master's, comprehensive exam (for some programs), thesis (for some programs). *Entrance requirements:* For master's, GMAT, minimum GPA of 3.0. Additional exam requirements/recommendations for international students: Required—TOEFL (minimum score 500 paper-based; 173 computer-based; 61 iBT). *Application deadline:* For fall admission, 7/1 for domestic students, 4/1 for international students; for spring admission, 11/1 for domestic students, 9/1 for international students. Applications are processed on a rolling basis. Application fee: $45 ($80 for international students). Electronic applications accepted. *Expenses:* Tuition, state resident: full-time $3975; part-time $221 per contact hour. Tuition, nonresident: full-time $13,947; part-time $775 per contact hour. Required fees: $1853. *Financial support:* In 2009–10, 13 students received support, including 16 research assistantships (averaging $12,703 per year), 15 teaching assistantships (averaging $8,400 per year). *Faculty research:* Applied statistics, biostatistics, supply chain management. Total annual research expenditures: $23,518. *Unit head:* Dr. Nandini Kannan, Head, 210-458-5691, Fax: 210-458-6350, E-mail: nandini.kannan@utsa.edu. *Application contact:* Dr. Dorothy A. Flannagan, Dean of the Graduate School, 210-458-4330, Fax: 210-458-4332, E-mail: dorothy.flannagan@utsa.edu.

University of the District of Columbia, College of Arts and Sciences, Department of Mathematics, Program in Applied Statistics, Washington, DC 20008-1175. Offers MS. *Degree requirements:* For master's, internship or thesis. *Expenses:* Tuition, state resident: full-time $7580. Tuition, nonresident: full-time $14,580. Required fees: $620. *Unit head:* Dr. Vernise Steadman, Chair (This is a new program—No students as yet), 202-274-5153. *Application contact:* Ann Marie Waterman, Associate Vice President of Admission, Recruitment and Financial Aid, 202-274-6069.

University of West Florida, College of Arts and Sciences: Sciences, Department of Mathematics and Statistics, Pensacola, FL 32514-5750. Offers applied statistics (MS); mathematical sciences (MS). Part-time and evening/weekend programs available. *Faculty:* 9 full-time (1 woman). *Students:* 9 full-time (4 women), 26 part-time (17 women); includes 5 minority (3 African Americans, 1 Asian American or Pacific Islander, 1 Hispanic American), 2 international. Average age 32. 16 applicants, 88% accepted, 10 enrolled. In 2009, 14 master's awarded. *Degree requirements:* For master's, thesis optional. *Entrance requirements:* For master's, GRE General Test, minimum GPA of 3.0. Additional exam requirements/recommendations for international students: Required—TOEFL (minimum score 550 paper-based; 213 computer-based). *Application deadline:* For fall admission, 6/1 for domestic students, 5/15 for international students; for spring admission, 11/1 for domestic students, 10/1 for international students. Applications are processed on a rolling basis. Application fee: $30. *Expenses:* Tuition, state resident: full-time $4982; part-time $260 per credit hour. Tuition, nonresident: full-time $20,059; part-time $919 per credit hour. Required fees: $1247; $52 per credit hour. *Financial support:* In 2009–10, 14 teaching assistantships with partial tuition reimbursements (averaging $4,006 per year) were awarded; unspecified assistantships also available. Financial award application deadline: 4/15; financial award applicants required to submit FAFSA. *Unit head:* Dr. Kuiyuan Li, Chairperson, 850-474-2287, E-mail: mathstat@uwf.edu. *Application contact:* Terry McCray, Assistant Director of Graduate Admissions, 850-473-7718, Fax: 850-473-7714, E-mail: gradadmissions@uwf.edu.

Villanova University, Graduate School of Liberal Arts and Sciences, Department of Mathematical Sciences, Program in Applied Statistics, Villanova, PA 19085-1699. Offers MS. Part-time and evening/weekend programs available. *Students:* 2 full-time (1 woman), 21 part-time (8 women); includes 4 minority (all Asian Americans or Pacific Islanders), 2 international. Average age 31. 10 applicants. In 2009, 9 master's awarded. *Degree requirements:* For master's, comprehensive exam. *Entrance requirements:* For master's, GRE, minimum GPA of 3.0. Additional exam requirements/recommendations for international students: Required—TOEFL. *Application deadline:* For fall admission, 3/1 priority date for domestic and international students; for spring admission, 11/15 priority date for domestic and international students. Applications are processed on a rolling basis. Application fee: $50. Electronic applications accepted. *Expenses:* Tuition: Part-time $630 per credit. Required fees: $60 per credit. Part-time tuition and fees vary according to degree level and program. *Financial support:* Research assistantships, Federal Work-Study available. Financial award applicants required to submit FAFSA. *Unit head:* Dr. Michael Levitan, Director, 610-519-4818. *Application contact:* Dr. Adele Lindenmeyr, Dean, Graduate School of Liberal Arts and Sciences, 610-519-7093, Fax: 610-519-7096.

Washington State University, Graduate School, College of Agricultural, Human, and Natural Resource Sciences, Department of Statistics, Pullman, WA 99164. Offers applied statistics (MS); theoretical statistics (MS). *Faculty:* 12. *Students:* 9 full-time (5 women), 4 part-time (1 woman), 12 international. Average age 30. 74 applicants, 23% accepted, 6 enrolled. In 2009, 12 master's awarded. *Degree requirements:* For master's, comprehensive exam (for some programs), thesis (for some programs), project. *Entrance requirements:* For master's, GRE, Submit a letter of application stating qualifications, personal goals, and objectives of graduate study; three letters of reference; application for admission to the Graduate School; official GRE scores (official TOEFL or IELTS scores for international students); and official copies of all college transcripts. Additional exam requirements/recommendations for international students: Required—TOEFL (minimum score 560 paper-based; 220 computer-based), IELTS. *Application deadline:* For fall admission, 1/10 for domestic and international students; for spring admission, 7/1 for domestic and international students. Application fee: $50. *Financial support:* In 2009–10, 10 students received support, including 2 research assistantships (averaging $13,917 per year), 6 teaching assistantships with tuition reimbursements available (averaging $13,056 per year). *Faculty research:* Environmental statistics, logistic regression, statistical methods for ecology and wildlife, spatial data analysis, linear and non-linear models. Total annual research expenditures: $15,000. *Unit head:* Dr. Michael A. Jacroux, Professor/Chair, 509-335-8645, Fax: 509-335-8369, E-mail: jacroux@wsu.edu. *Application contact:* Graduate School Admissions, 800-GRADWSU, Fax: 509-335-1949, E-mail: gradsch@wsu.edu.

West Chester University of Pennsylvania, Office of Graduate Studies, College of Arts and Sciences, Department of Mathematics, West Chester, PA 19383. Offers applied statistics (MS, Certificate); mathematics (MA, Teaching Certificate). Part-time and evening/weekend programs available. *Students:* 1 full-time (0 women), 89 part-time (37 women); includes 33 minority (14 African Americans, 17 Asian Americans or Pacific Islanders, 2 Hispanic Americans), 5 international. Average age 32. 55 applicants, 93% accepted, 37 enrolled. In 2009, 34 master's awarded. *Entrance requirements:* For master's, GMAT, GRE General Test, or MAT (mathematics), interview; for other advanced degree, GMAT, GRE General Test, or MAT (for mathematics). Additional exam requirements/recommendations for international students: Required—TOEFL (minimum score 550 paper-based; 213 computer-based; 80 iBT). *Application deadline:* For fall admission, 4/15 priority date for domestic students, 3/15 for international students; for spring admission, 10/15 for domestic students, 9/1 for international students. Applications are processed on a rolling basis. Application fee: $35. Electronic applications accepted. *Expenses:* Tuition, state resident: full-time $6666; part-time $370 per credit. Tuition, nonresident: full-time $10,666; part-time $593 per credit. Required fees: $122.56 per credit. *Financial support:* In 2009–10, 6 research assistantships with full and partial tuition reimbursements (averaging $5,000 per year) were awarded; unspecified assistantships also available. Support available to part-time students. Financial award application deadline: 2/15; financial award applicants required to submit FAFSA. *Faculty research:* Teachers teaching with technology in service training program. *Unit head:* Dr. Kathleen Jackson, Chair, 610-436-2537, E-mail: kjackson@wcupa.edu. *Application contact:* Dr. John Kerrigan, Graduate Coordinator, 610-436-2351, E-mail: jkerrigan@wcupa.edu.

Western Michigan University, Graduate College, College of Arts and Sciences, Department of Statistics, Kalamazoo, MI 49008. Offers applied statistics (MS); statistics (PhD).

Worcester Polytechnic Institute, Graduate Studies and Research, Department of Mathematical Sciences, Worcester, MA 01609-2280. Offers applied mathematics (MS); applied statistics (MS); financial mathematics (MS); industrial mathematics (MS); mathematical sciences (PhD); mathematics (MME). Part-time and evening/weekend programs available. *Faculty:* 15 full-time (2 women), 7 part-time/adjunct (1 woman). *Students:* 28 full-time (13 women), 36 part-time (17 women). 172 applicants, 77% accepted, 32 enrolled. In 2009, 29 master's, 1 doctorate awarded. *Degree requirements:* For master's, thesis (for some programs); for doctorate, comprehensive exam, thesis/dissertation. *Entrance requirements:* For master's and doctorate, GRE General Test, GRE Subject Test in math (recommended), 3 letters of recommendation. Additional exam requirements/recommendations for international students: Required—TOEFL (minimum score 550 paper-based; 213 computer-based; 79 iBT), IELTS (minimum score 6.5). *Application deadline:* For fall admission, 1/15 priority date for domestic students, 1/15 for international students; for spring admission, 10/15 priority date for domestic students, 10/15 for international students. Applications are processed on a rolling basis. Application fee: $70. Electronic applications accepted. *Financial support:* Career-related internships or fieldwork, institutionally sponsored loans, scholarships/grants, and unspecified assistantships available. Financial award application deadline: 1/15. *Faculty research:* Applied analysis and differential equations, computational mathematics, discrete mathematics, applied and computational statistics, industrial and financial mathematics. *Unit head:* Dr. Bogdan Vernescu, Head, 508-831-5241, Fax: 508-831-5824, E-mail: vernescu@wpi.edu. *Application contact:* Dr. Joseph Petruccelli, Graduate Coordinator, 508-831-5241, Fax: 508-831-5824, E-mail: jdp@wpi.edu.

Wright State University, School of Graduate Studies, College of Science and Mathematics, Department of Mathematics and Statistics, Program in Applied Statistics, Dayton, OH 45435. Offers MS. *Degree requirements:* For master's, comprehensive exam. *Entrance requirements:* For master's, 1 year of course work in calculus and matrix algebra, previous course work in computer programming and statistics. Additional exam requirements/recommendations for international students: Required—TOEFL. *Faculty research:* Reliability theory, stochastic process, nonparametric statistics, design of experiments, multivariate statistics.

Biomathematics

North Carolina State University, Graduate School, College of Physical and Mathematical Sciences, Program in Biomathematics, Raleigh, NC 27695. Offers M Biomath, MS, PhD. Part-time programs available. Terminal master's awarded for partial completion of doctoral program. *Degree requirements:* For master's, thesis (for some programs); for doctorate, thesis/dissertation. *Entrance requirements:* For master's and doctorate, GRE General Test. Additional exam requirements/recommendations for international students: Required—TOEFL. Electronic applications accepted. *Faculty research:* Theory and methods of biological modeling, theoretical biology (genetics, ecology, neurobiology), applied biology (wildlife).

University of California, Los Angeles, David Geffen School of Medicine and Graduate Division, Graduate Programs in Medicine, Department of Biomathematics, Los Angeles, CA 90095. Offers biomathematics (MS, PhD); clinical research (MS). *Degree requirements:* For master's, comprehensive exam or thesis; for doctorate, thesis/dissertation, oral and written qualifying exams. *Entrance requirements:* For master's and doctorate, GRE General Test, GRE Subject Test.

The University of Texas Health Science Center at Houston, Graduate School of Biomedical Sciences, Program in Biomathematics and Biostatistics, Houston, TX 77225-0036. Offers MS, PhD, MD/PhD. Terminal master's awarded for partial completion of doctoral program. *Degree requirements:* For master's, thesis; for doctorate, thesis/dissertation. *Entrance requirements:* For master's and doctorate, GRE General Test. Additional exam requirements/recommendations for international students: Required—TOEFL. Electronic applications accepted. *Faculty research:* Biostatistics, biomarkers, epidemiology, bioinformatics, computational biology.

Biometry

Cornell University, Graduate School, Graduate Fields of Agriculture and Life Sciences, Field of Biometry, Ithaca, NY 14853-0001. Offers MS, PhD. *Faculty:* 13 full-time (0 women). *Students:* 2 full-time (1 woman); includes 1 minority (Asian American or Pacific Islander). Average age 33. 6 applicants, 0% accepted, 0 enrolled. In 2009, 1 master's awarded. Terminal master's awarded for partial completion of doctoral program. *Degree requirements:* For master's, thesis; for doctorate, comprehensive exam, thesis/dissertation. *Entrance requirements:* For master's and doctorate, GRE General Test, 2 letters of recommendation. Additional exam requirements/recommendations for international students: Required—TOEFL (minimum score 550 paper-based; 213 computer-based; 77 iBT). *Application deadline:* For fall admission, 1/15 for domestic students. Application fee: $70. Electronic applications accepted. *Expenses:* Tuition: Full-time $29,500. Required fees: $70. Full-time tuition and fees vary according to degree level, program and student level. *Financial support:* Fellowships with full tuition reimbursements, research assistantships with full tuition reimbursements, teaching assistantships with full tuition reimbursements, institutionally sponsored loans, scholarships/grants, health care benefits, tuition waivers (full and partial), and unspecified assistantships available. Financial award applicants required to submit FAFSA. *Faculty research:* Environmental, agricultural, and biological statistics; biomathematics; modern nonparametric statistics; statistical genetics; computational statistics. *Unit head:* Director of Graduate Studies, 607-255-8066. *Application contact:* Graduate Field Assistant, 607-255-8066, E-mail: bscb@cornell.edu.

Cornell University, Graduate School, Graduate Fields of Engineering, Field of Statistics, Ithaca, NY 14853-0001. Offers applied statistics (MPS); biometry (MS, PhD); decision theory (MS, PhD); economic and social statistics (MS, PhD); engineering statistics (MS, PhD); experimental design (MS, PhD); mathematical statistics (MS, PhD); probability (MS, PhD); sampling (MS, PhD); statistical computing (MS, PhD); stochastic processes (MS, PhD). *Faculty:* 33 full-time (4 women). *Students:* 62 full-time (22 women); includes 5 minority (4 Asian Americans or Pacific Islanders, 1 Hispanic American), 37 international. Average age 27. 306 applicants, 24% accepted, 31 enrolled. In 2009, 36 master's, 3 doctorates awarded. Terminal master's awarded for partial completion of doctoral program. *Degree requirements:* For master's, project (MPS), thesis (MS); for doctorate, one foreign language, thesis/dissertation. *Entrance requirements:* For master's, GRE General Test (MS), 2 letters of recommendation (MS, MPS); for doctorate, GRE General Test, 2 letters of recommendation. Additional exam requirements/recommendations for international students: Required—TOEFL (minimum score 550 paper-based; 213 computer-based; 77 iBT). *Application deadline:* For fall admission, 1/15 for domestic students. Applications are processed on a rolling basis. Application fee: $70. Electronic applications accepted. *Expenses:* Tuition: Full-time $29,500. Required fees: $70. Full-time tuition and fees vary according to degree level, program and student level. *Financial support:* In 2009–10, 26 students received support, including 1 fellowship with full tuition reimbursement available, 3 teaching assistantships with full tuition reimbursements available; research assistantships with full tuition reimbursements available, institutionally sponsored loans, scholarships/grants, tuition waivers (full and partial), and unspecified assistantships also available. Financial award applicants required to submit FAFSA. *Faculty research:* Bayesian analysis, survival analysis, nonparametric statistics, stochastic processes, mathematical statistics. *Unit head:* Director of Graduate Studies, 607-255-8066. *Application contact:* Graduate Field Assistant, 607-255-8066, E-mail: csc@cornell.edu.

San Diego State University, Graduate and Research Affairs, College of Health and Human Services, Program in Biostatistics and Biometry, San Diego, CA 92182. Offers biometry (MPH). Electronic applications accepted.

University of California, Los Angeles, David Geffen School of Medicine and Graduate Division, Graduate Programs in Medicine, Department of Biomathematics, Los Angeles, CA 90095. Offers biomathematics (MS, PhD); clinical research (MS). *Degree requirements:* For master's, comprehensive exam or thesis; for doctorate, thesis/dissertation, oral and written qualifying exams. *Entrance requirements:* For master's and doctorate, GRE General Test, GRE Subject Test.

University of Wisconsin–Madison, Graduate School, College of Letters and Science, Department of Statistics, Biometry Program, Madison, WI 53706-1380. Offers MS. *Expenses:* Tuition, state resident: part-time $594 per credit. Tuition, nonresident: part-time $1504 per credit. Required fees: $65 per credit. Tuition and fees vary according to course load, program and reciprocity agreements.

Biostatistics

American University of Beirut, Graduate Programs, Faculty of Health Sciences, Beirut, Lebanon. Offers environmental sciences (MSES), including environmental health; epidemiology (MS); epidemiology and biostatistics (MPH); health behavior and education (MPH); population health (MS); public health (MPH). Part-time programs available. *Degree requirements:* For master's, one foreign language, comprehensive exam, thesis (for some programs). *Entrance requirements:* For master's, 2 letters of recommendation. Additional exam requirements/recommendations for international students: Required—TOEFL (minimum score 573 paper-based; 230 computer-based; 98 iBT), IELTS (minimum score 7.5). Electronic applications accepted. *Faculty research:* Urban health, childbirth, tobacco control, HIV/AIDS surveillance, health finance and policies.

Boston University, Graduate School of Arts and Sciences, Intercollegiate Program in Biostatistics, Boston, MA 02215. Offers MA, PhD. *Students:* 60 full-time (39 women), 34 part-time (19 women); includes 14 minority (3 African Americans, 1 American Indian/Alaska Native, 9 Asian Americans or Pacific Islanders, 1 Hispanic American), 26 international. Average age 31. 114 applicants, 36% accepted, 11 enrolled. In 2009, 30 master's, 6 doctorates awarded. Terminal master's awarded for partial completion of doctoral program. *Degree requirements:* For master's, one foreign language, comprehensive exam; for doctorate, one foreign language, comprehensive exam, thesis/dissertation. *Entrance requirements:* For master's and doctorate, GRE General Test, 2 letters of recommendation. Additional exam requirements/recommendations for international students: Required—TOEFL (minimum score 550 paper-based; 213 computer-based). *Application deadline:* For fall admission, 3/1 for domestic and international students; for spring admission, 10/15 for domestic and international students. Application fee: $70. Electronic applications accepted. *Expenses:* Tuition: Full-time $37,910; part-time $1184 per credit hour. Required fees: $386; $40 per semester. Part-time tuition and fees vary according to class time, course level, degree level and program. *Financial support:* In 2009–10, 40 students received support, including 40 research assistantships with full tuition reimbursements available (averaging $18,400 per year); fellowships, teaching assistantships also available. Support available to part-time students. Financial award application deadline: 1/15; financial award applicants required to submit FAFSA. *Unit head:* Lisa Sullivan, Chairman, 617-638-5047, Fax: 617-638-4458, E-mail: lsull@bu.edu. *Application contact:* MyHanh SloatTran, Curriculum Coordinator, 617-638-5207, Fax: 617-638-6484, E-mail: msloat@bu.edu.

Boston University, School of Public Health, Biostatistics Department, Boston, MA 02215. Offers MA, MPH, PhD. Part-time and evening/weekend programs available. *Students:* 11 full-time (8 women), 12 part-time (9 women); includes 5 minority (1 African American, 1 American Indian/Alaska Native, 3 Asian Americans or Pacific Islanders), 4 international. Average age 27. In 2009, 16 master's, 5 doctorates awarded. *Entrance requirements:* For master's, GRE, GMAT, LSAT, DAT, or MCAT; for doctorate, GRE. Additional exam requirements/recommendations for international students: Required—TOEFL (minimum score 600 paper-based; 250 computer-based; 100 iBT), IELTS (minimum score 6). *Application deadline:* For fall admission, 2/1 priority date for domestic and international students; for spring admission, 10/15 priority date for domestic and international students. Applications are processed on a rolling basis. Application fee: $95. Electronic applications accepted. *Expenses:* Tuition: Full-time $37,910; part-time $1184 per credit hour. Required fees: $386; $40 per semester. Part-time tuition and fees vary according to class time, course level, degree level and program. *Financial support:* Career-related internships or fieldwork, Federal Work-Study, institutionally sponsored loans, scholarships/grants, traineeships, health care benefits, and unspecified assistantships available. Support available to part-time students. Financial award application deadline: 3/1; financial award applicants required to submit FAFSA. *Unit head:* Lisa Sullivan, Chairman, 617-638-5176, Fax: 617-638-4458. *Application contact:* LePhan Quan, Assistant Director of Admissions, 617-638-4640, Fax: 617-638-5299, E-mail: asksph@bu.edu.

Brown University, Graduate School, Division of Biology and Medicine, Department of Community Health, Providence, RI 02912. Offers health services research (MS, PhD); public health (MPH); statistical science (MS, PhD), including biostatistics, epidemiology; MD/PhD. *Accreditation:* CEPH. *Degree requirements:* For doctorate, thesis/dissertation, preliminary exam. *Entrance requirements:* For master's and doctorate, GRE General Test. Additional exam requirements/recommendations for international students: Required—TOEFL.

Brown University, Graduate School, Division of Biology and Medicine, Department of Community Health, Center for Statistical Science, Program in Biostatistics, Providence, RI 02912. Offers MS, PhD, MD/PhD. *Degree requirements:* For doctorate, thesis/dissertation, preliminary exam. *Entrance requirements:* For master's and doctorate, GRE General Test.

California State University, East Bay, Academic Programs and Graduate Studies, College of Science, Department of Statistics and Biostatistics, Biostatistics Program, Hayward, CA 94542-3000. Offers MS. Part-time and evening/weekend programs available. *Faculty:* 7 full-time (3 women). *Students:* 4 full-time (all women), 34 part-time (21 women); includes 19 minority (1 African American, 17 Asian Americans or Pacific Islanders, 1 Hispanic American), 7 international. Average age 33. 41 applicants, 56% accepted, 15 enrolled. In 2009, 8 master's awarded. *Degree requirements:* For master's, comprehensive exam. *Entrance requirements:* For master's, minimum GPA of 3.0; math through lower-division calculus. Additional exam requirements/recommendations for international students: Required—TOEFL (minimum score 550 paper-based; 213 computer-based). *Application deadline:* For fall admission, 6/30 for domestic and international students. Application fee: $55. Electronic applications accepted. *Financial support:* Fellowships, career-related internships or fieldwork, Federal Work-Study, scholarships/grants, and unspecified assistantships available. Support available to part-time students. Financial award application deadline: 3/1; financial award applicants required to submit FAFSA. *Unit head:* Dr. Eric Suess, Chair, 510-885-3435, Fax: 510-885-4714, E-mail: eric.suess@csueastbay.edu. *Application contact:* Donna Wiley, Interim Associate Director, 510-885-2928, Fax: 510-885-4777, E-mail: donna.wiley@csueastbay.edu.

Case Western Reserve University, School of Medicine and School of Graduate Studies, Graduate Programs in Medicine, Department of Epidemiology and Biostatistics, Program in

Biostatistics, Cleveland, OH 44106. Offers MS, PhD. Part-time programs available. Terminal master's awarded for partial completion of doctoral program. *Degree requirements:* For master's, comprehensive exam, thesis, exam/practicum; for doctorate, comprehensive exam, thesis/dissertation. *Entrance requirements:* For master's, GRE General Test or MCAT, 3 recommendations; for doctorate, GRE General Test, 3 recommendations. Additional exam requirements/recommendations for international students: Required—TOEFL (minimum score 550 paper-based; 213 computer-based). Electronic applications accepted. *Faculty research:* Survey sampling and statistical computing, generalized linear models, statistical modeling, models in breast cancer survival.

Columbia University, Columbia University Mailman School of Public Health, Division of Biostatistics, New York, NY 10032. Offers MPH, MS, Dr PH, PhD. PhD offered in cooperation with the Graduate School of Arts and Sciences. Part-time programs available. *Students:* 15 full-time (11 women), 74 part-time (36 women); includes 15 minority (1 African American, 10 Asian Americans or Pacific Islanders, 4 Hispanic Americans), 31 international. Average age 32. 147 applicants, 48% accepted, 18 enrolled. In 2009, 30 master's, 4 doctorates awarded. *Degree requirements:* For doctorate, thesis/dissertation. *Entrance requirements:* For master's, GRE General Test; for doctorate, GRE General Test, MPH or equivalent (Dr PH). Additional exam requirements/recommendations for international students: Required—TOEFL (minimum score 600 paper-based; 250 computer-based; 100 iBT). *Application deadline:* For fall admission, 1/5 for domestic students. Applications are processed on a rolling basis. Application fee: $60. Electronic applications accepted. *Financial support:* Research assistantships, teaching assistantships, career-related internships or fieldwork and Federal Work-Study available. Financial award application deadline: 2/1; financial award applicants required to submit FAFSA. *Faculty research:* Statistical methods and public health implications of: biomedical experiments, clinical trials, functional data analysis, statistical genetics, and observational studies. *Unit head:* Dr. Bruce Levin, Acting Head, 212-305-4901, Fax: 212-305-9408. *Application contact:* Dr. Bruce Levin, Acting Head, 212-305-4901, Fax: 212-305-9408.

Drexel University, School of Biomedical Engineering, Science and Health Systems, Philadelphia, PA 19104-2875. Offers biomedical engineering (MS, PhD); biomedical science (MS, PhD); biostatistics (MS); clinical/rehabilitation engineering (MS); MD/PhD. *Degree requirements:* For doctorate, thesis/dissertation, 1 year of residency, qualifying exam. *Entrance requirements:* For master's, minimum GPA of 3.0; for doctorate, minimum GPA of 3.0, MS. Additional exam requirements/recommendations for international students: Required—TOEFL. Electronic applications accepted. *Faculty research:* Cardiovascular dynamics, diagnostic and therapeutic ultrasound.

Drexel University, School of Public Health, Department of Epidemiology and Biostatistics, Philadelphia, PA 19104-2875. Offers biostatistics (MS); epidemiology (PhD); epidemiology and biostatistics (Certificate).

Emory University, Graduate School of Arts and Sciences, Department of Biostatistics, Atlanta, GA 30322-1100. Offers biostatistics (MPH, MSPH, PhD); public health informatics (MSPH). *Degree requirements:* For doctorate, comprehensive exam, thesis/dissertation. *Entrance requirements:* For doctorate, GRE General Test. Additional exam requirements/recommendations for international students: Required—TOEFL (minimum score 550 paper-based; 220 computer-based). Electronic applications accepted. *Faculty research:* Vaccine efficacy, clinical trials, spatial statistics, statistical genetics, neuroimaging.

Emory University, Rollins School of Public Health, Department of Biostatistics and Bioinformatics, Atlanta, GA 30322-1100. Offers MPH, MSPH. Part-time programs available. *Degree requirements:* For master's, thesis, practicum. *Entrance requirements:* For master's, GRE General Test. Additional exam requirements/recommendations for international students: Required—TOEFL (minimum score 550 paper-based; 213 computer-based; 80 iBT). Electronic applications accepted.

Florida International University, Stempel College of Public Health and Social Work, Programs in Public Health, Miami, FL 33199. Offers biostatistics (MPH); environmental and occupational health (MPH, PhD); epidemiology (MPH, PhD); health policy and management (MPH); health promotion and disease prevention (PhD); health promotion and diseases prevention (MPH). PhD only admits in Fall. *Accreditation:* CEPH. Part-time and evening/weekend programs available. Postbaccalaureate distance learning degree programs offered (no on-campus study). *Faculty:* 18 full-time (6 women). *Students:* 249 full-time (186 women), 185 part-time (144 women); includes 309 minority (154 African Americans, 2 American Indian/Alaska Native, 26 Asian Americans or Pacific Islanders, 127 Hispanic Americans), 48 international. Average age 35. 484 applicants, 29% accepted, 123 enrolled. In 2009, 79 master's, 1 doctorate awarded. *Degree requirements:* For master's, thesis optional; for doctorate, comprehensive exam, thesis/dissertation. *Entrance requirements:* For master's, minimum GPA of 3.0, letters of recommendation; for doctorate, GRE, resume, minimum GPA of 3.0, letters of recommendation, letter of intent;. Additional exam requirements/recommendations for international students: Required—TOEFL (minimum score 550 paper-based; 80 iBT). *Application deadline:* For fall admission, 6/1 for domestic students, 4/1 for international students; for spring admission, 10/1 for domestic students, 9/1 for international students. Applications are processed on a rolling basis. Application fee: $30. Electronic applications accepted. *Expenses:* Contact institution. *Financial support:* Institutionally sponsored loans, scholarships/grants, and tuition waivers (full) available. Financial award application deadline: 3/1; financial award applicants required to submit FAFSA. *Faculty research:* Drugs/AIDS intervention among migrant workers, provision of services for active/recovering drug users with HIV. *Unit head:* Dr. Gilbert Ramirez, Associate Dean for Academic and Student Affairs, 305-348-7442, E-mail: ph@fiu.edu. *Application contact:* Nanett Rojas, Assistant Director of Graduate Admissions, 305-348-7442, Fax: 305-348-7441, E-mail: gradadm@fiu.edu.

Florida State University, The Graduate School, College of Arts and Sciences, Department of Statistics, Tallahassee, FL 32306-4330. Offers applied statistics (MS); biostatistics (MS, PhD); mathematical statistics (MS, PhD). Part-time programs available. *Faculty:* 15 full-time (2 women). *Students:* 51 full-time (22 women), 6 part-time (1 woman); includes 18 minority (8 African Americans, 5 Asian Americans or Pacific Islanders, 5 Hispanic Americans), 23 international. Average age 31. 139 applicants, 19% accepted, 14 enrolled. In 2009, 12 master's, 10 doctorates awarded. Terminal master's awarded for partial completion of doctoral program. *Degree requirements:* For doctorate, thesis/dissertation, departmental qualifying exam. *Entrance requirements:* For master's, GRE General Test, previous course work in calculus, minimum GPA of 3.0; for doctorate, GRE General Test, minimum GPA of 3.0, 1 course in linear algebra (preferred), Calculus I-III, Real Analysis. Additional exam requirements/recommendations for international students: Required—TOEFL (minimum score 600 paper-based; 250 computer-based; 100 iBT). *Application deadline:* For fall admission, 7/1 for domestic and international students; for spring admission, 11/1 for domestic and international students. Applications are processed on a rolling basis. Application fee: $30. Electronic applications accepted. *Expenses:* Tuition, state resident: full-time $7413.36. Tuition, nonresident: full-time $22,567. *Financial support:* In 2009–10, 48 students received support, including 7 research assistantships with full tuition reimbursements available (averaging $19,575 per year), 41 teaching assistantships with full tuition reimbursements available (averaging $19,575 per year); fellowships with full tuition reimbursements available, Federal Work-Study, institutionally sponsored loans, scholarships/grants, health care benefits, and unspecified assistantships also available. Support available to part-time students. Financial award application deadline: 2/15; financial award applicants required to submit FAFSA. *Faculty research:* Statistical inference, probability theory, biostatistics, nonparametric estimation, automatic target recognition. Total annual research expenditures: $747,131. *Unit head:* Dr. Dan McGee, Chairman, 850-644-3218, Fax: 850-644-5271, E-mail: info@stat.fsu.edu. *Application contact:* Chauncey Richburg, Academic Support Assistant, 850-644-3514, Fax: 850-644-5271, E-mail: richburg@stat.fsu.edu.

George Mason University, College of Health and Human Services, Department of Global and Community Health, Fairfax, VA 22030. Offers biostatistics (Certificate); epidemiology (Certificate); epidemiology and biostatistics (MS); gerontology (Certificate); global health (MS, Certificate); nutrition (Certificate); public health (MPH, Certificate); rehabilitation science (Certificate). *Faculty:* 14 full-time (8 women), 12 part-time/adjunct (8 women). *Students:* 93 full-time (75 women), 106 part-time (92 women); includes 87 minority (46 African Americans, 1 American Indian/Alaska Native, 31 Asian Americans or Pacific Islanders, 9 Hispanic Americans), 22 international. Average age 31. 269 applicants, 69% accepted, 146 enrolled. In 2009, 17 master's, 2 other advanced degrees awarded. *Degree requirements:* For master's, comprehensive exam (for some programs), thesis or practicum. *Entrance requirements:* For master's, GRE, BA with minimum GPA of 3.0, 2 letters of recommendation. Additional exam requirements/recommendations for international students: Required—TOEFL. *Application deadline:* For fall admission, 4/1 priority date for domestic students, 4/1 for international students; for spring admission, 11/1 for domestic and international students. Applications are processed on a rolling basis. Application fee: $75. Electronic applications accepted. *Expenses:* Tuition, state resident: full-time $7568; part-time $315.33 per credit hour. Tuition, nonresident: full-time $21,704; part-time $904.33 per credit hour. Required fees: $2184; $91 per credit hour. *Financial support:* In 2009–10, 4 students received support, including 2 research assistantships with full and partial tuition reimbursements available (averaging $3,500 per year), 2 teaching assistantships with full and partial tuition reimbursements available (averaging $2,790 per year); Federal Work-Study, scholarships/grants, unspecified assistantships, and research awards, health care benefits health care benefits (full-time research or teaching assistantship recipients) also available. Support available to part-time students. Financial award application deadline: 3/1. *Faculty research:* Providing introductory and advanced degrees in health-related disciplines centered in global and community issues, health issues and the needs of affected populations at the regional and global level. *Unit head:* Dr. Shirley S. Travis, Dean, 703-993-1918. *Application contact:* Allan Weiss, Office Manager, 703-993-3126, E-mail: aweiss2@gmu.edu.

George Mason University, Volgenau School of Information Technology and Engineering, Department of Statistics, Fairfax, VA 22030. Offers biostatistics (Certificate); federal statistics (Certificate); statistical science (MS, PhD). Part-time and evening/weekend programs available. *Faculty:* 11 full-time (2 women), 6 part-time/adjunct (0 women). *Students:* 6 full-time (2 women), 61 part-time (32 women); includes 11 minority (4 African Americans, 4 Asian Americans or Pacific Islanders, 3 Hispanic Americans), 17 international. Average age 31. 52 applicants, 65% accepted, 20 enrolled. In 2009, 12 master's, 1 doctorate, 2 other advanced degrees awarded. Terminal master's awarded for partial completion of doctoral program. *Degree requirements:* For master's, comprehensive exam, thesis optional, qualifying exams; for doctorate, comprehensive exam, thesis/dissertation, qualifying exams. *Entrance requirements:* For master's, GRE (recommended), letters of recommendation, resume; for doctorate, GRE (recommended), personal goal statement, resume, 2 transcripts, letters of recommendation. Additional exam requirements/recommendations for international students: Required—TOEFL (minimum score 575 paper-based; 230 computer-based), IELTS (minimum score 6.5). *Application deadline:* For fall admission, 3/15 priority date for domestic students, 12/15 priority date for international students; for spring admission, 10/1 for domestic and international students. Applications are processed on a rolling basis. Application fee: $75. Electronic applications accepted. *Expenses:* Tuition, state resident: full-time $7568; part-time $315.33 per credit hour. Tuition, nonresident: full-time $21,704; part-time $904.33 per credit hour. Required fees: $2184; $91 per credit hour. *Financial support:* In 2009–10, 19 students received support, including 2 fellowships with full tuition reimbursements available (averaging $18,000 per year), 5 research assistantships with full and partial tuition reimbursements available (averaging $11,043 per year), 12 teaching assistantships with full and partial tuition reimbursements available (averaging $9,866 per year); Federal Work-Study, scholarships/grants, unspecified assistantships, and health care benefits (full-time research or teaching assistantship recipients) also available. Financial award application deadline: 3/1; financial award applicants required to submit FAFSA. *Faculty research:* Computational statistics, nonparametric function estimation, scientific and statistical visualization, statistical applications to engineering, survey research. Total annual research expenditures: $228,993. *Unit head:* Dr. William Rosenberger, Chair, 703-993-3645, Fax: 703-993-1700, E-mail: satistics@gmu.edu. *Application contact:* Elizabeth Quigley, Administrative Assitant, 703-993-9107, E-mail: equigley@gmu.edu.

Georgetown University, Graduate School of Arts and Sciences, Programs in Biomedical Sciences, Department of Biostatistics, Bioinformatics and Biomathematics, Washington, DC 20057-1484. Offers biostatistics (MS), including bioinformatics, epidemiology. *Entrance requirements:* For master's, GRE General Test. Additional exam requirements/recommendations for international students: Required—TOEFL. *Faculty research:* Occupation epidemiology, cancer.

The George Washington University, Columbian College of Arts and Sciences, Program in Biostatistics, Washington, DC 20052. Offers MS, PhD. *Students:* 6 full-time (4 women), 14 part-time (9 women); includes 5 minority (1 African American, 4 Asian Americans or Pacific Islanders), 6 international. Average age 33. 41 applicants, 51% accepted, 3 enrolled. In 2009, 3 master's, 1 doctorate awarded. *Degree requirements:* For master's, comprehensive exam; for doctorate, thesis/dissertation, general exam. *Entrance requirements:* For master's and doctorate, GRE General Test, minimum GPA of 3.0. Additional exam requirements/recommendations for international students: Required—TOEFL (minimum score 550 paper-based; 213 computer-based; 80 iBT). *Application deadline:* For fall admission, 1/15 priority date for domestic and international students; for spring admission, 10/1 priority date for domestic students, 9/1 priority date for international students. Applications are processed on a rolling basis. Application fee: $60. Electronic applications accepted. *Financial support:* In 2009–10, 1 student received support; fellowships with full tuition reimbursements available, teaching assistantships, tuition waivers available. *Unit head:* Dr. Zhaohai Li, Director, 202-994-7844, Fax: 202-994-6917, E-mail: zli@gwu.edu. *Application contact:* Dr. Zhaohai Li, Director, 202-994-7844, Fax: 202-994-6917, E-mail: zli@gwu.edu.

The George Washington University, School of Public Health and Health Services, Department of Epidemiology and Biostatistics, Washington, DC 20052. Offers biostatistics (MPH); epidemiology (MPH); microbiology and emerging infectious diseases (MSPH). *Faculty:* 16 full-time (7 women), 14 part-time/adjunct (8 women). *Students:* 52 full-time (40 women), 53 part-time (37 women); includes 44 minority (14 African Americans, 25 Asian Americans or Pacific Islanders, 5 Hispanic Americans), 5 international. Average age 28. 165 applicants, 85% accepted, 37 enrolled. In 2009, 28 master's awarded. *Degree requirements:* For master's, case study or special project. *Entrance requirements:* For master's, GMAT, GRE General Test, or MCAT. Additional exam requirements/recommendations for international students: Required—TOEFL. *Application deadline:* For fall admission, 4/15 priority date for domestic students, 4/15 for international students; for spring admission, 11/1 for domestic and international students. Applications are processed on a rolling basis. Application fee: $60. *Financial support:* In 2009–10, 6 students received support. Tuition waivers available. Financial award application deadline: 2/15. *Unit head:* Dr. Alan E. Greenberg, Chair, 202-994-0612, E-mail: aeg1@gwu.edu. *Application contact:* Jane Smith, Director of Admissions, 202-994-0248, Fax: 202-994-1860, E-mail: sphhsinfo@gwumc.edu.

Georgia Southern University, Jack N. Averitt College of Graduate Studies, Jiann-Ping Hsu College of Public Health, Program in Public Health, Statesboro, GA 30460. Offers biostatistics (MPH, Dr PH); community health behavior and education (Dr PH); community health education (MPH); environmental health sciences (MPH); epidemiology (MPH); health services policy management (MPH); public health leadership (Dr PH). Part-time programs available. *Students:* 75 full-time (47 women), 23 part-time (15 women); includes 39 minority (36 African Americans, 3 Asian Americans or Pacific Islanders), 24 international. Average age 30. 50 applicants, 80% accepted, 20 enrolled. In 2009, 20 master's awarded. *Degree requirements:* For master's,

Biostatistics

Georgia Southern University (continued)
thesis optional, practicum; for doctorate, comprehensive exam, thesis/dissertation, practicum. *Entrance requirements:* For master's, GRE General Test, minimum GPA of 2.75, resume, 3 letters of reference; for doctorate, GRE, GMAT, MCAT, LSAT, 3 letters of reference, statement of purpose, resume or curriculum vitae. Additional exam requirements/recommendations for international students: Required—TOEFL (minimum score 550 paper-based; 213 computer-based; 80 iBT). *Application deadline:* For fall admission, 3/1 priority date for domestic and international students; for spring admission, 10/1 priority date for domestic students, 10/1 for international students. Applications are processed on a rolling basis. Application fee: $50. Electronic applications accepted. *Expenses:* Contact institution. *Financial support:* In 2009–10, 83 students received support, including research assistantships with partial tuition reimbursements available (averaging $7,200 per year), teaching assistantships with partial tuition reimbursements available (averaging $7,200 per year); career-related internships or fieldwork, Federal Work-Study, scholarships/grants, tuition waivers (partial), and unspecified assistantships also available. Support available to part-time students. Financial award application deadline: 4/15; financial award applicants required to submit FAFSA. *Faculty research:* Biostatistics, community health, environmental health sciences, epidemiology, health policy and management, community health behavior and education, public health leadership. *Unit head:* Dr. Charles Hardy, Dean, 912-478-2674, Fax: 912-478-5811, E-mail: chardy@georgiasouthern.edu. *Application contact:* Dr. Charles Ziglar, Coordinator for Graduate Student Recruitment, 912-478-5635, Fax: 912-478-0740, E-mail: gradadmissions@georgiasouthern.edu.

Grand Valley State University, College of Liberal Arts and Sciences, Program in Biostatistics, Allendale, MI 49401-9403. Offers MS. *Faculty:* 5 full-time (1 woman). *Students:* 13 full-time (9 women), 11 part-time (3 women); includes 1 minority (Asian American or Pacific Islander), 2 international. Average age 29. 15 applicants, 73% accepted, 8 enrolled. In 2009, 9 master's awarded. *Entrance requirements:* For master's, minimum GPA of 3.0. Application fee: $30. *Financial support:* In 2009–10, 14 students received support, including 2 fellowships (averaging $1,610 per year), 14 research assistantships with tuition reimbursements available (averaging $7,851 per year); unspecified assistantships also available. *Faculty research:* Biometrical models, spatial methods, medical statistics, design of experiments. *Unit head:* Dr. Robert Downer, Director, 616-331-2247. *Application contact:* Dr. David Elrod, PSM Coordinator, 616-331-8643, E-mail: elrodd@gvsu.edu.

Harvard University, Graduate School of Arts and Sciences, Department of Biostatistics, Cambridge, MA 02138. Offers PhD. *Expenses:* Tuition: Full-time $33,696. Required fees: $1126. Full-time tuition and fees vary according to program.

Harvard University, School of Public Health, Department of Biostatistics, Boston, MA 02115-6096. Offers SM, PhD. Part-time programs available. *Faculty:* 46 full-time (15 women), 7 part-time/adjunct (3 women). *Students:* 77 full-time, 1 part-time; includes 18 minority (4 African Americans, 1 American Indian/Alaska Native, 10 Asian Americans or Pacific Islanders, 3 Hispanic Americans), 33 international. Average age 29. 44 applicants, 36% accepted, 6 enrolled. In 2009, 8 master's, 8 doctorates awarded. *Degree requirements:* For doctorate, thesis/dissertation, oral and written qualifying exams. *Entrance requirements:* For master's and doctorate, GRE, prior training in mathematics and/or statistics. Additional exam requirements/recommendations for international students: Required—TOEFL (minimum score 590 paper-based; 240 computer-based; 95 iBT); Recommended—IELTS (minimum score 7). *Application deadline:* For fall admission, 12/15 for domestic and international students. Application fee: $115. Electronic applications accepted. *Expenses:* Tuition: Full-time $33,696. Required fees: $1126. Full-time tuition and fees vary according to program. *Financial support:* Fellowships, research assistantships, teaching assistantships, Federal Work-Study, scholarships/grants, traineeships, tuition waivers (partial), and unspecified assistantships available. Support available to part-time students. Financial award application deadline: 2/8; financial award applicants required to submit FAFSA. *Faculty research:* Statistical genetics, clinical trials, cancer and AIDS research, environmental and mental health, dose response modeling. *Unit head:* Dr. Victor DeGruttola, Chair, 617-432-1056, Fax: 617-432-5619, E-mail: degrut@hsph.harvard.edu. *Application contact:* Vincent W. James, Director of Admissions, 617-432-1031, Fax: 617-432-7080, E-mail: admisofc@hsph.harvard.edu.

Hunter College of the City University of New York, Graduate School, Schools of the Health Professions, School of Health Sciences, Programs in Urban Public Health, Program in Epidemiology and Biostatistics, New York, NY 10021-5085. Offers MPH. Part-time and evening/weekend programs available. *Faculty:* 27 full-time (17 women), 3 part-time/adjunct (2 women). *Students:* 8 full-time (7 women), 16 part-time (10 women); includes 12 minority (6 African Americans, 5 Asian Americans or Pacific Islanders, 1 Hispanic American). Average age 32. 31 applicants, 61% accepted, 11 enrolled. *Degree requirements:* For master's, comprehensive exam, thesis optional, internship. *Entrance requirements:* For master's, GRE General Test, previous course work in calculus and statistics. Additional exam requirements/recommendations for international students: Required—TOEFL. *Application deadline:* For fall admission, 4/1 for domestic students; for spring admission, 11/1 for domestic students. Application fee: $125. *Expenses:* Tuition, state resident: full-time $7360; part-time $310 per credit. Required fees: $250 per semester. *Financial support:* In 2009–10, 6 fellowships were awarded; career-related internships or fieldwork, Federal Work-Study, institutionally sponsored loans, and tuition waivers (partial) also available. Support available to part-time students. Financial award application deadline: 3/1. *Unit head:* Victoria Frye, Coordinator, 212-481-7580, Fax: 212-481-5260, E-mail: vfrye@hunter.cuny.edu. *Application contact:* Milena Solo, Director for Graduate Admissions, 212-772-4288, Fax: 212-650-3336, E-mail: milena.solo@hunter.cuny.edu.

Iowa State University of Science and Technology, Graduate College, Interdisciplinary Programs, Bioinformatics and Computational Biology Program, Ames, IA 50011. Offers MS, PhD. *Students:* 52 full-time (19 women), 2 part-time (1 woman); includes 3 minority (all Asian Americans or Pacific Islanders), 34 international. In 2009, 2 master's, 11 doctorates awarded. *Degree requirements:* For doctorate, thesis/dissertation. *Entrance requirements:* For doctorate, GRE General Test. Additional exam requirements/recommendations for international students: Required—TOEFL (minimum score 550 paper-based; 213 computer-based; 79 iBT) or IELTS (minimum score 6.5). *Application deadline:* For fall admission, 1/15 priority date for domestic students, 1/15 for international students; for spring admission, 10/15 for domestic and international students. Application fee: $40 ($90 for international students). Electronic applications accepted. *Expenses:* Tuition, state resident: full-time $6716. Tuition, nonresident: full-time $8908. Tuition and fees vary according to course level, course load, program and student level. *Financial support:* In 2009–10, 48 research assistantships with full and partial tuition reimbursements (averaging $18,330 per year), 3 teaching assistantships (averaging $17,000 per year) were awarded; fellowships with full tuition reimbursements, scholarships/grants, traineeships, health care benefits, and unspecified assistantships also available. *Faculty research:* Functional and structural genomics, genome evolution, macromolecular structure and function, mathematical biology and biological statistics, metabolic and developmental networks. *Unit head:* Dr. Volker Brendel, Chair, Supervising Committee, 515-294-5122, Fax: 515-294-6790, E-mail: bcb@iastate.edu. *Application contact:* Dr. Volker Brendel, Chair, Supervising Committee, 515-294-5122, Fax: 515-294-6790, E-mail: bcb@iastate.edu.

The Johns Hopkins University, Bloomberg School of Public Health, Department of Biostatistics, Baltimore, MD 21205-2179. Offers bioinformatics (MHS); biostatistics (MHS, Sc M, PhD). Part-time programs available. *Faculty:* 34 full-time (11 women), 16 part-time/adjunct (3 women). *Students:* 47 full-time (22 women), 2 part-time (1 woman); includes 9 minority (3 African Americans, 5 Asian Americans or Pacific Islanders, 1 Hispanic American), 20 international. Average age 25. 197 applicants, 22% accepted, 22 enrolled. In 2009, 18 master's, 5 doctorates awarded. *Degree requirements:* For master's, comprehensive exam (for some programs), thesis (for some programs), written exam, final project; for doctorate, comprehensive exam, thesis/dissertation, 1 year full-time residency, oral and written exams. *Entrance requirements:* For master's and doctorate, GRE General Test, course work in calculus and matrix algebra, 3 letters of recommendation, curriculum vitae. Additional exam requirements/recommendations for international students: Required—TOEFL (minimum score 600 paper-based; 250 computer-based). *Application deadline:* For fall admission, 1/15 for domestic and international students. Applications are processed on a rolling basis. Application fee: $45. Electronic applications accepted. *Financial support:* In 2009–10, 49 students received support, including 33 research assistantships (averaging $22,000 per year); fellowships, Federal Work-Study, institutionally sponsored loans, scholarships/grants, traineeships, health care benefits, and unspecified assistantships also available. Financial award application deadline: 3/15; financial award applicants required to submit FAFSA. *Faculty research:* Statistical genetics, bioinformatics, statistical computing, statistical methods, environmental statistics. Total annual research expenditures: $4.2 million. *Unit head:* Dr. Karen Bandeen-Roche, Chair, 410-955-3067, Fax: 410-955-0958, E-mail: kbandeen@jhsph.edu. *Application contact:* Mary Joy Argo, Academic Administrator, 410-614-4454, Fax: 410-955-0958, E-mail: margo@jhsph.edu.

Loma Linda University, School of Public Health, Programs in Epidemiology and Biostatistics, Loma Linda, CA 92350. Offers MPH, MSPH, Dr PH, Postbaccalaureate Certificate. *Entrance requirements:* Additional exam requirements/recommendations for international students: Required—Michigan English Language Assessment Battery or TOEFL.

Louisiana State University Health Sciences Center, School of Graduate Studies in New Orleans, Department of Biostatistics, New Orleans, LA 70112-2223. Offers MPH, MS, PhD. Terminal master's awarded for partial completion of doctoral program. *Degree requirements:* For master's, comprehensive exam, thesis; for doctorate, comprehensive exam, thesis/dissertation. *Entrance requirements:* For master's and doctorate, GRE General Test. Additional exam requirements/recommendations for international students: Required—TOEFL. *Faculty research:* Longitudinal data, repeated measures, missing data, generalized estimating equations, multivariate methods.

McGill University, Faculty of Graduate and Postdoctoral Studies, Faculty of Medicine, Department of Epidemiology and Biostatistics, Montréal, QC H3A 2T5, Canada. Offers community health (M Sc); environmental health (M Sc); epidemiology and biostatistics (M Sc, PhD, Diploma); health care evaluation (M Sc); medical statistics (M Sc). *Accreditation:* CEPH (one or more programs are accredited).

Medical College of Georgia, School of Graduate Studies, Program in Biostatistics, Augusta, GA 30912. Offers MS, PhD. *Degree requirements:* For master's, thesis or alternative. *Entrance requirements:* For master's, GRE General Test, substantial mathematics background, computer literacy. Additional exam requirements/recommendations for international students: Required—TOEFL (minimum score 550 paper-based; 213 computer-based; 79 iBT). Electronic applications accepted. Full-time tuition and fees vary according to campus/location, program and student level. *Faculty research:* Computational biology, clinical trials, statistical genetics, statistical epidemiology, survival analysis.

Medical College of Wisconsin, Graduate School of Biomedical Sciences, Department of Population Health, Division of Biostatistics, Milwaukee, WI 53226-0509. Offers PhD. Part-time programs available. *Degree requirements:* For doctorate, comprehensive exam, thesis/dissertation. *Entrance requirements:* For doctorate, GRE General Test. Additional exam requirements/recommendations for international students: Required—TOEFL. Electronic applications accepted. *Faculty research:* Survival analysis, spatial statistics, time series, genetic statistics, Bayesian statistics.

See Close-Up on page 317.

Medical University of South Carolina, College of Graduate Studies, Division of Biostatistics and Epidemiology, Charleston, SC 29425. Offers biostatistics (MS, PhD); epidemiology (MS, PhD); DMD/PhD; MD/PhD. *Faculty:* 21 full-time (14 women), 1 part-time/adjunct (0 women). *Students:* 20 full-time (15 women), 1 (woman) part-time; includes 4 minority (3 African Americans, 1 Hispanic American), 4 international. Average age 29. 8 applicants, 63% accepted, 2 enrolled. In 2009, 6 master's, 9 doctorates awarded. Terminal master's awarded for partial completion of doctoral program. *Degree requirements:* For master's, thesis; for doctorate, thesis/dissertation, oral and written exams. *Entrance requirements:* For master's, GRE General Test; for doctorate, GRE General Test, interview, minimum GPA of 3.0. Additional exam requirements/recommendations for international students: Required—TOEFL (minimum score 600 paper-based; 250 computer-based; 100 iBT). *Application deadline:* For fall admission, 1/15 priority date for domestic and international students. Applications are processed on a rolling basis. Application fee: $0 ($85 for international students). Electronic applications accepted. *Financial support:* In 2009–10, 18 research assistantships with partial tuition reimbursements (averaging $23,000 per year) were awarded; Federal Work-Study and scholarships/grants also available. Support available to part-time students. Financial award application deadline: 3/10; financial award applicants required to submit FAFSA. *Faculty research:* Health disparities, central nervous system injuries, radiation exposure, analysis of clinical trial data, biomedical information. *Unit head:* Dr. Yuko Y. Palesch, Professor/Director, 843-876-1917, Fax: 843-792-6590, E-mail: paleschy@musc.edu. *Application contact:* Dr. Anbesaw Selassie, Associate Professor, 843-876-1140, Fax: 843-792-6590, E-mail: selassie@musc.edu.

Middle Tennessee State University, College of Graduate Studies, College of Basic and Applied Sciences, Program in Professional Science, Murfreesboro, TN 37132. Offers biostatistics (MS); health care informatics (MS). Part-time and evening/weekend programs available. Postbaccalaureate distance learning degree programs offered. *Students:* 5 full-time (2 women), 52 part-time (32 women); includes 27 minority (11 African Americans, 14 Asian Americans or Pacific Islanders, 2 Hispanic Americans). Average age 28. 40 applicants, 55% accepted, 22 enrolled. In 2009, 21 master's awarded. *Degree requirements:* For master's, comprehensive exam. *Entrance requirements:* For master's, GRE. Additional exam requirements/recommendations for international students: Required—TOEFL (minimum score 525 paper-based; 195 computer-based; 71 iBT) or IELTS (minimum score 6). *Application deadline:* For fall admission, 6/1 for domestic and international students. Applications are processed on a rolling basis. Application fee: $25 ($30 for international students). *Expenses:* Tuition, state resident: full-time $4404. Tuition, nonresident: full-time $10,956. *Financial support:* In 2009–10, 7 students received support. Institutionally sponsored loans available. Support available to part-time students. Financial award application deadline: 5/1. *Unit head:* Dr. Thomas Cheatham, Dean, 615-898-5508, Fax: 615-898-2615. *Application contact:* Dr. Michael Allen, Dean and Vice Provost for Research, 615-898-2840, Fax: 615-904-8020, E-mail: mallen@mtsu.edu.

New Jersey Institute of Technology, Office of Graduate Studies, College of Science and Liberal Arts, Department of Mathematical Science, Program in Biostatistics, Newark, NJ 07102. Offers MS. Part-time and evening/weekend programs available. Postbaccalaureate distance learning degree programs offered. Terminal master's awarded for partial completion of doctoral program. *Degree requirements:* For master's, thesis optional. *Entrance requirements:* For master's, GRE General Test. Additional exam requirements/recommendations for international students: Required—TOEFL (minimum score 550 paper-based; 213 computer-based; 79 iBT). Electronic applications accepted.

The Ohio State University, Graduate School, College of Mathematical and Physical Sciences, Department of Statistics, Program in Biostatistics, Columbus, OH 43210. Offers PhD. *Faculty:* 14. *Students:* 10 full-time (5 women), 5 part-time (all women); includes 1 minority (Asian American or Pacific Islander), 7 international. Average age 28. In 2009, 3 doctorates awarded. *Degree requirements:* For doctorate, thesis/dissertation. *Entrance requirements:* For doctorate, GRE General Test. Additional exam requirements/recommendations for international students: Required—TOEFL (minimum score 600 paper-based; 250 computer-based). *Application deadline:* For fall admission, 8/15 priority date for domestic students, 7/1 priority date for international students; for winter admission, 12/1 priority date for domestic students, 11/1 priority date for international students; for spring admission, 3/1 priority date for domestic students, 2/1 priority date for international students. Applications are processed on a rolling basis. Application fee: $40 ($50 for international students). Electronic applications accepted. *Expenses:* Tuition, state resident: full-time $10,683. Tuition, nonresident: full-time $25,923. Tuition and fees vary according to course load and program. *Financial support:* Fellowships, research assistantships, teaching assistantships, Federal Work-Study and institutionally sponsored loans available. Support available to part-time students. *Unit head:* Elizabeth A. Stasny, Graduate Studies Committee Chair, 614-292-0784, Fax: 614-292-2096, E-mail: stasny.1@osu.edu. *Application contact:* 614-292-9444, Fax: 614-292-3895, E-mail: domestic.grad@osu.edu.

Oregon Health & Science University, School of Medicine, Department of Public Health and Preventive Medicine, Portland, OR 97239-3098. Offers epidemiology and biostatistics (MPH). *Accreditation:* CEPH. Part-time programs available. *Degree requirements:* For master's, thesis, fieldwork/internship. *Entrance requirements:* For master's, GRE General Test, previous undergraduate course work in statistics. Additional exam requirements/recommendations for international students: Required—TOEFL. Tuition and fees vary according to course level, course load, degree level, program and reciprocity agreements. *Faculty research:* Health services, health care access, health policy, environmental and occupational health.

Rice University, Graduate Programs, George R. Brown School of Engineering, Department of Statistics, Houston, TX 77251-1892. Offers bioinformatics (PhD); biostatistics (PhD); computational finance (PhD); general statistics (PhD); statistics (M Stat, MA); MBA/M Stat. Part-time programs available. *Faculty:* 16 full-time (6 women), 1 part-time/adjunct (0 women). *Students:* 45 full-time (20 women), 3 part-time (2 women); includes 12 minority (1 African American, 5 Asian Americans or Pacific Islanders, 6 Hispanic Americans), 16 international. Average age 28. 112 applicants, 41% accepted, 20 enrolled. In 2009, 9 master's, 7 doctorates awarded. *Degree requirements:* For master's, comprehensive exam; for doctorate, comprehensive exam, thesis/dissertation. *Entrance requirements:* For master's and doctorate, GRE General Test, minimum GPA of 3.0. Additional exam requirements/recommendations for international students: Required—TOEFL (minimum score 630 paper-based; 250 computer-based; 90 iBT). *Application deadline:* For fall admission, 1/15 priority date for domestic and international students; for spring admission, 11/1 for international students. Applications are processed on a rolling basis. Application fee: $70. Electronic applications accepted. *Financial support:* In 2009–10, 13 students received support, including 1 fellowship with full tuition reimbursement available (averaging $15,000 per year), 19 research assistantships with full tuition reimbursements available (averaging $23,000 per year), 9 teaching assistantships with full tuition reimbursements available (averaging $17,250 per year); career-related internships or fieldwork, institutionally sponsored loans, scholarships/grants, traineeships, health care benefits, tuition waivers (full), and unspecified assistantships also available. *Faculty research:* Statistical genetics, non parametric function estimation, computational statistics and visualization, stochastic processes. Total annual research expenditures: $800,000. *Unit head:* Carolyn Duhon, Sr. Department Administrator, 713-348-6032, Fax: 713-348-5476, E-mail: stat@rice.edu. *Application contact:* Margaret Poon, Department Coordinator, 713-348-6032, Fax: 713-348-5476, E-mail: poon@rice.edu.

Rutgers, The State University of New Jersey, New Brunswick, Graduate School-New Brunswick, BioMaPS Institute for Quantitative Biology, Piscataway, NJ 08854-8097. Offers computational biology and molecular biophysics (PhD). *Degree requirements:* For doctorate, comprehensive exam, thesis/dissertation. *Entrance requirements:* For doctorate, GRE. Additional exam requirements/recommendations for international students: Required—TOEFL. Electronic applications accepted. *Faculty research:* Structural biology, systems biology, bioinformatics, translational medicine, genomics.

Rutgers, The State University of New Jersey, New Brunswick, Graduate School-New Brunswick, Program in Statistics, Piscataway, NJ 08854-8097. Offers applied statistics (MS); biostatistics (MS); data mining (MS); quality and productivity management (MS); statistics (MS, PhD). Part-time programs available. Terminal master's awarded for partial completion of doctoral program. *Degree requirements:* For master's, comprehensive exam, essay, exam, non-thesis essay paper; for doctorate, one foreign language, thesis/dissertation, qualifying oral and written exams. *Entrance requirements:* For master's, GRE General Test; for doctorate, GRE General Test, GRE Subject Test (recommended). Additional exam requirements/recommendations for international students: Required—TOEFL (minimum score 550 paper-based; 213 computer-based). Electronic applications accepted. *Faculty research:* Probability, decision theory, linear models, multivariate statistics, statistical computing.

San Diego State University, Graduate and Research Affairs, College of Health and Human Services, Graduate School of Public Health, San Diego, CA 92182. Offers environmental health (MPH); epidemiology (MPH, PhD), including biostatistics (MPH); global emergency preparedness and response (MS); global health (PhD); health behavior (PhD); health promotion (MPH); health services administration (MPH); toxicology (MS); MPH/MA; MSW/MPH. *Accreditation:* ABET (one or more programs are accredited); CAHME (one or more programs are accredited); CEPH (one or more programs are accredited). Part-time programs available. *Degree requirements:* For master's, comprehensive exam (for some programs), thesis (for some programs); for doctorate, thesis/dissertation. *Entrance requirements:* For master's, GMAT (MPH in health services administration), GRE General Test; for doctorate, GRE General Test. Additional exam requirements/recommendations for international students: Required—TOEFL. *Faculty research:* Evaluation of tobacco, AIDS prevalence and prevention, mammography, infant death project, Alzheimer's in elderly Chinese.

Tufts University, Sackler School of Graduate Biomedical Sciences, Division of Clinical Care Research, Medford, MA 02155. Offers MS, PhD. *Faculty:* 37 full-time (11 women). *Students:* 23 full-time (15 women), 1 part-time (0 women); includes 5 minority (1 African American, 4 Asian Americans or Pacific Islanders), 10 international. Average age 33. 32 applicants, 41% accepted, 13 enrolled. In 2009, 7 master's awarded. Terminal master's awarded for partial completion of doctoral program. *Degree requirements:* For master's, thesis; for doctorate, thesis/dissertation. *Entrance requirements:* For master's and doctorate, MD or PhD, strong clinical research background. Additional exam requirements/recommendations for international students: Required—TOEFL. *Application deadline:* For fall admission, 12/15 for domestic and international students. Applications are processed on a rolling basis. Application fee: $70. Electronic applications accepted. *Expenses:* Tuition: Full-time $38,096; part-time $3962 per credit. Required fees: $686; $40 per year. Tuition and fees vary according to course level, course load, degree level, program and student level. *Financial support:* In 2009–10, 27 fellowships with full tuition reimbursements were awarded. Financial award application deadline: 12/15. *Faculty research:* Clinical study design, mathematical modeling, meta analysis, epidemiologic research, coronary heart disease. *Unit head:* Dr. Harry P. Selker, Program Director, 617-636-5009, Fax: 617-636-8023, E-mail: hselker@lifespan.org. *Application contact:* Kellie Johnston, Associate Director of Admissions, 617-636-6767, Fax: 617-636-0375, E-mail: sackler-school@tufts.edu.

Tulane University, School of Public Health and Tropical Medicine, Department of Biostatistics, New Orleans, LA 70118-5669. Offers MS, MSPH, PhD, Sc D. MS and PhD offered through the Graduate School. Part-time programs available. *Degree requirements:* For doctorate, comprehensive exam, thesis/dissertation. *Entrance requirements:* For master's and doctorate, GRE General Test. Additional exam requirements/recommendations for international students: Required—TOEFL. Electronic applications accepted. *Faculty research:* Clinical trials, measurement, longitudinal analyses.

University at Albany, State University of New York, School of Public Health, Department of Epidemiology and Biostatistics, Albany, NY 12222-0001. Offers MS, PhD. *Degree requirements:* For master's, thesis; for doctorate, thesis/dissertation. *Entrance requirements:* For master's and doctorate, GRE General Test. Additional exam requirements/recommendations for international students: Required—TOEFL (minimum score 550 paper-based; 213 computer-based). Electronic applications accepted.

University at Buffalo, the State University of New York, Graduate School, School of Public Health and Health Professions, Department of Biostatistics, Buffalo, NY 14260. Offers MA, PhD. *Faculty:* 10 full-time (3 women), 2 part-time/adjunct (0 women). *Students:* 32 full-time (19 women), 7 part-time (3 women); includes 8 minority (2 African Americans, 6 Asian Americans or Pacific Islanders), 21 international. Average age 31. 99 applicants, 58% accepted, 24 enrolled. In 2009, 11 master's, 2 doctorates awarded. Terminal master's awarded for partial completion of doctoral program. *Degree requirements:* For master's, comprehensive exam, thesis optional, final oral exam, practical data analysis experience; for doctorate, comprehensive exam, thesis/dissertation, final oral exam. *Entrance requirements:* For master's, GRE, 3 semesters of course work in calculus (mathematics), course work in real analysis (preferred), course work in linear algebra; for doctorate, GRE, master's degree in statistics, biostatistics or equivalent. Additional exam requirements/recommendations for international students: Required—TOEFL (minimum score 640 paper-based; 250 computer-based; 79 iBT). *Application deadline:* For fall admission, 4/1 priority date for domestic and international students. Application fee: $50. Electronic applications accepted. *Financial support:* In 2009–10, 2 fellowships (averaging $4,000 per year), 8 research assistantships with full tuition reimbursements (averaging $15,000 per year), 5 teaching assistantships with full tuition reimbursements (averaging $12,000 per year) were awarded; tuition waivers (partial) also available. Financial award application deadline: 2/1; financial award applicants required to submit FAFSA. *Faculty research:* Biostatistics, longitudinal data analysis, nonparametrics, statistical genetics, epidemiology. Total annual research expenditures: $1.9 million. *Unit head:* Dr. Alan D. Hutson, Chair and Associate Professor, 716-829-2594, Fax: 716-829-2200, E-mail: ahutson@buffalo.edu. *Application contact:* Dr. Randolph L. Carter, Associate Chair and Professor, 716-829-2884, Fax: 716-829-2200, E-mail: rcarter@buffalo.edu.

The University of Alabama at Birmingham, School of Public Health, Program in Biostatistics, Birmingham, AL 35294. Offers MS, PhD. *Degree requirements:* For master's, variable foreign language requirement, thesis, fieldwork, research project; for doctorate, variable foreign language requirement, comprehensive exam, thesis/dissertation. *Entrance requirements:* For master's, GRE General Test or MAT, minimum GPA of 3.0; for doctorate, GRE General Test or MAT, MPH or MSPH, minimum GPA of 3.0, interview. Electronic applications accepted. *Expenses:* Contact institution.

University of Alberta, Faculty of Graduate Studies and Research, Department of Mathematical and Statistical Sciences, Edmonton, AB T6G 2E1, Canada. Offers applied mathematics (M Sc, PhD); biostatistics (M Sc); mathematical finance (M Sc, PhD); mathematical physics (M Sc, PhD); mathematics (M Sc, PhD); statistics (M Sc, PhD, Postgraduate Diploma). Part-time programs available. *Faculty:* 48 full-time (4 women). *Students:* 112 full-time (41 women), 5 part-time (0 women). Average age 24. 776 applicants, 5% accepted, 34 enrolled. In 2009, 12 master's, 10 doctorates awarded. Terminal master's awarded for partial completion of doctoral program. *Degree requirements:* For master's, thesis (for some programs); for doctorate, comprehensive exam, thesis/dissertation. *Entrance requirements:* Additional exam requirements/recommendations for international students: Required—TOEFL (minimum score 580 paper-based; 237 computer-based). *Application deadline:* For fall admission, 3/1 for domestic students, 2/1 for international students. Applications are processed on a rolling basis. Application fee: $0. Electronic applications accepted. Tuition and fees charges are reported in Canadian dollars. *Expenses:* Tuition, area resident: Full-time $4626.24 Canadian dollars; part-time $99.72 Canadian dollars per unit. International tuition: $8216 Canadian dollars full-time. Required fees: $3589.92 Canadian dollars; $99.72 Canadian dollars per unit. $215 Canadian dollars per term. *Financial support:* In 2009–10, 51 research assistantships, 88 teaching assistantships with full and partial tuition reimbursements were awarded; scholarships/grants also available. Financial award application deadline: 5/1. *Faculty research:* Classical and functional analysis, algebra, differential equations, geometry. *Unit head:* Dr. Anthony To-Ming Lau, Chair, 403-492-5141, E-mail: tlau@math.ualberta.ca. *Application contact:* Dr. Yau Shu Wong, Associate Chair, Graduate Studies, 403-492-5799, Fax: 403-492-6828, E-mail: gradmail@math.ualberta.ca.

The University of Arizona, Mel and Enid Zuckerman College of Public Health, Program in Biostatistics, Tucson, AZ 85721. Offers PhD. *Students:* 4 full-time (2 women), 3 part-time (all women); includes 2 minority (1 African American, 1 Hispanic American), 2 international. Average age 36. 18 applicants, 28% accepted, 2 enrolled. *Entrance requirements:* Additional exam requirements/recommendations for international students: Required—TOEFL (minimum score 550 paper-based; 213 computer-based; 79 iBT). *Application deadline:* For fall admission, 1/1 for domestic and international students. Applications are processed on a rolling basis. Application fee: $75. Electronic applications accepted. *Expenses:* Tuition, state resident: full-time $9028. Tuition, nonresident: full-time $24,890. *Unit head:* Dr. Iman Hakim, Interim Dean, 520-626-7083, E-mail: ihakim@email.arizona.edu. *Application contact:* Lorraine Varela, Special Assistant to the Dean, 520-626-3201, E-mail: varelal@coph.arizona.edu.

University of California, Berkeley, Graduate Division, School of Public Health, Group in Biostatistics, Berkeley, CA 94720-1500. Offers MA, PhD. *Accreditation:* CEPH (one or more programs are accredited). *Faculty:* 5. *Students:* 38 full-time (23 women). Average age 31. 58 applicants, 11 enrolled. In 2009, 8 master's, 7 doctorates awarded. *Degree requirements:* For master's, oral exam; for doctorate, thesis/dissertation, oral exam. *Entrance requirements:* For master's and doctorate, GRE General Test, minimum GPA of 3.0, 3 letters of recommendation. Additional exam requirements/recommendations for international students: Required—TOEFL. *Application deadline:* For fall admission, 12/1 for domestic students. Applications are processed on a rolling basis. Application fee: $70 ($90 for international students). *Financial support:* Fellowships with full tuition reimbursements, career-related internships or fieldwork, Federal Work-Study, institutionally sponsored loans, and unspecified assistantships available. Financial award applicants required to submit FAFSA. *Unit head:* Prof. Sandrine Dudoit, Chair, 510-642-3241, E-mail: biostat@berkeley.edu. *Application contact:* Matthew Lau, Receptionist, 510-643-0881, Fax: 510-643-4404, E-mail: sphinfo@berkeley.edu.

University of California, Davis, Graduate Studies, Graduate Group in Biostatistics, Davis, CA 95616. Offers MS, PhD. *Degree requirements:* For master's, comprehensive exam; for doctorate, thesis/dissertation. *Entrance requirements:* Additional exam requirements/recommendations for international students: Required—TOEFL (minimum score 550 paper-based; 213 computer-based). Electronic applications accepted.

University of California, Los Angeles, Graduate Division, School of Public Health, Department of Biostatistics, Los Angeles, CA 90095. Offers MPH, MS, Dr PH, PhD. *Degree requirements:* For master's, comprehensive exam; for doctorate, thesis/dissertation, oral and written qualifying exams. *Entrance requirements:* For master's, GRE General Test, minimum GPA of 3.0; for doctorate, GRE General Test, minimum undergraduate GPA of 3.0. Electronic applications accepted.

University of Cincinnati, Graduate School, College of Medicine, Graduate Programs in Biomedical Sciences, Department of Environmental Health, Cincinnati, OH 45221. Offers environmental and industrial hygiene (MS, PhD); environmental and occupational medicine (MS); environmental genetics and molecular toxicology (MS, PhD); epidemiology and biostatistics (MS, PhD); occupational safety and ergonomics (MS, PhD). *Accreditation:* ABET (one or more programs are accredited). Terminal master's awarded for partial completion of doctoral program. *Degree requirements:* For master's, thesis; for doctorate, thesis/dissertation,

Biostatistics

University of Cincinnati (continued)

qualifying exam. *Entrance requirements:* For master's, GRE General Test, bachelor's degree in science; for doctorate, GRE General Test. Additional exam requirements/recommendations for international students: Required—TOEFL (minimum score 600 paper-based; 250 computer-based; 100 iBT). Electronic applications accepted. *Faculty research:* Carcinogens and mutagenesis, pulmonary studies, reproduction and development.

University of Colorado Denver, Colorado School of Public Health, Program in Biostatistics, Denver, CO 80262. Offers MS, PhD. *Students:* 20 full-time (9 women), 14 part-time (7 women); includes 5 minority (1 American Indian/Alaska Native, 3 Asian Americans or Pacific Islanders, 1 Hispanic American), 2 international. In 2009, 7 master's awarded. *Degree requirements:* For master's, comprehensive exam, thesis; for doctorate, comprehensive exam, thesis/dissertation. *Entrance requirements:* For master's, GRE General Test, minimum GPA of 3.0, 2 semesters of course work in calculus; for doctorate, GRE General Test, minimum GPA of 3.0; 2 semesters of calculus; MS in biometrics, biostatistics, statistics or equivalent. Additional exam requirements/recommendations for international students: Required—TOEFL (minimum score 550 paper-based; 213 computer-based). *Application deadline:* For fall admission, 2/1 for domestic students. Application fee: $50. *Financial support:* Application deadline: 3/1; *Faculty research:* Health policy research, nonlinear mixed effects models for longitudinal data, statistical methods in nutrition, clinical trials. *Unit head:* Dr. Gary Grunwald, Director, 303-724-4360, Fax: 303-724-4620, E-mail: gary.grunwald@ucdenver.edu. *Application contact:* Fayette Augillard, Program Coordinator, 303-724-4442, Fax: 303-724-4620, E-mail: fayette.augillard@ucdenver.edu.

University of Florida, Graduate School, College of Public Health and Health Professions and College of Medicine, Programs in Public Health, Gainesville, FL 32611. Offers biostatistics (MPH); environmental health (MPH); epidemiology (MPH); public health management and policy (MPH); public health practice (MPH); social and behavioral sciences (MPH). *Entrance requirements:* For master's, GRE General Test, minimum GPA of 3.0. Additional exam requirements/recommendations for international students: Required—TOEFL (minimum score 550 paper-based; 213 computer-based).

University of Illinois at Chicago, Graduate College, School of Public Health, Biostatistics Section, Chicago, IL 60607-7128. Offers biostatistics (MS, PhD); quantitative methods (MPH). Part-time programs available. Terminal master's awarded for partial completion of doctoral program. *Degree requirements:* For master's, thesis, field practicum; for doctorate, thesis/dissertation, independent research, internship. *Entrance requirements:* For master's and doctorate, GRE General Test, minimum GPA of 2.75. Additional exam requirements/recommendations for international students: Required—TOEFL. Electronic applications accepted.

The University of Iowa, Graduate College, College of Public Health, Department of Biostatistics, Iowa City, IA 52242-1316. Offers MS, PhD. *Degree requirements:* For master's, thesis optional, exam; for doctorate, comprehensive exam, thesis/dissertation. *Entrance requirements:* For master's and doctorate, GRE General Test, minimum GPA of 3.0. Additional exam requirements/recommendations for international students: Required—TOEFL (minimum score 600 paper-based; 250 computer-based; 100 iBT). Electronic applications accepted.

The University of Kansas, University of Kansas Medical Center, School of Medicine, Department of Biostatistics, Kansas City, KS 66160. Offers MS, PhD. *Faculty:* 10 full-time. *Entrance requirements:* For master's, GRE, Calculus I-III, computer programming, linear algebra, differential equations, numerical analysis; for doctorate, Master's. Additional exam requirements/recommendations for international students: Required—TOEFL. *Expenses:* Tuition, state resident: full-time $6492; part-time $270.50 per credit hour. Tuition, nonresident: full-time $15,510; part-time $646.25 per credit hour. Required fees: $847; $70.56 per credit hour. Tuition and fees vary according to course load and program. *Financial support:* Scholarships/grants, traineeships, and unspecified assistantships available. *Faculty research:* Biostatistics, clinical trials. *Unit head:* Dr. Matthew Mayo, Chair and Professor, 913-588-4735 Ext. 913, Fax: 913-588-0252, E-mail: mmayo@kumc.edu. *Application contact:* Tami Walz, Marketing, Recruitment and Graduate Education Coordinator, 913-588-2757, Fax: 913-588-0252, E-mail: twalz@kumc.edu.

University of Louisville, Graduate School, School of Public Health and Information Sciences, Department of Bioinformatics and Biostatistics, Louisville, KY 40292-0001. Offers biostatistics (MS, PhD); decision science (MS). Part-time programs available. *Faculty:* 10 full-time (3 women), 1 part-time/adjunct (0 women). *Students:* 16 full-time (6 women), 6 part-time (4 women); includes 2 minority (both Asian Americans or Pacific Islanders), 10 international. Average age 33. 22 applicants, 64% accepted, 9 enrolled. In 2009, 1 master's, 4 doctorates awarded. *Entrance requirements:* For master's, GRE (minimum 85th percentile quantitative), 2 letters of recommendation; for doctorate, GRE (85% or higher in Quantitative section), 2 letters of recommendation. Additional exam requirements/recommendations for international students: Required—TOEFL (minimum score 547 paper-based; 210 computer-based; 78 iBT). *Application deadline:* For fall admission, 3/1 for domestic and international students. Application fee: $50. Electronic applications accepted. *Financial support:* In 2009–10, 9 students received support, including 3 research assistantships with full tuition reimbursements available (averaging $20,000 per year); unspecified assistantships also available. Financial award application deadline: 5/1; financial award applicants required to submit FAFSA. *Faculty research:* Bioinformatics, compound decision problems, infectious disease modeling, inference, statistical genetics, genomics, clinical trials, information theory, utility theory and measurement. Total annual research expenditures: $222,000. *Unit head:* Dr. Robert Esterhay, Interim Department Chair, 502-852-6135, Fax: 502-852-3294, E-mail: robert.esterhay@louisville.edu. *Application contact:* Vicki Lewis, Administrative Assistant, 502-852-1798, Fax: 502-852-3294, E-mail: vicki.lewis@louisville.edu.

University of Maryland, Baltimore, School of Medicine, Department of Epidemiology and Preventive Medicine, Baltimore, MD 21201. Offers biostatistics (MS); clinical research (MS); epidemiology (PhD); epidemiology and preventive medicine (MPH, MS); gerontology (PhD); human genetics and genomic (MS, PhD); molecular epidemiology (PhD); toxicology (MS, PhD); JD/MS; MD/PhD; MS/PhD. *Accreditation:* CEPH. Part-time programs available. *Students:* 64 full-time (42 women), 60 part-time (40 women); includes 40 minority (17 African Americans, 19 Asian Americans or Pacific Islanders, 4 Hispanic Americans), 16 international. Average age 31. 207 applicants, 48% accepted, 50 enrolled. In 2009, 24 master's, 9 doctorates awarded. *Entrance requirements:* For master's and doctorate, GRE General Test, minimum GPA of 3.0. Additional exam requirements/recommendations for international students: Required—TOEFL; Recommended—IELTS. *Application deadline:* For fall admission, 1/15 for domestic and international students. Application fee: $50. Electronic applications accepted. *Expenses:* Tuition, state resident: full-time $7290; part-time $405 per credit hour. Tuition, nonresident: full-time $12,780; part-time $710 per credit hour. Required fees: $774; $10 per credit hour. $297 per semester. Tuition and fees vary according to course load, degree level and program. *Financial support:* In 2009–10, research assistantships with partial tuition reimbursements (averaging $25,000 per year); fellowships also available. Financial award application deadline: 3/1. *Unit head:* Dr. Patricia Langenberg, Program Director, 410-706-3251, Fax: 410-706-8013. *Application contact:* Rachael Holmes, Academic Coordinator, 410-706-8492, Fax: 410-706-4225, E-mail: rholmes@epi.umaryland.edu.

University of Maryland, Baltimore County, Graduate School, College of Natural and Mathematical Sciences, Department of Mathematics and Statistics, Program in Statistics, Baltimore, MD 21250. Offers biostatistics (PhD); environmental statistics (MS); statistics (MS, PhD). Part-time and evening/weekend programs available. *Faculty:* 9 full-time (2 women). *Students:* 28 full-time (16 women), 20 part-time (4 women); includes 9 minority (3 African Americans, 6 Asian Americans or Pacific Islanders), 19 international. Average age 30. 51 applicants, 61% accepted, 16 enrolled. In 2009, 7 master's awarded. Terminal master's awarded for partial completion of doctoral program. *Degree requirements:* For master's, comprehensive exam (for some programs), thesis (for some programs); for doctorate, comprehensive exam, thesis/dissertation. *Entrance requirements:* For master's and doctorate, GRE General Test, minimum GPA of 3.0. Additional exam requirements/recommendations for international students: Required—TOEFL (minimum score 600 paper-based; 250 computer-based; 100 iBT). *Application deadline:* For fall admission, 2/15 priority date for domestic students, 1/1 priority date for international students; for spring admission, 10/15 priority date for domestic students, 5/1 priority date for international students. Applications are processed on a rolling basis. Application fee: $50. Electronic applications accepted. *Financial support:* In 2009–10, 21 students received support, including 3 research assistantships with full tuition reimbursements available (averaging $15,500 per year), 18 teaching assistantships with full tuition reimbursements available (averaging $15,500 per year); fellowships with full tuition reimbursements available, career-related internships or fieldwork, scholarships/grants, health care benefits, tuition waivers (full and partial), and unspecified assistantships also available. Support available to part-time students. Financial award application deadline: 2/15. *Faculty research:* Design of experiments, statistical decision theory and inference, time series analysis, biostatistics and environmental statistics, bioinformatics. Total annual research expenditures: $496,334. *Unit head:* Dr. Anindya Roy, Director, 410-455-2435, Fax: 410-455-1066, E-mail: anindya@math.umbc.edu. *Application contact:* Dr. Anindya Roy, Director, 410-455-2435, Fax: 410-455-1066, E-mail: anindya@math.umbc.edu.

University of Maryland, College Park, Academic Affairs, School of Public Health, Department of Epidemiology and Biostatistics, College Park, MD 20742. Offers biostatistics (MPH); epidemiology (MPH, PhD). *Faculty:* 12 full-time (9 women), 2 part-time/adjunct (1 woman). *Students:* 5 full-time (3 women); includes 2 minority (1 Asian American or Pacific Islander, 1 Hispanic American). 37 applicants, 8% accepted, 3 enrolled. *Application deadline:* For fall admission, 1/15 for domestic and international students; for spring admission, 6/1 for international students. *Expenses:* Tuition, area resident: Part-time $471 per credit hour. Tuition, state resident: part-time $471 per credit hour. Tuition, nonresident: part-time $1016 per credit hour. Required fees: $337.04 per term. *Financial support:* In 2009–10, 3 fellowships with full tuition reimbursements (averaging $22,544 per year), 2 research assistantships (averaging $15,878 per year), 1 teaching assistantship (averaging $15,694 per year) were awarded. Total annual research expenditures: $988,635. *Unit head:* Dr. Deborah Young, Chair, 301-405-2496, E-mail: dryoung@umd.edu. *Application contact:* Dean of Graduate School, 301-405-0358.

University of Maryland, College Park, Academic Affairs, School of Public Health, Department of Public and Community Health, College Park, MD 20742. Offers biostatistics (MPH); community health education (MPH); environmental health sciences (MPH); epidemiology (MPH); public/community health (PhD). *Accreditation:* CEPH. Part-time and evening/weekend programs available. *Faculty:* 26 full-time (16 women), 7 part-time/adjunct (6 women). *Students:* 56 full-time (47 women), 31 part-time (29 women); includes 25 minority (19 African Americans, 4 Asian Americans or Pacific Islanders, 2 Hispanic Americans), 12 international. 252 applicants, 25% accepted, 25 enrolled. In 2009, 14 master's, 4 doctorates awarded. *Degree requirements:* For master's, thesis optional; for doctorate, comprehensive exam, thesis/dissertation. *Entrance requirements:* For master's, GRE General Test, minimum GPA of 3.0, 3 letters of recommendation; for doctorate, GRE General Test, minimum GPA of 3.5, 3 letters of recommendation. Additional exam requirements/recommendations for international students: Required—TOEFL. *Application deadline:* For fall admission, 1/15 for domestic and international students; for spring admission, 6/1 for international students. Applications are processed on a rolling basis. Application fee: $60. Electronic applications accepted. *Expenses:* Tuition, area resident: Part-time $471 per credit hour. Tuition, state resident: part-time $471 per credit hour. Tuition, nonresident: part-time $1016 per credit hour. Required fees: $337.04 per term. *Financial support:* In 2009–10, 14 research assistantships with tuition reimbursements (averaging $15,827 per year), 21 teaching assistantships with tuition reimbursements (averaging $16,363 per year) were awarded; fellowships, career-related internships or fieldwork, Federal Work-Study, and scholarships/grants also available. Support available to part-time students. Financial award applicants required to submit FAFSA. *Faculty research:* Controlling stress and tension, women's health, aging and public policy, adolescent health, long-term care. Total annual research expenditures: $3.2 million. *Unit head:* Dr. Elbert Glover, Chair, 301-405-2467, Fax: 301-314-9167, E-mail: eglover1@umd.edu. *Application contact:* Dean of Graduate School, 301-405-0358.

University of Massachusetts Amherst, Graduate School, School of Public Health and Health Sciences, Department of Public Health, Amherst, MA 01003. Offers biostatistics (MS, PhD); community health education (MS); environmental health sciences (MPH, MS); epidemiology (MPH, MS); health policy and management (MPH, MS); nutrition (PhD); public health practice (MPH). *Accreditation:* CEPH (one or more programs are accredited). Part-time and evening/weekend programs available. Postbaccalaureate distance learning degree programs offered (no on-campus study). *Faculty:* 38 full-time (23 women). *Students:* 96 full-time (71 women), 232 part-time (153 women); includes 41 minority (14 African Americans, 17 Asian Americans or Pacific Islanders, 10 Hispanic Americans), 65 international. Average age 36. 316 applicants, 61% accepted, 79 enrolled. In 2009, 91 master's, 5 doctorates awarded. Terminal master's awarded for partial completion of doctoral program. *Degree requirements:* For master's, thesis (for some programs); for doctorate, comprehensive exam, thesis/dissertation. *Entrance requirements:* For master's and doctorate, GRE General Test. Additional exam requirements/recommendations for international students: Required—TOEFL (minimum score 550 paper-based; 213 computer-based; 80 iBT), IELTS (minimum score 6.5). *Application deadline:* For fall admission, 2/1 for domestic and international students. Applications are processed on a rolling basis. Application fee: $40 ($65 for international students). Electronic applications accepted. *Expenses:* Tuition, state resident: full-time $2640; part-time $110 per credit. Tuition, nonresident: full-time $9936; part-time $414 per credit. Tuition and fees vary according to course load. *Financial support:* In 2009–10, 3 fellowships with full tuition reimbursements (averaging $2,791 per year), 32 research assistantships with full tuition reimbursements (averaging $9,196 per year), 24 teaching assistantships with full tuition reimbursements (averaging $5,789 per year) were awarded; career-related internships or fieldwork, Federal Work-Study, scholarships/grants, traineeships, health care benefits, tuition waivers (full), and unspecified assistantships also available. Support available to part-time students. Financial award application deadline: 2/1. *Unit head:* Dr. Paula Stamps, Graduate Program Director, 413-545-2861, Fax: 413-545-0964. *Application contact:* Jean M. Ames, Supervisor of Admissions, 413-545-0722, Fax: 413-577-0010, E-mail: gradadm@grad.umass.edu.

University of Medicine and Dentistry of New Jersey, UMDNJ–School of Public Health (UMDNJ, Rutgers, NJIT) Piscataway/New Brunswick Campus, Piscataway, NJ 08854. Offers biostatistics (MS); epidemiology (Certificate); general public health (Certificate); public health (MPH, Dr PH, PhD); DO/MPH; MD/MPH; MPH/MBA; MPH/MSPA; Psy D/MPH. *Degree requirements:* For master's, internship; for doctorate, thesis/dissertation. *Entrance requirements:* For master's, GRE General Test; for doctorate, GRE General Test, MPH (Dr PH); MA, MPH, or MS (PhD). Additional exam requirements/recommendations for international students: Required—TOEFL. Electronic applications accepted.

University of Memphis, Graduate School, School of Public Health, Memphis, TN 38152. Offers biostatistics (MPH); environmental health (MPH); epidemiology (MPH); health systems management (MPH); public health (MHA); social and behavioral sciences (MPH). Part-time and evening/weekend programs available. Postbaccalaureate distance learning degree programs offered. *Faculty:* 5 full-time (2 women), 4 part-time/adjunct (2 women). *Students:* 45 full-time (23 women), 29 part-time (14 women); includes 19 African Americans, 6 Asian Americans or Pacific Islanders, 2 Hispanic Americans, 7 international. Average age 32. 57 applicants, 70% accepted, 22 enrolled. In 2009, 17 master's awarded. *Degree requirements:* For master's, comprehensive exam, thesis. *Entrance requirements:* For master's, GRE, MAT, DAT, GMAT or LSAT, letters of recommendation. Additional exam requirements/recommendations for international students: Required—TOEFL. *Application deadline:* For fall admission, 11/1 for domestic students; for spring admission, 4/1 for domestic students. Application fee: $35 ($60 for international students). Electronic applications accepted. *Expenses:* Tuition, state resident: full-time $6246; part-time $347 per credit hour. Tuition, nonresident: full-time $15,894; part-time $883 per credit hour. Required fees: $1160. Full-time tuition and fees vary according to course load, degree level and program. *Financial support:* In 2009–10, 46 students received support; research assistantships with full tuition reimbursements available, Federal Work-Study, scholarships/grants, and unspecified assistantships available. Financial award application deadline: 2/15; financial award applicants required to submit FAFSA. *Faculty research:* Health and medical savings accounts, adoption rates, health informatics, Telehealth technologies, biostatistics, environmental health, epidemiology, health systems management, social and behavioral sciences. *Unit head:* Dr. Lisa M. Klesges, Director, 901-678-4637, E-mail: lmklsges@memphis.edu. *Application contact:* Dr. Lisa M. Klesges, Director, 901-678-4637, E-mail: lmklsges@memphis.edu.

University of Michigan, School of Public Health, Department of Biostatistics, Ann Arbor, MI 48109. Offers MPH, MS, PhD. MS and PhD offered through the Horace H. Rackham School of Graduate Studies. *Faculty:* 27 full-time (11 women), 10 part-time/adjunct (3 women). *Students:* 120 full-time (60 women); includes 78 minority (all Asian Americans or Pacific Islanders), 76 international. Average age 27. 226 applicants, 43% accepted, 31 enrolled. In 2009, 30 master's, 7 doctorates awarded. Terminal master's awarded for partial completion of doctoral program. *Degree requirements:* For doctorate, oral defense of dissertation, preliminary exam. *Entrance requirements:* For master's, GRE General Test; for doctorate, GRE General Test, master's degree. Additional exam requirements/recommendations for international students: Required—TOEFL (minimum score 560 paper-based; 220 computer-based; 84 iBT). *Application deadline:* For fall admission, 1/15 priority date for domestic and international students. Applications are processed on a rolling basis. Application fee: $60 ($75 for international students). Electronic applications accepted. *Expenses:* Tuition, state resident: full-time $17,286; part-time $1099 per credit hour. Tuition, nonresident: full-time $34,944; part-time $2080 per credit hour. Required fees: $95 per semester. Tuition and fees vary according to course load, degree level and program. *Financial support:* In 2009–10, 101 students received support, including 13 fellowships with full tuition reimbursements available (averaging $20,976 per year), 65 research assistantships with full tuition reimbursements available (averaging $25,041 per year), 10 teaching assistantships with partial tuition reimbursements available (averaging $16,694 per year); scholarships/grants, traineeships, and tuition waivers (full) also available. Financial award application deadline: 1/15. *Faculty research:* Statistical genetics, categorical data analysis, incomplete data, survival analysis, modeling. Total annual research expenditures: $14.4 million. *Unit head:* Dr. Trivellore Raghunathan, Chair, 734-615-9832, Fax: 734-763-2215, E-mail: teraghu@umich.edu. *Application contact:* Nicole Fenech, Student Services Coordinator, 734-615-9817, Fax: 734-763-2215, E-mail: sph.bio.inquiries@umich.edu.

University of Michigan, School of Public Health, Program in Clinical Research Design and Statistical Analysis, Ann Arbor, MI 48109. Offers MS. Offered through the Horace H. Rackham School of Graduate Studies. Program admits applicants in odd-numbered calendar years only. Evening/weekend programs available. *Faculty:* 11 full-time (4 women), 1 part-time/adjunct (0 women). *Students:* 36 full-time (14 women); includes 8 minority (1 African American, 7 Asian Americans or Pacific Islanders), 4 international. Average age 33. 44 applicants, 84% accepted, 30 enrolled. In 2009, 36 master's awarded. *Degree requirements:* For master's, comprehensive exam. *Entrance requirements:* For master's, GRE General Test or MCAT. Additional exam requirements/recommendations for international students: Recommended—TOEFL (minimum score 560 paper-based; 220 computer-based; 84 iBT). *Application deadline:* For fall admission, 3/1 priority date for international students. Applications are processed on a rolling basis. Application fee: $60 ($75 for international students). Electronic applications accepted. *Expenses:* Contact institution. *Financial support:* Institutionally sponsored loans and scholarships/grants available. Financial award application deadline: 3/15; financial award applicants required to submit FAFSA. *Faculty research:* Survival analysis, missing data, Bayesian inference, health economics, quality of life. Total annual research expenditures: $14.4 million. *Unit head:* Dr. Trivellore Raghunathan, Director, 734-615-9832, E-mail: teraghu@umich.edu. *Application contact:* Fatma Nedjari, Information Contact, 734-615-9812, Fax: 734-763-2215, E-mail: sph.bio.inquiries@umich.edu.

University of Minnesota, Twin Cities Campus, School of Public Health, Major in Biostatistics, Minneapolis, MN 55455-0213. Offers MPH, MS, PhD. Part-time programs available. Terminal master's awarded for partial completion of doctoral program. *Degree requirements:* For master's, comprehensive exam; for doctorate, comprehensive exam, thesis/dissertation. *Entrance requirements:* For master's, GRE General Test, course work in applied statistics, computer programming, multivariable calculus, linear algebra; for doctorate, GRE General Test, bachelor's or master's degree in statistics, biostatistics or mathematics. Additional exam requirements/recommendations for international students: Required—TOEFL (minimum score 600 paper-based; 250 computer-based; 90 iBT). Electronic applications accepted. *Faculty research:* Analysis of spatial and longitudinal data, Bayes/Empirical Bayes methods, survival analysis, longitudinal models, generalized linear models.

The University of North Carolina at Chapel Hill, Graduate School, School of Public Health, Department of Biostatistics, Chapel Hill, NC 27599. Offers MPH, MS, Dr PH, PhD. Part-time programs available. *Degree requirements:* For master's, comprehensive exam, thesis, major paper; for doctorate, comprehensive exam, thesis/dissertation. *Entrance requirements:* For master's and doctorate, GRE General Test, minimum GPA of 3.0. Additional exam requirements/recommendations for international students: Required—TOEFL. Electronic applications accepted. *Faculty research:* Cancer, cardiovascular, environmental biostatistics; AIDS and other infectious diseases; statistical genetics; demography and population studies.

University of North Texas Health Science Center at Fort Worth, School of Public Health, Fort Worth, TX 76107-2699. Offers biostatistics (MPH); community health (MPH); disease control and prevention (Dr PH); environmental and occupational health sciences (MPH); epidemiology (MPH); health administration (MHA); health policy and management (MPH, Dr PH); DO/MPH; MS/MPH; MSN/MPH. *Accreditation:* CEPH. Part-time and evening/weekend programs available. *Degree requirements:* For master's, thesis or alternative, supervised internship; for doctorate, thesis/dissertation, supervised internship. *Entrance requirements:* For master's, GRE General Test. Additional exam requirements/recommendations for international students: Required—TOEFL. Electronic applications accepted.

University of Oklahoma Health Sciences Center, Graduate College, College of Public Health, Program in Biostatistics and Epidemiology, Oklahoma City, OK 73190. Offers biostatistics (MPH, MS, Dr PH, PhD); epidemiology (MPH, MS, Dr PH, PhD). *Accreditation:* CEPH (one or more programs are accredited). Part-time programs available. *Degree requirements:* For master's, comprehensive exam, thesis (for some programs); for doctorate, comprehensive exam, thesis/dissertation. *Entrance requirements:* For master's, 3 letters of recommendation, resume; for doctorate, GRE General Test, letters of recommendation. Additional exam requirements/recommendations for international students: Required—TOEFL (minimum score 570 paper-based; 230 computer-based), TWE. *Expenses:* Tuition, state resident: full-time $3120; part-time $156 per credit hour. Tuition, nonresident: full-time $11,314; part-time $409.70 per credit hour. Required fees: $1471; $51.20 per credit hour. $223.25 per term. *Faculty research:* Statistical methodology, applied statistics, acute and chronic disease epidemiology.

University of Pennsylvania, School of Medicine, Biomedical Graduate Studies, Graduate Group in Epidemiology and Biostatistics, Philadelphia, PA 19104. Offers biostatistics (MS, PhD). Part-time programs available. *Faculty:* 110 full-time (44 women). *Students:* 22 full-time (14 women), 7 part-time (4 women); includes 18 minority (all Asian Americans or Pacific Islanders). Average age 25. 45 applicants, 36% accepted, 6 enrolled. In 2009, 7 master's, 6 doctorates awarded. Terminal master's awarded for partial completion of doctoral program. *Degree requirements:* For master's, thesis, evaluations examination; for doctorate, thesis/dissertation, evaluations exam, preliminary exam. *Entrance requirements:* For master's and doctorate, GRE, 1 year of course work in calculus, 1 semester of course work in linear algebra, working knowledge of programming language. Additional exam requirements/recommendations for international students: Required—TOEFL. *Application deadline:* For fall admission, 12/1 for domestic and international students. Application fee: $70. *Expenses:* Tuition: Full-time $25,660; part-time $4758 per course. Required fees: $2152; $270 per course. Tuition and fees vary according to course load, degree level and program. *Financial support:* In 2009–10, 22 students received support, including 12 fellowships with full and partial tuition reimbursements available (averaging $21,500 per year), 9 research assistantships with full and partial tuition reimbursements available (averaging $21,500 per year), 1 teaching assistantship with full and partial tuition reimbursement available (averaging $21,500 per year); career-related internships or fieldwork, institutionally sponsored loans, scholarships/grants, traineeships, health care benefits, and unspecified assistantships also available. Financial award application deadline: 12/1. *Faculty research:* Randomized clinical trials, data coordinating centers, methodological approaches to non-experimental epidemiologic studies, theoretical research in biostatistics. Total annual research expenditures: $38.6 million. *Unit head:* Dr. Daniel F. Heitjan, Chair, 215-573-7328, Fax: 215-573-4865, E-mail: dheitjan@mail.med.upenn.edu. *Application contact:* Ann R. Facciolo, Program Manager, 215-573-3881, Fax: 215-573-4865, E-mail: facciolo@mail.med.upenn.edu.

University of Pittsburgh, Graduate School of Public Health, Department of Biostatistics, Pittsburgh, PA 15260. Offers MPH, MS, Dr PH, PhD. Part-time programs available. *Faculty:* 25 full-time (9 women), 1 part-time/adjunct (0 women). *Students:* 82 full-time (53 women), 13 part-time (8 women); includes 15 minority (3 African Americans, 11 Asian Americans or Pacific Islanders, 1 Hispanic American), 62 international. Average age 32. 181 applicants, 71% accepted, 22 enrolled. In 2009, 11 master's, 7 doctorates awarded. Terminal master's awarded for partial completion of doctoral program. *Degree requirements:* For master's, thesis; for doctorate, one foreign language, thesis/dissertation. *Entrance requirements:* For master's and doctorate, GRE General Test, previous course work in biology, calculus, and Fortran. Additional exam requirements/recommendations for international students: Required—TOEFL (minimum score 550 paper-based; 213 computer-based; 80 iBT). *Application deadline:* For fall admission, 3/30 priority date for domestic students, 3/1 priority date for international students; for spring admission, 11/30 for domestic students, 4/5 priority date for international students. Applications are processed on a rolling basis. Application fee: $95. Electronic applications accepted. *Expenses:* Tuition, state resident: full-time $16,402; part-time $665 per credit. Tuition, nonresident: full-time $28,694; part-time $1175 per credit. Required fees: $690; $175 per term. Tuition and fees vary according to program. *Financial support:* In 2009–10, 51 students received support, including 41 research assistantships with full tuition reimbursements available (averaging $21,240 per year), 4 teaching assistantships with full tuition reimbursements available (averaging $22,598 per year); traineeships and tuition waivers (full and partial) also available. Financial award application deadline: 4/15. *Faculty research:* Survival analysis, environmental risk assessment, statistical computing, longitudinal data analysis, experimental design. Total annual research expenditures: $2.7 million. *Unit head:* Dr. Gary M. Marsh, Interim Chair, 412-624-3022, Fax: 412-624-9969, E-mail: gmarsh@pitt.edu. *Application contact:* Dr. Lisa Weissfeld, Professor, 412-624-3023, Fax: 412-624-2183, E-mail: lweis@pitt.edu.

University of Puerto Rico, Medical Sciences Campus, Graduate School of Public Health, Program in Biostatistics, San Juan, PR 00936-5067. Offers MPH. Part-time programs available. *Entrance requirements:* For master's, GRE, previous course work in algebra. *Expenses:* Contact institution.

University of Rochester, School of Medicine and Dentistry, Graduate Programs in Medicine and Dentistry, Department of Biostatistics and Computational Biology, Rochester, NY 14627. Offers medical statistics (MS); statistics (MA, PhD). Terminal master's awarded for partial completion of doctoral program. *Degree requirements:* For doctorate, thesis/dissertation, qualifying exam. *Entrance requirements:* For master's and doctorate, GRE General Test. Additional exam requirements/recommendations for international students: Required—TOEFL.

University of South Carolina, The Graduate School, Arnold School of Public Health, Department of Epidemiology and Biostatistics, Program in Biostatistics, Columbia, SC 29208. Offers MPH, MSPH, Dr PH, PhD. Part-time programs available. *Degree requirements:* For master's, comprehensive exam, thesis (for some programs), practicum (MPH); for doctorate, comprehensive exam, thesis/dissertation (for some programs), practicum (Dr PH). *Entrance requirements:* For master's, GRE General Test; for doctorate, GRE General Test, master's degree. Additional exam requirements/recommendations for international students: Required—TOEFL (minimum score 570 paper-based; 230 computer-based; 88 iBT). Electronic applications accepted. *Faculty research:* Bayesian methods, biometric modeling, nonlinear regression, health survey methodology, measurement of health status.

University of Southern California, Keck School of Medicine and Graduate School, Graduate Programs in Medicine, Department of Preventive Medicine, Division of Biostatistics, Los Angeles, CA 90089. Offers applied biostatistics/epidemiology (MS); biostatistics (MS, PhD); epidemiology (PhD); genetic epidemiology and statistical genetics (PhD); molecular epidemiology (MS, PhD). *Faculty:* 71 full-time (30 women). *Students:* 108 full-time (63 women); includes 24 minority (18 Asian Americans or Pacific Islanders, 6 Hispanic Americans), 58 international. Average age 29. 79 applicants, 52% accepted, 18 enrolled. In 2009, 12 master's, 4 doctorates awarded. Terminal master's awarded for partial completion of doctoral program. *Degree requirements:* For master's, thesis; for doctorate, thesis/dissertation. *Entrance requirements:* For master's and doctorate, GRE General Test, GRE Subject Test, minimum GPA of 3.0. Additional exam requirements/recommendations for international students: Required—TOEFL (minimum score 600 paper-based; 250 computer-based; 100 iBT). *Application deadline:* For fall admission, 12/1 priority date for domestic students, 12/1 for international students. Application fee: $85. Electronic applications accepted. *Expenses:* Tuition: Full-time $25,980; part-time $1315 per unit. Required fees: $554. One-time fee: $35 full-time. Full-time tuition and fees vary according to degree level and program. *Financial support:* In 2009–10, 3 fellowships with full tuition reimbursements (averaging $27,060 per year), 55 research assistantships with full tuition reimbursements (averaging $27,060 per year), 19 teaching assistantships with full and partial tuition reimbursements (averaging $13,530 per year) were awarded; career-related internships or fieldwork, Federal Work-Study, institutionally sponsored loans, scholarships/grants, health care benefits, and unspecified assistantships also available. Financial award application deadline: 5/5. *Faculty research:* Clinical trials in ophthalmology and cancer research, methods of analysis for epidemiological studies, genetic epidemiology. Total annual research expenditures: $1.3 million. *Unit head:* Dr. Stanley P. Azen, Co-Director, 323-442-1810, Fax: 323-442-2993, E-mail: mtrujill@usc.edu. *Application contact:* Mary L. Trujillo, Student Adviser, 323-442-1810, Fax: 323-442-2993, E-mail: mtrujill@usc.edu.

See Close-Up on page 325.

University of Southern California, Keck School of Medicine and Graduate School, Graduate Programs in Medicine, Department of Preventive Medicine, Master of Public Health Program, Alhambra, CA 91803. Offers biostatistics/epidemiology (MPH); child and family health (MPH); global health leadership (MPH); health communication (MPH); health promotion (MPH). *Accreditation:* CEPH. Part-time programs available. *Faculty:* 22 full-time (12 women), 3 part-time/adjunct (0 women). *Students:* 215 full-time (158 women), 3 part-time (2 women); includes 148 minority (13 African Americans, 3 American Indian/Alaska Native, 114 Asian Americans or Pacific Islanders, 18 Hispanic Americans), 25 international. Average age 26. 208 applicants,

Biostatistics

University of Southern California (continued)

74% accepted, 76 enrolled. In 2009, 60 master's awarded. *Degree requirements:* For master's, practicum, final report, oral presentation. *Entrance requirements:* For master's, GRE General Test, MCAT, GMAT, minimum GPA of 3.0. Additional exam requirements/recommendations for international students: Required—TOEFL (minimum score 600 paper-based; 250 computer-based; 100 iBT). *Application deadline:* For fall admission, 6/1 priority date for domestic and international students; for spring admission, 11/1 priority date for domestic students, 10/1 priority date for international students. Applications are processed on a rolling basis. Application fee: $85. Electronic applications accepted. *Expenses:* Tuition: Full-time $25,980; part-time $1315 per unit. Required fees: $554. One-time fee: $35 full-time. Full-time tuition and fees vary according to degree level and program. *Financial support:* In 2009–10, 175 students received support, including 20 fellowships (averaging $3,200 per year); career-related internships or fieldwork, Federal Work-Study, institutionally sponsored loans, and scholarships/grants also available. Support available to part-time students. Financial award application deadline: 5/1; financial award applicants required to submit CSS PROFILE or FAFSA. *Faculty research:* Substance abuse prevention, cancer and heart disease prevention, mass media and health communication research, health promotion, treatment compliance. *Unit head:* Dr. Thomas W. Valente, Director, 626-457-4139, Fax: 626-457-6699, E-mail: tvalente@usc.edu. *Application contact:* Chrystal Romero, Admissions Counselor, 626-457-6676, Fax: 626-457-6699, E-mail: ccromero@usc.edu.

University of Southern Mississippi, Graduate School, College of Health, Department of Community Health Sciences, Hattiesburg, MS 39406-0001. Offers epidemiology and biostatistics (MPH); health education (MPH); health policy/administration (MPH); occupational/environmental health (MPH); public health nutrition (MPH). *Accreditation:* CEPH. Part-time and evening/weekend programs available. *Faculty:* 8 full-time (4 women), 1 part-time/adjunct (0 women). *Students:* 92 full-time (59 women), 20 part-time (14 women); includes 40 minority (36 African Americans, 1 Asian American or Pacific Islander, 3 Hispanic Americans), 13 international. Average age 32. 90 applicants, 73% accepted, 47 enrolled. In 2009, 4 master's awarded. *Degree requirements:* For master's, comprehensive exam, thesis (for some programs). *Entrance requirements:* For master's, GRE General Test, minimum GPA of 2.75 in last 60 hours. Additional exam requirements/recommendations for international students: Required—TOEFL. *Application deadline:* For fall admission, 3/1 for domestic and international students. Applications are processed on a rolling basis. Application fee: $35. *Expenses:* Tuition, state resident: full-time $5096; part-time $284 per hour. Tuition, nonresident: full-time $13,052; part-time $726 per hour. Required fees: $402. Tuition and fees vary according to course level and course load. *Financial support:* In 2009–10, 5 research assistantships with full tuition reimbursements (averaging $7,000 per year), 1 teaching assistantship with full tuition reimbursement (averaging $8,263 per year) were awarded; career-related internships or fieldwork and Federal Work-Study also available. Financial award application deadline: 3/15; financial award applicants required to submit FAFSA. *Faculty research:* Rural health care delivery, school health, nutrition of pregnant teens, risk factor reduction, sexually transmitted diseases. *Unit head:* Dr. James McGuire, Chair, 601-266-5437, Fax: 601-266-5043. *Application contact:* Shonna Breland, Manager of Graduate Admissions, 601-266-6563, Fax: 601-266-5138.

University of South Florida, Graduate School, College of Public Health, Department of Epidemiology and Biostatistics, Tampa, FL 33620-9951. Offers MPH, MSPH, PhD. *Accreditation:* CEPH (one or more programs are accredited). Part-time and evening/weekend programs available. *Faculty:* 12 full-time (5 women), 7 part-time/adjunct (5 women). *Students:* 71 full-time (43 women), 67 part-time (51 women); includes 36 minority (12 African Americans, 1 American Indian/Alaska Native, 12 Asian Americans or Pacific Islanders, 11 Hispanic Americans), 26 international. Average age 31. 115 applicants, 68% accepted, 30 enrolled. In 2009, 24 master's awarded. *Degree requirements:* For master's, comprehensive exam, thesis (for some programs); for doctorate, comprehensive exam, thesis/dissertation. *Entrance requirements:* For master's, GRE General Test, minimum GPA of 3.0 in upper-level course work Goal statement letter Two professional letters of recommendation Resume/CV ; for doctorate, GRE General Test, minimum GPA of 3.0 in upper-level course work, 3 professional letters of recommendation, resume/curriculum vitae, writing sample. Additional exam requirements/recommendations for international students: Required—TOEFL (minimum score 550 paper-based; 213 computer-based; 79 iBT). *Application deadline:* For fall admission, 6/1 for domestic students, 1/2 for international students; for spring admission, 10/15 for domestic students, 7/1 for international students. Applications are processed on a rolling basis. Application fee: $30. Electronic applications accepted. *Financial support:* In 2009–10, 3 fellowships with full tuition reimbursements (averaging $3,800 per year), 11 research assistantships with full and partial tuition reimbursements (averaging $3,324 per year), 19 teaching assistantships (averaging $3,044 per year) were awarded; career-related internships or fieldwork, Federal Work-Study, institutionally sponsored loans, scholarships/grants, traineeships, and unspecified assistantships also available. Support available to part-time students. Financial award applicants required to submit FAFSA. *Faculty research:* Dementia, mental illness, mental health preventative trails, rural health outreach, clinical and administrative studies. Total annual research expenditures: $1.5 million. *Unit head:* Dr. Heather Stockwell, Chairperson, 813-974-4860, Fax: 813-974-4719, E-mail: stockwell@hsc.usf.edu. *Application contact:* Michelle Hodge, Academic Advisor, 813-974-6665, Fax: 813-974-8121, E-mail: mhodge1@health.usf.edu.

The University of Texas Health Science Center at Houston, Graduate School of Biomedical Sciences, Program in Biomathematics and Biostatistics, Houston, TX 77225-0036. Offers MS, PhD, MD/PhD. Terminal master's awarded for partial completion of doctoral program. *Degree requirements:* For master's, thesis; for doctorate, thesis/dissertation. *Entrance requirements:* For master's and doctorate, GRE General Test. Additional exam requirements/recommendations for international students: Required—TOEFL. Electronic applications accepted. *Faculty research:* Biostatistics, biomarkers, epidemiology, bioinformatics, computational biology.

The University of Toledo, College of Graduate Studies, College of Medicine, Department of Public Health and Homeland Security, Program in Public Health, Toledo, OH 43606-3390. Offers biostatistics and epidemiology (Certificate); emergency response (Certificate); global health (Certificate); public health (MPH); MD/MPH.

University of Utah, The Graduate School, Interdepartmental Program in Statistics, Salt Lake City, UT 84112-1107. Offers biostatistics (MST); business (MST); econometrics (MST); educational psychology (MST); mathematics (MST); sociology (MST); statistics (M Stat). Part-time programs available. *Students:* 25 full-time (11 women), 15 part-time (6 women); includes 4 minority (3 Asian Americans or Pacific Islanders, 1 Hispanic American), 12 international. Average age 30. 59 applicants, 44% accepted, 12 enrolled. In 2009, 15 master's awarded. *Degree requirements:* For master's, comprehensive exam, projects. *Entrance requirements:* For master's, GMAT (business), GRE General Test (sociology and educational psychology), minimum GPA of 3.0; course work in calculus, matrix theory, statistics. Additional exam requirements/recommendations for international students: Required—TOEFL (minimum score 500 paper-based; 173 computer-based). *Application deadline:* For fall admission, 7/1 for domestic students, 4/1 for international students. Applications are processed on a rolling basis. Application fee: $55 ($65 for international students). *Expenses:* Tuition, state resident: full-time $4004; part-time $1674 per semester. Tuition, nonresident: full-time $14,134; part-time $5915 per semester. Required fees: $324 per semester. Tuition and fees vary according to course load, degree level and program. *Financial support:* Career-related internships or fieldwork available. *Faculty research:* Biostatistics, management, economics, educational psychology, mathematics. *Unit head:* Tariq Mughal, Chair, University Statistics Committee, 801-585-9547, E-mail: tariaq.mughal@business.utah.edu. *Application contact:* Laura Egbert, MSTAT Program Coordinator, 801-585-6853, E-mail: laura.demattia@utah.edu.

University of Utah, School of Medicine and The Graduate School, Graduate Programs in Medicine, Programs in Public Health, Salt Lake City, UT 84112-1107. Offers biostatistics (M Stat); public health (MPH, MSPH, PhD). *Accreditation:* CEPH (one or more programs are accredited). Part-time programs available. *Degree requirements:* For master's, comprehensive exam, thesis or project (MSPH); for doctorate, comprehensive exam, thesis/dissertation. *Entrance requirements:* For master's and doctorate, GRE General Test, 3 letters of reference, in-person interviews, minimum GPA of 3.0. Additional exam requirements/recommendations for international students: Required—TOEFL (minimum score 550 paper-based; 175 computer-based). Electronic applications accepted. *Expenses:* Tuition, state resident: full-time $4004; part-time $1674 per semester. Tuition, nonresident: full-time $14,134; part-time $5915 per semester. Required fees: $324 per semester. Tuition and fees vary according to course load, degree level and program. *Faculty research:* Health services, health policy, epidemiology of chronic disease, infectious disease epidemiology, cancer epidemiology.

University of Vermont, Graduate College, College of Engineering and Mathematics, Department of Mathematics and Statistics, Program in Biostatistics, Burlington, VT 05405. Offers MS. *Students:* 4; includes 1 minority (Hispanic American). 11 applicants, 82% accepted, 1 enrolled. *Degree requirements:* For master's, thesis or alternative. *Entrance requirements:* Additional exam requirements/recommendations for international students: Required—TOEFL (minimum score 550 paper-based; 213 computer-based; 80 iBT). *Application deadline:* For fall admission, 4/1 priority date for domestic students. Applications are processed on a rolling basis. Application fee: $40. Electronic applications accepted. *Expenses:* Tuition, area resident: Part-time $508 per credit hour. Tuition, state resident: part-time $508 per credit hour. Tuition, nonresident: part-time $1281 per credit hour. *Financial support:* Fellowships, research assistantships, teaching assistantships available. Financial award application deadline: 3/1. *Unit head:* Dr. Jeff Buzas, Coordinator, 802-656-2940. *Application contact:* Dr. Jeff Buzas, Coordinator, 802-656-2940.

University of Washington, Graduate School, Interdisciplinary Graduate Program in Quantitative Ecology and Resource Management, Seattle, WA 98195. Offers MS, PhD. *Degree requirements:* For master's, thesis; for doctorate, thesis/dissertation. *Entrance requirements:* For master's and doctorate, GRE General Test, minimum GPA of 3.0. Additional exam requirements/recommendations for international students: Required—TOEFL. Electronic applications accepted. *Faculty research:* Population dynamics, statistical analysis, ecological modeling and systems analysis of aquatic and terrestrial ecosystems.

University of Washington, Graduate School, School of Public Health, Department of Biostatistics, Seattle, WA 98195. Offers biostatistics (MPH, MS, PhD); clinical research (MS), including biostatistics; statistical genetics (PhD). Part-time programs available. *Faculty:* 41 full-time (15 women), 8 part-time/adjunct (1 woman). *Students:* 80 full-time (47 women), 5 part-time (2 women); includes 8 minority (7 Asian Americans or Pacific Islanders, 1 Hispanic American), 31 international. Average age 30. 187 applicants, 20% accepted, 21 enrolled. In 2009, 4 master's, 8 doctorates awarded. Terminal master's awarded for partial completion of doctoral program. *Degree requirements:* For master's, comprehensive exam, thesis, computer proficiency, consulting, departmental qualifying exams; for doctorate, comprehensive exam, thesis/dissertation, computer proficiency, consulting, departmental qualifying exams. *Entrance requirements:* For master's and doctorate, GRE General Test, 2 years of course work in advanced calculus, 1 course in linear algebra, 1 course in mathematical probability, 30 credits math/statistics, minimum GPA of 3.0. Additional exam requirements/recommendations for international students: Required—TOEFL. *Application deadline:* For fall admission, 1/5 for domestic students. Application fee: $50. Electronic applications accepted. *Financial support:* In 2009–10, 79 students received support, including 75 research assistantships with full and partial tuition reimbursements available (averaging $22,000 per year), 10 teaching assistantships with full and partial tuition reimbursements available (averaging $22,000 per year); traineeships, health care benefits, and tuition waivers (partial) also available. *Faculty research:* Statistical methods for survival data analysis, clinical trials, epidemiological case control and cohort studies, statistical genetics. *Unit head:* Dr. Bruce Weir, Department Chair, 206-543-1044. *Application contact:* Alex Mackenzie, Counseling Services Coordinator, 206-543-1044, Fax: 206-543-3286, E-mail: alexam@u.washington.edu.

University of Waterloo, Graduate Studies, Faculty of Mathematics, Department of Statistics and Actuarial Science, Waterloo, ON N2L 3G1, Canada. Offers actuarial science (M Math, PhD); biostatistics (PhD); statistics (M Math, PhD); statistics-biostatistics (M Math); statistics-computing (M Math); statistics-finance (M Math). *Degree requirements:* For master's, research paper or thesis; for doctorate, comprehensive exam, thesis/dissertation. *Entrance requirements:* For master's, honors degree in field, minimum B+ average; for doctorate, master's degree, minimum B+ average. Additional exam requirements/recommendations for international students: Required—TOEFL (minimum score 600 paper-based; 250 computer-based; 90 iBT), TWE (minimum score 4.5). Electronic applications accepted. *Faculty research:* Data analysis, risk theory, inference, stochastic processes, quantitative finance.

The University of Western Ontario, Faculty of Graduate Studies, Biosciences Division, Department of Epidemiology and Biostatistics, London, ON N6A 5B8, Canada. Offers M Sc, PhD. *Accreditation:* CEPH (one or more programs are accredited). Part-time programs available. *Degree requirements:* For master's, thesis; for doctorate, comprehensive exam, thesis proposal defense. *Entrance requirements:* For master's, BA or B Sc honors degree, minimum B+ average in last 10 courses; for doctorate, M Sc or equivalent, minimum B+ average in last 10 courses. *Faculty research:* Chronic disease epidemiology, clinical epidemiology.

Virginia Commonwealth University, Medical College of Virginia-Professional Programs, School of Medicine, School of Medicine Graduate Programs, Department of Biostatistics, Richmond, VA 23284-9005. Offers MS, PhD, MD/PhD. Part-time programs available. Terminal master's awarded for partial completion of doctoral program. *Degree requirements:* For master's, thesis; for doctorate, thesis/dissertation, comprehensive oral and written exams. *Entrance requirements:* For master's, DAT, GRE General Test, or MCAT; for doctorate, GRE General Test, MCAT, DAT. *Faculty research:* Health services, linear models, response surfaces, design and analysis of drug/chemical combinations, clinical trials.

Yale University, School of Medicine, School of Public Health, Division of Biostatistics, New Haven, CT 06520. Offers MPH, MS, PhD. MS and PhD offered through the Graduate School. Part-time programs available. Terminal master's awarded for partial completion of doctoral program. *Degree requirements:* For master's, thesis, internship. *Entrance requirements:* For master's, GMAT, GRE, or MCAT, previous undergraduate course work in mathematics and science. Additional exam requirements/recommendations for international students: Required—TOEFL. Electronic applications accepted. *Expenses:* Contact institution. *Faculty research:* Statistical and genetic epidemiology, population models for chronic and infectious diseases, clinical trials, regression methods.

Computational Sciences

California Institute of Technology, Division of Engineering and Applied Science, Option in Computation and Neural Systems, Pasadena, CA 91125-0001. Offers MS, PhD. *Faculty:* 3 full-time (0 women). *Students:* 40 full-time (10 women). 114 applicants, 14% accepted, 7 enrolled. In 2009, 1 master's, 6 doctorates awarded. Terminal master's awarded for partial completion of doctoral program. *Degree requirements:* For doctorate, thesis/dissertation, qualifying exam. *Entrance requirements:* For doctorate, GRE General Test. *Application deadline:* For fall admission, 1/1 for domestic students. Application fee: $0. *Financial support:* In 2009–10, 10 fellowships, 23 research assistantships, 3 teaching assistantships were awarded; Federal Work-Study and institutionally sponsored loans also available. Financial award application deadline: 1/15. *Faculty research:* Biological and artificial computational devices, modeling of sensory processes and learning, theory of collective computation. *Unit head:* Dr. Pietro Perona, Executive Officer, 626-395-4867, E-mail: perona@its.caltech.edu. *Application contact:* Natalie Gilmore, Assistant Dean of Graduate Studies, 626-395-3812, Fax: 626-577-9246, E-mail: ngilmore@caltech.edu.

Carnegie Mellon University, Carnegie Institute of Technology, Department of Civil and Environmental Engineering, Pittsburgh, PA 15213. Offers civil and environmental engineering (PhD); advanced infrastructure systems (MS, PhD); civil and environmental engineering (MS); civil and environmental engineering/engineering and public policy (PhD); civil engineering (MS, PhD); computational mechanics (MS, PhD); computational science and engineering (MS, PhD); environmental engineering (MS, PhD); environmental management and science (MS, PhD). Part-time programs available. *Faculty:* 19 full-time (3 women), 13 part-time/adjunct (3 women). *Students:* 118 full-time (48 women), 12 part-time (6 women); includes 15 minority (4 African Americans, 10 Asian Americans or Pacific Islanders, 1 Hispanic American), 78 international. Average age 26. 294 applicants, 75% accepted, 78 enrolled. In 2009, 55 master's, 10 doctorates awarded. Terminal master's awarded for partial completion of doctoral program. *Degree requirements:* For master's, thesis optional; for doctorate, comprehensive exam, thesis/dissertation, qualifying exam, public defense of dissertation. *Entrance requirements:* For master's and doctorate, GRE General Test. Additional exam requirements/recommendations for international students: Required—TOEFL (minimum score 550 paper-based; 213 computer-based; 82 iBT). *Application deadline:* For fall admission, 1/15 priority date for domestic and international students; for spring admission, 9/30 priority date for domestic and international students. Application fee: $65. Electronic applications accepted. *Financial support:* In 2009–10, 102 students received support, including 18 fellowships with full and partial tuition reimbursements available (averaging $22,853 per year), 34 research assistantships with full and partial tuition reimbursements available (averaging $23,661 per year); tuition waivers (partial) and unspecified assistantships also available. Financial award application deadline: 1/15. *Faculty research:* Advanced infrastructure systems; environmental engineering science and management; mechanics, materials, and computing; green design; global sustainable construction. Total annual research expenditures: $4.5 million. *Unit head:* Dr. James H. Garrett, Head, 412-268-2941, Fax: 412-268-7813, E-mail: garrett@cmu.edu. *Application contact:* Maxine A. Leffard, Graduate Program Administrator, 412-268-5673, Fax: 412-268-7813, E-mail: ce-admissions@andrew.cmu.edu.

Carnegie Mellon University, Tepper School of Business, Program in Algorithms, Combinatorics, and Optimization, Pittsburgh, PA 15213-3891. Offers PhD. *Degree requirements:* For doctorate, thesis/dissertation. *Entrance requirements:* For doctorate, GRE General Test.

Claremont Graduate University, Graduate Programs, School of Mathematical Sciences, Claremont, CA 91711-6160. Offers computational and systems biology (PhD); computational mathematics and numerical analysis (MA, MS); computational science (PhD); engineering and industrial applied mathematics (PhD); mathematics (PhD); operations research and statistics (MA, MS); physical applied mathematics (MA, MS); pure mathematics (MA, MS); scientific computing (MA, MS); systems and control theory (MA, MS). Part-time programs available. *Faculty:* 5 full-time (0 women), 2 part-time/adjunct (0 women). *Students:* 56 full-time (20 women), 12 part-time (3 women); includes 13 minority (2 African Americans, 6 Asian Americans or Pacific Islanders, 5 Hispanic Americans), 25 international. Average age 33. In 2009, 7 master's, 7 doctorates awarded. Terminal master's awarded for partial completion of doctoral program. *Entrance requirements:* For master's and doctorate, GRE General Test. Additional exam requirements/recommendations for international students: Required—TOEFL (minimum score 550 paper-based; 213 computer-based; 80 iBT). *Application deadline:* For fall admission, 2/1 priority date for domestic students. Applications are processed on a rolling basis. Application fee: $60. Electronic applications accepted. *Expenses:* Tuition: Full-time $35,046; part-time $1524 per credit. Required fees: $161 per semester. *Financial support:* Fellowships, research assistantships, Federal Work-Study, institutionally sponsored loans, scholarships/grants, and tuition waivers (full and partial) available. Support available to part-time students. Financial award application deadline: 2/15; financial award applicants required to submit FAFSA. *Unit head:* John Angus, Dean, 909-621-8080, Fax: 909-607-8261, E-mail: john.angus@cgu.edu. *Application contact:* Susan Townzen, Program Coordinator, 909-621-8080, Fax: 909-607-8261, E-mail: susan.n.townzen@cgu.edu.

Clemson University, Graduate School, College of Engineering and Science, Department of Mathematical Sciences, Clemson, SC 29634. Offers applied and pure mathematics (MS, PhD); computational mathematics (MS, PhD); operations research (MS, PhD); statistics (MS, PhD). Part-time programs available. *Faculty:* 51 full-time (14 women), 9 part-time/adjunct (2 women). *Students:* 92 full-time (39 women), 1 part-time (0 women); includes 3 minority (2 African Americans, 1 American Indian/Alaska Native), 31 international. Average age 26. 134 applicants, 76% accepted, 20 enrolled. In 2009, 36 master's, 13 doctorates awarded. *Degree requirements:* For master's, thesis optional, final project; for doctorate, thesis/dissertation, qualifying exams. *Entrance requirements:* For master's and doctorate, GRE General Test. Additional exam requirements/recommendations for international students: Required—TOEFL. *Application deadline:* For fall admission, 1/15 priority date for domestic students, 2/15 priority date for international students; for spring admission, 10/1 priority date for domestic students, 9/15 priority date for international students. Applications are processed on a rolling basis. Application fee: $70 ($80 for international students). Electronic applications accepted. *Expenses:* Tuition, state resident: full-time $8684; part-time $528 per credit hour. Tuition, nonresident: full-time $15,330; part-time $1078 per credit hour. Required fees: $736; $37 per semester. Part-time tuition and fees vary according to course load and program. *Financial support:* In 2009–10, 85 students received support, including 1 fellowship with full and partial tuition reimbursement available (averaging $10,000 per year), 7 research assistantships with partial tuition reimbursements available (averaging $17,591 per year), 66 teaching assistantships with partial tuition reimbursements available (averaging $18,593 per year); career-related internships or fieldwork, institutionally sponsored loans, scholarships/grants, health care benefits, and unspecified assistantships also available. Support available to part-time students. Financial award application deadline: 4/15. *Faculty research:* Applied and computational analysis, cryptography, discrete mathematics, optimization, statistics. Total annual research expenditures: $535,985. *Unit head:* Dr. Robert L. Taylor, Chair, 864-656-5240, Fax: 864-656-5230, E-mail: rtaylo2@clemson.edu. *Application contact:* Dr. K. B. Kulasekera, Graduate Coordinator, 864-656-5231, Fax: 864-656-5230, E-mail: kk@clemson.edu.

The College at Brockport, State University of New York, School of Science and Mathematics, Department of Computational Science, Brockport, NY 14420-2997. Offers MS. Part-time programs available. *Students:* 2 full-time (0 women), 4 part-time (0 women). 1 applicant, 100% accepted, 0 enrolled. In 2009, 1 master's awarded. *Degree requirements:* For master's, thesis. *Entrance requirements:* For master's, minimum GPA of 3.0, letters of recommendation. Additional exam requirements/recommendations for international students: Required—TOEFL (minimum score 550 paper-based; 213 computer-based; 79 iBT). *Application deadline:* For fall admission, 7/15 priority date for domestic and international students; for spring admission, 11/15 priority date for domestic and international students. Application fee: $50. Electronic applications accepted. *Expenses:* Tuition, state resident: full-time $8370; part-time $349 per credit. Tuition, nonresident: full-time $13,250; part-time $522 per credit. *Financial support:* Federal Work-Study, scholarships/grants, and unspecified assistantships available. Support available to part-time students. Financial award application deadline: 3/15; financial award applicants required to submit FAFSA. *Faculty research:* Parallel computing; fluid and particle dynamics; molecular simulation; engine combustion; computational mathematics, science, and technology education. *Unit head:* Dr. Robert Tuzun, Chairman, 585-395-5368, Fax: 585-395-5020, E-mail: rtuzun@brockport.edu. *Application contact:* Dr. Robert Tuzun, Chairman, 585-395-5368, Fax: 585-395-5020, E-mail: rtuzun@brockport.edu.

The College of William and Mary, Faculty of Arts and Sciences, Department of Computer Science, Program in Computational Operations Research, Williamsburg, VA 23187-8795. Offers computer science (MS), including operations research. Part-time programs available. *Students:* 17 full-time (4 women); includes 1 minority (Hispanic American), 5 international. Average age 26. 19 applicants, 79% accepted, 10 enrolled. In 2009, 6 master's awarded. *Degree requirements:* For master's, research project. *Entrance requirements:* For master's, GRE General Test, minimum GPA of 2.5. Additional exam requirements/recommendations for international students: Required—TOEFL. *Application deadline:* For fall admission, 3/1 priority date for domestic students, 3/15 priority date for international students; for spring admission, 11/1 for domestic and international students. Applications are processed on a rolling basis. Application fee: $45. Electronic applications accepted. *Expenses:* Tuition, state resident: full-time $6400; part-time $315 per credit hour. Tuition, nonresident: full-time $19,720; part-time $840 per credit hour. Required fees: $4114. *Financial support:* In 2009–10, 13 students received support, including 6 fellowships (averaging $9,000 per year), 7 teaching assistantships with full tuition reimbursements available (averaging $11,500 per year); scholarships/grants, tuition waivers (full), and unspecified assistantships also available. Financial award application deadline: 3/1; financial award applicants required to submit FAFSA. *Faculty research:* Metaheuristics, reliability, optimization, statistics, networks. *Unit head:* Dr. Rex Kincaid, Professor, 757-221-2038, Fax: 757-221-1717, E-mail: rrkinc@math.wm.edu. *Application contact:* Vanessa Godwin, Administrative Director, 757-221-3455, Fax: 757-221-1717, E-mail: cor@cs.wm.edu.

Cornell University, Graduate School, Graduate Fields of Engineering, Field of Chemical Engineering, Ithaca, NY 14853-0001. Offers advanced materials processing (M Eng, MS, PhD); applied mathematics and computational methods (M Eng, MS, PhD); biochemical engineering (M Eng, MS, PhD); chemical reaction engineering (M Eng, MS, PhD); classical and statistical thermodynamics (M Eng, MS, PhD); fluid dynamics, rheology and biorheology (M Eng, MS, PhD); heat and mass transfer (M Eng, MS, PhD); kinetics and catalysis (M Eng, MS, PhD); polymers (M Eng, MS, PhD); surface science (M Eng, MS, PhD). *Faculty:* 29 full-time (2 women). *Students:* 95 full-time (30 women); includes 9 minority (1 African American, 5 Asian Americans or Pacific Islanders, 3 Hispanic Americans), 41 international. Average age 25. 317 applicants, 38% accepted, 46 enrolled. In 2009, 22 master's, 17 doctorates awarded. *Degree requirements:* For master's, thesis (MS); for doctorate, comprehensive exam, thesis/dissertation. *Entrance requirements:* For master's and doctorate, GRE General Test, 2 letters of recommendation. Additional exam requirements/recommendations for international students: Required—TOEFL (minimum score 600 paper-based; 237 computer-based; 77 iBT). *Application deadline:* For fall admission, 1/15 priority date for domestic students. Application fee: $70. Electronic applications accepted. *Expenses:* Tuition: Full-time $29,500. Required fees: $70. Full-time tuition and fees vary according to degree level, program and student level. *Financial support:* In 2009–10, 67 students received support, including 3 fellowships with full tuition reimbursements available, 3 research assistantships with full tuition reimbursements available; teaching assistantships with full tuition reimbursements available, institutionally sponsored loans, scholarships/grants, health care benefits, tuition waivers (full and partial), and unspecified assistantships also available. Financial award applicants required to submit FAFSA. *Faculty research:* Biochemical, biomedical and metabolic engineering; fluid and polymer dynamics; surface science and chemical kinetics; electronics materials; microchemical systems and nanotechnology. *Unit head:* Director of Graduate Studies, 607-255-4550. *Application contact:* Graduate Field Assistant, 607-255-4550, E-mail: dgs@cheme.cornell.edu.

George Mason University, College of Science, Fairfax, VA 22030. Offers biodefense (MS, PhD); bioinformatics and computational biology (MS, PhD, Certificate); biology (MS, PhD), including bioinformatics (MS), ecology, systematics and evolution (MS), interpretive biology (MS), molecular and cellular biology (MS), molecular and microbiology (PhD), organismal biology (MS); chemistry and biochemistry (MS), including chemistry; climate dynamics (PhD); computational and data sciences (MS, PhD, Certificate); computational social science (PhD); computational techniques and applications (Certificate); earth systems and geoinformation sciences (MS, PhD, Certificate); environmental science and policy (MS, PhD); geography (MS), including geographic and cartographic sciences; mathematical sciences (MS, PhD), including mathematics; nanotechnology and nanoscience (Certificate); neuroscience (PhD); physical sciences (PhD); physics and astronomy (MS), including applied and engineering physics; remote sensing and earth image processing (Certificate). Part-time and evening/weekend programs available. *Degree requirements:* For doctorate, comprehensive exam, thesis/dissertation. *Entrance requirements:* For master's and doctorate, GRE General Test, minimum GPA of 3.0 in last 60 hours. Additional exam requirements/recommendations for international students: Required—TOEFL. Electronic applications accepted. *Expenses:* Tuition, state resident: full-time $7568; part-time $315.33 per credit hour. Tuition, nonresident: full-time $21,704; part-time $904.33 per credit hour. Required fees: $2184; $91 per credit hour. *Faculty research:* Space sciences and astrophysics, fluid dynamics, materials modeling and simulation, bioinformatics, global changes and statistics.

Hampton University, Graduate College, Program in Applied Mathematics, Hampton, VA 23668. Offers computational mathematics (MS); nonlinear science (MS); statistics and probability (MS). *Degree requirements:* For master's, thesis optional. *Entrance requirements:* For master's, GRE General Test.

Kean University, College of Natural, Applied and Health Sciences, Program in Computing, Statistics and Mathematics, Union, NJ 07083. Offers MS. Part-time and evening/weekend programs available. *Faculty:* 13 full-time (4 women). *Students:* 2 full-time (1 woman), 5 part-time (0 women); includes 5 minority (2 African Americans, 2 Asian Americans or Pacific Islanders, 1 Hispanic American), 1 international. Average age 30. 2 applicants, 50% accepted, 1 enrolled. In 2009, 1 master's awarded. *Degree requirements:* For master's, thesis or alternative, research component. *Entrance requirements:* For master's, GRE General Test, minimum GPA of 3.0, 2 letters of recommendation, interview, 24-27 credits in prerequisites, official transcripts from all institutions attended. *Application deadline:* For fall admission, 5/1 for domestic students; for spring admission, 11/1 for domestic students. Application fee: $60 ($150 for international students). Electronic applications accepted. *Expenses:* Tuition, state resident: full-time $10,440; part-time $435 per credit. Tuition, nonresident: full-time $14,160; part-time $590 per credit. Required fees: $2642; $110 per credit. Part-time tuition and fees vary according to course load and degree level. *Financial support:* In 2009–10, 2 research assistantships with full tuition reimbursements (averaging $3,263 per year) were awarded; unspecified assistantships also available. *Unit head:* Dr. Wolde Woubneh, Program Coordinator, 908-737-3700, E-mail: wwoubneh@kean.edu. *Application contact:* Reenat Hasan, Pre-Admissions Coordinator, 908-737-5923, Fax: 908-737-5965, E-mail: rhasan@exchange.kean.edu.

Computational Sciences

Lehigh University, P.C. Rossin College of Engineering and Applied Science, Department of Mechanical Engineering and Mechanics, Bethlehem, PA 18015. Offers applied mathematics (MS, PhD); computational engineering and mechanics (MS, PhD); mechanical engineering (M Eng, MS, PhD, MBA/E); polymer science/engineering (M Eng, MS, PhD, MBA/E); MBA/E. Part-time and evening/weekend programs available. Postbaccalaureate distance learning degree programs offered. *Faculty:* 20 full-time (0 women). *Students:* 85 full-time (12 women), 32 part-time (3 women); includes 4 minority (1 African American, 2 Asian Americans or Pacific Islanders, 1 Hispanic American), 51 international. Average age 27. 320 applicants, 29% accepted, 45 enrolled. In 2009, 23 master's, 6 doctorates awarded. Terminal master's awarded for partial completion of doctoral program. *Degree requirements:* For master's, thesis; for doctorate, thesis/dissertation, general exam. *Entrance requirements:* Additional exam requirements/recommendations for international students: Required—TOEFL (minimum score 550 paper-based; 213 computer-based; 79 iBT). *Application deadline:* For fall admission, 7/15 for domestic and international students; for spring admission, 12/1 for domestic and international students. Applications are processed on a rolling basis. Application fee: $75. Electronic applications accepted. *Financial support:* In 2009–10, 30 students received support, including 8 fellowships with full and partial tuition reimbursements available (averaging $21,060 per year), 24 research assistantships with full and partial tuition reimbursements available (averaging $20,700 per year), 18 teaching assistantships with full and partial tuition reimbursements available (averaging $21,060 per year); unspecified assistantships also available. Financial award application deadline: 1/15. *Faculty research:* Thermofluids, dynamic systems, CAD/CAM, computational mechanics, solid mechanics. Total annual research expenditures: $3.1 million. *Unit head:* Dr. D. Gary Harlow, Chairman, 610-758-4102, Fax: 610-758-6224, E-mail: dgh0@lehigh.edu. *Application contact:* Jo Ann M. Casciano, Graduate Coordinator, 610-758-4107, Fax: 610-758-6224, E-mail: jmc4@lehigh.edu.

Louisiana Tech University, Graduate School, College of Engineering and Science, Department of Physics, Ruston, LA 71272. Offers applied computational analysis and modeling (PhD); physics (MS). Part-time programs available. *Degree requirements:* For master's, thesis or alternative; for doctorate, thesis/dissertation. *Entrance requirements:* For master's, GRE General Test, minimum GPA of 3.0 in last 60 hours. Additional exam requirements/recommendations for international students: Required—TOEFL. *Faculty research:* Experimental high energy physics, laser/optics, computational physics, quantum gravity.

Marquette University, Graduate School, College of Arts and Sciences, Department of Mathematics, Statistics, and Computer Science, Milwaukee, WI 53201-1881. Offers bioinformatics (MS); computational sciences (PhD); computers (MS); mathematics education (MS). Part-time programs available. *Faculty:* 28 full-time (12 women), 7 part-time/adjunct (2 women). *Students:* 20 full-time (4 women), 25 part-time (4 women); includes 2 minority (both Asian Americans or Pacific Islanders), 20 international. Average age 31. 68 applicants, 47% accepted, 15 enrolled. In 2009, 16 master's, 1 doctorate awarded. Terminal master's awarded for partial completion of doctoral program. *Degree requirements:* For master's, comprehensive exam, thesis or alternative; for doctorate, 2 foreign languages, comprehensive exam, thesis/dissertation. *Entrance requirements:* For doctorate, sample of scholarly writing. Additional exam requirements/recommendations for international students: Required—TOEFL. Application fee: $40. *Financial support:* In 2009–10, 2 research assistantships, 20 teaching assistantships were awarded; Federal Work-Study, institutionally sponsored loans, scholarships/grants, and tuition waivers (full and partial) also available. Support available to part-time students. Financial award application deadline: 2/15. *Faculty research:* Models of physiological systems, mathematical immunology, computational group theory, mathematical logic, computational science. *Unit head:* Dr. Peter Jones, Chair, 414-288-3263, Fax: 414-288-1578. *Application contact:* Dr. Gary Krenz, Director of Graduate Studies, 414-288-6345.

Massachusetts Institute of Technology, School of Engineering and School of Science and MIT Sloan School of Management, Program in Computation for Design and Optimization, Cambridge, MA 02139. Offers SM. *Faculty:* 36 full-time (4 women). *Students:* 29 full-time (8 women), 23 international. Average age 24. 127 applicants, 26% accepted, 21 enrolled. In 2009, 21 master's awarded. *Degree requirements:* For master's, thesis. *Entrance requirements:* For master's, GRE General Test, 3 letters of reference. Additional exam requirements/recommendations for international students: Required—IELTS (minimum score 7). *Application deadline:* For fall admission, 1/10 for domestic and international students. Application fee: $75. Electronic applications accepted. *Financial support:* In 2009–10, 25 students received support, including 16 fellowships with full tuition reimbursements available (averaging $6,725 per year), 6 research assistantships with full tuition reimbursements available (averaging $19,561 per year), 1 teaching assistantship with full tuition reimbursement available (averaging $32,560 per year); health care benefits and unspecified assistantships also available. Financial award application deadline: 1/10. *Faculty research:* Computational methods, partial differential equations, optimization, uncertainty quantification, computational mechanics and materials. *Unit head:* Prof. Anthony Patera, Co-Director, Center for Computational Engineering, and Computation for Design and Optimization Program, 617-253-3725, E-mail: cdo_info@mit.edu. *Application contact:* Laura F. Koller, Academic Administrator, 617-253-3725, E-mail: cdo_info@mit.edu.

McGill University, Faculty of Graduate and Postdoctoral Studies, Faculty of Science, Department of Mathematics and Statistics, Montréal, QC H3A 2T5, Canada. Offers computational science and engineering (M Sc); mathematics and statistics (M Sc, MA, PhD), including applied mathematics (M Sc, MA), pure mathematics (M Sc, MA), statistics (M Sc, MA).

Memorial University of Newfoundland, School of Graduate Studies, Interdisciplinary Program in Computational Science, St. John's, NL A1C 5S7, Canada. Offers computational science (M Sc); computational science (cooperative) (M Sc). *Degree requirements:* For master's, thesis optional. *Entrance requirements:* For master's, honors B Sc or significant background in the field. Electronic applications accepted. *Faculty research:* Scientific computing, modeling and simulation, computational fluid dynamics, polymer physics, computational chemistry.

Miami University, Graduate School, School of Engineering and Applied Science, Computational Science and Engineering Program, Oxford, OH 45056. Offers MS. *Students:* 8 full-time (1 woman), 2 part-time (1 woman); includes 1 minority (Asian American or Pacific Islander), 3 international. *Entrance requirements:* For master's, GRE. Additional exam requirements/recommendations for international students: Required—TOEFL. *Application deadline:* For fall admission, 2/1 for domestic and international students. Application fee: $50. *Expenses:* Tuition, state resident: full-time $11,280. Tuition, nonresident: full-time $24,912. Required fees: $516. *Financial support:* Fellowships, research assistantships, teaching assistantships, health care benefits and unspecified assistantships available. Financial award application deadline: 3/1; financial award applicants required to submit FAFSA. *Unit head:* Dr. Marek Dollar, Dean, 513-529-0700, E-mail: seasfyi@muohio.edu. *Application contact:* Mary York, Domestic Graduate Admission Coordinator or Janet Miller, International Graduate Admission Coordinator, 513-529-3734, Fax: 513-529-3734, E-mail: gradschool@muohio.edu.

Michigan Technological University, Graduate School, College of Engineering, Program in Computational Science and Engineering, Houghton, MI 49931. Offers PhD. Part-time programs available. *Degree requirements:* For doctorate, comprehensive exam, thesis/dissertation. *Entrance requirements:* For doctorate, MS in relevant discipline. Additional exam requirements/recommendations for international students: Required—TOEFL (minimum score 550 paper-based; 213 computer-based). Electronic applications accepted. *Expenses:* Contact institution.

Northwestern University, McCormick School of Engineering and Applied Science, Program in Computational Biology and Bioinformatics, Evanston, IL 60208. Offers MS. Part-time programs available. *Degree requirements:* For master's, thesis. *Entrance requirements:* For master's, GRE General Test, 2 letters of reference. Additional exam requirements/recommendations for international students: Required—TOEFL (minimum score 600 paper-based; 250 computer-based). Electronic applications accepted. *Faculty research:* Mathematical models of protein signaling, high throughput DNA sequencing, macromolecule interactions, chemoinformatics, genome DNA sequence evolution.

Princeton University, Graduate School, Program in Applied and Computational Mathematics, Princeton, NJ 08544-1019. Offers PhD. *Degree requirements:* For doctorate, thesis/dissertation. *Entrance requirements:* For doctorate, GRE General Test, GRE Subject Test. Additional exam requirements/recommendations for international students: Required—TOEFL (minimum score 600 paper-based; 250 computer-based). Electronic applications accepted.

Rice University, Graduate Programs, George R. Brown School of Engineering, Department of Computational and Applied Mathematics, Houston, TX 77251-1892. Offers computational and applied mathematics (MA, MCAM, PhD); computational science and engineering (MCSE, PhD). *Degree requirements:* For master's, comprehensive exam (for some programs), thesis (for some programs); for doctorate, comprehensive exam, thesis/dissertation. *Entrance requirements:* For master's and doctorate, GRE General Test, minimum GPA of 3.0. Additional exam requirements/recommendations for international students: Required—TOEFL (minimum score 600 paper-based; 250 computer-based). Electronic applications accepted. *Faculty research:* Inverse problems, partial differential equations, computer algorithms, computational modeling, optimization theory.

Rice University, Graduate Programs, George R. Brown School of Engineering, Program in Computational Science and Engineering, Houston, TX 77251-1892. Offers MCSE.

Sam Houston State University, College of Arts and Sciences, Department of Computer Science, Huntsville, TX 77341. Offers computing and information science (MS). Part-time programs available. *Faculty:* 8 full-time (3 women). *Students:* 31 full-time (8 women), 24 part-time (6 women); includes 1 minority (African American), 31 international. Average age 29. 29 applicants, 83% accepted, 15 enrolled. In 2009, 9 master's awarded. *Entrance requirements:* For master's, GRE General Test. Additional exam requirements/recommendations for international students: Required—TOEFL (minimum score 550 paper-based; 213 computer-based; 79 iBT). *Application deadline:* For fall admission, 8/1 for domestic and international students; for spring admission, 12/1 for domestic and international students. Application fee: $20. *Expenses:* Tuition, state resident: full-time $3690; part-time $205 per credit hour. Tuition, nonresident: full-time $8676; part-time $482 per credit hour. Required fees: $1474. Tuition and fees vary according to course load and campus/location. *Financial support:* Research assistantships, teaching assistantships, Federal Work-Study, institutionally sponsored loans, and tuition waivers (partial) available. Support available to part-time students. Financial award application deadline: 5/31; financial award applicants required to submit FAFSA. *Unit head:* Dr. Peter Cooper, Chair, 936-294-1569, Fax: 936-294-4312, E-mail: css_pac@shsu.edu. *Application contact:* Dr. Jiuhung Ji, Advisor, 936-294-1579, E-mail: csc_jxj@shsu.edu.

San Diego State University, Graduate and Research Affairs, College of Sciences, Program in Computational Science, San Diego, CA 92182. Offers MS, PhD. *Degree requirements:* For master's, thesis; for doctorate, thesis/dissertation. *Entrance requirements:* For master's, GRE General Test, 3 letters of recommendation; for doctorate, GRE, 3 letters of recommendation. Additional exam requirements/recommendations for international students: Required—TOEFL. Electronic applications accepted.

Simon Fraser University, Graduate Studies, Faculty of Science, Department of Mathematics, Burnaby, BC V5A 1S6, Canada. Offers applied and computational mathematics (M Sc, PhD); mathematics (M Sc, PhD). *Degree requirements:* For master's, thesis; for doctorate, thesis/dissertation. *Entrance requirements:* For master's, GRE General Test, minimum GPA of 3.0, 3 letters of reference; for doctorate, GRE General Test, minimum GPA of 3.5, 3 letters of reference. Additional exam requirements/recommendations for international students: Required—TWE or IELTS. Electronic applications accepted. *Faculty research:* Semi-groups, number theory, optimization, combinations.

South Dakota State University, Graduate School, College of Engineering, Department of Mathematics and Statistics, Brookings, SD 57007. Offers computational science and statistics (PhD); geospatial science and engineering (PhD); mathematics (MS). Part-time programs available. *Degree requirements:* For master's, thesis (for some programs), oral exam; for doctorate, comprehensive exam, thesis/dissertation, oral and written exams. *Entrance requirements:* Additional exam requirements/recommendations for international students: Required—TOEFL (minimum score 550 paper-based; 213 computer-based; 80 iBT); Recommended—IELTS. *Faculty research:* Mathematics, biostatistics, computational science, numerical linear algebra, statistics, applied quality number theory, abstract algebra.

Southern Methodist University, Dedman College, Department of Mathematics, Dallas, TX 75275. Offers computational and applied mathematics (MS, PhD). *Faculty:* 17 full-time (2 women). *Students:* 18 full-time (6 women); includes 9 minority (5 Asian Americans or Pacific Islanders, 4 Hispanic Americans). Average age 26. 18 applicants, 44% accepted, 7 enrolled. In 2009, 3 master's, 4 doctorates awarded. *Degree requirements:* For master's, oral and written exams; for doctorate, thesis/dissertation, oral and written exams. *Entrance requirements:* For master's and doctorate, GRE General Test, minimum GPA of 3.0, 18 undergraduate hours in mathematics beyond first and second year calculus. Additional exam requirements/recommendations for international students: Required—TOEFL. *Application deadline:* For fall admission, 2/1 priority date for domestic students, 2/1 for international students; for spring admission, 11/30 for domestic students. Applications are processed on a rolling basis. Application fee: $75. Electronic applications accepted. *Financial support:* In 2009–10, 18 students received support, including 6 research assistantships with full tuition reimbursements available (averaging $16,500 per year), 12 teaching assistantships with full tuition reimbursements available (averaging $16,500 per year); career-related internships or fieldwork, scholarships/grants, health care benefits, tuition waivers, and unspecified assistantships also available. Support available to part-time students. Financial award application deadline: 2/1; financial award applicants required to submit FAFSA. *Faculty research:* Numerical analysis, scientific computation, fluid dynamics, software development, differential equations. Total annual research expenditures: $92,000. *Unit head:* Dr. Douglas A. Reinelt, Chairman, 214-768-2506, Fax: 214-768-2355, E-mail: mathchair@mail.smu.edu. *Application contact:* Dr. Thomas W. Carr, Director of Graduate Studies, 214-768-3460, E-mail: math@mail.smu.edu.

Stanford University, School of Engineering, Program in Scientific Computing and Computational Mathematics, Stanford, CA 94305-9991. Offers MS, PhD. Terminal master's awarded for partial completion of doctoral program. *Degree requirements:* For doctorate, thesis/dissertation, qualifying exam. *Entrance requirements:* For master's, GRE General Test; for doctorate, GRE General Test, GRE Subject Test. Additional exam requirements/recommendations for international students: Required—TOEFL. Electronic applications accepted. *Expenses:* Tuition: Full-time $37,380; part-time $2760 per quarter. Required fees: $501.

Temple University, Graduate School, College of Science and Technology, Department of Mathematics, Philadelphia, PA 19122-6096. Offers applied mathematics (MA); mathematics (PhD); pure mathematics (MA). Part-time and evening/weekend programs available. Terminal master's awarded for partial completion of doctoral program. *Degree requirements:* For master's, thesis optional, written exam; for doctorate, 2 foreign languages, thesis/dissertation, oral and written exams. *Entrance requirements:* For master's, GRE General Test, minimum GPA of 3.0; for doctorate, GRE General Test, GRE Subject Test, minimum GPA of 3.0. Additional exam requirements/recommendations for international students: Required—TOEFL (minimum score 550 paper-based; 213 computer-based; 79 iBT). Electronic applications accepted. *Faculty research:* Differential geometry, numerical analysis.

University of Alaska Fairbanks, College of Natural Sciences and Mathematics, Department of Physics, Fairbanks, AK 99775-5920. Offers computational physics (MS); physics (MAT, MS, PhD); space physics (MS, PhD). Part-time programs available. *Faculty:* 10 full-time (1 woman). *Students:* 23 full-time (3 women), 2 part-time (0 women); includes 1 minority (American Indian/Alaska Native), 8 international. Average age 31. 24 applicants, 25% accepted, 6 enrolled. In 2009, 2 master's awarded. Terminal master's awarded for partial completion of doctoral program. *Degree requirements:* For master's, comprehensive exam, thesis or alternative; for doctorate, comprehensive exam, thesis/dissertation, oral defense. *Entrance requirements:* Additional exam requirements/recommendations for international students: Required—TOEFL (minimum score 550 paper-based; 213 computer-based; 80 iBT). *Application deadline:* For fall admission, 6/1 for domestic students, 3/1 for international students; for spring admission, 10/15 for domestic students, 9/1 for international students. Applications are processed on a rolling basis. Application fee: $60. Electronic applications accepted. *Expenses:* Tuition, state resident: full-time $7584; part-time $316 per credit. Tuition, nonresident: full-time $15,504; part-time $646 per credit. Required fees: $23 per credit. $135 per semester. Tuition and fees vary according to course level, course load and reciprocity agreements. *Financial support:* In 2009–10, 1 fellowship (averaging $16,454 per year), 11 research assistantships (averaging $16,320 per year), 7 teaching assistantships (averaging $15,451 per year) were awarded; Federal Work-Study, scholarships/grants, health care benefits, and unspecified assistantships also available. Support available to part-time students. Financial award application deadline: 2/15; financial award applicants required to submit FAFSA. *Faculty research:* Atmospheric and ionospheric radar studies, space plasma theory, magnetospheric dynamics, space weather and auroral studies, turbulence and complex systems. *Unit head:* John Olson, Chair, 907-474-7339, Fax: 907-474-6130, E-mail: physics@uaf.edu. *Application contact:* John Olson, Chair, 907-474-7339, Fax: 907-474-6130, E-mail: physics@uaf.edu.

University of California, Santa Barbara, Graduate Division, College of Engineering, Department of Chemical Engineering, Santa Barbara, CA 93106-5080. Offers chemical engineering (MS, PhD); computational science and engineering (PhD). *Faculty:* 21 full-time (1 woman). *Students:* 69 full-time (18 women). Average age 25. 285 applicants, 23% accepted, 16 enrolled. In 2009, 2 master's, 15 doctorates awarded. Terminal master's awarded for partial completion of doctoral program. *Degree requirements:* For master's, thesis or comprehensive exam; for doctorate, thesis/dissertation, candidacy exam, dissertation defense, defense exam, seminar presentation. *Entrance requirements:* For master's, GRE General Test, 3 letters of recommendation, resume/curriculum vitae; for doctorate, GRE General Test, 3 letters of recommendation, statement of purpose, personal achievements/contributions statement, resume/curriculum vitae, transcripts for post-secondary institutions attended. Additional exam requirements/recommendations for international students: Required—TOEFL (minimum score 560 paper-based; 220 computer-based; 83 iBT) or IELTS (minimum score 7). *Application deadline:* For fall admission, 1/15 priority date for domestic and international students. Application fee: $70 ($90 for international students). Electronic applications accepted. *Financial support:* In 2009–10, 68 students received support, including 32 fellowships with full and partial tuition reimbursements available (averaging $8,200 per year), 63 research assistantships with full and partial tuition reimbursements available (averaging $10,800 per year), 41 teaching assistantships with partial tuition reimbursements available (averaging $3,400 per year); Federal Work-Study, institutionally sponsored loans, scholarships/grants, health care benefits, tuition waivers (full and partial), and unspecified assistantships also available. Financial award application deadline: 1/15; financial award applicants required to submit FAFSA. *Faculty research:* Fluid transport, complex fluid and polymers, biomaterials/bioengineering, catalysis and reaction engineering, systems process design and control. Total annual research expenditures: $7.4 million. *Unit head:* Prof. Michael Doherty, Chair, 805-893-5309, Fax: 805-893-4731, E-mail: mfd@engineering.ucsb.edu. *Application contact:* Laura Crownover, Student Affairs Officer, 805-893-8671, Fax: 805-893-4731, E-mail: laura@engineering.ucsb.edu.

University of California, Santa Barbara, Graduate Division, College of Engineering, Department of Computer Science, Santa Barbara, CA 93106-5110. Offers computational science and engineering (PhD); computer science (MS, PhD). *Faculty:* 33 full-time (5 women), 4 part-time/adjunct (0 women). *Students:* 147 full-time (30 women). Average age 27. 559 applicants, 23% accepted, 45 enrolled. In 2009, 26 master's, 19 doctorates awarded. Terminal master's awarded for partial completion of doctoral program. *Degree requirements:* For master's, comprehensive exam (for some programs), thesis (for some programs), project (for some programs); for doctorate, thesis/dissertation. *Entrance requirements:* For master's, GRE, 3 letters of recommendation, resume/curriculum vitae; for doctorate, GRE, 3 letters of recommendation, statement of purpose, personal achievements/contributions statement, resume/curriculum vitae, transcripts for post-secondary institutions attended. Additional exam requirements/recommendations for international students: Required—TOEFL (minimum score 600 paper-based; 250 computer-based; 100 iBT) or IELTS (minimum score 7). *Application deadline:* For fall admission, 12/15 for domestic and international students. Application fee: $70 ($90 for international students). Electronic applications accepted. *Financial support:* In 2009–10, 115 students received support, including 18 fellowships with full and partial tuition reimbursements available (averaging $17,300 per year), 73 research assistantships with full and partial tuition reimbursements available (averaging $9,600 per year), 54 teaching assistantships with partial tuition reimbursements available (averaging $7,200 per year); career-related internships or fieldwork, Federal Work-Study, institutionally sponsored loans, scholarships/grants, traineeships, health care benefits, tuition waivers (full and partial), and unspecified assistantships also available. Financial award application deadline: 12/15; financial award applicants required to submit FAFSA. *Faculty research:* Networking and security, database systems, computational science and engineering, programming languages and software engineering, human computer interaction. Total annual research expenditures: $5.8 million. *Unit head:* Prof. Amr El Abbadi, Chair, 805-893-5334, Fax: 805-893-8553, E-mail: amr@cs.ucsb.edu. *Application contact:* Amanda Hoagland, Graduate Program Assistant, 805-893-4322, Fax: 805-893-8553, E-mail: gradhelp@cs.ucsb.edu.

University of California, Santa Barbara, Graduate Division, College of Engineering, Department of Electrical and Computer Engineering, Santa Barbara, CA 93106-9560. Offers computational science and engineering (PhD); electrical and computer engineering (PhD); MS/PhD. *Faculty:* 39 full-time (3 women), 1 part-time/adjunct (0 women). *Students:* 277 full-time (52 women). Average age 26. 1,135 applicants, 19% accepted, 50 enrolled. In 2009, 58 master's, 26 doctorates awarded. Terminal master's awarded for partial completion of doctoral program. *Degree requirements:* For master's, comprehensive exam, thesis; for doctorate, thesis/dissertation, screening exam, qualifying exam, dissertation defense exam. *Entrance requirements:* For master's, GRE General Test, 3 letters of recommendation, resume/curriculum vitae; for doctorate, GRE General Test, 3 letters of recommendation, statement of purpose, personal achievements/contributions statement, resume/curriculum vitae, transcripts for post-secondary institutions attended. Additional exam requirements/recommendations for international students: Required—TOEFL (minimum score 550 paper-based; 213 computer-based; 80 iBT) or IELTS (minimum score 7). *Application deadline:* For fall admission, 12/15 for domestic and international students; for winter admission, 11/1 for domestic and international students; for spring admission, 1/1 for domestic and international students. Application fee: $70 ($90 for international students). Electronic applications accepted. *Financial support:* In 2009–10, 209 students received support, including 52 fellowships with full and partial tuition reimbursements available (averaging $8,600 per year), 163 research assistantships with full and partial tuition reimbursements available (averaging $12,100 per year), 54 teaching assistantships with partial tuition reimbursements available (averaging $7,400 per year); career-related internships or fieldwork, Federal Work-Study, institutionally sponsored loans, scholarships/grants, traineeships, health care benefits, tuition waivers (full and partial), and unspecified assistantships also available. Financial award application deadline: 12/15; financial award applicants required to submit FAFSA. *Faculty research:* Communications, signal processing, computer engineering, control, electronics and photonics. Total annual research expenditures: $21.6 million. *Unit head:* Prof. Jerry Gibson, Chair, 805-893-3821, Fax: 805-893-3262, E-mail: gibson@ece.ucsb.edu. *Application contact:* Erika Raquel Klukovich, Graduate Admissions Coordinator, 805-893-3114, Fax: 805-893-5402, E-mail: erika@ece.ucsb.edu.

University of California, Santa Barbara, Graduate Division, College of Engineering, Department of Mechanical Engineering, Santa Barbara, CA 93106-5070. Offers computational science and engineering (PhD); mechanical engineering (MS, PhD); MS/PhD. *Faculty:* 33 full-time (4 women), 5 part-time/adjunct (0 women). *Students:* 74 full-time (15 women). Average age 27. 204 applicants, 21% accepted, 15 enrolled. In 2009, 2 master's, 15 doctorates awarded. *Degree requirements:* For master's, thesis; for doctorate, comprehensive exam, thesis/dissertation. *Entrance requirements:* For master's, GRE, 3 letters of recommendation, statement of purpose, personal achievements/contributions statement, resume/curriculum vitae, transcripts for post-secondary institutions attended; for doctorate, GRE General Test, 3 letters of recommendation, resume/curriculum vitae. Additional exam requirements/recommendations for international students: Required—TOEFL (minimum score 550 paper-based; 213 computer-based; 80 iBT) or IELTS (minimum score 7). *Application deadline:* For fall admission, 1/1 for domestic and international students. Application fee: $70 ($90 for international students). Electronic applications accepted. *Financial support:* In 2009–10, 72 students received support, including 29 fellowships with full and partial tuition reimbursements available (averaging $11,500 per year), 55 research assistantships with full and partial tuition reimbursements available (averaging $10,800 per year), 40 teaching assistantships with partial tuition reimbursements available (averaging $7,100 per year); Federal Work-Study, institutionally sponsored loans, scholarships/grants, health care benefits, tuition waivers (full and partial), and unspecified assistantships also available. Financial award application deadline: 1/1; financial award applicants required to submit FAFSA. *Faculty research:* Micro/nanoscale technology; computational science and engineering; dynamics, controls and robotics; thermofluid sciences, solid mechanics, materials, and structures. Total annual research expenditures: $4.9 million. *Unit head:* Prof. Kimberly Turner, Chair, 805-893-5106, Fax: 805-893-8486, E-mail: turner@engineering.ucsb.edu. *Application contact:* Laura Reynolds, Staff Graduate Program Advisor, 805-893-2239, Fax: 805-893-8651, E-mail: meegrad@engineering.ucsb.edu.

University of California, Santa Barbara, Graduate Division, College of Letters and Sciences, Division of Mathematics, Life, and Physical Sciences, Department of Earth Science, Santa Barbara, CA 93106-9620. Offers geological sciences (MS, PhD), including computational science and engineering (MS), geological sciences; geophysics (MS), including computational science and engineering, geophysics. *Faculty:* 20 full-time (4 women). *Students:* 35 full-time (15 women). Average age 27. 90 applicants, 27% accepted, 9 enrolled. In 2009, 3 master's, 4 doctorates awarded. *Degree requirements:* For master's, comprehensive exam, thesis; for doctorate, comprehensive exam, thesis/dissertation. *Entrance requirements:* For master's, GRE General Test, 3 letters of recommendation, resume/curriculum vitae; for doctorate, GRE General Test, 3 letters of recommendation, statement of purpose, personal achievements/contributions statement, resume/curriculum vitae, transcripts for post-secondary institutions attended. Additional exam requirements/recommendations for international students: Required—TOEFL (minimum score 550 paper-based; 213 computer-based; 80 iBT) or IELTS (minimum score 7). *Application deadline:* For fall admission, 2/1 for domestic students, 1/1 for international students. Application fee: $70 ($90 for international students). Electronic applications accepted. *Financial support:* In 2009–10, 35 students received support, including 21 fellowships with full and partial tuition reimbursements available (averaging $6,200 per year), 17 research assistantships with full and partial tuition reimbursements available (averaging $6,000 per year), 28 teaching assistantships with partial tuition reimbursements available (averaging $7,600 per year); career-related internships or fieldwork, Federal Work-Study, institutionally sponsored loans, scholarships/grants, traineeships, health care benefits, and unspecified assistantships also available. Financial award applicants required to submit FAFSA. *Faculty research:* Tectonics, geochronology, paleontology, volcanology, geomorphology. *Unit head:* Dr. Ralph Archuleta, Chair, 805-893-8441, E-mail: ralph@crustal.ucsb.edu. *Application contact:* Samuel C. Rifkin, Graduate Program Assistant, 805-893-3329, Fax: 805-893-2314, E-mail: rifkin@geol.ucsb.edu.

University of California, Santa Barbara, Graduate Division, College of Letters and Sciences, Division of Mathematics, Life, and Physical Sciences, Department of Ecology, Evolution, and Marine Biology, Santa Barbara, CA 93106-9620. Offers computational science and engineering (PhD); MA/PhD. *Faculty:* 39 full-time (8 women). *Students:* 56 full-time (35 women). Average age 30. 135 applicants, 13% accepted, 7 enrolled. In 2009, 7 master's, 15 doctorates awarded. Terminal master's awarded for partial completion of doctoral program. *Degree requirements:* For master's, comprehensive exam (for some programs), thesis (for some programs); for doctorate, comprehensive exam, thesis/dissertation. *Entrance requirements:* For master's, GRE General Test, 3 letters of recommendation, resume/curriculum vitae; for doctorate, GRE General Test, 3 letters of recommendation, statement of purpose, personal achievements/contributions statement, resume/curriculum vitae, transcripts for post-secondary institutions attended. Additional exam requirements/recommendations for international students: Required—TOEFL (minimum score 550 paper-based; 213 computer-based; 80 iBT) or IELTS. *Application deadline:* For fall admission, 12/15 for domestic and international students. Application fee: $70 ($90 for international students). Electronic applications accepted. *Financial support:* In 2009–10, 54 students received support, including 26 fellowships with full and partial tuition reimbursements available (averaging $17,900 per year), 16 research assistantships with full and partial tuition reimbursements available (averaging $7,300 per year), 35 teaching assistantships with partial tuition reimbursements available (averaging $9,100 per year); Federal Work-Study, institutionally sponsored loans, scholarships/grants, traineeships, health care benefits, tuition waivers (full and partial), and unspecified assistantships also available. Financial award applicants required to submit FAFSA. *Faculty research:* Ecology, population genetics, stream ecology, evolution, marine biology. *Unit head:* Robert Warner, Chair, 805-893-2415, Fax: 805-893-4724, E-mail: eembchair@lifesci.ucsb.edu. *Application contact:* Alina Haas, Staff Graduate Advisor, 805-893-3023, Fax: 805-893-5885, E-mail: haas@lifesci.ucsb.edu.

University of California, Santa Barbara, Graduate Division, College of Letters and Sciences, Division of Mathematics, Life, and Physical Sciences, Department of Mathematics, Santa Barbara, CA 93106-3080. Offers applied mathematics (MA); computational science and engineering (PhD); mathematics (MA, PhD); MA/PhD. *Faculty:* 31 full-time (3 women). *Students:* 54 full-time (14 women). Average age 26. 151 applicants, 26% accepted, 14 enrolled. In 2009, 5 master's, 14 doctorates awarded. Terminal master's awarded for partial completion of doctoral program. *Degree requirements:* For master's, comprehensive exam (for some programs), thesis (for some programs); for doctorate, comprehensive exam, thesis/dissertation. *Entrance requirements:* For master's, GRE General Test, GRE Subject Test (mathematics), 3 letters of recommendation, resume/curriculum vitae; for doctorate, GRE General Test, GRE Subject Test (math), 3 letters of recommendation, statement of purpose, personal achievements/contributions statement, resume/curriculum vitae, transcripts for post-secondary institutions attended. Additional exam requirements/recommendations for international students: Required—TOEFL (minimum score 575 paper-based; 231 computer-based; 80 iBT) or IELTS (7). *Application deadline:* For fall admission, 1/1 for domestic and international students. Application fee: $70 ($90 for international students). Electronic applications accepted. *Financial support:* In 2009–10, 54 students received support, including 13 fellowships with full and partial tuition reimbursements available (averaging $13,200 per year), 13 research assistantships with full and partial tuition reimbursements available (averaging $6,500 per year), 48 teaching assistantships with partial tuition reimbursements available (averaging $10,600 per year); Federal Work-Study, institutionally sponsored loans, scholarships/grants, health care benefits, and unspecified assistantships also available. Financial award applicants required to submit FAFSA. *Faculty research:* Topology, differential geometry, algebra, applied mathematics, partial differential equations. Total annual research expenditures: $204,214. *Unit head:* Prof. Jeffrey Stopple,

Computational Sciences

University of California, Santa Barbara (continued)
Chair, 805-893-8330, Fax: 805-893-2385, E-mail: stopple@math.ucsb.edu. *Application contact:* Medina Price, Graduate Advisor, 805-893-8192, Fax: 805-893-2385, E-mail: price@math.ucsb.edu.

University of Central Florida, College of Graduate Studies, Program in Modeling and Simulation, Orlando, FL 32816. Offers MS, PhD. *Students:* 40 full-time (11 women), 56 part-time (12 women); includes 20 minority (6 African Americans, 1 American Indian/Alaska Native, 4 Asian Americans or Pacific Islanders, 9 Hispanic Americans), 10 international. Average age 35. 45 applicants, 67% accepted, 21 enrolled. In 2009, 17 master's, 5 doctorates awarded. *Expenses:* Tuition, state resident: part-time $306.31 per credit hour. Tuition, nonresident: part-time $1099.01 per credit hour. Part-time tuition and fees vary according to degree level and program. *Financial support:* In 2009–10, 19 students received support, including 3 fellowships (averaging $8,900 per year), 21 research assistantships (averaging $9,600 per year). *Unit head:* Dr. Peter Kincaid, Coordinator, 407-882-1330, E-mail: pkincaid@ist.ucf.edu. *Application contact:* Dr. Peter Kincaid, Coordinator, 407-882-1330, E-mail: pkincaid@ist.ucf.edu.

The University of Iowa, Graduate College, Program in Applied Mathematical and Computational Sciences, Iowa City, IA 52242-1316. Offers PhD. *Degree requirements:* For doctorate, comprehensive exam, thesis/dissertation. *Entrance requirements:* For doctorate, GRE General Test, minimum GPA of 3.0. Additional exam requirements/recommendations for international students: Required—TOEFL (minimum score 620 paper-based; 260 computer-based; 105 iBT). Electronic applications accepted.

The University of Kansas, Graduate Studies, College of Liberal Arts and Sciences, Department of Physics and Astronomy, Lawrence, KS 66045. Offers computational physics and astronomy (MS); physics (MS, PhD). *Students:* 40 full-time (7 women), 3 part-time (1 woman); includes 3 minority (1 African American, 2 Hispanic Americans), 13 international. Average age 28. 47 applicants, 26% accepted, 6 enrolled. In 2009, 12 master's, 6 doctorates awarded. *Degree requirements:* For master's, thesis (for some programs); for doctorate, comprehensive exam, thesis/dissertation, computer skills, undergraduate certification, communication skills. *Entrance requirements:* For master's and doctorate, GRE Subject Test (physics), undergraduate degree. Additional exam requirements/recommendations for international students: Required—TOEFL. *Application deadline:* For fall admission, 5/1 priority date for domestic and international students; for spring admission, 11/15 for domestic and international students. Applications are processed on a rolling basis. Application fee: $45 ($55 for international students). Electronic applications accepted. *Expenses:* Tuition, state resident: full-time $6492; part-time $270.50 per credit hour. Tuition, nonresident: full-time $15,510; part-time $646.25 per credit hour. Required fees: $847; $70.56 per credit hour. Tuition and fees vary according to course load and program. *Financial support:* Fellowships with full and partial tuition reimbursements, research assistantships with full and partial tuition reimbursements, teaching assistantships with full and partial tuition reimbursements, health care benefits and unspecified assistantships available. Financial award application deadline: 5/1. *Faculty research:* Condensed-matter, cosmology, elementary particles, nuclear physics, space physics, astrophysics, astrobiology, biophysics, high energy. *Unit head:* Dr. Stephen J. Sanders, Chair, 785-864-4626, Fax: 785-864-5262. *Application contact:* Tess Gratton, Graduate Admission Specialist, 785-864-4626, Fax: 785-864-5262, E-mail: physics@ku.edu.

See Close-Up on page 231.

University of Lethbridge, School of Graduate Studies, Lethbridge, AB T1K 3M4, Canada. Offers accounting (MScM); addictions counseling (M Sc); agricultural biotechnology (M Sc); agricultural studies (M Sc, MA); anthropology (MA); archaeology (MA); art (MA, MFA); biochemistry (M Sc); biological sciences (M Sc); biomolecular science (PhD); biosystems and biodiversity (PhD); Canadian studies (MA); chemistry (M Sc); computer science (M Sc); computer science and geographical information science (M Sc); counseling psychology (M Ed); dramatic arts (MA); earth, space, and physical science (PhD); economics (MA); educational leadership (M Ed); English (MA); environmental science (M Sc); evolution and behavior (PhD); exercise science (M Sc); finance (MScM); French (MA); French/German (MA); French/Spanish (MA); general education (M Ed); general management (MScM); geography (M Sc, MA); German (MA); health science (M Sc); health sciences (MA); history (MA); human resource management and labour relations (MScM); individualized multidisciplinary (M Sc, MA); information systems (MScM); international management (MScM); kinesiology (M Sc, MA); management (M Sc, MA); marketing (MScM); mathematics (M Sc); music (M Mus, MA); Native American studies (MA); neuroscience (M Sc, PhD); new media (MA); nursing (M Sc); philosophy (MA); physics (M Sc); policy and strategy (MScM); political science (MA); psychology (M Sc, MA); religious studies (MA); social sciences (MA); sociology (MA); theatre and dramatic arts (MFA); theoretical and computational science (PhD); urban and regional studies (MA); women's studies (MA). Part-time and evening/weekend programs available. *Degree requirements:* For doctorate, comprehensive exam, thesis/dissertation. *Entrance requirements:* For master's, GMAT (M Sc in management), bachelor's degree in related field, minimum GPA of 3.0 during previous 20 graded semester courses, 2 years teaching or related experience (M Ed); for doctorate, master's degree, minimum graduate GPA of 3.5. Additional exam requirements/recommendations for international students: Required—TOEFL. *Faculty research:* Movement and brain plasticity, gibberellin physiology, photosynthesis, carbon cycling, molecular properties of main-group ring components.

University of Manitoba, Faculty of Graduate Studies, Faculty of Science, Program in Mathematical, Computational and Statistical Sciences, Winnipeg, MB R3T 2N2, Canada. Offers MMCSS.

University of Massachusetts Lowell, College of Arts and Sciences, Department of Mathematical Sciences, Lowell, MA 01854-2881. Offers applied mathematics (MS); computational mathematics (PhD); mathematics (MS). Part-time programs available. *Entrance requirements:* For master's, GRE General Test.

University of Michigan–Dearborn, College of Arts, Sciences, and Letters, Master of Science in Applied and Computational Mathematics Program, Dearborn, MI 48128. Offers MS. Part-time and evening/weekend programs available. *Faculty:* 9 full-time (3 women). *Students:* 17 part-time (8 women); includes 2 minority (1 African American, 1 Asian American or Pacific Islander). Average age 38. 4 applicants, 50% accepted, 2 enrolled. In 2009, 3 master's awarded. *Degree requirements:* For master's, thesis or alternative, project. *Entrance requirements:* For master's, 3 letters of recommendation, minimum GPA of 3.0, 2 years course work in math. Additional exam requirements/recommendations for international students: Required—TOEFL (minimum score 560 paper-based; 220 computer-based). *Application deadline:* For fall admission, 8/1 priority date for domestic students, 4/1 for international students; for winter admission, 12/1 priority date for domestic students, 11/1 for international students; for spring admission, 4/1 for domestic students, 3/1 for international students. Applications are processed on a rolling basis. Application fee: $60 ($75 for international students). Electronic applications accepted. *Expenses:* Tuition, area resident: Part-time $504.10 per credit hour. Tuition, state resident: part-time $504.10 per credit hour. Tuition, nonresident: part-time $957.90 per credit hour. *Financial support:* Federal Work-Study and scholarships/grants available. Support available to part-time students. Financial award application deadline: 4/1; financial award applicants required to submit FAFSA. *Faculty research:* Partial differential equations, statistics, discrete optimization, approximation theory, stochastic processes. *Unit head:* Dr. Joan Remski, Director, 313-593-4994, E-mail: remski@umd.umich.edu. *Application contact:* Carol Ligienza, Graduate Program Coordinator, CASL Graduate Programs, 313-593-1183, Fax: 313-583-6700, E-mail: caslgrad@umd.umich.edu.

University of Minnesota, Duluth, Graduate School, Swenson College of Science and Engineering, Department of Mathematics and Statistics, Duluth, MN 55812-2496. Offers applied and computational mathematics (MS). Part-time programs available. *Faculty:* 17 full-time (3 women). *Students:* 30 full-time (14 women); includes 13 minority (all Asian Americans or Pacific Islanders), 15 international. Average age 24. 22 applicants, 95% accepted, 11 enrolled. In 2009, 15 master's awarded. *Degree requirements:* For master's, thesis or alternative. *Entrance requirements:* For master's, GRE General Test, minimum GPA of 3.0. Additional exam requirements/recommendations for international students: Required—TOEFL (minimum score 550 paper-based; 213 computer-based; 79 iBT); Recommended—TWE. *Application deadline:* For fall admission, 2/15 priority date for domestic and international students; for spring admission, 11/1 for domestic and international students. Applications are processed on a rolling basis. Application fee: $75 ($95 for international students). Electronic applications accepted. *Financial support:* In 2009–10, 24 students received support, including 1 research assistantship with full tuition reimbursement available (averaging $13,120 per year), 22 teaching assistantships with full tuition reimbursements available (averaging $13,120 per year); fellowships, scholarships/grants, health care benefits, and unspecified assistantships also available. Financial award application deadline: 2/15. *Faculty research:* Discrete mathematics, diagnostic markers, combinatorics, biostatistics, mathematical modeling and scientific computation. Total annual research expenditures: $680,763. *Unit head:* Dr. Dalibor Froncek, Director of Graduate Studies, 218-726-7598, Fax: 218-726-8399, E-mail: dfroncek@d.umn.edu. *Application contact:* Jenny Kroft, Principal Office Administrative Specialist, 218-726-8747, Fax: 218-726-8399, E-mail: mkroft@d.umn.edu.

See Display on page 253.

University of Minnesota, Twin Cities Campus, Graduate School, Scientific Computation Program, Minneapolis, MN 55455-0213. Offers MS, PhD. Part-time programs available. *Degree requirements:* For master's, thesis; for doctorate, thesis/dissertation. *Entrance requirements:* For doctorate, GRE General Test. Additional exam requirements/recommendations for international students: Required—TOEFL (minimum score 550 paper-based; 213 computer-based; 79 iBT), IELTS (minimum score 6.5). Electronic applications accepted. *Faculty research:* Parallel computations, quantum mechanical dynamics, computational materials science, computational fluid dynamics, computational neuroscience.

University of Mississippi, Graduate School, School of Engineering, Oxford, University, MS 38677. Offers computational engineering science (MS, PhD); engineering science (MS, PhD). *Faculty:* 46 full-time (3 women), 2 part-time/adjunct (1 woman). *Students:* 122 full-time (31 women), 37 part-time (7 women); includes 14 minority (9 African Americans, 4 Asian Americans or Pacific Islanders, 1 Hispanic American), 82 international. In 2009, 36 master's, 14 doctorates awarded. *Degree requirements:* For master's, thesis (for some programs); for doctorate, thesis/dissertation. *Entrance requirements:* For master's, GRE General Test, minimum GPA of 3.0; for doctorate, GRE General Test. Additional exam requirements/recommendations for international students: Required—TOEFL. *Application deadline:* For fall admission, 4/1 for domestic students; for spring admission, 10/1 for domestic students. Applications are processed on a rolling basis. Application fee: $25. Electronic applications accepted. *Financial support:* Scholarships/grants available. Financial award application deadline: 3/1; financial award applicants required to submit FAFSA. *Unit head:* Alexander Cheng, 662-915-7407, Fax: 662-915-1287, E-mail: engineer@olemiss.edu. *Application contact:* Dr. Christy M. Wyandt, Associate Dean, 662-915-7474, Fax: 662-915-7577, E-mail: cwyandt@olemiss.edu.

University of New Haven, Graduate School, Tagliatela College of Engineering, Program in Computer and Information Science, West Haven, CT 06516-1916. Offers computer science (MS, Certificate), including advanced applications (MS), computer applications (Certificate), computer programming (Certificate), computer systems (MS), computing (Certificate), database and information systems (MS), network administration (Certificate), network systems (MS), software engineering and development (MS). Part-time and evening/weekend programs available. *Faculty:* 9 full-time (2 women), 5 part-time/adjunct (0 women). *Students:* 21 full-time (8 women), 32 part-time (8 women); includes 5 minority (2 African Americans, 1 Asian American or Pacific Islander, 2 Hispanic Americans), 26 international. Average age 30. 163 applicants, 88% accepted, 18 enrolled. In 2009, 24 master's awarded. *Degree requirements:* For master's, thesis or alternative. *Entrance requirements:* Additional exam requirements/recommendations for international students: Required—TOEFL (minimum score 520 paper-based; 190 computer-based; 70 iBT); Recommended—IELTS (minimum score 5.5). *Application deadline:* For fall admission, 5/31 for international students; for winter admission, 10/15 for international students; for spring admission, 1/15 for international students. Applications are processed on a rolling basis. Application fee: $50. Electronic applications accepted. *Expenses:* Tuition: Part-time $700 per credit. Required fees: $45 per term. One-time fee: $390 part-time. *Financial support:* Research assistantships with partial tuition reimbursements, teaching assistantships with partial tuition reimbursements, career-related internships or fieldwork, Federal Work-Study, scholarships/grants, tuition waivers, and unspecified assistantships available. Support available to part-time students. Financial award applicants required to submit FAFSA. *Unit head:* Dr. Tahany Fergany, Coordinator, 203-932-7067. *Application contact:* Eloise Gormley, Director of Graduate Admissions, 203-932-7449, Fax: 203-932-7137, E-mail: gradinfo@newhaven.edu.

University of New Mexico, Graduate School, Program in Computational Science and Engineering, Albuquerque, NM 87131-2039. Offers Post-Doctoral Certificate. *Application deadline:* For fall admission, 6/30 for domestic students; for spring admission, 11/15 for domestic students. Application fee: $50. Electronic applications accepted. *Expenses:* Tuition, state resident: full-time $2098.80; part-time $233.20 per credit hour. Tuition, nonresident: full-time $6650. Required fees: $25 per semester. Tuition and fees vary according to course load, program and reciprocity agreements. *Financial support:* Application deadline: 3/1; *Faculty research:* Arts technology, biophysics and nanoscale systems, chemistry and chemical biology, civil engineering, climate and weather modeling, computational biology and bioinformatics, cyberinfrastructure, digital arts and humanities, electromagnetics, energy grid modeling, high performance computing and scalable systems, image processing, materials physics, visualization and virtual environments, observational astronomy, open science grid, particle physics, quantum materials and devices, systems biology. *Unit head:* Dr. Susan Rachel Atlas, Unit Administrator, 505-277-0727, Fax: 505-277-8235, E-mail: director@hpc.unm.edu. *Application contact:* Stephanie Grant, Associate Director, Admissions, 505-277-0727, Fax: 505-277-8235, E-mail: slgrant@unm.edu.

University of Pennsylvania, School of Arts and Sciences, Graduate Group in Applied Mathematics and Computational Science, Philadelphia, PA 19104. Offers PhD. *Faculty:* 46 full-time (3 women), 1 part-time/adjunct (0 women). *Students:* 14 full-time (8 women), 13 international. 92 applicants, 15% accepted, 7 enrolled. *Application deadline:* For fall admission, 1/15 for domestic students. *Expenses:* Tuition: Full-time $25,660; part-time $4758 per course. Required fees: $2152; $270 per course. Tuition and fees vary according to course load, degree level and program. *Financial support:* Institutionally sponsored loans, scholarships/grants, traineeships, health care benefits, and unspecified assistantships available.

University of Puerto Rico, Mayagüez Campus, Graduate Studies, College of Arts and Sciences, Department of Mathematics, Mayagüez, PR 00681-9000. Offers applied mathematics (MS); computational sciences (MS); pure mathematics (MS); statistics (MS). Part-time programs available. *Degree requirements:* For master's, one foreign language, comprehensive exam, thesis optional. *Entrance requirements:* For master's, undergraduate degree in mathematics or its equivalent. *Faculty research:* Automata theory, linear algebra, logic.

The University of South Dakota, Graduate School, College of Arts and Sciences, Department of Computer Science, Vermillion, SD 57069-2390. Offers computational sciences and statistics (PhD); computer science (MS). Part-time programs available. *Degree requirements:* For master's, thesis optional. *Entrance requirements:* For master's, GRE General Test, GRE Subject Test (recommended), minimum GPA of 2.7. Additional exam requirements/recommendations for international students: Required—TOEFL (minimum score 550 paper-based; 213 computer-based; 79 iBT). Electronic applications accepted.

University of Southern Mississippi, Graduate School, College of Science and Technology, Department of Mathematics, Hattiesburg, MS 39406-0001. Offers computational science: mathematics (PhD); mathematics (MS). Part-time programs available. *Faculty:* 11 full-time (3 women), 1 part-time/adjunct (0 women). *Students:* 7 full-time (4 women), 1 (woman) part-time; includes 1 minority (African American), 3 international. Average age 29. 10 applicants, 90% accepted, 6 enrolled. In 2009, 5 master's awarded. *Degree requirements:* For master's, comprehensive exam, thesis or alternative. *Entrance requirements:* For master's, GRE General Test, minimum GPA of 2.75 in last 60 hours. Additional exam requirements/recommendations for international students: Required—TOEFL. *Application deadline:* For fall admission, 3/15 priority date for domestic students, 3/15 for international students. Applications are processed on a rolling basis. Application fee: $35. *Expenses:* Tuition, state resident: full-time $5096; part-time $284 per hour. Tuition, nonresident: full-time $13,052; part-time $726 per hour. Required fees: $402. Tuition and fees vary according to course level and course load. *Financial support:* In 2009–10, 1 fellowship (averaging $18,000 per year), 10 teaching assistantships with full tuition reimbursements (averaging $11,408 per year) were awarded; research assistantships with full tuition reimbursements, Federal Work-Study and institutionally sponsored loans also available. Financial award application deadline: 3/15; financial award applicants required to submit FAFSA. *Faculty research:* Dynamical systems, numerical analysis and multigrid methods, random number generation, matrix theory, group theory. *Unit head:* Dr. C. S. Chen, Chair, 601-266-4289, Fax: 601-266-5818. *Application contact:* Shonna Breland, Manager of Graduate Admissions, 601-266-6563, Fax: 601-266-5138.

University of Southern Mississippi, Graduate School, College of Science and Technology, Department of Physics and Astronomy, Hattiesburg, MS 39406-0001. Offers computational science (PhD); physics (MS). *Faculty:* 10 full-time (1 woman). *Students:* 7 full-time (3 women), 1 part-time (0 women), 4 international. Average age 31. 17 applicants, 29% accepted, 3 enrolled. In 2009, 6 master's awarded. *Degree requirements:* For master's, comprehensive exam, thesis. *Entrance requirements:* For master's, GRE General Test, minimum GPA of 2.75 in last 60 hours. Additional exam requirements/recommendations for international students: Required—TOEFL. *Application deadline:* For fall admission, 3/1 priority date for domestic students, 3/1 for international students. Applications are processed on a rolling basis. Application fee: $35. *Expenses:* Tuition, state resident: full-time $5096; part-time $284 per hour. Tuition, nonresident: full-time $13,052; part-time $726 per hour. Required fees: $402. Tuition and fees vary according to course level and course load. *Financial support:* In 2009–10, 15 teaching assistantships with full tuition reimbursements (averaging $11,745 per year) were awarded; research assistantships, Federal Work-Study also available. Financial award application deadline: 3/15; financial award applicants required to submit FAFSA. *Faculty research:* Polymers, atomic physics, fluid mechanics, liquid crystals, refractory materials. *Unit head:* Dr. Khin Maung, Chair, 601-266-4934, Fax: 601-266-5149. *Application contact:* Shonna Breland, Manager of Graduate Admissions, 601-266-6563, Fax: 601-266-5138.

University of Southern Mississippi, Graduate School, College of Science and Technology, School of Computing, Hattiesburg, MS 39406-0001. Offers computational science (MS, PhD); computer science (MS, PhD); engineering technology (MS). *Faculty:* 18 full-time (3 women), 1 (woman) part-time/adjunct. *Students:* 72 full-time (20 women), 21 part-time (6 women); includes 7 minority (5 African Americans, 2 Hispanic Americans), 51 international. Average age 29. 101 applicants, 61% accepted, 24 enrolled. In 2009, 15 master's awarded. *Degree requirements:* For master's, comprehensive exam, thesis; for doctorate, comprehensive exam, thesis/dissertation. *Entrance requirements:* For master's, GRE General Test, minimum GPA of 2.75 in last 60 hours. Additional exam requirements/recommendations for international students: Required—TOEFL. *Application deadline:* For fall admission, 3/15 priority date for domestic students, 3/15 for international students. Applications are processed on a rolling basis. Application fee: $35. *Expenses:* Tuition, state resident: full-time $5096; part-time $284 per hour. Tuition, nonresident: full-time $13,052; part-time $726 per hour. Required fees: $402. Tuition and fees vary according to course level and course load. *Financial support:* In 2009–10, 29 research assistantships with full tuition reimbursements (averaging $8,750 per year), 7 teaching assistantships with full tuition reimbursements (averaging $9,944 per year) were awarded; Federal Work-Study and institutionally sponsored loans also available. Financial award application deadline: 3/15; financial award applicants required to submit FAFSA. *Faculty research:* Satellite telecommunications, advanced life-support systems, artificial intelligence. *Unit head:* Dr. Adel Ali, Chair, 601-266-4949, Fax: 601-266-6452. *Application contact:* Shonna Breland, Manager of Graduate Admissions, 601-266-6563, Fax: 601-266-5138.

The University of Tennessee at Chattanooga, Graduate School, College of Engineering and Computer Science, Program in Computational Engineering, Chattanooga, TN 37403. Offers PhD. *Faculty:* 6 full-time (0 women). *Students:* 9 full-time (2 women), 8 part-time (1 woman); includes 2 minority (both Asian Americans or Pacific Islanders), 5 international. Average age 32. 6 applicants, 83% accepted, 5 enrolled. In 2009, 4 doctorates awarded. *Degree requirements:* For doctorate, comprehensive exam, thesis/dissertation. *Entrance requirements:* For doctorate, GRE General Test. Additional exam requirements/recommendations for international students: Required—TOEFL (minimum score 550 paper-based; 213 computer-based; 79 iBT), IELTS (minimum score 6). *Application deadline:* For fall admission, 8/1 priority date for domestic students, 6/1 for international students; for spring admission, 12/1 priority date for domestic students, 10/1 for international students. Applications are processed on a rolling basis. Application fee: $35. Electronic applications accepted. *Expenses:* Tuition, state resident: full-time $5404; part-time $300 per credit hour. Tuition, nonresident: full-time $16,702; part-time $928 per credit hour. Required fees: $1150; $130 per credit hour. *Financial support:* In 2009–10, 8 research assistantships with full and partial tuition reimbursements (averaging $5,500 per year) were awarded; career-related internships or fieldwork, scholarships/grants, and unspecified assistantships also available. Support available to part-time students. *Faculty research:* Computational fluid dynamics, design optimization, solution algorithms, hydronamics and propulsion. Total annual research expenditures: $4 million. *Unit head:* Dr. Tim Swafford, Director, 423-425-5497, Fax: 423-425-5517, E-mail: tim-swafford@utc.edu. *Application contact:* Dr. Stephanie Bellar, Dean of Graduate Studies, 423-425-4666, Fax: 423-425-5223, E-mail: stephanie-bellar@utc.edu.

The University of Tennessee at Chattanooga, Graduate School, College of Engineering and Computer Science, Program in Engineering, Chattanooga, TN 37403. Offers chemical (MS Engr); civil (MS Engr); computational (MS Engr); electrical (MS Engr); industrial (MS Engr); mechanical (MS Engr). Part-time and evening/weekend programs available. *Faculty:* 8 full-time (0 women). *Students:* 22 full-time (7 women), 30 part-time (3 women); includes 9 minority (4 African Americans, 4 Asian Americans or Pacific Islanders, 1 Hispanic American), 9 international. Average age 29. 59 applicants, 59% accepted, 19 enrolled. In 2009, 9 master's awarded. *Degree requirements:* For master's, comprehensive exam, thesis or alternative, engineering project. *Entrance requirements:* For master's, GRE General Test, minimum undergraduate GPA of 2.5 or 3.0 in last 30 hours of coursework. Additional exam requirements/recommendations for international students: Required—TOEFL (minimum score 550 paper-based; 213 computer-based; 79 iBT), IELTS (minimum score 6). *Application deadline:* For fall admission, 8/1 priority date for domestic students, 6/1 for international students; for spring admission, 12/1 priority date for domestic students, 10/1 for international students. Applications are processed on a rolling basis. Application fee: $35. Electronic applications accepted. *Expenses:* Tuition, state resident: full-time $5404; part-time $300 per credit hour. Tuition, nonresident: full-time $16,702; part-time $928 per credit hour. Required fees: $1150; $130 per credit hour. *Financial support:* In 2009–10, 23 research assistantships with full and partial tuition reimbursements (averaging $5,500 per year) were awarded; career-related internships or fieldwork, scholarships/grants, and unspecified assistantships also available. Support available to part-time students. *Faculty research:* Quality control and reliability engineering, financial management, thermal science, energy conservation, structural analysis. Total annual research expenditures: $2.6 million. *Unit head:* Dr. Neslihan Alp, Director, 423-425-4032, Fax: 423-425-5229, E-mail: neslihan-alp@utc.edu. *Application contact:* Dr. Stephanie Bellar, Dean of Graduate Studies, 423-425-4666, Fax: 423-425-5223, E-mail: stephanie-bellar@utc.edu.

The University of Texas at Austin, Graduate School, Program in Computational and Applied Mathematics, Austin, TX 78712-1111. Offers MA, PhD. Terminal master's awarded for partial completion of doctoral program. *Degree requirements:* For master's, thesis optional; for doctorate, thesis/dissertation, 3 area qualifying exams. Electronic applications accepted.

The University of Texas at El Paso, Graduate School, College of Science, Computational Science Program, El Paso, TX 79968-0001. Offers MS, PhD. *Students:* 16 (2 women); includes 6 minority (1 African American, 5 Hispanic Americans), 10 international. *Degree requirements:* For master's, thesis or internship; for doctorate, thesis/dissertation. *Entrance requirements:* For master's, Contact Director; for doctorate, GRE, Statement of Purpose, Letters of Recommendation. Additional exam requirements/recommendations for international students: Required—TOEFL; Recommended—IELTS. *Application deadline:* For fall admission, 8/1 for domestic students, 3/1 for international students; for spring admission, 11/1 for domestic students, 9/1 for international students. Applications are processed on a rolling basis. Application fee: $45 ($80 for international students). Electronic applications accepted. *Financial support:* Fellowships with partial tuition reimbursements, research assistantships with partial tuition reimbursements, teaching assistantships with partial tuition reimbursements, institutionally sponsored loans, scholarships/grants, health care benefits, tuition waivers (partial), and unspecified assistantships available. Support available to part-time students. Financial award application deadline: 3/15; financial award applicants required to submit FAFSA. *Unit head:* Dr. Leticia Velazquez, Director, 915-747-6768, Fax: 915-747-6502, E-mail: leti@utep.edu. *Application contact:* Dr. Patricia D. Witherspoon, Dean of the Graduate School, 915-747-5491, Fax: 915-747-5788, E-mail: withersp@utep.edu.

University of Utah, The Graduate School, College of Engineering, School of Computing, Computational Engineering and Science Program, Salt Lake City, UT 84112. Offers MS. *Students:* 4 full-time (1 woman), 4 part-time (2 women); includes 1 minority (Asian American or Pacific Islander), 6 international. Average age 29. 21 applicants, 48% accepted, 8 enrolled. In 2009, 7 master's awarded. *Degree requirements:* For master's, comprehensive exam, thesis (for some programs). *Entrance requirements:* For master's, minimum GPA of 3.0. Additional exam requirements/recommendations for international students: Required—TOEFL (minimum score 500 paper-based; 173 computer-based; 61 iBT), IELTS (minimum score 5). *Application deadline:* For fall admission, 1/15 priority date for domestic and international students. Application fee: $55 ($65 for international students). Electronic applications accepted. *Expenses:* Tuition, state resident: full-time $4004; part-time $1674 per semester. Tuition, nonresident: full-time $14,134; part-time $5915 per semester. Required fees: $324 per semester. Tuition and fees vary according to course load, degree level and program. *Financial support:* In 2009–10, 1 teaching assistantship with full tuition reimbursement (averaging $11,000 per year) was awarded; health care benefits and unspecified assistantships also available. Financial award application deadline: 12/15; financial award applicants required to submit FAFSA. *Faculty research:* Mathematical modeling, the formulation of the numerical methodology for solving the problem, the selection of the appropriate computer architecture and algorithms, and the effective interpretation of the results through visualization and/or statistical reduction. *Unit head:* Dr. Kris Sikorski, Director, 801-581-8579, Fax: 801-581-5843, E-mail: sikorski@cs.utah.edu. *Application contact:* Dr. Kris Sikorski, 801-581-8579, Fax: 801-581-5843, E-mail: sikorski@cs.utah.edu.

University of Utah, The Graduate School, Professional Master of Science and Technology Program, Salt Lake City, UT 84112-1107. Offers biotechnology (PSM); computational science (PSM); environmental science (PSM); science instrumentation (PSM). Part-time programs available. *Students:* 32 full-time (17 women), 38 part-time (13 women); includes 5 minority (1 African American, 3 Asian Americans or Pacific Islanders, 1 Hispanic American), 19 international. Average age 31. 84 applicants, 33% accepted, 16 enrolled. In 2009, 7 master's awarded. *Degree requirements:* For master's, internship. *Entrance requirements:* For master's, GRE (recommended), minimum undergraduate GPA of 3.0, bachelor's degree from accredited university or college. Additional exam requirements/recommendations for international students: Required—TOEFL (minimum score 500 paper-based; 173 computer-based). *Application deadline:* For fall admission, 3/1 for domestic and international students. Application fee: $55 ($65 for international students). Electronic applications accepted. *Expenses:* Tuition, state resident: full-time $4004; part-time $1674 per semester. Tuition, nonresident: full-time $14,134; part-time $5915 per semester. Required fees: $324 per semester. Tuition and fees vary according to course load, degree level and program. *Financial support:* In 2009–10, 4 fellowships with full and partial tuition reimbursements (averaging $12,000 per year), 3 research assistantships with full tuition reimbursements (averaging $13,000 per year) were awarded; unspecified assistantships also available. Financial award applicants required to submit FAFSA. *Unit head:* Jennifer Schmidt, Program Director, 801-585-5630, E-mail: jennifer.schmidt@gradschool.utah.edu. *Application contact:* Francine Stirling, Project Coordinator, 801-585-3650, Fax: 801-585-6749, E-mail: francine.stirling@gradschool.utah.edu.

University of Washington, Graduate School, College of Arts and Sciences, Department of Mathematics, Seattle, WA 98195. Offers mathematics (MA, MS, PhD); numerical analysis (MS); optimization (MS). Part-time programs available. Terminal master's awarded for partial completion of doctoral program. *Degree requirements:* For master's, thesis optional; for doctorate, 2 foreign languages, thesis/dissertation. *Entrance requirements:* For master's, GRE, minimum GPA of 3.0; for doctorate, GRE General Test, GRE Subject Test (mathematics), minimum GPA of 3.0. Additional exam requirements/recommendations for international students: Required—TOEFL. Electronic applications accepted. *Faculty research:* Algebra, analysis, probability, combinatorics and geometry.

Western Michigan University, Graduate College, College of Arts and Sciences, Department of Mathematics, Program in Applied and Computational Mathematics, Kalamazoo, MI 49008. Offers MS.

Mathematical and Computational Finance

Bernard M. Baruch College of the City University of New York, Weissman School of Arts and Sciences, Program in Financial Engineering, New York, NY 10010-5585. Offers MS. *Entrance requirements:* For master's, GRE General Test or GMAT, 3 recommendations. Additional exam requirements/recommendations for international students: Required—TOEFL, TWE.

Boston University, Graduate School of Arts and Sciences, Department of Mathematics and Statistics, Boston, MA 02215. Offers mathematical finance (MA); mathematics (MA, PhD). *Students:* 41 full-time (11 women), 2 part-time (0 women); includes 2 minority (1 African American, 1 Hispanic American), 20 international. Average age 27. 198 applicants, 17% accepted, 12 enrolled. In 2009, 9 master's, 7 doctorates awarded. Terminal master's awarded for partial completion of doctoral program. *Degree requirements:* For master's, one foreign language, comprehensive exam; for doctorate, one foreign language, comprehensive exam, thesis/dissertation. *Entrance requirements:* For master's and doctorate, GRE General Test, GRE Subject Test, 3 letters of recommendation. Additional exam requirements/recommendations for international students: Required—TOEFL (minimum score 600 paper-based; 250 computer-based). *Application deadline:* For fall admission, 1/15 for domestic and international students; for spring admission, 10/15 for domestic and international students. Application fee: $70. Electronic applications accepted. *Expenses:* Tuition: Full-time $37,910; part-time $1184 per credit hour. Required fees: $386; $40 per semester. Part-time tuition and fees vary according to class time, course level, degree level and program. *Financial support:* In 2009–10, 3 fellowships with full tuition reimbursements (averaging $18,900 per year), 17 research assistantships with full tuition reimbursements (averaging $18,400 per year), 28 teaching assistantships with full tuition reimbursements (averaging $18,400 per year) were awarded; Federal Work-Study and scholarships/grants also available. Support available to part-time students. Financial award application deadline: 1/15; financial award applicants required to submit FAFSA. *Unit head:* Ralph D'Agostino, Chairman, 617-353-2767, Fax: 617-353-8100, E-mail: ralph@bu.edu. *Application contact:* Kathleen Heavey, Staff Coordinator, 617-353-2560, Fax: 617-353-8100, E-mail: kheavey@bu.edu.

Boston University, School of Management, Program in Mathematical Finance, Boston, MA 02215. Offers MS, PhD. Part-time programs available. *Students:* 56 full-time (20 women), 51 international. Average age 24. *Degree requirements:* For doctorate, thesis/dissertation. *Entrance requirements:* For master's, GMAT or GRE, 2 Letters of Recommendation, Essays, Resume, Personal Statement, Official Transcripts; for doctorate, GMAT or GRE, 3 Letters of Recommendation, Essays, Resume, Personal Statement, Official Transcripts. Additional exam requirements/recommendations for international students: Required—TOEFL, IELTS. *Application deadline:* For fall admission, 4/15 for domestic and international students. Application fee: $125. Electronic applications accepted. *Expenses:* Tuition: Full-time $37,910; part-time $1184 per credit hour. Required fees: $386; $40 per semester. Part-time tuition and fees vary according to class time, course level, degree level and program. *Financial support:* Career-related internships or fieldwork, Federal Work-Study, institutionally sponsored loans, and scholarships/grants available. Financial award applicants required to submit FAFSA. *Faculty research:* Equilibrium asset pricing in incomplete financial markets with heterogeneous agents interactions; numerical methods for free boundary value problems in higher dimensions; market imperfections, frictions and corrections; topics in corporate finance; economic and financial modeling. *Unit head:* Andrew Lyasoff, Faculty Director, 617-353-5785, Fax: 617-353-4415, E-mail: mathfn@bu.edu. *Application contact:* Hayden Estrada, Assistant Dean, Admissions, 617-353-2670, Fax: 617-353-7368, E-mail: mathfn@bu.edu.

Carnegie Mellon University, Mellon College of Science, Department of Mathematical Sciences, Pittsburgh, PA 15213-3891. Offers algorithms, combinatorics, and optimization (PhD); applied mathematics (PhD); computational finance (MS); mathematical finance (PhD); mathematical sciences (MS, DA, PhD); pure and applied logic (PhD). Part-time programs available. Terminal master's awarded for partial completion of doctoral program. *Degree requirements:* For doctorate, thesis/dissertation. *Entrance requirements:* For master's and doctorate, GRE General Test, GRE Subject Test. Additional exam requirements/recommendations for international students: Required—TOEFL. Electronic applications accepted. *Faculty research:* Continuum mechanics, discrete mathematics, applied and computational mathematics.

Carnegie Mellon University, Tepper School of Business, Pittsburgh, PA 15213-3891. Offers accounting (PhD); algorithms, combinatorics, and optimization (MS, PhD); business management and software engineering (MBMSE); civil engineering and industrial management (MS); computational finance (MSCF); economics (MS, PhD); electronic commerce (MS); environmental engineering and management (MEEM); finance (PhD); financial economics (PhD); industrial administration (MBA), including administration and public management; information systems (PhD); management of manufacturing and automation (PhD); marketing (PhD); mathematical finance (PhD); operations research (PhD); organizational behavior and theory (PhD); political economy (PhD); production and operations management (PhD); public policy and management (MS, MSED); software engineering and business management (MS); JD/MS; JD/MSIA; M Div/MS; MOM/MSIA; MSCF/MSIA. Part-time programs available. Terminal master's awarded for partial completion of doctoral program. *Degree requirements:* For doctorate, thesis/dissertation. *Entrance requirements:* For master's, GMAT. Additional exam requirements/recommendations for international students: Required—TOEFL. *Expenses:* Contact institution.

DePaul University, Charles H. Kellstadt Graduate School of Business, Department of Finance, Chicago, IL 60604-2287. Offers behavioral finance (MBA); computational finance (MS); finance (MBA, MSF); financial analysis (MBA); financial management and control (MBA); international marketing and finance (MBA); managerial finance (MBA); real estate (MS); real estate finance and investment (MBA); strategy, execution and valuation (MBA). Part-time and evening/weekend programs available. *Faculty:* 26 full-time (5 women), 23 part-time/adjunct (2 women). *Students:* 432 full-time (120 women), 197 part-time (47 women); includes 94 minority (13 African Americans, 1 American Indian/Alaska Native, 55 Asian Americans or Pacific Islanders, 25 Hispanic Americans), 82 international. In 2009, 239 master's awarded. *Entrance requirements:* For master's, GMAT, 2 letters of recommendation, resume. Additional exam requirements/recommendations for international students: Required—TOEFL (minimum score 550 paper-based; 213 computer-based; 80 iBT). *Application deadline:* For fall admission, 7/1 for domestic students, 6/1 for international students; for winter admission, 10/1 for domestic students, 9/1 for international students; for spring admission, 2/1 for domestic students, 1/1 for international students. Applications are processed on a rolling basis. Application fee: $60. Electronic applications accepted. *Expenses:* Tuition: Full-time $37,525; part-time $620 per credit hour. *Financial support:* In 2009–10, 8 students received support, including 6 research assistantships with partial tuition reimbursements available (averaging $4,340 per year); scholarships/grants and unspecified assistantships also available. Financial award application deadline: 4/1; financial award applicants required to submit FAFSA. *Faculty research:* Derivatives, valuation, international finance, real estate, corporate finance. *Unit head:* Ali M. Fatemi, Professor and Chair, 312-362-8826, Fax: 312-362-6566, E-mail: afatemi@depaul.edu. *Application contact:* Christopher E. Kinsella, Director of Cohort MBA Programs, 312-362-8810, Fax: 312-362-6677, E-mail: kgsb@depaul.edu.

DePaul University, College of Computing and Digital Media, Chicago, IL 60604. Offers business information technology (MS); computational finance (MS); computer and information sciences (PhD); computer game development (MS); computer graphics and motion technology (MS); computer science (MS); computer, information and network security (MS), including applied technology; digital cinema (MFA, MS), including information technology project management (MS); e-commerce technology (MS); human-computer interaction (MS); information systems (MS); information technology (MA); information technology project management (MS); software engineering (MS); telecommunications systems (MS); JD/MS. Part-time and evening/weekend programs available. Postbaccalaureate distance learning degree programs offered (no on-campus study). *Faculty:* 78 full-time (16 women), 191 part-time/adjunct (51 women). *Students:* 922 full-time (239 women), 887 part-time (209 women); includes 466 minority (193 African Americans, 3 American Indian/Alaska Native, 162 Asian Americans or Pacific Islanders, 108 Hispanic Americans), 276 international. Average age 31. 853 applicants, 67% accepted, 294 enrolled. In 2009, 444 master's, 4 doctorates awarded. *Degree requirements:* For master's, thesis (for some programs); for doctorate, comprehensive exam, thesis/dissertation. *Entrance requirements:* For master's, GRE or GMAT (MS in computational finance only), bachelor's degree; for doctorate, GRE, master's degree in computer science. Additional exam requirements/recommendations for international students: Required—TOEFL (minimum score 550 paper-based; 213 computer-based), IELTS (minimum score 6.5), Pearson Test of English (minimum score 53). *Application deadline:* For fall admission, 8/15 priority date for domestic students, 6/1 priority date for international students; for winter admission, 12/15 priority date for domestic students, 9/15 priority date for international students; for spring admission, 3/1 priority date for domestic students, 12/15 priority date for international students. Applications are processed on a rolling basis. Application fee: $25. Electronic applications accepted. *Expenses:* Contact institution. *Financial support:* In 2009–10, 69 students received support, including 6 fellowships with full tuition reimbursements available (averaging $25,858 per year), 75 teaching assistantships with full and partial tuition reimbursements available (averaging $5,780 per year); research assistantships, Federal Work-Study, scholarships/grants, tuition waivers (full and partial), and unspecified assistantships also available. Support available to part-time students. Financial award application deadline: 4/30; financial award applicants required to submit FAFSA. *Faculty research:* Bioinformatics, visual computing, graphics and animation, high performance and scientific computing, databases. Total annual research expenditures: $790,000. *Unit head:* Dr. David Miller, Dean, 312-362-8381, Fax: 312-362-5185. *Application contact:* Dr. Liz Friedman, Assistant Dean of Student Services, 312-362-5384, Fax: 312-362-5327, E-mail: efriedm2@cdm.depaul.edu.

Florida State University, The Graduate School, College of Arts and Sciences, Department of Mathematics, Tallahassee, FL 32306-4510. Offers applied computational mathematics (MS, PhD); biomedical mathematics (MS, PhD); financial mathematics (MS, PhD); pure mathematics (MS, PhD). Part-time programs available. *Faculty:* 57 full-time (14 women). *Students:* 140 full-time (35 women), 9 part-time (2 women); includes 8 minority (2 African Americans, 2 Asian Americans or Pacific Islanders, 4 Hispanic Americans), 84 international. Average age 26. 273 applicants, 38% accepted, 34 enrolled. In 2009, 36 master's, 6 doctorates awarded. Terminal master's awarded for partial completion of doctoral program. *Degree requirements:* For master's, comprehensive exam (for some programs), thesis optional; for doctorate, comprehensive exam (for some programs), thesis/dissertation, candidacy exam. *Entrance requirements:* For master's and doctorate, GRE General Test, minimum upper-division GPA of 3.0, 4-year bachelor's degree. Additional exam requirements/recommendations for international students: Required—TOEFL (minimum score 550 paper-based; 213 computer-based; 80 iBT), or IELTS. *Application deadline:* For fall admission, 1/10 priority date for domestic students, 12/15 priority date for international students; for spring admission, 11/1 for domestic and international students. Applications are processed on a rolling basis. Application fee: $30. Electronic applications accepted. *Expenses:* Tuition, state resident: full-time $7413.36. Tuition, nonresident: full-time $22,567. *Financial support:* In 2009–10, 102 students received support, including 4 fellowships with full tuition reimbursements available (averaging $19,000 per year), 12 research assistantships with full tuition reimbursements available (averaging $20,000 per year), 84 teaching assistantships with full tuition reimbursements available (averaging $17,000 per year); career-related internships or fieldwork, scholarships/grants, and unspecified assistantships also available. Financial award application deadline: 4/1. *Faculty research:* Geometric topology, algebraic geometry, fluid dynamics, financial mathematics, biomedical mathematics. *Unit head:* Dr. Philip L. Bowers, Chairperson, 850-645-3338, Fax: 850-644-4053, E-mail: bowers@math.fsu.edu. *Application contact:* Dr. Bettye Anne Case, Associate Chair for Graduate Studies, 850-644-1586, Fax: 850-644-4053, E-mail: case@math.fsu.edu.

Georgia Institute of Technology, Graduate Studies and Research, College of Management, Program in Management, Atlanta, GA 30332-0001. Offers accounting (PhD); finance (PhD); information technology management (PhD); marketing (PhD); operations management (PhD); organizational behavior (PhD); quantitative and computational finance (MS); strategic management (PhD). *Accreditation:* AACSB. *Degree requirements:* For doctorate, comprehensive exam, thesis/dissertation, oral exams. *Entrance requirements:* For master's and doctorate, GMAT. Additional exam requirements/recommendations for international students: Required—TOEFL. *Faculty research:* MIS, management of technology, international business, entrepreneurship, operations management.

Georgia Institute of Technology, Graduate Studies and Research, College of Sciences, School of Mathematics, Atlanta, GA 30332-0001. Offers algorithms, combinatorics, and optimization (PhD); applied mathematics (MS); bioinformatics (PhD); mathematics (PhD); quantitative and computational finance (MS); statistics (MS Stat). Terminal master's awarded for partial completion of doctoral program. *Degree requirements:* For master's, thesis or alternative; for doctorate, one foreign language, thesis/dissertation. *Entrance requirements:* For master's, GRE General Test, minimum GPA of 3.0; for doctorate, GRE General Test, GRE Subject Test, minimum GPA of 3.0. Additional exam requirements/recommendations for international students: Required—TOEFL. Electronic applications accepted. *Faculty research:* Dynamical systems, discrete mathematics, probability and statistics, mathematical physics.

Illinois Institute of Technology, Stuart School of Business, Program in Mathematical Finance, Chicago, IL 60616-3793. Offers MMF. Part-time and evening/weekend programs available. *Entrance requirements:* For master's, GMAT or GRE General Test. Additional exam requirements/recommendations for international students: Required—TOEFL (minimum score 600 paper-based; 250 computer-based; 100 iBT). Electronic applications accepted. *Expenses:* Tuition: Full-time $17,550; part-time $888 per credit hour. Required fees: $850; $7.50 per credit hour. One-time fee: $50 full-time. Full-time tuition and fees vary according to program. *Faculty research:* Factor models for investment management, credit rating and credit risk management, hedge fund performance analysis, option trading and risk management, global asset allocation strategies.

The Johns Hopkins University, G. W. C. Whiting School of Engineering, Department of Applied Mathematics and Statistics, Baltimore, MD 21218-2699. Offers computational medicine (PhD); discrete mathematics (MA, MSE, PhD); financial mathematics (MSE); operations research/optimization/decision science (MA, MSE, PhD); statistics/probability/stochastic processes (MA, MSE, PhD). *Faculty:* 17 full-time (3 women), 4 part-time/adjunct (0 women). *Students:* 56 full-time (19 women), 5 part-time (2 women); includes 7 minority (1 African American, 6 Asian Americans or Pacific Islanders), 37 international. Average age 27. 213 applicants, 51% accepted, 16 enrolled. In 2009, 24 master's, 4 doctorates awarded. Terminal master's awarded for partial completion of doctoral program. *Degree requirements:* For master's, thesis (for some programs); for doctorate, thesis/dissertation, oral exam, introductory exam. *Entrance requirements:* For master's and doctorate, GRE General Test, GRE Subject Test. Additional exam requirements/recommendations for international students: Required—TOEFL (minimum score 600 paper-based; 250 computer-based; 100 iBT). *Application deadline:* For fall admission, 1/15 for domestic and international students; for spring admission, 9/15 for domestic and international students. Application fee: $75. Electronic applications accepted. *Financial support:* In 2009–10, 40 students received support, including 3 fellowships with full tuition reimbursements available (averaging $3,000 per year), 13 research assistantships with full tuition reimbursements available (averaging $22,333 per year), 15 teaching assistantships with full tuition reimbursements available (averaging $16,750 per year); Federal Work-Study, institutionally sponsored loans, scholarships/grants, health care benefits, tuition waivers (partial), and unspecified assistantships also available. Financial award application deadline: 1/15. *Faculty research:* Discrete mathematics, probability, statistics, optimization and operations research, scientific computation, financial mathematics. Total annual research expenditures: $1.1 million. *Unit head:* Dr. Daniel Q. Naiman, Chair, 410-516-7203, Fax: 410-516-7459, E-mail: daniel.naiman@jhu.edu. *Application contact:* Kristin Bechtel, Academic Program Coordinator, 410-516-7198, Fax: 410-516-7459, E-mail: kbechtel@jhu.edu.

Monmouth University, Graduate School, Department of Mathematics, West Long Branch, NJ 07764-1898. Offers financial mathematics (MS). Part-time and evening/weekend programs available. *Faculty:* 2 full-time (0 women). *Students:* 1 full-time (0 women), 6 part-time (3 women); includes 3 minority (1 African American, 1 Asian American or Pacific Islander, 1 Hispanic American). Average age 35. 14 applicants, 64% accepted, 3 enrolled. *Degree requirements:* For master's, 6 credits of financial mathematics practicum. *Entrance requirements:* For master's, minimum GPA of 3.0 in major, 2.5 overall; undergraduate degree in mathematics or related field with substantial component of math; coursework in calculus, linear algebra, differential equations (with some exposure to partial differential equations), and a course in calculus-based statistics. Additional exam requirements/recommendations for international students: Required—TOEFL (minimum score 550 paper-based; 213 computer-based; 79 iBT), IELTS (minimum score 5), or Michigan English Language Assessment Battery (minimum score 77) Cambridge A, B, C. *Application deadline:* For fall admission, 7/15 priority date for domestic students, 6/1 for international students; for spring admission, 10/15 priority date for domestic students, 11/1 for international students. Application fee: $50. *Expenses:* Tuition: Part-time $773 per credit. Required fees: $157 per semester. *Financial support:* In 2009–10, 7 students received support, including 7 fellowships (averaging $1,857 per year); career-related internships or fieldwork, scholarships/grants, and unspecified assistantships also available. Support available to part-time students. Financial award applicants required to submit FAFSA. *Faculty research:* Mathematics and computational finance, economics, Monte Carlo methods. *Unit head:* Dr. Suneal Chaudhary, Program Director, 732-263-5413, E-mail: schaudha@monmouth.edu. *Application contact:* Kevin Roane, Director, Office of Graduate Admission, 732-571-3452, Fax: 732-263-5123, E-mail: gradadm@monmouth.edu.

New York University, Graduate School of Arts and Science, Courant Institute of Mathematical Sciences, Department of Mathematics, New York, NY 10012-1019. Offers atmosphere ocean science and mathematics (PhD); mathematics (MS, PhD); mathematics and statistics/operations research (MS); mathematics in finance (MS); scientific computing (MS). Part-time and evening/weekend programs available. *Faculty:* 46 full-time (0 women). *Students:* 179 full-time (35 women), 111 part-time (20 women); includes 40 minority (1 African American, 33 Asian Americans or Pacific Islanders, 6 Hispanic Americans), 139 international. Average age 29. 1,071 applicants, 29% accepted, 72 enrolled. In 2009, 88 master's, 19 doctorates awarded. *Degree requirements:* For master's, thesis optional; for doctorate, one foreign language, thesis/dissertation, oral and written exams. *Entrance requirements:* For master's and doctorate, GRE General Test, GRE Subject Test. Additional exam requirements/recommendations for international students: Required—TOEFL. *Application deadline:* For fall admission, 1/4 for domestic students; for spring admission, 11/1 for domestic students. Application fee: $90. *Expenses:* Tuition: Full-time $30,528; part-time $1272 per credit. Required fees: $2177. *Financial support:* Fellowships with tuition reimbursements, research assistantships with tuition reimbursements, teaching assistantships with tuition reimbursements, Federal Work-Study, institutionally sponsored loans, scholarships/grants, health care benefits, and unspecified assistantships available. Financial award application deadline: 1/4; financial award applicants required to submit FAFSA. *Faculty research:* Partial differential equations, computational science, applied mathematics, geometry and topology, probability and stochastic processes. *Unit head:* Fedor Bogomolov, Director of Graduate Studies, 212-998-3238, Fax: 212-995-4195, E-mail: admissions@math.nyu.edu. *Application contact:* Tamar Arnon, Application Contact, 212-998-3238, Fax: 212-995-4195, E-mail: admissions@math.nyu.edu.

North Carolina State University, Graduate School, College of Agriculture and Life Sciences and College of Engineering and College of Physical and Mathematical Sciences, Program in Financial Mathematics, Raleigh, NC 27695. Offers MFM. Part-time programs available. *Degree requirements:* For master's, thesis optional, project/internship. *Entrance requirements:* For master's, GRE General Test. Additional exam requirements/recommendations for international students: Required—TOEFL (minimum score 550 paper-based; 213 computer-based). Electronic applications accepted. *Faculty research:* Financial mathematics modeling and computation, futures, options and commodities markets, real options, credit risk, portfolio optimization.

Polytechnic Institute of NYU, Department of Finance and Risk Engineering, Brooklyn, NY 11201-2990. Offers financial engineering (MS, Advanced Certificate), including capital markets (MS), computational finance (MS), financial technology (MS); financial technology management (Advanced Certificate); organizational behavior (Advanced Certificate); risk management (Advanced Certificate); technology management (Advanced Certificate). Part-time and evening/weekend programs available. *Faculty:* 6 full-time (1 woman), 20 part-time/adjunct (4 women). *Students:* 196 full-time (71 women), 79 part-time (15 women); includes 28 minority (5 African Americans, 23 Asian Americans or Pacific Islanders), 202 international. Average age 26. 497 applicants, 45% accepted, 85 enrolled. In 2009, 102 master's awarded. *Degree requirements:* For master's, comprehensive exam (for some programs), thesis (for some programs). *Entrance requirements:* For master's, GMAT, minimum B average in undergraduate course work. Additional exam requirements/recommendations for international students: Required—TOEFL (minimum score 550 paper-based; 213 computer-based; 80 iBT); Recommended—IELTS (minimum score 6.5). *Application deadline:* For fall admission, 7/31 priority date for domestic students, 4/30 priority date for international students; for spring admission, 12/31 priority date for domestic students, 11/30 priority date for international students. Applications are processed on a rolling basis. Application fee: $75. Electronic applications accepted. *Expenses:* Tuition: Full-time $21,492; part-time $1194 per credit hour. Required fees: $1160; $204 per course. *Financial support:* Institutionally sponsored loans, scholarships/grants, and unspecified assistantships available. Support available to part-time students. Financial award applicants required to submit FAFSA. *Unit head:* Prof. Charles S. Tapiero, Academic Director, 718-260-3653, Fax: 718-260-3874, E-mail: ctapiero@poly.edu. *Application contact:* JeanCarlo Bonilla, Director of Graduate Enrollment Management, 718-260-3182, Fax: 718-260-3624.

Polytechnic Institute of NYU, Westchester Graduate Center, Graduate Programs, Department of Finance and Risk Engineering, Major in Financial Engineering, Hawthorne, NY 10532-1507. Offers capital markets (MS); computational finance (MS); financial engineering (AC); financial technology (MS); financial technology management (AC); information management (AC). *Students:* 9 full-time (6 women), 8 international. *Degree requirements:* For master's, comprehensive exam (for some programs), thesis (for some programs). *Entrance requirements:* Additional exam requirements/recommendations for international students: Required—TOEFL (minimum score 550 paper-based; 213 computer-based; 80 iBT); Recommended—IELTS (minimum score 6.5). *Application deadline:* For fall admission, 7/31 priority date for domestic students, 4/30 priority date for international students; for spring admission, 12/31 priority date for domestic students, 11/30 priority date for international students. Applications are processed on a rolling basis. Application fee: $75. Electronic applications accepted. *Financial support:* Institutionally sponsored loans, scholarships/grants, and unspecified assistantships available. Support available to part-time students. *Unit head:* Dr. Charles S. Tapiero, Department Head, 718-260-3653, E-mail: ctapiero@poly.edu. *Application contact:* JeanCarlo Bonilla, Director of Graduate Enrollment Management, 718-260-3182, Fax: 718-260-3624, E-mail: gradinfo@poly.edu.

Rice University, Graduate Programs, George R. Brown School of Engineering, Department of Statistics, Houston, TX 77251-1892. Offers bioinformatics (PhD); biostatistics (PhD); computational finance (PhD); general statistics (PhD); statistics (M Stat, MA); MBA/M Stat. Part-time programs available. *Faculty:* 16 full-time (6 women), 1 part-time/adjunct (0 women). *Students:* 45 full-time (20 women), 3 part-time (2 women); includes 12 minority (1 African American, 5 Asian Americans or Pacific Islanders, 6 Hispanic Americans), 16 international. Average age 28. 112 applicants, 41% accepted, 20 enrolled. In 2009, 9 master's, 7 doctorates awarded. *Degree requirements:* For master's, comprehensive exam; for doctorate, comprehensive exam, thesis/dissertation. *Entrance requirements:* For master's and doctorate, GRE General Test, minimum GPA of 3.0. Additional exam requirements/recommendations for international students: Required—TOEFL (minimum score 630 paper-based; 250 computer-based; 90 iBT). *Application deadline:* For fall admission, 1/15 priority date for domestic and international students; for spring admission, 11/1 for international students. Applications are processed on a rolling basis. Application fee: $70. Electronic applications accepted. *Financial support:* In 2009–10, 13 students received support, including 1 fellowship with full tuition reimbursement available (averaging $15,000 per year), 19 research assistantships with full tuition reimbursements available (averaging $23,000 per year), 9 teaching assistantships with full tuition reimbursements available (averaging $17,250 per year); career-related internships or fieldwork, institutionally sponsored loans, scholarships/grants, traineeships, health care benefits, tuition waivers (full), and unspecified assistantships also available. *Faculty research:* Statistical genetics, non parametric function estimation, computational statistics and visualization, stochastic processes. Total annual research expenditures: $800,000. *Unit head:* Carolyn Duhon, Sr. Department Administrator, 713-348-6032, Fax: 713-348-5476, E-mail: stat@rice.edu. *Application contact:* Margaret Poon, Department Coordinator, 713-348-6032, Fax: 713-348-5476, E-mail: poon@rice.edu.

Stanford University, School of Humanities and Sciences, Department of Mathematics, Stanford, CA 94305-9991. Offers financial mathematics (MS); mathematics (MS, PhD). Terminal master's awarded for partial completion of doctoral program. *Degree requirements:* For doctorate, 2 foreign languages, thesis/dissertation, oral exam. *Entrance requirements:* For master's, GRE General Test; for doctorate, GRE General Test, GRE Subject Test. Additional exam requirements/recommendations for international students: Required—TOEFL. Electronic applications accepted. *Expenses:* Tuition: Full-time $37,380; part-time $2760 per quarter. Required fees: $501.

University of Alberta, Faculty of Graduate Studies and Research, Department of Mathematical and Statistical Sciences, Edmonton, AB T6G 2E1, Canada. Offers applied mathematics (M Sc, PhD); biostatistics (M Sc); mathematical finance (M Sc, PhD); mathematical physics (M Sc, PhD); mathematics (M Sc, PhD); statistics (M Sc, PhD, Postgraduate Diploma). Part-time programs available. *Faculty:* 48 full-time (4 women). *Students:* 112 full-time (41 women), 5 part-time (0 women). Average age 24. 776 applicants, 5% accepted, 34 enrolled. In 2009, 12 master's, 10 doctorates awarded. Terminal master's awarded for partial completion of doctoral program. *Degree requirements:* For master's, thesis (for some programs); for doctorate, comprehensive exam, thesis/dissertation. *Entrance requirements:* Additional exam requirements/recommendations for international students: Required—TOEFL (minimum score 580 paper-based; 237 computer-based). *Application deadline:* For fall admission, 3/1 for domestic students, 2/1 for international students. Applications are processed on a rolling basis. Application fee: $0. Electronic applications accepted. Tuition and fees charges are reported in Canadian dollars. *Expenses:* Tuition, area resident: Full-time $4626.24 Canadian dollars; part-time $99.72 Canadian dollars per unit. International tuition: $8216 Canadian dollars full-time. Required fees: $3589.92 Canadian dollars; $99.72 Canadian dollars per unit. $215 Canadian dollars per term. *Financial support:* In 2009–10, 51 research assistantships, 88 teaching assistantships with full and partial tuition reimbursements were awarded; scholarships/grants also available. Financial award application deadline: 5/1. *Faculty research:* Classical and functional analysis, algebra, differential equations, geometry. *Unit head:* Dr. Anthony To-Ming Lau, Chair, 403-492-5141, E-mail: tlau@math.ualberta.ca. *Application contact:* Dr. Yau Shu Wong, Associate Chair, Graduate Studies, 403-492-5799, Fax: 403-492-6828, E-mail: gradmail@math.ualberta.ca.

University of California, Santa Barbara, Graduate Division, College of Letters and Sciences, Division of Mathematics, Life, and Physical Sciences, Department of Statistics and Applied Probability, Santa Barbara, CA 93106-3110. Offers financial mathematics and statistics (PhD); quantitative methods in the social sciences (PhD); statistics (MA), including applied statistics, mathematical statistics; statistics and applied probability (PhD); MA/PhD. *Faculty:* 12 full-time (3 women), 4 part-time/adjunct (1 woman). *Students:* 42 full-time (12 women). Average age 28. 218 applicants, 39% accepted, 14 enrolled. In 2009, 20 master's, 1 doctorate awarded. Terminal master's awarded for partial completion of doctoral program. *Degree requirements:* For master's, comprehensive exam, thesis or alternative; for doctorate, comprehensive exam, thesis/dissertation. *Entrance requirements:* For master's, GRE General Test, 3 letters of recommendation, resume/curriculum vitae; for doctorate, GRE General Test, 3 letters of recommendation, statement of purpose, personal achievements/contributions statement, resume/curriculum vitae, transcripts for post-secondary institutions attended. Additional exam requirements/recommendations for international students: Required—TOEFL (minimum score 550 paper-based; 213 computer-based; 80 iBT), or IELTS (minimum score 7). *Application deadline:* For fall admission, 1/1 for domestic and international students; for winter admission, 11/1 for domestic and international students; for spring admission, 2/1 for domestic and international students. Application fee: $70 ($90 for international students). Electronic applications accepted. *Financial support:* In 2009–10, 29 students received support, including 5 fellowships with full and partial tuition reimbursements available (averaging $7,400 per year), 28 teaching assistantships with partial tuition reimbursements available (averaging $10,300 per year); Federal Work-Study, institutionally sponsored loans, scholarships/grants, health care benefits, and unspecified assistantships also available. Financial award application deadline: 1/1; financial award applicants required to submit FAFSA. *Faculty research:* Bayesian inference, financial mathematics, stochastic processes, environmental statistics, biostatistical modeling. *Unit head:* Dr. Yuedong Wang, Chair, 805-893-4870, Fax: 805-893-2334, E-mail: yeudong@pstat.ucsb.edu. *Application contact:* Rickie R. Lazzerini, Graduate Program Assistant, 805-893-4857, Fax: 805-893-2334, E-mail: gradinfo@pstat.ucsb.edu.

University of Chicago, Division of the Physical Sciences, Department of Mathematics, Program on Financial Mathematics, Chicago, IL 60637-1513. Offers MS. Part-time and evening/weekend programs available. Postbaccalaureate distance learning degree programs offered (no on-campus study). *Entrance requirements:* For master's, GRE General Test, GRE Subject Test. Additional exam requirements/recommendations for international students: Required—TOEFL (minimum score 600 paper-based; 250 computer-based). Electronic applications accepted.

University of Connecticut, Graduate School, College of Liberal Arts and Sciences, Department of Mathematics, Field of Applied Financial Mathematics, Storrs, CT 06269. Offers MS. *Faculty:* 49 full-time (10 women). *Students:* 18 full-time (3 women), 3 part-time (0 women); includes 1 minority (African American), 14 international. Average age 29. 105 applicants, 7% accepted, 5 enrolled. In 2009, 6 master's awarded. *Degree requirements:* For master's, comprehensive exam. *Entrance requirements:* Additional exam requirements/recommendations for international students: Required—TOEFL (minimum score 550 paper-based; 213 computer-based). *Application deadline:* For fall admission, 2/1 priority date for domestic and international students; for spring admission, 11/1 for domestic students, 10/1 for international students. Applications are processed on a rolling basis. Application fee: $55. Electronic applications accepted. *Expenses:* Tuition, state resident: full-time $4725; part-time $525 per credit. Tuition, nonresident: full-time $12,267; part-time $1363 per credit. Required fees: $346 per semester. Tuition and fees vary according to course load. *Financial support:* In 2009–10, 6 research assistantships with full tuition reimbursements, 6 teaching assistantships with full tuition reimbursements were awarded; Federal Work-Study and scholarships/grants also available.

Mathematical and Computational Finance

University of Connecticut (continued)
Financial award application deadline: 2/1; financial award applicants required to submit FAFSA. *Unit head:* James Bridgeman, Program Director, 860-486-8382, Fax: 860-486-4283, E-mail: james.bridgeman@uconn.edu. *Application contact:* Sharon McDermott, Administrative Assistant, 860-486-6452, Fax: 860-486-4283, E-mail: gradadm@math.uconn.edu.

University of Dayton, Graduate School, College of Arts and Sciences, Department of Mathematics, Dayton, OH 45469-1300. Offers applied mathematics (MAS); financial mathematics (MFM); mathematics (MME). Part-time and evening/weekend programs available. *Faculty:* 15 full-time (5 women). *Students:* 15 full-time (5 women), 5 part-time (2 women), 10 international. Average age 31. 51 applicants, 57% accepted, 8 enrolled. In 2009, 4 master's awarded. *Entrance requirements:* For master's, minimum undergraduate GPA of 2.8 (MAS), 3.0 (MFM, MME). Additional exam requirements/recommendations for international students: Required—TOEFL (minimum score 550 paper-based; 213 computer-based; 80 iBT). *Application deadline:* For fall admission, 3/1 priority date for domestic students, 7/1 priority date for international students; for winter admission, 7/1 priority date for international students; for spring admission, 1/1 priority date for international students. Application fee: $0 ($50 for international students). Electronic applications accepted. *Expenses:* Tuition: Full-time $8412; part-time $701 per credit hour. Required fees: $325; $65 per course. $25 per semester. Tuition and fees vary according to course load, degree level and program. *Financial support:* In 2009–10, 7 teaching assistantships with full tuition reimbursements (averaging $12,755 per year) were awarded; institutionally sponsored loans, health care benefits, and unspecified assistantships also available. Financial award applicants required to submit FAFSA. *Faculty research:* Differential equations, integral equations, general topology, measure theory, graph theory, financial math, math education, numerical analysis. *Unit head:* Dr. Joe D. Mashburn, Chair, 937-229-2511, Fax: 937-229-2566, E-mail: joe.mashburn@notes.udayton.edu. *Application contact:* Associate Director of Graduate Admissions, 937-229-4411, Fax: 937-229-4729, E-mail: gradadmission@udayton.edu.

University of Illinois at Chicago, Graduate College, College of Liberal Arts and Sciences, Department of Mathematics, Statistics, and Computer Science, Chicago, IL 60607-7128. Offers applied mathematics (MS, PhD); computational finance (MS, PhD); computer science (MS, PhD); mathematics (DA); mathematics and information sciences for industry (MS); probability and statistics (PhD); pure mathematics (MS, PhD); statistics (MS); teaching of mathematics (MST), including elementary, secondary. Part-time programs available. *Degree requirements:* For master's, comprehensive exam; for doctorate, one foreign language, thesis/dissertation. *Entrance requirements:* For master's and doctorate, GRE General Test, minimum GPA of 2.75. Additional exam requirements/recommendations for international students: Required—TOEFL. Electronic applications accepted.

The University of North Carolina at Charlotte, Graduate School, Belk College of Business, Program in Mathematical Finance, Charlotte, NC 28223-0001. Offers MS. Part-time and evening/weekend programs available. *Faculty:* 13 full-time (1 woman). *Students:* 25 full-time (8 women), 41 part-time (6 women); includes 4 African Americans, 10 Asian Americans or Pacific Islanders, 22 international. Average age 29. 66 applicants, 86% accepted, 15 enrolled. In 2009, 26 master's awarded. *Entrance requirements:* For master's, GRE General Test or GMAT, minimum GPA of 2.75 overall. Additional exam requirements/recommendations for international students: Required—TOEFL (minimum score 557 paper-based; 220 computer-based; 83 iBT). *Application deadline:* For fall admission, 7/15 for domestic students, 5/1 for international students; for spring admission, 11/15 for domestic students, 10/1 for international students. Applications are processed on a rolling basis. Application fee: $55. Electronic applications accepted. *Financial support:* In 2009–10, 7 students received support, including 3 research assistantships (averaging $8,000 per year), 4 teaching assistantships (averaging $6,750 per year); career-related internships or fieldwork, Federal Work-Study, institutionally sponsored loans, scholarships/grants, and unspecified assistantships also available. Support available to part-time students. Financial award application deadline: 4/1; financial award applicants required to submit FAFSA. *Unit head:* Dr. Judson Russell, Director, 704-687-7618, Fax: 704-687-4014, E-mail: belkgradprograms@uncc.edu. *Application contact:* Kathy B. Giddings, Director of Graduate Admissions, 704-687-5503, Fax: 704-687-3279, E-mail: gradadm@uncc.edu.

University of Southern California, Graduate School, College of Letters, Arts and Sciences, Department of Economics, Los Angeles, CA 90089. Offers economic development programming (MA, PhD); mathematical finance (MS); M Pl/MA; MA/JD. *Faculty:* 18 full-time (2 women), 14 part-time/adjunct (0 women). *Students:* 128 full-time (47 women), 6 part-time (2 women); includes 12 minority (1 African American, 8 Asian Americans or Pacific Islanders, 3 Hispanic Americans), 105 international. 355 applicants, 28% accepted, 32 enrolled. In 2009, 34 master's, 9 doctorates awarded. Terminal master's awarded for partial completion of doctoral program. *Degree requirements:* For master's, comprehensive exam, thesis optional; for doctorate, comprehensive exam, thesis/dissertation. *Entrance requirements:* For master's and doctorate, GRE. Additional exam requirements/recommendations for international students: Required—TOEFL (minimum score 93 iBT). *Application deadline:* For fall admission, 12/1 for domestic and international students; for spring admission, 11/1 for domestic and international students. Application fee: $85. *Expenses:* Tuition: Full-time $25,980; part-time $1315 per unit. Required fees: $554. One-time fee: $35 full-time. Full-time tuition and fees vary according to degree level and program. *Financial support:* In 2009–10, 61 students received support, including 14 fellowships with full tuition reimbursements available (averaging $21,000 per year), 4 research assistantships with full tuition reimbursements available (averaging $19,000 per year), 41 teaching assistantships with full tuition reimbursements available (averaging $19,000 per year). *Faculty research:* Applied micro/io, development, econometrics, finance, international finance, macroeconomic theory, microeconomic theory. *Unit head:* Prof. Simon Wilkie, Chair, 213-740-8335, Fax: 213-740-4595, E-mail: swilkie@usc.edu. *Application contact:* Morgan Ponder, Graduate Advisor, 213-740-3507, E-mail: ponder@usc.edu.

University of Southern California, Graduate School, College of Letters, Arts and Sciences, Department of Mathematics, Los Angeles, CA 90089. Offers applied mathematics (MA, MS, PhD); mathematical finance (MS); mathematics (MA, PhD); statistics (MS). Part-time programs available. *Faculty:* 50 full-time (5 women). *Students:* 102 full-time (33 women), 16 part-time (8 women); includes 10 minority (9 Asian Americans or Pacific Islanders, 1 Hispanic American), 87 international. 500 applicants, 20% accepted, 28 enrolled. In 2009, 37 master's, 7 doctorates awarded. Terminal master's awarded for partial completion of doctoral program. *Degree requirements:* For master's, comprehensive exam (for some programs), thesis (for some programs); for doctorate, 2 foreign languages, comprehensive exam, thesis/dissertation. *Entrance requirements:* For master's, GRE General Test, GMAT; for doctorate, GRE General Test. Additional exam requirements/recommendations for international students: Recommended—TOEFL (minimum score 100 iBT). *Application deadline:* For fall admission, 12/1 for domestic students, 2/15 for international students; for spring admission, 9/1 for domestic and international students. Applications are processed on a rolling basis. Application fee: $85. Electronic applications accepted. *Expenses:* Tuition: Full-time $25,980; part-time $1315 per unit. Required fees: $554. One-time fee: $35 full-time. Full-time tuition and fees vary according to degree level and program. *Financial support:* In 2009–10, 67 students received support, including 5 fellowships with full tuition reimbursements available (averaging $19,000 per year), 9 research assistantships with full tuition reimbursements available (averaging $19,000 per year), 53 teaching assistantships with full tuition reimbursements available (averaging $19,000 per year). Financial award application deadline: 12/1. *Faculty research:* Algebra, algebraic geometry and number theory, analysis/partial differential equations, applied mathematics, financial mathematics, probability, combinatorics and statistics. Total annual research expenditures: $2 million. *Unit head:* Prof. Gary Rosen, Chair, 213-740-1717, Fax: 213-740-2424, E-mail: grosen@usc.edu. *Application contact:* Amy Yung, Department Coordinator, 213-740-8168, Fax: 213-740-2424, E-mail: amy@usc.edu.

Mathematics

Alabama State University, School of Graduate Studies, College of Arts and Sciences, Department of Mathematics and Computer Science, Montgomery, AL 36101-0271. Offers mathematics (M Ed, MS, Ed S). Part-time programs available. *Degree requirements:* For Ed S, thesis. *Entrance requirements:* For master's, GRE, GRE Subject Test, graduate writing competence test; for Ed S, GRE General Test, MAT, graduate writing competency test. Additional exam requirements/recommendations for international students: Required—TOEFL (minimum score 500 paper-based; 173 computer-based). *Faculty research:* Discrete mathematics, symbolic dynamics, mathematical social sciences.

American University, College of Arts and Sciences, Department of Mathematics and Statistics, Program in Mathematics, Washington, DC 22016-8050. Offers MA. Part-time and evening/weekend programs available. *Students:* 5 full-time (2 women), 4 part-time (1 woman); includes 1 minority (African American), 1 international. Average age 33. 13 applicants, 85% accepted, 5 enrolled. *Degree requirements:* For master's, comprehensive exam, thesis or alternative, foreign language or computer language. *Entrance requirements:* For master's, GRE, BA in mathematics. Additional exam requirements/recommendations for international students: Required—TOEFL. *Application deadline:* For fall admission, 2/1 for domestic students; for spring admission, 10/1 for domestic students. Application fee: $80. *Expenses:* Tuition: Full-time $22,266; part-time $1237 per credit hour. Required fees: $430. Tuition and fees vary according to program. *Financial support:* Fellowships, teaching assistantships, career-related internships or fieldwork, Federal Work-Study, and institutionally sponsored loans available. Support available to part-time students. Financial award application deadline: 2/1. *Unit head:* Dr. Jeffrey Hakim, Chair, 202-885-3131, Fax: 202-885-3155. *Application contact:* Kathleen Clowery, Director, Graduate Admissions, 202-885-3621, Fax: 202-885-1505.

American University of Beirut, Graduate Programs, Faculty of Arts and Sciences, Beirut, Lebanon. Offers anthropology (MA); Arabic language and literature (MA); archaeology (MA); biology (MS); chemistry (MS); computer science (MS); economics (MA); education (MA); English language (MA); English literature (MA); environmental policy planning (MSES); financial economics (MAFE); geology (MS); history (MA); mathematics (MA, MS); Middle Eastern studies (MA); philosophy (MA); physics (MS); political studies (MA); psychology (MA); public administration (MA); sociology (MA); statistics (MA, MS). Part-time programs available. *Degree requirements:* For master's, one foreign language, comprehensive exam, thesis (for some programs). *Entrance requirements:* For master's, GRE, letter of recommendation. Additional exam requirements/recommendations for international students: Required—TOEFL (minimum score 600 paper-based; 250 computer-based; 100 iBT), IELTS (minimum score 7.5). *Faculty research:* String theory and supergravity; computer graphics; algebra and number theory; popular Arabic literature; marine and freshwater biology; integrating science, math and technology.

Andrews University, School of Graduate Studies, College of Arts and Sciences, Interdisciplinary Studies in Mathematics and Physical Science Program, Berrien Springs, MI 49104. Offers MS. *Students:* 2 full-time (1 woman), both international. Average age 27. 1 applicant, 100% accepted, 1 enrolled. *Application deadline:* Applications are processed on a rolling basis. Application fee: $43. *Unit head:* Dr. Margarita Mattingly, Chairman, 269-471-3431. *Application contact:* Carolyn Hurst, Supervisor of Graduate Admission, 800-253-3430, Fax: 269-471-3228, E-mail: enroll@andrews.edu.

Appalachian State University, Cratis D. Williams Graduate School, Department of Mathematical Sciences, Boone, NC 28608. Offers mathematics (MA); mathematics education (MA). Part-time programs available. Postbaccalaureate distance learning degree programs offered (no on-campus study). *Faculty:* 27 full-time (10 women). *Students:* 7 full-time (4 women), 11 part-time (10 women). 7 applicants, 100% accepted, 5 enrolled. In 2009, 11 master's awarded. *Degree requirements:* For master's, comprehensive exam, thesis optional. *Entrance requirements:* For master's, GRE General Test, 3 letters of recommendation. Additional exam requirements/recommendations for international students: Required—TOEFL (minimum score 570 paper-based; 230 computer-based; 79 iBT), IELTS (minimum score 6.5). *Application deadline:* For fall admission, 7/1 for domestic students, 2/1 for international students; for spring admission, 11/1 for domestic students, 7/1 for international students. Applications are processed on a rolling basis. Application fee: $50. Electronic applications accepted. *Expenses:* Tuition, state resident: full-time $2960. Tuition, nonresident: full-time $14,051. Required fees: $2320. *Financial support:* In 2009–10, 14 teaching assistantships (averaging $9,500 per year) were awarded; fellowships, research assistantships, career-related internships or fieldwork, Federal Work-Study, scholarships/grants, and unspecified assistantships also available. Financial award application deadline: 4/1; financial award applicants required to submit FAFSA. *Faculty research:* Graph theory, differential equations, logic, geometry, complex analysis, topology, algebra, mathematics education. Total annual research expenditures: $482,500. *Unit head:* Dr. Mark Ginn, Chair, 828-262-3050, Fax: 828-265-8617, E-mail: ginnmc@appstate.edu. *Application contact:* Dr. Greg Rhoads, Graduate Director, 828-262-3050, E-mail: rhoadsgs@appstate.edu.

Arizona State University, Graduate College, College of Liberal Arts and Sciences, Division of Natural Sciences, Department of Mathematics and Statistics, Tempe, AZ 85287. Offers computational biosciences (PSM, PhD); mathematics (MA, MNS, PhD). *Degree requirements:* For master's, thesis or alternative; for doctorate, one foreign language, thesis/dissertation. *Entrance requirements:* For master's and doctorate, GRE General Test.

Arkansas State University—Jonesboro, Graduate School, College of Sciences and Mathematics, Department of Mathematics and Statistics, Jonesboro, State University, AR 72467. Offers mathematics (MS); mathematics education (MSE). Part-time programs available. *Faculty:* 7 full-time (2 women). *Students:* 9 full-time (4 women), 12 part-time (6 women), 2 international. Average age 31. 12 applicants, 100% accepted, 11 enrolled. In 2009, 5 master's awarded. *Degree requirements:* For master's, comprehensive exam, thesis or alternative. *Entrance requirements:* For master's, GRE General Test or MAT, appropriate bachelor's degree. Additional exam requirements/recommendations for international students: Required—TOEFL (minimum score 550 paper-based; 213 computer-based; 79 iBT), IELTS (minimum score 6). *Application deadline:* For fall admission, 7/1 for domestic and international students; for spring admission, 11/15 for domestic students, 11/13 for international students. Applications are processed on a rolling basis. Application fee: $30 ($40 for international students). Electronic applications accepted. *Expenses:* Tuition, state resident: full-time $3744; part-time $208 per credit hour. Tuition, nonresident: full-time $9540; part-time $530 per credit hour. Required fees: $896; $47 per credit hour. $25 per term. One-time fee: $50. Tuition and fees vary according to course load and program. *Financial support:* In 2009–10, 8 students received support; teaching assistantships, career-related internships or fieldwork, scholarships/grants, and unspecified assistantships available. Financial award application deadline: 7/1; financial award applicants required to submit FAFSA. *Unit head:* Dr. Debra Ingram, Chair, 870-972-3090, Fax: 870-972-3950, E-mail: dingram@astate.edu. *Application contact:* Dr. Andrew Sustich, Dean of the Graduate School, 870-972-3029, Fax: 870-972-3857, E-mail: sustich@astate.edu.

Auburn University, Graduate School, College of Sciences and Mathematics, Department of Mathematics and Statistics, Auburn University, AL 36849. Offers applied mathematics (MAM, MS); mathematics (MS, PhD); probability and statistics (M Prob S); statistics (MS). *Faculty:* 54 full-time (8 women), 4 part-time/adjunct (1 woman). *Students:* 50 full-time (8 women), 44 part-time (17 women); includes 4 minority (2 African Americans, 1 Asian American or Pacific Islander, 1 Hispanic American), 46 international. Average age 28. 212 applicants, 52% accepted, 20 enrolled. In 2009, 16 master's, 10 doctorates awarded. *Degree requirements:* For doctorate, thesis/dissertation. *Entrance requirements:* For master's, GRE General Test, undergraduate mathematics background; for doctorate, GRE General Test, GRE Subject Test. *Application deadline:* For fall admission, 7/7 priority date for domestic students; for spring admission, 11/24 for domestic students. Applications are processed on a rolling basis. Application fee: $50 ($60 for international students). Electronic applications accepted. *Expenses:* Tuition, state resident: full-time $6240. Tuition, nonresident: full-time $18,720. International tuition: $18,938 full-time. Required fees: $492. Tuition and fees vary according to course load, program and reciprocity agreements. *Financial support:* Fellowships, teaching assistantships, special tuition awards available. Financial award applicants required to submit FAFSA. *Faculty research:* Pure and applied mathematics. *Unit head:* Dr. Michel Smith, Chair, 334-844-4290, Fax: 334-844-6655. *Application contact:* Dr. George Flowers, Dean of the Graduate School, 334-844-2125.

Aurora University, College of Arts and Sciences, Aurora, IL 60506-4892. Offers mathematics (MS). Part-time and evening/weekend programs available. *Entrance requirements:* Additional exam requirements/recommendations for international students: Required—TOEFL (minimum score 550 paper-based; 213 computer-based). Electronic applications accepted. *Expenses:* Contact institution.

Ball State University, Graduate School, College of Sciences and Humanities, Department of Mathematical Sciences, Program in Mathematics, Muncie, IN 47306-1099. Offers mathematics (MA, MS); mathematics education (MAE).

Baylor University, Graduate School, College of Arts and Sciences, Department of Mathematics, Waco, TX 76798. Offers MS, PhD. *Students:* 26 full-time (7 women); includes 2 minority (both Asian Americans or Pacific Islanders), 6 international. In 2009, 4 master's, 6 doctorates awarded. *Degree requirements:* For master's, final oral exam. *Entrance requirements:* For master's, GRE General Test. *Application deadline:* For fall admission, 8/1 for domestic students. Applications are processed on a rolling basis. Application fee: $25. *Financial support:* Teaching assistantships, career-related internships or fieldwork, Federal Work-Study, and institutionally sponsored loans available. Support available to part-time students. Financial award application deadline: 5/1. *Faculty research:* Algebra, statistics, probability, applied mathematics, numerical analysis. *Unit head:* Dr. Ronald Stanke, Graduate Program Director, 254-710-6577, Fax: 254-710-3569, E-mail: ronald_stanke@baylor.edu. *Application contact:* Rita Massey, Administrative Assistant, 254-710-3146, Fax: 254-710-3870, E-mail: rita_massey@baylor.edu.

Boston College, Graduate School of Arts and Sciences, Department of Mathematics, Chestnut Hill, MA 02467-3800. Offers PhD, MBA/MA. Part-time programs available. *Students:* 10 full-time (4 women); includes 1 minority (African American), 3 international. 60 applicants, 28% accepted, 10 enrolled. *Entrance requirements:* Additional exam requirements/recommendations for international students: Required—TOEFL (minimum score 600 paper-based; 250 computer-based; 100 iBT). *Application deadline:* For fall admission, 1/2 priority date for domestic students. Application fee: $70. Electronic applications accepted. *Financial support:* Fellowships with full tuition reimbursements, teaching assistantships with full tuition reimbursements, Federal Work-Study and scholarships/grants available. Support available to part-time students. Financial award application deadline: 3/1; financial award applicants required to submit FAFSA. *Faculty research:* Abstract algebra and number theory, topology, probability and statistics, computer science, analysis. *Unit head:* Dr. Sol Friedberg, Chairperson, 917-552-3750. *Application contact:* Dr. Robert Meyerholt, Graduate Program Director, 617-552-3759, E-mail: meyerhog@bc.edu.

Boston University, Graduate School of Arts and Sciences, Department of Mathematics and Statistics, Boston, MA 02215. Offers mathematical finance (MA); mathematics (MA, PhD). *Students:* 41 full-time (11 women), 2 part-time (0 women); includes 2 minority (1 African American, 1 Hispanic American), 20 international. Average age 27. 198 applicants, 17% accepted, 12 enrolled. In 2009, 9 master's, 7 doctorates awarded. Terminal master's awarded for partial completion of doctoral program. *Degree requirements:* For master's, one foreign language, comprehensive exam; for doctorate, one foreign language, comprehensive exam, thesis/dissertation. *Entrance requirements:* For master's and doctorate, GRE General Test, GRE Subject Test, 3 letters of recommendation. Additional exam requirements/recommendations for international students: Required—TOEFL (minimum score 600 paper-based; 250 computer-based). *Application deadline:* For fall admission, 1/15 for domestic and international students; for spring admission, 10/15 for domestic and international students. Application fee: $70. Electronic applications accepted. *Expenses:* Tuition: Full-time $37,910; part-time $1184 per credit hour. Required fees: $386; $40 per semester. Part-time tuition and fees vary according to class time, course level, degree level and program. *Financial support:* In 2009–10, 3 fellowships with full tuition reimbursements (averaging $18,900 per year), 17 research assistantships with full tuition reimbursements (averaging $18,400 per year), 28 teaching assistantships with full tuition reimbursements (averaging $18,400 per year) were awarded; Federal Work-Study and scholarships/grants also available. Support available to part-time students. Financial award application deadline: 1/15; financial award applicants required to submit FAFSA. *Unit head:* Ralph D'Agostino, Chairman, 617-353-2767, Fax: 617-353-8100, E-mail: ralph@bu.edu. *Application contact:* Kathleen Heavey, Staff Coordinator, 617-353-2560, Fax: 617-353-8100, E-mail: kheavey@bu.edu.

Bowling Green State University, Graduate College, College of Arts and Sciences, Department of Mathematics and Statistics, Bowling Green, OH 43403. Offers applied statistics (MS); mathematics (MA, MAT, PhD); statistics (PhD). Part-time programs available. *Degree requirements:* For master's, thesis or alternative; for doctorate, comprehensive exam, thesis/dissertation. *Entrance requirements:* For master's and doctorate, GRE General Test. Additional exam requirements/recommendations for international students: Required—TOEFL. Electronic applications accepted. *Faculty research:* Statistics and probability, algebra, analysis.

Brandeis University, Graduate School of Arts and Sciences, Department of Mathematics, Waltham, MA 02454-9110. Offers MA, PhD, Postbaccalaureate Certificate. Part-time programs available. *Faculty:* 13 full-time (2 women), 1 part-time/adjunct (0 women). *Students:* 32 full-time (8 women), 1 part-time (0 women); includes 2 minority (1 Asian American or Pacific Islander, 1 Hispanic American), 11 international. Average age 25. 9 applicants, 33% accepted, 3 enrolled. In 2009, 1 master's, 3 doctorates awarded. *Degree requirements:* For doctorate, 2 foreign languages, thesis/dissertation. *Entrance requirements:* For master's, GRE General Test and GRE Subject Test (recommended), resume, letters of recommendation; for doctorate, GRE General Test, GRE Subject Test, resume, letters of recommendation. Additional exam requirements/recommendations for international students: Required—TOEFL (minimum score 600 paper-based; 250 computer-based; 100 iBT); Recommended—IELTS (minimum score 7). *Application deadline:* For fall admission, 1/15 priority date for domestic students. Applications are processed on a rolling basis. Application fee: $75. Electronic applications accepted. *Financial support:* In 2009–10, 25 fellowships with full tuition reimbursements (averaging $20,000 per year), 2 teaching assistantships with partial tuition reimbursements (averaging $3,200 per year) were awarded; scholarships/grants, health care benefits, and tuition waivers (full) also available. Financial award application deadline: 4/15; financial award applicants required to submit FAFSA. *Faculty research:* Algebra, analysis, number theory, combinatorics, topology. *Unit head:* Prof. Dmitry Kleinbock, Director of Graduate Studies, 781-736-3059, Fax: 781-736-3085, E-mail: kleinboc@brandeis.edu. *Application contact:* Janet Ledda, Department Administrator, 781-736-3051, Fax: 781-736-3085, E-mail: ledda@brandeis.edu.

Brigham Young University, Graduate Studies, College of Physical and Mathematical Sciences, Department of Mathematics, Provo, UT 84602-1001. Offers MS, PhD. Part-time programs available. *Faculty:* 30 full-time (2 women). *Students:* 21 full-time (3 women), 16 part-time (1 woman); includes 2 minority (both Asian Americans or Pacific Islanders), 9 international. Average age 23. 27 applicants, 67% accepted, 16 enrolled. In 2009, 12 master's, 1 doctorate awarded. Terminal master's awarded for partial completion of doctoral program. *Degree requirements:* For master's, comprehensive exam, thesis (for some programs), project; written exam; for doctorate, one foreign language, comprehensive exam, thesis/dissertation, qualifying exams. *Entrance requirements:* For master's, GRE General Test, GRE Subject Test (math), minimum GPA of 3.0 in last 60 hours, bachelor's degree in mathematics; for doctorate, GRE General Test, GRE Subject Test (math), master's degree in mathematics or related field. Additional exam requirements/recommendations for international students: Required—TOEFL (minimum score 600 paper-based; 240 computer-based; 85 iBT). *Application deadline:* For fall admission, 3/1 priority date for domestic and international students; for winter admission, 9/15 for domestic students, 3/1 priority date for international students; for spring admission, 2/15 for domestic and international students. Applications are processed on a rolling basis. Application fee: $50. Electronic applications accepted. *Expenses:* Tuition: Full-time $5580; part-time $301 per credit hour. Tuition and fees vary according to student's religious affiliation. *Financial support:* In 2009–10, 30 students received support, including 30 teaching assistantships with full tuition reimbursements available (averaging $16,000 per year); institutionally sponsored loans also available. Support available to part-time students. Financial award application deadline: 3/1. *Faculty research:* Algebraic geometry/number theory, applied math/nonlinear PDEs, combinatorics/matrix theory, geometric group theory/topology. Total annual research expenditures: $6,950. *Unit head:* Dr. Tyler J. Jarvis, Chairperson, 801-422-5925, Fax: 801-422-0504, E-mail: jarvis@math.byu.edu. *Application contact:* Lonette Stoddard, Graduate Secretary, 801-422-2062, Fax: 801-422-0504, E-mail: gradschool@math.byu.edu.

Brock University, Faculty of Graduate Studies, Faculty of Mathematics and Science, Program in Mathematics and Statistics, St. Catharines, ON L2S 3A1, Canada. Offers M Sc. Part-time programs available. *Degree requirements:* For master's, thesis or project. *Entrance requirements:* For master's, honors degree. Additional exam requirements/recommendations for international students: Required—TOEFL (minimum score 550 paper-based; 213 computer-based; 80 iBT), IELTS (minimum score 6.5), TWE (minimum score 4). Electronic applications accepted.

Brooklyn College of the City University of New York, Division of Graduate Studies, Department of Mathematics, Brooklyn, NY 11210-2889. Offers mathematics (MA, PhD). The department offers courses at Brooklyn College that are creditable toward the CUNY doctoral degree (with permission of the executive officer of the doctoral program). Part-time and evening/weekend programs available. *Degree requirements:* For master's, comprehensive exam (mathematics). *Entrance requirements:* For master's, minimum GPA of 3.0, 2 letters of recommendation. Additional exam requirements/recommendations for international students: Required—TOEFL. Electronic applications accepted. *Faculty research:* Differential geometry, gauge theory, complex analysis, orthogonal functions.

Brown University, Graduate School, Department of Mathematics, Providence, RI 02912. Offers M Sc, MA, PhD. *Faculty:* 26 full-time (3 women). *Students:* 37 full-time (7 women); includes 2 minority (both Asian Americans or Pacific Islanders), 25 international. Average age 25. 229 applicants, 13% accepted, 10 enrolled. In 2009, 6 master's, 6 doctorates awarded. *Degree requirements:* For doctorate, one foreign language, thesis/dissertation. *Entrance requirements:* For doctorate, GRE. Additional exam requirements/recommendations for international students: Required—TOEFL (minimum score 500 paper-based; 173 computer-based). *Application deadline:* For fall admission, 1/10 priority date for domestic and international students. Application fee: $75. Electronic applications accepted. *Financial support:* In 2009–10, 36 students received support, including 9 fellowships with full tuition reimbursements available (averaging $19,500 per year), 9 research assistantships with full tuition reimbursements available (averaging $19,000 per year), 19 teaching assistantships with full tuition reimbursements available (averaging $19,500 per year); Federal Work-Study, institutionally sponsored loans, and tuition waivers (full and partial) also available. Financial award application deadline: 1/10; financial award applicants required to submit FAFSA. *Faculty research:* Algebraic geometry, number theory, functional analysis, geometry, topology, theoretical PDE. Total annual research expenditures: $1 million. *Unit head:* Prof. Jeffrey Hoffstein, Chair, 401-863-3319, Fax: 401-863-9471, E-mail: jhoff@math.brown.edu. *Application contact:* Prof. Dan Abramovich, Director of Graduate Studies, 401-863-7968, Fax: 401-863-9471, E-mail: abrmovic@math.brown.edu.

Bryn Mawr College, Graduate School of Arts and Sciences, Department of Mathematics, Bryn Mawr, PA 19010-2899. Offers MA, PhD. Part-time programs available. *Degree requirements:* For master's, one foreign language, thesis; for doctorate, 2 foreign languages, comprehensive exam, thesis/dissertation. *Entrance requirements:* For master's and doctorate, GRE General Test. Additional exam requirements/recommendations for international students: Required—TOEFL (minimum score 600 paper-based; 200 computer-based). *Expenses:* Tuition: Full-time $31,340. Required fees: $430.

Bucknell University, Graduate Studies, College of Arts and Sciences, Department of Mathematics, Lewisburg, PA 17837. Offers MA, MS. Part-time programs available. *Entrance requirements:* For master's, GRE General Test, GRE Subject Test, minimum GPA of 2.8. Additional exam requirements/recommendations for international students: Required—TOEFL.

California Institute of Technology, Division of Physics, Mathematics and Astronomy, Department of Mathematics, Pasadena, CA 91125-0001. Offers PhD. *Degree requirements:* For doctorate, one foreign language, thesis/dissertation, candidacy and final exams. *Entrance requirements:* For doctorate, GRE General Test, GRE Subject Test. Additional exam requirements/recommendations for international students: Required—TOEFL. *Faculty research:* Number theory, combinatorics, differential geometry, dynamical systems, finite groups.

California Polytechnic State University, San Luis Obispo, College of Science and Mathematics, Department of Mathematics, San Luis Obispo, CA 93407. Offers MS. Part-time programs available. *Faculty:* 9 full-time (3 women), 1 (woman) part-time/adjunct. *Students:* 5 full-time (1 woman), 11 part-time (4 women); includes 4 minority (1 American Indian/Alaska Native, 2 Asian Americans or Pacific Islanders, 1 Hispanic American). Average age 27. 20 applicants, 45% accepted, 5 enrolled. In 2009, 1 master's awarded. *Degree requirements:* For master's, comprehensive exam, qualifying exams. *Entrance requirements:* For master's, minimum GPA of 2.5 in last 90 quarter units of course work. Additional exam requirements/recommendations for international students: Required—TOEFL (minimum score 550 paper-based; 213 computer-based), or IELTS (minimum score 6). *Application deadline:* For fall admission, 7/1 for domestic students, 11/30 for international students; for winter admission, 11/1 for domestic students, 6/30 for international students; for spring admission, 2/1 for domestic students. Applications are processed on a rolling basis. Application fee: $55. *Expenses:* Tuition, nonresident: full-time $11,160; part-time $248 per unit. Required fees: $7134; $1553 per quarter. *Financial support:* Fellowships, teaching assistantships, career-related internships

Mathematics

California Polytechnic State University, San Luis Obispo (continued)
or fieldwork, Federal Work-Study, and scholarships/grants available. Support available to part-time students. Financial award application deadline: 3/2; financial award applicants required to submit FAFSA. *Faculty research:* Combinatorics, dynamical systems, ordinary and partial differential equations, operator theory, topology. *Unit head:* Dr. Dylan Retsek, Graduate Coordinator, 805-756-2072, Fax: 805-756-6537, E-mail: dretsek@calpoly.edu. *Application contact:* Dr. Dylan Retsek, Graduate Coordinator, 805-756-2072, Fax: 805-756-6537, E-mail: dretsek@calpoly.edu.

California State Polytechnic University, Pomona, Academic Affairs, College of Science, Program in Mathematics, Pomona, CA 91768-2557. Offers applied mathematics (MS); pure mathematics (MS). Part-time programs available. *Students:* 27 full-time (16 women), 31 part-time (14 women); includes 30 minority (18 Asian Americans or Pacific Islanders, 12 Hispanic Americans), 5 international. Average age 32. 55 applicants, 69% accepted, 26 enrolled. In 2009, 11 master's awarded. *Degree requirements:* For master's, thesis or alternative. *Entrance requirements:* For master's, GRE General Test. *Application deadline:* For fall admission, 5/1 priority date for domestic students; for winter admission, 10/15 priority date for domestic students; for spring admission, 1/20 priority date for domestic students. Applications are processed on a rolling basis. Application fee: $55. Electronic applications accepted. *Expenses:* Tuition, nonresident: full-time $6696; part-time $248 per credit. Required fees: $5487; $3237 per term. Tuition and fees vary according to course load, degree level and program. *Financial support:* Career-related internships or fieldwork, Federal Work-Study, and institutionally sponsored loans available. Support available to part-time students. Financial award application deadline: 3/2; financial award applicants required to submit FAFSA. *Unit head:* Dr. Amber Rosin, Assistant Professor, 909-869-2426, Fax: 909-869-4904, E-mail: arrosin@csupomona.edu. *Application contact:* Scott J. Duncan, Director, Admissions, 909-869-3258, Fax: 909-869-4529, E-mail: sjduncan@csupomona.edu.

California State University Channel Islands, Extended Education, Program in Mathematics, Camarillo, CA 93012. Offers MS. Part-time and evening/weekend programs available. *Degree requirements:* For master's, thesis. *Entrance requirements:* For master's, BA in math. Additional exam requirements/recommendations for international students: Required—TOEFL (minimum score 550 paper-based).

California State University, East Bay, Academic Programs and Graduate Studies, College of Science, Department of Mathematics and Computer Science, Mathematics Program, Hayward, CA 94542-3000. Offers MS. Part-time and evening/weekend programs available. *Faculty:* 6 full-time (4 women). *Students:* 34 full-time (13 women), 50 part-time (20 women); includes 38 minority (6 African Americans, 26 Asian Americans or Pacific Islanders, 6 Hispanic Americans), 3 international. Average age 36. 51 applicants, 80% accepted, 25 enrolled. In 2009, 12 master's awarded. *Degree requirements:* For master's, comprehensive exam or thesis. *Entrance requirements:* For master's, minimum GPA of 3.0 in field. Additional exam requirements/recommendations for international students: Required—TOEFL (minimum score 550 paper-based; 213 computer-based). *Application deadline:* For fall admission, 6/30 for domestic and international students. Application fee: $55. Electronic applications accepted. *Financial support:* Fellowships, teaching assistantships, Federal Work-Study, institutionally sponsored loans, and scholarships/grants available. Support available to part-time students. Financial award application deadline: 3/1; financial award applicants required to submit FAFSA. *Unit head:* Prof. Kevin Callahan, Chair, 510-885-4011, Fax: 510-885-4169, E-mail: kevin.callahan@csueastbay.edu. *Application contact:* Donna Wiley, Interim Associate Director, 510-885-2928, Fax: 510-885-4777, E-mail: donna.wiley@csueastbay.edu.

California State University, Fresno, Division of Graduate Studies, College of Science and Mathematics, Department of Mathematics, Fresno, CA 93740-8027. Offers mathematics (MA); teaching (MA). Part-time programs available. *Degree requirements:* For master's, thesis or alternative. *Entrance requirements:* For master's, GRE General Test. Additional exam requirements/recommendations for international students: Required—TOEFL. Electronic applications accepted. *Faculty research:* Diagnostic testing project.

California State University, Fullerton, Graduate Studies, College of Natural Science and Mathematics, Department of Mathematics, Fullerton, CA 92834-9480. Offers applied mathematics (MA); mathematics (MA); mathematics for secondary school teachers (MA). Part-time programs available. *Students:* 15 full-time (8 women), 58 part-time (31 women); includes 30 minority (25 Asian Americans or Pacific Islanders, 5 Hispanic Americans), 3 international. Average age 30. 62 applicants, 76% accepted, 31 enrolled. In 2009, 25 master's awarded. *Degree requirements:* For master's, comprehensive exam or project. *Entrance requirements:* For master's, minimum GPA of 2.5 in last 60 units of course work, major in mathematics or related field. Application fee: $55. *Expenses:* Tuition, nonresident: full-time $11,160; part-time $373 per credit. Required fees: $1440 per term. Tuition and fees vary according to course load, degree level and program. *Financial support:* Research assistantships, teaching assistantships, career-related internships or fieldwork, Federal Work-Study, institutionally sponsored loans, and scholarships/grants available. Support available to part-time students. Financial award application deadline: 3/1; financial award applicants required to submit FAFSA. *Unit head:* Dr. Paul Deland, Chair, 657-278-3631. *Application contact:* Admissions/Applications, 657-278-2371.

California State University, Long Beach, Graduate Studies, College of Natural Sciences and Mathematics, Department of Mathematics and Statistics, Long Beach, CA 90840. Offers mathematics (MS), including applied mathematics, applied statistics, mathematics education for secondary school teachers. Part-time programs available. *Faculty:* 11 full-time (5 women). *Students:* 73 full-time (30 women), 90 part-time (36 women); includes 75 minority (6 African Americans, 47 Asian Americans or Pacific Islanders, 22 Hispanic Americans), 15 international. Average age 30. 123 applicants, 69% accepted, 44 enrolled. *Degree requirements:* For master's, comprehensive exam or thesis. *Application deadline:* For fall admission, 7/1 for domestic students; for spring admission, 12/1 for domestic students. Applications are processed on a rolling basis. Application fee: $55. Electronic applications accepted. *Expenses:* Required fees: $1802 per semester. Part-time tuition and fees vary according to course load. *Financial support:* Teaching assistantships, Federal Work-Study, institutionally sponsored loans, scholarships/grants, and traineeships available. Financial award application deadline: 3/2. *Faculty research:* Algebra, functional analysis, partial differential equations, operator theory, numerical analysis. *Unit head:* Dr. Robert Mena, Chair, 562-985-4721, Fax: 562-985-8227, E-mail: rmena@csulb.edu. *Application contact:* Dr. Ngo Viet, Graduate Associate Chair, 562-985-4721, Fax: 562-985-8227, E-mail: viet@csulb.edu.

California State University, Los Angeles, Graduate Studies, College of Natural and Social Sciences, Department of Mathematics, Los Angeles, CA 90032-8530. Offers mathematics (MS), including applied mathematics, mathematics. Part-time and evening/weekend programs available. *Faculty:* 8 full-time (1 woman), 2 part-time/adjunct (1 woman). *Students:* 26 full-time (12 women), 34 part-time (14 women); includes 29 minority (3 African Americans, 17 Asian Americans or Pacific Islanders, 9 Hispanic Americans), 11 international. Average age 34. 32 applicants, 100% accepted, 13 enrolled. In 2009, 18 master's awarded. *Degree requirements:* For master's, comprehensive exam or thesis. *Entrance requirements:* For master's, previous course work in mathematics. Additional exam requirements/recommendations for international students: Required—TOEFL (minimum score 500 paper-based; 173 computer-based). *Application deadline:* For fall admission, 5/1 for domestic and international students. Applications are processed on a rolling basis. Application fee: $55. Electronic applications accepted. *Financial support:* Teaching assistantships, Federal Work-Study available. Support available to part-time students. Financial award application deadline: 3/1. *Faculty research:* Group theory, functional analysis, convexity theory, ordered geometry. *Unit head:* Dr. Silva Heubach, Chair, 323-343-2150, Fax: 323-343-5071, E-mail: sheubac@calstatela.edu. *Application contact:* Dr. Cheryl L. Ney, Associate Vice President for Academic Affairs and Dean of Graduate Studies, 323-343-3820, Fax: 323-343-5653, E-mail: cney@cslanet.calstatela.edu.

California State University, Northridge, Graduate Studies, College of Science and Mathematics, Department of Mathematics, Northridge, CA 91330. Offers applied mathematics (MS); mathematics (MS); mathematics for educational careers (MS). Part-time and evening/weekend programs available. *Faculty:* 34 full-time (9 women), 36 part-time/adjunct (17 women). *Students:* 19 full-time (11 women), 34 part-time (12 women); includes 1 African American, 4 Asian Americans or Pacific Islanders, 9 Hispanic Americans, 2 international. Average age 31. 86 applicants, 49% accepted, 27 enrolled. In 2009, 16 master's awarded. *Degree requirements:* For master's, thesis (for some programs). *Entrance requirements:* For master's, GRE (if cumulative undergraduate GPA less than 3.0). Additional exam requirements/recommendations for international students: Required—TOEFL. *Application deadline:* For fall admission, 4/15 priority date for domestic students. Application fee: $55. *Financial support:* Teaching assistantships, Federal Work-Study and institutionally sponsored loans available. Support available to part-time students. Financial award application deadline: 3/1. *Unit head:* Dr. Werner Horn, Graduate Coordinator, 818-677-7794, E-mail: werner.horn@csun.edu. *Application contact:* Dr. Werner Horn, Graduate Coordinator, 818-677-7794, E-mail: werner.horn@csun.edu.

California State University, Sacramento, Graduate Studies, College of Natural Sciences and Mathematics, Department of Mathematics and Statistics, Sacramento, CA 95819. Offers MA. Part-time programs available. *Degree requirements:* For master's, thesis or alternative, writing proficiency exam. *Entrance requirements:* For master's, minimum GPA of 3.0 in mathematics, 2.5 overall during previous 2 years; BA in mathematics or equivalent. Additional exam requirements/recommendations for international students: Required—TOEFL. Electronic applications accepted.

California State University, San Bernardino, Graduate Studies, College of Natural Sciences, Department of Mathematics, San Bernardino, CA 92407-2397. Offers mathematics (MA); teaching mathematics (MAT). Part-time programs available. *Faculty:* 13 full-time (4 women). *Students:* 36 full-time (15 women), 42 part-time (18 women); includes 36 minority (5 African Americans, 10 Asian Americans or Pacific Islanders, 21 Hispanic Americans), 2 international. Average age 34. 44 applicants, 75% accepted, 23 enrolled. In 2009, 11 master's awarded. *Degree requirements:* For master's, advancement to candidacy. *Entrance requirements:* For master's, writing exam, minimum GPA of 3.0 in math courses. Application fee: $55. *Financial support:* Teaching assistantships available. *Faculty research:* Mathematics education, technology in education, algebra, combinatorics, real analysis. *Unit head:* Dr. Peter D. Williams, Chair, 909-537-5361, Fax: 909-537-7119, E-mail: pwilliam@csusb.edu. *Application contact:* Olivia Rosas, Director of Admissions, 909-537-7577, Fax: 909-537-7034, E-mail: orosas@csusb.edu.

California State University, San Marcos, College of Arts and Sciences, Program in Mathematics, San Marcos, CA 92096-0001. Offers MS. Part-time and evening/weekend programs available. *Degree requirements:* For master's, thesis optional. *Entrance requirements:* Additional exam requirements/recommendations for international students: Required—TOEFL, TWE. *Faculty research:* Combinatorics, graph theory, partial differential equations, numerical analysis, computational linear algebra.

Carleton University, Faculty of Graduate Studies, Faculty of Science, School of Mathematics and Statistics, Ottawa, ON K1S 5B6, Canada. Offers mathematics (M Sc, PhD). *Degree requirements:* For master's, thesis optional; for doctorate, one foreign language, comprehensive exam, thesis/dissertation. *Entrance requirements:* For master's, honors degree; for doctorate, master's degree. Additional exam requirements/recommendations for international students: Required—TOEFL. *Faculty research:* Pure mathematics, applied mathematics, probability and statistics.

Carnegie Mellon University, Mellon College of Science, Department of Mathematical Sciences, Pittsburgh, PA 15213-3891. Offers algorithms, combinatorics, and optimization (PhD); applied mathematics (PhD); computational finance (MS); mathematical finance (PhD); mathematical sciences (MS, DA, PhD); pure and applied logic (PhD). Part-time programs available. Terminal master's awarded for partial completion of doctoral program. *Degree requirements:* For doctorate, thesis/dissertation. *Entrance requirements:* For master's and doctorate, GRE General Test, GRE Subject Test. Additional exam requirements/recommendations for international students: Required—TOEFL. Electronic applications accepted. *Faculty research:* Continuum mechanics, discrete mathematics, applied and computational mathematics.

Case Western Reserve University, School of Graduate Studies, Department of Mathematics, Cleveland, OH 44106. Offers applied mathematics (MS, PhD); mathematics (MS, PhD). Part-time programs available. *Faculty:* 18 full-time (5 women), 2 part-time/adjunct (1 woman). *Students:* 19 full-time (10 women), 1 part-time (0 women), 7 international. Average age 25. 55 applicants, 38% accepted, 8 enrolled. In 2009, 5 master's, 1 doctorate awarded. Terminal master's awarded for partial completion of doctoral program. *Degree requirements:* For master's, thesis or alternative, thesis (applied mathematics); for doctorate, thesis/dissertation. *Entrance requirements:* For master's and doctorate, GRE General Test. Additional exam requirements/recommendations for international students: Required—TOEFL (minimum score 550 paper-based; 213 computer-based; 79 iBT). *Application deadline:* For fall admission, 2/15 priority date for domestic students; for spring admission, 11/12 for domestic students. Applications are processed on a rolling basis. Application fee: $50. Electronic applications accepted. *Financial support:* Research assistantships, teaching assistantships available. Financial award application deadline: 2/15. *Faculty research:* Probability theory, differential equations and control theory, differential geometry and topology, Lie groups, functional and harmonic analysis. *Unit head:* Daniela Calvetti, Chair, 216-368-2880, Fax: 216-368-5163, E-mail: daniela.calvetti@case.edu. *Application contact:* Gaythresa Lewis, Admissions, 216-368-5014, Fax: 216-368-5163, E-mail: gxl34@case.edu.

Central Connecticut State University, School of Graduate Studies, School of Arts and Sciences, Department of Mathematical Sciences, New Britain, CT 06050-4010. Offers data mining (MS, Certificate); mathematics (MA, MS, Certificate, Sixth Year Certificate), including actuarial science (MA), computer science (MA), statistics (MA). Part-time and evening/weekend programs available. *Faculty:* 33 full-time (12 women), 60 part-time/adjunct (30 women). *Students:* 21 full-time (10 women), 129 part-time (76 women); includes 13 minority (4 African Americans, 1 American Indian/Alaska Native, 4 Asian Americans or Pacific Islanders, 4 Hispanic Americans), 13 international. Average age 37. 78 applicants, 64% accepted, 37 enrolled. In 2009, 27 master's, 13 other advanced degrees awarded. *Degree requirements:* For master's, comprehensive exam, thesis or alternative; for other advanced degree, qualifying exam. *Entrance requirements:* For master's, minimum undergraduate GPA of 2.7. Additional exam requirements/recommendations for international students: Required—TOEFL. *Application deadline:* For fall admission, 7/1 for domestic students; for spring admission, 12/1 for domestic students. Applications are processed on a rolling basis. Application fee: $50. Electronic applications accepted. *Expenses:* Tuition, area resident: Full-time $4662; part-time $440 per credit. Tuition, state resident: full-time $6994; part-time $440 per credit. Tuition, nonresident: full-time $12,988; part-time $440 per credit. Required fees: $3606. One-time fee: $62 part-time. *Financial support:* In 2009–10, 7 students received support, including 3 research assistantships; career-related internships or fieldwork, Federal Work-Study, scholarships/grants, and unspecified assistantships also available. Support available to part-time students. Financial award application deadline: 3/1; financial award applicants required to submit FAFSA. *Faculty research:* Statistics, actuarial mathematics, computer systems and engineering, computer programming techniques, operations research. *Unit head:* Dr. Jeffrey McGowan, Chair, 860-832-2835. *Application contact:* Dr. Jeffrey McGowan, Chair, 860-832-2835.

Central Michigan University, College of Graduate Studies, College of Science and Technology, Department of Mathematics, Mount Pleasant, MI 48859. Offers mathematics (MA, PhD), including teaching of college mathematics (PhD). Part-time programs available. *Degree requirements:* For master's, thesis or alternative; for doctorate, thesis/dissertation. *Entrance requirements:* For master's, minimum GPA of 2.7, 20 hours of course work in mathematics; for doctorate, GRE, minimum GPA of 3.0, 20 hours of course work in mathematics. Electronic applications accepted. *Faculty research:* Combinatorics, approximation theory, applied mathematics, statistics, functional analysis and operator theory.

Central Washington University, Graduate Studies and Research, College of the Sciences, Department of Mathematics, Ellensburg, WA 98926. Offers MAT. Program offered during summer only. *Faculty:* 14 full-time (4 women). *Students:* 2 full-time (both women). In 2009, 6 master's awarded. *Degree requirements:* For master's, thesis or alternative. *Entrance requirements:* For master's, minimum GPA of 3.0. Additional exam requirements/recommendations for international students: Required—TOEFL (minimum score 550 paper-based; 213 computer-based; 79 iBT). *Application deadline:* Applications are processed on a rolling basis. Application fee: $50. Electronic applications accepted. *Expenses:* Tuition, state resident: full-time $7353; part-time $245 per credit. Tuition, nonresident: full-time $16,383; part-time $546 per credit. Required fees: $882. Tuition and fees vary according to degree level. *Financial support:* Federal Work-Study and health care benefits available. Financial award application deadline: 3/1; financial award applicants required to submit FAFSA. *Unit head:* Dr. Aaron Montgomery, Chair, 509-963-2103. *Application contact:* Justine Eason, Admissions Program Coordinator, 509-963-3103, Fax: 509-963-1799, E-mail: masters@cwu.edu.

Chicago State University, School of Graduate and Professional Studies, College of Arts and Sciences, Department of Mathematics and Computer Science, Chicago, IL 60628. Offers computer science (MS); mathematics (MS). *Degree requirements:* For master's, thesis optional, oral exam. *Entrance requirements:* For master's, minimum GPA of 2.75.

City College of the City University of New York, Graduate School, College of Liberal Arts and Science, Division of Science, Department of Mathematics, New York, NY 10031-9198. Offers MA. Part-time programs available. *Degree requirements:* For master's, one foreign language. *Entrance requirements:* Additional exam requirements/recommendations for international students: Required—TOEFL (minimum score 500 paper-based; 61 iBT). Electronic applications accepted. *Faculty research:* Group theory, number theory, logic, statistics, computational geometry.

Claremont Graduate University, Graduate Programs, School of Mathematical Sciences, Claremont, CA 91711-6160. Offers computational and systems biology (PhD); computational mathematics and numerical analysis (MA, MS); computational science (PhD); engineering and industrial applied mathematics (PhD); mathematics (PhD); operations research and statistics (MA, MS); physical applied mathematics (MA, MS); pure mathematics (MA, MS); scientific computing (MA, MS); systems and control theory (MA, MS). Part-time programs available. *Faculty:* 5 full-time (0 women), 2 part-time/adjunct (0 women). *Students:* 56 full-time (20 women), 12 part-time (3 women); includes 13 minority (2 African Americans, 6 Asian Americans or Pacific Islanders, 5 Hispanic Americans), 25 international. Average age 33. In 2009, 7 master's, 7 doctorates awarded. Terminal master's awarded for partial completion of doctoral program. *Entrance requirements:* For master's and doctorate, GRE General Test. Additional exam requirements/recommendations for international students: Required—TOEFL (minimum score 550 paper-based; 213 computer-based; 80 iBT). *Application deadline:* For fall admission, 2/1 priority date for domestic students. Applications are processed on a rolling basis. Application fee: $60. Electronic applications accepted. *Expenses:* Tuition: Full-time $35,046; part-time $1524 per credit. Required fees: $161 per semester. *Financial support:* Fellowships, research assistantships, Federal Work-Study, institutionally sponsored loans, scholarships/grants, and tuition waivers (full and partial) available. Support available to part-time students. Financial award application deadline: 2/15; financial award applicants required to submit FAFSA. *Unit head:* John Angus, Dean, 909-621-8080, Fax: 909-607-8261, E-mail: john.angus@cgu.edu. *Application contact:* Susan Townzen, Program Coordinator, 909-621-8080, Fax: 909-607-8261, E-mail: susan.n.townzen@cgu.edu.

Clark Atlanta University, School of Arts and Sciences, Department of Mathematical Sciences, Atlanta, GA 30314. Offers MS. Part-time programs available. *Faculty:* 2 full-time (1 woman), 1 part-time/adjunct (0 women). *Students:* 2 full-time (both women), 2 part-time (both women); includes 3 minority (all African Americans), 1 international. Average age 32. 5 applicants, 100% accepted, 4 enrolled. *Degree requirements:* For master's, one foreign language, thesis optional. *Entrance requirements:* For master's, GRE General Test, minimum GPA of 2.5. Additional exam requirements/recommendations for international students: Required—TOEFL (minimum score 500 paper-based; 173 computer-based). *Application deadline:* For fall admission, 4/1 for domestic and international students; for spring admission, 11/1 for domestic and international students. Applications are processed on a rolling basis. Application fee: $40 ($55 for international students). *Expenses:* Tuition: Full-time $12,240; part-time $680 per credit hour. Required fees: $710; $355 per semester. *Financial support:* Scholarships/grants and unspecified assistantships available. Financial award application deadline: 4/30; financial award applicants required to submit FAFSA. *Faculty research:* Numerical methods for operator equations, Ada language development. *Unit head:* Dr. Charles Pierre, Chairperson, 404-880-8195, E-mail: cpierre@cau.edu. *Application contact:* Michelle Clark-Davis, Graduate Program Admissions, 404-880-6605, E-mail: cauadmissions@cau.edu.

Clarkson University, Graduate School, School of Arts and Sciences, Department of Mathematics, Potsdam, NY 13699. Offers MS, PhD. Part-time programs available. *Faculty:* 14 full-time (4 women), 1 part-time/adjunct (0 women). *Students:* 26 full-time (3 women), 14 international. Average age 29. 34 applicants, 50% accepted, 8 enrolled. In 2009, 1 master's, 6 doctorates awarded. Terminal master's awarded for partial completion of doctoral program. *Degree requirements:* For doctorate, thesis/dissertation, departmental qualifying exam. *Entrance requirements:* For master's, GRE, 3 letters of recommendation; resume (recommended); for doctorate, GRE, transcripts of all college coursework, three letters of recommendation; resume and personal statement (recommended). Additional exam requirements/recommendations for international students: Required—TOEFL, TSE (recommended). *Application deadline:* For fall admission, 1/30 priority date for domestic and international students; for spring admission, 9/1 priority date for domestic and international students. Applications are processed on a rolling basis. Application fee: $25 ($35 for international students). Electronic applications accepted. *Expenses:* Tuition: Part-time $1074 per credit hour. *Financial support:* In 2009–10, 24 students received support, including 2 fellowships (averaging $30,000 per year), 8 research assistantships (averaging $20,190 per year), 13 teaching assistantships (averaging $20,190 per year); scholarships/grants and unspecified assistantships also available. *Faculty research:* Dynamical systems, chaos theory, optimization, non-linear equations, atmospheric and environmental modeling. Total annual research expenditures: $770,369. *Unit head:* Dr. Christopher Lynch, Chair, 315-268-2384, Fax: 315-268-2371, E-mail: clynch@clarkson.edu. *Application contact:* Jennifer E. Reed, Graduate School Coordinator for School of Arts and Sciences, 315-268-3802, Fax: 315-268-3989, E-mail: jreed@clarkson.edu.

Clemson University, Graduate School, College of Engineering and Science, Department of Mathematical Sciences, Clemson, SC 29634. Offers applied and pure mathematics (MS, PhD); computational mathematics (MS, PhD); operations research (MS, PhD); statistics (MS, PhD). Part-time programs available. *Faculty:* 51 full-time (14 women), 9 part-time/adjunct (2 women). *Students:* 92 full-time (39 women), 1 part-time (0 women); includes 3 minority (2 African Americans, 1 American Indian/Alaska Native), 31 international. Average age 26. 134 applicants, 76% accepted, 20 enrolled. In 2009, 36 master's, 13 doctorates awarded. *Degree requirements:* For master's, thesis optional, final project; for doctorate, thesis/dissertation, qualifying exams. *Entrance requirements:* For master's and doctorate, GRE General Test. Additional exam requirements/recommendations for international students: Required—TOEFL. *Application deadline:* For fall admission, 1/15 priority date for domestic students, 2/15 priority date for international students; for spring admission, 10/1 priority date for domestic students, 9/15 priority date for international students. Applications are processed on a rolling basis. Application fee: $70 ($80 for international students). Electronic applications accepted. *Expenses:* Tuition, state resident: full-time $8684; part-time $528 per credit hour. Tuition, nonresident: full-time $15,330; part-time $1078 per credit hour. Required fees: $736; $37 per semester. Part-time tuition and fees vary according to course load and program. *Financial support:* In 2009–10, 85 students received support, including 1 fellowship with full and partial tuition reimbursement available (averaging $10,000 per year), 7 research assistantships with partial tuition reimbursements available (averaging $17,591 per year), 66 teaching assistantships with partial tuition reimbursements available (averaging $18,593 per year); career-related internships or fieldwork, institutionally sponsored loans, scholarships/grants, health care benefits, and unspecified assistantships also available. Support available to part-time students. Financial award application deadline: 4/15. *Faculty research:* Applied and computational analysis, cryptography, discrete mathematics, optimization, statistics. Total annual research expenditures: $535,985. *Unit head:* Dr. Robert L. Taylor, Chair, 864-656-5240, Fax: 864-656-5230, E-mail: rtaylo2@clemson.edu. *Application contact:* Dr. K. B. Kulasekera, Graduate Coordinator, 864-656-5231, Fax: 864-656-5230, E-mail: kk@clemson.edu.

Cleveland State University, College of Graduate Studies, College of Science, Department of Mathematics, Cleveland, OH 44115. Offers MA, MS. Part-time programs available. *Degree requirements:* For master's, exit project. *Entrance requirements:* For master's, GRE. Additional exam requirements/recommendations for international students: Required—TOEFL (minimum score 515 paper-based; 197 computer-based). Electronic applications accepted. *Faculty research:* Algebraic topology, probability and statistics, differential equations, geometry.

The College at Brockport, State University of New York, School of Science and Mathematics, Department of Mathematics, Brockport, NY 14420-2997. Offers MA. Part-time programs available. *Students:* 10 full-time (3 women), 4 part-time (1 woman). 8 applicants, 88% accepted, 5 enrolled. In 2009, 7 master's awarded. *Degree requirements:* For master's, comprehensive exam. *Entrance requirements:* For master's, minimum GPA of 3.0, letters of recommendation. Additional exam requirements/recommendations for international students: Required—TOEFL (minimum score 550 paper-based; 213 computer-based; 79 iBT). *Application deadline:* For fall admission, 7/15 priority date for domestic and international students; for spring admission, 11/15 priority date for domestic and international students. Application fee: $50. Electronic applications accepted. *Expenses:* Tuition, state resident: full-time $8370; part-time $349 per credit. Tuition, nonresident: full-time $13,250; part-time $522 per credit. *Financial support:* In 2009–10, 3 teaching assistantships with full tuition reimbursements (averaging $6,000 per year) were awarded; Federal Work-Study, scholarships/grants, and unspecified assistantships also available. Support available to part-time students. Financial award application deadline: 3/15; financial award applicants required to submit FAFSA. *Faculty research:* Mathematical modeling, dynamical systems, complex/functional analysis, graph theory and combinations, algebra and number theory. *Unit head:* Dr. Mihail Barbosu, Chairperson, 585-395-2194, Fax: 585-395-2304, E-mail: mbarbosu@brockport.edu. *Application contact:* Dr. Howard Skogman, Graduate Director, 585-395-2046, Fax: 585-395-2304, E-mail: hskogman@brockport.edu.

College of Charleston, Graduate School, School of Sciences and Mathematics, Program in Mathematics, Charleston, SC 29424-0001. Offers mathematics (MS). Evening/weekend programs available. *Faculty:* 27 full-time (6 women). *Students:* 4 full-time (2 women), 7 part-time (5 women); includes 3 minority (all African Americans), 1 international. Average age 32. 6 applicants, 100% accepted, 2 enrolled. In 2009, 6 master's awarded. *Entrance requirements:* For master's, GRE, BS in mathematics or equivalent, 2 letters of recommendation. Additional exam requirements/recommendations for international students: Required—TOEFL. *Application deadline:* For fall admission, 7/1 priority date for domestic students; for spring admission, 11/1 priority date for domestic students. Applications are processed on a rolling basis. Application fee: $45. Electronic applications accepted. *Financial support:* Federal Work-Study, scholarships/grants, and unspecified assistantships available. Support available to part-time students. Financial award applicants required to submit FAFSA. *Faculty research:* Algebra, dynamical systems, probability, analysis and topology, combinatorics. *Unit head:* Dr. Ben Cox, Director, 843-953-5715, Fax: 843-953-1410, E-mail: coxbl@cofc.edu. *Application contact:* Susan Hallatt, Director of Graduate Admissions, 843-953-5614, Fax: 843-953-1434, E-mail: hallatts@cofc.edu.

Colorado School of Mines, Graduate School, Department of Mathematical and Computer Sciences, Golden, CO 80401. Offers MS, PhD. Part-time programs available. *Faculty:* 33 full-time (15 women), 3 part-time/adjunct (0 women). *Students:* 42 full-time (12 women), 8 part-time (1 woman); includes 7 minority (1 American Indian/Alaska Native, 4 Asian Americans or Pacific Islanders, 2 Hispanic Americans), 8 international. Average age 30. 63 applicants, 60% accepted, 19 enrolled. In 2009, 10 master's, 2 doctorates awarded. *Degree requirements:* For master's, thesis (for some programs); for doctorate, comprehensive exam, thesis/dissertation. *Entrance requirements:* For master's and doctorate, GRE General Test. Additional exam requirements/recommendations for international students: Required—TOEFL (minimum score 550 paper-based; 213 computer-based; 80 iBT). *Application deadline:* For fall admission, 1/15 priority date for domestic and international students; for spring admission, 9/1 priority date for domestic and international students. Application fee: $50 ($70 for international students). Electronic applications accepted. *Expenses:* Tuition, state resident: full-time $10,584; part-time $588 per credit hour. Tuition, nonresident: full-time $24,750; part-time $1375 per credit hour. Required fees: $1654; $827.10 per semester. *Financial support:* In 2009–10, 30 students received support, including 2 fellowships with full tuition reimbursements available (averaging $20,000 per year), 15 research assistantships with full tuition reimbursements available (averaging $20,000 per year), 13 teaching assistantships with full tuition reimbursements available (averaging $20,000 per year); scholarships/grants, health care benefits, and unspecified assistantships also available. Financial award application deadline: 1/15; financial award applicants required to submit FAFSA. *Faculty research:* Applied statistics, numerical computation, artificial intelligence, linear optimization. Total annual research expenditures: $607,892. *Unit head:* Dr. Dinesh Mehta, Department Head, 303-273-3713, Fax: 303-273-3875, E-mail: dmehta@mines.edu. *Application contact:* William Navidi, Professor, 303-273-3489, Fax: 303-273-3875, E-mail: wnavidi@mines.edu.

Colorado State University, Graduate School, College of Natural Sciences, Department of Mathematics, Fort Collins, CO 80523-1874. Offers MAT, MS, PhD. Postbaccalaureate distance learning degree programs offered (no on-campus study). *Faculty:* 25 full-time (5 women), 1 part-time/adjunct (0 women). *Students:* 39 full-time (14 women), 14 part-time (7 women); includes 3 minority (1 African American, 2 Hispanic Americans), 7 international. Average age 28. 105 applicants, 30% accepted, 9 enrolled. In 2009, 14 master's, 6 doctorates awarded. Terminal master's awarded for partial completion of doctoral program. *Degree requirements:* For master's, comprehensive exam (for some programs), thesis (for some programs); for doctorate, comprehensive exam, thesis/dissertation. *Entrance requirements:* For master's and doctorate, GRE General Test or GMAT, minimum GPA of 3.0, 3 letters of recommendation. Additional exam requirements/recommendations for international students: Required—TOEFL (minimum score 550 paper-based; 213 computer-based; 80 iBT). *Application deadline:* For fall admission, 9/15 priority date for domestic and international students; for spring admission, 1/15 priority date for domestic and international students. Applications are processed on a rolling basis. Application fee: $50. Electronic applications accepted. *Expenses:* Tuition, state resident: full-time $6434; part-time $359.10 per credit. Tuition, nonresident: full-time $18,116;

Mathematics

Colorado State University (continued)
part-time $1006.45 per credit. Required fees: $1496; $83 per credit. *Financial support:* In 2009–10, 3 fellowships (averaging $59,667 per year), 16 research assistantships with full tuition reimbursements (averaging $10,211 per year), 42 teaching assistantships with full tuition reimbursements (averaging $13,603 per year) were awarded; health care benefits also available. Financial award application deadline: 1/15; financial award applicants required to submit FAFSA. *Faculty research:* Numerical analysis, algebraic geometry, combinatorics, number theory, computational mathematics. Total annual research expenditures: $1.2 million. *Unit head:* Dr. Simon Tavener, Chair, 970-491-6452, Fax: 970-491-2161, E-mail: tavener@math.colostate.edu. *Application contact:* Dr. Jeanne Duflot, Director, Graduate Program, 970-491-6453, Fax: 970-491-2161, E-mail: grad_program@math.colostate.edu.

Columbia University, Graduate School of Arts and Sciences, Division of Natural Sciences, Department of Mathematics, New York, NY 10027. Offers M Phil, MA, PhD. *Degree requirements:* For master's, written exam; for doctorate, 2 foreign languages, thesis/dissertation. *Entrance requirements:* For master's and doctorate, GRE General Test, major in mathematics. Additional exam requirements/recommendations for international students: Required—TOEFL. *Faculty research:* Algebra, topology, analysis.

Concordia University, School of Graduate Studies, Faculty of Arts and Science, Department of Mathematics and Statistics, Montréal, QC H3G 1M8, Canada. Offers mathematics (M Sc, MA, PhD); teaching of mathematics (MTM). *Degree requirements:* For master's, thesis optional; for doctorate, comprehensive exam, thesis/dissertation. *Entrance requirements:* For master's, honors degree in mathematics or equivalent. *Faculty research:* Number theory, computational algebra, mathematical physics, differential geometry, dynamical systems and statistics.

Cornell University, Graduate School, Graduate Fields of Arts and Sciences, Field of Mathematics, Ithaca, NY 14853-0001. Offers PhD. *Faculty:* 52 full-time (4 women). *Students:* 64 full-time (22 women); includes 2 minority (both Asian Americans or Pacific Islanders), 31 international. Average age 27. 265 applicants, 11% accepted, 12 enrolled. In 2009, 11 doctorates awarded. *Degree requirements:* For doctorate, one foreign language, comprehensive exam, thesis/dissertation, teaching experience. *Entrance requirements:* For doctorate, GRE General Test, GRE Subject Test (mathematics), 3 letters of recommendation. Additional exam requirements/recommendations for international students: Required—TOEFL (minimum score 600 paper-based; 250 computer-based; 95 iBT). *Application deadline:* For fall admission, 1/15 for domestic students. Application fee: $70. Electronic applications accepted. *Expenses:* Tuition: Full-time $29,500. Required fees: $70. Full-time tuition and fees vary according to degree level, program and student level. *Financial support:* In 2009–10, 5 fellowships with full tuition reimbursements, 1 research assistantship with full tuition reimbursement, 4 teaching assistantships with full tuition reimbursements were awarded; institutionally sponsored loans, scholarships/grants, health care benefits, tuition waivers (full and partial), and unspecified assistantships also available. Financial award applicants required to submit FAFSA. *Faculty research:* Analysis, dynamical systems, Lie theory, logic, topology and geometry. *Unit head:* Director of Graduate Studies, 607-255-6757, Fax: 607-255-7149. *Application contact:* Graduate Field Assistant, 607-255-6757, Fax: 607-255-7149, E-mail: gradinfo@math.cornell.edu.

Dalhousie University, Faculty of Science, Department of Mathematics and Statistics, Program in Mathematics, Halifax, NS B3H 4R2, Canada. Offers M Sc, PhD. In 2009, 8 master's, 5 doctorates awarded. *Degree requirements:* For master's, thesis; for doctorate, thesis/dissertation. *Entrance requirements:* Additional exam requirements/recommendations for international students: Required—TOEFL, IELTS, CANTEST, CAEL, or Michigan English Language Assessment Battery. Application fee: $70. Electronic applications accepted. *Financial support:* In 2009–10, research assistantships (averaging $10,000 per year), teaching assistantships (averaging $2,500 per year) were awarded; career-related internships or fieldwork, scholarships/grants, and health care benefits also available. *Faculty research:* Applied mathematics, category theory, algebra, analysis, graph theory. *Unit head:* Dr. Sara Faridi, Graduate Coordinator, 902-494-2658, Fax: 902-494-5130, E-mail: faridi@mathstat.dal.ca. *Application contact:* Paula Flemming, Graduate Secretary, 902-494-2572, Fax: 902-494-5130, E-mail: chair@mscs.dal.ca.

Dartmouth College, Arts and Sciences Graduate Programs, Department of Mathematics, Hanover, NH 03755. Offers PhD. *Faculty:* 20 full-time (6 women). *Students:* 26 full-time (8 women); includes 2 minority (1 Asian American or Pacific Islander, 1 Hispanic American), 4 international. Average age 26. 102 applicants, 10% accepted, 6 enrolled. In 2009, 4 doctorates awarded. *Degree requirements:* For doctorate, 2 foreign languages, thesis/dissertation. *Entrance requirements:* For doctorate, GRE General Test, GRE Subject Test. Additional exam requirements/recommendations for international students: Required—TOEFL. *Application deadline:* For fall admission, 2/15 priority date for domestic students. Application fee: $0. *Financial support:* In 2009–10, 23 students received support, including fellowships with full tuition reimbursements available (averaging $23,823 per year), research assistantships with full tuition reimbursements available (averaging $23,823 per year), teaching assistantships with full tuition reimbursements available (averaging $23,823 per year); institutionally sponsored loans, scholarships/grants, tuition waivers (full and partial), and unspecified assistantships also available. *Faculty research:* Mathematical logic, set theory, combinations, number theory. *Unit head:* Dr. Daniel N. Rockmore, Chair, 603-646-2415, Fax: 603-646-1312. *Application contact:* Traci Flynn-Moloney, Department Administration, 603-646-3723, Fax: 603-646-1312.

Delaware State University, Graduate Programs, Department of Mathematics, Program in Mathematics, Dover, DE 19901-2277. Offers MS. *Entrance requirements:* Additional exam requirements/recommendations for international students: Required—TOEFL (minimum score 550 paper-based). Electronic applications accepted.

DePaul University, College of Liberal Arts and Sciences, Department of Mathematical Sciences, Chicago, IL 60614. Offers applied mathematics (MS), including actuarial science or statistics; applied statistics (MS, Certificate); mathematics education (MA). Part-time and evening/weekend programs available. *Faculty:* 23 full-time (6 women), 18 part-time/adjunct (5 women). *Students:* 117 full-time (64 women), 67 part-time (37 women); includes 47 minority (22 African Americans, 15 Asian Americans or Pacific Islanders, 10 Hispanic Americans), 13 international. Average age 30. 40 applicants, 100% accepted. In 2009, 30 master's awarded. *Degree requirements:* For master's, comprehensive exam. *Entrance requirements:* Additional exam requirements/recommendations for international students: Required—TOEFL. *Application deadline:* For fall admission, 7/30 for domestic students, 6/30 for international students; for winter admission, 11/30 for domestic students, 10/31 for international students; for spring admission, 2/15 for domestic students. Applications are processed on a rolling basis. Application fee: $25. *Expenses:* Tuition: Full-time $37,525; part-time $620 per credit hour. *Financial support:* In 2009–10, 12 students received support, including research assistantships with partial tuition reimbursements available (averaging $6,000 per year); teaching assistantships, tuition waivers (full) also available. Financial award application deadline: 4/30. *Faculty research:* Verbally prime algebras, enveloping algebras of Lie, superalgebras and related rings, harmonic analysis, estimation theory. *Unit head:* Dr. Ahmed I. Zayed, Chairperson, 773-325-7806, Fax: 773-325-7807, E-mail: azayed@depaul.edu. *Application contact:* Ann Spittle, Director of Graduate Admissions, 312-362-8300, Fax: 312-362-5749, E-mail: admitdpu@depaul.edu.

Dowling College, Programs in Arts and Sciences, Oakdale, NY 11769-1999. Offers integrated math and science (MS); liberal studies (MA). Part-time and evening/weekend programs available. *Faculty:* 4 full-time (1 woman), 4 part-time/adjunct (1 woman). *Students:* 3 full-time (2 women), 9 part-time (5 women), 1 international. Average age 33. 9 applicants, 89% accepted, 2 enrolled. In 2009, 1 master's awarded. *Degree requirements:* For master's, comprehensive exam, thesis. *Entrance requirements:* For master's, minimum undergraduate GPA of 3.0, 2 letters of recommendation. Additional exam requirements/recommendations for international students: Required—TOEFL (minimum score 550 paper-based). *Application deadline:* For fall admission, 9/1 priority date for domestic students; for winter admission, 1/1 priority date for domestic students; for spring admission, 2/1 priority date for domestic students. Applications are processed on a rolling basis. Application fee: $50. Electronic applications accepted. *Expenses:* Tuition: Full-time $14,490; part-time $805 per credit. Required fees: $346 per term. *Financial support:* Federal Work-Study available. Support available to part-time students. Financial award application deadline: 6/30; financial award applicants required to submit FAFSA. *Unit head:* Dr. Paul Abramson, Dean, 631-244-3162, Fax: 631-244-1035, E-mail: abramsop@dowling.edu. *Application contact:* Glenn M. Berman, Assistant Vice President for Enrollment Services/Dean of Admissions, 631-244-3357, Fax: 631-244-1059, E-mail: glenn.berman@dowling.edu.

Drexel University, College of Arts and Sciences, Department of Mathematics, Program in Mathematics, Philadelphia, PA 19104-2875. Offers MS, PhD. *Degree requirements:* For doctorate, one foreign language, thesis/dissertation. *Entrance requirements:* For master's and doctorate, GRE. Additional exam requirements/recommendations for international students: Required—TOEFL. Electronic applications accepted.

Duke University, Graduate School, Department of Mathematics, Durham, NC 27708-0586. Offers PhD. *Faculty:* 27 full-time. *Students:* 46 full-time (10 women); includes 3 minority (1 African American, 2 Hispanic Americans), 16 international. 159 applicants, 19% accepted, 12 enrolled. In 2009, 9 doctorates awarded. *Degree requirements:* For doctorate, 2 foreign languages, thesis/dissertation. *Entrance requirements:* For doctorate, GRE General Test, GRE Subject Test. Additional exam requirements/recommendations for international students: Required—TOEFL (minimum score 550 paper-based; 213 computer-based; 83 iBT), IELTS (minimum score 7). *Application deadline:* For fall admission, 12/8 priority date for domestic and international students. Application fee: $75. Electronic applications accepted. *Financial support:* Fellowships, research assistantships, teaching assistantships, Federal Work-Study available. Financial award application deadline: 12/31. *Unit head:* Thomas Witelski, Director of Graduate Studies, Fax: 919-660-2801, E-mail: sholder@math.duke.edu. *Application contact:* Cynthia Robertson, Associate Dean for Enrollment Services, 919-684-3913, E-mail: grad-admissions@duke.edu.

Duquesne University, Graduate School of Liberal Arts, Program in Computational Mathematics, Pittsburgh, PA 15282-0001. Offers MA, MS. *Faculty:* 18 full-time (5 women), 19 part-time/adjunct (7 women). *Students:* 9 full-time (1 woman), 5 part-time (2 women); includes 1 minority (Hispanic American), 6 international. Average age 23. 12 applicants, 100% accepted, 6 enrolled. In 2009, 5 master's awarded. *Degree requirements:* For master's, thesis. *Entrance requirements:* For master's, GRE General Test. Additional exam requirements/recommendations for international students: Required—TOEFL. *Application deadline:* For fall admission, 8/1 for domestic students, 5/1 for international students. Applications are processed on a rolling basis. Electronic applications accepted. *Expenses:* Tuition: Part-time $851 per credit. Required fees: $81 per credit. *Financial support:* In 2009–10, 2 teaching assistantships with full tuition reimbursements (averaging $10,000 per year) were awarded; Federal Work-Study, institutionally sponsored loans, scholarships/grants, and unspecified assistantships also available. Financial award application deadline: 5/1. *Unit head:* Dr. Jeff Jackson, Chair, 412-396-6467. *Application contact:* Dr. Donald Simon, Professor, E-mail: compmath@mathcs.duq.edu.

East Carolina University, Graduate School, Thomas Harriot College of Arts and Sciences, Department of Mathematics, Greenville, NC 27858-4353. Offers applied mathematics (MA); mathematics (MA). Part-time and evening/weekend programs available. *Degree requirements:* For master's, comprehensive exam. *Entrance requirements:* For master's, GRE General Test, MAT. Additional exam requirements/recommendations for international students: Required—TOEFL.

Eastern Illinois University, Graduate School, College of Sciences, Department of Mathematics and Computer Science, Charleston, IL 61920-3099. Offers mathematics (MA); mathematics education (MA). *Faculty:* 30 full-time (6 women). In 2009, 9 master's awarded. *Entrance requirements:* For master's, GRE General Test. *Application deadline:* For fall admission, 3/31 priority date for domestic students. Applications are processed on a rolling basis. Application fee: $30. *Expenses:* Tuition, state resident: full-time $9434; part-time $239 per credit hour. Tuition, nonresident: full-time $23,774; part-time $717 per credit hour. Required fees: $802.63. *Financial support:* In 2009–10, research assistantships with tuition reimbursements (averaging $8,100 per year), 8 teaching assistantships with tuition reimbursements (averaging $8,100 per year) were awarded. *Unit head:* Dr. Peter Andrews, Chair, 217-581-6275, Fax: 217-581-6284, E-mail: pgandrews@eiu.edu. *Application contact:* Dr. Keith Wolcott, Coordinator, 217-581-6279, Fax: 217-581-6284, E-mail: kwolcott@eiu.edu.

Eastern Kentucky University, The Graduate School, College of Arts and Sciences, Department of Mathematics and Statistics, Richmond, KY 40475-3102. Offers mathematical sciences (MS). Part-time programs available. *Degree requirements:* For master's, comprehensive exam. *Entrance requirements:* For master's, GRE General Test, minimum GPA of 2.5. *Faculty research:* Graph theory, number theory, ring theory, topology, statistics, Abstract Algebra.

Eastern Michigan University, Graduate School, College of Arts and Sciences, Department of Mathematics, Ypsilanti, MI 48197. Offers applied statistics (MA); computer science (MA); mathematics (MA); mathematics education (MA). Part-time and evening/weekend programs available. Postbaccalaureate distance learning degree programs offered (minimal on-campus study). *Faculty:* 25 full-time (10 women). *Students:* 11 full-time (7 women), 39 part-time (17 women); includes 2 minority (1 African American, 1 Asian American or Pacific Islander), 11 international. Average age 35. 28 applicants, 75% accepted, 14 enrolled. In 2009, 15 master's awarded. *Degree requirements:* For master's, thesis optional. *Entrance requirements:* Additional exam requirements/recommendations for international students: Required—TOEFL. *Application deadline:* Applications are processed on a rolling basis. Application fee: $35. Tuition and fees vary according to course level. *Financial support:* Fellowships, research assistantships with full tuition reimbursements, teaching assistantships with full tuition reimbursements, career-related internships or fieldwork, Federal Work-Study, institutionally sponsored loans, scholarships/grants, tuition waivers (partial), and unspecified assistantships available. Support available to part-time students. Financial award applicants required to submit FAFSA. *Unit head:* Dr. Christopher Gardiner, Interim Department Head, 734-487-1444, Fax: 734-487-2489, E-mail: cgardiner@emich.edu. *Application contact:* Dr. Bingwu Wang, Graduate Coordinator, 734-487-5044, Fax: 734-487-2489, E-mail: bwang@emich.edu.

Eastern New Mexico University, Graduate School, College of Liberal Arts and Sciences, Department of Mathematical Sciences, Portales, NM 88130. Offers MA. Part-time programs available. *Faculty:* 6 full-time (2 women). *Students:* 4 part-time (2 women); includes 2 minority (both Hispanic Americans). Average age 29. 9 applicants, 67% accepted, 1 enrolled. In 2009, 2 master's awarded. *Degree requirements:* For master's, thesis optional, 3 comprehensive exams. *Entrance requirements:* For master's, minimum GPA of 3.0. Additional exam requirements/recommendations for international students: Required—TOEFL (minimum score 550 paper-based; 213 computer-based; 79 iBT), IELTS (minimum score 6). *Application deadline:* For fall admission, 7/20 priority date for domestic students, 6/20 for international students. Applications are processed on a rolling basis. Application fee: $10. Electronic applications accepted. *Expenses:* Tuition, state resident: full-time $2922; part-time $121.75 per credit hour. Tuition, nonresident: full-time $8454; part-time $352.25 per credit hour. Required fees: $1038; $43.25 per credit hour. *Financial support:* In 2009–10, 2 teaching assistantships with partial tuition reimbursements (averaging $8,500 per year) were awarded; research assistantships, career-related internships or fieldwork, tuition waivers (partial), and unspecified assistantships also available. Support available to part-time students. Financial award applicants required to submit FAFSA. *Faculty research:* Applied mathematics, graph theory. *Unit head:* Dr. Kristi

Jarman, Graduate Coordinator, 575-562-2336, E-mail: kristi.jarman@enmu.edu. *Application contact:* Dr. Kristi Jarman, Graduate Coordinator, 575-562-2336, E-mail: kristi.jarman@enmu.edu.

Eastern Washington University, Graduate Studies, College of Science, Health and Engineering, Department of Mathematics, Cheney, WA 99004-2431. Offers mathematics (MS); teaching mathematics (MA). *Accreditation:* NCATE. Part-time programs available. *Degree requirements:* For master's, comprehensive exam, thesis (for some programs). *Entrance requirements:* For master's, GRE General Test, departmental qualifying exam, minimum GPA of 3.0. *Expenses:* Tuition, state resident: full-time $7476; part-time $249 per quarter hour. Tuition, nonresident: full-time $18,030; part-time $601 per quarter hour. Required fees: $3.50 per quarter hour. $142 per quarter.

East Tennessee State University, School of Graduate Studies, College of Arts and Sciences, Department of Mathematics, Johnson City, TN 37614. Offers MS. Part-time and evening/weekend programs available. *Degree requirements:* For master's, comprehensive exam, thesis or alternative. *Entrance requirements:* For master's, GRE General Test. Additional exam requirements/recommendations for international students: Required—TOEFL (minimum score 550 paper-based; 213 computer-based). *Faculty research:* Graph theory and combinatorics, probability and statistics, analysis, numerical and applied math, algebra.

Elizabeth City State University, School of Mathematics, Science and Technology, Program in Mathematics, Elizabeth City, NC 27909-7806. Offers MS. Part-time and evening/weekend programs available. *Degree requirements:* For master's, thesis. *Entrance requirements:* For master's, MAT and/or GRE. Additional exam requirements/recommendations for international students: Required—TOEFL. Electronic applications accepted. *Faculty research:* Oceanic temperature effects, mathematics strategies in elementary schools, multimedia, Antarctic temperature mapping, computer networks, water quality, remote sensing, polar ice, satellite imagery.

Emory University, Graduate School of Arts and Sciences, Department of Mathematics and Computer Science, Atlanta, GA 30322-1100. Offers computer science (MS); mathematics (PhD). Terminal master's awarded for partial completion of doctoral program. *Degree requirements:* For master's, thesis; for doctorate, one foreign language, comprehensive exam, thesis/dissertation. *Entrance requirements:* For master's and doctorate, GRE General Test. Electronic applications accepted.

See Display above.

Emporia State University, School of Graduate Studies, College of Liberal Arts and Sciences, Department of Mathematics, Computer Science and Economics, Emporia, KS 66801-5087. Offers mathematics (MS). Part-time programs available. *Faculty:* 14 full-time (2 women), 2 part-time/adjunct (both women). *Students:* 8 full-time (4 women), 10 part-time (7 women); includes 3 minority (all Asian Americans or Pacific Islanders), 5 international. 10 applicants, 70% accepted, 7 enrolled. In 2009, 4 master's awarded. *Degree requirements:* For master's, comprehensive exam or thesis. *Entrance requirements:* For master's, appropriate undergraduate degree. Additional exam requirements/recommendations for international students: Required—TOEFL (minimum score 520 paper-based; 133 computer-based; 68 iBT). *Application deadline:* For fall admission, 8/15 priority date for domestic students. Applications are processed on a rolling basis. Application fee: $30 ($75 for international students). Electronic applications accepted. *Expenses:* Tuition, state resident: full-time $4154; part-time $173 per credit hour. Tuition, nonresident: full-time $12,864; part-time $536 per credit hour. Required fees: $948; $58 per credit hour. Tuition and fees vary according to campus/location. *Financial support:* In 2009–10, 1 research assistantship (averaging $7,059 per year), 3 teaching assistantships with full tuition reimbursements (averaging $7,809 per year) were awarded; career-related internships or fieldwork, Federal Work-Study, institutionally sponsored loans, health care benefits, and unspecified assistantships also available. Financial award application deadline: 3/15; financial award applicants required to submit FAFSA. *Unit head:* Dr. Larry Scott, Chair, 620-341-5281, Fax: 620-341-6055, E-mail: lscott@emporia.edu. *Application contact:* Dr. H. Joe Yanik, Graduate Coordinator, 620-341-5639, E-mail: hyanik@emporia.edu.

Fairfield University, College of Arts and Sciences, Fairfield, CT 06824-5195. Offers American studies (MA); communication (MA); creative writing (MFA); mathematics (MS). Part-time and evening/weekend programs available. *Degree requirements:* For master's, capstone research course. *Entrance requirements:* For master's, minimum GPA of 3.0, 2 letters of recommendation, resume. Additional exam requirements/recommendations for international students: Required—TOEFL (minimum score 550 paper-based; 213 computer-based; 80 iBT). Electronic applications accepted. *Faculty research:* Non-commutative algebra, partial differential equations, writing (fiction, non-fiction and poetry), communication for social change, comparative media systems, negotiation and management.

Fairleigh Dickinson University, Metropolitan Campus, University College: Arts, Sciences, and Professional Studies, School of Computer Sciences and Engineering, Program in Mathematical Foundation, Teaneck, NJ 07666-1914. Offers MS. *Students:* 31 part-time (27 women). Average age 37. In 2009, 12 master's awarded. *Application deadline:* Applications are processed on a rolling basis. Application fee: $40. *Application contact:* Susan Brooman, University Director of Graduate Admissions, 201-692-2554, Fax: 201-692-2560, E-mail: globaleducation@fdu.edu.

Fayetteville State University, Graduate School, Department of Mathematics and Computer Science, Fayetteville, NC 28301-4298. Offers mathematics (MS). Part-time and evening/weekend programs available. *Faculty:* 6 full-time (1 woman). *Students:* 2 full-time (1 woman), 1 part-time (0 women); all minorities (2 African Americans, 1 Asian American or Pacific Islander). Average age 29. 1 applicant, 100% accepted, 1 enrolled. In 2009, 2 master's awarded. *Degree requirements:* For master's, comprehensive exam, thesis or alternative, internship. *Entrance requirements:* For master's, GRE General Test. *Application deadline:* For fall admission, 4/15 for domestic students; for spring admission, 10/15 for domestic students. Applications are processed on a rolling basis. Application fee: $35. Electronic applications accepted. *Unit head:* Dr. Vinod Arya, Chairperson, 910-672-1294, E-mail: varya@uncfsu.edu. *Application contact:* Roxie Shabazz, Associate Vice-Chancellor for Enrollment Management, 910-672-1784, Fax: 910-672-2209, E-mail: rshabazz@uncfsu.edu.

Florida Atlantic University, Charles E. Schmidt College of Science, Department of Mathematical Sciences, Boca Raton, FL 33431-0991. Offers applied mathematics and statistics (MS); mathematical sciences (MS, MST, PhD). Part-time programs available. *Faculty:* 36 full-time (5 women), 5 part-time/adjunct (1 woman). *Students:* 52 full-time (14 women), 31 part-time (19 women); includes 13 minority (5 African Americans, 5 Asian Americans or Pacific Islanders, 3 Hispanic Americans), 29 international. Average age 32. 62 applicants, 58% accepted, 18 enrolled. In 2009, 23 master's, 4 doctorates awarded. Terminal master's awarded for partial completion of doctoral program. *Degree requirements:* For master's, comprehensive exam (for some programs), thesis (for some programs); for doctorate, comprehensive exam, thesis/dissertation. *Entrance requirements:* For master's and doctorate, GRE General Test, minimum GPA of 3.0. Additional exam requirements/recommendations for international students: Required—TOEFL (minimum score 500 paper-based; 173 computer-based). *Application deadline:* For fall admission, 7/1 priority date for domestic students, 2/15 priority date for international students; for spring admission, 11/1 priority date for domestic students, 7/15 priority date for international students. Applications are processed on a rolling basis. Application fee: $30. Electronic applications accepted. *Expenses:* Tuition, state resident: full-time $7055; part-time $293.94 per credit hour. Tuition, nonresident: full-time $22,096; part-time $920.66 per credit hour. *Financial support:* In 2009–10, fellowships with partial tuition reimbursements (averaging $20,000 per year), teaching assistantships with partial tuition reimbursements (averaging $20,000 per year) were awarded; Federal Work-Study also available. Financial award application deadline: 4/1. *Faculty research:* Cryptography, statistics, algebra, analysis, combinatorics. *Unit head:* Dr. Lee Klingler, Chair, 561-297-0274, Fax: 561-297-2436, E-mail: klingler@fau.edu. *Application contact:* Dr. Heinrich Niederhausen, Graduate Director, 561-297-3237, Fax: 561-297-2436, E-mail: niederha@fau.edu.

Mathematics

Florida International University, College of Arts and Sciences, Department of Mathematics and Statistics, Program in Mathematical Sciences, Miami, FL 33199. Offers MS. Part-time and evening/weekend programs available. *Students:* 11 full-time (4 women), 4 part-time (2 women); includes 9 minority (2 African Americans, 2 Asian Americans or Pacific Islanders, 5 Hispanic Americans), 2 international. Average age 26. 22 applicants, 55% accepted, 12 enrolled. In 2009, 10 master's awarded. *Entrance requirements:* For master's, GRE, Letter of intent; three letters of recommendation; A 3.0 average or higher in upper division mathematics courses. Additional exam requirements/recommendations for international students: Required—TOEFL (minimum score 550 paper-based; 80 iBT). *Application deadline:* For fall admission, 6/1 for domestic students, 3/1 for international students; for spring admission, 10/1 for domestic students, 9/1 for international students. Applications are processed on a rolling basis. Application fee: $30. Electronic applications accepted. *Expenses:* Tuition, state resident: full-time $8008; part-time $4004 per year. Tuition, nonresident: full-time $20,104; part-time $10,052 per year. Required fees: $298; $149 per term. *Financial support:* Institutionally sponsored loans and scholarships/grants available. Financial award application deadline: 3/1; financial award applicants required to submit FAFSA. *Unit head:* Dr. Bao Qin Li, Chair, Mathematics and Statistics Department, 305-348-2743, Fax: 305-348-6158, E-mail: bao.li@fiu.edu. *Application contact:* Dr. Zhenmin Chen, Graduate Director, 305-348-2743, Fax: 305-348-6158, E-mail: gradadm@fiu.edu.

Florida State University, The Graduate School, College of Arts and Sciences, Department of Mathematics, Tallahassee, FL 32306-4510. Offers applied computational mathematics (MS, PhD); biomedical mathematics (MS, PhD); financial mathematics (MS, PhD); pure mathematics (MS, PhD). Part-time programs available. *Faculty:* 57 full-time (14 women). *Students:* 140 full-time (35 women), 9 part-time (2 women); includes 8 minority (2 African Americans, 2 Asian Americans or Pacific Islanders, 4 Hispanic Americans), 84 international. Average age 26. 273 applicants, 38% accepted, 34 enrolled. In 2009, 36 master's, 6 doctorates awarded. Terminal master's awarded for partial completion of doctoral program. *Degree requirements:* For master's, comprehensive exam (for some programs), thesis optional; for doctorate, comprehensive exam (for some programs), thesis/dissertation, candidacy exam. *Entrance requirements:* For master's and doctorate, GRE General Test, minimum upper-division GPA of 3.0, 4-year bachelor's degree. Additional exam requirements/recommendations for international students: Required—TOEFL (minimum score 550 paper-based; 213 computer-based; 80 iBT), or IELTS. *Application deadline:* For fall admission, 1/10 priority date for domestic students, 12/15 priority date for international students; for spring admission, 11/1 for domestic and international students. Applications are processed on a rolling basis. Application fee: $30. Electronic applications accepted. *Expenses:* Tuition, state resident: full-time $7413.36. Tuition, nonresident: full-time $22,567. *Financial support:* In 2009–10, 102 students received support, including 4 fellowships with full tuition reimbursements available (averaging $19,000 per year), 12 research assistantships with full tuition reimbursements available (averaging $20,000 per year), 84 teaching assistantships with full tuition reimbursements available (averaging $17,000 per year); career-related internships or fieldwork, scholarships/grants, and unspecified assistantships also available. Financial award application deadline: 4/1. *Faculty research:* Geometric topology, algebraic geometry, fluid dynamics, financial mathematics, biomedical mathematics. *Unit head:* Dr. Philip L. Bowers, Chairperson, 850-645-3338, Fax: 850-644-4053, E-mail: bowers@math.fsu.edu. *Application contact:* Dr. Bettye Anne Case, Associate Chair for Graduate Studies, 850-644-1586, Fax: 850-644-4053, E-mail: case@math.fsu.edu.

George Mason University, College of Science, Department of Mathematical Sciences, Fairfax, VA 22030. Offers mathematics (MS, PhD). Evening/weekend programs available. *Degree requirements:* For master's, comprehensive exam, thesis optional. *Entrance requirements:* For master's, minimum GPA of 3.0 in last 60 hours of course work. Electronic applications accepted. *Expenses:* Tuition, state resident: full-time $7568; part-time $315.33 per credit hour. Tuition, nonresident: full-time $21,704; part-time $904.33 per credit hour. Required fees: $2184; $91 per credit hour.

Georgetown University, Graduate School of Arts and Sciences, Department of Mathematics, Washington, DC 20057. Offers mathematics and statistics (MS).

The George Washington University, Columbian College of Arts and Sciences, Department of Mathematics, Washington, DC 20052. Offers applied mathematics (MA, MS, PhD); pure mathematics (MA, MS, PhD). Part-time and evening/weekend programs available. *Faculty:* 18 full-time (3 women), 5 part-time/adjunct (1 woman). *Students:* 16 full-time (4 women), 11 part-time (6 women); includes 4 minority (all Asian Americans or Pacific Islanders), 10 international. Average age 27. 62 applicants, 81% accepted, 9 enrolled. In 2009, 2 master's, 2 doctorates awarded. Terminal master's awarded for partial completion of doctoral program. *Degree requirements:* For master's, comprehensive exam; for doctorate, one foreign language, thesis/dissertation, general exam. *Entrance requirements:* For master's and doctorate, GRE General Test, minimum GPA of 3.0, interview. Additional exam requirements/recommendations for international students: Required—TOEFL (minimum score 550 paper-based; 213 computer-based; 80 iBT). *Application deadline:* For fall admission, 1/15 priority date for domestic and international students; for spring admission, 10/1 priority date for domestic students, 9/1 priority date for international students. Applications are processed on a rolling basis. Application fee: $60. Electronic applications accepted. *Financial support:* In 2009–10, 17 students received support; fellowships with full tuition reimbursements available, teaching assistantships with tuition reimbursements available, Federal Work-Study and tuition waivers available. Financial award application deadline: 1/15. *Unit head:* John B. Conway, Chair, 202-994-0553, E-mail: conway@gwu.edu. *Application contact:* John B. Conway, Chair, 202-994-0553, E-mail: conway@gwu.edu.

Georgia Institute of Technology, Graduate Studies and Research, College of Sciences, School of Mathematics, Atlanta, GA 30332-0001. Offers algorithms, combinatorics, and optimization (PhD); applied mathematics (MS); bioinformatics (PhD); mathematics (PhD); quantitative and computational finance (MS); statistics (MS Stat). Terminal master's awarded for partial completion of doctoral program. *Degree requirements:* For master's, thesis or alternative; for doctorate, one foreign language, thesis/dissertation. *Entrance requirements:* For master's, GRE General Test, minimum GPA of 3.0; for doctorate, GRE General Test, GRE Subject Test, minimum GPA of 3.0. Additional exam requirements/recommendations for international students: Required—TOEFL. Electronic applications accepted. *Faculty research:* Dynamical systems, discrete mathematics, probability and statistics, mathematical physics.

Georgia Institute of Technology, Graduate Studies and Research, Multidisciplinary Program in Algorithms, Combinatorics, and Optimization, Atlanta, GA 30332-0001. Offers PhD. *Degree requirements:* For doctorate, thesis/dissertation. *Entrance requirements:* For doctorate, GRE General Test, GRE Subject Test (computer science or mathematics). Additional exam requirements/recommendations for international students: Required—TOEFL. Electronic applications accepted. *Faculty research:* Complexity, graph minors, combinatorial optimization, mathematical programming, probabilistic methods.

Georgian Court University, School of Sciences and Mathematics, Lakewood, NJ 08701-2697. Offers biology (MS); counseling psychology (MA); holistic health (Certificate); holistic health studies (MA); mathematics (MA); professional counselor (Certificate); school psychology (Certificate). Part-time and evening/weekend programs available. *Faculty:* 18 full-time (11 women), 9 part-time/adjunct (6 women). *Students:* 74 full-time (67 women), 79 part-time (67 women); includes 19 minority (8 African Americans, 1 American Indian/Alaska Native, 2 Asian Americans or Pacific Islanders, 8 Hispanic Americans), 2 international. Average age 32. 137 applicants, 50% accepted, 54 enrolled. In 2009, 27 master's, 2 other advanced degrees awarded. *Degree requirements:* For master's, comprehensive exam (for some programs), thesis (for some programs). *Entrance requirements:* For master's, GRE General Test, GRE Subject Test in biology (MS), 3 letters of recommendation. Additional exam requirements/recommendations for international students: Required—TOEFL (minimum score 550 paper-based; 213 computer-based). *Application deadline:* For fall admission, 8/1 priority date for domestic students, 4/1 for international students; for spring admission, 1/1 priority date for domestic students, 7/1 for international students. Applications are processed on a rolling basis. Application fee: $40. Electronic applications accepted. *Expenses:* Tuition: Full-time $12,510; part-time $695 per credit. Required fees: $416 per year. Tuition and fees vary according to campus/location. *Financial support:* Scholarships/grants, health care benefits, and unspecified assistantships available. Financial award application deadline: 4/15; financial award applicants required to submit FAFSA. *Unit head:* Dr. Linda James, Dean, 732-987-2617, Fax: 732-987-2007. *Application contact:* Eugene Soltys, Director of Graduate Admissions, 732-987-2770, Fax: 732-987-2084, E-mail: graduateadmissions@georgian.edu.

Georgia Southern University, Jack N. Averitt College of Graduate Studies, Allen E. Paulson College of Science and Technology, Department of Mathematical Sciences, Statesboro, GA 30460. Offers mathematics (MS). Part-time programs available. *Students:* 23 full-time (8 women), 6 part-time (2 women); includes 7 minority (5 African Americans, 1 Asian American or Pacific Islander, 1 Hispanic American), 11 international. Average age 27. 13 applicants, 85% accepted, 8 enrolled. In 2009, 4 master's awarded. *Degree requirements:* For master's, comprehensive exam, thesis, terminal exam, project. *Entrance requirements:* For master's, GRE, BS in engineering, science, or mathematics; course work in calculus, probability, linear algebra; proficiency in a computer programming language. Additional exam requirements/recommendations for international students: Required—TOEFL (minimum score 550 paper-based; 213 computer-based; 80 iBT). *Application deadline:* For fall admission, 3/1 priority date for domestic and international students; for spring admission, 10/1 priority date for domestic students, 10/1 for international students. Applications are processed on a rolling basis. Application fee: $50. Electronic applications accepted. *Expenses:* Tuition, state resident: full-time $5040; part-time $210 per credit hour. Tuition, nonresident: full-time $20,136; part-time $839 per credit hour. Required fees: $1644. *Financial support:* In 2009–10, 25 students received support, including research assistantships with partial tuition reimbursements available (averaging $7,200 per year), teaching assistantships with partial tuition reimbursements available (averaging $7,200 per year); career-related internships or fieldwork, Federal Work-Study, scholarships/grants, tuition waivers (partial), and unspecified assistantships also available. Support available to part-time students. Financial award application deadline: 4/15; financial award applicants required to submit FAFSA. *Faculty research:* Optimization, approximation theory, computed tomography, matrix analysis, applied statistics. Total annual research expenditures: $2,200. *Unit head:* Dr. Martha Abell, Chair, 912-478-5390, Fax: 912-478-0654, E-mail: xli@georgiasouthern.edu. *Application contact:* Dr. Charles Ziglar, Coordinator for Graduate Student Recruitment, 912-478-5384, Fax: 912-478-0740, E-mail: gradadmissions@georgiasouthern.edu.

Georgia State University, College of Arts and Sciences, Department of Mathematics and Statistics, Atlanta, GA 30302-3083. Offers mathematics (MA, MS); mathematics and statistics (PhD). Part-time and evening/weekend programs available. *Degree requirements:* For master's, comprehensive exam (for some programs), thesis (for some programs), exam; for doctorate, comprehensive exam, thesis/dissertation. *Entrance requirements:* For master's and doctorate, GRE. Additional exam requirements/recommendations for international students: Required TOEFL. Electronic applications accepted. *Faculty research:* Analysis, biostatistics, discrete mathematics, linear algebra, statistics.

Graduate School and University Center of the City University of New York, Graduate Studies, Program in Mathematics, New York, NY 10016-4039. Offers PhD. *Faculty:* 43 full-time (2 women). *Students:* 123 full-time (23 women), 4 part-time (2 women); includes 13 minority (1 African American, 5 Asian Americans or Pacific Islanders, 7 Hispanic Americans), 35 international. Average age 32. 95 applicants, 60% accepted, 21 enrolled. In 2009, 8 doctorates awarded. *Degree requirements:* For doctorate, 2 foreign languages, thesis/dissertation. *Entrance requirements:* For doctorate, GRE General Test. Additional exam requirements/recommendations for international students: Required—TOEFL. *Application deadline:* For fall admission, 2/1 priority date for domestic students; for spring admission, 11/15 for domestic students. Application fee: $125. Electronic applications accepted. *Financial support:* In 2009–10, 83 students received support, including 82 fellowships, 2 research assistantships, 10 teaching assistantships; career-related internships or fieldwork, Federal Work-Study, institutionally sponsored loans, and tuition waivers (full and partial) also available. Financial award application deadline: 2/1; financial award applicants required to submit FAFSA. *Unit head:* Dr. Jozef Dodzuik, Executive Officer, 212-817-8531, Fax: 212-817-1527. *Application contact:* Les Gribben, Director of Admissions, 212-817-7470, Fax: 212-817-1624, E-mail: lgribben@gc.cuny.edu.

Hardin-Simmons University, Graduate School, Holland School of Sciences and Mathematics, Abilene, TX 79698-0001. Offers MS, DPT. Part-time programs available. *Faculty:* 4 full-time (0 women). *Students:* 6 full-time (1 woman), 1 (woman) part-time; includes 1 minority (Hispanic American). Average age 29. 6 applicants, 83% accepted, 5 enrolled. In 2009, 2 master's awarded. *Degree requirements:* For master's, comprehensive exam, thesis or alternative, internship; for doctorate, comprehensive exam, thesis/dissertation or alternative. *Entrance requirements:* For master's, minimum undergraduate GPA of 3.0 in major, 2.7 overall; 2 semesters of course work each in biology, chemistry and geology; interview; writing sample; occupational experience; for doctorate, letters of recommendation, interview, writing sample. Additional exam requirements/recommendations for international students: Required—TOEFL (minimum score 550 paper-based; 213 computer-based; 75 iBT). *Application deadline:* For fall admission, 8/15 priority date for domestic students, 4/1 for international students; for spring admission, 1/5 priority date for domestic students, 9/1 for international students. Applications are processed on a rolling basis. Application fee: $50. *Expenses:* Tuition: Full-time $11,430; part-time $635 per credit hour. Required fees: $650; $110 per semester. Tuition and fees vary according to degree level. *Financial support:* Fellowships, career-related internships or fieldwork and scholarships/grants available. Support available to part-time students. Financial award application deadline: 6/30; financial award applicants required to submit FAFSA. *Unit head:* Dr. Christopher McNair, Dean, 325-670-1401, Fax: 325-670-1385, E-mail: cmcnair@hsutx.edu. *Application contact:* Dr. Gary Stanlake, Dean of Graduate Studies, 325-670-1298, Fax: 325-670-1564, E-mail: gradoff@hsutx.edu.

Harvard University, Graduate School of Arts and Sciences, Department of Mathematics, Cambridge, MA 02138. Offers PhD. *Degree requirements:* For doctorate, 2 foreign languages, thesis/dissertation, qualifying exam. *Entrance requirements:* For doctorate, GRE General Test, GRE Subject Test. Additional exam requirements/recommendations for international students: Required—TOEFL. *Expenses:* Tuition: Full-time $33,696. Required fees: $1126. Full-time tuition and fees vary according to program.

Hofstra University, College of Liberal Arts and Sciences, Department of Mathematics, Hempstead, NY 11549. Offers applied mathematics (MS); mathematics (MA). Part-time and evening/weekend programs available. *Faculty:* 3 full-time (2 women). *Students:* 7 full-time (3 women), 6 part-time (3 women); includes 1 minority (Asian American or Pacific Islander), 1 international. Average age 28. 11 applicants, 100% accepted, 6 enrolled. In 2009, 4 master's awarded. *Degree requirements:* For master's, thesis or alternative. *Entrance requirements:* For master's, bachelor's degree with strong background in math. Additional exam requirements/recommendations for international students: Required—TOEFL (minimum score 550 paper-based; 213 computer-based; 80 iBT). *Application deadline:* Applications are processed on a rolling basis. Application fee: $60. Electronic applications accepted. *Expenses:* Tuition: Full-time $16,200; part-time $900 per credit hour. Required fees: $970; $145 per term. Tuition and fees vary according to program. *Financial support:* In 2009–10, 9 students received support; fellowships with full and partial tuition reimbursements available, research assistantships with full and partial tuition reimbursements available, Federal Work-Study, institutionally sponsored loans, scholarships/grants, and tuition waivers (full and partial) available. Support available to part-time students. Financial award applicants required to submit FAFSA. *Faculty research:* Number theory; topology; discrete geometry, combinatorics; functional analysis, real analysis; set theory, logic. *Unit head:* Dr. Sylvia Silberger, Chairperson, 516-463-5580, Fax: 516-463-6596, E-mail: matsbs@hofstra.edu. *Application contact:* Carol Drummer, Dean of Graduate Admissions, 516-463-4876, Fax: 516-463-4664, E-mail: gradstudent@hofstra.edu.

Howard University, Graduate School, Department of Mathematics, Washington, DC 20059-0002. Offers applied mathematics (MS, PhD); mathematics (MS, PhD). Part-time programs available. Terminal master's awarded for partial completion of doctoral program. *Degree requirements:* For master's, comprehensive exam, thesis or alternative, qualifying exam; for doctorate, 2 foreign languages, comprehensive exam, thesis/dissertation, qualifying exams. *Entrance requirements:* For master's, GRE General Test, minimum GPA of 3.0; for doctorate, GRE General Test. Additional exam requirements/recommendations for international students: Required—TOEFL. Electronic applications accepted.

Hunter College of the City University of New York, Graduate School, School of Arts and Sciences, Department of Mathematics and Statistics, New York, NY 10021-5085. Offers applied mathematics (MA); mathematics for secondary education (MA); pure mathematics (MA). Part-time and evening/weekend programs available. *Faculty:* 7 full-time (1 woman). *Students:* 19 full-time (7 women), 56 part-time (26 women); includes 24 minority (3 African Americans, 18 Asian Americans or Pacific Islanders, 3 Hispanic Americans). Average age 31. 43 applicants, 77% accepted, 21 enrolled. In 2009, 35 master's awarded. *Degree requirements:* For master's, one foreign language, comprehensive exam, thesis (for some programs). *Entrance requirements:* For master's, GRE General Test, 24 credits in mathematics. Additional exam requirements/recommendations for international students: Required—TOEFL. *Application deadline:* For fall admission, 4/1 for domestic students, 2/1 for international students; for spring admission, 11/1 for domestic students, 9/1 for international students. Application fee: $125. *Expenses:* Tuition, state resident: full-time $7360; part-time $310 per credit. Required fees: $250 per semester. *Financial support:* Federal Work-Study, institutionally sponsored loans, scholarships/grants, and tuition waivers (partial) available. Support available to part-time students. *Faculty research:* Data analysis, dynamical systems, computer graphics, topology, statistical decision theory. *Unit head:* Ada Peluso, Chairperson, 212-772-5300, Fax: 212-772-4858, E-mail: peluso@math.hunter.cuny.edu. *Application contact:* William Zlata, Director for Graduate Admissions, 212-772-4482, Fax: 212-650-3336, E-mail: admissions@hunter.cuny.edu.

Idaho State University, Office of Graduate Studies, College of Arts and Sciences, Department of Mathematics, Pocatello, ID 83209-8085. Offers mathematics (MS, DA); mathematics for secondary teachers (MA). Part-time programs available. *Faculty:* 18 full-time (3 women), 1 part-time/adjunct (0 women). *Students:* 13 full-time (3 women), 8 part-time (3 women); includes 2 minority (1 American Indian/Alaska Native, 1 Hispanic American), 3 international. Average age 35. *Degree requirements:* For master's, comprehensive exam, thesis (for some programs), oral and written exams; for doctorate, comprehensive exam, thesis/dissertation, teaching internships. *Entrance requirements:* For master's, GRE General Test, GRE Subject Test, course work in modern algebra, differential equations, advanced calculus, introductory analysis; for doctorate, GRE General Test, GRE Subject Test, minimum graduate GPA of 3.5, MS in mathematics, teaching experience, 3 letters of recommendation. Additional exam requirements/recommendations for international students: Required—TOEFL (minimum score 550 paper-based; 213 computer-based; 80 iBT). *Application deadline:* For fall admission, 7/1 for domestic students, 6/1 for international students; for spring admission, 12/1 for domestic students, 11/1 for international students. Applications are processed on a rolling basis. Application fee: $55. Electronic applications accepted. *Expenses:* Tuition, state resident: full-time $3318; part-time $297 per credit hour. Tuition, nonresident: full-time $13,120; part-time $437 per credit hour. Required fees: $2530. Tuition and fees vary according to program. *Financial support:* In 2009–10, 13 teaching assistantships with full and partial tuition reimbursements (averaging $10,841 per year) were awarded; fellowships with full and partial tuition reimbursements, career-related internships or fieldwork, Federal Work-Study, institutionally sponsored loans, scholarships/grants, health care benefits, tuition waivers (full and partial), and unspecified assistantships also available. Support available to part-time students. Financial award application deadline: 1/1; financial award applicants required to submit FAFSA. *Faculty research:* Algebra, analysis geometry, statistics, applied mathematics. *Unit head:* Dr. Robert Fisher, Chairman, 208-282-3604, Fax: 208-282-2636, E-mail: fishrobe@isu.edu. *Application contact:* Tami Carson, Graduate School Technical Records Specialist, 208-282-2150, Fax: 208-282-4847, E-mail: carstami@isu.edu.

Illinois State University, Graduate School, College of Arts and Sciences, Department of Mathematics, Program in Mathematics, Normal, IL 61790-2200. Offers MA, MS. *Degree requirements:* For master's, thesis or alternative. *Entrance requirements:* For master's, GRE General Test, minimum GPA of 2.8 in last 60 hours of course work.

Indiana State University, School of Graduate Studies, College of Arts and Sciences, Department of Mathematics and Computer Science, Terre Haute, IN 47809. Offers math teaching (MA, MS); mathematics and computer science (MA); mathematics and computer sciences (MS). Part-time programs available. *Degree requirements:* For master's, thesis or alternative. *Entrance requirements:* For master's, 24 semester hours of course work in undergraduate mathematics. Electronic applications accepted.

Indiana University Bloomington, University Graduate School, College of Arts and Sciences, Department of Mathematics, Bloomington, IN 47405-7000. Offers applied mathematics–numerical analysis (MA, PhD); mathematics education (MAT); probability-statistics (MA, PhD); pure mathematics (MA). *Faculty:* 46 full-time (4 women). *Students:* 131 full-time (26 women); includes 10 minority (1 African American, 1 American Indian/Alaska Native, 7 Asian Americans or Pacific Islanders, 1 Hispanic American), 67 international. Average age 28. 211 applicants, 29% accepted, 26 enrolled. In 2009, 13 master's, 18 doctorates awarded. Terminal master's awarded for partial completion of doctoral program. *Degree requirements:* For doctorate, one foreign language, thesis/dissertation. *Entrance requirements:* For master's and doctorate, GRE General Test, GRE Subject Test. Additional exam requirements/recommendations for international students: Required—TOEFL. *Application deadline:* For fall admission, 1/15 priority date for domestic and international students. Applications are processed on a rolling basis. Application fee: $55 ($65 for international students). Electronic applications accepted. *Financial support:* In 2009–10, 9 fellowships with full tuition reimbursements (averaging $20,000 per year), 5 research assistantships with full tuition reimbursements (averaging $16,440 per year), 106 teaching assistantships with full tuition reimbursements (averaging $15,940 per year) were awarded; scholarships/grants, health care benefits, and unspecified assistantships also available. Financial award application deadline: 1/15. *Faculty research:* Topology, geometry, algebra. *Unit head:* James F. Davis, Chair, 812-855-2200. *Application contact:* Kate Bowman, Graduate Secretary, 812-855-2645, Fax: 812-855-0046, E-mail: gradmath@indiana.edu.

Indiana University of Pennsylvania, School of Graduate Studies and Research, College of Natural Sciences and Mathematics, Department of Mathematics, Indiana, PA 15705-1087. Offers applied mathematics (MS); elementary and middle school mathematics education (M Ed); mathematics education (M Ed). Part-time programs available. *Faculty:* 10 full-time (3 women). *Students:* 20 full-time (5 women), 23 part-time (16 women); includes 4 minority (2 African Americans, 2 Asian Americans or Pacific Islanders), 7 international. Average age 30. 44 applicants, 55% accepted, 14 enrolled. In 2009, 16 master's awarded. *Degree requirements:* For master's, thesis optional. *Entrance requirements:* For master's, 2 letters of recommendation. Additional exam requirements/recommendations for international students: Required—TOEFL. *Application deadline:* For fall admission, 7/1 priority date for domestic students; for spring admission, 11/1 for domestic students. Applications are processed on a rolling basis. Application fee: $40. *Expenses:* Tuition, state resident: full-time $6666; part-time $370 per credit hour. Tuition, nonresident: full-time $10,666; part-time $593 per credit hour. Required fees: $813 per semester. *Financial support:* In 2009–10, 10 research assistantships with full and partial tuition reimbursements (averaging $4,042 per year) were awarded; career-related internships or fieldwork and Federal Work-Study also available. Support available to part-time students. Financial award application deadline: 3/15; financial award applicants required to submit FAFSA. *Unit head:* Dr. Gary S. Stoudt, Chairperson, 724-357-2608, E-mail: gsstoudt@iup.edu. *Application contact:* Dr. Jacqueline Gorman, Dean's Associate, 724-357-2609, E-mail: jgorman@iup.edu.

Indiana University–Purdue University Fort Wayne, College of Arts and Sciences, Department of Mathematical Sciences, Fort Wayne, IN 46805-1499. Offers applied mathematics (MS); applied statistics (Certificate); mathematics (MS); operations research (MS); teaching (MAT). Part-time and evening/weekend programs available. *Faculty:* 17 full-time (4 women), 2 part-time/adjunct (1 woman). *Students:* 2 full-time (0 women), 15 part-time (6 women); includes 2 minority (1 American Indian/Alaska Native, 1 Asian American or Pacific Islander), 1 international. Average age 35. 5 applicants, 60% accepted, 3 enrolled. In 2009, 2 master's, 2 other advanced degrees awarded. *Entrance requirements:* For master's, minimum GPA of 3.0, major or minor in mathematics, three letters of recommendation. Additional exam requirements/recommendations for international students: Required—TOEFL (minimum score 550 paper-based; 213 computer-based; 77 iBT); Recommended—TWE. *Application deadline:* For fall admission, 8/1 priority date for domestic students, 7/1 priority date for international students; for spring admission, 12/1 for domestic students, 10/1 for international students. Applications are processed on a rolling basis. Application fee: $55 ($60 for international students). Electronic applications accepted. *Expenses:* Tuition, state resident: full-time $4595; part-time $255 per credit. Tuition, nonresident: full-time $10,963; part-time $609 per credit. Required fees: $528; $29.35 per credit. Tuition and fees vary according to course load. *Financial support:* In 2009–10, 1 research assistantship with partial tuition reimbursement (averaging $12,740 per year), 6 teaching assistantships with partial tuition reimbursements (averaging $12,740 per year) were awarded; scholarships/grants and unspecified assistantships also available. Support available to part-time students. Financial award application deadline: 3/1; financial award applicants required to submit FAFSA. *Faculty research:* Target value, toroidal queen's graph, holomorphic maps. *Unit head:* Dr. David A. Legg, Chair, 260-481-6222, Fax: 260-481-0155, E-mail: legg@ipfw.edu. *Application contact:* Dr. W. Douglas Weakley, Director of Graduate Studies, 260-481-6233, Fax: 260-481-0155, E-mail: weakley@ipfw.edu.

Indiana University–Purdue University Indianapolis, School of Science, Department of Mathematical Sciences, Doctoral Program in Mathematics, Indianapolis, IN 46202-2896. Offers applied mathematics (PhD); mathematics (PhD). Application fee: $50 ($60 for international students). *Unit head:* Slawomir Klimek, Director of Graduate Programs, 317-274-6918, E-mail: grad-program@math.iupui.edu. *Application contact:* Slawomir Klimek, Director of Graduate Programs, 317-274-6918, E-mail: grad-program@math.iupui.edu.

Indiana University–Purdue University Indianapolis, School of Science, Department of Mathematical Sciences, Master's Program in Mathematics, Indianapolis, IN 46202-2896. Offers applied mathematics (MS); applied statistics (MS); mathematics (MS). Application fee: $50 ($60 for international students). *Unit head:* Slawomir Klimek, Director of Graduate Programs, 317-274-6918, E-mail: grad-program@math.iupui.edu. *Application contact:* Slawomir Klimek, Director of Graduate Programs, 317-274-6918, E-mail: grad-program@math.iupui.edu.

Instituto Tecnologico de Santo Domingo, Graduate School, Santo Domingo, Dominican Republic. Offers applied linguistics (MA); construction administration (M Mgmt); corporate finance (M Mgmt); education (M Ed); engineering (M Eng), including data telecommunications, industrial engineering, logistics and supply chain, maintenance engineering, sanitary and environmental engineering, structural engineering; environmental science (M En S), including environmental education, environmental management, marine and coastal ecosystems, natural resources management; family therapy (MA); food science and technology (MS); human development (MA); human resources administration (M Mgmt); international business (M Mgmt); labor risks (M Mgmt); management (M Mgmt); marketing (M Mgmt); mathematics (MS); organizational development (M Mgmt); planning and taxation (M Mgmt); psychology (MA); social science (M Ed); upper management (M Mgmt). *Entrance requirements:* For master's, birth certificate, minimum GPA of 2.0.

Iowa State University of Science and Technology, Graduate College, College of Liberal Arts and Sciences, Department of Mathematics, Ames, IA 50011. Offers applied mathematics (MS, PhD); mathematics (MS, PhD); school mathematics (MSM). *Faculty:* 44 full-time (5 women), 2 part-time/adjunct (1 woman). *Students:* 76 full-time (18 women), 10 part-time (2 women); includes 4 minority (1 African American, 2 Asian Americans or Pacific Islanders, 1 Hispanic American), 38 international. 133 applicants, 25% accepted, 24 enrolled. In 2009, 12 master's, 10 doctorates awarded. *Degree requirements:* For master's, thesis or alternative; for doctorate, thesis/dissertation. *Entrance requirements:* For master's and doctorate, GRE General Test. Additional exam requirements/recommendations for international students: Required—TOEFL (minimum score 550 paper-based; 79 iBT) or IELTS (minimum score 6.5). *Application deadline:* For fall admission, 2/1 priority date for domestic and international students; for spring admission, 10/1 priority date for domestic and international students. Application fee: $40 ($90 for international students). Electronic applications accepted. *Expenses:* Tuition, state resident: full-time $6716. Tuition, nonresident: full-time $8908. Tuition and fees vary according to course level, course load, program and student level. *Financial support:* In 2009–10, 15 research assistantships with full and partial tuition reimbursements (averaging $13,500 per year), 66 teaching assistantships with full and partial tuition reimbursements (averaging $16,400 per year) were awarded; fellowships, scholarships/grants, health care benefits, and unspecified assistantships also available. *Unit head:* Dr. Wolfgang Kliemann, Chair, 515-294-1752, Fax: 515-294-5454, E-mail: gradmath@iastate.edu. *Application contact:* Dr. Paul Sacks, Director of Graduate Education, 515-294-0393, E-mail: gradmath@iastate.edu.

Jackson State University, Graduate School, School of Science and Technology, Department of Mathematics, Jackson, MS 39217. Offers mathematics (MS); mathematics education (MST). Part-time and evening/weekend programs available. *Degree requirements:* For master's, comprehensive exam, thesis (for some programs). *Entrance requirements:* For master's, GRE General Test. Additional exam requirements/recommendations for international students: Required—TOEFL.

Jacksonville State University, College of Graduate Studies and Continuing Education, College of Arts and Sciences, Department of Mathematics, Jacksonville, AL 36265-1602. Offers MS. Part-time and evening/weekend programs available. *Degree requirements:* For master's, comprehensive exam, thesis (for some programs). *Entrance requirements:* For master's, GRE General Test or MAT. Electronic applications accepted.

James Madison University, The Graduate School, College of Science and Mathematics, Department of Mathematics and Statistics, Harrisonburg, VA 22807. Offers M Ed. Part-time programs available. *Students:* 7 part-time (5 women). Average age 27. In 2009, 3 master's awarded. *Degree requirements:* For master's, comprehensive exam. *Entrance requirements:* For master's, undergraduate major in mathematics. *Application deadline:* For fall admission, 5/1 priority date for domestic students; for spring admission, 9/1 priority date for domestic students. Application fee: $55. *Expenses:* Tuition, area resident: Part-time $305 per credit hour. Tuition, state resident: part-time $305 per credit hour. Tuition, nonresident: part-time $890 per credit hour. *Financial support:* Application deadline: 3/1; *Unit head:* Dr. David C. Carothers, Academic Unit Head, 540-568-6184. *Application contact:* Lynette M. Bible, Director of Graduate Admissions, 540-568-6395, Fax: 540-568-7860, E-mail: biblelm@jmu.edu.

John Carroll University, Graduate School, Department of Mathematics, University Heights, OH 44118-4581. Offers MA, MS. Part-time and evening/weekend programs available. *Degree*

Mathematics

John Carroll University (continued)

requirements: For master's, comprehensive exam, thesis (for some programs), research essay. *Entrance requirements:* For master's, minimum GPA of 2.5, teaching certificate (MA). Electronic applications accepted. *Faculty research:* Algebraic topology, algebra, differential geometry, combinatorics, Lie groups.

The Johns Hopkins University, Zanvyl Krieger School of Arts and Sciences, Department of Mathematics, Baltimore, MD 21218-2699. Offers PhD. *Faculty:* 25 full-time (5 women), 11 part-time/adjunct (3 women). *Students:* 30 full-time (8 women); includes 2 minority (1 African American, 1 Asian American or Pacific Islander), 15 international. Average age 26. 103 applicants, 11% accepted, 11 enrolled. In 2009, 11 doctorates awarded. *Degree requirements:* For doctorate, one foreign language, thesis/dissertation, 3 qualifying exams. *Entrance requirements:* For doctorate, GRE General Test, GRE Subject Test. Additional exam requirements/recommendations for international students: Required—TOEFL (minimum score 600 paper-based; 250 computer-based; 100 iBT), IELTS. *Application deadline:* For fall admission, 1/15 for domestic and international students. Application fee: $75. Electronic applications accepted. *Financial support:* In 2009–10, 32 teaching assistantships with full tuition reimbursements were awarded; fellowships with full tuition reimbursements, research assistantships, Federal Work-Study and institutionally sponsored loans also available. Financial award application deadline: 4/15; financial award applicants required to submit FAFSA. *Faculty research:* Algebraic geometry, number theory, algebraic topology, differential geometry, partial differential equations. Total annual research expenditures: $907,848. *Unit head:* Dr. Richard Wentworth, Chair, 410-516-4518, Fax: 410-516-5549, E-mail: cmese@math.jhu.edu. *Application contact:* Sabrina Raymond, Graduate Program Coordinator, 410-516-4178, Fax: 410-516-5549, E-mail: sraymond@jhu.edu.

Kansas State University, Graduate School, College of Arts and Sciences, Department of Mathematics, Manhattan, KS 66506. Offers MS, PhD. Part-time programs available. *Faculty:* 31 full-time (4 women), 1 part-time/adjunct (0 women). *Students:* 56 applicants, 14% accepted. In 2009, 5 master's, 1 doctorate awarded. Terminal master's awarded for partial completion of doctoral program. *Degree requirements:* For master's, thesis or alternative; for doctorate, one foreign language, thesis/dissertation. *Entrance requirements:* For master's, GRE, bachelor's degree in mathematics; for doctorate, master's degree in mathematics. Additional exam requirements/recommendations for international students: Required—TOEFL (minimum score 600 paper-based; 250 computer-based). *Application deadline:* For fall admission, 2/1 priority date for domestic and international students; for spring admission, 8/1 priority date for domestic and international students. Applications are processed on a rolling basis. Application fee: $40 ($55 for international students). Electronic applications accepted. *Financial support:* In 2009–10, 38 teaching assistantships with full tuition reimbursements (averaging $14,389 per year) were awarded; research assistantships, Federal Work-Study, institutionally sponsored loans, and scholarships/grants also available. Support available to part-time students. Financial award application deadline: 3/1; financial award applicants required to submit FAFSA. *Faculty research:* Low-dimensional topology, geometry, complex and harmonic analysis, group and representation theory, noncommunicative spaces. Total annual research expenditures: $190,983. *Unit head:* Louis Pigno, Head, 785-532-0559, Fax: 785-532-0546, E-mail: lpigno@ksu.edu. *Application contact:* David Yetter, Director, 785-532-0590, Fax: 785-532-0546, E-mail: dyetter@math.ksu.edu.

Kean University, College of Natural, Applied and Health Sciences, Program in Computing, Statistics and Mathematics, Union, NJ 07083. Offers MS. Part-time and evening/weekend programs available. *Faculty:* 13 full-time (4 women). *Students:* 2 full-time (1 woman), 5 part-time (0 women); includes 5 minority (2 African Americans, 2 Asian Americans or Pacific Islanders, 1 Hispanic American), 1 international. Average age 30. 2 applicants, 50% accepted, 1 enrolled. In 2009, 1 master's awarded. *Degree requirements:* For master's, thesis or alternative, research component. *Entrance requirements:* For master's, GRE General Test, minimum GPA of 3.0, 2 letters of recommendation, interview, 24-27 credits in prerequisites, official transcripts from all institutions attended. *Application deadline:* For fall admission, 5/1 for domestic students; for spring admission, 11/1 for domestic students. Application fee: $60 ($150 for international students). Electronic applications accepted. *Expenses:* Tuition, state resident: full-time $10,440; part-time $435 per credit. Tuition, nonresident: full-time $14,160; part-time $590 per credit. Required fees: $2642; $110 per credit. Part-time tuition and fees vary according to course load and degree level. *Financial support:* In 2009–10, 2 research assistantships with full tuition reimbursements (averaging $3,263 per year) were awarded; unspecified assistantships also available. *Unit head:* Dr. Wolde Woubneh, Program Coordinator, 908-737-3700, E-mail: wwoubneh@kean.edu. *Application contact:* Reenat Hasan, Pre-Admissions Coordinator, 908-737-5923, Fax: 908-737-5965, E-mail: rhasan@exchange.kean.edu.

Kent State University, College of Arts and Sciences, Department of Mathematical Sciences, Kent, OH 44242-0001. Offers applied mathematics (MA, MS, PhD); pure mathematics (MA, MS, PhD). Part-time programs available. *Degree requirements:* For master's, thesis optional; for doctorate, one foreign language, thesis/dissertation. Electronic applications accepted. *Faculty research:* Approximation theory, measure theory, ring theory, functional analysis, complex analysis.

Kent State University, Graduate School of Education, Health, and Human Services, School of Teaching, Learning and Curriculum Studies, Program in Math Specialization, Kent, OH 44242-0001. Offers M Ed, MA. Part-time programs available. *Faculty:* 4 full-time (3 women). *Students:* 5 part-time (4 women). 2 applicants, 0% accepted. In 2009, 3 master's awarded. *Entrance requirements:* Additional exam requirements/recommendations for international students: Required—TOEFL. *Application deadline:* Applications are processed on a rolling basis. Application fee: $30 ($60 for international students). Electronic applications accepted. *Financial support:* In 2009–10, research assistantships (averaging $9,000 per year). *Unit head:* Dr. Trish Koontz, Coordinator, 330-672-0640, E-mail: tkoontz@kent.edu. *Application contact:* Nancy Miller, Academic Program Coordinator, Office of Graduate Student Services, 330-672-2576, Fax: 330-672-9162, E-mail: ogs@kent.edu.

Lakehead University, Graduate Studies, School of Mathematical Sciences, Thunder Bay, ON P7B 5E1, Canada. Offers computer science (M Sc); mathematical science (MA). Part-time and evening/weekend programs available. *Degree requirements:* For master's, thesis optional. *Entrance requirements:* For master's, minimum B average, honours degree in mathematics or computer science. Additional exam requirements/recommendations for international students: Required—TOEFL. *Faculty research:* Numerical analysis, classical analysis, theoretical computer science, abstract harmonic analysis, functional analysis.

Lamar University, College of Graduate Studies, College of Arts and Sciences, Department of Mathematics, Beaumont, TX 77710. Offers MS. *Faculty:* 7 full-time (1 woman). *Students:* 5 full-time (3 women), 5 part-time (1 woman); includes 1 minority (African American), 4 international. Average age 26. 10 applicants, 40% accepted, 3 enrolled. In 2009, 1 master's awarded. *Degree requirements:* For master's, comprehensive exam (for some programs), thesis optional. *Entrance requirements:* For master's, GRE General Test, minimum GPA of 2.5 in last 60 hours of undergraduate course work. Additional exam requirements/recommendations for international students: Required—TOEFL. *Application deadline:* For fall admission, 5/15 priority date for domestic students; for spring admission, 10/1 priority date for domestic students. Applications are processed on a rolling basis. Application fee: $25 ($50 for international students). *Financial support:* In 2009–10, 4 teaching assistantships (averaging $12,000 per year) were awarded; fellowships, research assistantships also available. Financial award application deadline: 4/1. *Faculty research:* Complex analysis, differential equations, algebra, topology statistics. Total annual research expenditures: $43,585. *Unit head:* Charles F. Coppin, Chair, 409-880-8792, Fax: 409-880-8794, E-mail: chair@math.lamar.edu. *Application contact:* Dr. Paul Chiou, Professor, 409-880-8800, Fax: 409-880-8794, E-mail: chiou@math.lamar.edu.

Lehigh University, College of Arts and Sciences, Department of Mathematics, Bethlehem, PA 18015. Offers applied mathematics (MS, PhD); mathematics (MS, PhD); statistics (MS). Part-time programs available. *Faculty:* 21 full-time (1 woman), 1 part-time/adjunct (0 women). *Students:* 35 full-time (18 women), 5 part-time (1 woman); includes 3 minority (1 African American, 1 Asian American or Pacific Islander, 1 Hispanic American), 15 international. Average age 28. 85 applicants, 42% accepted, 10 enrolled. In 2009, 12 master's, 3 doctorates awarded. Terminal master's awarded for partial completion of doctoral program. *Degree requirements:* For master's, comprehensive exam, thesis optional; for doctorate, comprehensive exam, thesis/dissertation, qualifying exams, general exam. *Entrance requirements:* For master's and doctorate, minimum undergraduate GPA of 2.75, 3.0 for last two semesters; adequate background in math. Additional exam requirements/recommendations for international students: Required—TOEFL (minimum score 550 paper-based; 213 computer-based; 85 iBT). *Application deadline:* For fall admission, 1/15 priority date for domestic and international students; for spring admission, 12/1 priority date for domestic and international students. Applications are processed on a rolling basis. Application fee: $75. Electronic applications accepted. *Financial support:* In 2009–10, 28 students received support, including 2 fellowships with full tuition reimbursements available (averaging $22,000 per year), 23 teaching assistantships with full tuition reimbursements available (averaging $16,900 per year); research assistantships with full tuition reimbursements available, scholarships/grants and tuition waivers (partial) also available. Financial award application deadline: 1/15. *Faculty research:* Probability and statistics, geometry and topology, number theory, algebra, differential equations. Total annual research expenditures: $196,010. *Unit head:* Dr. Wei-Min Huang, Chairman, 610-758-3730, Fax: 610-758-3767, E-mail: wh02@lehigh.edu. *Application contact:* Dr. Terry Napier, Graduate Coordinator, 610-758-3755, E-mail: mathgrad@lehigh.edu.

Lehman College of the City University of New York, Division of Natural and Social Sciences, Department of Mathematics and Computer Science, Program in Mathematics, Bronx, NY 10468-1589. Offers MA. Part-time and evening/weekend programs available. *Degree requirements:* For master's, one foreign language, thesis or alternative.

Long Island University, C.W. Post Campus, College of Liberal Arts and Sciences, Department of Mathematics, Brookville, NY 11548-1300. Offers applied mathematics (MS); mathematics education (MS); mathematics for secondary school teachers (MS). Part-time and evening/weekend programs available. *Degree requirements:* For master's, thesis or alternative, oral presentation. *Entrance requirements:* Additional exam requirements/recommendations for international students: Required—TOEFL. Electronic applications accepted. *Faculty research:* Differential geometry, topological groups, general topology, number theory, analysis and statistics, numerical analysis.

Louisiana State University and Agricultural and Mechanical College, Graduate School, College of Basic Sciences, Department of Mathematics, Baton Rouge, LA 70803. Offers MS, PhD. *Faculty:* 58 full-time (4 women). *Students:* 97 full-time (27 women), 4 part-time (1 woman); includes 5 minority (2 African Americans, 1 Asian American or Pacific Islander, 2 Hispanic Americans), 43 international. Average age 27. 128 applicants, 65% accepted, 22 enrolled. In 2009, 4 master's, 15 doctorates awarded. Terminal master's awarded for partial completion of doctoral program. *Degree requirements:* For doctorate, 2 foreign languages, thesis/dissertation. *Entrance requirements:* For master's and doctorate, GRE General Test, minimum GPA of 3.0. Additional exam requirements/recommendations for international students: Required—TOEFL (minimum score 550 paper-based; 213 computer-based; 79 iBT) or IELTS (minimum score 6.5). *Application deadline:* For fall admission, 1/25 priority date for domestic students, 5/15 for international students; for spring admission, 10/15 for international students. Applications are processed on a rolling basis. Application fee: $50 ($70 for international students). Electronic applications accepted. *Financial support:* In 2009–10, 97 students received support, including 24 fellowships with full and partial tuition reimbursements available (averaging $28,305 per year), 8 research assistantships with full and partial tuition reimbursements available (averaging $22,142 per year), 62 teaching assistantships with full and partial tuition reimbursements available (averaging $18,760 per year); Federal Work-Study, institutionally sponsored loans, scholarships/grants, health care benefits, tuition waivers (full), and unspecified assistantships also available. Financial award application deadline: 3/1; financial award applicants required to submit FAFSA. *Faculty research:* Algebra, graph theory and combinatorics, algebraic topology, analysis and probability, topological algebra. Total annual research expenditures: $1.5 million. *Unit head:* Dr. Lawrence Smolinksy, Chair, 225-578-1570, Fax: 225-578-4276, E-mail: mmsmol@lsu.edu. *Application contact:* Dr. Leonard F. Richardson, Director of Graduate Studies and Assistant Chairman, 225-578-1568, Fax: 225-578-4276, E-mail: rich@math.lsu.edu.

Louisiana Tech University, Graduate School, College of Engineering and Science, Department of Mathematics and Statistics, Ruston, LA 71272. Offers MS. Part-time programs available. *Degree requirements:* For master's, thesis or alternative. *Entrance requirements:* For master's, GRE General Test, minimum GPA of 3.0 in last 60 hours. Additional exam requirements/recommendations for international students: Required—TOEFL.

Loyola University Chicago, Graduate School, Department of Mathematical Sciences and Statistics, Chicago, IL 60660. Offers applied statistics (MS); mathematics and statistics (MS), including pure mathematics. Part-time programs available. *Faculty:* 19 full-time (4 women). *Students:* 24 full-time (16 women), 8 part-time (3 women); includes 7 minority (3 African Americans, 4 Asian Americans or Pacific Islanders), 8 international. Average age 28. 49 applicants, 63% accepted, 16 enrolled. In 2009, 11 master's awarded. *Entrance requirements:* For master's, GRE General Test. Additional exam requirements/recommendations for international students: Required—TOEFL. *Application deadline:* For fall admission, 8/1 for domestic students; for spring admission, 12/1 for domestic students. Applications are processed on a rolling basis. Application fee: $0. Electronic applications accepted. *Expenses:* Tuition: Full-time $14,220; part-time $790 per credit hour. Required fees: $60 per semester hour. Tuition and fees vary according to program. *Financial support:* In 2009–10, 13 students received support, including 6 teaching assistantships with tuition reimbursements available (averaging $10,000 per year); career-related internships or fieldwork, Federal Work-Study, institutionally sponsored loans, and tuition waivers (partial) also available. Financial award application deadline: 3/15. *Faculty research:* Probability and statistics, differential equations, algebra, combinations. Total annual research expenditures: $10,000. *Unit head:* Dr. Robert Jensen, Chair, 773-508-3578, Fax: 773-508-2123, E-mail: rjensen@luc.edu. *Application contact:* Dr. Joseph Mayne, Director, 773-508-3574, Fax: 773-508-2123, E-mail: jmayne@luc.edu.

Marquette University, Graduate School, College of Arts and Sciences, Department of Mathematics, Statistics, and Computer Science, Milwaukee, WI 53201-1881. Offers bioinformatics (MS); computational sciences (PhD); computers (MS); mathematics education (MS). Part-time programs available. *Faculty:* 28 full-time (12 women), 7 part-time/adjunct (2 women). *Students:* 20 full-time (4 women), 25 part-time (4 women); includes 2 minority (both Asian Americans or Pacific Islanders), 20 international. Average age 31. 68 applicants, 47% accepted, 15 enrolled. In 2009, 16 master's, 1 doctorate awarded. Terminal master's awarded for partial completion of doctoral program. *Degree requirements:* For master's, comprehensive exam, thesis or alternative; for doctorate, 2 foreign languages, comprehensive exam, thesis/dissertation. *Entrance requirements:* For doctorate, sample of scholarly writing. Additional exam requirements/recommendations for international students: Required—TOEFL. Application fee: $40. *Financial support:* In 2009–10, 2 research assistantships, 20 teaching assistantships were awarded; Federal Work-Study, institutionally sponsored loans, scholarships/grants, and tuition waivers (full and partial) also available. Support available to part-time students. Financial award application deadline: 2/15. *Faculty research:* Models of physiological systems, mathematical immunology, computational group theory, mathematical logic, computational science. *Unit head:* Dr. Peter Jones, Chair, 414-288-3263, Fax: 414-288-1578. *Application contact:* Dr. Gary Krenz, Director of Graduate Studies, 414-288-6345.

Marshall University, Academic Affairs Division, College of Science, Department of Mathematics, Huntington, WV 25755. Offers MA, MS. *Faculty:* 14 full-time (5 women), 17 part-time/adjunct (7 women). *Students:* 20 full-time (8 women), 3 part-time (1 woman); includes 2 minority (1 Asian American or Pacific Islander, 1 Hispanic American), 6 international. Average age 26. In 2009, 5 master's awarded. *Degree requirements:* For master's, thesis (for some programs). *Entrance requirements:* For master's, GRE General Test. Application fee: $40. *Unit head:* Dr. Ralph Oberste-Vorth, Chairperson, 304-696-6010, E-mail: oberstevorth@marshall.edu. *Application contact:* Dr. Alfred Akinsete, Information Contact, 304-696-4646, Fax: 304-746-1902, E-mail: akinsete@marshall.edu.

Massachusetts Institute of Technology, School of Science, Department of Mathematics, Cambridge, MA 02139-4307. Offers PhD. *Faculty:* 49 full-time (4 women), 1 part-time/adjunct (0 women). *Students:* 115 full-time (26 women); includes 11 minority (2 African Americans, 9 Asian Americans or Pacific Islanders), 59 international. Average age 25. 440 applicants, 7% accepted, 15 enrolled. In 2009, 19 doctorates awarded. *Degree requirements:* For doctorate, comprehensive exam, thesis/dissertation. *Entrance requirements:* For doctorate, GRE General Test, GRE Subject Test (mathematics). Additional exam requirements/recommendations for international students: Required—IELTS (minimum score 6). *Application deadline:* For fall admission, 12/15 for domestic and international students. Application fee: $75. Electronic applications accepted. *Financial support:* In 2009–10, 114 students received support, including 43 fellowships with tuition reimbursements available (averaging $27,039 per year), 20 research assistantships with tuition reimbursements available (averaging $29,502 per year), 49 teaching assistantships with tuition reimbursements available (averaging $29,829 per year); Federal Work-Study, institutionally sponsored loans, scholarships/grants, health care benefits, and unspecified assistantships also available. *Faculty research:* Analysis, algebra and number theory, representation theory, combinatorics, physical applied mathematics and computational science, theoretical computer science and computational biology, geometry and topology. Total annual research expenditures: $3.7 million. *Unit head:* Prof. Michael Sipser, Department Head, 617-253-4381, Fax: 617-253-4358, E-mail: math@mit.edu. *Application contact:* Graduate Education, 617-253-2689, Fax: 617-253-4358, E-mail: gradofc@math.mit.edu.

McGill University, Faculty of Graduate and Postdoctoral Studies, Faculty of Science, Department of Mathematics and Statistics, Montréal, QC H3A 2T5, Canada. Offers computational science and engineering (M Sc); mathematics and statistics (M Sc, MA, PhD), including applied mathematics (M Sc, MA), pure mathematics (M Sc, MA), statistics (M Sc, MA).

McMaster University, School of Graduate Studies, Faculty of Science, Department of Mathematics and Statistics, Hamilton, ON L8S 4M2, Canada. Offers mathematics (M Sc, PhD); statistics (M Sc), including applied statistics, medical statistics, statistical theory. Part-time programs available. *Degree requirements:* For master's, thesis or alternative, oral exam; for doctorate, comprehensive exam, thesis/dissertation. *Entrance requirements:* For master's, minimum B+ average in last year of honors degree; for doctorate, minimum B+ average, M Sc in mathematics or statistics. Additional exam requirements/recommendations for international students: Required—TOEFL (minimum score 550 paper-based; 213 computer-based). *Faculty research:* Algebra, analysis, applied mathematics, geometry and topology, probability and statistics.

McNeese State University, Doré School of Graduate Studies, College of Science, Department of Mathematics, Computer Science, and Statistics, Lake Charles, LA 70609. Offers mathematical science (MS), including computer science, mathematics, statistics. Evening/weekend programs available. *Degree requirements:* For master's, comprehensive exam, thesis or alternative, written exam. *Entrance requirements:* For master's, GRE.

Memorial University of Newfoundland, School of Graduate Studies, Department of Mathematics and Statistics, St. John's, NL A1C 5S7, Canada. Offers mathematics (M Sc, PhD); statistics (M Sc, MAS, PhD). Part-time programs available. *Degree requirements:* For master's, thesis, practicum and report (MAS); for doctorate, comprehensive exam, thesis/dissertation, oral defense of thesis. *Entrance requirements:* For master's, 2nd class honors degree (MAS); for doctorate, MAS or M Sc in mathematics and statistics. Electronic applications accepted. *Faculty research:* Algebra, topology, applied mathematics, mathematical statistics, applied statistics and probability.

Miami University, Graduate School, College of Arts and Sciences, Department of Mathematics, Oxford, OH 45056. Offers MA, MAT, MS. *Students:* 23 full-time (12 women), 2 part-time (1 woman), 1 international. *Entrance requirements:* Additional exam requirements/recommendations for international students: Required—TOEFL. Application fee: $50. *Expenses:* Tuition, state resident: full-time $11,280. Tuition, nonresident: full-time $24,912. Required fees: $516. *Financial support:* Research assistantships, teaching assistantships, health care benefits and unspecified assistantships available. Financial award application deadline: 3/1; financial award applicants required to submit FAFSA. *Unit head:* Dr. Patrick Dowling, Department Chair, 513-529-5818, E-mail: dowlinpn@muohio.edu. *Application contact:* Dr. Doug Ward, Director of Graduate Studies, 513-529-3534, E-mail: wardde@muohio.edu.

Michigan State University, The Graduate School, College of Natural Science, Department of Mathematics, East Lansing, MI 48824. Offers applied mathematics (MS, PhD); industrial mathematics (MS); mathematics (MAT, MS, PhD). *Entrance requirements:* Additional exam requirements/recommendations for international students: Required—TOEFL. Electronic applications accepted.

Michigan Technological University, Graduate School, College of Sciences and Arts, Department of Mathematical Sciences, Houghton, MI 49931. Offers MS, PhD. Part-time programs available. Terminal master's awarded for partial completion of doctoral program. *Degree requirements:* For master's, comprehensive exam (for some programs), thesis (for some programs); for doctorate, comprehensive exam, thesis/dissertation, proficiency exam. *Entrance requirements:* For master's and doctorate, GRE General Test, GRE Subject Test (recommended). Additional exam requirements/recommendations for international students: Required—TOEFL (minimum score 550 paper-based; 213 computer-based). Electronic applications accepted. *Faculty research:* Fluid dynamics, mathematical modeling, design theory, coding theory, statistical genetics.

Middle Tennessee State University, College of Graduate Studies, College of Basic and Applied Sciences, Department of Mathematical Sciences, Murfreesboro, TN 37132. Offers mathematics (MS, MST). Part-time and evening/weekend programs available. Postbaccalaureate distance learning degree programs offered. *Faculty:* 21 full-time (9 women). *Students:* 3 full-time (2 women), 38 part-time (22 women); includes 11 minority (5 African Americans, 6 Asian Americans or Pacific Islanders). Average age 27. 17 applicants, 82% accepted, 14 enrolled. In 2009, 12 master's awarded. *Degree requirements:* For master's, comprehensive exam. *Entrance requirements:* For master's, GRE General Test or MAT. Additional exam requirements/recommendations for international students: Required—TOEFL (minimum score 525 paper-based; 195 computer-based; 71 iBT) or IELTS (minimum score 6). *Application deadline:* For fall admission, 6/1 for domestic and international students. Applications are processed on a rolling basis. Application fee: $25 ($30 for international students). Electronic applications accepted. *Expenses:* Tuition, state resident: full-time $4404. Tuition, nonresident: full-time $10,956. *Financial support:* In 2009–10, 11 students received support. Institutionally sponsored loans available. Support available to part-time students. Financial award application deadline: 5/1; financial award applicants required to submit FAFSA. *Unit head:* Dr. Donald Nelson, Interim Chair, 615-898-2704, Fax: 615-898-5422, E-mail: dnelson@mtsu.edu. *Application contact:* Dr. Michael Allen, Dean and Vice Provost for Research, 615-898-2840, Fax: 615-904-8020, E-mail: mallen@mtsu.edu.

Minnesota State University Mankato, College of Graduate Studies, College of Science, Engineering and Technology, Department of Mathematics and Statistics, Program in Mathematics, Mankato, MN 56001. Offers MA, MS. *Students:* 4 full-time (1 woman), 7 part-time (3 women). *Degree requirements:* For master's, one foreign language, comprehensive exam, thesis or alternative. *Entrance requirements:* For master's, GRE General Test, minimum GPA of 3.0 during previous 2 years. Additional exam requirements/recommendations for international students: Required—TOEFL. *Application deadline:* For fall admission, 7/1 priority date for domestic students; for spring admission, 11/1 for domestic students. Applications are processed on a rolling basis. Application fee: $40. Electronic applications accepted. *Expenses:* Tuition, state resident: full-time $5364. Tuition, nonresident: full-time $8314. *Financial support:* Research assistantships with partial tuition reimbursements, teaching assistantships with partial tuition reimbursements, unspecified assistantships available. Financial award application deadline: 3/15; financial award applicants required to submit FAFSA. *Unit head:* Dr. Deepak Sanjel, Graduate Coordinator, 507-389-2319. *Application contact:* 507-389-2321, E-mail: grad@mnsu.edu.

Mississippi College, Graduate School, College of Arts and Sciences, School of Science and Mathematics, Department of Mathematics, Clinton, MS 39058. Offers M Ed, MCS, MS. Part-time programs available. *Faculty:* 4 full-time (2 women). *Students:* 3 full-time (1 woman). Average age 31. In 2009, 3 master's awarded. *Degree requirements:* For master's, comprehensive exam, thesis optional. *Entrance requirements:* For master's, GRE or NTE, minimum GPA of 2.5. Additional exam requirements/recommendations for international students: Recommended—IELTS. *Application deadline:* For fall admission, 8/15 priority date for domestic students. Applications are processed on a rolling basis. Application fee: $30. Electronic applications accepted. *Expenses:* Tuition: Part-time $452 per credit hour. Required fees: $101 per semester. Tuition and fees vary according to degree level, campus/location, program and student level. *Financial support:* Federal Work-Study and unspecified assistantships available. Support available to part-time students. Financial award application deadline: 4/1; financial award applicants required to submit FAFSA. *Unit head:* Dr. John Travis, Chair, 601-925-3817, E-mail: travis@mc.edu. *Application contact:* Elnora Lewis, Secretary, 601-925-3225, Fax: 601-925-3889, E-mail: lewis09@mc.edu.

Mississippi State University, College of Arts and Sciences, Department of Mathematics and Statistics, Mississippi State, MS 39762. Offers mathematical sciences (PhD); mathematics (MS); statistics (MS). Part-time programs available. *Faculty:* 21 full-time (4 women). *Students:* 36 full-time (15 women), 2 part-time (1 woman); includes 3 minority (all African Americans), 24 international. Average age 28. 66 applicants, 39% accepted, 15 enrolled. In 2009, 11 master's, 2 doctorates awarded. Terminal master's awarded for partial completion of doctoral program. *Degree requirements:* For master's, thesis optional, comprehensive oral or written exam; for doctorate, one foreign language, thesis/dissertation, comprehensive oral and written exam. *Entrance requirements:* For master's, minimum GPA of 2.75 on last two years of undergraduate courses; for doctorate, GRE. Additional exam requirements/recommendations for international students: Required—TOEFL (minimum score 475 paper-based; 153 computer-based; 53 iBT); Recommended—IELTS (minimum score 4.5). *Application deadline:* For fall admission, 3/15 priority date for domestic students, 5/1 for international students; for spring admission, 11/1 for domestic students, 9/1 for international students. Applications are processed on a rolling basis. Application fee: $40. Electronic applications accepted. *Expenses:* Tuition, state resident: full-time $2575.50; part-time $286.25 per credit hour. Tuition, nonresident: full-time $6510; part-time $723.50 per credit hour. Tuition and fees vary according to course load. *Financial support:* In 2009–10, 2 research assistantships (averaging $12,379 per year), 27 teaching assistantships with full tuition reimbursements (averaging $13,142 per year) were awarded; Federal Work-Study, institutionally sponsored loans, tuition waivers (partial), and unspecified assistantships also available. Financial award applicants required to submit FAFSA. *Faculty research:* Differential equations, algebra, numerical analysis, functional analysis, applied statistics. Total annual research expenditures: $1.9 million. *Unit head:* Dr. Mohsen Razzaghi, Interim Head, 662-325-3414, Fax: 662-325-0005, E-mail: razzaghi@math.msstate.edu. *Application contact:* Dr. Corlis Johnson, Associate Head/Graduate Coordinator, 662-325-3414, Fax: 662-325-0005, E-mail: cjohnson@math.msstate.edu.

Missouri State University, Graduate College, College of Natural and Applied Sciences, Department of Mathematics, Springfield, MO 65897. Offers mathematics (MS); natural and applied science (MNAS), including mathematics (MNAS, MS Ed); secondary education (MS Ed), including mathematics (MNAS, MS Ed). Part-time programs available. *Faculty:* 23 full-time (5 women). *Students:* 15 full-time (1 woman), 7 part-time (1 woman), 1 international. Average age 25. 12 applicants, 100% accepted, 9 enrolled. In 2009, 4 master's awarded. *Degree requirements:* For master's, comprehensive exam, thesis or alternative. *Entrance requirements:* For master's, GRE (MS, MNAS), minimum undergraduate GPA of 3.0 (MS, MNAS), 9-12 teacher certification (MS Ed). Additional exam requirements/recommendations for international students: Required—TOEFL (minimum score 550 paper-based; 213 computer-based; 79 iBT). *Application deadline:* For fall admission, 7/20 priority date for domestic students, 5/1 for international students; for spring admission, 12/20 priority date for domestic students, 9/1 for international students. Applications are processed on a rolling basis. Application fee: $35 ($50 for international students). Electronic applications accepted. *Expenses:* Tuition, state resident: full-time $3852; part-time $214 per credit hour. Tuition, nonresident: full-time $7524; part-time $418 per credit hour. Required fees: $696; $172 per semester. Tuition and fees vary according to course level, course load, degree level and program. *Financial support:* In 2009–10, 7 teaching assistantships with full tuition reimbursements (averaging $9,730 per year) were awarded; Federal Work-Study, institutionally sponsored loans, scholarships/grants, and unspecified assistantships also available. Financial award application deadline: 3/31; financial award applicants required to submit FAFSA. *Faculty research:* Harmonic analysis, commutative algebra, number theory, K-theory, probability. *Unit head:* Dr. Yungchen Cheng, Head, 417-836-5112, Fax: 417-836-6966, E-mail: yungchencheng@missouristate.edu. *Application contact:* Eric Eckert, Director of Admissions and Recruitment, 417-836-5331, Fax: 417-836-6200, E-mail: ericeckert@missouristate.edu.

Missouri University of Science and Technology, Graduate School, Department of Mathematics and Statistics, Rolla, MO 65409. Offers applied mathematics (MS); mathematics (MST, PhD), including mathematics (PhD), mathematics education (MST), statistics (PhD). Terminal master's awarded for partial completion of doctoral program. *Degree requirements:* For master's, thesis or alternative; for doctorate, one foreign language, thesis/dissertation. *Entrance requirements:* For master's and doctorate, GRE General Test, GRE Subject Test. Electronic applications accepted. *Faculty research:* Analysis, differential equations, topology, statistics.

Montana State University, College of Graduate Studies, College of Letters and Science, Department of Mathematical Sciences, Bozeman, MT 59717. Offers mathematics (MS, PhD), including mathematics education option (MS); statistics (MS, PhD). Part-time programs available. Postbaccalaureate distance learning degree programs offered (minimal on-campus study). *Faculty:* 35 full-time (11 women), 7 part-time/adjunct (3 women). *Students:* 17 full-time (6 women), 71 part-time (33 women); includes 3 minority (1 American Indian/Alaska Native, 1 Asian American or Pacific Islander, 1 Hispanic American), 6 international. Average age 31. 53 applicants, 36% accepted, 15 enrolled. In 2009, 18 master's, 3 doctorates awarded. *Degree requirements:* For master's, comprehensive exam, thesis (for some programs); for doctorate, comprehensive exam, thesis/dissertation. *Entrance requirements:* For master's and doctorate, GRE General Test. Additional exam requirements/recommendations for international students: Required—TOEFL (minimum score 550 paper-based; 213 computer-based). *Application*

Mathematics

Montana State University (continued)

deadline: For fall admission, 7/15 priority date for domestic students, 5/15 priority date for international students; for spring admission, 12/1 priority date for domestic students, 10/1 priority date for international students. Applications are processed on a rolling basis. Application fee: $30. Electronic applications accepted. *Expenses:* Tuition, state resident: full-time $5635; part-time $3492 per year. Tuition, nonresident: full-time $17,212; part-time $7865.10 per year. Required fees: $1441.05; $153.15 per credit. Tuition and fees vary according to course load and program. *Financial support:* In 2009–10, 58 students received support, including 4 research assistantships with tuition reimbursements available (averaging $15,650 per year), 54 teaching assistantships with tuition reimbursements available (averaging $15,450 per year); career-related internships or fieldwork, scholarships/grants, tuition waivers (full), and unspecified assistantships also available. Support available to part-time students. Financial award application deadline: 3/1; financial award applicants required to submit FAFSA. *Faculty research:* Applied mathematics, dynamical systems, statistics, mathematics education, mathematical and computational biology. Total annual research expenditures: $248,209. *Unit head:* Dr. Kenneth Bowers, Head, 406-994-3604, Fax: 406-994-1789, E-mail: bowers@math.montana.edu. *Application contact:* Dr. Carl A. Fox, Vice Provost for Graduate Education, 406-994-4145, Fax: 406-994-7433, E-mail: gradstudy@montana.edu.

Montclair State University, The Graduate School, College of Science and Mathematics, Department of Mathematics, Montclair, NJ 07043-1624. Offers math pedagogy (Ed D); mathematics (MS), including computer science, mathematics education, pure and applied mathematics, statistics; physical science (Certificate); teaching middle grades math (MS, Certificate). Part-time and evening/weekend programs available. *Faculty:* 30 full-time (10 women), 39 part-time/adjunct (19 women). *Students:* 15 full-time (7 women), 101 part-time (75 women). Average age 32. 55 applicants, 76% accepted, 31 enrolled. In 2009, 32 master's, 2 doctorates, 9 other advanced degrees awarded. *Degree requirements:* For master's, comprehensive exam. *Entrance requirements:* For master's, GRE General Test, 2 letters of recommendation. Additional exam requirements/recommendations for international students: Required—TOEFL (minimum score 83 computer-based), or IELTS. *Application deadline:* For fall admission, 6/1 for international students; for spring admission, 10/1 for international students. Applications are processed on a rolling basis. Application fee: $60. *Expenses:* Tuition, area resident: Part-time $486.74 per credit. Tuition, state resident: part-time $486.74 per credit. Tuition, nonresident: part-time $751.34 per credit. Tuition and fees vary according to degree level and program. *Financial support:* In 2009–10, 9 research assistantships with full tuition reimbursements (averaging $7,000 per year), 1 teaching assistantship with full tuition reimbursement (averaging $15,000 per year) were awarded; Federal Work-Study, scholarships/grants, and unspecified assistantships also available. Support available to part-time students. Financial award application deadline: 3/1; financial award applicants required to submit FAFSA. *Faculty research:* Infectious disease. *Unit head:* Dr. Helen Roberts, Chairperson, 973-655-5132. *Application contact:* Amy Aiello, Director of Graduate Admissions and Operations, 973-655-5147, Fax: 973-655-7869, E-mail: graduate.school@montclair.edu.

Morgan State University, School of Graduate Studies, School of Computer, Mathematical, and Natural Sciences, Department of Mathematics, Baltimore, MD 21251. Offers MA. Part-time and evening/weekend programs available. *Degree requirements:* For master's, comprehensive exam, thesis. *Entrance requirements:* For master's, GRE. Additional exam requirements/recommendations for international students: Required—TOEFL (minimum score 550 paper-based; 213 computer-based). *Faculty research:* Number theory, semigroups, analysis, operations research.

Murray State University, College of Science, Engineering and Technology, Program in Mathematics and Statistics, Murray, KY 42071. Offers MA, MAT, MS. Part-time programs available. *Degree requirements:* For master's, comprehensive exam, thesis optional. *Entrance requirements:* For master's, GRE General Test. Additional exam requirements/recommendations for international students: Required—TOEFL. *Faculty research:* Algebraic structures, mathematical biology, topolgy.

Naval Postgraduate School, Graduate Programs, Department of Mathematics, Monterey, CA 93943. Offers applied mathematics (MS, PhD). Program only open to commissioned officers of the United States and friendly nations and selected United States federal civilian employees. Part-time programs available. *Degree requirements:* For master's, thesis; for doctorate, one foreign language, thesis/dissertation.

New Jersey Institute of Technology, Office of Graduate Studies, College of Science and Liberal Arts, Department of Mathematical Science, Program in Mathematics Science, Newark, NJ 07102. Offers PhD. Part-time and evening/weekend programs available. *Entrance requirements:* For doctorate, GRE General Test, minimum graduate GPA of 3.5. Additional exam requirements/recommendations for international students: Required—TOEFL (minimum score 550 paper-based; 213 computer-based; 79 iBT). Electronic applications accepted.

New Mexico Institute of Mining and Technology, Graduate Studies, Department of Mathematics, Socorro, NM 87801. Offers applied math (PhD); mathematics (MS); operations research (MS). *Degree requirements:* For master's, thesis optional; for doctorate, thesis/dissertation. *Entrance requirements:* For master's, GRE General Test. Additional exam requirements/recommendations for international students: Required—TOEFL (minimum score 540 paper-based; 207 computer-based). *Faculty research:* Applied mathematics, differential equations, industrial mathematics, numerical analysis, stochastic processes.

New Mexico State University, Graduate School, College of Arts and Sciences, Department of Mathematical Sciences, Las Cruces, NM 88003-8001. Offers MS, PhD. Part-time programs available. *Faculty:* 12 full-time (2 women). *Students:* 42 full-time (12 women), 9 part-time (5 women); includes 7 minority (1 African American, 6 Hispanic Americans), 29 international. Average age 32. 87 applicants, 80% accepted, 13 enrolled. In 2009, 9 master's, 5 doctorates awarded. *Degree requirements:* For master's, thesis optional, final oral exam; for doctorate, one foreign language, comprehensive exam, thesis/dissertation, final oral exam. *Entrance requirements:* Additional exam requirements/recommendations for international students: Required—TOEFL (minimum score 530 paper-based; 197 computer-based). *Application deadline:* For fall admission, 2/1 priority date for domestic and international students; for spring admission, 10/1 for domestic and international students. Applications are processed on a rolling basis. Application fee: $30 ($50 for international students). Electronic applications accepted. *Expenses:* Tuition, state resident: full-time $4080; part-time $223 per credit. Tuition, nonresident: full-time $14,256; part-time $647 per credit. Required fees: $1278; $639 per semester. *Financial support:* In 2009–10, 3 research assistantships (averaging $16,587 per year), 32 teaching assistantships (averaging $14,997 per year) were awarded; fellowships, scholarships/grants, health care benefits, and unspecified assistantships also available. Financial award application deadline: 2/1. *Faculty research:* Commutative algebra, dynamical systems, harmonic analysis and applications, algebraic topology, statistics. *Unit head:* Dr. Patrick Morandi, Head, 575-646-3901, Fax: 575-646-1064, E-mail: pmorandi@nmsu.edu. *Application contact:* Dr. David Finston, Professor, 575-646-2637, Fax: 575-646-1064, E-mail: dfinston@nmsu.edu.

New York University, Graduate School of Arts and Science, Courant Institute of Mathematical Sciences, Department of Mathematics, New York, NY 10012-1019. Offers atmosphere ocean science and mathematics (PhD); mathematics (MS, PhD); mathematics and statistics/operations research (MS); mathematics in finance (MS); scientific computing (MS). Part-time and evening/weekend programs available. *Faculty:* 46 full-time (0 women). *Students:* 179 full-time (35 women), 111 part-time (20 women); includes 40 minority (1 African American, 33 Asian Americans or Pacific Islanders, 6 Hispanic Americans), 139 international. Average age 29. 1,071 applicants, 29% accepted, 72 enrolled. In 2009, 88 master's, 19 doctorates awarded. *Degree requirements:* For master's, thesis optional; for doctorate, one foreign language, thesis/dissertation, oral and written exams. *Entrance requirements:* For master's and doctorate, GRE General Test, GRE Subject Test. Additional exam requirements/recommendations for international students: Required—TOEFL. *Application deadline:* For fall admission, 1/4 for domestic students; for spring admission, 11/1 for domestic students. Application fee: $90. *Expenses:* Tuition: Full-time $30,528; part-time $1272 per credit. Required fees: $2177. *Financial support:* Fellowships with tuition reimbursements, research assistantships with tuition reimbursements, teaching assistantships with tuition reimbursements, Federal Work-Study, institutionally sponsored loans, scholarships/grants, health care benefits, and unspecified assistantships available. Financial award application deadline: 1/4; financial award applicants required to submit FAFSA. *Faculty research:* Partial differential equations, computational science, applied mathematics, geometry and topology, probability and stochastic processes. *Unit head:* Fedor Bogomolov, Director of Graduate Studies, 212-998-3238, Fax: 212-995-4195, E-mail: admissions@math.nyu.edu. *Application contact:* Tamar Arnon, Application Contact, 212-998-3238, Fax: 212-995-4195, E-mail: admissions@math.nyu.edu.

Nicholls State University, Graduate Studies, College of Arts and Sciences, Department of Mathematics and Computer Science, Thibodaux, LA 70310. Offers community/technical college mathematics (MS). Part-time and evening/weekend programs available. *Degree requirements:* For master's, comprehensive exam. *Entrance requirements:* For master's, GRE General Test. Electronic applications accepted. *Faculty research:* Operations research, statistics, numerical analysis, algebra, topology.

North Carolina Central University, Division of Academic Affairs, College of Science and Technology, Department of Mathematics and Computer Science, Durham, NC 27707-3129. Offers applied mathematics (MS); mathematics education (MS); pure mathematics (MS). Part-time and evening/weekend programs available. *Degree requirements:* For master's, one foreign language, comprehensive exam, thesis. *Entrance requirements:* For master's, minimum GPA of 3.0 in major, 2.5 overall. Additional exam requirements/recommendations for international students: Required—TOEFL. *Faculty research:* Structure theorems for Lie algebra, Kleene monoids and semi-groups, theoretical computer science, mathematics education.

North Carolina State University, Graduate School, College of Agriculture and Life Sciences and College of Engineering and College of Physical and Mathematical Sciences, Program in Financial Mathematics, Raleigh, NC 27695. Offers MFM. Part-time programs available. *Degree requirements:* For master's, thesis optional, project/internship. *Entrance requirements:* For master's, GRE General Test. Additional exam requirements/recommendations for international students: Required—TOEFL (minimum score 550 paper-based; 213 computer-based). Electronic applications accepted. *Faculty research:* Financial mathematics modeling and computation, futures, options and commodities markets, real options, credit risk, portfolio optimization.

North Carolina State University, Graduate School, College of Physical and Mathematical Sciences, Department of Mathematics, Program in Mathematics, Raleigh, NC 27695. Offers MS, PhD. *Degree requirements:* For master's, thesis (for some programs); for doctorate, thesis/dissertation. *Entrance requirements:* For master's and doctorate, GRE, GRE Subject Test (recommended). Electronic applications accepted.

North Dakota State University, College of Graduate and Interdisciplinary Studies, College of Science and Mathematics, Department of Mathematics, Fargo, ND 58108. Offers applied mathematics (MS, PhD); mathematics (MS, PhD). *Faculty:* 15 full-time, 4 part-time/adjunct. *Students:* 22 full-time (6 women), 7 part-time (4 women), 7 international. Average age 28. 7 applicants, 100% accepted, 5 enrolled. In 2009, 1 master's, 2 doctorates awarded. *Degree requirements:* For master's, comprehensive exam, thesis; for doctorate, one foreign language, comprehensive exam, thesis/dissertation, computer proficiency. *Entrance requirements:* For master's and doctorate, GRE General Test. Additional exam requirements/recommendations for international students: Required—TOEFL (minimum score 525 paper-based; 197 computer-based; 71 iBT), IELTS. *Application deadline:* For fall admission, 5/1 priority date for domestic and international students; for spring admission, 8/1 for domestic students, 8/1 priority date for international students. Applications are processed on a rolling basis. Application fee: $45 ($60 for international students). Electronic applications accepted. *Financial support:* In 2009–10, 5 fellowships with full tuition reimbursements (averaging $18,000 per year), 1 research assistantship with tuition reimbursement (averaging $14,000 per year), 17 teaching assistantships with full tuition reimbursements (averaging $9,300 per year) were awarded; Federal Work-Study, institutionally sponsored loans, and tuition waivers (full) also available. Support available to part-time students. Financial award application deadline: 3/31. *Faculty research:* Discrete mathematics, number theory, analysis theory, algebra, applied math. Total annual research expenditures: $33,227. *Unit head:* Dr. Warren Shreve, Chair, 701-231-8171, Fax: 701-231-7598, E-mail: warren.shreve@ndsu.edu. *Application contact:* Dr. Jim Coykendall, Graduate Program Director, 701-231-8079, Fax: 701-231-7598, E-mail: jim.coykendall@ndsu.edu.

Northeastern Illinois University, Graduate College, College of Arts and Sciences, Department of Mathematics, Programs in Mathematics, Chicago, IL 60625-4699. Offers mathematics (MS); mathematics for elementary school teachers (MA). Part-time and evening/weekend programs available. *Degree requirements:* For master's, comprehensive exam, thesis optional, project. *Entrance requirements:* For master's, minimum GPA of 2.75, 6 undergraduate courses in mathematics. Additional exam requirements/recommendations for international students: Required—TOEFL (minimum score 550 paper-based; 213 computer-based; 80 iBT). Electronic applications accepted. *Faculty research:* Numerical analysis, mathematical biology, operations research, statistics, geometry and mathematics of finance.

Northeastern University, College of Science, Department of Mathematics, Boston, MA 02115-5096. Offers applied mathematics (MS); mathematics (MS, PhD); operations research (MSOR). Part-time and evening/weekend programs available. *Faculty:* 39 full-time (5 women), 15 part-time/adjunct (7 women). *Students:* 52 full-time (17 women), 4 part-time (1 woman); includes 2 Asian Americans or Pacific Islanders, 1 Hispanic American, 28 international. 146 applicants, 76% accepted, 23 enrolled. In 2009, 8 master's, 6 doctorates awarded. *Degree requirements:* For master's, thesis (for some programs); for doctorate, thesis/dissertation, qualifying exams. *Entrance requirements:* For master's and doctorate, GRE Subject Test, GRE General Test. Additional exam requirements/recommendations for international students: Required—TOEFL. *Application deadline:* For fall admission, 2/1 priority date for domestic and international students. Applications are processed on a rolling basis. Application fee: $50. Electronic applications accepted. *Financial support:* In 2009–10, 26 teaching assistantships with tuition reimbursements (averaging $17,345 per year) were awarded; research assistantships with tuition reimbursements, Federal Work-Study, institutionally sponsored loans, tuition waivers (full and partial), and unspecified assistantships also available. Financial award application deadline: 3/1; financial award applicants required to submit FAFSA. *Faculty research:* Algebra and singularities, combinatorics, topology, probability and statistics, geometric analysis and partial differential equations. *Unit head:* Dr. Jerzy Weyman, Graduate Coordinator, 617-373-5513, Fax: 617-373-5658, E-mail: j.weyman@neu.edu. *Application contact:* Jo-Anne Dickinson, Admissions Contact, 617-373-5990, Fax: 617-373-7281, E-mail: gsas@neu.edu.

Northern Arizona University, Graduate College, College of Engineering, Forestry and Natural Sciences, Department of Mathematics and Statistics, Flagstaff, AZ 86011. Offers mathematics (MAT, MS); statistics (MS). Part-time programs available. *Faculty:* 32 full-time (10 women). *Students:* 21 full-time (9 women), 22 part-time (14 women); includes 5 minority (3 Asian Americans or Pacific Islanders, 2 Hispanic Americans), 3 international. Average age 28. 34 applicants, 62% accepted, 14 enrolled. In 2009, 9 master's awarded. *Degree requirements:* For master's, comprehensive exam, thesis optional. *Entrance requirements:* For master's, minimum GPA of 3.0. Additional exam requirements/recommendations for international students: Required—TOEFL (minimum score 550 paper-based; 213 computer-based; 80 iBT), IELTS (minimum score 7), or a bachelor's degree from an English-speaking university and demonstrated proficiency. *Application deadline:* For fall admission, 3/15 priority date for domestic students, 9/1 priority date for international students; for spring admission, 10/15 priority date for domestic students. Applications are processed on a rolling basis. Application fee: $65. Electronic applications accepted. *Financial support:* In 2009–10, 22 teaching assistantships with partial tuition reimbursements (averaging $14,213 per year) were awarded; career-related internships or fieldwork, Federal Work-Study, tuition waivers (full and partial), and unspecified assistantships also available. Support available to part-time students. Financial award application deadline: 3/30; financial award applicants required to submit FAFSA. *Faculty research:* Topology, statistics, groups, ring theory, number theory. *Unit head:* Dr. Janet M. McShane, Chair, 928-523-1252, Fax: 928-523-5847, E-mail: janet.mcshane@nau.edu. *Application contact:* Dr. Jeffrey Allen Hovermill, Chair, 928-523-6897, Fax: 928-523-5847, E-mail: jeff.hovermill@nau.edu.

Northern Illinois University, Graduate School, College of Liberal Arts and Sciences, Department of Mathematical Sciences, De Kalb, IL 60115-2854. Offers mathematical sciences (PhD); mathematics (MS); statistics (MS). Part-time programs available. *Faculty:* 43 full-time (10 women), 4 part-time/adjunct (0 women). *Students:* 51 full-time (21 women), 39 part-time (18 women); includes 11 minority (2 African Americans, 7 Asian Americans or Pacific Islanders, 2 Hispanic Americans), 22 international. Average age 29. 65 applicants, 63% accepted, 14 enrolled. In 2009, 11 master's, 6 doctorates awarded. Terminal master's awarded for partial completion of doctoral program. *Degree requirements:* For master's, comprehensive exam, thesis optional; for doctorate, one foreign language, thesis/dissertation, candidacy exam, dissertation defense, internship. *Entrance requirements:* For master's, GRE General Test, minimum GPA of 2.75; for doctorate, GRE General Test, minimum GPA of 2.75 (undergraduate), 3.2 (graduate). Additional exam requirements/recommendations for international students: Required—TOEFL (minimum score 550 paper-based; 213 computer-based). *Application deadline:* For fall admission, 6/1 for domestic students, 5/1 for international students; for spring admission, 11/1 for domestic students, 10/1 for international students. Applications are processed on a rolling basis. Application fee: $30. Electronic applications accepted. *Expenses:* Tuition, state resident: full-time $6576; part-time $274 per credit hour. Tuition, nonresident: full-time $13,152; part-time $548 per credit hour. Required fees: $1813; $75.53 per credit hour. Part-time tuition and fees vary according to course load. *Financial support:* In 2009–10, 40 teaching assistantships with full tuition reimbursements were awarded; fellowships with full tuition reimbursements, research assistantships with full tuition reimbursements, career-related internships or fieldwork, Federal Work-Study, scholarships/grants, tuition waivers (full), and unspecified assistantships also available. Support available to part-time students. Financial award applicants required to submit FAFSA. *Faculty research:* Numerical linear algebra, noncommutative rings, nonlineal partial differential equations, finite group theory, abstract harmonic analysis. *Unit head:* Dr. William D. Blair, Chair, 815-753-0566, Fax: 815-753-1112, E-mail: blair@math.niu.edu. *Application contact:* Dr. Bernard Harris, Director, Graduate Studies, 815-753-6775, E-mail: harris@math.niu.edu.

Northwestern University, The Graduate School, Judd A. and Marjorie Weinberg College of Arts and Sciences, Department of Mathematics, Evanston, IL 60208. Offers PhD. Admissions and degrees offered through The Graduate School. Part-time programs available. *Degree requirements:* For doctorate, thesis/dissertation, preliminary exam. *Entrance requirements:* For doctorate, GRE General Test, GRE Subject Test. Additional exam requirements/recommendations for international students: Required—TOEFL. *Faculty research:* Algebra, algebraic topology, analysis dynamical systems, partial differential equations.

Oakland University, Graduate Study and Lifelong Learning, College of Arts and Sciences, Department of Mathematics and Statistics, Program in Mathematics, Rochester, MI 48309-4401. Offers MA. *Entrance requirements:* Additional exam requirements/recommendations for international students: Required—TOEFL (minimum score 550 paper-based; 213 computer-based). Electronic applications accepted. *Expenses:* Contact institution.

The Ohio State University, Graduate School, College of Mathematical and Physical Sciences, Department of Mathematics, Columbus, OH 43210. Offers MA, MS, PhD. *Faculty:* 68. *Students:* 45 full-time (7 women), 79 part-time (23 women); includes 5 minority (1 Asian American or Pacific Islander, 4 Hispanic Americans), 67 international. Average age 27. In 2009, 7 master's, 19 doctorates awarded. *Degree requirements:* For master's, thesis optional; for doctorate, 2 foreign languages, thesis/dissertation. *Entrance requirements:* For master's and doctorate, GRE General Test, GRE Subject Test in mathematics. Additional exam requirements/recommendations for international students: Required—TOEFL. *Application deadline:* For fall admission, 8/15 priority date for domestic students, 7/1 priority date for international students; for winter admission, 12/1 priority date for domestic students, 11/1 priority date for international students; for spring admission, 3/1 priority date for domestic students, 2/1 priority date for international students. Applications are processed on a rolling basis. Application fee: $40 ($50 for international students). Electronic applications accepted. *Expenses:* Tuition, state resident: full-time $10,683. Tuition, nonresident: full-time $25,923. Tuition and fees vary according to course load and program. *Financial support:* Fellowships, research assistantships, teaching assistantships, Federal Work-Study, institutionally sponsored loans, and unspecified assistantships available. Support available to part-time students. *Unit head:* Thomas Kerler, Graduate Studies Committee Chair, E-mail: kerler.2@osu.edu. *Application contact:* 614-292-9444, Fax: 614-292-3895, E-mail: domestic.grad@osu.edu.

Ohio University, Graduate College, College of Arts and Sciences, Department of Mathematics, Athens, OH 45701-2979. Offers MS, PhD. Part-time and evening/weekend programs available. *Faculty:* 25 full-time (3 women). *Students:* 41 full-time (11 women), 3 part-time (0 women); includes 2 minority (1 American Indian/Alaska Native, 1 Asian American or Pacific Islander), 14 international. 77 applicants, 62% accepted, 17 enrolled. In 2009, 27 master's, 2 doctorates awarded. Terminal master's awarded for partial completion of doctoral program. *Degree requirements:* For master's, thesis optional; for doctorate, comprehensive exam, thesis/dissertation. *Entrance requirements:* For master's and doctorate, minimum GPA of 3.0. Additional exam requirements/recommendations for international students: Required—TOEFL (minimum score 550 paper-based; 80 iBT) or IELTS Academic (minimum score 6.5). *Application deadline:* For fall admission, 2/1 priority date for domestic and international students. Applications are processed on a rolling basis. Application fee: $50 ($55 for international students). Electronic applications accepted. *Expenses:* Tuition, state resident: full-time $7839; part-time $323 per quarter hour. Tuition, nonresident: full-time $15,831; part-time $654 per quarter hour. Required fees: $2931. *Financial support:* Fellowships with full tuition reimbursements, teaching assistantships with full tuition reimbursements, Federal Work-Study and institutionally sponsored loans available. Financial award application deadline: 2/1. *Faculty research:* Algebra (group and ring theory), functional analysis, topology, differential equations, computational math. *Unit head:* Dr. Jeff Connor, Chair, 740-593-1254, Fax: 740-593-9805, E-mail: connor@math.ohiou.edu. *Application contact:* Dr. Martin Mohlenkamp, Graduate Chair, 740-593-1259, E-mail: mjm@math.ohiou.edu.

Oklahoma State University, College of Arts and Sciences, Department of Mathematics, Stillwater, OK 74078. Offers mathematics (pure and applied) (PhD); mathematics (pure) (MS). *Faculty:* 36 full-time (7 women), 8 part-time/adjunct (6 women). *Students:* 5 full-time (2 women), 24 part-time (9 women); includes 1 minority (Asian American or Pacific Islander), 21 international. Average age 32. 72 applicants, 19% accepted, 6 enrolled. In 2009, 6 master's, 4 doctorates awarded. *Degree requirements:* For master's, comprehensive exam, creative component, report or thesis; for doctorate, comprehensive exam, thesis/dissertation. *Entrance requirements:* For master's, GRE; for doctorate, GRE. Additional exam requirements/recommendations for international students: Required—TOEFL (minimum score 550 paper-based; 79 iBT). *Application deadline:* For fall admission, 3/1 priority date for international students; for spring admission, 8/1 priority date for international students. Applications are processed on a rolling basis. Application fee: $40 ($75 for international students). Electronic applications accepted. *Expenses:* Tuition, state resident: full-time $3716; part-time $154.85 per credit hour. Tuition, nonresident: full-time $14,448; part-time $602 per credit hour. Required fees: $1772; $73.85 per credit hour. One-time fee: $50. Tuition and fees vary according to course load and campus/location. *Financial support:* In 2009–10, 25 teaching assistantships (averaging $19,087 per year) were awarded; career-related internships or fieldwork, Federal Work-Study, scholarships/grants, health care benefits, tuition waivers (partial), and unspecified assistantships also available. Support available to part-time students. Financial award application deadline: 3/1; financial award applicants required to submit FAFSA. *Unit head:* Dr. Dale Alspach, Head, 405-744-5688, Fax: 405-744-8275. *Application contact:* Dr. Gordon Emslie, Dean, 405-744-6368, Fax: 405-744-0355, E-mail: grad-i@okstate.edu.

See Close-Up on page 319.

Old Dominion University, College of Sciences, Programs in Computational and Applied Mathematics, Norfolk, VA 23529. Offers MS, PhD. Part-time programs available. *Faculty:* 22 full-time (0 women), 2 part-time/adjunct (0 women). *Students:* 29 full-time (15 women), 17 part-time (10 women); includes 5 minority (2 African Americans, 3 Asian Americans or Pacific Islanders), 17 international. Average age 28. 31 applicants, 55% accepted, 8 enrolled. In 2009, 5 master's, 2 doctorates awarded. Terminal master's awarded for partial completion of doctoral program. *Degree requirements:* For master's, project; for doctorate, comprehensive exam, thesis/dissertation, candidacy exam. *Entrance requirements:* For master's, minimum GPA of 3.0 in major, 2.5 overall; for doctorate, GRE General Test, 3 recommendation letters, transcripts, essay. Additional exam requirements/recommendations for international students: Required—TOEFL. *Application deadline:* For fall admission, 6/1 for domestic students, 5/15 for international students; for winter admission, 11/1 for domestic students, 10/1 for international students; for spring admission, 3/1 for domestic students, 2/1 for international students. Applications are processed on a rolling basis. Application fee: $40. Electronic applications accepted. *Expenses:* Tuition, state resident: full-time $8112; part-time $338 per credit. Tuition, nonresident: full-time $20,256; part-time $844 per credit. Required fees: $119 per semester. One-time fee: $50. *Financial support:* In 2009–10, 4 fellowships with full tuition reimbursements (averaging $17,000 per year), 4 research assistantships with full tuition reimbursements (averaging $16,000 per year), 12 teaching assistantships with full tuition reimbursements (averaging $15,000 per year) were awarded; scholarships/grants also available. Financial award application deadline: 2/15; financial award applicants required to submit FAFSA. *Faculty research:* Numerical analysis, integral equations, continuum mechanics. Total annual research expenditures: $506,890. *Unit head:* Dr. Richard Noren, Graduate Program Director, 757-683-3882, Fax: 757-683-3885, E-mail: rnoren@odu.edu. *Application contact:* Dr. Richard Noren, Graduate Program Director, 757-683-3882, Fax: 757-683-3885, E-mail: rnoren@odu.edu.

Oregon State University, Graduate School, College of Science, Department of Mathematics, Corvallis, OR 97331. Offers MA, MAIS, MS, PhD. *Faculty:* 32 full-time (13 women), 3 part-time/adjunct (1 woman). *Students:* 53 full-time (18 women), 3 part-time (1 woman); includes 2 minority (both Asian Americans or Pacific Islanders), 20 international. Average age 28. In 2009, 12 master's, 6 doctorates awarded. Terminal master's awarded for partial completion of doctoral program. *Degree requirements:* For master's, variable foreign language requirement, thesis or alternative; for doctorate, one foreign language, thesis/dissertation, qualifying exams. *Entrance requirements:* For master's and doctorate, minimum GPA of 3.0 in last 90 hours. Additional exam requirements/recommendations for international students: Required—TOEFL. *Application deadline:* For fall admission, 3/1 for domestic students. Applications are processed on a rolling basis. Application fee: $50. *Expenses:* Tuition, state resident: full-time $9774; part-time $362 per credit. Tuition, nonresident: full-time $15,849; part-time $587 per credit. Required fees: $1639. Full-time tuition and fees vary according to course load and program. *Financial support:* Research assistantships, teaching assistantships, Federal Work-Study and institutionally sponsored loans available. Support available to part-time students. Financial award application deadline: 2/1. *Unit head:* Dr. Dennis J. Garity, Chair, 541-737-5138, Fax: 541-737-0517, E-mail: garity@math.orst.edu. *Application contact:* Dr. Mary Ann Matzke, Head Advisor, 541-737-3880, Fax: 541-737-1009, E-mail: maryann.matzke@oregonstate.edu.

Penn State University Park, Graduate School, Eberly College of Science, Department of Mathematics, State College, University Park, PA 16802-1503. Offers mathematics (MA), including applied mathematics. *Unit head:* Dr. John Roe, Head, 814-865-7527, Fax: 814-865-3735, E-mail: roe@math.psu.edu. *Application contact:* Dr. Dimitri Burago, Associate Head of Graduate Studies, 814-865-7741, E-mail: burago@math.psu.edu.

Pittsburg State University, Graduate School, College of Arts and Sciences, Department of Mathematics, Pittsburg, KS 66762. Offers MS. *Degree requirements:* For master's, thesis or alternative. *Expenses:* Tuition, state resident: full-time $4212; part-time $176 per credit. Tuition, nonresident: full-time $11,530; part-time $480 per credit. Required fees: $940; $43 per credit. Tuition and fees vary according to course level, course load, degree level, campus/location, reciprocity agreements and student level. *Faculty research:* Operations research, numerical analysis, applied analysis, applied algebra.

Polytechnic Institute of NYU, Department of Mathematics, Brooklyn, NY 11201-2990. Offers MS, PhD. Part-time and evening/weekend programs available. *Faculty:* 3 full-time (0 women), 1 part-time/adjunct (0 women). *Students:* 10 full-time (3 women), 15 part-time (5 women); includes 6 minority (2 African Americans, 3 Asian Americans or Pacific Islanders, 1 Hispanic American), 10 international. Average age 32. 47 applicants, 64% accepted, 12 enrolled. In 2009, 5 master's awarded. *Degree requirements:* For master's, comprehensive exam (for some programs), thesis (for some programs); for doctorate, comprehensive exam, thesis/dissertation. *Entrance requirements:* Additional exam requirements/recommendations for international students: Required—TOEFL (minimum score 550 paper-based; 213 computer-based; 80 iBT); Recommended—IELTS (minimum score 6.5). *Application deadline:* For fall admission, 7/31 priority date for domestic students, 4/30 priority date for international students; for spring admission, 12/31 priority date for domestic students, 11/30 priority date for international students. Applications are processed on a rolling basis. Application fee: $75. Electronic applications accepted. *Expenses:* Tuition: Full-time $21,492; part-time $1194 per credit hour. Required fees: $1160; $204 per course. *Financial support:* In 2009–10, 5 fellowships (averaging $35,280 per year), 5 teaching assistantships (averaging $47,554 per year) were awarded; research assistantships, institutionally sponsored loans, scholarships/grants, and unspecified assistantships also available. Support available to part-time students. Financial award applicants required to submit FAFSA. Total annual research expenditures: $125,063. *Unit head:* Dr. Erwin Lutwak, Head, 718-260-3366, Fax: 718-260-3139, E-mail: lutwak@magnus.poly.edu. *Application contact:* JeanCarlo Bonilla, Director of Graduate Enrollment Management, 718-260-3182, Fax: 718-260-3624, E-mail: gradinfo@poly.edu.

Portland State University, Graduate Studies, College of Liberal Arts and Sciences, Department of Mathematics and Statistics, Portland, OR 97207-0751. Offers mathematical sciences (PhD); mathematics education (PhD); statistics (MS); MA/MS. *Degree requirements:* For master's, thesis or alternative, exams; for doctorate, 2 foreign languages, thesis/dissertation, exams. *Entrance requirements:* For master's, GRE General Test, GRE Subject Test, minimum GPA of 3.0 in upper-division course work or 2.75 overall; for doctorate, GRE General Test. Additional exam requirements/recommendations for international students: Required—TOEFL (minimum score 550 paper-based; 213 computer-based). *Faculty research:* Algebra, topology, statistical distribution theory, control theory, statistical robustness.

Portland State University, Graduate Studies, Systems Science Program, Portland, OR 97207-0751. Offers computational intelligence (Certificate); computer modeling and simulation (Certificate); systems science (MS); systems science/anthropology (PhD); systems science/business administration (PhD); systems science/civil engineering (PhD); systems science/

Mathematics

Portland State University (continued)
economics (PhD); systems science/engineering management (PhD); systems science/general (PhD); systems science/mathematical sciences (PhD); systems science/mechanical engineering (PhD); systems science/psychology (PhD); systems science/sociology (PhD). *Degree requirements:* For doctorate, variable foreign language requirement, thesis/dissertation. *Entrance requirements:* For master's, 2 letters of recommendation; for doctorate, GMAT, GRE General Test, minimum undergraduate GPA of 3.0. Additional exam requirements/recommendations for international students: Required—TOEFL. *Faculty research:* Systems theory and methodology, artificial intelligence neural networks, information theory, nonlinear dynamics/chaos, modeling and simulation.

Prairie View A&M University, College of Arts and Sciences, Department of Mathematics, Prairie View, TX 77446-0519. Offers MS. Part-time and evening/weekend programs available. *Faculty:* 2 full-time (1 woman). *Students:* 2 full-time (1 woman), 3 part-time (1 woman); includes 4 minority (all African Americans). Average age 40. 3 applicants, 100% accepted, 3 enrolled. In 2009, 2 master's awarded. *Degree requirements:* For master's, comprehensive exam, thesis. *Entrance requirements:* For master's, GRE General Test, bachelor's degree in mathematics. *Application deadline:* Applications are processed on a rolling basis. Application fee: $50. *Expenses:* Tuition, state resident: full-time $2200. Tuition, nonresident: full-time $5600. Required fees: $1720. Tuition and fees vary according to course load. *Financial support:* In 2009–10, 5 students received support, including 2 research assistantships with tuition reimbursements available (averaging $14,400 per year), 1 teaching assistantship with tuition reimbursement available (averaging $14,400 per year); fellowships, career-related internships or fieldwork, Federal Work-Study, and institutionally sponsored loans also available. Support available to part-time students. Financial award application deadline: 4/1; financial award applicants required to submit FAFSA. *Faculty research:* Stochastic processor, queuing theory, waveler numeric analyses, delay systems mathematic modeling. Total annual research expenditures: $43,413. *Unit head:* Dr. Aliakbar Montazer Haghighi, Head, 936-261-1970, Fax: 936-261-2088, E-mail: amhaghighi@pvamu.edu. *Application contact:* Dr. Arona R. Davies, Graduate Advisor, 936-261-1972, Fax: 936-261-2088, E-mail: andavies@pvamu.edu.

Princeton University, Graduate School, Department of Mathematics, Princeton, NJ 08544-1019. Offers PhD. *Degree requirements:* For doctorate, 2 foreign languages, thesis/dissertation. *Entrance requirements:* For doctorate, GRE General Test, GRE Subject Test, 3 letters of recommendation. Additional exam requirements/recommendations for international students: Required—TOEFL (minimum score 600 paper-based; 250 computer-based). Electronic applications accepted.

Purdue University, Graduate School, College of Science, Department of Mathematics, West Lafayette, IN 47907. Offers MS, PhD. Terminal master's awarded for partial completion of doctoral program. *Degree requirements:* For doctorate, one foreign language, thesis/dissertation, oral and written exams. *Entrance requirements:* For master's and doctorate, GRE. Additional exam requirements/recommendations for international students: Required—TOEFL (minimum score 570 paper-based; 230 computer-based). Electronic applications accepted. *Faculty research:* Algebra, analysis, topology, differential equations, applied mathematics.

Purdue University Calumet, Graduate School, School of Engineering, Mathematics, and Science, Department of Mathematics, Computer Science, and Statistics, Hammond, IN 46323-2094. Offers mathematics (MAT, MS). Part-time programs available. *Entrance requirements:* Additional exam requirements/recommendations for international students: Required—TOEFL. *Faculty research:* Topology, analysis, algebra, mathematics education.

Queens College of the City University of New York, Division of Graduate Studies, Mathematics and Natural Sciences Division, Department of Mathematics, Flushing, NY 11367-1597. Offers MA. Part-time and evening/weekend programs available. *Faculty:* 31 full-time (6 women). *Students:* 3 full-time (1 woman), 45 part-time (22 women). 49 applicants, 47% accepted, 16 enrolled. In 2009, 17 master's awarded. *Degree requirements:* For master's, comprehensive exam. *Entrance requirements:* For master's, minimum GPA of 3.0. Additional exam requirements/recommendations for international students: Required—TOEFL. *Application deadline:* For fall admission, 4/1 for domestic students; for spring admission, 11/1 for domestic students. Applications are processed on a rolling basis. Application fee: $125. *Expenses:* Tuition, state resident: full-time $7360; part-time $310 per credit. Tuition, nonresident: part-time $575 per credit. One-time fee: $195.25 full-time; $145.25 part-time. *Financial support:* Career-related internships or fieldwork, Federal Work-Study, institutionally sponsored loans, and tuition waivers (partial) available. Support available to part-time students. Financial award application deadline: 4/1; financial award applicants required to submit FAFSA. *Faculty research:* Topology, differential equations, combinatorics. *Unit head:* Dr. Wallace Goldberg, Chairperson, 718-997-5800, E-mail: wallace_goldberg@qc.edu. *Application contact:* Dr. Nick Metas, Graduate Adviser, 718-997-5800, E-mail: nick_metas@qc.edu.

Queen's University at Kingston, School of Graduate Studies and Research, Faculty of Arts and Sciences, Department of Mathematics and Statistics, Kingston, ON K7L 3N6, Canada. Offers mathematics (M Sc, M Sc Eng, PhD); statistics (M Sc, M Sc Eng, PhD). Part-time programs available. *Degree requirements:* For master's, thesis; for doctorate, comprehensive exam, thesis/dissertation. *Entrance requirements:* Additional exam requirements/recommendations for international students: Required—TOEFL. *Faculty research:* Algebra, analysis, applied mathematics, statistics.

Rensselaer Polytechnic Institute, Graduate School, School of Science, Department of Mathematical Sciences, Program in Mathematics, Troy, NY 12180-3590. Offers MS, PhD. Part-time programs available. *Faculty:* 23 full-time (3 women), 4 part-time/adjunct (1 woman). *Students:* 45 full-time (18 women), 3 part-time (2 women); includes 3 African Americans, 5 Asian Americans or Pacific Islanders, 1 Hispanic American. Average age 22. 87 applicants, 52% accepted, 15 enrolled. In 2009, 9 master's, 7 doctorates awarded. Terminal master's awarded for partial completion of doctoral program. *Degree requirements:* For doctorate, comprehensive exam, thesis/dissertation, preliminary exam, candidacy presentation. *Entrance requirements:* For master's and doctorate, GRE General Test. Additional exam requirements/recommendations for international students: Required—TOEFL. *Application deadline:* For fall admission, 1/15 priority date for domestic students. Applications are processed on a rolling basis. Application fee: $75. Electronic applications accepted. *Expenses:* Tuition: Full-time $38,100. *Financial support:* In 2009–10, 42 students received support, including fellowships with full tuition reimbursements available (averaging $18,000 per year), 5 research assistantships with full tuition reimbursements available (averaging $21,000 per year), 34 teaching assistantships with full tuition reimbursements available (averaging $14,500 per year); institutionally sponsored loans also available. Financial award application deadline: 2/1. *Faculty research:* Inverse problems, biomathematics, operations research, applied mathematics, mathematical modeling. *Unit head:* Dr. Donald A. Drew, Chair, 518-276-6345, Fax: 518-276-4824, E-mail: drewd@rpi.edu. *Application contact:* Dawnmarie Robens, Graduate Student Coordinator, 518-276-6414, Fax: 518-276-4824, E-mail: robensd@rpi.edu.

Rhode Island College, School of Graduate Studies, Faculty of Arts and Sciences, Department of Mathematics and Computer Science, Providence, RI 02908-1991. Offers mathematics (MA). Part-time and evening/weekend programs available. *Faculty:* 2 full-time (0 women). *Students:* 1 (woman) full-time, 4 part-time (1 woman). Average age 29. In 2009, 2 master's awarded. *Degree requirements:* For master's, comprehensive exam. *Entrance requirements:* For master's, GRE General Test or MAT, minimum of 30 hours beyond pre-calculus math, 3 letters of recommendation, interview. Additional exam requirements/recommendations for international students: Recommended—TOEFL (minimum score 550 paper-based; 213 computer-based; 79 iBT). *Application deadline:* For fall admission, 4/1 for domestic students; for spring admission, 11/1 for domestic students. Applications are processed on a rolling basis. Application fee: $50. *Expenses:* Tuition, state resident: full-time $7440; part-time $310 per credit hour. Tuition, nonresident: full-time $14,784; part-time $616 per credit hour. Required fees: $552; $20 per credit. $70 per term. *Financial support:* In 2009–10, 2 teaching assistantships with full tuition reimbursements (averaging $4,550 per year) were awarded; Federal Work-Study, scholarships/grants, health care benefits, and unspecified assistantships also available. Support available to part-time students. Financial award application deadline: 5/15; financial award applicants required to submit FAFSA. *Unit head:* Dr. Raimundo Kovac, Chair, 401-456-8038. *Application contact:* Graduate Studies, 401-456-8700.

Rice University, Graduate Programs, Wiess School of Natural Sciences, Department of Mathematics, Houston, TX 77251-1892. Offers PhD. *Faculty:* 23 full-time (5 women). *Students:* 31 full-time (12 women); includes 6 minority (all Asian Americans or Pacific Islanders), 3 international. 76 applicants, 26% accepted, 6 enrolled. In 2009, 6 degrees awarded. Terminal master's awarded for partial completion of doctoral program. *Median time to degree:* Of those who began their doctoral program in fall 2001, 100% received their degree in 8 years or less. *Degree requirements:* For doctorate, one foreign language, comprehensive exam, thesis/dissertation. *Entrance requirements:* For doctorate, GRE Subject GRE Analytical GRE Math GRE Verbal. Additional exam requirements/recommendations for international students: Required—TOEFL (minimum score 600 paper-based; 90 iBT). *Application deadline:* For fall admission, 2/1 priority date for domestic students, 2/1 for international students. Application fee: $70. Electronic applications accepted. *Financial support:* In 2009–10, 31 students received support, including 23 fellowships (averaging $17,000 per year), 7 research assistantships (averaging $17,000 per year). *Faculty research:* Algebraic geometry/algebra, complex analysis and Teichmuller theory, dynamical systems and Ergodic theory, topology, differential geometry and geometric analysis. *Unit head:* Marie Magee, Department Administrator, 713-348-5714, Fax: 713-348-5231, E-mail: mageemd@rice.edu.

Rivier College, School of Graduate Studies, Department of Computer Science and Mathematics, Nashua, NH 03060. Offers computer science (MS); mathematics (MAT). Part-time and evening/weekend programs available. *Faculty:* 6 full-time (3 women), 4 part-time/adjunct (0 women). *Students:* 2 full-time (both women), 16 part-time (10 women); includes 1 minority (African American). Average age 36. In 2009, 10 master's awarded. *Entrance requirements:* For master's, GRE Subject Test. *Application deadline:* Applications are processed on a rolling basis. Application fee: $25. Electronic applications accepted. *Expenses:* Tuition: Part-time $447 per credit. *Financial support:* Available to part-time students. Application deadline: 2/1; *Unit head:* Dr. Paul Cunningham, Director, 603-897-8272, E-mail: pcunningham@rivier.edu. *Application contact:* Mathew Kittredge, Director of Graduate Admissions, 603-897-8129, Fax: 603-897-8810, E-mail: mkittredge@rivier.edu.

Roosevelt University, Graduate Division, College of Arts and Sciences, Department of Mathematics and Actuarial Science, Program in Mathematics, Chicago, IL 60605. Offers mathematical sciences (MS), including actuarial science. Part-time and evening/weekend programs available. *Faculty research:* Statistics, mathematics education, finite groups, computers in mathematics.

Rowan University, Graduate School, College of Liberal Arts and Sciences, Department of Mathematics, Glassboro, NJ 08028-1701. Offers MA. Part-time and evening/weekend programs available. *Faculty:* 7 full-time (1 woman). *Students:* 3 full-time (0 women), 44 part-time (32 women); includes 9 minority (6 African Americans, 1 Asian American or Pacific Islander, 2 Hispanic Americans). Average age 39. 20 applicants, 100% accepted, 14 enrolled. In 2009, 2 master's awarded. *Degree requirements:* For master's, thesis. *Entrance requirements:* For master's, GRE General Test. Additional exam requirements/recommendations for international students: Required—TOEFL. *Application deadline:* Applications are processed on a rolling basis. Application fee: $50. Electronic applications accepted. *Expenses:* Tuition, state resident: full-time $10,624; part-time $590 per semester hour. Tuition, nonresident: full-time $10,624; part-time $590 per semester hour. Required fees: $2320; $125 per semester hour. *Financial support:* Career-related internships or fieldwork, scholarships/grants, health care benefits, and unspecified assistantships available. Support available to part-time students. *Unit head:* Dr. Mira Lalovic-Hand, Interim Associate Provost/Director of Graduate School, 856-256-5120 Ext. 3888, E-mail: lalovic-hand@rowan.edu. *Application contact:* Karen Haynes, Graduate Coordinator, 856-256-4052, Fax: 856-256-4436, E-mail: haynes@rowan.edu.

Royal Military College of Canada, Division of Graduate Studies and Research, Science Division, Department of Mathematics and Computer Science, Kingston, ON K7K 7B4, Canada. Offers computer science (M Sc); mathematics (M Sc). *Degree requirements:* For master's, thesis. *Entrance requirements:* For master's, honours degree with second-class standing. Electronic applications accepted.

Rutgers, The State University of New Jersey, Camden, Graduate School of Arts and Sciences, Program in Mathematical Sciences, Camden, NJ 08102-1401. Offers mathematics (MS). Part-time and evening/weekend programs available. *Degree requirements:* For master's, comprehensive exam, thesis optional, survey paper. *Entrance requirements:* For master's, GRE, BS/BA in math or related subject, 2 letters of recommendation. Additional exam requirements/recommendations for international students: Required—TOEFL (minimum score 550 paper-based; 213 computer-based), IELTS. Electronic applications accepted. *Faculty research:* Differential geometry, dynamical systems, vertex operator algebra, automorphic forms, CR-structures.

Rutgers, The State University of New Jersey, Newark, Graduate School, Program in Mathematical Sciences, Newark, NJ 07102. Offers PhD. *Degree requirements:* For doctorate, thesis/dissertation, written qualifying exam. *Entrance requirements:* For doctorate, GRE General Test, minimum B average. Additional exam requirements/recommendations for international students: Required—TOEFL. Electronic applications accepted. *Faculty research:* Number theory, automorphic form, low-dimensional topology, Kleinian groups, representation theory.

Rutgers, The State University of New Jersey, New Brunswick, Graduate School-New Brunswick, Department of Mathematics, Piscataway, NJ 08854-8097. Offers applied mathematics (MS, PhD); mathematics (MS, PhD). Part-time programs available. *Degree requirements:* For doctorate, one foreign language, comprehensive exam, thesis/dissertation. *Entrance requirements:* For master's and doctorate, GRE General Test, GRE Subject Test. Additional exam requirements/recommendations for international students: Required—TOEFL. *Faculty research:* Logic and set theory, number theory, mathematical physics, control theory, partial differential equations.

St. Cloud State University, School of Graduate Studies, College of Science and Engineering, Department of Mathematics, St. Cloud, MN 56301-4498. Offers MS. *Faculty:* 19 full-time (5 women). *Students:* 1 part-time (0 women). 10 applicants, 100% accepted, 0 enrolled. *Degree requirements:* For master's, comprehensive exam (for some programs), thesis or alternative. *Entrance requirements:* For master's, GRE General Test, minimum GPA of 2.75. Additional exam requirements/recommendations for international students: Required—Michigan English Language Assessment Battery; Recommended—TOEFL (minimum score 550 paper-based; 213 computer-based), IELTS (minimum score 6.5). *Application deadline:* For fall admission, 6/1 priority date for domestic students, 4/1 for international students; for spring admission, 10/1 priority date for domestic students, 8/1 for international students. Applications are processed on a rolling basis. Application fee: $35. Electronic applications accepted. *Financial support:* Federal Work-Study and unspecified assistantships available. Financial award application deadline: 3/1. *Unit head:* Dr. Daniel Scully, Chairperson, 320-308-3001, E-mail: mathdept@stcloudstate.edu. *Application contact:* Linda Lou Krueger, School of Graduate Studies, 320-308-2113, Fax: 320-308-5371, E-mail: lekrueger@stcloudstate.edu.

St. John's University, St. John's College of Liberal Arts and Sciences, Department of Mathematics and Computer Science, Queens, NY 11439. Offers algebra (MA); analysis (MA);

applied mathematics (MA); computer science (MA); geometry-topology (MA); logic and foundations (MA); probability and statistics (MA). Part-time and evening/weekend programs available. *Students:* 3 full-time (0 women), 2 part-time (1 woman); includes 1 minority (Hispanic American), 1 international. Average age 25. 21 applicants, 67% accepted, 3 enrolled. In 2009, 2 master's awarded. *Degree requirements:* For master's, comprehensive exam, thesis optional. *Entrance requirements:* For master's, minimum GPA of 3.0. Additional exam requirements/recommendations for international students: Required—TOEFL (minimum score 500 paper-based; 173 computer-based; 61 iBT), IELTS (minimum score 5.5). *Application deadline:* For fall admission, 5/1 priority date for domestic and international students; for spring admission, 11/1 priority date for domestic and international students. Applications are processed on a rolling basis. Application fee: $70. Electronic applications accepted. *Expenses:* Tuition: Full-time $16,290; part-time $905 per credit. Required fees: $300; $150 per semester. Tuition and fees vary according to program. *Financial support:* Research assistantships, scholarships/grants available. Support available to part-time students. Financial award application deadline: 3/1; financial award applicants required to submit FAFSA. *Faculty research:* Functional analysis and operator theory, algebraic K-theory, applied mathematics, measure theory, differential geometry and mathematics education. *Unit head:* Dr. Charles Traina, Chair, 718-990-6166, E-mail: trainac@stjohns.edu. *Application contact:* Kathleen Davis, Director of Graduate Admission, 718-990-2790, Fax: 718-990-5686, E-mail: gradhelp@stjohns.edu.

Saint Joseph's University, College of Arts and Sciences, Department of Mathematics and Computer Science, Philadelphia, PA 19131-1395. Offers computer science (MS); mathematics and computer science (Post-Master's Certificate). Part-time and evening/weekend programs available. *Students:* 49 full-time (18 women), 20 part-time (4 women); includes 7 minority (5 African Americans, 2 Asian Americans or Pacific Islanders), 49 international. Average age 25. In 2009, 18 master's awarded. *Entrance requirements:* For master's, 2 letters of recommendation. Additional exam requirements/recommendations for international students: Required—or IELTS. *Application deadline:* For fall admission, 7/15 priority date for domestic students, 4/15 for international students; for winter admission, 4/15 for domestic students, 1/15 for international students; for spring admission, 11/15 priority date for domestic students, 10/15 for international students. Applications are processed on a rolling basis. Application fee: $35. Electronic applications accepted. *Expenses:* Tuition: Part-time $729 per credit hour. Tuition and fees vary according to degree level and program. *Financial support:* Teaching assistantships with partial tuition reimbursements, unspecified assistantships available. Financial award applicants required to submit FAFSA. *Faculty research:* Computer vision, pathways to careers. Total annual research expenditures: $175,000. *Unit head:* Dr. Jonathan Hodgson, Director, Graduate Computer Science, 610-660-1517, Fax: 610-660-3082, E-mail: jhodgson@sju.edu. *Application contact:* Kate McConnell, Director, Graduate College of Arts and Sciences Admissions and Retention, 610-660-3184, Fax: 610-660-3230, E-mail: kate.mcconnell@sju.edu.

Saint Louis University, Graduate School, College of Arts and Sciences and Graduate School, Department of Mathematics and Computer Science, St. Louis, MO 63103-2097. Offers mathematics (MA, MA-R, PhD). Part-time programs available. *Degree requirements:* For master's, comprehensive exam, thesis (for some programs); for doctorate, one foreign language, thesis/dissertation, preliminary exams. *Entrance requirements:* For master's, GRE General Test, letters of recommendation, resume, interview; for doctorate, GRE General Test, letters of recommendation, resumé, interview, transcripts, goal statement. Additional exam requirements/recommendations for international students: Required—TOEFL (minimum score 525 paper-based; 194 computer-based). Electronic applications accepted. *Faculty research:* Algebra, groups and rings, analysis, differential geometry, topology.

Saint Xavier University, Graduate Studies, School of Arts and Sciences, Department of Mathematics and Computer Science, Chicago, IL 60655-3105. Offers applied computer science in Internet information systems (MS); mathematics and computer science (MA); MBA/MS. *Degree requirements:* For master's, thesis optional. *Expenses:* Tuition: Part-time $743 per credit hour. Required fees: $135 per semester.

Salem State College, School of Graduate Studies, Program in Mathematics, Salem, MA 01970-5353. Offers MAT, MS. Part-time and evening/weekend programs available. *Students:* 12 part-time (6 women), 1 international. Average age 32. 7 applicants, 86% accepted, 6 enrolled. In 2009, 6 master's awarded. *Entrance requirements:* For master's, GRE or MAT. Additional exam requirements/recommendations for international students: Required—TOEFL (minimum score 550 paper-based; 80 iBT), or IELTS (minimum score 5.5). *Application deadline:* For fall admission, 5/1 for domestic students; for spring admission, 10/1 for domestic students. Applications are processed on a rolling basis. Application fee: $50. *Expenses:* Tuition, state resident: full-time $2520; part-time $275 per credit hour. Tuition, nonresident: full-time $4140; part-time $365 per credit hour. Required fees: $2430. *Financial support:* In 2009–10, 3 students received support. Career-related internships or fieldwork, Federal Work-Study, scholarships/grants, health care benefits, and unspecified assistantships available. Financial award application deadline: 5/1; financial award applicants required to submit FAFSA. *Unit head:* Julie Belock, Program Coordinator, 978-542-6321, Fax: 978-542-7175, E-mail: jbelock@salemstate.edu. *Application contact:* Dr. Lee A. Brossoit, Assistant Dean of Graduate Admissions, 978-542-6675, Fax: 978-542-7215, E-mail: lbrossoit@salemstate.edu.

Sam Houston State University, College of Arts and Sciences, Department of Mathematics and Statistics, Huntsville, TX 77341. Offers mathematics (MA, MS); statistics (MS). Part-time programs available. *Faculty:* 11 full-time (3 women). *Students:* 19 full-time (10 women), 7 part-time (6 women); includes 1 minority (Asian American or Pacific Islander), 8 international. Average age 30. 24 applicants, 92% accepted, 10 enrolled. In 2009, 8 master's awarded. *Entrance requirements:* For master's, GRE General Test. Additional exam requirements/recommendations for international students: Required—TOEFL (minimum score 550 paper-based; 213 computer-based; 79 iBT). *Application deadline:* For fall admission, 8/1 for domestic and international students; for spring admission, 12/1 for domestic and international students. Applications are processed on a rolling basis. Application fee: $20. *Expenses:* Tuition, state resident: full-time $3690; part-time $205 per credit hour. Tuition, nonresident: full-time $8676; part-time $482 per credit hour. Required fees: $1474. Tuition and fees vary according to course load and campus/location. *Financial support:* Teaching assistantships, institutionally sponsored loans available. Support available to part-time students. Financial award application deadline: 5/31; financial award applicants required to submit FAFSA. *Unit head:* Dr. Mark Klespis, Chair, 936-294-1577, Fax: 936-294-1882, E-mail: klespis@shsu.edu. *Application contact:* Dr. Jianzhong Wang, Advisor, 936-294-3521, Fax: 936-294-1882, E-mail: mth_jxw@shsu.edu.

San Diego State University, Graduate and Research Affairs, College of Sciences, Department of Mathematics and Statistics, San Diego, CA 92182. Offers applied mathematics (MS); mathematics (MA); mathematics and science education (PhD); statistics (MS). Part-time programs available. *Degree requirements:* For doctorate, thesis/dissertation. *Entrance requirements:* For master's, GRE General Test; for doctorate, GRE, minimum GPA of 3.25 in last 30 undergraduate semester units, minimum graduate GPA of 3.5, MSE recommendation form, 3 letters of recommendation. Additional exam requirements/recommendations for international students: Required—TOEFL. Electronic applications accepted. *Faculty research:* Teacher education in mathematics.

San Francisco State University, Division of Graduate Studies, College of Science and Engineering, Department of Mathematics, San Francisco, CA 94132-1722. Offers MA.

San Jose State University, Graduate Studies and Research, College of Science, Department of Mathematics, San Jose, CA 95192-0001. Offers applied mathematics (MS); mathematics (MA, MS); mathematics education (MA); statistics (MA). Part-time and evening/weekend programs available. *Students:* 13 full-time (7 women), 22 part-time (8 women); includes 17 minority (1 African American, 12 Asian Americans or Pacific Islanders, 4 Hispanic Americans), 5 international. Average age 34. 50 applicants, 30% accepted, 10 enrolled. In 2009, 7 master's awarded. *Degree requirements:* For master's, comprehensive exam, thesis (for some programs). *Entrance requirements:* For master's, GRE Subject Test. *Application deadline:* For fall admission, 6/29 for domestic students; for spring admission, 11/30 for domestic students. Applications are processed on a rolling basis. Application fee: $59. Electronic applications accepted. *Financial support:* Teaching assistantships, career-related internships or fieldwork and Federal Work-Study available. Support available to part-time students. Financial award applicants required to submit FAFSA. *Faculty research:* Artificial intelligence, algorithms, numerical analysis, software database, number theory. *Unit head:* Dr. Bradley Jackson, Chair, 408-924-5100, Fax: 408-924-5080. *Application contact:* Prof. Richard Kubelka, Graduate Coordinator, 408-924-5132, E-mail: kubelka@math.sjsu.edu.

Simon Fraser University, Graduate Studies, Faculty of Science, Department of Mathematics, Burnaby, BC V5A 1S6, Canada. Offers applied and computational mathematics (M Sc, PhD); mathematics (M Sc, PhD). *Degree requirements:* For master's, thesis; for doctorate, thesis/dissertation. *Entrance requirements:* For master's, GRE General Test, minimum GPA of 3.0, 3 letters of reference; for doctorate, GRE General Test, minimum GPA of 3.5, 3 letters of reference. Additional exam requirements/recommendations for international students: Required—TWE or IELTS. Electronic applications accepted. *Faculty research:* Semi-groups, number theory, optimization, combinations.

Smith College, Graduate and Special Programs, Center for Women in Mathematics Post-Baccalaureate Program, Northampton, MA 01063. Offers Postbaccalaureate Certificate. Part-time programs available. *Faculty:* 12 full-time (5 women). *Students:* 10 full-time (all women); includes 3 minority (1 African American, 1 Asian American or Pacific Islander, 1 Hispanic American). Average age 26. 17 applicants, 59% accepted, 8 enrolled. In 2009, 7 Postbaccalaureate Certificates awarded. *Entrance requirements:* Additional exam requirements/recommendations for international students: Required—TOEFL. *Application deadline:* For fall admission, 7/1 for domestic students; for spring admission, 12/15 for domestic students. Applications are processed on a rolling basis. Application fee: $60. *Financial support:* In 2009–10, 10 students received support. Scholarships/grants and tuition waivers (full) available. Support available to part-time students. *Unit head:* Ruth Haas, Director, 413-585-3872, E-mail: rhaas@smith.edu. *Application contact:* Jim Henle, Director, 413-585-3867, E-mail: jhenle@smith.edu.

South Dakota State University, Graduate School, College of Engineering, Department of Mathematics and Statistics, Brookings, SD 57007. Offers computational science and statistics (PhD); geospatial science and engineering (PhD); mathematics (MS). Part-time programs available. *Degree requirements:* For master's, thesis (for some programs), oral exam; for doctorate, comprehensive exam, thesis/dissertation, oral and written exams. *Entrance requirements:* Additional exam requirements/recommendations for international students: Required—TOEFL (minimum score 550 paper-based; 213 computer-based; 80 iBT); Recommended—IELTS. *Faculty research:* Mathematics, biostatistics, computational science, numerical linear algebra, statistics, applied quality number theory, abstract algebra.

Southeast Missouri State University, School of Graduate Studies, Department of Mathematics, Cape Girardeau, MO 63701-4799. Offers MNS. Part-time and evening/weekend programs available. *Degree requirements:* For master's, comprehensive exam (for some programs), thesis (for some programs). *Entrance requirements:* For master's, minimum undergraduate GPA of 2.75 in last 30 hours in mathematics and science, major in mathematics or completion of certain courses. Additional exam requirements/recommendations for international students: Required—TOEFL (minimum score 550 paper-based; 213 computer-based); Recommended—IELTS (minimum score 6). Electronic applications accepted. *Expenses:* Tuition, state resident: full-time $4266; part-time $237 per credit hour. Tuition, nonresident: full-time $7506; part-time $417 per credit hour. Required fees: $427; $427. *Faculty research:* Applied mathematics, algebraic geometry, differential equations, mathematics education, statistics.

Southern Connecticut State University, School of Graduate Studies, School of Arts and Sciences, Department of Mathematics, New Haven, CT 06515-1355. Offers MS. Part-time and evening/weekend programs available. *Faculty:* 2 full-time. *Students:* 14 full-time (6 women), 22 part-time (9 women); includes 2 minority (both Hispanic Americans). 24 applicants, 63% accepted, 12 enrolled. In 2009, 4 master's awarded. *Degree requirements:* For master's, thesis or alternative. *Entrance requirements:* For master's, interview. *Application deadline:* For fall admission, 7/15 priority date for domestic students. Applications are processed on a rolling basis. Application fee: $50. Electronic applications accepted. Tuition and fees vary according to program. *Financial support:* Application deadline: 4/15; *Unit head:* Dr. Alain D'Amour, Chairperson, 203-392-5579, Fax: 203-392-6805, E-mail: damoura1@southernct.edu. *Application contact:* Dr. Therese Bennett, Graduate Coordinator, 203-392-6997, Fax: 203-392-6805, E-mail: bennettt1@southernct.edu.

Southern Illinois University Carbondale, Graduate School, College of Science, Department of Mathematics, Carbondale, IL 62901-4701. Offers mathematics (MA, MS, PhD); statistics (MS). Part-time programs available. *Degree requirements:* For master's, thesis; for doctorate, 2 foreign languages, thesis/dissertation. *Entrance requirements:* For master's, minimum GPA of 2.7; for doctorate, minimum GPA of 3.25. Additional exam requirements/recommendations for international students: Required—TOEFL. *Faculty research:* Differential equations, combinatorics, probability, algebra, numerical analysis.

Southern Illinois University Edwardsville, Graduate Studies and Research, College of Arts and Sciences, Department of Mathematics and Statistics, Edwardsville, IL 62026-0001. Offers mathematics (MS). Part-time programs available. *Faculty:* 17 full-time (6 women). *Students:* 9 full-time (4 women), 14 part-time (4 women), 6 international. Average age 26. 32 applicants, 44% accepted. In 2009, 8 master's awarded. *Degree requirements:* For master's, thesis (for some programs), research paper/project. *Entrance requirements:* Additional exam requirements/recommendations for international students: Required—TOEFL (minimum score 550 paper-based; 213 computer-based; 79 iBT), IELTS (minimum score 6.5). *Application deadline:* For fall admission, 7/23 for domestic students, 6/1 for international students; for spring admission, 12/11 for domestic students, 10/1 for international students. Applications are processed on a rolling basis. Application fee: $30. Electronic applications accepted. *Expenses:* Tuition, state resident: part-time $1252.50 per semester. Tuition, nonresident: part-time $3131.25 per semester. Required fees: $586.85 per semester. Tuition and fees vary according to course load. *Financial support:* In 2009–10, 15 teaching assistantships with full tuition reimbursements (averaging $8,064 per year) were awarded; fellowships with full tuition reimbursements, research assistantships with full tuition reimbursements, career-related internships or fieldwork, Federal Work-Study, institutionally sponsored loans, scholarships/grants, traineeships, and unspecified assistantships also available. Support available to part-time students. Financial award application deadline: 3/1; financial award applicants required to submit FAFSA. *Unit head:* Dr. Krzysztof Jarosz, Chair, 618-650-2354, E-mail: kjarosz@siue.edu. *Application contact:* Dr. Adam Weyhaupt, Director, 618-650-2220, E-mail: aweyhau@siue.edu.

Southern Methodist University, Dedman College, Department of Mathematics, Dallas, TX 75275. Offers computational and applied mathematics (MS, PhD). *Faculty:* 17 full-time (2 women). *Students:* 18 full-time (6 women); includes 9 minority (5 Asian Americans or Pacific Islanders, 4 Hispanic Americans). Average age 26. 18 applicants, 44% accepted, 7 enrolled. In 2009, 3 master's, 4 doctorates awarded. *Degree requirements:* For master's, oral and written exams; for doctorate, thesis/dissertation, oral and written exams. *Entrance requirements:* For master's and doctorate, GRE General Test, minimum GPA of 3.0, 18 undergraduate hours in mathematics beyond first and second year calculus. Additional exam requirements/recommendations for international students: Required—TOEFL. *Application deadline:* For fall admission, 2/1 priority date for domestic students, 2/1 for international students; for spring

Mathematics

Southern Methodist University (continued)
admission, 11/30 for domestic students. Applications are processed on a rolling basis. Application fee: $75. Electronic applications accepted. *Financial support:* In 2009–10, 18 students received support, including 6 research assistantships with full tuition reimbursements available (averaging $16,500 per year), 12 teaching assistantships with full tuition reimbursements available (averaging $16,500 per year); career-related internships or fieldwork, scholarships/grants, health care benefits, tuition waivers, and unspecified assistantships also available. Support available to part-time students. Financial award application deadline: 2/1; financial award applicants required to submit FAFSA. *Faculty research:* Numerical analysis, scientific computation, fluid dynamics, software development, differential equations. Total annual research expenditures: $92,000. *Unit head:* Dr. Douglas A. Reinelt, Chairman, 214-768-2506, Fax: 214-768-2355, E-mail: mathchair@mail.smu.edu. *Application contact:* Dr. Thomas W. Carr, Director of Graduate Studies, 214-768-3460, E-mail: math@mail.smu.edu.

Southern University and Agricultural and Mechanical College, Graduate School, College of Sciences, Department of Mathematics, Baton Rouge, LA 70813. Offers MS. *Degree requirements:* For master's, comprehensive exam, thesis optional. *Entrance requirements:* For master's, GMAT, GRE General Test. Additional exam requirements/recommendations for international students: Required—TOEFL. *Faculty research:* Algebraic number theory, abstract algebra, computer analysis, probability, mathematics education.

Stanford University, School of Engineering, Program in Scientific Computing and Computational Mathematics, Stanford, CA 94305-9991. Offers MS, PhD. Terminal master's awarded for partial completion of doctoral program. *Degree requirements:* For doctorate, thesis/dissertation, qualifying exam. *Entrance requirements:* For master's, GRE General Test; for doctorate, GRE General Test, GRE Subject Test. Additional exam requirements/recommendations for international students: Required—TOEFL. Electronic applications accepted. *Expenses:* Tuition: Full-time $37,380; part-time $2760 per quarter. Required fees: $501.

Stanford University, School of Humanities and Sciences, Department of Mathematics, Stanford, CA 94305-9991. Offers financial mathematics (MS); mathematics (MS, PhD). Terminal master's awarded for partial completion of doctoral program. *Degree requirements:* For doctorate, 2 foreign languages, thesis/dissertation, oral exam. *Entrance requirements:* For master's, GRE General Test; for doctorate, GRE General Test, GRE Subject Test. Additional exam requirements/recommendations for international students: Required—TOEFL. Electronic applications accepted. *Expenses:* Tuition: Full-time $37,380; part-time $2760 per quarter. Required fees: $501.

State University of New York at Binghamton, Graduate School, School of Arts and Sciences, Department of Mathematical Sciences, Binghamton, NY 13902-6000. Offers computer science (MA, PhD); probability and statistics (MA, PhD). Part-time programs available. *Faculty:* 24 full-time (4 women), 11 part-time/adjunct (6 women). *Students:* 43 full-time (14 women), 25 part-time (10 women); includes 8 minority (4 African Americans, 1 Asian American or Pacific Islander, 3 Hispanic Americans), 29 international. Average age 27. 79 applicants, 47% accepted, 19 enrolled. In 2009, 8 master's, 3 doctorates awarded. Terminal master's awarded for partial completion of doctoral program. *Degree requirements:* For master's, thesis or alternative; for doctorate, 2 foreign languages, thesis/dissertation. *Entrance requirements:* For master's and doctorate, GRE General Test, GRE Subject Test. Additional exam requirements/recommendations for international students: Required—TOEFL (minimum score 550 paper-based; 213 computer-based; 80 iBT). *Application deadline:* For fall admission, 4/15 priority date for domestic and international students; for spring admission, 11/30 priority date for domestic and international students. Applications are processed on a rolling basis. Application fee: $60. Electronic applications accepted. *Financial support:* In 2009–10, 60 students received support, including 3 fellowships with full tuition reimbursements available (averaging $16,500 per year), 5 research assistantships with full tuition reimbursements available (averaging $16,500 per year), 48 teaching assistantships with full tuition reimbursements available (averaging $16,500 per year); career-related internships or fieldwork, Federal Work-Study, institutionally sponsored loans, scholarships/grants, health care benefits, and unspecified assistantships also available. Financial award application deadline: 2/15; financial award applicants required to submit FAFSA. *Unit head:* Dr. Fernando Guzman, Chairperson, 607-777-2148, E-mail: fer@math.binghamton.edu. *Application contact:* Victoria Williams, Recruiting and Admissions Coordinator, 607-777-2151, Fax: 607-777-2501, E-mail: vwilliam@binghamton.edu.

State University of New York at Fredonia, Graduate Studies, Department of Mathematical Sciences, Fredonia, NY 14063-1136. Offers MS Ed. Part-time and evening/weekend programs available. *Degree requirements:* For master's, thesis optional. *Expenses:* Tuition, state resident: full-time $8370; part-time $349 per credit. Tuition, nonresident: full-time $13,250; part-time $552 per credit. Required fees: $1289; $53.55 per credit.

State University of New York College at Cortland, Graduate Studies, School of Arts and Sciences, Department of Mathematics, Cortland, NY 13045. Offers MAT, MS Ed.

State University of New York College at Potsdam, School of Arts and Sciences, Department of Mathematics, Potsdam, NY 13676. Offers MA. Part-time and evening/weekend programs available. *Faculty:* 6 full-time (2 women). *Students:* 3 full-time (1 woman), 1 (woman) part-time. 5 applicants, 100% accepted, 4 enrolled. In 2009, 6 master's awarded. *Degree requirements:* For master's, comprehensive exam. *Entrance requirements:* For master's, minimum GPA of 3.0 in all undergraduate math courses, 2.75 in last 60 hours of undergraduate coursework. Additional exam requirements/recommendations for international students: Required—TOEFL (minimum score 550 paper-based; 213 computer-based; 80 iBT), IELTS (minimum score 6). *Application deadline:* For fall admission, 4/1 priority date for domestic and international students; for spring admission, 10/15 priority date for domestic and international students. Applications are processed on a rolling basis. Application fee: $50. *Expenses:* Tuition, state resident: full-time $8370; part-time $349 per credit hour. Tuition, nonresident: full-time $13,250; part-time $552 per credit hour. Required fees: $942; $38.70 per credit hour. *Financial support:* In 2009–10, 1 student received support; teaching assistantships with full tuition reimbursements available, Federal Work-Study and unspecified assistantships available. Support available to part-time students. Financial award application deadline: 3/1; financial award applicants required to submit FAFSA. *Unit head:* Dr. Joel Foisy, Chairperson, 315-267-2084, Fax: 315-267-3176, E-mail: foisyjs@potsdam.edu. *Application contact:* Peter Cutler, Graduate Admissions Counselor, 315-267-3154, Fax: 315-267-4802, E-mail: cutlerpj@potsdam.edu.

Stephen F. Austin State University, Graduate School, College of Sciences and Mathematics, Department of Mathematics and Statistics, Nacogdoches, TX 75962. Offers mathematics (MS); mathematics education (MS); statistics (MS). *Degree requirements:* For master's, comprehensive exam, thesis optional. *Entrance requirements:* For master's, GRE General Test, minimum GPA of 2.8 in last 60 hours, 2.5 overall. Additional exam requirements/recommendations for international students: Required—TOEFL. *Faculty research:* Kernel type estimators, fractal mappings, spline curve fitting, robust regression continua theory.

Stevens Institute of Technology, Graduate School, Charles V. Schaefer Jr. School of Engineering, Department of Mathematical Sciences, Program in Mathematics, Hoboken, NJ 07030. Offers MS, PhD. *Degree requirements:* For master's, thesis optional; for doctorate, one foreign language, thesis/dissertation. *Entrance requirements:* For master's and doctorate, GRE. Additional exam requirements/recommendations for international students: Required—TOEFL. Electronic applications accepted. *Expenses:* Tuition: Full-time $9900; part-time $1100 per credit. Required fees: $286 per semester.

Stony Brook University, State University of New York, Graduate School, College of Arts and Sciences, Department of Mathematics, Stony Brook, NY 11794. Offers MA, MAT, PhD. *Faculty:* 26 full-time (4 women), 3 part-time/adjunct (0 women). *Students:* 73 full-time (11 women), 38 part-time (22 women); includes 5 minority (4 Asian Americans or Pacific Islanders, 1 Hispanic American), 40 international. Average age 27. 207 applicants, 31% accepted. In 2009, 23 master's, 11 doctorates awarded. *Degree requirements:* For doctorate, 2 foreign languages, thesis/dissertation. *Entrance requirements:* For master's and doctorate, GRE General Test. Additional exam requirements/recommendations for international students: Required—TOEFL. *Application deadline:* For fall admission, 1/15 for domestic students. Application fee: $60. *Expenses:* Tuition, state resident: full-time $8370; part-time $349 per credit. Tuition, nonresident: full-time $13,250; part-time $552 per credit. Required fees: $933. *Financial support:* In 2009–10, 8 research assistantships, 53 teaching assistantships were awarded; fellowships also available. *Faculty research:* Real analysis, relativity and mathematical physics, complex analysis, topology, combinatorics. Total annual research expenditures: $1 million. *Unit head:* Dr. David Ebin, Chair, 631-632-8290. *Application contact:* Dr. Leon Takhtajan, Director, 631-632-8258, Fax: 631-632-7631, E-mail: leontak@math.sunysb.edu.

Syracuse University, College of Arts and Sciences, Program in Mathematics, Syracuse, NY 13244. Offers MS, PhD. Part-time programs available. *Students:* 47 full-time (15 women), 17 international. Average age 27. 90 applicants, 21% accepted, 16 enrolled. In 2009, 16 master's, 6 doctorates awarded. Terminal master's awarded for partial completion of doctoral program. *Degree requirements:* For doctorate, 2 foreign languages, thesis/dissertation, qualifying exam. *Entrance requirements:* For master's and doctorate, GRE General Test, GRE Subject Test (recommended). Additional exam requirements/recommendations for international students: Required—TOEFL (minimum score 100 iBT). *Application deadline:* For fall admission, 2/28 priority date for domestic and international students. Application fee: $75. Electronic applications accepted. *Expenses:* Tuition: Full-time $26,808; part-time $1117 per credit. Required fees: $1024. *Financial support:* Fellowships with full tuition reimbursements, research assistantships with full tuition reimbursements, teaching assistantships with full and partial tuition reimbursements, tuition waivers (partial) available. Financial award application deadline: 1/1; financial award applicants required to submit FAFSA. *Faculty research:* Pure mathematics, numerical mathematics, computing statistics. *Unit head:* Dr. Mark Kleiner, Associate Chair for Graduate Studies, 315-443-1499, Fax: 315-443-1475. *Application contact:* Dr. Mark Kleiner, Associate Chair for Graduate Studies, 315-443-1499, Fax: 315-443-1475, E-mail: mkleiner@syr.edu.

Tarleton State University, College of Graduate Studies, College of Science and Technology, Department of Mathematics, Stephenville, TX 76402. Offers mathematics (MS). Part-time and evening/weekend programs available. *Degree requirements:* For master's, comprehensive exam, thesis (for some programs). *Entrance requirements:* For master's, GRE General Test, minimum GPA of 3.0. Additional exam requirements/recommendations for international students: Required—TOEFL (minimum score 550 paper-based; 213 computer-based; 80 iBT). Electronic applications accepted.

Temple University, Graduate School, College of Science and Technology, Department of Mathematics, Philadelphia, PA 19122-6096. Offers applied mathematics (MA); mathematics (PhD); pure mathematics (MA). Part-time and evening/weekend programs available. Terminal master's awarded for partial completion of doctoral program. *Degree requirements:* For master's, thesis optional, written exam; for doctorate, 2 foreign languages, thesis/dissertation, oral and written exams. *Entrance requirements:* For master's, GRE General Test, minimum GPA of 3.0; for doctorate, GRE General Test, GRE Subject Test, minimum GPA of 3.0. Additional exam requirements/recommendations for international students: Required—TOEFL (minimum score 550 paper-based; 213 computer-based; 79 iBT). Electronic applications accepted. *Faculty research:* Differential geometry, numerical analysis.

Tennessee State University, The School of Graduate Studies and Research, College of Arts and Sciences, Department of Physics and Mathematics, Nashville, TN 37209-1561. Offers mathematical sciences (MS). *Entrance requirements:* For master's, GRE General Test. Electronic applications accepted.

Tennessee Technological University, Graduate School, College of Arts and Sciences, Department of Mathematics, Cookeville, TN 38505. Offers MS. Part-time programs available. *Faculty:* 17 full-time (4 women). *Students:* 8 full-time (1 woman), 1 (woman) part-time; includes 2 minority (both Asian Americans or Pacific Islanders). Average age 27. 19 applicants, 37% accepted, 5 enrolled. In 2009, 5 master's awarded. *Degree requirements:* For master's, thesis or alternative. *Entrance requirements:* For master's, GRE General Test. Additional exam requirements/recommendations for international students: Required—TOEFL (minimum score 550 paper-based; 79 iBT), IELTS (minimum score 5.5). *Application deadline:* For fall admission, 8/1 for domestic students, 5/1 for international students; for spring admission, 12/1 for domestic students, 10/1 for international students. Application fee: $25 ($30 for international students). Electronic applications accepted. *Expenses:* Tuition, state resident: full-time $7034; part-time $368 per credit hour. *Financial support:* In 2009–10, 3 research assistantships (averaging $7,500 per year), 7 teaching assistantships (averaging $7,500 per year) were awarded. Financial award application deadline: 4/1. *Unit head:* Dr. Allan Mills, Interim Chairperson, 931-372-3441, Fax: 931-372-6353. *Application contact:* Shelia K. Kendrick, Coordinator of Graduate Studies, 931-372-3808, Fax: 931-372-3497, E-mail: skendrick@tntech.edu.

Texas A&M International University, Office of Graduate Studies and Research, College of Arts and Sciences, Department of Mathematical and Physical Science, Laredo, TX 78041-1900. Offers MA. *Faculty:* 3 full-time (0 women). *Students:* 2 full-time (0 women), 9 part-time (2 women); includes 9 minority (all Hispanic Americans), 1 international. Average age 31. 9 applicants, 56% accepted, 4 enrolled. In 2009, 1 master's awarded. *Entrance requirements:* For master's, GRE General Test. Additional exam requirements/recommendations for international students: Required—TOEFL (minimum score 550 paper-based; 213 computer-based). *Application deadline:* For fall admission, 4/30 priority date for domestic students; for spring admission, 11/30 for domestic students. Applications are processed on a rolling basis. Application fee: $25. *Financial support:* In 2009–10, 1 student received support. Application deadline: 11/1. *Unit head:* Dr. Hoonandara Goonatilake, Interim Chair, 956-326-2588, E-mail: rbachnak@tamiu.edu. *Application contact:* Rosie Espinoza-Dickinson, Director of Admissions, 956-326-2200, Fax: 956-326-2199, E-mail: enroll@tamiu.edu.

Texas A&M University, College of Science, Department of Mathematics, College Station, TX 77843. Offers MS, PhD. Part-time programs available. Postbaccalaureate distance learning degree programs offered (minimal on-campus study). *Faculty:* 49. *Students:* 114 full-time (37 women), 20 part-time (9 women); includes 11 minority (1 African American, 5 Asian Americans or Pacific Islanders, 5 Hispanic Americans), 69 international. Average age 27. In 2009, 24 master's, 15 doctorates awarded. Terminal master's awarded for partial completion of doctoral program. *Degree requirements:* For master's, comprehensive exam, thesis optional; for doctorate, one foreign language, comprehensive exam, thesis/dissertation. *Entrance requirements:* For master's and doctorate, GRE General Test. Additional exam requirements/recommendations for international students: Required—TOEFL (minimum score 550 paper-based; 213 computer-based). *Application deadline:* For fall admission, 3/1 for domestic and international students; for spring admission, 8/1 for domestic and international students. Applications are processed on a rolling basis. Application fee: $50 ($75 for international students). Electronic applications accepted. *Expenses:* Tuition, state resident: full-time $3991.32; part-time $221.74 per credit hour. Tuition, nonresident: full-time $9049; part-time $502.74 per credit hour. *Financial support:* In 2009–10, fellowships with partial tuition reimbursements (averaging $17,850 per year), research assistantships with partial tuition reimbursements (averaging $17,850 per year), teaching assistantships with partial tuition reimbursements (averaging $17,850 per year) were awarded; career-related internships or fieldwork, institutionally sponsored loans, scholarships/grants, and unspecified assistantships also available. Financial award application deadline: 3/1; financial award applicants required to submit FAFSA. *Faculty research:* Functional analysis, numerical analysis, algebra, geometry/topology, applied mathematics. *Unit head:* Dr. Albert Boggess, Head, 979-845-3261, Fax: 979-845-6028, E-mail: mathdept@tamu.edu. *Application contact:* Monique Stewart, Academic Advisor I, 979-862-4137, Fax: 979-862-4190, E-mail: gstudies@math.tamu.edu.

Texas A&M University–Commerce, Graduate School, College of Arts and Sciences, Department of Mathematics, Commerce, TX 75429-3011. Offers MA, MS. Part-time programs available. *Degree requirements:* For master's, comprehensive exam, thesis (for some programs). *Entrance requirements:* For master's, GRE General Test. Electronic applications accepted.

Texas A&M University–Corpus Christi, Graduate Studies and Research, College of Science and Technology, Program in Mathematics, Corpus Christi, TX 78412-5503. Offers applied and computational mathematics (MS); curriculum content (MS). Part-time programs available. *Degree requirements:* For master's, thesis (for some programs). *Entrance requirements:* For master's, 2 letters of recommendation.

Texas A&M University–Kingsville, College of Graduate Studies, College of Arts and Sciences, Department of Mathematics, Kingsville, TX 78363. Offers MS. Part-time programs available. *Degree requirements:* For master's, comprehensive exam, thesis or alternative. *Entrance requirements:* For master's, GRE General Test. Additional exam requirements/recommendations for international students: Required—TOEFL. *Faculty research:* Complex analysis, multivariate analysis, algebra, numerical analysis, applied statistics.

Texas Christian University, College of Science and Engineering, Department of Mathematics, Fort Worth, TX 76129-0002. Offers MAT, MS, PhD. Part-time and evening/weekend programs available. *Faculty:* 12 full-time (2 women). In 2009, 4 master's awarded. Terminal master's awarded for partial completion of doctoral program. *Degree requirements:* For master's, thesis optional; for doctorate, comprehensive exam, thesis/dissertation, 72 hours of full-time graduate study with minimum GPA of 2.75. *Entrance requirements:* For master's and doctorate, GRE, 24 hours of math, including courses in elementary calculus of one and several variables, linear algebra, abstract algebra and real analysis. Additional exam requirements/recommendations for international students: Required—TOEFL. *Application deadline:* For fall admission, 3/1 for domestic and international students; for spring admission, 12/1 for domestic and international students. Applications are processed on a rolling basis. Application fee: $50. Electronic applications accepted. *Expenses:* Tuition: Full-time $17,640; part-time $980 per credit hour. Tuition and fees vary according to program. *Financial support:* In 2009–10, 7 students received support, including 2 teaching assistantships (averaging $10,000 per year); tuition waivers also available. Financial award application deadline: 3/1. *Faculty research:* Topology, analysis, number theory. *Unit head:* Dr. Bob Doran, Chairperson, 817-257-7335, E-mail: r.doran@tcu.edu. *Application contact:* Dr. Bob Doran, Chairperson, 817-257-7335, E-mail: r.doran@tcu.edu.

Texas Southern University, School of Science and Technology, Department of Mathematics, Houston, TX 77004-4584. Offers MS. Part-time and evening/weekend programs available. *Faculty:* 6 full-time (1 woman), 1 part-time/adjunct (0 women). *Students:* 1 full-time (0 women), 11 part-time (6 women); includes 11 minority (9 African Americans, 2 Asian Americans or Pacific Islanders). Average age 33. 5 applicants, 100% accepted, 4 enrolled. In 2009, 1 master's awarded. *Degree requirements:* For master's, comprehensive exam, thesis. *Entrance requirements:* For master's, GRE General Test, minimum GPA of 2.5. Additional exam requirements/recommendations for international students: Required—TOEFL. *Application deadline:* For fall admission, 7/1 for domestic and international students; for spring admission, 11/1 for domestic and international students. Applications are processed on a rolling basis. Application fee: $50 ($75 for international students). Electronic applications accepted. *Expenses:* Tuition, state resident: full-time $1805; part-time $100 per credit hour. Tuition, nonresident: full-time $6470; part-time $343 per credit hour. Tuition and fees vary according to course level, course load and degree level. *Financial support:* In 2009–10, 1 research assistantship (averaging $6,000 per year), 4 teaching assistantships (averaging $7,492 per year) were awarded; fellowships, scholarships/grants and unspecified assistantships also available. Financial award application deadline: 5/1. *Faculty research:* Statistics, number theory, topology, differential equations, numerical analysis. *Unit head:* Dr. Della Bell, Chair, 713-313-7839, E-mail: bell_d@tsu.edu. *Application contact:* Ami Bush, Secretary, 713-313-7002, E-mail: bushar@tsu.edu.

Texas State University–San Marcos, Graduate School, College of Science, Department of Mathematics, San Marcos, TX 78666. Offers industrial mathematics (MS); mathematics (MS); mathematics education (PhD); middle school mathematics teaching (M Ed). Part-time programs available. *Faculty:* 18 full-time (6 women), 1 part-time/adjunct (0 women). *Students:* 33 full-time (18 women), 39 part-time (25 women); includes 19 minority (5 African Americans, 1 American Indian/Alaska Native, 4 Asian Americans or Pacific Islanders, 9 Hispanic Americans), 2 international. Average age 35. 28 applicants, 79% accepted, 18 enrolled. In 2009, 17 master's awarded. *Degree requirements:* For master's, comprehensive exam, thesis (for some programs). *Entrance requirements:* For master's, GRE General Test, minimum GPA of 2.75 in last 60 hours of course work. Additional exam requirements/recommendations for international students: Required—TOEFL (minimum score 550 paper-based; 213 computer-based). *Application deadline:* For fall admission, 6/15 priority date for domestic students, 6/1 priority date for international students; for spring admission, 10/15 priority date for domestic students, 10/1 priority date for international students. Applications are processed on a rolling basis. Application fee: $40 ($90 for international students). Electronic applications accepted. *Expenses:* Tuition, state resident: full-time $5784; part-time $241 per credit hour. Tuition, nonresident: part-time $551 per credit hour. Required fees: $1728; $48 per credit hour. $306. Tuition and fees vary according to course load. *Financial support:* In 2009–10, 59 students received support, including 4 research assistantships (averaging $9,389 per year), 24 teaching assistantships (averaging $10,296 per year); Federal Work-Study and institutionally sponsored loans also available. Support available to part-time students. Financial award application deadline: 4/1; financial award applicants required to submit FAFSA. *Faculty research:* Differential equations, geometric topology, number theory, mathematics education, graph theory. Total annual research expenditures: $330,689. *Unit head:* Dr. Stanley G. Wayment, Chair, 512-245-3555, Fax: 512-245-3425, E-mail: sw05@txstate.edu. *Application contact:* Dr. Gregory Passty, Graduate Adviser, 512-245-3446, Fax: 512-245-3425, E-mail: passty@txstate.edu.

Texas Tech University, Graduate School, College of Arts and Sciences, Department of Mathematics and Statistics, Lubbock, TX 79409. Offers mathematics (MA, MS, PhD); statistics (MS). Part-time programs available. *Faculty:* 35 full-time (5 women). *Students:* 101 full-time (42 women), 18 part-time (7 women); includes 7 minority (1 African American, 1 Asian American or Pacific Islander, 5 Hispanic Americans), 64 international. Average age 28. 123 applicants, 80% accepted, 27 enrolled. In 2009, 14 master's, 6 doctorates awarded. *Degree requirements:* For master's, thesis or alternative; for doctorate, one foreign language, thesis/dissertation. *Entrance requirements:* For master's and doctorate, GRE General Test. Additional exam requirements/recommendations for international students: Required—TOEFL (minimum score 550 paper-based; 213 computer-based). *Application deadline:* For fall admission, 3/1 priority date for international students; for spring admission, 11/1 priority date for international students. Applications are processed on a rolling basis. Application fee: $50 ($75 for international students). Electronic applications accepted. *Expenses:* Tuition, state resident: full-time $5100; part-time $213 per credit hour. Tuition, nonresident: full-time $11,748; part-time $490 per credit hour. Required fees: $2298; $50 per credit hour. $555 per semester. *Financial support:* In 2009–10, 1 research assistantship with partial tuition reimbursement (averaging $56,250 per year), 12 teaching assistantships with partial tuition reimbursements (averaging $15,097 per year) were awarded; fellowships, Federal Work-Study and institutionally sponsored loans also available. Support available to part-time students. Financial award application deadline: 4/15; financial award applicants required to submit FAFSA. *Faculty research:* Numerical analysis, mathematical biology, complex analysis, algebra and geometry; ordinary and partial differential equations. Total annual research expenditures: $910,237. *Unit head:* Dr. Kent Pearce, Chair, 806-742-2566, Fax: 806-742-1112, E-mail: kent.pearce@ttu.edu. *Application contact:* Dr. Ram Iyer, Graduate Adviser, 806-742-2566, Fax: 806-742-1112, E-mail: ram.iyer@ttu.edu.

Texas Woman's University, Graduate School, College of Arts and Sciences, Department of Mathematics and Computer Science, Denton, TX 76201. Offers mathematics (MA, MS); mathematics teaching (MS). Part-time and evening/weekend programs available. *Faculty:* 10 full-time (7 women), 3 part-time/adjunct (2 women). *Students:* 9 full-time (6 women), 20 part-time (17 women); includes 9 minority (1 African American, 4 Asian Americans or Pacific Islanders, 4 Hispanic Americans), 2 international. Average age 37. 19 applicants, 89% accepted, 8 enrolled. In 2009, 9 master's awarded. *Degree requirements:* For master's, comprehensive exam, thesis (for some programs). *Entrance requirements:* For master's, 2 letters of reference. Additional exam requirements/recommendations for international students: Required—TOEFL (minimum score 550 paper-based; 213 computer-based; 79 iBT). *Application deadline:* For fall admission, 7/1 priority date for domestic students, 3/1 for international students; for spring admission, 12/1 priority date for domestic students, 7/1 for international students. Applications are processed on a rolling basis. Application fee: $50. Electronic applications accepted. *Expenses:* Tuition, state resident: full-time $3564; part-time $198 per credit hour. Tuition, nonresident: full-time $8550; part-time $475 per credit hour. Required fees: $69.26 per credit hour. Tuition and fees vary according to course load. *Financial support:* In 2009–10, 4 students received support, including 7 research assistantships (averaging $10,440 per year), 3 teaching assistantships (averaging $10,440 per year); career-related internships or fieldwork, Federal Work-Study, institutionally sponsored loans, scholarships/grants, traineeships, health care benefits, and unspecified assistantships also available. Support available to part-time students. Financial award application deadline: 3/1; financial award applicants required to submit FAFSA. *Faculty research:* Biopharmaceutical statistics, dynamic systems and control theory, Bayesian inference, math and computer science curriculum innovation, computer modeling of physical phenomenon. *Unit head:* Dr. Don E. Edwards, Chair, 940-898-2166, Fax: 940-898-2179, E-mail: mathcs@twu.edu. *Application contact:* Samuel Wheeler, Assistant Director of Admissions, 940-898-3188, Fax: 940-898-3081, E-mail: wheelersr@twu.edu.

Tufts University, Graduate School of Arts and Sciences, Department of Mathematics, Medford, MA 02155. Offers MA, MS, PhD. *Faculty:* 20 full-time, 5 part-time/adjunct. *Students:* 27 full-time (10 women); includes 1 minority (Asian American or Pacific Islander), 8 international. Average age 27. 66 applicants, 33% accepted, 9 enrolled. In 2009, 5 master's, 4 doctorates awarded. Terminal master's awarded for partial completion of doctoral program. *Degree requirements:* For master's, one foreign language, thesis; for doctorate, 2 foreign languages, thesis/dissertation. *Entrance requirements:* For master's, GRE General Test; for doctorate, GRE General Test, GRE Subject Tests. Additional exam requirements/recommendations for international students: Required—TOEFL (minimum score 550 paper-based; 213 computer-based; 80 iBT). *Application deadline:* For fall admission, 1/15 for domestic students, 12/15 for international students. Applications are processed on a rolling basis. Application fee: $75. Electronic applications accepted. *Expenses:* Tuition: Full-time $38,096; part-time $3962 per credit. Required fees: $686; $40 per year. Tuition and fees vary according to course level, course load, degree level, program and student level. *Financial support:* Fellowships, research assistantships, teaching assistantships with full tuition reimbursements, Federal Work-Study, scholarships/grants, tuition waivers (partial), and unspecified assistantships available. Financial award application deadline: 1/15; financial award applicants required to submit FAFSA. *Unit head:* Bruce Boghosian, Chair, 617-627-3234, E-mail: mathgrad@tufts.edu. *Application contact:* Zbigniew Nitecki, Graduate Advisor, 617-627-3234, E-mail: mathgrad@tufts.edu.

Tulane University, School of Science and Engineering, Department of Mathematics, New Orleans, LA 70118-5669. Offers applied mathematics (MS); mathematics (MS, PhD); statistics (MS). *Degree requirements:* For master's, thesis (for some programs); for doctorate, thesis/dissertation. *Entrance requirements:* For master's, GRE General Test, minimum B average in undergraduate course work; for doctorate, GRE General Test. Additional exam requirements/recommendations for international students: Required—TOEFL. Electronic applications accepted.

Université de Moncton, Faculty of Science, Department of Mathematics and Statistics, Moncton, NB E1A 3E9, Canada. Offers mathematics (M Sc). *Degree requirements:* For master's, one foreign language, thesis. *Entrance requirements:* For master's, minimum GPA of 3.0. Electronic applications accepted. *Faculty research:* Statistics, numerical analysis, fixed point theory, mathematical physics.

Université de Montréal, Faculty of Arts and Sciences, Department of Mathematics and Statistics, Montréal, QC H3C 3J7, Canada. Offers mathematics (M Sc, PhD); statistics (M Sc, PhD). *Degree requirements:* For master's, thesis; for doctorate, thesis/dissertation, general exam. *Entrance requirements:* For master's and doctorate, proficiency in French. Electronic applications accepted. *Faculty research:* Pure and applied mathematics, actuarial mathematics.

Université de Sherbrooke, Faculty of Sciences, Department of Mathematics, Sherbrooke, QC J1K 2R1, Canada. Offers M Sc, PhD. *Degree requirements:* For master's, thesis; for doctorate, comprehensive exam, thesis/dissertation. *Entrance requirements:* For doctorate, master's degree. Electronic applications accepted. *Faculty research:* Measure theory, differential equations, probability, statistics, error control codes.

Université du Québec à Montréal, Graduate Programs, Program in Mathematics, Montréal, QC H3C 3P8, Canada. Offers M Sc, PhD. Part-time programs available. *Degree requirements:* For master's, thesis; for doctorate, thesis/dissertation. *Entrance requirements:* For master's, appropriate bachelor's degree or equivalent, proficiency in French; for doctorate, appropriate master's degree or equivalent, proficiency in French.

Université du Québec à Trois-Rivières, Graduate Programs, Program in Mathematics and Computer Science, Trois-Rivières, QC G9A 5H7, Canada. Offers M Sc. *Faculty research:* Probability, statistics.

Université Laval, Faculty of Sciences and Engineering, Department of Mathematics and Statistics, Programs in Mathematics, Québec, QC G1K 7P4, Canada. Offers M Sc, PhD. Terminal master's awarded for partial completion of doctoral program. *Degree requirements:* For master's, thesis (for some programs); for doctorate, comprehensive exam, thesis/dissertation. *Entrance requirements:* For master's and doctorate, knowledge of French and English. Electronic applications accepted.

University at Albany, State University of New York, College of Arts and Sciences, Department of Mathematics and Statistics, Albany, NY 12222-0001. Offers mathematics (PhD); secondary teaching (MA); statistics (MA). *Degree requirements:* For doctorate, one foreign language, thesis/dissertation. *Entrance requirements:* For doctorate, GRE General Test. Additional exam requirements/recommendations for international students: Required—TOEFL (minimum score 550 paper-based; 213 computer-based). Electronic applications accepted.

University at Buffalo, the State University of New York, Graduate School, College of Arts and Sciences, Department of Mathematics, Buffalo, NY 14260. Offers MA, PhD. *Faculty:* 36 full-time (4 women), 18 part-time/adjunct (3 women). *Students:* 74 full-time (25 women), 5 part-time (0 women); includes 30 minority (29 Asian Americans or Pacific Islanders, 1 Hispanic American), 2 international. Average age 29. 98 applicants, 59% accepted, 23 enrolled. In 2009, 16 master's, 6 doctorates awarded. Terminal master's awarded for partial completion of doctoral program. *Degree requirements:* For master's, comprehensive exam (for some programs), thesis (for some programs), Project-S; for doctorate, comprehensive exam, thesis/dissertation. *Entrance requirements:* Additional exam requirements/recommendations for international students: Required—TOEFL (minimum score 550 paper-based; 213 computer-based;

Mathematics

University at Buffalo, the State University of New York (continued)

79 iBT). *Application deadline:* For fall admission, 1/15 priority date for domestic and international students; for spring admission, 9/15 priority date for domestic and international students. Applications are processed on a rolling basis. Application fee: $50. Electronic applications accepted. *Financial support:* In 2009–10, 33 students received support, including fellowships with full tuition reimbursements available (averaging $4,000 per year), 50 teaching assistantships with full tuition reimbursements available (averaging $16,188 per year); research assistantships, Federal Work-Study, institutionally sponsored loans, and unspecified assistantships also available. Financial award application deadline: 1/15; financial award applicants required to submit FAFSA. *Faculty research:* Algebra, analysis, applied mathematics, logic, number theory, topology. Total annual research expenditures: $154,500. *Unit head:* Dr. Brian D. Hassard, Chairman, 716-645-6284 Ext. 103, Fax: 716-645-5039, E-mail: chair@math.buffalo.edu. *Application contact:* Dr. Clifford Bloom, Director of Graduate Studies, 716-645-6284 Ext. 109, Fax: 716-645-5039, E-mail: graduatedirector@math.buffalo.edu.

The University of Akron, Graduate School, Buchtel College of Arts and Sciences, Department of Theoretical and Applied Mathematics, Program in Mathematics, Akron, OH 44325. Offers MS. Part-time and evening/weekend programs available. *Students:* 8 full-time (3 women), 5 part-time (2 women), 1 international. Average age 34. 8 applicants, 50% accepted, 2 enrolled. In 2009, 4 master's awarded. *Degree requirements:* For master's, seminar and comprehensive exam or thesis. *Entrance requirements:* For master's, minimum GPA of 2.75, letters of recommendation. Additional exam requirements/recommendations for international students: Required—TOEFL (minimum score 550 paper-based; 213 computer-based; 79 iBT). *Application deadline:* Applications are processed on a rolling basis. Application fee: $30 ($40 for international students). Electronic applications accepted. *Expenses:* Tuition, state resident: full-time $6570; part-time $365 per credit hour. Tuition, nonresident: full-time $11,250; part-time $625 per credit hour. *Unit head:* Dr. Gerald Young, Coordinator, 330-972-5731, E-mail: gwyoung@uakron.edu. *Application contact:* Associate Dean.

The University of Alabama, Graduate School, College of Arts and Sciences, Department of Mathematics, Tuscaloosa, AL 35487. Offers applied mathematics (PhD); mathematics (MA, PhD); pure mathematics (PhD). *Faculty:* 23 full-time (1 woman). *Students:* 32 full-time (11 women), 10 part-time (2 women); includes 2 minority (both African Americans), 27 international. Average age 29. 34 applicants, 47% accepted, 12 enrolled. In 2009, 8 master's, 7 doctorates awarded. Terminal master's awarded for partial completion of doctoral program. *Median time to degree:* Of those who began their doctoral program in fall 2001, 85% received their degree in 8 years or less. *Degree requirements:* For master's, thesis or alternative; for doctorate, thesis/dissertation. *Entrance requirements:* For master's and doctorate, GRE General Test, minimum GPA of 3.0. Additional exam requirements/recommendations for international students: Required—TOEFL (minimum score 550 paper-based; 79 iBT). *Application deadline:* For fall admission, 7/1 for domestic students, 5/31 for international students; for spring admission, 11/30 for domestic students, 10/31 for international students. Applications are processed on a rolling basis. Application fee: $50 ($60 for international students). Electronic applications accepted. *Expenses:* Tuition, state resident: full-time $7000. Tuition, nonresident: full-time $19,200. *Financial support:* In 2009–10, 1 fellowship with full tuition reimbursement (averaging $30,000 per year), 35 teaching assistantships with full tuition reimbursements (averaging $12,258 per year) were awarded; research assistantships with full tuition reimbursements, Federal Work-Study, institutionally sponsored loans, scholarships/grants, and unspecified assistantships also available. Support available to part-time students. Financial award application deadline: 7/1. *Faculty research:* Analysis, topology, algebra, fluid mechanics and system control theory, optimization, stochastic processes, numerical analysis. Total annual research expenditures: $25,303. *Unit head:* Dr. Zhijian Wu, Chairperson and Professor, 205-348-5080, Fax: 205-348-7067, E-mail: zwu@as.ua.edu. *Application contact:* Dr. Vo Liem, Director, 205-348-4898, Fax: 205-348-7067, E-mail: vliem@as.ua.edu.

The University of Alabama at Birmingham, College of Arts and Sciences, Program in Mathematics, Birmingham, AL 35294. Offers MS. Terminal master's awarded for partial completion of doctoral program. *Degree requirements:* For master's, thesis optional. *Entrance requirements:* For master's, GRE General Test. Electronic applications accepted. *Faculty research:* Differential equations, topology, mathematical physics, dynamic systems.

The University of Alabama in Huntsville, School of Graduate Studies, College of Science, Department of Mathematical Sciences, Huntsville, AL 35899. Offers applied mathematics (PhD); mathematics (MA, MS). Part-time and evening/weekend programs available. *Faculty:* 13 full-time (0 women). *Students:* 19 full-time (9 women), 15 part-time (6 women); includes 6 minority (4 African Americans, 2 Asian Americans or Pacific Islanders), 6 international. Average age 30. 38 applicants, 55% accepted, 12 enrolled. In 2009, 4 master's, 2 doctorates awarded. *Degree requirements:* For master's, comprehensive exam, thesis or alternative, oral and written exams; for doctorate, comprehensive exam, thesis/dissertation, oral and written exams. *Entrance requirements:* For master's and doctorate, GRE General Test, minimum GPA of 3.0. Additional exam requirements/recommendations for international students: Required—TOEFL (minimum score 550 paper-based; 213 computer-based; 62 iBT). *Application deadline:* For fall admission, 7/15 for domestic students, 4/1 for international students; for spring admission, 11/30 for domestic students, 9/1 for international students. Applications are processed on a rolling basis. Application fee: $40 ($50 for international students). Electronic applications accepted. *Expenses:* Tuition, state resident: part-time $355.75 per credit hour. Tuition, nonresident: part-time $847.10 per credit hour. Required fees: $210.80 per semester. Tuition and fees vary according to course load and program. *Financial support:* In 2009–10, 16 students received support, including 16 teaching assistantships with full and partial tuition reimbursements available (averaging $10,793 per year); career-related internships or fieldwork, Federal Work-Study, institutionally sponsored loans, scholarships/grants, health care benefits, and unspecified assistantships also available. Support available to part-time students. Financial award application deadline: 4/1; financial award applicants required to submit FAFSA. *Faculty research:* Dynamical systems, mathematical biology, stochastic processes, numerical analysis, combinatorics. Total annual research expenditures: $290,027. *Unit head:* Dr. Jia Li, Chair, 256-824-6470, Fax: 256-824-6173, E-mail: li@math.uah.edu. *Application contact:* Kathy Biggs, Graduate Studies Admissions Manager, 256-824-6199, Fax: 256-824-6405, E-mail: deangrad@uah.edu.

University of Alaska Fairbanks, College of Natural Sciences and Mathematics, Department of Mathematics and Statistics, Fairbanks, AK 99775-6660. Offers mathematics (MAT, PhD); statistics (MS). Part-time programs available. *Faculty:* 15 full-time (5 women), 3 part-time/adjunct (0 women). *Students:* 10 full-time (3 women), 6 part-time (all women); includes 2 minority (both Asian Americans or Pacific Islanders), 2 international. Average age 31. 16 applicants, 50% accepted, 5 enrolled. In 2009, 4 master's, 4 doctorates awarded. Terminal master's awarded for partial completion of doctoral program. *Degree requirements:* For master's, comprehensive exam, thesis or alternative; for doctorate, comprehensive exam, thesis/dissertation, oral defense. *Entrance requirements:* Additional exam requirements/recommendations for international students: Required—TOEFL (minimum score 550 paper-based; 213 computer-based; 80 iBT). *Application deadline:* For fall admission, 6/1 for domestic students, 3/1 for international students; for spring admission, 10/15 for domestic students, 9/1 for international students. Applications are processed on a rolling basis. Application fee: $60. Electronic applications accepted. *Expenses:* Tuition, state resident: full-time $7584; part-time $316 per credit. Tuition, nonresident: full-time $15,504; part-time $646 per credit. Required fees: $23 per credit. $135 per semester. Tuition and fees vary according to course level, course load and reciprocity agreements. *Financial support:* In 2009–10, 1 fellowship (averaging $15,284 per year), 3 research assistantships (averaging $12,497 per year), 10 teaching assistantships (averaging $12,723 per year) were awarded; career-related internships or fieldwork, Federal Work-Study, scholarships/grants, health care benefits, and unspecified assistantships also available. Support available to part-time students. Financial award application deadline: 2/15; financial award applicants required to submit FAFSA. *Faculty research:* Kriging, arrangements of hyperplanes, bifurcation analysis of time-periodic differential-delay equations, inverse problems, phylogenic tree construction. *Unit head:* Dr. John Rhodes, Department Chair, 907-474-7332, Fax: 907-474-5394, E-mail: fymath@uaf.edu. *Application contact:* Dr. John Rhodes, Department Chair, 907-474-7332, Fax: 907-474-5394, E-mail: fymath@uaf.edu.

University of Alberta, Faculty of Graduate Studies and Research, Department of Mathematical and Statistical Sciences, Edmonton, AB T6G 2E1, Canada. Offers applied mathematics (M Sc, PhD); biostatistics (M Sc); mathematical finance (M Sc, PhD); mathematical physics (M Sc, PhD); mathematics (M Sc, PhD); statistics (M Sc, PhD, Postgraduate Diploma). Part-time programs available. *Faculty:* 48 full-time (4 women). *Students:* 112 full-time (41 women), 5 part-time (0 women). Average age 24. 776 applicants, 5% accepted, 34 enrolled. In 2009, 12 master's, 10 doctorates awarded. Terminal master's awarded for partial completion of doctoral program. *Degree requirements:* For master's, thesis (for some programs); for doctorate, comprehensive exam, thesis/dissertation. *Entrance requirements:* Additional exam requirements/recommendations for international students: Required—TOEFL (minimum score 580 paper-based; 237 computer-based). *Application deadline:* For fall admission, 3/1 for domestic students, 2/1 for international students. Applications are processed on a rolling basis. Application fee: $0. Electronic applications accepted. Tuition and fees charges are reported in Canadian dollars. *Expenses:* Tuition, area resident: Full-time $4626.24 Canadian dollars; part-time $99.72 Canadian dollars per unit. International tuition: $8216 Canadian dollars full-time. Required fees: $3589.92 Canadian dollars; $99.72 Canadian dollars per unit. $215 Canadian dollars per term. *Financial support:* In 2009–10, 51 research assistantships, 88 teaching assistantships with full and partial tuition reimbursements were awarded; scholarships/grants also available. Financial award application deadline: 5/1. *Faculty research:* Classical and functional analysis, algebra, differential equations, geometry. *Unit head:* Dr. Anthony To-Ming Lau, Chair, 403-492-5141, E-mail: tlau@math.ualberta.ca. *Application contact:* Dr. Yau Shu Wong, Associate Chair, Graduate Studies, 403-492-5799, Fax: 403-492-6828, E-mail: gradmail@math.ualberta.ca.

The University of Arizona, Graduate College, College of Science, Department of Mathematics, Tucson, AZ 85721. Offers mathematical sciences (PMS), including applied science and business; mathematics (MA, MS, PhD). Part-time programs available. *Faculty:* 60. *Students:* 51 full-time (13 women), 46 part-time (31 women); includes 7 minority (2 African Americans, 1 American Indian/Alaska Native, 2 Asian Americans or Pacific Islanders, 2 Hispanic Americans), 15 international. Average age 33. 98 applicants, 31% accepted, 13 enrolled. In 2009, 4 master's, 4 doctorates awarded. *Degree requirements:* For master's, thesis; for doctorate, 2 foreign languages, thesis/dissertation. *Entrance requirements:* For master's, GRE; for doctorate, GRE, statement of purpose. Additional exam requirements/recommendations for international students: Required—TOEFL (minimum score 550 paper-based; 213 computer-based; 79 iBT). *Application deadline:* For fall admission, 2/1 for domestic students, 12/1 for international students; for spring admission, 10/1 for domestic students, 6/1 for international students. Applications are processed on a rolling basis. Application fee: $75. Electronic applications accepted. *Expenses:* Tuition, state resident: full-time $9028. Tuition, nonresident: full-time $24,890. *Financial support:* In 2009–10, 20 research assistantships (averaging $16,568 per year), 59 teaching assistantships (averaging $16,391 per year) were awarded; scholarships/grants, health care benefits, tuition waivers (full and partial), and unspecified assistantships also available. Financial award application deadline: 3/5. *Faculty research:* Algebra/number theory, computational science, dynamical systems, geometry, analysis. Total annual research expenditures: $6.8 million. *Unit head:* Department Head's Office, 520-621-2713. *Application contact:* Sandy Sutton, Graduate Coordinator, 520-621-2068, Fax: 520-621-8322, E-mail: gradoffice@math.arizona.edu.

The University of Arizona, Graduate College, Graduate Interdisciplinary Programs, Graduate Interdisciplinary Program in Applied Mathematics, Tucson, AZ 85721. Offers applied mathematics (MS, PhD); mathematical sciences (PMS). *Faculty:* 1. *Students:* 35 full-time (4 women), 12 part-time (6 women); includes 9 minority (3 Asian Americans or Pacific Islanders, 6 Hispanic Americans), 8 international. Average age 28. 108 applicants, 10% accepted, 11 enrolled. In 2009, 9 master's, 7 doctorates awarded. Terminal master's awarded for partial completion of doctoral program. *Degree requirements:* For master's, thesis (for some programs); for doctorate, comprehensive exam, thesis/dissertation. *Entrance requirements:* For master's, GRE, 3 letters of recommendation; for doctorate, GRE, 3 letters of recommendation, statement of purpose. Additional exam requirements/recommendations for international students: Required—TOEFL (minimum score 575 paper-based; 230 computer-based; 80 iBT). *Application deadline:* For fall admission, 1/23 for domestic students, 1/30 for international students. Applications are processed on a rolling basis. Application fee: $65. Electronic applications accepted. *Expenses:* Tuition, state resident: full-time $9028. Tuition, nonresident: full-time $24,890. *Financial support:* In 2009–10, 1 research assistantship with full tuition reimbursement (averaging $17,120 per year) was awarded; institutionally sponsored loans, scholarships/grants, health care benefits, tuition waivers (full), and unspecified assistantships also available. Financial award application deadline: 3/1; financial award applicants required to submit FAFSA. *Faculty research:* Dynamical systems and chaos, partial differential equations, pattern formation, fluid dynamics and turbulence, scientific computation, mathematical physics, mathematical biology, medical imaging, applied probability and stochastic processes. Total annual research expenditures: $22,526. *Unit head:* Dr. Michael Tabor, Head, 520-621-4664, Fax: 520-626-5048, E-mail: tabor@math.arizona.edu. *Application contact:* Graduate Coordinator, 520-621-2016, Fax: 520-626-5048, E-mail: applmath@u.arizona.edu.

University of Arkansas, Graduate School, J. William Fulbright College of Arts and Sciences, Department of Mathematical Sciences, Program in Mathematics, Fayetteville, AR 72701-1201. Offers MS, PhD. *Students:* 18 full-time (5 women), 24 part-time (13 women); includes 1 minority (African American), 15 international. In 2009, 7 master's, 1 doctorate awarded. *Degree requirements:* For master's, thesis or alternative; for doctorate, 2 foreign languages, thesis/dissertation. Application fee: $40 ($50 for international students). *Expenses:* Tuition, state resident: full-time $7355; part-time $356.58 per hour. Tuition, nonresident: full-time $17,401; part-time $775.17 per hour. Required fees: $1203. *Financial support:* In 2009–10, 3 fellowships with tuition reimbursements, 4 research assistantships, 34 teaching assistantships were awarded; career-related internships or fieldwork and Federal Work-Study also available. Support available to part-time students. Financial award application deadline: 4/1; financial award applicants required to submit FAFSA. *Unit head:* Dr. Chaim Goodman-Strauss, Chair, 479-575-3351, Fax: 479-575-8630, E-mail: strauss@uark.edu. *Application contact:* Dr. Mark Johnson, Graduate Coordinator, 479-575-3351, Fax: 479-575-8630, E-mail: markj@uark.edu.

University of Arkansas at Little Rock, Graduate School, College of Science and Mathematics, Department of Mathematics and Statistics, Little Rock, AR 72204-1099. Offers applied statistics (Graduate Certificate); mathematical sciences (MS). Part-time and evening/weekend programs available. *Degree requirements:* For master's, comprehensive exam. *Entrance requirements:* For master's, GRE General Test, GRE Subject Test, minimum GPA of 2.7, previous course work in advanced mathematics.

University of Arkansas at Little Rock, Graduate School, College of Science and Mathematics, Program in Integrated Science and Mathematics, Little Rock, AR 72204-1099. Offers MS.

The University of British Columbia, Faculty of Science, Program in Mathematics, Vancouver, BC V6T 1Z2, Canada. Offers M Sc, MA, PhD. Part-time programs available. *Degree requirements:* For master's, thesis or alternative, essay, qualifying exam; for doctorate, comprehensive exam, thesis/dissertation, qualifying exam, thesis proposal. *Entrance requirements:* Additional exam requirements/recommendations for international students: Required—TOEFL (minimum score 600 paper-based; 250 computer-based; 100 iBT). Electronic applications accepted. *Faculty research:* Applied mathematics, financial mathematics, pure mathematics.

University of Calgary, Faculty of Graduate Studies, Faculty of Science, Department of Mathematics and Statistics, Calgary, AB T2N 1N4, Canada. Offers M Sc, PhD. *Degree requirements:* For master's, comprehensive exam, thesis; for doctorate, thesis/dissertation, candidacy exam, preliminary exams. *Entrance requirements:* For master's, honors degree in applied math, pure math, or statistics; for doctorate, MA or M Sc. Additional exam requirements/recommendations for international students: Required—TOEFL (minimum score 600 paper-based; 250 computer-based), IELTS (minimum score 7), TOEFL (paper-based 600; computer-based 250) or IELTS (paper-based 7). *Faculty research:* Combinatorics, applied mathematics, statistics, probability, analysis.

University of California, Berkeley, Graduate Division, College of Letters and Science, Department of Mathematics, Berkeley, CA 94720-1500. Offers applied mathematics (PhD); mathematics (MA, PhD). *Students:* 148 full-time (19 women). Average age 26. 411 applicants, 25 enrolled.Terminal master's awarded for partial completion of doctoral program. *Degree requirements:* For master's, exam or thesis; for doctorate, 2 foreign languages, thesis/dissertation, qualifying exam. *Entrance requirements:* For master's and doctorate, GRE General Test, GRE Subject Test, minimum GPA of 3.0, 3 letters of recommendation. *Application deadline:* For fall admission, 12/10 for domestic students. Application fee: $70 ($90 for international students). *Financial support:* Fellowships, research assistantships, teaching assistantships, institutionally sponsored loans and unspecified assistantships available. *Faculty research:* Algebra, analysis, logic, geometry/topology. *Unit head:* Prof. Theodore A. Slaman, Chair, 510-642-6550, E-mail: ch_math@ls.berkeley.edu. *Application contact:* Barbara F. Waller, Student Affairs Officer, 510-642-0665, E-mail: barb@math.berkeley.edu.

University of California, Davis, Graduate Studies, Program in Mathematics, Davis, CA 95616. Offers MA, MAT, PhD. Terminal master's awarded for partial completion of doctoral program. *Degree requirements:* For master's, comprehensive exam; for doctorate, one foreign language, thesis/dissertation. *Entrance requirements:* For master's and doctorate, GRE General Test, GRE Subject Test, minimum GPA of 3.0. Additional exam requirements/recommendations for international students: Required—TOEFL (minimum score 550 paper-based; 213 computer-based). Electronic applications accepted. *Faculty research:* Mathematical physics, geometric topology, probability, partial differential equations, applied mathematics.

University of California, Irvine, Office of Graduate Studies, School of Physical Sciences, Department of Mathematics, Irvine, CA 92697. Offers MS, PhD. *Students:* 101 full-time (27 women); includes 19 minority (1 African American, 15 Asian Americans or Pacific Islanders, 3 Hispanic Americans), 40 international. Average age 27. 172 applicants, 31% accepted, 20 enrolled. In 2009, 29 master's, 11 doctorates awarded. *Degree requirements:* For doctorate, thesis/dissertation. *Entrance requirements:* For master's and doctorate, GRE General Test, GRE Subject Test, minimum GPA of 3.0. Additional exam requirements/recommendations for international students: Required—TOEFL (minimum score 550 paper-based; 213 computer-based). *Application deadline:* For fall admission, 1/15 priority date for domestic and international students. Applications are processed on a rolling basis. Application fee: $70 ($90 for international students). Electronic applications accepted. *Financial support:* Fellowships, research assistantships with full tuition reimbursements, teaching assistantships, institutionally sponsored loans, traineeships, health care benefits, and unspecified assistantships available. Financial award application deadline: 3/1; financial award applicants required to submit FAFSA. *Faculty research:* Algebra and logic, geometry and topology, probability, mathematical physics. *Unit head:* Bernard Russo, Chair, 949-824-5510, Fax: 949-824-7993, E-mail: brusso@uci.edu. *Application contact:* Jennifer Dugan, Graduate Coordinator, 949-824-5544, Fax: 949-824-7993, E-mail: jdugan@math.uci.edu.

University of California, Los Angeles, Graduate Division, College of Letters and Science, Department of Mathematics, Los Angeles, CA 90095. Offers MA, MAT, PhD. *Students:* 175 full-time (26 women); includes 23 minority (1 African American, 15 Asian Americans or Pacific Islanders, 7 Hispanic Americans), 60 international. Average age 26. 334 applicants, 25% accepted, 37 enrolled. In 2009, 19 master's, 19 doctorates awarded. Terminal master's awarded for partial completion of doctoral program. *Degree requirements:* For master's, comprehensive exam or thesis; for doctorate, one foreign language, thesis/dissertation, oral and written qualifying exams. *Entrance requirements:* For master's, GRE General Test, GRE Subject Test, minimum GPA of 3.2 in mathematics, 12 quarter courses of upper division math; for doctorate, GRE General Test, GRE Subject Test, minimum GPA of 3.5 in mathematics, 12 quarter courses of upper division math. *Application deadline:* For fall admission, 12/15 for domestic students, 11/15 for international students. Application fee: $70 ($90 for international students). Electronic applications accepted. *Financial support:* In 2009–10, 91 fellowships with full and partial tuition reimbursements, 72 research assistantships with full and partial tuition reimbursements, 132 teaching assistantships with full and partial tuition reimbursements were awarded; Federal Work-Study, institutionally sponsored loans, scholarships/grants, health care benefits, tuition waivers (full and partial), and unspecified assistantships also available. Financial award application deadline: 3/1; financial award applicants required to submit FAFSA. *Unit head:* Dr. Sorin Popa, Chair, 310-825-8502. *Application contact:* Departmental Office, 310-825-4971, E-mail: gradapps@math.ucla.edu.

University of California, Riverside, Graduate Division, Department of Mathematics, Riverside, CA 92521-0102. Offers MA, MS, PhD. Part-time programs available. *Faculty:* 24 full-time (3 women). *Students:* 65 full-time (13 women), 1 part-time (0 women); includes 15 minority (2 African Americans, 7 Asian Americans or Pacific Islanders, 6 Hispanic Americans), 4 international. Average age 28. 71 applicants, 44% accepted, 13 enrolled. In 2009, 13 master's, 5 doctorates awarded. Terminal master's awarded for partial completion of doctoral program. *Degree requirements:* For master's, comprehensive exam; for doctorate, thesis/dissertation, qualifying exams. *Entrance requirements:* For master's and doctorate, GRE General Test, minimum GPA of 3.2. Additional exam requirements/recommendations for international students: Required—TOEFL (minimum score 550 paper-based; 213 computer-based; 80 iBT). *Application deadline:* For fall admission, 5/1 for domestic students, 2/1 for international students; for winter admission, 9/1 for domestic students, 7/1 for international students; for spring admission, 12/1 for domestic students, 10/1 for international students. Applications are processed on a rolling basis. Application fee: $60 ($75 for international students). Electronic applications accepted. *Financial support:* In 2009–10, fellowships with tuition reimbursements (averaging $12,000 per year), teaching assistantships with full and partial tuition reimbursements (averaging $16,500 per year) were awarded; research assistantships, career-related internships or fieldwork, Federal Work-Study, institutionally sponsored loans, health care benefits, and tuition waivers (full and partial) also available. Financial award application deadline: 1/5; financial award applicants required to submit FAFSA. *Faculty research:* Algebraic geometry, commutative algebra, Lie algebra, differential equations, differential geometry. *Unit head:* Dr. Vyjayanthi Chari, Chair, 951-827-6463, Fax: 951-827-7314, E-mail: chari@math.ucr.edu. *Application contact:* Melissa Gomez, Graduate Program Assistant, 951-827-7378, Fax: 951-827-7314, E-mail: gradprog@math.ucr.edu.

University of California, San Diego, Office of Graduate Studies, Department of Mathematics, La Jolla, CA 92093. Offers applied mathematics (MA); mathematics (MA, PhD); statistics (MS). *Degree requirements:* For doctorate, thesis/dissertation. *Entrance requirements:* For master's and doctorate, GRE General Test, GRE Subject Test. Electronic applications accepted.

University of California, Santa Barbara, Graduate Division, College of Letters and Sciences, Division of Mathematics, Life, and Physical Sciences, Department of Mathematics, Santa Barbara, CA 93106-3080. Offers applied mathematics (MA); computational science and engineering (PhD); mathematics (MA, PhD); MA/PhD. *Faculty:* 31 full-time (3 women). *Students:* 54 full-time (14 women). Average age 26. 151 applicants, 26% accepted, 14 enrolled. In 2009, 5 master's, 14 doctorates awarded. Terminal master's awarded for partial completion of doctoral program. *Degree requirements:* For master's, comprehensive exam (for some programs), thesis (for some programs); for doctorate, comprehensive exam, thesis/dissertation. *Entrance requirements:* For master's, GRE General Test, GRE Subject Test (mathematics), 3 letters of recommendation, resume/curriculum vitae; for doctorate, GRE General Test, GRE Subject Test (math), 3 letters of recommendation, statement of purpose, personal achievements/contributions statement, resume/curriculum vitae, transcripts for post-secondary institutions attended. Additional exam requirements/recommendations for international students: Required—TOEFL (minimum score 575 paper-based; 231 computer-based; 80 iBT) or IELTS (7). *Application deadline:* For fall admission, 1/1 for domestic and international students. Application fee: $70 ($90 for international students). Electronic applications accepted. *Financial support:* In 2009–10, 54 students received support, including 13 fellowships with full and partial tuition reimbursements available (averaging $13,200 per year), 13 research assistantships with full and partial tuition reimbursements available (averaging $6,500 per year), 48 teaching assistantships with partial tuition reimbursements available (averaging $10,600 per year); Federal Work-Study, institutionally sponsored loans, scholarships/grants, health care benefits, and unspecified assistantships also available. Financial award applicants required to submit FAFSA. *Faculty research:* Topology, differential geometry, algebra, applied mathematics, partial differential equations. Total annual research expenditures: $204,214. *Unit head:* Prof. Jeffrey Stopple, Chair, 805-893-8330, Fax: 805-893-2385, E-mail: stopple@math.ucsb.edu. *Application contact:* Medina Price, Graduate Advisor, 805-893-8192, Fax: 805-893-2385, E-mail: price@math.ucsb.edu.

University of California, Santa Cruz, Division of Graduate Studies, Division of Physical and Biological Sciences, Department of Mathematics, Santa Cruz, CA 95064. Offers MA, PhD. Terminal master's awarded for partial completion of doctoral program. *Degree requirements:* For master's, thesis; for doctorate, one foreign language, thesis/dissertation, qualifying exam. *Entrance requirements:* For doctorate, GRE General Test, GRE Subject Test.

University of Central Arkansas, Graduate School, College of Natural Sciences and Math, Department of Mathematics, Conway, AR 72035-0001. Offers applied mathematics (MS); math education (MA). Part-time programs available. *Faculty:* 16 full-time (4 women). *Students:* 17 full-time (10 women), 8 part-time (6 women); includes 2 minority (1 African American, 1 Asian American or Pacific Islander), 2 international. Average age 28. 8 applicants, 100% accepted, 4 enrolled. In 2009, 5 master's awarded. *Degree requirements:* For master's, comprehensive exam, thesis optional. *Entrance requirements:* For master's, GRE General Test, minimum GPA of 2.7. Additional exam requirements/recommendations for international students: Required—TOEFL (minimum score 550 paper-based; 213 computer-based). *Application deadline:* For fall admission, 3/1 priority date for domestic students; for spring admission, 10/1 priority date for domestic students. Applications are processed on a rolling basis. Application fee: $25 ($50 for international students). *Expenses:* Tuition, state resident: full-time $5136; part-time $214 per credit hour. Required fees: $379.50; $127 per term. Tuition and fees vary according to course level, course load and campus/location. *Financial support:* In 2009–10, 11 teaching assistantships with partial tuition reimbursements (averaging $8,500 per year) were awarded; Federal Work-Study, scholarships/grants, and unspecified assistantships also available. Financial award application deadline: 2/15; financial award applicants required to submit FAFSA. *Unit head:* Dr. Ramesh Garimella, Chair, 501-450-3147, Fax: 501-450-5662, E-mail: rameshg@uca.edu. *Application contact:* Brenda Herring, Admissions Assistant, 501-450-5065, Fax: 501-450-5678, E-mail: bherring@uca.edu.

University of Central Florida, College of Sciences, Department of Mathematics, Orlando, FL 32816. Offers applied mathematics (Certificate); mathematical science (MS); mathematics (PhD). Part-time and evening/weekend programs available. *Faculty:* 31 full-time (10 women), 10 part-time/adjunct (0 women). *Students:* 36 full-time (10 women), 14 part-time (7 women); includes 9 minority (1 African American, 3 Asian Americans or Pacific Islanders, 5 Hispanic Americans), 12 international. Average age 32. 55 applicants, 53% accepted, 16 enrolled. In 2009, 8 master's, 8 doctorates awarded. *Degree requirements:* For master's, thesis or alternative; for doctorate, thesis/dissertation, candidacy exam. *Entrance requirements:* For master's, GRE General Test, minimum GPA of 3.0 in last 60 hours; for doctorate, GRE Subject Test, minimum GPA of 3.0 in last 60 hours or master's qualifying exam. Additional exam requirements/recommendations for international students: Required—TOEFL. *Application deadline:* For fall admission, 7/15 for domestic students; for spring admission, 12/1 for domestic students. Application fee: $30. Electronic applications accepted. *Expenses:* Tuition, state resident: part-time $306.31 per credit hour. Tuition, nonresident: part-time $1099.01 per credit hour. Part-time tuition and fees vary according to degree level and program. *Financial support:* In 2009–10, 27 students received support, including 1 fellowship with partial tuition reimbursement available (averaging $18,000 per year), 3 research assistantships with partial tuition reimbursements available (averaging $13,000 per year), 23 teaching assistantships with partial tuition reimbursements available (averaging $14,400 per year); career-related internships or fieldwork, Federal Work-Study, institutionally sponsored loans, tuition waivers (partial), and unspecified assistantships also available. Financial award application deadline: 3/1; financial award applicants required to submit FAFSA. *Faculty research:* Applied mathematics, analysis, approximation theory, graph theory, mathematical statistics. *Unit head:* Dr. Piotr Mikusinski, Chair, 407-823-0445, Fax: 407-823-6253, E-mail: piotrm@mail.ucf.edu. *Application contact:* Dr. Piotr Mikusinski, Chair, 407-823-0445, Fax: 407-823-6253, E-mail: piotrm@mail.ucf.edu.

University of Central Missouri, The Graduate School, College of Science and Technology, Warrensburg, MO 64093. Offers applied mathematics (MS); aviation safety (MS); biology (MS); computer science (MS); environmental studies (MA); industrial management (MS); mathematics (MS); technology (MS); technology management (PhD). Part-time programs available. Postbaccalaureate distance learning degree programs offered. *Faculty:* 59. *Students:* 99 full-time (31 women), 85 part-time (37 women). Average age 33. 45 applicants, 96% accepted, 42 enrolled. In 2009, 68 master's awarded. *Entrance requirements:* Additional exam requirements/recommendations for international students: Required—TOEFL (minimum score 550 paper-based; 79 computer-based). *Application deadline:* For fall admission, 6/1 priority date for domestic students, 5/1 for international students; for spring admission, 10/1 priority date for domestic students, 10/1 for international students. Applications are processed on a rolling basis. Application fee: $30 ($75 for international students). Electronic applications accepted. *Expenses:* Tuition, area resident: Part-time $245.80 per credit hour. Tuition, nonresident: part-time $491.60 per credit hour. Required fees: $24.20 per credit hour. Full-time tuition and fees vary according to course load, degree level, campus/location and reciprocity agreements. *Financial support:* In 2009–10, 15 students received support; fellowships with full and partial tuition reimbursements available, research assistantships with full and partial tuition reimbursements available, teaching assistantships with full and partial tuition reimbursements available, career-related internships or fieldwork, Federal Work-Study, scholarships/grants, and administrative and laboratory assistantships available. Support available to part-time students. Financial award application deadline: 3/1; financial award applicants required to submit FAFSA. *Unit head:* Dr. Alice Greife, Dean, 660-543-4450, Fax: 660-543-8031, E-mail: greife@ucmo.edu. *Application contact:* Laurie Delap, Admissions Coordinator, 660-543-4621, Fax: 660-543-4778, E-mail: gradinfo@ucmo.edu.

University of Central Oklahoma, College of Graduate Studies and Research, College of Mathematics and Science, Department of Mathematics and Statistics, Edmond, OK 73034-5209. Offers applied mathematical sciences (MS), including computer science, mathematics, mathematics/computer science teaching, statistics. Part-time programs available. *Degree requirements:* For master's, thesis. *Entrance requirements:* Additional exam requirements/recommendations for international students: Required—TOEFL (minimum score 550 paper-based; 213 computer-based). Electronic applications accepted. *Faculty research:* Curvature, FAA, math education.

University of Chicago, Division of the Physical Sciences, Department of Mathematics, Chicago, IL 60637-1513. Offers applied mathematics (SM, PhD); financial mathematics (MS); mathematics

Mathematics

University of Chicago (continued)
(SM, PhD). *Faculty:* 57 full-time (3 women). *Students:* 84 full-time (19 women), 39 international. 342 applicants, 13% accepted, 16 enrolled. In 2009, 19 master's, 13 doctorates awarded. *Degree requirements:* For master's, one foreign language; for doctorate, one foreign language, thesis/dissertation, 2 qualifying exams, oral topic presentation. *Entrance requirements:* For master's and doctorate, GRE General Test, GRE Subject Test. Additional exam requirements/recommendations for international students: Required—TOEFL (minimum score 600 paper-based; 250 computer-based). *Application deadline:* For fall admission, 1/5 for domestic and international students. Application fee: $55. Electronic applications accepted. *Financial support:* In 2009–10, 24 fellowships, 44 teaching assistantships were awarded; research assistantships, career-related internships or fieldwork, institutionally sponsored loans, and scholarships/grants also available. Financial award application deadline: 1/5; financial award applicants required to submit CSS PROFILE or FAFSA. *Faculty research:* Analysis, differential geometry, algebra number theory, topology, algebraic geometry. *Unit head:* Dr. Peter Constantin, Chair, 773-702-7399, Fax: 773-702-9787. *Application contact:* Laurie Wail, Graduate Studies Assistant, 773-702-7358, Fax: 773-702-9787, E-mail: lwail@math.uchicago.edu.

University of Cincinnati, Graduate School, McMicken College of Arts and Sciences, Department of Mathematical Sciences, Cincinnati, OH 45221. Offers applied mathematics (MS, PhD); mathematics education (MAT); pure mathematics (MS, PhD); statistics (MS, PhD). Part-time programs available. Terminal master's awarded for partial completion of doctoral program. *Degree requirements:* For master's, comprehensive exam, thesis or alternative; for doctorate, one foreign language, comprehensive exam, thesis/dissertation. *Entrance requirements:* For master's, GRE, teacher certification (MAT); for doctorate, GRE. Additional exam requirements/recommendations for international students: Required—TOEFL. Electronic applications accepted. *Faculty research:* Algebra, analysis, differential equations, numerical analysis, statistics.

University of Colorado at Boulder, Graduate School, College of Arts and Sciences, Department of Mathematics, Boulder, CO 80309. Offers MA, MS, PhD. *Faculty:* 27 full-time (4 women). *Students:* 70 full-time (15 women), 3 part-time (1 woman); includes 10 minority (3 African Americans, 2 American Indian/Alaska Native, 1 Asian American or Pacific Islander, 4 Hispanic Americans), 7 international. Average age 28. 117 applicants, 17% accepted, 14 enrolled. In 2009, 7 master's, 3 doctorates awarded. Terminal master's awarded for partial completion of doctoral program. *Degree requirements:* For master's, comprehensive exam, thesis or alternative; for doctorate, one foreign language, comprehensive exam, thesis/dissertation, 2 preliminary exams. *Entrance requirements:* For master's, minimum undergraduate GPA of 3.0. *Application deadline:* For fall admission, 1/15 priority date for domestic students, 1/15 for international students; for spring admission, 11/1 for domestic and international students. Applications are processed on a rolling basis. Application fee: $50 ($60 for international students). *Financial support:* In 2009–10, 42 fellowships (averaging $6,054 per year), 10 research assistantships (averaging $6,092 per year) were awarded; scholarships/grants and tuition waivers (full) also available. Support available to part-time students. Financial award application deadline: 2/1. *Faculty research:* Pure mathematics, applied mathematics and mathematical physics (including algebra, algebraic geometry, differential equations, differential geometry, logic and foundations). Total annual research expenditures: $125,290.

University of Colorado at Colorado Springs, Graduate School, College of Letters, Arts and Sciences, Department of Mathematics, Colorado Springs, CO 80933-7150. Offers applied mathematics (MS); mathematics (M Sc). Part-time and evening/weekend programs available. *Faculty:* 12 full-time (2 women). *Students:* 12 full-time (7 women), 16 part-time (8 women); includes 3 minority (1 Asian American or Pacific Islander, 2 Hispanic Americans). Average age 38. 12 applicants, 75% accepted, 6 enrolled. In 2009, 7 master's awarded. *Degree requirements:* For master's, thesis, qualifying exam. *Entrance requirements:* For master's, GRE General Test, minimum GPA of 3.0. Additional exam requirements/recommendations for international students: Required—TOEFL. *Application deadline:* For fall admission, 6/15 for domestic students. Application fee: $60 ($75 for international students). *Expenses:* Tuition, state resident: full-time $8922; part-time $639 per credit hour. Tuition, nonresident: full-time $19,372; part-time $1154 per credit hour. Tuition and fees vary according to course level, course load, degree level, program, reciprocity agreements and student level. *Financial support:* Teaching assistantships, Federal Work-Study and scholarships/grants available. Support available to part-time students. Financial award application deadline: 3/1; financial award applicants required to submit FAFSA. *Faculty research:* Abelian groups and noncommutative rings, hormone analysis and computer vision, probability and mathematical physics, stochastic dynamics, probability models. *Unit head:* Dr. Rinaldo Schinazi, Chair, 719-255-3920, Fax: 719-255-3605. *Application contact:* Dr. James Daly, Director of Graduate Studies, 719-255-3428, Fax: 719-255-3605, E-mail: jdaly@uccs.edu.

University of Colorado Denver, College of Liberal Arts and Sciences, Program in Integrated Sciences, Denver, CO 80217-3364. Offers applied science (MIS); computer science (MIS); mathematics (MIS). *Students:* 3 part-time (1 woman); includes 1 minority (African American). 1 applicant, 0% accepted, 0 enrolled. In 2009, 4 master's awarded. *Financial support:* Research assistantships, teaching assistantships available. Financial award application deadline: 4/1; financial award applicants required to submit FAFSA. *Application contact:* Tammy Stone, Associate Dean, Curriculum and Student Affairs, 303-556-3063, Fax: 303-556-4861.

University of Connecticut, Graduate School, College of Liberal Arts and Sciences, Department of Mathematics, Field of Mathematics, Storrs, CT 06269. Offers actuarial science (MS, PhD); mathematics (MS, PhD). *Faculty:* 51 full-time (10 women). *Students:* 93 full-time (41 women), 18 part-time (6 women); includes 9 minority (3 African Americans, 6 Asian Americans or Pacific Islanders), 62 international. Average age 27. 237 applicants, 15% accepted, 26 enrolled. In 2009, 34 master's, 10 doctorates awarded. Terminal master's awarded for partial completion of doctoral program. *Degree requirements:* For master's, comprehensive exam; for doctorate, thesis/dissertation. *Entrance requirements:* For master's and doctorate, GRE General Test. Additional exam requirements/recommendations for international students: Required—TOEFL (minimum score 550 paper-based; 213 computer-based). *Application deadline:* For fall admission, 2/1 priority date for domestic and international students; for spring admission, 11/1 for domestic students, 10/1 for international students. Applications are processed on a rolling basis. Application fee: $55. Electronic applications accepted. *Expenses:* Tuition, state resident: full-time $4725; part-time $525 per credit. Tuition, nonresident: full-time $12,267; part-time $1363 per credit. Required fees: $346 per semester. Tuition and fees vary according to course load. *Financial support:* In 2009–10, 13 research assistantships with full tuition reimbursements, 47 teaching assistantships with full tuition reimbursements were awarded; fellowships, Federal Work-Study, scholarships/grants, health care benefits, and unspecified assistantships also available. Financial award application deadline: 2/1; financial award applicants required to submit FAFSA. *Application contact:* Sharon McDermott, Administrative Assistant, 860-486-6452, Fax: 860-486-4283, E-mail: gradadm@math.uconn.edu.

University of Delaware, College of Arts and Sciences, Department of Mathematical Sciences, Newark, DE 19716. Offers applied mathematics (MS, PhD); mathematics (MS, PhD). Part-time programs available. Terminal master's awarded for partial completion of doctoral program. *Degree requirements:* For master's, thesis (for some programs); for doctorate, one foreign language, thesis/dissertation, qualifying exam. *Entrance requirements:* For master's and doctorate, GRE General Test. Additional exam requirements/recommendations for international students: Required—TOEFL. Electronic applications accepted. *Faculty research:* Scattering theory, inverse problems, fluid dynamics, numerical analysis, combinatorics.

See Close-Up on page 323.

University of Denver, Faculty of Natural Sciences and Mathematics, Department of Mathematics, Denver, CO 80208. Offers applied mathematics (MA, MS); computer science (MS); mathematics (PhD). Part-time programs available. *Faculty:* 14 full-time (5 women), 1 part-time/adjunct (0 women). *Students:* 4 full-time (1 woman), 9 part-time (4 women); includes 2 minority (both Hispanic Americans), 4 international. Average age 27. 33 applicants, 82% accepted, 8 enrolled. In 2009, 4 master's awarded. Terminal master's awarded for partial completion of doctoral program. *Degree requirements:* For master's, computer language, foreign language, or laboratory experience; for doctorate, one foreign language, thesis/dissertation, oral and written exams. *Entrance requirements:* For master's and doctorate, GRE General Test. Additional exam requirements/recommendations for international students: Required—TOEFL. *Application deadline:* Applications are processed on a rolling basis. Application fee: $50. Electronic applications accepted. *Expenses:* Tuition: Full-time $34,596; part-time $961 per quarter hour. Required fees: $4 per quarter hour. Tuition and fees vary according to course load, campus/location and program. *Financial support:* In 2009–10, 1 research assistantship with full and partial tuition reimbursement (averaging $17,000 per year), 11 teaching assistantships with full and partial tuition reimbursements (averaging $17,000 per year) were awarded; career-related internships or fieldwork, Federal Work-Study, institutionally sponsored loans, and scholarships/grants also available. Support available to part-time students. Financial award application deadline: 3/1; financial award applicants required to submit FAFSA. *Faculty research:* Real-time software, convex bodies, multidimensional data, parallel computer clusters. *Unit head:* Dr. Alvaro Arias, Chairperson, 303-871-3559. *Application contact:* Information Contact, 303-871-2911, E-mail: info@math.du.edu.

University of Florida, Graduate School, College of Liberal Arts and Sciences, Department of Mathematics, Gainesville, FL 32611. Offers MA, MAT, MS, MST, PhD. Part-time programs available. Terminal master's awarded for partial completion of doctoral program. *Degree requirements:* For master's, thesis optional; for doctorate, one foreign language, thesis/dissertation. *Entrance requirements:* For master's and doctorate, GRE General Test, minimum GPA of 3.0. Additional exam requirements/recommendations for international students: Required—TOEFL (minimum score 550 paper-based; 213 computer-based). Electronic applications accepted. *Faculty research:* Combinatorics and number theory, group theory, probability theory, logic, differential geometry and mathematical physics.

University of Georgia, Graduate School, College of Arts and Sciences, Department of Mathematics, Athens, GA 30602. Offers applied mathematical science (MAMS); mathematics (MA, PhD). *Faculty:* 32 full-time (4 women). *Students:* 43 full-time (14 women), 1 part-time (0 women); includes 2 minority (both Hispanic Americans), 13 international. 119 applicants, 18% accepted, 9 enrolled. In 2009, 9 master's, 6 doctorates awarded. *Degree requirements:* For master's, one foreign language, thesis (for some programs); for doctorate, 2 foreign languages, thesis/dissertation. *Entrance requirements:* For master's and doctorate, GRE General Test. *Application deadline:* For fall admission, 7/1 priority date for domestic students; for spring admission, 11/15 for domestic students. Application fee: $50. Electronic applications accepted. *Expenses:* Tuition, state resident: full-time $6000; part-time $250 per credit hour. Tuition, nonresident: full-time $20,904; part-time $871 per credit hour. Required fees: $730 per semester. *Financial support:* Fellowships, research assistantships, teaching assistantships, unspecified assistantships available. *Unit head:* Dr. Joseph H. G. Fu, Head, 706-542-2564, Fax: 706-542-2573, E-mail: fu@math.uga.edu. *Application contact:* Dr. Brian D. Boe, Graduate Coordinator, 706-542-2547, Fax: 706-542-2573, E-mail: grad@math.uga.edu.

University of Guelph, Graduate Program Services, College of Physical and Engineering Science, Department of Mathematics and Statistics, Guelph, ON N1G 2W1, Canada. Offers applied mathematics (PhD); applied statistics (PhD); mathematics and statistics (M Sc). Part-time programs available. *Degree requirements:* For master's, thesis (for some programs); for doctorate, thesis/dissertation. *Entrance requirements:* For master's, minimum B- average during previous 2 years of course work; for doctorate, minimum B average. Additional exam requirements/recommendations for international students: Required—TOEFL (minimum score 550 paper-based; 213 computer-based; 89 iBT), IELTS (minimum score 6.5). *Faculty research:* Dynamical systems, mathematical biology, numerical analysis, linear and nonlinear models, reliability and bioassay.

University of Hawaii at Manoa, Graduate Division, College of Natural Sciences, Department of Mathematics, Honolulu, HI 96822. Offers MA, PhD. Part-time programs available. *Faculty:* 22 full-time (1 woman), 5 part-time/adjunct (1 woman). *Students:* 19 full-time (5 women), 15 part-time (7 women); includes 11 minority (1 African American, 8 Asian Americans or Pacific Islanders, 2 Hispanic Americans), 5 international. Average age 28. 39 applicants, 67% accepted, 11 enrolled. In 2009, 5 master's awarded. *Degree requirements:* For doctorate, one foreign language, comprehensive exam, thesis/dissertation. *Entrance requirements:* For master's and doctorate, GRE General Test, minimum GPA of 3.0. Additional exam requirements/recommendations for international students: Required—TOEFL (minimum score 500 paper-based; 173 computer-based; 61 iBT), IELTS (minimum score 5). *Application deadline:* For fall admission, 3/1 for domestic students, 2/1 for international students; for spring admission, 9/1 for domestic students, 8/1 for international students. Applications are processed on a rolling basis. Application fee: $60. *Expenses:* Tuition, state resident: full-time $8900; part-time $372 per credit. Tuition, nonresident: full-time $21,400; part-time $898 per credit. Required fees: $207 per semester. *Financial support:* In 2009–10, 1 student received support, including 7 fellowships (averaging $1,214 per year), 1 research assistantship (averaging $18,198 per year), 13 teaching assistantships (averaging $16,045 per year); institutionally sponsored loans, tuition waivers (full and partial), and unspecified assistantships also available. Support available to part-time students. Financial award application deadline: 3/1. *Faculty research:* Analysis, algebra, lattice theory, logic topology, differential geometry. Total annual research expenditures: $492,000. *Application contact:* James Nation, Graduate Chair, 808-956-7951, Fax: 808-956-9139, E-mail: jb@math.hawaii.edu.

University of Houston, College of Natural Sciences and Mathematics, Department of Mathematics, Houston, TX 77204. Offers MA, MS, PhD. Part-time and evening/weekend programs available. *Faculty:* 26 full-time (2 women), 1 (woman) part-time/adjunct. *Students:* 78 full-time (33 women), 39 part-time (19 women); includes 21 minority (2 African Americans, 11 Asian Americans or Pacific Islanders, 8 Hispanic Americans), 54 international. Average age 31. 44 applicants, 98% accepted, 29 enrolled. In 2009, 26 master's, 7 doctorates awarded. *Degree requirements:* For master's, thesis optional; for doctorate, thesis/dissertation. *Entrance requirements:* For master's, GRE General Test, minimum GPA of 3.0 in last 60 hours, bachelor's degree in mathematics or related area; for doctorate, GRE General Test, MS in mathematics or equivalent, minimum GPA of 3.0 in last 60 hours of course work. Additional exam requirements/recommendations for international students: Required—TOEFL. *Application deadline:* For fall admission, 7/1 for domestic students; for spring admission, 12/1 for domestic students. Applications are processed on a rolling basis. Application fee: $0 ($75 for international students). Electronic applications accepted. *Expenses:* Tuition, state resident: full-time $7676; part-time $320 per credit hour. Tuition, nonresident: full-time $14,324; part-time $597 per credit hour. Required fees: $3034. *Financial support:* In 2009–10, 12 research assistantships with full tuition reimbursements (averaging $12,750 per year), 54 teaching assistantships with full tuition reimbursements (averaging $12,750 per year) were awarded; career-related internships or fieldwork, Federal Work-Study, institutionally sponsored loans, scholarships/grants, health care benefits, and unspecified assistantships also available. Support available to part-time students. Financial award application deadline: 2/1. *Faculty research:* Applied mathematics, modern analysis, computational science, geometry, dynamical systems. *Unit head:* Dr. Jeffery E. Morgan, Chairperson, 713-743-3500, Fax: 713-743-3505, E-mail: jmorgan@math.uh.edu. *Application contact:* Dr. Jeffery E. Morgan, Chairperson, 713-743-3500, Fax: 713-743-3505, E-mail: jmorgan@math.uh.edu.

University of Houston–Clear Lake, School of Science and Computer Engineering, Program in Mathematical Sciences, Houston, TX 77058-1098. Offers MS. Part-time and evening/

weekend programs available. *Entrance requirements:* For master's, GRE General Test. Additional exam requirements/recommendations for international students: Required—TOEFL (minimum score 550 paper-based; 213 computer-based).

University of Idaho, College of Graduate Studies, College of Science, Department of Mathematics, Moscow, ID 83844-2282. Offers MAT, MS, PhD. *Faculty:* 5 full-time, 2 part-time/adjunct. *Students:* 17 full-time (8 women), 22 part-time (10 women). In 2009, 11 master's, 3 doctorates awarded. *Degree requirements:* For doctorate, 2 foreign languages, thesis/dissertation. *Entrance requirements:* For master's, minimum GPA of 2.8; for doctorate, minimum undergraduate GPA of 2.8, 3.0 graduate. *Application deadline:* For fall admission, 8/1 for domestic students; for spring admission, 12/15 for domestic students. Application fee: $55 ($60 for international students). *Expenses:* Tuition, state resident: full-time $6120. Tuition, nonresident: full-time $17,712. *Financial support:* Research assistantships, teaching assistantships available. Financial award application deadline: 2/15. *Faculty research:* Bioinformatics and mathematical biology, analysis and differential equations, combinatorics, probability and stochastic processes, discrete geometry. *Unit head:* Dr. Monte Boisen, Chair, 208-885-6742. *Application contact:* Dr. Monte Boisen, Chair, 208-885-6742.

University of Illinois at Chicago, Graduate College, College of Liberal Arts and Sciences, Department of Mathematics, Statistics, and Computer Science, Chicago, IL 60607-7128. Offers applied mathematics (MS, PhD); computational finance (MS, PhD); computer science (MS, PhD); mathematics (DA); mathematics and information sciences for industry (MS); probability and statistics (PhD); pure mathematics (MS, PhD); statistics (MS); teaching of mathematics (MST), including elementary, secondary. Part-time programs available. *Degree requirements:* For master's, comprehensive exam; for doctorate, one foreign language, thesis/dissertation. *Entrance requirements:* For master's and doctorate, GRE General Test, minimum GPA of 2.75. Additional exam requirements/recommendations for international students: Required—TOEFL. Electronic applications accepted.

University of Illinois at Urbana–Champaign, Graduate College, College of Liberal Arts and Sciences, Department of Mathematics, Champaign, IL 61820. Offers applied mathematics (MS); applied mathematics: actuarial science (MS); mathematics (MA, MS, PhD); teaching of mathematics (MS). *Faculty:* 67 full-time (5 women), 3 part-time/adjunct (0 women). *Students:* 161 full-time (40 women), 25 part-time (8 women); includes 13 minority (1 African American, 10 Asian Americans or Pacific Islanders, 2 Hispanic Americans), 107 international. 361 applicants, 25% accepted, 37 enrolled. In 2009, 41 master's, 23 doctorates awarded. *Entrance requirements:* For master's, GRE General Test, GRE Subject Test (mathematics), minimum GPA of 3.0; for doctorate, GRE General Test, GRE Subject Test (math), minimum GPA of 3.0. Additional exam requirements/recommendations for international students: Required—TOEFL (minimum score 550 paper-based; 213 computer-based). *Application deadline:* Applications are processed on a rolling basis. Application fee: $60 ($75 for international students). Electronic applications accepted. *Financial support:* In 2009–10, 22 fellowships, 44 research assistantships, 148 teaching assistantships were awarded; tuition waivers (full and partial) also available. *Unit head:* Sheldon Katz, Chair, 217-265-6258, Fax: 217-333-9576, E-mail: katzs@illinois.edu. *Application contact:* Marci Blocher, Office Support Specialist, 217-333-3350, Fax: 217-333-9576, E-mail: mblocher@illinois.edu.

The University of Iowa, Graduate College, College of Liberal Arts and Sciences, Department of Mathematics, Iowa City, IA 52242-1316. Offers MS, PhD. *Degree requirements:* For master's, thesis optional, exam; for doctorate, comprehensive exam, thesis/dissertation. *Entrance requirements:* For master's and doctorate, GRE General Test, minimum GPA of 3.0. Additional exam requirements/recommendations for international students: Required—TOEFL (minimum score 620 paper-based; 260 computer-based; 105 iBT). Electronic applications accepted.

The University of Kansas, Graduate Studies, College of Liberal Arts and Sciences, Department of Mathematics, Lawrence, KS 66045. Offers mathematics (MA, PhD). *Students:* 50 full-time (6 women), 11 part-time (3 women); includes 6 minority (2 African Americans, 2 Asian Americans or Pacific Islanders, 2 Hispanic Americans), 22 international. Average age 28. 68 applicants, 50% accepted, 10 enrolled. In 2009, 11 master's, 5 doctorates awarded. Terminal master's awarded for partial completion of doctoral program. *Degree requirements:* For master's, thesis or alternative; for doctorate, one foreign language, comprehensive exam, thesis/dissertation, 1 computer language. *Entrance requirements:* For master's and doctorate, GRE. Additional exam requirements/recommendations for international students: Required—TOEFL. *Application deadline:* For fall admission, 1/31 priority date for domestic and international students. Applications are processed on a rolling basis. Application fee: $45 ($55 for international students). Electronic applications accepted. *Expenses:* Tuition, state resident: full-time $6492; part-time $270.50 per credit hour. Tuition, nonresident: full-time $15,510; part-time $646.25 per credit hour. Required fees: $847; $70.56 per credit hour. Tuition and fees vary according to course load and program. *Financial support:* Fellowships with full tuition reimbursements, research assistantships with full and partial tuition reimbursements, teaching assistantships with full tuition reimbursements, institutionally sponsored loans, scholarships/grants, health care benefits, and unspecified assistantships available. Support available to part-time students. Financial award application deadline: 1/31. *Faculty research:* Commutative algebra, algebraic geometry, combinatronics, stochastic adaptive control, probability analysis, operator algebras, harmonic analysis, PDES, numerical analysis, dynamical systems, topology, set theory. *Unit head:* Prof. Satya Mandal, Chair, 785-864-3651, Fax: 785-864-5255, E-mail: mandal@math.ku.edu. *Application contact:* Prof. Yaozhong Hu, Admissions Director of Graduate Studies, 785-864-3651, E-mail: admissions@math.ku.edu.

University of Kentucky, Graduate School, College of Arts and Sciences, Program in Mathematics, Lexington, KY 40506-0032. Offers applied mathematics (MS); mathematics (MA, MS, PhD). *Degree requirements:* For master's, comprehensive exam, thesis optional; for doctorate, one foreign language, comprehensive exam, thesis/dissertation. *Entrance requirements:* For master's, GRE General Test, minimum undergraduate GPA of 2.75; for doctorate, GRE General Test, minimum graduate GPA of 3.0. Additional exam requirements/recommendations for international students: Required—TOEFL (minimum score 550 paper-based; 213 computer-based). Electronic applications accepted. *Faculty research:* Numerical analysis, combinatorics, partial differential equations, algebra and number theory, real and complex analysis.

University of Lethbridge, School of Graduate Studies, Lethbridge, AB T1K 3M4, Canada. Offers accounting (MScM); addictions counseling (M Sc); agricultural biotechnology (M Sc); agricultural studies (M Sc, MA); anthropology (MA); archaeology (MA); art (MA, MFA); biochemistry (M Sc); biological sciences (M Sc); biomolecular science (PhD); biosystems and biodiversity (PhD); Canadian studies (MA); chemistry (M Sc); computer science (M Sc); computer science and geographical information science (M Sc); counseling psychology (M Ed); dramatic arts (MA); earth, space, and physical science (PhD); economics (MA); educational leadership (M Ed); English (MA); environmental science (M Sc); evolution and behavior (PhD); exercise science (M Sc); finance (MScM); French (MA); French/German (MA); French/Spanish (MA); general education (M Ed); general management (MScM); geography (M Sc, MA); German (MA); health science (M Sc); health sciences (MA); history (MA); human resource management and labour relations (MScM); individualized multidisciplinary (M Sc, MA); information systems (MScM); international management (MScM); kinesiology (M Sc, MA); management (M Sc, MA); marketing (MScM); mathematics (M Sc); music (M Mus, MA); Native American studies (MA); neuroscience (M Sc, PhD); new media (MA); nursing (M Sc); philosophy (MA); physics (M Sc); policy and strategy (MScM); political science (MA); psychology (M Sc, MA); religious studies (MA); social sciences (MA); sociology (MA); theatre and dramatic arts (MFA); theoretical and computational science (PhD); urban and regional studies (MA); women's studies (MA). Part-time and evening/weekend programs available. *Degree requirements:* For doctorate, comprehensive exam, thesis/dissertation. *Entrance requirements:* For master's, GMAT (M Sc in management), bachelor's degree in related field, minimum GPA of 3.0 during previous 20 graded semester courses, 2 years teaching or related experience (M Ed); for doctorate, master's degree, minimum graduate GPA of 3.5. Additional exam requirements/recommendations for international students: Required—TOEFL. *Faculty research:* Movement and brain plasticity, gibberellin physiology, photosynthesis, carbon cycling, molecular properties of main-group ring components.

University of Louisiana at Lafayette, College of Sciences, Department of Mathematics, Lafayette, LA 70504. Offers MS, PhD. Terminal master's awarded for partial completion of doctoral program. *Degree requirements:* For master's, thesis or alternative; for doctorate, 2 foreign languages, comprehensive exam, thesis/dissertation. *Entrance requirements:* For master's, GRE General Test, minimum GPA of 2.75; for doctorate, GRE General Test, minimum GPA of 3.0. Additional exam requirements/recommendations for international students: Required—TOEFL (minimum score 550 paper-based; 213 computer-based). Electronic applications accepted. *Faculty research:* Topology, algebra, applied mathematics, analysis.

University of Louisville, Graduate School, College of Arts and Sciences, Department of Mathematics, Louisville, KY 40292. Offers applied and industrial mathematics (PhD); mathematics (MA). Part-time programs available. *Faculty:* 30 full-time (8 women), 3 part-time/adjunct (1 woman). *Students:* 28 full-time (12 women), 6 part-time (2 women); includes 2 minority (both African Americans), 7 international. Average age 29. 29 applicants, 52% accepted, 12 enrolled. In 2009, 6 master's, 3 doctorates awarded. Terminal master's awarded for partial completion of doctoral program. *Degree requirements:* For master's, comprehensive exam (for some programs), thesis optional; for doctorate, comprehensive exam, thesis/dissertation, internship, project. *Entrance requirements:* For master's and doctorate, GRE General Test. Additional exam requirements/recommendations for international students: Required—TOEFL (minimum score 550 paper-based; 215 computer-based; 79 iBT). *Application deadline:* For fall admission, 3/15 priority date for domestic students, 3/31 priority date for international students; for winter admission, 8/15 priority date for domestic students, 8/31 priority date for international students. Applications are processed on a rolling basis. Application fee: $50. Electronic applications accepted. *Financial support:* In 2009–10, 2 fellowships with tuition reimbursements (averaging $20,000 per year), 1 research assistantship (averaging $20,000 per year), 25 teaching assistantships with tuition reimbursements (averaging $20,000 per year) were awarded; health care benefits and unspecified assistantships also available. *Faculty research:* Algebra, analysis, biomathematics, combinatorics, math financial. *Unit head:* Dr. Thomas Riedel, Chair, 502-852-6826, Fax: 502-852-7132, E-mail: thomas.riedel@louisville.edu. *Application contact:* Dr. Bingtuan Li, Graduate Studies Director, 502-852-6826, Fax: 502-852-7132, E-mail: bing.li@louisville.edu.

University of Maine, Graduate School, College of Liberal Arts and Sciences, Department of Mathematics and Statistics, Orono, ME 04469. Offers mathematics (MA). *Faculty:* 16 full-time (3 women), 8 part-time/adjunct (2 women). *Students:* 7 full-time (2 women), 3 part-time (0 women), 1 international. Average age 27. 11 applicants, 64% accepted, 7 enrolled. In 2009, 2 master's awarded. *Degree requirements:* For master's, thesis optional. *Entrance requirements:* For master's, GRE General Test. Additional exam requirements/recommendations for international students: Required—TOEFL. *Application deadline:* For fall admission, 2/1 priority date for domestic students. Applications are processed on a rolling basis. Application fee: $65. Electronic applications accepted. *Financial support:* In 2009–10, 7 teaching assistantships with tuition reimbursements (averaging $12,790 per year) were awarded; tuition waivers (full and partial) also available. Financial award application deadline: 3/1. *Unit head:* Dr. David Bradley, Chair, 207-581-3920, Fax: 207-581-4977. *Application contact:* Scott G. Delcourt, Associate Dean of the Graduate School, 207-581-3291, Fax: 207-581-3232, E-mail: graduate@maine.edu.

University of Manitoba, Faculty of Graduate Studies, Faculty of Science, Department of Mathematics, Winnipeg, MB R3T 2N2, Canada. Offers M Sc, PhD. *Degree requirements:* For master's, one foreign language, thesis or alternative; for doctorate, one foreign language, thesis/dissertation.

University of Manitoba, Faculty of Graduate Studies, Faculty of Science, Program in Mathematical, Computational and Statistical Sciences, Winnipeg, MB R3T 2N2, Canada. Offers MMCSS.

University of Maryland, College Park, Academic Affairs, College of Computer, Mathematical and Physical Sciences, Department of Mathematics, Program in Mathematics, College Park, MD 20742. Offers MA, PhD. Part-time and evening/weekend programs available. *Students:* 73 full-time (15 women), 11 part-time (0 women); includes 6 minority (4 Asian Americans or Pacific Islanders, 2 Hispanic Americans), 26 international. 233 applicants, 12% accepted, 10 enrolled. In 2009, 6 master's, 10 doctorates awarded. Terminal master's awarded for partial completion of doctoral program. *Degree requirements:* For master's, thesis or alternative; for doctorate, one foreign language, thesis/dissertation, written exam, oral exam. *Entrance requirements:* For master's, GRE General Test, GRE Subject Test, minimum GPA of 3.0, 3 letters of recommendation; for doctorate, GRE General Test, GRE Subject Test, 3 letters of recommendation. *Application deadline:* For fall admission, 1/15 priority date for domestic students, 2/1 for international students; for spring admission, 10/1 for domestic students, 6/1 for international students. Applications are processed on a rolling basis. Application fee: $60. Electronic applications accepted. *Expenses:* Tuition, area resident: Part-time $471 per credit hour. Tuition, state resident: part-time $471 per credit hour. Tuition, nonresident: part-time $1016 per credit hour. Required fees: $337.04 per term. *Financial support:* In 2009–10, 8 fellowships with partial tuition reimbursements (averaging $11,208 per year), 7 research assistantships (averaging $18,131 per year), 52 teaching assistantships (averaging $17,435 per year) were awarded. Financial award applicants required to submit FAFSA. *Unit head:* James Yorke, 301-405-5048, E-mail: yorke@umd.edu. *Application contact:* Dean of Graduate School, 301-405-0358, Fax: 301-314-9305.

University of Massachusetts Amherst, Graduate School, College of Natural Sciences, Department of Mathematics and Statistics, Program in Mathematics and Statistics, Amherst, MA 01003. Offers MS, PhD. *Students:* 53 full-time (18 women), 4 part-time (2 women); includes 2 minority (1 Asian American or Pacific Islander, 1 Hispanic American), 21 international. Average age 28. 286 applicants, 13% accepted, 20 enrolled. In 2009, 14 master's, 4 doctorates awarded. Terminal master's awarded for partial completion of doctoral program. *Degree requirements:* For master's, thesis or alternative; for doctorate, comprehensive exam, thesis/dissertation. *Entrance requirements:* For master's and doctorate, GRE General Test, GRE Subject Test (mathematics). Additional exam requirements/recommendations for international students: Required—TOEFL (minimum score 550 paper-based; 213 computer-based; 80 iBT), IELTS (minimum score 6.5). *Application deadline:* For fall admission, 2/1 for domestic and international students; for spring admission, 10/1 for domestic and international students. Applications are processed on a rolling basis. Application fee: $50 ($65 for international students). Electronic applications accepted. *Expenses:* Tuition, state resident: full-time $2640; part-time $110 per credit. Tuition, nonresident: full-time $9936; part-time $414 per credit. Tuition and fees vary according to course load. *Financial support:* Fellowships, research assistantships, teaching assistantships, career-related internships or fieldwork, Federal Work-Study, scholarships/grants, traineeships, health care benefits, tuition waivers (full), and unspecified assistantships available. Support available to part-time students. Financial award application deadline: 2/1. *Unit head:* Dr. Siman Wong, Graduate Program Director, 413-545-2282, Fax: 413-545-1801. *Application contact:* Jean M. Ames, Supervisor of Admissions, 413-545-0722, Fax: 413-577-0010, E-mail: gradadm@grad.umass.edu.

University of Massachusetts Lowell, College of Arts and Sciences, Department of Mathematical Sciences, Lowell, MA 01854-2881. Offers applied mathematics (MS); computational

Mathematics

University of Massachusetts Lowell (continued)
mathematics (PhD); mathematics (MS). Part-time programs available. *Entrance requirements:* For master's, GRE General Test.

University of Memphis, Graduate School, College of Arts and Sciences, Department of Mathematical Sciences, Memphis, TN 38152. Offers applied mathematics (MS); applied statistics (PhD); bioinformatics (MS); computer science (PhD); computer sciences (MS); mathematics (MS, PhD); statistics (MS, PhD). Part-time programs available. *Faculty:* 19 full-time (4 women), 3 part-time/adjunct (0 women). *Students:* 38 full-time (19 women), 25 part-time (9 women); includes 4 minority (2 African Americans, 2 Asian Americans or Pacific Islanders), 29 international. Average age 34. 26 applicants, 96% accepted, 11 enrolled. In 2009, 6 master's, 5 doctorates awarded. Terminal master's awarded for partial completion of doctoral program. *Degree requirements:* For master's, comprehensive exam; for doctorate, one foreign language, thesis/dissertation, oral exams. *Entrance requirements:* For master's and doctorate, GRE General Test, minimum GPA of 2.5. Additional exam requirements/recommendations for international students: Required—TOEFL (minimum score 550 paper-based; 210 computer-based). *Application deadline:* For fall admission, 8/1 for domestic students, 5/1 priority date for international students; for spring admission, 12/1 for domestic students, 9/1 priority date for international students. Applications are processed on a rolling basis. Application fee: $35 ($60 for international students). Electronic applications accepted. *Expenses:* Tuition, state resident: full-time $6246; part-time $347 per credit hour. Tuition, nonresident: full-time $15,894; part-time $883 per credit hour. Required fees: $1160. Full-time tuition and fees vary according to course load, degree level and program. *Financial support:* In 2009–10, 22 students received support; fellowships with full tuition reimbursements available, research assistantships with full tuition reimbursements available, teaching assistantships with full tuition reimbursements available, career-related internships or fieldwork, Federal Work-Study, scholarships/grants, and unspecified assistantships available. Financial award application deadline: 2/15; financial award applicants required to submit FAFSA. *Faculty research:* Combinatorics, ergodic theory, graph theory, Ramsey theory, applied statistics. *Unit head:* Dr. James E. Jamison, Chairman, 901-678-2482, Fax: 901-678-2480, E-mail: jjamison@memphis.edu. *Application contact:* Dr. Anna Kaminska, Coordinator of Graduate Studies, 901-678-2494, Fax: 901-678-2480.

University of Miami, Graduate School, College of Arts and Sciences, Department of Mathematics, Coral Gables, FL 33124. Offers MA, MS, PhD. Part-time and evening/weekend programs available. Terminal master's awarded for partial completion of doctoral program. *Degree requirements:* For master's, comprehensive exam, qualifying exams; for doctorate, one foreign language, thesis/dissertation, qualifying exams. *Entrance requirements:* For master's and doctorate, GRE General Test, minimum GPA of 3.0. Additional exam requirements/recommendations for international students: Required—TOEFL (minimum score 550 paper-based; 213 computer-based; 59 iBT). Electronic applications accepted. *Faculty research:* Applied mathematics, probability, geometric analysis, differential equations, algebraic combinatorics.

University of Michigan, Horace H. Rackham School of Graduate Studies, College of Literature, Science, and the Arts, Department of Mathematics, Ann Arbor, MI 48109. Offers applied and interdisciplinary mathematics (AM, MS, PhD); mathematics (AM, MS, PhD). Part-time programs available. *Faculty:* 62 full-time (10 women), 1 part-time/adjunct (0 women). *Students:* 134 full-time (32 women), 2 part-time (0 women); includes 16 minority (2 African Americans, 8 Asian Americans or Pacific Islanders, 6 Hispanic Americans), 55 international. Average age 26. 545 applicants, 15% accepted, 33 enrolled. In 2009, 27 master's, 29 doctorates awarded. *Degree requirements:* For doctorate, one foreign language, comprehensive exam, thesis/dissertation, oral defense of dissertation, preliminary exam. *Entrance requirements:* For master's and doctorate, GRE General Test, GRE Subject Test. Additional exam requirements/recommendations for international students: Required—TOEFL (minimum score 580 paper-based; 220 computer-based; 84 iBT). *Application deadline:* For fall admission, 1/22 for domestic students, 1/15 for international students. Applications are processed on a rolling basis. Application fee: $60 ($75 for international students). Electronic applications accepted. *Expenses:* Tuition, state resident: full-time $17,286; part-time $1099 per credit hour. Tuition, nonresident: full-time $34,944; part-time $2080 per credit hour. Required fees: $95 per semester. Tuition and fees vary according to course load, degree level and program. *Financial support:* In 2009–10, 126 students received support, including 18 fellowships with full tuition reimbursements available (averaging $25,000 per year), 11 research assistantships with full tuition reimbursements available (averaging $16,694 per year), 97 teaching assistantships with full tuition reimbursements available (averaging $16,694 per year). Financial award application deadline: 3/15. *Faculty research:* Algebra, analysis, topology, applied mathematics, geometry. *Unit head:* Prof. Mel Hochster, Chair, 734-936-1310, Fax: 734-763-0937, E-mail: math-chair@umich.edu. *Application contact:* Prof. Sergey Fomin, Associate Chairman for Graduate Studies, 734-764-7436, Fax: 734-763-0937, E-mail: math.acgs@umich.edu.

University of Minnesota, Twin Cities Campus, Institute of Technology, School of Mathematics, Minneapolis, MN 55455-0213. Offers MS, PhD. Part-time programs available. Terminal master's awarded for partial completion of doctoral program. *Degree requirements:* For master's, thesis (for some programs); for doctorate, 2 foreign languages, thesis/dissertation. *Entrance requirements:* For master's, GRE Subject Test (recommended); for doctorate, GRE Subject Test. Additional exam requirements/recommendations for international students: Required—TOEFL. *Faculty research:* Partial and ordinary differential equations, algebra and number theory, geometry, combinatorics, numerical analysis.

University of Mississippi, Graduate School, College of Liberal Arts, Department of Mathematics, Oxford, University, MS 38677. Offers MA, MS, PhD. *Faculty:* 28 full-time (9 women). *Students:* 31 full-time (15 women), 1 (woman) part-time; includes 8 minority (7 African Americans, 1 Asian American or Pacific Islander), 4 international. In 2009, 4 master's awarded. *Degree requirements:* For master's, thesis (for some programs); for doctorate, thesis/dissertation. *Entrance requirements:* For master's, GRE General Test, minimum GPA of 3.0; for doctorate, GRE General Test. Additional exam requirements/recommendations for international students: Required—TOEFL. *Application deadline:* For fall admission, 4/1 for domestic students; for spring admission, 10/1 for domestic students. Applications are processed on a rolling basis. Application fee: $25. Electronic applications accepted. *Financial support:* Scholarships/grants available. Financial award application deadline: 3/1; financial award applicants required to submit FAFSA. *Unit head:* Dr. Iwo M. Labuda, Interim Chairman, 662-915-7071, Fax: 662-915-5491, E-mail: mdepart@olemiss.edu. *Application contact:* Dr. Christy M. Wyandt, Associate Dean, 662-915-7474, Fax: 662-915-7577, E-mail: cwyandt@olemiss.edu.

University of Missouri, Graduate School, College of Arts and Sciences, Department of Mathematics, Columbia, MO 65211. Offers applied mathematics (MS); mathematics (MA, MST, PhD). *Faculty:* 47 full-time (9 women), 11 part-time/adjunct (6 women). *Students:* 59 full-time (6 women), 14 part-time (5 women); includes 2 minority (both Hispanic Americans), 25 international. Average age 27. 107 applicants, 23% accepted, 16 enrolled. In 2009, 8 master's, 4 doctorates awarded. *Degree requirements:* For doctorate, 2 foreign languages, comprehensive exam, thesis/dissertation. *Entrance requirements:* For master's and doctorate, GRE General Test, minimum GPA of 3.0; bachelor's degree from an accredited institution, does not have to be in math as long as have sufficient math training. Additional exam requirements/recommendations for international students: Required—TOEFL (minimum score 500 paper-based; 173 computer-based; 61 iBT). *Application deadline:* For fall admission, 1/15 for domestic students. Applications are processed on a rolling basis. Application fee: $45 ($60 for international students). Electronic applications accepted. *Financial support:* In 2009–10, 7 fellowships with full tuition reimbursements, 4 research assistantships with full tuition reimbursements, 64 teaching assistantships with full tuition reimbursements were awarded; institutionally sponsored loans, health care benefits, and unspecified assistantships also available. Financial award applicants required to submit FAFSA. *Faculty research:* Algebraic geometry, analysis (real, complex, functional and harmonic), analytic functions, applied mathematics, financial mathematics and mathematics of insurance, commutative rings, scattering theory, differential equations (ordinary and partial), differential geometry, dynamical systems, general relativity, mathematical physics, number theory, probabilistic analysis and topology. *Unit head:* Dr. Glen Himmelberg, Department Chair, E-mail: himmelbergg@missouri.edu. *Application contact:* Dr. Jan Segert, Director of Graduate Studies, 573-882-4926, E-mail: segertj@missouri.edu.

University of Missouri–Kansas City, College of Arts and Sciences, Department of Mathematics and Statistics, Kansas City, MO 64110-2499. Offers MA, MS, PhD. PhD (interdisciplinary) offered through the School of Graduate Studies. Part-time programs available. *Faculty:* 10 full-time (3 women), 6 part-time/adjunct (1 woman). *Students:* 7 full-time (6 women), 22 part-time (6 women); includes 3 minority (1 African American, 2 Asian Americans or Pacific Islanders), 6 international. Average age 29. 25 applicants, 92% accepted, 14 enrolled. In 2009, 10 master's awarded. Terminal master's awarded for partial completion of doctoral program. *Degree requirements:* For master's, written exam; for doctorate, 2 foreign languages, thesis/dissertation, oral and written exams. *Entrance requirements:* For master's, bachelor's degree in mathematics, minimum GPA of 3.0; for doctorate, GMAT or GRE General Test. Additional exam requirements/recommendations for international students: Required—TOEFL (minimum score 550 paper-based; 213 computer-based; 80 iBT). *Application deadline:* For fall admission, 3/15 for domestic students, 3/15 priority date for international students; for spring admission, 10/15 for domestic and international students. Applications are processed on a rolling basis. Application fee: $45 ($50 for international students). Electronic applications accepted. *Expenses:* Tuition, state resident: full-time $5378; part-time $299 per credit hour. Tuition, nonresident: full-time $13,881; part-time $771 per credit hour. Required fees: $641; $71 per credit hour. Tuition and fees vary according to course load and program. *Financial support:* In 2009–10, 10 teaching assistantships with full tuition reimbursements (averaging $17,460 per year) were awarded; Federal Work-Study, institutionally sponsored loans, and tuition waivers (full and partial) also available. Support available to part-time students. Financial award application deadline: 3/1; financial award applicants required to submit FAFSA. *Faculty research:* Numerical analysis, statistics, biostatistics commutative algebra, differential equations. Total annual research expenditures: $28,737. *Unit head:* Dr. Jie Chen, Chair/Professor, 816-235-1641, Fax: 816-235-5517, E-mail: umkcmathdept@umkc.edu. *Application contact:* Dr. Yong Zeng, Associate Professor, 816-235-1641, Fax: 816-235-5517, E-mail: umkcmathdept@umkc.edu.

University of Missouri–St. Louis, College of Arts and Sciences, Department of Mathematics and Computer Science, St. Louis, MO 63121. Offers applied mathematics (PhD), including computer science; computer science (MS); mathematics (MA). Part-time and evening/weekend programs available. *Faculty:* 16 full-time (2 women), 1 part-time/adjunct (0 women). *Students:* 24 full-time (11 women), 47 part-time (11 women); includes 7 minority (5 African Americans, 1 American Indian/Alaska Native, 1 Asian American or Pacific Islander), 27 international. Average age 30. 88 applicants, 53% accepted, 20 enrolled. In 2009, 23 master's, 1 doctorate awarded. *Degree requirements:* For master's, thesis optional; for doctorate, thesis/dissertation. *Entrance requirements:* For master's, 2 letters of recommendation; for doctorate, GRE General Test, 3 letters of recommendation. Additional exam requirements/recommendations for international students: Required—TOEFL (minimum score 550 paper-based; 213 computer-based). *Application deadline:* For fall admission, 7/1 priority date for domestic and international students; for spring admission, 12/1 priority date for domestic and international students. Applications are processed on a rolling basis. Application fee: $35 ($40 for international students). Electronic applications accepted. *Expenses:* Tuition, state resident: full-time $5377; part-time $297.70 per credit hour. Tuition, nonresident: full-time $13,882; part-time $771.20 per credit hour. Required fees: $220; $12.20 per credit hour. One-time fee: $12. Tuition and fees vary according to course level, campus/location and program. *Financial support:* In 2009–10, 3 research assistantships with full and partial tuition reimbursements (averaging $9,563 per year), 5 teaching assistantships with full and partial tuition reimbursements (averaging $13,500 per year) were awarded; fellowships with full tuition reimbursements also available. Financial award applicants required to submit FAFSA. *Faculty research:* Statistics, algebra, analysis. *Unit head:* Dr. Shiying Zhao, Director of Graduate Studies, 314-516-5741, Fax: 314-516-5400, E-mail: zhao@arch.cs.umsl.edu. *Application contact:* 314-516-5458, Fax: 314-516-6996, E-mail: gradadm@umsl.edu.

The University of Montana, Graduate School, College of Arts and Sciences, Department of Mathematical Sciences, Missoula, MT 59812-0002. Offers mathematics (MA, PhD), including college teaching (PhD), traditional mathematics research (PhD); mathematics education (MA). Part-time programs available. Terminal master's awarded for partial completion of doctoral program. *Degree requirements:* For doctorate, thesis/dissertation. *Entrance requirements:* For master's and doctorate, GRE General Test. Additional exam requirements/recommendations for international students: Required—TOEFL (minimum score 525 paper-based; 195 computer-based).

University of Nebraska at Omaha, Graduate Studies, College of Arts and Sciences, Department of Mathematics, Omaha, NE 68182. Offers MA, MAT, MS. Part-time programs available. *Faculty:* 17 full-time (5 women). *Students:* 19 full-time (6 women), 18 part-time (15 women); includes 4 minority (2 African Americans, 1 Asian American or Pacific Islander, 1 Hispanic American), 7 international. Average age 33. 21 applicants, 62% accepted, 10 enrolled. In 2009, 10 master's awarded. *Degree requirements:* For master's, comprehensive exam, thesis (for some programs). *Entrance requirements:* For master's, minimum GPA of 3.0, 15 undergraduate math hours. Additional exam requirements/recommendations for international students: Required—TOEFL (minimum score 500 paper-based; 173 computer-based; 61 iBT). *Application deadline:* For fall admission, 7/1 priority date for domestic students; for spring admission, 12/1 priority date for domestic students. Applications are processed on a rolling basis. Application fee: $45. Electronic applications accepted. *Financial support:* In 2009–10, 24 students received support; research assistantships with tuition reimbursements available, teaching assistantships with tuition reimbursements available, Federal Work-Study, institutionally sponsored loans, traineeships, tuition waivers (partial), and unspecified assistantships available. Support available to part-time students. Financial award application deadline: 3/1; financial award applicants required to submit FAFSA. *Unit head:* Dr. Jack W. Heidel, Chairperson, 402-554-3430. *Application contact:* Penny Harmoney, Director, Graduate Studies, 402-554-2341, Fax: 402-554-3143, E-mail: graduate@unomaha.edu.

University of Nebraska–Lincoln, Graduate College, College of Arts and Sciences, Department of Mathematics, Lincoln, NE 68588. Offers mathematics (MA, MAT, MS, PhD); mathematics and computer science (PhD). *Degree requirements:* For master's, thesis optional; for doctorate, variable foreign language requirement, comprehensive exam, thesis/dissertation. *Entrance requirements:* Additional exam requirements/recommendations for international students: Required—TOEFL (minimum score 550 paper-based; 213 computer-based), GRE General Test. Electronic applications accepted. *Faculty research:* Applied mathematics, commutative algebra, algebraic geometry, Bayesian statistics, biostatistics.

University of Nevada, Las Vegas, Graduate College, College of Science, Department of Mathematical Sciences, Las Vegas, NV 89154-4020. Offers MS, PhD. Part-time programs available. *Faculty:* 31 full-time (5 women). *Students:* 34 full-time (10 women), 9 part-time (5 women); includes 1 minority (Asian American or Pacific Islander), 15 international. Average age 32. 65 applicants, 57% accepted, 16 enrolled. In 2009, 3 master's, 1 doctorate awarded. *Degree requirements:* For master's, comprehensive exam (for some programs), thesis (for some programs), oral exam. *Entrance requirements:* For master's and doctorate, GRE General Test. Additional exam requirements/recommendations for international students: Required—TOEFL (minimum score 550 paper-based; 213 computer-based; 80 iBT), IELTS (minimum score 7). *Application deadline:* For fall admission, 2/1 priority date for domestic and international students; for spring admission, 10/1 priority date for domestic and international students. Applications are processed on a rolling basis. Application fee: $60 ($75 for international students). Electronic applications accepted. *Financial support:* In 2009–10, 46 teaching assistantships with partial tuition reimbursements (averaging $10,739 per year) were awarded; institutionally sponsored loans, scholarships/grants, health care benefits, and unspecified assistantships also available. Financial award application deadline: 3/1. *Faculty research:* Statistics, pure mathematics; applied mathematics; teaching mathematics; computational mathematics. *Unit head:* Dr. Derrick Dubose, Chair/ Professor, 702-895-0382, Fax: 702-895-4343, E-mail: dubose@unlv.nevada.edu. *Application contact:* Graduate College Admissions Evaluator, 702-895-3320, Fax: 702-895-4180, E-mail: gradcollege@unlv.edu.

University of Nevada, Reno, Graduate School, College of Science, Department of Mathematics and Statistics, Reno, NV 89557. Offers mathematics (MS); teaching mathematics (MATM). *Degree requirements:* For master's, thesis optional. *Entrance requirements:* For master's, GRE General Test, minimum GPA of 2.75. Additional exam requirements/recommendations for international students: Required—TOEFL (minimum score 500 paper-based; 173 computer-based; 61 iBT), IELTS (minimum score 6). Electronic applications accepted. *Faculty research:* Operator algebra, nonlinear systems, differential equations.

University of New Brunswick Fredericton, School of Graduate Studies, Faculty of Science, Department of Mathematics and Statistics, Fredericton, NB E3B 5A3, Canada. Offers M Sc, PhD. *Faculty:* 21 full-time (5 women). *Students:* 22 full-time (7 women). In 2009, 5 master's awarded. *Degree requirements:* For master's, thesis; for doctorate, comprehensive exam, thesis/dissertation. *Entrance requirements:* For master's and doctorate, minimum GPA of 3.0. Additional exam requirements/recommendations for international students: Required—TOEFL (minimum score 550 paper-based; 80 computer-based), TWE (minimum score 4); Recommended—IELTS (minimum score 7). *Application deadline:* For fall admission, 3/1 priority date for domestic students. Applications are processed on a rolling basis. Application fee: $50 Canadian dollars. Tuition and fees charges are reported in Canadian dollars. *Expenses:* Tuition, area resident: Full-time $5562 Canadian dollars; part-time $2781 Canadian dollars per year. Required fees: $49.75 Canadian dollars per term. *Financial support:* In 2009–10, 1 fellowship, 16 research assistantships (averaging $12,000 per year), 12 teaching assistantships (averaging $4,996 per year) were awarded. *Faculty research:* Algebra, general relativity, mechanical biology, sampling theory. *Unit head:* Dr. James Watmough, Director of Graduate Studies, 506-458-7363, Fax: 506-453-4705, E-mail: watmough@unb.ca. *Application contact:* Marilyn Hetherington, Graduate Secretary, 506-458-7373, Fax: 506-453-4705, E-mail: mhetheri@unb.ca.

University of New Hampshire, Graduate School, College of Engineering and Physical Sciences, Department of Mathematics and Statistics, Durham, NH 03824. Offers applied mathematics (MS); industrial statistics (Postbaccalaureate Certificate); mathematics (MS, MST, PhD); mathematics education (PhD); statistics (MS). *Faculty:* 21 full-time (5 women). *Students:* 34 full-time (21 women), 24 part-time (8 women); includes 4 minority (1 Asian American or Pacific Islander, 3 Hispanic Americans), 20 international. Average age 29. 76 applicants, 50% accepted, 17 enrolled. In 2009, 17 master's, 7 doctorates, 1 other advanced degree awarded. Terminal master's awarded for partial completion of doctoral program. *Degree requirements:* For doctorate, 2 foreign languages, thesis/dissertation. *Entrance requirements:* Additional exam requirements/recommendations for international students: Required—TOEFL (minimum score 550 paper-based; 213 computer-based; 80 iBT). *Application deadline:* For fall admission, 4/1 priority date for domestic students, 4/1 for international students; for spring admission, 12/1 for domestic students. Applications are processed on a rolling basis. Application fee: $65. Electronic applications accepted. *Expenses:* Tuition, state resident: full-time $10,380; part-time $577 per credit hour. Tuition, nonresident: full-time $24,350; part-time $1002 per credit hour. Required fees: $1550; $387.50 per semester. Tuition and fees vary according to course load and program. *Financial support:* In 2009–10, 35 students received support, including 2 fellowships, 1 research assistantship, 32 teaching assistantships; Federal Work-Study, scholarships/grants, and tuition waivers (full and partial) also available. Support available to part-time students. Financial award application deadline: 2/15. *Faculty research:* Operator theory, complex analysis, algebra, nonlinear dynamics, statistics. *Unit head:* Dr. Eric Grinberg, Chairperson, 603-862-5772. *Application contact:* Jan Jankowski, Administrative Assistant, 603-862-2320, E-mail: jan.jankowski@unh.edu.

University of New Mexico, Graduate School, College of Arts and Sciences, Department of Mathematics and Statistics, Albuquerque, NM 87131-2039. Offers mathematics (MS, PhD); statistics (MS, PhD). Part-time programs available. *Faculty:* 33 full-time (10 women), 35 part-time/adjunct (10 women). *Students:* 60 full-time (20 women), 29 part-time (9 women); includes 15 minority (3 Asian Americans or Pacific Islanders, 12 Hispanic Americans), 33 international. Average age 33. 71 applicants, 42% accepted, 15 enrolled. In 2009, 17 master's, 8 doctorates awarded. Terminal master's awarded for partial completion of doctoral program. *Degree requirements:* For master's, comprehensive exam (for some programs), thesis or alternative; for doctorate, one foreign language, comprehensive exam, thesis/dissertation, 4 department seminars. *Entrance requirements:* For master's and doctorate, minimum GPA of 3.0, 3 letters of recommendation, letter of intent. Additional exam requirements/recommendations for international students: Required—TOEFL (minimum score 550 paper-based; 213 computer-based). *Application deadline:* For fall admission, 2/15 for domestic students; for spring admission, 11/1 for domestic students. Application fee: $50. Electronic applications accepted. *Expenses:* Tuition, state resident: full-time $2098.80; part-time $233.20 per credit hour. Tuition, nonresident: full-time $6650. Required fees: $25 per semester. Tuition and fees vary according to course load, program and reciprocity agreements. *Financial support:* In 2009–10, 20 students received support, including 4 fellowships (averaging $4,000 per year), 24 research assistantships with tuition reimbursements available (averaging $17,000 per year), 45 teaching assistantships with tuition reimbursements available (averaging $17,300 per year); health care benefits and unspecified assistantships also available. Financial award application deadline: 2/15; financial award applicants required to submit FAFSA. *Faculty research:* Pure and applied mathematics, applied statistics, numerical analysis, biostatistics, differential geometry, fluid dynamics, nonparametric curve estimation. Total annual research expenditures: $1.5 million. *Unit head:* Dr. Alexander Stone, Chair, 505-277-4613, Fax: 505-277-5505, E-mail: astone@math.unm.edu. *Application contact:* Rozanne Littlefield, Program Advisement Coordinator, 505-277-5250, Fax: 505-277-5505, E-mail: rxlitfil@unm.edu.

University of New Orleans, Graduate School, College of Sciences, Department of Mathematics, New Orleans, LA 70148. Offers MS. Part-time programs available. *Entrance requirements:* For master's, BA or BS in mathematics. Additional exam requirements/recommendations for international students: Required—TOEFL (minimum score 550 paper-based; 213 computer-based; 79 iBT). Electronic applications accepted. *Faculty research:* Differential equations, combinatorics, statistics, complex analysis, algebra.

The University of North Carolina at Chapel Hill, Graduate School, College of Arts and Sciences, Department of Mathematics, Chapel Hill, NC 27599. Offers MA, MS, PhD. *Degree requirements:* For master's, comprehensive exam, thesis or alternative, computer proficiency; for doctorate, 2 foreign languages, thesis/dissertation, 3 comprehensive exams, computer proficiency. *Entrance requirements:* For master's and doctorate, GRE General Test, minimum GPA of 3.0. Additional exam requirements/recommendations for international students: Required—TOEFL. Electronic applications accepted. *Faculty research:* Algebraic geometry, topology, analysis, lie theory, applied math.

The University of North Carolina at Charlotte, Graduate School, College of Arts and Sciences, Department of Mathematics and Statistics, Charlotte, NC 28223-0001. Offers applied mathematics (MS, PhD); mathematics (MS); mathematics education (MA). Part-time and evening/weekend programs available. *Faculty:* 43 full-time (5 women). *Students:* 48 full-time (19 women), 35 part-time (16 women); includes 7 African Americans, 4 Asian Americans or Pacific Islanders, 35 international. Average age 29. 45 applicants, 96% accepted, 16 enrolled. In 2009, 13 master's, 5 doctorates awarded. *Degree requirements:* For master's, comprehensive exam; for doctorate, thesis/dissertation. *Entrance requirements:* For master's, GRE General Test, minimum GPA of 3.0 in undergraduate major, 2.75 overall; for doctorate, GRE General Test, minimum overall GPA of 3.0. Additional exam requirements/recommendations for international students: Required—TOEFL (minimum score 557 paper-based; 220 computer-based; or 83 iBT), Michigan English Language Assessment Battery (minimum score 78), IELTS (minimum 6.5), or post-secondary degree earned in a country or province where English is the primary spoken language. *Application deadline:* For fall admission, 7/1 for domestic students, 5/1 for international students; for spring admission, 11/1 for domestic students, 10/1 for international students. Applications are processed on a rolling basis. Application fee: $55. Electronic applications accepted. *Financial support:* In 2009–10, 41 students received support, including 5 fellowships (averaging $26,412 per year), 4 research assistantships (averaging $14,075 per year), 32 teaching assistantships (averaging $14,680 per year); career-related internships or fieldwork, Federal Work-Study, institutionally sponsored loans, scholarships/grants, and unspecified assistantships also available. Support available to part-time students. Financial award application deadline: 4/1; financial award applicants required to submit FAFSA. *Faculty research:* Numerical analysis, differential equations, probability, algebra, analysis, mathematics education, statistics. Total annual research expenditures: $997,165. *Unit head:* Dr. Alan S. Dow, Chair, 704-687-4560, Fax: 704-687-6415, E-mail: adow@uncc.edu. *Application contact:* Kathy B. Giddings, Director of Graduate Admissions, 704-687-5503, Fax: 704-687-3279, E-mail: gradadm@uncc.edu.

The University of North Carolina at Greensboro, Graduate School, College of Arts and Sciences, Department of Mathematics and Statistics, Greensboro, NC 27412-5001. Offers mathematics (MA, PhD). Part-time programs available. *Degree requirements:* For master's, comprehensive exam, thesis (for some programs). *Entrance requirements:* For master's, GRE General Test. Additional exam requirements/recommendations for international students: Required—TOEFL. Electronic applications accepted. *Faculty research:* General and geometric topology, statistics, computer networks, symbolic logic, mathematics education.

The University of North Carolina Wilmington, College of Arts and Sciences, Department of Mathematical Sciences, Wilmington, NC 28403-3297. Offers MS. *Degree requirements:* For master's, comprehensive exam, thesis. *Entrance requirements:* For master's, GRE General Test, GRE Subject Test, minimum B average in undergraduate major. Additional exam requirements/recommendations for international students: Required—TOEFL (minimum score 550 paper-based; 217 computer-based; 79 iBT), IELTS (minimum score 6.5).

University of North Dakota, Graduate School, College of Arts and Sciences, Department of Mathematics, Grand Forks, ND 58202. Offers M Ed, MS. Part-time programs available. *Degree requirements:* For master's, thesis or alternative, final exam. *Entrance requirements:* For master's, minimum GPA of 3.0. Additional exam requirements/recommendations for international students: Required—TOEFL (minimum score 550 paper-based; 213 computer-based; 79 iBT), IELTS (minimum score 6.5). Electronic applications accepted. *Faculty research:* Statistics, measure theory, topological vector spaces, algebra, applied math.

University of Northern British Columbia, Office of Graduate Studies, Prince George, BC V2N 4Z9, Canada. Offers business administration (Diploma); community health science (M Sc); disability management (MA); education (M Ed); first nations studies (MA); gender studies (MA); history (MA); interdisciplinary studies (MA); international studies (MA); mathematical, computer and physical sciences (M Sc); natural resources and environmental studies (M Sc, MA, MNRES, PhD); political science (MA); psychology (M Sc, PhD); social work (MSW). Part-time and evening/weekend programs available. Postbaccalaureate distance learning degree programs offered (no on-campus study). *Degree requirements:* For master's, thesis; for doctorate, thesis/dissertation. *Entrance requirements:* For master's, GRE, minimum B average in undergraduate course work; for doctorate, candidacy exam, minimum A average in graduate course work.

University of Northern Colorado, Graduate School, College of Natural and Health Sciences, School of Mathematical Sciences, Greeley, CO 80639. Offers mathematical teaching (MA); mathematics (MA, PhD); mathematics education (PhD); mathematics: liberal arts (MA). Part-time programs available. *Faculty:* 14 full-time (4 women). *Students:* 15 full-time (9 women), 16 part-time (12 women); includes 2 minority (1 American Indian/Alaska Native, 1 Hispanic American), 3 international. Average age 34. 15 applicants, 100% accepted, 7 enrolled. In 2009, 4 master's, 2 doctorates awarded. *Degree requirements:* For master's, comprehensive exam, thesis or alternative; for doctorate, comprehensive exam, thesis/dissertation. *Entrance requirements:* For master's, GRE General Test (liberal arts), 3 letters of recommendation; for doctorate, GRE General Test, 3 letters of recommendation. *Application deadline:* Applications are processed on a rolling basis. Application fee: $50 ($60 for international students). Electronic applications accepted. *Expenses:* Tuition, state resident: full-time $5770; part-time $320.55 per credit hour. Tuition, nonresident: full-time $13,847; part-time $769.27 per credit hour. Required fees: $948.78; $52.72 per credit. *Financial support:* In 2009–10, 3 research assistantships (averaging $7,835 per year), 13 teaching assistantships (averaging $12,032 per year) were awarded; fellowships, unspecified assistantships also available. Financial award application deadline: 3/1; financial award applicants required to submit FAFSA. *Unit head:* Dr. Dean Allison, Director, 970-351-2820, Fax: 970-351-2155. *Application contact:* Linda Sisson, Graduate Student Admission Coordinator, 970-351-1807, Fax: 970-351-2371, E-mail: linda.sisson@unco.edu.

University of Northern Iowa, Graduate College, College of Natural Sciences, Department of Mathematics, Cedar Falls, IA 50614. Offers mathematics (MA); mathematics for middle grades (MA). Part-time programs available. *Students:* 16 full-time (9 women), 41 part-time (27 women); includes 3 minority (1 African American, 2 Hispanic Americans), 5 international. 23 applicants, 78% accepted, 8 enrolled. In 2009, 13 master's awarded. *Degree requirements:* For master's, comprehensive exam (for some programs), thesis or alternative. *Entrance requirements:* For master's, minimum GPA of 3.0. Additional exam requirements/recommendations for international students: Required—TOEFL (minimum score 600 paper-based; 250 computer-based; 100 iBT). *Application deadline:* For fall admission, 8/1 priority date for domestic students. Applications are processed on a rolling basis. Application fee: $30 ($50 for international students). Electronic applications accepted. *Financial support:* Career-related internships or fieldwork, Federal Work-Study, scholarships/grants, and tuition waivers (full and partial) available. Support available to part-time students. Financial award application deadline: 2/1. *Unit head:* Dr. Douglas Mupasiri, Interim Head, 319-273-2012, Fax: 319-273-2546, E-mail: douglas.mupasiri@uni.edu. *Application contact:* Laurie S. Russell, Record Analyst, 319-273-2623, Fax: 319-273-6792, E-mail: laurie.russell@uni.edu.

University of North Florida, College of Arts and Sciences, Department of Mathematics and Statistics, Jacksonville, FL 32224. Offers mathematical sciences (MS); statistics (MS). Part-time and evening/weekend programs available. *Faculty:* 20 full-time (8 women). *Students:* 12 full-time (4 women), 14 part-time (6 women); includes 3 minority (2 African Americans, 1 Hispanic American), 5 international. Average age 31. 21 applicants, 57% accepted, 5 enrolled. In 2009, 15 master's awarded. *Degree requirements:* For master's, comprehensive exam, thesis optional. *Entrance requirements:* For master's, GRE General Test, minimum GPA of 3.0 in last 60 hours of course work. Additional exam requirements/recommendations for international students: Required—TOEFL (minimum score 500 paper-based; 173 computer-based). *Application deadline:* For fall admission, 7/1 priority date for domestic students, 5/1 for international students; for spring admission, 11/1 priority date for domestic students, 10/1 for international students. Applications are processed on a rolling basis. Application fee: $30. Electronic applications accepted. *Expenses:* Tuition, state resident: full-time $6649.20; part-time

University of North Florida (continued)

$277.05 per credit hour. Tuition, nonresident: full-time $22,970; part-time $957.08 per credit hour. Required fees: $985; $41.03 per credit hour. *Financial support:* In 2009–10, 15 students received support, including 2 teaching assistantships (averaging $6,000 per year); Federal Work-Study and tuition waivers (partial) also available. Support available to part-time students. Financial award application deadline: 4/1; financial award applicants required to submit FAFSA. *Faculty research:* Real analysis, number theory, Euclidean geometry. Total annual research expenditures: $58,348. *Unit head:* Dr. Scott H. Hochwald, Chair, 904-620-2653, Fax: 904-620-2818, E-mail: shochwal@unf.edu. *Application contact:* Dr. Pali Sen, Graduate Coordinator, 904-620-3724, Fax: 904-620-2818, E-mail: psen@unf.edu.

University of North Texas, Robert B. Toulouse School of Graduate Studies, College of Arts and Sciences, Department of Mathematics, Denton, TX 76203. Offers MA, MS, PhD. Part-time programs available. Terminal master's awarded for partial completion of doctoral program. *Degree requirements:* For master's, thesis (for some programs); for doctorate, one foreign language, comprehensive exam, thesis/dissertation. *Entrance requirements:* For master's and doctorate, GRE General Test. Additional exam requirements/recommendations for international students: Required—proof of English language proficiency required for non-native English speakers; Recommended—TOEFL (minimum score 550 paper-based; 213 computer-based). *Application deadline:* For fall admission, 7/15 for domestic students; for spring admission, 11/15 for domestic students. Application fee: $50 ($75 for international students). *Expenses:* Tuition, state resident: full-time $4298; part-time $239 per contact hour. Tuition, nonresident: full-time $9878; part-time $549 per contact hour. Required fees: $265 per contact hour. *Financial support:* In 2009–10, teaching assistantships (averaging $1 per year); fellowships with tuition reimbursements, research assistantships, Federal Work-Study and institutionally sponsored loans also available. Financial award application deadline: 4/1; financial award applicants required to submit FAFSA. *Faculty research:* Differential equations, descriptive set theory, combinatorics, functional analysis, algebra. *Application contact:* Graduate Advisor, 940-565-4304, Fax: 940-565-4805, E-mail: brojovic@unt.edu.

University of Notre Dame, Graduate School, College of Science, Department of Mathematics, Notre Dame, IN 46556. Offers algebra (PhD); algebraic geometry (PhD); applied mathematics (MSAM); complex analysis (PhD); differential geometry (PhD); logic (PhD); partial differential equations (PhD); topology (PhD). Terminal master's awarded for partial completion of doctoral program. *Degree requirements:* For doctorate, one foreign language, thesis/dissertation, qualifying exam. *Entrance requirements:* For master's and doctorate, GRE General Test, GRE Subject Test. Additional exam requirements/recommendations for international students: Required—TOEFL (minimum score 600 paper-based; 250 computer-based; 80 iBT). Electronic applications accepted. *Faculty research:* Algebra, analysis, geometry/topology, logic, applied math.

University of Oklahoma, Graduate College, College of Arts and Sciences, Department of Mathematics, Norman, OK 73019. Offers MA, MS, PhD, MBA/MS. Part-time programs available. *Faculty:* 33 full-time (3 women). *Students:* 65 full-time (28 women), 8 part-time (2 women); includes 11 minority (3 African Americans, 1 American Indian/Alaska Native, 4 Asian Americans or Pacific Islanders, 3 Hispanic Americans), 31 international. 22 applicants, 68% accepted, 9 enrolled. In 2009, 16 master's, 6 doctorates awarded. Terminal master's awarded for partial completion of doctoral program. *Degree requirements:* For master's, comprehensive exam, thesis optional; for doctorate, 2 foreign languages, thesis/dissertation, qualifying exam. *Entrance requirements:* Additional exam requirements/recommendations for international students: Required—TOEFL (minimum score 550 paper-based; 213 computer-based). *Application deadline:* For fall admission, 4/1 priority date for domestic students, 4/1 for international students; for spring admission, 11/1 for domestic students, 9/1 for international students. Applications are processed on a rolling basis. Application fee: $40 ($90 for international students). Electronic applications accepted. *Expenses:* Tuition, state resident: full-time $3744; part-time $156 per credit hour. Tuition, nonresident: full-time $13,577; part-time $565.70 per credit hour. Required fees: $2415; $90.10 per credit hour. *Financial support:* In 2009–10, 62 students received support, including 12 fellowships with full tuition reimbursements available (averaging $3,696 per year), 62 teaching assistantships with partial tuition reimbursements available (averaging $14,807 per year); scholarships/grants and unspecified assistantships also available. Financial award applicants required to submit FAFSA. *Faculty research:* Topology, geometry, algebra, analysis, mathematics pedagogy. Total annual research expenditures: $507,771. *Unit head:* Paul Goodey, Chair, 405-325-6711, Fax: 405-325-7484, E-mail: pgoodey@ou.edu. *Application contact:* Anne Jones, Assistant to Graduate Director, 405-325-6711, Fax: 405-325-7484, E-mail: ajones@math.ou.edu.

See Display above.

University of Oregon, Graduate School, College of Arts and Sciences, Department of Mathematics, Eugene, OR 97403. Offers MA, MS, PhD. Part-time programs available. Terminal master's awarded for partial completion of doctoral program. *Degree requirements:* For doctorate, 2 foreign languages, thesis/dissertation. *Entrance requirements:* For master's and doctorate, GRE General Test, GRE Subject Test. Additional exam requirements/recommendations for international students: Required—TOEFL. *Faculty research:* Algebra, topology, analytic geometry, numerical analysis, statistics.

University of Ottawa, Faculty of Graduate and Postdoctoral Studies, Faculty of Science, Ottawa-Carleton Institute of Mathematics and Statistics, Ottawa, ON K1N 6N5, Canada. Offers M Sc, PhD. Part-time programs available. *Degree requirements:* For master's, thesis optional; for doctorate, one foreign language, comprehensive exam, thesis/dissertation. *Entrance requirements:* For master's, honors B Sc degree or equivalent, minimum B average; for doctorate, M Sc, minimum B+ average. Electronic applications accepted. *Faculty research:* Pure mathematics, applied mathematics, probability and statistics.

University of Pennsylvania, School of Arts and Sciences, Graduate Group in Mathematics, Philadelphia, PA 19104. Offers AM, PhD. *Faculty:* 31 full-time (3 women), 4 part-time/adjunct (0 women). *Students:* 63 full-time (7 women), 2 part-time (0 women); includes 1 minority (Asian American or Pacific Islander), 36 international. 210 applicants, 18% accepted, 19 enrolled. In 2009, 7 master's, 14 doctorates awarded. Terminal master's awarded for partial completion of doctoral program. *Degree requirements:* For master's, one foreign language, thesis or alternative; for doctorate, 2 foreign languages, thesis/dissertation. *Entrance requirements:* For master's and doctorate, GRE General Test, GRE Subject Test. Additional exam requirements/recommendations for international students: Required—TOEFL. *Application deadline:* For fall admission, 12/1 priority date for domestic students. Application fee: $70. Electronic applications accepted. *Expenses:* Tuition: Full-time $25,660; part-time $4758 per course. Required fees: $2152; $270 per course. Tuition and fees vary according to course load, degree level and program. *Financial support:* In 2009–10, 13 fellowships, 27 teaching assistantships were awarded; institutionally sponsored loans, scholarships/grants, traineeships, health care benefits, and unspecified assistantships also available. Financial award application deadline: 12/15. *Faculty research:* Geometry-topology, analysis, algebra, logic, combinatorics.

University of Pittsburgh, School of Arts and Sciences, Department of Mathematics, Pittsburgh, PA 15260. Offers applied mathematics (MA, MS); mathematics (MA, MS, PhD). Part-time programs available. *Faculty:* 33 full-time (5 women), 16 part-time/adjunct (2 women). *Students:* 83 full-time (23 women), 7 part-time (4 women); includes 3 minority (2 African Americans, 1 Asian American or Pacific Islander), 40 international. 250 applicants, 31% accepted, 14 enrolled. In 2009, 13 master's, 3 doctorates awarded. Terminal master's awarded for partial completion of doctoral program. *Degree requirements:* For master's, comprehensive exam, thesis (for some programs); for doctorate, comprehensive exam, thesis/dissertation, preliminary exams, defense of dissertation. *Entrance requirements:* For master's, GRE General Test, GRE Subject Test (recommended), minimum GPA of 3.0; for doctorate, GRE General Test, GRE Subject Test (recommended), minimum GPA of 3.0, minimum QPA of 3.25 in math curriculum. Additional exam requirements/recommendations for international students: Required—TOEFL (minimum score 550 paper-based; 213 computer-based; 80 iBT), IELTS (minimum score 6.5). *Application deadline:* For fall admission, 1/4 priority date for domestic and international students; for spring admission, 9/1 priority date for domestic students, 9/1 for international students. Applications are processed on a rolling basis. Application fee: $50. Electronic applications accepted. *Expenses:* Tuition, state resident: full-time $16,402; part-time $665 per credit. Tuition, nonresident: full-time $28,694; part-time $1175 per credit. Required fees: $690; $175 per term. Tuition and fees vary according to program. *Financial support:* In 2009–10, 84 students received support, including 8 fellowships with full and partial tuition reimbursements available (averaging $18,200 per year), 14 research assistantships with full and partial tuition reimbursements available (averaging $16,000 per year), 50 teaching assistantships with full and partial tuition reimbursements available (averaging $15,300 per year); institutionally sponsored loans, scholarships/grants, traineeships, health care benefits, tuition waivers (partial), and unspecified assistantships also available. Financial award application deadline: 1/4. *Faculty research:* Algebra, analysis, computational math, geometry/topology, math biology. Total annual research expenditures: $1 million. *Unit head:* Ivan Yotov, Chair, 412-624-8361, Fax: 412-624-8397, E-mail: yotov@math.pitt.edu. *Application contact:* Molly Williams, Administrator, 412-624-1175, Fax: 412-624-8397, E-mail: mollyw@pitt.edu.

University of Puerto Rico, Mayagüez Campus, Graduate Studies, College of Arts and Sciences, Department of Mathematics, Mayagüez, PR 00681-9000. Offers applied mathematics (MS); computational sciences (MS); pure mathematics (MS); statistics (MS). Part-time programs available. *Degree requirements:* For master's, one foreign language, comprehensive exam, thesis optional. *Entrance requirements:* For master's, undergraduate degree in mathematics or its equivalent. *Faculty research:* Automata theory, linear algebra, logic.

University of Puerto Rico, Río Piedras, College of Natural Sciences, Department of Mathematics, San Juan, PR 00931-3300. Offers MS, PhD. Part-time programs available. *Degree requirements:* For master's, comprehensive exam, thesis; for doctorate, comprehensive exam, thesis/dissertation. *Entrance requirements:* For master's and doctorate, GRE General Test and GRE Subject Test, interview, minimum GPA of 3.0, 3 letters of recommendation. *Faculty research:* Investigation of database logistics, cryptograph systems, distribution and spectral theory, Boolean function, differential equations.

University of Regina, Faculty of Graduate Studies and Research, Faculty of Science, Department of Mathematics and Statistics, Regina, SK S4S 0A2, Canada. Offers mathematics (M Sc, MA, PhD); statistics (M Sc, MA). *Faculty:* 22 full-time (4 women), 3 part-time/adjunct (0 women). *Students:* 20 full-time (8 women). 23 applicants, 78% accepted. In 2009, 4 master's awarded. *Degree requirements:* For doctorate, comprehensive exam, thesis/dissertation. *Entrance requirements:* Additional exam requirements/recommendations for international students: Required—TOEFL (minimum score 580 paper-based; 237 computer-based; 80 iBT). *Application deadline:* Applications are processed on a rolling basis. Application fee: $90 ($100 for international students). *Financial support:* In 2009–10, 3 fellowships (averaging $19,000 per year), 2 research assistantships (averaging $16,910 per year), 10 teaching assistantships (averaging $6,650 per year) were awarded; scholarships/grants also available. Financial award application deadline: 6/15. *Faculty research:* Pure and applied mathematics, statistics and probability. *Unit head:* Dr. Nader Mobed, Head, 306-585-4359, E-mail: nader.mobed@uregina.ca. *Application contact:* Dr. Shaun Fallat, Graduate Program Coordinator, 306-585-4107, E-mail: sfallat@math.uregina.ca.

University of Rhode Island, Graduate School, College of Arts and Sciences, Department of Mathematics, Kingston, RI 02881. Offers applied mathematical sciences (MS, PhD); mathematics (MS, PhD). Part-time programs available. *Faculty:* 19 full-time (4 women). *Students:* 24 full-time (5 women), 10 part-time (5 women), 4 international. In 2009, 4 master's, 2 doctorates awarded. *Degree requirements:* For master's, comprehensive exam (for some programs), thesis optional; for doctorate, one foreign language, comprehensive exam, thesis/dissertation optional. *Entrance requirements:* For master's and doctorate, 2 letters of recommendation. Additional exam requirements/recommendations for international students: Required—TOEFL (minimum score 550 paper-based; 213 computer-based). *Application deadline:* For fall admission, 7/15 for domestic students, 2/1 for international students; for spring admission, 11/15 for domestic students, 7/15 for international students. Application fee: $65. Electronic applications accepted. *Expenses:* Tuition, state resident: full-time $8828; part-time $490 per credit hour. Tuition, nonresident: full-time $22,100; part-time $1228 per credit hour. Required fees: $1118; $57 per semester. Tuition and fees vary according to program. *Financial support:* In 2009–10, 2 research assistantships with full tuition reimbursements (averaging $13,894 per year), 13 teaching assistantships with full and partial tuition reimbursements (averaging $13,560 per year) were awarded. Financial award application deadline: 7/15; financial award applicants required to submit FAFSA. *Unit head:* Dr. Nancy Eaton, Chairman, 401-874-2709, Fax: 401-874-4454, E-mail: eaton@math.uri.edu. *Application contact:* Dr. Woong Kook, Director of Graduate Studies, 401-874-4421, Fax: 401-874-4454, E-mail: andrewk@math.uri.edu.

University of Rochester, The College, Arts and Sciences, Department of Mathematics, Rochester, NY 14627. Offers MA, MS, PhD. Terminal master's awarded for partial completion of doctoral program. *Degree requirements:* For master's, thesis (for some programs); for doctorate, thesis/dissertation, qualifying exam. *Entrance requirements:* For master's and doctorate, GRE General Test. Additional exam requirements/recommendations for international students: Required—TOEFL.

University of Saskatchewan, College of Graduate Studies and Research, College of Arts and Sciences, Department of Mathematics and Statistics, Saskatoon, SK S7N 5A2, Canada. Offers M Math, MA, PhD. *Faculty:* 22. *Students:* 17. In 2009, 2 master's, 1 doctorate awarded. *Degree requirements:* For master's, thesis (for some programs); for doctorate, comprehensive exam (for some programs), thesis/dissertation. *Entrance requirements:* Additional exam requirements/recommendations for international students: Required—TOEFL (minimum score 80 iBT); Recommended—IELTS (minimum score 6.5). *Application deadline:* For fall admission, 7/1 priority date for domestic students. Applications are processed on a rolling basis. Application fee: $75. Electronic applications accepted. Tuition and fees charges are reported in Canadian dollars. *Expenses:* Tuition, area resident: Full-time $3000 Canadian dollars; part-time $500 Canadian dollars per term. Required fees: $700 Canadian dollars; $100 Canadian dollars per term. *Financial support:* Fellowships, research assistantships, teaching assistantships available. Financial award application deadline: 1/31. *Unit head:* Dr. Raj Srinivasan, Head, 306-966-6089, Fax: 306-966-6086, E-mail: raj.srinivasan@usask.ca. *Application contact:* Dr. Christine Soteros, Graduate Chair, 306-966-6104, Fax: 306-966-6086, E-mail: chris.soteros@usask.ca.

University of South Alabama, Graduate School, College of Arts and Sciences, Department of Mathematics and Statistics, Mobile, AL 36688-0002. Offers mathematics (MS). Part-time and evening/weekend programs available. *Degree requirements:* For master's, comprehensive exam, thesis optional. *Entrance requirements:* For master's, GRE, BS in mathematics or a mathematics-related field. *Expenses:* Tuition, state resident: part-time $218 per contact hour. Required fees: $1102 per year. *Faculty research:* Knot theory, chaos theory.

University of South Carolina, The Graduate School, College of Arts and Sciences, Department of Mathematics, Columbia, SC 29208. Offers mathematics (MA, MS, PhD); mathematics education (M Math, MAT). MAT offered in cooperation with the College of Education. Part-time programs available. Terminal master's awarded for partial completion of doctoral program. *Degree requirements:* For master's, comprehensive exam, thesis (for some programs); for doctorate, one foreign language, comprehensive exam, thesis/dissertation, admission to candidacy exam, residency. *Entrance requirements:* For master's and doctorate, GRE General Test. Additional exam requirements/recommendations for international students: Required—TOEFL (minimum score 600 paper-based; 250 computer-based; 100 iBT). Electronic applications accepted. *Faculty research:* Computational mathematics, analysis (classical/modern), discrete mathematics, algebra, number theory.

The University of South Dakota, Graduate School, College of Arts and Sciences, Department of Mathematics, Vermillion, SD 57069-2390. Offers MA, MNS, MS. Part-time programs available. *Degree requirements:* For master's, thesis (for some programs). *Entrance requirements:* For master's, GRE, minimum GPA of 2.7. Additional exam requirements/recommendations for international students: Required—TOEFL (minimum score 550 paper-based; 213 computer-based; 79 iBT). Electronic applications accepted.

University of Southern California, Graduate School, College of Letters, Arts and Sciences, Department of Mathematics, Los Angeles, CA 90089. Offers applied mathematics (MA, MS, PhD); mathematical finance (MS); mathematics (MA, PhD); statistics (MS). Part-time programs available. *Faculty:* 50 full-time (5 women). *Students:* 102 full-time (33 women), 16 part-time (8 women); includes 10 minority (9 Asian Americans or Pacific Islanders, 1 Hispanic American), 87 international. 500 applicants, 20% accepted, 28 enrolled. In 2009, 37 master's, 7 doctorates awarded. Terminal master's awarded for partial completion of doctoral program. *Degree requirements:* For master's, comprehensive exam (for some programs), thesis (for some programs); for doctorate, 2 foreign languages, comprehensive exam, thesis/dissertation. *Entrance requirements:* For master's, GRE General Test, GMAT; for doctorate, GRE General Test. Additional exam requirements/recommendations for international students: Recommended—TOEFL (minimum score 100 iBT). *Application deadline:* For fall admission, 12/1 for domestic students, 2/15 for international students; for spring admission, 9/1 for domestic and international students. Applications are processed on a rolling basis. Application fee: $85. Electronic applications accepted. *Expenses:* Tuition: Full-time $25,980; part-time $1315 per unit. Required fees: $554. One-time fee: $35 full-time. Full-time tuition and fees vary according to degree level and program. *Financial support:* In 2009–10, 67 students received support, including 5 fellowships with full tuition reimbursements available (averaging $19,000 per year), 9 research assistantships with full tuition reimbursements available (averaging $19,000 per year), 53 teaching assistantships with full tuition reimbursements available (averaging $19,000 per year). Financial award application deadline: 12/1. *Faculty research:* Algebra, algebraic geometry and number theory, analysis/partial differential equations, applied mathematics, financial mathematics, probability, combinatorics and statistics. Total annual research expenditures: $2 million. *Unit head:* Prof. Gary Rosen, Chair, 213-740-1717, Fax: 213-740-2424, E-mail: grosen@usc.edu. *Application contact:* Amy Yung, Department Coordinator, 213-740-8168, Fax: 213-740-2424, E-mail: amy@usc.edu.

University of Southern Mississippi, Graduate School, College of Science and Technology, Department of Mathematics, Hattiesburg, MS 39406-0001. Offers computational science: mathematics (PhD); mathematics (MS). Part-time programs available. *Faculty:* 11 full-time (3 women), 1 part-time/adjunct (0 women). *Students:* 7 full-time (4 women), 1 (woman) part-time; includes 1 minority (African American), 3 international. Average age 29. 10 applicants, 90% accepted, 6 enrolled. In 2009, 5 master's awarded. *Degree requirements:* For master's, comprehensive exam, thesis or alternative. *Entrance requirements:* For master's, GRE General Test, minimum GPA of 2.75 in last 60 hours. Additional exam requirements/recommendations for international students: Required—TOEFL. *Application deadline:* For fall admission, 3/15 priority date for domestic students, 3/15 for international students. Applications are processed on a rolling basis. Application fee: $35. *Expenses:* Tuition, state resident: full-time $5096; part-time $284 per hour. Tuition, nonresident: full-time $13,052; part-time $726 per hour. Required fees: $402. Tuition and fees vary according to course level and course load. *Financial support:* In 2009–10, 1 fellowship (averaging $18,000 per year), 10 teaching assistantships with full tuition reimbursements (averaging $11,408 per year) were awarded; research assistantships with full tuition reimbursements, Federal Work-Study and institutionally sponsored loans also available. Financial award application deadline: 3/15; financial award applicants required to submit FAFSA. *Faculty research:* Dynamical systems, numerical analysis and multigrid methods, random number generation, matrix theory, group theory. *Unit head:* Dr. C. S. Chen, Chair, 601-266-4289, Fax: 601-266-5818. *Application contact:* Shonna Breland, Manager of Graduate Admissions, 601-266-6563, Fax: 601-266-5138.

University of South Florida, Graduate School, College of Arts and Sciences, Department of Mathematics and Statistics, Tampa, FL 33620-9951. Offers mathematics (MA, PhD); statistics (MA). Part-time and evening/weekend programs available. *Faculty:* 24 full-time (3 women), 15 part-time/adjunct (6 women). *Students:* 70 full-time (20 women), 17 part-time (3 women); includes 14 minority (4 African Americans, 6 Asian Americans or Pacific Islanders, 4 Hispanic Americans), 41 international. Average age 32. 99 applicants, 57% accepted, 24 enrolled. In 2009, 12 master's, 3 doctorates awarded. Terminal master's awarded for partial completion of doctoral program. *Degree requirements:* For master's, one foreign language, comprehensive exam, thesis optional; for doctorate, 2 foreign languages, comprehensive exam, thesis/dissertation. *Entrance requirements:* For master's, GRE General Test, minimum GPA of 3.0; for doctorate, GRE General Test, minimum GPA of 3.5 in undergraduate/graduate mathematics courses. Additional exam requirements/recommendations for international students: Required—TOEFL (minimum score 550 paper-based; 213 computer-based; 79 iBT). *Application deadline:* For fall admission, 2/1 for domestic students, 1/2 for international students; for spring admission, 8/1 for domestic students, 6/1 for international students. Application fee: $30. Electronic applications accepted. *Financial support:* In 2009–10, 57 students received support, including teaching assistantships with partial tuition reimbursements available (averaging $14,000 per year); unspecified assistantships also available. Financial award application deadline: 2/1. *Faculty research:* Approximation theory, differential equations, discrete mathematics, functional analysis topology. Total annual research expenditures: $481,106. *Unit head:* Dr. Marcus McWaters, Chairperson, 813-974-3838, Fax: 813-974-2700, E-mail: mmm@usf.edu. *Application contact:* Dr. Xiang-Dong Hou, Graduate Admissions Director, 813-974-2561, Fax: 813-974-2700, E-mail: xhou@cas.usf.edu.

The University of Tennessee, Graduate School, College of Arts and Sciences, Department of Mathematics, Knoxville, TN 37996. Offers applied mathematics (MS); mathematical ecology (PhD); mathematics (M Math, MS, PhD). Part-time programs available. *Degree requirements:* For master's, thesis or alternative; for doctorate, one foreign language, thesis/dissertation. *Entrance requirements:* For master's and doctorate, minimum GPA of 2.7. Additional exam requirements/recommendations for international students: Required—TOEFL. Electronic applications accepted. *Expenses:* Tuition, state resident: full-time $6826; part-time $380 per semester hour. Tuition, nonresident: full-time $21,844; part-time $1147 per semester hour. Tuition and fees vary according to program.

The University of Texas at Arlington, Graduate School, College of Science, Department of Mathematics, Arlington, TX 76019. Offers MA, MS, PhD. Part-time and evening/weekend programs available. *Faculty:* 26 full-time (7 women), 2 part-time/adjunct (0 women). *Students:* 54 full-time (19 women), 75 part-time (32 women); includes 32 minority (13 African Americans, 7 Asian Americans or Pacific Islanders, 12 Hispanic Americans), 31 international. 86 applicants, 99% accepted, 63 enrolled. In 2009, 11 master's, 9 doctorates awarded. *Degree requirements:* For master's, comprehensive exam, thesis or alternative; for doctorate, comprehensive exam, thesis/dissertation. *Entrance requirements:* For master's, GRE General Test (minimum score 350 verbal, 650 quantitative); for doctorate, GRE General Test (minimum score: 350 verbal, 700 quantitative), 30 hours of graduate course work in mathematics, minimum GPA of 3.0 in last 60 hours of course work. Additional exam requirements/recommendations for international students: Required—TOEFL (minimum score 550 paper-based; 213 computer-based; 79 iBT). *Application deadline:* For fall admission, 6/16 priority date for domestic students; for winter admission, 10/17 priority date for domestic students. Applications are processed on a rolling basis. Application fee: $35 ($50 for international students). Electronic applications accepted. *Financial support:* In 2009–10, 36 students received support, including 1 fellowship (averaging $1,000 per year), 2 research assistantships, 23 teaching assistantships (averaging $15,600 per year); Federal Work-Study, institutionally sponsored loans, scholarships/grants, health care benefits, and unspecified assistantships also available. Financial award application deadline: 6/1; financial award applicants required to submit FAFSA. *Faculty research:* Algebra, combinatorics and geometry, applied mathematics and mathematical biology, computational mathematics, mathematics education, probability and statistics. *Unit head:* Dr. Zhu Jiaping,

Mathematics

The University of Texas at Arlington (continued)

Chair, 817-272-1114, E-mail: jpzhu@uta.edu. *Application contact:* Dr. Jianzhong Su, Graduate Advisor, 817-272-5684, Fax: 817-272-5802, E-mail: su@uta.edu.

The University of Texas at Austin, Graduate School, College of Natural Sciences, Department of Mathematics, Austin, TX 78712-1111. Offers mathematics (MA, PhD); statistics (MS Stat). *Entrance requirements:* For master's and doctorate, GRE General Test. Electronic applications accepted.

The University of Texas at Brownsville, Graduate Studies, College of Science, Mathematics and Technology, Brownsville, TX 78520-4991. Offers biological sciences (MS, MSIS); mathematics (MS); physics (MS). Part-time and evening/weekend programs available. *Degree requirements:* For master's, comprehensive exam, thesis optional. *Entrance requirements:* For master's, GRE General Test. Additional exam requirements/recommendations for international students: Required—TOEFL. *Faculty research:* Fish, insects, barrier islands, algae, curlits.

The University of Texas at Dallas, School of Natural Sciences and Mathematics, Programs in Mathematical Sciences, Richardson, TX 75080. Offers applied mathematics (MS, PhD); engineering mathematics (MS); mathematical science (MS); statistics (MS, PhD). Part-time and evening/weekend programs available. *Faculty:* 13 full-time (1 woman), 1 (woman) part-time/adjunct. *Students:* 35 full-time (14 women), 25 part-time (6 women); includes 20 minority (4 African Americans, 15 Asian Americans or Pacific Islanders, 1 Hispanic American), 22 international. Average age 32. 79 applicants, 44% accepted, 13 enrolled. In 2009, 17 master's, 1 doctorate awarded. *Degree requirements:* For master's, thesis optional; for doctorate, thesis/dissertation. *Entrance requirements:* For master's, GRE General Test, minimum GPA of 3.0 in upper-level course work in field; for doctorate, GRE General Test, minimum GPA of 3.5 in upper-level course work in field. Additional exam requirements/recommendations for international students: Required—TOEFL (minimum score 550 paper-based; 213 computer-based). *Application deadline:* For fall admission, 7/15 for domestic students, 5/1 priority date for international students; for spring admission, 11/15 for domestic students, 9/1 priority date for international students. Applications are processed on a rolling basis. Application fee: $50 ($100 for international students). Electronic applications accepted. *Expenses:* Tuition, state resident: full-time $11,068; part-time $461 per credit hour. Tuition, nonresident: full-time $21,178; part-time $882 per credit hour. Tuition and fees vary according to course load. *Financial support:* In 2009–10, 30 teaching assistantships with full tuition reimbursements (averaging $13,500 per year) were awarded; fellowships, research assistantships, career-related internships or fieldwork, Federal Work-Study, institutionally sponsored loans, scholarships/grants, and unspecified assistantships also available. Support available to part-time students. Financial award application deadline: 4/30; financial award applicants required to submit FAFSA. *Faculty research:* Statistical methods, control theory, mathematical modeling and analyses of biological and physical systems. *Unit head:* Dr. Wieslaw Z. Krawcewicz, Department Head, 972-883-2161, Fax: 972-883-6622, E-mail: utdmath@utdallas.edu. *Application contact:* Dr. Michael Baron, Graduate Advisor, 972-883-6874, Fax: 972-883-6622, E-mail: mbaron@utdallas.edu.

See Close-Up on page 327.

The University of Texas at El Paso, Graduate School, College of Science, Department of Mathematical Sciences, El Paso, TX 79968-0001. Offers mathematical sciences (MS); mathematics (teaching) (MAT); statistics (MS). Part-time and evening/weekend programs available. *Students:* 61 (30 women); includes 39 minority (1 Asian American or Pacific Islander, 38 Hispanic Americans), 13 international. Average age 34. In 2009, 17 master's awarded. *Degree requirements:* For master's, thesis optional. *Entrance requirements:* For master's, minimum GPA of 3.0, letters of recommendation. Additional exam requirements/recommendations for international students: Required—TOEFL; Recommended—IELTS. *Application deadline:* For fall admission, 8/1 priority date for domestic students, 3/1 for international students; for spring admission, 11/1 priority date for domestic students, 9/1 for international students. Applications are processed on a rolling basis. Application fee: $45 ($80 for international students). Electronic applications accepted. *Financial support:* In 2009–10, research assistantships with partial tuition reimbursements (averaging $21,812 per year), teaching assistantships with partial tuition reimbursements (averaging $17,450 per year) were awarded; fellowships with tuition reimbursements, institutionally sponsored loans, scholarships/grants, health care benefits, tuition waivers (partial), and unspecified assistantships also available. Support available to part-time students. Financial award application deadline: 3/15; financial award applicants required to submit FAFSA. *Unit head:* Dr. Maria C. Mariani, Chair, 915-747-5761, Fax: 915-747-6502, E-mail: mcmariani@utep.edu. *Application contact:* Dr. Patricia D. Witherspoon, Dean of the Graduate School, 915-747-5491, Fax: 915-747-5788, E-mail: withersp@utep.edu.

The University of Texas at San Antonio, College of Sciences, Department of Mathematics, San Antonio, TX 78249-0617. Offers applied/industrial mathematics (MS); mathematics (MS). Part-time and evening/weekend programs available. *Faculty:* 10 full-time (2 women). *Students:* 15 full-time (6 women), 36 part-time (17 women); includes 22 minority (4 African Americans, 1 Asian American or Pacific Islander, 17 Hispanic Americans), 7 international. Average age 31. 34 applicants, 79% accepted, 16 enrolled. In 2009, 13 master's awarded. *Degree requirements:* For master's, comprehensive exam (for some programs), thesis (for some programs). *Entrance requirements:* For master's, GRE General Test, minimum GPA of 3.0 in last 60 hours. Additional exam requirements/recommendations for international students: Required—TOEFL (minimum score 500 paper-based; 173 computer-based; 61 iBT), IELTS (minimum score 5). *Application deadline:* For fall admission, 7/1 for domestic students, 4/1 for international students; for spring admission, 11/1 for domestic students, 9/1 for international students. Applications are processed on a rolling basis. Application fee: $45 ($80 for international students). Electronic applications accepted. *Expenses:* Tuition, state resident: full-time $3975; part-time $221 per contact hour. Tuition, nonresident: full-time $13,947; part-time $775 per contact hour. Required fees: $1853. *Financial support:* In 2009–10, 9 students received support, including 22 teaching assistantships (averaging $12,682 per year); research assistantships, scholarships/grants, tuition waivers, and unspecified assistantships also available. Support available to part-time students. *Faculty research:* Computational statistics, deterministic and stochastic differential equations, applications of mathematics to architecture and urbanism, mathematical biology, numerical analysis. Total annual research expenditures: $117,596. *Unit head:* Dr. Francis A. Norman, Interim Chair, 210-458-4494, Fax: 210-458-4439, E-mail: sandy.norman@utsa.edu. *Application contact:* Dr. Dorothy A. Flannagan, Dean of the Graduate School, 210-458-4330, Fax: 210-458-4332, E-mail: dorothy.flannagan@utsa.edu.

The University of Texas at Tyler, College of Arts and Sciences, Department of Mathematics, Tyler, TX 75799-0001. Offers MS, MSIS. *Faculty:* 10 full-time (3 women). *Students:* 6 full-time (1 woman), 1 (woman) part-time; includes 1 minority (Hispanic American), 3 international. Average age 26. 4 applicants, 100% accepted, 4 enrolled. In 2009, 2 master's awarded. *Degree requirements:* For master's, comprehensive exam, thesis optional. *Entrance requirements:* For master's, GRE General Test. Additional exam requirements/recommendations for international students: Required—TOEFL (minimum score 79 computer-based). *Application deadline:* For fall admission, 8/17 priority date for domestic students, 7/1 priority date for international students; for spring admission, 12/21 priority date for domestic students, 11/1 priority date for international students. Applications are processed on a rolling basis. Application fee: $25 ($50 for international students). *Expenses:* Tuition, state resident: part-time $665 per semester hour. Tuition, nonresident: part-time $942 per semester hour. Part-time tuition and fees vary according to degree level and program. *Financial support:* In 2009–10, 7 students received support, including 7 teaching assistantships (averaging $10,000 per year); fellowships, research assistantships, unspecified assistantships also available. Financial award application deadline: 7/1; financial award applicants required to submit FAFSA. *Faculty research:* Discrete geometry, knot theory, commutative algebra, noncommutative rings, group theory, mathematical biology, mathematical physics. *Unit head:* Dr. Sheldon Davis, Chair, 903-566-7210, Fax: 903-565-5781. *Application contact:* Dr. Sheldon Davis.

The University of Texas–Pan American, College of Science and Engineering, Department of Mathematics, Edinburg, TX 78539. Offers mathematical science (MS); mathematics teaching (MS). Part-time and evening/weekend programs available. *Degree requirements:* For master's, comprehensive exam. *Entrance requirements:* For master's, GRE General Test, minimum GPA of 3.0. *Expenses:* Tuition, state resident: full-time $3630.60; part-time $201.70 per credit hour. Tuition, nonresident: full-time $8617; part-time $478.70 per credit hour. Required fees: $806.50. *Faculty research:* Boundary value problems in differential equations, training of public school teachers in methods of presenting mathematics, harmonic analysis, inverse problems, commulative algebra.

University of the Incarnate Word, School of Graduate Studies and Research, School of Mathematics, Science, and Engineering, Program in Mathematics, San Antonio, TX 78209-6397. Offers mathematics teaching (MA); research statistics (MS). Part-time and evening/weekend programs available. *Students:* 1 full-time (0 women), 1 (woman) part-time; includes 1 minority (Hispanic American). Average age 49. In 2009, 2 master's awarded. *Degree requirements:* For master's, capstone or prerequisite knowledge for research statistics. *Entrance requirements:* For master's, GRE (minimum score 800 verbal and quantitative), 18 hours of undergraduate mathematics with minimum GPA of 3.0; letter of recommendation by a professional in the field, writing sample, teaching experience at the precollege level. Additional exam requirements/recommendations for international students: Required—TOEFL (minimum score 560 paper-based; 220 computer-based; 83 iBT). *Application deadline:* Applications are processed on a rolling basis. Application fee: $20. Electronic applications accepted. *Expenses:* Tuition: Full-time $12,150; part-time $675 per credit hour. Required fees: $83 per credit hour. *Financial support:* Federal Work-Study and scholarships/grants available. Financial award applicants required to submit FAFSA. *Unit head:* Dr. Zhanbo Yang, Graduate Programs Coordinator, 210-283-5008, Fax: 210-829-3153, E-mail: yang@uiwtx.edu. *Application contact:* Andrea Cyterski-Acosta, Dean of Enrollment, 210-829-6005, Fax: 210-829-3921, E-mail: admis@uiwtx.edu.

The University of Toledo, College of Graduate Studies, College of Arts and Sciences, Department of Mathematics, Toledo, OH 43606-3390. Offers applied mathematics (MS, PhD); mathematics (MA, PhD); statistics (MS, PhD). Part-time programs available. *Degree requirements:* For doctorate, 2 foreign languages, thesis/dissertation. *Entrance requirements:* For master's and doctorate, GRE General Test, GRE Subject Test. Electronic applications accepted. *Faculty research:* Topology.

University of Toronto, School of Graduate Studies, Physical Sciences Division, Department of Mathematics, Toronto, ON M5S 1A1, Canada. Offers M Sc, MMF, PhD. Part-time programs available. *Degree requirements:* For master's, thesis optional, research project; for doctorate, thesis/dissertation. *Entrance requirements:* For master's, minimum B average in final year, bachelor's degree in mathematics or a related area, 3 letters of reference; for doctorate, master's degree in mathematics or a related area, minimum A– average, 3 letters of reference.

University of Tulsa, Graduate School, College of Engineering and Natural Sciences, Department of Mathematical and Computer Sciences, Program in Mathematical Sciences, Tulsa, OK 74104-3189. Offers MS, MTA, MSF/MSAM. Part-time programs available. *Faculty:* 11 full-time (2 women). *Students:* 3 full-time (2 women), 3 part-time (1 woman); includes 1 minority (American Indian/Alaska Native), 1 international. Average age 27. 8 applicants, 38% accepted, 2 enrolled. In 2009, 1 master's awarded. *Degree requirements:* For master's, thesis (for some programs). *Entrance requirements:* For master's, GRE General Test. Additional exam requirements/recommendations for international students: Required—TOEFL (minimum score 550 paper-based; 213 computer-based; 80 iBT), IELTS (minimum score 6). *Application deadline:* Applications are processed on a rolling basis. Application fee: $40. Electronic applications accepted. *Expenses:* Tuition: Full-time $16,182; part-time $899 per credit hour. Required fees: $4 per credit hour. Tuition and fees vary according to course load. *Financial support:* In 2009–10, 3 students received support, including 3 teaching assistantships with full and partial tuition reimbursements available (averaging $9,661 per year); fellowships with full and partial tuition reimbursements available, research assistantships with full and partial tuition reimbursements available, Federal Work-Study, scholarships/grants, health care benefits, tuition waivers (full and partial), and unspecified assistantships also available. Financial award application deadline: 2/1; financial award applicants required to submit FAFSA. *Faculty research:* Optimization theory, numerical analysis, mathematical physics, modeling, Bayesian statistical inference. *Application contact:* Dr. Christian Constanda, Advisor, 918-631-3088, Fax: 918-631-3077, E-mail: christian-constanda@utulsa.edu.

University of Utah, The Graduate School, College of Science, Department of Mathematics, Salt Lake City, UT 84112-0090. Offers M Phil, M Stat, MA, MS, PhD. Part-time programs available. *Faculty:* 44 full-time (3 women). *Students:* 82 full-time (25 women), 32 part-time (16 women); includes 7 minority (2 African Americans, 3 Asian Americans or Pacific Islanders, 2 Hispanic Americans), 31 international. Average age 30. 182 applicants, 23% accepted, 21 enrolled. In 2009, 12 master's, 4 doctorates awarded. Terminal master's awarded for partial completion of doctoral program. *Degree requirements:* For master's, thesis or alternative, written or oral exam; for doctorate, thesis/dissertation, written and oral exams. *Entrance requirements:* For master's and doctorate, minimum undergraduate GPA of 3.0. Additional exam requirements/recommendations for international students: Required—TOEFL (minimum score 500 paper-based; 173 computer-based; 61 iBT). *Application deadline:* For fall admission, 1/15 for domestic and international students; for spring admission, 11/1 for domestic and international students. Application fee: $55 ($65 for international students). Electronic applications accepted. *Expenses:* Tuition, state resident: full-time $4004; part-time $1674 per semester. Tuition, nonresident: full-time $14,134; part-time $5915 per semester. Required fees: $324 per semester. Tuition and fees vary according to course load, degree level and program. *Financial support:* In 2009–10, 82 students received support, including 19 fellowships with full tuition reimbursements available (averaging $26,250 per year), 5 research assistantships with full tuition reimbursements available (averaging $15,800 per year), 44 teaching assistantships with full tuition reimbursements available (averaging $15,300 per year). Financial award application deadline: 1/15. *Faculty research:* Algebraic geometry; geometry and topology materials and microstructure; mathematical biology; probability and statistics. Total annual research expenditures: $2.7 million. *Unit head:* Dr. Aaron Bertram, Chairman, 801-581-6851, Fax: 801-581-4148, E-mail: bertram@math.utah.edu. *Application contact:* Dr. Andrejs Treibergs, Graduate Advisor, 801-581-8350, Fax: 801-581-4148, E-mail: treiberg@math.utah.edu.

See Close-Up on page 329.

University of Utah, The Graduate School, Interdepartmental Program in Statistics, Salt Lake City, UT 84112-1107. Offers biostatistics (MST); business (MST); econometrics (MST); educational psychology (MST); mathematics (MST); sociology (MST); statistics (M Stat). Part-time programs available. *Students:* 25 full-time (11 women), 15 part-time (6 women); includes 4 minority (3 Asian Americans or Pacific Islanders, 1 Hispanic American), 12 international. Average age 30. 59 applicants, 44% accepted, 12 enrolled. In 2009, 15 master's awarded. *Degree requirements:* For master's, comprehensive exam, projects. *Entrance requirements:* For master's, GMAT (business), GRE General Test (sociology and educational psychology), minimum GPA of 3.0; course work in calculus, matrix theory, statistics. Additional exam requirements/recommendations for international students: Required—TOEFL (minimum score 500 paper-based; 173 computer-based). *Application deadline:* For fall admission, 7/1 for domestic students, 4/1 for international students. Applications are processed on a rolling basis. Application fee: $55 ($65 for international students). *Expenses:* Tuition, state resident: full-time $4004; part-time $1674 per semester. Tuition, nonresident: full-time $14,134; part-time $5915 per semester. Required fees: $324 per semester. Tuition and fees vary according to course load, degree level and program. *Financial support:* Career-related internships or fieldwork available. *Faculty research:* Biostatistics, management, economics, educational psychology, mathematics. *Unit head:* Tariq Mughal, Chair, University Statistics Committee, 801-585-9547, E-mail: tariq.mughal@business.utah.edu. *Application contact:* Laura Egbert, MSTAT Program Coordinator, 801-585-6853, E-mail: laura.demattia@utah.edu.

University of Vermont, Graduate College, College of Engineering and Mathematics, Department of Mathematics and Statistics, Program in Mathematics, Burlington, VT 05405. Offers mathematics (MS, PhD); mathematics education (MST). *Students:* 24 (8 women), 1 international. 39 applicants, 41% accepted, 6 enrolled. In 2009, 6 master's, 1 doctorate awarded. *Degree requirements:* For doctorate, thesis/dissertation. *Entrance requirements:* For master's and doctorate, GRE General Test. Additional exam requirements/recommendations for international students: Required—TOEFL (minimum score 550 paper-based; 213 computer-based; 80 iBT). *Application deadline:* For fall admission, 4/1 priority date for domestic students. Applications are processed on a rolling basis. Application fee: $40. Electronic applications accepted. *Expenses:* Tuition, area resident: Part-time $508 per credit hour. Tuition, state resident: part-time $508 per credit hour. Tuition, nonresident: part-time $1281 per credit hour. *Financial support:* Fellowships, research assistantships, teaching assistantships available. Financial award application deadline: 3/1. *Unit head:* Dr. M. Wilson, Coordinator, 802-656-2940. *Application contact:* Dr. M. Wilson, Coordinator, 802-656-2940.

University of Victoria, Faculty of Graduate Studies, Faculty of Science, Department of Mathematics and Statistics, Victoria, BC V8W 2Y2, Canada. Offers M Sc, MA, PhD. Part-time programs available. *Degree requirements:* For master's, thesis; for doctorate, one foreign language, thesis/dissertation, 3 qualifying exams, candidacy exam. *Entrance requirements:* Additional exam requirements/recommendations for international students: Required—TOEFL (minimum score 575 paper-based; 233 computer-based), IELTS (minimum score 7). Electronic applications accepted. *Faculty research:* Functional analysis and operator theory, applied ordinary and partial differential equations, discrete mathematics and graph theory.

University of Virginia, College and Graduate School of Arts and Sciences, Department of Mathematics, Charlottesville, VA 22903. Offers math education (MA); mathematics (MA, PhD). *Faculty:* 31 full-time (5 women), 5 part-time/adjunct (2 women). *Students:* 49 full-time (14 women), 1 (woman) part-time; includes 1 minority (Asian American or Pacific Islander), 11 international. Average age 25. 105 applicants, 15% accepted, 5 enrolled. In 2009, 8 master's, 7 doctorates awarded. *Degree requirements:* For master's, one foreign language, comprehensive exam, thesis optional; for doctorate, one foreign language, comprehensive exam, thesis/dissertation. *Entrance requirements:* For master's and doctorate, GRE General Test, GRE Subject Test, 2-3 letters of recommendation. Additional exam requirements/recommendations for international students: Required—TOEFL (minimum score 600 paper-based; 250 computer-based; 90 iBT), IELTS. *Application deadline:* For fall admission, 1/15 for domestic and international students. Applications are processed on a rolling basis. Application fee: $60. Electronic applications accepted. *Financial support:* Fellowships, teaching assistantships, unspecified assistantships available. Financial award application deadline: 1/15; financial award applicants required to submit FAFSA. *Unit head:* Don Ramirez, Chair, 434-924-4919, Fax: 434-982-3084, E-mail: math-help@virginia.edu. *Application contact:* Don Ramirez, Chair, 434-924-4919, Fax: 434-982-3084, E-mail: math-help@virginia.edu.

University of Washington, Graduate School, College of Arts and Sciences, Department of Mathematics, Seattle, WA 98195. Offers mathematics (MA, MS, PhD); numerical analysis (MS); optimization (MS). Part-time programs available. Terminal master's awarded for partial completion of doctoral program. *Degree requirements:* For master's, thesis optional; for doctorate, 2 foreign languages, thesis/dissertation. *Entrance requirements:* For master's, GRE, minimum GPA of 3.0; for doctorate, GRE General Test, GRE Subject Test (mathematics), minimum GPA of 3.0. Additional exam requirements/recommendations for international students: Required—TOEFL. Electronic applications accepted. *Faculty research:* Algebra, analysis, probability, combinatorics and geometry.

University of Washington, Graduate School, Interdisciplinary Graduate Program in Quantitative Ecology and Resource Management, Seattle, WA 98195. Offers MS, PhD. *Degree requirements:* For master's, thesis; for doctorate, thesis/dissertation. *Entrance requirements:* For master's and doctorate, GRE General Test, minimum GPA of 3.0. Additional exam requirements/recommendations for international students: Required—TOEFL. Electronic applications accepted. *Faculty research:* Population dynamics, statistical analysis, ecological modeling and systems analysis of aquatic and terrestrial ecosystems.

University of Waterloo, Graduate Studies, Faculty of Mathematics, Department of Combinatorics and Optimization, Waterloo, ON N2L 3G1, Canada. Offers M Math, PhD. *Degree requirements:* For master's, research paper or thesis; for doctorate, comprehensive exam, thesis/dissertation. *Entrance requirements:* For master's, GRE General Test, honors degree in field, minimum B+ average; for doctorate, GRE General Test, master's degree, minimum A average. Additional exam requirements/recommendations for international students: Required—TOEFL, TWE. Electronic applications accepted. *Faculty research:* Algebraic and enumerative combinatorics, continuous optimization, cryptography, discrete optimization and graph theory.

University of Waterloo, Graduate Studies, Faculty of Mathematics, Department of Pure Mathematics, Waterloo, ON N2L 3G1, Canada. Offers M Math, PhD. Part-time programs available. Terminal master's awarded for partial completion of doctoral program. *Degree requirements:* For master's, thesis optional; for doctorate, comprehensive exam, thesis/dissertation. *Entrance requirements:* For master's, honors degree in field, minimum B+ average; for doctorate, master's degree, minimum B+ average. Additional exam requirements/recommendations for international students: Required—TOEFL (minimum score 580 paper-based; 237 computer-based; 92 iBT), TWE (minimum score 4). Electronic applications accepted. *Faculty research:* Algebra, algebraic and differential geometry, functional and harmonic analysis, logic and universal algebra, number theory.

The University of Western Ontario, Faculty of Graduate Studies, Physical Sciences Division, Department of Mathematics, London, ON N6A 5B8, Canada. Offers M Sc, PhD. Terminal master's awarded for partial completion of doctoral program. *Degree requirements:* For master's, thesis or alternative; for doctorate, one foreign language, comprehensive exam, thesis/dissertation, qualifying exam. *Entrance requirements:* For master's, minimum B average, honors degree; for doctorate, master's degree. Additional exam requirements/recommendations for international students: Required—TOEFL (minimum score 550 paper-based; 213 computer-based). *Faculty research:* Algebra and number theory, analysis, geometry and topology.

University of West Florida, College of Arts and Sciences: Sciences, Department of Mathematics and Statistics, Pensacola, FL 32514-5750. Offers applied statistics (MS); mathematical sciences (MS). Part-time and evening/weekend programs available. *Faculty:* 9 full-time (1 woman). *Students:* 9 full-time (4 women), 26 part-time (17 women); includes 5 minority (3 African Americans, 1 Asian American or Pacific Islander, 1 Hispanic American), 2 international. Average age 32. 16 applicants, 88% accepted, 10 enrolled. In 2009, 14 master's awarded. *Degree requirements:* For master's, thesis optional. *Entrance requirements:* For master's, GRE General Test, minimum GPA of 3.0. Additional exam requirements/recommendations for international students: Required—TOEFL (minimum score 550 paper-based; 213 computer-based). *Application deadline:* For fall admission, 6/1 for domestic students, 5/15 for international students; for spring admission, 11/1 for domestic students, 10/1 for international students. Applications are processed on a rolling basis. Application fee: $30. *Expenses:* Tuition, state resident: full-time $4982; part-time $260 per credit hour. Tuition, nonresident: full-time $20,059; part-time $919 per credit hour. Required fees: $1247; $52 per credit hour. *Financial support:* In 2009–10, 14 teaching assistantships with partial tuition reimbursements (averaging $4,006 per year) were awarded; unspecified assistantships also available. Financial award application deadline: 4/15; financial award applicants required to submit FAFSA. *Unit head:* Dr. Kuiyuan Li, Chairperson, 850-474-2287, E-mail: mathstat@uwf.edu. *Application contact:* Terry McCray, Assistant Director of Graduate Admissions, 850-473-7718, Fax: 850-473-7714, E-mail: gradadmissions@uwf.edu.

University of West Georgia, Graduate School, College of Arts and Sciences, Department of Mathematics, Carrollton, GA 30118. Offers mathematics (MSM); teaching and applied mathematics (MS). *Faculty:* 13 full-time (2 women). *Students:* 3 full-time (1 woman), 3 part-time (1 woman); includes 1 minority (African American), 1 international. Average age 25. 6 applicants, 50% accepted, 1 enrolled. *Application deadline:* For fall admission, 7/17 for domestic students; for spring admission, 11/20 for domestic students. Applications are processed on a rolling basis. Application fee: $30. Electronic applications accepted. *Expenses:* Tuition, state resident: full-time $2952; part-time $164 per semester hour. Tuition, nonresident: full-time $11,808; part-time $656 per semester hour. Required fees: $42.90 per semester hour. $307 per semester. Tuition and fees vary according to course load. *Unit head:* Dr. Bruce Landman, Chair, 678-839-6489, E-mail: landman@westga.edu. *Application contact:* Dr. Charles W. Clark, Dean, 678-839-6508, E-mail: cclark@westga.edu.

University of Windsor, Faculty of Graduate Studies, Faculty of Science, Department of Mathematics and Statistics, Windsor, ON N9B 3P4, Canada. Offers mathematics (M Sc); statistics (M Sc, PhD). *Degree requirements:* For master's, thesis or alternative; for doctorate, comprehensive exam, thesis/dissertation. *Entrance requirements:* For master's, minimum B average; for doctorate, minimum A average. Additional exam requirements/recommendations for international students: Required—TOEFL (minimum score 560 paper-based; 220 computer-based). Electronic applications accepted. *Faculty research:* Applied mathematics, operational research, fluid dynamics.

University of Wisconsin–Madison, Graduate School, College of Letters and Science, Department of Mathematics, Madison, WI 53706. Offers PhD. *Faculty:* 54 full-time (3 women). *Students:* 130 full-time (39 women); includes 33 minority (1 African American, 26 Asian Americans or Pacific Islanders, 6 Hispanic Americans). Average age 24. 425 applicants, 11% accepted, 22 enrolled. In 2009, 19 doctorates awarded. *Degree requirements:* For doctorate, comprehensive exam, thesis/dissertation, classes in a minor field. *Entrance requirements:* For doctorate, GRE General Test, GRE Math Subject Test. Additional exam requirements/recommendations for international students: Required—TOEFL (minimum score 580 paper-based; 237 computer-based; 92 iBT). *Application deadline:* For fall admission, 12/31 priority date for domestic and international students. Application fee: $56. Electronic applications accepted. *Expenses:* Tuition, state resident: part-time $594 per credit. Tuition, nonresident: part-time $1504 per credit. Required fees: $65 per credit. Tuition and fees vary according to course load, program and reciprocity agreements. *Financial support:* In 2009–10, 2 students received support, including 11 fellowships with full tuition reimbursements available (averaging $23,000 per year), 5 research assistantships with full tuition reimbursements available (averaging $16,500 per year), 131 teaching assistantships with full tuition reimbursements available (averaging $14,088 per year); institutionally sponsored loans, scholarships/grants, and unspecified assistantships also available. Financial award application deadline: 12/31. *Faculty research:* Analysis, applied/computational mathematics, geometry/topology, logic, algebra/number theory, probability. Total annual research expenditures: $2.3 million. *Unit head:* Shi Jin, Chair, 608-263-3051, Fax: 608-263-8891, E-mail: jin@math.wisc.edu. *Application contact:* Mary Rice, Graduate Program Administrator, 608-263-8884, Fax: 608-263-8891, E-mail: grad_program@math.wisc.edu.

University of Wisconsin–Milwaukee, Graduate School, College of Letters and Sciences, Department of Mathematical Sciences, Milwaukee, WI 53201-0413. Offers mathematics (MS, PhD). *Faculty:* 36 full-time (4 women). *Students:* 66 full-time (28 women), 17 part-time (8 women); includes 4 minority (3 Asian Americans or Pacific Islanders, 1 Hispanic American), 32 international. Average age 30. 110 applicants, 54% accepted, 23 enrolled. In 2009, 21 master's, 10 doctorates awarded. *Degree requirements:* For master's, comprehensive exam, thesis optional; for doctorate, 2 foreign languages, thesis/dissertation. *Entrance requirements:* Additional exam requirements/recommendations for international students: Required—TOEFL (minimum score 550 paper-based; 79 iBT), IELTS (minimum score 6.5). *Application deadline:* For fall admission, 1/1 priority date for domestic students; for spring admission, 9/1 for domestic students. Applications are processed on a rolling basis. Application fee: $45 ($75 for international students). *Expenses:* Tuition, state resident: full-time $8800. Tuition, nonresident: full-time $20,760. Tuition and fees vary according to program and reciprocity agreements. *Financial support:* In 2009–10, 9 fellowships, 4 research assistantships, 53 teaching assistantships were awarded; career-related internships or fieldwork also available. Support available to part-time students. Financial award application deadline: 4/15. *Faculty research:* Algebra, applied mathematics, atmospheric science, probability and statistics, topology. Total annual research expenditures: $535,523. *Unit head:* Craig Guilbault, Representative, 414-229-5110, Fax: 414-229-4907, E-mail: craigg@uwm.edu. *Application contact:* General Information Contact, 414-229-4982, Fax: 414-229-6967, E-mail: gradschool@uwm.edu.

University of Wyoming, College of Arts and Sciences, Department of Mathematics, Laramie, WY 82071. Offers mathematics (MA, MAT, MS, MST, PhD); mathematics/computer science (PhD). Part-time programs available. Terminal master's awarded for partial completion of doctoral program. *Degree requirements:* For master's, comprehensive exam, thesis, qualifying exam; for doctorate, comprehensive exam, thesis/dissertation, preliminary exam. *Entrance requirements:* For master's and doctorate, GRE General Test, minimum GPA of 3.0. Additional exam requirements/recommendations for international students: Required—TOEFL (minimum score 540 paper-based; 76 iBT). *Faculty research:* Numerical analysis, classical analysis, mathematical modeling, algebraic combinations.

Utah State University, School of Graduate Studies, College of Science, Department of Mathematics and Statistics, Logan, UT 84322. Offers industrial mathematics (MS); mathematical sciences (PhD); mathematics (M Math, MS); statistics (MS). Part-time programs available. Terminal master's awarded for partial completion of doctoral program. *Degree requirements:* For master's, thesis optional, qualifying exam; for doctorate, one foreign language, comprehensive exam, thesis/dissertation. *Entrance requirements:* For master's and doctorate, GRE General Test, minimum GPA of 3.0. Additional exam requirements/recommendations for international students: Required—TOEFL. *Faculty research:* Differential equations, computational mathematics, dynamical systems, probability and statistics, pure mathematics.

Vanderbilt University, Graduate School, Department of Mathematics, Nashville, TN 37240-1001. Offers MA, MAT, MS, PhD. *Faculty:* 53 full-time (6 women). *Students:* 35 full-time (11 women); includes 1 minority (Hispanic American), 16 international. Average age 26. 133 applicants, 6% accepted, 4 enrolled. In 2009, 9 master's, 3 doctorates awarded. *Degree requirements:* For master's, one foreign language, thesis or alternative; for doctorate, one foreign language, comprehensive exam, thesis/dissertation. *Entrance requirements:* For master's and doctorate, GRE General Test, GRE Subject Test. Additional exam requirements/recommendations for international students: Required—TOEFL (minimum score 570 paper-based; 230 computer-based; 88 iBT). *Application deadline:* For fall admission, 1/15 for domestic and international students. Application fee: $0. Electronic applications accepted. *Financial support:* Fellowships with full and partial tuition reimbursements, research assistantships with full tuition reimbursements, teaching assistantships with full tuition reimbursements, Federal Work-Study, institutionally sponsored loans, scholarships/grants, and health care benefits available. Financial award application deadline: 1/15; financial award applicants required to submit CSS PROFILE or FAFSA. *Faculty research:* Algebra, topology, applied mathematics, graph theory, analytical mathematics. *Unit head:* Dietmar Bisch, Chair, 615-322-6672, Fax:

Mathematics

Vanderbilt University (continued)
615-343-0215. *Application contact:* Mike Neamtu, Director of Graduate Studies, 615-322-6672, Fax: 315-343-0215, E-mail: mathgrad@vanderbilt.edu.

Villanova University, Graduate School of Liberal Arts and Sciences, Department of Mathematical Sciences, Program in Mathematical Sciences, Villanova, PA 19085-1699. Offers MA. Part-time and evening/weekend programs available. *Students:* 4 full-time (1 woman), 28 part-time (9 women); includes 1 minority (Asian American or Pacific Islander). Average age 32. 16 applicants, 100% accepted, 11 enrolled. In 2009, 11 master's awarded. *Degree requirements:* For master's, comprehensive exam. *Entrance requirements:* For master's, GRE, minimum GPA of 3.0. Additional exam requirements/recommendations for international students: Required—TOEFL. *Application deadline:* For fall admission, 3/1 priority date for domestic and international students; for spring admission, 11/15 priority date for domestic and international students. Applications are processed on a rolling basis. Application fee: $50. Electronic applications accepted. *Expenses:* Tuition: Part-time $630 per credit. Required fees: $60 per credit. Part-time tuition and fees vary according to degree level and program. *Financial support:* Research assistantships, Federal Work-Study available. Financial award applicants required to submit FAFSA. *Unit head:* Dr. Douglas Norton, Chair, 610-519-4850. *Application contact:* Dr. Adele Lindenmeyr, Dean, Graduate School of Liberal Arts and Sciences, 610-519-7093, Fax: 610-519-7096.

See Close-Up on page 331.

Virginia Commonwealth University, Graduate School, College of Humanities and Sciences, Department of Mathematics and Applied Mathematics, Richmond, VA 23284-9005. Offers applied mathematics (MS); mathematics (MS); operations research (MS); statistical sciences and operations research (MS, Certificate). *Degree requirements:* For master's, thesis optional. *Entrance requirements:* For master's, GRE General Test, GRE Subject Test. Additional exam requirements/recommendations for international students: Required—TOEFL.

Virginia Polytechnic Institute and State University, Graduate School, College of Science, Department of Mathematics, Blacksburg, VA 24061. Offers applied mathematics (MS, PhD); mathematical physics (MS, PhD); pure mathematics (MS, PhD). *Entrance requirements:* For master's and doctorate, GRE. Additional exam requirements/recommendations for international students: Required—TOEFL (minimum score 550 paper-based; 213 computer-based). Electronic applications accepted. *Faculty research:* Differential equations, operator theory, numerical analysis, algebra, control theory.

Virginia State University, School of Graduate Studies, Research, and Outreach, School of Engineering, Science and Technology, Department of Mathematics and Computer Science, Petersburg, VA 23806-0001. Offers computer science (MS); mathematics (MS); mathematics education (M Ed). *Degree requirements:* For master's, thesis (for some programs).

Wake Forest University, Graduate School of Arts and Sciences, Department of Mathematics, Winston-Salem, NC 27109. Offers MA. Part-time programs available. *Degree requirements:* For master's, one foreign language, thesis optional. *Entrance requirements:* For master's, GRE General Test. Additional exam requirements/recommendations for international students: Required—TOEFL (minimum score 213 computer-based; 79 iBT). Electronic applications accepted. *Faculty research:* Algebra, ring theory, topology, differential equations.

Washington State University, Graduate School, College of Sciences, Department of Mathematics, Pullman, WA 99164. Offers applied mathematics (MS, PhD); mathematics teaching (MS, PhD). Part-time programs available. *Faculty:* 26. *Students:* 33 full-time (11 women), 5 part-time (3 women); includes 3 minority (1 African American, 2 Asian Americans or Pacific Islanders), 10 international. Average age 29. 84 applicants, 29% accepted, 9 enrolled. In 2009, 7 master's, 1 doctorate awarded. *Degree requirements:* For master's, comprehensive exam (for some programs), thesis (for some programs), oral exam, project; for doctorate, 2 foreign languages, comprehensive exam, thesis/dissertation, oral exam, written exam. *Entrance requirements:* For master's and doctorate, minimum GPA of 3.0, 3 letters of recommendation. Additional exam requirements/recommendations for international students: Required—TOEFL (minimum score 600 paper-based; 250 computer-based), IELTS. *Application deadline:* For fall admission, 1/10 for domestic and international students; for spring admission, 7/1 for domestic and international students. Applications are processed on a rolling basis. Application fee: $50. Electronic applications accepted. *Financial support:* In 2009–10, 33 students received support, including 2 fellowships with tuition reimbursements available (averaging $2,500 per year), 3 research assistantships with full and partial tuition reimbursements available (averaging $14,634 per year), 27 teaching assistantships with full and partial tuition reimbursements available (averaging $13,383 per year); career-related internships or fieldwork, Federal Work-Study, institutionally sponsored loans, health care benefits, and tuition waivers (partial) also available. Financial award application deadline: 2/15; financial award applicants required to submit FAFSA. *Faculty research:* Computational mathematics, operations research, modeling in the natural sciences, applied statistics. *Unit head:* Dr. K. A. Ariyawansa, Chair, 509-335-4918, Fax: 509-335-1188, E-mail: ari@wsu.edu. *Application contact:* Graduate School Admissions, 800-GRADWSU, Fax: 509-335-1949, E-mail: gradsch@wsu.edu.

See Close-Up on page 333.

Washington University in St. Louis, Graduate School of Arts and Sciences, Department of Mathematics, St. Louis, MO 63130-4899. Offers mathematics (MA, PhD); statistics (MA). Terminal master's awarded for partial completion of doctoral program. *Degree requirements:* For master's, thesis or alternative; for doctorate, thesis/dissertation. *Entrance requirements:* For master's and doctorate, GRE General Test. Electronic applications accepted.

Washington University in St. Louis, Henry Edwin Sever Graduate School of Engineering and Applied Science, Department of Electrical and Systems Engineering, St. Louis, MO 63130-4899. Offers electrical engineering (MS, D Sc, PhD); systems science and mathematics (MS, D Sc, PhD). Part-time programs available. *Faculty:* 17 full-time (2 women), 5 part-time/adjunct (1 woman). *Students:* 75 full-time (33 women), 21 part-time (2 women); includes 10 minority (1 African American, 8 Asian Americans or Pacific Islanders, 1 Hispanic American), 45 international. Average age 23. 281 applicants, 29% accepted, 25 enrolled. In 2009, 16 master's, 4 doctorates awarded. Terminal master's awarded for partial completion of doctoral program. *Degree requirements:* For master's, thesis or alternative; for doctorate, comprehensive exam, thesis/dissertation. *Entrance requirements:* For master's, minimum GPA of 3.0 in the last 2 years of undergraduate course work; for doctorate, GRE. Additional exam requirements/recommendations for international students: Required—TOEFL (minimum score 550 paper-based; 213 computer-based; 80 iBT). *Application deadline:* For fall admission, 1/15 for domestic and international students. Applications are processed on a rolling basis. Application fee: $60. Electronic applications accepted. *Financial support:* In 2009–10, 8 fellowships with full tuition reimbursements (averaging $20,000 per year), 29 research assistantships with full tuition reimbursements (averaging $26,950 per year) were awarded; teaching assistantships with full tuition reimbursements, career-related internships or fieldwork, Federal Work-Study, institutionally sponsored loans, scholarships/grants, and unspecified assistantships also available. Financial award application deadline: 1/15; financial award applicants required to submit FAFSA. *Faculty research:* Applied physics and electronics, signal and image processing, systems analysis, biomedicine, and energy. Total annual research expenditures: $1 million. *Unit head:* Dr. Arye Nehorai, Chair, 314-935-5565, Fax: 314-935-7500, E-mail: nehorai@ese.wustl.edu. *Application contact:* Shauna Dollison, Director of Graduate Programs, 314-935-4830, Fax: 314-935-7500.

Wayne State University, College of Liberal Arts and Sciences, Department of Mathematics, Program in Mathematics, Detroit, MI 48202. Offers MA, MS, PhD. *Degree requirements:* For master's, thesis or alternative; for doctorate, 2 foreign languages, thesis/dissertation. *Entrance requirements:* For master's, successful completion of 12 semester credits in mathematics beyond sophmore calculus; for doctorate, Master's degree in mathematics or equivalent level of advancement. Additional exam requirements/recommendations for international students: Required—TOEFL (minimum score 550 paper-based; 213 computer-based); Recommended—TWE (minimum score 6). Electronic applications accepted.

Wesleyan University, Graduate Programs, Department of Mathematics, Middletown, CT 06459. Offers MA, PhD. *Faculty:* 16 full-time (3 women). *Students:* 20 full-time (5 women), 5 international. Average age 28. 47 applicants, 9% accepted, 2 enrolled. In 2009, 3 master's, 4 doctorates awarded. Terminal master's awarded for partial completion of doctoral program. *Degree requirements:* For master's, one foreign language, thesis; for doctorate, 2 foreign languages, thesis/dissertation. *Entrance requirements:* For master's, GRE General Test, GRE Subject Test; for doctorate, GRE Subject Test. Additional exam requirements/recommendations for international students: Required—TOEFL. *Application deadline:* For fall admission, 2/15 for domestic and international students. Applications are processed on a rolling basis. Application fee: $0. Electronic applications accepted. *Financial support:* In 2009–10, 18 teaching assistantships with full tuition reimbursements were awarded; tuition waivers (full and partial) also available. Financial award application deadline: 4/15; financial award applicants required to submit FAFSA. *Faculty research:* Topology, analysis. *Unit head:* Dr. Mark Hovey, Chair, 860-685-2169, E-mail: mhovey@wesleyan.edu. *Application contact:* Caryn Canalia, Administrative Assistant, 860-685-2182, Fax: 860-685-2571, E-mail: ccanalia@wesleyan.edu.

See Close-Up on page 337.

West Chester University of Pennsylvania, Office of Graduate Studies, College of Arts and Sciences, Department of Mathematics, West Chester, PA 19383. Offers applied statistics (MS, Certificate); mathematics (MA, Teaching Certificate). Part-time and evening/weekend programs available. *Students:* 1 full-time (0 women), 89 part-time (37 women); includes 33 minority (14 African Americans, 17 Asian Americans or Pacific Islanders, 2 Hispanic Americans), 5 international. Average age 32. 55 applicants, 93% accepted, 37 enrolled. In 2009, 34 master's awarded. *Entrance requirements:* For master's, GMAT, GRE General Test, or MAT (mathematics), interview; for other advanced degree, GMAT, GRE General Test, or MAT (for mathematics). Additional exam requirements/recommendations for international students: Required—TOEFL (minimum score 550 paper-based; 213 computer-based; 80 iBT). *Application deadline:* For fall admission, 4/15 priority date for domestic students, 3/15 for international students; for spring admission, 10/15 for domestic students, 9/1 for international students. Applications are processed on a rolling basis. Application fee: $35. Electronic applications accepted. *Expenses:* Tuition, state resident: full-time $6666; part-time $370 per credit. Tuition, nonresident: full-time $10,666; part-time $593 per credit. Required fees: $122.56 per credit. *Financial support:* In 2009–10, 6 research assistantships with full and partial tuition reimbursements (averaging $5,000 per year) were awarded; unspecified assistantships also available. Support available to part-time students. Financial award application deadline: 2/15; financial award applicants required to submit FAFSA. *Faculty research:* Teachers teaching with technology in service training program. *Unit head:* Dr. Kathleen Jackson, Chair, 610-436-2537, E-mail: kjackson@wcupa.edu. *Application contact:* Dr. John Kerrigan, Graduate Coordinator, 610-436-2351, E-mail: jkerrigan@wcupa.edu.

Western Carolina University, Graduate School, College of Arts and Sciences, Department of Mathematics and Computer Science, Cullowhee, NC 28723. Offers applied mathematics (MS). Part-time and evening/weekend programs available. *Students:* 10 full-time (4 women). Average age 28. 6 applicants, 67% accepted, 3 enrolled. In 2009, 9 master's awarded. *Degree requirements:* For master's, thesis or alternative. *Entrance requirements:* For master's, GRE General Test, appropriate undergraduate degree, 3 letters of recommendation. Additional exam requirements/recommendations for international students: Required—TOEFL (minimum score 550 paper-based; 270 computer-based; 79 iBT). *Application deadline:* For fall admission, 5/1 priority date for domestic students; for spring admission, 9/1 priority date for domestic students. Applications are processed on a rolling basis. Application fee: $45. *Financial support:* In 2009–10, 7 students received support, including 7 teaching assistantships with full and partial tuition reimbursements available (averaging $9,000 per year); fellowships, research assistantships with full and partial tuition reimbursements available, career-related internships or fieldwork, institutionally sponsored loans, scholarships/grants, and unspecified assistantships also available. Financial award application deadline: 3/31; financial award applicants required to submit FAFSA. *Unit head:* Dr. Mark Holliday, Head, 828-227-7245, Fax: 828-227-7240, E-mail: holliday@email.wcu.edu. *Application contact:* Admissions Specialist for Applied Mathematics, 828-227-7398, Fax: 828-227-7480, E-mail: gradsch@email.wcu.edu.

Western Connecticut State University, Division of Graduate Studies, School of Arts and Sciences, Department of Mathematics, Danbury, CT 06810-6885. Offers mathematics (MA); theoretical mathematics (MA). Part-time programs available. *Faculty:* 4 full-time (1 woman), 1 (woman) part-time/adjunct. *Students:* 18 part-time (8 women); includes 1 minority (Asian American or Pacific Islander). Average age 32. 11 applicants, 91% accepted, 10 enrolled. In 2009, 2 master's awarded. *Degree requirements:* For master's, thesis or research project, completion of program in 6 years. *Entrance requirements:* For master's, minimum GPA of 2.5. Additional exam requirements/recommendations for international students: Recommended—TOEFL (minimum score 550 paper-based; 213 computer-based; 79 iBT), IELTS (minimum score 6). *Application deadline:* For fall admission, 8/5 priority date for domestic students; for spring admission, 1/5 priority date for domestic students. Applications are processed on a rolling basis. Application fee: $50. *Expenses:* Tuition, state resident: full-time $5012; part-time $278 per credit hour. Tuition, nonresident: full-time $13,962; part-time $284 per credit hour. Required fees: $3886; $139 per credit hour. Full-time tuition and fees vary according to course load and program. Part-time tuition and fees vary according to course level, degree level and program. *Financial support:* Application deadline: 5/1; *Unit head:* Dr. Sam Lightwood, Graduate Coordinator, 203-837-9369, Fax: 203-837-8525, E-mail: lightwoods@wcsu.edu. *Application contact:* Chris Shankle, Associate Director of Graduate Studies, 203-837-9005, Fax: 203-837-8326, E-mail: shanklec@wcsu.edu.

Western Illinois University, School of Graduate Studies, College of Arts and Sciences, Department of Mathematics, Macomb, IL 61455-1390. Offers applied math (Certificate); mathematics (MS). Part-time programs available. *Students:* 13 full-time (5 women), 3 part-time (2 women), 5 international. Average age 31. 11 applicants, 91% accepted. In 2009, 3 master's awarded. *Degree requirements:* For master's, thesis or alternative. *Entrance requirements:* Additional exam requirements/recommendations for international students: Required—TOEFL (minimum score 500 paper-based; 173 computer-based; 61 iBT). *Application deadline:* Applications are processed on a rolling basis. Application fee: $30. Electronic applications accepted. *Expenses:* Tuition, state resident: full-time $4486; part-time $249.21 per credit hour. Tuition, nonresident: full-time $8972; part-time $498.42 per credit hour. Required fees: $72.62 per credit hour. *Financial support:* In 2009–10, 12 students received support, including 9 research assistantships with full tuition reimbursements available (averaging $7,280 per year), 3 teaching assistantships with full tuition reimbursements available (averaging $8,400 per year). Financial award applicants required to submit FAFSA. *Unit head:* Dr. Iraj Kalantari, Chairperson, 309-298-1054. *Application contact:* Evelyn Hoing, Assistant Director of Graduate Studies, 309-298-1806, Fax: 309-298-2345, E-mail: grad-office@wiu.edu.

Western Kentucky University, Graduate Studies, Ogden College of Science and Engineering, Department of Mathematics, Bowling Green, KY 42101. Offers MA Ed, MS. *Degree requirements:* For master's, comprehensive exam, thesis optional, written exam. *Entrance requirements:* For master's, GRE General Test, minimum GPA of 2.75. Additional exam requirements/recommendations for international students: Required—TOEFL (minimum score 555 paper-based; 213 computer-based; 79 iBT). *Expenses:* Tuition, state resident: full-time $4160; part-time $416 per credit hour. Tuition, nonresident: full-time $9550; part-time $506 per credit hour. Tuition and fees vary according to campus/location and reciprocity agreements.

Faculty research: Differential equations numerical analysis, probability statistics, algebra, typology, knot theory.

Western Michigan University, Graduate College, College of Arts and Sciences, Department of Mathematics, Programs in Mathematics, Kalamazoo, MI 49008. Offers mathematics (MA); mathematics education (MA, PhD). *Degree requirements:* For master's, oral exams; for doctorate, one foreign language, thesis/dissertation, oral exams, 3 comprehensive exams, internship. *Entrance requirements:* For doctorate, GRE General Test.

Western Washington University, Graduate School, College of Sciences and Technology, Department of Mathematics, Bellingham, WA 98225-5996. Offers MS. Part-time programs available. *Degree requirements:* For master's, thesis (for some programs), project, qualifying examination. *Entrance requirements:* For master's, GRE General Test, minimum GPA of 3.0 in last 60 semester hours or last 90 quarter hours. Additional exam requirements/recommendations for international students: Required—TOEFL (minimum score 567 paper-based; 227 computer-based). Electronic applications accepted. *Faculty research:* Numerical analysis, combinatorics, harmonic analysis, inverse problems, reliability testing.

West Texas A&M University, College of Agriculture, Nursing, and Natural Sciences, Department of Mathematics, Physical Sciences and Engineering Technology, Program in Mathematics, Canyon, TX 79016-0001. Offers MS. Part-time programs available. *Degree requirements:* For master's, comprehensive exam, thesis optional. *Entrance requirements:* For master's, GRE General Test. Additional exam requirements/recommendations for international students: Required—TOEFL (minimum score 550 paper-based). Electronic applications accepted.

West Virginia University, Eberly College of Arts and Sciences, Department of Mathematics, Morgantown, WV 26506. Offers applied mathematics (MS, PhD); discrete mathematics (PhD); interdisciplinary mathematics (MS); mathematics for secondary education (MS); pure mathematics (MS). Part-time programs available. Terminal master's awarded for partial completion of doctoral program. *Degree requirements:* For master's, comprehensive exam (for some programs), thesis optional; for doctorate, one foreign language, comprehensive exam, thesis/dissertation. *Entrance requirements:* For master's, GRE Subject Test (recommended), minimum GPA of 2.5; for doctorate, GRE Subject Test (recommended), master's degree in mathematics. Additional exam requirements/recommendations for international students: Required—TOEFL (paper-based 550; computer-based 213) or IELTS (paper-based 6). *Faculty research:* Combinatorics and graph theory, differential equations, applied and computational mathematics.

Wichita State University, Graduate School, Fairmount College of Liberal Arts and Sciences, Department of Mathematics and Statistics, Wichita, KS 67260. Offers applied mathematics (PhD); mathematics (MS). Part-time programs available. *Expenses:* Tuition, state resident: full-time $4247; part-time $235.95 per credit hour. Tuition, nonresident: full-time $11,171; part-time $620.60 per credit hour. Required fees: $34; $3.60 per credit hour. $17 per term. Tuition and fees vary according to campus/location and program. *Unit head:* Dr. Buma Fridman, Chair, 316-978-3160, Fax: 316-978-3748, E-mail: buma.fridman@wichita.edu. *Application contact:* Dr. Buma Fridman, Chair, 316-978-3160, Fax: 316-978-3748, E-mail: buma.fridman@wichita.edu.

Wilfrid Laurier University, Faculty of Graduate Studies, Faculty of Science, Department of Mathematics, Waterloo, ON N2L 3C5, Canada. Offers M Sc. *Degree requirements:* For master's, thesis optional. *Entrance requirements:* For master's, 4 year honors degree in mathematics, minimum B+ average. Additional exam requirements/recommendations for international students: Required—TOEFL (minimum score 230 computer-based; 89 iBT). Electronic applications accepted. *Faculty research:* Modeling, analysis, resolution, and generalization of financial and scientific problems.

Wilkes University, College of Graduate and Professional Studies, College of Science and Engineering, Department of Mathematics and Computer Science, Wilkes-Barre, PA 18766-0002. Offers mathematics (MS, MS Ed). Part-time programs available. *Students:* 1 full-time (0 women), 1 part-time (0 women). Average age 33. In 2009, 2 master's awarded. *Degree requirements:* For master's, thesis or alternative. *Entrance requirements:* For master's, GRE General Test. Additional exam requirements/recommendations for international students: Required—TOEFL (minimum score 500 paper-based; 173 computer-based; 79 iBT). *Application deadline:* Applications are processed on a rolling basis. Application fee: $45. *Financial support:* Federal Work-Study and unspecified assistantships available. Financial award application deadline: 3/1; financial award applicants required to submit FAFSA. *Unit head:* Dr. John Harrison, Chair, 570-408-4845, Fax: 570-408-7883, E-mail: john.harrison@wilkes.edu. *Application contact:* Kathleen Houlihan, Director of Graduate Studies, 570-408-3235, Fax: 570-408-7846, E-mail: kathleen.houlihan@wilkes.edu.

Worcester Polytechnic Institute, Graduate Studies and Research, Department of Mathematical Sciences, Worcester, MA 01609-2280. Offers applied mathematics (MS); applied statistics (MS); financial mathematics (MS); industrial mathematics (MS); mathematical sciences (PhD); mathematics (MME). Part-time and evening/weekend programs available. *Faculty:* 15 full-time (2 women), 7 part-time/adjunct (1 woman). *Students:* 28 full-time (13 women), 36 part-time (17 women). 172 applicants, 77% accepted, 32 enrolled. In 2009, 29 master's, 1 doctorate awarded. *Degree requirements:* For master's, thesis (for some programs); for doctorate, comprehensive exam, thesis/dissertation. *Entrance requirements:* For master's and doctorate, GRE General Test, GRE Subject Test in math (recommended), 3 letters of recommendation. Additional exam requirements/recommendations for international students: Required—TOEFL (minimum score 550 paper-based; 213 computer-based; 79 iBT), IELTS (minimum score 6.5). *Application deadline:* For fall admission, 1/15 priority date for domestic students, 1/15 for international students; for spring admission, 10/15 priority date for domestic students, 10/15 for international students. Applications are processed on a rolling basis. Application fee: $70. Electronic applications accepted. *Financial support:* Career-related internships or fieldwork, institutionally sponsored loans, scholarships/grants, and unspecified assistantships available. Financial award application deadline: 1/15. *Faculty research:* Applied analysis and differential equations, computational mathematics, discrete mathematics, applied and computational statistics, industrial and financial mathematics. *Unit head:* Dr. Bogdan Vernescu, Head, 508-831-5241, Fax: 508-831-5824, E-mail: vernescu@wpi.edu. *Application contact:* Dr. Joseph Petruccelli, Graduate Coordinator, 508-831-5241, Fax: 508-831-5824, E-mail: jdp@wpi.edu.

Wright State University, School of Graduate Studies, College of Science and Mathematics, Department of Mathematics and Statistics, Program in Mathematics, Dayton, OH 45435. Offers MS. *Degree requirements:* For master's, comprehensive exam. *Entrance requirements:* For master's, previous course work in mathematics beyond calculus. Additional exam requirements/recommendations for international students: Required—TOEFL. *Faculty research:* Analysis, algebraic combinatorics, graph theory, operator theory.

Yale University, Graduate School of Arts and Sciences, Department of Mathematics, New Haven, CT 06520. Offers M Phil, MS, PhD. *Degree requirements:* For doctorate, 2 foreign languages, thesis/dissertation. *Entrance requirements:* For doctorate, GRE General Test, GRE Subject Test.

York University, Faculty of Graduate Studies, Faculty of Science and Engineering, Program in Mathematics and Statistics, Toronto, ON M3J 1P3, Canada. Offers industrial and applied mathematics (M Sc); mathematics and statistics (MA, PhD). Part-time programs available. *Degree requirements:* For master's, thesis optional; for doctorate, one foreign language, comprehensive exam, thesis/dissertation. Electronic applications accepted.

Youngstown State University, Graduate School, College of Science, Technology, Engineering and Mathematics, Department of Mathematics and Statistics, Youngstown, OH 44555-0001. Offers applied mathematics (MS); computer science (MS); secondary mathematics (MS); statistics (MS). Part-time programs available. *Degree requirements:* For master's, comprehensive exam, thesis optional. *Entrance requirements:* For master's, minimum GPA of 2.7 in computer science and mathematics. Additional exam requirements/recommendations for international students: Required—TOEFL. *Faculty research:* Regression analysis, numerical analysis, statistics, Markov chain, topology and fuzzy sets.

Statistics

Acadia University, Faculty of Pure and Applied Science, Department of Mathematics and Statistics, Wolfville, NS B4P 2R6, Canada. Offers applied mathematics and statistics (M Sc). *Faculty:* 13 full-time (2 women). *Students:* 3 full-time (1 woman), 1 part-time (0 women). 6 applicants, 17% accepted, 1 enrolled. In 2009, 6 master's awarded. *Degree requirements:* For master's, thesis. *Entrance requirements:* For master's, honors degree in mathematics, statistics or equivalent. Additional exam requirements/recommendations for international students: Required—TOEFL (minimum score 580 paper-based; 237 computer-based; 93 iBT), IELTS (minimum score 6.5). *Application deadline:* For fall admission, 2/1 priority date for domestic and international students. Applications are processed on a rolling basis. Application fee: $50. *Financial support:* Research assistantships, teaching assistantships, career-related internships or fieldwork and unspecified assistantships available. Financial award application deadline: 2/1. *Faculty research:* Geophysical fluid dynamics, machine scheduling problems, control theory, stochastic optimization, survival analysis. *Unit head:* Dr. Jeff Hooper, Head, 902-585-1382, Fax: 902-585-1074, E-mail: jeff.hooper@acadiau.ca. *Application contact:* Dr. Richard Karsten, Professor, 902-585-1608, Fax: 902-585-1074, E-mail: richard.karsten@acadiau.ca.

American University, College of Arts and Sciences, Department of Mathematics and Statistics, Program in Statistics, Washington, DC 22016-8050. Offers applied statistics (Certificate); statistics (MS). Part-time and evening/weekend programs available. *Students:* 6 full-time (2 women), 7 part-time (6 women); includes 1 minority (Asian American or Pacific Islander), 6 international. Average age 27. 26 applicants, 46% accepted, 5 enrolled. In 2009, 4 master's awarded. *Degree requirements:* For master's, comprehensive exam, thesis or alternative, tools of research; foreign language, computer language, or analytic skill. *Entrance requirements:* For master's, GRE; for Certificate, bachelor's degree. Additional exam requirements/recommendations for international students: Required—TOEFL. *Application deadline:* For fall admission, 2/1 for domestic students; for spring admission, 10/1 for domestic students. Application fee: $80. *Expenses:* Tuition: Full-time $22,266; part-time $1237 per credit hour. Required fees: $430. Tuition and fees vary according to program. *Financial support:* Fellowships, teaching assistantships, career-related internships or fieldwork, Federal Work-Study, and institutionally sponsored loans available. Support available to part-time students. Financial award application deadline: 2/1. *Faculty research:* Statistical computing; data analysis; random processes; environmental, meteorological, and biological applications. *Unit head:* Dr. Jeffrey Hakim, Chair, 202-885-3131, Fax: 202-885-3155. *Application contact:* Dr. Jeffrey Hakim, Chair, 202-885-3131, Fax: 202-885-3155.

American University of Beirut, Graduate Programs, Faculty of Arts and Sciences, Beirut, Lebanon. Offers anthropology (MA); Arabic language and literature (MA); archaeology (MA); biology (MS); chemistry (MS); computer science (MS); economics (MA); education (MA); English language (MA); English literature (MA); environmental policy planning (MSES); financial economics (MAFE); geology (MS); history (MA); mathematics (MA, MS); Middle Eastern studies (MA); philosophy (MA); physics (MS); political studies (MA); psychology (MA); public administration (MA); sociology (MA); statistics (MA, MS). Part-time programs available. *Degree requirements:* For master's, one foreign language, comprehensive exam, thesis (for some programs). *Entrance requirements:* For master's, GRE, letter of recommendation. Additional exam requirements/recommendations for international students: Required—TOEFL (minimum score 600 paper-based; 250 computer-based; 100 iBT), IELTS (minimum score 7.5). *Faculty research:* String theory and supergravity; computer graphics; algebra and number theory; popular Arabic literature; marine and freshwater biology; integrating science, math and technology.

Arizona State University, Graduate College, College of Liberal Arts and Sciences, Division of Natural Sciences, Department of Mathematics and Statistics, Tempe, AZ 85287. Offers computational biosciences (PSM, PhD); mathematics (MA, MNS, PhD). *Degree requirements:* For master's, thesis or alternative; for doctorate, one foreign language, thesis/dissertation. *Entrance requirements:* For master's and doctorate, GRE General Test.

Arizona State University, Graduate College, Interdisciplinary Program in Statistics, Tempe, AZ 85287. Offers MS. *Entrance requirements:* For master's, GRE.

Auburn University, Graduate School, College of Sciences and Mathematics, Department of Mathematics and Statistics, Auburn University, AL 36849. Offers applied mathematics (MAM, MS); mathematics (MS, PhD); probability and statistics (M Prob S); statistics (MS). *Faculty:* 54 full-time (8 women), 4 part-time/adjunct (1 woman). *Students:* 50 full-time (8 women), 44 part-time (17 women); includes 4 minority (2 African Americans, 1 Asian American or Pacific Islander, 1 Hispanic American), 46 international. Average age 28. 212 applicants, 52% accepted, 20 enrolled. In 2009, 16 master's, 10 doctorates awarded. *Degree requirements:* For doctorate, thesis/dissertation. *Entrance requirements:* For master's, GRE General Test, undergraduate mathematics background; for doctorate, GRE General Test, GRE Subject Test. *Application deadline:* For fall admission, 7/7 priority date for domestic students; for spring admission, 11/24 for domestic students. Applications are processed on a rolling basis. Application fee: $50 ($60 for international students). Electronic applications accepted. *Expenses:* Tuition, state resident: full-time $6240. Tuition, nonresident: full-time $18,720. International tuition: $18,938 full-time. Required fees: $492. Tuition and fees vary according to course load, program and reciprocity agreements. *Financial support:* Fellowships, teaching assistantships, special tuition awards available. Financial award applicants required to submit FAFSA. *Faculty research:* Pure and applied mathematics. *Unit head:* Dr. Michel Smith, Chair, 334-844-4290, Fax: 334-844-6655. *Application contact:* Dr. George Flowers, Dean of the Graduate School, 334-844-2125.

Ball State University, Graduate School, College of Sciences and Humanities, Department of Mathematical Sciences, Program in Mathematical Statistics, Muncie, IN 47306-1099. Offers MA. *Faculty research:* Robust methods.

Statistics

Baylor University, Graduate School, College of Arts and Sciences, Department of Statistics, Waco, TX 76798. Offers MA, PhD. *Faculty:* 7 full-time (1 woman), 4 part-time/adjunct (1 woman). *Students:* 27 full-time (17 women), 1 part-time (0 women); includes 4 minority (2 African Americans, 2 Asian Americans or Pacific Islanders), 5 international. Average age 24. 38 applicants, 16% accepted. In 2009, 6 master's, 3 doctorates awarded. *Degree requirements:* For doctorate, thesis/dissertation. *Entrance requirements:* For master's, GRE General Test, 3 semesters of course work in calculus; for doctorate, GRE General Test. *Application deadline:* Applications are processed on a rolling basis. Application fee: $25. *Financial support:* In 2009–10, 1 fellowship, 5 research assistantships, 7 teaching assistantships were awarded; institutionally sponsored loans also available. *Faculty research:* Mathematical statistics, probability theory, biostatistics, linear models, time series. *Unit head:* Dr. Tom Bratcher, Graduate Program Director, 254-710-6573, Fax: 254-710-3033, E-mail: tom_bratcher@baylor.edu. *Application contact:* Dr. Tom Bratcher, Graduate Program Director, 254-710-6573, Fax: 254-710-3870, E-mail: tom_bratcher@baylor.edu.

Bernard M. Baruch College of the City University of New York, Zicklin School of Business, Department of Statistics and Computer Information Systems, Program in Statistics, New York, NY 10010-5585. Offers MBA, MS. Part-time and evening/weekend programs available. *Entrance requirements:* For master's, GMAT, 2 letters of recommendation, resume, 2 years of work experience. Additional exam requirements/recommendations for international students: Required—TOEFL (minimum score 590 paper-based; 243 computer-based), TWE.

Bowling Green State University, Graduate College, College of Arts and Sciences, Department of Mathematics and Statistics, Bowling Green, OH 43403. Offers applied statistics (MS); mathematics (MA, MAT, PhD); statistics (PhD). Part-time programs available. *Degree requirements:* For master's, thesis or alternative; for doctorate, comprehensive exam, thesis/dissertation. *Entrance requirements:* For master's and doctorate, GRE General Test. Additional exam requirements/recommendations for international students: Required—TOEFL. Electronic applications accepted. *Faculty research:* Statistics and probability, algebra, analysis.

Brigham Young University, Graduate Studies, College of Physical and Mathematical Sciences, Department of Statistics, Provo, UT 84602-1001. Offers applied statistics (MS). *Faculty:* 15 full-time (2 women). *Students:* 20 full-time (9 women); includes 1 minority (Asian American or Pacific Islander). Average age 26. 25 applicants, 68% accepted, 13 enrolled. In 2009, 9 master's awarded. *Degree requirements:* For master's, comprehensive exam, thesis (for some programs). *Entrance requirements:* For master's, GRE General Test, minimum undergraduate GPA of 3.3; course work in statistical methods, theory, multivariable calculus and linear algebra with minimum B- average. Additional exam requirements/recommendations for international students: Required—TOEFL (minimum score 580 paper-based; 237 computer-based; 85 iBT). *Application deadline:* For fall admission, 2/1 for domestic and international students. Application fee: $50. Electronic applications accepted. *Expenses:* Tuition: Full-time $5580; part-time $301 per credit hour. Tuition and fees vary according to student's religious affiliation. *Financial support:* In 2009–10, 20 students received support, including 2 research assistantships with full and partial tuition reimbursements available (averaging $10,000 per year), 18 teaching assistantships with full and partial tuition reimbursements available (averaging $10,000 per year); scholarships/grants and unspecified assistantships also available. Financial award application deadline: 2/1. *Faculty research:* Statistical genetics, reliability and pollution monitoring, Bayesian methods. Total annual research expenditures: $50,000. *Unit head:* Dr. Del T. Scott, Chair, 801-422-7054, Fax: 801-422-0635, E-mail: scottd@byu.edu. *Application contact:* Dr. Scott D. Grimshaw, Graduate Coordinator, 801-422-6251, Fax: 801-422-0635, E-mail: grimshaw@byu.edu.

Brock University, Faculty of Graduate Studies, Faculty of Mathematics and Science, Program in Mathematics and Statistics, St. Catharines, ON L2S 3A1, Canada. Offers M Sc. Part-time programs available. *Degree requirements:* For master's, thesis or project. *Entrance requirements:* For master's, honors degree. Additional exam requirements/recommendations for international students: Required—TOEFL (minimum score 550 paper-based; 213 computer-based; 80 iBT), IELTS (minimum score 6.5), TWE (minimum score 4). Electronic applications accepted.

California State University, East Bay, Academic Programs and Graduate Studies, College of Science, Department of Statistics and Biostatistics, Statistics Program, Hayward, CA 94542-3000. Offers MS. Part-time and evening/weekend programs available. *Faculty:* 7 full-time (3 women). *Students:* 24 full-time (11 women), 64 part-time (33 women); includes 1 African American, 32 Asian Americans or Pacific Islanders, 1 Hispanic American, 22 international. Average age 32. 70 applicants, 74% accepted, 34 enrolled. In 2009, 24 master's awarded. *Degree requirements:* For master's, comprehensive exam. *Entrance requirements:* For master's, letters of recommendation, minimum GPA of 3.0, math through lower-division calculus. Additional exam requirements/recommendations for international students: Required—TOEFL (minimum score 550 paper-based; 213 computer-based). *Application deadline:* For fall admission, 6/30 for domestic and international students. Application fee: $55. Electronic applications accepted. *Financial support:* Fellowships, career-related internships or fieldwork, Federal Work-Study, institutionally sponsored loans, scholarships/grants, and unspecified assistantships available. Support available to part-time students. Financial award application deadline: 3/1; financial award applicants required to submit FAFSA. *Unit head:* Dr. Eric Suess, Chair, 510-885-3435, Fax: 510-885-4714, E-mail: eric.suess@csueastbay.edu. *Application contact:* Donna Wiley, Interim Associate Director, 510-885-3286, Fax: 510-885-4777, E-mail: donna.wiley@csueastbay.edu.

California State University, Sacramento, Graduate Studies, College of Natural Sciences and Mathematics, Department of Mathematics and Statistics, Sacramento, CA 95819. Offers MA. Part-time programs available. *Degree requirements:* For master's, thesis or alternative, writing proficiency exam. *Entrance requirements:* For master's, minimum GPA of 3.0 in mathematics, 2.5 overall during previous 2 years; BA in mathematics or equivalent. Additional exam requirements/recommendations for international students: Required—TOEFL. Electronic applications accepted.

Carnegie Mellon University, College of Humanities and Social Sciences, Department of Statistics, Pittsburgh, PA 15213-3891. Offers machine learning and statistics (PhD); mathematical finance (PhD); statistics (MS, PhD), including applied statistics (PhD), computational statistics (PhD), theoretical statistics (PhD); statistics and public policy (PhD). Terminal master's awarded for partial completion of doctoral program. *Degree requirements:* For doctorate, comprehensive exam, thesis/dissertation. *Entrance requirements:* For master's and doctorate, GRE General Test. Additional exam requirements/recommendations for international students: Required—TOEFL. *Faculty research:* Stochastic processes, Bayesian statistics, statistical computing, decision theory, psychiatric statistics.

Case Western Reserve University, School of Graduate Studies, Department of Statistics, Cleveland, OH 44106. Offers MS, PhD. *Degree requirements:* For master's, thesis (for some programs); for doctorate, thesis/dissertation. *Entrance requirements:* Additional exam requirements/recommendations for international students: Required—TOEFL (minimum score 550 paper-based; 213 computer-based; 79 iBT). Electronic applications accepted. *Faculty research:* Generalized linear models, asymptotics for restricted MLE Bayesian inference, sample survey theory, statistical computing, nonparametric inference, projection pursuit, stochastic processes, dynamical systems and chaotic behavior.

Central Connecticut State University, School of Graduate Studies, School of Arts and Sciences, Department of Mathematical Sciences, New Britain, CT 06050-4010. Offers data mining (MS, Certificate); mathematics (MA, MS, Certificate, Sixth Year Certificate), including actuarial science (MA), computer science (MA), statistics (MA). Part-time and evening/weekend programs available. *Faculty:* 33 full-time (12 women), 60 part-time/adjunct (30 women). *Students:* 21 full-time (10 women), 129 part-time (76 women); includes 13 minority (4 African Americans, 1 American Indian/Alaska Native, 4 Asian Americans or Pacific Islanders, 4 Hispanic Americans), 13 international. Average age 37. 78 applicants, 64% accepted, 37 enrolled. In 2009, 27 master's, 13 other advanced degrees awarded. *Degree requirements:* For master's, comprehensive exam, thesis or alternative; for other advanced degree, qualifying exam. *Entrance requirements:* For master's, minimum undergraduate GPA of 2.7. Additional exam requirements/recommendations for international students: Required—TOEFL. *Application deadline:* For fall admission, 7/1 for domestic students; for spring admission, 12/1 for domestic students. Applications are processed on a rolling basis. Application fee: $50. Electronic applications accepted. *Expenses:* Tuition, area resident: Full-time $4662; part-time $440 per credit. Tuition, state resident: full-time $6994; part-time $440 per credit. Tuition, nonresident: full-time $12,988; part-time $440 per credit. Required fees: $3606. One-time fee: $62 part-time. *Financial support:* In 2009–10, 7 students received support, including 3 research assistantships; career-related internships or fieldwork, Federal Work-Study, scholarships/grants, and unspecified assistantships also available. Support available to part-time students. Financial award application deadline: 3/1; financial award applicants required to submit FAFSA. *Faculty research:* Statistics, actuarial mathematics, computer systems and engineering, computer programming techniques, operations research. *Unit head:* Dr. Jeffrey McGowan, Chair, 860-832-2835. *Application contact:* Dr. Jeffrey McGowan, Chair, 860-832-2835.

Claremont Graduate University, Graduate Programs, School of Mathematical Sciences, Claremont, CA 91711-6160. Offers computational and systems biology (PhD); computational mathematics and numerical analysis (MA, MS); computational science (PhD); engineering and industrial applied mathematics (PhD); mathematics (PhD); operations research and statistics (MA, MS); physical applied mathematics (MA, MS); pure mathematics (MA, MS); scientific computing (MA, MS); systems and control theory (MA, MS). Part-time programs available. *Faculty:* 5 full-time (0 women), 2 part-time/adjunct (0 women). *Students:* 56 full-time (20 women), 12 part-time (3 women); includes 13 minority (2 African Americans, 6 Asian Americans or Pacific Islanders, 5 Hispanic Americans), 25 international. Average age 33. In 2009, 7 master's, 7 doctorates awarded. Terminal master's awarded for partial completion of doctoral program. *Entrance requirements:* For master's and doctorate, GRE General Test. Additional exam requirements/recommendations for international students: Required—TOEFL (minimum score 550 paper-based; 213 computer-based; 80 iBT). *Application deadline:* For fall admission, 2/1 priority date for domestic students. Applications are processed on a rolling basis. Application fee: $60. Electronic applications accepted. *Expenses:* Tuition: Full-time $35,046; part-time $1524 per credit. Required fees: $161 per semester. *Financial support:* Fellowships, research assistantships, Federal Work-Study, institutionally sponsored loans, scholarships/grants, and tuition waivers (full and partial) available. Support available to part-time students. Financial award application deadline: 2/15; financial award applicants required to submit FAFSA. *Unit head:* John Angus, Dean, 909-621-8080, Fax: 909-607-8261, E-mail: john.angus@cgu.edu. *Application contact:* Susan Townzen, Program Coordinator, 909-621-8080, Fax: 909-607-8261, E-mail: susan.n.townzen@cgu.edu.

Clemson University, Graduate School, College of Engineering and Science, Department of Mathematical Sciences, Clemson, SC 29634. Offers applied and pure mathematics (MS, PhD); computational mathematics (MS, PhD); operations research (MS, PhD); statistics (MS, PhD). Part-time programs available. *Faculty:* 51 full-time (14 women), 9 part-time/adjunct (2 women). *Students:* 92 full-time (39 women), 1 part-time (0 women); includes 3 minority (2 African Americans, 1 American Indian/Alaska Native), 31 international. Average age 26. 134 applicants, 76% accepted, 20 enrolled. In 2009, 36 master's, 13 doctorates awarded. *Degree requirements:* For master's, thesis optional, final project; for doctorate, thesis/dissertation, qualifying exams. *Entrance requirements:* For master's and doctorate, GRE General Test. Additional exam requirements/recommendations for international students: Required—TOEFL. *Application deadline:* For fall admission, 1/15 priority date for domestic students, 2/15 priority date for international students; for spring admission, 10/1 priority date for domestic students, 9/15 priority date for international students. Applications are processed on a rolling basis. Application fee: $70 ($80 for international students). Electronic applications accepted. *Expenses:* Tuition, state resident: full-time $8684; part-time $528 per credit hour. Tuition, nonresident: full-time $15,330; part-time $1078 per credit hour. Required fees: $736; $37 per semester. Part-time tuition and fees vary according to course load and program. *Financial support:* In 2009–10, 85 students received support, including 1 fellowship with full and partial tuition reimbursement available (averaging $10,000 per year), 7 research assistantships with partial tuition reimbursements available (averaging $17,591 per year), 66 teaching assistantships with partial tuition reimbursements available (averaging $18,593 per year); career-related internships or fieldwork, institutionally sponsored loans, scholarships/grants, health care benefits, and unspecified assistantships also available. Support available to part-time students. Financial award application deadline: 4/15. *Faculty research:* Applied and computational analysis, cryptography, discrete mathematics, optimization, statistics. Total annual research expenditures: $535,985. *Unit head:* Dr. Robert L. Taylor, Chair, 864-656-5240, Fax: 864-656-5230, E-mail: rtaylo2@clemson.edu. *Application contact:* Dr. K. B. Kulasekera, Graduate Coordinator, 864-656-5231, Fax: 864-656-5230, E-mail: kk@clemson.edu.

Colorado State University, Graduate School, College of Natural Sciences, Department of Statistics, Fort Collins, CO 80523-1877. Offers MS, PhD. Postbaccalaureate distance learning degree programs offered (no on-campus study). *Faculty:* 12 full-time (5 women). *Students:* 26 full-time (8 women), 51 part-time (18 women); includes 9 minority (1 African American, 5 Asian Americans or Pacific Islanders, 3 Hispanic Americans), 18 international. Average age 33. 137 applicants, 14% accepted, 11 enrolled. In 2009, 17 master's, 7 doctorates awarded. Terminal master's awarded for partial completion of doctoral program. *Degree requirements:* For master's, comprehensive exam (for some programs), thesis (for some programs), project, seminar; for doctorate, comprehensive exam, thesis/dissertation, candidacy exam, preliminary exam, seminar. *Entrance requirements:* For master's and doctorate, GRE General Test, minimum GPA of 3.0, background in math and statistics. Additional exam requirements/recommendations for international students: Required—TOEFL (minimum score 550 paper-based; 213 computer-based; 80 iBT). *Application deadline:* For fall admission, 9/15 priority date for domestic students, 8/15 priority date for international students; for spring admission, 1/15 priority date for domestic and international students. Applications are processed on a rolling basis. Application fee: $50. Electronic applications accepted. *Expenses:* Tuition, state resident: full-time $6434; part-time $359.10 per credit. Tuition, nonresident: full-time $18,116; part-time $1006.45 per credit. Required fees: $1496; $83 per credit. *Financial support:* In 2009–10, 29 students received support, including 2 research assistantships with full tuition reimbursements available (averaging $7,650 per year), 27 teaching assistantships with full tuition reimbursements available (averaging $13,904 per year); fellowships, health care benefits also available. Financial award application deadline: 1/15; financial award applicants required to submit FAFSA. *Faculty research:* Applied probability, linear models and experimental design, time-series analysis, non-parametric statistical inference, statistical consulting. Total annual research expenditures: $521,016. *Unit head:* Dr. F. Jay Breidt, Professor and Chair, 970-491-6786, Fax: 970-491-7895, E-mail: jbreidt@stat.colostate.edu. *Application contact:* Jennifer Tallchief, Graduate Admissions Coordinator, 970-491-5269, Fax: 970-491-7895, E-mail: tallchie@stat.colostate.edu.

Columbia University, Graduate School of Arts and Sciences, Division of Natural Sciences, Department of Statistics, New York, NY 10027. Offers M Phil, MA, PhD, MD/PhD. Part-time programs available. *Degree requirements:* For doctorate, thesis/dissertation. *Entrance requirements:* For master's and doctorate, GRE General Test, GRE Subject Test. Additional exam requirements/recommendations for international students: Required—TOEFL.

Columbia University, Graduate School of Arts and Sciences, Program in Quantitative Methods in the Social Sciences, New York, NY 10027. Offers MA. Part-time programs available.

Cornell University, Graduate School, Graduate Fields of Engineering, Field of Operations Research and Information Engineering, Ithaca, NY 14853-0001. Offers applied probability and statistics (PhD); manufacturing systems engineering (PhD); mathematical programming (PhD); operations research and industrial engineering (M Eng). *Faculty:* 46 full-time (9 women). *Students:* 163 full-time (46 women); includes 20 minority (2 African Americans, 12 Asian Americans or Pacific Islanders, 6 Hispanic Americans), 103 international. Average age 25. 774 applicants, 29% accepted, 91 enrolled. In 2009, 85 master's, 6 doctorates awarded. *Degree requirements:* For doctorate, comprehensive exam, thesis/dissertation. *Entrance requirements:* For master's and doctorate, GRE General Test, 3 letters of recommendation. Additional exam requirements/recommendations for international students: Required—TOEFL (minimum score 600 paper-based; 250 computer-based; 77 iBT). *Application deadline:* For fall admission, 1/15 for domestic students. Application fee: $70. Electronic applications accepted. *Expenses:* Tuition: Full-time $29,500. Required fees: $70. Full-time tuition and fees vary according to degree level, program and student level. *Financial support:* In 2009–10, 44 students received support, including 6 fellowships with full tuition reimbursements available, 5 teaching assistantships with full tuition reimbursements available; research assistantships with full tuition reimbursements available, institutionally sponsored loans, scholarships/grants, health care benefits, tuition waivers (full and partial), and unspecified assistantships also available. Financial award applicants required to submit FAFSA. *Faculty research:* Mathematical programming and combinatorial optimization, statistics, stochastic processes, mathematical finance, simulation, manufacturing, e-commerce. *Unit head:* Director of Graduate Studies, 607-255-9128, Fax: 607-255-9129. *Application contact:* Graduate Field Assistant, 607-255-9128, Fax: 607-255-9129, E-mail: orie@cornell.edu.

Cornell University, Graduate School, Graduate Fields of Engineering, Field of Statistics, Ithaca, NY 14853-0001. Offers applied statistics (MPS); biometry (MS, PhD); decision theory (MS, PhD); economic and social statistics (MS, PhD); engineering statistics (MS, PhD); experimental design (MS, PhD); mathematical statistics (MS, PhD); probability (MS, PhD); sampling (MS, PhD); statistical computing (MS, PhD); stochastic processes (MS, PhD). *Faculty:* 33 full-time (4 women). *Students:* 62 full-time (22 women); includes 5 minority (4 Asian Americans or Pacific Islanders, 1 Hispanic American), 37 international. Average age 27. 306 applicants, 24% accepted, 31 enrolled. In 2009, 36 master's, 3 doctorates awarded. Terminal master's awarded for partial completion of doctoral program. *Degree requirements:* For master's, project (MPS), thesis (MS); for doctorate, one foreign language, thesis/dissertation. *Entrance requirements:* For master's, GRE General Test (MS), 2 letters of recommendation (MS, MPS); for doctorate, GRE General Test, 2 letters of recommendation. Additional exam requirements/recommendations for international students: Required—TOEFL (minimum score 550 paper-based; 213 computer-based; 77 iBT). *Application deadline:* For fall admission, 1/15 for domestic students. Applications are processed on a rolling basis. Application fee: $70. Electronic applications accepted. *Expenses:* Tuition: Full-time $29,500. Required fees: $70. Full-time tuition and fees vary according to degree level, program and student level. *Financial support:* In 2009–10, 26 students received support, including 1 fellowship with full tuition reimbursement available, 3 teaching assistantships with full tuition reimbursements available; research assistantships with full tuition reimbursements available, institutionally sponsored loans, scholarships/grants, tuition waivers (full and partial), and unspecified assistantships also available. Financial award applicants required to submit FAFSA. *Faculty research:* Bayesian analysis, survival analysis, nonparametric statistics, stochastic processes, mathematical statistics. *Unit head:* Director of Graduate Studies, 607-255-8066. *Application contact:* Graduate Field Assistant, 607-255-8066, E-mail: csc@cornell.edu.

Dalhousie University, Faculty of Science, Department of Mathematics and Statistics, Program in Statistics, Halifax, NS B3H 4R2, Canada. Offers M Sc, PhD. *Faculty:* 7 full-time (0 women). *Students:* 8 full-time (4 women), 1 international. 10 applicants, 40% accepted. In 2009, 1 master's, 1 doctorate awarded. *Degree requirements:* For master's, thesis, 50 hours of consulting; for doctorate, thesis/dissertation, 50 hours of consulting. *Entrance requirements:* Additional exam requirements/recommendations for international students: Required—TOEFL, IELTS, CANTEST, CAEL, or Michigan English Language Assessment Battery. Application fee: $70. Electronic applications accepted. *Financial support:* In 2009–10, 8 students received support, including 5 teaching assistantships with full tuition reimbursements available (averaging $10,000 per year); career-related internships or fieldwork, scholarships/grants, and health care benefits also available. Financial award application deadline: 1/31. *Faculty research:* Data analysis, multivariate analysis, robustness, time series, statistical genetics. *Unit head:* Dr. Ed Susko, Graduate Coordinator, 902-494-8865, Fax: 902-494-5130, E-mail: susko@mathstat.dal.ca. *Application contact:* Paula Flemming, Graduate Secretary, 902-494-2572, Fax: 902-494-5130, E-mail: chair@mscs.dal.ca.

Duke University, Graduate School, Institute of Statistics and Decision Sciences, Durham, NC 27708-0586. Offers PhD. Part-time programs available. *Faculty:* 20 full-time. *Students:* 35 full-time (13 women), 24 international. 168 applicants, 9% accepted, 10 enrolled. In 2009, 9 doctorates awarded. *Degree requirements:* For doctorate, thesis/dissertation. *Entrance requirements:* For doctorate, GRE General Test. Additional exam requirements/recommendations for international students: Required—TOEFL (minimum score 550 paper-based; 213 computer-based; 83 iBT), IELTS (minimum score 7). *Application deadline:* For fall admission, 12/8 priority date for domestic and international students. Application fee: $75. Electronic applications accepted. *Financial support:* Fellowships, research assistantships, teaching assistantships available. Financial award application deadline: 12/31. *Unit head:* Mike West, Director of Graduate Studies, 919-684-4210, Fax: 91-684-8594, E-mail: anne@stat.duke.edu. *Application contact:* Cynthia Robertson, imn-app-tst-01.oit.duke.edu, 919-684-3913, E-mail: grad-admissions@duke.edu.

Florida Atlantic University, Charles E. Schmidt College of Science, Department of Mathematical Sciences, Boca Raton, FL 33431-0991. Offers applied mathematics and statistics (MS); mathematical sciences (MS, MST, PhD). Part-time programs available. *Faculty:* 36 full-time (5 women), 5 part-time/adjunct (1 woman). *Students:* 52 full-time (14 women), 31 part-time (19 women); includes 13 minority (5 African Americans, 5 Asian Americans or Pacific Islanders, 3 Hispanic Americans), 29 international. Average age 32. 62 applicants, 58% accepted, 18 enrolled. In 2009, 23 master's, 4 doctorates awarded. Terminal master's awarded for partial completion of doctoral program. *Degree requirements:* For master's, comprehensive exam (for some programs), thesis (for some programs); for doctorate, comprehensive exam, thesis/dissertation. *Entrance requirements:* For master's and doctorate, GRE General Test, minimum GPA of 3.0. Additional exam requirements/recommendations for international students: Required—TOEFL (minimum score 500 paper-based; 173 computer-based). *Application deadline:* For fall admission, 7/1 priority date for domestic students, 2/15 priority date for international students; for spring admission, 11/1 priority date for domestic students, 7/15 priority date for international students. Applications are processed on a rolling basis. Application fee: $30. Electronic applications accepted. *Expenses:* Tuition, state resident: full-time $7055; part-time $293.94 per credit hour. Tuition, nonresident: full-time $22,096; part-time $920.66 per credit hour. *Financial support:* In 2009–10, fellowships with partial tuition reimbursements (averaging $20,000 per year), teaching assistantships with partial tuition reimbursements (averaging $20,000 per year) were awarded; Federal Work-Study also available. Financial award application deadline: 4/1. *Faculty research:* Cryptography, statistics, algebra, analysis, combinatorics. *Unit head:* Dr. Lee Klingler, Chair, 561-297-0274, Fax: 561-297-2436, E-mail: klingler@fau.edu. *Application contact:* Dr. Heinrich Niederhausen, Graduate Director, 561-297-3237, Fax: 561-297-2436, E-mail: niederha@fau.edu.

Florida International University, College of Arts and Sciences, Department of Mathematics and Statistics, Department of Statistics, Miami, FL 33199. Offers MS. Part-time and evening/weekend programs available. *Students:* 4 full-time (1 woman), 10 part-time (5 women); includes 5 minority (1 Asian American or Pacific Islander, 4 Hispanic Americans), 8 international. Average age 32. 11 applicants, 45% accepted, 5 enrolled. In 2009, 4 master's awarded. *Degree requirements:* For master's, thesis optional. *Entrance requirements:* For master's, GRE General Test, minimum GPA of 3.0, 3 letters of recommendation, resume. Additional exam requirements/recommendations for international students: Required—TOEFL (minimum score 550 paper-based; 80 iBT). *Application deadline:* For fall admission, 6/1 for domestic students, 4/1 for international students; for spring admission, 10/1 for domestic students, 9/1 for international students. Applications are processed on a rolling basis. Application fee: $30. Electronic applications accepted. *Expenses:* Tuition, state resident: full-time $8008; part-time $4004 per year. Tuition, nonresident: full-time $20,104; part-time $10,052 per year. Required fees: $298; $149 per term. *Financial support:* Institutionally sponsored loans and scholarships/grants available. Financial award application deadline: 3/1; financial award applicants required to submit FAFSA. *Unit head:* Dr. Bao Qin Li, Chair, Mathematics and Statistics Department, 305-348-2743, Fax: 305-348-6158, E-mail: bao.li@fiu.edu. *Application contact:* Dr. Zhenmin Chen, Director of Graduate Programs, 305-348-2743, Fax: 305-348-6158, E-mail: zhenmin.Chen@fiu.edu.

Florida State University, The Graduate School, College of Arts and Sciences, Department of Statistics, Tallahassee, FL 32306-4330. Offers applied statistics (MS); biostatistics (MS, PhD); mathematical statistics (MS, PhD). Part-time programs available. *Faculty:* 15 full-time (2 women). *Students:* 51 full-time (22 women), 6 part-time (1 woman); includes 18 minority (8 African Americans, 5 Asian Americans or Pacific Islanders, 5 Hispanic Americans), 23 international. Average age 31. 139 applicants, 19% accepted, 14 enrolled. In 2009, 12 master's, 10 doctorates awarded. Terminal master's awarded for partial completion of doctoral program. *Degree requirements:* For doctorate, thesis/dissertation, departmental qualifying exam. *Entrance requirements:* For master's, GRE General Test, previous course work in calculus, minimum GPA of 3.0; for doctorate, GRE General Test, minimum GPA of 3.0, 1 course in linear algebra (preferred), Calculus I-III, Real Analysis. Additional exam requirements/recommendations for international students: Required—TOEFL (minimum score 600 paper-based; 250 computer-based; 100 iBT). *Application deadline:* For fall admission, 7/1 for domestic and international students; for spring admission, 11/1 for domestic and international students. Applications are processed on a rolling basis. Application fee: $30. Electronic applications accepted. *Expenses:* Tuition, state resident: full-time $7413.36. Tuition, nonresident: full-time $22,567. *Financial support:* In 2009–10, 48 students received support, including 7 research assistantships with full tuition reimbursements available (averaging $19,575 per year), 41 teaching assistantships with full tuition reimbursements available (averaging $19,575 per year); fellowships with full tuition reimbursements available, Federal Work-Study, institutionally sponsored loans, scholarships/grants, health care benefits, and unspecified assistantships also available. Support available to part-time students. Financial award application deadline: 2/15; financial award applicants required to submit FAFSA. *Faculty research:* Statistical inference, probability theory, biostatistics, nonparametric estimation, automatic target recognition. Total annual research expenditures: $747,131. *Unit head:* Dr. Dan McGee, Chairman, 850-644-3218, Fax: 850-644-5271, E-mail: info@stat.fsu.edu. *Application contact:* Chauncey Richburg, Academic Support Assistant, 850-644-3514, Fax: 850-644-5271, E-mail: richburg@stat.fsu.edu.

Florida State University, The Graduate School, College of Education, Department of Educational Psychology and Learning Systems, Program in Measurement and Statistics, Tallahassee, FL 32306. Offers MS, PhD, Ed S. *Faculty:* 4 full-time (2 women), 1 (woman) part-time/adjunct. *Students:* 23 full-time (18 women), 4 part-time (2 women); includes 3 minority (1 African American, 2 Asian Americans or Pacific Islanders), 19 international. 31 applicants, 29% accepted, 6 enrolled. In 2009, 1 master's, 3 doctorates awarded. *Degree requirements:* For master's, comprehensive exam; for doctorate, thesis/dissertation, preliminary exam, prospectus. *Entrance requirements:* Additional exam requirements/recommendations for international students: Required—TOEFL (minimum score 550 paper-based; 213 computer-based; 80 iBT). *Application deadline:* For fall admission, 6/1 priority date for domestic and international students; for spring admission, 10/1 priority date for domestic and international students. Application fee: $30. *Expenses:* Tuition, state resident: full-time $7413.36. Tuition, nonresident: full-time $22,567. *Financial support:* In 2009–10, 11 research assistantships with full and partial tuition reimbursements were awarded; fellowships with full and partial tuition reimbursements, teaching assistantships with full and partial tuition reimbursements also available. *Faculty research:* Methods for meta analysis; IRT/mixIRT; CBT; modeling, especially of large data sets. *Unit head:* Dr. Betsy Becker, Program Leader, 850-645-2371, Fax: 850-644-8776, E-mail: bjbecker@coe.fsu.edu. *Application contact:* Sally Gadson, Program Assistant, 850-644-8046, Fax: 850-644-5067, E-mail: gadson@coe.fsu.edu.

George Mason University, Volgenau School of Information Technology and Engineering, Department of Statistics, Fairfax, VA 22030. Offers biostatistics (Certificate); federal statistics (Certificate); statistical science (MS, PhD). Part-time and evening/weekend programs available. *Faculty:* 11 full-time (2 women), 6 part-time/adjunct (0 women). *Students:* 6 full-time (2 women), 61 part-time (32 women); includes 11 minority (4 African Americans, 4 Asian Americans or Pacific Islanders, 3 Hispanic Americans), 17 international. Average age 31. 52 applicants, 65% accepted, 20 enrolled. In 2009, 12 master's, 1 doctorate, 2 other advanced degrees awarded. Terminal master's awarded for partial completion of doctoral program. *Degree requirements:* For master's, comprehensive exam, thesis optional, qualifying exams; for doctorate, comprehensive exam, thesis/dissertation, qualifying exams. *Entrance requirements:* For master's, GRE (recommended), letters of recommendation, resume; for doctorate, GRE (recommended), personal goal statement, resume, 2 transcripts, letters of recommendation. Additional exam requirements/recommendations for international students: Required—TOEFL (minimum score 575 paper-based; 230 computer-based), IELTS (minimum score 6.5). *Application deadline:* For fall admission, 3/15 priority date for domestic students, 12/15 priority date for international students; for spring admission, 10/1 for domestic and international students. Applications are processed on a rolling basis. Application fee: $75. Electronic applications accepted. *Expenses:* Tuition, state resident: full-time $7568; part-time $315.33 per credit hour. Tuition, nonresident: full-time $21,704; part-time $904.33 per credit hour. Required fees: $2184; $91 per credit hour. *Financial support:* In 2009–10, 19 students received support, including 2 fellowships with full tuition reimbursements available (averaging $18,000 per year), 5 research assistantships with full and partial tuition reimbursements available (averaging $11,043 per year), 12 teaching assistantships with full and partial tuition reimbursements available (averaging $9,866 per year); Federal Work-Study, scholarships/grants, unspecified assistantships, and health care benefits (full-time research or teaching assistantship recipients) also available. Financial award application deadline: 3/1; financial award applicants required to submit FAFSA. *Faculty research:* Computational statistics, nonparametric function estimation, scientific and statistical visualization, statistical applications to engineering, survey research. Total annual research expenditures: $228,993. *Unit head:* Dr. William Rosenberger, Chair, 703-993-3645, Fax: 703-993-1700, E-mail: satistics@gmu.edu. *Application contact:* Elizabeth Quigley, Administrative Assitant, 703-993-9107, E-mail: equigley@gmu.edu.

Georgetown University, Graduate School of Arts and Sciences, Department of Mathematics, Washington, DC 20057. Offers mathematics and statistics (MS).

The George Washington University, Columbian College of Arts and Sciences, Department of Statistics, Washington, DC 20052. Offers statistics (MS, PhD); survey design and data analysis (Graduate Certificate). Part-time and evening/weekend programs available. *Faculty:* 16 full-time (4 women), 18 part-time/adjunct (3 women). *Students:* 28 full-time (14 women), 50 part-time (23 women); includes 9 minority (2 African Americans, 5 Asian Americans or Pacific Islanders, 2 Hispanic Americans), 35 international. Average age 30. 166 applicants, 86% accepted, 37 enrolled. In 2009, 9 master's, 1 doctorate, 14 other advanced degrees awarded. Terminal master's awarded for partial completion of doctoral program. *Degree requirements:* For master's, comprehensive exam; for doctorate, thesis/dissertation, general exam. *Entrance requirements:* For master's and doctorate, GRE General Test, interview, minimum GPA of 3.0.

Statistics

The George Washington University (continued)

Additional exam requirements/recommendations for international students: Required—TOEFL (minimum score 550 paper-based; 213 computer-based; 80 iBT). *Application deadline:* For fall admission, 1/15 priority date for domestic and international students; for spring admission, 10/1 priority date for domestic students, 9/1 priority date for international students. Applications are processed on a rolling basis. Application fee: $60. Electronic applications accepted. *Financial support:* In 2009–10, 13 students received support; fellowships with tuition reimbursements available, teaching assistantships with tuition reimbursements available, Federal Work-Study and tuition waivers available. Financial award application deadline: 1/15. *Unit head:* Dr. Reza Modarres, Chair, 202-994-6888, E-mail: reza@gwu.edu. *Application contact:* Information Contact, 202-994-6356, Fax: 202-994-6917.

Georgia Institute of Technology, Graduate Studies and Research, College of Sciences, School of Mathematics, Atlanta, GA 30332-0001. Offers algorithms, combinatorics, and optimization (PhD); applied mathematics (MS); bioinformatics (PhD); mathematics (PhD); quantitative and computational finance (MS); statistics (MS Stat). Terminal master's awarded for partial completion of doctoral program. *Degree requirements:* For master's, thesis or alternative; for doctorate, one foreign language, thesis/dissertation. *Entrance requirements:* For master's, GRE General Test, minimum GPA of 3.0; for doctorate, GRE General Test, GRE Subject Test, minimum GPA of 3.0. Additional exam requirements/recommendations for international students: Required—TOEFL. Electronic applications accepted. *Faculty research:* Dynamical systems, discrete mathematics, probability and statistics, mathematical physics.

Georgia Institute of Technology, Graduate Studies and Research, Multidisciplinary Program in Statistics, Atlanta, GA 30332-0001. Offers MS Stat. Part-time programs available. *Degree requirements:* For master's, thesis optional. *Entrance requirements:* For master's, GRE General Test, minimum GPA of 3.0. Additional exam requirements/recommendations for international students: Required—TOEFL. *Faculty research:* Statistical control procedures, statistical modeling of transportation systems.

Georgia State University, College of Arts and Sciences, Department of Mathematics and Statistics, Atlanta, GA 30302-3083. Offers mathematics (MA, MS); mathematics and statistics (PhD). Part-time and evening/weekend programs available. *Degree requirements:* For master's, comprehensive exam (for some programs), thesis (for some programs), exam; for doctorate, comprehensive exam, thesis/dissertation. *Entrance requirements:* For master's and doctorate, GRE. Additional exam requirements/recommendations for international students: Required—TOEFL. Electronic applications accepted. *Faculty research:* Analysis, biostatistics, discrete mathematics, linear algebra, statistics.

Hampton University, Graduate College, Program in Applied Mathematics, Hampton, VA 23668. Offers computational mathematics (MS); nonlinear science (MS); statistics and probability (MS). *Degree requirements:* For master's, thesis optional. *Entrance requirements:* For master's, GRE General Test.

Harvard University, Graduate School of Arts and Sciences, Department of Statistics, Cambridge, MA 02138. Offers AM, PhD. Terminal master's awarded for partial completion of doctoral program. *Degree requirements:* For master's, one foreign language; for doctorate, one foreign language, thesis/dissertation, exam, qualifying paper. *Entrance requirements:* For master's and doctorate, GRE General Test, GRE Subject Test (recommended). Additional exam requirements/recommendations for international students: Required—TOEFL. *Expenses:* Tuition: Full-time $33,696. Required fees: $1126. Full-time tuition and fees vary according to program. *Faculty research:* Interactive graphic analysis of multidimensional data, data analysis, modeling and inference, statistical modeling of U.S. economic time series.

Indiana University Bloomington, University Graduate School, College of Arts and Sciences, Department of Mathematics, Bloomington, IN 47405-7000. Offers applied mathematics–numerical analysis (MA, PhD); mathematics education (MAT); probability-statistics (MA, PhD); pure mathematics (MA). *Faculty:* 46 full-time (4 women). *Students:* 131 full-time (26 women); includes 10 minority (1 African American, 1 American Indian/Alaska Native, 7 Asian Americans or Pacific Islanders, 1 Hispanic American), 67 international. Average age 28. 211 applicants, 29% accepted, 26 enrolled. In 2009, 13 master's, 18 doctorates awarded. Terminal master's awarded for partial completion of doctoral program. *Degree requirements:* For doctorate, one foreign language, thesis/dissertation. *Entrance requirements:* For master's and doctorate, GRE General Test, GRE Subject Test. Additional exam requirements/recommendations for international students: Required—TOEFL. *Application deadline:* For fall admission, 1/15 priority date for domestic and international students. Applications are processed on a rolling basis. Application fee: $55 ($65 for international students). Electronic applications accepted. *Financial support:* In 2009–10, 9 fellowships with full tuition reimbursements (averaging $20,000 per year), 5 research assistantships with full tuition reimbursements (averaging $16,440 per year), 106 teaching assistantships with full tuition reimbursements (averaging $15,940 per year) were awarded; scholarships/grants, health care benefits, and unspecified assistantships also available. Financial award application deadline: 1/15. *Faculty research:* Topology, geometry, algebra. *Unit head:* James F. Davis, Chair, 812-855-2200. *Application contact:* Kate Bowman, Graduate Secretary, 812-855-2645, Fax: 812-855-0046, E-mail: gradmath@indiana.edu.

Iowa State University of Science and Technology, Graduate College, College of Liberal Arts and Sciences, Department of Statistics, Ames, IA 50011. Offers MS, PhD, MBA/MS. *Faculty:* 33 full-time (11 women), 1 part-time/adjunct (0 women). *Students:* 109 full-time (46 women), 19 part-time (11 women); includes 19 minority (13 African Americans, 6 Asian Americans or Pacific Islanders), 50 international. 324 applicants, 13% accepted, 21 enrolled. In 2009, 26 master's, 11 doctorates awarded. *Degree requirements:* For master's, thesis or alternative; for doctorate, thesis/dissertation. *Entrance requirements:* For master's and doctorate, GRE General Test. Additional exam requirements/recommendations for international students: Required—TOEFL (minimum score 550 paper-based; 80 iBT) or IELTS (minimum score 6.5). *Application deadline:* For fall admission, 3/15 priority date for domestic and international students; for spring admission, 10/31 for domestic and international students. Applications are processed on a rolling basis. Application fee: $40 ($90 for international students). *Expenses:* Tuition, state resident: full-time $6716. Tuition, nonresident: full-time $8908. Tuition and fees vary according to course level, course load, program and student level. *Financial support:* In 2009–10, 45 research assistantships with full and partial tuition reimbursements (averaging $17,000 per year), 52 teaching assistantships with full and partial tuition reimbursements (averaging $17,000 per year) were awarded; fellowships, scholarships/grants, health care benefits, and unspecified assistantships also available. *Unit head:* Dr. Kenneth Koehler, Chair, 515-294-4181, Fax: 515-294-4040, E-mail: statistics@iastate.edu. *Application contact:* Dr. Alicia Carriguiry, Director of Graduate Education, 515-294-3440, E-mail: statistics@iastate.edu.

James Madison University, The Graduate School, College of Science and Mathematics, Department of Mathematics and Statistics, Harrisonburg, VA 22807. Offers M Ed. Part-time programs available. *Students:* 7 part-time (5 women). Average age 27. In 2009, 3 master's awarded. *Degree requirements:* For master's, comprehensive exam. *Entrance requirements:* For master's, undergraduate major in mathematics. *Application deadline:* For fall admission, 5/1 priority date for domestic students; for spring admission, 9/1 priority date for domestic students. Application fee: $55. *Expenses:* Tuition, area resident: Part-time $305 per credit hour. Tuition, state resident: part-time $305 per credit hour. Tuition, nonresident: part-time $890 per credit hour. *Financial support:* Application deadline: 3/1; *Unit head:* Dr. David C. Carothers, Academic Unit Head, 540-568-6184. *Application contact:* Lynette M. Bible, Director of Graduate Admissions, 540-568-6395, Fax: 540-568-7860, E-mail: biblelm@jmu.edu.

The Johns Hopkins University, G. W. C. Whiting School of Engineering, Department of Applied Mathematics and Statistics, Baltimore, MD 21218-2699. Offers computational medicine (PhD); discrete mathematics (MA, MSE, PhD); financial mathematics (MSE); operations research/optimization/decision science (MA, MSE, PhD); statistics/probability/stochastic processes (MA, MSE, PhD). *Faculty:* 17 full-time (3 women), 4 part-time/adjunct (0 women). *Students:* 56 full-time (19 women), 5 part-time (2 women); includes 7 minority (1 African American, 6 Asian Americans or Pacific Islanders), 37 international. Average age 27. 213 applicants, 51% accepted, 16 enrolled. In 2009, 24 master's, 4 doctorates awarded. Terminal master's awarded for partial completion of doctoral program. *Degree requirements:* For master's, thesis (for some programs); for doctorate, thesis/dissertation, oral exam, introductory exam. *Entrance requirements:* For master's and doctorate, GRE General Test, GRE Subject Test. Additional exam requirements/recommendations for international students: Required—TOEFL (minimum score 600 paper-based; 250 computer-based; 100 iBT). *Application deadline:* For fall admission, 1/15 for domestic and international students; for spring admission, 9/15 for domestic and international students. Application fee: $75. Electronic applications accepted. *Financial support:* In 2009–10, 40 students received support, including 3 fellowships with full tuition reimbursements available (averaging $3,000 per year), 13 research assistantships with full tuition reimbursements available (averaging $22,333 per year), 15 teaching assistantships with full tuition reimbursements available (averaging $16,750 per year); Federal Work-Study, institutionally sponsored loans, scholarships/grants, health care benefits, tuition waivers (partial), and unspecified assistantships also available. Financial award application deadline: 1/15. *Faculty research:* Discrete mathematics, probability, statistics, optimization and operations research, scientific computation, financial mathematics. Total annual research expenditures: $1.1 million. *Unit head:* Dr. Daniel Q. Naiman, Chair, 410-516-7203, Fax: 410-516-7459, E-mail: daniel.naiman@jhu.edu. *Application contact:* Kristin Bechtel, Academic Program Coordinator, 410-516-7198, Fax: 410-516-7459, E-mail: kbechtel@jhu.edu.

The Johns Hopkins University, G. W. C. Whiting School of Engineering, Program in Engineering Management, Baltimore, MD 21218-2699. Offers biomaterials (MSEM); communications science (MSEM); computer science (MSEM); fluid mechanics (MSEM); materials science and engineering (MSEM); mechanical engineering (MSEM); mechanics and materials (MSEM); nano-biotechnology (MSEM); nanomaterials and nanotechnology (MSEM); probability and statistics (MSEM); smart product and device design (MSEM); systems analysis, management and environmental policy (MSEM). *Students:* 12 full-time (0 women), 3 international. Average age 23. 66 applicants, 67% accepted. *Entrance requirements:* For master's, GRE, 3 letters of recommendation, resume. Additional exam requirements/recommendations for international students: Required—TOEFL (minimum score 600 paper-based; 250 computer-based; 100 iBT) or IELTS (minimum score 7). *Application deadline:* For fall admission, 1/15 priority date for domestic students, 1/15 for international students; for spring admission, 9/15 priority date for domestic students, 9/15 for international students. Applications are processed on a rolling basis. Application fee: $75. Electronic applications accepted. *Financial support:* Fellowships, health care benefits available. *Unit head:* Dr. Edward R. Scheinerman, Interim Director/Vice Dean for Education, School of Engineering/Professor, Applied Mathematics and Statistics, 410-516-7395, Fax: 410-516-4880, E-mail: ers@jhu.edu. *Application contact:* Dennis McIver, Coordinator of Graduate Admissions, 410-516-8174, Fax: 410-516-0780, E-mail: graduateadmissions@jhu.edu.

Kansas State University, Graduate School, College of Arts and Sciences, Department of Statistics, Manhattan, KS 66506. Offers MS, PhD. *Faculty:* 11 full-time (4 women), 1 part-time/adjunct (0 women). *Students:* 49 full-time (25 women); includes 5 minority (2 African Americans, 3 Asian Americans or Pacific Islanders), 22 international. Average age 32. 155 applicants, 6% accepted, 9 enrolled. In 2009, 5 master's, 9 doctorates awarded. Terminal master's awarded for partial completion of doctoral program. *Degree requirements:* For master's, thesis optional; for doctorate, thesis/dissertation, qualifying and preliminary exams. *Entrance requirements:* For master's, GRE; for doctorate, previous course work in statistics and mathematics. Additional exam requirements/recommendations for international students: Required—TOEFL (minimum score 550 paper-based; 213 computer-based). *Application deadline:* For fall admission, 2/1 priority date for domestic and international students; for spring admission, 7/1 priority date for domestic students, 8/1 priority date for international students. Applications are processed on a rolling basis. Application fee: $40 ($55 for international students). Electronic applications accepted. *Financial support:* In 2009–10, 18 research assistantships (averaging $22,305 per year), 30 teaching assistantships with full tuition reimbursements (averaging $14,705 per year) were awarded; Federal Work-Study, institutionally sponsored loans, and scholarships/grants also available. Support available to part-time students. Financial award application deadline: 3/1; financial award applicants required to submit FAFSA. *Faculty research:* Linear and nonlinear statistical models, design analysis of experiments, nonparametric methods for reliability and survival data, resampling methods and their application, categorical data analysis. Total annual research expenditures: $2,558. *Unit head:* David Rintoul, Head, 785-532-6615, Fax: 785-532-7336, E-mail: drintoul@ksu.edu. *Application contact:* S. Keith Chapes, Director, 785-532-6795, Fax: 785-532-7336, E-mail: skcbiol@ksu.edu.

Kean University, College of Natural, Applied and Health Sciences, Program in Computing, Statistics and Mathematics, Union, NJ 07083. Offers MS. Part-time and evening/weekend programs available. *Faculty:* 13 full-time (4 women). *Students:* 2 full-time (1 woman), 5 part-time (0 women); includes 5 minority (2 African Americans, 2 Asian Americans or Pacific Islanders, 1 Hispanic American), 1 international. Average age 30. 2 applicants, 50% accepted, 1 enrolled. In 2009, 1 master's awarded. *Degree requirements:* For master's, thesis or alternative, research component. *Entrance requirements:* For master's, GRE General Test, minimum GPA of 3.0, 2 letters of recommendation, interview, 24-27 credits in prerequisites, official transcripts from all institutions attended. *Application deadline:* For fall admission, 5/1 for domestic students; for spring admission, 11/1 for domestic students. Application fee: $60 ($150 for international students). Electronic applications accepted. *Expenses:* Tuition, state resident: full-time $10,440; part-time $435 per credit. Tuition, nonresident: full-time $14,160; part-time $590 per credit. Required fees: $2642; $110 per credit. Part-time tuition and fees vary according to course load and degree level. *Financial support:* In 2009–10, 2 research assistantships with full tuition reimbursements (averaging $3,263 per year) were awarded; unspecified assistantships also available. *Unit head:* Dr. Wolde Woubneh, Program Coordinator, 908-737-3700, E-mail: wwoubneh@kean.edu. *Application contact:* Reenat Hasan, Pre-Admissions Coordinator, 908-737-5923, Fax: 908-737-5965, E-mail: rhasan@exchange.kean.edu.

Lehigh University, College of Arts and Sciences, Department of Mathematics, Bethlehem, PA 18015. Offers applied mathematics (MS, PhD); mathematics (MS, PhD); statistics (MS). Part-time programs available. *Faculty:* 21 full-time (1 woman), 1 part-time/adjunct (0 women). *Students:* 35 full-time (18 women), 5 part-time (1 woman); includes 3 minority (1 African American, 1 Asian American or Pacific Islander, 1 Hispanic American), 15 international. Average age 28. 85 applicants, 42% accepted, 10 enrolled. In 2009, 12 master's, 3 doctorates awarded. Terminal master's awarded for partial completion of doctoral program. *Degree requirements:* For master's, comprehensive exam, thesis optional; for doctorate, comprehensive exam, thesis/dissertation, qualifying exams, general exam. *Entrance requirements:* For master's and doctorate, minimum undergraduate GPA of 2.75, 3.0 for last two semesters; adequate background in math. Additional exam requirements/recommendations for international students: Required—TOEFL (minimum score 550 paper-based; 213 computer-based; 85 iBT). *Application deadline:* For fall admission, 1/15 priority date for domestic and international students; for spring admission, 12/1 priority date for domestic and international students. Applications are processed on a rolling basis. Application fee: $75. Electronic applications accepted. *Financial support:* In 2009–10, 28 students received support, including 2 fellowships with full tuition reimbursements available (averaging $22,000 per year), 23 teaching assistantships with full tuition reimbursements available (averaging $16,900 per year); research assistantships with full tuition reimbursements available, scholarships/grants and tuition waivers (partial) also available. Financial award application deadline: 1/15. *Faculty research:* Probability and statistics, geometry and topology, number theory, algebra, differential equations. Total annual research expenditures: $196,010. *Unit head:* Dr. Wei-Min Huang, Chairman, 610-758-3730, Fax: 610-758-3767, E-mail: wh02@lehigh.edu. *Application contact:* Dr. Terry Napier, Graduate Coordinator, 610-758-3755, E-mail: mathgrad@lehigh.edu.

Louisiana State University and Agricultural and Mechanical College, Graduate School, College of Agriculture, Department of Experimental Statistics, Baton Rouge, LA 70803. Offers applied statistics (M App St). Part-time programs available. *Faculty:* 9 full-time (1 woman). *Students:* 13 full-time (11 women), 3 part-time (1 woman); includes 1 Asian American or Pacific Islander, 9 international. Average age 29. 13 applicants, 38% accepted, 3 enrolled. In 2009, 10 master's awarded. *Degree requirements:* For master's, project. *Entrance requirements:* For master's, GRE General Test, minimum GPA of 3.0. Additional exam requirements/recommendations for international students: Required—TOEFL (minimum score 550 paper-based; 213 computer-based; 79 iBT) or IELTS (minimum score 6.5). *Application deadline:* For fall admission, 1/25 priority date for domestic students, 5/15 for international students; for spring admission, 10/15 priority date for domestic students, 10/15 for international students. Applications are processed on a rolling basis. Application fee: $50 ($70 for international students). Electronic applications accepted. *Financial support:* In 2009–10, 14 students received support, including 1 research assistantship with partial tuition reimbursement available (averaging $12,000 per year), 11 teaching assistantships with partial tuition reimbursements available (averaging $10,800 per year); fellowships, career-related internships or fieldwork, Federal Work-Study, institutionally sponsored loans, tuition waivers (full and partial), and unspecified assistantships also available. Financial award application deadline: 4/1; financial award applicants required to submit FAFSA. *Faculty research:* Linear models, statistical computing, ecological statistics. Total annual research expenditures: $1,511. *Unit head:* Dr. James Geaghan, Head, 225-578-8303, Fax: 225-578-8344, E-mail: head@stat.lsu.edu. *Application contact:* Dr. James Geaghan, Graduate Adviser, 225-578-8303, E-mail: jgeaghan@lsu.edu.

Louisiana Tech University, Graduate School, College of Engineering and Science, Department of Mathematics and Statistics, Ruston, LA 71272. Offers MS. Part-time programs available. *Degree requirements:* For master's, thesis or alternative. *Entrance requirements:* For master's, GRE General Test, minimum GPA of 3.0 in last 60 hours. Additional exam requirements/recommendations for international students: Required—TOEFL.

Loyola University Chicago, Graduate School, Department of Mathematical Sciences and Statistics, Chicago, IL 60660. Offers applied statistics (MS); mathematics and statistics (MS), including pure mathematics. Part-time programs available. *Faculty:* 19 full-time (4 women). *Students:* 24 full-time (16 women), 8 part-time (3 women); includes 7 minority (3 African Americans, 4 Asian Americans or Pacific Islanders), 8 international. Average age 28. 49 applicants, 63% accepted, 16 enrolled. In 2009, 11 master's awarded. *Entrance requirements:* For master's, GRE General Test. Additional exam requirements/recommendations for international students: Required—TOEFL. *Application deadline:* For fall admission, 8/1 for domestic students; for spring admission, 12/1 for domestic students. Applications are processed on a rolling basis. Application fee: $0. Electronic applications accepted. *Expenses:* Tuition: Full-time $14,220; part-time $790 per credit hour. Required fees: $60 per semester hour. Tuition and fees vary according to program. *Financial support:* In 2009–10, 13 students received support, including 6 teaching assistantships with tuition reimbursements available (averaging $10,000 per year); career-related internships or fieldwork, Federal Work-Study, institutionally sponsored loans, and tuition waivers (partial) also available. Financial award application deadline: 3/15. *Faculty research:* Probability and statistics, differential equations, algebra, combinations. Total annual research expenditures: $10,000. *Unit head:* Dr. Robert Jensen, Chair, 773-508-3578, Fax: 773-508-2123, E-mail: rjensen@luc.edu. *Application contact:* Dr. Joseph Mayne, Director, 773-508-3574, Fax: 773-508-2123, E-mail: jmayne@luc.edu.

McGill University, Faculty of Graduate and Postdoctoral Studies, Faculty of Arts, Department of Economics, Montréal, QC H3A 2T5, Canada. Offers economics (MA, PhD); social statistics (MA).

McGill University, Faculty of Graduate and Postdoctoral Studies, Faculty of Arts, Department of Sociology, Montréal, QC H3A 2T5, Canada. Offers medical sociology (MA); neo-tropical environment (MA); social statistics (MA); sociology (MA, PhD, Diploma).

McGill University, Faculty of Graduate and Postdoctoral Studies, Faculty of Science, Department of Mathematics and Statistics, Montréal, QC H3A 2T5, Canada. Offers computational science and engineering (M Sc); mathematics and statistics (M Sc, MA, PhD), including applied mathematics (M Sc, MA), pure mathematics (M Sc, MA), statistics (M Sc, MA).

McMaster University, School of Graduate Studies, Faculty of Science, Department of Mathematics and Statistics, Program in Statistics, Hamilton, ON L8S 4M2, Canada. Offers applied statistics (M Sc); medical statistics (M Sc); statistical theory (M Sc). *Degree requirements:* For master's, thesis or alternative. *Entrance requirements:* For master's, honors degree background in mathematics and statistics. Additional exam requirements/recommendations for international students: Required—TOEFL (minimum score 550 paper-based; 213 computer-based). *Faculty research:* Development of polymer production technology, quality of life in patients who use pharmaceutical agents, mathematical modeling, order statistics from progressively censored samples, nonlinear stochastic model in genetics.

McNeese State University, Doré School of Graduate Studies, College of Science, Department of Mathematics, Computer Science, and Statistics, Lake Charles, LA 70609. Offers mathematical science (MS), including computer science, mathematics, statistics. Evening/weekend programs available. *Degree requirements:* For master's, comprehensive exam, thesis or alternative, written exam. *Entrance requirements:* For master's, GRE.

Memorial University of Newfoundland, School of Graduate Studies, Department of Mathematics and Statistics, St. John's, NL A1C 5S7, Canada. Offers mathematics (M Sc, PhD); statistics (M Sc, MAS, PhD). Part-time programs available. *Degree requirements:* For master's, thesis, practicum and report (MAS); for doctorate, comprehensive exam, thesis/dissertation, oral defense of thesis. *Entrance requirements:* For master's, 2nd class honors degree (MAS); for doctorate, MAS or M Sc in mathematics and statistics. Electronic applications accepted. *Faculty research:* Algebra, topology, applied mathematics, mathematical statistics, applied statistics and probability.

Miami University, Graduate School, College of Arts and Sciences, Department of Statistics, Oxford, OH 45056. Offers MS. *Students:* 13 full-time (4 women), 1 part-time (0 women); includes 3 minority (2 African Americans, 1 Asian American or Pacific Islander), 7 international. *Entrance requirements:* Additional exam requirements/recommendations for international students: Required—TOEFL. Application fee: $50. *Expenses:* Tuition, state resident: full-time $11,280. Tuition, nonresident: full-time $24,912. Required fees: $516. *Financial support:* Research assistantships, teaching assistantships, health care benefits and unspecified assistantships available. Financial award application deadline: 3/1; financial award applicants required to submit FAFSA. *Unit head:* Dr. A. John Bailer, Distinguished University Professor and Chair, 513-529-3538, E-mail: baileraj@muohio.edu. *Application contact:* Dr. David J. Groggel, Associate Professor and Director of Graduate Studies, 513-529-6087, E-mail: groggedj@muohio.edu.

Michigan State University, The Graduate School, College of Natural Science, Department of Statistics and Probability, East Lansing, MI 48824. Offers applied statistics (MS); statistics (MS, PhD). *Entrance requirements:* Additional exam requirements/recommendations for international students: Required—TOEFL. Electronic applications accepted.

Minnesota State University Mankato, College of Graduate Studies, College of Science, Engineering and Technology, Department of Mathematics and Statistics, Program in Statistics, Mankato, MN 56001. Offers MS. *Students:* 4 full-time (2 women), 4 part-time (0 women). *Degree requirements:* For master's, one foreign language, comprehensive exam, thesis or alternative. *Entrance requirements:* For master's, GRE General Test, minimum GPA of 3.0 during previous 2 years. Additional exam requirements/recommendations for international students: Required—TOEFL. *Application deadline:* For fall admission, 7/1 priority date for domestic students; for spring admission, 11/1 for domestic students. Applications are processed on a rolling basis. Application fee: $40. Electronic applications accepted. *Expenses:* Tuition, state resident: full-time $5364. Tuition, nonresident: full-time $8314. *Financial support:* Research assistantships with partial tuition reimbursements, teaching assistantships with partial tuition reimbursements, unspecified assistantships available. Financial award application deadline: 3/15; financial award applicants required to submit FAFSA. *Unit head:* Dr. Ernest Boyd, Chairperson, 507-389-1453. *Application contact:* 507-389-2321, E-mail: grad@mnsu.edu.

Mississippi State University, College of Arts and Sciences, Department of Mathematics and Statistics, Mississippi State, MS 39762. Offers mathematical sciences (PhD); mathematics (MS); statistics (MS). Part-time programs available. *Faculty:* 21 full-time (4 women). *Students:* 36 full-time (15 women), 2 part-time (1 woman); includes 3 minority (all African Americans), 24 international. Average age 28. 66 applicants, 39% accepted, 15 enrolled. In 2009, 11 master's, 2 doctorates awarded. Terminal master's awarded for partial completion of doctoral program. *Degree requirements:* For master's, thesis optional, comprehensive oral or written exam; for doctorate, one foreign language, thesis/dissertation, comprehensive oral and written exam. *Entrance requirements:* For master's, minimum GPA of 2.75 on last two years of undergraduate courses; for doctorate, GRE. Additional exam requirements/recommendations for international students: Required—TOEFL (minimum score 475 paper-based; 153 computer-based; 53 iBT); Recommended—IELTS (minimum score 4.5). *Application deadline:* For fall admission, 3/15 priority date for domestic students, 5/1 for international students; for spring admission, 11/1 for domestic students, 9/1 for international students. Applications are processed on a rolling basis. Application fee: $40. Electronic applications accepted. *Expenses:* Tuition, state resident: full-time $2575.50; part-time $286.25 per credit hour. Tuition, nonresident: full-time $6510; part-time $723.50 per credit hour. Tuition and fees vary according to course load. *Financial support:* In 2009–10, 2 research assistantships (averaging $12,379 per year), 27 teaching assistantships with full tuition reimbursements (averaging $13,142 per year) were awarded; Federal Work-Study, institutionally sponsored loans, tuition waivers (partial), and unspecified assistantships also available. Financial award applicants required to submit FAFSA. *Faculty research:* Differential equations, algebra, numerical analysis, functional analysis, applied statistics. Total annual research expenditures: $1.9 million. *Unit head:* Dr. Mohsen Razzaghi, Interim Head, 662-325-3414, Fax: 662-325-0005, E-mail: razzaghi@math.msstate.edu. *Application contact:* Dr. Corlis Johnson, Associate Head/Graduate Coordinator, 662-325-3414, Fax: 662-325-0005, E-mail: cjohnson@math.msstate.edu.

Missouri University of Science and Technology, Graduate School, Department of Mathematics and Statistics, Rolla, MO 65409. Offers applied mathematics (MS); mathematics (MST, PhD), including mathematics (PhD), mathematics education (MST), statistics (PhD). Terminal master's awarded for partial completion of doctoral program. *Degree requirements:* For master's, thesis or alternative; for doctorate, one foreign language, thesis/dissertation. *Entrance requirements:* For master's and doctorate, GRE General Test, GRE Subject Test. Electronic applications accepted. *Faculty research:* Analysis, differential equations, topology, statistics.

Montana State University, College of Graduate Studies, College of Letters and Science, Department of Ecology, Bozeman, MT 59717. Offers ecological and environmental statistics (MS); ecology and environmental sciences (PhD); fish and wildlife biology (PhD); fish and wildlife management (MS). Part-time programs available. *Faculty:* 12 full-time (2 women), 2 part-time/adjunct (0 women). *Students:* 8 full-time (2 women), 48 part-time (18 women). Average age 31. 18 applicants, 33% accepted, 6 enrolled. In 2009, 6 master's, 7 doctorates awarded. *Degree requirements:* For master's, comprehensive exam, thesis (for some programs); for doctorate, comprehensive exam, thesis/dissertation. *Entrance requirements:* For master's, GRE General Test, GPA, Letters of Recommendation, Essay; for doctorate, GRE General Test, letters of recommendation. Additional exam requirements/recommendations for international students: Required—TOEFL (minimum score 550 paper-based; 213 computer-based). *Application deadline:* For fall admission, 7/15 priority date for domestic students, 5/15 priority date for international students; for spring admission, 12/1 priority date for domestic students, 10/1 priority date for international students. Applications are processed on a rolling basis. Application fee: $30. Electronic applications accepted. *Expenses:* Tuition, state resident: full-time $5635; part-time $3492 per year. Tuition, nonresident: full-time $17,212; part-time $7865.10 per year. Required fees: $1441.05; $153.15 per credit. Tuition and fees vary according to course load and program. *Financial support:* In 2009–10, 2 fellowships with full tuition reimbursements (averaging $17,725 per year), 29 research assistantships with full and partial tuition reimbursements (averaging $19,500 per year), 20 teaching assistantships with full tuition reimbursements (averaging $12,321 per year) were awarded; career-related internships or fieldwork, scholarships/grants, health care benefits, tuition waivers (partial), and unspecified assistantships also available. Support available to part-time students. Financial award application deadline: 3/1; financial award applicants required to submit FAFSA. *Faculty research:* Evolutionary biology, conservation ecology, human impact on ecosystems, biodiversity, applied wildlife and fisheries research, plant and animal community ecology. Total annual research expenditures: $2.6 million. *Unit head:* Dr. David Roberts, Head, 406-994-4548, Fax: 406-994-3190, E-mail: droberts@montana.edu. *Application contact:* Dr. Carl A. Fox, Vice Provost for Graduate Education, 406-994-4145, Fax: 406-994-7433, E-mail: gradstudy@montana.edu.

Montana State University, College of Graduate Studies, College of Letters and Science, Department of Mathematical Sciences, Bozeman, MT 59717. Offers mathematics (MS, PhD), including mathematics education option (MS); statistics (MS, PhD). Part-time programs available. Postbaccalaureate distance learning degree programs offered (minimal on-campus study). *Faculty:* 35 full-time (11 women), 7 part-time/adjunct (3 women). *Students:* 17 full-time (6 women), 71 part-time (33 women); includes 3 minority (1 American Indian/Alaska Native, 1 Asian American or Pacific Islander, 1 Hispanic American), 6 international. Average age 31. 53 applicants, 36% accepted, 15 enrolled. In 2009, 18 master's, 3 doctorates awarded. *Degree requirements:* For master's, comprehensive exam, thesis (for some programs); for doctorate, comprehensive exam, thesis/dissertation. *Entrance requirements:* For master's and doctorate, GRE General Test. Additional exam requirements/recommendations for international students: Required—TOEFL (minimum score 550 paper-based; 213 computer-based). *Application deadline:* For fall admission, 7/15 priority date for domestic students, 5/15 priority date for international students; for spring admission, 12/1 priority date for domestic students, 10/1 priority date for international students. Applications are processed on a rolling basis. Application fee: $30. Electronic applications accepted. *Expenses:* Tuition, state resident: full-time $5635; part-time $3492 per year. Tuition, nonresident: full-time $17,212; part-time $7865.10 per year. Required fees: $1441.05; $153.15 per credit. Tuition and fees vary according to course load and program. *Financial support:* In 2009–10, 58 students received support, including 4 research assistantships with tuition reimbursements available (averaging $15,650 per year), 54 teaching assistantships with tuition reimbursements available (averaging $15,450 per year); career-related internships or fieldwork, scholarships/grants, tuition waivers (full), and unspecified assistantships also available. Support available to part-time students. Financial award application deadline: 3/1; financial award applicants required to submit FAFSA. *Faculty research:* Applied mathematics, dynamical systems, statistics, mathematics education, mathematical and computational biology. Total annual research expenditures: $248,209. *Unit head:* Dr. Kenneth Bowers, Head, 406-994-3604, Fax: 406-994-1789, E-mail: bowers@math.montana.edu. *Application contact:* Dr. Carl A. Fox, Vice Provost for Graduate Education, 406-994-4145, Fax: 406-994-7433, E-mail: gradstudy@montana.edu.

Montclair State University, The Graduate School, College of Science and Mathematics, Department of Mathematics, Montclair, NJ 07043-1624. Offers math pedagogy (Ed D);

Statistics

Montclair State University (continued)
mathematics (MS), including computer science, mathematics education, pure and applied mathematics, statistics; physical science (Certificate); teaching middle grades math (MS, Certificate). Part-time and evening/weekend programs available. *Faculty:* 30 full-time (10 women), 39 part-time/adjunct (19 women). *Students:* 15 full-time (7 women), 101 part-time (75 women). Average age 32. 55 applicants, 76% accepted, 31 enrolled. In 2009, 32 master's, 2 doctorates, 9 other advanced degrees awarded. *Degree requirements:* For master's, comprehensive exam. *Entrance requirements:* For master's, GRE General Test, 2 letters of recommendation. Additional exam requirements/recommendations for international students: Required—TOEFL (minimum score 83 computer-based), or IELTS. *Application deadline:* For fall admission, 6/1 for international students; for spring admission, 10/1 for international students. Applications are processed on a rolling basis. Application fee: $60. *Expenses:* Tuition, area resident: Part-time $486.74 per credit. Tuition, state resident: part-time $486.74 per credit. Tuition, nonresident: part-time $751.34 per credit. Tuition and fees vary according to degree level and program. *Financial support:* In 2009–10, 9 research assistantships with full tuition reimbursements (averaging $7,000 per year), 1 teaching assistantship with full tuition reimbursement (averaging $15,000 per year) were awarded; Federal Work-Study, scholarships/grants, and unspecified assistantships also available. Support available to part-time students. Financial award application deadline: 3/1; financial award applicants required to submit FAFSA. *Faculty research:* Infectious disease. *Unit head:* Dr. Helen Roberts, Chairperson, 973-655-5132. *Application contact:* Amy Aiello, Director of Graduate Admissions and Operations, 973-655-5147, Fax: 973-655-7869, E-mail: graduate.school@montclair.edu.

Murray State University, College of Science, Engineering and Technology, Program in Mathematics and Statistics, Murray, KY 42071. Offers MA, MAT, MS. Part-time programs available. *Degree requirements:* For master's, comprehensive exam, thesis optional. *Entrance requirements:* For master's, GRE General Test. Additional exam requirements/recommendations for international students: Required—TOEFL. *Faculty research:* Algebraic structures, mathematical biology, topolgy.

New York University, Leonard N. Stern School of Business, Department of Information, Operations and Management Sciences, New York, NY 10012-1019. Offers information systems (MBA, PhD); operations management (MBA, PhD); statistics (MBA, PhD). *Expenses:* Tuition: Full-time $30,528; part-time $1272 per credit. Required fees: $2177. *Faculty research:* Knowledge management, economics of information, computer-supported groups and communities financial information systems, data mining and business intelligence.

North Carolina State University, Graduate School, College of Physical and Mathematical Sciences, Department of Statistics, Raleigh, NC 27695. Offers M Stat, MS, PhD. Part-time programs available. *Degree requirements:* For master's, comprehensive exam, thesis (for some programs), final oral exam; for doctorate, thesis/dissertation, final oral and written exams, written and oral preliminary exams. *Entrance requirements:* For master's and doctorate, GRE General Test. Additional exam requirements/recommendations for international students: Required—TOEFL. Electronic applications accepted. *Faculty research:* Biostatistics; time series; spatial, inference, environmental, industrial, genetics applications; nonlinear models; DOE.

North Dakota State University, College of Graduate and Interdisciplinary Studies, College of Science and Mathematics, Department of Statistics, Fargo, ND 58108. Offers applied statistics (MS, Certificate); statistics (PhD); MS/MS. *Faculty:* 4 full-time (2 women), 1 part-time/adjunct (0 women). *Students:* 24 full-time (10 women), 1 (woman) part-time; includes 1 minority (African American), 16 international. Average age 24. 14 applicants, 79% accepted, 5 enrolled. In 2009, 7 master's awarded. *Degree requirements:* For master's, comprehensive exam, thesis; for doctorate, comprehensive exam, thesis/dissertation. *Entrance requirements:* For master's and doctorate, minimum GPA of 3.0. Additional exam requirements/recommendations for international students: Required—TOEFL (minimum score 550 paper-based; 213 computer-based; 79 iBT). *Application deadline:* Applications are processed on a rolling basis. Application fee: $45 ($60 for international students). *Financial support:* In 2009–10, 2 fellowships with full tuition reimbursements, 7 research assistantships with full tuition reimbursements, 9 teaching assistantships with full tuition reimbursements were awarded; career-related internships or fieldwork, Federal Work-Study, institutionally sponsored loans, and tuition waivers (full) also available. Financial award application deadline: 4/15. *Faculty research:* Nonparametric statistics, survival analysis, multivariate analysis, distribution theory, inference modeling, biostatistics. *Unit head:* Dr. Rhonda Magel, Chair, 701-231-7532, Fax: 701-231-8734, E-mail: ndsu.stats@ndsu.edu. *Application contact:* Judy Normann, Academic Assistant, 701-231-7532, Fax: 702-231-8734, E-mail: ndsu.stats@ndsu.edu.

Northern Arizona University, Graduate College, College of Engineering, Forestry and Natural Sciences, Department of Mathematics and Statistics, Flagstaff, AZ 86011. Offers mathematics (MAT, MS); statistics (MS). Part-time programs available. *Faculty:* 32 full-time (10 women). *Students:* 21 full-time (9 women), 22 part-time (14 women); includes 5 minority (3 Asian Americans or Pacific Islanders, 2 Hispanic Americans), 3 international. Average age 28. 34 applicants, 62% accepted, 14 enrolled. In 2009, 9 master's awarded. *Degree requirements:* For master's, comprehensive exam, thesis optional. *Entrance requirements:* For master's, minimum GPA of 3.0. Additional exam requirements/recommendations for international students: Required—TOEFL (minimum score 550 paper-based; 213 computer-based; 80 iBT), IELTS (minimum score 7), or a bachelor's degree from an English-speaking university and demonstrated proficiency. *Application deadline:* For fall admission, 3/15 priority date for domestic students, 9/1 priority date for international students; for spring admission, 10/15 priority date for domestic students. Applications are processed on a rolling basis. Application fee: $65. Electronic applications accepted. *Financial support:* In 2009–10, 22 teaching assistantships with partial tuition reimbursements (averaging $14,213 per year) were awarded; career-related internships or fieldwork, Federal Work-Study, tuition waivers (full and partial), and unspecified assistantships also available. Support available to part-time students. Financial award application deadline: 3/30; financial award applicants required to submit FAFSA. *Faculty research:* Topology, statistics, groups, ring theory, number theory. *Unit head:* Dr. Janet M. McShane, Chair, 928-523-1252, Fax: 928-523-5847, E-mail: janet.mcshane@nau.edu. *Application contact:* Dr. Jeffrey Allen Hovermill, Chair, 928-523-6897, Fax: 928-523-5847, E-mail: jeff.hovermill@nau.edu.

Northern Illinois University, Graduate School, College of Liberal Arts and Sciences, Department of Mathematical Sciences, Division of Statistics, De Kalb, IL 60115-2854. Offers MS. Part-time programs available. *Faculty:* 8 full-time (1 woman), 1 part-time/adjunct (0 women). *Students:* 16 full-time (4 women), 6 part-time (3 women); includes 4 minority (all Asian Americans or Pacific Islanders), 8 international. Average age 29. 28 applicants, 68% accepted, 9 enrolled. In 2009, 16 master's awarded. *Degree requirements:* For master's, comprehensive exam, thesis optional. *Entrance requirements:* For master's, GRE General Test, minimum GPA of 2.75, course work in statistics, calculus, linear algebra. Additional exam requirements/recommendations for international students: Required—TOEFL (minimum score 550 paper-based; 213 computer-based). *Application deadline:* For fall admission, 6/1 for domestic students, 5/1 for international students; for spring admission, 11/1 for domestic students, 10/1 for international students. Applications are processed on a rolling basis. Application fee: $30. Electronic applications accepted. *Expenses:* Tuition, state resident: full-time $6576; part-time $274 per credit hour. Tuition, nonresident: full-time $13,152; part-time $548 per credit hour. Required fees: $1813; $75.53 per credit hour. Part-time tuition and fees vary according to course load. *Financial support:* In 2009–10, 2 research assistantships with full tuition reimbursements, 14 teaching assistantships with full tuition reimbursements were awarded; fellowships with full tuition reimbursements, career-related internships or fieldwork, Federal Work-Study, scholarships/grants, tuition waivers (full), and unspecified assistantships also available. Support available to part-time students. Financial award applicants required to submit FAFSA. *Faculty research:* Reality and life testing, quality control, statistical inference from stochastic process, nonparametric statistics. *Unit head:* Dr. Rama T. Lingham, Director, 815-753-6773, Fax: 815-753-6776. *Application contact:* Dr. Alan Polansky, Director, Graduate Studies, 815-753-6864, E-mail: polansky@math.niu.edu.

Northwestern University, The Graduate School, Judd A. and Marjorie Weinberg College of Arts and Sciences, Department of Statistics, Evanston, IL 60208. Offers MS, PhD. Admissions and degrees offered through The Graduate School. Part-time programs available. Terminal master's awarded for partial completion of doctoral program. *Degree requirements:* For master's, final exam; for doctorate, thesis/dissertation, preliminary exam, final exam. *Entrance requirements:* For master's and doctorate, GRE General Test. Additional exam requirements/recommendations for international students: Required—TOEFL. *Faculty research:* Theoretical statistics, applied statistics, computational methods, statistical designs, complex models.

Oakland University, Graduate Study and Lifelong Learning, College of Arts and Sciences, Department of Mathematics and Statistics, Program in Statistical Methods, Rochester, MI 48309-4401. Offers Certificate. *Entrance requirements:* Additional exam requirements/recommendations for international students: Required—TOEFL (minimum score 550 paper-based; 213 computer-based). *Expenses:* Contact institution.

The Ohio State University, Graduate School, College of Mathematical and Physical Sciences, Department of Statistics, Columbus, OH 43210. Offers biostatistics (PhD); statistics (M Appl Stat, MS, PhD). *Faculty:* 29. *Students:* 74 full-time (33 women), 39 part-time (16 women); includes 9 minority (2 African Americans, 6 Asian Americans or Pacific Islanders, 1 Hispanic American), 51 international. Average age 27. In 2009, 40 master's, 11 doctorates awarded. *Degree requirements:* For master's, thesis optional; for doctorate, thesis/dissertation. *Entrance requirements:* For master's and doctorate, GRE General Test. Additional exam requirements/recommendations for international students: Required—TOEFL (minimum score 600 paper-based; 250 computer-based). *Application deadline:* For fall admission, 8/15 priority date for domestic students, 7/1 priority date for international students; for winter admission, 12/1 priority date for domestic students, 11/1 priority date for international students; for spring admission, 3/1 priority date for domestic students, 2/1 priority date for international students. Applications are processed on a rolling basis. Application fee: $40 ($50 for international students). Electronic applications accepted. *Expenses:* Tuition, state resident: full-time $10,683. Tuition, nonresident: full-time $25,923. Tuition and fees vary according to course load and program. *Financial support:* Fellowships, research assistantships, teaching assistantships, Federal Work-Study and institutionally sponsored loans available. Support available to part-time students. *Unit head:* Elizabeth A. Stasny, Graduate Studies Committee Chair, 614-292-2866, Fax: 614-292-2096, E-mail: stasny.1@osu.edu. *Application contact:* 614-292-9444, Fax: 614-292-3895, E-mail: domestic.grad@osu.edu.

Oklahoma State University, College of Arts and Sciences, Department of Statistics, Stillwater, OK 74078. Offers MS, PhD. *Faculty:* 7 full-time (3 women), 2 part-time/adjunct (1 woman). *Students:* 12 full-time (5 women), 10 part-time (6 women), 15 international. Average age 31. 67 applicants, 25% accepted, 8 enrolled. In 2009, 6 master's, 1 doctorate awarded. *Degree requirements:* For master's, comprehensive exam, thesis optional; for doctorate, comprehensive exam, thesis/dissertation. *Entrance requirements:* For master's and doctorate, GRE. Additional exam requirements/recommendations for international students: Required—TOEFL (minimum score 550 paper-based; 7 iBT). *Application deadline:* For fall admission, 3/1 priority date for international students; for spring admission, 8/1 priority date for international students. Applications are processed on a rolling basis. Application fee: $40 ($75 for international students). Electronic applications accepted. *Expenses:* Tuition, state resident: full-time $3716; part-time $154.85 per credit hour. Tuition, nonresident: full-time $14,448; part-time $602 per credit hour. Required fees: $1772; $73.85 per credit hour. One-time fee: $50. Tuition and fees vary according to course load and campus/location. *Financial support:* In 2009–10, 2 research assistantships (averaging $15,714 per year), 20 teaching assistantships (averaging $15,402 per year) were awarded; career-related internships or fieldwork, Federal Work-Study, scholarships/grants, health care benefits, tuition waivers (partial), and unspecified assistantships also available. Support available to part-time students. Financial award application deadline: 3/1; financial award applicants required to submit FAFSA. *Faculty research:* Linear models, sampling methods, ranking and selections procedures, categorical data, multiple comparisons. *Unit head:* Dr. Ibrahim Ahmad, Head, 405-744-5684, Fax: 405-744-3533. *Application contact:* Dr. Gordon Emslie, Dean, 405-744-6368, Fax: 405-744-0355, E-mail: grad-i@okstate.edu.

Oregon State University, Graduate School, College of Science, Department of Statistics, Corvallis, OR 97331. Offers operations research (MA, MS); statistics (MA, MS, PhD). Part-time programs available. *Faculty:* 10 full-time (4 women). *Students:* 25 full-time (10 women), 2 part-time (both women); includes 3 minority (2 Asian Americans or Pacific Islanders, 1 Hispanic American), 6 international. Average age 30. In 2009, 14 master's, 2 doctorates awarded. *Degree requirements:* For master's, consulting experience; for doctorate, thesis/dissertation, consulting experience. *Entrance requirements:* For master's and doctorate, minimum GPA of 3.0 in last 90 hours. Additional exam requirements/recommendations for international students: Required—TOEFL. *Application deadline:* For fall admission, 2/15 for domestic students. Applications are processed on a rolling basis. Application fee: $50. *Expenses:* Tuition, state resident: full-time $9774; part-time $362 per credit. Tuition, nonresident: full-time $15,849; part-time $587 per credit. Required fees: $1639. Full-time tuition and fees vary according to course load and program. *Financial support:* In 2009–10, 8 research assistantships, 19 teaching assistantships were awarded; Federal Work-Study and institutionally sponsored loans also available. Financial award application deadline: 2/15. *Faculty research:* Analysis of enumerative data, nonparametric statistics, asymptotics, experimental design, generalized regression models, linear model theory, reliability theory, survival analysis, wildlife and general survey methodology. *Unit head:* Dr. Robert T. Smythe, Chair, 541-737-3480, Fax: 541-737-3489, E-mail: smythe@science.oregonstate.edu. *Application contact:* Dr. Alix I. Gitelman, Director of Graduate Studies, 541-737-1987, Fax: 541-737-3489, E-mail: gitelman@science.oregonstate.edu.

Penn State University Park, Graduate School, Eberly College of Science, Department of Statistics, State College, University Park, PA 16802-1503. Offers MA, MAS, MS, PhD. *Unit head:* Dr. Bruce G. Lindsay, Head, 814-865-1348, Fax: 814-863-7114, E-mail: bgl@psu.edu. *Application contact:* Information Contact, E-mail: b2a@psu.edu.

Portland State University, Graduate Studies, College of Liberal Arts and Sciences, Department of Mathematics and Statistics, Portland, OR 97207-0751. Offers mathematical sciences (PhD); mathematics education (PhD); statistics (MS); MA/MS. *Degree requirements:* For master's, thesis or alternative, exams; for doctorate, 2 foreign languages, thesis/dissertation, exams. *Entrance requirements:* For master's, GRE General Test, GRE Subject Test, minimum GPA of 3.0 in upper-division course work or 2.75 overall; for doctorate, GRE General Test. Additional exam requirements/recommendations for international students: Required—TOEFL (minimum score 550 paper-based; 213 computer-based). *Faculty research:* Algebra, topology, statistical distribution theory, control theory, statistical robustness.

Purdue University, Graduate School, College of Science, Department of Statistics, West Lafayette, IN 47907. Offers MS, PhD, Certificate. *Degree requirements:* For doctorate, thesis/dissertation, qualifying exams. *Entrance requirements:* For master's and doctorate, GRE General Test. Additional exam requirements/recommendations for international students: Required—TOEFL (minimum score 250 computer-based); Recommended—TWE. Electronic applications accepted. *Faculty research:* Nonparametric models, computational finance, design of experiments, probability theory, bioinformatics.

Queen's University at Kingston, School of Graduate Studies and Research, Faculty of Arts and Sciences, Department of Mathematics and Statistics, Kingston, ON K7L 3N6, Canada.

Offers mathematics (M Sc, M Sc Eng, PhD); statistics (M Sc, M Sc Eng, PhD). Part-time programs available. *Degree requirements:* For master's, thesis; for doctorate, comprehensive exam, thesis/dissertation. *Entrance requirements:* Additional exam requirements/recommendations for international students: Required—TOEFL. *Faculty research:* Algebra, analysis, applied mathematics, statistics.

Rice University, Graduate Programs, George R. Brown School of Engineering, Department of Statistics, Houston, TX 77251-1892. Offers bioinformatics (PhD); biostatistics (PhD); computational finance (PhD); general statistics (PhD); statistics (M Stat, MA); MBA/M Stat. Part-time programs available. *Faculty:* 16 full-time (6 women), 1 part-time/adjunct (0 women). *Students:* 45 full-time (20 women), 3 part-time (2 women); includes 12 minority (1 African American, 5 Asian Americans or Pacific Islanders, 6 Hispanic Americans), 16 international. Average age 28. 112 applicants, 41% accepted, 20 enrolled. In 2009, 9 master's, 7 doctorates awarded. *Degree requirements:* For master's, comprehensive exam; for doctorate, comprehensive exam, thesis/dissertation. *Entrance requirements:* For master's and doctorate, GRE General Test, minimum GPA of 3.0. Additional exam requirements/recommendations for international students: Required—TOEFL (minimum score 630 paper-based; 250 computer-based; 90 iBT). *Application deadline:* For fall admission, 1/15 priority date for domestic and international students; for spring admission, 11/1 for international students. Applications are processed on a rolling basis. Application fee: $70. Electronic applications accepted. *Financial support:* In 2009–10, 13 students received support, including 1 fellowship with full tuition reimbursement available (averaging $15,000 per year), 19 research assistantships with full tuition reimbursements available (averaging $23,000 per year), 9 teaching assistantships with full tuition reimbursements available (averaging $17,250 per year); career-related internships or fieldwork, institutionally sponsored loans, scholarships/grants, traineeships, health care benefits, tuition waivers (full), and unspecified assistantships also available. *Faculty research:* Statistical genetics, non parametric function estimation, computational statistics and visualization, stochastic processes. Total annual research expenditures: $800,000. *Unit head:* Carolyn Duhon, Sr. Department Administrator, 713-348-6032, Fax: 713-348-5476, E-mail: stat@rice.edu. *Application contact:* Margaret Poon, Department Coordinator, 713-348-6032, Fax: 713-348-5476, E-mail: poon@rice.edu.

Rochester Institute of Technology, Graduate Enrollment Services, Kate Gleason College of Engineering, Center of Quality and Applied Statistics, Rochester, NY 14623-5603. Offers applied statistics (MS); statistical quality (AC). Part-time and evening/weekend programs available. Postbaccalaureate distance learning degree programs offered (no on-campus study). *Students:* 17 full-time (11 women), 31 part-time (10 women); includes 9 minority (2 African Americans, 4 Asian Americans or Pacific Islanders, 3 Hispanic Americans), 11 international. Average age 32. 46 applicants, 67% accepted, 21 enrolled. In 2009, 21 master's, 3 other advanced degrees awarded. *Degree requirements:* For master's, oral exam. *Entrance requirements:* For master's, course work in calculus, minimum GPA of 3.0. Additional exam requirements/recommendations for international students: Required—TOEFL (minimum score 570 paper-based; 230 computer-based; 88 iBT), or IELTS (minimum score 6.5). *Application deadline:* For fall admission, 2/15 priority date for domestic and international students; for winter admission, 10/15 for domestic students; for spring admission, 2/1 for domestic students. Applications are processed on a rolling basis. Application fee: $50. *Expenses:* Tuition: Full-time $31,533; part-time $876 per credit hour. Required fees: $210. *Financial support:* In 2009–10, 33 students received support; research assistantships with partial tuition reimbursements available, career-related internships or fieldwork, institutionally sponsored loans, scholarships/grants, and unspecified assistantships available. Support available to part-time students. Financial award applicants required to submit FAFSA. *Faculty research:* Industrial statistics, quality control. *Unit head:* Dr. Donald Baker, Director, 585-475-6990, Fax: 585-475-5959, E-mail: cqas@rit.edu. *Application contact:* Diane Ellison, Assistant Vice President, Graduate Enrollment Services, 585-475-2229, Fax: 585-475-7164, E-mail: gradinfo@rit.edu.

Rutgers, The State University of New Jersey, New Brunswick, Graduate School-New Brunswick, Program in Statistics, Piscataway, NJ 08854-8097. Offers applied statistics (MS); biostatistics (MS); data mining (MS); quality and productivity management (MS); statistics (MS, PhD). Part-time programs available. Terminal master's awarded for partial completion of doctoral program. *Degree requirements:* For master's, comprehensive exam, essay, exam, non-thesis essay paper; for doctorate, one foreign language, thesis/dissertation, qualifying oral and written exams. *Entrance requirements:* For master's, GRE General Test; for doctorate, GRE General Test, GRE Subject Test (recommended). Additional exam requirements/recommendations for international students: Required—TOEFL (minimum score 550 paper-based; 213 computer-based). Electronic applications accepted. *Faculty research:* Probability, decision theory, linear models, multivariate statistics, statistical computing.

St. John's University, St. John's College of Liberal Arts and Sciences, Department of Mathematics and Computer Science, Queens, NY 11439. Offers algebra (MA); analysis (MA); applied mathematics (MA); computer science (MA); geometry-topology (MA); logic and foundations (MA); probability and statistics (MA). Part-time and evening/weekend programs available. *Students:* 3 full-time (0 women), 2 part-time (1 woman); includes 1 minority (Hispanic American), 1 international. Average age 25. 21 applicants, 67% accepted, 3 enrolled. In 2009, 2 master's awarded. *Degree requirements:* For master's, comprehensive exam, thesis optional. *Entrance requirements:* For master's, minimum GPA of 3.0. Additional exam requirements/recommendations for international students: Required—TOEFL (minimum score 500 paper-based; 173 computer-based; 61 iBT), IELTS (minimum score 5.5). *Application deadline:* For fall admission, 5/1 priority date for domestic and international students; for spring admission, 11/1 priority date for domestic and international students. Applications are processed on a rolling basis. Application fee: $70. Electronic applications accepted. *Expenses:* Tuition: Full-time $16,290; part-time $905 per credit. Required fees: $300; $150 per semester. Tuition and fees vary according to program. *Financial support:* Research assistantships, scholarships/grants available. Support available to part-time students. Financial award application deadline: 3/1; financial award applicants required to submit FAFSA. *Faculty research:* Functional analysis and operator theory, algebraic K-theory, applied mathematics, measure theory, differential geometry and mathematics education. *Unit head:* Dr. Charles Traina, Chair, 718-990-6166, E-mail: trainac@stjohns.edu. *Application contact:* Kathleen Davis, Director of Graduate Admission, 718-990-2790, Fax: 718-990-5686, E-mail: gradhelp@stjohns.edu.

Sam Houston State University, College of Arts and Sciences, Department of Mathematics and Statistics, Huntsville, TX 77341. Offers mathematics (MA, MS); statistics (MS). Part-time programs available. *Faculty:* 11 full-time (3 women). *Students:* 19 full-time (10 women), 7 part-time (6 women); includes 1 minority (Asian American or Pacific Islander), 8 international. Average age 30. 24 applicants, 92% accepted, 10 enrolled. In 2009, 8 master's awarded. *Entrance requirements:* For master's, GRE General Test. Additional exam requirements/recommendations for international students: Required—TOEFL (minimum score 550 paper-based; 213 computer-based; 79 iBT). *Application deadline:* For fall admission, 8/1 for domestic and international students; for spring admission, 12/1 for domestic and international students. Applications are processed on a rolling basis. Application fee: $20. *Expenses:* Tuition, state resident: full-time $3690; part-time $205 per credit hour. Tuition, nonresident: full-time $8676; part-time $482 per credit hour. Required fees: $1474. Tuition and fees vary according to course load and campus/location. *Financial support:* Teaching assistantships, institutionally sponsored loans available. Support available to part-time students. Financial award application deadline: 5/31; financial award applicants required to submit FAFSA. *Unit head:* Dr. Mark Klespis, Chair, 936-294-1577, Fax: 936-294-1882, E-mail: klespis@shsu.edu. *Application contact:* Dr. Jianzhong Wang, Advisor, 936-294-3521, Fax: 936-294-1882, E-mail: mth_jxw@shsu.edu.

San Diego State University, Graduate and Research Affairs, College of Sciences, Department of Mathematics and Statistics, Program in Statistics, San Diego, CA 92182. Offers MS. Part-time programs available. *Degree requirements:* For master's, comprehensive exam. *Entrance requirements:* For master's, GRE General Test. Additional exam requirements/recommendations for international students: Required—TOEFL. Electronic applications accepted.

San Jose State University, Graduate Studies and Research, College of Science, Department of Mathematics, San Jose, CA 95192-0001. Offers applied mathematics (MS); mathematics (MA, MS); mathematics education (MA); statistics (MA). Part-time and evening/weekend programs available. *Students:* 13 full-time (7 women), 22 part-time (8 women); includes 17 minority (1 African American, 12 Asian Americans or Pacific Islanders, 4 Hispanic Americans), 5 international. Average age 34. 50 applicants, 30% accepted, 10 enrolled. In 2009, 7 master's awarded. *Degree requirements:* For master's, comprehensive exam, thesis (for some programs). *Entrance requirements:* For master's, GRE Subject Test. *Application deadline:* For fall admission, 6/29 for domestic students; for spring admission, 11/30 for domestic students. Applications are processed on a rolling basis. Application fee: $59. Electronic applications accepted. *Financial support:* Teaching assistantships, career-related internships or fieldwork and Federal Work-Study available. Support available to part-time students. Financial award applicants required to submit FAFSA. *Faculty research:* Artificial intelligence, algorithms, numerical analysis, software database, number theory. *Unit head:* Dr. Bradley Jackson, Chair, 408-924-5100, Fax: 408-924-5080. *Application contact:* Prof. Richard Kubelka, Graduate Coordinator, 408-924-5132, E-mail: kubelka@math.sjsu.edu.

Simon Fraser University, Graduate Studies, Faculty of Science, Department of Statistics and Actuarial Science, Burnaby, BC V5A 1S6, Canada. Offers M Sc, PhD. Part-time programs available. *Degree requirements:* For master's, participation in consulting, project; for doctorate, comprehensive exam, thesis/dissertation. *Entrance requirements:* For master's, minimum GPA of 3.0; for doctorate, minimum GPA of 3.5. Additional exam requirements/recommendations for international students: Required—TOEFL. Electronic applications accepted. *Faculty research:* Biostatistics, experimental design, envirometrics, statistical computing, statistical theory.

South Dakota State University, Graduate School, College of Engineering, Department of Mathematics and Statistics, Brookings, SD 57007. Offers computational science and statistics (PhD); geospatial science and engineering (PhD); mathematics (MS). Part-time programs available. *Degree requirements:* For master's, thesis (for some programs), oral exam; for doctorate, comprehensive exam, thesis/dissertation, oral and written exams. *Entrance requirements:* Additional exam requirements/recommendations for international students: Required—TOEFL (minimum score 550 paper-based; 213 computer-based; 80 iBT); Recommended—IELTS. *Faculty research:* Mathematics, biostatistics, computational science, numerical linear algebra, statistics, applied quality number theory, abstract algebra.

Southern Illinois University Carbondale, Graduate School, College of Science, Department of Mathematics, Carbondale, IL 62901-4701. Offers mathematics (MA, MS, PhD); statistics (MS). Part-time programs available. *Degree requirements:* For master's, thesis; for doctorate, 2 foreign languages, thesis/dissertation. *Entrance requirements:* For master's, minimum GPA of 2.7; for doctorate, minimum GPA of 3.25. Additional exam requirements/recommendations for international students: Required—TOEFL. *Faculty research:* Differential equations, combinatorics, probability, algebra, numerical analysis.

Southern Methodist University, Dedman College, Department of Statistical Science, Dallas, TX 75080. Offers MS, PhD. Part-time programs available. *Faculty:* 10 full-time (4 women), 2 part-time/adjunct (1 woman). *Students:* 27 full-time (11 women), 2 part-time (1 woman); includes 2 minority (1 African American, 1 Asian American or Pacific Islander), 20 international. Average age 29. 47 applicants, 77% accepted. In 2009, 4 master's, 1 doctorate awarded. *Degree requirements:* For master's, thesis, oral and written exams; for doctorate, thesis/dissertation, oral and written exams. *Entrance requirements:* For master's, GRE General Test, 12 hours of advanced math courses; for doctorate, GRE General Test, minimum GPA of 3.0. Additional exam requirements/recommendations for international students: Required—TOEFL. *Application deadline:* For fall admission, 6/30 priority date for domestic students; for spring admission, 11/30 priority date for domestic students. Applications are processed on a rolling basis. Application fee: $60. Electronic applications accepted. *Financial support:* In 2009–10, 25 students received support, including 4 research assistantships with full tuition reimbursements available (averaging $19,000 per year), 21 teaching assistantships with full tuition reimbursements available (averaging $15,000 per year). Financial award application deadline: 4/30; financial award applicants required to submit FAFSA. *Faculty research:* Regression, time series, linear models sampling, nonparametrics, biostatistics. Total annual research expenditures: $500,000. *Unit head:* Dr. Wayne A. Woodward, Chair, 214-768-2457, Fax: 214-768-4035, E-mail: waynew@mail.smu.edu. *Application contact:* Dr. Richard Gunst, Graduate Advisor, 214-768-2441, Fax: 214-768-4035, E-mail: rgunst@smu.edu.

Stanford University, School of Humanities and Sciences, Department of Statistics, Stanford, CA 94305-9991. Offers MS, PhD. Terminal master's awarded for partial completion of doctoral program. *Degree requirements:* For doctorate, thesis/dissertation, oral exam, qualifying exams. *Entrance requirements:* For master's, GRE General Test; for doctorate, GRE General Test, GRE Subject Test. Additional exam requirements/recommendations for international students: Required—TOEFL. Electronic applications accepted. *Expenses:* Tuition: Full-time $37,380; part-time $2760 per quarter. Required fees: $501.

State University of New York at Binghamton, Graduate School, School of Arts and Sciences, Department of Mathematical Sciences, Binghamton, NY 13902-6000. Offers computer science (MA, PhD); probability and statistics (MA, PhD). Part-time programs available. *Faculty:* 24 full-time (4 women), 11 part-time/adjunct (6 women). *Students:* 43 full-time (14 women), 25 part-time (10 women); includes 8 minority (4 African Americans, 1 Asian American or Pacific Islander, 3 Hispanic Americans), 29 international. Average age 27. 79 applicants, 47% accepted, 19 enrolled. In 2009, 8 master's, 3 doctorates awarded. Terminal master's awarded for partial completion of doctoral program. *Degree requirements:* For master's, thesis or alternative; for doctorate, 2 foreign languages, thesis/dissertation. *Entrance requirements:* For master's and doctorate, GRE General Test, GRE Subject Test. Additional exam requirements/recommendations for international students: Required—TOEFL (minimum score 550 paper-based; 213 computer-based; 80 iBT). *Application deadline:* For fall admission, 4/15 priority date for domestic and international students; for spring admission, 11/30 priority date for domestic and international students. Applications are processed on a rolling basis. Application fee: $60. Electronic applications accepted. *Financial support:* In 2009–10, 60 students received support, including 3 fellowships with full tuition reimbursements available (averaging $16,500 per year), 5 research assistantships with full tuition reimbursements available (averaging $16,500 per year), 48 teaching assistantships with full tuition reimbursements available (averaging $16,500 per year); career-related internships or fieldwork, Federal Work-Study, institutionally sponsored loans, scholarships/grants, health care benefits, and unspecified assistantships also available. Financial award application deadline: 2/15; financial award applicants required to submit FAFSA. *Unit head:* Dr. Fernando Guzman, Chairperson, 607-777-2148, E-mail: fer@math.binghamton.edu. *Application contact:* Victoria Williams, Recruiting and Admissions Coordinator, 607-777-2151, Fax: 607-777-2501, E-mail: vwilliam@binghamton.edu.

Stephen F. Austin State University, Graduate School, College of Sciences and Mathematics, Department of Mathematics and Statistics, Nacogdoches, TX 75962. Offers mathematics (MS); mathematics education (MS); statistics (MS). *Degree requirements:* For master's, comprehensive exam, thesis optional. *Entrance requirements:* For master's, GRE General Test, minimum GPA of 2.8 in last 60 hours, 2.5 overall. Additional exam requirements/recommendations for international students: Required—TOEFL. *Faculty research:* Kernel type estimators, fractal mappings, spline curve fitting, robust regression continua theory.

Statistics

Stevens Institute of Technology, Graduate School, Charles V. Schaefer Jr. School of Engineering, Department of Mathematical Sciences, Program in Stochastic Systems, Hoboken, NJ 07030. Offers MS, Certificate. *Expenses:* Tuition: Full-time $9900; part-time $1100 per credit. Required fees: $286 per semester.

Stony Brook University, State University of New York, Graduate School, College of Engineering and Applied Sciences, Department of Applied Mathematics and Statistics, Stony Brook, NY 11794. Offers MS, PhD. *Faculty:* 19 full-time (3 women), 1 part-time/adjunct (0 women). *Students:* 179 full-time (60 women), 20 part-time (9 women); includes 28 minority (6 African Americans, 18 Asian Americans or Pacific Islanders, 4 Hispanic Americans), 132 international. Average age 28. 275 applicants, 41% accepted. In 2009, 35 master's, 21 doctorates awarded. *Degree requirements:* For master's, thesis or alternative; for doctorate, one foreign language, comprehensive exam, thesis/dissertation. *Entrance requirements:* For master's and doctorate, GRE General Test. Additional exam requirements/recommendations for international students: Required—TOEFL. *Application deadline:* For fall admission, 1/15 for domestic students. Application fee: $60. *Expenses:* Tuition, state resident: full-time $8370; part-time $349 per credit. Tuition, nonresident: full-time $13,250; part-time $552 per credit. Required fees: $933. *Financial support:* In 2009–10, 32 research assistantships, 42 teaching assistantships were awarded; fellowships also available. *Faculty research:* Biostatistics, combinatorial analysis, differential equations, modeling. Total annual research expenditures: $2.7 million. *Unit head:* Dr. Jim Glimm, Chairman, 631-632-8360. *Application contact:* Dr. Xiaolin Li, Graduate Director, 631-632-8354, Fax: 631-632-8490, E-mail: linli@ams.sunysb.edu.

Temple University, Graduate School, Fox School of Business, Doctoral Programs in Business, Philadelphia, PA 19122-6096. Offers accounting (PhD); entrepreneurship (PhD); finance (PhD); human resource administration (PhD); international business (PhD); management information systems (PhD); marketing (PhD); risk management and insurance (PhD); statistics (PhD); strategic management (PhD); tourism and sport (PhD). *Accreditation:* AACSB. *Degree requirements:* For doctorate, thesis/dissertation. *Entrance requirements:* For doctorate, GRE General Test, GMAT, minimum GPA of 3.0, master's degree. Additional exam requirements/recommendations for international students: Required—TOEFL (minimum score 600 paper-based; 250 computer-based; 100 iBT), IELTS (minimum score 7.5). Electronic applications accepted.

Temple University, Graduate School, Fox School of Business, Specialized Master's Programs, Philadelphia, PA 19122-6096. Offers accounting and financial management (MS); actuarial science (MS); finance (MS); financial engineering (MS); healthcare financial management (MS); healthcare management (MHM); human resource management (MS); management information systems (MS); marketing (MS); statistics (MS). *Accreditation:* AACSB. Part-time programs available. *Entrance requirements:* For master's, GRE General Test or GMAT, minimum undergraduate GPA of 3.0. Additional exam requirements/recommendations for international students: Required—TOEFL (minimum score 600 paper-based; 250 computer-based; 100 iBT), IELTS (minimum score 7.5).

Texas A&M University, College of Science, Department of Statistics, College Station, TX 77843. Offers MS, PhD. Part-time programs available. *Faculty:* 31. *Students:* 106 full-time (50 women), 64 part-time (20 women); includes 18 minority (3 African Americans, 9 Asian Americans or Pacific Islanders, 6 Hispanic Americans), 76 international. Average age 29. In 2009, 22 master's, 5 doctorates awarded. Terminal master's awarded for partial completion of doctoral program. *Degree requirements:* For doctorate, thesis/dissertation. *Entrance requirements:* For master's and doctorate, GRE General Test. Additional exam requirements/recommendations for international students: Required—TOEFL. *Application deadline:* For fall admission, 3/1 priority date for domestic students; for spring admission, 8/1 for domestic students. Applications are processed on a rolling basis. Application fee: $50 ($75 for international students). *Expenses:* Tuition, state resident: full-time $3991.32; part-time $221.74 per credit hour. Tuition, nonresident: full-time $9049; part-time $502.74 per credit hour. *Financial support:* Fellowships, research assistantships, teaching assistantships, career-related internships or fieldwork available. Financial award application deadline: 3/1. *Faculty research:* Time series, chemometrics, biometrics, smoothing, linear models. *Unit head:* Dr. Simon Sheather, Head, 979-845-3141, Fax: 979-845-3144, E-mail: tamustat@stat.tamu.edu. *Application contact:* P. Fred Dahm, Graduate Director, 800-826-8009, Fax: 979-845-3144, E-mail: tamustat@stat.tamu.edu.

Texas Tech University, Jerry S. Rawls College of Business Administration, Programs in Business Administration, Lubbock, TX 79409. Offers agricultural business (MBA); business administration (IMBA); entrepreneurship (MBA); finance (MBA); general business (MBA); health organization management (MBA); international business (MBA); management and leadership skills (MBA); management information systems (MBA); marketing (MBA); statistics (MBA); JD/MBA; MBA/M Arch; MBA/MA; MBA/MD; MBA/MS; MBA/Pharm D. Part-time and evening/weekend programs available. *Faculty:* 54 full-time (9 women), 5 part-time/adjunct (0 women). *Students:* 59 full-time (15 women), 487 part-time (148 women); includes 107 minority (24 African Americans, 4 American Indian/Alaska Native, 30 Asian Americans or Pacific Islanders, 49 Hispanic Americans), 51 international. Average age 30. 477 applicants, 81% accepted, 302 enrolled. In 2009, 185 master's awarded. *Degree requirements:* For master's, capstone course. *Entrance requirements:* For master's, GMAT, holistic review of academic credentials. Additional exam requirements/recommendations for international students: Required—TOEFL (minimum score 550 paper-based; 213 computer-based; 79 iBT). *Application deadline:* For fall admission, 4/1 priority date for domestic students, 1/15 priority date for international students; for spring admission, 9/1 priority date for domestic students, 7/15 priority date for international students. Applications are processed on a rolling basis. Application fee: $50 ($75 for international students). Electronic applications accepted. *Expenses:* Tuition, state resident: full-time $5100; part-time $213 per credit hour. Tuition, nonresident: full-time $11,748; part-time $490 per credit hour. Required fees: $2298; $50 per credit hour. $555 per semester. *Financial support:* In 2009–10, 13 research assistantships (averaging $8,000 per year) were awarded; teaching assistantships, career-related internships or fieldwork, Federal Work-Study, scholarships/grants, health care benefits, and unspecified assistantships also available. Support available to part-time students. Financial award applicants required to submit FAFSA. *Unit head:* Dr. W. Jay Conover, Director, 806-742-1546, Fax: 806-742-3958, E-mail: jay.conover@ttu.edu. *Application contact:* Cynthia D. Barnes, Director, Graduate Services Center, 806-742-3184, Fax: 806-742-3958, E-mail: ba_grad@ttu.edu.

Tulane University, School of Science and Engineering, Department of Mathematics, New Orleans, LA 70118-5669. Offers applied mathematics (MS); mathematics (MS, PhD); statistics (MS). *Degree requirements:* For master's, thesis (for some programs); for doctorate, thesis/dissertation. *Entrance requirements:* For master's, GRE General Test, minimum B average in undergraduate course work; for doctorate, GRE General Test. Additional exam requirements/recommendations for international students: Required—TOEFL. Electronic applications accepted.

Université de Montréal, Faculty of Arts and Sciences, Department of Mathematics and Statistics, Montréal, QC H3C 3J7, Canada. Offers mathematics (M Sc, PhD); statistics (M Sc, PhD). *Degree requirements:* For master's, thesis; for doctorate, thesis/dissertation, general exam. *Entrance requirements:* For master's and doctorate, proficiency in French. Electronic applications accepted. *Faculty research:* Pure and applied mathematics, actuarial mathematics.

Université Laval, Faculty of Sciences and Engineering, Department of Mathematics and Statistics, Program in Statistics, Québec, QC G1K 7P4, Canada. Offers M Sc. *Degree requirements:* For master's, thesis (for some programs). *Entrance requirements:* For master's, knowledge of French and English. Electronic applications accepted.

University at Albany, State University of New York, College of Arts and Sciences, Department of Mathematics and Statistics, Albany, NY 12222-0001. Offers mathematics (PhD); secondary teaching (MA); statistics (MA). *Degree requirements:* For doctorate, one foreign language, thesis/dissertation. *Entrance requirements:* For doctorate, GRE General Test. Additional exam requirements/recommendations for international students: Required—TOEFL (minimum score 550 paper-based; 213 computer-based). Electronic applications accepted.

University at Albany, State University of New York, School of Education, Department of Educational and Counseling Psychology, Albany, NY 12222-0001. Offers counseling psychology (MS, PhD, CAS); educational psychology (Ed D); educational psychology and statistics (MS); measurements and evaluation (Ed D); rehabilitation counseling (MS), including counseling psychology; school counselor (CAS); school psychology (Psy D, CAS); special education (MS); statistics and research design (Ed D). *Accreditation:* APA (one or more programs are accredited). Evening/weekend programs available. *Degree requirements:* For doctorate, thesis/dissertation. *Entrance requirements:* For doctorate, GRE General Test. Additional exam requirements/recommendations for international students: Required—TOEFL (minimum score 550 paper-based; 213 computer-based). Electronic applications accepted.

The University of Akron, Graduate School, Buchtel College of Arts and Sciences, Department of Statistics, Akron, OH 44325. Offers MS. Part-time and evening/weekend programs available. *Faculty:* 8 full-time (1 woman), 2 part-time/adjunct (0 women). *Students:* 25 full-time (13 women), 3 part-time (2 women); includes 2 minority (1 American Indian/Alaska Native, 1 Asian American or Pacific Islander), 15 international. Average age 28. 16 applicants, 63% accepted, 4 enrolled. In 2009, 10 master's awarded. *Degree requirements:* For master's, comprehensive exam, thesis optional. *Entrance requirements:* For master's, minimum GPA of 2.75, letters of recommendation, one semester of applied statistics, completion of three semesters of calculus, linear algebra, or equivalent. Additional exam requirements/recommendations for international students: Required—TOEFL (minimum score 550 paper-based; 213 computer-based; 79 iBT). *Application deadline:* Applications are processed on a rolling basis. Application fee: $30 ($40 for international students). Electronic applications accepted. *Expenses:* Tuition, state resident: full-time $6570; part-time $365 per credit hour. Tuition, nonresident: full-time $11,250; part-time $625 per credit hour. *Financial support:* In 2009–10, 17 teaching assistantships with full tuition reimbursements were awarded; research assistantships. *Faculty research:* Experimental design, sampling, actuarial science, biostatistics. Total annual research expenditures: $41,155. *Unit head:* Dr. Chand Midha, Chair, 330-972-6886, E-mail: cmidha@uakron.edu. *Application contact:* Associate Dean.

University of Alaska Fairbanks, College of Natural Sciences and Mathematics, Department of Mathematics and Statistics, Fairbanks, AK 99775-6660. Offers mathematics (MAT, PhD); statistics (MS). Part-time programs available. *Faculty:* 15 full-time (5 women), 3 part-time/adjunct (0 women). *Students:* 10 full-time (3 women), 6 part-time (all women); includes 2 minority (both Asian Americans or Pacific Islanders), 2 international. Average age 31. 16 applicants, 50% accepted, 5 enrolled. In 2009, 4 master's, 4 doctorates awarded. Terminal master's awarded for partial completion of doctoral program. *Degree requirements:* For master's, comprehensive exam, thesis or alternative; for doctorate, comprehensive exam, thesis/dissertation, oral defense. *Entrance requirements:* Additional exam requirements/recommendations for international students: Required—TOEFL (minimum score 550 paper-based; 213 computer-based; 80 iBT). *Application deadline:* For fall admission, 6/1 for domestic students, 3/1 for international students; for spring admission, 10/15 for domestic students, 9/1 for international students. Applications are processed on a rolling basis. Application fee: $60. Electronic applications accepted. *Expenses:* Tuition, state resident: full-time $7584; part-time $316 per credit. Tuition, nonresident: full-time $15,504; part-time $646 per credit. Required fees: $23 per credit. $135 per semester. Tuition and fees vary according to course level, course load and reciprocity agreements. *Financial support:* In 2009–10, 1 fellowship (averaging $15,284 per year), 3 research assistantships (averaging $12,497 per year), 10 teaching assistantships (averaging $12,723 per year) were awarded; career-related internships or fieldwork, Federal Work-Study, scholarships/grants, health care benefits, and unspecified assistantships also available. Support available to part-time students. Financial award application deadline: 2/15; financial award applicants required to submit FAFSA. *Faculty research:* Kriging, arrangements of hyperplanes, bifurcation analysis of time-periodic differential-delay equations, inverse problems, phylogenic tree construction. *Unit head:* Dr. John Rhodes, Department Chair, 907-474-7332, Fax: 907-474-5394, E-mail: fymath@uaf.edu. *Application contact:* Dr. John Rhodes, Department Chair, 907-474-7332, Fax: 907-474-5394, E-mail: fymath@uaf.edu.

University of Alberta, Faculty of Graduate Studies and Research, Department of Mathematical and Statistical Sciences, Edmonton, AB T6G 2E1, Canada. Offers applied mathematics (M Sc, PhD); biostatistics (M Sc); mathematical finance (M Sc, PhD); mathematical physics (M Sc, PhD); mathematics (M Sc, PhD); statistics (M Sc, PhD, Postgraduate Diploma). Part-time programs available. *Faculty:* 48 full-time (4 women). *Students:* 112 full-time (41 women), 5 part-time (0 women). Average age 24. 776 applicants, 5% accepted, 34 enrolled. In 2009, 12 master's, 10 doctorates awarded. Terminal master's awarded for partial completion of doctoral program. *Degree requirements:* For master's, thesis (for some programs); for doctorate, comprehensive exam, thesis/dissertation. *Entrance requirements:* Additional exam requirements/recommendations for international students: Required—TOEFL (minimum score 580 paper-based; 237 computer-based). *Application deadline:* For fall admission, 3/1 for domestic students, 2/1 for international students. Applications are processed on a rolling basis. Application fee: $0. Electronic applications accepted. Tuition and fees charges are reported in Canadian dollars. *Expenses:* Tuition, area resident: Full-time $4626.24 Canadian dollars; part-time $99.72 Canadian dollars per unit. International tuition: $8216 Canadian dollars full-time. Required fees: $3589.92 Canadian dollars; $99.72 Canadian dollars per unit. $215 Canadian dollars per term. *Financial support:* In 2009–10, 51 research assistantships, 88 teaching assistantships with full and partial tuition reimbursements were awarded; scholarships/grants also available. Financial award application deadline: 5/1. *Faculty research:* Classical and functional analysis, algebra, differential equations, geometry. *Unit head:* Dr. Anthony To-Ming Lau, Chair, 403-492-5141, E-mail: tlau@math.ualberta.ca. *Application contact:* Dr. Yau Shu Wong, Associate Chair, Graduate Studies, 403-492-5799, Fax: 403-492-6828, E-mail: gradmail@math.ualberta.ca.

The University of Arizona, Graduate College, Graduate Interdisciplinary Programs, Graduate Interdisciplinary Program in Statistics, Tucson, AZ 85721. Offers MS, PhD. *Students:* 8 full-time (2 women), 1 (woman) part-time, 3 international. Average age 31. 19 applicants, 63% accepted, 5 enrolled. *Application deadline:* For fall admission, 2/1 for domestic and international students; for spring admission, 8/1 for domestic and international students. *Expenses:* Tuition, state resident: full-time $9028. Tuition, nonresident: full-time $24,890. *Application contact:* Jolene M. Gruener, Associate Director, 520-621-8368, E-mail: gidp@email.arizona.edu.

University of Arkansas, Graduate School, J. William Fulbright College of Arts and Sciences, Department of Mathematical Sciences, Program in Statistics, Fayetteville, AR 72701-1201. Offers MS. *Students:* 16 full-time (9 women), 1 part-time (0 women); includes 1 minority (Hispanic American), 13 international. In 2009, 5 master's awarded. *Degree requirements:* For master's, thesis. Application fee: $40 ($50 for international students). *Expenses:* Tuition, state resident: full-time $7355; part-time $356.58 per hour. Tuition, nonresident: full-time $17,401; part-time $775.17 per hour. Required fees: $1203. *Financial support:* In 2009–10, 5 research assistantships, 9 teaching assistantships were awarded; fellowships, career-related internships or fieldwork and Federal Work-Study also available. Support available to part-time students. Financial award application deadline: 4/1; financial award applicants required to submit FAFSA. *Unit head:* Dr. Laurie Meaux, Chair of Studies, 479-575-3352, Fax: 479-575-8630, E-mail: lmeaux@uark.edu. *Application contact:* Dr. Mark Johnson, Graduate Coordinator, 479-575-3351, Fax: 479-575-8630, E-mail: markj@uark.edu.

The University of British Columbia, Faculty of Science, Department of Statistics, Vancouver, BC V6T 1Z2, Canada. Offers M Sc, PhD. *Degree requirements:* For master's, thesis or alternative; for doctorate, comprehensive exam, thesis/dissertation. *Entrance requirements:*

Additional exam requirements/recommendations for international students: Required—TOEFL (600 paper, 250 computer, 100 Internet-based), IELTS (minimum overall score of 7.5, no component less than 6.5). Electronic applications accepted. *Faculty research:* Theoretical, applied, biostatistical, and computational statistics.

University of Calgary, Faculty of Graduate Studies, Faculty of Science, Department of Mathematics and Statistics, Calgary, AB T2N 1N4, Canada. Offers M Sc, PhD. *Degree requirements:* For master's, comprehensive exam, thesis; for doctorate, thesis/dissertation, candidacy exam, preliminary exams. *Entrance requirements:* For master's, honors degree in applied math, pure math, or statistics; for doctorate, MA or M Sc. Additional exam requirements/ recommendations for international students: Required—TOEFL (minimum score 600 paper-based; 250 computer-based), IELTS (minimum score 7), TOEFL (paper-based 600; computer-based 250) or IELTS (paper-based 7). *Faculty research:* Combinatorics, applied mathematics, statistics, probability, analysis.

University of California, Berkeley, Graduate Division, College of Letters and Science, Department of Statistics, Berkeley, CA 94720-1500. Offers MA, PhD. *Students:* 53 full-time (20 women). Average age 28. 301 applicants, 11 enrolled. In 2009, 15 master's, 7 doctorates awarded. *Degree requirements:* For doctorate, thesis/dissertation, qualifying exam, written preliminary exam. *Entrance requirements:* For master's and doctorate, GRE General Test, minimum GPA of 3.0, 3 letters of recommendation. *Application deadline:* For fall admission, 12/15 for domestic students. Application fee: $70 ($90 for international students). *Financial support:* Fellowships, research assistantships, teaching assistantships, unspecified assistantships available. *Unit head:* Prof. Bin Yu, Chair, 510-642-2781, E-mail: ch_statistics@ls.berkeley.edu. *Application contact:* Angie Fong, Student Affairs Officer, 510-642-5361, Fax: 510-642-7892, E-mail: statinfo@stat.berkeley.edu.

University of California, Davis, Graduate Studies, Program in Statistics, Davis, CA 95616. Offers MS, PhD. Terminal master's awarded for partial completion of doctoral program. *Degree requirements:* For master's, comprehensive exam; for doctorate, thesis/dissertation. *Entrance requirements:* For master's and doctorate, GRE General Test, minimum GPA of 3.0. Additional exam requirements/recommendations for international students: Required—TOEFL (minimum score 550 paper-based; 213 computer-based). Electronic applications accepted. *Faculty research:* Nonparametric analysis, time series analysis, biostatistics, curve estimation, reliability.

University of California, Los Angeles, Graduate Division, College of Letters and Science, Department of Statistics, Los Angeles, CA 90095. Offers MS, PhD. *Students:* 69 full-time (24 women); includes 19 minority (12 Asian Americans or Pacific Islanders, 7 Hispanic Americans), 24 international. Average age 28. 214 applicants, 22% accepted, 21 enrolled. In 2009, 17 master's, 9 doctorates awarded. Terminal master's awarded for partial completion of doctoral program. *Degree requirements:* For master's, comprehensive exam or thesis; for doctorate, thesis/dissertation, oral and written exams, student teaching. *Entrance requirements:* For master's, GRE General Test, minimum GPA of 3.2, 12 quarter or 8 semester courses in upper-division quantitative work; for doctorate, GRE General Test, minimum GPA of 3.5, 12 quarter or 8 semester courses in upper-division quantitative work. Application fee: $70 ($90 for international students). Electronic applications accepted. *Financial support:* In 2009–10, 41 fellowships with full and partial tuition reimbursements, 34 research assistantships with full and partial tuition reimbursements, 52 teaching assistantships with full and partial tuition reimbursements were awarded; Federal Work-Study, institutionally sponsored loans, scholarships/grants, health care benefits, tuition waivers (full and partial), and unspecified assistantships also available. Financial award application deadline: 3/1; financial award applicants required to submit FAFSA. *Unit head:* Dr. Jan DeLeeuw, Chair, 310-825-9550. *Application contact:* Department Office, 310-206-3742, E-mail: glenda@stat.ucla.edu.

University of California, Riverside, Graduate Division, Department of Statistics, Riverside, CA 92521-0102. Offers applied statistics (PhD); statistics (MS). *Faculty:* 10 full-time (4 women), 1 (woman) part-time/adjunct. *Students:* 47 full-time (18 women); includes 32 minority (30 Asian Americans or Pacific Islanders, 2 Hispanic Americans), 5 international. Average age 26. 141 applicants, 20% accepted, 10 enrolled. In 2009, 18 master's, 7 doctorates awarded. Terminal master's awarded for partial completion of doctoral program. *Degree requirements:* For master's, comprehensive exam; for doctorate, comprehensive exam, thesis/dissertation. *Entrance requirements:* For master's and doctorate, GRE General Test. Additional exam requirements/ recommendations for international students: Required—TOEFL (minimum score 550 paper-based; 213 computer-based; 80 iBT). *Application deadline:* For fall admission, 5/1 priority date for domestic and international students; for winter admission, 9/1 for domestic students, 7/1 for international students; for spring admission, 12/1 for domestic students, 10/1 for international students. Applications are processed on a rolling basis. Application fee: $80 ($100 for international students). Electronic applications accepted. *Financial support:* In 2009–10, 5 students received support, including 5 fellowships with full tuition reimbursements available (averaging $23,150 per year), 4 research assistantships with partial tuition reimbursements available (averaging $16,405 per year), 24 teaching assistantships with partial tuition reimbursements available (averaging $16,637 per year); tuition waivers also available. Financial award application deadline: 1/5; financial award applicants required to submit FAFSA. *Faculty research:* Design and analysis of gene expression experiments using DNA microarrays, statistical design and analysis of experiments, linear models, probability models and statistical inference, SNP/SFP discovery using DNA microarray, genetic mapping. *Unit head:* Dr. Subir Ghosh, Graduate Advisor for Admissions and Recruitment, 951-827-3781, Fax: 951-827-3286. *Application contact:* Perla Fabelo, Graduate Student Affairs Assistant, 951-827-4716, Fax: 951-827-5517, E-mail: fabelo@ucr.edu.

University of California, San Diego, Office of Graduate Studies, Department of Mathematics, La Jolla, CA 92093. Offers applied mathematics (MA); mathematics (MA, PhD); statistics (MS). *Degree requirements:* For doctorate, thesis/dissertation. *Entrance requirements:* For master's and doctorate, GRE General Test, GRE Subject Test. Electronic applications accepted.

University of California, Santa Barbara, Graduate Division, College of Letters and Sciences, Division of Mathematics, Life, and Physical Sciences, Department of Statistics and Applied Probability, Santa Barbara, CA 93106-3110. Offers financial mathematics and statistics (PhD); quantitative methods in the social sciences (PhD); statistics (MA), including applied statistics, mathematical statistics; statistics and applied probability (PhD); MA/PhD. *Faculty:* 12 full-time (3 women), 4 part-time/adjunct (1 woman). *Students:* 42 full-time (12 women). Average age 28. 218 applicants, 39% accepted, 14 enrolled. In 2009, 20 master's, 1 doctorate awarded. Terminal master's awarded for partial completion of doctoral program. *Degree requirements:* For master's, comprehensive exam, thesis or alternative; for doctorate, comprehensive exam, thesis/dissertation. *Entrance requirements:* For master's, GRE General Test, 3 letters of recommendation, resume/curriculum vitae; for doctorate, GRE General Test, 3 letters of recommendation, statement of purpose, personal achievements/contributions statement, resume/ curriculum vitae, transcripts for post-secondary institutions attended. Additional exam requirements/recommendations for international students: Required—TOEFL (minimum score 550 paper-based; 213 computer-based; 80 iBT), or IELTS (minimum score 7). *Application deadline:* For fall admission, 1/1 for domestic and international students; for winter admission, 11/1 for domestic and international students; for spring admission, 2/1 for domestic and international students. Application fee: $70 ($90 for international students). Electronic applications accepted. *Financial support:* In 2009–10, 29 students received support, including 5 fellowships with full and partial tuition reimbursements available (averaging $7,400 per year), 28 teaching assistantships with partial tuition reimbursements available (averaging $10,300 per year); Federal Work-Study, institutionally sponsored loans, scholarships/grants, health care benefits, and unspecified assistantships also available. Financial award application deadline: 1/1; financial award applicants required to submit FAFSA. *Faculty research:* Bayesian inference, financial mathematics, stochastic processes, environmental statistics, biostatistical modeling. *Unit head:* Dr. Yuedong Wang, Chair, 805-893-4870, Fax: 805-893-2334, E-mail: yeudong@pstat.ucsb.edu. *Application contact:* Rickie R. Lazzerini, Graduate Program Assistant, 805-893-4857, Fax: 805-893-2334, E-mail: gradinfo@pstat.ucsb.edu.

University of California, Santa Cruz, Division of Graduate Studies, Jack Baskin School of Engineering, Program in Statistics and Applied Mathematics, Santa Cruz, CA 95064. Offers MS, PhD. *Degree requirements:* For master's, seminar, qualifying exam, capstone project; for doctorate, thesis/dissertation, seminar, qualifying exam.

University of Central Florida, College of Sciences, Department of Statistics and Actuarial Science, Orlando, FL 32816. Offers SAS data mining (Certificate); statistical computing (MS). Part-time and evening/weekend programs available. *Faculty:* 11 full-time (3 women), 2 part-time/adjunct (0 women). *Students:* 30 full-time (14 women), 19 part-time (5 women); includes 8 minority (5 African Americans, 1 Asian American or Pacific Islander, 2 Hispanic Americans), 26 international. Average age 30. 62 applicants, 74% accepted, 21 enrolled. In 2009, 18 master's, 1 other advanced degree awarded. *Degree requirements:* For master's, comprehensive exam. *Entrance requirements:* For master's, GRE General Test, minimum GPA of 3.0 in last 60 hours. Additional exam requirements/recommendations for international students: Required—TOEFL. *Application deadline:* For fall admission, 7/15 for domestic students; for spring admission, 12/1 for domestic students. Application fee: $30. Electronic applications accepted. *Expenses:* Tuition, state resident: part-time $306.31 per credit hour. Tuition, nonresident: part-time $1099.01 per credit hour. Part-time tuition and fees vary according to degree level and program. *Financial support:* In 2009–10, 14 students received support, including 2 fellowships with partial tuition reimbursements available (averaging $5,300 per year), 1 research assistantship with partial tuition reimbursement available (averaging $12,600 per year), 11 teaching assistantships with partial tuition reimbursements available (averaging $10,500 per year); career-related internships or fieldwork, Federal Work-Study, institutionally sponsored loans, tuition waivers (partial), and unspecified assistantships also available. Financial award application deadline: 3/1; financial award applicants required to submit FAFSA. *Faculty research:* Multivariate analysis, quality control, shrinkage estimation. *Unit head:* Dr. David Nickerson, Chair, 407-823-2289, Fax: 407-823-5419, E-mail: nickerson@mail.ucf.edu. *Application contact:* Dr. David Nickerson, Chair, 407-823-2289, Fax: 407-823-5419, E-mail: nickerson@mail.ucf.edu.

University of Central Oklahoma, College of Graduate Studies and Research, College of Mathematics and Science, Department of Mathematics and Statistics, Edmond, OK 73034-5209. Offers applied mathematical sciences (MS), including computer science, mathematics, mathematics/computer science teaching, statistics. Part-time programs available. *Degree requirements:* For master's, thesis. *Entrance requirements:* Additional exam requirements/ recommendations for international students: Required—TOEFL (minimum score 550 paper-based; 213 computer-based). Electronic applications accepted. *Faculty research:* Curvature, FAA, math education.

University of Chicago, Division of the Physical Sciences, Department of Statistics, Chicago, IL 60637-1513. Offers SM, PhD. Part-time programs available. *Faculty:* 18 full-time (4 women), 1 part-time/adjunct (0 women). *Students:* 72 full-time (26 women), 2 part-time (0 women); includes 10 minority (1 African American, 7 Asian Americans or Pacific Islanders, 2 Hispanic Americans), 46 international. Average age 27. 406 applicants, 31 enrolled. In 2009, 11 master's, 3 doctorates awarded. Terminal master's awarded for partial completion of doctoral program. *Degree requirements:* For master's, thesis; for doctorate, thesis/dissertation. *Entrance requirements:* For master's and doctorate, GRE General Test, GRE Subject Test. Additional exam requirements/recommendations for international students: Required—TOEFL. *Application deadline:* For fall admission, 6/15 for domestic and international students. Applications are processed on a rolling basis. Application fee: $55. Electronic applications accepted. *Financial support:* In 2009–10, fellowships with full tuition reimbursements (averaging $21,030 per year), research assistantships with full tuition reimbursements (averaging $21,030 per year), teaching assistantships with full tuition reimbursements (averaging $21,030 per year) were awarded; tuition waivers (partial) also available. Financial award application deadline: 2/1. *Faculty research:* Genetics, econometrics, generalized linear models, history of statistics, probability theory. *Unit head:* Dr. Stephen M. Stigler, Chairman, 773-702-8335. *Application contact:* Dr. Michael J. Wichura, Admissions Chair, 773-702-8329, E-mail: wichura@galton.uchicago.edu.

University of Cincinnati, Graduate School, McMicken College of Arts and Sciences, Department of Mathematical Sciences, Cincinnati, OH 45221. Offers applied mathematics (MS, PhD); mathematics education (MAT); pure mathematics (MS, PhD); statistics (MS, PhD). Part-time programs available. Terminal master's awarded for partial completion of doctoral program. *Degree requirements:* For master's, comprehensive exam, thesis or alternative; for doctorate, one foreign language, comprehensive exam, thesis/dissertation. *Entrance requirements:* For master's, GRE, teacher certification (MAT); for doctorate, GRE. Additional exam requirements/ recommendations for international students: Required—TOEFL. Electronic applications accepted. *Faculty research:* Algebra, analysis, differential equations, numerical analysis, statistics.

University of Connecticut, Graduate School, College of Liberal Arts and Sciences, Department of Statistics, Storrs, CT 06269. Offers MS, PhD. *Faculty:* 14 full-time (3 women). *Students:* 59 full-time (37 women), 7 part-time (1 woman); includes 8 minority (1 African American, 5 Asian Americans or Pacific Islanders, 2 Hispanic Americans), 42 international. Average age 29. 198 applicants, 12% accepted, 8 enrolled. In 2009, 8 master's, 7 doctorates awarded. Terminal master's awarded for partial completion of doctoral program. *Degree requirements:* For master's, comprehensive exam; for doctorate, thesis/dissertation. *Entrance requirements:* For master's and doctorate, GRE General Test. Additional exam requirements/recommendations for international students: Required—TOEFL (minimum score 550 paper-based; 213 computer-based). *Application deadline:* For fall admission, 2/1 priority date for domestic and international students; for spring admission, 11/1 for domestic students, 10/1 for international students. Applications are processed on a rolling basis. Application fee: $55. Electronic applications accepted. *Expenses:* Tuition, state resident: full-time $4725; part-time $525 per credit. Tuition, nonresident: full-time $12,267; part-time $1363 per credit. Required fees: $346 per semester. Tuition and fees vary according to course load. *Financial support:* In 2009–10, 24 research assistantships with full tuition reimbursements, 19 teaching assistantships with full tuition reimbursements were awarded; fellowships, Federal Work-Study, scholarships/grants, health care benefits, and unspecified assistantships also available. Financial award application deadline: 2/1; financial award applicants required to submit FAFSA. *Unit head:* Dipak K. Dey, Head, 860-486-4196, Fax: 860-486-4113, E-mail: dipak.dey@uconn.edu. *Application contact:* Lynn Kuo, Director, 860-486-2951, Fax: 860-486-4113, E-mail: lynn.kuo@uconn.edu.

University of Delaware, College of Agriculture and Natural Resources, Program in Statistics, Newark, DE 19716. Offers MS. Part-time programs available. *Entrance requirements:* For master's, GRE General Test, 3 letters of recommendation. Additional exam requirements/ recommendations for international students: Required—TOEFL (minimum score 550 paper-based; 213 computer-based). Electronic applications accepted.

University of Denver, Daniels College of Business, Department of Statistics and Operations Technology, Denver, CO 80208. Offers business intelligence (MS); data mining (MS). *Faculty:* 7 full-time (2 women). *Students:* 6 full-time (0 women), 8 part-time (4 women); includes 1 minority (Hispanic American), 1 international. Average age 33. 23 applicants, 78% accepted, 11 enrolled. In 2009, 6 master's awarded. *Application deadline:* For fall admission, 1/15 priority date for domestic students. Applications are processed on a rolling basis. Application fee: $50. Electronic applications accepted. *Expenses:* Tuition: Full-time $34,596; part-time $961 per quarter hour. Required fees: $4 per quarter hour. Tuition and fees vary according to course load, campus/location and program. *Financial support:* Career-related internships or fieldwork, Federal Work-Study, institutionally sponsored loans, and scholarships/grants available. Support available to part-time students. Financial award application deadline: 2/15; financial award

Statistics

University of Denver (continued)
applicants required to submit FAFSA. *Unit head:* Dr. Anthony Hayter, Chair, 303-871-4341. *Application contact:* Information Contact, 303-871-3416, Fax: 303-871-4466, E-mail: daniels@du.edu.

University of Florida, Graduate School, College of Liberal Arts and Sciences, Department of Statistics, Gainesville, FL 32611. Offers M Stat, MS Stat, PhD. *Degree requirements:* For master's, variable foreign language requirement, comprehensive exam, thesis or alternative, final oral exam; for doctorate, thesis/dissertation. *Entrance requirements:* For master's and doctorate, GRE General Test, minimum GPA of 3.0. Additional exam requirements/recommendations for international students: Required—TOEFL (minimum score 550 paper-based; 213 computer-based). Electronic applications accepted. *Faculty research:* Categorical data, time series, Bayesian analysis, nonparametrics, sampling.

University of Georgia, Graduate School, College of Arts and Sciences, Department of Statistics, Athens, GA 30602. Offers MS, PhD. *Faculty:* 17 full-time (5 women). *Students:* 45 full-time (23 women), 11 part-time (8 women); includes 5 minority (2 African Americans, 3 Asian Americans or Pacific Islanders), 35 international. 114 applicants, 22% accepted, 17 enrolled. In 2009, 21 master's, 7 doctorates awarded. *Degree requirements:* For master's, thesis (for some programs); for doctorate, one foreign language, thesis/dissertation. *Entrance requirements:* For master's and doctorate, GRE General Test. *Application deadline:* For fall admission, 7/1 priority date for domestic students; for spring admission, 11/15 for domestic students. Application fee: $50. Electronic applications accepted. *Expenses:* Tuition, state resident: full-time $6000; part-time $250 per credit hour. Tuition, nonresident: full-time $20,904; part-time $871 per credit hour. Required fees: $730 per semester. *Financial support:* Fellowships, research assistantships, teaching assistantships, unspecified assistantships available. *Unit head:* Dr. John Stufken, Head, 706-542-8218, Fax: 706-542-3391, E-mail: jstufken@stat.uga.edu. *Application contact:* Dr. Lynn Seymour, Graduate Coordinator, 706-542-3307, Fax: 706-542-3391, E-mail: seymour@stat.uga.edu.

University of Guelph, Graduate Program Services, College of Physical and Engineering Science, Department of Mathematics and Statistics, Guelph, ON N1G 2W1, Canada. Offers applied mathematics (PhD); applied statistics (PhD); mathematics and statistics (M Sc). Part-time programs available. *Degree requirements:* For master's, thesis (for some programs); for doctorate, thesis/dissertation. *Entrance requirements:* For master's, minimum B- average during previous 2 years of course work; for doctorate, minimum B average. Additional exam requirements/recommendations for international students: Required—TOEFL (minimum score 550 paper-based; 213 computer-based; 89 iBT), IELTS (minimum score 6.5). *Faculty research:* Dynamical systems, mathematical biology, numerical analysis, linear and nonlinear models, reliability and bioassay.

University of Houston–Clear Lake, School of Science and Computer Engineering, Program in Statistics, Houston, TX 77058-1098. Offers MS. *Entrance requirements:* For master's, GRE General Test. Additional exam requirements/recommendations for international students: Required—TOEFL (minimum score 550 paper-based; 213 computer-based).

University of Idaho, College of Graduate Studies, College of Science, Department of Statistics, Moscow, ID 83844-2282. Offers MS. *Faculty:* 6 full-time, 4 part-time/adjunct. *Students:* 16 full-time, 3 part-time. In 2009, 7 master's awarded. *Entrance requirements:* For master's, minimum GPA of 2.8. *Application deadline:* For fall admission, 8/1 for domestic students; for spring admission, 12/15 for domestic students. Application fee: $55 ($60 for international students). *Expenses:* Tuition, state resident: full-time $6120. Tuition, nonresident: full-time $17,712. *Financial support:* Research assistantships, teaching assistantships available. Financial award application deadline: 2/15. *Faculty research:* Statistical genetics, biostatistics, nonlinear population dynamics, multivariate and computational statistics, Six Sigma innovation and design. *Unit head:* Dr. Rick Edgeman, Chair, 208-885-2929. *Application contact:* Dr. Rick Edgeman, Chair, 208-885-2929.

University of Illinois at Chicago, Graduate College, College of Liberal Arts and Sciences, Department of Mathematics, Statistics, and Computer Science, Chicago, IL 60607-7128. Offers applied mathematics (MS, PhD); computational finance (MS, PhD); computer science (MS, PhD); mathematics (DA); mathematics and information sciences for industry (MS); probability and statistics (PhD); pure mathematics (MS, PhD); statistics (MS); teaching of mathematics (MST), including elementary, secondary. Part-time programs available. *Degree requirements:* For master's, comprehensive exam; for doctorate, one foreign language, thesis/dissertation. *Entrance requirements:* For master's and doctorate, GRE General Test, minimum GPA of 2.75. Additional exam requirements/recommendations for international students: Required—TOEFL. Electronic applications accepted.

University of Illinois at Urbana–Champaign, Graduate College, College of Liberal Arts and Sciences, Department of Statistics, Champaign, IL 61820. Offers applied statistics (MS); statistics (PhD). *Faculty:* 12 full-time (4 women). *Students:* 50 full-time (29 women), 11 part-time (3 women); includes 3 minority (1 African American, 2 Asian Americans or Pacific Islanders), 45 international. 230 applicants, 11% accepted, 17 enrolled. In 2009, 38 master's, 2 doctorates awarded. *Entrance requirements:* For master's and doctorate, GRE, minimum GPA of 3.0. Additional exam requirements/recommendations for international students: Required—TOEFL (minimum score 590 paper-based; 243 computer-based). *Application deadline:* Applications are processed on a rolling basis. Application fee: $60 ($75 for international students). Electronic applications accepted. *Financial support:* In 2009–10, 1 fellowship, 24 research assistantships, 38 teaching assistantships were awarded; tuition waivers (full and partial) also available. *Faculty research:* Statistical decision theory, sequential analysis, computer-aided stochastic modeling. *Unit head:* Douglas G. Simpson, Chair, 217-244-0885, Fax: 217-244-7190, E-mail: dgs@illinois.edu. *Application contact:* Melissa Banks, Office Support Specialist, 217-333-2167, Fax: 217-244-7190, E-mail: mdbanks@illinois.edu.

The University of Iowa, Graduate College, College of Education, Department of Psychological and Quantitative Foundations, Iowa City, IA 52242-1316. Offers counseling psychology (PhD); educational measurement and statistics (MA, PhD); educational psychology (MA, PhD); school psychology (PhD, Ed S); JD/PhD. *Accreditation:* APA. *Degree requirements:* For master's, thesis optional, exam; for doctorate, comprehensive exam, thesis/dissertation; for Ed S, exam. *Entrance requirements:* For master's, doctorate, and Ed S, GRE General Test, minimum GPA of 3.0. Additional exam requirements/recommendations for international students: Required—TOEFL (minimum score 550 paper-based; 213 computer-based; 81 iBT). Electronic applications accepted.

The University of Iowa, Graduate College, College of Liberal Arts and Sciences, Department of Statistics and Actuarial Science, Iowa City, IA 52242-1316. Offers MS, PhD. *Degree requirements:* For master's, thesis optional, exam; for doctorate, comprehensive exam, thesis/dissertation. *Entrance requirements:* For master's and doctorate, GRE General Test, minimum GPA of 3.0. Additional exam requirements/recommendations for international students: Required—TOEFL (minimum score 550 paper-based; 213 computer-based; 81 iBT). Electronic applications accepted.

University of Kentucky, Graduate School, College of Arts and Sciences, Program in Statistics, Lexington, KY 40506-0032. Offers MS, PhD. *Degree requirements:* For master's, comprehensive exam, thesis optional; for doctorate, comprehensive exam, thesis/dissertation. *Entrance requirements:* For master's, GRE General Test, minimum undergraduate GPA of 2.75; for doctorate, GRE General Test, minimum graduate GPA of 3.0. Additional exam requirements/recommendations for international students: Required—TOEFL (minimum score 550 paper-based; 213 computer-based). Electronic applications accepted. *Faculty research:* Computer intensive statistical inference, biostatistics, mathematical and applied statistics, applied probability.

University of Manitoba, Faculty of Graduate Studies, Faculty of Science, Department of Statistics, Winnipeg, MB R3T 2N2, Canada. Offers M Sc, PhD. *Degree requirements:* For master's, thesis or alternative; for doctorate, one foreign language, thesis/dissertation.

University of Manitoba, Faculty of Graduate Studies, Faculty of Science, Program in Mathematical, Computational and Statistical Sciences, Winnipeg, MB R3T 2N2, Canada. Offers MMCSS.

University of Maryland, Baltimore County, Graduate School, College of Natural and Mathematical Sciences, Department of Mathematics and Statistics, Program in Statistics, Baltimore, MD 21250. Offers biostatistics (PhD); environmental statistics (MS); statistics (MS, PhD). Part-time and evening/weekend programs available. *Faculty:* 9 full-time (2 women). *Students:* 28 full-time (16 women), 20 part-time (4 women); includes 9 minority (3 African Americans, 6 Asian Americans or Pacific Islanders), 19 international. Average age 30. 51 applicants, 61% accepted, 16 enrolled. In 2009, 7 master's awarded. Terminal master's awarded for partial completion of doctoral program. *Degree requirements:* For master's, comprehensive exam (for some programs), thesis (for some programs); for doctorate, comprehensive exam, thesis/dissertation. *Entrance requirements:* For master's and doctorate, GRE General Test, minimum GPA of 3.0. Additional exam requirements/recommendations for international students: Required—TOEFL (minimum score 600 paper-based; 250 computer-based; 100 iBT). *Application deadline:* For fall admission, 2/15 priority date for domestic students, 1/1 priority date for international students; for spring admission, 10/15 priority date for domestic students, 5/1 priority date for international students. Applications are processed on a rolling basis. Application fee: $50. Electronic applications accepted. *Financial support:* In 2009–10, 21 students received support, including 3 research assistantships with full tuition reimbursements available (averaging $15,500 per year), 18 teaching assistantships with full tuition reimbursements available (averaging $15,500 per year); fellowships with full tuition reimbursements available, career-related internships or fieldwork, scholarships/grants, health care benefits, tuition waivers (full and partial), and unspecified assistantships also available. Support available to part-time students. Financial award application deadline: 2/15. *Faculty research:* Design of experiments, statistical decision theory and inference, time series analysis, biostatistics and environmental statistics, bioinformatics. Total annual research expenditures: $496,334. *Unit head:* Dr. Anindya Roy, Director, 410-455-2435, Fax: 410-455-1066, E-mail: anindya@math.umbc.edu. *Application contact:* Dr. Anindya Roy, Director, 410-455-2435, Fax: 410-455-1066, E-mail: anindya@math.umbc.edu.

University of Maryland, College Park, Academic Affairs, College of Computer, Mathematical and Physical Sciences, Department of Mathematics, Program in Mathematical Statistics, College Park, MD 20742. Offers MA, PhD. Part-time and evening/weekend programs available. *Students:* 23 full-time (13 women), 11 part-time (4 women); includes 8 minority (2 African Americans, 6 Asian Americans or Pacific Islanders), 20 international. 104 applicants, 13% accepted, 4 enrolled. In 2009, 8 master's, 4 doctorates awarded. Terminal master's awarded for partial completion of doctoral program. *Degree requirements:* For master's, thesis or comprehensive exams, scholarly paper; for doctorate, one foreign language, thesis/dissertation, written and oral exams. *Entrance requirements:* For master's and doctorate, GRE General Test, GRE Subject Test (mathematics), minimum GPA of 3.0, 3 letters of recommendation. *Application deadline:* For fall admission, 5/1 for domestic students, 2/1 for international students; for spring admission, 10/1 for domestic students, 6/1 for international students. Applications are processed on a rolling basis. Application fee: $60. Electronic applications accepted. *Expenses:* Tuition, area resident: Part-time $471 per credit hour. Tuition, state resident: part-time $471 per credit hour. Tuition, nonresident: part-time $1016 per credit hour. Required fees: $337.04 per term. *Financial support:* In 2009–10, 1 research assistantship (averaging $24,865 per year), 10 teaching assistantships (averaging $17,471 per year) were awarded; fellowships also available. Financial award applicants required to submit FAFSA. *Faculty research:* Statistics and probability, stochastic processes, nonparametric statistics, space-time statistics. *Unit head:* Dr. Paul Smith, Director, 301-405-5061, Fax: 301-314-0827, E-mail: pjs@math.umd.edu. *Application contact:* Dean of Graduate School, 301-405-0358, Fax: 301-314-9305.

University of Massachusetts Amherst, Graduate School, College of Natural Sciences, Department of Mathematics and Statistics, Program in Mathematics and Statistics, Amherst, MA 01003. Offers MS, PhD. *Students:* 53 full-time (18 women), 4 part-time (2 women); includes 2 minority (1 Asian American or Pacific Islander, 1 Hispanic American), 21 international. Average age 28. 286 applicants, 13% accepted, 20 enrolled. In 2009, 14 master's, 4 doctorates awarded. Terminal master's awarded for partial completion of doctoral program. *Degree requirements:* For master's, thesis or alternative; for doctorate, comprehensive exam, thesis/dissertation. *Entrance requirements:* For master's and doctorate, GRE General Test, GRE Subject Test (mathematics). Additional exam requirements/recommendations for international students: Required—TOEFL (minimum score 550 paper-based; 213 computer-based; 80 iBT), IELTS (minimum score 6.5). *Application deadline:* For fall admission, 2/1 for domestic and international students; for spring admission, 10/1 for domestic and international students. Applications are processed on a rolling basis. Application fee: $50 ($65 for international students). Electronic applications accepted. *Expenses:* Tuition, state resident: full-time $2640; part-time $110 per credit. Tuition, nonresident: full-time $9936; part-time $414 per credit. Tuition and fees vary according to course load. *Financial support:* Fellowships, research assistantships, teaching assistantships, career-related internships or fieldwork, Federal Work-Study, scholarships/grants, traineeships, health care benefits, tuition waivers (full), and unspecified assistantships available. Support available to part-time students. Financial award application deadline: 2/1. *Unit head:* Dr. Siman Wong, Graduate Program Director, 413-545-2282, Fax: 413-545-1801. *Application contact:* Jean M. Ames, Supervisor of Admissions, 413-545-0722, Fax: 413-577-0010, E-mail: gradadm@grad.umass.edu.

University of Memphis, Graduate School, College of Arts and Sciences, Department of Mathematical Sciences, Memphis, TN 38152. Offers applied mathematics (MS); applied statistics (PhD); bioinformatics (MS); computer science (PhD); computer sciences (MS); mathematics (MS, PhD); statistics (MS, PhD). Part-time programs available. *Faculty:* 19 full-time (4 women), 3 part-time/adjunct (0 women). *Students:* 38 full-time (19 women), 25 part-time (9 women); includes 4 minority (2 African Americans, 2 Asian Americans or Pacific Islanders), 29 international. Average age 34. 26 applicants, 96% accepted, 11 enrolled. In 2009, 6 master's, 5 doctorates awarded. Terminal master's awarded for partial completion of doctoral program. *Degree requirements:* For master's, comprehensive exam; for doctorate, one foreign language, thesis/dissertation, oral exams. *Entrance requirements:* For master's and doctorate, GRE General Test, minimum GPA of 2.5. Additional exam requirements/recommendations for international students: Required—TOEFL (minimum score 550 paper-based; 210 computer-based). *Application deadline:* For fall admission, 8/1 for domestic students, 5/1 priority date for international students; for spring admission, 12/1 for domestic students, 9/1 priority date for international students. Applications are processed on a rolling basis. Application fee: $35 ($60 for international students). Electronic applications accepted. *Expenses:* Tuition, state resident: full-time $6246; part-time $347 per credit hour. Tuition, nonresident: full-time $15,894; part-time $883 per credit hour. Required fees: $1160. Full-time tuition and fees vary according to course load, degree level and program. *Financial support:* In 2009–10, 22 students received support; fellowships with full tuition reimbursements available, research assistantships with full tuition reimbursements available, teaching assistantships with full tuition reimbursements available, career-related internships or fieldwork, Federal Work-Study, scholarships/grants, and unspecified assistantships available. Financial award application deadline: 2/15; financial award applicants required to submit FAFSA. *Faculty research:* Combinatorics, ergodic theory, graph theory,

Ramsey theory, applied statistics. *Unit head:* Dr. James E. Jamison, Chairman, 901-678-2482, Fax: 901-678-2480, E-mail: jjamison@memphis.edu. *Application contact:* Dr. Anna Kaminska, Coordinator of Graduate Studies, 901-678-2494, Fax: 901-678-2480.

University of Michigan, Horace H. Rackham School of Graduate Studies, College of Literature, Science, and the Arts, Department of Statistics, Ann Arbor, MI 48109. Offers applied statistics (AM); statistics (AM, PhD). *Faculty:* 32 full-time (8 women), 1 part-time/adjunct (0 women). *Students:* 92 full-time (44 women); includes 5 minority (1 African American, 1 American Indian/Alaska Native, 2 Asian Americans or Pacific Islanders, 1 Hispanic American), 54 international. Average age 24. 327 applicants, 17% accepted, 20 enrolled. In 2009, 23 master's, 11 doctorates awarded. Terminal master's awarded for partial completion of doctoral program. *Degree requirements:* For master's, thesis; for doctorate, thesis/dissertation, oral defense of dissertation, preliminary exam. *Entrance requirements:* For master's and doctorate, GRE General Test. Additional exam requirements/recommendations for international students: Required—TOEFL (minimum score 560 paper-based; 220 computer-based; 84 iBT), IELTS (minimum score 6.5). *Application deadline:* For fall admission, 1/31 priority date for domestic students, 1/15 priority date for international students. Applications are processed on a rolling basis. Application fee: $60 ($75 for international students). Electronic applications accepted. *Expenses:* Tuition, state resident: full-time $17,286; part-time $1099 per credit hour. Tuition, nonresident: full-time $34,944; part-time $2080 per credit hour. Required fees: $95 per semester. Tuition and fees vary according to course load, degree level and program. *Financial support:* In 2009–10, 62 students received support, including 4 fellowships with full and partial tuition reimbursements available (averaging $23,000 per year), 15 research assistantships with full and partial tuition reimbursements available (averaging $16,694 per year), 43 teaching assistantships with full and partial tuition reimbursements available (averaging $16,694 per year); career-related internships or fieldwork, Federal Work-Study, institutionally sponsored loans, scholarships/grants, health care benefits, and unspecified assistantships also available. Financial award application deadline: 1/31. *Faculty research:* Reliability and degradation modeling, biological and legal applications, bioinformatics, statistical computing, covariance estimation. *Unit head:* Prof. Vijay Nair, Chair, 734-763-3520, Fax: 734-763-4676, E-mail: statchair@umich.edu. *Application contact:* Lu Ann Custer, Graduate Secretary, 734-763-3520, Fax: 734-763-4676, E-mail: stat-admiss-ques@umich.edu.

University of Minnesota, Twin Cities Campus, Graduate School, College of Liberal Arts, School of Statistics, Minneapolis, MN 55455-0213. Offers MS, PhD. Part-time programs available. *Faculty:* 16 full-time (2 women), 1 part-time/adjunct (0 women). *Students:* 51 full-time (19 women), 13 part-time (8 women); includes 6 minority (5 Asian Americans or Pacific Islanders, 1 Hispanic American), 36 international. Average age 24. 201 applicants, 17% accepted, 16 enrolled. In 2009, 10 master's, 5 doctorates awarded. Terminal master's awarded for partial completion of doctoral program. *Degree requirements:* For doctorate, comprehensive exam, thesis/dissertation. *Entrance requirements:* For master's and doctorate, GRE General Test. Additional exam requirements/recommendations for international students: Required—TOEFL (minimum score 100 iBT). *Application deadline:* For fall admission, 12/1 priority date for domestic and international students. Applications are processed on a rolling basis. Application fee: $75 ($95 for international students). Electronic applications accepted. *Financial support:* In 2009–10, 51 students received support, including 3 fellowships with full tuition reimbursements available (averaging $14,485 per year), 7 research assistantships with full tuition reimbursements available (averaging $14,485 per year), 41 teaching assistantships with full tuition reimbursements available (averaging $14,485 per year); scholarships/grants and health care benefits also available. Financial award application deadline: 12/15. *Faculty research:* Data analysis, statistical computing, experimental design, probability theory, Bayesian inference. Total annual research expenditures: $413,751. *Unit head:* Prof. Glen Meeden, Director, 612-625-8321, Fax: 612-624-8868, E-mail: glen@stat.umn.edu. *Application contact:* Mary Hildre, Executive Administrative Specialist, 612-625-7300, Fax: 612-624-8868, E-mail: mary@stat.umn.edu.

University of Missouri, Graduate School, College of Arts and Sciences, Department of Statistics, Columbia, MO 65211. Offers MA, PhD. *Faculty:* 17 full-time (7 women), 2 part-time/adjunct (0 women). *Students:* 35 full-time (11 women), 12 part-time (5 women); includes 2 minority (1 African American, 1 Asian American or Pacific Islander), 32 international. Average age 27. 150 applicants, 12% accepted, 9 enrolled. In 2009, 10 master's, 1 doctorate awarded. *Degree requirements:* For doctorate, comprehensive exam, thesis/dissertation. *Entrance requirements:* For master's, GRE General Test, minimum GPA of 3.0 in math and statistics courses; bachelor's degree from accredited college/university in related area; for doctorate, GRE General Test, minimum GPA of 3.0; min of 3.5 in math/stats. Additional exam requirements/recommendations for international students: Required—TOEFL (minimum score 535 paper-based; 200 computer-based; 73 iBT). *Application deadline:* For fall admission, 1/15 priority date for domestic students; for winter admission, 10/15 priority date for domestic students. Applications are processed on a rolling basis. Application fee: $45 ($60 for international students). Electronic applications accepted. *Financial support:* In 2009–10, 7 fellowships with full tuition reimbursements, 8 research assistantships with full tuition reimbursements, 26 teaching assistantships with full tuition reimbursements were awarded; institutionally sponsored loans, health care benefits, and tuition waivers (full and partial) also available. *Faculty research:* Statistical problems in the fields of ecology, genetics, economics, meteorology, wildlife management, epidemiology, AIDS research, geophysics, and climatology. *Unit head:* Dr. Nancy Flournoy, Department Chair, E-mail: flournoyn@missouri.edu. *Application contact:* Tracy Pickens, Office Support Staff IV, 573-882-6377, E-mail: pickenst@missouri.edu.

University of Missouri–Kansas City, College of Arts and Sciences, Department of Mathematics and Statistics, Kansas City, MO 64110-2499. Offers MA, MS, PhD. PhD (interdisciplinary) offered through the School of Graduate Studies. Part-time programs available. *Faculty:* 10 full-time (3 women), 6 part-time/adjunct (1 woman). *Students:* 7 full-time (6 women), 22 part-time (6 women); includes 3 minority (1 African American, 2 Asian Americans or Pacific Islanders), 6 international. Average age 29. 25 applicants, 92% accepted, 14 enrolled. In 2009, 10 master's awarded. Terminal master's awarded for partial completion of doctoral program. *Degree requirements:* For master's, written exam; for doctorate, 2 foreign languages, thesis/dissertation, oral and written exams. *Entrance requirements:* For master's, bachelor's degree in mathematics, minimum GPA of 3.0; for doctorate, GMAT or GRE General Test. Additional exam requirements/recommendations for international students: Required—TOEFL (minimum score 550 paper-based; 213 computer-based; 80 iBT). *Application deadline:* For fall admission, 3/15 for domestic students, 3/15 priority date for international students; for spring admission, 10/15 for domestic and international students. Applications are processed on a rolling basis. Application fee: $45 ($50 for international students). Electronic applications accepted. *Expenses:* Tuition, state resident: full-time $5378; part-time $299 per credit hour. Tuition, nonresident: full-time $13,881; part-time $771 per credit hour. Required fees: $641; $71 per credit hour. Tuition and fees vary according to course load and program. *Financial support:* In 2009–10, 10 teaching assistantships with full tuition reimbursements (averaging $17,460 per year) were awarded; Federal Work-Study, institutionally sponsored loans, and tuition waivers (full and partial) also available. Support available to part-time students. Financial award application deadline: 3/1; financial award applicants required to submit FAFSA. *Faculty research:* Numerical analysis, statistics, biostatistics commutative algebra, differential equations. Total annual research expenditures: $28,737. *Unit head:* Dr. Jie Chen, Chair/Professor, 816-235-1641, Fax: 816-235-5517, E-mail: umkcmathdept@umkc.edu. *Application contact:* Dr. Yong Zeng, Associate Professor, 816-235-1641, Fax: 816-235-5517, E-mail: umkcmathdept@umkc.edu.

University of Nebraska–Lincoln, Graduate College, College of Agricultural Sciences and Natural Resources, Department of Statistics, Lincoln, NE 68588. Offers MS, PhD. *Degree requirements:* For master's, thesis optional. *Entrance requirements:* For master's, GRE General Test. Additional exam requirements/recommendations for international students: Required—TOEFL (minimum score 550 paper-based; 213 computer-based). Electronic applications accepted. *Faculty research:* Design of experiments, linear models, spatial variability, statistical modeling and inference, sampling.

University of New Brunswick Fredericton, School of Graduate Studies, Faculty of Science, Department of Mathematics and Statistics, Fredericton, NB E3B 5A3, Canada. Offers M Sc, PhD. *Faculty:* 21 full-time (5 women). *Students:* 22 full-time (7 women). In 2009, 5 master's awarded. *Degree requirements:* For master's, thesis; for doctorate, comprehensive exam, thesis/dissertation. *Entrance requirements:* For master's and doctorate, minimum GPA of 3.0. Additional exam requirements/recommendations for international students: Required—TOEFL (minimum score 550 paper-based; 80 computer-based), TWE (minimum score 4); Recommended—IELTS (minimum score 7). *Application deadline:* For fall admission, 3/1 priority date for domestic students. Applications are processed on a rolling basis. Application fee: $50 Canadian dollars. Tuition and fees charges are reported in Canadian dollars. *Expenses:* Tuition, area resident: Full-time $5562 Canadian dollars; part-time $2781 Canadian dollars per year. Required fees: $49.75 Canadian dollars per term. *Financial support:* In 2009–10, 1 fellowship, 16 research assistantships (averaging $12,000 per year), 12 teaching assistantships (averaging $4,996 per year) were awarded. *Faculty research:* Algebra, general relativity, mechanical biology, sampling theory. *Unit head:* Dr. James Watmough, Director of Graduate Studies, 506-458-7363, Fax: 506-453-4705, E-mail: watmough@unb.ca. *Application contact:* Marilyn Hetherington, Graduate Secretary, 506-458-7373, Fax: 506-453-4705, E-mail: mhetheri@unb.ca.

University of New Hampshire, Center for Graduate and Professional Studies, Manchester, NH 03101. Offers business administration (MBA); counseling (M Ed); education (M Ed, MAT); educational administration and supervision (M Ed, CAGS); industrial statistics (Certificate); public administration (MPA); public health (MPH, Certificate); social work (MSW). Part-time and evening/weekend programs available. *Students:* 86 full-time (57 women), 150 part-time (87 women); includes 13 minority (3 African Americans, 6 Asian Americans or Pacific Islanders, 4 Hispanic Americans), 7 international. 127 applicants, 73% accepted, 60 enrolled. In 2009, 81 master's, 5 other advanced degrees awarded. *Degree requirements:* For master's, thesis or alternative. *Entrance requirements:* Additional exam requirements/recommendations for international students: Required—TOEFL (minimum score 550 paper-based; 213 computer-based; 80 iBT), TOEIC, TSE. *Application deadline:* For fall admission, 6/1 for domestic students, 4/1 for international students; for spring admission, 12/1 for domestic students. Applications are processed on a rolling basis. Application fee: $65. Electronic applications accepted. *Expenses:* Tuition, state resident: full-time $10,380; part-time $577 per credit hour. Tuition, nonresident: full-time $24,350; part-time $1002 per credit hour. Required fees: $1550; $387.50 per semester. Tuition and fees vary according to course load and program. *Financial support:* In 2009–10, 20 students received support, including 1 fellowship, 1 teaching assistantship; research assistantships, Federal Work-Study, scholarships/grants, health care benefits, and unspecified assistantships also available. Support available to part-time students. Financial award application deadline: 3/1; financial award applicants required to submit FAFSA. *Unit head:* Kate Ferreira, Director, 603-641-4313, E-mail: unhm.gradcenter@unh.edu. *Application contact:* Graduate Admissions Office, 603-862-3000, Fax: 603-862-0275, E-mail: grad.school@unh.edu.

University of New Hampshire, Graduate School, College of Engineering and Physical Sciences, Department of Mathematics and Statistics, Durham, NH 03824. Offers applied mathematics (MS); industrial statistics (Postbaccalaureate Certificate); mathematics (MS, MST, PhD); mathematics education (PhD); statistics (MS). *Faculty:* 21 full-time (5 women). *Students:* 34 full-time (21 women), 24 part-time (8 women); includes 4 minority (1 Asian American or Pacific Islander, 3 Hispanic Americans), 20 international. Average age 29. 76 applicants, 50% accepted, 17 enrolled. In 2009, 17 master's, 7 doctorates, 1 other advanced degree awarded. Terminal master's awarded for partial completion of doctoral program. *Degree requirements:* For doctorate, 2 foreign languages, thesis/dissertation. *Entrance requirements:* Additional exam requirements/recommendations for international students: Required—TOEFL (minimum score 550 paper-based; 213 computer-based; 80 iBT). *Application deadline:* For fall admission, 4/1 priority date for domestic students, 4/1 for international students; for spring admission, 12/1 for domestic students. Applications are processed on a rolling basis. Application fee: $65. Electronic applications accepted. *Expenses:* Tuition, state resident: full-time $10,380; part-time $577 per credit hour. Tuition, nonresident: full-time $24,350; part-time $1002 per credit hour. Required fees: $1550; $387.50 per semester. Tuition and fees vary according to course load and program. *Financial support:* In 2009–10, 35 students received support, including 2 fellowships, 1 research assistantship, 32 teaching assistantships; Federal Work-Study, scholarships/grants, and tuition waivers (full and partial) also available. Support available to part-time students. Financial award application deadline: 2/15. *Faculty research:* Operator theory, complex analysis, algebra, nonlinear dynamics, statistics. *Unit head:* Dr. Eric Grinberg, Chairperson, 603-862-5772. *Application contact:* Jan Jankowski, Administrative Assistant, 603-862-2320, E-mail: jan.jankowski@unh.edu.

University of New Mexico, Graduate School, College of Arts and Sciences, Department of Mathematics and Statistics, Albuquerque, NM 87131-2039. Offers mathematics (MS, PhD); statistics (MS, PhD). Part-time programs available. *Faculty:* 33 full-time (10 women), 35 part-time/adjunct (10 women). *Students:* 60 full-time (20 women), 29 part-time (9 women); includes 15 minority (3 Asian Americans or Pacific Islanders, 12 Hispanic Americans), 33 international. Average age 33. 71 applicants, 42% accepted, 15 enrolled. In 2009, 17 master's, 8 doctorates awarded. Terminal master's awarded for partial completion of doctoral program. *Degree requirements:* For master's, comprehensive exam (for some programs), thesis or alternative; for doctorate, one foreign language, comprehensive exam, thesis/dissertation, 4 department seminars. *Entrance requirements:* For master's and doctorate, minimum GPA of 3.0, 3 letters of recommendation, letter of intent. Additional exam requirements/recommendations for international students: Required—TOEFL (minimum score 550 paper-based; 213 computer-based). *Application deadline:* For fall admission, 2/15 for domestic students; for spring admission, 11/1 for domestic students. Application fee: $50. Electronic applications accepted. *Expenses:* Tuition, state resident: full-time $2098.80; part-time $233.20 per credit hour. Tuition, nonresident: full-time $6650. Required fees: $25 per semester. Tuition and fees vary according to course load, program and reciprocity agreements. *Financial support:* In 2009–10, 20 students received support, including 4 fellowships (averaging $4,000 per year), 24 research assistantships with tuition reimbursements available (averaging $17,000 per year), 45 teaching assistantships with tuition reimbursements available (averaging $17,300 per year); health care benefits and unspecified assistantships also available. Financial award application deadline: 2/15; financial award applicants required to submit FAFSA. *Faculty research:* Pure and applied mathematics, applied statistics, numerical analysis, biostatistics, differential geometry, fluid dynamics, nonparametric curve estimation. Total annual research expenditures: $1.5 million. *Unit head:* Dr. Alexander Stone, Chair, 505-277-4613, Fax: 505-277-5505, E-mail: astone@math.unm.edu. *Application contact:* Rozanne Littlefield, Program Advisement Coordinator, 505-277-5250, Fax: 505-277-5505, E-mail: rxlitfil@unm.edu.

The University of North Carolina at Chapel Hill, Graduate School, College of Arts and Sciences, Department of Statistics, Chapel Hill, NC 27599. Offers MS, PhD. *Degree requirements:* For master's, comprehensive exam, essay or thesis; for doctorate, comprehensive exam, thesis/dissertation. *Entrance requirements:* For master's and doctorate, GRE General Test, GRE Subject Test, minimum GPA of 3.0. Additional exam requirements/recommendations for international students: Required—TOEFL.

University of North Florida, College of Arts and Sciences, Department of Mathematics and Statistics, Jacksonville, FL 32224. Offers mathematical sciences (MS); statistics (MS). Part-time and evening/weekend programs available. *Faculty:* 20 full-time (8 women). *Students:* 12 full-time (4 women), 14 part-time (6 women); includes 3 minority (2 African Americans, 1 Hispanic American), 5 international. Average age 31. 21 applicants, 57% accepted, 5 enrolled.

Statistics

University of North Florida (continued)
In 2009, 15 master's awarded. *Degree requirements:* For master's, comprehensive exam, thesis optional. *Entrance requirements:* For master's, GRE General Test, minimum GPA of 3.0 in last 60 hours of course work. Additional exam requirements/recommendations for international students: Required—TOEFL (minimum score 500 paper-based; 173 computer-based). *Application deadline:* For fall admission, 7/1 priority date for domestic students, 5/1 for international students; for spring admission, 11/1 priority date for domestic students, 10/1 for international students. Applications are processed on a rolling basis. Application fee: $30. Electronic applications accepted. *Expenses:* Tuition, state resident: full-time $6649.20; part-time $277.05 per credit hour. Tuition, nonresident: full-time $22,970; part-time $957.08 per credit hour. Required fees: $985; $41.03 per credit hour. *Financial support:* In 2009–10, 15 students received support, including 2 teaching assistantships (averaging $6,000 per year); Federal Work-Study and tuition waivers (partial) also available. Support available to part-time students. Financial award application deadline: 4/1; financial award applicants required to submit FAFSA. *Faculty research:* Real analysis, number theory, Euclidean geometry. Total annual research expenditures: $58,348. *Unit head:* Dr. Scott H. Hochwald, Chair, 904-620-2653, Fax: 904-620-2818, E-mail: shochwal@unf.edu. *Application contact:* Dr. Pali Sen, Graduate Coordinator, 904-620-3724, Fax: 904-620-2818, E-mail: psen@unf.edu.

University of Ottawa, Faculty of Graduate and Postdoctoral Studies, Faculty of Science, Ottawa-Carleton Institute of Mathematics and Statistics, Ottawa, ON K1N 6N5, Canada. Offers M Sc, PhD. Part-time programs available. *Degree requirements:* For master's, thesis optional; for doctorate, one foreign language, comprehensive exam, thesis/dissertation. *Entrance requirements:* For master's, honors B Sc degree or equivalent, minimum B average; for doctorate, M Sc, minimum B+ average. Electronic applications accepted. *Faculty research:* Pure mathematics, applied mathematics, probability and statistics.

University of Pennsylvania, Wharton School, Department of Statistics, Philadelphia, PA 19104. Offers MBA, PhD. *Degree requirements:* For doctorate, comprehensive exam, thesis/dissertation. *Entrance requirements:* For master's and doctorate, GRE. Additional exam requirements/recommendations for international students: Required—TOEFL, TWE. *Expenses:* Tuition: Full-time $25,660; part-time $4758 per course. Required fees: $2152; $270 per course. Tuition and fees vary according to course load, degree level and program. *Faculty research:* Nonparametric function estimation, analysis of algorithms, time series analysis, observational studies, inference.

University of Pittsburgh, School of Arts and Sciences, Department of Statistics, Pittsburgh, PA 15260. Offers applied statistics (MA, MS); statistics (MA, MS, PhD). Part-time programs available. *Faculty:* 8 full-time (1 woman). *Students:* 29 full-time (14 women), 6 part-time (2 women); includes 1 African American, 26 international. Average age 23. 219 applicants, 18% accepted, 3 enrolled. In 2009, 7 master's, 2 doctorates awarded. Terminal master's awarded for partial completion of doctoral program. *Degree requirements:* For master's, comprehensive exam, thesis (for some programs); for doctorate, comprehensive exam, thesis/dissertation. *Entrance requirements:* For master's, 3 semesters of calculus, 1 semester of linear algebra, 1 year of mathematical statistics; for doctorate, 3 semesters of calculus, 1 semester of linear algebra, 1 year of mathematical statistics, 1 semester of advanced calculus. Additional exam requirements/recommendations for international students: Required—TOEFL (minimum score 550 paper-based; 213 computer-based; 80 iBT). *Application deadline:* For fall admission, 1/15 priority date for domestic and international students; for spring admission, 10/1 priority date for domestic students, 9/1 priority date for international students. Applications are processed on a rolling basis. Application fee: $50. Electronic applications accepted. *Expenses:* Tuition, state resident: full-time $16,402; part-time $665 per credit. Tuition, nonresident: full-time $28,694; part-time $1175 per credit. Required fees: $690; $175 per term. Tuition and fees vary according to program. *Financial support:* In 2009–10, 1 fellowship with full tuition reimbursement (averaging $17,822 per year), 7 research assistantships with full tuition reimbursements (averaging $15,675 per year), 13 teaching assistantships with full tuition reimbursements (averaging $15,065 per year) were awarded; career-related internships or fieldwork, Federal Work-Study, institutionally sponsored loans, scholarships/grants, health care benefits, and unspecified assistantships also available. Financial award application deadline: 1/15. *Faculty research:* Multivariate statistics, time series, reliability, meta-analysis, linear and nonlinear regression modeling. *Unit head:* Henry Block, Chairman, 412-624-8369, Fax: 412-648-8814, E-mail: hwb@pitt.edu. *Application contact:* Leon J. Gleser, Director of Graduate Studies, 412-624-3925, Fax: 412-648-8814, E-mail: gleser@pitt.edu.

University of Puerto Rico, Mayagüez Campus, Graduate Studies, College of Arts and Sciences, Department of Mathematics, Mayagüez, PR 00681-9000. Offers applied mathematics (MS); computational sciences (MS); pure mathematics (MS); statistics (MS). Part-time programs available. *Degree requirements:* For master's, one foreign language, comprehensive exam, thesis optional. *Entrance requirements:* For master's, undergraduate degree in mathematics or its equivalent. *Faculty research:* Automata theory, linear algebra, logic.

University of Regina, Faculty of Graduate Studies and Research, Faculty of Science, Department of Mathematics and Statistics, Regina, SK S4S 0A2, Canada. Offers mathematics (M Sc, MA, PhD); statistics (M Sc, MA). *Faculty:* 22 full-time (4 women), 3 part-time/adjunct (0 women). *Students:* 20 full-time (8 women). 23 applicants, 78% accepted. In 2009, 4 master's awarded. *Degree requirements:* For doctorate, comprehensive exam, thesis/dissertation. *Entrance requirements:* Additional exam requirements/recommendations for international students: Required—TOEFL (minimum score 580 paper-based; 237 computer-based; 80 iBT). *Application deadline:* Applications are processed on a rolling basis. Application fee: $90 ($100 for international students). *Financial support:* In 2009–10, 3 fellowships (averaging $19,000 per year), 2 research assistantships (averaging $16,910 per year), 10 teaching assistantships (averaging $6,650 per year) were awarded; scholarships/grants also available. Financial award application deadline: 6/15. *Faculty research:* Pure and applied mathematics, statistics and probability. *Unit head:* Dr. Nader Mobed, Head, 306-585-4359, E-mail: nader.mobed@uregina.ca. *Application contact:* Dr. Shaun Fallat, Graduate Program Coordinator, 306-585-4107, E-mail: sfallat@math.uregina.ca.

University of Rhode Island, Graduate School, College of Arts and Sciences, Department of Computer Science and Statistics, Kingston, RI 02881. Offers applied mathematics (PhD), including computer science, statistics; computer science (MS, PhD); digital forensics (Graduate Certificate); statistics (MS). Part-time programs available. *Faculty:* 10 full-time (3 women), 3 part-time/adjunct (1 woman). *Students:* 18 full-time (5 women), 20 part-time (6 women); includes 4 minority (2 Asian Americans or Pacific Islanders, 2 Hispanic Americans), 7 international. In 2009, 7 master's awarded. *Degree requirements:* For master's, comprehensive exam (for some programs), thesis optional; for doctorate, comprehensive exam, thesis/dissertation. *Entrance requirements:* For master's and doctorate, GRE, 2 letters of recommendation. Additional exam requirements/recommendations for international students: Required—TOEFL (minimum score 550 paper-based; 213 computer-based). *Application deadline:* For fall admission, 7/15 for domestic students, 2/1 for international students; for spring admission, 11/15 for domestic students, 7/15 for international students. Application fee: $65. Electronic applications accepted. *Expenses:* Tuition, state resident: full-time $8828; part-time $490 per credit hour. Tuition, nonresident: full-time $22,100; part-time $1228 per credit hour. Required fees: $1118; $57 per semester. Tuition and fees vary according to program. *Financial support:* In 2009–10, 10 teaching assistantships with full and partial tuition reimbursements (averaging $11,094 per year) were awarded. Financial award application deadline: 2/1; financial award applicants required to submit FAFSA. *Faculty research:* Bioinformatics, computer and digital forensics, behavioral model of pedestrian dynamics, real-time distributed object computing, cryptography. Total annual research expenditures: $694,026. *Unit head:* Dr. James G. Kowalski, Chair, 401-874-2510, Fax: 401-874-4617, E-mail: kowalski@cs.uri.edu. *Application contact:* Dr. Victor Fay-Wolfe, Director of Graduate Studies, 401-874-2701, Fax: 401-874-4617, E-mail: wolfe@cs.uri.edu.

University of Rochester, School of Medicine and Dentistry, Graduate Programs in Medicine and Dentistry, Department of Biostatistics and Computational Biology, Rochester, NY 14627. Offers medical statistics (MS); statistics (MA, PhD). Terminal master's awarded for partial completion of doctoral program. *Degree requirements:* For doctorate, thesis/dissertation, qualifying exam. *Entrance requirements:* For master's and doctorate, GRE General Test. Additional exam requirements/recommendations for international students: Required—TOEFL.

University of Saskatchewan, College of Graduate Studies and Research, College of Arts and Sciences, Department of Mathematics and Statistics, Saskatoon, SK S7N 5A2, Canada. Offers M Math, MA, PhD. *Faculty:* 22. *Students:* 17. In 2009, 2 master's, 1 doctorate awarded. *Degree requirements:* For master's, thesis (for some programs); for doctorate, comprehensive exam (for some programs), thesis/dissertation. *Entrance requirements:* Additional exam requirements/recommendations for international students: Required—TOEFL (minimum score 80 iBT); Recommended—IELTS (minimum score 6.5). *Application deadline:* For fall admission, 7/1 priority date for domestic students. Applications are processed on a rolling basis. Application fee: $75. Electronic applications accepted. Tuition and fees charges are reported in Canadian dollars. *Expenses:* Tuition, area resident: Full-time $3000 Canadian dollars; part-time $500 Canadian dollars per term. Required fees: $700 Canadian dollars; $100 Canadian dollars per term. *Financial support:* Fellowships, research assistantships, teaching assistantships available. Financial award application deadline: 1/31. *Unit head:* Dr. Raj Srinivasan, Head, 306-966-6089, Fax: 306-966-6086, E-mail: raj.srinivasan@usask.ca. *Application contact:* Dr. Christine Soteros, Graduate Chair, 306-966-6104, Fax: 306-966-6086, E-mail: chris.soteros@usask.ca.

University of South Africa, College of Economic and Management Sciences, Pretoria, South Africa. Offers accounting (D Admin, D Com); accounting science (DA); auditing (D Admin, D Com); business administration (M Tech); business economics (D Admin); business leadership (DBL); business management (D Admin, D Com); economic management analysis (M Tech); economics (D Admin, D Com, PhD); human resource development (M Tech); industrial psychology (D Admin, D Com, PhD); logistics (D Com); marketing (M Tech); public administration (D Admin, D Com, DPA, PhD); public management (M Tech); quantitative management (D Admin, D Com); real estate (M Tech); statistics (D Admin, PhD); tourism management (D Admin, D Com); transport economics (D Admin, D Com).

University of South Carolina, The Graduate School, College of Arts and Sciences, Department of Statistics, Columbia, SC 29208. Offers applied statistics (CAS); industrial statistics (MIS); statistics (MS, PhD). Part-time and evening/weekend programs available. Postbaccalaureate distance learning degree programs offered (minimal on-campus study). Terminal master's awarded for partial completion of doctoral program. *Degree requirements:* For master's, thesis; for doctorate, comprehensive exam, thesis/dissertation. *Entrance requirements:* For master's, GRE General Test or GMAT, 2 years of work experience (MIS); for doctorate, GRE General Test; for CAS, GRE General Test or GMAT. Additional exam requirements/recommendations for international students: Required—TOEFL (minimum score 600 paper-based; 250 computer-based; 100 iBT). Electronic applications accepted. *Expenses:* Contact institution. *Faculty research:* Reliability, environmentrics, statistics computing, psychometrics, bioinformatics.

The University of South Dakota, Graduate School, College of Arts and Sciences, Department of Computer Science, Vermillion, SD 57069-2390. Offers computational sciences and statistics (PhD); computer science (MS). Part-time programs available. *Degree requirements:* For master's, thesis optional. *Entrance requirements:* For master's, GRE General Test, GRE Subject Test (recommended), minimum GPA of 2.7. Additional exam requirements/recommendations for international students: Required—TOEFL (minimum score 550 paper-based; 213 computer-based; 79 iBT). Electronic applications accepted.

University of Southern California, Graduate School, College of Letters, Arts and Sciences, Department of Mathematics, Los Angeles, CA 90089. Offers applied mathematics (MA, MS, PhD); mathematical finance (MS); mathematics (MA, PhD); statistics (MS). Part-time programs available. *Faculty:* 50 full-time (5 women). *Students:* 102 full-time (33 women), 16 part-time (8 women); includes 10 minority (9 Asian Americans or Pacific Islanders, 1 Hispanic American), 87 international. 500 applicants, 20% accepted, 28 enrolled. In 2009, 37 master's, 7 doctorates awarded. Terminal master's awarded for partial completion of doctoral program. *Degree requirements:* For master's, comprehensive exam (for some programs), thesis (for some programs); for doctorate, 2 foreign languages, comprehensive exam, thesis/dissertation. *Entrance requirements:* For master's, GRE General Test, GMAT; for doctorate, GRE General Test. Additional exam requirements/recommendations for international students: Recommended—TOEFL (minimum score 100 iBT). *Application deadline:* For fall admission, 12/1 for domestic students, 2/15 for international students; for spring admission, 9/1 for domestic and international students. Applications are processed on a rolling basis. Application fee: $85. Electronic applications accepted. *Expenses:* Tuition: Full-time $25,980; part-time $1315 per unit. Required fees: $554. One-time fee: $35 full-time. Full-time tuition and fees vary according to degree level and program. *Financial support:* In 2009–10, 67 students received support, including 5 fellowships with full tuition reimbursements available (averaging $19,000 per year), 9 research assistantships with full tuition reimbursements available (averaging $19,000 per year), 53 teaching assistantships with full tuition reimbursements available (averaging $19,000 per year). Financial award application deadline: 12/1. *Faculty research:* Algebra, algebraic geometry and number theory, analysis/partial differential equations, applied mathematics, financial mathematics, probability, combinatorics and statistics. Total annual research expenditures: $2 million. *Unit head:* Prof. Gary Rosen, Chair, 213-740-1717, Fax: 213-740-2424, E-mail: grosen@usc.edu. *Application contact:* Amy Yung, Department Coordinator, 213-740-8168, Fax: 213-740-2424, E-mail: amy@usc.edu.

University of Southern Maine, College of Arts and Sciences, Program in Statistics, Portland, ME 04104-9300. Offers MS.

University of South Florida, Graduate School, College of Arts and Sciences, Department of Mathematics and Statistics, Tampa, FL 33620-9951. Offers mathematics (MA, PhD); statistics (MA). Part-time and evening/weekend programs available. *Faculty:* 24 full-time (3 women), 15 part-time/adjunct (6 women). *Students:* 70 full-time (20 women), 17 part-time (3 women); includes 14 minority (4 African Americans, 6 Asian Americans or Pacific Islanders, 4 Hispanic Americans), 41 international. Average age 32. 99 applicants, 57% accepted, 24 enrolled. In 2009, 12 master's, 3 doctorates awarded. Terminal master's awarded for partial completion of doctoral program. *Degree requirements:* For master's, one foreign language, comprehensive exam, thesis optional; for doctorate, 2 foreign languages, comprehensive exam, thesis/dissertation. *Entrance requirements:* For master's, GRE General Test, minimum GPA of 3.0; for doctorate, GRE General Test, minimum GPA of 3.5 in undergraduate/graduate mathematics courses. Additional exam requirements/recommendations for international students: Required—TOEFL (minimum score 550 paper-based; 213 computer-based; 79 iBT). *Application deadline:* For fall admission, 2/1 for domestic students, 1/2 for international students; for spring admission, 8/1 for domestic students, 6/1 for international students. Application fee: $30. Electronic applications accepted. *Financial support:* In 2009–10, 57 students received support, including teaching assistantships with partial tuition reimbursements available (averaging $14,000 per year); unspecified assistantships also available. Financial award application deadline: 2/1. *Faculty research:* Approximation theory, differential equations, discrete mathematics, functional analysis topology. Total annual research expenditures: $481,106. *Unit head:* Dr. Marcus McWaters, Chairperson, 813-974-3838, Fax: 813-974-2700, E-mail: mmm@usf.edu. *Application* *contact:* Dr. Xiang-Dong Hou, Graduate Admissions Director, 813-974-2561, Fax: 813-974-2700, E-mail: xhou@cas.usf.edu.

The University of Tennessee, Graduate School, College of Business Administration, Department of Statistics, Knoxville, TN 37996. Offers industrial statistics (MS); statistics (MS). Part-time programs available. *Degree requirements:* For master's, thesis or alternative. *Entrance requirements:* For master's, GMAT or GRE General Test, minimum GPA of 2.7. Additional exam requirements/recommendations for international students: Required—TOEFL. Electronic applications accepted. *Expenses:* Tuition, state resident: full-time $6826; part-time $380 per semester hour. Tuition, nonresident: full-time $21,844; part-time $1147 per semester hour. Tuition and fees vary according to program.

The University of Tennessee, Graduate School, College of Business Administration, Program in Business Administration, Knoxville, TN 37996. Offers accounting (PhD); finance (MBA, PhD); logistics and transportation (MBA, PhD); management (PhD); marketing (MBA, PhD); operations management (MBA); professional business administration (MBA); statistics (PhD); JD/MBA; MS/MBA. *Accreditation:* AACSB. Postbaccalaureate distance learning degree programs offered. *Degree requirements:* For master's, thesis or alternative; for doctorate, thesis/dissertation. *Entrance requirements:* For master's and doctorate, GMAT, minimum GPA of 2.7. Additional exam requirements/recommendations for international students: Required—TOEFL. Electronic applications accepted. *Expenses:* Tuition, state resident: full-time $6826; part-time $380 per semester hour. Tuition, nonresident: full-time $21,844; part-time $1147 per semester hour. Tuition and fees vary according to program.

The University of Texas at Austin, Graduate School, College of Natural Sciences, Department of Mathematics, Program in Statistics, Austin, TX 78712-1111. Offers MS Stat. *Entrance requirements:* For master's, GRE General Test.

The University of Texas at Dallas, School of Natural Sciences and Mathematics, Programs in Mathematical Sciences, Richardson, TX 75080. Offers applied mathematics (MS, PhD); engineering mathematics (MS); mathematical science (MS); statistics (MS, PhD). Part-time and evening/weekend programs available. *Faculty:* 13 full-time (1 woman), 1 (woman) part-time/adjunct. *Students:* 35 full-time (14 women), 25 part-time (6 women); includes 20 minority (4 African Americans, 15 Asian Americans or Pacific Islanders, 1 Hispanic American), 22 international. Average age 32. 79 applicants, 44% accepted, 13 enrolled. In 2009, 17 master's, 1 doctorate awarded. *Degree requirements:* For master's, thesis optional; for doctorate, thesis/dissertation. *Entrance requirements:* For master's, GRE General Test, minimum GPA of 3.0 in upper-level course work in field; for doctorate, GRE General Test, minimum GPA of 3.5 in upper-level course work in field. Additional exam requirements/recommendations for international students: Required—TOEFL (minimum score 550 paper-based; 213 computer-based). *Application deadline:* For fall admission, 7/15 for domestic students, 5/1 priority date for international students; for spring admission, 11/15 for domestic students, 9/1 priority date for international students. Applications are processed on a rolling basis. Application fee: $50 ($100 for international students). Electronic applications accepted. *Expenses:* Tuition, state resident: full-time $11,068; part-time $461 per credit hour. Tuition, nonresident: full-time $21,178; part-time $882 per credit hour. Tuition and fees vary according to course load. *Financial support:* In 2009–10, 30 teaching assistantships with full tuition reimbursements (averaging $13,500 per year) were awarded; fellowships, research assistantships, career-related internships or fieldwork, Federal Work-Study, institutionally sponsored loans, scholarships/grants, and unspecified assistantships also available. Support available to part-time students. Financial award application deadline: 4/30; financial award applicants required to submit FAFSA. *Faculty research:* Statistical methods, control theory, mathematical modeling and analyses of biological and physical systems. *Unit head:* Dr. Wieslaw Z. Krawcewicz, Department Head, 972-883-2161, Fax: 972-883-6622, E-mail: utdmath@utdallas.edu. *Application contact:* Dr. Michael Baron, Graduate Advisor, 972-883-6874, Fax: 972-883-6622, E-mail: mbaron@utdallas.edu.

See Close-Up on page 327.

The University of Texas at El Paso, Graduate School, College of Science, Department of Mathematical Sciences, El Paso, TX 79968-0001. Offers mathematical sciences (MS); mathematics (teaching) (MAT); statistics (MS). Part-time and evening/weekend programs available. *Students:* 61 (30 women); includes 39 minority (1 Asian American or Pacific Islander, 38 Hispanic Americans), 13 international. Average age 34. In 2009, 17 master's awarded. *Degree requirements:* For master's, thesis optional. *Entrance requirements:* For master's, minimum GPA of 3.0, letters of recommendation. Additional exam requirements/recommendations for international students: Required—TOEFL; Recommended—IELTS. *Application deadline:* For fall admission, 8/1 priority date for domestic students, 3/1 for international students; for spring admission, 11/1 priority date for domestic students, 9/1 for international students. Applications are processed on a rolling basis. Application fee: $45 ($80 for international students). Electronic applications accepted. *Financial support:* In 2009–10, research assistantships with partial tuition reimbursements (averaging $21,812 per year), teaching assistantships with partial tuition reimbursements (averaging $17,450 per year) were awarded; fellowships with tuition reimbursements, institutionally sponsored loans, scholarships/grants, health care benefits, tuition waivers (partial), and unspecified assistantships also available. Support available to part-time students. Financial award application deadline: 3/15; financial award applicants required to submit FAFSA. *Unit head:* Dr. Maria C. Mariani, Chair, 915-747-5761, Fax: 915-747-6502, E-mail: mcmariani@utep.edu. *Application contact:* Dr. Patricia D. Witherspoon, Dean of the Graduate School, 915-747-5491, Fax: 915-747-5788, E-mail: withersp@utep.edu.

The University of Texas at San Antonio, College of Business, Department of Management Science and Statistics, San Antonio, TX 78249-0617. Offers applied statistics (PhD); management science (MBA); statistics (MS). *Accreditation:* AACSB. Part-time and evening/weekend programs available. *Faculty:* 14 full-time (4 women), 1 part-time/adjunct (0 women). *Students:* 16 full-time (5 women), 88 part-time (22 women); includes 33 minority (4 African Americans, 1 American Indian/Alaska Native, 6 Asian Americans or Pacific Islanders, 22 Hispanic Americans), 8 international. Average age 34. 29 applicants, 59% accepted, 14 enrolled. In 2009, 14 master's awarded. *Degree requirements:* For master's, comprehensive exam (for some programs), thesis (for some programs). *Entrance requirements:* For master's, GMAT, minimum GPA of 3.0. Additional exam requirements/recommendations for international students: Required—TOEFL (minimum score 500 paper-based; 173 computer-based; 61 iBT). *Application deadline:* For fall admission, 7/1 for domestic students, 4/1 for international students; for spring admission, 11/1 for domestic students, 9/1 for international students. Applications are processed on a rolling basis. Application fee: $45 ($80 for international students). Electronic applications accepted. *Expenses:* Tuition, state resident: full-time $3975; part-time $221 per contact hour. Tuition, nonresident: full-time $13,947; part-time $775 per contact hour. Required fees: $1853. *Financial support:* In 2009–10, 13 students received support, including 16 research assistantships (averaging $12,703 per year), 15 teaching assistantships (averaging $8,400 per year). *Faculty research:* Applied statistics, biostatistics, supply chain management. Total annual research expenditures: $23,518. *Unit head:* Dr. Nandini Kannan, Head, 210-458-5691, Fax: 210-458-6350, E-mail: nandini.kannan@utsa.edu. *Application contact:* Dr. Dorothy A. Flannagan, Dean of the Graduate School, 210-458-4330, Fax: 210-458-4332, E-mail: dorothy.flannagan@utsa.edu.

University of the Incarnate Word, School of Graduate Studies and Research, School of Mathematics, Science, and Engineering, Program in Mathematics, San Antonio, TX 78209-6397. Offers mathematics teaching (MA); research statistics (MS). Part-time and evening/weekend programs available. *Students:* 1 full-time (0 women), 1 (woman) part-time; includes 1 minority (Hispanic American). Average age 49. In 2009, 2 master's awarded. *Degree requirements:* For master's, capstone or prerequisite knowledge for research statistics. *Entrance requirements:* For master's, GRE (minimum score 800 verbal and quantitative), 18 hours of undergraduate mathematics with minimum GPA of 3.0; letter of recommendation by a professional in the field, writing sample, teaching experience at the precollege level. Additional exam requirements/recommendations for international students: Required—TOEFL (minimum score 560 paper-based; 220 computer-based; 83 iBT). *Application deadline:* Applications are processed on a rolling basis. Application fee: $20. Electronic applications accepted. *Expenses:* Tuition: Full-time $12,150; part-time $675 per credit hour. Required fees: $83 per credit hour. *Financial support:* Federal Work-Study and scholarships/grants available. Financial award applicants required to submit FAFSA. *Unit head:* Dr. Zhanbo Yang, Graduate Programs Coordinator, 210-283-5008, Fax: 210-829-3153, E-mail: yang@uiwtx.edu. *Application contact:* Andrea Cyterski-Acosta, Dean of Enrollment, 210-829-6005, Fax: 210-829-3921, E-mail: admis@uiwtx.edu.

University of the Incarnate Word, School of Graduate Studies and Research, School of Mathematics, Science, and Engineering, Program in Research Statistics, San Antonio, TX 78209-6397. Offers MS. *Expenses:* Tuition: Full-time $12,150; part-time $675 per credit hour. Required fees: $83 per credit hour. *Unit head:* Dr. Glen Edward James, Dean, 210-829-3152, Fax: 210-829-3153, E-mail: gjames@uiwtx.edu. *Application contact:* Andrea Cyterski-Acosta, Dean of Enrollment, 210-829-6005, Fax: 210-829-3921, E-mail: admis@uiwtx.edu.

The University of Toledo, College of Graduate Studies, College of Arts and Sciences, Department of Mathematics, Toledo, OH 43606-3390. Offers applied mathematics (MS, PhD); mathematics (MA, PhD); statistics (MS, PhD). Part-time programs available. *Degree requirements:* For doctorate, 2 foreign languages, thesis/dissertation. *Entrance requirements:* For master's and doctorate, GRE General Test, GRE Subject Test. Electronic applications accepted. *Faculty research:* Topology.

University of Toronto, School of Graduate Studies, Physical Sciences Division, Department of Statistics, Toronto, ON M5S 1A1, Canada. Offers M Sc, PhD. Part-time programs available. *Degree requirements:* For doctorate, comprehensive exam, thesis/dissertation. *Entrance requirements:* For master's, GRE (recommended for students educated outside of Canada), 3 letters of reference; for doctorate, GRE (recommended for students educated outside of Canada), 3 letters of reference, M Stat or equivalent, minimum B+ average.

University of Utah, The Graduate School, College of Education, Department of Educational Psychology, Salt Lake City, UT 84112. Offers counseling psychology (PhD); educational psychology (MA); instructional design and educational technology (M Ed); learning and cognition (MS, PhD); professional counseling (MS); professional psychology (M Ed); reading and literacy (M Ed, PhD); school counseling (M Ed, MS); school psychology (MS, PhD); statistics (M Stat). *Accreditation:* APA (one or more programs are accredited). Evening/weekend programs available. Postbaccalaureate distance learning degree programs offered (minimal on-campus study). *Faculty:* 21 full-time (11 women), 8 part-time/adjunct (5 women). *Students:* 92 full-time (67 women), 74 part-time (43 women); includes 16 minority (4 Asian Americans or Pacific Islanders, 12 Hispanic Americans), 2 international. Average age 33. 177 applicants, 34% accepted, 50 enrolled. In 2009, 44 master's, 9 doctorates awarded. *Degree requirements:* For master's, variable foreign language requirement, comprehensive exam, thesis (for some programs); for doctorate, variable foreign language requirement, thesis/dissertation, oral exam. *Entrance requirements:* For master's and doctorate, GRE General Test, minimum GPA of 3.0. Additional exam requirements/recommendations for international students: Required—TOEFL (minimum score 500 paper-based; 173 computer-based). *Application deadline:* For fall admission, 4/1 for domestic and international students; for spring admission, 11/1 for domestic and international students. Application fee: $55 ($65 for international students). *Expenses:* Tuition, state resident: full-time $4004; part-time $1674 per semester. Tuition, nonresident: full-time $14,134; part-time $5915 per semester. Required fees: $324 per semester. Tuition and fees vary according to course load, degree level and program. *Financial support:* In 2009–10, 55 students received support, including 20 fellowships with full tuition reimbursements available (averaging $11,000 per year), 5 research assistantships with full tuition reimbursements available (averaging $11,000 per year), 32 teaching assistantships with full and partial tuition reimbursements available (averaging $11,000 per year); career-related internships or fieldwork, Federal Work-Study, institutionally sponsored loans, scholarships/grants, and unspecified assistantships also available. Financial award application deadline: 2/1; financial award applicants required to submit FAFSA. *Faculty research:* Autism, computer technology and instruction, cognitive behavior, aging, group counseling. Total annual research expenditures: $151,911. *Unit head:* Dr. Elaine Clark, Chair, 801-581-7148, Fax: 801-581-5566, E-mail: clark@ed.utah.edu. *Application contact:* Jenna Atkinson, Academic Program Specialist, 801-581-7148, Fax: 801-581-5566, E-mail: jenna.atkinson@utah.edu.

University of Utah, The Graduate School, David Eccles School of Business, Business Administration Program, Salt Lake City, UT 84112, United Arab Emirates. Offers accounting (PhD); business administration (EMBA, MBA, PMBA); statistics (M Stat). Part-time and evening/weekend programs available. *Faculty:* 18 full-time (8 women). *Students:* 525 full-time (97 women), 91 part-time (18 women); includes 44 minority (3 African Americans, 1 American Indian/Alaska Native, 27 Asian Americans or Pacific Islanders, 13 Hispanic Americans), 47 international. Average age 32. 936 applicants, 47% accepted, 337 enrolled. In 2009, 258 master's, 6 doctorates awarded. Terminal master's awarded for partial completion of doctoral program. *Degree requirements:* For doctorate, thesis/dissertation, oral qualifying exams, written qualifying exams. *Entrance requirements:* For master's, GMAT, statistics course with minimum B grade, minimum undergraduate GPA of 3.0; for doctorate, GMAT or GRE General Test. Additional exam requirements/recommendations for international students: Required—TOEFL (minimum score 600 paper-based; 250 computer-based; 100 iBT), IELTS (minimum score 7). *Application deadline:* For fall admission, 2/15 priority date for domestic and international students. Applications are processed on a rolling basis. Application fee: $55 ($65 for international students). Electronic applications accepted. *Expenses:* Contact institution. *Financial support:* In 2009–10, 20 students received support, including 1 fellowship with partial tuition reimbursement available (averaging $9,000 per year), 58 teaching assistantships with partial tuition reimbursements available (averaging $6,350 per year); scholarships/grants and unspecified assistantships also available. Financial award application deadline: 2/15; financial award applicants required to submit FAFSA. *Faculty research:* Corporate finance, strategy services, consumer behavior, financial disclosures, operations. Total annual research expenditures: $60,805. *Unit head:* Don Wardell, 801-581-8774, Fax: 801-581-3666, E-mail: don.wardell@utah.edu. *Application contact:* Andrea Chmelik, Coordinator, 801-581-1719, Fax: 801-581-3666, E-mail: andrea.chmelik@business.utah.edu.

University of Utah, The Graduate School, Interdepartmental Program in Statistics, Salt Lake City, UT 84112-1107. Offers biostatistics (MST); business (MST); econometrics (MST); educational psychology (MST); mathematics (MST); sociology (MST); statistics (M Stat). Part-time programs available. *Students:* 25 full-time (11 women), 15 part-time (6 women); includes 4 minority (3 Asian Americans or Pacific Islanders, 1 Hispanic American), 12 international. Average age 30. 59 applicants, 44% accepted, 12 enrolled. In 2009, 15 master's awarded. *Degree requirements:* For master's, comprehensive exam, projects. *Entrance requirements:* For master's, GMAT (business), GRE General Test (sociology and educational psychology), minimum GPA of 3.0; course work in calculus, matrix theory, statistics. Additional exam requirements/recommendations for international students: Required—TOEFL (minimum score 500 paper-based; 173 computer-based). *Application deadline:* For fall admission, 7/1 for domestic students, 4/1 for international students. Applications are processed on a rolling basis. Application fee: $55 (for international students). *Expenses:* Tuition, state resident: full-time $4004; part-time $1674 per semester. Tuition, nonresident: full-time $14,134; part-time $5915 per semester. Required fees: $324 per semester. Tuition and fees vary according to course load, degree level and program. *Financial support:* Career-related internships or fieldwork

Statistics

University of Utah (continued)
available. *Faculty research:* Biostatistics, management, economics, educational psychology, mathematics. *Unit head:* Tariq Mughal, Chair, University Statistics Committee, 801-585-9547, E-mail: tariq.mughal@business.utah.edu. *Application contact:* Laura Egbert, MSTAT Program Coordinator, 801-585-6853, E-mail: laura.demattia@utah.edu.

University of Utah, The Graduate School, Professional Master of Science and Technology Program, Salt Lake City, UT 84112-1107. Offers biotechnology (PSM); computational science (PSM); environmental science (PSM); science instrumentation (PSM). Part-time programs available. *Students:* 32 full-time (17 women), 38 part-time (13 women); includes 5 minority (1 African American, 3 Asian Americans or Pacific Islanders, 1 Hispanic American), 19 international. Average age 31. 84 applicants, 33% accepted, 16 enrolled. In 2009, 7 master's awarded. *Degree requirements:* For master's, internship. *Entrance requirements:* For master's, GRE (recommended), minimum undergraduate GPA of 3.0, bachelor's degree from accredited university or college. Additional exam requirements/recommendations for international students: Required—TOEFL (minimum score 500 paper-based; 173 computer-based). *Application deadline:* For fall admission, 3/1 for domestic and international students. Application fee: $55 ($65 for international students). Electronic applications accepted. *Expenses:* Tuition, state resident: full-time $4004; part-time $1674 per semester. Tuition, nonresident: full-time $14,134; part-time $5915 per semester. Required fees: $324 per semester. Tuition and fees vary according to course load, degree level and program. *Financial support:* In 2009–10, 4 fellowships with full and partial tuition reimbursements (averaging $12,000 per year), 3 research assistantships with full tuition reimbursements (averaging $13,000 per year) were awarded; unspecified assistantships also available. Financial award applicants required to submit FAFSA. *Unit head:* Jennifer Schmidt, Program Director, 801-585-5630, E-mail: jennifer.schmidt@gradschool.utah.edu. *Application contact:* Francine Stirling, Project Coordinator, 801-585-3650, Fax: 801-585-6749, E-mail: francine.stirling@gradschool.utah.edu.

University of Vermont, Graduate College, College of Engineering and Mathematics, Department of Mathematics and Statistics, Program in Statistics, Burlington, VT 05405. Offers MS. *Students:* 15 (9 women); includes 2 minority (both Asian Americans or Pacific Islanders), 7 international. 27 applicants, 70% accepted, 5 enrolled. *Entrance requirements:* Additional exam requirements/recommendations for international students: Required—TOEFL (minimum score 550 paper-based; 213 computer-based). *Application deadline:* For fall admission, 4/1 priority date for domestic students. Applications are processed on a rolling basis. Application fee: $40. Electronic applications accepted. *Expenses:* Tuition, area resident: Part-time $508 per credit hour. Tuition, state resident: part-time $508 per credit hour. Tuition, nonresident: part-time $1281 per credit hour. *Financial support:* Fellowships, research assistantships, teaching assistantships available. Financial award application deadline: 3/1. *Faculty research:* Applied statistics. *Unit head:* Dr. Jeff Buzas, Coordinator, 802-656-2940. *Application contact:* Dr. Jeff Buzas, Coordinator, 802-656-2940.

University of Victoria, Faculty of Graduate Studies, Faculty of Science, Department of Mathematics and Statistics, Victoria, BC V8W 2Y2, Canada. Offers M Sc, MA, PhD. Part-time programs available. *Degree requirements:* For master's, thesis; for doctorate, one foreign language, thesis/dissertation, 3 qualifying exams, candidacy exam. *Entrance requirements:* Additional exam requirements/recommendations for international students: Required—TOEFL (minimum score 575 paper-based; 233 computer-based), IELTS (minimum score 7). Electronic applications accepted. *Faculty research:* Functional analysis and operator theory, applied ordinary and partial differential equations, discrete mathematics and graph theory.

University of Virginia, College and Graduate School of Arts and Sciences, Department of Statistics, Charlottesville, VA 22903. Offers MS, PhD. *Faculty:* 8 full-time (2 women). *Students:* 34 full-time (18 women), 3 part-time (0 women); includes 3 minority (all Asian Americans or Pacific Islanders), 24 international. Average age 26. 100 applicants, 35% accepted, 18 enrolled. In 2009, 13 master's, 2 doctorates awarded. *Degree requirements:* For master's, exam; for doctorate, comprehensive exam, thesis/dissertation. *Entrance requirements:* For master's and doctorate, GRE General Test, 3 letters of recommendation. Additional exam requirements/recommendations for international students: Required—TOEFL (minimum score 600 paper-based; 250 computer-based; 90 iBT), IELTS (minimum score 7). *Application deadline:* For fall admission, 2/1 for domestic and international students. Applications are processed on a rolling basis. Application fee: $60. Electronic applications accepted. *Financial support:* Fellowships, teaching assistantships available. Financial award applicants required to submit FAFSA. *Unit head:* Ted Chang, Chairman, 434-924-3222, Fax: 434-924-3076, E-mail: gradapp1@pitman.stat.virginia.edu. *Application contact:* Feifang Hu, Director of Graduate Program, 434-924-3222, Fax: 434-924-3076, E-mail: gradapp1@pitman.stat.virginia.edu.

University of Washington, Graduate School, College of Arts and Sciences, Department of Statistics, Seattle, WA 98195. Offers MS, PhD. Terminal master's awarded for partial completion of doctoral program. *Degree requirements:* For master's, thesis optional; for doctorate, one foreign language, thesis/dissertation. *Entrance requirements:* For master's and doctorate, GRE General Test, minimum GPA of 3.0. Additional exam requirements/recommendations for international students: Required—TOEFL. *Faculty research:* Mathematical statistics, stochastic modeling, spatial statistics, statistical computing.

University of Washington, Graduate School, School of Public Health, Department of Biostatistics, Seattle, WA 98195. Offers biostatistics (MPH, MS, PhD); clinical research (MS), including biostatistics; statistical genetics (PhD). Part-time programs available. *Faculty:* 41 full-time (15 women), 8 part-time/adjunct (1 woman). *Students:* 80 full-time (47 women), 5 part-time (2 women); includes 8 minority (7 Asian Americans or Pacific Islanders, 1 Hispanic American), 31 international. Average age 30. 187 applicants, 20% accepted, 21 enrolled. In 2009, 4 master's, 8 doctorates awarded. Terminal master's awarded for partial completion of doctoral program. *Degree requirements:* For master's, comprehensive exam, thesis, computer proficiency, consulting, departmental qualifying exams; for doctorate, comprehensive exam, thesis/dissertation, computer proficiency, consulting, departmental qualifying exams. *Entrance requirements:* For master's and doctorate, GRE General Test, 2 years of course work in advanced calculus, 1 course in linear algebra, 1 course in mathematical probability, 30 credits math/statistics, minimum GPA of 3.0. Additional exam requirements/recommendations for international students: Required—TOEFL. *Application deadline:* For fall admission, 1/5 for domestic students. Application fee: $50. Electronic applications accepted. *Financial support:* In 2009–10, 79 students received support, including 75 research assistantships with full and partial tuition reimbursements available (averaging $22,000 per year), 10 teaching assistantships with full and partial tuition reimbursements available (averaging $22,000 per year); traineeships, health care benefits, and tuition waivers (partial) also available. *Faculty research:* Statistical methods for survival data analysis, clinical trials, epidemiological case control and cohort studies, statistical genetics. *Unit head:* Dr. Bruce Weir, Department Chair, 206-543-1044. *Application contact:* Alex Mackenzie, Counseling Services Coordinator, 206-543-1044, Fax: 206-543-3286, E-mail: alexam@u.washington.edu.

University of Waterloo, Graduate Studies, Faculty of Mathematics, Department of Statistics and Actuarial Science, Waterloo, ON N2L 3G1, Canada. Offers actuarial science (M Math, PhD); biostatistics (PhD); statistics (M Math, PhD); statistics-biostatistics (M Math); statistics-computing (M Math); statistics-finance (M Math). *Degree requirements:* For master's, research paper or thesis; for doctorate, comprehensive exam, thesis/dissertation. *Entrance requirements:* For master's, honors degree in field, minimum B+ average; for doctorate, master's degree, minimum B+ average. Additional exam requirements/recommendations for international students: Required—TOEFL (minimum score 600 paper-based; 250 computer-based; 90 iBT), TWE (minimum score 4.5). Electronic applications accepted. *Faculty research:* Data analysis, risk theory, inference, stochastic processes, quantitative finance.

The University of Western Ontario, Faculty of Graduate Studies, Physical Sciences Division, Department of Statistical and Actuarial Sciences, London, ON N6A 5B8, Canada. Offers M Sc, PhD. *Degree requirements:* For master's, thesis (for some programs); for doctorate, comprehensive exam, thesis/dissertation. *Entrance requirements:* For master's, honours BA with B+ average. Additional exam requirements/recommendations for international students: Required—TOEFL. *Faculty research:* Statistical theory, statistical applications, probability, actuarial science.

University of Windsor, Faculty of Graduate Studies, Faculty of Science, Department of Mathematics and Statistics, Windsor, ON N9B 3P4, Canada. Offers mathematics (M Sc); statistics (M Sc, PhD). *Degree requirements:* For master's, thesis or alternative; for doctorate, comprehensive exam, thesis/dissertation. *Entrance requirements:* For master's, minimum B average; for doctorate, minimum A average. Additional exam requirements/recommendations for international students: Required—TOEFL (minimum score 560 paper-based; 220 computer-based). Electronic applications accepted. *Faculty research:* Applied mathematics, operational research, fluid dynamics.

University of Wisconsin–Madison, Graduate School, College of Letters and Science, Department of Statistics, Madison, WI 53706-1380. Offers biometry (MS); statistics (MS, PhD). Part-time programs available. *Degree requirements:* For master's, exam; for doctorate, thesis/dissertation. *Entrance requirements:* For master's and doctorate, GRE. Additional exam requirements/recommendations for international students: Required—TOEFL. Electronic applications accepted. *Expenses:* Tuition, state resident: part-time $594 per credit. Tuition, nonresident: part-time $1504 per credit. Required fees: $65 per credit. Tuition and fees vary according to course load, program and reciprocity agreements. *Faculty research:* Biostatistics, bootstrap and other resampling theory and methods, linear and nonlinear models, nonparametrics, time series and stochastic processes.

University of Wyoming, College of Arts and Sciences, Department of Statistics, Laramie, WY 82070. Offers MS, PhD. Terminal master's awarded for partial completion of doctoral program. *Degree requirements:* For master's, comprehensive exam (for some programs), thesis (for some programs); for doctorate, comprehensive exam, thesis/dissertation. *Entrance requirements:* For master's, GMAT, GRE General Test, minimum GPA of 3.0; for doctorate, GRE General Test, minimum GPA of 3.0. Additional exam requirements/recommendations for international students: Required—TOEFL; Recommended—TWE. Electronic applications accepted. *Faculty research:* Linear models categorical, Baysain, spatial biological sciences and engineering, multi-variate.

Utah State University, School of Graduate Studies, College of Science, Department of Mathematics and Statistics, Logan, UT 84322. Offers industrial mathematics (MS); mathematical sciences (PhD); mathematics (M Math, MS); statistics (MS). Part-time programs available. Terminal master's awarded for partial completion of doctoral program. *Degree requirements:* For master's, thesis optional, qualifying exam; for doctorate, one foreign language, comprehensive exam, thesis/dissertation. *Entrance requirements:* For master's and doctorate, GRE General Test, minimum GPA of 3.0. Additional exam requirements/recommendations for international students: Required—TOEFL. *Faculty research:* Differential equations, computational mathematics, dynamical systems, probability and statistics, pure mathematics.

Virginia Commonwealth University, Graduate School, College of Humanities and Sciences, Department of Mathematics and Applied Mathematics, Program in Statistical Sciences and Operations Research, Richmond, VA 23284-9005. Offers MS, Certificate. *Entrance requirements:* For master's, GRE General Test, GRE Subject Test. Additional exam requirements/recommendations for international students: Required—TOEFL.

Virginia Polytechnic Institute and State University, Graduate School, College of Science, Department of Statistics, Blacksburg, VA 24061. Offers MS, PhD. *Entrance requirements:* Additional exam requirements/recommendations for international students: Required—TOEFL (minimum score 600 paper-based; 250 computer-based). Electronic applications accepted. *Faculty research:* Design and sampling theory, computing and simulation, nonparametric statistics, robust and multivariate methods, biostatistics quality.

Washington State University, Graduate School, College of Agricultural, Human, and Natural Resource Sciences, Department of Statistics, Pullman, WA 99164. Offers applied statistics (MS); theoretical statistics (MS). *Faculty:* 12. *Students:* 9 full-time (5 women), 4 part-time (1 woman), 12 international. Average age 30. 74 applicants, 23% accepted, 6 enrolled. In 2009, 12 master's awarded. *Degree requirements:* For master's, comprehensive exam (for some programs), thesis (for some programs), project. *Entrance requirements:* For master's, GRE, Submit a letter of application stating qualifications, personal goals, and objectives of graduate study; three letters of reference; application for admission to the Graduate School; official GRE scores (official TOEFL or IELTS scores for international students); and official copies of all college transcripts. Additional exam requirements/recommendations for international students: Required—TOEFL (minimum score 560 paper-based; 220 computer-based), IELTS. *Application deadline:* For fall admission, 1/10 for domestic and international students; for spring admission, 7/1 for domestic and international students. Application fee: $50. *Financial support:* In 2009–10, 10 students received support, including 2 research assistantships (averaging $13,917 per year), 6 teaching assistantships with tuition reimbursements available (averaging $13,056 per year). *Faculty research:* Environmental statistics, logistic regression, statistical methods for ecology and wildlife, spatial data analysis, linear and non-linear models. Total annual research expenditures: $15,000. *Unit head:* Dr. Michael A. Jacroux, Professor/Chair, 509-335-8645, Fax: 509-335-8369, E-mail: jacroux@wsu.edu. *Application contact:* Graduate School Admissions, 800-GRADWSU, Fax: 509-335-1949, E-mail: gradsch@wsu.edu.

Washington University in St. Louis, Graduate School of Arts and Sciences, Department of Mathematics, St. Louis, MO 63130-4899. Offers mathematics (MA, PhD); statistics (MA). Terminal master's awarded for partial completion of doctoral program. *Degree requirements:* For master's, thesis or alternative; for doctorate, thesis/dissertation. *Entrance requirements:* For master's and doctorate, GRE General Test. Electronic applications accepted.

Wayne State University, College of Liberal Arts and Sciences, Department of Mathematics, Program in Mathematical Statistics, Detroit, MI 48202. Offers MA, PhD. *Degree requirements:* For doctorate, thesis/dissertation. *Entrance requirements:* Additional exam requirements/recommendations for international students: Required—TOEFL (minimum score 550 paper-based; 213 computer-based); Recommended—TWE (minimum score 6). Electronic applications accepted.

Western Michigan University, Graduate College, College of Arts and Sciences, Department of Statistics, Kalamazoo, MI 49008. Offers applied statistics (MS); statistics (PhD).

West Virginia University, College of Business and Economics, Division of Economics and Finance, Morgantown, WV 26506. Offers business analysis (MA); developmental financial economics (PhD); environmental and resource economics (PhD); international economics (PhD); mathematical economics (MA); monetary economics (PhD); public finance (PhD); public policy (MA); regional and urban economics (PhD); statistics and economics (MA). Terminal master's awarded for partial completion of doctoral program. *Degree requirements:* For master's, thesis optional; for doctorate, comprehensive exam, thesis/dissertation. *Entrance requirements:* For master's and doctorate, GRE General Test, minimum GPA of 3.0; course work in intermediate microeconomics, intermediate macroeconomics, calculus, and statistics. Additional exam requirements/recommendations for international students: Required—TOEFL. Electronic applications accepted. *Faculty research:* Financial economics, regional/urban development, public economics, international trade/international finance/development economics, monetary economics.

West Virginia University, Eberly College of Arts and Sciences, Department of Statistics, Morgantown, WV 26506. Offers MS. *Degree requirements:* For master's, comprehensive exam, thesis. *Entrance requirements:* For master's, minimum GPA of 3.0, course work in linear algebra and multivariable calculus. Additional exam requirements/recommendations for international students: Required—TOEFL. *Faculty research:* Linear models, categorical data analysis, statistical computing, experimental design, non parametric analysis.

Yale University, Graduate School of Arts and Sciences, Department of Statistics, New Haven, CT 06520. Offers MA, PhD. Terminal master's awarded for partial completion of doctoral program. *Degree requirements:* For doctorate, thesis/dissertation. *Entrance requirements:* For doctorate, GRE General Test, GRE Subject Test.

York University, Faculty of Graduate Studies, Faculty of Science and Engineering, Program in Mathematics and Statistics, Toronto, ON M3J 1P3, Canada. Offers industrial and applied mathematics (M Sc); mathematics and statistics (MA, PhD). Part-time programs available. *Degree requirements:* For master's, thesis optional; for doctorate, one foreign language, comprehensive exam, thesis/dissertation. Electronic applications accepted.

Youngstown State University, Graduate School, College of Science, Technology, Engineering and Mathematics, Department of Mathematics and Statistics, Youngstown, OH 44555-0001. Offers applied mathematics (MS); computer science (MS); secondary mathematics (MS); statistics (MS). Part-time programs available. *Degree requirements:* For master's, comprehensive exam, thesis optional. *Entrance requirements:* For master's, minimum GPA of 2.7 in computer science and mathematics. Additional exam requirements/recommendations for international students: Required—TOEFL. *Faculty research:* Regression analysis, numerical analysis, statistics, Markov chain, topology and fuzzy sets.

MEDICAL COLLEGE OF WISCONSIN

MEDICAL COLLEGE OF WISCONSIN

Graduate School of Biomedical Sciences
Division of Biostatistics

Program of Study

The Division of Biostatistics offers a Ph.D. degree program designed for students with strong undergraduate preparation in mathematics and trains students in biostatistical methodology, theory, and practice. Emphasis is placed on sound theoretical understanding of statistical principles, research in the development of applied methodology, and collaborative research with biomedical scientists and clinicians. In addition, students gain substantial training and experience in statistical computing and in the use of software packages. Courses in the program are offered in collaboration with the Department of Mathematics at the University of Wisconsin–Milwaukee. The degree requirements, including dissertation research, are typically completed in five years beyond a bachelor's degree.

Faculty members are engaged in a number of collaborative research projects at the Center for International Blood and Marrow Transplant Research, the Clinical and Translational Science Institute, the Center for Patient Care and Outcomes Research, the Human and Molecular Genetics Center, the Clinical Cancer Center, and Marquette University. Dissertation research topics in statistical methodology often evolve from the faculty collaborative research projects, and students usually become coauthors on professional periodicals.

Research Facilities

The Division of Biostatistics is located in the Department of Population Health at the Medical College of Wisconsin (MCW). The Medical College has extensive research laboratories and facilities available for faculty and student use. The Division has an up-to-date network of Sun workstations, PCs, and peripherals. The Division's network is equipped with all leading statistical software and tools needed for the development of statistical methodology. Students are afforded access to multiple library collections including MCW, the University of Wisconsin–Milwaukee, and the Division of Biostatistics. The Epidemiology Data Service provides access to national data on health, health care, and special clinical data sets collected locally. The Medical College is a repository for the National Center for Health Statistics. The Biostatistics program also houses the Biostatistics Consulting Service, which affords students the opportunity to experience extensive biomedical research.

Financial Aid

Students are supported by fellowships for the first 18 months and then by research assistantships. Each includes tuition, stipend, and health insurance. The stipend for 2008–09 was $25,750 per year. The research assistantships provide students with the opportunity to gain experience in statistical consulting and collaborative research.

Living and Housing Costs

Many rental units are available in pleasant residential neighborhoods surrounding the Medical College. Housing costs begin at about $550 per month for a shared apartment.

Student Group

There are 525 degree-seeking graduate students, 715 residents and fellows, and 796 medical students at the Medical College. A low student-faculty ratio fosters individual attention and a close working relationship between students and faculty members.

Alumni of the MCW Biostatistics program are typically employed in academia and biomedical sciences. Alumni are employed at Georgia State University, Johns Hopkins University, the University of Pittsburgh, the Medical College of Wisconsin, GlaxoSmithKline, Takeda Global Research and Development, Teva Pharmaceuticals, and many other private- and public-sector organizations.

Location

Milwaukee has long been noted for its old-world image. Its many ethnic traditions, especially from Middle Europe, give the city this distinction. Cultural opportunities are numerous and include museums, concert halls, art centers, and theaters. Milwaukee has a well-administered government, a low crime rate, and excellent schools. It borders Lake Michigan and lies within commuting distance of 200 inland lakes. Outdoor activities may be pursued year-round.

The College

Founded in 1893, the College became the Marquette University School of Medicine in 1913. It was reorganized in 1967 as an independent corporation and renamed the Medical College of Wisconsin in 1970. There are more than 1,300 faculty members. MCW is one of six organizations working in partnership on the Milwaukee Regional Medical Complex (MRMC) campus. Full-time students in any department may enroll in graduate courses in other departments and in programs of the University of Wisconsin–Milwaukee and Marquette University without any increase in basic tuition. The College ranks in the top 34 percent of U.S. medical schools in National Institute of Health research funding.

Applying

Prerequisites include an undergraduate degree in mathematics or closely related fields, an overall grade point average of B or better, B average or better in mathematics and science, and an average of 60th percentile score on the quantitative and verbal sections of the GRE. Foreign students are also required to submit their TOEFL score. The application deadline is February 15 but students are encouraged to complete applications by early January.

Correspondence and Information

Division of Biostatistics
Medical College of Wisconsin
8701 Watertown Plank Road
Milwaukee, Wisconsin 53227
Phone: 414-456-6513
E-mail: biostat@mcw.edu
Web site: http://www.mcw.edu/biostatistics.htm

For application forms and information:
Graduate School of Biomedical Sciences
Medical College of Wisconsin
8701 Watertown Plank Road
Milwaukee, Wisconsin 53227
Phone: 414-456-8218
E-mail: gradschool@mcw.edu
Web site: http://www.mcw.edu/gradschool

Medical College of Wisconsin

THE FACULTY AND THEIR RESEARCH

Kwang Woo Ahn, Assistant Professor, Ph.D., Iowa.
Web site: http://www.mcw.edu/biostatistics/Faculty/Faculty/KwangWooAhnPhD.htm.
Ruta Bajorunaite, Assistant Professor; Ph.D., Medical College of Wisconsin.
Web site: http://www.mcw.edu/biostatistics/Faculty/Faculty/RutaBajorunaitePhD.htm.
John P. Klein, Professor and Director; Ph.D., Missouri–Columbia.
Web site: http://www.mcw.edu/biostatistics/Faculty/Faculty/JohnPKleinPhD.htm.
Purushottam (Prakash) W. Laud, Professor; Ph.D., Missouri–Columbia.
Web site: http://www.mcw.edu/biostatistics/Faculty/Faculty/PrakashLaudPhD.htm.
Jennifer Le-Rademacher, Assistant Professor, Ph.D., Georgia.
Web site: http://www.mcw.edu/biostatistics/Faculty/Faculty/JenniferLeRademacherPhD.htm.
Brent R. Logan, Associate Professor; Ph.D., Northwestern.
Web site: http://www.mcw.edu/biostatistics/Faculty/Faculty/BrentLoganPhD.htm.
Aniko Szabo, Associate Professor; Ph.D., Memphis.
Web site: http://www.mcw.edu/biostatistics/Faculty/Faculty/AnikoSzaboPhD.htm.
Sergey Tarima, Assistant Professor; Ph.D., Kentucky.
Web site: http://www.mcw.edu/biostatistics/Faculty/Faculty/SergeyTarimaPhD.htm.
Tao Wang, Assistant Professor; Ph.D., North Carolina State.
Web site: http://www.mcw.edu/biostatistics/Faculty/Faculty/TaoWangPhD.htm.
Mei-Jie Zhang, Professor; Ph.D., Florida State.
Web site: http://www.mcw.edu/biostatistics/Faculty/Faculty/MeiJieZhangPhD.htm.

Adjunct Faculty (University of Wisconsin–Milwaukee and Marquette University)
Jay Beder, Professor; Ph.D., George Washington.
Web site: https://pantherfile.uwm.edu/beder/www/.
Vytaras Brazauskas, Associate Professor; Ph.D., Texas at Dallas.
Web site: https://pantherfile.uwm.edu/vytaras/www/.
Daniel Gervini, Associate Professor; Ph.D., Buenos Aires.
Web site: https://pantherfile.uwm.edu/gervini/www/.
Jugal Ghorai, Professor; Ph.D., Purdue.
Web site: https://pantherfile.uwm.edu/jugal/www/.
Eric Key, Professor; Ph.D., Cornell.
Web site: http://www.uwm.edu/~ericskey/.
Tom O'Bryan, Associate Professor; Ph.D., Michigan State.
Daniel B. Rowe, Associate Professor, Ph.D., California, Riverside.
Web site: http://www.mscs.mu.edu/mscs/faculty/rowe.html.
Gil Walter, Professor Emeritus; Ph.D., Wisconsin–Madison.
Web site: https://pantherfile.uwm.edu/ggw/www/.

OSU

OKLAHOMA STATE UNIVERSITY

Department of Mathematics

Programs of Study

The Department of Mathematics offers programs leading to the Master of Science and Doctor of Philosophy degrees. There are three Master of Science degree options—pure mathematics, applied mathematics, and mathematics education—each requiring 32 credit hours of graduate course work in mathematics and/or related subjects. Students must receive a grade of A or B in 18 hours of core courses of the appropriate option and write a thesis, a report, or a creative component. Students with a good background in mathematics should expect to complete all requirements within two years. The Doctor of Philosophy program accepts only students with superior records in their graduate or undergraduate study. There are three options in the doctoral program: pure mathematics, applied mathematics, and mathematics education. All three options are designed to prepare students for faculty positions at major research universities or for positions in industry. The Ph.D. degree with specialization in mathematics education at Oklahoma State University is designed to prepare a student for a career where instruction in mathematics and research in mathematics education are of primary importance and is especially intended for students with an interest in teaching mathematics at the college level. A minimum of 90 credit hours of graduate credit beyond the bachelor's degree or 60 hours beyond the master's degree is required for each option, with 15 to 24 hours credited for a thesis. Students must pass a written comprehensive exam covering core courses and embark on a study of a chosen area of mathematics, pass an oral qualifying examination, and, for some options, complete the foreign language or computer language requirement. The most important requirement is the preparation of an acceptable thesis, which must demonstrate the candidate's ability to do independent, original work in mathematics or mathematics education. A well-prepared, motivated student should expect to complete all requirements within five to six years (or three to four years beyond the master's).

Research Facilities

The Department operates a network of microcomputer workstations and personal computers with several file servers. Computing is available for all graduate students. Through this network, access to the University Computer Center is available. The Department also houses current issues of important mathematics journals in a reading room. This makes about 100 journals available in a very convenient location. Electronic access is available for the Math Reviews, many journals, and the library catalog and database resources.

Financial Aid

Teaching assistantships are available to qualified students, with appointments covering the fall and spring semesters (renewed each year based on satisfactory progress). Students without prior teaching experience do not teach in their first semester and are provided with training to enhance their instructional skills. Some reduction in teaching is available to doctoral candidates making good progress toward their degree. Nine-month stipends are $12,987 for pre-master's students and $14,600 for students who have a master's degree or have passed the doctoral comprehensive exam. Some summer appointments, as well as scholarships, fellowships, and stipend enhancements of up to $10,000 are available.

Cost of Study

For all assistants, tuition is reduced to the in-state level. For those employed full-time, 12 credit hours of in-state tuition for the academic year are waived, and three credit hours in the summer term are waived. Full tuition waivers are given to some exceptional incoming students.

Living and Housing Costs

On-campus housing is available in residence halls and in several apartment complexes. It is recommended that prospective students contact the Office of Residential Life (phone: 405-744-5592; e-mail: reslife@okway.okstate.edu; Web site: http://www.reslife.okstate.edu) for information. Most students live in apartment complexes in the surrounding community.

Student Group

Of the current student body of about 30 students, with a 1:1 ratio of faculty to graduate students, half are women, and half are international students. Almost all are full-time students on teaching assistantships. The Department seeks highly motivated students without regard to race, color, national origin, religion, sex, or disability.

Student Outcomes

The Department has been very successful in having all its recent doctoral students obtain positions in higher education institutions across the country. Master's students have placed very well in industry, community colleges, and schools. Many master's students go on to pursue doctoral degrees.

Location

Stillwater, a small city of about 45,000, is a safe, friendly, and lively community. The cost of living is relatively low, and affordable housing is plentiful. The city offers most of the cultural and recreational opportunities of a college town and is just an hour's drive from both Oklahoma City and Tulsa.

The University

Oklahoma State University, a comprehensive research university with more than 22,000 students and almost 1,000 faculty members, is located on a scenic campus in Stillwater, Oklahoma. Founded in 1890, the University has developed an international reputation for excellence in teaching and research, especially in the basic and applied sciences. Students come to OSU from fifty states and more than fifty countries. The Graduate College has about 4,000 students.

Applying

An application package may be obtained from the Department of Mathematics. Applicants should plan to have three letters of recommendation sent to the Department. GRE scores are not required, but they are strongly recommended. The Graduate Committee in the Department begins deliberations in early December and continues the process until March. It is recommended that applicants read the Department's Web page for a detailed description.

Correspondence and Information

Director of Graduate Studies
Department of Mathematics
Oklahoma State University
Stillwater, Oklahoma 74078-1058
E-mail: graddir@math.okstate.edu
Web site: http://math.okstate.edu

Oklahoma State University

THE FACULTY AND THEIR RESEARCH

Alan Adolphson, Regents Professor; Ph.D., Princeton, 1973. Number theory, arithmetical algebraic geometry.
Douglas Aichele, Professor; Ed.D., Missouri, 1969. Mathematics education.
Dale Alspach, Professor and Head; Ph.D., Ohio State, 1976. Functional analysis, Banach space theory.
Mahdi Asgari, Assistant Professor; Ph.D., Purdue, 2000. Number theory, automorphic forms, representation theory.
Leticia Barchini, Ph.D., National University (Argentina), 1987. Representations of Lie groups.
Birne Binegar, Professor; Ph.D., UCLA, 1982. Representations of Lie groups and Lie algebras, mathematical physics.
James Choike, Noble Professor; Ph.D., Wayne State, 1970. Complex analysis, mathematics education.
Bruce Crauder, Professor; Ph.D., Columbia, 1981. Algebraic geometry.
Benny Evans, Professor; Ph.D., Michigan, 1971. Topology of low-dimensional manifolds, mathematics education.
Christopher Francisco, Assistant Professor; Ph.D., Cornell, 2004. Commutative algebra, combinatorics, algebraic geometry.
Amit Ghosh, Professor; Ph.D., Nottingham, 1981. Number theory, automorphic forms.
R. Paul Horja, Assistant Professor; Ph.D., Duke, 1999. Algebraic geometry and mirror symmetry.
William Jaco, G. B. Kerr Professor; Ph.D., Wisconsin, 1968. Topology of low-dimensional manifolds.Jesse Johnson, Assistant Professor, Ph.D., California, Davis, 2006. Topology.
Ning Ju, Associate Professor; Ph.D., Indiana, 1999. Applied mathematics, partial differential equations.
Anthony Kable, Associate Professor; Ph.D., Oklahoma State, 1997. Number theory.
JaEun Ku, Assistant Professor; Ph.D., Cornell, 2004. Partial differential equations, numerical analysis.
Weiping Li, Professor; Ph.D., Michigan State, 1992. Low-dimensional topology, gauge theory, differential geometry.
Lisa Mantini, Professor; Ph.D., Harvard, 1983. Representations of Lie groups, integral geometry.
Anvar Mavlyutov, Assistant Professor; Ph.D., Massachusetts, 2002. Algebraic geometry and mirror symmetry.Jeffery Mermin, Assistant Professor; Ph.D., Cornell, 2006. Computative algebra.
Robert Myers, Professor; Ph.D., Rice, 1977. Topology of low-dimensional manifolds.
Alan Noell, Professor; Ph.D., Princeton, 1983. Several complex variables.
Igor Pritsker, Professor; Ph.D., South Florida, 1995. Complex analysis, potential theory, approximation theory.
A. Raghuram, Assistant Professor; Ph.D., Tata Institute (India), 2001. Algebra, number theory, and representation theory.
Mathias Schulze, Assistant Professor; Ph.D., Kaiserslautern (Germany), 2002. Several complex variables, algebraic geometry.
David Ullrich, Professor; Ph.D., Wisconsin, 1986. Harmonic analysis.
Yanqiu Wang, Assistant Professor; Ph.D., Texas A&M, 2004. Numerical analysis, applied mathematics.
David J. Wright, Professor; Ph.D., Harvard, 1982. Algebraic number theory, Riemann surfaces.
Jiahong Wu, AT&T Professor; Ph.D., Chicago, 1996. Fluid mechanics, partial differential equations.
Roger Zierau, Professor; Ph.D., Berkeley, 1985. Representations of Lie groups.

RESEARCH ACTIVITIES

Algebraic Geometry: three-dimensional algebraic varieties, birational geometry, degenerations of surfaces, geometry of resolutions, birational geometry of projective spaces; enumerative geometry, interaction of algebraic geometry with theoretical physics; complex holomorphic vector bundles over algebraic varieties, intersection theory on the moduli space of curves.

Analysis: functional analysis, geometry of Banach spaces; approximation theory, numerical analysis, optimization; several complex variables, convexity properties of pseudoconvex domains; harmonic analysis, random Fourier series, boundary behavior of harmonic and analytic functions; Riemann surfaces.

Lie Groups: representation theory of semisimple and reductive Lie groups, analysis and geometry of homogeneous spaces, symmetry and groups of transformations, algebraic aspects of the study of Lie groups and arithmetic groups.

Mathematics Education: school mathematics curriculum, professional development of mathematics teachers, technology in the classroom and applications in the curriculum, mathematics reform issues, equity and minority issues, early intervention testing programs.

Number Theory: L-functions of algebraic varieties over finite fields and cohomological techniques, automorphic representations and L-functions, analytic number theory and the distribution of zeros of the Riemann zeta function, algebraic number theory and cubic extensions of number fields, algebraic groups over algebraic number fields and geometric invariant theory.

Partial Differential Equations: theoretical and numerical studies of the Navier-Stokes equations, the 2-D quasi-geostrophic equations, nonlinear wave equations, and other model equations arising in fluid mechanics; qualitative and quantitative analysis of turbulent dynamics.

Topology: structure and classification of compact 3-manifolds; normal, incompressible, and Heegaard surfaces; algorithms and computation in low-dimensional topology; relations with combinatorial and geometric group theory; structure of noncompact 3-manifolds; covering spaces of 3-manifolds; Casson invariants, Floer homology, symplectic topology, dynamical systems.

SELECTED PUBLICATIONS

Adolphson, A., and S. Sperber. Exponential sums on A^n, III. *Manuscripta Math.* 102(4):429–46, 2000.

Adolphson, A., and S. Sperber. Dwork cohomology, de Rham cohomology, and hypergeometric functions. *Am. J. Math.* 122(2):319–48, 2000.

Adolphson, A. Higher solutions of hypergeometric systems and Dwork cohomology. *Rend. Sem. Mat. Univ. Padova* 101:179–90, 1999.

Adolphson, A., and S. Sperber. A remark on local cohomology. *J. Algebra* 206(2):555–67, 1998.

Adolphson, A., and S. Sperber. On twisted de Rham cohomology. *Nagoya Math. J.* 146:55–81, 1997.

Adolphson, A., and S. Sperber. On the zeta function of a complete intersection. *Ann. Sci. Ecole Norm. Suppl. (4)* 29(3), 1996.

Adolphson, A., and B. Dwork. Contiguity relations for generalized hypergeometric functions. *Trans. Am. Math. Soc.* 347(2), 1995.

Aichele, D. B., and J. Wolfe. *Geometric Structures–An Inquiry Based Approach for Prospective Elementary Teachers.* Prentice Hall, 2008.

Aichele, D. B. Geometric structures—An inquiry-based approach to geometry for prospective elementary and middle school teachers through study teams. In *2007 Conference Proceedings of the Hawaii International Conference on Education,* pp. 19–41, 2007.

Aichele, D. B., et al. *Geometry—Explorations and Applications.* Boston: Houghton Mifflin/McDougal Littell, 1997.

Aichele, D. B., and S. Gay. Middle school students' understanding of number sense related to percent. *Sch. Sci. Math.* 97(1):27–36, 1997.

Aichele, D. B., ed. *Professional Development for Teachers of Mathematics—1994 Yearbook.* Reston, Va.: NCTM, 1994.

Alspach, D., and S. Tong. Subspaces of L_p, $p \geq 2$, with unconditional bases have equivalent partition and weight norms. *Arch. Math.* 86:73–8, 2006.

Alspach, D., R. Judd, and E. Odell. The Szlenk index and local l_1-indices. *Positivity* 9:1–44, 2005.

Alspach, D., and S. Tong. Subspaces of L_p, $p \geq 2$, determined by partitions and weights. *Studia Math.* 159:207–27, 2003.

Alspach, D., and E. Odell. L_p spaces. In *Handbook of the Geometry of Banach Spaces,* vol. 1, pp. 123–60, eds. W. B. Johnson and J. Lindenstrauss. Amsterdam: North-Holland, 2001.

Alspach, D. The dual of the Bourgain-Delbaen space. *Israel J. Math.* 117:239–59, 2000.

Alspach, D. Tensor products and independent sums of L_p-spaces, $1<p<\infty$. *Mem. Am. Math. Soc.* 138(660):77, 1999.

Asgari, M., and F. Shahidi. Generic transfer from GSp(4) to GL(4). *Compos. Math.* 142(3):541–50, 2006.

Asgari, M., and F. Shahidi. Generic transfer for general spin groups. *Duke Math. J.* 132(1):137–90, 2006.

Asgari, M. Local L-functions for split spinor groups. *Can. J. Math.* 54(4):673–93, 2002.

Asgari, M., and R. Schmidt. Siegel-Modular formas and representations. *Manuscripta Math.* 104(2):173–200, 2001.

Barchini L., A. Kable, and **R. Zierau.** Conformally invariant systems of differential operators. *Adv. Math.* 221:788–811, 2009.

Barchini, L., A. C. Kable, and **R. Zierau.** Conformally invariant systems of differential equations and prehomogeneous vector spaces of Heisenberg parabolic type. *Publ. RIMS* 44:749–835, 2008.

Barchini, L., and **R. Zierau.** Certain components of the Springer fibers and associated cycles for discrete series representations of SU(p,q). *Represent. Theor.* 12:403–34, 2008.

Barchini, L. Zeto distributions and boundary values of Paissan transforms. *J. Funct. Anal.* 216:47–70, 2004.

Barchini, L. Stein extensions of real symmetric spaces and the geometry of the flag manifold. *Math. Ann.* 326:331–46, 2003.

Barchini, L., C. Leslie, and **R. Zierau.** Domains of holomorphy and representations of SL (n,**R**). *Manuscripta Math.* 106:411–27, 2001.

Barchini, L. Strongly harmonic forms for representations in the discrete series. *J. Funct. Anal.* 161(1):111–31, 1999.

Barchini, L., and **R. Zierau.** Square integrable harmonic forms and representation theory. *Duke Math. J.* 92(3):645–64, 1998.

Binegar, B. On the evaluation of some Selberg-like integrals. *J. Math. Anal. Appl.* 343:601–20, 2008.

Binegar, B. On a family of multiplicity-free K_c-orbits. *J. Math. Kyoto Univ.* 47:735–66, 2007.

Binegar, B., and **R. Zierau.** A singular representation of E_6. *Trans. Am. Math. Soc.* 341(2):771–85, 1994.

Binegar, B., and **R. Zierau.** Unitarization of a singular representation of $SO_{(p,q)}$. *Comm. Math. Phys.* 138(2):245–58, 1991.

Binegar, B. Cohomology and deformations of Lie superalgebras. *Lett. Math. Phys.* 12(4):201–308, 1986.

Binegar, B. Conformal superalgebras, massless representations, and hidden symmetries. *Phys. Rev. D* 3-34(2):525–32, 1986.

Binegar, B. Unitarity of conformal supergravity. *Phys. Rev. D* 3-31(10):2497–502, 1985.

Binegar, B. On the state space of the dipole ghost. *Lett. Math. Phys.* 8(2):149–58, 1984.

Binegar, B., C. Fronsdal, and W. Heidenreich. Conformal QED. *J. Math. Phys.* 24(12):2828–46, 1983.

Binegar, B., C. Fronsdal, and W. Heidenreich. Linear conformal quantum gravity. *Phys. Rev. D* 3(10):2249–61, 1983.

Binegar, B., C. Fronsdal, and W. Heidenreich. de Sitter QED. *Ann. Phys.* 149(2):254–72, 1983.

Binegar, B. Relativistic field theories in three dimensions. *J. Math. Phys.* 23(8):1511–7, 1982.

Binegar, B., C. Fronsdal, M. Flato, and S. Salamo. de Sitter and conformal field theories. In *Proceedings of the International Symposium "Selected Topics in Quantum Field Theory and Mathematics Physics"* (Bechnyle, 1981). *Czechoslovak J. Phys. B* 32(4):439–71, 1982.

Crauder, B., and R. Miranda. Quantum cohomology of rational surfaces. In *The Moduli Space of Curves* (Texel Island, 1994) *Progr. Math.*, 129. Boston: Birkhäuser Boston, 1995.

Crauder, B., and D. R. Morrison. Minimal models and degenerations of surfaces with Kodaira number zero. *Trans. Am. Math. Soc.* 343(2), 1994.

Crauder, B., and S. Katz. Cremona transformers and Hartshorne's conjecture. *Am. J. Math.* 113(2), 1991.

Evans, B., B. Crauder, J. Johnson, and **A. Noell.** *Quantitative Literacy Text* (with accompanying materials). Addison Wesley, in press.

Evans, B., B. Crauder, and **A. Noell.** *College Algebra and Trigonometry.* Boston: Houghton Mifflin, in press.

Evans, B. Rethinking college algebra. In *A Fresh Start for Collegiate Mathematics,* pp. 441–6, ed. J. Poinsett. MAA, 2006.

Evans, B., B. Crauder, and **A. Noell.** *Functions and Change,* 2nd ed. Boston: Houghton Mifflin, 2003.

Evans, B. The long annulus theorem. *Can. Math. Bull.* 29(3), 1986.

Francisco, C. Tetrahedral curves via graphs and Alexander duality. *J. Pure Appl. Algebra* 212:364–75, 2008.

Francisco, C., and H. T. Hà. Whiskers and sequentially Cohen-Macaulay graphs. *J. Combin. Theory, Ser.* A 115:304–16, 2008.

Francisco, C., and B. Richert. Lex-plus-powers ideals. In *Syzygies and Hilbert Functions (Lecture Notes in Pure and Applied Mathematics),* 254:113–44, ed. I. Peeva. Virginia Beach: Chapman & Hall/CRC Press. 2007.

Francisco, C., and A. Van Tuyl. Sequentially Cohen-Macaulay edge ideals. *Proc. Amer. Math. Soc.* 135:2327–37, 2007.

Francisco, C., and A. Van Tuyl. Some families of componentwise linear monomial ideals. *Nagoya Math. J.* 187:115–56, 2007.

Francisco, C., J. Migliore, and U. Nagel. On the componentwise linearity and the minimal free resolution of a tetrahedral curve. *J. Algebra* 299:535–69, 2006.

Francisco, C. New approaches to bounding the multiplicity of an ideal. *J. Algebra* 299:309–28, 2006.

Francisco, C. Resolutions of small sets of fat points. *J. Pure Appl. Algebra* 203:220–36, 2005.

Francisco, C. Almost complete intersections and the Lex-Plus-Powell Conjecture. *J. Algebra* 31:4971–87, 2003.

Francisco, C. Minimal graded Betti numbers and stable ideals. *Comm. Algebra* 31:4971–87, 2003.

Borisov, L. A., and **R. P. Horja.** Mellin-Barnes integrals as Fourier-Mukai transforms. *Adv. Math.* 207:876–927, 2006.

Borisov, L. A., and **R. P. Horja.** On the K-theory of smooth toric DM stacks, Snowbird lectures on string geometry. *Contemp. Math.* 401:21–42, 2006.

Aspinwall, P. S., **R. P. Horja,** and R. L. Karp. Massless D-Branes and Calabi-Yau threefolds and monodromy. *Comm. Math. Phys.* 259(1):45–69, 2005.

Horja, R. P. Derived category automorphisms from mirror symmetry. *Duke Math. J.* 127(1):1–34, 2005.

Jaco, W., and J. H. Rubinstein. 0-efficient triangulations of 3-manifolds. *J. Differential Geom.* 65, 2003.

Jaco, W., and E. Sedgwick. Decision problems in the space of Dehn fillings. *Topology* 42, 2003.

Jaco, W., D. Letscher, and J. H. Rubinstein. Algorithms for essential surfaces in 3-manifolds. *Contemp. Math.* 314, 2002.

Jaco, W., and J. L. Tollefson. Algorithms for the complete decomposition of a closed 3-manifold. *Illinois J. Math.* 39(3), 1995.

Jaco, W., and J. H. Rubinstein. PL equivariant surgery and invariant decompositions of 3-manifolds. *Adv. Math.* 73(2), 1989.

Jaco, W. Lectures on three-manifold topology. *CBMS Reg. Conf. Ser. Math. 43.* Providence, R.I.: American Mathematical Society, 1980.

Ju, N. Geometric constrains for global regularity of 2D quasi-geostrophic flow. *J. Differential Equations* 226:54–79, 2006.

Ju, N. Geometric depletion of vortex stretch in 3D viscous incompressible flow. *J. Math. Anal. Appl.* 321:412–25, 2006.

Ju, N. Global solutions to the two dimensional quasi-geostrophic equation with critical or super-critical dissipation. *Math. Ann.* 334(3):627–42, 2006.

Ju, N. On the 2D dissipative quasi-geostrophic equations. *Indiana Univ. Math. J.* 54(3):897, 2005.

Barchini L., A. Kable, and **R. Zierau.** Conformally invariant systems of differential operators. *Adv. Math.* 221:788–811, 2009.

Kable, A., and **D. J. Wright.** Uniform distribution of the Steinitz invariants of quadratic and cubic extensions. *Compos. Math.* 142:84–100, 2006.

Kable, A. C. Asai L-functions and Jacquet's conjecture. *Am. J. Math.* 126:789–820, 2004.

Kable, A. C. The tensor product of exceptional representations on the general linear group. *Ann. Sci. Ecole Norm. Suppl.* 34(5):741–69, 2001.

Ku, J. Weak coupling of solutions of first-order least-squares method. *Math. Comp.* 77(263):1323–32, 2008.

Ku, J. A least-squares method for second order non-coercive elliptic partial differential equations. *Math. Comp.* 76:97–114, 2007.

Ku, J. A remark on the coercivity for a first-order least-squares method. *Numer. Methods Partial Differential Equations* 23(6):1577–81, 2007.

Cai, Z., and **J. Ku.** The L^2 norm error estimates for the div least-squares method. *SIAM J. Numer. Anal.* 44:1721–34, 2006.

Li, W., and Z. Weiping. An L^2-Alexander invariant for knots. *Commun. Contemp. Math.* 8(2):167–87, 2006.

Li, W. Instanton Floer homology for connected sums of Poincare spheres. *Math. Zeit.* 251(1):215–31, 2005.

Li, W. The Z-graded symplectic Floer cohomology of monotone Lagrangian sub-manifolds. *Alg. Geom. Topol.* 4(30):647–84, 2004.

Li, W., and L. Xu. Counting $SL_2(F_q)$-representations of torus knot groups. *J. Knot Theory Ramifications* 13(3):401–26, 2004.

Oklahoma State University

Li, W., and L. Xu. Counting $SL_2(F_q)$-representations of torus knot groups. *Acta Math Sinica, Eng. Ser.* 19(2):233–44, 2003.

Mantini, L. A. Intertwining ladder representations for SU(*p,q*) into Dolbeault cohomology. In *Non-commutative Harmonic Analysis, Progr. Math.*, vol. 220, pp. 295–418. Boston: Birkhäuser, 2004. With Lorch and Novak.

Mantini, L. A. Teaching mathematics in colleges and universities: Case studies for today's classroom. In CBMS series *Issues in Mathematics Education, Am. Math. Soc.*, vol. 10, 2001. With Friedberg et al.

Lorch, J. D., and **L. A. Mantini.** Inversion of an integral transform and ladder representations of U(1,*q*). In *Representation Theory and Harmonic Analysis* (Cincinnati, Ohio, 1994); *Contemp. Math.*, 191; *Am. Math. Soc.* Providence, R.I., 1995.

Mantini, L. A. An L^2-cohomology construction of unitary highest weight modules for U(*p,q*). *Trans. Am. Math. Soc.* 323(2), 1991.

Myers, R. End reductions, fundamental groups, and covering spaces of irreducible open 3-manifolds. *Geom. Topol.* 9:971–90, 2005.

Myers, R. Splitting homomorphisms and the geometrization conjecture. *Math. Proc. Cambridge Philos. Soc.* 129(2):291–300, 2000.

Myers, R. Uncountably many arcs in S^3 whose complements have non-isomorphic, indecomposable fundamental groups. *J. Knot Theory Ramifications* 9(4):505–21, 2000.

Myers, R. On covering translations and homeotopy groups of contractible open *n*-manifolds. *Proc. Am. Math. Soc.* 128(5):1563–6, 2000.

Myers, R. Compactifying sufficiently regular covering spaces of compact 3-manifolds. *Proc. Am. Math. Soc.* 128:1507–13, 2000.

Myers, R. Contractible open 3-manifolds which non-trivially cover only non-compact 3-manifolds. *Topology* 38(1):85–94, 1999.

Myers, R. Contractible open 3-manifolds with free covering translation groups. *Topol. Appl.* 96(2):97–108, 1999.

Noell, A. Peake points for pseudo convex domains: a survey. *J. Geomet. Anal.* 18:1058–87, 2008.

Noell, A., and R. Belhachemi. Global plurisubharmonic defining functions. *Mich. Math. J.* 47:377–84, 2000.

Noell, A. Local and global plurisubharmonic defining functions. *Pacific J. Math.* 176(2):421–6, 1996.

Noell, A. Peak functions for pseudoconvex domains in C^n. In *Several Complex Variables: Proceedings of the Mittag-leffler Institute,* 1987–88, *Math. Notes* 38. Princeton, N.J.: Princeton University Press, 1993.

Noell, A. Local versus global convexity of pseudoconvex domains. In *Several Complex Variables and Complex Geometry, Proc. Sympos. Pure Math.*, vol. 52. Providence, R.I.: American Mathematics Society, 1991.

Noell, A., and B. Stensones. Proper holomorphic maps from weakly pseudoconvex domains. *Duke Math. J.* 60:363–88, 1990.

Noell, A., and T. Wolff. On peak sets for Lip α classes. *J. Funct. Anal.* 86:136–79, 1989.

Pritsker, E. Means of algebraic numbers in the unit disk. *C. R. Acad. Sci. Paris* Series I, 347:119–22, 2009.

Borwein, P. B., and I. E. Pritsker. The multivariate integer Chebyshev problem. *Constr. Approx.* 30:299–310, 2009.

Pritsker, I. E. and S. Ruscheweyh. Inequalities for products of polynomials I. *Math. Scand.* 104:147–60, 2009.

Pritsker, I. E. An areal analog of Mahler's measure. *Illinois J. Math* 52:347–63, 2008.

Pritsker, I. E. Weighted energy problem on the unit circle. *Constr. Approx.* 23:103–20, 2006.

Pritsker, I. E. Small polynomials with integer coefficients. *J. d'Analyse Math.* 96:151–90, 2005.

Pritsker, I. E. The Gelfond-Schnirelman method in prime number theory. *Can. J. Math.* 57:1080–101, 2005.

Pritsker, I. E. Convergence of Julia polynomials. *J. d'Analyse Math.* 94:343–61, 2004.

Lansky, J., and **A. Raghuram.** On conductors and newforms for SL(2). *Pacific J. Math.* 231:127–53, 2007.

Raghuram, A. On representations p-adic GL_2(D). *Pacific J. Math.* 206:451–64, 2002.

Murty, M. R., and **A. Raghuram.** Some variations on the Dedekind conjecture. *J. Ramanujan Math. Soc.* 14:75–95, 2000.

Prasad, D., and **A. Raghuram.** Kirillov theory for GL_2(D) where D is a division algebra over a non-Archimedean local field. *Duke Math. J.* 104:19–44, 2000.

Granger, M., D. Mond, A. Nieto-Reyes, and **M. Schulze.** Linear free divisors and the global logarithmic comparison theorem. *Ann. Inst. Fourier.* 59(2):811–50, 2009.

Schulze, M., and U. Walther. Cohen-Macaulayness and computation of Newton graded toric rings. *J. Pure App. Alg.* 213:1522–35, 2009.

Schulze, M., and U. Walther. Irregularity of hypergeometric systems via slopes along coordinate subspaces. *Duke Math. J.* 143(3):465–509, 2008.

Schulze, M. Maximal multihomogeneity of algebraic hypersurface singularities. *Manuscr. Math.* 123(4):373–9, 2007.

Granger, M., and **M. Schulze.** On the formal structure of lagarithmic vector fields. *Comp. Math.* 143:765–78, 2006.

Granger, M., and **M. Schulze.** Quasihomogeneity of isolated hypersurface singularities and logarithmic cohomology. *Manuscripta Math.* 121:411–6, 2006.

Granger, M., and **M. Schulze.** On the formal structure of logarithmic vector fields. *Comp. Math.* 142:765–78, 2006.

Schulze, M. Good bases for tame polynomials. *J. Symbolic Comput.* 39(1):103–26, 2005.

Schulze, M. A normal form algorithm for the Brieskorn lattice. *J. Symbolic Comput.* 38(4):1207–25, 2004.

Schulze, M. Monodromy of hypersurface singularities. *Acta Appl. Math.* 75:3–13, 2003.

Ullrich, D. C. *Complex Made Simple (Graduate Studies in Mathematics),* American Mathematical Society, 2008.

Choe, B. R., W. Ramey, and **D. C. Ullrich.** Bloch-to-BMOA pullbacks on the disk. *Proc. Am. Math. Soc.* 125(10):2987–96, 1997.

Stegenga, D. A., and **D. C. Ullrich.** Superharmonic functions in Hölder domains. *Rocky Mountain J. Math.* 25(4), 1995.

Ullrich, D. C. Radial divergence in BMOA. *Proc. London Math. Soc. (3)* 68(1), 1994.

Ullrich, D. C. Recurrence for lacunary cosine series. In *The Madison Symposium on Complex Analysis* (Madison, Wisc., 1991); *Contemp. Math.*, 137; *Am. Math. Soc.* Providence, R.I., 1992.

Pasciak, J. E., and **Y. Wang.** A multigrid preconditioner for the mixed formulation of linear plane elasticity. *SIAM J. Numer. Anal.* 44:478–93, 2006.

Wang, Y. Overlapping Schwarz preconditioner for the mixed formulation of plane elasticity. *Appl. Numer. Math.* 54:292–309, 2005.

Series, C., and **D. J. Wright.** Non- Euclidean symmetry and Indra's pearls. In *Proceedings of the 2006 Bridges Conference on Mathematics Connections in Art, Music, and Science,* pp. 25–32, Institute of Education. London Knowledge Lab, 2007.

Series, C., and **D. J. Wright.** Non- Euclidean symmetry and Indra's pearls. *+Plus Magazine,* 2007, http://plus.maths.org/issue43/features/serieswright/.

Wright, D. J. Searching for the cusp. In *Spaces of Kleinian Groups (London Mathematical Society Lecture Note Series,* 329:301-36, eds. Y. Minsky, M. Sakuma, and C. Series. London: Cambridge University Press, 2006.

Wright, D. J. Double cusp group. *Notices AMS* 51:1332–3, 2004.

Matthews, C., and **D. J. Wright.** Cycle decomposition and train tracks. *Proc. Am. Math. Soc.* 132:283–314, 2004.

Mumford, D., C. Series, and **D. J. Wright.** *Indra's Pearls: The Vision of Felix Klein.* Cambridge University Press, 2002.

Bona, J. L., and **J. Wu.** Temporal growth and eventual periodicity for dispersive wave equations in a quarter plane. *Discrete and Continuous Dynamical Systems-Series A* 23(4):1141–68, 2009.

Constantin, P., and **J. Wu.** Regularity of Hlder continuous solutions of the supercritical quasi-geostrophic equation. *Annales de l'Institut Henri Poincare (C) Nonlinear Anal.* 25(6):1103–10, 2008.

Khanal, N., **J. Wu,** and J. M. Yuan. Regularity criteria for the generalized MHD equations. *Commun. Part. Diff. Equat.* 33(1–3):285–306, 2008.

Yuan, J. M., J. Shen and **J. Wu.** A dual-Petrov-Galerkin method for the Kawahara-type equations. *SIAM J. Sci. Comput.* 34(1):48–63, 2008.

Wu, J., and J. M. Yuan. Local well-posedness and local (in space) regularity results for the complex Korteweg-de Vries equation. *Proc. Math. Roy. Soc. Edinb.* 137(1):203–23, 2007.

Wu, J. Existence and uniqueness results for the 2-D dissipative quasi-geostrophic equation. *Nonlinear Anal. Theor. Meth. Appl.* 67(11):3013–36, 2007.

Shen, J., **J. Wu,** and J. M. Yuan. Eventual periodicity for the KdV equation on a half-line. *Phys. Nonlinear Phenom.* 227(2):105–19, 2007.

Wu, J. Lower bounds for an integral involving fractional Laplacians and the generalized Navier-Stokes equations in Besov spaces. *Comm. Math. Phys.* 263(3):803-31, 2006.

Alazman, A. A., et al. and **J. Wu.** Comparisons between the BBM equation and a Boussinesq system. *Adv. Differ. Equat.* 11(2):121–166, 2006.

Wu, J., and J. M. Yuan. The effect of dissipation on solutions of the complex KdV equation. *Mathematics and Computers in Simulation* 69(5-6):589–99, 2005.

Wu, J. Solutions of the 2D quasi-geostrophic equation in Hlder spaces, *Nonlinear Anal. Theor. Meth. Appl.* 62(4):579–94, 2005.

Yuan, J. M. and **J. Wu.**, The complex KdV equation with or without dissipation, **Discrete and Continuous Dynamical Systems-Series** *B* 5(2):489-512, 2005.

Mehdi, S., and **R. Zierau.** Principal series representations and harmonic spinors. *Adv. Math.* 199:1–28, 2006.

Mehdi, S., and **R. Zierau.** Harmonic spinors on semisimple symmetric spaces. *J. Funct. Anal.* 198(2):536–57, 2003.

Zierau, R. Representations in Dolbeault cohomology. In *Representation Theory of Lie Groups,* Park City Math Institute, vol. 8; *Am. Math. Soc.* Providence, R.I., 2000.

Wolf, J. A., and **R. Zierau.** Linear cycle spaces in flag domains. *Math. Ann.* 316(3):529–45, 2000.

Dunne, E. G., and **R. Zierau.** The automorphism groups of complex homogeneous spaces. *Math. Ann.* 307(3):489–503, 1997.

UNIVERSITY OF DELAWARE

Department of Mathematical Sciences

Programs of Study

The Department of Mathematical Sciences offers master's and Ph.D. programs in mathematics and applied mathematics. Students receive instruction in a broad range of courses and may specialize in many areas of mathematics. Strong Departmental research groups exist in analysis, applied mathematics, partial differential equations, combinatorics, inverse problems, probability, and numerical analysis. Master's programs normally require two years for completion, while the Ph.D. usually takes five years.

Research Facilities

The University libraries contain 2 million volumes and documents and subscribe to 24,000 periodicals and serials. The University library belongs to the Association of Research Libraries.

The University Information Technologies Department provides e-mail and network access via central Sun servers. The Department of Mathematical Sciences has its own network and three computer classrooms and a 24-node cluster parallel computer. All graduate students have personal workstations in their offices with network access.

The Department fosters an active research environment, with numerous seminars and colloquia and many national and international visitors.

Financial Aid

Graduate assistantships and fellowships are available on a competitive basis. Teaching assistantships in 2010–11 range from $15,500 to $16,000 for nine months (two semesters), plus tuition remission. Additional winter and summer session teaching stipends are available. Currently, most full-time students receive full financial support. Research assistantships and fellowships are also available.

Cost of Study

Tuition for full-time graduate students was $22,240 for the 2009–10 academic year.

Living and Housing Costs

While prices vary widely throughout the area, average monthly rent for a one-bedroom apartment is $750 plus utilities.

Student Group

There are approximately 60 full-time graduate students in the Department of Mathematical Sciences. One half of these are international students and one third are women.

Location

The University is located in Newark, Delaware, a pleasant college community of about 30,000 residents. Newark is 14 miles southwest of Wilmington and halfway between Philadelphia and Baltimore. It offers the advantages of a small community yet is within easy driving distance of Philadelphia, New York, Baltimore, and Washington, D.C. It is also close to the recreational areas on the Atlantic Ocean and Chesapeake Bay.

The University

The University of Delaware grew out of a small academy founded in 1743. It has been a degree-granting institution since 1834. In 1867, an act of the Delaware General Assembly made the University a part of the nationwide system of land-grant colleges and universities. Delaware College and the Women's College, an affiliate, were combined under the name of the University of Delaware in 1921. In 1950, the Graduate College was organized to administer the existing graduate programs and develop new ones.

Applying

Application forms may be obtained online at http://www.udel.edu/gradoffice/applicants/. Completed applications, including letters of recommendation, a $75 application fee, GRE General Test scores, a subject GRE score, and transcripts of previous work, should be submitted as early as possible but no later than February 1 to be considered for financial aid for the fall semester.

Correspondence and Information

Coordinator of Graduate Studies
Department of Mathematical Sciences
University of Delaware
Newark, Delaware 19716
Phone: 302-831-2346
E-mail: see@math.udel.edu
Web site: http://www.math.udel.edu

University of Delaware

THE FACULTY AND THEIR RESEARCH

Thomas S. Angell, Professor; Ph.D., Michigan. Optimal control theory, differential equations.
Constantin Bacuta, Associate Professor; Ph.D., Texas A&M. Numerical analysis.
David P. Bellamy, Professor; Ph.D., Michigan State. Topology.
Richard J. Braun, Professor; Ph.D., Northwestern. Applied mathematics, mathematical biology.
Jinfa Cai, Professor; Ph.D., Pittsburgh. Mathematics education.
Fioralba Cakoni, Professor; Ph.D., Tirana University (Albania). Direct and inverse scattering theory.
Michelle Cirillo, Assistant Professor; Ph.D., Iowa State. Mathematics education.
Antonio Ciro, Instructor; M.S., Drexel. Mathematics education.
David L. Colton, Unidel Professor; Ph.D., D.Sc., Edinburgh. Partial differential equations, integral equations.
L. Pamela Cook-Ioannidis, Professor; Ph.D., Cornell. Applied mathematics, perturbation theory, transonic flow.
Robert Coulter, Associate Professor; Queensland (Australia). Finite fields, combinatorics.
Bryan Crissinger, Instructor; M.S., Penn State. Statistics.
Bettyann Daley, Assistant Professor; Ed.D., Delaware. Education leadership.
Margaret Donlan, Instructor; M.S., Toledo. Mathematics for the liberal arts student, quantitative literacy.
Tobin A. Driscoll, Professor; Ph.D., Cornell. Numerical analysis, applied mathematics.
Christine Ebert, Assistant Professor; Ph.D., Delaware. Investigation of pedagogical content knowledge for preservice and in-service teachers, cognitive development of the concept of function, use of technology.
David A. Edwards, Professor and Interim Chair; Ph.D., Caltech. Math biology, financial math.
Alfinio Flores, Hollowell Professorship Chair; Ph.D., Ohio State. Mathematics education.
Pak-Wing Fok, Assistant Professor; Ph.D., MIT. Mathematical biology, applied mathematics.
Robert P. Gilbert, Unidel Chair Professor; Ph.D., Carnegie Mellon. Homogenization, inverse problems, partial differential equations.
Philippe J. Guyenne, Associate Professor; Ph.D., Nice–Sophia Antipolis (France). Applied mathematics, fluid mechanics, differential equations, nonlinear waves, numerical analysis.
George C. Hsiao, Carl J. Rees Professor; Ph.D., Carnegie Mellon. Differential and integral equations, perturbation theory, fluid dynamics and elasticity.
Felix Lazebnik, Professor; Ph.D., Pennsylvania. Graph theory, combinatorics, algebra.
Yuk J. Leung, Associate Professor; Ph.D., Michigan. Function theory.
Wenbo Li, Professor; Ph.D., Wisconsin–Madison. Probability theory, stochastic processes, statistics.
Peter Monk, Unidel Professor; Ph.D., Rutgers. Numerical analysis.
Patrick F. Mwerinde, Assistant Professor; Ph.D., Columbia. Math education, conceptual learning theory, active learning, experimental design, statistical inference.
David Olagunju, Professor; Ph.D., Northwestern. Applied mathematics.
John A. Pelesko, Associate Professor and Director of Graduate Studies; Ph.D., NJIT. Applied mathematics.
Geraldine Prange, Instructor; M.S., Saint Louis. Math education for liberal arts majors, cooperative learning.
Georgia B. Pyrros, Instructor; M.S., McMaster. Nuclear physics.
Rakesh, Associate Professor; Ph.D., Cornell. Partial differential equations.
Louis F. Rossi, Associate Professor and Director of Undergraduate Studies; Ph.D., Arizona. Fluid dynamics, numerical analysis, vorticity dynamics.
Gilberto Schleiniger, Associate Professor and Associate Chair; Ph.D., UCLA. Scientific computing, numerical analysis.
Patricia Schwarzkopf, Instructor; M.A., Ohio State. Mathematics education.
Anthony Seraphin, Associate Professor; Ph.D., Delaware. Boundary-layer flow, turbulent diffusion and dispersion within and above canopies, wind and water tunnel flow simulations, air pollution climatology and its precursors.
Qing Xiang, Professor; Ph.D., Ohio State. Combinatorics.
Shangyou Zhang, Associate Professor; Ph.D., Penn State. Numerical analysis and scientific computation.

Emeritus Professors
Willard E. Baxter, Ph.D., Pennsylvania. Algebra.
Richard J. Libera, Ph.D., Rutgers. Function theory.
Albert E. Livingston, Ph.D., Rutgers. Function theory.
David P. Roselle, Ph.D., Duke. Combinatorics.
Ivar Stakgold, Ph.D., Harvard. Nonlinear boundary-value problems.
Robert M. Stark, Ph.D., Delaware. Applied probability, operations research, civil engineering systems.
Richard J. Weinacht, Ph.D., Maryland. Partial differential equations.

Joint Appointments with Other Departments
Kay Biondi, Ph.D., Delaware; Center for Secondary Education. Curriculum and instruction.
Morris W. Brooks, Ph.D., Harvard. Computer-based instruction.
Bobby F. Caviness, Ph.D., Carnegie Mellon. Computer algebra.
Prasad Dhurjati, Ph.D., Purdue. Chemical engineering
Jon Manon, Ph.D., Delaware. Mathematics education.
William B. Moody, Ed.D., Maryland. Mathematics education.
Dick Sacher, Ph.D., Stanford. Optimization.
David Saunders, Ph.D., Wisconsin–Madison. Computer algebra.
Leonard W. Schwartz, Ph.D., Stanford. Fluid mechanics.
Stephen Siegel, Ph.D., Chicago. Computer and information sciences.
Xiang-Gen Xia, Ph.D., USC. Electrical engineering.

Adjunct Faculty and Their Affiliations
Patrick S. Hagan, Ph.D. Bloomberg L.P.
Rainer Kress, Ph.D. University of Göttingen. Integral equations, scattering theory.
Emeka Nwanko, Ph.D. DuPont Company.
Lassi Paivarinta, Ph.D. University of Oulu (Finland).
Wolfgang Wendland, Ph.D. University of Stuttgart (Germany). Integral equations and analysis.

UNIVERSITY OF SOUTHERN CALIFORNIA

Division of Biostatistics

Programs of Study

Graduate education at the University of Southern California (USC) prepares students for leadership in research, teaching, or professional practice in the private or public sector. Rigorous individually tailored course work and research forms the basis for the graduate programs.

Graduate studies in biostatistics, epidemiology, molecular epidemiology, and statistical genetics and genetic epidemiology are contained within USC's Keck School of Medicine. The University offers the Master of Science (M.S.) and Doctor of Philosophy (Ph.D.) degrees. The Ph.D. in biostatistics is designed to produce a biostatistician with a deep knowledge of statistical theory and methodology. The Ph.D. in statistical genetics and genetic epidemiology is a joint effort to combine biostatistics, epidemiology, statistical and molecular genetics, and computational methods in order to develop new and cutting-edge statistical methodology that is appropriate for human genomic studies.

Master's degree studies in biostatistics focus on the theory of biostatistics, data analytic methods, experimental design (including clinical trials), statistical methods in human genetics, biomedical informatics, and statistical computing methods. The master's degree in applied biostatistics and epidemiology includes applied biostatistics, epidemiological research methods, and research applications, including cancer, infectious disease, chronic disease, and environmental epidemiology. Doctoral studies cover the areas of biostatistics and data analysis; descriptive, genetic, and molecular epidemiology; computational methods; clinical trial methodology; and related fields of field research, such as population disease and treatment trials.

The Division of Biostatistics also offers a joint-degree program in either the M.S. or Ph.D. in molecular epidemiology in conjunction with the Department of Biochemistry and Molecular Biology. The objective of the M.S. degree is to train students in the application of statistical methods to the design of biomedical research. The objective of the doctoral degree is to produce a molecular epidemiologist with in-depth laboratory, statistical, and analytical skills in both epidemiology and the molecular biosciences.

Research Facilities

Hands-on research alongside a faculty mentor is the norm at USC. Graduate students work alongside colleagues as coinvestigators on epidemiological, clinical trial, and environmental research projects. Graduate students have myriad opportunities to participate in the latest clinical and biomedical research projects. Research teams gain expertise on study design as well as statistical methodology, data analysis, and manuscript preparation. The University's Health Sciences Campus contains the Norris Cancer Center, the General Clinical Research Center, the Zilkha Neurogenetic Research Institute, and the Doheny Eye Institute Vision Research Center.

USC has a dozen libraries to serve all the varied needs of its graduate students. Primary source materials include ongoing research projects and recent faculty and staff members' publications. In addition, electronic resources in hundreds of subjects plus online archives and Internet access are available for students through the library system.

Financial Aid

Most graduate students who demonstrate financial need qualify for low-interest loans or assistantships. Graduate assistantships are awarded on the basis of scholastic accomplishment and competence. Students exchange teaching and laboratory assistant time for tuition waivers and stipends.

The Sponsored Projects Information Network (SPIN) is a computerized database of funding opportunities—federal, private, and corporate—created to help faculty members identify external financial support for research and education. SPIN funds that are directed toward USC programs in biostatistics result in research funds and fellowships for graduate students.

Cost of Study

Estimated costs for 2010–11 are as follows: tuition, $40,384; books and supplies, $2500; and other miscellaneous expenses, $5000.

Living and Housing Costs

Estimated housing costs for the Los Angeles area are approximately $18,000 per year. Housing costs vary greatly, depending on the location and type of accommodation. There are ample housing facilities in the many communities surrounding the medical school.

Student Group

There are approximately 3,000 graduate students at USC and 120 in the biostatistics, epidemiology, and genetics programs. The relatively small size of the programs facilitates student–faculty member interchange and good accessibility for students to their professors and mentors.

Location

University of Southern California campuses are mostly centered around Los Angeles, with other facilities in nearby Alhambra, Pasadena, and Marina del Rey; on Catalina Island; and further away in Orange County to the south and Sacramento to the north. Los Angeles is the second-largest city in the U.S. and the nucleus of southern California. The scenic, sunny, and culturally diverse area of Los Angeles offers miles of beaches, acres of recreational and park areas, and some of the finest arts and cultural opportunities in the nation.

The University

USC is the oldest and largest independent coeducational university in the West. The campus is composed of 169 buildings located in a 150-acre parklike setting near downtown Los Angeles. USC is among the ten most successful private universities in the country in attracting research support from external sources (more than $100 million annually). Graduate students in the Division of Biostatistics take the majority of their courses at the Health Sciences Campus, 3 miles northeast of downtown Los Angeles and 7 miles from the USC University Park Campus. The Health Sciences Campus is adjacent to the Los Angeles County–USC Medical Center, one of the nation's largest teaching hospitals. The surrounding neighborhoods are among the most historically significant in the city, with rich educational resources.

Applying

For the M.S. degree, an undergraduate degree in mathematics, statistics, biostatistics, or computer science is most helpful. Undergraduate preparation should include differential and integral calculus, mathematical statistics, and basic computer programming. The Ph.D. requires successful scores on a screening examination (the M.S. prepares students for this exam). Applicants must apply online through USC's general Web site. They must also get the department's preapplication via the graduate program's direct Web site at http://www.usc.edu/medicine/biostats.

Correspondence and Information

Graduate Programs in Biostatistics, Epidemiology, Molecular Epidemiology, and Statistical Genetics and Genetic Epidemiology
Division of Biostatistics
Department of Preventive Medicine
Keck School of Medicine
Center for Health Professions, 222
University of Southern California
1540 Alcazar
Los Angeles, California 90089-9010
Phone: 323-442-1810
Fax: 323-442-2993
E-mail: mtrujill@usc.edu
Web site: http://www.usc.edu/medicine/biostats

University of Southern California

THE FACULTY AND THEIR RESEARCH

Hooman Allayee, Assistant Professor.
Todd Alonzo, Assistant Professor; Ph.D., Washington (Seattle), 2000. Design and analysis of clinical trials, pediatric oncology, statistical methodology, and missing data methodology.
Susan Ames, Assistant Professor of Research.
Edward Avol, Associate Professor; M.S., Caltech, 1974. Chronic respiratory effects of airborne pollutants in populations.
Stanley Azen, Professor and Codirector; Ph.D., UCLA, 1969. Biostatistical methodology.
Lourdes Baezconde-Garbanati, Associate Professor; Ph.D., UCLA, 1994. Cancer control research.
Kiros Berhane, Associate Professor; Ph.D., Toronto, 1994. Analysis of health effects of environmental exposures.
Jonathan Buckley, Professor of Research (also with Pediatrics, CHLA); Ph.D., Melbourne, 1981. Epidemiology of childhood cancer, clinical trials, molecular epidemiology.
John Casagrande, Clinical Associate Professor; D.Ph., UCLA, 1978. Computer applications in research.
Jiu-Chiuan Chen, Associate Professor; Sc.D., Harvard, 2002. Cardiovascular and neurological effects of air pollution, characterization of individual susceptibility to health effects of air pollution.
Lu Chen, Assistant Professor of Research.
Chih-Ping Chou, Associate Professor of Research; Ph.D., UCLA, 1983. Evaluation of approaches to substance-abuse prevention among adolescents, statistical methods in prevention research.
Myles Cockburn, Assistant Professor of Research; Ph.D., Otago (New Zealand), 1998. Epidemiology of melanoma, gastric cancer, and *Helicobacter pylori;* computational methods; geographical information systems (GIS).
David Conti, Assistant Professor; Ph.D., Case Western Reserve, 2002. Statistical methods in genetic association studies, use of hierarchical models in epidemiology.
Victoria Cortessis, Assistant Professor; Ph.D., UCLA, 1993. Genetic-epidemiologic and molecular genetic studies of congenital disorders, adult-onset cancers and etiologic relationships among these entities.
Wendy Cozen, Associate Professor of Research; M.P.H., UCLA, 1989. Epidemiology of hematologic neoplasms, Hodgkin's disease, non-Hodgkin's lymphoma.
N. Tess Cruz, Assistant Professor of Clinical; Ph.D., Massachusetts, 1993. Public health communications research, anti-tobacco media and pro-tobacco marketing effects.
Dennis Deapen, Professor; Dr.Ph., UCLA, 1982. Cancer outcomes among breast implant patients; lupus erythematosus, diabetes, multiple sclerosis, and Alzheimer's disease.
Manuela Gago, Assistant Professor of Research.
Peggy Gallaher, Assistant Professor of Research.
W. James Gauderman, Professor; Ph.D., USC, 1992. Biostatistical methodology, genetic-epidemiological analysis of pedigree data, health outcomes to environmental exposure.
Frank Gilliland, Professor; M.D., Minnesota, 1992. Environmental exposures on air pollution.
Michael I. Goran, Professor (also with Physiology and Biophysics); Ph.D., Manchester (England), 1986. Biophysics etiology prevention of obesity, type 2 diabetes in children.
Susan Groshen, Professor of Research; Ph.D., Rutgers, 1980. New drugs and treating cancer.
Robert Haile, Professor; Ph.D., UCLA, 1979. Genetic epidemiology of breast, colon, and prostate cancers.
Christopher Haiman, Associate Professor; Sc.D. Genetics and molecular epidemiology.
Ann Hamilton, Associate Professor; Ph.D., UCLA, 1987. Breast, prostate, and testicular cancer; Kaposi's sarcoma; cancers in twins.
Brian Henderson, Professor; M.D., Chicago, 1962. Cancers of the breast, prostate, ovary, testes, and endometrium in different ethnic groups.
Andrea Hricko, Associate Professor; M.P.H., North Carolina, 1971. Outreach and education techniques, translational and community-based participatory research.
Sue A. Ingles, Associate Professor; D.P.H., UCLA, 1993. Nutritional genetics and breast, prostate, and colorectal cancer.
Carol Koprowski, Assistant Professor; Ph.D., USC, 1998. Diet and physical activity.
Mark Krailo, Professor of Research; Ph.D., Waterloo, 1981. Clinical trials on cancer treatment.
Peter W. Laird, Associate Professor; Ph.D., Amsterdam (Netherlands Cancer Institute), 1988. Biochemistry and molecular biology, cancer genetics, gene regulation.
Bryan Langholz, Professor of Research; Ph.D., Washington (Seattle), 1984. Cancer and other chronic diseases, cohort studies.
Thomas Mack, Professor (also with Pathology); M.P.H., Harvard, 1969. Chronic disease in twins.
Wendy Mack, Professor (also with Pathology); Ph.D., USC, 1989. Biostatistical methodology in cardiovascular research, clinical trials using angiographic and ultrasound endpoints.
Paul Marjoram, Associate Professor of Research; Ph.D., University College (London), 1992. Computational biology; the coalescent, probabilistic models; microarray data.
Rob McConnell, Professor; M.D., California, San Francisco, 1980. Environmental exposures, air pollution.
Roberta McKean-Cowdin, Assistant Professor of Research; Ph.D., 1996. Breast, brain, and endometrial cancer.
Joel Milam, Assistant Professor of Research.
Elaine Nezami, Associate Professor; Ph.D., USC, 1994. Chronic disease, cancer, cardiovascular.
Celeste Pearce, Assistant Professor of Research.
Mary Ann Pentz, Professor; Ph.D., Syracuse, 1978. Development and testing of school/community-based prevention intervention for adolescents.
Malcolm Pike, Professor; Ph.D., Aberdeen (England), 1963. Hormonal, endometrial, and ovarian cancer.
Jean Richardson, Professor; M.P.H., UCLA, 1971. Cancer control, behavioral and epidemiological research methods.
Louise Rohrbach, Associate Professor of Research; Ph.D., USC, 1989. Community-based interventions for disease prevention and health promotion; prevention of tobacco, alcohol, and other drug abuse.
Jonathan Samet, Professor and Chair of Preventive Medicine; M.D., M.S., Harvard School of Public Health.
Fredrick Schumacher, Assistant Professor; Ph.D., Case Western Reserve, 2006. Genetic epidemiology (cancer, obesity); cancer genetics; gene-environment interactions; biostatistics.
Kimberly Siegmund, Associate Professor; Ph.D., Washington (Seattle), 1995. Statistical methods for genetics.
Richard Sposto, Professor of Research; Ph.D., UCLA, 1981. Biostatistics, clinical trials in pediatric oncology, Bayesian analysis of survival data.
Donna Spruijt-Metz, Associate Professor of Research; Ph.D., Amsterdam Vrije, 1996. Obesity and type 2 diabetes, smoking prevention.
Michael R. Stallcup, Professor; Ph.D., Berkeley, 1977. Cancer cell biology, signal transduction, genes.
Mariana Stern, Assistant Professor; Ph.D., Texas Health Science Center, 1997. Colorectal and breast cancer, genes–diet, genes–smoking.
Daniel Stram, Professor; Ph.D., Temple, 1983. Modern statistical methods, measurement error methods in cancer epidemiology, repeated measures data, human genetics data.
Ping Sun, Assistant Professor of Research; Ph.D., USC, 1999. Cardiovascular disease and cancer.
Steven Sussman, Professor; Ph.D., Illinois at Chicago, 1984. Drug abuse, cessation, school-based alcohol, tobacco.
Duncan Thomas, Professor; Ph.D., McGill, 1976. Statistical methods, occupational and environmental health.
Paul D. Thomas, Associate Professor and Director of Bioinformatics; Ph.D., Development and application of computational methods for reconstructing gene evolution to understand the function of human genes.
Jennifer Unger, Associate Professor; Ph.D., USC, 1996. Psychosocial and cultural factors in adolescent.
Thomas Valente, Professor; Ph.D., USC, 1991. Health promotion, substance abuse.
Richard Watanabe, Associate Professor; Ph.D., USC, 1995. Type 2 diabetes, biologic systems, positional cloning and gene characterization in complex disease.
Anna Wu, Professor; Ph.D., UCLA, 1983. Various cancers among Asian migrants to the U.S.
Tianni Zhou, Assistant Professor of Research; Ph.D., 2002. Clinical trials in pediatric oncology.

THE UNIVERSITY OF TEXAS AT DALLAS

Mathematical Sciences

Programs of Study

The mathematical sciences department at the University of Texas at Dallas (UT Dallas) offers the Master of Science degree in five specializations: applied mathematics, bioinformatics and computational biology, engineering mathematics, mathematics, and statistics. The Doctor of Philosophy degree is offered in applied mathematics and in statistics. The program has major research faculty members and thrusts in the latter two areas. The degree programs are designed to prepare graduates for careers in mathematical sciences or in related fields for which these disciplines provide indispensable foundations and tools. There is no language requirement.

The Master of Science degree requires 33–36 hours of course work, consisting of core courses and approved electives. The student may choose a thesis plan or a nonthesis plan. In the thesis plan, the thesis replaces 6 hours of course work.

The Ph.D. program is tailored to the student, who arranges a course program with the guidance and approval of the graduate adviser. Adjustments can be made as the student's interests develop and a specific dissertation topic is chosen. Approximately 39 hours of core courses and 18–24 hours of elective courses are required for a typical degree program. After completion of about two years of course work, the student must undertake and pass a Ph.D. qualifying examination in order to continue in the program. The program culminates in the preparation of a dissertation, which must be approved by the graduate program. The topic may be in mathematical sciences exclusively or may involve considerable work in an area of application. Typical areas of concentration within applied mathematics include, but are not restricted to, applied analysis, computational and mathematical biology, relativity theory, differential equations, scattering theory, systems theory, control theory, signal processing, and differential geometry. In the area of statistics, concentrations are offered in mathematical statistics, applied statistics, statistical computing, probability, stochastic processes, linear models, time-series analysis, statistical classification, multivariate analysis, robust statistics, statistical inference, sequential analysis, and asymptotic theory.

In addition to a wide range of courses in mathematics and statistics, the mathematical sciences program offers a unique selection of courses that consider theoretical and computational aspects of engineering and scientific problems.

Research Facilities

Faculty, staff, and research/teaching assistant offices are equipped with the latest generation of computers. The department also has a classroom equipped with state-of-the-art computers for classroom and research use. All of the department's machines are connected via Ethernet to the campus network, giving faculty members and students access to all of the software tools and machines on campus for research and educational use.

Financial Aid

The Graduate Tuition Scholarship (GTS) covers the full cost of tuition and fees for up to 9 hours per semester; the total value is $9400 per academic year. In addition to the GTS, full-time graduate students qualify for teaching assistantships. The full teaching assistantship stipend for 2009–10 was $13,500; the value of the total package is $22,900 per academic year. Support for summer study is usually available. In addition to the GTS and teaching assistantships, applicants may also be awarded an Excellence in Education Fellowship for up to two years at a rate of $8000 per year. UT Dallas has also developed a comprehensive program of grants, scholarships, loans, and employment opportunities to assist students in meeting the cost of their education.

Cost of Study

Effective fall 2007, there are two different tuition and fee plans. The non-guaranteed rate will be assessed to all students who have an open matriculation prior to fall 2007 and did not opt-in to the guaranteed tuition plan. All new students at UT Dallas will automatically be included in the guaranteed tuition plan. This plan freezes tuition rates at the rate applicable to the first semester they enroll, and remains valid for a period of four years. For more information regarding these two tuition plans, please visit the guaranteed tuition Web page at http://www.utdallas.edu/tuition/guarantee/.

Living and Housing Costs

Graduate students attending UT Dallas have two options when considering on-campus housing: University Village, operated by American Campus Communities, and Waterview Park, operated by University Partners. The two communities offer several housing-style options; more information is available by following the links from the residential life Web page at http://www.utdallas.edu/housing/general/.

Student Group

The total enrollment at the University is 15,783, including 5,982 graduate students. The mathematical sciences program has 35 master's students and 34 Ph.D. candidates, some of whom attend part-time while employed full-time with companies in the Dallas area.

Student Outcomes

The program's most recent Ph.D. graduates have secured employment in both industrial and academic positions. Of the most recent Ph.D. students in applied mathematics, one is on the faculty at the University of North Texas at Dallas, and another has joined the faculty of Collin County Community College in McKinney, Texas. Of the program's most recent Ph.D. students in statistics, one is on the faculty at the Universidad de Sonora, Hermosillo, Sonora, Mexico; one is a Senior Statistician in a biostatistics research group at Sanofi Pasteur in Beijing, China; and the third has accepted a position as a Senior Statistician/Consultant with Straight Line Performance Solutions, LLC, based in Ithaca, New York.

Location

UT Dallas is located in Richardson, a quiet suburb of North Dallas, which is easily accessible to the more than 800 high-technology companies located in the Dallas–Fort Worth area. Many of these companies are located within 10 miles of UT Dallas, providing graduates with numerous career opportunities. The Dallas metropolitan area also offers a wide range of cultural, social, and sports activities.

The University and The Program

The University of Texas at Dallas was created in 1969 when the privately funded Southwest Center for Advanced Studies was transferred to the state of Texas. In 1972, the Program in Mathematical Sciences was introduced and in 1975 became part of the School of Natural Sciences and Mathematics. Research at the graduate level has continued to represent a major thrust of the University and of the program.

Applying

Applications are considered at any time until vacancies are filled. For consideration for teaching assistantships, the deadline of January 15 is set for first-round consideration. Applicants should arrange for GRE scores and (for international students) TOEFL scores to be included as early as possible in the application materials. Applications not complete before March 15 receive relatively late consideration for teaching assistantships.

Correspondence and Information

Head
Mathematical Sciences
The University of Texas at Dallas
P.O. Box 830688, MS EC35
Richardson, Texas 75083-0688

Phone: 972-883-2161
Fax: 972-883-6622
E-mail: utdmath@utdallas.edu
Web site: http://www.utdallas.edu/dept/math

The University of Texas at Dallas

THE FACULTY AND THEIR RESEARCH

Larry P. Ammann, Professor; Ph.D., Florida State, 1976. Robust multivariate statistical methods, signal processing, statistical computing, applied probability, remote sensing.
Zalman Balanov, Ph.D., Belarusian State University, Minsk. Nonlinear analysis (especially equivariant degree), dynamical systems with symmetries (especially bifurcation theory), mathematical theory of hysteresis, nonassociative algebras.
Michael Baron, Professor; Ph.D., Maryland, 1995. Sequential analysis, Bayesian inference, change-point problems, applications in semiconductor manufacturing, psychology, energy finance.
Yan Cao, Assistant Professor; Ph.D., Brown, 2003. Medical image analysis, computational anatomy, computer vision, pattern theory, shape analysis and shape models.
Pankaj Choudhary, Associate Professor; Ph.D., Ohio State, 2002. Biostatistics, statistical inference, method comparison studies.
Mieczyslaw K. Dabkowski, Associate Professor; Ph.D., George Washington, 2003. Knot invariants and 3-manifold invariants, applications of topology to biology, recursion theory.
Sam Efromovich, Professor; Ph.D., Moscow, 1986. Information theory, optimization, probability, statistical inference, nonparametric curve estimation, time-series analysis, multivariate regression, signal processing, images, wavelets, statistics of finance.
Tobias Hagge, Assistant Professor, Ph.D., Indiana, 2008. Quantum topology, topological quautum computing, fusion categories, knot theory.
M. Ali Hooshyar, Professor; Ph.D., Indiana, 1970. Scattering theory, inverse scattering theory with geophysical and optical applications, fission.
Natalia A. Humphreys, Clinical Associate Professor, Associate Head of Actuarial Program, and Undergraduate Adviser in Actuarial Science; Ph.D., Ohio State, 1999, FSA, 2005. Actuarial science, applied complex variable, analysis, probability.
Wieslaw Krawcewicz, Professor; Ph.D., Montreal, 1985. Topological methods in nonlinear analysis, symmetric differential equations and bifurcation problems.
Istvan Ozsvath, Professor; Ph.D., Hamburg, 1960. Relativistic cosmology, differential geometry.
Viswanath Ramakrishna, Professor; Ph.D., Washington (St. Louis), 1991. Control, optimization, computation, applications in material and molecular sciences.
Ivor Robinson, Emeritus Professor; B.A., Cambridge, 1947. General relativity theory, particularly exact solutions to Einstein's equations of gravitation.
Robert Serfling, Professor; Ph.D., North Carolina, 1967. Probability theory, statistical inference, robust and nonparametric methods, asymptotic theory, stochastic processes, applications in bioscience and finance. (Web site: http://www.utdallas.edu/~serfling)
Qiongxia Song, Ph.D., Michigan State, Statistical inference, nonparametric methods, confidence bands problems, time-series analysis, probability theory.
Janos Turi, Professor; Ph.D., Virginia Tech, 1986. Functional differential equations, integral equations, approximation theory, optimal control theory, numerical analysis, applied functional analysis.
John Van Ness, Emeritus Professor; Ph.D., Brown, 1964. Robust linear models, statistical classification, measurement error models, applications of statistics to the physical and medical sciences.
John Wiorkowski, Professor; Ph.D., Chicago, 1972. Statistical time series, forecasting, applied statistics, regression analysis, multivariate techniques.

SELECTED PUBLICATIONS

Ammann, L., E. M. Dowling, and R. D. DeGroat. A TQR-iteration based adaptive SVD for real-time angle and frequency tracking. *IEEE Trans. Signal Processing* 42:914–26, 1994.
Ammann, L. Robust singular value decompositions: A new approach to projection pursuit. *J. Am. Stat. Assoc.* 88:504–14, 1993.
Balanov, Z., W. Krawcesicz, and H. Steinlein. *Applied Equivariant Degree (Differential Equations and Dynamical Systems).* Springfield, Mo.: American Institute of Mathematical Sciences, 2006.
Balanov, Z., and Y. Krasnov. Complex structures in real algebras. Part I: Two-dimensional commutative case. *Comm. Algebra* 31(9):4571–609, 2003.
Balanov, Z., and Y. Schwartzman. Morse complex, even functionals and buckling of a thin elastic plate. *Compt. Rendus Acad. Sci. Math.* 320(3):273–8, 1995.
Baron, M., A. Takken, E. Yashchin, and M. Lanzerotti, Modeling and forecasting of defect-limited yield in semiconductor manufacturing. *IEEE Trans. Semicond. Manuf.* 21(4):614–24, 2008.
Schmegner, C., and **Baron, M.** Sequential plans and risk evaluation. *Sequential Analysis* 26(4):335–54, 2007.
Baron, M., and A. G. Tartakovsky. Asymptotic optimality of change-point detection schemes in general continuous-time models. *Sequential Analysis* 25(3):257–96, 2006.
Baron, M. Bayes stopping rules in a change-point model with a random hazard rate. *Sequential Analysis* 20(3):147–63, 2001.
Cao, Y., et al. Diffeomorphic matching of diffusion tensor images. In *Proceedings of MMBIA 2006: IEEE Computer Society Workshop on Mathematical Methods in Biomedical Image Analysis.* New York, 2006.
Cao, Y., M. I. Miller, R. L. Winslow, and L. Younes. Large deformation diffeomorphic metric mapping of vector fields. *IEEE Trans. Med. Imaging* 24(9):1216–30, 2005.
Lu, C., **Y. Cao,** and D. Mumford. Surface evolution under curvature flows. *J. Vis. Commun. Image Representation* 13:65–81, 2002.
Choudhary, P. K., and K. Yin. Bayesian and frequentist methodologies for analyzing method comparison studies with multiple methods. *Statistics in Biopharmaceutical Research* 2(1):122–32, 2010.
Yin, K., **P. K. Choudhary,** D. Varghese, and S. R. Goodman. A Bayesian approach for sample size determination in method comparison studies. *Stat. Med.* 27(13):2273–89, 2008.
Choudhary, P. K., A tolerance interval approach for assessment of agreement in method comparison studies with repeated measurements. *J. Stat. Plann. Infer.* 138(4):1102–15, 2008.
Dabkowski, M. K., J. H. Przytycki, and A. Togha. Non-left-orderable 3-manifold groups. *Can. Math. Bull.* 48X(1):32–40, 2005.
Dabkowski, M. K., and J. H. Przytycki. Unexpected connections between Burnside groups and knot theory. *Proc. Natl. Acad. Sci. U.S.A.* 101(50):17357–60, 2004.
Dabkowski, M. K., and J. H. Przytycki. Burnside obstructions to the Montesinos-Nakanishi 3-move conjecture. *Geom. Topol.* 6:355–60, 2002.
Efromovich, S. Oracle inequality for conditional density estimation and an actuarial example. *Ann. Inst. Math. Stat.* 62(2):249–75, 2010.
Efromovich, S. Adaptive estimation of and oracle inequalities for probability densities and characteristic functions. *Ann. Stat.* 36(3):1127–55, 2008.
Hooshyar, M. A. Electromagnetic scattering from a dielectric cylinder and the method of lines. *Microw. Opt. Tech. Lett.* 51(4):1046–9, 2009.
Haque, M., I. Reichshstein, **M. A. Hooshyar,** and F. B. Malik. Energy-density functional approach to fission-, cluster-, and alpha-radioactivity. In *Condensed Matter Theories,* vol. 21, pp. 45–54, eds. H. Akai, et al. New York: Nova Science Publishers, Inc., 2007.
Hooshyar, M. A., and L. V. Lasater. Shape and impedance recovery of obstacles from electromagnetic scattering data. *Microw. Opt. Tech. Lett.* 48(3):596–600, 2006.
Humphreys, N., A central limit theorem for some special complex-valued probability densities. *J. Math. Anal. Appl.* 248(1):1–28, 2000.
Krawcewicz, W., and J. Wu. *Theory of Degrees with Applications to Bifurcations and Differential Equations.* New York: John Wiley and Sons, Inc, 1997.
Ozsvath, I., J. Ehlers, E. L. Schucking, and Y. Shang. Pressure as a source of gravity. *Phys. Rev. D* 72:124003-1–8, 2005.
Ozsvath, I., and E. Schucking. Godel's trip. *Am. J. Phys.* 71:801–5, 2003.
Ramakrishna, V. Local solvability of degenerate, overdetermined systems: A control-theoretic perspective. *J. Differ. Equat.*, in press.
Ramakrishna, V. Controlled invariance for singular distributions. *SIAM J. Contr. Optim.* 32:790–807, 1994.
Robinson, I., and I. Trautman. The conformal geometry of complex quadrics and the fractional-linear form of Mobius transformations. *J. Math. Phys.* 34:5391, 1993.
Serfling, R. Equivariance and invariance properties of multivariate quantile and related functions, and the role of standardization. *Journal of Nonparametric Statistics.* 2010. doi:10.1080/10485250903431710.
Dang, X., and **R. Serfling.** Nonparametric depth-based multivariate outlier identifiers, and masking robustness properties. *J. Stat. Plann. Infer.* 140(1):198–213, 2010.
Serfling, R., and Satyaki Mazumder. Exponential probability inequality and convergence results for the median absolute deviation and its modifications. *Stat. Probab. Lett.* 79(16):1767–73, 2009.
Song, Q., and L. Yang. Oracally efficient spline smoothing of nonlinear additive autoregression model with simultaneous confidence bands. *J. Multivariate Anal.*, in press.
Song, Q., and L. Yang. Spline confidence bands for variance functions. *Journal of Nonparametric Statistics* 21(5):589–09, 2009.
Ma, Y., **Q. Song,** and L. Wu. Large deviation principles with respect to the [tau]-topology for exchangeable sequences: A necessary and sufficient condition. *Statist. Probab. Lett.* 77(3): 239–46, 2007.
Turi, J., and F. Hartung. Linearized stability in functional differential equations with state-dependent delays. *Dynamical Syst. Differential Equations* (an added volume to *Discrete Continuous Dynamical Syst.*) 416–25, 2001.
Turi, J., F. Hartung, and T. L. Herdman. Parameter identification in classes of neutral differential equations with state-dependent delays. *J. Nonlinear Anal. Theory Methods Appl.* 39:305–25, 2000.
Turi, J., and W. Desch. The stop operator related to a convex polyhedron. *J. Differ. Equat.* 157:329–47, 1999.
Van Ness, J. Recent results in clustering admissibility. In *Applied Stochastic Models and Data Analysis.* Lisbon: Instituto Nacional del Estastistica, 1999.
Van Ness, J., and C. L. Cheng. *Statistical Regression with Measurement Error.* London: Edward Arnold Publishers, 1999.
Van Ness, J., and J. Yang. Robust discriminant analysis: Training data breakdown point. *J. Stat. Plann. Inference* 1:67–84, 1998.
Wiorkowski, J., and V. Gylis. An empirical real-time test for take off with applications to cellular telephony. *Rev. Marketing Sci.* 4(1), 2006.
Wiorkowski, J. A lightly annotated bibliography of the publications of the American Statistical Association. *Am. Stat.* 44:106–13, 1990.
Wiorkowski, J. Fitting of growth curves over time when the data are obtained from a single realization. *J. Forecasting* 7:259–72, 1988.

UNIVERSITY OF UTAH

Department of Mathematics

Programs of Study

The Department of Mathematics offers programs leading to the degrees of Doctor of Philosophy, Master of Arts, Master of Statistics, Master of Science in mathematics, Master Science in mathematics (teaching), and Master of Science in computational engineering and science. A Professional Master of Science and Technology degree is also offered.

The master's degrees require 30 hours of course work beyond certain basic prerequisites, and passing qualifying examinations or doing nine credits of a curriculum project.

The doctoral degree carries a minimum course requirement designed to provide a broad exposure to related fields and good preparation in the area of specialization. Three written qualifying examinations in the basic fields of mathematics and an oral examination, with emphasis on the candidate's area of specialization, are also required. A dissertation describing independent and original work is required. The Department of Mathematics stresses excellence in research.

Research Facilities

The Mathematics Branch Library collection consists of 190 journal subscriptions, 15,000 bound journals, and 12,000 books. In addition, the Marriott Library collection includes numerous books and journals of interest to mathematics researchers and scholars. There are extensive interactive computing and computer graphics facilities available in the Department.

Financial Aid

Approximately 70 percent of the mathematics graduate students are supported by fellowships. There are teaching fellowships that range from $15,000 to $16,000, plus tuition and health insurance. The Graduate School and the Department provide each funded graduate student with a premium subsidy that covers the full cost of group health insurance offered through GMSouthwest.

The normal teaching load for a teaching assistant and teaching fellow is one course per semester. Summer teaching is available. The stipend for one course during the summer ranges from $3500 to $4500.

Cost of Study

For the 2010–11 academic year, tuition is $3141 per semester for Utah residents and $10,042 per semester for nonresidents (12 credit hours). The Graduate Tuition Benefit Program administered by the Graduate School waives tuition fees for teaching fellows, teaching assistants, and research assistants.

Living and Housing Costs

A wide variety of housing is offered by the University on or near the campus. University Village, for married students, is operated by the University. Privately owned housing near the campus is also available. For details and complete listings of on-campus housing, students should visit the Web site at http://www.housing.utah.edu.

Student Group

The University's total enrollment is currently 29,285. The Department of Mathematics has 113 graduate students; 70 receive financial support.

Student Outcomes

Graduates typically go on to postdoctoral research appointments followed by academic careers in teaching and research or careers in government and industry. In the past two years, 15 graduates took positions at various universities, including Duke University; Ohio State University; Princeton University; the Universities of Calgary; Maryland, Pittsburgh, and Ottawa; and several other institutions with National Science Foundation postdoctoral fellowships.

Location

The Salt Lake City metropolitan area has a population of about 1 million and is the cultural, economic, and educational center of the Intermountain West. Climate and geography combine in the Salt Lake environs to provide ideal conditions for outdoor sports. Some of the world's best skiing is available less than an hour's drive from the University campus.

The University and The Department

The University of Utah is a state-supported coeducational public institution. Founded in 1850, it is the oldest state university west of the Missouri River.

In the last five years, the Department of Mathematics has awarded 140 graduate degrees. In recent years, the Graduate School has been awarding about 600 doctoral degrees per year. The University faculty has 2,700 members.

Applying

Admission to graduate status requires that students hold a bachelor's degree or its equivalent and that they show promise for success in graduate work. Applicants are required to take the mathematics Subject Test of the Graduate Record Examinations.

Students are normally admitted at the beginning of the fall semester. Applications for teaching fellowships should be submitted as early as possible (after December 15). All applications received before January 15 are automatically considered for financial assistance. Applications received after January 15 will be considered for admission only. The deadline to apply for admission only is March 15. All program information and application materials can be accessed from the Department's Web site.

Correspondence and Information

Graduate Admissions
Department of Mathematics
University of Utah
155 South 1400 East, JWB 233
Salt Lake City, Utah 84112-0090

Phone: 801-581-6851
Fax: 801-581-4148
E-mail: treibergs@math.utah.edu
Web site: http://www.math.utah.edu/grad

University of Utah

THE FACULTY AND THEIR RESEARCH

Distinguished Professors
M. Bestvina, Ph.D., Tennessee, 1984. Topology.
C. Hacon, Ph.D., UCLA, 1998. Algebraic geometry.
J. P. Keener, Ph.D., Caltech, 1972. Applied mathematics.
G. W. Milton, Ph.D., Cornell, 1985. Materials science.

Professors
F. R. Adler, Ph.D., Cornell, 1991. Mathematical biology.
P. W. Alfeld, Ph.D., Dundee (Scotland), 1977. Numerical analysis.
A. Balk, Ph.D., Moscow Institute of Physics, 1988. Nonlinear phenomena.
A. Bertram, Ph.D., UCLA, 1989. Algebraic geometry and physics.
P. C. Bressloff, Ph.D., King's College (London), 1988. Mathematical biology.
R. M. Brooks, Ph.D., LSU, 1963. Topological algebras.
A. V. Cherkaev, Ph.D., St. Petersburg Technical (Russia), 1979. Applied mathematics.
E. Cherkaev, Ph.D., Leningrad, 1988. Partial differential equations.
D. C. Dobson, Ph.D., Rice, 1990. Partial differential equations.
S. N. Ethier, Ph.D., Wisconsin–Madison, 1975. Probability and statistics.
A. L. Fogelson, Ph.D., NYU, 1982. Computational fluids.
K. M. Golden, Ph.D., NYU, 1984. Applied math.
G. B. Gustafson, Ph.D., Arizona State, 1968. Ordinary differential equations.
H. Hecht, Ph.D., Columbia, 1974. Lie groups.
L. Horvath, Ph.D., Szeged (Hungary), 1982. Probability, statistics.
D. Khoshnevisan, Ph.D., Berkeley, 1989. Probability.
N. J. Korevaar, Ph.D., Stanford, 1981. Partial differential equations.
D. Milicic, Ph.D., Zagreb (Yugoslavia), 1973. Lie groups.
G. Savin, Ph.D., Harvard, 1988. Group representation.
N. Smale, Ph.D., Berkeley, 1987. Differential geometry.
J. L. Taylor, Ph.D., LSU, 1964. Abstract analysis.
D. Toledo, Ph.D., Cornell, 1972. Algebraic and differential geometry.
A. E. Treibergs, Ph.D., Stanford, 1980. Differential geometry.
P. C. Trombi, Ph.D., Illinois at Urbana-Champaign, 1970. Lie groups.
D. H. Tucker, Ph.D., Texas, 1958. Differential equations, functional analysis.

Emeritus Professors
J. A. Carlson, Ph.D., Princeton, 1971. Algebraic geometry.
W. J. Coles, Ph.D., Duke, 1954. Ordinary differential equations.
P. Fife, Ph.D., NYU, 1959. Applied mathematics.
E. S. Folias, Ph.D., Caltech, 1963. Applied mathematics, elasticity.
S. M. Gersten, Ph.D., Cambridge, 1965. Algebra.
L. C. Glaser, Ph.D., Wisconsin–Madison, 1964. Geometric topology.
F. I. Gross, Ph.D., Caltech, 1964. Algebra.
J. D. Mason, Ph.D., California, Riverside, 1968. Probability.
A. D. Roberts, Ph.D., McGill, 1972. Analysis.
P. C. Roberts, Ph.D., McGill, 1974. Commutative algebra, algebraic geometry.
H. Rossi, Ph.D., MIT, 1960. Complex analysis.
K. Schmitt, Ph.D., Nebraska, 1967. Differential equations.

Associate Professors
K. Bromberg, Berkeley, 1998. Topology.
T. de Fernex, Ph.D., Illinois at Chicago, 2002. Algegbraic geometry.
Y. P. Lee, Ph.D., Berkeley, 1999. Algebraic geometry.
W. Niziol, Ph.D., Chicago, 1991. Arithmetical algebraic geometry.
F. Rassoul-Agha, Ph.D., NYU (Courant), 2003. Probability theory.
A. Singh, Ph.D., Michigan, 1998. Commutative algebra.
P. Trapa, Ph.D., MIT, 1998. Representation theory.
J. Zhu, Ph.D., NYU (Courant), 1989. Mathematical finance.

Assistant Professors
A. Borisyuk, Ph.D., NYU (Courant), 2002. Mathematical biology.
D. Ciubotaru, Ph.D., Cornell, 2003. Topological groups, Lie groups.
Y. Epshteyn, Ph.D., Pittsburgh, 2007. Numerical analysis.
F. Guevara Vasquez, Ph.D., Rice, 2006. Partial differential equations.
C. Hohenegger, Ph.D., Georgia Tech, 2006. Fluid mechanics. .
K. Wortman, Ph.D., Chicago, 2003. Geometric group theory.

Research Professors
N. Beebe, Ph.D., Florida, 1972. Numerical analysis.
R. Horn, Ph.D., Stanford, 1967. Matrix analysis.
R. Palais, Ph.D., Berkeley, 1986. Mathematical modeling.

Research Associate Professor
H.-P. Huang, Ph.D., Berkeley, 2000. Functional analysis.

Assistant Professors (Lecturers)
B. Q. Alali, Ph.D., LSU, 2008. Partial differential equations.
C. Cashen, Ph.D., Illinois at Chicago, 2007. Geometric group theory.
D. Conus, Ph.D., Swiss Federal Institute of Technology, 2008. Probability.
J. Dillies, Ph.D., Pennsylvania, 2006. Algebraic geometry.
R. Docampo-Alvarez, Ph.D., Illinois at Chicago, 2009. Algebraic geometry.
R. Easton, Ph.D., Stanford, 2007. Algebraic geometry.
M. Joseph, Ph.D., Wisconsin–Madison, 2009. Probability.
P. S. Kim, Ph.D., Stanford, 2007. Mathematical biology.
E. K. Lakuriqi, Ph.D., Pennsylvania, 2008. Algebraic geometry.
J. Lin, Ph.D., North Carolina, 2009. Applied mathematics.
R. S. Lodh, Ph.D., Bonn, 2007. Algebraic geometry.
D. Onofrei, Ph.D., Worcester Polytechnic, 2007. Partial differential equations.
S. Stirling, Ph.D., Texas at Austin, 2008. Mathematical physics.
J. Tao, Ph.D., Illinois at Chicago, 2009. Geometric group theory.
D. Toth, Ph.D., Washington (Seattle), 2006. Mathematical biology.
L. Yao, Ph.D., North Carolina at Chapel Hill, 2007. Numerical analysis.
M. Zajac, Ph.D., Notre Dame, 2002. Math biology.

VILLANOVA UNIVERSITY

College of Liberal Arts and Sciences
Department of Mathematical Sciences

Programs of Study

The Department of Mathematical Sciences at Villanova University is committed to exemplary teaching, learning, scholarship, and service. Courses are designed to provide every student with the technical background they need and to inculcate a love for the *veritas* of logical thought and elegant reasoning—specifically formalizing, defining, analyzing, proving, and communicating mathematical skills.

Mathematics plays an essential part in every area of modern technology. Recognizing this diverse and important role of mathematics, the Department offers a very flexible Master of Arts (M.A.) in mathematics program built on a core of basic courses and a wide range of specialized electives. Each student is required to complete 30 credit hours, including two courses in analysis, a graduate math seminar, and electives. Graduates can advance their careers in actuarial and accounting firms, the pharmaceutical industry, teaching, and other fields. Some choose to complete their master's degree and enter a doctoral program.

The Master of Science in Applied Statistics (M.S.A.S.) program began as an outgrowth of an earlier certificate in the quality control program. Candidates have six years to complete their degree program, which includes ten courses and a comprehensive exam. Students should consult with the director to formulate a program of study suitable to their individual needs. By the proper selection of electives, a degree candidate may train for work as a systems analyst for a management consulting firm, a statistician for a drug corporation, an operations research analyst, a high school teacher, a two-year-college teacher, a candidate for a doctoral program in mathematics, an actuary for an insurance company, or a number of other careers in mathematics,

The Certificate of Graduate Study in the Teaching of Secondary School Mathematics is explicitly intended for individuals who currently teach secondary school. This 15-credit program consists of five graduate courses that cover geometry, the history of mathematics, statistics, and using technology in the classroom, as well as a special topic. There is at least one course in the certificate program offered during each of the fall and spring semesters and usually two in the summer.

Research Facilities

The University library contains more than 780,000 volumes and 5,600 current periodicals. Special library holdings include the collection of the Augustinian Historical Institute and an extensive collection of works in contemporary Continental philosophy. The Office of University Information Technologies provides data and voice communication, computing services, and access to remote computing and information services over the Internet; offers noncredit seminars and workshops on popular computer software and the use of the Villanova phone system; and maintains state-of-the-art computer labs for students on campus.

The Mathematics Learning Resource Center (MLRC) is a tutoring lab where students can work on individual and group assignments. The modest computer lab has twelve computers, which have mathematical software (Maple, Minitab, SAS, Excel), as well as mathematical tutorial software.

Financial Aid

Graduate assistantships are awarded on a competitive basis. The assistantship stipend began at approximately $13,100 in 2009–10 and carried with it a waiver of all tuition and academic fees. A few research fellowships are also awarded each year. A number of tuition scholarships are available; they provide a waiver of all tuition and academic fees. For priority consideration, those applying for assistantship or scholarship for the academic year should submit credentials by March 15 to be considered for fall of that year. In addition, the Office of the Director of Financial Aid administers the Federal Stafford Student Loan Program.

Cost of Study

Graduate tuition ranged from approximately $630 to $700 per credit hour in 2009–10. In addition, there is a University fee of $30 each semester.

Living and Housing Costs

Although on-campus housing is not available, ample apartments/rooms are available in the suburban neighborhoods surrounding Villanova. The Office of Residence Life offers assistance by providing rental lists to students. Living expenses for a single student are estimated at $13,000 per year.

Student Group

Approximately 2,200 graduate students were enrolled for the fall 2008 term, and 985 were in liberal arts and sciences programs. Total University enrollment is approximately 12,000, including 7,577 full-time undergraduates, 1,000 part-time evening (undergraduate and continuing studies) students, and 1,000 students in the School of Law. There are about equal numbers of men and women graduate students.

Student Outcomes

Some graduates are employed by the nine major pharmaceutical firms in the Philadelphia area. Others choose employment at smaller companies, and some continue their studies in doctoral programs in chemistry and related areas.

Location

Located in a safe, suburban community 12 miles west of Philadelphia, the picturesque 254-acre campus features sixty buildings. Bryn Mawr and Haverford Colleges are nearby, and major universities in Philadelphia (Penn, Temple, Drexel, and others) are easily accessible by public transportation. Philadelphia supports many cultural opportunities including theater, opera, symphony concerts, and ballet, as well as professional sports teams of every variety.

The University

Founded in 1842 by the priests and brothers of the Order of St. Augustine, Villanova University is the oldest and largest Catholic university in the Commonwealth of Pennsylvania. The University's commitment to love and service is reflected in the Latin words of its seal, which translate into truth, unity, and love.

Applying

Applicants for admission to the graduate programs must hold a bachelor's degree, with a 3.0 GPA or higher. Those with degrees in areas other than mathematics and statistics are encouraged to apply. M.A. candidates must have completed undergraduate work in calculus through differential equations and one semester of linear algebra; M.S. candidates must have completed mathematics through multivariable calculus (usually calculus III) and linear algebra. Students with graduate degrees may have the GRE requirement waived with the approval of the Director of the Applied Statistics program.

Students must submit the completed application and nonrefundable $50 fee (online), official GRE scores, and two official undergraduate transcripts, as well as TOEFL scores (if applicable) to the Office of Graduate Studies. In addition, applicants must submit three letters of recommendation to the graduate program director. Deadlines for the fall, spring, and summer semesters are August 1, November 15, and May 1, respectively.

Correspondence and Information

David Sprows, M.A. Program Director
Michael Levitan, M.S.A.S. Program Director
Mathematics Graduate Program
St. Augustine, Room 305
Villanova University
800 Lancaster Avenue
Villanova, Pennsylvania 19085-1699

Phone: 610-519-7339 (M.A. Program)
610-519-4818 (M.S.A.S. Program)
Fax: 610-519-7167
E-mail: david.sprows@villanova.edu
michael.levitan@villanova.edu
Web site: http://www.villanova.edu/artsci/mathematics/graduate/

Villanova University

THE FACULTY AND THEIR RESEARCH

Charles Ashley, Assistant Professor and Assistant Chair; Ph.D., Rensselaer.
Thomas Bartlow, Assistant Professor; Ph.D. History of mathematics.
Marilyn Belkin, Assistant Professor; M.S., Carnegie-Mellon.
Steven Chiacchiere, Instructor; M.A., Villanova. Calculus and statistics.
Alice Deanin, Assistant Professor; Ph.D., Maryland. Number theory, mathematics education.
Robert DeVos, Associate Dean for Enrollment and External Transfer Services and Professor; Ph.D., Lehigh.
Timothy Feeman, Professor; Ph.D., Michigan. Theory of operators on Hilbert spaces, connections between mathematics and cartography.
William Fleischman, Professor; Ph.D., Lehigh.
Jesse C. Frey, Assistant Professor; Ph.D., Ohio State.
Alan Gluchoff, Professor; Ph.D., Wisconsin–Madison. Complex variables (function spaces and operators), univalent functions, inner functions.
Frederick Hartmann, Professor; Ph.D., Lehigh. Problems in classical geometric function theory, computer-aided classroom and laboratory facilities.
Robert Jantzen, Professor; Ph.D., Berkeley. General relativity, differential geometry, Lie groups, CAS educational use.
Martin Kleiber, Associate Professor; Ph.D., Wisconsin–Milwaukee. Topology.
Michael L. Levitan, Associate Professor and Director of the Graduate Program; Ph.D., Minnesota. Statistics, operations research, modeling.
Joyce Longman, Associate Professor; Ph.D., Temple. Math analysis, calculus, linear algebra/differential equations.
R. Edel Lukens, Instructor; M.A., Villanova.
Paul J. Lupinacci, Associate Professor; Ph.D., Temple. Statistics.
Roger Lynn, Associate Professor; Ph.D., NYU. Linear goal programming, mathematical programming with data perturbations.
Osvaldo Marrero, Professor; M.P.H., Ph.D., Miami.
Douglas E. Norton, Associate Professor and Chair; Ph.D., Minnesota. Dynamical systems, mathematical applications in the life sciences, undergraduate mathematics curriculum, encouraging participation of underrepresented groups in science and mathematics, interactions of mathematics with the arts and humanities, pedagogical linkages between secondary and early collegiate mathematics.
Paul Pasles, Associate Professor; Ph.D., Temple. Benjamin Franklin as mathematician.
Joseph Pigeon, Professor; Ph.D., Temple.
Bruce Pollack-Johnson, Associate Professor; Ph.D., Pennsylvania. Operations research, applied math, math modeling, project management.
Michael A. Posner, Assistant Professor; Ph.D., Boston University. Statistical education research, observational studies, biostatistics and public health research, statistics education.
John Santomas, Instructor; M.A., Villanova. Mathematics education and games.
Miriam Seliktar, Assistant Professor; Ph.D., Drexel. Applied mathematics, mathematics education.
Melissa Simone, Instructor and Director of the Mathematics Learning Resource Center.
David Sprows, Professor and Director of the Graduate Program; Ph.D., Pennsylvania. Low dimensional topology, mathematics education.
Robert Styer, Associate Professor; Ph.D., MIT. Analytic and elementary number theory.
Klaus Volpert, Associate Professor; Ph.D., Oregon. Algebraic topology and differential geometry, financial derivatives, specifically volatility.
Andrew Woldar, Professor; Ph.D., Ohio State. Group theory, algebraic combinatorics, graph theory.

WASHINGTON STATE UNIVERSITY

WASHINGTON STATE UNIVERSITY

College of Sciences
Department of Mathematics

Programs of Study

The Department of Mathematics offers graduate programs leading to the M.S., Ph.D., and Ph.D. with teaching emphasis. The M.S. degree program includes an option in applied mathematics, which is tailored to industrial employment, and an option in mathematics teaching. The Ph.D. degree program includes an option in applied mathematics, which allows students from a range of backgrounds to pursue a traditional applied mathematics program while retaining the option to thoroughly learn an area of application. Courses of study are available in all of the principal branches of mathematics, with special emphases in the applied areas of computational mathematics, operations research, discrete mathematics, applied analysis, and mathematical modeling as well as in the more traditional fields of number theory, geometry, algebra, and analysis. The Ph.D. program combines the more traditional orientations usually associated with university teaching and research with options specifically directed toward careers in industry and government. The Ph.D. with teaching emphasis program is designed to prepare exceptionally well-qualified teachers of undergraduate mathematics. The degree program is distinguished from that of the traditional Ph.D. by a greater emphasis on breadth of course work and a critical, historical, or expository thesis.

Research Facilities

All mathematics faculty members and graduate students are housed in Neill Hall. These modern and spacious facilities include offices, seminar rooms, classrooms, consulting rooms, student computer laboratories, and computing facilities. An outstanding collection of mathematics books and journals is housed in the nearby Owen Science and Engineering Library. The Department operates a high-speed network of UNIX and Windows computers for research and instruction. Offices of the graduate students are equipped with computers connected to the network. The University operates a gigabit backbone with high-speed connection to the Internet.

Financial Aid

More than 85 percent of the mathematics graduate students are supported by teaching assistantships; stipends range from $15,075 to $15,858 for the 2009–10 academic year. The teaching assistantships include a full tuition waiver. Normal duties are 20 hours per week teaching classes or assisting a faculty member. Summer teaching assignments for an additional stipend are usually available, as are a few annual research assistantships for advanced students. Federal and state-supported work-study and loan programs are also available. Outstanding applicants receive special scholarships of varying amounts in addition to the assistantship stipend.

Cost of Study

Tuition for full-time study (based on 10 to 18 credit hours per term) is $8456 per academic year for Washington residents and $20,644 per academic year for nonresidents. Part-time and summer students pay on a per-credit-hour basis. There are tuition waivers for teaching and research assistants. In addition to tuition, both resident and nonresident students pay mandatory fees of $1833 per academic year.

Living and Housing Costs

The University maintains a residence center strictly for graduate students as well as a wide variety of single-student and family apartments. Private apartments are readily available at slightly higher rates. An estimate of indirect costs is $14,466 (consisting of $1104 for books and supplies, $9820 for rent/food/utilities, $1434 for transportation expenses, and $2108 for miscellaneous expenses) per academic year.

Student Group

Washington State University (WSU) has four campuses with an enrollment of 23,908, including about 3,400 graduate students; 40 of the latter are in mathematics. The mathematics graduate students come from many areas of the United States and several other countries, and about a dozen complete an advanced degree each year.

Student Outcomes

Recent recipients of advanced degrees have taken positions in academic institutions, in the private sector, and in governmental agencies. The academic appointments include teaching and research at both comprehensive universities and four-year liberal arts colleges. The nonacademic positions include systems analyst, actuary, program manager, senior scientist, research mathematician, reliability analyst, and computer consultant.

Location

Pullman, a city of about 27,600, is located in the heart of the Palouse region in southeastern Washington. It is a rich agricultural area that enjoys clean air and a generally dry, "continental" climate. The area offers easy access to outdoor recreational opportunities such as fishing, hiking, camping, sailing, skiing, and white-water rafting in three states—Washington, Idaho, and Oregon. The on-campus activities both at WSU and at the University of Idaho (8 miles away) contribute greatly to the cultural, athletic, and scientific life of the area.

The University and The Department

The University was founded in 1890 and was the first land-grant institution to establish a chapter of Phi Beta Kappa. Today, the core of the Pullman campus covers nearly 600 acres, and some 100 major buildings house the faculty members and students associated with the more than fifty academic disciplines. Mathematics is the largest department in the Division of Sciences, with a faculty of 27. Master's degrees were first awarded in 1912, and more than 150 mathematics Ph.D.'s have been hooded since 1960.

Applying

Requests for information or applications for admission and financial support should be directed to the Graduate Program Coordinator. Completed applications and other necessary credentials should be submitted as early as possible, preferably by January 10 for fall admission. Applicants are advised to take the Graduate Record Examinations General Test and the Subject Test in mathematics. Also required are copies of transcripts of all previous college work and three letters of recommendation. TOEFL scores must be submitted to the Graduate School by all students whose native language is not English.

Correspondence and Information

Graduate Program Coordinator
Department of Mathematics
Washington State University
Pullman, Washington 99164-3113

Phone: 509-335-6868
E-mail: gradinfo@math.wsu.edu
Web site: http://www.math.wsu.edu

Washington State University

THE FACULTY AND THEIR RESEARCH

Algebra and Number Theory
Bala Krishnamoorthy, Ph.D., North Carolina at Chapel Hill, 2004. Applied algebraic topology, lattice-based approaches in discrete optimization, public key cryptography.
J. J. McDonald, Ph.D., Wisconsin–Madison, 1993. Matrix analysis, linear algebra.
M. J. Tsatsomeros, Ph.D., Connecticut, 1990. Linear algebra, matrix analysis, dynamical systems.
W. A. Webb, Ph.D., Penn State, 1968. Number theory, fair division problems, combinatorics, cryptography.

Analysis
K. R. Vixie, Ph.D., Portland State, 2001. Geometric analysis (geometric measure theory, with pieces of variational analysis, harmonic analysis, and PDEs), geometry in high and infinite dimensions (e.g., concentration of measure, random projections).

Computational Mathematics and Optimization
K. A. Ariyawansa, Ph.D., Toronto, 1983. Mathematical programming and optimization, high-performance computing, operations research, statistical inference methodologies.
Tom Asaki, Ph.D., Washington State, 1995. Mixed variable and direct search optimization with applications to expensive and time-critical problems in engineering design, tomography, and security.
A. Genz, Ph.D., Kent (England), 1976. Numerical analysis, numerical integration, scientific computing, statistical computation.
Bala Krishnamoorthy, Ph.D., North Carolina at Chapel Hill, 2004. Integer optimization, linear programming, computation approaches to protein structure and function.
S. Lapin, Ph.D., Houston, 2005. Scientific computing, mathematical modeling, biomathematics.
R. B. Mifflin, Ph.D., Berkeley, 1971. Operations research, nonsmooth optimization.
D. S. Watkins, Ph.D., Calgary, 1974. Numerical analysis, scientific computing.

Financial Mathematics
H. Li, Ph.D., Arizona, 1994. Stochastic inequalities and multivariate dependence, stochastic processes, reliability, financial risk.
Hong-Ming Yin, Ph. D., Washington State, 1988. Analysis of option pricing models in financial markets.

Geometry
M. Hudelson, Ph.D., Washington (Seattle), 1995. Combinatorics, discrete geometry.
M. J. Kallaher, Ph.D., Syracuse, 1967. Algebra, projective geometry, finite geometries.

Mathematical Data Science
Tom Asaki, Ph.D., Washington State, 1995. Algorithms and optimization techniques for image analysis with applications in dimension reduction, classification, noise removal, segmentation and object identification.
E. J. Schwartz, Ph.D., CUNY, Mount Sinai, 2001. Coupling mathematical approaches with experimental methods in biology.
K. R. Vixie, Ph.D., Portland State, 2001. Image analysis, prototyping data analysis algorithms.

Mathematics Education
S. C. Cooper, Ph.D., Colorado State, 1988. Mathematics education 9–20, transition from secondary to tertiary mathematics, role of mathematics in retention in STEM majors.
L. Knott, Ph.D., Oregon State, 1996. K–16 mathematics education and professional development, mathematics education: conceptual understanding of mathematics, use of representation, proof and justification in mathematics, mathematical discourse.
D. Slavit, Ph.D., Delaware, 1994. Mathematics education, student learning, collaborative teacher professional development.

Modeling
Tom Asaki, Ph.D., Washington State, 1995. Software engineering and algorithm design, mixed-variable optimization, special-application X-ray tomography, image registration and warping, high-dimensional data analysis.
R. H. Dillon, Ph.D., Utah, 1993. Computational biofluids, mathematical biology.
Bala Krishnamoorthy, Ph.D., North Carolina at Chapel Hill, 2004. Geometric models for protein structure and function, models for neck muscle anatomy, habitat reserve management.
V. S. Manoranjan, Ph.D., Dundee (Scotland), 1982. Mathematical modeling, biomathematics, numerical analysis, nonlinear waves.
M. F. Schumaker, Ph.D., Texas at Austin, 1987. Mathematical modeling, biomathematics.
E. J. Schwartz, Ph.D., CUNY, Mount Sinai, 2001. Mathematical biology, infectious disease dynamics, computational biology, epidemiolgoy.
D. J. Wollkind, Ph.D., Rensselaer, 1968. Continuum mechanics, asymptotic methods, stability techniques and mathematical modeling.

Partial Differential Equations and Applications
A. Y. Khapalov, Ph.D., Russian Academy of Sciences, 1982. Control theory for linear and nonlinear PDE's, modeling and motion capabilities for swimming phenomenon, granular material formation problem.
A. N. Panchenko, Ph.D., Delaware, 2000. Partial differential equations of continuum mechanics, homogenization, inverse problems.
Hong-Ming Yin, Ph. D., Washington State, 1988. Partial differential equations with applications to inverse problems, free boundary problems, electromagnetic fields and various industrial problems.

Thesis Titles and Current Positions of Recent Graduates
R. Drake. *A Dynamically Adaptive Method and Spectrum Enveloping Technique.* Research Scientist, Sandia National Laboratories.
A. J. Felt. *A Computational Evaluation of Interior Point Cutting Plane Algorithms for Stochastic Programs.* Assistant Professor of Mathematics, University of Wisconsin–Stevens Point.
C. Gómez-Wulschner. *Compactness of Inductive Limits.* Assistant Professor of Mathematics, Departamento de Mathematicas, Instituto Technológico Autónomo de México.
K. Griffin. *Solving the Principal Minor Assignment Problem and Related Computations.* Senior Principal Software Engineer, Symantec Research Laboratories.
P. Nag. Associate Professor of Mathematics, Black Hills State University.
B. E. Peterson. *Integer Polyhedra and the Perfect Box.* Associate Professor of Mathematics Education, Brigham Young University.
M. Tian. *Pattern Formation Analysis of Thin Liquid Films.* Assistant Professor of Mathematics, Wright State University.
Amy Yielding. *Spectrally Arbitrary Zero-Nonzero Patterns.* Assistant Professor of Mathematics at Eastern Oregon University.
Y. Zhu. *Semidefinite Programming Under Uncertainty.* Assistant Professor of Mathematical Sciences and Applied Computing, Arizona State University–Phoenix.

Washington State University

SELECTED PUBLICATIONS

K. A. Ariyawansa

A class of polynomial volumetric barrier decomposition algorithms for stochastic semidefinite programming. *Math. Comput.,* in press.

A class of collinear scaling algorithms for bound-constrained optimization: Derivation and computational results. *J. Comput. Appl. Math.* 230(1):143–63, 2009.

A class of collinear scaling algorithms for bound-constrained optimization: Convergence theorems. *J. Math. Anal. Appl.* 334(1):716–37, 2007.

A characterization of convexity-preserving maps from a subset of a vector space into another. *J. London Math. Soc.* 64:179–90, 2001.

S. C. Cooper

Influence of teaching approaches and class size on undergraduate mathematical learning. *Primus,* in press.

The strong Chebyshev and orthogonal Laurent polynomials. *J. Approx. Theor.* 92:361–78, 1998.

Extremal properties of strong quadrative weights and maximal mass results for truncated strong moment problems. *JCAM* 80:197–208, 1997.

R. Dillon

A 3D motile rod-shaped monotrichous bacterial model. *Bull. Math. Biol.* 71(5):1228–63, 2009.

A single cell–based model of multicellular growth using the immersed boundary method. In *AMS Contemporary Mathematics: Moving Interface Problems and Applications in Fluid Dynamics,* pp. 1–15, 2008.

An integrative computational model of multiciliary beating. *Bull. Math. Biol.* 70(4):1192–215, 2008.

A single cell–based model of the ductal tumor microarchitecture. *Computational and Mathematical Methods in Medicine* 8(1):51–69, 2007.

A. Genz

Efficient computation of confidence intervals for Bayesian model predictions based on multidimensional parameter space. In *Methods in Enzymology #454: Computer Methods,* pp. 214–30, 2009.

MCQMC methods for multivariate statistical distributions. In *Monte Carlo and Quasi-Monte Carlo Methods,* pp. 35–52, 2008.

Approximation of multiple integrals over hyperboloids with application to a quadratic portfolio with options. *Comput. Stat. Data Anal.,* 52(7):3389–407, 2008.

M. Hudelson

Recurrences Modulo P. *Fibonacci Q.,* in press.

Periodic omnihedral billiards in regular polyhedra and polytopes. *J. Geometry,* in press.

A solution to the generalized Cevian problem using forest polynomials. *J. Comb. Theory Ser. A* 88:297–305, 1999.

M. Kallaher

Translation planes. In *Handbook of Geometry,* pp. 137–92, 1995 (an invited review chapter).

Finite Bol quasifields are nearfields. *Utilitas Math.* 37:45–64, 1990.

A. Y. Khapalov

Multiplicative controllability for the one dimensional parabolic equation with target states admitting finitely many changes of sign. *Discrete and Continuous Dynamical Systems–Series B,* in press.

Controllability of Partial Differential Equations Governed by Multiplicative Controls. Heidelberg-Dordrecht-London-New York: Springer, 2010.

Geometric aspects of force controllability for a swimming model. *Appl. Math. Optim.* 57(1):98–124, 2008.

Local controllability for a "swimming" model. *SIAM J. Contr. Optim.* 46(2):655–82, 2007.

B. Krishnamoorthy

Optimal homologous cycles, total unimodularity, and linear programming. In *Proceedings of the 42nd ACM Symposium on Theory of Computing,* pp. 221–30, 2010.

Column basis reduction and decomposable knapsack problems. *Discrete Optim.* 6(3):242–70, 2009.

Four-body scoring function for mutagenesis. *Bioinformatics* 23(22):3009–15, 2007.

Development of a four-body statistical pseudo-potential to discriminate native from non-native protein conformations. *Bioinformatics* 19(12):1540–8, 2003.

S. Lapin

Non-uniform decay of predictability and return of skill in stochastic oscillatory models. *Phys. Nonlinear Phenom.* 232(2):116–27, 2007.

Design of optimal endprosthesis using mathematical modeling. *Endovasc. Today* 48–50, 2006.

A penalty approach to the numerical solution of the constrained motion. *J. Numer. Math.* 11(4):289–300, 2003.

H. Li

Orthant tail dependence of multivariate extreme value distributions. *J. Multivariate Anal.* 100(1):243–56, 2009.

Conditional tail expectations for multivariate phase type distributions. *J. Appl. Probab.* 42(3):810–25, 2005.

On the coordinated random group replacement policy in multivariate repairable systems. *Oper. Res.* 52(3):464–77, 2004.

Stochastic models for dependent life lengths induced by common pure jump shock environments. *J. Appl. Probab.* 37(2):453–69, 2000.

V. S. Manoranjan

Fuzzy cell mapping applied to autonomous systems. *ASME J. Comput. Information Sci. Eng.,* in press.

On a two-phase Stefan problem arising from a microwave heating process. *Dynamics Continuous Discrete Impulsive Syst. Ser. A* 15:1155–68, 2006.

Plate formation at the surface of a convecting fluid. *Proc. XIII Int. Congress Rheology, Br. Soc. Rheology* 167–9, 2000.

Qualitative study of differential equations. In *MAA Notes No. 50, Revolutions in Differential Equations—Exploring ODEs with Modern Technology,* pp. 59–65, 1999.

J. J. McDonald

On a generalization of soules bases. *SIAM J. Matrix Anal. Appl.* 31(3):1227–34, 2009.

Level characteristics corresponding to peripheral eigenvalues of a nonnegative matrix. *Lin. Algebra Appl.* 429(7):1719–29, 2008.

Spectrally arbitrary zero-nonzero patterns of order 4. *Linear and Multilinear Algebra* 55(3):249–73, 2007.

Inertias of zero-nonzero patterns. *Linear and Multilinear Algebra* 55(3):229–38, 2007.

R. Mifflin

A VU-algorithm for convex minimization. *Math. Program.* 104:583–608, 2005.

VU-smoothness and proximal point results for some nonconvex functions. *Optim. Meth. Software* 19(5):463–78, 2004.

Primal-dual gradient structured functions: Second-order results; links to epi-derivatives and partly smooth functions. *SIAM J. Optim.* 13(4):1174–94, 2002.

Proximal points are on the fast track. *J. Convex Anal.* 9:563–80, 2002.

M. F. Schumaker

Single-occupancy binding in simple bounded and unbounded systems. *Bull. Math. Biol.* 69(6):1979–2003, 2007.

Washington State University

Framework models of ion permeation through membrane channels and the generalized King-Altman method. *Bull. Math. Biol.* 68(7):1429–60, 2006.

A framework model based on the Smoluchowski equation in two reaction coordinates. *J. Chem. Phys.* 121(13):6134–44, 2004.

The role of Trp side chains in tuning single proton conduction through gramicidin channels. *Biophys. J.* 83(2):880–98, 2002.

E. J. Schwartz

Transmission-dynamic model to capture the indirect effects of infant vaccination with Prevnar (7-valent pneumococcal conjugate vaccine (PCV7)) in older populations *Vaccine* 27(34):4694–703, 2009.

Predicting the potential impact of a cytotoxic T-lymphocyte HIV vaccine: How often should you vaccinate and how strong should the vaccine be?. *Math. Biosci.* 212(2):180–7, 2008.

Effectiveness and efficiency of imperfect therapeutic HSV-2 vaccines. *Hum. Vaccine.* 3(6):231–8, 2007.

Predicting the potential individual- and population-level effects of imperfect herpes simplex virus type 2 vaccines. *J. Infect. Dis.* 191(10):1734–46, 2005.

D. Slavit

Perspectives on Supported Collaborative Teacher Inquiry, New York: Routledge, 2009.

Connecting research to teaching: Collaborative teacher inquiry through the use of rich mathematics tasks. *Math. Teach.* 102(7):546–51, 2009.

A culture of collaborative inquiry: Learning to develop and support professional learning communities. *Teachers Coll. Rec.* 110(6):1269–303, 2008.

Teaching mathematics and English to English language learners simultaneously. *Middle Sch. J.* 39(2):4–11, 2007.

M. J. Tsatsomeros

Reachability and holdability of nonnegative states. *SIAM J. Matrix Anal. Appl.,* 30(2):700–12, 2008.

Noncirculant Toeplitz matrices all of whose powers are Toeplitz. *Czech. Math. J.* 58(4):1185–93, 2008.

Mapping and preserver properties of principal pivot transform. *Linear Multilinear Algebra.* 56(3):279–92, 2008.

K. Vixie

A gradient descent solution to the Monge-Kantorovich problem. *Appl. Math. Sci.* 3(22):1071–80, 2009.

Graduated adaptive image denoising: Local compromise between total variation and isotropic diffusion. *Adv. Comput. Math.,* 2008. doi:10.1007/s10444-008-9082-7.

L^1TV computes the flat norm for boundaries. *Abstr. Appl. Anal.* 2007:45153, 2007.

Review of: Deblurring images: Matrices, spectra and filtering. *SIAM Rev.* 49(4):722–5, 2007.

D. S. Watkins

A new block method for computing the Hamiltonian Schur form. *Lin. Algebra Appl.* 431(3-4):350–68, 2009.

Optimizing the hyperpolarizability tensor using external electromagnetic fields and nuclear placement. *J. Chem. Phys.* 131(6):064110, 2009.

Implicit QR algorithms for palindromic and even eigenvalue problems. *Numer. Algorithm.* 51(2):209–38, 2009.

The Matrix Eigenvalue Problem: GR and Krylov Subspace Methods. Philadelphia: SIAM, 2007.

W. Webb

Polynomial Pell's equation II. *J. Number Theory* 106(1):128–41, 2004.

Polynomial Pell's equation. *Proc. Am. Math. Soc.* 131(4):993–1006, 2003.

An algorithm for proving arbitrary identities involving linear recurrences. In *Applications of Fibonacci Numbers,* vol. 10.

Cake Cutting Algorithms. Natick, Mass.: A. K. Peters, 1998.

D. J. Wollkind

Nonlinear stability analyses of vegetative pattern formation in an arid environment. *J. Biol. Dynam.* 4(4):346–80, 2010.

Non-linear stability analyses of optical pattern formation in an atomic sodium vapour ring cavity. *IMA J. Appl. Math.* 73(6):902–35, 2008.

Nonlinear stability analyses of pattern formation on solid surfaces during ion-sputtered erosion. *Mathematical and Computer Modelling* 41:939–64, 2005.

A nonlinear stability analysis of pattern formation in thin liquid films. *Interfaces Free Boundaries* 5:1–25, 2003.

H. Yin

On a degenerate parabolic system. *J. Differ. Equat.* 245(3):722–36, 2008.

On a free boundary problem modelling inductive-heating processes. *Interfaces and Free Boundaries* 10(3):361–76, 2008.

On a phase-change problem arising from inductive heating. *Nonlinear Differ. Equat. Appl.* 13:735–57, 2007.

Existence and regularity of a weak solution to Maxwell's equations with a thermal effect. *Math. Methods Appl. Sci.* 29(10):1199–213, 2006.

WESLEYAN UNIVERSITY

Department of Mathematics

Programs of Study

The Department offers a program of courses and research leading to the degrees of Master of Arts and Doctor of Philosophy.

The Ph.D. degree demands breadth of knowledge, intensive specialization in one field, original contribution to that field, and expository skill. First-year courses are designed to provide a strong foundation in algebra, analysis, and topology. Written preliminary examinations are normally taken after the first year. During the second year, the student continues with a variety of courses, sampling areas of possible concentration. By the start of the third year, the student chooses a specialty and begins research work under the guidance of a thesis adviser. Also required is the ability to read mathematics in at least two of the following languages: French, German, and Russian. The usual time required for completion of all requirements for a Ph.D., including the dissertation, is four to five years.

After passing the preliminary examinations, most Ph.D. candidates teach one course per year, typically a small section (fewer than 20 students) of calculus.

The M.A. degree is designed to ensure basic knowledge and the capacity for sustained scholarly study; requirements are six semester courses at the graduate level and the writing and oral presentation of a thesis. The thesis requires (at least) independent search and study of the literature.

Students are also involved in a variety of Departmental activities, including seminars and colloquiums. The small size of the program contributes to an atmosphere of informality and accessibility.

The emphasis at Wesleyan is in pure mathematics and theoretical computer science, and most Wesleyan Ph.D.'s have chosen academic careers.

Research Facilities

The Department is housed in the Science Center, where all graduate students and faculty members have offices. Computer facilities are available for both learning and research purposes. The Science Library collection has about 120,000 volumes, with extensive mathematics holdings; there are more than 200 subscriptions to mathematics journals, and approximately sixty new mathematics books arrive each month. The proximity of students and faculty and the daily gatherings at teatime are also key elements of the research environment.

Financial Aid

Each applicant for admission is automatically considered for appointment to an assistantship. For the 2010–11 academic year, the stipend is $17,599, plus a dependency allowance when appropriate, and a higher twelve-month stipend is usually available for the student who wishes to remain on campus to study during the summer. Costs of tuition and health fees are borne by the University. All students in good standing are given financial support for the duration of their studies.

Cost of Study

The only academic costs to the student are books and other educational materials.

Living and Housing Costs

The University provides some subsidized housing and assists in finding private housing. The academic-year cost of a single student's housing (a private room in a 2- or 4-person house, with common kitchen and living area) is about $5600.

Student Group

The number of graduate students in mathematics ranges from 18 to 24, with an entering class of 5 to 10 each year. There have always been both male and female students, graduates of small colleges and large universities, and U.S. and international students, including, in recent years, students from Chile, China, India, Iran, Mexico, and Poland.

All of the Department's recent Ph.D. recipients have obtained academic employment. Some of these have subsequently taken positions as industrial mathematicians.

Location

Middletown, Connecticut, is a small city of 40,000 by the Connecticut River, about 19 miles southeast of Hartford and 25 miles northeast of New Haven, midway between New York and Boston. The University provides many cultural and recreational opportunities, supplemented by those in the countryside and in larger cities nearby. Several members of the mathematical community are actively involved in sports, including distance running, golf, handball, hiking, softball, squash, table tennis, volleyball, and cycling.

The University

Founded in 1831, Wesleyan is an independent coeducational institution of liberal arts and sciences, with Ph.D. programs in biology, chemistry, ethnomusicology, mathematics, and physics and master's programs in a number of departments. Current enrollments show about 2,800 undergraduates and 145 graduate students.

Applying

No specific courses are required for admission, but it is expected that the equivalent of an undergraduate major in mathematics will have been completed. The complete application consists of the application form, transcripts of all previous academic work at or beyond the college level, letters of recommendation from 3 college instructors familiar with the applicant's mathematical ability and performance, and GRE scores (if available). Applications should be submitted by February 15 in order to receive adequate consideration, but requests for admission from outstanding candidates are welcome at any time. Preference is given to Ph.D. candidates. A visit to the campus is strongly recommended for its value in determining the suitability of the program for the applicant.

Correspondence and Information

Department of Mathematics and Computer Science
Graduate Education Committee
Wesleyan University
Middletown, Connecticut 06459-0128
Phone: 860-685-2620
E-mail: ccanalia@wesleyan.edu
Web site: http://www.math.wesleyan.edu

Wesleyan University

THE FACULTY AND THEIR RESEARCH

Professors
Karen Collins, Ph.D., MIT. Combinatorics.
Adam Fieldsteel, Ph.D., Berkeley. Ergodic theory.
Mark Hovey, Ph.D., MIT. Algebraic topology and homological algebra.
Michael S. Keane, Dr.rer.nat., Erlangen-Nuremberg. Ergodic theory, random walks, statistical physics.
Philip H. Scowcroft, Ph.D., Cornell. Foundations of mathematics, model-theoretic algebra.
Carol Wood, Ph.D., Yale. Mathematical logic, applications of model theory to algebra.

Associate Professors
Petra Bonfert-Taylor, Ph.D., Berlin Technical. Complex analysis, complex dynamics, geometric function theory, discrete groups.
Wai Kiu Chan, Ph.D., Ohio State. Number theory, quadratic forms.
David Pollack, Ph.D., Harvard. Number theory, automorphic forms, representation of p-adic groups.
Edward C. Taylor, Ph.D., SUNY at Stony Brook. Analysis, low-dimensional geometry and topology.

Assistant Professors
Constance Leidy, Ph.D., Rice. Knot theory, low-dimensional topology.
Christopher Rasmussen, Ph.D., Arizona. Algebraic geometry.

Visiting Professor of Mathematics
James D. Reid, Ph.D., Washington (Seattle). Abelian groups, module theory.

Visiting Instructor of Mathematics
James Frugale, M.A., Wesleyan.

Professors of Computer Science
Danny Krizanc, Ph.D., Harvard. Theoretical computer science.
Michael Rice, Ph.D., Wesleyan. Parallel computing, formal specification methods.

Associate Professors of Computer Science
James Lipton, Ph.D., Cornell. Logic and computation, logic programming, type theory, linear logic.
Norman Danner, Ph.D., Indiana Bloomington. Logic, theoretical computer science.

Assistant Professor of Computer Science
Eric Aaron, Ph.D., Cornell. Intelligent virtual agents, reasoning about navigation, hybrid systems, game artificial intelligence, behavioral animation/robotics, applied logic, cognitive modeling, attention, automated verification, tumor modeling.

Professors Emeriti
W. Wistar Comfort, Ph.D., Washington (Seattle). Point-set topology, ultrafilters, set theory, topological groups.
Ethan M. Coven, Ph.D., Yale. Dynamical systems.
Anthony W. Hager, Ph.D., Penn State. Lattice-ordered algebraic structures, general and categorical topology.
F. E. J. Linton, Ph.D., Columbia. Categorical algebra, functorial semantics, topoi.
James D. Reid, Ph.D., Washington (Seattle). Abelian groups, module theory.
Lewis C. Robertson, Ph.D., UCLA. Lie groups, topological groups, representation theory.
Robert A. Rosenbaum, Ph.D., Yale. Geometry, mathematics and science education.

Faculty-student conferences, daily gatherings at teatime, and discussions in graduate students' offices are key ingredients of the research environment in the Department of Mathematics.

ACADEMIC AND PROFESSIONAL PROGRAMS IN THE AGRICULTURAL SCIENCES

Section 8
Agricultural and Food Sciences

This section contains a directory of institutions offering graduate work in agricultural and food sciences, followed by in-depth entries submitted by institutions that chose to prepare detailed program descriptions. Additional information about programs listed in the directory but not augmented by an in-depth entry may be obtained by writing directly to the dean of a graduate school or chair of a department at the address given in the directory.

For programs offering related work, see also in this book *Natural Resources.* In the other guides in this series:

Graduate Programs in the Humanities, Arts & Social Sciences

See *Architecture (Landscape Architecture)* and *Economics (Agricultural Economics and Agribusiness)*

Graduate Programs in the Biological Sciences

See *Biological and Biomedical Sciences; Botany and Plant Biology; Ecology, Environmental Biology, and Evolutionary Biology; Entomology; Genetics, Developmental Biology, and Reproductive Biology; Nutrition; Pathology and Pathobiology; Physiology;* and *Zoology*

Graduate Programs in Engineering & Applied Sciences

See *Agricultural Engineering and Bioengineering* and *Biomedical Engineering and Biotechnology*

Graduate Programs in Business, Education, Health, Information Studies, Law & Social Work

See *Education (Agricultural Education)* and *Veterinary Medicine and Sciences*

CONTENTS

Program Directories

Agricultural Sciences—General

Alabama Agricultural and Mechanical University, School of Graduate Studies, School of Agricultural and Environmental Sciences, Huntsville, AL 35811. Offers MS, MURP, PhD. Part-time and evening/weekend programs available. Terminal master's awarded for partial completion of doctoral program. *Degree requirements:* For doctorate, one foreign language, thesis/dissertation. *Entrance requirements:* For master's, GRE General Test; for doctorate, GRE General Test, MS. Additional exam requirements/recommendations for international students: Required—TOEFL (minimum score 500 paper-based; 173 computer-based; 61 iBT). Electronic applications accepted. *Faculty research:* Remote sensing, environmental pollutants, food biotechnology, plant growth.

Alcorn State University, School of Graduate Studies, School of Agriculture and Applied Science, Alcorn State, MS 39096-7500. Offers agricultural economics (MS Ag); agronomy (MS Ag); animal science (MS Ag). *Degree requirements:* For master's, thesis optional. *Faculty research:* Aquatic systems, dairy herd improvement, fruit production, alternative farming practices.

Angelo State University, College of Graduate Studies, College of Sciences, Department of Agriculture, San Angelo, TX 76909. Offers animal science (MS). Part-time and evening/weekend programs available. *Faculty:* 4 full-time (0 women). *Students:* 17 full-time (7 women), 4 part-time (2 women); includes 1 minority (Hispanic American). Average age 23. 7 applicants, 100% accepted, 5 enrolled. In 2009, 5 master's awarded. *Degree requirements:* For master's, comprehensive exam, thesis optional. *Entrance requirements:* For master's, GRE General Test. Additional exam requirements/recommendations for international students: Required—TOEFL or IELTS. *Application deadline:* For fall admission, 7/15 priority date for domestic students, 6/10 for international students; for spring admission, 12/1 priority date for domestic students, 11/1 for international students. Applications are processed on a rolling basis. Application fee: $40 ($50 for international students). Electronic applications accepted. *Expenses:* Tuition, state resident: full-time $3396; part-time $142 per credit hour. Tuition, nonresident: full-time $10,152; part-time $423 per credit hour. Required fees: $1786; $36.25 per credit hour. $494 per semester. Full-time tuition and fees vary according to course load, degree level and program. *Financial support:* In 2009–10, 10 students received support, including 9 research assistantships (averaging $9,887 per year); Federal Work-Study, scholarships/grants, and unspecified assistantships also available. Support available to part-time students. Financial award application deadline: 3/1. *Faculty research:* Effect of protein and energy on feedlot performance, bitterweed toxicosis in sheep, meat laboratory, North Concho watershed project, baseline vegetation. *Unit head:* Dr. Gilbert R. Engdahl, Department Head, 325-942-2027 Ext. 227, E-mail: gil.engdahl@angelo.edu. *Application contact:* Dr. Cody B. Scott, Graduate Advisor, 325-942-2027 Ext. 284, E-mail: cody.scott@angelo.edu.

Arkansas State University—Jonesboro, Graduate School, College of Agriculture and Technology, Jonesboro, State University, AR 72467. Offers agricultural education (MSA, SCCT); agriculture (MSA); vocational-technical administration (MS, SCCT). Part-time programs available. *Faculty:* 8 full-time (0 women), 3 part-time/adjunct (1 woman). *Students:* 7 full-time (1 woman), 24 part-time (14 women); includes 3 minority (all African Americans), 10 international. Average age 28. 19 applicants, 74% accepted, 11 enrolled. In 2009, 10 master's awarded. *Degree requirements:* For master's, comprehensive exam, thesis or alternative; for SCCT, comprehensive exam. *Entrance requirements:* For master's, GRE General Test or MAT, appropriate bachelor's degree; for SCCT, GRE General Test or MAT, interview, master's degree, official transcript, immunization records. Additional exam requirements/recommendations for international students: Required—TOEFL (minimum score 550 paper-based; 213 computer-based; 79 iBT), IELTS (minimum score 6). *Application deadline:* For fall admission, 7/15 for domestic students, 7/1 for international students; for spring admission, 12/1 for domestic students, 11/13 for international students. Applications are processed on a rolling basis. Application fee: $30 ($40 for international students). Electronic applications accepted. *Expenses:* Tuition, state resident: full-time $3744; part-time $208 per credit hour. Tuition, nonresident: full-time $9540; part-time $530 per credit hour. Required fees: $896; $47 per credit hour. $25 per term. One-time fee: $50. Tuition and fees vary according to course load and program. *Financial support:* In 2009–10, 8 students received support; teaching assistantships, career-related internships or fieldwork, scholarships/grants, and unspecified assistantships available. Financial award application deadline: 7/1; financial award applicants required to submit FAFSA. *Unit head:* Dr. Gregory Phillips, Dean, 870-972-2085, Fax: 870-972-3885, E-mail: gphillips@astate.edu. *Application contact:* Dr. Andrew Sustich, Dean of the Graduate School, 870-972-3029, Fax: 870-972-3857, E-mail: sustich@astate.edu.

Auburn University, Graduate School, College of Agriculture, Auburn University, AL 36849. Offers M Ag, M Aq, MS, PhD. Part-time programs available. *Faculty:* 150 full-time (30 women), 1 part-time/adjunct (0 women). *Students:* 133 full-time (54 women), 123 part-time (48 women); includes 19 minority (8 African Americans, 2 American Indian/Alaska Native, 6 Asian Americans or Pacific Islanders, 3 Hispanic Americans), 106 international. Average age 29. 204 applicants, 45% accepted, 55 enrolled. In 2009, 48 master's, 17 doctorates awarded. *Degree requirements:* For doctorate, thesis/dissertation. *Entrance requirements:* For master's and doctorate, GRE General Test. *Application deadline:* For fall admission, 7/7 for domestic students; for spring admission, 11/24 for domestic students. Applications are processed on a rolling basis. Application fee: $50 ($60 for international students). Electronic applications accepted. *Expenses:* Tuition, state resident: full-time $6240. Tuition, nonresident: full-time $18,720. International tuition: $18,938 full-time. Required fees: $492. Tuition and fees vary according to course load, program and reciprocity agreements. *Financial support:* Fellowships, research assistantships, teaching assistantships, Federal Work-Study available. Support available to part-time students. Financial award application deadline: 3/15; financial award applicants required to submit FAFSA. *Unit head:* Dr. Richard Guthrie, Dean, 334-844-2345. *Application contact:* Dr. George Flowers, Dean of the Graduate School, 334-844-2125.

Brigham Young University, Graduate Studies, College of Life Sciences, Provo, UT 84602-1001. Offers MPH, MS, PhD. Part-time programs available. *Faculty:* 124 full-time (15 women), 15 part-time/adjunct (3 women). *Students:* 174 full-time (82 women), 69 part-time (31 women); includes 30 minority (2 African Americans, 2 American Indian/Alaska Native, 14 Asian Americans or Pacific Islanders, 12 Hispanic Americans), 11 international. Average age 29. 158 applicants, 57% accepted, 73 enrolled. In 2009, 59 master's, 13 doctorates awarded. *Degree requirements:* For master's, comprehensive exam, thesis; for doctorate, comprehensive exam, thesis/dissertation. *Entrance requirements:* For master's and doctorate, GRE General Test, minimum GPA of 3.0 for last 60 hours of course work. Additional exam requirements/recommendations for international students: Required—TOEFL (minimum score 580 paper-based; 237 computer-based; 85 iBT), IELTS (minimum score 7). *Application deadline:* For fall admission, 1/31 for domestic and international students. Application fee: $50. Electronic applications accepted. *Expenses:* Tuition: Full-time $5580; part-time $301 per credit hour. Tuition and fees vary according to student's religious affiliation. *Financial support:* In 2009–10, 144 students received support, including 26 fellowships with partial tuition reimbursements available (averaging $4,322 per year), 64 research assistantships with full and partial tuition reimbursements available (averaging $12,840 per year), 94 teaching assistantships with full and partial tuition reimbursements available (averaging $15,996 per year); career-related internships or fieldwork, institutionally sponsored loans, scholarships/grants, tuition waivers (full and partial), unspecified assistantships, and tuition awards also available. Financial award application deadline: 2/1. Total annual research expenditures: $4.3 million. *Unit head:* Dr. Rodney J. Brown, Dean, 801-422-3963, Fax: 801-422-0050. *Application contact:* Sue Pratley, Application Contact, 801-422-3963, Fax: 801-422-0050, E-mail: sue_pratley@byu.edu.

California Polytechnic State University, San Luis Obispo, College of Agriculture, Food and Environmental Sciences, Department of Agriculture, San Luis Obispo, CA 93407. Offers MS. Part-time programs available. *Faculty:* 29 full-time (8 women), 4 part-time/adjunct (1 woman). *Students:* 57 full-time (34 women), 50 part-time (27 women); includes 16 minority (1 African American, 1 Asian American or Pacific Islander, 14 Hispanic Americans), 4 international. Average age 27. 69 applicants, 49% accepted, 29 enrolled. In 2009, 36 master's awarded. *Degree requirements:* For master's, comprehensive exam, thesis. *Entrance requirements:* For master's, GRE, minimum GPA of 2.75 in last 90 quarter units of course work. Additional exam requirements/recommendations for international students: Required—TOEFL (minimum score 550 paper-based; 213 computer-based), or IELTS (minimum score 6). *Application deadline:* For fall admission, 2/1 for domestic students, 11/30 for international students; for winter admission, 11/1 for domestic students, 6/30 for international students; for spring admission, 2/1 for domestic students. Applications are processed on a rolling basis. Application fee: $55. Electronic applications accepted. *Expenses:* Tuition, nonresident: full-time $11,160; part-time $248 per unit. Required fees: $7134; $1553 per quarter. *Financial support:* Fellowships, research assistantships, teaching assistantships, career-related internships or fieldwork, Federal Work-Study, institutionally sponsored loans, scholarships/grants, and unspecified assistantships available. Support available to part-time students. Financial award application deadline: 3/2; financial award applicants required to submit FAFSA. *Unit head:* Dr. Mark Shelton, Associate Dean/Graduate Coordinator, 805-756-2161, Fax: 805-756-6577, E-mail: mshelton@calpoly.edu. *Application contact:* Dr. Mark Shelton, Associate Dean/Graduate Coordinator, 805-756-2161, Fax: 805-756-6577, E-mail: mshelton@calpoly.edu.

California State Polytechnic University, Pomona, Academic Affairs, College of Agriculture, Pomona, CA 91768-2557. Offers MS. Part-time programs available. *Faculty:* 36 full-time (13 women), 13 part-time/adjunct (7 women). *Students:* 20 full-time (17 women), 49 part-time (41 women); includes 26 minority (2 African Americans, 13 Asian Americans or Pacific Islanders, 11 Hispanic Americans), 7 international. Average age 29. 69 applicants, 54% accepted, 30 enrolled. In 2009, 12 master's awarded. *Degree requirements:* For master's, thesis or alternative. *Application deadline:* For fall admission, 5/1 priority date for domestic students; for winter admission, 10/15 priority date for domestic students; for spring admission, 1/2 priority date for domestic students. Applications are processed on a rolling basis. Application fee: $55. Electronic applications accepted. *Expenses:* Tuition, nonresident: full-time $6696; part-time $248 per credit. Required fees: $5487; $3237 per term. Tuition and fees vary according to course load, degree level and program. *Financial support:* Career-related internships or fieldwork, Federal Work-Study, and institutionally sponsored loans available. Support available to part-time students. Financial award application deadline: 3/2; financial award applicants required to submit FAFSA. *Faculty research:* Equine nutrition, physiology, and reproduction; leadership development; bioartificial pancreas; plant science; ruminant and human nutrition. *Unit head:* Dr. Lester C. Young, Interim Dean, 909-869-2203, E-mail: lcyoung@csupomona.edu. *Application contact:* Dan Hostetler, Chair/Professor, 909-869-2189, Fax: 909-869-5036, E-mail: dghostetler@csupomona.edu.

Clemson University, Graduate School, College of Agriculture, Forestry and Life Sciences, Clemson, SC 29634. Offers M Ag Ed, MFR, MS, PhD. Part-time programs available. *Faculty:* 187 full-time (53 women), 18 part-time/adjunct (6 women). *Students:* 372 full-time (193 women), 75 part-time (30 women); includes 22 minority (10 African Americans, 1 American Indian/Alaska Native, 6 Asian Americans or Pacific Islanders, 5 Hispanic Americans), 121 international. Average age 28. 498 applicants, 36% accepted, 99 enrolled. In 2009, 73 master's, 50 doctorates awarded. Terminal master's awarded for partial completion of doctoral program. *Degree requirements:* For master's, thesis (for some programs); for doctorate, thesis/dissertation. *Entrance requirements:* For master's and doctorate, GRE General Test. Additional exam requirements/recommendations for international students: Required—TOEFL. *Application deadline:* For fall admission, 4/15 for domestic and international students; for spring admission, 10/1 for domestic students, 9/15 for international students. Applications are processed on a rolling basis. Application fee: $70 ($80 for international students). Electronic applications accepted. *Expenses:* Contact institution. *Financial support:* In 2009–10, 333 students received support, including 59 fellowships with full and partial tuition reimbursements available (averaging $9,554 per year), 145 research assistantships with partial tuition reimbursements available (averaging $16,670 per year), 149 teaching assistantships with partial tuition reimbursements available (averaging $16,303 per year); career-related internships or fieldwork, Federal Work-Study, institutionally sponsored loans, scholarships/grants, and unspecified assistantships also available. Financial award applicants required to submit FAFSA. Total annual research expenditures: $9.4 million. *Unit head:* Dr. Thomas Scott, Dean, 864-656-7592, Fax: 864-656-1286. *Application contact:* Dr. Joseph Culin, Associate Dean for Research and Graduate Studies, 864-656-2810, E-mail: jculin@clemson.edu.

Colorado State University, Graduate School, College of Agricultural Sciences, Fort Collins, CO 80523-1101. Offers M Agr, MS, PhD. Part-time and evening/weekend programs available. Postbaccalaureate distance learning degree programs offered (no on-campus study). *Faculty:* 93 full-time (17 women), 3 part-time/adjunct (0 women). *Students:* 137 full-time (71 women), 116 part-time (48 women); includes 20 minority (4 African Americans, 7 American Indian/Alaska Native, 1 Asian American or Pacific Islander, 8 Hispanic Americans), 39 international. Average age 30. 238 applicants, 56% accepted, 69 enrolled. In 2009, 60 master's, 13 doctorates awarded. *Degree requirements:* For master's, thesis (for some programs); for doctorate, comprehensive exam (for some programs), thesis/dissertation. *Entrance requirements:* For master's and doctorate, GRE General Test, minimum GPA of 3.0, 3 letters of recommendation, bachelor's degree. Additional exam requirements/recommendations for international students: Recommended—TOEFL (minimum score 550 paper-based; 150 computer-based). *Application deadline:* For fall admission, 7/1 for domestic and international students; for spring admission, 1/1 for domestic and international students. Applications are processed on a rolling basis. Application fee: $50. Electronic applications accepted. *Expenses:* Tuition, state resident: full-time $6434; part-time $359.10 per credit. Tuition, nonresident: full-time $18,116; part-time $1006.45 per credit. Required fees: $1496; $83 per credit. *Financial support:* In 2009–10, 134 students received support, including 13 fellowships (averaging $32,554 per year), 97 research assistantships (averaging $13,827 per year), 24 teaching assistantships (averaging $11,101 per year); scholarships/grants and unspecified assistantships also available. Financial award applicants required to submit FAFSA. *Faculty research:* Systems methodology, biotechnology, plant and animal breeding, water management, plant protection. Total annual research expenditures: $11.9 million. *Unit head:* Dr. Lee Sommers, Interim Dean, 970-491-1421, Fax: 970-491-4895, E-mail: lee.sommers@colostate.edu. *Application contact:* Pam Schell, Administrative Assistant, 970-491-2410, Fax: 970-491-4895, E-mail: pam.schell@colostate.edu.

Dalhousie University, Faculty of Graduate Studies, Nova Scotia Agricultural College, Truro, NS B2N 5E3, Canada. Offers M Sc. Part-time programs available. *Degree requirements:* For master's, thesis, candidacy exam. *Entrance requirements:* For master's, minimum GPA of 3.0. Additional exam requirements/recommendations for international students: Required—TOEFL, IELTS, 1 of the following 5 approved tests: TOEFL, IELTS, CANTEST, CAEL, Michigan English Language Assessment Battery. Electronic applications accepted. *Faculty research:* Agribiology, soil science, animal science, plant science, and agricultural chemistry.

Florida Agricultural and Mechanical University, Division of Graduate Studies, Research, and Continuing Education, College of Engineering Science, Technology, and Agriculture, Division of Agricultural Sciences, Tallahassee, FL 32307-3200. Offers agribusiness (MS); animal science (MS); engineering technology (MS); entomology (MS); food science (MS); international programs (MS); plant science (MS). *Faculty:* 31 full-time (2 women). *Students:* 14

full-time (8 women), 8 part-time (4 women); includes 17 minority (16 African Americans, 1 Asian American or Pacific Islander), 3 international. In 2009, 7 master's awarded. *Degree requirements:* For master's, thesis. *Entrance requirements:* For master's, GRE General Test, minimum GPA of 3.0. Additional exam requirements/recommendations for international students: Required—TOEFL (minimum score 500 paper-based). *Application deadline:* For fall admission, 5/18 for domestic students, 12/18 for international students; for spring admission, 11/12 for domestic students, 5/12 for international students. Application fee: $20. *Financial support:* Application deadline: 2/15. *Unit head:* Dr. Mitwe N. Musingo, Graduate Coordinator, 850-561-2309, Fax: 850-599-8821. *Application contact:* Dr. Chanta M. Haywood, Dean of Graduate Studies, Research, and Continuing Education, 850-599-3315, Fax: 850-599-3727.

Illinois State University, Graduate School, College of Applied Science and Technology, Department of Agriculture, Normal, IL 61790-2200. Offers agribusiness (MS). *Degree requirements:* For master's, thesis optional. *Entrance requirements:* For master's, GRE General Test, minimum GPA of 3.0 in last 60 hours. *Faculty research:* Engineering-economic system models for rural ethanol production facilities, development and evaluation of a propane-fueled, production scale, on-site thermal destruction system C-FAR 2007; field scale evaluation and technology transfer of economically, ecologically systems; sound liquid swine manure treatment and application.

Instituto Tecnológico y de Estudios Superiores de Monterrey, Campus Monterrey, Graduate and Research Division, Program in Agriculture, Monterrey, Mexico. Offers agricultural parasitology (PhD); agricultural sciences (MS); farming productivity (MS); food processing engineering (MS); phytopathology (MS). Part-time programs available. *Degree requirements:* For master's, one foreign language, thesis; for doctorate, one foreign language, thesis/dissertation. *Entrance requirements:* For master's, EXADEP; for doctorate, GMAT or GRE, master's degree in related field. Additional exam requirements/recommendations for international students: Required—TOEFL. *Faculty research:* Animal embryos and reproduction, crop entomology, tropical agriculture, agricultural productivity, induced mutation in oleaginous plants.

Iowa State University of Science and Technology, Graduate College, College of Agriculture, Ames, IA 50011. Offers M Ag, MS, PhD. Part-time programs available. Postbaccalaureate distance learning degree programs offered (no on-campus study). *Faculty:* 309 full-time (63 women), 29 part-time/adjunct (11 women). *Students:* 422 full-time (179 women), 198 part-time (65 women); includes 37 minority (15 African Americans, 3 American Indian/Alaska Native, 10 Asian Americans or Pacific Islanders, 9 Hispanic Americans), 181 international. 436 applicants, 35% accepted, 124 enrolled. In 2009, 76 master's, 34 doctorates awarded. *Degree requirements:* For doctorate, thesis/dissertation. *Entrance requirements:* Additional exam requirements/recommendations for international students: Required—TOEFL. *Application deadline:* Applications are processed on a rolling basis. Application fee: $40 ($90 for international students). Electronic applications accepted. *Expenses:* Tuition, state resident: full-time $6716. Tuition, nonresident: full-time $8908. Tuition and fees vary according to course level, course load, program and student level. *Financial support:* In 2009–10, 215 research assistantships with full and partial tuition reimbursements (averaging $15,870 per year), 24 teaching assistantships with full and partial tuition reimbursements (averaging $16,000 per year) were awarded; fellowships, Federal Work-Study, scholarships/grants, health care benefits, and unspecified assistantships also available. Support available to part-time students. *Unit head:* Dr. Wendy Wintersteen, Dean, 515-294-2518, Fax: 515-294-6800. *Application contact:* Information Contact, 515-294-5836, Fax: 515-294-2592, E-mail: grad_admissions@iastate.edu.

Iowa State University of Science and Technology, Graduate College, Interdisciplinary Programs, Program in Sustainable Agriculture, Ames, IA 50011. Offers MS, PhD. *Students:* 26 full-time (16 women), 7 part-time (3 women); includes 2 minority (1 Asian American or Pacific Islander, 1 Hispanic American), 7 international. In 2009, 5 master's, 1 doctorate awarded. *Degree requirements:* For master's, thesis or alternative; for doctorate, thesis/dissertation. *Entrance requirements:* For master's and doctorate, GRE General Test. Additional exam requirements/recommendations for international students: Required—TOEFL (minimum score 570 paper-based; 80 iBT) or IELTS (minimum score 6.5). *Application deadline:* For fall admission, 2/1 for domestic and international students; for spring admission, 6/1 priority date for domestic and international students. Application fee: $40 ($90 for international students). *Expenses:* Tuition, state resident: full-time $6716. Tuition, nonresident: full-time $8908. Tuition and fees vary according to course level, course load, program and student level. *Financial support:* In 2009–10, 23 research assistantships with full and partial tuition reimbursements (averaging $15,870 per year), 3 teaching assistantships with full and partial tuition reimbursements (averaging $15,860 per year) were awarded. *Unit head:* Dr. Mary Wiedenhoeft, Chair, Supervising Committee, 515-294-6518, E-mail: gpsa@iastate.edu. *Application contact:* Charles Sauer, Information Contact, 515-294-6518, E-mail: gpsa@iastate.edu.

Kansas State University, Graduate School, College of Agriculture, Manhattan, KS 66506. Offers MAB, MS, PhD. Part-time programs available. Postbaccalaureate distance learning degree programs offered (minimal on-campus study). *Faculty:* 173 full-time (30 women), 42 part-time/adjunct (6 women). *Students:* 297 full-time (122 women), 138 part-time (82 women); includes 30 minority (16 African Americans, 4 American Indian/Alaska Native, 10 Hispanic Americans), 130 international. Average age 30. 249 applicants, 52% accepted, 78 enrolled. In 2009, 92 master's, 24 doctorates awarded. Terminal master's awarded for partial completion of doctoral program. *Degree requirements:* For doctorate, thesis/dissertation. *Entrance requirements:* For master's, GRE, minimum undergraduate GPA of 3.0; for doctorate, GRE, minimum undergraduate GPA of 3.5. Additional exam requirements/recommendations for international students: Required—TOEFL (minimum score 550 paper-based; 213 computer-based). *Application deadline:* For fall admission, 2/1 priority date for domestic and international students; for spring admission, 8/1 priority date for domestic and international students. Applications are processed on a rolling basis. Application fee: $40 ($55 for international students). Electronic applications accepted. *Financial support:* In 2009–10, 258 research assistantships (averaging $14,892 per year), 8 teaching assistantships (averaging $14,523 per year) were awarded; career-related internships or fieldwork, Federal Work-Study, institutionally sponsored loans, scholarships/grants, and tuition waivers (partial) also available. Support available to part-time students. Financial award application deadline: 3/1; financial award applicants required to submit FAFSA. *Unit head:* Gary M. Pierzynski, Interim Dean, 785-532-6101, Fax: 785-532-6563, E-mail: gmp@ksu.edu. *Application contact:* Gary M. Pierzynski, Interim Dean, 785-532-6101, Fax: 785-532-6563, E-mail: gmp@ksu.edu.

Louisiana State University and Agricultural and Mechanical College, Graduate School, College of Agriculture, Baton Rouge, LA 70803. Offers M App St, MS, MSBAE, PhD. Part-time programs available. *Students:* 332 full-time (152 women), 137 part-time (83 women); includes 46 minority (27 African Americans, 1 American Indian/Alaska Native, 7 Asian Americans or Pacific Islanders, 11 Hispanic Americans), 153 international. Average age 31. 275 applicants, 54% accepted, 79 enrolled. In 2009, 73 master's, 39 doctorates awarded. Terminal master's awarded for partial completion of doctoral program. *Degree requirements:* For doctorate, thesis/dissertation. *Entrance requirements:* For master's and doctorate, GRE General Test, minimum GPA of 3.0. Additional exam requirements/recommendations for international students: Required—TOEFL (minimum score 550 paper-based; 213 computer-based; 79 iBT) or IELTS (minimum score 6.5). *Application deadline:* For fall admission, 5/15 for domestic and international students; for spring admission, 10/15 for domestic and international students. Applications are processed on a rolling basis. Application fee: $50 ($70 for international students). Electronic applications accepted. *Financial support:* In 2009–10, 348 students received support, including 12 fellowships with full tuition reimbursements available (averaging $26,530 per year), 226 research assistantships with partial tuition reimbursements available (averaging $17,455 per year), 47 teaching assistantships with partial tuition reimbursements available (averaging $13,072 per year); career-related internships or fieldwork, Federal Work-Study, institutionally sponsored loans, health care benefits, tuition waivers (full), and unspecified assistantships also available. Support available to part-time students. Financial award applicants required to submit FAFSA. *Faculty research:* Biotechnology, resource economics and marketing, aquaculture, food science and technology. Total annual research expenditures: $340,773. *Unit head:* Dr. Kenneth Koonce, Dean, 225-578-2362, Fax: 225-578-2526, E-mail: kkoonce@lsu.edu. *Application contact:* Paula Beecher, Recruiting Coordinator, 225-578-2468, E-mail: pbeeche@lsu.edu.

McGill University, Faculty of Graduate and Postdoctoral Studies, Faculty of Agricultural and Environmental Sciences, Montréal, QC H3A 2T5, Canada. Offers M Sc, M Sc A, PhD, Certificate, Graduate Diploma.

McNeese State University, Doré School of Graduate Studies, College of Science, Department of Agricultural Sciences, Program in Environmental and Chemical Sciences, Lake Charles, LA 70609. Offers agricultural sciences (MS); environmental and chemical science (MS). Evening/weekend programs available. *Degree requirements:* For master's, comprehensive exam, thesis or alternative. *Entrance requirements:* For master's, GRE.

Michigan State University, The Graduate School, College of Agriculture and Natural Resources, East Lansing, MI 48824. Offers MA, MIPS, MS, MURP, PhD. *Faculty research:* Plant science, animal sciences, forestry, fisheries and wildlife, recreation and tourism.

Mississippi State University, College of Agriculture and Life Sciences, Department of Biochemistry and Molecular Biology, Mississippi State, MS 39762. Offers agriculture life sciences (MS), including biochemistry; molecular biology (PhD). *Faculty:* 7 full-time (0 women). *Students:* 23 full-time (7 women), 4 part-time (3 women); includes 3 minority (1 African American, 1 American Indian/Alaska Native, 1 Asian American or Pacific Islander), 14 international. Average age 27. 20 applicants, 40% accepted, 2 enrolled. In 2009, 2 master's, 3 doctorates awarded. Terminal master's awarded for partial completion of doctoral program. *Degree requirements:* For master's, thesis (for some programs), comprehensive oral or written exam; for doctorate, thesis/dissertation, comprehensive oral and written exam. *Entrance requirements:* For master's, GRE General Test, minimum GPA of 2.75; for doctorate, GRE. Additional exam requirements/recommendations for international students: Required—TOEFL (minimum score 550 paper-based; 213 computer-based; 79 iBT); Recommended—IELTS (minimum score 6.5). *Application deadline:* For fall admission, 7/1 for domestic students, 5/1 for international students; for spring admission, 11/1 for domestic students, 9/1 for international students. Applications are processed on a rolling basis. Application fee: $40. Electronic applications accepted. *Expenses:* Tuition, state resident: full-time $2575.50; part-time $286.25 per credit hour. Tuition, nonresident: full-time $6510; part-time $723.50 per credit hour. Tuition and fees vary according to course load. *Financial support:* In 2009–10, 16 research assistantships with full tuition reimbursements (averaging $11,115 per year) were awarded; Federal Work-Study, institutionally sponsored loans, and unspecified assistantships also available. Financial award applicants required to submit FAFSA. *Faculty research:* Fish nutrition, plant and animal molecular biology, plant biochemistry, enzymology, lipid metabolism. *Unit head:* Dr. Scott T. Willard, Professor and Department Head, 662-325-2640, Fax: 662-325-8664, E-mail: swilliard@ads.msstate.edu. *Application contact:* Dr. Din-Pow Ma, Professor/Graduate Coordinator, 662-325-7739, Fax: 662-325-8664, E-mail: dm1@ra.msstate.edu.

Mississippi State University, College of Agriculture and Life Sciences, Department of Entomology and Plant Pathology, Mississippi State, MS 39762. Offers agricultural life sciences (MS), including entomology and plant pathology (MS, PhD); life sciences (PhD), including entomology and plant pathology (MS, PhD). *Faculty:* 18 full-time (1 woman). *Students:* 16 full-time (5 women), 5 part-time (3 women); includes 2 minority (1 Asian American or Pacific Islander, 1 Hispanic American), 4 international. Average age 35. 12 applicants, 33% accepted, 2 enrolled. In 2009, 3 master's, 3 doctorates awarded. *Degree requirements:* For master's, thesis; for doctorate, thesis/dissertation. *Entrance requirements:* For master's, GRE General Test, minimum GPA of 2.75; for doctorate, GRE General Test. Additional exam requirements/recommendations for international students: Required—TOEFL (minimum score 475 paper-based; 153 computer-based; 53 iBT); Recommended—IELTS (minimum score 4.5). *Application deadline:* For fall admission, 7/1 for domestic students, 5/1 for international students; for spring admission, 11/1 for domestic students, 9/1 for international students. Applications are processed on a rolling basis. Application fee: $40. Electronic applications accepted. *Expenses:* Tuition, state resident: full-time $2575.50; part-time $286.25 per credit hour. Tuition, nonresident: full-time $6510; part-time $723.50 per credit hour. Tuition and fees vary according to course load. *Financial support:* In 2009–10, 15 research assistantships (averaging $13,924 per year) were awarded; Federal Work-Study, institutionally sponsored loans, and unspecified assistantships also available. Financial award applicants required to submit FAFSA. *Unit head:* Dr. Clarence H. Collison, Professor and Department Head, 662-325-2085, Fax: 662-325-8837, E-mail: ccollison@entomology.msstate.edu. *Application contact:* Dr. Clarence H. Collison, Professor and Department Head, 662-325-2085, Fax: 662-325-8837, E-mail: ccollison@entomology.msstate.edu.

Mississippi State University, College of Agriculture and Life Sciences, Department of Plant and Soil Sciences, Mississippi State, MS 39762. Offers agricultural sciences (PhD), including agronomy (MS, PhD), horticulture (MS, PhD), weed science (MS, PhD); agriculture (MS), including agronomy (MS, PhD), horticulture (MS, PhD), weed science (MS, PhD). *Faculty:* 24 full-time (1 woman), 1 part-time/adjunct (0 women). *Students:* 26 full-time (8 women), 30 part-time (8 women); includes 1 minority (American Indian/Alaska Native), 16 international. Average age 30. 31 applicants, 39% accepted, 12 enrolled. In 2009, 7 master's, 1 doctorate awarded. *Degree requirements:* For master's, thesis, exit seminar describing thesis research; for doctorate, comprehensive exam, thesis/dissertation, two departmental seminars. *Entrance requirements:* For master's, GRE (weed science), minimum GPA of 2.75 (agronomy/horticulture), 3.0 (weed science); for doctorate, GRE (weed science), minimum GPA of 3.0 (agronomy/horticulture), 3.25 (weed science). Additional exam requirements/recommendations for international students: Required—TOEFL (minimum score 550 paper-based; 213 computer-based; 79 iBT); Recommended—IELTS (minimum score 6.5). *Application deadline:* For fall admission, 7/1 for domestic students, 5/1 for international students; for spring admission, 10/1 for domestic students, 9/1 for international students. Applications are processed on a rolling basis. Application fee: $40. Electronic applications accepted. *Expenses:* Tuition, state resident: full-time $2575.50; part-time $286.25 per credit hour. Tuition, nonresident: full-time $6510; part-time $723.50 per credit hour. Tuition and fees vary according to course load. *Financial support:* In 2009–10, 25 research assistantships (averaging $11,626 per year), 3 teaching assistantships (averaging $12,379 per year) were awarded; Federal Work-Study, institutionally sponsored loans, scholarships/grants, and unspecified assistantships also available. Financial award application deadline: 4/1; financial award applicants required to submit FAFSA. *Unit head:* Dr. Daniel Reynolds, Professor/Interim Head, 662-325-2311, Fax: 662-325-8742, E-mail: dreynolds@pss.msstate.edu. *Application contact:* Dr. William Kingery, Graduate Coordinator, 662-325-2748, Fax: 662-325-8742, E-mail: wkingery@pss.msstate.edu.

Mississippi State University, College of Agriculture and Life Sciences, Department of Poultry Science, Mississippi State, MS 39762. Offers agriculture (MS), including poultry science (MS, PhD); agriculture sciences (PhD), including poultry science (MS, PhD). *Faculty:* 5 full-time (1 woman). *Students:* 13 full-time (5 women); includes 2 minority (both African Americans), 4 international. Average age 27. 8 applicants, 38% accepted, 3 enrolled. In 2009, 5 master's awarded. *Degree requirements:* For master's, comprehensive exam, thesis optional; for doctorate, comprehensive exam, thesis/dissertation. *Entrance requirements:* Additional exam requirements/recommendations for international students: Required—TOEFL (minimum score 475 paper-based; 153 computer-based; 53 iBT); Recommended—IELTS (minimum score 4.5). *Application deadline:* For fall admission, 7/1 for domestic students, 5/1 for international

Agricultural Sciences—General

Mississippi State University (continued)

students; for spring admission, 10/1 for domestic students, 11/1 for international students. Applications are processed on a rolling basis. Application fee: $40. Electronic applications accepted. *Expenses:* Tuition, state resident: full-time $2575.50; part-time $286.25 per credit hour. Tuition, nonresident: full-time $6510; part-time $723.50 per credit hour. Tuition and fees vary according to course load. *Financial support:* In 2009–10, 11 research assistantships with partial tuition reimbursements (averaging $10,524 per year), 1 teaching assistantship with partial tuition reimbursement (averaging $8,029 per year) were awarded; Federal Work-Study, institutionally sponsored loans, scholarships/grants, and unspecified assistantships also available. Financial award application deadline: 4/1; financial award applicants required to submit FAFSA. *Unit head:* Dr. Yvonne Thaxton, Interim Department Head and Professor, 662-325-9087, Fax: 662-325-8292, E-mail: yvizzier@poultry.msstate.edu. *Application contact:* Dr. Yvonne Thaxton, Interim Department Head and Professor, 662-325-9087, Fax: 662-325-8292, E-mail: yvizzier@poultry.msstate.edu.

Mississippi State University, College of Agriculture and Life Sciences, School of Human Sciences, Mississippi State, MS 39762. Offers agricultural sciences (PhD), including agriculture and extension education; agriculture and extension education (MS). *Accreditation:* NCATE (one or more programs are accredited). Part-time programs available. *Faculty:* 13 full-time (8 women). *Students:* 9 full-time (6 women), 42 part-time (24 women); includes 12 minority (all African Americans). Average age 33. 23 applicants, 78% accepted, 17 enrolled. In 2009, 11 master's, 3 doctorates awarded. *Degree requirements:* For master's, thesis optional, comprehensive oral or written exam. *Entrance requirements:* For master's, GRE, minimum GPA of 2.75 in last 4 semesters of course work; for doctorate, minimum GPA of 3.0 on prior graduate work. Additional exam requirements/recommendations for international students: Required—TOEFL (minimum score 475 paper-based; 153 computer-based; 53 iBT); Recommended—IELTS (minimum score 4.5). *Application deadline:* For fall admission, 7/1 for domestic students, 5/1 for international students; for spring admission, 11/1 for domestic students, 9/1 for international students. Applications are processed on a rolling basis. Application fee: $40. Electronic applications accepted. *Expenses:* Tuition, state resident: full-time $2575.50; part-time $286.25 per credit hour. Tuition, nonresident: full-time $6510; part-time $723.50 per credit hour. Tuition and fees vary according to course load. *Financial support:* In 2009–10, 2 research assistantships (averaging $8,351 per year), 5 teaching assistantships with full tuition reimbursements (averaging $9,081 per year) were awarded; Federal Work-Study, institutionally sponsored loans, and unspecified assistantships also available. Financial award application deadline: 4/1; financial award applicants required to submit FAFSA. *Faculty research:* Animal welfare, agroscience, information technology, learning styles, problem solving. *Unit head:* Dr. Gary Jackson, Director, 662-325-8593, E-mail: gjackson@humansci.msstate.edu. *Application contact:* Dr. Jacquelyn Deeds, Professor and Graduate Coordinator, 662-325-7834, E-mail: jdeeds@ais.msstate.edu.

Missouri State University, Graduate College, College of Natural and Applied Sciences, Department of Agriculture, Springfield, MO 65897. Offers natural and applied science (MNAS), including agriculture (MNAS, MS Ed); plant science (MS); secondary education (MS Ed), including agriculture (MNAS, MS Ed). Part-time programs available. *Faculty:* 16 full-time (3 women). *Students:* 10 full-time (7 women), 16 part-time (10 women), 2 international. Average age 31. 7 applicants, 71% accepted, 3 enrolled. In 2009, 9 master's awarded. *Degree requirements:* For master's, comprehensive exam, thesis or alternative. *Entrance requirements:* For master's, GRE (MS plant science, MNAS), 9-12 teacher certification (MS Ed), minimum GPA of 3.0 (MS plant science, MNAS). Additional exam requirements/recommendations for international students: Required—TOEFL (minimum score 550 paper-based; 213 computer-based; 79 iBT). *Application deadline:* For fall admission, 7/20 priority date for domestic students, 5/1 for international students; for spring admission, 12/20 priority date for domestic students, 9/1 for international students. Applications are processed on a rolling basis. Application fee: $35 ($50 for international students). Electronic applications accepted. *Expenses:* Tuition, state resident: full-time $3852; part-time $214 per credit hour. Tuition, nonresident: full-time $7524; part-time $418 per credit hour. Required fees: $696; $172 per semester. Tuition and fees vary according to course level, course load, degree level and program. *Financial support:* In 2009–10, 6 research assistantships with full tuition reimbursements (averaging $8,535 per year), 6 teaching assistantships with full tuition reimbursements (averaging $8,535 per year) were awarded; Federal Work-Study, institutionally sponsored loans, scholarships/grants, and unspecified assistantships also available. Financial award application deadline: 3/31; financial award applicants required to submit FAFSA. *Faculty research:* Grapevine biotechnology, agricultural marketing, Asian elephant reproduction, poultry science, integrated pest management. *Unit head:* Dr. W. Anson Elliott, Head, 417-836-5638, E-mail: ansonelliot@missouristate.edu. *Application contact:* Eric Eckert, Coordinator of Graduate Admissions and Recruitment, 417-836-5331, Fax: 417-836-6200.

Montana State University, College of Graduate Studies, College of Agriculture, Bozeman, MT 59717. Offers MS, PhD. Part-time programs available. Postbaccalaureate distance learning degree programs offered (minimal on-campus study). *Faculty:* 86 full-time (19 women), 13 part-time/adjunct (5 women). *Students:* 32 full-time (17 women), 85 part-time (31 women); includes 2 minority (1 American Indian/Alaska Native, 1 Hispanic American), 14 international. Average age 27. 67 applicants, 37% accepted, 22 enrolled. In 2009, 31 master's, 12 doctorates awarded. *Degree requirements:* For master's, comprehensive exam; for doctorate, comprehensive exam, thesis/dissertation. *Entrance requirements:* For master's and doctorate, GRE General Test. Additional exam requirements/recommendations for international students: Required—TOEFL (minimum score 550 paper-based; 213 computer-based). *Application deadline:* For fall admission, 7/15 priority date for domestic students, 5/15 priority date for international students; for spring admission, 12/1 priority date for domestic students, 10/1 priority date for international students. Applications are processed on a rolling basis. Application fee: $30. Electronic applications accepted. *Expenses:* Tuition, state resident: full-time $5635; part-time $3492 per year. Tuition, nonresident: full-time $17,212; part-time $7865.10 per year. Required fees: $1441.05; $153.15 per credit. Tuition and fees vary according to course load and program. *Financial support:* Application deadline: 3/1; Total annual research expenditures: $18.8 million. *Unit head:* Dr. Jeffrey S. Jacobsen, Dean, 406-994-7060, Fax: 406-994-3933, E-mail: jefj@montana.edu. *Application contact:* Dr. Carl A. Fox, Vice Provost for Graduate Education, 406-994-4145, Fax: 406-994-7433, E-mail: gradstudy@montana.edu.

Morehead State University, Graduate Programs, College of Science and Technology, Department of Agricultural Sciences, Morehead, KY 40351. Offers career and technical agricultural education (MS). Part-time and evening/weekend programs available. *Faculty:* 2 full-time (0 women). *Students:* 5 full-time (3 women), 5 part-time (2 women). Average age 27. 5 applicants, 100% accepted, 3 enrolled. In 2009, 2 master's awarded. *Degree requirements:* For master's, comprehensive exam, thesis or alternative, exit exam. *Entrance requirements:* For master's, GRE, minimum GPA of 3.0 for undergraduate major. Additional exam requirements/recommendations for international students: Required—TOEFL (minimum score 500 paper-based; 173 computer-based). *Application deadline:* For fall admission, 8/1 priority date for domestic and international students; for spring admission, 12/1 priority date for domestic and international students. Applications are processed on a rolling basis. Application fee: $30. Electronic applications accepted. *Expenses:* Tuition, state resident: full-time $6318; part-time $351 per credit hour. Tuition, nonresident: full-time $15,804; part-time $878 per credit hour. *Financial support:* In 2009–10, 2 teaching assistantships (averaging $10,000 per year) were awarded; career-related internships or fieldwork, Federal Work-Study, and unspecified assistantships also available. Financial award application deadline: 3/15; financial award applicants required to submit FAFSA. *Unit head:* Dr. Gerald DeMoss, Dean, 606-783-2158, Fax: 606-783-5039, E-mail: g.demoss@moreheadstate.edu. *Application contact:* Michelle Barber, Graduate Recruitment and Retention Assistant Director, 606-783-5127, Fax: 606-783-5061, E-mail: m.barber@moreheadstate.edu.

Murray State University, School of Agriculture, Murray, KY 42071. Offers agriculture (MS); agriculture education (MS). Evening/weekend programs available. Postbaccalaureate distance learning degree programs offered (minimal on-campus study). *Degree requirements:* For master's, comprehensive exam, thesis (for some programs). *Entrance requirements:* Additional exam requirements/recommendations for international students: Required—TOEFL. *Faculty research:* Ultrasound in beef, corn and soybean research, tobacco research.

New Mexico State University, Graduate School, College of Agricultural, Consumer and Environmental Sciences, Department of Entomology, Plant Pathology and Weed Science, Las Cruces, NM 88003-8001. Offers agricultural biology (MS). Part-time programs available. *Faculty:* 8 full-time (2 women). *Students:* 8 full-time (2 women), 2 part-time (1 woman); includes 2 minority (both Hispanic Americans), 2 international. Average age 26. 8 applicants, 88% accepted, 3 enrolled. In 2009, 4 master's awarded. *Degree requirements:* For master's, comprehensive exam, thesis. *Entrance requirements:* For master's, GRE General Test. *Application deadline:* For fall admission, 7/1 priority date for domestic students; for spring admission, 11/1 priority date for domestic students. Applications are processed on a rolling basis. Application fee: $30 ($50 for international students). Electronic applications accepted. *Expenses:* Tuition, state resident: full-time $4080; part-time $223 per credit. Tuition, nonresident: full-time $14,256; part-time $647 per credit. Required fees: $1278; $639 per semester. *Financial support:* In 2009–10, 5 research assistantships with partial tuition reimbursements (averaging $18,450 per year), 1 teaching assistantship with partial tuition reimbursement (averaging $20,500 per year) were awarded; career-related internships or fieldwork and health care benefits also available. Financial award application deadline: 3/1. *Faculty research:* Integrated pest management, pesticide application and safety, livestock ectoparasite research, biotechnology, nematology. *Unit head:* Dr. David Thompson, Head, 575-646-3225, Fax: 575-646-8087, E-mail: dathomps@nmsu.edu. *Application contact:* Dr. David Thompson, Head, 575-646-3225, Fax: 575-646-8087, E-mail: dathomps@nmsu.edu.

North Carolina Agricultural and Technical State University, Graduate School, School of Agriculture and Environmental Sciences, Greensboro, NC 27411. Offers MS. Part-time and evening/weekend programs available. *Degree requirements:* For master's, comprehensive exam, qualifying exam. *Entrance requirements:* For master's, GRE General Test. *Faculty research:* Aid for small farmers, agricultural technology, housing, food science, nutrition.

North Carolina State University, Graduate School, College of Agriculture and Life Sciences, Raleigh, NC 27695. Offers M Tox, MAE, MB, MBAE, MFG, MFM, MFS, MG, MMB, MN, MP, MS, MZS, Ed D, PhD, Certificate. Part-time programs available. Electronic applications accepted.

North Dakota State University, College of Graduate and Interdisciplinary Studies, College of Agriculture, Food Systems, and Natural Resources, Fargo, ND 58108. Offers MS, PhD. Part-time programs available. *Faculty:* 126. *Students:* 92 full-time (39 women), 45 part-time (19 women); includes 31 minority (4 African Americans, 1 American Indian/Alaska Native, 17 Asian Americans or Pacific Islanders, 9 Hispanic Americans), 30 international. *Degree requirements:* For doctorate, thesis/dissertation. *Entrance requirements:* Additional exam requirements/recommendations for international students: Required—TOEFL. *Application deadline:* Applications are processed on a rolling basis. Application fee: $45 ($60 for international students). Electronic applications accepted. *Financial support:* Fellowships with full tuition reimbursements, research assistantships with full tuition reimbursements, teaching assistantships with full tuition reimbursements, career-related internships or fieldwork, Federal Work-Study, and institutionally sponsored loans available. Support available to part-time students. *Faculty research:* Horticulture and forestry, plant and wheat breeding, diseases of insects, animal and range sciences, soil science, veterinary medicine. *Unit head:* Dr. Kenneth F. Grafton, Dean, 701-231-8790, Fax: 701-231-8520, E-mail: k.grafton@ndsu.edu. *Application contact:* Dr. Kenneth F. Grafton, Dean, 701-231-8790, Fax: 701-231-8520, E-mail: k.grafton@ndsu.edu.

Northwest Missouri State University, Graduate School, Melvin and Valorie Booth College of Business and Professional Studies, Department of Agriculture, Maryville, MO 64468-6001. Offers agricultural economics (MBA); agriculture (MS); teaching agriculture (MS Ed). Part-time programs available. *Faculty:* 7 full-time (2 women). *Students:* 8 full-time (3 women), 4 part-time (1 woman), 2 international. 10 applicants, 80% accepted, 5 enrolled. In 2009, 3 master's awarded. *Degree requirements:* For master's, comprehensive exam, thesis (for some programs). *Entrance requirements:* For master's, GRE General Test, minimum undergraduate GPA of 2.5, writing sample. Additional exam requirements/recommendations for international students: Required—TOEFL (minimum score 550 paper-based; 213 computer-based). *Application deadline:* For fall admission, 7/1 for domestic and international students; for spring admission, 11/15 for domestic and international students. Applications are processed on a rolling basis. Application fee: $0 ($50 for international students). *Expenses:* Tuition, state resident: part-time $296.34 per credit hour. Tuition, nonresident: part-time $510.43 per credit hour. *Financial support:* In 2009–10, 3 research assistantships with full tuition reimbursements (averaging $6,000 per year), 2 teaching assistantships with full tuition reimbursements (averaging $6,000 per year) were awarded; unspecified assistantships also available. Financial award application deadline: 4/1; financial award applicants required to submit FAFSA. *Unit head:* Dr. Arley Larson, Chairperson, 660-562-1161. *Application contact:* Dr. Gregory Haddock, Dean of Graduate School, 660-562-1145, Fax: 660-562-1096, E-mail: gradsch@nwmissouri.edu.

Nova Scotia Agricultural College, Research and Graduate Studies, Truro, NS B2N 5E3, Canada. Offers agriculture (M Sc), including air quality, animal behavior, animal molecular genetics, animal nutrition, animal technology, aquaculture, botany, crop management, crop physiology, ecology, environmental microbiology, food science, horticulture, nutrient management, pest management, physiology, plant biotechnology, plant pathology, soil chemistry, soil fertility, waste management and composting, water quality. Part-time programs available. *Degree requirements:* For master's, thesis, ATC Exam Teaching Assistantship. *Entrance requirements:* For master's, honors B Sc, minimum GPA of 3.0. Additional exam requirements/recommendations for international students: Required—TOEFL (minimum score 580 paper-based; 237 computer-based; 92 iBT), IELTS, Michigan English Language Assessment Battery, CanTEST, CAEL. *Faculty research:* Bio-product development, organic agriculture, nutrient management, air and water quality, agricultural biotechnology.

The Ohio State University, Graduate School, College of Food, Agricultural, and Environmental Sciences, Columbus, OH 43210. Offers M Ed, MS, PhD. Part-time programs available. *Faculty:* 313. *Students:* 343 full-time (196 women), 134 part-time (64 women); includes 32 minority (7 African Americans, 1 American Indian/Alaska Native, 10 Asian Americans or Pacific Islanders, 14 Hispanic Americans), 195 international. Average age 28. In 2009, 92 master's, 48 doctorates awarded. *Degree requirements:* For doctorate, thesis/dissertation. *Entrance requirements:* Additional exam requirements/recommendations for international students: Required—TOEFL (minimum score 550 paper-based; 213 computer-based) or IELTS (minimum score 7) or Michigan English Language Assessment Battery (minimum score 83). *Application deadline:* For fall admission, 8/15 priority date for domestic students, 7/1 priority date for international students; for winter admission, 12/1 priority date for domestic students, 11/1 priority date for international students; for spring admission, 3/1 priority date for domestic students, 2/1 priority date for international students. Applications are processed on a rolling basis. Application fee: $40 ($50 for international students). Electronic applications accepted. *Expenses:* Tuition, state resident: full-time $10,683. Tuition, nonresident: full-time $25,923. Tuition and fees vary according to course load and program. *Financial support:* Fellowships, research assistantships, teaching assistantships, career-related internships or fieldwork, Federal Work-Study, institutionally sponsored loans, and unspecified assistantships available. Support available to part-time students. *Unit head:* Dr. Bobby Moser, Dean, 614-292-6891, Fax: 614-292-1218, E-mail: moser.2@osu.edu. *Application contact:* Graduate Admissions, 614-292-9444, Fax: 614-292-3895, E-mail: domestic.grad@osu.edu.

Oklahoma State University, College of Agricultural Science and Natural Resources, Stillwater, OK 74078. Offers M Ag, MS, PhD. Postbaccalaureate distance learning degree programs offered. *Faculty:* 262 full-time (59 women), 11 part-time/adjunct (2 women). *Students:* 153 full-time (66 women), 308 part-time (145 women); includes 39 minority (8 African Americans, 19 American Indian/Alaska Native, 7 Asian Americans or Pacific Islanders, 5 Hispanic Americans), 174 international. Average age 29. 527 applicants, 33% accepted, 107 enrolled. In 2009, 109 master's, 34 doctorates awarded. *Degree requirements:* For master's, thesis (for some programs); for doctorate, comprehensive exam, thesis/dissertation. *Entrance requirements:* For master's and doctorate, GRE or GMAT. Additional exam requirements/recommendations for international students: Required—TOEFL (minimum score 550 paper-based; 79 iBT). *Application deadline:* For fall admission, 3/1 priority date for international students; for spring admission, 8/1 priority date for international students. Applications are processed on a rolling basis. Application fee: $40 ($75 for international students). Electronic applications accepted. *Expenses:* Tuition, state resident: full-time $3716; part-time $154.85 per credit hour. Tuition, nonresident: full-time $14,448; part-time $602 per credit hour. Required fees: $1772; $73.85 per credit hour. One-time fee: $50. Tuition and fees vary according to course load and campus/location. *Financial support:* In 2009–10, 285 research assistantships (averaging $15,491 per year), 25 teaching assistantships (averaging $13,252 per year) were awarded; fellowships, career-related internships or fieldwork, Federal Work-Study, scholarships/grants, health care benefits, tuition waivers (partial), and unspecified assistantships also available. Support available to part-time students. Financial award application deadline: 3/1; financial award applicants required to submit FAFSA. *Unit head:* Dr. Robert E. Whitson, Dean, 405-744-5398, Fax: 405-744-2480. *Application contact:* Dr. Gordon Emslie, Dean, 405-744-6368, Fax: 405-744-0355, E-mail: grad-i@okstate.edu.

Oregon State University, Graduate School, College of Agricultural Sciences, Corvallis, OR 97331. Offers M Ag, M Agr, MA, MAIS, MAT, MS, PhD. Part-time programs available. *Faculty:* 127 full-time (31 women), 11 part-time/adjunct (6 women). *Students:* 217 full-time (113 women), 29 part-time (12 women); includes 26 minority (1 African American, 5 American Indian/Alaska Native, 10 Asian Americans or Pacific Islanders, 10 Hispanic Americans), 64 international. Average age 32. In 2009, 53 master's, 24 doctorates awarded. Terminal master's awarded for partial completion of doctoral program. *Degree requirements:* For doctorate, thesis/dissertation. *Entrance requirements:* For master's and doctorate, GRE, minimum GPA of 3.0 in last 90 hours of course work. Additional exam requirements/recommendations for international students: Required—TOEFL. Application fee: $50. *Expenses:* Tuition, state resident: full-time $9774; part-time $362 per credit. Tuition, nonresident: full-time $15,849; part-time $587 per credit. Required fees: $1639. Full-time tuition and fees vary according to course load and program. *Financial support:* Fellowships, research assistantships, teaching assistantships, career-related internships or fieldwork, Federal Work-Study, and institutionally sponsored loans available. Support available to part-time students. Financial award application deadline: 2/1. *Faculty research:* Fish and wildlife biology, food science, soil/water/plant relationships, natural resources, animal biochemistry. *Unit head:* Dr. Thayne R. Dutson, Dean, 541-737-5812, Fax: 541-737-4574, E-mail: thayne.dutson@orst.edu. *Application contact:* Dr. Stella Coakley, Associate Dean, 541-737-5264, Fax: 541-737-3178, E-mail: stella.coakley@oregonstate.edu.

Penn State University Park, Graduate School, College of Agricultural Sciences, State College, University Park, PA 16802-1503. Offers M Agr, M Ed, MFR, MPS, MS, PhD, Postbaccalaureate Certificate. *Students:* 322 full-time (180 women), 51 part-time (23 women). Average age 29. 507 applicants, 33% accepted, 99 enrolled. In 2009, 67 master's, 40 doctorates awarded. *Entrance requirements:* Additional exam requirements/recommendations for international students: Required—TOEFL (minimum score 550 paper-based; 213 computer-based; 80 iBT). *Application deadline:* Applications are processed on a rolling basis. Application fee: $65. Electronic applications accepted. *Financial support:* Fellowships, research assistantships, teaching assistantships available. Financial award applicants required to submit FAFSA. *Unit head:* Dr. Bruce A. McPheron, Dean, 814-865-2541, Fax: 814-865-3103, E-mail: bam10@psu.edu. *Application contact:* Cynthia E. Nicosia, Director, Graduate Enrollment Services, 814-865-1834, E-mail: cey1@psu.edu.

Prairie View A&M University, College of Agriculture and Human Sciences, Prairie View, TX 77446-0519. Offers agricultural economics (MS); animal sciences (MS); interdisciplinary human sciences (MS); soil science (MS). Part-time and evening/weekend programs available. *Faculty:* 11 full-time (4 women). *Students:* 36 full-time (27 women), 40 part-time (29 women); includes 57 African Americans, 1 Hispanic American, 6 international. Average age 31. 147 applicants, 100% accepted. In 2009, 23 master's awarded. *Degree requirements:* For master's, comprehensive exam, thesis (for some programs), field placement. *Entrance requirements:* For master's, GRE General Test, minimum GPA of 2.45. Additional exam requirements/recommendations for international students: Required—TOEFL (minimum score 550 paper-based). *Application deadline:* For fall admission, 6/1 for domestic and international students; for spring admission, 10/1 for domestic and international students. Applications are processed on a rolling basis. Application fee: $50. *Expenses:* Tuition, state resident: full-time $2200. Tuition, nonresident: full-time $5600. Required fees: $1720. Tuition and fees vary according to course load. *Financial support:* In 2009–10, 57 students received support, including 8 fellowships with tuition reimbursements available (averaging $12,000 per year), 10 research assistantships with tuition reimbursements available (averaging $15,000 per year); career-related internships or fieldwork, Federal Work-Study, institutionally sponsored loans, scholarships/grants, tuition waivers (partial), and unspecified assistantships also available. Support available to part-time students. Financial award application deadline: 4/1; financial award applicants required to submit FAFSA. *Faculty research:* Domestic violence prevention, water quality, food growth regulators, wetland dynamics, biochemistry, obesity and nutrition, family therapy. Total annual research expenditures: $4 million. *Unit head:* Dr. Freddie Richards, Dean, 936-261-2528, Fax: 936-261-5143, E-mail: flrichards@pvamu.edu. *Application contact:* Dr. Richard W. Griffin, Interim Department Head, 936-261-5019, Fax: 936-261-5148, E-mail: rwgriffin@pvamu.edu.

Purdue University, Graduate School, College of Agriculture, West Lafayette, IN 47907. Offers EMBA, M Agr, MA, MS, MSF, PhD. Part-time programs available. *Degree requirements:* For doctorate, thesis/dissertation. *Entrance requirements:* Additional exam requirements/recommendations for international students: Required—TOEFL. Electronic applications accepted.

Sam Houston State University, College of Arts and Sciences, Department of Agricultural Sciences, Huntsville, TX 77341. Offers agriculture (MS); industrial technology (MA). Part-time and evening/weekend programs available. *Faculty:* 8 full-time (1 woman), 2 part-time/adjunct (0 women). *Students:* 26 full-time (13 women), 16 part-time (5 women); includes 1 minority (Hispanic American), 1 international. Average age 27. 18 applicants, 100% accepted, 17 enrolled. In 2009, 12 master's awarded. *Degree requirements:* For master's, thesis optional. *Entrance requirements:* For master's, GRE General Test, minimum GPA of 2.5. Additional exam requirements/recommendations for international students: Required—TOEFL (minimum score 550 paper-based; 213 computer-based; 79 iBT). *Application deadline:* For fall admission, 8/1 for domestic and international students; for spring admission, 12/1 for domestic and international students. Application fee: $20. Electronic applications accepted. *Expenses:* Tuition, state resident: full-time $3690; part-time $205 per credit hour. Tuition, nonresident: full-time $8676; part-time $482 per credit hour. Required fees: $1474. Tuition and fees vary according to course load and campus/location. *Financial support:* Teaching assistantships, career-related internships or fieldwork available. Financial award application deadline: 5/31; financial award applicants required to submit FAFSA. *Unit head:* Dr. Stanley F. Kelley, Chair, 936-294-1189, Fax: 936-294-1232, E-mail: sfkelley@shsu.edu. *Application contact:* Tammy Gray, Advisor, 936-294-1230, E-mail: dca_tag@shsu.edu.

South Dakota State University, Graduate School, College of Agriculture and Biological Sciences, Brookings, SD 57007. Offers MS, PhD. Part-time programs available. *Degree requirements:* For master's, thesis, oral exam; for doctorate, thesis/dissertation, preliminary oral and written exams. *Entrance requirements:* Additional exam requirements/recommendations for international students: Required—TOEFL.

Southern Arkansas University–Magnolia, Graduate Programs, Magnolia, AR 71753. Offers agriculture (MS); business administration (MBA); computer and information sciences (MS); counseling (MS); education (M Ed), including counseling and development, curriculum and instruction emphasis, educational administration and supervision, elementary education, middle level emphasis, reading emphasis, secondary education, TESOL emphasis; kinesiology (MS); library media and information specialist (M Ed); mental health and clinical counseling (MS); public administration (EMPA); school counseling (M Ed); teaching (MAT). *Accreditation:* NCATE. Part-time and evening/weekend programs available. *Faculty:* 43 full-time (24 women), 12 part-time/adjunct (7 women). *Students:* 116 full-time (78 women), 333 part-time (255 women); includes 105 minority (98 African Americans, 3 American Indian/Alaska Native, 3 Asian Americans or Pacific Islanders, 1 Hispanic American), 11 international. Average age 33. In 2009, 88 master's awarded. *Degree requirements:* For master's, comprehensive exam, thesis optional. *Entrance requirements:* For master's, GRE, MAT or GMAT, minimum GPA of 2.75. *Application deadline:* For fall admission, 8/15 for domestic students; for winter admission, 1/8 for domestic students; for spring admission, 1/8 for domestic students. Applications are processed on a rolling basis. Application fee: $0. *Expenses:* Tuition, state resident: full-time $3798; part-time $211 per hour. Tuition, nonresident: full-time $5580; part-time $310 per hour. Required fees: $584. *Financial support:* Career-related internships or fieldwork, Federal Work-Study, scholarships/grants, tuition waivers (full), and unspecified assistantships available. Financial award applicants required to submit FAFSA. *Faculty research:* Alternative certification for teachers, supervision of instruction, instructional leadership, counseling. *Unit head:* Dr. Kim Bloss, Dean, Graduate Studies, 870-235-4150, Fax: 870-235-5227, E-mail: kkbloss@saumag.edu. *Application contact:* Dr. Kim Bloss, Dean, Graduate Studies, 870-235-4150, Fax: 870-235-5227, E-mail: kkbloss@saumag.edu.

Southern Illinois University Carbondale, Graduate School, College of Agriculture, Carbondale, IL 62901-4701. Offers MS, MBA/MS. Part-time programs available. *Entrance requirements:* For master's, minimum GPA of 2.7. Additional exam requirements/recommendations for international students: Required—TOEFL. *Faculty research:* Production and studies in crops, animal nutrition, agribusiness economics and management, forest biology and ecology, microcomputers in agriculture.

Southern University and Agricultural and Mechanical College, Graduate School, College of Agricultural, Family and Consumer Sciences, Baton Rouge, LA 70813. Offers urban forestry (MS). *Degree requirements:* For master's, thesis. *Entrance requirements:* For master's, GRE, minimum GPA of 3.0. Additional exam requirements/recommendations for international students: Required—TOEFL (minimum score 525 paper-based; 193 computer-based). *Faculty research:* Urban forest interactions with environment, social and economic impacts of urban forests, tree biology/pathology, development of urban forest management tools.

Tarleton State University, College of Graduate Studies, College of Agriculture and Human Sciences, Department of Agribusiness, Agronomy, Horticulture, and Range Management, Stephenville, TX 76402. Offers agriculture (MS). Part-time and evening/weekend programs available. *Degree requirements:* For master's, comprehensive exam. *Entrance requirements:* For master's, GRE, minimum GPA of 3.0. Additional exam requirements/recommendations for international students: Required—TOEFL (minimum score 550 paper-based; 213 computer-based; 80 iBT). Electronic applications accepted.

Tarleton State University, College of Graduate Studies, College of Agriculture and Human Sciences, Department of Agricultural Services and Development, Stephenville, TX 76402. Offers agriculture education (MS). Part-time and evening/weekend programs available. Postbaccalaureate distance learning degree programs offered (minimal on-campus study). *Degree requirements:* For master's, comprehensive exam. *Entrance requirements:* For master's, GRE General Test, minimum GPA of 3.0. Additional exam requirements/recommendations for international students: Required—TOEFL (minimum score 550 paper-based; 213 computer-based; 80 iBT). Electronic applications accepted.

Tennessee State University, The School of Graduate Studies and Research, School of Agriculture and Consumer Sciences, Nashville, TN 37209-1561. Offers agricultural sciences (MS), including agribusiness, agricultural education, animal science, plant science. Part-time and evening/weekend programs available. *Degree requirements:* For master's, thesis. *Entrance requirements:* For master's, GRE General Test, GRE Subject Test, MAT. *Faculty research:* Small farm economics, ornamental horticulture, beef cattle production, rural elderly.

Texas A&M University, College of Agriculture and Life Sciences, College Station, TX 77843. Offers M Agr, M Ed, M Eng, MAB, MS, DE, Ed D, PhD. Part-time programs available. Postbaccalaureate distance learning degree programs offered (minimal on-campus study). *Faculty:* 314. *Students:* 1,020 full-time (511 women), 291 part-time (127 women); includes 174 minority (43 African Americans, 6 American Indian/Alaska Native, 17 Asian Americans or Pacific Islanders, 108 Hispanic Americans), 425 international. Average age 29. In 2009, 173 master's, 83 doctorates awarded. *Entrance requirements:* Additional exam requirements/recommendations for international students: Required—TOEFL (minimum score 550 paper-based; 213 computer-based). *Application deadline:* For fall admission, 7/21 priority date for domestic students, 6/1 priority date for international students; for spring admission, 12/1 priority date for domestic students, 10/1 priority date for international students. Applications are processed on a rolling basis. Application fee: $50 ($75 for international students). Electronic applications accepted. *Expenses:* Tuition, state resident: full-time $3991.32; part-time $221.74 per credit hour. Tuition, nonresident: full-time $9049; part-time $502.74 per credit hour. *Financial support:* Fellowships, research assistantships, teaching assistantships, career-related internships or fieldwork, Federal Work-Study, institutionally sponsored loans, scholarships/grants, tuition waivers (partial), and unspecified assistantships available. Support available to part-time students. Financial award applicants required to submit FAFSA. *Faculty research:* Plant sciences, animal sciences, environmental natural resources, biological and agricultural engineering, agricultural economics. *Unit head:* Dr. Mark Hussey, Vice Chancellor/Dean, 979-845-4747, Fax: 979-845-9938, E-mail: mhussey@tamu.edu. *Application contact:* Graduate Admissions, 979-845-1044, E-mail: admissions@tamu.edu.

Texas A&M University–Commerce, Graduate School, College of Arts and Sciences, Department of Agriculture, Commerce, TX 75429-3011. Offers agricultural education (M Ed, MS); agricultural sciences (M Ed, MS). Part-time programs available. *Degree requirements:* For master's, comprehensive exam, thesis (for some programs). *Entrance requirements:* For master's, GRE General Test. Electronic applications accepted. *Faculty research:* Soil conservation, retention.

Texas A&M University–Kingsville, College of Graduate Studies, College of Agriculture and Home Economics, Kingsville, TX 78363. Offers MS, PhD. Part-time and evening/weekend programs available. *Degree requirements:* For master's, comprehensive exam, thesis or alternative; for doctorate, one foreign language, comprehensive exam, thesis/dissertation. *Entrance requirements:* For master's, GRE General Test, minimum GPA of 3.0; for doctorate, GRE General Test, minimum GPA of 3.5. Additional exam requirements/recommendations for international students: Required—TOEFL. *Faculty research:* Mesquite cloning; genesis of soil salinity; dove management; bone development; egg, meat, and milk consumption versus price.

Texas Tech University, Graduate School, College of Agricultural Sciences and Natural Resources, Lubbock, TX 79409. Offers M Agr, MAB, MLA, MS, Ed D, PhD, JD/MS. Part-time and evening/weekend programs available. *Faculty:* 57 full-time (9 women), 7 part-time/adjunct

Agricultural Sciences—General

Texas Tech University (continued)
(0 women). *Students:* 208 full-time (100 women), 116 part-time (46 women); includes 25 minority (7 African Americans, 2 American Indian/Alaska Native, 1 Asian American or Pacific Islander, 15 Hispanic Americans), 79 international. Average age 31. 302 applicants, 59% accepted, 83 enrolled. In 2009, 72 master's, 14 doctorates awarded. *Degree requirements:* For master's, thesis or alternative; for doctorate, thesis/dissertation. *Entrance requirements:* For master's and doctorate, GRE General Test. Additional exam requirements/recommendations for international students: Required—TOEFL (minimum score 550 paper-based; 213 computer-based). *Application deadline:* For fall admission, 3/1 priority date for international students; for spring admission, 11/1 priority date for international students. Applications are processed on a rolling basis. Application fee: $50 ($75 for international students). Electronic applications accepted. *Expenses:* Contact institution. *Financial support:* In 2009–10, 65 research assistantships with partial tuition reimbursements (averaging $19,920 per year), 6 teaching assistantships with partial tuition reimbursements (averaging $11,577 per year) were awarded; career-related internships or fieldwork, Federal Work-Study, and institutionally sponsored loans also available. Support available to part-time students. Financial award application deadline: 4/15; financial award applicants required to submit FAFSA. *Faculty research:* Biotechnology and genomics, water management, food safety, policy, ecology. Total annual research expenditures: $10 million. *Unit head:* Dr. John M. Burns, Dean, 806-742-2810, E-mail: john.burns@ttu.edu. *Application contact:* Dr. Cindy Akers, Director, Student Services Center, 806-742-2808, Fax: 806-742-2836, E-mail: cindy.akers@ttu.edu.

Tropical Agriculture Research and Higher Education Center, Graduate School, Turrialba, Costa Rica. Offers agribusiness management (MS); agroforestry systems (PhD); ecological agriculture (MS); environmental socioeconomics (MS); forestry in tropical and subtropical zones (PhD); integrated watershed management (MS); management and conservation of tropical rainforests and biodiversity (MS); tropical agriculture (PhD); tropical agroforestry (MS). *Entrance requirements:* For master's, GRE, 2 years of related professional experience, letters of recommendation; for doctorate, GRE, 4 letters of recommendation, letter of support from employing organization, master's degree in agronomy, biological sciences, forestry, natural resources or related field. Additional exam requirements/recommendations for international students: Required—TOEFL (minimum score 550 paper-based; 213 computer-based). Electronic applications accepted. *Faculty research:* Biodiversity in fragmented landscapes, ecosystem management, integrated pest management, environmental livestock production, biotechnology carbon balances in diverse land uses.

Université Laval, Faculty of Agricultural and Food Sciences, Program in Agricultural Microbiology, Québec, QC G1K 7P4, Canada. Offers agricultural microbiology (M Sc); agro-food microbiology (PhD). Terminal master's awarded for partial completion of doctoral program. *Degree requirements:* For master's, thesis; for doctorate, comprehensive exam, thesis/dissertation. *Entrance requirements:* For master's and doctorate, knowledge of French and English. Electronic applications accepted.

University of Alberta, Faculty of Graduate Studies and Research, Department of Agricultural, Food and Nutritional Science, Edmonton, AB T6G 2E1, Canada. Offers M Ag, M Eng, M Sc, PhD, MBA/M Ag. *Faculty:* 44 full-time (14 women). *Students:* 209 full-time (119 women), 34 part-time (19 women). In 2009, 16 master's, 6 doctorates awarded. *Degree requirements:* For master's, thesis; for doctorate, comprehensive exam, thesis/dissertation. *Entrance requirements:* For master's, minimum GPA of 3.3; for doctorate, minimum GPA of 3.5. Additional exam requirements/recommendations for international students: Required—TOEFL (minimum score of 550 paper-based or a total score of 88 with a score of at least 20 on each of the individual skill areas iBT), Michigan English Language Assessment Battery (minimum score 85); IELTS (minimum overall band score 6.5), CAEL (overall minimum score 60). *Application deadline:* For fall admission, 5/15 for international students; for winter admission, 9/15 for international students. Applications are processed on a rolling basis. Tuition and fees charges are reported in Canadian dollars. *Expenses:* Tuition, area resident: Full-time $4626.24 Canadian dollars; part-time $99.72 Canadian dollars per unit. International tuition: $8216 Canadian dollars full-time. Required fees: $3589.92 Canadian dollars; $99.72 Canadian dollars per unit. $215 Canadian dollars per term. *Financial support:* In 2009–10, 65 students received support, including 6 fellowships, 17 research assistantships with partial tuition reimbursements available (averaging $7,000 per year), 37 teaching assistantships (averaging $3,600 per year); scholarships/grants and unspecified assistantships also available. *Faculty research:* Animal science, food science, nutrition and metabolism, bioresource engineering, plant science and range management. *Application contact:* Jody Forslund, Student Support, 780-492-5131, Fax: 780-492-4265, E-mail: afns.grad@ualberta.ca.

The University of Arizona, Graduate College, College of Agriculture and Life Sciences, Tucson, AZ 85721. Offers M Ag Ed, MHE Ed, MS, PhD. Part-time programs available. *Faculty:* 111. *Students:* 253 full-time (140 women), 134 part-time (65 women); includes 48 minority (9 African Americans, 5 American Indian/Alaska Native, 9 Asian Americans or Pacific Islanders, 25 Hispanic Americans), 112 international. Average age 32. 298 applicants, 43% accepted, 85 enrolled. In 2009, 73 master's, 32 doctorates awarded. *Degree requirements:* For doctorate, thesis/dissertation. *Entrance requirements:* For master's, GRE, GMAT, or MAT, bachelor's degree or equivalent, minimum GPA of 3.0. Additional exam requirements/recommendations for international students: Required—TOEFL. *Application deadline:* For fall admission, 1/1 for domestic students, 12/1 for international students. Applications are processed on a rolling basis. Application fee: $75. Electronic applications accepted. *Expenses:* Tuition, state resident: full-time $9028. Tuition, nonresident: full-time $24,890. *Financial support:* In 2009–10, 126 research assistantships with full and partial tuition reimbursements (averaging $16,919 per year), 47 teaching assistantships with full and partial tuition reimbursements (averaging $15,942 per year) were awarded; fellowships with full and partial tuition reimbursements, career-related internships or fieldwork, Federal Work-Study, institutionally sponsored loans, scholarships/grants, traineeships, health care benefits, tuition waivers (full and partial), and unspecified assistantships also available. *Faculty research:* Regulation of skeletal muscle mass during growth, bone health and osteoporosis prevention, regulation of gene expression, development of new crops for arid and semi-arid lands, molecular genetics and pathogenesis of the opportunistic pathogen. Total annual research expenditures: $36.4 million. *Unit head:* Dr. Eugene G. Sander, Dean, 520-621-7621, Fax: 520-621-7196. *Application contact:* Dr. David E. Cox, Associate Dean, 520-621-3612, Fax: 520-621-8662.

University of Arkansas, Graduate School, Dale Bumpers College of Agricultural, Food and Life Sciences, Fayetteville, AR 72701-1201. Offers MS, PhD. *Students:* 89 full-time (45 women), 218 part-time (99 women); includes 24 minority (9 African Americans, 3 American Indian/Alaska Native, 6 Asian Americans or Pacific Islanders, 6 Hispanic Americans), 87 international. In 2009, 69 master's, 14 doctorates awarded. *Degree requirements:* For doctorate, thesis/dissertation. Application fee: $40 ($50 for international students). *Expenses:* Tuition, state resident: full-time $7355; part-time $356.58 per hour. Tuition, nonresident: full-time $17,401; part-time $775.17 per hour. Required fees: $1203. *Financial support:* In 2009–10, 10 fellowships with tuition reimbursements, 174 research assistantships, 5 teaching assistantships were awarded; career-related internships or fieldwork, Federal Work-Study, scholarships/grants, and unspecified assistantships also available. Support available to part-time students. Financial award application deadline: 4/1; financial award applicants required to submit FAFSA. *Unit head:* Dr. Lalit Verma, Interim Dean, 479-575-2252, Fax: 479-575-7273, E-mail: lverma@uark.edu. *Application contact:* Graduate Admissions, 479-575-6246, Fax: 479-575-5908, E-mail: gradinfo@uark.edu.

The University of British Columbia, Faculty of Land and Food Systems, Vancouver, BC V6T 1Z1, Canada. Offers M Sc, MFS, PhD. *Degree requirements:* For master's, thesis; for doctorate, comprehensive exam, thesis/dissertation. *Entrance requirements:* Additional exam requirements/recommendations for international students: Required—TOEFL (minimum score 577 paper-based; 233 computer-based; 90 iBT), IELTS (minimum score 6.5). Electronic applications accepted.

University of California, Davis, Graduate Studies, Graduate Group in International Agricultural Development, Davis, CA 95616. Offers MS. *Degree requirements:* For master's, comprehensive exam (for some programs), thesis (for some programs). *Entrance requirements:* For master's, GRE General Test, minimum GPA of 3.0. Additional exam requirements/recommendations for international students: Required—TOEFL (minimum score 550 paper-based; 213 computer-based). Electronic applications accepted. *Faculty research:* Aspects of agricultural, environmental and social sciences on agriculture and related issues in developing countries.

University of Connecticut, Graduate School, College of Agriculture and Natural Resources, Storrs, CT 06269. Offers MS, PhD. *Faculty:* 99 full-time (29 women). *Students:* 175 full-time (96 women), 35 part-time (18 women); includes 24 minority (6 African Americans, 2 American Indian/Alaska Native, 8 Asian Americans or Pacific Islanders, 8 Hispanic Americans), 77 international. Average age 31. 228 applicants, 19% accepted, 28 enrolled. In 2009, 42 master's, 23 doctorates awarded. Terminal master's awarded for partial completion of doctoral program. *Degree requirements:* For master's, comprehensive exam; for doctorate, comprehensive exam, thesis/dissertation. *Entrance requirements:* For master's and doctorate, GRE General Test. Additional exam requirements/recommendations for international students: Required—TOEFL (minimum score 550 paper-based; 213 computer-based). *Application deadline:* For fall admission, 2/1 priority date for domestic and international students; for spring admission, 11/1 for domestic students, 10/1 for international students. Applications are processed on a rolling basis. Application fee: $55. Electronic applications accepted. *Expenses:* Tuition, state resident: full-time $4725; part-time $525 per credit. Tuition, nonresident: full-time $12,267; part-time $1363 per credit. Required fees: $346 per semester. Tuition and fees vary according to course load. *Financial support:* In 2009–10, 134 research assistantships with full tuition reimbursements, 20 teaching assistantships with full tuition reimbursements were awarded; fellowships, Federal Work-Study, scholarships/grants, health care benefits, and unspecified assistantships also available. Financial award application deadline: 2/1; financial award applicants required to submit FAFSA. *Unit head:* Kirklyn M. Kerr, Dean, 860-486-2917, Fax: 860-486-5113, E-mail: kirklyn.ker@uconn.edu. *Application contact:* Kirklyn M. Kerr, Dean, 860-486-2917, Fax: 860-486-5113, E-mail: kirklyn.ker@uconn.edu.

University of Delaware, College of Agriculture and Natural Resources, Newark, DE 19716. Offers MA, MS, PhD. Part-time programs available. *Degree requirements:* For master's, thesis; for doctorate, thesis/dissertation. *Entrance requirements:* For master's and doctorate, GRE General Test. Electronic applications accepted.

University of Florida, Graduate School, College of Agricultural and Life Sciences, Gainesville, FL 32611. Offers MAB, MFAS, MFRC, MFYCS, MS, DPM, PhD, JD/MFRC, JD/MS, JD/PhD. Part-time programs available. *Degree requirements:* For doctorate, thesis/dissertation. *Entrance requirements:* For master's and doctorate, GRE General Test, minimum GPA of 3.0. Additional exam requirements/recommendations for international students: Required—TOEFL. Electronic applications accepted.

University of Georgia, Graduate School, College of Agricultural and Environmental Sciences, Athens, GA 30602. Offers MA Ext, MADS, MAE, MAL, MCCS, MFT, MPPPM, MS, PhD. *Faculty:* 207 full-time (37 women), 18 part-time/adjunct (4 women). *Students:* 327 full-time (161 women), 90 part-time (35 women); includes 34 minority (14 African Americans, 9 Asian Americans or Pacific Islanders, 11 Hispanic Americans), 145 international. 262 applicants, 57% accepted, 98 enrolled. In 2009, 70 master's, 34 doctorates awarded. *Degree requirements:* For doctorate, thesis/dissertation. *Entrance requirements:* For master's and doctorate, GRE General Test. *Application deadline:* For fall admission, 7/1 priority date for domestic students; for spring admission, 11/15 for domestic students. Application fee: $50. Electronic applications accepted. *Expenses:* Tuition, state resident: full-time $6000; part-time $250 per credit hour. Tuition, nonresident: full-time $20,904; part-time $871 per credit hour. Required fees: $730 per semester. *Financial support:* Fellowships, research assistantships, teaching assistantships, career-related internships or fieldwork and unspecified assistantships available. *Unit head:* Dr. J. Scott Angle, Dean, 706-542-3924, Fax: 706-542-0803, E-mail: caesdean@uga.edu. *Application contact:* Krista Haynes, Director of Enrolled Student Services, 706-425-1789, Fax: 706-425-3094, E-mail: gradoff@uga.edu.

University of Guelph, Graduate Program Services, Ontario Agricultural College, Guelph, ON N1G 2W1, Canada. Offers M Sc, MLA, PhD, Diploma, MA/M Sc. Part-time programs available. Postbaccalaureate distance learning degree programs offered (minimal on-campus study). *Degree requirements:* For doctorate, thesis/dissertation.

University of Hawaii at Manoa, Graduate Division, College of Tropical Agriculture and Human Resources, Honolulu, HI 96822. Offers MS, PhD. Part-time programs available. *Entrance requirements:* Additional exam requirements/recommendations for international students: Required—TOEFL or IELTS. *Expenses:* Tuition, state resident: full-time $8900; part-time $372 per credit. Tuition, nonresident: full-time $21,400; part-time $898 per credit. Required fees: $207 per semester.

University of Illinois at Urbana–Champaign, Graduate College, College of Agricultural, Consumer and Environmental Sciences, Champaign, IL 61820. Offers MS, PhD, MS/JD, MS/MSW. *Faculty:* 218 full-time (56 women), 6 part-time/adjunct (1 woman). *Students:* 479 full-time (246 women), 155 part-time (73 women); includes 48 minority (13 African Americans, 23 Asian Americans or Pacific Islanders, 12 Hispanic Americans), 239 international. 632 applicants, 32% accepted, 155 enrolled. In 2009, 117 master's, 55 doctorates awarded. *Entrance requirements:* For master's, minimum GPA of 3.0. *Application deadline:* Applications are processed on a rolling basis. Application fee: $60 ($75 for international students). Electronic applications accepted. *Financial support:* In 2009–10, 119 fellowships, 408 research assistantships, 118 teaching assistantships were awarded; tuition waivers (full and partial) also available. *Unit head:* Robert Hauser, Interim Dean, 217-244-2807, Fax: 217-244-2911, E-mail: r-hauser@illinois.edu. *Application contact:* Robert Hauser, Interim Dean, 217-244-2807, Fax: 217-244-2911, E-mail: r-hauser@illinois.edu.

University of Kentucky, Graduate School, College of Agriculture, Lexington, KY 40506-0032. Offers MS, MSFAM, MSFOR, PhD. Part-time programs available. Terminal master's awarded for partial completion of doctoral program. *Degree requirements:* For master's, comprehensive exam, thesis (for some programs); for doctorate, comprehensive exam, thesis/dissertation. *Entrance requirements:* For master's, GRE General Test, minimum undergraduate GPA of 2.75; for doctorate, GRE General Test, minimum undergraduate GPA of 2.75, graduate 3.0. Additional exam requirements/recommendations for international students: Required—TOEFL (minimum score 550 paper-based; 213 computer-based). Electronic applications accepted.

University of Lethbridge, School of Graduate Studies, Lethbridge, AB T1K 3M4, Canada. Offers accounting (MScM); addictions counseling (M Sc); agricultural biotechnology (M Sc); agricultural studies (M Sc, MA); anthropology (MA); archaeology (MA); art (MA, MFA); biochemistry (M Sc); biological sciences (M Sc); biomolecular science (PhD); biosystems and biodiversity (PhD); Canadian studies (MA); chemistry (M Sc); computer science (M Sc); computer science and geographical information science (M Sc); counseling psychology (M Ed); dramatic arts (MA); earth, space, and physical science (PhD); economics (MA); educational leadership (M Ed); English (MA); environmental science (M Sc); evolution and behavior (PhD); exercise science (M Sc); finance (MScM); French (MA); French/German (MA); French/Spanish (MA); general education (M Ed); general management (MScM); geography (M Sc, MA); German (MA); health science (M Sc); health sciences (MA); history (MA); human resource management and labour relations (MScM); individualized multidisciplinary (M Sc, MA); information systems

(MScM); international management (MScM); kinesiology (M Sc, MA); management (M Sc, MA); marketing (MScM); mathematics (M Sc); music (M Mus, MA); Native American studies (MA); neuroscience (M Sc, PhD); new media (MA); nursing (M Sc); philosophy (MA); physics (M Sc); policy and strategy (MScM); political science (MA); psychology (M Sc, MA); religious studies (MA), social sciences (MA); sociology (MA); theatre and dramatic arts (MFA); theoretical and computational science (PhD); urban and regional studies (MA); women's studies (MA). Part-time and evening/weekend programs available. *Degree requirements:* For doctorate, comprehensive exam, thesis/dissertation. *Entrance requirements:* For master's, GMAT (M Sc in management), bachelor's degree in related field, minimum GPA of 3.0 during previous 20 graded semester courses, 2 years teaching or related experience (M Ed); for doctorate, master's degree, minimum graduate GPA of 3.5. Additional exam requirements/recommendations for international students: Required—TOEFL. *Faculty research:* Movement and brain plasticity, gibberellin physiology, photosynthesis, carbon cycling, molecular properties of main-group ring components.

University of Maine, Graduate School, College of Natural Sciences, Forestry, and Agriculture, Orono, ME 04469. Offers MF, MPS, MS, MWC, PhD, CAS. *Accreditation:* SAF (one or more programs are accredited). Part-time and evening/weekend programs available. *Faculty:* 137 full-time (50 women), 57 part-time/adjunct (34 women). *Students:* 210 full-time (120 women), 114 part-time (69 women); includes 9 minority (2 African Americans, 2 American Indian/Alaska Native, 2 Asian Americans or Pacific Islanders, 3 Hispanic Americans), 43 international. Average age 30. 368 applicants, 31% accepted, 72 enrolled. In 2009, 66 master's, 19 doctorates awarded. *Degree requirements:* For doctorate, thesis/dissertation. *Entrance requirements:* For master's and doctorate, GRE General Test. Additional exam requirements/recommendations for international students: Required—TOEFL. *Application deadline:* For fall admission, 2/1 priority date for domestic students. Applications are processed on a rolling basis. Application fee: $65. Electronic applications accepted. *Financial support:* Career-related internships or fieldwork, Federal Work-Study, institutionally sponsored loans, scholarships/grants, tuition waivers (full and partial), and unspecified assistantships available. Support available to part-time students. Financial award application deadline: 3/1. *Unit head:* Dr. Edward Ashworth, Dean, 207-581-3206, Fax: 207-581-3207. *Application contact:* Scott G. Delcourt, Associate Dean of the Graduate School, 207-581-3291, Fax: 207-581-3232, E-mail: graduate@maine.edu.

University of Manitoba, Faculty of Graduate Studies, Faculty of Agricultural and Food Sciences, Winnipeg, MB R3T 2N2, Canada. Offers M Sc, PhD. *Degree requirements:* For master's, thesis or alternative; for doctorate, variable foreign language requirement, thesis/dissertation.

University of Maryland, College Park, Academic Affairs, College of Agriculture and Natural Resources, College Park, MD 20742. Offers DVM, MS, PhD. Part-time and evening/weekend programs available. *Faculty:* 336 full-time (151 women), 37 part-time/adjunct (20 women). *Students:* 332 full-time (198 women), 28 part-time (20 women); includes 7 African Americans, 9 Asian Americans or Pacific Islanders, 8 Hispanic Americans, 105 international. 463 applicants, 27% accepted, 90 enrolled. In 2009, 30 first professional degrees, 32 master's, 27 doctorates awarded. *Degree requirements:* For doctorate, thesis/dissertation; for DVM, thesis/dissertation, oral exam, public seminar. *Entrance requirements:* For DVM, GRE General Test; for master's, minimum GPA of 3.0. Additional exam requirements/recommendations for international students: Required—TOEFL. *Application deadline:* For fall admission, 12/15 for domestic and international students; for spring admission, 6/1 for international students. Applications are processed on a rolling basis. Application fee: $60. Electronic applications accepted. *Expenses:* Tuition, area resident: Part-time $471 per credit hour. Tuition, state resident: part-time $471 per credit hour. Tuition, nonresident: part-time $1016 per credit hour. Required fees: $337.04 per term. *Financial support:* In 2009–10, 5 fellowships with full and partial tuition reimbursements (averaging $10,888 per year), 93 research assistantships with tuition reimbursements (averaging $17,455 per year), 68 teaching assistantships with tuition reimbursements (averaging $16,345 per year) were awarded; career-related internships or fieldwork, Federal Work-Study, and scholarships/grants also available. Support available to part-time students. Financial award applicants required to submit FAFSA. Total annual research expenditures: $32.9 million. *Unit head:* Dr. Cheng-i Wei, Dean, 301-405-2072, Fax: 301-314-9146, E-mail: wei@umd.edu. *Application contact:* Dean of Graduate School, 301-405-0376, Fax: 301-314-9305.

University of Maryland Eastern Shore, Graduate Programs, Department of Agriculture, Princess Anne, MD 21853-1299. Offers food and agricultural sciences (MS); food science and technology (PhD). *Degree requirements:* For master's, comprehensive exam, thesis (for some programs), oral exam; for doctorate, comprehensive exam, thesis/dissertation. *Entrance requirements:* For master's, GRE, minimum GPA of 3.0. Additional exam requirements/recommendations for international students: Required—TOEFL (minimum score 213 computer-based; 80 iBT). Electronic applications accepted. *Faculty research:* Poultry and swine nutrition and management, soybean specialty products, farm management practices, aquaculture technology.

University of Minnesota, Twin Cities Campus, Graduate School, College of Food, Agricultural and Natural Resource Sciences, Minneapolis, MN 55455-0213. Offers MS, PhD. Part-time and evening/weekend programs available. Terminal master's awarded for partial completion of doctoral program. *Degree requirements:* For master's, comprehensive exam, thesis; for doctorate, comprehensive exam, thesis/dissertation. *Entrance requirements:* Additional exam requirements/recommendations for international students: Required—TOEFL (minimum score 550 paper-based; 213 computer-based; 70 iBT). Electronic applications accepted.

University of Missouri, Graduate School, College of Agriculture, Food and Natural Resources, Columbia, MO 65211. Offers MS, PhD, Graduate Certificate, MD/PhD. Part-time programs available. *Faculty:* 431 full-time (121 women), 40 part-time/adjunct (11 women). *Students:* 173 full-time (86 women), 118 part-time (56 women); includes 13 minority (6 African Americans, 1 American Indian/Alaska Native, 4 Asian Americans or Pacific Islanders, 2 Hispanic Americans), 90 international. Average age 29. 268 applicants, 37% accepted, 70 enrolled. In 2009, 13 master's, 9 doctorates awarded. Terminal master's awarded for partial completion of doctoral program. *Degree requirements:* For master's, thesis (for some programs); for doctorate, variable foreign language requirement, comprehensive exam (for some programs), thesis/dissertation. *Entrance requirements:* For master's and doctorate, GRE General Test, minimum GPA of 3.0. Additional exam requirements/recommendations for international students: Required—TOEFL (minimum score 500 paper-based; 173 computer-based; 61 iBT), IELTS (minimum score 5.5). *Application deadline:* Applications are processed on a rolling basis. Application fee: $45 ($60 for international students). Electronic applications accepted. *Financial support:* Fellowships with tuition reimbursements, research assistantships with tuition reimbursements, teaching assistantships with tuition reimbursements, institutionally sponsored loans available. *Unit head:* Dr. Thomas L. Payne, Dean, 573-882-3846, E-mail: paynet@missouri.edu. *Application contact:* Dr. Bryan L. Garton, Associate Dean, E-mail: gartonb@missouri.edu.

University of Nebraska–Lincoln, Graduate College, College of Agricultural Sciences and Natural Resources, Lincoln, NE 68588. Offers M Ag, MA, MBA, MS, PhD. *Degree requirements:* For doctorate, comprehensive exam, thesis/dissertation. *Entrance requirements:* Additional exam requirements/recommendations for international students: Required—TOEFL. Electronic applications accepted. *Faculty research:* Environmental sciences, animal sciences, human resources and family sciences, plant breeding and genetics, food and nutrition.

University of Nevada, Reno, Graduate School, College of Agriculture, Biotechnology and Natural Resources, Reno, NV 89557. Offers MS, PhD. Terminal master's awarded for partial completion of doctoral program. *Degree requirements:* For master's, thesis optional; for doctorate, thesis/dissertation. *Entrance requirements:* For master's, GRE General Test, minimum GPA of 2.75; for doctorate, GRE General Test, minimum GPA of 3.0. Additional exam requirements/recommendations for international students: Required—TOEFL (minimum score 500 paper-based; 173 computer-based; 61 iBT), IELTS (minimum score 6). Electronic applications accepted.

University of Puerto Rico, Mayagüez Campus, Graduate Studies, College of Agricultural Sciences, Mayagüez, PR 00681-9000. Offers MS. Part-time programs available. *Degree requirements:* For master's, comprehensive exam, thesis.

University of Saskatchewan, College of Graduate Studies and Research, College of Agriculture, Saskatoon, SK S7N 5A2, Canada. Offers M Ag, M Sc, MA, PhD, Diploma, PGD. Part-time programs available. *Faculty:* 136. *Students:* 228. *Degree requirements:* For master's, thesis (for some programs); for doctorate, comprehensive exam (for some programs), thesis/dissertation. *Entrance requirements:* Additional exam requirements/recommendations for international students: Required—TOEFL (minimum score 80 iBT); Recommended—IELTS (minimum score 6.5). *Application deadline:* For fall admission, 7/1 priority date for domestic students. Applications are processed on a rolling basis. Application fee: $75. Tuition and fees charges are reported in Canadian dollars. *Expenses:* Tuition, area resident: Full-time $3000 Canadian dollars; part-time $500 Canadian dollars per term. Required fees: $700 Canadian dollars; $100 Canadian dollars per term. *Financial support:* Fellowships, research assistantships, teaching assistantships, career-related internships or fieldwork available. Financial award application deadline: 1/31. *Unit head:* Dr. M. Buhr, Dean, 306-966-4050, Fax: 306-966-8894, E-mail: ernie.barber@usask.ca. *Application contact:* Dr. M. Buhr, Dean, 306-966-4050, Fax: 306-966-8894, E-mail: ernie.barber@usask.ca.

University of South Africa, College of Agriculture and Environmental Sciences, Pretoria, South Africa. Offers agriculture (MS); consumer science (MCS); environmental management (MA, MS, PhD); environmental science (MA, MS, PhD); geography (MA, MS, PhD); horticulture (M Tech); human ecology (MHE); life sciences (MS); nature conservation (M Tech).

The University of Tennessee, Graduate School, College of Agricultural Sciences and Natural Resources, Knoxville, TN 37996. Offers MS, PhD. Part-time programs available. Postbaccalaureate distance learning degree programs offered (minimal on-campus study). *Degree requirements:* For master's, thesis (for some programs); for doctorate, thesis/dissertation. *Entrance requirements:* For master's and doctorate, minimum GPA of 2.7. Additional exam requirements/recommendations for international students: Required—TOEFL. Electronic applications accepted. *Expenses:* Tuition, state resident: full-time $6826; part-time $380 per semester hour. Tuition, nonresident: full-time $21,844; part-time $1147 per semester hour. Tuition and fees vary according to program.

The University of Tennessee at Martin, Graduate Programs, College of Agriculture and Applied Sciences, Program in Agricultural and Natural Resources Management, Martin, TN 38238-1000. Offers MSANR. Part-time programs available. Postbaccalaureate distance learning degree programs offered (no on-campus study). *Faculty:* 22. *Students:* 31 (13 women). 20 applicants, 65% accepted, 8 enrolled. In 2009, 7 master's awarded. *Degree requirements:* For master's, comprehensive exam, thesis optional. *Entrance requirements:* For master's, GRE General Test, minimum GPA of 2.5. Additional exam requirements/recommendations for international students: Required—TOEFL (minimum score 525 paper-based; 197 computer-based; 71 iBT). *Application deadline:* For fall admission, 8/1 priority date for domestic students, 7/15 priority date for international students; for spring admission, 12/15 priority date for domestic students, 12/1 priority date for international students. Applications are processed on a rolling basis. Application fee: $30 ($130 for international students). Electronic applications accepted. *Expenses:* Tuition, state resident: full-time $6660; part-time $372 per hour. Tuition, nonresident: full-time $18,000; part-time $1005 per hour. *Financial support:* In 2009–10, 2 students received support, including 2 research assistantships with full tuition reimbursements available (averaging $8,200 per year); scholarships/grants and unspecified assistantships also available. Support available to part-time students. Financial award application deadline: 2/15; financial award applicants required to submit FAFSA. *Unit head:* Dr. Tim Burcham, Coordinator, 731-881-7275, Fax: 731-881-7968, E-mail: tburcham@utm.edu. *Application contact:* Linda S. Arant, Student Services Specialist, 731-881-7012, Fax: 731-881-7499, E-mail: larant@utm.edu.

University of Vermont, Graduate College, College of Agriculture and Life Sciences, Burlington, VT 05405. Offers MPA, MS, MSD, PhD, MD/MS, MD/PhD. Part-time programs available. *Students:* 158 (96 women); includes 7 minority (6 Asian Americans or Pacific Islanders, 1 Hispanic American), 20 international. 216 applicants, 54% accepted, 46 enrolled. In 2009, 36 master's, 6 doctorates awarded. *Degree requirements:* For doctorate, one foreign language, thesis/dissertation. *Entrance requirements:* For master's and doctorate, GRE General Test. Additional exam requirements/recommendations for international students: Required—TOEFL (minimum score 550 paper-based; 213 computer-based; 80 iBT). Application fee: $40. Electronic applications accepted. *Expenses:* Tuition, area resident: Part-time $508 per credit hour. Tuition, state resident: part-time $508 per credit hour. Tuition, nonresident: part-time $1281 per credit hour. *Financial support:* Fellowships, research assistantships, teaching assistantships, career-related internships or fieldwork, Federal Work-Study, and tuition waivers (full and partial) available. Financial award application deadline: 3/1. *Unit head:* Dr. Thomas C. Vogelmann, Dean, 802-656-2980. *Application contact:* Dr. Thomas C. Vogelmann, Dean, 802-656-2980.

University of Wisconsin–Madison, Graduate School, College of Agricultural and Life Sciences, Madison, WI 53706-1380. Offers MA, MPS, MS, PhD. Part-time programs available. *Entrance requirements:* For master's and doctorate, GRE. Additional exam requirements/recommendations for international students: Required—TOEFL. Electronic applications accepted. *Expenses:* Tuition, state resident: part-time $594 per credit. Tuition, nonresident: part-time $1504 per credit. Required fees: $65 per credit. Tuition and fees vary according to course load, program and reciprocity agreements.

University of Wisconsin–River Falls, Outreach and Graduate Studies, College of Agriculture, Food, and Environmental Sciences, River Falls, WI 54022. Offers MS. Part-time programs available. *Degree requirements:* For master's, comprehensive exam, thesis (for some programs). *Entrance requirements:* For master's, minimum GPA of 2.75. Additional exam requirements/recommendations for international students: Required—TOEFL (minimum score 500 paper-based; 65 iBT), IELTS (minimum score 5.4). Electronic applications accepted.

University of Wyoming, College of Agriculture, Laramie, WY 82070. Offers MS, PhD. Part-time programs available. Terminal master's awarded for partial completion of doctoral program. *Degree requirements:* For doctorate, thesis/dissertation. *Entrance requirements:* For master's and doctorate, GRE General Test, minimum GPA of 3.0. Electronic applications accepted. *Faculty research:* Nutrition, molecular biology, animal science, plant science, entomology.

Utah State University, School of Graduate Studies, College of Agriculture, Logan, UT 84322. Offers MDA, MFMS, MS, PhD. Part-time programs available. Postbaccalaureate distance learning degree programs offered (minimal on-campus study). Terminal master's awarded for partial completion of doctoral program. *Degree requirements:* For doctorate, thesis/dissertation. *Entrance requirements:* For master's and doctorate, GRE General Test, minimum GPA of 3.0. Additional exam requirements/recommendations for international students: Required—TOEFL. *Faculty research:* Low-input agriculture, anti-viral chemotherapy, lactic culture, environmental biophysics and climate.

Virginia Polytechnic Institute and State University, Graduate School, College of Agriculture and Life Sciences, Blacksburg, VA 24061. Offers MS, PhD. *Entrance requirements:* Additional exam requirements/recommendations for international students: Required—TOEFL. Electronic applications accepted. *Faculty research:* Biotechnology, plant pathology, animal nutrition, agribusiness.

Virginia State University, School of Graduate Studies, Research, and Outreach, School of Agriculture, Petersburg, VA 23806-0001. Offers MS.

Agricultural Sciences—General

Washington State University, Graduate School, College of Agricultural, Human, and Natural Resource Sciences, Department of Crop and Soil Sciences, Program in Agriculture, Pullman, WA 99164. Offers MS. *Faculty:* 18. *Students:* 2 full-time (0 women), 22 part-time (13 women); includes 2 minority (1 American Indian/Alaska Native, 1 Asian American or Pacific Islander). 16 applicants, 44% accepted, 2 enrolled. In 2009, 12 master's awarded. *Degree requirements:* For master's, comprehensive exam (for some programs), thesis (for some programs), oral defense. *Entrance requirements:* For master's, Fill out the online application at the WSU Graduate School and send transcripts of all college course work to the Graduate School. In addition, submit three letters of reference and a personal statement describing your intent and interest area(s). Additional exam requirements/recommendations for international students: Required—TOEFL, IELTS. *Application deadline:* For fall admission, 1/10 for domestic and international students; for spring admission, 7/1 for domestic and international students. Application fee: $50. *Financial support:* In 2009–10, 1 fellowship (averaging $2,850 per year), research assistantships (averaging $13,917 per year), teaching assistantships (averaging $13,056 per year) were awarded. *Unit head:* Dr. Kim Kidwell, Interim Director, 509-335-2899, Fax: 509-335-2722, E-mail: mswan@wsu.edu. *Application contact:* Graduate School Admissions, 800-GRADWSU, Fax: 509-335-1949, E-mail: gradsch@wsu.edu.

Western Kentucky University, Graduate Studies, Ogden College of Science and Engineering, Department of Agriculture, Bowling Green, KY 42101. Offers MA Ed, MS. Part-time and evening/weekend programs available. *Degree requirements:* For master's, comprehensive exam, thesis optional. *Entrance requirements:* For master's, GRE General Test, minimum GPA of 2.75. Additional exam requirements/recommendations for international students: Required—TOEFL (minimum score 555 paper-based; 213 computer-based; 79 iBT). *Expenses:* Tuition, state resident: full-time $4160; part-time $416 per credit hour. Tuition, nonresident: full-time $9550; part-time $506 per credit hour. Tuition and fees vary according to campus/location and reciprocity agreements. *Faculty research:* Establishment of warm season grasses, heat composting, enrichment activities in agricultural education.

West Texas A&M University, College of Agriculture, Nursing, and Natural Sciences, Division of Agriculture, Canyon, TX 79016-0001. Offers agricultural business and economics (MS); agriculture (PhD); animal science (MS); plant science (MS). Part-time programs available. *Degree requirements:* For master's, comprehensive exam, thesis optional. *Entrance requirements:* For master's, GRE General Test. Additional exam requirements/recommendations for international students: Required—TOEFL (minimum score 550 paper-based). Electronic applications accepted.

West Virginia University, Davis College of Agriculture, Forestry and Consumer Sciences, Morgantown, WV 26506. Offers M Agr, MS, MSF, PhD. Part-time programs available. *Degree requirements:* For master's, thesis; for doctorate, thesis/dissertation. *Entrance requirements:* Additional exam requirements/recommendations for international students: Required—TOEFL. Electronic applications accepted. *Faculty research:* Reproductive physiology, soil and water quality, human nutrition, aquaculture, wildlife management.

Agronomy and Soil Sciences

Alabama Agricultural and Mechanical University, School of Graduate Studies, School of Agricultural and Environmental Sciences, Department of Plant and Soil Science, Huntsville, AL 35811. Offers animal sciences (MS); environmental science (MS); plant and soil science (PhD). Evening/weekend programs available. Terminal master's awarded for partial completion of doctoral program. *Degree requirements:* For master's, thesis; for doctorate, one foreign language, thesis/dissertation. *Entrance requirements:* For master's, GRE General Test, BS in agriculture; for doctorate, GRE General Test, master's degree. Additional exam requirements/recommendations for international students: Required—TOEFL (minimum score 500 paper-based; 173 computer-based; 61 iBT). Electronic applications accepted. *Faculty research:* Plant breeding, cytogenetics, crop production, soil chemistry and fertility, remote sensing.

Alcorn State University, School of Graduate Studies, School of Agriculture and Applied Science, Alcorn State, MS 39096-7500. Offers agricultural economics (MS Ag); agronomy (MS Ag); animal science (MS Ag). *Degree requirements:* For master's, thesis optional. *Faculty research:* Aquatic systems, dairy herd improvement, fruit production, alternative farming practices.

American University of Beirut, Graduate Programs, Faculty of Agricultural and Food Sciences, Beirut, Lebanon. Offers agricultural economics (MS); animal sciences (MS); ecosystem management (MSES); food technology (MS); irrigation (MS); mechanization (MS); nutrition (MS); plant protection (MS); plant science (MS); poultry science (MS); soils (MS). Part-time programs available. *Degree requirements:* For master's, one foreign language, comprehensive exam, thesis (for some programs). *Entrance requirements:* For master's, letter of recommendation. Additional exam requirements/recommendations for international students: Required—TOEFL (minimum score 600 paper-based; 250 computer-based; 100 iBT), IELTS (minimum score 7.5). *Faculty research:* Sustainable animal systems/agriculture; natural resource management; community nutrition, obesity and food safety; integrated pest management; ecosystem management.

Auburn University, Graduate School, College of Agriculture, Department of Agronomy and Soils, Auburn University, AL 36849. Offers M Ag, MS, PhD. Part-time programs available. *Faculty:* 26 full-time (6 women). *Students:* 20 full-time (7 women), 21 part-time (5 women); includes 1 minority (Asian American or Pacific Islander), 20 international. Average age 28. 19 applicants, 47% accepted, 7 enrolled. In 2009, 11 master's, 4 doctorates awarded. *Degree requirements:* For master's, thesis (for some programs); for doctorate, thesis/dissertation. *Entrance requirements:* For master's and doctorate, GRE General Test. *Application deadline:* For fall admission, 7/7 for domestic students; for spring admission, 11/24 for domestic students. Applications are processed on a rolling basis. Application fee: $50 ($60 for international students). Electronic applications accepted. *Expenses:* Tuition, state resident: full-time $6240. Tuition, nonresident: full-time $18,720. International tuition: $18,938 full-time. Required fees: $492. Tuition and fees vary according to course load, program and reciprocity agreements. *Financial support:* Research assistantships, teaching assistantships, Federal Work-Study available. Support available to part-time students. Financial award application deadline: 3/15; financial award applicants required to submit FAFSA. *Faculty research:* Plant breeding and genetics; weed science; crop production; soil fertility and plant nutrition; soil genesis, morphology, and classification. *Unit head:* Dr. Joseph T. Touchton, Head, 334-844-4100, E-mail: jtouchto@ag.auburn.edu. *Application contact:* Dr. George Flowers, Dean of the Graduate School, 334-844-2125.

Colorado State University, Graduate School, College of Agricultural Sciences, Department of Soil and Crop Sciences, Fort Collins, CO 80523-1170. Offers MS, PhD. Part-time programs available. *Faculty:* 20 full-time (5 women), 2 part-time/adjunct (0 women). *Students:* 16 full-time (7 women), 17 part-time (4 women); includes 2 minority (1 African American, 1 American Indian/Alaska Native), 12 international. Average age 32. 23 applicants, 43% accepted, 6 enrolled. In 2009, 6 master's, 3 doctorates awarded. Terminal master's awarded for partial completion of doctoral program. *Degree requirements:* For master's, thesis; for doctorate, comprehensive exam, thesis/dissertation, student teaching, 2 seminar courses. *Entrance requirements:* For master's, GRE, minimum GPA of 3.0, appropriate bachelor's degree, letters of recommendation, statement of purpose; for doctorate, GRE, minimum GPA of 3.0, appropriate master's degree, letters of recommendation. Additional exam requirements/recommendations for international students: Required—TOEFL (minimum score 550 paper-based; 213 computer-based; 80 iBT). *Application deadline:* For fall admission, 4/1 priority date for domestic and international students; for spring admission, 9/1 priority date for domestic and international students. Application fee: $50. Electronic applications accepted. *Expenses:* Tuition, state resident: full-time $6434; part-time $359.10 per credit. Tuition, nonresident: full-time $18,116; part-time $1006.45 per credit. Required fees: $1496; $83 per credit. *Financial support:* In 2009–10, 15 students received support, including 1 fellowship with full tuition reimbursement available (averaging $17,341 per year), 14 research assistantships with full tuition reimbursements available (averaging $17,591 per year); teaching assistantships with full tuition reimbursements available, scholarships/grants, unspecified assistantships, and fellowships also available. Financial award application deadline: 2/15; financial award applicants required to submit FAFSA. *Faculty research:* Water quality, soil fertility, soil/plant ecosystems, plant breeding and genetics, cropping systems. Total annual research expenditures: $2.4 million. *Unit head:* Dr. Gary A. Peterson, Head, 970-491-6501, Fax: 970-491-0564, E-mail: gary.peterson@colostate.edu. *Application contact:* Dr. Pat F. Byrne, Graduate Studies Coordinator, 970-491-6985, Fax: 970-491-0564, E-mail: pbyrne@lamar.colostate.edu.

Cornell University, Graduate School, Graduate Fields of Agriculture and Life Sciences, Field of Soil and Crop Sciences, Ithaca, NY 14853-0001. Offers agronomy (MS, PhD); environmental information science (MS, PhD); environmental management (MPS); field crop science (MS, PhD); soil science (MS, PhD). *Faculty:* 40 full-time (9 women). *Students:* 32 full-time (17 women); includes 5 minority (1 American Indian/Alaska Native, 4 Hispanic Americans), 9 international. Average age 33. 42 applicants, 24% accepted, 5 enrolled. In 2009, 2 master's, 8 doctorates awarded. *Degree requirements:* For master's, thesis (MS); for doctorate, comprehensive exam, thesis/dissertation. *Entrance requirements:* For master's and doctorate, GRE General Test, 2 letters of recommendation. Additional exam requirements/recommendations for international students: Required—TOEFL (minimum score 550 paper-based; 213 computer-based; 77 iBT). *Application deadline:* For fall admission, 2/1 priority date for domestic students. Applications are processed on a rolling basis. Application fee: $70. Electronic applications accepted. *Expenses:* Tuition: Full-time $29,500. Required fees: $70. Full-time tuition and fees vary according to degree level, program and student level. *Financial support:* In 2009–10, 26 students received support, including 1 fellowship with full tuition reimbursement available, 1 research assistantship with full tuition reimbursement available, 1 teaching assistantship with full tuition reimbursement available; institutionally sponsored loans, traineeships, health care benefits, tuition waivers (full and partial), and unspecified assistantships also available. *Faculty research:* Soil chemistry, physics and biology; crop physiology and management; environmental information science and modeling; international agriculture; weed science. *Unit head:* Director of Graduate Studies, 607-255-3267, Fax: 607-255-8615. *Application contact:* Graduate Field Assistant, 607-255-3267, Fax: 607-255-8615, E-mail: ljh4@cornell.edu.

Iowa State University of Science and Technology, Graduate College, College of Agriculture, Department of Agronomy, Ames, IA 50011. Offers agricultural meteorology (MS, PhD); agronomy (MS); crop production and physiology (MS, PhD); plant breeding (MS, PhD); soil science (MS, PhD). Postbaccalaureate distance learning degree programs offered (no on-campus study). *Faculty:* 60 full-time (9 women), 6 part-time/adjunct (0 women). *Students:* 93 full-time (32 women), 101 part-time (24 women); includes 12 minority (4 African Americans, 5 Asian Americans or Pacific Islanders, 3 Hispanic Americans), 40 international. 93 applicants, 52% accepted, 45 enrolled. In 2009, 21 master's, 7 doctorates awarded. *Degree requirements:* For master's, thesis or alternative; for doctorate, thesis/dissertation. *Entrance requirements:* Additional exam requirements/recommendations for international students: Required—TOEFL (minimum score 550 paper-based; 79 iBT) or IELTS (minimum score 6.5). *Application deadline:* For fall admission, 5/8 priority date for domestic and international students; for spring admission, 10/1 priority date for domestic and international students. Applications are processed on a rolling basis. Application fee: $40 ($90 for international students). Electronic applications accepted. *Expenses:* Tuition, state resident: full-time $6716. Tuition, nonresident: full-time $8908. Tuition and fees vary according to course level, course load, program and student level. *Financial support:* In 2009–10, 58 research assistantships with full and partial tuition reimbursements (averaging $15,870 per year), 2 teaching assistantships with full and partial tuition reimbursements (averaging $15,870 per year) were awarded; fellowships, scholarships/grants, health care benefits, and unspecified assistantships also available. *Unit head:* Dr. Kendall Lamkey, Head, 515-294-7636, Fax: 515-294-3163. *Application contact:* Dr. Thomas E. Loynachan, Director of Graduate Education, 515-294-2999, E-mail: gradprograms@agron.iastate.edu.

Kansas State University, Graduate School, College of Agriculture, Department of Agronomy, Manhattan, KS 66506. Offers crop science (MS, PhD); range management (MS, PhD); soil science (MS, PhD); weed science (MS, PhD). Part-time programs available. *Faculty:* 32 full-time (4 women), 11 part-time/adjunct (1 woman). *Students:* 72 full-time (17 women); includes 1 minority (African American), 28 international. Average age 34. 16 applicants, 38% accepted, 6 enrolled. In 2009, 13 master's, 5 doctorates awarded. Terminal master's awarded for partial completion of doctoral program. *Degree requirements:* For master's, thesis or alternative, oral exam; for doctorate, thesis/dissertation, preliminary exams. *Entrance requirements:* For master's, minimum GPA of 3.0 in BS; for doctorate, minimum GPA of 3.5 in master's program. Additional exam requirements/recommendations for international students: Required—TOEFL (minimum score 500 paper-based; 250 computer-based). *Application deadline:* For fall admission, 2/1 priority date for domestic and international students; for spring admission, 8/1 priority date for domestic and international students. Applications are processed on a rolling basis. Application fee: $40 ($55 for international students). Electronic applications accepted. *Financial support:* In 2009–10, 60 research assistantships (averaging $16,061 per year) were awarded; teaching assistantships with partial tuition reimbursements, institutionally sponsored loans and scholarships/grants also available. Support available to part-time students. Financial award application deadline: 3/1; financial award applicants required to submit FAFSA. *Faculty research:* Range and forage science, soil and environmental science, crop physiology, weed science, plant breeding and genetics. Total annual research expenditures: $4.6 million. *Unit head:* Dr. Gary Pierzynski, Head, 785-532-6101, Fax: 785-532-6094, E-mail: gmp@ksu.edu. *Application contact:* Dr. Bill Schapaugh, Director, 785-532-7242, Fax: 785-532-6094, E-mail: wts@ksu.edu.

Louisiana State University and Agricultural and Mechanical College, Graduate School, College of Agriculture, School of Plant, Environmental and Soil Science, Department of Agronomy and Environmental Management, Baton Rouge, LA 70803. Offers agronomy (MS, PhD). Part-time programs available. *Faculty:* 32 full-time (4 women). *Students:* 31 full-time (9 women), 5 part-time (1 woman); includes 3 minority (2 Asian Americans or Pacific Islanders, 1 Hispanic American), 16 international. Average age 31. 22 applicants, 45% accepted, 7 enrolled. In 2009, 2 master's, 7 doctorates awarded. *Degree requirements:* For master's, thesis or alternative; for doctorate, thesis/dissertation. *Entrance requirements:* For master's and doctorate,

GRE General Test, minimum GPA of 3.0. Additional exam requirements/recommendations for international students: Required—TOEFL (minimum score 550 paper-based; 213 computer-based; 79 iBT) or IELTS (minimum score 6.5). *Application deadline:* For fall admission, 1/25 priority date for domestic students, 5/15 for international students; for spring admission, 10/15 for international students. Applications are processed on a rolling basis. Application fee: $50 ($70 for international students). Electronic applications accepted. *Financial support:* In 2009–10, 33 students received support, including 26 research assistantships with partial tuition reimbursements available (averaging $18,606 per year); fellowships, teaching assistantships with partial tuition reimbursements available, Federal Work-Study, scholarships/grants, tuition waivers (full), and unspecified assistantships also available. Support available to part-time students. Financial award applicants required to submit FAFSA. *Faculty research:* Crop production, resource management, environmental studies, soil science, plant genetics. Total annual research expenditures: $20,107. *Unit head:* Dr. Don LaBonte, Director, 225-578-2110, Fax: 225-578-1403, E-mail: dlabont@lsu.edu. *Application contact:* Dr. Magdi Selim, Graduate Coordinator, Agronomy, 225-578-1332, Fax: 225-578-1403, E-mail: mselim@agctr.lsu.edu.

McGill University, Faculty of Graduate and Postdoctoral Studies, Faculty of Agricultural and Environmental Sciences, Department of Bioresource Engineering, Montréal, QC H3A 2T5, Canada. Offers computer applications (M Sc, M Sc A, PhD); food engineering (M Sc, M Sc A, PhD); grain drying (M Sc, M Sc A, PhD); irrigation and drainage (M Sc, M Sc A, PhD); machinery (M Sc, M Sc A, PhD); pollution control (M Sc, M Sc A, PhD); post-harvest technology (M Sc, M Sc A, PhD); soil dynamics (M Sc, M Sc A, PhD); structure and environment (M Sc, M Sc A, PhD); vegetable and fruit storage (M Sc, M Sc A, PhD).

McGill University, Faculty of Graduate and Postdoctoral Studies, Faculty of Agricultural and Environmental Sciences, Department of Natural Resource Sciences, Montréal, QC H3A 2T5, Canada. Offers entomology (M Sc, PhD); environmental assessment (M Sc); forest science (M Sc, PhD); microbiology (M Sc, PhD); micrometeorology (M Sc, PhD); neotropical environment (M Sc, PhD); soil science (M Sc, PhD); wildlife biology (M Sc, PhD).

Michigan State University, The Graduate School, College of Agriculture and Natural Resources, Department of Crop and Soil Sciences, East Lansing, MI 48824. Offers crop and soil sciences (MS, PhD); crop and soil sciences-environmental toxicology (PhD); plant breeding and genetics-crop and soil sciences (MS); plant breeding, genetics and biotechnology-crop and soil sciences (PhD). *Entrance requirements:* Additional exam requirements/recommendations for international students: Required—TOEFL (minimum score 550 paper-based; 213 computer-based), Michigan State University ELT (85), Michigan ELAB (83). Electronic applications accepted.

Mississippi State University, College of Agriculture and Life Sciences, Department of Plant and Soil Sciences, Mississippi State, MS 39762. Offers agricultural sciences (PhD), including agronomy (MS, PhD), horticulture (MS, PhD), weed science (MS, PhD); agriculture (MS), including agronomy (MS, PhD), horticulture (MS, PhD), weed science (MS, PhD). *Faculty:* 24 full-time (1 woman), 1 part-time/adjunct (0 women). *Students:* 26 full-time (8 women), 30 part-time (8 women); includes 1 minority (American Indian/Alaska Native), 16 international. Average age 30. 31 applicants, 39% accepted, 12 enrolled. In 2009, 7 master's, 1 doctorate awarded. *Degree requirements:* For master's, thesis, exit seminar describing thesis research; for doctorate, comprehensive exam, thesis/dissertation, two departmental seminars. *Entrance requirements:* For master's, GRE (weed science), minimum GPA of 2.75 (agronomy/horticulture), 3.0 (weed science); for doctorate, GRE (weed science), minimum GPA of 3.0 (agronomy/horticulture), 3.25 (weed science). Additional exam requirements/recommendations for international students: Required—TOEFL (minimum score 550 paper-based; 213 computer-based; 79 iBT); Recommended—IELTS (minimum score 6.5). *Application deadline:* For fall admission, 7/1 for domestic students, 5/1 for international students; for spring admission, 10/1 for domestic students, 9/1 for international students. Applications are processed on a rolling basis. Application fee: $40. Electronic applications accepted. *Expenses:* Tuition, state resident: full-time $2575.50; part-time $286.25 per credit hour. Tuition, nonresident: full-time $6510; part-time $723.50 per credit hour. Tuition and fees vary according to course load. *Financial support:* In 2009–10, 25 research assistantships (averaging $11,626 per year), 3 teaching assistantships (averaging $12,379 per year) were awarded; Federal Work-Study, institutionally sponsored loans, scholarships/grants, and unspecified assistantships also available. Financial award application deadline: 4/1; financial award applicants required to submit FAFSA. *Unit head:* Dr. Daniel Reynolds, Professor/Interim Head, 662-325-2311, Fax: 662-325-8742, E-mail: dreynolds@pss.msstate.edu. *Application contact:* Dr. William Kingery, Graduate Coordinator, 662-325-2748, Fax: 662-325-8742, E-mail: wkingery@pss.msstate.edu.

North Carolina Agricultural and Technical State University, Graduate School, School of Agriculture and Environmental Sciences, Department of Natural Resources and Environmental Design, Greensboro, NC 27411. Offers plant, soil and environmental science (MS). Part-time and evening/weekend programs available. *Degree requirements:* For master's, comprehensive exam, thesis optional, qualifying exam. *Entrance requirements:* For master's, GRE General Test, minimum GPA of 3.0. *Faculty research:* Soil parameters and compaction of forest site, controlled traffic effects on soil, improving soybean and vegetable crops.

North Carolina State University, Graduate School, College of Agriculture and Life Sciences, Department of Crop Science, Raleigh, NC 27695. Offers MS, PhD. Part-time programs available. Terminal master's awarded for partial completion of doctoral program. *Degree requirements:* For master's, thesis; for doctorate, thesis/dissertation. *Entrance requirements:* For master's and doctorate, GRE. Electronic applications accepted. *Faculty research:* Crop breeding and genetics, application of biotechnology to crop improvement, plant physiology, crop physiology and management, agroecology.

North Carolina State University, Graduate School, College of Agriculture and Life Sciences, Department of Soil Science, Raleigh, NC 27695. Offers MS, PhD. Part-time programs available. Postbaccalaureate distance learning degree programs offered. *Degree requirements:* For master's, thesis (for some programs); for doctorate, thesis/dissertation. *Entrance requirements:* For master's and doctorate, GRE, minimum GPA of 3.0. Additional exam requirements/recommendations for international students: Required—TOEFL (minimum score 75 iBT). Electronic applications accepted. *Faculty research:* Soil management, soil-environmental relations, chemical and physical properties of soils, nutrient and water management, land use.

North Dakota State University, College of Graduate and Interdisciplinary Studies, College of Agriculture, Food Systems, and Natural Resources, Department of Soil Science, Fargo, ND 58108. Offers environmental and conservation science (PhD); environmental conservation science (MS); natural resource management (MS, PhD); soil sciences (MS, PhD). Part-time programs available. *Faculty:* 8 full-time (1 woman), 6 part-time/adjunct (0 women). *Students:* 6 full-time (4 women), 3 part-time (1 woman). Average age 23. 3 applicants, 67% accepted, 2 enrolled. In 2009, 2 master's, 1 doctorate awarded. *Degree requirements:* For master's, comprehensive exam, thesis, classroom teaching; for doctorate, comprehensive exam, thesis/dissertation, classroom teaching. *Entrance requirements:* Additional exam requirements/recommendations for international students: Required—TOEFL (minimum score 525 paper-based; 193 computer-based; 71 iBT). *Application deadline:* Applications are processed on a rolling basis. Application fee: $45 ($60 for international students). Electronic applications accepted. *Financial support:* In 2009–10, 7 research assistantships with full tuition reimbursements (averaging $14,300 per year) were awarded; fellowships, Federal Work-Study, institutionally sponsored loans, and scholarships/grants also available. Financial award application deadline: 3/15. *Faculty research:* Microclimate, nitrogen management, landscape studies, water quality, soil management. *Unit head:* Dr. Donald Kirby, Interim Chair, 701-231-8901, Fax: 701-231-7861. *Application contact:* Dr. Donald Kirby, Interim Chair, 701-231-8901, Fax: 701-231-7861.

Nova Scotia Agricultural College, Research and Graduate Studies, Truro, NS B2N 5E3, Canada. Offers agriculture (M Sc), including air quality, animal behavior, animal molecular genetics, animal nutrition, animal technology, aquaculture, botany, crop management, crop physiology, ecology, environmental microbiology, food science, horticulture, nutrient management, pest management, physiology, plant biotechnology, plant pathology, soil chemistry, soil fertility, waste management and composting, water quality. Part-time programs available. *Degree requirements:* For master's, thesis, ATC Exam Teaching Assistantship. *Entrance requirements:* For master's, honors B Sc, minimum GPA of 3.0. Additional exam requirements/recommendations for international students: Required—TOEFL (minimum score 580 paper-based; 237 computer-based; 92 iBT), IELTS, Michigan English Language Assessment Battery, CanTEST, CAEL. *Faculty research:* Bio-product development, organic agriculture, nutrient management, air and water quality, agricultural biotechnology.

The Ohio State University, Graduate School, College of Food, Agricultural, and Environmental Sciences, School of Environment and Natural Resources, Program in Soil Science, Columbus, OH 43210. Offers MS, PhD. *Faculty:* 17. *Students:* 7 full-time (3 women), 4 part-time (3 women); includes 1 minority (Hispanic American), 3 international. Average age 29. In 2009, 4 master's, 3 doctorates awarded. *Degree requirements:* For doctorate, thesis/dissertation. *Entrance requirements:* For master's and doctorate, GRE General Test. Additional exam requirements/recommendations for international students: Required—TOEFL (minimum score 550 paper-based; 213 computer-based) or IELTS (minimum score 7) or Michigan English Language Assessment Battery (minimum score 90). *Application deadline:* For fall admission, 8/15 priority date for domestic students, 7/1 priority date for international students; for winter admission, 12/1 priority date for domestic students, 11/1 priority date for international students; for spring admission, 3/1 priority date for domestic students, 2/1 priority date for international students. Applications are processed on a rolling basis. Application fee: $40 ($50 for international students). Electronic applications accepted. *Expenses:* Tuition, state resident: full-time $10,683. Tuition, nonresident: full-time $25,923. Tuition and fees vary according to course load and program. *Unit head:* Richard Dick, Graduate Studies Committee Chair, 614-263-3877, Fax: 614-292-7432, E-mail: dick.78@osu.edu. *Application contact:* 614-292-9444, Fax: 614-292-3895, E-mail: domestic.grad@osu.edu.

Oklahoma State University, College of Agricultural Science and Natural Resources, Department of Horticulture and Landscape Architecture, Stillwater, OK 74078. Offers agriculture (M Ag); crop science (PhD); environmental science (PhD); horticulture (MS); plant science (PhD). *Accreditation:* ASLA. *Faculty:* 21 full-time (2 women), 2 part-time/adjunct (1 woman). *Students:* 14 part-time (6 women); includes 2 minority (1 African American, 1 American Indian/Alaska Native), 6 international. Average age 28. 23 applicants, 48% accepted, 7 enrolled. In 2009, 3 master's awarded. *Degree requirements:* For master's, thesis (for some programs); for doctorate, comprehensive exam, thesis/dissertation. *Entrance requirements:* For master's and doctorate, GRE or GMAT. Additional exam requirements/recommendations for international students: Required—TOEFL (minimum score 550 paper-based; 79 iBT). *Application deadline:* For fall admission, 3/1 priority date for international students; for spring admission, 8/1 priority date for international students. Applications are processed on a rolling basis. Application fee: $40 ($75 for international students). Electronic applications accepted. *Expenses:* Tuition, state resident: full-time $3716; part-time $154.85 per credit hour. Tuition, nonresident: full-time $14,448; part-time $602 per credit hour. Required fees: $1772; $73.85 per credit hour. One-time fee: $50. Tuition and fees vary according to course load and campus/location. *Financial support:* In 2009–10, 12 research assistantships (averaging $15,748 per year) were awarded; career-related internships or fieldwork, Federal Work-Study, scholarships/grants, health care benefits, tuition waivers (partial), and unspecified assistantships also available. Support available to part-time students. Financial award application deadline: 3/1; financial award applicants required to submit FAFSA. *Faculty research:* Stress and postharvest physiology; water utilization and runoff; IPM systems and nursery, turf, floriculture, vegetable, net and fruit produces and natural resources, food extraction, and processing; public garden management. *Unit head:* Dr. Dale Maronek, Head, 405-744-5414, Fax: 405-744-9709. *Application contact:* Dr. Gordon Emslie, Dean, 405-744-6368, Fax: 405-744-0355, E-mail: grad-i@okstate.edu.

Oklahoma State University, College of Agricultural Science and Natural Resources, Department of Plant and Soil Sciences, Stillwater, OK 74078. Offers crop science (PhD); environmental science (PhD); plant and soil sciences (MS); plant science (PhD); soil science (M Ag, PhD). *Faculty:* 33 full-time (4 women), 2 part-time/adjunct (0 women). *Students:* 15 full-time (4 women), 37 part-time (13 women); includes 1 minority (Asian American or Pacific Islander), 20 international. Average age 28. 34 applicants, 38% accepted, 7 enrolled. In 2009, 9 master's, 3 doctorates awarded. *Degree requirements:* For master's, thesis; for doctorate, comprehensive exam, thesis/dissertation. *Entrance requirements:* For master's and doctorate, GRE or GMAT. Additional exam requirements/recommendations for international students: Required—TOEFL (minimum score 550 paper-based; 79 iBT). *Application deadline:* For fall admission, 3/1 priority date for international students; for spring admission, 8/1 priority date for international students. Applications are processed on a rolling basis. Application fee: $40 ($75 for international students). Electronic applications accepted. *Expenses:* Tuition, state resident: full-time $3716; part-time $154.85 per credit hour. Tuition, nonresident: full-time $14,448; part-time $602 per credit hour. Required fees: $1772; $73.85 per credit hour. One-time fee: $50. Tuition and fees vary according to course load and campus/location. *Financial support:* In 2009–10, 38 research assistantships (averaging $14,373 per year), 1 teaching assistantship (averaging $13,920 per year) were awarded; career-related internships or fieldwork, Federal Work-Study, scholarships/grants, health care benefits, tuition waivers (partial), and unspecified assistantships also available. Support available to part-time students. Financial award application deadline: 3/1; financial award applicants required to submit FAFSA. *Faculty research:* Crop science, weed science, rangeland ecology and management, biotechnology, breeding and genetics. *Unit head:* Dr. David R. Porter, Head, 405-744-6130, Fax: 405-744-5269. *Application contact:* Dr. Gordon Emslie, Dean, 405-744-6368, Fax: 405-744-0355, E-mail: grad-i@okstate.edu.

Oregon State University, Graduate School, College of Agricultural Sciences, Department of Crop and Soil Science, Program in Crop Science, Corvallis, OR 97331. Offers M Agr, MAIS, MS, PhD. Part-time programs available. *Students:* 18 full-time (10 women), 2 part-time (0 women), 10 international. Average age 32. In 2009, 1 master's awarded. *Degree requirements:* For master's, thesis (for some programs); for doctorate, variable foreign language requirement, thesis/dissertation. *Entrance requirements:* For master's and doctorate, GRE, minimum GPA of 3.0 in last 90 hours of course work. Additional exam requirements/recommendations for international students: Required—TOEFL. *Application deadline:* For fall admission, 3/1 for domestic students. Applications are processed on a rolling basis. Application fee: $50. *Expenses:* Tuition, state resident: full-time $9774; part-time $362 per credit. Tuition, nonresident: full-time $15,849; part-time $587 per credit. Required fees: $1639. Full-time tuition and fees vary according to course load and program. *Financial support:* Fellowships, research assistantships, teaching assistantships, career-related internships or fieldwork, Federal Work-Study, and institutionally sponsored loans available. Support available to part-time students. Financial award application deadline: 2/1. *Faculty research:* Cereal and new crops breeding and genetics; weed science; seed technology and production; potato, new crops, and general crop production; plant physiology. *Unit head:* Dr. Patrick M. Hayes, Head, 541-737-5878, Fax: 541-737-1589, E-mail: patrick.m.hayes@oregonstate.edu. *Application contact:* Dr. Patrick M. Hayes, Head, 541-737-5878, Fax: 541-737-1589, E-mail: patrick.m.hayes@oregonstate.edu.

Oregon State University, Graduate School, College of Agricultural Sciences, Department of Crop and Soil Science, Program in Soil Science, Corvallis, OR 97331. Offers M Agr, MAIS, MS, PhD. Part-time programs available. *Students:* 10 full-time (4 women), 5 part-time (all women); includes 1 minority (Asian American or Pacific Islander), 3 international. Average age 33. In 2009, 4 master's awarded. *Degree requirements:* For master's, thesis (for some programs); for doctorate, variable foreign language requirement, thesis/dissertation. *Entrance requirements:*

Agronomy and Soil Sciences

Oregon State University (continued)

For master's and doctorate, GRE, minimum GPA of 3.0 in last 90 hours of course work. Additional exam requirements/recommendations for international students: Required—TOEFL. *Application deadline:* For fall admission, 3/1 for domestic students. Applications are processed on a rolling basis. Application fee: $50. *Expenses:* Tuition, state resident: full-time $9774; part-time $362 per credit. Tuition, nonresident: full-time $15,849; part-time $587 per credit. Required fees: $1639. Full-time tuition and fees vary according to course load and program. *Financial support:* Fellowships, research assistantships, teaching assistantships, career-related internships or fieldwork, Federal Work-Study, and institutionally sponsored loans available. Support available to part-time students. Financial award application deadline: 2/1. *Faculty research:* Soil physics, chemistry, biology, fertility, and genesis. *Unit head:* Dr. David D. Myrold, Associate Head, 541-737-5737, Fax: 541-737-5725, E-mail: david.myrold@oregonstate.edu. *Application contact:* Dr. Neil W. Christensen, Professor, 541-737-5733, Fax: 541-737-5725, E-mail: neil.w.christensen@orst.edu.

Penn State University Park, Graduate School, College of Agricultural Sciences, Department of Crop and Soil Sciences, State College, University Park, PA 16802-1503. Offers MS, PhD.

Prairie View A&M University, College of Agriculture and Human Sciences, Prairie View, TX 77446-0519. Offers agricultural economics (MS); animal sciences (MS); interdisciplinary human sciences (MS); soil science (MS). Part-time and evening/weekend programs available. *Faculty:* 11 full-time (4 women). *Students:* 36 full-time (27 women), 40 part-time (29 women); includes 57 African Americans, 1 Hispanic American, 6 international. Average age 31. 147 applicants, 100% accepted. In 2009, 23 master's awarded. *Degree requirements:* For master's, comprehensive exam, thesis (for some programs), field placement. *Entrance requirements:* For master's, GRE General Test, minimum GPA of 2.45. Additional exam requirements/recommendations for international students: Required—TOEFL (minimum score 550 paper-based). *Application deadline:* For fall admission, 6/1 for domestic and international students; for spring admission, 10/1 for domestic and international students. Applications are processed on a rolling basis. Application fee: $50. *Expenses:* Tuition, state resident: full-time $2200. Tuition, nonresident: full-time $5600. Required fees: $1720. Tuition and fees vary according to course load. *Financial support:* In 2009–10, 57 students received support, including 8 fellowships with tuition reimbursements available (averaging $12,000 per year), 10 research assistantships with tuition reimbursements available (averaging $15,000 per year); career-related internships or fieldwork, Federal Work-Study, institutionally sponsored loans, scholarships/grants, tuition waivers (partial), and unspecified assistantships also available. Support available to part-time students. Financial award application deadline: 4/1; financial award applicants required to submit FAFSA. *Faculty research:* Domestic violence prevention, water quality, food growth regulators, wetland dynamics, biochemistry, obesity and nutrition, family therapy. Total annual research expenditures: $4 million. *Unit head:* Dr. Freddie Richards, Dean, 936-261-2528, Fax: 936-261-5143, E-mail: flrichards@pvamu.edu. *Application contact:* Dr. Richard W. Griffin, Interim Department Head, 936-261-5019, Fax: 936-261-5148, E-mail: rwgriffin@pvamu.edu.

Purdue University, Graduate School, College of Agriculture, Department of Agronomy, West Lafayette, IN 47907. Offers MS, PhD. Part-time programs available. *Degree requirements:* For doctorate, thesis/dissertation. *Entrance requirements:* For master's and doctorate, GRE General Test. Electronic applications accepted. *Faculty research:* Plant genetics and breeding, crop physiology and ecology, agricultural meteorology, soil microbiology.

South Dakota State University, Graduate School, College of Agriculture and Biological Sciences, Department of Plant Science, Brookings, SD 57007. Offers agronomy (PhD); biological sciences (PhD); plant science (MS). *Degree requirements:* For master's, thesis (for some programs), oral exam; for doctorate, comprehensive exam, thesis/dissertation, preliminary oral and written exams. *Entrance requirements:* Additional exam requirements/recommendations for international students: Required—TOEFL (minimum score 560 paper-based; 220 computer-based; 83 iBT).

Southern Illinois University Carbondale, Graduate School, College of Agriculture, Department of Plant, Soil, and General Agriculture, Carbondale, IL 62901-4701. Offers horticultural science (MS); plant and soil science (MS). *Degree requirements:* For master's, thesis. *Entrance requirements:* For master's, minimum GPA of 2.7. Additional exam requirements/recommendations for international students: Required—TOEFL. *Faculty research:* Herbicides, fertilizers, agriculture education, landscape design, plant breeding.

Texas A&M University, College of Agriculture and Life Sciences, Department of Soil and Crop Sciences, College Station, TX 77843. Offers agronomy (M Agr, MS, PhD); genetics (PhD); molecular and environmental plant sciences (MS, PhD); soil science (MS, PhD). *Faculty:* 36. *Students:* 82 full-time (28 women), 25 part-time (6 women); includes 16 minority (4 African Americans, 1 American Indian/Alaska Native, 1 Asian American or Pacific Islander, 10 Hispanic Americans), 33 international. Average age 26. In 2009, 6 master's, 2 doctorates awarded. *Degree requirements:* For master's, thesis; for doctorate, thesis/dissertation. *Entrance requirements:* For master's and doctorate, GRE General Test. Additional exam requirements/recommendations for international students: Required—TOEFL. *Application deadline:* For fall admission, 3/1 priority date for domestic students; for spring admission, 8/1 for domestic students. Applications are processed on a rolling basis. Application fee: $50 ($75 for international students). *Expenses:* Tuition, state resident: full-time $3991.32; part-time $221.74 per credit hour. Tuition, nonresident: full-time $9049; part-time $502.74 per credit hour. *Financial support:* In 2009–10, fellowships (averaging $16,000 per year), research assistantships with partial tuition reimbursements (averaging $15,000 per year) were awarded; career-related internships or fieldwork, Federal Work-Study, and institutionally sponsored loans also available. *Faculty research:* Soil and crop management, turfgrass science, weed science, cereal chemistry, food protein chemistry. *Unit head:* Department Head, 979-845-3041, E-mail: soilcrop@tamu.edu. *Application contact:* Department Head, 979-845-3041, E-mail: soilcrop@tamu.edu.

Texas A&M University–Kingsville, College of Graduate Studies, College of Agriculture and Home Economics, Program in Plant and Soil Sciences, Kingsville, TX 78363. Offers MS, PhD. *Degree requirements:* For master's, comprehensive exam, thesis or alternative. *Entrance requirements:* For master's, GRE General Test, minimum GPA of 3.0. Additional exam requirements/recommendations for international students: Required—TOEFL.

Texas Tech University, Graduate School, College of Agricultural Sciences and Natural Resources, Department of Plant and Soil Science, Lubbock, TX 79409. Offers crop science (MS); entomology (MS); horticulture (MS); plant and soil science (PhD); soil science (MS); JD/MS. Part-time programs available. *Faculty:* 15 full-time (3 women), 6 part-time/adjunct (0 women). *Students:* 48 full-time (21 women), 42 part-time (18 women); includes 6 minority (2 African Americans, 4 Hispanic Americans), 26 international. Average age 33. 58 applicants, 72% accepted, 27 enrolled. In 2009, 13 master's, 4 doctorates awarded. *Degree requirements:* For master's, thesis or alternative; for doctorate, thesis/dissertation. *Entrance requirements:* For master's and doctorate, GRE General Test. Additional exam requirements/recommendations for international students: Required—TOEFL (minimum score 550 paper-based; 213 computer-based). *Application deadline:* For fall admission, 3/1 priority date for international students; for spring admission, 11/1 priority date for international students. Applications are processed on a rolling basis. Application fee: $50 ($75 for international students). Electronic applications accepted. *Expenses:* Tuition, state resident: full-time $5100; part-time $213 per credit hour. Tuition, nonresident: full-time $11,748; part-time $490 per credit hour. Required fees: $2298; $50 per credit hour. $555 per semester. *Financial support:* In 2009–10, 23 research assistantships with partial tuition reimbursements (averaging $20,991 per year) were awarded; teaching assistantships with partial tuition reimbursements, Federal Work-Study and institutionally sponsored loans also available. Support available to part-time students. Financial award application deadline: 4/15; financial award applicants required to submit FAFSA. *Faculty research:* Molecular and cellular biology of plant stress, physiology/genetics of crop production in semiarid conditions, agricultural bioterrorism, improvement of native plants, soil science and management. Total annual research expenditures: $3.4 million. *Unit head:* Dr. Thomas Thompson, Chair, 806-742-2837, Fax: 806-742-0775, E-mail: thomas.thompson@ttu.edu. *Application contact:* Dr. Eric Hequet, Graduate Adviser, 806-742-2837, Fax: 806-742-0775, E-mail: eric.hequet@ttu.edu.

Tuskegee University, Graduate Programs, College of Agricultural, Environmental and Natural Sciences, Department of Agricultural Sciences, Program in Plant and Soil Sciences, Tuskegee, AL 36088. Offers MS. *Faculty:* 13 full-time (1 woman), 2 part-time/adjunct (1 woman). *Students:* 8 full-time (2 women), 1 (woman) part-time; includes 3 minority (all African Americans), 6 international. Average age 30. In 2009, 1 master's awarded. *Degree requirements:* For master's, thesis. *Entrance requirements:* For master's, GRE General Test. Additional exam requirements/recommendations for international students: Required—TOEFL (minimum score 500 paper-based; 69 computer-based). *Application deadline:* For fall admission, 7/15 for domestic students. Applications are processed on a rolling basis. Application fee: $25 ($35 for international students). *Expenses:* Tuition: Full-time $15,630; part-time $940 per credit hour. Required fees: $650. *Financial support:* Application deadline: 4/15. *Application contact:* Dr. Robert L. Laney, Vice President/Director of Admissions and Enrollment Management, 334-727-8580, Fax: 334-727-5750, E-mail: planey@tuskegee.edu.

Université Laval, Faculty of Agricultural and Food Sciences, Department of Soils and Agricultural Engineering, Programs in Soils and Environment Science, Québec, QC G1K 7P4, Canada. Offers environmental technology (M Sc); soils and environment science (M Sc, PhD). Terminal master's awarded for partial completion of doctoral program. *Degree requirements:* For master's, thesis (for some programs); for doctorate, comprehensive exam, thesis/dissertation. *Entrance requirements:* For master's and doctorate, knowledge of French and English. Electronic applications accepted.

Université Laval, Faculty of Forestry and Geomatics, Program in Agroforestry, Québec, QC G1K 7P4, Canada. Offers M Sc. *Degree requirements:* For master's, thesis (for some programs). *Entrance requirements:* For master's, English exam (comprehension of English), knowledge of French, knowledge of a third language. Electronic applications accepted.

University of Alberta, Faculty of Graduate Studies and Research, Department of Renewable Resources, Edmonton, AB T6G 2E1, Canada. Offers agroforestry (M Ag, M Sc, MF); conservation biology (M Sc, PhD); forest biology and management (M Sc, PhD); land reclamation and remediation (M Sc, PhD); protected areas and wildlands management (M Sc, PhD); soil science (M Ag, M Sc, PhD); water and land resources (M Ag, M Sc, PhD); wildlife ecology and management (M Sc, PhD); MBA/M Ag; MBA/MF. Part-time programs available. *Faculty:* 26 full-time (4 women), 22 part-time/adjunct (3 women). *Students:* 63 full-time (33 women), 50 part-time (20 women), 14 international. 122 applicants, 24% accepted, 22 enrolled. In 2009, 16 master's, 8 doctorates awarded. *Degree requirements:* For master's, thesis (for some programs); for doctorate, comprehensive exam, thesis/dissertation. *Entrance requirements:* For master's, minimum 2 years of relevant professional experiences, minimum GPA of 3.0; for doctorate, minimum GPA of 3.0. Additional exam requirements/recommendations for international students: Required—TOEFL (minimum score 550 paper-based; 213 computer-based). *Application deadline:* For fall admission, 7/1 priority date for domestic students, 6/1 priority date for international students. Applications are processed on a rolling basis. Application fee: $0. Electronic applications accepted. Tuition and fees charges are reported in Canadian dollars. *Expenses:* Tuition, area resident: Full-time $4626.24 Canadian dollars; part-time $99.72 Canadian dollars per unit. International tuition: $8216 Canadian dollars full-time. Required fees: $3589.92 Canadian dollars; $99.72 Canadian dollars per unit. $215 Canadian dollars per term. *Financial support:* In 2009–10, 63 students received support, including 21 research assistantships with partial tuition reimbursements available (averaging $2,800 per year), 28 teaching assistantships with partial tuition reimbursements available (averaging $1,900 per year); scholarships/grants and unspecified assistantships also available. *Faculty research:* Natural and managed landscapes. Total annual research expenditures: $6.1 million. *Unit head:* Dr. John R. Spence, Chair, 780-492-2820, Fax: 780-492-4323, E-mail: john.spence@ualberta.ca. *Application contact:* Sandy Nakashima, Graduate Program Secretary, 780-492-2820, Fax: 780-492-4323, E-mail: rrgrads.inquiry@ualberta.ca.

The University of Arizona, Graduate College, College of Agriculture and Life Sciences, Department of Soil, Water and Environmental Science, Tucson, AZ 85721. Offers MS, PhD. *Faculty:* 11. *Students:* 50 full-time (33 women), 8 part-time (5 women); includes 14 minority (3 African Americans, 1 American Indian/Alaska Native, 10 Hispanic Americans), 16 international. Average age 32. 37 applicants, 54% accepted, 13 enrolled. In 2009, 12 master's, 6 doctorates awarded. *Degree requirements:* For master's, thesis; for doctorate, comprehensive exam, thesis/dissertation. *Entrance requirements:* For master's, GRE (recommended), minimum GPA of 3.0, letter of interest, 3 letters of recommendation; for doctorate, GRE (recommended), MS, minimum GPA of 3.0, letter of interest, 3 letters of recommendation. Additional exam requirements/recommendations for international students: Required—TOEFL (minimum score 550 paper-based; 213 computer-based; 80 iBT). *Application deadline:* For fall admission, 6/1 for domestic students, 12/1 for international students; for spring admission, 10/1 for domestic students, 6/1 for international students. Applications are processed on a rolling basis. Application fee: $75. *Expenses:* Tuition, state resident: full-time $9028. Tuition, nonresident: full-time $24,890. *Financial support:* In 2009–10, 14 students received support, including 25 research assistantships with full and partial tuition reimbursements available (averaging $18,090 per year), 5 teaching assistantships with full and partial tuition reimbursements available (averaging $17,669 per year); fellowships, Federal Work-Study, institutionally sponsored loans, scholarships/grants, health care benefits, tuition waivers (full and partial), and unspecified assistantships also available. Financial award application deadline: 5/1. *Faculty research:* Plant production, environmental microbiology, contaminant flow and transport, aquaculture. Total annual research expenditures: $3.6 million. *Unit head:* Dr. Jeffery C. Silvertooth, Head, 520-621-7228, Fax: 520-621-1647, E-mail: silver@ag.arizona.edu. *Application contact:* Alicia Velasquez, 520-621-1606, Fax: 520-621-1647, E-mail: avelasqu@ag.arizona.edu.

University of Arkansas, Graduate School, Dale Bumpers College of Agricultural, Food and Life Sciences, Department of Crop, Soil and Environmental Sciences, Fayetteville, AR 72701-1201. Offers agronomy (MS, PhD). *Students:* 11 full-time (3 women), 41 part-time (10 women), 16 international. In 2009, 7 master's, 6 doctorates awarded. *Degree requirements:* For master's, thesis optional; for doctorate, variable foreign language requirement, thesis/dissertation. Application fee: $40 ($50 for international students). *Expenses:* Tuition, state resident: full-time $7355; part-time $356.58 per hour. Tuition, nonresident: full-time $17,401; part-time $775.17 per hour. Required fees: $1203. *Financial support:* In 2009–10, 1 fellowship with tuition reimbursement, 45 research assistantships were awarded; teaching assistantships, career-related internships or fieldwork and Federal Work-Study also available. Support available to part-time students. Financial award application deadline: 4/1; financial award applicants required to submit FAFSA. *Unit head:* Dr. Robert Bacon, Interim Departmental Chairperson, 479-575-2347, Fax: 479-575-7465, E-mail: rbacon@uark.edu. *Application contact:* Dr. Derrick Oosterhuis, Graduate Coordinator, 479-575-3979, E-mail: oosterhu@uark.edu.

The University of British Columbia, Faculty of Land and Food Systems, Program in Soil Science, Vancouver, BC V6T 1Z1, Canada. Offers M Sc, PhD. *Degree requirements:* For master's, thesis; for doctorate, comprehensive exam, thesis/dissertation. *Entrance requirements:* Additional exam requirements/recommendations for international students: Required—TOEFL (minimum score 577 paper-based; 233 computer-based; 90 iBT), IELTS (minimum score 6.5). Electronic applications accepted. *Faculty research:* Soil and water conservation, land use, land use and land classification, soil physics, soil chemistry and mineralogy.

University of California, Davis, Graduate Studies, Graduate Group in Horticulture and Agronomy, Davis, CA 95616. Offers MS. *Degree requirements:* For master's, comprehensive exam (for some programs), thesis (for some programs). *Entrance requirements:* For master's, GRE General Test. Additional exam requirements/recommendations for international students: Required—TOEFL (minimum score 550 paper-based; 213 computer-based). Electronic applications accepted. *Faculty research:* Postharvest physiology, mineral nutrition, crop improvement, plant growth and development.

University of California, Davis, Graduate Studies, Graduate Group in Soils and Biogeochemistry, Davis, CA 95616. Offers MS, PhD. Terminal master's awarded for partial completion of doctoral program. *Degree requirements:* For master's, comprehensive exam (for some programs), thesis (for some programs); for doctorate, thesis/dissertation. *Entrance requirements:* For master's, minimum GPA of 3.3; for doctorate, GRE, minimum GPA of 3.3. Additional exam requirements/recommendations for international students: Required—TOEFL (minimum score 550 paper-based; 213 computer-based). Electronic applications accepted. *Faculty research:* Rhizosphere ecology, soil transport processes, biogeochemical cycling, sustainable agriculture.

University of California, Riverside, Graduate Division, Program in Soil and Water Sciences, Riverside, CA 92521-0102. Offers MS, PhD. *Faculty:* 27 full-time (4 women). *Students:* 17 full-time (10 women); includes 8 minority (6 Asian Americans or Pacific Islanders, 2 Hispanic Americans), 10 international. Average age 29. 63 applicants, 19% accepted, 9 enrolled. In 2009, 4 master's awarded. *Entrance requirements:* For master's and doctorate, minimum GPA of 3.2. Additional exam requirements/recommendations for international students: Required—TOEFL (minimum score 550 paper-based; 213 computer-based; 80 iBT). *Application deadline:* For fall admission, 5/1 for domestic students, 2/1 for international students; for winter admission, 9/1 for domestic students, 7/1 for international students; for spring admission, 12/1 for domestic students, 10/1 for international students. Application fee: $60 ($75 for international students). Electronic applications accepted. *Financial support:* In 2009–10, fellowships with tuition reimbursements (averaging $12,000 per year), research assistantships with tuition reimbursements (averaging $18,000 per year) were awarded. *Unit head:* Dr. Jay Gan, Chair, 951-827-2712, Fax: 951-827-3993. *Application contact:* Mari Ridgeway, Program Assistant, 951-827-5103, Fax: 951-827-3993, E-mail: soilwater@ucr.edu.

University of Connecticut, Graduate School, College of Agriculture and Natural Resources, Department of Plant Science, Storrs, CT 06269. Offers plant and soil sciences (MS, PhD). *Faculty:* 18 full-time (5 women). *Students:* 23 full-time (7 women), 2 part-time (0 women); includes 4 minority (2 African Americans, 1 Asian American or Pacific Islander, 1 Hispanic American), 10 international. Average age 33. 20 applicants, 20% accepted, 3 enrolled. In 2009, 2 master's, 3 doctorates awarded. Terminal master's awarded for partial completion of doctoral program. *Degree requirements:* For master's, comprehensive exam; for doctorate, thesis/dissertation. *Entrance requirements:* For master's and doctorate, GRE General Test, GRE Subject Test. Additional exam requirements/recommendations for international students: Required—TOEFL (minimum score 550 paper-based; 213 computer-based). *Application deadline:* For fall admission, 2/1 priority date for domestic and international students; for spring admission, 11/1 for domestic students, 10/1 for international students. Applications are processed on a rolling basis. Application fee: $55. Electronic applications accepted. *Expenses:* Tuition, state resident: full-time $4725; part-time $525 per credit. Tuition, nonresident: full-time $12,267; part-time $1363 per credit. Required fees: $346 per semester. Tuition and fees vary according to course load. *Financial support:* In 2009–10, 18 research assistantships with full tuition reimbursements, 4 teaching assistantships with full tuition reimbursements were awarded; fellowships, Federal Work-Study, scholarships/grants, health care benefits, and unspecified assistantships also available. Financial award application deadline: 2/1; financial award applicants required to submit FAFSA. *Unit head:* Mary Musgrave, Head, 860-486-2925, Fax: 860-486-0682, E-mail: mary.musgrave@uconn.edu. *Application contact:* George C. Elliott, Chairperson, 860-486-1938, Fax: 860-486-0682, E-mail: george.elliott@uconn.edu.

University of Delaware, College of Agriculture and Natural Resources, Department of Plant and Soil Sciences, Newark, DE 19716. Offers MS, PhD. Part-time programs available. Terminal master's awarded for partial completion of doctoral program. *Degree requirements:* For master's, thesis; for doctorate, thesis/dissertation. *Entrance requirements:* For master's and doctorate, GRE General Test. Additional exam requirements/recommendations for international students: Required—TOEFL (minimum score 550 paper-based; 213 computer-based). Electronic applications accepted. *Faculty research:* Soil chemistry, plant and cell tissue culture, plant breeding and genetics, soil physics, soil biochemistry, plant molecular biology, soil microbiology.

University of Florida, Graduate School, College of Agricultural and Life Sciences, Department of Agronomy, Gainesville, FL 32611. Offers MS, PhD. *Degree requirements:* For master's, thesis optional; for doctorate, thesis/dissertation. *Entrance requirements:* For master's and doctorate, GRE General Test, minimum GPA of 3.0. Additional exam requirements/recommendations for international students: Required—TOEFL. Electronic applications accepted. *Faculty research:* Genetics and plant breeding, aquatic and terrestrial weed science, plant physiology, molecular biology, forage and crop production.

University of Florida, Graduate School, College of Agricultural and Life Sciences, Department of Soil and Water Science, Gainesville, FL 32611. Offers MS, PhD. Part-time programs available. Postbaccalaureate distance learning degree programs offered. Terminal master's awarded for partial completion of doctoral program. *Degree requirements:* For master's, thesis optional; for doctorate, thesis/dissertation. *Entrance requirements:* For master's and doctorate, GRE General Test, minimum GPA of 3.0. Additional exam requirements/recommendations for international students: Required—TOEFL. Electronic applications accepted. *Faculty research:* Environmental fate and transport of pesticides, conservation, wetlands, land application of nonhazardous waste, soil/water agrochemical management.

University of Georgia, Graduate School, College of Agricultural and Environmental Sciences, Department of Crop and Soil Sciences, Athens, GA 30602. Offers crop and soil science (MS, PhD); crop and soil sciences (MCCS); plant protection and pest management (MPPPM). Part-time programs available. *Faculty:* 29 full-time (2 women), 1 (woman) part-time/adjunct. *Students:* 32 full-time (14 women), 9 part-time (0 women); includes 2 minority (1 African American, 1 Asian American or Pacific Islander), 13 international. Average age 24. 30 applicants, 63% accepted, 17 enrolled. In 2009, 11 master's, 2 doctorates awarded. *Degree requirements:* For master's, thesis (MS); for doctorate, comprehensive exam, thesis/dissertation. *Entrance requirements:* For master's and doctorate, GRE General Test. Additional exam requirements/recommendations for international students: Required—TOEFL (minimum score 550 paper-based; 213 computer-based). *Application deadline:* For fall admission, 7/1 priority date for domestic students, 4/15 priority date for international students; for spring admission, 11/15 for domestic students, 10/15 priority date for international students. Applications are processed on a rolling basis. Application fee: $50. Electronic applications accepted. *Expenses:* Tuition, state resident: full-time $6000; part-time $250 per credit hour. Tuition, nonresident: full-time $20,904; part-time $871 per credit hour. Required fees: $730 per semester. *Financial support:* In 2009–10, research assistantships with full tuition reimbursements (averaging $14,600 per year), teaching assistantships with full tuition reimbursements (averaging $15,350 per year) were awarded; fellowships, scholarships/grants, tuition waivers (full), and unspecified assistantships also available. *Faculty research:* Plant breeding, genomics, nutrient management, water quality, soil chemistry. *Unit head:* Dr. Donn Graham Shilling, Head, 706-542-0900, Fax: 706-542-0914, E-mail: cropsoil@uga.edu. *Application contact:* Dr. Miguel L. Cabrera, Graduate Coordinator, 706-542-1242, Fax: 706-542-0914, E-mail: mcabrera@uga.edu.

University of Guelph, Graduate Program Services, Ontario Agricultural College, Department of Land Resource Science, Guelph, ON N1G 2W1, Canada. Offers atmospheric science (M Sc, PhD); environmental and agricultural earth sciences (M Sc, PhD); land resources management (M Sc, PhD); soil science (M Sc, PhD). Part-time programs available. *Degree requirements:* For master's, thesis (for some programs), research project (non-thesis track); for doctorate, comprehensive exam, thesis/dissertation. *Entrance requirements:* For master's, minimum B- average during previous 2 years of course work; for doctorate, minimum B average during previous 2 years of course work. Additional exam requirements/recommendations for international students: Required—TOEFL (minimum score 550 paper-based; 213 computer-based). Electronic applications accepted. *Faculty research:* Soil science, environmental earth science, land resource management.

University of Idaho, College of Graduate Studies, College of Agricultural and Life Sciences, Department of Plant, Soil, and Entomological Sciences, Program in Soil and Land Resources, Moscow, ID 83844-2282. Offers MS, PhD. *Students:* 8 full-time, 1 part-time. In 2009, 1 master's, 1 doctorate awarded. *Degree requirements:* For doctorate, thesis/dissertation. *Entrance requirements:* For master's and doctorate, GRE General Test, minimum GPA of 3.0. *Application deadline:* For fall admission, 8/1 for domestic students; for spring admission, 12/15 for domestic students. Application fee: $55 ($60 for international students). *Expenses:* Tuition, state resident: full-time $6120. Tuition, nonresident: full-time $17,712. *Financial support:* Application deadline: 2/15. *Faculty research:* Pedology, soil biology and biochemistry, soil chemistry, soil fertility and plant nutrition, soil physics. *Unit head:* Dr. Robert Mahler, Chair, 208-885-7025. *Application contact:* Dr. Robert Mahler, Chair, 208-885-7025.

University of Illinois at Urbana–Champaign, Graduate College, College of Agricultural, Consumer and Environmental Sciences, Department of Crop Sciences, Champaign, IL 61820. Offers agricultural production (MS), including professional science; bioinformatics: crop sciences (MS); crop sciences (MS, PhD). Postbaccalaureate distance learning degree programs offered (no on-campus study). *Faculty:* 46 full-time (6 women). *Students:* 56 full-time (17 women), 35 part-time (10 women); includes 4 minority (1 African American, 1 Asian American or Pacific Islander, 2 Hispanic Americans), 30 international. 64 applicants, 33% accepted, 15 enrolled. In 2009, 18 master's, 5 doctorates awarded. *Entrance requirements:* For master's and doctorate, GRE, minimum GPA of 3.0. Additional exam requirements/recommendations for international students: Required—TOEFL (minimum score 570 paper-based). *Application deadline:* Applications are processed on a rolling basis. Application fee: $60 ($75 for international students). Electronic applications accepted. *Financial support:* In 2009–10, 32 fellowships, 60 research assistantships, 17 teaching assistantships were awarded; tuition waivers (full and partial) also available. *Faculty research:* Plant breeding and genetics, molecular biology, crop production, plant physiology, weed science. *Unit head:* German A. Bollero, Head, 217-333-9475, Fax: 217-333-9817, E-mail: gbollero@illinois.edu. *Application contact:* S. Dianne Carson, Secretary, 217-244-0396, Fax: 217-333-9817, E-mail: sdcarson@illinois.edu.

University of Kentucky, Graduate School, College of Agriculture, Program in Crop Science, Lexington, KY 40506-0032. Offers MS, PhD. *Degree requirements:* For master's, comprehensive exam, thesis optional; for doctorate, comprehensive exam, thesis/dissertation. *Entrance requirements:* For master's, GRE General Test, minimum GPA of 2.75; for doctorate, GRE General Test, minimum GPA of 3.0. Additional exam requirements/recommendations for international students: Required—TOEFL (minimum score 550 paper-based; 213 computer-based). Electronic applications accepted. *Faculty research:* Crop physiology, crop ecology, crop management, crop breeding and genetics, weed science.

University of Kentucky, Graduate School, College of Agriculture, Program in Plant and Soil Science, Lexington, KY 40506-0032. Offers MS. *Degree requirements:* For master's, comprehensive exam, thesis optional. *Entrance requirements:* For master's, GRE General Test, minimum undergraduate GPA of 2.75, graduate 3.0. Additional exam requirements/recommendations for international students: Required—TOEFL (minimum score 550 paper-based; 213 computer-based). Electronic applications accepted.

University of Kentucky, Graduate School, College of Agriculture, Program in Soil Science, Lexington, KY 40506-0032. Offers PhD. *Degree requirements:* For doctorate, comprehensive exam, thesis/dissertation. *Entrance requirements:* For doctorate, GRE General Test, minimum graduate GPA of 3.0, undergraduate 2.75. Additional exam requirements/recommendations for international students: Required—TOEFL (minimum score 550 paper-based; 213 computer-based). Electronic applications accepted. *Faculty research:* Soil fertility and plant nutrition, soil chemistry and physics, soil genesis and morphology, soil management and conservation, water and environmental quality.

University of Maine, Graduate School, College of Natural Sciences, Forestry, and Agriculture, Department of Plant, Soil, and Environmental Sciences, Orono, ME 04469. Offers biological sciences (PhD); ecology and environmental sciences (MS, PhD); forest resources (PhD); horticulture (MS); plant science (PhD); plant, soil, and environmental sciences (MS); resource utilization (MS). *Faculty:* 8 full-time (2 women), 9 part-time/adjunct (3 women). *Students:* 6 full-time (3 women), 3 part-time (2 women), 1 international. Average age 31. 6 applicants, 17% accepted, 0 enrolled. In 2009, 2 master's awarded. *Entrance requirements:* For master's and doctorate, GRE General Test. Additional exam requirements/recommendations for international students: Required—TOEFL. *Application deadline:* Applications are processed on a rolling basis. Application fee: $65. Electronic applications accepted. *Financial support:* In 2009–10, 16 research assistantships with tuition reimbursements (averaging $16,260 per year), 3 teaching assistantships with tuition reimbursements (averaging $12,790 per year) were awarded; scholarships/grants, tuition waivers (full and partial), and unspecified assistantships also available. *Unit head:* Dr. Gregory Porter, Chair, 207-581-2943, Fax: 207-581-3207. *Application contact:* Scott G. Delcourt, Associate Dean of the Graduate School, 207-581-3291, Fax: 207-581-3232, E-mail: graduate@maine.edu.

University of Manitoba, Faculty of Graduate Studies, Faculty of Agricultural and Food Sciences, Department of Plant Science, Winnipeg, MB R3T 2N2, Canada. Offers agronomy and plant protection (M Sc, PhD); horticulture (M Sc, PhD); plant breeding and genetics (M Sc, PhD); plant physiology-biochemistry (M Sc, PhD). *Degree requirements:* For master's, thesis; for doctorate, one foreign language, thesis/dissertation.

University of Manitoba, Faculty of Graduate Studies, Faculty of Agricultural and Food Sciences, Department of Soil Science, Winnipeg, MB R3T 2N2, Canada. Offers M Sc, PhD. *Degree requirements:* For master's, thesis; for doctorate, one foreign language, thesis/dissertation.

University of Maryland, College Park, Academic Affairs, College of Agriculture and Natural Resources, Department of Plant Science and Landscape Architecture, Program in Agronomy, College Park, MD 20742. Offers MS, PhD. *Degree requirements:* For doctorate, written and oral exams. *Entrance requirements:* Additional exam requirements/recommendations for international students: Required—TOEFL. *Application deadline:* Applications are processed on a rolling basis. Application fee: $60. Electronic applications accepted. *Expenses:* Tuition, area resident: Part-time $471 per credit hour. Tuition, state resident: part-time $471 per credit hour. Tuition, nonresident: part-time $1016 per credit hour. Required fees: $337.04 per term. *Financial support:* Fellowships, research assistantships, teaching assistantships, career-related internships or fieldwork available. Financial award applicants required to submit FAFSA. *Faculty research:* Cereal crop production, soil and water conservation, turf management, x-ray defraction. *Unit head:* Dr. William Kenworthy, Acting Chair, 301-405-6244, Fax: 301-314-9308, E-mail: wkenwort@umd.edu. *Application contact:* Dean of Graduate School, 301-405-0376, Fax: 301-314-9305.

University of Massachusetts Amherst, Graduate School, College of Natural Sciences, Department of Plant, Soil and Insect Sciences, Program in Plant and Soil Sciences, Amherst, MA 01003. Offers plant and soil sciences (MS, PhD); soil science (MS). Postbaccalaureate distance learning degree programs offered (minimal on-campus study). *Faculty:* 28 full-time (7

Agronomy and Soil Sciences

University of Massachusetts Amherst (continued)
women). *Students:* 16 full-time (8 women), 21 part-time (10 women); includes 2 minority (1 African American, 1 Asian American or Pacific Islander), 12 international. Average age 32. 20 applicants, 25% accepted, 4 enrolled. In 2009, 11 master's, 1 doctorate awarded. Terminal master's awarded for partial completion of doctoral program. *Degree requirements:* For master's, thesis optional; for doctorate, comprehensive exam, thesis/dissertation. *Entrance requirements:* For master's and doctorate, GRE General Test. Additional exam requirements/recommendations for international students: Required—TOEFL (minimum score 550 paper-based; 213 computer-based; 80 iBT), IELTS (minimum score 6.5). *Application deadline:* For fall admission, 1/2 for domestic and international students; for spring admission, 10/1 for domestic and international students. Applications are processed on a rolling basis. Application fee: $50 ($65 for international students). Electronic applications accepted. *Expenses:* Tuition, state resident: full-time $2640; part-time $110 per credit. Tuition, nonresident: full-time $9936; part-time $414 per credit. Tuition and fees vary according to course load. *Financial support:* Fellowships, research assistantships, teaching assistantships, career-related internships or fieldwork, Federal Work-Study, scholarships/grants, traineeships, health care benefits, tuition waivers (full), and unspecified assistantships available. Support available to part-time students. Financial award application deadline: 1/2. *Unit head:* Dr. Geunhwa Jung, Graduate Program Director, 413-545-1059, Fax: 413-545-2115. *Application contact:* Jean M. Ames, Supervisor of Admissions, 413-545-0722, Fax: 413-577-0010, E-mail: gradadm@grad.umass.edu.

University of Minnesota, Twin Cities Campus, Graduate School, College of Food, Agricultural and Natural Resource Sciences, Program in Soil Science, Minneapolis, MN 55455-0213. Offers MS, PhD. *Degree requirements:* For master's, comprehensive exam, thesis or alternative; for doctorate, comprehensive exam, thesis/dissertation. *Entrance requirements:* For master's and doctorate, GRE General Test, minimum GPA of 3.0. Additional exam requirements/recommendations for international students: Required—TOEFL (minimum score 550 paper-based; 213 computer-based). Electronic applications accepted. *Faculty research:* Soil water and atmospheric resources, soil physical management, agricultural chemicals and their management, plant nutrient management, biological nitrogen fixation.

University of Missouri, Graduate School, College of Agriculture, Food and Natural Resources, Division of Plant Sciences, Columbia, MO 65211. Offers crop, soil and pest management (MS, PhD); entomology (MS, PhD); horticulture (MS, PhD); plant biology and genetics (MS, PhD); plant stress biology (MS, PhD). *Faculty:* 103 full-time (24 women), 5 part-time/adjunct (1 woman). *Students:* 41 full-time (21 women), 28 part-time (14 women); includes 1 minority (African American), 26 international. Average age 29. 39 applicants, 41% accepted, 16 enrolled. In 2009, 2 master's, 1 doctorate awarded. Terminal master's awarded for partial completion of doctoral program. *Degree requirements:* For master's, thesis; for doctorate, comprehensive exam, thesis/dissertation. *Entrance requirements:* For master's and doctorate, GRE General Test, minimum GPA of 3.0; bachelor's degree from an accredited college; demonstrated capability to perform graduate-level work. Additional exam requirements/recommendations for international students: Required—TOEFL (minimum score 500 paper-based; 173 computer-based; 61 iBT), IELTS (minimum score 5.5). *Application deadline:* For fall admission, 1/15 priority date for domestic students. Applications are processed on a rolling basis. Application fee: $45 ($60 for international students). Electronic applications accepted. *Financial support:* In 2009–10, 2 fellowships with tuition reimbursements, 59 research assistantships with tuition reimbursements, 1 teaching assistantship with tuition reimbursement were awarded; institutionally sponsored loans and health care benefits also available. *Faculty research:* Crop, soil and pest management; entomology; horticulture; plant biology and genetics; plant microbiology and pathology. *Unit head:* Dr. Michael Collins, Director, E-mail: collinsm@missouri.edu. *Application contact:* Dr. James Schoelz, Director of Graduate Studies, 573-882-1185, E-mail: schoelzj@missouri.edu.

University of Missouri, Graduate School, School of Natural Resources, Department of Soil, Environmental, and Atmospheric Sciences, Columbia, MO 65211. Offers atmospheric science (MS, PhD); soil science (MS, PhD). *Degree requirements:* For doctorate, thesis/dissertation. *Entrance requirements:* For master's and doctorate, GRE General Test, minimum GPA of 3.0. Additional exam requirements/recommendations for international students: Required—TOEFL (minimum score 530 paper-based; 197 computer-based; 71 iBT).

University of Nebraska–Lincoln, Graduate College, College of Agricultural Sciences and Natural Resources, Department of Agronomy and Horticulture, Program in Agronomy, Lincoln, NE 68588. Offers MS, PhD. *Degree requirements:* For master's, thesis; for doctorate, comprehensive exam, thesis/dissertation. *Entrance requirements:* Additional exam requirements/recommendations for international students: Required—TOEFL (minimum score 500 paper-based; 173 computer-based). Electronic applications accepted. *Faculty research:* Crop physiology and production, plant breeding and genetics, range and forage management, soil and water science, weed science.

University of New Hampshire, Graduate School, College of Life Sciences and Agriculture, Department of Natural Resources, Durham, NH 03824. Offers environmental conservation (MS); forestry (MS); soil science (MS); water resources management (MS); wildlife (MS). Part-time programs available. *Faculty:* 40 full-time. *Students:* 22 full-time (12 women), 29 part-time (19 women); includes 1 minority (Asian American or Pacific Islander), 1 international. Average age 31. 41 applicants, 34% accepted, 10 enrolled. In 2009, 19 master's awarded. *Degree requirements:* For master's, thesis or alternative. *Entrance requirements:* For master's, GRE General Test. Additional exam requirements/recommendations for international students: Required—TOEFL (minimum score 550 paper-based; 213 computer-based; 80 iBT). *Application deadline:* For fall admission, 6/1 for domestic students, 4/1 for international students; for spring admission, 12/1 for domestic students. Applications are processed on a rolling basis. Application fee: $65. Electronic applications accepted. *Expenses:* Tuition, state resident: full-time $10,380; part-time $577 per credit hour. Tuition, nonresident: full-time $24,350; part-time $1002 per credit hour. Required fees: $1550; $387.50 per semester. Tuition and fees vary according to course load and program. *Financial support:* In 2009–10, 24 students received support, including 2 fellowships, 11 research assistantships, 11 teaching assistantships; career-related internships or fieldwork, Federal Work-Study, scholarships/grants, and tuition waivers (full and partial) also available. Support available to part-time students. Financial award application deadline: 2/15. *Unit head:* Dr. John Halstead, Chairperson, 603-862-3950, E-mail: natural.resources@unh.edu. *Application contact:* Linda Scogin, Administrative Assistant, 603-862-3932, E-mail: natural.resources@unh.edu.

University of Puerto Rico, Mayagüez Campus, Graduate Studies, College of Agricultural Sciences, Department of Agronomy and Soils, Mayagüez, PR 00681-9000. Offers agronomy (MS); soils (MS). Part-time programs available. *Degree requirements:* For master's, comprehensive exam, thesis. *Faculty research:* Soil physics and chemistry, soil management, plant physiology, ecology, plant breeding.

University of Puerto Rico, Mayagüez Campus, Graduate Studies, College of Agricultural Sciences, Department of Crop Protection, Mayagüez, PR 00681-9000. Offers MS. Part-time programs available. *Degree requirements:* For master's, comprehensive exam, thesis. *Entrance requirements:* For master's, minimum GPA of 2.75, BS degree in agricultural science or its equivalent. *Faculty research:* Nematology, virology, plant pathology, weed control, peas and soybean seed diseases.

University of Saskatchewan, College of Graduate Studies and Research, College of Agriculture, Department of Soil Science, Saskatoon, SK S7N 5A2, Canada. Offers M Ag, M Sc, PhD, Diploma. *Faculty:* 26. *Students:* 44. In 2009, 6 master's, 2 doctorates awarded. *Degree requirements:* For master's, thesis (for some programs); for doctorate, comprehensive exam (for some programs), thesis/dissertation. *Entrance requirements:* Additional exam requirements/recommendations for international students: Required—TOEFL (minimum score 80 iBT); Recommended—IELTS (minimum score 6.5). *Application deadline:* For fall admission, 7/1 priority date for domestic students. Applications are processed on a rolling basis. Application fee: $75. Tuition and fees charges are reported in Canadian dollars. *Expenses:* Tuition, area resident: Full-time $3000 Canadian dollars; part-time $500 Canadian dollars per term. Required fees: $700 Canadian dollars; $100 Canadian dollars per term. *Financial support:* Fellowships, research assistantships, teaching assistantships available. Financial award application deadline: 1/31. *Unit head:* Dr. Fran Walley, Head, 306-966-6848, Fax: 306-966-6881, E-mail: germida@sask.usask.ca. *Application contact:* Dr. Steven Siciliano, Graduate Chair, 306-966-6848, Fax: 306-966-6881, E-mail: steven.siciliano@usask.ca.

University of Vermont, Graduate College, College of Agriculture and Life Sciences, Department of Plant and Soil Science, Burlington, VT 05405. Offers MS, PhD. *Students:* 25 (14 women); includes 1 minority (Asian American or Pacific Islander), 4 international. 25 applicants, 68% accepted, 7 enrolled. In 2009, 3 master's, 3 doctorates awarded. *Degree requirements:* For master's, thesis; for doctorate, one foreign language, thesis/dissertation. *Entrance requirements:* For master's and doctorate, GRE General Test. Additional exam requirements/recommendations for international students: Required—TOEFL (minimum score 550 paper-based; 213 computer-based; 80 iBT). *Application deadline:* For fall admission, 3/1 priority date for domestic students. Applications are processed on a rolling basis. Application fee: $40. Electronic applications accepted. *Expenses:* Tuition, area resident: Part-time $508 per credit hour. Tuition, state resident: part-time $508 per credit hour. Tuition, nonresident: part-time $1281 per credit hour. *Financial support:* Fellowships, research assistantships, teaching assistantships available. Financial award application deadline: 3/1. *Faculty research:* Soil chemistry, plant nutrition. *Unit head:* Dr. Deborah Neher, Chairperson, 802-656-2630. *Application contact:* Dr. Josef Gorres, Coordinator, 802-656-2630.

University of Wisconsin–Madison, Graduate School, College of Agricultural and Life Sciences, Department of Agronomy, Madison, WI 53706-1380. Offers agronomy (MS, PhD); plant breeding and plant genetics (MS, PhD). *Degree requirements:* For master's, thesis or alternative; for doctorate, thesis/dissertation. *Entrance requirements:* For master's and doctorate, GRE, minimum GPA of 3.0. Additional exam requirements/recommendations for international students: Required—TOEFL (minimum score 580 paper-based; 213 computer-based). Electronic applications accepted. *Expenses:* Tuition, state resident: part-time $594 per credit. Tuition, nonresident: part-time $1504 per credit. Required fees: $65 per credit. Tuition and fees vary according to course load, program and reciprocity agreements. *Faculty research:* Plant breeding and genetics, plant molecular biology and physiology, cropping systems and management, weed science.

University of Wisconsin–Madison, Graduate School, College of Agricultural and Life Sciences, Department of Soil Science, Madison, WI 53706-1380. Offers MS, PhD. *Degree requirements:* For master's, comprehensive exam, thesis; for doctorate, comprehensive exam, thesis/dissertation. *Entrance requirements:* For master's and doctorate, GRE General Test. Additional exam requirements/recommendations for international students: Required—TOEFL. Electronic applications accepted. *Expenses:* Tuition, state resident: part-time $594 per credit. Tuition, nonresident: part-time $1504 per credit. Required fees: $65 per credit. Tuition and fees vary according to course load, program and reciprocity agreements. *Faculty research:* Physical chemistry of soil colloids/surfaces, forest biogeochemistry, soil-plant-atmosphere interactions, organic byproducts recycling, microbial metabolism in soil, environmental chemistry.

University of Wyoming, College of Agriculture, Department of Plant Sciences, Laramie, WY 82070. Offers agronomy (MS, PhD). *Degree requirements:* For master's, thesis; for doctorate, thesis/dissertation. *Entrance requirements:* For master's and doctorate, GRE General Test, minimum GPA of 3.0. Additional exam requirements/recommendations for international students: Required—TOEFL (minimum score 525 paper-based; 197 computer-based). Electronic applications accepted. *Faculty research:* Crops, weeds, plant diseases.

University of Wyoming, College of Agriculture, Department of Renewable Resources, Laramie, WY 82070. Offers agroecology (MS); entomology (MS, PhD); entomology/water resources (MS, PhD); rangeland ecology and watershed management (MS, PhD), including soil sciences (PhD), soil sciences and water resources (MS); rangeland ecology and watershed management/water resources (MS, PhD); soil science (MS); soil science/water resources (PhD). Part-time programs available. *Degree requirements:* For master's, comprehensive exam, thesis, oral examination; for doctorate, comprehensive exam, thesis/dissertation, preliminary oral and written exam, oral final exam. *Entrance requirements:* For master's and doctorate, GRE General Test, minimum GPA of 3.0. Additional exam requirements/recommendations for international students: Required—TOEFL. Electronic applications accepted. *Faculty research:* Plant control, grazing management, riparian restoration, riparian management, reclamation.

Utah State University, School of Graduate Studies, College of Agriculture, Department of Plants, Soils, and Biometeorology, Logan, UT 84322. Offers biometeorology (MS, PhD); ecology (MS, PhD); plant science (MS, PhD); soil science (MS, PhD). Part-time programs available. Terminal master's awarded for partial completion of doctoral program. *Degree requirements:* For master's, thesis; for doctorate, thesis/dissertation. *Entrance requirements:* For master's, GRE General Test, BS in plant, soil, atmospheric science, or related field; minimum GPA of 3.0; for doctorate, GRE General Test, minimum GPA of 3.0. Additional exam requirements/recommendations for international students: Required—TOEFL. Electronic applications accepted. *Faculty research:* Biotechnology and genomics, plant physiology and biology, nutrient and water efficient landscapes, physical-chemical-biological processes in soil, environmental biophysics and climate.

Virginia Polytechnic Institute and State University, Graduate School, College of Agriculture and Life Sciences, Department of Crop and Soil Environmental Sciences, Blacksburg, VA 24061. Offers MS, PhD. *Entrance requirements:* For master's and doctorate, GRE. Additional exam requirements/recommendations for international students: Required—TOEFL (minimum score 550 paper-based; 213 computer-based). Electronic applications accepted. *Faculty research:* Environmental soil chemistry, waste management, soil fertility, plant molecular genetics, turfgrass management.

Washington State University, Graduate School, College of Agricultural, Human, and Natural Resource Sciences, Department of Crop and Soil Sciences, Program in Crop Sciences, Pullman, WA 99164. Offers MS, PhD. *Faculty:* 44. *Students:* 22 full-time (8 women), 2 part-time (both women), 11 international. Average age 30. 38 applicants, 16% accepted, 3 enrolled. In 2009, 2 master's, 3 doctorates awarded. Terminal master's awarded for partial completion of doctoral program. *Degree requirements:* For master's, comprehensive exam (for some programs), thesis (for some programs), oral exam; for doctorate, comprehensive exam, thesis/dissertation, oral exam, written exam. *Entrance requirements:* For master's and doctorate, GRE General Test, In addition to the Graduate School admission requirements, the Department of Crop and Soil Sciences requires a personal statement of the applicant???s educational goals and professional expectations. Additional exam requirements/recommendations for international students: Required—TOEFL (minimum score 550 paper-based; 213 computer-based), IELTS. *Application deadline:* For fall admission, 1/10 priority date for domestic and international students; for spring admission, 7/1 priority date for domestic and international students. Applications are processed on a rolling basis. Application fee: $50. Electronic applications accepted. *Financial support:* In 2009–10, 5 fellowships (averaging $7,580 per year), 15 research assistantships with full and partial tuition reimbursements (averaging $13,917 per year), 1 teaching assistantship with full and partial tuition reimbursement (averaging $13,056 per year) were awarded; career-related internships or fieldwork, Federal Work-Study, institutionally sponsored loans, tuition waivers (partial), and teaching associateships also available. Financial award application deadline: 2/1; financial award applicants required to submit FAFSA. *Faculty research:* Barley genetics, soil biology, soil fertility, winter wheat breeding, weed science. *Unit head:* Dr. Kimberlee Kidwell, Interim Director, 509-335-4562, Fax: 509-335-8674, E-mail: kidwell@wsu.edu. *Application contact:* Graduate School Admissions, 800-GRADWSU, Fax: 509-335-1949, E-mail: gradsch@wsu.edu.

Washington State University, Graduate School, College of Agricultural, Human, and Natural Resource Sciences, Department of Crop and Soil Sciences, Program in Soil Sciences, Pullman, WA 99164. Offers MS, PhD. *Faculty:* 44. *Students:* 20 full-time (7 women), 5 part-time (2 women); includes 1 minority (Asian American or Pacific Islander), 4 international. Average age 30. 38 applicants, 45% accepted, 7 enrolled. In 2009, 3 master's, 1 doctorate awarded. Terminal master's awarded for partial completion of doctoral program. *Degree requirements:* For master's, comprehensive exam (for some programs), thesis (for some programs), oral exam; for doctorate, comprehensive exam, thesis/dissertation, oral exam, written exam. *Entrance requirements:* For master's and doctorate, GRE. Additional exam requirements/recommendations for international students: Required—TOEFL (minimum score 550 paper-based; 213 computer-based), IELTS. *Application deadline:* For fall admission, 1/10 priority date for domestic and international students; for spring admission, 7/1 priority date for domestic and international students. Applications are processed on a rolling basis. Application fee: $50. Electronic applications accepted. *Financial support:* In 2009–10, 1 fellowship (averaging $4,000 per year), 11 research assistantships with full and partial tuition reimbursements (averaging $13,917 per year), 1 teaching assistantship with full and partial tuition reimbursement (averaging $13,056 per year) were awarded; career-related internships or fieldwork, Federal Work-Study, institutionally sponsored loans, tuition waivers (partial), and teaching associateships also available. Financial award application deadline: 4/1; financial award applicants required to submit FAFSA. *Faculty research:* Environmental soils, soil/water quality, soil microbiology, soil physics. Total annual research expenditures: $5.8 million. *Unit head:* Dr. Kimberlee Kidwell, Interim Director, 509-335-4562, Fax: 509-335-8674, E-mail: kidwell@wsu.edu. *Application contact:* Graduate School Admissions, 800-GRADWSU, Fax: 509-335-1949, E-mail: gradsch@wsu.edu.

West Virginia University, Davis College of Agriculture, Forestry and Consumer Sciences, Division of Plant and Soil Sciences, Program in Agricultural Sciences, Morgantown, WV 26506. Offers animal and food sciences (PhD); plant and soil sciences (PhD). *Degree requirements:* For doctorate, thesis/dissertation, oral and written exams. *Entrance requirements:* Additional exam requirements/recommendations for international students: Required—TOEFL. *Faculty research:* Ruminant nutrition, metabolism, forage utilization, physiology, reproduction.

Animal Sciences

Alabama Agricultural and Mechanical University, School of Graduate Studies, School of Agricultural and Environmental Sciences, Department of Plant and Soil Science, Huntsville, AL 35811. Offers animal sciences (MS); environmental science (MS); plant and soil science (PhD). Evening/weekend programs available. Terminal master's awarded for partial completion of doctoral program. *Degree requirements:* For master's, thesis; for doctorate, one foreign language, thesis/dissertation. *Entrance requirements:* For master's, GRE General Test, BS in agriculture; for doctorate, GRE General Test, master's degree. Additional exam requirements/recommendations for international students: Required—TOEFL (minimum score 500 paper-based; 173 computer-based; 61 iBT). Electronic applications accepted. *Faculty research:* Plant breeding, cytogenetics, crop production, soil chemistry and fertility, remote sensing.

Alcorn State University, School of Graduate Studies, School of Agriculture and Applied Science, Alcorn State, MS 39096-7500. Offers agricultural economics (MS Ag); agronomy (MS Ag); animal science (MS Ag). *Degree requirements:* For master's, thesis optional. *Faculty research:* Aquatic systems, dairy herd improvement, fruit production, alternative farming practices.

American University of Beirut, Graduate Programs, Faculty of Agricultural and Food Sciences, Beirut, Lebanon. Offers agricultural economics (MS); animal sciences (MS); ecosystem management (MSES); food technology (MS); irrigation (MS); mechanization (MS); nutrition (MS); plant protection (MS); plant science (MS); poultry science (MS); soils (MS). Part-time programs available. *Degree requirements:* For master's, one foreign language, comprehensive exam, thesis (for some programs). *Entrance requirements:* For master's, letter of recommendation. Additional exam requirements/recommendations for international students: Required—TOEFL (minimum score 600 paper-based; 250 computer-based; 100 iBT), IELTS (minimum score 7.5). *Faculty research:* Sustainable animal systems/agriculture; natural resource management; community nutrition, obesity and food safety; integrated pest management; ecosystem management.

Angelo State University, College of Graduate Studies, College of Sciences, Department of Agriculture, San Angelo, TX 76909. Offers animal science (MS). Part-time and evening/weekend programs available. *Faculty:* 4 full-time (0 women). *Students:* 17 full-time (7 women), 4 part-time (2 women); includes 1 minority (Hispanic American). Average age 23. 7 applicants, 100% accepted, 5 enrolled. In 2009, 5 master's awarded. *Degree requirements:* For master's, comprehensive exam, thesis optional. *Entrance requirements:* For master's, GRE General Test. Additional exam requirements/recommendations for international students: Required—TOEFL or IELTS. *Application deadline:* For fall admission, 7/15 priority date for domestic students, 6/10 for international students; for spring admission, 12/1 priority date for domestic students, 11/1 for international students. Applications are processed on a rolling basis. Application fee: $40 ($50 for international students). Electronic applications accepted. *Expenses:* Tuition, state resident: full-time $3396; part-time $142 per credit hour. Tuition, nonresident: full-time $10,152; part-time $423 per credit hour. Required fees: $1786; $36.25 per credit hour. $494 per semester. Full-time tuition and fees vary according to course load, degree level and program. *Financial support:* In 2009–10, 10 students received support, including 9 research assistantships (averaging $9,887 per year); Federal Work-Study, scholarships/grants, and unspecified assistantships also available. Support available to part-time students. Financial award application deadline: 3/1. *Faculty research:* Effect of protein and energy on feedlot performance, bitterweed toxicosis in sheep, meat laboratory, North Concho watershed project, baseline vegetation. *Unit head:* Dr. Gilbert R. Engdahl, Department Head, 325-942-2027 Ext. 227, E-mail: gil.engdahl@angelo.edu. *Application contact:* Dr. Cody B. Scott, Graduate Advisor, 325-942-2027 Ext. 284, E-mail: cody.scott@angelo.edu.

Auburn University, Graduate School, College of Agriculture, Department of Animal Sciences, Auburn University, AL 36849. Offers M Ag, MS, PhD. Part-time programs available. *Faculty:* 23 full-time (5 women), 1 part-time/adjunct (0 women). *Students:* 5 full-time (2 women), 20 part-time (11 women); includes 4 minority (2 African Americans, 1 American Indian/Alaska Native, 1 Hispanic American). Average age 27. 28 applicants, 14% accepted, 2 enrolled. In 2009, 8 master's awarded. *Degree requirements:* For master's, thesis (for some programs); for doctorate, thesis/dissertation. *Entrance requirements:* For master's and doctorate, GRE General Test. *Application deadline:* For fall admission, 7/7 for domestic students; for spring admission, 11/24 for domestic students. Applications are processed on a rolling basis. Application fee: $50 ($60 for international students). Electronic applications accepted. *Expenses:* Tuition, state resident: full-time $6240. Tuition, nonresident: full-time $18,720. International tuition: $18,938 full-time. Required fees: $492. Tuition and fees vary according to course load, program and reciprocity agreements. *Financial support:* Research assistantships, teaching assistantships, Federal Work-Study available. Support available to part-time students. Financial award application deadline: 3/15; financial award applicants required to submit FAFSA. *Faculty research:* Animal breeding and genetics, animal biochemistry and nutrition, physiology of reproduction, animal production. *Unit head:* Dr. L. Wayne Greene, Head, 334-844-1528. *Application contact:* Dr. George Flowers, Dean of the Graduate School, 334-844-2125.

Auburn University, Graduate School, College of Agriculture, Department of Poultry Science, Auburn University, AL 36849. Offers M Ag, MS, PhD. Part-time programs available. *Faculty:* 16 full-time (3 women). *Students:* 9 full-time (3 women), 9 part-time (all women); includes 2 minority (both Asian Americans or Pacific Islanders), 7 international. Average age 29. 12 applicants, 33% accepted, 3 enrolled. In 2009, 3 master's, 3 doctorates awarded. *Degree requirements:* For master's, thesis (for some programs); for doctorate, thesis/dissertation. *Entrance requirements:* For master's, GRE General Test; for doctorate, GRE General Test, MS. *Application deadline:* For fall admission, 7/7 for domestic students; for spring admission, 11/24 for domestic students. Applications are processed on a rolling basis. Application fee: $50 ($60 for international students). Electronic applications accepted. *Expenses:* Tuition, state resident: full-time $6240. Tuition, nonresident: full-time $18,720. International tuition: $18,938 full-time. Required fees: $492. Tuition and fees vary according to course load, program and reciprocity agreements. *Financial support:* Research assistantships, Federal Work-Study available. Support available to part-time students. Financial award application deadline: 3/15; financial award applicants required to submit FAFSA. *Faculty research:* Poultry nutrition, poultry breeding, poultry physiology, poultry diseases and parasites, processing/food science. *Unit head:* Dr. Donald E. Conner, Head, 334-844-4133, E-mail: connede@auburn.edu. *Application contact:* Dr. George Flowers, Dean of the Graduate School, 334-844-2125.

Boise State University, Graduate College, College of Arts and Sciences, Department of Biology, Program in Raptor Biology, Boise, ID 83725-0399. Offers MS. Part-time programs available. *Degree requirements:* For master's, thesis. *Entrance requirements:* For master's, GRE General Test, minimum GPA of 3.0. Electronic applications accepted. *Expenses:* Tuition, state resident: full-time $3106; part-time $209 per credit. Tuition, nonresident: part-time $284 per credit. *Faculty research:* Avian ecology.

Brigham Young University, Graduate Studies, College of Life Sciences, Department of Plant and Wildlife Sciences, Provo, UT 84602-1001. Offers environmental science (MS); genetics and biotechnology (MS); wildlife and wildlands conservation (MS, PhD). *Faculty:* 21 full-time (1 woman), 15 part-time/adjunct (3 women). *Students:* 35 full-time (13 women), 18 part-time (5 women); includes 7 minority (2 Asian Americans or Pacific Islanders, 5 Hispanic Americans), 5 international. Average age 29. 34 applicants, 68% accepted, 21 enrolled. In 2009, 9 master's, 1 doctorate awarded. *Degree requirements:* For master's, thesis; for doctorate, comprehensive exam, thesis/dissertation, minimum GPA of 3.0, 54 hours (18 dissertation, 36 coursework). *Entrance requirements:* For master's, GRE General Test, minimum GPA of 3.0 during last 60 hours of course work; for doctorate, GRE, minimum GPA of 3.0. Additional exam requirements/recommendations for international students: Required—TOEFL (minimum score 580 paper-based; 237 computer-based; 85 iBT). *Application deadline:* 2/1 for domestic and international students. Applications are processed on a rolling basis. Application fee: $50. Electronic applications accepted. *Expenses:* Tuition: Full-time $5580; part-time $301 per credit hour. Tuition and fees vary according to student's religious affiliation. *Financial support:* In 2009–10, 22 students received support, including 2 research assistantships with partial tuition reimbursements available (averaging $16,650 per year), 37 teaching assistantships with partial tuition reimbursements available (averaging $16,650 per year); scholarships/grants and tuition waivers (partial) also available. Financial award application deadline: 2/1. *Faculty research:* environmental science, plant genetics, plant ecology, plant nutrition and pathology, wildlife and wildlands conservation. Total annual research expenditures: $1.1 million. *Unit head:* Dr. Val J. Anderson, Chair, 801-422-3527, Fax: 801-422-0008, E-mail: val_anderson@byu.edu. *Application contact:* Dr. Loreen Allphin, Graduate Coordinator, 801-422-5603, Fax: 801-422-0008, E-mail: loreen_allphin@byu.edu.

California State University, Fresno, Division of Graduate Studies, College of Agricultural Sciences and Technology, Department of Animal Science and Agricultural Education, Fresno, CA 93740-8027. Offers animal science (MS). Part-time and evening/weekend programs available. *Degree requirements:* For master's, thesis. *Entrance requirements:* For master's, GRE General Test, minimum GPA of 3.0 in last 60 hours. Additional exam requirements/recommendations for international students: Required—TOEFL. Electronic applications accepted. *Faculty research:* Horse nutrition, animal health and welfare, electronic monitoring.

Clemson University, Graduate School, College of Agriculture, Forestry and Life Sciences, Department of Animal and Veterinary Sciences, Clemson, SC 29634. Offers animal and veterinary sciences (MS, PhD). *Faculty:* 13 full-time (5 women), 1 part-time/adjunct (0 women). *Students:* 17 full-time (13 women), 4 part-time (2 women), 4 international. Average age 26. 19 applicants, 42% accepted, 5 enrolled. In 2009, 1 master's, 1 doctorate awarded. *Degree requirements:* For doctorate, thesis/dissertation. *Entrance requirements:* For master's and doctorate, GRE General Test. Additional exam requirements/recommendations for international students: Required—TOEFL. *Application deadline:* For fall admission, 4/15 for international students; for spring admission, 9/15 for international students. Applications are processed on a rolling basis. Application fee: $70 ($80 for international students). Electronic applications accepted. *Expenses:* Contact institution. *Financial support:* In 2009–10, 13 students received support, including 5 fellowships with full and partial tuition reimbursements available (averaging $8,533 per year), 6 research assistantships with partial tuition reimbursements available (averaging $16,578 per year), 7 teaching assistantships with partial tuition reimbursements available (averaging $14,643 per year); career-related internships or fieldwork, Federal Work-Study, institutionally sponsored loans, scholarships/grants, and unspecified assistantships also available. Financial award applicants required to submit FAFSA. Total annual research expenditures: $574,478. *Unit head:* Dr. Susan K. Duckett, Chair, 864-656-2570, Fax: 864-656-3131, E-mail: sducket@clemson.edu. *Application contact:* Dr. Denzil Maurice, 864-656-4023, E-mail: dmrc@clemson.edu.

Colorado State University, Graduate School, College of Agricultural Sciences, Department of Animal Sciences, Fort Collins, CO 80523-1171. Offers MS, PhD. *Faculty:* 20 full-time (3 women). *Students:* 35 full-time (20 women), 26 part-time (11 women); includes 2 minority (both American Indian/Alaska Native), 9 international. Average age 28. 64 applicants, 30% accepted, 15 enrolled. In 2009, 9 master's, 3 doctorates awarded. *Degree requirements:* For master's, comprehensive exam, thesis, 4 seminar department presentations and 1 professional program; for doctorate, comprehensive exam, thesis/dissertation, 4 seminar department presentations and 1 professional program. *Entrance requirements:* For master's, GRE General Test (minimum score 1000 verbal and quantitative), minimum GPA of 3.0; reference letters; department

Animal Sciences

Colorado State University (continued)
questionnaire; for doctorate, GRE General Test (combined minimum score of 1000 on the Verbal and Quantitative sections), minimum GPA of 3.0; reference letters; department questionnaire. Additional exam requirements/recommendations for international students: Required—TOEFL (minimum score 550 paper-based; 80 iBT), IELTS (minimum score 6). *Application deadline:* For fall admission, 4/1 priority date for domestic and international students; for spring admission, 10/1 priority date for domestic and international students. Applications are processed on a rolling basis. Application fee: $50. Electronic applications accepted. *Expenses:* Tuition, state resident: full-time $6434; part-time $359.10 per credit. Tuition, nonresident: full-time $18,116; part-time $1006.45 per credit. Required fees: $1496; $83 per credit. *Financial support:* In 2009–10, 44 students received support, including 3 fellowships with full tuition reimbursements available (averaging $33,520 per year), 36 research assistantships with full tuition reimbursements available (averaging $13,490 per year), 5 teaching assistantships with full tuition reimbursements available (averaging $12,251 per year); career-related internships or fieldwork, scholarships/grants, health care benefits, tuition waivers (full and partial), and unspecified assistantships also available. Support available to part-time students. Financial award applicants required to submit FAFSA. *Faculty research:* Efficiency, food safety, beef management, equine science, breeding and genetics. Total annual research expenditures: $3 million. *Unit head:* William R. Wailes, Department Head, 970-491-5390, Fax: 970-491-5326, E-mail: w.wailes@colostate.edu. *Application contact:* Melissa Weiss, Administrative Assistant, 970-491-1442, Fax: 970-491-5326, E-mail: m.weiss@colostate.edu.

Cornell University, Graduate School, Graduate Fields of Agriculture and Life Sciences, Field of Animal Science, Ithaca, NY 14853-0001. Offers animal breeding (MS, PhD); animal genetics (MS, PhD). *Faculty:* 42 full-time (8 women). *Students:* 33 full-time (20 women); includes 3 minority (1 Asian American or Pacific Islander, 2 Hispanic Americans), 10 international. Average age 28. 40 applicants. In 2009, 9 master's, 4 doctorates awarded. *Degree requirements:* For master's, thesis, teaching experience; for doctorate, comprehensive exam, thesis/dissertation, teaching experience. *Entrance requirements:* For master's and doctorate, 2 letters of recommendation. Additional exam requirements/recommendations for international students: Required—TOEFL (minimum score 550 paper-based; 213 computer-based; 77 iBT). *Application deadline:* For fall admission, 4/1 for domestic students; for spring admission, 9/1 for domestic students. Application fee: $70. Electronic applications accepted. *Expenses:* Tuition: Full-time $29,500. Required fees: $70. Full-time tuition and fees vary according to degree level, program and student level. *Financial support:* In 2009–10, 2 fellowships with full tuition reimbursements, 1 research assistantship with full tuition reimbursement, 2 teaching assistantships with full tuition reimbursements were awarded; institutionally sponsored loans, scholarships/grants, health care benefits, tuition waivers (full and partial), and unspecified assistantships also available. Financial award applicants required to submit FAFSA. *Faculty research:* Quantitative genetics, genetic improvement of animal populations, statistical genetics. *Unit head:* Director of Graduate Studies, 607-255-4416, Fax: 607-254-5413, E-mail: shh4@cornell.edu. *Application contact:* Graduate Field Assistant, 607-255-4416, Fax: 607-254-5413, E-mail: shh4@cornell.edu.

Florida Agricultural and Mechanical University, Division of Graduate Studies, Research, and Continuing Education, College of Engineering Science, Technology, and Agriculture, Division of Agricultural Sciences, Tallahassee, FL 32307-3200. Offers agribusiness (MS); animal science (MS); engineering technology (MS); entomology (MS); food science (MS); international programs (MS); plant science (MS). *Faculty:* 31 full-time (2 women). *Students:* 14 full-time (8 women), 8 part-time (4 women); includes 17 minority (16 African Americans, 1 Asian American or Pacific Islander), 3 international. In 2009, 7 master's awarded. *Degree requirements:* For master's, thesis. *Entrance requirements:* For master's, GRE General Test, minimum GPA of 3.0. Additional exam requirements/recommendations for international students: Required—TOEFL (minimum score 500 paper-based). *Application deadline:* For fall admission, 5/18 for domestic students, 12/18 for international students; for spring admission, 11/12 for domestic students, 5/12 for international students. Application fee: $20. *Financial support:* Application deadline: 2/15. *Unit head:* Dr. Mitwe N. Musingo, Graduate Coordinator, 850-561-2309, Fax: 850-599-8821. *Application contact:* Dr. Chanta M. Haywood, Dean of Graduate Studies, Research, and Continuing Education, 850-599-3315, Fax: 850-599-3727.

Fort Valley State University, College of Graduate Studies and Extended Education, Program in Animal Science, Fort Valley, GA 31030. Offers MS. *Degree requirements:* For master's, thesis. *Entrance requirements:* For master's, GRE General Test.

Iowa State University of Science and Technology, Graduate College, College of Agriculture, Department of Animal Science, Ames, IA 50011. Offers animal breeding and genetics (MS, PhD); animal physiology (MS); animal psychology (PhD); animal science (MS, PhD); meat science (MS, PhD). *Faculty:* 56 full-time (8 women), 2 part-time/adjunct (0 women). *Students:* 67 full-time (35 women), 13 part-time (5 women); includes 5 minority (3 African Americans, 1 Asian American or Pacific Islander, 1 Hispanic American), 28 international. 50 applicants, 34% accepted, 17 enrolled. In 2009, 9 master's, 4 doctorates awarded. *Degree requirements:* For master's, thesis or alternative; for doctorate, thesis/dissertation. *Entrance requirements:* For master's and doctorate, GRE General Test. Additional exam requirements/recommendations for international students: Required—TOEFL (minimum score 550 paper-based; 80 iBT) or IELTS (minimum score 6.5). *Application deadline:* For fall admission, 2/1 priority date for domestic and international students; for spring admission, 9/1 priority date for domestic and international students. Application fee: $40 ($90 for international students). Electronic applications accepted. *Expenses:* Tuition, state resident: full-time $6716. Tuition, nonresident: full-time $8908. Tuition and fees vary according to course level, course load, program and student level. *Financial support:* In 2009–10, 31 research assistantships with full and partial tuition reimbursements (averaging $15,260 per year), 1 teaching assistantship with full and partial tuition reimbursement (averaging $15,260 per year) were awarded; fellowships, scholarships/grants, health care benefits, and unspecified assistantships also available. *Faculty research:* Animal breeding, animal nutrition, meat science, muscle biology, nutritional physiology. *Unit head:* Dr. Maynard Hogberg, Head, 515-294-2160, Fax: 515-294-6994. *Application contact:* Dr. Joseph Sebranek, Director of Graduate Education, 515-294-2160.

Kansas State University, Graduate School, College of Agriculture, Department of Animal Sciences and Industry, Manhattan, KS 66506. Offers animal breeding and genetics (MS, PhD); meat science (MS, PhD); monogastric nutrition (MS, PhD); physiology (MS, PhD); ruminant nutrition (MS, PhD). *Faculty:* 36 full-time (7 women), 7 part-time/adjunct (1 woman). *Students:* 53 full-time (24 women), 14 part-time (6 women); includes 2 minority (both Hispanic Americans), 10 international. Average age 32. 29 applicants, 59% accepted, 11 enrolled. In 2009, 17 master's, 4 doctorates awarded. *Degree requirements:* For master's, thesis, oral exam; for doctorate, thesis/dissertation, preliminary exams. *Entrance requirements:* Additional exam requirements/recommendations for international students: Required—TOEFL (minimum score 550 paper-based; 213 computer-based). *Application deadline:* For fall admission, 2/1 priority date for domestic and international students; for spring admission, 8/1 priority date for domestic and international students. Applications are processed on a rolling basis. Application fee: $40 ($55 for international students). Electronic applications accepted. *Financial support:* In 2009–10, 65 research assistantships (averaging $13,154 per year), 4 teaching assistantships with full tuition reimbursements (averaging $13,632 per year) were awarded; fellowships, Federal Work-Study, institutionally sponsored loans, and scholarships/grants also available. Support available to part-time students. Financial award application deadline: 3/1; financial award applicants required to submit FAFSA. *Faculty research:* Animal nutrition, animal physiology, meat science, animal genetics. Total annual research expenditures: $2.1 million. *Unit head:* Ken Odde, Head, 785-532-1227, Fax: 785-532-7059, E-mail: kenodde@ksu.edu. *Application contact:* Evan Titgemeyer, Director, 785-532-1220, Fax: 785-532-7059, E-mail: etitgeme@ksu.edu.

Louisiana State University and Agricultural and Mechanical College, Graduate School, College of Agriculture, School of Animal Sciences, Baton Rouge, LA 70803. Offers MS, PhD. Part-time programs available. *Faculty:* 19 full-time (2 women). *Students:* 25 full-time (14 women), 7 part-time (5 women); includes 1 African American, 1 Hispanic American, 8 international. Average age 27. 16 applicants, 44% accepted, 4 enrolled. In 2009, 13 master's, 2 doctorates awarded. Terminal master's awarded for partial completion of doctoral program. *Degree requirements:* For master's, thesis; for doctorate, thesis/dissertation. *Entrance requirements:* For master's and doctorate, GRE General Test, minimum GPA of 3.0. Additional exam requirements/recommendations for international students: Required—TOEFL (minimum score 550 paper-based; 213 computer-based; 79 iBT) or IELTS (minimum score 6.5). *Application deadline:* For fall admission, 1/25 priority date for domestic students, 5/15 for international students; for spring admission, 10/15 for international students. Applications are processed on a rolling basis. Application fee: $50 ($70 for international students). Electronic applications accepted. *Financial support:* In 2009–10, 30 students received support, including 1 fellowship (averaging $6,261 per year), 2 research assistantships with partial tuition reimbursements available (averaging $12,500 per year), 20 teaching assistantships with partial tuition reimbursements available (averaging $15,676 per year); Federal Work-Study, institutionally sponsored loans, scholarships/grants, health care benefits, tuition waivers (full and partial), and unspecified assistantships also available. Support available to part-time students. Financial award applicants required to submit FAFSA. *Faculty research:* Reproductive physiology, biotechnology, meats, non-ruminant and ruminant nutrition, daily science. Total annual research expenditures: $18,307. *Unit head:* Dr. Gary Hay, Head, 225-578-3241, Fax: 225-578-3279, E-mail: ghay@agctr.lsu.edu. *Application contact:* Dr. Donald L. Thompson, Graduate Coordinator, 225-578-3445, Fax: 225-578-3279, E-mail: dthomp1@lsu.edu.

McGill University, Faculty of Graduate and Postdoctoral Studies, Faculty of Agricultural and Environmental Sciences, Department of Animal Science, Montréal, QC H3A 2T5, Canada. Offers M Sc, M Sc A, PhD.

Michigan State University, College of Veterinary Medicine and The Graduate School, Graduate Programs in Veterinary Medicine, Department of Large Animal Clinical Sciences, East Lansing, MI 48824. Offers MS, PhD. *Entrance requirements:* Additional exam requirements/recommendations for international students: Required—TOEFL (minimum score 550 paper-based; 213 computer-based), Michigan State University ELT (85), Michigan ELAB (83). Electronic applications accepted.

Michigan State University, College of Veterinary Medicine and The Graduate School, Graduate Programs in Veterinary Medicine, Department of Small Animal Clinical Sciences, East Lansing, MI 48824. Offers MS. *Degree requirements:* For master's, thesis. *Entrance requirements:* Additional exam requirements/recommendations for international students: Required—TOEFL, Michigan State University ELT (85), Michigan ELAB (83).

Michigan State University, The Graduate School, College of Agriculture and Natural Resources, Department of Animal Science, East Lansing, MI 48824. Offers animal science (MS, PhD); animal science-environmental toxicology (PhD). *Entrance requirements:* Additional exam requirements/recommendations for international students: Required—TOEFL (minimum score 550 paper-based; 213 computer-based), Michigan State University ELT (85), Michigan ELAB (83). Electronic applications accepted.

Mississippi State University, College of Agriculture and Life Sciences, Department of Animal Dairy Sciences, Mississippi State, MS 39762. Offers agricultural life sciences (MS), including animal physiology (MS, PhD), genetics (MS, PhD); agricultural science (PhD), including animal dairy sciences, animal nutrition (MS, PhD); agriculture (MS), including animal nutrition (MS, PhD); life sciences (PhD), including animal physiology (MS, PhD), genetics (MS, PhD). *Faculty:* 13 full-time (4 women). *Students:* 28 full-time (10 women), 12 part-time (7 women); includes 4 minority (2 African Americans, 2 Hispanic Americans), 7 international. Average age 29. 25 applicants, 36% accepted, 9 enrolled. In 2009, 8 master's, 1 doctorate awarded. *Degree requirements:* For master's, thesis, comprehensive oral or written exam; for doctorate, thesis/dissertation, comprehensive oral or written exam. *Entrance requirements:* For master's, GRE General Test, minimum GPA of 3.0; for doctorate, GRE General Test. Additional exam requirements/recommendations for international students: Required—TOEFL (minimum score 575 paper-based). *Application deadline:* For fall admission, 7/1 for domestic students, 5/1 for international students; for spring admission, 11/1 for domestic students, 9/1 for international students. Applications are processed on a rolling basis. Application fee: $40. Electronic applications accepted. *Expenses:* Tuition, state resident: full-time $2575.50; part-time $286.25 per credit hour. Tuition, nonresident: full-time $6510; part-time $723.50 per credit hour. Tuition and fees vary according to course load. *Financial support:* In 2009–10, 13 research assistantships (averaging $10,389 per year), 2 teaching assistantships (averaging $8,110 per year) were awarded; Federal Work-Study, institutionally sponsored loans, and unspecified assistantships also available. Financial award applicants required to submit FAFSA. *Faculty research:* Ecology and population dynamics, physiology, biochemistry and behavior, systematics. *Unit head:* Dr. Terry Kiser, Professor and Department Head, 662-325-2802, Fax: 662-325-8873, E-mail: tkiser@ads.msstate.edu. *Application contact:* Dr. Peter Ryan, Graduate Coordinator, 662-325-2802, Fax: 662-325-8873, E-mail: pryan@ads.msstate.edu.

Mississippi State University, College of Agriculture and Life Sciences, Department of Poultry Science, Mississippi State, MS 39762. Offers agriculture (MS), including poultry science (MS, PhD); agriculture sciences (PhD), including poultry science (MS, PhD). *Faculty:* 5 full-time (1 woman). *Students:* 13 full-time (5 women); includes 2 minority (both African Americans), 4 international. Average age 27. 8 applicants, 38% accepted, 3 enrolled. In 2009, 5 master's awarded. *Degree requirements:* For master's, comprehensive exam, thesis optional; for doctorate, comprehensive exam, thesis/dissertation. *Entrance requirements:* Additional exam requirements/recommendations for international students: Required—TOEFL (minimum score 475 paper-based; 153 computer-based; 53 iBT); Recommended—IELTS (minimum score 4.5). *Application deadline:* For fall admission, 7/1 for domestic students, 5/1 for international students; for spring admission, 10/1 for domestic students, 11/1 for international students. Applications are processed on a rolling basis. Application fee: $40. Electronic applications accepted. *Expenses:* Tuition, state resident: full-time $2575.50; part-time $286.25 per credit hour. Tuition, nonresident: full-time $6510; part-time $723.50 per credit hour. Tuition and fees vary according to course load. *Financial support:* In 2009–10, 11 research assistantships with partial tuition reimbursements (averaging $10,524 per year), 1 teaching assistantship with partial tuition reimbursement (averaging $8,029 per year) were awarded; Federal Work-Study, institutionally sponsored loans, scholarships/grants, and unspecified assistantships also available. Financial award application deadline: 4/1; financial award applicants required to submit FAFSA. *Unit head:* Dr. Yvonne Thaxton, Interim Department Head and Professor, 662-325-9087, Fax: 662-325-8292, E-mail: yvizzier@poultry.msstate.edu. *Application contact:* Dr. Yvonne Thaxton, Interim Department Head and Professor, 662-325-9087, Fax: 662-325-8292, E-mail: yvizzier@poultry.msstate.edu.

Montana State University, College of Graduate Studies, College of Agriculture, Department of Animal and Range Sciences, Bozeman, MT 59717. Offers MS, PhD. Part-time programs available. *Faculty:* 13 full-time (4 women), 5 part-time/adjunct (0 women). *Students:* 5 full-time (3 women), 13 part-time (5 women), 1 international. Average age 33. 12 applicants, 33% accepted, 3 enrolled. In 2009, 1 doctorate awarded. *Degree requirements:* For master's, comprehensive exam; for doctorate, comprehensive exam, thesis/dissertation. *Entrance requirements:* For master's, GRE General Test, minimum GPA of 3.0; undergraduate course work in animal science, range science or a closely-related field; faculty adviser; for doctorate, GRE General Test. Additional exam requirements/recommendations for international students: Required—TOEFL (minimum score 550 paper-based; 213 computer-based). *Application deadline:* For fall admission, 7/15 priority date for domestic students, 5/15 priority date for international students; for spring admission, 12/1 priority date for domestic students, 10/1 priority date for international students. Applications are processed on a rolling basis. Application fee: $30. Electronic applications accepted. *Expenses:* Tuition, state resident: full-time $5635; part-time $3492 per year. Tuition, nonresident: full-time $17,212; part-time $7865.10 per year. Required fees: $1441.05; $153.15 per credit. Tuition and fees vary according to course load and program. *Financial support:* In 2009–10, 10 students received support, including 9 research assistantships with partial tuition reimbursements available (averaging $1,000 per year), 1 teaching assistantship with partial tuition reimbursement available (averaging $1,000 per year); scholarships/grants, health care benefits, tuition waivers (partial), and unspecified assistantships also available. Financial award application deadline: 3/1; financial award applicants required to submit FAFSA. *Faculty research:* Ruminant nutrition, ruminant reproductive physiology, wildlife habitat ecology, grazing ecology and management. Total annual research expenditures: $1.9 million. *Unit head:* Bret Olson, Interim Department Head, 406-994-3721, Fax: 406-994-5589, E-mail: bolson@montana.edu. *Application contact:* Dr. Carl A. Fox, Vice Provost for Graduate Education, 406-994-4145, Fax: 406-994-7433, E-mail: gradstudy@montana.edu.

New Mexico State University, Graduate School, College of Agricultural, Consumer and Environmental Sciences, Department of Animal and Range Sciences, Las Cruces, NM 88003-8001. Offers animal science (M Ag, MS, PhD); range science (M Ag, MS, PhD). Part-time programs available. *Faculty:* 5 full-time (1 woman). *Students:* 35 full-time (23 women), 7 part-time (1 woman); includes 7 minority (2 American Indian/Alaska Native, 5 Hispanic Americans), 4 international. Average age 28. 32 applicants, 88% accepted, 18 enrolled. In 2009, 6 master's, 4 doctorates awarded. Terminal master's awarded for partial completion of doctoral program. *Degree requirements:* For master's, thesis, seminar; for doctorate, thesis/dissertation, research tool. *Entrance requirements:* For master's, minimum GPA of 3.0 in last 60 hours of undergraduate course work (MS); for doctorate, minimum graduate GPA of 3.2. Additional exam requirements/recommendations for international students: Required—TOEFL (minimum score 530 paper-based; 197 computer-based). *Application deadline:* For fall admission, 7/1 priority date for domestic students; for spring admission, 11/1 for domestic students. Applications are processed on a rolling basis. Application fee: $30 ($50 for international students). Electronic applications accepted. *Expenses:* Tuition, state resident: full-time $4080; part-time $223 per credit. Tuition, nonresident: full-time $14,256; part-time $647 per credit. Required fees: $1278; $639 per semester. *Financial support:* In 2009–10, 2 research assistantships (averaging $20,760 per year), 23 teaching assistantships (averaging $20,624 per year) were awarded; Federal Work-Study and health care benefits also available. Support available to part-time students. Financial award application deadline: 3/1. *Faculty research:* Reproductive physiology, ruminant nutrition, nutrition toxicology, range ecology, wildland hydrology. *Unit head:* Dr. Tim Ross, Interim Head, 575-646-2514, Fax: 575-646-5441, E-mail: tross@nmsu.edu. *Application contact:* Dr. Tim Ross, Interim Head, 575-646-2514, Fax: 575-646-5441, E-mail: tross@nmsu.edu.

North Carolina Agricultural and Technical State University, Graduate School, School of Agriculture and Environmental Sciences, Department of Animal Sciences, Greensboro, NC 27411. Offers animal health science (MS).

North Carolina State University, Graduate School, College of Agriculture and Life Sciences, Department of Animal Science, Raleigh, NC 27695. Offers animal and poultry science (PhD); animal science (MS). *Degree requirements:* For master's, thesis optional. *Entrance requirements:* For master's, GRE, minimum GPA of 3.0. Electronic applications accepted. *Faculty research:* Nutrient utilization, mineral nutrition, genomics, endocrinology, reproductive physiology.

North Carolina State University, Graduate School, College of Agriculture and Life Sciences, Department of Poultry Science, Raleigh, NC 27695. Offers MS. Part-time programs available. *Degree requirements:* For master's, thesis. Electronic applications accepted. *Faculty research:* Reproductive physiology, nutrition, toxicology, immunology, molecular biology.

North Dakota State University, College of Graduate and Interdisciplinary Studies, College of Agriculture, Food Systems, and Natural Resources, Department of Animal and Range Sciences, Fargo, ND 58108. Offers animal science (MS, PhD); natural resource management (MS, PhD); range sciences (MS, PhD). *Faculty:* 32. *Students:* 18 full-time (10 women), 7 part-time (6 women); includes 1 American Indian/Alaska Native, 1 Asian American or Pacific Islander. Average age 25. 13 applicants, 62% accepted. In 2009, 17 master's, 2 doctorates awarded. *Degree requirements:* For master's, thesis; for doctorate, comprehensive exam, thesis/dissertation. *Entrance requirements:* For master's and doctorate, GRE General Test. Additional exam requirements/recommendations for international students: Required—TOEFL (minimum score 71 iBT). *Application deadline:* Applications are processed on a rolling basis. Application fee: $45 ($60 for international students). *Financial support:* In 2009–10, 1 fellowship with tuition reimbursement (averaging $18,000 per year), 29 research assistantships with tuition reimbursements (averaging $13,000 per year) were awarded; teaching assistantships, Federal Work-Study, institutionally sponsored loans, and tuition waivers (partial) also available. Financial award application deadline: 3/15. *Faculty research:* Reproduction, nutrition, meat and muscle biology, breeding/genetics. Total annual research expenditures: $1.5 million. *Unit head:* Dr. David Buchanan, Chair, 701-231-7643, Fax: 701-231-7590, E-mail: david.buchanan@ndsu.edu. *Application contact:* Dr. David Buchanan, Chair, 701-231-7643, Fax: 701-231-7590, E-mail: david.buchanan@ndsu.edu.

Nova Scotia Agricultural College, Research and Graduate Studies, Truro, NS B2N 5E3, Canada. Offers agriculture (M Sc), including air quality, animal behavior, animal molecular genetics, animal nutrition, animal technology, aquaculture, botany, crop management, crop physiology, ecology, environmental microbiology, food science, horticulture, nutrient management, pest management, physiology, plant biotechnology, plant pathology, soil chemistry, soil fertility, waste management and composting, water quality. Part-time programs available. *Degree requirements:* For master's, thesis, ATC Exam Teaching Assistantship. *Entrance requirements:* For master's, honors B Sc, minimum GPA of 3.0. Additional exam requirements/recommendations for international students: Required—TOEFL (minimum score 580 paper-based; 237 computer-based; 92 iBT), IELTS, Michigan English Language Assessment Battery, CanTEST, CAEL. *Faculty research:* Bio-product development, organic agriculture, nutrient management, air and water quality, agricultural biotechnology.

The Ohio State University, Graduate School, College of Food, Agricultural, and Environmental Sciences, Department of Animal Sciences, Columbus, OH 43210. Offers MS, PhD. *Faculty:* 47. *Students:* 29 full-time (20 women), 14 part-time (9 women); includes 6 minority (1 African American, 1 American Indian/Alaska Native, 4 Hispanic Americans), 14 international. Average age 27. In 2009, 9 master's, 1 doctorate awarded. *Degree requirements:* For master's, thesis; for doctorate, thesis/dissertation. *Entrance requirements:* For master's and doctorate, GRE General Test. Additional exam requirements/recommendations for international students: Required—TOEFL (minimum score 550 paper-based; 213 computer-based) or IELTS (minimum score 7) or Michigan English Language Assessment Battery (minimum score 84). *Application deadline:* For fall admission, 8/15 priority date for domestic students, 7/1 priority date for international students; for winter admission, 12/1 priority date for domestic students, 11/1 priority date for international students; for spring admission, 3/1 priority date for domestic students, 2/1 priority date for international students. Applications are processed on a rolling basis. Application fee: $40 ($50 for international students). Electronic applications accepted. *Expenses:* Tuition, state resident: full-time $10,683. Tuition, nonresident: full-time $25,923. Tuition and fees vary according to course load and program. *Financial support:* Fellowships, research assistantships, teaching assistantships, Federal Work-Study and institutionally sponsored loans available. Support available to part-time students. *Unit head:* Michael Day, Graduate Studies Committee Chair, 614-292-6401, Fax: 614-292-2929, E-mail: day.5@osu.edu. *Application contact:* Graduate Admissions, 614-292-9444, Fax: 614-292-3895, E-mail: domestic.grad@osu.edu.

Oklahoma State University, College of Agricultural Science and Natural Resources, Department of Animal Science, Stillwater, OK 74078. Offers animal sciences (M Ag, MS); food science (MS, PhD). *Faculty:* 29 full-time (6 women), 3 part-time/adjunct (1 woman). *Students:* 22 full-time (15 women), 52 part-time (30 women); includes 4 minority (1 African American, 1 American Indian/Alaska Native, 2 Hispanic Americans), 35 international. Average age 28. 115 applicants, 12% accepted, 11 enrolled. In 2009, 24 master's, 16 doctorates awarded. *Degree requirements:* For master's, thesis; for doctorate, comprehensive exam, thesis/dissertation. *Entrance requirements:* For master's and doctorate, GRE or GMAT. Additional exam requirements/recommendations for international students: Required—TOEFL (minimum score 550 paper-based; 79 iBT). *Application deadline:* For fall admission, 3/1 priority date for international students; for spring admission, 8/1 priority date for international students. Applications are processed on a rolling basis. Application fee: $40 ($75 for international students). Electronic applications accepted. *Expenses:* Tuition, state resident: full-time $3716; part-time $154.85 per credit hour. Tuition, nonresident: full-time $14,448; part-time $602 per credit hour. Required fees: $1772; $73.85 per credit hour. One-time fee: $50. Tuition and fees vary according to course load and campus/location. *Financial support:* In 2009–10, 30 research assistantships (averaging $14,084 per year), 7 teaching assistantships (averaging $12,470 per year) were awarded; career-related internships or fieldwork, Federal Work-Study, scholarships/grants, health care benefits, tuition waivers (partial), and unspecified assistantships also available. Support available to part-time students. Financial award application deadline: 3/1; financial award applicants required to submit FAFSA. *Faculty research:* Quantitative trait loci identification for economical traits in swing/beef; waste management strategies in livestock; endocrine control of reproductive processes in farm animals; cholesterol synthesis, inhibition, and reduction; food safety research. *Unit head:* Dr. Ronald Kensinger, Head, 405-744-6062, Fax: 405-744-7390. *Application contact:* Dr. Gerald Horn, Information Contact, 405-744-6070, Fax: 405-744-6621, E-mail: gerald.horn@okstate.edu.

Oregon State University, Graduate School, College of Agricultural Sciences, Department of Animal Sciences, Corvallis, OR 97331. Offers animal science (M Agr, MAIS, MS, PhD); poultry science (M Agr, MAIS, MS, PhD). *Faculty:* 11 full-time (4 women), 1 (woman) part-time/adjunct. *Students:* 13 full-time (8 women), 1 (woman) part-time, 1 international. Average age 27. In 2009, 1 master's awarded. Terminal master's awarded for partial completion of doctoral program. *Degree requirements:* For master's, thesis (for some programs); for doctorate, thesis/dissertation. *Entrance requirements:* For master's and doctorate, GRE General Test, minimum GPA of 3.0 in last 90 hours. Additional exam requirements/recommendations for international students: Required—TOEFL. *Application deadline:* For fall admission, 3/1 for domestic students. Applications are processed on a rolling basis. Application fee: $50. *Expenses:* Tuition, state resident: full-time $9774; part-time $362 per credit. Tuition, nonresident: full-time $15,849; part-time $587 per credit. Required fees: $1639. Full-time tuition and fees vary according to course load and program. *Financial support:* Fellowships, research assistantships, career-related internships or fieldwork, Federal Work-Study, and institutionally sponsored loans available. Support available to part-time students. Financial award application deadline: 2/1. *Faculty research:* Reproductive physiology, population genetics, general nutrition of ruminants and nonruminants, embryo physiology, endocrinology. *Unit head:* Dr. James R. Males, Head, 541-737-3431, Fax: 541-737-4174, E-mail: james.males@orst.edu. *Application contact:* Dr. Stella Coakley, Associate Dean, 541-737-5264, Fax: 541-737-3178, E-mail: stella.coakley@oregonstate.edu.

Penn State University Park, Graduate School, College of Agricultural Sciences, Department of Dairy and Animal Science, State College, University Park, PA 16802-1503. Offers MPS, MS, PhD.

Prairie View A&M University, College of Agriculture and Human Sciences, Prairie View, TX 77446-0519. Offers agricultural economics (MS); animal sciences (MS); interdisciplinary human sciences (MS); soil science (MS). Part-time and evening/weekend programs available. *Faculty:* 11 full-time (4 women). *Students:* 36 full-time (27 women), 40 part-time (29 women); includes 57 African Americans, 1 Hispanic American, 6 international. Average age 31. 147 applicants, 100% accepted. In 2009, 23 master's awarded. *Degree requirements:* For master's, comprehensive exam, thesis (for some programs), field placement. *Entrance requirements:* For master's, GRE General Test, minimum GPA of 2.45. Additional exam requirements/recommendations for international students: Required—TOEFL (minimum score 550 paper-based). *Application deadline:* For fall admission, 6/1 for domestic and international students; for spring admission, 10/1 for domestic and international students. Applications are processed on a rolling basis. Application fee: $50. *Expenses:* Tuition, state resident: full-time $2200. Tuition, nonresident: full-time $5600. Required fees: $1720. Tuition and fees vary according to course load. *Financial support:* In 2009–10, 57 students received support, including 8 fellowships with tuition reimbursements available (averaging $12,000 per year), 10 research assistantships with tuition reimbursements available (averaging $15,000 per year); career-related internships or fieldwork, Federal Work-Study, institutionally sponsored loans, scholarships/grants, tuition waivers (partial), and unspecified assistantships also available. Support available to part-time students. Financial award application deadline: 4/1; financial award applicants required to submit FAFSA. *Faculty research:* Domestic violence prevention, water quality, food growth regulators, wetland dynamics, biochemistry, obesity and nutrition, family therapy. Total annual research expenditures: $4 million. *Unit head:* Dr. Freddie Richards, Dean, 936-261-2528, Fax: 936-261-5143, E-mail: flrichards@pvamu.edu. *Application contact:* Dr. Richard W. Griffin, Interim Department Head, 936-261-5019, Fax: 936-261-5148, E-mail: rwgriffin@pvamu.edu.

Purdue University, Graduate School, College of Agriculture, Department of Animal Sciences, West Lafayette, IN 47907. Offers MS, PhD. Part-time programs available. Terminal master's awarded for partial completion of doctoral program. *Degree requirements:* For master's, thesis optional; for doctorate, thesis/dissertation. *Entrance requirements:* For master's and doctorate, GRE General Test. Additional exam requirements/recommendations for international students: Required—TOEFL; Recommended—TWE. Electronic applications accepted. *Faculty research:* Genetics, meat science, nutrition, management, ethology.

Rutgers, The State University of New Jersey, New Brunswick, Graduate School-New Brunswick, Program in Endocrinology and Animal Biosciences, Piscataway, NJ 08854-8097. Offers MS, PhD. Terminal master's awarded for partial completion of doctoral program. *Degree requirements:* For master's, thesis; for doctorate, comprehensive exam, thesis/dissertation. *Entrance requirements:* For master's and doctorate, GRE General Test. Additional exam requirements/recommendations for international students: Required—TOEFL. Electronic applications accepted. *Faculty research:* Comparative and behavioral endocrinology, epigenetic regulation of the endocrine system, exercise physiology and immunology, fetal and neonatal developmental programming, mammary gland biology and breast cancer, neuroendocrinology and alcohol studies, reproductive and developmental toxicology.

South Dakota State University, Graduate School, College of Agriculture and Biological Sciences, Department of Animal and Range Sciences, Brookings, SD 57007. Offers animal science (MS, PhD); biological sciences (PhD). Part-time programs available. *Degree requirements:* For master's, thesis, oral exam; for doctorate, comprehensive exam, thesis/dissertation, preliminary oral and written exams. *Entrance requirements:* Additional exam requirements/recommendations for international students: Required—TOEFL (minimum score 550 paper-based; 213 computer-based; 79 iBT). *Faculty research:* Ruminant and nonruminant nutrition, meat science, reproductive physiology, range utilization, ecology genetics, muscle biology, animal production.

Animal Sciences

South Dakota State University, Graduate School, College of Agriculture and Biological Sciences, Department of Dairy Science, Brookings, SD 57007. Offers animal sciences (MS, PhD); biological sciences (MS, PhD). Part-time programs available. *Degree requirements:* For master's, thesis, oral exam; for doctorate, comprehensive exam, thesis/dissertation, preliminary oral and written exams. *Entrance requirements:* Additional exam requirements/recommendations for international students: Required—TOEFL (minimum score 550 paper-based; 213 computer-based). *Faculty research:* Dairy cattle nutrition, energy metabolism, food safety, dairy processing technology.

Southern Illinois University Carbondale, Graduate School, College of Agriculture, Department of Animal Science, Food and Nutrition, Program in Animal Science, Carbondale, IL 62901-4701. Offers MS. *Degree requirements:* For master's, thesis. *Entrance requirements:* For master's, minimum GPA of 2.7. Additional exam requirements/recommendations for international students: Required—TOEFL. *Faculty research:* Nutrition, reproductive physiology, animal biotechnology, phytoestrogens and animal reproduction.

Sul Ross State University, Division of Agricultural and Natural Resource Science, Program in Animal Science, Alpine, TX 79832. Offers M Ag, MS. Part-time programs available. *Degree requirements:* For master's, thesis (for some programs). *Entrance requirements:* For master's, GRE General Test, minimum GPA of 2.5 in last 60 hours of undergraduate work. *Faculty research:* Reproductive physiology, meat processing, animal nutrition, equine foot and motion studies, Spanish goat and Barbido sheep studies.

Texas A&M University, College of Agriculture and Life Sciences, Department of Animal Science, College Station, TX 77843. Offers animal breeding (MS, PhD); animal science (M Agr, MS, PhD); dairy science (M Agr, MS); physiology of reproduction (MS, PhD). *Faculty:* 31. *Students:* 99 full-time (55 women), 28 part-time (15 women); includes 13 minority (3 African Americans, 1 Asian American or Pacific Islander, 9 Hispanic Americans), 16 international. Average age 26. In 2009, 22 master's, 10 doctorates awarded. *Degree requirements:* For master's, thesis; for doctorate, thesis/dissertation. *Entrance requirements:* For master's and doctorate, GRE General Test. Additional exam requirements/recommendations for international students: Required—TOEFL. *Application deadline:* For fall admission, 2/1 priority date for domestic students; for spring admission, 10/1 priority date for domestic students. Applications are processed on a rolling basis. Application fee: $50 ($75 for international students). *Expenses:* Tuition, state resident: full-time $3991.32; part-time $221.74 per credit hour. Tuition, nonresident: full-time $9049; part-time $502.74 per credit hour. *Financial support:* In 2009–10, fellowships (averaging $15,000 per year), research assistantships (averaging $12,950 per year), teaching assistantships (averaging $11,500 per year) were awarded; career-related internships or fieldwork, Federal Work-Study, institutionally sponsored loans, and scholarships/grants also available. Financial award application deadline: 2/1; financial award applicants required to submit FAFSA. *Faculty research:* Genetic engineering/gene markers, dietary effects on colon cancer, biotechnology. *Unit head:* Head, 979-845-1541, Fax: 979-845-6433, E-mail: anscience@mail.ansc.ad.tamu.edu. *Application contact:* Graduate Advisor, 979-845-1542, Fax: 979-845-6433.

Texas A&M University, College of Agriculture and Life Sciences, Department of Poultry Science, College Station, TX 77843. Offers M Agr, MS, PhD. Part-time and evening/weekend programs available. Postbaccalaureate distance learning degree programs offered (no on-campus study). *Faculty:* 14. *Students:* 42 full-time (23 women), 8 part-time (3 women); includes 6 minority (1 African American, 3 Asian Americans or Pacific Islanders, 2 Hispanic Americans), 26 international. Average age 29. In 2009, 7 master's, 5 doctorates awarded. Terminal master's awarded for partial completion of doctoral program. *Degree requirements:* For master's, thesis (for some programs); for doctorate, thesis/dissertation. *Entrance requirements:* For master's and doctorate, GRE General Test. Additional exam requirements/recommendations for international students: Required—TOEFL. Application fee: $50 ($75 for international students). Electronic applications accepted. *Expenses:* Tuition, state resident: full-time $3991.32; part-time $221.74 per credit hour. Tuition, nonresident: full-time $9049; part-time $502.74 per credit hour. *Financial support:* In 2009–10, fellowships with partial tuition reimbursements (averaging $18,000 per year); research assistantships with partial tuition reimbursements, teaching assistantships, scholarships/grants and unspecified assistantships also available. Financial award application deadline: 4/1; financial award applicants required to submit FAFSA. *Faculty research:* Poultry diseases and immunology, avian genetics and physiology, nutrition and metabolism, poultry processing and food safety, waste management. *Unit head:* Head, 979-845-4318, E-mail: www@poultry.tamu.edu. *Application contact:* Dr., Advisor/Lecturer, 979-845-1654, Fax: 979-845-1931, E-mail: www@poultry.tamu.edu.

Texas A&M University–Kingsville, College of Graduate Studies, College of Agriculture and Home Economics, Program in Animal Sciences, Kingsville, TX 78363. Offers MS. *Degree requirements:* For master's, comprehensive exam, thesis or alternative. *Entrance requirements:* For master's, GRE General Test, minimum GPA of 3.0. Additional exam requirements/recommendations for international students: Required—TOEFL.

Texas Tech University, Graduate School, College of Agricultural Sciences and Natural Resources, Department of Animal and Food Sciences, Lubbock, TX 79409-2141. Offers animal science (MS, PhD); food science (MS). Part-time programs available. *Faculty:* 10 full-time (4 women). *Students:* 46 full-time (25 women), 12 part-time (4 women); includes 3 minority (1 African American, 2 Hispanic Americans), 15 international. Average age 27. 72 applicants, 31% accepted, 11 enrolled. In 2009, 18 master's, 4 doctorates awarded. *Degree requirements:* For master's, thesis or alternative, internship (M Agr); for doctorate, thesis/dissertation. *Entrance requirements:* For master's and doctorate, GRE General Test. Additional exam requirements/recommendations for international students: Required—TOEFL (minimum score 550 paper-based; 213 computer-based). *Application deadline:* For fall admission, 3/1 priority date for international students; for spring admission, 11/1 priority date for international students. Applications are processed on a rolling basis. Application fee: $50 ($75 for international students). Electronic applications accepted. *Expenses:* Tuition, state resident: full-time $5100; part-time $213 per credit hour. Tuition, nonresident: full-time $11,748; part-time $490 per credit hour. Required fees: $2298; $50 per credit hour. $555 per semester. *Financial support:* In 2009–10, 15 research assistantships with partial tuition reimbursements (averaging $18,621 per year), 2 teaching assistantships with partial tuition reimbursements (averaging $9,675 per year) were awarded; Federal Work-Study and institutionally sponsored loans also available. Support available to part-time students. Financial award application deadline: 4/15; financial award applicants required to submit FAFSA. *Faculty research:* Animal growth composition and product acceptability, animal nutrition and utilization, animal physiology and adaptation to stress, food microbiology, meat science safety and security. Total annual research expenditures: $2.7 million. *Unit head:* Dr. Kevin R. Pond, Chairman, 806-742-2805 Ext. 223, Fax: 806-742-0898, E-mail: kevin.pond@ttu.edu. *Application contact:* Sandy Gellner, Graduate Secretary, 806-742-2805 Ext. 221, Fax: 806-742-0898, E-mail: sandra.gellner@ttu.edu.

Tuskegee University, Graduate Programs, College of Agricultural, Environmental and Natural Sciences, Department of Agricultural Sciences, Program in Animal and Poultry Sciences, Tuskegee, AL 36088. Offers MS. *Faculty:* 13 full-time (1 woman), 2 part-time/adjunct (1 woman). *Students:* 8 full-time (6 women), 2 part-time (1 woman); includes 8 minority (all African Americans). Average age 27. In 2009, 4 master's awarded. *Degree requirements:* For master's, thesis. *Entrance requirements:* For master's, GRE General Test. Additional exam requirements/recommendations for international students: Required—TOEFL (minimum score 500 paper-based; 69 computer-based). *Application deadline:* For fall admission, 7/15 for domestic students. Applications are processed on a rolling basis. Application fee: $25 ($35 for international students). *Expenses:* Tuition: Full-time $15,630; part-time $940 per credit hour. Required fees: $650. *Financial support:* Application deadline: 4/15. *Unit head:* Dr. P. K. Biswas, Head, 334-727-8446. *Application contact:* Dr. Robert L. Laney, Vice President/Director of Admissions and Enrollment Management, 334-727-8580, Fax: 334-727-5750, E-mail: planey@tuskegee.edu.

Université Laval, Faculty of Agricultural and Food Sciences, Department of Animal Sciences, Programs in Animal Sciences, Québec, QC G1K 7P4, Canada. Offers M Sc, PhD. Part-time programs available. Terminal master's awarded for partial completion of doctoral program. *Degree requirements:* For master's, thesis; for doctorate, comprehensive exam, thesis/dissertation. *Entrance requirements:* For master's and doctorate, knowledge of French and English. Electronic applications accepted.

The University of Arizona, Graduate College, College of Agriculture and Life Sciences, Department of Animal Sciences, Tucson, AZ 85721. Offers MS, PhD. Part-time programs available. *Faculty:* 9. *Students:* 25 full-time (14 women), 7 part-time (4 women); includes 3 minority (1 American Indian/Alaska Native, 1 Asian American or Pacific Islander, 1 Hispanic American), 6 international. Average age 27. 26 applicants, 65% accepted, 12 enrolled. In 2009, 6 master's, 1 doctorate awarded. *Degree requirements:* For master's, thesis; for doctorate, thesis/dissertation. *Entrance requirements:* For master's, GRE Subject Test, 3 letters of recommendation, minimum GPA of 3.0; for doctorate, GRE Subject Test (biology or chemistry recommended), 3 letters of recommendation, statement of purpose, minimum GPA of 3.0. Additional exam requirements/recommendations for international students: Required—TOEFL (minimum score 550 paper-based; 213 computer-based; 80 iBT). *Application deadline:* Applications are processed on a rolling basis. Application fee: $75. *Expenses:* Tuition, state resident: full-time $9028. Tuition, nonresident: full-time $24,890. *Financial support:* In 2009–10, 10 students received support, including 7 research assistantships with partial tuition reimbursements available (averaging $19,431 per year); fellowships, teaching assistantships with partial tuition reimbursements available, scholarships/grants, health care benefits, and unspecified assistantships also available. Financial award application deadline: 4/1. *Faculty research:* Nutrition of beef and dairy cattle, reproduction and breeding, muscle growth and function, animal stress, meat science. Total annual research expenditures: $793,069. *Unit head:* Dr. Ronald E. Allen, Professor and Head, 520-621-7626, Fax: 520-621-9435, E-mail: rallen@ag.arizona.edu. *Application contact:* Dr. Lance Baumgard, Grad, Committee Chair, 520-621-1487, Fax: 520-621-9435, E-mail: baumgard@ag.arizona.edu.

University of Arkansas, Graduate School, Dale Bumpers College of Agricultural, Food and Life Sciences, Department of Animal Science, Fayetteville, AR 72701-1201. Offers MS, PhD. *Students:* 8 full-time (5 women), 19 part-time (8 women); includes 3 minority (1 American Indian/Alaska Native, 1 Asian American or Pacific Islander, 1 Hispanic American), 3 international. In 2009, 4 master's awarded. *Degree requirements:* For master's, thesis; for doctorate, variable foreign language requirement, thesis/dissertation. *Entrance requirements:* For master's, GRE General Test or minimum GPA of 2.7. Application fee: $40 ($50 for international students). *Expenses:* Tuition, state resident: full-time $7355; part-time $356.58 per hour. Tuition, nonresident: full-time $17,401; part-time $775.17 per hour. Required fees: $1203. *Financial support:* In 2009–10, 15 research assistantships, 3 teaching assistantships were awarded; fellowships with tuition reimbursements, career-related internships or fieldwork and Federal Work-Study also available. Support available to part-time students. Financial award application deadline: 4/1; financial award applicants required to submit FAFSA. *Unit head:* Dr. Keith Lusby, Chair, 479-575-4351, E-mail: klusby@uark.edu. *Application contact:* Dr. David Kreider, Graduate Coordinator, 479-575-6323, E-mail: dkreider@uark.edu.

University of Arkansas, Graduate School, Dale Bumpers College of Agricultural, Food and Life Sciences, Department of Poultry Science, Fayetteville, AR 72701-1201. Offers MS, PhD. *Faculty:* 15 full-time (3 women). *Students:* 8 full-time (2 women), 24 part-time (11 women); includes 4 minority (1 African American, 3 Hispanic Americans), 16 international. In 2009, 6 master's, 5 doctorates awarded. *Degree requirements:* For master's, thesis; for doctorate, variable foreign language requirement, thesis/dissertation. Application fee: $40 ($50 for international students). *Expenses:* Tuition, state resident: full-time $7355; part-time $356.58 per hour. Tuition, nonresident: full-time $17,401; part-time $775.17 per hour. Required fees: $1203. *Financial support:* In 2009–10, 2 fellowships with tuition reimbursements, 22 research assistantships were awarded; teaching assistantships, career-related internships or fieldwork and Federal Work-Study also available. Support available to part-time students. Financial award application deadline: 4/1; financial award applicants required to submit FAFSA. *Unit head:* Dr. Mike Kidd, Department Head, 479-575-4952, E-mail: mkidd@uark.edu. *Application contact:* Dr. Mike Slavik, Graduate Coordinator, 479-575-4952, E-mail: mslavik@uark.edu.

The University of British Columbia, Faculty of Land and Food Systems, Animal Science Graduate Program, Vancouver, BC V6T 1Z1, Canada. Offers M Sc, PhD. *Degree requirements:* For master's, thesis; for doctorate, comprehensive exam, thesis/dissertation. *Entrance requirements:* Additional exam requirements/recommendations for international students: Required—TOEFL (minimum score 577 paper-based; 233 computer-based; 90 iBT), IELTS (minimum score 6.5). Electronic applications accepted. *Faculty research:* Animal production, animal behavior and welfare, reproductive physiology, animal genetics, aquaculture and fish physiology.

University of California, Davis, Graduate Studies, Graduate Group in Animal Biology, Davis, CA 95616. Offers MAM, MS, PhD. Terminal master's awarded for partial completion of doctoral program. *Degree requirements:* For master's, comprehensive exam (for some programs), thesis (for some programs); for doctorate, thesis/dissertation. *Entrance requirements:* For master's, GRE General Test, minimum GPA of 3.0. Additional exam requirements/recommendations for international students: Required—TOEFL (minimum score 550 paper-based; 213 computer-based). Electronic applications accepted. *Faculty research:* Genetics, nutrition, physiology and behavior in domestic and aquatic animals.

University of Connecticut, Graduate School, College of Agriculture and Natural Resources, Department of Animal Science, Storrs, CT 06269. Offers MS, PhD. *Faculty:* 19 full-time (4 women). *Students:* 32 full-time (19 women), 3 part-time (2 women); includes 1 minority (Asian American or Pacific Islander), 16 international. Average age 30. 23 applicants, 26% accepted, 3 enrolled. In 2009, 6 master's, 4 doctorates awarded. Terminal master's awarded for partial completion of doctoral program. *Degree requirements:* For master's, comprehensive exam, thesis; for doctorate, comprehensive exam, thesis/dissertation. *Entrance requirements:* For master's and doctorate, GRE General Test, GRE Subject Test. Additional exam requirements/recommendations for international students: Required—TOEFL (minimum score 550 paper-based; 213 computer-based). *Application deadline:* For fall admission, 2/1 priority date for domestic and international students; for spring admission, 11/1 for domestic students, 10/1 for international students. Applications are processed on a rolling basis. Application fee: $55. Electronic applications accepted. *Expenses:* Tuition, state resident: full-time $4725; part-time $525 per credit. Tuition, nonresident: full-time $12,267; part-time $1363 per credit. Required fees: $346 per semester. Tuition and fees vary according to course load. *Financial support:* In 2009–10, 25 research assistantships with full tuition reimbursements, 1 teaching assistantship with full tuition reimbursement were awarded; fellowships, Federal Work-Study, scholarships/grants, health care benefits, and unspecified assistantships also available. Financial award application deadline: 2/1; financial award applicants required to submit FAFSA. *Unit head:* Daniel L. Fletcher, Head, 860-486-2413, Fax: 860-486-4375, E-mail: daniel.fletcher@uconn.edu. *Application contact:* Theodore Rasmussen, Chairperson, 860-486-8339, Fax: 860-486-4375, E-mail: theodore.rasmussen@uconn.edu.

University of Delaware, College of Agriculture and Natural Resources, Department of Animal and Food Sciences, Newark, DE 19716. Offers animal sciences (MS, PhD); food sciences (MS). Part-time programs available. Terminal master's awarded for partial completion of doctoral program. *Degree requirements:* For master's, thesis; for doctorate, comprehensive exam, thesis/dissertation. *Entrance requirements:* For master's and doctorate, GRE General Test. Additional exam requirements/recommendations for international students: Required—TOEFL. Electronic applications accepted. *Faculty research:* Food chemistry, food microbiology, process engineering technology, packaging, food analysis, microbial genetics, molecular endocrinology, growth physiology, avian immunology and virology, monogastric nutrition, avian genomics.

University of Florida, Graduate School, College of Agricultural and Life Sciences, Department of Animal Sciences, Gainesville, FL 32611. Offers MS, PhD. *Degree requirements:* For master's, variable foreign language requirement, thesis optional; for doctorate, thesis/dissertation. *Entrance requirements:* For master's and doctorate, GRE General Test, minimum GPA of 3.0. Additional exam requirements/recommendations for international students: Required—TOEFL. Electronic applications accepted. *Faculty research:* Meat science, breeding and genetics, animal physiology, molecular biology, animal nutrition.

University of Florida, Interdisciplinary Concentration in Animal Molecular and Cellular Biology, Gainesville, FL 32611. Offers MS, PhD. Program offered by College of Agricultural and Life Sciences, College of Liberal Arts and Sciences, College of Medicine, and College of Veterinary Medicine.

University of Georgia, Graduate School, College of Agricultural and Environmental Sciences, Department of Animal and Dairy Sciences, Athens, GA 30602. Offers animal and dairy science (PhD); animal and dairy sciences (MADS); animal science (MS); dairy science (MS). *Faculty:* 19 full-time (2 women), 2 part-time/adjunct (0 women). *Students:* 32 full-time (22 women), 9 part-time (4 women); includes 2 minority (1 African American, 1 American Indian/Alaska Native), 9 international. 25 applicants, 60% accepted, 12 enrolled. In 2009, 13 master's, 3 doctorates awarded. *Degree requirements:* For master's, thesis; for doctorate, one foreign language, thesis/dissertation. *Entrance requirements:* For master's and doctorate, GRE General Test. *Application deadline:* For fall admission, 7/1 priority date for domestic students; for spring admission, 11/15 for domestic students. Application fee: $50. Electronic applications accepted. *Expenses:* Tuition, state resident: full-time $6000; part-time $250 per credit hour. Tuition, nonresident: full-time $20,904; part-time $871 per credit hour. Required fees: $730 per semester. *Financial support:* Fellowships, research assistantships, teaching assistantships, unspecified assistantships available. *Unit head:* Dr. J. Keith Bertrand, Interim Head, 706-542-6259, Fax: 706-542-2465, E-mail: adshead@uga.edu. *Application contact:* Dr. Mark A. Froetschel, Graduate Coordinator, 706-542-0985, Fax: 706-583-0274, E-mail: markf@uga.edu.

University of Georgia, Graduate School, College of Agricultural and Environmental Sciences, Department of Poultry Science, Athens, GA 30602. Offers animal nutrition (PhD); poultry science (MS, PhD). *Faculty:* 14 full-time (3 women), 2 part-time/adjunct (1 woman). *Students:* 23 full-time (13 women), 2 part-time (1 woman); includes 4 minority (2 Asian Americans or Pacific Islanders, 2 Hispanic Americans), 6 international. 16 applicants, 75% accepted, 9 enrolled. In 2009, 1 doctorate awarded. *Degree requirements:* For master's, thesis; for doctorate, one foreign language, thesis/dissertation. *Entrance requirements:* For master's and doctorate, GRE General Test. *Application deadline:* For fall admission, 7/1 priority date for domestic students; for spring admission, 11/15 for domestic students. Application fee: $50. Electronic applications accepted. *Expenses:* Tuition, state resident: full-time $6000; part-time $250 per credit hour. Tuition, nonresident: full-time $20,904; part-time $871 per credit hour. Required fees: $730 per semester. *Financial support:* Fellowships, research assistantships, teaching assistantships, unspecified assistantships available. *Unit head:* Dr. Michael Lacy, Head, 706-542-1351, Fax: 706-542-8383, E-mail: mlacy@uga.edu. *Application contact:* Dr. Larry R. McDougald, Graduate Coordinator, 706-542-1367, Fax: 706-542-1827, E-mail: rmcd@uga.edu.

University of Guelph, Graduate Program Services, Ontario Agricultural College, Department of Animal and Poultry Science, Guelph, ON N1G 2W1, Canada. Offers M Sc, PhD. Part-time programs available. *Degree requirements:* For master's, thesis (for some programs); for doctorate, comprehensive exam, thesis/dissertation. *Entrance requirements:* For master's, minimum B- average during previous 2 years of course work; for doctorate, minimum B-average. Additional exam requirements/recommendations for international students: Required—TOEFL (minimum score 550 paper-based; 213 computer-based; 89 iBT), IELTS (minimum score 6.5). *Faculty research:* Animal breeding and genetics (quantitative or molecular), animal nutrition (monogastric or ruminant), animal physiology (environmental, reproductive or behavioral), behavior and welfare.

University of Hawaii at Manoa, Graduate Division, College of Tropical Agriculture and Human Resources, Department of Human Nutrition, Food and Animal Sciences, Program in Animal Sciences, Honolulu, HI 96822. Offers MS. Part-time programs available. *Faculty:* 24 full-time (7 women), 3 part-time/adjunct (1 woman). *Students:* 9 full-time (8 women), 5 part-time (4 women); includes 7 minority (all Asian Americans or Pacific Islanders), 2 international. Average age 26. 5 applicants, 20% accepted, 1 enrolled. In 2009, 1 master's awarded. *Entrance requirements:* For master's, GRE General Test. Additional exam requirements/recommendations for international students: Required—TOEFL (minimum score 580 paper-based; 237 computer-based; 92 iBT), IELTS (minimum score 5). *Application deadline:* For fall admission, 2/1 for domestic and international students; for spring admission, 9/1 for domestic and international students. Application fee: $60. *Expenses:* Tuition, state resident: full-time $8900; part-time $372 per credit. Tuition, nonresident: full-time $21,400; part-time $898 per credit. Required fees: $207 per semester. *Financial support:* In 2009–10, 1 fellowship (averaging $3,000 per year), 2 research assistantships (averaging $16,824 per year) were awarded; tuition waivers (full) also available. *Faculty research:* Nutritional biochemistry, food composition, nutrition education, nutritional epidemiology, international nutrition, food toxicology. Total annual research expenditures: $330,000. *Application contact:* Jinzeng Yang, Graduate Chairperson, 808-956-7095, Fax: 808-956-4024, E-mail: jinzeng@hawaii.edu.

University of Idaho, College of Graduate Studies, College of Agricultural and Life Sciences, Department of Animal and Veterinary Science, Moscow, ID 83844-2282. Offers animal physiology (PhD); animal science (MS, PhD), including production. *Faculty:* 7 full-time. *Students:* 23 full-time, 13 part-time, 8 international. In 2009, 3 master's, 2 doctorates awarded. *Degree requirements:* For doctorate, thesis/dissertation. *Entrance requirements:* For master's, GRE General Test, minimum GPA of 2.8; for doctorate, minimum undergraduate GPA of 2.8, graduate 3.0. *Application deadline:* For fall admission, 8/1 for domestic students; for spring admission, 12/15 for domestic students. Application fee: $55 ($60 for international students). *Expenses:* Tuition, state resident: full-time $6120. Tuition, nonresident: full-time $17,712. *Financial support:* Research assistantships, teaching assistantships available. Financial award application deadline: 2/15. *Faculty research:* Reproductive biology, muscle and growth physiology, meat science, aquaculture, ruminant nutrition. *Unit head:* Dr. Carl W. Hunt, Head, 208-885-6932. *Application contact:* Dr. Carl W. Hunt, Head, 208-885-6932.

University of Illinois at Urbana–Champaign, Graduate College, College of Agricultural, Consumer and Environmental Sciences, Department of Animal Sciences, Champaign, IL 61820. Offers animal sciences (MS, PhD); bioinformatics: animal sciences (MS). *Faculty:* 42 full-time (5 women), 3 part-time/adjunct (0 women). *Students:* 97 full-time (46 women), 5 part-time (2 women); includes 4 minority (1 African American, 2 Asian Americans or Pacific Islanders, 1 Hispanic American), 42 international. 69 applicants, 39% accepted, 24 enrolled. In 2009, 12 master's, 12 doctorates awarded. *Entrance requirements:* For master's and doctorate, GRE General Test, GRE Subject Test (biology), minimum GPA of 3.0. Additional exam requirements/recommendations for international students: Required—TOEFL (minimum score 590 paper-based; 243 computer-based), TWE. *Application deadline:* Applications are processed on a rolling basis. Application fee: $60 ($75 for international students). Electronic applications accepted. *Financial support:* In 2009–10, 12 fellowships, 90 research assistantships, 7 teaching assistantships were awarded; tuition waivers (full and partial) also available. *Unit head:* Neal R. Merchen, Head, 217-333-3462, Fax: 217-244-2871, E-mail: nmerchen@illinois.edu. *Application contact:* Allison Mosley, Resource and Policy Analyst, 217-333-1044, Fax: 217-333-5044, E-mail: amosley@illinois.edu.

University of Kentucky, Graduate School, College of Agriculture, Program in Animal Sciences, Lexington, KY 40506-0032. Offers MS, PhD. Terminal master's awarded for partial completion of doctoral program. *Degree requirements:* For master's, comprehensive exam, thesis optional; for doctorate, comprehensive exam, thesis/dissertation. *Entrance requirements:* For master's, GRE General Test, minimum undergraduate GPA of 2.75; for doctorate, GRE General Test, minimum graduate GPA of 3.0. Additional exam requirements/recommendations for international students: Required—TOEFL (minimum score 550 paper-based; 213 computer-based). Electronic applications accepted. *Faculty research:* Nutrition of horses, cattle, swine, poultry, and sheep; physiology of reproduction and lactation; food science; microbiology.

University of Maine, Graduate School, College of Natural Sciences, Forestry, and Agriculture, Department of Animal and Veterinary Sciences, Orono, ME 04469. Offers animal sciences (MPS, MS). Part-time programs available. *Faculty:* 6 full-time (0 women), 2 part-time/adjunct (1 woman). *Students:* 3 full-time (2 women), 3 part-time (2 women); includes 1 minority (American Indian/Alaska Native). Average age 34. 11 applicants, 18% accepted, 1 enrolled. In 2009, 2 master's awarded. *Entrance requirements:* For master's, GRE General Test. Additional exam requirements/recommendations for international students: Required—TOEFL. *Application deadline:* For fall admission, 2/1 priority date for domestic students. Applications are processed on a rolling basis. Application fee: $65. Electronic applications accepted. *Financial support:* In 2009–10, 3 research assistantships with tuition reimbursements (averaging $14,887 per year), 1 teaching assistantship with tuition reimbursement (averaging $12,790 per year) were awarded; Federal Work-Study, institutionally sponsored loans, and tuition waivers (full and partial) also available. Financial award application deadline: 3/1. *Faculty research:* Animal nutrition, parasitology, veterinary pathology, reproductive physiology, marine life nutrition and management. *Unit head:* Dr. Martin Stokes, Chair, 207-581-2770, Fax: 207-581-2770. *Application contact:* Scott G. Delcourt, Associate Dean of the Graduate School, 207-581-3291, Fax: 207-581-3232, E-mail: graduate@maine.edu.

University of Manitoba, Faculty of Graduate Studies, Faculty of Agricultural and Food Sciences, Department of Animal Science, Winnipeg, MB R3T 2N2, Canada. Offers M Sc, PhD. *Degree requirements:* For master's, thesis; for doctorate, one foreign language, thesis/dissertation.

University of Maryland, College Park, Academic Affairs, College of Agriculture and Natural Resources, Department of Animal and Avian Sciences, Program in Animal Sciences, College Park, MD 20742. Offers MS, PhD. *Students:* 29 full-time (14 women), 4 part-time (all women); includes 2 minority (1 Asian American or Pacific Islander, 1 Hispanic American), 14 international. 50 applicants, 22% accepted, 10 enrolled. In 2009, 8 master's, 5 doctorates awarded. *Degree requirements:* For master's, thesis, oral exam or written comprehensive exam; for doctorate, thesis/dissertation, journal publication, scientific paper. *Entrance requirements:* For master's, GRE General Test, minimum GPA of 3.0; for doctorate, GRE General Test. Additional exam requirements/recommendations for international students: Required—TOEFL. *Application deadline:* For fall admission, 5/15 for domestic students, 2/1 for international students; for spring admission, 10/1 for domestic students, 6/1 for international students. Applications are processed on a rolling basis. Application fee: $60. Electronic applications accepted. *Expenses:* Tuition, area resident: Part-time $471 per credit hour. Tuition, state resident: part-time $471 per credit hour. Tuition, nonresident: part-time $1016 per credit hour. Required fees: $337.04 per term. *Financial support:* In 2009–10, 2 research assistantships (averaging $18,359 per year), 27 teaching assistantships (averaging $16,403 per year) were awarded; fellowships also available. Financial award applicants required to submit FAFSA. *Faculty research:* Animal physiology, cell biology and biochemistry, reproduction, biometrics, animal behavior. *Unit head:* Dr. Tom Porter, Chairman, 301-405-1366, Fax: 301-314-9059, E-mail: teporter@umd.edu. *Application contact:* Dean of Graduate School, 301-405-0376, Fax: 301-314-9305.

University of Massachusetts Amherst, Graduate School, College of Natural Sciences, Department of Animal Biotechnology and Biomedical Sciences, Amherst, MA 01003. Offers MS, PhD. Part-time programs available. *Faculty:* 21 full-time (8 women). *Students:* 22 full-time (15 women); includes 2 minority (1 African American, 1 Hispanic American), 8 international. Average age 30. 41 applicants, 7% accepted, 3 enrolled. In 2009, 1 master's, 4 doctorates awarded. Terminal master's awarded for partial completion of doctoral program. *Degree requirements:* For master's, thesis or alternative; for doctorate, comprehensive exam, thesis/dissertation. *Entrance requirements:* For master's and doctorate, GRE General Test. Additional exam requirements/recommendations for international students: Required—TOEFL (minimum score 550 paper-based; 213 computer-based; 80 iBT), IELTS (minimum score 6.5). *Application deadline:* For fall admission, 2/1 for domestic and international students; for spring admission, 10/1 for domestic and international students. Applications are processed on a rolling basis. Application fee: $50 ($65 for international students). Electronic applications accepted. *Expenses:* Tuition, state resident: full-time $2640; part-time $110 per credit. Tuition, nonresident: full-time $9936; part-time $414 per credit. Tuition and fees vary according to course load. *Financial support:* In 2009–10, 42 research assistantships with full tuition reimbursements (averaging $11,650 per year), 11 teaching assistantships with full tuition reimbursements (averaging $11,217 per year) were awarded; fellowships, career-related internships or fieldwork, Federal Work-Study, scholarships/grants, traineeships, health care benefits, tuition waivers (full), and unspecified assistantships also available. Support available to part-time students. Financial award application deadline: 2/1. *Unit head:* Dr. Pablo E. Visconti, Graduate Program Director, 413-577-1193, Fax: 413-577-1150. *Application contact:* Jean M. Ames, Supervisor of Admissions, 413-545-0722, Fax: 413-577-0010, E-mail: gradadm@grad.umass.edu.

University of Minnesota, Twin Cities Campus, Graduate School, College of Food, Agricultural and Natural Resource Sciences, Program in Animal Science, Minneapolis, MN 55455-0213. Offers MS, PhD. Part-time programs available. *Degree requirements:* For master's, comprehensive exam, thesis; for doctorate, comprehensive exam, thesis/dissertation. *Entrance requirements:* For master's and doctorate, GRE. Additional exam requirements/recommendations for international students: Required—TOEFL. Electronic applications accepted. *Faculty research:* Physiology, growth biology, nutrition, genetics, production systems.

University of Missouri, Graduate School, College of Agriculture, Food and Natural Resources, Department of Animal Sciences, Columbia, MO 65211. Offers MS, PhD. *Faculty:* 71 full-time (12 women), 6 part-time/adjunct (1 woman). *Students:* 43 full-time (23 women), 10 part-time (5 women), 8 international. Average age 25. 44 applicants, 34% accepted, 15 enrolled. In 2009, 16 master's awarded. Terminal master's awarded for partial completion of doctoral program. *Degree requirements:* For doctorate, 2 foreign languages, comprehensive exam, thesis/dissertation. *Entrance requirements:* For master's, GRE General Test, minimum GPA of 3.0; for doctorate, GRE General Test: V=400; Q=550, minimum GPA of 3.0. Additional exam requirements/recommendations for international students: Required—TOEFL (minimum score 500 paper-based; 173 computer-based; 61 iBT), IELTS (minimum score 5.5). *Application deadline:* Applications are processed on a rolling basis. Application fee: $45 ($60 for international students). Electronic applications accepted. *Financial support:* Research assistantships with tuition reimbursements, teaching assistantships with tuition reimbursements, institutionally sponsored loans available. *Unit head:* Dr. Rod Geisert, Department Chair, E-mail: geisertr@missouri.edu. *Application contact:* Cinda Hudlow, Administrative Assistant, 573-882-7446, E-mail: hudlowc@missouri.edu.

University of Nebraska–Lincoln, Graduate College, College of Agricultural Sciences and Natural Resources, Department of Animal Science, Lincoln, NE 68588. Offers MS, PhD. *Degree requirements:* For master's, thesis; for doctorate, comprehensive exam, thesis/

Animal Sciences

University of Nebraska–Lincoln (continued)
dissertation. *Entrance requirements:* For master's and doctorate, GRE General Test. Additional exam requirements/recommendations for international students: Required—TOEFL (minimum score 525 paper-based; 195 computer-based). Electronic applications accepted. *Faculty research:* Animal breeding and genetics, meat and poultry products, nonruminant and ruminant nutrition, physiology.

University of Nevada, Reno, Graduate School, College of Agriculture, Biotechnology and Natural Resources, Department of Animal Science, Reno, NV 89557. Offers MS. *Degree requirements:* For master's, thesis optional. *Entrance requirements:* For master's, GRE, minimum GPA of 2.75. Additional exam requirements/recommendations for international students: Required—TOEFL (minimum score 500 paper-based; 173 computer-based; 61 iBT), IELTS (minimum score 6). Electronic applications accepted. *Faculty research:* Sperm fertility, embryo development, ruminant utilization of forages.

University of New Hampshire, Graduate School, College of Life Sciences and Agriculture, Department of Biological Sciences, Program in Animal Science, Durham, NH 03824. Offers MS. Part-time programs available. *Faculty:* 23 full-time. *Students:* 7 full-time (5 women), 4 part-time (3 women); includes 1 minority (Hispanic American). Average age 27. 15 applicants, 20% accepted, 2 enrolled. *Entrance requirements:* For master's, GRE General Test. Additional exam requirements/recommendations for international students: Required—TOEFL (minimum score 550 paper-based; 213 computer-based; 80 iBT). *Application deadline:* For fall admission, 6/1 priority date for domestic students, 4/1 for international students; for spring admission, 12/1 for domestic students. Applications are processed on a rolling basis. Application fee: $65. Electronic applications accepted. *Expenses:* Tuition, state resident: full-time $10,380; part-time $577 per credit hour. Tuition, nonresident: full-time $24,350; part-time $1002 per credit hour. Required fees: $1550; $387.50 per semester. Tuition and fees vary according to course load and program. *Financial support:* In 2009–10, 7 students received support, including 2 research assistantships, 5 teaching assistantships; fellowships, career-related internships or fieldwork, Federal Work-Study, scholarships/grants, and tuition waivers (full and partial) also available. Support available to part-time students. Financial award application deadline: 2/15. *Unit head:* Dr. Chris Neefus, Chair, 603-862-3205. *Application contact:* Diane Lavalliere, Administrative Assistant, 603-862-2100.

University of New Hampshire, Graduate School, College of Life Sciences and Agriculture, Department of Molecular, Cellular and Biomedical Sciences, Program in Animal and Nutritional Sciences, Durham, NH 03824. Offers PhD. Part-time programs available. *Faculty:* 23 full-time. *Students:* 5 full-time (2 women), 1 (woman) part-time. Average age 37. 4 applicants, 25% accepted, 1 enrolled. *Entrance requirements:* For doctorate, GRE. Additional exam requirements/recommendations for international students: Required—TOEFL (minimum score 550 paper-based; 213 computer-based; 80 iBT). *Application deadline:* For fall admission, 6/1 priority date for domestic students, 4/1 priority date for international students; for spring admission, 12/1 for domestic students. Application fee: $65. Electronic applications accepted. *Expenses:* Tuition, state resident: full-time $10,380; part-time $577 per credit hour. Tuition, nonresident: full-time $24,350; part-time $1002 per credit hour. Required fees: $1550; $387.50 per semester. Tuition and fees vary according to course load and program. *Financial support:* In 2009–10, 4 students received support, including 1 fellowship, 1 research assistantship, 2 teaching assistantships; scholarships/grants, traineeships, and unspecified assistantships also available. Support available to part-time students. *Unit head:* Dr. Rick Cote, Chairperson, 603-862-2458. *Application contact:* Flora Joyal, Administrative Assistant, 603-862-4095, E-mail: ansc.grad.program.info@unh.edu.

University of Puerto Rico, Mayagüez Campus, Graduate Studies, College of Agricultural Sciences, Department of Cattle Industry, Mayagüez, PR 00681-9000. Offers MS. Part-time programs available. *Degree requirements:* For master's, comprehensive exam, thesis. *Entrance requirements:* For master's, minimum GPA of 2.75, BS degree in agricultural science or a closely related field. *Faculty research:* Swine production and nutrition, poultry production, dairy science and technology, microbiology.

University of Rhode Island, Graduate School, College of the Environment and Life Sciences, Department of Fisheries, Animal and Veterinary Science, Kingston, RI 02881. Offers animal health and disease (MS); animal science (MS); aquaculture (MS); aquatic pathology (MS); environmental sciences (PhD), including animal science, aquacultural science, aquatic pathology, fisheries science; fisheries (MS). *Faculty:* 10 full-time (4 women). *Students:* 14 full-time (7 women), 12 part-time (7 women); includes 5 minority (2 African Americans, 3 Hispanic Americans), 3 international. In 2009, 3 master's, 2 doctorates awarded. *Degree requirements:* For master's, comprehensive exam (for some programs), thesis optional; for doctorate, comprehensive exam, thesis/dissertation. *Entrance requirements:* For master's and doctorate, GRE, 2 letters of recommendation. Additional exam requirements/recommendations for international students: Required—TOEFL (minimum score 550 paper-based; 213 computer-based). *Application deadline:* For fall admission, 7/15 for domestic students, 2/1 for international students; for spring admission, 11/15 for domestic students, 7/15 for international students. Application fee: $65. Electronic applications accepted. *Expenses:* Tuition, state resident: full-time $8828; part-time $490 per credit hour. Tuition, nonresident: full-time $22,100; part-time $1228 per credit hour. Required fees: $1118; $57 per semester. Tuition and fees vary according to program. *Financial support:* In 2009–10, 4 research assistantships with full and partial tuition reimbursements (averaging $11,386 per year), 7 teaching assistantships with full and partial tuition reimbursements (averaging $10,940 per year) were awarded. Financial award application deadline: 7/15; financial award applicants required to submit FAFSA. Total annual research expenditures: $2.1 million. *Unit head:* Dr. David Bengtson, Chair, 401-874-2668, Fax: 401-874-7575, E-mail: bengtson@uri.edu. *Application contact:* Dr. Marta Gomez-Chiarra, Director of Graduate Studies, 401-874-2917, Fax: 401-874-7575, E-mail: gomezchi@uri.edu.

University of Saskatchewan, College of Graduate Studies and Research, College of Agriculture, Department of Animal and Poultry Science, Saskatoon, SK S7N 5A2, Canada. Offers M Ag, M Sc, PhD. *Faculty:* 28. *Students:* 58. In 2009, 10 master's, 1 doctorate awarded. *Degree requirements:* For master's, thesis; for doctorate, thesis/dissertation. *Entrance requirements:* Additional exam requirements/recommendations for international students: Required—TOEFL. *Application deadline:* For fall admission, 7/1 priority date for domestic students. Applications are processed on a rolling basis. Application fee: $75. Tuition and fees charges are reported in Canadian dollars. *Expenses:* Tuition, area resident: Full-time $3000 Canadian dollars; part-time $500 Canadian dollars per term. Required fees: $700 Canadian dollars; $100 Canadian dollars per term. *Financial support:* Fellowships, research assistantships, teaching assistantships available. Financial award application deadline: 1/31. *Unit head:* Dr. Hank Classen, Head, 306-966-4972, Fax: 306-966-4151, E-mail: hank.classen@usask.ca. *Application contact:* Dr. Bernard Laarveld, Graduate Chair, 306-966-4972, Fax: 306-966-4151, E-mail: bernard.laarveld@usask.ca.

University of Saskatchewan, Western College of Veterinary Medicine and College of Graduate Studies and Research, Graduate Programs in Veterinary Medicine, Department of Large Animal Clinical Sciences, Saskatoon, SK S7N 5A2, Canada. Offers M Sc, M Vet Sc, PhD. *Faculty:* 30. *Students:* 20; includes 1 minority (African American). In 2009, 7 master's, 2 doctorates awarded. *Degree requirements:* For master's, thesis (for some programs); for doctorate, comprehensive exam (for some programs), thesis/dissertation. *Entrance requirements:* Additional exam requirements/recommendations for international students: Required—TOEFL (minimum score 80 iBT); Recommended—IELTS (minimum score 6.5). Electronic applications accepted. Tuition and fees charges are reported in Canadian dollars. *Expenses:* Tuition, area resident: Full-time $3000 Canadian dollars; part-time $500 Canadian dollars per term. Required fees: $700 Canadian dollars; $100 Canadian dollars per term. *Faculty research:* Reproduction, infectious diseases, epidemiology, food safety. *Unit head:* Dr. David Wilson, Head, 306-966-7145, Fax: 306-966-7159, E-mail: david.wilson@usask.ca. *Application contact:* Dr. Joseph Stookey, Associate Dean, Research, 306-966-7145, Fax: 306-966-7159, E-mail: joseph.stookey@usask.ca.

University of Saskatchewan, Western College of Veterinary Medicine and College of Graduate Studies and Research, Graduate Programs in Veterinary Medicine, Department of Small Animal Clinical Sciences, Saskatoon, SK S7N 5A2, Canada. Offers small animal clinical sciences (M Sc, PhD); veterinary anesthesiology, radiology and surgery (M Vet Sc); veterinary internal medicine (M Vet Sc). *Faculty:* 6 full-time (4 women). *Students:* 7. In 2009, 5 master's awarded. *Degree requirements:* For master's, thesis (for some programs); for doctorate, comprehensive exam (for some programs), thesis/dissertation. *Entrance requirements:* Additional exam requirements/recommendations for international students: Required—TOEFL (minimum score 80 iBT); Recommended—IELTS (minimum score 6.5). Application fee: $75. Electronic applications accepted. Tuition and fees charges are reported in Canadian dollars. *Expenses:* Tuition, area resident: Full-time $3000 Canadian dollars; part-time $500 Canadian dollars per term. Required fees: $700 Canadian dollars; $100 Canadian dollars per term. *Faculty research:* Orthopedics, wildlife, cardiovascular exercise/myelopathy, ophthalmology. *Unit head:* Dr. Klaas Post, Head, 306-966-7084, Fax: 306-966-7174, E-mail: klaas.post@usask.ca. *Application contact:* Dr. Klaas Post, Graduate Chair, 306-966-7084, Fax: 306-966-7174, E-mail: klaas.post@usask.ca.

The University of Tennessee, Graduate School, College of Agricultural Sciences and Natural Resources, Department of Animal Science, Knoxville, TN 37996. Offers animal anatomy (PhD); breeding (MS, PhD); management (MS, PhD); nutrition (MS, PhD); physiology (MS, PhD). Part-time programs available. *Degree requirements:* For master's, thesis; for doctorate, thesis/dissertation. *Entrance requirements:* For master's and doctorate, GRE General Test, minimum GPA of 2.7. Additional exam requirements/recommendations for international students: Required—TOEFL. Electronic applications accepted. *Expenses:* Tuition, state resident: full-time $6826; part-time $380 per semester hour. Tuition, nonresident: full-time $21,844; part-time $1147 per semester hour. Tuition and fees vary according to program.

University of Vermont, Graduate College, College of Agriculture and Life Sciences, Department of Animal Sciences, Burlington, VT 05405. Offers MS, PhD. *Students:* 6 (3 women), 1 international. 13 applicants, 15% accepted, 2 enrolled. In 2009, 3 master's, 2 doctorates awarded. *Degree requirements:* For master's, thesis; for doctorate, one foreign language, thesis/dissertation. *Entrance requirements:* For master's and doctorate, GRE General Test. Additional exam requirements/recommendations for international students: Required—TOEFL (minimum score 550 paper-based; 213 computer-based; 80 iBT). *Application deadline:* For fall admission, 4/1 priority date for domestic students. Applications are processed on a rolling basis. Application fee: $40. Electronic applications accepted. *Expenses:* Tuition, area resident: Part-time $508 per credit hour. Tuition, state resident: part-time $508 per credit hour. Tuition, nonresident: part-time $1281 per credit hour. *Financial support:* Fellowships, research assistantships, teaching assistantships available. Financial award application deadline: 3/1. *Faculty research:* Animal nutrition, dairy production. *Unit head:* Dr. John M. Burke, Interim Chairperson, 802-656-2070. *Application contact:* Dr. David Kerr, Coordinator, 802-656-2070.

University of Vermont, Graduate College, College of Agriculture and Life Sciences, Program in Animal, Nutrition and Food Sciences, Burlington, VT 05405. Offers PhD. *Students:* 11 (4 women), 7 international. 21 applicants, 33% accepted, 3 enrolled. In 2009, 1 doctorate awarded. *Degree requirements:* For doctorate, one foreign language, thesis/dissertation. *Entrance requirements:* For doctorate, GRE General Test. Additional exam requirements/recommendations for international students: Required—TOEFL (minimum score 550 paper-based; 213 computer-based; 80 iBT). *Application deadline:* For fall admission, 4/1 priority date for domestic students. Applications are processed on a rolling basis. Application fee: $40. Electronic applications accepted. *Expenses:* Tuition, area resident: Part-time $508 per credit hour. Tuition, state resident: part-time $508 per credit hour. Tuition, nonresident: part-time $1281 per credit hour. *Financial support:* Application deadline: 3/1. *Unit head:* Dr. R. K. Johnson, Dean, 802-656-2070. *Application contact:* Dr. David Kerr, Coordinator, 802-656-2070.

University of Wisconsin–Madison, Graduate School, College of Agricultural and Life Sciences, Department of Animal Sciences, Madison, WI 53706-1380. Offers MS, PhD. Part-time programs available. Terminal master's awarded for partial completion of doctoral program. *Degree requirements:* For master's, thesis; for doctorate, thesis/dissertation. *Entrance requirements:* For master's and doctorate, GRE. Additional exam requirements/recommendations for international students: Required—TOEFL (minimum score 550 paper-based; 213 computer-based). Electronic applications accepted. *Expenses:* Tuition, state resident: part-time $594 per credit. Tuition, nonresident: part-time $1504 per credit. Required fees: $65 per credit. Tuition and fees vary according to course load, program and reciprocity agreements. *Faculty research:* Animal biology, immunity and toxicology, endocrinology and reproductive physiology, genetics-animal breeding, meat science muscle biology.

University of Wisconsin–Madison, Graduate School, College of Agricultural and Life Sciences, Department of Dairy Science, Madison, WI 53706-1380. Offers MS, PhD. Part-time programs available. *Degree requirements:* For master's, thesis (for some programs); for doctorate, thesis/dissertation. *Entrance requirements:* For master's and doctorate, GRE General Test. Additional exam requirements/recommendations for international students: Required—TOEFL. Electronic applications accepted. *Expenses:* Tuition, state resident: part-time $594 per credit. Tuition, nonresident: part-time $1504 per credit. Required fees: $65 per credit. Tuition and fees vary according to course load, program and reciprocity agreements. *Faculty research:* Genetics, nutrition, lactation, reproduction, management of dairy cattle.

University of Wyoming, College of Agriculture, Department of Animal Sciences, Program in Animal Sciences, Laramie, WY 82070. Offers MS, PhD. *Degree requirements:* For master's, comprehensive exam, thesis; for doctorate, comprehensive exam, thesis/dissertation. *Entrance requirements:* For master's, GRE General Test, minimum GPA of 3.0; for doctorate, GRE General Test or MS degree, minimum GPA of 3.0. Additional exam requirements/recommendations for international students: Required—TOEFL (minimum score 525 paper-based). *Faculty research:* Reproductive biology, ruminant nutrition meat science, muscle biology, food microbiology, lipid metabolism.

Utah State University, School of Graduate Studies, College of Agriculture, Department of Animal, Dairy and Veterinary Sciences, Logan, UT 84322. Offers animal science (MS, PhD); bioveterinary science (MS, PhD); dairy science (MS). Part-time programs available. *Degree requirements:* For master's, thesis (for some programs); for doctorate, comprehensive exam, thesis/dissertation. *Entrance requirements:* For master's and doctorate, GRE General Test, minimum GPA of 3.0. Additional exam requirements/recommendations for international students: Required—TOEFL. Electronic applications accepted. *Faculty research:* Monoclonal antibodies, antiviral chemotherapy, management systems, biotechnology, rumen fermentation manipulation.

Virginia Polytechnic Institute and State University, Graduate School, College of Agriculture and Life Sciences, Department of Animal and Poultry Sciences, Blacksburg, VA 24061. Offers animal science (MS, PhD); poultry science (MS, PhD), including behavior, genetics, management, nutrition, physiology. *Entrance requirements:* For master's and doctorate, GRE. Additional exam requirements/recommendations for international students: Required—TOEFL (minimum score 550 paper-based; 213 computer-based). Electronic applications accepted. *Faculty research:* Quantitative genetics of cattle and sheep, swine nutrition and management, animal molecular biology, nutrition of grazing livestock.

Virginia Polytechnic Institute and State University, Graduate School, College of Agriculture and Life Sciences, Department of Dairy Science, Blacksburg, VA 24061. Offers animal science (MS, PhD). *Entrance requirements:* For master's and doctorate, GRE. Additional exam requirements/recommendations for international students: Required—TOEFL (minimum score 550 paper-based; 213 computer-based). Electronic applications accepted. *Faculty research:* Genetics, nutrition, reproduction, lactation.

Washington State University, Graduate School, College of Agricultural, Human, and Natural Resource Sciences, Department of Animal Sciences, Pullman, WA 99164. Offers MS, PhD. Part-time programs available. *Faculty:* 19. *Students:* 14 full-time (10 women), 3 part-time (2 women); includes 1 African American, 1 Asian American or Pacific Islander, 7 international. Average age 32. 48 applicants, 23% accepted, 5 enrolled. In 2009, 6 master's, 2 doctorates awarded. *Degree requirements:* For master's, comprehensive exam (for some programs), thesis (for some programs), oral exam; for doctorate, comprehensive exam, thesis/dissertation, oral and written exam. *Entrance requirements:* For master's, GRE, minimum GPA of 3.0, 3 letters of recommendation, department questionnaire; for doctorate, GRE General Test, minimum GPA of 3.0. Additional exam requirements/recommendations for international students: Required—TOEFL, IELTS. *Application deadline:* For fall admission, 1/10 priority date for domestic students, 1/10 for international students; for spring admission, 7/1 priority date for domestic students, 7/1 for international students. Applications are processed on a rolling basis. Application fee: $50. Electronic applications accepted. *Financial support:* In 2009–10, fellowships (averaging $5,000 per year), research assistantships with full and partial tuition reimbursements (averaging $14,634 per year), teaching assistantships with full and partial tuition reimbursements (averaging $13,383 per year) were awarded; career-related internships or fieldwork, Federal Work-Study, institutionally sponsored loans, scholarships/grants, health care benefits, tuition waivers (partial), and teaching associateships also available. Financial award application deadline: 4/1; financial award applicants required to submit FAFSA. *Faculty research:* Reproduction, genetics, equine cytokines, fish diseases and vaccines. Total annual research expenditures: $397,512. *Unit head:* Dr. Margaret Benson, Professor and Chair, 509-335-5523, Fax: 509-335-1082, E-mail: m_benson@wsu.edu. *Application contact:* Graduate School Admissions, 800-GRADWSU, Fax: 509-335-1949, E-mail: gradsch@wsu.edu.

West Texas A&M University, College of Agriculture, Nursing, and Natural Sciences, Division of Agriculture, Emphasis in Animal Science, Canyon, TX 79016-0001. Offers MS. Part-time programs available. *Degree requirements:* For master's, comprehensive exam, thesis optional. *Entrance requirements:* For master's, GRE General Test. Additional exam requirements/recommendations for international students: Required—TOEFL (minimum score 550 paper-based). Electronic applications accepted. *Faculty research:* Nutrition, animal breeding, meat science, reproduction physiology, feedlots.

West Virginia University, Davis College of Agriculture, Forestry and Consumer Sciences, Division of Animal and Nutritional Sciences, Program in Animal and Nutritional Sciences, Morgantown, WV 26506. Offers breeding (MS); food sciences (MS); nutrition (MS); physiology (MS); production management (MS); reproduction (MS). Part-time programs available. *Degree requirements:* For master's, thesis, oral and written exams. *Entrance requirements:* For master's, GRE, minimum GPA of 2.5. Additional exam requirements/recommendations for international students: Required—TOEFL. *Faculty research:* Animal nutrition, reproductive physiology, food science.

West Virginia University, Davis College of Agriculture, Forestry and Consumer Sciences, Division of Plant and Soil Sciences, Program in Agricultural Sciences, Morgantown, WV 26506. Offers animal and food sciences (PhD); plant and soil sciences (PhD). *Degree requirements:* For doctorate, thesis/dissertation, oral and written exams. *Entrance requirements:* Additional exam requirements/recommendations for international students: Required—TOEFL. *Faculty research:* Ruminant nutrition, metabolism, forage utilization, physiology, reproduction.

Aquaculture

American University of Beirut, Graduate Programs, Faculty of Agricultural and Food Sciences, Beirut, Lebanon. Offers agricultural economics (MS); animal sciences (MS); ecosystem management (MSES); food technology (MS); irrigation (MS); mechanization (MS); nutrition (MS); plant protection (MS); plant science (MS); poultry science (MS); soils (MS). Part-time programs available. *Degree requirements:* For master's, one foreign language, comprehensive exam, thesis (for some programs). *Entrance requirements:* For master's, letter of recommendation. Additional exam requirements/recommendations for international students: Required—TOEFL (minimum score 600 paper-based; 250 computer-based; 100 iBT), IELTS (minimum score 7.5). *Faculty research:* Sustainable animal systems/agriculture; natural resource management; community nutrition, obesity and food safety; integrated pest management; ecosystem management.

Auburn University, Graduate School, College of Agriculture, Department of Fisheries and Allied Aquacultures, Auburn University, AL 36849. Offers M Aq, MS, PhD. Part-time programs available. *Faculty:* 20 full-time (3 women). *Students:* 37 full-time (16 women), 31 part-time (10 women); includes 4 minority (2 African Americans, 1 American Indian/Alaska Native, 1 Hispanic American), 33 international. Average age 28. 49 applicants, 49% accepted, 21 enrolled. In 2009, 12 master's, 5 doctorates awarded. *Degree requirements:* For master's, thesis (for some programs); for doctorate, 2 foreign languages, thesis/dissertation. *Entrance requirements:* For master's and doctorate, GRE General Test. *Application deadline:* For fall admission, 7/7 for domestic students; for spring admission, 11/24 for domestic students. Applications are processed on a rolling basis. Application fee: $50 ($60 for international students). Electronic applications accepted. *Expenses:* Tuition, state resident: full-time $6240. Tuition, nonresident: full-time $18,720. International tuition: $18,938 full-time. Required fees: $492. Tuition and fees vary according to course load, program and reciprocity agreements. *Financial support:* Fellowships, research assistantships, teaching assistantships, Federal Work-Study available. Support available to part-time students. Financial award application deadline: 3/15; financial award applicants required to submit FAFSA. *Faculty research:* Channel catfish production; aquatic animal health; community and population ecology; pond management; production hatching, breeding and genetics. Total annual research expenditures: $8 million. *Unit head:* Dr. David B. Rouse, Head, 334-844-4786. *Application contact:* Dr. George Flowers, Dean of the Graduate School, 334-844-2125.

Clemson University, Graduate School, College of Agriculture, Forestry and Life Sciences, Department of Forestry and Natural Resources, Program in Wildlife and Fisheries Biology, Clemson, SC 29634. Offers MS, PhD. *Students:* 28 full-time (20 women), 8 part-time (6 women); includes 3 minority (2 African Americans, 1 American Indian/Alaska Native), 1 international. Average age 31. 27 applicants, 33% accepted, 7 enrolled. In 2009, 6 master's, 3 doctorates awarded. *Degree requirements:* For master's, thesis; for doctorate, thesis/dissertation. *Entrance requirements:* For master's, GRE General Test, minimum undergraduate GPA of 3.0; for doctorate, GRE General Test. Additional exam requirements/recommendations for international students: Required—TOEFL, IELTS. *Application deadline:* For fall admission, 6/1 for domestic students, 4/15 for international students; for spring admission, 9/15 for international students. Applications are processed on a rolling basis. Application fee: $70 ($80 for international students). Electronic applications accepted. *Expenses:* Contact institution. *Financial support:* In 2009–10, 26 students received support, including 6 fellowships with full and partial tuition reimbursements available (averaging $4,916 per year), 21 research assistantships with partial tuition reimbursements available (averaging $17,050 per year), 4 teaching assistantships with partial tuition reimbursements available (averaging $11,000 per year); career-related internships or fieldwork, institutionally sponsored loans, scholarships/grants, health care benefits, and unspecified assistantships also available. Support available to part-time students. Financial award applicants required to submit FAFSA. *Faculty research:* Intensive freshwater culture systems, conservation biology, stream management, applied wildlife management. *Unit head:* Dr. Patricia Layton, Chair, 864-656-3303, Fax: 864-656-3304, E-mail: playton@clemson.edu. *Application contact:* Dr. David Guynn, Graduate Program Coordinator, 864-656-4830, Fax: 864-656-5344, E-mail: dguynn@clemson.edu.

Kentucky State University, College of Mathematics, Sciences, Technology and Health, Frankfort, KY 40601. Offers aquaculture (MS); computer science (MS), including computer science theory, information assurance, information technology. Part-time and evening/weekend programs available. *Faculty:* 8 full-time (0 women), 1 part-time/adjunct (0 women). *Students:* 18 full-time (6 women), 18 part-time (4 women); includes 11 minority (8 African Americans, 1 Asian American or Pacific Islander, 2 Hispanic Americans), 7 international. Average age 35. 42 applicants, 55% accepted, 12 enrolled. In 2009, 8 master's awarded. *Degree requirements:* For master's, comprehensive exam, thesis optional. *Entrance requirements:* For master's, GRE, GMAT. Additional exam requirements/recommendations for international students: Required—TOEFL (minimum score 525 paper-based; 173 computer-based). *Application deadline:* For fall admission, 7/1 priority date for domestic students, 4/15 priority date for international students; for spring admission, 11/15 priority date for domestic students, 8/1 priority date for international students. Applications are processed on a rolling basis. Application fee: $30 ($100 for international students). Electronic applications accepted. *Expenses:* Tuition, state resident: full-time $5634; part-time $313 per credit hour. Tuition, nonresident: full-time $14,598; part-time $811 per credit hour. Required fees: $450; $25 per credit hour. *Financial support:* In 2009–10, 28 students received support, including 10 research assistantships (averaging $10,505 per year); career-related internships or fieldwork, scholarships/grants, tuition waivers (partial), and unspecified assistantships also available. Financial award application deadline: 4/15; financial award applicants required to submit FAFSA. *Unit head:* Dr. Charles Bennett, Dean, 502-597-6926, E-mail: charles.bennett@kysu.edu. *Application contact:* Cedric Cunningham, Administrative Assistant, Office of Graduate Studies, 502-597-6536, Fax: 502-597-6432, E-mail: cedric.cunningham@kysu.edu.

Memorial University of Newfoundland, School of Graduate Studies, Interdisciplinary Program in Aquaculture, St. John's, NL A1C 5S7, Canada. Offers M Sc. Part-time programs available. *Degree requirements:* For master's, thesis, seminar or thesis topic. *Entrance requirements:* For master's, honors B Sc or diploma in aquaculture from the Marine Institute of Memorial University of Newfoundland. Electronic applications accepted. *Faculty research:* Marine fish larval biology, fin fish nutrition, shellfish culture, fin fish virology, fin fish reproductive biology.

Nova Scotia Agricultural College, Research and Graduate Studies, Truro, NS B2N 5E3, Canada. Offers agriculture (M Sc), including air quality, animal behavior, animal molecular genetics, animal nutrition, animal technology, aquaculture, botany, crop management, crop physiology, ecology, environmental microbiology, food science, horticulture, nutrient management, pest management, physiology, plant biotechnology, plant pathology, soil chemistry, soil fertility, waste management and composting, water quality. Part-time programs available. *Degree requirements:* For master's, thesis, ATC Exam Teaching Assistantship. *Entrance requirements:* For master's, honors B Sc, minimum GPA of 3.0. Additional exam requirements/recommendations for international students: Required—TOEFL (minimum score 580 paper-based; 237 computer-based; 92 iBT), IELTS, Michigan English Language Assessment Battery, CanTEST, CAEL. *Faculty research:* Bio-product development, organic agriculture, nutrient management, air and water quality, agricultural biotechnology.

Purdue University, Graduate School, College of Agriculture, Department of Forestry and Natural Resources, West Lafayette, IN 47907. Offers aquaculture, fisheries, aquatic science (MSF); aquaculture, fisheries, aquatic sciences (MS, PhD); forest biology (MS, MSF, PhD); natural resources and environmental policy (MS, MSF); natural resources environmental policy (PhD); quantitative resource analysis (MS, MSF, PhD); wildlife science (MS, MSF, PhD); wood science and technology (MS, MSF, PhD). *Degree requirements:* For master's, thesis; for doctorate, thesis/dissertation. *Entrance requirements:* For master's and doctorate, GRE General Test, minimum B+ average in undergraduate course work. Additional exam requirements/recommendations for international students: Required—TOEFL. Electronic applications accepted. *Faculty research:* Wildlife management, forest management, forest ecology, forest soils, limnology.

Texas A&M University–Corpus Christi, Graduate Studies and Research, College of Science and Technology, Program in Mariculture, Corpus Christi, TX 78412-5503. Offers MS.

University of Arkansas at Pine Bluff, School of Agriculture, Fisheries and Human Sciences, Pine Bluff, AR 71601-2799. Offers aquaculture and fisheries (MS).

University of Florida, Graduate School, College of Agricultural and Life Sciences, Department of Fisheries and Aquatic Sciences, Gainesville, FL 32611. Offers MFAS, MS, PhD. *Degree requirements:* For master's, thesis optional; for doctorate, thesis/dissertation. *Entrance requirements:* For master's and doctorate, GRE General Test, minimum GPA of 3.0. Additional exam requirements/recommendations for international students: Required—TOEFL. Electronic applications accepted.

University of Guelph, Graduate Program Services, Ontario Agricultural College, Program in Aquaculture, Guelph, ON N1G 2W1, Canada. Offers M Sc. *Degree requirements:* For master's, practicum, research project. *Entrance requirements:* For master's, minimum B- average during previous 2 years of course work. *Faculty research:* Protein and amino acid metabolism, genetics, gamete cryogenics, pathology, epidemiology.

University of Rhode Island, Graduate School, College of the Environment and Life Sciences, Department of Fisheries, Animal and Veterinary Science, Kingston, RI 02881. Offers animal health and disease (MS); animal science (MS); aquaculture (MS); aquatic pathology (MS); environmental sciences (PhD), including animal science, aquacultural science, aquatic pathology, fisheries science; fisheries (MS). *Faculty:* 10 full-time (4 women). *Students:* 14 full-time (7 women), 12 part-time (7 women); includes 5 minority (2 African Americans, 3 Hispanic Americans), 3 international. In 2009, 3 master's, 2 doctorates awarded. *Degree requirements:* For master's, comprehensive exam (for some programs), thesis optional; for doctorate, comprehensive exam, thesis/dissertation. *Entrance requirements:* For master's and doctorate, GRE, 2 letters of recommendation. Additional exam requirements/recommendations for international students: Required—TOEFL (minimum score 550 paper-based; 213 computer-based). *Application deadline:* For fall admission, 7/15 for domestic students, 2/1 for international

Aquaculture

University of Rhode Island (continued)
students; for spring admission, 11/15 for domestic students, 7/15 for international students. Application fee: $65. Electronic applications accepted. *Expenses:* Tuition, state resident: full-time $8828; part-time $490 per credit hour. Tuition, nonresident: full-time $22,100; part-time $1228 per credit hour. Required fees: $1118; $57 per semester. Tuition and fees vary according to program. *Financial support:* In 2009–10, 4 research assistantships with full and partial tuition reimbursements (averaging $11,386 per year), 7 teaching assistantships with full and partial tuition reimbursements (averaging $10,940 per year) were awarded. Financial award application deadline: 7/15; financial award applicants required to submit FAFSA. Total annual research expenditures: $2.1 million. *Unit head:* Dr. David Bengtson, Chair, 401-874-2668, Fax: 401-874-7575, E-mail: bengtson@uri.edu. *Application contact:* Dr. Marta Gomez-Chiarra, Director of Graduate Studies, 401-874-2917, Fax: 401-874-7575, E-mail: gomezchi@uri.edu.

Food Science and Technology

Alabama Agricultural and Mechanical University, School of Graduate Studies, School of Agricultural and Environmental Sciences, Department of Family and Consumer Sciences, Huntsville, AL 35811. Offers family and consumer sciences (MS); food science (MS, PhD). Part-time and evening/weekend programs available. *Degree requirements:* For master's, comprehensive exam, thesis optional; for doctorate, one foreign language, thesis/dissertation. *Entrance requirements:* For master's, GRE General Test; for doctorate, GRE General Test, MS. Additional exam requirements/recommendations for international students: Required—TOEFL (minimum score 500 paper-based; 173 computer-based; 61 iBT). Electronic applications accepted. *Faculty research:* Food biotechnology, nutrition, food microbiology, food engineering, food chemistry.

Alabama Agricultural and Mechanical University, School of Graduate Studies, School of Agricultural and Environmental Sciences, Department of Food and Animal Sciences, Huntsville, AL 35811. Offers food science (MS, PhD). *Entrance requirements:* Additional exam requirements/recommendations for international students: Required—TOEFL (minimum score 500 paper-based; 173 computer-based; 61 iBT).

American University of Beirut, Graduate Programs, Faculty of Agricultural and Food Sciences, Beirut, Lebanon. Offers agricultural economics (MS); animal sciences (MS); ecosystem management (MSES); food technology (MS); irrigation (MS); mechanization (MS); nutrition (MS); plant protection (MS); plant science (MS); poultry science (MS); soils (MS). Part-time programs available. *Degree requirements:* For master's, one foreign language, comprehensive exam, thesis (for some programs). *Entrance requirements:* For master's, letter of recommendation. Additional exam requirements/recommendations for international students: Required—TOEFL (minimum score 600 paper-based; 250 computer-based; 100 iBT), IELTS (minimum score 7.5). *Faculty research:* Sustainable animal systems/agriculture; natural resource management; community nutrition, obesity and food safety; integrated pest management; ecosystem management.

Auburn University, Graduate School, College of Human Sciences, Department of Nutrition and Food Science, Auburn University, AL 36849. Offers MS, PhD. Part-time programs available. *Faculty:* 16 full-time (7 women). *Students:* 16 full-time (11 women), 13 part-time (6 women); includes 4 minority (all African Americans), 7 international. Average age 31. 79 applicants, 37% accepted, 9 enrolled. In 2009, 10 master's, 5 doctorates awarded. *Degree requirements:* For master's, thesis (for some programs); for doctorate, thesis/dissertation. *Entrance requirements:* For master's and doctorate, GRE General Test. *Application deadline:* For fall admission, 7/7 for domestic students; for spring admission, 11/24 for domestic students. Applications are processed on a rolling basis. Application fee: $50 ($60 for international students). Electronic applications accepted. *Expenses:* Tuition, state resident: full-time $6240. Tuition, nonresident: full-time $18,720. International tuition: $18,938 full-time. Required fees: $492. Tuition and fees vary according to course load, program and reciprocity agreements. *Financial support:* Research assistantships, teaching assistantships, career-related internships or fieldwork and Federal Work-Study available. Support available to part-time students. Financial award application deadline: 3/15; financial award applicants required to submit FAFSA. *Faculty research:* Food quality and safety, diet, food supply, physical activity in maintenance of health, prevention of selected chronic disease states. *Unit head:* Dr. Douglas B. White, Head, 334-844-4261. *Application contact:* Dr. George Flowers, Dean of the Graduate School, 334-844-2125.

Boston University, Metropolitan College, Program in Gastronomy, Boston, MA 02215. Offers MLA. Part-time and evening/weekend programs available. *Faculty:* 18 part-time/adjunct (11 women). *Students:* 36 part-time (29 women); includes 2 minority (1 American Indian/Alaska Native, 1 Asian American or Pacific Islander). Average age 31. 30 applicants, 93% accepted, 26 enrolled. In 2009, 8 master's awarded. *Degree requirements:* For master's, thesis. Application fee: $70. *Expenses:* Tuition: Full-time $37,910; part-time $1184 per credit hour. Required fees: $386; $40 per semester. Part-time tuition and fees vary according to class time, course level, degree level and program. *Financial support:* Teaching assistantships with partial tuition reimbursements, scholarships/grants and unspecified assistantships available. *Faculty research:* Food studies. *Unit head:* Rebecca Alssid, Chairman, 617-353-9852, Fax: 617-353-4130, E-mail: ralssid@bu.edu. *Application contact:* Rebecca Alssid, Chairman, 617-353-9852, Fax: 617-353-4130, E-mail: ralssid@bu.edu.

Brigham Young University, Graduate Studies, College of Life Sciences, Department of Nutrition, Dietetics and Food Science, Provo, UT 84602-1001. Offers food science (MS); nutrition (MS). *Faculty:* 13 full-time (5 women). *Students:* 14 full-time (10 women), 2 part-time (both women); includes 2 minority (1 African American, 1 Asian American or Pacific Islander). Average age 24. 5 applicants, 60% accepted, 1 enrolled. In 2009, 6 master's awarded. *Degree requirements:* For master's, comprehensive exam, thesis. *Entrance requirements:* For master's, GRE General Test. Additional exam requirements/recommendations for international students: Required—TOEFL (minimum score 550 paper-based; 213 computer-based). *Application deadline:* For fall admission, 2/1 for domestic students, 2/1 priority date for international students; for winter admission, 6/30 for domestic students, 6/30 priority date for international students. Application fee: $50. Electronic applications accepted. *Expenses:* Tuition: Full-time $5580; part-time $301 per credit hour. Tuition and fees vary according to student's religious affiliation. *Financial support:* In 2009–10, 9 students received support, including 4 research assistantships (averaging $20,325 per year), 3 teaching assistantships (averaging $20,325 per year); career-related internships or fieldwork, institutionally sponsored loans, and scholarships/grants also available. Financial award application deadline: 4/1. *Faculty research:* Dairy foods, lipid oxidation, food processes, magnesium and selenium nutrition, nutrient effect on gene expression. Total annual research expenditures: $398,048. *Unit head:* Dr. Miochael L. Dunn, Chair, 801-422-6670, Fax: 801-422-0258, E-mail: michael_dunn@byu.edu. *Application contact:* Dr. Susan Fullmer, Graduate Coordinator, 801-422-3349, Fax: 801-422-0258, E-mail: susan_fullmer@byu.edu.

California State University, Fresno, Division of Graduate Studies, College of Agricultural Sciences and Technology, Department of Food Science and Nutritional Sciences, Fresno, CA 93740-8027. Offers MS. Part-time programs available. *Degree requirements:* For master's, thesis. *Entrance requirements:* For master's, GRE General Test, minimum GPA of 3.0 in last 60 units. Additional exam requirements/recommendations for international students: Required—TOEFL. Electronic applications accepted. *Faculty research:* Liquid foods, analysis, mushrooms, gaseous ozone, natamycin.

California State University, Long Beach, Graduate Studies, College of Health and Human Services, Department of Family and Consumer Sciences, Master of Science in Nutritional Science Program, Long Beach, CA 90840. Offers food science (MS); hospitality foodservice and hotel management (MS); nutritional science (MS). Part-time programs available. *Students:* 25 full-time (24 women), 22 part-time (all women); includes 14 minority (1 African American, 10 Asian Americans or Pacific Islanders, 3 Hispanic Americans), 1 international. Average age 26. 50 applicants, 62% accepted, 17 enrolled. *Degree requirements:* For master's, thesis, oral presentation of thesis or directed project. *Entrance requirements:* For master's, GRE, minimum GPA of 2.5 in last 60 units. *Application deadline:* For fall admission, 5/1 for domestic students. Applications are processed on a rolling basis. Application fee: $55. Electronic applications accepted. *Expenses:* Required fees: $1802 per semester. Part-time tuition and fees vary according to course load. *Financial support:* Federal Work-Study, institutionally sponsored loans, and scholarships/grants available. Financial award application deadline: 3/2. *Faculty research:* Protein and water-soluble vitamins, sensory evaluation of foods, mineral deficiencies in humans, child nutrition, minerals and blood pressure. *Unit head:* Dr. M. Sue Stanley, Chair, 562-985-4484, Fax: 562-985-4414, E-mail: stanleym@csulb.edu. *Application contact:* Dr. Mary Jacob, Graduate Coordinator, 562-985-4484, Fax: 562-985-4414, E-mail: marjacob@csulb.edu.

Chapman University, Graduate Studies, Schmid College of Science, Food Science Program, Orange, CA 92866. Offers MS, MBA/MS. Part-time and evening/weekend programs available. *Faculty:* 3 full-time (2 women). *Students:* 12 full-time (8 women), 20 part-time (14 women); includes 7 minority (1 African American, 5 Asian Americans or Pacific Islanders, 1 Hispanic American), 14 international. Average age 25. 35 applicants, 63% accepted, 11 enrolled. In 2009, 12 master's awarded. *Degree requirements:* For master's, comprehensive exam, thesis optional. *Entrance requirements:* For master's, GRE, minimum undergraduate GPA of 2.5. Additional exam requirements/recommendations for international students: Required—TOEFL (minimum score 550 paper-based; 213 computer-based; 80 iBT). *Application deadline:* Applications are processed on a rolling basis. Application fee: $50. Electronic applications accepted. Tuition and fees vary according to course load, degree level and program. *Financial support:* Fellowships, Federal Work-Study and scholarships/grants available. Financial award application deadline: 6/30; financial award applicants required to submit FAFSA. *Unit head:* Dr. Anuradha Prakash, Director, 714-744-7895, E-mail: prakash@chapman.edu. *Application contact:* Priscilla Garcia Powers, Graduate Admission Counselor, 714-997-6711, E-mail: pgarcia@chapman.edu.

Clemson University, Graduate School, College of Agriculture, Forestry and Life Sciences, Department of Food Science and Human Nutrition, Program in Food, Nutrition, and Culinary Science, Clemson, SC 29634. Offers MS. *Students:* 12 full-time (6 women), 10 part-time (3 women); includes 1 minority (African American), 5 international. Average age 28. 53 applicants, 15% accepted, 5 enrolled. In 2009, 5 master's awarded. *Degree requirements:* For master's, thesis. *Entrance requirements:* For master's, GRE General Test. Additional exam requirements/recommendations for international students: Required—TOEFL, IELTS. *Application deadline:* For fall admission, 6/1 for domestic students, 4/15 for international students; for spring admission, 9/15 for international students. Applications are processed on a rolling basis. Application fee: $70 ($80 for international students). Electronic applications accepted. *Expenses:* Contact institution. *Financial support:* In 2009–10, 8 students received support, including 2 research assistantships with partial tuition reimbursements available (averaging $12,000 per year), 6 teaching assistantships with partial tuition reimbursements available (averaging $15,444 per year); fellowships with full and partial tuition reimbursements available, career-related internships or fieldwork, institutionally sponsored loans, scholarships/grants, health care benefits, and unspecified assistantships also available. Support available to part-time students. Financial award applicants required to submit FAFSA. *Unit head:* Dr. Anthony L. Pometto, Chair, 864-656-4382, Fax: 864-656-3131, E-mail: pometto@clemson.edu. *Application contact:* Dr. Paul Dawson, Coordinator, 864-656-1138, Fax: 864-656-3131, E-mail: pdawson@clemson.edu.

Clemson University, Graduate School, College of Agriculture, Forestry and Life Sciences, Department of Food Science and Human Nutrition and Department of Animal and Veterinary Sciences, Program in Food Technology, Clemson, SC 29634. Offers PhD. *Students:* 8 full-time (6 women), 7 part-time (4 women); includes 2 minority (1 African American, 1 Asian American or Pacific Islander), 7 international. Average age 38. 21 applicants, 19% accepted, 2 enrolled. In 2009, 3 doctorates awarded. *Degree requirements:* For doctorate, thesis/dissertation. *Entrance requirements:* For doctorate, GRE General Test. Additional exam requirements/recommendations for international students: Required—TOEFL, IELTS. *Application deadline:* For fall admission, 6/1 for domestic students, 4/15 for international students; for spring admission, 9/15 for international students. Applications are processed on a rolling basis. Application fee: $70 ($80 for international students). Electronic applications accepted. *Expenses:* Contact institution. *Financial support:* In 2009–10, 9 students received support, including 1 fellowship with full and partial tuition reimbursement available (averaging $12,500 per year), 5 research assistantships with partial tuition reimbursements available (averaging $14,753 per year), 4 teaching assistantships with partial tuition reimbursements available (averaging $18,667 per year); career-related internships or fieldwork, institutionally sponsored loans, scholarships/grants, health care benefits, and unspecified assistantships also available. Support available to part-time students. Financial award applicants required to submit FAFSA. *Unit head:* Dr. Anthony Pometto, Coordinator, 864-656-4382, Fax: 864-656-3131, E-mail: pometto@clemson.edu. *Application contact:* Dr. Paul Dawson, Coordinator, 864-656-1138, Fax: 864-656-3131, E-mail: pdawson@clemson.edu.

Colorado State University, Graduate School, College of Applied Human Sciences, Department of Food Science and Human Nutrition, Fort Collins, CO 80523-1571. Offers MS, PhD. *Accreditation:* ADtA. Part-time programs available. *Faculty:* 15 full-time (6 women), 3 part-time/adjunct (2 women). *Students:* 47 full-time (35 women), 36 part-time (26 women); includes 9 minority (1 African American, 3 Asian Americans or Pacific Islanders, 5 Hispanic Americans), 6 international. Average age 30. 85 applicants, 52% accepted, 23 enrolled. In 2009, 23 master's, 4 doctorates awarded. *Degree requirements:* For master's, thesis; for doctorate, thesis/dissertation. *Entrance requirements:* For master's and doctorate, GRE General Test, minimum GPA of 3.0, resume, 3 letters of recommendation. Additional exam requirements/recommendations for international students: Required—TOEFL (minimum score 550 paper-based; 213 computer-based; 80 iBT). *Application deadline:* For fall admission, 2/1 priority date for domestic and international students; for spring admission, 8/1 priority date for domestic and international students. Application fee: $50. Electronic applications accepted. *Expenses:* Tuition, state resident: full-time $6434; part-time $359.10 per credit. Tuition, nonresident: full-time $18,116; part-time $1006.45 per credit. Required fees: $1496; $83 per credit. *Financial support:* In 2009–10, 19 students received support, including 1 fellowship (averaging $41,500 per year), 9 research assistantships with full and partial tuition reimbursements available (averaging $9,342 per year), 9 teaching assistantships with full and partial tuition reimbursements available (averaging $8,215 per year); Federal Work-Study and scholarships/grants also available. Financial award application deadline: 3/1; financial award applicants required to submit FAFSA. *Faculty research:* Metabolic regulation, nutrition education, food safety, obesity and diabetes, metabolism. Total annual research expenditures: $6 million. *Unit head:* Dr. Christopher Melby, Head, 970-491-6736, Fax: 970-491-7252, E-mail: christopher.melby@colostate.edu. *Application contact:* Paula Coleman, Graduate Coordinator, 970-491-3819, Fax: 970-491-3875, E-mail: pcoleman@cahs.colostate.edu.

Cornell University, Graduate School, Graduate Fields of Agriculture and Life Sciences, Field of Food Science and Technology, Ithaca, NY 14853-0001. Offers dairy science (MPS, MS, PhD); food chemistry (MPS, MS, PhD); food engineering (MPS, MS, PhD); food microbiology (MPS, MS, PhD); food processing waste technology (MPS, MS, PhD); food science (MFS, MPS, MS, PhD); international food science (MPS, MS, PhD); sensory evaluation (MPS, MS, PhD). *Faculty:* 46 full-time (9 women). *Students:* 72 full-time (41 women); includes 7 minority (3 African Americans, 3 Asian Americans or Pacific Islanders, 1 Hispanic American), 37 international. Average age 27. 175 applicants, 21% accepted, 30 enrolled. In 2009, 8 master's, 8 doctorates awarded. Terminal master's awarded for partial completion of doctoral program. *Degree requirements:* For master's, thesis (MS), teaching experience; for doctorate, comprehensive exam, thesis/dissertation, teaching experience. *Entrance requirements:* For master's and doctorate, GRE General Test, 3 letters of recommendation. Additional exam requirements/recommendations for international students: Required—TOEFL (minimum score 550 paper-based; 213 computer-based; 77 iBT). *Application deadline:* For fall admission, 1/30 priority date for domestic students. Application fee: $70. Electronic applications accepted. *Expenses:* Tuition: Full-time $29,500. Required fees: $70. Full-time tuition and fees vary according to degree level, program and student level. *Financial support:* In 2009–10, 41 students received support, including 4 fellowships with full tuition reimbursements available, 5 research assistantships with full tuition reimbursements available, 7 teaching assistantships with full tuition reimbursements available; institutionally sponsored loans, scholarships/grants, health care benefits, tuition waivers (full and partial), and unspecified assistantships also available. Financial award applicants required to submit FAFSA. *Faculty research:* Food microbiology/biotechnology, food engineering/processing, food safety/toxicology, sensory science/flavor chemistry, food packaging. *Unit head:* Director of Graduate Studies, 607-255-7637, Fax: 607-254-4868. *Application contact:* Graduate Field Assistant, 607-255-7637, Fax: 607-254-4868, E-mail: fdscigrad@cornell.edu.

Dalhousie University, Faculty of Engineering, Department of Food Science and Technology, Halifax, NS B3J 1Z1, Canada. Offers M Sc, PhD. *Faculty:* 5 full-time (0 women), 2 part-time/adjunct (0 women). *Students:* 17 full-time (7 women), 5 international. 10 applicants, 100% accepted. In 2009, 2 master's, 1 doctorate awarded. *Degree requirements:* For master's, thesis; for doctorate, thesis/dissertation. *Entrance requirements:* Additional exam requirements/recommendations for international students: Required—TOEFL, IELTS, CANTEST, CAEL, or Michigan English Language Assessment Battery. *Application deadline:* For fall admission, 6/1 for domestic students, 4/1 for international students; for winter admission, 11/15 for domestic students, 8/31 for international students; for spring admission, 2/28 for domestic students, 12/31 for international students. Application fee: $70. Electronic applications accepted. *Financial support:* Fellowships, research assistantships, teaching assistantships, scholarships/grants and unspecified assistantships available. *Faculty research:* Food microbiology, food safety/HALLP, rheology and rheometry, food processing, seafood processing. *Unit head:* Dr. Michael Pegg, Head, 902-494-3252, Fax: 902-420-0219, E-mail: michael.pegg@dal.ca. *Application contact:* Dr. Georges Kipouros, Graduate Coordinator, 902-494-6100, Fax: 902-494-0219, E-mail: abdel.ghaly@dal.ca.

Drexel University, School of Technology and Professional Studies, Philadelphia, PA 19104-2875. Offers construction management (MS); engineering technology (MS); food science (MS); hospitality management (MS); professional studies: creativity studies (MS); professional studies: e-learning leadership (MS); professional studies: homeland security management (MS); project management (MS); property management (MS); sport management (MS). Postbaccalaureate distance learning degree programs offered.

Florida Agricultural and Mechanical University, Division of Graduate Studies, Research, and Continuing Education, College of Engineering Science, Technology, and Agriculture, Division of Agricultural Sciences, Tallahassee, FL 32307-3200. Offers agribusiness (MS); animal science (MS); engineering technology (MS); entomology (MS); food science (MS); international programs (MS); plant science (MS). *Faculty:* 31 full-time (2 women). *Students:* 14 full-time (8 women), 8 part-time (4 women); includes 17 minority (16 African Americans, 1 Asian American or Pacific Islander), 3 international. In 2009, 7 master's awarded. *Degree requirements:* For master's, thesis. *Entrance requirements:* For master's, GRE General Test, minimum GPA of 3.0. Additional exam requirements/recommendations for international students: Required—TOEFL (minimum score 500 paper-based). *Application deadline:* For fall admission, 5/18 for domestic students, 12/18 for international students; for spring admission, 11/12 for domestic students, 5/12 for international students. Application fee: $20. *Financial support:* Application deadline: 2/15. *Unit head:* Dr. Mitwe N. Musingo, Graduate Coordinator, 850-561-2309, Fax: 850-599-8821. *Application contact:* Dr. Chanta M. Haywood, Dean of Graduate Studies, Research, and Continuing Education, 850-599-3315, Fax: 850-599-3727.

Florida State University, The Graduate School, College of Human Sciences, Department of Nutrition, Food, and Exercise Sciences, Tallahassee, FL 32306-1493. Offers exercise science (MS, PhD), including exercise physiology; nutrition and food sciences (MS, PhD), including clinical nutrition (MS), food science, human nutrition (PhD), nutrition and sport (MS), nutrition science (MS), nutrition, education and health promotion (MS). Part-time programs available. *Faculty:* 13 full-time (8 women). *Students:* 88 full-time (58 women), 21 part-time (14 women); includes 28 minority (10 African Americans, 5 Asian Americans or Pacific Islanders, 13 Hispanic Americans), 23 international. 128 applicants, 52% accepted, 35 enrolled. In 2009, 30 master's, 8 doctorates awarded. *Degree requirements:* For master's, comprehensive exam (for some programs), thesis optional; for doctorate, thesis/dissertation. *Entrance requirements:* For master's, GRE General Test, minimum upper division GPA of 3.0; for doctorate, GRE General Test, minimum upper division GPA of 3.0 and MS degree. Additional exam requirements/recommendations for international students: Required—TOEFL (minimum score 570 paper-based; 80 iBT). *Application deadline:* For fall admission, 7/1 for domestic students, 3/1 for international students; for spring admission, 11/1 for domestic students, 5/1 for international students. Application fee: $30. Electronic applications accepted. *Expenses:* Tuition, state resident: full-time $7413.36. Tuition, nonresident: full-time $22,567. *Financial support:* In 2009–10, 42 students received support, including 5 fellowships with partial tuition reimbursements available (averaging $10,000 per year), 8 research assistantships with partial tuition reimbursements available (averaging $8,000 per year), 31 teaching assistantships with partial tuition reimbursements available (averaging $8,000 per year); career-related internships or fieldwork, Federal Work-Study, institutionally sponsored loans, scholarships/grants, and unspecified assistantships also available. Financial award application deadline: 1/15; financial award applicants required to submit FAFSA. *Faculty research:* Body composition, functional food, chronic disease and aging response; food safety, food allergy, and safety/quality detection methods; sports nutrition, energy and human performance. *Unit head:* Dr. Bahram H. Arjmandi, Margaret A. Sitton Professor and Chair, 850-645-1517, Fax: 850-645-5000, E-mail: barjmandi@fsu.edu. *Application contact:* Ursula M. Tate, Administrative Support Assistant, 850-644-4800, Fax: 850-645-5000, E-mail: utate@fsu.edu.

Framingham State College, Division of Graduate and Continuing Education, Programs in Food and Nutrition, Food Science and Nutrition Science Program, Framingham, MA 01701-9101. Offers MS. Part-time and evening/weekend programs available. *Entrance requirements:* For master's, GRE General Test.

Illinois Institute of Technology, Graduate College, College of Science and Letters, Program in Food Safety and Technology, Chicago, IL 60616-3793. Offers MFST, MS. Part-time and evening/weekend programs available. *Degree requirements:* For master's, comprehensive exam, thesis (for some programs), project. *Entrance requirements:* For master's, GRE General Test, minimum undergraduate GPA of 3.0. Additional exam requirements/recommendations for international students: Required—TOEFL (minimum score 550 paper-based; 213 computer-based; 80 iBT). Electronic applications accepted. *Expenses:* Tuition: Full-time $17,550; part-time $888 per credit hour. Required fees: $850; $7.50 per credit hour. One-time fee: $50 full-time. Full-time tuition and fees vary according to program. *Faculty research:* Food microbiology, food processing, food packaging, chemical constituents and allergens, food defense.

Instituto Tecnologico de Santo Domingo, Graduate School, Santo Domingo, Dominican Republic. Offers applied linguistics (MA); construction administration (M Mgmt); corporate finance (M Mgmt); education (M Ed); engineering (M Eng), including data telecommunications, industrial engineering, logistics and supply chain, maintenance engineering, sanitary and environmental engineering, structural engineering; environmental science (M En S), including environmental education, environmental management, marine and coastal ecosystems, natural resources management; family therapy (MA); food science and technology (MS); human development (MA); human resources administration (M Mgmt); international business (M Mgmt); labor risks (M Mgmt); management (M Mgmt); marketing (M Mgmt); mathematics (MS); organizational development (M Mgmt); planning and taxation (M Mgmt); psychology (MA); social science (M Ed); upper management (M Mgmt). *Entrance requirements:* For master's, birth certificate, minimum GPA of 2.0.

Iowa State University of Science and Technology, Graduate College, College of Human Sciences and College of Agriculture, Department of Food Science and Human Nutrition, Ames, IA 50011. Offers food science and technology (MS, PhD); nutrition (MS, PhD). *Faculty:* 31 full-time (19 women), 1 (woman) part-time/adjunct. *Students:* 54 full-time (37 women), 4 part-time (2 women); includes 5 minority (2 African Americans, 2 Asian Americans or Pacific Islanders, 1 Hispanic American), 24 international. 74 applicants, 22% accepted, 15 enrolled. In 2009, 3 master's, 5 doctorates awarded. *Degree requirements:* For master's, thesis; for doctorate, thesis/dissertation. *Entrance requirements:* For master's and doctorate, GRE General Test. Additional exam requirements/recommendations for international students: Required—TOEFL (minimum score 550 paper-based; 79 iBT) or IELTS (minimum score 6.5). *Application deadline:* For fall admission, 1/15 priority date for domestic and international students. Applications are processed on a rolling basis. Application fee: $40 ($90 for international students). Electronic applications accepted. *Expenses:* Tuition, state resident: full-time $6716. Tuition, nonresident: full-time $8908. Tuition and fees vary according to course level, course load, program and student level. *Financial support:* In 2009–10, 21 research assistantships with full and partial tuition reimbursements (averaging $16,240 per year) were awarded; fellowships, teaching assistantships with full and partial tuition reimbursements, scholarships/grants also available. *Unit head:* Dr. Ruth S. MacDonald, Chair, 515-294-5991, Fax: 515-294-8181, E-mail: ruthmacd@iastate.edu. *Application contact:* Dr. Patricia Murphy, Director of Graduate Education, 515-294-6442, E-mail: gradsecretary@iastate.edu.

Kansas State University, Graduate School, College of Agriculture, Food Science Institute, Manhattan, KS 66506. Offers MS, PhD. Part-time programs available. Postbaccalaureate distance learning degree programs offered (minimal on-campus study). *Faculty:* 3 full-time (2 women). *Students:* 35 full-time (20 women), 92 part-time (61 women); includes 11 minority (2 African Americans, 1 American Indian/Alaska Native, 5 Asian Americans or Pacific Islanders, 3 Hispanic Americans), 14 international. Average age 33. 71 applicants, 41% accepted, 29 enrolled. In 2009, 18 master's, 1 doctorate awarded. *Degree requirements:* For master's, thesis, residency; for doctorate, thesis/dissertation, preliminary exams, residency. *Entrance requirements:* For master's, GRE General Test, minimum GPA of 3.0 in undergraduate course work, course work in mathematics; for doctorate, GRE General Test, minimum GPA of 3.5 in master's course work. Additional exam requirements/recommendations for international students: Required—TOEFL (minimum score 550 paper-based; 213 computer-based). *Application deadline:* For fall admission, 2/1 priority date for domestic and international students; for spring admission, 8/1 priority date for domestic and international students. Applications are processed on a rolling basis. Application fee: $40 ($55 for international students). Electronic applications accepted. *Financial support:* In 2009–10, 1 research assistantship with partial tuition reimbursement (averaging $20,766 per year) was awarded; teaching assistantships with partial tuition reimbursements, Federal Work-Study, institutionally sponsored loans, and scholarships/grants also available. Support available to part-time students. Financial award application deadline: 3/1; financial award applicants required to submit FAFSA. *Faculty research:* Systems to insure food safety and security, determining nutrients and bioactive compounds, evaluate new processes and agricultural ingredients into higher food values, sensory evaluation strategies for foods. Total annual research expenditures: $656,839. *Unit head:* Curtis Kastner, Head, 785-532-4057, Fax: 785-532-5681, E-mail: ckastner@ksu.edu. *Application contact:* J. Scott Smith, Director, 785-532-1219, Fax: 785-532-5681, E-mail: jsschem@ksu.edu.

Louisiana State University and Agricultural and Mechanical College, Graduate School, College of Agriculture, Department of Food Science, Baton Rouge, LA 70803. Offers MS, PhD. Part-time programs available. *Faculty:* 11 full-time (6 women). *Students:* 38 full-time (26 women), 5 part-time (2 women); includes 2 African Americans, 2 Hispanic Americans, 30 international. Average age 28. 63 applicants, 43% accepted, 13 enrolled. In 2009, 5 master's, 3 doctorates awarded. *Degree requirements:* For master's, thesis; for doctorate, thesis/dissertation. *Entrance requirements:* For master's and doctorate, GRE General Test, minimum GPA of 3.0. Additional exam requirements/recommendations for international students: Required—TOEFL (minimum score 550 paper-based; 213 computer-based; 79 iBT), IELTS (minimum score 6.5). *Application deadline:* For fall admission, 1/25 priority date for domestic students, 5/15 for international students; for spring admission, 10/15 for international students. Applications are processed on a rolling basis. Application fee: $50 ($70 for international students). Electronic applications accepted. *Financial support:* In 2009–10, 42 students received support, including 1 fellowship (averaging $29,011 per year), 33 research assistantships with partial tuition reimbursements available (averaging $17,234 per year), 1 teaching assistantship with partial tuition reimbursement available (averaging $13,500 per year); Federal Work-Study, institutionally sponsored loans, scholarships/grants, health care benefits, tuition waivers (full and partial), and unspecified assistantships also available. Support available to part-time students. Financial award application deadline: 4/1; financial award applicants required to submit FAFSA. *Faculty research:* Food chemistry/analysis, food microbiology, food processing/engineering, sensory science, product development. *Unit head:* Dr. John W. Finley, Head, 225-578-5206, Fax: 225-578-5300, E-mail: jfinley@agcenter.lsu.edu. *Application contact:* Dr. Kenneth McMillan, Graduate Coordinator, 225-578-5207, Fax: 225-578-5300, E-mail: kmcmill@agcenter.lsu.edu.

McGill University, Faculty of Graduate and Postdoctoral Studies, Faculty of Agricultural and Environmental Sciences, Department of Food Science and Agricultural Chemistry, Montréal, QC H3A 2T5, Canada. Offers M Sc, PhD.

Memorial University of Newfoundland, School of Graduate Studies, Department of Biochemistry, St. John's, NL A1C 5S7, Canada. Offers biochemistry (M Sc, PhD); food science (M Sc, PhD). Part-time programs available. *Degree requirements:* For master's, thesis; for doctorate, comprehensive exam, thesis/dissertation, oral defense of thesis. *Entrance requirements:* For master's, 2nd class degree in related field; for doctorate, M Sc. Electronic

Food Science and Technology

Memorial University of Newfoundland (continued)
applications accepted. *Faculty research:* Toxicology, cell and molecular biology, food engineering, marine biotechnology, lipid biology.

Michigan State University, College of Veterinary Medicine and The Graduate School, Graduate Programs in Veterinary Medicine, National Food Safety and Toxicology Center, East Lansing, MI 48824. Offers food safety (MS). *Entrance requirements:* Additional exam requirements/recommendations for international students: Required—TOEFL, Michigan State University ELT (85), Michigan ELAB (83). Electronic applications accepted.

Michigan State University, The Graduate School, College of Agriculture and Natural Resources and College of Natural Science, Department of Food Science and Human Nutrition, East Lansing, MI 48824. Offers food science (MS, PhD); food science—environmental toxicology (PhD); human nutrition (MS, PhD); human nutrition-environmental toxicology (PhD). *Entrance requirements:* Additional exam requirements/recommendations for international students: Required—TOEFL (minimum score 550 paper-based; 213 computer-based), Michigan State University ELT (85), Michigan ELAB (83). Electronic applications accepted.

Middle Tennessee State University, College of Graduate Studies, College of Education and Behavioral Science, Department of Human Sciences, Murfreesboro, TN 37132. Offers child development and family studies (MS); nutrition and food science (MS). Part-time and evening/weekend programs available. Postbaccalaureate distance learning degree programs offered. *Faculty:* 7 full-time (all women). *Students:* 24 part-time (all women); includes 5 minority (4 African Americans, 1 Asian American or Pacific Islander). Average age 27. 22 applicants, 82% accepted, 18 enrolled. In 2009, 3 master's awarded. *Degree requirements:* For master's, comprehensive exam, thesis. *Entrance requirements:* For master's, GRE or MAT. Additional exam requirements/recommendations for international students: Required—TOEFL (minimum score 525 paper-based; 195 computer-based; 71 iBT) or IELTS (minimum score 6). *Application deadline:* For fall admission, 6/1 for domestic and international students. Applications are processed on a rolling basis. Application fee: $25 ($30 for international students). Electronic applications accepted. *Expenses:* Tuition, state resident: full-time $4404. Tuition, nonresident: full-time $10,956. *Financial support:* In 2009–10, 5 students received support. Application deadline: 5/1. *Faculty research:* Courtship relationships, feminist methodology and epistemology in family studies, school uniforms, body fat in elderly, asynchronous distance education. *Unit head:* Dr. Dellmar Walker, Chair, 615-898-2884. *Application contact:* Dr. Michael Allen, Dean and Vice Provost for Research, 615-898-2840, Fax: 615-904-8020, E-mail: mallen@mtsu.edu.

Mississippi State University, College of Agriculture and Life Sciences, Department of Food Science, Nutrition and Health Promotion, MS State, MS 39762. Offers food science and technology (PhD); nutrition (MS). Postbaccalaureate distance learning degree programs offered (no on-campus study). *Faculty:* 12 full-time (5 women), 2 part-time/adjunct (0 women). *Students:* 50 full-time (35 women), 28 part-time (20 women); includes 14 minority (10 African Americans, 2 Asian Americans or Pacific Islanders, 2 Hispanic Americans), 18 international. Average age 29. 88 applicants, 48% accepted, 28 enrolled. In 2009, 16 master's, 1 doctorate awarded. *Degree requirements:* For master's, comprehensive exam, thesis; for doctorate, comprehensive exam, thesis/dissertation. *Entrance requirements:* For master's, GRE General Test, minimum GPA of 2.8; for doctorate, GRE General Test, minimum GPA of 3.0. Additional exam requirements/recommendations for international students: Required—TOEFL (minimum score 475 paper-based; 153 computer-based; 53 iBT); Recommended—IELTS (minimum score 4.5). *Application deadline:* For fall admission, 7/1 for domestic students, 5/1 for international students; for spring admission, 11/1 for domestic students, 9/1 for international students. Applications are processed on a rolling basis. Application fee: $40. Electronic applications accepted. *Expenses:* Tuition, state resident: full-time $2575.50; part-time $286.25 per credit hour. Tuition, nonresident: full-time $6510; part-time $723.50 per credit hour. Tuition and fees vary according to course load. *Financial support:* In 2009–10, 13 research assistantships with full tuition reimbursements (averaging $9,766 per year), 4 teaching assistantships with full tuition reimbursements (averaging $9,943 per year) were awarded; Federal Work-Study, institutionally sponsored loans, scholarships/grants, and unspecified assistantships also available. Financial award application deadline: 4/1; financial award applicants required to submit FAFSA. *Faculty research:* Food preservation, food chemistry, food safety, food processing, product development. *Unit head:* Dr. Benjy Mikel, Professor and Head, 662-325-3200, Fax: 662-325-8728, E-mail: wmikel@fsnhp.msstate.edu. *Application contact:* Dr. Juan Silva, Professor and Graduate Coordinator, 662-325-3200, Fax: 662-325-8728, E-mail: jls@ra.msstate.edu.

Montclair State University, The Graduate School, College of Education and Human Services, Department of Health and Nutrition Sciences, Montclair, NJ 07043-1624. Offers American Dietetic Association (Certificate); community health education (MPH); food safety instructor (Certificate); health education (MA); nutrition and exercise science (MS); nutrition and food science (MS). Part-time and evening/weekend programs available. *Faculty:* 15 full-time (10 women), 55 part-time/adjunct (40 women). *Students:* 38 full-time (32 women), 78 part-time (68 women). Average age 32. 53 applicants, 64% accepted, 23 enrolled. In 2009, 19 master's, 2 other advanced degrees awarded. *Degree requirements:* For master's, comprehensive exam, thesis optional. *Entrance requirements:* For master's, GRE, 2 letters of recommendation. Additional exam requirements/recommendations for international students: Required—TOEFL (minimum score 83 computer-based), or IELTS. *Application deadline:* For fall admission, 6/1 for international students; for spring admission, 10/1 for international students. Application fee: $60. *Expenses:* Tuition, area resident: Part-time $486.74 per credit. Tuition, state resident: part-time $486.74 per credit. Tuition, nonresident: part-time $751.34 per credit. Tuition and fees vary according to degree level and program. *Financial support:* In 2009–10, 8 research assistantships with full tuition reimbursements (averaging $7,000 per year) were awarded; Federal Work-Study, scholarships/grants, and unspecified assistantships also available. Support available to part-time students. Financial award application deadline: 3/1; financial award applicants required to submit FAFSA. *Faculty research:* Adolescent physical activity. *Unit head:* Dr. Eva Goldfarb, Chairperson, 973-655-4154. *Application contact:* Amy Aiello, Director of Graduate Admissions and Operations, 973-655-5147, Fax: 973-655-7869, E-mail: graduate.school@montclair.edu.

New York University, Steinhardt School of Culture, Education, and Human Development, Department of Nutrition, Food Studies, and Public Health, Program in Food Studies and Food Management, New York, NY 10012-1019. Offers food studies (MA), including food culture, food systems; food studies and food management (PhD). Part-time programs available. *Students:* 28 full-time (26 women), 107 part-time (89 women); includes 24 minority (5 African Americans, 13 Asian Americans or Pacific Islanders, 6 Hispanic Americans), 15 international. Average age 31. 107 applicants, 66% accepted, 50 enrolled. In 2009, 25 master's, 1 doctorate awarded. *Degree requirements:* For master's, thesis (for some programs); for doctorate, thesis/dissertation. *Entrance requirements:* For doctorate, GRE General Test, interview. Additional exam requirements/recommendations for international students: Required—TOEFL. *Application deadline:* For fall admission, 12/15 priority date for domestic students, 12/15 for international students; for spring admission, 11/1 for domestic and international students. Applications are processed on a rolling basis. Application fee: $75. Electronic applications accepted. *Expenses:* Tuition: Full-time $30,528; part-time $1272 per credit. Required fees: $2177. *Financial support:* Fellowships with full and partial tuition reimbursements, career-related internships or fieldwork, Federal Work-Study, institutionally sponsored loans, scholarships/grants, tuition waivers (partial), and unspecified assistantships available. Financial award application deadline: 2/1; financial award applicants required to submit FAFSA. *Faculty research:* Cultural and social history of food; food systems and agriculture; food and aesthetics; political economy of food. *Unit head:* Dr. Jennifer Berg, Director, 212-998-5580, Fax: 212-995-4194. *Application contact:* 212-998-5030, Fax: 212-995-4328, E-mail: steinhardt.gradadmissions@nyu.edu.

North Carolina State University, Graduate School, College of Agriculture and Life Sciences, Department of Food Science, Raleigh, NC 27695. Offers MFS, MS, PhD. *Degree requirements:* For master's, thesis (for some programs); for doctorate, thesis/dissertation. *Entrance requirements:* For master's and doctorate, GRE. Electronic applications accepted. *Faculty research:* Food safety, value-added food products, environmental quality, nutrition and health, biotechnology.

North Dakota State University, College of Graduate and Interdisciplinary Studies, College of Agriculture, Food Systems, and Natural Resources, Department of Cereal and Food Sciences, Fargo, ND 58108. Offers cereal science (MS, PhD). Part-time programs available. *Faculty:* 8 full-time (2 women), 2 part-time/adjunct (0 women). *Students:* 7 full-time (4 women), 6 part-time (3 women), 11 international. 5 applicants, 20% accepted, 1 enrolled. In 2009, 2 master's awarded. Terminal master's awarded for partial completion of doctoral program. *Degree requirements:* For master's, comprehensive exam, thesis; for doctorate, comprehensive exam, thesis/dissertation. *Entrance requirements:* Additional exam requirements/recommendations for international students: Required—TOEFL (minimum score 550 paper-based; 213 computer-based; 79 iBT), IELTS (minimum score 6). *Application deadline:* For fall admission, 5/1 priority date for domestic students. Application fee: $45 ($60 for international students). *Financial support:* In 2009–10, 15 research assistantships with full tuition reimbursements (averaging $12,000 per year) were awarded; career-related internships or fieldwork and unspecified assistantships also available. Support available to part-time students. *Faculty research:* Legume food products, cereal proteins and product quality, oilseeds functional components. Total annual research expenditures: $500,000. *Unit head:* Dr. Deland Myers, Chair, 701-231-7711, Fax: 701-231-5171, E-mail: deland.myers@ndsu.edu. *Application contact:* Dr. Deland Myers, Chair, 701-231-7711, Fax: 701-231-5171, E-mail: deland.myers@ndsu.edu.

North Dakota State University, College of Graduate and Interdisciplinary Studies, Interdisciplinary Program in Food Safety, Fargo, ND 58108. Offers MS, PhD. Part-time programs available. Postbaccalaureate distance learning degree programs offered (minimal on-campus study). *Faculty:* 10 full-time (5 women), 3 part-time/adjunct (2 women). *Students:* 10 full-time (5 women), 3 part-time (1 woman), 9 international. Average age 25. 10 applicants, 60% accepted, 5 enrolled. In 2009, 2 doctorates awarded. Terminal master's awarded for partial completion of doctoral program. *Degree requirements:* For master's, thesis; for doctorate, comprehensive exam, thesis/dissertation. *Entrance requirements:* For doctorate, preliminary exam. Additional exam requirements/recommendations for international students: Required—TOEFL (minimum score 525 paper-based; 197 computer-based; 71 iBT), TWE (minimum score 5). *Application deadline:* Applications are processed on a rolling basis. Application fee: $45 ($60 for international students). Electronic applications accepted. *Financial support:* In 2009–10, 9 research assistantships with full tuition reimbursements (averaging $16,000 per year) were awarded; scholarships/grants also available. *Faculty research:* Mycotoxins in grain, pathogens in meat systems, sensor development for food pathogens. *Unit head:* Dr. Deland Myers, Chair, 701-231-7711, Fax: 701-231-5171, E-mail: deland.myers@ndsu.edu. *Application contact:* Dr. Deland Myers, Chair, 701-231-7711, Fax: 701-231-5171, E-mail: deland.myers@ndsu.edu.

Nova Scotia Agricultural College, Research and Graduate Studies, Truro, NS B2N 5E3, Canada. Offers agriculture (M Sc), including air quality, animal behavior, animal molecular genetics, animal nutrition, animal technology, aquaculture, botany, crop management, crop physiology, ecology, environmental microbiology, food science, horticulture, nutrient management, pest management, physiology, plant biotechnology, plant pathology, soil chemistry, soil fertility, waste management and composting, water quality. Part-time programs available. *Degree requirements:* For master's, thesis, ATC Exam Teaching Assistantship. *Entrance requirements:* For master's, honors B Sc, minimum GPA of 3.0. Additional exam requirements/recommendations for international students: Required—TOEFL (minimum score 580 paper-based; 237 computer-based; 92 iBT), IELTS, Michigan English Language Assessment Battery, CanTEST, CAEL. *Faculty research:* Bio-product development, organic agriculture, nutrient management, air and water quality, agricultural biotechnology.

The Ohio State University, Graduate School, College of Food, Agricultural, and Environmental Sciences, Department of Food Science and Nutrition, Columbus, OH 43210. Offers MS, PhD. *Accreditation:* ADtA. *Faculty:* 23. *Students:* 40 full-time (28 women), 32 part-time (12 women); includes 9 minority (2 African Americans, 5 Asian Americans or Pacific Islanders, 2 Hispanic Americans), 37 international. Average age 27. In 2009, 21 master's, 5 doctorates awarded. *Degree requirements:* For master's, thesis optional; for doctorate, thesis/dissertation. *Entrance requirements:* For master's and doctorate, GRE General Test. Additional exam requirements/recommendations for international students: Required—TOEFL (minimum score 550 paper-based; 213 computer-based) or IELTS (minimum score 7) or Michigan English Language Assessment Battery (minimum score 89). *Application deadline:* For fall admission, 8/15 priority date for domestic students, 7/1 priority date for international students; for winter admission, 12/1 priority date for domestic students, 11/1 priority date for international students; for spring admission, 3/1 priority date for domestic students, 2/1 priority date for international students. Applications are processed on a rolling basis. Application fee: $40 ($50 for international students). Electronic applications accepted. *Expenses:* Tuition, state resident: full-time $10,683. Tuition, nonresident: full-time $25,923. Tuition and fees vary according to course load and program. *Financial support:* Fellowships, research assistantships, Federal Work-Study and institutionally sponsored loans available. Support available to part-time students. *Application contact:* Graduate Admissions, 614-292-9444, Fax: 614-292-3895, E-mail: domestic.grad@osu.edu.

Oklahoma State University, College of Agricultural Science and Natural Resources, Department of Animal Science, Stillwater, OK 74078. Offers animal sciences (M Ag, MS); food science (MS, PhD). *Faculty:* 29 full-time (6 women), 3 part-time/adjunct (1 woman). *Students:* 22 full-time (15 women), 52 part-time (30 women); includes 4 minority (1 African American, 1 American Indian/Alaska Native, 2 Hispanic Americans), 35 international. Average age 28. 115 applicants, 12% accepted, 11 enrolled. In 2009, 24 master's, 16 doctorates awarded. *Degree requirements:* For master's, thesis; for doctorate, comprehensive exam, thesis/dissertation. *Entrance requirements:* For master's and doctorate, GRE or GMAT. Additional exam requirements/recommendations for international students: Required—TOEFL (minimum score 550 paper-based; 79 iBT). *Application deadline:* For fall admission, 3/1 priority date for international students; for spring admission, 8/1 priority date for international students. Applications are processed on a rolling basis. Application fee: $40 ($75 for international students). Electronic applications accepted. *Expenses:* Tuition, state resident: full-time $3716; part-time $154.85 per credit hour. Tuition, nonresident: full-time $14,448; part-time $602 per credit hour. Required fees: $1772; $73.85 per credit hour. One-time fee: $50. Tuition and fees vary according to course load and campus/location. *Financial support:* In 2009–10, 30 research assistantships (averaging $14,084 per year), 7 teaching assistantships (averaging $12,470 per year) were awarded; career-related internships or fieldwork, Federal Work-Study, scholarships/grants, health care benefits, tuition waivers (partial), and unspecified assistantships also available. Support available to part-time students. Financial award application deadline: 3/1; financial award applicants required to submit FAFSA. *Faculty research:* Quantitative trait loci identification for economical traits in swing/beef; waste management strategies in livestock; endocrine control of reproductive processes in farm animals; cholesterol synthesis, inhibition, and reduction; food safety research. *Unit head:* Dr. Ronald Kensinger, Head, 405-744-6062, Fax: 405-744-7390. *Application contact:* Dr. Gerald Horn, Information Contact, 405-744-6070, Fax: 405-744-6621, E-mail: gerald.horn@okstate.edu.

Oregon State University, Graduate School, College of Agricultural Sciences, Department of Food Science and Technology, Corvallis, OR 97331. Offers M Agr, MAIS, MS, PhD. *Faculty:* 10 full-time (2 women). *Students:* 26 full-time (18 women), 4 part-time (2 women); includes 5 minority (4 Asian Americans or Pacific Islanders, 1 Hispanic American), 15 international.

Average age 29. In 2009, 6 master's, 1 doctorate awarded. *Degree requirements:* For master's, thesis (for some programs); for doctorate, thesis/dissertation. *Entrance requirements:* For master's and doctorate, GRE General Test, minimum GPA of 3.0 in last 90 hours. Additional exam requirements/recommendations for international students: Required—TOEFL. *Application deadline:* For fall admission, 3/1 for domestic students. Applications are processed on a rolling basis. Application fee: $50. *Expenses:* Tuition, state resident: full-time $9774; part-time $362 per credit. Tuition, nonresident: full-time $15,849; part-time $587 per credit. Required fees: $1639. Full-time tuition and fees vary according to course load and program. *Financial support:* Fellowships, research assistantships, teaching assistantships, career-related internships or fieldwork, Federal Work-Study, and institutionally sponsored loans available. Support available to part-time students. Financial award application deadline: 2/1. *Faculty research:* Diet, cancer, and anticarcinogenesis; sensory analysis; chemistry and biochemistry. *Unit head:* Dr. Robert McGorrin, Head, 541-737-3131, Fax: 541-737-1877, E-mail: robert.mcgorrin@orst.edu. *Application contact:* 541-737-6486, Fax: 541-737-1877.

Penn State University Park, Graduate School, College of Agricultural Sciences, Department of Food Science, State College, University Park, PA 16802-1503. Offers MS, PhD.

Purdue University, Graduate School, College of Agriculture, Department of Food Science, West Lafayette, IN 47907. Offers MS, PhD. *Degree requirements:* For master's, thesis (for some programs); for doctorate, thesis/dissertation, teaching assistantship. *Entrance requirements:* For master's and doctorate, GRE General Test. Additional exam requirements/recommendations for international students: Required—TOEFL, TWE. Electronic applications accepted. *Faculty research:* Processing, technology, microbiology, chemistry of foods, carbohydrate chemistry.

Rutgers, The State University of New Jersey, New Brunswick, Graduate School-New Brunswick, Program in Food Science, Piscataway, NJ 08854-8097. Offers M Phil, MS, PhD. Part-time and evening/weekend programs available. Postbaccalaureate distance learning degree programs offered (minimal on-campus study). *Degree requirements:* For master's, thesis or alternative; for doctorate, thesis/dissertation. *Entrance requirements:* For master's and doctorate, GRE General Test. *Faculty research:* Nutraceuticals and functional foods, food and flavor analysis, food chemistry and biochemistry, food nanotechnology, food engineering and processing.

South Dakota State University, Graduate School, College of Education and Human Sciences, Department of Nutrition, Food Science and Hospitality, Brookings, SD 57007. Offers dietetics (MS); nutrition, food science and hospitality (MFCS); nutritional sciences (MS, PhD). Part-time programs available. *Degree requirements:* For master's, comprehensive exam (for some programs), thesis (for some programs), oral exam. *Entrance requirements:* Additional exam requirements/recommendations for international students: Required—TOEFL (minimum score 525 paper-based). *Faculty research:* Food chemistry, bone density, functional food, nutrition education, nutrition biochemistry.

Texas A&M University, College of Agriculture and Life Sciences, Department of Nutrition and Food Science, College Station, TX 77843. Offers M Agr, MS, PhD. *Faculty:* 15. *Students:* 62 full-time (51 women), 4 part-time (all women); includes 7 minority (2 African Americans, 2 Asian Americans or Pacific Islanders, 3 Hispanic Americans), 28 international. *Degree requirements:* For master's, thesis; for doctorate, thesis/dissertation. *Entrance requirements:* For master's and doctorate, GRE General Test. Additional exam requirements/recommendations for international students: Required—TOEFL. *Application deadline:* For fall admission, 2/1 priority date for domestic students; for spring admission, 10/1 priority date for domestic students. Applications are processed on a rolling basis. Application fee: $50 ($75 for international students). *Expenses:* Tuition, state resident: full-time $3991.32; part-time $221.74 per credit hour. Tuition, nonresident: full-time $9049; part-time $502.74 per credit hour. *Financial support:* Fellowships, research assistantships, teaching assistantships, career-related internships or fieldwork and scholarships/grants available. *Faculty research:* Food safety, microbiology, product development. *Unit head:* Department Head, 979-845-3975, E-mail: nfsc@tamu.edu. *Application contact:* Department Head, 979-845-3975, E-mail: nfsc@tamu.edu.

Texas Tech University, Graduate School, College of Agricultural Sciences and Natural Resources, Department of Animal and Food Sciences, Lubbock, TX 79409-2141. Offers animal science (MS, PhD); food science (MS). Part-time programs available. *Faculty:* 10 full-time (4 women). *Students:* 46 full-time (25 women), 12 part-time (4 women); includes 3 minority (1 African American, 2 Hispanic Americans), 15 international. Average age 27. 72 applicants, 31% accepted, 11 enrolled. In 2009, 18 master's, 4 doctorates awarded. *Degree requirements:* For master's, thesis or alternative, internship (M Agr); for doctorate, thesis/dissertation. *Entrance requirements:* For master's and doctorate, GRE General Test. Additional exam requirements/recommendations for international students: Required—TOEFL (minimum score 550 paper-based; 213 computer-based). *Application deadline:* For fall admission, 3/1 priority date for international students; for spring admission, 11/1 priority date for international students. Applications are processed on a rolling basis. Application fee: $50 ($75 for international students). Electronic applications accepted. *Expenses:* Tuition, state resident: full-time $5100; part-time $213 per credit hour. Tuition, nonresident: full-time $11,748; part-time $490 per credit hour. Required fees: $2298; $50 per credit hour. $555 per semester. *Financial support:* In 2009–10, 15 research assistantships with partial tuition reimbursements (averaging $18,621 per year), 2 teaching assistantships with partial tuition reimbursements (averaging $9,675 per year) were awarded; Federal Work-Study and institutionally sponsored loans also available. Support available to part-time students. Financial award application deadline: 4/15; financial award applicants required to submit FAFSA. *Faculty research:* Animal growth composition and product acceptability, animal nutrition and utilization, animal physiology and adaptation to stress, food microbiology, meat science safety and security. Total annual research expenditures: $2.7 million. *Unit head:* Dr. Kevin R. Pond, Chairman, 806-742-2805 Ext. 223, Fax: 806-742-0898, E-mail: kevin.pond@ttu.edu. *Application contact:* Sandy Gellner, Graduate Secretary, 806-742-2805 Ext. 221, Fax: 806-742-0898, E-mail: sandra.gellner@ttu.edu.

Texas Woman's University, Graduate School, College of Health Sciences, Department of Nutrition and Food Sciences, Denton, TX 76201. Offers exercise and sports nutrition (MS); food science (MS); food systems administration (MS); nutrition (MS, PhD). Part-time and evening/weekend programs available. *Faculty:* 15 full-time (7 women). *Students:* 88 full-time (78 women), 90 part-time (81 women); includes 44 minority (13 African Americans, 1 American Indian/Alaska Native, 16 Asian Americans or Pacific Islanders, 14 Hispanic Americans), 25 international. Average age 28. 121 applicants, 76% accepted, 57 enrolled. In 2009, 55 master's, 3 doctorates awarded. *Degree requirements:* For master's, comprehensive exam; for doctorate, comprehensive exam, thesis/dissertation, qualifying exam. *Entrance requirements:* For master's, GRE General Test (minimum score 350 verbal, 450 quantitative), minimum GPA of 3.25, resume; for doctorate, GRE General Test (minimum score: 450 Verbal, 550 Quantitative), minimum GPA of 3.5, 2 letters of reference, resume. Additional exam requirements/recommendations for international students: Required—TOEFL (minimum score 550 paper-based; 213 computer-based; 79 iBT). *Application deadline:* For fall admission, 7/1 priority date for domestic students, 3/1 for international students; for spring admission, 12/1 priority date for domestic students, 7/1 for international students. Applications are processed on a rolling basis. Application fee: $50. Electronic applications accepted. *Expenses:* Tuition, state resident: full-time $3564; part-time $198 per credit hour. Tuition, nonresident: full-time $8550; part-time $475 per credit hour. Required fees: $69.26 per credit hour. Tuition and fees vary according to course load. *Financial support:* In 2009–10, 47 students received support, including 18 research assistantships (averaging $10,746 per year), 1 teaching assistantship (averaging $10,746 per year); career-related internships or fieldwork, Federal Work-Study, institutionally sponsored loans, scholarships/grants, traineeships, health care benefits, and unspecified assistantships also available. Support available to part-time students. Financial award application deadline: 3/1; financial award applicants required to submit FAFSA. *Faculty research:* Food science, food safety, clinical nutrition, nutrition and cancer, weight management, chemical and toxicological evaluations, food waste management, nutrition education, processing models and parfrying, elimination of transfats, impact of d-delta-tocotienol on osteoclasts and osteoblasts, osteoarthritis, markers for protective for Diabetes, melanomas. Total annual research expenditures: $1 million. *Unit head:* Dr. Chandan Prasad, Chair, 940-898-2636, Fax: 940-898-2634, E-mail: nutrfdsci@twu.edu. *Application contact:* Samuel Wheeler, Assistant Director of Admissions, 940-898-3188, Fax: 940-898-3081, E-mail: wheelersr@twu.edu.

Tuskegee University, Graduate Programs, College of Agricultural, Environmental and Natural Sciences, Department of Food and Nutritional Sciences, Tuskegee, AL 36088. Offers MS. *Faculty:* 4 full-time (3 women). *Students:* 16 full-time (14 women), 1 (woman) part-time; includes 14 minority (all African Americans), 1 international. Average age 28. In 2009, 5 master's awarded. *Degree requirements:* For master's, thesis. *Entrance requirements:* For master's, GRE General Test. Additional exam requirements/recommendations for international students: Required—TOEFL (minimum score 500 paper-based; 69 computer-based). *Application deadline:* For fall admission, 7/15 for domestic students. Applications are processed on a rolling basis. Application fee: $25 ($35 for international students). *Expenses:* Tuition: Full-time $15,630; part-time $940 per credit hour. Required fees: $650. *Financial support:* Application deadline: 4/15. *Unit head:* Dr. Ralphenia Pace, Head, 334-727-8162. *Application contact:* Dr. Robert L. Laney, Vice President/Director of Admissions and Enrollment Management, 334-727-8580, Fax: 334-727-5750, E-mail: planey@tuskegee.edu.

Universidad de las Américas–Puebla, Division of Graduate Studies, School of Engineering, Program in Chemical Engineering, Puebla, Mexico. Offers chemical engineering (MS); food technology (MS). Part-time and evening/weekend programs available. *Degree requirements:* For master's, one foreign language, thesis. *Faculty research:* Food science, reactors, oil industry, biotechnology.

Universidad de las Américas–Puebla, Division of Graduate Studies, School of Engineering, Program in Food Sciences, Puebla, Mexico. Offers MS.

Université de Moncton, School of Food Science, Nutrition and Family Studies, Moncton, NB E1A 3E9, Canada. Offers foods/nutrition (M Sc). Part-time programs available. *Degree requirements:* For master's, one foreign language, thesis. *Entrance requirements:* For master's, previous course work in statistics. Electronic applications accepted. *Faculty research:* Clinic nutrition (anemia, elderly, osteoporosis), applied nutrition, metabolic activities of lactic bacteria, solubility of low density lipoproteins, bile acids.

Université Laval, Faculty of Agricultural and Food Sciences, Department of Food Sciences and Nutrition, Programs in Food Sciences and Technology, Québec, QC G1K 7P4, Canada. Offers M Sc, PhD. Terminal master's awarded for partial completion of doctoral program. *Degree requirements:* For master's, thesis (for some programs); for doctorate, comprehensive exam, thesis/dissertation. *Entrance requirements:* For master's and doctorate, knowledge of French and English. Electronic applications accepted.

University of Arkansas, Graduate School, Dale Bumpers College of Agricultural, Food and Life Sciences, Department of Food Science, Fayetteville, AR 72701-1201. Offers MS, PhD. *Students:* 10 full-time (5 women), 39 part-time (24 women); includes 6 minority (3 African Americans, 2 Asian Americans or Pacific Islanders, 1 Hispanic American), 19 international. In 2009, 6 master's, 1 doctorate awarded. *Degree requirements:* For master's, thesis; for doctorate, thesis/dissertation. Application fee: $40 ($50 for international students). *Expenses:* Tuition, state resident: full-time $7355; part-time $356.58 per hour. Tuition, nonresident: full-time $17,401; part-time $775.17 per hour. Required fees: $1203. *Financial support:* In 2009–10, 3 fellowships with tuition reimbursements, 32 research assistantships were awarded; teaching assistantships, career-related internships or fieldwork, Federal Work-Study, scholarships/grants, and unspecified assistantships also available. Support available to part-time students. Financial award application deadline: 4/1; financial award applicants required to submit FAFSA. *Unit head:* Dr. Jean-Francois Meullenet, Department Head, 479-575-4605, E-mail: jfmeull@uark.edu. *Application contact:* Dr. Jean-Francois Meullenet, Department Head, 479-575-4605, E-mail: jfmeull@uark.edu.

University of Arkansas, Graduate School, Dale Bumpers College of Agricultural, Food and Life Sciences, Program in Agricultural, Food and Life Sciences, Fayetteville, AR 72701-1201. Offers MS. Part-time and evening/weekend programs available. Postbaccalaureate distance learning degree programs offered (minimal on-campus study). *Students:* 3 full-time (2 women), 23 part-time (8 women); includes 2 minority (1 African American, 1 American Indian/Alaska Native). In 2009, 6 master's awarded. *Degree requirements:* For master's, thesis optional. Application fee: $40 ($50 for international students). *Expenses:* Tuition, state resident: full-time $7355; part-time $356.58 per hour. Tuition, nonresident: full-time $17,401; part-time $775.17 per hour. Required fees: $1203. *Financial support:* Fellowships, research assistantships, teaching assistantships, career-related internships or fieldwork and Federal Work-Study available. Support available to part-time students. Financial award application deadline: 4/1; financial award applicants required to submit FAFSA. *Unit head:* Dr. Donna Graham, Associate Dean for Academic Programs, 479-575-4433, E-mail: dgraham@uark.edu. *Application contact:* Diana Bisbee, Program Coordinator, 479-575-2025, E-mail: dbisbee@uark.edu.

The University of British Columbia, Faculty of Land and Food Systems, Program in Food Science, Vancouver, BC V6T 1Z1, Canada. Offers M Sc, MFS, PhD. *Degree requirements:* For master's, thesis; for doctorate, comprehensive exam, thesis/dissertation. *Entrance requirements:* Additional exam requirements/recommendations for international students: Required—TOEFL (minimum score 577 paper-based; 233 computer-based; 90 iBT), IELTS (minimum score 6.5). Electronic applications accepted. *Faculty research:* Food chemistry and biochemistry, food process science, food toxicology and safety, food microbiology, food biotechnology.

University of California, Davis, Graduate Studies, Graduate Group in Food Science, Davis, CA 95616. Offers MS, PhD. Terminal master's awarded for partial completion of doctoral program. *Degree requirements:* For master's, comprehensive exam (for some programs), thesis (for some programs); for doctorate, thesis/dissertation. *Entrance requirements:* For master's and doctorate, GRE General Test, minimum GPA of 3.0. Additional exam requirements/recommendations for international students: Required—TOEFL (minimum score 550 paper-based; 213 computer-based). Electronic applications accepted.

University of Delaware, College of Agriculture and Natural Resources, Department of Animal and Food Sciences, Newark, DE 19716. Offers animal sciences (MS, PhD); food sciences (MS). Part-time programs available. Terminal master's awarded for partial completion of doctoral program. *Degree requirements:* For master's, thesis; for doctorate, comprehensive exam, thesis/dissertation. *Entrance requirements:* For master's and doctorate, GRE General Test. Additional exam requirements/recommendations for international students: Required—TOEFL. Electronic applications accepted. *Faculty research:* Food chemistry, food microbiology, process engineering technology, packaging, food analysis, microbial genetics, molecular endocrinology, growth physiology, avian immunology and virology, monogastric nutrition, avian genomics.

University of Florida, Graduate School, College of Agricultural and Life Sciences, Department of Food Science and Human Nutrition, Gainesville, FL 32611. Offers food science (MS, PhD); nutritional sciences (MS, PhD). *Degree requirements:* For master's, thesis optional; for doctorate, thesis/dissertation. *Entrance requirements:* For master's and doctorate, GRE General Test, minimum GPA of 3.0. Additional exam requirements/recommendations for international students: Required—TOEFL. Electronic applications accepted. *Faculty research:* Pesticide research, nutritional biochemistry and microbiology, food safety and toxicology assessment and dietetics, food chemistry.

Food Science and Technology

University of Georgia, Graduate School, College of Agricultural and Environmental Sciences, Department of Food Science and Technology, Athens, GA 30602. Offers food science (MS, PhD); food technology (MFT). Part-time programs available. *Faculty:* 19 full-time (7 women), 2 part-time/adjunct (0 women). *Students:* 48 full-time (33 women), 10 part-time (6 women); includes 12 minority (3 African Americans, 4 Asian Americans or Pacific Islanders, 5 Hispanic Americans), 28 international. 68 applicants, 59% accepted, 11 enrolled. In 2009, 15 master's, 10 doctorates awarded. *Degree requirements:* For master's, thesis; for doctorate, thesis/dissertation. *Entrance requirements:* For master's and doctorate, GRE General Test. Additional exam requirements/recommendations for international students: Required—TOEFL (minimum score 550 paper-based; 213 computer-based). *Application deadline:* For fall admission, 7/1 for domestic students, 5/1 priority date for international students; for spring admission, 11/15 for domestic students, 10/1 priority date for international students. Applications are processed on a rolling basis. Application fee: $50. Electronic applications accepted. *Expenses:* Tuition, state resident: full-time $6000; part-time $250 per credit hour. Tuition, nonresident: full-time $20,904; part-time $871 per credit hour. Required fees: $730 per semester. *Financial support:* Fellowships, research assistantships, teaching assistantships, unspecified assistantships available. Total annual research expenditures: $1.5 million. *Unit head:* Dr. Rakesh K. Singh, Head, 706-542-2286, E-mail: rsingh@uga.edu. *Application contact:* Dr. Mark A. Harrison, Graduate Coordinator, 706-542-1088, Fax: 706-542-1050, E-mail: mahfst@uga.edu.

University of Guelph, Graduate Program Services, Ontario Agricultural College, Department of Food Science, Guelph, ON N1G 2W1, Canada. Offers food safety and quality assurance (M Sc); food science (M Sc, PhD). *Degree requirements:* For master's, thesis; for doctorate, comprehensive exam, thesis/dissertation. *Entrance requirements:* For master's, minimum B-average during previous 2 years of honors B Sc degree; for doctorate, minimum B average. Additional exam requirements/recommendations for international students: Required—TOEFL (minimum score 550 paper-based; 213 computer-based), IELTS (minimum score 6.5). Electronic applications accepted. *Faculty research:* Food chemistry, food microbiology, food processing, preservation and utilization.

University of Hawaii at Manoa, Graduate Division, College of Tropical Agriculture and Human Resources, Department of Human Nutrition, Food and Animal Sciences, Program in Food Science, Honolulu, HI 96822. Offers MS. Part-time programs available. *Faculty:* 15 full-time (2 women), 3 part-time/adjunct (0 women). *Students:* 3 full-time (2 women), 1 part-time (0 women); includes 2 minority (both Asian Americans or Pacific Islanders), 2 international. Average age 29. 6 applicants, 67% accepted, 1 enrolled. In 2009, 1 master's awarded. *Degree requirements:* For master's, thesis optional. *Entrance requirements:* For master's, GRE General Test. Additional exam requirements/recommendations for international students: Required—TOEFL (minimum score 580 paper-based; 237 computer-based; 92 iBT), IELTS (minimum score 5). *Application deadline:* For fall admission, 2/1 for domestic and international students; for spring admission, 9/1 for domestic and international students. Application fee: $50. *Expenses:* Tuition, state resident: full-time $8900; part-time $372 per credit. Tuition, nonresident: full-time $21,400; part-time $898 per credit. Required fees: $207 per semester. *Financial support:* In 2009–10, 3 fellowships (averaging $5,174 per year), 3 research assistantships (averaging $17,740 per year) were awarded. *Faculty research:* Biochemistry of natural products, sensory evaluation, food processing, food chemistry, food safety. Total annual research expenditures: $10,000. *Application contact:* Yong Li, Graduate Chairperson, 808-956-7095, Fax: 808-956-4024, E-mail: liyong@hawaii.edu.

University of Idaho, College of Graduate Studies, College of Agricultural and Life Sciences, Bistate School of Food Science, Moscow, ID 83844-2282. Offers MS, PhD. *Faculty:* 4 full-time, 5 part-time/adjunct. *Students:* 4 full-time, 5 part-time. Average age 28. *Entrance requirements:* For master's, minimum GPA of 2.8. *Application deadline:* For fall admission, 8/1 for domestic students; for spring admission, 12/15 for domestic students. Application fee: $55 ($60 for international students). *Expenses:* Tuition, state resident: full-time $6120. Tuition, nonresident: full-time $17,712. *Financial support:* Research assistantships, teaching assistantships available. Financial award application deadline: 2/15. *Faculty research:* Food biotechnology, food and environmental toxicology, bio-preservation of food products, conversion of biomass. *Unit head:* Barry Swanson, Interim Chair, 208-885-0345. *Application contact:* Barry Swanson, Interim Chair, 208-885-0345.

University of Illinois at Urbana–Champaign, Graduate College, College of Agricultural, Consumer and Environmental Sciences, Department of Food Science and Human Nutrition, Champaign, IL 61820. Offers food science (MS); food science and human nutrition (MS, PhD), including professional science (MS); human nutrition (MS). Part-time programs available. Postbaccalaureate distance learning degree programs offered (minimal on-campus study). *Faculty:* 28 full-time (12 women), 1 (woman) part-time/adjunct. *Students:* 62 full-time (43 women), 32 part-time (22 women); includes 5 minority (1 African American, 3 Asian Americans or Pacific Islanders, 1 Hispanic American), 44 international. 147 applicants, 28% accepted, 31 enrolled. In 2009, 15 master's, 3 doctorates awarded. *Entrance requirements:* For master's and doctorate, GRE, minimum GPA of 3.0. Additional exam requirements/recommendations for international students: Required—TOEFL (minimum score 550 paper-based; 213 computer-based; 79 iBT), or IELTS (minimum score 6.5). *Application deadline:* Applications are processed on a rolling basis. Application fee: $60 ($75 for international students). Electronic applications accepted. *Financial support:* In 2009–10, 14 fellowships, 38 research assistantships, 18 teaching assistantships were awarded; tuition waivers (full and partial) also available. *Unit head:* Faye L. Dong, Head, 217-244-4498, Fax: 217-265-0925, E-mail: fayedong@illinois.edu. *Application contact:* Barb J. Vandeventer, Office Administrator, 217-333-1324, Fax: 217-265-0925, E-mail: vandvntr@illinois.edu.

University of Maine, Graduate School, College of Natural Sciences, Forestry, and Agriculture, Department of Food Science and Human Nutrition, Orono, ME 04469. Offers food and nutritional sciences (PhD); food science and human nutrition (MS). Part-time programs available. *Faculty:* 8 full-time (6 women), 2 part-time/adjunct (1 woman). *Students:* 25 full-time (21 women), 6 part-time (all women); includes 1 minority (African American), 4 international. Average age 28. 36 applicants, 44% accepted, 9 enrolled. In 2009, 6 master's, 1 doctorate awarded. *Degree requirements:* For master's, thesis; for doctorate, thesis/dissertation. *Entrance requirements:* For master's, GRE General Test, minimum GPA of 3.0; for doctorate, GRE General Test. Additional exam requirements/recommendations for international students: Required—TOEFL. *Application deadline:* For fall admission, 2/1 priority date for domestic students. Applications are processed on a rolling basis. Application fee: $65. Electronic applications accepted. *Financial support:* In 2009–10, 9 research assistantships with tuition reimbursements (averaging $13,500 per year), 4 teaching assistantships with tuition reimbursements (averaging $12,000 per year) were awarded; scholarships/grants and tuition waivers (full and partial) also available. Financial award application deadline: 3/1. *Faculty research:* Product development of fruit and vegetables, lipid oxidation in fish and meat, analytical methods development, metabolism of potato glycoalkaloids, seafood quality. *Unit head:* Dr. Denise Skonberg, 207-581-1639. *Application contact:* Scott G. Delcourt, Associate Dean of the Graduate School, 207-581-3291, Fax: 207-581-3232, E-mail: graduate@maine.edu.

University of Manitoba, Faculty of Graduate Studies, Faculty of Agricultural and Food Sciences, Department of Food Science, Winnipeg, MB R3T 2N2, Canada. Offers food and nutritional sciences (PhD); food science (M Sc); foods and nutrition (M Sc). *Degree requirements:* For master's, thesis.

University of Maryland, College Park, Academic Affairs, College of Agriculture and Natural Resources, Department of Nutrition and Food Science, Program in Food Science, College Park, MD 20742. Offers MS, PhD. *Students:* 25 full-time (11 women), 3 part-time (all women); includes 4 minority (2 African Americans, 2 Hispanic Americans), 15 international. 48 applicants, 21% accepted, 8 enrolled. In 2009, 4 master's, 2 doctorates awarded. *Degree requirements:* For master's, comprehensive exam, research-based thesis or equivalent paper; for doctorate, comprehensive exam, thesis/dissertation. *Entrance requirements:* For master's, GRE General Test, minimum GPA of 3.0, professional experience, 3 letters of recommendation; for doctorate, GRE General Test, minimum GPA of 3.0. Additional exam requirements/recommendations for international students: Required—TOEFL. *Application deadline:* For fall admission, 12/15 for domestic and international students; for spring admission, 6/1 for domestic and international students. Applications are processed on a rolling basis. Application fee: $60. Electronic applications accepted. *Expenses:* Tuition, area resident: Part-time $471 per credit hour. Tuition, state resident: part-time $471 per credit hour. Tuition, nonresident: part-time $1016 per credit hour. Required fees: $337.04 per term. *Financial support:* In 2009–10, 2 fellowships (averaging $9,680 per year), 7 research assistantships (averaging $16,178 per year), 15 teaching assistantships (averaging $15,862 per year) were awarded. Financial award applicants required to submit FAFSA. *Faculty research:* Food chemistry, engineering, microbiology, and processing technology; quality assurance; membrane separations, rheology and texture measurement. *Unit head:* Lucy Yu, Acting Chair, 301-405-0773, E-mail: lyu5@umd.edu. *Application contact:* Dean of Graduate School, 301-405-0376, Fax: 301-314-9305.

University of Maryland Eastern Shore, Graduate Programs, Department of Agriculture, Program in Food and Agricultural Sciences, Princess Anne, MD 21853-1299. Offers MS. *Degree requirements:* For master's, comprehensive exam, thesis or alternative, oral exams. *Entrance requirements:* For master's, GRE General Test, minimum GPA of 3.0. Additional exam requirements/recommendations for international students: Required—TOEFL (minimum score 213 computer-based; 80 iBT). Electronic applications accepted. *Faculty research:* Poultry and swine nutrition and management, soybean specialty products, farm management practices, agriculture technology.

University of Maryland Eastern Shore, Graduate Programs, Department of Agriculture, Program in Food Science and Technology, Princess Anne, MD 21853-1299. Offers PhD. *Degree requirements:* For doctorate, comprehensive exam, thesis/dissertation. *Entrance requirements:* For doctorate, minimum GPA of 3.0, strong background in food science and related fields, intended dissertation research. Additional exam requirements/recommendations for international students: Required—TOEFL (minimum score 213 computer-based; 80 iBT). Electronic applications accepted. *Faculty research:* Prevalence, growth, survival and control of listeria; microbial models of the effect of storage temperature.

University of Massachusetts Amherst, Graduate School, College of Natural Sciences, Department of Food Science, Amherst, MA 01003. Offers MS, PhD. Part-time programs available. *Faculty:* 15 full-time (4 women). *Students:* 24 full-time (14 women), 7 part-time (4 women); includes 2 minority (both Asian Americans or Pacific Islanders), 21 international. Average age 26. 95 applicants, 26% accepted, 12 enrolled. In 2009, 3 master's, 4 doctorates awarded. Terminal master's awarded for partial completion of doctoral program. *Degree requirements:* For master's, thesis or alternative; for doctorate, comprehensive exam, thesis/dissertation. *Entrance requirements:* For master's and doctorate, GRE General Test. Additional exam requirements/recommendations for international students: Required—TOEFL (minimum score 550 paper-based; 213 computer-based; 80 iBT), IELTS (minimum score 6.5). *Application deadline:* For fall admission, 2/1 for domestic and international students; for spring admission, 10/1 for domestic and international students. Applications are processed on a rolling basis. Application fee: $50 ($65 for international students). Electronic applications accepted. *Expenses:* Tuition, state resident: full-time $2640; part-time $110 per credit. Tuition, nonresident: full-time $9936; part-time $414 per credit. Tuition and fees vary according to course load. *Financial support:* In 2009–10, 16 research assistantships with full tuition reimbursements (averaging $9,822 per year), 10 teaching assistantships with full tuition reimbursements (averaging $8,957 per year) were awarded; fellowships, career-related internships or fieldwork, Federal Work-Study, scholarships/grants, traineeships, health care benefits, tuition waivers (full), and unspecified assistantships also available. Support available to part-time students. Financial award application deadline: 2/1. *Unit head:* Dr. Ronald G. Labbe, Graduate Program Director, 413-545-2276, Fax: 413-545-1262. *Application contact:* Jean M. Ames, Supervisor of Admissions, 413-545-0721, Fax: 413-577-0010, E-mail: gradadm@grad.umass.edu.

University of Minnesota, Twin Cities Campus, Graduate School, College of Food, Agricultural and Natural Resource Sciences, Program in Food Science, Minneapolis, MN 55455-0213. Offers MS, PhD. *Accreditation:* ADtA. Part-time programs available. *Faculty:* 18 full-time (4 women), 7 part-time/adjunct (4 women). *Students:* 36 full-time (22 women), 20 part-time (13 women); includes 1 African American, 14 Asian Americans or Pacific Islanders, 2 Hispanic Americans. Average age 31. 87 applicants, 17% accepted, 13 enrolled. In 2009, 10 master's, 12 doctorates awarded. Terminal master's awarded for partial completion of doctoral program. *Degree requirements:* For master's, comprehensive exam, thesis (for some programs); for doctorate, comprehensive exam, thesis/dissertation. *Entrance requirements:* For master's and doctorate, GRE General Test, previous course work in general chemistry, organic chemistry, calculus, physics, and biology. Additional exam requirements/recommendations for international students: Required—TOEFL (minimum score 550 paper-based; 213 computer-based; 79 iBT). *Application deadline:* For fall admission, 12/15 for domestic and international students; for spring admission, 10/15 for domestic and international students. Applications are processed on a rolling basis. Application fee: $75 ($95 for international students). Electronic applications accepted. *Financial support:* In 2009–10, 28 students received support, including 1 fellowship with full tuition reimbursement available (averaging $20,000 per year), 24 research assistantships with full and partial tuition reimbursements available (averaging $17,500 per year), 3 teaching assistantships with full and partial tuition reimbursements available (averaging $17,500 per year); career-related internships or fieldwork, Federal Work-Study, institutionally sponsored loans, scholarships/grants, traineeships, health care benefits, and unspecified assistantships also available. Support available to part-time students. *Faculty research:* Food chemistry, food microbiology, food technology, grain science, dairy science, food safety. Total annual research expenditures: $1.8 million. *Unit head:* Dr. David E. Smith, Director of Graduate Studies, 612-624-3260, Fax: 612-625-5272, E-mail: desmith@umn.edu. *Application contact:* Nancy L. Toedt, Program Coordinator, 612-624-6753, Fax: 612-625-5272, E-mail: ntoedt@umn.edu.

University of Missouri, Graduate School, College of Agriculture, Food and Natural Resources, Department of Food and Hospitality Systems, Columbia, MO 65211. Offers food science (MS, PhD); foods and food systems management (MS); human nutrition (MS). *Faculty:* 17 full-time (4 women), 2 part-time/adjunct (0 women). *Students:* 18 full-time (11 women), 13 part-time (6 women), 15 international. Average age 27. 44 applicants, 36% accepted, 9 enrolled. In 2009, 1 master's awarded. Terminal master's awarded for partial completion of doctoral program. *Degree requirements:* For doctorate, comprehensive exam, thesis/dissertation. *Entrance requirements:* For master's, GRE General Test; V+Q=1000 with neither section below 400, A=3.5, minimum GPA of 3.0; BS in Food Science from accredited university; for doctorate, GRE General Test; V+Q = 1000 with neither section below 400; A=3.5, minimum GPA of 3.0; BS and MS in Food Science from accredited university. Additional exam requirements/recommendations for international students: Required—TOEFL (minimum score 550 paper-based; 79 iBT). *Application deadline:* For fall admission, 4/1 priority date for domestic students; for winter admission, 10/1 priority date for domestic students. Applications are processed on a rolling basis. Application fee: $45 ($60 for international students). Electronic applications accepted. *Financial support:* Research assistantships with tuition reimbursements, teaching assistantships with tuition reimbursements, institutionally sponsored loans available. *Unit head:* Dr. Jinglu Tan, Department Chair, E-mail: tanj@missouri.edu. *Application contact:* JoAnn Lewis, 573-882-4113, E-mail: lewisj@missouri.edu.

University of Nebraska–Lincoln, Graduate College, College of Agricultural Sciences and Natural Resources, Department of Food Science and Technology, Lincoln, NE 68588. Offers MS, PhD. *Degree requirements:* For master's, thesis optional; for doctorate, comprehensive exam, thesis/dissertation. *Entrance requirements:* For master's and doctorate, GRE General Test. Additional exam requirements/recommendations for international students: Required—TOEFL (minimum score 505 paper-based; 213 computer-based). Electronic applications accepted. *Faculty research:* Food chemistry, microbiology, processing, engineering, and biotechnology.

University of Puerto Rico, Mayagüez Campus, Graduate Studies, College of Agricultural Sciences, Department of Food Science and Technology, Mayagüez, PR 00681-9000. Offers MS. Part-time programs available. *Degree requirements:* For master's, comprehensive exam, thesis. *Entrance requirements:* For master's, minimum GPA of 2.5. *Faculty research:* Food microbiology, food science, seafood technology, food engineering and packaging, fermentation.

University of Rhode Island, Graduate School, College of the Environment and Life Sciences, Department of Nutrition and Food Sciences, Kingston, RI 02881. Offers food science (MS, PhD); nutrition (MS, PhD). Part-time programs available. *Faculty:* 8 full-time (5 women), 1 (woman) part-time/adjunct. *Students:* 15 full-time (14 women), 13 part-time (12 women); includes 2 minority (1 Asian American or Pacific Islander, 1 Hispanic American), 1 international. In 2009, 5 master's, 2 doctorates awarded. *Degree requirements:* For master's, comprehensive exam (for some programs), thesis optional; for doctorate, thesis/dissertation. *Entrance requirements:* For master's and doctorate, GRE, 2 letters of recommendation. Additional exam requirements/recommendations for international students: Required—TOEFL (minimum score 550 paper-based; 213 computer-based). *Application deadline:* For fall admission, 7/15 for domestic students, 2/1 for international students; for spring admission, 11/15 for domestic students, 7/15 for international students. Application fee: $65. Electronic applications accepted. *Expenses:* Tuition, state resident: full-time $8828; part-time $490 per credit hour. Tuition, nonresident: full-time $22,100; part-time $1228 per credit hour. Required fees: $1118; $57 per semester. Tuition and fees vary according to program. *Financial support:* In 2009–10, 6 research assistantships with full and partial tuition reimbursements (averaging $12,736 per year), 8 teaching assistantships with full and partial tuition reimbursements (averaging $12,350 per year) were awarded. Financial award application deadline: 7/15; financial award applicants required to submit FAFSA. *Faculty research:* Food safety and quality, marine resource utilization, nutrition in underserved populations, eating behavior, lipid metabolism. Total annual research expenditures: $1.5 million. *Unit head:* Dr. Catherine English, Chair, 401-874-5869, Fax: 401-874-5974, E-mail: cathy@uri.edu. *Application contact:* Dr. Linda T. Green, Director of Graduate Studies, 401-874-2905, Fax: 401-874-4561, E-mail: lgreen@uri.edu.

University of Saskatchewan, College of Graduate Studies and Research, College of Agriculture, Department of Applied Microbiology and Food Science, Saskatoon, SK S7N 5A2, Canada. Offers M Ag, M Sc, PhD. *Faculty:* 19. *Students:* 40. In 2009, 2 master's, 1 doctorate awarded. *Degree requirements:* For master's, thesis; for doctorate, comprehensive exam (for some programs), thesis/dissertation. *Entrance requirements:* Additional exam requirements/recommendations for international students: Required—TOEFL (minimum score 80 iBT); Recommended—IELTS (minimum score 6.5). *Application deadline:* For fall admission, 7/1 priority date for domestic students. Applications are processed on a rolling basis. Application fee: $50. Tuition and fees charges are reported in Canadian dollars. *Expenses:* Tuition, area resident: Full-time $3000 Canadian dollars; part-time $500 Canadian dollars per term. Required fees: $700 Canadian dollars; $100 Canadian dollars per term. *Financial support:* Fellowships, research assistantships, teaching assistantships available. Financial award application deadline: 1/31. *Unit head:* Dr. N. Low, Chair, 306-966-5034, Fax: 306-966-8898, E-mail: george.khachatourians@usask.ca. *Application contact:* Dr. Tak Tanaka, Graduate Chair, 306-966-1697, Fax: 306-966-8898, E-mail: tak.tanaka@usask.ca.

University of Southern California, Graduate School, School of Pharmacy, Regulatory Science Programs, Los Angeles, CA 90089. Offers clinical research design and management (Graduate Certificate); food safety (Graduate Certificate); patient and product safety (Graduate Certificate); preclinical drug development (Graduate Certificate); regulatory and clinical affairs (Graduate Certificate); regulatory science (MS, DRSc). Part-time and evening/weekend programs available. Postbaccalaureate distance learning degree programs offered (minimal on-campus study). *Faculty:* 6 full-time (2 women), 7 part-time/adjunct (5 women). *Students:* 23 full-time (11 women), 80 part-time (52 women); includes 38 minority (7 African Americans, 1 American Indian/Alaska Native, 25 Asian Americans or Pacific Islanders, 5 Hispanic Americans), 19 international. 57 applicants, 54% accepted, 31 enrolled. In 2009, 32 master's, 28 other advanced degrees awarded. Terminal master's awarded for partial completion of doctoral program. *Degree requirements:* For master's, thesis optional; for doctorate, comprehensive exam, thesis/dissertation. *Entrance requirements:* For master's, GRE. Additional exam requirements/recommendations for international students: Required—TOEFL (minimum score 250 computer-based; 100 iBT). *Application deadline:* For fall admission, 6/15 priority date for domestic and international students; for winter admission, 2/15 priority date for domestic and international students; for spring admission, 10/15 priority date for domestic and international students. Application fee: $85. Electronic applications accepted. *Expenses:* Tuition: Full-time $25,980; part-time $1315 per unit. Required fees: $554. One-time fee: $35 full-time. Full-time tuition and fees vary according to degree level and program. *Unit head:* Dr. Frances J. R. Richmond, Director, 323-442-3531, Fax: 323-442-2333, E-mail: fjr@hsc.usc.edu. *Application contact:* Dr. Kathy Rolle, Program Manager, 323-442-3102, Fax: 323-442-2333, E-mail: regsci@usc.edu.

University of Southern Mississippi, Graduate School, College of Health, Department of Nutrition and Food Systems, Hattiesburg, MS 39406-0001. Offers MS, PhD. *Faculty:* 6 full-time (5 women). *Students:* 14 full-time (all women), 31 part-time (29 women); includes 9 minority (8 African Americans, 1 Asian American or Pacific Islander). Average age 30. 23 applicants, 35% accepted, 3 enrolled. In 2009, 15 master's awarded. *Degree requirements:* For master's, comprehensive exam, thesis (for some programs); for doctorate, comprehensive exam, thesis/dissertation. *Application deadline:* For fall admission, 3/1 for domestic and international students. Application fee: $35. *Expenses:* Tuition, state resident: full-time $5096; part-time $284 per hour. Tuition, nonresident: full-time $13,052; part-time $726 per hour. Required fees: $402. Tuition and fees vary according to course level and course load. *Financial support:* In 2009–10, 2 research assistantships with full tuition reimbursements (averaging $12,069 per year), 6 teaching assistantships with full tuition reimbursements (averaging $7,676 per year) were awarded. Financial award applicants required to submit FAFSA. *Unit head:* Dr. Kathleen Yadrick, Chair, 601-266-5377, Fax: 601-266-6343. *Application contact:* Belinda Brock, Manager of Graduate Admissions, 601-266-5377, Fax: 601-266-5138.

The University of Tennessee, Graduate School, College of Agricultural Sciences and Natural Resources, Department of Food Science and Technology, Knoxville, TN 37996. Offers food science and technology (MS, PhD), including food chemistry (PhD), food microbiology (PhD), food processing (PhD), sensory evaluation of foods (PhD). Part-time programs available. *Degree requirements:* For master's, thesis or alternative; for doctorate, thesis/dissertation. *Entrance requirements:* For master's and doctorate, GRE General Test, minimum GPA of 2.7. Additional exam requirements/recommendations for international students: Required—TOEFL. Electronic applications accepted. *Expenses:* Tuition, state resident: full-time $6826; part-time $380 per semester hour. Tuition, nonresident: full-time $21,844; part-time $1147 per semester hour. Tuition and fees vary according to program.

The University of Tennessee at Martin, Graduate Programs, College of Agriculture and Applied Sciences, Department of Family and Consumer Sciences, Martin, TN 38238-1000. Offers dietetics (MSFCS); general family and consumer sciences (MSFCS). Part-time programs available. Postbaccalaureate distance learning degree programs offered (minimal on-campus study). *Faculty:* 6. *Students:* 47 (43 women). 5,430 applicants, 1% accepted, 23 enrolled. In 2009, 10 master's awarded. *Degree requirements:* For master's, comprehensive exam, thesis optional. *Entrance requirements:* For master's, GRE General Test, minimum GPA of 2.5. Additional exam requirements/recommendations for international students: Required—TOEFL (minimum score 525 paper-based; 197 computer-based; 71 iBT). *Application deadline:* For fall admission, 8/1 priority date for domestic students, 6/15 priority date for international students; for spring admission, 12/15 priority date for domestic students, 12/1 priority date for international students. Applications are processed on a rolling basis. Application fee: $30 ($130 for international students). Electronic applications accepted. *Expenses:* Tuition, state resident: full-time $6660; part-time $372 per hour. Tuition, nonresident: full-time $18,000; part-time $1005 per hour. *Financial support:* In 2009–10, 3 students received support, including 3 research assistantships with full tuition reimbursements available (averaging $7,234 per year); scholarships/grants and unspecified assistantships also available. Support available to part-time students. Financial award application deadline: 2/15; financial award applicants required to submit FAFSA. *Faculty research:* Children with developmental disabilities, regional food product development and marketing, parent education. *Unit head:* Dr. Lisa LeBleu, Coordinator, 731-881-7116, Fax: 731-881-7106, E-mail: llebleu@utm.edu. *Application contact:* Linda S. Arant, Student Services Specialist, 731-881-7012, Fax: 731-881-7499, E-mail: larant@utm.edu.

University of Vermont, Graduate College, College of Agriculture and Life Sciences, Program in Animal, Nutrition and Food Sciences, Burlington, VT 05405. Offers PhD. *Students:* 11 (4 women), 7 international. 21 applicants, 33% accepted, 3 enrolled. In 2009, 1 doctorate awarded. *Degree requirements:* For doctorate, one foreign language, thesis/dissertation. *Entrance requirements:* For doctorate, GRE General Test. Additional exam requirements/recommendations for international students: Required—TOEFL (minimum score 550 paper-based; 213 computer-based; 80 iBT). *Application deadline:* For fall admission, 4/1 priority date for domestic students. Applications are processed on a rolling basis. Application fee: $40. Electronic applications accepted. *Expenses:* Tuition, area resident: Part-time $508 per credit hour. Tuition, state resident: part-time $508 per credit hour. Tuition, nonresident: part-time $1281 per credit hour. *Financial support:* Application deadline: 3/1. *Unit head:* Dr. R. K. Johnson, Dean, 802-656-2070. *Application contact:* Dr. David Kerr, Coordinator, 802-656-2070.

University of Wisconsin–Madison, Graduate School, College of Agricultural and Life Sciences, Department of Food Science, Madison, WI 53706-1380. Offers MS, PhD. Part-time programs available. *Degree requirements:* For master's, thesis; for doctorate, thesis/dissertation. *Entrance requirements:* For master's and doctorate, GRE General Test. Additional exam requirements/recommendations for international students: Required—TOEFL. Electronic applications accepted. *Expenses:* Tuition, state resident: part-time $594 per credit. Tuition, nonresident: part-time $1504 per credit. Required fees: $65 per credit. Tuition and fees vary according to course load, program and reciprocity agreements. *Faculty research:* Food chemistry, food engineering, food microbiology, food processing.

University of Wisconsin–Stout, Graduate School, College of Human Development, Program in Food and Nutritional Sciences, Menomonie, WI 54751. Offers MS. Part-time programs available. *Degree requirements:* For master's, thesis. *Entrance requirements:* For master's, minimum GPA of 3.0. Additional exam requirements/recommendations for international students: Required—TOEFL (minimum score 500 paper-based; 173 computer-based; 61 iBT). Electronic applications accepted. *Faculty research:* Disease states and nutrition, childhood obesity, nutraceuticals, food safety, nanotechnology.

University of Wyoming, College of Agriculture, Department of Animal Sciences, Program in Food Science and Human Nutrition, Laramie, WY 82070. Offers MS. *Degree requirements:* For master's, thesis. *Entrance requirements:* For master's, GRE General Test, minimum GPA of 3.0. Additional exam requirements/recommendations for international students: Required—TOEFL (minimum score 525 paper-based). Electronic applications accepted. *Faculty research:* Protein and lipid metabolism, food microbiology, food safety, meat science.

Utah State University, School of Graduate Studies, College of Agriculture, Department of Nutrition and Food Sciences, Logan, UT 84322. Offers dietetic administration (MDA); food microbiology and safety (MFMS); nutrition and food sciences (MS, PhD); nutrition science (MS, PhD), including molecular biology. Postbaccalaureate distance learning degree programs offered. *Degree requirements:* For master's, thesis; for doctorate, comprehensive exam, thesis/dissertation, teaching experience. *Entrance requirements:* For master's, GRE General Test, minimum GPA of 3.0, course work in chemistry, biochemistry, physics, math, bacteriology, physiology; for doctorate, GRE General Test, minimum GPA of 3.2, course work in chemistry, MS or manuscript in referred journal. Additional exam requirements/recommendations for international students: Required—TOEFL (minimum score 550 paper-based). Electronic applications accepted. *Faculty research:* Mineral balance, meat microbiology and nitrate interactions, milk ultrafiltration, lactic culture, milk coagulation.

Virginia Polytechnic Institute and State University, Graduate School, College of Agriculture and Life Sciences, Department of Food Science and Technology, Blacksburg, VA 24061. Offers MS, PhD. *Entrance requirements:* For master's and doctorate, GRE General Test. Additional exam requirements/recommendations for international students: Required—TOEFL (minimum score 570 paper-based; 230 computer-based). Electronic applications accepted. *Faculty research:* Food microbiology, food chemistry, food processing, engineering, muscle foods.

Washington State University, Graduate School, College of Agricultural, Human, and Natural Resource Sciences, Department of Food Science and Human Nutrition, Program in Food Science, Pullman, WA 99164. Offers MS, PhD. *Faculty:* 22. *Students:* 30 full-time (17 women), 3 part-time (1 woman), 13 international. Average age 29. 135 applicants, 14% accepted, 14 enrolled. In 2009, 5 master's, 1 doctorate awarded. *Degree requirements:* For master's, comprehensive exam (for some programs), thesis (for some programs), oral exam, written exam; for doctorate, comprehensive exam, thesis/dissertation, oral exam, written exam. *Entrance requirements:* For master's, GRE General Test, Apply to the Graduate School, and submit all official transcripts, letter of interest, resume, GRE and TOEFL scores (minimum 213-computer test and 80-Internet test), and the names of three references. minimum GPA of 3.0; resume; 3 letters of recommendation, 1 from major advisor; for doctorate, GRE General Test, A PhD requires a MS degree that demonstrates the ability to conduct and report research. Exceptional students may by-pass the MS degree. minimum GPA of 3.0; resume; 3 letters of recommendation, 1 from major advisor. Additional exam requirements/recommendations for international students: Required—TOEFL (minimum score 550 paper-based; 213 computer-based), IELTS. *Application deadline:* For fall admission, 1/10 priority date for domestic students, 1/10 for international students; for spring admission, 7/1 priority date for domestic students, 7/1 for international students. Applications are processed on a rolling basis. Application fee: $50. Electronic applications accepted. *Financial support:* In 2009–10, 21 students received support, including 2 fellowships with tuition reimbursements available (averaging $4,250 per year), 14 research assistantships with full and partial tuition reimbursements available (averaging $13,917 per year), 5 teaching assistantships with full and partial tuition reimbursements available (averaging $13,506 per year); career-related internships or fieldwork, Federal Work-Study, institutionally sponsored loans, scholarships/grants, tuition waivers (partial), and unspecified assistantships also available. Financial award application deadline: 2/1; financial award applicants required to submit FAFSA. *Faculty research:* Sports anemia, lipid chemistry, malfunction of edible oils and fats, malolactic fermentation, wine microbiology. *Unit head:* Dr. Barry Swanson, Interim Director, 509-335-3793, Fax: 509-335-4815, E-mail: swansonb@wsu.edu. *Application contact:* Graduate School Admissions, 800-GRADWSU, Fax: 509-335-1949, E-mail: gradsch@wsu.edu.

Wayne State University, College of Liberal Arts and Sciences, Department of Nutrition and Food Science, Detroit, MI 48202. Offers MA, MS, PhD. Terminal master's awarded for partial completion of doctoral program. *Degree requirements:* For master's, thesis (for some programs);

Food Science and Technology

Wayne State University (continued)

for doctorate, thesis/dissertation. *Entrance requirements:* For master's, GRE General Test, minimum GPA of 3.0; for doctorate, GRE General Test, minimum GPA of 3.0; letters of recommendation; personal statement. Additional exam requirements/recommendations for international students: Required—TOEFL (minimum score 550 paper-based; 213 computer-based); Recommended—TWE (minimum score 6). Electronic applications accepted. *Faculty research:* Nutrition, cancer and gene expression, food microbiology and food safety, lipids, lipoprotein and cholesterol metabolism, obesity and diabetes, metabolomics.

West Virginia University, Davis College of Agriculture, Forestry and Consumer Sciences, Division of Animal and Nutritional Sciences, Program in Animal and Nutritional Sciences, Morgantown, WV 26506. Offers breeding (MS); food sciences (MS); nutrition (MS); physiology (MS); production management (MS); reproduction (MS). Part-time programs available. *Degree requirements:* For master's, thesis, oral and written exams. *Entrance requirements:* For master's, GRE, minimum GPA of 2.5. Additional exam requirements/recommendations for international students: Required—TOEFL. *Faculty research:* Animal nutrition, reproductive physiology, food science.

West Virginia University, Davis College of Agriculture, Forestry and Consumer Sciences, Division of Plant and Soil Sciences, Program in Agricultural Sciences, Morgantown, WV 26506. Offers animal and food sciences (PhD); plant and soil sciences (PhD). *Degree requirements:* For doctorate, thesis/dissertation, oral and written exams. *Entrance requirements:* Additional exam requirements/recommendations for international students: Required—TOEFL. *Faculty research:* Ruminant nutrition, metabolism, forage utilization, physiology, reproduction.

Horticulture

Auburn University, Graduate School, College of Agriculture, Department of Horticulture, Auburn University, AL 36849. Offers M Ag, MS, PhD. Part-time programs available. *Faculty:* 19 full-time (4 women). *Students:* 10 full-time (7 women), 24 part-time (6 women); includes 3 minority (2 African Americans, 1 Hispanic American), 5 international. Average age 29. 20 applicants, 45% accepted, 6 enrolled. In 2009, 6 master's, 3 doctorates awarded. *Degree requirements:* For master's, thesis (for some programs); for doctorate, thesis/dissertation. *Entrance requirements:* For master's and doctorate, GRE General Test. *Application deadline:* For fall admission, 7/7 for domestic students; for spring admission, 11/24 for domestic students. Applications are processed on a rolling basis. Application fee: $50 ($60 for international students). Electronic applications accepted. *Expenses:* Tuition, state resident: full-time $6240. Tuition, nonresident: full-time $18,720. International tuition: $18,938 full-time. Required fees: $492. Tuition and fees vary according to course load, program and reciprocity agreements. *Financial support:* Research assistantships, teaching assistantships, Federal Work-Study available. Support available to part-time students. Financial award application deadline: 3/15; financial award applicants required to submit FAFSA. *Faculty research:* Environmental regulators, water quality, weed control, growth regulators, plasticulture. *Unit head:* Dr. J. David Williams, Chair, 334-844-4862. *Application contact:* Dr. George Flowers, Dean of the Graduate School, 334-844-2125.

Colorado State University, Graduate School, College of Agricultural Sciences, Department of Horticulture and Landscape Architecture, Fort Collins, CO 80523-1173. Offers horticulture (MS, PhD). Part-time programs available. *Faculty:* 18 full-time (3 women), 1 part-time/adjunct (0 women). *Students:* 12 full-time (5 women), 13 part-time (4 women); includes 3 minority (2 African Americans, 1 Hispanic American), 4 international. Average age 34. 27 applicants, 48% accepted, 8 enrolled. In 2009, 2 master's, 3 doctorates awarded. *Degree requirements:* For master's, thesis (for some programs); for doctorate, comprehensive exam, thesis/dissertation. *Entrance requirements:* For master's, GRE General Test (minimum upper 50th percentile, minimum score 1100 verbal and quantitative), minimum GPA of 3.0, letters of reference, related bachelor's degree or experience; for doctorate, GRE General Test (upper 50th percentile and combined minimum score of 1100 for the Verbal and Quantitative sections), minimum GPA of 3.0, letters of reference, statement of purpose, related bachelor's degree or experience. Additional exam requirements/recommendations for international students: Required—TOEFL (minimum score 550 paper-based; 213 computer-based; 80 iBT). *Application deadline:* Applications are processed on a rolling basis. Application fee: $50. Electronic applications accepted. *Expenses:* Tuition, state resident: full-time $6434; part-time $359.10 per credit. Tuition, nonresident: full-time $18,116; part-time $1006.45 per credit. Required fees: $1496; $83 per credit. *Financial support:* In 2009–10, 9 students received support, including 1 fellowship with full tuition reimbursement available (averaging $44,000 per year), 3 research assistantships with partial tuition reimbursements available (averaging $11,147 per year), 5 teaching assistantships with partial tuition reimbursements available (averaging $12,786 per year); scholarships/grants, unspecified assistantships, and fellowships also available. Financial award application deadline: 3/1; financial award applicants required to submit FAFSA. *Faculty research:* Antioxidants in food crops, environmental physiology, water conservation, tissue culture, rhizosphere biology, cancer prevention through dietary intervention. Total annual research expenditures: $1.8 million. *Unit head:* Dr. Stephen J. Wallner, Head, 970-491-7018, Fax: 970-491-7745, E-mail: stephen.wallner@colostate.edu. *Application contact:* Kathi Nietfeld, Coordinator, 970-491-7018, Fax: 970-491-7745, E-mail: kathi.nietfeld@colostate.edu.

Cornell University, Graduate School, Graduate Fields of Agriculture and Life Sciences, Field of Horticulture, Ithaca, NY 14853-0001. Offers controlled environment agriculture (MPS, PhD); controlled environment horticulture (MS); greenhouse crops (MPS, MS, PhD); horticultural business management (MPS, MS, PhD); horticultural physiology (MPS, MS, PhD); landscape horticulture (MPS, MS, PhD); nursery crops (MPS, MS, PhD); nutrition of horticultural crops (MPS, MS, PhD); plant propagation (MPS, MS, PhD); public garden management (MPS, MS, PhD); restoration ecology (MPS, MS, PhD); taxonomy of ornamental plants (MPS, MS, PhD); turfgrass science (MPS, MS, PhD); urban horticulture (MPS, MS, PhD); weed science (MPS, MS, PhD). *Faculty:* 51 full-time (13 women). *Students:* 44 full-time (20 women); includes 1 minority (African American), 16 international. Average age 31. 43 applicants, 28% accepted, 10 enrolled. In 2009, 6 master's, 6 doctorates awarded. *Degree requirements:* For master's, thesis (MS); for doctorate, comprehensive exam, thesis/dissertation. *Entrance requirements:* For master's and doctorate, GRE General Test, 3 letters of recommendation. Additional exam requirements/recommendations for international students: Required—TOEFL (minimum score 550 paper-based; 213 computer-based; 77 iBT). *Application deadline:* For fall admission, 1/15 for domestic students; for spring admission, 8/15 for domestic students. Application fee: $70. Electronic applications accepted. *Expenses:* Tuition: Full-time $29,500. Required fees: $70. Full-time tuition and fees vary according to degree level, program and student level. *Financial support:* In 2009–10, 42 students received support, including 1 fellowship with full tuition reimbursement available, 3 research assistantships with full tuition reimbursements available, 1 teaching assistantship with full tuition reimbursement available; institutionally sponsored loans, scholarships/grants, health care benefits, tuition waivers (full and partial), and unspecified assistantships also available. Financial award applicants required to submit FAFSA. *Faculty research:* Plant selection/plant materials, greenhouse management, greenhouse crop production, urban landscape management, turfgrass management. *Unit head:* Director of Graduate Studies, 607-255-4568, Fax: 607-255-0599. *Application contact:* Graduate Field Assistant, 607-255-4568, Fax: 607-255-0599, E-mail: hortgrad@cornell.edu.

Iowa State University of Science and Technology, Graduate College, College of Agriculture, Department of Horticulture, Ames, IA 50011. Offers MS, PhD. *Faculty:* 15 full-time (4 women), 1 (woman) part-time/adjunct. *Students:* 19 full-time (9 women), 4 part-time (1 woman); includes 1 minority (African American), 6 international. 16 applicants, 38% accepted, 6 enrolled. In 2009, 8 master's awarded. *Degree requirements:* For master's, thesis; for doctorate, thesis/dissertation. *Entrance requirements:* For master's and doctorate, GRE General Test. Additional exam requirements/recommendations for international students: Required—TOEFL (minimum score 550 paper-based; 79 iBT) or IELTS (minimum score 6.5). *Application deadline:* For fall admission, 12/15 priority date for domestic and international students; for spring admission, 9/1 priority date for domestic and international students. Applications are processed on a rolling basis. Application fee: $40 ($90 for international students). Electronic applications accepted. *Expenses:* Tuition, state resident: full-time $6716. Tuition, nonresident: full-time $8908. Tuition and fees vary according to course level, course load, program and student level. *Financial support:* In 2009–10, 12 research assistantships with partial tuition reimbursements (averaging $15,380 per year) were awarded; fellowships, teaching assistantships with full and partial tuition reimbursements, scholarships/grants, health care benefits, and unspecified assistantships also available. *Unit head:* Dr. Jeffrey Iles, Head, 515-294-3718, E-mail: hortgrad@iastate.edu. *Application contact:* Dr. William R. Graves, Director of Graduate Education, 515-294-2751, E-mail: hortgrade@iastate.edu.

Kansas State University, Graduate School, College of Agriculture, Department of Horticulture, Forestry and Recreation Resources, Manhattan, KS 66506. Offers horticulture (MS, PhD). *Faculty:* 18 full-time (6 women). *Students:* 21 full-time (7 women), 3 international. Average age 40. 7 applicants, 86% accepted, 6 enrolled. In 2009, 3 master's, 1 doctorate awarded. *Degree requirements:* For master's, thesis, oral exam; for doctorate, thesis/dissertation, preliminary exams. *Entrance requirements:* For master's and doctorate, GRE General Test. Additional exam requirements/recommendations for international students: Required—TOEFL (minimum score 550 paper-based; 213 computer-based). *Application deadline:* For fall admission, 2/1 priority date for domestic and international students; for spring admission, 8/1 priority date for domestic and international students. Applications are processed on a rolling basis. Application fee: $40 ($55 for international students). Electronic applications accepted. *Financial support:* In 2009–10, 13 research assistantships (averaging $12,415 per year), 1 teaching assistantship (averaging $12,423 per year) were awarded; career-related internships or fieldwork, Federal Work-Study, institutionally sponsored loans, and scholarships/grants also available. Support available to part-time students. Financial award application deadline: 3/1; financial award applicants required to submit FAFSA. *Faculty research:* Environmental stress, phytochemicals and health, crop nutrition, sustainable horticulture, turfgrass science. Total annual research expenditures: $515,640. *Unit head:* Stuart Warren, Head, 785-532-6170, Fax: 785-532-6949, E-mail: slwarren@ksu.edu. *Application contact:* Dr. Stuart Warren, Director, 785-532-6170, Fax: 785-532-6949, E-mail: slwarren@ksu.edu.

Louisiana State University and Agricultural and Mechanical College, Graduate School, College of Agriculture, School of Plant, Environmental and Soil Science, Department of Horticulture, Baton Rouge, LA 70803. Offers MS, PhD. Part-time programs available. *Faculty:* 11 full-time (1 woman). *Students:* 6 full-time (2 women), 2 part-time (1 woman); includes 1 African American, 2 international. Average age 31. 4 applicants, 25% accepted, 1 enrolled. In 2009, 5 master's, 2 doctorates awarded. Terminal master's awarded for partial completion of doctoral program. *Degree requirements:* For master's, thesis (for some programs); for doctorate, thesis/dissertation. *Entrance requirements:* For master's and doctorate, GRE General Test, minimum GPA of 3.0. Additional exam requirements/recommendations for international students: Required—TOEFL (minimum score 550 paper-based; 213 computer-based; 79 iBT) or IELTS (minimum score 6.5). *Application deadline:* For fall admission, 7/1 priority date for domestic students, 5/15 for international students; for spring admission, 10/15 for international students. Applications are processed on a rolling basis. Application fee: $50 ($70 for international students). Electronic applications accepted. *Financial support:* In 2009–10, 5 research assistantships with partial tuition reimbursements (averaging $18,400 per year), 1 teaching assistantship with partial tuition reimbursement (averaging $16,000 per year) were awarded; fellowships, Federal Work-Study, health care benefits, tuition waivers (full and partial), and unspecified assistantships also available. Financial award application deadline: 4/15; financial award applicants required to submit FAFSA. *Faculty research:* Plant breeding, stress physiology, postharvest physiology, biotechnology. *Unit head:* Dr. Don LaBonte, Director, 225-578-1043, Fax: 225-578-1068, E-mail: dlabont@lsu.edu. *Application contact:* Dr. David Weindorf, Graduate Coordinator, 225-578-0396, Fax: 225-578-1068, E-mail: dweindorf@agcenter.lsu.edu.

Michigan State University, The Graduate School, College of Agriculture and Natural Resources, Department of Horticulture, East Lansing, MI 48824. Offers horticulture (MS, PhD); plant breeding, genetics and biotechnology-horticulture (MS, PhD). *Entrance requirements:* Additional exam requirements/recommendations for international students: Required—TOEFL. Electronic applications accepted.

Mississippi State University, College of Agriculture and Life Sciences, Department of Plant and Soil Sciences, Mississippi State, MS 39762. Offers agricultural sciences (PhD), including agronomy (MS, PhD), horticulture (MS, PhD), weed science (MS, PhD); agriculture (MS), including agronomy (MS, PhD), horticulture (MS, PhD), weed science (MS, PhD). *Faculty:* 24 full-time (1 woman), 1 part-time/adjunct (0 women). *Students:* 26 full-time (8 women), 30 part-time (8 women); includes 1 minority (American Indian/Alaska Native), 16 international. Average age 30. 31 applicants, 39% accepted, 12 enrolled. In 2009, 7 master's, 1 doctorate awarded. *Degree requirements:* For master's, thesis, exit seminar describing thesis research; for doctorate, comprehensive exam, thesis/dissertation, two departmental seminars. *Entrance requirements:* For master's, GRE (weed science), minimum GPA of 2.75 (agronomy/horticulture), 3.0 (weed science); for doctorate, GRE (weed science), minimum GPA of 3.0 (agronomy/horticulture), 3.25 (weed science). Additional exam requirements/recommendations for international students: Required—TOEFL (minimum score 550 paper-based; 213 computer-based; 79 iBT); Recommended—IELTS (minimum score 6.5). *Application deadline:* For fall admission, 7/1 for domestic students, 5/1 for international students; for spring admission, 10/1 for domestic students, 9/1 for international students. Applications are processed on a rolling basis. Application fee: $40. Electronic applications accepted. *Expenses:* Tuition, state resident: full-time $2575.50; part-time $286.25 per credit hour. Tuition, nonresident: full-time $6510; part-time $723.50 per credit hour. Tuition and fees vary according to course load. *Financial support:* In 2009–10, 25 research assistantships (averaging $11,626 per year), 3 teaching assistantships (averaging $12,379 per year) were awarded; Federal Work-Study, institutionally sponsored loans, scholarships/grants, and unspecified assistantships also available. Financial award application deadline: 4/1; financial award applicants required to submit FAFSA. *Unit head:* Dr. Daniel Reynolds, Professor/Interim Head, 662-325-2311, Fax: 662-325-8742, E-mail: dreynolds@pss.msstate.edu. *Application contact:* Dr. William Kingery, Graduate Coordinator, 662-325-2748, Fax: 662-325-8742, E-mail: wkingery@pss.msstate.edu.

New Mexico State University, Graduate School, College of Agricultural, Consumer and Environmental Sciences, Department of Plant and Environmental Sciences, Las Cruces, NM 88003-8001. Offers horticulture (MS); plant and environmental sciences (MS, PhD). Part-time programs available. *Faculty:* 11 full-time (3 women). *Students:* 45 full-time (17 women), 9 part-time (3 women); includes 11 minority (1 American Indian/Alaska Native, 10 Hispanic Americans), 17 international. Average age 31. 29 applicants, 97% accepted, 16 enrolled. In 2009, 5 master's, 2 doctorates awarded. *Degree requirements:* For master's, thesis; for doctorate, one foreign language, thesis/dissertation. *Entrance requirements:* For master's, minimum GPA of 3.0; for doctorate, minimum GPA of 3.3. Additional exam requirements/recommendations for international students: Required—TOEFL. *Application deadline:* For fall admission, 7/1 priority date for domestic students; for spring admission, 11/1 priority date for domestic students. Applications are processed on a rolling basis. Application fee: $30 ($50 for international students). Electronic applications accepted. *Expenses:* Tuition, state resident: full-time $4080; part-time $223 per credit. Tuition, nonresident: full-time $14,256; part-time $647 per credit. Required fees: $1278; $639 per semester. *Financial support:* In 2009–10, 29 research assistantships with partial tuition reimbursements (averaging $19,764 per year), 9 teaching assistantships with partial tuition reimbursements (averaging $15,733 per year) were awarded; career-related internships or fieldwork, Federal Work-Study, scholarships/grants, health care benefits, and unspecified assistantships also available. Support available to part-time students. Financial award application deadline: 3/1. *Faculty research:* Plant breeding and genetics, molecular biology, plant physiology, soil science and environmental remediation, urban horticulture and turfgrass management. *Unit head:* Dr. John G. Mexal, Interim Head, 575-646-3406, Fax: 575-646-6041, E-mail: jmexal@nmsu.edu. *Application contact:* Esther Ramirez, Information Contact, 575-646-3406, Fax: 575-646-6041, E-mail: esramire@nmsu.edu.

North Carolina State University, Graduate School, College of Agriculture and Life Sciences, Department of Horticultural Science, Raleigh, NC 27695. Offers MS, PhD, Certificate. Post-baccalaureate distance learning degree programs offered. Terminal master's awarded for partial completion of doctoral program. *Degree requirements:* For master's, thesis (for some programs); for doctorate, thesis/dissertation. *Entrance requirements:* For master's and doctorate, GRE General Test, bachelor's degree in agriculture or biology, minimum GPA of 3.0. Electronic applications accepted. *Faculty research:* Plant physiology, breeding and genetics, tissue culture, herbicide physiology, propagation.

Nova Scotia Agricultural College, Research and Graduate Studies, Truro, NS B2N 5E3, Canada. Offers agriculture (M Sc), including air quality, animal behavior, animal molecular genetics, animal nutrition, animal technology, aquaculture, botany, crop management, crop physiology, ecology, environmental microbiology, food science, horticulture, nutrient management, pest management, physiology, plant biotechnology, plant pathology, soil chemistry, soil fertility, waste management and composting, water quality. Part-time programs available. *Degree requirements:* For master's, thesis, ATC Exam Teaching Assistantship. *Entrance requirements:* For master's, honors B Sc, minimum GPA of 3.0. Additional exam requirements/recommendations for international students: Required—TOEFL (minimum score 580 paper-based; 237 computer-based; 92 iBT), IELTS, Michigan English Language Assessment Battery, CanTEST, CAEL. *Faculty research:* Bio-product development, organic agriculture, nutrient management, air and water quality, agricultural biotechnology.

The Ohio State University, Graduate School, College of Food, Agricultural, and Environmental Sciences, Department of Horticulture and Crop Science, Columbus, OH 43210. Offers MS, PhD. *Faculty:* 51. *Students:* 40 full-time (20 women), 9 part-time (2 women); includes 3 minority (1 Asian American or Pacific Islander, 2 Hispanic Americans), 22 international. Average age 29. In 2009, 5 master's, 5 doctorates awarded. *Degree requirements:* For master's, thesis optional; for doctorate, thesis/dissertation. *Entrance requirements:* For master's and doctorate, GRE General Test. Additional exam requirements/recommendations for international students: Required—TOEFL (minimum score 550 paper-based; 213 computer-based) or IELTS (minimum score 7) or Michigan English Language Assessment Battery (minimum score 86). *Application deadline:* For fall admission, 8/15 priority date for domestic students, 7/1 priority date for international students; for winter admission, 12/1 priority date for domestic students, 11/1 priority date for international students; for spring admission, 3/1 priority date for domestic students, 2/1 priority date for international students. Applications are processed on a rolling basis. Application fee: $40 ($50 for international students). Electronic applications accepted. *Expenses:* Tuition, state resident: full-time $10,683. Tuition, nonresident: full-time $25,923. Tuition and fees vary according to course load and program. *Financial support:* Fellowships, research assistantships, teaching assistantships, Federal Work-Study and institutionally sponsored loans available. Support available to part-time students. *Unit head:* Richard Pratt, Graduate Studies Committee Chair, E-mail: pratt.3@osu.edu. *Application contact:* Graduate Admissions, 614-292-9444, Fax: 614-292-3895, E-mail: domestic.grad@osu.edu.

Oklahoma State University, College of Agricultural Science and Natural Resources, Department of Horticulture and Landscape Architecture, Stillwater, OK 74078. Offers agriculture (M Ag); crop science (PhD); environmental science (PhD); horticulture (MS); plant science (PhD). *Accreditation:* ASLA. *Faculty:* 21 full-time (2 women), 2 part-time/adjunct (1 woman). *Students:* 14 part-time (6 women); includes 2 minority (1 African American, 1 American Indian/Alaska Native), 6 international. Average age 28. 23 applicants, 48% accepted, 7 enrolled. In 2009, 3 master's awarded. *Degree requirements:* For master's, thesis (for some programs); for doctorate, comprehensive exam, thesis/dissertation. *Entrance requirements:* For master's and doctorate, GRE or GMAT. Additional exam requirements/recommendations for international students: Required—TOEFL (minimum score 550 paper-based; 79 iBT). *Application deadline:* For fall admission, 3/1 priority date for international students; for spring admission, 8/1 priority date for international students. Applications are processed on a rolling basis. Application fee: $40 ($75 for international students). Electronic applications accepted. *Expenses:* Tuition, state resident: full-time $3716; part-time $154.85 per credit hour. Tuition, nonresident: full-time $14,448; part-time $602 per credit hour. Required fees: $1772; $73.85 per credit hour. One-time fee: $50. Tuition and fees vary according to course load and campus/location. *Financial support:* In 2009–10, 12 research assistantships (averaging $15,748 per year) were awarded; career-related internships or fieldwork, Federal Work-Study, scholarships/grants, health care benefits, tuition waivers (partial), and unspecified assistantships also available. Support available to part-time students. Financial award application deadline: 3/1; financial award applicants required to submit FAFSA. *Faculty research:* Stress and postharvest physiology; water utilization and runoff; IPM systems and nursery, turf, floriculture, vegetable, net and fruit produces and natural resources, food extraction, and processing; public garden management. *Unit head:* Dr. Dale Maronek, Head, 405-744-5414, Fax: 405-744-9709. *Application contact:* Dr. Gordon Emslie, Dean, 405-744-6368, Fax: 405-744-0355, E-mail: grad-i@okstate.edu.

Oregon State University, Graduate School, College of Agricultural Sciences, Department of Horticulture, Corvallis, OR 97331. Offers M Ag, MAIS, MS, PhD. *Faculty:* 12 full-time (1 woman), 1 part-time/adjunct (0 women). *Students:* 15 full-time (6 women), 2 part-time (0 women); includes 1 minority (Asian American or Pacific Islander), 6 international. Average age 32. In 2009, 1 master's, 3 doctorates awarded. *Degree requirements:* For master's, thesis (for some programs); for doctorate, thesis/dissertation. *Entrance requirements:* For master's and doctorate, GRE General Test, minimum GPA of 3.0 in last 90 hours. Additional exam requirements/recommendations for international students: Required—TOEFL. *Application deadline:* For fall admission, 3/1 for domestic students. Applications are processed on a rolling basis. Application fee: $50. *Expenses:* Tuition, state resident: full-time $9774; part-time $362 per credit. Tuition, nonresident: full-time $15,849; part-time $587 per credit. Required fees: $1639. Full-time tuition and fees vary according to course load and program. *Financial support:* Research assistantships, teaching assistantships, career-related internships or fieldwork, Federal Work-Study, and institutionally sponsored loans available. Support available to part-time students. Financial award application deadline: 2/1. *Unit head:* Dr. Anita Azarenko, Head, 541-737-5475, Fax: 541-737-3479, E-mail: azarenko@hort.oregonstate.edu. *Application contact:* Dr. Shawn Mehlenbacher, Graduate Coordinator, 541-737-5467, Fax: 541-737-3479, E-mail: mehlenbs@oregonstate.edu.

Penn State University Park, Graduate School, College of Agricultural Sciences, Department of Horticulture, State College, University Park, PA 16802-1503. Offers M Agr, MS, PhD.

Purdue University, Graduate School, College of Agriculture, Department of Horticulture and Landscape Architecture, West Lafayette, IN 47907. Offers horticulture (M Agr, MS, PhD). Part-time programs available. Terminal master's awarded for partial completion of doctoral program. *Degree requirements:* For doctorate, thesis/dissertation. *Entrance requirements:* For master's and doctorate, GRE. Additional exam requirements/recommendations for international students: Required—TOEFL. Electronic applications accepted. *Faculty research:* Plant physiology, plant genetics and breeding, plant molecular biology and cell physiology, environmental and production horticulture.

Rutgers, The State University of New Jersey, New Brunswick, Graduate School-New Brunswick, Program in Plant Biology, Piscataway, NJ 08854-8097. Offers horticulture and plant technology (MS, PhD); molecular and cellular biology (MS, PhD); organismal and population biology (MS, PhD); plant pathology (MS, PhD). Part-time programs available. Terminal master's awarded for partial completion of doctoral program. *Degree requirements:* For master's, comprehensive exam, thesis or alternative; for doctorate, comprehensive exam, thesis/dissertation. *Entrance requirements:* For master's and doctorate, GRE General Test, GRE Subject Test (recommended). Additional exam requirements/recommendations for international students: Required—TOEFL (minimum score 600 paper-based; 250 computer-based). Electronic applications accepted. *Faculty research:* Molecular biology and biochemistry of plants, plant development and genomics, plant protection, plant improvement, plant management of horticultural and field crops.

Southern Illinois University Carbondale, Graduate School, College of Agriculture, Department of Plant, Soil, and General Agriculture, Carbondale, IL 62901-4701. Offers horticultural science (MS); plant and soil science (MS). *Degree requirements:* For master's, thesis. *Entrance requirements:* For master's, minimum GPA of 2.7. Additional exam requirements/recommendations for international students: Required—TOEFL. *Faculty research:* Herbicides, fertilizers, agriculture education, landscape design, plant breeding.

Texas A&M University, College of Agriculture and Life Sciences, Department of Horticultural Sciences, College Station, TX 77843. Offers horticulture (PhD); horticulture and floriculture (M Agr, MS). *Faculty:* 13. *Students:* 28 full-time (16 women), 11 part-time (6 women); includes 1 minority (Hispanic American), 19 international. Average age 29. In 2009, 2 master's, 3 doctorates awarded. Terminal master's awarded for partial completion of doctoral program. *Degree requirements:* For master's, thesis (for some programs), professional internship; for doctorate, thesis/dissertation. *Entrance requirements:* For master's and doctorate, GRE General Test. Additional exam requirements/recommendations for international students: Required—TOEFL. Application fee: $50 ($75 for international students). Electronic applications accepted. *Expenses:* Tuition, state resident: full-time $3991.32; part-time $221.74 per credit hour. Tuition, nonresident: full-time $9049; part-time $502.74 per credit hour. *Financial support:* In 2009–10, 30 students received support, including fellowships with full tuition reimbursements available (averaging $15,000 per year), research assistantships with partial tuition reimbursements available (averaging $14,000 per year), teaching assistantships with partial tuition reimbursements available (averaging $14,000 per year); career-related internships or fieldwork and tuition waivers (partial) also available. Financial award application deadline: 4/1. *Faculty research:* Plant breeding, molecular biology, plant nutrition, postharvest physiology, plant physiology. *Unit head:* Head, 979-845-0139, Fax: 979-845-0627, E-mail: dan-lineberger@tamu.edu. *Application contact:* Dr. Michael A. Arnold, Associate Head for Research, 979-845-1499, Fax: 979-845-0627, E-mail: ma-arnold@tamu.edu.

Texas Tech University, Graduate School, College of Agricultural Sciences and Natural Resources, Department of Plant and Soil Science, Lubbock, TX 79409. Offers crop science (MS); entomology (MS); horticulture (MS); plant and soil science (PhD); soil science (MS); JD/MS. Part-time programs available. *Faculty:* 15 full-time (3 women), 6 part-time/adjunct (0 women). *Students:* 48 full-time (21 women), 42 part-time (18 women); includes 6 minority (2 African Americans, 4 Hispanic Americans), 26 international. Average age 33. 58 applicants, 72% accepted, 27 enrolled. In 2009, 13 master's, 4 doctorates awarded. *Degree requirements:* For master's, thesis or alternative; for doctorate, thesis/dissertation. *Entrance requirements:* For master's and doctorate, GRE General Test. Additional exam requirements/recommendations for international students: Required—TOEFL (minimum score 550 paper-based; 213 computer-based). *Application deadline:* For fall admission, 3/1 priority date for international students; for spring admission, 11/1 priority date for international students. Applications are processed on a rolling basis. Application fee: $50 ($75 for international students). Electronic applications accepted. *Expenses:* Tuition, state resident: full-time $5100; part-time $213 per credit hour. Tuition, nonresident: full-time $11,748; part-time $490 per credit hour. Required fees: $2298; $50 per credit hour. $555 per semester. *Financial support:* In 2009–10, 23 research assistantships with partial tuition reimbursements (averaging $20,991 per year) were awarded; teaching assistantships with partial tuition reimbursements, Federal Work-Study and institutionally sponsored loans also available. Support available to part-time students. Financial award application deadline: 4/15; financial award applicants required to submit FAFSA. *Faculty research:* Molecular and cellular biology of plant stress, physiology/genetics of crop production in semiarid conditions, agricultural bioterrorism, improvement of native plants, soil science and management. Total annual research expenditures: $3.4 million. *Unit head:* Dr. Thomas Thompson, Chair, 806-742-2837, Fax: 806-742-0775, E-mail: thomas.thompson@ttu.edu. *Application contact:* Dr. Eric Hequet, Graduate Adviser, 806-742-2837, Fax: 806-742-0775, E-mail: eric.hequet@ttu.edu.

University of Arkansas, Graduate School, Dale Bumpers College of Agricultural, Food and Life Sciences, Department of Horticulture, Fayetteville, AR 72701-1201. Offers MS. *Students:* 3 full-time (all women), 6 part-time (2 women), 3 international. In 2009, 3 master's awarded. *Degree requirements:* For master's, thesis. Application fee: $40 ($50 for international students). *Expenses:* Tuition, state resident: full-time $7355; part-time $356.58 per hour. Tuition, nonresident: full-time $17,401; part-time $775.17 per hour. Required fees: $1203. *Financial support:* In 2009–10, 4 research assistantships were awarded; fellowships, teaching assistantships, career-related internships or fieldwork and Federal Work-Study also available. Support available to part-time students. Financial award application deadline: 4/1; financial award applicants required to submit FAFSA. *Unit head:* Dr. David Hensley, Department Head, 479-575-2603, E-mail: dhensley@uark.edu. *Application contact:* Dr. J. Brad Murphy, Graduate Coordinator, 479-575-2603, E-mail: jbmurph@comp.uark.edu.

University of California, Davis, Graduate Studies, Graduate Group in Horticulture and Agronomy, Davis, CA 95616. Offers MS. *Degree requirements:* For master's, comprehensive exam (for some programs), thesis (for some programs). *Entrance requirements:* For master's, GRE General Test. Additional exam requirements/recommendations for international students: Required—TOEFL (minimum score 550 paper-based; 213 computer-based). Electronic applications accepted. *Faculty research:* Postharvest physiology, mineral nutrition, crop improvement, plant growth and development.

University of Delaware, College of Agriculture and Natural Resources, Longwood Graduate Program in Public Horticulture, Newark, DE 19716. Offers MS. *Degree requirements:* For master's, thesis, internship. *Entrance requirements:* For master's, GRE General Test, introductory taxonomy course. Additional exam requirements/recommendations for international students:

Horticulture

University of Delaware (continued)

Required—TOEFL. Electronic applications accepted. *Faculty research:* Management and development of publicly oriented horticultural institutions.

University of Florida, Graduate School, College of Agricultural and Life Sciences, Department of Environmental Horticulture, Gainesville, FL 32611. Offers anatomy and development (MS, PhD); breeding and genetics (MS, PhD); ecology (MS, PhD); plant biotechnology (MS, PhD); stress physiology (MS, PhD); taxonomy (MS, PhD); tissue culture (MS, PhD). *Degree requirements:* For master's, thesis optional; for doctorate, thesis/dissertation. *Entrance requirements:* For master's and doctorate, GRE General Test, minimum GPA of 3.0. Electronic applications accepted. *Faculty research:* Production and genetics, landscape horticulture, turf grass, foliage, floriculture.

University of Florida, Graduate School, College of Agricultural and Life Sciences, Department of Horticultural Sciences, Gainesville, FL 32611. Offers plant breeding and genetics (MS, PhD); plant production and nutrient management (MS, PhD); postharvest biology (MS, PhD); sustainable/organic practice (MS, PhD); weed science (MS, PhD). *Degree requirements:* For master's, variable foreign language requirement, thesis optional; for doctorate, variable foreign language requirement, thesis/dissertation. *Entrance requirements:* For master's and doctorate, GRE General Test, minimum GPA of 3.0. Electronic applications accepted. *Faculty research:* Genetics, plant nutrition, stress physiology, biotechnology, postharvest physiology.

University of Georgia, Graduate School, College of Agricultural and Environmental Sciences, Department of Horticulture, Athens, GA 30602. Offers horticulture (MS, PhD); plant protection and pest management (MPPPM). Part-time programs available. *Faculty:* 23 full-time (6 women). *Students:* 14 full-time (7 women), 8 part-time (4 women); includes 1 minority (Hispanic American), 7 international. 15 applicants, 67% accepted, 7 enrolled. In 2009, 4 master's, 2 doctorates awarded. *Degree requirements:* For master's, thesis (MS); for doctorate, one foreign language, thesis/dissertation. *Entrance requirements:* For master's and doctorate, GRE General Test. *Application deadline:* For fall admission, 7/1 priority date for domestic students; for spring admission, 11/15 for domestic students. Application fee: $50. Electronic applications accepted. *Expenses:* Tuition, state resident: full-time $6000; part-time $250 per credit hour. Tuition, nonresident: full-time $20,904; part-time $871 per credit hour. Required fees: $730 per semester. *Financial support:* In 2009–10, fellowships with partial tuition reimbursements (averaging $1,338 per year), research assistantships with partial tuition reimbursements (averaging $1,338 per year), teaching assistantships with partial tuition reimbursements (averaging $1,338 per year) were awarded; unspecified assistantships also available. *Unit head:* Dr. Douglas A. Bailey, Head, 706-542-2471, Fax: 706-542-0624, E-mail: dabailey@uga.edu. *Application contact:* Dr. Marc W. VanIersel, Graduate Coordinator, 706-583-0284, Fax: 706-542-0624, E-mail: mvanier@uga.edu.

University of Guelph, Graduate Program Services, Ontario Agricultural College, Department of Plant Agriculture, Guelph, ON N1G 2W1, Canada. Offers M Sc, PhD. Part-time programs available. *Degree requirements:* For master's, thesis; for doctorate, comprehensive exam, thesis/dissertation. *Entrance requirements:* For master's, minimum B average during previous 2 years of course work; for doctorate, minimum B average. Additional exam requirements/recommendations for international students: Required—TOEFL (minimum score 550 paper-based; 213 computer-based; 89 iBT), IELTS (minimum score 6.5), Michigan English Language Assessment Battery (minimum score: 85). Electronic applications accepted. *Faculty research:* Plant physiology, biochemistry, taxonomy, morphology, genetics, production, ecology, breeding and biotechnology.

University of Hawaii at Manoa, Graduate Division, College of Tropical Agriculture and Human Resources, Department of Tropical Plant and Soil Sciences, Honolulu, HI 96822. Offers MS, PhD. Part-time programs available. *Faculty:* 31 full-time (4 women), 14 part-time/adjunct (3 women). *Students:* 21 full-time (11 women), 8 part-time (4 women); includes 8 minority (all Asian Americans or Pacific Islanders), 11 international. Average age 32. 18 applicants, 67% accepted, 9 enrolled. In 2009, 2 master's awarded. *Degree requirements:* For master's, thesis optional; for doctorate, comprehensive exam, thesis/dissertation. *Entrance requirements:* For master's and doctorate, GRE General Test. Additional exam requirements/recommendations for international students: Required—TOEFL (minimum score 520 paper-based; 213 computer-based; 79 iBT), IELTS (minimum score 5). *Application deadline:* For fall admission, 3/1 for domestic students, 1/15 for international students; for spring admission, 9/1 for domestic students, 8/1 for international students. Application fee: $60. *Expenses:* Tuition, state resident: full-time $8900; part-time $372 per credit. Tuition, nonresident: full-time $21,400; part-time $898 per credit. Required fees: $207 per semester. *Financial support:* In 2009–10, 18 fellowships (averaging $5,037 per year), 18 research assistantships (averaging $17,899 per year) were awarded; tuition waivers (full and partial) also available. *Faculty research:* Genetics and breeding; physiology, culture, and management; weed science; turfgrass and landscape; sensory evaluation. Total annual research expenditures: $2.5 million. *Application contact:* Joseph DeFrank, Graduate Chair, 808-956-5900, Fax: 808-956-3894, E-mail: defrank@hawaii.edu.

University of Maine, Graduate School, College of Natural Sciences, Forestry, and Agriculture, Department of Plant, Soil, and Environmental Sciences, Program in Horticulture, Orono, ME 04469. Offers MS. *Students:* 2 full-time (1 woman), 2 part-time (1 woman), 1 international. Average age 30. 4 applicants, 25% accepted, 0 enrolled. In 2009, 1 master's awarded. *Entrance requirements:* For master's, GRE General Test. Additional exam requirements/recommendations for international students: Required—TOEFL. *Application deadline:* For fall admission, 2/1 priority date for domestic students. Applications are processed on a rolling basis. Application fee: $65. Electronic applications accepted. *Financial support:* Tuition waivers (full and partial) available. Financial award application deadline: 3/1. *Unit head:* Dr. Tsutomu Ohno, Coordinator, 207-584-2975. *Application contact:* Scott G. Delcourt, Associate Dean of the Graduate School, 207-581-3291, Fax: 207-581-3232, E-mail: graduate@maine.edu.

University of Manitoba, Faculty of Graduate Studies, Faculty of Agricultural and Food Sciences, Department of Plant Science, Winnipeg, MB R3T 2N2, Canada. Offers agronomy and plant protection (M Sc, PhD); horticulture (M Sc, PhD); plant breeding and genetics (M Sc, PhD); plant physiology-biochemistry (M Sc, PhD). *Degree requirements:* For master's, thesis; for doctorate, one foreign language, thesis/dissertation.

University of Maryland, College Park, Academic Affairs, College of Agriculture and Natural Resources, Department of Plant Science and Landscape Architecture, Program in Horticulture, College Park, MD 20742. Offers PhD. *Entrance requirements:* For doctorate, GRE General Test. Additional exam requirements/recommendations for international students: Required—TOEFL. *Application deadline:* For fall admission, 2/1 for domestic and international students; for spring admission, 6/1 for international students. Applications are processed on a rolling basis. Application fee: $60. Electronic applications accepted. *Expenses:* Tuition, area resident: Part-time $471 per credit hour. Tuition, state resident: part-time $471 per credit hour. Tuition, nonresident: part-time $1016 per credit hour. Required fees: $337.04 per term. *Financial support:* Fellowships, research assistantships, teaching assistantships, career-related internships or fieldwork available. Financial award applicants required to submit FAFSA. *Faculty research:* Mineral nutrition, genetics and breeding, chemical growth, histochemistry, postharvest physiology. *Unit head:* Dr. William Kenworthy, Acting Chair, 301-405-6244, Fax: 301-314-9308, E-mail: wkenwort@umd.edu. *Application contact:* Dean of Graduate School, 301-405-0358, Fax: 301-314-9305.

University of Missouri, Graduate School, College of Agriculture, Food and Natural Resources, Division of Plant Sciences, Program in Horticulture, Columbia, MO 65211. Offers MS, PhD. *Degree requirements:* For master's, thesis; for doctorate, variable foreign language requirement, thesis/dissertation. *Entrance requirements:* For master's and doctorate, GRE General Test, minimum GPA of 3.0. *Application deadline:* Applications are processed on a rolling basis. Application fee: $45 ($60 for international students). *Financial support:* Research assistantships, teaching assistantships, institutionally sponsored loans available. *Application contact:* Dr. Jeanne Mihail, Director of Graduate Studies, 573-882-0574, E-mail: mihailj@missouri.edu.

University of Nebraska–Lincoln, Graduate College, College of Agricultural Sciences and Natural Resources, Department of Agronomy and Horticulture, Program in Horticulture, Lincoln, NE 68588. Offers MS, PhD. *Degree requirements:* For master's, thesis optional. *Entrance requirements:* For master's, GRE General Test. Additional exam requirements/recommendations for international students: Required—TOEFL (minimum score 600 paper-based; 250 computer-based). Electronic applications accepted. *Faculty research:* Horticultural crops: production, management, cultural, and ecological aspects; tissue and cell culture; plant nutrition and anatomy; postharvest physiology and ecology.

University of Puerto Rico, Mayagüez Campus, Graduate Studies, College of Agricultural Sciences, Department of Horticulture, Mayagüez, PR 00681-9000. Offers MS. Part-time programs available. *Degree requirements:* For master's, comprehensive exam, thesis. *Entrance requirements:* For master's, BS degree in agricultural science or its equivalent. *Faculty research:* Growth regulators, floriculture, starchy crops, coffee and fruit technology.

University of South Africa, College of Agriculture and Environmental Sciences, Pretoria, South Africa. Offers agriculture (MS); consumer science (MCS); environmental management (MA, MS, PhD); environmental science (MA, MS, PhD); geography (MA, MS, PhD); horticulture (M Tech); human ecology (MHE); life sciences (MS); nature conservation (M Tech).

University of Vermont, Graduate College, College of Agriculture and Life Sciences, Department of Plant and Soil Science, Burlington, VT 05405. Offers MS, PhD. *Students:* 25 (14 women); includes 1 minority (Asian American or Pacific Islander), 4 international. 25 applicants, 68% accepted, 7 enrolled. In 2009, 3 master's, 3 doctorates awarded. *Degree requirements:* For master's, thesis; for doctorate, one foreign language, thesis/dissertation. *Entrance requirements:* For master's and doctorate, GRE General Test. Additional exam requirements/recommendations for international students: Required—TOEFL (minimum score 550 paper-based; 213 computer-based; 80 iBT). *Application deadline:* For fall admission, 3/1 priority date for domestic students. Applications are processed on a rolling basis. Application fee: $40. Electronic applications accepted. *Expenses:* Tuition, area resident: Part-time $508 per credit hour. Tuition, state resident: part-time $508 per credit hour. Tuition, nonresident: part-time $1281 per credit hour. *Financial support:* Fellowships, research assistantships, teaching assistantships available. Financial award application deadline: 3/1. *Faculty research:* Soil chemistry, plant nutrition. *Unit head:* Dr. Deborah Neher, Chairperson, 802-656-2630. *Application contact:* Dr. Josef Gorres, Coordinator, 802-656-2630.

University of Washington, Graduate School, College of Forest Resources, Seattle, WA 98195. Offers bioresource science and engineering (MS, PhD); environmental horticulture (MEH); environmental horticulture and urban forestry (MS, PhD); forest ecology (MS, PhD); forest management (MFR); forest soils (MS, PhD); forest systems and bioenergy (MS, PhD); restoration ecology (MS, PhD); social sciences (MS, PhD); sustainable resource management (MS, PhD); wildlife science (MS, PhD); MFR/MAIS; MPA/MS. *Accreditation:* SAF. *Degree requirements:* For master's, thesis (for some programs); for doctorate, comprehensive exam (for some programs), thesis/dissertation. *Entrance requirements:* For master's and doctorate, GRE, minimum GPA of 3.0. Additional exam requirements/recommendations for international students: Required—TOEFL. Electronic applications accepted. *Faculty research:* Ecosystem analysis, silviculture and forest protection, paper science and engineering, environmental horticulture and urban forestry, natural resource policy and economics.

University of Wisconsin–Madison, Graduate School, College of Agricultural and Life Sciences, Department of Horticulture, Madison, WI 53706-1380. Offers MS, PhD. Part-time programs available. Terminal master's awarded for partial completion of doctoral program. *Degree requirements:* For master's, comprehensive exam, thesis (for some programs); for doctorate, comprehensive exam, thesis/dissertation. *Entrance requirements:* For master's and doctorate, minimum GPA of 3.0. Additional exam requirements/recommendations for international students: Required—TOEFL (minimum score 580 paper-based; 213 computer-based). Electronic applications accepted. *Expenses:* Tuition, state resident: part-time $594 per credit. Tuition, nonresident: part-time $1504 per credit. Required fees: $65 per credit. Tuition and fees vary according to course load, program and reciprocity agreements. *Faculty research:* Biotechnology, crop breeding/genetics, environmental physiology, crop management, cytogenetics.

Virginia Polytechnic Institute and State University, Graduate School, College of Agriculture and Life Sciences, Department of Horticulture, Blacksburg, VA 24061. Offers MS, PhD. *Entrance requirements:* For master's and doctorate, GRE. Additional exam requirements/recommendations for international students: Required—TOEFL (minimum score 550 paper-based; 213 computer-based). Electronic applications accepted.

Washington State University, Graduate School, College of Agricultural, Human, and Natural Resource Sciences, Department of Horticulture and Landscape Architecture, Pullman, WA 99164. Offers horticulture (MS, PhD); landscape architecture (MSLA). *Accreditation:* ASLA. Part-time programs available. *Degree requirements:* For master's, comprehensive exam (for some programs), thesis (for some programs), oral exam; for doctorate, comprehensive exam, thesis/dissertation, oral exam, written exam. *Entrance requirements:* For master's and doctorate, GRE General Test, GRE Subject Test, minimum GPA of 3.0, 3 letters of recommendation. Additional exam requirements/recommendations for international students: Required—TOEFL (minimum score 550 paper-based). Electronic applications accepted. *Faculty research:* Postharvest physiology, genetics/plant breeding, molecular biology.

West Virginia University, Davis College of Agriculture, Forestry and Consumer Sciences, Division of Plant and Soil Sciences, Morgantown, WV 26506. Offers agricultural sciences (PhD), including animal and food sciences, plant and soil sciences; agronomy (MS); entomology (MS); environmental microbiology (MS); horticulture (MS); plant pathology (MS). *Degree requirements:* For master's, thesis. *Entrance requirements:* For master's, GRE, minimum GPA of 2.5. Additional exam requirements/recommendations for international students: Required—TOEFL. *Faculty research:* Water quality, reclamation of disturbed land, crop production, pest control, environmental protection.

Plant Sciences

Alabama Agricultural and Mechanical University, School of Graduate Studies, School of Agricultural and Environmental Sciences, Department of Plant and Soil Science, Huntsville, AL 35811. Offers animal sciences (MS); environmental science (MS); plant and soil science (PhD). Evening/weekend programs available. Terminal master's awarded for partial completion of doctoral program. *Degree requirements:* For master's, thesis; for doctorate, one foreign language, thesis/dissertation. *Entrance requirements:* For master's, GRE General Test, BS in agriculture; for doctorate, GRE General Test, master's degree. Additional exam requirements/recommendations for international students: Required—TOEFL (minimum score 500 paper-based; 173 computer-based; 61 iBT). Electronic applications accepted. *Faculty research:* Plant breeding, cytogenetics, crop production, soil chemistry and fertility, remote sensing.

American University of Beirut, Graduate Programs, Faculty of Agricultural and Food Sciences, Beirut, Lebanon. Offers agricultural economics (MS); animal sciences (MS); ecosystem management (MSES); food technology (MS); irrigation (MS); mechanization (MS); nutrition (MS); plant protection (MS); plant science (MS); poultry science (MS); soils (MS). Part-time programs available. *Degree requirements:* For master's, one foreign language, comprehensive exam, thesis (for some programs). *Entrance requirements:* For master's, letter of recommendation. Additional exam requirements/recommendations for international students: Required—TOEFL (minimum score 600 paper-based; 250 computer-based; 100 iBT), IELTS (minimum score 7.5). *Faculty research:* Sustainable animal systems/agriculture; natural resource management; community nutrition, obesity and food safety; integrated pest management; ecosystem management.

Brigham Young University, Graduate Studies, College of Life Sciences, Department of Plant and Wildlife Sciences, Provo, UT 84602-1001. Offers environmental science (MS); genetics and biotechnology (MS); wildlife and wildlands conservation (MS, PhD). *Faculty:* 21 full-time (1 woman), 15 part-time/adjunct (3 women). *Students:* 35 full-time (13 women), 18 part-time (5 women); includes 7 minority (2 Asian Americans or Pacific Islanders, 5 Hispanic Americans), 5 international. Average age 29. 34 applicants, 68% accepted, 21 enrolled. In 2009, 9 master's, 1 doctorate awarded. *Degree requirements:* For master's, thesis; for doctorate, comprehensive exam, thesis/dissertation, minimum GPA of 3.0, 54 hours (18 dissertation, 36 coursework). *Entrance requirements:* For master's, GRE General Test, minimum GPA of 3.0 during last 60 hours of course work; for doctorate, GRE, minimum GPA of 3.0. Additional exam requirements/recommendations for international students: Required—TOEFL (minimum score 580 paper-based; 237 computer-based; 85 iBT). *Application deadline:* 2/1 for domestic and international students. Applications are processed on a rolling basis. Application fee: $50. Electronic applications accepted. *Expenses:* Tuition: Full-time $5580; part-time $301 per credit hour. Tuition and fees vary according to student's religious affiliation. *Financial support:* In 2009–10, 22 students received support, including 2 research assistantships with partial tuition reimbursements available (averaging $16,650 per year), 37 teaching assistantships with partial tuition reimbursements available (averaging $16,650 per year); scholarships/grants and tuition waivers (partial) also available. Financial award application deadline: 2/1. *Faculty research:* environmental science, plant genetics, plant ecology, plant nutrition and pathology, wildlife and wildlands conservation. Total annual research expenditures: $1.1 million. *Unit head:* Dr. Val J. Anderson, Chair, 801-422-3527, Fax: 801-422-0008, E-mail: val_anderson@byu.edu. *Application contact:* Dr. Loreen Allphin, Graduate Coordinator, 801-422-5603, Fax: 801-422-0008, E-mail: loreen_allphin@byu.edu.

California State University, Fresno, Division of Graduate Studies, College of Agricultural Sciences and Technology, Department of Plant Science, Fresno, CA 93740-8027. Offers MS. Part-time programs available. *Degree requirements:* For master's, thesis. *Entrance requirements:* For master's, GRE General Test, minimum GPA of 2.5. Additional exam requirements/recommendations for international students: Required—TOEFL. Electronic applications accepted. *Faculty research:* Crop patterns, small watershed management, electronic monitoring of feedlot cattle, disease control, dairy operations.

Clemson University, Graduate School, College of Agriculture, Forestry and Life Sciences, Department of Entomology, Soils, and Plant Sciences, Program in Plant and Environmental Sciences, Clemson, SC 29634. Offers MS, PhD. *Students:* 34 full-time (14 women), 10 part-time (1 woman); includes 2 minority (both Hispanic Americans), 11 international. Average age 29. 35 applicants, 49% accepted, 14 enrolled. In 2009, 9 master's, 6 doctorates awarded. *Degree requirements:* For master's, thesis; for doctorate, thesis/dissertation. *Entrance requirements:* For master's, GRE General Test, bachelor's degree in biological science or chemistry; for doctorate, GRE General Test. Additional exam requirements/recommendations for international students: Required—TOEFL, IELTS. *Application deadline:* Applications are processed on a rolling basis. Application fee: $70 ($80 for international students). Electronic applications accepted. *Expenses:* Contact institution. *Financial support:* In 2009–10, 28 students received support, including 3 fellowships with full and partial tuition reimbursements available (averaging $11,033 per year), 21 research assistantships with partial tuition reimbursements available (averaging $16,366 per year), 7 teaching assistantships with partial tuition reimbursements available (averaging $14,566 per year); career-related internships or fieldwork, institutionally sponsored loans, scholarships/grants, health care benefits, and unspecified assistantships also available. Support available to part-time students. Financial award application deadline: 3/15; financial award applicants required to submit FAFSA. *Faculty research:* Systematics, aquatic botany, plant ecology, plant-fungus interactions, plant developmental genetics. *Unit head:* Dr. Patricia A. Zungoli, Chair, 864-656-3137, Fax: 864-656-5065, E-mail: pzngl@clemson.edu. *Application contact:* Dr. Halina Knap, Plant and Environmental Sciences Graduate Coordinator, 864-656-3102, Fax: 864-656-5065, E-mail: hskrpsk@clemson.edu.

Colorado State University, Graduate School, College of Agricultural Sciences, Department of Bioagricultural Sciences and Pest Management, Fort Collins, CO 80523-1177. Offers entomology (MS, PhD); plant pathology and weed science (MS, PhD). Part-time programs available. *Faculty:* 19 full-time (3 women). *Students:* 19 full-time (8 women), 13 part-time (5 women); includes 3 minority (2 American Indian/Alaska Native, 1 Hispanic American), 2 international. Average age 31. 26 applicants, 31% accepted, 4 enrolled. In 2009, 5 master's, 1 doctorate awarded. *Degree requirements:* For master's, comprehensive exam, thesis; for doctorate, comprehensive exam, thesis/dissertation, 72 credits. *Entrance requirements:* For master's, GRE General Test, minimum GPA of 3.0, letters of recommendation; for doctorate, GRE General Test, minimum GPA of 3.0, letters of recommendation, essay. Additional exam requirements/recommendations for international students: Required—TOEFL (minimum score 550 paper-based; 213 computer-based). *Application deadline:* For fall admission, 1/15 priority date for domestic and international students; for spring admission, 9/1 priority date for domestic and international students. Applications are processed on a rolling basis. Application fee: $50. Electronic applications accepted. *Expenses:* Tuition, state resident: full-time $6434; part-time $359.10 per credit. Tuition, nonresident: full-time $18,116; part-time $1006.45 per credit. Required fees: $1496; $83 per credit. *Financial support:* In 2009–10, 7 fellowships with partial tuition reimbursements (averaging $32,685 per year), 22 research assistantships with full tuition reimbursements (averaging $14,370 per year), 8 teaching assistantships with full tuition reimbursements (averaging $11,230 per year) were awarded; career-related internships or fieldwork, scholarships/grants, unspecified assistantships, and fellowships also available. Financial award application deadline: 1/15; financial award applicants required to submit FAFSA. *Faculty research:* Biological control of post-insect plant pathogens and weeds, integrated pest management, weed ecology and biology, pest genomes of plants. Total annual research expenditures: $2.6 million. *Unit head:* Thomas O. Holtzer, Head, 970-491-5261, Fax: 970-491-3862, E-mail: tholtzer@lamar.colostate.edu. *Application contact:* Janet Dill, Education Coordinator, 970-491-0402, Fax: 970-491-3862, E-mail: janet.dill@colostate.edu.

Colorado State University, Graduate School, College of Agricultural Sciences, Department of Soil and Crop Sciences, Fort Collins, CO 80523-1170. Offers MS, PhD. Part-time programs available. *Faculty:* 20 full-time (5 women), 2 part-time/adjunct (0 women). *Students:* 16 full-time (7 women), 17 part-time (4 women); includes 2 minority (1 African American, 1 American Indian/Alaska Native), 12 international. Average age 32. 23 applicants, 43% accepted, 6 enrolled. In 2009, 6 master's, 3 doctorates awarded. Terminal master's awarded for partial completion of doctoral program. *Degree requirements:* For master's, thesis; for doctorate, comprehensive exam, thesis/dissertation, student teaching, 2 seminar courses. *Entrance requirements:* For master's, GRE, minimum GPA of 3.0, appropriate bachelor's degree, letters of recommendation, statement of purpose; for doctorate, GRE, minimum GPA of 3.0, appropriate master's degree, letters of recommendation. Additional exam requirements/recommendations for international students: Required—TOEFL (minimum score 550 paper-based; 213 computer-based; 80 iBT). *Application deadline:* For fall admission, 4/1 priority date for domestic and international students; for spring admission, 9/1 priority date for domestic and international students. Application fee: $50. Electronic applications accepted. *Expenses:* Tuition, state resident: full-time $6434; part-time $359.10 per credit. Tuition, nonresident: full-time $18,116; part-time $1006.45 per credit. Required fees: $1496; $83 per credit. *Financial support:* In 2009–10, 15 students received support, including 1 fellowship with full tuition reimbursement available (averaging $17,341 per year), 14 research assistantships with full tuition reimbursements available (averaging $17,591 per year); teaching assistantships with full tuition reimbursements available, scholarships/grants, unspecified assistantships, and fellowships also available. Financial award application deadline: 2/15; financial award applicants required to submit FAFSA. *Faculty research:* Water quality, soil fertility, soil/plant ecosystems, plant breeding and genetics, cropping systems. Total annual research expenditures: $2.4 million. *Unit head:* Dr. Gary A. Peterson, Head, 970-491-6501, Fax: 970-491-0564, E-mail: gary.peterson@colostate.edu. *Application contact:* Dr. Pat F. Byrne, Graduate Studies Coordinator, 970-491-6985, Fax: 970-491-0564, E-mail: pbyrne@lamar.colostate.edu.

Cornell University, Graduate School, Graduate Fields of Agriculture and Life Sciences, Field of Plant Breeding, Ithaca, NY 14853-0001. Offers plant breeding (MPS, MS, PhD); plant genetics (MPS, MS, PhD). *Faculty:* 31 full-time (8 women). *Students:* 32 full-time (17 women); includes 2 minority (1 Asian American or Pacific Islander, 1 Hispanic American), 15 international. Average age 27. 45 applicants, 31% accepted, 10 enrolled. In 2009, 1 master's, 4 doctorates awarded. Terminal master's awarded for partial completion of doctoral program. *Degree requirements:* For master's, thesis (MS), project paper (MPS); for doctorate, comprehensive exam, thesis/dissertation. *Entrance requirements:* For master's and doctorate, GRE General Test, GRE Subject Test (recommended), 3 letters of recommendation. Additional exam requirements/recommendations for international students: Required—TOEFL (minimum score 550 paper-based; 213 computer-based; 77 iBT). *Application deadline:* For fall admission, 1/15 priority date for domestic students. Application fee: $70. Electronic applications accepted. *Expenses:* Tuition: Full-time $29,500. Required fees: $70. Full-time tuition and fees vary according to degree level, program and student level. *Financial support:* In 2009–10, 28 students received support, including 2 fellowships with full tuition reimbursements available, 1 research assistantship with full tuition reimbursement available; teaching assistantships with full tuition reimbursements available, institutionally sponsored loans, scholarships/grants, health care benefits, tuition waivers (full and partial), and unspecified assistantships also available. Financial award applicants required to submit FAFSA. *Faculty research:* Crop breeding for improved yield, stress resistance and quality; genetics and genomics of crop plants; applications of molecular biology and bioinformatics to crop improvement; genetic diversity and utilization of wild germplasm; international agriculture. *Unit head:* Director of Graduate Studies, 607-255-2180. *Application contact:* Graduate Field Assistant, 607-255-2180, E-mail: plbrgrad@cornell.edu.

Cornell University, Graduate School, Graduate Fields of Agriculture and Life Sciences, Field of Plant Protection, Ithaca, NY 14853-0001. Offers MPS. *Degree requirements:* For master's, internship, final exam. *Entrance requirements:* For master's, GRE General Test, 3 letters of recommendation. Additional exam requirements/recommendations for international students: Required—TOEFL (minimum score 550 paper-based; 213 computer-based; 77 iBT). *Application deadline:* For fall admission, 4/1 for domestic students. Application fee: $70. Electronic applications accepted. *Expenses:* Tuition: Full-time $29,500. Required fees: $70. Full-time tuition and fees vary according to degree level, program and student level. *Financial support:* Fellowships with full tuition reimbursements, research assistantships with full tuition reimbursements, teaching assistantships with full tuition reimbursements, institutionally sponsored loans, scholarships/grants, health care benefits, tuition waivers (full and partial), and unspecified assistantships available. Financial award applicants required to submit FAFSA. *Faculty research:* Fruit and vegetable crop insects and diseases, systems modeling, biological control, plant protection economics, integrated pest management. *Unit head:* Director of Graduate Studies, 315-787-2323, Fax: 315-787-2326. *Application contact:* Graduate Field Assistant, 315-787-2323, Fax: 315-787-2326, E-mail: plprotection@cornell.edu.

Delaware State University, Graduate Programs, Department of Agriculture and Natural Resources, Program in Plant Science, Dover, DE 19901-2277. Offers MS. *Entrance requirements:* For master's, GRE. Additional exam requirements/recommendations for international students: Required—TOEFL (minimum score 550 paper-based).

Florida Agricultural and Mechanical University, Division of Graduate Studies, Research, and Continuing Education, College of Engineering Science, Technology, and Agriculture, Division of Agricultural Sciences, Tallahassee, FL 32307-3200. Offers agribusiness (MS); animal science (MS); engineering technology (MS); entomology (MS); food science (MS); international programs (MS); plant science (MS). *Faculty:* 31 full-time (2 women). *Students:* 14 full-time (8 women), 8 part-time (4 women); includes 17 minority (16 African Americans, 1 Asian American or Pacific Islander), 3 international. In 2009, 7 master's awarded. *Degree requirements:* For master's, thesis. *Entrance requirements:* For master's, GRE General Test, minimum GPA of 3.0. Additional exam requirements/recommendations for international students: Required—TOEFL (minimum score 500 paper-based). *Application deadline:* For fall admission, 5/18 for domestic students, 12/18 for international students; for spring admission, 11/12 for domestic students, 5/12 for international students. Application fee: $20. *Financial support:* Application deadline: 2/15. *Unit head:* Dr. Mitwe N. Musingo, Graduate Coordinator, 850-561-2309, Fax: 850-599-8821. *Application contact:* Dr. Chanta M. Haywood, Dean of Graduate Studies, Research, and Continuing Education, 850-599-3315, Fax: 850-599-3727.

Illinois State University, Graduate School, College of Arts and Sciences, Department of Biological Sciences, Normal, IL 61790-2200. Offers animal behavior (MS); bacteriology (MS); biochemistry (MS); biological sciences (MS); biology (PhD); biophysics (MS); biotechnology (MS); botany (MS, PhD); cell biology (MS); conservation biology (MS); developmental biology (MS); ecology (MS, PhD); entomology (MS); evolutionary biology (MS); genetics (MS, PhD); immunology (MS); microbiology (MS, PhD); molecular biology (MS); molecular genetics (MS); neurobiology (MS); neuroscience (MS); parasitology (MS); physiology (MS, PhD); plant biology (MS); plant molecular biology (MS); plant sciences (MS); structural biology (MS); zoology (MS, PhD). Part-time programs available. *Degree requirements:* For master's, thesis or alternative; for doctorate, variable foreign language requirement, thesis/dissertation, 2 terms of residency. *Entrance requirements:* For master's, GRE General Test, minimum GPA of 2.6 in last 60 hours of course work; for doctorate, GRE General Test. *Faculty research:* Redoc balance and drug development in schistosoma mansoni, control of the growth of listeria monocytogenes at low temperature, regulation of cell expansion and microtubule function by SPRI, CRUI: physiology and fitness consequences of different life history phenotypes.

Plant Sciences

Lehman College of the City University of New York, Division of Natural and Social Sciences, Department of Biological Sciences, Program in Plant Sciences, Bronx, NY 10468-1589. Offers PhD. *Degree requirements:* For doctorate, 2 foreign languages, thesis/dissertation. *Entrance requirements:* For doctorate, GRE General Test.

McGill University, Faculty of Graduate and Postdoctoral Studies, Faculty of Agricultural and Environmental Sciences, Department of Plant Science, Montréal, QC H3A 2T5, Canada. Offers M Sc, M Sc A, PhD, Certificate.

Miami University, Graduate School, College of Arts and Sciences, Department of Botany, Oxford, OH 45056. Offers MA, MAT, MS, PhD. *Students:* 29 full-time (17 women), 14 international. *Entrance requirements:* For master's, GRE General Test, GRE Subject Test (recommended), minimum undergraduate GPA of 3.0 during previous 2 years or 2.75 overall; for doctorate, GRE General Test, GRE Subject Test (recommended), minimum undergraduate GPA of 2.75, 3.0 graduate. Additional exam requirements/recommendations for international students: Required—TOEFL (minimum score 550 paper-based). *Application deadline:* Applications are processed on a rolling basis. Application fee: $50. Electronic applications accepted. *Expenses:* Tuition, state resident: full-time $11,280. Tuition, nonresident: full-time $24,912. Required fees: $516. *Financial support:* Research assistantships, teaching assistantships with full tuition reimbursements, Federal Work-Study, institutionally sponsored loans, health care benefits, and unspecified assistantships available. Financial award application deadline: 3/1; financial award applicants required to submit FAFSA. *Faculty research:* Evolution of plants, fungi and algae; bioinformatics; molecular biology of plants and cyanobacteria; food web dynamics; plant science education. *Unit head:* Dr. John Kiss, Chair, 513-529-4200, E-mail: kissjz@muohio.edu. *Application contact:* Dr. R. James Hickey, Graduate Coordinator, 513-529-6000, E-mail: hickeyrj@muohio.edu.

Michigan State University, The Graduate School, College of Agriculture and Natural Resources, Program in Plant Breeding and Genetics, East Lansing, MI 48824. Offers MS, PhD. *Entrance requirements:* Additional exam requirements/recommendations for international students: Required—TOEFL. Electronic applications accepted. *Faculty research:* Applied plant breeding and genetics; disease, insect and herbicide resistances; gene isolation and genomics; abiotic stress factors; molecular mapping.

Mississippi State University, College of Agriculture and Life Sciences, Department of Plant and Soil Sciences, Mississippi State, MS 39762. Offers agricultural sciences (PhD), including agronomy (MS, PhD), horticulture (MS, PhD), weed science (MS, PhD); agriculture (MS), including agronomy (MS, PhD), horticulture (MS, PhD), weed science (MS, PhD). *Faculty:* 24 full-time (1 woman), 1 part-time/adjunct (0 women). *Students:* 26 full-time (8 women), 30 part-time (8 women); includes 1 minority (American Indian/Alaska Native), 16 international. Average age 30. 31 applicants, 39% accepted, 12 enrolled. In 2009, 7 master's, 1 doctorate awarded. *Degree requirements:* For master's, thesis, exit seminar describing thesis research; for doctorate, comprehensive exam, thesis/dissertation, two departmental seminars. *Entrance requirements:* For master's, GRE (weed science), minimum GPA of 2.75 (agronomy/horticulture), 3.0 (weed science); for doctorate, GRE (weed science), minimum GPA of 3.0 (agronomy/horticulture), 3.25 (weed science). Additional exam requirements/recommendations for international students: Required—TOEFL (minimum score 550 paper-based; 213 computer-based; 79 iBT); Recommended—IELTS (minimum score 6.5). *Application deadline:* For fall admission, 7/1 for domestic students, 5/1 for international students; for spring admission, 10/1 for domestic students, 9/1 for international students. Applications are processed on a rolling basis. Application fee: $40. Electronic applications accepted. *Expenses:* Tuition, state resident: full-time $2575.50; part-time $286.25 per credit hour. Tuition, nonresident: full-time $6510; part-time $723.50 per credit hour. Tuition and fees vary according to course load. *Financial support:* In 2009–10, 25 research assistantships (averaging $11,626 per year), 3 teaching assistantships (averaging $12,379 per year) were awarded; Federal Work-Study, institutionally sponsored loans, scholarships/grants, and unspecified assistantships also available. Financial award application deadline: 4/1; financial award applicants required to submit FAFSA. *Unit head:* Dr. Daniel Reynolds, Professor/Interim Head, 662-325-2311, Fax: 662-325-8742, E-mail: dreynolds@pss.msstate.edu. *Application contact:* Dr. William Kingery, Graduate Coordinator, 662-325-2748, Fax: 662-325-8742, E-mail: wkingery@pss.msstate.edu.

Missouri State University, Graduate College, College of Natural and Applied Sciences, Department of Agriculture, Springfield, MO 65897. Offers natural and applied science (MNAS), including agriculture (MNAS, MS Ed); plant science (MS); secondary education (MS Ed), including agriculture (MNAS, MS Ed). Part-time programs available. *Faculty:* 16 full-time (3 women). *Students:* 10 full-time (7 women), 16 part-time (10 women), 2 international. Average age 31. 7 applicants, 71% accepted, 3 enrolled. In 2009, 9 master's awarded. *Degree requirements:* For master's, comprehensive exam, thesis or alternative. *Entrance requirements:* For master's, GRE (MS plant science, MNAS), 9-12 teacher certification (MS Ed), minimum GPA of 3.0 (MS plant science, MNAS). Additional exam requirements/recommendations for international students: Required—TOEFL (minimum score 550 paper-based; 213 computer-based; 79 iBT). *Application deadline:* For fall admission, 7/20 priority date for domestic students, 5/1 for international students; for spring admission, 12/20 priority date for domestic students, 9/1 for international students. Applications are processed on a rolling basis. Application fee: $35 ($50 for international students). Electronic applications accepted. *Expenses:* Tuition, state resident: full-time $3852; part-time $214 per credit hour. Tuition, nonresident: full-time $7524; part-time $418 per credit hour. Required fees: $696; $172 per semester. Tuition and fees vary according to course level, course load, degree level and program. *Financial support:* In 2009–10, 6 research assistantships with full tuition reimbursements (averaging $8,535 per year), 6 teaching assistantships with full tuition reimbursements (averaging $8,535 per year) were awarded; Federal Work-Study, institutionally sponsored loans, scholarships/grants, and unspecified assistantships also available. Financial award application deadline: 3/31; financial award applicants required to submit FAFSA. *Faculty research:* Grapevine biotechnology, agricultural marketing, Asian elephant reproduction, poultry science, integrated pest management. *Unit head:* Dr. W. Anson Elliott, Head, 417-836-5638, E-mail: ansonelliot@missouristate.edu. *Application contact:* Eric Eckert, Coordinator of Graduate Admissions and Recruitment, 417-836-5331, Fax: 417-836-6200.

Montana State University, College of Graduate Studies, College of Agriculture, Department of Plant Sciences and Plant Pathology, Bozeman, MT 59717. Offers plant pathology (MS); plant sciences (MS, PhD), including plant genetics (PhD), plant pathology (PhD). Part-time programs available. *Faculty:* 23 full-time (4 women), 3 part-time/adjunct (1 woman). *Students:* 7 full-time (3 women), 11 part-time (5 women), 6 international. Average age 30. 19 applicants, 16% accepted, 3 enrolled. In 2009, 5 master's, 2 doctorates awarded. *Degree requirements:* For master's, comprehensive exam; for doctorate, comprehensive exam, thesis/dissertation. *Entrance requirements:* For master's, GRE General Test, minimum GPA of 3.0; for doctorate, GRE General Test. Additional exam requirements/recommendations for international students: Required—TOEFL (minimum score 550 paper-based; 213 computer-based). *Application deadline:* For fall admission, 7/15 priority date for domestic students, 5/15 priority date for international students; for spring admission, 12/1 priority date for domestic students, 10/1 priority date for international students. Applications are processed on a rolling basis. Application fee: $30. Electronic applications accepted. *Expenses:* Tuition, state resident: full-time $5635; part-time $3492 per year. Tuition, nonresident: full-time $17,212; part-time $7865.10 per year. Required fees: $1441.05; $153.15 per credit. Tuition and fees vary according to course load and program. *Financial support:* In 2009–10, 9 students received support, including 5 research assistantships with tuition reimbursements available (averaging $36,000 per year), 4 teaching assistantships with tuition reimbursements available (averaging $17,000 per year); health care benefits and unspecified assistantships also available. Financial award application deadline: 3/1; financial award applicants required to submit FAFSA. *Faculty research:* Plant genetics, plant metabolism, plant microbe interactions, plant pathology, entomology. Total annual research expenditures: $2.9 million. *Unit head:* Dr. John Sherwood, Head, 406-994-5153, Fax: 406-994-7600, E-mail: sherwood@montana.edu. *Application contact:* Dr. Carl A. Fox, Vice Provost for Graduate Education, 406-994-4145, Fax: 406-994-7433, E-mail: gradstudy@montana.edu.

New Mexico State University, Graduate School, College of Agricultural, Consumer and Environmental Sciences, Department of Entomology, Plant Pathology and Weed Science, Las Cruces, NM 88003-8001. Offers agricultural biology (MS). Part-time programs available. *Faculty:* 8 full-time (2 women). *Students:* 8 full-time (2 women), 2 part-time (1 woman); includes 2 minority (both Hispanic Americans), 2 international. Average age 26. 8 applicants, 88% accepted, 3 enrolled. In 2009, 4 master's awarded. *Degree requirements:* For master's, comprehensive exam, thesis. *Entrance requirements:* For master's, GRE General Test. *Application deadline:* For fall admission, 7/1 priority date for domestic students; for spring admission, 11/1 priority date for domestic students. Applications are processed on a rolling basis. Application fee: $30 ($50 for international students). Electronic applications accepted. *Expenses:* Tuition, state resident: full-time $4080; part-time $223 per credit. Tuition, nonresident: full-time $14,256; part-time $647 per credit. Required fees: $1278; $639 per semester. *Financial support:* In 2009–10, 5 research assistantships with partial tuition reimbursements (averaging $18,450 per year), 1 teaching assistantship with partial tuition reimbursement (averaging $20,500 per year) were awarded; career-related internships or fieldwork and health care benefits also available. Financial award application deadline: 3/1. *Faculty research:* Integrated pest management, pesticide application and safety, livestock ectoparasite research, biotechnology, nematology. *Unit head:* Dr. David Thompson, Head, 575-646-3225, Fax: 575-646-8087, E-mail: dathomps@nmsu.edu. *Application contact:* Dr. David Thompson, Head, 575-646-3225, Fax: 575-646-8087, E-mail: dathomps@nmsu.edu.

New Mexico State University, Graduate School, College of Agricultural, Consumer and Environmental Sciences, Department of Plant and Environmental Sciences, Las Cruces, NM 88003-8001. Offers horticulture (MS); plant and environmental sciences (MS, PhD). Part-time programs available. *Faculty:* 11 full-time (3 women). *Students:* 45 full-time (17 women), 9 part-time (3 women); includes 11 minority (1 American Indian/Alaska Native, 10 Hispanic Americans), 17 international. Average age 31. 29 applicants, 97% accepted, 16 enrolled. In 2009, 5 master's, 2 doctorates awarded. *Degree requirements:* For master's, thesis; for doctorate, one foreign language, thesis/dissertation. *Entrance requirements:* For master's, minimum GPA of 3.0; for doctorate, minimum GPA of 3.3. Additional exam requirements/recommendations for international students: Required—TOEFL. *Application deadline:* For fall admission, 7/1 priority date for domestic students; for spring admission, 11/1 priority date for domestic students. Applications are processed on a rolling basis. Application fee: $30 ($50 for international students). Electronic applications accepted. *Expenses:* Tuition, state resident: full-time $4080; part-time $223 per credit. Tuition, nonresident: full-time $14,256; part-time $647 per credit. Required fees: $1278; $639 per semester. *Financial support:* In 2009–10, 29 research assistantships with partial tuition reimbursements (averaging $19,764 per year), 9 teaching assistantships with partial tuition reimbursements (averaging $15,733 per year) were awarded; career-related internships or fieldwork, Federal Work-Study, scholarships/grants, health care benefits, and unspecified assistantships also available. Support available to part-time students. Financial award application deadline: 3/1. *Faculty research:* Plant breeding and genetics, molecular biology, plant physiology, soil science and environmental remediation, urban horticulture and turfgrass management. *Unit head:* Dr. John G. Mexal, Interim Head, 575-646-3406, Fax: 575-646-6041, E-mail: jmexal@nmsu.edu. *Application contact:* Esther Ramirez, Information Contact, 575-646-3406, Fax: 575-646-6041, E-mail: esramire@nmsu.edu.

North Carolina Agricultural and Technical State University, Graduate School, School of Agriculture and Environmental Sciences, Department of Natural Resources and Environmental Design, Greensboro, NC 27411. Offers plant, soil and environmental science (MS). Part-time and evening/weekend programs available. *Degree requirements:* For master's, comprehensive exam, thesis optional, qualifying exam. *Entrance requirements:* For master's, GRE General Test, minimum GPA of 3.0. *Faculty research:* Soil parameters and compaction of forest site, controlled traffic effects on soil, improving soybean and vegetable crops.

North Dakota State University, College of Graduate and Interdisciplinary Studies, College of Agriculture, Food Systems, and Natural Resources, Department of Plant Sciences, Fargo, ND 58108. Offers crop and weed sciences (MS); horticulture (MS); natural resource management (MS); plant sciences (PhD). Part-time programs available. *Faculty:* 36 full-time (3 women), 23 part-time/adjunct (3 women). *Students:* 25 full-time (10 women), 17 part-time (6 women); includes 4 minority (all Hispanic Americans), 19 international. Average age 26. 44 applicants, 45% accepted. In 2009, 11 master's, 6 doctorates awarded. *Degree requirements:* For master's, thesis; for doctorate, thesis/dissertation. *Entrance requirements:* Additional exam requirements/recommendations for international students: Required—TOEFL (minimum score 525 paper-based; 197 computer-based; 71 iBT). *Application deadline:* Applications are processed on a rolling basis. Application fee: $45 ($60 for international students). Electronic applications accepted. *Financial support:* In 2009–10, 2 fellowships (averaging $19,950 per year), 64 research assistantships were awarded; teaching assistantships, Federal Work-Study and institutionally sponsored loans also available. Financial award application deadline: 4/15. *Faculty research:* Biotechnology, weed control science, plant breeding, plant genetics, crop physiology. Total annual research expenditures: $880,000. *Unit head:* Dr. Al Schneiter, Head, 701-231-7971, Fax: 701-231-8474, E-mail: albert.schneiter@ndsu.edu. *Application contact:* Dr. Al Schneiter, Head, 701-231-7971, Fax: 701-231-8474, E-mail: albert.schneiter@ndsu.edu.

Oklahoma State University, College of Agricultural Science and Natural Resources, Department of Horticulture and Landscape Architecture, Stillwater, OK 74078. Offers agriculture (M Ag); crop science (PhD); environmental science (PhD); horticulture (MS); plant science (PhD). *Accreditation:* ASLA. *Faculty:* 21 full-time (2 women), 2 part-time/adjunct (1 woman). *Students:* 14 part-time (6 women); includes 2 minority (1 African American, 1 American Indian/Alaska Native), 6 international. Average age 28. 23 applicants, 48% accepted, 7 enrolled. In 2009, 3 master's awarded. *Degree requirements:* For master's, thesis (for some programs); for doctorate, comprehensive exam, thesis/dissertation. *Entrance requirements:* For master's and doctorate, GRE or GMAT. Additional exam requirements/recommendations for international students: Required—TOEFL (minimum score 550 paper-based; 79 iBT). *Application deadline:* For fall admission, 3/1 priority date for international students; for spring admission, 8/1 priority date for international students. Applications are processed on a rolling basis. Application fee: $40 ($75 for international students). Electronic applications accepted. *Expenses:* Tuition, state resident: full-time $3716; part-time $154.85 per credit hour. Tuition, nonresident: full-time $14,448; part-time $602 per credit hour. Required fees: $1772; $73.85 per credit hour. One-time fee: $50. Tuition and fees vary according to course load and campus/location. *Financial support:* In 2009–10, 12 research assistantships (averaging $15,748 per year) were awarded; career-related internships or fieldwork, Federal Work-Study, scholarships/grants, health care benefits, tuition waivers (partial), and unspecified assistantships also available. Support available to part-time students. Financial award application deadline: 3/1; financial award applicants required to submit FAFSA. *Faculty research:* Stress and postharvest physiology; water utilization and runoff; IPM systems and nursery, turf, floriculture, vegetable, net and fruit produces and natural resources, food extraction, and processing; public garden management. *Unit head:* Dr. Dale Maronek, Head, 405-744-5414, Fax: 405-744-9709. *Application contact:* Dr. Gordon Emslie, Dean, 405-744-6368, Fax: 405-744-0355, E-mail: grad-i@okstate.edu.

Oklahoma State University, College of Agricultural Science and Natural Resources, Department of Plant and Soil Sciences, Stillwater, OK 74078. Offers crop science (PhD); environmental science (PhD); plant and soil sciences (MS); plant science (PhD); soil science (M Ag, PhD). *Faculty:* 33 full-time (4 women), 2 part-time/adjunct (0 women). *Students:* 15 full-time (4 women), 37 part-time (13 women); includes 1 minority (Asian American or Pacific Islander), 20 international. Average age 28. 34 applicants, 38% accepted, 7 enrolled. In 2009, 9 master's, 3 doctorates awarded. *Degree requirements:* For master's, thesis; for doctorate, comprehensive exam, thesis/dissertation. *Entrance requirements:* For master's and doctorate, GRE or GMAT. Additional exam requirements/recommendations for international students: Required—TOEFL (minimum score 550 paper-based; 79 iBT). *Application deadline:* For fall admission, 3/1 priority date for international students; for spring admission, 8/1 priority date for international students. Applications are processed on a rolling basis. Application fee: $40 ($75 for international students). Electronic applications accepted. *Expenses:* Tuition, state resident: full-time $3716; part-time $154.85 per credit hour. Tuition, nonresident: full-time $14,448; part-time $602 per credit hour. Required fees: $1772; $73.85 per credit hour. One-time fee: $50. Tuition and fees vary according to course load and campus/location. *Financial support:* In 2009–10, 38 research assistantships (averaging $14,373 per year), 1 teaching assistantship (averaging $13,920 per year) were awarded; career-related internships or fieldwork, Federal Work-Study, scholarships/grants, health care benefits, tuition waivers (partial), and unspecified assistantships also available. Support available to part-time students. Financial award application deadline: 3/1; financial award applicants required to submit FAFSA. *Faculty research:* Crop science, weed science, rangeland ecology and management, biotechnology, breeding and genetics. *Unit head:* Dr. David R. Porter, Head, 405-744-6130, Fax: 405-744-5269. *Application contact:* Dr. Gordon Emslie, Dean, 405-744-6368, Fax: 405-744-0355, E-mail: grad-i@okstate.edu.

Oklahoma State University, College of Arts and Sciences, Department of Botany, Stillwater, OK 74078. Offers botany (MS); environmental science (MS, PhD); plant science (PhD). *Faculty:* 17 full-time (5 women). *Students:* 12 part-time (4 women); includes 1 minority (American Indian/Alaska Native), 2 international. Average age 31. 10 applicants, 40% accepted, 4 enrolled. In 2009, 1 master's awarded. *Degree requirements:* For master's, thesis; for doctorate, comprehensive exam, thesis/dissertation. *Entrance requirements:* For master's and doctorate, GRE or GMAT. Additional exam requirements/recommendations for international students: Required—TOEFL (minimum score 550 paper-based; 79 iBT). *Application deadline:* For fall admission, 3/1 priority date for international students; for spring admission, 8/1 priority date for international students. Applications are processed on a rolling basis. Application fee: $40 ($75 for international students). Electronic applications accepted. *Expenses:* Tuition, state resident: full-time $3716; part-time $154.85 per credit hour. Tuition, nonresident: full-time $14,448; part-time $602 per credit hour. Required fees: $1772; $73.85 per credit hour. One-time fee: $50. Tuition and fees vary according to course load and campus/location. *Financial support:* In 2009–10, 3 research assistantships (averaging $15,770 per year), 10 teaching assistantships (averaging $15,469 per year) were awarded; career-related internships or fieldwork, Federal Work-Study, scholarships/grants, health care benefits, tuition waivers (partial), and unspecified assistantships also available. Support available to part-time students. Financial award application deadline: 3/1; financial award applicants required to submit FAFSA. *Faculty research:* Ethnobotany, developmental genetics of Arabidopsis, biological roles of Plasmodesmata, community ecology and biodiversity, nutrient cycling in grassland ecosystems. *Unit head:* Dr. Linda Watson, Head, 405-744-5559, Fax: 405-744-7074. *Application contact:* Dr. Gordon Emslie, Dean, 405-744-6368, Fax: 405-744-0355, E-mail: grad-i@okstate.edu.

Oklahoma State University, Graduate College, Stillwater, OK 74078. Offers environmental science (MS); international studies (MS); natural and applied science (MS); photonics (PhD); plant science (PhD). Programs are interdisciplinary. *Faculty:* 2 full-time (0 women). *Students:* 82 full-time (47 women), 156 part-time (75 women); includes 49 minority (15 African Americans, 17 American Indian/Alaska Native, 10 Asian Americans or Pacific Islanders, 7 Hispanic Americans), 60 international. Average age 32. 779 applicants, 68% accepted, 87 enrolled. In 2009, 77 master's, 8 doctorates awarded. *Degree requirements:* For master's, thesis (for some programs); for doctorate, comprehensive exam, thesis/dissertation. *Entrance requirements:* For master's and doctorate, GRE or GMAT. Additional exam requirements/recommendations for international students: Required—TOEFL (minimum score 550 paper-based; 79 iBT). *Application deadline:* For fall admission, 3/1 priority date for international students; for spring admission, 8/1 priority date for international students. Applications are processed on a rolling basis. Application fee: $40 ($75 for international students). Electronic applications accepted. *Expenses:* Tuition, state resident: full-time $3716; part-time $154.85 per credit hour. Tuition, nonresident: full-time $14,448; part-time $602 per credit hour. Required fees: $1772; $73.85 per credit hour. One-time fee: $50. Tuition and fees vary according to course load and campus/location. *Financial support:* In 2009–10, 2 research assistantships (averaging $10,200 per year) were awarded; career-related internships or fieldwork, Federal Work-Study, scholarships/grants, health care benefits, tuition waivers (partial), and unspecified assistantships also available. Support available to part-time students. Financial award application deadline: 3/1; financial award applicants required to submit FAFSA. *Unit head:* Dr. Gordon Emslie, Dean, 405-744-6368, Fax: 405-744-0355, E-mail: grad-i@okstate.edu. *Application contact:* Dr. Susan Mathew, Coordinator of Admissions, 405-744-6368, Fax: 405-744-0355, E-mail: grad-i@okstate.edu.

South Dakota State University, Graduate School, College of Agriculture and Biological Sciences, Department of Plant Science, Brookings, SD 57007. Offers agronomy (PhD); biological sciences (PhD); plant science (MS). *Degree requirements:* For master's, thesis (for some programs), oral exam; for doctorate, comprehensive exam, thesis/dissertation, preliminary oral and written exams. *Entrance requirements:* Additional exam requirements/recommendations for international students: Required—TOEFL (minimum score 560 paper-based; 220 computer-based; 83 iBT).

Southern Illinois University Carbondale, Graduate School, College of Agriculture, Department of Plant, Soil, and General Agriculture, Carbondale, IL 62901-4701. Offers horticultural science (MS); plant and soil science (MS). *Degree requirements:* For master's, thesis. *Entrance requirements:* For master's, minimum GPA of 2.7. Additional exam requirements/recommendations for international students: Required—TOEFL. *Faculty research:* Herbicides, fertilizers, agriculture education, landscape design, plant breeding.

State University of New York College of Environmental Science and Forestry, Department of Environmental and Forest Biology, Syracuse, NY 13210-2779. Offers applied ecology (MPS); chemical ecology (MPS, MS, PhD); conservation biology (MPS, MS, PhD); ecology (MPS, MS, PhD); entomology (MPS, MS, PhD); environmental interpretation (MPS, MS, PhD); environmental physiology (MPS, MS, PhD); fish and wildlife biology (MPS, MS, PhD); forest pathology and mycology (MPS, MS, PhD); plant biotechnology (MPS); plant science and biotechnology (MPS, MS, PhD). *Degree requirements:* For master's, thesis (for some programs); for doctorate, comprehensive exam, thesis/dissertation. *Entrance requirements:* For master's and doctorate, GRE General Test, GRE Subject Test, minimum GPA of 3.0. Additional exam requirements/recommendations for international students: Required—TOEFL (minimum score 550 paper-based; 213 computer-based; 80 iBT), IELTS (minimum score 6). *Faculty research:* Ecology, fish and wildlife biology and management, plant science, entomology.

Texas A&M University, College of Agriculture and Life Sciences, Department of Soil and Crop Sciences, College Station, TX 77843. Offers agronomy (M Agr, MS, PhD); genetics (PhD); molecular and environmental plant sciences (MS, PhD); soil science (MS, PhD). *Faculty:* 36. *Students:* 82 full-time (28 women), 25 part-time (6 women); includes 16 minority (4 African Americans, 1 American Indian/Alaska Native, 1 Asian American or Pacific Islander, 10 Hispanic Americans), 33 international. Average age 26. In 2009, 6 master's, 2 doctorates awarded. *Degree requirements:* For master's, thesis; for doctorate, thesis/dissertation. *Entrance requirements:* For master's and doctorate, GRE General Test. Additional exam requirements/recommendations for international students: Required—TOEFL. *Application deadline:* For fall admission, 3/1 priority date for domestic students; for spring admission, 8/1 for domestic students. Applications are processed on a rolling basis. Application fee: $50 ($75 for international students). *Expenses:* Tuition, state resident: full-time $3991.32; part-time $221.74 per credit hour. Tuition, nonresident: full-time $9049; part-time $502.74 per credit hour. *Financial support:* In 2009–10, fellowships (averaging $16,000 per year), research assistantships with partial tuition reimbursements (averaging $15,000 per year) were awarded; career-related internships or fieldwork, Federal Work-Study, and institutionally sponsored loans also available. *Faculty research:* Soil and crop management, turfgrass science, weed science, cereal chemistry, food protein chemistry. *Unit head:* Department Head, 979-845-3041, E-mail: soilcrop@tamu.edu. *Application contact:* Department Head, 979-845-3041, E-mail: soilcrop@tamu.edu.

Texas A&M University–Kingsville, College of Graduate Studies, College of Agriculture and Home Economics, Program in Plant and Soil Sciences, Kingsville, TX 78363. Offers MS, PhD. *Degree requirements:* For master's, comprehensive exam, thesis or alternative. *Entrance requirements:* For master's, GRE General Test, minimum GPA of 3.0. Additional exam requirements/recommendations for international students: Required—TOEFL.

Texas Tech University, Graduate School, College of Agricultural Sciences and Natural Resources, Department of Plant and Soil Science, Lubbock, TX 79409. Offers crop science (MS); entomology (MS); horticulture (MS); plant and soil science (PhD); soil science (MS); JD/MS. Part-time programs available. *Faculty:* 15 full-time (3 women), 6 part-time/adjunct (0 women). *Students:* 48 full-time (21 women), 42 part-time (18 women); includes 6 minority (2 African Americans, 4 Hispanic Americans), 26 international. Average age 33. 58 applicants, 72% accepted, 27 enrolled. In 2009, 13 master's, 4 doctorates awarded. *Degree requirements:* For master's, thesis or alternative; for doctorate, thesis/dissertation. *Entrance requirements:* For master's and doctorate, GRE General Test. Additional exam requirements/recommendations for international students: Required—TOEFL (minimum score 550 paper-based; 213 computer-based). *Application deadline:* For fall admission, 3/1 priority date for international students; for spring admission, 11/1 priority date for international students. Applications are processed on a rolling basis. Application fee: $50 ($75 for international students). Electronic applications accepted. *Expenses:* Tuition, state resident: full-time $5100; part-time $213 per credit hour. Tuition, nonresident: full-time $11,748; part-time $490 per credit hour. Required fees: $2298; $50 per credit hour. $555 per semester. *Financial support:* In 2009–10, 23 research assistantships with partial tuition reimbursements (averaging $20,991 per year) were awarded; teaching assistantships with partial tuition reimbursements, Federal Work-Study and institutionally sponsored loans also available. Support available to part-time students. Financial award application deadline: 4/15; financial award applicants required to submit FAFSA. *Faculty research:* Molecular and cellular biology of plant stress, physiology/genetics of crop production in semiarid conditions, agricultural bioterrorism, improvement of native plants, soil science and management. Total annual research expenditures: $3.4 million. *Unit head:* Dr. Thomas Thompson, Chair, 806-742-2837, Fax: 806-742-0775, E-mail: thomas.thompson@ttu.edu. *Application contact:* Dr. Eric Hequet, Graduate Adviser, 806-742-2837, Fax: 806-742-0775, E-mail: eric.hequet@ttu.edu.

Tuskegee University, Graduate Programs, College of Agricultural, Environmental and Natural Sciences, Department of Agricultural Sciences, Program in Plant and Soil Sciences, Tuskegee, AL 36088. Offers MS. *Faculty:* 13 full-time (1 woman), 2 part-time/adjunct (1 woman). *Students:* 8 full-time (2 women), 1 (woman) part-time; includes 3 minority (all African Americans), 6 international. Average age 30. In 2009, 1 master's awarded. *Degree requirements:* For master's, thesis. *Entrance requirements:* For master's, GRE General Test. Additional exam requirements/recommendations for international students: Required—TOEFL (minimum score 500 paper-based; 69 computer-based). *Application deadline:* For fall admission, 7/15 for domestic students. Applications are processed on a rolling basis. Application fee: $25 ($35 for international students). *Expenses:* Tuition: Full-time $15,630; part-time $940 per credit hour. Required fees: $650. *Financial support:* Application deadline: 4/15. *Application contact:* Dr. Robert L. Laney, Vice President/Director of Admissions and Enrollment Management, 334-727-8580, Fax: 334-727-5750, E-mail: planey@tuskegee.edu.

The University of Arizona, Graduate College, College of Agriculture and Life Sciences, Department of Plant Sciences, Tucson, AZ 85721. Offers plant pathology (PhD); plant sciences (MS, PhD). Part-time programs available. *Faculty:* 18. *Students:* 23 full-time (13 women), 4 part-time (0 women), 17 international. Average age 32. 41 applicants, 22% accepted, 5 enrolled. In 2009, 3 master's, 4 doctorates awarded. *Degree requirements:* For master's, thesis or alternative; for doctorate, thesis/dissertation. *Entrance requirements:* For master's, GRE General Test, GRE Subject Test (biology or chemistry recommended), minimum GPA of 3.0, academic resume, 3 letters of recommendation; for doctorate, GRE General Test, GRE Subject Test (biology or chemistry recommended), minimum GPA of 3.0, academic resume, statement of interest, 3 letters of recommendation. Additional exam requirements/recommendations for international students: Required—TOEFL. *Application deadline:* For fall admission, 12/1 for domestic and international students; for spring admission, 6/1 for domestic and international students. Applications are processed on a rolling basis. Application fee: $75. Electronic applications accepted. *Expenses:* Tuition, state resident: full-time $9028. Tuition, nonresident: full-time $24,890. *Financial support:* In 2009–10, 15 research assistantships with full tuition reimbursements (averaging $18,419 per year), 7 teaching assistantships with full tuition reimbursements (averaging $16,235 per year) were awarded; fellowships, career-related internships or fieldwork, Federal Work-Study, scholarships/grants, health care benefits, tuition waivers (partial), and unspecified assistantships also available. *Faculty research:* Molecular/cell biology, plant genetics and physiology, agronomic and horticultural production (including turf and ornamentals). Total annual research expenditures: $6.8 million. *Unit head:* Dr. Robert T. Leonard, Head, 520-621-1945. *Application contact:* Dr. Rachel W. Pfister, Graduate Coordinator/Advisor, 520-621-8423, Fax: 520-621-7186, E-mail: pfister@ag.arizona.edu.

University of Arkansas, Graduate School, Dale Bumpers College of Agricultural, Food and Life Sciences, Interdepartmental Program in Plant Science, Fayetteville, AR 72701-1201. Offers PhD. *Students:* 1 (woman) full-time, 13 part-time (4 women), 7 international. In 2009, 1 doctorate awarded. *Degree requirements:* For doctorate, thesis/dissertation. Application fee: $40 ($50 for international students). *Expenses:* Tuition, state resident: full-time $7355; part-time $356.58 per hour. Tuition, nonresident: full-time $17,401; part-time $775.17 per hour. Required fees: $1203. *Financial support:* In 2009–10, 9 research assistantships were awarded; fellowships with tuition reimbursements, teaching assistantships, career-related internships or fieldwork and Federal Work-Study also available. Support available to part-time students. Financial award application deadline: 4/1; financial award applicants required to submit FAFSA. *Unit head:* Dr. A. Rick Bennett, Department Head, 479-575-2445, E-mail: rbennett@uark.edu. *Application contact:* Dr. Craig S. Rothrock, Graduate Coordinator, 479-575-6687, E-mail: rothrock@uark.edu.

The University of British Columbia, Faculty of Land and Food Systems, Plant Science Program, Vancouver, BC V6T 1Z1, Canada. Offers M Sc, PhD. Part-time programs available. *Degree requirements:* For master's, thesis; for doctorate, comprehensive exam, thesis/dissertation. *Entrance requirements:* Additional exam requirements/recommendations for international students: Required—TOEFL (minimum score 577 paper-based; 233 computer-based; 90 iBT), IELTS (minimum score 6.5). Electronic applications accepted. *Faculty research:* Plant physiology and biochemistry, biotechnology, plant protection (insect, weeds, and diseases), plant breeding, plant-environment interaction.

University of California, Riverside, Graduate Division, Department of Botany and Plant Sciences, Riverside, CA 92521-0102. Offers plant biology (MS, PhD), including plant genetics (PhD). Part-time programs available. *Faculty:* 40 full-time (13 women). *Students:* 52 full-time (34 women); includes 7 minority (1 African American, 4 Asian Americans or Pacific Islanders, 2 Hispanic Americans), 22 international. Average age 29. In 2009, 3 master's, 3 doctorates awarded. Terminal master's awarded for partial completion of doctoral program. *Degree requirements:* For master's, comprehensive exams or thesis; for doctorate, thesis/dissertation, qualifying exams. *Entrance requirements:* For master's and doctorate, GRE General Test,

Plant Sciences

University of California, Riverside (continued)
minimum GPA of 3.2. Additional exam requirements/recommendations for international students: Required—TOEFL (minimum score 550 paper-based; 213 computer-based; 80 iBT). *Application deadline:* For fall admission, 5/1 for domestic students, 2/1 for international students; for winter admission, 2/1 for domestic students, 7/1 for international students; for spring admission, 12/1 for domestic students, 10/1 for international students. Applications are processed on a rolling basis. Application fee: $80 ($100 for international students). Electronic applications accepted. *Financial support:* In 2009–10, fellowships with tuition reimbursements (averaging $12,000 per year), research assistantships with tuition reimbursements (averaging $23,000 per year), teaching assistantships with tuition reimbursements (averaging $16,500 per year) were awarded; career-related internships or fieldwork, Federal Work-Study, institutionally sponsored loans, scholarships/grants, and tuition waivers (full and partial) also available. Financial award application deadline: 2/1; financial award applicants required to submit FAFSA. *Faculty research:* Agricultural plant biology; biochemistry and physiology; cellular, molecular and developmental biology; ecology, evolution, systematics and ethnobotany; genetics, genomics and bioinformatics. *Unit head:* Dr. Jodie S. Holt, Chair, 951-827-3801. *Application contact:* Deidra Kornfeld, Graduate Program Assistant, 800-735-0717, Fax: 951-827-5517, E-mail: deidra.kornfeld@ucr.edu.

University of Connecticut, Graduate School, College of Agriculture and Natural Resources, Department of Plant Science, Storrs, CT 06269. Offers plant and soil sciences (MS, PhD). *Faculty:* 18 full-time (5 women). *Students:* 23 full-time (7 women), 2 part-time (0 women); includes 4 minority (2 African Americans, 1 Asian American or Pacific Islander, 1 Hispanic American), 10 international. Average age 33. 20 applicants, 20% accepted, 3 enrolled. In 2009, 2 master's, 3 doctorates awarded. Terminal master's awarded for partial completion of doctoral program. *Degree requirements:* For master's, comprehensive exam; for doctorate, thesis/dissertation. *Entrance requirements:* For master's and doctorate, GRE General Test, GRE Subject Test. Additional exam requirements/recommendations for international students: Required—TOEFL (minimum score 550 paper-based; 213 computer-based). *Application deadline:* For fall admission, 2/1 priority date for domestic and international students; for spring admission, 11/1 for domestic students, 10/1 for international students. Applications are processed on a rolling basis. Application fee: $55. Electronic applications accepted. *Expenses:* Tuition, state resident: full-time $4725; part-time $525 per credit. Tuition, nonresident: full-time $12,267; part-time $1363 per credit. Required fees: $346 per semester. Tuition and fees vary according to course load. *Financial support:* In 2009–10, 18 research assistantships with full tuition reimbursements, 4 teaching assistantships with full tuition reimbursements were awarded; fellowships, Federal Work-Study, scholarships/grants, health care benefits, and unspecified assistantships also available. Financial award application deadline: 2/1; financial award applicants required to submit FAFSA. *Unit head:* Mary Musgrave, Head, 860-486-2925, Fax: 860-486-0682, E-mail: mary.musgrave@uconn.edu. *Application contact:* George C. Elliott, Chairperson, 860-486-1938, Fax: 860-486-0682, E-mail: george.elliott@uconn.edu.

University of Delaware, College of Agriculture and Natural Resources, Department of Plant and Soil Sciences, Newark, DE 19716. Offers MS, PhD. Part-time programs available. Terminal master's awarded for partial completion of doctoral program. *Degree requirements:* For master's, thesis; for doctorate, thesis/dissertation. *Entrance requirements:* For master's and doctorate, GRE General Test. Additional exam requirements/recommendations for international students: Required—TOEFL (minimum score 550 paper-based; 213 computer-based). Electronic applications accepted. *Faculty research:* Soil chemistry, plant and cell tissue culture, plant breeding and genetics, soil physics, soil biochemistry, plant molecular biology, soil microbiology.

University of Florida, Graduate School, College of Agricultural and Life Sciences, Program in Plant Medicine, Gainesville, FL 32611. Offers DPM.

University of Hawaii at Manoa, Graduate Division, College of Tropical Agriculture and Human Resources, Department of Plant and Environmental Protection Sciences, Honolulu, HI 96822. Offers entomology (MS, PhD); tropical plant pathology (MS, PhD). Part-time programs available. Terminal master's awarded for partial completion of doctoral program. *Degree requirements:* For master's, thesis optional; for doctorate, comprehensive exam, thesis/dissertation. *Entrance requirements:* For master's and doctorate, GRE General Test. Additional exam requirements/recommendations for international students: Required—TOEFL (minimum score 500 paper-based; 173 computer-based; 61 iBT), IELTS (minimum score 5). *Expenses:* Tuition, state resident: full-time $8900; part-time $372 per credit. Tuition, nonresident: full-time $21,400; part-time $898 per credit. Required fees: $207 per semester. *Faculty research:* Nematology, virology, mycology, bacteriology, epidemiology.

University of Idaho, College of Graduate Studies, College of Agricultural and Life Sciences, Department of Plant, Soil, and Entomological Sciences, Program in Plant Science, Moscow, ID 83844-2282. Offers MS, PhD. *Students:* 16 full-time, 6 part-time. In 2009, 6 master's, 1 doctorate awarded. *Degree requirements:* For doctorate, thesis/dissertation. *Entrance requirements:* For master's and doctorate, GRE General Test, minimum GPA of 3.0. *Application deadline:* For fall admission, 8/1 for domestic students; for spring admission, 12/15 for domestic students. Application fee: $55 ($60 for international students). *Expenses:* Tuition, state resident: full-time $6120. Tuition, nonresident: full-time $17,712. *Financial support:* Application deadline: 2/15. *Faculty research:* Controlling root diseases in wheat and barley, sustainable agriculture, horticulture and urban landscape management, reduced herbicide rates control weeds in grain, wheat breeding program. *Unit head:* Jeffrey Stark, Chair, 208-885-8376. *Application contact:* Jeffrey Stark, Chair, 208-885-8376.

University of Kentucky, Graduate School, College of Agriculture, Program in Plant and Soil Science, Lexington, KY 40506-0032. Offers MS. *Degree requirements:* For master's, comprehensive exam, thesis optional. *Entrance requirements:* For master's, GRE General Test, minimum undergraduate GPA of 2.75, graduate 3.0. Additional exam requirements/recommendations for international students: Required—TOEFL (minimum score 550 paper-based; 213 computer-based). Electronic applications accepted.

University of Maine, Graduate School, College of Natural Sciences, Forestry, and Agriculture, Department of Biological Sciences, Orono, ME 04469. Offers biological sciences (PhD); botany and plant pathology (MS); ecology and environmental science (MS, PhD); entomology (MS); plant science (PhD); zoology (MS, PhD). Part-time programs available. *Faculty:* 20 full-time (7 women), 4 part-time/adjunct (2 women). *Students:* 40 full-time (31 women), 21 part-time (10 women), 5 international. Average age 30. 84 applicants, 17% accepted, 12 enrolled. In 2009, 8 master's, 7 doctorates awarded. *Degree requirements:* For doctorate, thesis/dissertation. *Entrance requirements:* For master's and doctorate, GRE General Test. Additional exam requirements/recommendations for international students: Required—TOEFL. *Application deadline:* For fall admission, 2/1 priority date for domestic students. Applications are processed on a rolling basis. Application fee: $65. Electronic applications accepted. *Financial support:* In 2009–10, 5 research assistantships with tuition reimbursements (averaging $17,995 per year), 19 teaching assistantships with tuition reimbursements (averaging $12,790 per year) were awarded; career-related internships or fieldwork, Federal Work-Study, institutionally sponsored loans, and tuition waivers (full and partial) also available. Financial award application deadline: 3/1. *Unit head:* Dr. Jody Jellison, Chair, 207-581-2551, Fax: 207-581-2537. *Application contact:* Scott G. Delcourt, Associate Dean of the Graduate School, 207-581-3291, Fax: 207-581-3232, E-mail: graduate@maine.edu.

University of Maine, Graduate School, College of Natural Sciences, Forestry, and Agriculture, Department of Plant, Soil, and Environmental Sciences, Orono, ME 04469. Offers biological sciences (PhD); ecology and environmental sciences (MS, PhD); forest resources (PhD); horticulture (MS); plant science (PhD); plant, soil, and environmental sciences (MS); resource utilization (MS). *Faculty:* 8 full-time (2 women), 9 part-time/adjunct (3 women). *Students:* 6 full-time (3 women), 3 part-time (2 women), 1 international. Average age 31. 6 applicants, 17% accepted, 0 enrolled. In 2009, 2 master's awarded. *Entrance requirements:* For master's and doctorate, GRE General Test. Additional exam requirements/recommendations for international students: Required—TOEFL. *Application deadline:* Applications are processed on a rolling basis. Application fee: $65. Electronic applications accepted. *Financial support:* In 2009–10, 16 research assistantships with tuition reimbursements (averaging $16,260 per year), 3 teaching assistantships with tuition reimbursements (averaging $12,790 per year) were awarded; scholarships/grants, tuition waivers (full and partial), and unspecified assistantships also available. *Unit head:* Dr. Gregory Porter, Chair, 207-581-2943, Fax: 207-581-3207. *Application contact:* Scott G. Delcourt, Associate Dean of the Graduate School, 207-581-3291, Fax: 207-581-3232, E-mail: graduate@maine.edu.

University of Manitoba, Faculty of Graduate Studies, Faculty of Agricultural and Food Sciences, Department of Plant Science, Winnipeg, MB R3T 2N2, Canada. Offers agronomy and plant protection (M Sc, PhD); horticulture (M Sc, PhD); plant breeding and genetics (M Sc, PhD); plant physiology-biochemistry (M Sc, PhD). *Degree requirements:* For master's, thesis; for doctorate, one foreign language, thesis/dissertation.

University of Massachusetts Amherst, Graduate School, College of Natural Sciences, Department of Plant, Soil and Insect Sciences, Program in Plant and Soil Sciences, Amherst, MA 01003. Offers plant and soil sciences (MS, PhD); soil science (MS). Postbaccalaureate distance learning degree programs offered (minimal on-campus study). *Faculty:* 28 full-time (7 women). *Students:* 16 full-time (8 women), 21 part-time (10 women); includes 2 minority (1 African American, 1 Asian American or Pacific Islander), 12 international. Average age 32. 20 applicants, 25% accepted, 4 enrolled. In 2009, 11 master's, 1 doctorate awarded. Terminal master's awarded for partial completion of doctoral program. *Degree requirements:* For master's, thesis optional; for doctorate, comprehensive exam, thesis/dissertation. *Entrance requirements:* For master's and doctorate, GRE General Test. Additional exam requirements/recommendations for international students: Required—TOEFL (minimum score 550 paper-based; 213 computer-based; 80 iBT), IELTS (minimum score 6.5). *Application deadline:* For fall admission, 1/2 for domestic and international students; for spring admission, 10/1 for domestic and international students. Applications are processed on a rolling basis. Application fee: $50 ($65 for international students). Electronic applications accepted. *Expenses:* Tuition, state resident: full-time $2640; part-time $110 per credit. Tuition, nonresident: full-time $9936; part-time $414 per credit. Tuition and fees vary according to course load. *Financial support:* Fellowships, research assistantships, teaching assistantships, career-related internships or fieldwork, Federal Work-Study, scholarships/grants, traineeships, health care benefits, tuition waivers (full), and unspecified assistantships available. Support available to part-time students. Financial award application deadline: 1/2. *Unit head:* Dr. Geunhwa Jung, Graduate Program Director, 413-545-1059, Fax: 413-545-2115. *Application contact:* Jean M. Ames, Supervisor of Admissions, 413-545-0722, Fax: 413-577-0010, E-mail: gradadm@grad.umass.edu.

University of Massachusetts Amherst, Graduate School, Interdisciplinary Programs, Program in Plant Biology, Amherst, MA 01003. Offers biochemistry and metabolism (MS, PhD); cell biology and physiology (MS, PhD); environmental, ecological and integrative (MS, PhD); genetics and evolution (MS, PhD). *Students:* 3 full-time (2 women), 12 part-time (5 women); includes 2 minority (both Asian Americans or Pacific Islanders), 8 international. Average age 27. 32 applicants, 41% accepted, 3 enrolled. In 2009, 3 master's, 1 doctorate awarded. *Degree requirements:* For master's, thesis; for doctorate, 2 foreign languages, comprehensive exam, thesis/dissertation. *Entrance requirements:* For master's and doctorate, GRE General Test. Additional exam requirements/recommendations for international students: Required—TOEFL (minimum score 550 paper-based; 213 computer-based; 80 iBT), IELTS (minimum score 6.5). *Application deadline:* For fall admission, 12/15 for domestic and international students; for spring admission, 10/1 for domestic and international students. Applications are processed on a rolling basis. Application fee: $50 ($65 for international students). Electronic applications accepted. *Expenses:* Tuition, state resident: full-time $2640; part-time $110 per credit. Tuition, nonresident: full-time $9936; part-time $414 per credit. Tuition and fees vary according to course load. *Financial support:* In 2009–10, 11 research assistantships with full tuition reimbursements (averaging $8,884 per year) were awarded; fellowships, teaching assistantships, career-related internships or fieldwork, Federal Work-Study, scholarships/grants, traineeships, health care benefits, tuition waivers (full), and unspecified assistantships also available. Support available to part-time students. Financial award application deadline: 12/15. *Unit head:* Dr. Elsbeth L. Walker, Graduate Program Director, 413-577-3217, Fax: 413-545-3243. *Application contact:* Jean M. Ames, Supervisor of Admissions, 413-545—0722, Fax: 413-577-0010, E-mail: gradadm@grad.umass.edu.

University of Minnesota, Twin Cities Campus, Graduate School, College of Food, Agricultural and Natural Resource Sciences, Program in Applied Plant Sciences, Minneapolis, MN 55455-0213. Offers MS, PhD. Part-time programs available. *Faculty:* 58 full-time (12 women). *Students:* 51 full-time (22 women), 6 part-time (2 women); includes 5 minority (1 African American, 4 Hispanic Americans), 9 international. Average age 24. 36 applicants, 33% accepted, 12 enrolled. In 2009, 8 master's, 8 doctorates awarded. *Degree requirements:* For master's, comprehensive exam, thesis; for doctorate, comprehensive exam, thesis/dissertation. *Entrance requirements:* For master's and doctorate, GRE General Test. Additional exam requirements/recommendations for international students: Required—TOEFL (minimum score 550 paper-based; 239 computer-based; 79 iBT). *Application deadline:* For fall admission, 12/1 priority date for domestic and international students; for spring admission, 10/15 priority date for domestic and international students. Applications are processed on a rolling basis. Application fee: $75 ($95 for international students). Electronic applications accepted. *Financial support:* In 2009–10, 38 students received support, including fellowships with full tuition reimbursements available (averaging $24,000 per year), research assistantships with full and partial tuition reimbursements available (averaging $21,000 per year); scholarships/grants, health care benefits, and unspecified assistantships also available. *Faculty research:* Weed science, horticulture, crop management, sustainable agriculture, biotechnology, plant breeding. *Unit head:* Dr. Jim Anderson, Director of Graduate Studies, 612-625-9763, Fax: 612-625-1268, E-mail: ander319@umn.edu. *Application contact:* Lynne Medgaarden, Assistant to the Director of Graduate Studies, 612-625-4742, Fax: 612-625-1268, E-mail: medga001@umn.edu.

University of Missouri, Graduate School, College of Agriculture, Food and Natural Resources, Division of Plant Sciences, Program in Plant Biology and Genetics, Columbia, MO 65211. Offers MS, PhD. Terminal master's awarded for partial completion of doctoral program. *Degree requirements:* For master's, thesis; for doctorate, thesis/dissertation. *Entrance requirements:* For master's and doctorate, GRE General Test, minimum GPA of 3.0. *Application deadline:* For fall admission, 3/1 priority date for domestic students. Applications are processed on a rolling basis. Application fee: $45 ($60 for international students). *Financial support:* Research assistantships, teaching assistantships, institutionally sponsored loans available. *Unit head:* Dr. Jeanne Mihail, Director of Graduate Studies, 573-882-0574, E-mail: mihailj@missouri.edu. *Application contact:* Dr. Jeanne Mihail, Director of Graduate Studies, 573-882-0574, E-mail: mihailj@missouri.edu.

University of Rhode Island, Graduate School, College of the Environment and Life Sciences, Department of Plant Sciences, Kingston, RI 02881. Offers entomology (MS, PhD); plant sciences (MS, PhD). Part-time programs available. *Faculty:* 9 full-time (2 women). *Students:* 1 full-time (0 women), all international. *Degree requirements:* For master's, comprehensive exam (for some programs), thesis optional; for doctorate, comprehensive exam, thesis/dissertation. *Entrance requirements:* For master's and doctorate, GRE, 2 letters of recommendation. Additional exam requirements/recommendations for international students: Required—TOEFL (minimum score 550 paper-based; 213 computer-based). *Application deadline:* For fall admission, 7/15 for domestic students, 2/1 for international students; for spring admission, 11/15 for domestic students, 7/15 for international students. Application fee: $65. Electronic applications accepted. *Expenses:* Tuition, state resident: full-time $8828; part-time $490 per credit hour. Tuition, nonresident: full-time $22,100; part-time $1228 per credit hour. Required fees: $1118; $57 per semester. Tuition and fees vary according to program. *Financial support:* In 2009–10, 2 research assistantships with full and partial tuition reimbursements (averaging $9,263 per year), 4 teaching assistantships with full and partial tuition reimbursements (averaging $11,389 per year) were awarded. Financial award application deadline: 7/15; financial award applicants required to submit FAFSA. *Faculty research:* Plant development and management; pest management; tick biology, ecology, and control; identification and replacement of invasive ornamentals. Total annual research expenditures: $1.3 million. *Unit head:* Dr. Brian K. Maynard, Interim Chair, 401-874-2928, Fax: 401-874-2494, E-mail: bmaynard@uri.edu. *Application contact:* Dr. Thomas Mather, Director of Graduate Studies, 401-874-5616, Fax: 401-874-2494, E-mail: tmather@uri.edu.

University of Saskatchewan, College of Graduate Studies and Research, College of Agriculture, Department of Plant Sciences, Saskatoon, SK S7N 5A2, Canada. Offers M Sc, PhD. *Faculty:* 35. *Students:* 44. In 2009, 6 master's, 5 doctorates awarded. *Degree requirements:* For master's, thesis; for doctorate, comprehensive exam (for some programs), thesis/dissertation. *Entrance requirements:* Additional exam requirements/recommendations for international students: Required—TOEFL (minimum score 80 iBT); Recommended—IELTS (minimum score 6.5). *Application deadline:* For fall admission, 7/1 priority date for domestic students. Applications are processed on a rolling basis. Application fee: $75. Tuition and fees charges are reported in Canadian dollars. *Expenses:* Tuition, area resident: Full-time $3000 Canadian dollars; part-time $500 Canadian dollars per term. Required fees: $700 Canadian dollars; $100 Canadian dollars per term. *Financial support:* Fellowships, research assistantships, teaching assistantships available. Financial award application deadline: 1/31. *Unit head:* Dr. Bruce Coulman, Head, 306-966-4951, Fax: 306-966-5015, E-mail: bruce.coulman@usask.ca. *Application contact:* Dr. Pierre Hucl, Graduate Chair, 306-966-4951, Fax: 306-966-5015, E-mail: pierre.hucl@usask.ca.

The University of Tennessee, Graduate School, College of Agricultural Sciences and Natural Resources, Department of Plant Sciences, Knoxville, TN 37996. Offers floriculture (MS); landscape design (MS); public horticulture (MS); turfgrass (MS); woody ornamentals (MS). Part-time programs available. *Degree requirements:* For master's, thesis or alternative. *Entrance requirements:* For master's, minimum GPA of 2.7. Additional exam requirements/recommendations for international students: Required—TOEFL. Electronic applications accepted. *Expenses:* Tuition, state resident: full-time $6826; part-time $380 per semester hour. Tuition, nonresident: full-time $21,844; part-time $1147 per semester hour. Tuition and fees vary according to program.

University of Vermont, Graduate College, College of Agriculture and Life Sciences, Department of Plant and Soil Science, Burlington, VT 05405. Offers MS, PhD. *Students:* 25 (14 women); includes 1 minority (Asian American or Pacific Islander), 4 international. 25 applicants, 68% accepted, 7 enrolled. In 2009, 3 master's, 3 doctorates awarded. *Degree requirements:* For master's, thesis; for doctorate, one foreign language, thesis/dissertation. *Entrance requirements:* For master's and doctorate, GRE General Test. Additional exam requirements/recommendations for international students: Required—TOEFL (minimum score 550 paper-based; 213 computer-based; 80 iBT). *Application deadline:* For fall admission, 3/1 priority date for domestic students. Applications are processed on a rolling basis. Application fee: $40. Electronic applications accepted. *Expenses:* Tuition, area resident: Part-time $508 per credit hour. Tuition, state resident: part-time $508 per credit hour. Tuition, nonresident: part-time $1281 per credit hour. *Financial support:* Fellowships, research assistantships, teaching assistantships available. Financial award application deadline: 3/1. *Faculty research:* Soil chemistry, plant nutrition. *Unit head:* Dr. Deborah Neher, Chairperson, 802-656-2630. *Application contact:* Dr. Josef Gorres, Coordinator, 802-656-2630.

The University of Western Ontario, Faculty of Graduate Studies, Biosciences Division, Department of Plant Sciences, London, ON N6A 5B8, Canada. Offers plant and environmental sciences (M Sc); plant sciences (M Sc, PhD); plant sciences and environmental sciences (PhD); plant sciences and molecular biology (M Sc, PhD). *Degree requirements:* For master's, thesis; for doctorate, thesis/dissertation. *Entrance requirements:* For doctorate, M Sc or equivalent. Additional exam requirements/recommendations for international students: Required—TOEFL. *Faculty research:* Ecology systematics, plant biochemistry and physiology, yeast genetics, molecular biology.

University of Wisconsin–Madison, Graduate School, College of Agricultural and Life Sciences, Department of Agronomy, Plant Breeding and Plant Genetics Program, Madison, WI 53706-1380. Offers MS, PhD. Part-time programs available. Terminal master's awarded for partial completion of doctoral program. *Degree requirements:* For master's, comprehensive exam, thesis (for some programs); for doctorate, comprehensive exam, thesis/dissertation. *Entrance requirements:* For master's and doctorate, GRE, minimum GPA of 3.0. Additional exam requirements/recommendations for international students: Required—TOEFL (minimum score 580 paper-based; 213 computer-based). Electronic applications accepted. *Expenses:* Tuition, state resident: part-time $594 per credit. Tuition, nonresident: part-time $1504 per credit. Required fees: $65 per credit. Tuition and fees vary according to course load, program and reciprocity agreements. *Faculty research:* Classical and molecular genetics.

Utah State University, School of Graduate Studies, College of Agriculture, Department of Plants, Soils, and Biometeorology, Logan, UT 84322. Offers biometeorology (MS, PhD); ecology (MS, PhD); plant science (MS, PhD); soil science (MS, PhD). Part-time programs available. Terminal master's awarded for partial completion of doctoral program. *Degree requirements:* For master's, thesis; for doctorate, thesis/dissertation. *Entrance requirements:* For master's, GRE General Test, BS in plant, soil, atmospheric science, or related field; minimum GPA of 3.0; for doctorate, GRE General Test, minimum GPA of 3.0. Additional exam requirements/recommendations for international students: Required—TOEFL. Electronic applications accepted. *Faculty research:* Biotechnology and genomics, plant physiology and biology, nutrient and water efficient landscapes, physical-chemical-biological processes in soil, environmental biophysics and climate.

Virginia State University, School of Graduate Studies, Research, and Outreach, School of Agriculture, Department of Agriculture and Human Ecology, Petersburg, VA 23806-0001. Offers plant science (MS).

West Texas A&M University, College of Agriculture, Nursing, and Natural Sciences, Division of Agriculture, Emphasis in Plant Science, Canyon, TX 79016-0001. Offers MS. Part-time programs available. *Degree requirements:* For master's, comprehensive exam, thesis optional. *Entrance requirements:* For master's, GRE General Test. Additional exam requirements/recommendations for international students: Required—TOEFL (minimum score 550 paper-based). Electronic applications accepted. *Faculty research:* Crop and soil disciplines.

West Virginia University, Davis College of Agriculture, Forestry and Consumer Sciences, Division of Plant and Soil Sciences, Program in Agricultural Sciences, Morgantown, WV 26506. Offers animal and food sciences (PhD); plant and soil sciences (PhD). *Degree requirements:* For doctorate, thesis/dissertation, oral and written exams. *Entrance requirements:* Additional exam requirements/recommendations for international students: Required—TOEFL. *Faculty research:* Ruminant nutrition, metabolism, forage utilization, physiology, reproduction.

Viticulture and Enology

California State University, Fresno, Division of Graduate Studies, College of Agricultural Sciences and Technology, Department of Viticulture and Enology, Fresno, CA 93740-8027. Offers MS. Part-time and evening/weekend programs available. *Degree requirements:* For master's, comprehensive exam (for some programs), thesis (for some programs). *Entrance requirements:* For master's, GRE General Test, minimum GPA of 2.5. Additional exam requirements/recommendations for international students: Required—TOEFL. Electronic applications accepted. *Faculty research:* Ethel carbonate formation, clinical an physiological characterization, grape and wine quality.

University of California, Davis, Graduate Studies, Graduate Group in Viticulture and Enology, Davis, CA 95616. Offers MS, PhD. *Degree requirements:* For master's, comprehensive exam (for some programs), thesis (for some programs). *Entrance requirements:* Additional exam requirements/recommendations for international students: Required—TOEFL (minimum score 550 paper-based; 213 computer-based).

ACADEMIC AND PROFESSIONAL PROGRAMS IN THE ENVIRONMENT AND NATURAL RESOURCES

Section 9
Environmental Sciences and Management

This section contains a directory of institutions offering graduate work in environmental sciences and management, followed by in-depth entries submitted by institutions that chose to prepare detailed program descriptions. Additional information about programs listed in the directory but not augmented by an in-depth entry may be obtained by writing directly to the dean of a graduate school or chair of a department at the address given in the directory.

For programs offering related work, see also in this book *Natural Resources.* In the other guides in this series:

Graduate Programs in the Humanities, Arts & Social Sciences
See *Political Science and International Affairs* and *Public, Regional, and Industrial Affairs*

Graduate Programs in the Biological Sciences
See *Ecology, Environmental Biology,* and *Evolutionary Biology*

Graduate Programs in Engineering & Applied Sciences
See *Management of Engineering and Technology*

CONTENTS

Program Directories

Close-Ups

See also:

Environmental Management and Policy

Adelphi University, Graduate School of Arts and Sciences, Program in Environmental Studies, Garden City, NY 11530-0701. Offers MS. *Students:* 9 full-time (7 women), 13 part-time (7 women); includes 4 minority (3 African Americans, 1 Hispanic American), 1 international. Average age 27. In 2009, 4 master's awarded. *Degree requirements:* For master's, thesis optional. *Entrance requirements:* For master's, GRE General Test, 2 letters of recommendation; course work in microeconomics, political science, statistics/calculus, and either chemistry or physics; computer literacy. Additional exam requirements/recommendations for international students: Required—TOEFL (minimum score 550 paper-based; 213 computer-based; 80 iBT). *Application deadline:* For fall admission, 5/1 for international students; for spring admission, 11/1 for international students. Applications are processed on a rolling basis. Application fee: $50. Electronic applications accepted. *Expenses:* Tuition: Full-time $28,340; part-time $830 per credit. Required fees: $600; $250 per credit. Full-time tuition and fees vary according to course load and program. *Financial support:* Research assistantships with full and partial tuition reimbursements, teaching assistantships, career-related internships or fieldwork, Federal Work-Study, institutionally sponsored loans, and unspecified assistantships available. Financial award application deadline: 2/15; financial award applicants required to submit FAFSA. *Faculty research:* Contaminates sites, workplace exposure level of contaminants, climate change and human health. *Unit head:* Dr. Anagnostis Agelarakis, Director, 516-877-4112, E-mail: agelarak@adelphi.edu. *Application contact:* Christine Murphy, Director of Admissions, 516-877-3050, Fax: 516-877-3039, E-mail: graduateadmissions@adelphi.edu.

Air Force Institute of Technology, Graduate School of Engineering and Management, Department of Systems and Engineering Management, Dayton, OH 45433-7765. Offers cost analysis (MS); environmental and engineering management (MS); environmental engineering science (MS); information resource/systems management (MS). *Accreditation:* ABET. Part-time programs available. *Degree requirements:* For master's, thesis. *Entrance requirements:* For master's, GRE, GMAT, minimum GPA of 3.0.

American Public University System, AMU/APU Graduate Programs, Charles Town, WV 25414. Offers air warfare (MA Military Studies); American Revolution (MA Military Studies); business administration (MBA); Civil War (MA Military Studies); criminal justice (MA); defense management (MA Military Studies); emergency and disaster management (MA); environmental policy and management (MS); fire science management (MA); global engagement (MA); history (MA); homeland security (MA); humanities (MA); intelligence (MA Military Studies, MA Strategic Intelligence); international peace and conflict resolution (MA); international relations and conflict resolution (MA); joint warfare (MA Military Studies); land warfare international perspective (MA Military Studies); management (MA); military history (MA); military leadership (MA Military Studies); national security studies (MA); naval warfare international (MA Military Studies); naval warfare US (MA Military Studies); political science (MA); public administration (MA); public health (MA); security management (MA); space studies (MS); special ops/LIC (MA Military Studies); sports management (MA); transportation and logistics management (MA); transportation management (MA); unconventional warfare (MA Military Studies); World War II (MA Military Studies). Programs offered via distance learning only. Part-time and evening/weekend programs available. Postbaccalaureate distance learning degree programs offered (no on-campus study). *Degree requirements:* For master's, comprehensive exam. *Entrance requirements:* For master's, bachelor's degree or equivalent, minimum GPA of 2.7 in last 60 hours of course work. Electronic applications accepted. *Faculty research:* Military history, criminal justice, management performance, national security.

American University, College of Arts and Sciences, Department of Environmental Science, Washington, DC 20016-8001. Offers environmental assessment (Graduate Certificate); environmental science (MS). *Faculty:* 3 full-time (0 women). *Students:* 9 full-time (6 women), 3 part-time (all women), 1 international. Average age 30. 20 applicants, 70% accepted, 6 enrolled. In 2009, 6 master's awarded. *Degree requirements:* For master's, comprehensive exam, thesis (for some programs). *Entrance requirements:* For master's, GRE General Test, GRE Subject Test, minimum GPA of 3.0. Additional exam requirements/recommendations for international students: Required—TOEFL. *Application deadline:* For fall admission, 2/1 for domestic students; for spring admission, 10/1 for domestic students. Application fee: $80. *Expenses:* Tuition: Full-time $22,266; part-time $1237 per credit hour. Required fees: $430. Tuition and fees vary according to program. *Financial support:* Research assistantships, teaching assistantships available. Financial award application deadline: 2/1. *Unit head:* Dr. Kiho Kim, Chair, 202-885-2182, E-mail: kiho@american.edu. *Application contact:* Kathleen Clowery, Director, Graduate Admissions, 202-885-3621, Fax: 202-885-1505.

American University, School of International Service, Washington, DC 20016-8071. Offers comparative and regional studies (Certificate); cross-cultural communication (Certificate); development management (MS); ethics, peace, and global affairs (MA); European studies (Certificate); global environmental policy (MA, Certificate); international affairs (MA), including comparative and regional studies, environmental policy, international economic policy, international politics, natural resources and sustainable development, U.S. foreign policy; international communication (MA, Certificate); international development (MA, Certificate); international development management (Certificate); international economic policy (Certificate); international economic relations (Certificate); international media (MA); international peace and conflict resolution (MA, Certificate); international relations (PhD); international service (MIS); peace building (Certificate); the Americas (Certificate); United States foreign policy (Certificate); JD/MA. Part-time and evening/weekend programs available. *Faculty:* 98 full-time (42 women), 48 part-time/adjunct (13 women). *Students:* 565 full-time (349 women), 329 part-time (189 women); includes 128 minority (44 African Americans, 2 American Indian/Alaska Native, 37 Asian Americans or Pacific Islanders, 45 Hispanic Americans), 102 international. Average age 27. 2,034 applicants, 63% accepted, 344 enrolled. In 2009, 326 master's, 6 doctorates, 9 other advanced degrees awarded. Terminal master's awarded for partial completion of doctoral program. *Degree requirements:* For master's, one foreign language, comprehensive exam, thesis or alternative; for doctorate, one foreign language, comprehensive exam, thesis/dissertation, research practicum; for Certificate, minimum 15 credit hours related course work. *Entrance requirements:* For master's, GRE, 24 credits of course work in related social sciences, minimum GPA of 3.5, 2 letters of recommendation, bachelor's degree, resume; for doctorate, GRE, 2 letters of recommendation, 24 credits in related social sciences; for Certificate, bachelor's degree. Additional exam requirements/recommendations for international students: Required—TOEFL (minimum score 600 paper-based; 250 computer-based; 100 iBT). *Application deadline:* For fall admission, 1/15 priority date for domestic students; for spring admission, 10/1 priority date for domestic students. Applications are processed on a rolling basis. Application fee: $50. *Expenses:* Tuition: Full-time $22,266; part-time $1237 per credit hour. Required fees: $430. Tuition and fees vary according to program. *Financial support:* Career-related internships or fieldwork, Federal Work-Study, and institutionally sponsored loans available. Financial award application deadline: 1/15. *Faculty research:* International intellectual property, international environmental issues, international law and legal order, international telecommunications/technology, international sustainable development. *Unit head:* Dr. Louis W. Goodman, Dean, 202-885-1600, Fax: 202-885-2494. *Application contact:* Yasmin Quianzon, Director of Graduate Admissions and Financial Aid, 202-885-2496, Fax: 202-885-1109.

American University of Beirut, Graduate Programs, Faculty of Arts and Sciences, Beirut, Lebanon. Offers anthropology (MA); Arabic language and literature (MA); archaeology (MA); biology (MS); chemistry (MS); computer science (MS); economics (MA); education (MA); English language (MA); English literature (MA); environmental policy planning (MSES); financial economics (MAFE); geology (MS); history (MA); mathematics (MA, MS); Middle Eastern studies (MA); philosophy (MA); physics (MS); political studies (MA); psychology (MA); public administration (MA); sociology (MA); statistics (MA, MS). Part-time programs available. *Degree requirements:* For master's, one foreign language, comprehensive exam, thesis (for some programs). *Entrance requirements:* For master's, GRE, letter of recommendation. Additional exam requirements/recommendations for international students: Required—TOEFL (minimum score 600 paper-based; 250 computer-based; 100 iBT), IELTS (minimum score 7.5). *Faculty research:* String theory and supergravity; computer graphics; algebra and number theory; popular Arabic literature; marine and freshwater biology; integrating science, math and technology.

Antioch University New England, Graduate School, Department of Environmental Studies, Doctoral Program in Environmental Studies, Keene, NH 03431-3552. Offers PhD. *Degree requirements:* For doctorate, thesis/dissertation, practicum. *Entrance requirements:* For doctorate, master's degree and previous experience in the environmental field. Additional exam requirements/recommendations for international students: Required—TOEFL (minimum score 600 paper-based; 250 computer-based). Electronic applications accepted. *Expenses:* Contact institution. *Faculty research:* Environmental history, green politics, ecopsychology.

Antioch University New England, Graduate School, Department of Environmental Studies, Individualized Program, Keene, NH 03431-3552. Offers MS. *Degree requirements:* For master's, practicum, seminar, thesis or project. *Entrance requirements:* For master's, detailed proposal.

Antioch University New England, Graduate School, Department of Environmental Studies, Program in Environmental Advocacy and Organizing, Keene, NH 03431-3552. Offers MS. *Degree requirements:* For master's, practicum, seminar. *Entrance requirements:* For master's, samples of written work, portfolio, letters of recommendation, interview.

Antioch University New England, Graduate School, Department of Environmental Studies, Program in Resource Management and Conservation, Keene, NH 03431-3552. Offers MS. *Degree requirements:* For master's, thesis optional, practicum. *Entrance requirements:* For master's, previous undergraduate course work in science and math. Additional exam requirements/recommendations for international students: Required—TOEFL (minimum score 600 paper-based; 250 computer-based). Electronic applications accepted. *Expenses:* Contact institution. *Faculty research:* Waste management, land use.

Antioch University New England, Graduate School, Department of Organization and Management, Program in Organizational and Environmental Sustainability (Green MBA), Keene, NH 03431-3552. Offers MBA. Part-time programs available. *Entrance requirements:* For master's, GRE, resume, 3 letters of recommendation. Additional exam requirements/recommendations for international students: Required—TOEFL (minimum score 600 paper-based; 250 computer-based).

Antioch University Seattle, Graduate Programs, Center for Creative Change, Seattle, WA 98121-1814. Offers environment and community (MA); management (MS); organizational psychology (MA); strategic communications (MA); whole system design (MA). Evening/weekend programs available. Electronic applications accepted. *Expenses:* Contact institution.

Appalachian State University, Cratis D. Williams Graduate School, Department of Government and Justice Studies, Boone, NC 28608. Offers criminal justice (MS); political science (MA), including American government, environmental politics and policy analysis, international relations; public administration (MPA), including public management, town, city and county management. Part-time programs available. Postbaccalaureate distance learning degree programs offered (no on-campus study). *Faculty:* 27 full-time (5 women), 12 part-time/adjunct (1 woman). *Students:* 65 full-time (26 women), 62 part-time (22 women); includes 6 minority (5 African Americans, 1 American Indian/Alaska Native), 1 international. 100 applicants, 93% accepted, 53 enrolled. In 2009, 45 master's awarded. *Degree requirements:* For master's, variable foreign language requirement, comprehensive exam, thesis optional. *Entrance requirements:* For master's, GRE General Test, 3 letters of recommendation. Additional exam requirements/recommendations for international students: Required—TOEFL (minimum score 570 paper-based; 230 computer-based; 79 iBT), IELTS (minimum score 6.5). *Application deadline:* For fall admission, 7/1 for domestic students, 2/1 for international students; for spring admission, 11/1 for domestic students, 7/1 for international students. Applications are processed on a rolling basis. Application fee: $50. Electronic applications accepted. *Expenses:* Tuition, state resident: full-time $2960. Tuition, nonresident: full-time $14,051. Required fees: $2320. *Financial support:* In 2009–10, 20 research assistantships (averaging $8,000 per year) were awarded; fellowships, teaching assistantships, career-related internships or fieldwork, Federal Work-Study, scholarships/grants, and unspecified assistantships also available. Financial award application deadline: 4/1; financial award applicants required to submit FAFSA. *Faculty research:* Campaign finance, emerging democracies, bureaucratic politics, judicial behavior, administration of justice. Total annual research expenditures: $320,000. *Unit head:* Dr. Brian Ellison, Chairperson, 828-262-3085, E-mail: ellisonba@appstate.edu. *Application contact:* Sandy Krause, Director of Admissions and Recruiting, 828-262-2130, Fax: 828-262-2709, E-mail: krausesl@appstate.edu.

Arizona State University, Graduate College, W.P. Carey School of Business, Morrison School of Management and Agribusiness, Tempe, AZ 85287. Offers agribusiness (MS). Part-time and evening/weekend programs available. *Degree requirements:* For master's, thesis, oral defense. *Entrance requirements:* For master's, GMAT, GRE General Test, MAT, minimum GPA of 3.0, 3 letters of recommendation, resume. Additional exam requirements/recommendations for international students: Required—TOEFL (minimum score 550 paper-based; 213 computer-based); Recommended—TWE. Electronic applications accepted. *Faculty research:* Agribusiness marketing, management and financial structuring.

Bard College, Bard Center for Environmental Policy, Annandale-on-Hudson, NY 12504. Offers MS, Professional Certificate, MS/JD, MS/MA. *Degree requirements:* For master's, thesis, 4-month, full-time internship. *Entrance requirements:* For master's, GRE, course work in statistics, chemistry and 1 other semester of college science; curriculum vitae; 3 letters of recommendation; sample of written work. Additional exam requirements/recommendations for international students: Required—TOEFL (minimum score 600 paper-based; 250 computer-based; 100 iBT). Electronic applications accepted. *Expenses:* Contact institution. *Faculty research:* Climate and agriculture, alternative energy, environmental economics, environmental toxicology, EPA law, sustainable development, international relations, literature and composition.

Baylor University, Graduate School, College of Arts and Sciences, Department of Environmental Studies, Waco, TX 76798. Offers MES, MS. *Students:* 9 full-time (5 women), 2 part-time (0 women); includes 3 minority (1 African American, 1 American Indian/Alaska Native, 1 Hispanic American), 2 international. In 2009, 7 master's awarded. *Degree requirements:* For master's, thesis. *Entrance requirements:* For master's, GRE General Test. *Application deadline:* For fall admission, 8/1 priority date for domestic students; for spring admission, 1/1 for domestic students. Applications are processed on a rolling basis. Application fee: $25. *Financial support:* Research assistantships, teaching assistantships, career-related internships or fieldwork, Federal Work-Study, and institutionally sponsored loans available. *Faculty research:* Renewable energy/waste management policies, Third World environmental problem solving, ecotourism. *Unit head:* Dr. Joe Yelderman, Graduate Program Director, 254-710-1385, Fax: 254-710-3409, E-mail: joe_yelderman@baylor.edu. *Application contact:* Glenda Plemons, Administrative Assistant, 254-710-3405, Fax: 254-710-3870, E-mail: glenda_plemons@baylor.edu.

Baylor University, Graduate School, College of Arts and Sciences, Program in Air Science and Environment, Waco, TX 76798. Offers IMES. *Application contact:* Suzanne Keener, Administrative Assistant, 254-710-3588, Fax: 254-710-3870.

Bemidji State University, School of Graduate Studies, College of Social and Natural Sciences, Center for Environmental Studies, Bemidji, MN 56601-2699. Offers MS. Part-time programs available. *Degree requirements:* For master's, thesis or alternative. *Entrance requirements:* For master's, GRE General Test. Additional exam requirements/recommendations for international students: Required—TOEFL. Electronic applications accepted. *Faculty research:* Biofuels, waste systems, environmental changes.

Boise State University, Graduate College, College of Social Sciences and Public Affairs, Department of Public Policy and Administration, Boise, ID 83725-0399. Offers environmental and natural resources policy and administration (MPA); general public administration (MPA); state and local government policy and administration (MPA). *Accreditation:* NASPAA. Part-time programs available. *Degree requirements:* For master's, comprehensive exam, directed research project, internship. *Entrance requirements:* For master's, GRE General Test, minimum GPA of 3.0. Additional exam requirements/recommendations for international students: Required—TOEFL. Electronic applications accepted. *Expenses:* Tuition, state resident: full-time $3106; part-time $209 per credit. Tuition, nonresident: part-time $284 per credit.

Boston University, Graduate School of Arts and Sciences, Department of Geography and Environment, Boston, MA 02215. Offers energy and environmental analysis (MA); environmental remote sensing and GIs (MA); geography (MA); geography and environment (PhD); international relations and environmental policy (MA). *Students:* 50 full-time (22 women), 15 part-time (6 women); includes 2 minority (1 Asian American or Pacific Islander, 1 Hispanic American), 19 international. Average age 30. 64 applicants, 23% accepted, 5 enrolled. In 2009, 4 master's, 6 doctorates awarded. Terminal master's awarded for partial completion of doctoral program. *Degree requirements:* For master's, one foreign language, comprehensive exam, thesis; for doctorate, one foreign language, comprehensive exam, thesis/dissertation. *Entrance requirements:* For master's and doctorate, GRE General Test, GRE Subject Test, 3 letters of recommendation. Additional exam requirements/recommendations for international students: Required—TOEFL (minimum score 600 paper-based; 250 computer-based). *Application deadline:* For fall admission, 7/1 for domestic and international students; for spring admission, 11/15 for domestic and international students. Application fee: $70. Electronic applications accepted. *Expenses:* Tuition: Full-time $37,910; part-time $1184 per credit hour. Required fees: $386; $40 per semester. Part-time tuition and fees vary according to class time, course level, degree level and program. *Financial support:* In 2009–10, 33 students received support, including 2 fellowships with full tuition reimbursements available (averaging $18,900 per year), 20 research assistantships with full tuition reimbursements available (averaging $18,400 per year), 11 teaching assistantships with full tuition reimbursements available (averaging $18,400 per year); Federal Work-Study and unspecified assistantships also available. Support available to part-time students. Financial award application deadline: 1/15; financial award applicants required to submit FAFSA. Total annual research expenditures: $1.2 million. *Unit head:* Robert Kaufmann, Chairman, 617-353-3940, Fax: 617-353-8399, E-mail: kaufmann@bu.edu. *Application contact:* Christopher DeVits, Graduate Program Coordinator, 617-353-7554, Fax: 617-353-8399, E-mail: cdevits@bu.edu.

Boston University, Graduate School of Arts and Sciences, Department of International Relations, Boston, MA 02215. Offers African studies (Certificate); international relations (MA); international relations and environmental policy management (MA); international relations and international communication (MA); JD/MA; MBA/MA. *Students:* 66 full-time (41 women), 16 part-time (10 women); includes 7 minority (3 African Americans, 3 Asian Americans or Pacific Islanders, 1 Hispanic American), 16 international. Average age 27. 417 applicants, 59% accepted, 50 enrolled. In 2009, 43 master's awarded. *Degree requirements:* For master's, one foreign language, comprehensive exam, thesis. *Entrance requirements:* For master's, GRE General Test, 3 letters of recommendation; for Certificate, GRE General Test. Additional exam requirements/recommendations for international students: Required—TOEFL (minimum score 600 paper-based; 250 computer-based). *Application deadline:* For fall admission, 4/15 for domestic and international students; for spring admission, 10/15 for domestic and international students. Application fee: $70. Electronic applications accepted. *Expenses:* Tuition: Full-time $37,910; part-time $1184 per credit hour. Required fees: $386; $40 per semester. Part-time tuition and fees vary according to class time, course level, degree level and program. *Financial support:* In 2009–10, 17 students received support. Federal Work-Study, scholarships/grants, and unspecified assistantships available. Support available to part-time students. Financial award application deadline: 1/15; financial award applicants required to submit FAFSA. *Unit head:* Dr. Erik Goldstein, Chairman, 617-353-9280, Fax: 617-353-9290, E-mail: goldstee@bu.edu. *Application contact:* Michael Williams, Graduate Program Administrator, 617-353-9349, Fax: 617-353-9290; E-mail: mawillia@bu.edu.

Brown University, Graduate School, Center for Environmental Studies, Providence, RI 02912. Offers AM. Part-time programs available. *Degree requirements:* For master's, thesis. *Entrance requirements:* For master's, GRE, writing sample. Additional exam requirements/recommendations for international students: Required—TOEFL. Electronic applications accepted. *Faculty research:* Solid waste management, risk management policy (environmental health), resource management policy (water/fisheries), climate change, environmental justice, sustainable design, marine ecosystems.

California State University, Fullerton, Graduate Studies, College of Humanities and Social Sciences, Program in Environmental Studies, Fullerton, CA 92834-9480. Offers environmental sciences (MS). Part-time programs available. *Students:* 28 full-time (15 women), 45 part-time (26 women); includes 18 minority (2 African Americans, 7 Asian Americans or Pacific Islanders, 9 Hispanic Americans), 3 international. Average age 29. 76 applicants, 34% accepted, 17 enrolled. In 2009, 19 master's awarded. *Degree requirements:* For master's, thesis. *Entrance requirements:* For master's, minimum GPA of 2.5 in last 60 units of course work. Application fee: $55. *Expenses:* Tuition, nonresident: full-time $11,160; part-time $373 per credit. Required fees: $1440 per term. Tuition and fees vary according to course load, degree level and program. *Financial support:* Career-related internships or fieldwork, Federal Work-Study, institutionally sponsored loans, and scholarships/grants available. Support available to part-time students. Financial award application deadline: 3/1; financial award applicants required to submit FAFSA. *Unit head:* Dr. John Bock, Coordinator, 657-278-4373. *Application contact:* Admissions/Applications, 657-278-2371.

The Catholic University of America, School of Engineering, Department of Civil Engineering, Washington, DC 20064. Offers environmental engineering (MCE, MSE, D Engr, PhD, Certificate); environmental engineering and management (MCE, MSE, PhD, Certificate); environmental engineering and management (D Engr); fluid and solid mechanics (MCE, MSE, PhD, Certificate); geotechnical engineering (MCE, MSE, PhD, Certificate); management of construction (MCE, MSE, D Engr, PhD); structural engineering (MSE, D Engr, PhD); systems engineering (MSE, D Engr, PhD, Certificate). Part-time programs available. *Faculty:* 5 full-time (0 women), 7 part-time/adjunct (1 woman). *Students:* 7 full-time (3 women), 18 part-time (5 women); includes 6 minority (3 African Americans, 3 Hispanic Americans), 11 international. Average age 32. 36 applicants, 47% accepted, 9 enrolled. In 2009, 8 master's, 2 doctorates awarded. *Degree requirements:* For master's, thesis optional; for doctorate, comprehensive exam, thesis/dissertation. *Entrance requirements:* For master's and doctorate, statement of purpose, official copies of academic transcripts, three letters of recommendation. Additional exam requirements/recommendations for international students: Required—TOEFL (minimum score 580 paper-based; 237 computer-based). *Application deadline:* For fall admission, 8/1 priority date for domestic students, 7/15 for international students; for spring admission, 12/1 priority date for domestic students, 10/15 for international students. Applications are processed on a rolling basis. Application fee: $55. Electronic applications accepted. *Expenses:* Contact institution. *Financial support:* Fellowships, research assistantships, teaching assistantships, Federal Work-Study, scholarships/grants, tuition waivers (full and partial), and unspecified assistantships available. Financial award application deadline: 2/1; financial award applicants required to submit FAFSA. *Faculty research:* Geotechnical engineering, solid mechanics, construction engineering and management, environmental engineering, structural engineering. Total annual research expenditures: $438,834. *Unit head:* Dr. Lu Sun, Chair, 202-319-5164, Fax: 202-319-6677, E-mail: sunl@cua.edu. *Application contact:* Julie Schwing, Director of Graduate Admissions, 202-319-5057, Fax: 202-319-6533, E-mail: cua-admissions@cua.edu.

Central European University, Graduate Studies, Department of Environmental Sciences and Policy, Budapest, Hungary. Offers MS, PhD. *Degree requirements:* For master's, one foreign language, thesis; for doctorate, one foreign language, comprehensive exam, thesis/dissertation. *Entrance requirements:* For master's and doctorate, interview. Additional exam requirements/recommendations for international students: Required—TOEFL (minimum score 570 paper-based; 230 computer-based). Electronic applications accepted. *Faculty research:* Management of ecological systems, environmental impact assessment, energy conservation, climate change policy, forest policy in countries in transition.

Clark University, Graduate School, Department of International Development, Community, and Environment, Program in Environmental Science and Policy, Worcester, MA 01610-1477. Offers MA, MA/MBA. Part-time programs available. *Faculty:* 3 full-time (2 women), 2 part-time/adjunct (0 women). *Students:* 37 full-time (22 women), 7 part-time (3 women); includes 1 minority (African American), 20 international. Average age 29. 73 applicants, 73% accepted, 21 enrolled. In 2009, 22 master's awarded. *Degree requirements:* For master's, thesis. *Entrance requirements:* For master's, 3 references, resume or curriculum vitae. Additional exam requirements/recommendations for international students: Required—TOEFL (minimum score 575 paper-based; 233 computer-based; 90 iBT) or IELTS (minimum score 6.5). *Application deadline:* For fall admission, 1/15 for domestic students. Application fee: $50. *Expenses:* Tuition: Full-time $34,900; part-time $4362.50 per course. *Financial support:* Fellowships, institutionally sponsored loans and scholarships/grants available. *Faculty research:* Environmental justice, health and risk assessment, media content analysis of energy technologies, uncertainty-risk analysis, inventory of major sources of greenhouse gas emissions. *Unit head:* Dr. William F. Fisher, Director, 508-421-3765, Fax: 508-793-8820, E-mail: wfisher@clarku.edu. *Application contact:* Paula Hall, Department of International Development, Community, and Environment Graduate Admissions Office, 508-793-7201, Fax: 508-793-8820, E-mail: idce@clarku.edu.

Clark University, Graduate School, Department of International Development, Community, and Environment, Program in Geographic Information Science for Development and Environment, Worcester, MA 01610-1477. Offers MA. *Faculty:* 2 full-time (1 woman). *Students:* 32 full-time (17 women); includes 2 minority (1 African American, 1 Asian American or Pacific Islander), 19 international. Average age 26. 50 applicants, 80% accepted, 23 enrolled. In 2009, 7 master's awarded. *Degree requirements:* For master's, thesis. *Entrance requirements:* For master's, 3 references, resume or curriculum vitae. Additional exam requirements/recommendations for international students: Required—TOEFL (minimum score 575 paper-based; 233 computer-based; 90 iBT) or IELTS (minimum score 6.5). *Application deadline:* For fall admission, 1/15 for domestic students. Application fee: $50. *Expenses:* Tuition: Full-time $34,900; part-time $4362.50 per course. *Financial support:* Fellowships, institutionally sponsored loans and scholarships/grants available. *Faculty research:* Land-use change, the effects of environmental influences on child health and development, quantitative methods, watershed management, brownfields redevelopment, human/environment interactions, biodiversity conservation, climate change. *Unit head:* Department of International Development, Community, and Environment, 508-793-7201, Fax: 508-793-8820. *Application contact:* Paula Hall, Department of International Development, Community, and Environment Graduate Admissions Office, 508-793-7205, E-mail: idce@clarku.edu.

Clemson University, Graduate School, College of Agriculture, Forestry and Life Sciences, Department of Entomology, Soils, and Plant Sciences, Program in Plant and Environmental Sciences, Clemson, SC 29634. Offers MS, PhD. *Students:* 34 full-time (14 women), 10 part-time (1 woman); includes 2 minority (both Hispanic Americans), 11 international. Average age 29. 35 applicants, 49% accepted, 14 enrolled. In 2009, 9 master's, 6 doctorates awarded. *Degree requirements:* For master's, thesis; for doctorate, thesis/dissertation. *Entrance requirements:* For master's, GRE General Test, bachelor's degree in biological science or chemistry; for doctorate, GRE General Test. Additional exam requirements/recommendations for international students: Required—TOEFL, IELTS. *Application deadline:* Applications are processed on a rolling basis. Application fee: $70 ($80 for international students). Electronic applications accepted. *Expenses:* Contact institution. *Financial support:* In 2009–10, 28 students received support, including 3 fellowships with full and partial tuition reimbursements available (averaging $11,033 per year), 21 research assistantships with partial tuition reimbursements available (averaging $16,366 per year), 7 teaching assistantships with partial tuition reimbursements available (averaging $14,566 per year); career-related internships or fieldwork, institutionally sponsored loans, scholarships/grants, health care benefits, and unspecified assistantships also available. Support available to part-time students. Financial award application deadline: 3/15; financial award applicants required to submit FAFSA. *Faculty research:* Systematics, aquatic botany, plant ecology, plant-fungus interactions, plant developmental genetics. *Unit head:* Dr. Patricia A. Zungoli, Chair, 864-656-3137, Fax: 864-656-5065, E-mail: pzngl@clemson.edu. *Application contact:* Dr. Halina Knap, Plant and Environmental Sciences Graduate Coordinator, 864-656-3102, Fax: 864-656-5065, E-mail: hskrpsk@clemson.edu.

Cleveland State University, College of Graduate Studies, Maxine Goodman Levin College of Urban Affairs, Program in Environmental Studies, Cleveland, OH 44115. Offers environmental studies (MAES); geographic information systems (Certificate); urban real estate development and finance (Certificate); JD/MAES. Part-time and evening/weekend programs available. *Degree requirements:* For master's, thesis or alternative, exit project. *Entrance requirements:* For master's, GRE General Test (minimum score: verbal and quantitative 40th percentile, analytical writing 4.0), minimum GPA of 3.0. Additional exam requirements/recommendations for international students: Required—TOEFL (minimum score 525 paper-based; 197 computer-based; 65 iBT). Electronic applications accepted. *Faculty research:* Environmental policy and administration, environmental planning, geographic information systems (GIS), nonprofit management.

College of the Atlantic, Program in Human Ecology, Bar Harbor, ME 04609-1198. Offers M Phil. *Degree requirements:* For master's, thesis. *Faculty research:* Conservation of endangered species, public policy/community planning, environmental education, history, philosophy.

Columbia University, Graduate School of Arts and Sciences, Program in Climate and Society, New York, NY 10027. Offers MA.

Columbia University, School of International and Public Affairs, Program in Environmental Science and Policy, New York, NY 10027. Offers MPA. Program admits applicants for late May/early June start only. *Faculty:* 8 full-time (3 women), 10 part-time/adjunct (6 women). *Students:* 67 full-time (45 women); includes 13 minority (1 African American, 11 Asian Americans or Pacific Islanders, 1 Hispanic American). Average age 27. 262 applicants, 49% accepted, 67 enrolled. In 2009, 58 master's awarded. *Degree requirements:* For master's, workshops. *Entrance requirements:* For master's, GRE (recommended), previous course work in biology and chemistry, or earth sciences (recommended); previous course work in economics strongly recommended. Additional exam requirements/recommendations for international students: Required—TOEFL. *Application deadline:* For fall admission, 11/1 priority date for domestic and international students; for winter admission, 1/14 priority date for domestic students, 1/15

Environmental Management and Policy

Columbia University (continued)
priority date for international students; for spring admission, 2/15 priority date for domestic and international students. Applications are processed on a rolling basis. Application fee: $85. Electronic applications accepted. *Financial support:* In 2009–10, 21 students received support, including 21 fellowships with partial tuition reimbursements available (averaging $11,667 per year); Federal Work-Study and scholarships/grants also available. Financial award application deadline: 1/15; financial award applicants required to submit FAFSA. *Faculty research:* Ecological management of enclosed ecosystems vegetation dynamics, environmental policy and management, energy policy, nuclear waste policy, environmental and natural resource economics and policy, carbon sequestration, urban planning, environmental risk assessment/toxicology, environmental justice. *Unit head:* Dr. Steven A. Cohen, Director, 212-854-3142, Fax: 212-864-4847, E-mail: sc32@columbia.edu. *Application contact:* Louise A. Rosen, Associate Director, 212-854-0643, Fax: 212-864-4847, E-mail: lar46@columbia.edu.

Concordia University, School of Graduate Studies, Faculty of Arts and Science, Department of Geography, Planning and Environment, Montréal, QC H3G 1M8, Canada. Offers environmental impact assessment (Diploma); geography, urban and environmental studies (M Sc).

Cornell University, Graduate School, Graduate Fields of Agriculture and Life Sciences, Field of Natural Resources, Ithaca, NY 14853-0001. Offers aquatic science (MPS, MS, PhD); environmental management (MPS); fishery science (MPS, MS, PhD); forest science (MPS, MS, PhD); resource policy and management (MPS, MS, PhD); wildlife science (MPS, MS, PhD). *Faculty:* 39 full-time (7 women). *Students:* 60 full-time (28 women); includes 4 minority (2 American Indian/Alaska Native, 1 Asian American or Pacific Islander, 1 Hispanic American), 13 international. Average age 31. 63 applicants, 32% accepted, 19 enrolled. In 2009, 6 master's, 7 doctorates awarded. *Degree requirements:* For master's, thesis (MS), project paper (MPS); for doctorate, comprehensive exam, thesis/dissertation. *Entrance requirements:* For master's and doctorate, GRE General Test, 2 letters of recommendation. Additional exam requirements/recommendations for international students: Required—TOEFL (minimum score 550 paper-based; 213 computer-based; 77 iBT). *Application deadline:* For spring admission, 10/30 for domestic students. Applications are processed on a rolling basis. Application fee: $70. Electronic applications accepted. *Expenses:* Tuition: Full-time $29,500. Required fees: $70. Full-time tuition and fees vary according to degree level, program and student level. *Financial support:* In 2009–10, 39 students received support, including 12 research assistantships with full tuition reimbursements available, 5 teaching assistantships with full tuition reimbursements available; fellowships with full tuition reimbursements available, institutionally sponsored loans, scholarships/grants, health care benefits, tuition waivers (full and partial), and unspecified assistantships also available. Financial award applicants required to submit FAFSA. *Faculty research:* Ecosystem-level dynamics, systems modeling, conservation biology/management, resource management's human dimensions, biogeochemistry. *Unit head:* Director of Graduate Studies, 607-255-2807, Fax: 607-255-0349. *Application contact:* Graduate Field Assistant, 607-255-2807, Fax: 607-255-0349, E-mail: nrgrad@cornell.edu.

Cornell University, Graduate School, Graduate Fields of Agriculture and Life Sciences, Field of Soil and Crop Sciences, Ithaca, NY 14853-0001. Offers agronomy (MS, PhD); environmental information science (MS, PhD); environmental management (MPS); field crop science (MS, PhD); soil science (MS, PhD). *Faculty:* 40 full-time (9 women). *Students:* 32 full-time (17 women); includes 5 minority (1 American Indian/Alaska Native, 4 Hispanic Americans), 9 international. Average age 33. 42 applicants, 24% accepted, 5 enrolled. In 2009, 2 master's, 8 doctorates awarded. *Degree requirements:* For master's, thesis (MS); for doctorate, comprehensive exam, thesis/dissertation. *Entrance requirements:* For master's and doctorate, GRE General Test, 2 letters of recommendation. Additional exam requirements/recommendations for international students: Required—TOEFL (minimum score 550 paper-based; 213 computer-based; 77 iBT). *Application deadline:* For fall admission, 2/1 priority date for domestic students. Applications are processed on a rolling basis. Application fee: $70. Electronic applications accepted. *Expenses:* Tuition: Full-time $29,500. Required fees: $70. Full-time tuition and fees vary according to degree level, program and student level. *Financial support:* In 2009–10, 26 students received support, including 1 fellowship with full tuition reimbursement available, 1 research assistantship with full tuition reimbursement available, 1 teaching assistantship with full tuition reimbursement available; institutionally sponsored loans, traineeships, health care benefits, tuition waivers (full and partial), and unspecified assistantships also available. *Faculty research:* Soil chemistry, physics and biology; crop physiology and management; environmental information science and modeling; international agriculture; weed science. *Unit head:* Director of Graduate Studies, 607-255-3267, Fax: 607-255-8615. *Application contact:* Graduate Field Assistant, 607-255-3267, Fax: 607-255-8615, E-mail: ljh4@cornell.edu.

Cornell University, Graduate School, Graduate Fields of Architecture, Art and Planning, Field of Regional Science, Ithaca, NY 14853-0001. Offers environmental studies (MA, MS, PhD); international spatial problems (MA, MS, PhD); location theory (MA, MS, PhD); multiregional economic analysis (MA, MS, PhD); peace science (MA, MS, PhD); planning methods (MA, MS, PhD); urban and regional economics (MA, MS, PhD). *Faculty:* 22 full-time (5 women). *Students:* 21 full-time (8 women); includes 2 minority (1 African American, 1 Asian American or Pacific Islander), 18 international. Average age 35. 15 applicants, 53% accepted, 4 enrolled. In 2009, 1 master's, 4 doctorates awarded. Terminal master's awarded for partial completion of doctoral program. *Degree requirements:* For master's, thesis; for doctorate, comprehensive exam, thesis/dissertation. *Entrance requirements:* For master's and doctorate, GRE General Test, 2 letters of recommendation. Additional exam requirements/recommendations for international students: Required—TOEFL (minimum score 600 paper-based; 250 computer-based; 77 iBT). *Application deadline:* For fall admission, 1/15 priority date for domestic students. Application fee: $70. Electronic applications accepted. *Expenses:* Tuition: Full-time $29,500. Required fees: $70. Full-time tuition and fees vary according to degree level, program and student level. *Financial support:* In 2009–10, 7 students received support; fellowships with full tuition reimbursements available, research assistantships with full tuition reimbursements available, teaching assistantships with full tuition reimbursements available, institutionally sponsored loans, scholarships/grants, health care benefits, tuition waivers (full and partial), and unspecified assistantships available. Financial award applicants required to submit FAFSA. *Faculty research:* Urban and regional growth, spatial economics, formation of spatial patterns by socioeconomic systems, non-linear dynamics and complex systems, environmental-economic systems. *Unit head:* Director of Graduate Studies, 607-255-6848, Fax: 607-255-1971. *Application contact:* Graduate Field Assistant, 607-255-6848, Fax: 607-255-1971, E-mail: regsci@cornell.edu.

Cornell University, Graduate School, Graduate Fields of Arts and Sciences, Field of Archaeology, Ithaca, NY 14853-0001. Offers environmental archaeology (MA); historical archaeology (MA); Latin American archaeology (MA); medieval archaeology (MA); Mediterranean and Near Eastern archaeology (MA); Stone Age archaeology (MA). *Faculty:* 13 full-time (3 women). *Students:* 7 full-time (5 women). Average age 25. 20 applicants, 35% accepted, 4 enrolled. *Degree requirements:* For master's, one foreign language, thesis. *Entrance requirements:* For master's, GRE General Test, 3 letters of recommendation, sample of written work. Additional exam requirements/recommendations for international students: Required—TOEFL (minimum score 550 paper-based; 213 computer-based; 77 iBT). *Application deadline:* For fall admission, 1/15 for domestic students. Application fee: $70. Electronic applications accepted. *Expenses:* Tuition: Full-time $29,500. Required fees: $70. Full-time tuition and fees vary according to degree level, program and student level. *Financial support:* In 2009–10, 4 students received support; fellowships with full tuition reimbursements available, research assistantships with full tuition reimbursements available, teaching assistantships with full tuition reimbursements available, institutionally sponsored loans, scholarships/grants, health care benefits, tuition waivers (full and partial), and unspecified assistantships available. Financial award applicants required to submit FAFSA. *Faculty research:* Anatolia, Lydia, Sardis, classical and Hellenistic Greece; science in archaeology; North American Indians; Stone Age Africa; Maya trade. *Unit head:* Director of Graduate Studies, 607-255-6768, E-mail: blj7@cornell.edu. *Application contact:* Graduate Field Assistant, 607-255-6768, E-mail: dsd6@cornell.edu.

Dalhousie University, Faculty of Management, School for Resource and Environmental Studies, Halifax, NS B3H 3J5, Canada. Offers MES, MREM, MLIS/MREM. Part-time programs available. *Students:* 50 full-time (35 women), 10 part-time (6 women); includes 3 minority (1 African American, 2 Asian Americans or Pacific Islanders), 2 international. Average age 28. 70 applicants, 50% accepted. In 2009, 15 master's awarded. *Degree requirements:* For master's, thesis. *Entrance requirements:* For master's, honors degree, proof of funding (for international students). Additional exam requirements/recommendations for international students: Required—TOEFL, IELTS, CANTEST, CAEL, or Michigan English Language Assessment Battery. *Application deadline:* For fall admission, 2/1 for domestic and international students. Applications are processed on a rolling basis. Application fee: $70. Electronic applications accepted. *Financial support:* In 2009–10, 17 students received support, including 15 fellowships (averaging $9,000 per year), 5 teaching assistantships; scholarships/grants also available. Financial award application deadline: 2/1. *Faculty research:* Resource management and ecology, aboriginal resource rights, management of toxic substances, environmental impact assessment, forest management, policy, coastal zone management. Total annual research expenditures: $200,000. *Unit head:* Dr. Peter Tyedmers, Graduate Coordinator, 902-494-6517, Fax: 902-494-3728, E-mail: sres@dal.ca. *Application contact:* Mary MacGillvray, Graduate Secretary, 902-494-3632, Fax: 902-494-3728, E-mail: mary.macgillvray@dal.ca.

Drexel University, College of Arts and Sciences, Program in Environmental Policy, Philadelphia, PA 19104-2875. Offers MS. Part-time and evening/weekend programs available. *Degree requirements:* For master's, thesis optional. Electronic applications accepted.

Duke University, Graduate School, Department of Environment, Durham, NC 27708. Offers natural resource economics/policy (AM, PhD); natural resource science/ecology (AM, PhD); natural resource systems science (AM, PhD); JD/AM. Part-time programs available. *Faculty:* 28 full-time. *Students:* 66 full-time (39 women); includes 3 minority (2 African Americans, 1 Asian American or Pacific Islander), 25 international. 126 applicants, 26% accepted, 19 enrolled. In 2009, 4 master's, 11 doctorates awarded. *Degree requirements:* For doctorate, variable foreign language requirement, thesis/dissertation. *Entrance requirements:* For master's and doctorate, GRE General Test. Additional exam requirements/recommendations for international students: Required—TOEFL (minimum score 550 paper-based; 213 computer-based; 83 iBT), IELTS (minimum score 7). *Application deadline:* For fall admission, 12/8 priority date for domestic and international students. Application fee: $75. Electronic applications accepted. *Financial support:* Fellowships, research assistantships, teaching assistantships, Federal Work-Study available. Financial award application deadline: 12/31. *Unit head:* Kenneth Reckhow, Director of Graduate Studies, Fax: 919-660-1884, E-mail: meg.stephens@duke.edu. *Application contact:* Cynthia Robertson, Associate Dean for Enrollment Services, 919-684-3913, E-mail: grad-admissions@duke.edu.

Duke University, Nicholas School of the Environment, Durham, NC 27708-0328. Offers coastal environmental management (MEM); DEL-environmental leadership (MEM); energy and environment (MEM); environmental economics and policy (MEM); environmental health and security (MEM); forest resource management (MF); global environmental change (MEM); resource ecology (MEM); water and air resources (MEM); JD/AM; JD/MEM; JD/MF; MAT/MEM; MBA/MEM; MBA/MF; MEM/MPP; MF/MPP. *Accreditation:* SAF (one or more programs are accredited). Part-time programs available. *Degree requirements:* For master's, thesis. *Entrance requirements:* For master's, GRE General Test, previous course work in biology or ecology, calculus, statistics, and microeconomics; computer familiarity with word processing and data analysis. Additional exam requirements/recommendations for international students: Required—TOEFL (minimum score 550 paper-based; 213 computer-based). Electronic applications accepted. *Expenses:* Contact institution. *Faculty research:* Ecosystem management, conservation ecology, earth systems, risk assessment.

Duquesne University, Bayer School of Natural and Environmental Sciences, Environmental Science and Management Program, Pittsburgh, PA 15282-0001. Offers environmental management (MEM, Certificate); environmental science (Certificate); environmental science and management (MS); JD/MS; MBA/MS; MS/MS. Part-time and evening/weekend programs available. Postbaccalaureate distance learning degree programs offered (minimal on-campus study). *Faculty:* 4 full-time (0 women), 10 part-time/adjunct (1 woman). *Students:* 16 full-time (10 women), 21 part-time (12 women), 3 international. Average age 27. 35 applicants, 51% accepted, 11 enrolled. In 2009, 16 master's, 2 other advanced degrees awarded. *Degree requirements:* For master's, thesis (for some programs); for Certificate, minimum of 18 credit hours (for certificate). *Entrance requirements:* For master's, GRE General Test, course work in biology, chemistry, and calculus or statistics; 3 letters of reference. Additional exam requirements/recommendations for international students: Required—TOEFL (minimum score 80 iBT). *Application deadline:* For fall admission, 4/1 priority date for domestic students, 4/1 for international students; for spring admission, 10/1 priority date for domestic students, 10/1 for international students. Applications are processed on a rolling basis. Application fee: $40. *Expenses:* Contact institution. *Financial support:* In 2009–10, 7 students received support, including 1 fellowship (averaging $16,500 per year), 1 research assistantship, 5 teaching assistantships with full and partial tuition reimbursements available (averaging $12,000 per year); career-related internships or fieldwork, scholarships/grants, and unspecified assistantships also available. Financial award application deadline: 5/31. *Faculty research:* Watershed management systems, environmental analytical chemistry, environmental endocrinology, environmental microbiology, aquatic biology. *Unit head:* Dr. John Stolz, Director, 412-396-4367, Fax: 412-396-4092, E-mail: stolz@duq.edu. *Application contact:* Heather Costello, Graduate Academic Advisor, 412-396-6339, Fax: 412-396-4881, E-mail: costelloh@duq.edu.

The Evergreen State College, Graduate Programs, Program in Environmental Studies, Olympia, WA 98505. Offers MES, MES/MPA. Part-time and evening/weekend programs available. *Faculty:* 5 full-time (2 women), 2 part-time/adjunct (1 woman). *Students:* 34 full-time (19 women), 41 part-time (25 women); includes 9 minority (2 African Americans, 1 American Indian/Alaska Native, 2 Asian Americans or Pacific Islanders, 4 Hispanic Americans). Average age 33. 55 applicants, 91% accepted, 34 enrolled. In 2009, 24 master's awarded. *Degree requirements:* For master's, thesis. *Entrance requirements:* For master's, GRE, minimum GPA of 3.0 in last 90 quarter hours toward BA/BS; 15 quarter hours in social sciences and biological or physical science; 4 in statistics, biology, and microeconomics; 3 letters of recommendation. Additional exam requirements/recommendations for international students: Required—TOEFL (minimum score 600 paper-based; 250 computer-based). *Application deadline:* For fall admission, 11/15 priority date for domestic and international students. Applications are processed on a rolling basis. Application fee: $50. Electronic applications accepted. *Expenses:* Contact institution. *Financial support:* In 2009–10, 13 students received support, including 13 fellowships (averaging $1,072 per year); research assistantships, career-related internships or fieldwork, Federal Work-Study, scholarships/grants, tuition waivers (partial), and unspecified assistantships also available. Support available to part-time students. Financial award application deadline: 3/15; financial award applicants required to submit FAFSA. *Faculty research:* Marine ecology, sustainable design, cultural geography, environmental political economy, environmental policy/education, fluvial geomorphology, forest practices. *Unit head:* Dr. Martha Henderson, Director, 360-867-6225, Fax: 360-867-5430, E-mail: mhenders@evergreen.edu. *Application contact:* Gail Wootan, Assistant Director, 360-867-6225, Fax: 360-867-5430, E-mail: wootang@evergreen.edu.

Florida Atlantic University, Dorothy F. Schmidt College of Arts and Letters, Department of History, Boca Raton, FL 33431-0991. Offers environmental studies (Certificate); history (MA).

Part-time programs available. *Faculty:* 19 full-time (8 women), 1 part-time/adjunct (0 women). *Students:* 15 full-time (4 women), 14 part-time (6 women); includes 3 minority (all Hispanic Americans), 1 international. Average age 33. 30 applicants, 40% accepted, 2 enrolled. In 2009, 13 master's awarded. *Degree requirements:* For master's, one foreign language, thesis optional. *Entrance requirements:* For master's, GRE General Test, minimum GPA of 3.0. *Application deadline:* For fall admission, 6/1 priority date for domestic students, 2/15 for international students; for spring admission, 10/15 for domestic students, 8/15 for international students. Applications are processed on a rolling basis. Application fee: $30. Electronic applications accepted. *Expenses:* Tuition, state resident: full-time $7055; part-time $293.94 per credit hour. Tuition, nonresident: full-time $22,096; part-time $920.66 per credit hour. *Financial support:* Fellowships, research assistantships, teaching assistantships with tuition reimbursements, career-related internships or fieldwork, Federal Work-Study, and tuition waivers (partial) available. Support available to part-time students. Financial award application deadline: 3/1. *Faculty research:* Twentieth century America, U.S. urban history, Florida history, history of socialism, Latin America. *Unit head:* Dr. Patricia Kollander, Chair, 561-297-3841, Fax: 561-297-2704, E-mail: kollande@fau.edu. *Application contact:* Ben Lowe, Director of Graduate Programs, 561-297-3846, Fax: 561-297-2704, E-mail: bplowe@fau.edu.

Florida Gulf Coast University, College of Professional Studies, Program in Public Administration, Fort Myers, FL 33965-6565. Offers criminal justice (MPA); environmental policy (MPA); general public administration (MPA); management (MPA). *Accreditation:* NASPAA. Part-time programs available. *Entrance requirements:* For master's, GRE General Test, MAT, minimum GPA of 3.0. Additional exam requirements/recommendations for international students: Required—TOEFL (minimum score 550 paper-based; 213 computer-based). Electronic applications accepted. *Faculty research:* Personnel, public policy, public finance, housing policy.

Florida Institute of Technology, Graduate Programs, College of Engineering, Department of Marine and Environmental Systems, Melbourne, FL 32901-6975. Offers earth remote sensing (MS); environmental resource management (MS); environmental science (MS, PhD); meteorology (MS); ocean engineering (MS, PhD); oceanography (MS, PhD), including biological oceanography (MS), chemical oceanography (MS), coastal zone management (MS), geological oceanography (MS), oceanography (PhD), physical oceanography (MS). Part-time programs available. *Faculty:* 12 full-time (1 woman), 1 part-time/adjunct (0 women). *Students:* 42 full-time (18 women), 23 part-time (9 women); includes 2 minority (1 African American, 1 Asian American or Pacific Islander), 11 international. Average age 28. 103 applicants, 50% accepted, 16 enrolled. In 2009, 22 master's, 1 doctorate awarded. *Degree requirements:* For master's, comprehensive exam (for some programs), thesis (for some programs), seminar, field project, written final exam, internship, technical paper, oral presentation or internship; for doctorate, comprehensive exam, thesis/dissertation, seminar, internships (oceanography and environmental science), publications. *Entrance requirements:* For master's, GRE General Test (environmental science, oceanography, environmental resource management, meteorology, earth remote sensing), 3 letters of recommendation, minimum GPA of 3.0, resume; for doctorate, GRE General Test (oceanography, environmental science), resume, 3 letters of recommendation, minimum GPA of 3.3, statement of objectives, on campus interview (highly recommended). Additional exam requirements/recommendations for international students: Required—TOEFL (minimum score 550 paper-based; 213 computer-based; 79 iBT). *Application deadline:* For fall admission, 4/1 for international students; for spring admission, 9/30 for international students. Applications are processed on a rolling basis. Application fee: $50. Electronic applications accepted. *Expenses:* Tuition: Part-time $1015 per credit. Tuition and fees vary according to campus/location and program. *Financial support:* In 2009–10, 19 students received support, including 5 fellowships with full and partial tuition reimbursements available (averaging $7,240 per year), 9 research assistantships with full and partial tuition reimbursements available (averaging $5,542 per year), 10 teaching assistantships with full and partial tuition reimbursements available (averaging $5,411 per year); career-related internships or fieldwork, institutionally sponsored loans, tuition waivers (partial), unspecified assistantships, and tuition remissions also available. Support available to part-time students. Financial award application deadline: 3/1; financial award applicants required to submit FAFSA. Total annual research expenditures: $1.7 million. *Unit head:* Dr. George Maul, Department Head, 321-674-7453, Fax: 321-674-7212, E-mail: gmaul@fit.edu. *Application contact:* Thomas M. Shea, Director of Graduate Admissions, 321-674-7577, Fax: 321-723-9468, E-mail: tshea@fit.edu.

See Close-Up on page 411.

Florida International University, College of Arts and Sciences, Department of Earth and Environment, Department of Environmental Studies, Miami, FL 33199. Offers MS. Part-time programs available. *Students:* 18 full-time (8 women), 20 part-time (13 women); includes 10 minority (1 African American, 9 Hispanic Americans), 8 international. Average age 28. 25 applicants, 40% accepted, 10 enrolled. In 2009, 12 master's awarded. *Degree requirements:* For master's, thesis or alternative. *Entrance requirements:* For master's, GRE General Test, minimum GPA of 3.0, 3 letters of recommendation, letter of intent. Additional exam requirements/recommendations for international students: Required—TOEFL (minimum score 550 paper-based; 80 iBT). *Application deadline:* For fall admission, 3/1 for domestic and international students; for spring admission, 10/1 for domestic students, 9/1 for international students. Applications are processed on a rolling basis. Application fee: $30. Electronic applications accepted. *Expenses:* Tuition, state resident: full-time $8008; part-time $4004 per year. Tuition, nonresident: full-time $20,104; part-time $10,052 per year. Required fees: $298; $149 per term. *Financial support:* Institutionally sponsored loans and scholarships/grants available. Financial award application deadline: 3/1; financial award applicants required to submit FAFSA. *Unit head:* Dr. Rosemary Hickey-Vargas, Chair, Earth and Environment Department, 305-348-1930, Fax: 305-348-6137, E-mail: rosemary.hickey-vargas@fiu.edu. *Application contact:* Dr. Krishnaswamy Jayachandran, Director, Graduate Program, 305-348-1930, Fax: 305-348-6137, E-mail: jayachan@fiu.edu.

The George Washington University, Columbian College of Arts and Sciences, Trachtenberg School of Public Policy and Public Administration, Washington, DC 20052. Offers public administration (MPA), including budget and public finance, federal policy, politics, and management, international development management, managing public organizations, managing state and local governments, nonprofit management, policy analysis and evaluation, public administration, public-private policy and management; public policy (MA, MPP), including environmental and resource policy (MA), philosophy and social policy (MA), women's studies (MA); public policy and administration (PhD); JD/MPP; MPA/JD; PhD/MPP. Part-time and evening/weekend programs available. *Faculty:* 35 full-time (12 women), 19 part-time/adjunct (10 women). *Students:* 187 full-time (114 women), 232 part-time (151 women); includes 62 minority (15 African Americans, 3 American Indian/Alaska Native, 29 Asian Americans or Pacific Islanders, 15 Hispanic Americans), 23 international. Average age 26. 913 applicants, 56% accepted, 186 enrolled. In 2009, 106 master's, 9 doctorates awarded. *Degree requirements:* For doctorate, thesis/dissertation, general exam. *Entrance requirements:* For master's, GRE General Test, minimum GPA of 3.0; for doctorate, GRE General Test, interview, minimum GPA of 3.0. Additional exam requirements/recommendations for international students: Required—TOEFL (minimum score 600 paper-based; 250 computer-based; 100 iBT). *Application deadline:* For fall admission, 1/15 priority date for domestic and international students; for spring admission, 10/1 priority date for domestic students, 9/1 priority date for international students. Applications are processed on a rolling basis. Application fee: $60. Electronic applications accepted. *Financial support:* In 2009–10, 87 students received support; fellowships, research assistantships, teaching assistantships, institutionally sponsored loans available. Financial award application deadline: 1/15. *Unit head:* Dr. Kathyrn E. Newcomer, Director, 202-994-3959, Fax: 202-994-3959, E-mail: newcomer@gwu.edu. *Application contact:* Information Contact, 202-994-6295, Fax: 202-994-6295, E-mail: tspppa@gwu.edu.

The George Washington University, Columbian College of Arts and Sciences, Trachtenberg School of Public Policy and Public Administration, Interdisciplinary Programs in Public Policy, Program in Environmental and Resource Policy, Washington, DC 20052. Offers MA. *Students:* 3 full-time (2 women), 17 part-time (14 women); includes 4 minority (1 African American, 2 Asian Americans or Pacific Islanders, 1 Hispanic American). Average age 28. 38 applicants, 68% accepted, 5 enrolled. In 2009, 6 master's awarded. *Degree requirements:* For master's, comprehensive exam, project. *Entrance requirements:* For master's, GRE General Test, minimum GPA of 3.0. Additional exam requirements/recommendations for international students: Required—TOEFL (minimum score 600 paper-based; 250 computer-based; 100 iBT). *Application deadline:* For fall admission, 4/1 priority date for domestic and international students; for spring admission, 10/1 priority date for domestic students, 9/1 priority date for international students. Applications are processed on a rolling basis. Application fee: $60. Electronic applications accepted. *Financial support:* In 2009–10, 2 students received support; fellowships with tuition reimbursements available, institutionally sponsored loans and tuition waivers available. Financial award application deadline: 1/15. *Unit head:* Dr. Henry C. Merchant, Director, 202-994-7123, E-mail: hmerchnt@gwu.edu. *Application contact:* Information Contact, 202-994-8500, Fax: 202-994-8913, E-mail: pubpol@gwu.edu.

Georgia Institute of Technology, Graduate Studies and Research, College of Architecture, City and Regional Planning Program, Atlanta, GA 30332-0001. Offers city and regional planning (PhD); economic development (MCRP); environmental planning and management (MCRP); geographic information systems (MCRP); land and community development (MCRP); land use planning (MCRP); transportation (MCRP); urban design (MCRP); MCP/MSCE. *Accreditation:* ACSP. *Degree requirements:* For master's, thesis, internship. *Entrance requirements:* For master's, GRE General Test, minimum GPA of 2.7. Additional exam requirements/recommendations for international students: Required—TOEFL. Electronic applications accepted.

Goddard College, Graduate Division, Master of Arts in Individualized Studies Program, Plainfield, VT 05667-9432. Offers consciousness studies (MA); environmental studies (MA); transformative language arts (MA). Postbaccalaureate distance learning degree programs offered (minimal on-campus study). *Faculty:* 10 part-time/adjunct (7 women). *Students:* 42. Average age 37. 31 applicants, 81% accepted, 17 enrolled. *Degree requirements:* For master's, thesis. *Entrance requirements:* For master's, 3 letters of recommendation, study plan, bibliography/ resource list, interview. *Application deadline:* Applications are processed on a rolling basis. Application fee: $40. Electronic applications accepted. *Expenses:* Contact institution. *Financial support:* In 2009–10, 36 students received support. Applicants required to submit FAFSA. *Unit head:* Prof. Ruth Farmer, Director, 802-454-8311, Fax: 802-454-7835, E-mail: ruth.farmer@goddard.edu. *Application contact:* Jamie Kline, Admissions Counselor, 800-468-4888 Ext. 311, Fax: 802-454-1029, E-mail: jamie.kline@goddard.edu.

Green Mountain College, Program in Environmental Studies, Poultney, VT 05764-1199. Offers MS. Distance learning only. Part-time and evening/weekend programs available. Postbaccalaureate distance learning degree programs offered (no on-campus study). *Entrance requirements:* For master's, portfolio, curriculum vitae, 3 recommendations. Electronic applications accepted. *Faculty research:* Herbarium specimen, solar electricity's value, environmental politics.

Hardin-Simmons University, Graduate School, Holland School of Sciences and Mathematics, Program in Environmental Management, Abilene, TX 79698-0001. Offers MS. Part-time programs available. *Faculty:* 4 full-time (0 women). *Students:* 6 full-time (1 woman), 1 (woman) part-time; includes 1 minority (Hispanic American). Average age 29. 6 applicants, 83% accepted, 5 enrolled. In 2009, 2 master's awarded. *Degree requirements:* For master's, comprehensive exam, thesis or alternative, internship. *Entrance requirements:* For master's, minimum undergraduate GPA of 3.0 in major, 2.7 overall; 2 semesters of course work each in biology, chemistry, and geology; interview; writing sample; occupational experience. Additional exam requirements/recommendations for international students: Required—TOEFL (minimum score 550 paper-based; 213 computer-based; 75 iBT). *Application deadline:* For fall admission, 8/15 priority date for domestic students, 4/1 for international students; for spring admission, 1/5 priority date for domestic students, 9/1 for international students. Applications are processed on a rolling basis. Application fee: $50. *Expenses:* Tuition: Full-time $11,430; part-time $635 per credit hour. Required fees: $650; $110 per semester. Tuition and fees vary according to degree level. *Financial support:* Fellowships, career-related internships or fieldwork and scholarships/grants available. Support available to part-time students. Financial award application deadline: 6/30; financial award applicants required to submit FAFSA. *Faculty research:* South American history, herpetology, geology, environmental education, petroleum biodegradation, environmental ecology and microbiology. *Unit head:* Dr. Mark Ouimette, Director, 325-670-1383, Fax: 325-670-1391, E-mail: ouimette@hsutx.edu. *Application contact:* Dr. Gary Stanlake, Dean of Graduate Studies, 325-670-1298, Fax: 325-670-1564, E-mail: gradoff@hsutx.edu.

Harvard University, Extension School, Cambridge, MA 02138-3722. Offers applied sciences (CAS); biotechnology (ALM); educational technologies (ALM); educational technology (CET); English for graduate and professional studies (DGP); environmental management (ALM, CEM); information technology (ALM); journalism (ALM); liberal arts (ALM); management (ALM, CM); mathematics for teaching (ALM); museum studies (ALM); premedical studies (Diploma); publication and communication (CPC). Part-time and evening/weekend programs available. *Degree requirements:* For master's, thesis. *Entrance requirements:* For master's, 3 completed graduate courses with grade of B or higher. Additional exam requirements/recommendations for international students: Required—TOEFL (minimum score 600 paper-based; 250 computer-based), TWE (minimum score 5). *Expenses:* Contact institution.

Humboldt State University, Graduate Studies, College of Natural Resources and Sciences, Programs in Environmental Systems, Arcata, CA 95521-8299. Offers environmental systems (MS), including energy, environment and society, environmental resources engineering, geology, math modeling. *Students:* 31 full-time (11 women), 7 part-time (1 woman); includes 4 minority (2 Asian Americans or Pacific Islanders, 2 Hispanic Americans), 1 international. Average age 30. 54 applicants, 57% accepted, 17 enrolled. In 2009, 13 master's awarded. *Degree requirements:* For master's, thesis. *Entrance requirements:* For master's, GRE, appropriate bachelor's degree, minimum GPA of 2.5, 3 letters of recommendation. Additional exam requirements/recommendations for international students: Required—TOEFL. *Application deadline:* For fall admission, 3/15 for domestic students; for spring admission, 10/15 for domestic students. Applications are processed on a rolling basis. Application fee: $55. *Expenses:* Tuition, nonresident: full-time $8928. Required fees: $6102. Tuition and fees vary according to program. *Financial support:* Application deadline: 3/1; *Faculty research:* Mathematical modeling, international development technology, geology, environmental resources engineering. *Unit head:* Dr. Chris Dugaw, Chair, 707-826-4251, Fax: 707-826-4145, E-mail: dugaw@humboldt.edu. *Application contact:* Julie Tucker, Administrative Support, 707-826-3256, Fax: 707-826-3140, E-mail: jlt7002@humboldt.edu.

Idaho State University, Office of Graduate Studies, College of Engineering, Civil and Environmental Engineering Department, Pocatello, ID 83209-8060. Offers civil engineering (MS); environmental engineering (MS); environmental science and management (MS). Part-time programs available. *Faculty:* 1 full-time (0 women). *Students:* 9 full-time (1 woman), 17 part-time (6 women); includes 2 minority (both Asian Americans or Pacific Islanders), 12 international. Average age 31. In 2009, 9 master's awarded. *Degree requirements:* For master's, comprehensive exam (for some programs), thesis optional, thesis project, 2 semesters of seminar. *Entrance requirements:* For master's, GRE. Additional exam requirements/recommendations for international students: Required—TOEFL (minimum score 550 paper-based; 213 computer-based; 80 iBT). *Application deadline:* For fall admission, 7/1 for domestic students, 6/1 for international students; for spring admission, 12/1 for domestic students, 11/1 for international students. Applications are processed on a rolling basis. Application fee: $55. Electronic applications accepted. *Expenses:* Tuition, state resident: full-time $3318; part-time $297 per credit hour. Tuition, nonresident: full-time $13,120; part-time $437 per credit hour.

Environmental Management and Policy

Idaho State University (continued)

Required fees: $2530. Tuition and fees vary according to program. *Financial support:* Research assistantships with full and partial tuition reimbursements, teaching assistantships with full and partial tuition reimbursements, career-related internships or fieldwork, Federal Work-Study, institutionally sponsored loans, scholarships/grants, traineeships, health care benefits, tuition waivers (full and partial), and unspecified assistantships available. Support available to part-time students. Financial award application deadline: 1/1; financial award applicants required to submit FAFSA. *Faculty research:* Floor vibration investigations, earthquake engineering, base isolation systems and seismic risk assessment, infrastructure revitalization (building foundations and damage, bridge structures, highways, and dams), slope stability and soil erosion, pavement rehabilitation, computational fluid dynamics and flood control structures, microbial fuel cells, water treatment and water quality modeling, environmental risk assessment, biotechnology, nanotechnology. *Unit head:* Dr. Arya Ebrahimpour, Chair, 208-282-4695, Fax: 208-282-4538, E-mail: ebraaryai@isu.edu. *Application contact:* Tami Carson, Graduate School Technical Records Specialist, 208-282-2150, Fax: 208-282-4847, E-mail: carstami@isu.edu.

Illinois Institute of Technology, Stuart School of Business, Program in Environmental Management and Sustainability, Chicago, IL 60616-3793. Offers MS, JD/MS, MBA/MS. Part-time and evening/weekend programs available. *Entrance requirements:* For master's, GMAT or GRE General Test. Additional exam requirements/recommendations for international students: Required—TOEFL (minimum score 600 paper-based; 250 computer-based; 100 iBT). Electronic applications accepted. *Expenses:* Contact institution. *Faculty research:* Wind energy, carbon footprint reduction, critical asset management, solar energy, water quality management.

Indiana University Bloomington, School of Public and Environmental Affairs, Public Affairs Programs, Bloomington, IN 47405-7000. Offers comparative and international affairs (MPA); economic development (MPA); energy (MPA); environmental policy and natural resource management (MPA); information systems (MPA); local government management (MPA); nonprofit management (MPA); policy analysis (MPA); public financial administration (MPA); public management (MPA); sustainability and sustainable development (MPA); JD/MPA; MPA/MA; MPA/MIS; MPA/MLS; MSES/MPA. *Accreditation:* NASPAA (one or more programs are accredited). Part-time programs available. *Faculty:* 75 full-time (22 women), 91 part-time/adjunct (24 women). *Students:* 389 full-time (222 women), 45 part-time (24 women); includes 38 minority (18 African Americans, 1 American Indian/Alaska Native, 12 Asian Americans or Pacific Islanders, 7 Hispanic Americans), 72 international. Average age 26. 474 applicants, 206 enrolled. In 2009, 190 master's, 11 doctorates, 3 other advanced degrees awarded. Terminal master's awarded for partial completion of doctoral program. *Degree requirements:* For master's, thesis optional; for doctorate, comprehensive exam, thesis/dissertation or alternative, A thesis is required for the Public Affairs and Public Policy degree. *Entrance requirements:* For master's, GRE, LSAT (if also applying for the Law School), 3 letters of recommendation, resume or curriculum vitae; for doctorate, GRE General Test. Additional exam requirements/recommendations for international students: Required—TOEFL (minimum score 590 paper-based; 243 computer-based; 96 iBT). *Application deadline:* For fall admission, 2/1 priority date for domestic students, 12/1 priority date for international students; for spring admission, 9/1 for international students. Application fee: $55 ($65 for international students). Electronic applications accepted. *Financial support:* Fellowships with full tuition reimbursements, research assistantships with partial tuition reimbursements, teaching assistantships with partial tuition reimbursements, career-related internships or fieldwork, Federal Work-Study, institutionally sponsored loans, unspecified assistantships, and Service Corps programs available. Financial award application deadline: 2/1; financial award applicants required to submit FAFSA. *Faculty research:* Comparative and international affairs, environmental policy and resource management, policy analysis, public finance, public management, urban management, nonprofit management. *Unit head:* Dean John Graham, Dean, School of Public and Environmental Affairs, 812-855-1432, E-mail: grahamjd@indiana.edu. *Application contact:* Jennifer Medlin, Assistant Director of Admissions and Financial Aid, 812-855-3784, Fax: 812-856-3665, E-mail: jlmedlin@indiana.edu.

Indiana University–Purdue University Indianapolis, School of Public and Environmental Affairs, Indianapolis, IN 46202-2896. Offers health administration (MHA); public affairs (MPA), including criminal justice, environmental management, nonprofit management, policy analysis, public management; JD/MHA; MBA/MHA; MLS/NMC; MLS/PMC; MSN/MHA. *Accreditation:* CAHME (one or more programs are accredited); NASPAA. Part-time and evening/weekend programs available. *Faculty:* 17 full-time (6 women). *Students:* 126 full-time (71 women), 283 part-time (164 women); includes 58 minority (29 African Americans, 1 American Indian/Alaska Native, 17 Asian Americans or Pacific Islanders, 11 Hispanic Americans), 20 international. Average age 33. 255 applicants, 77% accepted, 136 enrolled. In 2009, 77 master's awarded. *Entrance requirements:* For master's, GRE General Test, minimum GPA of 3.0 (preferred). Additional exam requirements/recommendations for international students: Required—TOEFL. *Application deadline:* For fall admission, 7/15 priority date for domestic students; for spring admission, 11/15 for domestic students. Applications are processed on a rolling basis. Application fee: $55 ($65 for international students). *Financial support:* In 2009–10, 11 fellowships with full and partial tuition reimbursements (averaging $5,890 per year), 10 teaching assistantships (averaging $9,900 per year) were awarded; research assistantships with full and partial tuition reimbursements, career-related internships or fieldwork, Federal Work-Study, institutionally sponsored loans, and scholarships/grants also available. Support available to part-time students. Financial award application deadline: 3/1. *Faculty research:* Economic development, water and air quality, ethics, financing, organization design and structure. Total annual research expenditures: $1.9 million. *Unit head:* Dr. Greg Lindsey, Associate Dean, 317-274-4656, Fax: 317-274-5153. *Application contact:* 317-274-4656, Fax: 317-274-5153, E-mail: speainfo@speanet.iupui.edu.

Instituto Tecnológico y de Estudios Superiores de Monterrey, Campus Estado de México, Professional and Graduate Division, Estado de Mexico, Mexico. Offers administration of information technologies (MITA); architecture (M Arch); business administration (GMBA, MBA); computer sciences (MCS, PhD); education (M Ed); educational institution administration (MAD); educational technology and innovation (PhD); electronic commerce (MEC); environmental systems (MS); finance (MAF); humanistic studies (MHS); information sciences and knowledge management (MISKM); information systems (MS); manufacturing systems (MS); marketing (MEM); quality systems and productivity (MS); science and materials engineering (PhD); telecommunications management (MTM). Part-time programs available. Postbaccalaureate distance learning degree programs offered (minimal on-campus study). *Degree requirements:* For master's, one foreign language, thesis (for some programs); for doctorate, one foreign language, thesis/dissertation. *Entrance requirements:* For master's, E-PAEP 500, interview; for doctorate, E-PAEP 500, research proposal. Additional exam requirements/recommendations for international students: Required—TOEFL (minimum score 550 paper-based). *Faculty research:* Surface treatments by plasmas, mechanical properties, robotics, graphical computing, mechatronics security protocols.

Instituto Tecnológico y de Estudios Superiores de Monterrey, Campus Irapuato, Graduate Programs, Irapuato, Mexico. Offers administration (MBA); administration of information technology (MAIT); administration of telecommunications (MAT); architecture (M Arch); computer science (MCS); education (M Ed); educational administration (MEA); educational innovation and technology (DEIT); educational technology (MET); electronic commerce (MBA); environmental administration and planning (MEAP); environmental systems (MES); finances (MBA); humanistic studies (MHS); international management for Latin American executives (MIMLAE); library and information science (MLIS); manufacturing quality management (MMQM); marketing research (MBA).

Inter American University of Puerto Rico, Metropolitan Campus, Graduate Programs, Program in Environmental Evaluation and Protection, San Juan, PR 00919-1293. Offers MS.

The Johns Hopkins University, Engineering for Professionals, Part-Time Program in Environmental Planning and Management, Baltimore, MD 21218-2699. Offers MS, Post-Master's Certificate. Part-time and evening/weekend programs available. Postbaccalaureate distance learning degree programs offered (no on-campus study). *Students:* 1 full-time (0 women), 40 part-time (24 women); includes 12 minority (3 African Americans, 6 Asian Americans or Pacific Islanders, 3 Hispanic Americans), 2 international. Average age 30. In 2009, 7 master's awarded. Application fee: $75. *Unit head:* Dr. Hedy Alavi, Program Chair, 410-516-7091, Fax: 410-516-8996, E-mail: hedy.alavi@jhu.edu. *Application contact:* Priyanka Dwivedi, Admissions Manager, 410-516-2300, Fax: 410-579-8049, E-mail: pdwived1@jhu.edu.

The Johns Hopkins University, G. W. C. Whiting School of Engineering, Program in Engineering Management, Baltimore, MD 21218-2699. Offers biomaterials (MSEM); communications science (MSEM); computer science (MSEM); fluid mechanics (MSEM); materials science and engineering (MSEM); mechanical engineering (MSEM); mechanics and materials (MSEM); nano-biotechnology (MSEM); nanomaterials and nanotechnology (MSEM); probability and statistics (MSEM); smart product and device design (MSEM); systems analysis, management and environmental policy (MSEM). *Students:* 12 full-time (0 women), 3 international. Average age 23. 66 applicants, 67% accepted. *Entrance requirements:* For master's, GRE, 3 letters of recommendation, resume. Additional exam requirements/recommendations for international students: Required—TOEFL (minimum score 600 paper-based; 250 computer-based; 100 iBT) or IELTS (minimum score 7). *Application deadline:* For fall admission, 1/15 priority date for domestic students, 1/15 for international students; for spring admission, 9/15 priority date for domestic students, 9/15 for international students. Applications are processed on a rolling basis. Application fee: $75. Electronic applications accepted. *Financial support:* Fellowships, health care benefits available. *Unit head:* Dr. Edward R. Scheinerman, Interim Director/Vice Dean for Education, School of Engineering/Professor, Applied Mathematics and Statistics, 410-516-7395, Fax: 410-516-4880, E-mail: ers@jhu.edu. *Application contact:* Dennis McIver, Coordinator of Graduate Admissions, 410-516-8174, Fax: 410-516-0780, E-mail: graduateadmissions@jhu.edu.

The Johns Hopkins University, Zanvyl Krieger School of Arts and Sciences, Advanced Academic Programs, Program in Environmental Sciences and Policy, Baltimore, MD 21218-2699. Offers MS. Part-time and evening/weekend programs available. Postbaccalaureate distance learning degree programs offered (minimal on-campus study). *Faculty:* 1 (woman) full-time, 37 part-time/adjunct (3 women). *Students:* 16 full-time (13 women), 200 part-time (125 women); includes 25 minority (7 African Americans, 1 American Indian/Alaska Native, 9 Asian Americans or Pacific Islanders, 8 Hispanic Americans), 9 international. Average age 31. 126 applicants, 63% accepted, 55 enrolled. In 2009, 68 master's awarded. *Degree requirements:* For master's, thesis (for some programs). *Entrance requirements:* For master's, minimum GPA of 3.0, coursework in chemistry and calculus. Additional exam requirements/recommendations for international students: Required—TOEFL (minimum score 250 computer-based). *Application deadline:* For fall admission, 5/31 priority date for domestic students, 4/30 priority date for international students; for spring admission, 10/31 priority date for domestic and international students. Application fee: $75. *Financial support:* Applicants required to submit FAFSA. *Unit head:* Dr. Eileen McGurty, Associate Program Chair, 410-516-7049, E-mail: emgurty@jhu.edu. *Application contact:* Valana M. McMickens, Admissions Manager, 202-452-1941, Fax: 202-452-1970, E-mail: aapadmissions@jhu.edu.

Kean University, College of Business and Public Administration, Program in Public Administration, Union, NJ 07083. Offers environmental management (MPA); health services administration (MPA); non-profit management (MPA); public administration (MPA). *Accreditation:* NASPAA. Part-time and evening/weekend programs available. *Faculty:* 8 full-time (4 women). *Students:* 48 full-time (33 women), 92 part-time (53 women); includes 85 minority (62 African Americans, 9 Asian Americans or Pacific Islanders, 14 Hispanic Americans), 9 international. Average age 31. 80 applicants, 74% accepted, 34 enrolled. In 2009, 49 master's awarded. *Degree requirements:* For master's, thesis, internship, research seminar. *Entrance requirements:* For master's, minimum GPA of 3.0, 2 letters of recommendation, interview. *Application deadline:* For fall admission, 5/1 for domestic students; for spring admission, 11/1 for domestic students. Application fee: $60 ($150 for international students). Electronic applications accepted. *Expenses:* Tuition, state resident: full-time $10,440; part-time $435 per credit. Tuition, nonresident: full-time $14,160; part-time $590 per credit. Required fees: $2642; $110 per credit. Part-time tuition and fees vary according to course load and degree level. *Financial support:* In 2009–10, 10 research assistantships with full tuition reimbursements (averaging $3,263 per year) were awarded; unspecified assistantships also available. *Unit head:* Dr. Patricia Moore, Program Coordinator, 908-737-4300, E-mail: pmoore@kean.edu. *Application contact:* Steven Koch, Pre-Admissions Coordinator, 908-737-5924, Fax: 908-737-5965, E-mail: skoch@kean.edu.

Lamar University, College of Graduate Studies, College of Engineering, Department of Civil Engineering, Beaumont, TX 77710. Offers civil engineering (ME, MES, DE); environmental engineering (MS); environmental studies (MS). Part-time programs available. *Faculty:* 6 full-time (1 woman), 3 part-time/adjunct (0 women). *Students:* 55 full-time (12 women), 16 part-time (4 women); includes 2 minority (both African Americans), 41 international. Average age 26. 94 applicants, 40% accepted, 17 enrolled. In 2009, 49 master's, 2 doctorates awarded. *Degree requirements:* For master's, thesis optional; for doctorate, thesis/dissertation. *Entrance requirements:* For master's and doctorate, GRE General Test. Additional exam requirements/recommendations for international students: Required—TOEFL. *Application deadline:* For fall admission, 5/15 priority date for domestic students; for spring admission, 10/1 priority date for domestic students. Applications are processed on a rolling basis. Application fee: $25 ($50 for international students). *Financial support:* In 2009–10, 45 fellowships with partial tuition reimbursements (averaging $1,000 per year), 10 research assistantships with partial tuition reimbursements (averaging $7,200 per year), 3 teaching assistantships with partial tuition reimbursements (averaging $7,200 per year) were awarded; scholarships/grants and tuition waivers (partial) also available. Financial award application deadline: 4/1. *Faculty research:* Environmental remediations, construction productivity, geotechnical soil stabilization, lake/reservoir hydrodynamics, air pollution. *Unit head:* Dr. Enno Koehn, Chair, 409-880-8759, Fax: 409-880-8121, E-mail: koehneu@hal.lamar.edu. *Application contact:* Sandy Drane, Coordinator of Graduate Admissions, 409-880-8356, Fax: 409-880-8414, E-mail: gradmissions@hal.lamar.edu.

Lehigh University, College of Arts and Sciences, Program in Environmental Initiative, Bethlehem, PA 18015. Offers environmental policy design (MA). Part-time programs available. *Students:* 8 full-time (7 women), 7 part-time (4 women); includes 2 minority (1 African American, 1 Asian American or Pacific Islander). Average age 26. 11 applicants, 73% accepted, 7 enrolled. In 2009, 2 master's awarded. *Degree requirements:* For master's, thesis optional. *Entrance requirements:* For master's, GRE. Additional exam requirements/recommendations for international students: Required—TOEFL. *Application deadline:* For fall admission, 1/15 for domestic and international students; for spring admission, 12/1 for domestic and international students. Application fee: $75. *Financial support:* Teaching assistantships with full tuition reimbursements available. Financial award application deadline: 1/15. *Unit head:* Dr. John Gilroy, Director, 610-758-5964, Fax: 610-758-6377, E-mail: ei@lehigh.edu. *Application contact:* Dr. John Gilroy, Director, 610-758-5964, Fax: 610-758-6377, E-mail: ei@lehigh.edu.

Long Island University, C.W. Post Campus, College of Liberal Arts and Sciences, Department of Earth and Environmental Science, Brookville, NY 11548-1300. Offers earth science (MS); earth science education (MS); environmental studies (MS).

Louisiana State University and Agricultural and Mechanical College, Graduate School, School of the Coast and Environment, Department of Environmental Sciences, Baton Rouge, LA 70803. Offers environmental planning and management (MS); environmental toxicology (MS). *Faculty:* 10 full-time (4 women). *Students:* 21 full-time (13 women), 6 part-time (2 women); includes 4 African Americans, 6 international. Average age 28. 22 applicants, 86% accepted, 12 enrolled. In 2009, 8 master's awarded. *Degree requirements:* For master's, thesis (for some programs). *Entrance requirements:* For master's, GRE General Test, minimum GPA of 3.0. Additional exam requirements/recommendations for international students: Required—TOEFL (minimum score 550 paper-based; 213 computer-based; 79 iBT) or IELTS (minimum score 6.5). *Application deadline:* For fall admission, 1/25 priority date for domestic students, 5/15 for international students; for spring admission, 10/15 for international students. Applications are processed on a rolling basis. Application fee: $50 ($70 for international students). Electronic applications accepted. *Financial support:* In 2009–10, 21 students received support, including 14 research assistantships with full and partial tuition reimbursements available (averaging $13,171 per year), 1 teaching assistantship with full and partial tuition reimbursement available (averaging $15,740 per year); fellowships with full and partial tuition reimbursements available, career-related internships or fieldwork, Federal Work-Study, institutionally sponsored loans, scholarships/grants, health care benefits, and unspecified assistantships also available. Support available to part-time students. Financial award applicants required to submit FAFSA. *Faculty research:* Environmental toxicology, environmental policy and law, microbial ecology, bioremediation, genetic toxicology. Total annual research expenditures: $656,188. *Unit head:* Dr. Nina Lam, Chair, 225-578-3030, Fax: 225-578-4286, E-mail: nlam@lsu.edu. *Application contact:* Charlotte G. St. Romain, Academic Coordinator, 225-578-8522, Fax: 225-578-4286, E-mail: cstrom4@lsu.edu.

Marylhurst University, Department of Business Administration, Marylhurst, OR 97036-0261. Offers finance (MBA); general management (MBA); government policy and administration (MBA); green development (MBA); health care management (MBA); marketing (MBA); natural and organic resources (MBA); nonprofit management (MBA); organizational behavior (MBA); real estate (MBA); renewable energy (MBA); sustainable business (MBA). Part-time and evening/weekend programs available. Postbaccalaureate distance learning degree programs offered (no on-campus study). *Faculty:* 2 full-time (1 woman), 28 part-time/adjunct (5 women). *Students:* 30 full-time (12 women), 627 part-time (323 women); includes 79 minority (28 African Americans, 3 American Indian/Alaska Native, 17 Asian Americans or Pacific Islanders, 31 Hispanic Americans), 9 international. Average age 37. 299 applicants, 80% accepted, 209 enrolled. In 2009, 193 master's awarded. *Degree requirements:* For master's, comprehensive exam, capstone course. *Entrance requirements:* For master's, GMAT (if GPA less than 3.0 and fewer than 5 years of work experience), interview, resume, 2 letters of recommendation. Additional exam requirements/recommendations for international students: Recommended—TOEFL (minimum score 550 paper-based; 213 computer-based; 80 iBT). *Application deadline:* For fall admission, 9/11 priority date for domestic and international students; for winter admission, 12/15 priority date for domestic and international students; for spring admission, 3/17 priority date for domestic and international students. Applications are processed on a rolling basis. Application fee: $40 ($50 for international students). Electronic applications accepted. *Financial support:* Scholarships/grants available. Support available to part-time students. Financial award applicants required to submit FAFSA. *Unit head:* Bob Hanks, Director of Business and Real Estate Programs, 503-636-8141, Fax: 503-697-5597, E-mail: mba@marylhurst.edu. *Application contact:* Kathleen Schneff, Admissions Specialist, 800-634-9982 Ext. 3322, Fax: 503-635-6585, E-mail: admissions@marylhurst.edu.

McGill University, Faculty of Graduate and Postdoctoral Studies, Faculty of Agricultural and Environmental Sciences, Department of Natural Resource Sciences, Montréal, QC H3A 2T5, Canada. Offers entomology (M Sc, PhD); environmental assessment (M Sc); forest science (M Sc, PhD); microbiology (M Sc, PhD); micrometeorology (M Sc, PhD); neotropical environment (M Sc, PhD); soil science (M Sc, PhD); wildlife biology (M Sc, PhD).

Michigan Technological University, Graduate School, College of Sciences and Arts, Department of Social Sciences, Program in Environmental Policy, Houghton, MI 49931. Offers MS. Part-time programs available. *Degree requirements:* For master's, comprehensive exam, project or thesis. *Entrance requirements:* Additional exam requirements/recommendations for international students: Required—TOEFL (minimum score 550 paper-based; 213 computer-based). Electronic applications accepted.

Missouri State University, Graduate College, Interdisciplinary Program in Administrative Studies, Springfield, MO 65897. Offers applied communication (MS); criminal justice (MS); environmental management (MS); project management (MS); sports management (MS). Part-time and evening/weekend programs available. Postbaccalaureate distance learning degree programs offered (no on-campus study). *Students:* 17 full-time (11 women), 60 part-time (26 women); includes 6 minority (4 African Americans, 1 Asian American or Pacific Islander, 1 Hispanic American), 2 international. Average age 35. 24 applicants, 100% accepted, 19 enrolled. In 2009, 16 master's awarded. *Degree requirements:* For master's, comprehensive exam, thesis or alternative. *Entrance requirements:* For master's, GRE, GMAT, 3 years of work experience. Additional exam requirements/recommendations for international students: Required—TOEFL (minimum score 550 paper-based; 213 computer-based; 79 iBT). *Application deadline:* For fall admission, 7/20 priority date for domestic students; for spring admission, 12/20 priority date for domestic students. Applications are processed on a rolling basis. Application fee: $35 ($50 for international students). Electronic applications accepted. *Expenses:* Tuition, state resident: full-time $3852; part-time $214 per credit hour. Tuition, nonresident: full-time $7524; part-time $418 per credit hour. Required fees: $696; $172 per semester. Tuition and fees vary according to course level, course load, degree level and program. *Financial support:* In 2009–10, 1 teaching assistantship with full tuition reimbursement (averaging $7,340 per year) was awarded; career-related internships or fieldwork, Federal Work-Study, institutionally sponsored loans, scholarships/grants, and unspecified assistantships also available. Support available to part-time students. Financial award application deadline: 3/31; financial award applicants required to submit FAFSA. *Unit head:* John Bourhis, Director, 417-836-6390, E-mail: johnbourhis@missouristate.edu. *Application contact:* Eric Eckert, Coordinator of Graduate Admissions and Recruitment, 417-836-5331, Fax: 417-836-6200, E-mail: ericeckert@missouristate.edu.

Montclair State University, The Graduate School, College of Science and Mathematics, Department of Earth and Environmental Studies, Program in Environmental Management, Montclair, NJ 07043-1624. Offers MA, D Env M. *Degree requirements:* For master's, comprehensive exam. *Entrance requirements:* For master's, GRE General Test, 2 letters of recommendation; for doctorate, GRE General Test, 3 letters of recommendation. Additional exam requirements/recommendations for international students: Required—TOEFL (minimum score 83 computer-based), or IELTS. Application fee: $60. *Expenses:* Tuition, area resident: Part-time $486.74 per credit. Tuition, state resident: part-time $486.74 per credit. Tuition, nonresident: part-time $751.34 per credit. Tuition and fees vary according to degree level and program. *Financial support:* Tuition waivers (full) and unspecified assistantships available. *Faculty research:* Spatial environmental data analysis, water resource management in northern New Jersey and Long Island drainage basins, marine geochemistry of the Newark Bay and New York Harbor. *Unit head:* Dr. Michael Kruge, Director, 973-655-5423, Fax: 973-655-6810. *Application contact:* Dr. Michael Kruge, Director, 973-655-5423, Fax: 973-655-6810.

Monterey Institute of International Studies, Graduate School of International Policy and Management, Program in International Environmental Policy, Monterey, CA 93940-2691. Offers MA. *Students:* 67 full-time (40 women), 2 part-time (0 women); includes 11 minority (2 African Americans, 1 American Indian/Alaska Native, 6 Asian Americans or Pacific Islanders, 2 Hispanic Americans), 11 international. Average age 27. In 2009, 37 master's awarded. *Degree requirements:* For master's, one foreign language. *Entrance requirements:* For master's, minimum GPA of 3.0, proficiency in a foreign language. Additional exam requirements/recommendations for international students: Required—TOEFL (minimum score 550 paper-based; 213 computer-based; 80 iBT). *Application deadline:* For fall admission, 3/15 priority date for domestic students, 3/5 priority date for international students; for spring admission, 10/1 priority date for domestic and international students. Applications are processed on a rolling basis. Application fee: $50. Electronic applications accepted. *Expenses:* Tuition: Full-time $31,000; part-time $1500 per credit. Required fees: $56. *Financial support:* Application deadline: 3/15; *Application contact:* 831-647-4123, Fax: 831-647-6405, E-mail: admit@miis.edu.

Morehead State University, Graduate Programs, College of Science and Technology, Department of Biology and Chemistry, Morehead, KY 40351. Offers biology (MS); biology regional analysis (MS). Part-time programs available. *Faculty:* 8 full-time (2 women). *Students:* 10 full-time (6 women), 2 part-time (both women); includes 1 minority (African American), 4 international. Average age 26. 12 applicants, 83% accepted, 7 enrolled. In 2009, 8 master's awarded. *Degree requirements:* For master's, comprehensive exam, thesis optional, oral and written final exams. *Entrance requirements:* For master's, GRE General Test, minimum GPA of 3.0 in biology, 2.5 overall; undergraduate major/minor in biology, environmental science, or equivalent. Additional exam requirements/recommendations for international students: Required—TOEFL (minimum score 525 paper-based; 173 computer-based). *Application deadline:* For fall admission, 8/1 priority date for domestic and international students; for spring admission, 12/1 priority date for domestic and international students. Applications are processed on a rolling basis. Application fee: $30. Electronic applications accepted. *Expenses:* Tuition, state resident: full-time $6318; part-time $351 per credit hour. Tuition, nonresident: full-time $15,804; part-time $878 per credit hour. *Financial support:* In 2009–10, 7 teaching assistantships (averaging $10,000 per year) were awarded; career-related internships or fieldwork, Federal Work-Study, and unspecified assistantships also available. Financial award application deadline: 3/15; financial award applicants required to submit FAFSA. *Faculty research:* Atherosclerosis, RNA evolution, cancer biology, water quality/ecology, immunoparasitology. *Unit head:* Dr. Doug Dennis, Chair, 606-783-2944, Fax: 606-783-5002, E-mail: d.dennis@moreheadstate.edu. *Application contact:* Michelle Barber, Graduate Recruitment and Retention Assistant Director, 606-783-5127, Fax: 606-783-5061, E-mail: m.barber@moreheadstate.edu.

Naropa University, Graduate Programs, Program in Environmental Leadership, Boulder, CO 80302-6697. Offers MA. *Degree requirements:* For master's, comprehensive exam, applied leadership project. *Entrance requirements:* For master's, in-person interview, writing sample, letter of interest, resume, 3 letters of recommendation. Additional exam requirements/recommendations for international students: Required—TOEFL (minimum score 600 paper-based; 250 computer-based). Electronic applications accepted.

New Jersey Institute of Technology, Office of Graduate Studies, College of Science and Liberal Arts, Department of Chemistry and Environmental Science, Program in Environmental Policy Studies, Newark, NJ 07102. Offers MS. Part-time and evening/weekend programs available. Terminal master's awarded for partial completion of doctoral program. *Degree requirements:* For master's, thesis or alternative. *Entrance requirements:* For master's, GRE General Test. Additional exam requirements/recommendations for international students: Required—TOEFL (minimum score 550 paper-based; 213 computer-based; 79 iBT). Electronic applications accepted.

New York Institute of Technology, Graduate Division, School of Engineering and Computing Sciences, Program in Energy Management, Old Westbury, NY 11568-8000. Offers energy management (MS); energy technology (Advanced Certificate); environmental management (Advanced Certificate); facilities management (Advanced Certificate). Part-time and evening/weekend programs available. Postbaccalaureate distance learning degree programs offered. *Students:* 53 full-time (8 women), 105 part-time (14 women); includes 38 minority (13 African Americans, 1 American Indian/Alaska Native, 9 Asian Americans or Pacific Islanders, 15 Hispanic Americans), 33 international. Average age 33. In 2009, 25 master's, 15 other advanced degrees awarded. *Degree requirements:* For master's, comprehensive exam, thesis or alternative. *Entrance requirements:* For master's, minimum QPA of 2.85. Additional exam requirements/recommendations for international students: Required—TOEFL (minimum score 550 paper-based; 213 computer-based). *Application deadline:* For fall admission, 7/1 priority date for domestic students; for spring admission, 12/1 priority date for domestic students. Applications are processed on a rolling basis. Application fee: $50. Electronic applications accepted. *Expenses:* Tuition: Part-time $825 per credit. *Financial support:* Fellowships, research assistantships with partial tuition reimbursements, institutionally sponsored loans, tuition waivers (full and partial), and unspecified assistantships available. Support available to part-time students. Financial award applicants required to submit FAFSA. *Unit head:* Dr. Frank Zeman, Director, 212-261-1656, Fax: 212-261-1748, E-mail: fzeman@nyit.edu. *Application contact:* Dr. Jacquelyn Nealon, Vice President for Enrollment Services, 516-686-7925, Fax: 516-686-7597, E-mail: jnealon@nyit.edu.

New York University, School of Continuing and Professional Studies, Center for Global Affairs, New York, NY 10012-1019. Offers global affairs (MS), including environment/energy policy, human rights and humanitarian assistance, international law, dispute settlement, and institutions, international relations, peace building, private sector: international business, economics, and development, transnational security. Part-time and evening/weekend programs available. *Faculty:* 9 full-time (3 women), 31 part-time/adjunct (14 women). *Students:* 120 full-time (82 women), 179 part-time (121 women); includes 22 minority (1 American Indian/Alaska Native, 21 Asian Americans or Pacific Islanders), 27 international. Average age 30. 419 applicants, 59% accepted, 94 enrolled. In 2009, 86 master's awarded. *Degree requirements:* For master's, thesis. *Entrance requirements:* For master's, GRE General Test or GMAT (for recent graduates), 2 letters of recommendation, resume. Additional exam requirements/recommendations for international students: Required—TOEFL (minimum score 600 paper-based; 250 computer-based; 100 iBT), TWE. *Application deadline:* For fall admission, 2/1 priority date for domestic and international students; for spring admission, 10/15 priority date for domestic students, 8/15 priority date for international students. Applications are processed on a rolling basis. Application fee: $75. Electronic applications accepted. *Expenses:* Tuition: Full-time $30,528; part-time $1272 per credit. Required fees: $2177. *Financial support:* In 2009–10, 159 students received support, including 159 fellowships (averaging $2,932 per year); institutionally sponsored loans, scholarships/grants, and tuition waivers (partial) also available. Support available to part-time students. Financial award application deadline: 3/1; financial award applicants required to submit FAFSA. *Unit head:* Dr. Vera Jelinek, Assistant Dean and Director, 212-992-8380, Fax: 212-995-3638, E-mail: vera.jelinek@nyu.edu. *Application contact:* Mykellan Ledden, Associate Director, 212-992-8380, Fax: 212-995-3638, E-mail: mykellan.ledden@nyu.edu.

Northeastern Illinois University, Graduate College, College of Arts and Sciences, Department of Geography, Environmental Studies and Economics, Program in Geography and Environmental Studies, Chicago, IL 60625-4699. Offers MA. Part-time and evening/weekend programs available. *Degree requirements:* For master's, comprehensive exam, thesis optional. *Entrance requirements:* For master's, undergraduate minor in geography or environmental studies, minimum GPA of 2.75. Additional exam requirements/recommendations for international students: Required—TOEFL (minimum score 550 paper-based; 213 computer-based; 80 iBT). Electronic applications accepted. *Faculty research:* Segregation and urbanization of minority groups in the Chicago area, scale dependence and parameterization in nonpoint source pollution modeling, ecological land classification and mapping, ecosystem restoration, soil-vegetation relationships.

Northern Arizona University, Graduate College, College of Engineering, Forestry and Natural Sciences, Center for Sustainable Environments, Flagstaff, AZ 86011. Offers environmental sciences and policy (MS). *Faculty:* 5 full-time (3 women). *Students:* 18 full-time (12 women), 6 part-time (3 women); includes 5 minority (1 American Indian/Alaska Native, 1 Asian American or Pacific Islander, 3 Hispanic Americans), 3 international. Average age 28. 42 applicants, 17% accepted, 5 enrolled. In 2009, 7 master's awarded. *Degree requirements:* For master's, thesis optional. *Entrance requirements:* For master's, GRE General Test. Additional exam requirements/

Environmental Management and Policy

Northern Arizona University (continued)

recommendations for international students: Required—TOEFL (minimum score 550 paper-based; 213 computer-based; 80 iBT), IELTS (minimum score 7), or a bachelor's degree from an English-speaking university and demonstrated proficiency. *Application deadline:* For fall admission, 3/13 priority date for domestic students, 9/1 for international students. Application fee: $65. Electronic applications accepted. *Financial support:* In 2009–10, 2 teaching assistantships with partial tuition reimbursements (averaging $10,439 per year) were awarded; Federal Work-Study, scholarships/grants, health care benefits, and unspecified assistantships also available. Support available to part-time students. Financial award application deadline: 2/15; financial award applicants required to submit FAFSA. *Unit head:* Dr. Tom Sisk, Interim Director, 928-523-7283, E-mail: tom.sisk@nau.edu. *Application contact:* Information Contact, E-mail: esf.program@nau.edu.

Northern Arizona University, Graduate College, College of Engineering, Forestry and Natural Sciences, School of Earth Sciences and Environmental Sustainability, Flagstaff, AZ 86011. Offers climate science and solutions (MS); environmental sciences and policy (MS); geology (MS). *Faculty:* 22 full-time (5 women). *Students:* 28 full-time (17 women), 25 part-time (21 women); includes 6 minority (2 American Indian/Alaska Native, 1 Asian American or Pacific Islander, 3 Hispanic Americans). 70 applicants, 36% accepted, 17 enrolled. In 2009, 19 master's awarded. *Entrance requirements:* Additional exam requirements/recommendations for international students: Required—TOEFL (minimum score 550 paper-based; 213 computer-based; 80 iBT), IELTS (minimum score 7), or a bachelor's degree from an English-speaking university and demonstrated proficiency. *Application deadline:* For fall admission, 2/15 for domestic and international students. Application fee: $65. *Financial support:* In 2009–10, 32 students received support, including 7 research assistantships with partial tuition reimbursements available, 26 teaching assistantships with partial tuition reimbursements available; Federal Work-Study, scholarships/grants, health care benefits, and unspecified assistantships also available. Support available to part-time students. Financial award applicants required to submit FAFSA. *Unit head:* Dr. Abe Springer, Director, 928-523-7198. *Application contact:* Dr. Abe Springer, Director, 928-523-7198.

Nova Scotia Agricultural College, Research and Graduate Studies, Truro, NS B2N 5E3, Canada. Offers agriculture (M Sc), including air quality, animal behavior, animal molecular genetics, animal nutrition, animal technology, aquaculture, botany, crop management, crop physiology, ecology, environmental microbiology, food science, horticulture, nutrient management, pest management, physiology, plant biotechnology, plant pathology, soil chemistry, soil fertility, waste management and composting, water quality. Part-time programs available. *Degree requirements:* For master's, thesis, ATC Exam Teaching Assistantship. *Entrance requirements:* For master's, honors B Sc, minimum GPA of 3.0. Additional exam requirements/recommendations for international students: Required—TOEFL (minimum score 580 paper-based; 237 computer-based; 92 iBT), IELTS, Michigan English Language Assessment Battery, CanTEST, CAEL. *Faculty research:* Bio-product development, organic agriculture, nutrient management, air and water quality, agricultural biotechnology.

Ohio University, Graduate College, College of Arts and Sciences, Department of Geological Sciences, Athens, OH 45701-2979. Offers environmental geochemistry (MS); environmental geology (MS); environmental/hydrology (MS); geology (MS); geology education (MS); geomorphology/surficial processes (MS); geophysics (MS); hydrogeology (MS); sedimentology (MS); structure/tectonics (MS). Part-time programs available. *Faculty:* 10 full-time (4 women), 4 part-time/adjunct (1 woman). *Students:* 18 full-time (13 women), 1 part-time (0 women), 9 international. 15 applicants, 67% accepted, 6 enrolled. In 2009, 5 master's awarded. *Degree requirements:* For master's, thesis. *Entrance requirements:* Additional exam requirements/recommendations for international students: Required—TOEFL (minimum score 550 paper-based; 80 iBT) or IELTS Academic (minimum score 6.5). *Application deadline:* For fall admission, 2/1 priority date for domestic and international students. Application fee: $50 ($55 for international students). Electronic applications accepted. *Expenses:* Tuition, state resident: full-time $7839; part-time $323 per quarter hour. Tuition, nonresident: full-time $15,831; part-time $654 per quarter hour. Required fees: $2931. *Financial support:* Research assistantships with full tuition reimbursements, teaching assistantships with full tuition reimbursements, Federal Work-Study, institutionally sponsored loans, scholarships/grants, tuition waivers (partial), and unspecified assistantships available. Financial award application deadline: 2/1. *Faculty research:* Geoscience education, tectonics, fluvial geomorphology, invertebrate paleontology, mine/hydrology. Total annual research expenditures: $649,020. *Unit head:* Dr. Gregory Nadon, Chair, 740-593-4212, Fax: 740-593-0486, E-mail: nadon@ohio.edu. *Application contact:* Dr. Douglas Green, Graduate Chair, 740-593-1843, Fax: 740-593-0486, E-mail: green@ohio.edu.

Ohio University, Graduate College, College of Arts and Sciences, Program in Environmental Studies, Athens, OH 45701-2979. Offers MS. Part-time programs available. *Faculty:* 79 full-time (24 women). *Students:* 55 full-time, 11 part-time; includes 1 minority (African American), 15 international. Average age 28. 33 applicants, 48% accepted, 10 enrolled. In 2009, 19 master's awarded. *Degree requirements:* For master's, comprehensive exam (for some programs), written exams or thesis, research project. *Entrance requirements:* For master's, minimum GPA of 3.0. Additional exam requirements/recommendations for international students: Required—TOEFL (minimum score 600 paper-based; 100 iBT) or IELTS Academic (minimum score 7). *Application deadline:* For fall admission, 1/1 priority date for domestic and international students; for winter admission, 10/1 for domestic and international students; for spring admission, 2/1 for domestic and international students. Application fee: $50 ($55 for international students). Electronic applications accepted. *Expenses:* Tuition, state resident: full-time $7839; part-time $323 per quarter hour. Tuition, nonresident: full-time $15,831; part-time $654 per quarter hour. Required fees: $2931. *Financial support:* Fellowships with tuition reimbursements, research assistantships with tuition reimbursements, teaching assistantships with tuition reimbursements, career-related internships or fieldwork, Federal Work-Study, institutionally sponsored loans, scholarships/grants, tuition waivers (full and partial), and unspecified assistantships available. Financial award application deadline: 1/1. *Faculty research:* Air quality modeling, conservation biology, environmental policy, geographical information systems, land management and watershed restoration. *Unit head:* Dr. Michele Morrone, Director, 740-593-9526, Fax: 740-593-0924, E-mail: morrone@ohio.edu. *Application contact:* Graduate Admissions, 740-593-2800, Fax: 740-593-4625, E-mail: graduate@ohio.edu.

Pace University, Dyson College of Arts and Sciences, Department of Public Administration, New York, NY 10038. Offers environmental management (MPA); government management (MPA); health care administration (MPA); management for public safety and homeland security (MA); nonprofit management (MPA); JD/MPA. Offered at White Plains, NY location only. Part-time and evening/weekend programs available. *Faculty:* 4 full-time, 6 part-time/adjunct. *Students:* 52 full-time (31 women), 75 part-time (49 women); includes 47 minority (28 African Americans, 1 American Indian/Alaska Native, 1 Asian American or Pacific Islander, 17 Hispanic Americans), 8 international. Average age 30. 75 applicants, 100% accepted, 43 enrolled. In 2009, 38 master's awarded. *Degree requirements:* For master's, capstone project. *Entrance requirements:* For master's, GRE General Test. Additional exam requirements/recommendations for international students: Required—TOEFL. *Application deadline:* For fall admission, 8/1 priority date for domestic students; for spring admission, 12/1 priority date for domestic students. Applications are processed on a rolling basis. Application fee: $70. Electronic applications accepted. *Expenses:* Tuition: Part-time $954 per credit. Tuition and fees vary according to course load, degree level and program. *Financial support:* Research assistantships, career-related internships or fieldwork, Federal Work-Study, and tuition waivers (partial) available. Support available to part-time students. Financial award applicants required to submit FAFSA. *Unit head:* Dr. Farrokh Hormozi, Chairperson, 914-422-4285, E-mail: fhormozi@pace.edu. *Application contact:* Joanna Broda, Director of Admissions, 914-422-4283, Fax: 914-422-4287, E-mail: gradwp@pace.edu.

Penn State University Park, Graduate School, Intercollege Graduate Programs, Intercollege Program in Environmental Pollution Control, State College, University Park, PA 16802-1503. Offers MEPC, MS. *Unit head:* Dr. Herschel A. Elliott, Chair, 814-865-1417, Fax: 814-863-1031, E-mail: helliott3@psu.edu. *Application contact:* Dr. Herschel A. Elliott, Chair, 814-865-1417, Fax: 814-863-1031, E-mail: helliott3@psu.edu.

Plymouth State University, College of Graduate Studies, Graduate Studies in Education, Program in Science, Plymouth, NH 03264-1595. Offers applied meteorology (MS); environmental science and policy (MS); science education (MS).

Polytechnic University of Puerto Rico, Graduate School, Hato Rey, PR 00919. Offers business administration (MBA), including general studies, management of information systems, management of international enterprises; civil engineering (ME, MS); computer engineering (ME, MS); computer science (MS); electrical engineering (ME, MS); engineering management (MEM); environmental management (MEPM); landscape architecture (M Land Arch); manufacturing competitiveness (MMC, MS); manufacturing engineering (ME, MS). Part-time and evening/weekend programs available. *Entrance requirements:* For master's, 3 letters of recommendation.

Pontificia Universidad Catolica Madre y Maestra, Graduate School, Santiago, Dominican Republic. Offers administration (M Adm); architecture of interiors (M Arch); architecture of tourist lodgings (M Arch); banking and financial management (M Mgmt); civil law (LL M); construction administration (ME); corporate business law (LL M); criminal procedure law (LL M); environmental engineering (ME, MEE); finance (M Mgmt); history applied to education (M Ed); human resources (EMBA); insurance (M Mgmt); international business (M Mgmt); labor law and Social Security (LL M); logistics management (ME); marketing (M Mgmt); renewable energy (ME); strategic cost management (M Mgmt). *Entrance requirements:* For master's, curriculum vitae, interview.

Portland State University, Graduate Studies, College of Liberal Arts and Sciences, Interdisciplinary Program in Environmental Sciences and Management, Portland, OR 97207-0751. Offers environmental management (MEM); environmental sciences/biology (PhD); environmental sciences/chemistry (PhD); environmental sciences/civil engineering (PhD); environmental sciences/geography (PhD); environmental sciences/geology (PhD); environmental sciences/physics (PhD); environmental studies (MS); science/environmental science (MST). Part-time programs available. *Degree requirements:* For master's, thesis or alternative; for doctorate, variable foreign language requirement, comprehensive exam, thesis/dissertation, oral and qualifying exams. *Entrance requirements:* For master's, GRE General Test, 3 letters of recommendation; for doctorate, minimum GPA of 3.0 in upper-division course work or 2.75 overall. Additional exam requirements/recommendations for international students: Required—TOEFL (minimum score 550 paper-based; 213 computer-based). *Faculty research:* Environmental aspects of biology, chemistry, civil engineering, geology, physics.

Prescott College, Graduate Programs, Program in Environmental Studies, Prescott, AZ 86301. Offers environmental studies (MA); student-directed independent study (MA). Part-time programs available. Postbaccalaureate distance learning degree programs offered (minimal on-campus study). *Faculty:* 1 full-time (0 women), 31 part-time/adjunct (16 women). *Students:* 16 full-time (11 women), 27 part-time (17 women); includes 2 minority (1 African American, 1 American Indian/Alaska Native), 1 international. Average age 35. 30 applicants, 77% accepted, 13 enrolled. In 2009, 21 master's awarded. *Degree requirements:* For master's, thesis, fieldwork or internship, practicum. *Entrance requirements:* For master's, 2 letters of recommendation, resume. Additional exam requirements/recommendations for international students: Required—TOEFL (minimum score 500 paper-based; 173 computer-based). *Application deadline:* For fall admission, 4/15 priority date for domestic and international students; for spring admission, 9/15 priority date for domestic and international students. Applications are processed on a rolling basis. Application fee: $40. Electronic applications accepted. *Expenses:* Tuition: Full-time $14,712; part-time $613 per credit. Required fees: $50 per term. One-time fee: $150. Tuition and fees vary according to course load and degree level. *Financial support:* Career-related internships or fieldwork, Federal Work-Study, and scholarships/grants available. Financial award applicants required to submit FAFSA. *Unit head:* Dr. Ed Grumbine, Interim Chair, 928-350-2259, Fax: 928-776-5151, E-mail: egrumbine@prescott.edu. *Application contact:* Kerstin Alicki, Admissions Counselor, 877-412-8705, Fax: 928-277-4695, E-mail: admissions@prescott.edu.

Purdue University, Graduate School, College of Agriculture, Department of Forestry and Natural Resources, West Lafayette, IN 47907. Offers aquaculture, fisheries, aquatic science (MSF); aquaculture, fisheries, aquatic sciences (MS, PhD); forest biology (MS, MSF, PhD); natural resources and environmental policy (MS, MSF); natural resources environmental policy (PhD); quantitative resource analysis (MS, MSF, PhD); wildlife science (MS, MSF, PhD); wood science and technology (MS, MSF, PhD). *Degree requirements:* For master's, thesis; for doctorate, thesis/dissertation. *Entrance requirements:* For master's and doctorate, GRE General Test, minimum B+ average in undergraduate course work. Additional exam requirements/recommendations for international students: Required—TOEFL. Electronic applications accepted. *Faculty research:* Wildlife management, forest management, forest ecology, forest soils, limnology.

Rensselaer Polytechnic Institute, Graduate School, School of Humanities and Social Sciences, Department of Economics, Interdisciplinary Program in Ecological Economics, Troy, NY 12180-3590. Offers PhD. *Faculty:* 7 full-time (1 woman). *Students:* 11 full-time (7 women); includes 4 Asian Americans or Pacific Islanders, 3 Hispanic Americans. Average age 29. 30 applicants, 30% accepted, 2 enrolled. In 2009, 3 doctorates awarded. *Degree requirements:* For doctorate, comprehensive exam, thesis/dissertation. *Entrance requirements:* For doctorate, GRE General Test or GMAT, 2 recommendation letters, resume or curriculum vitae. Additional exam requirements/recommendations for international students: Required—TOEFL or IELTS. *Application deadline:* For fall admission, 1/15 priority date for domestic and international students. Applications are processed on a rolling basis. Application fee: $75. Electronic applications accepted. *Expenses:* Tuition: Full-time $38,100. *Financial support:* In 2009–10, 9 students received support, including 2 fellowships with full tuition reimbursements available (averaging $22,000 per year), 3 research assistantships with full tuition reimbursements available (averaging $17,500 per year), 4 teaching assistantships with full tuition reimbursements available (averaging $17,500 per year); scholarships/grants and unspecified assistantships also available. Financial award application deadline: 1/15. *Faculty research:* Economic development and trade with a focus on technology, lifestyles, and environment; input-output analysis; pollution policy in the electric power sector; electricity market design; renewable energy integration in the power grid; experimental economics; law and economics; environmental economics; behavioral economics; technology change; applied econometrics. Total annual research expenditures: $100,000. *Unit head:* Prof. Faye Duchin, Professor of Economics/Director, 518-276-2038, Fax: 518-276-2235, E-mail: duchin@rpi.edu. *Application contact:* Betty Jean Kaufman, Administrative Assistant, 518-276-6387, Fax: 518-276-2235, E-mail: kaufmb@rpi.edu.

Rice University, Graduate Programs, Wiess School–Professional Science Master's Programs, Professional Master's Program in Environmental Analysis and Decision Making, Houston, TX 77251-1892. Offers MS. Part-time programs available. *Degree requirements:* For master's, internship. *Entrance requirements:* For master's, GRE General Test, letters of recommendation (4). Additional exam requirements/recommendations for international students: Required—TOEFL (minimum score 600 paper-based; 250 computer-based; 90 iBT). Electronic applications accepted. *Faculty research:* Environmental biotechnology, environmental nanochemistry, environmental statistics, remote sensing.

Rochester Institute of Technology, Graduate Enrollment Services, College of Applied Science and Technology, Department of Civil Engineering Technology, Environmental Management and Safety, Rochester, NY 14623-5603. Offers MS. Part-time and evening/weekend programs available. Postbaccalaureate distance learning degree programs offered (minimal on-campus study). *Students:* 18 full-time (9 women), 31 part-time (10 women); includes 5 minority (3 African Americans, 1 Asian American or Pacific Islander, 1 Hispanic American), 13 international. Average age 35. 46 applicants, 57% accepted, 17 enrolled. In 2009, 15 master's awarded. *Degree requirements:* For master's, thesis or project. *Entrance requirements:* For master's, minimum GPA of 3.0. Additional exam requirements/recommendations for international students: Required—TOEFL (minimum score 550 paper-based; 213 computer-based; 79 iBT), or IELTS (minimum score 6.5). *Application deadline:* For fall admission, 2/15 priority date for domestic and international students; for winter admission, 11/1 priority date for domestic students; for spring admission, 2/1 priority date for domestic students, 1/1 priority date for international students. Applications are processed on a rolling basis. Application fee: $50. Electronic applications accepted. *Expenses:* Tuition: Full-time $31,533; part-time $876 per credit hour. Required fees: $210. *Financial support:* In 2009–10, 31 students received support; research assistantships with partial tuition reimbursements available, teaching assistantships with partial tuition reimbursements available, career-related internships or fieldwork, scholarships/grants, and unspecified assistantships available. Support available to part-time students. Financial award applicants required to submit FAFSA. *Faculty research:* Environmental, health and safety (EHS) issues; regulatory, voluntary and business drivers for EHS programs; design and implementation of effective EHS management systems and programs; design and implementation of performance measurement processes. *Unit head:* Joseph Rosenbeck, Graduate Program Chair, 585-475-6469, E-mail: jmrcem@rit.edu. *Application contact:* Diane Ellison, Assistant Vice President, Graduate Enrollment Services, 585-475-2229, Fax: 585-475-7164, E-mail: gradinfo@rit.edu.

Royal Roads University, Graduate Studies, Environment and Sustainability Program, Victoria, BC V9B 5Y2, Canada. Offers environment and management (M Sc, MA); environmental education and communication (MA, G Dip, Graduate Certificate); MA/MS. Postbaccalaureate distance learning degree programs offered (minimal on-campus study). *Degree requirements:* For master's, thesis. *Entrance requirements:* For master's, 5-7 years of related work experience. Electronic applications accepted. *Faculty research:* Sustainable development, atmospheric processes, sustainable communities, chemical fate and transport of persistent organic pollutants, educational technology.

St. Cloud State University, School of Graduate Studies, College of Science and Engineering, Department of Environmental and Technological Studies, St. Cloud, MN 56301-4498. Offers MS. *Faculty:* 7 full-time (0 women). *Students:* 9 part-time (4 women); includes 1 minority (African American), 2 international. 21 applicants, 90% accepted. In 2009, 14 master's awarded. *Degree requirements:* For master's, thesis or alternative. *Entrance requirements:* For master's, minimum GPA of 2.75. Additional exam requirements/recommendations for international students: Required—TOEFL (minimum score 550 paper-based; 213 computer-based), Michigan English Language Assessment Battery; Recommended—IELTS (minimum score 6.5). *Application deadline:* For fall admission, 6/1 priority date for domestic students, 4/1 for international students; for spring admission, 10/1 priority date for domestic students, 8/1 for international students. Applications are processed on a rolling basis. Application fee: $35. Electronic applications accepted. *Financial support:* Federal Work-Study, scholarships/grants, and unspecified assistantships available. Financial award application deadline: 3/1. *Unit head:* Dr. Michner Bender, Interim Chairperson, 320-308-3891, Fax: 320-308-5122, E-mail: ets@stcloudstate.edu. *Application contact:* Linda Lou Krueger, School of Graduate Studies, 320-308-2113, Fax: 320-308-5371, E-mail: lckrueger@stcloudstate.edu.

Saint Mary-of-the-Woods College, Program in Earth Literacy, Saint Mary-of-the-Woods, IN 47876. Offers MA. Part-time programs available. Postbaccalaureate distance learning degree programs offered (minimal on-campus study). *Degree requirements:* For master's, thesis. Electronic applications accepted. *Faculty research:* Ecology, art, spirituality.

Samford University, Howard College of Arts and Sciences, Birmingham, AL 35229. Offers MSEM, JD/MSEM. Part-time and evening/weekend programs available. *Faculty:* 7 full-time (1 woman), 6 part-time/adjunct (0 women). *Students:* 16 full-time (8 women), 16 part-time (7 women); includes 3 minority (all African Americans), 1 international. Average age 36. 10 applicants, 100% accepted, 10 enrolled. In 2009, 10 master's awarded. *Entrance requirements:* For master's, GRE General Test (minimum score 1000) or MAT (minimum score 50), minimum GPA of 3.0, 3 years of work experience. Additional exam requirements/recommendations for international students: Required—TOEFL (minimum score 550 paper-based; 213 computer-based). *Application deadline:* For fall admission, 8/1 for domestic and international students; for spring admission, 1/2 for domestic students, 12/14 for international students. Applications are processed on a rolling basis. Application fee: $35. *Expenses:* Contact institution. *Faculty research:* Mosquito fish as an environmental model for pollutants, PCB contamination, environmental epidemiology and toxicology, GIS, geology and natural resource management. *Unit head:* Dr. David W. Chapman, Dean, 205-726-2771, Fax: 205-726-2279. *Application contact:* Dr. Ronald N. Hunsinger, Professor/Chair, 205-726-2944, Fax: 205-726-2479, E-mail: rnhunsin@samford.edu.

San Francisco State University, Division of Graduate Studies, College of Behavioral and Social Sciences, Department of Geography and Human Environmental Studies, San Francisco, CA 94132-1722. Offers geography (MA), including resource management and environmental planning.

San Jose State University, Graduate Studies and Research, College of Social Sciences, Department of Environmental Studies, San Jose, CA 95192-0001. Offers MS. Part-time programs available. *Students:* 16 full-time (11 women), 22 part-time (11 women); includes 7 minority (1 African American, 3 Asian Americans or Pacific Islanders, 3 Hispanic Americans), 2 international. Average age 34. 27 applicants, 37% accepted, 7 enrolled. In 2009, 6 master's awarded. *Degree requirements:* For master's, comprehensive exam, thesis or alternative. *Entrance requirements:* Additional exam requirements/recommendations for international students: Required—TOEFL (minimum score 580 paper-based). *Application deadline:* For fall admission, 6/29 for domestic students; for spring admission, 11/30 for domestic students. Applications are processed on a rolling basis. Application fee: $59. Electronic applications accepted. *Financial support:* Teaching assistantships, career-related internships or fieldwork, Federal Work-Study, and institutionally sponsored loans available. Support available to part-time students. Financial award applicants required to submit FAFSA. *Faculty research:* Remote sensing, land use/land cover mapping. *Unit head:* Lynne Trulio, Acting Chair, 408-924-5445, Fax: 408-924-5477. *Application contact:* Lynne Trulio, Acting Chair, 408-924-5445, Fax: 408-924-5477.

Shippensburg University of Pennsylvania, School of Graduate Studies, College of Arts and Sciences, Department of Geography and Earth Science, Shippensburg, PA 17257-2299. Offers geoenvironmental studies (MS). Part-time and evening/weekend programs available. *Degree requirements:* For master's, comprehensive exam, thesis (6 credits) or a 1 semester research project (3 credits) and internship (6 credits), departmental practicum exam. *Entrance requirements:* For master's, GRE (if GPA less than 2.75), 12 credit hours in geography or earth sciences (including 6 in geography) and 15 credit hours in natural sciences (including 6 in the earth sciences) or a combined total of 18 credits in geography and earth science. Additional exam requirements/recommendations for international students: Required—TOEFL (minimum score 560 paper-based; 220 computer-based); Recommended—IELTS (minimum score 6). Electronic applications accepted.

Shippensburg University of Pennsylvania, School of Graduate Studies, College of Arts and Sciences, Department of Sociology and Anthropology, Shippensburg, PA 17257-2299. Offers organizational development and leadership (MS), including business, communications, education, environmental management, higher education, historical administration, individual and organizational development, public organizations, social structures and organizations. Part-time and evening/weekend programs available. *Degree requirements:* For master's, capstone experience. *Entrance requirements:* For master's, interview (if GPA less than 2.75), resume. Additional exam requirements/recommendations for international students: Required—TOEFL (minimum score 560 paper-based, 220 computer-based); Recommended—IELTS (minimum score 6). Electronic applications accepted.

Simon Fraser University, Graduate Studies, Faculty of Applied Sciences, School of Resource and Environmental Management, Burnaby, BC V5A 1S6, Canada. Offers MRM, PhD. *Degree requirements:* For master's, thesis or alternative, research project; for doctorate, comprehensive exam, thesis/dissertation. *Entrance requirements:* For master's, minimum GPA of 3.0; for doctorate, GRE Writing Assessment, minimum GPA of 3.5. Additional exam requirements/recommendations for international students: Required—TOEFL or IELTS. *Faculty research:* Management of resources, resource economics, regional planning, public policy analysis, tourism and parks.

Slippery Rock University of Pennsylvania, Graduate Studies (Recruitment), College of Health, Environment, and Science, Department of Parks, Recreation, and Environmental Education, Slippery Rock, PA 16057-1383. Offers environmental education (M Ed); resource management (MS). Part-time and evening/weekend programs available. *Degree requirements:* For master's, comprehensive exam (for some programs), thesis (for some programs). *Entrance requirements:* For master's, GRE General Test, MAT, minimum GPA of 2.75. Additional exam requirements/recommendations for international students: Required—TOEFL (minimum score 550 paper-based; 213 computer-based). *Application deadline:* For fall admission, 3/1 priority date for domestic students, 5/1 priority date for international students; for spring admission, 11/1 priority date for domestic students, 9/1 priority date for international students. Applications are processed on a rolling basis. Application fee: $25 ($30 for international students). Electronic applications accepted. *Expenses:* Tuition, state resident: full-time $6666; part-time $370 per credit. Tuition, nonresident: full-time $10,666; part-time $593 per credit. Required fees: $2184; $182 per credit. *Financial support:* Career-related internships or fieldwork, Federal Work-Study, scholarships/grants, and unspecified assistantships available. Support available to part-time students. Financial award application deadline: 5/1; financial award applicants required to submit FAFSA. *Unit head:* Dr. Daniel Dziubek, Graduate Coordinator, 724-738-2958, Fax: 724-738-2938, E-mail: daniel.dziubek@sru.edu. *Application contact:* Angela Piverotto, Interim Director of Graduate Studies, 724-738-2051, Fax: 724-738-2146, E-mail: graduate.admissions@sru.edu.

Southeast Missouri State University, School of Graduate Studies, Department of Human Environmental Studies, Cape Girardeau, MO 63701-4799. Offers human environmental studies (MA). Part-time programs available. *Degree requirements:* For master's, thesis or alternative. *Entrance requirements:* For master's, GRE General Test, MAT, minimum undergraduate GPA of 2.75. Additional exam requirements/recommendations for international students: Required—TOEFL (minimum score 550 paper-based; 213 computer-based); Recommended—IELTS (minimum score 6). Electronic applications accepted. *Expenses:* Tuition, state resident: full-time $4266; part-time $237 per credit hour. Tuition, nonresident: full-time $7506; part-time $417 per credit hour. Required fees: $427; $427.

Southeast Missouri State University, School of Graduate Studies, Harrison College of Business, Cape Girardeau, MO 63701-4799. Offers accounting (MBA); entrepreneurship (MBA); environmental management (MBA); financial management (MBA); general management (MBA); health administration (MBA); industrial management (MBA); international business (MBA); sport management (MBA). *Accreditation:* AACSB. Part-time and evening/weekend programs available. Postbaccalaureate distance learning degree programs offered (no on-campus study). *Degree requirements:* For master's, applied research project. *Entrance requirements:* For master's, GMAT, minimum undergraduate GPA of 2.5. Additional exam requirements/recommendations for international students: Required—TOEFL (minimum score 550 paper-based; 213 computer-based); Recommended—IELTS (minimum score 6). *Expenses:* Tuition, state resident: full-time $4266; part-time $237 per credit hour. Tuition, nonresident: full-time $7506; part-time $417 per credit hour. Required fees: $427; $427. *Faculty research:* Human resources, laws impacting accounting, advertising.

Southern Illinois University Edwardsville, Graduate Studies and Research, College of Arts and Sciences, Program in Environmental Science Management, Edwardsville, IL 62026-0001. Offers MS. Part-time programs available. *Students:* 4 full-time (0 women), 5 part-time (4 women); includes 1 minority (African American), 1 international. Average age 26. 21 applicants, 29% accepted. In 2009, 1 master's awarded. *Degree requirements:* For master's, thesis, internship. *Entrance requirements:* For master's, GRE. Additional exam requirements/recommendations for international students: Required—TOEFL (minimum score 550 paper-based; 213 computer-based; 79 iBT), IELTS (minimum score 6.5). *Application deadline:* For fall admission, 7/23 for domestic students, 6/1 for international students; for spring admission, 12/11 for domestic students, 10/1 for international students. Applications are processed on a rolling basis. Application fee: $30. Electronic applications accepted. *Expenses:* Tuition, state resident: part-time $1252.50 per semester. Tuition, nonresident: part-time $3131.25 per semester. Required fees: $586.85 per semester. Tuition and fees vary according to course load. *Financial support:* Fellowships with full tuition reimbursements, research assistantships with full tuition reimbursements, teaching assistantships with full tuition reimbursements, career-related internships or fieldwork, Federal Work-Study, institutionally sponsored loans, scholarships/grants, traineeships, and unspecified assistantships available. Support available to part-time students. Financial award application deadline: 3/1; financial award applicants required to submit FAFSA. *Unit head:* Dr. Zhi-Qing Lin, Program Director, 618-650-2650, E-mail: zhlin@siue.edu. *Application contact:* Dr. Zhi-Qing Lin, Program Director, 618-650-2650, E-mail: zhlin@siue.edu.

Stanford University, School of Earth Sciences, Earth Systems Program, Stanford, CA 94305-9991. Offers MS. Students admitted at the undergraduate level. Electronic applications accepted. *Expenses:* Tuition: Full-time $37,380; part-time $2760 per quarter. Required fees: $501.

State University of New York College of Environmental Science and Forestry, Department of Environmental Studies, Syracuse, NY 13210-2779. Offers MPS, MS. *Degree requirements:* For master's, thesis (for some programs). *Entrance requirements:* For master's, GRE General Test.

State University of New York College of Environmental Science and Forestry, Department of Forest and Natural Resources Management, Syracuse, NY 13210-2779. Offers environmental and natural resource policy (MS, PhD); environmental and natural resources policy (MPS); forest management and operations (MF); forestry ecosystems science and applications (MPS, MS, PhD); natural resources management (MPS, MS, PhD); quantitative methods and management in forest science (MPS, MS, PhD); recreation and resource management (MPS, MS, PhD); watershed management and forest hydrology (MPS, MS, PhD). *Degree requirements:* For master's, thesis (for some programs); for doctorate, comprehensive exam, thesis/dissertation. *Entrance requirements:* For master's and doctorate, GRE General Test, minimum GPA of 3.0. Additional exam requirements/recommendations for international students: Required—TOEFL (minimum score 550 paper-based; 213 computer-based; 80 iBT), IELTS (minimum score 6). *Faculty research:* Silviculture recreation management, tree improvement, operations management, economics.

State University of New York College of Environmental Science and Forestry, Program in Environmental Science, Syracuse, NY 13210-2779. Offers environmental and community land planning (MPS, MS, PhD); environmental and natural resources policy (PhD); environmental communication and participatory processes (MPS, MS, PhD); environmental policy and democratic processes (MPS, MS, PhD); environmental systems and risk management (MPS,

Environmental Management and Policy

State University of New York College of Environmental Science and Forestry (continued)

MS, PhD); water and wetland resource studies (MPS, MS, PhD). Part-time programs available. *Degree requirements:* For master's, thesis (for some programs); for doctorate, comprehensive exam, thesis/dissertation. *Entrance requirements:* For master's and doctorate, GRE General Test, minimum GPA of 3.0. Additional exam requirements/recommendations for international students: Required—TOEFL (minimum score 550 paper-based; 213 computer-based; 80 iBT), IELTS (minimum score 6). *Faculty research:* Environmental education/communications, water resources, land resources, waste management.

Stony Brook University, State University of New York, Graduate School, College of Engineering and Applied Sciences, Department of Technology and Society, Program in Energy and Environmental Systems, Stony Brook, NY 11794. Offers MS, Advanced Certificate. Part-time programs available. *Degree requirements:* For master's, thesis, project. *Application deadline:* For fall admission, 5/1 for domestic students; for spring admission, 11/1 for domestic students. Electronic applications accepted. *Expenses:* Tuition, state resident: full-time $8370; part-time $349 per credit. Tuition, nonresident: full-time $13,250; part-time $552 per credit. Required fees: $933. *Financial support:* Research assistantships, teaching assistantships, career-related internships or fieldwork available. *Unit head:* David Ferguson, Chairman, 631-632-8770, E-mail: david.ferguson@stonybrook.edu. *Application contact:* Sheldon Reaven, 631-632-8770, E-mail: sheldon.raven@sunysb.edu.

Stony Brook University, State University of New York, School of Professional Development, Stony Brook, NY 11794. Offers biology-grade 7-12 (MAT); chemistry-grade 7-12 (MAT); coaching (Graduate Certificate); computer integrated engineering (Graduate Certificate); earth science-grade 7-12 (MAT); educational computing (Graduate Certificate); educational leadership (Advanced Certificate); English-grade 7-12 (MAT); environmental management (Graduate Certificate); environmental/occupational health and safety (Graduate Certificate); French-grade 7-12 (MAT); German-grade 7-12 (MAT); human resource management (Graduate Certificate); information systems management (Graduate Certificate); Italian-grade 7-12 (MAT); liberal studies (MA); mathematics-grade 7-12 (MAT); operation research (Graduate Certificate); physics-grade 7-12 (MAT); school administration and supervision (Graduate Certificate); school building leadership (Graduate Certificate); school district administration (Graduate Certificate); school district business leadership (Advanced Certificate); school district leadership (Graduate Certificate); social science and the professions (MPS), including environmental waste management, human resource management; social studies-grade 7-12 (MAT); Spanish-grade 7-12 (MAT); waste management (Graduate Certificate). Part-time and evening/weekend programs available. Postbaccalaureate distance learning degree programs offered. *Faculty:* 5 full-time (3 women), 131 part-time/adjunct (53 women). *Students:* 317 full-time (187 women), 1,200 part-time (773 women); includes 187 minority (77 African Americans, 2 American Indian/Alaska Native, 22 Asian Americans or Pacific Islanders, 86 Hispanic Americans), 11 international. Average age 28. In 2009, 597 master's, 234 other advanced degrees awarded. *Degree requirements:* For master's, one foreign language, thesis or alternative. *Application deadline:* Applications are processed on a rolling basis. Application fee: $62. *Expenses:* Tuition, state resident: full-time $8370; part-time $349 per credit. Tuition, nonresident: full-time $13,250; part-time $552 per credit. Required fees: $933. *Financial support:* Fellowships, research assistantships, teaching assistantships, career-related internships or fieldwork available. Support available to part-time students. *Unit head:* Dr. Paul J. Edelson, Dean, 631-632-7052, Fax: 631-632-9046, E-mail: paul.edelson@stonybrook.edu. *Application contact:* Dr. Paul J. Edelson, Dean, 631-632-7052, Fax: 631-632-9046, E-mail: paul.edelson@stonybrook.edu.

Texas State University–San Marcos, Graduate School, College of Liberal Arts, Department of Geography, Program in Resource and Environmental Studies, San Marcos, TX 78666. Offers MAG. Part-time and evening/weekend programs available. *Faculty:* 5 full-time (3 women), 2 part-time/adjunct (0 women). *Students:* 14 full-time (4 women), 22 part-time (10 women); includes 5 minority (1 Asian American or Pacific Islander, 4 Hispanic Americans). Average age 30. 15 applicants, 93% accepted, 14 enrolled. In 2009, 5 master's awarded. *Degree requirements:* For master's, comprehensive exam. *Entrance requirements:* For master's, GRE General Test, minimum GPA of 3.0 in last 60 hours of course work; letter of interest; 2 letters of recommendation; Vita/resume. Additional exam requirements/recommendations for international students: Required—TOEFL. *Application deadline:* For fall admission, 6/15 priority date for domestic students; for spring admission, 10/15 priority date for domestic students. Applications are processed on a rolling basis. Application fee: $40 ($90 for international students). *Expenses:* Tuition, state resident: full-time $5784; part-time $241 per credit hour. Tuition, nonresident: part-time $551 per credit hour. Required fees: $1728; $48 per credit hour. $306. Tuition and fees vary according to course load. *Financial support:* In 2009–10, 13 students received support, including 2 research assistantships (averaging $4,200 per year), 5 teaching assistantships (averaging $5,357 per year); career-related internships or fieldwork, Federal Work-Study, institutionally sponsored loans, and scholarships/grants also available. Support available to part-time students. Financial award application deadline: 4/1; financial award applicants required to submit FAFSA. *Unit head:* Dr. David Butler, Graduate Adviser, 512-245-2170, Fax: 512-245-8353, E-mail: db25@txstate.edu. *Application contact:* Dr. J. Michael Willoughby, Dean of Graduate School, 512-245-2581, Fax: 512-245-8365, E-mail: gradcollege@txstate.edu.

Texas Tech University, Graduate School, College of Architecture, PhD Program in Land-Use Planning, Management, and Design, Lubbock, TX 79409. Offers PhD. *Students:* 5 full-time (2 women), 3 part-time (1 woman), 3 international. Average age 39. 16 applicants, 50% accepted, 2 enrolled. In 2009, 1 doctorate awarded. *Degree requirements:* For doctorate, thesis/dissertation. *Entrance requirements:* For doctorate, GRE General Test. Additional exam requirements/recommendations for international students: Required—TOEFL (minimum score 550 paper-based; 213 computer-based). *Application deadline:* For fall admission, 3/1 priority date for international students; for spring admission, 11/1 priority date for international students. Applications are processed on a rolling basis. Application fee: $50 ($75 for international students). Electronic applications accepted. *Expenses:* Tuition, state resident: full-time $5100; part-time $213 per credit hour. Tuition, nonresident: full-time $11,748; part-time $490 per credit hour. Required fees: $2298; $50 per credit hour. $555 per semester. *Financial support:* Research assistantships with partial tuition reimbursements, teaching assistantships with partial tuition reimbursements, career-related internships or fieldwork, Federal Work-Study, and institutionally sponsored loans available. Support available to part-time students. Financial award application deadline: 4/15; financial award applicants required to submit FAFSA. *Faculty research:* Architecture, landscape architecture, urban planning, environmental engineering, environmental policy planning. *Unit head:* Dr. Saif Haq, Program Director, 806-742-3136 Ext. 265, Fax: 806-742-1400, E-mail: saif.haq@ttu.edu. *Application contact:* Lori Rodriguez, Academic Program Assistant, 806-742-3136 Ext. 247, Fax: 806-742-1400, E-mail: lori.rodriguez@ttu.edu.

Towson University, College of Graduate Studies and Research, Program in Geography and Environmental Planning, Towson, MD 21252-0001. Offers MA. Part-time and evening/weekend programs available. *Degree requirements:* For master's, thesis optional. *Entrance requirements:* For master's, 9 credits of course work in geography, minimum GPA of 3.0 in geography, 2 narrative letters of recomendation. Additional exam requirements/recommendations for international students: Required—TOEFL. Electronic applications accepted. *Faculty research:* Geographic information systems, regional planning, hazards, development issues, urban fluvial systems.

Trent University, Graduate Studies, Program in Environmental and Life Sciences, Environmental and Resource Studies Program, Peterborough, ON K9J 7B8, Canada. Offers M Sc, PhD. *Degree requirements:* For master's, thesis; for doctorate, thesis/dissertation. *Entrance requirements:* For master's, honours degree; for doctorate, master's degree. *Faculty research:* Environmental biogeochemistry, aquatic organic contaminants, fisheries, wetland ecology, renewable resource management.

Tropical Agriculture Research and Higher Education Center, Graduate School, Turrialba, Costa Rica. Offers agribusiness management (MS); agroforestry systems (PhD); ecological agriculture (MS); environmental socioeconomics (MS); forestry in tropical and subtropical zones (PhD); integrated watershed management (MS); management and conservation of tropical rainforests and biodiversity (MS); tropical agriculture (PhD); tropical agroforestry (MS). *Entrance requirements:* For master's, GRE, 2 years of related professional experience, letters of recommendation; for doctorate, GRE, 4 letters of recommendation, letter of support from employing organization, master's degree in agronomy, biological sciences, forestry, natural resources or related field. Additional exam requirements/recommendations for international students: Required—TOEFL (minimum score 550 paper-based; 213 computer-based). Electronic applications accepted. *Faculty research:* Biodiversity in fragmented landscapes, ecosystem management, integrated pest management, environmental livestock production, biotechnology carbon balances in diverse land uses.

Troy University, Graduate School, College of Arts and Sciences, Program in Environmental Analysis and Management, Troy, AL 36082. Offers MS. Part-time and evening/weekend programs available. *Students:* 13 full-time (7 women), 18 part-time (13 women); includes 8 minority (5 African Americans, 1 Asian American or Pacific Islander, 2 Hispanic Americans). Average age 25. 49 applicants, 24% accepted. In 2009, 10 master's awarded. *Degree requirements:* For master's, comprehensive exam or thesis. *Entrance requirements:* For master's, GRE or MAT, minimum undergraduate GPA of 2.5, 2 letters of recommendation. Additional exam requirements/recommendations for international students: Required—TOEFL (minimum score 523 paper-based; 193 computer-based; 70 iBT), IELTS (minimum score 6). *Application deadline:* Applications are processed on a rolling basis. Application fee: $50. Electronic applications accepted. *Unit head:* Dr. Glenn Cohen, Chairman, 334-670-3660, Fax: 334-670-3662, E-mail: gcohen@troy.edu. *Application contact:* Brenda K. Campbell, Director of Graduate Admissions, 334-670-3178, Fax: 334-670-3733, E-mail: bcamp@troy.edu.

Troy University, Graduate School, College of Arts and Sciences, Program in Public Administration, Troy, AL 36082. Offers education (MPA); environmental management (MPA); government contracting (MPA); health care administration (MPA); justice administration (MPA); management information systems (MPA); national security affairs (MPA); nonprofit management (MPA); public human resources management (MPA); public management (MPA). *Accreditation:* NASPAA. Part-time and evening/weekend programs available. Postbaccalaureate distance learning degree programs offered (no on-campus study). *Students:* 239 full-time (161 women), 652 part-time (416 women); includes 596 minority (547 African Americans, 11 American Indian/Alaska Native, 6 Asian Americans or Pacific Islanders, 32 Hispanic Americans). Average age 34. 415 applicants, 80% accepted. In 2009, 247 master's awarded. *Degree requirements:* For master's, capstone course, research methodologies course. *Entrance requirements:* For master's, GRE, MAT or GMAT, minimum undergraduate GPA of 2.5, letter of recommendation. Additional exam requirements/recommendations for international students: Required—TOEFL (minimum score 523 paper-based; 193 computer-based; 70 iBT), IELTS (minimum score 6). *Application deadline:* Applications are processed on a rolling basis. Application fee: $50. Electronic applications accepted. *Financial support:* Available to part-time students. Applicants required to submit FAFSA. *Unit head:* Dr. Ellen Rosell, Chairman, 334-670-3758, Fax: 334-670-5647, E-mail: erosell@troy.edu. *Application contact:* Brenda K. Campbell, Director of Graduate Admissions, 334-670-3178, Fax: 334-670-3733, E-mail: bcamp@troy.edu.

Tufts University, Graduate School of Arts and Sciences, Department of Urban and Environmental Policy and Planning, Medford, MA 02155. Offers community development (MA); environmental policy (MA); health and human welfare (MA); housing policy (MA); international environment/development policy (MA); public policy (MPP); MA/MS; MALD/MA. *Accreditation:* ACSP (one or more programs are accredited). Part-time programs available. *Faculty:* 11 full-time, 9 part-time/adjunct. *Students:* 133 (83 women); includes 26 minority (15 African Americans, 5 Asian Americans or Pacific Islanders, 6 Hispanic Americans), 2 international. Average age 27. 200 applicants, 63% accepted, 53 enrolled. In 2009, 44 master's awarded. *Degree requirements:* For master's, thesis, internship. *Entrance requirements:* For master's, GRE General Test. Additional exam requirements/recommendations for international students: Required—TOEFL (minimum score 550 paper-based; 213 computer-based; 80 iBT). *Application deadline:* For fall admission, 1/15 for domestic students, 12/15 for international students. Applications are processed on a rolling basis. Application fee: $75. Electronic applications accepted. *Expenses:* Contact institution. *Financial support:* Teaching assistantships with partial tuition reimbursements, career-related internships or fieldwork, Federal Work-Study, scholarships/grants, tuition waivers (partial), and unspecified assistantships available. Support available to part-time students. Financial award application deadline: 1/15; financial award applicants required to submit FAFSA. *Unit head:* Julian Agyeman, Chair, 617-627-3394, Fax: 617-627-3377. *Application contact:* Ann Urosevich, Department Administrator, 617-627-3394.

Tufts University, Graduate School of Arts and Sciences, Graduate Certificate Programs, Community Environmental Studies Program, Medford, MA 02155. Offers Certificate. Part-time and evening/weekend programs available. Electronic applications accepted. *Expenses:* Contact institution.

Tufts University, Graduate School of Arts and Sciences, Graduate Certificate Programs, Environmental Management Program, Medford, MA 02155. Offers Certificate. Part-time and evening/weekend programs available. Electronic applications accepted. *Expenses:* Tuition: Full-time $38,096; part-time $3962 per credit. Required fees: $686; $40 per year. Tuition and fees vary according to course level, course load, degree level, program and student level.

Tufts University, School of Engineering, Department of Civil and Environmental Engineering, Medford, MA 02155. Offers civil engineering (ME, MS, PhD), including geotechnical engineering, structural engineering; environmental engineering (ME, MS, PhD), including environmental engineering and environmental sciences, environmental geotechnology, environmental health, environmental science and management, hazardous materials management, water resources engineering. Part-time programs available. *Faculty:* 17 full-time, 7 part-time/adjunct. *Students:* 72 (33 women); includes 6 minority (2 African Americans, 4 Asian Americans or Pacific Islanders), 17 international. Average age 27. 170 applicants, 59% accepted, 20 enrolled. In 2009, 17 master's, 3 doctorates awarded. Terminal master's awarded for partial completion of doctoral program. *Degree requirements:* For master's, thesis or alternative; for doctorate, thesis/dissertation. *Entrance requirements:* For master's and doctorate, GRE General Test. Additional exam requirements/recommendations for international students: Required—TOEFL (minimum score 550 paper-based; 213 computer-based; 80 iBT). *Application deadline:* For fall admission, 1/15 priority date for domestic students, 12/15 for international students; for spring admission, 10/15 for domestic students, 9/15 for international students. Applications are processed on a rolling basis. Application fee: $75. Electronic applications accepted. *Expenses:* Tuition: Full-time $38,096; part-time $3962 per credit. Required fees: $686; $40 per year. Tuition and fees vary according to course level, course load, degree level, program and student level. *Financial support:* Fellowships with full tuition reimbursements, research assistantships with full and partial tuition reimbursements, teaching assistantships with full and partial tuition reimbursements, Federal Work-Study, scholarships/grants, tuition waivers (partial), and unspecified assistantships available. Financial award application deadline: 1/15; financial award applicants required to submit FAFSA. *Unit head:* Dr. Kurt Pennell, Chair, 617-627-3211, Fax: 617-627-3994. *Application contact:* Laura Sacco, Information Contact, 617-627-3211.

Universidad Autonoma de Guadalajara, Graduate Programs, Guadalajara, Mexico. Offers administrative law and justice (LL M); advertising and corporate communications (MA);

architecture (M Arch); business (MBA); computational science (MCC); education (Ed M, Ed D); English-Spanish translation (MA); fiscal law (MA); integrated management of digital animation (MA); international business (MIB); international corporate law (LL M); internet technologies (MS); labor health (MS); manufacturing systems (MMS); philosophy (MA, PhD); power electronics (MS); quality systems (MQS); renewable energy (MS); social evaluation of projects (MBA); strategic market research (MBA); teaching mathematics (MA).

Universidad del Turabo, Graduate Programs, Programs in Science and Technology, Gurabo, PR 00778-3030. Offers environmental analysis (MSE), including environmental chemistry; environmental management (MSE), including pollution management; environmental science (D Sc), including environmental biology. *Students:* 8 full-time (7 women), 110 part-time (76 women); includes 115 Hispanic Americans. Average age 37. 52 applicants, 65% accepted, 30 enrolled. In 2009, 6 master's awarded. *Entrance requirements:* For master's, GRE, EXADEP, interview. *Application deadline:* For fall admission, 8/5 for domestic students. Application fee: $25. *Application contact:* Virginia Gonzalez, Admissions Officer, 787-746-3009.

Universidad Metropolitana, School of Environmental Affairs, Program in Environmental Planning, San Juan, PR 00928-1150. Offers MSEM. Part-time programs available. *Degree requirements:* For master's, thesis. *Entrance requirements:* For master's, EXADEP, interview. Electronic applications accepted.

Universidad Metropolitana, School of Environmental Affairs, Program in Environmental Risk and Assessment Management, San Juan, PR 00928-1150. Offers MSEM. Part-time programs available. *Degree requirements:* For master's, thesis. Electronic applications accepted.

Université de Montréal, Faculty of Medicine, Programs in Environment and Prevention, Montréal, QC H3C 3J7, Canada. Offers environment and prevention (DESS); environment, health and disaster management (DESS). Electronic applications accepted. *Faculty research:* Health, environment, pollutants, protection, waste.

Université du Québec à Chicoutimi, Graduate Programs, Program in Renewable Resources, Chicoutimi, QC G7H 2B1, Canada. Offers M Sc. Part-time programs available. *Degree requirements:* For master's, thesis. *Entrance requirements:* For master's, appropriate bachelor's degree, proficiency in French.

Université du Québec, Institut National de la Recherche Scientifique, Graduate Programs, Research Center—Water, Earth and Environment, Québec, QC G1K 9A9, Canada. Offers earth sciences (M Sc, PhD); earth sciences-environmental technologies (M Sc); water sciences (M Sc, PhD). Part-time programs available. *Faculty:* 42. *Students:* 181 full-time (70 women), 9 part-time (1 woman), 74 international. Average age 30. In 2009, 19 master's, 10 doctorates awarded. *Degree requirements:* For master's, thesis optional; for doctorate, thesis/dissertation. *Entrance requirements:* For master's, appropriate bachelor's degree, proficiency in French; for doctorate, appropriate master's degree, proficiency in French. *Application deadline:* For fall admission, 3/30 for domestic and international students; for winter admission, 11/1 for domestic and international students. Application fee: $30. *Financial support:* Fellowships, research assistantships, teaching assistantships available. *Faculty research:* Land use, impacts of climate change, adaptation to climate change, integrated management of resources (mineral and water). *Unit head:* Yves Begin, Director, 418-654-2524, Fax: 418-654-2600, E-mail: info@ete.inrs.ca. *Application contact:* Yvonne Boisvert, Registrar, 418-654-3861, Fax: 418-654-3858, E-mail: registrariat@adm.inrs.ca.

Université Laval, Faculty of Administrative Sciences, Programs in Business Administration, Québec, QC G1K 7P4, Canada. Offers accounting (MBA); agri-food management (MBA); electronic business (MBA, Diploma); factory management and logistics (MBA); finance (MBA); firm management (MBA); geomatic management (MBA); information technology management (MBA); international management (MBA); management (MBA); management accounting (MBA, Diploma); marketing (MBA); modeling and organizational decision (MBA); occupational health and safety management (MBA); pharmacy management (MBA); social and environmental responsibility (MBA); technological entrepreneurship (Diploma). *Accreditation:* AACSB. Part-time and evening/weekend programs available. Postbaccalaureate distance learning degree programs offered (no on-campus study). *Entrance requirements:* For master's and Diploma, knowledge of French and English. Electronic applications accepted.

Université Laval, Faculty of Agricultural and Food Sciences, Department of Soils and Agricultural Engineering, Programs in Agri-Food Engineering, Québec, QC G1K 7P4, Canada. Offers agri-food engineering (M Sc); environmental technology (M Sc). *Degree requirements:* For master's, thesis (for some programs). *Entrance requirements:* For master's, knowledge of French. Electronic applications accepted.

Université Laval, Faculty of Agricultural and Food Sciences, Department of Soils and Agricultural Engineering, Programs in Soils and Environment Science, Québec, QC G1K 7P4, Canada. Offers environmental technology (M Sc); soils and environment science (M Sc, PhD). Terminal master's awarded for partial completion of doctoral program. *Degree requirements:* For master's, thesis (for some programs); for doctorate, comprehensive exam, thesis/dissertation. *Entrance requirements:* For master's and doctorate, knowledge of French and English. Electronic applications accepted.

University at Albany, State University of New York, College of Arts and Sciences, Department of Biological Sciences, Program in Biodiversity, Conservation, and Policy, Albany, NY 12222-0001. Offers MS. *Degree requirements:* For master's, one foreign language. *Entrance requirements:* For master's, GRE General Test. *Faculty research:* Aquatic ecology, plant community ecology, biodiversity and public policy, restoration ecology, coastal and estuarine science.

University of Alaska Fairbanks, College of Engineering and Mines, Department of Civil and Environmental Engineering, Program in Environmental Engineering, Fairbanks, AK 99775-5900. Offers engineering (PhD), including environmental engineering; environmental engineering (MS), including environmental contaminants, environmental science and management, water supply and waste treatment. Part-time programs available. *Students:* 4 full-time (3 women), 3 part-time (2 women). Average age 28. 5 applicants, 60% accepted, 1 enrolled. In 2009, 3 master's, 1 doctorate awarded. *Degree requirements:* For master's, comprehensive exam, thesis or alternative; for doctorate, comprehensive exam, thesis/dissertation, oral exam, oral defense. *Entrance requirements:* For master's, basic computer techniques; for doctorate, GRE General Test. Additional exam requirements/recommendations for international students: Required—TOEFL (minimum score 575 paper-based; 213 computer-based). *Application deadline:* For fall admission, 5/1 for domestic students, 3/1 for international students; for spring admission, 10/15 for domestic students, 9/1 for international students. Applications are processed on a rolling basis. Application fee: $60. Electronic applications accepted. *Expenses:* Tuition, state resident: full-time $7584; part-time $316 per credit. Tuition, nonresident: full-time $15,504; part-time $646 per credit. Required fees: $23 per credit. $135 per semester. Tuition and fees vary according to course level, course load and reciprocity agreements. *Financial support:* In 2009–10, 4 research assistantships (averaging $13,290 per year), 1 teaching assistantship (averaging $7,088 per year) were awarded; fellowships, career-related internships or fieldwork, Federal Work-Study, scholarships/grants, health care benefits, and unspecified assistantships also available. Support available to part-time students. Financial award application deadline: 7/1; financial award applicants required to submit FAFSA. *Unit head:* Dr. David Barnes, Department Chair, 907-474-7241, Fax: 907-474-6087, E-mail: fyeqe@uaf.edu. *Application contact:* Dr. David Barnes, Department Chair, 907-474-7241, Fax: 907-474-6087, E-mail: fyeqe@uaf.edu.

University of Alaska Fairbanks, College of Liberal Arts, Department of Northern Studies, Fairbanks, AK 99775-6460. Offers environmental politics and policy (MA); Northern history (MA). Part-time programs available. *Faculty:* 9 full-time (5 women), 1 part-time/adjunct (0 women). *Students:* 14 full-time (6 women), 21 part-time (15 women); includes 2 minority (1 African American, 1 American Indian/Alaska Native), 5 international. Average age 39. 19 applicants, 63% accepted, 9 enrolled. In 2009, 11 master's awarded. *Degree requirements:* For master's, comprehensive exam, thesis or alternative. *Entrance requirements:* Additional exam requirements/recommendations for international students: Required—TOEFL (minimum score 550 paper-based; 213 computer-based; 80 iBT). *Application deadline:* For fall admission, 6/1 for domestic students, 3/1 for international students; for spring admission, 10/15 for domestic students, 9/1 for international students. Applications are processed on a rolling basis. Application fee: $60. Electronic applications accepted. *Expenses:* Tuition, state resident: full-time $7584; part-time $316 per credit. Tuition, nonresident: full-time $15,504; part-time $646 per credit. Required fees: $23 per credit. $135 per semester. Tuition and fees vary according to course level, course load and reciprocity agreements. *Financial support:* In 2009–10, 3 research assistantships (averaging $7,517 per year), 11 teaching assistantships (averaging $7,671 per year) were awarded; fellowships, career-related internships or fieldwork, Federal Work-Study, scholarships/grants, health care benefits, and unspecified assistantships also available. Support available to part-time students. Financial award application deadline: 1/1; financial award applicants required to submit FAFSA. *Faculty research:* Canadian history, environmental history, Native Alaskan history and art, fetal alcohol syndrome. *Unit head:* Dr. Judith S. Kleinfeld, Co-Director, 907-474-7126, Fax: 907-474-5817, E-mail: fynors@uaf.edu. *Application contact:* Dr. Judith S. Kleinfeld, Co-Director, 907-474-7126, Fax: 907-474-5817, E-mail: fynors@uaf.edu.

University of Alberta, Faculty of Graduate Studies and Research, Department of Economics, Edmonton, AB T6G 2E1, Canada. Offers economics (MA, PhD); economics and finance (MA); environmental and natural resource economics (PhD). Part-time programs available. *Faculty:* 25 full-time (5 women), 3 part-time/adjunct (0 women). *Students:* 33 full-time (7 women), 7 part-time (3 women). Average age 26. 112 applicants, 58% accepted, 22 enrolled. In 2009, 8 master's, 1 doctorate awarded. *Degree requirements:* For doctorate, thesis/dissertation. *Entrance requirements:* For master's and doctorate, GRE. Additional exam requirements/recommendations for international students: Required—TOEFL. *Application deadline:* For fall admission, 6/15 for domestic students. Applications are processed on a rolling basis. Tuition and fees charges are reported in Canadian dollars. *Expenses:* Tuition, area resident: Full-time $4626.24 Canadian dollars; part-time $99.72 Canadian dollars per unit. International tuition: $8216 Canadian dollars full-time. Required fees: $3589.92 Canadian dollars; $99.72 Canadian dollars per unit. $215 Canadian dollars per term. *Financial support:* In 2009–10, 19 students received support, including 6 research assistantships with partial tuition reimbursements available (averaging $14,300 per year), 5 teaching assistantships with partial tuition reimbursements available (averaging $11,200 per year); career-related internships or fieldwork and scholarships/grants also available. Financial award application deadline: 3/1. *Faculty research:* Public finance, international trade, industrial organization, Pacific Rim economics, monetary economics. *Unit head:* Henry van Egteren, Graduate Coordinator, 780-492-7634, Fax: 780-492-3300. *Application contact:* Audrey Jackson, Graduate Program Administrator, 780-492-7634, Fax: 780-492-3300, E-mail: econapps@ualberta.ca.

University of Calgary, Faculty of Graduate Studies, Interdisciplinary Graduate Programs, Calgary, AB T2N 1N4, Canada. Offers interdisciplinary research (M Sc, MA, PhD); resources and the environment (M Sc, MA, PhD). Part-time programs available. *Degree requirements:* For master's, thesis; for doctorate, thesis/dissertation, written and oral candidacy exam. *Entrance requirements:* Additional exam requirements/recommendations for international students: Required—TOEFL (minimum score 600 paper-based; 250 computer-based).

University of Calgary, Faculty of Law, Programs in Natural Resources, Energy and Environmental Law, Calgary, AB T2N 1N4, Canada. Offers LL M, Graduate Certificate. *Entrance requirements:* Additional exam requirements/recommendations for international students: Required—TOEFL.

University of California, Berkeley, Graduate Division, College of Natural Resources, Department of Environmental Science, Policy, and Management, Berkeley, CA 94720-1500. Offers environmental science, policy, and management (MS, PhD); forestry (MF). *Students:* 270 full-time (185 women). Average age 31. 281 applicants, 27 enrolled. In 2009, 8 master's, 24 doctorates awarded. Terminal master's awarded for partial completion of doctoral program. *Degree requirements:* For master's, thesis optional; for doctorate, thesis/dissertation, qualifying exam. *Entrance requirements:* For master's and doctorate, GRE General Test, minimum GPA of 3.0, 3 letters of recommendation. Additional exam requirements/recommendations for international students: Required—TOEFL. *Application deadline:* For fall admission, 12/1 for domestic students. Application fee: $70 ($90 for international students). Electronic applications accepted. *Financial support:* Fellowships with full tuition reimbursements, research assistantships with full tuition reimbursements, teaching assistantships with full tuition reimbursements, unspecified assistantships available. Financial award application deadline: 12/1; financial award applicants required to submit FAFSA. *Faculty research:* Biology and ecology of insects; ecosystem function and environmental issues of soils; plant health/interactions from molecular to ecosystem levels; range management and ecology; forest and resource policy, sustainability, and management. *Unit head:* Prof. Allen Goldstein, Chair, 510-643-7430, Fax: 510-643-5438, E-mail: espmgrad@berkeley.edu. *Application contact:* Richard M. Battrick, Student Affairs Officer, 510-642-6410, Fax: 510-642-4034, E-mail: espmgrad@nature.berkeley.edu.

University of California, Berkeley, UC Berkeley Extension, Certificate Programs in Sustainability Studies, Berkeley, CA 94720-1500. Offers leadership in sustainability and environmental management (Professional Certificate); solar energy and green building (Professional Certificate); sustainable design (Professional Certificate). *Unit head:* Diana Wu, Dean, 510-642-4181. *Application contact:* Sustainability Studies, 510-642-4151, E-mail: course@unex.berkeley.edu.

University of California, Santa Barbara, Graduate Division, Donald Bren School of Environmental Science and Management, Santa Barbara, CA 93106-5131. Offers MESM, PhD. *Faculty:* 18 full-time (4 women), 24 part-time/adjunct (7 women). *Students:* 187 full-time (112 women); includes 21 minority (1 African American, 1 American Indian/Alaska Native, 11 Asian Americans or Pacific Islanders, 8 Hispanic Americans), 15 international. Average age 27. 335 applicants, 61% accepted, 89 enrolled. In 2009, 63 master's, 8 doctorates awarded. *Degree requirements:* For master's, thesis optional, group project as student thesis; for doctorate, comprehensive exam, thesis/dissertation. *Entrance requirements:* For master's, GRE, 3 letters of recommendation, resume/curriculum vitae; for doctorate, GRE, 3 letters of recommendation, statement of purpose, personal achievements/contributions statement, resume/curriculum vitae, transcripts for post-secondary institutions attended. Additional exam requirements/recommendations for international students: Required—TOEFL (minimum score 550 paper-based; 213 computer-based; 80 iBT), or IELTS (minimum score 7). *Application deadline:* For fall admission, 1/10 priority date for domestic and international students. Application fee: $70 ($90 for international students). Electronic applications accepted. *Financial support:* In 2009–10, 68 students received support, including 44 fellowships with full and partial tuition reimbursements available (averaging $8,400 per year), 20 research assistantships with full and partial tuition reimbursements available (averaging $6,600 per year), 28 teaching assistantships with partial tuition reimbursements available (averaging $6,900 per year); career-related internships or fieldwork, Federal Work-Study, institutionally sponsored loans, scholarships/grants, health care benefits, and unspecified assistantships also available. Financial award application deadline: 12/15; financial award applicants required to submit FAFSA. *Faculty research:* Ecological processes, environmental politics and policy, sustainability, conservation science and planning, water resources management. *Unit head:* Dr. John Melack, Acting Dean, 805-

Environmental Management and Policy

University of California, Santa Barbara (continued)
893-3879, Fax: 805-893-6113, E-mail: melack@bren.ucsb.edu. *Application contact:* Kristen Robinson, Graduate Program Advisor, 805-893-7611, Fax: 805-893-6113, E-mail: gradasst@bren.ucsb.edu.

University of California, Santa Cruz, Division of Graduate Studies, Division of Social Sciences, Program in Environmental Studies, Santa Cruz, CA 95064. Offers PhD. *Degree requirements:* For doctorate, thesis/dissertation, qualifying exam. *Entrance requirements:* For doctorate, GRE General Test. Additional exam requirements/recommendations for international students: Required—TOEFL (minimum score 550 paper-based; 220 computer-based). *Faculty research:* Political economy and sustainability, conservation biology, agroecology.

University of Central Missouri, The Graduate School, College of Science and Technology, Warrensburg, MO 64093. Offers applied mathematics (MS); aviation safety (MS); biology (MS); computer science (MS); environmental studies (MA); industrial management (MS); mathematics (MS); technology (MS); technology management (PhD). Part-time programs available. Postbaccalaureate distance learning degree programs offered. *Faculty:* 59. *Students:* 99 full-time (31 women), 85 part-time (37 women). Average age 33. 45 applicants, 96% accepted, 42 enrolled. In 2009, 68 master's awarded. *Entrance requirements:* Additional exam requirements/recommendations for international students: Required—TOEFL (minimum score 550 paper-based; 79 computer-based). *Application deadline:* For fall admission, 6/1 priority date for domestic students, 5/1 for international students; for spring admission, 10/1 priority date for domestic students, 10/1 for international students. Applications are processed on a rolling basis. Application fee: $30 ($75 for international students). Electronic applications accepted. *Expenses:* Tuition, area resident: Part-time $245.80 per credit hour. Tuition, nonresident: part-time $491.60 per credit hour. Required fees: $24.20 per credit hour. Full-time tuition and fees vary according to course load, degree level, campus/location and reciprocity agreements. *Financial support:* In 2009–10, 15 students received support; fellowships with full and partial tuition reimbursements available, research assistantships with full and partial tuition reimbursements available, teaching assistantships with full and partial tuition reimbursements available, career-related internships or fieldwork, Federal Work-Study, scholarships/grants, and administrative and laboratory assistantships available. Support available to part-time students. Financial award application deadline: 3/1; financial award applicants required to submit FAFSA. *Unit head:* Dr. Alice Greife, Dean, 660-543-4450, Fax: 660-543-8031, E-mail: greife@ucmo.edu. *Application contact:* Laurie Delap, Admissions Coordinator, 660-543-4621, Fax: 660-543-4778, E-mail: gradinfo@ucmo.edu.

University of Chicago, Irving B. Harris Graduate School of Public Policy Studies, Chicago, IL 60637-1513. Offers environmental science and policy (MS); public policy studies (AM, MPP, PhD); JD/MPP; MBA/MPP; MPP/M Div; MPP/MA. Part-time programs available. *Degree requirements:* For doctorate, thesis/dissertation. *Entrance requirements:* Additional exam requirements/recommendations for international students: Required—TOEFL. Electronic applications accepted. *Expenses:* Contact institution. *Faculty research:* Family and child policy, international security, health policy, social policy.

University of Colorado at Boulder, Graduate School, College of Arts and Sciences, Program in Environmental Studies, Boulder, CO 80309. Offers MS, PhD. *Faculty:* 9 full-time (4 women). *Students:* 45 full-time (28 women), 6 part-time (4 women); includes 8 minority (1 African American, 3 American Indian/Alaska Native, 4 Asian Americans or Pacific Islanders). Average age 31. 271 applicants, 6% accepted, 7 enrolled. In 2009, 6 master's, 3 doctorates awarded. *Entrance requirements:* For master's, minimum undergraduate GPA of 3.0. *Application deadline:* For fall admission, 1/15 for domestic students, 12/1 for international students. *Financial support:* In 2009–10, 19 fellowships (averaging $13,158 per year), 13 research assistantships (averaging $13,454 per year) were awarded. *Faculty research:* Climate and atmospheric chemistry, water sciences, environmental policy and sustainability, waste management and environmental remediation, biogeochemical cycles. Total annual research expenditures: $831,855.

University of Dayton, Graduate School, School of Engineering, Department of Mechanical and Aerospace Engineering, Dayton, OH 45469-1300. Offers aerospace engineering (MSAE, DE, PhD); mechanical engineering (MSME, DE, PhD); renewable and clean energy (MS). Part-time programs available. Postbaccalaureate distance learning degree programs offered (no on-campus study). *Faculty:* 15 full-time (2 women), 13 part-time/adjunct (1 woman). *Students:* 83 full-time (16 women), 29 part-time (5 women); includes 13 minority (6 African Americans, 3 Asian Americans or Pacific Islanders, 4 Hispanic Americans), 32 international. Average age 30. 80 applicants, 50% accepted, 24 enrolled. In 2009, 24 master's, 5 doctorates awarded. Terminal master's awarded for partial completion of doctoral program. *Degree requirements:* For master's, thesis optional; for doctorate, variable foreign language requirement, thesis/dissertation, departmental qualifying exam. *Entrance requirements:* Additional exam requirements/recommendations for international students: Required—TOEFL (minimum score 550 paper-based; 213 computer-based; 80 iBT). *Application deadline:* For fall admission, 8/1 priority date for domestic students, 6/1 priority date for international students; for winter admission, 9/1 priority date for international students; for spring admission, 3/1 priority date for international students. Applications are processed on a rolling basis. Application fee: $0. Electronic applications accepted. *Expenses:* Tuition: Full-time $8412; part-time $701 per credit hour. Required fees: $325; $65 per course. $25 per semester. Tuition and fees vary according to course load, degree level and program. *Financial support:* In 2009–10, 25 students received support, including 2 fellowships with full tuition reimbursements available (averaging $27,500 per year), 22 research assistantships with full tuition reimbursements available (averaging $12,000 per year), 1 teaching assistantship (averaging $9,000 per year). Financial award applicants required to submit FAFSA. *Faculty research:* Jet engine combustion, surface coating friction and wear, aircraft thermal management, aerospace fuels, energy efficient buildings, energy efficient manufacturing, renewable energy. Total annual research expenditures: $1.2 million. *Unit head:* Dr. Kevin Hallinan, Chair, 937-229-2835, Fax: 937-229-4766, E-mail: kevin.hallinan@udayton.edu. *Application contact:* Graduate Admissions, 937-229-4411, Fax: 937-229-4729, E-mail: gradadmission@udayton.edu.

University of Delaware, College of Human Services, Education and Public Policy, Center for Energy and Environmental Policy, Newark, DE 19716. Offers environmental and energy policy (MEEP, PhD); urban affairs and public policy (MA, PhD), including community development and nonprofit leadership (MA), energy and environmental policy (MA), governance, planning and management (PhD), historic preservation (MA), social and urban policy (PhD), technology, environment and society (PhD). *Degree requirements:* For master's, analytical paper or thesis; for doctorate, comprehensive exam, thesis/dissertation. *Entrance requirements:* For master's, GRE General Test, minimum GPA of 3.0; for doctorate, GRE General Test, minimum GPA of 3.5. Additional exam requirements/recommendations for international students: Required—TOEFL. Electronic applications accepted. *Faculty research:* Sustainable development, renewable energy, climate change, environmental policy, environmental justice, disaster policy.

University of Denver, University College, Denver, CO 80208. Offers applied communication (MAS, MPS, Certificate); computer information systems (MAS, Certificate); environmental policy and management (MAS, Certificate); geographic information systems (MAS, Certificate); human resource administration (MPS, Certificate); knowledge and information technologies (MAS); liberal studies (MLS, Certificate); modern languages (MLS, Certificate); organizational leadership (MPS, Certificate); security management (Certificate); technology management (MAS, Certificate), including 21st century strategic management (MAS), international markets (MAS), project management (MAS), research and development management (MAS); telecommunications (MAS, Certificate), including broadband (MAS), telecommunications management and policy (MAS), telecommunications technology (MAS), wireless networks (MAS). Part-time and evening/weekend programs available. Postbaccalaureate distance learning degree programs offered (no on-campus study). *Faculty:* 160 part-time/adjunct (64 women). *Students:* 53 full-time (25 women), 984 part-time (551 women); includes 171 minority (72 African Americans, 10 American Indian/Alaska Native, 33 Asian Americans or Pacific Islanders, 56 Hispanic Americans), 75 international. Average age 36. 537 applicants, 96% accepted, 494 enrolled. In 2009, 229 master's, 109 Certificates awarded. *Entrance requirements:* Additional exam requirements/recommendations for international students: Required—TOEFL (minimum score 550 paper-based; 213 computer-based). *Application deadline:* Applications are processed on a rolling basis. Application fee: $75. Electronic applications accepted. *Expenses:* Contact institution. *Financial support:* Applicants required to submit FAFSA. *Unit head:* Dr. James Davis, Dean, 303-871-2291, Fax: 303-871-4047, E-mail: jdavis@du.edu. *Application contact:* Information Contact, 303-871-3155.

The University of Findlay, Graduate and Professional Studies, College of Sciences, Master of Science Program in Environmental, Safety and Health Management, Findlay, OH 45840-3653. Offers MSEM. Part-time and evening/weekend programs available. Postbaccalaureate distance learning degree programs offered (no on-campus study). *Degree requirements:* For master's, cumulative project. *Entrance requirements:* For master's, GRE, minimum undergraduate GPA of 3.0 in last 60 hours of course work. Additional exam requirements/recommendations for international students: Required—TOEFL (minimum score 550 paper-based; 213 computer-based; 80 iBT). Electronic applications accepted.

University of Guelph, Graduate Program Services, Ontario Agricultural College, Department of Land Resource Science, Guelph, ON N1G 2W1, Canada. Offers atmospheric science (M Sc, PhD); environmental and agricultural earth sciences (M Sc, PhD); land resources management (M Sc, PhD); soil science (M Sc, PhD). Part-time programs available. *Degree requirements:* For master's, thesis (for some programs), research project (non-thesis track); for doctorate, comprehensive exam, thesis/dissertation. *Entrance requirements:* For master's, minimum B- average during previous 2 years of course work; for doctorate, minimum B average during previous 2 years of course work. Additional exam requirements/recommendations for international students: Required—TOEFL (minimum score 550 paper-based; 213 computer-based). Electronic applications accepted. *Faculty research:* Soil science, environmental earth science, land resource management.

University of Hawaii at Manoa, Graduate Division, College of Social Sciences, Department of Urban and Regional Planning, Honolulu, HI 96822. Offers community planning and social policy (MURP); disaster preparedness and emergency management (Graduate Certificate); environmental planning and management (MURP); land use and infrastructure planning (MURP); urban and regional planning (PhD, Graduate Certificate); urban and regional planning in Asia and Pacific (MURP). *Accreditation:* ACSP. Part-time programs available. *Faculty:* 19 full-time (6 women), 17 part-time/adjunct (3 women). *Students:* 51 full-time (26 women), 45 part-time (22 women); includes 28 minority (1 American Indian/Alaska Native, 26 Asian Americans or Pacific Islanders, 1 Hispanic American), 25 international. Average age 32. 67 applicants, 66% accepted, 21 enrolled. In 2009, 27 master's, 4 doctorates, 1 other advanced degree awarded. *Entrance requirements:* For master's, GRE General Test, minimum GPA of 3.0; for doctorate, GRE General Test. Additional exam requirements/recommendations for international students: Required—TOEFL (minimum score 500 paper-based; 173 computer-based; 61 iBT), IELTS (minimum score 5). *Application deadline:* For fall admission, 3/1 for domestic and international students; for spring admission, 9/1 for domestic and international students. Application fee: $60. *Expenses:* Tuition, state resident: full-time $8900; part-time $372 per credit. Tuition, nonresident: full-time $21,400; part-time $898 per credit. Required fees: $207 per semester. *Financial support:* In 2009–10, 4 students received support, including 8 fellowships (averaging $1,625 per year), 23 research assistantships (averaging $16,551 per year), 1 teaching assistantship (averaging $15,558 per year); career-related internships or fieldwork, Federal Work-Study, institutionally sponsored loans, and tuition waivers (full) also available. Total annual research expenditures: $423,000. *Application contact:* Dolores Foley, Graduate Chair, 808-956-7381, Fax: 808-956-6870, E-mail: dolores@hawaii.edu.

University of Hawaii at Manoa, Graduate Division, College of Tropical Agriculture and Human Resources, Department of Natural Resources and Environmental Management, Honolulu, HI 96822. Offers MS, PhD. Part-time programs available. *Faculty:* 28 full-time (3 women), 10 part-time/adjunct (3 women). *Students:* 52 full-time (28 women), 13 part-time (5 women); includes 12 minority (11 Asian Americans or Pacific Islanders, 1 Hispanic American), 23 international. Average age 29. 60 applicants, 62% accepted, 24 enrolled. In 2009, 10 master's, 4 doctorates awarded. Terminal master's awarded for partial completion of doctoral program. *Degree requirements:* For master's, thesis optional; for doctorate, comprehensive exam, thesis/dissertation. *Entrance requirements:* For master's and doctorate, GRE General Test, minimum GPA of 3.0 in last 4 semesters of course work. Additional exam requirements/recommendations for international students: Required—TOEFL (minimum score 600 paper-based; 250 computer-based; 100 iBT), IELTS (minimum score 7). *Application deadline:* For fall admission, 3/1 for domestic students, 1/15 for international students; for spring admission, 9/1 for domestic students, 8/1 for international students. Applications are processed on a rolling basis. Application fee: $60. *Expenses:* Tuition, state resident: full-time $8900; part-time $372 per credit. Tuition, nonresident: full-time $21,400; part-time $898 per credit. Required fees: $207 per semester. *Financial support:* In 2009–10, 1 student received support, including 5 fellowships (averaging $3,860 per year), 21 research assistantships (averaging $17,968 per year), 3 teaching assistantships (averaging $14,382 per year); career-related internships or fieldwork and tuition waivers (full and partial) also available. *Faculty research:* Bioeconomics, natural resource management. Total annual research expenditures: $3.1 million. *Application contact:* Ali Fares, Graduate Chair, 808-956-7530, Fax: 808-956-6539, E-mail: afares@hawaii.edu.

University of Houston–Clear Lake, School of Business, Program in Administrative Science, Houston, TX 77058-1098. Offers environmental management (MS); human resource management (MA). *Accreditation:* CAHME (one or more programs are accredited). Part-time and evening/weekend programs available. *Degree requirements:* For master's, thesis optional. *Entrance requirements:* For master's, GMAT. Additional exam requirements/recommendations for international students: Required—TOEFL (minimum score 550 paper-based; 213 computer-based). Electronic applications accepted.

University of Illinois at Springfield, Graduate Programs, College of Public Affairs and Administration, Program in Environmental Studies, Springfield, IL 62703-5407. Offers environmental science (MS); environmental studies (MA). Part-time and evening/weekend programs available. Postbaccalaureate distance learning degree programs offered (no on-campus study). *Faculty:* 4 full-time (1 woman), 3 part-time/adjunct (0 women). *Students:* 13 full-time (7 women), 77 part-time (50 women); includes 5 minority (1 African American, 2 Asian Americans or Pacific Islanders, 2 Hispanic Americans), 2 international. Average age 36. 76 applicants, 55% accepted, 26 enrolled. In 2009, 7 master's awarded. *Degree requirements:* For master's, thesis or project. *Entrance requirements:* For master's, minimum undergraduate GPA of 3.0, 2 letters of recommendation. Additional exam requirements/recommendations for international students: Required—TOEFL (minimum score 500 paper-based; 176 computer-based; 61 iBT). *Application deadline:* Applications are processed on a rolling basis. Application fee: $50 ($60 for international students). Electronic applications accepted. *Expenses:* Tuition, state resident: full-time $6390; part-time $266.25 per credit hour. Tuition, nonresident: full-time $14,226; part time $592.75 per credit hour. Required fees: $2044; $14.36 per credit hour. $722.50 per term. *Financial support:* In 2009–10, research assistantships with full tuition reimbursements (averaging $8,109 per year), teaching assistantships with full tuition reimbursements (averaging $8,109 per year) were awarded; career-related internships or fieldwork, Federal Work-Study, scholarships/grants, health care benefits, and unspecified assistantships also available. Support available to part-time students. Financial award application deadline: 11/15; financial award applicants required to submit FAFSA. *Unit head:* Dr. Dennis Ruez, Program Administrator, 217-206-8424, E-mail: druez2@uis.edu. *Application contact:* Dr. Lynn Pardie, Office of Graduate Studies, 800-252-8533, Fax: 217-206-7623, E-mail: pardie.lynn@uis.edu.

University of Maryland, Baltimore County, Graduate School, College of Arts, Humanities and Social Sciences, Department of Geography and Environmental Systems, Program in Geography and Environmental Systems, Baltimore, MD 21250. Offers MS, PhD. *Faculty:* 11 full-time (4 women), 6 part-time/adjunct (1 woman). *Students:* 18 full-time (12 women), 4 part-time (3 women); includes 2 African Americans, 1 Asian American or Pacific Islander, 2 international. Average age 32. 32 applicants, 28% accepted, 7 enrolled.Terminal master's awarded for partial completion of doctoral program. *Degree requirements:* For master's, thesis optional, annual faculty evaluation, research paper; for doctorate, comprehensive exam, thesis/dissertation, annual faculty evaluation, qualifying exams, proposal and dissertation defense. *Entrance requirements:* For master's and doctorate, GRE, minimum GPA of 3.0 overall, 3.3 in major. Additional exam requirements/recommendations for international students: Required—TOEFL (minimum score 550 paper-based; 213 computer-based; 80 iBT). *Application deadline:* For fall admission, 2/1 for domestic and international students. Application fee: $50. Electronic applications accepted. *Financial support:* In 2009–10, 15 students received support, including 1 fellowship with full tuition reimbursement available (averaging $30,000 per year), 8 research assistantships with full tuition reimbursements available (averaging $18,392 per year), 6 teaching assistantships with full tuition reimbursements available (averaging $18,392 per year); scholarships/grants, traineeships, and unspecified assistantships also available. Financial award application deadline: 2/1. *Faculty research:* Watershed processes, climate and weather systems; ecology and biogeography; landscape ecology and land-use change; human geography, urban sustainability and environmental health; environmental policy; geographic information science and remote sensing. *Unit head:* Dr. Christopher M. Swan, Graduate Program Director, 410-455-2002, E-mail: gpd.ges@umbc.edu. *Application contact:* Kathryn Nee, Coordinator of Domestic Admissions, 410-455-2944, E-mail: nee@umbc.edu.

University of Maryland University College, Graduate School of Management and Technology, Program in Environmental Management, Adelphi, MD 20783. Offers MS, Certificate. Offered evenings and weekends only. Part-time and evening/weekend programs available. Postbaccalaureate distance learning degree programs offered (no on-campus study). *Students:* 6 full-time (all women), 361 part-time (181 women); includes 98 minority (64 African Americans, 3 American Indian/Alaska Native, 11 Asian Americans or Pacific Islanders, 20 Hispanic Americans), 4 international. Average age 35. 224 applicants, 100% accepted, 84 enrolled. In 2009, 59 master's, 14 other advanced degrees awarded. *Degree requirements:* For master's, thesis or alternative. *Application deadline:* Applications are processed on a rolling basis. Application fee: $50. Electronic applications accepted. *Expenses:* Tuition, state resident: full-time $7704; part-time $428 per credit hour. Tuition, nonresident: full-time $11,862; part-time $659 per credit hour. *Financial support:* Federal Work-Study and scholarships/grants available. Support available to part-time students. Financial award application deadline: 6/1; financial award applicants required to submit FAFSA. *Unit head:* Dr. Robert Beauchamp, Director, 240-684-2400, Fax: 240-684-2401, E-mail: rbeauchamp@umuc.edu. *Application contact:* Coordinator, Graduate Admissions, 800-888-UMUC, Fax: 240-684-2151, E-mail: newgrad@umuc.edu.

University of Massachusetts Dartmouth, Graduate School, School of Education, Public Policy, and Civic Engagement, Department of Public Policy, North Dartmouth, MA 02747-2300. Offers environmental policy (Postbaccalaureate Certificate); public policy (MPP). Part-time programs available. Postbaccalaureate distance learning degree programs offered. *Faculty:* 4 full-time (1 woman). *Students:* 12 full-time (8 women), 28 part-time (16 women); includes 5 minority (all African Americans). Average age 35. 26 applicants, 92% accepted, 13 enrolled. In 2009, 9 master's awarded. *Entrance requirements:* For master's, GRE or GMAT. Additional exam requirements/recommendations for international students: Required—TOEFL (minimum score 500 paper-based; 213 computer-based). *Application deadline:* For fall admission, 4/20 for domestic students, 2/20 for international students; for spring admission, 11/15 for domestic students, 9/15 for international students. Applications are processed on a rolling basis. Application fee: $40 ($60 for international students). Electronic applications accepted. *Expenses:* Tuition, state resident: full-time $2071; part-time $86.29 per credit. Tuition, nonresident: full-time $8099; part-time $337.46 per credit. Required fees: $9446. Tuition and fees vary according to class time, course load and reciprocity agreements. *Financial support:* In 2009–10, 3 research assistantships with full tuition reimbursements (averaging $5,333 per year) were awarded; Federal Work-Study and unspecified assistantships also available. Support available to part-time students. Financial award application deadline: 3/1. *Faculty research:* International human rights, international political economy, gender and politics. Total annual research expenditures: $128,000. *Unit head:* Dr. Michael Goodmon, 508-990-9660, E-mail: mgoodmon@umassd.edu. *Application contact:* Elan Turcotte-Shamski, Graduate Admissions Officer, 508-999-8604, Fax: 508-999-8183, E-mail: graduate@umassd.edu.

University of Massachusetts Lowell, School of Health and Environment, Department of Work Environment, Lowell, MA 01854-2881. Offers cleaner production and pollution prevention (MS, Sc D); environmental risk assessment (Certificate); epidemiology (MS, Sc D); ergonomics and safety (MS, Sc D); identification and control of ergonomic hazards (Certificate); job stress and healthy job redesign (Certificate); occupational and environmental hygiene (MS, Sc D); radiological health physics and general work environment protection (Certificate); work environment policy (MS, Sc D). *Accreditation:* ABET (one or more programs are accredited). Part-time programs available. Terminal master's awarded for partial completion of doctoral program. *Degree requirements:* For master's, thesis optional; for doctorate, thesis/dissertation. *Entrance requirements:* For master's and doctorate, GRE General Test. Additional exam requirements/recommendations for international students: Required—TOEFL.

University of Miami, Graduate School, School of Business Administration, Department of Economics, Coral Gables, FL 33124. Offers economic development (MA, PhD); environmental economics (PhD); human resource economics (MA, PhD); international economics (MA, PhD); macroeconomics (PhD). Students admitted every two years in the fall semester. Terminal master's awarded for partial completion of doctoral program. *Degree requirements:* For master's, comprehensive exam; for doctorate, comprehensive exam, thesis/dissertation. *Entrance requirements:* For master's and doctorate, GRE General Test, minimum GPA of 3.0. Additional exam requirements/recommendations for international students: Required—TOEFL (minimum score 550 paper-based). *Faculty research:* International economics/trade, applied microeconomics, development.

University of Michigan, School of Natural Resources and Environment, Program in Natural Resources and Environment, Ann Arbor, MI 48109. Offers aquatic sciences: research and management (MS); behavior, education and communication (MS); conservation biology (MS); environmental informatics (MS); environmental justice (MS); environmental policy and planning (MS); natural resources and environment (PhD); sustainable systems (MS); terrestrial ecosystems (MS); MS/AM; MS/JD; MS/MBA. *Students:* Average age 27. In 2009, 87 master's, 14 doctorates awarded. Terminal master's awarded for partial completion of doctoral program. *Degree requirements:* For master's, practicum or group project; for doctorate, comprehensive exam, thesis/dissertation, oral defense of dissertation, preliminary exam. *Entrance requirements:* For master's, GRE General Test; for doctorate, GRE General Test, master's degree. Additional exam requirements/recommendations for international students: Required—TOEFL (minimum score 560 paper-based; 220 computer-based; 84 iBT). *Application deadline:* For fall admission, 1/5 priority date for domestic and international students. Applications are processed on a rolling basis. Application fee: $60 ($75 for international students). Electronic applications accepted. *Expenses:* Tuition, state resident: full-time $17,286; part-time $1099 per credit hour. Tuition, nonresident: full-time $34,944; part-time $2080 per credit hour. Required fees: $95 per semester. Tuition and fees vary according to course load, degree level and program. *Financial support:* Fellowships with tuition reimbursements, research assistantships with tuition reimbursements, teaching assistantships with tuition reimbursements, career-related internships or fieldwork, Federal Work-Study, institutionally sponsored loans, scholarships/grants, health care benefits, and unspecified assistantships available. Support available to part-time students. Financial award application deadline: 1/5; financial award applicants required to submit FAFSA. *Faculty research:* Stream ecology, plant-insect interactions, fish biology, resource control and reproductive success, remote sensing. *Application contact:* Graduate Admissions Team, 734-764-6453, Fax: 734-936-2195, E-mail: snre.admissions@umich.edu.

University of Minnesota, Twin Cities Campus, Graduate School, Hubert H. Humphrey Institute of Public Affairs, Program in Science, Technology, and Environmental Policy, Minneapolis, MN 55455-0213. Offers MS, JD/MS. Part-time programs available. *Faculty:* 33 full-time (14 women), 29 part-time/adjunct (15 women). *Students:* 15 full-time (5 women), 9 part-time (4 women); includes 3 minority (all Asian Americans or Pacific Islanders), 2 international. Average age 26. 24 applicants, 75% accepted, 12 enrolled. In 2009, 10 master's awarded. *Degree requirements:* For master's, thesis. *Entrance requirements:* For master's, GRE General Test, undergraduate training in the biological or physical sciences or engineering, minimum undergraduate GPA of 3.0. Additional exam requirements/recommendations for international students: Required—TOEFL (minimum score 600 paper-based; 250 computer-based; 100 iBT). *Application deadline:* For fall admission, 4/1 for domestic and international students. Applications are processed on a rolling basis. Application fee: $75 ($95 for international students). Electronic applications accepted. *Financial support:* In 2009–10, 6 students received support, including fellowships with full and partial tuition reimbursements available (averaging $8,500 per year), research assistantships with full and partial tuition reimbursements available (averaging $5,270 per year), teaching assistantships with full and partial tuition reimbursements available (averaging $5,270 per year); career-related internships or fieldwork, Federal Work-Study, scholarships/grants, health care benefits, tuition waivers (full and partial), and unspecified assistantships also available. Financial award application deadline: 1/5. *Faculty research:* Economics, history, philosophy, and politics of science and technology; organization and management of science and technology. Total annual research expenditures: $5.1 million. *Unit head:* Dr. Deborah Swackhamer, Head, 612-624-3800, Fax: 612-626-0002, E-mail: hhhadmit@umn.edu. *Application contact:* Julie Harrold, Director of Admissions, 612-626-7229, Fax: 612-626-0002, E-mail: hhhadmit@umn.edu.

University of Missouri–St. Louis, College of Arts and Sciences, Department of Biology, St. Louis, MO 63121. Offers biology (MS, PhD), including animal behavior (MS), biochemistry, biochemistry and biotechnology (MS), biotechnology (MS), conservation biology (MS), development (MS), ecology (MS), environmental studies (PhD), evolution (MS), genetics (MS), molecular biology and biochemistry (PhD), molecular/cellular biology (MS), physiology (MS), plant systematics, population biology (MS), tropical biology (MS); biotechnology (Certificate); tropical biology and conservation (Certificate). Part-time programs available. *Faculty:* 43 full-time (13 women), 2 part-time/adjunct (1 woman). *Students:* 54 full-time (27 women), 79 part-time (43 women); includes 15 minority (6 African Americans, 7 Asian Americans or Pacific Islanders, 2 Hispanic Americans), 47 international. Average age 29. 193 applicants, 44% accepted, 44 enrolled. In 2009, 30 master's, 7 doctorates, 9 other advanced degrees awarded. *Degree requirements:* For master's, thesis or alternative; for doctorate, thesis/dissertation, 1 semester of teaching experience. *Entrance requirements:* For master's, 3 letters of recommendation; for doctorate, GRE General Test, 3 letters of recommendation. Additional exam requirements/recommendations for international students: Required—TOEFL. *Application deadline:* For fall admission, 12/1 priority date for domestic and international students; for spring admission, 10/15 priority date for domestic and international students. Applications are processed on a rolling basis. Application fee: $35 ($40 for international students). Electronic applications accepted. *Expenses:* Tuition, state resident: full-time $5377; part-time $297.70 per credit hour. Tuition, nonresident: full-time $13,882; part-time $771.20 per credit hour. Required fees: $220; $12.20 per credit hour. One-time fee: $12. Tuition and fees vary according to course level, campus/location and program. *Financial support:* In 2009–10, 22 research assistantships with full and partial tuition reimbursements (averaging $16,300 per year), 14 teaching assistantships with full and partial tuition reimbursements (averaging $16,727 per year) were awarded; fellowships with full tuition reimbursements, career-related internships or fieldwork and Federal Work-Study also available. Support available to part-time students. Financial award application deadline: 2/1. *Faculty research:* Molecular biology, microbial genetics, animal behavior, tropical ecology, plant systematics. *Unit head:* Dr. Elizabeth Kellogg, Director of Graduate Studies, 314-516-6200, Fax: 314-516-6233, E-mail: tkellogg@umsl.edu. *Application contact:* 314-516-5458, Fax: 314-516-6996, E-mail: gradadm@umsl.edu.

The University of Montana, Graduate School, College of Arts and Sciences, Program in Environmental Studies (EVST), Missoula, MT 59812-0002. Offers MS, JD/MS. Part-time programs available. *Faculty:* 5 full-time (2 women), 3 part-time/adjunct (1 woman). *Students:* 36 full-time (23 women), 34 part-time (19 women); includes 3 minority (1 American Indian/Alaska Native, 1 Asian American or Pacific Islander, 1 Hispanic American), 1 international. Average age 30. 76 applicants, 61% accepted, 23 enrolled. In 2009, 30 master's awarded. *Degree requirements:* For master's, thesis, portfolio or professional paper. *Entrance requirements:* For master's, GRE General Test, minimum 500 verbal GRE. Additional exam requirements/recommendations for international students: Required—TOEFL (minimum score 580 paper-based; 237 computer-based; 92 iBT). *Application deadline:* For fall admission, 2/1 priority date for domestic and international students. Application fee: $51. *Financial support:* In 2009–10, 14 students received support, including 4 fellowships with partial tuition reimbursements available (averaging $5,000 per year), 6 teaching assistantships with full tuition reimbursements available (averaging $9,000 per year); career-related internships or fieldwork, Federal Work-Study, and scholarships/grants also available. Support available to part-time students. Financial award application deadline: 4/15. *Faculty research:* Pollution ecology, sustainable agriculture, environmental writing, environmental policy, environmental justice, habitat-land management. Total annual research expenditures: $185,000. *Unit head:* Dr. Len Broberg, Director, 406-243-5209, Fax: 406-243-6090, E-mail: len.broberg@mso.umt.edu. *Application contact:* Karen Hurd, Administrative Assistant, 406-243-6273, Fax: 406-243-6090, E-mail: karen.hurd@mso.umt.edu.

University of Nevada, Reno, Graduate School, College of Science, Mackay School of Earth Sciences and Engineering, Department of Geography, Program in Land Use Planning, Reno, NV 89557. Offers MS. *Degree requirements:* For master's, thesis. *Entrance requirements:* For master's, GRE General Test, minimum GPA of 3.0. Additional exam requirements/recommendations for international students: Required—TOEFL (minimum score 500 paper-based; 173 computer-based; 61 iBT), IELTS (minimum score 6). Electronic applications accepted. *Faculty research:* Contemporary planning, environmental planning.

University of New Brunswick Fredericton, School of Graduate Studies, Faculty of Engineering, Department of Civil Engineering, Fredericton, NB E3B 5A3, Canada. Offers construction engineering and management (M Eng, M Sc E, PhD); environmental engineering (M Eng, M Sc E, PhD); environmental studies (M Eng); geotechnical engineering (M Eng, M Sc E, PhD); groundwater/hydrology (M Eng, M Sc E, PhD); materials (M Eng, M Sc E, PhD); pavements (M Eng, M Sc E, PhD); structures (M Eng, M Sc E, PhD); transportation (M Eng, M Sc E, PhD). Part-time programs available. *Faculty:* 18 full-time (1 woman), 1 (woman) part-time/adjunct. *Students:* 42 full-time (9 women), 18 part-time (2 women). In 2009, 11 master's, 4 doctorates awarded. *Degree requirements:* For master's, thesis, proposal; for doctorate, comprehensive exam, thesis/dissertation, Qualifying exam; Proposal; 27 credit hours of courses. *Entrance requirements:* For master's, Minimum GPA of 3.0; BScE in Civil Engineering or related engineering degree.; for doctorate, Minimum GPA of 3.0; Candidates are normally

Environmental Management and Policy

University of New Brunswick Fredericton (continued)
required to have a graduate degree in engineering or applied science. Additional exam requirements/recommendations for international students: Required—TOEFL (minimum score 580 paper-based; 237 computer-based), TWE (minimum score 4), or IELTS (minimum score 7.5). *Application deadline:* For fall admission, 5/1 priority date for domestic students; for winter admission, 11/1 priority date for domestic students. Applications are processed on a rolling basis. Application fee: $50 Canadian dollars. Tuition and fees charges are reported in Canadian dollars. *Expenses:* Tuition, area resident: Full-time $5562 Canadian dollars; part-time $2781 Canadian dollars per year. Required fees: $49.75 Canadian dollars per term. *Financial support:* In 2009–10, 51 research assistantships (averaging $7,000 per year), 43 teaching assistantships (averaging $2,000 per year) were awarded; career-related internships or fieldwork and scholarships/grants also available. *Faculty research:* Construction engineering and management, concrete materials and structural engineering, transportation and asset management, geotechnical engineering, water and environmental engineering. *Unit head:* Dr. Eric Hildebrand, Director of Graduate Studies, 506-453-5113, Fax: 506-453-3568, E-mail: ktm@unb.ca. *Application contact:* Joyce Moore, Graduate Secretary, 506-452-6127, Fax: 506-453-3568, E-mail: civil-grad@unb.ca.

University of New Brunswick Fredericton, School of Graduate Studies, Faculty of Forestry and Environmental Management, Fredericton, NB E3B 5A3, Canada. Offers ecological foundations of forest management (PhD); environmental management (MEM); forest engineering (M Sc FE, MFE); forest products marketing (MBA); forest resources (M Sc F, MF, PhD). Part-time programs available. *Faculty:* 32 full-time (2 women). *Students:* 87 full-time (47 women), 11 part-time (4 women). In 2009, 10 master's, 5 doctorates awarded. *Degree requirements:* For master's, thesis; for doctorate, thesis/dissertation. *Entrance requirements:* For master's and doctorate, minimum GPA of 3.0. Additional exam requirements/recommendations for international students: Required—TOEFL (minimum score 580 paper-based), TWE (minimum score 4), or IELTS. *Application deadline:* For fall admission, 3/1 priority date for domestic students. Application fee: $50 Canadian dollars. Electronic applications accepted. Tuition and fees charges are reported in Canadian dollars. *Expenses:* Tuition, area resident: Full-time $5562 Canadian dollars; part-time $2781 Canadian dollars per year. Required fees: $49.75 Canadian dollars per term. *Financial support:* Research assistantships, teaching assistantships available. *Faculty research:* Forest management, forest ecology, wildlife ecology, wood tech, human dimensions in forestry. *Unit head:* Dr. John Kershaw, Director of Graduate Studies, 506-453-4933, Fax: 506-453-3538, E-mail: kershaw@unb.ca. *Application contact:* Faith Sharpe, Graduate Secretary, 506-458-7520, Fax: 506-453-3538, E-mail: fsharpe@unb.ca.

University of New Hampshire, Graduate School, College of Life Sciences and Agriculture, Department of Natural Resources, Durham, NH 03824. Offers environmental conservation (MS); forestry (MS); soil science (MS); water resources management (MS); wildlife (MS). Part-time programs available. *Faculty:* 40 full-time. *Students:* 22 full-time (12 women), 29 part-time (19 women); includes 1 minority (Asian American or Pacific Islander), 1 international. Average age 31. 41 applicants, 34% accepted, 10 enrolled. In 2009, 19 master's awarded. *Degree requirements:* For master's, thesis or alternative. *Entrance requirements:* For master's, GRE General Test. Additional exam requirements/recommendations for international students: Required—TOEFL (minimum score 550 paper-based; 213 computer-based; 80 iBT). *Application deadline:* For fall admission, 6/1 for domestic students, 4/1 for international students; for spring admission, 12/1 for domestic students. Applications are processed on a rolling basis. Application fee: $65. Electronic applications accepted. *Expenses:* Tuition, state resident: full-time $10,380; part-time $577 per credit hour. Tuition, nonresident: full-time $24,350; part-time $1002 per credit hour. Required fees: $1550; $387.50 per semester. Tuition and fees vary according to course load and program. *Financial support:* In 2009–10, 24 students received support, including 2 fellowships, 11 research assistantships, 11 teaching assistantships; career-related internships or fieldwork, Federal Work-Study, scholarships/grants, and tuition waivers (full and partial) also available. Support available to part-time students. Financial award application deadline: 2/15. *Unit head:* Dr. John Halstead, Chairperson, 603-862-3950, E-mail: natural.resources@unh.edu. *Application contact:* Linda Scogin, Administrative Assistant, 603-862-3932, E-mail: natural.resources@unh.edu.

University of New Haven, Graduate School, College of Arts and Sciences, Program in Environmental Sciences, West Haven, CT 06516-1916. Offers environmental ecology (Certificate); environmental geoscience (MS); environmental health and management (MS); environmental science (MS); geographical information systems (Certificate). Part-time and evening/weekend programs available. *Faculty:* 6 full-time (3 women), 8 part-time/adjunct (2 women). *Students:* 8 full-time (5 women), 21 part-time (9 women); includes 2 minority (both African Americans), 4 international. Average age 27. 28 applicants, 79% accepted, 4 enrolled. In 2009, 7 master's, 5 other advanced degrees awarded. *Degree requirements:* For master's, thesis or alternative. *Entrance requirements:* Additional exam requirements/recommendations for international students: Required—TOEFL (minimum score 520 paper-based; 190 computer-based; 70 iBT); Recommended—IELTS (minimum score 5.5). *Application deadline:* For fall admission, 5/31 for international students; for winter admission, 10/15 for international students; for spring admission, 1/15 for international students. Applications are processed on a rolling basis. Application fee: $50. Electronic applications accepted. *Expenses:* Tuition: Part-time $700 per credit. Required fees: $45 per term. One-time fee: $390 part-time. *Financial support:* Research assistantships with partial tuition reimbursements, teaching assistantships with partial tuition reimbursements, career-related internships or fieldwork, Federal Work-Study, scholarships/grants, tuition waivers, and unspecified assistantships available. Support available to part-time students. Financial award applicants required to submit FAFSA. *Faculty research:* Mapping and assessing geological and living resources in Long Island Sound, geology, San Salvador Island, Bahamas. *Unit head:* Dr. Roman Zajac, Coordinator, 203-932-7108. *Application contact:* Eloise Gormley, Director of Graduate Admissions, 203-932-7449, Fax: 203-932-7137, E-mail: gradinfo@newhaven.edu.

The University of North Carolina at Chapel Hill, Graduate School, School of Public Health, Department of Environmental Sciences and Engineering, Chapel Hill, NC 27599. Offers air, radiation and industrial hygiene (MPH, MS, MSEE, MSPH, PhD); aquatic and atmospheric sciences (MPH, MS, MSPH, PhD); environmental engineering (MPH, MS, MSEE, MSPH, PhD); environmental health sciences (MPH, MS, MSPH, PhD); environmental management and policy (MPH, MS, MSPH, PhD). Terminal master's awarded for partial completion of doctoral program. *Degree requirements:* For master's, comprehensive exam, thesis (for some programs), research paper; for doctorate, comprehensive exam, thesis/dissertation. *Entrance requirements:* For master's and doctorate, GRE General Test, minimum GPA of 3.0. Additional exam requirements/recommendations for international students: Required—TOEFL. Electronic applications accepted. *Faculty research:* Air, radiation and industrial hygiene, aquatic and atmospheric sciences, environmental health sciences, environmental management and policy, water resources engineering.

The University of North Carolina Wilmington, College of Arts and Sciences, Department of Environmental Studies, Wilmington, NC 28403-3297. Offers coastal management (MA); environmental education and interpretation (MA); environmental management (MA); individualized study (MA). Part-time programs available. *Degree requirements:* For master's, comprehensive exam, thesis or alternative, final project, practicum. *Entrance requirements:* For master's, GRE, 3 letters of recommendation. Additional exam requirements/recommendations for international students: Required—TOEFL (minimum score 550 paper-based; 217 computer-based; 79 iBT), IELTS (minimum score 6.5). Electronic applications accepted. *Faculty research:* Coastal management, environmental management, environmental education, environmental law, natural resource management.

University of Northern British Columbia, Office of Graduate Studies, Prince George, BC V2N 4Z9, Canada. Offers business administration (Diploma); community health science (M Sc); disability management (MA); education (M Ed); first nations studies (MA); gender studies (MA); history (MA); interdisciplinary studies (MA); international studies (MA); mathematical, computer and physical sciences (M Sc); natural resources and environmental studies (M Sc, MA, MNRES, PhD); political science (MA); psychology (M Sc, PhD); social work (MSW). Part-time and evening/weekend programs available. Postbaccalaureate distance learning degree programs offered (no on-campus study). *Degree requirements:* For master's, thesis; for doctorate, thesis/dissertation. *Entrance requirements:* For master's, GRE, minimum B average in undergraduate course work; for doctorate, candidacy exam, minimum A average in graduate course work.

University of Oregon, Graduate School, College of Arts and Sciences, Environmental Studies Program, Eugene, OR 97403. Offers environmental science, studies, and policy (PhD); environmental studies (MA, MS). *Degree requirements:* For master's, one foreign language, thesis; for doctorate, comprehensive exam, thesis/dissertation. *Entrance requirements:* For master's, GRE General Test, minimum GPA of 3.0; for doctorate, GRE General Test. Additional exam requirements/recommendations for international students: Required—TOEFL (minimum score 550 paper-based; 213 computer-based). Electronic applications accepted.

University of Pennsylvania, School of Arts and Sciences, College of Liberal and Professional Studies, Philadelphia, PA 19104. Offers environmental studies (MES); individualized study (MLA). *Students:* 98 full-time (67 women), 300 part-time (185 women); includes 23 minority (11 African Americans, 6 Asian Americans or Pacific Islanders, 6 Hispanic Americans), 30 international. 441 applicants, 50% accepted, 157 enrolled. In 2009, 175 master's awarded. *Application deadline:* For fall admission, 12/1 priority date for domestic students. Application fee: $70. Electronic applications accepted. *Expenses:* Tuition: Full-time $25,660; part-time $4758 per course. Required fees: $2152; $270 per course. Tuition and fees vary according to course load, degree level and program. *Unit head:* Dr. Kristine Billmyer, Associate Dean and Director, College of Liberal and Professional Studies, 215-898-8681, E-mail: gdasdmis@sas.upenn.edu. *Application contact:* Patricia Rea, Coordinator for Admissions, 215-573-5816, Fax: 215-573-8068, E-mail: gdasadmis@sas.upenn.edu.

University of Pittsburgh, Graduate School of Public and International Affairs, Division of International Development, Pittsburgh, PA 15260. Offers development planning and environmental sustainability (MID); human security (MID); nongovernmental organizations and civil society (MID); MID/JD; MID/MBA; MID/MPH; MID/MPIA; MID/MSIS; MID/MSW. Part-time programs available. *Faculty:* 28 full-time (8 women), 56 part-time/adjunct (20 women). *Students:* 47 full-time (34 women), 4 part-time (3 women); includes 8 minority (3 African Americans, 2 Asian Americans or Pacific Islanders, 3 Hispanic Americans), 4 international. Average age 25. 123 applicants, 87% accepted, 37 enrolled. In 2009, 26 master's awarded. *Degree requirements:* For master's, thesis optional, internship, capstone seminar. *Entrance requirements:* For master's, GRE General Test, 3 letters of recommendation, minimum GPA of 3.2. Additional exam requirements/recommendations for international students: Required—TOEFL (minimum score 550 paper-based; 213 computer-based; 80 iBT), TWE (minimum score 4); Recommended—IELTS (minimum score 7). *Application deadline:* For fall admission, 2/1 for domestic students, 1/5 for international students; for spring admission, 11/1 for domestic students, 8/1 for international students. Application fee: $50. Electronic applications accepted. *Expenses:* Tuition, state resident: full-time $16,402; part-time $665 per credit. Tuition, nonresident: full-time $28,694; part-time $1175 per credit. Required fees: $690; $175 per term. Tuition and fees vary according to program. *Financial support:* In 2009–10, 27 students received support, including 4 fellowships (averaging $30,000 per year); scholarships/grants, tuition waivers (full and partial), and unspecified assistantships also available. Financial award application deadline: 2/1. *Faculty research:* Nongovernmental organizations, religion and civil society, international development, development economics and policy, human rights and development, humanitarian intervention, ethnic conflict and civil war, post-conflict peace building, corruption and transnational governance, civil society and public affairs, political constraints on rural development. Total annual research expenditures: $357,117. *Unit head:* Dr. Louis Picard, Director, 412-648-7659, Fax: 412-648-2605, E-mail: picard@pitt.edu. *Application contact:* Elizabeth Hruby, Graduate Enrollment Counselor, 412-648-7640, Fax: 412-648-7641, E-mail: eah44@pitt.edu.

University of Rhode Island, Graduate School, College of the Environment and Life Sciences, Department of Environmental and Natural Resource Economics, Kingston, RI 02881. Offers MESM, MS, PhD. Part-time programs available. *Faculty:* 6 full-time (2 women), 2 part-time/adjunct (0 women). *Students:* 24 full-time (9 women), 8 part-time (4 women); includes 3 minority (1 African American, 2 Hispanic Americans), 11 international. In 2009, 4 master's, 4 doctorates awarded. *Degree requirements:* For master's, comprehensive exam (for some programs), thesis optional; for doctorate, comprehensive exam, thesis/dissertation. *Entrance requirements:* For master's, GRE, 2 letters of recommendation; for doctorate, GRE, 3 letters of recommendation. Additional exam requirements/recommendations for international students: Required—TOEFL (minimum score 550 paper-based; 213 computer-based). *Application deadline:* For fall admission, 7/15 for domestic students, 2/1 for international students; for spring admission, 11/15 for domestic students, 7/15 for international students. Application fee: $65. Electronic applications accepted. *Expenses:* Tuition, state resident: full-time $8828; part-time $490 per credit hour. Tuition, nonresident: full-time $22,100; part-time $1228 per credit hour. Required fees: $1118; $57 per semester. Tuition and fees vary according to program. *Financial support:* In 2009–10, 1 research assistantship with partial tuition reimbursement (averaging $6,947 per year), 6 teaching assistantships with full and partial tuition reimbursements (averaging $11,145 per year) were awarded. Financial award application deadline: 7/15; financial award applicants required to submit FAFSA. *Faculty research:* The Policy Simulation Laboratory utilizes computer technologies to help understand the consequences of policy actions, experimental economics. Total annual research expenditures: $654,763. *Unit head:* Dr. James L. Anderson, Chair, 401-874-4568, Fax: 401-874-4766, E-mail: jla@uri.edu. *Application contact:* Dr. Christopher M. Anderson, Director of Graduate Studies, 401-874-4587, Fax: 401-874-4766, E-mail: cma@uri.edu.

University of South Africa, College of Agriculture and Environmental Sciences, Pretoria, South Africa. Offers agriculture (MS); consumer science (MCS); environmental management (MA, MS, PhD); environmental science (MA, MS, PhD); geography (MA, MS, PhD); horticulture (M Tech); human ecology (MHE); life sciences (MS); nature conservation (M Tech).

University of South Carolina, The Graduate School, School of the Environment, Program in Earth and Environmental Resources Management, Columbia, SC 29208. Offers MEERM, JD/MEERM. Part-time programs available. Postbaccalaureate distance learning degree programs offered (no on-campus study). *Degree requirements:* For master's, thesis optional. *Entrance requirements:* For master's, GRE General Test. Additional exam requirements/recommendations for international students: Required—TOEFL. Electronic applications accepted. *Faculty research:* Hydrology, sustainable development, environmental geology and engineering, energy/environmental resources management.

University of South Florida, Graduate School, College of Arts and Sciences, Department of Environmental Science and Policy, Tampa, FL 33620-9951. Offers MS. *Students:* 9 full-time (5 women), 11 part-time (5 women); includes 5 minority (1 African American, 4 Hispanic Americans). Average age 32. 21 applicants, 38% accepted, 6 enrolled. In 2009, 5 master's awarded. *Degree requirements:* For master's, comprehensive exam, thesis (for some programs). *Entrance requirements:* For master's, minimum GPA of 3.0. Additional exam requirements/recommendations for international students: Required—TOEFL (minimum score 600 paper-based; 213 computer-based). *Application deadline:* For fall admission, 2/15 for domestic students, 1/2 for international students; for spring admission, 10/15 for domestic students. Application fee: $30. *Financial support:* Scholarships/grants and unspecified assistantships available. Support available to part-time students. Financial award application deadline: 5/1. Total annual research expenditures: $434,251. *Unit head:* Robert Brinkmann, Interim Director, 813-974-4939, Fax: 813-974-4808, E-mail: rbrinkmann@cas.usf.edu. *Application contact:* Philip Van Beynen, Program Director, 813-974-3026, Fax: 813-974-4808, E-mail: vanbeyne@cas.usf.edu.

The University of Tennessee, Graduate School, College of Arts and Sciences, Department of Sociology, Knoxville, TN 37996. Offers criminology (MA, PhD); energy, environment, and resource policy (MA, PhD); political economy (MA, PhD). Part-time programs available. *Degree requirements:* For master's, thesis or alternative; for doctorate, thesis/dissertation. *Entrance requirements:* For master's, GRE General Test, minimum GPA of 3.0; for doctorate, GRE General Test, minimum GPA of 3.5. Additional exam requirements/recommendations for international students: Required—TOEFL. Electronic applications accepted. *Expenses:* Tuition, state resident: full-time $6826; part-time $380 per semester hour. Tuition, nonresident: full-time $21,844; part-time $1147 per semester hour. Tuition and fees vary according to program.

University of Washington, Graduate School, Interdisciplinary Graduate Program in Quantitative Ecology and Resource Management, Seattle, WA 98195. Offers MS, PhD. *Degree requirements:* For master's, thesis; for doctorate, thesis/dissertation. *Entrance requirements:* For master's and doctorate, GRE General Test, minimum GPA of 3.0. Additional exam requirements/recommendations for international students: Required—TOEFL. Electronic applications accepted. *Faculty research:* Population dynamics, statistical analysis, ecological modeling and systems analysis of aquatic and terrestrial ecosystems.

University of Waterloo, Graduate Studies, Faculty of Environmental Studies, Department of Environment and Resource Studies, Waterloo, ON N2L 3G1, Canada. Offers MES. Part-time programs available. *Degree requirements:* For master's, thesis. *Entrance requirements:* For master's, honors degree, minimum B average, resume. Additional exam requirements/recommendations for international students: Required—TOEFL, TWE. Electronic applications accepted. *Faculty research:* Applied sustainability; sustainable water policy; food, agriculture, and the environment; biology studies; environment and business; ecological monitoring; soil ecosystem dynamics; urban water demand management; demand response.

University of Waterloo, Graduate Studies, Faculty of Environmental Studies, Program in Tourism Policy and Planning, Waterloo, ON N2L 3G1, Canada. Offers MAES. Part-time programs available. *Degree requirements:* For master's, research paper. *Entrance requirements:* For master's, honors degree in related field, minimum B average. Additional exam requirements/recommendations for international students: Required—TOEFL, TWE. Electronic applications accepted. *Faculty research:* Urban and regional economics, regional economic development, strategic planning, environmental economics, economic geography.

University of Wisconsin–Green Bay, Graduate Studies, Program in Environmental Science and Policy, Green Bay, WI 54311-7001. Offers MS. Part-time programs available. *Faculty:* 22 full-time (5 women), 4 part-time/adjunct (0 women). *Students:* 11 full-time (3 women), 17 part-time (8 women); includes 5 minority (2 American Indian/Alaska Native, 2 Asian Americans or Pacific Islanders, 1 Hispanic American), 1 international. Average age 33. 27 applicants, 56% accepted, 10 enrolled. In 2009, 11 master's awarded. *Degree requirements:* For master's, thesis. *Entrance requirements:* For master's, GRE General Test, minimum GPA of 3.0. *Application deadline:* For fall admission, 8/1 for domestic students; for spring admission, 11/1 for domestic students. Applications are processed on a rolling basis. Application fee: $56. Electronic applications accepted. *Expenses:* Tuition, state resident: full-time $6706; part-time $373 per credit. Tuition, nonresident: full-time $16,722; part-time $932 per credit. Required fees: $1250; $52 per credit. Tuition and fees vary according to degree level and reciprocity agreements. *Financial support:* In 2009–10, 1 research assistantship with full tuition reimbursement, 4 teaching assistantships with full tuition reimbursements were awarded; career-related internships or fieldwork, Federal Work-Study, and institutionally sponsored loans also available. Financial award application deadline: 7/15; financial award applicants required to submit FAFSA. *Faculty research:* Bald eagle, parasitic population of domestic and wild animals, resource recovery, anaerobic digestion of organic waste. *Unit head:* Dr. Patricia Terry, Coordinator, 920-465-2749, E-mail: terryp@uwgb.edu. *Application contact:* Pam Harvey-Jacobs, Director of Admissions, E-mail: harveyp@uwgb.edu.

Utah State University, School of Graduate Studies, College of Natural Resources, Department of Environment and Society, Logan, UT 84322. Offers bioregional planning (MS); geography (MA, MS); human dimensions of ecosystem science and management (MS, PhD); recreation resource management (MS, PhD). *Degree requirements:* For master's, comprehensive exam, thesis (for some programs). *Entrance requirements:* For master's and doctorate, GRE General Test, minimum GPA of 3.0. Additional exam requirements/recommendations for international students: Required—TOEFL. Electronic applications accepted. *Faculty research:* Geographic information systems/geographic and environmental education, bioregional planning, natural resource and environmental policy, outdoor recreation and tourism, natural resource and environmental management.

Vanderbilt University, School of Engineering, Department of Civil and Environmental Engineering, Program in Environmental Engineering, Nashville, TN 37240-1001. Offers environmental engineering (M Eng); environmental management (MS, PhD). MS and PhD offered through Graduate School. Part-time programs available. *Faculty:* 9 full-time (0 women), 1 (woman) part-time/adjunct. *Students:* 24 full-time (13 women); includes 2 minority (1 African American, 1 Asian American or Pacific Islander), 4 international. Average age 30. 75 applicants, 17% accepted, 8 enrolled. In 2009, 5 master's awarded. Terminal master's awarded for partial completion of doctoral program. *Degree requirements:* For master's, thesis or alternative; for doctorate, thesis/dissertation. *Entrance requirements:* For master's and doctorate, GRE General Test. Additional exam requirements/recommendations for international students: Required—TOEFL. *Application deadline:* For fall admission, 1/15 for domestic students; for spring admission, 11/1 for domestic students. Applications are processed on a rolling basis. Application fee: $0. Electronic applications accepted. *Financial support:* In 2009–10, 5 fellowships with full tuition reimbursements (averaging $30,000 per year), 12 research assistantships with full tuition reimbursements (averaging $25,200 per year), 7 teaching assistantships with full tuition reimbursements (averaging $21,600 per year) were awarded; career-related internships or fieldwork, institutionally sponsored loans, scholarships/grants, traineeships, and tuition waivers (full and partial) also available. Financial award application deadline: 1/15. *Faculty research:* Waste treatment, hazardous waste management, chemical waste treatment, water quality. *Unit head:* Dr. David S. Kosson, Chair, 615-322-2697, Fax: 615-322-3365, E-mail: david.kosson@vanderbilt.edu. *Application contact:* Dr. James H. Clarke, Graduate Program Administrator, 615-322-3897, Fax: 615-322-3365.

Vermont Law School, Law School, Environmental Law Center, South Royalton, VT 05068-0096. Offers LL M, MELP, JD/MELP. Part-time programs available. *Faculty:* 11 full-time (3 women), 13 part-time/adjunct (7 women). *Students:* 38 full-time (20 women), 2 part-time (1 woman); includes 1 Asian American or Pacific Islander, 1 Hispanic American. Average age 30. 86 applicants, 88% accepted, 40 enrolled. In 2009, 65 master's awarded. *Entrance requirements:* Additional exam requirements/recommendations for international students: Required—TOEFL. *Application deadline:* For fall admission, 3/1 priority date for domestic students. Applications are processed on a rolling basis. Application fee: $60. *Expenses:* Tuition: Full-time $40,420. *Financial support:* In 2009–10, 2 fellowships with full tuition reimbursements (averaging $5,000 per year) were awarded; career-related internships or fieldwork, Federal Work-Study, institutionally sponsored loans, scholarships/grants, and tuition waivers (partial) also available. Support available to part-time students. Financial award application deadline: 3/1; financial award applicants required to submit FAFSA. *Faculty research:* Environment and technology; takings; international environmental law; interaction among science, law, and environmental policy; air pollution. Total annual research expenditures: $52,000. *Unit head:* Marc Mihaly, Associate Dean, 802-831-1342, Fax: 802-763-2490, E-mail: admiss@vermontlaw.edu. *Application contact:* Anne Mansfield, Associate Director, 802-831-1338, Fax: 802-763-2940, E-mail: admiss@vermontlaw.edu.

Virginia Commonwealth University, Graduate School, School of Life Sciences, Center for Environmental Studies, Richmond, VA 23284-9005. Offers environmental communication (MIS); environmental health (MIS); environmental policy (MIS); environmental sciences (MIS). *Degree requirements:* For master's, thesis. *Entrance requirements:* For master's, GRE General Test.

Virginia Polytechnic Institute and State University, Graduate School, College of Architecture and Urban Studies, School of Public and International Affairs, Blacksburg, VA 24061. Offers environmental planning and policy (MURP); government and international affairs (MPIA); housing, community and economic development (MURP); international development planning (MURP); land use and physical planning (MURP); planning, governance and globalization (PhD), including environmental planning and landscape analysis, physical planning and urban design, public and international affairs, urban and environmental design and planning; urban and regional planning (MURP). *Accreditation:* ACSP. *Entrance requirements:* Additional exam requirements/recommendations for international students: Required—TOEFL (minimum score 550 paper-based; 213 computer-based). Electronic applications accepted. *Faculty research:* Design theory, environmental planning, town planning, transportation planning.

Virginia Polytechnic Institute and State University, VT Online, Blacksburg, VA 24061. Offers aerospace engineering (MS); business information systems (Graduate Certificate); career and technical education (MS); computer engineering (M Eng, MS); decision support systems (Graduate Certificate); eLearning leadership (MA); electrical engineering (M Eng, MS); engineering administration (MEA); environmental politics and policy (Graduate Certificate); foundations of political analysis (Graduate Certificate); health product risk management (Graduate Certificate); information policy and society (Graduate Certificate); information security (Graduate Certificate); instructional technology (MA); liberal arts (Graduate Certificate); life sciences: health product risk management (MS); natural resources (MNR, Graduate Certificate); networking (Graduate Certificate); nonprofit and nongovernmental organization management (Graduate Certificate); ocean engineering (MS); political science (MA); security studies (Graduate Certificate); software development (Graduate Certificate).

Webster University, College of Arts and Sciences, Department of Biological Sciences, St. Louis, MO 63119-3194. Offers environmental management (MS); nurse anesthesia (MS); professional science management and leadership (MA). Part-time programs available. Postbaccalaureate distance learning degree programs offered (no on-campus study). *Faculty:* 6 full-time, 20 part-time/adjunct. *Students:* 83 full-time (39 women), 120 part-time (61 women); includes 55 minority (40 African Americans, 6 Asian Americans or Pacific Islanders, 9 Hispanic Americans). Average age 33. In 2009, 58 master's awarded. *Degree requirements:* For master's, comprehensive exam (for some programs), thesis (for some programs). *Entrance requirements:* Additional exam requirements/recommendations for international students: Required—TOEFL. Application fee: $25 ($50 for international students). *Expenses:* Tuition: Part-time $565 per credit hour. Tuition and fees vary according to degree level, campus/location and program. *Financial support:* Application deadline: 4/1; *Unit head:* Dr. Stephanie Schroeder, Chair, 314-968-7518. *Application contact:* Matt Nolan, Assoc. V.P.—Enrollment Management / Dean of Admissions, Fax: 314-968-7116, E-mail: gadmit@webster.edu.

Webster University, George Herbert Walker School of Business and Technology, Department of Business, St. Louis, MO 63119-3194. Offers business (MA); business and organizational security management (MA); computer resources and information management (MBA); environmental management (MBA); finance (MA, MBA); health services management (MBA); human resources development (MBA); human resources management (MBA); international business (MA, MBA); management and leadership (MBA); marketing (MBA); procurement and acquisitions management (MBA); telecommunications management (MBA). Part-time and evening/weekend programs available. Postbaccalaureate distance learning degree programs offered (no on-campus study). *Faculty:* 9 full-time, 430 part-time/adjunct. *Students:* 1,190 full-time (543 women), 4,226 part-time (2,159 women); includes 2,110 minority (1,448 African Americans, 20 American Indian/Alaska Native, 310 Asian Americans or Pacific Islanders, 332 Hispanic Americans), 2,176 international. Average age 34. In 2009, 2,021 master's awarded. *Degree requirements:* For master's, comprehensive exam (for some programs), thesis (for some programs). *Entrance requirements:* Additional exam requirements/recommendations for international students: Required—TOEFL. *Application deadline:* Applications are processed on a rolling basis. Application fee: $35 ($50 for international students). *Expenses:* Tuition: Part-time $565 per credit hour. Tuition and fees vary according to degree level, campus/location and program. *Financial support:* Federal Work-Study available. Support available to part-time students. Financial award application deadline: 4/1; financial award applicants required to submit FAFSA. *Unit head:* Dr. Debbie Psihountas, Chair, 314-246-7553 Ext. 7017, Fax: 314-968-7077, E-mail: buschair@webster.edu. *Application contact:* Matt Nolan, Assoc., V.P.—Enrollment Management / Dean of Admissions, Fax: 314-968-7116, E-mail: gadmit@webster.edu.

Webster University, George Herbert Walker School of Business and Technology, Department of Management, St. Louis, MO 63119-3194. Offers business and organizational security management (MA); computer resources and information management (MA); environmental management (MS); government contracting (Certificate); health care management (MA); health services management (MA); human resources development (MA); human resources management (MA); management (DM); management and leadership (MA); marketing (MA); nonprofit management (Certificate); procurement and acquisitions management (MA); public administration (MA); quality management (MA); space systems operations management (MS); telecommunications management (MA). Part-time and evening/weekend programs available. Postbaccalaureate distance learning degree programs offered (no on-campus study). *Faculty:* 16 full-time, 781 part-time/adjunct. *Students:* 1,369 full-time (610 women), 5,182 part-time (3,047 women); includes 3,460 minority (2,835 African Americans, 38 American Indian/Alaska Native, 169 Asian Americans or Pacific Islanders, 418 Hispanic Americans), 80 international. Average age 37. In 2009, 2,491 master's, 13 doctorates, 68 other advanced degrees awarded. *Degree requirements:* For master's, thesis (for some programs); for doctorate, thesis/dissertation, written exam. *Entrance requirements:* For doctorate, GMAT, 3 years of work experience, MBA. Additional exam requirements/recommendations for international students: Required—TOEFL. *Application deadline:* Applications are processed on a rolling basis. Application fee: $25 ($50 for international students). *Expenses:* Tuition: Part-time $565 per credit hour. Tuition and fees vary according to degree level, campus/location and program. *Financial support:* Federal Work-Study available. Support available to part-time students. Financial award application deadline: 4/1; financial award applicants required to submit FAFSA. *Unit head:* Jim Brasfield, Chair, 314-961-2660 Ext. 7063, Fax: 314-968-7077, E-mail: mgtchair@webster.edu. *Application contact:* Matt Nolan, Assoc. V.P.—Enrollment Management / Dean of Admissions, Fax: 314-968-7116, E-mail: gadmit@webster.edu.

Wesley College, Business Program, Dover, DE 19901-3875. Offers environmental management (MBA); executive leadership (MBA); management (MBA). Executive leadership concentration also offered at New Castle, DE location. Part-time and evening/weekend programs available. *Entrance requirements:* For master's, GMAT or GRE, minimum undergraduate GPA of 2.75.

Wesley College, Environmental Studies Program, Dover, DE 19901-3875. Offers MS. Part-time and evening/weekend programs available. *Entrance requirements:* For master's, BA/BSM in science or engineering field, portfolio.

Environmental Management and Policy

West Virginia University, Davis College of Agriculture, Forestry and Consumer Sciences, Division of Resource Management and Sustainable Development, Morgantown, WV 26506. Offers agricultural and extension education (MS, PhD), including agricultural and extension education, teaching vocational-agriculture (MS); agricultural and resource economics (MS); human and community development (PhD); natural resource economics (PhD); resource management (PhD); resource management and sustainable development (PhD). Part-time programs available. *Degree requirements:* For master's, thesis; for doctorate, comprehensive exam, thesis/dissertation. *Entrance requirements:* For master's, GRE General Test. Additional exam requirements/recommendations for international students: Required—TOEFL. *Faculty research:* Environmental economics, energy economics, agriculture.

West Virginia University, Eberly College of Arts and Sciences, Department of Geology and Geography, Program in Geography, Morgantown, WV 26506. Offers energy and environmental resources (MA); geographic information systems (PhD); geography-regional development (PhD); GIS/cartographic analysis (MA); regional development (MA). Part-time programs available. *Degree requirements:* For master's, thesis, oral and written exams; for doctorate, comprehensive exam, thesis/dissertation, oral and written exams. *Entrance requirements:* For master's and doctorate, GRE General Test, minimum GPA of 3.0. Additional exam requirements/recommendations for international students: Required—TOEFL. Electronic applications accepted. *Faculty research:* Space, place and development, geographic information science, environmental geography.

Yale University, Graduate School of Arts and Sciences, Department of Forestry and Environmental Studies, New Haven, CT 06520. Offers environmental sciences (PhD); forestry (PhD). *Degree requirements:* For doctorate, thesis/dissertation. *Entrance requirements:* For doctorate, GRE General Test.

Yale University, School of Forestry and Environmental Studies, New Haven, CT 06511. Offers MEM, MES, MF, MFS, PhD, JD/MEM, MBA/MEM, MBA/MF, MEM/M Arch, MEM/MA, MEM/MPH, MF/MA. *Accreditation:* SAF (one or more programs are accredited). Part-time programs available. Terminal master's awarded for partial completion of doctoral program. *Degree requirements:* For master's, thesis (for some programs); for doctorate, thesis/dissertation. *Entrance requirements:* For master's, GRE General Test, GMAT or LSAT; for doctorate, GRE General Test. Additional exam requirements/recommendations for international students: Required—TOEFL (minimum score 600 paper-based; 250 computer-based; 100 iBT). Electronic applications accepted. *Expenses:* Contact institution. *Faculty research:* Environmental policy, social ecology, industrial environmental management, forestry, environmental health, urban ecology, water science policy.

York University, Faculty of Graduate Studies, Program in Environmental Studies, Toronto, ON M3J 1P3, Canada. Offers MES, PhD, MES/LL B, MES/MA. Part-time programs available. *Degree requirements:* For master's, thesis optional; for doctorate, comprehensive exam, thesis/dissertation, research seminar. Electronic applications accepted.

Youngstown State University, Graduate School, College of Liberal Arts and Social Sciences, Program in Environmental Studies, Youngstown, OH 44555-0001. Offers environmental studies (MS); industrial/institutional management (Certificate); risk management (Certificate). *Degree requirements:* For master's, comprehensive exam, thesis, oral defense of dissertation. *Entrance requirements:* For master's, GRE General Test or minimum GPA of 2.7. Additional exam requirements/recommendations for international students: Required—TOEFL.

Environmental Sciences

Alabama Agricultural and Mechanical University, School of Graduate Studies, School of Agricultural and Environmental Sciences, Department of Plant and Soil Science, Huntsville, AL 35811. Offers animal sciences (MS); environmental science (MS); plant and soil science (PhD). Evening/weekend programs available. Terminal master's awarded for partial completion of doctoral program. *Degree requirements:* For master's, thesis; for doctorate, one foreign language, thesis/dissertation. *Entrance requirements:* For master's, GRE General Test, BS in agriculture; for doctorate, GRE General Test, master's degree. Additional exam requirements/recommendations for international students: Required—TOEFL (minimum score 500 paper-based; 173 computer-based; 61 iBT). Electronic applications accepted. *Faculty research:* Plant breeding, cytogenetics, crop production, soil chemistry and fertility, remote sensing.

Alaska Pacific University, Graduate Programs, Environmental Science Department, Program in Environmental Science, Anchorage, AK 99508-4672. Offers MSES. Part-time programs available. *Degree requirements:* For master's, thesis. *Entrance requirements:* For master's, GRE General Test, minimum GPA of 3.0. Additional exam requirements/recommendations for international students: Required—TOEFL (minimum score 550 paper-based; 213 computer-based).

American University, College of Arts and Sciences, Department of Biology, Washington, DC 20016-8007. Offers applied science (MS); biology (MA, MS); environmental science (MS), including environmental science, marine science. Part-time programs available. *Faculty:* 7 full-time (3 women), 3 part-time/adjunct (1 woman). *Students:* 20 full-time (11 women), 17 part-time (15 women); includes 4 minority (2 African Americans, 2 Asian Americans or Pacific Islanders), 6 international. Average age 27. 55 applicants, 60% accepted, 15 enrolled. In 2009, 12 master's awarded. *Degree requirements:* For master's, comprehensive exam, thesis (for some programs). *Entrance requirements:* For master's, GRE General Test, GRE Subject Test. Additional exam requirements/recommendations for international students: Required—TOEFL. *Application deadline:* For fall admission, 2/1 for domestic students; for spring admission, 10/1 for domestic students. Application fee: $80. *Expenses:* Tuition: Full-time $22,266; part-time $1237 per credit hour. Required fees: $430. Tuition and fees vary according to program. *Financial support:* Fellowships, research assistantships with tuition reimbursements, teaching assistantships with tuition reimbursements, career-related internships or fieldwork, Federal Work-Study, and institutionally sponsored loans available. Financial award application deadline: 2/1. *Faculty research:* Neurobiology, cave biology, population genetics, vertebrate physiology. *Unit head:* Victoria Connaughton, Chair, 202-885-2194, Fax: 202-885-2182, E-mail: vconn@american.edu. *Application contact:* Kathleen Clowery, Director, Graduate Admissions, 202-885-3621, Fax: 202-885-1505.

American University, College of Arts and Sciences, Department of Environmental Science, Washington, DC 20016-8001. Offers environmental assessment (Graduate Certificate); environmental science (MS). *Faculty:* 3 full-time (0 women). *Students:* 9 full-time (6 women), 3 part-time (all women), 1 international. Average age 30. 20 applicants, 70% accepted, 6 enrolled. In 2009, 6 master's awarded. *Degree requirements:* For master's, comprehensive exam, thesis (for some programs). *Entrance requirements:* For master's, GRE General Test, GRE Subject Test, minimum GPA of 3.0. Additional exam requirements/recommendations for international students: Required—TOEFL. *Application deadline:* For fall admission, 2/1 for domestic students; for spring admission, 10/1 for domestic students. Application fee: $80. *Expenses:* Tuition: Full-time $22,266; part-time $1237 per credit hour. Required fees: $430. Tuition and fees vary according to program. *Financial support:* Research assistantships, teaching assistantships available. Financial award application deadline: 2/1. *Unit head:* Dr. Kiho Kim, Chair, 202-885-2182, E-mail: kiho@american.edu. *Application contact:* Kathleen Clowery, Director, Graduate Admissions, 202-885-3621, Fax: 202-885-1505.

American University of Beirut, Graduate Programs, Faculty of Agricultural and Food Sciences, Beirut, Lebanon. Offers agricultural economics (MS); animal sciences (MS); ecosystem management (MSES); food technology (MS); irrigation (MS); mechanization (MS); nutrition (MS); plant protection (MS); plant science (MS); poultry science (MS); soils (MS). Part-time programs available. *Degree requirements:* For master's, one foreign language, comprehensive exam, thesis (for some programs). *Entrance requirements:* For master's, letter of recommendation. Additional exam requirements/recommendations for international students: Required—TOEFL (minimum score 600 paper-based; 250 computer-based; 100 iBT), IELTS (minimum score 7.5). *Faculty research:* Sustainable animal systems/agriculture; natural resource management; community nutrition, obesity and food safety; integrated pest management; ecosystem management.

American University of Beirut, Graduate Programs, Faculty of Engineering and Architecture, Beirut, Lebanon. Offers civil engineering (ME, PhD); electrical and computer engineering (ME, PhD); engineering management (MEM); environmental and water resources (ME); environmental and water resources engineering (PhD); environmental technology (MSES); mechanical engineering (ME, PhD); urban design (MUD); urban planning and policy (MUP). Part-time programs available. *Degree requirements:* For master's, one foreign language, comprehensive exam, thesis (for some programs); for doctorate, one foreign language, comprehensive exam, thesis/dissertation, publications. *Entrance requirements:* For master's, letters of recommendation; for doctorate, letters of recommendation, master's degree, transcripts, curriculum vitae, interview. Additional exam requirements/recommendations for international students: Required—TOEFL (minimum score 600 paper-based; 250 computer-based; 100 iBT), IELTS (minimum score 7.5). Electronic applications accepted.

American University of Beirut, Graduate Programs, Faculty of Health Sciences, Beirut, Lebanon. Offers environmental sciences (MSES), including environmental health; epidemiology (MS); epidemiology and biostatistics (MPH); health behavior and education (MPH); population health (MS); public health (MPH). Part-time programs available. *Degree requirements:* For master's, one foreign language, comprehensive exam, thesis (for some programs). *Entrance requirements:* For master's, 2 letters of recommendation. Additional exam requirements/recommendations for international students: Required—TOEFL (minimum score 573 paper-based; 230 computer-based; 98 iBT), IELTS (minimum score 7.5). Electronic applications accepted. *Faculty research:* Urban health, childbirth, tobacco control, HIV/AIDS surveillance, health finance and policies.

Antioch University New England, Graduate School, Department of Environmental Studies, Doctoral Program in Environmental Studies, Keene, NH 03431-3552. Offers PhD. *Degree requirements:* For doctorate, thesis/dissertation, practicum. *Entrance requirements:* For doctorate, master's degree and previous experience in the environmental field. Additional exam requirements/recommendations for international students: Required—TOEFL (minimum score 600 paper-based; 250 computer-based). Electronic applications accepted. *Expenses:* Contact institution. *Faculty research:* Environmental history, green politics, ecopsychology.

Antioch University New England, Graduate School, Department of Environmental Studies, Program in Environmental Education, Keene, NH 03431-3552. Offers MS. *Degree requirements:* For master's, practicum. *Entrance requirements:* For master's, previous undergraduate course work in biology, chemistry, mathematics (environmental biology); resume; 3 letters of recommendation. Additional exam requirements/recommendations for international students: Required—TOEFL (minimum score 550 paper-based; 213 computer-based). Electronic applications accepted. *Expenses:* Contact institution. *Faculty research:* Sustainability, natural resources inventory.

Arizona State University, Graduate College, College of Liberal Arts and Sciences, Division of Social Sciences, School of Human Evolution and Social Change, Tempe, AZ 85287. Offers anthropology (PhD); applied mathematics for the life and social sciences (PhD); environmental social science (PhD); museum studies in anthropology (MA); social science and health (PhD). *Degree requirements:* For master's, thesis or alternative; for doctorate, thesis/dissertation. *Entrance requirements:* For master's and doctorate, GRE.

Arkansas State University—Jonesboro, Graduate School, College of Sciences and Mathematics, Program in Environmental Sciences, Jonesboro, State University, AR 72467. Offers MS, PhD. Part-time programs available. *Faculty:* 2 full-time (1 woman), 1 (woman) part-time/adjunct. *Students:* 14 full-time (7 women), 9 part-time (5 women); includes 3 minority (2 African Americans, 1 Hispanic American), 6 international. Average age 32. 11 applicants, 82% accepted, 7 enrolled. In 2009, 6 master's, 4 doctorates awarded. *Degree requirements:* For master's, comprehensive exam, thesis (for some programs); for doctorate, comprehensive exam, thesis/dissertation. *Entrance requirements:* For master's, GRE General Test, appropriate bachelor's degree, letters of reference, interview; for doctorate, GRE, appropriate bachelor's or master's degree, interview, letters of reference, personal statement, official transcript, immunization records. Additional exam requirements/recommendations for international students: Required—TOEFL (minimum score 550 paper-based; 213 computer-based; 79 iBT), IELTS (minimum score 6). *Application deadline:* For fall admission, 2/15 for domestic and international students; for spring admission, 8/15 for domestic and international students. Applications are processed on a rolling basis. Application fee: $50. Electronic applications accepted. *Expenses:* Tuition, state resident: full-time $3744; part-time $208 per credit hour. Tuition, nonresident: full-time $9540; part-time $530 per credit hour. Required fees: $896; $47 per credit hour. $25 per term. One-time fee: $50. Tuition and fees vary according to course load and program. *Financial support:* In 2009–10, 11 students received support; fellowships, research assistantships, teaching assistantships, career-related internships or fieldwork, scholarships/grants, and unspecified assistantships available. Financial award application deadline: 7/1; financial award applicants required to submit FAFSA. *Unit head:* Dr. Thomas Risch, Director, 870-972-2007, Fax: 870-972-2008, E-mail: trisch@astate.edu. *Application contact:* Dr. Andrew Sustich, Dean of the Graduate School, 870-972-3029, Fax: 870-972-3857, E-mail: sustich@astate.edu.

Baylor University, Graduate School, College of Arts and Sciences, The Institute of Ecological, Earth and Environmental Sciences, Waco, TX 76798. Offers PhD. *Students:* 5 full-time (2 women), 3 international. *Unit head:* Dr. Joseph D. White, Director, 254-710-2911, E-mail: joseph_d_white@baylor.edu. *Application contact:* Suzanne Keener, Administrative Assistant, 254-710-3588, Fax: 254-710-3870.

Brigham Young University, Graduate Studies, College of Life Sciences, Department of Plant and Wildlife Sciences, Provo, UT 84602-1001. Offers environmental science (MS); genetics and biotechnology (MS); wildlife and wildlands conservation (MS, PhD). *Faculty:* 21 full-time (1 woman), 15 part-time/adjunct (3 women). *Students:* 35 full-time (13 women), 18 part-time (5 women); includes 7 minority (2 Asian Americans or Pacific Islanders, 5 Hispanic Americans), 5 international. Average age 29. 34 applicants, 68% accepted, 21 enrolled. In 2009, 9 master's, 1 doctorate awarded. *Degree requirements:* For master's, thesis; for doctorate, comprehensive exam, thesis/dissertation, minimum GPA of 3.0, 54 hours (18 dissertation, 36 coursework). *Entrance requirements:* For master's, GRE General Test, minimum GPA of 3.0 during last 60 hours of course work; for doctorate, GRE, minimum GPA of 3.0. Additional exam requirements/recommendations for international students: Required—TOEFL (minimum score 580 paper-based; 237 computer-based; 85 iBT). *Application deadline:* 2/1 for domestic and international students. Applications are processed on a rolling basis. Application fee: $50. Electronic applications accepted. *Expenses:* Tuition: Full-time $5580; part-time $301 per credit hour. Tuition and fees vary according to student's religious affiliation. *Financial support:* In 2009–10, 22 students received support, including 2 research assistantships with partial tuition reimbursements available (averaging $16,650 per year), 37 teaching assistantships with partial tuition reimbursements available (averaging $16,650 per year); scholarships/grants and tuition waivers (partial) also available. Financial award application deadline: 2/1. *Faculty research:* environmental science, plant genetics, plant ecology, plant nutrition and pathology, wildlife and wildlands conservation. Total annual research expenditures: $1.1 million. *Unit head:* Dr. Val J. Anderson, Chair, 801-422-3527, Fax: 801-422-0008, E-mail: val_anderson@byu.edu. *Application contact:* Dr. Loreen Allphin, Graduate Coordinator, 801-422-5603, Fax: 801-422-0008, E-mail: loreen_allphin@byu.edu.

California State Polytechnic University, Pomona, Academic Affairs, College of Environmental Design, John T. Lyle Center for Regenerative Studies, Pomona, CA 91768-2557. Offers MS. Part-time programs available. *Students:* 17 full-time (7 women), 17 part-time (12 women); includes 4 minority (2 Asian Americans or Pacific Islanders, 2 Hispanic Americans). Average age 31. 31 applicants, 71% accepted, 16 enrolled. In 2009, 4 master's awarded. *Application deadline:* For fall admission, 5/1 priority date for domestic students; for winter admission, 10/15 priority date for domestic students; for spring admission, 1/20 priority date for domestic students. Applications are processed on a rolling basis. Application fee: $55. Electronic applications accepted. *Expenses:* Tuition, nonresident: full-time $6696; part-time $248 per credit. Required fees: $5487; $3237 per term. Tuition and fees vary according to course load, degree level and program. *Financial support:* Application deadline: 3/2; *Unit head:* Dr. Kyle D. Brown, Director, 909-869-5178, E-mail: kdbrown@csupomona.edu. *Application contact:* Scott J. Duncan, Director, Admissions, 909-869-3258, Fax: 909-869-4529, E-mail: sjduncan@csupomona.edu.

California State University, Chico, Graduate School, College of Natural Sciences, Department of Geological and Environmental Sciences, Program in Environmental Science, Chico, CA 95929-0722. Offers MS. Part-time programs available. *Students:* 10 full-time (4 women), 4 part-time (3 women); includes 1 minority (Asian American or Pacific Islander), 2 international. Average age 27. 12 applicants, 92% accepted, 6 enrolled. In 2009, 1 master's awarded. *Degree requirements:* For master's, thesis. *Entrance requirements:* For master's, GRE. Additional exam requirements/recommendations for international students: Required—TOEFL (minimum score 550 paper-based; 213 computer-based; 80 iBT), IELTS (minimum score 6.5). *Application deadline:* For fall admission, 3/1 priority date for domestic students, 3/1 for international students; for spring admission, 9/15 priority date for domestic students, 9/15 for international students. Applications are processed on a rolling basis. Application fee: $55. Electronic applications accepted. *Unit head:* Dr. William Murphy, Graduate Coordinator, 530-898-5163. *Application contact:* Dr. William Murphy, Graduate Coordinator, 530-898-5163.

California State University, Dominguez Hills, College of Natural and Behavioral Sciences, Program in Environmental Science, Carson, CA 90747-0001. Offers MS. *Faculty:* 1 full-time (0 women). *Students:* 2 full-time (1 woman), 5 part-time (1 woman); includes 5 minority (2 African Americans, 1 Asian American or Pacific Islander, 2 Hispanic Americans). Average age 29. 8 applicants, 100% accepted, 6 enrolled.Application fee: $55. *Expenses:* Tuition, nonresident: full-time $6696; part-time $372 per unit. Required fees: $5946; $1752 per semester. *Unit head:* Dr. Laura Robles, Interim Dean, 310-243-2547, E-mail: lrobles@csudh.edu. *Application contact:* Dr. Gayle Ball-Parker, Director of Admissions, 310-243-3645, E-mail: gball@csudh.edu.

California State University, East Bay, Academic Programs and Graduate Studies, College of Science, Department of Earth and Environmental Sciences, Hayward, CA 94542-3000. Offers geology (MS). Evening/weekend programs available. *Faculty:* 3 full-time (0 women), 2 part-time/adjunct (1 woman). *Students:* 6 full-time (3 women), 8 part-time (3 women); includes 1 minority (African American), 1 international. Average age 32. 12 applicants, 100% accepted, 10 enrolled. *Degree requirements:* For master's, thesis. *Entrance requirements:* For master's, GRE, minimum GPA of 2.75 in field, 2.5 overall. Additional exam requirements/recommendations for international students: Required—TOEFL (minimum score 550 paper-based; 213 computer-based). *Application deadline:* For fall admission, 6/30 for domestic and international students. Application fee: $55. Electronic applications accepted. *Financial support:* Career-related internships or fieldwork, Federal Work-Study, and institutionally sponsored loans available. Support available to part-time students. Financial award application deadline: 3/1; financial award applicants required to submit FAFSA. *Unit head:* Dr. Jeffrey Seitz, Chair/Graduate Coordinator, 510-885-3486, Fax: 510-885-2526, E-mail: jeffrey.seitz@csueastbay.edu. *Application contact:* Donna Wiley, Interim Associate Director, 510-885-2928, Fax: 510-885-4777, E-mail: donna.wiley@csueastbay.edu.

California State University, Fullerton, Graduate Studies, College of Humanities and Social Sciences, Program in Environmental Studies, Fullerton, CA 92834-9480. Offers environmental sciences (MS). Part-time programs available. *Students:* 28 full-time (15 women), 45 part-time (26 women); includes 18 minority (2 African Americans, 7 Asian Americans or Pacific Islanders, 9 Hispanic Americans), 3 international. Average age 29. 76 applicants, 34% accepted, 17 enrolled. In 2009, 19 master's awarded. *Degree requirements:* For master's, thesis. *Entrance requirements:* For master's, minimum GPA of 2.5 in last 60 units of course work. Application fee: $55. *Expenses:* Tuition, nonresident: full-time $11,160; part-time $373 per credit. Required fees: $1440 per term. Tuition and fees vary according to course load, degree level and program. *Financial support:* Career-related internships or fieldwork, Federal Work-Study, institutionally sponsored loans, and scholarships/grants available. Support available to part-time students. Financial award application deadline: 3/1; financial award applicants required to submit FAFSA. *Unit head:* Dr. John Bock, Coordinator, 657-278-4373. *Application contact:* Admissions/Applications, 657-278-2371.

California State University, Northridge, Graduate Studies, College of Science and Mathematics, Department of Chemistry and Biochemistry, Northridge, CA 91330. Offers biochemistry (MS); chemistry (MS), including chemistry, environmental chemistry. *Faculty:* 14 full-time (4 women), 12 part-time/adjunct (6 women). *Students:* 15 full-time (6 women), 29 part-time (10 women); includes 2 African Americans, 4 Asian Americans or Pacific Islanders, 6 Hispanic Americans, 11 international. Average age 29. 68 applicants, 38% accepted, 12 enrolled. In 2009, 5 master's awarded. *Degree requirements:* For master's, thesis. *Entrance requirements:* For master's, GRE General Test or minimum GPA of 3.0. Additional exam requirements/recommendations for international students: Required—TOEFL. *Application deadline:* For fall admission, 11/30 for domestic students. Application fee: $55. Electronic applications accepted. *Financial support:* Teaching assistantships available. Support available to part-time students. Financial award application deadline: 3/1. *Unit head:* Dr. Taeboem Oh, Chair, 818-677-3381, E-mail: taeboem.oh@csun.edu. *Application contact:* Dr. Taeboem Oh, Chair, 818-677-3381, E-mail: taeboem.oh@csun.edu.

California State University, San Bernardino, Graduate Studies, College of Social and Behavioral Sciences, Program in Environmental Sciences, San Bernardino, CA 92407-2397. Offers MS. *Faculty:* 3 full-time (1 woman). *Students:* 3 full-time (2 women), 4 part-time (1 woman); includes 1 minority (Hispanic American). Average age 40. 3 applicants, 100% accepted, 1 enrolled.*Unit head:* Dr. Jeff Hackel, Chair, 909-537-5562, E-mail: jhackel@csusb.edu. *Application contact:* Olivia Rosas, Director of Admissions, 909-537-7577, Fax: 909-537-7034, E-mail: orosas@csusb.edu.

Christopher Newport University, Graduate Studies, Department of Biology, Chemistry and Environmental Science, Newport News, VA 23606-2998. Offers environmental science (MS). Part-time and evening/weekend programs available. *Faculty:* 6 full-time (1 woman), 1 part-time/adjunct (0 women). *Students:* 10 full-time (4 women), 23 part-time (14 women); includes 2 minority (1 African American, 1 Hispanic American). Average age 27. 18 applicants, 89% accepted, 14 enrolled. In 2009, 3 master's awarded. *Degree requirements:* For master's, comprehensive exam; thesis optional. *Entrance requirements:* For master's, GRE General Test, minimum GPA of 3.0. Additional exam requirements/recommendations for international students: Required—TOEFL (minimum score 580 paper-based; 237 computer-based; 92 iBT). *Application deadline:* For fall admission, 8/15 priority date for domestic students, 4/1 for international students; for spring admission, 10/15 for domestic students, 10/1 for international students. Applications are processed on a rolling basis. Application fee: $45. Electronic applications accepted. *Expenses:* Tuition, area resident: Part-time $384 per credit hour. Tuition, state resident: part-time $384 per credit hour. Tuition, nonresident: part-time $701 per credit hour. *Financial support:* In 2009–10, 3 research assistantships with full tuition reimbursements (averaging $2,000 per year) were awarded; fellowships with full tuition reimbursements, teaching assistantships, career-related internships or fieldwork, Federal Work-Study, institutionally sponsored loans, scholarships/grants, and unspecified assistantships also available. Support available to part-time students. Financial award application deadline: 2/1; financial award applicants required to submit FAFSA. *Faculty research:* Wetlands ecology and restoration, aquatic ecology, wetlands mitigation, greenhouse gases. *Unit head:* Dr. Gary Whiting, Coordinator, 757-594-7613, Fax: 757-594-7209, E-mail: gwhiting@cnu.edu. *Application contact:* Lyn Sawyer, Associate Director, Graduate Admissions and Records, 757-594-7544, Fax: 757-594-7649, E-mail: gradstdy@cnu.edu.

City College of the City University of New York, Graduate School, College of Liberal Arts and Science, Division of Science, Department of Earth and Atmospheric Sciences, New York, NY 10031-9198. Offers earth and environmental science (PhD); earth systems science (MA). *Degree requirements:* For master's, comprehensive exam, thesis. *Entrance requirements:* Additional exam requirements/recommendations for international students: Required—TOEFL (minimum score 500 paper-based; 61 iBT). Electronic applications accepted. *Faculty research:* Water resources, high-temperature geochemistry, sedimentary basin analysis, tectonics.

Clarkson University, Graduate School, Wallace H. Coulter School of Engineering, Program in Environmental Science and Engineering, Potsdam, NY 13699. Offers MS, PhD. Part-time programs available. *Students:* 28 full-time (12 women), 2 part-time (both women), 16 international. Average age 28. 68 applicants, 44% accepted, 10 enrolled. In 2009, 3 master's, 1 doctorate awarded. Terminal master's awarded for partial completion of doctoral program. *Degree requirements:* For master's, thesis; for doctorate, comprehensive exam, thesis/dissertation, proposal/defense. *Entrance requirements:* For master's, GRE, transcripts of all college coursework, resume, personal statement, three letters of recommendation; for doctorate, GRE, resume, 3 letters of recommendation. Additional exam requirements/recommendations for international students: Required—TOEFL (minimum score 550 paper-based; 213 computer-based; 80 iBT), IELTS (minimum score 6.5). *Application deadline:* For fall admission, 1/30 priority date for domestic and international students; for spring admission, 9/1 priority date for domestic and international students. Applications are processed on a rolling basis. Application fee: $25 ($35 for international students). Electronic applications accepted. *Expenses:* Tuition: Part-time $1074 per credit hour. *Financial support:* In 2009–10, 26 students received support, including 1 fellowship (averaging $30,000 per year), 18 research assistantships (averaging $20,190 per year), 4 teaching assistantships (averaging $20,190 per year); scholarships/grants, tuition waivers (partial), and unspecified assistantships also available. *Faculty research:* Biological, chemical, physical and social systems, renewable energy, environmental health. *Unit head:* Dr. Susan E. Powers, Associate Dean, 315-268-6542, Fax: 315-268-4291, E-mail: sep@clarkson.edu. *Application contact:* Kelly Sharlow, Assistant to the Dean, 315-268-7929, Fax: 315-268-4494, E-mail: ksharlow@clarkson.edu.

Clemson University, Graduate School, College of Agriculture, Forestry and Life Sciences, Program in Environmental Toxicology, Clemson, SC 29634. Offers MS, PhD. *Students:* 23 full-time (10 women), 4 part-time (0 women); includes 1 minority (Hispanic American), 7 international. Average age 29. 40 applicants, 10% accepted, 4 enrolled. In 2009, 2 master's, 5 doctorates awarded. *Degree requirements:* For master's, thesis; for doctorate, one foreign language, thesis/dissertation. *Entrance requirements:* For master's and doctorate, GRE General Test. Additional exam requirements/recommendations for international students: Required—TOEFL. *Application deadline:* For fall admission, 2/1 for domestic students, 4/15 for international students; for spring admission, 9/15 for international students. Applications are processed on a rolling basis. Application fee: $70 ($80 for international students). Electronic applications accepted. *Expenses:* Contact institution. *Financial support:* In 2009–10, 25 students received support, including 5 fellowships with full and partial tuition reimbursements available (averaging $10,962 per year), 12 research assistantships with partial tuition reimbursements available (averaging $17,249 per year), 11 teaching assistantships with partial tuition reimbursements available (averaging $15,682 per year); career-related internships or fieldwork, Federal Work-Study, institutionally sponsored loans, scholarships/grants, health care benefits, and unspecified assistantships also available. Financial award applicants required to submit FAFSA. *Faculty research:* Biochemical toxicology, analytical toxicology, ecological risk assessment, wildlife toxicology, mathematical modeling. Total annual research expenditures: $3 million. *Unit head:* Dr. Steve Klaine, Interim Director, 864-656-2188, E-mail: sklaine@clemson.edu. *Application contact:* Dr. Lisa J. Bain, Graduate Program Director, 864-656-5050, E-mail: lbain@clemson.edu.

Cleveland State University, College of Graduate Studies, College of Science, Department of Biological, Geological, and Environmental Sciences, Cleveland, OH 44115. Offers biology (MS); environmental science (MS); museum studies for natural historians (MS); regulatory biology (PhD); JD/MS. Part-time programs available. Terminal master's awarded for partial completion of doctoral program. *Degree requirements:* For master's, comprehensive exam (for some programs), thesis (for some programs); for doctorate, comprehensive exam, thesis/dissertation. *Entrance requirements:* For master's, GRE General Test, 2 letters of recommendation; for doctorate, GRE General Test, 2 letters of recommendation; 1-2 page essay statement of career goals and research interests. Additional exam requirements/recommendations for international students: Required—TOEFL (minimum score 525 paper-based; 197 computer-based). Electronic applications accepted. *Faculty research:* Molecular and cell biology, immunology, urban ecology.

The College at Brockport, State University of New York, School of Science and Mathematics, Department of Environmental Science and Biology, Brockport, NY 14420-2997. Offers MS. Part-time programs available. *Students:* 9 full-time (2 women), 9 part-time (4 women); includes 2 minority (1 Asian American or Pacific Islander, 1 Hispanic American). 17 applicants, 82% accepted, 12 enrolled. *Degree requirements:* For master's, comprehensive exam, thesis. *Entrance requirements:* For master's, minimum GPA of 3.0, letters of recommendation, sample of scientific writing. Additional exam requirements/recommendations for international students: Required—TOEFL (minimum score 550 paper-based; 213 computer-based; 79 iBT). *Application deadline:* For fall admission, 3/15 priority date for domestic and international students; for spring admission, 11/15 priority date for domestic and international students. Application fee: $50. Electronic applications accepted. *Expenses:* Tuition, state resident: full-time $8370; part-time $349 per credit. Tuition, nonresident: full-time $13,250; part-time $522 per credit. *Financial support:* In 2009–10, 1 research assistantship with full tuition reimbursement was awarded; Federal Work-Study, scholarships/grants, and unspecified assistantships also available. Support available to part-time students. Financial award application deadline: 3/15; financial

Environmental Sciences

The College at Brockport, State University of New York (continued)
award applicants required to submit FAFSA. *Faculty research:* Aquatic and terrestrial ecology/organismal biology, watersheds and wetlands, persistent toxic chemicals, soil-plant interactions, aquaculture. *Unit head:* Dr. James Haynes, Chairperson, 585-395-5975, Fax: 585-395-5969, E-mail: jhaynes@brockport.edu. *Application contact:* Dr. Christopher Norment, Graduate Director, 585-395-5748, Fax: 585-395-5969, E-mail: cnorment@brockport.edu.

College of Charleston, Graduate School, School of Sciences and Mathematics, Program in Environmental Studies, Charleston, SC 29424-0001. Offers MS. *Faculty:* 24 full-time (7 women), 10 part-time/adjunct (3 women). *Students:* 50 full-time (31 women), 29 part-time (15 women); includes 2 minority (1 African American, 1 Asian American or Pacific Islander), 2 international. Average age 27. 47 applicants, 68% accepted, 22 enrolled. In 2009, 18 master's awarded. *Degree requirements:* For master's, thesis or research internship. *Entrance requirements:* For master's, GRE, minimum GPA of 3.0, 3 letters of recommendation. Additional exam requirements/recommendations for international students: Required—TOEFL. *Application deadline:* For fall admission, 4/1 for domestic students; for spring admission, 11/1 for domestic students. Application fee: $45. Electronic applications accepted. *Expenses:* Contact institution. *Financial support:* In 2009–10, 5 research assistantships (averaging $17,000 per year), 6 teaching assistantships (averaging $13,300 per year) were awarded; fellowships, scholarships/grants and unspecified assistantships also available. Financial award application deadline: 6/1; financial award applicants required to submit FAFSA. *Unit head:* Dr. Kem Fronabarger, Director, 843-953-2002, Fax: 843-953-2001, E-mail: fronabargera@cofc.edu. *Application contact:* Susan Hallatt, Director of Graduate Admissions, 843-953-5614, Fax: 843-953-1434, E-mail: hallatts@cofc.edu.

College of Staten Island of the City University of New York, Graduate Programs, Center for Environmental Science, Staten Island, NY 10314-6600. Offers MS. Part-time and evening/weekend programs available. *Faculty:* 2 full-time (1 woman), 2 part-time/adjunct (1 woman). *Students:* 29 part-time (12 women); includes 8 minority (4 African Americans, 3 Asian Americans or Pacific Islanders, 1 Hispanic American), 4 international. Average age 32. 18 applicants, 83% accepted, 9 enrolled. In 2009, 5 master's awarded. Terminal master's awarded for partial completion of doctoral program. *Degree requirements:* For master's, thesis. *Entrance requirements:* For master's, GRE General Test, 1 year of course work in chemistry, physics, calculus, and ecology; minimum GPA of 3.0 in undergraduate science and engineering; bachelor's degree in a natural science or engineering; interview. Additional exam requirements/recommendations for international students: Required—TOEFL (minimum score 550 paper-based; 213 computer-based; 79 iBT). *Application deadline:* Applications are processed on a rolling basis. Application fee: $125. Electronic applications accepted. *Expenses:* Tuition, state resident: full-time $7360; part-time $310 per credit. Tuition, nonresident: part-time $575 per credit. Required fees: $378; $113 per semester. *Financial support:* In 2009–10, 1 student received support. Career-related internships or fieldwork, Federal Work-Study, and scholarships/grants available. Support available to part-time students. Financial award applicants required to submit FAFSA. Total annual research expenditures: $10,000. *Unit head:* Dr. Alfred Levine, Director, 718-982-2822, Fax: 718-982-3923, E-mail: envirscimasters@mail.csi.cuny.edu. *Application contact:* Sasha Spence, Assistant Director of Graduate Recruitment and Admissions, 718-982-2699, Fax: 718-982-2500, E-mail: sasha.spence@csi.cuny.edu.

Colorado School of Mines, Graduate School, Division of Environmental Science and Engineering, Golden, CO 80401. Offers MS, PhD. Part-time programs available. *Faculty:* 27 full-time (8 women), 6 part-time/adjunct (1 woman). *Students:* 74 full-time (44 women), 21 part-time (6 women); includes 15 minority (4 African Americans, 4 Asian Americans or Pacific Islanders, 7 Hispanic Americans), 5 international. Average age 30. 127 applicants, 65% accepted, 38 enrolled. In 2009, 34 master's, 1 doctorate awarded. *Degree requirements:* For master's, thesis (for some programs); for doctorate, comprehensive exam, thesis/dissertation. *Entrance requirements:* For master's and doctorate, GRE General Test. Additional exam requirements/recommendations for international students: Required—TOEFL (minimum score 550 paper-based; 213 computer-based; 80 iBT). *Application deadline:* For fall admission, 1/15 priority date for domestic and international students; for spring admission, 9/1 priority date for domestic and international students. Application fee: $50 ($70 for international students). Electronic applications accepted. *Expenses:* Tuition, state resident: full-time $10,584; part-time $588 per credit hour. Tuition, nonresident: full-time $24,750; part-time $1375 per credit hour. Required fees: $1654; $827.10 per semester. *Financial support:* In 2009–10, 35 students received support, including 2 fellowships with full tuition reimbursements available (averaging $20,000 per year), 30 research assistantships with full tuition reimbursements available (averaging $20,000 per year), 3 teaching assistantships with full tuition reimbursements available (averaging $20,000 per year); scholarships/grants, health care benefits, and unspecified assistantships also available. Financial award application deadline: 1/15; financial award applicants required to submit FAFSA. *Faculty research:* Treatment of water and wastes, environmental law: policy and practice, natural environment systems, hazardous waste management, environmental data analysis. Total annual research expenditures: $5.3 million. *Unit head:* Dr. Robert Siegrist, Division Director, 303-384-2158, Fax: 303-273-3413, E-mail: siegrist@mines.edu. *Application contact:* Tim VanHaverbeke, Research Faculty, 303-273-3467, Fax: 303-273-3413, E-mail: tvanhave@mines.edu.

Columbia University, Graduate School of Arts and Sciences, Program in Climate and Society, New York, NY 10027. Offers MA.

Columbia University, School of International and Public Affairs, Program in Environmental Science and Policy, New York, NY 10027. Offers MPA. Program admits applicants for late May/early June start only. *Faculty:* 8 full-time (3 women), 10 part-time/adjunct (6 women). *Students:* 67 full-time (45 women); includes 13 minority (1 African American, 11 Asian Americans or Pacific Islanders, 1 Hispanic American). Average age 27. 262 applicants, 49% accepted, 67 enrolled. In 2009, 58 master's awarded. *Degree requirements:* For master's, workshops. *Entrance requirements:* For master's, GRE (recommended), previous course work in biology and chemistry, or earth sciences (recommended); previous course work in economics strongly recommended. Additional exam requirements/recommendations for international students: Required—TOEFL. *Application deadline:* For fall admission, 11/1 priority date for domestic and international students; for winter admission, 1/14 priority date for domestic students, 1/15 priority date for international students; for spring admission, 2/15 priority date for domestic and international students. Applications are processed on a rolling basis. Application fee: $85. Electronic applications accepted. *Financial support:* In 2009–10, 21 students received support, including 21 fellowships with partial tuition reimbursements available (averaging $11,667 per year); Federal Work-Study and scholarships/grants also available. Financial award application deadline: 1/15; financial award applicants required to submit FAFSA. *Faculty research:* Ecological management of enclosed ecosystems vegetation dynamics, environmental policy and management, energy policy, nuclear waste policy, environmental and natural resource economics and policy, carbon sequestration, urban planning, environmental risk assessment/toxicology, environmental justice. *Unit head:* Dr. Steven A. Cohen, Director, 212-854-3142, Fax: 212-864-4847, E-mail: sc32@columbia.edu. *Application contact:* Louise A. Rosen, Associate Director, 212-854-0643, Fax: 212-864-4847, E-mail: lar46@columbia.edu.

Columbus State University, Graduate Studies, College of Letters and Sciences, Environmental Science Program, Columbus, GA 31907-5645. Offers environmental science (MS). Part-time and evening/weekend programs available. *Faculty:* 4 full-time (0 women), 1 part-time/adjunct (0 women). *Students:* 11 full-time (7 women), 13 part-time (4 women); includes 8 minority (6 African Americans, 1 Asian American or Pacific Islander, 1 Hispanic American), 1 international. Average age 34. 16 applicants, 69% accepted, 6 enrolled. In 2009, 11 master's awarded. *Degree requirements:* For master's, thesis. *Entrance requirements:* For master's, GRE General Test, minimum GPA of 3.0. Additional exam requirements/recommendations for international students: Required—TOEFL (minimum score 550 paper-based; 213 computer-based; 79 iBT). *Application deadline:* For fall admission, 5/1 priority date for domestic students, 5/1 for international students; for spring admission, 11/1 for domestic and international students. Applications are processed on a rolling basis. Application fee: $30. Electronic applications accepted. *Financial support:* In 2009–10, 8 students received support, including 11 research assistantships with partial tuition reimbursements available (averaging $3,000 per year); career-related internships or fieldwork, Federal Work-Study, institutionally sponsored loans, scholarships/grants, and unspecified assistantships also available. Support available to part-time students. Financial award application deadline: 5/1; financial award applicants required to submit FAFSA. *Unit head:* Dr. Shawn Cruzen, Department Chair, 706-649-1785, E-mail: cruzen_shawn@colstate.edu. *Application contact:* Katie Thornton, Graduate Admissions Specialist, 706-568-2035, Fax: 706-568-2462, E-mail: thornton_katie@colstate.edu.

Cornell University, Graduate School, Graduate Fields of Agriculture and Life Sciences, Field of Soil and Crop Sciences, Ithaca, NY 14853-0001. Offers agronomy (MS, PhD); environmental information science (MS, PhD); environmental management (MPS); field crop science (MS, PhD); soil science (MS, PhD). *Faculty:* 40 full-time (9 women). *Students:* 32 full-time (17 women); includes 5 minority (1 American Indian/Alaska Native, 4 Hispanic Americans), 9 international. Average age 33. 42 applicants, 24% accepted, 5 enrolled. In 2009, 2 master's, 8 doctorates awarded. *Degree requirements:* For master's, thesis (MS); for doctorate, comprehensive exam, thesis/dissertation. *Entrance requirements:* For master's and doctorate, GRE General Test, 2 letters of recommendation. Additional exam requirements/recommendations for international students: Required—TOEFL (minimum score 550 paper-based; 213 computer-based; 77 iBT). *Application deadline:* For fall admission, 2/1 priority date for domestic students. Applications are processed on a rolling basis. Application fee: $70. Electronic applications accepted. *Expenses:* Tuition: Full-time $29,500. Required fees: $70. Full-time tuition and fees vary according to degree level, program and student level. *Financial support:* In 2009–10, 26 students received support, including 1 fellowship with full tuition reimbursement available, 1 research assistantship with full tuition reimbursement available, 1 teaching assistantship with full tuition reimbursement available; institutionally sponsored loans, traineeships, health care benefits, tuition waivers (full and partial), and unspecified assistantships also available. *Faculty research:* Soil chemistry, physics and biology; crop physiology and management; environmental information science and modeling; international agriculture; weed science. *Unit head:* Director of Graduate Studies, 607-255-3267, Fax: 607-255-8615. *Application contact:* Graduate Field Assistant, 607-255-3267, Fax: 607-255-8615, E-mail: ljh4@cornell.edu.

Drexel University, College of Arts and Sciences, Program in Environmental Science, Philadelphia, PA 19104-2875. Offers MS, PhD. Part-time and evening/weekend programs available. Terminal master's awarded for partial completion of doctoral program. *Degree requirements:* For master's, thesis optional; for doctorate, thesis/dissertation. Electronic applications accepted.

Duke University, Graduate School, Department of Environment, Durham, NC 27708. Offers natural resource economics/policy (AM, PhD); natural resource science/ecology (AM, PhD); natural resource systems science (AM, PhD); JD/AM. Part-time programs available. *Faculty:* 28 full-time. *Students:* 66 full-time (39 women); includes 3 minority (2 African Americans, 1 Asian American or Pacific Islander), 25 international. 126 applicants, 26% accepted, 19 enrolled. In 2009, 4 master's, 11 doctorates awarded. *Degree requirements:* For doctorate, variable foreign language requirement, thesis/dissertation. *Entrance requirements:* For master's and doctorate, GRE General Test. Additional exam requirements/recommendations for international students: Required—TOEFL (minimum score 550 paper-based; 213 computer-based; 83 iBT), IELTS (minimum score 7). *Application deadline:* For fall admission, 12/8 priority date for domestic and international students. Application fee: $75. Electronic applications accepted. *Financial support:* Fellowships, research assistantships, teaching assistantships, Federal Work-Study available. Financial award application deadline: 12/31. *Unit head:* Kenneth Reckhow, Director of Graduate Studies, Fax: 919-660-1884, E-mail: meg.stephens@duke.edu. *Application contact:* Cynthia Robertson, Associate Dean for Enrollment Services, 919-684-3913, E-mail: grad-admissions@duke.edu.

Duke University, Nicholas School of the Environment, Durham, NC 27708-0328. Offers coastal environmental management (MEM); DEL-environmental leadership (MEM); energy and environment (MEM); environmental economics and policy (MEM); environmental health and security (MEM); forest resource management (MF); global environmental change (MEM); resource ecology (MEM); water and air resources (MEM); JD/AM; JD/MEM; JD/MF; MAT/MEM; MBA/MEM; MBA/MF; MEM/MPP; MF/MPP. *Accreditation:* SAF (one or more programs are accredited). Part-time programs available. *Degree requirements:* For master's, thesis. *Entrance requirements:* For master's, GRE General Test, previous course work in biology or ecology, calculus, statistics, and microeconomics; computer familiarity with word processing and data analysis. Additional exam requirements/recommendations for international students: Required—TOEFL (minimum score 550 paper-based; 213 computer-based). Electronic applications accepted. *Expenses:* Contact institution. *Faculty research:* Ecosystem management, conservation ecology, earth systems, risk assessment.

Duquesne University, Bayer School of Natural and Environmental Sciences, Environmental Science and Management Program, Pittsburgh, PA 15282-0001. Offers environmental management (MEM, Certificate); environmental science (Certificate); environmental science and management (MS); JD/MS; MBA/MS; MS/MS. Part-time and evening/weekend programs available. Postbaccalaureate distance learning degree programs offered (minimal on-campus study). *Faculty:* 4 full-time (0 women), 10 part-time/adjunct (1 woman). *Students:* 16 full-time (10 women), 21 part-time (12 women), 3 international. Average age 27. 35 applicants, 51% accepted, 11 enrolled. In 2009, 16 master's, 2 other advanced degrees awarded. *Degree requirements:* For master's, thesis (for some programs); for Certificate, minimum of 18 credit hours (for certificate). *Entrance requirements:* For master's, GRE General Test, course work in biology, chemistry, and calculus or statistics; 3 letters of reference. Additional exam requirements/recommendations for international students: Required—TOEFL (minimum score 80 iBT). *Application deadline:* For fall admission, 4/1 priority date for domestic students, 4/1 for international students; for spring admission, 10/1 priority date for domestic students, 10/1 for international students. Applications are processed on a rolling basis. Application fee: $40. *Expenses:* Contact institution. *Financial support:* In 2009–10, 7 students received support, including 1 fellowship (averaging $16,500 per year), 1 research assistantship, 5 teaching assistantships with full and partial tuition reimbursements available (averaging $12,000 per year); career-related internships or fieldwork, scholarships/grants, and unspecified assistantships also available. Financial award application deadline: 5/31. *Faculty research:* Watershed management systems, environmental analytical chemistry, environmental endocrinology, environmental microbiology, aquatic biology. *Unit head:* Dr. John Stolz, Director, 412-396-4367, Fax: 412-396-4092, E-mail: stolz@duq.edu. *Application contact:* Heather Costello, Graduate Academic Advisor, 412-396-6339, Fax: 412-396-4881, E-mail: costelloh@duq.edu.

Florida Agricultural and Mechanical University, Environmental Sciences Institute, Tallahassee, FL 32307. Offers MS, PhD. *Faculty:* 10 full-time (2 women). *Students:* 30 full-time (21 women), 1 (woman) part-time; includes 24 minority (all African Americans), 7 international. Average age 25. 15 applicants, 13% accepted, 2 enrolled. In 2009, 4 master's, 1 doctorate awarded. *Degree requirements:* For master's, thesis; for doctorate, comprehensive exam, thesis/dissertation, oral exam. *Entrance requirements:* For master's and doctorate, GRE General Test, minimum GPA of 3.0. Additional exam requirements/recommendations for international students: Required—TOEFL. *Application deadline:* For fall admission, 6/1 priority date for domestic students, 4/1 priority date for international students; for spring admission, 11/1 priority date for domestic and international students. Application fee: $25 for international students. *Financial support:* In 2009–10, 10 fellowships with full and partial tuition reimbursements, 21 research assistantships with tuition reimbursements were awarded; career-related internships or fieldwork, institutionally sponsored loans, scholarships/grants, and unspecified assistantships also available. Financial award application deadline: 6/1; financial award applicants required to submit FAFSA. *Faculty research:* Environmental chemistry, environmental policy and risk management, aquatic and terrestrial ecology, biomolecular sciences. *Unit head:* Dr. Michael Abazinge, Director, 850-599-3550, Fax: 850-599-8183, E-mail: michael.abazinge@famu.edu. *Application contact:* Ora S. Mukes, Coordinator Academic Support Services, 850-561-2641, Fax: 850-412-5504, E-mail: ora.mukes@famu.edu.

Florida Atlantic University, Charles E. Schmidt College of Science, Environmental Sciences Program, Boca Raton, FL 33431-0991. Offers MS. *Students:* 10 full-time (6 women), 3 part-time (all women); includes 1 minority (Hispanic American), 1 international. Average age 27. 13 applicants, 38% accepted, 1 enrolled. In 2009, 2 master's awarded. *Degree requirements:* For master's, thesis. *Entrance requirements:* For master's, GRE General Test, minimum GPA of 3.0. Additional exam requirements/recommendations for international students: Required—TOEFL. *Application deadline:* For fall admission, 3/15 for domestic and international students; for spring admission, 10/1 for domestic and international students. Application fee: $30. *Expenses:* Tuition, state resident: full-time $7055; part-time $293.94 per credit hour. Tuition, nonresident: full-time $22,096; part-time $920.66 per credit hour. *Financial support:* Teaching assistantships, career-related internships or fieldwork and Federal Work-Study available. *Faculty research:* Tropical and terrestrial ecology, coastal/marine/wetlands ecology, hydrogeology, tropical botany. *Unit head:* Dr. Dale Gawlik, Director, 561-297-3333, Fax: 561-297-2067, E-mail: dgawlik@fau.edu. *Application contact:* Dr. Dale Gawlik, Director, 561-297-3333, Fax: 561-297-2067, E-mail: dgawlik@fau.edu.

Florida Gulf Coast University, College of Arts and Sciences, Program in Environmental Science, Fort Myers, FL 33965-6565. Offers MS. Part-time programs available. *Entrance requirements:* For master's, GRE General Test, minimum GPA of 3.0. Additional exam requirements/recommendations for international students: Required—TOEFL (minimum score 550 paper-based; 213 computer-based). Electronic applications accepted. *Faculty research:* Political issues in environmental science, recycling, environmental friendly buildings, pathophysiology, immunotoxicology of marine organisms.

Florida Institute of Technology, Graduate Programs, College of Engineering, Department of Marine and Environmental Systems, Melbourne, FL 32901-6975. Offers earth remote sensing (MS); environmental resource management (MS); environmental science (MS, PhD); meteorology (MS); ocean engineering (MS, PhD); oceanography (MS, PhD), including biological oceanography (MS), chemical oceanography (MS), coastal zone management (MS), geological oceanography (MS), oceanography (PhD), physical oceanography (MS). Part-time programs available. *Faculty:* 12 full-time (1 woman), 1 part-time/adjunct (0 women). *Students:* 42 full-time (18 women), 23 part-time (9 women); includes 2 minority (1 African American, 1 Asian American or Pacific Islander), 11 international. Average age 28. 103 applicants, 50% accepted, 16 enrolled. In 2009, 22 master's, 1 doctorate awarded. *Degree requirements:* For master's, comprehensive exam (for some programs), thesis (for some programs), seminar, field project, written final exam, internship, technical paper, oral presentation or internship; for doctorate, comprehensive exam, thesis/dissertation, seminar, internships (oceanography and environmental science), publications. *Entrance requirements:* For master's, GRE General Test (environmental science, oceanography, environmental resource management, meteorology, earth remote sensing), 3 letters of recommendation, minimum GPA of 3.0, resume; for doctorate, GRE General Test (oceanography, environmental science), resume, 3 letters of recommendation, minimum GPA of 3.3, statement of objectives, on campus interview (highly recommended). Additional exam requirements/recommendations for international students: Required—TOEFL (minimum score 550 paper-based; 213 computer-based; 79 iBT). *Application deadline:* For fall admission, 4/1 for international students; for spring admission, 9/30 for international students. Applications are processed on a rolling basis. Application fee: $50. Electronic applications accepted. *Expenses:* Tuition: Part-time $1015 per credit. Tuition and fees vary according to campus/location and program. *Financial support:* In 2009–10, 19 students received support, including 5 fellowships with full and partial tuition reimbursements available (averaging $7,240 per year), 9 research assistantships with full and partial tuition reimbursements available (averaging $5,542 per year), 10 teaching assistantships with full and partial tuition reimbursements available (averaging $5,411 per year); career-related internships or fieldwork, institutionally sponsored loans, tuition waivers (partial), unspecified assistantships, and tuition remissions also available. Support available to part-time students. Financial award application deadline: 3/1; financial award applicants required to submit FAFSA. Total annual research expenditures: $1.7 million. *Unit head:* Dr. George Maul, Department Head, 321-674-7453, Fax: 321-674-7212, E-mail: gmaul@fit.edu. *Application contact:* Thomas M. Shea, Director of Graduate Admissions, 321-674-7577, Fax: 321-723-9468, E-mail: tshea@fit.edu.

See Close-Up on page 411.

Florida International University, College of Arts and Sciences, Department of Earth and Environment, Department of Environmental Studies, Miami, FL 33199. Offers MS. Part-time programs available. *Students:* 18 full-time (8 women), 20 part-time (13 women); includes 10 minority (1 African American, 9 Hispanic Americans), 8 international. Average age 28. 25 applicants, 40% accepted, 10 enrolled. In 2009, 12 master's awarded. *Degree requirements:* For master's, thesis or alternative. *Entrance requirements:* For master's, GRE General Test, minimum GPA of 3.0, 3 letters of recommendation, letter of intent. Additional exam requirements/recommendations for international students: Required—TOEFL (minimum score 550 paper-based; 80 iBT). *Application deadline:* For fall admission, 3/1 for domestic and international students; for spring admission, 10/1 for domestic students, 9/1 for international students. Applications are processed on a rolling basis. Application fee: $30. Electronic applications accepted. *Expenses:* Tuition, state resident: full-time $8008; part-time $4004 per year. Tuition, nonresident: full-time $20,104; part-time $10,052 per year. Required fees: $298; $149 per term. *Financial support:* Institutionally sponsored loans and scholarships/grants available. Financial award application deadline: 3/1; financial award applicants required to submit FAFSA. *Unit head:* Dr. Rosemary Hickey-Vargas, Chair, Earth and Environment Department, 305-348-1930, Fax: 305-348-6137, E-mail: rosemary.hickey-vargas@fiu.edu. *Application contact:* Dr. Krishnaswamy Jayachandran, Director, Graduate Program, 305-348-1930, Fax: 305-348-6137, E-mail: jayachan@fiu.edu.

Gannon University, School of Graduate Studies, College of Engineering and Business, School of Engineering and Computer Science, Program in Environmental and Occupational Science and Health, Erie, PA 16541-0001. Offers Certificate. Part-time and evening/weekend programs available. *Entrance requirements:* Additional exam requirements/recommendations for international students: Required—TOEFL (minimum score 79 iBT). *Application deadline:* Applications are processed on a rolling basis. Application fee: $25. Electronic applications accepted. *Expenses:* Tuition: Full-time $13,590; part-time $755 per credit. Required fees: $524; $17 per credit. Tuition and fees vary according to course load, degree level, campus/location and program. *Financial support:* Scholarships/grants available. Financial award application deadline: 7/1; financial award applicants required to submit FAFSA. *Unit head:* Dr. Harry Diz, Chair, 814-871-7633, E-mail: diz001@gannon.edu. *Application contact:* Kara Morgan, Assistant Director of Graduate Admissions, 814-871-5831, Fax: 814-871-5827, E-mail: graduate@gannon.edu.

Gannon University, School of Graduate Studies, College of Engineering and Business, School of Engineering and Computer Science, Program in Environmental Science and Engineering, Erie, PA 16541-0001. Offers MS. Part-time and evening/weekend programs available. *Students:* 8 full-time (2 women), 4 part-time (2 women); includes 1 minority (African American), 1 international. Average age 28. 24 applicants, 42% accepted, 1 enrolled. In 2009, 4 master's awarded. *Degree requirements:* For master's, thesis, internship, research paper or project. *Entrance requirements:* For master's, GRE. Additional exam requirements/recommendations for international students: Required—TOEFL (minimum score 79 iBT). *Application deadline:* Applications are processed on a rolling basis. Application fee: $25. Electronic applications accepted. *Expenses:* Tuition: Full-time $13,590; part-time $755 per credit. Required fees: $524; $17 per credit. Tuition and fees vary according to course load, degree level, campus/location and program. *Financial support:* Scholarships/grants and unspecified assistantships available. Financial award application deadline: 7/1; financial award applicants required to submit FAFSA. *Unit head:* Dr. Harry Diz, Chair, 814-871-7633, E-mail: diz001@gannon.edu. *Application contact:* Kara Morgan, Assistant Director of Graduate Admissions, 814-871-5831, Fax: 814-871-5827, E-mail: graduate@gannon.edu.

George Mason University, College of Science, Department of Environmental Science and Policy, Fairfax, VA 22030. Offers MS, PhD. Part-time programs available. *Degree requirements:* For doctorate, thesis/dissertation, internship. *Entrance requirements:* For doctorate, GRE General Test, GRE Subject Test. Electronic applications accepted. *Expenses:* Tuition, state resident: full-time $7568; part-time $315.33 per credit hour. Tuition, nonresident: full-time $21,704; part-time $904.33 per credit hour. Required fees: $2184; $91 per credit hour.

Georgia Institute of Technology, Graduate Studies and Research, College of Sciences, School of Earth and Atmospheric Sciences, Atlanta, GA 30332-0340. Offers atmospheric chemistry, aerosols and clouds (MS, PhD); dynamics of weather and climate (MS, PhD); geochemistry (MS, PhD); geophysics (MS, PhD); oceanography (MS, PhD); paleoclimate (MS, PhD); planetary science (MS, PhD); remote sensing (MS, PhD). Part-time programs available. Terminal master's awarded for partial completion of doctoral program. *Degree requirements:* For master's, thesis or alternative; for doctorate, comprehensive exam, thesis/dissertation. *Entrance requirements:* For master's, GRE, letters of recommendation; for doctorate, GRE, academic transcripts, letters of recommendation, personal statement. Additional exam requirements/recommendations for international students: Required—TOEFL (minimum score 550 paper-based; 213 computer-based; 79 iBT). *Faculty research:* Geophysics; atmospheric chemistry, aerosols and clouds; dynamics of weather and climate; geochemistry; oceanography; paleoclimate; planetary science; remote sensing.

Graduate School and University Center of the City University of New York, Graduate Studies, Program in Earth and Environmental Sciences, New York, NY 10016-4039. Offers PhD. *Faculty:* 36 full-time (5 women). *Students:* 76 full-time (35 women), 5 part-time (3 women); includes 11 minority (2 African Americans, 5 Asian Americans or Pacific Islanders, 4 Hispanic Americans), 18 international. Average age 36. 49 applicants, 55% accepted, 14 enrolled. In 2009, 5 doctorates awarded. *Degree requirements:* For doctorate, one foreign language, comprehensive exam, thesis/dissertation. *Entrance requirements:* For doctorate, GRE General Test. Additional exam requirements/recommendations for international students: Required—TOEFL. *Application deadline:* For fall admission, 1/15 priority date for domestic students. Application fee: $125. Electronic applications accepted. *Financial support:* In 2009–10, 52 students received support, including 51 fellowships, 2 research assistantships, 1 teaching assistantship; career-related internships or fieldwork, Federal Work-Study, institutionally sponsored loans, and tuition waivers (full and partial) also available. Financial award application deadline: 2/1; financial award applicants required to submit FAFSA. *Unit head:* Dr. Yehuda Klein, Executive Officer, 212-817-8241, Fax: 212-817-1513. *Application contact:* Les Gribben, Director of Admissions, 212-817-7470, Fax: 212-817-1624, E-mail: lgribben@gc.cuny.edu.

Harvard University, Cyprus International Institute for the Environment and Public Health in Association with Harvard School of Public Health, Cambridge, MA 02138. Offers environmental health (MS). *Entrance requirements:* For master's, GRE, resume, 3 letters of recommendation, BA or BS. Additional exam requirements/recommendations for international students: Required—TOEFL (minimum score 220 computer-based), IELTS (minimum score 7). Electronic applications accepted. *Expenses:* Tuition: Full-time $33,696. Required fees: $1126. Full-time tuition and fees vary according to program. *Faculty research:* Air pollution, climate change, biostatistics, sustainable development, environmental management.

Howard University, Graduate School, Department of Chemistry, Washington, DC 20059-0002. Offers analytical chemistry (MS, PhD); atmospheric (MS, PhD); biochemistry (MS, PhD); environmental (MS, PhD); inorganic chemistry (MS, PhD); organic chemistry (MS, PhD); physical chemistry (MS, PhD). Terminal master's awarded for partial completion of doctoral program. *Degree requirements:* For master's, comprehensive exam, thesis, teaching experience; for doctorate, comprehensive exam, thesis/dissertation, teaching experience. *Entrance requirements:* For master's, GRE General Test, minimum GPA of 2.7; for doctorate, GRE General Test, minimum GPA of 3.0. Additional exam requirements/recommendations for international students: Required—TOEFL. Electronic applications accepted. *Faculty research:* Synthetic organics, materials, natural products, mass spectrometry.

Humboldt State University, Graduate Studies, College of Natural Resources and Sciences, Programs in Environmental Systems, Arcata, CA 95521-8299. Offers environmental systems (MS), including energy, environment and society, environmental resources engineering, geology, math modeling. *Students:* 31 full-time (11 women), 7 part-time (1 woman); includes 4 minority (2 Asian Americans or Pacific Islanders, 2 Hispanic Americans), 1 international. Average age 30. 54 applicants, 57% accepted, 17 enrolled. In 2009, 13 master's awarded. *Degree requirements:* For master's, thesis. *Entrance requirements:* For master's, GRE, appropriate bachelor's degree, minimum GPA of 2.5, 3 letters of recommendation. Additional exam requirements/recommendations for international students: Required—TOEFL. *Application deadline:* For fall admission, 3/15 for domestic students; for spring admission, 10/15 for domestic students. Applications are processed on a rolling basis. Application fee: $55. *Expenses:* Tuition, nonresident: full-time $8928. Required fees: $6102. Tuition and fees vary according to program. *Financial support:* Application deadline: 3/1; *Faculty research:* Mathematical modeling, international development technology, geology, environmental resources engineering. *Unit head:* Dr. Chris Dugaw, Chair, 707-826-4251, Fax: 707-826-4145, E-mail: dugaw@humboldt.edu. *Application contact:* Julie Tucker, Administrative Support, 707-826-3256, Fax: 707-826-3140, E-mail: jlt7002@humboldt.edu.

Hunter College of the City University of New York, Graduate School, School of Arts and Sciences, Department of Geography, New York, NY 10021-5085. Offers analytical geography (MA); earth system science (MA); environmental and social issues (MA); geographic information science (Certificate); geographic information systems (MA); teaching earth science (MA). Part-time and evening/weekend programs available. *Faculty:* 12 full-time (5 women), 4 part-time/adjunct (0 women). *Students:* 17 full-time (16 women), 20 part-time (19 women); includes 9 minority (1 African American, 1 American Indian/Alaska Native, 4 Asian Americans or Pacific Islanders, 3 Hispanic Americans). Average age 31. 13 applicants, 92% accepted, 9 enrolled. In 2009, 10 master's, 3 other advanced degrees awarded. *Degree requirements:* For master's, comprehensive exam or thesis. *Entrance requirements:* For master's, GRE General Test, minimum B average in major, B- overall; 18 credits of course work in geography; 2 letters of recommendation; for Certificate, minimum B average in major, B- overall. Additional exam requirements/recommendations for international students: Required—TOEFL. *Application deadline:* For fall admission, 4/1 for domestic students; for spring admission, 11/1 for domestic students. Applications are processed on a rolling basis. Application fee: $125. *Expenses:* Tuition, state resident: full-time $7360; part-time $310 per credit. Required fees: $250 per semester. *Financial support:* In 2009–10, 1 fellowship (averaging $3,000 per year), 2 research assistantships (averaging $10,000 per year), 10 teaching assistantships (averaging $6,000 per year) were awarded; career-related internships or fieldwork, Federal Work-Study, institutionally sponsored loans, and unspecified assistantships also available. Financial award application deadline: 3/1. *Faculty research:* Urban geography, economic geography, geographic information science, demographic methods, climate change. *Unit head:* Prof. William Solecki, Chair, 212-772-4536, Fax: 212-772-5268, E-mail: wsolecki@hunter.cuny.edu. *Application contact:*

Environmental Sciences

Hunter College of the City University of New York (continued)
Prof. Marianna Pavlovskaya, Graduate Adviser, 212-772-5320, Fax: 212-772-5268, E-mail: mpavlov@geo.hunter.cuny.edu.

Idaho State University, Office of Graduate Studies, College of Arts and Sciences, Department of Geosciences, Pocatello, ID 83209-8072. Offers geographic information science (MS); geology (MNS, MS); geology emphasis environmental geoscience (MS); geophysics/hydrology/geology (MS); geotechnology (Postbaccalaureate Certificate). Part-time programs available. *Faculty:* 8 full-time (1 woman). *Students:* 25 full-time (12 women), 20 part-time (6 women); includes 1 minority (Asian American or Pacific Islander), 4 international. Average age 33. In 2009, 7 master's, 2 other advanced degrees awarded. *Degree requirements:* For master's, comprehensive exam, thesis, oral colloquium; for Postbaccalaureate Certificate, thesis optional, minimum 19 credits. *Entrance requirements:* For master's, GRE General Test (minimum 50th percentile in 2 sections), 3 letters of recommendation; for Postbaccalaureate Certificate, GRE General Test, 3 letters of recommendation, bachelor's degree, statement of goals. Additional exam requirements/recommendations for international students: Required—TOEFL (minimum score 550 paper-based; 213 computer-based; 80 iBT). *Application deadline:* For fall admission, 7/1 for domestic students, 6/1 for international students; for spring admission, 12/1 for domestic students, 11/1 for international students. Applications are processed on a rolling basis. Application fee: $55. Electronic applications accepted. *Expenses:* Tuition, state resident: full-time $3318; part-time $297 per credit hour. Tuition, nonresident: full-time $13,120; part-time $437 per credit hour. Required fees: $2530. Tuition and fees vary according to program. *Financial support:* In 2009–10, 20 research assistantships with full and partial tuition reimbursements (averaging $9,713 per year), 7 teaching assistantships with full and partial tuition reimbursements (averaging $10,841 per year) were awarded; career-related internships or fieldwork, Federal Work-Study, institutionally sponsored loans, scholarships/grants, health care benefits, tuition waivers (full and partial), and unspecified assistantships also available. Support available to part-time students. Financial award application deadline: 1/1; financial award applicants required to submit FAFSA. *Faculty research:* Quantitative field mapping and sampling: microscopic, geochemical, and isotopic analysis of rocks, minerals and water; remote sensing, geographic information systems, and global positioning systems: environmental and watershed management; surficial and fluvial processes: landscape change; regional tectonics, structural geology; planetary geology. *Unit head:* Dr. David Rodgers, Chairman, 208-282-3365, Fax: 208-282-4414, E-mail: rodgdavi@isu.edu. *Application contact:* Tami Carson, Graduate School Technical Records Specialist, 208-282-2150, Fax: 208-282-4847, E-mail: carstami@isu.edu.

Idaho State University, Office of Graduate Studies, College of Engineering, Civil and Environmental Engineering Department, Pocatello, ID 83209-8060. Offers civil engineering (MS); environmental engineering (MS); environmental science and management (MS). Part-time programs available. *Faculty:* 1 full-time (0 women). *Students:* 9 full-time (1 woman), 17 part-time (6 women); includes 2 minority (both Asian Americans or Pacific Islanders), 12 international. Average age 31. In 2009, 9 master's awarded. *Degree requirements:* For master's, comprehensive exam (for some programs), thesis optional, thesis project, 2 semesters of seminar. *Entrance requirements:* For master's, GRE. Additional exam requirements/recommendations for international students: Required—TOEFL (minimum score 550 paper-based; 213 computer-based; 80 iBT). *Application deadline:* For fall admission, 7/1 for domestic students, 6/1 for international students; for spring admission, 12/1 for domestic students, 11/1 for international students. Applications are processed on a rolling basis. Application fee: $55. Electronic applications accepted. *Expenses:* Tuition, state resident: full-time $3318; part-time $297 per credit hour. Tuition, nonresident: full-time $13,120; part-time $437 per credit hour. Required fees: $2530. Tuition and fees vary according to program. *Financial support:* Research assistantships with full and partial tuition reimbursements, teaching assistantships with full and partial tuition reimbursements, career-related internships or fieldwork, Federal Work-Study, institutionally sponsored loans, scholarships/grants, traineeships, health care benefits, tuition waivers (full and partial), and unspecified assistantships available. Support available to part-time students. Financial award application deadline: 1/1; financial award applicants required to submit FAFSA. *Faculty research:* Floor vibration investigations, earthquake engineering, base isolation systems and seismic risk assessment, infrastructure revitalization (building foundations and damage, bridge structures, highways, and dams), slope stability and soil erosion, pavement rehabilitation, computational fluid dynamics and flood control structures, microbial fuel cells, water treatment and water quality modeling, environmental risk assessment, biotechnology, nanotechnology. *Unit head:* Dr. Arya Ebrahimpour, Chair, 208-282-4695, Fax: 208-282-4538, E-mail: ebraaryai@isu.edu. *Application contact:* Tami Carson, Graduate School Technical Records Specialist, 208-282-2150, Fax: 208-282-4847, E-mail: carstami@isu.edu.

Idaho State University, Office of Graduate Studies, Department of Interdisciplinary Studies, Pocatello, ID 83209. Offers general interdisciplinary (M Ed, MA, MNS); waste management and environmental science (MS). Part-time programs available. *Faculty:* 2 full-time (1 woman). In 2009, 2 master's awarded. *Degree requirements:* For master's, comprehensive exam, thesis optional. *Entrance requirements:* For master's, GRE General Test or MAT, minimum GPA of 3.0. Additional exam requirements/recommendations for international students: Required—TOEFL (minimum score 550 paper-based; 213 computer-based; 80 iBT). *Application deadline:* For fall admission, 7/1 for domestic students, 6/1 for international students; for spring admission, 12/1 for domestic students, 11/1 for international students. Applications are processed on a rolling basis. Application fee: $55. *Expenses:* Tuition, state resident: full-time $3318; part-time $297 per credit hour. Tuition, nonresident: full-time $13,120; part-time $437 per credit hour. Required fees: $2530. Tuition and fees vary according to program. *Financial support:* Career-related internships or fieldwork, Federal Work-Study, scholarships/grants, and unspecified assistantships available. Support available to part-time students. Financial award application deadline: 1/1; financial award applicants required to submit FAFSA. *Unit head:* Dr. Pamela Crowell, Vice President for Research, 208-282-2714, Fax: 208-282-4529. *Application contact:* Ellen Combs, Graduate School Technical Records Specialist, 208-282-2150, Fax: 208-282-4847.

Indiana University Bloomington, School of Public and Environmental Affairs, Environmental Science Programs, Bloomington, IN 47405-7000. Offers environmental science (MSES, PhD). *Students:* 61 full-time (32 women), 5 part-time (1 woman); includes 3 minority (1 African American, 1 Asian American or Pacific Islander, 1 Hispanic American), 20 international. Average age 28. 129 applicants, 83% accepted, 49 enrolled. In 2009, 44 master's, 3 doctorates awarded. *Degree requirements:* For doctorate, comprehensive exam, thesis/dissertation or alternative. *Entrance requirements:* For master's, GRE General Test; for doctorate, GRE General Test, statement of purpose, 3 letters of recommendation. Additional exam requirements/recommendations for international students: Required—TOEFL. *Application deadline:* For fall admission, 1/15 priority date for domestic students, 12/1 priority date for international students; for spring admission, 11/1 priority date for domestic students, 9/1 priority date for international students. Applications are processed on a rolling basis. Application fee: $55 ($65 for international students). Electronic applications accepted. *Financial support:* In 2009–10, 16 students received support; fellowships with full tuition reimbursements available, research assistantships, teaching assistantships, career-related internships or fieldwork, Federal Work-Study, institutionally sponsored loans, and unspecified assistantships available. Financial award application deadline: 1/15; financial award applicants required to submit FAFSA. *Faculty research:* Applied ecology, bio-geo chemistry, toxicology, wetlands ecology, environmental microbiology, forest ecology, environmental chemistry. *Unit head:* Charles Kurt Zorn, Interim Dean, 812-855-5058, Fax: 812-855-6234, E-mail: zorn@indiana.edu. *Application contact:* Charles A. Johnson, Coordinator of Student Recruitment, 800-765-7755, Fax: 812-855-7802, E-mail: speainfo@indiana.edu.

See Close-Up on page 413.

Indiana University Northwest, School of Public and Environmental Affairs, Gary, IN 46408-1197. Offers criminal justice (MPA); environmental affairs (Graduate Certificate); health services administration (MPA); human services administration (MPA); nonprofit management (Graduate Certificate); public management (MPA, Graduate Certificate). *Accreditation:* NASPAA (one or more programs are accredited). Part-time programs available. *Faculty:* 5 full-time (3 women). *Students:* 19 full-time (14 women), 121 part-time (100 women); includes 100 minority (84 African Americans, 1 American Indian/Alaska Native, 1 Asian American or Pacific Islander, 14 Hispanic Americans). Average age 39. In 2009, 29 master's, 27 other advanced degrees awarded. *Entrance requirements:* For master's, GRE General Test or GMAT, letters of recommendation. *Application deadline:* For fall admission, 8/15 priority date for domestic students. Applications are processed on a rolling basis. Application fee: $25. *Financial support:* Career-related internships or fieldwork, Federal Work-Study, and tuition waivers (partial) available. Support available to part-time students. Financial award application deadline: 3/1. *Faculty research:* Employment in income security policies, evidence in criminal justice, equal employment law, social welfare policy and welfare reform, public finance in developing countries. *Unit head:* George Assibey-Mensah, Interim Dean/Division Director, 219-980-6695, Fax: 219-980-6737. *Application contact:* Sandra Hall Smith, Secretary, 219-980-6695, Fax: 219-980-6737, E-mail: shsmith@iun.edu.

Instituto Tecnologico de Santo Domingo, Graduate School, Santo Domingo, Dominican Republic. Offers applied linguistics (MA); construction administration (M Mgmt); corporate finance (M Mgmt); education (M Ed); engineering (M Eng), including data telecommunications, industrial engineering, logistics and supply chain, maintenance engineering, sanitary and environmental engineering, structural engineering; environmental science (M En S), including environmental education, environmental management, marine and coastal ecosystems, natural resources management; family therapy (MA); food science and technology (MS); human development (MA); human resources administration (M Mgmt); international business (M Mgmt); labor risks (M Mgmt); management (M Mgmt); marketing (M Mgmt); mathematics (MS); organizational development (M Mgmt); planning and taxation (M Mgmt); psychology (MA); social science (M Ed); upper management (M Mgmt). *Entrance requirements:* For master's, birth certificate, minimum GPA of 2.0.

Instituto Tecnológico y de Estudios Superiores de Monterrey, Campus Ciudad de México, Virtual University Division, Ciudad de Mexico, Mexico. Offers administration of information technologies (MA); computer sciences (MA); education (MA, PhD); educational technology (MA); environmental engineering (MA); environmental systems (MA); humanistic studies (MA); industrial engineering (MA); international business for Latin America (MA); quality systems (MA); quality systems and productivity (MA). Part-time and evening/weekend programs available. Postbaccalaureate distance learning degree programs offered (minimal on-campus study). *Entrance requirements:* For master's and doctorate, Instituto entrance exam. Additional exam requirements/recommendations for international students: Required—TOEFL.

Inter American University of Puerto Rico, San Germán Campus, Graduate Studies Center, Program in Environmental Sciences, San Germán, PR 00683-5008. Offers environmental biology (MS); environmental chemistry (MS); water analysis (MS). Part-time and evening/weekend programs available. *Degree requirements:* For master's, comprehensive exam, thesis. *Entrance requirements:* For master's, GRE General Test or EXADEP, minimum GPA of 3.0. *Faculty research:* Environmental biology, environmental chemistry, water resources and unit operations.

Iowa State University of Science and Technology, Graduate College, College of Liberal Arts and Sciences, Department of Geological and Atmospheric Sciences, Ames, IA 50011. Offers earth science (MS, PhD); environmental science (MS, PhD); geology (MS, PhD); meteorology (MS, PhD). *Faculty:* 15 full-time (2 women), 1 part-time/adjunct (0 women). *Students:* 31 full-time (6 women), 3 part-time (0 women); includes 1 minority (Asian American or Pacific Islander), 8 international. 33 applicants, 55% accepted, 9 enrolled. In 2009, 3 master's, 2 doctorates awarded. *Degree requirements:* For master's, thesis (for some programs); for doctorate, thesis/dissertation. *Entrance requirements:* For master's and doctorate, GRE General Test. Additional exam requirements/recommendations for international students: Required—TOEFL (minimum score 550 paper-based; 79 iBT) or IELTS (minimum score 6.5). *Application deadline:* For fall admission, 1/1 priority date for domestic students. Applications are processed on a rolling basis. Application fee: $40 ($90 for international students). Electronic applications accepted. *Expenses:* Tuition, state resident: full-time $6716. Tuition, nonresident: full-time $8908. Tuition and fees vary according to course level, course load, program and student level. *Financial support:* In 2009–10, 21 research assistantships with full and partial tuition reimbursements (averaging $14,610 per year), 7 teaching assistantships with full and partial tuition reimbursements (averaging $14,610 per year) were awarded; fellowships, scholarships/grants, health care benefits, and unspecified assistantships also available. *Unit head:* Dr. Carl E. Jacobson, Chair, 515-294-4477. *Application contact:* Dr. Carl E. Jacobson, Chair, 515-294-4477.

Iowa State University of Science and Technology, Graduate College, Interdisciplinary Programs, Program in Environmental Sciences, Ames, IA 50011. Offers MS, PhD. *Students:* 17 full-time (12 women), 1 part-time (0 women), 9 international. In 2009, 3 master's, 1 doctorate awarded. *Degree requirements:* For master's, thesis; for doctorate, thesis/dissertation. *Entrance requirements:* For master's and doctorate, GRE General Test. Additional exam requirements/recommendations for international students: Required—TOEFL (minimum score 550 paper-based; 79 iBT) or IELTS (minimum score 6.5). *Application deadline:* For fall admission, 2/1 for domestic and international students; for spring admission, 6/1 for domestic and international students. Applications are processed on a rolling basis. Application fee: $40 ($90 for international students). Electronic applications accepted. *Expenses:* Tuition, state resident: full-time $6716. Tuition, nonresident: full-time $8908. Tuition and fees vary according to course level, course load, program and student level. *Financial support:* In 2009–10, 14 research assistantships with partial tuition reimbursements (averaging $15,870 per year), 1 teaching assistantship with partial tuition reimbursement (averaging $15,870 per year) were awarded; scholarships/grants, health care benefits, and unspecified assistantships also available. *Unit head:* Dr. John Downing, Supervisory Committee Chair, 515-294-6518, Fax: 515-294-9573. *Application contact:* Charles Sauer, Information Contact, 515-294-6518, E-mail: eeboffice@iastate.edu.

Jackson State University, Graduate School, School of Science and Technology, Department of Biology, Jackson, MS 39217. Offers biology education (MST); environmental science (MS, PhD). Part-time and evening/weekend programs available. *Degree requirements:* For master's, comprehensive exam, thesis (alternative accepted for MST); for doctorate, comprehensive exam, thesis/dissertation. *Entrance requirements:* For master's, GRE General Test; for doctorate, MAT. Additional exam requirements/recommendations for international students: Required—TOEFL. *Faculty research:* Comparative studies on the carbohydrate composition of marine macroalgae, host-parasite relationship between the spruce budworm and entomepathogen fungus.

The Johns Hopkins University, Zanvyl Krieger School of Arts and Sciences, Advanced Academic Programs, Program in Environmental Sciences and Policy, Baltimore, MD 21218-2699. Offers MS. Part-time and evening/weekend programs available. Postbaccalaureate distance learning degree programs offered (minimal on-campus study). *Faculty:* 1 (woman) full-time, 37 part-time/adjunct (3 women). *Students:* 16 full-time (13 women), 200 part-time (125 women); includes 25 minority (7 African Americans, 1 American Indian/Alaska Native, 9 Asian Americans or Pacific Islanders, 8 Hispanic Americans), 9 international. Average age 31. 126 applicants, 63% accepted, 55 enrolled. In 2009, 68 master's awarded. *Degree requirements:* For master's, thesis (for some programs). *Entrance requirements:* For master's, minimum GPA of 3.0, coursework in chemistry and calculus. Additional exam requirements/recommendations for international students: Required—TOEFL (minimum score 250 computer-based). *Application deadline:* For fall admission, 5/31 priority date for domestic students, 4/30 priority date for international students; for spring admission, 10/31 priority date for domestic and international students. Application fee: $75. *Financial support:* Applicants required to submit FAFSA. *Unit head:* Dr. Eileen McGurty, Associate Program Chair, 410-516-7049, E-mail: emgurty@jhu.edu. *Application contact:* Valana M. McMickens, Admissions Manager, 202-452-1941, Fax: 202-452-1970, E-mail: aapadmissions@jhu.edu.

Laurentian University, School of Graduate Studies and Research, Programme in Chemistry and Biochemistry, Sudbury, ON P3E 2C6, Canada. Offers analytical chemistry (M Sc); biochemistry (M Sc); environmental chemistry (M Sc); organic chemistry (M Sc); physical/theoretical chemistry (M Sc). Part-time programs available. *Degree requirements:* For master's, thesis or alternative. *Entrance requirements:* For master's, honors degree with minimum second class. *Faculty research:* Cell cycle checkpoints, kinetic modeling, toxicology to metal stress, quantum chemistry, biogeochemistry metal speciation.

Lehigh University, College of Arts and Sciences, Department of Earth and Environmental Sciences, Bethlehem, PA 18015. Offers MS, PhD. *Faculty:* 14 full-time (1 woman), 1 (woman) part-time/adjunct. *Students:* 25 full-time (12 women), 4 international. Average age 26. 55 applicants, 42% accepted, 7 enrolled. In 2009, 8 master's, 3 doctorates awarded. *Degree requirements:* For doctorate, comprehensive exam, thesis/dissertation. *Entrance requirements:* For master's and doctorate, GRE General Test. Additional exam requirements/recommendations for international students: Required—TOEFL. *Application deadline:* For fall admission, 1/15 for domestic and international students. Applications are processed on a rolling basis. Application fee: $65. Electronic applications accepted. *Financial support:* In 2009–10, 13 students received support, including 3 fellowships with full tuition reimbursements available (averaging $15,400 per year), 12 research assistantships with full tuition reimbursements available (averaging $15,400 per year), 10 teaching assistantships with full tuition reimbursements available (averaging $15,400 per year); career-related internships or fieldwork, Federal Work-Study, institutionally sponsored loans, scholarships/grants, tuition waivers (full and partial), and unspecified assistantships also available. Support available to part-time students. Financial award application deadline: 1/15. *Faculty research:* Tectonics, surficial processes, aquatic ecology. Total annual research expenditures: $866,591. *Unit head:* Dr. Frank J. Pazzaglia, Chairman, 610-758-3671, Fax: 610-758-3677, E-mail: fjp3@lehigh.edu. *Application contact:* Dr. Zicheng Yu, Graduate Coordinator, 610-758-3660 Ext. 6751, Fax: 610-758-3677, E-mail: ziy2@lehigh.edu.

Louisiana State University and Agricultural and Mechanical College, Graduate School, College of Agriculture, School of Renewable Natural Resources, Baton Rouge, LA 70803. Offers fisheries (MS); forestry (MS, PhD); wildlife (MS); wildlife and fisheries science (PhD). *Faculty:* 32 full-time (3 women). *Students:* 73 full-time (17 women), 9 part-time (4 women); includes 1 Hispanic American, 26 international. Average age 29. 31 applicants, 48% accepted, 14 enrolled. In 2009, 11 master's, 2 doctorates awarded. *Degree requirements:* For master's, thesis; for doctorate, thesis/dissertation. *Entrance requirements:* For master's, GRE General Test, minimum GPA of 3.0; for doctorate, GRE General Test, MS, minimum GPA of 3.0. Additional exam requirements/recommendations for international students: Required—TOEFL (minimum score 550 paper-based; 213 computer-based; 79 iBT), IELTS (minimum score 6.5). *Application deadline:* For fall admission, 1/25 priority date for domestic students, 5/15 for international students; for spring admission, 10/15 for international students. Applications are processed on a rolling basis. Application fee: $50 ($70 for international students). Electronic applications accepted. *Financial support:* In 2009–10, 80 students received support, including 7 fellowships (averaging $36,514 per year), 61 research assistantships with partial tuition reimbursements available (averaging $18,686 per year), 1 teaching assistantship with partial tuition reimbursement available (averaging $10,800 per year); Federal Work-Study, institutionally sponsored loans, scholarships/grants, health care benefits, tuition waivers (full and partial), and unspecified assistantships also available. Financial award application deadline: 4/15; financial award applicants required to submit FAFSA. *Faculty research:* Forest biology and management, aquaculture, fisheries biology and ecology, upland and wetlands wildlife. Total annual research expenditures: $3,308. *Unit head:* Dr. Allen Rutherford, Director, 225-578-4131, Fax: 225-578-4227, E-mail: druther@lsu.edu. *Application contact:* Dr. William Kelso, Coordinator of Graduate Studies, 225-578-4176, Fax: 225-578-4227, E-mail: wkelso@lsu.edu.

Louisiana State University and Agricultural and Mechanical College, Graduate School, School of the Coast and Environment, Department of Environmental Sciences, Baton Rouge, LA 70803. Offers environmental planning and management (MS); environmental toxicology (MS). *Faculty:* 10 full-time (4 women). *Students:* 21 full-time (13 women), 6 part-time (2 women); includes 4 African Americans, 6 international. Average age 28. 22 applicants, 86% accepted, 12 enrolled. In 2009, 8 master's awarded. *Degree requirements:* For master's, thesis (for some programs). *Entrance requirements:* For master's, GRE General Test, minimum GPA of 3.0. Additional exam requirements/recommendations for international students: Required—TOEFL (minimum score 550 paper-based; 213 computer-based; 79 iBT) or IELTS (minimum score 6.5). *Application deadline:* For fall admission, 1/25 priority date for domestic students, 5/15 for international students; for spring admission, 10/15 for international students. Applications are processed on a rolling basis. Application fee: $50 ($70 for international students). Electronic applications accepted. *Financial support:* In 2009–10, 21 students received support, including 14 research assistantships with full and partial tuition reimbursements available (averaging $13,171 per year), 1 teaching assistantship with full and partial tuition reimbursement available (averaging $15,740 per year); fellowships with full and partial tuition reimbursements available, career-related internships or fieldwork, Federal Work-Study, institutionally sponsored loans, scholarships/grants, health care benefits, and unspecified assistantships also available. Support available to part-time students. Financial award applicants required to submit FAFSA. *Faculty research:* Environmental toxicology, environmental policy and law, microbial ecology, bioremediation, genetic toxicology. Total annual research expenditures: $656,188. *Unit head:* Dr. Nina Lam, Chair, 225-578-3030, Fax: 225-578-4286, E-mail: nlam@lsu.edu. *Application contact:* Charlotte G. St. Romain, Academic Coordinator, 225-578-8522, Fax: 225-578-4286, E-mail: cstrom4@lsu.edu.

Loyola Marymount University, College of Science and Engineering, Department of Civil Engineering and Environmental Science, Program in Environmental Science, Los Angeles, CA 90045. Offers MS. Part-time programs available. *Faculty:* 6 full-time (1 woman), 3 part-time/adjunct (0 women). *Students:* 4 full-time (all women), 22 part-time (12 women); includes 10 minority (3 African Americans, 5 Asian Americans or Pacific Islanders, 2 Hispanic Americans), 2 international. Average age 31. 13 applicants, 69% accepted, 5 enrolled. In 2009, 1 master's awarded. *Degree requirements:* For master's, comprehensive exam, thesis or alternative. *Entrance requirements:* For master's, 2 letters of recommendation; bachelor of science degree or undergraduate engineering degree; 3 semester hours of general chemistry; course work in mathematics through one year of college calculus; 12 semester hours or 4 courses in science including biology, microbiology, chemistry, or physics. Additional exam requirements/recommendations for international students: Required—TOEFL (minimum score 550 paper-based; 213 computer-based; 80 iBT). *Application deadline:* Applications are processed on a rolling basis. Application fee: $50. Electronic applications accepted. *Financial support:* In 2009–10, 3 students received support. Scholarships/grants and unspecified assistantships available. Support available to part-time students. Financial award application deadline: 6/1; financial award applicants required to submit FAFSA. Total annual research expenditures: $14,321. *Unit head:* Prof. Joe J. Reichenberger, Graduate Director, 310-338-2830, E-mail: jreichenberger@lmu.edu. *Application contact:* Chake H. Kouyoumjian, Associate Dean of Graduate Studies, 310-338-2721, Fax: 310-338-6086, E-mail: ckouyoum@lmu.edu.

Marshall University, Academic Affairs Division, College of Information Technology and Engineering, Division of Applied Science and Technology, Program in Environmental Science, Huntington, WV 25755. Offers MS. Part-time and evening/weekend programs available. *Faculty:* 3 full-time (0 women). *Students:* 18 full-time (5 women), 16 part-time (6 women), 6 international. Average age 30. In 2009, 13 master's awarded. *Degree requirements:* For master's, final project, oral exam. *Entrance requirements:* For master's, GRE General Test or MAT, minimum GPA of 2.5, course work in calculus. Application fee: $40. *Financial support:* Tuition waivers (full) available. Support available to part-time students. Financial award application deadline: 8/1; financial award applicants required to submit FAFSA. *Unit head:* Dr. D. Scott Simonton, Associate Professor, 304-746-2045, E-mail: simonton@marshall.edu. *Application contact:* Information Contact, 304-746-1900, Fax: 304-746-1902, E-mail: services@marshall.edu.

Massachusetts Institute of Technology, School of Engineering, Department of Civil and Environmental Engineering, Cambridge, MA 02139-4307. Offers biological oceanography (PhD, Sc D); chemical oceanography (PhD, Sc D); civil and environmental engineering (M Eng, SM, PhD, Sc D); civil and environmental systems (PhD, Sc D); civil engineering (PhD, Sc D, CE); coastal engineering (PhD, Sc D); construction engineering and management (PhD, Sc D); environmental biology (PhD, Sc D); environmental chemistry (PhD, Sc D); environmental engineering (PhD, Sc D); environmental fluid mechanics (PhD, Sc D); geotechnical and geoenvironmental engineering (PhD, Sc D); hydrology (PhD, Sc D); information technology (PhD, Sc D); oceanographic engineering (PhD, Sc D); structures and materials (PhD, Sc D); transportation (PhD, Sc D); SM/MBA. *Faculty:* 36 full-time (5 women). *Students:* 190 full-time (59 women); includes 22 minority (2 African Americans, 14 Asian Americans or Pacific Islanders, 6 Hispanic Americans), 103 international. Average age 26. 478 applicants, 25% accepted, 76 enrolled. In 2009, 72 master's, 14 doctorates awarded. *Degree requirements:* For master's and CE, thesis; for doctorate, comprehensive exam, thesis/dissertation. *Entrance requirements:* For master's and doctorate, GRE General Test. Additional exam requirements/recommendations for international students: Required—TOEFL (minimum score 577 paper-based; 233 computer-based; 90 iBT), IELTS (minimum score 7). *Application deadline:* For fall admission, 1/2 for domestic and international students. Application fee: $75. Electronic applications accepted. *Financial support:* In 2009–10, 185 students received support, including 40 fellowships with tuition reimbursements available (averaging $27,725 per year), 97 research assistantships with tuition reimbursements available (averaging $28,035 per year), 21 teaching assistantships with tuition reimbursements available (averaging $24,802 per year); career-related internships or fieldwork, Federal Work-Study, institutionally sponsored loans, scholarships/grants, health care benefits, and unspecified assistantships also available. *Faculty research:* Environmental chemistry, environmental microbiology, environmental fluid mechanics and coastal engineering, geotechnical engineering and geomechanics, hydrology and hydroclimatology, mechanics of materials and structures, operations research/supply chain, transportation. Total annual research expenditures: $16.6 million. *Unit head:* Prof. Andrew Whittle, Department Head, 617-253-7101. *Application contact:* Patricia Glidden, Graduate Admissions Coordinator, 617-253-7119, Fax: 617-258-6775, E-mail: cee-admissions@mit.edu.

Memorial University of Newfoundland, School of Graduate Studies, Interdisciplinary Program in Environmental Science, St. John's, NL A1C 5S7, Canada. Offers M Env Sc, M Sc. Part-time programs available. *Degree requirements:* For master's, thesis (M Sc), project (M Env Sci). *Entrance requirements:* For master's, honors B Sc or 2nd class B Eng. Electronic applications accepted. *Faculty research:* Earth and ocean systems, environmental chemistry and toxicology, environmental engineering.

Mercer University, Graduate Studies, Macon Campus, School of Engineering, Macon, GA 31207-0003. Offers biomedical engineering (MSE); computer engineering (MSE); electrical engineering (MSE); engineering management (MSE); environmental engineering (MSE); environmental systems (MS); mechanical engineering (MSE); software engineering (MSE); software systems (MS); technical communications management (MS); technical management (MS). Part-time and evening/weekend programs available. Postbaccalaureate distance learning degree programs offered (no on-campus study). *Faculty:* 19 full-time (4 women), 1 part-time/adjunct (0 women). *Students:* 6 full-time (1 woman), 95 part-time (22 women); includes 22 minority (5 African Americans, 13 Asian Americans or Pacific Islanders, 4 Hispanic Americans), 3 international. Average age 33. In 2009, 42 master's awarded. *Degree requirements:* For master's, thesis or alternative. *Entrance requirements:* For master's, minimum undergraduate GPA of 3.0. Additional exam requirements/recommendations for international students: Required—TOEFL. *Application deadline:* For fall admission, 7/1 for domestic students; for spring admission, 11/15 for domestic students. Applications are processed on a rolling basis. Application fee: $35 ($50 for international students). Electronic applications accepted. *Expenses:* Contact institution. *Financial support:* Federal Work-Study available. *Unit head:* Dr. Wade H. Shaw, Dean, 478-301-2459, Fax: 478-301-5593, E-mail: shaw_wh@mercer.edu. *Application contact:* Greg Lofton, Graduate Program Coordinator, 478-301-5480, Fax: 478-301-5434, E-mail: lofton_g@mercer.edu.

Miami University, Graduate School, Institute of Environmental Sciences, Oxford, OH 45056. Offers M En. Part-time programs available. *Students:* 54 full-time (32 women), 1 (woman) part-time; includes 5 minority (3 African Americans, 1 American Indian/Alaska Native, 1 Asian American or Pacific Islander), 8 international. *Entrance requirements:* For master's, minimum undergraduate GPA of 3.0 during previous 2 years or 2.75 overall. Additional exam requirements/recommendations for international students: Required—TOEFL. Application fee: $50. *Expenses:* Tuition, state resident: full-time $11,280. Tuition, nonresident: full-time $24,912. Required fees: $516. *Financial support:* Fellowships with tuition reimbursements, research assistantships, teaching assistantships, career-related internships or fieldwork, Federal Work-Study, health care benefits, tuition waivers (full), and unspecified assistantships available. Financial award application deadline: 3/1; financial award applicants required to submit FAFSA. *Unit head:* Dr. Doug Miekle, Co-Director, 513-529-5811, Fax: 513-529-5814, E-mail: ies@muohio.edu. *Application contact:* Dr. Doug Miekle, Co-Director, 513-529-5811, Fax: 513-529-5814, E-mail: ies@muohio.edu.

Michigan State University, The Graduate School, College of Natural Science, Department of Geological Sciences, East Lansing, MI 48824. Offers environmental geosciences (MS, PhD); environmental geosciences-environmental toxicology (PhD); geological sciences (MS, PhD). *Degree requirements:* For master's, thesis (for those without prior thesis work); for doctorate, thesis/dissertation. *Entrance requirements:* For master's, GRE General Test, minimum GPA of 3.0, course work in geoscience, 3 letters of recommendation; for doctorate, GRE General Test, 3 letters of recommendation. Additional exam requirements/recommendations for international students: Required—TOEFL (minimum score 550 paper-based; 213 computer-based), Michigan State University ELT (85), Michigan English Language Assessment Battery (83). Electronic applications accepted. *Faculty research:* Water in the environment, global and biological change, crystal dynamics.

Minnesota State University Mankato, College of Graduate Studies, College of Science, Engineering and Technology, Department of Biological Sciences, Program in Environmental Sciences, Mankato, MN 56001. Offers MS. *Students:* 3 full-time (2 women), 9 part-time (3 women). *Degree requirements:* For master's, one foreign language, comprehensive exam, thesis or alternative. *Entrance requirements:* For master's, minimum GPA of 3.0 during previous 2 years. Additional exam requirements/recommendations for international students: Required—TOEFL. *Application deadline:* For fall admission, 7/1 priority date for domestic students; for spring admission, 11/1 for domestic students. Applications are processed on a rolling basis. Application fee: $40. Electronic applications accepted. *Expenses:* Tuition, state resident: full-time $5364. Tuition, nonresident: full-time $8314. *Financial support:* Research assistantships with partial tuition reimbursements, teaching assistantships with partial tuition reimbursements, career-related internships or fieldwork, Federal Work-Study, institutionally sponsored loans, and unspecified assistantships available. Financial award application deadline: 3/15;

Environmental Sciences

Minnesota State University Mankato (continued)
financial award applicants required to submit FAFSA. *Unit head:* Dr. Bertha Proctor, Graduate Coordinator, 507-389-5697. *Application contact:* 507-389-2321, E-mail: grad@mnsu.edu.

Montana State University, College of Graduate Studies, College of Agriculture, Department of Land Resources and Environmental Sciences, Bozeman, MT 59717. Offers land rehabilitation (interdisciplinary) (MS); land resources and environmental sciences (MS), including land rehabilitation (interdisciplinary), land resources and environmental sciences. Part-time programs available. *Faculty:* 22 full-time (5 women), 1 part-time/adjunct (0 women). *Students:* 8 full-time (5 women), 39 part-time (13 women); includes 2 minority (1 American Indian/Alaska Native, 1 Hispanic American), 5 international. Average age 31. 22 applicants. In 2009, 11 master's awarded. *Degree requirements:* For master's, comprehensive exam. *Entrance requirements:* For master's, GRE General Test. Additional exam requirements/recommendations for international students: Required—TOEFL (minimum score 550 paper-based; 213 computer-based). *Application deadline:* For fall admission, 7/15 priority date for domestic students, 5/15 priority date for international students; for spring admission, 12/1 priority date for domestic students, 10/1 priority date for international students. Applications are processed on a rolling basis. Application fee: $30. Electronic applications accepted. *Expenses:* Tuition, state resident: full-time $5635; part-time $3492 per year. Tuition, nonresident: full-time $17,212; part-time $7865.10 per year. Required fees: $1441.05; $153.15 per credit. Tuition and fees vary according to course load and program. *Financial support:* In 2009–10, 5 fellowships with partial tuition reimbursements (averaging $25,000 per year), 38 research assistantships with full and partial tuition reimbursements (averaging $17,000 per year), 15 teaching assistantships with full and partial tuition reimbursements (averaging $2,000 per year) were awarded; scholarships/grants, health care benefits, tuition waivers (partial), and unspecified assistantships also available. Financial award application deadline: 3/1; financial award applicants required to submit FAFSA. *Faculty research:* Soil nutrient management and plant nutrition, isotope biogeochemistry of soils, biodegradation of hydrocarbons in soils and natural waters, remote sensing, GIS systems, managed and natural ecosystems, microbial and metabolic diversity in geothermally heated soils, integrated management of weeds, diversified cropping systems, insect behavior and ecology, river ecology, microbial biogeochemistry, weed ecology. Total annual research expenditures: $4.7 million. *Unit head:* Dr. Tracy M. Sterling, Head, 406-994-7060, Fax: 406-994-3933, E-mail: tracy.sterling@montana.edu. *Application contact:* Dr. Carl A. Fox, Vice Provost for Graduate Education, 406-994-4145, Fax: 406-994-7433, E-mail: gradstudy@montana.edu.

Montana State University, College of Graduate Studies, College of Letters and Science, Department of Ecology, Bozeman, MT 59717. Offers ecological and environmental statistics (MS); ecology and environmental sciences (PhD); fish and wildlife biology (PhD); fish and wildlife management (MS). Part-time programs available. *Faculty:* 12 full-time (2 women), 2 part-time/adjunct (0 women). *Students:* 8 full-time (2 women), 48 part-time (18 women). Average age 31. 18 applicants, 33% accepted, 6 enrolled. In 2009, 6 master's, 7 doctorates awarded. *Degree requirements:* For master's, comprehensive exam, thesis (for some programs); for doctorate, comprehensive exam, thesis/dissertation. *Entrance requirements:* For master's, GRE General Test, GPA, Letters of Recommendation, Essay; for doctorate, GRE General Test, letters of recommendation. Additional exam requirements/recommendations for international students: Required—TOEFL (minimum score 550 paper-based; 213 computer-based). *Application deadline:* For fall admission, 7/15 priority date for domestic students, 5/15 priority date for international students; for spring admission, 12/1 priority date for domestic students, 10/1 priority date for international students. Applications are processed on a rolling basis. Application fee: $30. Electronic applications accepted. *Expenses:* Tuition, state resident: full-time $5635; part-time $3492 per year. Tuition, nonresident: full-time $17,212; part-time $7865.10 per year. Required fees: $1441.05; $153.15 per credit. Tuition and fees vary according to course load and program. *Financial support:* In 2009–10, 2 fellowships with full tuition reimbursements (averaging $17,725 per year), 29 research assistantships with full and partial tuition reimbursements (averaging $19,500 per year), 20 teaching assistantships with full tuition reimbursements (averaging $12,321 per year) were awarded; career-related internships or fieldwork, scholarships/grants, health care benefits, tuition waivers (partial), and unspecified assistantships also available. Support available to part-time students. Financial award application deadline: 3/1; financial award applicants required to submit FAFSA. *Faculty research:* Evolutionary biology, conservation ecology, human impact on ecosystems, biodiversity, applied wildlife and fisheries research, plant and animal community ecology. Total annual research expenditures: $2.6 million. *Unit head:* Dr. David Roberts, Head, 406-994-4548, Fax: 406-994-3190, E-mail: droberts@montana.edu. *Application contact:* Dr. Carl A. Fox, Vice Provost for Graduate Education, 406-994-4145, Fax: 406-994-7433, E-mail: gradstudy@montana.edu.

Montclair State University, The Graduate School, College of Science and Mathematics, Department of Earth and Environmental Studies, Montclair, NJ 07043-1624. Offers earth science (Certificate); environmental management (MA, D Env M); environmental studies (MS), including environmental education, environmental health, environmental management, environmental science; geographic information science (Certificate); geoscience (MS, Certificate), including geoscience (MS), water resource management (Certificate). Part-time and evening/weekend programs available. *Faculty:* 16 full-time (2 women), 13 part-time/adjunct (4 women). *Students:* 36 full-time (17 women), 60 part-time (26 women). Average age 34. 42 applicants, 60% accepted, 17 enrolled. In 2009, 11 degrees awarded. *Degree requirements:* For master's, comprehensive exam, thesis or alternative; for doctorate, thesis/dissertation. *Entrance requirements:* For master's, GRE General Test, 2 letters of recommendation; for doctorate, GRE General Test, 3 letters of recommendation. Additional exam requirements/recommendations for international students: Required—TOEFL (minimum score 83 computer-based), or IELTS. *Application deadline:* For fall admission, 6/1 for international students; for spring admission, 10/1 for international students. Applications are processed on a rolling basis. Application fee: $60. Electronic applications accepted. *Expenses:* Tuition, area resident: Part-time $486.74 per credit. Tuition, state resident: part-time $486.74 per credit. Tuition, nonresident: part-time $751.34 per credit. Tuition and fees vary according to degree level and program. *Financial support:* In 2009–10, 3 fellowships (averaging $15,000 per year), 12 research assistantships with full tuition reimbursements (averaging $8,500 per year), 11 teaching assistantships with full tuition reimbursements (averaging $15,000 per year) were awarded; Federal Work-Study, scholarships/grants, and unspecified assistantships also available. Support available to part-time students. Financial award application deadline: 3/1; financial award applicants required to submit FAFSA. *Faculty research:* Antarctica, carbon pools, contaminated sediments, wetlands. *Unit head:* Dr. Duke Ophori, Chairperson, 973-655-7558. *Application contact:* Amy Aiello, Director of Graduate Admissions and Operations, 973-655-5147, Fax: 973-655-7869, E-mail: graduate.school@montclair.edu.

Murray State University, College of Health Sciences and Human Services, Program in Occupational Safety and Health, Murray, KY 42071. Offers environmental science (MS); industrial hygiene (MS); safety management (MS). *Accreditation:* ABET. Part-time programs available. *Degree requirements:* For master's, comprehensive exam, thesis optional, professional internship. Electronic applications accepted. *Faculty research:* Light effects on plant growth, ergonomics, toxic effects of pets' pesticides, traffic safety.

New Jersey Institute of Technology, Office of Graduate Studies, College of Science and Liberal Arts, Department of Chemistry and Environmental Science, Program in Environmental Science, Newark, NJ 07102. Offers MS, PhD. Part-time and evening/weekend programs available. *Degree requirements:* For doctorate, thesis/dissertation. *Entrance requirements:* For master's, GRE General Test; for doctorate, GRE General Test, minimum graduate GPA of 3.5. Additional exam requirements/recommendations for international students: Required—TOEFL (minimum score 550 paper-based; 213 computer-based; 79 iBT). Electronic applications accepted.

New Mexico Institute of Mining and Technology, Graduate Studies, Department of Chemistry, Socorro, NM 87801. Offers biochemistry (MS); chemistry (MS); environmental chemistry (PhD); explosives technology and atmospheric chemistry (PhD). Part-time programs available. *Degree requirements:* For master's, thesis; for doctorate, thesis/dissertation. *Entrance requirements:* For master's, GRE General Test; for doctorate, GRE General Test, GRE Subject Test. Additional exam requirements/recommendations for international students: Required—TOEFL (minimum score 540 paper-based; 207 computer-based). Electronic applications accepted. *Faculty research:* Organic, analytical, environmental, and explosives chemistry.

New Mexico State University, Graduate School, College of Agricultural, Consumer and Environmental Sciences, Department of Plant and Environmental Sciences, Las Cruces, NM 88003-8001. Offers horticulture (MS); plant and environmental sciences (MS, PhD). Part-time programs available. *Faculty:* 11 full-time (3 women). *Students:* 45 full-time (17 women), 9 part-time (3 women); includes 11 minority (1 American Indian/Alaska Native, 10 Hispanic Americans), 17 international. Average age 31. 29 applicants, 97% accepted, 16 enrolled. In 2009, 5 master's, 2 doctorates awarded. *Degree requirements:* For master's, thesis; for doctorate, one foreign language, thesis/dissertation. *Entrance requirements:* For master's, minimum GPA of 3.0; for doctorate, minimum GPA of 3.3. Additional exam requirements/recommendations for international students: Required—TOEFL. *Application deadline:* For fall admission, 7/1 priority date for domestic students; for spring admission, 11/1 priority date for domestic students. Applications are processed on a rolling basis. Application fee: $30 ($50 for international students). Electronic applications accepted. *Expenses:* Tuition, state resident: full-time $4080; part-time $223 per credit. Tuition, nonresident: full-time $14,256; part-time $647 per credit. Required fees: $1278; $639 per semester. *Financial support:* In 2009–10, 29 research assistantships with partial tuition reimbursements (averaging $19,764 per year), 9 teaching assistantships with partial tuition reimbursements (averaging $15,733 per year) were awarded; career-related internships or fieldwork, Federal Work-Study, scholarships/grants, health care benefits, and unspecified assistantships also available. Support available to part-time students. Financial award application deadline: 3/1. *Faculty research:* Plant breeding and genetics, molecular biology, plant physiology, soil science and environmental remediation, urban horticulture and turfgrass management. *Unit head:* Dr. John G. Mexal, Interim Head, 575-646-3406, Fax: 575-646-6041, E-mail: jmexal@nmsu.edu. *Application contact:* Esther Ramirez, Information Contact, 575-646-3406, Fax: 575-646-6041, E-mail: esramire@nmsu.edu.

North Carolina Agricultural and Technical State University, Graduate School, School of Agriculture and Environmental Sciences, Greensboro, NC 27411. Offers MS. Part-time and evening/weekend programs available. *Degree requirements:* For master's, comprehensive exam, qualifying exam. *Entrance requirements:* For master's, GRE General Test. *Faculty research:* Aid for small farmers, agricultural technology, housing, food science, nutrition.

North Dakota State University, College of Graduate and Interdisciplinary Studies, College of Agriculture, Food Systems, and Natural Resources, Department of Soil Science, Fargo, ND 58108. Offers environmental and conservation science (PhD); environmental conservation science (MS); natural resource management (MS, PhD); soil sciences (MS, PhD). Part-time programs available. *Faculty:* 8 full-time (1 woman), 6 part-time/adjunct (0 women). *Students:* 6 full-time (4 women), 3 part-time (1 woman). Average age 23. 3 applicants, 67% accepted, 2 enrolled. In 2009, 2 master's, 1 doctorate awarded. *Degree requirements:* For master's, comprehensive exam, thesis, classroom teaching; for doctorate, comprehensive exam, thesis/dissertation, classroom teaching. *Entrance requirements:* Additional exam requirements/recommendations for international students: Required—TOEFL (minimum score 525 paper-based; 193 computer-based; 71 iBT). *Application deadline:* Applications are processed on a rolling basis. Application fee: $45 ($60 for international students). Electronic applications accepted. *Financial support:* In 2009–10, 7 research assistantships with full tuition reimbursements (averaging $14,300 per year) were awarded; fellowships, Federal Work-Study, institutionally sponsored loans, and scholarships/grants also available. Financial award application deadline: 3/15. *Faculty research:* Microclimate, nitrogen management, landscape studies, water quality, soil management. *Unit head:* Dr. Donald Kirby, Interim Chair, 701-231-8901, Fax: 701-231-7861. *Application contact:* Dr. Donald Kirby, Interim Chair, 701-231-8901, Fax: 701-231-7861.

North Dakota State University, College of Graduate and Interdisciplinary Studies, College of Science and Mathematics, Department of Biological Sciences, Fargo, ND 58108. Offers biology (MS); botany (MS, PhD); cellular and molecular biology (PhD); environmental and conservation sciences (MS, PhD); genomics (PhD); natural resources management (MS, PhD); zoology (MS, PhD). *Students:* 32 full-time (21 women), 14 part-time (10 women); includes 1 Asian American or Pacific Islander, 14 international. In 2009, 12 master's, 9 doctorates awarded. *Degree requirements:* For master's, thesis; for doctorate, thesis/dissertation. *Entrance requirements:* For master's and doctorate, GRE General Test. Additional exam requirements/recommendations for international students: Required—TOEFL. *Application deadline:* For fall admission, 3/15 priority date for domestic students; for spring admission, 10/30 priority date for domestic students. Applications are processed on a rolling basis. Application fee: $45 ($60 for international students). Electronic applications accepted. *Financial support:* Fellowships with full tuition reimbursements, research assistantships with full tuition reimbursements, teaching assistantships with full tuition reimbursements, career-related internships or fieldwork, Federal Work-Study, institutionally sponsored loans, scholarships/grants, tuition waivers (full), and unspecified assistantships available. Support available to part-time students. Financial award application deadline: 4/15; financial award applicants required to submit FAFSA. *Faculty research:* Comparative endocrinology, physiology, behavioral ecology, plant cell biology, aquatic biology. Total annual research expenditures: $675,000. *Unit head:* Dr. Marinus L. Otte, Head, 701-231-7087, E-mail: marinus.otte@ndsu.edu. *Application contact:* Dr. Marinus L. Otte, Head, 701-231-7087, E-mail: marinus.otte@ndsu.edu.

North Dakota State University, College of Graduate and Interdisciplinary Studies, Interdisciplinary Program in Environmental and Conservation Sciences, Fargo, ND 58108. Offers MS, PhD. *Faculty:* 59. *Students:* 3 full-time (0 women), 2 part-time (0 women). *Degree requirements:* For master's, comprehensive exam, thesis. *Entrance requirements:* Additional exam requirements/recommendations for international students: Required—TOEFL (minimum score 550 paper-based; 213 computer-based; 79 iBT). *Unit head:* Dr. Wei Lin, Director, 701-231-8785, Fax: 701-231-7149, E-mail: wei.lin@ndsu.edu. *Application contact:* Ruth Ann Faulkner, Administrative Assistant, 701-231-6727, E-mail: ruthann.faulkner@ndsu.edu.

Northern Arizona University, Graduate College, College of Engineering, Forestry and Natural Sciences, Center for Sustainable Environments, Flagstaff, AZ 86011. Offers environmental sciences and policy (MS). *Faculty:* 5 full-time (3 women). *Students:* 18 full-time (12 women), 6 part-time (3 women); includes 5 minority (1 American Indian/Alaska Native, 1 Asian American or Pacific Islander, 3 Hispanic Americans), 3 international. Average age 28. 42 applicants, 17% accepted, 5 enrolled. In 2009, 7 master's awarded. *Degree requirements:* For master's, thesis optional. *Entrance requirements:* For master's, GRE General Test. Additional exam requirements/recommendations for international students: Required—TOEFL (minimum score 550 paper-based; 213 computer-based; 80 iBT), IELTS (minimum score 7), or a bachelor's degree from an English-speaking university and demonstrated proficiency. *Application deadline:* For fall admission, 3/13 priority date for domestic students, 9/1 for international students. Application fee: $65. Electronic applications accepted. *Financial support:* In 2009–10, 2 teaching assistantships with partial tuition reimbursements (averaging $10,439 per year) were awarded; Federal Work-Study, scholarships/grants, health care benefits, and unspecified assistantships also available. Support available to part-time students. Financial award application deadline: 2/15; financial award applicants required to submit FAFSA. *Unit head:* Dr. Tom Sisk, Interim Director, 928-523-7283, E-mail: tom.sisk@nau.edu. *Application contact:* Information Contact, E-mail: esf.program@nau.edu.

Northern Arizona University, Graduate College, College of Engineering, Forestry and Natural Sciences, School of Earth Sciences and Environmental Sustainability, Flagstaff, AZ 86011. Offers climate science and solutions (MS); environmental sciences and policy (MS); geology (MS). *Faculty:* 22 full-time (5 women). *Students:* 28 full-time (17 women), 25 part-time (21 women); includes 6 minority (2 American Indian/Alaska Native, 1 Asian American or Pacific Islander, 3 Hispanic Americans). 70 applicants, 36% accepted, 17 enrolled. In 2009, 10 master's awarded. *Entrance requirements:* Additional exam requirements/recommendations for international students: Required—TOEFL (minimum score 550 paper-based; 213 computer-based; 80 iBT), IELTS (minimum score 7), or a bachelor's degree from an English-speaking university and demonstrated proficiency. *Application deadline:* For fall admission, 2/15 for domestic and international students. Application fee: $65. *Financial support:* In 2009–10, 32 students received support, including 7 research assistantships with partial tuition reimbursements available, 26 teaching assistantships with partial tuition reimbursements available; Federal Work-Study, scholarships/grants, health care benefits, and unspecified assistantships also available. Support available to part-time students. Financial award applicants required to submit FAFSA. *Unit head:* Dr. Abe Springer, Director, 928-523-7198. *Application contact:* Dr. Abe Springer, Director, 928-523-7198.

Nova Scotia Agricultural College, Research and Graduate Studies, Truro, NS B2N 5E3, Canada. Offers agriculture (M Sc), including air quality, animal behavior, animal molecular genetics, animal nutrition, animal technology, aquaculture, botany, crop management, crop physiology, ecology, environmental microbiology, food science, horticulture, nutrient management, pest management, physiology, plant biotechnology, plant pathology, soil chemistry, soil fertility, waste management and composting, water quality. Part-time programs available. *Degree requirements:* For master's, thesis, ATC Exam Teaching Assistantship. *Entrance requirements:* For master's, honors B Sc, minimum GPA of 3.0. Additional exam requirements/ recommendations for international students: Required—TOEFL (minimum score 580 paper-based; 237 computer-based; 92 iBT), IELTS, Michigan English Language Assessment Battery, CanTEST, CAEL. *Faculty research:* Bio-product development, organic agriculture, nutrient management, air and water quality, agricultural biotechnology.

Nova Southeastern University, Oceanographic Center, Program in Marine Environmental Science, Fort Lauderdale, FL 33314-7796. Offers MS. *Faculty:* 15 full-time (1 woman), 5 part-time/adjunct (0 women). *Students:* 4 full-time (3 women), 4 part-time (3 women). 10 applicants, 100% accepted, 3 enrolled. In 2009, 1 master's awarded. *Degree requirements:* For master's, thesis. *Entrance requirements:* For master's, GRE. Additional exam requirements/ recommendations for international students: Required—TOEFL (minimum score 550 paper-based). *Application deadline:* Applications are processed on a rolling basis. Application fee: $50. *Unit head:* Dr. Richard Dodge, Dean, 954-262-3600, Fax: 954-262-4020, E-mail: dodge@nsu.nova.edu. *Application contact:* Dr. Richard Spieler, Director of Academic Programs, 954-262-3600, Fax: 954-262-4020, E-mail: spieler@nova.edu.

Oakland University, Graduate Study and Lifelong Learning, College of Arts and Sciences, Department of Chemistry, Rochester, MI 48309-4401. Offers biological sciences: health and environmental chemistry (PhD); chemistry (MS). *Degree requirements:* For master's, thesis; for doctorate, thesis/dissertation. *Entrance requirements:* For master's, minimum GPA of 3.0 for unconditional admission; for doctorate, GRE Subject Test, minimum GPA of 3.0 for unconditional admission. Additional exam requirements/recommendations for international students: Required—TOEFL (minimum score 550 paper-based; 213 computer-based). Electronic applications accepted. *Faculty research:* Chemistry of free radical species generated from biological intermediates; fate of toxic organic compounds in the environment; electroanalytical and surface chemistry at solid/liquid interface; computational modeling of intermolecular interactions and surface phenomena; metabolism and biological activity of modified fatty acids and xenobiotic carboxylic acids; physiologic and pathologic mechanisms that modulate immune responses.

OGI School of Science & Engineering at Oregon Health & Science University, Graduate Studies, Department of Environmental and Biomolecular Systems, Beaverton, OR 97006-8921. Offers biochemistry and molecular biology (MS, PhD); environmental health systems (MS); environmental information technology (MS, PhD); environmental science and engineering (MS, PhD). Part-time programs available. Terminal master's awarded for partial completion of doctoral program. *Degree requirements:* For master's, thesis optional; for doctorate, comprehensive exam, oral defense of dissertation. *Entrance requirements:* For master's and doctorate, GRE General Test. Additional exam requirements/recommendations for international students: Required—TOEFL. Electronic applications accepted. *Faculty research:* Air and water science, hydrogeology, estuarine and coastal modeling, environmental microbiology, contaminant transport, biochemistry, biomolecular systems.

The Ohio State University, Graduate School, College of Biological Sciences, Program in Environmental Science, Columbus, OH 43210. Offers MS, PhD. *Faculty:* 89. *Students:* 38 full-time (22 women), 18 part-time (11 women), 28 international. Average age 28. In 2009, 10 master's, 6 doctorates awarded. *Degree requirements:* For master's, one foreign language, thesis optional; for doctorate, one foreign language, thesis/dissertation. *Entrance requirements:* For master's and doctorate, GRE General Test. Additional exam requirements/recommendations for international students: Required—TOEFL (minimum score 600 paper-based; 250 computer-based). *Application deadline:* For fall admission, 8/15 priority date for domestic students, 7/1 priority date for international students; for winter admission, 12/1 priority date for domestic students, 11/1 priority date for international students; for spring admission, 3/1 priority date for domestic students, 2/1 priority date for international students. Applications are processed on a rolling basis. Application fee: $40 ($50 for international students). Electronic applications accepted. *Expenses:* Tuition, state resident: full-time $10,683. Tuition, nonresident: full-time $25,923. Tuition and fees vary according to course load and program. *Financial support:* Fellowships, research assistantships, teaching assistantships, Federal Work-Study and institutionally sponsored loans available. Support available to part-time students. *Unit head:* Richard H. Moore, Graduate Studies Committee Chair, 614-292-9762, Fax: 614-292-7432, E-mail: moore.11@osu.edu. *Application contact:* 614-292-9444, Fax: 614-292-3895, E-mail: domestic.grad@osu.edu.

The Ohio State University, Graduate School, College of Food, Agricultural, and Environmental Sciences, School of Environment and Natural Resources, Columbus, OH 43210. Offers MS, PhD. *Students:* 58 full-time (29 women), 17 part-time (7 women); includes 5 minority (1 African American, 1 Asian American or Pacific Islander, 3 Hispanic Americans), 14 international. Average age 29. In 2009, 16 master's, 7 doctorates awarded. *Application deadline:* Applications are processed on a rolling basis. Application fee: $40 ($50 for international students). Electronic applications accepted. *Expenses:* Tuition, state resident: full-time $10,683. Tuition, nonresident: full-time $25,923. Tuition and fees vary according to course load and program. *Unit head:* Ronald Hendrick, Director, E-mail: hendrick.15@osu.edu. *Application contact:* Graduate Admissions, 614-292-9444, Fax: 614-292-3895, E-mail: domestic.grad@osu.edu.

Oklahoma State University, College of Agricultural Science and Natural Resources, Department of Horticulture and Landscape Architecture, Stillwater, OK 74078. Offers agriculture (M Ag); crop science (PhD); environmental science (PhD); horticulture (MS); plant science (PhD). *Accreditation:* ASLA. *Faculty:* 21 full-time (2 women), 2 part-time/adjunct (1 woman). *Students:* 14 part-time (6 women); includes 2 minority (1 African American, 1 American Indian/Alaska Native), 6 international. Average age 28. 23 applicants, 48% accepted, 7 enrolled. In 2009, 3 master's awarded. *Degree requirements:* For master's, thesis (for some programs); for doctorate, comprehensive exam, thesis/dissertation. *Entrance requirements:* For master's and doctorate, GRE or GMAT. Additional exam requirements/recommendations for international students: Required—TOEFL (minimum score 550 paper-based; 79 iBT). *Application deadline:* For fall admission, 3/1 priority date for international students; for spring admission, 8/1 priority date for international students. Applications are processed on a rolling basis. Application fee: $40 ($75 for international students). Electronic applications accepted. *Expenses:* Tuition, state resident: full-time $3716; part-time $154.85 per credit hour. Tuition, nonresident: full-time $14,448; part-time $602 per credit hour. Required fees: $1772; $73.85 per credit hour. One-time fee: $50. Tuition and fees vary according to course load and campus/location. *Financial support:* In 2009–10, 12 research assistantships (averaging $15,748 per year) were awarded; career-related internships or fieldwork, Federal Work-Study, scholarships/grants, health care benefits, tuition waivers (partial), and unspecified assistantships also available. Support available to part-time students. Financial award application deadline: 3/1; financial award applicants required to submit FAFSA. *Faculty research:* Stress and postharvest physiology; water utilization and runoff; IPM systems and nursery, turf, floriculture, vegetable, net and fruit produces and natural resources, food extraction, and processing; public garden management. *Unit head:* Dr. Dale Maronek, Head, 405-744-5414, Fax: 405-744-9709. *Application contact:* Dr. Gordon Emslie, Dean, 405-744-6368, Fax: 405-744-0355, E-mail: grad-i@okstate.edu.

Oklahoma State University, College of Agricultural Science and Natural Resources, Department of Plant and Soil Sciences, Stillwater, OK 74078. Offers crop science (PhD); environmental science (PhD); plant and soil sciences (MS); plant science (PhD); soil science (M Ag, PhD). *Faculty:* 33 full-time (4 women), 2 part-time/adjunct (0 women). *Students:* 15 full-time (4 women), 37 part-time (13 women); includes 1 minority (Asian American or Pacific Islander), 20 international. Average age 28. 34 applicants, 38% accepted, 7 enrolled. In 2009, 9 master's, 3 doctorates awarded. *Degree requirements:* For master's, thesis; for doctorate, comprehensive exam, thesis/dissertation. *Entrance requirements:* For master's and doctorate, GRE or GMAT. Additional exam requirements/recommendations for international students: Required—TOEFL (minimum score 550 paper-based; 79 iBT). *Application deadline:* For fall admission, 3/1 priority date for international students; for spring admission, 8/1 priority date for international students. Applications are processed on a rolling basis. Application fee: $40 ($75 for international students). Electronic applications accepted. *Expenses:* Tuition, state resident: full-time $3716; part-time $154.85 per credit hour. Tuition, nonresident: full-time $14,448; part-time $602 per credit hour. Required fees: $1772; $73.85 per credit hour. One-time fee: $50. Tuition and fees vary according to course load and campus/location. *Financial support:* In 2009–10, 38 research assistantships (averaging $14,373 per year), 1 teaching assistantship (averaging $13,920 per year) were awarded; career-related internships or fieldwork, Federal Work-Study, scholarships/ grants, health care benefits, tuition waivers (partial), and unspecified assistantships also available. Support available to part-time students. Financial award application deadline: 3/1; financial award applicants required to submit FAFSA. *Faculty research:* Crop science, weed science, rangeland ecology and management, biotechnology, breeding and genetics. *Unit head:* Dr. David R. Porter, Head, 405-744-6130, Fax: 405-744-5269. *Application contact:* Dr. Gordon Emslie, Dean, 405-744-6368, Fax: 405-744-0355, E-mail: grad-i@okstate.edu.

Oklahoma State University, College of Arts and Sciences, Department of Botany, Stillwater, OK 74078. Offers botany (MS); environmental science (MS, PhD); plant science (PhD). *Faculty:* 17 full-time (5 women). *Students:* 12 part-time (4 women); includes 1 minority (American Indian/Alaska Native), 2 international. Average age 31. 10 applicants, 40% accepted, 4 enrolled. In 2009, 1 master's awarded. *Degree requirements:* For master's, thesis; for doctorate, comprehensive exam, thesis/dissertation. *Entrance requirements:* For master's and doctorate, GRE or GMAT. Additional exam requirements/recommendations for international students: Required—TOEFL (minimum score 550 paper-based; 79 iBT). *Application deadline:* For fall admission, 3/1 priority date for international students; for spring admission, 8/1 priority date for international students. Applications are processed on a rolling basis. Application fee: $40 ($75 for international students). Electronic applications accepted. *Expenses:* Tuition, state resident: full-time $3716; part-time $154.85 per credit hour. Tuition, nonresident: full-time $14,448; part-time $602 per credit hour. Required fees: $1772; $73.85 per credit hour. One-time fee: $50. Tuition and fees vary according to course load and campus/location. *Financial support:* In 2009–10, 3 research assistantships (averaging $15,770 per year), 10 teaching assistantships (averaging $15,469 per year) were awarded; career-related internships or fieldwork, Federal Work-Study, scholarships/grants, health care benefits, tuition waivers (partial), and unspecified assistantships also available. Support available to part-time students. Financial award application deadline: 3/1; financial award applicants required to submit FAFSA. *Faculty research:* Ethnobotany, developmental genetics of Arabidopsis, biological roles of Plasmodesmata, community ecology and biodiversity, nutrient cycling in grassland ecosystems. *Unit head:* Dr. Linda Watson, Head, 405-744-5559, Fax: 405-744-7074. *Application contact:* Dr. Gordon Emslie, Dean, 405-744-6368, Fax: 405-744-0355, E-mail: grad-i@okstate.edu.

Oklahoma State University, Graduate College, Stillwater, OK 74078. Offers environmental science (MS); international studies (MS); natural and applied science (MS); photonics (PhD); plant science (PhD). Programs are interdisciplinary. *Faculty:* 2 full-time (0 women). *Students:* 82 full-time (47 women), 156 part-time (75 women); includes 49 minority (15 African Americans, 17 American Indian/Alaska Native, 10 Asian Americans or Pacific Islanders, 7 Hispanic Americans), 68 international. Average age 32. 779 applicants, 68% accepted, 87 enrolled. In 2009, 77 master's, 8 doctorates awarded. *Degree requirements:* For master's, thesis (for some programs); for doctorate, comprehensive exam, thesis/dissertation. *Entrance requirements:* For master's and doctorate, GRE or GMAT. Additional exam requirements/recommendations for international students: Required—TOEFL (minimum score 550 paper-based; 79 iBT). *Application deadline:* For fall admission, 3/1 priority date for international students; for spring admission, 8/1 priority date for international students. Applications are processed on a rolling basis. Application fee: $40 ($75 for international students). Electronic applications accepted. *Expenses:* Tuition, state resident: full-time $3716; part-time $154.85 per credit hour. Tuition, nonresident: full-time $14,448; part-time $602 per credit hour. Required fees: $1772; $73.85 per credit hour. One-time fee: $50. Tuition and fees vary according to course load and campus/location. *Financial support:* In 2009–10, 2 research assistantships (averaging $10,200 per year) were awarded; career-related internships or fieldwork, Federal Work-Study, scholarships/grants, health care benefits, tuition waivers (partial), and unspecified assistantships also available. Support available to part-time students. Financial award application deadline: 3/1; financial award applicants required to submit FAFSA. *Unit head:* Dr. Gordon Emslie, Dean, 405-744-6368, Fax: 405-744-0355, E-mail: grad-i@okstate.edu. *Application contact:* Dr. Susan Mathew, Coordinator of Admissions, 405-744-6368, Fax: 405-744-0355, E-mail: grad-i@okstate.edu.

Oregon Health & Science University, OGI School of Science and Engineering, Department of Environmental and Biomolecular Systems, Portland, OR 97239-3098. Offers biochemistry and molecular biology (MS, PhD); environmental science and engineering (MS, PhD). Tuition and fees vary according to course level, course load, degree level, program and reciprocity agreements.

Oregon State University, Graduate School, College of Agricultural Sciences, Department of Environmental and Molecular Toxicology, Corvallis, OR 97331. Offers toxicology (MS, PhD). *Faculty:* 13 full-time (5 women), 1 part-time/adjunct (0 women). *Students:* 23 full-time (14 women), 2 part-time (1 woman); includes 6 minority (1 African American, 2 American Indian/ Alaska Native, 1 Asian American or Pacific Islander, 2 Hispanic Americans), 2 international. Average age 29. In 2009, 5 doctorates awarded. Application fee: $50. *Expenses:* Tuition, state resident: full-time $9774; part-time $362 per credit. Tuition, nonresident: full-time $15,849; part-time $587 per credit. Required fees: $1639. Full-time tuition and fees vary according to course load and program. *Unit head:* Dr. Nancy I. Kerkvliet, Interim Head, 541-737-4387, Fax: 541-737-0497, E-mail: nancy.kerkvliet@oregonstate.edu. *Application contact:* Dr. Stella Coakley, Associate Dean, 541-737-5264, Fax: 541-737-3178, E-mail: stella.coakley@oregonstate.edu.

Oregon State University, Graduate School, Program in Environmental Sciences, Corvallis, OR 97331. Offers MA, MS, PhD. *Students:* 40 full-time (27 women), 10 part-time (6 women);

Environmental Sciences

Oregon State University (continued)

includes 4 minority (2 American Indian/Alaska Native, 1 Asian American or Pacific Islander, 1 Hispanic American), 8 international. Average age 32. In 2009, 7 master's, 3 doctorates awarded. Application fee: $50. *Expenses:* Tuition, state resident: full-time $9774; part-time $362 per credit. Tuition, nonresident: full-time $15,849; part-time $587 per credit. Required fees: $1639. Full-time tuition and fees vary according to course load and program. *Unit head:* Dr. Andrew R. Blaustein, Director, 541-737-9869, Fax: 541-737-9858, E-mail: blaustea@science.oregonstate.edu. *Application contact:* Rosemary Garagnani, Assistant Dean, 541-737-1465, Fax: 541-737-3313.

Pace University, Dyson College of Arts and Sciences, Program in Environmental Science, New York, NY 10038. Offers MS. Offered at Pleasantville, NY location only. *Faculty:* 7 full-time (3 women), 4 part-time/adjunct (0 women). *Students:* 11 full-time (6 women), 9 part-time (5 women); includes 2 minority (1 Asian American or Pacific Islander, 1 Hispanic American), 3 international. Average age 31. 24 applicants, 71% accepted, 5 enrolled. In 2009, 5 master's awarded. *Degree requirements:* For master's, research project. *Entrance requirements:* For master's, GRE. Additional exam requirements/recommendations for international students: Required—TOEFL. *Application deadline:* For fall admission, 8/1 priority date for domestic students; for spring admission, 12/1 priority date for domestic students. Applications are processed on a rolling basis. Application fee: $70. Electronic applications accepted. *Expenses:* Tuition: Part-time $954 per credit. Tuition and fees vary according to course load, degree level and program. *Unit head:* Dr. Richard Schlesinger, Director, 914-773-3707, Fax: 914-773-3634, E-mail: rschlesinger@pace.edu. *Application contact:* Joanna Broda, Director of Graduate Admissions, 914-422-4283, Fax: 914-422-4287, E-mail: gradwp@pace.edu.

Penn State Harrisburg, Graduate School, School of Science, Engineering and Technology, Middletown, PA 17057-4898. Offers M Eng, MEPC, MPS, MS, MEPC/JD. Evening/weekend programs available. *Unit head:* Dr. Omid Ansary, Director, 717-948-6353, E-mail: axa8@psu.edu. *Application contact:* Robert Coffman, Director of Admissions, 717-948-6250, Fax: 717-948-6325, E-mail: ric1@psu.edu.

Penn State University Park, Graduate School, Intercollege Graduate Programs, Intercollege Program in Environmental Pollution Control, State College, University Park, PA 16802-1503. Offers MEPC, MS. *Unit head:* Dr. Herschel A. Elliott, Chair, 814-865-1417, Fax: 814-863-1031, E-mail: helliott3@psu.edu. *Application contact:* Dr. Herschel A. Elliott, Chair, 814-865-1417, Fax: 814-863-1031, E-mail: helliott3@psu.edu.

Polytechnic Institute of NYU, Department of Civil Engineering, Major in Environmental Science, Brooklyn, NY 11201-2990. Offers MS. Part-time and evening/weekend programs available. *Students:* 1 full-time (0 women), 1 (woman) part-time; includes 1 minority (African American), 1 international. 3 applicants, 0% accepted. In 2009, 1 master's awarded. *Degree requirements:* For master's, comprehensive exam (for some programs), thesis (for some programs). *Entrance requirements:* Additional exam requirements/recommendations for international students: Required—TOEFL (minimum score 550 paper-based; 213 computer-based; 80 iBT); Recommended—IELTS (minimum score 6.5). *Application deadline:* For fall admission, 7/31 priority date for domestic students, 4/30 priority date for international students; for spring admission, 12/31 priority date for domestic students, 10/30 priority date for international students. Applications are processed on a rolling basis. Application fee: $75. Electronic applications accepted. *Expenses:* Tuition: Full-time $21,492; part-time $1194 per credit hour. Required fees: $1160; $204 per course. *Financial support:* Fellowships, research assistantships, teaching assistantships, institutionally sponsored loans, scholarships/grants, and unspecified assistantships available. Support available to part-time students. Financial award applicants required to submit FAFSA. *Unit head:* Dr. Lawrence Chiarelli, Head, 718-260-4040, Fax: 718-260-3433, E-mail: lchiarel@poly.edu. *Application contact:* JeanCarlo Bonilla, Director of Graduate Enrollment Management, 718-260-3182, Fax: 718-260-3624, E-mail: gradinfo@poly.edu.

Pontifical Catholic University of Puerto Rico, College of Sciences, Department of Biology, Ponce, PR 00717-0777. Offers environmental sciences (MS). *Degree requirements:* For master's, thesis. *Entrance requirements:* For master's, GRE, 2 letters of recommendation, interview, minimum GPA of 2.75.

Portland State University, Graduate Studies, College of Liberal Arts and Sciences, Department of Geology, Portland, OR 97207-0751. Offers environmental sciences and resources (PhD); geology (MA, MS); science/geology (MAT, MST). Part-time programs available. *Degree requirements:* For master's, comprehensive exam, thesis, field comprehensive; for doctorate, thesis/dissertation, 2 years of residency. *Entrance requirements:* For master's, GRE General Test, GRE Subject Test, BA/BS in geology, minimum GPA of 3.0 in upper-division course work or 2.75 overall. Additional exam requirements/recommendations for international students: Required—TOEFL (minimum score 550 paper-based; 213 computer-based). *Faculty research:* Sediment transport, volcanic environmental geology, coastal and fluvial processes.

Portland State University, Graduate Studies, College of Liberal Arts and Sciences, Interdisciplinary Program in Environmental Sciences and Management, Portland, OR 97207-0751. Offers environmental management (MEM); environmental sciences/biology (PhD); environmental sciences/chemistry (PhD); environmental sciences/civil engineering (PhD); environmental sciences/geography (PhD); environmental sciences/geology (PhD); environmental sciences/physics (PhD); environmental studies (MS); science/environmental science (MST). Part-time programs available. *Degree requirements:* For master's, thesis or alternative; for doctorate, variable foreign language requirement, comprehensive exam, thesis/dissertation, oral and qualifying exams. *Entrance requirements:* For master's, GRE General Test, 3 letters of recommendation; for doctorate, minimum GPA of 3.0 in upper-division course work or 2.75 overall. Additional exam requirements/recommendations for international students: Required—TOEFL (minimum score 550 paper-based; 213 computer-based). *Faculty research:* Environmental aspects of biology, chemistry, civil engineering, geology, physics.

Queens College of the City University of New York, Division of Graduate Studies, Mathematics and Natural Sciences Division, School of Earth and Environmental Sciences, Flushing, NY 11367-1597. Offers MA. Part-time and evening/weekend programs available. *Faculty:* 14 full-time (4 women). *Students:* 2 full-time (both women), 10 part-time (5 women). 13 applicants, 38% accepted, 3 enrolled. In 2009, 3 master's awarded. *Degree requirements:* For master's, comprehensive exam, thesis. *Entrance requirements:* For master's, GRE, previous course work in calculus, physics, and chemistry; minimum GPA of 3.0. Additional exam requirements/recommendations for international students: Required—TOEFL. *Application deadline:* For fall admission, 4/1 for domestic students; for spring admission, 11/1 for domestic students. Applications are processed on a rolling basis. Application fee: $125. *Expenses:* Tuition, state resident: full-time $7360; part-time $310 per credit. Tuition, nonresident: part-time $575 per credit. One-time fee: $195.25 full-time; $145.25 part-time. *Financial support:* Career-related internships or fieldwork, Federal Work-Study, institutionally sponsored loans, tuition waivers (partial), and unspecified assistantships available. Support available to part-time students. Financial award application deadline: 4/1; financial award applicants required to submit FAFSA. *Faculty research:* Sedimentology/stratigraphy, paleontology, field petrology. *Unit head:* Dr. Yan Zheng, Chairperson, 718-997-3300. *Application contact:* Dr. Hannes Brueckner, Graduate Adviser, 718-997-3300, E-mail: hannes_brueckner@qc.edu.

Rensselaer Polytechnic Institute, Graduate School, School of Science, Department of Earth and Environmental Sciences, Troy, NY 12180-3590. Offers geochemistry (MS, PhD); geology (MS, PhD); geophysics (MS, PhD); petrology (MS, PhD). Part-time programs available. *Faculty:* 8 full-time (1 woman), 1 part-time/adjunct (0 women). *Students:* 8 full-time (5 women), 1 (woman) part-time; includes 1 minority (Asian American or Pacific Islander). Average age 24. 48 applicants, 15% accepted. In 2009, 2 master's, 3 doctorates awarded. Terminal master's awarded for partial completion of doctoral program. *Degree requirements:* For master's, comprehensive exam, thesis (for some programs); for doctorate, comprehensive exam, thesis/dissertation. *Entrance requirements:* For master's and doctorate, GRE General Test. Additional exam requirements/recommendations for international students: Required—TOEFL. *Application deadline:* For fall admission, 1/15 priority date for domestic students. Applications are processed on a rolling basis. Application fee: $75. Electronic applications accepted. *Expenses:* Tuition: Full-time $38,100. *Financial support:* In 2009–10, 7 research assistantships with full tuition reimbursements (averaging $23,000 per year), 4 teaching assistantships with full tuition reimbursements (averaging $23,000 per year) were awarded; fellowships with full tuition reimbursements, career-related internships or fieldwork, institutionally sponsored loans, and scholarships/grants also available. Financial award application deadline: 2/1; financial award applicants required to submit FAFSA. *Faculty research:* Mantel geochemistry, contaminant geochemistry, seismology, GPS geodesy, remote sensing petrology. Total annual research expenditures: $2.3 million. *Unit head:* Dr. Frank Spear, Chair, 518-276-6474, Fax: 518-276-2012, E-mail: ees@rpi.edu. *Application contact:* Dr. Steven Roecker, Professor, 518-276-6773, Fax: 518-276-2012, E-mail: ees@rpi.edu.

Rice University, Graduate Programs, George R. Brown School of Engineering, Department of Civil and Environmental Engineering, Houston, TX 77251-1892. Offers civil engineering (MCE, MS, PhD); environmental engineering (MEE, MES, MS, PhD); environmental science (MEE, MES, MS, PhD). Part-time programs available. *Degree requirements:* For master's, thesis (for some programs); for doctorate, thesis/dissertation. *Entrance requirements:* For master's and doctorate, GRE General Test, GRE Subject Test, minimum GPA of 3.25. Additional exam requirements/recommendations for international students: Required—TOEFL (minimum score 600 paper-based; 250 computer-based; 90 iBT). Electronic applications accepted. *Faculty research:* Biology and chemistry of groundwater, pollutant fate in groundwater systems, water quality monitoring, urban storm water runoff, urban air quality.

Rice University, Graduate Programs, Wiess School–Professional Science Master's Programs, Houston, TX 77251-1892. Offers MS.

Rochester Institute of Technology, Graduate Enrollment Services, College of Science, Department of Biological Sciences, Program in Environmental Science, Rochester, NY 14623-5603. Offers MS. Part-time and evening/weekend programs available. *Students:* 9 full-time (6 women), 1 (woman) part-time, 1 international. Average age 24. 18 applicants, 17% accepted, 3 enrolled. In 2009, 3 master's awarded. *Degree requirements:* For master's, thesis. *Entrance requirements:* For master's, GRE General Test (recommended), minimum GPA of 3.0. Additional exam requirements/recommendations for international students: Required—TOEFL (minimum score 550 paper-based; 213 computer-based; 79 iBT) or IELTS (minimum score 6.5). *Application deadline:* For fall admission, 2/15 priority date for domestic and international students; for winter admission, 11/1 for domestic students; for spring admission, 2/1 for domestic students. Applications are processed on a rolling basis. Application fee: $50. Electronic applications accepted. *Expenses:* Tuition: Full-time $31,533; part-time $876 per credit hour. Required fees: $210. *Financial support:* In 2009–10, 7 students received support; fellowships with partial tuition reimbursements available, research assistantships with partial tuition reimbursements available, teaching assistantships with partial tuition reimbursements available, career-related internships or fieldwork, scholarships/grants, and unspecified assistantships available. Support available to part-time students. Financial award applicants required to submit FAFSA. *Faculty research:* Environmental chemistry, digital imaging, environmental biology, remote sensing, mathematics and statistics, environmental public policy, environmental economics. *Unit head:* Dr. Karl Korfmacher, Director, 585-475-7577, Fax: 585-475-5000, E-mail: ncbsbi@rit.edu. *Application contact:* Diane Ellison, Assistant Vice President, Graduate Enrollment Services, 585-475-2229, Fax: 585-475-7164, E-mail: gradinfo@rit.edu.

Royal Military College of Canada, Division of Graduate Studies and Research, Engineering Division, Program in Environmental Science, Kingston, ON K7K 7B4, Canada. Offers M Sc, PhD. *Degree requirements:* For master's, thesis; for doctorate, comprehensive exam, thesis/dissertation. *Entrance requirements:* For master's, honours degree with second-class standing; for doctorate, master's degree. Electronic applications accepted.

Rutgers, The State University of New Jersey, Newark, Graduate School, Program in Environmental Science, Newark, NJ 07102. Offers MS, PhD. *Entrance requirements:* For master's and doctorate, GRE, minimum B average.

Rutgers, The State University of New Jersey, New Brunswick, Graduate School-New Brunswick, Department of Environmental Sciences, Piscataway, NJ 08854-8097. Offers air pollution and resources (MS, PhD); aquatic biology (MS, PhD); aquatic chemistry (MS, PhD); atmospheric science (MS, PhD); chemistry and physics of aerosol and hydrosol systems (MS, PhD); environmental chemistry (MS, PhD); environmental microbiology (MS, PhD); environmental toxicology (PhD); exposure assessment (PhD); fate and effects of pollutants (MS, PhD); pollution prevention and control (MS, PhD); water and wastewater treatment (MS, PhD); water resources (MS, PhD). Terminal master's awarded for partial completion of doctoral program. *Degree requirements:* For master's, comprehensive exam, thesis or alternative, oral final exam; for doctorate, comprehensive exam, thesis/dissertation, thesis defense, qualifying exam. *Entrance requirements:* For master's and doctorate, GRE General Test. Additional exam requirements/recommendations for international students: Required—TOEFL. Electronic applications accepted. *Faculty research:* Biological waste treatment; contaminant fate and transport; air, soil and water quality.

South Dakota School of Mines and Technology, Graduate Division, College of Science and Letters, Department of Atmospheric Sciences, PhD Program in Atmospheric and Environmental Sciences, Rapid City, SD 57701-3995. Offers PhD. *Faculty:* 9 full-time (0 women), 1 (woman) part-time/adjunct. *Students:* 3 full-time (0 women), 4 part-time (1 woman), 1 international. Average age 34. 2 applicants, 50% accepted, 0 enrolled. In 2009, 2 doctorates awarded. *Degree requirements:* For doctorate, comprehensive exam, thesis/dissertation. *Entrance requirements:* For doctorate, GRE General Test, GRE Subject Test. Additional exam requirements/recommendations for international students: Required—TOEFL, TWE. *Application deadline:* For fall admission, 7/1 priority date for domestic students, 4/1 for international students; for spring admission, 11/1 for domestic students, 9/1 for international students. Applications are processed on a rolling basis. Application fee: $35. Electronic applications accepted. *Expenses:* Tuition, state resident: full-time $3340; part-time $139 per credit hour. Tuition, nonresident: full-time $7060; part-time $294 per credit hour. Required fees: $3270. *Financial support:* In 2009–10, 3 fellowships (averaging $4,000 per year), 4 teaching assistantships with partial tuition reimbursements (averaging $6,774 per year) were awarded; research assistantships with partial tuition reimbursements, unspecified assistantships also available. *Unit head:* Dr. P. V. Sundareshwar, Director, 605-394-2492, E-mail: pv.sundareshwar@sdsmt.edu. *Application contact:* Jeannette R. Nilson, Administrative Support Coordinator, Graduate Education, 800-454-8162 Ext. 1206, Fax: 605-394-5360, E-mail: graduate_admissions@sdsmt.edu.

Southern Illinois University Carbondale, Graduate School, College of Science, Department of Geology and Department of Geography, Program in Environmental Resources and Policy, Carbondale, IL 62901-4701. Offers PhD. *Entrance requirements:* For doctorate, GRE.

Southern Illinois University Edwardsville, Graduate Studies and Research, College of Arts and Sciences, Program in Environmental Sciences, Edwardsville, IL 62026-0001. Offers MS. Part-time programs available. *Students:* 4 full-time (2 women), 24 part-time (11 women), 6 international. Average age 26. 31 applicants, 52% accepted, 0 enrolled. In 2009, 7 master's awarded. *Degree requirements:* For master's, thesis (for some programs), final exam, oral exam. *Entrance requirements:* For master's, GRE. Additional exam requirements/

recommendations for international students: Required—TOEFL (minimum score 550 paper-based; 213 computer-based; 79 iBT), IELTS (minimum score 6.5). *Application deadline:* For fall admission, 7/23 for domestic students, 6/1 for international students; for spring admission, 12/11 for domestic students, 10/1 for international students. Applications are processed on a rolling basis. Application fee: $30. Electronic applications accepted. *Expenses:* Tuition, state resident: part-time $1252.50 per semester. Tuition, nonresident: part-time $3131.25 per semester. Required fees: $586.85 per semester. Tuition and fees vary according to course load. *Financial support:* In 2009–10, 1 research assistantship with full tuition reimbursement (averaging $8,064 per year), 11 teaching assistantships with full tuition reimbursements (averaging $8,064 per year) were awarded; fellowships with full tuition reimbursements, career-related internships or fieldwork, Federal Work-Study, institutionally sponsored loans, scholarships/grants, traineeships, and unspecified assistantships also available. Support available to part-time students. Financial award application deadline: 3/1; financial award applicants required to submit FAFSA. *Unit head:* Dr. Zhi-Qing Lin, Program Director, 618-650-2650, E-mail: zhlin@siue.edu. *Application contact:* Dr. Zhi-Qing Lin, Program Director, 618-650-2650, E-mail: zhlin@siue.edu.

Southern Methodist University, Bobby B. Lyle School of Engineering, Department of Environmental and Civil Engineering, Dallas, TX 75275-0340. Offers applied science (MS, PhD); civil engineering (MS, PhD); environmental engineering (MS); environmental science (MS), including environmental systems management, hazardous and waste materials management; facilities management (MS). Part-time and evening/weekend programs available. Postbaccalaureate distance learning degree programs offered (no on-campus study). *Faculty:* 7 full-time (0 women), 13 part-time/adjunct (4 women). *Students:* 19 full-time (8 women), 50 part-time (17 women); includes 13 minority (9 African Americans, 2 Asian Americans or Pacific Islanders, 2 Hispanic Americans), 7 international. Average age 34. 50 applicants, 86% accepted, 28 enrolled. In 2009, 17 master's, 1 doctorate awarded. Terminal master's awarded for partial completion of doctoral program. *Degree requirements:* For master's, thesis optional; for doctorate, thesis/dissertation, oral and written qualifying exams. *Entrance requirements:* For master's, GRE General Test, minimum GPA of 3.0 in last 2 years; bachelor's degree in engineering, mathematics, or sciences; for doctorate, GRE, BS and MS in related field, minimum GPA of 3.3. Additional exam requirements/recommendations for international students: Required—TOEFL. *Application deadline:* For fall admission, 7/1 for domestic students, 5/15 for international students; for spring admission, 11/15 for domestic students, 9/1 for international students. Applications are processed on a rolling basis. Application fee: $75. Electronic applications accepted. *Financial support:* In 2009–10, 9 students received support, including 2 research assistantships with full tuition reimbursements available (averaging $18,000 per year), 7 teaching assistantships with full tuition reimbursements available (averaging $18,000 per year); career-related internships or fieldwork, tuition waivers (full and partial), and unspecified assistantships also available. *Faculty research:* Human and environmental health effects of endocrine disrupters, development of air pollution control systems for diesel engines, structural analysis and design, modeling and design of waste treatment systems. Total annual research expenditures: $100,000. *Unit head:* Prof. Bijan Mohraz, Chair, 214-768-3894, Fax: 214-768-2164, E-mail: bmohraz@lyle.smu.edu. *Application contact:* Marc Valerin, Director of Graduate and Executive Admissions, 214-768-3042, Fax: 214-768-3778, E-mail: valerin@lyle.smu.edu.

Southern University and Agricultural and Mechanical College, Graduate School, College of Sciences, Department of Chemistry, Baton Rouge, LA 70813. Offers analytical chemistry (MS); biochemistry (MS); environmental sciences (MS); inorganic chemistry (MS); organic chemistry (MS); physical chemistry (MS). *Degree requirements:* For master's, thesis. *Entrance requirements:* For master's, GMAT or GRE General Test. Additional exam requirements/recommendations for international students: Required—TOEFL (minimum score 525 paper-based; 193 computer-based). *Faculty research:* Synthesis of macrocyclic ligands, latex accelerators, anticancer drugs, biosensors, absorption isotheums, isolation of specific enzymes from plants.

Stanford University, School of Earth Sciences, Department of Geological and Environmental Sciences, Stanford, CA 94305-9991. Offers MS, PhD, Eng. Terminal master's awarded for partial completion of doctoral program. *Degree requirements:* For master's and Eng, thesis; for doctorate, thesis/dissertation. *Entrance requirements:* For master's, doctorate, and Eng, GRE General Test. Additional exam requirements/recommendations for international students: Required—TOEFL. Electronic applications accepted. *Expenses:* Tuition: Full-time $37,380; part-time $2760 per quarter. Required fees: $501.

Stanford University, School of Earth Sciences, Earth Systems Program, Stanford, CA 94305-9991. Offers MS. Students admitted at the undergraduate level. Electronic applications accepted. *Expenses:* Tuition: Full-time $37,380; part-time $2760 per quarter. Required fees: $501.

State University of New York College of Environmental Science and Forestry, Department of Environmental and Forest Biology, Syracuse, NY 13210-2779. Offers applied ecology (MPS); chemical ecology (MPS, MS, PhD); conservation biology (MPS, MS, PhD); ecology (MPS, MS, PhD); entomology (MPS, MS, PhD); environmental interpretation (MPS, MS, PhD); environmental physiology (MPS, MS, PhD); fish and wildlife biology (MPS, MS, PhD); forest pathology and mycology (MPS, MS, PhD); plant biotechnology (MPS); plant science and biotechnology (MPS, MS, PhD). *Degree requirements:* For master's, thesis (for some programs); for doctorate, comprehensive exam, thesis/dissertation. *Entrance requirements:* For master's and doctorate, GRE General Test, GRE Subject Test, minimum GPA of 3.0. Additional exam requirements/recommendations for international students: Required—TOEFL (minimum score 550 paper-based; 213 computer-based; 80 iBT), IELTS (minimum score 6). *Faculty research:* Ecology, fish and wildlife biology and management, plant science, entomology.

State University of New York College of Environmental Science and Forestry, Program in Environmental Science, Syracuse, NY 13210-2779. Offers environmental and community land planning (MPS, MS, PhD); environmental and natural resources policy (PhD); environmental communication and participatory processes (MPS, MS, PhD); environmental policy and democratic processes (MPS, MS, PhD); environmental systems and risk management (MPS, MS, PhD); water and wetland resource studies (MPS, MS, PhD). Part-time programs available. *Degree requirements:* For master's, thesis (for some programs); for doctorate, comprehensive exam, thesis/dissertation. *Entrance requirements:* For master's and doctorate, GRE General Test, minimum GPA of 3.0. Additional exam requirements/recommendations for international students: Required—TOEFL (minimum score 550 paper-based; 213 computer-based; 80 iBT), IELTS (minimum score 6). *Faculty research:* Environmental education/communications, water resources, land resources, waste management.

Stephen F. Austin State University, Graduate School, College of Sciences and Mathematics, Division of Environmental Science, Nacogdoches, TX 75962. Offers MS. *Degree requirements:* For master's, comprehensive exam. *Entrance requirements:* For master's, GRE General Test, minimum GPA of 2.8 in last 60 hours, 2.5 overall. Additional exam requirements/recommendations for international students: Required—TOEFL.

Syracuse University, L. C. Smith College of Engineering and Computer Science, Program in Environmental Engineering, Syracuse, NY 13244. Offers environmental engineering (MS, PhD); environmental science (MS). Part-time programs available. *Students:* 8 full-time (5 women), 1 part-time (0 women), 8 international. Average age 24. 23 applicants, 57% accepted, 4 enrolled. In 2009, 2 master's awarded. *Entrance requirements:* For master's and doctorate, GRE General Test. Additional exam requirements/recommendations for international students: Required—TOEFL (minimum score 100 iBT). *Application deadline:* For fall admission, 6/1 priority date for domestic students, 5/1 priority date for international students. Applications are processed on a rolling basis. Application fee: $75. Electronic applications accepted. *Expenses:* Tuition: Full-time $26,808; part-time $1117 per credit. Required fees: $1024. *Financial support:* Fellowships with tuition reimbursements, research assistantships with tuition reimbursements, teaching assistantships with tuition reimbursements, tuition waivers (partial) available. Financial award application deadline: 1/1. *Unit head:* Dr. Chris E. Johnson, Interim Chair, 315-443-4425, E-mail: cejohns@syr.edu. *Application contact:* Elizabeth Buchanan, Information Contact, 314-443-2558, E-mail: topgrads@syr.edu.

Tarleton State University, College of Graduate Studies, College of Science and Technology, Department of Chemistry, Geosciences and Environmental Sciences, Stephenville, TX 76402. Offers environmental science (MS). Part-time and evening/weekend programs available. *Degree requirements:* For master's, comprehensive exam, thesis optional. *Entrance requirements:* For master's, GRE General Test, minimum GPA of 3.0. Additional exam requirements/recommendations for international students: Required—TOEFL (minimum score 550 paper-based; 213 computer-based; 80 iBT). Electronic applications accepted.

Taylor University, Master of Environmental Science Program, Upland, IN 46989-1001. Offers MES. *Faculty:* 3 part-time/adjunct (0 women). *Students:* 19 full-time (8 women); includes 1 minority (Asian American or Pacific Islander). Average age 26. 25 applicants, 44% accepted, 11 enrolled. In 2009, 5 master's awarded. *Degree requirements:* For master's, thesis (for some programs). *Application deadline:* Applications are processed on a rolling basis. Application fee: $0. *Expenses:* Contact institution. *Financial support:* In 2009–10, 19 students received support, including 19 fellowships (averaging $10,000 per year), 7 teaching assistantships (averaging $6,000 per year); scholarships/grants also available. Financial award applicants required to submit FAFSA. *Faculty research:* Environmental assessment. *Unit head:* Dr. Edwin Richard Squiers, Graduate Chair, 765-998-5386, Fax: 765-998-4976, E-mail: rcsquiers@taylor.edu. *Application contact:* Becky Taylor, Program Assistant, 765-998-4960, Fax: 765-998-4976, E-mail: mes@taylor.edu.

Tennessee Technological University, Graduate School, College of Arts and Sciences, Department of Environmental Sciences, Cookeville, TN 38505. Offers biology (PhD); chemistry (PhD). *Students:* 9 full-time (5 women), 8 part-time (3 women); includes 9 minority (3 African Americans, 3 Asian Americans or Pacific Islanders, 3 Hispanic Americans). 12 applicants, 50% accepted, 3 enrolled. In 2009, 1 doctorate awarded. *Degree requirements:* For doctorate, comprehensive exam, thesis/dissertation. *Entrance requirements:* For doctorate, GRE. Additional exam requirements/recommendations for international students: Required—TOEFL (minimum score 550 paper-based; 79 iBT), IELTS (minimum score 5.5). *Application deadline:* For fall admission, 8/1 for domestic students, 5/1 for international students; for spring admission, 12/1 for domestic students, 10/2 for international students. Application fee: $25 ($30 for international students). Electronic applications accepted. *Expenses:* Tuition, state resident: full-time $7034; part-time $368 per credit hour. *Financial support:* In 2009–10, 5 research assistantships (averaging $10,000 per year), 3 teaching assistantships (averaging $10,000 per year) were awarded; fellowships also available. Financial award application deadline: 4/1. *Unit head:* Dr. Dal Ensor, Director. *Application contact:* Shelia K. Kendrick, Coordinator of Graduate Studies, 931-372-3808, Fax: 931-372-3497, E-mail: skendrick@tntech.edu.

Texas A&M University–Corpus Christi, Graduate Studies and Research, College of Science and Technology, Program in Environmental Science, Corpus Christi, TX 78412-5503. Offers MS. Part-time and evening/weekend programs available. *Degree requirements:* For master's, comprehensive exam, thesis (for some programs). *Entrance requirements:* For master's, GRE General Test. Additional exam requirements/recommendations for international students: Required—TOEFL. Electronic applications accepted.

Texas Christian University, College of Science and Engineering, Department of Environmental Science, Fort Worth, TX 76129-0002. Offers MA, MS, MBA/MEM. Part-time programs available. *Degree requirements:* For master's, comprehensive exam, thesis (MS). *Entrance requirements:* For master's, GRE General Test, 1 year each of course work in biology and chemistry, 1 semester each in calculus and statistics. Additional exam requirements/recommendations for international students: Required—TOEFL (minimum score 80 iBT). *Application deadline:* For fall admission, 2/28 for domestic and international students. Applications are processed on a rolling basis. Application fee: $50. *Expenses:* Tuition: Full-time $17,640; part-time $980 per credit hour. Tuition and fees vary according to program. *Financial support:* In 2009–10, 8 teaching assistantships with full and partial tuition reimbursements (averaging $14,000 per year) were awarded; career-related internships or fieldwork, tuition waivers, and unspecified assistantships also available. Support available to part-time students. Financial award application deadline: 2/28. *Unit head:* Dr. Mike Slattery, Chair, 817-257-7506. *Application contact:* Prof. Becky Richards, Professor of Professional Practice, 817-257-7271.

Texas Tech University, Graduate School, College of Arts and Sciences, Department of Environmental Toxicology, Lubbock, TX 79409. Offers MS, PhD. Part-time programs available. *Faculty:* 9 full-time (1 woman). *Students:* 47 full-time (24 women), 2 part-time (0 women), 26 international. Average age 28. 48 applicants, 71% accepted, 19 enrolled. In 2009, 5 master's, 6 doctorates awarded. *Degree requirements:* For master's, thesis; for doctorate, thesis/dissertation. *Entrance requirements:* For master's and doctorate, GRE General Test. Additional exam requirements/recommendations for international students: Required—TOEFL (minimum score 550 paper-based; 213 computer-based). *Application deadline:* For fall admission, 3/1 priority date for international students; for spring admission, 11/1 priority date for international students. Applications are processed on a rolling basis. Application fee: $50 ($75 for international students). Electronic applications accepted. *Expenses:* Tuition, state resident: full-time $5100; part-time $213 per credit hour. Tuition, nonresident: full-time $11,748; part-time $490 per credit hour. Required fees: $2298; $50 per credit hour. $555 per semester. *Financial support:* Teaching assistantships with partial tuition reimbursements available. Financial award application deadline: 4/15. *Faculty research:* Terrestrial and aquatic toxicology, biochemical and developmental toxicology, advanced materials, countermeasures to biologic and chemical threats, molecular epidemiology and modeling. Total annual research expenditures: $1.9 million. *Unit head:* Dr. Ronald J. Kendall, Director and Chairman, 806-885-4567, Fax: 806-885-2132, E-mail: ron.kendall@tiehh.ttu.edu. *Application contact:* Dr. Steve Cox, Graduate Program Adviser, 806-885-4567, Fax: 806-885-2132, E-mail: stephen.cox@ttu.edu.

Thompson Rivers University, Program in Environmental Science, Kamloops, BC V2C 5N3, Canada. Offers MS. *Entrance requirements:* For master's, personal resume, 2 letters of recommendation. Additional exam requirements/recommendations for international students: Required—TOEFL.

Towson University, College of Graduate Studies and Research, Program in Environmental Science, Towson, MD 21252-0001. Offers MS, Certificate. Part-time and evening/weekend programs available. *Entrance requirements:* For master's, GRE (recommended), bachelor's degree in related field, minimum GPA of 3.0. Electronic applications accepted.

Tufts University, School of Engineering, Department of Civil and Environmental Engineering, Medford, MA 02155. Offers civil engineering (ME, MS, PhD), including geotechnical engineering, structural engineering; environmental engineering (ME, MS, PhD), including environmental engineering and environmental sciences, environmental geotechnology, environmental health, environmental science and management, hazardous materials management, water resources engineering. Part-time programs available. *Faculty:* 17 full-time, 7 part-time/adjunct. *Students:* 72 (33 women); includes 6 minority (2 African Americans, 4 Asian Americans or Pacific Islanders), 17 international. Average age 27. 170 applicants, 59% accepted, 20 enrolled. In 2009, 17 master's, 3 doctorates awarded. Terminal master's awarded for partial completion of doctoral program. *Degree requirements:* For master's, thesis or alternative; for doctorate, thesis/dissertation. *Entrance requirements:* For master's and doctorate, GRE General Test. Additional exam requirements/recommendations for international students: Required—TOEFL (minimum score 550 paper-based; 213 computer-based; 80 iBT). *Application deadline:* For fall

Environmental Sciences

Tufts University (continued)

admission, 1/15 priority date for domestic students, 12/15 for international students; for spring admission, 10/15 for domestic students, 9/15 for international students. Applications are processed on a rolling basis. Application fee: $75. Electronic applications accepted. *Expenses:* Tuition: Full-time $38,096; part-time $3962 per credit. Required fees: $686; $40 per year. Tuition and fees vary according to course level, course load, degree level, program and student level. *Financial support:* Fellowships with full tuition reimbursements, research assistantships with full and partial tuition reimbursements, teaching assistantships with full and partial tuition reimbursements, Federal Work-Study, scholarships/grants, tuition waivers (partial), and unspecified assistantships available. Financial award application deadline: 1/15; financial award applicants required to submit FAFSA. *Unit head:* Dr. Kurt Penell, Chair, 617-627-3211, Fax: 617-627-3994. *Application contact:* Laura Sacco, Information Contact, 617-627-3211.

Tulane University, School of Science and Engineering, Department of Earth and Environmental Sciences, New Orleans, LA 70118-5669. Offers MS, PhD. *Degree requirements:* For master's, one foreign language, thesis or alternative; for doctorate, one foreign language, thesis/dissertation. *Entrance requirements:* For master's, GRE General Test, minimum B average in undergraduate course work; for doctorate, GRE General Test. Additional exam requirements/recommendations for international students: Required—TOEFL. Electronic applications accepted. *Faculty research:* Sedimentation, isotopes, biogeochemistry, marine geology, structural geology.

Tuskegee University, Graduate Programs, College of Agricultural, Environmental and Natural Sciences, Department of Agricultural Sciences, Program in Environmental Sciences, Tuskegee, AL 36088. Offers MS. *Faculty:* 13 full-time (1 woman), 2 part-time/adjunct (1 woman). *Students:* 4 full-time (2 women); includes 2 African Americans, 2 international. Average age 31. In 2009, 4 master's awarded. *Degree requirements:* For master's, thesis. *Entrance requirements:* For master's, GRE General Test. Additional exam requirements/recommendations for international students: Required—TOEFL (minimum score 500 paper-based; 69 computer-based). *Application deadline:* For fall admission, 7/15 for domestic students. Applications are processed on a rolling basis. Application fee: $25 ($35 for international students). *Expenses:* Tuition: Full-time $15,630; part-time $940 per credit hour. Required fees: $650. *Financial support:* Application deadline: 4/15. *Unit head:* Dr. P. K. Biswas, Head, 334-727-8446. *Application contact:* Dr. Robert L. Laney, Vice President/Director of Admissions and Enrollment Management, 334-727-8580, Fax: 334-727-5750, E-mail: planey@tuskegee.edu.

Universidad del Turabo, Graduate Programs, Programs in Science and Technology, Gurabo, PR 00778-3030. Offers environmental analysis (MSE), including environmental chemistry; environmental management (MSE), including pollution management; environmental science (D Sc), including environmental biology. *Students:* 8 full-time (7 women), 110 part-time (76 women); includes 115 Hispanic Americans. Average age 37. 52 applicants, 65% accepted, 30 enrolled. In 2009, 6 master's awarded. *Entrance requirements:* For master's, GRE, EXADEP, interview. *Application deadline:* For fall admission, 8/5 for domestic students. Application fee: $25. *Application contact:* Virginia Gonzalez, Admissions Officer, 787-746-3009.

Université de Sherbrooke, Faculty of Sciences, Centre Universitaire de Formation en Environnement, Sherbrooke, QC J1K 2R1, Canada. Offers M Sc, Diploma. Postbaccalaureate distance learning degree programs offered (no on-campus study). Electronic applications accepted. *Faculty research:* Environmental studies.

Université du Québec à Montréal, Graduate Programs, Program in Environmental Sciences, Montréal, QC H3C 3P8, Canada. Offers M Sc, PhD, Certificate. Part-time programs available. *Degree requirements:* For master's, research report; for doctorate, thesis/dissertation. *Entrance requirements:* For master's, appropriate bachelor's degree or equivalent, proficiency in French; for doctorate, appropriate master's degree or equivalent, proficiency in French.

Université du Québec à Trois-Rivières, Graduate Programs, Program in Environmental Sciences, Trois-Rivières, QC G9A 5H7, Canada. Offers M Sc, PhD. Part-time programs available. *Degree requirements:* For master's, thesis. *Entrance requirements:* For master's, appropriate bachelor's degree, proficiency in French.

Université du Québec en Abitibi-Témiscamingue, Graduate Programs, Program in Environmental Sciences, Rouyn-Noranda, QC J9X 5E4, Canada. Offers biology (MS); environmental sciences (PhD); sustainable forest ecosystem management (MS).

Université Laval, Faculty of Sciences and Engineering, Department of Geology and Geological Engineering, Programs in Earth Sciences, Québec, QC G1K 7P4, Canada. Offers earth sciences (M Sc, PhD); environmental technologies (M Sc). Offered jointly with INRS-Géressources. Terminal master's awarded for partial completion of doctoral program. *Degree requirements:* For master's, thesis (for some programs); for doctorate, comprehensive exam, thesis/dissertation. *Entrance requirements:* For master's and doctorate, knowledge of French. Electronic applications accepted.

University at Albany, State University of New York, College of Arts and Sciences, Department of Biological Sciences, Program in Biodiversity, Conservation, and Policy, Albany, NY 12222-0001. Offers MS. *Degree requirements:* For master's, one foreign language. *Entrance requirements:* For master's, GRE General Test. *Faculty research:* Aquatic ecology, plant community ecology, biodiversity and public policy, restoration ecology, coastal and estuarine science.

University at Buffalo, the State University of New York, Graduate School, College of Arts and Sciences, Department of Geography, Buffalo, NY 14260. Offers earth systems science (MA); economic geography and international business and world trade (MA); environmental and earth systems science (MS); environmental modeling and analysis (MA); geographic information science (MA, Certificate); geographic information systems and science (MS); geography (MA, PhD); urban and regional geography (MA); MA/MBA. *Faculty:* 14 full-time (6 women), 2 part-time/adjunct (0 women). *Students:* 63 full-time (16 women), 32 part-time (8 women); includes 31 minority (3 African Americans, 26 Asian Americans or Pacific Islanders, 2 Hispanic Americans), 3 international. Average age 29. 154 applicants, 42% accepted, 24 enrolled. In 2009, 18 master's, 6 doctorates awarded. *Degree requirements:* For master's, thesis (for some programs), project; for doctorate, thesis/dissertation. *Entrance requirements:* For master's, GRE General Test, minimum GPA of 2.9; for doctorate, GRE General Test, minimum GPA of 3.0. Additional exam requirements/recommendations for international students: Required—TOEFL (minimum score 550 paper-based; 213 computer-based; 79 iBT). *Application deadline:* For fall admission, 7/1 priority date for domestic students, 1/10 priority date for international students; for spring admission, 12/1 priority date for domestic students, 10/1 priority date for international students. Applications are processed on a rolling basis. Application fee: $75. Electronic applications accepted. *Financial support:* In 2009–10, 19 students received support, including 6 fellowships with full tuition reimbursements available (averaging $4,333 per year), 14 teaching assistantships with full tuition reimbursements available (averaging $13,361 per year); research assistantships with full tuition reimbursements available, career-related internships or fieldwork, Federal Work-Study, institutionally sponsored loans, traineeships, health care benefits, and unspecified assistantships also available. Financial award application deadline: 1/10. *Faculty research:* International business and world trade, geographic information systems and cartography, transportation, urban and regional analysis, physical and environmental geography. Total annual research expenditures: $944,614. *Unit head:* Dr. Peter Rogerson, Chairman, 716-645-0473, Fax: 716-645-2329, E-mail: rogerson@buffalo.edu. *Application contact:* Betsy Abraham, Graduate Secretary, 716-645-0471, Fax: 716-645-2329, E-mail: babraham@buffalo.edu.

The University of Alabama in Huntsville, School of Graduate Studies, College of Science, Department of Atmospheric and Environmental Science, Huntsville, AL 35899. Offers MS, PhD. Part-time and evening/weekend programs available. *Faculty:* 8 full-time (0 women), 1 part-time/adjunct (0 women). *Students:* 31 full-time (14 women), 12 part-time (4 women); includes 3 minority (2 African Americans, 1 Hispanic American), 9 international. Average age 28. 25 applicants, 80% accepted, 8 enrolled. In 2009, 15 master's, 3 doctorates awarded. *Degree requirements:* For master's, comprehensive exam, thesis or alternative, oral and written exams; for doctorate, comprehensive exam, thesis/dissertation, oral and written exams. *Entrance requirements:* For master's, GRE General Test, minimum GPA of 3.0; sequence of courses in calculus (including the calculus of vector-valued functions); course in linear algebra; course in ordinary differential equations; two semesters of chemistry; two semesters of calculus-based physics; proficiency in at least one high-level computer programming language; for doctorate, GRE General Test, minimum GPA of 3.0. Additional exam requirements/recommendations for international students: Required—TOEFL (minimum score 550 paper-based; 213 computer-based; 62 iBT). *Application deadline:* For fall admission, 7/15 for domestic students, 4/1 for international students; for spring admission, 11/30 for domestic students, 9/1 for international students. Applications are processed on a rolling basis. Application fee: $40 ($50 for international students). Electronic applications accepted. *Expenses:* Tuition, state resident: part-time $355.75 per credit hour. Tuition, nonresident: part-time $847.10 per credit hour. Required fees: $210.80 per semester. Tuition and fees vary according to course load and program. *Financial support:* In 2009–10, 34 students received support, including 32 research assistantships with full and partial tuition reimbursements available (averaging $1,480 per year), 1 teaching assistantship with full and partial tuition reimbursement available (averaging $13,500 per year); career-related internships or fieldwork, Federal Work-Study, institutionally sponsored loans, scholarships/grants, health care benefits, tuition waivers, and unspecified assistantships also available. Support available to part-time students. Financial award application deadline: 4/1; financial award applicants required to submit FAFSA. *Faculty research:* Satellite remote sensing, severe weather, mesoscale modeling, atmospheric chemistry, data assimilation. Total annual research expenditures: $10.7 million. *Unit head:* Dr. John Christy, Chair, 256-922-7789, Fax: 256-922-7755, E-mail: christy@nsstc.uah.edu. *Application contact:* Kathy Biggs, Graduate Studies Admissions Manager, 256-824-6199, Fax: 256-824-6405, E-mail: deangrad@uah.edu.

University of Alaska Anchorage, School of Engineering, Program in Applied Environmental Science and Technology, Anchorage, AK 99508. Offers M AEST, MS. Part-time and evening/weekend programs available. *Degree requirements:* For master's, comprehensive exam, thesis (for some programs). *Entrance requirements:* For master's, GRE General Test. Additional exam requirements/recommendations for international students: Required—TOEFL (minimum score 550 paper-based; 213 computer-based). *Faculty research:* Wastewater treatment, environmental regulations, water resources management, justification of public facilities, rural sanitation, biological treatment process.

University of Alaska Fairbanks, College of Engineering and Mines, Department of Civil and Environmental Engineering, Program in Environmental Engineering, Fairbanks, AK 99775-5900. Offers engineering (PhD), including environmental engineering; environmental engineering (MS), including environmental contaminants, environmental science and management, water supply and waste treatment. Part-time programs available. *Students:* 4 full-time (3 women), 3 part-time (2 women). Average age 28. 5 applicants, 60% accepted, 1 enrolled. In 2009, 3 master's, 1 doctorate awarded. *Degree requirements:* For master's, comprehensive exam, thesis or alternative; for doctorate, comprehensive exam, thesis/dissertation, oral exam, oral defense. *Entrance requirements:* For master's, basic computer techniques; for doctorate, GRE General Test. Additional exam requirements/recommendations for international students: Required—TOEFL (minimum score 575 paper-based; 213 computer-based). *Application deadline:* For fall admission, 5/1 for domestic students, 3/1 for international students; for spring admission, 10/15 for domestic students, 9/1 for international students. Applications are processed on a rolling basis. Application fee: $60. Electronic applications accepted. *Expenses:* Tuition, state resident: full-time $7584; part-time $316 per credit. Tuition, nonresident: full-time $15,504; part-time $646 per credit. Required fees: $23 per credit. $135 per semester. Tuition and fees vary according to course level, course load and reciprocity agreements. *Financial support:* In 2009–10, 4 research assistantships (averaging $13,290 per year), 1 teaching assistantship (averaging $7,088 per year) were awarded; fellowships, career-related internships or fieldwork, Federal Work-Study, scholarships/grants, health care benefits, and unspecified assistantships also available. Support available to part-time students. Financial award application deadline: 7/1; financial award applicants required to submit FAFSA. *Unit head:* Dr. David Barnes, Department Chair, 907-474-7241, Fax: 907-474-6087, E-mail: fyeqe@uaf.edu. *Application contact:* Dr. David Barnes, Department Chair, 907-474-7241, Fax: 907-474-6087, E-mail: fyeqe@uaf.edu.

University of Alaska Fairbanks, College of Engineering and Mines, Department of Civil and Environmental Engineering, Program in Environmental Quality Science, Fairbanks, AK 99775-5900. Offers MS. Part-time programs available. *Students:* 2 full-time (both women). Average age 24. 2 applicants, 0% accepted, 0 enrolled. *Degree requirements:* For master's, comprehensive exam, thesis or alternative. *Entrance requirements:* For master's, calculus, chemistry, basic computer techniques. Additional exam requirements/recommendations for international students: Required—TOEFL (minimum score 575 paper-based; 213 computer-based). *Application deadline:* For fall admission, 6/1 for domestic students, 3/1 for international students; for spring admission, 10/15 for domestic students, 9/1 for international students. Applications are processed on a rolling basis. Application fee: $60. Electronic applications accepted. *Expenses:* Tuition, state resident: full-time $7584; part-time $316 per credit. Tuition, nonresident: full-time $15,504; part-time $646 per credit. Required fees: $23 per credit. $135 per semester. Tuition and fees vary according to course level, course load and reciprocity agreements. *Financial support:* Fellowships, research assistantships, teaching assistantships, career-related internships or fieldwork, Federal Work-Study, scholarships/grants, health care benefits, and unspecified assistantships available. Support available to part-time students. Financial award application deadline: 7/1; financial award applicants required to submit FAFSA. *Unit head:* Dr. David Barnes, Department Chair, 907-474-7241, Fax: 907-474-6087, E-mail: fyeqe@uaf.edu. *Application contact:* Dr. David Barnes, Department Chair, 907-474-7241, Fax: 907-474-6087, E-mail: fyeqe@uaf.edu.

University of Alaska Fairbanks, College of Natural Sciences and Mathematics, Department of Chemistry and Biochemistry, Fairbanks, AK 99775-6160. Offers biochemistry and molecular biology (MS, PhD); chemistry (MA, MS); environmental chemistry (MS, PhD). Part-time programs available. *Faculty:* 12 full-time (4 women), 2 part-time/adjunct (1 woman). *Students:* 32 full-time (21 women), 9 part-time (5 women); includes 9 minority (2 African Americans, 2 American Indian/Alaska Native, 2 Asian Americans or Pacific Islanders, 3 Hispanic Americans), 5 international. Average age 35. 26 applicants, 38% accepted, 8 enrolled. In 2009, 3 master's, 3 doctorates awarded. *Degree requirements:* For master's, comprehensive exam, thesis or alternative; for doctorate, comprehensive exam, thesis/dissertation, oral defense. *Entrance requirements:* Additional exam requirements/recommendations for international students: Required—TOEFL (minimum score 550 paper-based; 213 computer-based). *Application deadline:* For fall admission, 6/1 for domestic students, 3/1 for international students; for spring admission, 10/15 for domestic students, 9/1 for international students. Applications are processed on a rolling basis. Application fee: $60. Electronic applications accepted. *Expenses:* Tuition, state resident: full-time $7584; part-time $316 per credit. Tuition, nonresident: full-time $15,504; part-time $646 per credit. Required fees: $23 per credit. $135 per semester. Tuition and fees vary according to course level, course load and reciprocity agreements. *Financial support:* In 2009–10, 1 fellowship (averaging $13,500 per year), 15 research assistantships (averaging $14,179 per year), 11 teaching assistantships (averaging $13,937 per year) were awarded; Federal Work-Study, scholarships/grants, health care benefits, and unspecified assistantships also available. Support available to part-time students. Financial award application deadline: 7/1; financial award applicants required to submit FAFSA. *Faculty research:* Atmospheric aerosols, cold adaptation, hibernation and neuroprotection, liganogated ion channels, arctic contaminants. *Unit head:* Dr. John Keller, Department Chair, 907-474-5510, Fax: 907-474-5640, E-mail: fychem@uaf.edu. *Application contact:* Dr. John Keller, Department Chair, 907-474-5510, Fax: 907-474-5640, E-mail: fychem@uaf.edu.

University of Alberta, Faculty of Graduate Studies and Research, Department of Civil and Environmental Engineering, Edmonton, AB T6G 2E1, Canada. Offers construction engineering and management (M Eng, M Sc, PhD); environmental engineering (M Eng, M Sc, PhD); environmental science (M Sc, PhD); geoenvironmental engineering (M Eng, M Sc, PhD); geotechnical engineering (M Eng, M Sc, PhD); mining engineering (M Eng, M Sc, PhD); petroleum engineering (M Eng, M Sc, PhD); structural engineering (M Eng, M Sc, PhD); water resources (M Eng, M Sc, PhD). Part-time programs available. Postbaccalaureate distance learning degree programs offered (minimal on-campus study). *Faculty:* 44 full-time (3 women), 2 part-time/adjunct (0 women). *Students:* 215 full-time (49 women), 99 part-time (19 women). 1,428 applicants, 15% accepted, 123 enrolled. In 2009, 124 master's, 34 doctorates awarded. *Degree requirements:* For master's, thesis (for some programs); for doctorate, thesis/dissertation. *Entrance requirements:* For master's, minimum GPA of 3.0 in last 2 years of undergraduate studies; for doctorate, minimum GPA of 3.0. Additional exam requirements/recommendations for international students: Required—TOEFL (minimum score 550 paper-based; 213 computer-based). *Application deadline:* For fall admission, 6/1 priority date for domestic students, 6/1 for international students; for winter admission, 11/1 for domestic students, 9/15 for international students. Applications are processed on a rolling basis. Application fee: $0 Canadian dollars. Electronic applications accepted. Tuition and fees charges are reported in Canadian dollars. *Expenses:* Tuition, area resident: Full-time $4626.24 Canadian dollars; part-time $99.72 Canadian dollars per unit. International tuition: $8216 Canadian dollars full-time. Required fees: $3589.92 Canadian dollars; $99.72 Canadian dollars per unit. $215 Canadian dollars per term. *Financial support:* In 2009–10, 88 research assistantships with full and partial tuition reimbursements, 134 teaching assistantships with full and partial tuition reimbursements were awarded; scholarships/grants and tuition waivers (full and partial) also available. Financial award application deadline: 4/1. *Faculty research:* Mining. Total annual research expenditures: $6,791 Canadian dollars. *Unit head:* Dr. David Zhu, Associate Chair, Graduate Studies, 780-492-1198, Fax: 403-492-8198. *Application contact:* Gwen Mendoza, Student Services Officer, 403-492-1539, Fax: 403-492-0249, E-mail: civegrad@ualberta.ca.

The University of Arizona, Graduate College, College of Agriculture and Life Sciences, Department of Soil, Water and Environmental Science, Tucson, AZ 85721. Offers MS, PhD. *Faculty:* 11. *Students:* 50 full-time (33 women), 8 part-time (5 women); includes 14 minority (3 African Americans, 1 American Indian/Alaska Native, 10 Hispanic Americans), 16 international. Average age 32. 37 applicants, 54% accepted, 13 enrolled. In 2009, 12 master's, 6 doctorates awarded. *Degree requirements:* For master's, thesis; for doctorate, comprehensive exam, thesis/dissertation. *Entrance requirements:* For master's, GRE (recommended), minimum GPA of 3.0, letter of interest, 3 letters of recommendation; for doctorate, GRE (recommended), MS, minimum GPA of 3.0, letter of interest, 3 letters of recommendation. Additional exam requirements/recommendations for international students: Required—TOEFL (minimum score 550 paper-based; 213 computer-based; 80 iBT). *Application deadline:* For fall admission, 6/1 for domestic students, 12/1 for international students; for spring admission, 10/1 for domestic students, 6/1 for international students. Applications are processed on a rolling basis. Application fee: $75. *Expenses:* Tuition, state resident: full-time $9028. Tuition, nonresident: full-time $24,890. *Financial support:* In 2009–10, 14 students received support, including 25 research assistantships with full and partial tuition reimbursements available (averaging $18,090 per year), 5 teaching assistantships with full and partial tuition reimbursements available (averaging $17,669 per year); fellowships, Federal Work-Study, institutionally sponsored loans, scholarships/grants, health care benefits, tuition waivers (full and partial), and unspecified assistantships also available. Financial award application deadline: 5/1. *Faculty research:* Plant production, environmental microbiology, contaminant flow and transport, aquaculture. Total annual research expenditures: $3.6 million. *Unit head:* Dr. Jeffery C. Silvertooth, Head, 520-621-7228, Fax: 520-621-1647, E-mail: silver@ag.arizona.edu. *Application contact:* Alicia Velasquez, 520-621-1606, Fax: 520-621-1647, E-mail: avelasqu@ag.arizona.edu.

The University of Arizona, Graduate College, College of Agriculture and Life Sciences, Graduate Interdisciplinary Program in Arid Lands Resource Sciences, Tucson, AZ 85721. Offers PhD. *Faculty:* 5. *Students:* 10 full-time (3 women), 20 part-time (10 women); includes 1 minority (American Indian/Alaska Native), 10 international. Average age 42. 7 applicants, 57% accepted, 4 enrolled. *Degree requirements:* For doctorate, one foreign language, comprehensive exam, thesis/dissertation. *Entrance requirements:* For doctorate, GRE. Additional exam requirements/recommendations for international students: Required—TOEFL (minimum score 550 paper-based; 213 computer-based). *Application deadline:* For fall admission, 2/15 priority date for domestic and international students; for spring admission, 8/1 priority date for domestic students, 8/15 priority date for international students. Applications are processed on a rolling basis. Application fee: $75. *Expenses:* Tuition, state resident: full-time $9028. Tuition, nonresident: full-time $24,890. *Financial support:* In 2009–10, 2 research assistantships with full tuition reimbursements (averaging $14,670 per year), 1 teaching assistantship with full tuition reimbursement (averaging $14,164 per year) were awarded; fellowships, career-related internships or fieldwork, scholarships/grants, health care benefits, and unspecified assistantships also available. Financial award application deadline: 4/1. *Faculty research:* International development; famine, famine early warning systems, and food security; land use, history, change, degradation, desertification, management, and policy; sustainable agriculture and farming systems; remote sensing and spatial analysis; carbon sequestration; political-ecology of natural resources; ethnoecology and other ethno-sciences; economic and agricultural policy and development; economic botany; borderlands issues; globalization; civil conflict; urban development. Total annual research expenditures: $2.3 million. *Unit head:* Dr. Stuart E. Marsh, Chair, 520-621-8574, E-mail: smarsh@ag.arizona.edu. *Application contact:* Anita E. Finnell, Graduate Coordinator, 520-621-9111, Fax: 520-621-3816, E-mail: alrsgidp@email.arizona.edu.

University of California, Berkeley, Graduate Division, College of Natural Resources, Department of Environmental Science, Policy, and Management, Berkeley, CA 94720-1500. Offers environmental science, policy, and management (MS, PhD); forestry (MF). *Students:* 270 full-time (185 women). Average age 31. 281 applicants, 27 enrolled. In 2009, 8 master's, 24 doctorates awarded. Terminal master's awarded for partial completion of doctoral program. *Degree requirements:* For master's, thesis optional; for doctorate, thesis/dissertation, qualifying exam. *Entrance requirements:* For master's and doctorate, GRE General Test, minimum GPA of 3.0, 3 letters of recommendation. Additional exam requirements/recommendations for international students: Required—TOEFL. *Application deadline:* For fall admission, 12/1 for domestic students. Application fee: $70 ($90 for international students). Electronic applications accepted. *Financial support:* Fellowships with full tuition reimbursements, research assistantships with full tuition reimbursements, teaching assistantships with full tuition reimbursements, unspecified assistantships available. Financial award application deadline: 12/1; financial award applicants required to submit FAFSA. *Faculty research:* Biology and ecology of insects; ecosystem function and environmental issues of soils; plant health/interactions from molecular to ecosystem levels; range management and ecology; forest and resource policy, sustainability, and management. *Unit head:* Prof. Allen Goldstein, Chair, 510-643-7430, Fax: 510-643-5438, E-mail: espmgrad@berkeley.edu. *Application contact:* Richard M. Battrick, Student Affairs Officer, 510-642-6410, Fax: 510-642-4034, E-mail: espmgrad@nature.berkeley.edu.

University of California, Davis, Graduate Studies, Graduate Group in Soils and Biogeochemistry, Davis, CA 95616. Offers MS, PhD. Terminal master's awarded for partial completion of doctoral program. *Degree requirements:* For master's, comprehensive exam (for some programs), thesis (for some programs); for doctorate, thesis/dissertation. *Entrance requirements:* For master's, minimum GPA of 3.3; for doctorate, GRE, minimum GPA of 3.3. Additional exam requirements/recommendations for international students: Required—TOEFL (minimum score 550 paper-based; 213 computer-based). Electronic applications accepted. *Faculty research:* Rhizosphere ecology, soil transport processes, biogeochemical cycling, sustainable agriculture.

University of California, Los Angeles, Graduate Division, School of Public Health, Department of Environmental Health Sciences, Los Angeles, CA 90095. Offers environmental health sciences (MS, PhD); environmental science and engineering (D Env); molecular toxicology (PhD); JD/MPH. *Accreditation:* ABET (one or more programs are accredited). *Degree requirements:* For master's, comprehensive exam or thesis; for doctorate, thesis/dissertation, oral and written qualifying exams. *Entrance requirements:* For master's, GRE General Test, minimum GPA of 3.0; for doctorate, GRE General Test, minimum undergraduate GPA of 3.0. Electronic applications accepted.

University of California, Los Angeles, Graduate Division, School of Public Health, Program in Environmental Science and Engineering, Los Angeles, CA 90095. Offers D Env. *Degree requirements:* For doctorate, thesis/dissertation, oral and written qualifying exams. *Entrance requirements:* For doctorate, GRE General Test, minimum undergraduate GPA of 3.0, master's degree or equivalent in a natural science, engineering, or public health. *Faculty research:* Toxic and hazardous substances, air and water pollution, risk assessment/management, water resources, marine science.

University of California, Merced, Division of Graduate Studies, School of Natural Sciences, Merced, CA 95343. Offers applied mathematics (MS, PhD); biological engineering and small-scale technologies (MS, PhD); environmental systems (MS, PhD); mechanical engineering and applied mechanics (MS, PhD); physics and chemistry (PhD); quantitative and systems biology (MS, PhD). *Expenses:* Tuition, nonresident: full-time $15,102. Required fees: $10,919.

University of California, Riverside, Graduate Division, Graduate Materials Science and Engineering Program, Riverside, CA 92521-0102. Offers MS, PhD.

University of California, Santa Barbara, Graduate Division, Donald Bren School of Environmental Science and Management, Santa Barbara, CA 93106-5131. Offers MESM, PhD. *Faculty:* 18 full-time (4 women), 24 part-time/adjunct (7 women). *Students:* 187 full-time (112 women); includes 21 minority (1 African American, 1 American Indian/Alaska Native, 11 Asian Americans or Pacific Islanders, 8 Hispanic Americans), 15 international. Average age 27. 335 applicants, 61% accepted, 89 enrolled. In 2009, 63 master's, 8 doctorates awarded. *Degree requirements:* For master's, thesis optional, group project as student thesis; for doctorate, comprehensive exam, thesis/dissertation. *Entrance requirements:* For master's, GRE, 3 letters of recommendation, resume/curriculum vitae; for doctorate, GRE, 3 letters of recommendation, statement of purpose, personal achievements/contributions statement, resume/curriculum vitae, transcripts for post-secondary institutions attended. Additional exam requirements/recommendations for international students: Required—TOEFL (minimum score 550 paper-based; 213 computer-based; 80 iBT), or IELTS (minimum score 7). *Application deadline:* For fall admission, 1/10 priority date for domestic and international students. Application fee: $70 ($90 for international students). Electronic applications accepted. *Financial support:* In 2009–10, 68 students received support, including 44 fellowships with full and partial tuition reimbursements available (averaging $8,400 per year), 20 research assistantships with full and partial tuition reimbursements available (averaging $6,600 per year), 28 teaching assistantships with partial tuition reimbursements available (averaging $6,900 per year); career-related internships or fieldwork, Federal Work-Study, institutionally sponsored loans, scholarships/grants, health care benefits, and unspecified assistantships also available. Financial award application deadline: 12/15; financial award applicants required to submit FAFSA. *Faculty research:* Ecological processes, environmental politics and policy, sustainability, conservation science and planning, water resources management. *Unit head:* Dr. John Melack, Acting Dean, 805-893-3879, Fax: 805-893-6113, E-mail: melack@bren.ucsb.edu. *Application contact:* Kristen Robinson, Graduate Program Advisor, 805-893-7611, Fax: 805-893-6113, E-mail: gradasst@bren.ucsb.edu.

University of Chicago, Irving B. Harris Graduate School of Public Policy Studies, Chicago, IL 60637-1513. Offers environmental science and policy (MS); public policy studies (AM, MPP, PhD); JD/MPP; MBA/MPP; MPP/M Div; MPP/MA. Part-time programs available. *Degree requirements:* For doctorate, thesis/dissertation. *Entrance requirements:* Additional exam requirements/recommendations for international students: Required—TOEFL. Electronic applications accepted. *Expenses:* Contact institution. *Faculty research:* Family and child policy, international security, health policy, social policy.

University of Cincinnati, Graduate School, College of Engineering, Department of Civil and Environmental Engineering, Program in Environmental Sciences, Cincinnati, OH 45221. Offers MS, PhD. Part-time programs available. *Degree requirements:* For master's, thesis or alternative; for doctorate, one foreign language, thesis/dissertation. *Entrance requirements:* For master's and doctorate, GRE General Test. Additional exam requirements/recommendations for international students: Required—TOEFL (minimum score 580 paper-based; 237 computer-based; 92 iBT). Electronic applications accepted. *Faculty research:* Environmental microbiology, solid-waste management, air pollution control, water pollution control, aerosols.

University of Colorado at Colorado Springs, Graduate School, College of Letters, Arts and Sciences, Department of Geography and Environmental Studies, Colorado Springs, CO 80933-7150. Offers MA. Part-time programs available. *Faculty:* 11 full-time (2 women), 1 part-time/adjunct (0 women). *Students:* 11 full-time (2 women), 6 part-time (2 women); includes 1 minority (Hispanic American). Average age 36. 13 applicants, 85% accepted, 8 enrolled. In 2009, 3 master's awarded. *Degree requirements:* For master's, thesis (for some programs). *Entrance requirements:* For master's, GRE. *Application deadline:* For fall admission, 4/1 for domestic students. Application fee: $60. *Expenses:* Tuition, state resident: full-time $8922; part-time $639 per credit hour. Tuition, nonresident: full-time $19,372; part-time $1154 per credit hour. Tuition and fees vary according to course level, course load, degree level, program, reciprocity agreements and student level. *Financial support:* Federal Work-Study and scholarships/grants available. Support available to part-time students. Financial award application deadline: 3/1; financial award applicants required to submit FAFSA. *Faculty research:* Natural hazard mitigation and policy issues, applied geography, geographic information systems, population geography. *Unit head:* Dr. Robert Larkin, Associate Professor, 719-255-4053, Fax: 719-255-4066, E-mail: rlarkin@uccs.edu. *Application contact:* Mary McGill, Program Assistant, 719-255-3016, E-mail: mmcgill@uccs.edu.

University of Colorado Denver, College of Liberal Arts and Sciences, Department of Environmental Sciences, Denver, CO 80217-3364. Offers MS. Part-time and evening/weekend programs available. *Students:* 26 full-time (15 women), 30 part-time (17 women); includes 6 minority (1 African American, 2 Asian Americans or Pacific Islanders, 3 Hispanic Americans), 5 international. 35 applicants, 57% accepted, 14 enrolled. In 2009, 13 master's awarded. *Degree requirements:* For master's, thesis or alternative. *Entrance requirements:* For master's, GRE General Test. Additional exam requirements/recommendations for international students: Required—TOEFL (minimum score 525 paper-based; 197 computer-based). *Application deadline:* For fall admission, 4/1 for domestic students; for spring admission, 10/1 for domestic students. Applications are processed on a rolling basis. Application fee: $50 ($75 for international students). Electronic applications accepted. *Financial support:* Research assistantships, teaching assistantships, Federal Work-Study available. Financial award application deadline: 4/1; financial award applicants required to submit FAFSA. *Unit head:* Dr. John Wyckoff, Director, 303-556-2590, Fax: 303-556-6197, E-mail: john.wyckoff@cudenver.edu. *Application contact:* Dr. John Wyckoff, Director, 303-556-2590, Fax: 303-556-6197, E-mail: john.wyckoff@cudenver.edu.

Environmental Sciences

University of Guam, Office of Graduate Studies, College of Natural and Applied Sciences, Program in Environmental Science, Mangilao, GU 96923. Offers MS. Part-time programs available. *Degree requirements:* For master's, thesis. *Entrance requirements:* For master's, GRE General Test. Additional exam requirements/recommendations for international students: Required—TOEFL. *Faculty research:* Water resources, ecology, karst formations, hydrogeology, meteorology.

University of Guelph, Graduate Program Services, Ontario Agricultural College, Department of Land Resource Science, Guelph, ON N1G 2W1, Canada. Offers atmospheric science (M Sc, PhD); environmental and agricultural earth sciences (M Sc, PhD); land resources management (M Sc, PhD); soil science (M Sc, PhD). Part-time programs available. *Degree requirements:* For master's, thesis (for some programs), research project (non-thesis track); for doctorate, comprehensive exam, thesis/dissertation. *Entrance requirements:* For master's, minimum B- average during previous 2 years of course work; for doctorate, minimum B average during previous 2 years of course work. Additional exam requirements/recommendations for international students: Required—TOEFL (minimum score 550 paper-based; 213 computer-based). Electronic applications accepted. *Faculty research:* Soil science, environmental earth science, land resource management.

University of Hawaii at Hilo, Program in Tropical Conservation Biology and Environmental Science, Hilo, HI 96720-4091. Offers MS.

University of Houston–Clear Lake, School of Science and Computer Engineering, Program in Environmental Science, Houston, TX 77058-1098. Offers MS. Part-time and evening/weekend programs available. *Entrance requirements:* For master's, GRE General Test. Additional exam requirements/recommendations for international students: Required—TOEFL (minimum score 550 paper-based; 213 computer-based).

University of Idaho, College of Graduate Studies, Program in Environmental Science, Moscow, ID 83844-2282. Offers MS, PhD. *Students:* 37 full-time (17 women), 35 part-time (22 women). In 2009, 3 doctorates awarded. *Application deadline:* For fall admission, 8/1 for domestic students; for spring admission, 12/15 for domestic students. Applications are processed on a rolling basis. Application fee: $55 ($60 for international students). *Expenses:* Tuition, state resident: full-time $6120. Tuition, nonresident: full-time $17,712. *Financial support:* Research assistantships, teaching assistantships available. Financial award application deadline: 2/15. *Unit head:* Dr. Stephen S. Mulkey, Director, 208-885-6113, Fax: 208-885-6198, E-mail: uigrad@uidaho.edu. *Application contact:* Dr. Stephen S. Mulkey, Director, 208-885-6113, Fax: 208-885-6198, E-mail: uigrad@uidaho.edu.

University of Illinois at Springfield, Graduate Programs, College of Public Affairs and Administration, Program in Environmental Studies, Springfield, IL 62703-5407. Offers environmental science (MS); environmental studies (MA). Part-time and evening/weekend programs available. Postbaccalaureate distance learning degree programs offered (no on-campus study). *Faculty:* 4 full-time (1 woman), 3 part-time/adjunct (0 women). *Students:* 13 full-time (7 women), 77 part-time (50 women); includes 5 minority (1 African American, 2 Asian Americans or Pacific Islanders, 2 Hispanic Americans), 2 international. Average age 36. 76 applicants, 55% accepted, 26 enrolled. In 2009, 7 master's awarded. *Degree requirements:* For master's, thesis or project. *Entrance requirements:* For master's, minimum undergraduate GPA of 3.0, 2 letters of recommendation. Additional exam requirements/recommendations for international students: Required—TOEFL (minimum score 500 paper-based; 176 computer-based; 61 iBT). *Application deadline:* Applications are processed on a rolling basis. Application fee: $50 ($60 for international students). Electronic applications accepted. *Expenses:* Tuition, state resident: full-time $6390; part-time $266.25 per credit hour. Tuition, nonresident: full-time $14,226; part-time $592.75 per credit hour. Required fees: $2044; $14.36 per credit hour. $722.50 per term. *Financial support:* In 2009–10, research assistantships with full tuition reimbursements (averaging $8,109 per year), teaching assistantships with full tuition reimbursements (averaging $8,109 per year) were awarded; career-related internships or fieldwork, Federal Work-Study, scholarships/grants, health care benefits, and unspecified assistantships also available. Support available to part-time students. Financial award application deadline: 11/15; financial award applicants required to submit FAFSA. *Unit head:* Dr. Dennis Ruez, Program Administrator, 217-206-8424, E-mail: druez2@uis.edu. *Application contact:* Dr. Lynn Pardie, Office of Graduate Studies, 800-252-8533, Fax: 217-206-7623, E-mail: pardie.lynn@uis.edu.

University of Illinois at Urbana–Champaign, Graduate College, College of Agricultural, Consumer and Environmental Sciences, Department of Natural Resources and Environmental Science, Champaign, IL 61820. Offers MS, PhD, MS/JD. Part-time programs available. Postbaccalaureate distance learning degree programs offered (no on-campus study). *Faculty:* 24 full-time (6 women), 1 part-time/adjunct (0 women). *Students:* 70 full-time (27 women), 47 part-time (26 women); includes 6 minority (3 Asian Americans or Pacific Islanders, 3 Hispanic Americans), 25 international. 102 applicants, 46% accepted, 32 enrolled. In 2009, 21 master's, 9 doctorates awarded. *Entrance requirements:* For master's and doctorate, GRE, minimum GPA of 3.0. Additional exam requirements/recommendations for international students: Required—TOEFL (minimum score 600 paper-based; 250 computer-based). *Application deadline:* Applications are processed on a rolling basis. Application fee: $60 ($75 for international students). Electronic applications accepted. *Financial support:* In 2009–10, 8 fellowships, 59 research assistantships, 20 teaching assistantships were awarded; tuition waivers (full and partial) also available. *Unit head:* Jeffrey D. Brawn, Head, 217-244-5937, Fax: 217-244-3219, E-mail: jbrawn@illinois.edu. *Application contact:* Karen M. Claus, Secretary, 217-333-5824, Fax: 217-244-3219, E-mail: kclaus@illinois.edu.

University of Illinois at Urbana–Champaign, Graduate College, College of Engineering, Department of Civil and Environmental Engineering, Champaign, IL 61820. Offers civil engineering (MS); environmental engineering in civil engineering (MS, PhD); environmental science in civil engineering (MS, PhD); M Arch/MS; MBA/MS. *Faculty:* 48 full-time (6 women), 4 part-time/adjunct (1 woman). *Students:* 349 full-time (88 women), 69 part-time (23 women); includes 37 minority (3 African Americans, 22 Asian Americans or Pacific Islanders, 12 Hispanic Americans), 212 international. 803 applicants, 35% accepted, 140 enrolled. In 2009, 83 master's, 24 doctorates awarded. *Entrance requirements:* For master's and doctorate, GRE. Additional exam requirements/recommendations for international students: Required—TOEFL (minimum score 550 paper-based; 213 computer-based; 79 iBT), or IELTS (minimum score 6.5). *Application deadline:* Applications are processed on a rolling basis. Application fee: $60 ($75 for international students). Electronic applications accepted. *Financial support:* In 2009–10, 58 fellowships, 253 research assistantships, 66 teaching assistantships were awarded; tuition waivers (full and partial) also available. *Unit head:* Amr S. Elnashai, Head, 217-265-5497, Fax: 217-265-8040, E-mail: aelnash@illinois.edu. *Application contact:* Mary Pearson, Administrative Secretary, 217-333-3811, Fax: 217-333-9464, E-mail: mkpearso@illinois.edu.

The University of Kansas, Graduate Studies, School of Engineering, Department of Civil, Environmental, and Architectural Engineering, Program in Environmental Science, Lawrence, KS 66045. Offers MS, PhD. Part-time and evening/weekend programs available. *Faculty:* 9 full-time (1 woman), 1 part-time/adjunct (0 women). *Students:* 1 full-time (0 women), 2 part-time (0 women); includes 1 minority (American Indian/Alaska Native). Average age 32. 4 applicants, 75% accepted, 0 enrolled. In 2009, 2 master's awarded. *Degree requirements:* For master's, thesis or alternative, exam; for doctorate, comprehensive exam, thesis/dissertation. *Entrance requirements:* For master's, GRE, minimum GPA of 3.0; for doctorate, GRE, minimum GPA of 3.5. Additional exam requirements/recommendations for international students: Required—TOEFL. *Application deadline:* For fall admission, 3/1 priority date for domestic students, 3/15 priority date for international students; for spring admission, 12/1 priority date for domestic students, 8/15 priority date for international students. Applications are processed on a rolling basis. Application fee: $45 ($55 for international students). Electronic applications accepted. *Expenses:* Tuition, state resident: full-time $6492; part-time $270.50 per credit hour. Tuition, nonresident: full-time $15,510; part-time $646.25 per credit hour. Required fees: $847; $70.56 per credit hour. Tuition and fees vary according to course load and program. *Financial support:* Fellowships with full tuition reimbursements, research assistantships with full tuition reimbursements, teaching assistantships, career-related internships or fieldwork available. Financial award application deadline: 2/7. *Faculty research:* Water quality, water treatment, wastewater treatment, air quality, air pollution control, solid waste, hazardous waste, water resources engineering, water resources science. *Unit head:* Craig D. Adams, Professor and Chair, 785-864-2700, Fax: 785-864-5631, E-mail: adamscd@ku.edu. *Application contact:* Bruce M. McEnroe, Professor and Graduate Advisor, 785-864-2925, Fax: 785-864-5631, E-mail: mcenroe@ku.edu.

University of Lethbridge, School of Graduate Studies, Lethbridge, AB T1K 3M4, Canada. Offers accounting (MScM); addictions counseling (M Sc); agricultural biotechnology (M Sc); agricultural studies (M Sc, MA); anthropology (MA); archaeology (MA); art (MA, MFA); biochemistry (M Sc); biological sciences (M Sc); biomolecular science (PhD); biosystems and biodiversity (PhD); Canadian studies (MA); chemistry (M Sc); computer science (M Sc); computer science and geographical information science (M Sc); counseling psychology (M Ed); dramatic arts (MA); earth, space, and physical science (PhD); economics (MA); educational leadership (M Ed); English (MA); environmental science (M Sc); evolution and behavior (PhD); exercise science (M Sc); finance (MScM); French (MA); French/German (MA); French/Spanish (MA); general education (M Ed); general management (MScM); geography (M Sc, MA); German (MA); health science (M Sc); health sciences (MA); history (MA); human resource management and labour relations (MScM); individualized multidisciplinary (M Sc, MA); information systems (MScM); international management (MScM); kinesiology (M Sc, MA); management (M Sc, MA); marketing (MScM); mathematics (M Sc); music (M Mus, MA); Native American studies (MA); neuroscience (M Sc, PhD); new media (MA); nursing (M Sc); philosophy (MA); physics (M Sc); policy and strategy (MScM); political science (MA); psychology (M Sc, MA); religious studies (MA); social sciences (MA); sociology (MA); theatre and dramatic arts (MFA); theoretical and computational science (PhD); urban and regional studies (MA); women's studies (MA). Part-time and evening/weekend programs available. *Degree requirements:* For doctorate, comprehensive exam, thesis/dissertation. *Entrance requirements:* For master's, GMAT (M Sc in management), bachelor's degree in related field, minimum GPA of 3.0 during previous 20 graded semester courses, 2 years teaching or related experience (M Ed); for doctorate, master's degree, minimum graduate GPA of 3.5. Additional exam requirements/recommendations for international students: Required—TOEFL. *Faculty research:* Movement and brain plasticity, gibberellin physiology, photosynthesis, carbon cycling, molecular properties of main-group ring components.

University of Maine, Graduate School, College of Natural Sciences, Forestry, and Agriculture, Department of Biological Sciences, Program in Ecology and Environmental Science, Orono, ME 04469. Offers MS, PhD. Part-time programs available. *Students:* 28 full-time (23 women), 9 part-time (6 women). Average age 29. 67 applicants, 16% accepted, 10 enrolled. In 2009, 5 master's, 1 doctorate awarded. *Degree requirements:* For doctorate, thesis/dissertation. *Entrance requirements:* For master's and doctorate, GRE General Test. Additional exam requirements/recommendations for international students: Required—TOEFL. *Application deadline:* For fall admission, 2/1 priority date for domestic students. Applications are processed on a rolling basis. Application fee: $65. Electronic applications accepted. *Financial support:* Career-related internships or fieldwork, Federal Work-Study, institutionally sponsored loans, and tuition waivers (full) available. Financial award application deadline: 3/1. *Unit head:* Dr. Chris Cronan, Coordinator, 207-581-3235. *Application contact:* Scott G. Delcourt, Associate Dean of the Graduate School, 207-581-3291, Fax: 207-581-3232, E-mail: graduate@maine.edu.

University of Maine, Graduate School, College of Natural Sciences, Forestry, and Agriculture, Department of Plant, Soil, and Environmental Sciences, Orono, ME 04469. Offers biological sciences (PhD); ecology and environmental sciences (MS, PhD); forest resources (PhD); horticulture (MS); plant science (PhD); plant, soil, and environmental sciences (MS); resource utilization (MS). *Faculty:* 8 full-time (2 women), 9 part-time/adjunct (3 women). *Students:* 6 full-time (3 women), 3 part-time (2 women), 1 international. Average age 31. 6 applicants, 17% accepted, 0 enrolled. In 2009, 2 master's awarded. *Entrance requirements:* For master's and doctorate, GRE General Test. Additional exam requirements/recommendations for international students: Required—TOEFL. *Application deadline:* Applications are processed on a rolling basis. Application fee: $65. Electronic applications accepted. *Financial support:* In 2009–10, 16 research assistantships with tuition reimbursements (averaging $16,260 per year), 3 teaching assistantships with tuition reimbursements (averaging $12,790 per year) were awarded; scholarships/grants, tuition waivers (full and partial), and unspecified assistantships also available. *Unit head:* Dr. Gregory Porter, Chair, 207-581-2943, Fax: 207-581-3207. *Application contact:* Scott G. Delcourt, Associate Dean of the Graduate School, 207-581-3291, Fax: 207-581-3232, E-mail: graduate@maine.edu.

University of Manitoba, Faculty of Graduate Studies, Clayton H. Riddell Faculty of Environment, Earth, and Resources, Department of Environment and Geography, Winnipeg, MB R3T 2N2, Canada. Offers environment (M Env); environment and geography (M Sc); geography (MA, PhD). *Degree requirements:* For master's, thesis; for doctorate, one foreign language, thesis/dissertation.

University of Maryland, Baltimore, Graduate School, Program in Marine-Estuarine-Environmental Sciences, Baltimore, MD 21201. Offers MS, PhD. Part-time programs available. *Faculty:* 8. Terminal master's awarded for partial completion of doctoral program. *Degree requirements:* For master's, thesis, oral defense; for doctorate, comprehensive exam, thesis/dissertation, proposal defense, oral defense. *Entrance requirements:* For master's and doctorate, GRE General Test, minimum GPA of 3.0. Additional exam requirements/recommendations for international students: Required—TOEFL. *Application deadline:* For fall admission, 2/1 for domestic students, 1/1 for international students; for spring admission, 9/1 for domestic students. Applications are processed on a rolling basis. Application fee: $50. Electronic applications accepted. *Expenses:* Tuition, state resident: full-time $7290; part-time $405 per credit hour. Tuition, nonresident: full-time $12,780; part-time $710 per credit hour. Required fees: $774; $10 per credit hour. $297 per semester. Tuition and fees vary according to course load, degree level and program. *Financial support:* Fellowships with tuition reimbursements, research assistantships with tuition reimbursements, teaching assistantships with tuition reimbursements, scholarships/grants and unspecified assistantships available. *Unit head:* Dr. Kennedy T. Paynter, Director, 301-405-6938, Fax: 301-314-4139, E-mail: mees@umd.edu. *Application contact:* Dr. Kennedy T. Paynter, Director, 301-405-6938, Fax: 301-314-4139, E-mail: mees@umd.edu.

See Close-Up on page 169 and Display on page 161.

University of Maryland, Baltimore County, Graduate School, Program in Marine-Estuarine-Environmental Sciences, Baltimore, MD 21250. Offers MS, PhD. Part-time programs available. *Faculty:* 16. *Students:* 7 full-time (4 women), 1 part-time (0 women); includes 2 minority (1 African American, 1 Hispanic American), 1 international. 12 applicants, 8% accepted, 1 enrolled. In 2009, 1 doctorate awarded. *Degree requirements:* For master's, thesis, oral defense; for doctorate, comprehensive exam, thesis/dissertation, proposal defense, oral defense. *Entrance requirements:* For master's and doctorate, GRE General Test, minimum GPA of 3.0. Additional exam requirements/recommendations for international students: Required—TOEFL. *Application deadline:* For fall admission, 2/1 for domestic students, 1/1 for international students; for spring admission, 9/1 for domestic students. Applications are processed on a rolling basis. Application fee: $50. Electronic applications accepted. *Financial support:* In 2009–10, 3 fellowships with tuition reimbursements (averaging $22,500 per year), 2 research assistantships with tuition reimbursements (averaging $21,000 per year), 2 teaching assistantships with tuition reimbursements (averaging $20,000 per year) were awarded; career-related internships or fieldwork, scholarships/grants, and unspecified assistantships also available. Financial award application deadline: 12/1. *Unit head:* Dr. Kennedy T. Paynter, Director, 301-405-6938, Fax: 301-314-4139, E-mail: mees@umd.edu. *Application contact:* Dr. Kennedy T. Paynter, Director, 301-405-6938, Fax: 301-314-4139, E-mail: mees@umd.edu.

See Close-Up on page 169 and Display on page 161.

University of Maryland, College Park, Academic Affairs, College of Agriculture and Natural Resources, Department of Environmental Science and Technology, College Park, MD 20742. Offers MS, PhD. *Faculty:* 36 full-time (9 women), 4 part-time/adjunct (0 women). *Students:* 27 full-time (12 women), 2 part-time (0 women); includes 2 minority (1 African American, 1 Hispanic American), 5 international. 58 applicants, 36% accepted, 9 enrolled. In 2009, 1 master's, 7 doctorates awarded. *Application deadline:* For fall admission, 2/1 for domestic and international students; for spring admission, 8/15 for domestic students, 6/1 for international students. *Expenses:* Tuition, area resident: Part-time $471 per credit hour. Tuition, state resident: part-time $471 per credit hour. Tuition, nonresident: part-time $1016 per credit hour. Required fees: $337.04 per term. *Financial support:* In 2009–10, 1 fellowship with full tuition reimbursement (averaging $15,390 per year), 13 research assistantships (averaging $17,159 per year), 7 teaching assistantships (averaging $16,885 per year) were awarded. *Unit head:* Dr. Frank Coale, Chair, 301-405-1306, E-mail: fjcoale@umd.edu. *Application contact:* Dean of Graduate School, 301-405-0376, Fax: 301-314-9305.

University of Maryland, College Park, Academic Affairs, College of Chemical and Life Sciences, Program in Marine-Estuarine-Environmental Sciences, College Park, MD 20742. Offers MS, PhD. Intercampus, interdisciplinary program. Part-time programs available. *Faculty:* 133. *Students:* 114 (69 women); includes 9 minority (4 African Americans, 2 Asian Americans or Pacific Islanders, 3 Hispanic Americans), 24 international. 99 applicants, 33% accepted, 24 enrolled. In 2009, 21 master's, 11 doctorates awarded. Terminal master's awarded for partial completion of doctoral program. *Degree requirements:* For master's, thesis, oral defense; for doctorate, comprehensive exam, thesis/dissertation, proposal defense, oral defense. *Entrance requirements:* For master's and doctorate, GRE General Test, minimum GPA of 3.0. Additional exam requirements/recommendations for international students: Required—TOEFL. *Application deadline:* For fall admission, 2/1 for domestic and international students; for spring admission, 9/1 for domestic students, 6/1 for international students. Applications are processed on a rolling basis. Application fee: $60. Electronic applications accepted. *Expenses:* Tuition, area resident: Part-time $471 per credit hour. Tuition, state resident: part-time $471 per credit hour. Tuition, nonresident: part-time $1016 per credit hour. Required fees: $337.04 per term. *Financial support:* In 2009–10, 9 teaching assistantships with full tuition reimbursements were awarded; fellowships with full tuition reimbursements, research assistantships with full tuition reimbursements, Federal Work-Study, scholarships/grants, traineeships, health care benefits, and unspecified assistantships also available. Financial award application deadline: 1/1; financial award applicants required to submit FAFSA. *Faculty research:* Marine and estuarine organisms, terrestrial and freshwater ecology, remote environmental sensing. *Unit head:* Dr. Kennedy T. Paynter, Director, 301-405-6938, Fax: 301-314-4139, E-mail: mees@umd.edu. *Application contact:* Dean of Graduate School, 301-405-0376, Fax: 301-314-9305.

See Close-Up on page 169 and Display on page 161.

University of Maryland Eastern Shore, Graduate Programs, Department of Natural Sciences, Program in Marine-Estuarine-Environmental Sciences, Princess Anne, MD 21853-1299. Offers MS, PhD. Part-time programs available. *Faculty:* 28. *Students:* 30 (19 women); includes 15 minority (all African Americans), 8 international. 15 applicants, 47% accepted, 6 enrolled. In 2009, 3 master's, 1 doctorate awarded. *Degree requirements:* For master's, thesis; for doctorate, comprehensive exam, thesis/dissertation, proposal defense. *Entrance requirements:* For master's and doctorate, GRE General Test, minimum GPA of 3.0. Additional exam requirements/recommendations for international students: Required—TOEFL. *Application deadline:* For fall admission, 2/1 for domestic and international students; for spring admission, 9/1 for domestic students, 8/1 for international students. Applications are processed on a rolling basis. Application fee: $30. Electronic applications accepted. *Financial support:* In 2009–10, 30 students received support; fellowships with tuition reimbursements available, research assistantships with tuition reimbursements available, teaching assistantships with tuition reimbursements available, career-related internships or fieldwork, scholarships/grants, and unspecified assistantships available. Support available to part-time students. Financial award application deadline: 1/1. *Unit head:* Dr. Kennedy T. Paynter, Director, 301-405-6938, Fax: 301-314-4139, E-mail: mees@umd.edu. *Application contact:* Dr. Kennedy T. Paynter, Director, 301-405-6938, Fax: 301-314-4139, E-mail: mees@umd.edu.

See Close-Up on page 169 and Display on page 161.

University of Massachusetts Boston, Office of Graduate Studies, College of Science and Mathematics, Department of Environmental, Earth and Ocean Sciences, Track in Environmental, Earth and Ocean Sciences, Boston, MA 02125-3393. Offers PhD. Part-time and evening/weekend programs available. *Degree requirements:* For doctorate, comprehensive exam, thesis/dissertation, oral exams. *Entrance requirements:* For doctorate, GRE General Test, minimum GPA of 2.75. *Faculty research:* Conservation genetics, anthropogenic and natural influences on community structures of coral reef factors, geographical variation in mitochondrial DNA, protein chemistry and enzymology pertaining to insect cuticle.

University of Massachusetts Lowell, College of Arts and Sciences, Department of Chemistry, Lowell, MA 01854-2881. Offers analytical chemistry (PhD); biochemistry (PhD); chemistry (MS, PhD); environmental studies (PhD); green chemistry (PhD); inorganic chemistry (PhD); organic chemistry (PhD); polymer science (MS). Terminal master's awarded for partial completion of doctoral program. *Degree requirements:* For master's, thesis; for doctorate, 2 foreign languages, thesis/dissertation. *Entrance requirements:* For master's and doctorate, GRE General Test. Electronic applications accepted.

University of Massachusetts Lowell, James B. Francis College of Engineering, Department of Civil and Environmental Engineering and College of Arts and Sciences, Program in Environmental Studies, Lowell, MA 01854-2881. Offers environmental engineering (MSES); environmental studies (PhD, Certificate). Part-time programs available. *Degree requirements:* For master's, thesis optional. *Entrance requirements:* For master's, GRE General Test. *Faculty research:* Remote sensing of air pollutants, atmospheric deposition of toxic metals, contaminant transport in groundwater, soil remediation.

University of Massachusetts Lowell, School of Health and Environment, Department of Work Environment, Lowell, MA 01854-2881. Offers cleaner production and pollution prevention (MS, Sc D); environmental risk assessment (Certificate); epidemiology (MS, Sc D); ergonomics and safety (MS, Sc D); identification and control of ergonomic hazards (Certificate); job stress and healthy job redesign (Certificate); occupational and environmental hygiene (MS, Sc D); radiological health physics and general work environment protection (Certificate); work environment policy (MS, Sc D). *Accreditation:* ABET (one or more programs are accredited). Part-time programs available. Terminal master's awarded for partial completion of doctoral program. *Degree requirements:* For master's, thesis optional; for doctorate, thesis/dissertation. *Entrance requirements:* For master's and doctorate, GRE General Test. Additional exam requirements/recommendations for international students: Required—TOEFL.

University of Medicine and Dentistry of New Jersey, Graduate School of Biomedical Sciences, Graduate Programs in Biomedical Sciences–Piscataway, Program in Environmental Sciences/Exposure Assessment, Piscataway, NJ 08854-5635. Offers PhD, MD/PhD. *Entrance requirements:* Additional exam requirements/recommendations for international students: Required—TOEFL. *Application deadline:* For fall admission, 1/5 for domestic students. Applications are processed on a rolling basis. Application fee: $40. Electronic applications accepted. *Financial support:* Application deadline: 5/1; *Unit head:* Dr. Clifford Weisel, Director, 732-445-0154, Fax: 732-445-0116, E-mail: weisel@eohsi.rutgers.edu. *Application contact:* University Registrar, 973-972-5338.

University of Michigan, School of Natural Resources and Environment, Program in Natural Resources and Environment, Ann Arbor, MI 48109. Offers aquatic sciences: research and management (MS); behavior, education and communication (MS); conservation biology (MS); environmental informatics (MS); environmental justice (MS); environmental policy and planning (MS); natural resources and environment (PhD); sustainable systems (MS); terrestrial ecosystems (MS); MS/AM; MS/JD; MS/MBA. *Students:* Average age 27. In 2009, 87 master's, 14 doctorates awarded. Terminal master's awarded for partial completion of doctoral program. *Degree requirements:* For master's, practicum or group project; for doctorate, comprehensive exam, thesis/dissertation, oral defense of dissertation, preliminary exam. *Entrance requirements:* For master's, GRE General Test; for doctorate, GRE General Test, master's degree. Additional exam requirements/recommendations for international students: Required—TOEFL (minimum score 560 paper-based; 220 computer-based; 84 iBT). *Application deadline:* For fall admission, 1/5 priority date for domestic and international students. Applications are processed on a rolling basis. Application fee: $60 ($75 for international students). Electronic applications accepted. *Expenses:* Tuition, state resident: full-time $17,286; part-time $1099 per credit hour. Tuition, nonresident: full-time $34,944; part-time $2080 per credit hour. Required fees: $95 per semester. Tuition and fees vary according to course load, degree level and program. *Financial support:* Fellowships with tuition reimbursements, research assistantships with tuition reimbursements, teaching assistantships with tuition reimbursements, career-related internships or fieldwork, Federal Work-Study, institutionally sponsored loans, scholarships/grants, health care benefits, and unspecified assistantships available. Support available to part-time students. Financial award application deadline: 1/5; financial award applicants required to submit FAFSA. *Faculty research:* Stream ecology, plant-insect interactions, fish biology, resource control and reproductive success, remote sensing. *Application contact:* Graduate Admissions Team, 734-764-6453, Fax: 734-936-2195, E-mail: snre.admissions@umich.edu.

University of Michigan–Dearborn, College of Arts, Sciences, and Letters, Master of Science in Environmental Science Program, Dearborn, MI 48128. Offers MS. Part-time and evening/weekend programs available. *Faculty:* 9 full-time (2 women), 3 part-time/adjunct (0 women). *Students:* 31 part-time (20 women); includes 3 minority (1 African American, 1 Asian American or Pacific Islander, 1 Hispanic American). Average age 33. 8 applicants, 100% accepted, 8 enrolled. In 2009, 10 master's awarded. *Degree requirements:* For master's, thesis optional. *Entrance requirements:* For master's, 2 letters of reference, minimum GPA of 3.0. Additional exam requirements/recommendations for international students: Required—TOEFL (minimum score 560 paper-based; 220 computer-based). *Application deadline:* For fall admission, 8/1 priority date for domestic students, 4/1 for international students; for winter admission, 12/1 priority date for domestic students, 11/1 for international students; for spring admission, 4/1 for domestic students, 3/1 for international students. Applications are processed on a rolling basis. Application fee: $60 ($75 for international students). *Expenses:* Tuition, area resident: Part-time $504.10 per credit hour. Tuition, state resident: part-time $504.10 per credit hour. Tuition, nonresident: part-time $957.90 per credit hour. *Financial support:* In 2009–10, 1 fellowship (averaging $2,500 per year), 2 research assistantships (averaging $2,500 per year) were awarded. Financial award application deadline: 4/1; financial award applicants required to submit FAFSA. *Faculty research:* Heavy metal and PAH containment/remediation, land use and impact on ground water and surface water quality, ecosystems and management, natural resources, plant and animal diversity. *Unit head:* Dr. Robert Simpson, Director, 313-593-5277, E-mail: rlsumd@umich.edu. *Application contact:* Carol Ligienza, Administrative Coordinator, CASL Graduate Programs, 313-593-1183, Fax: 313-583-6700, E-mail: caslgrad@umd.umich.edu.

The University of Montana, Graduate School, College of Arts and Sciences, Program in Environmental Studies (EVST), Missoula, MT 59812-0002. Offers MS, JD/MS. Part-time programs available. *Faculty:* 5 full-time (2 women), 3 part-time/adjunct (1 woman). *Students:* 36 full-time (23 women), 34 part-time (19 women); includes 3 minority (1 American Indian/Alaska Native, 1 Asian American or Pacific Islander, 1 Hispanic American), 1 international. Average age 30. 76 applicants, 61% accepted, 23 enrolled. In 2009, 30 master's awarded. *Degree requirements:* For master's, thesis, portfolio or professional paper. *Entrance requirements:* For master's, GRE General Test, minimum 500 verbal GRE. Additional exam requirements/recommendations for international students: Required—TOEFL (minimum score 580 paper-based; 237 computer-based; 92 iBT). *Application deadline:* For fall admission, 2/1 priority date for domestic and international students. Application fee: $51. *Financial support:* In 2009–10, 14 students received support, including 4 fellowships with partial tuition reimbursements available (averaging $5,000 per year), 6 teaching assistantships with full tuition reimbursements available (averaging $9,000 per year); career-related internships or fieldwork, Federal Work-Study, and scholarships/grants also available. Support available to part-time students. Financial award application deadline: 4/15. *Faculty research:* Pollution ecology, sustainable agriculture, environmental writing, environmental policy, environmental justice, habitat-land management. Total annual research expenditures: $185,000. *Unit head:* Dr. Len Broberg, Director, 406-243-5209, Fax: 406-243-6090, E-mail: len.broberg@mso.umt.edu. *Application contact:* Karen Hurd, Administrative Assistant, 406-243-6273, Fax: 406-243-6090, E-mail: karen.hurd@mso.umt.edu.

University of Nevada, Las Vegas, Graduate College, Greenspun College of Urban Affairs, Department of Environmental Studies, Las Vegas, NV 89154-4030. Offers crisis and emergency management (MS); environmental science (MS, PhD); non-profit management (Certificate); public administration (MPA); public affairs (PhD). Part-time programs available. *Faculty:* 6 full-time (2 women). *Students:* 39 full-time (18 women), 145 part-time (79 women); includes 47 minority (22 African Americans, 4 American Indian/Alaska Native, 3 Asian Americans or Pacific Islanders, 18 Hispanic Americans), 7 international. Average age 39. 16 applicants, 31% accepted, 2 enrolled. In 2009, 50 master's, 3 doctorates, 27 other advanced degrees awarded. *Degree requirements:* For master's, comprehensive exam (for some programs), thesis; for doctorate, comprehensive exam (for some programs), thesis/dissertation. *Entrance requirements:* Additional exam requirements/recommendations for international students: Required—TOEFL (minimum score 550 paper-based; 213 computer-based; 80 iBT), IELTS (minimum score 7). *Application deadline:* For fall admission, 6/1 priority date for domestic students, 2/15 priority date for international students; for spring admission, 11/15 priority date for domestic students, 10/1 for international students. Applications are processed on a rolling basis. Application fee: $60 ($95 for international students). Electronic applications accepted. *Financial support:* In 2009–10, 9 students received support, including 6 research assistantships with partial tuition reimbursements available (averaging $13,850 per year), 3 teaching assistantships with partial tuition reimbursements available (averaging $10,666 per year); institutionally sponsored loans, scholarships/grants, health care benefits, and unspecified assistantships also available. Financial award application deadline: 3/1. *Faculty research:* Environmental chemistry, environmental policy and management. *Unit head:* Dr. Ed Weber, Chair/ Associate Professor, 702-895-4440, Fax: 702-895-4436, E-mail: edward.weber@unlv.edu. *Application contact:* Graduate College Admissions Evaluator, 702-895-3320, Fax: 702-895-4180, E-mail: gradcollege@unlv.edu.

University of Nevada, Reno, Graduate School, College of Agriculture, Biotechnology and Natural Resources, Department of Natural Resources and Environmental Sciences, Reno, NV 89557. Offers MS. *Degree requirements:* For master's, thesis optional. *Entrance requirements:* For master's, GRE, minimum GPA of 2.75. Additional exam requirements/recommendations for international students: Required—TOEFL (minimum score 500 paper-based; 173 computer-based; 61 iBT), IELTS (minimum score 6). Electronic applications accepted. *Faculty research:* Range management, plant physiology, remote sensing, soils, wildlife.

Environmental Sciences

University of Nevada, Reno, Graduate School, Interdisciplinary Program in Environmental Sciences and Health, Reno, NV 89557. Offers MS, PhD. Terminal master's awarded for partial completion of doctoral program. *Degree requirements:* For master's, thesis; for doctorate, thesis/dissertation. *Entrance requirements:* For master's, GRE General Test, minimum GPA of 2.75; for doctorate, GRE General Test, minimum GPA of 3.0. Additional exam requirements/recommendations for international students: Required—TOEFL (minimum score 500 paper-based; 173 computer-based; 61 iBT), IELTS (minimum score 6). Electronic applications accepted. *Faculty research:* Environmental chemistry, environmental toxicology, ecological toxicology.

University of New Haven, Graduate School, College of Arts and Sciences, Program in Environmental Sciences, West Haven, CT 06516-1916. Offers environmental ecology (Certificate); environmental geoscience (MS); environmental health and management (MS); environmental science (MS); geographical information systems (Certificate). Part-time and evening/weekend programs available. *Faculty:* 6 full-time (3 women), 8 part-time/adjunct (2 women). *Students:* 8 full-time (5 women), 21 part-time (9 women); includes 2 minority (both African Americans), 4 international. Average age 27. 28 applicants, 79% accepted, 4 enrolled. In 2009, 7 master's, 5 other advanced degrees awarded. *Degree requirements:* For master's, thesis or alternative. *Entrance requirements:* Additional exam requirements/recommendations for international students: Required—TOEFL (minimum score 520 paper-based; 190 computer-based; 70 iBT); Recommended—IELTS (minimum score 5.5). *Application deadline:* For fall admission, 5/31 for international students; for winter admission, 10/15 for international students; for spring admission, 1/15 for international students. Applications are processed on a rolling basis. Application fee: $50. Electronic applications accepted. *Expenses:* Tuition: Part-time $700 per credit. Required fees: $45 per term. One-time fee: $390 part-time. *Financial support:* Research assistantships with partial tuition reimbursements, teaching assistantships with partial tuition reimbursements, career-related internships or fieldwork, Federal Work-Study, scholarships/grants, tuition waivers, and unspecified assistantships available. Support available to part-time students. Financial award applicants required to submit FAFSA. *Faculty research:* Mapping and assessing geological and living resources in Long Island Sound, geology, San Salvador Island, Bahamas. *Unit head:* Dr. Roman Zajac, Coordinator, 203-932-7108. *Application contact:* Eloise Gormley, Director of Graduate Admissions, 203-932-7449, Fax: 203-932-7137, E-mail: gradinfo@newhaven.edu.

University of New Orleans, Graduate School, College of Sciences, Department of Earth and Environmental Sciences, New Orleans, LA 70148. Offers MS. Evening/weekend programs available. *Degree requirements:* For master's, thesis. *Entrance requirements:* For master's, GRE General Test. Additional exam requirements/recommendations for international students: Required—TOEFL (minimum score 550 paper-based; 213 computer-based; 79 iBT). Electronic applications accepted. *Faculty research:* Continental margin structure and seismology, burial diagenesis of siliclastic sediments, tectonics at convergent plate margins, continental shelf sediment stability, early diagenesis of carbonates.

The University of North Carolina at Chapel Hill, Graduate School, School of Public Health, Department of Environmental Sciences and Engineering, Chapel Hill, NC 27599. Offers air, radiation and industrial hygiene (MPH, MS, MSEE, MSPH, PhD); aquatic and atmospheric sciences (MPH, MS, MSPH, PhD); environmental engineering (MPH, MS, MSEE, MSPH, PhD); environmental health sciences (MPH, MS, MSPH, PhD); environmental management and policy (MPH, MS, MSPH, PhD). Terminal master's awarded for partial completion of doctoral program. *Degree requirements:* For master's, comprehensive exam, thesis (for some programs), research paper; for doctorate, comprehensive exam, thesis/dissertation. *Entrance requirements:* For master's and doctorate, GRE General Test, minimum GPA of 3.0. Additional exam requirements/recommendations for international students: Required—TOEFL. Electronic applications accepted. *Faculty research:* Air, radiation and industrial hygiene, aquatic and atmospheric sciences, environmental health sciences, environmental management and policy, water resources engineering.

University of Northern Iowa, Graduate College, College of Natural Sciences, Environmental Programs, Cedar Falls, IA 50614. Offers environmental health (MS); environmental science (MS); environmental technology (MS). *Students:* 6 full-time (3 women), 4 part-time (2 women), 4 international. 13 applicants, 15% accepted, 2 enrolled. In 2009, 2 master's awarded. *Degree requirements:* For master's, comprehensive exam, thesis or alternative. *Entrance requirements:* For master's, minimum GPA of 3.0; 3 letters of recommendation. Additional exam requirements/recommendations for international students: Required—TOEFL (minimum score 500 paper-based; 180 computer-based; 61 iBT). *Application deadline:* For fall admission, 8/1 priority date for domestic students. Applications are processed on a rolling basis. Application fee: $30 ($50 for international students). Electronic applications accepted. *Financial support:* Application deadline: 2/1. *Unit head:* Dr. Maureen Clayton, Head, 319-273-7147, Fax: 319-273-7125, E-mail: maureen.clayton@uni.edu. *Application contact:* Laurie S. Russell, Record Analyst, 319-273-2623, Fax: 319-273-6792, E-mail: laurie.russell@uni.edu.

University of North Texas, Robert B. Toulouse School of Graduate Studies, College of Arts and Sciences, Department of Biological Sciences, Program in Environmental Science, Denton, TX 76203. Offers MS, PhD. *Degree requirements:* For master's, oral defense of thesis; for doctorate, one foreign language, comprehensive exam, thesis/dissertation. *Entrance requirements:* For master's and doctorate, GRE General Test. Additional exam requirements/recommendations for international students: Required—proof of English language proficiency required for non-native English speakers; Recommended—TOEFL (minimum score 550 paper-based; 213 computer-based; 79 iBT). Application fee: $50 ($75 for international students). *Expenses:* Tuition, state resident: full-time $4298; part-time $239 per contact hour. Tuition, nonresident: full-time $9878; part-time $549 per contact hour. Required fees: $265 per contact hour. *Financial support:* Applicants required to submit FAFSA. *Application contact:* Graduate Advisor, 940-565-2011, Fax: 940-565-3821.

University of Oklahoma, Graduate College, College of Engineering, School of Civil Engineering and Environmental Science, Program in Environmental Science, Norman, OK 73019-0390. Offers air (M Env Sc); environmental science (PhD); groundwater management (M Env Sc); hazardous solid waste (M Env Sc); occupational safety and health (M Env Sc); process design (M Env Sc); water quality resources (M Env Sc). *Students:* 9 full-time (4 women), 8 part-time (6 women); includes 3 minority (1 African American, 2 American Indian/Alaska Native), 2 international. 9 applicants, 67% accepted, 4 enrolled. In 2009, 4 master's, 2 doctorates awarded. Terminal master's awarded for partial completion of doctoral program. *Degree requirements:* For master's, comprehensive exam, oral exams; for doctorate, comprehensive exam, thesis/dissertation, oral and qualifying exams. *Entrance requirements:* For master's, minimum GPA of 3.0; for doctorate, minimum graduate GPA of 3.5. Additional exam requirements/recommendations for international students: Required—TOEFL (minimum score 600 paper-based; 250 computer-based). *Application deadline:* For fall admission, 4/1 priority date for domestic students, 4/1 for international students; for spring admission, 11/1 for domestic students, 9/1 for international students. Applications are processed on a rolling basis. Application fee: $40 ($90 for international students). Electronic applications accepted. *Expenses:* Tuition, state resident: full-time $3744; part-time $156 per credit hour. Tuition, nonresident: full-time $13,577; part-time $565.70 per credit hour. Required fees: $2415; $90.10 per credit hour. *Financial support:* In 2009–10, 10 students received support. Scholarships/grants available. Financial award application deadline: 3/1; financial award applicants required to submit FAFSA. *Faculty research:* Treatment wetlands, soil remediation, biomediation. *Unit head:* Robert C. Knox, Director, 405-325-5911, Fax: 405-325-4217, E-mail: rknox@ou.edu. *Application contact:* Robert C. Knox, Director, 405-325-5911, Fax: 405-325-4217, E-mail: rknox@ou.edu.

University of Pennsylvania, School of Arts and Sciences, Graduate Group in Earth and Environmental Science, Philadelphia, PA 19104. Offers MS, PhD. Part-time programs available. *Faculty:* 8 full-time (0 women), 3 part-time/adjunct (0 women). *Students:* 17 full-time (9 women), 6 international. 27 applicants, 22% accepted, 6 enrolled. In 2009, 5 doctorates awarded. *Degree requirements:* For master's, one foreign language, thesis; for doctorate, one foreign language, thesis/dissertation. *Entrance requirements:* For master's and doctorate, GRE General Test. Additional exam requirements/recommendations for international students: Required—TOEFL. *Application deadline:* For fall admission, 12/1 priority date for domestic students. Application fee: $70. Electronic applications accepted. *Expenses:* Tuition: Full-time $25,660; part-time $4758 per course. Required fees: $2152; $270 per course. Tuition and fees vary according to course load, degree level and program. *Financial support:* Fellowships, research assistantships, teaching assistantships, institutionally sponsored loans, scholarships/grants, traineeships, health care benefits, and unspecified assistantships available. Financial award application deadline: 12/15. *Faculty research:* Isotope geochemistry, regional tectonics, environmental geology, metamorphic and igneous petrology, paleontology.

University of Puerto Rico, Río Piedras, College of Natural Sciences, Department of Environmental Sciences, San Juan, PR 00931-3300. Offers MS.

University of Rhode Island, Graduate School, College of the Environment and Life Sciences, Department of Fisheries, Animal and Veterinary Science, Kingston, RI 02881. Offers animal health and disease (MS); animal science (MS); aquaculture (MS); aquatic pathology (MS); environmental sciences (PhD), including animal science, aquacultural science, aquatic pathology, fisheries science; fisheries (MS). *Faculty:* 10 full-time (4 women). *Students:* 14 full-time (7 women), 12 part-time (7 women); includes 5 minority (2 African Americans, 3 Hispanic Americans), 3 international. In 2009, 3 master's, 2 doctorates awarded. *Degree requirements:* For master's, comprehensive exam (for some programs), thesis optional; for doctorate, comprehensive exam, thesis/dissertation. *Entrance requirements:* For master's and doctorate, GRE, 2 letters of recommendation. Additional exam requirements/recommendations for international students: Required—TOEFL (minimum score 550 paper-based; 213 computer-based). *Application deadline:* For fall admission, 7/15 for domestic students, 2/1 for international students; for spring admission, 11/15 for domestic students, 7/15 for international students. Application fee: $65. Electronic applications accepted. *Expenses:* Tuition, state resident: full-time $8828; part-time $490 per credit hour. Tuition, nonresident: full-time $22,100; part-time $1228 per credit hour. Required fees: $1118; $57 per semester. Tuition and fees vary according to program. *Financial support:* In 2009–10, 4 research assistantships with full and partial tuition reimbursements (averaging $11,386 per year), 7 teaching assistantships with full and partial tuition reimbursements (averaging $10,940 per year) were awarded. Financial award application deadline: 7/15; financial award applicants required to submit FAFSA. Total annual research expenditures: $2.1 million. *Unit head:* Dr. David Bengtson, Chair, 401-874-2668, Fax: 401-874-7575, E-mail: bengtson@uri.edu. *Application contact:* Dr. Marta Gomez-Chiarra, Director of Graduate Studies, 401-874-2917, Fax: 401-874-7575, E-mail: gomezchi@uri.edu.

University of Saskatchewan, College of Graduate Studies and Research, School of Environment and Sustainability, Saskatoon, SK S7N 5A2, Canada. Offers MES. Tuition and fees charges are reported in Canadian dollars. *Expenses:* Tuition, area resident: Full-time $3000 Canadian dollars; part-time $500 Canadian dollars per term. Required fees: $700 Canadian dollars; $100 Canadian dollars per term.

University of South Africa, College of Agriculture and Environmental Sciences, Pretoria, South Africa. Offers agriculture (MS); consumer science (MCS); environmental management (MA, MS, PhD); environmental science (MA, MS, PhD); geography (MA, MS, PhD); horticulture (M Tech); human ecology (MHE); life sciences (MS); nature conservation (M Tech).

University of South Florida, Graduate School, College of Arts and Sciences, Department of Chemistry, Tampa, FL 33620-9951. Offers computational chemistry (PhD); analytical chemistry (MS, PhD); biochemistry (MS, PhD); computational chemistry (MS); environmental chemistry (MS, PhD); inorganic chemistry (MS, PhD); organic chemistry (MS); physical chemistry (MS, PhD); polymer chemistry (PhD). Part-time programs available. *Faculty:* 25 full-time (4 women). *Students:* 113 full-time (36 women), 15 part-time (11 women); includes 19 minority (5 African Americans, 6 Asian Americans or Pacific Islanders, 8 Hispanic Americans), 58 international. Average age 32. 112 applicants, 30% accepted, 21 enrolled. In 2009, 8 master's, 11 doctorates awarded. Terminal master's awarded for partial completion of doctoral program. *Degree requirements:* For master's, comprehensive exam, thesis (for some programs); for doctorate, 2 foreign languages, comprehensive exam, thesis/dissertation. *Entrance requirements:* For master's, GRE General Test or GMAT, minimum GPA of 3.0. Additional exam requirements/recommendations for international students: Required—TOEFL (minimum score 550 paper-based; 213 computer-based). *Application deadline:* For fall admission, 2/15 priority date for domestic students, 1/2 priority date for international students; for spring admission, 10/1 priority date for domestic students, 6/1 priority date for international students. Applications are processed on a rolling basis. Application fee: $30. Electronic applications accepted. *Financial support:* In 2009–10, teaching assistantships with tuition reimbursements (averaging $27,522 per year); unspecified assistantships also available. Financial award application deadline: 6/30. *Faculty research:* Synthesis, bio-organic chemistry, bioinorganic chemistry, environmental chemistry, NMR. Total annual research expenditures: $3.2 million. *Unit head:* Dr. Randy Larsen, Chairperson, 813-974-4129, Fax: 813-974-3203, E-mail: rlarsen@cas.usf.edu. *Application contact:* Patricia Muisener, Director, 813-974-1730, Fax: 813-974-3203, E-mail: muisener@cas.usf.edu.

University of South Florida, Graduate School, College of Arts and Sciences, Department of Environmental Science and Policy, Tampa, FL 33620-9951. Offers MS. *Students:* 9 full-time (5 women), 11 part-time (5 women); includes 5 minority (1 African American, 4 Hispanic Americans). Average age 32. 21 applicants, 38% accepted, 6 enrolled. In 2009, 5 master's awarded. *Degree requirements:* For master's, comprehensive exam, thesis (for some programs). *Entrance requirements:* For master's, minimum GPA of 3.0. Additional exam requirements/recommendations for international students: Required—TOEFL (minimum score 600 paper-based; 213 computer-based). *Application deadline:* For fall admission, 2/15 for domestic students, 1/2 for international students; for spring admission, 10/15 for domestic students. Application fee: $30. *Financial support:* Scholarships/grants and unspecified assistantships available. Support available to part-time students. Financial award application deadline: 5/1. Total annual research expenditures: $434,251. *Unit head:* Robert Brinkmann, Interim Director, 813-974-4939, Fax: 813-974-4808, E-mail: rbrinkmann@cas.usf.edu. *Application contact:* Philip Van Beynen, Program Director, 813-974-3026, Fax: 813-974-4808, E-mail: vanbeyne@cas.usf.edu.

The University of Tennessee at Chattanooga, Graduate School, College of Arts and Sciences, Department of Biological and Environmental Sciences, Chattanooga, TN 37403. Offers environmental sciences (MS). Part-time and evening/weekend programs available. *Faculty:* 8 full-time (1 woman). *Students:* 13 full-time (8 women), 14 part-time (10 women), 1 international. Average age 31. 13 applicants, 92% accepted, 6 enrolled. In 2009, 14 master's awarded. *Degree requirements:* For master's, thesis optional. *Entrance requirements:* For master's, GRE General Test, minimum undergraduate GPA of 2.75; undergraduate course work in ecology or knowledge equivalent. Additional exam requirements/recommendations for international students: Required—TOEFL (minimum score 550 paper-based; 213 computer-based; 79 iBT), IELTS (minimum score 6). *Application deadline:* For fall admission, 8/1 priority date for domestic students, 6/1 for international students; for spring admission, 12/1 priority date for domestic students, 10/1 for international students. Applications are processed on a rolling basis. Application fee: $35. Electronic applications accepted. *Expenses:* Tuition, state resident: full-time $5404; part-time $300 per credit hour. Tuition, nonresident: full-time $16,702; part-time $928 per credit hour. Required fees: $1150; $130 per credit hour. *Financial support:* In 2009–10, 5 research assistantships with full and partial tuition reimbursements (averaging $5,500 per year), 6 teaching assistantships with full and partial tuition reimbursements (averaging $5,500 per year) were awarded; career-related internships or fieldwork, scholarships/grants, and unspecified assistantships also available. Support available to part-time students. *Faculty research:* Bioremediation, stream fish ecology and conservation, environmental law and policy, avian conservation and management. Total annual research expenditures: $574,605. *Unit head:* Dr. John Tucker, Department Head, 423-425-4341, Fax: 423-425-2285, E-mail: john-tucker@utc.edu. *Application contact:* Dr. Stephanie Bellar, Dean of Graduate Studies, 423-425-4666, Fax: 423-425-5223, E-mail: stephanie-bellar@utc.edu.

The University of Texas at Arlington, Graduate School, College of Science, Department of Earth and Environmental Sciences, Program in Environmental and Earth Sciences, Arlington, TX 76019. Offers environmental science (MS, PhD); geology (MS, PhD). Part-time and evening/weekend programs available. *Faculty:* 7 full-time (0 women), 5 part-time/adjunct (0 women). *Students:* 22 full-time (13 women), 25 part-time (12 women); includes 9 minority (2 African Americans, 1 American Indian/Alaska Native, 2 Asian Americans or Pacific Islanders, 4 Hispanic Americans), 11 international. 23 applicants, 74% accepted, 10 enrolled. In 2009, 11 master's, 1 doctorate awarded. Terminal master's awarded for partial completion of doctoral program. *Degree requirements:* For master's, thesis optional; for doctorate, comprehensive exam, thesis/dissertation. *Entrance requirements:* For master's, GRE General Test. Additional exam requirements/recommendations for international students: Required—TOEFL (minimum score 550 paper-based; 213 computer-based). *Financial support:* In 2009–10, 4 fellowships (averaging $1,000 per year), 7 teaching assistantships (averaging $14,700 per year) were awarded; career-related internships or fieldwork, Federal Work-Study, institutionally sponsored loans, scholarships/grants, health care benefits, and unspecified assistantships also available. *Unit head:* Dr. John S. Wickham, Chair, 817-272-2987, Fax: 817-272-2628, E-mail: wickham@uta.edu. *Application contact:* Dr. Andrew Hunt, Graduate Advisor, 817-272-2987, Fax: 817-272-2628, E-mail: hunt@uta.edu.

The University of Texas at El Paso, Graduate School, College of Science, Environmental Science Program, El Paso, TX 79968-0001. Offers MS. *Degree requirements:* For master's, thesis. *Entrance requirements:* For master's, GRE, bachelor's degree in a science or engineering discipline, 3 letters of recommendation. Additional exam requirements/recommendations for international students: Required—TOEFL.

The University of Texas at El Paso, Graduate School, Interdisciplinary Program in Environmental Science and Engineering, El Paso, TX 79968-0001. Offers PhD. Part-time and evening/weekend programs available. *Students:* 41 (15 women); includes 13 minority (3 Asian Americans or Pacific Islanders, 10 Hispanic Americans), 21 international. Average age 34. In 2009, 4 doctorates awarded. *Degree requirements:* For doctorate, thesis/dissertation. *Entrance requirements:* For doctorate, GRE, letters of recommendation. Additional exam requirements/recommendations for international students: Required—TOEFL; Recommended—IELTS. *Application deadline:* For fall admission, 8/1 for domestic students, 3/1 for international students; for spring admission, 11/1 for domestic students, 9/1 for international students. Applications are processed on a rolling basis. Application fee: $45 ($80 for international students). Electronic applications accepted. *Financial support:* In 2009–10, research assistantships with partial tuition reimbursements (averaging $22,500 per year), teaching assistantships with partial tuition reimbursements (averaging $18,000 per year) were awarded; fellowships with partial tuition reimbursements, institutionally sponsored loans, scholarships/grants, health care benefits, tuition waivers (partial), and unspecified assistantships also available. Support available to part-time students. Financial award application deadline: 3/15; financial award applicants required to submit FAFSA. *Unit head:* Dr. Barry A. Benedict, Director, 915-747-5604, Fax: 915-747-5145, E-mail: babenedict@utep.edu. *Application contact:* Dr. Patricia D. Witherspoon, Dean of the Graduate School, 915-747-5491, Fax: 915-747-5788, E-mail: withersp@utep.edu.

The University of Texas at San Antonio, College of Engineering, Department of Civil and Environmental Engineering, San Antonio, TX 78249-0617. Offers civil engineering (MSCE); environmental science and engineering (PhD). Part-time and evening/weekend programs available. *Faculty:* 11 full-time (1 woman), 1 part-time/adjunct (0 women). *Students:* 34 full-time (8 women), 28 part-time (5 women); includes 16 minority (4 African Americans, 4 Asian Americans or Pacific Islanders, 8 Hispanic Americans), 24 international. Average age 33. 56 applicants, 55% accepted, 19 enrolled. In 2009, 12 master's, 4 doctorates awarded. *Degree requirements:* For master's, comprehensive exam (for some programs), thesis (for some programs); for doctorate, comprehensive exam, thesis/dissertation. *Entrance requirements:* For master's, GRE General Test, minimum GPA of 3.0 in last 60 hours of undergraduate degree. Additional exam requirements/recommendations for international students: Required—TOEFL (minimum score 500 paper-based; 173 computer-based; 61 iBT), IELTS (minimum score 5). *Application deadline:* For fall admission, 7/1 for domestic students, 4/1 for international students; for spring admission, 11/1 for domestic students, 9/1 for international students. Applications are processed on a rolling basis. Application fee: $45 ($80 for international students). Electronic applications accepted. *Expenses:* Tuition, state resident: full-time $3975; part-time $221 per contact hour. Tuition, nonresident: full-time $13,947; part-time $775 per contact hour. Required fees: $1853. *Financial support:* In 2009–10, 29 students received support, including 15 research assistantships (averaging $18,213 per year); career-related internships or fieldwork, scholarships/grants, tuition waivers, and unspecified assistantships also available. Support available to part-time students. Financial award application deadline: 3/31. Total annual research expenditures: $475,434. *Unit head:* Dr. Athanassio T. Papagiannakis, Chair, 210-458-7071, Fax: 210-458-6475, E-mail: at.papagiannakis@utsa.edu. *Application contact:* Dr. Dorothy A. Flannagan, Dean of the Graduate School, 210-458-4330, Fax: 210-458-4332, E-mail: dorothy.flannagan@utsa.edu.

The University of Texas at San Antonio, College of Sciences, Department of Geological Sciences, San Antonio, TX 78249-0617. Offers MS. Part-time programs available. *Faculty:* 9 full-time (2 women). *Students:* 11 full-time (3 women), 5 part-time (2 women); includes 3 minority (1 Asian American or Pacific Islander, 2 Hispanic Americans), 2 international. Average age 28. 13 applicants, 77% accepted, 6 enrolled. In 2009, 4 master's awarded. *Degree requirements:* For master's, comprehensive exam (for some programs), thesis (for some programs). *Entrance requirements:* For master's, GRE General Test, minimum GPA of 3.0 in last 60 hours. Additional exam requirements/recommendations for international students: Required—TOEFL (minimum score 500 paper-based; 173 computer-based; 61 iBT), IELTS (minimum score 5). *Application deadline:* For fall admission, 7/1 for domestic students, 4/1 for international students; for spring admission, 11/1 for domestic students, 9/1 for international students. Applications are processed on a rolling basis. Application fee: $45 ($80 for international students). Electronic applications accepted. *Expenses:* Tuition, state resident: full-time $3975; part-time $221 per contact hour. Tuition, nonresident: full-time $13,947; part-time $775 per contact hour. Required fees: $1853. *Financial support:* In 2009–10, 7 students received support, including 2 fellowships (averaging $31,999 per year), 10 teaching assistantships (averaging $9,463 per year); scholarships/grants, tuition waivers, and unspecified assistantships also available. Support available to part-time students. *Faculty research:* Water resources/hydrogeology, low-temperature geochemistry, petrology and tectonics, energy resources, paleoclimatology, landscape dynamics. Total annual research expenditures: $396,687. *Unit head:* Dr. Allan R. Dutton, Interim Chair, 210-458-5746, E-mail: allan.dutton@utsa.edu. *Application contact:* Dorothy A. Flannagan, Dean of the Graduate School, 210-458-4330, Fax: 210-458-4332, E-mail: dorothy.flannagan@utsa.edu.

University of the Virgin Islands, Graduate Programs, Division of Science and Mathematics, Program in Environmental and Marine Science, Saint Thomas, VI 00802-9990. Offers MS. *Entrance requirements:* For master's, GRE. Additional exam requirements/recommendations for international students: Required—TOEFL (minimum score 550 paper-based; 213 computer-based).

The University of Toledo, College of Graduate Studies, College of Arts and Sciences, Department of Environmental Sciences, Toledo, OH 43606-3390. Offers biology (ecology track) (MS, PhD); geology (MS), including earth surface processes, general geology. Part-time programs available. *Degree requirements:* For master's, thesis. *Entrance requirements:* For master's, GRE General Test. Additional exam requirements/recommendations for international students: Required—TOEFL. Electronic applications accepted. *Faculty research:* Environmental geochemistry, geophysics, petrology and mineralogy, paleontology, geohydrology.

University of Utah, The Graduate School, Professional Master of Science and Technology Program, Salt Lake City, UT 84112-1107. Offers biotechnology (PSM); computational science (PSM); environmental science (PSM); science instrumentation (PSM). Part-time programs available. *Students:* 32 full-time (17 women), 38 part-time (13 women); includes 5 minority (1 African American, 3 Asian Americans or Pacific Islanders, 1 Hispanic American), 19 international. Average age 31. 84 applicants, 33% accepted, 16 enrolled. In 2009, 7 master's awarded. *Degree requirements:* For master's, internship. *Entrance requirements:* For master's, GRE (recommended), minimum undergraduate GPA of 3.0, bachelor's degree from accredited university or college. Additional exam requirements/recommendations for international students: Required—TOEFL (minimum score 500 paper-based; 173 computer-based). *Application deadline:* For fall admission, 3/1 for domestic and international students. Application fee: $55 ($65 for international students). Electronic applications accepted. *Expenses:* Tuition, state resident: full-time $4004; part-time $1674 per semester. Tuition, nonresident: full-time $14,134; part-time $5915 per semester. Required fees: $324 per semester. Tuition and fees vary according to course load, degree level and program. *Financial support:* In 2009–10, 4 fellowships with full and partial tuition reimbursements (averaging $12,000 per year), 3 research assistantships with full tuition reimbursements (averaging $13,000 per year) were awarded; unspecified assistantships also available. Financial award applicants required to submit FAFSA. *Unit head:* Jennifer Schmidt, Program Director, 801-585-5630, E-mail: jennifer.schmidt@gradschool.utah.edu. *Application contact:* Francine Stirling, Project Coordinator, 801-585-3650, Fax: 801-585-6749, E-mail: francine.stirling@gradschool.utah.edu.

University of Virginia, College and Graduate School of Arts and Sciences, Department of Environmental Sciences, Charlottesville, VA 22903. Offers MA, MS, PhD. *Faculty:* 30 full-time (4 women), 4 part-time/adjunct (all women). *Students:* 68 full-time (38 women), 2 part-time (0 women); includes 3 minority (2 Asian Americans or Pacific Islanders, 1 Hispanic American), 9 international. Average age 29. 57 applicants, 47% accepted, 13 enrolled. In 2009, 6 master's, 8 doctorates awarded. *Degree requirements:* For master's, thesis; for doctorate, comprehensive exam, thesis/dissertation. *Entrance requirements:* For master's and doctorate, GRE General Test, 2 letters of recommendation. Additional exam requirements/recommendations for international students: Required—TOEFL (minimum score 600 paper-based; 250 computer-based; 90 iBT), IELTS (minimum score 7). *Application deadline:* For fall admission, 12/1 for domestic and international students; for winter admission, 10/15 for domestic and international students. Applications are processed on a rolling basis. Electronic applications accepted. *Financial support:* Fellowships, research assistantships, teaching assistantships available. Financial award application deadline: 12/1; financial award applicants required to submit FAFSA. *Unit head:* Patricia Wiberg, Chairman, 434-924-7761, Fax: 434-982-2137, E-mail: jcz@virginia.edu. *Application contact:* Graduate Admissions Chair, 434-924-7761, Fax: 434-982-2137.

The University of Western Ontario, Faculty of Graduate Studies, Biosciences Division, Department of Plant Sciences, London, ON N6A 5B8, Canada. Offers plant and environmental sciences (M Sc); plant sciences (M Sc, PhD); plant sciences and environmental sciences (PhD); plant sciences and molecular biology (M Sc, PhD). *Degree requirements:* For master's, thesis; for doctorate, thesis/dissertation. *Entrance requirements:* For doctorate, M Sc or equivalent. Additional exam requirements/recommendations for international students: Required—TOEFL. *Faculty research:* Ecology systematics, plant biochemistry and physiology, yeast genetics, molecular biology.

The University of Western Ontario, Faculty of Graduate Studies, Physical Sciences Division, Department of Earth Sciences, London, ON N6A 5B8, Canada. Offers environment and sustainability (MES); geology (M Sc, PhD); geology and environmental science (M Sc, PhD); geophysics (M Sc, PhD); geophysics and environmental science (M Sc, PhD). *Degree requirements:* For master's, thesis; for doctorate, thesis/dissertation, qualifying exam. *Entrance requirements:* For master's, honors in B Sc; for doctorate, M Sc. Additional exam requirements/recommendations for international students: Required—TOEFL. *Faculty research:* Geophysics, geochemistry, paleontology, sedimentology/stratigraphy, glaciology/quaternary.

University of West Florida, College of Arts and Sciences: Sciences, Department of Environmental Studies, Pensacola, FL 32514-5750. Offers environmental science (MS). Part-time programs available. *Faculty:* 2 full-time (0 women), 1 part-time/adjunct (0 women). *Students:* 7 full-time (3 women), 10 part-time (5 women), 2 international. Average age 28. 11 applicants, 73% accepted, 4 enrolled. In 2009, 9 master's awarded. *Entrance requirements:* For master's, GRE General Test. Additional exam requirements/recommendations for international students: Required—TOEFL (minimum score 550 paper-based; 213 computer-based). *Application deadline:* For fall admission, 6/1 for domestic students, 5/15 for international students; for spring admission, 11/1 for domestic students, 10/1 for international students. Application fee: $30. *Expenses:* Tuition, state resident: full-time $4982; part-time $260 per credit hour. Tuition, nonresident: full-time $20,059; part-time $919 per credit hour. Required fees: $1247; $52 per credit hour. *Financial support:* In 2009–10, 3 teaching assistantships with partial tuition reimbursements (averaging $4,006 per year) were awarded; unspecified assistantships also available. Financial award application deadline: 4/15; financial award applicants required to submit FAFSA. *Unit head:* Dr. Klaus Meyer-Arendt, Chairperson, 850-474-2746. *Application contact:* Terry McCray, Assistant Director of Graduate Admissions, 850-473-7718, Fax: 850-473-7714, E-mail: gradadmissions@uwf.edu.

University of Windsor, Faculty of Graduate Studies, GLIER-Great Lakes Institute for Environmental Research, Windsor, ON N9B 3P4, Canada. Offers environmental science (M Sc, PhD). *Degree requirements:* For master's, thesis; for doctorate, thesis/dissertation. *Entrance requirements:* For master's, minimum B+ average; for doctorate, M Sc degree, minimum B+ average. Additional exam requirements/recommendations for international students: Required—TOEFL (minimum score 560 paper-based; 220 computer-based). Electronic applications accepted. *Faculty research:* Environmental chemistry and toxicology, conservation and resource management, iron formation geochemistry.

University of Wisconsin–Green Bay, Graduate Studies, Program in Environmental Science and Policy, Green Bay, WI 54311-7001. Offers MS. Part-time programs available. *Faculty:* 22 full-time (5 women), 4 part-time/adjunct (0 women). *Students:* 11 full-time (3 women), 17 part-time (8 women); includes 5 minority (2 American Indian/Alaska Native, 2 Asian Americans or Pacific Islanders, 1 Hispanic American), 1 international. Average age 33. 27 applicants, 56% accepted, 10 enrolled. In 2009, 11 master's awarded. *Degree requirements:* For master's, thesis. *Entrance requirements:* For master's, GRE General Test, minimum GPA of 3.0. *Application deadline:* For fall admission, 8/1 for domestic students; for spring admission, 11/1 for domestic students. Applications are processed on a rolling basis. Application fee: $56. Electronic applications accepted. *Expenses:* Tuition, state resident: full-time $6706; part-time $373 per credit. Tuition, nonresident: full-time $16,722; part-time $932 per credit. Required fees: $1250; $52 per credit. Tuition and fees vary according to degree level and reciprocity agreements. *Financial support:* In 2009–10, 1 research assistantship with full tuition reimbursement, 4 teaching assistantships with full tuition reimbursements were awarded; career-related internships or

Environmental Sciences

University of Wisconsin–Green Bay (continued)
fieldwork, Federal Work-Study, and institutionally sponsored loans also available. Financial award application deadline: 7/15; financial award applicants required to submit FAFSA. *Faculty research:* Bald eagle, parasitic population of domestic and wild animals, resource recovery, anaerobic digestion of organic waste. *Unit head:* Dr. Patricia Terry, Coordinator, 920-465-2749, E-mail: terryp@uwgb.edu. *Application contact:* Pam Harvey-Jacobs, Director of Admissions, E-mail: harveyp@uwgb.edu.

University of Wisconsin–Madison, Graduate School, Gaylord Nelson Institute for Environmental Studies, Environmental Monitoring Program, Madison, WI 53706-1380. Offers MS, PhD. Part-time programs available. *Degree requirements:* For master's, thesis or alternative; for doctorate, thesis/dissertation. *Entrance requirements:* For master's and doctorate, GRE General Test. Additional exam requirements/recommendations for international students: Required—TOEFL (minimum score 600 paper-based; 250 computer-based; 100 iBT). Electronic applications accepted. *Expenses:* Tuition, state resident: part-time $594 per credit. Tuition, nonresident: part-time $1504 per credit. Required fees: $65 per credit. Tuition and fees vary according to course load, program and reciprocity agreements. *Faculty research:* Remote sensing, geographic information systems, climate modeling, natural resource management.

Vanderbilt University, Graduate School, Department of Earth and Environmental Sciences, Nashville, TN 37240-1001. Offers MAT, MS. *Faculty:* 13 full-time (2 women). *Students:* 7 full-time (4 women), 2 part-time (1 woman); includes 1 minority (Hispanic American), 1 international. Average age 25. 23 applicants, 26% accepted, 3 enrolled. In 2009, 5 master's awarded. *Degree requirements:* For master's, thesis. *Entrance requirements:* For master's, GRE General Test, GRE Subject Test (recommended). Additional exam requirements/recommendations for international students: Required—TOEFL (minimum score 570 paper-based; 230 computer-based; 88 iBT). *Application deadline:* For fall admission, 1/15 for domestic and international students. Application fee: $0. Electronic applications accepted. *Financial support:* Fellowships with full and partial tuition reimbursements, research assistantships with full and partial tuition reimbursements, teaching assistantships with full tuition reimbursements, career-related internships or fieldwork, Federal Work-Study, institutionally sponsored loans, and health care benefits available. Financial award application deadline: 1/15; financial award applicants required to submit CSS PROFILE or FAFSA. *Faculty research:* Geochemical processes, magmatic processes and crustal evolution, paleoecology and paleoenvironments, sedimentary systems, transport phenomena, environmental policy. *Unit head:* Dr. David J. Furbish, Chair, 615-322-2976, Fax: 615-322-2138. *Application contact:* Calvin F. Miller, Director of Graduate Studies, 615-322-2232, Fax: 615-322-2138, E-mail: calvin.f.miller@vanderbilt.edu.

Virginia Commonwealth University, Graduate School, School of Life Sciences, Center for Environmental Studies, Richmond, VA 23284-9005. Offers environmental communication (MIS); environmental health (MIS); environmental policy (MIS); environmental sciences (MIS). *Degree requirements:* For master's, thesis. *Entrance requirements:* For master's, GRE General Test.

Virginia Polytechnic Institute and State University, Graduate School, College of Engineering, Department of Civil and Environmental Engineering, Blacksburg, VA 24061. Offers civil engineering (M Eng, MS, PhD); environmental engineering (M Eng, MS); environmental sciences and engineering (MS). *Accreditation:* ABET (one or more programs are accredited). *Entrance requirements:* For master's and doctorate, GRE. Additional exam requirements/recommendations for international students: Required—TOEFL (minimum score 570 paper-based; 230 computer-based). Electronic applications accepted. *Faculty research:* Construction, environmental geotechnical hydrosystems, structures and transportation engineering.

Virginia Polytechnic Institute and State University, Graduate School, College of Natural Resources, Program in Geospatial and Environmental Analysis, Blacksburg, VA 24061. Offers PhD.

Washington State University, Graduate School, College of Sciences, Programs in Environmental Science and Regional Planning, Program in Environmental and Natural Resource Sciences, Pullman, WA 99164. Offers PhD.

Washington State University, Graduate School, College of Sciences, School of Earth and Environmental Sciences, Pullman, WA 99164. Offers MS, PhD.

Washington State University, Graduate School, College of Sciences, School of Earth and Environmental Sciences, Department of Natural Resource Sciences, Program in Environmental Science, Pullman, WA 99164. Offers environmental and natural resource sciences (PhD); environmental science (MS). *Faculty:* 7. *Students:* 42 full-time (24 women), 34 part-time (17 women); includes 8 minority (1 African American, 2 American Indian/Alaska Native, 3 Asian Americans or Pacific Islanders, 2 Hispanic Americans), 2 international. Average age 29. 76 applicants, 32% accepted, 18 enrolled. In 2009, 15 master's awarded. *Degree requirements:* For master's, comprehensive exam (for some programs), thesis (for some programs), oral exam; for doctorate, comprehensive exam, thesis/dissertation, oral exam, written exam. *Entrance requirements:* For doctorate, minimum GPA of 3.0. Additional exam requirements/recommendations for international students: Required—TOEFL, IELTS. *Application deadline:* For fall admission, 1/10 priority date for domestic students, 1/10 for international students. Applications are processed on a rolling basis. Application fee: $50. *Financial support:* In 2009–10, 16 students received support, including 1 fellowship (averaging $3,000 per year), 4 research assistantships with full and partial tuition reimbursements available (averaging $13,917 per year), 4 teaching assistantships with full and partial tuition reimbursements available (averaging $13,506 per year); Federal Work-Study, institutionally sponsored loans, and tuition waivers (partial) also available. Financial award application deadline: 2/15; financial award applicants required to submit FAFSA. *Unit head:* Dr. John A. Wolff, Head, 509-335-2825, E-mail: jawolff@mail.wsu.edu. *Application contact:* Graduate School Admissions, 800-GRADWSU, Fax: 509-335-1949, E-mail: gradsch@wsu.edu.

Washington State University Tri-Cities, Graduate Programs, Program in Environmental Science, Richland, WA 99352-1671. Offers applied environmental science (MS); environmental science (PhD). Part-time programs available. *Faculty:* 40. *Students:* 5 full-time (1 woman), 37 part-time (17 women); includes 3 minority (1 African American, 1 American Indian/Alaska Native, 1 Hispanic American). *Degree requirements:* For master's, comprehensive exam, thesis (for some programs), oral exam; for doctorate, comprehensive exam, thesis/dissertation. *Entrance requirements:* For master's, GRE General Test, minimum GPA of 3.0, 3 letters of recommendation. Additional exam requirements/recommendations for international students: Required—TOEFL (minimum score 550 paper-based; 213 computer-based). *Application deadline:* For fall admission, 1/10 priority date for domestic students, 1/10 for international students; for spring admission, 7/1 priority date for domestic students, 7/1 for international students. Application fee: $50. *Expenses:* Tuition, state resident: part-time $423 per credit. Tuition, nonresident: part-time $1032 per credit. *Financial support:* In 2009–10, 8 students received support, including research assistantships with full and partial tuition reimbursements available (averaging $14,634 per year), teaching assistantships with full and partial tuition reimbursements available (averaging $13,383 per year); fellowships, Federal Work-Study, scholarships/grants, health care benefits, and unspecified assistantships also available. Financial award application deadline: 1/15. *Faculty research:* Radiation ecology, cytogenetics. *Unit head:* John Strand, Graduate Advisor, 509-372-7326, E-mail: jstrand@tricity.wsu.edu. *Application contact:* Bonnie Bates, Graduate School Admissions, 800-GRADWSU, Fax: 509-372-7171, E-mail: bbates@tricity.wsu.edu.

Washington State University Vancouver, Graduate Programs, Program in Environmental Science, Vancouver, WA 98686. Offers MS. *Faculty:* 16. *Students:* 22 full-time (12 women); includes 3 minority (1 American Indian/Alaska Native, 1 Asian American or Pacific Islander, 1 Hispanic American). Average age 38. In 2009, 5 master's awarded. *Degree requirements:* For master's, comprehensive exam, thesis (for some programs). *Entrance requirements:* For master's, GRE General Test, minimum GPA of 3.0, 3 letters of recommendation. Additional exam requirements/recommendations for international students: Required—TOEFL (minimum score 550 paper-based; 213 computer-based). *Application deadline:* For fall admission, 1/10 priority date for domestic students, 1/10 for international students; for spring admission, 7/1 priority date for domestic students, 7/1 for international students. Application fee: $50. *Expenses:* Tuition, state resident: full-time $4228; part-time $423 per credit. Tuition, nonresident: full-time $10,322; part-time $1032 per credit. *Financial support:* In 2009–10, research assistantships with tuition reimbursements (averaging $14,634 per year), teaching assistantships (averaging $13,383 per year) were awarded. Financial award application deadline: 2/15. *Faculty research:* Conservation biology, environmental chemistry. *Unit head:* Dr. Stephen Bollens, Graduate Program Coordinator, 360-546-9611, Fax: 360-546-9064, E-mail: tissot@vancouver.wsu.edu. *Application contact:* Dawn Banker, Academic Coordinator, 360-546-9478, Fax: 360-546-9064, E-mail: bankerd@vancouver.wsu.edu.

Wesleyan University, Graduate Programs, Department of Earth and Environmental Sciences, Middletown, CT 06459. Offers MA. *Faculty:* 10 full-time (3 women). *Students:* 4 full-time (2 women). Average age 25. 6 applicants, 50% accepted, 1 enrolled. In 2009, 1 master's awarded. *Degree requirements:* For master's, thesis. *Entrance requirements:* For master's, GRE General Test, GRE Subject Test. Additional exam requirements/recommendations for international students: Required—TOEFL. *Application deadline:* For fall admission, 1/15 for domestic and international students. Applications are processed on a rolling basis. Application fee: $0. Electronic applications accepted. *Financial support:* In 2009–10, 3 teaching assistantships with full tuition reimbursements were awarded; tuition waivers (full and partial) also available. Financial award application deadline: 4/15; financial award applicants required to submit FAFSA. *Faculty research:* Tectonics, volcanology, stratigraphy, coastal processes, geochemistry. *Unit head:* Dr. Peter Patton, Chair, 860-685-2268, E-mail: ppatton@wesleyan.edu. *Application contact:* Ginny Harris, Administrative Assistant, 860-685-2244, E-mail: vharris@wesleyan.edu.

Western Connecticut State University, Division of Graduate Studies, School of Arts and Sciences, Department of Biological and Environmental Sciences, Danbury, CT 06810-6885. Offers MA. Part-time programs available. *Faculty:* 3 full-time (1 woman), 1 part-time/adjunct (0 women). *Students:* 2 full-time (1 woman), 19 part-time (11 women); includes 2 minority (1 African American, 1 American Indian/Alaska Native). Average age 39. 15 applicants, 73% accepted, 10 enrolled. In 2009, 2 master's awarded. *Degree requirements:* For master's, comprehensive exam or thesis, completion of program in 6 years. *Entrance requirements:* For master's, minimum GPA of 2.5. Additional exam requirements/recommendations for international students: Recommended—TOEFL (minimum score 550 paper-based; 213 computer-based; 79 iBT), IELTS (minimum score 6). *Application deadline:* For fall admission, 8/5 priority date for domestic students; for spring admission, 1/5 priority date for domestic students. Applications are processed on a rolling basis. Application fee: $50. *Expenses:* Tuition, state resident: full-time $5012; part-time $278 per credit hour. Tuition, nonresident: full-time $13,962; part-time $284 per credit hour. Required fees: $3886; $139 per credit hour. Full-time tuition and fees vary according to course load and program. Part-time tuition and fees vary according to course level, degree level and program. *Financial support:* Application deadline: 5/1; *Unit head:* Dr. Richard Halliburton, Graduate Coordinator, 203-837-8233, Fax: 203-837-8525, E-mail: halliburtonr@wcsu.edu. *Application contact:* Chris Shankle, Associate Director of Graduate Studies, 203-837-9005, Fax: 203-837-8326, E-mail: shanklec@wcsu.edu.

Western Washington University, Graduate School, Huxley College of the Environment, Department of Environmental Sciences, Bellingham, WA 98225-5996. Offers environmental science (MS); marine and estuarine science (MS). Part-time programs available. *Degree requirements:* For master's, thesis. *Entrance requirements:* For master's, GRE General Test, minimum GPA of 3.0 in last 60 semester hours or last 90 quarter hours. Additional exam requirements/recommendations for international students: Required—TOEFL (minimum score 567 paper-based; 227 computer-based). Electronic applications accepted. *Faculty research:* Landscape ecology, climate change, watershed studies, environmental toxicology and risk assessment, aquatic toxicology, toxic algae, invasive species.

Western Washington University, Graduate School, Huxley College of the Environment, Department of Environmental Studies, Bellingham, WA 98225-5996. Offers environmental education (M Ed); geography (MS). Part-time programs available. *Degree requirements:* For master's, thesis. *Entrance requirements:* For master's, GRE General Test, minimum GPA of 3.0 in last 60 semester hours or last 90 quarter hours. Additional exam requirements/recommendations for international students: Required—TOEFL (minimum score 567 paper-based; 227 computer-based). Electronic applications accepted. *Faculty research:* Geomorphology; pedogenesis; quaternary studies and climate change in the western U.S. landscape ecology, biogeography, pyrogeography, and spatial analysis.

West Texas A&M University, College of Agriculture, Nursing, and Natural Sciences, Department of Life, Earth, and Environmental Sciences, Program in Environmental Science, Canyon, TX 79016-0001. Offers MS. Part-time programs available. *Degree requirements:* For master's, comprehensive exam, thesis optional. *Entrance requirements:* For master's, GRE General Test. Additional exam requirements/recommendations for international students: Required—TOEFL (minimum score 550 paper-based). Electronic applications accepted. *Faculty research:* Degradation of presistant pesticides in soils and ground water, air quality.

Wichita State University, Graduate School, Fairmount College of Liberal Arts and Sciences, Department of Geology, Wichita, KS 67260. Offers earth, environmental, and physical sciences (MS). Part-time programs available. *Expenses:* Tuition, state resident: full-time $4247; part-time $235.95 per credit hour. Tuition, nonresident: full-time $11,171; part-time $620.60 per credit hour. Required fees: $34; $3.60 per credit hour. $17 per term. Tuition and fees vary according to campus/location and program. *Unit head:* Dr. William Parcell, Chair, 316-978-3140, E-mail: william.parcell@wichita.edu. *Application contact:* Dr. William Parcell, Chair, 316-978-3140, E-mail: william.parcell@wichita.edu.

Wright State University, School of Graduate Studies, College of Science and Mathematics, Department of Biological Sciences, Dayton, OH 45435. Offers biological sciences (MS); environmental sciences (MS). *Degree requirements:* For master's, thesis optional. *Entrance requirements:* Additional exam requirements/recommendations for international students: Required—TOEFL.

Wright State University, School of Graduate Studies, College of Science and Mathematics, Department of Chemistry, Dayton, OH 45435. Offers chemistry (MS); environmental sciences (MS). Part-time and evening/weekend programs available. *Degree requirements:* For master's, oral defense of thesis, seminar. *Entrance requirements:* Additional exam requirements/recommendations for international students: Required—TOEFL. *Faculty research:* Polymer synthesis and characterization, laser kinetics, organic and inorganic synthesis, analytical and environmental chemistry.

Wright State University, School of Graduate Studies, College of Science and Mathematics, Program in Environmental Sciences, Dayton, OH 45435. Offers PhD.

Yale University, Graduate School of Arts and Sciences, Department of Forestry and Environmental Studies, New Haven, CT 06520. Offers environmental sciences (PhD); forestry (PhD). *Degree requirements:* For doctorate, thesis/dissertation. *Entrance requirements:* For doctorate, GRE General Test.

Yale University, School of Forestry and Environmental Studies, New Haven, CT 06511. Offers MEM, MES, MF, MFS, PhD, JD/MEM, MBA/MEM, MBA/MF, MEM/M Arch, MEM/MA, MEM/MPH, MF/MA. *Accreditation:* SAF (one or more programs are accredited). Part-time programs available. Terminal master's awarded for partial completion of doctoral program. *Degree requirements:* For master's, thesis (for some programs); for doctorate, thesis/dissertation. *Entrance requirements:* For master's, GRE General Test, GMAT or LSAT; for doctorate, GRE General Test. Additional exam requirements/recommendations for international students: Required—TOEFL (minimum score 600 paper-based; 250 computer-based; 100 iBT). Electronic applications accepted. *Expenses:* Contact institution. *Faculty research:* Environmental policy, social ecology, industrial environmental management, forestry, environmental health, urban ecology, water science policy.

Marine Affairs

Dalhousie University, Faculty of Management, Marine Affairs Program, Halifax, NS B3H 3J5, Canada. Offers MMM. *Faculty:* 2 full-time (0 women), 2 part-time/adjunct (0 women). *Students:* 18 full-time (10 women). Average age 31. 67 applicants, 34% accepted. In 2009, 20 master's awarded. *Degree requirements:* For master's, project. *Entrance requirements:* For master's, minimum GPA of 3.0. Additional exam requirements/recommendations for international students: Required—TOEFL, IELTS, CANTEST, CAEL, or Michigan English Language Assessment Battery. *Application deadline:* For fall admission, 2/28 for domestic and international students. Application fee: $70. Electronic applications accepted. *Financial support:* In 2009–10, 6 students received support. Scholarships/grants available. Financial award application deadline: 1/31. *Faculty research:* Coastal zone management, sea use planning, development of non-living resources, protection and preservation of the coastal and marine environment, marine law and policy, fisheries management, maritime transport, conflict management. Total annual research expenditures: $45,550. *Unit head:* Dr. Lucia Fanning, Graduate Coordinator, 902-494-8390, Fax: 902-494-1001, E-mail: marine.affairs@dal.ca. *Application contact:* Becky Field, Administrator, 902-494-3555, Fax: 902-494-1001, E-mail: marine.affairs@dal.ca.

Duke University, Nicholas School of the Environment, Durham, NC 27708-0328. Offers coastal environmental management (MEM); DEL-environmental leadership (MEM); energy and environment (MEM); environmental economics and policy (MEM); environmental health and security (MEM); forest resource management (MF); global environmental change (MEM); resource ecology (MEM); water and air resources (MEM); JD/AM; JD/MEM; JD/MF; MAT/MEM; MBA/MEM; MBA/MF; MEM/MPP; MF/MPP. *Accreditation:* SAF (one or more programs are accredited). Part-time programs available. *Degree requirements:* For master's, thesis. *Entrance requirements:* For master's, GRE General Test, previous course work in biology or ecology, calculus, statistics, and microeconomics; computer familiarity with word processing and data analysis. Additional exam requirements/recommendations for international students: Required—TOEFL (minimum score 550 paper-based; 213 computer-based). Electronic applications accepted. *Expenses:* Contact institution. *Faculty research:* Ecosystem management, conservation ecology, earth systems, risk assessment.

East Carolina University, Graduate School, Program in Coastal Resources Management, Greenville, NC 27858-4353. Offers PhD. *Degree requirements:* For doctorate, comprehensive exam, thesis/dissertation, internship. *Entrance requirements:* For doctorate, GRE. Additional exam requirements/recommendations for international students: Required—TOEFL. *Faculty research:* Coastal geology, wetlands and coastal ecology, ecological and social networks, submerged cultural resources, coastal resources economics.

Florida Institute of Technology, Graduate Programs, College of Engineering, Department of Marine and Environmental Systems, Program in Oceanography, Melbourne, FL 32901-6975. Offers biological oceanography (MS); chemical oceanography (MS); coastal zone management (MS); geological oceanography (MS); oceanography (PhD); physical oceanography (MS). Part-time programs available. *Students:* Average age 30.Terminal master's awarded for partial completion of doctoral program. *Degree requirements:* For master's, thesis (for some programs); for doctorate, one foreign language, comprehensive exam, thesis/dissertation, departmental qualifying exams. *Entrance requirements:* For master's, GRE General Test, minimum GPA of 3.0; for doctorate, GRE General Test, minimum GPA of 3.3, resume. *Application deadline:* Applications are processed on a rolling basis. Electronic applications accepted. *Expenses:* Tuition: Part-time $1015 per credit. Tuition and fees vary according to campus/location and program. *Financial support:* Research assistantships with full and partial tuition reimbursements, teaching assistantships with full and partial tuition reimbursements, career-related internships or fieldwork and tuition remissions available. Financial award application deadline: 3/1; financial award applicants required to submit FAFSA. *Faculty research:* Marine geochemistry, ecosystem dynamics, coastal processes, marine pollution, environmental modeling. Total annual research expenditures: $938,395. *Unit head:* Dr. Dean R. Norris, Chair, 321-674-7377, Fax: 321-674-7212, E-mail: norris@fit.edu. *Application contact:* Carolyn P. Shea.

See Close-Ups on pages 167 and 411.

Louisiana State University and Agricultural and Mechanical College, Graduate School, School of the Coast and Environment, Department of Oceanography and Coastal Sciences, Baton Rouge, LA 70803. Offers MS, PhD. *Faculty:* 29 full-time (4 women), 2 part-time/adjunct (0 women). *Students:* 53 full-time (32 women), 8 part-time (3 women); includes 2 Hispanic Americans, 15 international. Average age 30. 33 applicants, 42% accepted, 9 enrolled. In 2009, 9 master's, 11 doctorates awarded. *Degree requirements:* For master's, thesis (for some programs); for doctorate, one foreign language, thesis/dissertation. *Entrance requirements:* For master's, GRE General Test, minimum GPA of 3.0; for doctorate, GRE General Test, MA or MS, minimum GPA of 3.0. Additional exam requirements/recommendations for international students: Required—TOEFL (minimum score 550 paper-based; 213 computer-based; 79 iBT) or IELTS (minimum score 6.5). *Application deadline:* For fall admission, 1/25 priority date for domestic students, 5/15 for international students; for spring admission, 10/15 for international students. Applications are processed on a rolling basis. Application fee: $50 ($70 for international students). *Financial support:* In 2009–10, 55 students received support, including 8 fellowships (averaging $24,370 per year), 42 research assistantships with full and partial tuition reimbursements available (averaging $19,799 per year), 5 teaching assistantships with full and partial tuition reimbursements available (averaging $15,533 per year); Federal Work-Study, institutionally sponsored loans, scholarships/grants, health care benefits, tuition waivers (full and partial), and unspecified assistantships also available. Support available to part-time students. Financial award applicants required to submit FAFSA. *Faculty research:* Physical and geological oceanography, wetland sustainability and restoration fisheries, coastal ecology and biogeochemistry. Total annual research expenditures: $8.9 million. *Unit head:* Dr. Donald Baltz, Chair, 225-578-6308, Fax: 225-578-6307, E-mail: dbaltz@lsu.edu. *Application contact:* Dr. Charles Lindau, Graduate Adviser, 225-578-8766, Fax: 225-578-6423, E-mail: clinda1@lsu.edu.

Memorial University of Newfoundland, School of Graduate Studies, Department of Sociology, St. John's, NL A1C 5S7, Canada. Offers gender (PhD); maritime sociology (PhD); sociology (M Phil, MA); work and development (PhD). Part-time programs available. *Degree requirements:* For master's, comprehensive exam, thesis optional, program journal (M Phil); for doctorate, one foreign language, comprehensive exam, thesis/dissertation, oral defense of thesis. *Entrance requirements:* For master's, 2nd class degree from university of recognized standing in area of study; for doctorate, MA, M Phil, or equivalent. Electronic applications accepted. *Faculty research:* Work and development, gender, maritime sociology.

Memorial University of Newfoundland, School of Graduate Studies, Interdisciplinary Program in Marine Studies, St. John's, NL A1C 5S7, Canada. Offers fisheries resource management (MMS, Advanced Diploma). Part-time programs available. *Degree requirements:* For master's, report. *Entrance requirements:* For master's and Advanced Diploma, high 2nd class degree from a recognized university. *Faculty research:* Biological, ecological and oceanographic aspects of world fisheries; economics; political science; sociology.

Nova Southeastern University, Oceanographic Center, Program in Coastal Zone Management, Dania Beach, FL 33004. Offers MS. *Faculty:* 15 full-time (1 woman), 5 part-time/adjunct (0 women). *Students:* 16 full-time (11 women), 50 part-time (34 women); includes 10 minority (6 African Americans, 1 Asian American or Pacific Islander, 3 Hispanic Americans). Average age 28. 35 applicants, 86% accepted, 20 enrolled. In 2009, 5 master's awarded. *Entrance requirements:* For master's, GRE. Additional exam requirements/recommendations for international students: Required—TOEFL (minimum score 550 paper-based). *Application deadline:* Applications are processed on a rolling basis. Application fee: $50. *Financial support:* Career-related internships or fieldwork, Federal Work-Study, scholarships/grants, and unspecified assistantships available. Financial award applicants required to submit FAFSA. *Unit head:* Dr. Richard Spieler, Director of Academic Programs, 954-262-3600, Fax: 954-262-4020, E-mail: spieler@nova.edu. *Application contact:* Dr. Richard Spieler, Director of Academic Programs, 954-262-3600, Fax: 954-262-4020, E-mail: spieler@nova.edu.

Old Dominion University, College of Business and Public Administration, Master's Program in Business Administration, Norfolk, VA 23529. Offers business and economic forecasting (MBA); financial analysis and valuation (MBA); information technology and enterprise integration (MBA); international business (MBA); maritime and port management (MBA); public administration (MBA). *Accreditation:* AACSB. Part-time and evening/weekend programs available. *Faculty:* 66 full-time (15 women), 6 part-time/adjunct (1 woman). *Students:* 81 full-time (27 women), 198 part-time (92 women); includes 46 minority (25 African Americans, 1 American Indian/Alaska Native, 13 Asian Americans or Pacific Islanders, 7 Hispanic Americans), 31 international. Average age 30. 169 applicants, 52% accepted, 61 enrolled. In 2009, 81 master's awarded. *Entrance requirements:* For master's, GMAT, letters of reference, resume, coursework in calculus. Additional exam requirements/recommendations for international students: Required—TOEFL (minimum score 550 paper-based; 213 computer-based; 80 iBT). *Application deadline:* For fall admission, 6/1 priority date for domestic students, 4/15 priority date for international students; for spring admission, 11/1 priority date for domestic students, 10/1 priority date for international students. Applications are processed on a rolling basis. Application fee: $50. Electronic applications accepted. *Expenses:* Tuition, state resident: full-time $8112; part-time $338 per credit. Tuition, nonresident: full-time $20,256; part-time $844 per credit. Required fees: $119 per semester. One-time fee: $50. *Financial support:* In 2009–10, 46 students received support, including 31 research assistantships with partial tuition reimbursements available (averaging $7,000 per year), 3 teaching assistantships with partial tuition reimbursements available (averaging $6,300 per year); career-related internships or fieldwork, scholarships/grants, and unspecified assistantships also available. Support available to part-time students. Financial award application deadline: 2/15; financial award applicants required to submit FAFSA. *Faculty research:* International business, buyer behavior, financial markets, strategy, operations research. *Unit head:* Dr. Bruce Rubin, Graduate Program Director, 757-683-3585, E-mail: mbainfo@odu.edu. *Application contact:* Shanna Wood, MBA Program Manager, 757-683-3585, Fax: 757-683-5750, E-mail: mbainfo@odu.edu.

Oregon State University, Graduate School, College of Oceanic and Atmospheric Sciences, Program in Marine Resource Management, Corvallis, OR 97331. Offers MA, MS. *Students:* 26 full-time (15 women), 3 part-time (all women); includes 3 minority (2 Asian Americans or Pacific Islanders, 1 Hispanic American), 2 international. Average age 30. In 2009, 9 master's awarded. *Degree requirements:* For master's, thesis optional. *Entrance requirements:* For master's, GRE General Test, minimum GPA of 3.0 in last 90 hours of course work. Additional exam requirements/recommendations for international students: Required—TOEFL. *Application deadline:* For fall admission, 2/1 priority date for domestic students. Applications are processed on a rolling basis. Application fee: $50. *Expenses:* Tuition, state resident: full-time $9774; part-time $362 per credit. Tuition, nonresident: full-time $15,849; part-time $587 per credit. Required fees: $1639. Full-time tuition and fees vary according to course load and program. *Financial support:* Fellowships, research assistantships, teaching assistantships, career-related internships or fieldwork, Federal Work-Study, and institutionally sponsored loans available. Support available to part-time students. Financial award application deadline: 2/1. *Faculty research:* Ocean and coastal resources, fisheries resources, marine pollution, marine recreation and tourism. *Unit head:* Dr. Robert S. Allan, Assistant Director, Student Programs, 541-737-1340, Fax: 541-737-2064, E-mail: rallan@coas.oregonstate.edu. *Application contact:* Dr. Robert S. Allan, Assistant Director, Student Programs, 541-737-1340, Fax: 541-737-2064, E-mail: rallan@coas.oregonstate.edu.

Stevens Institute of Technology, Graduate School, Charles V. Schaefer Jr. School of Engineering, Department of Civil, Environmental, and Ocean Engineering, Program in Maritime Systems, Hoboken, NJ 07030. Offers MS. *Expenses:* Tuition: Full-time $9900; part-time $1100 per credit. Required fees: $286 per semester.

Université du Québec à Rimouski, Graduate Programs, Program in Management of Marine Resources, Rimouski, QC G5L 3A1, Canada. Offers M Sc, Diploma. Part-time programs available. *Entrance requirements:* For master's, appropriate bachelor's degree, proficiency in French.

University of Delaware, College of Marine and Earth Studies, School of Marine Science and Policy, Newark, DE 19716. Offers MMM, MMP, MS, PhD.

University of Maine, Graduate School, College of Natural Sciences, Forestry, and Agriculture, School of Marine Sciences, Program in Marine Policy, Orono, ME 04469. Offers MS. *Students:* 6 full-time (4 women), 3 part-time (2 women), 1 international. Average age 31. 13 applicants, 15% accepted, 1 enrolled. In 2009, 5 master's awarded. *Degree requirements:* For master's, thesis. *Entrance requirements:* For master's, GRE General Test. Additional exam requirements/recommendations for international students: Required—TOEFL. *Application deadline:* For fall

Marine Affairs

University of Maine (continued)
admission, 2/1 priority date for domestic students. Applications are processed on a rolling basis. Application fee: $65. Electronic applications accepted. *Financial support:* Fellowships with tuition reimbursements, research assistantships with tuition reimbursements, teaching assistantships with tuition reimbursements, career-related internships or fieldwork, Federal Work-Study, and tuition waivers (full and partial) available. Support available to part-time students. Financial award application deadline: 3/1. *Unit head:* Dr. James Wilson, Coordinator, 207-581-4368. *Application contact:* Scott G. Delcourt, Associate Dean of the Graduate School, 207-581-3219, Fax: 207-581-3232, E-mail: graduate@maine.edu.

University of Miami, Graduate School, Rosenstiel School of Marine and Atmospheric Science, Division of Marine Affairs and Policy, Coral Gables, FL 33124. Offers MA, MS, JD/MA. Part-time programs available. *Degree requirements:* For master's, comprehensive exam, thesis (for some programs), internship, paper. *Entrance requirements:* For master's, GRE General Test. Additional exam requirements/recommendations for international students: Required—TOEFL (minimum score 550 paper-based; 213 computer-based). Electronic applications accepted.

University of Rhode Island, Graduate School, College of the Environment and Life Sciences, Department of Marine Affairs, Kingston, RI 02881. Offers MA, MESM, MMA, PhD, JD/MMA. Part-time programs available. *Faculty:* 7 full-time (1 woman). *Students:* 30 full-time (17 women), 17 part-time (9 women); includes 2 minority (1 Asian American or Pacific Islander, 1 Hispanic American), 3 international. In 2009, 9 master's awarded. *Degree requirements:* For master's, comprehensive exam (for some programs), thesis optional; for doctorate, comprehensive exam, thesis/dissertation. *Entrance requirements:* For master's, GRE (for MA), 2 letters of recommendation (for MMA); for doctorate, GRE, 2 letters of recommendation, writing sample. Additional exam requirements/recommendations for international students: Required—TOEFL (minimum score 550 paper-based; 213 computer-based). *Application deadline:* For fall admission, 4/7 for domestic students, 2/1 for international students. Application fee: $65. Electronic applications accepted. *Expenses:* Tuition, state resident: full-time $8828; part-time $490 per credit hour. Tuition, nonresident: full-time $22,100; part-time $1228 per credit hour. Required fees: $1118; $57 per semester. Tuition and fees vary according to program. *Financial support:* In 2009–10, 3 research assistantships with full tuition reimbursements (averaging $13,894 per year), 5 teaching assistantships with full and partial tuition reimbursements (averaging $9,213 per year) were awarded. Financial award application deadline: 2/1; financial award applicants required to submit FAFSA. *Faculty research:* Assessing change in coastal ecosystems and its impact to society. Total annual research expenditures: $207,297. *Unit head:* Dr. Richard Pollnac, Chair, 401-874-5107, Fax: 401-874-2156, E-mail: pollnac3@gmail.com. *Application contact:* Dr. Richard Burroughs, Director of Master's Studies, 401-874-4045, Fax: 401-874-2156, E-mail: rburroughs@uri.edu.

University of San Diego, College of Arts and Sciences, Department of Marine Science and Environmental Studies, San Diego, CA 92110-2492. Offers marine science (MS). Part-time programs available. *Faculty:* 3 full-time (2 women). *Students:* 5 full-time (4 women), 14 part-time (7 women); includes 1 minority (Hispanic American). Average age 27. 14 applicants, 64% accepted, 4 enrolled. In 2009, 3 master's awarded. *Degree requirements:* For master's, thesis. *Entrance requirements:* For master's, GRE General Test, minimum GPA of 3.0, undergraduate major in science. Additional exam requirements/recommendations for international students: Required—TOEFL (minimum score 580 paper-based; 237 computer-based; 83 iBT), TWE. *Application deadline:* For fall admission, 4/1 for domestic and international students. Applications are processed on a rolling basis. Application fee: $45. Electronic applications accepted. *Expenses:* Tuition: Full-time $21,042; part-time $1169 per unit. Required fees: $224. Full-time tuition and fees vary according to course load and degree level. *Financial support:* In 2009–10, 9 students received support. Career-related internships or fieldwork, Federal Work-Study, institutionally sponsored loans, and unspecified assistantships available. Support available to part-time students. Financial award application deadline: 4/1; financial award applicants required to submit FAFSA. *Faculty research:* Bioacoustics, aquaculture, molecular genetics, ecology, physiology. *Unit head:* Dr. Ronald S. Kaufmann, Director, 619-260-5904, Fax: 619-260-6874, E-mail: kaufmann@sandiego.edu. *Application contact:* Dr. John Mosby, Associate Director of Graduate Admissions, 619-260-4524, Fax: 619-260-4158, E-mail: grads@sandiego.edu.

University of Washington, Graduate School, College of Ocean and Fishery Sciences, School of Marine Affairs, Seattle, WA 98195. Offers MMA, Graduate Certificate. *Degree requirements:* For master's, thesis. *Entrance requirements:* For master's, GRE General Test, minimum GPA of 3.0. Additional exam requirements/recommendations for international students: Required—TOEFL. Electronic applications accepted. *Faculty research:* Marine pollution, port authorities, fisheries management, global climate change, marine environmental protection.

University of West Florida, College of Arts and Sciences: Arts, Division of Anthropology and Archaeology, Pensacola, FL 32514-5750. Offers anthropology (MA); historical archaeology (MA); maritime studies (MA). *Faculty:* 7 full-time (2 women). *Students:* 40 full-time (24 women), 20 part-time (15 women); includes 8 minority (2 African Americans, 2 Asian Americans or Pacific Islanders, 4 Hispanic Americans). Average age 28. 59 applicants, 54% accepted, 20 enrolled. In 2009, 10 master's awarded. *Degree requirements:* For master's, internship or thesis. *Entrance requirements:* For master's, GRE, bachelor's degree in anthropology, minimum GPA of 3.0, 3 letters of recommendation, writing sample. Additional exam requirements/recommendations for international students: Required—TOEFL (minimum score 550 paper-based; 213 computer-based). *Application deadline:* For fall admission, 6/1 for domestic students, 5/15 for international students; for spring admission, 11/1 for domestic students, 10/1 for international students. Application fee: $30. *Expenses:* Tuition, state resident: full-time $4982; part-time $260 per credit hour. Tuition, nonresident: full-time $20,059; part-time $919 per credit hour. Required fees: $1247; $52 per credit hour. *Financial support:* In 2009–10, 10 research assistantships with partial tuition reimbursements (averaging $3,760 per year), 7 teaching assistantships with partial tuition reimbursements (averaging $3,938 per year) were awarded; unspecified assistantships also available. Financial award application deadline: 4/15; financial award applicants required to submit FAFSA. *Unit head:* Dr. John Bratten, Interim Chair, 850-857-6278, E-mail: anthropology@uwf.edu. *Application contact:* Terry McCray, Assistant Director of Graduate Admissions, 850-473-7718, Fax: 850-473-7714, E-mail: gradadmissions@uwf.edu.

University of West Florida, College of Arts and Sciences: Sciences, School of Allied Health and Life Sciences, Department of Biology, Pensacola, FL 32514-5750. Offers biological chemistry (MS); biology (MS); biology education (MST); biotechnology (MS); coastal zone studies (MS); environmental biology (MS). *Faculty:* 7 full-time (2 women), 1 (woman) part-time/adjunct. *Students:* 5 full-time (1 woman), 21 part-time (14 women); includes 2 minority (1 Asian American or Pacific Islander, 1 Hispanic American), 1 international. Average age 28. 19 applicants, 58% accepted, 7 enrolled. In 2009, 12 master's awarded. *Degree requirements:* For master's, thesis. *Entrance requirements:* For master's, GRE General Test. Additional exam requirements/recommendations for international students: Required—TOEFL (minimum score 550 paper-based; 213 computer-based). *Application deadline:* For fall admission, 6/1 for domestic students, 5/15 for international students; for spring admission, 11/1 for domestic students, 10/1 for international students. Applications are processed on a rolling basis. Application fee: $30. *Expenses:* Tuition, state resident: full-time $4982; part-time $260 per credit hour. Tuition, nonresident: full-time $20,059; part-time $919 per credit hour. Required fees: $1247; $52 per credit hour. *Financial support:* In 2009–10, 2 research assistantships with partial tuition reimbursements (averaging $8,500 per year), 10 teaching assistantships with partial tuition reimbursements (averaging $8,176 per year) were awarded; unspecified assistantships also available. Financial award application deadline: 4/15; financial award applicants required to submit FAFSA. *Unit head:* Dr. George L. Stewart, Chairperson, 850-474-2748. *Application contact:* Terry McCray, Assistant Director of Graduate Admissions, 850-473-7718, Fax: 850-473-7714, E-mail: gradadmissions@uwf.edu.

FLORIDA INSTITUTE OF TECHNOLOGY

College of Engineering, Department of Marine and Environmental Systems Programs in Environmental Sciences, Meteorology, Earth Remote Sensing, and Environmental Resource Management

Programs of Study

Florida Institute of Technology offers programs of study leading to Master of Science and Doctor of Philosophy degrees in environmental science, the M.S. degree in meteorology, the M.S. degree in environmental resource management, and the M.S. degree in Earth remote sensing. These programs are designed to prepare students for careers in industry, government, colleges and universities, or consulting firms. Emphasis is on the application of scientific principles to the maintenance and wise use of the environment. The environmental science curriculum provides a thorough background in the biological and chemical fundamentals of natural systems and water and wastewater treatment systems. The principal areas of emphasis in environmental science are related to freshwater and estuarine problems in areas such as eutrophication, toxic wastes, aquatic ecology, and hydrology; to groundwater contamination problems from sources such as septic tanks, landfills, and underground storage tanks; to air pollution, such as air quality monitoring and impacts of air pollutants on natural systems; to renewable energy, environmental and marine remote sensing, and real-time spectral monitoring of environmental systems using in situ sensors, aircraft, and ships as well as satellites and geographic information systems (GIS). Atmospheric science is focused on understanding Earth's gaseous envelope, predicting its evolution, and mitigating human impacts. The M.S. program at Florida Tech is uniquely interdisciplinary, drawing on expertise from the College of Engineering, the College of Aeronautics, the College of Science, and the College of Psychology and Liberal Arts. As such, the M.S. in meteorology can have special emphasis in areas such as marine meteorology, water resources, atmospheric chemistry, aviation meteorology, or remote sensing.

The Department also offers an M.S. program in coastal zone management and M.S. and Ph.D. programs in the marine sciences of biological, chemical, geological, and physical oceanography, with specializations in geophysical remote sensing of the environment and in ocean engineering. A highly interdisciplinary education is emphasized in this program.

Degree requirements and additional information may be found at http://coe.fit.edu/dmes/oceanography.php.

Research Facilities

The programs offer extensive facilities for instruction and research, such as an environmental optics laboratory and satellite data reception, as part of the Florida Tech Center for Remote Sensing and the Geographical Information System (GIS) facility. The marine and environmental sciences laboratory is equipped with such standard water analysis equipment as balances, ovens, muffle furnaces, a chemical oxygen-demand apparatus, a macro-Kjeldahl apparatus, pH meters, and spectrophotometers. Analytical instruments provided for advanced study include an ion chromatograph, a total organic carbon analyzer, an atomic absorption spectrophotometer, and an auto analyzer. For the M.S. in meteorology, collaborative research is conducted with specialists from the nearby NASA Kennedy Space Center, the USAF 45th Weather Squadron, the NOAA National Weather Service, the Harbor Branch Oceanographic Institute, WHIRL (Wind and Hurricane Impacts Research Laboratory), and local government agencies and corporations. The synoptic meteorology laboratory is equipped to download and analyze weather data and is a node for SuomiNet.

Financial Aid

Graduate teaching and research assistantships and endowed fellowships are available to a limited number of qualified students. For 2010–11, typical financial support ranges from $16,000 upward, including stipend and tuition, per academic year for approximately half-time duties. Stipend-only assistantships are sometimes awarded for less time commitment. Students with internships may receive an hourly salary.

Cost of Study

Tuition is $1040 per graduate semester hour in 2010–11. New students must pay a tuition deposit of $300, which is deducted from the first semester's tuition charge.

Living and Housing Costs

Room and board on campus cost approximately $4500 per semester in 2010–11. On-campus housing (dormitories and apartments) is available for full-time single and married graduate students, but priority for dormitory rooms is given to undergraduate students. Many apartment complexes and rental houses are available near the campus.

Student Group

Graduate students constitute more than one quarter of the approximately 4,000 students on the Melbourne campus. They come from all parts of the United States and from many other countries.

Student Outcomes

Graduates of the program obtain positions in places such as the U.S Environmental Protection Agency, the Florida Department of Environmental Protection; St. John's River Water Management District; Brevard County; Sarasota County; Volusia County; South Florida Water Management District; U.S. Army Corps of Engineers; National Park Service; Lockheed Martin; NASA; Dynamac; Bionetics; Jordan, Jones and Goulding, Inc.; Florida Groundwater Services; Harris Corp.; Walt Disney World; NOAA National Weather Service; and the U.S. Air Force.

Location

Melbourne is located on the east coast of Florida. The climate is extremely pleasant, and opportunities for outdoor recreation abound. The John F. Kennedy Space Center and Disney World/EPCOT Center are nearby and the Atlantic beaches are within 3 miles of the campus.

The Institute

Florida Institute of Technology was founded in 1958 by a group of scientists and engineers pioneering America's space program at Cape Canaveral. The environmental remote sensing program utilizes the technology developed by the space program. Florida Tech has rapidly developed into a residential institution and is the only independent technological university in the Southeast. It is supported by the community and industry and is the recipient of many research grants and contracts, a number of which provide financial support for graduate students. The campus covers 175 acres and includes a beautiful botanical garden and an internationally known collection of palm trees.

Applying

Forms and instructions for applying for admission and assistantships are sent on request. Admission is possible at the beginning of any semester, but admission in the fall semester is recommended. It is advantageous to apply early. Entering students are expected to have had courses in chemistry, calculus, physics, and biology as well as a year or more of advanced science courses. The GRE General Test is required for admission.

Correspondence and Information

Dr. John G. Windsor Jr., Program Chair
Environmental Sciences Program
Florida Institute of Technology
Melbourne, Florida 32901
Phone: 321-674-8096
Fax: 321-984-8461
E-mail: dmes@fit.edu
Web site: http://www.fit.edu/AcadRes/dmes

Office of Graduate Admissions
Florida Institute of Technology
Melbourne, Florida 32901
Phone: 321-674-8027
800-944-4348 (toll-free in the U.S.)
Fax: 321-723-9468
E-mail: grad-admissions@fit.edu
Web site: http://www.fit.edu

Florida Institute of Technology

THE FACULTY AND RESEARCH AREAS

(For additional information see http://www.fit.edu/faculty/profile)

Thomas V. Belanger, Professor; Ph.D., Florida. Limonology, oxygen budgets, groundwater/surface water interaction, eutrophication.
Charles R. Bostater, Associate Professor; Ph.D., Delaware. Remote sensing, hydrologic optics, modeling of toxic substances, coastal physical oceanography, numerical modeling.
Sen Chaio, Ph.D., North Carolina State. Numerical weather prediction, boundary layer meteorology, mesoscale meteorology, tropical weather systems.
Iver W. Duedall, Professor Emeritus; Ph.D., Dalhousie. Chemical oceanography, physical chemistry of seawater, marine pollution, ocean management.
Joseph Dwyer, Professor; Ph.D., Chicago. Physics and space sciences, lightning, atmospheric electricity, thunderstorms.
Howell H. Heck, Associate Professor; Ph.D., Arkansas. Hazardous wastes, permitting regulations, waste water.
Steven M. Lazarus, Assistant Professor; Ph.D., Oklahoma. Mesoscale predictability, coastal meteorology, atmospheric modeling, data assimilation.
George A. Maul, Professor; Ph.D., Miami. Coastal physical oceanography, climate and sea change, Atlantic tsunamis, Earth system science.
Jean-Paul Pinelli, Professor; Ph.D., Georgia Tech. Energy dissipation, structures, wind.
Hamid K. Rassoul, Professor; Ph.D., Texas at Dallas. Lightning, space weather, aeronomy, auroras.
John H. Trefry, Professor; Ph.D., Texas A&M. Marine geochemistry, trace metals, deep-sea hydrothermal vents, marine pollution.
Tom Utley, Associate Professor; Ph.D., Florida Tech. Aviation meteorology, military meteorology, atmospheric pollution mediation.
John G. Windsor Jr., Professor and Program Chair, Environmental Sciences; Ph.D., William and Mary. Environmental analysis, organic compounds, water quality, air quality, environmental education, environmental management.

Adjunct Faculty
Frank R. Leslie, M.S., Harris Corporation.
Carlton R. Parks, M.S., Acta, Inc.
Michael Splitt, M.S., University of Utah.
Robert W. Virnstein, Ph.D. St. John's River Water Management District.

RESEARCH INTERESTS
Within the broad discipline of environmental science are areas of specialization that focus on physical, biological, or chemical issues of natural and human-made systems. Because of the interdisciplinary nature of the environmental sciences, the Department offers programs that link the following areas in an integrated systems approach, focusing on quantitative techniques:

Environmental Biology. Aquatic ecology, eutrophication of lakes, water quality indicator organisms, microbiology of wastewater treatment, wetlands systems, limnology, environmental planning, and impact statements.

Environmental Chemistry. Chemistry of natural waters, wetlands, nutrient cycling, nitrogen transformations, biogeochemical mass balance modeling, management models for water quality control, non-point-source pollution, and waste treatment.

Environmental Modeling. Specialized environmental climatological environmental systems, theoretical studies and numerical modeling of coastal processes, water quality modeling and toxic chemical modeling, and hazard assessments of chemicals in the environment.

Environmental Resource Management. Applied management practicums in internship opportunities are offered, such as EIS development and review, policy analysis, and natural resource management in developing countries.

Global Change. Global temperature change and sea level rise, carbon flux, and ozone depletion.

Remote Sensing and Real-Time Optical Spectral Monitoring. Earth remote sensing utilizing optical and microwave radiometry based on aircraft and ships and in estuarine, coastal, and inland waters and satellite altimetry. The program maintains the Center for Remote Sensing, with an image processing/remote sensing facility and an environmental optics laboratory.

Sustainable Development. Population control, wise use of resources, and environmental economics, with a special focus on islands.

SCHOOL OF PUBLIC AND ENVIRONMENTAL AFFAIRS
INDIANA UNIVERSITY

INDIANA UNIVERSITY BLOOMINGTON

School of Public and Environmental Affairs Environmental Science Graduate Programs

Programs of Study

The School of Public and Environmental Affairs (SPEA) offers graduate degree programs leading to the Master of Science in Environmental Science (M.S.E.S.).

The M.S.E.S. program educates professionals who combine specialization in an area of environmental science with the analytical and policy skills necessary to apply that knowledge in a broader context. This degree program includes an experiential requirement, usually fulfilled by an internship, but also allows for a research focus culminating in a traditional master's thesis.

For students desiring more in-depth study in environmental science, the M.S.E.S. program is an excellent preparation for entry into the Ph.D. in Environmental Science Program. Alternatively, students desiring more in-depth preparation in policy, law, or other related fields can combine their M.S.E.S. degree with a degree in public affairs (M.P.A./M.S.E.S.), law (M.S.E.S./J.D.), or a number of other disciplines in biology, chemistry, physics, geography, geological sciences, or journalism.

The M.S.E.S. program requires 48 credit hours distributed among four sets of courses: science courses, policy and management courses, tool-skill courses, and an experiential requirement. There are no required courses per se; however, each student is expected to demonstrate several competencies, depending on his or her concentration. These competencies include relevant natural and physical sciences, economics, policy or law, and quantitative problem solving. Concentrations include applied ecology; energy policy; environmental chemistry, toxicology, and risk assessment; environmental management; and water resources. Faculty adviser(s) work with the student to ensure that these competencies are met and that the student is pursuing a suitable plan of study. This curriculum provides students with a general knowledge of environmental science, tool skills to allow them to apply that knowledge, and a specialized area of expertise.

Research Facilities

Complementing the School's own resources, Indiana University maintains eight nationally prominent area studies centers and sixty language programs to facilitate international research and career interests. SPEA has affiliations with several research centers on both the Bloomington and Indianapolis campuses, including the Center for Research in Environmental Science; the Indiana University Research and Teaching Preserve; and the Center for the Study of Institutions, Population, and Environmental Change. In addition, IU's new multidisciplinary science building opened in October 2009. This 65,000-square-foot, five-story facility brings together IU researchers in environmental science, biogeochemistry, and other life sciences that cross disciplinary boundaries.

SPEA is committed to meeting the research needs of its students. PCs, mainframe computers, and a geographic information system (GIS) computing laboratory are available. More than forty additional computing sites on the Bloomington campus are available for student use. Libraries on the Bloomington campus house more than 6 million volumes, and another 3.2 million are available through the University's seven other campuses. SPEA houses an Information Commons, which provides convenient access to rich library resources, individual and group workstations, and student-centered services that support individual and collaborative learning and research.

Financial Aid

Departmental assistance for qualified students is awarded on a competitive basis and is determined by merit. Awards include fellowships, scholarships, and teaching and research assistantships. Prospective students may apply for merit-based awards by checking the appropriate box on the admission application form. Students may apply for need-based aid through the University Office of Student Financial Assistance (OSFA).

SPEA hosts a one-of-a-kind, collaborative program called Service Corps, which enables M.S.E.S. and M.P.A. students to apply their classroom learning directly to the field in both the public and nonprofit sectors. Service Corps is a financial aid mechanism that offers students real-world experience working in an array of governmental and nonprofit agencies while concurrently pursuing their academic plans. The program is a partnership among the University, the School, and a number of valued external stakeholders in the community and region. Students are selected for participation during the merit aid allocation process.

Cost of Study

In-state residents pay $391.55 per credit hour and nonresidents pay $850.33 per credit hour for master's programs in 2010–11.

Living and Housing Costs

The 1,139 on-campus apartments for graduate students range in monthly rent from $519 for a furnished efficiency to $1099 for an unfurnished three-bedroom apartment. Rates include all utilities as well as local telephone service, cable TV, and Internet connection. A variety of off-campus apartments are available near the University. Rents are generally inexpensive, with the average two-bedroom unit renting for $550 to $800 per month.

Student Group

About 45 students are enrolled in the M.S.E.S. program, 77 students are in the joint M.P.A./M.S.E.S. program, and 21 students are in the Ph.D. program in environmental science. About 9 percent of these students are international, and more than half are women.

SPEA recognizes service in AmeriCorps, Teach for America, and Peace Corps, hosting both Peace Corps Fellows/USA and Master's International (MI) Programs. Volunteers receive a waiver of the experiential component which is a part of the academic design and a reduction of the total number of credit hours required for degree completion. Peace Corps Fellows and MIs also receive a competitive merit aid package in addition to the benefits described above.

Student Outcomes

SPEA maintains an outstanding placement record, attributed to a well-rounded curriculum, national prestige, and strong alumni support. Within six months of the close of the 2008–09 academic year, approximately 76 percent of students responding to SPEA's annual employment survey indicated that they had procured full-time professional positions or were continuing their education. The SPEA Office of Career Services (OCS) is staffed with professionals who assist graduate students with all of their career development needs. With so many resources at their disposal, SPEA students annually compete for many of the most prestigious and competitive positions in federal and state government and top-tier nonprofits and foundations. Recent placements include positions with the Environmental Protection Agency; Department of State; National Forest Service; National Oceanographic and Atmospheric Institute; Nature Conservancy; Indiana Department of Environmental Management; U.S. Geological Survey; U.S. Agency for International Development; U.S. Department of Agriculture; Federal Highway Administration; ICF International; National Park Service; ABT Associates, Inc.; GEI Consultants, Inc.; Tetra Tech, Inc.; Federal Energy Regulatory Commission; U.S. Department of Energy; U.S. Peace Corps; NTH Consultants, Ltd.; and U.S. Fish and Wildlife Service.

Location

Bloomington, a college town with a population of 110,000, was chosen as one of the top 10 college towns in America for its "rich mixture of atmospherics and academia" by Edward Fiske, former education editor of the *New York Times.* It is a culturally vibrant community settled among southern Indiana's rolling hills, just 45 miles south of Indianapolis, the state capital. Mild winters and warm summers are ideal for outdoor recreation in the two state forests, one national forest, three state parks, and an array of lakes and streams that surround Bloomington.

The University and The School

Established in 1820, Indiana University has more than 7,500 graduate students and more than 38,000 students, total, enrolled on the Bloomington campus. SPEA is the top-ranked graduate program on the campus. Fifty-five other academic departments are ranked in the top 20 in the country, including music, business, biology, foreign languages, political science, and chemistry. Attractions include nearly 1,000 musical performances each year, including eight full-length operas and professional Broadway plays; the IU Art Museum, designed by I. M. Pei, with more than 30,000 art objects; fifty campus and community volunteer agencies; more than 700 student clubs and organizations; two indoor student recreational facilities; and Big Ten athletics.

SPEA, founded in 1972, was the first school to combine public management, policy, and administration with the environmental sciences.

Applying

Application files must include the SPEA admission application form, transcripts, GRE General Test scores, and three letters of recommendation. Priority is given to applications received by February 1. Students applying for awards must submit a complete application file by the priority deadline, February 1. School visits are encouraged. Applicants can access the School's Web site at http://www.spea.indiana.edu.

Correspondence and Information

For master's programs:
Master's Program Office
SPEA 260
Indiana University
Bloomington, Indiana 47405
Phone: 812-855-2840
800-765-7755 (toll-free in U.S. only)
E-mail: speainfo@indiana.edu
Web site: http://www.spea.indiana.edu

For doctoral programs:
Ph.D. Programs Office
SPEA 441
Indiana University
Bloomington, Indiana 47405
Phone: 812-855-2457
800-765-7755 (toll-free in U.S. only)
E-mail: speainfo@indiana.edu

Indiana University Bloomington

THE FACULTY AND THEIR RESEARCH

Osita G. Afoaku, Ph.D., Washington State, 1991. Human rights, sustainable development, democratization, and state reconstruction in Africa; U.S.-African/Third World relations; UN Security Council reform.
David B. Audretsch, Ph.D., Wisconsin, 1980. Economics policy, entrepreneurship, innovation, globalization, regional economic policy, industrial restructuring and government policy, small enterprises in Europe and the United States.
Matthew R. Auer, Ph.D., Yale, 1996. Intersection of foreign aid and sustainable development, international forest politics, energy efficiency, environmental education.
Matthew Bagetta, Ph.D., Harvard, 2009. Governance and management, time commitment of leaders in voluntary associations and special ties formed by associations in metropolitan regions, citizen engagement with politics and community and the subsequent influence on society's major institutions.
James Barnes, J.D., Harvard, 1967. Environmental law, domestic and international environmental policy, ethics and the public official, mediation and alternative dispute resolution, law and public policy.
Lisa Blomgren Bingham, J.D., Connecticut, 1979. Collaborative governance, comparative governance, dispute resolution, dispute system design, mediation, administrative law, labor and employment law.
Jennifer Brass, Ph.D., Berkeley, 2010. Governance and management, research on corruption, poverty reduction, international livestock policy; role of NGOs in public management in post-conflict countries.
Charles F. Bonser, Emeritus; D.B.A., Indiana, 1965. Regional economic development, the role of nongovernmental organizations, public policy, transatlantic education and policy.
Sanya Carley, Ph.D. candidate, North Carolina at Chapel Hill. Energy policy; energy technology innovation policy including sustainability of the electricity sector, effectiveness of energy policy incentives and regulatory efforts to alter states' electricity generation and operations, and the use of distributed generation and micro-grid electricity systems to compliment traditional macro-operations.
Melissa A. L. Clark, M.S., Indiana, 1999. Aquatic and terrestrial habitats, Indiana Clean Lakes Program, water resources and water quality.
Christopher B. Craft, Ph.D., North Carolina State, 1987. Wetland restoration and ecosystem development; wetlands and water quality; wetlands and climate change, including carbon sequestration and peat accretion.
Sameeksha Desai, Ph.D., George Mason, 2008. Entrepreneurship and economic development, focus on areas of violence, conflict, and disaster.
Denvil Duncan, Ph.D. candidate. Georgia State. Public finance, personal income taxation and income inequality.
Michael A. Edwards, Ph.D., North Dakota State, 1999. Atmospheric chemistry research: mechanistic studies of terpenes reacting with ozone, future regulation of hydrogen storage materials.
Sergio Fernandez, Ph.D., Georgia, 2004. Public management and organization theory, with focus on privatization and contracting out, public-sector leadership, and organizational change.
Burnell C. Fischer, Ph.D., Purdue, 1974. Forestry, particularly silviculture and urban forestry; growth and development of Central Hardwood Forest stands and response to various silvicultural practices; community and urban forestry issues; forest resources policy and state government management; human factors relating to forests and forest products, particularly with regard to collaborative forestry.
Beth Gazley, Ph.D., Georgia, 2004. Nonprofit management and governance, volunteerism, collaboration, intersectoral relations, role of the voluntary sector in emergency planning.
David Good, Ph.D., Pennsylvania, 1985. Quantitative policy modeling, productivity measurement in public and regulated industries, urban policy analysis.
John D. Graham, Ph.D., Carnegie Mellon, 1983. Government reform, energy and the environment, future of the automobile in both developed and developing countries.
Kirsten Grønbjerg, Ph.D., Chicago, 1974. Nonprofit and public-sector relationships, examining scope and community dimensions of the Indiana nonprofit sector, the American welfare system, nonprofit funding relations, nonprofit data sources.
Hendrik M. Haitjema, Ph.D., Minnesota, 1982. Groundwater flow modeling, including regional groundwater flow systems, conjunctive surface-water and groundwater flow modeling, 3-D groundwater flow, and saltwater intrusion problems, with emphasis on application of analytic functions to modeling groundwater flow, specifically analytic-element method.
Bradley T. Heim, Ph.D., Northwestern, 2002. Financial Economist in the Office of Tax Analysis at the U.S. Department of the Treasury. Public finance, focusing on behavioral impact of tax policies on labor supply, consumption, income and earnings, employment mode, health insurance purchases, charitable giving, and retirement savings.
Diane S. Henshel, Ph.D., Washington (St. Louis), 1987. Sublethal health effects of environmental pollutants, especially pollutant effects on the developing organism, including the effects of polychlorinated dibenzo-p-dioxins (PCDDs) and related congeners on the developing nervous system of birds exposed in the wild and under controlled laboratory conditions.
Monika Herzig, D.M.E., Indiana, 1997. Concert promotion, music industry, jazz education.
Ronald Hites, Ph.D., MIT, 1968. Applying organic analytical chemistry techniques to the analysis of trace levels of toxic pollutants, such as polychlorinated biphenyls and pesticides, with focus on understanding behavior of these compounds in the atmosphere and in the Great Lakes.
Cheryl Hughes, M.B.A., Indiana Wesleyan. Business, management, human resources.
Christopher Hunt, M.A., Cambridge, 1961. Programming and presentation of the performing and visual arts and entertainment.
Chaman Jain, Ph.D., Indiana, 1975. Governmental and nonprofit accounting and reporting, financial management in nonprofit organizations, governmental budgeting and finance, financial (corporate) management.
Craig Johnson, Ph.D., SUNY at Albany, 1993. Capital markets and financial intermediation, financial management, public budgeting and finance, financing e-government, financing economic development, environmental and infrastructure finance.
William W. Jones, M.S., Wisconsin–Madison, 1977. Lake and watershed management, especially diagnosing lake and watershed water-quality problems; preparing management plans to address problems identified; stream ecology; Caribbean coral reef ecology and underwater archaeology; certified lake manager (CLM).
Haeil Jung, Ph.D., Chicago, 2009. Applied econometrics and program evaluation, crime policy, public policy for low-income families.
Al Lyons, Ph.D., Indiana–Purdue at Indianapolis, 2009. Fundraising and engagement practices of nonprofit organizations, philanthropy, social entrepreneurship.
Kerry Krutilla, Ph.D., Duke, 1988. Theory and practice of benefit-cost analysis, environmental policy analysis, evaluation of environmental programs, natural resource management in developing countries.
Marc L. Lame, Ph.D., Arizona State, 1992. Implementation of integrated pest-management programs in schools and day-care facilities.
Leslie Lenkowsky, Ph.D., Harvard, 1982. Nonprofits and public policy, civil society in comparative perspective, institutional grant makers, volunteering and civic engagement, education and social welfare policy, social entrepreneurship.
Joyce Y. Man, Ph.D., Johns Hopkins, 1993. Public finance, urban and regional economics, international trade, economic development, public budgeting and financial management.
Eugene B. McGregor Jr., Ph.D., Syracuse, 1968. Interaction of public policy, organizational structure, and management practice; special interest in the relationship between education and economic development and in impacts of information technology on structure and management of public and nonprofit enterprise.
Michael McGuire, Ph.D., Indiana, 1995. Intergovernmental and interorganizational collaboration and networks, federalism and intergovernmental relations, public management, emergency management.
Vicky J. Meretsky, Ph.D., Arizona, 1995. Ecology and management of rare species, biocomplexity, landscape-level species and community conservation, temporal patterns in biodiversity, integrating ecosystem research and endangered species management within adaptive management.
John L. Mikesell, Ph.D., Illinois, 1969. Governmental finance, especially questions of policy and administration of sales and property taxation; state lotteries; public budgeting; public finance in countries of the former Soviet Union.
Alfredo Minetti, Ph.D., Indiana, 2007. Social dynamics of music: how music groups organize themselves, their social aesthetics, how they foster creativity, how different music styles and genres are embodied by individuals, audience development, and arts organizations.
Ashlyn Aiko Nelson, Ph.D., Stanford, 2005. Housing finance, education finance, education policy, the mortgage crisis.
Patrick O'Meara, Ph.D., Indiana, 1970. Comparative politics and development, Southern African politics, ethics and politics.
Clinton V. Oster Jr., Ph.D., Harvard, 1978. Aviation safety, airline economics and competition policy, international aviation, aviation infrastructure, environmental and natural resource policy, government regulation, business-government relations.
Elinor Ostrom, Ph.D., UCLA, 1965. How institutional rules affect the structure of action situations within which individuals face incentives, make choices, and jointly affect each other; problems involving collective goods and common-pool resource systems, and how various types of institutions enhance or detract from the capabilities of individuals to achieve equitable, workable, efficient solutions.
James Perry, Ph.D., Syracuse, 1974. Public service motivation, government and civil service reform, public management, public human resource management, national and community service, performance-related pay, public organizational behavior.
Flynn W. Picardal, Ph.D., Arizona, 1992. Bioremediation, environmental microbiology, and biogeochemistry, with a focus on the microbial reduction of iron oxides and nitrate, transformation of metals and chlorinated hydrocarbons, and combined microbial-geochemical interactions.
Maureen A. Pirog, Ph.D., Pennsylvania, 1981. Poverty and income maintenance, with emphasis on child support enforcement, welfare reform, and adolescent parenting.
Orville W. Powell, M.P.A., Penn State, 1963. Local government and the U.S. Constitution.
Jonathan Raff, Ph.D., Indiana. Interdisciplinary approaches to understand how heterogeneous photochemistry affects the fate of pollutants in the environment and impacts global climate.
J. C. Randolph, Ph.D., Carleton (Ottawa), 1972. Forest ecology; ecological aspects of global environmental change, with particular interests in forestry and agriculture; applications of geographic information systems (GIS) and remote sensing in environmental and natural resources management; landscape ecology and regional-scale modeling; physiological ecology of woody plants and of small mammals.
David A. Reingold, Ph.D., Chicago, 1996. Urban poverty, economic development, social welfare policy, low-income housing policy, government performance.
Terri L. Renner, M.B.A., Indiana, 1985. Financial management, information systems, entrepreneurship.
Rafael Reuveny, Ph.D., Indiana, 1997. International political economy, with emphasis on globalization; rise and fall of major powers; political conflict and how it interacts with international trade, democracy, and the environment; sustainable development; Middle East political economy.
Edwardo L. Rhodes, Ph.D., Carnegie-Mellon, 1978. Public policy analysis, particularly public-sector applications of management science in the evaluation and assessment of the efficiency or organization performance of public activities, including environmental and natural resource policy implementation.
Kenneth R. Richards, J.D./Ph.D., Pennsylvania, 1997. Domestic and international climate change policy, environmental policy implementation, carbon sequestration economics and law, energy law, U.S. Forest Service organizational design and management.
Evan J. Ringquist, Ph.D., Wisconsin–Madison, 1990. Public policy (environmental, energy, natural resources, and regulation), research methodology, American political institutions.
Justin Ross, Ph.D., West Virginia, 2007. Public economics, urban/regional economics, spatial econometrics, applied microeconomics, quantile regressions, public finance, political economy, game theory.
Todd V. Royer, Ph.D., Idaho State, 1999. Aquatic biogeochemistry, water resources, nutrient and carbon cycling in streams and rivers, water quality and nutrient standards.
Barry Rubin, Ph.D., Wisconsin–Madison, 1977. Urban and regional economic development and impact analysis, quantitative analysis of local government management and labor relations issues, statistics and quantitative methods, econometric modeling, public management information systems, strategic planning and management.
Michael Rushton, Ph.D., British Columbia, 1990. Cultural economics, policy and administration, nonprofit and public organizations and management, tax policy, government funding for the arts and other policies toward nonprofit organizations, cultural districts, relationships between the arts and economic growth.
Yue (Jen) Shang, Ph.D., Indiana, 2008. Nonprofit marketing, marketing communications for nonprofit organizations, donor behavior, fund development, philanthropic psychology.
Joseph Shaw, Ph.D., Kentucky, 2001. Environmental toxicology, comparative physiology, functional genomics.
Nan Stager, M.S., Indiana, 1978. Mediation, negotiation, alternative dispute resolution, public input processes.
Philip S. Stevens, Ph.D., Harvard, 1990. Characterization of chemical mechanisms that influence regional air quality and global climate change.
Anh Tran, Ph.D., Harvard, 2009. Economic and public administration policies for developing countries, evaluation of public policies and social programs.
Terry Usrey, M.S., Indiana, 1983. E-government, information technology policy, and information technology management.
Henry K. Wakhungu, Ph.D., Indiana, 2004. Development of growth simulation models for sustainable management of indigenous community forests; experimental designs in tropical forestry research; how preservice teachers conceptualize mathematics (philosophically), indexed with mathematics learning and teaching.
Jeffrey R. White, Ph.D., Syracuse, 1984. Environmental biogeochemistry, aquatic chemistry, limnology.
Lois R. Wise, Ph.D., Indiana, 1982. Public management and employment policies and practices.
Wenli Yan, Ph.D., Kentucky, 2008. Public and nonprofit financial management, state and local finance, quantitative methods.
C. Kurt Zorn, Ph.D., Syracuse, 1981. State and local finance, transportation safety, economic development, gaming policy.

Section 10
Natural Resources

This section contains a directory of institutions offering graduate work in natural resources, followed by in-depth entries submitted by institutions that chose to prepare detailed program descriptions. Additional information about programs listed in the directory but not augmented by an in-depth entry may be obtained by writing directly to the dean of a graduate school or chair of a department at the address given in the directory.

For programs offering related work, see also in this book *Environmental Sciences and Management* and *Meteorology and Atmospheric Sciences*. In the other guides in this series:

Graduate Programs in the Humanities, Arts & Social Sciences
See *Architecture (Landscape Architecture)* and *Public, Regional, and Industrial Affairs*

Graduate Programs in the Biological Sciences
See *Biological and Biomedical Sciences; Botany and Plant Biology; Ecology, Environmental Biology, and Evolutionary Biology; Entomology; Genetics, Developmental Biology, and Reproductive Biology; Nutrition; Pathology and Pathobiology; Pharmacology and Toxicology; Physiology;* and *Zoology*

Graduate Programs in Engineering & Applied Sciences
See *Agricultural Engineering and Bioengineering; Civil and Environmental Engineering; Geological, Mineral/Mining, and Petroleum Engineering; Management of Engineering and Technology;* and *Ocean Engineering*

Graduate Programs in Business, Education, Health, Information Studies, Law & Social Work
See *Veterinary Medicine and Sciences*

CONTENTS

Program Directories

Fish, Game, and Wildlife Management

Arkansas Tech University, Graduate College, College of Natural and Health Sciences, Russellville, AR 72801. Offers fisheries and wildlife biology (MS); health informatics (MS); nursing (MSN). *Students:* 6 full-time (5 women), 12 part-time (6 women). Average age 31. In 2009, 1 master's awarded. *Degree requirements:* For master's, thesis, project. *Entrance requirements:* For master's, GRE General Test. Additional exam requirements/recommendations for international students: Required—TOEFL (minimum score 550 paper-based; 213 computer-based; 79 iBT), IELTS (minimum score 6). *Application deadline:* For fall admission, 3/1 priority date for domestic students, 5/1 priority date for international students; for spring admission, 10/1 priority date for domestic and international students. Applications are processed on a rolling basis. Application fee: $0 ($30 for international students). Electronic applications accepted. *Expenses:* Tuition, state resident: full-time $3438; part-time $191 per hour. Tuition, nonresident: full-time $6876; part-time $382 per hour. Required fees: $482; $9 per credit hour. $140 per semester. Tuition and fees vary according to course load. *Financial support:* In 2009–10, teaching assistantships with full tuition reimbursements (averaging $4,000 per year); research assistantships, career-related internships or fieldwork, Federal Work-Study, scholarships/grants, health care benefits, and unspecified assistantships also available. Support available to part-time students. Financial award application deadline: 4/15; financial award applicants required to submit FAFSA. *Faculty research:* Fisheries, warblers, fish movement, darter populations, bob white studies. *Unit head:* Dr. Richard Cohoon, Dean, 479-964-0816, E-mail: richard.cohoon@atu.edu. *Application contact:* Dr. Mary B. Gunter, Dean of Graduate College, 479-968-0398, Fax: 479-964-0542, E-mail: graduate.school@atu.edu.

Auburn University, Graduate School, College of Agriculture, Department of Fisheries and Allied Aquacultures, Auburn University, AL 36849. Offers M Aq, MS, PhD. Part-time programs available. *Faculty:* 20 full-time (3 women). *Students:* 37 full-time (16 women), 31 part-time (10 women); includes 4 minority (2 African Americans, 1 American Indian/Alaska Native, 1 Hispanic American), 33 international. Average age 28. 49 applicants, 49% accepted, 21 enrolled. In 2009, 12 master's, 5 doctorates awarded. *Degree requirements:* For master's, thesis (for some programs); for doctorate, 2 foreign languages, thesis/dissertation. *Entrance requirements:* For master's and doctorate, GRE General Test. *Application deadline:* For fall admission, 7/7 for domestic students; for spring admission, 11/24 for domestic students. Applications are processed on a rolling basis. Application fee: $50 ($60 for international students). Electronic applications accepted. *Expenses:* Tuition, state resident: full-time $6240. Tuition, nonresident: full-time $18,720. International tuition: $18,938 full-time. Required fees: $492. Tuition and fees vary according to course load, program and reciprocity agreements. *Financial support:* Fellowships, research assistantships, teaching assistantships, Federal Work-Study available. Support available to part-time students. Financial award application deadline: 3/15; financial award applicants required to submit FAFSA. *Faculty research:* Channel catfish production; aquatic animal health; community and population ecology; pond management; production hatching, breeding and genetics. Total annual research expenditures: $8 million. *Unit head:* Dr. David B. Rouse, Head, 334-844-4786. *Application contact:* Dr. George Flowers, Dean of the Graduate School, 334-844-2125.

Auburn University, Graduate School, School of Forestry and Wildlife Sciences, Auburn University, AL 36849. Offers forest economics (PhD); forestry (MS, PhD); natural resource conservation (MNR); wildlife sciences (MS, PhD). *Accreditation:* SAF. Part-time programs available. *Faculty:* 28 full-time (5 women), 2 part-time/adjunct (0 women). *Students:* 29 full-time (12 women), 53 part-time (17 women); includes 3 minority (1 African American, 1 Asian American or Pacific Islander, 1 Hispanic American), 28 international. Average age 28. 55 applicants, 44% accepted, 17 enrolled. In 2009, 5 master's, 3 doctorates awarded. *Degree requirements:* For master's, thesis (MS); for doctorate, thesis/dissertation. *Entrance requirements:* For master's and doctorate, GRE General Test. *Application deadline:* For fall admission, 7/7 for domestic students; for spring admission, 11/24 for domestic students. Applications are processed on a rolling basis. Application fee: $50 ($60 for international students). Electronic applications accepted. *Expenses:* Tuition, state resident: full-time $6240. Tuition, nonresident: full-time $18,720. International tuition: $18,938 full-time. Required fees: $492. Tuition and fees vary according to course load, program and reciprocity agreements. *Financial support:* Fellowships, research assistantships, teaching assistantships, Federal Work-Study available. Support available to part-time students. Financial award application deadline: 3/15; financial award applicants required to submit FAFSA. *Faculty research:* Forest nursery management, silviculture and vegetation management, biological processes and ecological relationships, growth and yield of plantations and natural stands, urban forestry, forest taxation, law and policy. *Unit head:* Dr. Richard W. Brinker, Dean, 334-844-1007, Fax: 334-844-1084, E-mail: brinker@forestry.auburn.edu. *Application contact:* Dr. George Flowers, Dean of the Graduate School, 334-844-2125.

Brigham Young University, Graduate Studies, College of Life Sciences, Department of Plant and Wildlife Sciences, Provo, UT 84602-1001. Offers environmental science (MS); genetics and biotechnology (MS); wildlife and wildlands conservation (MS, PhD). *Faculty:* 21 full-time (1 woman), 15 part-time/adjunct (3 women). *Students:* 35 full-time (13 women), 18 part-time (5 women); includes 7 minority (2 Asian Americans or Pacific Islanders, 5 Hispanic Americans), 5 international. Average age 29. 34 applicants, 68% accepted, 21 enrolled. In 2009, 9 master's, 1 doctorate awarded. *Degree requirements:* For master's, thesis; for doctorate, comprehensive exam, thesis/dissertation, minimum GPA of 3.0, 54 hours (18 dissertation, 36 coursework). *Entrance requirements:* For master's, GRE General Test, minimum GPA of 3.0 during last 60 hours of course work; for doctorate, GRE, minimum GPA of 3.0. Additional exam requirements/recommendations for international students: Required—TOEFL (minimum score 580 paper-based; 237 computer-based; 85 iBT). *Application deadline:* 2/1 for domestic and international students. Applications are processed on a rolling basis. Application fee: $50. Electronic applications accepted. *Expenses:* Tuition: Full-time $5580; part-time $301 per credit hour. Tuition and fees vary according to student's religious affiliation. *Financial support:* In 2009–10, 22 students received support, including 2 research assistantships with partial tuition reimbursements available (averaging $16,650 per year), 37 teaching assistantships with partial tuition reimbursements available (averaging $16,650 per year); scholarships/grants and tuition waivers (partial) also available. Financial award application deadline: 2/1. *Faculty research:* environmental science, plant genetics, plant ecology, plant nutrition and pathology, wildlife and wildlands conservation. Total annual research expenditures: $1.1 million. *Unit head:* Dr. Val J. Anderson, Chair, 801-422-3527, Fax: 801-422-0008, E-mail: val_anderson@byu.edu. *Application contact:* Dr. Loreen Allphin, Graduate Coordinator, 801-422-5603, Fax: 801-422-0008, E-mail: loreen_allphin@byu.edu.

Clemson University, Graduate School, College of Agriculture, Forestry and Life Sciences, Department of Forestry and Natural Resources, Program in Wildlife and Fisheries Biology, Clemson, SC 29634. Offers MS, PhD. *Students:* 28 full-time (20 women), 8 part-time (6 women); includes 3 minority (2 African Americans, 1 American Indian/Alaska Native), 1 international. Average age 31. 27 applicants, 33% accepted, 7 enrolled. In 2009, 6 master's, 3 doctorates awarded. *Degree requirements:* For master's, thesis; for doctorate, thesis/dissertation. *Entrance requirements:* For master's, GRE General Test, minimum undergraduate GPA of 3.0; for doctorate, GRE General Test. Additional exam requirements/recommendations for international students: Required—TOEFL, IELTS. *Application deadline:* For fall admission, 6/1 for domestic students, 4/15 for international students; for spring admission, 9/15 for international students. Applications are processed on a rolling basis. Application fee: $70 ($80 for international students). Electronic applications accepted. *Expenses:* Contact institution. *Financial support:* In 2009–10, 26 students received support, including 6 fellowships with full and partial tuition reimbursements available (averaging $4,916 per year), 21 research assistantships with partial tuition reimbursements available (averaging $17,050 per year), 4 teaching assistantships with partial tuition reimbursements available (averaging $11,000 per year); career-related internships or fieldwork, institutionally sponsored loans, scholarships/grants, health care benefits, and unspecified assistantships also available. Support available to part-time students. Financial award applicants required to submit FAFSA. *Faculty research:* Intensive freshwater culture systems, conservation biology, stream management, applied wildlife management. *Unit head:* Dr. Patricia Layton, Chair, 864-656-3303, Fax: 864-656-3304, E-mail: playton@clemson.edu. *Application contact:* Dr. David Guynn, Graduate Program Coordinator, 864-656-4830, Fax: 864-656-5344, E-mail: dguynn@clemson.edu.

Colorado State University, Graduate School, Warner College of Natural Resources, Department of Fishery and Wildlife Biology, Fort Collins, CO 80523-1474. Offers fish, wildlife and conservation biology (MFWCB); fishery and wildlife biology (MFWB, MS, PhD). *Faculty:* 15 full-time (4 women). *Students:* 11 full-time (3 women), 12 part-time (5 women). Average age 31. 23 applicants, 17% accepted, 4 enrolled. In 2009, 9 master's, 1 doctorate awarded. Terminal master's awarded for partial completion of doctoral program. *Degree requirements:* For master's, comprehensive exam, thesis (for some programs); for doctorate, comprehensive exam, thesis/dissertation. *Entrance requirements:* For master's, GRE General Test (combined minimum score of 1200 on the Verbal and Quantitative sections), minimum GPA of 3.0, BA or BS in related field, letters of recommendation, personal narrative, resume, transcripts; for doctorate, GRE General Test (minimum score 1000 verbal and quantitative), minimum GPA of 3.0, MS in related field. Additional exam requirements/recommendations for international students: Required—TOEFL (minimum score 550 paper-based; 213 computer-based; 80 iBT). *Application deadline:* For fall admission, 2/15 priority date for domestic and international students. Applications are processed on a rolling basis. Application fee: $50. Electronic applications accepted. *Expenses:* Tuition, state resident: full-time $6434; part-time $359.10 per credit. Tuition, nonresident: full-time $18,116; part-time $1006.45 per credit. Required fees: $1496; $83 per credit. *Financial support:* In 2009–10, 21 students received support, including 3 fellowships with full and partial tuition reimbursements available (averaging $32,645 per year), 15 research assistantships with full and partial tuition reimbursements available (averaging $13,957 per year), 3 teaching assistantships with full and partial tuition reimbursements available (averaging $7,524 per year); institutionally sponsored loans, scholarships/grants, tuition waivers (full and partial), and unspecified assistantships also available. Financial award application deadline: 3/1; financial award applicants required to submit FAFSA. *Faculty research:* Conservation biology, aquatic ecology, animal behavior, population modeling, habitat evaluation and management. Total annual research expenditures: $3.5 million. *Unit head:* Dr. Kenneth R. Wilson, Head, 970-491-7755, Fax: 970-491-5091, E-mail: kenneth.wilson@colostate.edu. *Application contact:* Kathy Bowers, Graduate Affairs Coordinator, 970-491-5020, Fax: 970-491-5091, E-mail: fwb@cnr.colostate.edu.

Cornell University, Graduate School, Graduate Fields of Agriculture and Life Sciences, Field of Natural Resources, Ithaca, NY 14853-0001. Offers aquatic science (MPS, MS, PhD); environmental management (MPS); fishery science (MPS, MS, PhD); forest science (MPS, MS, PhD); resource policy and management (MPS, MS, PhD); wildlife science (MPS, MS, PhD). *Faculty:* 39 full-time (7 women). *Students:* 60 full-time (28 women); includes 4 minority (2 American Indian/Alaska Native, 1 Asian American or Pacific Islander, 1 Hispanic American), 13 international. Average age 31. 63 applicants, 32% accepted, 19 enrolled. In 2009, 6 master's, 7 doctorates awarded. *Degree requirements:* For master's, thesis (MS), project paper (MPS); for doctorate, comprehensive exam, thesis/dissertation. *Entrance requirements:* For master's and doctorate, GRE General Test, 2 letters of recommendation. Additional exam requirements/recommendations for international students: Required—TOEFL (minimum score 550 paper-based; 213 computer-based; 77 iBT). *Application deadline:* For spring admission, 10/30 for domestic students. Applications are processed on a rolling basis. Application fee: $70. Electronic applications accepted. *Expenses:* Tuition: Full-time $29,500. Required fees: $70. Full-time tuition and fees vary according to degree level, program and student level. *Financial support:* In 2009–10, 39 students received support, including 12 research assistantships with full tuition reimbursements available, 5 teaching assistantships with full tuition reimbursements available; fellowships with full tuition reimbursements available, institutionally sponsored loans, scholarships/grants, health care benefits, tuition waivers (full and partial), and unspecified assistantships also available. Financial award applicants required to submit FAFSA. *Faculty research:* Ecosystem-level dynamics, systems modeling, conservation biology/management, resource management's human dimensions, biogeochemistry. *Unit head:* Director of Graduate Studies, 607-255-2807, Fax: 607-255-0349. *Application contact:* Graduate Field Assistant, 607-255-2807, Fax: 607-255-0349, E-mail: nrgrad@cornell.edu.

Frostburg State University, Graduate School, College of Liberal Arts and Sciences, Department of Biology, Program in Fisheries and Wildlife Management, Frostburg, MD 21532-1099. Offers MS. Part-time and evening/weekend programs available. *Faculty:* 10. *Students:* 9 full-time (7 women), 2 part-time (both women), 1 international. Average age 26. 7 applicants, 14% accepted, 0 enrolled. *Degree requirements:* For master's, thesis. *Entrance requirements:* For master's, GRE General Test, resume. Additional exam requirements/recommendations for international students: Required—TOEFL. *Application deadline:* For fall admission, 7/15 priority date for domestic students. Applications are processed on a rolling basis. Application fee: $30. Electronic applications accepted. *Expenses:* Tuition, state resident: full-time $5706; part-time $317 per credit hour. Tuition, nonresident: full-time $6948; part-time $386 per credit hour. Required fees: $1476; $82 per credit hour. $11 per term. One-time fee: $30 full-time. *Financial support:* In 2009–10, 6 research assistantships with full tuition reimbursements (averaging $5,000 per year) were awarded; Federal Work-Study also available. Financial award application deadline: 4/1; financial award applicants required to submit FAFSA. *Faculty research:* Evolution and systematics of freshwater fishes, biochemical mechanisms of temperature adaptation in freshwater fishes, wildlife and fish parasitology, biology of freshwater invertebrates, remote sensing. *Unit head:* Dr. R. Scott Fritz, Coordinator, 301-687-4166, E-mail: rfritz@frostburg.edu. *Application contact:* Vickie Mazer, Director, Graduate Services, 301-687-7053, Fax: 301-687-4597, E-mail: vmmazer@frostburg.edu.

Humboldt State University, Graduate Studies, College of Natural Resources and Sciences, Programs in Natural Resources, Arcata, CA 95521-8299. Offers natural resources (MS), including fisheries, forestry, natural resources planning and interpretation, rangeland resources and wildland soils, wastewater utilization, watershed management, wildlife. *Students:* 51 full-time (22 women), 26 part-time (10 women); includes 4 minority (1 American Indian/Alaska Native, 1 Asian American or Pacific Islander, 2 Hispanic Americans), 1 international. Average age 31. 81 applicants, 26% accepted, 15 enrolled. In 2009, 25 master's awarded. *Degree requirements:* For master's, thesis or alternative. *Entrance requirements:* For master's, GRE, appropriate bachelor's degree, minimum GPA of 2.5, 3 letters of recommendation, resume. Additional exam requirements/recommendations for international students: Required—TOEFL (minimum score 500 paper-based; 173 computer-based). *Application deadline:* For fall admission, 2/1 for domestic and international students; for spring admission, 9/30 for domestic and international students. Applications are processed on a rolling basis. Application fee: $55. *Expenses:* Tuition, nonresident: full-time $8928. Required fees: $6102. Tuition and fees vary according to program. *Financial support:* Fellowships, career-related internships or fieldwork and Federal Work-Study available. Support available to part-time students. Financial award application deadline: 3/1; financial award applicants required to submit FAFSA. *Faculty research:* Spotted owl habitat, pre-settlement vegetation, hardwood utilization, tree physiology, fisheries. *Unit head:* Dr. Gary Hendrickson, Coordinator, 707-826-4233, E-mail: thiesfel@humboldt.edu. *Application contact:* Julie Tucker, Administrative Support Coordinator, 707-826-3256, E-mail: jlt7002@humboldt.edu.

Iowa State University of Science and Technology, Graduate College, College of Agriculture, Department of Natural Resource Ecology and Management, Ames, IA 50011. Offers forestry (MS, PhD); wildlife ecology (MS). *Faculty:* 18 full-time (4 women), 7 part-time/adjunct (2 women). *Students:* 40 full-time (13 women), 2 part-time (1 woman); includes 3 minority (1 American Indian/Alaska Native, 2 Hispanic Americans), 6 international. 28 applicants, 29% accepted, 8 enrolled. In 2009, 9 master's, 2 doctorates awarded. *Degree requirements:* For master's, thesis (for some programs); for doctorate, thesis/dissertation. *Entrance requirements:* For master's and doctorate, GRE General Test. Additional exam requirements/recommendations for international students: Required—TOEFL (minimum score 550 paper-based; 79 iBT) or IELTS (minimum score 6.5). *Application deadline:* For fall admission, 4/1 priority date for domestic and international students; for spring admission, 10/1 priority date for domestic and international students. Application fee: $40 ($90 for international students). Electronic applications accepted. *Expenses:* Tuition, state resident: full-time $6716. Tuition, nonresident: full-time $8908. Tuition and fees vary according to course level, course load, program and student level. *Financial support:* In 2009–10, 23 research assistantships with full and partial tuition reimbursements (averaging $15,420 per year), 2 teaching assistantships with full and partial tuition reimbursements (averaging $15,420 per year) were awarded. *Unit head:* Dr. Stephen Jungst, Interim Chair, 515-294-1166. *Application contact:* Dr. Janette Thompson, Director of Graduate Education, 515-294-1626, E-mail: nremgrad@iastate.edu.

Louisiana State University and Agricultural and Mechanical College, Graduate School, College of Agriculture, School of Renewable Natural Resources, Baton Rouge, LA 70803. Offers fisheries (MS); forestry (MS, PhD); wildlife (MS); wildlife and fisheries science (PhD). *Faculty:* 32 full-time (3 women). *Students:* 73 full-time (17 women), 9 part-time (4 women); includes 1 Hispanic American, 26 international. Average age 29. 31 applicants, 48% accepted, 14 enrolled. In 2009, 11 master's, 2 doctorates awarded. *Degree requirements:* For master's, thesis; for doctorate, thesis/dissertation. *Entrance requirements:* For master's, GRE General Test, minimum GPA of 3.0; for doctorate, GRE General Test, MS, minimum GPA of 3.0. Additional exam requirements/recommendations for international students: Required—TOEFL (minimum score 550 paper-based; 213 computer-based; 79 iBT), IELTS (minimum score 6.5). *Application deadline:* For fall admission, 1/25 priority date for domestic students, 5/15 for international students; for spring admission, 10/15 for international students. Applications are processed on a rolling basis. Application fee: $50 ($70 for international students). Electronic applications accepted. *Financial support:* In 2009–10, 80 students received support, including 7 fellowships (averaging $36,514 per year), 61 research assistantships with partial tuition reimbursements available (averaging $18,686 per year), 1 teaching assistantship with partial tuition reimbursement available (averaging $10,800 per year); Federal Work-Study, institutionally sponsored loans, scholarships/grants, health care benefits, tuition waivers (full and partial), and unspecified assistantships also available. Financial award application deadline: 4/15; financial award applicants required to submit FAFSA. *Faculty research:* Forest biology and management, aquaculture, fisheries biology and ecology, upland and wetlands wildlife. Total annual research expenditures: $3,308. *Unit head:* Dr. Allen Rutherford, Director, 225-578-4131, Fax: 225-578-4227, E-mail: druther@lsu.edu. *Application contact:* Dr. William Kelso, Coordinator of Graduate Studies, 225-578-4176, Fax: 225-578-4227, E-mail: wkelso@lsu.edu.

McGill University, Faculty of Graduate and Postdoctoral Studies, Faculty of Agricultural and Environmental Sciences, Department of Natural Resource Sciences, Montréal, QC H3A 2T5, Canada. Offers entomology (M Sc, PhD); environmental assessment (M Sc); forest science (M Sc, PhD); microbiology (M Sc, PhD); micrometeorology (M Sc, PhD); neotropical environment (M Sc, PhD); soil science (M Sc, PhD); wildlife biology (M Sc, PhD).

Memorial University of Newfoundland, School of Graduate Studies, Interdisciplinary Program in Marine Studies, St. John's, NL A1C 5S7, Canada. Offers fisheries resource management (MMS, Advanced Diploma). Part-time programs available. *Degree requirements:* For master's, report. *Entrance requirements:* For master's and Advanced Diploma, high 2nd class degree from a recognized university. *Faculty research:* Biological, ecological and oceanographic aspects of world fisheries; economics; political science; sociology.

Michigan State University, The Graduate School, College of Agriculture and Natural Resources, Department of Fisheries and Wildlife, East Lansing, MI 48824. Offers fisheries and wildlife (MS, PhD); fisheries and wildlife—environmental toxicology (PhD). *Entrance requirements:* Additional exam requirements/recommendations for international students: Required—TOEFL (minimum score 550 paper-based; 213 computer-based), Michigan State University ELT (85), Michigan ELAB (83). Electronic applications accepted.

Mississippi State University, College of Forest Resources, Department of Wildlife, Fisheries and Aquaculture, Mississippi State, MS 39762. Offers forest resources (PhD), including wildlife and fisheries; wildlife and fisheries science (MS). Part-time programs available. *Faculty:* 19 full-time (1 woman). *Students:* 54 full-time (17 women), 17 part-time (6 women); includes 3 minority (1 Asian American or Pacific Islander, 2 Hispanic Americans), 4 international. Average age 28. 23 applicants, 65% accepted, 14 enrolled. In 2009, 7 master's, 4 doctorates awarded. *Degree requirements:* For master's, comprehensive exam, thesis, comprehensive oral or written exam; for doctorate, comprehensive exam, thesis/dissertation. *Entrance requirements:* For master's, GRE or minimum GPA of 3.0 on last 60 hours of undergraduate courses, bachelor's degree; for doctorate, GRE or minimum GPA of 3.2 on prior graduate studies, master's degree. Additional exam requirements/recommendations for international students: Required—TOEFL (minimum score 550 paper-based; 213 computer-based; 79 iBT); Recommended—IELTS (minimum score 6.5). *Application deadline:* For fall admission, 7/1 for domestic students, 5/1 for international students; for spring admission, 11/1 for domestic students, 9/1 for international students. Applications are processed on a rolling basis. Application fee: $40. Electronic applications accepted. *Expenses:* Tuition, state resident: full-time $2575.50; part-time $286.25 per credit hour. Tuition, nonresident: full-time $6510; part-time $723.50 per credit hour. Tuition and fees vary according to course load. *Financial support:* In 2009–10, 52 research assistantships with partial tuition reimbursements (averaging $11,195 per year), 1 teaching assistantship with partial tuition reimbursement (averaging $10,037 per year) were awarded; Federal Work-Study, institutionally sponsored loans, and unspecified assistantships also available. Financial award application deadline: 4/1; financial award applicants required to submit FAFSA. *Faculty research:* Spatial technology, habitat restoration, aquaculture, fisheries, wildlife management. *Unit head:* Dr. Bruce D. Leopold, Department Head and Graduate Coordinator, 662-325-2619, Fax: 662-325-8726, E-mail: bleopold@cfr.msstate.edu. *Application contact:* Dr. Bruce D. Leopold, Department Head and Graduate Coordinator, 662-325-2619, Fax: 662-325-8726, E-mail: bleopold@cfr.msstate.edu.

Montana State University, College of Graduate Studies, College of Letters and Science, Department of Ecology, Bozeman, MT 59717. Offers ecological and environmental statistics (MS); ecology and environmental sciences (PhD); fish and wildlife biology (PhD); fish and wildlife management (MS). Part-time programs available. *Faculty:* 12 full-time (2 women), 2 part-time/adjunct (0 women). *Students:* 8 full-time (2 women), 48 part-time (18 women). Average age 31. 18 applicants, 33% accepted, 6 enrolled. In 2009, 6 master's, 7 doctorates awarded. *Degree requirements:* For master's, comprehensive exam, thesis (for some programs); for doctorate, comprehensive exam, thesis/dissertation. *Entrance requirements:* For master's, GRE General Test, GPA, Letters of Recommendation, Essay; for doctorate, GRE General Test, letters of recommendation. Additional exam requirements/recommendations for international students: Required—TOEFL (minimum score 550 paper-based; 213 computer-based). *Application deadline:* For fall admission, 7/15 priority date for domestic students, 5/15 priority date for international students; for spring admission, 12/1 priority date for domestic students, 10/1 priority date for international students. Applications are processed on a rolling basis. Application fee: $30. Electronic applications accepted. *Expenses:* Tuition, state resident: full-time $5635; part-time $3492 per year. Tuition, nonresident: full-time $17,212; part-time $7865.10 per year. Required fees: $1441.05; $153.15 per credit. Tuition and fees vary according to course load and program. *Financial support:* In 2009–10, 2 fellowships with full tuition reimbursements (averaging $17,725 per year), 29 research assistantships with full and partial tuition reimbursements (averaging $19,500 per year), 20 teaching assistantships with full tuition reimbursements (averaging $12,321 per year) were awarded; career-related internships or fieldwork, scholarships/grants, health care benefits, tuition waivers (partial), and unspecified assistantships also available. Support available to part-time students. Financial award application deadline: 3/1; financial award applicants required to submit FAFSA. *Faculty research:* Evolutionary biology, conservation ecology, human impact on ecosystems, biodiversity, applied wildlife and fisheries research, plant and animal community ecology. Total annual research expenditures: $2.6 million. *Unit head:* Dr. David Roberts, Head, 406-994-4548, Fax: 406-994-3190, E-mail: droberts@montana.edu. *Application contact:* Dr. Carl A. Fox, Vice Provost for Graduate Education, 406-994-4145, Fax: 406-994-7433, E-mail: gradstudy@montana.edu.

New Mexico Highlands University, Graduate Studies, College of Arts and Sciences, Department of Natural Sciences, Las Vegas, NM 87701. Offers chemistry (MS); life science (MS). Part-time programs available. *Degree requirements:* For master's, comprehensive exam, thesis. *Entrance requirements:* For master's, minimum undergraduate GPA of 3.0. Additional exam requirements/recommendations for international students: Required—TOEFL (minimum score 540 paper-based; 207 computer-based). *Faculty research:* Invasive organisms in managed and wildland ecosystems, juniper and pinyon ecology and management, vegetation and community structure, big game management, quantitative forestry.

New Mexico State University, Graduate School, College of Agricultural, Consumer and Environmental Sciences, Department of Fish, Wildlife and Conservation Ecology, Las Cruces, NM 88003-8001. Offers wildlife science (MS). *Faculty:* 9 full-time (4 women). *Students:* 19 full-time (6 women), 5 part-time (3 women); includes 3 minority (1 American Indian/Alaska Native, 2 Hispanic Americans), 2 international. Average age 28. 12 applicants, 100% accepted, 4 enrolled. In 2009, 3 master's awarded. *Degree requirements:* For master's, thesis (for some programs). *Entrance requirements:* For master's, GRE General Test, minimum GPA of 3.0. Additional exam requirements/recommendations for international students: Required—TOEFL. *Application deadline:* For fall admission, 4/1 priority date for domestic students; for spring admission, 11/1 priority date for domestic students. Applications are processed on a rolling basis. Application fee: $30 ($50 for international students). Electronic applications accepted. *Expenses:* Tuition, state resident: full-time $4080; part-time $223 per credit. Tuition, nonresident: full-time $14,256; part-time $647 per credit. Required fees: $1278; $639 per semester. *Financial support:* In 2009–10, 12 research assistantships with partial tuition reimbursements (averaging $18,100 per year), 4 teaching assistantships with partial tuition reimbursements (averaging $7,900 per year) were awarded; career-related internships or fieldwork, Federal Work-Study, scholarships/grants, and health care benefits also available. Support available to part-time students. Financial award application deadline: 4/1. *Faculty research:* Ecosystems analyses, landscape and wildlife ecology, wildlife and fish population dynamics, management models, wildlife and fish habitat relationships. *Unit head:* Dr. Raul Valdez, Head, 575-646-3719, Fax: 575-646-1281, E-mail: rvaldez@nmsu.edu. *Application contact:* Doris J. Morgan, Administrative Secretary III, 575-646-7051, Fax: 575-646-1281, E-mail: domorgan@nmsu.edu.

North Carolina State University, Graduate School, College of Natural Resources, Program in Fisheries and Wildlife Sciences, Raleigh, NC 27695. Offers MFWS, MS, PhD. *Degree requirements:* For master's, thesis optional. *Entrance requirements:* For master's, GRE General Test. Additional exam requirements/recommendations for international students: Required—TOEFL. Electronic applications accepted. *Faculty research:* Fisheries biology; ecology of marine, estuarine, and anadromous fishes; aquaculture pond water quality; larviculture of freshwater and marine finfish; predator/prey interactions.

Oregon State University, Graduate School, College of Agricultural Sciences, Department of Fisheries and Wildlife, Program in Fisheries Science, Corvallis, OR 97331. Offers M Agr, MAIS, MS, PhD. Part-time programs available. *Students:* 39 full-time (18 women), 4 part-time (1 woman); includes 5 minority (1 American Indian/Alaska Native, 2 Asian Americans or Pacific Islanders, 2 Hispanic Americans), 4 international. Average age 33. In 2009, 8 master's, 7 doctorates awarded. *Degree requirements:* For master's, thesis (for some programs); for doctorate, thesis/dissertation. *Entrance requirements:* For master's and doctorate, GRE, minimum GPA of 3.0 in last 90 hours. Additional exam requirements/recommendations for international students: Required—TOEFL. *Application deadline:* For fall admission, 3/15 for domestic students; for spring admission, 12/15 for domestic students. Applications are processed on a rolling basis. Application fee: $50. *Expenses:* Tuition, state resident: full-time $9774; part-time $362 per credit. Tuition, nonresident: full-time $15,849; part-time $587 per credit. Required fees: $1639. Full-time tuition and fees vary according to course load and program. *Financial support:* Fellowships, research assistantships, teaching assistantships, career-related internships or fieldwork, Federal Work-Study, and institutionally sponsored loans available. Support available to part-time students. Financial award application deadline: 2/1. *Faculty research:* Fisheries ecology, fish toxicology, stream ecology, quantitative analyses of marine and freshwater fish populations. *Unit head:* Dr. Nancy Allen, Head Advisor, 541-737-2910, Fax: 541-737-3590, E-mail: nancy.allen@oregonstate.edu. *Application contact:* Dr. Nancy Allen, Head Advisor, 541-737-2910, Fax: 541-737-3590, E-mail: nancy.allen@oregonstate.edu.

Oregon State University, Graduate School, College of Agricultural Sciences, Department of Fisheries and Wildlife, Program in Wildlife Science, Corvallis, OR 97331. Offers MAIS, MS, PhD. *Students:* 35 full-time (17 women), 2 part-time (1 woman); includes 3 minority (1 Asian American or Pacific Islander, 2 Hispanic Americans), 7 international. Average age 33. In 2009, 6 master's, 2 doctorates awarded. *Degree requirements:* For master's, thesis (for some programs); for doctorate, thesis/dissertation. *Entrance requirements:* For master's and doctorate, GRE, minimum GPA of 3.0 in last 90 hours. Additional exam requirements/recommendations for international students: Required—TOEFL. Application fee: $50. *Expenses:* Tuition, state resident: full-time $9774; part-time $362 per credit. Tuition, nonresident: full-time $15,849; part-time $587 per credit. Required fees: $1639. Full-time tuition and fees vary according to course load and program. *Financial support:* Fellowships, research assistantships, teaching assistantships, career-related internships or fieldwork, Federal Work-Study, and institutionally sponsored loans available. Financial award application deadline: 2/1. *Unit head:* Dr. Nancy Allen, Head Advisor, 541-737-2910, Fax: 541-737-3590, E-mail: nancy.allen@oregonstate.edu. *Application contact:* Dr. Nancy Allen, Head Advisor, 541-737-2910, Fax: 541-737-3590, E-mail: nancy.allen@oregonstate.edu.

Purdue University, Graduate School, College of Agriculture, Department of Forestry and Natural Resources, West Lafayette, IN 47907. Offers aquaculture, fisheries, aquatic science (MSF); aquaculture, fisheries, aquatic sciences (MS, PhD); forest biology (MS, MSF, PhD); natural resources and environmental policy (MS, MSF); natural resources environmental policy (PhD); quantitative resource analysis (MS, MSF, PhD); wildlife science (MS, MSF, PhD); wood science and technology (MS, MSF, PhD). *Degree requirements:* For master's, thesis; for doctorate, thesis/dissertation. *Entrance requirements:* For master's and doctorate, GRE General Test, minimum B+ average in undergraduate course work. Additional exam requirements/recommendations for international students: Required—TOEFL. Electronic applications accepted. *Faculty research:* Wildlife management, forest management, forest ecology, forest soils, limnology.

South Dakota State University, Graduate School, College of Agriculture and Biological Sciences, Department of Wildlife and Fisheries Sciences, Brookings, SD 57007. Offers MS, PhD. Part-time programs available. *Degree requirements:* For master's, thesis, oral exam; for doctorate, comprehensive exam, thesis/dissertation, interim exam, oral and written comprehensive exams. *Entrance requirements:* For master's and doctorate, GRE. Additional exam requirements/recommendations for international students: Required—TOEFL (minimum score 525 paper-

Fish, Game, and Wildlife Management

South Dakota State University (continued)
based; 197 computer-based; 71 iBT). *Faculty research:* Agriculture interactions, wetland conservation, biostress, wildlife and fisheries ecology and techniques.

State University of New York College of Environmental Science and Forestry, Department of Environmental and Forest Biology, Syracuse, NY 13210-2779. Offers applied ecology (MPS); chemical ecology (MPS, MS, PhD); conservation biology (MPS, MS, PhD); ecology (MPS, MS, PhD); entomology (MPS, MS, PhD); environmental interpretation (MPS, MS, PhD); environmental physiology (MPS, MS, PhD); fish and wildlife biology (MPS, MS, PhD); forest pathology and mycology (MPS, MS, PhD); plant biotechnology (MPS); plant science and biotechnology (MPS, MS, PhD). *Degree requirements:* For master's, thesis (for some programs); for doctorate, comprehensive exam, thesis/dissertation. *Entrance requirements:* For master's and doctorate, GRE General Test, GRE Subject Test, minimum GPA of 3.0. Additional exam requirements/recommendations for international students: Required—TOEFL (minimum score 550 paper-based; 213 computer-based; 80 iBT), IELTS (minimum score 6). *Faculty research:* Ecology, fish and wildlife biology and management, plant science, entomology.

Sul Ross State University, Division of Agricultural and Natural Resource Science, Program in Range and Wildlife Management, Alpine, TX 79832. Offers M Ag, MS. Part-time programs available. *Degree requirements:* For master's, thesis (for some programs). *Entrance requirements:* For master's, GRE General Test, minimum undergraduate GPA of 2.5 in last 60 hours.

Tennessee Technological University, Graduate School, College of Arts and Sciences, Department of Biology, Cookeville, TN 38505. Offers fish, game, and wildlife management (MS). Part-time programs available. *Faculty:* 22 full-time (2 women). *Students:* 15 full-time (4 women), 13 part-time (6 women); includes 1 minority (African American). Average age 25. 23 applicants, 52% accepted, 12 enrolled. In 2009, 14 master's awarded. *Degree requirements:* For master's, thesis. *Entrance requirements:* For master's, GRE. Additional exam requirements/recommendations for international students: Required—TOEFL (minimum score 550 paper-based; 79 iBT), IELTS (minimum score 5.5). *Application deadline:* For fall admission, 8/1 for domestic students, 5/1 for international students; for spring admission, 12/1 for domestic students, 10/1 for international students. Application fee: $25 ($30 for international students). Electronic applications accepted. *Expenses:* Tuition, state resident: full-time $7034; part-time $368 per credit hour. *Financial support:* In 2009–10, 17 research assistantships (averaging $9,000 per year), 8 teaching assistantships (averaging $7,500 per year) were awarded. Financial award application deadline: 4/1. *Faculty research:* Aquatics, environmental studies. *Unit head:* Dr. Daniel Combs, Interim Chairperson, 931-372-3134, Fax: 931-372-6257, E-mail: dcombs@tntech.edu. *Application contact:* Shelia K. Kendrick, Coordinator of Graduate Studies, 931-372-3808, Fax: 931-372-3497, E-mail: skendrick@tntech.edu.

Texas A&M University, College of Agriculture and Life Sciences, Department of Wildlife and Fisheries Sciences, College Station, TX 77843. Offers M Agr, MS, PhD. Part-time programs available. Postbaccalaureate distance learning degree programs offered (no on-campus study). *Faculty:* 28. *Students:* 97 full-time (60 women), 47 part-time (24 women); includes 30 minority (5 African Americans, 2 American Indian/Alaska Native, 1 Asian American or Pacific Islander, 22 Hispanic Americans), 20 international. Average age 26. In 2009, 31 master's, 12 doctorates awarded. Terminal master's awarded for partial completion of doctoral program. *Degree requirements:* For master's, thesis, final oral defense; for doctorate, thesis/dissertation, final oral defense. *Entrance requirements:* For master's and doctorate, GRE General Test, minimum GPA of 3.0. Additional exam requirements/recommendations for international students: Required—TOEFL (minimum score 550 paper-based; 213 computer-based). *Application deadline:* For fall admission, 3/1 for international students; for spring admission, 8/1 for international students. Applications are processed on a rolling basis. Application fee: $50 ($75 for international students). Electronic applications accepted. *Expenses:* Tuition, state resident: full-time $3991.32; part-time $221.74 per credit hour. Tuition, nonresident: full-time $9049; part-time $502.74 per credit hour. *Financial support:* In 2009–10, fellowships with partial tuition reimbursements (averaging $22,000 per year), research assistantships (averaging $14,400 per year), teaching assistantships (averaging $14,400 per year) were awarded; career-related internships or fieldwork, institutionally sponsored loans, and scholarships/grants also available. Financial award application deadline: 3/1; financial award applicants required to submit FAFSA. *Faculty research:* Wildlife ecology and management, fisheries ecology and management, aquaculture, biological inventories and museum collections, biosystematics and genome analysis. *Unit head:* Dr. Thomas Lacher, Professor and Head, 979-845-5777, Fax: 979-845-3786, E-mail: tlacher@tamu.edu. *Application contact:* Felix Arnold, Senior Academic Advisor I, 979-845-5777, Fax: 979-845-3786, E-mail: fwarnold@tamu.edu.

Texas A&M University–Kingsville, College of Graduate Studies, College of Agriculture and Home Economics, Program in Range and Wildlife Management, Kingsville, TX 78363. Offers MS. *Degree requirements:* For master's, comprehensive exam, thesis or alternative. *Entrance requirements:* For master's, GRE General Test, minimum GPA of 3.0. Additional exam requirements/recommendations for international students: Required—TOEFL.

Texas A&M University–Kingsville, College of Graduate Studies, College of Agriculture and Home Economics, Program in Wildlife Science, Kingsville, TX 78363. Offers PhD. *Degree requirements:* For doctorate, one foreign language, comprehensive exam, thesis/dissertation. *Entrance requirements:* For doctorate, GRE General Test, minimum GPA of 3.5.

Texas State University–San Marcos, Graduate School, College of Science, Department of Biology, Program in Wildlife Ecology, San Marcos, TX 78666. Offers MS. *Faculty:* 7 full-time (1 woman), 2 part-time/adjunct (0 women). *Students:* 23 full-time (11 women), 14 part-time (7 women); includes 9 minority (1 African American, 2 Asian Americans or Pacific Islanders, 6 Hispanic Americans). Average age 27. 10 applicants, 90% accepted, 9 enrolled. In 2009, 7 master's awarded. *Degree requirements:* For master's, thesis. *Entrance requirements:* For master's, GRE General Test, Bachelor's degree in biology or related discipline, minimum GPA of 3.0 in last 60 hours of undergraduate work, preferred GRE (1000 v&q). Additional exam requirements/recommendations for international students: Required—TOEFL (minimum score 550 paper-based; 213 computer-based). *Application deadline:* For fall admission, 6/15 priority date for domestic students, 6/1 priority date for international students; for spring admission, 10/15 priority date for domestic students, 10/1 priority date for international students. Applications are processed on a rolling basis. Application fee: $40 ($90 for international students). Electronic applications accepted. *Expenses:* Tuition, state resident: full-time $5784; part-time $241 per credit hour. Tuition, nonresident: part-time $551 per credit hour. Required fees: $1728; $48 per credit hour. $306. Tuition and fees vary according to course load. *Financial support:* In 2009–10, 19 students received support, including 3 research assistantships (averaging $5,310 per year), 21 teaching assistantships (averaging $7,076 per year); Federal Work-Study and institutionally sponsored loans also available. Support available to part-time students. Financial award application deadline: 4/1; financial award applicants required to submit FAFSA. *Unit head:* Dr. John Baccus, Graduate Advisor, 512-245-2178, Fax: 512-245-8713, E-mail: jb02@txstate.edu. *Application contact:* Dr. J. Michael Willoughby, Dean of the Graduate School, 512-245-2581, Fax: 512-245-8365, E-mail: jw02@swt.edu.

Texas Tech University, Graduate School, College of Agricultural Sciences and Natural Resources, Department of Natural Resources Management, Lubbock, TX 79409. Offers fisheries science (MS, PhD); range science (MS, PhD); wildlife science (MS, PhD). Part-time programs available. *Faculty:* 9 full-time (0 women), 1 part-time/adjunct (0 women). *Students:* 33 full-time (11 women), 1 part-time (0 women); includes 4 minority (1 Asian American or Pacific Islander, 3 Hispanic Americans), 4 international. Average age 28. 22 applicants, 50% accepted, 8 enrolled. In 2009, 8 master's, 2 doctorates awarded. *Degree requirements:* For master's, thesis; for doctorate, thesis/dissertation. *Entrance requirements:* For master's and doctorate, GRE General Test. Additional exam requirements/recommendations for international students: Required—TOEFL (minimum score 550 paper-based; 213 computer-based). *Application deadline:* For fall admission, 3/1 priority date for international students; for spring admission, 11/1 priority date for international students. Applications are processed on a rolling basis. Application fee: $50 ($75 for international students). Electronic applications accepted. *Expenses:* Tuition, state resident: full-time $5100; part-time $213 per credit hour. Tuition, nonresident: full-time $11,748; part-time $490 per credit hour. Required fees: $2298; $50 per credit hour. $555 per semester. *Financial support:* In 2009–10, 7 research assistantships with partial tuition reimbursements (averaging $18,972 per year), 2 teaching assistantships with partial tuition reimbursements (averaging $15,975 per year) were awarded; Federal Work-Study and institutionally sponsored loans also available. Support available to part-time students. Financial award application deadline: 4/15; financial award applicants required to submit FAFSA. *Faculty research:* Use of fire on range lands, big game, upland game, and waterfowl; playa lakes in the southern Great Plains; conservation biology; fish ecology and physiology. Total annual research expenditures: $509,586. *Unit head:* Dr. Philip S. Gipson, Chairman, 806-742-2841 Ext. 223, Fax: 806-742-2280, E-mail: philip.gipson@ttu.edu. *Application contact:* Renee Dillon, Sr. Business Assistant, 806-742-2841, E-mail: renee.dillon@ttu.edu.

Université du Québec à Rimouski, Graduate Programs, Program in Wildlife Resources Management, Rimouski, QC G5L 3A1, Canada. Offers biology (PhD); wildlife resources management (M Sc, Diploma). *Entrance requirements:* For degree, appropriate bachelor's degree, proficiency in French.

University of Alaska Fairbanks, College of Natural Sciences and Mathematics, Department of Biology and Wildlife, Fairbanks, AK 99775-6100. Offers biological sciences (MS, PhD), including biology, botany, wildlife biology (PhD), zoology; biology (MAT, MS); wildlife biology (MS). Part-time programs available. *Faculty:* 27 full-time (9 women), 2 part-time/adjunct (0 women). *Students:* 95 full-time (61 women), 32 part-time (18 women); includes 13 minority (1 African American, 3 American Indian/Alaska Native, 4 Asian Americans or Pacific Islanders, 5 Hispanic Americans), 9 international. Average age 35. 76 applicants, 32% accepted, 24 enrolled. In 2009, 10 master's, 13 doctorates awarded. *Degree requirements:* For master's, comprehensive exam, thesis, oral exam, oral defense; for doctorate, comprehensive exam, thesis/dissertation, oral exam, oral defense. *Entrance requirements:* For master's and doctorate, GRE General Test, GRE Subject Test (biology). Additional exam requirements/recommendations for international students: Required—TOEFL (minimum score 550 paper-based; 213 computer-based; 80 iBT), TWE. *Application deadline:* For fall admission, 6/1 for domestic students, 3/1 for international students; for spring admission, 10/15 for domestic students, 9/1 for international students. Applications are processed on a rolling basis. Application fee: $60. Electronic applications accepted. *Expenses:* Tuition, state resident: full-time $7584; part-time $316 per credit. Tuition, nonresident: full-time $15,504; part-time $646 per credit. Required fees: $23 per credit. $135 per semester. Tuition and fees vary according to course level, course load and reciprocity agreements. *Financial support:* In 2009–10, 46 research assistantships (averaging $13,543 per year), 24 teaching assistantships (averaging $7,495 per year) were awarded; fellowships, career-related internships or fieldwork, Federal Work-Study, scholarships/grants, health care benefits, and unspecified assistantships also available. Support available to part-time students. Financial award application deadline: 7/1; financial award applicants required to submit FAFSA. *Faculty research:* Plant-herbivore interactions, plant metabolic defenses, insect manufacture of glycerol, ice nucleators, structure and functions of arctic and subarctic freshwater ecosystems. *Unit head:* Dr. Richard E. Boone, Chair, 907-474-7671, Fax: 907-474-6716, E-mail: fybio@uaf.edu. *Application contact:* Dr. Richard E. Boone, Chair, 907-474-7671, Fax: 907-474-6716, E-mail: fybio@uaf.edu.

University of Alaska Fairbanks, School of Fisheries and Ocean Sciences, Program in Marine Sciences and Limnology, Fairbanks, AK 99775-7220. Offers marine biology (MS, PhD); oceanography (PhD), including biological oceanography, chemical oceanography, fisheries, geological oceanography, physical oceanography. Part-time programs available. *Faculty:* 12 full-time (5 women), 2 part-time/adjunct (0 women). *Students:* 29 full-time (17 women), 14 part-time (9 women); includes 4 minority (2 Asian Americans or Pacific Islanders, 2 Hispanic Americans), 2 international. Average age 33. 45 applicants, 18% accepted, 8 enrolled. In 2009, 8 master's, 2 doctorates awarded. *Degree requirements:* For master's, comprehensive exam, thesis, oral defense; for doctorate, comprehensive exam, thesis/dissertation, oral defense. *Entrance requirements:* For master's and doctorate, GRE General Test. Additional exam requirements/recommendations for international students: Required—TOEFL (minimum score 550 paper-based; 213 computer-based; 80 iBT). *Application deadline:* For fall admission, 6/1 for domestic students, 3/1 for international students; for spring admission, 10/15 for domestic students, 8/1 for international students. Applications are processed on a rolling basis. Application fee: $60. Electronic applications accepted. *Expenses:* Tuition, state resident: full-time $7584; part-time $316 per credit. Tuition, nonresident: full-time $15,504; part-time $646 per credit. Required fees: $23 per credit. $135 per semester. Tuition and fees vary according to course level, course load and reciprocity agreements. *Financial support:* In 2009–10, 3 fellowships (averaging $10,865 per year), 18 research assistantships (averaging $10,454 per year), 6 teaching assistantships (averaging $10,748 per year) were awarded; career-related internships or fieldwork, Federal Work-Study, scholarships/grants, health care benefits, and unspecified assistantships also available. Support available to part-time students. Financial award application deadline: 7/1; financial award applicants required to submit FAFSA. *Unit head:* Dr. Denis Wiesenberg, Dean, 907-474-7824, Fax: 907-474-7204, E-mail: info@sfos.uaf.edu. *Application contact:* Katie Straub, Recruitment and Retention Coordinator, 907-474-6786, Fax: 907-474-5863, E-mail: kmstraub@alaska.edu.

The University of Arizona, Graduate College, College of Agriculture and Life Sciences, School of Natural Resources, Program in Wildlife, Fisheries Conservation, and Management, Tucson, AZ 85721. Offers MS, PhD. *Students:* 10 part-time (3 women); includes 1 Hispanic American, 4 international. Average age 39. *Degree requirements:* For master's, thesis; for doctorate, comprehensive exam, thesis/dissertation. *Entrance requirements:* For master's, GRE General Test, GRE Subject Test (biology), minimum GPA of 3.0, 3 letters of recommendation; for doctorate, GRE General Test, GRE Subject Test (biology), minimum GPA of 3.0, 3 letters of recommendation, MA or MS degree. Additional exam requirements/recommendations for international students: Required—TOEFL (minimum score 550 paper-based; 213 computer-based). *Application deadline:* For fall admission, 8/1 priority date for domestic students, 12/1 for international students; for spring admission, 7/1 for international students. Applications are processed on a rolling basis. Application fee: $75. *Expenses:* Tuition, state resident: full-time $9028. Tuition, nonresident: full-time $24,890. *Financial support:* Research assistantships with partial tuition reimbursements, teaching assistantships with partial tuition reimbursements, scholarships/grants, health care benefits, tuition waivers (partial), and unspecified assistantships available. *Faculty research:* Short-term effects of artificial oases on Arizona wildlife, elk response to cattle in northern Arizona, effect of reservoir operation on tailwaters, conservation of wildlife. *Unit head:* Dr. R. William Mannan, Chair, 520-621-7283, E-mail: mannan@ag.arizona.edu. *Application contact:* Cheryl L. Craddock, Academic Coordinator, 520-621-7260, Fax: 520-621-8801, E-mail: ccraddoc@email.arizona.edu.

University of Arkansas at Pine Bluff, School of Agriculture, Fisheries and Human Sciences, Pine Bluff, AR 71601-2799. Offers aquaculture and fisheries (MS).

University of Delaware, College of Agriculture and Natural Resources, Department of Entomology and Wildlife Ecology, Newark, DE 19716. Offers entomology and applied ecology (MS, PhD), including avian ecology, evolution and taxonomy, insect biological control, insect ecology and behavior (MS), insect genetics, pest management, plant-insect interactions, wildlife ecology and management. Part-time programs available. *Degree requirements:* For master's, comprehensive exam, thesis, oral exam, seminar; for doctorate, comprehensive exam, thesis/dissertation, qualifying exam, seminar. *Entrance requirements:* For master's, GRE General Test, minimum GPA of 3.0 in field, 2.8 overall; for doctorate, GRE General Test, GRE Subject Test (biology), minimum GPA of 3.0 in field, 2.8 overall. Additional exam requirements/recommendations for international students: Required—TOEFL. Electronic applications accepted. *Faculty research:* Ecology and evolution of plant-insect interactions, ecology of wildlife conservation management, habitat restoration, biological control, applied ecosystem management.

University of Florida, Graduate School, College of Agricultural and Life Sciences, Department of Wildlife Ecology and Conservation, Gainesville, FL 32611. Offers MS, PhD. *Degree requirements:* For master's, thesis optional; for doctorate, thesis/dissertation. *Entrance requirements:* For master's and doctorate, GRE General Test, minimum GPA of 3.3. Electronic applications accepted. *Faculty research:* Wildlife biology and management, tropical ecology and conservation, conservation biology, landscape ecology and restoration, conservation education.

University of Idaho, College of Graduate Studies, College of Natural Resources, Department of Fish and Wildlife Resources, Program in Fishery Resources, Moscow, ID 83844-2282. Offers MS. *Students:* 8 full-time, 3 part-time. In 2009, 5 master's awarded. *Entrance requirements:* For master's, minimum GPA of 2.8. *Application deadline:* For fall admission, 8/1 for domestic students; for spring admission, 12/15 for domestic students. Application fee: $55 ($60 for international students). *Expenses:* Tuition, state resident: full-time $6120. Tuition, nonresident: full-time $17,712. *Financial support:* Research assistantships available. Financial award application deadline: 2/15. *Unit head:* Dr. Kerry Reese, Head, 208-885-6435. *Application contact:* Dr. Kerry Reese, Head, 208-885-6435.

University of Idaho, College of Graduate Studies, College of Natural Resources, Department of Fish and Wildlife Resources, Program in Wildlife Resources, Moscow, ID 83844-2282. Offers MS. *Students:* 4 full-time, 1 part-time. In 2009, 3 master's awarded. *Entrance requirements:* For master's, minimum GPA of 2.8. *Application deadline:* For fall admission, 8/1 for domestic students; for spring admission, 12/15 for domestic students. Application fee: $55 ($60 for international students). *Expenses:* Tuition, state resident: full-time $6120. Tuition, nonresident: full-time $17,712. *Financial support:* Research assistantships, teaching assistantships available. Financial award application deadline: 2/15. *Unit head:* Dr. Kerry Reese, Head, 208-885-6435. *Application contact:* Dr. Kerry Reese, Head, 208-885-6435.

University of Maine, Graduate School, College of Natural Sciences, Forestry, and Agriculture, Department of Wildlife Ecology, Orono, ME 04469. Offers wildlife conservation (MWC); wildlife ecology (MS, PhD). Part-time programs available. *Faculty:* 7 full-time (3 women), 1 (woman) part-time/adjunct. *Students:* 15 full-time (3 women), 2 part-time (1 woman); includes 1 minority (Asian American or Pacific Islander), 1 international. Average age 31. 14 applicants, 21% accepted, 3 enrolled. In 2009, 2 master's, 1 doctorate awarded. *Degree requirements:* For master's, thesis (for some programs); for doctorate, one foreign language, thesis/dissertation. *Entrance requirements:* For master's and doctorate, GRE General Test. Additional exam requirements/recommendations for international students: Required—TOEFL. *Application deadline:* For fall admission, 2/1 priority date for domestic students. Applications are processed on a rolling basis. Application fee: $65. Electronic applications accepted. *Financial support:* In 2009–10, 19 research assistantships with tuition reimbursements (averaging $18,218 per year), 2 teaching assistantships with tuition reimbursements (averaging $12,790 per year) were awarded; career-related internships or fieldwork, Federal Work-Study, institutionally sponsored loans, and tuition waivers (full and partial) also available. Financial award application deadline: 3/1. *Faculty research:* Integration of wildlife and forest management; population dynamics; behavior, physiology and nutrition; wetland ecology and influence of environmental disturbances. *Unit head:* Dr. James Gilbert, Chair, 207-581-2872, Fax: 207-581-2858. *Application contact:* Scott G. Delcourt, Associate Dean of the Graduate School, 207-581-3291, Fax: 207-581-3232, E-mail: graduate@maine.edu.

University of Massachusetts Amherst, Graduate School, College of Natural Sciences, Department of Natural Resources Conservation, Program in Wildlife and Fisheries Conservation, Amherst, MA 01003. Offers MS, PhD. Part-time programs available. *Students:* 32 full-time (17 women), 32 part-time (11 women); includes 2 minority (1 African American, 1 American Indian/Alaska Native), 10 international. Average age 32. 43 applicants, 26% accepted, 9 enrolled. In 2009, 8 master's, 3 doctorates awarded. Terminal master's awarded for partial completion of doctoral program. *Degree requirements:* For master's, thesis optional; for doctorate, comprehensive exam, thesis/dissertation. *Entrance requirements:* For master's and doctorate, GRE General Test. Additional exam requirements/recommendations for international students: Required—TOEFL (minimum score 550 paper-based; 213 computer-based; 80 iBT), IELTS (minimum score 6.5). *Application deadline:* For fall admission, 2/1 for domestic and international students; for spring admission, 10/1 for domestic and international students. Applications are processed on a rolling basis. Application fee: $50 ($65 for international students). Electronic applications accepted. *Expenses:* Tuition, state resident: full-time $2640; part-time $110 per credit. Tuition, nonresident: full-time $9936; part-time $414 per credit. Tuition and fees vary according to course load. *Financial support:* Fellowships, research assistantships, teaching assistantships, career-related internships or fieldwork, Federal Work-Study, scholarships/grants, traineeships, health care benefits, tuition waivers (full), and unspecified assistantships available. Support available to part-time students. Financial award application deadline: 2/1. *Unit head:* Dr. Kevin McGarigal, Graduate Program Director, 413-545-2666, Fax: 413-545-4358. *Application contact:* Jean M. Ames, Supervisor of Admissions, 413-545-0722, Fax: 413-577-0010, E-mail: gradadm@grad.umass.edu.

University of Miami, Graduate School, Rosenstiel School of Marine and Atmospheric Science, Division of Marine Biology and Fisheries, Coral Gables, FL 33124. Offers MA, MS, PhD. Terminal master's awarded for partial completion of doctoral program. *Degree requirements:* For master's, comprehensive exam, thesis; for doctorate, comprehensive exam, thesis/dissertation. *Entrance requirements:* For master's and doctorate, GRE General Test. Additional exam requirements/recommendations for international students: Required—TOEFL (minimum score 550 paper-based; 213 computer-based). Electronic applications accepted. *Faculty research:* Biochemistry, physiology, plankton, coral, biology.

University of Missouri, Graduate School, School of Natural Resources, Department of Fisheries and Wildlife, Columbia, MO 65211. Offers MS, PhD. *Degree requirements:* For doctorate, thesis/dissertation. *Entrance requirements:* For master's and doctorate, GRE General Test, minimum GPA of 3.0. Additional exam requirements/recommendations for international students: Required—TOEFL (minimum score 550 paper-based; 213 computer-based; 79 iBT).

The University of Montana, Graduate School, College of Forestry and Conservation, Missoula, MT 59812-0002. Offers ecosystem management (MEM, MS); fish and wildlife biology (PhD); forestry (MS, PhD); recreation management (MS); resource conservation (MS); wildlife biology (MS). *Degree requirements:* For doctorate, thesis/dissertation. *Entrance requirements:* For master's and doctorate, GRE General Test. Additional exam requirements/recommendations for international students: Required—TOEFL (minimum score 575 paper-based; 213 computer-based).

University of New Hampshire, Graduate School, College of Life Sciences and Agriculture, Department of Natural Resources, Durham, NH 03824. Offers environmental conservation (MS); forestry (MS); soil science (MS); water resources management (MS); wildlife (MS). Part-time programs available. *Faculty:* 40 full-time. *Students:* 22 full-time (12 women), 29 part-time (19 women); includes 1 minority (Asian American or Pacific Islander), 1 international. Average age 31. 41 applicants, 34% accepted, 10 enrolled. In 2009, 19 master's awarded. *Degree requirements:* For master's, thesis or alternative. *Entrance requirements:* For master's, GRE General Test. Additional exam requirements/recommendations for international students: Required—TOEFL (minimum score 550 paper-based; 213 computer-based; 80 iBT). *Application deadline:* For fall admission, 6/1 for domestic students, 4/1 for international students; for spring admission, 12/1 for domestic students. Applications are processed on a rolling basis. Application fee: $65. Electronic applications accepted. *Expenses:* Tuition, state resident: full-time $10,380; part-time $577 per credit hour. Tuition, nonresident: full-time $24,350; part-time $1002 per credit hour. Required fees: $1550; $387.50 per semester. Tuition and fees vary according to course load and program. *Financial support:* In 2009–10, 24 students received support, including 2 fellowships, 11 research assistantships, 11 teaching assistantships; career-related internships or fieldwork, Federal Work-Study, scholarships/grants, and tuition waivers (full and partial) also available. Support available to part-time students. Financial award application deadline: 2/15. *Unit head:* Dr. John Halstead, Chairperson, 603-862-3950, E-mail: natural.resources@unh.edu. *Application contact:* Linda Scogin, Administrative Assistant, 603-862-3932, E-mail: natural.resources@unh.edu.

University of North Dakota, Graduate School, College of Arts and Sciences, Department of Biology, Grand Forks, ND 58202. Offers botany (MS, PhD); ecology (MS, PhD); entomology (MS, PhD); environmental biology (MS, PhD); fisheries/wildlife (MS, PhD); genetics (MS, PhD); zoology (MS, PhD). Terminal master's awarded for partial completion of doctoral program. *Degree requirements:* For master's, thesis, final exam; for doctorate, comprehensive exam, thesis/dissertation, final exam. *Entrance requirements:* For master's, GRE General Test, GRE Subject Test, minimum GPA of 3.0; for doctorate, GRE General Test, GRE Subject Test, minimum GPA of 3.5. Additional exam requirements/recommendations for international students: Required—TOEFL (minimum score 550 paper-based; 213 computer-based; 79 iBT), IELTS (minimum score 6.5). Electronic applications accepted. *Faculty research:* Population biology, wildlife ecology, RNA processing, hormonal control of behavior.

University of Rhode Island, Graduate School, College of the Environment and Life Sciences, Department of Fisheries, Animal and Veterinary Science, Kingston, RI 02881. Offers animal health and disease (MS); animal science (MS); aquaculture (MS); aquatic pathology (MS); environmental sciences (PhD), including animal science, aquacultural science, aquatic pathology, fisheries science; fisheries (MS). *Faculty:* 10 full-time (4 women). *Students:* 14 full-time (7 women), 12 part-time (7 women); includes 5 minority (2 African Americans, 3 Hispanic Americans), 3 international. In 2009, 3 master's, 2 doctorates awarded. *Degree requirements:* For master's, comprehensive exam (for some programs), thesis optional; for doctorate, comprehensive exam, thesis/dissertation. *Entrance requirements:* For master's and doctorate, GRE, 2 letters of recommendation. Additional exam requirements/recommendations for international students: Required—TOEFL (minimum score 550 paper-based; 213 computer-based). *Application deadline:* For fall admission, 7/15 for domestic students, 2/1 for international students; for spring admission, 11/15 for domestic students, 7/15 for international students. Application fee: $65. Electronic applications accepted. *Expenses:* Tuition, state resident: full-time $8828; part-time $490 per credit hour. Tuition, nonresident: full-time $22,100; part-time $1228 per credit hour. Required fees: $1118; $57 per semester. Tuition and fees vary according to program. *Financial support:* In 2009–10, 4 research assistantships with full and partial tuition reimbursements (averaging $11,386 per year), 7 teaching assistantships with full and partial tuition reimbursements (averaging $10,940 per year) were awarded. Financial award application deadline: 7/15; financial award applicants required to submit FAFSA. Total annual research expenditures: $2.1 million. *Unit head:* Dr. David Bengtson, Chair, 401-874-2668, Fax: 401-874-7575, E-mail: bengtson@uri.edu. *Application contact:* Dr. Marta Gomez-Chiarra, Director of Graduate Studies, 401-874-2917, Fax: 401-874-7575, E-mail: gomezchi@uri.edu.

The University of Tennessee, Graduate School, College of Agricultural Sciences and Natural Resources, Department of Forestry, Wildlife, and Fisheries, Program in Wildlife and Fisheries Science, Knoxville, TN 37996. Offers MS. *Degree requirements:* For master's, thesis. *Entrance requirements:* For master's, GRE General Test, minimum GPA of 2.7. Additional exam requirements/recommendations for international students: Required—TOEFL. Electronic applications accepted. *Expenses:* Tuition, state resident: full-time $6826; part-time $380 per semester hour. Tuition, nonresident: full-time $21,844; part-time $1147 per semester hour. Tuition and fees vary according to program.

University of Washington, Graduate School, College of Forest Resources, Seattle, WA 98195. Offers bioresource science and engineering (MS, PhD); environmental horticulture (MEH); environmental horticulture and urban forestry (MS, PhD); forest ecology (MS, PhD); forest management (MFR); forest soils (MS, PhD); forest systems and bioenergy (MS, PhD); restoration ecology (MS, PhD); social sciences (MS, PhD); sustainable resource management (MS, PhD); wildlife science (MS, PhD); MFR/MAIS; MPA/MS. *Accreditation:* SAF. *Degree requirements:* For master's, thesis (for some programs); for doctorate, comprehensive exam (for some programs), thesis/dissertation. *Entrance requirements:* For master's and doctorate, GRE, minimum GPA of 3.0. Additional exam requirements/recommendations for international students: Required—TOEFL. Electronic applications accepted. *Faculty research:* Ecosystem analysis, silviculture and forest protection, paper science and engineering, environmental horticulture and urban forestry, natural resource policy and economics.

University of Washington, Graduate School, College of Ocean and Fishery Sciences, School of Aquatic and Fishery Sciences, Seattle, WA 98195. Offers MS, PhD. *Degree requirements:* For master's, thesis; for doctorate, thesis/dissertation. *Entrance requirements:* For master's and doctorate, GRE General Test, minimum GPA of 3.0. Additional exam requirements/recommendations for international students: Required—TOEFL. Electronic applications accepted. *Faculty research:* Fish and shellfish ecology, fisheries management, aquatic ecology, conservation biology, genetics.

University of Wisconsin–Madison, Graduate School, College of Agricultural and Life Sciences, Department of Forest and Wildlife Ecology, Madison, WI 53706-1380. Offers MS, PhD. Part-time programs available. *Degree requirements:* For master's, thesis (for some programs); for doctorate, thesis/dissertation. *Entrance requirements:* For master's and doctorate, GRE. Additional exam requirements/recommendations for international students: Required—TOEFL. Electronic applications accepted. *Expenses:* Tuition, state resident: part-time $594 per credit. Tuition, nonresident: part-time $1504 per credit. Required fees: $65 per credit. Tuition and fees vary according to course load, program and reciprocity agreements. *Faculty research:* Forest and landscape ecology, forest biology, social forestry, recreation resources, wood science.

Utah State University, School of Graduate Studies, College of Natural Resources, Department of Aquatic, Watershed, and Earth Resources, Logan, UT 84322. Offers ecology (MS, PhD); fisheries biology (MS, PhD); watershed science (MS, PhD). *Degree requirements:* For master's, thesis (for some programs); for doctorate, thesis/dissertation. *Entrance requirements:* For master's and doctorate, GRE General Test, minimum GPA of 3.2. Additional exam requirements/recommendations for international students: Required—TOEFL. Electronic applications accepted. *Faculty research:* Behavior, population ecology, habitat, conservation biology, restoration, aquatic ecology, fisheries management, fluvial geomorphology, remote sensing, conservation biology.

Utah State University, School of Graduate Studies, College of Natural Resources, Department of Wildland Resources, Logan, UT 84322. Offers ecology (MS, PhD); forestry (MS, PhD); range science (MS, PhD); wildlife biology (MS, PhD). Part-time programs available. *Degree requirements:* For master's, thesis; for doctorate, comprehensive exam, thesis/dissertation. *Entrance requirements:* For master's and doctorate, GRE General Test, minimum GPA of 3.0. Additional exam requirements/recommendations for international students: Required—TOEFL. *Faculty research:* Range plant ecophysiology, plant community ecology, ruminant nutrition, population ecology.

Fish, Game, and Wildlife Management

Virginia Polytechnic Institute and State University, Graduate School, College of Natural Resources, Department of Fisheries and Wildlife Sciences, Blacksburg, VA 24061. Offers MS, PhD. *Entrance requirements:* Additional exam requirements/recommendations for international students: Required—TOEFL (minimum score 550 paper-based; 213 computer-based). Electronic applications accepted. *Faculty research:* Fisheries management, wildlife management, wildlife toxicology and physiology, endangered species, computer applications.

West Virginia University, Davis College of Agriculture, Forestry and Consumer Sciences, Division of Forestry, Program in Wildlife and Fisheries Resources, Morgantown, WV 26506. Offers MS. Part-time programs available. *Degree requirements:* For master's, comprehensive exam, thesis. *Entrance requirements:* For master's, GRE, minimum GPA of 3.0. Additional exam requirements/recommendations for international students: Required—TOEFL. Electronic applications accepted. *Faculty research:* Managing habitat for game, nongame, and fish; fish ecology; wildlife ecology.

Forestry

Auburn University, Graduate School, School of Forestry and Wildlife Sciences, Auburn University, AL 36849. Offers forest economics (PhD); forestry (MS, PhD); natural resource conservation (MNR); wildlife sciences (MS, PhD). *Accreditation:* SAF. Part-time programs available. *Faculty:* 28 full-time (5 women), 2 part-time/adjunct (0 women). *Students:* 29 full-time (12 women), 53 part-time (17 women); includes 3 minority (1 African American, 1 Asian American or Pacific Islander, 1 Hispanic American), 28 international. Average age 28. 55 applicants, 44% accepted, 17 enrolled. In 2009, 5 master's, 3 doctorates awarded. *Degree requirements:* For master's, thesis (MS); for doctorate, thesis/dissertation. *Entrance requirements:* For master's and doctorate, GRE General Test. *Application deadline:* For fall admission, 7/7 for domestic students; for spring admission, 11/24 for domestic students. Applications are processed on a rolling basis. Application fee: $50 ($60 for international students). Electronic applications accepted. *Expenses:* Tuition, state resident: full-time $6240. Tuition, nonresident: full-time $18,720. International tuition: $18,938 full-time. Required fees: $492. Tuition and fees vary according to course load, program and reciprocity agreements. *Financial support:* Fellowships, research assistantships, teaching assistantships, Federal Work-Study available. Support available to part-time students. Financial award application deadline: 3/15; financial award applicants required to submit FAFSA. *Faculty research:* Forest nursery management, silviculture and vegetation management, biological processes and ecological relationships, growth and yield of plantations and natural stands, urban forestry, forest taxation, law and policy. *Unit head:* Dr. Richard W. Brinker, Dean, 334-844-1007, Fax: 334-844-1084, E-mail: brinker@forestry.auburn.edu. *Application contact:* Dr. George Flowers, Dean of the Graduate School, 334-844-2125.

California Polytechnic State University, San Luis Obispo, College of Agriculture, Food and Environmental Sciences, Department of Natural Resources Management, San Luis Obispo, CA 93407. Offers forestry sciences (MS). Part-time programs available. *Faculty:* 8 full-time (2 women). *Students:* 2 full-time (1 woman), 4 part-time (0 women), 1 international. Average age 29. 3 applicants, 67% accepted, 1 enrolled. In 2009, 2 master's awarded. *Degree requirements:* For master's, comprehensive exam, thesis. *Entrance requirements:* For master's, minimum GPA of 2.75 in last 90 quarter units of course work. Additional exam requirements/recommendations for international students: Required—TOEFL (minimum score 550 paper-based; 213 computer-based), or IELTS (minimum score 6). *Application deadline:* For fall admission, 2/1 for domestic students, 11/30 for international students; for winter admission, 11/1 for domestic students, 6/30 for international students; for spring admission, 2/1 for domestic students. Applications are processed on a rolling basis. Application fee: $55. Electronic applications accepted. *Expenses:* Tuition, nonresident: full-time $11,160; part-time $248 per unit. Required fees: $7134; $1553 per quarter. *Financial support:* Fellowships, research assistantships, career-related internships or fieldwork, Federal Work-Study, institutionally sponsored loans, scholarships/grants, and unspecified assistantships available. Support available to part-time students. Financial award application deadline: 3/2; financial award applicants required to submit FAFSA. *Faculty research:* Hydrology, biometrics, forest health and management, fire science, urban and community forestry. *Unit head:* Dr. Doug Piirto, Department Head/Graduate Coordinator, 805-756-2968, Fax: 805-756-1402, E-mail: dpiirto@calpoly.edu. *Application contact:* Dr. Mark Shelton, Associate Dean/Graduate Coordinator, 805-756-2161, Fax: 805-756-6577, E-mail: mshelton@calpoly.edu.

Clemson University, Graduate School, College of Agriculture, Forestry and Life Sciences, Department of Forestry and Natural Resources, Program in Forest Resources, Clemson, SC 29634. Offers MFR, MS, PhD. Part-time programs available. *Students:* 27 full-time (5 women), 8 part-time (2 women); includes 1 minority (African American), 4 international. Average age 28. 28 applicants, 64% accepted, 12 enrolled. In 2009, 11 master's, 2 doctorates awarded. *Degree requirements:* For master's, thesis; for doctorate, thesis/dissertation. *Entrance requirements:* For master's, GRE General Test, minimum B average in last 2 years of undergraduate course work; for doctorate, GRE General Test, minimum B average in graduate course work. Additional exam requirements/recommendations for international students: Required—TOEFL, IELTS. *Application deadline:* For fall admission, 3/1 priority date for domestic students, 4/15 for international students; for spring admission, 10/1 for domestic students, 9/15 for international students. Applications are processed on a rolling basis. Application fee: $70 ($80 for international students). Electronic applications accepted. *Expenses:* Contact institution. *Financial support:* In 2009–10, 21 students received support, including 2 fellowships with full and partial tuition reimbursements available (averaging $11,133 per year), 14 research assistantships with partial tuition reimbursements available (averaging $14,934 per year), 5 teaching assistantships with partial tuition reimbursements available (averaging $23,000 per year); career-related internships or fieldwork, institutionally sponsored loans, scholarships/grants, health care benefits, and unspecified assistantships also available. Support available to part-time students. Financial award application deadline: 5/1; financial award applicants required to submit FAFSA. *Faculty research:* Wetlands management, wood technology, forest management, silviculture, economics. *Unit head:* Dr. Patricia Layton, Chair, 864-656-3303, Fax: 864-656-3304, E-mail: playton@clemson.edu. *Application contact:* Dr. David Guynn, Graduate Program Coordinator, 864-656-4830, E-mail: dguynn@clemson.edu.

Colorado State University, Graduate School, Warner College of Natural Resources, Department of Forest, Rangeland, and Watershed Stewardship, Fort Collins, CO 80523-1472. Offers forest sciences (MS, PhD); natural resources stewardship (MNRS); rangeland ecosystem science (MS, PhD); watershed science (MS). Part-time programs available. Postbaccalaureate distance learning degree programs offered (no on-campus study). *Faculty:* 21 full-time (5 women), 1 part-time/adjunct (0 women). *Students:* 47 full-time (23 women), 76 part-time (21 women); includes 9 minority (3 American Indian/Alaska Native, 1 Asian American or Pacific Islander, 5 Hispanic Americans), 7 international. Average age 33. 53 applicants, 81% accepted, 33 enrolled. In 2009, 26 master's, 7 doctorates awarded. *Degree requirements:* For master's, thesis (for some programs); for doctorate, comprehensive exam, thesis/dissertation. *Entrance requirements:* For master's, GRE General Test (minimum score 1000 verbal and quantitative), minimum GPA of 3.0, 3 letters of recommendation; for doctorate, GRE General Test (combined minimum score of 1100 on the Verbal and Quantitative sections), minimum GPA of 3.0, 3 letters of recommendation, statement of research interest. Additional exam requirements/recommendations for international students: Required—TOEFL (minimum score 550 paper-based; 213 computer-based; 80 iBT), IELTS (minimum score 6). *Application deadline:* For fall admission, 8/1 priority date for domestic students, 6/25 priority date for international students; for spring admission, 12/1 priority date for domestic students, 11/25 priority date for international students. Applications are processed on a rolling basis. Application fee: $50. Electronic applications accepted. *Expenses:* Tuition, state resident: full-time $6434; part-time $359.10 per credit. Tuition, nonresident: full-time $18,116; part-time $1006.45 per credit. Required fees: $1496; $83 per credit. *Financial support:* In 2009–10, 43 students received support, including 3 fellowships (averaging $40,417 per year), 33 research assistantships with full and partial tuition reimbursements available (averaging $15,898 per year), 7 teaching assistantships with full and partial tuition reimbursements available (averaging $6,506 per year); Federal Work-Study, scholarships/grants, and unspecified assistantships also available. Financial award applicants required to submit FAFSA. *Faculty research:* Ecology, natural resource management, hydrology, restoration, human dimensions. Total annual research expenditures: $3.7 million. *Unit head:* Dr. N. Thompson Hobbs, Head, 970-491-6911, Fax: 970-491-6754, E-mail: nthobbs@warnercnr@colostate.edu. *Application contact:* Sonya LeFebre, Coordinator, 970-491-1907, Fax: 970-491-6754, E-mail: sonya.lefebre@colostate.edu.

Cornell University, Graduate School, Graduate Fields of Agriculture and Life Sciences, Field of Natural Resources, Ithaca, NY 14853-0001. Offers aquatic science (MPS, MS, PhD); environmental management (MPS); fishery science (MPS, MS, PhD); forest science (MPS, MS, PhD); resource policy and management (MPS, MS, PhD); wildlife science (MPS, MS, PhD). *Faculty:* 39 full-time (7 women). *Students:* 60 full-time (28 women); includes 4 minority (2 American Indian/Alaska Native, 1 Asian American or Pacific Islander, 1 Hispanic American), 13 international. Average age 31. 63 applicants, 32% accepted, 19 enrolled. In 2009, 6 master's, 7 doctorates awarded. *Degree requirements:* For master's, thesis (MS), project paper (MPS); for doctorate, comprehensive exam, thesis/dissertation. *Entrance requirements:* For master's and doctorate, GRE General Test, 2 letters of recommendation. Additional exam requirements/recommendations for international students: Required—TOEFL (minimum score 550 paper-based; 213 computer-based; 77 iBT). *Application deadline:* For spring admission, 10/30 for domestic students. Applications are processed on a rolling basis. Application fee: $70. Electronic applications accepted. *Expenses:* Tuition: Full-time $29,500. Required fees: $70. Full-time tuition and fees vary according to degree level, program and student level. *Financial support:* In 2009–10, 39 students received support, including 12 research assistantships with full tuition reimbursements available, 5 teaching assistantships with full tuition reimbursements available; fellowships with full tuition reimbursements available, institutionally sponsored loans, scholarships/grants, health care benefits, tuition waivers (full and partial), and unspecified assistantships also available. Financial award applicants required to submit FAFSA. *Faculty research:* Ecosystem-level dynamics, systems modeling, conservation biology/management, resource management's human dimensions, biogeochemistry. *Unit head:* Director of Graduate Studies, 607-255-2807, Fax: 607-255-0349. *Application contact:* Graduate Field Assistant, 607-255-2807, Fax: 607-255-0349, E-mail: nrgrad@cornell.edu.

Duke University, Nicholas School of the Environment, Durham, NC 27708-0328. Offers coastal environmental management (MEM); DEL-environmental leadership (MEM); energy and environment (MEM); environmental economics and policy (MEM); environmental health and security (MEM); forest resource management (MF); global environmental change (MEM); resource ecology (MEM); water and air resources (MEM); JD/AM; JD/MEM; JD/MF; MAT/MEM; MBA/MEM; MBA/MF; MEM/MPP; MF/MPP. *Accreditation:* SAF (one or more programs are accredited). Part-time programs available. *Degree requirements:* For master's, thesis. *Entrance requirements:* For master's, GRE General Test, previous course work in biology or ecology, calculus, statistics, and microeconomics; computer familiarity with word processing and data analysis. Additional exam requirements/recommendations for international students: Required—TOEFL (minimum score 550 paper-based; 213 computer-based). Electronic applications accepted. *Expenses:* Contact institution. *Faculty research:* Ecosystem management, conservation ecology, earth systems, risk assessment.

Harvard University, Graduate School of Arts and Sciences, Department of Forestry, Cambridge, MA 02138. Offers forest science (MFS). *Degree requirements:* For master's, thesis. *Entrance requirements:* For master's, GRE General Test, bachelor's degree in biology or forestry. Additional exam requirements/recommendations for international students: Required—TOEFL. *Expenses:* Tuition: Full-time $33,696. Required fees: $1126. Full-time tuition and fees vary according to program. *Faculty research:* Forest ecology, planning, and physiology; forest microbiology.

Humboldt State University, Graduate Studies, College of Natural Resources and Sciences, Programs in Natural Resources, Arcata, CA 95521-8299. Offers natural resources (MS), including fisheries, forestry, natural resources planning and interpretation, rangeland resources and wildland soils, wastewater utilization, watershed management, wildlife. *Students:* 51 full-time (22 women), 26 part-time (10 women); includes 4 minority (1 American Indian/Alaska Native, 1 Asian American or Pacific Islander, 2 Hispanic Americans), 1 international. Average age 31. 81 applicants, 26% accepted, 15 enrolled. In 2009, 25 master's awarded. *Degree requirements:* For master's, thesis or alternative. *Entrance requirements:* For master's, GRE, appropriate bachelor's degree, minimum GPA of 2.5, 3 letters of recommendation, resume. Additional exam requirements/recommendations for international students: Required—TOEFL (minimum score 500 paper-based; 173 computer-based). *Application deadline:* For fall admission, 2/1 for domestic and international students; for spring admission, 9/30 for domestic and international students. Applications are processed on a rolling basis. Application fee: $55. *Expenses:* Tuition, nonresident: full-time $8928. Required fees: $6102. Tuition and fees vary according to program. *Financial support:* Fellowships, career-related internships or fieldwork and Federal Work-Study available. Support available to part-time students. Financial award application deadline: 3/1; financial award applicants required to submit FAFSA. *Faculty research:* Spotted owl habitat, pre-settlement vegetation, hardwood utilization, tree physiology, fisheries. *Unit head:* Dr. Gary Hendrickson, Coordinator, 707-826-4233, E-mail: thiesfel@humboldt.edu. *Application contact:* Julie Tucker, Administrative Support Coordinator, 707-826-3256, E-mail: jlt7002@humboldt.edu.

Iowa State University of Science and Technology, Graduate College, College of Agriculture, Department of Natural Resource Ecology and Management, Ames, IA 50011. Offers forestry (MS, PhD); wildlife ecology (MS). *Faculty:* 18 full-time (4 women), 7 part-time/adjunct (2 women). *Students:* 40 full-time (13 women), 2 part-time (1 woman); includes 3 minority (1 American Indian/Alaska Native, 2 Hispanic Americans), 6 international. 28 applicants, 29% accepted, 8 enrolled. In 2009, 9 master's, 2 doctorates awarded. *Degree requirements:* For master's, thesis (for some programs); for doctorate, thesis/dissertation. *Entrance requirements:*

For master's and doctorate, GRE General Test. Additional exam requirements/recommendations for international students: Required—TOEFL (minimum score 550 paper-based; 79 iBT) or IELTS (minimum score 6.5). *Application deadline:* For fall admission, 4/1 priority date for domestic and international students; for spring admission, 10/1 priority date for domestic and international students. Application fee: $40 ($90 for international students). Electronic applications accepted. *Expenses:* Tuition, state resident: full-time $6716. Tuition, nonresident: full-time $8908. Tuition and fees vary according to course level, course load, program and student level. *Financial support:* In 2009–10, 23 research assistantships with full and partial tuition reimbursements (averaging $15,420 per year), 2 teaching assistantships with full and partial tuition reimbursements (averaging $15,420 per year) were awarded. *Unit head:* Dr. Stephen Jungst, Interim Chair, 515-294-1166. *Application contact:* Dr. Janette Thompson, Director of Graduate Education, 515-294-1626, E-mail: nremgrad@iastate.edu.

Lakehead University, Graduate Studies, Faculty of Forestry, Thunder Bay, ON P7B 5E1, Canada. Offers forest sciences (PhD); forestry (M Sc F, MF). Part-time programs available. *Degree requirements:* For master's, report (MF), thesis (M Sc F). *Entrance requirements:* For master's, minimum B average. Additional exam requirements/recommendations for international students: Required—TOEFL. *Faculty research:* Soils, silviculture, wildlife, ecology, genetics.

Louisiana State University and Agricultural and Mechanical College, Graduate School, College of Agriculture, School of Renewable Natural Resources, Baton Rouge, LA 70803. Offers fisheries (MS); forestry (MS, PhD); wildlife (MS); wildlife and fisheries science (PhD). *Faculty:* 32 full-time (3 women). *Students:* 73 full-time (17 women), 9 part-time (4 women); includes 1 Hispanic American, 26 international. Average age 29. 31 applicants, 48% accepted, 14 enrolled. In 2009, 11 master's, 2 doctorates awarded. *Degree requirements:* For master's, thesis; for doctorate, thesis/dissertation. *Entrance requirements:* For master's, GRE General Test, minimum GPA of 3.0; for doctorate, GRE General Test, MS, minimum GPA of 3.0. Additional exam requirements/recommendations for international students: Required—TOEFL (minimum score 550 paper-based; 213 computer-based; 79 iBT), IELTS (minimum score 6.5). *Application deadline:* For fall admission, 1/25 priority date for domestic students, 5/15 for international students; for spring admission, 10/15 for international students. Applications are processed on a rolling basis. Application fee: $50 ($70 for international students). Electronic applications accepted. *Financial support:* In 2009–10, 80 students received support, including 7 fellowships (averaging $36,514 per year), 61 research assistantships with partial tuition reimbursements available (averaging $18,686 per year), 1 teaching assistantship with partial tuition reimbursement available (averaging $10,800 per year); Federal Work-Study, institutionally sponsored loans, scholarships/grants, health care benefits, tuition waivers (full and partial), and unspecified assistantships also available. Financial award application deadline: 4/15; financial award applicants required to submit FAFSA. *Faculty research:* Forest biology and management, aquaculture, fisheries biology and ecology, upland and wetlands wildlife. Total annual research expenditures: $3,308. *Unit head:* Dr. Allen Rutherford, Director, 225-578-4131, Fax: 225-578-4227, E-mail: druther@lsu.edu. *Application contact:* Dr. William Kelso, Coordinator of Graduate Studies, 225-578-4176, Fax: 225-578-4227, E-mail: wkelso@lsu.edu.

McGill University, Faculty of Graduate and Postdoctoral Studies, Faculty of Agricultural and Environmental Sciences, Department of Natural Resource Sciences, Montréal, QC H3A 2T5, Canada. Offers entomology (M Sc, PhD); environmental assessment (M Sc); forest science (M Sc, PhD); microbiology (M Sc, PhD); micrometeorology (M Sc, PhD); neotropical environment (M Sc, PhD); soil science (M Sc, PhD); wildlife biology (M Sc, PhD).

Michigan State University, The Graduate School, College of Agriculture and Natural Resources, Department of Forestry, East Lansing, MI 48824. Offers forestry (MS, PhD); forestry-environmental toxicology (PhD); plant breeding, genetics and biotechnology-forestry (MS, PhD). *Entrance requirements:* Additional exam requirements/recommendations for international students: Required—TOEFL (minimum score 550 paper-based; 213 computer-based), Michigan State University ELT (85), Michigan ELAB (83). Electronic applications accepted.

Michigan Technological University, Graduate School, School of Forest Resources and Environmental Science, Program in Forest Ecology and Management, Houghton, MI 49931. Offers MS. Part-time programs available. *Degree requirements:* For master's, thesis (for some programs). *Entrance requirements:* For master's, GRE. Additional exam requirements/recommendations for international students: Required—TOEFL (minimum score 550 paper-based; 213 computer-based). Electronic applications accepted.

Michigan Technological University, Graduate School, School of Forest Resources and Environmental Science, Program in Forest Molecular Genetics and Biotechnology, Houghton, MI 49931. Offers MS, PhD. Part-time programs available. Terminal master's awarded for partial completion of doctoral program. *Degree requirements:* For master's, thesis (for some programs); for doctorate, comprehensive exam, thesis/dissertation. *Entrance requirements:* For master's, GRE. Additional exam requirements/recommendations for international students: Required—TOEFL (minimum score 550 paper-based; 213 computer-based). Electronic applications accepted.

Michigan Technological University, Graduate School, School of Forest Resources and Environmental Science, Program in Forestry, Houghton, MI 49931. Offers MF, MS. Part-time programs available. *Degree requirements:* For master's, thesis (for some programs). *Entrance requirements:* For master's, GRE. Additional exam requirements/recommendations for international students: Required—TOEFL (minimum score 550 paper-based; 213 computer-based). Electronic applications accepted.

Michigan Technological University, Graduate School, School of Forest Resources and Environmental Science, Program in Forest Science, Houghton, MI 49931. Offers PhD. Part-time programs available. *Degree requirements:* For doctorate, comprehensive exam, thesis/dissertation. *Entrance requirements:* Additional exam requirements/recommendations for international students: Required—TOEFL (minimum score 550 paper-based; 213 computer-based). Electronic applications accepted.

Mississippi State University, College of Forest Resources, Department of Forest Products, Mississippi State, MS 39762. Offers forest products (MS); forest resources (PhD), including forest products. *Faculty:* 11 full-time (2 women), 2 part-time/adjunct (0 women). *Students:* 29 full-time (9 women), 4 part-time (0 women); includes 3 minority (1 African American, 1 Asian American or Pacific Islander, 1 Hispanic American), 18 international. Average age 30. 22 applicants, 45% accepted, 10 enrolled. In 2009, 6 master's awarded. *Degree requirements:* For master's, thesis optional; for doctorate, comprehensive exam, thesis/dissertation. *Entrance requirements:* For master's, GRE (if undergraduate GPA of last two years less than 3.0); for doctorate, GRE if undergraduate GPA of last two years is below 3.0. Additional exam requirements/recommendations for international students: Required—TOEFL (minimum score 550 paper-based; 213 computer-based; 79 iBT); Recommended—IELTS (minimum score 6.5). *Application deadline:* For fall admission, 7/1 for domestic students, 5/1 for international students; for spring admission, 11/1 for domestic students, 9/1 for international students. Applications are processed on a rolling basis. Application fee: $40. Electronic applications accepted. *Expenses:* Tuition, state resident: full-time $2575.50; part-time $286.25 per credit hour. Tuition, nonresident: full-time $6510; part-time $723.50 per credit hour. Tuition and fees vary according to course load. *Financial support:* In 2009–10, 21 research assistantships with full tuition reimbursements (averaging $10,818 per year), 1 teaching assistantship (averaging $13,784 per year) were awarded; Federal Work-Study, institutionally sponsored loans, and unspecified assistantships also available. Financial award application deadline: 4/1; financial award applicants required to submit FAFSA. *Faculty research:* Wood property enhancement and durability, environmental science and chemistry, wood-based composites, primary wood production, furniture manufacturing and management. *Unit head:* Dr. Robin Shmulsky, Department Head and Graduate Coordinator, 662-325-2116, Fax: 662-325-8126, E-mail: rshmulsky@cfr.msstate.edu. *Application contact:* Dr. Robin Shmulsky, Department Head and Graduate Coordinator, 662-325-2116, Fax: 662-325-8126, E-mail: rshmulsky@cfr.msstate.edu.

Mississippi State University, College of Forest Resources, Department of Forestry, Mississippi State, MS 39762. Offers forest resources (PhD), including forestry; forestry (MS). Part-time programs available. *Faculty:* 19 full-time (3 women), 1 part-time/adjunct (0 women). *Students:* 41 full-time (7 women), 10 part-time (2 women); includes 3 minority (2 African Americans, 1 Asian American or Pacific Islander), 10 international. Average age 31. 18 applicants, 67% accepted, 11 enrolled. In 2009, 11 master's awarded. *Degree requirements:* For master's, comprehensive exam, thesis optional, comprehensive oral or written exam; for doctorate, comprehensive exam, thesis/dissertation. *Entrance requirements:* For master's, GRE (if undergraduate GPA of last two years less than 3.0), minimum GPA of 2.5; for doctorate, minimum GPA of 3.1 on prior graduate courses. Additional exam requirements/recommendations for international students: Required—TOEFL (minimum score 550 paper-based; 213 computer-based; 79 iBT); Recommended—IELTS (minimum score 6.5). *Application deadline:* For fall admission, 7/1 for domestic students, 5/1 for international students; for spring admission, 11/1 for domestic students, 9/1 for international students. Applications are processed on a rolling basis. Application fee: $40. Electronic applications accepted. *Expenses:* Tuition, state resident: full-time $2575.50; part-time $286.25 per credit hour. Tuition, nonresident: full-time $6510; part-time $723.50 per credit hour. Tuition and fees vary according to course load. *Financial support:* In 2009–10, 28 research assistantships with full tuition reimbursements (averaging $11,757 per year), 4 teaching assistantships with full tuition reimbursements (averaging $10,093 per year) were awarded; Federal Work-Study, institutionally sponsored loans, and unspecified assistantships also available. Financial award application deadline: 4/1; financial award applicants required to submit FAFSA. *Faculty research:* Forest hydrology, forest biometry, forest management/economics, forest biology, industrial forest operations. *Unit head:* Dr. Andrew Ezell, Professor/Head/Graduate Coordinator, 662-325-2949, Fax: 662-325-8126, E-mail: aezell@cfr.msstate.edu. *Application contact:* Dr. Andrew Ezell, Professor/Head/Graduate Coordinator, 662-325-2949, Fax: 662-325-8126, E-mail: aezell@cfr.msstate.edu.

Mississippi State University, College of Forest Resources, Department of Wildlife, Fisheries and Aquaculture, Mississippi State, MS 39762. Offers forest resources (PhD), including wildlife and fisheries; wildlife and fisheries science (MS). Part-time programs available. *Faculty:* 19 full-time (1 woman). *Students:* 54 full-time (17 women), 17 part-time (6 women); includes 3 minority (1 Asian American or Pacific Islander, 2 Hispanic Americans), 4 international. Average age 28. 23 applicants, 65% accepted, 14 enrolled. In 2009, 7 master's, 4 doctorates awarded. *Degree requirements:* For master's, comprehensive exam, thesis, comprehensive oral or written exam; for doctorate, comprehensive exam, thesis/dissertation. *Entrance requirements:* For master's, GRE or minimum GPA of 3.0 on last 60 hours of undergraduate courses, bachelor's degree; for doctorate, GRE or minimum GPA of 3.2 on prior graduate studies, master's degree. Additional exam requirements/recommendations for international students: Required—TOEFL (minimum score 550 paper-based; 213 computer-based; 79 iBT); Recommended—IELTS (minimum score 6.5). *Application deadline:* For fall admission, 7/1 for domestic students, 5/1 for international students; for spring admission, 11/1 for domestic students, 9/1 for international students. Applications are processed on a rolling basis. Application fee: $40. Electronic applications accepted. *Expenses:* Tuition, state resident: full-time $2575.50; part-time $286.25 per credit hour. Tuition, nonresident: full-time $6510; part-time $723.50 per credit hour. Tuition and fees vary according to course load. *Financial support:* In 2009–10, 52 research assistantships with partial tuition reimbursements (averaging $11,195 per year), 1 teaching assistantship with partial tuition reimbursement (averaging $10,037 per year) were awarded; Federal Work-Study, institutionally sponsored loans, and unspecified assistantships also available. Financial award application deadline: 4/1; financial award applicants required to submit FAFSA. *Faculty research:* Spatial technology, habitat restoration, aquaculture, fisheries, wildlife management. *Unit head:* Dr. Bruce D. Leopold, Department Head and Graduate Coordinator, 662-325-2619, Fax: 662-325-8726, E-mail: bleopold@cfr.msstate.edu. *Application contact:* Dr. Bruce D. Leopold, Department Head and Graduate Coordinator, 662-325-2619, Fax: 662-325-8726, E-mail: bleopold@cfr.msstate.edu.

North Carolina State University, Graduate School, College of Natural Resources, Department of Forestry and Environmental Resources, Raleigh, NC 27695. Offers MF, MS, PhD. Part-time programs available. *Degree requirements:* For master's, thesis (for some programs), teaching experience; for doctorate, thesis/dissertation, teaching experience. *Entrance requirements:* For master's and doctorate, GRE General Test. Additional exam requirements/recommendations for international students: Required—TOEFL. Electronic applications accepted. *Faculty research:* Forest genetics, forest ecology and silviculture, forest economics/management/policy, international forestry, remote sensing/geographic information systems.

Northern Arizona University, Graduate College, College of Engineering, Forestry and Natural Sciences, School of Forestry, Flagstaff, AZ 86011. Offers forest science (MF, MSF); forestry (PhD). Part-time programs available. *Faculty:* 22 full-time (9 women). *Students:* 49 full-time (30 women), 16 part-time (9 women). Average age 33. 36 applicants, 64% accepted, 21 enrolled. In 2009, 13 master's, 5 doctorates awarded. *Degree requirements:* For master's, thesis optional; for doctorate, thesis/dissertation. *Entrance requirements:* For master's, GRE General Test; for doctorate, GRE General Test. Additional exam requirements/recommendations for international students: Required—TOEFL (minimum score 550 paper-based; 213 computer-based; 80 iBT), IELTS (minimum score 7), or a bachelor's degree from an English-speaking university and demonstrated proficiency. *Application deadline:* For fall admission, 3/15 priority date for domestic students, 9/1 for international students; for spring admission, 10/15 for domestic students. Applications are processed on a rolling basis. Application fee: $65. Electronic applications accepted. *Financial support:* In 2009–10, 38 teaching assistantships with partial tuition reimbursements (averaging $16,000 per year) were awarded; career-related internships or fieldwork, Federal Work-Study, scholarships/grants, traineeships, health care benefits, tuition waivers (full and partial), and unspecified assistantships also available. Support available to part-time students. Financial award application deadline: 3/30; financial award applicants required to submit FAFSA. *Faculty research:* Multiresource management, ecology, entomology, recreation, hydrology. Total annual research expenditures: $1.4 million. *Unit head:* Dr. James Allen, Graduate Coordinator, 928-523-5894, Fax: 928-523-1080, E-mail: james.allen@nau.edu. *Application contact:* Dr. Tom Kolb, Coordinator, 928-523-7491, Fax: 928-523-1080, E-mail: tom.kolb@nau.edu.

Oklahoma State University, College of Agricultural Science and Natural Resources, Department of Natural Resource Ecology and Management, Stillwater, OK 74078. Offers M Ag, MS, PhD. *Faculty:* 19 full-time (3 women). *Students:* 7 full-time (4 women), 43 part-time (11 women); includes 5 minority (1 African American, 2 American Indian/Alaska Native, 2 Asian Americans or Pacific Islanders), 3 international. Average age 31. 26 applicants, 46% accepted, 10 enrolled. In 2009, 17 master's, 2 doctorates awarded. *Degree requirements:* For master's, comprehensive exam (for some programs), thesis; for doctorate, comprehensive exam, thesis/dissertation. *Entrance requirements:* For master's and doctorate, GRE or GMAT. Additional exam requirements/recommendations for international students: Required—TOEFL (minimum score 550 paper-based; 79 iBT). *Application deadline:* For fall admission, 3/1 priority date for international students; for spring admission, 8/1 priority date for international students. Applications are processed on a rolling basis. Application fee: $40 ($75 for international students). Electronic applications accepted. *Expenses:* Tuition, state resident: full-time $3716; part-time $154.85 per credit hour. Tuition, nonresident: full-time $14,448; part-time $602 per credit hour. Required fees: $1772; $73.85 per credit hour. One-time fee: $50. Tuition and fees vary according to course load and campus/location. *Financial support:* In 2009–10, 36 research

Forestry

Oklahoma State University (continued)

assistantships (averaging $15,436 per year), 1 teaching assistantship (averaging $15,504 per year) were awarded; career-related internships or fieldwork, Federal Work-Study, scholarships/grants, health care benefits, tuition waivers (partial), and unspecified assistantships also available. Support available to part-time students. Financial award application deadline: 3/1; financial award applicants required to submit FAFSA. *Faculty research:* Forest ecology, upland bird ecology, forest ecophysiology, urban forestry, molecular forest genetics/biotechnology/tree breeding. *Unit head:* Dr. Keith Owens, Head, 405-744-5438, Fax: 405-744-3530. *Application contact:* Dr. Gordon Emslie, Dean, 405-744-6368, Fax: 405-744-0355, E-mail: grad-i@okstate.edu.

Oregon State University, Graduate School, College of Forestry, Department of Forest Ecosystems and Society, Corvallis, OR 97331. Offers MAIS, MF, MS, PhD. *Accreditation:* SAF (one or more programs are accredited). Part-time programs available. *Faculty:* 21 full-time (6 women), 4 part-time/adjunct (2 women). *Students:* 26 full-time (18 women), 4 part-time (2 women); includes 5 minority (4 Asian Americans or Pacific Islanders, 1 Hispanic American), 15 international. Average age 29. In 2009, 10 master's, 7 doctorates awarded. *Degree requirements:* For master's, thesis (for some programs); for doctorate, thesis/dissertation. *Entrance requirements:* For master's and doctorate, GRE General Test, minimum GPA of 3.0 in last 90 hours. Additional exam requirements/recommendations for international students: Required—TOEFL. *Application deadline:* For fall admission, 8/25 priority date for domestic students; for spring admission, 3/1 for domestic students. Applications are processed on a rolling basis. Application fee: $50. *Expenses:* Tuition, state resident: full-time $9774; part-time $362 per credit. Tuition, nonresident: full-time $15,849; part-time $587 per credit. Required fees: $1639. Full-time tuition and fees vary according to course load and program. *Financial support:* Fellowships, research assistantships, career-related internships or fieldwork, Federal Work-Study, and institutionally sponsored loans available. Support available to part-time students. Financial award application deadline: 2/1. *Faculty research:* Ecosystem structure and function, nutrient cycling, biotechnology, vegetation management, integrated forest protection. *Unit head:* Dr. W. Thomas Adams, Head, 541-737-6583, Fax: 541-737-1393. *Application contact:* Clay W. Torset, Head Advisor, 541-737-1542, Fax: 541-737-2668, E-mail: clay.torset@oregonstate.edu.

Oregon State University, Graduate School, College of Forestry, Department of Forest Engineering, Resources and Management, Corvallis, OR 97331. Offers forest engineering (MF, MS); forest hydrology (MF, MS, PhD); forest operations (MF); forest soil science (MF, MS, PhD); timber harvesting (PhD). *Faculty:* 15 full-time (1 woman), 2 part-time/adjunct (1 woman). *Students:* 50 full-time (18 women), 5 part-time (4 women); includes 2 minority (both Hispanic Americans), 6 international. Average age 32. In 2009, 12 master's, 11 doctorates awarded. *Expenses:* Tuition, state resident: full-time $9774; part-time $362 per credit. Tuition, nonresident: full-time $15,849; part-time $587 per credit. Required fees: $1639. Full-time tuition and fees vary according to course load and program. *Unit head:* Hal J. Salwasser, Dean, 541-737-5704, Fax: 541-737-2906, E-mail: hal.salwasser@oregonstate.edu. *Application contact:* Clay W. Torset, Head Advisor, 541-737-1542, Fax: 541-737-2668, E-mail: clay.torset@oregonstate.edu.

Oregon State University, Graduate School, College of Forestry, Department of Wood Science and Engineering, Corvallis, OR 97331. Offers forest products (MAIS, MF, MS, PhD); wood science and technology (MF, MS, PhD). *Accreditation:* SAF (one or more programs are accredited). Part-time programs available. *Faculty:* 9 full-time (1 woman). *Students:* 35 full-time (17 women), 2 part-time (1 woman); includes 3 minority (1 Asian American or Pacific Islander, 2 Hispanic Americans), 7 international. Average age 33. In 2009, 7 master's, 4 doctorates awarded. *Degree requirements:* For master's, thesis (for some programs); for doctorate, thesis/dissertation. *Entrance requirements:* For master's and doctorate, GRE General Test, minimum GPA of 3.0 in last 90 hours. Additional exam requirements/recommendations for international students: Required—TOEFL. *Application deadline:* For fall admission, 3/1 priority date for domestic students. Applications are processed on a rolling basis. Application fee: $50. *Expenses:* Tuition, state resident: full-time $9774; part-time $362 per credit. Tuition, nonresident: full-time $15,849; part-time $587 per credit. Required fees: $1639. Full-time tuition and fees vary according to course load and program. *Financial support:* Fellowships, research assistantships, career-related internships or fieldwork, Federal Work-Study, and institutionally sponsored loans available. Support available to part-time students. Financial award application deadline: 2/1. *Faculty research:* Biodeterioration and preservation, timber engineering, process engineering and control, composite materials science, anatomy, chemistry and physical properties. *Unit head:* Dr. Thomas E. McLain, Head, 541-737-4224, Fax: 541-737-3385, E-mail: thomas.mclain@oregonstate.edu. *Application contact:* George Swanson, Program Support Coordinator, 541-737-4206, Fax: 541-737-3385, E-mail: george.swanson@oregonstate.edu.

Penn State University Park, Graduate School, College of Agricultural Sciences, School of Forest Resources, State College, University Park, PA 16802-1503. Offers M Agr, MFR, MS, PhD.

Purdue University, Graduate School, College of Agriculture, Department of Forestry and Natural Resources, West Lafayette, IN 47907. Offers aquaculture, fisheries, aquatic science (MSF); aquaculture, fisheries, aquatic sciences (MS, PhD); forest biology (MS, MSF, PhD); natural resources and environmental policy (MS, MSF); natural resources environmental policy (PhD); quantitative resource analysis (MS, MSF, PhD); wildlife science (MS, MSF, PhD); wood science and technology (MS, MSF, PhD). *Degree requirements:* For master's, thesis; for doctorate, thesis/dissertation. *Entrance requirements:* For master's and doctorate, GRE General Test, minimum B+ average in undergraduate course work. Additional exam requirements/recommendations for international students: Required—TOEFL. Electronic applications accepted. *Faculty research:* Wildlife management, forest management, forest ecology, forest soils, limnology.

Southern Illinois University Carbondale, Graduate School, College of Agriculture, Department of Forestry, Carbondale, IL 62901-4701. Offers MS. Part-time programs available. *Degree requirements:* For master's, thesis. *Entrance requirements:* For master's, minimum GPA of 2.7. Additional exam requirements/recommendations for international students: Required—TOEFL. *Faculty research:* Forest recreation, forest ecology, remote sensing, forest management and economics.

Southern University and Agricultural and Mechanical College, Graduate School, College of Agricultural, Family and Consumer Sciences, Department of Urban Forestry, Baton Rouge, LA 70813. Offers MS. *Degree requirements:* For master's, thesis. *Entrance requirements:* For master's, GRE, minimum GPA of 3.0. Additional exam requirements/recommendations for international students: Required—TOEFL (minimum score 525 paper-based; 193 computer-based). *Faculty research:* Biology of plant pathogen, water resources, plant pathology.

State University of New York College of Environmental Science and Forestry, Department of Environmental and Forest Biology, Syracuse, NY 13210-2779. Offers applied ecology (MPS); chemical ecology (MPS, MS, PhD); conservation biology (MPS, MS, PhD); ecology (MPS, MS, PhD); entomology (MPS, MS, PhD); environmental interpretation (MPS, MS, PhD); environmental physiology (MPS, MS, PhD); fish and wildlife biology (MPS, MS, PhD); forest pathology and mycology (MPS, MS, PhD); plant biotechnology (MPS); plant science and biotechnology (MPS, MS, PhD). *Degree requirements:* For master's, thesis (for some programs); for doctorate, comprehensive exam, thesis/dissertation. *Entrance requirements:* For master's and doctorate, GRE General Test, GRE Subject Test, minimum GPA of 3.0. Additional exam requirements/recommendations for international students: Required—TOEFL (minimum score 550 paper-based; 213 computer-based; 80 iBT), IELTS (minimum score 6). *Faculty research:* Ecology, fish and wildlife biology and management, plant science, entomology.

State University of New York College of Environmental Science and Forestry, Department of Forest and Natural Resources Management, Syracuse, NY 13210-2779. Offers environmental and natural resource policy (MS, PhD); environmental and natural resources policy (MPS); forest management and operations (MF); forestry ecosystems science and applications (MPS, MS, PhD); natural resources management (MPS, MS, PhD); quantitative methods and management in forest science (MPS, MS, PhD); recreation and resource management (MPS, MS, PhD); watershed management and forest hydrology (MPS, MS, PhD). *Degree requirements:* For master's, thesis (for some programs); for doctorate, comprehensive exam, thesis/dissertation. *Entrance requirements:* For master's and doctorate, GRE General Test, minimum GPA of 3.0. Additional exam requirements/recommendations for international students: Required—TOEFL (minimum score 550 paper-based; 213 computer-based; 80 iBT), IELTS (minimum score 6). *Faculty research:* Silviculture recreation management, tree improvement, operations management, economics.

Stephen F. Austin State University, Graduate School, College of Forestry and Agriculture, Department of Forestry, Nacogdoches, TX 75962. Offers MF, MS, PhD. Part-time programs available. *Degree requirements:* For master's, thesis; for doctorate, thesis/dissertation. *Entrance requirements:* For master's and doctorate, GRE General Test. Additional exam requirements/recommendations for international students: Required—TOEFL. *Faculty research:* Wildlife management, basic plant science, forest recreation, multipurpose land management.

Texas A&M University, College of Agriculture and Life Sciences, Department of Ecosystem Science and Management, College Station, TX 77843. Offers forestry (MS, PhD); natural resources development (M Agr). Part-time programs available. *Faculty:* 26. *Students:* 54 full-time (27 women), 15 part-time (8 women); includes 17 minority (3 African Americans, 14 Hispanic Americans), 10 international. Average age 27. In 2009, 9 master's, 2 doctorates awarded. Terminal master's awarded for partial completion of doctoral program. *Degree requirements:* For master's, thesis (for some programs); for doctorate, thesis/dissertation. *Entrance requirements:* For master's and doctorate, GRE General Test. Additional exam requirements/recommendations for international students: Required—TOEFL. *Application deadline:* For fall admission, 3/1 priority date for domestic students; for spring admission, 11/1 priority date for domestic students. Applications are processed on a rolling basis. Application fee: $50 ($75 for international students). Electronic applications accepted. *Expenses:* Tuition, state resident: full-time $3991.32; part-time $221.74 per credit hour. Tuition, nonresident: full-time $9049; part-time $502.74 per credit hour. *Financial support:* In 2009–10, fellowships with partial tuition reimbursements (averaging $15,000 per year), research assistantships with partial tuition reimbursements (averaging $15,000 per year), teaching assistantships with partial tuition reimbursements (averaging $15,000 per year) were awarded; career-related internships or fieldwork and institutionally sponsored loans also available. Support available to part-time students. Financial award application deadline: 3/1; financial award applicants required to submit FAFSA. *Faculty research:* Expert systems, geographic information systems, economics, biology, genetics. *Unit head:* Dr. Steve Whisenant, Professor and Head, 979-845-5033, Fax: 979-845-6049, E-mail: s-whisenant@tamu.edu. *Application contact:* Dr. Carol Loopstra, Associate Head for Research and Graduate Studies, 979-862-2200, Fax: 979-845-6049, E-mail: c-loopstra@tamu.edu.

Tropical Agriculture Research and Higher Education Center, Graduate School, Turrialba, Costa Rica. Offers agribusiness management (MS); agroforestry systems (PhD); ecological agriculture (MS); environmental socioeconomics (MS); forestry in tropical and subtropical zones (PhD); integrated watershed management (MS); management and conservation of tropical rainforests and biodiversity (MS); tropical agriculture (PhD); tropical agroforestry (MS). *Entrance requirements:* For master's, GRE, 2 years of related professional experience, letters of recommendation; for doctorate, GRE, 4 letters of recommendation, letter of support from employing organization, master's degree in agronomy, biological sciences, forestry, natural resources or related field. Additional exam requirements/recommendations for international students: Required—TOEFL (minimum score 550 paper-based; 213 computer-based). Electronic applications accepted. *Faculty research:* Biodiversity in fragmented landscapes, ecosystem management, integrated pest management, environmental livestock production, biotechnology carbon balances in diverse land uses.

Université du Québec en Abitibi-Témiscamingue, Graduate Programs, Program in Environmental Sciences, Rouyn-Noranda, QC J9X 5E4, Canada. Offers biology (MS); environmental sciences (PhD); sustainable forest ecosystem management (MS).

Université Laval, Faculty of Forestry and Geomatics, Department of Wood and Forest Sciences, Programs in Forestry Sciences, Québec, QC G1K 7P4, Canada. Offers M Sc, PhD. Terminal master's awarded for partial completion of doctoral program. *Degree requirements:* For master's, thesis (for some programs); for doctorate, comprehensive exam, thesis/dissertation. *Entrance requirements:* For master's and doctorate, knowledge of French. Additional exam requirements/recommendations for international students: Required—TOEIC or TOEFL. Electronic applications accepted.

Université Laval, Faculty of Forestry and Geomatics, Department of Wood and Forest Sciences, Programs in Wood Sciences, Québec, QC G1K 7P4, Canada. Offers M Sc, PhD. Terminal master's awarded for partial completion of doctoral program. *Degree requirements:* For master's, thesis; for doctorate, comprehensive exam, thesis/dissertation. *Entrance requirements:* For master's and doctorate, knowledge of French. Electronic applications accepted.

Université Laval, Faculty of Forestry and Geomatics, Program in Agroforestry, Québec, QC G1K 7P4, Canada. Offers M Sc. *Degree requirements:* For master's, thesis (for some programs). *Entrance requirements:* For master's, English exam (comprehension of English), knowledge of French, knowledge of a third language. Electronic applications accepted.

University of Alberta, Faculty of Graduate Studies and Research, Department of Rural Economy, Edmonton, AB T6G 2E1, Canada. Offers agricultural economics (M Ag, M Sc, PhD); forest economics (M Ag, M Sc, PhD); rural sociology (M Ag, M Sc); MBA/M Ag. Part-time programs available. *Faculty:* 13 full-time (1 woman), 6 part-time/adjunct (0 women). *Students:* 31 full-time (13 women), 21 part-time (11 women). Average age 25. 35 applicants, 83% accepted. In 2009, 10 master's, 2 doctorates awarded. *Degree requirements:* For doctorate, thesis/dissertation. *Entrance requirements:* Additional exam requirements/recommendations for international students: Required—TOEFL. Application fee: $60. Tuition and fees charges are reported in Canadian dollars. *Expenses:* Tuition, area resident: Full-time $4626.24 Canadian dollars; part-time $99.72 Canadian dollars per unit. International tuition: $8216 Canadian dollars full-time. Required fees: $3589.92 Canadian dollars; $99.72 Canadian dollars per unit. $215 Canadian dollars per term. *Financial support:* In 2009–10, 4 fellowships, 12 research assistantships, 2 teaching assistantships were awarded; scholarships/grants also available. *Faculty research:* Agroforestry, development, extension education, marketing and trade, natural resources and environment, policy, production economics. Total annual research expenditures: $850,000. *Unit head:* Dr. V. Adamowicz, Graduate Coordinator, 403-492-4225, Fax: 403-492-0268. *Application contact:* Liz Bruce, Graduate Secretary, 780-492-4225, Fax: 780-492-0268, E-mail: rural.economy@ualberta.ca.

The University of Arizona, Graduate College, College of Agriculture and Life Sciences, School of Natural Resources, Watershed Resources Program, Tucson, AZ 85721. Offers MS, PhD. *Students:* 1 full-time (0 women), 6 part-time (4 women); includes 1 minority (Hispanic American), 1 international. Average age 39. *Degree requirements:* For master's, thesis; for doctorate, comprehensive exam, thesis/dissertation. *Entrance requirements:* For master's, GRE General Test, minimum GPA of 3.0, 3 letters of recommendation; for doctorate, GRE General Test, minimum GPA of 3.0, 3 letters of recommendation, MA or MS degree. Additional exam requirements/recommendations for international students: Required—TOEFL (minimum score 550 paper-based; 213 computer-based). *Application deadline:* For fall admission, 8/1 priority date for domestic students, 12/1 for international students; for spring admission, 7/1 for international students. Applications are processed on a rolling basis. Application fee: $75. *Expenses:* Tuition, state resident: full-time $9028. Tuition, nonresident: full-time $24,890. *Financial support:* Research assistantships with partial tuition reimbursements, teaching assistantships with partial tuition reimbursements, career-related internships or fieldwork, scholarships/grants, health care benefits, tuition waivers (partial), and unspecified assistantships available. *Faculty research:* Forest fuel characteristics, prescribed fire, tree ring-fire scar analysis, erosion, sedimentation. *Unit head:* Dr. Joseph G. Hiller, Chair, 520-621-7255, Fax: 520-621-8801, E-mail: jghiller@cals.arizona.edu. *Application contact:* Cheryl L. Craddock, Academic Coordinator, 520-621-7260, Fax: 520-621-8801, E-mail: ccraddoc@email.arizona.edu.

University of Arkansas at Monticello, School of Forest Resources, Monticello, AR 71656. Offers MS. Part-time programs available. *Degree requirements:* For master's, comprehensive exam, thesis. *Entrance requirements:* For master's, GRE General Test, minimum GPA of 2.7. Additional exam requirements/recommendations for international students: Required—TOEFL (minimum score 550 paper-based; 213 computer-based). Electronic applications accepted. *Faculty research:* Geographic information systems/remote sensing, forest ecology, wildlife ecology and management.

The University of British Columbia, Faculty of Forestry, Vancouver, BC V6T 1Z1, Canada. Offers M Sc, MA Sc, MF, PhD. Part-time programs available. *Degree requirements:* For master's, thesis (for some programs); for doctorate, comprehensive exam, thesis/dissertation, thesis exam. *Entrance requirements:* Additional exam requirements/recommendations for international students: Required—TOEFL (minimum score 550 paper-based; 213 computer-based; 80 iBT). Electronic applications accepted. *Faculty research:* Forest sciences, forest resources management, forest operations, wood sciences, conservation, forests and society.

University of California, Berkeley, Graduate Division, College of Natural Resources, Department of Environmental Science, Policy, and Management, Berkeley, CA 94720-1500. Offers environmental science, policy, and management (MS, PhD); forestry (MF). *Students:* 270 full-time (185 women). Average age 31. 281 applicants, 27 enrolled. In 2009, 8 master's, 24 doctorates awarded. Terminal master's awarded for partial completion of doctoral program. *Degree requirements:* For master's, thesis optional; for doctorate, thesis/dissertation, qualifying exam. *Entrance requirements:* For master's and doctorate, GRE General Test, minimum GPA of 3.0, 3 letters of recommendation. Additional exam requirements/recommendations for international students: Required—TOEFL. *Application deadline:* For fall admission, 12/1 for domestic students. Application fee: $70 ($90 for international students). Electronic applications accepted. *Financial support:* Fellowships with full tuition reimbursements, research assistantships with full tuition reimbursements, teaching assistantships with full tuition reimbursements, unspecified assistantships available. Financial award application deadline: 12/1; financial award applicants required to submit FAFSA. *Faculty research:* Biology and ecology of insects; ecosystem function and environmental issues of soils; plant health/interactions from molecular to ecosystem levels; range management and ecology; forest and resource policy, sustainability, and management. *Unit head:* Prof. Allen Goldstein, Chair, 510-643-7430, Fax: 510-643-5438, E-mail: espmgrad@berkeley.edu. *Application contact:* Richard M. Battrick, Student Affairs Officer, 510-642-6410, Fax: 510-642-4034, E-mail: espmgrad@nature.berkeley.edu.

University of Florida, Graduate School, College of Agricultural and Life Sciences, School of Forest Resources and Conservation, Gainesville, FL 32611. Offers MFRC, MS, PhD, JD/MFRC, JD/MS, JD/PhD. Part-time programs available. *Degree requirements:* For master's, comprehensive exam, project (MFRC), thesis defense (MS); for doctorate, thesis/dissertation, qualifying exams, defense. *Entrance requirements:* For master's and doctorate, GRE General Test, minimum GPA of 3.0. Additional exam requirements/recommendations for international students: Required—TOEFL. Electronic applications accepted. *Faculty research:* Forest biology and ecology; agroforestry and tropical forestry; forest management, economics, and policy; natural resource education and ecotourism.

University of Georgia, Graduate School, School of Forestry and Natural Resources, Athens, GA 30602. Offers MFR, MS, PhD. *Faculty:* 43 full-time (7 women), 8 part-time/adjunct (1 woman). *Students:* 147 full-time (47 women), 24 part-time (10 women); includes 3 minority (1 American Indian/Alaska Native, 1 Asian American or Pacific Islander, 1 Hispanic American), 23 international. 75 applicants, 60% accepted, 44 enrolled. In 2009, 27 master's, 12 doctorates awarded. *Degree requirements:* For master's, thesis (MS); for doctorate, one foreign language, thesis/dissertation. *Entrance requirements:* For master's and doctorate, GRE General Test. *Application deadline:* For fall admission, 7/1 priority date for domestic students; for spring admission, 11/15 for domestic students. Application fee: $50. Electronic applications accepted. *Expenses:* Tuition, state resident: full-time $6000; part-time $250 per credit hour. Tuition, nonresident: full-time $20,904; part-time $871 per credit hour. Required fees: $730 per semester. *Financial support:* Fellowships, research assistantships, teaching assistantships, unspecified assistantships available. *Unit head:* Dr. Michael C. Clutter, Dean, 706-542-4741, Fax: 706-542-2281, E-mail: mclutter@warnell.uga.edu. *Application contact:* Dr. Lawrence A. Morris, Graduate Coordinator, 706-542-2532, Fax: 706-542-2281, E-mail: lmorris@uga.edu.

University of Idaho, College of Graduate Studies, College of Natural Resources, Department of Forest Products, Moscow, ID 83844-2282. Offers MS. *Faculty:* 2 full-time. *Students:* 8 full-time, 1 part-time. In 2009, 3 master's awarded. *Entrance requirements:* For master's, minimum GPA of 2.8. *Application deadline:* For fall admission, 8/1 for domestic students; for spring admission, 12/15 for domestic students. Application fee: $55 ($60 for international students). *Expenses:* Tuition, state resident: full-time $6120. Tuition, nonresident: full-time $17,712. *Financial support:* Research assistantships, teaching assistantships available. Financial award application deadline: 2/15. *Faculty research:* Fuels reduction methods to lessen wildfire impacts, natural resource and environmental economics and policy, wood chemistry and composites, forest operations, forest products business management. *Unit head:* Dr. Thomas M. Gorman, Head, 208-885-7402. *Application contact:* Dr. Thomas M. Gorman, Head, 208-885-7402.

University of Idaho, College of Graduate Studies, College of Natural Resources, Department of Forest Resources, Moscow, ID 83844-2282. Offers MS. *Faculty:* 14 full-time, 1 part-time/adjunct. *Students:* 25 full-time (11 women), 24 part-time (11 women). In 2009, 9 master's awarded. *Entrance requirements:* For master's, minimum GPA of 2.8. *Application deadline:* For fall admission, 8/1 for domestic students; for spring admission, 12/15 for domestic students. Application fee: $55 ($60 for international students). *Expenses:* Tuition, state resident: full-time $6120. Tuition, nonresident: full-time $17,712. *Financial support:* Research assistantships, teaching assistantships available. Financial award application deadline: 2/15. *Faculty research:* Forest regeneration; forest, fire and landscape ecology; plant systematics; forest entomology; silviculture. *Unit head:* Dr. JoEllen Force, Head, 208-885-7311. *Application contact:* Dr. JoEllen Force, Head, 208-885-7311.

University of Kentucky, Graduate School, College of Agriculture, Program in Forestry, Lexington, KY 40506-0032. Offers MSFOR. *Degree requirements:* For master's, comprehensive exam, thesis optional. *Entrance requirements:* For master's, GRE General Test, minimum undergraduate GPA of 2.75. Additional exam requirements/recommendations for international students: Required—TOEFL (minimum score 550 paper-based; 213 computer-based). Electronic applications accepted. *Faculty research:* Forest ecology, silviculture, watershed management, forest products utilization, wildlife habitat management.

University of Maine, Graduate School, College of Natural Sciences, Forestry, and Agriculture, Department of Forest Management and Forest Ecosystem Science, Orono, ME 04469. Offers forest resources (PhD); forestry (MF, MS). *Accreditation:* SAF (one or more programs are accredited). Part-time programs available. *Faculty:* 18 full-time (1 woman), 3 part-time/adjunct (2 women). *Students:* 34 full-time (12 women), 12 part-time (5 women), 9 international. Average age 28. 44 applicants, 52% accepted, 11 enrolled. In 2009, 9 master's, 4 doctorates awarded. *Degree requirements:* For master's, thesis; for doctorate, one foreign language, thesis/dissertation. *Entrance requirements:* For master's and doctorate, GRE General Test. Additional exam requirements/recommendations for international students: Required—TOEFL. *Application deadline:* For fall admission, 2/1 priority date for domestic students. Applications are processed on a rolling basis. Application fee: $65. Electronic applications accepted. *Financial support:* In 2009–10, 28 research assistantships with tuition reimbursements (averaging $17,487 per year), 7 teaching assistantships with tuition reimbursements (averaging $12,790 per year) were awarded; career-related internships or fieldwork, Federal Work-Study, and institutionally sponsored loans also available. Financial award application deadline: 3/1. *Faculty research:* Forest economics, engineering and operations analysis, biometrics and remote sensing, timber management, wood technology. *Unit head:* Dr. Robert Wagner, Chair, 207-581-4737. *Application contact:* Scott G. Delcourt, Associate Dean of the Graduate School, 207-581-3291, Fax: 207-581-3232, E-mail: graduate@maine.edu.

University of Maine, Graduate School, College of Natural Sciences, Forestry, and Agriculture, Department of Plant, Soil, and Environmental Sciences, Orono, ME 04469. Offers biological sciences (PhD); ecology and environmental sciences (MS, PhD); forest resources (PhD); horticulture (MS); plant science (PhD); plant, soil, and environmental sciences (MS); resource utilization (MS). *Faculty:* 8 full-time (2 women), 9 part-time/adjunct (3 women). *Students:* 6 full-time (3 women), 3 part-time (2 women), 1 international. Average age 31. 6 applicants, 17% accepted, 0 enrolled. In 2009, 2 master's awarded. *Entrance requirements:* For master's and doctorate, GRE General Test. Additional exam requirements/recommendations for international students: Required—TOEFL. *Application deadline:* Applications are processed on a rolling basis. Application fee: $65. Electronic applications accepted. *Financial support:* In 2009–10, 16 research assistantships with tuition reimbursements (averaging $16,260 per year), 3 teaching assistantships with tuition reimbursements (averaging $12,790 per year) were awarded; scholarships/grants, tuition waivers (full and partial), and unspecified assistantships also available. *Unit head:* Dr. Gregory Porter, Chair, 207-581-2943, Fax: 207-581-3207. *Application contact:* Scott G. Delcourt, Associate Dean of the Graduate School, 207-581-3291, Fax: 207-581-3232, E-mail: graduate@maine.edu.

University of Massachusetts Amherst, Graduate School, College of Natural Sciences, Department of Natural Resources Conservation, Program in Forest Resources, Amherst, MA 01003. Offers MS, PhD. Part-time programs available. *Students:* 16 full-time (9 women), 7 part-time (3 women); includes 2 minority (1 African American, 1 Hispanic American), 3 international. Average age 31. 24 applicants, 63% accepted, 11 enrolled. In 2009, 2 master's, 2 doctorates awarded. Terminal master's awarded for partial completion of doctoral program. *Degree requirements:* For master's, thesis or alternative; for doctorate, comprehensive exam, thesis/dissertation. *Entrance requirements:* For master's and doctorate, GRE General Test. Additional exam requirements/recommendations for international students: Required—TOEFL (minimum score 550 paper-based; 213 computer-based; 80 iBT), IELTS (minimum score 6.5). *Application deadline:* For fall admission, 2/1 for domestic and international students; for spring admission, 10/1 for domestic and international students. Applications are processed on a rolling basis. Application fee: $50 ($65 for international students). Electronic applications accepted. *Expenses:* Tuition, state resident: full-time $2640; part-time $110 per credit. Tuition, nonresident: full-time $9936; part-time $414 per credit. Tuition and fees vary according to course load. *Financial support:* Fellowships, research assistantships, teaching assistantships, career-related internships or fieldwork, Federal Work-Study, scholarships/grants, traineeships, health care benefits, tuition waivers (full), and unspecified assistantships available. Support available to part-time students. Financial award application deadline: 2/1. *Unit head:* Dr. Brian C. P. Kane, Graduate Program Director, 413-545-2666, Fax: 413-545-4358. *Application contact:* Jean M. Ames, Supervisor of Admissions, 413-545-0722, Fax: 413-577-0010, E-mail: gradadm@grad.umass.edu.

University of Missouri, Graduate School, School of Natural Resources, Department of Forestry, Columbia, MO 65211. Offers MS, PhD. Terminal master's awarded for partial completion of doctoral program. *Degree requirements:* For master's, thesis; for doctorate, thesis/dissertation. *Entrance requirements:* For master's and doctorate, GRE General Test, minimum GPA of 3.0. Additional exam requirements/recommendations for international students: Required—TOEFL (minimum score 500 paper-based; 173 computer-based; 61 iBT).

The University of Montana, Graduate School, College of Forestry and Conservation, Missoula, MT 59812-0002. Offers ecosystem management (MEM, MS); fish and wildlife biology (PhD); forestry (MS, PhD); recreation management (MS); resource conservation (MS); wildlife biology (MS). *Degree requirements:* For doctorate, thesis/dissertation. *Entrance requirements:* For master's and doctorate, GRE General Test. Additional exam requirements/recommendations for international students: Required—TOEFL (minimum score 575 paper-based; 213 computer-based).

University of New Brunswick Fredericton, School of Graduate Studies, Faculty of Forestry and Environmental Management, Fredericton, NB E3B 5A3, Canada. Offers ecological foundations of forest management (PhD); environmental management (MEM); forest engineering (M Sc FE, MFE); forest products marketing (MBA); forest resources (M Sc F, MF, PhD). Part-time programs available. *Faculty:* 32 full-time (2 women). *Students:* 87 full-time (47 women), 11 part-time (4 women). In 2009, 10 master's, 5 doctorates awarded. *Degree requirements:* For master's, thesis; for doctorate, thesis/dissertation. *Entrance requirements:* For master's and doctorate, minimum GPA of 3.0. Additional exam requirements/recommendations for international students: Required—TOEFL (minimum score 580 paper-based), TWE (minimum score 4), or IELTS. *Application deadline:* For fall admission, 3/1 priority date for domestic students. Application fee: $50 Canadian dollars. Electronic applications accepted. Tuition and fees charges are reported in Canadian dollars. *Expenses:* Tuition, area resident: Full-time $5562 Canadian dollars; part-time $2781 Canadian dollars per year. Required fees: $49.75 Canadian dollars per term. *Financial support:* Research assistantships, teaching assistantships available. *Faculty research:* Forest management, forest ecology, wildlife ecology, wood tech, human dimensions in forestry. *Unit head:* Dr. John Kershaw, Director of Graduate Studies, 506-453-4933, Fax: 506-453-3538, E-mail: kershaw@unb.ca. *Application contact:* Faith Sharpe, Graduate Secretary, 506-458-7520, Fax: 506-453-3538, E-mail: fsharpe@unb.ca.

University of New Hampshire, Graduate School, College of Life Sciences and Agriculture, Department of Natural Resources, Durham, NH 03824. Offers environmental conservation (MS); forestry (MS); soil science (MS); water resources management (MS); wildlife (MS). Part-time programs available. *Faculty:* 40 full-time. *Students:* 22 full-time (12 women), 29 part-time (19 women); includes 1 minority (Asian American or Pacific Islander), 1 international. Average age 31. 41 applicants, 34% accepted, 10 enrolled. In 2009, 19 master's awarded. *Degree requirements:* For master's, thesis or alternative. *Entrance requirements:* For master's, GRE General Test. Additional exam requirements/recommendations for international students: Required—TOEFL (minimum score 550 paper-based; 213 computer-based; 80 iBT). *Application deadline:* For fall admission, 6/1 for domestic students, 4/1 for international students; for spring admission, 12/1 for domestic students. Applications are processed on a rolling basis. Application fee: $65. Electronic applications accepted. *Expenses:* Tuition, state resident: full-time $10,380; part-time $577 per credit hour. Tuition, nonresident: full-time $24,350; part-time $1002 per credit hour. Required fees: $1550; $387.50 per semester. Tuition and fees vary according to course load and program. *Financial support:* In 2009–10, 24 students received support, including 2 fellowships, 11 research assistantships, 11 teaching assistantships; career-related

Forestry

University of New Hampshire (continued)
internships or fieldwork, Federal Work-Study, scholarships/grants, and tuition waivers (full and partial) also available. Support available to part-time students. Financial award application deadline: 2/15. *Unit head:* Dr. John Halstead, Chairperson, 603-862-3950, E-mail: natural.resources@unh.edu. *Application contact:* Linda Scogin, Administrative Assistant, 603-862-3932, E-mail: natural.resources@unh.edu.

The University of Tennessee, Graduate School, College of Agricultural Sciences and Natural Resources, Department of Forestry, Wildlife, and Fisheries, Program in Forestry, Knoxville, TN 37996. Offers MS. *Degree requirements:* For master's, thesis or alternative. *Entrance requirements:* For master's, GRE General Test, minimum GPA of 2.7. Additional exam requirements/recommendations for international students: Required—TOEFL. Electronic applications accepted. *Expenses:* Tuition, state resident: full-time $6826; part-time $380 per semester hour. Tuition, nonresident: full-time $21,844; part-time $1147 per semester hour. Tuition and fees vary according to program.

University of Toronto, School of Graduate Studies, Life Sciences Division, Faculty of Forestry, Toronto, ON M5S 1A1, Canada. Offers M Sc F, MFC, PhD. *Degree requirements:* For master's, comprehensive exam, thesis, oral thesis/research paper defense; for doctorate, thesis/dissertation, oral defense of thesis. *Entrance requirements:* For master's, bachelor's degree in a related area, minimum B average in final year (M Sc F), final 2 years (MFC); resume, 3 letters of reference; for doctorate, writing sample, minimum A– average, master's in a related area, 3 letters of reference, resumé.

University of Vermont, Graduate College, The Rubenstein School of Environment and Natural Resources, Program in Natural Resources, Burlington, VT 05405. Offers natural resources (MS, PhD), including aquatic ecology and watershed science (MS), environment thought and culture (MS), environment, science and public affairs (MS), forestry (MS). *Students:* 108 (55 women); includes 14 minority (2 African Americans, 1 American Indian/Alaska Native, 7 Asian Americans or Pacific Islanders, 4 Hispanic Americans), 7 international. 167 applicants, 28% accepted, 12 enrolled. In 2009, 18 master's, 2 doctorates awarded. *Degree requirements:* For master's, thesis or alternative; for doctorate, thesis/dissertation. *Entrance requirements:* For master's and doctorate, GRE General Test. Additional exam requirements/recommendations for international students: Required—TOEFL (minimum score 550 paper-based; 213 computer-based; 80 iBT). *Application deadline:* For fall admission, 3/1 priority date for domestic students. Applications are processed on a rolling basis. Application fee: $40. Electronic applications accepted. *Expenses:* Tuition, area resident: Part-time $508 per credit hour. Tuition, state resident: part-time $508 per credit hour. Tuition, nonresident: part-time $1281 per credit hour. *Financial support:* Fellowships, research assistantships, teaching assistantships available. Financial award application deadline: 3/1. *Unit head:* Dr. Mary Watzin, Coordinator, 802-656-2620. *Application contact:* Dr. Mary Watzin, Coordinator, 802-656-2620.

University of Washington, Graduate School, College of Forest Resources, Seattle, WA 98195. Offers bioresource science and engineering (MS, PhD); environmental horticulture (MEH); environmental horticulture and urban forestry (MS, PhD); forest ecology (MS, PhD); forest management (MFR); forest soils (MS, PhD); forest systems and bioenergy (MS, PhD); restoration ecology (MS, PhD); social sciences (MS, PhD); sustainable resource management (MS, PhD); wildlife science (MS, PhD); MFR/MAIS; MPA/MS. *Accreditation:* SAF. *Degree requirements:* For master's, thesis (for some programs); for doctorate, comprehensive exam (for some programs), thesis/dissertation. *Entrance requirements:* For master's and doctorate, GRE, minimum GPA of 3.0. Additional exam requirements/recommendations for international students: Required—TOEFL. Electronic applications accepted. *Faculty research:* Ecosystem analysis, silviculture and forest protection, paper science and engineering, environmental horticulture and urban forestry, natural resource policy and economics.

University of Wisconsin–Madison, Graduate School, College of Agricultural and Life Sciences, Department of Forest and Wildlife Ecology, Madison, WI 53706-1380. Offers MS, PhD. Part-time programs available. *Degree requirements:* For master's, thesis (for some programs); for doctorate, thesis/dissertation. *Entrance requirements:* For master's and doctorate, GRE. Additional exam requirements/recommendations for international students: Required—TOEFL. Electronic applications accepted. *Expenses:* Tuition, state resident: part-time $594 per credit. Tuition, nonresident: part-time $1504 per credit. Required fees: $65 per credit. Tuition and fees vary according to course load, program and reciprocity agreements. *Faculty research:* Forest and landscape ecology, forest biology, social forestry, recreation resources, wood science.

Utah State University, School of Graduate Studies, College of Natural Resources, Department of Wildland Resources, Logan, UT 84322. Offers ecology (MS, PhD); forestry (MS, PhD); range science (MS, PhD); wildlife biology (MS, PhD). Part-time programs available. *Degree requirements:* For master's, thesis; for doctorate, comprehensive exam, thesis/dissertation. *Entrance requirements:* For master's and doctorate, GRE General Test, minimum GPA of 3.0. Additional exam requirements/recommendations for international students: Required—TOEFL. *Faculty research:* Range plant ecophysiology, plant community ecology, ruminant nutrition, population ecology.

Virginia Polytechnic Institute and State University, Graduate School, College of Natural Resources, Department of Forestry, Blacksburg, VA 24061. Offers forest biology (MF, MS, PhD); forest biometry (MF, MS, PhD); forest management/economics (MF, MS, PhD); industrial forestry operations (MF, MS, PhD); outdoor recreation (MF, MS, PhD). *Entrance requirements:* For master's and doctorate, GRE General Test. Additional exam requirements/recommendations for international students: Required—TOEFL (minimum score 550 paper-based; 213 computer-based). Electronic applications accepted.

Virginia Polytechnic Institute and State University, Graduate School, College of Natural Resources, Department of Wood Science and Forest Products, Blacksburg, VA 24061. Offers forest products marketing (MF, MS, PhD); wood science and engineering (MF, MS, PhD). *Entrance requirements:* For master's and doctorate, GRE General Test. Additional exam requirements/recommendations for international students: Required—TOEFL (minimum score 550 paper-based; 213 computer-based). Electronic applications accepted. *Faculty research:* Wood chemistry, wood engineering, wood composites, wood processing, forest products marketing/management, recycling.

West Virginia University, Davis College of Agriculture, Forestry and Consumer Sciences, Division of Forestry, Program in Forest Resource Science, Morgantown, WV 26506. Offers PhD. *Degree requirements:* For doctorate, comprehensive exam, thesis/dissertation. *Entrance requirements:* For doctorate, GRE, minimum GPA of 3.0. Additional exam requirements/recommendations for international students: Required—TOEFL. *Faculty research:* Impact of management on wildlife and fish, forest sampling designs, forest economics and policy, oak regeneration.

West Virginia University, Davis College of Agriculture, Forestry and Consumer Sciences, Division of Forestry, Program in Forestry, Morgantown, WV 26506. Offers MSF. *Degree requirements:* For master's, thesis. *Entrance requirements:* For master's, GRE, minimum GPA of 3.0. Additional exam requirements/recommendations for international students: Required—TOEFL. *Faculty research:* Health and productivity on Appalachian forests, wood industries in Appalachian forests, role of forestry in regional economics.

Yale University, Graduate School of Arts and Sciences, Department of Forestry and Environmental Studies, New Haven, CT 06520. Offers environmental sciences (PhD); forestry (PhD). *Degree requirements:* For doctorate, thesis/dissertation. *Entrance requirements:* For doctorate, GRE General Test.

Yale University, School of Forestry and Environmental Studies, New Haven, CT 06511. Offers MEM, MES, MF, MFS, PhD, JD/MEM, MBA/MEM, MBA/MF, MEM/M Arch, MEM/MA, MEM/MPH, MF/MA. *Accreditation:* SAF (one or more programs are accredited). Part-time programs available. Terminal master's awarded for partial completion of doctoral program. *Degree requirements:* For master's, thesis (for some programs); for doctorate, thesis/dissertation. *Entrance requirements:* For master's, GRE General Test, GMAT or LSAT; for doctorate, GRE General Test. Additional exam requirements/recommendations for international students: Required—TOEFL (minimum score 600 paper-based; 250 computer-based; 100 iBT). Electronic applications accepted. *Expenses:* Contact institution. *Faculty research:* Environmental policy, social ecology, industrial environmental management, forestry, environmental health, urban ecology, water science policy.

Natural Resources

American University, School of International Service, Washington, DC 20016-8071. Offers comparative and regional studies (Certificate); cross-cultural communication (Certificate); development management (MS); ethics, peace, and global affairs (MA); European studies (Certificate); global environmental policy (MA, Certificate); international affairs (MA), including comparative and regional studies, environmental policy, international economic policy, international politics, natural resources and sustainable development, U.S. foreign policy; international communication (MA, Certificate); international development (MA, Certificate); international development management (Certificate); international economic policy (Certificate); international economic relations (Certificate); international media (MA); international peace and conflict resolution (MA, Certificate); international relations (PhD); international service (MIS); peace building (Certificate); the Americas (Certificate); United States foreign policy (Certificate); JD/MA. Part-time and evening/weekend programs available. *Faculty:* 98 full-time (42 women), 48 part-time/adjunct (13 women). *Students:* 565 full-time (349 women), 329 part-time (189 women); includes 128 minority (44 African Americans, 2 American Indian/Alaska Native, 37 Asian Americans or Pacific Islanders, 45 Hispanic Americans), 102 international. Average age 27. 2,034 applicants, 63% accepted, 344 enrolled. In 2009, 326 master's, 6 doctorates, 9 other advanced degrees awarded. Terminal master's awarded for partial completion of doctoral program. *Degree requirements:* For master's, one foreign language, comprehensive exam, thesis or alternative; for doctorate, one foreign language, comprehensive exam, thesis/dissertation, research practicum; for Certificate, minimum 15 credit hours related course work. *Entrance requirements:* For master's, GRE, 24 credits of course work in related social sciences, minimum GPA of 3.5, 2 letters of recommendation, bachelor's degree, resume; for doctorate, GRE, 2 letters of recommendation, 24 credits in related social sciences; for Certificate, bachelor's degree. Additional exam requirements/recommendations for international students: Required—TOEFL (minimum score 600 paper-based; 250 computer-based; 100 iBT). *Application deadline:* For fall admission, 1/15 priority date for domestic students; for spring admission, 10/1 priority date for domestic students. Applications are processed on a rolling basis. Application fee: $50. *Expenses:* Tuition: Full-time $22,266; part-time $1237 per credit hour. Required fees: $430. Tuition and fees vary according to program. *Financial support:* Career-related internships or fieldwork, Federal Work-Study, and institutionally sponsored loans available. Financial award application deadline: 1/15. *Faculty research:* International intellectual property, international environmental issues, international law and legal order, international telecommunications/technology, international sustainable development. *Unit head:* Dr. Louis W. Goodman, Dean, 202-885-1600, Fax: 202-885-2494. *Application contact:* Yasmin Quianzon, Director of Graduate Admissions and Financial Aid, 202-885-2496, Fax: 202-885-1109.

Auburn University, Graduate School, School of Forestry and Wildlife Sciences, Auburn University, AL 36849. Offers forest economics (PhD); forestry (MS, PhD); natural resource conservation (MNR); wildlife sciences (MS, PhD). *Accreditation:* SAF. Part-time programs available. *Faculty:* 28 full-time (5 women), 2 part-time/adjunct (0 women). *Students:* 29 full-time (12 women), 53 part-time (17 women); includes 3 minority (1 African American, 1 Asian American or Pacific Islander, 1 Hispanic American), 28 international. Average age 28. 55 applicants, 44% accepted, 17 enrolled. In 2009, 5 master's, 3 doctorates awarded. *Degree requirements:* For master's, thesis (MS); for doctorate, thesis/dissertation. *Entrance requirements:* For master's and doctorate, GRE General Test. *Application deadline:* For fall admission, 7/7 for domestic students; for spring admission, 11/24 for domestic students. Applications are processed on a rolling basis. Application fee: $50 ($60 for international students). Electronic applications accepted. *Expenses:* Tuition, state resident: full-time $6240. Tuition, nonresident: full-time $18,720. International tuition: $18,938 full-time. Required fees: $492. Tuition and fees vary according to course load, program and reciprocity agreements. *Financial support:* Fellowships, research assistantships, teaching assistantships, Federal Work-Study available. Support available to part-time students. Financial award application deadline: 3/15; financial award applicants required to submit FAFSA. *Faculty research:* Forest nursery management, silviculture and vegetation management, biological processes and ecological relationships, growth and yield of plantations and natural stands, urban forestry, forest taxation, law and policy. *Unit head:* Dr. Richard W. Brinker, Dean, 334-844-1007, Fax: 334-844-1084, E-mail: brinker@forestry.auburn.edu. *Application contact:* Dr. George Flowers, Dean of the Graduate School, 334-844-2125.

Ball State University, Graduate School, College of Sciences and Humanities, Department of Natural Resources, Muncie, IN 47306-1099. Offers MA, MS. *Entrance requirements:* For master's, GRE General Test. *Faculty research:* Acid rain, indoor air pollution, land reclamation.

California Polytechnic State University, San Luis Obispo, College of Agriculture, Food and Environmental Sciences, Department of Natural Resources Management, San Luis Obispo, CA 93407. Offers forestry sciences (MS). Part-time programs available. *Faculty:* 8 full-time (2 women). *Students:* 2 full-time (1 woman), 4 part-time (0 women), 1 international. Average age 29. 3 applicants, 67% accepted, 1 enrolled. In 2009, 2 master's awarded. *Degree requirements:* For master's, comprehensive exam, thesis. *Entrance requirements:* For master's, minimum GPA of 2.75 in last 90 quarter units of course work. Additional exam requirements/recommendations for international students: Required—TOEFL (minimum score 550 paper-based; 213 computer-based), or IELTS (minimum score 6). *Application deadline:* For fall admission, 2/1 for domestic students, 11/30 for international students; for winter admission, 11/1 for domestic students, 6/30 for international students; for spring admission, 2/1 for domestic students. Applications are processed on a rolling basis. Application fee: $55. Electronic applications accepted. *Expenses:* Tuition, nonresident: full-time $11,160; part-time $248 per unit. Required fees: $7134; $1553 per quarter. *Financial support:* Fellowships, research assistantships, career-related internships or fieldwork, Federal Work-Study, institutionally sponsored loans, scholarships/grants, and unspecified assistantships available. Support available to part-time students. Financial award application deadline: 3/2; financial award applicants required to submit FAFSA. *Faculty research:* Hydrology, biometrics, forest health and management, fire science, urban and community forestry. *Unit head:* Dr. Doug Piirto, Department Head/Graduate Coordinator, 805-756-2968, Fax: 805-756-1402, E-mail: dpiirto@calpoly.edu. *Application contact:* Dr. Mark Shelton, Associate Dean/Graduate Coordinator, 805-756-2161, Fax: 805-756-6577, E-mail: mshelton@calpoly.edu.

Central Washington University, Graduate Studies and Research, College of the Sciences, Program in Resource Management, Ellensburg, WA 98926. Offers MS. *Faculty:* 44 full-time (12 women). *Students:* 44 full-time (27 women), 13 part-time (6 women); includes 8 minority (5 American Indian/Alaska Native, 2 Asian Americans or Pacific Islanders, 1 Hispanic American). In 2009, 10 master's awarded. *Degree requirements:* For master's, thesis. *Entrance requirements:* For master's, minimum GPA of 3.0. Additional exam requirements/recommendations for international students: Required—TOEFL (minimum score 550 paper-based; 213 computer-based; 79 iBT). *Application deadline:* For fall admission, 2/1 priority date for domestic students; for spring admission, 1/1 for domestic students. Applications are processed on a rolling basis. Application fee: $50. Electronic applications accepted. *Expenses:* Tuition, state resident: full-time $7353; part-time $245 per credit. Tuition, nonresident: full-time $16,383; part-time $546 per credit. Required fees: $882. Tuition and fees vary according to degree level. *Financial support:* In 2009–10, 16 research assistantships with full and partial tuition reimbursements (averaging $9,145 per year), 8 teaching assistantships with full and partial tuition reimbursements (averaging $9,145 per year) were awarded; career-related internships or fieldwork, Federal Work-Study, health care benefits, and unspecified assistantships also available. Financial award application deadline: 8/1; financial award applicants required to submit FAFSA. *Unit head:* Dr. Karl Lillquist, Co-Director, 509-963-1188, Fax: 509-963-3224, E-mail: lillquis@cwu.edu. *Application contact:* Justine Eason, Admissions Program Coordinator, 509-963-3103, Fax: 509-963-1799, E-mail: masters@cwu.edu.

Colorado State University, Graduate School, Warner College of Natural Resources, Department of Forest, Rangeland, and Watershed Stewardship, Fort Collins, CO 80523-1472. Offers forest sciences (MS, PhD); natural resources stewardship (MNRS); rangeland ecosystem science (MS, PhD); watershed science (MS). Part-time programs available. Postbaccalaureate distance learning degree programs offered (no on-campus study). *Faculty:* 21 full-time (5 women), 1 part-time/adjunct (0 women). *Students:* 47 full-time (23 women), 76 part-time (21 women); includes 9 minority (3 American Indian/Alaska Native, 1 Asian American or Pacific Islander, 5 Hispanic Americans), 7 international. Average age 33. 53 applicants, 81% accepted, 33 enrolled. In 2009, 26 master's, 7 doctorates awarded. *Degree requirements:* For master's, thesis (for some programs); for doctorate, comprehensive exam, thesis/dissertation. *Entrance requirements:* For master's, GRE General Test (minimum score 1000 verbal and quantitative), minimum GPA of 3.0, 3 letters of recommendation; for doctorate, GRE General Test (combined minimum score of 1100 on the Verbal and Quantitative sections), minimum GPA of 3.0, 3 letters of recommendation, statement of research interest. Additional exam requirements/recommendations for international students: Required—TOEFL (minimum score 550 paper-based; 213 computer-based; 80 iBT), IELTS (minimum score 6). *Application deadline:* For fall admission, 8/1 priority date for domestic students, 6/25 priority date for international students; for spring admission, 12/1 priority date for domestic students, 11/25 priority date for international students. Applications are processed on a rolling basis. Application fee: $50. Electronic applications accepted. *Expenses:* Tuition, state resident: full-time $6434; part-time $359.10 per credit. Tuition, nonresident: full-time $18,116; part-time $1006.45 per credit. Required fees: $1496; $83 per credit. *Financial support:* In 2009–10, 43 students received support, including 3 fellowships (averaging $40,417 per year), 33 research assistantships with full and partial tuition reimbursements available (averaging $15,898 per year), 7 teaching assistantships with full and partial tuition reimbursements available (averaging $6,506 per year); Federal Work-Study, scholarships/grants, and unspecified assistantships also available. Financial award applicants required to submit FAFSA. *Faculty research:* Ecology, natural resource management, hydrology, restoration, human dimensions. Total annual research expenditures: $3.7 million. *Unit head:* Dr. N. Thompson Hobbs, Head, 970-491-6911, Fax: 970-491-6754, E-mail: nthobbs@warnercnr@colostate.edu. *Application contact:* Sonya LeFebre, Coordinator, 970-491-1907, Fax: 970-491-6754, E-mail: sonya.lefebre@colostate.edu.

Colorado State University, Graduate School, Warner College of Natural Resources, Department of Human Dimensions of Natural Resources, Fort Collins, CO 80523-1480. Offers MS, PhD. Part-time programs available. *Faculty:* 10 full-time (3 women), 1 part-time/adjunct (0 women). *Students:* 21 full-time (11 women), 12 part-time (6 women); includes 5 minority (1 American Indian/Alaska Native, 1 Asian American or Pacific Islander, 3 Hispanic Americans), 2 international. Average age 31. 25 applicants, 32% accepted, 7 enrolled. In 2009, 9 master's, 1 doctorate awarded. Terminal master's awarded for partial completion of doctoral program. *Degree requirements:* For master's, comprehensive exam, thesis or alternative; for doctorate, comprehensive exam, thesis/dissertation. *Entrance requirements:* For master's, minimum GPA of 3.0, 3 letters of recommendation; for doctorate, GRE General Test (combined minimum score of 1000 on the Verbal and Quantitative sections), minimum GPA of 3.0, 3 letters of recommendation, copy of master's thesis or professional paper, interview, statement of interest. Additional exam requirements/recommendations for international students: Required—TOEFL. *Application deadline:* For fall admission, 3/1 priority date for domestic students. Applications are processed on a rolling basis. Application fee: $50. Electronic applications accepted. *Expenses:* Tuition, state resident: full-time $6434; part-time $359.10 per credit. Tuition, nonresident: full-time $18,116; part-time $1006.45 per credit. Required fees: $1496; $83 per credit. *Financial support:* In 2009–10, 19 students received support, including 1 fellowship (averaging $41,667 per year), 11 research assistantships with tuition reimbursements available (averaging $11,087 per year), 7 teaching assistantships with tuition reimbursements available (averaging $5,820 per year); career-related internships or fieldwork, Federal Work-Study, scholarships/grants, traineeships, and unspecified assistantships also available. Support available to part-time students. Financial award application deadline: 3/1; financial award applicants required to submit FAFSA. *Faculty research:* International tourism, wilderness preservation, resource interpretation, human dimensions in natural resources, protected areas management. Total annual research expenditures: $925,755. *Unit head:* Dr. Michael J. Manfredo, Head, 970-491-0474, Fax: 970-491-2255, E-mail: manfredo@cnr.colostate.edu. *Application contact:* Linda Adams, Coordinator of Administration, 970-491-6591, Fax: 970-491-2255, E-mail: linda.adams@colostate.edu.

Cornell University, Graduate School, Graduate Fields of Agriculture and Life Sciences, Field of Natural Resources, Ithaca, NY 14853-0001. Offers aquatic science (MPS, MS, PhD); environmental management (MPS); fishery science (MPS, MS, PhD); forest science (MPS, MS, PhD); resource policy and management (MPS, MS, PhD); wildlife science (MPS, MS, PhD). *Faculty:* 39 full-time (7 women). *Students:* 60 full-time (28 women); includes 4 minority (2 American Indian/Alaska Native, 1 Asian American or Pacific Islander, 1 Hispanic American), 13 international. Average age 31. 63 applicants, 32% accepted, 19 enrolled. In 2009, 6 master's, 7 doctorates awarded. *Degree requirements:* For master's, thesis (MS), project paper (MPS); for doctorate, comprehensive exam, thesis/dissertation. *Entrance requirements:* For master's and doctorate, GRE General Test, 2 letters of recommendation. Additional exam requirements/recommendations for international students: Required—TOEFL (minimum score 550 paper-based; 213 computer-based; 77 iBT). *Application deadline:* For spring admission, 10/30 for domestic students. Applications are processed on a rolling basis. Application fee: $70. Electronic applications accepted. *Expenses:* Tuition: Full-time $29,500. Required fees: $70. Full-time tuition and fees vary according to degree level, program and student level. *Financial support:* In 2009–10, 39 students received support, including 12 research assistantships with full tuition reimbursements available, 5 teaching assistantships with full tuition reimbursements available; fellowships with full tuition reimbursements available, institutionally sponsored loans, scholarships/grants, health care benefits, tuition waivers (full and partial), and unspecified assistantships also available. Financial award applicants required to submit FAFSA. *Faculty research:* Ecosystem-level dynamics, systems modeling, conservation biology/management, resource management's human dimensions, biogeochemistry. *Unit head:* Director of Graduate Studies, 607-255-2807, Fax: 607-255-0349. *Application contact:* Graduate Field Assistant, 607-255-2807, Fax: 607-255-0349, E-mail: nrgrad@cornell.edu.

Dalhousie University, Faculty of Management, Centre for Advanced Management Education, Halifax, NS B3H 3J5, Canada. Offers financial services (MBA); information management (MIM); management (MPA); natural resources (MBA). Part-time programs available. Postbaccalaureate distance learning degree programs offered. *Faculty:* 10 full-time (5 women). *Students:* 19 part-time (4 women). Average age 27. 50 applicants, 42% accepted. *Entrance requirements:* For master's, GMAT, minimum GPA of 3.0, resume. Additional exam requirements/recommendations for international students: Required—TOEFL, IELTS, CANTEST, CAEL, or Michigan English Language Assessment Battery. *Application deadline:* Applications are processed on a rolling basis. Application fee: $70. Electronic applications accepted. *Unit head:* Michelle Hunter, Associate Director (Administration), 902-494-1828, Fax: 902-494-7154, E-mail: mhunter@dal.ca. *Application contact:* Deborah McColl, Admissions and Registration Coordinator, 902-494-6391, E-mail: mbafs@dal.ca.

Delaware State University, Graduate Programs, Department of Agriculture and Natural Resources, Program in Natural Resources, Dover, DE 19901-2277. Offers MS. *Entrance requirements:* For master's, GRE. Additional exam requirements/recommendations for international students: Required—TOEFL (minimum score 550 paper-based).

Duke University, Graduate School, Department of Environment, Durham, NC 27708. Offers natural resource economics/policy (AM, PhD); natural resource science/ecology (AM, PhD); natural resource systems science (AM, PhD); JD/AM. Part-time programs available. *Faculty:* 28 full-time. *Students:* 66 full-time (39 women); includes 3 minority (2 African Americans, 1 Asian American or Pacific Islander), 25 international. 126 applicants, 26% accepted, 19 enrolled. In 2009, 4 master's, 11 doctorates awarded. *Degree requirements:* For doctorate, variable foreign language requirement, thesis/dissertation. *Entrance requirements:* For master's and doctorate, GRE General Test. Additional exam requirements/recommendations for international students: Required—TOEFL (minimum score 550 paper-based; 213 computer-based; 83 iBT), IELTS (minimum score 7). *Application deadline:* For fall admission, 12/8 priority date for domestic and international students. Application fee: $75. Electronic applications accepted. *Financial support:* Fellowships, research assistantships, teaching assistantships, Federal Work-Study available. Financial award application deadline: 12/31. *Unit head:* Kenneth Reckhow, Director of Graduate Studies, Fax: 919-660-1884, E-mail: meg.stephens@duke.edu. *Application contact:* Cynthia Robertson, Associate Dean for Enrollment Services, 919-684-3913, E-mail: grad-admissions@duke.edu.

Duke University, Nicholas School of the Environment, Durham, NC 27708-0328. Offers coastal environmental management (MEM); DEL-environmental leadership (MEM); energy and environment (MEM); environmental economics and policy (MEM); environmental health and security (MEM); forest resource management (MF); global environmental change (MEM); resource ecology (MEM); water and air resources (MEM); JD/AM; JD/MEM; JD/MF; MAT/MEM; MBA/MEM; MBA/MF; MEM/MPP; MF/MPP. *Accreditation:* SAF (one or more programs are accredited). Part-time programs available. *Degree requirements:* For master's, thesis. *Entrance requirements:* For master's, GRE General Test, previous course work in biology or ecology, calculus, statistics, and microeconomics; computer familiarity with word processing and data analysis. Additional exam requirements/recommendations for international students: Required—TOEFL (minimum score 550 paper-based; 213 computer-based). Electronic applications accepted. *Expenses:* Contact institution. *Faculty research:* Ecosystem management, conservation ecology, earth systems, risk assessment.

East Carolina University, Graduate School, Program in Coastal Resources Management, Greenville, NC 27858-4353. Offers PhD. *Degree requirements:* For doctorate, comprehensive exam, thesis/dissertation, internship. *Entrance requirements:* For doctorate, GRE. Additional exam requirements/recommendations for international students: Required—TOEFL. *Faculty research:* Coastal geology, wetlands and coastal ecology, ecological and social networks, submerged cultural resources, coastal resources economics.

Georgia Institute of Technology, Graduate Studies and Research, College of Engineering, School of Chemical and Biomolecular Engineering, Atlanta, GA 30332-0001. Offers bioengineering (MS Bio E, PhD); chemical engineering (MS Ch E, PhD); paper science and engineering (MS, PhD); polymers (MS Poly). *Degree requirements:* For master's, thesis; for doctorate, comprehensive exam, thesis/dissertation. *Entrance requirements:* For master's and doctorate, GRE, minimum GPA of 3.0. Additional exam requirements/recommendations for international students: Required—TOEFL (minimum score 550 paper-based; 213 computer-based). Electronic applications accepted. *Faculty research:* Biochemical engineering; process modeling, synthesis, and control; polymer science and engineering; thermodynamics and separations; surface and particle science.

Humboldt State University, Graduate Studies, College of Natural Resources and Sciences, Programs in Natural Resources, Arcata, CA 95521-8299. Offers natural resources (MS), including fisheries, forestry, natural resources planning and interpretation, rangeland resources and wildland soils, wastewater utilization, watershed management, wildlife. *Students:* 51 full-time (22 women), 26 part-time (10 women); includes 4 minority (1 American Indian/Alaska Native, 1 Asian American or Pacific Islander, 2 Hispanic Americans), 1 international. Average age 31. 81 applicants, 26% accepted, 15 enrolled. In 2009, 25 master's awarded. *Degree requirements:* For master's, thesis or alternative. *Entrance requirements:* For master's, GRE, appropriate bachelor's degree, minimum GPA of 2.5, 3 letters of recommendation, resume. Additional exam requirements/recommendations for international students: Required—TOEFL (minimum score 500 paper-based; 173 computer-based). *Application deadline:* For fall admission, 2/1 for domestic and international students; for spring admission, 9/30 for domestic and international students. Applications are processed on a rolling basis. Application fee: $55. *Expenses:* Tuition, nonresident: full-time $8928. Required fees: $6102. Tuition and fees vary according to program. *Financial support:* Fellowships, career-related internships or fieldwork and Federal Work-Study available. Support available to part-time students. Financial award application deadline: 3/1; financial award applicants required to submit FAFSA. *Faculty research:* Spotted owl habitat, pre-settlement vegetation, hardwood utilization, tree physiology, fisheries. *Unit head:* Dr. Gary Hendrickson, Coordinator, 707-826-4233, E-mail: thiesfel@humboldt.edu. *Application contact:* Julie Tucker, Administrative Support Coordinator, 707-826-3256, E-mail: jlt7002@humboldt.edu.

Iowa State University of Science and Technology, Graduate College, College of Agriculture, Department of Natural Resource Ecology and Management, Ames, IA 50011. Offers forestry (MS, PhD); wildlife ecology (MS). *Faculty:* 18 full-time (4 women), 7 part-time/adjunct (2 women). *Students:* 40 full-time (13 women), 2 part-time (1 woman); includes 3 minority (1 American Indian/Alaska Native, 2 Hispanic Americans), 6 international. 28 applicants, 29% accepted, 8 enrolled. In 2009, 9 master's, 2 doctorates awarded. *Degree requirements:* For master's, thesis (for some programs); for doctorate, thesis/dissertation. *Entrance requirements:* For master's and doctorate, GRE General Test. Additional exam requirements/recommendations for international students: Required—TOEFL (minimum score 550 paper-based; 79 iBT) or IELTS (minimum score 6.5). *Application deadline:* For fall admission, 4/1 priority date for domestic and international students; for spring admission, 10/1 priority date for domestic and international students. Application fee: $40 ($90 for international students). Electronic applications accepted. *Expenses:* Tuition, state resident: full-time $6716. Tuition, nonresident: full-time

Natural Resources

Iowa State University of Science and Technology (continued)
$8908. Tuition and fees vary according to course level, course load, program and student level. *Financial support:* In 2009–10, 23 research assistantships with full and partial tuition reimbursements (averaging $15,420 per year), 2 teaching assistantships with full and partial tuition reimbursements (averaging $15,420 per year) were awarded. *Unit head:* Dr. Stephen Jungst, Interim Chair, 515-294-1166. *Application contact:* Dr. Janette Thompson, Director of Graduate Education, 515-294-1626, E-mail: nremgrad@iastate.edu.

Iowa State University of Science and Technology, Graduate College, Interdisciplinary Programs, Program in Biorenewable Resources and Technology, Ames, IA 50011. Offers MS, PhD. *Students:* 6 full-time (2 women), 1 part-time (0 women), 6 international. In 2009, 1 doctorate awarded. *Degree requirements:* For master's, thesis or alternative; for doctorate, thesis/dissertation. *Entrance requirements:* For master's and doctorate, GRE General Test. Additional exam requirements/recommendations for international students: Required—TOEFL (minimum score 550 paper-based; 79 iBT) or IELTS (minimum score 6.5). *Application deadline:* For fall admission, 1/1 priority date for domestic and international students; for spring admission, 9/1 for domestic and international students. Applications are processed on a rolling basis. Application fee: $40 ($90 for international students). *Expenses:* Tuition, state resident: full-time $6716. Tuition, nonresident: full-time $8908. Tuition and fees vary according to course level, course load, program and student level. *Financial support:* In 2009–10, 4 research assistantships with full and partial tuition reimbursements (averaging $16,500 per year) were awarded. *Unit head:* Dr. Raj Raman, Chair, Supervising Committee, 515-294-6555, E-mail: brtgrad@iastate.edu. *Application contact:* Dr. Raj Raman, Chair, Supervising Committee, 515-294-6555, E-mail: brtgrad@iastate.edu.

Laurentian University, School of Graduate Studies and Research, School of Engineering, Sudbury, ON P3E 2C6, Canada. Offers mineral resources engineering (M Eng, MA Sc); natural resources engineering (PhD). Part-time programs available. *Faculty research:* Mining engineering, rock mechanics (tunneling, rockbursts, rock support), metallurgy (mineral processing, hydro and pyrometallurgy), simulations and remote mining, simulations and scheduling.

Louisiana State University and Agricultural and Mechanical College, Graduate School, College of Agriculture, School of Renewable Natural Resources, Baton Rouge, LA 70803. Offers fisheries (MS); forestry (MS, PhD); wildlife (MS); wildlife and fisheries science (PhD). *Faculty:* 32 full-time (3 women). *Students:* 73 full-time (17 women), 9 part-time (4 women); includes 1 Hispanic American, 26 international. Average age 29. 31 applicants, 48% accepted, 14 enrolled. In 2009, 11 master's, 2 doctorates awarded. *Degree requirements:* For master's, thesis; for doctorate, thesis/dissertation. *Entrance requirements:* For master's, GRE General Test, minimum GPA of 3.0; for doctorate, GRE General Test, MS, minimum GPA of 3.0. Additional exam requirements/recommendations for international students: Required—TOEFL (minimum score 550 paper-based; 213 computer-based; 79 iBT), IELTS (minimum score 6.5). *Application deadline:* For fall admission, 1/25 priority date for domestic students, 5/15 for international students; for spring admission, 10/15 for international students. Applications are processed on a rolling basis. Application fee: $50 ($70 for international students). Electronic applications accepted. *Financial support:* In 2009–10, 80 students received support, including 7 fellowships (averaging $36,514 per year), 61 research assistantships with partial tuition reimbursements available (averaging $18,686 per year), 1 teaching assistantship with partial tuition reimbursement available (averaging $10,800 per year); Federal Work-Study, institutionally sponsored loans, scholarships/grants, health care benefits, tuition waivers (full and partial), and unspecified assistantships also available. Financial award application deadline: 4/15; financial award applicants required to submit FAFSA. *Faculty research:* Forest biology and management, aquaculture, fisheries biology and ecology, upland and wetlands wildlife. Total annual research expenditures: $3,308. *Unit head:* Dr. Allen Rutherford, Director, 225-578-4131, Fax: 225-578-4227, E-mail: druther@lsu.edu. *Application contact:* Dr. William Kelso, Coordinator of Graduate Studies, 225-578-4176, Fax: 225-578-4227, E-mail: wkelso@lsu.edu.

Marylhurst University, Department of Business Administration, Marylhurst, OR 97036-0261. Offers finance (MBA); general management (MBA); government policy and administration (MBA); green development (MBA); health care management (MBA); marketing (MBA); natural and organic resources (MBA); nonprofit management (MBA); organizational behavior (MBA); real estate (MBA); renewable energy (MBA); sustainable business (MBA). Part-time and evening/weekend programs available. Postbaccalaureate distance learning degree programs offered (no on-campus study). *Faculty:* 2 full-time (1 woman), 28 part-time/adjunct (5 women). *Students:* 30 full-time (12 women), 627 part-time (323 women); includes 79 minority (28 African Americans, 3 American Indian/Alaska Native, 17 Asian Americans or Pacific Islanders, 31 Hispanic Americans), 9 international. Average age 37. 299 applicants, 80% accepted, 209 enrolled. In 2009, 193 master's awarded. *Degree requirements:* For master's, comprehensive exam, capstone course. *Entrance requirements:* For master's, GMAT (if GPA less than 3.0 and fewer than 5 years of work experience), interview, resume, 2 letters of recommendation. Additional exam requirements/recommendations for international students: Recommended—TOEFL (minimum score 550 paper-based; 213 computer-based; 80 iBT). *Application deadline:* For fall admission, 9/11 priority date for domestic and international students; for winter admission, 12/15 priority date for domestic and international students; for spring admission, 3/17 priority date for domestic and international students. Applications are processed on a rolling basis. Application fee: $40 ($50 for international students). Electronic applications accepted. *Financial support:* Scholarships/grants available. Support available to part-time students. Financial award applicants required to submit FAFSA. *Unit head:* Bob Hanks, Director of Business and Real Estate Programs, 503-636-8141, Fax: 503-697-5597, E-mail: mba@marylhurst.edu. *Application contact:* Kathleen Schneff, Admissions Specialist, 800-634-9982 Ext. 3322, Fax: 503-635-6585, E-mail: admissions@marylhurst.edu.

McGill University, Faculty of Graduate and Postdoctoral Studies, Faculty of Agricultural and Environmental Sciences, Department of Natural Resource Sciences, Montréal, QC H3A 2T5, Canada. Offers entomology (M Sc, PhD); environmental assessment (M Sc); forest science (M Sc, PhD); microbiology (M Sc, PhD); micrometeorology (M Sc, PhD); neotropical environment (M Sc, PhD); soil science (M Sc, PhD); wildlife biology (M Sc, PhD).

Michigan State University, The Graduate School, College of Agriculture and Natural Resources, Department of Community, Agriculture, Recreation, and Resource Studies, East Lansing, MI 48824. Offers MS, PhD. *Entrance requirements:* Additional exam requirements/recommendations for international students: Required—TOEFL. Electronic applications accepted.

Missouri State University, Graduate College, College of Natural and Applied Sciences, Department of Geography, Geology, and Planning, Springfield, MO 65897. Offers geospatial sciences (MS); natural and applied science (MNAS), including geography, geology and planning; secondary education (MS Ed), including earth science, geography. *Accreditation:* ACSP. Part-time and evening/weekend programs available. *Faculty:* 20 full-time (4 women). *Students:* 19 full-time (10 women), 12 part-time (5 women); includes 1 minority (American Indian/Alaska Native), 1 international. Average age 29. 19 applicants, 100% accepted, 13 enrolled. In 2009, 4 master's awarded. *Degree requirements:* For master's, comprehensive exam, thesis (for some programs). *Entrance requirements:* For master's, GRE General Test (MS, MNAS), minimum undergraduate GPA of 3.0 (MS, MNAS), 9-12 teacher certification (MS Ed). Additional exam requirements/recommendations for international students: Required—TOEFL (minimum score 550 paper-based; 213 computer-based; 79 iBT). *Application deadline:* For fall admission, 7/20 priority date for domestic students, 5/1 for international students; for spring admission, 12/20 priority date for domestic students, 9/1 for international students. Applications are processed on a rolling basis. Application fee: $35 ($50 for international students). Electronic applications accepted. *Expenses:* Tuition, state resident: full-time $3852; part-time $214 per credit hour. Tuition, nonresident: full-time $7524; part-time $418 per credit hour. Required fees: $696; $172 per semester. Tuition and fees vary according to course level, course load, degree level and program. *Financial support:* In 2009–10, 7 research assistantships with full tuition reimbursements (averaging $8,933 per year), 8 teaching assistantships with full tuition reimbursements (averaging $8,236 per year) were awarded; career-related internships or fieldwork, Federal Work-Study, institutionally sponsored loans, scholarships/grants, and unspecified assistantships also available. Financial award application deadline: 3/31; financial award applicants required to submit FAFSA. *Faculty research:* Stratigraphy and ancient meteorite impacts, environmental geochemistry of karst, hyperspectral image processing, water quality, small town planning. *Unit head:* Dr. Thomas Plymate, Head, 417-836-5800, Fax: 417-836-6934, E-mail: tomplymate@missouristate.edu. *Application contact:* Eric Eckert, Coordinator of Graduate Admissions and Recruitment, 417-836-5331, Fax: 417-836-6200, E-mail: ericeckert@missouristate.edu.

Montana State University, College of Graduate Studies, College of Agriculture, Department of Land Resources and Environmental Sciences, Bozeman, MT 59717. Offers land rehabilitation (interdisciplinary) (MS); land resources and environmental sciences (MS), including land rehabilitation (interdisciplinary), land resources and environmental sciences. Part-time programs available. *Faculty:* 22 full-time (5 women), 1 part-time/adjunct (0 women). *Students:* 8 full-time (5 women), 39 part-time (13 women); includes 2 minority (1 American Indian/Alaska Native, 1 Hispanic American), 5 international. Average age 31. 22 applicants. In 2009, 11 master's awarded. *Degree requirements:* For master's, comprehensive exam. *Entrance requirements:* For master's, GRE General Test. Additional exam requirements/recommendations for international students: Required—TOEFL (minimum score 550 paper-based; 213 computer-based). *Application deadline:* For fall admission, 7/15 priority date for domestic students, 5/15 priority date for international students; for spring admission, 12/1 priority date for domestic students, 10/1 priority date for international students. Applications are processed on a rolling basis. Application fee: $30. Electronic applications accepted. *Expenses:* Tuition, state resident: full-time $5635; part-time $3492 per year. Tuition, nonresident: full-time $17,212; part-time $7865.10 per year. Required fees: $1441.05; $153.15 per credit. Tuition and fees vary according to course load and program. *Financial support:* In 2009–10, 5 fellowships with partial tuition reimbursements (averaging $25,000 per year), 38 research assistantships with full and partial tuition reimbursements (averaging $17,000 per year), 15 teaching assistantships with full and partial tuition reimbursements (averaging $2,000 per year) were awarded; scholarships/grants, health care benefits, tuition waivers (partial), and unspecified assistantships also available. Financial award application deadline: 3/1; financial award applicants required to submit FAFSA. *Faculty research:* Soil nutrient management and plant nutrition, isotope biogeochemistry of soils, biodegradation of hydrocarbons in soils and natural waters, remote sensing, GIS systems, managed and natural ecosystems, microbial and metabolic diversity in geothermally heated soils, integrated management of weeds, diversified cropping systems, insect behavior and ecology, river ecology, microbial biogeochemistry, weed ecology. Total annual research expenditures: $4.7 million. *Unit head:* Dr. Tracy M. Sterling, Head, 406-994-7060, Fax: 406-994-3933, E-mail: tracy.sterling@montana.edu. *Application contact:* Dr. Carl A. Fox, Vice Provost for Graduate Education, 406-994-4145, Fax: 406-994-7433, E-mail: gradstudy@montana.edu.

North Carolina State University, Graduate School, College of Natural Resources, Department of Parks, Recreation and Tourism Management, Raleigh, NC 27695. Offers natural resource management (MPRTM, MS); park and recreation management (MPRTM, MS); parks, recreation and tourism management (PhD); recreational sport management (MPRTM, MS); spatial information science (MPRTM, MS); tourism policy and development (MPRTM, MS). *Degree requirements:* For master's, thesis (for some programs); for doctorate, thesis/dissertation. *Entrance requirements:* For master's and doctorate, GRE General Test. Additional exam requirements/recommendations for international students: Required—TOEFL. Electronic applications accepted. *Faculty research:* Tourism policy and development, spatial information systems, natural resource management, recreational sports management, park and recreation management.

North Carolina State University, Graduate School, College of Natural Resources and College of Agriculture and Life Sciences, Program in Natural Resources, Raleigh, NC 27695. Offers MNR, MS. *Degree requirements:* For master's, thesis optional. *Entrance requirements:* For master's, GRE. Electronic applications accepted.

North Dakota State University, College of Graduate and Interdisciplinary Studies, College of Agriculture, Food Systems, and Natural Resources, Department of Agribusiness and Applied Economics, Fargo, ND 58108. Offers agribusiness and applied economics (MS); international agribusiness (MS); natural resource management (MS). Part-time programs available. *Faculty:* 16 full-time (3 women), 5 part-time/adjunct (1 woman). *Students:* 16 full-time (5 women), 2 part-time (0 women); includes 3 African Americans, 4 Asian Americans or Pacific Islanders, 1 Hispanic American. Average age 24. 28 applicants, 68% accepted, 12 enrolled. In 2009, 13 master's awarded. *Degree requirements:* For master's, thesis. *Entrance requirements:* For master's, minimum GPA of 3.0. Additional exam requirements/recommendations for international students: Required—TOEFL (minimum score 525 paper-based; 225 computer-based; 71 iBT). *Application deadline:* For fall admission, 2/1 priority date for domestic students, 3/1 priority date for international students. Applications are processed on a rolling basis. Application fee: $45 ($60 for international students). Electronic applications accepted. *Financial support:* In 2009–10, 8 research assistantships with tuition reimbursements (averaging $14,520 per year) were awarded; Federal Work-Study and institutionally sponsored loans also available. Financial award application deadline: 4/15. *Faculty research:* Agribusiness, transportation, marketing, microeconomics, trade. Total annual research expenditures: $1 million. *Unit head:* Dr. Thomas I. Wahl, Chair, 701-231-7470, Fax: 701-231-7400. *Application contact:* Dr. Thomas I. Wahl, Chair, 701-231-7470, Fax: 701-231-7400.

North Dakota State University, College of Graduate and Interdisciplinary Studies, College of Agriculture, Food Systems, and Natural Resources, Department of Animal and Range Sciences, Fargo, ND 58108. Offers animal science (MS, PhD); natural resource management (MS, PhD); range sciences (MS, PhD). *Faculty:* 32. *Students:* 18 full-time (10 women), 7 part-time (6 women); includes 1 American Indian/Alaska Native, 1 Asian American or Pacific Islander. Average age 25. 13 applicants, 62% accepted. In 2009, 17 master's, 2 doctorates awarded. *Degree requirements:* For master's, thesis; for doctorate, comprehensive exam, thesis/dissertation. *Entrance requirements:* For master's and doctorate, GRE General Test. Additional exam requirements/recommendations for international students: Required—TOEFL (minimum score 71 iBT). *Application deadline:* Applications are processed on a rolling basis. Application fee: $45 ($60 for international students). *Financial support:* In 2009–10, 1 fellowship with tuition reimbursement (averaging $18,000 per year), 29 research assistantships with tuition reimbursements (averaging $13,000 per year) were awarded; teaching assistantships, Federal Work-Study, institutionally sponsored loans, and tuition waivers (partial) also available. Financial award application deadline: 3/15. *Faculty research:* Reproduction, nutrition, meat and muscle biology, breeding/genetics. Total annual research expenditures: $1.5 million. *Unit head:* Dr. David Buchanan, Chair, 701-231-7643, Fax: 701-231-7590, E-mail: david.buchanan@ndsu.edu. *Application contact:* Dr. David Buchanan, Chair, 701-231-7643, Fax: 701-231-7590, E-mail: david.buchanan@ndsu.edu.

North Dakota State University, College of Graduate and Interdisciplinary Studies, College of Agriculture, Food Systems, and Natural Resources, Department of Entomology, Fargo, ND 58108. Offers entomology (MS, PhD); environment and conservation science (MS, PhD); natural resource management (MS, PhD). Part-time programs available. *Faculty:* 7 full-time (3 women), 8 part-time/adjunct (0 women). *Students:* 2 full-time (1 woman), 12 part-time (8 women); includes 2 Asian Americans or Pacific Islanders, 4 international. Average age 34. 5

applicants, 20% accepted, 1 enrolled. In 2009, 5 doctorates awarded. *Degree requirements:* For master's, thesis; for doctorate, comprehensive exam, thesis/dissertation. *Entrance requirements:* For master's and doctorate, minimum GPA of 3.0. Additional exam requirements/recommendations for international students: Required—TOEFL (minimum score 550 paper-based; 213 computer-based; 79 iBT). *Application deadline:* Applications are processed on a rolling basis. Application fee: $45 ($60 for international students). Electronic applications accepted. *Financial support:* In 2009–10, 11 research assistantships with full tuition reimbursements (averaging $13,800 per year) were awarded; Federal Work-Study, institutionally sponsored loans, and unspecified assistantships also available. Financial award application deadline: 4/15. *Faculty research:* Insect systematics, conservation biology, integrated pest management, insect behavior, insect biology. *Unit head:* Dr. David A. Rider, Chair, 701-231-7908, Fax: 701-231-8557, E-mail: david.rider@ndsu.edu. *Application contact:* Dr. David A. Rider, Chair, 701-231-7908, Fax: 701-231-8557, E-mail: david.rider@ndsu.edu.

North Dakota State University, College of Graduate and Interdisciplinary Studies, College of Agriculture, Food Systems, and Natural Resources, Department of Plant Sciences, Fargo, ND 58108. Offers crop and weed sciences (MS); horticulture (MS); natural resource management (MS); plant sciences (PhD). Part-time programs available. *Faculty:* 36 full-time (3 women), 23 part-time/adjunct (3 women). *Students:* 25 full-time (10 women), 17 part-time (6 women); includes 4 minority (all Hispanic Americans), 19 international. Average age 26. 44 applicants, 45% accepted. In 2009, 11 master's, 6 doctorates awarded. *Degree requirements:* For master's, thesis; for doctorate, thesis/dissertation. *Entrance requirements:* Additional exam requirements/recommendations for international students: Required—TOEFL (minimum score 525 paper-based; 197 computer-based; 71 iBT). *Application deadline:* Applications are processed on a rolling basis. Application fee: $45 ($60 for international students). Electronic applications accepted. *Financial support:* In 2009–10, 2 fellowships (averaging $19,950 per year), 64 research assistantships were awarded; teaching assistantships, Federal Work-Study and institutionally sponsored loans also available. Financial award application deadline: 4/15. *Faculty research:* Biotechnology, weed control science, plant breeding, plant genetics, crop physiology. Total annual research expenditures: $880,000. *Unit head:* Dr. Al Schneiter, Head, 701-231-7971, Fax: 701-231-8474, E-mail: albert.schneiter@ndsu.edu. *Application contact:* Dr. Al Schneiter, Head, 701-231-7971, Fax: 701-231-8474, E-mail: albert.schneiter@ndsu.edu.

North Dakota State University, College of Graduate and Interdisciplinary Studies, College of Agriculture, Food Systems, and Natural Resources, Department of Soil Science, Fargo, ND 58108. Offers environmental and conservation science (PhD); environmental conservation science (MS); natural resource management (MS, PhD); soil sciences (MS, PhD). Part-time programs available. *Faculty:* 8 full-time (1 woman), 6 part-time/adjunct (0 women). *Students:* 6 full-time (4 women), 3 part-time (1 woman). Average age 23. 3 applicants, 67% accepted, 2 enrolled. In 2009, 2 master's, 1 doctorate awarded. *Degree requirements:* For master's, comprehensive exam, thesis, classroom teaching; for doctorate, comprehensive exam, thesis/dissertation, classroom teaching. *Entrance requirements:* Additional exam requirements/recommendations for international students: Required—TOEFL (minimum score 525 paper-based; 193 computer-based; 71 iBT). *Application deadline:* Applications are processed on a rolling basis. Application fee: $45 ($60 for international students). Electronic applications accepted. *Financial support:* In 2009–10, 7 research assistantships with full tuition reimbursements (averaging $14,300 per year) were awarded; fellowships, Federal Work-Study, institutionally sponsored loans, and scholarships/grants also available. Financial award application deadline: 3/15. *Faculty research:* Microclimate, nitrogen management, landscape studies, water quality, soil management. *Unit head:* Dr. Donald Kirby, Interim Chair, 701-231-8901, Fax: 701-231-7861. *Application contact:* Dr. Donald Kirby, Interim Chair, 701-231-8901, Fax: 701-231-7861.

North Dakota State University, College of Graduate and Interdisciplinary Studies, College of Science and Mathematics, Department of Biological Sciences, Fargo, ND 58108. Offers biology (MS); botany (MS, PhD); cellular and molecular biology (PhD); environmental and conservation sciences (MS, PhD); genomics (PhD); natural resources management (MS, PhD); zoology (MS, PhD). *Students:* 32 full-time (21 women), 14 part-time (10 women); includes 1 Asian American or Pacific Islander, 14 international. In 2009, 12 master's, 9 doctorates awarded. *Degree requirements:* For master's, thesis; for doctorate, thesis/dissertation. *Entrance requirements:* For master's and doctorate, GRE General Test. Additional exam requirements/recommendations for international students: Required—TOEFL. *Application deadline:* For fall admission, 3/15 priority date for domestic students; for spring admission, 10/30 priority date for domestic students. Applications are processed on a rolling basis. Application fee: $45 ($60 for international students). Electronic applications accepted. *Financial support:* Fellowships with full tuition reimbursements, research assistantships with full tuition reimbursements, teaching assistantships with full tuition reimbursements, career-related internships or fieldwork, Federal Work-Study, institutionally sponsored loans, scholarships/grants, tuition waivers (full), and unspecified assistantships available. Support available to part-time students. Financial award application deadline: 4/15; financial award applicants required to submit FAFSA. *Faculty research:* Comparative endocrinology, physiology, behavioral ecology, plant cell biology, aquatic biology. Total annual research expenditures: $675,000. *Unit head:* Dr. Marinus L. Otte, Head, 701-231-7087, E-mail: marinus.otte@ndsu.edu. *Application contact:* Dr. Marinus L. Otte, Head, 701-231-7087, E-mail: marinus.otte@ndsu.edu.

North Dakota State University, College of Graduate and Interdisciplinary Studies, Interdisciplinary Program in Natural Resources Management, Fargo, ND 58108. Offers MS, PhD. Part-time programs available. *Students:* 24 full-time (9 women), 21 part-time (11 women); includes 1 minority (African American), 9 international. In 2009, 9 master's, 2 doctorates awarded. *Degree requirements:* For master's, thesis; for doctorate, comprehensive exam, thesis/dissertation. *Entrance requirements:* Additional exam requirements/recommendations for international students: Required—TOEFL (minimum score 525 paper-based; 197 computer-based; 71 iBT). *Application deadline:* Applications are processed on a rolling basis. Application fee: $45 ($60 for international students). Electronic applications accepted. *Financial support:* In 2009–10, 25 students received support; research assistantships with full tuition reimbursements available, teaching assistantships with full tuition reimbursements available available. Support available to part-time students. Financial award application deadline: 3/15. *Faculty research:* Natural resources economics, wetlands issues, wildlife, prairie ecology, range management. Total annual research expenditures: $500,000. *Unit head:* Dr. Carolyn E. Grygiel, Director, 701-231-8180, Fax: 701-231-7590, E-mail: carolyn.grygiel@ndsu.edu. *Application contact:* Dr. Carolyn E. Grygiel, Director, 701-231-8180, Fax: 701-231-7590, E-mail: carolyn.grygiel@ndsu.edu.

The Ohio State University, Graduate School, College of Food, Agricultural, and Environmental Sciences, School of Environment and Natural Resources, Program in Human Dimensions in Natural Resources, Columbus, OH 43210. Offers MS, PhD. Electronic applications accepted. *Expenses:* Tuition, state resident: full-time $10,683. Tuition, nonresident: full-time $25,923. Tuition and fees vary according to course load and program.

The Ohio State University, Graduate School, College of Food, Agricultural, and Environmental Sciences, School of Environment and Natural Resources, Program in Natural Resources, Columbus, OH 43210. Offers MS, PhD. Part-time programs available. *Degree requirements:* For master's, thesis optional. *Entrance requirements:* For master's and doctorate, GRE General Test. Additional exam requirements/recommendations for international students: Required—TOEFL (paper-based 550; computer-based 213) or IELTS (7) or Michigan English Language Assessment Battery (91). Electronic applications accepted. *Expenses:* Tuition, state resident: full-time $10,683. Tuition, nonresident: full-time $25,923. Tuition and fees vary according to course load and program. *Faculty research:* Environmental education, natural resources development, fisheries and wildlife management.

Oklahoma State University, College of Agricultural Science and Natural Resources, Stillwater, OK 74078. Offers M Ag, MS, PhD. Postbaccalaureate distance learning degree programs offered. *Faculty:* 262 full-time (59 women), 11 part-time/adjunct (2 women). *Students:* 153 full-time (66 women), 308 part-time (145 women); includes 39 minority (8 African Americans, 19 American Indian/Alaska Native, 7 Asian Americans or Pacific Islanders, 5 Hispanic Americans), 174 international. Average age 29. 527 applicants, 33% accepted, 107 enrolled. In 2009, 109 master's, 34 doctorates awarded. *Degree requirements:* For master's, thesis (for some programs); for doctorate, comprehensive exam, thesis/dissertation. *Entrance requirements:* For master's and doctorate, GRE or GMAT. Additional exam requirements/recommendations for international students: Required—TOEFL (minimum score 550 paper-based; 79 iBT). *Application deadline:* For fall admission, 3/1 priority date for international students; for spring admission, 8/1 priority date for international students. Applications are processed on a rolling basis. Application fee: $40 ($75 for international students). Electronic applications accepted. *Expenses:* Tuition, state resident: full-time $3716; part-time $154.85 per credit hour. Tuition, nonresident: full-time $14,448; part-time $602 per credit hour. Required fees: $1772; $73.85 per credit hour. One-time fee: $50. Tuition and fees vary according to course load and campus/location. *Financial support:* In 2009–10, 285 research assistantships (averaging $15,491 per year), 25 teaching assistantships (averaging $13,252 per year) were awarded; fellowships, career-related internships or fieldwork, Federal Work-Study, scholarships/grants, health care benefits, tuition waivers (partial), and unspecified assistantships also available. Support available to part-time students. Financial award application deadline: 3/1; financial award applicants required to submit FAFSA. *Unit head:* Dr. Robert E. Whitson, Dean, 405-744-5398, Fax: 405-744-2480. *Application contact:* Dr. Gordon Emslie, Dean, 405-744-6368, Fax: 405-744-0355, E-mail: grad-i@okstate.edu.

Penn State University Park, Graduate School, Intercollege Graduate Programs, State College, University Park, PA 16802-1503. Offers acoustics (M Eng, MS, PhD); bioengineering (MS, PhD); biogeochemistry (dual) (PhD); business administration (MBA); cell and developmental biology (PhD); demography (dual) (MA); ecology (MS, PhD); environmental pollution control (MEPC, MS); genetics (MS, PhD); human dimensions of natural resources and the environment (dual) (MA, MS, PhD); immunology and infectious diseases (MS); integrative biosciences (MS, PhD), including integrative biosciences; materials science and engineering (PhD); operations research (dual) (M Eng, MA, MS, PhD); physiology (MS, PhD); plant physiology (MS, PhD); quality and manufacturing management (MMM). *Students:* 371 full-time (157 women), 22 part-time (7 women). Average age 27. 1,074 applicants, 18% accepted, 130 enrolled. *Entrance requirements:* Additional exam requirements/recommendations for international students: Required—TOEFL (minimum score 550 paper-based; 213 computer-based; 80 iBT). *Application deadline:* Applications are processed on a rolling basis. Application fee: $45. Electronic applications accepted. *Financial support:* Fellowships, research assistantships, teaching assistantships available. Financial award applicants required to submit FAFSA. *Unit head:* Dr. Regina Vasilatos-Younken, Senior Associate Dean, 814-865-2516, Fax: 814-863-4627, E-mail: rxv@psu.edu. *Application contact:* Cynthia E. Nicosia, Director, Graduate Enrollment Services, 814-865-1795, Fax: 814-865-4627, E-mail: cey1@psu.edu.

Purdue University, Graduate School, College of Agriculture, Department of Forestry and Natural Resources, West Lafayette, IN 47907. Offers aquaculture, fisheries, aquatic science (MSF); aquaculture, fisheries, aquatic sciences (MS, PhD); forest biology (MS, MSF, PhD); natural resources and environmental policy (MS, MSF); natural resources environmental policy (PhD); quantitative resource analysis (MS, MSF, PhD); wildlife science (MS, MSF, PhD); wood science and technology (MS, MSF, PhD). *Degree requirements:* For master's, thesis; for doctorate, thesis/dissertation. *Entrance requirements:* For master's and doctorate, GRE General Test, minimum B+ average in undergraduate course work. Additional exam requirements/recommendations for international students: Required—TOEFL. Electronic applications accepted. *Faculty research:* Wildlife management, forest management, forest ecology, forest soils, limnology.

San Francisco State University, Division of Graduate Studies, College of Behavioral and Social Sciences, Department of Geography and Human Environmental Studies, San Francisco, CA 94132-1722. Offers geography (MA), including resource management and environmental planning.

State University of New York College of Environmental Science and Forestry, Department of Construction Management and Wood Products Engineering, Syracuse, NY 13210-2779. Offers environmental and resources engineering (MPS, MS, PhD). *Degree requirements:* For master's, thesis (for some programs); for doctorate, comprehensive exam, thesis/dissertation. *Entrance requirements:* For master's and doctorate, GRE General Test, minimum GPA of 3.0. Additional exam requirements/recommendations for international students: Required—TOEFL (minimum score 550 paper-based; 213 computer-based; 80 iBT), IELTS (minimum score 6).

State University of New York College of Environmental Science and Forestry, Department of Environmental Resources and Forest Engineering, Syracuse, NY 13210-2779. Offers environmental and resources engineering (MPS, MS, PhD). *Degree requirements:* For master's, thesis (for some programs); for doctorate, comprehensive exam, thesis/dissertation. *Entrance requirements:* For master's and doctorate, GRE General Test, minimum GPA of 3.0. Additional exam requirements/recommendations for international students: Required—TOEFL (minimum score 550 paper-based; 213 computer-based; 80 iBT), IELTS (minimum score 6). *Faculty research:* Forest engineering, paper science and engineering, wood products engineering.

State University of New York College of Environmental Science and Forestry, Department of Forest and Natural Resources Management, Syracuse, NY 13210-2779. Offers environmental and natural resource policy (MS, PhD); environmental and natural resources policy (MPS); forest management and operations (MF); forestry ecosystems science and applications (MPS, MS, PhD); natural resources management (MPS, MS, PhD); quantitative methods and management in forest science (MPS, MS, PhD); recreation and resource management (MPS, MS, PhD); watershed management and forest hydrology (MPS, MS, PhD). *Degree requirements:* For master's, thesis (for some programs); for doctorate, comprehensive exam, thesis/dissertation. *Entrance requirements:* For master's and doctorate, GRE General Test, minimum GPA of 3.0. Additional exam requirements/recommendations for international students: Required—TOEFL (minimum score 550 paper-based; 213 computer-based; 80 iBT), IELTS (minimum score 6). *Faculty research:* Silviculture recreation management, tree improvement, operations management, economics.

Texas A&M University, College of Agriculture and Life Sciences, Department of Ecosystem Science and Management, College Station, TX 77843. Offers forestry (MS, PhD); natural resources development (M Agr). Part-time programs available. *Faculty:* 26. *Students:* 54 full-time (27 women), 15 part-time (8 women); includes 17 minority (3 African Americans, 14 Hispanic Americans), 10 international. Average age 27. In 2009, 9 master's, 2 doctorates awarded. Terminal master's awarded for partial completion of doctoral program. *Degree requirements:* For master's, thesis (for some programs); for doctorate, thesis/dissertation. *Entrance requirements:* For master's and doctorate, GRE General Test. Additional exam requirements/recommendations for international students: Required—TOEFL. *Application deadline:* For fall admission, 3/1 priority date for domestic students; for spring admission, 11/1 priority date for domestic students. Applications are processed on a rolling basis. Application fee: $50 ($75 for international students). Electronic applications accepted. *Expenses:* Tuition, state resident: full-time $3991.32; part-time $221.74 per credit hour. Tuition, nonresident: full-time $9049; part-time $502.74 per credit hour. *Financial support:* In 2009–10, fellowships with partial tuition reimbursements (averaging $15,000 per year), research assistantships with partial tuition reimbursements (averaging $15,000 per year), teaching assistantships with partial tuition reimbursements (averaging $15,000 per year) were awarded; career-related internships or fieldwork and institutionally sponsored loans also available. Support available to

Natural Resources

Texas A&M University (continued)
part-time students. Financial award application deadline: 3/1; financial award applicants required to submit FAFSA. *Faculty research:* Expert systems, geographic information systems, economics, biology, genetics. *Unit head:* Dr. Steve Whisenant, Professor and Head, 979-845-5033, Fax: 979-845-6049, E-mail: s-whisenant@tamu.edu. *Application contact:* Dr. Carol Loopstra, Associate Head for Research and Graduate Studies, 979-862-2200, Fax: 979-845-6049, E-mail: c-loopstra@tamu.edu.

Texas A&M University, College of Agriculture and Life Sciences, Department of Recreation, Park and Tourism Sciences, College Station, TX 77843. Offers natural resources development (M Agr); recreation resources development (M Agr); recreation, park, and tourism sciences (MS, PhD). *Faculty:* 15. *Students:* 46 full-time (28 women), 17 part-time (10 women); includes 7 minority (3 African Americans, 1 American Indian/Alaska Native, 3 Hispanic Americans), 26 international. Average age 28. In 2009, 8 master's, 15 doctorates awarded. *Degree requirements:* For master's, thesis (for some programs), internship and professional paper (M Agr); for doctorate, thesis/dissertation. *Entrance requirements:* For master's and doctorate, GRE General Test. Additional exam requirements/recommendations for international students: Required—TOEFL. *Application deadline:* For fall admission, 4/15 priority date for domestic students; for spring admission, 10/15 priority date for domestic students. Applications are processed on a rolling basis. Application fee: $50 ($75 for international students). Electronic applications accepted. *Expenses:* Tuition, state resident: full-time $3991.32; part-time $221.74 per credit hour. Tuition, nonresident: full-time $9049; part-time $502.74 per credit hour. *Financial support:* Fellowships, research assistantships, teaching assistantships, career-related internships or fieldwork, institutionally sponsored loans, and scholarships/grants available. Financial award application deadline: 4/15; financial award applicants required to submit FAFSA. *Faculty research:* Administration and tourism, outdoor recreation, commercial recreation, environmental law, system planning. *Unit head:* Head, 979-845-7324. *Application contact:* Graduate Recruitment Coordinator, 979-845-5412, Fax: 979-845-0446, E-mail: majohnson@ag.tamu.edu.

Texas Tech University, Graduate School, College of Agricultural Sciences and Natural Resources, Department of Natural Resources Management, Lubbock, TX 79409. Offers fisheries science (MS, PhD); range science (MS, PhD); wildlife science (MS, PhD). Part-time programs available. *Faculty:* 9 full-time (0 women), 1 part-time/adjunct (0 women). *Students:* 33 full-time (11 women), 1 part-time (0 women); includes 4 minority (1 Asian American or Pacific Islander, 3 Hispanic Americans), 4 international. Average age 28. 22 applicants, 50% accepted, 8 enrolled. In 2009, 8 master's, 2 doctorates awarded. *Degree requirements:* For master's, thesis; for doctorate, thesis/dissertation. *Entrance requirements:* For master's and doctorate, GRE General Test. Additional exam requirements/recommendations for international students: Required—TOEFL (minimum score 550 paper-based; 213 computer-based). *Application deadline:* For fall admission, 3/1 priority date for international students; for spring admission, 11/1 priority date for international students. Applications are processed on a rolling basis. Application fee: $50 ($75 for international students). Electronic applications accepted. *Expenses:* Tuition, state resident: full-time $5100; part-time $213 per credit hour. Tuition, nonresident: full-time $11,748; part-time $490 per credit hour. Required fees: $2298; $50 per credit hour. $555 per semester. *Financial support:* In 2009–10, 7 research assistantships with partial tuition reimbursements (averaging $18,972 per year), 2 teaching assistantships with partial tuition reimbursements (averaging $15,975 per year) were awarded; Federal Work-Study and institutionally sponsored loans also available. Support available to part-time students. Financial award application deadline: 4/15; financial award applicants required to submit FAFSA. *Faculty research:* Use of fire on range lands, big game, upland game, and waterfowl; playa lakes in the southern Great Plains; conservation biology; fish ecology and physiology. Total annual research expenditures: $509,586. *Unit head:* Dr. Philip S. Gipson, Chairman, 806-742-2841 Ext. 223, Fax: 806-742-2280, E-mail: philip.gipson@ttu.edu. *Application contact:* Renee Dillon, Sr. Business Assistant, 806-742-2841, E-mail: renee.dillon@ttu.edu.

Universidad Metropolitana, School of Environmental Affairs, Program in Conservation and Management of Natural Resources, San Juan, PR 00928-1150. Offers MSEM. Part-time programs available. *Degree requirements:* For master's, thesis. Electronic applications accepted.

Université du Québec à Montréal, Graduate Programs, Program in Earth Sciences, Montreal, QC H3C 3P8, Canada. Offers earth sciences (M Sc); mineral resources (PhD); non-renewable resources (DESS). Part-time programs available. Terminal master's awarded for partial completion of doctoral program. *Degree requirements:* For master's, thesis (for some programs); for doctorate, thesis/dissertation. *Entrance requirements:* For master's, appropriate bachelor's degree or equivalent, proficiency in French. *Faculty research:* Economic geology, structural geology, geochemistry, Quaternary geology, isotopic geochemistry.

Université du Québec en Abitibi-Témiscamingue, Graduate Programs, Program in Environmental Sciences, Rouyn-Noranda, QC J9X 5E4, Canada. Offers biology (MS); environmental sciences (PhD); sustainable forest ecosystem management (MS).

University of Alaska Fairbanks, School of Natural Resources and Agricultural Sciences, Fairbanks, AK 99775-7140. Offers natural resource and sustainability (PhD); natural resource management (MS); natural resource management and geography (MS). Part-time programs available. *Faculty:* 20 full-time (3 women), 2 part-time/adjunct (1 woman). *Students:* 31 full-time (21 women), 18 part-time (7 women); includes 2 minority (1 American Indian/Alaska Native, 1 Asian American or Pacific Islander), 5 international. Average age 32. 49 applicants, 45% accepted, 16 enrolled. In 2009, 7 master's, 3 doctorates awarded. *Degree requirements:* For master's, comprehensive exam, thesis or alternative. *Entrance requirements:* For master's, GRE General Test. Additional exam requirements/recommendations for international students: Required—TOEFL (minimum score 550 paper-based; 213 computer-based). *Application deadline:* For fall admission, 6/1 for domestic students, 3/1 for international students; for spring admission, 10/15 for domestic students, 9/1 for international students. Applications are processed on a rolling basis. Application fee: $60. Electronic applications accepted. *Expenses:* Tuition, state resident: full-time $7584; part-time $316 per credit. Tuition, nonresident: full-time $15,504; part-time $646 per credit. Required fees: $23 per credit. $135 per semester. Tuition and fees vary according to course level, course load and reciprocity agreements. *Financial support:* In 2009–10, 16 research assistantships (averaging $10,412 per year), 2 teaching assistantships (averaging $9,472 per year) were awarded; fellowships, career-related internships or fieldwork, Federal Work-Study, scholarships/grants, health care benefits, and unspecified assistantships also available. Support available to part-time students. Financial award application deadline: 2/15; financial award applicants required to submit FAFSA. *Faculty research:* Conservation biology, soil/water conservation, land use policy and planning in the arctic and subarctic, forest ecosystem management, subarctic agricultural production. Total annual research expenditures: $5.8 million. *Unit head:* Dr. Carol E. Lewis, Dean, 907-474-7083, Fax: 907-474-6567, E-mail: fysnras@uaf.edu. *Application contact:* Veazey David, Director of Enrollment Management, 907-474-5276, Fax: 907-474-6567, E-mail: dave.veazey@alaska.edu.

University of Alberta, Faculty of Graduate Studies and Research, Department of Renewable Resources, Edmonton, AB T6G 2E1, Canada. Offers agroforestry (M Ag, M Sc, MF); conservation biology (M Sc, PhD); forest biology and management (M Sc, PhD); land reclamation and remediation (M Sc, PhD); protected areas and wildlands management (M Sc, PhD); soil science (M Ag, M Sc, PhD); water and land resources (M Ag, M Sc, PhD); wildlife ecology and management (M Sc, PhD); MBA/M Ag; MBA/MF. Part-time programs available. *Faculty:* 26 full-time (4 women), 22 part-time/adjunct (3 women). *Students:* 63 full-time (33 women), 50 part-time (20 women), 14 international. 122 applicants, 24% accepted, 22 enrolled. In 2009, 16 master's, 8 doctorates awarded. *Degree requirements:* For master's, thesis (for some programs); for doctorate, comprehensive exam, thesis/dissertation. *Entrance requirements:* For master's, minimum 2 years of relevant professional experiences, minimum GPA of 3.0; for doctorate, minimum GPA of 3.0. Additional exam requirements/recommendations for international students: Required—TOEFL (minimum score 550 paper-based; 213 computer-based). *Application deadline:* For fall admission, 7/1 priority date for domestic students, 6/1 priority date for international students. Applications are processed on a rolling basis. Application fee: $0. Electronic applications accepted. Tuition and fees charges are reported in Canadian dollars. *Expenses:* Tuition, area resident: Full-time $4626.24 Canadian dollars; part-time $99.72 Canadian dollars per unit. International tuition: $8216 Canadian dollars full-time. Required fees: $3589.92 Canadian dollars; $99.72 Canadian dollars per unit. $215 Canadian dollars per term. *Financial support:* In 2009–10, 63 students received support, including 21 research assistantships with partial tuition reimbursements available (averaging $2,800 per year), 28 teaching assistantships with partial tuition reimbursements available (averaging $1,900 per year); scholarships/grants and unspecified assistantships also available. *Faculty research:* Natural and managed landscapes. Total annual research expenditures: $6.1 million. *Unit head:* Dr. John R. Spence, Chair, 780-492-2820, Fax: 780-492-4323, E-mail: john.spence@ualberta.ca. *Application contact:* Sandy Nakashima, Graduate Program Secretary, 780-492-2820, Fax: 780-492-4323, E-mail: rrgrads.inquiry@ualberta.ca.

University of Alberta, Faculty of Graduate Studies and Research, Program in Business Administration, Edmonton, AB T6G 2E1, Canada. Offers international business (MBA); leisure and sport management (MBA); natural resources and energy (MBA); technology commercialization (MBA); MBA/LL B; MBA/M Ag; MBA/M Eng; MBA/MF; MBA/PhD. *Accreditation:* AACSB. Part-time and evening/weekend programs available. *Faculty:* 77 full-time, 20 part-time/adjunct. *Students:* 131 full-time (56 women), 109 part-time (51 women). Average age 29. 525 applicants, 30% accepted, 90 enrolled. In 2009, 114 master's awarded. *Degree requirements:* For master's, thesis or alternative. *Entrance requirements:* For master's, GMAT. Additional exam requirements/recommendations for international students: Required—TOEFL (minimum score 600 paper-based; 250 computer-based). *Application deadline:* For fall admission, 4/30 priority date for domestic students, 4/30 for international students. Applications are processed on a rolling basis. Application fee: $0. Electronic applications accepted. Tuition and fees charges are reported in Canadian dollars. *Expenses:* Tuition, area resident: Full-time $4626.24 Canadian dollars; part-time $99.72 Canadian dollars per unit. International tuition: $8216 Canadian dollars full-time. Required fees: $3589.92 Canadian dollars; $99.72 Canadian dollars per unit. $215 Canadian dollars per term. *Financial support:* Fellowships, research assistantships, teaching assistantships, career-related internships or fieldwork, scholarships/grants, health care benefits, and unspecified assistantships available. *Faculty research:* Natural resources and energy/management and policy/family enterprise/international business/healthcare research management. Total annual research expenditures: $1 million. *Unit head:* Dr. Douglas Olsen, Associate Dean, 780-492-5412, Fax: 780-492-7825. *Application contact:* Joan A. White, Secretary, 780-492-3679, Fax: 780-492-2024, E-mail: mba@ualberta.ca.

University of Arkansas at Monticello, School of Forest Resources, Monticello, AR 71656. Offers MS. Part-time programs available. *Degree requirements:* For master's, comprehensive exam, thesis. *Entrance requirements:* For master's, GRE General Test, minimum GPA of 2.7. Additional exam requirements/recommendations for international students: Required—TOEFL (minimum score 550 paper-based; 213 computer-based). Electronic applications accepted. *Faculty research:* Geographic information systems/remote sensing, forest ecology, wildlife ecology and management.

The University of British Columbia, Program in Resource Management and Environmental Studies, Vancouver, BC, BC V6T 1Z4, Canada. Offers M Sc, MA, PhD. *Degree requirements:* For master's, thesis; for doctorate, comprehensive exam, thesis/dissertation. *Entrance requirements:* Additional exam requirements/recommendations for international students: Required—TOEFL (minimum score 600 paper-based; 250 computer-based; 100 iBT), GRE (optional). Electronic applications accepted. *Faculty research:* Land management, water resources, energy, environmental assessment, risk evaluation.

University of California, Berkeley, Graduate Division, Group in Energy and Resources, Berkeley, CA 94720-1500. Offers MA, MS, PhD. *Students:* 60 full-time (32 women). Average age 31. 189 applicants, 12 enrolled. In 2009, 12 master's, 6 doctorates awarded. *Degree requirements:* For master's, project or thesis; for doctorate, one foreign language, thesis/dissertation, qualifying exam. *Entrance requirements:* For master's and doctorate, GRE General Test, minimum GPA of 3.0, 3 letters of recommendation. *Application deadline:* For fall admission, 12/5 for domestic students. Application fee: $70 ($90 for international students). *Financial support:* Unspecified assistantships available. *Faculty research:* Technical, economic, environmental, and institutional aspects of energy conservation in residential and commercial buildings; international patterns of energy use; renewable energy sources; assessment of valuation of energy and environmental resources pricing. *Unit head:* Prof. Daniel Farber, Chair, 510-642-1640, E-mail: erggrad@berkeley.edu. *Application contact:* Bette L. Evans, Student Affairs Officer, 510-642-1750, Fax: 510-642-1085, E-mail: engbarrows@berkeley.edu.

University of Connecticut, Graduate School, College of Agriculture and Natural Resources, Department of Natural Resources Management and Engineering, Storrs, CT 06269. Offers MS, PhD. *Faculty:* 13 full-time (0 women). *Students:* 29 full-time (12 women), 13 part-time (2 women); includes 6 minority (1 African American, 2 American Indian/Alaska Native, 1 Asian American or Pacific Islander, 2 Hispanic Americans), 11 international. Average age 34. 36 applicants, 22% accepted, 4 enrolled. In 2009, 9 master's awarded. Terminal master's awarded for partial completion of doctoral program. *Degree requirements:* For master's, comprehensive exam. *Entrance requirements:* For master's, GRE General Test, GRE Subject Test. Additional exam requirements/recommendations for international students: Required—TOEFL (minimum score 550 paper-based; 213 computer-based). *Application deadline:* For fall admission, 2/1 priority date for domestic and international students; for spring admission, 11/1 for domestic students, 10/1 for international students. Applications are processed on a rolling basis. Application fee: $55. Electronic applications accepted. *Expenses:* Tuition, state resident: full-time $4725; part-time $525 per credit. Tuition, nonresident: full-time $12,267; part-time $1363 per credit. Required fees: $346 per semester. Tuition and fees vary according to course load. *Financial support:* In 2009–10, 22 research assistantships with full tuition reimbursements, 7 teaching assistantships with full tuition reimbursements were awarded; fellowships, Federal Work-Study, scholarships/grants, health care benefits, and unspecified assistantships also available. Financial award application deadline: 2/1; financial award applicants required to submit FAFSA. *Faculty research:* Forest management, forest protection, water resources, biometeorology. *Unit head:* John C. Volin, Head, 860-486-0137, Fax: 860-486-5408, E-mail: john.volin@uconn.edu. *Application contact:* Thomas Meyer, Chairman, 860-486-0145, Fax: 860-486-5408, E-mail: thomas.meyer@uconn.edu.

University of Delaware, College of Agriculture and Natural Resources, Department of Bioresources Engineering, Newark, DE 19716. Offers MS.

University of Florida, Graduate School, College of Agricultural and Life Sciences, School of Forest Resources and Conservation, Gainesville, FL 32611. Offers MFRC, MS, PhD, JD/MFRC, JD/MS, JD/PhD. Part-time programs available. *Degree requirements:* For master's, comprehensive exam, project (MFRC), thesis defense (MS); for doctorate, thesis/dissertation, qualifying exams, defense. *Entrance requirements:* For master's and doctorate, GRE General Test, minimum GPA of 3.0. Additional exam requirements/recommendations for international students: Required—TOEFL. Electronic applications accepted. *Faculty research:* Forest biology and ecology; agroforestry and tropical forestry; forest management, economics, and policy; natural resource education and ecotourism.

University of Florida, Graduate School, School of Natural Resources and Environment, Gainesville, FL 32611. Offers interdisciplinary ecology (MS, PhD). *Degree requirements:* For master's, thesis optional; for doctorate, thesis/dissertation. *Entrance requirements:* For master's and doctorate, GRE General Test, minimum GPA of 3.0. Additional exam requirements/ recommendations for international students: Required—TOEFL (minimum score 550 paper-based; 213 computer-based). Electronic applications accepted.

University of Georgia, Graduate School, School of Forestry and Natural Resources, Athens, GA 30602. Offers MFR, MS, PhD. *Faculty:* 43 full-time (7 women), 8 part-time/adjunct (1 woman). *Students:* 147 full-time (47 women), 24 part-time (10 women); includes 3 minority (1 American Indian/Alaska Native, 1 Asian American or Pacific Islander, 1 Hispanic American), 23 international. 75 applicants, 60% accepted, 44 enrolled. In 2009, 27 master's, 12 doctorates awarded. *Degree requirements:* For master's, thesis (MS); for doctorate, one foreign language, thesis/dissertation. *Entrance requirements:* For master's and doctorate, GRE General Test. *Application deadline:* For fall admission, 7/1 priority date for domestic students; for spring admission, 11/15 for domestic students. Application fee: $50. Electronic applications accepted. *Expenses:* Tuition, state resident: full-time $6000; part-time $250 per credit hour. Tuition, nonresident: full-time $20,904; part-time $871 per credit hour. Required fees: $730 per semester. *Financial support:* Fellowships, research assistantships, teaching assistantships, unspecified assistantships available. *Unit head:* Dr. Michael C. Clutter, Dean, 706-542-4741, Fax: 706-542-2281, E-mail: mclutter@warnell.uga.edu. *Application contact:* Dr. Lawrence A. Morris, Graduate Coordinator, 706-542-2532, Fax: 706-542-2281, E-mail: lmorris@uga.edu.

University of Guelph, Graduate Program Services, Ontario Agricultural College, Department of Land Resource Science, Guelph, ON N1G 2W1, Canada. Offers atmospheric science (M Sc, PhD); environmental and agricultural earth sciences (M Sc, PhD); land resources management (M Sc, PhD); soil science (M Sc, PhD). Part-time programs available. *Degree requirements:* For master's, thesis (for some programs), research project (non-thesis track); for doctorate, comprehensive exam, thesis/dissertation. *Entrance requirements:* For master's, minimum B- average during previous 2 years of course work; for doctorate, minimum B average during previous 2 years of course work. Additional exam requirements/recommendations for international students: Required—TOEFL (minimum score 550 paper-based; 213 computer-based). Electronic applications accepted. *Faculty research:* Soil science, environmental earth science, land resource management.

University of Hawaii at Manoa, Graduate Division, College of Tropical Agriculture and Human Resources, Department of Natural Resources and Environmental Management, Honolulu, HI 96822. Offers MS, PhD. Part-time programs available. *Faculty:* 28 full-time (3 women), 10 part-time/adjunct (3 women). *Students:* 52 full-time (28 women), 13 part-time (5 women); includes 12 minority (11 Asian Americans or Pacific Islanders, 1 Hispanic American), 23 international. Average age 29. 60 applicants, 62% accepted, 24 enrolled. In 2009, 10 master's, 4 doctorates awarded. Terminal master's awarded for partial completion of doctoral program. *Degree requirements:* For master's, thesis optional; for doctorate, comprehensive exam, thesis/dissertation. *Entrance requirements:* For master's and doctorate, GRE General Test, minimum GPA of 3.0 in last 4 semesters of course work. Additional exam requirements/ recommendations for international students: Required—TOEFL (minimum score 600 paper-based; 250 computer-based; 100 iBT), IELTS (minimum score 7). *Application deadline:* For fall admission, 3/1 for domestic students, 1/15 for international students; for spring admission, 9/1 for domestic students, 8/1 for international students. Applications are processed on a rolling basis. Application fee: $60. *Expenses:* Tuition, state resident: full-time $8900; part-time $372 per credit. Tuition, nonresident: full-time $21,400; part-time $898 per credit. Required fees: $207 per semester. *Financial support:* In 2009–10, 1 student received support, including 5 fellowships (averaging $3,860 per year), 21 research assistantships (averaging $17,968 per year), 3 teaching assistantships (averaging $14,382 per year); career-related internships or fieldwork and tuition waivers (full and partial) also available. *Faculty research:* Bioeconomics, natural resource management. Total annual research expenditures: $3.1 million. *Application contact:* Ali Fares, Graduate Chair, 808-956-7530, Fax: 808-956-6539, E-mail: afares@hawaii.edu.

University of Idaho, College of Graduate Studies, College of Natural Resources, Department of Conservation Social Sciences, Moscow, ID 83844-2282. Offers MS. *Faculty:* 10 full-time, 1 part-time/adjunct. *Students:* 20 full-time (12 women), 19 part-time (11 women). In 2009, 15 master's awarded. *Entrance requirements:* For master's, minimum GPA of 2.8. *Application deadline:* For fall admission, 8/1 for domestic students; for spring admission, 12/15 for domestic students. Application fee: $55 ($60 for international students). *Expenses:* Tuition, state resident: full-time $6120. Tuition, nonresident: full-time $17,712. *Financial support:* Research assistantships, teaching assistantships available. Financial award application deadline: 2/15. *Faculty research:* Parks, wilderness and protected areas policy, planning and management, recreation and tourism planning, urban and community forestry, resource-based tourism, ecotourism, human dimensions of ecosystem management. *Unit head:* Dr. Thomas M. Gorman, Acting Dean, 208-885-7911. *Application contact:* Dr. Thomas M. Gorman, Acting Dean, 208-885-7911.

University of Idaho, College of Graduate Studies, College of Natural Resources, Program in Natural Resources, Moscow, ID 83844-2282. Offers MNR, MS, PhD. *Students:* 9 full-time, 7 part-time. In 2009, 2 master's awarded. *Expenses:* Tuition, state resident: full-time $6120. Tuition, nonresident: full-time $17,712. *Unit head:* William McLaughlin, Dean, 208-885-8981, Fax: 208-885-5534. *Application contact:* Dr., Graduate Coordinator.

University of Illinois at Urbana–Champaign, Graduate College, College of Agricultural, Consumer and Environmental Sciences, Department of Natural Resources and Environmental Science, Champaign, IL 61820. Offers MS, PhD, MS/JD. Part-time programs available. Post-baccalaureate distance learning degree programs offered (no on-campus study). *Faculty:* 24 full-time (6 women), 1 part-time/adjunct (0 women). *Students:* 70 full-time (27 women), 47 part-time (26 women); includes 6 minority (3 Asian Americans or Pacific Islanders, 3 Hispanic Americans), 25 international. 102 applicants, 46% accepted, 32 enrolled. In 2009, 21 master's, 9 doctorates awarded. *Entrance requirements:* For master's and doctorate, GRE, minimum GPA of 3.0. Additional exam requirements/recommendations for international students: Required—TOEFL (minimum score 600 paper-based; 250 computer-based). *Application deadline:* Applications are processed on a rolling basis. Application fee: $60 ($75 for international students). Electronic applications accepted. *Financial support:* In 2009–10, 8 fellowships, 59 research assistantships, 20 teaching assistantships were awarded; tuition waivers (full and partial) also available. *Unit head:* Jeffrey D. Brawn, Head, 217-244-5937, Fax: 217-244-3219, E-mail: jbrawn@illinois.edu. *Application contact:* Karen M. Claus, Secretary, 217-333-5824, Fax: 217-244-3219, E-mail: kclaus@illinois.edu.

University of Maine, Graduate School, College of Natural Sciences, Forestry, and Agriculture, Department of Forest Management and Forest Ecosystem Science, Orono, ME 04469. Offers forest resources (PhD); forestry (MF, MS). *Accreditation:* SAF (one or more programs are accredited). Part-time programs available. *Faculty:* 18 full-time (1 woman), 3 part-time/adjunct (2 women). *Students:* 34 full-time (12 women), 12 part-time (5 women), 9 international. Average age 28. 44 applicants, 52% accepted, 11 enrolled. In 2009, 9 master's, 4 doctorates awarded. *Degree requirements:* For master's, thesis; for doctorate, one foreign language, thesis/dissertation. *Entrance requirements:* For master's and doctorate, GRE General Test. Additional exam requirements/recommendations for international students: Required—TOEFL. *Application deadline:* For fall admission, 2/1 priority date for domestic students. Applications are processed on a rolling basis. Application fee: $65. Electronic applications accepted. *Financial support:* In 2009–10, 28 research assistantships with tuition reimbursements (averaging $17,487 per year), 7 teaching assistantships with tuition reimbursements (averaging $12,790 per year) were awarded; career-related internships or fieldwork, Federal Work-Study, and institutionally sponsored loans also available. Financial award application deadline: 3/1. *Faculty research:* Forest economics, engineering and operations analysis, biometrics and remote sensing, timber management, wood technology. *Unit head:* Dr. Robert Wagner, Chair, 207-581-4737. *Application contact:* Scott G. Delcourt, Associate Dean of the Graduate School, 207-581-3291, Fax: 207-581-3232, E-mail: graduate@maine.edu.

University of Maine, Graduate School, College of Natural Sciences, Forestry, and Agriculture, Department of Plant, Soil, and Environmental Sciences, Orono, ME 04469. Offers biological sciences (PhD); ecology and environmental sciences (MS, PhD); forest resources (PhD); horticulture (MS); plant science (PhD); plant, soil, and environmental sciences (MS); resource utilization (MS). *Faculty:* 8 full-time (2 women), 9 part-time/adjunct (3 women). *Students:* 6 full-time (3 women), 3 part-time (2 women), 1 international. Average age 31. 6 applicants, 17% accepted, 0 enrolled. In 2009, 2 master's awarded. *Entrance requirements:* For master's and doctorate, GRE General Test. Additional exam requirements/recommendations for international students: Required—TOEFL. *Application deadline:* Applications are processed on a rolling basis. Application fee: $65. Electronic applications accepted. *Financial support:* In 2009–10, 16 research assistantships with tuition reimbursements (averaging $16,260 per year), 3 teaching assistantships with tuition reimbursements (averaging $12,790 per year) were awarded; scholarships/grants, tuition waivers (full and partial), and unspecified assistantships also available. *Unit head:* Dr. Gregory Porter, Chair, 207-581-2943, Fax: 207-581-3207. *Application contact:* Scott G. Delcourt, Associate Dean of the Graduate School, 207-581-3291, Fax: 207-581-3232, E-mail: graduate@maine.edu.

University of Manitoba, Faculty of Graduate Studies, Clayton H. Riddell Faculty of Environment, Earth, and Resources, Natural Resources Institute, Winnipeg, MB R3T 2N2, Canada. Offers natural resources and environmental management (PhD); natural resources management (MNRM).

University of Maryland, College Park, Academic Affairs, College of Agriculture and Natural Resources, Department of Plant Science and Landscape Architecture, Natural Resource Sciences Program, College Park, MD 20742. Offers MS, PhD. *Students:* 23 full-time (15 women), 9 part-time (5 women); includes 5 minority (1 African American, 1 Asian American or Pacific Islander, 3 Hispanic Americans), 7 international. 13 applicants, 62% accepted, 6 enrolled. In 2009, 6 master's, 2 doctorates awarded. *Degree requirements:* For master's, thesis optional; for doctorate, thesis/dissertation. *Entrance requirements:* For master's, GRE General Test, minimum GPA of 3.0, 3 letters of recommendation; for doctorate, GRE General Test. *Application deadline:* For fall admission, 1/15 for domestic students, 2/1 for international students; for spring admission, 8/1 for domestic students, 6/1 for international students. Applications are processed on a rolling basis. Application fee: $60. Electronic applications accepted. *Expenses:* Tuition, area resident: Part-time $471 per credit hour. Tuition, state resident: part-time $471 per credit hour. Tuition, nonresident: part-time $1016 per credit hour. Required fees: $337.04 per term. *Financial support:* In 2009–10, 18 research assistantships (averaging $17,009 per year), 2 teaching assistantships (averaging $17,251 per year) were awarded; fellowships also available. *Faculty research:* Wetland soils, acid mine drainage, acid sulfate soil. *Unit head:* Dr. William Kenworthy, Chair, 301-405-6244, Fax: 301-314-9308, E-mail: wkenwort@umd.edu. *Application contact:* Dean of Graduate School, 301-405-0376, Fax: 301-314-9305.

University of Michigan, School of Natural Resources and Environment, Program in Natural Resources and Environment, Ann Arbor, MI 48109. Offers aquatic sciences: research and management (MS); behavior, education and communication (MS); conservation biology (MS); environmental informatics (MS); environmental justice (MS); environmental policy and planning (MS); natural resources and environment (PhD); sustainable systems (MS); terrestrial ecosystems (MS); MS/AM; MS/JD; MS/MBA. *Students:* Average age 27. In 2009, 87 master's, 14 doctorates awarded. Terminal master's awarded for partial completion of doctoral program. *Degree requirements:* For master's, practicum or group project; for doctorate, comprehensive exam, thesis/dissertation, oral defense of dissertation, preliminary exam. *Entrance requirements:* For master's, GRE General Test; for doctorate, GRE General Test, master's degree. Additional exam requirements/recommendations for international students: Required—TOEFL (minimum score 560 paper-based; 220 computer-based; 84 iBT). *Application deadline:* For fall admission, 1/5 priority date for domestic and international students. Applications are processed on a rolling basis. Application fee: $60 ($75 for international students). Electronic applications accepted. *Expenses:* Tuition, state resident: full-time $17,286; part-time $1099 per credit hour. Tuition, nonresident: full-time $34,944; part-time $2080 per credit hour. Required fees: $95 per semester. Tuition and fees vary according to course load, degree level and program. *Financial support:* Fellowships with tuition reimbursements, research assistantships with tuition reimbursements, teaching assistantships with tuition reimbursements, career-related internships or fieldwork, Federal Work-Study, institutionally sponsored loans, scholarships/grants, health care benefits, and unspecified assistantships available. Support available to part-time students. Financial award application deadline: 1/5; financial award applicants required to submit FAFSA. *Faculty research:* Stream ecology, plant-insect interactions, fish biology, resource control and reproductive success, remote sensing. *Application contact:* Graduate Admissions Team, 734-764-6453, Fax: 734-936-2195, E-mail: snre.admissions@umich.edu.

University of Minnesota, Twin Cities Campus, Graduate School, College of Food, Agricultural and Natural Resource Sciences, Program in Natural Resources Science and Management, Minneapolis, MN 55455-0213. Offers MS, PhD. Part-time programs available. Terminal master's awarded for partial completion of doctoral program. *Degree requirements:* For master's, comprehensive exam, thesis (for some programs); for doctorate, comprehensive exam, thesis/ dissertation. *Entrance requirements:* For master's and doctorate, GRE. Additional exam requirements/recommendations for international students: Required—TOEFL (minimum score 500 paper-based; 213 computer-based; 70 iBT).

University of Missouri, Graduate School, School of Natural Resources, Natural Resources Master's Degree Program, Columbia, MO 65211. Offers MNR.

The University of Montana, Graduate School, College of Forestry and Conservation, Missoula, MT 59812-0002. Offers ecosystem management (MEM, MS); fish and wildlife biology (PhD); forestry (MS, PhD); recreation management (MS); resource conservation (MS); wildlife biology (MS). *Degree requirements:* For doctorate, thesis/dissertation. *Entrance requirements:* For master's and doctorate, GRE General Test. Additional exam requirements/recommendations for international students: Required—TOEFL (minimum score 575 paper-based; 213 computer-based).

University of Nebraska–Lincoln, Graduate College, College of Agricultural Sciences and Natural Resources, Department of Agricultural Economics, Lincoln, NE 68588. Offers agribusiness (MBA); agricultural economics (MS, PhD); community development (M Ag). *Degree requirements:* For master's, thesis optional; for doctorate, comprehensive exam, thesis/ dissertation. *Entrance requirements:* For master's and doctorate, GRE General Test. Additional exam requirements/recommendations for international students: Required—TOEFL (minimum score 550 paper-based; 213 computer-based). Electronic applications accepted. *Faculty research:* Marketing and agribusiness, production economics, resource law, international trade and development, rural policy and revitalization.

University of Nebraska–Lincoln, Graduate College, College of Agricultural Sciences and Natural Resources, School of Natural Resources, Lincoln, NE 68588. Offers geography (PhD); natural resources (MS, PhD). *Degree requirements:* For master's, thesis optional. *Entrance requirements:* For master's, GRE General Test. Additional exam requirements/recommendations for international students: Required—TOEFL. Electronic applications accepted. *Faculty research:* Wildlife biology, aquatic sciences, landscape ecology, agroforestry.

University of New Brunswick Saint John, Faculty of Business, Saint John, NB E2L 4L5, Canada. Offers administration (MBA); electronic commerce (MBA); international business (MBA); natural resource management (MBA). Part-time programs available. *Faculty:* 19 full-time

Natural Resources

University of New Brunswick Saint John (continued)
(4 women), 14 part-time/adjunct (8 women). *Students:* 45 full-time (14 women), 18 part-time (8 women). 93 applicants, 78% accepted, 25 enrolled. In 2009, 45 master's awarded. *Entrance requirements:* For master's, GMAT, minimum GPA of 3.0. Additional exam requirements/recommendations for international students: Required—TOEFL (minimum score 580 paper-based; 237 computer-based), IELTS (minimum score 7), TWE (minimum score 4.5). *Application deadline:* For fall admission, 5/15 for domestic and international students. Applications are processed on a rolling basis. Application fee: $100. Electronic applications accepted. *Expenses:* Contact institution. *Financial support:* In 2009–10, 4 students received support. Career-related internships or fieldwork and scholarships/grants available. *Faculty research:* Business use of weblogs and podcasts to communicate, corporate governance, high-involvement work systems, international competitiveness, supply chain management and logistics. *Unit head:* Henryk Sterniczuk, Director of Graduate Studies, 506-648-5573, Fax: 506-648-5574, E-mail: sternicz@unbsj.ca. *Application contact:* Tammy Morin, Secretary, 506-648-5746, Fax: 506-648-5574, E-mail: tmorin@unbsj.ca.

University of New Hampshire, Graduate School, College of Life Sciences and Agriculture, Department of Natural Resources, Durham, NH 03824. Offers environmental conservation (MS); forestry (MS); soil science (MS); water resources management (MS); wildlife (MS). Part-time programs available. *Faculty:* 40 full-time. *Students:* 22 full-time (12 women), 29 part-time (19 women); includes 1 minority (Asian American or Pacific Islander), 1 international. Average age 31. 41 applicants, 34% accepted, 10 enrolled. In 2009, 19 master's awarded. *Degree requirements:* For master's, thesis or alternative. *Entrance requirements:* For master's, GRE General Test. Additional exam requirements/recommendations for international students: Required—TOEFL (minimum score 550 paper-based; 213 computer-based; 80 iBT). *Application deadline:* For fall admission, 6/1 for domestic students, 4/1 for international students; for spring admission, 12/1 for domestic students. Applications are processed on a rolling basis. Application fee: $65. Electronic applications accepted. *Expenses:* Tuition, state resident: full-time $10,380; part-time $577 per credit hour. Tuition, nonresident: full-time $24,350; part-time $1002 per credit hour. Required fees: $1550; $387.50 per semester. Tuition and fees vary according to course load and program. *Financial support:* In 2009–10, 24 students received support, including 2 fellowships, 11 research assistantships, 11 teaching assistantships; career-related internships or fieldwork, Federal Work-Study, scholarships/grants, and tuition waivers (full and partial) also available. Support available to part-time students. Financial award application deadline: 2/15. *Unit head:* Dr. John Halstead, Chairperson, 603-862-3950, E-mail: natural.resources@unh.edu. *Application contact:* Linda Scogin, Administrative Assistant, 603-862-3932, E-mail: natural.resources@unh.edu.

University of New Hampshire, Graduate School, College of Life Sciences and Agriculture, Department of Resource Economics and Development, Program in Resource Administration, Durham, NH 03824. Offers MS. Part-time programs available. *Faculty:* 4 full-time (0 women), 1 (woman) part-time/adjunct. *Students:* 2 full-time (both women), 1 (woman) part-time. Average age 33. 4 applicants, 100% accepted, 2 enrolled. In 2009, 2 master's awarded. *Degree requirements:* For master's, thesis or alternative. *Entrance requirements:* For master's, GRE General Test. Additional exam requirements/recommendations for international students: Required—TOEFL (minimum score 550 paper-based; 213 computer-based; 80 iBT). *Application deadline:* For fall admission, 6/1 priority date for domestic students, 4/1 for international students; for spring admission, 12/1 for domestic students. Applications are processed on a rolling basis. Application fee: $65. Electronic applications accepted. *Expenses:* Tuition, state resident: full-time $10,380; part-time $577 per credit hour. Tuition, nonresident: full-time $24,350; part-time $1002 per credit hour. Required fees: $1550; $387.50 per semester. Tuition and fees vary according to course load and program. *Financial support:* In 2009–10, 2 students received support, including 2 teaching assistantships; fellowships, research assistantships, career-related internships or fieldwork, Federal Work-Study, and scholarships/grants also available. Support available to part-time students. Financial award application deadline: 2/15.

University of New Hampshire, Graduate School, College of Life Sciences and Agriculture, Department of Resource Economics and Development, Program in Resource Economics, Durham, NH 03824. Offers MS. Part-time programs available. *Faculty:* 6 full-time. *Students:* 1 full-time (0 women). Average age 23. 4 applicants, 0% accepted, 0 enrolled. *Degree requirements:* For master's, thesis or alternative. *Entrance requirements:* For master's, GRE General Test. Additional exam requirements/recommendations for international students: Required—TOEFL (minimum score 550 paper-based; 213 computer-based; 80 iBT). *Application deadline:* For fall admission, 6/1 for domestic students, 4/1 for international students; for spring admission, 12/1 for domestic students. Applications are processed on a rolling basis. Application fee: $65. Electronic applications accepted. *Expenses:* Tuition, state resident: full-time $10,380; part-time $577 per credit hour. Tuition, nonresident: full-time $24,350; part-time $1002 per credit hour. Required fees: $1550; $387.50 per semester. Tuition and fees vary according to course load and program. *Financial support:* Fellowships, research assistantships, teaching assistantships, career-related internships or fieldwork and Federal Work-Study available. Support available to part-time students. Financial award application deadline: 2/15. *Unit head:* Dr. John Halstea, Chairperson, 603-862-3914. *Application contact:* Dr. John Halstea, Chairperson, 603-862-3914.

University of New Hampshire, Graduate School, Interdisciplinary Programs, Doctoral Program in Natural Resources and Earth System Science, Durham, NH 03824. Offers earth and environmental science (PhD), including geology, oceanography; natural resources and environmental studies (PhD). *Faculty:* 59 full-time (11 women). *Students:* 61 full-time (34 women), 18 part-time (6 women); includes 4 minority (2 Asian Americans or Pacific Islanders, 2 Hispanic Americans), 11 international. Average age 37. 22 applicants, 59% accepted, 8 enrolled. In 2009, 6 doctorates awarded. *Degree requirements:* For doctorate, thesis/dissertation. *Entrance requirements:* For doctorate, GRE (if from a non-US university). Additional exam requirements/recommendations for international students: Required—TOEFL (minimum score 550 paper-based; 213 computer-based; 80 iBT). *Application deadline:* For fall admission, 6/1 priority date for domestic students, 4/1 for international students; for spring admission, 12/1 for domestic students. Applications are processed on a rolling basis. Application fee: $65. Electronic applications accepted. *Expenses:* Tuition, state resident: full-time $10,380; part-time $577 per credit hour. Tuition, nonresident: full-time $24,350; part-time $1002 per credit hour. Required fees: $1550; $387.50 per semester. Tuition and fees vary according to course load and program. *Financial support:* In 2009–10, 43 students received support, including 12 fellowships, 18 research assistantships, 8 teaching assistantships; Federal Work-Study, scholarships/grants, and tuition waivers (full and partial) also available. Financial award application deadline: 2/15. *Faculty research:* Environmental and natural resource studies and management. *Unit head:* Dr. John Halstead, Chairperson, 603-862-3914. *Application contact:* Dr. Linda Scogin, Administrative Assistant, 603-862-3932, E-mail: nress.phd.program@unh.edu.

University of Northern British Columbia, Office of Graduate Studies, Prince George, BC V2N 4Z9, Canada. Offers business administration (Diploma); community health science (M Sc); disability management (MA); education (M Ed); first nations studies (MA); gender studies (MA); history (MA); interdisciplinary studies (MA); international studies (MA); mathematical, computer and physical sciences (M Sc); natural resources and environmental studies (M Sc, MA, MNRES, PhD); political science (MA); psychology (M Sc, PhD); social work (MSW). Part-time and evening/weekend programs available. Postbaccalaureate distance learning degree programs offered (no on-campus study). *Degree requirements:* For master's, thesis; for doctorate, thesis/dissertation. *Entrance requirements:* For master's, GRE, minimum B average in undergraduate course work; for doctorate, candidacy exam, minimum A average in graduate course work.

University of Oklahoma, Graduate College, College of Earth and Energy, School of Petroleum and Geological Engineering, Program in Petroleum Engineering, Norman, OK 73019-0390. Offers natural gas engineering (MS); petroleum engineering (MS, PhD). Part-time programs available. Postbaccalaureate distance learning degree programs offered (minimal on-campus study). *Students:* 74 full-time (15 women), 13 part-time (1 woman); includes 4 minority (1 African American, 2 Asian Americans or Pacific Islanders, 1 Hispanic American), 73 international. 103 applicants, 25% accepted, 19 enrolled. In 2009, 11 master's, 2 doctorates awarded. Terminal master's awarded for partial completion of doctoral program. *Degree requirements:* For master's, thesis optional, industrial team project or thesis; for doctorate, thesis/dissertation. *Entrance requirements:* For master's, GRE General Test, bachelor's degree in engineering, 3 letters of recommendation, minimum GPA of 3.0 during final 60 hours of undergraduate course work; for doctorate, GRE General Test, minimum GPA of 3.0, 3 letters of recommendation. Additional exam requirements/recommendations for international students: Required—TOEFL (minimum score 550 paper-based; 213 computer-based). *Application deadline:* For fall admission, 6/1 priority date for domestic students, 4/1 for international students; for spring admission, 11/1 for domestic students, 9/1 for international students. Applications are processed on a rolling basis. Application fee: $40 ($90 for international students). Electronic applications accepted. *Expenses:* Tuition, state resident: full-time $3744; part-time $156 per credit hour. Tuition, nonresident: full-time $13,577; part-time $565.70 per credit hour. Required fees: $2415; $90.10 per credit hour. *Financial support:* In 2009–10, 67 students received support. Career-related internships or fieldwork, health care benefits, and unspecified assistantships available. Financial award application deadline: 4/15; financial award applicants required to submit FAFSA. *Faculty research:* Petrophysics, history watching, well-bore stimulation, unconventional reservoirs. *Unit head:* Dr. Chandra Rai, Director, 405-325-2921, Fax: 405-325-7477, E-mail: crai@ou.edu. *Application contact:* Dr. Dean Oliver, Professor, 405-325-0189, Fax: 405-325-7477, E-mail: dsoliver@ou.edu.

University of Rhode Island, Graduate School, College of the Environment and Life Sciences, Department of Environmental and Natural Resource Economics, Kingston, RI 02881. Offers MESM, MS, PhD. Part-time programs available. *Faculty:* 6 full-time (2 women), 2 part-time/adjunct (0 women). *Students:* 24 full-time (9 women), 8 part-time (4 women); includes 3 minority (1 African American, 2 Hispanic Americans), 11 international. In 2009, 4 master's, 4 doctorates awarded. *Degree requirements:* For master's, comprehensive exam (for some programs), thesis optional; for doctorate, comprehensive exam, thesis/dissertation. *Entrance requirements:* For master's, GRE, 2 letters of recommendation; for doctorate, GRE, 3 letters of recommendation. Additional exam requirements/recommendations for international students: Required—TOEFL (minimum score 550 paper-based; 213 computer-based). *Application deadline:* For fall admission, 7/15 for domestic students, 2/1 for international students; for spring admission, 11/15 for domestic students, 7/15 for international students. Application fee: $65. Electronic applications accepted. *Expenses:* Tuition, state resident: full-time $8828; part-time $490 per credit hour. Tuition, nonresident: full-time $22,100; part-time $1228 per credit hour. Required fees: $1118; $57 per semester. Tuition and fees vary according to program. *Financial support:* In 2009–10, 1 research assistantship with partial tuition reimbursement (averaging $6,947 per year), 6 teaching assistantships with full and partial tuition reimbursements (averaging $11,145 per year) were awarded. Financial award application deadline: 7/15; financial award applicants required to submit FAFSA. *Faculty research:* The Policy Simulation Laboratory utilizes computer technologies to help understand the consequences of policy actions, experimental economics. Total annual research expenditures: $654,763. *Unit head:* Dr. James L. Anderson, Chair, 401-874-4568, Fax: 401-874-4766, E-mail: jla@uri.edu. *Application contact:* Dr. Christopher M. Anderson, Director of Graduate Studies, 401-874-4587, Fax: 401-874-4766, E-mail: cma@uri.edu.

University of Rhode Island, Graduate School, College of the Environment and Life Sciences, Department of Natural Resources Science, Kingston, RI 02881. Offers MESM, MS, PhD. Part-time programs available. *Faculty:* 12 full-time (1 woman). *Students:* 31 full-time (22 women), 11 part-time (7 women); includes 1 minority (Hispanic American). In 2009, 11 master's, 3 doctorates awarded. *Degree requirements:* For master's, comprehensive exam (for some programs), thesis optional; for doctorate, comprehensive exam, thesis/dissertation. *Entrance requirements:* For master's and doctorate, GRE, 2 letters of recommendation. Additional exam requirements/recommendations for international students: Required—TOEFL (minimum score 550 paper-based; 213 computer-based). *Application deadline:* For fall admission, 7/15 for domestic students, 2/1 for international students; for spring admission, 11/15 for domestic students, 7/15 for international students. Application fee: $65. Electronic applications accepted. *Expenses:* Tuition, state resident: full-time $8828; part-time $490 per credit hour. Tuition, nonresident: full-time $22,100; part-time $1228 per credit hour. Required fees: $1118; $57 per semester. Tuition and fees vary according to program. *Financial support:* In 2009–10, 3 research assistantships with full and partial tuition reimbursements (averaging $10,649 per year), 8 teaching assistantships with full and partial tuition reimbursements (averaging $10,208 per year) were awarded. Financial award application deadline: 7/15; financial award applicants required to submit FAFSA. *Faculty research:* Spatial data modeling, ecological mapping, data integration for environmental applications. Total annual research expenditures: $2.9 million. *Unit head:* Dr. Peter Paton, Chair, 401-874-2986, Fax: 401-874-4561, E-mail: ppaton@uri.edu. *Application contact:* Dr. Francis C. Golet, Director of Graduate Studies, 401-874-2916, Fax: 401-874-4561, E-mail: fgswamps@uri.edu.

University of San Francisco, College of Arts and Sciences, Program in Environmental Management, San Francisco, CA 94117-1080. Offers MS, MS/MBA. Evening/weekend programs available. *Faculty:* 5 full-time (2 women), 4 part-time/adjunct (1 woman). *Students:* 67 full-time (39 women), 18 part-time (9 women); includes 19 minority (2 African Americans, 11 Asian Americans or Pacific Islanders, 6 Hispanic Americans), 2 international. Average age 30. 137 applicants, 43% accepted, 40 enrolled. In 2009, 21 master's awarded. *Degree requirements:* For master's, thesis. *Entrance requirements:* For master's, 3 semesters of course work in chemistry, minimum GPA of 2.7, work experience in environmental field. *Application deadline:* For fall admission, 3/1 priority date for domestic students. Applications are processed on a rolling basis. Application fee: $55 ($65 for international students). *Expenses:* Tuition: Full-time $19,710; part-time $1095 per unit. Part-time tuition and fees vary according to degree level, campus/location and program. *Financial support:* In 2009–10, 63 students received support; teaching assistantships, career-related internships or fieldwork available. Financial award application deadline: 3/2; financial award applicants required to submit FAFSA. *Faculty research:* Problems of environmental managers, water quality, hazardous materials, environmental health. *Unit head:* Dr. John Callaway, Chair, 415-422-6553, Fax: 415-422-6387. *Application contact:* Information Contact, 415-422-5135, Fax: 415-422-2217, E-mail: asgraduate@usfca.edu.

University of South Africa, College of Agriculture and Environmental Sciences, Pretoria, South Africa. Offers agriculture (MS); consumer science (MCS); environmental management (MA, MS, PhD); environmental science (MA, MS, PhD); geography (MA, MS, PhD); horticulture (M Tech); human ecology (MHE); life sciences (MS); nature conservation (M Tech).

The University of Texas at Austin, Graduate School, Cockrell School of Engineering, Department of Petroleum and Geosystems Engineering, Program in Energy and Earth Resources, Austin, TX 78712-1111. Offers MA. *Degree requirements:* For master's, thesis, seminar. *Entrance requirements:* For master's, GRE General Test. Additional exam requirements/recommendations for international students: Required—TOEFL. Electronic applications accepted.

University of Vermont, Graduate College, The Rubenstein School of Environment and Natural Resources, Program in Natural Resources, Burlington, VT 05405. Offers natural resources (MS, PhD), including aquatic ecology and watershed science (MS), environment thought and culture (MS), environment, science and public affairs (MS), forestry (MS). *Students:* 108 (55 women); includes 14 minority (2 African Americans, 1 American Indian/Alaska Native, 7 Asian Americans or Pacific Islanders, 4 Hispanic Americans), 7 international. 167 applicants, 28% accepted, 12 enrolled. In 2009, 18 master's, 2 doctorates awarded. *Degree requirements:* For master's, thesis or alternative; for doctorate, thesis/dissertation. *Entrance requirements:* For master's and doctorate, GRE General Test. Additional exam requirements/recommendations for international students: Required—TOEFL (minimum score 550 paper-based; 213 computer-based; 80 iBT). *Application deadline:* For fall admission, 3/1 priority date for domestic students. Applications are processed on a rolling basis. Application fee: $40. Electronic applications accepted. *Expenses:* Tuition, area resident: Part-time $508 per credit hour. Tuition, state resident: part-time $508 per credit hour. Tuition, nonresident: part-time $1281 per credit hour. *Financial support:* Fellowships, research assistantships, teaching assistantships available. Financial award application deadline: 3/1. *Unit head:* Dr. Mary Watzin, Coordinator, 802-656-2620. *Application contact:* Dr. Mary Watzin, Coordinator, 802-656-2620.

University of Washington, Graduate School, College of Forest Resources, Seattle, WA 98195. Offers bioresource science and engineering (MS, PhD); environmental horticulture (MEH); environmental horticulture and urban forestry (MS, PhD); forest ecology (MS, PhD); forest management (MFR); forest soils (MS, PhD); forest systems and bioenergy (MS, PhD); restoration ecology (MS, PhD); social sciences (MS, PhD); sustainable resource management (MS, PhD); wildlife science (MS, PhD); MFR/MAIS; MPA/MS. *Accreditation:* SAF. *Degree requirements:* For master's, thesis (for some programs); for doctorate, comprehensive exam (for some programs), thesis/dissertation. *Entrance requirements:* For master's and doctorate, GRE, minimum GPA of 3.0. Additional exam requirements/recommendations for international students: Required—TOEFL. Electronic applications accepted. *Faculty research:* Ecosystem analysis, silviculture and forest protection, paper science and engineering, environmental horticulture and urban forestry, natural resource policy and economics.

University of Wisconsin–Madison, Graduate School, Gaylord Nelson Institute for Environmental Studies, Environment and Resources Program, Madison, WI 53706-1380. Offers MS, PhD. Part-time programs available. *Degree requirements:* For master's, thesis; for doctorate, thesis/dissertation. *Entrance requirements:* For master's and doctorate, GRE General Test. Additional exam requirements/recommendations for international students: Required—TOEFL (minimum score 550 paper-based; 213 computer-based; 79 iBT). Electronic applications accepted. *Expenses:* Tuition, state resident: part-time $594 per credit. Tuition, nonresident: part-time $1504 per credit. Required fees: $65 per credit. Tuition and fees vary according to course load, program and reciprocity agreements. *Faculty research:* Land use issues, soil science/watershed management, geographic information systems, environmental law/justice, waste management.

University of Wisconsin–Stevens Point, College of Natural Resources, Stevens Point, WI 54481-3897. Offers MS. Part-time programs available. *Students:* 27 full-time (15 women), 35 part-time (17 women); includes 1 American Indian/Alaska Native. In 2009, 33 master's awarded. *Degree requirements:* For master's, thesis or alternative. *Entrance requirements:* For master's, GRE. *Application deadline:* For fall admission, 3/15 priority date for domestic students; for spring admission, 11/15 for domestic students. Applications are processed on a rolling basis. Application fee: $45. *Expenses:* Tuition, state resident: full-time $7740; part-time $430 per credit hour. Tuition, nonresident: full-time $17,804; part-time $989 per credit hour. Tuition and fees vary according to course load and reciprocity agreements. *Financial support:* Research assistantships, teaching assistantships, career-related internships or fieldwork, Federal Work-Study, and unspecified assistantships available. Support available to part-time students. Financial award application deadline: 5/1; financial award applicants required to submit FAFSA. *Faculty research:* Wildlife management, environmental education, fisheries, forestry, resource policy and planning. *Unit head:* Dr. Christine Thomas, Dean, 715-346-4617, Fax: 715-346-3624. *Application contact:* Catherine Glennon, Director of Admissions, 715-346-2441, E-mail: admiss@uwsp.edu.

University of Wyoming, College of Agriculture, Department of Renewable Resources, Laramie, WY 82070. Offers agroecology (MS); entomology (MS, PhD); entomology/water resources (MS, PhD); rangeland ecology and watershed management (MS, PhD), including soil sciences (PhD), soil sciences and water resources (MS); rangeland ecology and watershed management/water resources (MS, PhD); soil science (MS); soil science/water resources (PhD). Part-time programs available. *Degree requirements:* For master's, comprehensive exam, thesis, oral examination; for doctorate, comprehensive exam, thesis/dissertation, preliminary oral and written exam, oral final exam. *Entrance requirements:* For master's and doctorate, GRE General Test, minimum GPA of 3.0. Additional exam requirements/recommendations for international students: Required—TOEFL. Electronic applications accepted. *Faculty research:* Plant control, grazing management, riparian restoration, riparian management, reclamation.

University of Wyoming, College of Arts and Sciences, Department of Geography, Program in Rural Planning and Natural Resources, Laramie, WY 82070. Offers community and regional planning and natural resources (MP). *Degree requirements:* For master's, thesis or alternative. *Entrance requirements:* For master's, GRE General Test, minimum GPA of 3.0. Additional exam requirements/recommendations for international students: Required—TOEFL. *Faculty research:* Rural and small town planning, public land management.

Utah State University, School of Graduate Studies, College of Natural Resources, Interdisciplinary Program in Natural Resources, Logan, UT 84322. Offers MNR. *Entrance requirements:* For master's, GRE General Test, minimum GPA of 3.0. Additional exam requirements/recommendations for international students: Required—TOEFL. *Faculty research:* Ecosystem management, human dimensions, quantitative methods, informative management.

Virginia Polytechnic Institute and State University, Graduate School, College of Natural Resources, Program in Natural Resources, Blacksburg, VA 24061. Offers MNR. Program is interdisciplinary. *Entrance requirements:* Additional exam requirements/recommendations for international students: Required—TOEFL (minimum score 550 paper-based; 213 computer-based). Electronic applications accepted.

Virginia Polytechnic Institute and State University, VT Online, Blacksburg, VA 24061. Offers aerospace engineering (MS); business information systems (Graduate Certificate); career and technical education (MS); computer engineering (M Eng, MS); decision support systems (Graduate Certificate); eLearning leadership (MA); electrical engineering (M Eng, MS); engineering administration (MEA); environmental politics and policy (Graduate Certificate); foundations of political analysis (Graduate Certificate); health product risk management (Graduate Certificate); information policy and society (Graduate Certificate); information security (Graduate Certificate); instructional technology (MA); liberal arts (Graduate Certificate); life sciences: health product risk management (MS); natural resources (MNR, Graduate Certificate); networking (Graduate Certificate); nonprofit and nongovernmental organization management (Graduate Certificate); ocean engineering (MS); political science (MA); security studies (Graduate Certificate); software development (Graduate Certificate).

Washington State University, Graduate School, College of Sciences, Programs in Environmental Science and Regional Planning, Program in Environmental and Natural Resource Sciences, Pullman, WA 99164. Offers PhD.

Washington State University, Graduate School, College of Sciences, School of Earth and Environmental Sciences, Department of Natural Resource Sciences, Program in Environmental Science, Pullman, WA 99164. Offers environmental and natural resource sciences (PhD); environmental science (MS). *Faculty:* 7. *Students:* 42 full-time (24 women), 34 part-time (17 women); includes 8 minority (1 African American, 2 American Indian/Alaska Native, 3 Asian Americans or Pacific Islanders, 2 Hispanic Americans), 2 international. Average age 29. 76 applicants, 32% accepted, 18 enrolled. In 2009, 15 master's awarded. *Degree requirements:* For master's, comprehensive exam (for some programs), thesis (for some programs), oral exam; for doctorate, comprehensive exam, thesis/dissertation, oral exam, written exam. *Entrance requirements:* For doctorate, minimum GPA of 3.0. Additional exam requirements/recommendations for international students: Required—TOEFL, IELTS. *Application deadline:* For fall admission, 1/10 priority date for domestic students, 1/10 for international students. Applications are processed on a rolling basis. Application fee: $50. *Financial support:* In 2009–10, 16 students received support, including 1 fellowship (averaging $3,000 per year), 4 research assistantships with full and partial tuition reimbursements available (averaging $13,917 per year), 4 teaching assistantships with full and partial tuition reimbursements available (averaging $13,506 per year); Federal Work-Study, institutionally sponsored loans, and tuition waivers (partial) also available. Financial award application deadline: 2/15; financial award applicants required to submit FAFSA. *Unit head:* Dr. John A. Wolff, Head, 509-335-2825, E-mail: jawolff@mail.wsu.edu. *Application contact:* Graduate School Admissions, 800-GRADWSU, Fax: 509-335-1949, E-mail: gradsch@wsu.edu.

West Virginia University, College of Business and Economics, Division of Economics and Finance, Morgantown, WV 26506. Offers business analysis (MA); developmental financial economics (PhD); environmental and resource economics (PhD); international economics (PhD); mathematical economics (MA); monetary economics (PhD); public finance (PhD); public policy (MA); regional and urban economics (PhD); statistics and economics (MA). Terminal master's awarded for partial completion of doctoral program. *Degree requirements:* For master's, thesis optional; for doctorate, comprehensive exam, thesis/dissertation. *Entrance requirements:* For master's and doctorate, GRE General Test, minimum GPA of 3.0; course work in intermediate microeconomics, intermediate macroeconomics, calculus, and statistics. Additional exam requirements/recommendations for international students: Required—TOEFL. Electronic applications accepted. *Faculty research:* Financial economics, regional/urban development, public economics, international trade/international finance/development economics, monetary economics.

West Virginia University, Davis College of Agriculture, Forestry and Consumer Sciences, Division of Resource Management and Sustainable Development, Program in Resource Management and Sustainable Development, Morgantown, WV 26506. Offers PhD. Part-time programs available. *Degree requirements:* For doctorate, thesis/dissertation. *Entrance requirements:* For doctorate, GRE General Test. Additional exam requirements/recommendations for international students: Required—TOEFL.

Range Science

Colorado State University, Graduate School, Warner College of Natural Resources, Department of Forest, Rangeland, and Watershed Stewardship, Fort Collins, CO 80523-1472. Offers forest sciences (MS, PhD); natural resources stewardship (MNRS); rangeland ecosystem science (MS, PhD); watershed science (MS). Part-time programs available. Postbaccalaureate distance learning degree programs offered (no on-campus study). *Faculty:* 21 full-time (5 women), 1 part-time/adjunct (0 women). *Students:* 47 full-time (23 women), 76 part-time (21 women); includes 9 minority (3 American Indian/Alaska Native, 1 Asian American or Pacific Islander, 5 Hispanic Americans), 7 international. Average age 33. 53 applicants, 81% accepted, 33 enrolled. In 2009, 26 master's, 7 doctorates awarded. *Degree requirements:* For master's, thesis (for some programs); for doctorate, comprehensive exam, thesis/dissertation. *Entrance requirements:* For master's, GRE General Test (minimum score 1000 verbal and quantitative), minimum GPA of 3.0, 3 letters of recommendation; for doctorate, GRE General Test (combined minimum score of 1100 on the Verbal and Quantitative sections), minimum GPA of 3.0, 3 letters of recommendation, statement of research interest. Additional exam requirements/recommendations for international students: Required—TOEFL (minimum score 550 paper-based; 213 computer-based; 80 iBT), IELTS (minimum score 6). *Application deadline:* For fall admission, 8/1 priority date for domestic students, 6/25 priority date for international students; for spring admission, 12/1 priority date for domestic students, 11/25 priority date for international students. Applications are processed on a rolling basis. Application fee: $50. Electronic applications accepted. *Expenses:* Tuition, state resident: full-time $6434; part-time $359.10 per credit. Tuition, nonresident: full-time $18,116; part-time $1006.45 per credit. Required fees: $1496; $83 per credit. *Financial support:* In 2009–10, 43 students received support, including 3 fellowships (averaging $40,417 per year), 33 research assistantships with full and partial tuition reimbursements available (averaging $15,898 per year), 7 teaching assistantships with full and partial tuition reimbursements available (averaging $6,506 per year); Federal Work-Study, scholarships/grants, and unspecified assistantships also available. Financial award applicants required to submit FAFSA. *Faculty research:* Ecology, natural resource management, hydrology, restoration, human dimensions. Total annual research expenditures: $3.7 million. *Unit head:* Dr. N. Thompson Hobbs, Head, 970-491-6911, Fax: 970-491-6754, E-mail: nthobbs@warnercnr@colostate.edu. *Application contact:* Sonya LeFebre, Coordinator, 970-491-1907, Fax: 970-491-6754, E-mail: sonya.lefebre@colostate.edu.

Kansas State University, Graduate School, College of Agriculture, Department of Agronomy, Manhattan, KS 66506. Offers crop science (MS, PhD); range management (MS, PhD); soil science (MS, PhD); weed science (MS, PhD). Part-time programs available. *Faculty:* 32 full-time (4 women), 11 part-time/adjunct (1 woman). *Students:* 72 full-time (17 women); includes 1 minority (African American), 28 international. Average age 34. 16 applicants, 38% accepted, 6 enrolled. In 2009, 13 master's, 5 doctorates awarded. Terminal master's awarded for partial completion of doctoral program. *Degree requirements:* For master's, thesis or alternative, oral exam; for doctorate, thesis/dissertation, preliminary exams. *Entrance requirements:* For master's, minimum GPA of 3.0 in BS; for doctorate, minimum GPA of 3.5 in master's program. Additional exam requirements/recommendations for international students: Required—TOEFL (minimum score 500 paper-based; 250 computer-based). *Application deadline:* For fall admission, 2/1 priority date for domestic and international students; for spring admission, 8/1 priority date for domestic and international students. Applications are processed on a rolling basis. Application fee: $40 ($55 for international students). Electronic applications accepted. *Financial support:* In 2009–10, 60 research assistantships (averaging $16,061 per year) were awarded; teaching assistantships with partial tuition reimbursements, institutionally sponsored loans and scholarships/grants also available. Support available to part-time students. Financial award application deadline: 3/1; financial award applicants required to submit FAFSA. *Faculty research:* Range and forage science, soil and environmental science, crop physiology, weed science, plant breeding and genetics. Total annual research expenditures: $4.6 million. *Unit head:* Dr. Gary Pierzynski, Head, 785-532-6101, Fax: 785-532-6094, E-mail: gmp@ksu.edu. *Application contact:* Dr. Bill Schapaugh, Director, 785-532-7242, Fax: 785-532-6094, E-mail: wts@ksu.edu.

Range Science

Montana State University, College of Graduate Studies, College of Agriculture, Department of Animal and Range Sciences, Bozeman, MT 59717. Offers MS, PhD. Part-time programs available. *Faculty:* 13 full-time (4 women), 5 part-time/adjunct (0 women). *Students:* 5 full-time (3 women), 13 part-time (5 women), 1 international. Average age 33. 12 applicants, 33% accepted, 3 enrolled. In 2009, 1 doctorate awarded. *Degree requirements:* For master's, comprehensive exam; for doctorate, comprehensive exam, thesis/dissertation. *Entrance requirements:* For master's, GRE General Test, minimum GPA of 3.0; undergraduate course work in animal science, range science or a closely-related field; faculty adviser; for doctorate, GRE General Test. Additional exam requirements/recommendations for international students: Required—TOEFL (minimum score 550 paper-based; 213 computer-based). *Application deadline:* For fall admission, 7/15 priority date for domestic students, 5/15 priority date for international students; for spring admission, 12/1 priority date for domestic students, 10/1 priority date for international students. Applications are processed on a rolling basis. Application fee: $30. Electronic applications accepted. *Expenses:* Tuition, state resident: full-time $5635; part-time $3492 per year. Tuition, nonresident: full-time $17,212; part-time $7865.10 per year. Required fees: $1441.05; $153.15 per credit. Tuition and fees vary according to course load and program. *Financial support:* In 2009–10, 10 students received support, including 9 research assistantships with partial tuition reimbursements available (averaging $1,000 per year), 1 teaching assistantship with partial tuition reimbursement available (averaging $1,000 per year); scholarships/grants, health care benefits, tuition waivers (partial), and unspecified assistantships also available. Financial award application deadline: 3/1; financial award applicants required to submit FAFSA. *Faculty research:* Ruminant nutrition, ruminant reproductive physiology, wildlife habitat ecology, grazing ecology and management. Total annual research expenditures: $1.9 million. *Unit head:* Bret Olson, Interim Department Head, 406-994-3721, Fax: 406-994-5589, E-mail: bolson@montana.edu. *Application contact:* Dr. Carl A. Fox, Vice Provost for Graduate Education, 406-994-4145, Fax: 406-994-7433, E-mail: gradstudy@montana.edu.

New Mexico State University, Graduate School, College of Agricultural, Consumer and Environmental Sciences, Department of Animal and Range Sciences, Las Cruces, NM 88003-8001. Offers animal science (M Ag, MS, PhD); range science (M Ag, MS, PhD). Part-time programs available. *Faculty:* 5 full-time (1 woman). *Students:* 35 full-time (23 women), 7 part-time (1 woman); includes 7 minority (2 American Indian/Alaska Native, 5 Hispanic Americans), 4 international. Average age 28. 32 applicants, 88% accepted, 18 enrolled. In 2009, 6 master's, 4 doctorates awarded. Terminal master's awarded for partial completion of doctoral program. *Degree requirements:* For master's, thesis, seminar; for doctorate, thesis/dissertation, research tool. *Entrance requirements:* For master's, minimum GPA of 3.0 in last 60 hours of undergraduate course work (MS); for doctorate, minimum graduate GPA of 3.2. Additional exam requirements/recommendations for international students: Required—TOEFL (minimum score 530 paper-based; 197 computer-based). *Application deadline:* For fall admission, 7/1 priority date for domestic students; for spring admission, 11/1 for domestic students. Applications are processed on a rolling basis. Application fee: $30 ($50 for international students). Electronic applications accepted. *Expenses:* Tuition, state resident: full-time $4080; part-time $223 per credit. Tuition, nonresident: full-time $14,256; part-time $647 per credit. Required fees: $1278; $639 per semester. *Financial support:* In 2009–10, 2 research assistantships (averaging $20,760 per year), 23 teaching assistantships (averaging $20,624 per year) were awarded; Federal Work-Study and health care benefits also available. Support available to part-time students. Financial award application deadline: 3/1. *Faculty research:* Reproductive physiology, ruminant nutrition, nutrition toxicology, range ecology, wildland hydrology. *Unit head:* Dr. Tim Ross, Interim Head, 575-646-2514, Fax: 575-646-5441, E-mail: tross@nmsu.edu. *Application contact:* Dr. Tim Ross, Interim Head, 575-646-2514, Fax: 575-646-5441, E-mail: tross@nmsu.edu.

North Dakota State University, College of Graduate and Interdisciplinary Studies, College of Agriculture, Food Systems, and Natural Resources, Department of Animal and Range Sciences, Fargo, ND 58108. Offers animal science (MS, PhD); natural resource management (MS, PhD); range sciences (MS, PhD). *Faculty:* 32. *Students:* 18 full-time (10 women), 7 part-time (6 women); includes 1 American Indian/Alaska Native, 1 Asian American or Pacific Islander. Average age 25. 13 applicants, 62% accepted. In 2009, 17 master's, 2 doctorates awarded. *Degree requirements:* For master's, thesis; for doctorate, comprehensive exam, thesis/dissertation. *Entrance requirements:* For master's and doctorate, GRE General Test. Additional exam requirements/recommendations for international students: Required—TOEFL (minimum score 71 iBT). *Application deadline:* Applications are processed on a rolling basis. Application fee: $45 ($60 for international students). *Financial support:* In 2009–10, 1 fellowship with tuition reimbursement (averaging $18,000 per year), 29 research assistantships with tuition reimbursements (averaging $13,000 per year) were awarded; teaching assistantships, Federal Work-Study, institutionally sponsored loans, and tuition waivers (partial) also available. Financial award application deadline: 3/15. *Faculty research:* Reproduction, nutrition, meat and muscle biology, breeding/genetics. Total annual research expenditures: $1.5 million. *Unit head:* Dr. David Buchanan, Chair, 701-231-7643, Fax: 701-231-7590, E-mail: david.buchanan@ndsu.edu. *Application contact:* Dr. David Buchanan, Chair, 701-231-7643, Fax: 701-231-7590, E-mail: david.buchanan@ndsu.edu.

Oregon State University, Graduate School, College of Agricultural Sciences, Department of Rangeland Ecology and Management, Corvallis, OR 97331. Offers M Agr, MAIS, MS, PhD. *Faculty:* 8 full-time (0 women), 1 part-time/adjunct (0 women). *Students:* 7 full-time (3 women), 3 part-time (1 woman); includes 1 minority (American Indian/Alaska Native), 2 international. Average age 41. In 2009, 4 master's, 1 doctorate awarded. Terminal master's awarded for partial completion of doctoral program. *Degree requirements:* For master's, thesis (for some programs); for doctorate, thesis/dissertation. *Entrance requirements:* For master's and doctorate, GRE, minimum GPA of 3.0 in last 90 hours of course work. Additional exam requirements/recommendations for international students: Required—TOEFL. *Application deadline:* For fall admission, 6/1 priority date for domestic students; for spring admission, 12/15 for domestic students. Applications are processed on a rolling basis. Application fee: $50. *Expenses:* Tuition, state resident: full-time $9774; part-time $362 per credit. Tuition, nonresident: full-time $15,849; part-time $587 per credit. Required fees: $1639. Full-time tuition and fees vary according to course load and program. *Financial support:* Research assistantships, career-related internships or fieldwork, Federal Work-Study, and institutionally sponsored loans available. Support available to part-time students. Financial award application deadline: 2/1. *Faculty research:* Range ecology, watershed science, animal grazing, agroforestry. *Unit head:* Dr. Michael M. Borman, Interim Head, 541-737-1614, Fax: 541-737-0504, E-mail: michael.berman@oregonstate.edu. *Application contact:* Dr. Michael M. Borman, Interim Head, 541-737-1614, Fax: 541-737-0504, E-mail: michael.berman@oregonstate.edu.

Sul Ross State University, Division of Agricultural and Natural Resource Science, Program in Range and Wildlife Management, Alpine, TX 79832. Offers M Ag, MS. Part-time programs available. *Degree requirements:* For master's, thesis (for some programs). *Entrance requirements:* For master's, GRE General Test, minimum undergraduate GPA of 2.5 in last 60 hours.

Texas A&M University–Kingsville, College of Graduate Studies, College of Agriculture and Home Economics, Program in Range and Wildlife Management, Kingsville, TX 78363. Offers MS. *Degree requirements:* For master's, comprehensive exam, thesis or alternative. *Entrance requirements:* For master's, GRE General Test, minimum GPA of 3.0. Additional exam requirements/recommendations for international students: Required—TOEFL.

Texas Tech University, Graduate School, College of Agricultural Sciences and Natural Resources, Department of Natural Resources Management, Lubbock, TX 79409. Offers fisheries science (MS, PhD); range science (MS, PhD); wildlife science (MS, PhD). Part-time programs available. *Faculty:* 9 full-time (0 women), 1 part-time/adjunct (0 women). *Students:* 33 full-time (11 women), 1 part-time (0 women); includes 4 minority (1 Asian American or Pacific Islander, 3 Hispanic Americans), 4 international. Average age 28. 22 applicants, 50% accepted, 8 enrolled. In 2009, 8 master's, 2 doctorates awarded. *Degree requirements:* For master's, thesis; for doctorate, thesis/dissertation. *Entrance requirements:* For master's and doctorate, GRE General Test. Additional exam requirements/recommendations for international students: Required—TOEFL (minimum score 550 paper-based; 213 computer-based). *Application deadline:* For fall admission, 3/1 priority date for international students; for spring admission, 11/1 priority date for international students. Applications are processed on a rolling basis. Application fee: $50 ($75 for international students). Electronic applications accepted. *Expenses:* Tuition, state resident: full-time $5100; part-time $213 per credit hour. Tuition, nonresident: full-time $11,748; part-time $490 per credit hour. Required fees: $2298; $50 per credit hour. $555 per semester. *Financial support:* In 2009–10, 7 research assistantships with partial tuition reimbursements (averaging $18,972 per year), 2 teaching assistantships with partial tuition reimbursements (averaging $15,975 per year) were awarded; Federal Work-Study and institutionally sponsored loans also available. Support available to part-time students. Financial award application deadline: 4/15; financial award applicants required to submit FAFSA. *Faculty research:* Use of fire on range lands, big game, upland game, and waterfowl; playa lakes in the southern Great Plains; conservation biology; fish ecology and physiology. Total annual research expenditures: $509,586. *Unit head:* Dr. Philip S. Gipson, Chairman, 806-742-2841 Ext. 223, Fax: 806-742-2280, E-mail: philip.gipson@ttu.edu. *Application contact:* Renee Dillon, Sr. Business Assistant, 806-742-2841, E-mail: renee.dillon@ttu.edu.

The University of Arizona, Graduate College, College of Agriculture and Life Sciences, School of Natural Resources, Program in Rangeland Science and Management, Tucson, AZ 85721. Offers MS, PhD. *Students:* 1 (woman) part-time; minority (African American). Average age 39. *Degree requirements:* For master's, thesis; for doctorate, comprehensive exam, thesis/dissertation. *Entrance requirements:* For master's and doctorate, GRE General Test, minimum GPA of 3.0. Additional exam requirements/recommendations for international students: Required—TOEFL (minimum score 550 paper-based; 213 computer-based). *Application deadline:* Applications are processed on a rolling basis. Application fee: $75. *Expenses:* Tuition, state resident: full-time $9028. Tuition, nonresident: full-time $24,890. *Financial support:* Research assistantships, teaching assistantships, career-related internships or fieldwork, scholarships/grants, health care benefits, tuition waivers (partial), and unspecified assistantships available. *Faculty research:* Criteria for defining, mapping, and evaluating range sites; methods of establishing forage plants on southwestern range lands; plants for pollution and erosion control, beautification, and browse. *Application contact:* Cheryl L. Craddock, Academic Coordinator, 520-621-7260, Fax: 520-621-8801, E-mail: ccraddoc@email.arizona.edu.

University of California, Berkeley, Graduate Division, College of Natural Resources, Group in Range Management, Berkeley, CA 94720-1500. Offers MS. *Students:* 6 full-time (2 women). Average age 26. 7 applicants, 3 enrolled. *Degree requirements:* For master's, thesis. *Entrance requirements:* For master's, GRE General Test, minimum GPA of 3.0, 3 letters of recommendation. Additional exam requirements/recommendations for international students: Required—TOEFL. *Application deadline:* For fall admission, 12/1 for domestic students. Application fee: $70 ($90 for international students). *Financial support:* Fellowships, research assistantships with full tuition reimbursements, unspecified assistantships available. Financial award applicants required to submit FAFSA. *Faculty research:* Grassland and savannah ecology, wetland ecology, oak woodland classification, wildlife habitat management. *Unit head:* Prof. Barbara Allen-Diaz, Chair, 510-643-5438, E-mail: espmgrad@berkeley.edu. *Application contact:* Richard M. Battrick, Student Affairs Officer, 510-642-6410, Fax: 510-642-4034, E-mail: espmgrad@nature.berkeley.edu.

University of Idaho, College of Graduate Studies, College of Natural Resources, Department of Rangeland Ecology and Management, Moscow, ID 83844-2282. Offers MS, PhD. *Faculty:* 6 full-time, 1 part-time/adjunct. *Students:* 6 full-time, 7 part-time. In 2009, 6 master's awarded. *Degree requirements:* For doctorate, thesis/dissertation. *Entrance requirements:* For master's, minimum GPA of 2.8; for doctorate, minimum undergraduate GPA of 2.8, 3.0 graduate. *Application deadline:* For fall admission, 8/1 for domestic students; for spring admission, 12/15 for domestic students. Application fee: $55 ($60 for international students). *Expenses:* Tuition, state resident: full-time $6120. Tuition, nonresident: full-time $17,712. *Financial support:* Research assistantships, teaching assistantships available. Financial award application deadline: 2/15. *Faculty research:* Ecophysiology, fire ecology and management, invasive plant management, wildland restoration. *Unit head:* Dr. Karen L. Launchbaugh, Head, 208-885-4394. *Application contact:* Dr. Karen L. Launchbaugh, Head, 208-885-4394.

University of Wyoming, College of Agriculture, Department of Renewable Resources, Laramie, WY 82070. Offers agroecology (MS); entomology (MS, PhD); entomology/water resources (MS, PhD); rangeland ecology and watershed management (MS, PhD), including soil sciences (PhD), soil sciences and water resources (MS); rangeland ecology and watershed management/water resources (MS, PhD); soil science (MS); soil science/water resources (PhD). Part-time programs available. *Degree requirements:* For master's, comprehensive exam, thesis, oral examination; for doctorate, comprehensive exam, thesis/dissertation, preliminary oral and written exam, oral final exam. *Entrance requirements:* For master's and doctorate, GRE General Test, minimum GPA of 3.0. Additional exam requirements/recommendations for international students: Required—TOEFL. Electronic applications accepted. *Faculty research:* Plant control, grazing management, riparian restoration, riparian management, reclamation.

Utah State University, School of Graduate Studies, College of Natural Resources, Department of Wildland Resources, Logan, UT 84322. Offers ecology (MS, PhD); forestry (MS, PhD); range science (MS, PhD); wildlife biology (MS, PhD). Part-time programs available. *Degree requirements:* For master's, thesis; for doctorate, comprehensive exam, thesis/dissertation. *Entrance requirements:* For master's and doctorate, GRE General Test, minimum GPA of 3.0. Additional exam requirements/recommendations for international students: Required—TOEFL. *Faculty research:* Range plant ecophysiology, plant community ecology, ruminant nutrition, population ecology.

Water Resources

Albany State University, College of Arts and Humanities, Department of History, Political Science and Public Administration, Albany, GA 31705-2717. Offers community and economic development administration (MPA); criminal justice administration (MPA); fiscal management (MPA); general management (MPA); health administration and policy (MPA); human resources management (MPA); public policy (MPA); water resource management and policy (MPA). *Accreditation:* NASPAA. *Students:* 17 full-time (11 women), 43 part-time (29 women); includes 57 minority (56 African Americans, 1 Asian American or Pacific Islander). Average age 34. 21 applicants, 100% accepted, 17 enrolled. In 2009, 17 master's awarded. *Entrance requirements:* For master's, Graduate Record Examination (GRE) or Miller Analogies Test (MAT). *Application deadline:* For fall admission, 11/16 for domestic students, 9/16 for international students; for spring admission, 4/19 for domestic students, 2/19 for international students. Applications are processed on a rolling basis. Application fee: $20. Electronic applications accepted. *Expenses:* Tuition, state resident: full-time $2970; part-time $162 per credit hour. Tuition, nonresident: full-time $12,168; part-time $676 per credit hour. Required fees: $962; $75 per credit hour. *Financial support:* Application deadline: 6/30; *Faculty research:* Public policy, strategic public human resources and human capital management, diversity management in the public sector and collective bargaining and labor relations in the public sector, e-government and public sector information systems, public administration pedagogy and business process modeling simulation, funded research- community development, non profit organizations, civic engagement and civic participation, health care disparities among minorities and poverty. Total annual research expenditures: $26,000. *Unit head:* Dr. Peter Ngwafu, Director, 229-430-4873, Fax: 229-430-7895, E-mail: peter.ngwafu@asurams.edu. *Application contact:* Nicole Lane, Interim Graduate Admissions Officer, 229-430-4862, Fax: 229-430-6398, E-mail: nicole.lane@asurams.edu.

California State University, Monterey Bay, College of Science, Media Arts and Technology, Program in Coastal and Watershed Science and Policy, Seaside, CA 93955-8001. Offers MS. Part-time programs available. *Degree requirements:* For master's, thesis, thesis defense. *Entrance requirements:* For master's, GRE, ecommendations, interview. Additional exam requirements/recommendations for international students: Required—TOEFL (minimum score 525 paper-based; 213 computer-based; 71 iBT). Electronic applications accepted. *Faculty research:* Remote sensing and geospatial technology, MPA design, efficacy and management, marine science and ecology, watershed process, hydrology, restoration, sedim entology, ecosystem modeling.

Colorado State University, Graduate School, Warner College of Natural Resources, Department of Forest, Rangeland, and Watershed Stewardship, Fort Collins, CO 80523-1472. Offers forest sciences (MS, PhD); natural resources stewardship (MNRS); rangeland ecosystem science (MS, PhD); watershed science (MS). Part-time programs available. Postbaccalaureate distance learning degree programs offered (no on-campus study). *Faculty:* 21 full-time (5 women), 1 part-time/adjunct (0 women). *Students:* 47 full-time (23 women), 76 part-time (21 women); includes 9 minority (3 American Indian/Alaska Native, 1 Asian American or Pacific Islander, 5 Hispanic Americans), 7 international. Average age 33. 53 applicants, 81% accepted, 33 enrolled. In 2009, 26 master's, 7 doctorates awarded. *Degree requirements:* For master's, thesis (for some programs); for doctorate, comprehensive exam, thesis/dissertation. *Entrance requirements:* For master's, GRE General Test (minimum score 1000 verbal and quantitative), minimum GPA of 3.0, 3 letters of recommendation; for doctorate, GRE General Test (combined minimum score of 1100 on the Verbal and Quantitative sections), minimum GPA of 3.0, 3 letters of recommendation, statement of research interest. Additional exam requirements/recommendations for international students: Required—TOEFL (minimum score 550 paper-based; 213 computer-based; 80 iBT), IELTS (minimum score 6). *Application deadline:* For fall admission, 8/1 priority date for domestic students, 6/25 priority date for international students; for spring admission, 12/1 priority date for domestic students, 11/25 priority date for international students. Applications are processed on a rolling basis. Application fee: $50. Electronic applications accepted. *Expenses:* Tuition, state resident: full-time $6434; part-time $359.10 per credit. Tuition, nonresident: full-time $18,116; part-time $1006.45 per credit. Required fees: $1496; $83 per credit. *Financial support:* In 2009–10, 43 students received support, including 3 fellowships (averaging $40,417 per year), 33 research assistantships with full and partial tuition reimbursements available (averaging $15,898 per year), 7 teaching assistantships with full and partial tuition reimbursements available (averaging $6,506 per year); Federal Work-Study, scholarships/grants, and unspecified assistantships also available. Financial award applicants required to submit FAFSA. *Faculty research:* Ecology, natural resource management, hydrology, restoration, human dimensions. Total annual research expenditures: $3.7 million. *Unit head:* Dr. N. Thompson Hobbs, Head, 970-491-6911, Fax: 970-491-6754, E-mail: nthobbs@warnercnr@colostate.edu. *Application contact:* Sonya LeFebre, Coordinator, 970-491-1907, Fax: 970-491-6754, E-mail: sonya.lefebre@colostate.edu.

Duke University, Nicholas School of the Environment, Durham, NC 27708-0328. Offers coastal environmental management (MEM); DEL-environmental leadership (MEM); energy and environment (MEM); environmental economics and policy (MEM); environmental health and security (MEM); forest resource management (MF); global environmental change (MEM); resource ecology (MEM); water and air resources (MEM); JD/AM; JD/MEM; JD/MF; MAT/MEM; MBA/MEM; MBA/MF; MEM/MPP; MF/MPP. *Accreditation:* SAF (one or more programs are accredited). Part-time programs available. *Degree requirements:* For master's, thesis. *Entrance requirements:* For master's, GRE General Test, previous course work in biology or ecology, calculus, statistics, and microeconomics; computer familiarity with word processing and data analysis. Additional exam requirements/recommendations for international students: Required—TOEFL (minimum score 550 paper-based; 213 computer-based). Electronic applications accepted. *Expenses:* Contact institution. *Faculty research:* Ecosystem management, conservation ecology, earth systems, risk assessment.

Eastern Michigan University, Graduate School, College of Arts and Sciences, Department of Biology, Ypsilanti, MI 48197. Offers cell and molecular biology (MS); community college biology teaching (MS); ecology and organismal biology (MS); general biology (MS); water resources (MS). Part-time and evening/weekend programs available. Postbaccalaureate distance learning degree programs offered (minimal on-campus study). *Faculty:* 20 full-time (5 women). *Students:* 10 full-time (8 women), 35 part-time (21 women); includes 3 minority (2 African Americans, 1 Asian American or Pacific Islander), 7 international. Average age 28. 57 applicants, 63% accepted, 20 enrolled. In 2009, 17 master's awarded. *Entrance requirements:* For master's, GRE General Test, GRE Subject Test. Additional exam requirements/recommendations for international students: Required—TOEFL. *Application deadline:* Applications are processed on a rolling basis. Application fee: $35. Tuition and fees vary according to course level. *Financial support:* In 2009–10, 22 teaching assistantships with full tuition reimbursements (averaging $8,660 per year) were awarded; fellowships, research assistantships with full tuition reimbursements, career-related internships or fieldwork, Federal Work-Study, institutionally sponsored loans, scholarships/grants, tuition waivers (partial), and unspecified assistantships also available. Support available to part-time students. Financial award applicants required to submit FAFSA. *Unit head:* Dr. Marianne Laporte, Department Head, 734-487-4242, Fax: 734-487-9235, E-mail: mlaporte@emich.edu. *Application contact:* Dr. Marianne Laporte, Department Head, 734-487-4242, Fax: 734-487-9235, E-mail: mlaporte@emich.edu.

Eastern Michigan University, Graduate School, College of Arts and Sciences, Department of Geography and Geology, Programs in Geography and Geology, Ypsilanti, MI 48197. Offers geography (MA, MS); water resources (Graduate Certificate). Part-time and evening/weekend programs available. Postbaccalaureate distance learning degree programs offered (minimal on-campus study). *Degree requirements:* For master's, thesis optional. *Entrance requirements:* Additional exam requirements/recommendations for international students: Required—TOEFL. *Application deadline:* Applications are processed on a rolling basis. Application fee: $35. Tuition and fees vary according to course level. *Financial support:* Fellowships, research assistantships with full tuition reimbursements, teaching assistantships with full tuition reimbursements, career-related internships or fieldwork, Federal Work-Study, institutionally sponsored loans, traineeships, and unspecified assistantships available. Support available to part-time students. Financial award applicants required to submit FAFSA. *Application contact:* Dr. Andrew Nazzaro, Program Advisor, 734-487-0218, Fax: 734-487-6979, E-mail: andrew.nazzaro@emich.edu.

Humboldt State University, Graduate Studies, College of Natural Resources and Sciences, Programs in Natural Resources, Arcata, CA 95521-8299. Offers natural resources (MS), including fisheries, forestry, natural resources planning and interpretation, rangeland resources and wildland soils, wastewater utilization, watershed management, wildlife. *Students:* 51 full-time (22 women), 26 part-time (10 women); includes 4 minority (1 American Indian/Alaska Native, 1 Asian American or Pacific Islander, 2 Hispanic Americans), 1 international. Average age 31. 81 applicants, 26% accepted, 15 enrolled. In 2009, 25 master's awarded. *Degree requirements:* For master's, thesis or alternative. *Entrance requirements:* For master's, GRE, appropriate bachelor's degree, minimum GPA of 2.5, 3 letters of recommendation, resume. Additional exam requirements/recommendations for international students: Required—TOEFL (minimum score 500 paper-based; 173 computer-based). *Application deadline:* For fall admission, 2/1 for domestic and international students; for spring admission, 9/30 for domestic and international students. Applications are processed on a rolling basis. Application fee: $55. *Expenses:* Tuition, nonresident: full-time $8928. Required fees: $6102. Tuition and fees vary according to program. *Financial support:* Fellowships, career-related internships or fieldwork and Federal Work-Study available. Support available to part-time students. Financial award application deadline: 3/1; financial award applicants required to submit FAFSA. *Faculty research:* Spotted owl habitat, pre-settlement vegetation, hardwood utilization, tree physiology, fisheries. *Unit head:* Dr. Gary Hendrickson, Coordinator, 707-826-4233, E-mail: thiesfel@humboldt.edu. *Application contact:* Julie Tucker, Administrative Support Coordinator, 707-826-3256, E-mail: jlt7002@humboldt.edu.

Inter American University of Puerto Rico, San Germán Campus, Graduate Studies Center, Program in Environmental Sciences, San Germán, PR 00683-5008. Offers environmental biology (MS); environmental chemistry (MS); water analysis (MS). Part-time and evening/weekend programs available. *Degree requirements:* For master's, comprehensive exam, thesis. *Entrance requirements:* For master's, GRE General Test or EXADEP, minimum GPA of 3.0. *Faculty research:* Environmental biology, environmental chemistry, water resources and unit operations.

Missouri University of Science and Technology, Graduate School, Department of Geological Sciences and Engineering, Rolla, MO 65409. Offers geological engineering (MS, DE, PhD); geology and geophysics (MS, PhD), including geochemistry, geology, geophysics, groundwater and environmental geology; petroleum engineering (MS, DE, PhD). Part-time programs available. *Degree requirements:* For master's, thesis optional; for doctorate, comprehensive exam, thesis/dissertation. *Entrance requirements:* For master's, GRE General Test (minimum score 600 quantitative, writing 3.5), minimum GPA of 3.0 in last 4 semesters; for doctorate, GRE General Test (minimum: Q 600, GRE WR 3.5). Additional exam requirements/recommendations for international students: Required—TOEFL. Electronic applications accepted. *Faculty research:* Digital image processing and geographic information systems, mineralogy, igneous and sedimentary petrology-geochemistry, sedimentology groundwater hydrology and contaminant transport.

Montclair State University, The Graduate School, College of Science and Mathematics, Department of Earth and Environmental Studies, Montclair, NJ 07043-1624. Offers earth science (Certificate); environmental management (MA, D Env M); environmental studies (MS), including environmental education, environmental health, environmental management, environmental science; geographic information science (Certificate); geoscience (MS, Certificate), including geoscience (MS), water resource management (Certificate). Part-time and evening/weekend programs available. *Faculty:* 16 full-time (2 women), 13 part-time/adjunct (4 women). *Students:* 36 full-time (17 women), 60 part-time (26 women). Average age 34. 42 applicants, 60% accepted, 17 enrolled. In 2009, 11 degrees awarded. *Degree requirements:* For master's, comprehensive exam, thesis or alternative; for doctorate, thesis/dissertation. *Entrance requirements:* For master's, GRE General Test, 2 letters of recommendation; for doctorate, GRE General Test, 3 letters of recommendation. Additional exam requirements/recommendations for international students: Required—TOEFL (minimum score 83 computer-based), or IELTS. *Application deadline:* For fall admission, 6/1 for international students; for spring admission, 10/1 for international students. Applications are processed on a rolling basis. Application fee: $60. Electronic applications accepted. *Expenses:* Tuition, area resident: Part-time $486.74 per credit. Tuition, state resident: part-time $486.74 per credit. Tuition, nonresident: part-time $751.34 per credit. Tuition and fees vary according to degree level and program. *Financial support:* In 2009–10, 3 fellowships (averaging $15,000 per year), 12 research assistantships with full tuition reimbursements (averaging $8,500 per year), 11 teaching assistantships with full tuition reimbursements (averaging $15,000 per year) were awarded; Federal Work-Study, scholarships/grants, and unspecified assistantships also available. Support available to part-time students. Financial award application deadline: 3/1; financial award applicants required to submit FAFSA. *Faculty research:* Antarctica, carbon pools, contaminated sediments, wetlands. *Unit head:* Dr. Duke Ophori, Chairperson, 973-655-7558. *Application contact:* Amy Aiello, Director of Graduate Admissions and Operations, 973-655-5147, Fax: 973-655-7869, E-mail: graduate.school@montclair.edu.

Nova Scotia Agricultural College, Research and Graduate Studies, Truro, NS B2N 5E3, Canada. Offers agriculture (M Sc), including air quality, animal behavior, animal molecular genetics, animal nutrition, animal technology, aquaculture, botany, crop management, crop physiology, ecology, environmental microbiology, food science, horticulture, nutrient management, pest management, physiology, plant biotechnology, plant pathology, soil chemistry, soil fertility, waste management and composting, water quality. Part-time programs available. *Degree requirements:* For master's, thesis, ATC Exam Teaching Assistantship. *Entrance requirements:* For master's, honors B Sc, minimum GPA of 3.0. Additional exam requirements/recommendations for international students: Required—TOEFL (minimum score 580 paper-based; 237 computer-based; 92 iBT), IELTS, Michigan English Language Assessment Battery, CanTEST, CAEL. *Faculty research:* Bio-product development, organic agriculture, nutrient management, air and water quality, agricultural biotechnology.

Rutgers, The State University of New Jersey, New Brunswick, Graduate School-New Brunswick, Department of Environmental Sciences, Piscataway, NJ 08854-8097. Offers air pollution and resources (MS, PhD); aquatic biology (MS, PhD); aquatic chemistry (MS, PhD); atmospheric science (MS, PhD); chemistry and physics of aerosol and hydrosol systems (MS, PhD); environmental chemistry (MS, PhD); environmental microbiology (MS, PhD); environmental toxicology (PhD); exposure assessment (PhD); fate and effects of pollutants (MS, PhD); pollution prevention and control (MS, PhD); water and wastewater treatment (MS, PhD); water resources (MS, PhD). Terminal master's awarded for partial completion of doctoral program. *Degree requirements:* For master's, comprehensive exam, thesis or alternative, oral final exam; for doctorate, comprehensive exam, thesis/dissertation, thesis defense, qualifying exam. *Entrance requirements:* For master's and doctorate, GRE General Test. Additional exam requirements/recommendations for international students: Required—TOEFL. Electronic

Water Resources

Rutgers, The State University of New Jersey, New Brunswick (continued)
applications accepted. *Faculty research:* Biological waste treatment; contaminant fate and transport; air, soil and water quality.

State University of New York College of Environmental Science and Forestry, Department of Forest and Natural Resources Management, Syracuse, NY 13210-2779. Offers environmental and natural resource policy (MS, PhD); environmental and natural resources policy (MPS); forest management and operations (MF); forestry ecosystems science and applications (MPS, MS, PhD); natural resources management (MPS, MS, PhD); quantitative methods and management in forest science (MPS, MS, PhD); recreation and resource management (MPS, MS, PhD); watershed management and forest hydrology (MPS, MS, PhD). *Degree requirements:* For master's, thesis (for some programs); for doctorate, comprehensive exam, thesis/dissertation. *Entrance requirements:* For master's and doctorate, GRE General Test, minimum GPA of 3.0. Additional exam requirements/recommendations for international students: Required—TOEFL (minimum score 550 paper-based; 213 computer-based; 80 iBT), IELTS (minimum score 6). *Faculty research:* Silviculture recreation management, tree improvement, operations management, economics.

State University of New York College of Environmental Science and Forestry, Program in Environmental Science, Syracuse, NY 13210-2779. Offers environmental and community land planning (MPS, MS, PhD); environmental and natural resources policy (PhD); environmental communication and participatory processes (MPS, MS, PhD); environmental policy and democratic processes (MPS, MS, PhD); environmental systems and risk management (MPS, MS, PhD); water and wetland resource studies (MPS, MS, PhD). Part-time programs available. *Degree requirements:* For master's, thesis (for some programs); for doctorate, comprehensive exam, thesis/dissertation. *Entrance requirements:* For master's and doctorate, GRE General Test, minimum GPA of 3.0. Additional exam requirements/recommendations for international students: Required—TOEFL (minimum score 550 paper-based; 213 computer-based; 80 iBT), IELTS (minimum score 6). *Faculty research:* Environmental education/communications, water resources, land resources, waste management.

Tropical Agriculture Research and Higher Education Center, Graduate School, Turrialba, Costa Rica. Offers agribusiness management (MS); agroforestry systems (PhD); ecological agriculture (MS); environmental socioeconomics (MS); forestry in tropical and subtropical zones (PhD); integrated watershed management (MS); management and conservation of tropical rainforests and biodiversity (MS); tropical agriculture (PhD); tropical agroforestry (MS). *Entrance requirements:* For master's, GRE, 2 years of related professional experience, letters of recommendation; for doctorate, GRE, 4 letters of recommendation, letter of support from employing organization, master's degree in agronomy, biological sciences, forestry, natural resources or related field. Additional exam requirements/recommendations for international students: Required—TOEFL (minimum score 550 paper-based; 213 computer-based). Electronic applications accepted. *Faculty research:* Biodiversity in fragmented landscapes, ecosystem management, integrated pest management, environmental livestock production, biotechnology carbon balances in diverse land uses.

University of Alaska Fairbanks, College of Engineering and Mines, Department of Civil and Environmental Engineering, Program in Environmental Engineering, Fairbanks, AK 99775-5900. Offers engineering (PhD), including environmental engineering; environmental engineering (MS), including environmental contaminants, environmental science and management, water supply and waste treatment. Part-time programs available. *Students:* 4 full-time (3 women), 3 part-time (2 women). Average age 28. 5 applicants, 60% accepted, 1 enrolled. In 2009, 3 master's, 1 doctorate awarded. *Degree requirements:* For master's, comprehensive exam, thesis or alternative; for doctorate, comprehensive exam, thesis/dissertation, oral exam, oral defense. *Entrance requirements:* For master's, basic computer techniques; for doctorate, GRE General Test. Additional exam requirements/recommendations for international students: Required—TOEFL (minimum score 575 paper-based; 213 computer-based). *Application deadline:* For fall admission, 5/1 for domestic students, 3/1 for international students; for spring admission, 10/15 for domestic students, 9/1 for international students. Applications are processed on a rolling basis. Application fee: $60. Electronic applications accepted. *Expenses:* Tuition, state resident: full-time $7584; part-time $316 per credit. Tuition, nonresident: full-time $15,504; part-time $646 per credit. Required fees: $23 per credit. $135 per semester. Tuition and fees vary according to course level, course load and reciprocity agreements. *Financial support:* In 2009–10, 4 research assistantships (averaging $13,290 per year), 1 teaching assistantship (averaging $7,088 per year) were awarded; fellowships, career-related internships or fieldwork, Federal Work-Study, scholarships/grants, health care benefits, and unspecified assistantships also available. Support available to part-time students. Financial award application deadline: 7/1; financial award applicants required to submit FAFSA. *Unit head:* Dr. David Barnes, Department Chair, 907-474-7241, Fax: 907-474-6087, E-mail: fyeqe@uaf.edu. *Application contact:* Dr. David Barnes, Department Chair, 907-474-7241, Fax: 907-474-6087, E-mail: fyeqe@uaf.edu.

The University of Arizona, Graduate College, College of Agriculture and Life Sciences, Department of Soil, Water and Environmental Science, Tucson, AZ 85721. Offers MS, PhD. *Faculty:* 11. *Students:* 50 full-time (33 women), 8 part-time (5 women); includes 14 minority (3 African Americans, 1 American Indian/Alaska Native, 10 Hispanic Americans), 16 international. Average age 32. 37 applicants, 54% accepted, 13 enrolled. In 2009, 12 master's, 6 doctorates awarded. *Degree requirements:* For master's, thesis; for doctorate, comprehensive exam, thesis/dissertation. *Entrance requirements:* For master's, GRE (recommended), minimum GPA of 3.0, letter of interest, 3 letters of recommendation; for doctorate, GRE (recommended), MS, minimum GPA of 3.0, letter of interest, 3 letters of recommendation. Additional exam requirements/recommendations for international students: Required—TOEFL (minimum score 550 paper-based; 213 computer-based; 80 iBT). *Application deadline:* For fall admission, 6/1 for domestic students, 12/1 for international students; for spring admission, 10/1 for domestic students, 6/1 for international students. Applications are processed on a rolling basis. Application fee: $75. *Expenses:* Tuition, state resident: full-time $9028. Tuition, nonresident: full-time $24,890. *Financial support:* In 2009–10, 14 students received support, including 25 research assistantships with full and partial tuition reimbursements available (averaging $18,090 per year), 5 teaching assistantships with full and partial tuition reimbursements available (averaging $17,669 per year); fellowships, Federal Work-Study, institutionally sponsored loans, scholarships/grants, health care benefits, tuition waivers (full and partial), and unspecified assistantships also available. Financial award application deadline: 5/1. *Faculty research:* Plant production, environmental microbiology, contaminant flow and transport, aquaculture. Total annual research expenditures: $3.6 million. *Unit head:* Dr. Jeffery C. Silvertooth, Head, 520-621-7228, Fax: 520-621-1647, E-mail: silver@ag.arizona.edu. *Application contact:* Alicia Velasquez, 520-621-1606, Fax: 520-621-1647, E-mail: avelasqu@ag.arizona.edu.

The University of Arizona, Graduate College, College of Science, Department of Hydrology and Water Resources, Tucson, AZ 85721. Offers MS, PhD. Part-time programs available. *Faculty:* 14. *Students:* 44 full-time (16 women), 8 part-time (4 women); includes 4 minority (all Hispanic Americans), 17 international. Average age 32. 66 applicants, 14% accepted, 9 enrolled. In 2009, 6 master's, 4 doctorates awarded. *Degree requirements:* For master's, thesis; for doctorate, thesis/dissertation. *Entrance requirements:* For master's, GRE General Test, 3 letters of recommendation, bachelor's degree in related field; for doctorate, GRE General Test, minimum undergraduate GPA of 3.2, graduate 3.4; 3 letters of recommendation; master's degree in related field; master's thesis abstract. Additional exam requirements/recommendations for international students: Required—TOEFL (minimum score 550 paper-based; 213 computer-based; 79 iBT). *Application deadline:* For fall admission, 5/1 for domestic students, 12/1 for international students; for spring admission, 10/1 for domestic students, 6/1 for international students. Applications are processed on a rolling basis. Application fee: $75. Electronic applications accepted. *Expenses:* Tuition, state resident: full-time $9028. Tuition, nonresident: full-time $24,890. *Financial support:* In 2009–10, 25 research assistantships with full tuition reimbursements (averaging $18,532 per year), 4 teaching assistantships with full tuition reimbursements (averaging $18,074 per year) were awarded; institutionally sponsored loans, scholarships/grants, health care benefits, and unspecified assistantships also available. Financial award application deadline: 1/31. *Faculty research:* Subsurface and surface hydrology, hydrometeorology/climatology, applied remote sensing, water resource systems, environmental hydrology and water quality. Total annual research expenditures: $5.5 million. *Unit head:* Thomas Maddock, Department Head, 520-621-7120, E-mail: maddock@hwr.arizona.edu. *Application contact:* Terrie Thompson, Academic Advising Coordinator, 520-621-3131, Fax: 520-621-1422, E-mail: programs@hwr.arizona.edu.

University of California, Riverside, Graduate Division, Program in Soil and Water Sciences, Riverside, CA 92521-0102. Offers MS, PhD. *Faculty:* 27 full-time (4 women). *Students:* 17 full-time (10 women); includes 8 minority (6 Asian Americans or Pacific Islanders, 2 Hispanic Americans), 10 international. Average age 29. 63 applicants, 19% accepted, 9 enrolled. In 2009, 4 master's awarded. *Entrance requirements:* For master's and doctorate, minimum GPA of 3.2. Additional exam requirements/recommendations for international students: Required—TOEFL (minimum score 550 paper-based; 213 computer-based; 80 iBT). *Application deadline:* For fall admission, 5/1 for domestic students, 2/1 for international students; for winter admission, 9/1 for domestic students, 7/1 for international students; for spring admission, 12/1 for domestic students, 10/1 for international students. Application fee: $60 ($75 for international students). Electronic applications accepted. *Financial support:* In 2009–10, fellowships with tuition reimbursements (averaging $12,000 per year), research assistantships with tuition reimbursements (averaging $18,000 per year) were awarded. *Unit head:* Dr. Jay Gan, Chair, 951-827-2712, Fax: 951-827-3993. *Application contact:* Mari Ridgeway, Program Assistant, 951-827-5103, Fax: 951-827-3993, E-mail: soilwater@ucr.edu.

University of Florida, Graduate School, College of Agricultural and Life Sciences, Department of Soil and Water Science, Gainesville, FL 32611. Offers MS, PhD. Part-time programs available. Postbaccalaureate distance learning degree programs offered. Terminal master's awarded for partial completion of doctoral program. *Degree requirements:* For master's, thesis optional; for doctorate, thesis/dissertation. *Entrance requirements:* For master's and doctorate, GRE General Test, minimum GPA of 3.0. Additional exam requirements/recommendations for international students: Required—TOEFL. Electronic applications accepted. *Faculty research:* Environmental fate and transport of pesticides, conservation, wetlands, land application of nonhazardous waste, soil/water agrochemical management.

University of Idaho, College of Graduate Studies, Department of Water Resources, Moscow, ID 83844-2282. Offers MS, PhD. *Faculty:* 10 full-time, 3 part-time/adjunct. *Students:* 17 full-time, 3 part-time. In 2009, 1 master's awarded. *Expenses:* Tuition, state resident: full-time $6120. Tuition, nonresident: full-time $17,712. *Faculty research:* Water resource systems, biological wastewater treatment and water reclamation, invasive species, aquatics ecosystem restoration, watershed science and management. *Unit head:* Dr. Jan Boll, Director, 208-885-9694. *Application contact:* Dr. Jan Boll, Director, 208-885-9694.

University of Minnesota, Twin Cities Campus, Graduate School, College of Food, Agricultural and Natural Resource Sciences, Program in Water Resources Science, Minneapolis, MN 55455-0213. Offers MS, PhD. Part-time programs available. *Faculty:* 105 full-time (26 women), 16 part-time/adjunct (3 women). *Students:* 51 full-time (27 women), 22 part-time (10 women); includes 10 minority (2 African Americans, 7 Asian Americans or Pacific Islanders, 1 Hispanic American). 58 applicants, 33% accepted, 16 enrolled. In 2009, 18 master's, 4 doctorates awarded. *Degree requirements:* For master's, thesis; for doctorate, thesis/dissertation. *Entrance requirements:* For master's and doctorate, GRE, minimum GPA of 3.0, calculus, chemistry, biology, physics. Additional exam requirements/recommendations for international students: Required—TOEFL (minimum score 550 paper-based; 213 computer-based; 79 iBT). *Application deadline:* For fall and spring admission, 12/15 priority date for domestic and international students. Applications are processed on a rolling basis. Application fee: $75 ($95 for international students). Electronic applications accepted. *Financial support:* In 2009–10, 58 students received support, including 6 fellowships with full tuition reimbursements available (averaging $22,000 per year), 52 research assistantships with full and partial tuition reimbursements available (averaging $19,000 per year); scholarships/grants, health care benefits, and unspecified assistantships also available. Financial award application deadline: 12/15. *Faculty research:* Hydrology, limnology, water policy and economics, water quality, water chemistry. *Unit head:* Dr. Ray Newman, Director of Graduate Studies, 612-624-7456, E-mail: rnewman@umn.edu. *Application contact:* Bonnie R. Anderson, Director of Graduate Studies Assistant, 612-624-7456, Fax: 612-625-1263, E-mail: ander742@umn.edu.

University of Nevada, Las Vegas, Graduate College, College of Science, Program in Water Resources Management, Las Vegas, NV 89154-4029. Offers MS. Part-time programs available. *Faculty:* 2 part-time/adjunct (0 women). *Students:* 4 full-time (2 women), 13 part-time (3 women); includes 1 minority (Asian American or Pacific Islander), 2 international. Average age 37. 7 applicants, 86% accepted, 4 enrolled. In 2009, 4 master's awarded. *Degree requirements:* For master's, comprehensive exam, thesis. *Entrance requirements:* For master's, GRE Subject Test. Additional exam requirements/recommendations for international students: Required—TOEFL (minimum score 550 paper-based; 213 computer-based; 80 iBT), IELTS (minimum score 7). *Application deadline:* For fall admission, 2/1 priority date for domestic and international students; for spring admission, 10/1 priority date for domestic and international students. Applications are processed on a rolling basis. Application fee: $60 ($95 for international students). Electronic applications accepted. *Financial support:* In 2009–10, 1 student received support, including 1 research assistantship with partial tuition reimbursement available (averaging $14,000 per year); institutionally sponsored loans, scholarships/grants, health care benefits, and unspecified assistantships also available. Financial award application deadline: 3/1. *Faculty research:* Hydrogeology, water conservation, environmental chemistry, water resources planning, hydrology, waste management: hazardous materials management. *Unit head:* Dr. Michael Nicholl, Chair/Associate Professor, 702-895-4616, Fax: 702-895-4064, E-mail: michael.nicholl@unlv.edu. *Application contact:* Graduate College Admissions Evaluator, 702-895-3320, Fax: 702-895-4180, E-mail: gradcollege@unlv.edu.

University of New Brunswick Fredericton, School of Graduate Studies, Faculty of Engineering, Department of Civil Engineering, Fredericton, NB E3B 5A3, Canada. Offers construction engineering and management (M Eng, M Sc E, PhD); environmental engineering (M Eng, M Sc E, PhD); environmental studies (M Eng); geotechnical engineering (M Eng, M Sc E, PhD); groundwater/hydrology (M Eng, M Sc E, PhD); materials (M Eng, M Sc E, PhD); pavements (M Eng, M Sc E, PhD); structures (M Eng, M Sc E, PhD); transportation (M Eng, M Sc E, PhD). Part-time programs available. *Faculty:* 18 full-time (1 woman), 1 (woman) part-time/adjunct. *Students:* 42 full-time (9 women), 18 part-time (2 women). In 2009, 11 master's, 4 doctorates awarded. *Degree requirements:* For master's, thesis, proposal; for doctorate, comprehensive exam, thesis/dissertation, Qualifying exam; Proposal; 27 credit hours of courses. *Entrance requirements:* For master's, Minimum GPA of 3.0; BScE in Civil Engineering or related engineering degree.; for doctorate, Minimum GPA of 3.0; Candidates are normally required to have a graduate degree in engineering or applied science. Additional exam requirements/recommendations for international students: Required—TOEFL (minimum score 580 paper-based; 237 computer-based), TWE (minimum score 4), or IELTS (minimum score 7.5). *Application deadline:* For fall admission, 5/1 priority date for domestic students; for winter admission, 11/1 priority date for domestic students. Applications are processed on a rolling basis. Application fee: $50 Canadian dollars. Tuition and fees charges are reported in Canadian dollars. *Expenses:* Tuition, area resident: Full-time $5562 Canadian dollars; part-time $2781 Canadian dollars per year. Required fees: $49.75 Canadian dollars per term. *Financial support:*

In 2009–10, 51 research assistantships (averaging $7,000 per year), 43 teaching assistantships (averaging $2,000 per year) were awarded; career-related internships or fieldwork and scholarships/grants also available. *Faculty research:* Construction engineering and management, concrete materials and structural engineering, transportation and asset management, geotechnical engineering, water and environmental engineering. *Unit head:* Dr. Eric Hildebrand, Director of Graduate Studies, 506-453-5113, Fax: 506-453-3568, E-mail: ktm@unb.ca. *Application contact:* Joyce Moore, Graduate Secretary, 506-452-6127, Fax: 506-453-3568, E-mail: civil-grad@unb.ca.

University of New Hampshire, Graduate School, College of Life Sciences and Agriculture, Department of Natural Resources, Durham, NH 03824. Offers environmental conservation (MS); forestry (MS); soil science (MS); water resources management (MS); wildlife (MS). Part-time programs available. *Faculty:* 40 full-time. *Students:* 22 full-time (12 women), 29 part-time (19 women); includes 1 minority (Asian American or Pacific Islander), 1 international. Average age 31. 41 applicants, 34% accepted, 10 enrolled. In 2009, 19 master's awarded. *Degree requirements:* For master's, thesis or alternative. *Entrance requirements:* For master's, GRE General Test. Additional exam requirements/recommendations for international students: Required—TOEFL (minimum score 550 paper-based; 213 computer-based; 80 iBT). *Application deadline:* For fall admission, 6/1 for domestic students, 4/1 for international students; for spring admission, 12/1 for domestic students. Applications are processed on a rolling basis. Application fee: $65. Electronic applications accepted. *Expenses:* Tuition, state resident: full-time $10,380; part-time $577 per credit hour. Tuition, nonresident: full-time $24,350; part-time $1002 per credit hour. Required fees: $1550; $387.50 per semester. Tuition and fees vary according to course load and program. *Financial support:* In 2009–10, 24 students received support, including 2 fellowships, 11 research assistantships, 11 teaching assistantships; career-related internships or fieldwork, Federal Work-Study, scholarships/grants, and tuition waivers (full and partial) also available. Support available to part-time students. Financial award application deadline: 2/15. *Unit head:* Dr. John Halstead, Chairperson, 603-862-3950, E-mail: natural.resources@unh.edu. *Application contact:* Linda Scogin, Administrative Assistant, 603-862-3932, E-mail: natural.resources@unh.edu.

University of New Mexico, Graduate School, Program in Water Resources, Albuquerque, NM 87131-2039. Offers MWR. Part-time programs available. *Students:* 15 full-time (10 women), 25 part-time (16 women); includes 9 minority (6 American Indian/Alaska Native, 3 Hispanic Americans), 1 international. Average age 36. 29 applicants, 69% accepted, 13 enrolled. In 2009, 5 master's awarded. *Degree requirements:* For master's, professional project. *Entrance requirements:* For master's, minimum GPA of 3.0 during last 2 years of undergraduate work, 3 letters of reference, specific courses (see website). Additional exam requirements/recommendations for international students: Required—TOEFL (minimum score 550 paper-based; 213 computer-based). *Application deadline:* For fall admission, 7/15 for domestic students; for spring admission, 11/15 for domestic students. Applications are processed on a rolling basis. Application fee: $50. Electronic applications accepted. *Expenses:* Tuition, state resident: full-time $2098.80; part-time $233.20 per credit hour. Tuition, nonresident: full-time $6650. Required fees: $25 per semester. Tuition and fees vary according to course load, program and reciprocity agreements. *Financial support:* In 2009–10, 17 students received support; fellowships with partial tuition reimbursements available, career-related internships or fieldwork, institutionally sponsored loans, scholarships/grants, and unspecified assistantships available. Financial award application deadline: 3/1; financial award applicants required to submit FAFSA. *Faculty research:* Sustainable water resources, transboundary water resources, economics, water law, hydrology, developing countries, hydrogeology. Total annual research expenditures: $150,557. *Unit head:* Bruce M. Thompson, Head, 505-277-5249, Fax: 505-277-5226, E-mail: bthompson@unm.edu. *Application contact:* Annamarie Cordova, Administrative Assistant II, 505-277-7759, Fax: 505-277-5226, E-mail: acordova@unm.edu.

University of Oklahoma, Graduate College, College of Engineering, School of Civil Engineering and Environmental Science, Program in Environmental Science, Norman, OK 73019-0390. Offers air (M Env Sc); environmental science (PhD); groundwater management (M Env Sc); hazardous solid waste (M Env Sc); occupational safety and health (M Env Sc); process design (M Env Sc); water quality resources (M Env Sc). *Students:* 9 full-time (4 women), 8 part-time (6 women); includes 3 minority (1 African American, 2 American Indian/Alaska Native), 2 international. 9 applicants, 67% accepted, 4 enrolled. In 2009, 4 master's, 2 doctorates awarded. Terminal master's awarded for partial completion of doctoral program. *Degree requirements:* For master's, comprehensive exam, oral exams; for doctorate, comprehensive exam, thesis/dissertation, oral and qualifying exams. *Entrance requirements:* For master's, minimum GPA of 3.0; for doctorate, minimum graduate GPA of 3.5. Additional exam requirements/recommendations for international students: Required—TOEFL (minimum score 600 paper-based; 250 computer-based). *Application deadline:* For fall admission, 4/1 priority date for domestic students, 4/1 for international students; for spring admission, 11/1 for domestic students, 9/1 for international students. Applications are processed on a rolling basis. Application fee: $40 ($90 for international students). Electronic applications accepted. *Expenses:* Tuition, state resident: full-time $3744; part-time $156 per credit hour. Tuition, nonresident: full-time $13,577; part-time $565.70 per credit hour. Required fees: $2415; $90.10 per credit hour. *Financial support:* In 2009–10, 10 students received support. Scholarships/grants available. Financial award application deadline: 3/1; financial award applicants required to submit FAFSA. *Faculty research:* Treatment wetlands, soil remediation, biomediation. *Unit head:* Robert C. Knox, Director, 405-325-5911, Fax: 405-325-4217, E-mail: rknox@ou.edu. *Application contact:* Robert C. Knox, Director, 405-325-5911, Fax: 405-325-4217, E-mail: rknox@ou.edu.

University of the Pacific, McGeorge School of Law, Sacramento, CA 95817. Offers advocacy (JD); criminal justice (JD); experiential law teaching (LL M); intellectual property (JD); international legal studies (JD); international water resources law (LL M, JSD); law (JD); public law and policy (JD); public policy and law (LL M); tax (JD); transnational business practice (LL M); JD/MBA; JD/MPPA. *Accreditation:* ABA. Part-time and evening/weekend programs available. *Faculty:* 55 full-time (24 women), 57 part-time/adjunct (18 women). *Students:* 697 full-time (343 women), 377 part-time (197 women); includes 301 minority (33 African Americans, 11 American Indian/Alaska Native, 163 Asian Americans or Pacific Islanders, 94 Hispanic Americans). Average age 24. 2,659 applicants, 43% accepted, 236 enrolled. In 2009, 254 first professional degrees, 51 master's awarded. *Degree requirements:* For master's, thesis (for some programs); for doctorate, thesis/dissertation. *Entrance requirements:* For JD, LSAT; for master's, JD; for doctorate, LL M. Additional exam requirements/recommendations for international students: Required—TOEFL (minimum score 600 paper-based; 250 computer-based; 100 iBT). *Application deadline:* For fall admission, 3/15 priority date for domestic students. Applications are processed on a rolling basis. Application fee: $50. Electronic applications accepted. *Expenses:* Contact institution. *Financial support:* In 2009–10, 887 students received support, including 1 fellowship, 114 research assistantships (averaging $1,839 per year), 12 teaching assistantships (averaging $953 per year); career-related internships or fieldwork, Federal Work-Study, institutionally sponsored loans, and scholarships/grants also available. Support available to part-time students. Financial award applicants required to submit FAFSA. *Faculty research:* International legal studies, public policy and law, advocacy, intellectual property law, taxation, criminal law. *Unit head:* Elizabeth Rindskopf Parker, Dean, 916-739-7151, E-mail: elizabeth@pacific.edu. *Application contact:* 916-739-7105, Fax: 916-739-7301, E-mail: mcgeorge@pacific.edu.

University of Wisconsin–Madison, Graduate School, Gaylord Nelson Institute for Environmental Studies, Water Resources Management Program, Madison, WI 53706-1380. Offers MS. Part-time programs available. *Degree requirements:* For master's, practicum. *Entrance requirements:* For master's, GRE General Test. Additional exam requirements/recommendations for international students: Required—TOEFL (minimum score 550 paper-based; 213 computer-based). Electronic applications accepted. *Expenses:* Tuition, state resident: part-time $594 per credit. Tuition, nonresident: part-time $1504 per credit. Required fees: $65 per credit. Tuition and fees vary according to course load, program and reciprocity agreements. *Faculty research:* Geology, hydrogeology, water chemistry, limnology, oceanography.

University of Wyoming, College of Agriculture, Department of Renewable Resources, Laramie, WY 82070. Offers agroecology (MS); entomology (MS, PhD); entomology/water resources (MS, PhD); rangeland ecology and watershed management (MS, PhD), including soil sciences (PhD), soil sciences and water resources (MS); rangeland ecology and watershed management/water resources (MS, PhD); soil science (MS); soil science/water resources (PhD). Part-time programs available. *Degree requirements:* For master's, comprehensive exam, thesis, oral examination; for doctorate, comprehensive exam, thesis/dissertation, preliminary oral and written exam, oral final exam. *Entrance requirements:* For master's and doctorate, GRE General Test, minimum GPA of 3.0. Additional exam requirements/recommendations for international students: Required—TOEFL. Electronic applications accepted. *Faculty research:* Plant control, grazing management, riparian restoration, riparian management, reclamation.

Utah State University, School of Graduate Studies, College of Natural Resources, Department of Aquatic, Watershed, and Earth Resources, Logan, UT 84322. Offers ecology (MS, PhD); fisheries biology (MS, PhD); watershed science (MS, PhD). *Degree requirements:* For master's, thesis (for some programs); for doctorate, thesis/dissertation. *Entrance requirements:* For master's and doctorate, GRE General Test, minimum GPA of 3.2. Additional exam requirements/recommendations for international students: Required—TOEFL. Electronic applications accepted. *Faculty research:* Behavior, population ecology, habitat, conservation biology, restoration, aquatic ecology, fisheries management, fluvial geomorphology, remote sensing, conservation biology.

APPENDIXES

Institutional Changes Since the 2010 Edition

Following is an alphabetical listing of institutions that have recently closed, merged with other institutions, or changed their names or status. In the case of a name change, the former name appears first, followed by the new name.

Agnes Scott College (Decatur, GA): no longer offers graduate degrees

American Graduate School of International Relations and Diplomacy (Paris, France): name changed to American Graduate School in Paris

Antioch University McGregor (Yellow Springs, OH): name changed to Antioch University Midwest

Arizona State University at the Downtown Phoenix Campus (Phoenix, AZ): will be included with main campus Arizona State University (Tempe, AZ) by request from the institution

Arizona State University at the Polytechnic Campus (Mesa, AZ): will be included with main campus Arizona State University (Tempe, AZ) by request from the institution

Arizona State University at the West campus (Phoenix, AZ): [will be included with main campus Arizona State University (Tempe, AZ) by request from the institution

Arkansas State University (State University, AR): name changed to Arkansas State University–Jonesboro

Asbury College (Wilmore, KY): name changed to Asbury University

Australasian College of Health Sciences (Portland, OR): name changed to American College of Healthcare Sciences

Baker College Center for Graduate Studies (Flint, MI): name changed to Baker College Center for Graduate Studies–Online

Baltimore Hebrew University (Baltimore, MD): now a unit of Towson University (Towson, MD)

Beacon University (Columbus, GA): closed

Belhaven College (Jackson, MS): name changed to Belhaven University

Beth Benjamin Academy of Connecticut (Stamford, CT): no longer offers graduate degrees

Bethel College (McKenzie, TN): name changed to Bethel University

Bridgewater State College (Bridgewater, MA): name changed to Bridgewater State University

British American College London (London, United Kingdom): name changed to Regent's American College London

The Chicago School of Professional Psychology: Downtown Los Angeles Campus (Los Angeles, CA): name changed to The Chicago School of Professional Psychology at Downtown Los Angeles

The Chicago School of Professional Psychology: Grayslake Campus (Grayslake, IL): name changed to The Chicago School of Professional Psychology at Grayslake

The Cleveland Institute of Art (Cleveland, OH): no longer offers graduate degrees

Coleman College (San Diego, CA): name changed to Coleman University

Columbia Union College (Takoma Park, MD): name changed to Washington Adventist University

Dell'Arte School of Physical Theatre (Blue Lake, CA): name changed to Dell'Arte International School of Physical Theatre

DeVry University (San Francisco, CA): closed

Fitchburg State College (Fitchburg, MA): name changed to Fitchburg State University

George Meany Center for Labor Studies–The National Labor College (Silver Spring, MD): name changed to National Labor College

Hebrew Theological College (Skokie, IL): no longer offers graduate degrees

International University in Geneva (Geneva, Switzerland): no longer accredited by agency recognized by USDE or CHEA

Joint Military Intelligence College (Washington, DC): name changed to National Defense Intelligence College

Kent State University, Stark Campus (Canton, OH): name changed to Kent State University at Stark

Lancaster Bible College (Lancaster, PA): name changed to Lancaster Bible College & Graduate School

Leadership Institute of Seattle (Kenmore, WA): is now part of Saybrook University (San Francisco, CA)

New England School of Law (Boston, MA): name changed to New England Law-Boston

Otterbein College (Westerville, OH): name changed to Otterbein University

Pepperdine University (Los Angeles, CA): will be included with Pepperdine University (Malibu, CA) by request from the institution

The Protestant Episcopal Theological Seminary in Virginia (Alexandria, VA): name changed to Virginia Theological Seminary

Reinhardt College (Waleska, GA): name changed to Reinhardt University

Robert Morris College (Chicago, IL): name changed to Robert Morris University Illinois

St. Petersburg Theological Seminary (St. Petersburg, FL): no longer accredited by agency recognized by USDE or CHEA

Saybrook Graduate School and Research Center (San Francisco, CA): name changed to Saybrook University

Shorter College (Rome, GA): name changed to Shorter University

Southeastern University (Washington, DC): closed

Southern New England School of Law (North Dartmouth, MA): is now part of University of Massachusetts Dartmouth (North Dartmouth, MA)

Trinity Episcopal School for Ministry (Ambridge, PA): name changed to Trinity School for Ministry

University of Missouri–Columbia (Columbia, MO): name changed to University of Missouri

University of Phoenix–Renton Learning Center (Renton, WA): name changed to University of Phoenix–Western Washington Campus

University of Phoenix–Wisconsin Campus (Brookfield, WI): now listed as University of Phoenix–Madison Campus (Madison, WI)

West Liberty State University (West Liberty, WV): name changed to West Liberty University

World Medicine Institute: College of Acupuncture and Herbal Medicine (Honolulu, HI): name changed to World Medicine Institute of Acupuncture and Herbal Medicine

Abbreviations Used in the Guides

The following list includes abbreviations of degree names used in the profiles in the 2011 edition of the guides. Because some degrees (e.g., Doctor of Education) can be abbreviated in more than one way (e.g., D.Ed. or Ed.D.), and because the abbreviations used in the guides reflect the preferences of the individual colleges and universities, the list may include two or more abbreviations for a single degree.

Degrees

A Mus D	Doctor of Musical Arts
AC	Advanced Certificate
AD	Artist's Diploma Doctor of Arts
ADP	Artist's Diploma
Adv C	Advanced Certificate
Adv M	Advanced Master
AGC	Advanced Graduate Certificate
AGSC	Advanced Graduate Specialist Certificate
ALM	Master of Liberal Arts
AM	Master of Arts
AMBA	Accelerated Master of Business Administration
AMRS	Master of Arts in Religious Studies
APC	Advanced Professional Certificate
App Sc	Applied Scientist
App Sc D	Doctor of Applied Science
Au D	Doctor of Audiology
B Th	Bachelor of Theology
CAES	Certificate of Advanced Educational Specialization
CAGS	Certificate of Advanced Graduate Studies
CAL	Certificate in Applied Linguistics
CALS	Certificate of Advanced Liberal Studies
CAMS	Certificate of Advanced Management Studies
CAPS	Certificate of Advanced Professional Studies
CAS	Certificate of Advanced Studies
CASPA	Certificate of Advanced Study in Public Administration
CASR	Certificate in Advanced Social Research
CATS	Certificate of Achievement in Theological Studies
CBHS	Certificate in Basic Health Sciences
CBS	Graduate Certificate in Biblical Studies
CCJA	Certificate in Criminal Justice Administration
CCSA	Certificate in Catholic School Administration
CCTS	Certificate in Clinical and Translational Science
CE	Civil Engineer
CEM	Certificate of Environmental Management
CET	Certificate in Educational Technologies
CGS	Certificate of Graduate Studies
Ch E	Chemical Engineer
CM	Certificate in Management
CMH	Certificate in Medical Humanities
CMM	Master of Church Ministries
CMS	Certificate in Ministerial Studies
CNM	Certificate in Nonprofit Management
CP	Certificate in Performance
CPASF	Certificate Program for Advanced Study in Finance
CPC	Certificate in Professional Counseling Certificate in Publication and Communication
CPH	Certificate in Public Health
CPM	Certificate in Public Management
CPS	Certificate of Professional Studies
CScD	Doctor of Clinical Science
CSD	Certificate in Spiritual Direction
CSS	Certificate of Special Studies
CTS	Certificate of Theological Studies
CURP	Certificate in Urban and Regional Planning
D Admin	Doctor of Administration
D Arch	Doctor of Architecture
D Com	Doctor of Commerce
D Div	Doctor of Divinity
D Ed	Doctor of Education
D Ed Min	Doctor of Educational Ministry
D Eng	Doctor of Engineering
D Engr	Doctor of Engineering
D Env	Doctor of Environment
D Env M	Doctor of Environmental Management
D Law	Doctor of Law
D Litt	Doctor of Letters
D Med Sc	Doctor of Medical Science
D Min	Doctor of Ministry
D Miss	Doctor of Missiology
D Mus	Doctor of Music
D Mus A	Doctor of Musical Arts
D Phil	Doctor of Philosophy

D Ps	Doctor of Psychology
D Sc	Doctor of Science
D Sc D	Doctor of Science in Dentistry
D Sc IS	Doctor of Science in Information Systems
D Sc PA	Doctor of Science in Physician Assistant Studies
D Th	Doctor of Theology
D Th P	Doctor of Practical Theology
DA	Doctor of Accounting Doctor of Arts
DA Ed	Doctor of Arts in Education
DAH	Doctor of Arts in Humanities
DAOM	Doctorate in Acupuncture and Oriental Medicine
DAST	Diploma of Advanced Studies in Teaching
DBA	Doctor of Business Administration
DBL	Doctor of Business Leadership
DBS	Doctor of Buddhist Studies
DC	Doctor of Chiropractic
DCC	Doctor of Computer Science
DCD	Doctor of Communications Design
DCL	Doctor of Civil Law Doctor of Comparative Law
DCM	Doctor of Church Music
DCN	Doctor of Clinical Nutrition
DCS	Doctor of Computer Science
DDN	Diplôme du Droit Notarial
DDS	Doctor of Dental Surgery
DE	Doctor of Education Doctor of Engineering
DED	Doctor of Economic Development
DEIT	Doctor of Educational Innovation and Technology
DEL	Doctor of Executive Leadership
DEM	Doctor of Educational Ministry
DEPD	Diplôme Études Spécialisées
DES	Doctor of Engineering Science
DESS	Diplôme Études Supérieures Spécialisées
DFA	Doctor of Fine Arts
DGP	Diploma in Graduate and Professional Studies
DH Ed	Doctor of Health Education
DH Sc	Doctor of Health Sciences
DHA	Doctor of Health Administration
DHCE	Doctor of Health Care Ethics
DHL	Doctor of Hebrew Letters Doctor of Hebrew Literature
DHS	Doctor of Health Science Doctor of Human Services
DHSc	Doctor of Health Science
Dip CS	Diploma in Christian Studies
DIT	Doctor of Industrial Technology
DJ Ed	Doctor of Jewish Education
DJS	Doctor of Jewish Studies
DLS	Doctor of Liberal Studies
DM	Doctor of Management Doctor of Music
DMA	Doctor of Musical Arts
DMD	Doctor of Dental Medicine
DME	Doctor of Manufacturing Management Doctor of Music Education
DMEd	Doctor of Music Education
DMFT	Doctor of Marital and Family Therapy
DMH	Doctor of Medical Humanities
DML	Doctor of Modern Languages
DMM	Doctor of Music Ministry
DMP	Doctorate in Medical Physics
DMPNA	Doctor of Management Practice in Nurse Anesthesia
DN Sc	Doctor of Nursing Science
DNAP	Doctor of Nurse Anesthesia Practice
DNP	Doctor of Nursing Practice
DNS	Doctor of Nursing Science
DO	Doctor of Osteopathy
DPA	Doctor of Public Administration
DPC	Doctor of Pastoral Counseling
DPDS	Doctor of Planning and Development Studies
DPH	Doctor of Public Health
DPM	Doctor of Plant Medicine Doctor of Podiatric Medicine
DPPD	Doctor of Policy, Planning, and Development
DPS	Doctor of Professional Studies
DPT	Doctor of Physical Therapy
DPTSc	Doctor of Physical Therapy Science
Dr DES	Doctor of Design
Dr PH	Doctor of Public Health
Dr Sc PT	Doctor of Science in Physical Therapy
DRSc	Doctor of Regulatory Science
DS	Doctor of Science
DS Sc	Doctor of Social Science
DSJS	Doctor of Science in Jewish Studies

DSL	Doctor of Strategic Leadership
DSN	Doctor of Science in Nursing
DSW	Doctor of Social Work
DTL	Doctor of Talmudic Law
DV Sc	Doctor of Veterinary Science
DVM	Doctor of Veterinary Medicine
EAA	Engineer in Aeronautics and Astronautics
ECS	Engineer in Computer Science
Ed D	Doctor of Education
Ed DCT	Doctor of Education in College Teaching
Ed M	Master of Education
Ed S	Specialist in Education
Ed Sp	Specialist in Education
Ed Sp PTE	Specialist in Education in Professional Technical Education
EDM	Executive Doctorate in Management
EDSPC	Education Specialist
EE	Electrical Engineer
EJD	Executive Juris Doctor
EMBA	Executive Master of Business Administration
EMFA	Executive Master of Forensic Accounting
EMHA	Executive Master of Health Administration
EMIB	Executive Master of International Business
EML	Executive Master of Leadership
EMPA	Executive Master of Public Administration Executive Master of Public Affairs
EMS	Executive Master of Science
EMTM	Executive Master of Technology Management
Eng	Engineer
Eng Sc D	Doctor of Engineering Science
Engr	Engineer
Ex Doc	Executive Doctor of Pharmacy
Exec Ed D	Executive Doctor of Education
Exec MBA	Executive Master of Business Administration
Exec MPA	Executive Master of Public Administration
Exec MPH	Executive Master of Public Health
Exec MS	Executive Master of Science
G Dip	Graduate Diploma
GBC	Graduate Business Certificate
GCE	Graduate Certificate in Education
GDM	Graduate Diploma in Management
GDPA	Graduate Diploma in Public Administration
GDRE	Graduate Diploma in Religious Education
GEMBA	Global Executive Master of Business Administration
GEMPA	Gulf Executive Master of Public Administration
GM Acc	Graduate Master of Accountancy
GMBA	Global Master of Business Administration
GPD	Graduate Performance Diploma
GSS	Graduate Special Certificate for Students in Special Situations
IEMBA	International Executive Master of Business Administration
IM Acc	Integrated Master of Accountancy
IMA	Interdisciplinary Master of Arts
IMBA	International Master of Business Administration
IMES	International Masters in Environmental Studies
Ingeniero	Engineer
JCD	Doctor of Canon Law
JCL	Licentiate in Canon Law
JD	Juris Doctor
JSD	Doctor of Juridical Science Doctor of Jurisprudence Doctor of the Science of Law
JSM	Master of Science of Law
L Th	Licenciate in Theology
LL B	Bachelor of Laws
LL CM	Master of Laws in Comparative Law
LL D	Doctor of Laws
LL M	Master of Laws
LL M in Tax	Master of Laws in Taxation
LL M CL	Master of Laws (Common Law)
LL M/MBA	Master of Laws/Master of Business Administration
LL M/MNM	Master of Laws/Master of Nonprofit Management
M Ac	Master of Accountancy Master of Accounting Master of Acupuncture
M Ac OM	Master of Acupuncture and Oriental Medicine
M Acc	Master of Accountancy Master of Accounting
M Acct	Master of Accountancy Master of Accounting
M Accy	Master of Accountancy
M Actg	Master of Accounting
M Acy	Master of Accountancy
M Ad	Master of Administration
M Ad Ed	Master of Adult Education
M Adm	Master of Administration

M Adm Mgt	Master of Administrative Management
M Admin	Master of Administration
M ADU	Master of Architectural Design and Urbanism
M Adv	Master of Advertising
M Aero E	Master of Aerospace Engineering
M AEST	Master of Applied Environmental Science and Technology
M Ag	Master of Agriculture
M Ag Ed	Master of Agricultural Education
M Agr	Master of Agriculture
M Anesth Ed	Master of Anesthesiology Education
M App Comp Sc	Master of Applied Computer Science
M App St	Master of Applied Statistics
M Appl Stat	Master of Applied Statistics
M Aq	Master of Aquaculture
M Ar	Master of Architecture
M Arc	Master of Architecture
M Arch	Master of Architecture
M Arch I	Master of Architecture I
M Arch II	Master of Architecture II
M Arch E	Master of Architectural Engineering
M Arch H	Master of Architectural History
M Bioethics	Master in Bioethics
M Biomath	Master of Biomathematics
M Ch	Master of Chemistry
M Ch E	Master of Chemical Engineering
M Chem	Master of Chemistry
M Cl D	Master of Clinical Dentistry
M Cl Sc	Master of Clinical Science
M Comp E	Master of Computer Engineering
M Comp Sc	Master of Computer Science
M Coun	Master of Counseling
M Dent	Master of Dentistry
M Dent Sc	Master of Dental Sciences
M Des	Master of Design
M Des S	Master of Design Studies
M Div	Master of Divinity
M Ec	Master of Economics
M Econ	Master of Economics
M Ed	Master of Education
M Ed T	Master of Education in Teaching
M En	Master of Engineering Master of Environmental Science
M En S	Master of Environmental Sciences
M Eng	Master of Engineering
M Eng Mgt	Master of Engineering Management
M Engr	Master of Engineering
M Env	Master of Environment
M Env Des	Master of Environmental Design
M Env E	Master of Environmental Engineering
M Env Sc	Master of Environmental Science
M Fin	Master of Finance
M Geo E	Master of Geological Engineering
M Geoenv E	Master of Geoenvironmental Engineering
M Geog	Master of Geography
M Hum	Master of Humanities
M Hum Svcs	Master of Human Services
M IBD	Master of Integrated Building Delivery
M IDST	Master's in Interdisciplinary Studies
M Kin	Master of Kinesiology
M Land Arch	Master of Landscape Architecture
M Litt	Master of Letters
M Man	Master of Management
M Mat SE	Master of Material Science and Engineering
M Math	Master of Mathematics
M Med Sc	Master of Medical Science
M Mgmt	Master of Management
M Mgt	Master of Management
M Min	Master of Ministries
M Mtl E	Master of Materials Engineering
M Mu	Master of Music
M Mus	Master of Music
M Mus Ed	Master of Music Education
M Music	Master of Music
M Nat Sci	Master of Natural Science
M Oc E	Master of Oceanographic Engineering
M Pet E	Master of Petroleum Engineering
M Pharm	Master of Pharmacy
M Phil	Master of Philosophy
M Phil F	Master of Philosophical Foundations
M Pl	Master of Planning
M Plan	Master of Planning
M Pol	Master of Political Science
M Pr Met	Master of Professional Meteorology
M Prob S	Master of Probability and Statistics

M Psych	Master of Psychology
M Pub	Master of Publishing
M Rel	Master of Religion
M Sc	Master of Science
M Sc A	Master of Science (Applied)
M Sc AHN	Master of Science in Applied Human Nutrition
M Sc BMC	Master of Science in Biomedical Communications
M Sc CS	Master of Science in Computer Science
M Sc E	Master of Science in Engineering
M Sc Eng	Master of Science in Engineering
M Sc Engr	Master of Science in Engineering
M Sc F	Master of Science in Forestry
M Sc FE	Master of Science in Forest Engineering
M Sc Geogr	Master of Science in Geography
M Sc N	Master of Science in Nursing
M Sc OT	Master of Science in Occupational Therapy
M Sc P	Master of Science in Planning
M Sc Pl	Master of Science in Planning
M Sc PT	Master of Science in Physical Therapy
M Sc T	Master of Science in Teaching
M SEM	Master of Sustainable Environmental Management
M Serv Soc	Master of Social Service
M Soc	Master of Sociology
M Sp Ed	Master of Special Education
M Stat	Master of Statistics
M Sw En	Master of Software Engineering
M Sys Sc	Master of Systems Science
M Tax	Master of Taxation
M Tech	Master of Technology
M Th	Master of Theology
M Tox	Master of Toxicology
M Trans E	Master of Transportation Engineering
M Urb	Master of Urban Planning
M Vet Sc	Master of Veterinary Science
MA	Master of Administration Master of Arts
MA Comm	Master of Arts in Communication
MA Ed	Master of Arts in Education
MA Ed Ad	Master of Arts in Educational Administration
MA Ext	Master of Agricultural Extension
MA Islamic	Master of Arts in Islamic Studies
MA Military Studies	Master of Arts in Military Studies
MA Min	Master of Arts in Ministry
MA Miss	Master of Arts in Missiology
MA Past St	Master of Arts in Pastoral Studies
MA Ph	Master of Arts in Philosophy
MA Psych	Master of Arts in Psychology
MA Sc	Master of Applied Science
MA Sp	Master of Arts (Spirituality)
MA Strategic Intelligence	Master of Arts in Strategic Intelligence
MA Th	Master of Arts in Theology
MA-R	Master of Arts (Research)
MAA	Master of Administrative Arts Master of Applied Anthropology Master of Applied Arts Master of Arts in Administration
MAAAP	Master of Arts Administration and Policy
MAAE	Master of Arts in Art Education
MAAT	Master of Arts in Applied Theology Master of Arts in Art Therapy
MAB	Master of Agribusiness
MABC	Master of Arts in Biblical Counseling Master of Arts in Business Communication
MABE	Master of Arts in Bible Exposition
MABL	Master of Arts in Biblical Languages
MABM	Master of Agribusiness Management
MABS	Master of Arts in Biblical Studies
MABT	Master of Arts in Bible Teaching
MAC	Master of Accountancy Master of Accounting Master of Arts in Communication Master of Arts in Counseling
MACC	Master of Arts in Accountancy Master of Arts in Christian Counseling Master of Arts in Clinical Counseling
MACCM	Master of Arts in Church and Community Ministry
MACCT	Master of Accounting
MACE	Master of Arts in Christian Education
MACFM	Master of Arts in Children's and Family Ministry
MACH	Master of Arts in Church History
MACIS	Master of Accounting and Information Systems
MACJ	Master of Arts in Criminal Justice
MACL	Master of Arts in Christian Leadership

MACM	Master of Arts in Christian Ministries Master of Arts in Christian Ministry Master of Arts in Church Music Master of Arts in Counseling Ministries
MACN	Master of Arts in Counseling
MACO	Master of Arts in Counseling
MAcOM	Master of Acupuncture and Oriental Medicine
MACP	Master of Arts in Counseling Psychology
MACS	Master of Arts in Catholic Studies
MACSE	Master of Arts in Christian School Education
MACT	Master of Arts in Christian Thought Master of Arts in Communications and Technology
MAD	Master in Educational Institution Administration Master of Art and Design
MADR	Master of Arts in Dispute Resolution
MADS	Master of Animal and Dairy Science Master of Applied Disability Studies
MAE	Master of Aerospace Engineering Master of Agricultural Economics Master of Agricultural Education Master of Architectural Engineering Master of Art Education Master of Arts in Education Master of Arts in English Master of Automotive Engineering
MAECMS	Master of Aerospace Engineering in Composite Materials and Structures
MAEd	Master of Arts Education
MAEL	Master of Arts in Educational Leadership
MAEM	Master of Arts in Educational Ministries
MAEN	Master of Arts in English
MAEP	Master of Arts in Economic Policy
MAES	Master of Arts in Environmental Sciences
MAESL	Master of Arts in English as a Second Language
MAET	Master of Arts in English Teaching
MAF	Master of Arts in Finance
MAFE	Master of Arts in Financial Economics
MAFLL	Master of Arts in Foreign Language and Literature
MAFM	Master of Accounting and Financial Management
MAFS	Master of Arts in Family Studies
MAG	Master of Applied Geography
MAGU	Master of Urban Analysis and Management
MAH	Master of Arts in Humanities
MAHA	Master of Arts in Humanitarian Assistance Master of Arts in Humanitarian Studies
MAHCM	Master of Arts in Health Care Mission
MAHG	Master of American History and Government
MAHL	Master of Arts in Hebrew Letters
MAHN	Master of Applied Human Nutrition
MAHSR	Master of Applied Health Services Research
MAIA	Master of Arts in International Administration
MAIB	Master of Arts in International Business
MAICS	Master of Arts in Intercultural Studies
MAIDM	Master of Arts in Interior Design and Merchandising
MAIH	Master of Arts in Interdisciplinary Humanities
MAIPCR	Master of Arts in International Peace and Conflict Management
MAIR	Master of Arts in Industrial Relations
MAIS	Master of Arts in Intercultural Studies Master of Arts in Interdisciplinary Studies Master of Arts in International Studies
MAIT	Master of Administration in Information Technology Master of Applied Information Technology
MAJ	Master of Arts in Journalism
MAJ Ed	Master of Arts in Jewish Education
MAJCS	Master of Arts in Jewish Communal Service
MAJE	Master of Arts in Jewish Education
MAJS	Master of Arts in Jewish Studies
MAL	Master in Agricultural Leadership
MALA	Master of Arts in Liberal Arts
MALD	Master of Arts in Law and Diplomacy
MALED	Master of Arts in Literacy Education
MALER	Master of Arts in Labor and Employment Relations
MALM	Master of Applied Leadership and Management Master of Arts in Leadership Evangelical Mobilization
MALP	Master of Arts in Language Pedagogy
MALPS	Master of Arts in Liberal and Professional Studies
MALS	Master of Arts in Liberal Studies
MALT	Master of Arts in Learning and Teaching
MAM	Master of Acquisition Management Master of Agriculture and Management Master of Applied Mathematics Master of Arts in Management Master of Arts in Ministry Master of Arts Management Master of Avian Medicine
MAMB	Master of Applied Molecular Biology
MAMC	Master of Arts in Mass Communication Master of Arts in Ministry and Culture Master of Arts in Ministry for a Multicultural Church
MAME	Master of Arts in Missions/Evangelism

MAMFC	Master of Arts in Marriage and Family Counseling
MAMFCC	Master of Arts in Marriage, Family, and Child Counseling
MAMFT	Master of Arts in Marriage and Family Therapy
MAMM	Master of Arts in Ministry Management
MAMS	Master of Applied Mathematical Sciences Master of Arts in Ministerial Studies Master of Arts in Ministry and Spirituality
MAMT	Master of Arts in Mathematics Teaching
MAN	Master of Applied Nutrition
MANP	Master of Applied Natural Products
MANT	Master of Arts in New Testament
MAOM	Master of Acupuncture and Oriental Medicine Master of Arts in Organizational Management
MAOT	Master of Arts in Old Testament
MAP	Master of Applied Psychology Master of Arts in Planning Master of Public Administration Masters of Psychology
MAP Min	Master of Arts in Pastoral Ministry
MAPA	Master of Arts in Public Administration
MAPC	Master of Arts in Pastoral Counseling
MAPE	Master of Arts in Political Economy
MAPL	Master of Arts in Pastoral Leadership
MAPM	Master of Arts in Pastoral Ministry Master of Arts in Pastoral Music Master of Arts in Practical Ministry
MAPP	Master of Arts in Public Policy
MAPPS	Master of Arts in Asia Pacific Policy Studies
MAPS	Master of Arts in Pastoral Counseling/Spiritual Formation Master of Arts in Pastoral Studies Master of Arts in Public Service
MAPT	Master of Practical Theology
MAPW	Master of Arts in Professional Writing
MAR	Master of Arts in Religion
Mar Eng	Marine Engineer
MARC	Master of Arts in Rehabilitation Counseling
MARE	Master of Arts in Religious Education
MARL	Master of Arts in Religious Leadership
MARS	Master of Arts in Religious Studies
MAS	Master of Accounting Science Master of Actuarial Science Master of Administrative Science Master of Advanced Study Master of Aeronautical Science Master of American Studies Master of Applied Science Master of Applied Statistics Master of Architectural Studies Master of Archival Studies
MASA	Master of Advanced Studies in Architecture
MASD	Master of Arts in Spiritual Direction
MASE	Master of Arts in Special Education
MASF	Master of Arts in Spiritual Formation
MASJ	Master of Arts in Systems of Justice
MASL	Master of Arts in School Leadership
MASLA	Master of Advanced Studies in Landscape Architecture
MASM	Master of Aging Services Management Master of Arts in Specialized Ministries
MASP	Master of Applied Social Psychology Master of Arts in School Psychology
MASPAA	Master of Arts in Sports and Athletic Administration
MASS	Master of Applied Social Science Master of Arts in Social Science
MAST	Master of Arts in Science Teaching
MASW	Master of Aboriginal Social Work
MAT	Master of Arts in Teaching Master of Arts in Theology Master of Athletic Training Masters in Administration of Telecommunications
Mat E	Materials Engineer
MATCM	Master of Acupuncture and Traditional Chinese Medicine
MATDE	Master of Arts in Theology, Development, and Evangelism
MATDR	Master of Territorial Management and Regional Development
MATE	Master of Arts for the Teaching of English
MATESL	Master of Arts in Teaching English as a Second Language
MATESOL	Master of Arts in Teaching English to Speakers of Other Languages
MATF	Master of Arts in Teaching English as a Foreign Language/Intercultural Studies
MATFL	Master of Arts in Teaching Foreign Language
MATH	Master of Arts in Therapy
MATI	Master of Administration of Information Technology

MATL	Master of Arts in Teaching of Languages Master of Arts in Transformational Leadership
MATM	Master of Arts in Teaching of Mathematics
MATS	Master of Arts in Theological Studies Master of Arts in Transforming Spirituality
MATSL	Master of Arts in Teaching a Second Language
MAUA	Master of Arts in Urban Affairs
MAUD	Master of Arts in Urban Design
MAURP	Master of Arts in Urban and Regional Planning
MAW	Master of Arts in Worship
MAWL	Master of Arts in Worship Leadership
MAWSHP	Master of Arts in Worship
MAYM	Master of Arts in Youth Ministry
MB	Master of Bioinformatics
MBA	Master of Business Administration
MBA-EP	Master of Business Administration–Experienced Professionals
MBAA	Master of Business Administration in Aviation
MBAE	Master of Biological and Agricultural Engineering Master of Biosystems and Agricultural Engineering
MBAH	Master of Business Administration in Health
MBAi	Master of Business Administration–International
MBAICT	Master of Business Administration in Information and Communication Technology
MBAPA	Master of Business Administration–Physician Assistant
MBATM	Master of Business Administration in Technology Management
MBC	Master of Building Construction
MBE	Master of Bilingual Education Master of Bioengineering Master of Biological Engineering Master of Biomedical Engineering Master of Business and Engineering Master of Business Economics Master of Business Education
MBET	Master of Business, Entrepreneurship and Technology
MBiotech	Master of Biotechnology
MBIT	Master of Business Information Technology
MBL	Master of Business Law Master of Business Leadership
MBLE	Master in Business Logistics Engineering
MBMI	Master of Biomedical Imaging and Signals
MBMSE	Master of Business Management and Software Engineering
MBS	Master of Behavioral Science Master of Biblical Studies Master of Biological Science Master of Biomedical Sciences Master of Bioscience Master of Building Science
MBSI	Master of Business Information Science
MBT	Master of Biblical and Theological Studies Master of Biomedical Technology Master of Biotechnology Master of Business Taxation
MC	Master of Communication Master of Counseling Master of Cybersecurity
MC Ed	Master of Continuing Education
MC Sc	Master of Computer Science
MCA	Master of Arts in Applied Criminology Master of Commercial Aviation
MCAM	Master of Computational and Applied Mathematics
MCC	Master of Computer Science
MCCS	Master of Crop and Soil Sciences
MCD	Master of Communications Disorders Master of Community Development
MCE	Master in Electronic Commerce Master of Christian Education Master of Civil Engineering Master of Control Engineering
MCEM	Master of Construction Engineering Management
MCH	Master of Chemical Engineering
MCHE	Master of Chemical Engineering
MCIS	Master of Communication and Information Studies Master of Computer and Information Science Master of Computer Information Systems
MCIT	Master of Computer and Information Technology
MCJ	Master of Criminal Justice
MCJA	Master of Criminal Justice Administration
MCL	Master in Communication Leadership Master of Canon Law Master of Comparative Law
MCM	Master of Christian Ministry Master of Church Music Master of City Management Master of Communication Management Master of Community Medicine Master of Construction Management Master of Contract Management Masters of Corporate Media

MCMS	Master of Clinical Medical Science
MCP	Master in Science Master of City Planning Master of Community Planning Master of Counseling Psychology Master of Cytopathology Practice
MCPC	Master of Arts in Chaplaincy and Pastoral Care
MCPD	Master of Community Planning and Development
MCRP	Master of City and Regional Planning
MCRS	Master of City and Regional Studies
MCS	Master of Christian Studies Master of Clinical Science Master of Combined Sciences Master of Communication Studies Master of Computer Science Master of Consumer Science
MCSE	Master of Computer Science and Engineering
MCSL	Master of Catholic School Leadership
MCSM	Master of Construction Science/Management
MCST	Master of Science in Computer Science and Information Technology
MCTP	Master of Communication Technology and Policy
MCTS	Master of Clinical and Translational Science
MCVS	Master of Cardiovascular Science
MD	Doctor of Medicine
MDA	Master of Development Administration Master of Dietetic Administration
MDB	Master of Design-Build
MDE	Master of Developmental Economics Master of Distance Education Master of the Education of the Deaf
MDH	Master of Dental Hygiene
MDM	Master of Digital Media
MDP	Master of Development Practice
MDR	Master of Dispute Resolution
MDS	Master of Dental Surgery
ME	Master of Education Master of Engineering Master of Entrepreneurship Master of Evangelism
ME Sc	Master of Engineering Science
MEA	Master of Educational Administration Master of Engineering Administration
MEAP	Master of Environmental Administration and Planning
MEBT	Master in Electronic Business Technologies
MEC	Master of Electronic Commerce
MECE	Master of Electrical and Computer Engineering
Mech E	Mechanical Engineer
MED	Master of Education of the Deaf
MEDS	Master of Environmental Design Studies
MEE	Master in Education Master of Electrical Engineering Master of Energy Engineering Master of Environmental Engineering
MEEM	Master of Environmental Engineering and Management
MEENE	Master of Engineering in Environmental Engineering
MEEP	Master of Environmental and Energy Policy
MEERM	Master of Earth and Environmental Resource Management
MEH	Master in Humanistic Studies Master of Environmental Horticulture
MEHS	Master of Environmental Health and Safety
MEIM	Master of Entertainment Industry Management
MEL	Master of Educational Leadership Master of English Literature
MELP	Master of Environmental Law and Policy
MEM	Master of Ecosystem Management Master of Electricity Markets Master of Engineering Management Master of Environmental Management Master of Marketing
MEME	Master of Engineering in Manufacturing Engineering Master of Engineering in Mechanical Engineering
MEMS	Master of Engineering in Manufacturing Systems
MENG	Master of Arts in English
MENVEGR	Master of Environmental Engineering
MEP	Master of Engineering Physics
MEPC	Master of Environmental Pollution Control
MEPD	Master of Education–Professional Development Master of Environmental Planning and Design
MEPM	Master of Environmental Protection Management
MER	Master of Employment Relations
MES	Master of Education and Science Master of Engineering Science Master of Environmenta and Sustainability Master of Environmental Science Master of Environmental Studies Master of Environmental Systems Master of Special Education
MESM	Master of Environmental Science and Management
MET	Master of Education in Teaching Master of Educational Technology Master of Engineering Technology Master of Entertainment Technology Master of Environmental Toxicology
Met E	Metallurgical Engineer

METM	Master of Engineering and Technology Management
MF	Master of Finance Master of Forestry
MFA	Master of Financial Administration Master of Fine Arts
MFAM	Master in Food Animal Medicine
MFAS	Master of Fisheries and Aquatic Science
MFAW	Master of Fine Arts in Writing
MFC	Master of Forest Conservation
MFCS	Master of Family and Consumer Sciences
MFE	Master of Financial Economics Master of Financial Engineering Master of Forest Engineering
MFG	Master of Functional Genomics
MFHD	Master of Family and Human Development
MFM	Master of Financial Mathematics
MFMS	Masters in Food Microbiology and Safety
MFPE	Master of Food Process Engineering
MFR	Master of Forest Resources
MFRC	Master of Forest Resources and Conservation
MFS	Master of Food Science Master of Forensic Sciences Master of Forest Science Master of Forest Studies Master of French Studies
MFSA	Master of Forensic Sciences Administration
MFST	Master of Food Safety and Technology
MFT	Master of Family Therapy Master of Food Technology
MFWB	Master of Fishery and Wildlife Biology
MFWCB	Master of Fish, Wildlife and Conservation Biology
MFWS	Master of Fisheries and Wildlife Sciences
MFYCS	Master of Family, Youth and Community Sciences
MG	Master of Genetics
MGA	Master of Governmental Administration
MGD	Master of Graphic Design
MGE	Master of Gas Engineering Master of Geotechnical Engineering
MGEM	Master of Global Entrepreneurship and Management
MGH	Master of Geriatric Health
MGIS	Master of Geographic Information Science Master of Geographic Information Systems
MGM	Master of Global Management
MGP	Master of Gestion de Projet
MGPS	Master of Global Policy Studies
MGS	Master of Gerontological Studies Master of Global Studies
MH	Master of Humanities
MH Ed	Master of Health Education
MH Sc	Master of Health Sciences
MHA	Master of Health Administration Master of Healthcare Administration Master of Hospital Administration Master of Hospitality Administration
MHAD	Master of Health Administration
MHB	Master of Human Behavior
MHCA	Master of Health Care Administration
MHCI	Master of Human-Computer Interaction
MHCL	Master of Health Care Leadership
MHE	Master of Health Education Master of Human Ecology
MHE Ed	Master of Home Economics Education
MHEA	Masters of Higher Education Administration
MHHS	Master of Health and Human Services
MHI	Master of Health Informatics Master of Healthcare Innovation
MHIIM	Master of Health Informatics and Information Management
MHIS	Master of Health Information Systems
MHK	Master of Human Kinetics
MHL	Master of Hebrew Literature
MHMS	Master of Health Management Systems
MHP	Master of Health Physics Master of Heritage Preservation Master of Historic Preservation
MHPA	Master of Heath Policy and Administration
MHPE	Master of Health Professions Education
MHR	Master of Human Resources
MHRD	Master in Human Resource Development
MHRIR	Master of Human Resources and Industrial Relations
MHRLR	Master of Human Resources and Labor Relations
MHRM	Master of Human Resources Management
MHS	Master of Health Science Master of Health Sciences Master of Health Studies Master of Hispanic Studies Master of Human Services Master of Humanistic Studies
MHSA	Master of Health Services Administration
MHSM	Master of Health Sector Management Master of Health Systems Management
MI	Master of Instruction

MI Arch	Master of Interior Architecture
MI St	Master of Information Studies
MIA	Master of Interior Architecture Master of International Affairs
MIAA	Master of International Affairs and Administration
MIAM	Master of International Agribusiness Management
MIB	Master of International Business
MIBA	Master of International Business Administration
MICM	Master of International Construction Management
MID	Master of Industrial Design Master of Industrial Distribution Master of Interior Design Master of International Development
MIE	Master of Industrial Engineering
MIH	Master of Integrative Health
MIHTM	Master of International Hospitality and Tourism Management
MIJ	Master of International Journalism
MILR	Master of Industrial and Labor Relations
MiM	Master in Management
MIM	Master of Industrial Management Master of Information Management Master of International Management
MIMLAE	Master of International Management for Latin American Executives
MIMS	Master of Information Management and Systems Master of Integrated Manufacturing Systems
MIP	Master of Infrastructure Planning Master of Intellectual Property
MIPER	Master of International Political Economy of Resources
MIPP	Master of International Policy and Practice Master of International Public Policy
MIPS	Master of International Planning Studies
MIR	Master of Industrial Relations Master of International Relations
MIS	Master of Industrial Statistics Master of Information Science Master of Information Systems Master of Integrated Science Master of Interdisciplinary Studies Master of International Service Master of International Studies
MISE	Master of Industrial and Systems Engineering
MISKM	Master of Information Sciences and Knowledge Management
MISM	Master of Information Systems Management
MIT	Master in Teaching Master of Industrial Technology Master of Information Technology Master of Initial Teaching Master of International Trade Master of Internet Technology
MITA	Master of Information Technology Administration
MITM	Master of International Technology Management
MITO	Master of Industrial Technology and Operations
MJ	Master of Journalism Master of Jurisprudence
MJ Ed	Master of Jewish Education
MJA	Master of Justice Administration
MJM	Master of Justice Management
MJS	Master of Judicial Studies Master of Juridical Science
MKM	Master of Knowledge Management
ML	Master of Latin
ML Arch	Master of Landscape Architecture
MLA	Master of Landscape Architecture Master of Liberal Arts
MLAS	Master of Laboratory Animal Science Master of Liberal Arts and Sciences
MLAUD	Master of Landscape Architecture in Urban Development
MLD	Master of Leadership Development Master of Leadership Studies
MLE	Master of Applied Linguistics and Exegesis
MLER	Master of Labor and Employment Relations
MLERE	Master of Land Economics and Real Estate
MLHR	Master of Labor and Human Resources
MLI	Master of Legal Institutions
MLI Sc	Master of Library and Information Science
MLIS	Master of Library and Information Science Master of Library and Information Studies
MLM	Master of Library Media
MLOS	Masters in Leadership and Organizational Studies
MLRHR	Master of Labor Relations and Human Resources
MLS	Master of Leadership Studies Master of Legal Studies Master of Liberal Studies Master of Library Science Master of Life Sciences
MLSP	Master of Law and Social Policy
MLT	Master of Language Technologies

MM	Master of Management Master of Ministry Master of Missiology Master of Music
MM Ed	Master of Music Education
MM Sc	Master of Medical Science
MM St	Master of Museum Studies
MMA	Master of Marine Affairs Master of Media Arts Master of Musical Arts
MMAE	Master of Mechanical and Aerospace Engineering
MMAS	Master of Military Art and Science
MMB	Master of Microbial Biotechnology
MMBA	Managerial Master of Business Administration
MMC	Master of Manufacturing Competitiveness Master of Mass Communications Master of Music Conducting
MMCM	Master of Music in Church Music
MMCSS	Masters of Mathematical Computational and Statistical Sciences
MME	Master of Manufacturing Engineering Master of Mathematics Education Master of Mathematics for Educators Master of Mechanical Engineering Master of Medical Engineering Master of Mining Engineering Master of Music Education
MMF	Master of Mathematical Finance
MMFT	Master of Marriage and Family Therapy
MMG	Master of Management
MMH	Master of Management in Hospitality Master of Medical Humanities
MMI	Master of Management of Innovation
MMIS	Master of Management Information Systems
MMM	Master of Manufacturing Management Master of Marine Management Master of Medical Management
MMME	Master of Metallurgical and Materials Engineering
MMP	Master of Management Practice Master of Marine Policy Master of Medical Physics Master of Music Performance
MMPA	Master of Management and Professional Accounting
MMQM	Master of Manufacturing Quality Management
MMR	Master of Marketing Research
MMRM	Master of Marine Resources Management
MMS	Master of Management Science Master of Management Studies Master of Manufacturing Systems Master of Marine Studies Master of Materials Science Master of Medical Science Master of Medieval Studies Master of Modern Studies
MMSE	Master of Manufacturing Systems Engineering
MMSM	Master of Music in Sacred Music
MMT	Master in Marketing Master of Management Master of Music Teaching Master of Music Therapy Masters in Marketing Technology
MMus	Master of Music
MN	Master of Nursing Master of Nutrition
MN NP	Master of Nursing in Nurse Practitioner
MNA	Master of Nonprofit Administration Master of Nurse Anesthesia
MNAL	Master of Nonprofit Administration and Leadership
MNAS	Master of Natural and Applied Science
MNCM	Master of Network and Communications Management
MNE	Master of Network Engineering Master of Nuclear Engineering
MNL	Master in International Business for Latin America
MNM	Master of Nonprofit Management
MNO	Master of Nonprofit Organization
MNPL	Master of Not-for-Profit Leadership
MNPS	Master of New Professional Studies
MNpS	Master of Nonprofit Studies
MNR	Master of Natural Resources
MNRES	Master of Natural Resources and Environmental Studies
MNRM	Master of Natural Resource Management
MNRS	Master of Natural Resource Stewardship
MNS	Master of Natural Science
MO	Master of Oceanography
MOD	Master of Organizational Development
MOGS	Master of Oil and Gas Studies
MOH	Master of Occupational Health
MOL	Master of Organizational Leadership
MOM	Master of Oriental Medicine
MOR	Master of Operations Research

MOT	Master of Occupational Therapy
MP	Master of Physiology Master of Planning
MP Ac	Master of Professional Accountancy
MP Acc	Master of Professional Accountancy Master of Professional Accounting Master of Public Accounting
MP Aff	Master of Public Affairs
MP Th	Master of Pastoral Theology
MPA	Master of Physician Assistant Master of Professional Accountancy Master of Professional Accounting Master of Public Administration Master of Public Affairs
MPAC	Masters in Professional Accounting
MPAID	Master of Public Administration and International Development
MPAP	Master of Physician Assistant Practice Master of Public Affairs and Politics
MPAS	Master of Physician Assistant Science Master of Physician Assistant Studies Master of Public Art Studies
MPC	Master of Pastoral Counseling Master of Professional Communication Master of Professional Counseling
MPD	Master of Product Development Master of Public Diplomacy
MPDS	Master of Planning and Development Studies
MPE	Master of Physical Education Master of Power Engineering
MPEM	Master of Project Engineering and Management
MPH	Master of Public Health
MPHE	Master of Public Health Education
MPHTM	Master of Public Health and Tropical Medicine
MPIA	Master of Public and International Affairs Master Program in International Affairs
MPM	Master of Pastoral Ministry Master of Pest Management Master of Policy Management Master of Practical Ministries Master of Project Management Master of Public Management
MPNA	Master of Public and Nonprofit Administration
MPOD	Master of Positive Organizational Development
MPP	Master of Public Policy
MPPA	Master of Public Policy Administration Master of Public Policy and Administration
MPPAL	Master of Public Policy, Administration and Law
MPPM	Master of Public and Private Management Master of Public Policy and Management
MPPPM	Master of Plant Protection and Pest Management
MPPUP	Master of Public Policy and Urban Planning
MPRTM	Master of Parks, Recreation, and Tourism Management
MPS	Master of Pastoral Studies Master of Perfusion Science Master of Planning Studies Master of Political Science Master of Preservation Studies Master of Professional Studies Master of Public Service
MPSA	Master of Public Service Administration
MPSRE	Master of Professional Studies in Real Estate
MPT	Master of Pastoral Theology Master of Physical Therapy
MPVM	Master of Preventive Veterinary Medicine
MPW	Master of Professional Writing Master of Public Works
MQF	Master of Quantitative Finance
MQM	Master of Quality Management
MQS	Master of Quality Systems
MR	Master of Recreation Master of Retailing
MRA	Master in Research Administration
MRC	Master of Rehabilitation Counseling
MRCP	Master of Regional and City Planning Master of Regional and Community Planning
MRD	Master of Rural Development
MRE	Master of Religious Education
MRED	Master of Real Estate Development
MREM	Master of Resource and Environmental Management
MRLS	Master of Resources Law Studies
MRM	Master of Resources Management
MRP	Master of Regional Planning
MRS	Master of Religious Studies
MRSc	Master of Rehabilitation Science
MS	Master of Science
MS Cmp E	Master of Science in Computer Engineering
MS Kin	Master of Science in Kinesiology
MS Acct	Master of Science in Accounting
MS Accy	Master of Science in Accountancy
MS Aero E	Master of Science in Aerospace Engineering
MS Ag	Master of Science in Agriculture
MS Arch	Master of Science in Architecture
MS Arch St	Master of Science in Architectural Studies

MS Bio E	Master of Science in Bioengineering Master of Science in Biomedical Engineering
MS Bm E	Master of Science in Biomedical Engineering
MS Ch E	Master of Science in Chemical Engineering
MS Chem	Master of Science in Chemistry
MS Cp E	Master of Science in Computer Engineering
MS Eco	Master of Science in Economics
MS Econ	Master of Science in Economics
MS Ed	Master of Science in Education
MS El	Master of Science in Educational Leadership and Administration
MS En E	Master of Science in Environmental Engineering
MS Eng	Master of Science in Engineering
MS Engr	Master of Science in Engineering
MS Env E	Master of Science in Environmental Engineering
MS Exp Surg	Master of Science in Experimental Surgery
MS Int A	Master of Science in International Affairs
MS Mat E	Master of Science in Materials Engineering
MS Mat SE	Master of Science in Material Science and Engineering
MS Met E	Master of Science in Metallurgical Engineering
MS Metr	Master of Science in Meteorology
MS Mgt	Master of Science in Management
MS Min	Master of Science in Mining
MS Min E	Master of Science in Mining Engineering
MS Mt E	Master of Science in Materials Engineering
MS Otal	Master of Science in Otalrynology
MS Pet E	Master of Science in Petroleum Engineering
MS Phys	Master of Science in Physics
MS Phys Op	Master of Science in Physiological Optics
MS Poly	Master of Science in Polymers
MS Psy	Master of Science in Psychology
MS Pub P	Master of Science in Public Policy
MS Sc	Master of Science in Social Science
MS Sp Ed	Master of Science in Special Education
MS Stat	Master of Science in Statistics
MS Surg	Master of Science in Surgery
MS Tax	Master of Science in Taxation
MS Tc E	Master of Science in Telecommunications Engineering
MS-R	Master of Science (Research)
MSA	Master of School Administration Master of Science Administration Master of Science in Accountancy Master of Science in Accounting Master of Science in Administration Master of Science in Aeronautics Master of Science in Agriculture Master of Science in Anesthesia Master of Science in Architecture Master of Science in Aviation Master of Sports Administration
MSA Phy	Master of Science in Applied Physics
MSAA	Master of Science in Astronautics and Aeronautics
MSAAE	Master of Science in Aeronautical and Astronautical Engineering
MSABE	Master of Science in Agricultural and Biological Engineering
MSAC	Master of Science in Acupuncture
MSACC	Master of Science in Accounting
MSaCS	Master of Science in Applied Computer Science
MSAE	Master of Science in Aeronautical Engineering Master of Science in Aerospace Engineering Master of Science in Applied Economics Master of Science in Applied Engineering Master of Science in Architectural Engineering Master of Science in Art Education
MSAL	Master of Sport Administration and Leadership
MSAM	Master of Science in Applied Mathematics
MSANR	Master of Science in Agriculture and Natural Resources Systems Management
MSAPM	Master of Security Analysis and Portfolio Management
MSAS	Master of Science in Applied Statistics Master of Science in Architectural Studies
MSAT	Master of Science in Accounting and Taxation Master of Science in Advanced Technology Master of Science in Athletic Training
MSAUS	Master of Science in Architectural Urban Studies
MSB	Master of Science in Bible Master of Science in Business
MSBA	Master of Science in Business Administration
MSBAE	Master of Science in Biological and Agricultural Engineering Master of Science in Biosystems and Agricultural Engineering
MSBC	Master of Science in Building Construction
MSBE	Master of Science in Biological Engineering Master of Science in Biomedical Engineering
MSBENG	Master of Science in Bioengineering

MSBIT	Master of Science in Business Information Technology	
MSBM	Master of Sport Business Management	
MSBME	Master of Science in Biomedical Engineering	
MSBMS	Master of Science in Basic Medical Science	
MSBS	Master of Science in Biomedical Sciences	
MSC	Master of Science in Commerce Master of Science in Communication Master of Science in Computers Master of Science in Counseling Master of Science in Criminology	
MSCA	Master of Science in Construction Administration	
MSCC	Master of Science in Christian Counseling Master of Science in Community Counseling	
MSCD	Master of Science in Communication Disorders Master of Science in Community Development	
MSCE	Master of Science in Civil Engineering Master of Science in Clinical Epidemiology Master of Science in Computer Engineering Master of Science in Continuing Education	
MSCEE	Master of Science in Civil and Environmental Engineering	
MSCF	Master of Science in Computational Finance	
MSChE	Master of Science in Chemical Engineering	
MSCI	Master of Science in Clinical Investigation Master of Science in Curriculum and Instruction	
MSCIS	Master of Science in Computer and Information Systems Master of Science in Computer Information Science Master of Science in Computer Information Systems	
MSCIT	Master of Science in Computer Information Technology	
MSCJ	Master of Science in Criminal Justice	
MSCJA	Master of Science in Criminal Justice Administration	
MSCJS	Master of Science in Crime and Justice Studies	
MSCL	Master of Science in Collaborative Leadership	
MSCLS	Master of Science in Clinical Laboratory Studies	
MSCM	Master of Science in Conflict Management Master of Science in Construction Management	
MScM	Master of Science in Management	
MSCM	Master of Supply Chain Management	
MSCP	Master of Science in Clinical Psychology Master of Science in Computer Engineering Master of Science in Counseling Psychology	
MSCPE	Master of Science in Computer Engineering	
MSCPharm	Master of Science in Pharmacy	
MSCPI	Master in Strategic Planning for Critical Infrastructures	
MSCRP	Master of Science in City and Regional Planning Master of Science in Community and Regional Planning	
MSCS	Master of Science in Clinical Science Master of Science in Computer Science	
MSCSD	Master of Science in Communication Sciences and Disorders	
MSCSE	Master of Science in Computer Science and Engineering	
MSCTE	Master of Science in Career and Technical Education	
MSD	Master of Science in Dentistry Master of Science in Design Master of Science in Dietetics	
MSDD	Master of Software Design and Development	
MSDM	Master of Design Methods	
MSDR	Master of Dispute Resolution	
MSE	Master of Science Education Master of Science in Economics Master of Science in Education Master of Science in Engineering Master of Science in Engineering Management Master of Software Engineering Master of Special Education Master of Structural Engineering	
MSECE	Master of Science in Electrical and Computer Engineering	
MSED	Master of Sustainable Economic Development	
MSEE	Master of Science in Electrical Engineering Master of Science in Environmental Engineering	
MSEH	Master of Science in Environmental Health	
MSEL	Master of Science in Educational Leadership Master of Science in Executive Leadership	
MSEM	Master of Science in Engineering Management Master of Science in Engineering Mechanics Master of Science in Environmental Management	
MSENE	Master of Science in Environmental Engineering	
MSEO	Master of Science in Electro-Optics	
MSEP	Master of Science in Economic Policy Master of Science in Engineering Physics	
MSEPA	Masters of Science in Economics and Policy Analysis	
MSES	Master of Science in Embedded Software Engineering Master of Science in Engineering Science Master of Science in Environmental Science Master of Science in Environmental Studies	

MSESM	Master of Science in Engineering Science and Mechanics
MSET	Master of Science in Education in Educational Technology Master of Science in Engineering Technology
MSETM	Master of Science in Environmental Technology Management
MSEV	Master of Science in Environmental Engineering
MSEVH	Master of Science in Environmental Health and Safety
MSF	Master of Science in Finance Master of Science in Forestry
MSFA	Master of Science in Financial Analysis
MSFAM	Master of Science in Family Studies
MSFCS	Master of Science in Family and Consumer Science
MSFE	Master of Science in Financial Engineering
MSFOR	Master of Science in Forestry
MSFP	Master of Science in Financial Planning
MSFS	Master of Science in Financial Sciences Master of Science in Forensic Science
MSFSB	Master of Science in Financial Services and Banking
MSFT	Master of Science in Family Therapy
MSGC	Master of Science in Genetic Counseling
MSGL	Master of Science in Global Leadership
MSH	Master of Science in Health Master of Science in Hospice
MSHA	Master of Science in Health Administration
MSHCA	Master of Science in Health Care Administration
MSHCI	Master of Science in Human Computer Interaction
MSHCPM	Master of Science in Health Care Policy and Management
MSHE	Master of Science in Health Education
MSHES	Master of Science in Human Environmental Sciences
MSHFID	Master of Science in Human Factors in Information Design
MSHFS	Master of Science in Human Factors and Systems
MSHI	Master of Science in Health Informatics
MSHP	Master of Science in Health Professions Master of Science in Health Promotion
MSHR	Master of Science in Human Resources
MSHRL	Master of Science in Human Resource Leadership
MSHRM	Master of Science in Human Resource Management
MSHROD	Master of Science in Human Resources and Organizational Development
MSHS	Master of Science in Health Science Master of Science in Health Services Master of Science in Health Systems Master of Science in Homeland Security
MSHT	Master of Science in History of Technology
MSI	Master of Science in Instruction
MSIA	Master of Science in Industrial Administration Master of Science in Information Assurance and Computer Security
MSIB	Master of Science in International Business
MSIDM	Master of Science in Interior Design and Merchandising
MSIDT	Master of Science in Information Design and Technology
MSIE	Master of Science in Industrial Engineering Master of Science in International Economics
MSIEM	Master of Science in Information Engineering and Management
MSIID	Master of Science in Information and Instructional Design
MSIM	Master of Science in Information Management Master of Science in International Management Master of Science in Investment Management
MSIMC	Master of Science in Integrated Marketing Communications
MSIR	Master of Science in Industrial Relations
MSIS	Master of Science in Information Science Master of Science in Information Systems Master of Science in Interdisciplinary Studies
MSISE	Master of Science in Infrastructure Systems Engineering
MSISM	Master of Science in Information Systems Management
MSISPM	Master of Science in Information Security Policy and Management
MSIST	Master of Science in Information Systems Technology
MSIT	Master of Science in Industrial Technology Master of Science in Information Technology Master of Science in Instructional Technology
MSITM	Master of Science in Information Technology Management
MSJ	Master of Science in Journalism Master of Science in Jurisprudence
MSJE	Master of Science in Jewish Education
MSJFP	Master of Science in Juvenile Forensic Psychology
MSJJ	Master of Science in Juvenile Justice
MSJPS	Master of Science in Justice and Public Safety

MSJS	Master of Science in Jewish Studies
MSK	Master of Science in Kinesiology
MSKM	Master of Science in Knowledge Management
MSL	Master of School Leadership Master of Science in Leadership Master of Science in Limnology Master of Strategic Leadership Master of Studies in Law
MSLA	Master of Science in Landscape Architecture Master of Science in Legal Administration
MSLD	Master of Science in Land Development
MSLS	Master of Science in Legal Studies Master of Science in Library Science
MSLSCM	Master of Science in Logistics and Supply Chain Management
MSLT	Master of Second Language Teaching
MSM	Master of Sacred Ministry Master of Sacred Music Master of School Mathematics Master of Science in Management Master of Science in Mathematics Master of Science in Organization Management Master of Security Management
MSMA	Master of Science in Marketing Analysis
MSMAE	Master of Science in Materials Engineering
MSMC	Master of Science in Mass Communications
MSME	Master of Science in Mathematics Education Master of Science in Mechanical Engineering
MSMFE	Master of Science in Manufacturing Engineering
MSMFT	Master of Science in Marriage and Family Therapy
MSMIS	Master of Science in Management Information Systems
MSMIT	Master of Science in Management and Information Technology
MSMM	Master of Science in Manufacturing Management
MSMO	Master of Science in Manufacturing Operations
MSMOT	Master of Science in Management of Technology
MSMS	Master of Science in Management Science Master of Science in Medical Sciences
MSMSE	Master of Science in Manufacturing Systems Engineering Master of Science in Material Science and Engineering Master of Science in Mathematics and Science Education
MSMT	Master of Science in Management and Technology Master of Science in Medical Technology
MSMus	Master of Sacred Music
MSN	Master of Science in Nursing
MSN-R	Master of Science in Nursing (Research)
MSNA	Master of Science in Nurse Anesthesia
MSNE	Master of Science in Nuclear Engineering
MSNED	Master of Science in Nurse Education
MSNM	Master of Science in Nonprofit Management
MSNS	Master of Science in Natural Science Master's of Science in Nutritional Science
MSOD	Master of Science in Organizational Development
MSOEE	Master of Science in Outdoor and Environmental Education
MSOES	Master of Science in Occupational Ergonomics and Safety
MSOH	Master of Science in Occupational Health
MSOL	Master of Science in Organizational Leadership
MSOM	Master of Science in Operations Management Master of Science in Organization and Management Master of Science in Oriental Medicine
MSOR	Master of Science in Operations Research
MSOT	Master of Science in Occupational Technology Master of Science in Occupational Therapy
MSP	Master of Science in Pharmacy Master of Science in Planning Master of Science in Psychology Master of Speech Pathology
MSPA	Master of Science in Physician Assistant Master of Science in Professional Accountancy
MSPAS	Master of Science in Physician Assistant Studies
MSPC	Master of Science in Professional Communications Master of Science in Professional Counseling
MSPE	Master of Science in Petroleum Engineering
MSPG	Master of Science in Psychology
MSPH	Master of Science in Public Health
MSPHR	Master of Science in Pharmacy
MSPM	Master of Science in Professional Management Master of Science in Project Management
MSPNGE	Master of Science in Petroleum and Natural Gas Engineering
MSPS	Master of Science in Pharmaceutical Science Master of Science in Political Science Master of Science in Psychological Services
MSPT	Master of Science in Physical Therapy
MSpVM	Master of Specialized Veterinary Medicine
MSR	Master of Science in Radiology Master of Science in Reading
MSRA	Master of Science in Recreation Administration
MSRC	Master of Science in Resource Conservation

MSRE	Master of Science in Real Estate Master of Science in Religious Education
MSRED	Master of Science in Real Estate Development
MSRLS	Master of Science in Recreation and Leisure Studies
MSRMP	Master of Science in Radiological Medical Physics
MSRS	Master of Science in Rehabilitation Science
MSS	Master of Science in Software Master of Social Science Master of Social Services Master of Software Systems Master of Sports Science Master of Strategic Studies
MSSA	Master of Science in Social Administration
MSSCP	Master of Science in Science Content and Process
MSSE	Master of Science in Software Engineering Master of Science in Space Education Master of Science in Special Education
MSSEM	Master of Science in Systems and Engineering Management
MSSI	Master of Science in Security Informatics Master of Science in Strategic Intelligence
MSSL	Master of Science in Strategic Leadership
MSSLP	Master of Science in Speech-Language Pathology
MSSM	Master of Science in Sports Medicine
MSSP	Master of Science in Social Policy
MSSPA	Master of Science in Student Personnel Administration
MSSS	Master of Science in Safety Science Master of Science in Systems Science
MSST	Master of Science in Security Technologies
MSSW	Master of Science in Social Work
MSSWE	Master of Science in Software Engineering
MST	Master of Science and Technology Master of Science in Taxation Master of Science in Teaching Master of Science in Technology Master of Science in Telecommunications Master of Science Teaching
MSTC	Master of Science in Technical Communication Master of Science in Telecommunications
MSTCM	Master of Science in Traditional Chinese Medicine
MSTE	Master of Science in Telecommunications Engineering Master of Science in Transportation Engineering
MSTM	Master of Science in Technical Management
MSTOM	Master of Science in Traditional Oriental Medicine
MSUD	Master of Science in Urban Design
MSW	Master of Social Work
MSWE	Master of Software Engineering
MSWREE	Master of Science in Water Resources and Environmental Engineering
MSX	Master of Science in Exercise Science
MT	Master of Taxation Master of Teaching Master of Technology Master of Textiles
MTA	Master of Tax Accounting Master of Teaching Arts Master of Tourism Administration
MTCM	Master of Traditional Chinese Medicine
MTD	Master of Training and Development
MTE	Master in Educational Technology Master of Teacher Education
MTESOL	Master in Teaching English to Speakers of Other Languages
MTHM	Master of Tourism and Hospitality Management
MTI	Master of Information Technology
MTIM	Masters of Trust and Investment Management
MTL	Master of Talmudic Law
MTM	Master of Technology Management Master of Telecommunications Management Master of the Teaching of Mathematics
MTMH	Master of Tropical Medicine and Hygiene
MTOM	Master of Traditional Oriental Medicine
MTP	Master of Transpersonal Psychology
MTPC	Master of Technical and Professional Communication
MTS	Master of Theological Studies
MTSC	Master of Technical and Scientific Communication
MTSE	Master of Telecommunications and Software Engineering
MTT	Master in Technology Management
MTX	Master of Taxation
MUA	Master of Urban Affairs
MUD	Master of Urban Design
MUEP	Master of Urban and Environmental Planning
MUP	Master of Urban Planning
MUPDD	Master of Urban Planning, Design, and Development
MUPP	Master of Urban Planning and Policy
MUPRED	Masters of Urban Planning and Real Estate Development
MURP	Master of Urban and Regional Planning Master of Urban and Rural Planning

MUS	Master of Urban Studies
MVM	Master of VLSI and microelectronics
MVP	Master of Voice Pedagogy
MVPH	Master of Veterinary Public Health
MVS	Master of Visual Studies
MWC	Master of Wildlife Conservation
MWE	Master in Welding Engineering
MWPS	Master of Wood and Paper Science
MWR	Master of Water Resources
MWS	Master of Women's Studies
MZS	Master of Zoological Science
Nav Arch	Naval Architecture
Naval E	Naval Engineer
ND	Doctor of Naturopathic Medicine
NE	Nuclear Engineer
Nuc E	Nuclear Engineer
OD	Doctor of Optometry
OTD	Doctor of Occupational Therapy
PBME	Professional Master of Biomedical Engineering
PD	Professional Diploma
PGC	Post-Graduate Certificate
PGD	Postgraduate Diploma
Ph L	Licentiate of Philosophy
Pharm D	Doctor of Pharmacy
PhD	Doctor of Philosophy
PhD Otal	Doctor of Philosophy in Otalrynology
Phd Surg	Doctor of Philosophy in Surgery
PhDEE	Doctor of Philosophy in Electrical Engineering
PM Sc	Professional Master of Science
PMBA	Professional Master of Business Administration
PMC	Post Master Certificate
PMD	Post-Master's Diploma
PMS	Professional Master of Science Professional Master's Degree
Post-Doctoral MS	Post-Doctoral Master of Science
PPDPT	Postprofessional Doctor of Physical Therapy
PSM	Professional Master of Science Professional Science Master's
Psy D	Doctor of Psychology
Psy M	Master of Psychology
Psy S	Specialist in Psychology
Psya D	Doctor of Psychoanalysis
Re Dir	Director of Recreation
Rh D	Doctor of Rehabilitation
S Psy S	Specialist in Psychological Services
Sc D	Doctor of Science
Sc M	Master of Science
SCCT	Specialist in Community College Teaching
ScDPT	Doctor of Physical Therapy Science
SD	Doctor of Science Specialist Degree
SJD	Doctor of Juridical Science
SLPD	Doctor of Speech-Language Pathology
SLS	Specialist in Library Science
SM	Master of Science
SM Arch S	Master of Science in Architectural Studies
SM Vis S	Master of Science in Visual Studies
SMBT	Master of Science in Building Technology
SP	Specialist Degree
Sp C	Specialist in Counseling
Sp Ed	Specialist in Education
Sp LIS	Specialist in Library and Information Science
SPA	Specialist in Arts
SPCM	Special in Church Music
Spec	Specialist's Certificate
Spec M	Specialist in Music
SPEM	Special in Educational Ministries
SPS	School Psychology Specialist
Spt	Specialist Degree
SPTH	Special in Theology
SSP	Specialist in School Psychology
STB	Bachelor of Sacred Theology
STD	Doctor of Sacred Theology
STL	Licentiate of Sacred Theology
STM	Master of Sacred Theology
TDPT	Transitional Doctor of Physical Therapy
Th D	Doctor of Theology
Th M	Master of Theology
UA Undergraduate Associate	Aviation Master of Business Administration
VMD	Doctor of Veterinary Medicine
WEMBA	Weekend Executive Master of Business Administration
XMA	Executive Master of Arts
XMBA	Executive Master of Business Administration

INDEXES

Close-Ups and Displays

Directories and Subject Areas

Following is an alphabetical listing of directories and subject areas. Also listed are cross-references for subject area names not used in the directory structure of the guides, for example, "Arabic (*see* Near and Middle Eastern Languages)."

Graduate Programs in the Humanities, Arts & Social Sciences

Addictions/Substance Abuse Counseling
Administration (*see* Arts Administration; Public Administration)
African-American Studies
African Languages and Literatures (*see* African Studies)
African Studies
Agribusiness (*see* Agricultural Economics and Agribusiness)
Agricultural Economics and Agribusiness
Alcohol Abuse Counseling (*see* Addictions/Substance Abuse Counseling)
American Indian/Native American Studies
American Studies
Anthropology
Applied Arts and Design—General
Applied Economics
Applied History (*see* Public History)
Applied Social Research
Arabic (*see* Near and Middle Eastern Languages)
Arab Studies (*see* Near and Middle Eastern Studies)
Archaeology
Architectural History
Architecture
Archives Administration (*see* Public History)
Area and Cultural Studies (*see* African-American Studies; African Studies; American Indian/Native American Studies; American Studies; Asian-American Studies; Asian Studies; Canadian Studies; Cultural Studies; East European and Russian Studies; Ethnic Studies; Folklore; Gender Studies; Hispanic Studies; Holocaust Studies; Jewish Studies; Latin American Studies; Near and Middle Eastern Studies; Northern Studies; Pacific Area/Pacific Rim Studies; Western European Studies; Women's Studies)
Art/Fine Arts
Art History
Arts Administration
Arts Journalism
Art Therapy
Asian-American Studies
Asian Languages
Asian Studies
Behavioral Sciences (*see* Psychology)
Bible Studies (*see* Religion; Theology)
Biological Anthropology
Black Studies (*see* African-American Studies)
Broadcasting (*see* Communication; Film, Television, and Video Production)
Broadcast Journalism
Building Science
Canadian Studies
Celtic Languages
Ceramics (*see* Art/Fine Arts)
Child and Family Studies
Child Development
Chinese
Chinese Studies (*see* Asian Languages; Asian Studies)
Christian Studies (*see* Missions and Missiology; Religion; Theology)
Cinema (*see* Film, Television, and Video Production)
City and Regional Planning (*see* Urban and Regional Planning)
Classical Languages and Literatures (*see* Classics)
Classics
Clinical Psychology
Clothing and Textiles
Cognitive Psychology (*see* Psychology—General; Cognitive Sciences)
Cognitive Sciences
Communication—General
Community Affairs (*see* Urban and Regional Planning; Urban Studies)
Community Planning (*see* Architecture; Environmental Design; Urban and Regional Planning; Urban Design; Urban Studies)
Community Psychology (*see* Social Psychology)
Comparative and Interdisciplinary Arts
Comparative Literature
Composition (*see* Music)
Computer Art and Design
Conflict Resolution and Mediation/Peace Studies
Consumer Economics
Corporate and Organizational Communication
Corrections (*see* Criminal Justice and Criminology)
Counseling (*see* Counseling Psychology; Pastoral Ministry and Counseling)
Counseling Psychology
Crafts (*see* Art/Fine Arts)
Creative Arts Therapies (*see* Art Therapy; Therapies—Dance, Drama, and Music)
Criminal Justice and Criminology
Cultural Studies
Dance
Decorative Arts
Demography and Population Studies
Design (*see* Applied Arts and Design; Architecture; Art/Fine Arts; Environmental Design; Graphic Design; Industrial Design; Interior Design; Textile Design; Urban Design)
Developmental Psychology
Diplomacy (*see* International Affairs)
Disability Studies
Drama Therapy (*see* Therapies—Dance, Drama, and Music)
Dramatic Arts (*see* Theater)
Drawing (*see* Art/Fine Arts)
Drug Abuse Counseling (*see* Addictions/Substance Abuse Counseling)
Drug and Alcohol Abuse Counseling (*see* Addictions/Substance Abuse Counseling)
East Asian Studies (*see* Asian Studies)
East European and Russian Studies
Economic Development
Economics
Educational Theater (*see* Theater; Therapies—Dance, Drama, and Music)
Emergency Management
English
Environmental Design
Ethics
Ethnic Studies
Ethnomusicology (*see* Music)
Experimental Psychology
Family and Consumer Sciences—General
Family Studies (*see* Child and Family Studies)
Family Therapy (*see* Child and Family Studies; Clinical Psychology; Counseling Psychology; Marriage and Family Therapy)
Filmmaking (*see* Film, Television, and Video Production)
Film Studies (*see* Film, Television, and Video Production)
Film, Television, and Video Production
Film, Television, and Video Theory and Criticism
Fine Arts (*see* Art/Fine Arts)
Folklore

Foreign Languages (*see* specific language)
Foreign Service (*see* International Affairs; International Development)
Forensic Psychology
Forensic Sciences
Forensics (*see* Speech and Interpersonal Communication)
French
Gender Studies
General Studies (*see* Liberal Studies)
Genetic Counseling
Geographic Information Systems
Geography
German
Gerontology
Graphic Design
Greek (*see* Classics)
Health Communication
Health Psychology
Hebrew (*see* Near and Middle Eastern Languages)
Hebrew Studies (*see* Jewish Studies)
Hispanic Studies
Historic Preservation
History
History of Art (*see* Art History)
History of Medicine
History of Science and Technology
Holocaust and Genocide Studies
Home Economics (*see* Family and Consumer Sciences—General)
Homeland Security
Household Economics, Sciences, and Management (*see* Family and Consumer Sciences—General)
Human Development
Humanities
Illustration
Industrial and Labor Relations
Industrial and Organizational Psychology
Industrial Design
Interdisciplinary Studies
Interior Design
International Affairs
International Development
International Economics
International Service (*see* International Affairs; International Development)
International Trade Policy
Internet and Interactive Multimedia
Interpersonal Communication (*see* Speech and Interpersonal Communication)
Interpretation (*see* Translation and Interpretation)
Islamic Studies (*see* Near and Middle Eastern Studies; Religion)
Italian
Japanese
Japanese Studies (*see* Asian Languages; Asian Studies; Japanese)
Jewelry (*see* Art/Fine Arts)
Jewish Studies
Journalism
Judaic Studies (*see* Jewish Studies; Religion)
Labor Relations (*see* Industrial and Labor Relations)
Landscape Architecture
Latin American Studies
Latin (*see* Classics)
Law Enforcement (*see* Criminal Justice and Criminology)
Liberal Studies
Lighting Design
Linguistics
Literature (*see* Classics; Comparative Literature; specific language)
Marriage and Family Therapy
Mass Communication
Media Studies
Medical Illustration
Medieval and Renaissance Studies
Metalsmithing (*see* Art/Fine Arts)
Middle Eastern Studies (*see* Near and Middle Eastern Studies)
Military and Defense Studies
Mineral Economics
Ministry (*see* Pastoral Ministry and Counseling; Theology)
Missions and Missiology
Motion Pictures (*see* Film, Television, and Video Production)
Museum Studies
Music
Musicology (*see* Music)
Music Therapy (*see* Therapies—Dance, Drama, and Music)
National Security
Native American Studies (*see* American Indian/Native American Studies)
Near and Middle Eastern Languages
Near and Middle Eastern Studies
Near Environment (*see* Family and Consumer Sciences)
Northern Studies
Organizational Psychology (*see* Industrial and Organizational Psychology)
Oriental Languages (*see* Asian Languages)
Oriental Studies (*see* Asian Studies)
Pacific Area/Pacific Rim Studies
Painting (*see* Art/Fine Arts)
Pastoral Ministry and Counseling
Philanthropic Studies
Philosophy
Photography
Playwriting (*see* Theater; Writing)
Policy Studies (*see* Public Policy)
Political Science
Population Studies (*see* Demography and Population Studies)
Portuguese
Printmaking (*see* Art/Fine Arts)
Product Design (*see* Industrial Design)
Psychoanalysis and Psychotherapy
Psychology—General
Public Administration
Public Affairs
Public History
Public Policy
Public Speaking (*see* Mass Communication; Rhetoric; Speech and Interpersonal Communication)
Publishing
Regional Planning (*see* Architecture; Urban and Regional Planning; Urban Design; Urban Studies)
Rehabilitation Counseling
Religion
Renaissance Studies (*see* Medieval and Renaissance Studies)
Rhetoric
Romance Languages
Romance Literatures (*see* Romance Languages)
Rural Planning and Studies
Rural Sociology
Russian
Scandinavian Languages
School Psychology
Sculpture (*see* Art/Fine Arts)
Security Administration (*see* Criminal Justice and Criminology)
Slavic Languages
Slavic Studies (*see* East European and Russian Studies; Slavic Languages)
Social Psychology
Social Sciences
Sociology
Southeast Asian Studies (*see* Asian Studies)
Soviet Studies (*see* East European and Russian Studies; Russian)
Spanish
Speech and Interpersonal Communication
Sport Psychology
Studio Art (*see* Art/Fine Arts)
Substance Abuse Counseling (*see* Addictions/Substance Abuse Counseling)
Survey Methodology
Sustainable Development
Technical Communication
Technical Writing

Telecommunications (*see* Film, Television, and Video Production)
Television (*see* Film, Television, and Video Production)
Textile Design
Textiles (*see* Clothing and Textiles; Textile Design)
Thanatology
Theater
Theater Arts (*see* Theater)
Theology
Therapies—Dance, Drama, and Music
Translation and Interpretation
Transpersonal and Humanistic Psychology
Urban and Regional Planning
Urban Design
Urban Planning (*see* Architecture; Urban and Regional Planning; Urban Design; Urban Studies)
Urban Studies
Video (*see* Film, Television, and Video Production)
Visual Arts (*see* Applied Arts and Design; Art/Fine Arts; Film, Television, and Video Production; Graphic Design; Illustration; Photography)
Western European Studies
Women's Studies
World Wide Web (*see* Internet and Interactive Multimedia)
Writing

Graduate Programs in the Biological Sciences

Anatomy
Animal Behavior
Bacteriology
Behavioral Sciences (*see* Biopsychology; Neuroscience; Zoology)
Biochemistry
Biological and Biomedical Sciences—General
Biological Chemistry (*see* Biochemistry)
Biological Oceanography (*see* Marine Biology)
Biophysics
Biopsychology
Botany
Breeding (*see* Botany; Plant Biology; Genetics)
Cancer Biology/Oncology
Cardiovascular Sciences
Cell Biology
Cellular Physiology (*see* Cell Biology; Physiology)
Computational Biology
Conservation (*see* Conservation Biology; Environmental Biology)
Conservation Biology
Crop Sciences (*see* Botany; Plant Biology)
Cytology (*see* Cell Biology)
Developmental Biology
Dietetics (*see* Nutrition)
Ecology
Embryology (*see* Developmental Biology)
Endocrinology (*see* Physiology)
Entomology
Environmental Biology
Evolutionary Biology
Foods (*see* Nutrition)
Genetics
Genomic Sciences
Histology (*see* Anatomy; Cell Biology)
Human Genetics
Immunology
Infectious Diseases
Laboratory Medicine (*see* Immunology; Microbiology; Pathology)
Life Sciences (*see* Biological and Biomedical Sciences)
Marine Biology
Medical Microbiology
Medical Sciences (*see* Biological and Biomedical Sciences)
Medical Science Training Programs (*see* Biological and Biomedical Sciences)
Microbiology
Molecular Biology
Molecular Biophysics
Molecular Genetics
Molecular Medicine
Molecular Pathogenesis
Molecular Pathology
Molecular Pharmacology
Molecular Physiology
Molecular Toxicology
Neural Sciences (*see* Biopsychology; Neurobiology; Neuroscience)
Neurobiology
Neuroendocrinology (*see* Biopsychology; Neurobiology; Neuroscience; Physiology)
Neuropharmacology (*see* Biopsychology; Neurobiology; Neuroscience; Pharmacology)
Neurophysiology (*see* Biopsychology; Neurobiology; Neuroscience; Physiology)
Neuroscience
Nutrition
Oncology (*see* Cancer Biology/Oncology)
Organismal Biology (*see* Biological and Biomedical Sciences; Zoology)
Parasitology
Pathobiology
Pathology
Pharmacology
Photobiology of Cells and Organelles (*see* Botany; Cell Biology; Plant Biology)
Physiological Optics (*see* Physiology)
Physiology
Plant Biology
Plant Molecular Biology
Plant Pathology
Plant Physiology
Pomology (*see* Botany; Plant Biology)
Psychobiology (*see* Biopsychology)
Psychopharmacology (*see* Biopsychology; Neuroscience; Pharmacology)
Radiation Biology
Reproductive Biology
Sociobiology (*see* Evolutionary Biology)
Structural Biology
Systems Biology
Teratology
Theoretical Biology (*see* Biological and Biomedical Sciences)
Therapeutics (*see* Pharmacology)
Toxicology
Translational Biology
Tropical Medicine (*see* Parasitology)
Virology
Wildlife Biology (*see* Zoology)
Zoology

Graduate Programs in the Physical Sciences, Mathematics, Agricultural Sciences, the Environment & Natural Resources

Acoustics
Agricultural Sciences
Agronomy and Soil Sciences
Analytical Chemistry
Animal Sciences
Applied Mathematics
Applied Physics

Applied Statistics
Aquaculture
Astronomy
Astrophysical Sciences (*see* Astrophysics; Atmospheric Sciences; Meteorology; Planetary and Space Sciences)
Astrophysics
Atmospheric Sciences
Biological Oceanography (*see* Marine Affairs; Marine Sciences; Oceanography)
Biomathematics
Biometry
Biostatistics
Chemical Physics
Chemistry
Computational Sciences
Condensed Matter Physics
Dairy Science (*see* Animal Sciences)
Earth Sciences (*see* Geosciences)
Environmental Management and Policy
Environmental Sciences
Environmental Studies (*see* Environmental Management and Policy)
Experimental Statistics (*see* Statistics)
Fish, Game, and Wildlife Management
Food Science and Technology
Forestry
General Science (*see* specific topics)
Geochemistry
Geodetic Sciences
Geological Engineering (*see* Geology)
Geological Sciences (*see* Geology)
Geology
Geophysical Fluid Dynamics (*see* Geophysics)
Geophysics
Geosciences
Horticulture
Hydrogeology
Hydrology
Inorganic Chemistry
Limnology
Marine Affairs
Marine Geology
Marine Sciences
Marine Studies (*see* Marine Affairs; Marine Geology; Marine Sciences; Oceanography)
Mathematical and Computational Finance
Mathematical Physics
Mathematical Statistics (*see* Applied Statistics; Statistics)
Mathematics
Meteorology
Mineralogy
Natural Resource Management (*see* Environmental Management and Policy; Natural Resources)
Natural Resources
Nuclear Physics (*see* Physics)
Ocean Engineering (*see* Marine Affairs; Marine Geology; Marine Sciences; Oceanography)
Oceanography
Optical Sciences
Optical Technologies (*see* Optical Sciences)
Optics (*see* Applied Physics; Optical Sciences; Physics)
Organic Chemistry
Paleontology
Paper Chemistry (*see* Chemistry)
Photonics
Physical Chemistry
Physics
Planetary and Space Sciences
Plant Sciences
Plasma Physics
Poultry Science (*see* Animal Sciences)
Radiological Physics (*see* Physics)
Range Management (*see* Range Science)
Range Science
Resource Management (*see* Environmental Management and Policy; Natural Resources)
Solid-Earth Sciences (*see* Geosciences)
Space Sciences (*see* Planetary and Space Sciences)
Statistics
Theoretical Chemistry
Theoretical Physics
Viticulture and Enology
Water Resources

Graduate Programs in Engineering & Applied Sciences

Aeronautical Engineering (*see* Aerospace/Aeronautical Engineering)
Aerospace/Aeronautical Engineering
Aerospace Studies (*see* Aerospace/Aeronautical Engineering)
Agricultural Engineering
Applied Mechanics (*see* Mechanics)
Applied Science and Technology
Architectural Engineering
Artificial Intelligence/Robotics
Astronautical Engineering (*see* Aerospace/Aeronautical Engineering)
Automotive Engineering
Aviation
Biochemical Engineering
Bioengineering
Bioinformatics
Biological Engineering (*see* Bioengineering)
Biomedical Engineering
Biosystems Engineering
Biotechnology
Ceramic Engineering (*see* Ceramic Sciences and Engineering)
Ceramic Sciences and Engineering
Ceramics (*see* Ceramic Sciences and Engineering)
Chemical Engineering
Civil Engineering
Computer and Information Systems Security
Computer Engineering
Computer Science
Computing Technology (*see* Computer Science)
Construction Engineering
Construction Management
Database Systems
Electrical Engineering
Electronic Materials
Electronics Engineering (*see* Electrical Engineering)
Energy and Power Engineering
Energy Management and Policy
Engineering and Applied Sciences
Engineering and Public Affairs (*see* Technology and Public Policy)
Engineering and Public Policy (*see* Energy Management and Policy; Technology and Public Policy)
Engineering Design
Engineering Management
Engineering Mechanics (*see* Mechanics)
Engineering Metallurgy (*see* Metallurgical Engineering and Metallurgy)
Engineering Physics
Environmental Design (*see* Environmental Engineering)
Environmental Engineering
Ergonomics and Human Factors
Financial Engineering
Fire Protection Engineering
Food Engineering (*see* Agricultural Engineering)
Game Design and Development
Gas Engineering (*see* Petroleum Engineering)
Geological Engineering
Geophysics Engineering (*see* Geological Engineering)
Geotechnical Engineering
Hazardous Materials Management

Health Informatics
Health Systems (*see* Safety Engineering; Systems Engineering)
Highway Engineering (*see* Transportation and Highway Engineering)
Human-Computer Interaction
Human Factors (*see* Ergonomics and Human Factors)
Hydraulics
Hydrology (*see* Water Resources Engineering)
Industrial Engineering (*see* Industrial/Management Engineering)
Industrial/Management Engineering
Information Science
Internet Engineering
Macromolecular Science (*see* Polymer Science and Engineering)
Management Engineering (*see* Engineering Management; Industrial/Management Engineering)
Management of Technology
Manufacturing Engineering
Marine Engineering (*see* Civil Engineering)
Materials Engineering
Materials Sciences
Mechanical Engineering
Mechanics
Medical Informatics
Metallurgical Engineering and Metallurgy
Metallurgy (*see* Metallurgical Engineering and Metallurgy)
Mineral/Mining Engineering
Nanotechnology
Nuclear Engineering
Ocean Engineering
Operations Research
Paper and Pulp Engineering
Petroleum Engineering
Pharmaceutical Engineering
Plastics Engineering (*see* Polymer Science and Engineering)
Polymer Science and Engineering
Public Policy (*see* Energy Management and Policy; Technology and Public Policy)
Reliability Engineering
Robotics (*see* Artificial Intelligence/Robotics)
Safety Engineering
Software Engineering
Solid-State Sciences (*see* Materials Sciences)
Structural Engineering
Surveying Science and Engineering
Systems Analysis (*see* Systems Engineering)
Systems Engineering
Systems Science
Technology and Public Policy
Telecommunications
Telecommunications Management
Textile Sciences and Engineering
Textiles (*see* Textile Sciences and Engineering)
Transportation and Highway Engineering
Urban Systems Engineering (*see* Systems Engineering)
Waste Management (*see* Hazardous Materials Management)
Water Resources Engineering

Graduate Programs in Business, Education, Health, Information Studies, Law & Social Work

Accounting
Actuarial Science
Acupuncture and Oriental Medicine
Acute Care/Critical Care Nursing
Administration (*see* Business Administration and Management; Educational Administration; Health Services Management and Hospital Administration; Industrial and Manufacturing Management; Nursing and Healthcare Administration; Pharmaceutical Administration; Sports Management)
Adult Education
Adult Nursing
Advanced Practice Nursing (*see* Family Nurse Practitioner Studies)
Advertising and Public Relations
Agricultural Education
Alcohol Abuse Counseling (*see* Counselor Education)
Allied Health—General
Allied Health Professions (*see* Clinical Laboratory Sciences/Medical Technology; Clinical Research; Communication Disorders; Dental Hygiene; Emergency Medical Services; Occupational Therapy; Physical Therapy; Physician Assistant Studies; Rehabilitation Sciences)
Allopathic Medicine
Anesthesiologist Assistant Studies
Art Education
Athletics Administration (*see* Kinesiology and Movement Studies)
Athletic Training and Sports Medicine
Audiology (*see* Communication Disorders)
Aviation Management
Banking (*see* Finance and Banking)
Bioethics
Business Administration and Management—General
Business Education
Child-Care Nursing (*see* Maternal and Child/Neonatal Nursing)
Chiropractic
Clinical Laboratory Sciences/Medical Technology
Clinical Research
Communication Disorders
Community College Education
Community Health
Community Health Nursing
Computer Education
Continuing Education (*see* Adult Education)
Counseling (*see* Counselor Education)
Counselor Education
Curriculum and Instruction
Dental and Oral Surgery (*see* Oral and Dental Sciences)
Dental Assistant Studies (*see* Dental Hygiene)
Dental Hygiene
Dental Services (*see* Dental Hygiene)
Dentistry
Developmental Education
Distance Education Development
Drug Abuse Counseling (*see* Counselor Education)
Early Childhood Education
Educational Leadership and Administration
Educational Measurement and Evaluation
Educational Media/Instructional Technology
Educational Policy
Educational Psychology
Education—General
Education of the Blind (*see* Special Education)
Education of the Deaf (*see* Special Education)
Education of the Gifted
Education of the Hearing Impaired (*see* Special Education)
Education of the Learning Disabled (*see* Special Education)
Education of the Mentally Retarded (*see* Special Education)
Education of the Physically Handicapped (*see* Special Education)
Education of Students with Severe/Multiple Disabilities
Education of the Visually Handicapped (*see* Special Education)
Electronic Commerce
Elementary Education
Emergency Medical Services
English as a Second Language
English Education
Entertainment Management
Entrepreneurship
Environmental and Occupational Health
Environmental Education
Environmental Law
Epidemiology
Exercise and Sports Science
Exercise Physiology (*see* Kinesiology and Movement Studies)
Facilities and Entertainment Management

Directories and Subject Areas in This Book

NOTES

NOTES

NOTES

NOTES

NOTES

NOTES